P9-EIF-518

The Encyclopedia of Philosophy

Volumes 1 and 2
Complete and Unabridged

The ENCYCLOPEDIA *of* PHILOSOPHY

PAUL EDWARDS, *Editor in Chief*

VOLUME ONE

Macmillan Publishing Co., Inc. & The Free Press
NEW YORK
COLLIER MACMILLAN PUBLISHERS
LONDON

MACMILLAN PUBLISHING CO., INC.
COLLIER-MACMILLAN CANADA LTD.

MANUFACTURED IN THE UNITED STATES OF AMERICA

REPRINT EDITION 1972

Editorial Board

Introduction

The last and, in fact, the only previous major philosophical reference work in the English language, J. M. Baldwin's *Dictionary of Psychology and Philosophy*, appeared in 1901. While it was in many ways an admirable work (it numbered among its contributors men of such caliber as Charles Peirce and G. E. Moore), the scope of Baldwin's *Dictionary* was quite limited. The great majority of articles were exceedingly brief, providing concise definitions of technical terms sometimes accompanied by additional information of a historical nature. There were articles about individual philosophers, but these usually amounted to no more than a few lines. Baldwin himself insisted that his work was primarily a dictionary and not an encyclopedia, but he did feature several articles of "encyclopedic character" dealing with important movements in the history of philosophy and the general divisions of philosophy. Some of these "special" articles, as Baldwin called them, were of the highest quality and have become justly famous. Even they, however, were relatively brief—according to Baldwin's own estimate, they varied in length from 1,000 to 5,000 words—and many important questions were entirely neglected or treated in a very cursory fashion. In Baldwin's own day there was undoubtedly room for a philosophical reference work of more ambitious scope. Since then, especially in the light of the revolutionary developments in philosophy and related fields, the need for a truly encyclopedic presentation of philosophical theories and concepts has become increasingly acute.

The present encyclopedia is intended to fill this need. It has been our aim to cover the whole of philosophy as well as many of the points of contact between philosophy and other disciplines. The *Encyclopedia* treats Eastern and Western philosophy; it deals with ancient, medieval, and modern philosophy; and it discusses the theories of mathematicians, physicists, biologists, sociologists, psychologists, moral reformers, and religious thinkers where these have had an impact on philosophy. The *Encyclopedia* contains nearly 1,500 articles of ample length which can be of value to the specialist, while most of them are sufficiently explicit to be read with pleasure and profit by the intelligent nonspecialist. Some of the longer articles, such as those dealing with the history of the various fields of philosophical investigation or the work of the most influential philosophers, are in effect small books, and even the shorter articles are usually long enough to allow a reasonably comprehensive treatment of the subject under discussion. We believe that there is no philosophical concept or theory of any importance that is not identified and discussed in the *Encyclopedia,* although not every concept or theory has a separate article devoted to it. In apportioning the space at our disposal, we were guided by the thought that the majority of readers would derive more benefit from a smaller number of long and integrated articles than from a multitude of shorter entries.

Throughout we have aimed at presentations which are authoritative, clear, comprehensive, *and* interesting. Reference works have a reputation, not altogether undeserved, for being deadly dull. There are notable exceptions to this rule, but by and large it is true that the articles in both general and specialized encyclopedias are written in the most colorless prose and shy away from controversial issues. The authors frequently adopt a pose of complete neutrality and Olympian superiority to the conflicts of warring schools of thought, but in practice this usually amounts to an endorsement of safe positions and to neglect or even misrepresentation of radical thinkers, especially if they are contemporaries. Whatever else may be said about it, we do not believe that the present work will be condemned as either dull or timid. Radical movements and thinkers are given their full due, and the most controversial contemporary issues are discussed at great length. Moreover, the authors of the relevant articles were free and welcome to express their own views and in some instances to propose new solutions. It should be added that our contributors were not required to be serious and solemn at all costs, and some of our articles are certain to offend those who believe that philosophy and laughter are incompatible. As a consequence of our approach, the present work may in some respects have a greater resemblance to Dr. Johnson's *Dictionary* and even to Diderot's *Encyclopédie* than to the uncontroversial reference works to which the public has become accustomed in more recent times.

I have no doubt that in years to come a number of the articles in the *Encyclopedia* will be regarded as original contributions to philosophy. This comment refers in particular to articles which deal with controversial philosophical issues, but many of our historical articles also embody original research and in some instances treat topics which have not previously been the subject of thorough scholarly investigations. We have also made it a special point to rescue from obscurity unjustly neglected figures, and in such cases, where the reader would find it almost impossible to obtain reliable information in standard histories or in general encyclopedias, we have been particularly generous in our space allotments. In addition, the reader will find a number of articles on unexpected subjects—such as "Greek Drama," "If," "Nothing," and "Popular Arguments for the Existence of God"—that we considered sufficiently intriguing to be given individual attention.

In the attempt to make the articles interesting, we did not, however, lose sight of the basic goal of any reference work—to supply information in a clear and authoritative fashion. We have been fortunate in obtaining the collaboration of a large number of the foremost philosophers in the world, representing all shades of opinion. It is notorious that philosophy differs from the natural sciences in having no body of generally accepted conclusions. There are, for example, no answers to the problem of causation or the mind-body problem which have the endorsement of all competent students of the subjects; and the same is true of all or nearly all other philosophical problems. However, it is possible to provide an authoritative account of the nature of philosophical problems and of the various attempts to answer them. As far as exposition is concerned, the articles in the *Encyclopedia* are meant to be authoritative: although our contributors were free to express their own opinions, this was never done at the expense of providing the necessary information. To the attentive reader it will always be clear where a writer's exposition ends and the statement of his personal position begins.

Something should perhaps be said at this stage about the question of editorial bias, a subject on which there exists a great deal of confusion. It is important to distinguish two very different varieties of bias. The first is what we may call "polemical" bias—the kind that is operative in political campaigns, in the lower forms of journalism, and wherever fanatics of any kind discuss the views of their opponents. The stock in trade of this kind of partisanship is familiar: where the writer does not resort to deliberate forgery, he nevertheless frequently distorts his opponent's position by quoting out of context and in general by making him look as foolish as possible. Regrettably, philosophers, including some very great ones, have not been above employing such weapons, but in this *Encyclopedia* the use of such techniques has not been allowed. There is, however, another kind of bias which cannot be totally eliminated. No matter how fair and equitable an editor may try to be, his personal views and commitments are bound to affect the organization of the work, the space allotted to different subjects, and the criteria employed in judging the quality of contributions. If this kind of bias cannot be eliminated, its influence can at least be restricted, and it also can and should be openly acknowledged. One method that was used to limit the influence of editorial opinions was to assign articles, wherever possible, to authors who were to some considerable extent sympathetic to the theory or the figure they were to discuss. This rule was adhered to in most, though not in all, cases. It was not applied when there was a serious conflict with other criteria which were also relevant to the selection of contributors. If, for example, an author was in our opinion far superior to all other available writers in such qualifications as intellectual incisiveness and capacity for clear statement, he was chosen even if his sympathies for the subject of the article were limited. This happened in a few cases, but for the most part we succeeded in finding contributors who met all of our criteria.

It would, nevertheless, be idle to pretend that this *Encyclopedia* is free from bias and that my own ideological commitments have not significantly influenced its content. Like the majority of my closest advisers, I have been raised in the empirical and analytic tradition of Anglo-Saxon philosophy. There can be no doubt that if the *Encyclopedia* had been edited by a follower of Hegel or by a phenomenologist, assuming him to make every effort to be fair and equitable to other viewpoints, it would have looked very different. The topics chosen for separate articles would not have been the same, the space allotments would probably have been appreciably different, and there would undoubtedly have been a significantly different list of contributors. I doubt that an editor with such a background would have featured such articles as "Any and All," "Paradigm-case Argument," and "Proper Names and Descriptions," to give just a few illustrations, or that he would have devoted the same space to logic or to the philosophy of language. I am not here concerned with arguing that what we have done is right and that what other editors, with different commitments, would have done is wrong. I merely wish to remind the reader that in producing an encyclopedia one has to make a vast number of decisions and that one is not in the fortunate position of copying a pre-existing heavenly original. The decisions may be more or less justifiable, but in the last resort they always reflect the beliefs and sympathies of the editors.

We are presenting more than 900 articles on individual thinkers, and any responsible editor, no matter what his viewpoint, would have decided to include articles on the great majority of these. On the other hand, some figures have been omitted who, in the opinion of competent judges, have as good a claim to a separate article as some of those now included. We may as well here and now offer our apologies to all whose lists would have been different and who find that their favorites do not receive adequate attention. Some of these omissions can fairly be blamed on editorial judgment, but others are the result of accidental circumstances. For a number of relatively minor figures even the most diligent search failed to locate a contributor who could write an authoritative and readable article. In such cases it was decided that the space could be put to better use. Fortunately, these omissions are very few, and the ideas of most of the philosophers about whom we should have had separate articles are covered in various of our survey articles on the history of philosophy in different countries, in the articles on philosophical schools and movements, and sometimes also in those dealing with the history of the branches of philosophy. Nevertheless, there are some regrettable gaps, and we can only plead that if one works with over 500 contributors living in every corner of the globe, it is almost impossible that all one's plans should materialize.

One of the most difficult problems confronting the editor of any reference work is that of avoiding duplication without destroying the sense and continuity of individual articles. To be sure, not all duplication is undesirable, especially in a subject in which there is so much disagreement as in philosophy; and in the present work we have not tried to prevent discussions of the same topic in different contexts and from different viewpoints. To give one example, Zeno's paradoxes are discussed in the article bearing the philosopher's name and in the article "Infinity in Mathematics and Logic." The former article critically analyzes the paradoxes considered in the wider context of Greek thought, while in the latter the paradoxes are examined in order to cast light on problems concerning mathematical infinity. We have done our best, however, to avoid all duplication that would not serve a useful purpose. To achieve this end, it was necessary to be extremely flexible in the relative space provisions for various articles. It seemed unwise, for example, to have a lengthy review of the theories of Husserl once in the article bearing his name and then again in the article on phenomenology. In this particular instance we decided to feature a short article under "Husserl" but a very long one under "Phenomenology." This need for flexibility in order to use the available space to maximum advantage will account for many apparent disproportions in our space allotments. The articles on Marx and Engels, to give another illustration, are quite brief—much briefer than those on thinkers who have been far less influential; but this does not mean that Marxism has been neglected in the *Encyclopedia*. For, in addition to the biographical articles on Marx and Engels (and other Marxist thinkers), the *Encyclopedia* contains the very comprehensive articles "Dialectical Materialism," "Historical Materialism," and "Marxist Philosophy," as well as several shorter pieces, in all of which the theories of Marx and Engels are discussed. Our very elaborate index, prepared by a staff of specialists, and our system of cross references have made it possible to avoid a good deal of duplication.

The *Encyclopedia* is primarily the creation of the contributors, and I wish here to record our gratitude to the many fine scholars who have given so much of their time and energy to this enterprise. A certain type of reader drawn to philosophy is not happy unless he finds a plentiful supply of obscure and high-flown phraseology. Such readers will be disappointed by the present work. Those, on the other hand, who prefer simple and unpretentious language will (we hope) find our *Encyclopedia* to their liking. Nothing can make philosophy into an easy subject, but by taking very great pains it is possible to offer a lucid presentation even of extremely difficult and abstruse philosophical theories. If the majority of our articles are entirely intelligible to most educated readers, this is due to the special care taken by our contributors.

It should also be mentioned that although we were, unfortunately, compelled to reject a number of articles, this in no way reflects on their quality. Many of them were excellent studies and were excluded only for reasons pertaining to problems of space, duplication of material, or other technical considerations. The understanding and patience of all contributors as well as of all whose articles could not be used is greatly appreciated.

We are also very much indebted to the members of the editorial board, whose advice was constantly sought and always readily given. They aided us in a great many ways at all stages—they helped in mapping out the table of contents, in locating suitable contributors, and in evaluating manuscripts. When in the spring and summer of 1965 some absolutely indispensable articles had not arrived, it was chiefly through the intervention of members of the editorial board that outstanding scholars agreed to write the missing articles within the space of a few months. We would like to thank the following contributors for coming to our rescue at the last moment: William P. Alston, Stephen Barker, Thomas G. Bergin, George Boas, Vernon J. Bourke, Wing-tsit Chan, Arthur C. Danto, Phillip H. De Lacy, Ronald Grimsley, Philip P. Hallie, Peter L. Heath, John Hick, Paul O. Kristeller, Hugh R. MacCallum, James E. McClellan, Alasdair MacIntyre, John Macquarrie, F. S. Northedge, Robert G. Olson, John Passmore, Bede Rundle, Colin Smith, W. H. Walsh, and Edward Wasiolek. We are particularly grateful to Professor G. B. Kerferd for writing the article on Aristotle at incredibly short notice. That our extremely detailed and exhaustive article on the history of logic was completed in time is in large measure due to the tireless efforts of Professor A. N. Prior, who was wonderfully helpful in a great many other ways as well.

It would be impossible to praise too highly the performance of the members of the editorial staff. The best testimony to their skill and devotion is the fact that a work of this scope could be completed in a relatively short time by such a small group of people. Ann Trabulsi had the very difficult task of coordinating the work of contributors, editors, copy editors, and the production staff. Her admirable calm and self-possession resolved many a potentially explosive situation, while her tact and firmness worked wonders with even the most reluctant contributors. Philip Cummings, Donald Levy, Sandra Litt, and Margaret Miner were the four full-time editors. Their high standards of scholarship and accuracy, their fine feeling for language, and their unfailing good sense again and again evoked admiring comments and expressions of gratitude from our contributors. Their enthusiasm and their delightful and contagious sense of humor made my own share of the work not only less burdensome but frequently a great deal of fun. Dr. Albert Blumberg joined the editorial staff on a part-time basis early in 1964. It is largely owing to his rich knowledge and painstaking labors that our articles on logic and foundations of mathematics are, as we believe, of an exceedingly high quality. Alix Shulman assisted us during the last year in dealing with various tricky editorial problems, and we are most grateful to her for the excellence of her work. Dr. Murray Greene and Sheila Meyer worked for extended periods in the very onerous position of managing editor, and to both of them I wish to express my appreciation of their valuable contributions. I should also like to thank Mr. Sidney Solomon, who designed the *Encyclopedia* and who was involved in the project from the beginning, for giving valuable advice and assistance on many occasions. Finally, we are all indebted to our editorial secretary, Eunice Dean, whose careful management of our vast and complicated records and correspondence has been an indispensable aid to the production of the *Encyclopedia*.

I have left to the last obligations of a more personal nature. Four of my own articles—"Atheism," "Life, Meaning and Value of," "'My Death,'" and "Why"—were written during the academic year 1964/1965 while I held a John Simon Guggenheim Foundation Research Fellowship. The award of this fellowship made it possible for me to take a leave of absence from my teaching duties, and I wish to thank the Guggenheim Memorial Foundation for its generous aid. I should also like to thank the following friends and colleagues for reading one or more of my own articles and for offering criticism and suggestions: Reuben Abel, F. M. Barnard, Sandra Bartky, Milič Čapek, Gertrude Ezorsky, Antony Flew, Peter Heath, Martin Lean, Ruth Barcan Marcus, C. Douglas McGee, Sidney Morgenbesser, Mary Mothersill, Ernest Nagel, Andrew Oldenquist, Robert Olson, Richard Popkin, Bertrand Russell, J. B. Schneewind, Elmer Sprague, and Carl Wellman. In connection with the difficult article about Wilhelm Reich I am especially grateful for advice and comments to Mr. A. S. Neill, Drs. Allan Cott and Ola Raknes (all of whom knew Reich well), and to Sir Karl Popper, Alasdair MacIntyre, Sidney Hook, and Michael Scriven. Needless to say, none of those who kindly helped me with my articles is responsible for any of the views expressed in them. To my dear friend and teacher, Ernest Nagel, I am deeply grateful for his unfailing encouragement and moral support ever since I began to edit the *Encyclopedia*. In spite of his many obligations he always found time to listen to our problems and to offer suggestions based on his immense erudition and his acquaintance with scholars in the most diverse fields.

Brooklyn College
March, 1966

PAUL EDWARDS

Special Acknowledgments

We wish to thank the following persons who have given us advice and help in the preparation of the *Encyclopedia*: Professor F. M. Barnard of the University of Saskatchewan; Mr. Palle Birkeland, chief librarian of the Kongelige Bibliotek, Copenhagen; Professor Justus Buchler of Columbia University; Mr. Richard Cecil, formerly editor in chief of Collier Books; Professor Rosalie Colie of Iowa State University; Mother A. Fiske of the Manhattanville College of the Sacred Heart; Dr. Harry Frankfurt of the Rockefeller Institute; Dr. A. C. Graham of the University of London; Dr. L. H. Grunebaum of the New School for Social Research; Mr. Hector Hawton, editor of *The Humanist* and *The Rationalist Annual*; Father Thomas E. Henneberry, S.J., of Loyola Seminary; Professor R. J. Hirst of the University of Glasgow; Father Gerald A. McCool, S.J., of Loyola Seminary; Mr. Carl Morse of Collier Books; Dr: Eva Schaper of the University of Glasgow; Mr. Chad Walsh of Beloit College and the New York *Times*; Dr. W. Montgomery Watt of the University of Edinburgh; Mr. James R. C. Wright of Cambridge University.

The following institutions have courteously rendered us service: the Austrian Institute; the British Information Service; the Columbia University Library; the French Institute; the German Information Center; Humanities Press; the Israeli Consulate General; the Library of Congress, Loan Division; the New York Public Library; the New York *Times*; the New York University Library; the Public Library of the District of Columbia, Interlibrary Loan Service; Random House, Inc.; and the Wesley Theological Seminary Library.

Many others, too numerous to list here, have given us assistance, and we are grateful to them all.

P.E.

Editorial Staff

Jean Paradise MANAGING EDITOR, COPY DEPARTMENT

Barbara Bissell PRODUCTION COORDINATOR

Ann H. Trabulsi ADMINISTRATIVE EDITOR

Jane Rogers Tonero DIRECTOR OF INDEXING

Albert Blumberg SENIOR EDITOR
Philip Cummings SENIOR EDITOR
Donald Levy ASSOCIATE EDITOR

Sandra Litt ASSOCIATE EDITOR
Margaret Miner ASSOCIATE EDITOR
Alix Shulman CONSULTING EDITOR

COPY DEPARTMENT

Elizabeth I. Wilson COPY CHIEF
Pearl S. Greenberger ASSOCIATE COPY CHIEF
Judith Levey ASSOCIATE EDITOR
Maron Loeb ASSOCIATE EDITOR
Susan Day ASSISTANT EDITOR
Marshall De Bruhl ASSISTANT EDITOR

Joel Honig ASSISTANT EDITOR
Jane Jaffe ASSISTANT EDITOR
Martha R. Neufeld ASSISTANT EDITOR
Robert Schultz ASSISTANT EDITOR
George Shriver ASSISTANT EDITOR
Claire Sotnick ASSISTANT EDITOR

PRODUCTION DEPARTMENT

Gerald Vogt ASSISTANT PRODUCTION COORDINATOR
Arvella Edwards PRODUCTION ASSISTANT
Marva McAllister PRODUCTION ASSISTANT

INDEX DEPARTMENT

May Leavenworth INDEX ASSISTANT
Jane Ellen Rubin INDEX ASSISTANT
Susan Sheinman INDEX ASSISTANT

List of Contributors

Abbagnano, Nicola, Ph.D. (University of Naples). Professor of the History of Philosophy, Faculty of Letters and Philosophy, University of Turin; Member of the Accademia Nazionale dei Lincei, the Accademia delle Scienze di Torino, and the International Institute of Philosophy. Publications include *Guglielmo di Ockham* (1931); *Struttura dell'esistenza* (1939); *Introduzione all'esistenzialismo* (1942); *Storia della filosofia* (3 vols., 4th ed., 1963); *Possibilità e libertà* (1956); *Problemi di sociologia* (1959); *Dizionario di filosofia* (2d ed., 1964); and others. ALIOTTA, ANTONIO; ARDIGÒ, ROBERTO; FERRI, LUIGI; HUMANISM; LEONARDO DA VINCI; POSITIVISM; PSYCHOLOGISM; RENSI, GIUSEPPE; RIGNANO, EUGENIO.

Abel, Reuben, B.A. (Columbia); J.D. (New York University); M.S.Sc., Ph.D. (New School for Social Research). Adjunct Associate Professor of Philosophy, Graduate Faculty, New School for Social Research, and Chairman of the Division of Humanities, New School for Social Research. Editor, *Humanism: The Philosophy of Schiller* (1966). Author, *The Pragmatism of F. C. S. Schiller* (1955) and numerous articles and reviews in philosophical journals. SCHILLER, FERDINAND CANNING SCOTT.

Abelson, Raziel A., M.A. (University of Chicago); Ph.D. (New York University). Associate Professor and Chairman of the Department of Philosophy, University College, New York University. Formerly, Lecturer at Hunter College; Visiting Lecturer at Columbia University; Visiting Professor at the University of Hawaii. Editor, *Ethics and Metaethics* (1963). Author of many articles and reviews in philosophical journals, anthologies, and encyclopedias. DEFINITION; ETHICS, HISTORY OF (section on Greek ethics through 19th-century ethics).

Achinstein, Peter, A.B., A.M., Ph.D. (Harvard). Associate Professor of Philosophy at Johns Hopkins University. Assistant Professor of Philosophy at the University of Iowa (1961–1962); Visiting Professor of Philosophy at M.I.T. (1965–1966); Guggenheim Fellow (1966–1967). Publications include "Theoretical Terms and Partial Interpretation," *British Journal for the Philosophy of Science* (1963); "Variety and Analogy in Confirmation Theory," *Philosophy of Science* (1963); "The Problem of Theoretical Terms," *American Philosophical Quarterly* (1965). BRAITHWAITE, RICHARD BEVAN; REICHENBACH, HANS.

Acton, H. B., M.A., D.Phil. (Oxford). Professor of Moral Philosophy at the University of Edinburgh; Editor of *Philosophy*. Professor of Philosophy at the University of London (1945–1964); President of the Aristotelian Society (1952–1953); Dawes Hicks Lecturer at the British Academy (1959); Honorary Director of the Royal Institute of Philosophy (1961–1964). Author, *The Illusion of the Epoch: Marxism–Leninism as a Philosophical Creed* (1955); *The Philosophy of Language in Revolutionary France* (1959); and articles in *Mind, PAS,* and *Philosophy*. ABSOLUTE, THE; BERKELEY, GEORGE; BOSANQUET, BERNARD; BRADLEY, FRANCIS HERBERT; DIALECTICAL MATERIALISM; HEGEL, GEORG WILHELM FRIEDRICH; HISTORICAL MATERIALISM; IDEALISM.

Adams, E. M., A.B., M.A. (University of Richmond); B.D. (Colgate-Rochester Divinity School); M.A., Ph.D. (Harvard). Professor of Philosophy at the University of North Carolina. President of the North Carolina Philosophical Society (1953–1955); Chairman of the Program Committee of the Southern Society for Philosophy and Psychology (1963); Chairman of the Department of Philosophy at the University of North Carolina (1960–1965); Chairman of the Program Committee of the American Philosophical Association, Eastern Division (1965); Member of the Executive Council, Southern Society for Philosophy and Psychology (1963–1966). Editor, *Categorial Analysis: Selected Writings of Everett W. Hall . . .* (1964). Author, *Fundamentals of General Logic* (1954); *The Language of Value* (with others, 1957); *Ethical Naturalism and the Modern World-view* (1960). LEWIS, CLARENCE IRVING.

Aldridge, Alfred Owen, B.S. (Indiana University); M.A. (University of Georgia); Ph.D. (Duke); Docteur de l'Université de Paris. Head of the Department of Comparative

Literature at the University of Maryland. Formerly, Visiting Professor at the University of Toulouse, the University of Clermont-Ferrand, and the University of Brazil. Author, *Benjamin Franklin and His French Contemporaries* (1957); *Man of Reason: The Life of Thomas Paine* (1959); *Jonathan Edwards* (1964); *Benjamin Franklin: Philosopher and Man* (1965). PAINE, THOMAS.

Alexander, Peter, B.A., B.Sc. (University of London). Reader in Philosophy at the University of Bristol. Formerly, Lecturer in Philosophy at the University of Leeds; Visiting Lecturer at the University of Pennsylvania (1959); Visiting Associate Professor at the University of Maryland (1966). Author, *Sensationalism and Scientific Explanation* (1963); *A Preface to the Logic of Science* (1963); and articles in philosophical journals. CONVENTIONALISM; DUHEM, PIERRE MAURICE MARIE; HERTZ, HEINRICH RUDOLF; MACH, ERNST; PEARSON, KARL; POINCARÉ, JULES HENRI; SENSATIONALISM.

Alexander, W. M., A.B. (Davidson College); B.D. (Louisville Presbyterian Seminary); S.T.M. (Harvard); Th.D. (Princeton Theological Seminary). Associate Professor of Religion and Philosophy at St. Andrews College (North Carolina). Chaplain in the U.S. Army (1953–1956). Author, *Johann Georg Hamann: Philosophy and Faith* (1966). HAMANN, JOHANN GEORG.

Allen, R. E., A.B. (Haverford College); M.A. (Yale); B.Phil. (St. Andrews); Ph.D. (Yale). Professor of Philosophy and Classics at Indiana University. ANSELM, ST. (section on life and the proofs); GAUNILO.

Alluntis, Felix, O.F.M., M.A., Ph.D. (Catholic University of America). Ordinary Professor of Philosophy at the Catholic University of America. Formerly, Special Professor of Philosophy at the Catholic University of Villanueva (Havana); Professor of Philosophy at Siena College (Loudonville, N.Y.). Publications include *La filosofía cristiana de la propiedad* (1960); John Duns Scotus, *Del Primer Principio* (translated and edited in *Obras del Dr. Sutil Juan Duns Escoto, Dios Uno y Trino,* 1960); "Private Property and Natural Law," *Studies in Philosophy and the History of Philosophy* (1963). VITORIA, FRANCISCO DE.

Alston, William P., B.Mus. (Centenary College); Ph.D. (University of Chicago). Professor of Philosophy at the University of Michigan. Fellow of the American Philosophical Association, Western Division (1955–1956); Fellow of the Center for Advanced Study in the Behavioral Sciences (1965–1966). Author, *Philosophy of Language* (1964). EMOTION AND FEELING; EMOTIVE MEANING; LANGUAGE; LANGUAGE, PHILOSOPHY OF; MEANING; MOTIVES AND MOTIVATION; PHILOSOPHY OF RELIGION, PROBLEMS OF; PLEASURE; PSYCHOANALYTIC THEORIES, LOGICAL STATUS OF; RELIGION; RELIGION, NATURALISTIC RECONSTRUCTIONS OF; RELIGION, PSYCHOLOGICAL EXPLANATIONS OF; RELIGIOUS LANGUAGE; RUSSELL, BERTRAND ARTHUR WILLIAM (section on epistemology and metaphysics); SIGN AND SYMBOL; TELEOLOGICAL ARGUMENT FOR THE EXISTENCE OF GOD; TILLICH, PAUL; VAGUENESS.

Anastos, Milton V., A.B., S.T.B., Ph.D. (Harvard). Professor of Byzantine Greek at the University of California, Los Angeles; Member of the Board of Scholars, Dumbarton Oaks, Harvard University; Corresponding Member of the Society of Macedonian Studies (Thessalonike); Member of the Internationale Komitee für den Nachdruck griechischer Handschriftenkataloge (Berlin). Professor of Byzantine Theology at Harvard University (1962–1964). Author, "Some Aspects of Byzantine Influence on the Latin Culture of the Twelfth Century" (in *Twelfth Century Europe and the Foundations of Modern Society,* 1961) and many other scholarly papers. BYZANTINE PHILOSOPHY.

Anchor, Robert, Ph.D. (University of Rochester). Instructor of History at Yale University. Fulbright Scholar at the University of Göttingen (1960–1961). RICKERT, HEINRICH; RITSCHL, ALBRECHT BENJAMIN; SCHLEGEL, FRIEDRICH VON.

Arner, Douglas, A.B. (Creighton University); M.A., Ph.D. (University of Michigan). Professor of Philosophy at Arizona State University. Formerly taught at the University of Michigan and Princeton University. MCCOSH, JAMES.

Arway, Robert J., C.M., M.A. (Catholic University of America); Ph.D. (Institut Supérieur de Philosophie, Louvain, Belgium). Associate Professor of Philosophy at St. John's University. Past Vice-Rector of Our Lady of Angels Franciscan Seminary. GODFREY OF FONTAINES.

Ashby, R. W., B.A., Ph.D. Lecturer in Philosophy, King's College, University of London. Author, "Use and Verification," *PAS* (1955–1956); "Entailment and Modality," *PAS* (1962–1963). BASIC STATEMENTS; LINGUISTIC THEORY OF THE A PRIORI; VERIFIABILITY PRINCIPLE.

Atlas, Samuel, Ph.D. (University of Giessen). Professor of Philosophy at Hebrew Union College (New York). Author, *The Relevance of the Philosophy of Maimonides* (1954); *Maimon and Spinoza* (1959); *From Critical to Speculative Idealism: The Philosophy of Solomon Maimon* (1964). JACOBI, FRIEDRICH HEINRICH; MAIMON, SALOMON; SCHULZE, GOTTLOB ERNST.

Aune, Bruce, B.A., M.A., Ph.D. (University of Minnesota). Associate Professor of Philosophy at the University of Pittsburgh. Taught at Oberlin College (1960–1962); Guggenheim Fellow (1963–1964); Visiting Professor of Philosophy and Research Professor in the Minnesota Center for the Philosophy of Science (1965). Contributor to Max Black, ed., *Philosophy in America* (1965). CAN; IF; INTENTION; MUST; POSSIBILITY; THINKING.

Austeda, Franz, Ph.D. (University of Vienna). Councilor of the School Board of Vienna. Author, *Wörterbuch der Philosophie* (1954); *Axiomatische Philosophie (Ein Beitrag zur Selbstkritik der Philosophie)* (1962). AVENARIUS, RICHARD; CZOLBE, HEINRICH; DU BOIS-REYMOND, EMIL; FISCHER, KUNO; JODL, FRIEDRICH; PETZOLDT, JOSEPH; RORETZ, KARL; SCHULTZ, JULIUS; STÖHR, ADOLF; WAHLE, RICHARD; ZIEHEN, THEODOR.

Baier, A. C., M.A. (University of Otago, New Zealand); B.Phil. (Oxford). Lecturer in Philosophy at the Carnegie Institute of Technology. Formerly, Lecturer in Philosophy at the universities of Auckland (New Zealand) and Sydney. NONSENSE.

Baker, Keith Michael, M.A. (Cambridge); Ph.D. (University of London). Assistant Professor of History at the University of Chicago. Research Fellow, Institute of Historical Research, University of London (1963–1964). CONDORCET, MARQUIS DE.

Ballard, Edward G., M.A., Ph.D. (University of Virginia). Professor of Philosophy at Tulane University; President of the Southern Society for Philosophy and Psychology. Visiting Professor at Yale University (1963–1964). Publications include *Art and Analysis* (1957); *The Philosophy of Jules Lachelier* (translated with an introduction, 1960); *Socratic Ignorance, An Essay on Platonic Self-knowledge* (1965). LACHELIER, JULES.

Bambrough, Renford, M.A. (Cambridge). Fellow, Dean, and Director of Studies in Moral Sciences at St. John's College, Cambridge University, and University Lecturer in Classics. Visiting Associate Professor of Philosophy at Cornell University (1962); Stanton Lecturer in the Philosophy of Religion at Cambridge University (1962–1965). Contributor to Peter Laslett, ed., *Philosophy, Politics and Society* (1956), and to *Religion and Humanism* (1965). Other publications include *The Philosophy of Aristotle* (edited with commentary, 1963);

New Essays on Plato and Aristotle (1965). DEMIURGE; GREEK DRAMA.

Bar-Hillel, Yehoshua, M.A., Ph.D. Professor of Logic and Philosophy of Science at the Hebrew University of Jerusalem; President, Division of Logic, Methodology and Philosophy of Science, International Union of History and Philosophy of Science; President of the Israel Association for Information Processing; Member of the National Academy of Sciences and Humanities of Israel. Formerly, President of the Israel Society for Logic and Philosophy of Science; Member of the Council, Symbolic Logic Association; Visiting Professor at the University of Michigan and the University of California, Berkeley and San Diego. Publications include *An Outline of the Theory of Semantic Information* (with Rudolf Carnap, 1952); *Foundations of Set Theory* (with A. A. Fraenkel, 1957); *Language and Information: Selected Essays on Their Theory and Application* (1964). BOLZANO, BERNARD; LOGIC, HISTORY OF (section on Bolzano); SYNTACTICAL AND SEMANTICAL CATEGORIES; TYPES, THEORY OF.

Barker, Stephen F., B.A. (Swarthmore College); M.A., Ph.D. (Harvard). Professor of Philosophy at Johns Hopkins University. Author, *Induction and Hypothesis* (1957). *Philosophy of Mathematics* (1964); *Elements of Logic* (1965). GEOMETRY; NUMBER.

Barnard, Frederick M., B.A., M.A., Ph.D. Associate Professor of Political Science at the University of Saskatchewan (Canada). Formerly, Senior Lecturer in Social Studies at the University of Salford (England). Awarded Senior Research Fellowships by the German Academic Exchange Service, the Alexander von Humboldt Foundation, and the Canada Council. Publications include *Zwischen Aufklärung und Politischer Romantik* (1964); *Herder's Social and Political Thought* (1965); and various articles on the Enlightenment, political theory, and the philosophy of history. BACHOFEN, JOHANN JAKOB; MORGAN, LEWIS HENRY; REINHOLD, KARL LEONHARD; SPINOZISM; SUMNER, WILLIAM GRAHAM; WEBER, ALFRED.

Barricelli, Jean-Pierre, B.A., M.A., Ph.D. (Harvard). Associate Professor of Romance Languages and Comparative Literature and Chairman of the Department of French and Italian at the University of California, Riverside. Formerly, Director of the Wien International Scholarship Program at Brandeis University; Conductor of the Waltham Symphony Orchestra; Fulbright Professor to Norway (1962–1963). Coauthor (with Leo Weinstein), *Ernest Chausson* (1955). Author, *Dodecahedron* (1956); *Poems by Leopardi* (introduction and translation, 1963); *Demonic Souls: Three Essays on Balzac* (1964). LEOPARDI, COUNT GIACOMO.

Bartlett, Irving H., B.A. (Ohio Wesleyan); M.A., Ph.D. (Brown). Professor and Head of the Department of History at the Carnegie Institute of Technology. Formerly, Assistant Professor of History at M.I.T.; President of the Cape Cod Community College. Publications include *William Ellery Channing: Unitarian Christianity and Other Essays* (edited with an introduction, 1957); *Wendell Phillips, Brahmin Radical* (1961). CHANNING, WILLIAM ELLERY; PARKER, THEODORE.

Baylis, Charles A., A.B., A.M. (University of Washington); Ph.D. (Harvard). Professor and Chairman of the Department of Philosophy at Duke University; Chairman of the National Board of Officers of the American Philosophical Association (1965–1967). Sheldon Travelling Fellow (1926–1927); Member of the Department of Philosophy at Brown University (1927–1948); Managing Editor of the *Journal of Symbolic Logic* (1936–1942); Vice-President of the Association for Symbolic Logic (1942–1948); Professor and Head of the Department of Philosophy at the University of Maryland (1948–1952); Professor of Philosophy and Director of Graduate Studies at Duke University (1952–1956); Guggenheim Fellow and Senior Fulbright Scholar at Oxford University (1958–1959). Coauthor (with A. A. Bennett), *Formal Logic* (1938). Author, *Ethics* (1958); *Metaphysics* (1965). CONSCIENCE.

Beardsley, Monroe C., B.A., Ph.D. (Yale). Professor and Acting Chairman of the Department of Philosophy at Swarthmore College; Vice-President of the American Society for Aesthetics; Member of the Editorial Board of the *Monist.* Guggenheim Fellow (1950–1951). Coauthor (with Elizabeth Beardsley), *Philosophical Thinking: An Introduction* (1965). Author, *Aesthetics: Problems in the Philosophy of Criticism* (1958); *Aesthetics From Classical Greece to the Present: A Short History* (1965). AESTHETICS, HISTORY OF; METAPHOR.

Beck, Lewis White, A.B. (Emory); M.A., Ph.D. (Duke). Burbank Professor of Intellectual and Moral Philosophy at the University of Rochester. Professor of Philosophy at Lehigh University (1948–1949); Guggenheim Fellow (1957–1958); A.C.L.S. Fellow (1965). Publications include *Philosophic Inquiry* (1952); *A Commentary on Kant's Critique of Practical Reason* (1960); *Six Secular Philosophers* (1960); *Studies in the Philosophy of Kant* (1965); *Eighteenth-century Philosophy* (selections with an introduction, 1966). GERMAN PHILOSOPHY; NEO-KANTIANISM; STERN, LOUIS WILLIAM.

Beckner, Morton, A.B. (University of California); M.A., Ph.D. (Columbia). Associate Professor of Philosophy at Pomona College (Claremont, California). Author, *The Biological Way of Thought* (1959) and papers in the philosophy of biology. BIOLOGY; DARWINISM; MECHANISM IN BIOLOGY; ORGANISMIC BIOLOGY; TELEOLOGY; VITALISM.

Benn, Stanley I., B.Sc. (University of London). Senior Fellow in Philosophy at the Australian National University; Member of the Social Sciences Research Council of Australia. Formerly, Lecturer in Government at the University of Southampton (England). Coauthor (with R. S. Peters), *Social Principles and the Democratic State* (1959). Author of various papers on political and social philosophy in *Philosophy, Political Studies,* and *PAS.* AUTHORITY; DEMOCRACY; EQUALITY, MORAL AND SOCIAL; JUSTICE; NATIONALISM; POLITICAL PHILOSOPHY, NATURE OF; POWER; PROPERTY; PUNISHMENT; RIGHTS; SOCIETY; SOVEREIGNTY; STATE.

Berenda, Carlton W., B.Sc. (Villanova College); M.A., Ph.D. (Columbia). Professor of Philosophy at the University of Oklahoma. Chairman of the Philosophy Department of the University of Oklahoma (1950–1960); President of the Southwestern Philosophical Association (1953). Author, *World Visions and the Image of Man* (1965) and numerous articles in the *Journal of Philosophy, Philosophy of Science, Physical Review,* and others; WEYL, (CLAUS HUGO) HERMANN.

Bergin, Thomas Goddard, B.A., Ph.D. (Yale); Lit.D., D.H.L. Sterling Professor of Romance Languages and Master of Timothy Dwight College at Yale University. Professor of Romance Languages, Albany State College (1935–1941); Professor of Romance Languages and Chairman of the Department of Literature at Cornell University (1946–1948). Publications include *Anthology of the Provençal Troubadours* (edited with R. T. Hill, 1941); *The New Science of Giambattista Vico* (translated with M. H. Fisch, 1948); *Dante* (1965); *Concordance to the Divine Comedy* (with E. H. Wilkins, 1965). DANTE ALIGHIERI.

Bernays, Paul, Ph.D. Retired Professor at the Swiss Federal Institute of Technology (Zurich). Privatdozent at the University of Zurich (1913–1917); Assistant and Privatdozent (1917–1933) and Professor (1922) at the University of Göttingen. Privatdozent (1939–1945) and Extraordinary Professor (1945–1949) at the Swiss Federal Institute of Technology. Publications include *Grundlagen der Mathematik* (with

D. Hilbert, 2 vols., 1934, 1939); *Axiomatic Set Theory* (with A. A. Fraenkel, 1958); a series of papers on axiomatic set theory in the *Journal of Symbolic Logic* (1937–1954); and philosophical papers in *Abhandlungen der Fries'schen Schule, Dialectica, Synthese,* and *Ratio.* HILBERT, DAVID.

Berndtson, Arthur, A.B., Ph.D. (University of Chicago). Professor and Chairman of the Department of Philosophy at the University of Missouri. President of the Missouri State Philosophy Association (1955–1956). Contributor to V. T. A. Ferm, ed., *History of Philosophical Systems* (1953), and to W. L. Reese, ed., *Process and Divinity.* Author of papers in *Philosophy and Phenomenological Research, Journal of Aesthetics, Revue internationale de philosophie,* and other journals. CASO, ANTONIO; DEUSTUA, ALEJANDRO O.; INGENIEROS, JOSÉ; KORN, ALEJANDRO; LATIN AMERICAN PHILOSOPHY; ROMERO, FRANCISCO; VASCONCELOS, JOSÉ; VAZ FERREIRA, CARLOS.

Bernstein, Richard J., A.B. (University of Chicago); B.S. (Columbia); M.A., Ph.D. (Yale). Chairman of the Department of Philosophy at Haverford College; Editor of the *Review of Metaphysics.* Secretary of the Charles S. Peirce Society (1964). Editor, *John Dewey: On Experience, Nature and Freedom* (1959) and *Perspectives on Peirce* (1965). Author, *John Dewey* (1966). DEWEY, JOHN.

Bertocci, Peter Anthony, A.B. (Boston University); A.M. (Harvard); Ph.D. (Boston University). Formerly, Bowne Professor of Philosophy at Boston University; Fulbright Research Scholar in Italy (1951–1952) and in India (1960–1961); President of the Metaphysical Society of America (1962–1963); President of the American Theological Society (1962–1963). Editor, E. S. Brightman, *Person and Reality* (1958). Author, *The Human Venture in Sex, Love, and Marriage* (1949); *Personality and the Good* (with R. M. Millard, 1950); *Free Will, Responsibility, and Grace* (1956); *Religion as Creative Insecurity* (1958). BOWNE, BORDEN PARKER; HOWISON, GEORGE HOLMES.

Black, Max, Ph.D., D.Lit. (University of London). Professor of Philosophy at Cornell University; Fellow of the American Academy of Arts and Sciences; Member of the International Institute of Philosophy. President of the American Philosophical Association, Eastern Division (1958). Author, *The Nature of Mathematics* (1933); *Models and Metaphors* (1962); *A Companion to Wittgenstein's Tractatus* (1964); and many others. CRAIG'S THEOREM; INDUCTION; PROBABILITY; RAMSEY, FRANK PLUMPTON.

Blanché, Robert, Ancien élève de L'École Normale Supérieure, agrégé de philosophie, docteur ès lettres. Professor of Philosophy, Faculty of Letters and Humane Sciences, University of Toulouse (France); Corresponding Member of the Académie des sciences morales et politiques. Publications include *La Notion de fait physique* (1935); *Le Rationalisme de Whewell* (1935); *La Science physique et la réalité* (1948); *Le Attitudes idéalistes* (1949); *L'Axiomatique* (1955); *Introduction à la logique contemporaine* (1957); *Structures intellectuelles* (1966). COUTURAT, LOUIS; GOBLOT, EDMOND; HANNEQUIN, ARTHUR; MEYERSON, ÉMILE; MILHAUD, GASTON; ROUGIER, LOUIS; WHEWELL, WILLIAM.

Blanshard, Brand, M.A. (Columbia); Ph.D. (Harvard); B.Sc. (Oxford); LL.D. (St. Andrews); Litt.D., L.H.D. Sterling Professor Emeritus at Yale University. Formerly, Honorary Fellow of Merton College, Oxford University; Corresponding Fellow of the British Academy; President of the American Philosophical Association, Eastern Division (1942–1944); Gifford Lecturer (1952–1953); Carus Lecturer (1959). Author, *The Nature of Thought* (2 vols., 1939); *Reason and Goodness* (1960); *Reason and Analysis* (1961). WISDOM.

Blau, Joseph L., A.B., M.A., Ph.D. (Columbia). Professor of Religion at Columbia University. Author, *Men and Movements in American Philosophy* (1952): *The Story of Jewish Philosophy* (1962); *Modern Varieties of Judaism* (1966). ABBOT, FRANCIS ELLINGWOOD; ALBO, JOSEPH; BAHYA BEN JOSEPH IBN PAQUDA; CABALA; CORDOVERO, MOSES BEN JACOB; HICKOK, LAURENS PERSEUS; IBN-ZADDIK, JOSEPH BEN JACOB; ISRAELI, ISAAC BEN SOLOMON; JAMES, HENRY; KAPLAN, MORDECAI MENAHEM; MATHER, COTTON; MUKAMMAS, DAVID BEN MERWAN AL-; PORTER, NOAH; SAADIA BEN JOSEPH; SELLARS, ROY WOOD; WAYLAND, FRANCIS.

Bluhm, William T., A.B. (Brown); M.A. (Fletcher School of Law and Diplomacy); Ph.D. (University of Chicago). Associate Professor of Political Science at the University of Rochester. Fulbright Award for Research on Austrian Political Culture (1965–1966). Author, *Theories of the Political Systems* (1965) and articles in scholarly journals. HARRINGTON, JAMES; THUCYDIDES.

Blumberg, Albert E., A.B. (Johns Hopkins); M.A. (Yale); Ph.D. (University of Vienna). Assistant Professor of Philosophy at Rutgers University; Member of the Faculty of the New School for Social Research. One of the founding editors of *Philosophy of Science* (1934–1939); Instructor in Philosophy at Johns Hopkins University (1930–1935). Publications include "Logical Positivism" (with Herbert Feigl), *Journal of Philosophy* (1931); "Some Remarks in Defense of the Operational Theory of Meaning" (with George Boas), *Journal of Philosophy* (1931); "Émile Meyerson's Critique of Positivism," *Monist* (1932); and "The Nature of Philosophic Analysis," *Philosophy of Science* (1935). LOGIC, MODERN.

Boas, George, A.B., A.M., Ph.D., LL.D., L.H.D., D.F.A. Professor Emeritus of the History of Philosophy at Johns Hopkins University. Coauthor (with A. O. Lovejoy), *Primitivism in Antiquity* (1965). Author, *Rationalism in Greek Philosophy* (1961); *The Heaven of Invention* (1963); *French Philosophies of the Romantic Period* (1964); *The Challenge of Science* (1965); and many others. BAUTAIN, LOUIS EUGÈNE MARIE; BONALD, LOUIS GABRIEL AMBROISE, VICOMTE DE; BURTHOGGE, RICHARD; CHATEAUBRIAND, FRANÇOIS RENÉ DE; CORDEMOY, GÉRAUD DE; COUSIN, VICTOR; DESTUTT DE TRACY, COMTE ANTOINE LOUIS CLAUDE; FRENCH PHILOSOPHY; JOUFFROY, THÉODORE SIMON; LAMENNAIS, HUGUES FÉLICITÉ ROBERT DE; LAROMIGUIÈRE, PIERRE; LOVE; LOVEJOY, ARTHUR ONCKEN; MAISTRE, COMTE JOSEPH DE; RAVAISSON-MOLLIEN, JEAN GASPARD FÉLIX; RENOUVIER, CHARLES BERNARD; ROYER-COLLARD, PIERRE-PAUL; STAËL-HOLSTEIN, ANNE LOUISE GERMAINE NECKER, BARONNE DE; TRADITIONALISM.

Boeschenstein, Hermann, Ph.D. Head of the Department of German at the University of Toronto; Fellow of the Royal Society of Canada. Author of books and articles on 19th- and 20th-century German literature. OKEN, LORENZ.

Bonansea, Bernardine M., O.F.M., M.A., Ph.D. (Catholic University of America); Lector generalis (Hon.). Ordinary Professor of Philosophy at the Catholic University of America. Formerly, Superintendent of Catholic Schools, Archdiocese of Changsha, Hunan, China; Secretary of Hunan Province Catholic Relief Committee; Professor of Philosophy at Siena College (Loudonville, N.Y., 1955–1957). Translator and editor, Efrem Bettoni, *Duns Scotus: The Basic Principles of His Philosophy* (1961): Coeditor (with John K. Ryan), *John Duns Scotus, 1265–1965* (1965). Author, *The Theory of Knowledge of Tommaso Campanella: Exposition and Critique* (1954). CAMPANELLA, TOMMASO; SCOTISM; TELESIO, BERNARDINO.

Bourke, Vernon J., B.A., M.A., Ph.D. (University of Toronto). Professor of Philosophy at St. Louis University; President of the World Union of Catholic Philosophical Societies; Honorary Member of the Société Philosophique de Louvain. President of the American Catholic Philosophical Association

(1949); Director of the Thomistic Institute at St. Louis University (1958); Past Advisory Editor of *Speculum.* Recent publications include *The Pocket Aquinas* (edited with an introduction, 1960); *The Essential Augustine* (edited with an introduction, 1964); *Will in Western Thought* (1964); *Aquinas' Search for Wisdom* (1965). BANEZ, DOMINIC; BELLARMINE, ST. ROBERT; BIEL, GABRIEL; CAJETAN, CARDINAL; CAPREOLUS, JOHN; FONSECA, PETER; JOHN OF ST. THOMAS; MARIANA, JUAN DE; SOTO, DOMINIC DE; SYLVESTER OF FERRARA, FRANCIS; THOMAS AQUINAS, ST.; TOLETUS, FRANCIS; VASQUEZ, GABRIEL.

Bracken, Harry M., B.A. (Trinity College); M.A. (Johns Hopkins); Ph.D. (University of Iowa). Professor of Philosophy at Arizona State University. Formerly taught at the universities of Iowa and Minnesota. Publications include *The Early Reception of Berkeley's Immaterialism: 1710–1713* (1959); "Some Problems of Substance among the Cartesians," *American Philosophical Quarterly* (1964). ARNAULD, ANTOINE; NICOLE, PIERRE.

Brady, Ignatius Charles, O.F.M., B.A., M.A., S.M.L., Ph.D., Lector generalis. Prefect, Theological Commission, Collegio di S. Bonaventura, Franciscan International College of Research (Quaracchi, Italy). Formerly taught at Duns Scotus College (Detroit), St. Bonaventure University, and the Catholic University of America. Editor, William of Vaurouillon, *Liber de Anima* (1948–1949). Author, *History of Ancient Philosophy* (1959) and articles in the *New Scholasticism, Recherches de théologie ancienne et médi évale,* and *Antonianum.* ALEXANDER OF HALES; JOHN OF LA ROCHELLE; PETER LOMBARD.

Brandt, Frithiof, D.Phil. and others. Member of the Royal Danish Academy of Sciences and Letters. Formerly, Professor of Philosophy at the University of Copenhagen (1922–1958). Works include *The Mechanical Conception of Nature by Thomas Hobbes* (1928) and *Soeren Kierkegaard* (1963). HOFFDING, HARALD.

Brandt, R. B., B.A. (Denison); B.A. (Cambridge); Ph.D. (Yale). Professor of Philosophy at the University of Michigan; Vice-President of the American Philosophical Association, Eastern Division; President of the American Society for Political and Legal Philosophy. Guggenheim Fellow (1945–1946). Author, *The Philosophy of Schleiermacher* (1941); *Hopi Ethics: A Theoretical Analysis* (1954); *Ethical Theory* (1959). EMOTIVE THEORY OF ETHICS; EPISTEMOLOGY AND ETHICS, PARALLEL BETWEEN; ETHICAL RELATIVISM; HAPPINESS; HEDONISM.

Braybrooke, David, B.A. (Harvard); M.A., Ph.D. (Cornell). Professor of Philosophy and Politics at Dalhousie University (Canada). A.C.L.S. Advanced Graduate Fellowship at Oxford University (1952–1953); Rockefeller Foundation Grant in Legal and Political Philosophy at Oxford University (1959–1960); Guggenheim Fellow (1962–1963). Coauthor (with C. E. Lindblom), *A Strategy of Decision: Policy Evaluation as a Social Process* (1963). Editor, *Philosophical Problems of the Social Sciences* (with introduction and commentary, 1965). ECONOMICS AND RATIONAL CHOICE; IDEOLOGY.

Brée, Germaine, Agrégation (University of Paris); honorary degrees include D.Litt, D.H.L., LL.D. Vilas Professor at the Institute for Research in the Humanities (Madison, Wisconsin). Chairman of the Department of Romance Languages at New York University (1954–1960). Author, *Marcel Proust and Deliverance From Time* (English ed., 1955); *Camus* (1959); *An Age of Fiction* (with M. Guiton, 1957); *André Gide* (rev. English ed., 1963); *The World of Marcel Proust* (1966); and others. MALRAUX, GEORGES-ANDRÉ; WEIL, SIMONE.

Brimmer, Harvey H., II, Ph.D. Assistant Professor of Philosophy at the University of Maine. LEQUIER (JOSEPH LOUIS), JULES.

Brinton, Crane, A.B., D.Phil. (Oxford); L.H.D. (Hon., Ripon and Kenyon). McLean Professor of Ancient and Modern History at Harvard University; Member of the National Institute of Arts and Letters. Special Assistant with the O.S.S. (London and Paris, 1942–1944); President of the American Historical Association (1963). Publications include *English Political Thought in the Nineteenth Century* (1933); *Decade of Revolution: 1789–1799* (1934); *Anatomy of Revolution* (1938); *Nietzsche* (1941); *United States and Great Britain* (1945); *History of Western Morals* (1949); *The Fate of Man* (edited with an introduction and postscript, 1961). ENLIGHTENMENT; ROMANTICISM.

Brody, Boruch A., B.A. (Brooklyn College); M.A. (Princeton). Fulbright Fellow at Oxford University. Formerly, Assistant in Instruction at Princeton University; Lecturer at Brooklyn College; Princeton National Fellow (1962–1963); N.S.F. Fellow (1963–1965); Kent Fellow (1963–1965). LOGICAL TERMS, GLOSSARY OF.

Brown, Robert, B.A., Ph.D. (University of London). Senior Fellow, Philosophy Department, Institute of Advanced Studies, Australian National University. Author, *Explanation in Social Science* (1963) and papers in the *British Journal for the Philosophy of Science, Mind, Analysis,* and other philosophical journals. BROAD, CHARLIE DUNBAR.

Brummel, Leendert, Litt.Dr. Professor of Library Science at the University of Amsterdam. Past Director of the Royal Library (The Hague). Author, *Frans Hemsterhuis: Een philosofenleven* (Thesis, 1925); *Geschiedenis der Koninklijke Bibliotheek* (1939); *Union Catalogues: Their Problems and Organization* (1956); *Miscellanea Libraria* (1957). HEMSTERHUIS, FRANS.

Buchdahl, Gerd, B.A., M.A. (University of Melbourne and Cambridge). Lecturer in Philosophy of Science and Head of the Department of History and Philosophy of Science, Cambridge University. Formerly, Senior Lecturer-in-Charge, Department of History and Philosophy of Science, University of Melbourne; Lecturer in Philosophy of Science, Oxford University. Author, *The Image of Newton and Locke in the Age of Reason* (1961); *Aristotle, Induction and Necessity* (1963); and numerous philosophical papers in journals and cooperative volumes. CAMPBELL, NORMAN ROBERT.

Cahn, Steven M., A.B. (Columbia). Doctoral candidate at Columbia University. Author of articles in *Analysis, Journal of Philosophy,* and other philosophical journals. CHANCE.

Campbell, Archibald Hunter, M.A. (Edinburgh and Oxford); B.C.L. (Oxford); LL.M. (Birmingham); LL.D. (University of Aberdeen). Regius Professor of Public Law at the University of Edinburgh; Fellow of All Souls College, Oxford University; President of the Classical Association of Scotland. Stowell Fellow of University College, Oxford University (1930–1935); Barber Professor of Jurisprudence at the University of Birmingham (1935–1945); Dean of the Faculty of Law at the University of Edinburgh (1958–1964). Editor, Giorgio Del Vecchio, *Justice* (1952), and H. Kantorowicz, *The Definition of Law* (1958). Author of numerous articles and reviews, mainly on jurisprudence. DEL VECCHIO, GIORGIO.

Campbell, Keith, B.A., M.A. (University of New Zealand); B.Phil. (Oxford). Senior Lecturer in Philosophy at the University of Sydney. Formerly, Senior Lecturer at the University of Melbourne. Author of articles in *Mind, Analysis,* and other philosophical journals. MATERIALISM.

Campo, Mariano, Doctor of Letters. Professor Emeritus of the History of Philosophy at the University of Trieste. Formerly, Free Docent at the Catholic University of Milan; Ordinary Professor at the University of Trieste. Author, *Cristiano Wolff e il razionalismo precritico* (1939); *La genesi del criticismo Kantiano* (2 vols., 1953); *Schizzo storico della esegesi e critica Kantiana* (1959). LIEBMANN, OTTO; NATORP, PAUL; RIEHL, ALOIS.

Cannon, Walter F., M.A., Ph.D. Curator of Astronomy and Physics and Curator in Charge of the Division of Physical Sciences, Smithsonian Institution. Author of various articles on the history of science in Britain in the 19th century. HERSCHEL, JOHN.

Čapek, Milič, Ph.D., M.Sc. (Charles University of Prague). Professor of Philosophy at Boston University. Formerly, taught at the universities of Iowa, Nebraska, and Olmutz (Czechoslovakia); Professor of Philosophy at Carleton College (1948–1962). Author, *Bergson and the Trends of Contemporary Physics* (1938); *Philosophical Impact of Contemporary Physics* (1961); and numerous articles. AMPÈRE, ANDRÉ MARIE; CHANGE; CZECHOSLOVAK PHILOSOPHY; DYNAMISM; ETERNAL RETURN; OSTWALD, WILHELM; RIBOT, THÉODULE ARMAND; TAINE, HIPPOLYTE-ADOLPHE.

Caponigri, A. Robert, A.B., M.A., Ph.D. (University of Chicago). Professor of Philosophy at the University of Notre Dame. Visiting Lecturer at the Luigi Sturzo Institute in Rome (1961, 1964). Publications include *Time and Idea* (1953); *History and Liberty* (1955); *Modern Catholic Thinkers* (1960). CARLINI, ARMANDO; GALLARATE MOVEMENT; GIOBERTI, VINCENZO; MARTINETTI, PIERO; ROSMINI-SERBATI, ANTONIO; SCIACCA, MICHELE FEDERICO; STEFANINI, LUIGI.

Carré, Meyrick H., M.A. Formerly, Reader in Philosophy at the University of Bristol; now retired. Books include *Realists and Nominalists* and *Phases of Thought in England.* PHYSICOTHEOLOGY.

Castañeda, Héctor-Neri, B.A., M.A., Ph.D. (University of Minnesota). Professor of Philosophy and Acting Chairman (1965–1966) of the Philosophy Department of Wayne State University. Publications include *La dialéctica de la conciencia de Si Mismo* (1960); *Morality and the Language of Conduct* (edited with George Nakhnikian, 1963); *Studies in the Philosophy of Mind* (edited, 1966); "Arithmetic and the World," *Australasian Journal of Philosophy* (1959); "The Private Language Argument" (in C. D. Rollins, ed., *Knowledge and Experience,* 1963); and other articles. PRIVATE LANGUAGE PROBLEM.

Catania, Francis J., A.B., M.A. (Loyola); Ph.D. (St. Louis University). Associate Professor of Philosophy at Loyola University. Author of various papers on medieval philosophy. ALBERT THE GREAT.

Caton, Charles E., B.A. (Oberlin College); M.A., Ph.D. (University of Michigan). Associate Professor of Philosophy at the University of Illinois. Editor, *Philosophy and Ordinary Language* (1963). ARTIFICIAL AND NATURAL LANGUAGES.

Caws, Peter, B.Sc. (University of London); M.A., Ph.D. (Yale). Professor and Chairman of the Department of Philosophy, City University of New York, Hunter College; Consultant, Carnegie Corporation of New York. Formerly, Associate Professor and Chairman of the Department of Philosophy at the University of Kansas (to 1962); Executive Associate of the Carnegie Corporation (1962–1965). Translator, J. M. Bocheński, *The Method of Contemporary Thought* (1965). Author, *The Philosophy of Science, A Systematic Account* (1965). SCIENTIFIC METHOD.

Cerf, Walter, Dr.phil. (University of Bonn); Ph.D. (Princeton). Visiting Professor of Philosophy at the University of Wisconsin; Professor of Philosophy at the City University of New York, Brooklyn College. HARTMANN, NICOLAI.

Chadwick, Henry, D.D., Mus.B. Regius Professor of Divinity at Oxford University; Fellow of the British Academy. Gifford Lecturer (1962–1964). Publications include *Origen Contra Celsum* (2nd ed., 1965); *Lessing's Theological Writings* (1956); *The Sentences of Sextus* (1959); *Early Christian Thought and the Classical Tradition* (1966). LESSING, GOTTHOLD EPHRAIM.

Chan, Wing-tsit, Ph.D. (Harvard). Professor of Chinese Culture and Philosophy at Dartmouth College; Adjunct Professor of Chinese Thought at Columbia University. Dean of Faculty at Lingnan University (1929–1936); Chairman of the Division of the Humanities, Dartmouth College (1951–1955). Translator, *Instructions for Practical Living and Other Neo-Confucian Writings by Wang Yang-ming* (1963); translator and compiler, *A Source Book in Chinese Philosophy* (1963); translator, *The Way of Lao Tzu* (1963); Chu Hsi, *Reflections on Things at Hand* (1966). Author, *Religious Trends of Modern China* (1955); *An Outline and an Annotated Bibliography of Chinese Philosophy* (1965). CH'ENG HAO; CH'ENG I; CHINESE PHILOSOPHY; CHUANG TZU; CHU HSI; CONFUCIUS; HU SHIH; LAO TZU; WANG YANG-MING.

Chang, Carsun, B.A. (Waseda University, Japan). President of the Institute of Political Science in Shanghai (1923–1926); Chinese Delegate to the U.N. (1945); Visiting Professor at the University of Washington (1945, 1948); Research Associate at Stanford University (1955–1956); Visiting Professor in India (1950–1951). Publications include *Weltanschauung* (with R. Eucken); *Third Force in China* (1953); "Wang Yang-ming's Philosophy," *Philosophy East and West* (1955); *The Development of Neo-Confucian Thought* (2 vols., 1958). LU HSIANG-SHAN; MENCIUS.

Chisholm, Roderick M., A.B. (Brown); A.M. Ph.D. (Harvard). Romeo Elton Professor of Natural Theology and Professor of Philosophy at Brown University; Consulting Editor of *American Philosophical Quarterly* and *Philosophy and Phenomenological Research.* Publications include *Perceiving: A Philosophical Study* (1957); *Realism and the Background of Phenomenology* (1961); *Philosophy* (with Herbert Feigl, William Frankena, Manley Thompson, and John Passmore, 1965); *Theory of Knowledge* (1966). BRENTANO, FRANZ; INTENTIONALITY; MARTY, ANTON; MEINONG, ALEXIUS.

Christoff, Peter K., A.B. (Oberlin College); M.A., Ph.D. (Brown). Professor of Russian History at San Francisco State College. Visiting Fulbright Professor of Russian Intellectual History at the University of Leiden (1963–1964); also past Visiting Professor of Russian History at Cornell University, Stanford University, and Mills College. Author, *An Introduction to Nineteenth Century Slavophilism. A Study in Ideas,* Vol. I, *A. S. Xomjakov* (1961). KHOMYAKOV, ALEKSEI STEPANOVICH; KIREEVSKY, IVAN VASILIEVICH.

Clapp, James Gordon, A.B., M.A., Ph.D. (Columbia). Professor of Philosophy at the City University of New York, Hunter College. A.C.L.S. Fellow (1950). Author, *Locke's Conception of the Mind* (1937). Editor (with others), *Foundations of Western Thought* (1962). LOCKE, JOHN.

Cohen, Marshall, B.A. (Dartmouth College); M.A., (Harvard). Associate Professor of Philosophy at the University of Chicago; Drama Critic of the *Partisan Review.* Formerly, Junior Fellow, Society of Fellows, and Assistant Professor at Harvard University; Senior Fellow in Law at the Yale Law School; delivered the Lowell Institute Lectures (1957–1958) and the Christian Gauss Seminar in Criticism (Princeton University, 1964–1965). Editor, *The Philosophy of John Stuart Mill* (1965). Contributor to Max Black, ed., *Philosophy in Ameri-*

ca (1965). Author of numerous articles in learned journals and other periodicals. HART, HERBERT LIONEL ADOLPHUS.

Cohen, Robert S., B.A. (Wesleyan); M.S., Ph.D. (Yale). Professor and Chairman of the Department of Physics at Boston University; Chairman of the Boston Colloquium for the Philosophy of Science; Chairman of the American Institute for Marxist Studies. Author, "Alternate Interpretations of the History of Science" (in Philipp Frank, ed., *The Validation of Scientific Theories*); "Dialectical Materialism and Carnap's Logical Empiricism" (in P. A. Schilpp, ed., *The Philosophy of Rudolf Carnap*, 1963); and many other articles. NEURATH, OTTO.

Cole, Margaret, I Class Degree Certificate (Cambridge). President of the Fabian Society; Vice-Chairman of the Further and Higher Education Committee of the Inner London Education Authority. Alderman of the London County Council (1952); Chairman of the Higher Education Committee (1951–1960). Editor, *The Diaries of Beatrice Webb* (2 vols., 1952). Author, *Makers of the Labour Movement* (1948); *Growing up Into Revolution* (1949); *Robert Owen of New Lanark* (1953); *The Story of Fabian Socialism* (1961); and coauthor of many books with G. D. H. Cole. SOCIALISM.

Colie, Rosalie L., A.B. (Vassar College); A.M., Ph.D. (Columbia). Professor in the departments of History and English at the University of Iowa. Past A.C.L.S. Fellow, Fulbright Fellow, Guggenheim Fellow, and others. Publications include *English Influence Upon the Works of Constantijn Huygens* (1956); *Light and Enlightenment: A Study of Cambridge Platonism* (1957); *Paradoxia Epidemica* (1966). ARMINIUS AND ARMINIANISM.

Collins, James, A.B., A.M., Ph.D. (Catholic University of America); L.H.D. (Hon.), Litt.D. Professor of Philosophy at St. Louis University. Author, *The Existentialists: A Critical Study* (1952); *The Mind of Kierkegaard* (1954): *A History of Modern European Philosophy* (1954); *God in Modern Philosophy* (1960); *The Lure of Wisdom* (1962); *Three Paths in Philosophy* (1962). NEWMAN, JOHN HENRY.

Conway, James I., S.J. (1908–1962). Born in New York City, entered the Society of Jesus in Poughkeepsie, N.Y., in 1926. Studied philosophy at Woodstock College in Maryland (1930–1933), where he received his B.A.; instructor in Latin and Greek at St. Peter's College in Jersey City (1933–1936); studied theology in St. Albert's College in Louvain (1936–1940), where he received his S.T.L. Ordained in Belgium in 1939, he returned to the United States in 1940, studied ascetical theology at Auriesville, N.Y. (1940–1941), and philosophy at Fordham University, where he received his Ph.D. (1952). Taught history of philosophy at Woodstock College (1941–1942, 1943–1952), at Bellarmine College (1952–1955), and at Loyola Seminary, College of Philosophy and Letters of Fordham University (1955–1962), where he was Chairman of the Department of Philosophy. He was the author of various articles on the history of philosophy in scholarly journals and completed the manuscript for a book on Descartes, which is projected for publication. MARÉCHAL, JOSEPH.

Corbin, Henry, Dr. honoris causis (University of Teheran). Professor of Islamism at the École des Hautes Études, University of Paris at the Sorbonne; Director of the Department of Iranology, Institut franco-iranien (Teheran). Editor, *Bibliothèque iranienne* (14 vols., 1949–1966). Other publications include *L'Imagination créatrice dans le soufisme d'Ibn Arabi* (1958); *Avicenna and the Visionary Recital* (English translation, 1960); *Trilogie ismaélienne* (1961); *Histoire de la philosophie islamique* (Vol. 1, Paris, 1964). GHAZĀLĪ, ABŪ ḤĀMID MUHAMMAD; IBN BĀJJA; IBN TUFAYL; SOHRAWARDĪ, SHIHĀB AL-DIN YAHYĀ.

Cragg, Gerald R., M.A., Ph.D., Litt.D., D.D. Professor of Church History at the Andover Newton Theological School. Formerly, Professor of Theology at McGill University. Author, *From Puritanism to the Age of Reason: 1600–1700* (1951); *Puritanism in the Period of the Great Persecution: 1660–1688* (1957); *The Church and the Age of Reason* (1961); *Reason and Authority in the Eighteenth Century* (1964). LAW, WILLIAM; MELANCHTHON, PHILIPP.

Cranston, Maurice, B.Litt., M.A. (Oxford). Reader in Political Science at the University of London; Fellow of the Royal Society of Literature. Visiting Professor of Government at Harvard University (1965–1966). Author, *Freedom* (1963); *John Locke, A Biography* (1957); *Sartre* (1963); *What Are Human Rights?* (1964). BACON, FRANCIS; BURKE, EDMUND; FASCISM; LIBERALISM; MONTESQUIEU, BARON DE; TOLERATION.

Crites, Stephen D., B.A. (Ohio Wesleyan); B.D., M.A., Ph.D. (Yale). Assistant Professor of Religion at Wesleyan University. Fulbright Scholar in Germany (1959–1960); Instructor in Philosophy and Religion at Colgate University (1960–1961); Visiting Assistant Professor of Philosophy at the University of California, Berkeley (1965); Lilly Fellow (1965–1966). BAUER, BRUNO; HEGELIANISM; ROSENKRANZ, JOHANN KARL FRIEDRICH; VISCHER, FRIEDRICH THEODOR.

Crocker, Lester G., B.A., M.A., Ph.D. Dean of the Graduate School and W. G. Leutner Distinguished Professor of Romance Languages at Western Reserve University; Member and Correspondent of the Société d'Histoire Littéraire de la France and the Société francaise d'Étude du XVIIIe siècle. Past Member of the Institute for Advanced Study (Princeton, N.J.); past Visiting Professor, University College, University of London; former Guggenheim Fellow and Fulbright Research Fellow. Author, *Two Diderot Studies* (1953); *The Embattled Philosopher: A Biography of Denis Diderot* (1954); *An Age of Crisis: Man and World in Eighteenth Century French Thought* (1959); *Nature and Culture: Ethical Thought in the French Enlightenment* (1963). BONNET, CHARLES; CABANIS, PIERRE-JEAN GEORGES; NAIGEON, JACQUES ANDRÉ; ROBINET, JEAN-BAPTISTE-RENÉ; SAINT-HYACINTHE, THÉMISUEL DE; VAUVENARGUES, LUC DE CLAPIERS, MARQUIS DE; VOLNEY, CONSTANTIN-FRANÇOIS DE CHASSEBOEUF, COMTE DE.

Cummings, Philip W., B.A. (Bowdoin College). Lecturer in Philosophy at the City University of New York, Hunter College; Senior Editor of *The Encyclopedia of Philosophy*. Formerly, Assistant Editor of *Webster's Third New International Dictionary* and *Webster's Seventh Collegiate Dictionary*; Lecturer in Philosophy at the Bridgeport Engineering Institute. KIRCHHOFF, GUSTAV ROBERT; KÖHLER, WOLFGANG; POLITICAL PHILOSOPHY, HISTORY OF (section on Hegel through recent political thought); RACISM.

Cummins, Phillip D., B.A., M.A., Ph.D. Assistant Professor of Philosophy at the University of Iowa. LE CLERC, JEAN.

Curry, Haskell B., A.B., A.M., (Harvard); Ph.D. (University of Göttingen). Evan Pugh Research Professor at the University of Pennsylvania; Assesseur, Académie Internationale de Philosophie des Sciences; Honorary Visiting Professor at the University of Louvain. President of the Association for Symbolic Logic (1937–1939); Fulbright Research Scholar at the University of Louvain (1950–1951); Member of the Conference Board of the Mathematical Sciences (1958–1963); Member of the U.S. National Committee of the International Union for the History and Philosophy of Science (1959–1963). Author, *A Theory of Formal Deducibility* (1950); *Outlines of a Formalist Philosophy of Mathematics* (1951); *Leçons de logique algébrique* (1952); *Combinatory Logic* (with Robert Feys, 1958); *Foundations of Mathematical Logic* (1963). LOGIC, COMBINATORY.

Dales, Richard C., B.A. (University of Rochester); M.A., Ph.D. (University of Colorado). Associate Professor of History at the University of Southern California. A.C.L.S. Fellow (1960–1961). Publications include *Roberti Grossetesti Commentarius in VIII Libros Physicorum Aristotelis* (1963); "Robert Grosseteste's Scientific Works," *Isis* (1961); "The *Quaestio De Fluxu et Refluxu Maris* Attributed to Robert Grosseteste," *Speculum* (1962); "Anonymi *De Elementis*," *Isis* (1961). GROSSETESTE, ROBERT; PSEUDO-GROSSETESTE; THOMAS OF YORK.

Danto, Arthur C., A.B. (Wayne State); M.A., Ph.D. (Columbia). Associate Professor of History at Columbia University. Fulbright Fellow (1949); A.C.L.S. Fellow (1961). Coeditor (with Sidney Morgenbesser), *Philosophy of Science* (1960). Author, *Analytical Philosophy of History* (1965) and *Nietzsche as Philosopher* (1965). NATURALISM; PERSONS; PHILOSOPHY OF SCIENCE, PROBLEMS OF.

Dar, B. A., M.A. Director of the Iqbal Academy (Karachi); Managing Editor of the *Pakistan Philosophical Journal.* Formerly, Reader in Islamics at the Institute of Islamic Culture (Lahore); Honorary Assistant Editor of *Iqbal.* Author, *A Study in Iqbal's Philosophy; Iqbal and Post-Kantian Voluntarism; Religious Thought of Sayyid Ahmad Khan; Quranic Ethics.* IQBAL, MUHAMMAD.

Davie, G. E., M.A., D.Litt. (University of Edinburgh). Reader in Logic and Metaphysics, Department of Philosophy, University of Edinburgh. Formerly, Head of the Department of Moral Philosophy at Queen's University of Belfast. Author, *The Democratic Intellect* (2d ed., 1966). BAIN, ALEXANDER; FERRIER, JAMES FREDERICK; HODGSON, SHADWORTH HOLLOWAY; MANSEL, HENRY LONGUEVILLE.

Davis, Martin, B.S. (City College); M.A., Ph.D. (Princeton). Professor of Mathematics at New York University. Former academic positions at Yeshiva University, Rensselaer Polytechnic Institute, Ohio State University, University of California, Institute for Advanced Study (Princeton, N.J.), and the University of Illinois. Author, *Computability and Unsolvability* (1958). Editor, *The Undecidable* (1965). RECURSIVE FUNCTION THEORY.

De Lacy, Phillip H., B.A., M.A. (University of Washington); Ph.D. (Princeton). Professor of Classics at Cornell University. Professor of Classics at Washington University (St. Louis, 1949–1961); Guggenheim Fellow (1960–1961); Professor of Classics at Northwestern University (1961–1965). CICERO, MARCUS TULLIUS; EPICUREANISM AND THE EPICUREAN SCHOOL; EPICURUS; PLUTARCH OF CHAERONEA.

Desmonde, William H., B.A., M.A., Ph.D. Research Staff Member of the International Business Machines Corporation; Lecturer at the New School for Social Research. Author, "G. H. Mead and Freud: American Social Psychology and Psychoanalysis," *Journal of Psychoanalytic Psychology* (1956), and numerous other articles; *Magic, Myth, and Money* (1962); *Computers and Their Uses* (1964). MEAD, GEORGE HERBERT.

Diamandopoulos, P., B.A., M.A., Ph.D. (Harvard). Dean of Faculty and Associate Professor of Philosophy at Brandeis University. Formerly, Consultant in the History of Physics at the Smithsonian Institution; Chairman of the History of Ideas Program at Brandeis University. Author of papers and reviews in scholarly journals on the history of ancient philosophy. ALCMAEON OF CROTON; ANAXIMENES; ARCHE; ARCHYTAS OF TARENTUM; CHAOS AND COSMOS; DIOGENES OF APOLLONIA; NEMESIS; PHILOLAUS OF CROTON; THALES OF MILETUS.

Di Lascia, Alfred, B.A. (Queens College); M.A. (Fordham University). Associate Professor of Philosophy at Manhattan College; Associate Editor of *Cross Currents;* Ph.D. candidate at Fordham University. Past Editorial Advisor in American Philosophy for the *Enciclopedia filosofica.* Author of articles in *Thought* and *Cross Currents.* STURZO, LUIGI.

Donagan, Alan, A.B., A.M. (University of Melbourne); B.Phil. (Oxford). Professor of Philosophy at the University of Illinois. Associate Professor and Chairman of the Department of Philosophy at the University of Minnesota (1957–1961); Professor and Chairman of the Department of Philosophy at Indiana University (1961–1965). Author, *The Later Philosophy of R. G. Collingwood* (1962). COLLINGWOOD, ROBIN GEORGE.

Doney, Willis, B.A., M.A., Ph.D. (Princeton). Associate Professor of Philosophy at Dartmouth College. Formerly taught at Cornell University and Ohio State University; Visiting Lecturer at the University of Michigan and Harvard University. Author of papers in the *Philosophical Review, Journal of the History of Ideas, Philosophy and Phenomenological Research.* CARTESIANISM; GEULINCX, ARNOLD; MALEBRANCHE, NICOLAS.

Donnellan, Keith S., B.A. (University of Maryland); M.A., Ph.D. (Cornell). Associate Professor of Philosophy at Cornell University; Coeditor of the *Philosophical Review.* Author of papers in the *Journal of Philosophy* and the *Philosophical Review.* PARADIGM-CASE ARGUMENT; REASONS AND CAUSES.

Dowd, Douglas F., A.B., Ph.D. (University of California, Berkeley). Professor of Economics and Acting Chairman (1965–1966) of the Department of Economics at Cornell University. Editor and contributor, *Thorstein Veblen: A Critical Reappraisal* (1958). Author, *Modern Economic Problems in Historical Perspective* (1962); *Thorstein Veblen* (1964). VEBLEN, THORSTEIN BUNDE.

Drake, Stillman, A.B. (University of California, Berkeley). Municipal Finance Consultant, San Francisco. Publications include English translations of Galileo's scientific writings and various papers on Galileo and his scientific work. GALILEO GALILEI; STALLO, JOHN BERNARD.

Dray, William H., B.A. (University of Toronto); B.A., M.A., D.Phil. (Oxford). Professor of Philosophy at the University of Toronto. A.C.L.S. Fellow (1960–1961). Editor, *Philosophical Analysis and History* (1966). Author, *Laws and Explanation in History* (1957); *Philosophy of History* (1964). DETERMINISM IN HISTORY; HISTORY AND VALUE JUDGMENTS; HOLISM AND INDIVIDUALISM IN HISTORY AND SOCIAL SCIENCE; PHILOSOPHY OF HISTORY; SPENGLER, OSWALD.

Duggan, Timothy J., A.B., M.A. (Brown); M.A. (Harvard); Ph.D. (Brown). Associate Professor and Chairman of the Philosophy Department of Dartmouth College. Author of articles in the *Philosophical Review,* the *Philosophical Quarterly,* and the *Journal of Philosophy.* HAMILTON, WILLIAM.

Dummett, Michael, B.A., M.A. (Oxford). Reader in the Philosophy of Mathematics at Oxford University; Fellow of All Souls College, Oxford University. Harkness Fellow, University of California, Berkeley (1955–1956); Visiting Lecturer at the University of Ghana (1958); Visiting Professor at Stanford University (1961, 1962, 1964). Author, "Truth," *PAS* (1958–1959); "Wittgenstein's Philosophy of Mathematics," *Philosophical Review* (1959); "Bringing About the Past," *Philosophical Review* (1963); and others. FREGE, GOTTLOB.

Dunkel, Harold B., A.B., Ph.D. (University of Chicago). Professor of Education at the University of Chicago; Fellow of the Center for Advanced Study in the Behavioral Sciences (1965–1966). Publications include *General Education in the Humanities* (1947); *Second-language Learning* (1948);

French in the Elementary School (1962); *Whitehead on Education* (1965). HERBART, JOHANN FRIEDRICH.

Dye, James Wayne, A.B. (Carson-Newman College); B.D. (New Orleans Baptist Theological Seminary); Ph.D. (Tulane). Assistant Professor of Philosophy at Washington University (St. Louis); Secretary of the Missouri State Philosophical Association. Author, "Berdyaev on 'Creativity,'" *The Personalist* (1965), and other articles. BERDYAEV, NIKOLAI.

Earle, William James, A.B. Instructor in the Department of Philosophy at Long Island University; Graduate Student at Columbia University. JAMES, WILLIAM.

Easton, Loyd D., A.B. (DePauw); M.A., Ph.D. (Boston University). Professor and Chairman of the Department of Philosophy at Ohio Wesleyan University; Kent Fellow, Society for Religion in Higher Education; President of the Ohio Philosophical Association (1964–1967). Past Member of the Council of the American Association of University Professors; Visiting Professor of Philosophy at Ohio State University (1957). Coauthor, *Values and Policy in American Society* (1954). Author, *Ethics, Policy, and Social Ends* (1955); "Hegelianism in 19th Century Ohio," *Journal of the History of Ideas;* and other articles. HARRIS, WILLIAM TORREY.

Ebbinghaus, Julius, Dr.phil. Professor ordinarius emeritus at the University of Marburg. Acting Rector of the University of Marburg (1945–1946). Publications include *Relativer und absoluter Idealismus* (1919); *Zu Deutschlands Schicksalswende* (2d ed., 1947); *John Locke: Ein Brief über Toleranz* (translated with an introduction and commentary, 2d. ed., 1966); and numerous articles, chiefly on Kantian philosophy and the philosophy of law, in scholarly journals. COHEN, HERMANN.

Edelstein, Ludwig (1902–1965). Born in Berlin; attended the University of Berlin (1921–1924); received his Ph.D. from the University of Heidelberg (1929). Taught philosophy and the history of medicine at the University of Berlin (1930–1933); Associate (1934–1939) and Associate Professor (1939–1947) of the History of Medicine at Johns Hopkins University; Associate Professor of Classical Languages and Literature at the University of Washington (1947–1948); Professor of Greek at the University of California (1948–1950); Professor of Humanistic Studies at Johns Hopkins University (1952–1960); Professor of the History of Science and Philosophy at the Rockefeller Institute (1960–1965). Publications include *Peri Aeron und die Sammlung der Hippokratischen Schriften* (1931); "The Philosophical System of Posidonius," *American Journal of Philology* (1936); *The Hippocratic Oath* (the *Supplement* to the *Bulletin of the History of Medicine,* 1943). HIPPOCRATES OF COS; POSIDONIUS.

Edwards, Paul, B.A., M.A. (University of Melbourne); Ph.D. (Columbia). Associate Professor of Philosophy at the City University of New York, Brooklyn College; Lecturer in Philosophy at the New School for Social Research. Formerly taught at the University of Melbourne; Columbia University; City College of New York; the University of California, Berkeley; and New York University; Guggenheim Fellow (1964–1965). Coeditor (with Arthur Pap), *A Modern Introduction to Philosophy* (2d ed., 1965). Editor, Bertrand Russell, *Why I Am Not a Christian* (with an introduction and appendix, 1957). Author, "Bertrand Russell's Doubts About Induction," *Mind* (1949): *The Logic of Moral Discourse* (1955); "The Cosmological Argument," *The Rationalist Annual* (1959); "Professor Tillich's Confusions," *Mind* (1965); and other articles. ATHEISM; ATHEISMUSSTREIT; COMMON CONSENT ARGUMENTS FOR THE EXISTENCE OF GOD; LIFE, MEANING AND VALUE OF; "MY DEATH"; PANPSYCHISM; POPPER-LYNKEUS, JOSEF; REICH, WILHELM; RUSSELL, BERTRAND ARTHUR WILLIAM (sections on life and social theories; ethics and critique of religion); WHY.

Elevitch, Bernard, B.A., M.A. (University of Minnesota); Ph.D. (Columbia). Assistant Professor of Philosophy at the University of Massachusetts (Boston). Assistant Professor at Fairleigh Dickinson University (1962–1965). Author of articles and reviews on French literature and philosophy in the *Massachusetts Review* and the St. Louis *Post-Dispatch.* BRUNSCHVICG, LÉON.

Eliade, Mircea, M.A., Ph.D. (University of Bucharest). Sewell L. Avery Distinguished Service Professor of History of Religions and Professor of the Committee on Social Thought at the University of Chicago. Formerly, Assistant Professor at the University of Bucharest and Visiting Professor at the École des Hautes Études, University of Paris at the Sorbonne. Author, *The Myth of the Eternal Return* (1954); *Patterns in Comparative Religion* (1957); *Birth and Rebirth* (1958); *The Sacred and the Profane* (1958); *Yoga* (1958); *Images and Symbols* (1959); *Myths, Dreams, and Mysteries* (1960); *The Forge and the Crucible* (1961); *Shamanism* (1963); *Myth and Reality* (1963); *The One and the Two* (1965). IONESCU, NAE; RĂDULESCU-MOTRU, CONSTANTIN; RUMANIAN PHILOSOPHY.

Elias, Julius A., B.S. A.M., Ph.D. (Columbia). Assistant Professor of Philosophy at the City University of New York, City College. Author, "Friedrich Schiller—The Poet as Philosopher" (Thesis, 1963). Translator, J. C. F. Schiller, *On Naive and Sentimental Poetry* (1965). SCHILLER, FRIEDRICH.

Ellis, Brian, B.A., B.Sc. (University of Adelaide); B.Phil. (Oxford). Reader in the History and Philosophy of Science at the University of Melbourne. Visiting Associate Professor of Philosophy at the University of Pittsburgh (1962–1963). Author, *Basic Concepts of Measurement* (1966). MEASUREMENT.

Emery, Stephen A., A.B., Ph.D. (Cornell). Professor of Philosophy at Bishop College (Dallas). Professor of Philosophy at the University of North Carolina (1943–1963). Translator (with W. T. Emery), Wilhelm Dilthey, *The Essence of Philosophy* (1954). Author of numerous articles on philosophy in the *Encyclopedia International* and the *Universal Encyclopedia.* DESSOIR, MAX.

Emmen, James Antony (Father Aquilinus), O.F.M., Th.D. Member of the Theological Section, Collegio di S. Bonaventura, Franciscan International College of Research (Quaracchi, Italy). Member of the Commissio pro Edendis Operibus Ioannis Duns Scoti (1939–1942); Lector of Philosophy (1942–1949); Lector of Dogmatic Theology (1942–1945, 1949–1955). Author of several publications in the series Bibliotheca Franciscana Scholastica Medii Aevi and numerous articles in learned journals and encyclopedias. MATTHEW OF ACQUASPARTA; OLIVI, PETER JOHN; PETER AUREOL.

Emmet, Dorothy Mary, A.M. (Radcliffe College); M.A. (Oxford and the University of Manchester). Sir Samuel Hall Professor of Philosophy at the University of Manchester (to October 1966). Author, *Whitehead's Philosophy of Organism* (1932); *The Nature of Metaphysical Thinking* (1946); *Function, Purpose and Powers* (1958); *Rules, Roles and Relations* (1966). ALEXANDER, SAMUEL; FUNCTIONALISM IN SOCIOLOGY; WHITEHEAD, ALFRED NORTH.

Etzkorn, Ferdinand, O.F.M., Ph.D. Member of the Faculty at Our Lady of Angels Franciscan Seminary. Publications include "The Grades of Form According to Roger Marston, O.F.M.," *Franziskanische Studien* (1962). MARSTON, ROGER; PECKHAM, JOHN; RICHARD OF MEDIAVILLA.

Evans, Joseph W., B.A., M.A. (University of Western Ontario); Ph.D. (Notre Dame). Associate Professor of Philosophy at the University of Notre Dame; Director of the Jacques Maritain Center, Notre Dame. Ford Faculty Fellow at Yale University (1953–1954). Editor (with L. R. Ward), *The Social and Political Philosophy of Jacques Maritain: Selected Readings* (1955). Translator, Jacques Maritain, *Art and Scholasticism and The Frontiers of Poetry* (1962). Editor, *Jacques Maritain: The Man and His Achievement* (with an introduction, 1963). MARITAIN, JACQUES.

Ezorsky, Gertrude, M.A., Ph.D. (New York University). Assistant Professor of Philosophy at the City University of New York, Brooklyn College. Fellow of the American Association of University Women (1957). Publications include "Truth in Context," *Journal of Philosophy* (1963). PERFORMATIVE THEORY OF TRUTH; PRAGMATIC THEORY OF TRUTH.

Fairweather, Eugene R., B.A. (McGill); M.A., B.D. (University of Toronto); S.T.M., Th.D. (Union Theological Seminary). Keble Professor of Divinity, Trinity College, University of Toronto. Associate Professor of Dogmatic Theology and Ethics, Trinity College, University of Toronto (1949–1964); Bishop Paddock Lecturer, General Theological Seminary (1956); Hale Memorial Lecturer, Seabury-Western Theological Seminary (1963); Editor of the *Canadian Journal of Theology*. Editor, *A Scholastic Miscellany: Anselm to Ockham* (1956); *The Oxford Movement* (1964). ANSELM, ST. (section on theology); CAROLINGIAN RENAISSANCE; DAVID OF DINANT; ERIGENA, JOHN SCOTUS; HENRY OF GHENT; ISAAC OF STELLA; PETER DAMIAN; WILLIAM OF MOERBECKE.

Fay, Sidney B., A.B., Ph.D. (Harvard); Litt.D. (Smith College); D.H.L. (Columbia). Professor Emeritus at Harvard University. Professor of History at Dartmouth College (1902–1914), at Smith College (1914–1929), and at Harvard University (1929–1946). Author, *Origins of the World War* (1929) and many others. MEINECKE, FRIEDRICH.

Feigl, Herbert, Ph.D. (University of Vienna). Director of the Minnesota Center for Philosophy of Science, and Professor of Philosophy at the University of Minnesota; Member, Board of Directors, American Humanist Association; Member, Board of Governors, Philosophy of Science Association; Member, Académie Internationale de Philosophie des Sciences. Taught at the University of Iowa (1931–1940); Visiting Professor at the University of California (Berkeley), Columbia University, the University of Hawaii, the Institute for Advanced Studies (Vienna); President of the American Philosophical Association, Western Division (1962–1963); Rockefeller Fellow (1930–1931, 1940); Guggenheim Fellow (1947); Fulbright Fellow (1965); Gavin D. Young Lecturer at the University of Adelaide (1965). Coeditor (with Wilfrid Sellars), *Readings in Philosophical Analysis* (1949) and *Philosophical Studies;* (with May Brodbeck), *Readings in the Philosophy of Science* (1953); (with others), *Minnesota Studies in the Philosophy of Science*, Vols. I–III (1956–1962); (with George Maxwell), *Current Issues in the Philosophy of Science* (1960). Author of numerous articles in philosophical journals and collective books. MILLER, DICKINSON S.

Feinberg, Joel, Ph.D. (University of Michigan). Associate Professor of Philosophy at Princeton University. Assistant Professor of Philosophy at Brown University (1955–1962); Fellow of the Center for Advanced Studies in the Behavioral Sciences (Stanford, California, 1960–1961); Liberal Arts Fellow at Harvard Law School (1963–1964). Author of articles in *Nomos III, Nomos VI, Ethics, Philosophical Review,* and other journals and collective books, including Max Black, ed., *Philosophy in America* (1965). ANALYTIC JURISPRUDENCE.

Fellows, Otis, A.B. (American University); M.A., Ph.D. (Brown). Professor of French Literature and Chairman of the Italian Department at Columbia University; Member of the Board of Trustees and Cultural Advisor of the Lycée de Los Angeles. Formerly, Intelligence Officer with the Office of War Information (1943–1945); Member of the Board of Trustees of Horace Mann School for Boys; Guggenheim Fellow (1959–1960). Author, *French Opinion of Molière; The Periodical Press in Liberated Paris;* and numerous articles in scholarly journals. Founder and editor of *Diderot Studies.* BUFFON, GEORGES-LOUIS LECLERC, COMTE DE; CYRANO DE BERGERAC, SAVINIEN DE; FONTENELLE, BERNARD LE BOVIER DE; MAILLET, BENOÎT DE.

Ferré Frederick, A.B., M.A., Ph.D. Associate Professor of Philosophy at Dickinson College. Author, *Language, Logic and God* (1961) and *Exploring the Logic of Faith* (1962). Editor, *Paley's Natural Theology* (1963). ANALOGY IN THEOLOGY.

Feyerabend, Paul K., Ph.D. (University of Vienna). Professor of Philosophy at the University of California, Berkeley. BOLTZMANN, LUDWIG; HEISENBERG, WERNER; PLANCK, MAX; SCHRÖDINGER, ERWIN.

Filipović, Vladimir, D.Phil. Professor and Head of the Department of Philosophy, Faculty of Arts, University of Zagreb (Yugoslavia). Formerly, Dean of the Faculty of Arts, University of Zagreb; President of the Croatian Philosophical Society. Publications (in Croatian) include *Modern Trends in Psychology* (1935); *The Philosophy of the Renaissance* (1957); *German Idealism* (1962); *European Philosophy in the 19th Century* (1965). MARULIĆ, MARKO.

Fisher, Alden L., B.S., M.A., Lic. en Ps., Doc. en Ps. Associate Professor of Philosophy at St. Louis University; Associate Editor of the *Modern Schoolman* and the *New Scholasticism.* Fulbright Fellow at the University of Louvain (1953–1955); Director of the University Honors Program at St. Louis University (1961–1964). Translator, Maurice Merleau-Ponty, *The Structure of Behavior* (1963). Author, "Freud and the Image of Man," *Insight* (1963), and other articles. MERCIER, DÉSIRÉ JOSEPH.

Fishman, Sterling, B.A. (Washington University, St. Louis); M.S., Ph.D. (University of Wisconsin). Assistant Professor in the departments of History and Educational Policy Studies, University of Wisconsin. Awarded Gratitude Fellowship from the Federal Republic of Germany (1958–1959). Author, "Lassalle on Heraclitus of Ephesus," *Journal of the History of Ideas* (1962); "The Rise of Hitler as a Beer Hall Orator," *Review of Politics* (1964). LASSALLE, FERDINAND.

Flew, Antony, M.A. (Oxford). Professor of Philosophy at the University of Keele. Lecturer in Philosophy at Christ Church, Oxford University (1949–1950); Lecturer in Moral Philosophy at the University of Aberdeen (1950–1954); Visiting Professor of Philosophy at New York University (1958), Swarthmore College (1961), the universities of Adelaide and Melbourne (1963), and the University of Pittsburgh (1965). Author, *A New Approach to Psychical Research* (1953); *Hume's Philosophy of Belief* (1961); *God and Philosophy* (1966). ENDS AND MEANS; IMMORTALITY; MALTHUS, THOMAS ROBERT; MIDDLETON, CONYERS; MIRACLES; PRECOGNITION.

Flygt, Sten Gunnar, B.A., M.A., Ph.D. Professor of German at Vanderbilt University (Tennessee). Guggenheim Fellow (1958). Author, *Friedrich Hebbel's Conception of Movement in the Absolute and in History* (1952); *The Notorious Dr. Bahrdt* (1953). BAHRDT, CARL FRIEDRICH; HEBBEL, CHRISTIAN FRIEDRICH.

Fogelin, Robert J., B.A. (University of Rochester); M.A., Ph.D. (Yale). Associate Professor of Philosophy at Pomona College. BLANSHARD, BRAND.

Fraenkel, Abraham A., (1891–1965). Born in Munich; received his Ph.D. from the University of Marburg. Professor at the University of Marburg and the University of Kiel; immigrated to Israel in 1929; joined the Hebrew University of Jerusalem and helped to found the Institute of Mathematics, of which he was Chairman for many years; also helped to found the Adult Education Center at the Hebrew University and served as Chairman for 25 years. Rector of the Hebrew University (1938–1940); Chairman of the Israel Association for the Advancement of Science (1953–1956); Member of the Council of the Association for Symbolic Logic (1956–1959); Member of the Board of Governors of the Hebrew University (1959–1965). Publications include *Einleitung in die Mengenlehre* (3d ed., 1928; reprint, 1948); *Abstract Set Theory* (3d ed., 1965); *Foundations of Set Theory* (with Yehoshua Bar-Hillel, 1957). CANTOR, GEORG; SET THEORY.

Frankel, Charles, A.B., Ph.D. (Columbia). Assistant U.S. Secretary of State for Educational and Cultural Affairs; Chairman, Committee on Professional Ethics, American Association of University Professors. Member, Philosophy Department, Columbia University (1939–1965), Professor since 1956. Fulbright Professor, University of Paris (1953–1954); past Guggenheim Fellow and Carnegie Fellow; endowed lectureships at the University of Dublin, the New York School of Social Work, Bennington College, Ohio University, and Bowdoin College. General Editor, *Introduction to Contemporary Civilization in the West* (1941), Past Chief Consulting Editor of *Current*. Editor, Rousseau, *The Social Contract* (1947); *The Uses of Philosophy* (1955); *Issues in University Education* (1959); *The Golden Age of American Philosophy* (1960). Author, *The Faith of Reason* (1948); *The Bear and the Beaver* (1951); *The Case for Modern Man* (1956); *The Democratic Prospect* (1962); *The Love of Anxiety* (1965). PROGRESS, THE IDEA OF.

Frankena, William K., A.B. (Calvin College); A.M. (University of Michigan); Ph.D. (Harvard). Professor of Philosophy at the University of Michigan; President of the American Philosophical Association, Western Division. Guggenheim Fellow (1948–1949); Chairman of the Department of Philosophy at the University of Michigan (1947–1960); Chairman of the Board of Officers of the American Philosophical Association (1962–1964). Publications include *Ethics* (1963); *Philosophy of Education* (1965); *Three Historical Philosophies of Education* (1965). VALUE AND VALUATION.

Frankfurt, Harry G., B.A., M.A., Ph.D. (Johns Hopkins). Associate Professor at the Rockefeller University. Assistant Professor at Ohio State University (1959–1962); Associate Professor at Harpur College (1962–1963). Author of "Descartes' Validation of Reason," *American Philosophical Quarterly*; "Philosophical Certainty," *Philosophical Review*; "Meaning, Truth and Pragmatism," *Philosophical Quarterly*; and others. DOUBT.

Friedmann, Wolfgang, Dr.jur. (University of Berlin); LL.M., LL.D. (University of London); LL.M. (University of Melbourne); Barrister at Law, Middle Temple, England. Professor of Law and Director of International Legal Research at Columbia University. Reader in Law, University of London (1938–1947); served with the Allied Military Government of Germany (1944–1947); Professor of Public Law, University of Melbourne (1947–1950); Professor of Law at the University of Toronto (1950–1955); Visiting Professor, New York University Law School (1954, 1957, 1960); Director, Summer Seminars in International Law and Economic Development Problems for Civil Servants (Dar es Salaam, Tanganyika, 1964–1966). Editor, *The Public Corporation* (1954); *Anti-trust laws* (1956); *Joint International Business Ventures* (with George Kalmanoff, 1961); and others. Author, *Legal Theory* (4th ed., 1960); *Introduction to World Politics* (4th ed., 1960); *The Allied Military Government of Germany* (1947); *Principles of Australian Administrative Law* (with D. G. Benjafield, 2d ed., 1962); *Law and Social Change in Contemporary Britain* (1951); *Law in a Changing Society* (1959); *The Changing Structure of International Law* (1964). GROTIUS, HUGO; RADBRUCH, GUSTAV; STAMMLER, RUDOLF.

Friess, Horace L., A.B., Ph.D. (Columbia). J. L. Buttenwieser Professor of Human Relations; Member of the departments of Philosophy and Religion at Columbia University; Member of the Board of Leaders, New York Society for Ethical Culture. Editor of the *Review of Religion* (1943–1958); Chairman of the Department of Religion at Columbia University (1962–1965). Publications include *Schleiermacher's Soliloquies* (edited, 1926); *Religion in Various Cultures* (edited with H. W. Schneider, 1932). STEINER, RUDOLF.

Frye, Northrop, M.A., D.D., LL.D., D.Litt. Principal of Victoria College, University of Toronto; Fellow of the Royal Society of Canada. Chairman of the Department of English at Victoria College (1952–1959). Author, *Fearful Symmetry: A Study of William Blake* (1947); *Anatomy of Criticism* (1957); *The Return of Eden* (1963); *A Natural Perspective* (1963); *Fables of Identity* (1963); *The Well-tempered Critic* (1963); *T. S. Eliot* (1964); *The Educated Imagination* (1964). BLAKE, WILLIAM.

Furley, David J., M.A. (Cambridge). Reader in Greek and Latin, University College, University of London. Visiting Professor at the University of Minnesota (1960–1961); Member of the Institute for Advanced Study (Princeton, N.J., 1964). Editor, *Aristotle: On the Cosmos* (1956). HOMER; MELISSUS OF SAMOS; PARMENIDES.

Furlong, Edmund J., M.A. Professor of Moral Philosophy at the University of Dublin; Fellow of Trinity College, Dublin. Author, *A Study in Memory* (1951); *Imagination* (1961). WILSON, JOHN COOK.

Gale, Richard M., Ph.D. (New York University). Assistant Professor of Philosophy at the University of Pittsburgh. Author, "Is It Now Now?" *Mind* (1964); "The Egocentric Particular and Token-reflexive Analyses of Tense," *Philosophical Review* (1964); "Why a Cause Cannot Be Later Than Its Effect," *Review of Metaphysics* (1965); and others. INDEXICAL SIGNS, EGOCENTRIC PARTICULARS, AND TOKEN-REFLEXIVE WORDS; PROPOSITIONS, JUDGMENTS, SENTENCES, AND STATEMENTS.

Gardiner, Patrick, M.A. (Oxford). Fellow and Tutor in Philosophy, Magdalen College, Oxford University. Lecturer in Philosophy, Wadham College, Oxford University (1949–1952); Fellow of St. Antony's College, Oxford University (1953–1958); Visiting Professor in Philosophy, Columbia University (1955). Editor, *Theories in History* (1959). Author, *The Nature of Historical Explanation* (1952); *Schopenhauer* (1963); and articles in *Mind*, *Philosophy*, *PAS*, and others. BUCKLE, HENRY THOMAS; BURCKHARDT, JAKOB; HERDER, JOHANN GOTTFRIED; IRRATIONALISM; SAINT-SIMON, CLAUDE-HENRI DE ROUVROY, COMTE DE; SCHOPENHAUER, ARTHUR; SPECULATIVE SYSTEMS OF HISTORY; TOYNBEE, ARNOLD JOSEPH; VICO, GIAMBATTISTA.

Gardner, Martin, A.B. (University of Chicago). Editor and writer, Mathematical Games Department of *Scientific American*. Publications include *Great Essays in Science* (edited, 1957); *Logic Machines and Diagrams* (1958); *The Annotated Alice* (1960); *Relativity for the Million* (1962); *The Annotated Ancient Mariner* (1965). LOGIC DIAGRAMS; LOGIC MACHINES.

Garin, Eugenio, Dr.phil. Ordinary Professor of the History of Philosophy, Faculty of Letters and Philosophy, University of Florence. Publications include *Giovanni Pico della Mirandola* (1937); *L'illuminismo inglese* (1941); *Filosofi italiani del Quattrocento* (1940); *La filosofia* [*italiana*] (2 vols., 1947);

L'umanesimo italiano (1952); *Cronache di filosofia italiana* (1955); *L'educazione in Europa* (1957); *Studi sul platonismo medievale* (1958); *La cultura filosofica del Rinascimento italiano* (1961); *Scienza e vita civile nel Rinascimento* (1965). BANFI, ANTONIO; BONATELLI, FRANCESCO; GALLUPPI, PASQUALE; GENOVESI, ANTONIO; PASTORE, VALENTINO ANNIBALE; ROMAGNOSI, GIAN DOMENICO; VANINI, GIULIO CESARE.

Garver, Newton, A.B. (Swarthmore College); B.Phil. (Oxford); Ph.D. (Cornell). Lecturer in Philosophy at the State University of New York at Buffalo. Formerly, Instructor in Philosophy at the University of Minnesota. BLACK, MAX; RULES; SUBJECT AND PREDICATE.

Geanakoplos, Deno J., Ph.D. (Harvard); D.Litt. (University of Pisa). Professor of Medieval and Byzantine History at the University of Illinois; Coeditor, *Greek, Roman, Byzantine Studies;* Member of the Board of *Medieval and Renaissance Studies.* Past Visiting Lecturer at the universities of Paris, Rome, Athens, and others; former A.C.L.S. Fellow. Author, *Emperor Michael Palaeologus and the West: A Study in Byzantine–Latin Relations* (1959); *Greek Scholars in Venice: The Dissemination of Greek Learning From Byzantium to the West* (1962); *Byzantine East and Latin West: Two Worlds of Christendom* (1966). PLETHO, GIORGIUS GEMISTUS.

Gerber, William, B.A. (University of Pennsylvania); M.A. (George Washington University); Ph.D. (Columbia). Economist with the U.S. Department of Labor; Associate Professor of Philosophy at the University of Maryland; Secretary-Treasurer of the Washington Philosophy Club. Associate Professor of Philosophy at American University (1962). Publications include *The Domain of Reality* (1946); *The Mind of India* (1967). PHILOSOPHICAL BIBLIOGRAPHIES; PHILOSOPHICAL DICTIONARIES AND ENCYCLOPEDIAS; PHILOSOPHICAL JOURNALS; SUFI PHILOSOPHY; TAGORE, RABINDRANATH.

Gerrish, B. A., M.A. (Cambridge); S.T.M. (Union Theological Seminary); Ph.D. (Columbia). Associate Professor of Historical Theology at the Divinity School of the University of Chicago. Tutor at the Union Theological Seminary (1957–1958); Lecturer at the McCormick Theological Seminary (1958–1965), Associate Professor from 1963; American Association of Theological Schools Faculty Fellow in Germany (1961–1962). Author, *Grace and Reason: A Study in the Theology of Luther* (1962) and numerous articles in religious, historical, and theological journals. Editor, *The Faith of Christendom: A Source Book of Creeds and Confessions* (1963). LUTHER, MARTIN; REFORMATION.

Gewirth, Alan, A.B., Ph.D. (Columbia). Professor of Philosophy at the University of Chicago. Rockefeller Fellow (1946–1947, 1957–1958); Past Visiting Professor of Philosophy at Harvard University and the University of Michigan; Chairman of the Program Committee, American Philosophical Association (1954). Translator, Marsilius of Padua, *Defensor Pacis* (1956). Coauthor, *Social Justice* (1962). Author, *Marsilius of Padua and Medieval Political Philosophy* (1951); *Political Philosophy* (1965). MARSILIUS OF PADUA.

Gilbert, Felix, Ph.D. Professor in the School of Historical Studies at the Institute for Advanced Study (Princeton, N.J.). Professor of History at Bryn Mawr College (1946–1962). Author, *To the Farewell Address: Ideas of Early American Foreign Policy* (1961); *Machiavelli and Guicciardini, Politics and History in Sixteenth-century Florence* (1964); *History* (with John Higham and Leonard Krieger, 1965). MACHIAVELLI, NICCOLÒ.

Gilbert, Neal W., B.A. (Dartmouth College); Ph.D. (Columbia). Chairman of the Department of Philosophy at the University of California, Davis. Philosophy Representative on the Board of the Renaissance Society of America (1962–1963). Author, *Renaissance Concepts of Method* (1960). GALEN; JUNGIUS, JOACHIM; MAJOR, JOHN; RENAISSANCE; VALLA, LORENZO; VIVES, JUAN LUIS; ZABARELLA, JACOPO.

Gilby, Thomas, O.P., S.T.M., Ph.D. Blackfriars, Cambridge. ABELARD, PETER; ROSCELIN; THOMISM.

Gilman, Richard C., B.A. (Dartmouth College); Ph.D. (Boston University). President of Occidental College (Los Angeles). Associate Professor of Philosophy at Colby College (1955–1956); Dean of the College and Professor of Philosophy at Carleton College (1960–1965). HOCKING, WILLIAM ERNEST.

Glatzer, Nahum Norbert, Ph.D. Professor of Jewish History and Chairman of the Department of Near Eastern and Judaic Studies at Brandeis University. Formerly, Lecturer in Jewish Religious History at the University of Frankfurt; Chief Editor of Schocken Books (New York); Guggenheim Fellow (1959–1960). Publications include *Geschichtslehre der Tannaiten* (1932); *Geschichte der Talmudischen Zeit* (1938); *Franz Rosenzweig: His Life and Thought* (1953); *Leopold Zunz* (1958); *Jerusalem and Rome* (1960); *Texts in the Judaic Tradition* (3 vols., 1961–1965). ROSENZWEIG, FRANZ.

Golding, M. P., B.A., M.A. (University of California, Los Angeles); Ph.D. (Columbia). Associate Professor of Philosophy at Columbia University. KELSEN, HANS; PHILOSOPHY OF LAW, HISTORY OF.

Goldstine, Herman H., B.S., M.S., Ph.D. (University of Chicago). Director of Scientific Development, Data Processing Division, International Business Machines Corporation; Member of the Army Mathematics Steering Committee, the Advisory Committee for the Directorate of Information Sciences for the Air Force Office of Scientific Research, and the National Research Council Committee on Applications of Mathematics of Division of Mathematics; Member of the Board of Scientific Advisors for Cornell University/Sloan-Kettering Institute; Member of Advisory Council, Department of Mathematics, Princeton University; and advisor to other academic organizations. Past academic positions at the University of Chicago, the University of Michigan, and the Institute for Advanced Study (Princeton, N.J.). In charge of the development of the electronic computer for the U.S. Army (1942–1945); collaborated with John von Neumann in the design and development of the first computer at Princeton. NEUMANN, JOHN VON.

Gossman, Eva R., Ph.D. (Johns Hopkins). Lecturer in Philosophy at Goucher College (Towson, Maryland). Formerly, Member of Social Science Faculty at Sarah Lawrence College. FRANK, ERICH.

Gotesky, Rubin, B.S., M.A., Ph.D. (New York University). Professor of Philosophy at Northern Illinois University. Consultant to Human Resources Research Office (1958–1959); President of the Southern Society for Philosophy and Psychology (1961–1962); Past Visiting Professor at Tulane University, New York University, Emory University, Rutgers University, and the University of Chicago. Author, "Liberalism in Crisis" (in *European Ideologies,* Philosophical Library, 1948); *Excellence: Three Lectures* (Proceedings, Western Washington State College, 1965); "Aloneness, Loneliness, Isolation, Solitude" (in *Invitation to Phenomenology,* 1965); and other articles. CARUS, CARL GUSTAV; EUCKEN, RUDOLF CHRISTOPH; LOTZE, RUDOLPH HERMAN.

Goudge, T. A., M.A., Ph.D. Chairman of the Department of Philosophy at the University of Toronto; Fellow of the Royal Society of Canada. Past President of the Charles S. Peirce Society and of the Canadian Philosophical Association. Publications include *Bergson's Introduction to Metaphysics* (edited with an introduction, 1949); *The Thought of C. S. Peirce* (1950); *The Ascent of Life: A Philosophical Study of the*

Theory of Evolution (1961). Bergson, Henri; Bertalanffy, Ludwig von; Butler, Samuel; Darwin, Charles Robert; Darwin, Erasmus; Emergent evolutionism; Gray, Asa; Huxley, Thomas Henry; Lamarck, Chevalier de; Lecomte du Noüy, Pierre André; Life, Origin of; Loeb, Jacques; Morgan, C. Lloyd; Romanes, George John; Smuts, Jan Christian; Teilhard de Chardin, Pierre; Wallace, Alfred Russel; Woodger, Joseph Henry; Uexküll, Jakob Johann, Baron von.

Gould, Josiah B., Jr., A.B. (Lynchburg College); M.A. (Florida State University); Ph.D. (Johns Hopkins). Assistant Professor and Chairman of the Department of Philosophy at Claremont Graduate School (Claremont, California). Assistant Professor of Philosophy at the American University (Washington, D.C., 1960–1963). Author, "Reason in Seneca," *Journal of the History of Philosophy* (1965). Chrysippus.

Graham, A. C., M.A. (Oxford); Ph.D. (University of London). Lecturer in Chinese at the School of Oriental and African Studies, University of London. Publications include *Two Chinese Philosophers: Ch'eng Ming-tao and Ch'eng Yi-ch'uan* (1958); *The Problem of Value* (1961); *The Book of Lieh-tzu* (1961). Logic, history of (section on Chinese logic).

Grant, Edward, B.S.S. (City College of New York); M.A. (University of Chicago); Ph.D. (University of Wisconsin). Professor of the History of Science in the Department of History and Philosophy of Science, Indiana University; Member of the Governing Council of the History of Science Society (1964–1966); Member of the U.S. National Committee for the International Union of the History and Philosophy of Science. Guggenheim Fellow (1965–1966); Visiting Member of the Institute for Advanced Study (Princeton, N.J., 1965–1966). Translator and editor, *Nicole Oresme: "De proportionibus proportionum" and "Ad pauca respicientes"* (with introductions and critical notes, 1966). Author of various articles on the history of science in scholarly journals. Oresme, Nicholas.

Grant, Robert M., Th.D. Professor of New Testament and Early Christianity at the Divinity School of the University of Chicago. Apologists; Celsus; Eusebius; Nemesius of Emesa; Origen; Patristic philosophy; Tertullian, Quintus Septimius Florens.

Grave, S. A., M.A. (University of New Zealand); Ph.D. (St. Andrews). Professor of Philosophy at the University of Western Australia. Author, *The Scottish Philosophy of Common Sense* (1960). Brown, Thomas; Common sense; Reid, Thomas; Stewart, Dugald.

Greenberg, Daniel A., M.A., Ph.D. (Columbia). Associate Professor of History at Columbia University. Formerly, Assistant Professor of Physics at Columbia University. Coauthor (with D. E. Gershenson), *Anaxagoras and the Birth of Physics* (1964). Coeditor (with D. E. Gershenson), *The Natural Philosopher*, Vols. I–III. Author, *Mathematics for Introductory Science Courses* (1965). Extremal principles.

Grene, Marjorie, B.A. (Wellesley College); M.A., Ph.D. (Radcliffe). Professor of Philosophy at the University of California, Davis. Author, *Dreadful Freedom* (1948; reissued in paperback as *Introduction to Existentialism*, 1959); *Heidegger* (1957); *A Portrait of Aristotle* (1963); *The Knower and the Known* (1966). Heidegger, Martin.

Griffiths, A. Phillips, B.A. (University of Wales); B.Phil. (Oxford). Professor of Philosophy at the University of Warwick. Visiting Professor at the University of Wisconsin (1964). Ultimate moral principles: their justification.

Grimsley, Ronald, M.A., D.Phil. (Oxford); L. ès L. Professor of French at the University of Bristol. Formerly, Reader in French at the University College of North Wales, Bangor (until 1964). Author, *Existentialist Thought* (2d ed., 1960); *Jean-Jacques Rousseau: A Study in Self-awareness* (1961); *Jean d'Alembert (1717–83)* (1963); and others. Rousseau, Jean-Jacques.

Grünbaum, Adolph, B.A. (Wesleyan); M.S., Ph.D. (Yale). Andrew Mellon Professor of Philosophy and Director of the Center for Philosophy of Science at the University of Pittsburgh; President of the Philosophy of Science Association, U.S.A. (1965–1968); Member of the Executive Committee of the American Philosophical Association; Member of the Board of Editors of *Philosophy of Science* and the *American Philosophical Quarterly*. Vice-President of the American Association for the Advancement of Science, Section of the History and Philosophy of Science (1963). Author, *Philosophical Problems of Space and Time* (1963). Relativity theory, philosophical significance of.

Gunderson, Keith, B.A. (Macalester College and Oxford); Ph.D. (Princeton). Assistant Professor of Philosophy at the University of California, Los Angeles. Fulbright Fellow at Worcester College, Oxford University (1957–1959); Instructor in Philosophy at Princeton University (1962–1964). Author, "Interview with a Robot," *Analysis* (1963); "The Imitation Game," *Mind* (1964); "Descartes, La Mettrie, Language, and Machines," *Philosophy* (1964). Cybernetics.

Guthrie, W. K. C., Litt.D. (Cambridge); D.Litt. (Hon., University of Melbourne). Laurence Professor of Ancient Philosophy and Master of Downing College, Cambridge University; Fellow of the British Academy. Past Public Orator at Cambridge University. Author, *Orpheus and Greek Religion* (1935); *The Greeks and Their Gods* (1950); *In the Beginning* (1957); *A History of Greek Philosophy* (Vol. I, 1962; Vol. II, 1965; remaining volumes in progress). Pre-Socratic philosophy; Pythagoras and Pythagoreanism.

Hall, Roland, M.A., B.Phil. Lecturer in Philosophy at the University of St. Andrews and Assistant Editor of the *Philosophical Quarterly*. Frequent contributor to learned journals, including the *Philosophical Review, Mind, PAS, Analysis, Classical Quarterly,* and *Notes and Queries.* Contributor to *The Oxford English Dictionary Supplement* (New Edition). Dialectic; Monism and pluralism.

Hallie, Philip Paul, B.A., B.Litt. (Oxford); M.A., Ph.D. (Harvard). Griffin Professor of Philosophy and Chairman of the Philosophy Department at Wesleyan University; Member of the Editorial Board of the *American Scholar;* Member of the National Screening Board, Fulbright-Hays Fellowships. U.S. Representative at the International Congress of Philosophy at Mysore City (India, 1959); Fellow, Institute for Advanced Studies, Wesleyan University (1961–1962). Editor, *Scepticism, Man, and God* (1965). Author, *Maine de Biran, Reformer of Empiricism* (1959), and various articles in philosophical journals. Aenesidemus; Agrippa; Arcesilaus; Carneades; Condillac, Étienne Bonnot de; Epictetus; Maine de Biran; Panaetius of Rhodes; Pyrrho; Sextus Empiricus; Stoicism; Timon of Phlius; Zeno of Citium.

Hamblin, C. L., M.A., B.Sc. (University of Melbourne); Ph.D. (University of London). Associate Professor of Philosophy at the University of New South Wales. Nuffield Dominion Travelling Fellow (1962). Questions.

Hamlyn, D. W., M.A. (Oxford). Professor of Philosophy at Birkbeck College, University of London. Formerly, Research Fellow of Corpus Christi College, Oxford University; Lecturer, Jesus College, Oxford University; Lecturer and Reader, Birkbeck College, University of London. Author, *The Psychology of Perception* (1957); *Sensation and Perception* (1961);

"Greek Philosophy After Aristotle" (in D. J. O'Connor, ed., *A Critical History of Western Philosophy*, 1964); numerous articles in philosophical journals. ANALYTIC AND SYNTHETIC STATEMENTS; A PRIORI AND A POSTERIORI; CONTINGENT AND NECESSARY STATEMENTS; EMPIRICISM; EPISTEMOLOGY, HISTORY OF.

Hancock, Roger, A.B., M.A. (University of Chicago); Ph.D. (Yale). Assistant Professor of Philosophy at the University of Missouri. Visiting Assistant Professor of Philosophy at the University of Illinois (1963–1964). METAPHYSICS, HISTORY OF.

Handy, Rollo, B.A. (Carleton College); M.A. (Sarah Lawrence College); Ph.D. (University of Buffalo). Professor and Chairman of the Department of Philosophy and Chairman of the Division of Philosophy and the Social Sciences at the State University of New York at Buffalo. Assistant Professor, Professor, and Chairman of the Philosophy Department at the University of South Dakota (1954–1960); Associate Professor of Philosophy at Union College (1960–1961). Coauthor (with Paul Kurtz), *A Current Appraisal of the Behavioral Sciences* (1964). Author, *Methodology of the Behavioral Sciences: Problems and Controversies* (1964) and various articles in philosophical journals. BÜCHNER, LUDWIG; HAECKEL, ERNST HEINRICH; MOLESCHOTT, JACOB; VAIHINGER, HANS.

Hanson, Norwood Russell, B.A. (University of Chicago); B.Sc. (Columbia); M.A. (Columbia, Cambridge, and Yale); B.Phil., D.Phil. (Oxford); Ph.D. (Cambridge). Professor of Philosophy at Yale University. Past Chairman of the Department of History and Logic of Science at Indiana University; Fellow of St. John's College, Cambridge University (1956). Author, *Patterns of Discovery* (1958); *The Concept of the Positron* (1963). COPERNICUS, NICOLAS; QUANTUM MECHANICS, PHILOSOPHICAL IMPLICATIONS OF.

Harré, R., M.A., B.Sc., B.Phil. Fellow of Linacre College, Oxford University, and University Lecturer in the Philosophy of Science. Author, *Introduction to the Logic of the Sciences; Theories and Things; Matter and Method;* and *The Anticipation of Nature*. LAPLACE, PIERRE SIMON DE; PHILOSOPHY OF SCIENCE, HISTORY OF.

Harries, Karsten, B.A., Ph.D. (Yale). Assistant Professor of Philosophy at Yale University. Instructor in Philosophy at Yale University (1961–1963); Assistant Professor at the University of Texas (1963–1965), Guest Professor at the University of Bonn (1965–1966). Author of "Heidegger and Hölderlin—The Limits of Language," *Personalist* (1963); "Cusanus and the Platonic Idea," *New Scholasticism* (1963); "Heidegger's Conception of the Holy," *Personalist* (1966); and a number of papers on existential philosophy, especially on Heidegger. HÖLDERLIN, JOHANN CHRISTIAN FRIEDRICH; KEYSERLING, HERMANN ALEXANDER, GRAF VON; KLEIST, HEINRICH VON; NOVALIS; SOLGER, KARL WILHELM FERDINAND; ZIEGLER, LEOPOLD.

Harris, H. S., M.A. (Oxford); Ph.D. (University of Illinois). Professor of Philosophy, Glendom College, York University (Toronto). Author, *Social Philosophy of Giovanni Gentile* (1960). CARABELLESE, PANTALEO; CROCE, BENEDETTO; GENTILE, GIOVANNI; ITALIAN PHILOSOPHY; SPAVENTA, BERTRANDO; SPIRITO, UGO.

Harrison, Jonathan, M.A. Professor of Philosophy at the University of Nottingham. Formerly, Lecturer at the University of Durham and Edinburgh. Author of numerous articles in philosophical journals. ETHICAL NATURALISM; ETHICAL OBJECTIVISM; ETHICAL SUBJECTIVISM.

Hart, H. L. A., M.A. (Oxford). Professor of Jurisprudence at Oxford University. Formerly, Fellow and Tutor in Philosophy, New College, Oxford University. Coauthor (with A. M. Honoré), *Causation in the Law*. Author, *The Concept of Law; Law, Liberty and Morality*. LEGAL POSITIVISM; PHILOSOPHY OF LAW, PROBLEMS OF.

Hartmann, Klaus, Dr.Phil. (University of Bonn). Docent at Bonn University. Visiting Professor at the University of Texas (1965–1966). Editor, *Lebendiger Realismus (Festschrift* for Johannes Thyssen, 1962). Author, *Grundzüge der Ontologie Sartres in ihrem Verhältnis zu Hegels Logik* (1963); *Sartres Sozialphilosophie* (1966). EHRENFELS, CHRISTIAN FREIHERR VON; SCHUPPE, ERNST JULIUS WILHELM.

Hartnack, Justus, M.A., Dr.Phil. (University of Copenhagen). Professor of Philosophy at the University of Aarhus; Director of the Institute of Philosophy. Visiting Lecturer and Assistant Professor at Colgate University (1946–1954); Ford Fellow (1953–1954); Visiting Professor at Vassar College (1958–1959). Publications include *Problems of Perception in British Empiricism* (1950); *Philosophical Problems* (1956); *Philosophical Essays* (1957); *Logic—Classical and Modern* (1958); *Thinking and Reality* (1959); *Wittgenstein and Modern Philosophy* (1960); *Kant's Epistemology and Modern Philosophy*. PERFORMATIVE UTTERANCES; SCANDINAVIAN PHILOSOPHY.

Hay, W. H., A.B. (Haverford College); A.M. (Brown); Ph.D. (University of Illinois). Professor of Philosophy at the University of Wisconsin. Secretary of the American Philosophical Association, Western Division (1954–1957); Fellowship of the Committee to Advance Original Work in Philosophy, American Philosophical Association (1957–1958); Chairman of the Department of Philosophy at the University of Wisconsin (1958–1963); Faculty Professor at the Institute for Research in the Humanities, University of Wisconsin (1965–1966). Translator and editor, *Pomponazzi on Immortality* (1938); Editor, *Reason and the Common Good* (1963). Author of various essays on ethics, inductive logic, and the history of philosophy. CARUS, PAUL; MURPHY, ARTHUR EDWARD.

Heath, P. L., B.A. (Oxford). Professor of Philosophy at the University of Virginia. Formerly, Lecturer in Moral Philosophy at the University of Edinburgh; Senior Lecturer in Logic and Metaphysics at St. Andrews University. Translator, M. Scheler, *The Nature of Sympathy*; G. A. Wetter, *Dialectical Materialism;* M. von Senden, *Space and Sight;* G. A. Wetter, *Soviet Ideology Today*. Editor, A. de Morgan, *On the Syllogism*. Contributor to *PAS*, *Philosophical Quarterly*, and J. O. Urmson, ed., *The Concise Encyclopedia of Western Philosophy and Philosophers*. BALFOUR, ARTHUR JAMES; BOOLE, GEORGE; CARROLL, LEWIS; CONCEPT; DE MORGAN, AUGUSTUS; EXPERIENCE; JEVONS, WILLIAM STANLEY; LOGIC, HISTORY OF (part of the section on modern logic: the Boolean period); NOTHING; VENN, JOHN.

Hempel, Carl G., Ph.D. (University of Berlin). Stuart Professor of Philosophy at Princeton University. Guggenheim Fellow (1947–1948); Professor of Philosophy at Yale University (1948–1955); Fulbright Senior Research Fellow, Oxford University (1959–1960); President of the American Philosophical Association, Eastern Division (1961); Vice-President of the Association for Symbolic Logic (1962–1964); Fellow of the Center for Advanced Study in the Behavioral Sciences (1963–1964). Publications include *Fundamentals of Concept Formation in Empirical Science* (1952); *Aspects of Scientific Explanation* (1965); and numerous articles on the philosophy of science. CONFIRMATION: QUALITATIVE ASPECTS.

Henkin, Leon, A.B. (Columbia); Ph.D. (Princeton). Professor of Mathematics at the University of California, Berkeley. Editor of the *Journal of Symbolic Logic* (1949–1952); Fulbright Research Scholar at the University of Amsterdam (1954–1955); Guggenheim Fellow and Member of the Institute for Advanced Study (Princeton, N.J., 1961–1962). President of the Association for Symbolic Logic (1962–1964).

Author, *La Structure algébrique des théories mathématiques* (1955) and numerous articles. FORMAL SYSTEMS AND THEIR MODELS.

Henry, Desmond Paul, B.A. (University of Leeds); Ph.D. (University of Manchester). Senior Lecturer in Philosophy at the University of Manchester; Honorary Member of the Société Internationale pour l'Étude de la Philosophie Médiévale. Publications include *The 'De Grammatico' of Saint Anselm* (1964) and numerous articles on logic and its history in *Mind, Philosophical Quarterly, Ratio,* and other journals. MEDIEVAL PHILOSOPHY.

Henry-Hermann, Grete, Dr.phil. Professor at the Pädagogischen Hochschule in Bremen. NELSON, LEONARD.

Hepburn, Ronald, W., M.A., Ph.D. Professor of Philosophy at the University of Edinburgh. Visiting Associate Professor at New York University (1959–1960); Professor of Philosophy and Head of the Department of Philosophy at the University of Nottingham (1960–1964). Coauthor, *Metaphysical Beliefs* (1957). Author, *Christianity and Paradox* (1958); many articles in *Mind, PAS, Journal of the History of Ideas,* and others. AGNOSTICISM; BULTMANN, RUDOLF; COSMOLOGICAL ARGUMENT FOR THE EXISTENCE OF GOD; CREATION, RELIGIOUS DOCTRINE OF; MORAL ARGUMENTS FOR THE EXISTENCE OF GOD; MYSTICISM, NATURE AND ASSESSMENT OF; NATURE, PHILOSOPHICAL IDEAS OF; RELIGIOUS EXPERIENCE, ARGUMENT FOR THE EXISTENCE OF GOD.

Hesse, Mary, M.A., Ph.D. University Lecturer in Philosophy of Science at Cambridge University; Editor of the *British Journal for the Philosophy of Science.* Formerly, Lecturer in Mathematics at the University of Leeds; Lecturer in History and Philosophy of Science at University College, University of London. Author, *Forces and Fields* (1961); *Models and Analogies in Science* (1963). ACTION AT A DISTANCE AND FIELD THEORY; ETHER; LAWS AND THEORIES; MODELS AND ANALOGY IN SCIENCE; SIMPLICITY; VACUUM AND VOID.

Heyde, Joh's Erich, Dr.Phil. Ordinary Professor of Philosophy at the Technical University of Berlin. Past President of the Kant Society (Berlin); Past Director of the Johannes Rehmke Society. Publications include *Grundwissenschaftliche Philosophie* (1924); *Wert: Eine philosophische Grundlegung* (1926); *Grundlage und Gestalt: Ganzheitliche Unterrichtsweise* (1937); *Entwertung der Kausalität?* (1957); *Wege zur Klarheit: Gesammelte Aufsätze* (1960); *Technik des wissenschaftlichen Arbeitens* (9th ed., 1966). REHMKE, JOHANNES.

Hick, John, M.A. (University of Edinburgh); Ph.D. (Cambridge); D.Phil. (Oxford). Lecturer in the Philosophy of Religion at the University of Cambridge. Stuart Professor of Christian Philosophy, Princeton Theological Seminary (1959–1964); Guggenheim Fellow (1963–1964). Author, *Faith and Knowledge* (1957); *Evil and the God of Love; Philosophy of Religion* (1963). Editor, *Faith and the Philosopher* (1964); *The Existence of God* (1964); *Classical and Contemporary Readings in the Philosophy of Religion* (1964). CHRISTIANITY; EVIL, THE PROBLEM OF; FAITH; OMAN, JOHN WOOD; ONTOLOGICAL ARGUMENT FOR THE EXISTENCE OF GOD; REVELATION; TENNANT, FREDERICK ROBERT.

Hillgarth, Jocelyn Nigel, B.A., M.A., Ph.D. (Cambridge). Lecturer in History at Harvard University. Senior Research Fellow at the Warburg Institute, University of London (1959–1962); Member of the Institute for Advanced Study (Princeton, N.J., 1963-1964). Author, "Visigoth Spain and Early Christian Ireland," *Proceedings of the Royal Irish Academy* (1962); "The Position of Isidorian Studies," *Isidoriana* (1961); and many other articles. LULL, RAMON.

Hirst, R. J., B.A., M.A. (Oxford). Professor and Head of the Department of Logic at Glasgow University. Author, *The Problems of Perception* (1959). Coauthor (with G. M. Wyburn and R. W. Pickford), *Human Senses and Perception* (1964). Editor, *Perception and the External World* (1965). ILLUSIONS; PERCEPTION; PHENOMENALISM; PRIMARY AND SECONDARY QUALITIES; REALISM; SENSA.

Hiż, Henry, Ph.D. (Harvard). Professor of Linguistics at the University of Pennsylvania; Investigator for two N.S.F. Research Projects on Information Retrieval and Analysis of Chemical Notations. Formerly taught at Harvard University, Brooklyn College, the University of Utah, and Warsaw University. Author of numerous papers on semantics and formal logic. CHWISTEK, LEON.

Horowitz, Irving Louis, B.S.S., M.A., Ph.D. Professor of Sociology at Washington University (St. Louis); Director of Studies in Comparative International Development, Social Science Institute. Author, *Idea of War and Peace in Contemporary Philosophy* (1957); *Philosophy, Science and the Sociology of Knowledge* (1960); *Radicalism and the Revolt Against Reason* (1961); *The War Game* (1963); *The New Sociology* (1964); *Three Worlds of Development* (1966). DE SANCTIS, FRANCESCO.

Hospers, John, B.A., M.A. (Iowa State University); Ph.D. (Columbia); D.Litt. (Central College). Professor of Philosophy at the City University of New York, Brooklyn College. Former Fulbright Scholar at the University of London; Past Visiting Professor at the University of California, Los Angeles; Associate Professor of Philosophy at the University of Minnesota (1953–1956). Author, *Meaning and Truth in the Arts* (1946); *Readings in Ethical Theory* (with Wilfrid Sellars, 1952); *Introduction to Philosophical Analysis* (rev. ed., 1966); *Human Conduct* (1961). AESTHETICS, PROBLEMS OF.

Isham, Howard, M.A. (Columbia); M.F.A. (Princeton); Ph.D. (Columbia). Associate Professor of Humanities at San Francisco State College. Fulbright Scholar at the University of Freiburg im Breisgau (1959–1960). Publications include *The Idea in History: The Historical Thought of Wilhelm von Humboldt.* (1963). HUMBOLDT, WILHELM VON.

James, Theodore E., A.B., M.A. Associate Professor of Philosophy at Manhattan College; Associate Editor of the *New Scholasticism;* Ph.D. candidate. Chairman of the Department of Philosophy at Manhattan College (1949–1961). Author, introductory chapters to *Aristotle Dictionary* (1962), to Solomon Ibn Gabirol, *The Fountain of Life* (1962), to *Plato Dictionary* (1963), and to *Aquinas Dictionary* (1965). IBN-GABIROL, SOLOMON BEN JUDAH.

Jammer, Max, M.A., Ph.D. Rector, Head of the Department of Physics, and Professor of Physics and Philosophy of Science at Bar-Ilan University (Israel). Research Professor, or Visiting Professor, at Catholic University of America, Swiss Federal Institute of Technology, Boston University, University of Göttingen, and the University of Oklahoma; Visiting Lecturer at Harvard University; N.S.F. Fellow (1965). Author, *Concepts of Space; Foundations of Dynamics; The Concept of Mass in Classical and Modern Physics; The Conceptual Development of Quantum Mechanics.* ENERGY; FORCE; MASS; MOTION.

Jonas, Hans, Ph.D. (University of Marburg); D.H.L. (Hon., Hebrew Union College, Jewish Institute of Religion). Professor of Philosophy, Graduate Faculty of Political and Social Science, the New School for Social Research. Formerly Visiting Lecturer and Professor at the Hebrew University of Jerusalem, Carleton University, Princeton University, Columbia University, and Hunter College; Rockefeller Fellow (1959–1960); Fellow of the Center for Advanced Studies at Wesleyan University (1964–1965). Author, *Augustin und das paulinische Freiheitsproblem* (1930); *Gnosis und spätantiker Geist* (2 vols., 1934, 1954); *The Gnostic Religion* (1958); *The Phenomenon of Life: Toward a Philosophical Biology* (1966). GNOSTICISM.

Jonsson, Inge, Dr.phil. (University of Stockholm). Docent of the History of Literature at the University of Stockholm (since 1961). Author, *Swedenborgs Skapelsedrama de Cultu et Amore Dei* (1961). SWEDENBORG, EMANUEL.

Joravsky, David, B.A., M.A., Certificate of the Russian Institute, Ph.D. (Columbia). Professor of History at Northwestern University. Formerly, Instructor in History at the University of Connecticut; Associate Professor of History at Brown University; Guggenheim Fellow (1964–1965). Author, *Soviet Marxism and Natural Science* (1961) and numerous articles. DEBORIN, ABRAM MOISEEVICH.

Jordan, Z. A., M.A., Ph.D. (University of Poznan, Poland). Lecturer in the Philosophy of Social Sciences at the University of Reading. Senior Fellow at the Russian Institute, Columbia University (1962–1964). Publications include *The Development of Mathematical Logic and Logical Positivism in Poland Between the Two Wars* (1945); *Philosophy and Ideology* (1963). AJDUKIEWICZ, KAZIMIERZ; KOTARBIŃSKI, TADEUSZ.

Juhos, Béla, Dr.phil. Professor of Theological Philosophy at the University of Vienna; Member of the International Institute of Philosophy. Author, *Erkenntnisformen in Natur- und Geisteswissenschaften* (1940); *Theorie empirischer Sätze* (1945); *Die Erkenntnis und ihre Leistung* (1950); *Elemente der neuen Logik* (1954); *Das Wertgeschehen und seine Erfassung* (1956); *Probleme der Wissenschaftstheorie* (1960); *Die erkenntnislogischen Grundlagen der klassischen Physik* (with H. Schleichert, 1964); and many articles in scientific journals. SCHLICK, MORITZ.

Kahl, Russell, A.B. (University of California, Berkeley); Ph.D. (Columbia). Associate Professor of Philosophy at San Francisco State College. Formerly, Instructor in Philosophy at Columbia University. Editor, *Studies in Explanation* (1963). HELMHOLTZ, HERMANN LUDWIG VON.

Kahn, Charles H., B.A., M.A. (University of Chicago); Ph.D. (Columbia). Associate Professor of Philosophy at the University of Pennsylvania. Associate Professor of Greek and Latin at Columbia University (1962–1965); A.C.L.S. Research Fellow (1963–1964). Publications include *Anaximander and the Origins of Greek Cosmology* (1960) and various articles on Greek philosophy. ANAXIMANDER; EMPEDOCLES.

Kalish, Donald, B.A., M.A., Ph.D. (University of California, Berkeley). Professor and Chairman of the Department of Philosophy at the University of California, Los Angeles. Formerly taught at Swarthmore College and the University of California, Berkeley. Publications include *Logic–Techniques of Formal Reasoning* (with Richard Montague, 1964) and various articles and reviews. SEMANTICS.

Kamenka, Eugene, B.A. (University of Sydney); Ph.D. (Australian National University). Fellow (History of Ideas) in the Department of Philosophy at the Institute of Advanced Studies, Australian National University. Postdoctoral research with the Faculty of Philosophy at Moscow State University (1965–1966). Author, *The Ethical Foundations of Marxism* (1962). COMMUNISM, PHILOSOPHY UNDER; TOLSTOY, COUNT LEO NIKOLAEVICH.

Kaminsky, Alice R., B.A., M.A., Ph.D. Associate Professor of Philosophy at State University College (Cortland, New York). Formerly taught at New York University, Hunter College, and Cornell University. Author, "George Eliot, George H. Lewes, and the Novel," *PMLA* (1955). Editor, *The Literary Criticism of George Henry Lewes* (1964). LEWES, GEORGE HENRY.

Kaminsky, Jack, B.S. (City College of New York); M.A., Ph.D. (New York University). Professor of Philosophy, State University of New York at Binghamton. A.C.L.S. Fellow (1951–1952); Chairman, Department of Philosophy, State University of New York at Binghamton (1953–1965). Publications include *Logic and Language* (with B. F. Huppe, 1956); *Hegel on Art* (1962); and articles and reviews in the *Journal of Philosophy, Philosophy and Phenomenological Research, Philosophy of Science*, and others. SPENCER, HERBERT.

Kateb, George, A.B., A.M., Ph.D. (Columbia). Associate Professor of Political Science at Amherst College. Author, *Utopia and Its Enemies* (1963). UTOPIAS AND UTOPIANISM.

Kaufman, Arnold S., B.S.S. (City College of New York); Ph.D. (Columbia). Associate Professor of Philosophy at the University of Michigan. Fulbright Fellow in England (1953–1955). Fellow of the Center for Advanced Study in the Behavioral Sciences (1961–1962). Author of articles in the *Journal of Philosophy, Mind, Inquiry*, the *Philosophical Review*, and other scholarly journals. BEHAVIORISM; RESPONSIBILITY, MORAL AND LEGAL.

Kaufmann, Walter, B.A. (Williams College); A.M., Ph.D. (Harvard). Professor of Philosophy at Princeton University. Publications include *Nietzsche* (1950); *The Portable Nietzsche* (editor and translator, 1954); *Existentialism from Dostoevsky to Sartre* (edited with an introduction, 1956); *Critique of Religion and Philosophy* (1958); *From Shakespeare to Existentialism* (1959); *The Faith of a Heretic* (1961); *Goethe's Faust: A New Translation* (editor and translator, 1961); *Twenty German Poets* (editor and translator, 1962); *Cain and Other Poems* (1962); *Hegel: Reinterpretation, Texts, and Commentary* (1963). NIETZSCHE, FRIEDRICH.

Keen, Samuel McMurray, B.A., S.T.B., Th.M., Ph.D. Associate Professor of Philosophy and Christian Faith at the Louisville Presbyterian Seminary. MARCEL, GABRIEL.

Keeton, Morris T., B.A., M.A. (Southern Methodist University); M.A., Ph.D. (Harvard). Professor of Philosophy and Religion and Dean of the Faculty at Antioch College; Director of the Study of the Future of Liberal Arts Colleges (Carnegie Corporation Grant, 1965–1967); Chairman of the Carus Lectures Committee; Member of the Executive Committee, Association for Higher Education; Fellow of the Society for Religion in Higher Education. Ordained Deacon (1946) and Elder (1948), Methodist Episcopal Church; Guggenheim Fellow (1946); Head of Mission in Germany, American Friends Service Committee (1953–1955); Secretary-Treasurer of the American Philosophical Association, Western Division (1959–1961); Chairman, International Conferences and Seminars, American Friends Service Committee (1959–1963). Author, *The Philosophy of Edmund Montgomery* (1950); *Values Men Live By, An Invitation to Religious Inquiry* (1960). MONTGOMERY, EDMUND DUNCAN.

Kennick, W. E., B.A. (Oberlin College); Ph.D. (Cornell); M.A. (Hon., Amherst). Professor of Philosophy at Amherst College. Author, *Art and Philosophy* (1964). Coeditor (with Morris Lazerowitz), *Metaphysics: Readings and Reappraisals* (1965). APPEARANCE AND REALITY; INEFFABLE, THE.

Kenny, Anthony, M.A., D.Phil. Fellow of Balliol College, Oxford University. Publications include *Action, Emotion and Will*. CRITERION.

Kerferd, G. B., B.A. (University of Melbourne); M.A. (Oxford). Professor of Classics at the University College of Swansea, University of Wales (since 1956). Formerly, Lecturer in Classics at the University of Durham; Senior Lecturer in Classics at the University of Manchester. ANAXAGORAS OF CLAZOMENAE; APEIRON/PERAS; ARETĒ/AGATHON/KAKON; ARISTOTLE; CRATYLUS; GORGIAS OF LEONTINI; HEN/POLLA; HIPPIAS OF ELIS; KATHARSIS; LOGOS; MIMESIS; MOIRA/TYCHE/ANANKE; NOUS; PERIPATETICS; PHYSIS AND

# of Contributors

th Century Conteurs (1966). Bossuet, Jacques-Bénigne; énelon, François de Salignac de la Mothe; La Bruère, Jean de; La Rochefoucauld, Duc François de; abelais, François.

etzmann, Norman, B.A. (Valparaiso University); Ph.D. (Johns Hopkins). Associate Professor of Philosophy at Cornell University. Formerly, member of the philosophy departments of Bryn Mawr College, Ohio State University, the University of Illinois, and Wayne State University. Publications include *Elements of Formal Logic* (1965); *William of Sherwood's Introduction to Logic* (1966). Peter of Spain; Semantics, history of; William of Sherwood.

rikorian, Yervant H., A.B. (Robert College, Istanbul); M.A., Ph.D. (Harvard). Professor Emeritus of Philosophy at the City University of New York. Member of the faculty of the City University of New York, City College (1924–1962); Visiting Professor at George Washington University (1942), at Howard University (1948–1949), and at American University (1962–1964). Editor, *Naturalism and the Human Spirit* (1944). Coauthor, *Basic Problems of Philosophy* (1947); *Contemporary Philosophic Problems* (1959). Cohen, Morris Raphael.

Kristeller, Paul Oskar, Dr.phil. (University of Heidelberg); Dott. in filosofia (University of Pisa); Dott. in filosofia (Hon., University of Padua). Professor of Philosophy at Columbia University. Visiting Professor at the Scuola Normale Superiore (Pisa, 1949, 1952); Guggenheim Fellow (1958); Member of the Institute for Advanced Study (Princeton, N.J., 1954–1955, 1961). Author, *Der Begriff der Seele in der Ethik des Plotin* (1930); *Supplementum Ficinianum* (2 vols., 1937); *The Philosophy of Marsilio Ficino* (1943); *Studies in Renaissance Thought and Letters* (1956); *Eight Italian Philosophers of the Renaissance* (1964); *Iter Italicum I* (1963); *Renaissance Thought* (1961); *Renaissance Thought II* (1965). Ficino, Marsilio; Florentine Academy; Petrarch; Pico della Mirandola, Count Giovanni; Pomponazzi, Pietro.

Krzywicki-Herburt, George, Ph.D. (University of Brussels). Associate Professor of Philosophy at the City University of New York, Queens College. Polish philosophy; Twardowski, Kazimierz.

Kuhn, Helmut, Dr.phil. Ordinary University Professor and Head of the Philosophy Seminars at the University of Munich; Rector of the High School of Political Science in Munich. Past President of the Allgemeinen Gesellschaft für Philosophie, in Germany. Author, *Die Kulturfunktion der Kunst; Sokrates–Ein Versuch über den Ursprung der Metaphysik; A History of Esthetics* (with K. E. Gilbert); *Freedom Forgotten and Remembered; Begegnung mit dem Nichts–Ein Versuch über die Existenzphilosophie; Wesen und Wirken des Kunstwerkes; Romano Guardini; Das Sein und das Gute.* German philosophy and national socialism.

Kümmel, Friedrich, Dr.phil. Wissenschaftlicher Assistent at the University of Tübingen. Publications include *Über den Begriff der Zeit* (1962); *Verständnis und Vorverständnis* (1965). Bollnow, Otto Friedrich.

Kurtz, Paul, B.A. (New York University); M.A., Ph.D. (Columbia). Professor of Philosophy at the State University of New York at Buffalo; Coeditor of the *International Directory of Philosophy and Philosophers;* Director (for the U.S.A.) of the *Bibliography of Philosophy;* Member of the Editorial Advisory Board of the *Humanist;* Contributor to the *Encyclopedia Americana (Annual).* Formerly taught at the New School for Social Research, Vassar College, Union College (New York), Trinity College, the City University of New York, Queens College, and the University of Besançon (France). Editor, *American Thought Before 1900* (1966); *American Philosophy in the Twentieth Century* (1966). Coauthor, *A Current Appraisal of the Behavioral Sciences* (1964). Author, *Decision and Condition of Man* (1965). American philosophy; Colden, Cadwallader; Palmer, Elihu.

Ladd, John, A.B., A.M. (Harvard); M.A. (University of Virginia); Ph.D. (Harvard); M.A. ad eundem (Brown). Professor of Philosophy at Brown University; Secretary-Treasurer of the American Society for Political and Legal Science. Rockefeller Fellow (1948–1949); Guggenheim Fellow (1958–1959); Visiting Professor at Harvard University (1960). Publications include *The Structure of a Moral Code* (1957); *Kant's Metaphysical Elements of Justice* (translation with an introduction, 1965). Custom; Loyalty.

Lamprecht, Sterling P., A.B. (Williams College); A.M. (Harvard); B.D. (Union Theological Seminary); Ph.D. (Columbia); A.M. (Hon., Amherst College); Litt.D. (Hon., Williams College). Professor Emeritus of Philosophy at Amherst College. Professor of Philosophy at Amherst (1928–1956). Author, *Social and Political Philosophy of John Locke* (1918); *Our Religious Traditions* (1950); *Nature and History* (1950); *Our Philosophical Traditions* (1955). Woodbridge, Frederick James Eugene.

Landesman, Charles, Jr., B.A. (Wesleyan); M.A., Ph.D. (Yale). Associate Professor of Philosophy at the City University of New York, Hunter College. Author, "Philosophical Problems of Memory," *Journal of Philosophy* (1962); "Mental Events," *Philosophy and Phenomenological Research* (1964); and other articles. Consciousness.

Laslett, Peter, M.A. (Cambridge). Fellow of Trinity College, Cambridge, and Lecturer in History at the University of Cambridge. Cofounder of The Cambridge Group for the History of Population and Social Structure; Founder, editor, and contributor, the series *Philosophy, Politics and Society.* Publications include *"Patriarcha" and Other Political Works of Sir Robert Filmer* (1949); *Locke's Two Treatises of Government* (edited with an introduction and notes, 1960); *The Library of John Locke* (with John Harrison, 1965); *The World We Have Lost* (1965). Filmer, Robert; General will, the; Political philosophy, history of (sections from introduction through Kant and Bibliography); Social contract.

Latham, Ronald E., M.A. (Oxford). Principal Assistant Keeper, Public Record Office (London). Formerly, Lecturer in Latin at Queen's University of Belfast. Translator of the works of Lucretius and Marco Polo (Penguin Classics). Author of the Revised Medieval Latin Word List (British Academy). Lucretius.

Lavely, John H., A.B. (Allegheny College); S.T.B., Ph.D. (Boston University). Professor and Chairman of the Department of Philosophy at Boston University; Editor of the *Philosophical Forum* (since 1955). Associate Professor of Philosophy at Albion College (1947–1951). Brightman, Edgar Sheffield; Personalism.

Leff, Gordon, B.A., Ph.D. Reader in Medieval History at the University of York. Formerly, Senior Lecturer at Manchester University; Fellow of King's College, Cambridge University. Publications include *Bradwardine and the Pelagians; Medieval Thought; Gregory of Rimini; The Tyranny of Concepts; A Critique of Marxism; Richard FitzRalph.* Ailly, Pierre d'; Albert of Saxony; Bradwardine, Thomas; Burley, Walter; Giles of Rome; Gregory of Rimini; John of Mirecourt; Marsilius of Inghen; Swineshead, Richard.

Lejewski, Czesław, Magister Filozofii (University of Warsaw); Ph.D. (University of London). Senior Lecturer in Philosophy at the University of Manchester. Visiting Professor

NOMOS; PNEUMA; PRODICUS OF CEOS; PROTAGORAS OF ABDERA; PSYCHE; SOPHISTS; STRATO AND STRATONISM; THEOPHRASTUS; XENOPHANES OF COLOPHON.

Ketcham, Ralph, A.B. (Allegheny College); M.A. (Colgate); D.S.Sc. (Syracuse University). Professor of Political Science and American Studies at Syracuse University. Associate Editor of *The Papers of Benjamin Franklin* (1961–1963); Fulbright Lecturer in American Studies, Tokyo University (1965). Author, *Benjamin Franklin* (1965); *The Political Thought of Benjamin Franklin* (1965). FRANKLIN, BENJAMIN; JEFFERSON, THOMAS.

Kidd, Ian G., M.A. (St. Andrews); B.A. (Oxford). Senior Lecturer in Greek at the University of St. Andrews. Visiting Professor in Classics at the University of Texas (1965–1966). Contributor to J. O. Urmson, ed., *The Concise Encyclopedia of Western Philosophy and Philosophers* (1960), and to *Classical Quarterly, Classical Review, Philosophical Quarterly,* and *Gnomon.* ANTISTHENES; ARISTIPPUS OF CYRENE; CYNICS; CYRENAICS; DIOGENES OF SINOPE; GREEK ACADEMY; SOCRATES.

Kim, Jaegwon, A.B. (Dartmouth College); Ph.D. (Princeton). Assistant Professor of Philosophy at Brown University. Formerly, Instructor in Philosophy at Swarthmore College. Author of articles in *Philosophy of Science, Journal of Philosophy,* and the *American Philosophical Quarterly.* EXPLANATION IN SCIENCE; HEMPEL, CARL GUSTAV.

Kinghorn, A. M., M.A. (University of Aberdeen); Ph.D. (Cambridge). Senior Lecturer and Acting Head of the Department of English Literature at the University of the West Indies (Jamaica); Member of the Editorial Board of *Studies in Scottish Literature.* Coeditor, *Works of Allan Ramsay* (Scottish Text Society). Editor, *Barbour's Bruce* (Saltire Society). Author of many articles on medieval and 18th-century English and Scottish literature. FERGUSON, ADAM.

Kinnaird, John, B.A. (University of California, Berkeley); M.A., Ph.D. (Columbia). Assistant Professor of English at the University of Maryland. Assistant Professor of English at Vassar College (1959–1965). Author of articles on 19th- and 20th-century English and American literature. HAZLITT, WILLIAM.

Klappholz, Kurt, B.Sc. Senior Lecturer in Economics at the London School of Economics and Political Science, University of London. Publications include "Methodological Prescriptions in Economics" (with J. Agassi), *Economica* (1959); "Identities in Economic Models" (with E. J. Mishen), *Economica* (1962). ECONOMICS AND ETHICAL NEUTRALITY.

Kline, George L., A.B., M.A., Ph.D. (Columbia). Professor of Philosophy at Bryn Mawr College. Former Cutting Traveling Fellow, Fulbright Fellow, Ford Fellow, and Rockefeller Fellow. Translator, V. V. Zenkovsky, *A History of Russian Philosophy* (2 vols., 1953). Editor, *Alfred North Whitehead: Essays on His Philosophy* (1963); editor and contributor, *European Philosophy Today* (1965); coeditor and contributor, *Russian Philosophy* (3 vols., 1965). Author, *Spinoza in Soviet Philosophy* (1952). BAZAROV, VLADIMIR ALEKSANDROVICH; BOGDANOV, ALEXANDER ALEKSANDROVICH; CHICHERIN, BORIS NIKOLAYEVICH; FRANK, SIMON LYUDVIGOVICH; HERZEN, ALEXANDER IVANOVICH; KAREYEV, NICHOLAS IVANOVICH; KAVELIN, KONSTANTIN DMITRIEVICH; LEONTYEV, KONSTANTIN NIKOLAYEVICH; LUNACHARSKI, ANATOLI VASILYEVICH; PISAREV, DMITRI IVANOVICH; RUSSIAN PHILOSOPHY; SHESTOV, LEON; SKOVORODA, GREGORY SAVVICH; SOLOVYOV, VLADIMIR SERGEYEVICH; VOLSKI, STANISLAV.

Kneale, William C., M.A. (Oxford); LL.D. (Hon., University of Aberdeen). White's Professor of Moral Philosophy at the University of Oxford. Past Fellow and Tutor of Philosophy, Exeter College, Oxford University. Author, *Probability and Induction* (1949); *The Develop*... Kneale, 1962). ETERNITY.

Knowles, The Rev. David, M.A.; Li... torates. Honorary Fellow of Peterho... Cambridge University. Professor ... (1947–1954) and Regius Professo... (1954–1963) at Cambridge University. *Order in England; The Religious Or... Evolution of Medieval Thought.* BERN... ST.; BOETHIUS, ANICIUS MANLIUS SEVE... AURILLAC; JOHN OF SALISBURY; WILLIAM ...

Koestenbaum, Peter, B.A. (Stanford); M.A. ... (Boston University). Professor of Philoso... State College; Member of the Statewide Ac... California State Colleges; Member of the ed... the *Journal of Existentialism* and *Journal of ... chiatry.* Author of articles in *Philosophy and ... cal Research, Review internationale de philoso... Existential Psychiatry,* and others. JASPERS, K... MAX; UNAMUNO Y JUGO, MIGUEL DE.

Koestler, Arthur. Novelist, essayist, man of letter... the Royal Society of Literature; Member of the ... Patentees (Inc.). Author, *Darkness at Noon; T... Longing; Dialogue With Death; The Invisible W... God That Failed; The Yogi and the Commissar; ... on Hanging; The Sleepwalkers; The Act of Crea...* many others. KEPLER, JOHANNES.

Köhler, Eckehart, B.A. (Lehigh University). Member ... losophisches Seminar II at the University of Munich... candidate at New York University. SCHOLZ, HEINRICH.

Konvitz, Milton R., B.S., M.A., J.D. (New York Univers... Ph.D. (Cornell); Litt.D. (Hon., Rutgers); D.C.L. (H... University of Liberia). Professor of Law and Professor of ... dustrial and Labor Relations at Cornell University. Forme... General Counsel, Newark Housing Authority and N... Jersey State Housing Authority; Assistant General Couns... N.A.A.C.P.; member of the faculties of New York Universit... and the New School for Social Research. Author, *The Con... stitution and Civil Rights* (1947); *Fundamental Liberties o... a Free People* (1957); *A Century of Civil Rights* (1961); *Expanding Liberty* (1966); and other works. HISTORICAL SCHOOL OF JURISPRUDENCE; SAVIGNY, FRIEDRICH KARL VON.

Körner, Stephan, jur.Dr., M.A., Ph.D. Head of the Department of Philosophy at the University of Bristol; President of the British Society for the Philosophy of Science (1965–1967); President of the Aristotelian Society (1966). Visiting Professor of Philosophy at Brown University (1957), at Yale University (1960), and at the University of Texas (1964). Publications include *Conceptual Thinking* (2d ed., 1959); *Kant* (2d ed., 1960); *Philosophy of Mathematics* (1960); *Observation and Interpretation* (1959); *Experience and Theory* (1966). CASSIRER, ERNST; CONTINUITY; LAWS OF THOUGHT.

Kovesi, Julius, B.A. (University of Western Australia); B.Phil. (Oxford). Lecturer in Philosophy at the University of Western Australia. Formerly, Assistant Lecturer in Philosophy at the University of Edinburgh; Lecturer in Philosophy at the University of New England (Australia). HUNGARIAN PHILOSOPHY; PALÁGYI, MENYHERT; PAULER, AKOS.

Krailsheimer, Alban John, M.A. (Oxford); Ph.D. (University of Glasgow). University Lecturer and College Tutor in French, Christ Church, Oxford University. Formerly, Lecturer in French at the universities of Manchester and Glasgow. Publications include *Studies in Self Interest From Descartes to La Bruyère* (1962); *Rabelais and the Franciscans* (1963); Pascal's *Pensées* (translation, 1966); *Three* at the University of Notre Dame (1960–1961). Recent articles include "Logic and Existence," *British Journal for the Philosophy of Science* (1954–1955); "On Leśniewski's Ontology," *Ratio* (1957–1958); "A Re-examination of the Russellian Theory of Descriptions," *Philosophy* (1960); "Aristotle's Syllogistic and Its Extensions," *Synthese* (1963). LEŚNIEWSKI, STANISŁAW; LOGIC, HISTORY OF (section on ancient logic); ŁUKASIEWICZ, JAN.

Levy, Donald, B.A. (Cornell). Member of the Faculty at the New School for Social Research; Associate Editor of the *Encyclopedia of Philosophy;* Ph.D. candidate at Cornell University (1960–1961); Instructor in philosophy at Adelphi College (1962) and at Bard College (1962–1963). MACROCOSM AND MICROCOSM.

Lewis, H. D., M.A., B.Litt., D.D. (Hon., St. Andrews). Head of the Department of the History and Philosophy of Religion at King's College, University of London, and Fellow of King's College; Dean of the Faculty of Theology at the University of London; President of the Society for the Study of Theology; Chairman of the Council of the Royal Institute of Philosophy; Editor of the Muirhead Library of Philosophy; Editor of *Religious Studies.* President of the Mind Association (1948–1949) and the Aristotelian Society (1962–1963); has given the Edward Cadbury Lectures, the McMaster Lectures, the Owen Evans Lectures, the Wilde Lectures, the Firth Lectures, and the Gifford Lectures. Publications include *Morals and the New Theology; Morals and Revelation; Contemporary British Philosophy* (edited Vol. III); *Our Experience of God; Freedom and History; Teach Yourself: The Philosophy of Religion; World Religions* (with R. L. Slater). GUILT; PHILOSOPHY OF RELIGION, HISTORY OF.

Linsky, Leonard, B.A., M.A., Ph.D. Professor of Philosophy at the University of Illinois. Formerly, Visiting Professor at the universities of Wisconsin, Michigan, Amsterdam, and Chicago. Author, "Reference and Referents" (in C. E. Caton, ed., *Philosophy and Ordinary Language*). Editor, *Semantics and the Philosophy of Language* (1952). REFERRING; SYNONYMITY.

Liu, Wu-chi, B.A. (Lawrence College); Ph.D. (Yale). Professor of Chinese and Chairman of the Department of East Asian Languages and Literature at Indiana University. Formerly, Visiting Professor of Chinese at Yale University; Professor and Director of the Chinese Language and Area Center at the University of Pittsburgh. Author, *A Short History of Confucian Philosophy* (1955); *Confucius, His Life and Time* (1955). TUNG CHUNG-SHU; YANG CHU.

Lloyd, A. C., B.A. (Oxford). Professor of Philosophy at the University of Liverpool. Author, "The Later Neoplatonists" (in *Cambridge History of Later Greek and Early Medieval Philosophy*, 1966). ALEXANDER OF APHRODISIAS; IAMBLICHUS; PORPHYRY; SIMPLICIUS.

Lloyd, G. E. R., M.A., Ph.D. (Cambridge). University Assistant Lecturer in Classics and Fellow of King's College, Cambridge University. Publications include *Polarity and Analogy: Two Types of Argumentation in Early Greek Thought* (1966) and articles in *Phronesis, Journal of Hellenic Studies,* and *Proceedings of the Cambridge Philological Society.* LEUCIPPUS AND DEMOCRITUS.

Loemker, L. E., A.B. (University of Dubuque); S.T.B., Ph.D. (Boston University). Charles Howard Candler Professor of Philosophy at Emory University. Dean of the Graduate School at Emory University (1946–1952); Past Rosenwald, Fulbright, and Guggenheim Fellow. Translator and editor, Gottfried Wilhelm Leibniz, *Philosophical Papers and Letters* (2 vols., 1956). Author of articles in various philosophical journals. DEUSSEN, PAUL; HARTMANN, EDUARD VON; LIEBERT, ARTHUR; MONAD AND MONADOLOGY; PESSIMISM AND OPTIMISM; PAULSEN, FRIEDRICH; RINTELEN, FRITZ-JOACHIM VON; SPRANGER, (FRANZ ERNST) EDUARD.

Lombardi Franco, Ordinary Professor of Moral Philosophy at the University of Rome; Director of *De Homine.* Formerly, Professor of the History of Philosophy and Director of the Institute of Philosophy at the University of Rome; President of the Italian Philosophical Society; President of the Research Center in Moral and Social Sciences; Director of the Board of the Association for Cultural Liberty. Author of numerous works in French and German, including *Naissance du monde moderne.* BLOCH, ERNST.

Long, Herbert S., A.B. (Hamilton College); A.M., Ph.D. (Princeton). Edward North Professor of Greek at Hamilton College. Member of the Institute for Advanced Study (Princton, N.J., 1951–1951, 1965–1966); Visiting Professor at the American School of Classical Studies at Athens (1958–1959). Publications include *Diogenis Laertii Vitae Philosophorum* (2 vols., 1964). DIOGENES LAËRTIUS.

Loomis, Charles P., B.S. (New Mexico State University); M.S. (North Carolina State College); Ph.D. (Harvard). Research Professor at Michigan State University; Consultant in Rural Sociology and Program Specialist, Ford Foundation, India; President of the American Sociological Association. Visiting Lecturer at Harvard University (1932–1933) and the University of Wisconsin; Member of Morale Division, Strategic Bombing Survey, Germany (1943); Director of Extension and Training, Foreign Agricultural Relations, U.S. Department of Agriculture (1943–1944); Head of the Mission to Andean Countries, United Nations Refugee Organization (1947); Chairman of the Department of Sociology and Anthropology, Michigan State University (1944–1963). Numerous publications include *Rural Social Systems and Adult Education* (1953); *Turrialba* (edited with others, 1953); *Rural Sociology* (with J. A. Beegle, 1957); *Social Systems* (1960); *Modern Social Theories* (edited with Z. K. Loomis, 1961). TÖNNIES, FERDINAND.

Luckmann, Thomas, M.A., Ph.D. Professor at the University of Frankfurt; Visiting Professor, Graduate Faculty, the New School for Social Research. Past Associate Professor, Graduate Faculty, the New School for Social Research. Author, *Das Problem der Religion in der modernen Gesellschaft* PLESSNER, HELMUT.

Luscombe, D. E., M.A., Ph.D. (Cambridge). Fellow and Director of Studies in History at Churchill College, Cambridge University. Formerly, Fellow of King's College, Cambridge University. BERNARD OF CHARTRES; BERNARD OF TOURS; CHARTRES, SCHOOL OF; GILBERT OF POITIERS; SAINT VICTOR, SCHOOL OF; THEODORIC OF CHARTRES; WILLIAM OF CHAMPEAUX; WILLIAM OF CONCHES.

MacCallum, H. R., B.A., M.A., Ph.D. Associate Professor in the Department of English at the University of Toronto. MILTON, JOHN.

MacClintock, Stuart, A.B. (University of Chicago); Ph.D. (Columbia). Presently with the U.S. Government, Department of Defense. Assistant Professor of Philosophy at Indiana University (1952–1960); Visiting Assistant Professor of Philosophy at Columbia University (1953–1954); Visiting Lecturer at the University of Virginia (1959). Publications include "Heresy and Epithet," *Review of Metaphysics* (1954–1955); *Perversity and Error* (1956). AVERROËS; AVERROISM; JOHN OF JANDUN; SIGER OF BRABANT.

Mace, C. A., M.A. (Cambridge); D.Litt. (University of London). Emeritus Professor at the University of London; Honorary Fellow of Birbeck College, University of London; Honorary Fellow of the British Psychological Association.

Tarner Lecturer, Trinity College, Cambridge University (1940–1941); President of the Aristotelian Society (1948–1949); President of the British Psychology Society (1952–1953). Author, *The Psychology of Study* (rev. ed., 1962); *Principles of Logic* (1933); and papers in philosophical and psychological journals. PSYCHOLOGY (section on the transition from philosophy to science); STOUT, GEORGE FREDERICK; WARD, JAMES.

MacIntyre, Alasdair, B.A. (University of London); M.A. (University of Manchester and Oxford). Professor of Sociology at the University of Essex. Fellow of Nuffield College, Oxford University (1961–1962); Fellow of University College, Oxford University (1962–1966); Visiting Professor of Philosophy at Princeton University (1965–1966). Publications include *The Unconscious* (1957); *A Short History of Ethics* (1966). BEING; BRUNNER, EMIL; EGOISM AND ALTRUISM; ESSENCE AND EXISTENCE; EXISTENTIALISM; FREUD, SIGMUND; JUNG, CARL GUSTAV; KIERKEGAARD, SOREN AABYE; MYTH; ONTOLOGY; PANTHEISM; SPINOZA, BENEDICT (BARUCH).

Mackie, J. L., B.A. (University of Sydney); M.A. (Oxford). Professor of Philosophy at the University of York (England). Professor of Philosophy at the University of Otago (New Zealand, 1955–1959); Professor of Philosophy at the University of Sydney (1959–1963). Publications include "A Refutation of Morals" and "Responsibility and Language," *Australasian Journal of Philosophy;* "Evil and Omnipotence," *Mind;* "The Paradox of Confirmation," *British Journal for the Philosophy of Science;* "Causes and Conditions," *American Philosophical Quarterly.* FALLACIES; MILL'S METHODS OF INDUCTION; WESTERMARCK, EDWARD ALEXANDER.

MacNabb, Donald G. C., M.A. (Oxford). Fellow and Lecturer at Pembroke College, Oxford University. Author, *David Hume, His Theory of Knowledge and Morality* (1949). HUME, DAVID.

Macquarrie, John, M.A., B.D., Ph.D., D.Litt. Professor of Systematic Theology at Union Theological Seminary. Lecturer in Systematic Theology at the University of Glasgow (1953–1962). Author, *An Existentialist Theology* (1955); *The Scope of Demythologizing* (1960); *Twentieth-century Religious Thought* (1963). BLONDEL, MAURICE; DREWS, ARTHUR CHRISTIAN HEINRICH; GOGARTEN, FRIEDRICH; HARNACK, CARL GUSTAV ADOLF VON; HEIM, KARL; INGE, WILLIAM RALPH; LABERTHONNIERE, LUCIEN; PIETISM; SORLEY, WILLIAM RITCHIE; TAYLOR, ALFRED EDWARD; VARISCO, BERNARDINO.

Madden, Edward H., A.B., A.M. (Oberlin College); Ph.D. (University of Iowa). Professor of Philosophy at the State University of New York at Buffalo; General Editor of Source Books in the History of Science (Harvard University Press). Visiting Professor at Brown University (1954–1955) and at Amherst College (1962). Editor, *Philosophical Writings of Chauncey Wright* (1958). Coauthor (with R. M. Blake and C. J. Ducasse), *Theories of Scientific Method* (1960). Author, *The Structure of Scientific Thought* (1960); *Philosophical Problems of Psychology* (1962); *Chauncey Wright and the Foundations of Pragmatism* (1963); *Chauncey Wright* (1964). WRIGHT, CHAUNCEY.

Malcolm, Norman, B.A. (University of Nebraska); M.A., Ph.D. (Harvard). Susan Linn Sage Professor of Philosophy and Chairman of the Department of Philosophy at Cornell University; Managing Editor of the *Philosophical Review.* James Wood Fellow at Harvard University (1937–1939); Guggenheim Fellow (1946–1947); Hibben Research Fellow at Princeton University (1952); Fulbright Research Fellow at the University of Helsinki (1960–1961); Visiting Flint Professor of Philosophy at the University of California, Los Angeles (1964). Author, *Ludwig Wittgenstein: A Memoir* (1958); *Dreaming* (1959); *Knowledge and Certainty* (1963). WITTGENSTEIN, LUDWIG JOSEF JOHANN.

Mandelbaum, Maurice, A.B., M.A. (Dartmouth College); Ph.D. (Yale). Professor of Philosophy at Johns Hopkins University; Delegate to the American Council of Learned Societies from the American Philosophical Association. Guggenheim Fellow (1946); Secretary–Treasurer (1940–1942) and President (1962) of the American Philosophical Association, Eastern Division. Author, *The Problem of Historical Knowledge* (1938); *The Phenomenology of Moral Experience* (1955); *Philosophy, Science, and Sense Perception* (1964). HISTORICISM.

Manser, Anthony, M.A., B.Phil. (Oxford). Senior Lecturer in Philosophy at the University of Southampton (England). Publications include "Dreams," *Supplementary PAS* (1956); "The Concept of Evolution," *Philosophy* (1965); *Sartre: A Philosophic Study* (1966). DREAMS; IMAGES; IMAGINATION.

Margoshes, Adam (1922–1966). Born in New York, he received his B.A. from New York University and his M.A. from the New School for Social Research where he also completed the course work for his doctorate. At the time of his death he was Assistant Professor of Psychology at Shippensburg State College (Pennsylvania). He was the author of various essays, articles and reviews published in the *Village Voice* and elsewhere, and of fifteen articles on psychology published in scientific journals. BAADER, FRANZ XAVIER VON; SCHELLING, FRIEDRICH WILHELM JOSEPH VON.

Markovic, Mihailo, Ph.D. (University of Belgrade and University of London). Professor in the Philosophy Department at Belgrade University; Member-Correspondent of the Serbian Academy of Sciences; Head of the section for the Methodology of Science in the Institute for Social Sciences (Belgrade); Member of the Council for the Coordination of Scientific Research. Formerly, Head of the Philosophy Department and Vice-Dean of the Faculty of Philosophy, Belgrade University. Author, *Formalism in Contemporary Logic* (1958); *The Dialectical Theory of Meaning* (1961). YUGOSLAV PHILOSOPHY.

Markus, R. A., M.A., Ph.D. Senior Lecturer in Medieval History at the University of Liverpool. Coauthor (with A. H. Armstrong), *Christian Faith and Greek Philosophy* (1960). Author of articles in various theological journals and cooperative volumes. AUGUSTINE, ST.; ILLUMINATION.

Marmura, Michael E., B.A. (University of Wisconsin); M.A. Ph.D. (University of Michigan). Associate Professor in the Department of Islamic Studies at the University of Toronto. Publications include "Avicenna and the Problem of the Infinite Number of Souls," *Mediaeval Studies* (1960); "Avicenna's Psychological Proof of Prophecy," *Journal of Near Eastern Studies* (1963); "Ghazali and Demonstrative Science," *Journal of the History of Philosophy* (1965). AVICENNA.

Martin, Norman M., M.A. (University of Chicago); Ph.D. (University of California, Los Angeles). Associate Professor of Philosophy and Research Scientist in the Computation Center, University of Texas; Consultant, Logicon, Inc.; Member of the General Editorial Board of *Methodology and Science.* Formerly, Instructor at the universities of Illinois and California, Los Angeles; Research Associate at the University of Michigan (1953–1955); Head of the Logic and Techniques Group at the Technology Laboratories (1955–1961); Senior Staff Logician and Corporate Treasurer of Logicon, Inc. (1961–1965). Publications include "The Sheffer Functions of Three Valued Logic," *Journal of Symbolic Logic* (1954); "On Completeness of Decision Element Sets," *Journal of Computing Systems* (1953); "Deduction and Strict Implication," *Synthese* (1960). CARNAP, RUDOLF.

Marty, Martin E., A.B., B.D. (Concordia Seminary); S.T.M. (Union Theological Seminary); Ph.D. (University of Chicago); Litt.D. (Thiel College). Associate Professor of Church History, Divinity School, University of Chicago; Associate Editor of the *Christian Century*. Formerly, Minister at Christ Lutheran Church, Washington, D.C., and other parishes. Editor, *New Directions in Biblical Thought* (1960). Coeditor, *Handbook of Christian Theologians* (1964); *New Theology, No. 1, No. 2, No. 3* (1963, 1964, 1965). Author, *A Short History of Christianity* (1959); *The New Shape of American Religion* (1959); *The Infidel* (1961); *Second Chance for American Protestants* (1963); *Varieties of Unbelief* (1964). BONHOEFFER, DIETRICH.

Maurer, Armand, B.A., M.A., M.S.L. Ph.D. Professor of Philosophy at the Pontifical Institute of Mediaeval Studies and at the University of Toronto; Priest of the Congregation of St. Basil. Guggenheim Fellow (1954–1955). Author, *Medieval Philosophy* (1962). BOETIUS OF DACIA; BROWNSON, ORESTES AUGUSTUS; EDWARDS, JONATHAN; HENRY OF HARCLAY; JOHNSON, SAMUEL; NICHOLAS OF CUSA.

Mays, Wolfe, Ph.D. (Cambridge). Senior Lecturer in Philosophy at the University of Manchester; Visiting Professor of Philosophy at Northwestern University. Formerly, Assistant to Professor Jean Piaget and Member of the Centre International d'Epistémologie Génétique at the University of Geneva. Translator, Jean Piaget, *Logic and Psychology* (1953). Author, *The Philosophy of Whitehead* (1959), and numerous articles in philosophical and scientific journals. PIAGET, JEAN.

Mazlish, Bruce, A.B., A.M., Ph.D. (Columbia). Professor of History at M.I.T. Past Associate Editor of *History and Theory*. Editor, *Psychoanalysis and History* (1963); *The Railroad and the Space Program: An Exploration in Historical Analogy* (1965). Coauthor (with J. Bronowski), *The Western Intellectual Tradition: From Leonardo to Hegel* (1960). Author, *The Riddle of History: From Vico to Freud* (1966). COMTE, AUGUSTE.

McCall, Storrs, B.A. (McGill); B.Phil., D.Phil. (Oxford). Visiting Reader in Philosophy at Makerere University (Uganda, East Africa). Formerly taught at McGill University and the University of Pittsburgh. Author, *Aristotle's Modal Syllogisms* (1963); Editor, *Polish Logic* (1966). LOGIC, HISTORY OF (section on Hugh MacColl).

McClellan, James E., Jr., B.S. (University of Texas); M.A., Ph.D. (University of Illinois). Director of the Foundations of Education Department and The General Education Program for Teachers and Professor of Education at Temple University (Philadelphia). Formerly, Associate Professor at Columbia University; Guggenheim Fellow (1964–1965). Coauthor (with Solon T. Kimball), *Education and the New America* (1962). Author of numerous articles and reviews in journals and anthologies. PHILOSOPHY OF EDUCATION, INFLUENCE OF MODERN PSYCHOLOGY ON.

McInnes, Neil, B.S. (University of Sydney). Special writer in Paris for *Barron's Financial Weekly* and the *Wall Street Journal*. Formerly, writer for *Capital* and the *Statesman* in Calcutta; Investment Editor for the *Australian Financial Review*. Author, "An Examination of the Work of Wilhelm Reich," *Hermes* (1946), and other articles, and *Sorel on Violence* (forthcoming). COMMUNISM; ENGELS, FRIEDRICH; GRACIÁN Y MORALES, BALTASAR; GRAMSCI, ANTONIO; LABRIOLA, ANTONIO; LUKÁCS, GEORG; MARÍAS, JULIÁN; MARX, KARL; MARXIST PHILOSOPHY; ORTEGA Y GASSET, JOSÉ; PHILOSOPHER-KINGS; SOREL, GEORGES; SPANISH PHILOSOPHY; ZUBIRI, XAVIER.

Mei, Y. P., B.A. (Oberlin College); Ph.D. (University of Chicago); LL.D. (Oberlin College); L.H.D. (Wabash College). Professor and Chairman of the Department of Chinese and Oriental Studies and Director of the Center for Far Eastern Studies, University of Iowa. Professor of Philosophy (1934–1948), Dean of the College of Arts and Letters (1931–1934), and Acting President (1942–1946) of Yenching University (China). Publications include *The Ethical and Political Philosophy of Motse* (1929); *Motse, The Neglected Rival of Confucius* (1934); "The Basis of Social, Ethical, and Spiritual Values in Chinese Philosophy" (in C. A. Moore, ed., *Essays in East–West Philosophy,* 1951); and articles and translations in journals of Oriental studies. HSÜN TZU; MO TZU.

Merlan, Philip, Dr.phil., Dr.iur. (University of Vienna). Professor of German Philosophy and Literature at Scripps College and Claremont Graduate School (California). Guggenheim Fellow (1955); R. Merton Visiting Professor at the University of Würzburg (1958–1959); President of the American Philosophical Association, Pacific Division (1959–1960); President of the Society for Ancient Greek Philosophy (1958, 1961); Fulbright Senior Lecturer at Oxford University (1962); Acting Dean of Faculty, Scripps College (1963–1964); Visiting Professor and Fulbright Senior Lecturer at the University of Munich; Member of the Institute for Advanced Study (Princeton, N.J.). Numerous publications include *From Platonism to Neoplatonism* (1953); *Studies in Epicurus and Aristotle* (1960); *Monopsychism, Mysticism, Metaconsciousness* (1963). ALEXANDRIAN SCHOOL; ATHENIAN SCHOOL; EMANATIONISM; NEOPLATONISM; PLOTINUS.

Mesnard, Pierre, Agrégé de Philosophie, Licencié ès Sciences. Docteur ès Lettres. Professor of Philosophy, Faculty of Letters, University of Orléans-Tours; Director of Centre d'Études Supérieures de la Renaissance de Tours. Formerly, Professor in the Faculty of Letters at the University of Algiers. Author, *L'Essor de la philosophie politique au XVIe siècle; Le Vrai Visage de Kierkegaard; Éducation et caractère; Le Cas Diderot;* and others. BODIN, JEAN.

Miles, Leland, A.B. (Juniata College); M.A., Ph.D. (University of North Carolina). Dean of the College of Arts and Sciences, University of Bridgeport. Professor of English, University of Cincinnati (1960–1963); A.C.L.S. Fellow at Harvard University (1963–1964); Senior Fulbright Research Scholar, King's College, University of London (1964). Editor, Thomas More, *Dialogue of Comfort Against Tribulation* (1966). Author, *John Colet and the Platonic Tradition* (1961) and articles on Colet and More in scholarly journals. COLET, JOHN.

Miles, T. R., M.A., Ph.D. Professor of Psychology at the University College of North Wales, Bangor. Author, *Religion and the Scientific Outlook* (1959), Translator, E. A. Michotte, *The Perception of Causality* (with commentary, 1963). GESTALT THEORY; KOFFKA, KURT.

Miller, Robert G., C.S.B., B.A., M.A., Ph.D. (University of Toronto). Chairman of the Department of Philosophy at St. John Fisher College (New York). Formerly, Associate Editor of *New Scholasticism;* Chairman of the Canadian Philosophical Association; Director of Development, University of St. Thomas (Houston); Executive of the American Catholic Philosophical Association; Editor of *Canadian Priest's Magazine;* Carnegie Fellow (1934–1938); Assumption Fellow (1959). Author, *The Psychology of St. Albert the Great* (Thesis, 1938) and numerous articles in philosophical journals. GILSON, ÉTIENNE HENRI.

Minogue, Kenneth, B.A., B.Sc. (University of Sydney). Senior Lecturer in Political Science at the London School of Economics and Political Science. Author, *The Liberal Mind* (1963). Contributor to *Political Studies, American Scholar, Twentieth Century,* and others. CONSERVATISM.

Monro, D. H., M.A. (University of New Zealand). Professor of Philosophy at Monash University (Australia). Formerly, Lecturer at Otago University (New Zealand) and the University of Sydney. Publications include articles in philosophical journals; *Argument of Laughter* (1951); *Godwin's Moral Philosophy* (1953). Bentham, Jeremy; Godwin, William; Humor; Mill, James; Shelley, Percy Bysshe.

Montague, Roger, B.A. (University of Bristol); B.Phil. (Oxford). Lecturer in Philosophy at the University of Hull. Logic, History of (sections on F. H. Bradley and Bernard Bosanquet).

Montefiore, Alan, M.A. (Oxford). Samuel Fellow in Philosophy at Balliol College, Oxford University. Formerly, Senior Lecturer in Moral and Political Philosophy at the University of Keele. Publications include *A Modern Introduction to Moral Philosophy* (1958). Revel, Jean-François.

Moody, Ernest A., B.A. (Williams College); M.A., Ph.D. (Columbia). Professor of Philosophy at the University of California, Los Angeles; Member of the Council of the Mediaeval Academy of America. Chairman of the Department of Philosophy at the University of California, Los Angeles (1961–1964); President of the American Philosophical Association, Pacific Division (1963). Editor, *Joannis Buridani Quaestiones Super Libris De Caelo et Mundo* (1942); *Gulielmi Ockham Expositio in Librum Porphyrii De Praedicabilibus* (1965). Author, *The Logic of William Ockham* (1935); *The Medieval Science of Weights* (with Marshall Clagett, 1952); *Truth and Consequence in Mediaeval Logic* (1953). Logic, history of (section on medieval logic); Ockhamism; William of Ockham.

Moore, Merritt Hadden, B.A. (Occidental College); M.A., Ph.D. (University of Chicago). Professor and Head of the Department of Philosophy at the University of Tennessee. Professor (1936–1955) and Chairman (1933–1955) of the Department of Philosophy and Registrar (1944–1946) and Dean of Students (1946–1948) at Knox College; Fulbright Research Scholar in France (1951–1952). Translator, A. A. Cournot, *An Essay on the Foundations of Our Knowledge* (1956). Editor, G. H. Mead, *Movements of Thought in the Nineteenth Century* (1936). Author, "The Place of A. A. Cournot in the History of Philosophy," *Philosophical Review* (1934); "Truth and the Interest Theory of Knowledge," *Journal of Philosophy* (1935); "A Metaphysics of Design Without Purpose," *Philosophy of Science* (1936). Cournot, Antoine Augustin.

Moran, Michael, B.A. (University of Keele). Lecturer in Philosophy at the School of European Studies, University of Sussex. Ministry of Education Post-Graduate Student at the University of Bristol (1959–1960); Assistant Lecturer in Philosophy at the University of Keele (1960–1962). Carlyle, Thomas; Coleridge, Samuel Taylor; Emerson, Ralph Waldo; New England transcendentalism; Thoreau, Henry David.

Morris, Herbert, B.A. (University of California, Los Angeles); LL.B. (Yale); D.Phil. (Oxford). Professor of Philosophy and Law at the University of California, Los Angeles. Former Fulbright Scholar and Ford Fellow. Publications include "Verbal Disputes and the Legal Philosophy of John Austin," *U.C.L.A. Law Review* (1960); *Freedom and Responsibility: Readings in the Philosophy of Law* (1961); "Punishment for Thoughts," *Monist* (1965). Austin, John.

Morrison, John, M.A. President of University College, Cambridge University. Formerly, Fellow and Senior Tutor of Trinity College, Cambridge University; Fellow, Senior Tutor, and Vice-Master of Churchill College, Cambridge University; Leverhulme Research Fellow (1965). Orphism.

Mossner, Ernest Campbell, B.A. (City College of New York); M.A., Ph.D. (Columbia). Professor of English at the University of Texas, Austin; Joint Editor of "Texas Studies in Literature and Language." Formerly, Professor of English at Syracuse University, and twice a Guggenheim Fellow. Publications include *Bishop Butler and the Age of Reason* (1936); *New Letters of David Hume* (1954); *The Life of David Hume* (1955). Annet, Peter; Blount, Charles; Bolingbroke, Henry St. John; Chubb, Thomas; Collins, Anthony; Deism; Gibbon, Edward; Herbert of Cherbury; Johnson, Samuel; Morgan, Thomas; Pope, Alexander; Swift, Jonathan; Tindal, Matthew; Toland, John; Wollaston, William; Woolston, Thomas.

Mostowski, Andrzej, Professor of Mathematics at the University of Warsaw; Corresponding Member of the Polish Academy of Sciences. Author, *Sentences Undecidable in Formalized Arithmetic* (1952); *Undecidable Theories* (with Alfred Tarski and R. M. Robinson, 1953); and many other publications. Tarski, Alfred.

Mothersill, Mary, B.A. (University of Toronto); Ph.D. (Harvard). Professor and Chairman of the Department of Philosophy at Barnard College. Formerly taught at Vassar College, the University of Chicago, and the City University of New York, City College. Editor, *Ethics* (1965). Author of various articles on moral philosophy and aesthetics. Duty.

Mourant, John A., Ph.B. (University of Chicago); A.M. (Harvard); Ph.D. (University of Chicago). Professor of Philosophy at Pennsylvania State University. Editor, *Readings in the Philosophy of Religion* (1954); *Introduction to the Philosophy of St. Augustine* (1964); *Problems of Philosophy* (with E. H. Freund, 1964). Author, *Formal Logic* (1963) and numerous articles and reviews. Augustinianism; Pelagius and Pelagianism; Suárez, Francisco.

Mourelatos, Alexander P. D., B.A., M.A., Ph.D. (Yale). Assistant Professor of Philosophy at the University of Texas, Austin. Post-Doctoral Fellow at the Institute for Research in the Humanities, University of Wisconsin (1964–1965). Fries, Jakob Friedrich.

Mundle, C. W. K., M.A. (St. Andrews); B.A. (Oxford). Head of the Philosophy Department of University College of North Wales, University of Wales. Formerly, Shaw Fellow in Philosophy at the University of Edinburgh (1948–1950). Head of the Philosophy Department of Queen's College, St. Andrews University. ESP phenomena, their philosophical implications; Time, consciousness of.

Munitz, Milton K., B.A. (City College); M.A., Ph.D. (Columbia) Professor of Philosophy at New York University. Ford Faculty Fellow (1954); Guggenheim Fellow (1960); Fulbright Research Appointment (1960). Author, *The Moral Philosophy of Santayana* (1939); *Space, Time, and Creation* (1954); *The Mystery of Existence* (1965). Cosmology.

Munz, Peter, M.A., Ph.D. (Cambridge). Associate Professor of Philosophy at the University of Wellington (New Zealand). Author, *The Place of Hooker in the History of Thought* (1952); *Problems of Religious Knowledge* (1959); *The Origin of the Carolingian Empire* (1960); *Relationship and Solitude* (1964). Hooker, Richard.

Murphey, Murray G., A.B. (Harvard); Ph.D. (Yale). Associate Professor of American Civilization at the University of Pennsylvania. Publications include *The Development of Peirce's Philosophy* (1961); *Principales tendencias de la filosofía norteamericana* (with Elizabeth Flower, 1963). Peirce, Charles Sanders.

Musurillo, Herbert, S.J., B.A. (Georgetown); M.A. (Catholic University); Ph.L., S.T.L. (Woodstock College); Ph.D. (Fordham); D.Phil. (Oxford). Professor of Classics at Fordham University. Publications include *Acts of the Pagan Martyrs* (1954); *St. Methodius* (critical ed., 1963). Gregory of Nazianzus; Gregory of Nyssa.

Nasr, Seyyed Hossein, B.S., M.A., Ph.D. Professor of the History of Science and Philosophy at Tehran University. Visiting Lecturer at Harvard University (1962); Aga Khan Professor of Islamic Studies, American University of Beirut (1964–1965). Publications include *Three Muslim Sages* (1964); *An Introduction to Islamic Cosmological Doctrines* (1964); *Science and Civilization in Islam* (1966). Mullā Sadra.

Needleman, Jacob, Ph.D. (Yale). Associate Professor of Philosophy at San Francisco State College. Publications include *Being-in-the-world* (1963). Binswanger, Ludwig; Existential psychoanalysis.

Nelson, John O., A.B. (Princeton); M.A. (Colgate); Ph.D. (Cornell). Professor of Philosophy at the University of Colorado. Past Chairman of the Executive Committee, Mountain Plains Philosophical Association. Innate ideas; Moore, George Edward.

Nerlich, G. C., M.A., B.Phil. Senior Lecturer in Philosophy at the University of Sydney. Author, "On Evidence for Identity," *Australasian Journal of Philosophy* (1959); "Unexpected Examinations and Unprovable Statements," *Mind* (1961); "Presuppositions and Entailment," *American Philosophical Quarterly* (1965). Eddington, Arthur Stanley; Jeans, James Hopwood; Popular Arguments for the existence of God; Stebbing, Lizzie Susan.

Niebuhr, Richard R., A.B. (Harvard); B.D. (Union Theological Seminary); Ph.D. (Yale). Florence Corliss Lamont Professor of Divinity, Harvard Divinity School, Harvard University. Publications include *Schleiermacher on Christ and Religion* (1964). Schleiermacher, Friedrich Daniel Ernst.

Nielsen, Kai, A.B. (University of North Carolina); Ph.D. (Duke). Associate Professor of Philosophy at New York University. Formerly taught at Hamilton College, Mount Holyoke College, Amherst College, and the State University of New York, Harpur College. Author, "Justification and Moral Reasoning," *Methodos* (1957); "On Speaking of God," *Theoria* (1962); "Religion and Commitment" (in W. T Blackstone and R. H. Ayers, eds., *Problems of Religious Knowledge and Language*); "On Fixing the Reference Range of 'God,'" *Religious Studies* (1966); and others. Ethics, history of (section on contemporary ethics); Ethics, problems of.

Niklaus, Robert, B. ès L., L. ès L. (University of Lille); B.A., Ph.D. (University of London), Doctorat de l'Université de Rennes (Hon.). Professor of French and Italian and Deputy Vice-Chancellor at the University of Exeter; Member of the Executive Committees of the Modern Humanities Research Association and the Society for French Studies; General Editor, *Textes français classiques et modernes*. Dean of the Faculty of Arts, University of Exeter (1959–1962); Visiting Professor of French, University of California, Berkeley (1963–1964); President of the International Association of University Professors and Lecturers (1960–1964). Editor, *Denis Diderot, pensées philosophiques* (1950), *J.-J. Rousseau, Confessions* (2 vols., 1960); and many others. Author of numerous articles and reviews in journals and encyclopedias. Boulainvilliers, Henri, Comte de; Clandestine philosophical literature in France.

Northedge, F. S., B.Sc., Ph.D. (University of London). Reader in International Relations, London School of Economics and Political Science, University of London. Author, *British Foreign Policy: The Process of Readjustment, 1945–1961*. Peace, war, and philosophy.

Nowell-Smith, Patrick H., M.A. (Oxford); A.M. (Harvard). Professor of Philosophy at the University of Kent. Formerly, Fellow of Trinity College, Oxford University (1946–1957); Professor of Philosophy at the University of Leicester. Author, *Ethics* (1954). Religion and morality.

O'Brien, Thomas C., O.P. Dominican House of Studies, Washington, D.C. Garrigou-Lagrange, Réginald Marie.

O'Connor, D. J., M.A., Ph.D. Professor of Philosophy at the University of Exeter. Formerly, Commonwealth Fund Fellow at the University of Chicago (1946–1947); Professor of Philosophy at the universities of Natal (South Africa), Witwatersrand (South Africa), and Liverpool. Publications include *John Locke* (1952); *Introduction to Symbolic Logic* (with A. H. Basson, 1953); *Introduction to the Philosophy of Education* (1957); *A Critical History of Western Philosophy* (editor and contributor, 1964). Ayer, Alfred Jules; Substance and attribute.

Olafson, Frederick A., A.B., M.A., Ph.D. (Harvard). Professor of Education and Philosophy, Harvard Graduate School of Education, Harvard University. Associate Professor of Philosophy at Vassar College (1954–1960) and at the Johns Hopkins University (1960–1964); Hodder Fellow in the Humanities at Princeton University (1960–1961). Author, *Society, Law and Morality* (1961). Camus, Albert; Merleau-Ponty, Maurice; Santayana, George; Sartre, Jean-Paul.

Oldenquist, Andrew, B.S. (Northwestern); M.A. (Brown); Ph.D. (Ohio State University). Associate Professor of Philosophy at Ohio State University. Publications include "Causes, Predictions and Decisions," *Analysis* (1964); *Readings in Moral Philosophy* (1965). Choosing, deciding, and doing; Fiske, John; Palmer, George Herbert; Self-prediction.

Olson, Robert G., B.A. (University of Minnesota); docteur de l'université de Paris, Sorbonne; Ph.D. (University of Michigan). Associate Professor and Chairman of the Department of Philosophy, University College, Rutgers University. Instructor in Philosophy at the University of Michigan (1956–1958); Assistant Professor of Philosophy at Columbia University (1958–1961). Author, *An Introduction to Existentialism* (1962); *The Morality of Self-interest* (1965). Death; Deontological ethics; Good, the; Nihilism; Teleological ethics.

Ong, Walter J., S.J., B.A. (Rockhurst College); M.A., S.T.L. (St. Louis University); Ph.D. (Harvard). Professor of English at St. Louis University. Guggenheim Fellow (1949–1950); Visiting Professor at the University of California (1960); Fellow, Center for Advanced Studies, Wesleyan University (1961–1962); Visiting Lecturer, Centre d'Études Supérieres de la Renaissance (Tours, France); Terry Lecturer, Yale University (1963–1964); Fellow of the School of Letters, Indiana University (since 1955). Author, *Ramus, Method, and the Decay of Dialogue* (1958); *Ramus and Talon Inventory* (1958); *The Barbarian Within* (1962). Numerous contributions to books and international periodicals. Ramus, Peter.

Osborn, E. F., M.A., B.D. (University of Melbourne); Ph.D. (Cambridge). Professor of Biblical Studies, Queen's College, University of Melbourne; Editor of the *Australian Biblical Review*; Member of the Joint Commission for Church Union in Australia. Sims Travelling Scholar at the University of Melbourne (1952); Von Humboldt Research Fellow at the University of Tübingen (1964–1965). Publications include *The Philosophy of Clement of Alexandria* (1957); *The Faith of the Gospel* (1957); *Church Union Now* (1964); and articles and reviews in scholarly journals. Arius and Arianism; Clement of Alexandria; Pseudo-Dionysius.

Owen, H. P., M.A. Reader in the Philosophy of Religion at the University of London. Author, *Revelation and Existence* (1957); *The Moral Argument for Christian Theism* (1965).

DOGMA; ESCHATOLOGY; GOD, CONCEPTS OF; INFINITY IN THEOLOGY AND METAPHYSICS; PERFECTION; PROVIDENCE; THEISM.

Pappas, John N., B.A., M.A., Ph.D. (Columbia). Professor of French, Department of Romance Languages, University of Pennsylvania. Formerly taught at the University of Lille (1950–1951), Columbia University (1952–1956), and Indiana University (1956–1965). Publications include *Berthier's Journal de Trévoux and the Philosophes* (Vol. III of *Studies on Voltaire and the Eighteenth Century*, 1957); *Voltaire and D'Alembert* (1962); and many articles and reviews in scholarly journals. ALEMBERT, JEAN LE ROND D'.

Pappe, H. O., Ph.D. Member of the Faculty of the School of Social Sciences, University of Sussex. Formerly taught at the Australian National University. Publications include "On Philosophical Anthropology," *Australasian Journal of Philosophy* (1961). GEHLEN, ARNOLD; JÜNGER, ERNST; PHILOSOPHICAL ANTHROPOLOGY; SOMBART, WERNER.

Parsons, Charles, A.B., A.M., Ph.D. (Harvard). Associate Professor of Philosophy at Columbia University. Junior Fellow of the Society of Fellows, Harvard University (1958–1961); Assistant Professor of Philosophy at Cornell University (1961–1962) and at Harvard University (1962–1965). Author, "The ω-consistency of Ramified Analysis," *Archiv für mathematische Logik und Grundlagenforschung* (1962); "Infinity and Kant's Conception of the 'Possibility of Experience,'" *Philosophical Review* (1964); "Frege's Theory of Number" (in Max Black, ed., *Philosophy in America*, 1965). BROUWER, LUITZEN EGBERTUS JAN; MATHEMATICS, FOUNDATIONS OF.

Partridge, P. H., M.A. (University of Sydney). Director of the Research School of Social Sciences and Professor of Social Philosophy at the Australian National University. Formerly, Professor of Government at the University of Sydney. FREEDOM; MICHELS, ROBERT; MOSCA, GAETANO.

Passmore, John, M.A. (University of Sydney). Professor of Philosophy at the Institute of Advanced Studies, Australian National University. Professor of Philosophy at the University of Otago (New Zealand, 1950–1955); Visiting Professor of Philosophy at Brandeis University (1961). Author, *Ralph Cudworth; David Hume; A Hundred Years of Philosophy; Philosophical Reasoning.* ANDERSON, JOHN; BOYLE, ROBERT; CAMBRIDGE PLATONISTS; COLLIER, ARTHUR; CUDWORTH, RALPH; CULVERWEL, NATHANAEL; CUMBERLAND, RICHARD; FLUDD, ROBERT; HARVEY, WILLIAM; LOGICAL POSITIVISM; MORE, HENRY; NORRIS, JOHN; PHILOSOPHY; PHILOSOPHY, HISTORIOGRAPHY OF; PRIESTLEY, JOSEPH; SMITH, JOHN; WHICHCOTE, BENJAMIN.

Pavićević, Vuko, Ph.D. Professor of Ethics and Sociology at the University of Belgrade. Author, *Uvod u Etiku* ("Introduction to Ethics"); *Odnos Vrednosti i Stvarnosti u Nemačkoj Idealističkoj Nemačkoj Aksiologiji* ("Relation Between Values and Reality in the Idealistic German Axiology"); *O Dužnostima* ("Of Duties"). PETROVIĆ-NJEGOŠ, PETAR.

Penelhum, Terence, M.A. (University of Edinburgh); B. Phil. (Oxford). Professor and Head of the Department of Philosophy and Dean of Arts and Sciences, University of Alberta at Calgary. English-Speaking Union Visiting Fellow at Yale University (1952–1953). Author, "Hume on Personal Identity," *Philosophical Review* (1955); "The Logic of Pleasure," *Philosophy and Phenomenological Research* (1957); "Divine Necessity," *Mind* (1958); "Pleasure and Falsity," *American Philosophical Quarterly* (1964). PERSONAL IDENTITY.

Peters, R. S., B.A. (Oxford and the University of London); Ph.D. (University of London). Professor of the Philosophy of Education at the University of London Institute of Education. Formerly, Reader in Philosophy, Birkbeck College, University of London; Visiting Professor, Graduate School of Education, Harvard University. Publications include *Brett's History of Psychology* (revised and brought up to date, 2d ed., 1962); *Hobbes* (1956); *The Concept of Motivation* (2d ed., 1960); *Social Principles and the Democratic State* (with S. I. Benn, 1960). HOBBES, THOMAS; PSYCHOLOGY (section on the systematic philosophy of mind).

Petrović, Gajo, B.A., Ph.D. (University of Zagreb). Associate Professor of Philosophy at the University of Zagreb; President of the Yugoslav Philosophical Association. Editor in Chief of *Praxis.* President of the Croatian Philosophical Society (1963–1964). Publications include *Engleska Empiristička Filozofija* ("English Empirical Philosophy," 1955); *Filozofski Pogledi G. V. Plehanova* ("Philosophical Views of G. V. Plekhanov," 1957); *Logika* ("Logic," 1964); *Od Lockea do Ayera* ("From Locke to Ayer," 1964); *Filozofija i Marksizam* ("Philosophy and Marxism," 1965). ALIENATION; PLEKHANOV, GEORGI VALENTINOVICH.

Pines, Shlomo, Ph.D. (University of Berlin). Professor of General and Jewish Philosophy at the Hebrew University of Jerusalem. Publications include *Beiträge zur islamischen Atomenlehre; Nouvelles Études sur Abu'l-Barakāt al-Baghdādī; A New Fragment of Xenocrates and Its Implications; The Guide of the Perplexed, A Translation of Maimonides' Arabic Text.* JEWISH PHILOSOPHY; MAIMONIDES.

Piovesana, Gino K., S.J., Lit.D. (Keio University, Japan). Director of the Board of Regents and Professor of Philosophy at Sophia University (Japan). Formerly, Head of the Russian Department and Director of the Library at Sophia University. Author, *Recent Japanese Political Thought, 1862–1962* (1963). ANDŌ SHŌEKI; HATANO SEIICHI; HAYASHI RAZAN; ITŌ JINSAI; JAPANESE PHILOSOPHY; KAIBARA EKKEN; KUMAZAWA BANZAN; MIKI KIYOSHI; MINAGAWA KIEN; MIURA BAIEN; MURO KYŪSO; NAKAE TŌJU; NISHI AMANE; OGYŪ SORAI; TANABE HAJIME; WATSUJI TETSURŌ; YAMAGĀ SOKŌ; YAMAZAKI ANSAI.

Plantinga, Alvin, A.B. (Calvin College); A.M. (University of Michigan); Ph.D. (Yale). Professor of Philosophy at Calvin College. Instructor at Yale University (1957–1958); Visiting Lecturer at the University of Illinois (1960); Instructor, Assistant Professor, and Associate Professor at Wayne State University (1958–1963); Visiting Lecturer at Harvard University (1964–1965). Author of articles in books and journals. MALCOLM, NORMAN.

Popkin, Richard H., B.A., M.A., Ph.D. (Columbia). Professor and Chairman of the Department of Philosophy at the University of California, San Diego; Editor of the *Journal of the History of Philosophy;* Codirector of the International Archives of the History of Ideas. Fulbright Research Fellow in Paris (1952–1953) and Utrecht (1957–1958); Associate Professor of Philosophy at the University of Iowa (1954–1960); Professor of Philosophy at Harvey Mudd College (1960–1963). Publications include *History of Scepticism From Erasmus to Descartes* (1960); *Introduction to Philosophy* (with Avrum Stroll, 1961); *Pierre Bayle, Historical and Critical Dictionary* (Selections, translated and edited, 1965). AGRIPPA VON NETTESHEIM, HENRICUS CORNELIUS; BAYLE, PIERRE; CHARRON, PIERRE; COSTA, URIEL DA; ERASMUS, DESIDERIUS; FIDEISM; GASSENDI, PIERRE; GLANVIL, JOSEPH; HUET, PIERRE-DANIEL; LA MOTHE LE VAYER, FRANÇOIS DE; MENASSEH (MANASSEH) BEN ISRAEL; MERSENNE, MARIN; MONTAIGNE, MICHEL EYQUEM DE; OROBIO DE CASTRO, ISAAC; PASCAL, BLAISE; LA PEYRÈRE, ISAAC; SANCHES, FRANCISCO; SIMON, RICHARD; SKEPTICISM.

Presley, C. F., B.A. (University of Wales); B.Litt. (Oxford). Head of the Department of Philosophy at the University of Queensland (Australia). Author, "Laws and Theories in the

Sciences," *Australasian Journal of Philosophy* (1954); "Arguments About Meaninglessness," *British Journal for the Philosophy of Science* (1961). QUINE, WILLARD VAN ORMAN.

Price, Kingsley, A.B., M.A., Ph.D. (University of California). Professor of Philosophy at Johns Hopkins University. Publications include "Is a Philosophy of Education Necessary?," *Journal of Philosophy* (1955); "On Having an Education," *Harvard Educational Review* (1958); "The Work of Art and the Postures of the Mind," *Review of Metaphysics* (1959); *Education and Philosophical Thought* (1962). PHILOSOPHY OF EDUCATION, HISTORY OF.

Prior, A. N., M.A. (University of New Zealand and University of Manchester). Professor of Philosophy at the University of Manchester; Coeditor of the *Journal of Symbolic Logic;* Fellow of the British Academy. Formerly, Professor of Philosophy at the University of Canterbury (New Zealand); John Locke Lecturer at Oxford University (1956); Visiting Professor at the University of Chicago (1962); Flint Visiting Professor at the University of California, Los Angeles. Author, *Logic and the Basis of Ethics* (1949); *Formal Logic* (1955); *Time and Modality* (1957). CORRESPONDENCE THEORY OF TRUTH; EXISTENCE; LOGIC, DEONTIC; LOGIC, HISTORY OF (sections on W. E. Johnson, J. N. Keynes, C. S. Peirce, the heritage of Kant and Mill, Polish logicians); LOGIC, MANY-VALUED; LOGIC, MODAL; LOGIC, TRADITIONAL; NEGATION; RUSSELL, BERTRAND ARTHUR WILLIAM (section on logic and mathematics).

Prior, Mary, M.A. (University of New Zealand). Coauthor (with A. N. Prior), "Erotetic Logic," *Philosophical Review* (Vol. 64). WHATELY, RICHARD.

Quinton, Anthony, M.A. (Oxford). University Lecturer in Philosophy and Fellow of New College, Oxford University. Fellow of All Souls College, Oxford University (1949–1955); Visiting Professor of Philosophy at Swarthmore College (1960) and at Stanford University (1964). Author of numerous articles in philosophical periodicals and collective volumes. BRITISH PHILOSOPHY; KNOWLEDGE AND BELIEF; POPPER, KARL RAIMUND.

Rahman, Fazl-Ur-, M.A. (Panjab University, India); D.Phil. (Oxford). Director of the Central Institute of Islamic Research (Karachi); Formerly, Lecturer at the University of Durham; Associate Professor of Philosophy at McGill University, Publications include *Avicenna's Psychology* (1952); *Prophecy in Islam* (1958); *Avicenna's De Anima* (1959); *Islamic Methodology in History* (1965); *Islam* (1966). ISLAMIC PHILOSOPHY.

Ramsperger, Albert G., B.A., M.A., Ph.D. (University of California). Professor of Philosophy at the University of Wisconsin. Author, *Philosophies of Science* (1942). CRITICAL REALISM.

Reck, Andrew J., B.A., M.A. (Tulane); Ph.D. (Yale). Professor of Philosophy at Tulane University. Fulbright Scholar at St. Andrews University (1952–1953); Instructor of Philosophy at Yale University (1955–1958); Howard Fellow (1962–1963). Editor, George Herbert Mead, *Selected Writings* (1964). Author, *Recent American Philosophy* (1964). BOODIN, JOHN ELOF.

Rees, D. A., M.A., D.Phil. (Oxford). Fellow and Tutor in Philosophy at Jesus College, Oxford University. Formerly, Senior Lecturer in Philosophy at University College of North Wales; Member of the Institute for Advanced Study (Princeton, N.J., 1962–1963). PLATONISM AND THE PLATONIC TRADITION.

Reeves, Joan Wynn, B.A., Ph.D. (University of London). Reader in Psychology at Bedford College, University of London. Member of the Staff of the National Institute of Industrial Psychology (1936–1941, 1946–1950); Specialist Officer (psychology) in A.T.S. (Women's Service) War Office, London (1941–1946). Publications include *Body and Mind in Western Thought* (1958); *Thinking About Thinking* (1965). BINET, ALFRED.

Reeves, Marjorie E., M.A. (Oxford); Ph.D. (University of London). Vice-Principal and Fellow of St. Anne's College and University Lecturer, Oxford University. Coeditor (with L. Tondelli and B. Hirsch-Reich), *Il libro delle figure dell' abate Gioachino da Fiore* (1953). JOACHIM OF FIORE.

Rescher, Nicholas, Ph.D. (Princeton). Professor of Philosophy and Associate Director of the Center for Philosophy of Science at the University of Pittsburgh; Editor of the *American Philosophical Quarterly*. Publications include *The Development of Arabic Logic; Galen and the Syllogism; Hypothetical Reasoning; The Logic of Commands.* BURIDAN, JEAN; LOGIC, HISTORY OF (section on Arabic logic).

Riasanovsky, Nicholas, V., B.A. (University of Oregon); A.M. (Harvard); D.Phil. (Oxford). Professor of History at the University of California, Berkeley. Former Rhodes Scholar and Fulbright Scholar. Author, *Russia and the West in the Teachings of the Slavophiles: A Study of Romantic Ideology* (1952); *Nicholas I and Official Nationality in Russia 1825–1855* (1959); *A History of Russia* (1963); and numerous articles. FOURIER, FRANÇOIS MARIE CHARLES.

Rickman, Hans Peter, B.A., M.A. (University of London); D.Phil. (Oxford). Senior Lecturer in Philosophy at the Northampton College of Advanced Technology (London). Formerly, Staff Tutor in Philosophy at Hull University. Publications include *Meaning in History, Dilthey's Thought on History and Society* (1961; republished in the United States as *Pattern and Meaning in History,* 1962); *Preface to Philosophy* (1964); *Understanding and the Human Studies* (1966). DILTHEY, WILHELM; GEISTESWISSENSCHAFTEN.

Rintelen, Fritz Joachim von, Dr.phil., Dr. en artes (Hon.), Dr.Litt. (Hon.), Dr. phil. (Hon.). Professor of Philosophy at the University of Mainz. Formerly, Professor of Philosophy at the University of Bonn. Author, *Der Wertgedanke in der europäischen Geistesentwicklung* (1932); *Philosophie der Endlichkeit als Spiegel der Gegenwart* (2d ed., 1962); *Der Rang des Geistes: Goethes Weltverständnis* (1955); *Beyond Existentialism* (1961). GEYSER, JOSEPH.

Robinson, David B., B.Litt., M.A. (Oxford). Lecturer in Greek at the University of Edinburgh. MEGARIANS; XENOPHON.

Robischon, Thomas, B.S. (Montana State University); A.M., Ph.D. (Columbia). Associate Professor and Chairman of the Department of Philosophy at Tuskegee Institute. Member of the Summer Institute of the Council for Philosophical Studies (1966). HOLT, EDWIN BISSELL; MCGILVARY, EVANDER BRADLEY; MONTAGUE, WILLIAM PEPPERELL; NEW REALISM; PERRY, RALPH BARTON.

Rogat, Yosal, B.A., M.A. (Oxford); Ph.D. Associate Professor, Department of Political Science, University of Chicago; Visiting Professor, School of Law, Stanford University. Formerly, Fellow of the Center for Advanced Studies in the Behavioral Sciences (Stanford); Assistant Professor, Department of Political Science, University of California, Berkeley. Author, "The Eichmann Trial and the Role of Law"; contributor to the *University of Chicago Law Review* and the *Stanford Law Review*. LEGAL REALISM.

Rollins, C. D., D.Phil. (Oxford). Senior Fellow of the Institute of Advanced Studies, Australian National University. Former Rhodes Scholar and Rockefeller Postwar Fellow in the United Kingdom; Professor and Chairman of the Department of

Philosophy at Oberlin College (1962–1965). Editor, *Knowledge and Experience* (1963). CERTAINTY; SOLIPSISM.

Romanell, Patrick, B.A. (Brooklyn College); M.A., Ph.D. (Columbia). H. Y. Benedict Professor of Philosophy at the University of Texas, El Paso. Cutting Traveling Fellow and Carnegie Fellow in Mexico (1945–1946, Fulbright Lecturer in Italy (1952–1953); Smith-Mundt Lecturer in Mexico and Ecuador (1955–1956); Professor of Medical Philosophy at the University of Texas Medical Branch (1952–1962); Professor of Philosophy and Medical Philosophy at the University of Oklahoma (1962–1964). Author, *The Philosophy of Giovanni Gentile* (1938); *Can We Agree?* (1950); *Making of the Mexican Mind* (1952); *Toward a Critical Naturalism* (1958). ABBAGNANO, NICOLA.

Rorty, Richard M., B.A., M.A. (University of Chicago); Ph.D. (Yale). Associate Professor of Philosophy at Princeton University. INTUITION; RELATIONS, INTERNAL AND EXTERNAL.

Rosán, Laurence J., B.A., M.A., Ph.D. (Columbia). Lecturer in Philosophy and Religion at the City University of New York, Brooklyn College; Member of the International Mark Twain Society. Instructor in Philosophy and Religion at Pennsylvania State University (1948–1951); Assistant Professor of Religion at Alabama College (1952–1953). Author, *The Philosophy of Proclus* (1949); a series of articles on comparative and Oriental philosophy in *Philosophy East and West*. PROCLUS.

Rossi-Landi, Ferruccio, D.Lit. (University of Milan); D.Phil. (University of Pavia); Libero docente in theoretical philosophy. Research Member of the Staff of the State University of Milan. Research Student in Philosophy at Oxford University (1951–1953); Rockefeller Research Fellow (1959–1961); Lecturer in Philosophy at the State University of Milan (1955–1965); Associate Professor of Philosophy at the State University of Padua (1958–1961); Visiting Professor of Philosophy at the universities of Michigan (1962–1963) and Texas, Austin (1963). Editor, *Il pensiero americano contemporaneo* (2 vols., 1958). Author, *Significato, comunicazione e parlare comune* (1961), and many articles. CALDERONI, MARIO; CATTANEO, CARLO; COLORNI, EUGENIO; DINGLER, HUGO; ENRIQUES, FEDERIGO; PEANO, GIUSEPPE; VAILATI, GIOVANNI.

Rudner, Richard S., A.B. (Queens College); M.A., Ph.D. (University of Pennsylvania). Professor and Chairman of the Department of Philosophy at Washington University (St. Louis); Editor in Chief of *Philosophy of Science;* Member of the Governing Board of the Philosophy of Science Association. Former A.A.A.S. Fellow; N.S.F. Post-Doctoral Fellow at Cambridge University (1962–1963); Member of the N.S.F. Panel for the History and Philosophy of Science. Author, *Philosophy of Social Science* (1966) and articles on aesthetics, epistemology, and philosophy of science. GOODMAN, NELSON.

Rundle, Bede, M.A. (University of New Zealand and Oxford); B.Phil. (Oxford). Fellow and Lecturer in Philosophy at Trinity College, Oxford University. Formerly, Research Fellow at Queen's College, Oxford University. LOGIC, HISTORY OF (section on Frege to the present).

Russell, L. J., M.A., B.Sc., D.Phil., LL.D. (Hon., University of Glasgow). Emeritus Professor of Philosophy at the University of Birmingham; Fellow of the British Academy. Professor of Philosophy at the University of Bristol (1923–1925) and at the University of Birmingham (1925–1950); Visiting Professor at Stanford University (1932) and at Emory University (1963). Author of many articles in philosophical journals. LEIBNIZ, GOTTFRIED WILHELM.

Ryle, Gilbert, M.A. (Oxford). Waynflete Professor of Metaphysical Philosophy at Oxford University. Formerly, Student and Tutor of Christ Church, Oxford University. Author, *The Concept of Mind* (1949); *Dilemmas* (1954). PLATO.

Rynin, David, Ph.D. Professor of Philosophy at the University of California, Berkeley. Editor, Alexander Bryan Johnson, *A Treatise on Language* (1947). JOHNSON, ALEXANDER BRYAN.

Saab, Hassan, M.A. (University of Cairo); Ph.D. (Georgetown). Professor at the Lebanese University and at the Saint-Joseph University of Beirut. Lebanon's Cultural Counselor in North America. Member of the Lebanese Delegation to the Council and Commissions of the League of Arab States (1948, 1949, 1959); Secretary of the Embassy and Chargé d'Affaires of the Lebanese Embassy in Washington (1950–1956); Member of the Lebanese Delegation to the U.N. Security Council (1954–1955) and the General Assembly (1955); Director of Political Affairs at the Ministry of Foreign Affairs (1959–1960); Lecturer in Political Science at the American University of Beirut (1956–1960), the Lebanese University (1956–1961), and the Saint Joseph University of Beirut (1959–1960); Lecturer on the Institutional History of Arab Federalism at the Institute of Arab Studies in Cairo (1960). Author (in Arabic), *The UNESCO; The Ideological Conscience; The Modern Concept of the Statesman; Introduction to Political Science.* Author (in English), *The Arab Federalists of the Ottoman Empire.* IBN-KHALDŪN, AB-AR-RAHMAN.

Sambursky, Samuel, Ph.D. Professor of the History and Philosophy of Science at the Hebrew University of Jerusalem; Member of the Israel Academy of Science and Humanities. Formerly, Professor of Experimental Physics at the Hebrew University. Publications include *The Physical World of the Greeks* (1956); *Physics of the Stoics* (1959); *The Physical World of Late Antiquity* (1962). PHILOPONUS, JOHN.

Sandbach, Francis Henry, M.A. (Cambridge). Brereton Reader in Classics at Cambridge University. Formerly, Senior Tutor, Trinity College, Cambridge University. HELLENISTIC THOUGHT.

Sanford, David, B.A. (Wayne State University); Ph.D. (Cornell). Instructor in Philosophy at Dartmouth College. DEGREES OF PERFECTION, ARGUMENT FOR THE EXISTENCE OF GOD.

Santucci, Antonio. University Professor of the History of Modern and Contemporary Philosophy. Extraordinary Professor of the History of Philosophy, Faculty of Education, University of Bologna; Professor and Head of the Department of the History of Modern and Contemporary Philosophy, Faculty of Letters and Philosophy, University of Bologna. Author, *Esistenzialismo e filosofia italiana* (1959); *Le origini della sociologia* (1961); *Il pragmatismo in Italia* (1963); *L'umanismo scettico di David Hume* (1965). PAPINI, GIOVANNI.

Sassen, F. L. R., Ph.D. (University of Fribourg); Litt.D. (Hon., Laval University, Canada). Member of the Royal Netherlands Academy of Sciences and the Royal Flemish Academy of Sciences, Letters, and Arts of Belgium. Professor of Philosophy at the Catholic University of Nijmegen (1929–1945) and at the State University of Leiden (1946–1964); President of the Netherlands Council of Education (1956–1964). Publications (in Dutch) include *History of Philosophy* (5 vols.); *Philosophy in the Netherlands;* and numerous articles, particularly on philosophy in the Netherlands. BOLLAND, GERARD J. P. J.; DUTCH PHILOSOPHY.

Saunders, Jason, L., A.B. (Tufts); A.M., Ph.D. (Columbia). Professor of Philosophy at the University of California, San Diego. Member of the Faculty at Columbia University (1949–1951), Ripon College (1952–1954), and the University of North Carolina (1954–1963); Ford Fellow (1951–1952); Visiting Associate Professor of Philosophy at the Claremont Graduate School (1962–1963). Publications include *Justus Lipsius: The Philosophy of Renaissance Stoicism* (1955). CLEANTHES; LIPSIUS, JUSTUS; PATRIZI, FRANCESCO.

Scanlan, James P., B.A., M.A., Ph.D. (University of Chicago). Associate Professor of Philosophy at Goucher College. Research Fellow at the Institute for Philosophical Research (1953–1955); Ford Fellow at the Institute of Technology (1955–1956); Member of the Cultural Exchange Program, research in the history of Russian philosophy at the University of Moscow (1964–1965). Coeditor (with James Edie and Mary-Barbara Zeldin), *Russian Philosophy* (3 vols., 1965). BELINSKI, VISSARION GRIGORYEVICH; BULGAKOV, SERGEY NIKOLAYEVICH; CHERNYSHEVSKI, NIKOLAI GAVRILOVICH; FLORENSKY, PAUL; KOZLOV, ALEXEY ALEXANDROVICH; LAPSHIN, IVAN IVANOVICH; LAVROV, PETER LAVROVICH; LENIN, V. I.; LOPATIN, LEO MIKHAILOVICH; MIKHAILOVSKY, NICHOLAS KONSTANTINOVICH; RADISCHEV, ALEXANDER NIKOLAYEVICH; ROZANOV, VASILY VASILYEVICH; SHPET, GUSTAV GUSTAVOVICH; VYSHESLAVTSEV, BORIS PETROVICH.

Schaper, Eva, Dr. phil. Lecturer in Logic and Aesthetic Philosophy at the University of Glasgow. Formerly, Lecturer in Philosophy, University College of North Wales, Bangor. Author of articles and reviews, mainly on aesthetics and Kantian philosophy, in *Philosophical Quarterly, Review of Metaphysics, British Journal of Aesthetics, PAS,* and others. Translator, G. Martin, *General Metaphysics,* and others. PATER, WALTER HORATIO; TROELTSCH, ERNST.

Schick, Frederic, B.A., M.A., Ph.D. (Columbia). Associate Professor and Chairman of the Department of Philosophy at Rutgers University. Ford Fellow (1957–1958); Instructor in Philosophy at Columbia University (1958–1960); Assistant Professor of Philosophy at Brandeis University (1960–1962). Author of articles, reviews, and translations in various philosophical journals. CONFIRMATION: QUANTITATIVE ASPECTS.

Schlesinger, G., B.Sc., Ph.D. Professor of Philosophy at the University of North Carolina. Formerly, Fellow at the University of Pittsburgh; Visiting Professor at the Minnesota Center for the Philosophy of Science; Reader in Philosophy at the Australian National University. BRIDGMAN, PERCY WILLIAM; OPERATIONALISM.

Schlette, Antonia Ruth, Dr.phil. (University of Munich). Formerly, Scientific Assistant, History Seminar, University of Munich. Publications (under maiden name, A. R. Weiss) include *Friedrich Adolf Trendelenburg und das Naturrecht im 19. Jahrhundert* (Münchener Historische Studien, 1960); Maurice Blondel, *Histoire et Dogme* (German translation, 1963). CHAMBERLAIN, HOUSTON STEWART.

Schmitt, Richard, B.A., M.A. (University of Chicago); Ph.D. (Yale). Associate Professor of Philosophy at Brown University. Alfred Hodder Fellow at Princeton University (1963–1964); Guggenheim Fellow (1965–1966). Author, "In Search of Phenomenology," *Review of Metaphysics* (1962); "Phenomenology and Analysis," *Philosophy and Phenomenological Research* (1962); "Two Senses of 'Knowing,'" *Review of Metaphysics* (1965). HUSSERL, EDMUND; PHENOMENOLOGY.

Schneewind, J. B., B.A. (Cornell); M.A., Ph.D. (Princeton). Associate Professor of Philosophy at the University of Pittsburgh; Member of the Executive Committee of the American Philosophical Association, Eastern Division. Editor, J. S. Mill, *Essays on Literature and Society* (1965) and *Ethical Writings* (1965). Author of articles on Sidgwick's ethics and on philosophy and literature in the Victorian period. ELIOT, GEORGE; GROTE, JOHN; MCTAGGART, JOHN MCTAGGART ELLIS; MARTINEAU, JAMES; MILL, JOHN STUART; MYERS, FREDERICK W. H.; SIDGWICK, HENRY; STEPHEN, LESLIE.

Searle, John R., B.A., M.A., D.Phil. (Oxford). Associate Professor of Philosophy and Special Assistant to the Chancellor, University of California, Berkeley. Author of articles in *Mind, Philosophical Review,* and others. DETERMINABLES AND DETERMINATES; PROPER NAMES AND DESCRIPTIONS; STRAWSON, PETER FREDERICK.

Selznick, Philip, B.A. (City College of New York); M.A., Ph.D. (Columbia). Chairman of the Department of Sociology and of the Center for the Study of Law, University of California, Berkeley; Fellow of the American Academy of Arts and Sciences. Author, *TVA and the Grass Roots* (1949); *The Organizational Weapon* (1952); *Leadership in Administration* (1957); *Law, Society, and Industrial Justice* (1966). SOCIOLOGY OF LAW.

Šešić, Bogdan, Dr.phil. Ordinary Professor of Logic at the University of Belgrade. Publications in German include *Grundsätze der absoluten Wahrheit* (1937); *Die Katagorienlehren der Badischen philosophischen Schule* (1937). Publications in Serbo-Croat include *Dialectical Materialism of J. Dietzen* (1957); *Introduction to Dialectical Logic* (1957); *Logic* (2 vols., 1958, 1959); *Necessity and Freedom* (1962). PETRONIEVIĆ, BRANISLAV.

Shaffer, Jerome, B.A. (Cornell); Ph.D. (Princeton). Associate Professor of Philosophy at Swarthmore College; Executive Secretary of the Council for Philosophical Studies. Author, "Could Mental States Be Brain Processes?," *Journal of Philosophy* (1961); "Existence, Predication, and the Ontological Argument," *Mind* (1962); "Recent Work on the Mind–Body Problem," *American Philosophical Quarterly* (1965). MIND–BODY PROBLEM.

Shapere, Dudley, B.A., M.A., Ph.D. (Harvard). Associate Professor of Philosophy at the University of Chicago. Instructor in Philosophy at Ohio State University (1957–1960); Visiting Associate Professor at the Rockefeller Institute (1965–1966). Author, "Space, Time and Language" (in B. Baumrin, ed., *Philosophy of Science: The Delaware Seminar,* Vol. II, 1963); "The Causal Efficacy of Space," *Philosophy of Science* (1964); "The Structure of Scientific Revolutions," *Philosophical Review* (1964); and others. NEWTON, ISAAC; NEWTONIAN MECHANICS AND MECHANICAL EXPLANATION.

Shein, Louis J., B.A., M.A., B.D., Ph.D. Professor of Russian Literature and Chairman of the Department of Russian at McMaster University (Canada). Formerly, Special Lecturer in Philosophy and World Religions, University of Toronto and Carleton University (Canada); Canada Council Fellow (1963). Author of articles and reviews in scholarly journals. LOSSKY, NICHOLAS ONUFRIYEVICH.

Shih, Vincent Y. C., B.A. (Fukien Christian University, China); M.A. (Yenching University, China); Ph.D. (University of Southern California). Professor of Chinese Philosophy and Literature at the University of Washington. Formerly, Professor at the University of Honan, the National Chekiang University, and Yenching University in China. Author, *Prolegomena to Metaphysics* (1943); *Religious and Philosophical Topics in Ancient China* (1945); *The Literary Mind and the Carving of Dragons* (1959); and articles in scholarly journals. HUI SHIH; KUNG-SUN LUNG.

Shoemaker, Sydney, B.A. (Reed College); Ph.D. (Cornell). Associate Professor of Philosophy at Cornell University. Santayana Fellow at Harvard University (1960–1961); Coeditor of the *Philosophical Review* (1964–1966). Author, *Self-Knowledge and Self-Identity* (1963). MEMORY.

Shorter, J. M., M.A. (Oxford). Professor of Philosophy at the University of Canterbury (New Zealand). Visiting Professor at the University of Toronto (1964). Author, "Imagination," *Mind* (1952); "Meaning and Grammar," *Australasian Journal* *of Philosophy* (1956); "Facts, Logical Atomism and Reducibility," *Australasian Journal of Philosophy* (1962). OTHER MINDS.

Simon, W. M., B.A. (Wesleyan); M.A., Ph.D. (Yale). Professor of History at the University of Keele. Formerly, Professor of Modern European History at Cornell University; Guggenheim Fellow (1957–1958); Member of the Institute for Advanced Study (Princeton, N.J., 1960–1961). Publications include *Failure of the Prussian Reform Movement, 1807–1818* (1955); *European Positivism in the 19th Century* (1963); *Germany: A Brief History* (1966). BERNARD, CLAUDE; FOUILLÉE, ALFRED; LAAS, ERNST; LITTRÉ, ÉMILE; RENAN, JOSEPH ERNEST.

Singer, Marcus G., A.B. (University of Illinois); Ph.D. (Cornell). Professor and Chairman of the Department of Philosophy at the University of Wisconsin; Chairman of the Department of Philosophy of the University of Wisconsin Center System. Instructor in Philosophy at Cornell University (1951–1952); American Philosophical Association Fellow (1956–1957); Guggenheim Fellow and Visiting Fellow of Birbeck College, University of London (1962–1963). Coeditor, *Introductory Readings in Philosophy* (1962); *Reason and the Common Good: Selected Essays of Arthur E. Murphy* (1963). Contributor to A. I. Melden, ed., *Essays in Moral Philosophy* (1958). Author, *Generalization in Ethics* (1961). GOLDEN RULE.

Skolimowski, Henryk, M.Sc., M.A., D.Phil. Associate Professor of Philosophy at the University of Southern California. Formerly, Senior Lecturer at the Warsaw Institute of Technology. Author, *Polish Analytical Philosophy* (1966). INGARDEN, ROMAN.

Smart, J. J. C., M.A. (University of Glasgow); B.Phil. (Oxford). Hughes Professor of Philosophy at the University of Adelaide. Formerly, Junior Research Fellow, Corpus Christi College, Oxford University (1948–1950); Visiting Professor of Philosophy at Princeton University (1957), Harvard University (1963), and Yale University (1964). Editor, *Problems of Space and Time* (1964). Author, *An Outline of a System of Utilitarian Ethics* (1961); *Philosophy and Scientific Realism* (1963). RELIGION AND SCIENCE; SPACE; TIME; UTILITARIANISM.

Smart, Ninian, M.A., B.Phil. (Oxford). H. G. Wood Professor of Theology at the University of Birmingham. Formerly, Lecturer in the History and Philosophy of Religion at the University of London; Visiting Lecturer in Philosophy at Yale University; Visiting Professor in Philosophy and History at the University of Wisconsin. Author, *Reasons and Faiths* (1958); *A Dialogue of Religions* (1960); *Doctrine and Argument in Indian Philosophy* (1964). AUROBINDO GHOSE; BARTH, KARL; BOEHME, JAKOB; BUDDHISM; ECKHART, MEISTER; GERSON, JEAN DE; HINDUISM; HUGEL, BARON FRIEDRICH VON; INDIAN PHILOSOPHY; JAINISM; JOHN OF THE CROSS, ST.; KARMA; MADHVA; MYSTICISM, HISTORY OF; NĀGĀRJUNA; NIRVANA; RADHAKRISHNAN, SARVEPALLI; RĀMĀNUJA; REINCARNATION; RUYSBROECK, JAN VAN; ŚANKARA; SUSO, HEINRICH; TAULER, JOHANNES; TERESA OF ÁVILA, ST. THOMAS À KEMPIS; YOGA; ZEN; ZOROASTRIANISM.

Smith, Colin, M.A. (University of Manchester); Ph.D. (University of London). Reader in French at the University of London. Visiting Senior Professor, Department of Romance Languages, University of Western Ontario (1965–1966). Editor, E. Renan, *Caliban* (1954). Translator, M. Merleau-Ponty, *Phenomenology of Perception* (1962). Author, *Contemporary French Philosophy* (1964). BACHELARD, GASTON; BOUTROUX, ÉMILE; GUYAU, MARIE JEAN; HAMELIN, OCTAVE; JANKELEVITCH, VLADIMIR; LALANDE, ANDRÉ; LE ROY, ÉDOUARD; LE SENNE, RENÉ; LOISY, ALFRED; MODERNISM; MOUNIER, EMMANUEL.

Smith, James Ward, Ph.D. (Princeton). Professor of Philosophy at Princeton University. Coeditor (with A. L. Jamison), *Religion in American Life* (4 vols., 1961). Author, *Theme for Reason* (1957). STACE, WALTER TERENCE.

Smith, John E., A.B. (Columbia); B.D. (Union Theological Seminary); Ph.D. (Columbia); LL.D. (Notre Dame). Professor of Philosophy at Yale University; General Editor of the Yale Edition of *Works of Jonathan Edwards;* Member of the Editorial Board of the *Monist;* Member of the Advisory Board of *Religious Studies.* Dudleian Lecturer, Harvard University (1960); Suarez Lecturer, Fordham University (1962); Gates Lecturer, Grinnell College (1965). Editor, *The Philosophy of Religion* (1965). Author, *Royce's Social Infinite* (1950); *Reason and God* (1961); *The Spirit of American Philosophy* (1963). ROYCE, JOSIAH.

Smokler, Howard E., B.A. (Rutgers); M.A., Ph.D. (Columbia). Visiting Associate Professor of Philosophy at Stanford University. Formerly, Instructor in Philosophy at Rutgers University. Coeditor (with H. E. Kyburg), *Studies in Subjective Probability* (1964). Author, "W. K. Clifford's Conception of Geometry," *Philosophical Quarterly* (1966); "Goodman's Paradox and the Problem of Rules of Acceptance," *American Philosophical Quarterly* (1966). CLIFFORD, WILLIAM KINGDON; JOHNSON, WILLIAM ERNEST.

Smullyan, Raymond M., B.S. (University of Chicago); Ph.D. (Princeton). Associate Professor of Mathematics, Belfer Graduate School of Science, Yeshiva University. Instructor at Dartmouth College (1954–1956); Instructor and Lecturer at Princeton University (1956–1961). Publications include "Theory of Formal Systems," *Annals of Mathematics* (1961); "Analytic Natural Deduction," *Journal of Symbolic Logic* (1964); "On Transfinite Recursion," *Transactions of the New York Academy of Sciences* (1965). CONTINUUM PROBLEM.

Sprague, Elmer, B.A. (University of Nebraska); B.A., D.Phil. (Oxford). Associate Professor of Philosophy at the City University of New York, Brooklyn College. Author, *What Is Philosophy?* (1961). BALGUY, JOHN; BEATTIE, JAMES; BUTLER, JOSEPH; CLARKE, SAMUEL; GAY, JOHN; HARTLEY, DAVID; HOME, HENRY; HUTCHESON, FRANCIS; MANDEVILLE, BERNARD; MORAL SENSE; PALEY, WILLIAM; PRICE, RICHARD; SHAFTESBURY, THIRD EARL OF (ANTHONY ASHLEY COOPER); SMITH, ADAM.

Staal, J. F., Ph.D. Professor of General and Comparative Philosophy and Director of the Instituut voor Filosofie at the University of Amsterdam. Formerly, Lecturer in Sanskrit at the School of Oriental and African Studies, University of London; Visiting Lecturer in Indian Philosophy at the University of Pennsylvania, Publications include *Nambudiri Veda Recitation* (1961); *Advaita and Neoplatonism* (1961); *Euclides en Pāṇini* (1963). LOGIC, HISTORY OF (section on Indian logic).

Staniforth, Maxwell, M.A. (Oxford). Formerly, Rural Dean of Blandford and Vicar of Sixpenny Handley; Lecturer at Chichester Theological College. Now retired. Publications include *Marcus Aurelius: Meditations* (1964). MARCUS AURELIUS ANTONINUS.

Stark, Werner, Dr.rer.pol. (University of Hamburg); Dr.jur. (University of Prague); M.A. (University of Edinburgh). Professor of Sociology at Fordham University. Formerly, Lecturer in Social Theory at the University of Edinburgh; Reader in the History of the Social Sciences at the University of Manchester. Numerous publications include *Jeremy Bentham's Economic Writings; The Sociology of Knowledge; The Fundamental Forms of Social Thought.* MANNHEIM, KARL; SOCIOLOGY OF KNOWLEDGE.

Stern, J. P., M.A., Ph.D. (Cambridge). Fellow and Tutor of St. John's College and University Lecturer in German, Cambridge University. Visiting Professor of German at City College of New York (1958–1959), at the University of California, Berkeley (1964–1965), and at the University of Göttingen (1965). Author, *Ernst Jünger: A Writer of Our Time* (1953); *G. C. Lichtenberg: A Doctrine of Scattered Occasions* (1959); *Re-interpretations: Seven Studies in Nineteenth-century German Literature* (1964). BENN, GOTTFRIED; KAFKA, FRANZ; RILKE, RAINER MARIA (RENÉ).

Steinkraus, Warren E., A.B. (Baldwin-Wallace College); S.T.B., Ph.D. (Boston University). Professor of Philosophy at the State University of New York at Oswego. Jacob Sleeper Fellow at Boston University (1946–1947); Professor and Chairman of the Department of Philosophy at Union College (1959–1964). Publications include *New Studies in Berkeley's Philosophy* (1966) and articles in philosophical journals. CREIGHTON, JAMES EDWIN.

Stigen, Anfinn, M.A. (University of Chicago). Docent at the Institute of Philosophy and History of Ideas, University of Oslo; Philol. et Mag. Art. candidate at the University of Oslo. Formerly, Docent at Aarhus University (Denmark); Fulbright and Smith–Mundt Scholar at the University of Chicago (1951–1953); British Council Scholar at Oxford University (1958–1959); Boursier du Gouvernement français Award for study at the University of Paris at the Sorbonne (1956). Author, *The Structure of Aristotle's Thought* (Thesis, 1966). TRESCHOW, NIELS.

Stojković, Andrija, Dr.phil. Professor of Philosophy at the University of Belgrade. Publications include *Lenjin o Formalnoj Logici* (1959); *Bogdan Šešić & Andrija Stojković Dijalektički Materijalizam* (1962). MARKOVIĆ, SVETOZAR.

Stokes, Michael C., M.A. (Oxford and Cambridge). Lecturer in Greek at the University of Edinburgh. Lecturer in Classics, Balliol College, Oxford University (1955–1956); Junior Research Fellow of the Center for Hellenic Studies (Washington, D.C., 1962–1963). Author of articles in scholarly journals. HERACLITUS OF EPHESUS.

Stolnitz, Jerome, Ph.D. (Harvard). Professor of Philosophy at the University of Rochester. Editor, *Aesthetics* (1965). Author, *Aesthetics and Philosophy of Art* (1960). BEAUTY; UGLINESS.

Stout, A. K., M.A. (Oxford). Professor Emeritus and Fellow of the Senate at the University of Sydney. Independent Lecturer in Social Ethics at the University of Edinburgh (1934–1939); formerly, Professor and Head of the Department of Philosophy at the University of Sydney; Visiting Professor at the University of Wisconsin (1966); Editor of the *Australasian Journal of Philosophy*. Editor, G. F. Stout, *God and Nature* (1952). CAIRD, EDWARD; HOBHOUSE, LEONARD TRELAWNEY; PRINGLE-PATTISON, ANDREW SETH; RASHDALL, HASTINGS; ROSS, WILLIAM DAVID.

Stove, D., B.A. (University of Sydney). Senior Lecturer at the University of Sydney. Author of articles in *Australasian Journal of Philosophy, Philosophical Review, British Journal for the Philosophy of Science,* and others. KEYNES, JOHN MAYNARD.

Stover, Robert, Ph.D. (Columbia). Formerly, Assistant Professor of Philosophy at Vassar College. Coeditor (with J. Katz and P. Nochlin), *Writers on Ethics* (1962). GREAT MAN THEORY OF HISTORY.

Strasser, Michael W., B.S. (St. Louis University); M.A., Ph.D. (University of Toronto). Associate Professor of Philosophy at Duquesne University. President of the Western Pennsylvania Philosophical Society (1964–1965). Author, "The Thomistic Theory of Natural Law" (in Elwyn A. Smith, ed., *Church–State Relations in Ecumenical Perspective,* 1966). LIBER DE CAUSIS.

Stroll, Avrum, B.A., M.A., Ph.D. (University of California, Berkeley). Professor of Philosophy at the University of California, San Diego. Koerner Fellow (1957); Member of the Executive Committee of the American Philosophical Association, Pacific Division (1958–1961); Nuffield Fellow in England (1961–1962). Publications include *The Emotive Theory of Ethics* (1954); *Philosophy Made Simple* (with R. H. Popkin, 1956); *Reason and Religious Belief* (1958); *Introduction to Philosophy* (with R. H. Popkin, 1961); *Theory of Knowledge* (1966). IDENTITY; PRESUPPOSING.

Sturm, Fred Gillette, A.B. (Allegheny College); B.D. (Union Theological Seminary); A.M. (University of Rochester); Ph.D. (Columbia); diploma, Escola de Português (Brazil); certificate, Institute of Chinese Civilization, Tunghai University (Taiwan). Professor of Philosophy at the Western College for Women (Ohio); Visiting Professor of Philosophy at the Eastern Indiana Center of Indiana University. Professor of Greek and New Testament, Faculty of Theology, Methodist Theological Seminary of Brazil (1950–1951); Professor of Religion, Instituto Pôrto Alégre (1952); Visiting Professor of Religion, Miami University (1957–1958); Professor of Philosophy, Episcopal Theological Seminary of Brazil. Translator, Cruz Costa, *Panorama of the History of Philosophy* (1962). Author, *Existência em busca de essência: A filosofia de espírito de Raimundo de Farias Brito* (1966). FARIAS BRITO, RAIMUNDO DE; MOLINA GARMENDIA, ENRIQUE; REALE, MIGUEL; VARONA (Y PERA), ENRIQUE JOSÉ.

Suppes, Patrick, B.S. (University of Chicago); Ph.D. (Columbia). Director of the Institute for Mathematical Studies in the Social Sciences and Chairman of the Department of Philosophy, Stanford University. Coeditor (with Leon Henkin and Alfred Tarski), *The Axiomatic Method, With Special Reference to Geometry and Physics* (1959); (with K. J. Arrow and Samuel Karlin), *Mathematical Methods in the Social Sciences, 1959* (1960); (with Ernest Nagel and Alfred Tarski), *Logic, Methodology and Philosophy of Science* (1962); (with Joan Criswell and Herbert Solomon), *Mathematical Methods in Small Group Processes* (1962). Coauthor (with Donald Davidson and Sidney Siegel), *Decision Making: An Experimental Approach* (1957); (with R. C. Atkinson), *Markov Learning Models for Multiperson Interactions* (1960); (with Shirley Hill), *First Course in Mathematical Logic* (1964). Author, *Introduction to Logic* (1957); *Axiomatic Set Theory* (1960). DECISION THEORY.

Surtz, Edward, S.J., A.B. (John Carroll University); M.A. (Xavier University and Harvard); Ph.L., S.T.L. (West Baden College); Ph.D. (Harvard). Professor of English at Loyola University. Director of Upper-Division English (1951–1957) and Chairman of the Department of English (1957–1958) at Loyola University. Guggenheim Fellow (1954–1955); More Project Fellow (1959–1960); Weil Fellow (1964); A.C.L.S. Fellow (1964–1965). Publications include *The Praise of Pleasure: Philosophy, Education, and Communism in More's "Utopia"* (1957); *The Praise of Wisdom: A Commentary on the Religious and Moral Problems and Backgrounds of More's "Utopia"* (1957); *Utopia* (1964); *Utopia* (*Complete Works,* Vol. 4, edited with J. H. Hexter, 1965). MORE, THOMAS.

Sweeney, Leo, S.J., A.B., M.A. (St. Louis University); Ph.D. (University of Toronto). Associate Professor of Philosophy at St. Louis University; Chairman, Committee on Prepublication of Convention Papers, American Catholic Philosophical Association. A.C.L.S. Fellow (1963–1964); Secretary (1960–1963) and President (1965–1966) of the Jesuit Philosophical Association. Editor, *Proceedings of the Jesuit Philosophical Association* (1960–1963); *Wisdom in Death* (1966). Author, *A Metaphysics of Authentic Existentialism* (1965).

Contributor to C. O'Neil, ed., *An Étienne Gilson Tribute* (1959), and various scholarly journals. JOHN OF DAMASCUS.

Talmage, Frank, B.A., Ph.D. Assistant Professor of Hebrew Studies at the University of Wisconsin. CRESCAS, HASDAI; GERSONIDES.

Taylor, Charles, B.A. (McGill and Oxford); M.A., D.Phil. (Oxford). Associate Professor of Philosophy at the University of Montreal; Associate Professor of Political Science at McGill University. Fellow of All Souls College, Oxford University (1956–1961). Author, *The Explanation of Behaviour* (1964). PSYCHOLOGICAL BEHAVIORISM.

Taylor, Richard, A.B. (University of Illinois); M.A. (Oberlin College); Ph.D. (Brown). Professor of Philosophy at the University of Rochester. William H. P. Faunce Professor of Philosophy at Brown University (1959–1963); Visiting Professor of Philosophy at Ohio State University (1959, 1963); Professor of Philosophy, Graduate Faculties, Columbia University (1963–1965). Author, *Metaphysics* (1963); *Action and Purpose* (1966). CAUSATION; DETERMINISM; VOLUNTARISM.

Thalberg, Irving, B.A., Ph.D. (Stanford). Assistant Professor of Philosophy at the University of Illinois. Taught at Oberlin College (1960–1963); Visiting Assistant Professor at Stanford University (1963) and at the University of Washington (1963–1964). Author, "Remorse," *Mind* (1963): "Emotion and Thought," *American Philosophical Quarterly* (1964); "Freedom of Action and Freedom of Will," *Journal of Philosophy* (1964); and other articles. ERROR.

Thayer, H. S., A.B. (Bard College); A.M., Ph.D. (Columbia). Associate Professor and Chairman of the Department of Philosophy at the City University of New York, City College; Visiting Professor at the New York School of Psychiatry. Formerly, Assistant Professor of Philosophy at Columbia University; Wendell T. Bush Fellow at Columbia University (1947, 1948). Author, *The Logic of Pragmatism* (1952); *Newton's Philosophy of Nature* (1953); "Pragmatism" (in D. J. O'Connor, ed., *A Critical History of Western Philosophy,* 1964); *Meaning and Action: A Critical History of Pragmatism* (1966). NAGEL, ERNEST; PRAGMATISM.

Thomas, Ivo, O.P., M.A. (Oxford); S.T.M. Visiting Professor at Notre Dame University. Formerly, Prior of Blackfriars, Oxford; frequently Visiting Professor at Notre Dame and Ohio State universities. Translator and editor, J. M. Bocheński, *A History of Formal Logic* (1961). LOGIC, HISTORY OF (sections on interregnum; G. W. Leibniz; Leonhard Euler; J. H. Lambert; Gottfried Ploucquet; 19th-century mathematics).

Thompson, Manley, A.B., A.M., Ph.D. (University of Chicago). Professor and Chairman of the Department of Philosophy at the University of Chicago. Taught at the University of Toronto (1946–1949); Rockefeller Postwar Fellow in the Humanities (1948–1949); Visiting Lecturer at Harvard University (1954–1955). Author, *The Pragmatic Philosophy of C. S. Peirce* (2d ed., 1963); "Metaphysics" (in *Philosophy. The Princeton Studies: Humanistic Scholarship in America,* 1964); and numerous articles and reviews in journals and cooperative volumes. CATEGORIES.

Thomson, James, B.A. (University of London); M.A. (Cambridge and Oxford). Professor of Philosophy at M.I.T. Formerly, Fellow and Tutor, Corpus Christi College, Oxford University. INFINITY IN MATHEMATICS AND LOGIC.

Thomson, Judith Jarvis, B.A., B.A., M.A., Ph.D. Associate Professor of Philosophy at M.I.T. WISDOM, ARTHUR JOHN TERENCE DIBBEN.

Thomson, S. Harrison, A.B. (Princeton); Dr.phil. (Charles University of Prague); D.Litt. (Oxford University). Professor Emeritus of History at the University of Colorado. Visiting Professor at the University of Washington (1964–1965); Duke Professor of History, University of California, Los Angeles (1965–1966). Cultural Attaché, U.S. Embassies in Prague and Warsaw (1945–1946); Founder and Editor of the *Journal of Central European Affairs* (1936–1964) and of *Medievalia et Humanistica.* Publications include *Writings of Robert Grosseteste* (1940); *Czechoslovakia in European History* (2d ed., 1953); *Europe in Renaissance and Reformation* (1963). HUS, JOHN; SCOT, MICHAEL; WYCLYF, JOHN.

Tomas, Vincent, M.A., Ph.D. (Brown). William H. P. Faunce Professor of Philosophy at Brown University. Past Visiting Professor at the University of Minnesota, Northwestern University, Yale University, Harvard University, and Dartmouth College; former Guggenheim Fellow. Editor, C. S. Peirce, *Essays in the Philosophy of Science* and *Creativity in the Arts* (1964). Author of articles in philosophical journals and cooperative volumes. DUCASSE, JOHN CURT.

Tonelli, Giorgio, Dr.phil.; libero docente in History of Philosophy and in History of German Literature. Professor of History of German Literature and of History of Modern Philosophy at the University of Pisa. Publications include "Kant, dell'estetica metafisica all'estetica psicoempirica," *Memorie della Accademia delle Scienze di Torino* (1955); *Elementi metodologici e metafisici in Kant del 1745 al 1768* (Vol. I, 1958); *Heine e la Germania* (1963); *Poesia e pensiero in A. von Haller* (1965). ABBT, THOMAS; BASEDOW, JOHANN BERNHARD; BAUMGARTEN, ALEXANDER GOTTLIEB; BILFINGER, GEORG BERNHARD; BUDDE, JOHANN FRANZ; CLAUBERG, JOHANNES; CRUSIUS, CHRISTIAN AUGUST; EBERHARD, JOHANN AUGUST; GARVE, CHRISTIAN; HELMONT, JAN BAPTISTA VAN; KNUTZEN, MARTIN; LAMBERT, JOHANN HEINRICH; LAVATER, JOHANN KASPAR; MEIER, GEORG FRIEDRICH; MENDELSSOHN, MOSES; NICOLAI, CHRISTIAN FRIEDRICH; PLOUCQUET, GOTTFRIED; REIMARUS, HERMANN SAMUEL; RÜDIGER, ANDREAS; SULZER, JOHANN GEORG; TETENS, JOHANN NIKOLAS; THOMASIUS, CHRISTIAN; THÜMMIG, LUDWIG PHILIPP; TSCHIRNHAUSEN, EHRENFRIED WALTHER, GRAF VON; WINCKELMANN, JOHANN JOACHIM; WOLFF, CHRISTIAN.

Torrey, Norman L., Ph.D. (Harvard); Dr. honoris causa (University of Paris); Litt.D. (Middlebury College). Emeritus Professor of French at Columbia University. Formerly, Professor of French at Columbia University; Guggenheim Fellow (1932, 1955). Author, *Voltaire and the English Deists* (1930); *The Spirit of Voltaire* (1938); *The Censoring of Diderot's Encyclopédie* (with Douglas H. Gordon, 1947). DIDEROT, DENIS; VOLTAIRE, FRANÇOIS-MARIE AROUET DE.

Toulmin, Stephen E., B.A., M.A., Ph.D. (Cambridge). Professor of the History of Ideas and Philosophy at Brandeis University. Fellow of King's College, Cambridge University (1947–1951); University Lecturer in Philosophy of Science, Oxford University (1949–1955); Professor of Philosophy at Leeds University (1955–1959); Director of the Nuffield Foundation Unit for the History of Ideas (1960–1965). Publications include *An Examination of the Place of Reason in Ethics* (1949); *Philosophy of Science* (1953); *The Uses of Argument* (1958); *Foresight and Understanding* (1961); *The Ancestry of Science* (3 vols. to date, 1961–1965). MATTER.

Tranöy, Knut Erik, B.A. (University of Oslo); M.A. (University of North Carolina); Ph.D. (Cambridge). Professor of Philosophy at the University of Bergen (Norway). Associate Professor of Philosophy at the University of Oslo (1957–1959); Visiting Professor at the University of Wisconsin (1963–1964). Publications include *Thomas Aquinas as a Moral Philosopher* (in Norwegian, 1957); *Wholes and Struc-*

tures (1959); "Thomas Aquinas" (in D. J. O'Connor, ed., *A Critical History of Western Philosophy,* 1964). STEFFENS, HENRICH.

Tsanoff, Radoslav A., B.A. (Oberlin College); Ph.D. (Cornell). Trustee Distinguished Professor of Humanities at Rice University. Chairman of the Department of Philosophy at Rice University (1914–1956); Professor Emeritus (since 1956); Anderson Professor of Philosophy at the University of Houston (1959–1961). Publications include *The Problem of Immortality* (1924); *The Nature of Evil* (1931); *Religious Crossroads* (1942); *The Moral Ideals of Our Civilization* (1942); *Ethics* (rev. ed., 1955); *The Ways of Genius* (1949); *Worlds To Know* (also published in England as *Science and Human Perspectives,* 1962); *The Great Philosophers* (2d ed., 1964). BULGARIAN PHILOSOPHY; FICHTE, JOHANN GOTTLIEB.

Turner, Paul, M.A. (Cambridge). University Lecturer in English and Fellow of Linacre College, Oxford University. Formerly, Lecturer in English, University College, University of London; Professor of English at Ankara University. Publications include Lucian, *Satirical Sketches* (translated with an introduction, 1961); More, *Utopia* (translated with an introduction, 1965). LUCIAN OF SAMOSATA.

Tymieniecka, Anna-Teresa, Diplôme d'Études Supérieures (University of Paris at the Sorbonne); Ph.D. (University of Fribourg). Taught at Oregon State College, Pennsylvania State University, and Bryn Mawr College; Research Fellow, Yale University (1956–1957, 1958–1959); Associate Scholar, The Radcliffe Institute for Independent Study (1961–1964). Publications include *Essence and Existence* (1957); *Phenomenolgy and Science in Contemporary European Philosophy* (1961); *Leibniz' Cosmological Synthesis* (1965). LAVELLE, LOUIS.

Ulich, Robert, Dr.phil., Litt.D. James Bryant Conant Professor of Education Emeritus at Harvard University. Formerly, Professor in the Department of Philosophy at the Institute of Technology (Dresden); Counselor in charge of higher education in the Saxon Ministry of Education. Publications include various books on the philosophy, history, and policy of education, on comparative education, and on philosophical and sociological topics. APPERCEPTION; COMENIUS, JOHN AMOS; FROEBEL, FRIEDRICH; PESTALOZZI, JOHANN HEINRICH.

Urmson, James O., M.A. (Oxford). Fellow of Corpus Christi College, Oxford University. Formerly, Visiting Professor at the University of Michigan; Professor of Philosophy at St. Andrews University. Author, *Philosophical Analysis* (1956). AUSTIN, JOHN LANGSHAW; IDEAS; RYLE, GILBERT.

Uytman, John Douglas, M.B., Ch.B. (University of Glasgow); D.P.M. (University of London). Senior Lecturer in the Department of Psychiatry and Lecturer in Medical Psychology at St. Andrews University; Consultant Psychiatrist, Dundee Psychiatric and General Hospitals. ADLER, ALFRED; MCDOUGALL, WILLIAM; PAVLOV, IVAN PETROVICH; WATSON, JOHN BROADUS.

van Heijenoort, J., Ph.D. (New York University), Professor of Philosophy at Brandeis University. Formerly, Associate Professor of Mathematics at New York University and Visiting Professor of Philosophy at Columbia University. Publications include *From Frege to Gödel* (1966). GÖDEL'S THEOREM; LOGICAL PARADOXES.

van Melsen, Andrew G. M., Doctor of Science, Dr. honoris causis (Duquesne). Professor of Philosophy at the University of Nijmegen (Netherlands); Member of the International Institute of Philosophy and the Royal Academy of Science. Publications include *Natuurwetenschap en Wijsbegeerte* (1946); *From Atomos to Atom* (1952); *Philosophy of Nature* (1953); *Science and Technology* (1961); *Evolution and Philosophy* (1964). ATOMISM.

Van Norden, Linda, A.B., M.A. (Stanford); Ph.D. (University of California, Los Angeles). Professor of English at the University of California, Davis. Formerly, Assistant Professor of English at the College of Puget Sound (Tacoma, Washington); American Philosophical Society Fellow (1955); Guggenheim Fellow (1956). Author, *The Black Feet of the Peacock* (1966) and a number of articles on the antiquarian movement in England in the late Renaissance. PARACELSUS.

Vartanian, Aram, M.A., Ph.D. (Columbia). Professor of French at New York University. Assistant Professor of French, Harvard University (1952–1957); Professor of French, University of Minnesota (1957–1964); Ford Foundation Fellow (1951–1952); Fulbright Research Fellow and Guggenheim Fellow (1962–1963). Author, *Diderot and Descartes: A Study of Scientific Materialism in the Enlightenment* (1953); *La Mettrie's L'Homme Machine: A Study in the Origins of an Idea* (1960). HALLER, ALBRECHT VON; HELVÉTIUS, CLAUDE-ADRIEN; HOLBACH, PAUL HENRY THIRY, BARON D'; LA METTRIE, JULIEN OFFRAY DE; MAUPERTUIS, PIERRE LOUIS MOREAU DE; MESLIER, JEAN; STAHL, GEORG ERNST.

Vendler, Zeno, M.A., S.T.L. (Jesuit University at Maastricht, Netherlands); Ph.D. (Harvard). Associate Professor, Department of Linguistics, University of Alberta (Canada). Formerly, Assistant Professor of Philosophy at Cornell University and the City University of New York, Brooklyn College; N.S.F. Research Associate at the University of Pennsylvania. Author of articles in *Mind, Philosophical Review,* and other journals. ANY AND ALL.

Vesey, G. N. A., M.A., M.Litt. (Cambridge). Reader in Philosophy at the University of London; Honorary Director of The Royal Institute of Philosophy; Assistant Editor of *Philosophy.* Editor, *Body and Mind* (1964). Author, *The Embodied Mind* (1965), HEAT, SENSATIONS OF; SOUND; TOUCH; VISION; VOLITION.

Viglielmo, V. H., Ph.D. Assistant Professor in the Department of Oriental Studies of Princeton University. NISHIDA KITARŌ.

Vlastos, Gregory, Ph.D. (Harvard). Stuart Professor of Philosophy at Princeton University. Professor of Philosophy at Cornell University (1948–1955); Guggenheim Fellow (1953, 1960); Member of the Institute for Advanced Study (Princeton, N.J., 1954–1955); Chairman of the Department of Philosophy at Princeton University (1960–1964). ZENO OF ELEA.

von Wright, Georg Henrik, Ph.D. Fellow of the Academy of Finland; Professor-at-Large, Cornell University. Formerly, Professor of Philosophy at Helsingfors University and Cambridge University. Publications include *The Logical Problem of Induction* (rev. ed., 1957); *A Treatise on Induction and Probability* (1951); *An Essay in Modal Logic* (1951); *Logical Studies* (1957); *The Varieties of Goodness* (1963); *Norm and Action* (1963); *The Logic of Preference* (1963). LICHTENBERG, GEORG CHRISTOPH.

Vyverberg, Henry, B.A. (University of Rochester); M.A., Ph.D. (Harvard). Associate Professor of History at the University of Akron. Author, *Historical Pessimism in the French Enlightenment* (1958). TURGOT, ANNE ROBERT JACQUES, BARON DE L'AULNE.

Wainwright, William J., B.A. (Kenyon College); M.A., Ph.D. (University of Michigan). Assistant Professor of Philosophy at the University of Illinois. OTTO, RUDOLF.

Walsh, W. H., M.A. Professor of Logic and Metaphysics at the University of Edinburgh. Fellow and Tutor, Merton College, Oxford University (1947–1960); Lecturer, St. Andrews University (1946–1947); Visiting Professor at Ohio State University (1957–1958) and at Dartmouth College (1965); President of the Aristotelian Society (1964–1965). Author, *Reason and Experience* (1947); *An Introduction to Philosophy of History* (1951); *Metaphysics* (1963). GREEN, THOMAS HILL; KANT, IMMANUEL; METAPHYSICS, NATURE OF.

Walters, R. S., M.A. (University of Sydney). Senior Lecturer in Philosophy at the University of New South Wales (Australia). CONTRARY-TO-FACT CONDITIONAL; LAWS OF SCIENCE AND LAWLIKE STATEMENTS.

Walzer, Richard, D.phil. (University of Berlin); M.A. (Oxford). Honorary Professor and Reader at Oxford University; Fellow of the British Academy; Corresponding Member of the Academy of Mainz. KINDĪ, ABŪ-YŪSUF YAʿQUB IBN ISḤĀQ AL-.

Warnock, G. J., M.A. Fellow and Tutor of Philosophy, Magdalen College, Oxford University. Visiting Professor of Philosophy at Princeton University (1962). Editor, J. L. Austin, *Sense and Sensibilia* (1961). Author, *Berkeley* (1953); *English Philosophy Since 1900* (1957). REASON.

Wasiolek, Edward, A.B. (Rutgers); M.A., Ph.D. (Harvard). Professor of Russian and Comparative Literature at the University of Chicago. Publications include *Nine Soviet Portraits* (with Raymond Bauer, 1955); *Crime and Punishment and the Critics* (1961); *Dostoevsky: The Major Fiction* (1965). DOSTOYEVSKY, FYODOR MIKHAILOVICH.

Watson, Richard A., B.A., M.A., Ph.D. (University of Iowa); M.S. (University of Minnesota). Assistant Professor of Philosophy at Washington University (St. Louis). Instructor at the University of Michigan (1961–1964). Author, *The Downfall of Cartesianism 1673–1712* (1965); FOUCHER, SIMON; RÉGIS, PIERRE-SYLVAIN; ROHAULT, JACQUES.

Watt, W. Montgomery, M.A., B.Litt. (Oxford); M.A., Ph.D. (University of Edinburgh); D.D. (Hon., University of Aberdeen). Professor and Head of the Department of Islamic Studies, University of Edinburgh. Publications include *Muhammad at Mecca* (1953); *Muhammad at Medina* (1956); *Islam and the Integration of Society* (1961); *Islamic Philosophy and Theology* (1962); *Truth in the Religions* (1963); *Islamic Spain* (1965). FĀRĀBĪ, AL-.

Wedberg, Anders, Ph.D. (University of Stockholm). Professor of Philosophy at the University of Stockholm. Fellow of the American–Scandinavian Association (1939–1941). Author, *Plato's Philosophy of Mathematics* (1955) and various books in Swedish on philosophical topics. BOSTROM, CHRISTOPHER JACOB; HÄGERSTRÖM, AXEL.

Weiler, Gershon, M.A. (University of Jerusalem and University of Dublin); B.Phil. (Oxford). Research Fellow, Department of Philosophy, Institute of Advanced Studies, Australian National University. Author of articles in *Mind, Philosophy, Philosophical Quarterly,* and other journals. MAUTHNER, FRITZ.

Weinberg, Gerald M., Ph.D. (University of Michigan). Senior Staff Member of the I.B.M. Systems Research Institute. Coauthor (with H. D. Leeds), *Computer Programming Fundamentals* (2d ed., 1966). COMPUTING MACHINES.

Weinberg, Julius R., B.A., M.A. (Ohio State University); Ph.D. (Cornell). Vilas Professor of Philosophy and Member of the Institute for Research in the Humanities, University of Wisconsin. President of the American Philosophical Association, Western Division (1964–1965); Guggenheim Fellow (1965–1966). Author, *An Examination of Logical Positivism* (1936); *Nicolaus of Autrecourt* (1948); *Short History of Medieval Philosophy* (1964); *Abstraction, Relation, and Induction* (1965). NICOLAS OF AUTRECOURT.

Weinberg, Kurt, M.A. (Trinity College); Ph.D. (Yale). Professor of French and Comparative Literature at the University of Rochester. Guggenheim Fellow (1960). Publications include *Henri Heine* (1954); *Kafkas Dichtungen: Die Travestien des Mythos* (1963); and many articles in scholarly journals and reference works. PANTHEISMUSSTREIT.

Weingartner, Rudolph H., A.B., A.M., Ph.D. (Columbia). Associate Professor and Chairman of the Department of Philosophy, San Francisco State College. Social Science Research Council Fellow (1957–1958); Guggenheim Fellow (1965–1966). Coeditor (with Joseph Katz), *Philosophy in the West* (1965). Author, *Experience and Culture: The Philosophy of Georg Simmel* (1962). HISTORICAL EXPLANATION; SIMMEL, GEORG.

Weisheipl, James A., O. P., M.A., S.T.Lr. (River Forest); Ph.D. (University of Rome); D.Phil. (Oxford). Professor of Medieval Thought, School of Philosophy, Aquinas Institute (River Forest, Ill.); Director, Leonine Commission, U.S. sect., Yale University; Associate Professor of the History of Medieval Science, Institute of Mediaeval Studies (Toronto). President of the American Catholic Philosophical Association (1963–1964); Associate Editor of the *New Catholic Encyclopedia* (1963–1964). Editor, *The Dignity of Science* (1961). Author, *Nature and Gravitation* (1955); *Development of Physical Theory in the Middle Ages* (1959); "The *Problemata Determinata XLIII* ascribed to Albertus Magnus," *Medieval Studies* (1960). DURANDUS OF SAINT-POURÇAIN; JOHN OF PARIS; ULRICH (ENGELBERT) OF STRASBOURG.

Weiss, John, B.A. (Wayne State University); M.A., Ph.D. (Columbia). Associate Professor of History at Wayne State University. Editor, *The Origins of Modern Consciousness* (1965). Author, *Moses Hess, Utopian Socialist* (1960). HESS, MOSES; KAUTSKY, KARL; SABATIER, AUGUSTE.

Weitz, Morris, B.A. (Wayne State University); Ph.D. (University of Michigan). Professor of Philosophy at Ohio State University. Fulbright Research Fellow (1951–1952); Guggenheim Fellow (1959–1960). Author, "Analysis and the Unity of Russell's Philosophy" (in P. Schilpp, ed., *The Philosophy of Bertrand Russell,* 1944); *Philosophy in Literature* (1963); *Hamlet and the Philosophy of Literary Criticism* (1964); *Philosophy of the Arts* (1964). ANALYSIS, PHILOSOPHICAL; PROUST, MARCEL; TRAGEDY.

Wellek, Albert, Dr.phil., Dr.phil.habil. Professor and Director of the Department of Psychology at the University of Mainz. Professor at the Universities of Halle and Breslau (until 1945); Dean of the Faculty of Philosophy, University of Mainz (1957–1958). Author, *Das Absolute Gebör und seine Typen* (1938); *Typologie der Musikbegabung* (1939); *Das Problem des seelischen Seins* (2d ed., 1953); *Die Wiederherstellung der Seelenwissenschaften* (1950); *Die Polarität im Aufbau des Charakters* (3d ed., 1965); *Die genetische Ganzheitspsychologie* (1954); *Ganzheitspsychologie und Strukturtheorie* (1955); *Der Rückfall in die Methodenkrise der Psychologie* (1959); *Psychologie* (2d ed., 1965); *Musikpsychologie und Musikästhetik* (1963). KRUEGER, FELIX; WUNDT, WILHELM.

Wellek, René, Ph.D. (University of Prague); Hon. D.Litt. (Oxford, Harvard, University of Rome, University of Maryland); D.H.L. (Lawrence College), Sterling Professor and Chairman of the Department of Comparative Literature at Yale University. Docent in English Literature, University of Prague (1930–1935); Lecturer in Czech Language and Literature, University of London (1935–1939); Professor of Literature, University of Iowa (1939–1946); Professor of Slavic and Comparative Literature, Yale University (1952–1964). Author, *Immanuel Kant in England* (1931); *The Rise of English Literary History* (1941); *Theory of Literature* (with Austin Warren, 1949); *Concepts of Criticism* (1963); *Essays on*

Czech Literature (1963); *Confrontations* (1965); *History of Modern Criticism* (4 vols., 1965). MASARYK, TOMÁŠ GARRIGUE.

Wellman, Carl, B.A. (University of Arizona); M.A., Ph.D. (Harvard). Associate Professor and Chairman of the Department of Philosophy, Lawrence University. Author, *The Language of Ethics* (1961). ASCETICISM.

Werkmeister, William H., Ph.D. Director of the School of Philosophy, University of Southern California; Editor of the *Personalist*. Professor and Chairman of the Department of Philosophy, University of Nebraska (1945–1953); President of the American Philosophical Association, Pacific Division (1964–1965). Author, *A Philosophy of Science; The Basis and Structure of Knowledge; A History of Philosophical Ideas in America; Theories of Ethics; Outlines of a Theory of Value*. DRIESCH, HANS ADOLF EDUARD.

White, Alan R., B.A., Ph.D. Ferens Professor of Philosophy at the University of Hull; Honorary Secretary of the Mind Association. Author, *G. E. Moore: A Critical Exposition* (1958); *Attention* (1964). COHERENCE THEORY OF TRUTH.

White, Hayden V., B.A., M.A., Ph.D. (University of Michigan). Professor of History at the University of Rochester. Fulbright Scholar (1953–1955); Social Science Research Council Faculty Fellow (1961–1962). Coauthor (with W. H. Coates and J. S. Schapiro), *The Emergence of Liberal Humanism: An Intellectual History of Europe* (1966). FEUERBACH, LUDWIG ANDREAS; GOBINEAU, COMTE JOSEPH ARTHUR DE; KLAGES, LUDWIG; STRAUSS, DAVID FRIEDRICH; WINDELBAND, WILHELM.

Whitfield, Jacques J., Doctor of Law, Doctor of Economics (University of Würzburg), and other degrees. Author of articles on Michael Servetus and on the economic history of the 18th century. FRANCK, SEBASTIAN.

Whitrow, G. J., M.A., D.Phil. (Oxford). Reader in Applied Mathematics at the University of London; Vice-President of the Royal Astronomical Society. Formerly, Lecturer at Christ Church, Oxford University. Publications include *The Structure and Evolution of the Universe* (1959); *The Natural Philosophy of Time* (1961). EINSTEIN, ALBERT; ENTROPY.

Whyte, Lancelot Law, Author, *Next Development in Man; Unconscious Before Freud; Internal Factors in Evolution; Unitary Principle in Physics and Biology; Focus and Diversions; Accent on Form*. BOSCOVICH, ROGER JOSEPH; UNCONSCIOUS, THE.

Wick, Warner, B.A. (Williams College and Oxford); Ph.D. (University of Chicago). Professor of Philosophy and Dean of Students at the University of Chicago. Research Fellow, Committee to Advance Original Work in Philosophy, American Philosophical Association (1956–1957). Author, "Generalization and the Basis of Ethics," *Ethics* (1962); "Truth's Debt to Freedom," *Mind* (1964); "Kant's Moral Philosophy" (Introduction to *The Metaphysical Principles of Virtue*, translated by J. W. Ellington, 1964). ARISTOTELIANISM.

Wieman, Henry Nelson, A.B. (Park College); Ph.D. (Harvard); D.D. (Park College); D.Litt. (Occidental College and Grinnell College). Professor Emeritus at the University of Chicago; Distinguished Visiting Professor at Southern Illinois University. Past President of the American Theological Society and the Southern Society for Philosophy of Religion. Author, *Religious Experience and Scientific Method; The Source of Human Good; Man's Ultimate Commitment; Intellectual Foundation of Faith*. NIEBUHR, REINHOLD.

Williams, Bernard, M.A. (Oxford). Professor of Philosophy at the University of London. Fellow of All Souls College, Oxford University (1951–1954); Fellow of New College. Oxford University (1954–1959); Lecturer at University College, University of London (1959–1964); Visiting Professor at Princeton University (1963). Author of articles in various philosophical journals. DESCARTES, RENÉ; HAMPSHIRE, STUART NEWTON; RATIONALISM.

Williams, George Hunston, A.B. (St. Lawrence University); B.D., Th.D., D.D., A.M. (Hon.), Litt.D. Hollis Professor of Divinity, Divinity School, Harvard University; Director of the Foundation for Reformation Research. Past President of the American Society of Church History; Acting Dean of the Divinity School, Harvard University (1953–1955); Delegated Observer at the four sessions of the Vatican Council. Editor, *A History of the Harvard Divinity School 1811–1953* (1954); *Spiritual and Anabaptist Writers* (with A. M. Mergal, 1957). Author, *The Norman Anonymous of 1100 A.D.* (1951); *Anselm: Communion and Atonement* (1960); *Wilderness and Paradise in Christian Thought* (1962); *The Radical Reformation* (1962). SERVETUS, MICHAEL; SOCINIANISM.

Williams, Glanville, LL.D., F.B.A., and other degrees. Professor of English Law at Cambridge University. Formerly, Professor of Public Law and Quain Professor of Jurisprudence at the University of London; Carpentier Lecturer at Columbia University; Cohen Lecturer at the Hebrew University of Jerusalem; first Walter E. Meyer Visiting Research Professor at New York University. Author, *Liability for Animals* (1939); *Joint Torts and Contributory Negligence* (1950); *Criminal Law: The General Part* (2d ed., 1961); *The Proof of Guilt* (3d ed., 1963); *The Sanctity of Life and the Criminal Law* (1956). SUICIDE.

Williams, Raymond, M.A. (Cambridge and Oxford). Lecturer in English at Cambridge University, and Director of English Studies, Jesus College, Cambridge University. Author, *Drama From Ibsen to Eliot* (1952); *Culture and Society* (1958); *Border Country* (1960); *The Long Revolution* (1961); *Second Generation* (1964); *Modern Tragedy* (1966). ARNOLD, MATTHEW; CULTURE AND CIVILIZATION; ELIOT, THOMAS STEARNS; RUSKIN, JOHN.

Wilson, Arthur M., A.B. (Yankton College); B.A., B.Litt., M.A. (Oxford); M.A., Ph.D. (Harvard); L.H.D. (Yankton College). Daniel Webster Professor and Professor of Government and of Biography at Dartmouth College; Fellow of the Royal Historical Society (London). Rhodes Scholar (1924–1927); Guggenheim Fellow (1939–1940, 1956–1957); Past Member of the Editorial Board of the *Journal of Modern History*. Author, *French Foreign Policy Under the Administration of Cardinal Fleury* (1936); *Diderot: The Testing Years, 1713–1759* (1957). ENCYCLOPÉDIE.

Wilson, R. McL., M.A., B.D. (University of Edinburgh); Ph.D. (Cambridge). Senior Lecturer in New Testament Language and Literature, St. Mary's College, St. Andrews University. Visiting Professor, Divinity School, Vanderbilt University (1964–1965). Editor, English Edition, *Hennecke-Schneemelcher: New Testament Apocrypha*. Author, *The Gnostic Problem* (1958); *Studies in the Gospel of Thomas* (1960); *The Gospel of Philip* (1962). MANI AND MANICHAEISM; MARCION; NUMENIUS OF APAMEA; SIMON MAGUS; VALENTINUS AND VALENTINISM.

Winch, Peter, B.A., B.Phil. Oxford). Reader in Philosophy at the University of London; Editor of *Analysis*. Publications include *The Idea of a Social Science* (1958); "Understanding a Primitive Society," *American Philosophical Quarterly* (1964); "The Universalizability of Moral Judgements," *Monist* (1965); "Can a Good Man Be Harmed?," *PAS* (1966). DURKHEIM, ÉMILE; LÉVY-BRUHL, LUCIEN; PARETO, VILFREDO; SPANN, OTHMAR; WEBER, MAX.

Wisdom, J. O., B.A., Ph.D. Distinguished Visiting Professor of Philosophy of Science at the University of Southern California. Formerly, Reader in Logic and Scientific Method at the London School of Economics and Political Science; N.S.F. Senior Foreign Scientist Fellow; Associate Professor of Philosophy at the University of Alexandria. Author, *Foundations of Inference in Natural Science* (1952); *The Unconscious Origin of Berkeley's Philosophy* (1953). PSYCHOANALYTIC THEORIES OF THE UNCONSCIOUS.

Wolandt, Gerd, Dr.phil. Docent in philosophy at the University of Bonn. Publications include "Der Galileische Naturbegriff," *Philosophia Naturalis* (1964); "Cassirers Symbolbegriff," *Zeitschrift für philosophische Forschung* (1964); "Subjektstheoretische Ästhetik," *Jahrbuch für Ästhetik* (1964); *Philosophie der Dichtung* (1965). HÖNIGSWALD, RICHARD.

Wolf, Erik, Dr.iur., D.theol. (Hon.). Professor of Law, Director of the Philosophy of Law Seminar, University of Freiburg im Briesgau. Member of the Confessional Church (since 1933); Delegate to World Council of Churches (1948). Publications include *Grosse Rechtsdenker der deutschen Geistesgeschichte* (4th ed., 1963); *Das Problem der Naturrechtslehre* (3d ed., 1964); *Griechisches Rechtsdenken* (2 vols., 2d ed., 1950–1956); *Ordnung der Kirche* (1962). ALTHUSIUS, JOHANNES; PUFENDORF, SAMUEL VON.

Wolfgang, Marvin E., A.B., M.A., Ph.D. Professor and Graduate Chairman of the Department of Sociology at the University of Pennsylvania; Codirector of the Center of Criminal Research at the University of Pennsylvania; President of the Pennsylvania Prison Society. Past Associate Editor of the *Annals of the American Academy of Political and Social Science.* Author, *Patterns in Criminal Homicide* (1958); *The Sociology of Crime and Delinquency* (1962); *The Sociology of Punishment and Correction* (1962); *Crime and Race* (1964); *The Measurement of Delinquency* (1964). BECCARIA, CESARE BONESANA.

Wolfson, Harry A., A.B., A.M., Ph.D. (Harvard); D.H.Litt. (Hon., Jewish Theological Seminary); D.H.L. (Hon., Jewish Institute of Religion); L.H.D. (Hon., Yeshiva University and the University of Chicago); Litt.D. (Hon., Dropsie College). Nathan Littauer Professor Emeritus of Hebrew Literature and Philosophy at Harvard University. Author, *Crescas' Critique of Aristotle; The Philosophy of Spinoza; Philo; The Philosophy of the Church Fathers; Religious Philosophy.* PHILO JUDAEUS.

Wollheim, Richard, M.A. Grote Professor of Philosophy of Mind and Logic at the University of London. Reader in Philosophy at the University of London (1959–1963); Visiting Professor at Columbia University (1959–1960). Author, *F. H. Bradley* (1959); *Socialism and Culture* (1961); *On Drawing an Object* (1965); and articles in philosophical and literary journals. NATURAL LAW.

Wolman, Benjamin B., M.A., Ph.D. (University of Warsaw). Clinical Professor and Supervisor of Psychotherapy in Adelphi University's Post-Doctoral Program in Psychotherapy; Dean of Faculty at the Institute for Applied Psychoanalysis. Formerly, Director of Mental Health Clinic in Tel Aviv; Supervisor of Psychotherapy in the Post-Doctoral Program for psychiatrists and Lecturer in Psychiatry at the Albert Einstein College of Medicine. Chief Editor, *Handbook of Clinical Psychology;* Coeditor (with Ernest Nagel), *Scientific Psychology: Principles and Approaches;* Associate Editor, *American Imago;* Editor, *Historical Roots of Contemporary Psychology.* Author, *Contemporary Theories and Systems in Psychology* and *Mental Disorders: Their Theory and Classification.* LEWIN, KURT.

Wolter, Allan B., O.F.M., B.A. (Our Lady of Angels Franciscan Seminary); M.A., Ph.D. (Catholic University of America); Lector generalis (Franciscan Institute, St. Bonaventure University). Ordinary Professor of Philosophy at the Catholic University of America; Editor of Quincy College Publications. Taught at Our Lady of Angels Seminary (1943–1945) and the Franciscan Institute (1946–1962); Visiting Lecturer at Princeton University (1965); Associate Editor of the *New Scholasticism* (1949–1951); Editor of *Franciscan Studies* (1949–1952); Editor of *Franciscan Institute Publications,* Philosophy Series (1946–1962). Publications include *The Transcendentals and Their Function in the Metaphysics of Duns Scotus* (1946); *Summula Metaphysicae* (1958); *Duns Scotus: Philosophical Writings* (1962); *John Duns Scotus: A Treatise on God as First Principle* (1965). BACON, ROGER; BONAVENTURE, ST.; DUNS SCOTUS, JOHN.

Wolterstorff, Nicholas, A.B. (Calvin College); M.A., Ph.D. (Harvard). Professor of Philosophy at Calvin College. Past Visiting Associate Professor of Philosophy at the University of Chicago; former Sheldon Traveling Fellow. CALVIN, JOHN.

Woodcock, George. Editor of *Canadian Literature.* Formerly, Assistant Professor of English at the University of Washington; Associate Professor of English at the University of British Columbia; Guggenheim Fellow (1950); Canadian Government Overseas Fellow (1957). Author, *William Godwin* (1946); *The Anarchist Prince: A Life of Peter Kropotkin* (1950); *Pierre-Joseph Proudhon* (1956); *Anarchism* (1962); *Faces of India* (1963). ANARCHISM; BAKUNIN, MICHAEL; KROPOTKIN, PETER A.; PROUDHON, PIERRE-JOSEPH; STIRNER, MAX.

Woodruff, Arthur E., B.A., M.S. (Yale); Ph.D. (University of Rochester). Assistant Professor, Department of Mathematics and Science Education, Belfer Graduate School of Science, Yeshiva University. Taught at the University of Chicago (1955–1962); N.S.F. Faculty Fellow, Department of History of Science and Medicine, Yale University (1962–1963). Coeditor, *Proceedings of the 4th Annual Rochester Conference on High-Energy Physics* (1954). Author, "Proton-proton Scattering with Parity and Time-reversal Non-invariance," *Annals of Physics;* "Semi-Phenomenological Analysis of the Process $p + p \rightarrow d + \pi^+$ Near Threshold," *Physical Review;* "Action at a Distance in Nineteenth Century Electrodynamics," *Isis* (1962). FARADAY, MICHAEL; MAXWELL, JAMES CLERK; TYNDALL, JOHN.

Woozley, A. D., M.A. (Oxford). Professor of Moral Philosophy at St. Andrews University. Fellow of All Souls College, Oxford University (1935–1937); Fellow and Praelector in Philosophy, Queens College, Oxford University, and University Lecturer in Philosophy, Oxford University (1937–1954). Publications include *Thomas Reid's "Essays on the Intellectual Powers of Man"* (1941); *Theory of Knowledge* (1949); *Plato's Republic* (with R. C. Cross, 1964); *John Locke's "Essay Concerning Human Understanding"* (1964). UNIVERSALS, PROBLEMS OF.

Wright, James R. G., M.A. (University of Edinburgh); B.A. (Cambridge). Lecturer in Humanity (Latin) at the University of Edinburgh. Guthrie Fellow in Classical Literature and C. B. Black Scholar in New Testament Greek at the University of Edinburgh (1961); Henry Arthur Thomas Student at Cambridge University (1963). SENECA, LUCIUS ANNAEUS.

Wyschogrod, Michael, B.S.S., Ph.D. Assistant Professor of Philosophy, the City University of New York, City College. Publications include *Kierkegaard and Heidegger: The Ontology of Existence* (1954). BUBER, MARTIN; HALEVI, YEHUDA.

Yates, Frances A., M.A., D.Lit. Reader in the History of the Renaissance at the University of London; Fellow of the Royal Society of Literature. Gulbenkian Fellow, I Tatti (Italy,

1965). Author, *The French Academies of the Sixteenth Century* (1947); *Giordano Bruno and the Hermetic Tradition* (1964); *The Art of Memory* (1966). BRUNO, GIORDANO; HERMETICISM.

Young, Robert M., B.A. (Yale); M.A., Ph.D. (Cambridge). University Assistant Lecturer in the History and Philosophy of Science and Fellow of King's College, Cambridge University. Author of articles and reviews on the histories of biology, psychology, and the study of the nervous system. ANIMAL SOUL.

Zeldin, Mary-Barbara, A.B. (Bryn Mawr College); M.A., Ph.D. (Radcliffe). Associate Professor of Philosophy at Hollins College. Former Social Affairs Officer, Narcotic Drugs Division, United Nations. Coeditor (with James Edie and James Scanlan), *Russian Philosophy* (3 vols., 1965). Author of articles in *Journal of Philosophy* and *Journal of Criminal Psychodynamics.* CHAADAEV, PYOTR YAKOVLEVICH; SPIR, AFRIKAN ALEXANDROVICH.

Zia, Nai Z., M.A. Editor of Christian Classics Series. Former Professor at Lingnan University and the University of Nanking (China). Author of articles on the philosophy of religion and ethics. HAN FEI TZU.

Zweig, Arnulf, A.B. (University of Rochester); Ph.D. (Stanford). Assistant Professor of Philosophy at the University of Oregon. A.C.L.S. Fellow (1952–1953); Yale University Fellow (1952–1953); Stanford Graduate Honors Fellow (1953–1955); Visiting Professor at M.I.T. (1964–1965). Author of articles in *Philosophical Studies, Analysis,* and *Ethics.* BECK, JAKOB SIGISMUND; BENEKE, FRIEDRICH EDUARD; DÜHRING, EUGEN KARL; FECHNER, GUSTAV THEODOR; GOETHE, JOHANN WOLFGANG VON; KRAUSE, KARL CHRISTIAN FRIEDRICH; KÜLPE, OSWALD; LANGE, FRIEDRICH ALBERT; LIPPS, THEODOR; SIGWART, CHRISTOPH; STUMPF, KARL.

The Encyclopedia of Philosophy

ABBAGNANO, NICOLA, born in 1901 at Salerno, is the chief exponent of Italian existentialism, which he defines as a militant and rational "philosophy of the possible." Originally a pupil of Antonio Aliotta at the University of Naples, Abbagnano has been teaching since 1936 at the University of Turin, where he also for years has been coediting the influential *Rivista di filosofia*. Practically since his first book, *Le sorgenti irrazionali del pensiero* (Naples, 1923), Abbagnano has been advocating a change of philosophical horizon suitable to the problematic nature of human life. This advocacy is reflected in a notable series of historical studies, culminating in the monumental three-volume work *Storia della filosofia* (Turin, 1946–1950; 2d ed., 1963).

Reacting against the prevailing neo-Hegelianism of Croce and Gentile in Italy, Abbagnano was influenced, in turn, by Husserl's phenomenology and, later, by Kierkegaard, Heidegger, and Jaspers; but he revealed in his first attempt at existentialism, *La struttura dell'esistenza* (Turin, 1939), that he was no mere expositor or disciple of German existentialism. In that work he took a stand against Heidegger and Jaspers; and in subsequent writings his polemic was sharpened and extended to French existentialism, including Sartre on the one hand and Marcel, Lavelle, Le Senne on the other. He groups Sartre with Kierkegaard under German existentialism, and the others under "theological or ontological existentialism."

According to Abbagnano, all forms of existentialism in vogue since Kierkegaard have been self-defeating, since they lead, on examination, to the negation of what is basic to their whole interpretation of human existence: "the primacy of possibility." He discerns two principal directions within the contemporary existentialist movement. One (the left wing) is associated with the early Heidegger, Jaspers, and Sartre; the other (the right wing), with Marcel, Lavelle, and Le Senne. The first group of existentialists negates existence as possibility by reducing human possibilities to *impossibilities*, with everything projected by finite man inevitably foredoomed to fail; the second group negates existence by "surreptitiously" transforming human possibilities into *potentialities*, necessarily destined to succeed in the end.

Even though for Abbagnano the left and the right wings of the existentialist movement are founded, technically, on opposite principles—"the impossibility of the possible" and "the necessity of the possible," respectively—they at least share a common negative ground because each of them, in one way or another, ultimately makes possibility itself impossible. The only valid alternative to "negative existentialism," which for polemical reasons Abbagnano calls "positive existentialism," takes as its guiding principle "the possibility of the possible" or, in Kantian terminology, "transcendental possibility." In this view, an authentic possibility in human life is one that, once it has been chosen or realized, remains open to further choice or realization; that is, continues to be possible. In short, Abbagnano's alternative constitutes an *open possibilism.*

This alternative calls for a clarification and coherent use of the fundamental category of all existentialism: the modal category of possibility. It is perhaps here that Abbagnano has made his greatest contribution to the entire existentialist movement, especially since in contemporary logic, as he himself observes, the concept of modality has not been given sufficient "analytic elaboration."

Ever since Aristotle, Abbagnano maintains, there has been confusion concerning the modal categories, particularly with respect to the meaning of the term "possible." The possible in the empirical sense of what *may* be has been distinguished from the possible in the purely logical sense of the noncontradictory. But, unfortunately, it has been confused with the "potential" in Aristotle's sense and with the "contingent" in Avicenna's. Since potentiality signifies "*pre*-determination" of the actual, the potential excludes the possible, *ex hypothesi.* Aristotle did concede that not all potentialities are actualized, but this concession on his part was only introduced "surreptitiously." For, if the potential means what is destined to occur anyway, there is no room for possibility as such. As for Avicenna's concept of the contingent, there is no doubt about its necessitarian character. For he makes the contingent into a species of the necessary—the contingent being, by his own definition, whatever is necessary through another. Hence, it follows that the modal status of the potential and the contingent is not that of possibility, of what *may* be; but that of necessity, of what *must* be. Abbagnano concludes that those who think in such terms, including existentialists, are necessitarians in disguise.

Historically, Abbagnano sees his own version of existentialism as an attempt to relate Kant and Kierkegaard in a complementary way. In Kant's Table of Categories three pairs of categories are listed under modality: possibility–impossibility, existence–nonexistence, and necessity–contingency. Abbagnano virtually reduces Kant's three pairs of modality categories to one primary pair: the necessary and the nonnecessary. The reason he gives for doing so is that necessity and contingency are not really opposites. Neither are possibility and impossibility. For impossibility is the negative of necessity, not the negative of possibility; what *can't* be at all being the opposite of what *must* be of necessity.

As an existential possibilist, Abbagnano defines existence as possibility, and nonexistence as "non-possibility," not as impossibility. While the nonnecessary excludes the necessary and the impossible, it includes the possible and the nonpossible. This means that man can neither be sure of realizing his conflicting possibilities, nor be sure of the impossibility of their realization. It also means that every concrete possibility open to man has two aspects, a promising (positive) prospect and an inauspicious (negative) aspect. To illustrate, the possibility of knowledge implies the possibility of error. Errors are not "impossible," since we do in fact make them, but they *are* "non-possible" in the sense that they are unverifiable when put to test. Thus, a double-aspect theory of possibility lies at the heart of Abbagnano's "positive existentialism."

Another distinctive feature of Italian existentialism in general and of Abbagnano's philosophy in particular is the deliberate focus on a problem that was originally foreign to German existentialism; to wit, the problem of value.

Starting with the assumption that the problem of value is the problem of what man *ought to be,* Abbagnano argues in effect that, since the *ought-to-be* is the possible in the normative sense, it is therefore the moral equivalent of the *may-be,* which is the possible in the empirical sense. As a consequence, the logic of possibility coincides with the ethics of possibility, and these two phases of the same problem come together in Abbagnano's possibilistic interpretation of human conduct. This interpretation stresses the "normativity" of human existence, which involves the problem of freedom in all its dimensions. Thus, Abbagnano's existentialism logically unites the complementary categories of possibility and freedom, as is clear from his important volume *Possibilità e libertà* (Turin, 1956).

In recent years, Abbagnano has come to characterize what is living in contemporary philosophy as the "New Enlightenment," and has openly declared his affinities with the neopositivistic and neonaturalistic movements in the Anglo-American world. As a result, he has developed the empirical and naturalistic strains in his existentialism, emphasizing the methodological connections between possibility as a generic criterion of existence and verifiability as a specific criterion in scientific inquiry. This "transfiguration" of existentialism into scientific methodology is clearly evident in the article on Existentialism in *Dizionario di filosofia* (Turin, 1961). However, Abbagnano thinks that the romantic "myth of security" in Comte's positivism, typical of the nineteenth-century mentality, still survives in the scientific utopianism of the Vienna Circle; and although he sympathizes with the later Wittgenstein's thesis that the meaning of words depends on their use, he contends that the leader of the analytic movement failed to give a philosophical analysis of the notion of "use" itself. Abbagnano's sympathies with North American naturalism are reflected in his writings on John Dewey and in his review of P. Romanell's volume *Toward a Critical Naturalism* (*Rivista di filosofia,* Vol. 50, 1959, 108–109).

Additional Works by Abbagnano

HISTORICAL

Il nuovo idealismo inglese e americano. Naples, 1927.

La filosofia di E. Meyerson e la logica dell'identità. Naples, 1929.

Guglielmo di Ockham. Lanciano, 1931.

La nozione del tempo secondo Aristotele. Lanciano, 1933.

Bernardino Telesio. Milan, 1941.

SYSTEMATIC

Introduzione all'esistenzialismo. Milan, 1942.

Filosofia, religione, scienza. Turin, 1947.

Esistenzialismo positivo. Turin, 1948.

"Contemporary Science and Freedom," *Review of Metaphysics,* Vol. 5, No. 3 (1952), 361–378.

Problemi di sociologia. Turin, 1959.

"Existentialism in Italy," *Cesare Barbieri Courier,* Vol. 3, No. 2 (1961), 12–18.

Works on Abbagnano

Giannini, G., *L'esistenzialismo positivo di N. Abbagnano.* Brescia, 1956.

Santucci, Antonio, *Esistenzialismo e filosofia italiana.* Bologna, 1959.

Simona, Maria Angela, *La Notion de liberté dans l'existentialisme positif de Nicola Abbagnano.* Fribourg, Switzerland, 1962.

PATRICK ROMANELL

ABBOT, FRANCIS ELLINGWOOD (1836–1903), American philosopher and radical theologian. After his graduation from Harvard College and Meadville Theological Seminary, Abbot entered the Unitarian ministry. For some years he served a parish in Dover, New Hampshire. During this time he was one of the organizers of the Free Religious Association, composed originally of dissatisfied members of the Unitarian group who wanted the Unitarian Association to accept non-Christians as members. As time went on, the Free Religious Association developed a liberal theology, accepting the results of science in preference to dependence on revelation. It accepted into membership atheists like Benjamin F. Underwood and nontheists like Felix Adler. Abbot's sponsorship of this theology and his readiness to unite with non-Christians was a position much more radical than many of the members of his New Hampshire parish could tolerate, and he resigned his pastorate.

Debarred from an academic position in Boston, again because of his radical religious views, he returned to the ministry in Toledo, Ohio, in a congregation that was willing to follow him into independence and to finance a weekly journal of Free Religion, *The Index,* which was published under Abbot's editorship from 1870 to 1880. In the 1870s, in addition to his work with the Free Religious Association, Abbot became the leader of the National Liberal League, pledged to resist the erosion of religious freedom, and in 1880 he was named by a splinter party—the Conscience party—as candidate for vice-president of the United States.

In 1888 Abbot substituted for Josiah Royce during Royce's absence from Harvard. This led, on Royce's return, to considerable controversy, when Royce publicly attacked the realistic philosophy that Abbot had developed in his lectures. Royce's enthusiasm for idealism led him to extend his criticism beyond proper philosophical limits and to engage in personal attacks on Abbot. In view of twentieth-century philosophical developments, however, it is clear that Abbot was far more original than Royce would admit. The controversy embittered Abbot, and after his wife's death in 1893, he gave up all attempts to maintain contact with other thinkers and withdrew into solitude, preparing his major systematic work, *The Syllogistic Philosophy*. When it was completed, just ten years after his wife's death, he committed suicide at her grave.

As early as 1864 to 1868, Abbot had published a series of philosophical articles in the *North American Review* in which the germs of his later "scientific realism" were already discernible. In 1881, for his Harvard dissertation, and more fully in 1885, in a book called *Scientific Theism,* Abbot developed his position on the basis of a critical examination of Kantian epistemology which led him to reject modern nominalism and to accept in its stead a realistic position grounded in the objectivity of relations. Both his criticism of Kant and his affirmation of objective relativism are similar to the corresponding ideas of Hegel, yet Abbot claimed, with justice, that his version was free from idealistic presuppositions. To the degree that scientific realism allows the possibility of achieving a genuine knowledge of the objective world, it is, as Abbot declared it to be, a way out of the philosophical agnosticism of Kant's restriction of knowledge to phenomena.

Bibliography

Abbot's principal works are *Scientific Theism* (Boston, 1885); *The Way out of Agnosticism* (Boston, 1890); and *The Syllogistic Philosophy,* 2 vols. (Boston, 1906).

The only full-length study of Abbot's philosophy is an unpublished doctoral dissertation by William J. Callaghan, available in typescript in the Columbia University Library, New York. For other literature on Abbot, see Joseph L. Blau, *Men and Movements in American Philosophy* (New York, 1952), pp. 175–186; Stowe Persons, *Free Religion—An American Faith* (New Haven, 1947); and H. W. Schneider, *A History of American Philosophy* (New York, 1946), Chs. 6 and 8.

J. L. BLAU

ABBT, THOMAS (1738–1766), German moralist and popular philosopher, was born at Ulm, the son of a wigmaker. He studied theology at Halle, and taught philosophy at the University of Frankfurt an der Oder in 1760 and mathematics at Rinteln in 1761. He then lived for some time in Berlin, where he met Mendelssohn and Nicolai. After traveling in southern Germany, Switzerland, and France in 1763, he became surveyor of educational institutions for Count Wilhelm I von Schaumburg-Lippe at Bückeburg, where he died.

Abbt's first significant work—following a preliminary work also supporting Frederick II in 1761, *De Rege Philosopho*—was *Vom Tode fürs Vaterland* ("On Death for the Fatherland," Berlin, 1761), a pamphlet supporting Frederick II of Prussia in the Seven Years War. Abbt stated, against general opinion, that subjects of a monarchy—and not only citizens of a republic—should love their country. They should be loyal to their king and ready to die for him in a Stoic–Christian spirit. He complained that troops and even officers engaged in the war felt themselves to be only mercenaries and scoffed at patriotic ideas. Abbt thus was the first supporter of Prussian nationalism.

Abbt's second work, *Vom Verdienst* ("On Merit," Berlin, 1765), reflected his work as surveyor of educational institutions. He discussed the ideals of education appropriate to the different functions in society. He considered intellectual genius higher than the active or sentimental genius. According to Abbt, man is intended to be active and authoritarian; woman, to be passive and obedient. Education should direct moral goodness to its highest stage, benevolence (*Wohlwollen*). Merit may be either great, high, general, or beautiful (aesthetic). Abbt went on to distinguish various human types. Warriors are highest, followed by apostles of faith (*milites christiani*). Next come officials, writers, artists, and preachers. After describing the members of the elite classes, Abbt attempted a typology of the common people in terms of social and professional groups and analogous criteria of social function, rather than in terms of the traditional characterology of temperaments based on physiological and psychological elements.

Abbt, like Mendelssohn, Lessing, and Basedow, was a "popular philosopher" (*Popularphilosoph*), a writer who aimed at useful knowledge and the education of a wide public rather than at scholastic subtleties, and who discussed problems in a lively and easily understandable way in the fashion of the English and French Enlightenment philosophers. His main interest was in the analysis of human nature from a psychological and social viewpoint. He was influenced by Shaftesbury, Pope, and Hume; by La Rochefoucauld, La Bruyère, Montesquieu, and Helvétius; and by J. J. Spalding, Justus Möser, and Mendelssohn.

Additional Works by Abbt

Geschichte des menschlichens Geschlects. Halle, 1766.

Vermischte Schriften, C. F. Nicolai, ed., 6 vols. Berlin, 1768–1790.

Works on Abbt

Bender, A., *Thomas Abbt*. Bonn, 1922.

Bruck, Gertrud, *Die Bedeutung Justus Mösers fürs Leben und Denken Thomas Abbts*. Würzburg, 1937.

Herder, J. G., *Ueber Thomas Abbts Schriften*. Riga, 1768.

Nicolai, C. F., *Ehrengedächtnis Thomas Abbts*. Berlin, 1767.

Pentzhorn, E., *Thomas Abbt, ein Beitrag zu seiner Biographie*. Giessen, 1884.

Schuller, H., "Thomas Abbt." *Jahrbuch für Philosophie und Pädagogie,* (1887), Part 2, 65–92.

GIORGIO TONELLI

ABELARD, PETER (1079–1142), foremost logician and dialectician of his age, was called *peripateticus palatinus noster* ("our imperial paladin") by John of Salisbury in affection and in punning reference to Le Palais, near Nantes, where Abelard was born. Abelard studied the quadrivium, probably under Thierry of Chartres, and dialectics, first under Roscelin and then under William of Champeaux, archdeacon of Paris, two men holding opposite views on the status of universal ideas. He set up schools of his own at Melun, at Corbeil, and afterward at Paris. Following a retirement to Brittany because of illness, he turned to theology under the direction of Anselm of Laon and started teaching it himself at Paris in 1113. The love story of Abelard and Héloïse belongs to history and literature; after the atrocious revenge taken on him by her uncle, Abelard withdrew to the abbey of St. Denis, where he made his profession as a monk. Although he cared for regular discipline, he was too restless for monastic stability. His theological work, "On the Divine Unity and Trinity," was burned at an ecclesiastical council at Soissons in 1121 at the instance of a cabal of his enemies. These he was not backward at making; those who had taught him were not spared his ridicule, and his combativeness was answered with equal energy, if less penetration. Yet this fair and handsome man, slim and not tall, had stanch friends to protect him. He founded the school of the Paraclete near Nogent-sur-Seine in 1125, left to become abbot of St. Gildas in Brittany, and returned to Paris to lecture at St. Geneviève, where John of Salisbury, a major authority for the debates of the period, became his pupil in 1136. No more a rationalist than St. Anselm, his manner more than his matter made him a stormy petrel of theology, and St. Bernard, disliking Abelard's humanism and mistaking his intellectualism for a derogation from the obedience of faith, pushed through his condemnation at a council at Sens in 1141. An appeal to the pope brought another condemnation and an injunction against lecturing. The accusation of heresy, however, does not hold water. Abelard retired to Cluny, where the abbot, Peter the Venerable, extolled his piety, modesty, and dignity and also reconciled him to St. Bernard. He died at the Cluniac priory in St. Marcel-sur-Saône in 1142 and was buried with Héloïse.

Background and influence. Abelard stood for causes that later emerged, so much so that it is easy to read these back into him and see him out of proportion to his times. His seminal influence has been misrepresented as containing elements—notably rationalism, Scholasticism, and nominalism—that were, in fact, introduced afterward.

As for rationalism, Abelard's religious speculations were conducted in no neutral setting, still less on the assumption, which appeared in the next century with the "double truth" theory, that the truths of reason and faith could be in conflict. His effort was the same as St. Anselm's: to use the resources of philosophy for Christian defense and elucidation. To treat either man as simply a natural theologian calls for an abstraction more forced than that in the case of St. Thomas Aquinas, who inherited Abelard's rational hardiness but pressed it with quieter assurance and greater precision regarding the distinction between nature and grace.

Again, although Abelard set a standard of acuteness and severity in debate which Scholasticism was never to lose, the method of his famous *Sic et Non* was not new. It was written to sharpen the wits of the young reader by advancing a series of theological themes in an alternation of contrasting texts. These, however, were not harmonized, and, moreover, they stop at "authorities" taken from patristic anthologies without uncovering the "reasons" engaged, according to the method of thesis, antithesis, and synthesis found in the *Summa Theologiae* and, with more detailed development, in the *Quaestiones Disputatae* and *Quodlibetales* of Aquinas.

Whether one calls Abelard a nominalist, as John of Salisbury did, or, with later writers, a conceptualist or even a moderate realist, the questions he faced were not those of Ockham or of the fifteenth and later centuries, but the simpler extremes of nominalism and realism. The first, represented by Roscelin, Abelard considered of little account; against the second, he scored a tactical victory by pushing William of Champeaux from an early position. Yet a more refined Platonism persisted among thinkers no less humanistic than Abelard and more expert in natural science. Nobody knew then that William was the shadow of the formidable figure of Avicenna.

Although Plato was Abelard's hero, Abelard was nevertheless an Aristotelian before his time. His achievement is all the more surprising when it is considered that he knew at best only a little Greek and was familiar only with the *logica vetus*, which included, of Aristotle's works, only the *Categories* and *De Interpretatione* in translations by Boethius. He may have read *De Sophisticis Elenchis*, and he refers to the *Prior Analytics* and the *Posterior Analytics*, from the first of which he quotes twice. But he did not possess the *Organon* or the corpus of Aristotle's natural, moral, and metaphysical philosophy. He was like a man, unequipped with many subsequent technical tools, exploring a territory for which most of the maps have been lost. For instance, the terms "matter" and "form" relate to the distinction between the "thisness" of an individual thing and its "whatness" as a kind of thing without involving the doctrine of hylomorphism, or the notion of a primary matrix for, or substantial potentiality in, physical things; their various meanings and their bearings on the predicables and predicaments are not charted as they were by St. Thomas. Still, the reader of the *Summa* will note its debt to Abelard, most importantly in the general tenor of the dialogue, yet occasionally in a turn of phrase.

ABELARD'S PHILOSOPHY

Natural theology. Abelard did not treat natural theology as a special subject, and his teachings, like the much more systematic studies of St. Thomas, have to be extracted from his works on Christian theology. Faith is the beginning and, although not produced by reasoning, is neither forced nor blind. It seeks to understand (*intelligere*) what it cannot comprehend (*comprehendere*). Hence, the truths of revelation are to be reasoned about, since it is in our reason that we are made in the image of God and since it is there, through Christ who is the Word of Wisdom and the source of dialectic, that we receive divine truth. Abelard's interpretation of the assent of faith is intellectualist rather than voluntarist; his temper, dialectical rather than meditative. He admired the non-Christian philosophers for their observance of the natural law and welcomed their anticipations of the Christian mysteries; these were among the reasons why he incurred the hostility of the traditionalists, who considered theology more for reading in the cloister than for debate in the lecture hall.

He arrived at the existence of God by reflecting on the contrast between the eternal and transitory and enlarging on the dependence of body on mind gathered from Chalcidius' translation of the *Timaeus*. Other sources of argument for the grounds of Christian belief were St. Augustine, Boethius, and Macrobius. God's unity was shown by explaining the order of the universe in terms of monarchy. As for omnipotence, God was constrained by no force outside himself; nevertheless, creating is not an arbitrary exercise of will but an act that reflects a necessity of the divine nature in choosing what is best—an optimism Abelard's successors were to qualify. Abelard accepted Augustinian exemplarism; the world is made according to pre-existing Ideas, although these patterns are not things but concepts in the mind of God. What God is infinitely surpasses the analogies we use to think about him. Like St. Anselm, however, Abelard followed the tradition set by St. Augustine rather than the negative theology promoted by Erigena and spoke of the "Supreme Good," not the "Beyond Good."

Ethics. Abelard's *Scito Teipsum* ("Know Thyself") discusses topics not ordinarily included nowadays under ethics, such as the sacerdotal power of absolution. It is no less important in the history of moral theory than his commentaries on Porphyry in the history of logic. His teaching springs from the Gospels and is strengthened by St. Augustine. Morality does not consist in external observances but in the mind and heart. Sin is less an injury inflicted than a contempt of God; virtue, less doing what is respectable than living in love with God. Consider, St. Augustine had said, not what is done but in what mind it is done. Abelard took a leading part in the twelfth-century movement which brought out the capital importance of intention and which enabled moral theology to survive the later inroads of the canonists.

Here, again, it is too much to expect from Abelard the balanced statement St. Thomas gave of the interrelation of ends and means; of motives, objects, and circumstances; and of intentions and results in determining the morality of acts. But Abelard did go to the heart of the matter. There is vice in the concupiscence of the flesh and in the concupiscence of the soul; sin, however, does not lie in these inclinations but in the intentions and consents that grow out of them, and so virtue is also exercised by not consenting to what should not be done. The deed itself adds nothing to the morality, good or bad, of what is purposed. This is a matter of personal conscience, which is binding even when it is mistaken. Although a morality of pure intention was remote from the medieval temper, it seems that Abelard came very close to it. He did not think, however, that it was enough to follow what seems good, for he believed that we are obliged to strain after what is really good.

Logic and theory of knowledge. The problem of universals was the main philosophical topic of Abelard's period, partly because it was prompted by the only classical texts then available, partly because it seemed engaged by the dogma of one nature and three persons in God. Are species objective and real, or are they merely the mind's generalizations from individuals, which are the only existing things? Plato's own criticism in the *Parmenides* of his teaching on the Forms was taken up by Aristotle and repeated by Boethius in his commentaries on the *Isagoge* of Porphyry. The early medievals split into two wings. By all accounts, an extreme nominalism was represented by Roscelin: Only individuals exist, and a universal is just a word we breathe, *flatus vocis*. An extreme realism was represented by William of Champeaux: A real common nature is wholly present in each member of the species, and individuals differ from one another by their accidents, not their substance. Whether the views of either man were as simple as they were reported to be is not certain, but Abelard disposed of the suggestion that two men, for example, could be one and the same substance. William thereupon explained that he meant they were one and the same not essentially, *essentialiter*, but indeterminately, *indifferenter;* Peter and Paul are same in being man, for it belongs to man to be mortal and rational, but the humanity of each is not the same, but similar, because they are two men. Abelard had no difficulty in refuting an attempt by others to maintain that universals were real in that they existed in the collection of the many and that all men taken together are the species which is man. For this, as he pointed out, is not the universal of the discussion, which by definition is what can be predicated of many. What he was actually opposing in the ultrarealists was their habit of philosophizing as logicians of diction cradled in the grammar of Priscian and of assuming that things could be predicated of things or that the logical and real orders were so far parallel that because of the identity of predicate when we say, "Socrates is a man, and Plato is a man," there is a real substantial identity between the two men.

Abelard's own position was established not in grammar but in logic, which, as he observed, concerns the use of language in terms, propositions, and arguments and differs from natural science, which concerns the nature of things. He seems to have been acquainted with the work of the medical school of Salerno but took no part in the growth of experimental science, soon to be reinforced from across the frontier by Islam. Nor did he possess the metaphysical flair of St. Anselm. His critical analysis of the meaning of words rendered a lasting service, but he did more than that and should not be held responsible for the sterility, lamented by John of Salisbury, which resulted from the schools' being preoccupied with the meaning of meaning at the expense of the meaning of things.

Three questions were proposed by Porphyry, who refused to commit himself to an answer, and by Boethius, who, perhaps uneasy over the alternatives, took no definite stand. Do genera and species subsist, or are they bare thoughts? If they subsist, are they spiritual or material? Are they separate from or embodied in sensible things? In the epistemological frame of reference of Abelard and his contemporaries, these questions amounted to asking whether such universals were things, not whether they were real. To the early realists—the *antiqui doctores*, as they were called—a universal nature was extramental, in itself one, and diversified by individual forms below it; under pressure from Abelard such diversification of one substance by many accidents was abandoned, and realists spoke of one nature according to various states of existence or considered according to diverse respects of definition. To the nominalists, or *moderni*, universal natures were not *subsistentia* but *nuda intellecta*.

For Abelard a thing was always an individual. Nevertheless, a universal did name things which really existed, and, consequently, it was not a *flatus vocis*, a sound made from letters and syllables, but a word with a content of meaning, *vox significativa*, which he called a *nomen* and, in a revised edition of his logic, a *sermo*. This was imposed when individuals themselves were really like one another, *ipsi ad invicem conveniunt*. Such common likeness did not require us to ascribe universality to things but only to significant words. "I do not say that they agree in man, since no thing is man except an individual thing, but they agree in being man." The agreement was expressed in a shared predicate; there was no need to invoke a shared essence or nature as a thing distinct from what the individual was in itself. "To be a man" was a predicate and no more a thing than was a negative predicate—for instance, "not inhering in a subject."

To Porphyry's three questions, Abelard added a fourth. Does a universal refer to some thing, or if that thing is not in existence (as when, in winter, we say that there are no roses), does it consist in the mere meaning of the concept? His negative answer here and his treatment of propositions in which the referent is not a thing are enough to show that he was not a nominalist pure and simple. The proposition "If there is a rose, there is a flower" is logically true even if no rose exists. He saw a "quasi res" required by the necessity of such an implication, a reality indifferent to the presence or absence of a real subject; his thought here echoed St. Augustine's on the eternal laws ruling mathematics apart from any confirmation in point of fact. Our knowledge about inner forms not accessible to the senses—for instance, "rationality" and "paternity"—he called *opinio*, not a well-chosen term according to the vocabulary of classical and medieval philosophy and a term misleading to those who took him to entertain an element of uncertainty.

Abelard had no firsthand knowledge of Aristotle's psychology and epistemology of abstraction and could not draw on him in accounting for the formation of universal ideas, yet he came to some of the same conclusions, such as the distinction between empirical knowledge of a fact and rational knowledge of the cause of a fact and the intellect's difference from and dependence on the imagination. The intellect is incorporeal and constructs likenesses, *effigies*, of things outside it. Of these, some are particular and others universal; they are distinct both from the mind and from the things they designate.

Our use of universals supposes, first, that there is a real likeness among the individuals to which they are applied, for although universals are not things, they denominate things, and, second, that these common conceptions exist in consciousness. Abelard was aware that the abstract form in the mind was "otherwise" than the concrete form in the thing, yet there is no falsification when a particular thing which does not have only its form is considered as having only it, for the mind, although not attending to all that is there, sees nothing except what is there.

Abelard was a harbinger of causes that were later established, perhaps more so in theology than in philosophy. One forgets the deficiencies of his information in the vigor and energy of his inferences, his rudimentary apparatus in the exactness and incisiveness with which he used it, and even his animus and aggressiveness in the generosity and graciousness of his teaching. He founded no lasting school, but he left a lasting spirit. His character and work abound with the contrasts of a good debate; he was a linguistic philosopher, a poet, and a monk with a great love of the world. He confessed that he was bad at mathematics; it is said that he excelled at music. Indeed, he communicates a singing quality to topics ordinarily unmelodious. Few other Scholastics remain as readable and alive.

Bibliography

Patrologia Latina, Vol. 178, J. P. Migne, ed. (Paris, 1855), includes the theological, apologetical, and exegetical works and the letters and the biographical *Historia Calamitatum*. The main work, the *Christian Theology*, has been edited by H. Ostlender, *Theologia "Summi Boni," in Beiträge zur Geschichte der Philosophie des Mittelalters*, Vol. XXXVI, Nos. 2–3 (Münster, Germany, 1939), and translated by J. K. McCallum as *Abailard's Christian Theology* (London, 1948). McCallum also translated the *Scito Teipsum: Abailard's Ethics* (Oxford, 1935).

Victor Cousin made the philosophical works accessible with *Ouvrages inédits d'Abélard* (Paris, 1836) and the *Opera*, 2 vols. (Paris, 1848–1859). Literal glosses on isolated questions of logic will be found in M. Dal Pra, *Pietro Abelardo, scritti filosofici* (Rome and Milan, 1954). Glosses on the *Categories* and Porphyry, which, in effect, form systematic expositions, and on the *Logica Ingredientibus* and the *Logica Nostrorum Petitioni Sociorum* (so titled, like papal bulls, from their *incipit*'s) are in B. Geyer, ed., *Peter Abaelards philosophische Schriften*, in *Beiträge zur Geschichte der Philosophie des Mittelalters*, Vol. XXXI, Nos. 1–4 (Münster, Germany, 1919–1933). The *Dialectica*, in L. M. De Rijk, ed., *Petrus Abaelardus, Dialectica* (Assen, Netherlands, 1956), offers a complete methodological treatment of logic; the full and scientific introduction is most valuable.

Important texts from Abelard and others are translated by Richard McKeon, ed., *Selections from Medieval Philosophers* (New York, 1929; London, 1930). His influence in ethics is brought out by O. Lottin, *Psychologie et morale aux XIIe et XIIIe siècles*, 2 vols. (Louvain, Belgium, 1942–1948). For the debates on universals, see J. Reiners, *Der aristotelische Realismus in der Frühscholastik* (Bonn, 1907); see also *De Nominalismus in der Frühscholastik*, in *Beiträge zur Geschichte der Philosophie des Mittelalters*, Vol. VIII, No. 5 (Münster, Germany, 1910). There is a life by J. G. Sikes, *Peter Abailard* (Cambridge, 1932).

THOMAS GILBY, O.P.

ABSOLUTE, THE, is a term used by philosophers to signify the ultimate reality regarded as one and yet as the source of variety; as complete, or perfect, and yet as not divorced from the finite, imperfect world. The term was introduced into the philosophical vocabulary at the very end of the eighteenth century by Schelling and Hegel and was naturalized into English by Coleridge as early as 1809–1810 in *The Friend*. Later in the century it was an important term in the writings of such Idealist philosophers as Ferrier, Bradley, Bosanquet, and Royce.

Introduction of the term. One of the sources of the philosophy of the Absolute is the literature about Spinoza commencing with Moses Mendelssohn's *Morgenstunden* (1785) and F. H. Jacobi's *Ueber die Lehre des Spinoza in Briefen an den Herrn Moses Mendelssohn* (1785). The expression "the Absolute" does not appear in these books, but there is a discussion of Spinoza's view that God does not transcend the world but is the sole infinite substance in which everything has its being. In the second edition of his book (1789), Jacobi printed as an appendix passages from Bruno's *De la Causa, Principio et Uno* (1584) in order to call attention to a defense of pantheism that had, in Jacobi's view, influenced both Spinoza and Leibniz.

Another source of the philosophy of the Absolute is Kant's doctrine of the Reason as the faculty that aims at unified knowledge of the Unconditioned—"to find for the conditioned knowledge of the Understanding the Unconditioned that completes its unity" (*Critique of Pure Reason*, A307). In the Fourth Antinomy (A453) Kant writes of "an absolutely necessary being" (*ein Absolutnotwendiges*), and in the *Critique of Judgment*, in his account of the sublime, Kant distinguishes between what is great merely by comparison with something smaller (*comparative magnum*) and what is absolutely, not merely comparatively, great (*absolute magnum*). The former is a sensible concept, the latter is a concept of the Reason that "conducts the notion of nature to a supersensible substratum (underlying both nature and our faculty of thought) which is great beyond every standard of the senses" (§26). Kant, of course, warned against supposing that these concepts of absolute unity and the absolutely unconditioned were more than Ideas that direct and regulate the search for empirical knowledge. But he himself, in the *Critique of Practical Reason* (1788), claimed to show that the reality of an unconditioned cause, and hence of freedom, could be *proved* "by means of an apodeictic law of the practical reason, and becomes the keystone of the whole edifice of a system of pure, even of speculative reason. . . ." (Preface). Thus Kant himself went some way toward repairing the destruction he had wrought upon "the edifice of speculative reason," and during his last years Fichte and Schelling carried this work further in ways he by no means approved.

We have seen that Kant said that the Practical Reason provided proof of something Unconditioned, namely, of free, uncaused activity. Fichte, in his *Grundlage der gesammten Wissenschaftslehre* (1794), developed this aspect of Kant's teaching, arguing that a nonempirical, free, and active self must be regarded not merely as a condition of human knowledge, but also as the source and essence of all that is. (It is "All my I," as Coleridge derisively parodies it in the *Biographia Literaria.*) Thus the Transcendental Ego, which in Kant's philosophy was a logical or epistemological conception, was transformed by Fichte into the "absolute ego," a being that he later described as "the creator of all phenomena, including phenomenal individuals." Schelling's earliest writings were reinforcements of Fichte's views and shared his philosophical vocabulary. By 1800, however, Schelling was moving toward a position of his own, and in his *System des transzendentalen Idealismus* of that year he writes of "an Absolute," and even, once or twice, of "the Absolute." In his *Darstellung meines Systems der Philosophie* (1801) he writes that "there is no philosophy except from the standpoint of the Absolute," and "Reason is the Absolute." In Hegel's *Differenz des Fichtischen und Schellingschen Systems der Philosophie* (1801) the Absolute is constantly referred to. Hegel writes, for example: "Division and conflict [*Entzweiung*] is the source of the need for philosophy, and in the form of the culture of the age, is its unfree, merely given aspect. What is merely an appearance of the Absolute has isolated itself from the Absolute and set itself up as independent." It will be noticed that in this passage the Absolute is contrasted with appearances and with what is "unfree," and that there is a further contrast between appearances that are falsely regarded as independent and appearances viewed in relation to the Absolute.

In 1803, there appeared the second edition of the essay by Schelling entitled *Ideen zu einer Philosophie der Natur*, which had first appeared in 1797. In an appendix written for this new edition, Schelling argues that philosophy, as concerned with first principles, must be "an absolute science," that it is therefore concerned with what is absolute, and that, since all things (*Dinge*) are conditioned (*bedingt*), philosophy must be concerned with the activity of knowing rather than with things or objects. "Philosophy," he writes, "is the science of the Absolute," and the Absolute is the identity of the act of knowledge and of what is known. Schelling gives the name "Absolute Idealism" to the philosophy in which this identity is recognized. The exponent of Absolute Idealism, he argues, seeks out the intelligence that is necessarily embodied in nature, and he achieves by means of "intellectual intuition" a grasp of the identity between knower and known. "The Absolute" was now well established in the vocabulary of Idealist philosophy.

Some views about the nature of the Absolute. We have seen that Schelling regarded the Absolute as that which intellectual intuition revealed as the identity of the knower and the known. He argued, furthermore, that knowledge is inseparable from will, so that the ultimate whole is active and free. The Absolute is manifested not only in nature but also in human history, which is a progress toward self-consciousness. An important thesis of Schelling's philosophy of the Absolute is that whereas in nature the Absolute is embodied in an unconscious way, in works of art it is consciously embodied, so that through his productions the artistic genius reveals the Absolute to mankind. In *Philosophie und Religion* (1804) Schelling tried to show how the finite, phenomenal world is related to the Absolute. He here had recourse to the notion of a fall that is a consequence of freedom and is yet, like the Absolute itself, outside time. He recognized that his view might be regarded as pantheistic (it was so regarded by Coleridge), and he attempted to show that human selves are, although finite, divine by nature. Thus the philosophy of the Absolute is developed as a sort of theology with some kinship to the speculations of Nicholas of Cusa.

It is well known that in his *Phenomenology of Mind* (1807) Hegel, by his characterization, "a night in which all cows are black," insinuated that Schelling's Absolute had no positive ascertainable features. Schelling, for his part, regarded Hegel's Absolute as "panlogistical"; i.e., as nothing but an array of abstract categories. In his *Encyclopedia* Hegel presents various "definitions" of the Absolute in ascending order of complexity and adequacy. It is Being, he says, as Parmenides had held, but this is the least that can be said about it. It is also the self-identical, and, at a higher level, it is inference (*Schluss*—Wallace translates it "syllogism"). These definitions, from the *Logic*, appear to confirm Schelling's criticisms; but when Hegel comes to the *Philosophy of Mind,* the third part of the *Encyclopedia,* he writes that "the Absolute is mind: this is the highest definition of the Absolute." In his account of mind, Hegel shows how it develops as society moves toward higher levels of freedom in the course of human history, and how it reaches its fullest expression in the self-consciousness of the philosopher. Hegel's intention was to describe the Absolute in such a way that it would be seen to be infinite and yet comprise the finite within itself, and to be real and yet contain the apparent. But this intention was so ambitious that the result is ambiguity, and the Hegelian Absolute has been regarded by some, including Pringle-Pattison, as "a single self" in which finite selves are lost, and by others, such as McTaggart, as a society of individual, nontemporal selves. The ambiguity is also reflected in divergent interpretations of the religious significance of Hegel's Absolute, the majority of interpreters regarding it as equivalent to God, with others, *e.g.* Bruno Bauer and Kojève, taking the view that "the Absolute" is Hegel's designation for man as a progressing historical individual.

In the nineteenth century and the early twentieth century, Absolutism became an important influence in the philosophy of Great Britain and the United States. J. S. Ferrier, who had written a life of Schelling and who had studied Coleridge and was aware of Schelling's influence on him, expounded, in his *Institutes of Metaphysics* (1854), a pluralistic Absolutism according to which there is a plurality of contingent "Absolute Existences" that are "minds-together-with-that-which-they-apprehend," and one "Absolute Existence which is strictly *necessary* . . . a supreme, infinite and everlasting Mind in synthesis with all things." But the most influential version of Absolute Idealism to be published in English was F. H. Bradley's *Appearance and Reality* (1893). In this book Bradley argued that mere appearances are conflicting and self-contradictory and that reality or the Absolute must therefore be harmonious and consistent. The self-contradictory character of appearances is due to their relatedness, and therefore the Absolute must not contain relations. Bradley maintained that the nature and possibility of a harmonious nonrelational whole is adumbrated in "immediate experience," the prereflective experience from which the world of distinct and related things emerges as we learn to talk and to judge. In this prereflective experience, subject and object are not yet differentiated, and there is diversity without numerical plurality. "From such an experience of unity below relations," Bradley writes, "we can rise to the idea of a superior unity above them." In this view, the Absolute is a suprarelational, differentiated harmony of experience. It is not a self, and it is not God, for "short of the Absolute, God cannot rest, and having reached that goal, he is lost and religion with him." Some have thought that this view of the Absolute is less open to the charge of panlogism than is that of Hegel. Before the publication of *Appearance and Reality,* Andrew Seth (later Pringle-Pattison) had, from within the Idealist school, criticized the line of thought that submerged individual selves in an impersonal or suprapersonal Absolute. McTaggart, we have seen, did not interpret Hegel in this way, and endeavored on his own account to show that the unreality of the phenomenal world is consistent with the absolute existence of individual selves. Josiah Royce's solidly and persuasively argued *The World and the Individual* (1904) is another attempt to rescue individual minds from absorption in the Absolute.

Critical comments. It is remarkable that a line of philosophical argument that set out to defend the reality of mind and of freedom should end up with minds that are self-contradictory appearances and an Absolute that alone is free. The Absolute was to have been the seat of freedom, reality, truth, and harmony; yet if Bradley was right, harmony and reality shut out the possibility of truth and freedom. Like Spinoza he tried to meet the difficulty with a doctrine of degrees of truth and freedom; and the comparison is revealing, for Spinoza is often regarded as a determinist. What went wrong? Coleridge, although greatly impressed by Schelling, argued in *The Friend* that Schelling's view, like that of Spinoza, was pantheistic. We may agree that Schelling sought for truth and freedom in the universe at large instead of in the limited beings to which they really belong. Schelling continued Kant's error of locating freedom outside the only world in which it is of importance, the world in which individual men decide and act. The view of Absolute Idealists is, however, that this world is merely phenomenal and must be contrasted with an infinite reality that contains it. The critic will ask whether this infinite reality must exist or whether it is only a projection from the finite. In adopting the former view, Absolutists have used arguments analogous to the Ontological Argument and to the Argument from the Contingency of the World. It would be self-contradictory, that is, to suppose that the Perfect could fail to exist; and in any case contingent being could not *be* unless there were a Necessary Being. Gassendi, Kant, and others have brought forward arguments against these so-called proofs, but it will not do merely to move forward these "disproofs" in opposition to Absolute Idealism. For the defenders of the Absolute do not allow that the distinctions made in these objections, between thought and reality or between concepts and things, are tenable just as they stand. Absolute Idealists cannot be refuted by arguments in which common-sense distinctions or the terms of an opposed philosophical tradition are uncritically presupposed. It is true that the conceptual adventurousness of Absolute Idealism was the occasion for the extreme conceptual conservatism of G. E. Moore and of those philosophers who insist on the essential rightness of ordinary language. But in the course of philosophical argument it has emerged that facts and concepts, the world and the ways in which it is thought about, cannot be isolated from one another as dogmatic common sense says they can be. On this matter the Absolutists' prejudice in favor of unity seems to have caused them to look in the right direction and to see how closely associated with one another are our conceptual framework and the world it is used to describe and classify.

Bibliography

Historians of philosophy do not seem to say much about the introduction of the term "the Absolute." Information can be obtained from Richard Kroner, *Von Kant bis Hegel,* 2d ed. (Tübingen, 1961) and from Frederick Copleston, S. J., *A History of Philosophy,* Vol. VII, *Fichte to Nietzsche* (London, 1963).

On various views about the nature of the Absolute, see, in addition to the books mentioned in the text: Bruno Bauer, *Die Posaune des jüngsten Gerichts wider Hegel, den Atheisten und Antichristen* (Leipzig, 1841); Andrew Seth (later Pringle-Pattison), *Hegelianism and Personality* (London and Edinburgh, 1887); J. McT. E. McTaggart, *Studies in Hegelian Cosmology* (Cambridge, 1901); A. Kojève, *Introduction à la lecture de Hegel* (Paris, 1947).

For criticisms of Absolutism, see: William James, *A Pluralistic Universe* (New York and London, 1909), Chs. II and III; G. E. Moore, *Some Main Problems of Philosophy* (London, 1953), Chs. VIII–XII; A. C. Ewing, *Idealism, a Critical Survey* (London, 1936). In Ewing, Ch. VIII, §3 is headed "The Absolute" and contains a brief discussion of the views of Bradley and Bosanquet.

H. B. ACTON

ABSOLUTE IDEALISM. *See* IDEALISM.

ABUBACER. *See* IBN-TUFAYL.

ACADEMY. *See* FLORENTINE ACADEMY; *also* GREEK ACADEMY.

ACOSTA, GABRIEL. *See* COSTA, URIEL DA.

ACTION. *See* CHOOSING, DECIDING, AND DOING; DETERMINISM.

ACTION AT A DISTANCE AND FIELD THEORY. The question whether matter can act at a distance is one that can be discussed only in the context of a fairly definite theory of what constitutes "matter," "action," and even "distance." To superficial observation there are many kinds of interactions between things where it is not always obvious whether the concept of "action at a distance" or "action by contact" should be applied. For example, the impact of two billiard balls might seem a clear case of action by contact, but in classical electromagnetic theory such an action can be regarded as a repulsion at a distance. Again, magnetic attraction was recognized early in the Greek period as an action at a distance, and magnets were for that reason classified with animate rather than inanimate bodies; but in modern field theory it can be argued that magnetic action takes place continuously through an intervening medium. Human speech is superficially an action at a distance; and if there is such a thing as telepathic communication, this must certainly be regarded as an action at a distance in an even stronger sense, since it is inexplicable by any known continuous physical causes. It is noticeable in the early history of science and pre-science that actions at a distance were most frequently recognized in interactions involving human beings, as opposed to the apparently contiguous or continuous nature of most interactions of nonintelligent bodies. The association of action at a distance with human "sympathies" and "attractions"—and with magic, telepathy, clairvoyance, and the like—is perhaps one explanation of the intuitive suspicion that action at a distance must always retain overtones of anthropomorphism.

MATTER AND ACTION IN GREEK PHILOSOPHY

The problem of action at a distance first becomes explicit in Greek philosophy, where it is a corollary of fundamental theories of matter. In two of the most influential philosophies of nature—those of the atomists and of Aristotle—there is agreement that no action can take place at a distance, although there is conflict on almost every other basic issue. The grounds for the atomists' rejection of action at a distance are to be found in the Parmenidean origins of their doctrine of atoms and the void. Atoms are essentially the Parmenidean "pure Being," imperishable and homogeneous but without intrinsic qualities other than geometrical shape and size. The void, on the other hand, is interpreted as the "non-Being." Atoms can move in the void and may be separated by it from each other, but they cannot interact across it. The only interactions that can occur between them, therefore, must be the result of their essential nature as Beings, and must be impact actions. For no two Beings can interact without contact; and when they are in contact each must be impenetrable, since no two Beings can be in the same place. Thus, as Aristotle expresses the atomic doctrine in *Generation and Corruption,* the atoms "act and suffer action whenever they chance to be in contact . . . and they generate by being put together and becoming intertwined."

Aristotle is equally unsympathetic to the idea of action at a distance, although for different reasons. In his *Physics* he states explicitly that every object in local motion must have a mover continuously in contact with it, either pushing or pulling it. In his discussion of the alleged "suction of the vacuum," for example, it is clear that the only account that will satisfy him is one in which the apparent attraction at a distance is shown to be an external thrust of the air outside the vessel containing the "vacuum." Aristotle's physical explanations, and also Plato's, are clearly influenced to some extent by the use of mechanical analogues among both the pre-Socratic cosmologists and the Hippocratic medical writers. There are, especially in the writings of the Hippocratics, many examples of explanations of physical and physiological processes in terms of familiar mechanical gadgets—pumps, bellows, levers, irrigation channels, centrifuges, and the like—and most of these work by contact action. Thus, the desire to find comprehensive mechanical explanations has in Aristotle, as in later science, the incidental effect of eliminating the concept of action at a distance.

A more explicit philosophical defense of contact action might be expected from Aristotle, but it is not altogether forthcoming. His arguments against the void are not sufficient to provide this, for it is quite consistent to hold that two bodies separated from each other by a material medium nevertheless act at a distance upon one another without the active participation of the medium. Again, even if it be granted that the medium must be active in transmitting the action from one body to another at a distance from it, it does not follow that this transmission must take place by some particular kind of contact mechanism. Aristotle's "matter," which fills space, is in itself entirely undetermined as to form; and all that is required to save the action-by-contact principle is the postulate that *some* kind of efficient power informs the matter adjacent to a body in forced motion. Aristotle does not really attempt to specify this power further. Stoic theories later postulate the transmission of action through the pneumatic medium by "tension" as well as by pressure, and in the Aristotelian tradition itself many kinds of immaterial emanations and substantial forms were later postulated to account for distance transmission; all of these could claim to be at least consistent with Aristotle's fundamental doctrine. It is therefore not easy to find either in Aristotle or in his disciples any grounds for the view that action must necessarily be by "push" mechanisms, although this is frequently assumed to have been the Aristotelian view. This view should more properly be ascribed to atomism.

There is here an ambiguity that runs right through the history of concepts of action and raises two essential questions. There is first the metaphysical or methodological question of whether interaction at a distance can be understood at all without postulating some kind of medium as an agent in the interaction. However, in the absence of any specification of what the medium must be like, the assertion that action must be continuous through the medium may reduce to no more than a directive to look for some continuity of causes, no matter what, or for some means of introducing into the expression of the theory a reference to the intervening space, even if no "matter" comparable with that of gross bodies can be found there. Such a search for forms of theory that in some sense exhibit continuous action in a medium is often successful, although not always useful or economical. On the other hand, there is the question of what the medium that is postulated or discovered is like. That is to say, is the medium a substance similar to, or different from, gross observable matter, and how is it related to that matter? This is an empirical question whose answer cannot be determined by mere philosophic analysis of the concepts of matter and interaction. The failure to understand this point has been a weakness of much discussion in the Aristotelian tradition, and many writers have consequently appeared to be legislating a priori concerning the contents of the world.

THE MECHANIZATION OF MATTER

The significance of the scientific revolution of the seventeenth century lies not so much in the exploration of new domains of phenomena and the development of new theories, as in a new understanding of the nature of matter. This in turn gave sharper form to the problem of action at a distance, and provided a definitive answer to the second, empirical, question referred to in the last paragraph. The main philosophical influence on this new conception was undoubtedly the work of Descartes, although a revival of interest in Greek atomism also had its effect. The Cartesian and Greek atomist philosophies of matter differed primarily in the rejection and acceptance, respectively, of the void; but they were united in the assertion that there is no action at a distance and in their ascription to matter of a limited number of primary qualities in terms of which secondary qualities are to be explained. In the atomists' view, action is transmitted only by impact of atoms; for Descartes, it is transmitted by impact and by pressure exerted through the all-pervasive ethereal medium of subtle particles. Descartes' theory of continuous action was better grounded than Aristotle's because it depended on his fundamental argument that "body" is to be identified with extension, and has no intrinsic properties other than those of extension and motion relative to other bodies. It follows from this that no body can have the power to affect another body unless it is spatially adjacent to it. There are grave difficulties involved in Descartes' notion of "pieces of extension" in relative motion; but these difficulties are fundamental to his whole philosophy and will not be specially discussed here.

From the scientific point of view, any theory that forbids actions other than impact and pressure encounters serious problems in attempting to explain such phenomena as the cohesion of solid bodies, the elasticity of matter (including gases), and the apparent actions at a distance of magnets and gravitating bodies. Descartes and his disciples suggested ingenious mechanisms for reducing such phenomena to continuous pressures and vortex motions of the intervening ether. Many of these models were excessively elaborate and were criticized because of their unobservability and the indirectness and scarcity of the evidence supporting them. However, in the high period of the corpuscular philosophy, the mid-seventeenth century, it was unthinkable to postulate attractions and repulsions between particles at a distance to account for these interactions. Any such hypothesis seemed to involve a return to the quasi-animistic emanations and influences that had proliferated in medieval and Renaissance physics and that had been decisively banished by Descartes. Whatever criticisms there may have been of the details of Cartesian physics, to abandon the essential clarity and economy of his model of matter was bound to appear unnecessary and reactionary. Only a new synthesis that was potentially as comprehensive and even more economical than Descartes' could hope to replace it, and at the end of the century such a new synthesis did indeed emerge in the work of Newton.

The status of action at a distance is crucial to Newton's view of matter; but his discussions of it are few, brief, and occasionally inconsistent. During the period of his work on the *Principia Mathematica*, which was published in 1687, he seemed to hesitate between an orthodox mechanism and a new and more subtle mathematical interpretation of scientific theory. His early suggestions for a theory of gravitation made use of the motions and pressures of the ether in a manner not essentially different from Cartesianism. But in the *Principia* itself he professed agnosticism about the causal mechanism involved in gravitational attraction and claimed that the phenomena (in this context, Kepler's laws of planetary motion) imply that there is a mutual attraction between massive bodies and that this attraction can be expressed in terms of the general mathematical law of inverse squares without commitment either to a belief that action is at a distance or to belief in any particular contact mechanism. This particular problem elicited his well-known but much misunderstood remark that "I frame [or feign] no hypotheses" (*hypotheses non fingo*).

After 1687, however, it seems that Newton, although persisting in this minimum interpretation of the law of gravitation, began to introduce a less positivist view of the nature of the causes involved. Two aspects of this view can be detected. On the one hand, chiefly in Queries added to successive editions of the *Optics*, Newton spoke of "certain active principles, such as is that of gravity" that are "manifest qualities" of bodies to be added to the set of primary qualities of orthodox mechanism. These are not, he claimed, "occult qualities," because they are observable in the motions of bodies; but he admitted that their causes are so far unknown.

Once introduced, these active principles of attraction and repulsion at a distance became essential features of the Newtonian synthesis. Newton himself exploited them in suggested explanations of cohesion and chemical affinity, reflection and refraction of light corpuscles, and elasticity of gases, as well as of gravitation. His theory of gases became particularly influential in eighteenth-century physics, where the conception of elastic fluids, consisting of mutually repelling particles, provided a general explanatory model replacing the pervasive ethereal vortices of the previous century, and in which repulsive forces acting over at least short distances were accepted as fundamental and not in need of further analysis.

On the other hand, Newton himself never entirely abandoned the view that apparent actions at a distance required a medium of some sort, even if this was not material in the usual sense of the mechanical philosophy. This is clear in the controversy between Leibniz and Newton's disciple Samuel Clarke, in which it is likely that Clarke was acting directly as Newton's spokesman. Leibniz initiated an exchange of letters with Clarke in 1716 by attacking Newtonian philosophy on various grounds, including its admission of action at a distance. Leibniz' own metaphysical principles of continuity and sufficient reason provided him with arguments against the existence of void; and he asserted that an attraction across space, causing a free body to move in a curved line, would be a miracle. Clarke agreed that it is a contradiction for something to act where it is not, but went on to suggest that the means by which gravitating bodies attract each other may be "invisible and intangible, and of a different nature from mechanism." The argument between them was, therefore, not over the question of action at a distance—which both rejected—but rather over the kind of medium through which action takes place. Leibniz held the "modern" view that corporeal substance is mechanical and ridiculed the notion of nonmechanical causes, against which he brought scientific as well as philosophical arguments, for the idea that soul or spirit can act upon matter appeared to be a violation of the recently discovered mechanical law of conservation of *vis viva.* Clarke's (and Newton's) views, however, foreshadow the later development of field theories of matter, in which apparent action at a distance can be reduced to action through a nonmechanical continuum.

FIELD THEORIES

Field theories had two sources in eighteenth-century physics, one mathematical and the other metaphysical. The first was the mathematical theory of continuous material media, especially fluids, which was developed particularly by Leonhard Euler. Here the techniques of Newtonian point-particle mechanics were extended to deal with such variables as density, velocity, and pressure, which are continuous functions of position and time and satisfy appropriately generalized forms of the laws of motion. In this context a field may be said to be a region of space in which each point (possibly with isolated exceptions) is characterized by some quantity or quantities that are functions of the space coordinates and time, the nature of the quantities depending on the physical situation referred to. In the theory of fluid flow, and in the theory of continuous elastic solids developed in the early nineteenth century, the field quantities are mechanical properties of matter in the sense of seventeenth-century mechanism; but it is significant that the difficult problems of generalizing Newtonian mechanics to deal with continuous media were solved by Euler and his successors only through a process of deliberate neglect of the specific character of the material medium involved—of whether, for example, it was ultimately continuous or atomic. The mechanical quantities became just those variables that satisfied the laws of motion, without any further inquiry into their intrinsic material reference.

This tendency was reinforced by another application of mathematics to physics, namely the development by Joseph Louis Lagrange, Pierre Simon Laplace, and others of "potential" theories of gravitation, electricity, and magnetism. In these theories the intervening space between attracting and repelling particles is characterized by potential functions of space and time coordinates, and a continuous mathematical representation of the gravitational, electric, or magnetic "field" is given without implying anything about the nature of the variable called "potential." This may be a quantity characterizing some kind of medium; or it may merely be, in a literal sense, "potential," in that it refers to real causes or effects only when suitable material bodies (masses, charges, or magnetic poles) are present at the point. The first alternative would imply continuous action through some medium; the second would imply true action at a distance.

The formulation of these theories of motion in a continuum helped to clarify a puzzle about the concept of "contact" that had haunted previous theories of contact action. In the atomists' view, bodies interact when they are "together," but are the points of the bodies that are thus in "contact" in the same place or in different places? They cannot be in the same place, since no two parts of matter can occupy the same place; but if they are in different places, are they not acting at a distance? The solution of this problem seemed to demand a theory of "togetherness" involving the continuum; and the mathematics of continuous media provided the first framework for such a theory, without which careful discrimination of kinds of action would be impossible. And it followed from this analysis of "contact" that all contact actions, including impact, demand a theory of spatial, if not material, continuity.

The second, metaphysical, source of field theories is to be found in the work of Ruggiero Boscovich, whose *Theoria Philosophiae Naturalis* was published in 1758. Boscovich was a professed disciple of Leibniz' principle of continuity; but instead of concluding with Leibniz that this principle excludes the possibility of space void of mechanical matter, he used it to create a theory of continuous force functions and to reject the entire conception of matter as consisting of discrete, extended parts. For Boscovich, "matter" is reduced to point particles having inertia but interacting by distance forces of attraction and repulsion, whose magnitude depends on the distance between the particles. So far, this theory provides an extreme example of acceptance of action at a distance, since all properties of matter except inertia are the consequences of distance forces, even such previously intrinsic properties as impenetrability and shape. Extended bodies are pictured as collections of point masses attracting each other to preserve cohesion and repelling other bodies, which "hit" or "bounce off" them. But an alternative way of looking at this picture gives an entirely opposite result with regard to action at a distance. If attention is concentrated on the forces that are exerted in space between the point masses, it is possible to regard these as in some way constituting a medium, thus "substantializing" the force field itself and reducing the point masses to mere singularities in this field. This was essentially the step taken by Michael Faraday in transforming Boscovich's theory into field theory as it is understood in both classical and modern physics.

It is clear that by the early nineteenth century the comparatively simple alternatives discussed by the seventeenth-century mechanists had been elaborated into some fundamentally new views about the nature of interaction. Contact action was no longer restricted to the "push" mechanism of impact, but was allowed to consist of some modification of a field that is propagated continuously from agent to distant patient; and on the other hand, action at a distance could be represented mathematically by assigning values to field functions at points in space, without assuming a causally acting medium. It may be remarked here that the empiricist philosophers, especially Hume, had contributed to this multiplication of possible modes of action by arguing that the connections between the motions of bodies interacting by impact are no more intuitively evident or causally necessary than they are in other types of interaction. In all cases, according to this empiricist thesis, we are concerned in science with the sequences of observable motions, and not with the "inner" nature of their causes. Among those who were prepared to investigate causes, however, the effect of philosophical empiricism was to release them from the presupposition that causation is ultimately mechanical, and to leave the way open for exploration of such alternative fundamental models as were suggested by field theories.

One of the most important suggestions toward such alternatives occurred in Faraday's paper of 1844, entitled "A Speculation Touching Electrical Conduction and the Nature of Matter." Here, as a consequence of certain empirical findings concerning conduction, he adopted the Boscovichian view that an atom is a point with "an atmosphere of force grouped around it." But, he went on, this means that such properties as electric conduction, solidity, hardness, and specific gravity belong, not to the point atom abstracted from its powers (which is in any case inconceivable), but rather to the forces themselves. He concluded that "matter" is constituted as much by the forces as by the atoms. Thus, in radical contrast with the mechanical view, matter fills all space where there are forces, and different "matters" can interpenetrate. It also follows at once that no matter acts at a distance.

In papers of 1851 and 1852, Faraday withdrew somewhat from the view that all forces are continuously spread through space, and began to look for criteria for discriminating between different kinds of forces, some of which might still be said to act at a distance. He regarded three empirical characteristics as relevant to this distinction. First, if transmission of action is affected by changes in the intervening medium, as in the case of electric and magnetic induction, then this is an indication that the medium is causally active in transmission. This is not the case for gravity, which is therefore a typical action at a distance in this respect. Second, if the transmission of action takes time, this is an indication of an active medium; for it is unreasonable to postulate action "jumping" over an interval of time as well as space without being continuously propagated in the intervening space. Radiation is a clear case of continuous action according to this criterion, and gravity a case of action at a distance (since Faraday believed gravity is propagated instantaneously). Third, if the transmission is independent of the presence of any distant "receiving end," as in the case of light, it is a continuous action. By this criterion, electric, magnetic, and gravitational actions appear to be at a distance, since they need two poles of interaction for any effect to be observable. It may be remarked, however, that Faraday's argument here is question-begging, because it is not based strictly on the observable criteria, but upon our theories concerning observables. As soon as we detect the presence of light, we have *ipso facto* introduced a receiver. On the other hand, the electric and magnetic theories of Faraday's time did not compel postulation of an intervening medium; that is, they were action-at-a-distance theories. From these theories (not from the observed facts), it followed that any causal action required a receiving end. Thus, the question of action at a distance should be decided independently of Faraday's third criterion of a receiving end, for the satisfaction of this is entailed by action at a distance, but not conversely.

Eventually, the criterion of propagation in a finite time became the most important in distinguishing distance forces from continuous action. It was reinforced by the newly discovered principle of conservation of energy; for if an action—that is to say, energy of some kind—leaves the agent and does not make itself felt at the distant receiver until after a finite time, conservation demands that the energy should be located somewhere in the time interval. If it is not located in any observable bodies, it must be located somewhere in the intervening space; and so it follows that this space must be characterized by an energy function, even if no other material substratum can be found there. But can energy exist, as it were, disembodied? What is it the energy of? J. Clerk Maxwell gave the clearest discussion of this question. In the third of his great papers on the electromagnetic theory of light, in 1864, he explicitly abandoned his previous attempts to describe mechanical models of the light ether as carriers of the energy of light waves, and replaced them by a conception of a real energy pervading space, constituting in itself the "substratum" of the field. Since energy is quantitatively conserved, it has at least one of the traditional characteristics of substance. John H. Poynting later developed a representation of Maxwell's theory in which energy could be regarded as a fluid, although the further characteristic of having self-identical and persistent parts, traditionally ascribed to matter, cannot be ascribed to Poynting energy.

The Faraday-Maxwell conception of a substantial medium was not universally accepted, however; and some theorists, particularly in France and Germany, persisted in an action-at-a-distance view. As the argument developed, the point at issue became not so much a metaphysical one concerning the nature of matter and of the medium, but rather a methodological one concerning the propriety of introducing theoretical constructs of any kind over and above the observed motions. There has always been a tendency, which can be seen clearly in the discussions of Newtonian gravitation, to link action at a distance with a positivist view of theories, because the introduction of continuous media generally involves postulation of unobservable entities. In the late 1820s, André Ampère had deliberately modeled his theory of electromagnetic forces on Newton's theory of gravitational force and had shown that his forces could be derived mathematically from observables, independently of any assumption of a medium. The relation between this action-at-a-distance theory as it developed on the Continent, and the Faraday-Maxwell field theory, was complex. There was a sense in which the two theories could be said to be, at least potentially, intertranslatable and observationally identical, especially after the general recognition that Maxwell's field equations must be incorporated in any empirically adequate theory. Toward the end of the century, Heinrich Hertz made careful distinctions between the essentials of Maxwell's theory, which were Maxwell's equations, and what he called the "gay garment" of interpretation into field or distance forces, with which we clothe the equations. The issue was thus made to appear as merely one of convenience in mathematical expression, or of subjective preference for one kind of picture rather than another. But this was not a wholly adequate account, for the assumptions required in showing the observational equivalence of the two theories were different in each case, and not always plausible in either. The action-at-a-distance formulation, for example, ran into great difficulties in reconciling action transmitted at a finite speed with the conservation of energy. On the other hand, the Maxwell formulation led quite naturally to the propagation of electromagnetic waves with finite speed, but was not at all well adapted to deal with the discrete, atomic phenomena that demanded increasing attention at the end of the century, after the discovery of the elementary particles of electricity. In considering the forces between discrete moving charges, the action-at-a-distance formulations were successful in yielding results that did not follow from Maxwell's theory and had to be injected into it *ad hoc*.

These disputes provide good historical evidence for two important philosophical theses. First, two theories that apparently are observationally equivalent may contain radical theoretical differences that are not irrelevant to further observational development. Therefore, a positivist view of theories, in which these differences are held to be logically irrelevant, cannot in these cases be an adequate account of the logic of theoretical change, growth, and interaction. Second, there are empirical considerations to be taken into account in discussing the possibility of action at a distance, but these can never ultimately be decisive because it is open to a field theorist, at any stage, to hold that apparent action at a distance must be reducible to action in a still-hidden medium; and it is open to an action-at-a-distance theorist to hold that any field theory is compatible with action at a distance between still-hidden, subtle particles. Thus, a metaphysical question may remain after all empirical considerations have been taken into account; but it is difficult to see how such a question can be formulated without adopting some theory of matter and, except in neo-Aristotelian philosophies, it is not now fashionable to adopt theories of matter on nonempirical grounds. Thus there is at present no live metaphysical problem about action at a distance outside the Aristotelian tradition.

MODES OF ACTION IN MODERN PHYSICS

This last section will attempt to answer two questions: What kinds of action are in fact implied by the physical theories of matter of this century, and how much choice between various modes of action is left within the general framework of these theories? No more than a historical survey of the last sixty years can be attempted, since developments in this area are taking place at great speed; and any account is liable to be out of date before it is printed.

At the end of the nineteenth century, gravitation remained outside electromagnetic field theory, and was still generally held to be propagated instantaneously, or at least at a speed much greater than that of light. Einstein's special theory of relativity (1905), however, contained what appeared to be a proof that no causal action can be transmitted faster than light. This result applied to gravitation as well as to all other physical interactions. Nevertheless, it would not be correct to conclude that the result settles the question of action at a distance, even within the theory of relativity.

In the first place, the proof that the velocity of light is the absolute maximum for any causal action depends on more general assumptions about causality. What does follow from the relativistic (Lorentz) transformations for space-time coordinate frameworks is that if, in fact, some physical process were transmitted with a velocity greater than that of light, then for some observers the order of cause and effect in this process would be temporally reversed, as compared with the order for some other observers. That is to say, "effect" would temporally precede "cause" in some observational frameworks. Such a situation would certainly be contrary to our experience and general intuitions, but it is not immediately obvious that it is logically impossible. And if it is in fact logically possible, then so is the transmission of action at speeds greater than light, or indeed at an infinite speed. The possibility may be even stronger than the merely logical, for the fact that we do not observe such reversed causality does not imply that it may not, consistently with our present experience, be postulated in a theory, so long as this is done in such a way that the apparently anomalous features are in principle unobservable according to that theory. Quantum theory does, indeed, leave open such a possibility by setting lower limits to the observability of events on the microcosmic scale, and it would therefore be conceivable to incorporate into quantum theory the idea of instantaneous transmission across sufficiently short distances without becoming involved in causal anomalies on the observable scale. Whether it would under any circumstances be economical or expedient to do so is, of course, another question, to be settled only by the general state of the theory and its consistency with experiment.

The second reason why the prohibition of causal transmission faster than light in special relativity need not necessarily exclude all action-at-a-distance theories is that such a theory might be shown to be compatible with finite velocity of transmission. The question then arises: If transmission in a finite time is no longer a sufficient condition for rejecting action at a distance, what does it mean to say that action is transmitted at a distance, but at finite speed? The answer must be, as for Maxwell, that action takes place at a distance if no energy is present in the intervening space. It has usually been assumed that such action would violate the conservation of energy; but there have recently been some attempts, notably by J. A. Wheeler and R. P. Feynman, to show that this need not be the case for either classical or quantum electrodynamics when advanced as well as retarded solutions of Maxwell's and other equations are taken into account. These suggestions lead to some temporal reversals of causality, just as do attempts to introduce instantaneous propagation of action; and it seems indeed that the question of fields versus action at a distance in modern physics is closely bound up with our beliefs about the invariance of temporal order of the cause-effect relation. In the most recent theories of Feynman, even this belief is abandoned.

If, however, we examine the more traditional formulations of relativity and quantum theory, it is clear that these are field rather than action-at-a-distance theories. In general relativity, gravitation becomes a field action; and gravitational potentials, momentum, and energy densities satisfying conservation principles exist in the space between massive bodies. Indeed, here the geometrical curvature of space is determined by the gravitational potentials—and hence by the spatial distributions of mass—so that space itself becomes even more intimately associated with the field than in classical electromagnetics, where the field is produced by charged bodies in an independent Euclidean space. Attempts to formulate a "unified field theory," in which the electromagnetic field would share with gravitation this intimate association with the geometry of space, engaged Einstein to the end of his life, but so far no fully satisfactory theory of this kind has been forthcoming.

The question whether action is continuous or at a distance in quantum theory is more complicated. Since energy and time are complementary variables in this theory, it follows from the uncertainty principle that if passage of energy from one point to another is to be observed, a finite time interval is always required. Thus no action can be observed to be instantaneous. It also follows from the uncertainty principle, however, that no action can be observed to be continuous either. Moreover, it seems that there is not even any possibility of a continuous-action theory that is consistent with the uncertainty principle, either in terms of particles, or waves, or fields. The reaction of many quantum theorists to this situation has been a retreat from attempts to find any kind of theoretical interpretation of what Hans Reichenbach calls the "interphenomena"; that is, unobservable events taking place between phenomena. There has also been a widespread return to a positivist view that only mathematical relations between observable states are meaningful or acceptable. Thus there is, in this view, no causal action of one state on another, but only a description of the succession of states. Even the "quantum jump" of the electron is seen as a successive occupation of states, with no implication that "the same" electron is concerned in both states (electrons have no self-identity in quantum physics)—much less that it passes from point to point by some describable or intelligible process. Concerning the microcosmic realm, then, the most generally held view is that there is no continuous action and no action at a distance; there is just no action at all.

On the macroscopic scale, however, where the quantum of action is negligible it is possible to approximate continuous-action descriptions; these have been elaborated in the so-called quantum field theory. Some success has been attained here in assimilating quantum theory with the special theory of relativity, and in rationalizing the experimental results obtained in nuclear and other high-energy reactions, where particles and radiation interact in producing the multiplicity of mesons, hyperons, neutrinos, and other new particles that still go by the name of "elementary." But grave theoretical difficulties, and the rapid outstripping of limited theoretical explanations by experimental data, make this one of the least predictable regions of modern science. It would be rash to assume that the familiar field theoretic approach will long survive in anything like the present form. The empirical issue between field theory and action at a distance at the most fundamental level of physics seems to be as wide open as ever.

(See also ETHER; VACUUM AND VOID.)

General Historical Studies

Einstein, A., and Infeld, L., *The Evolution of Physics*. Cambridge, 1938.

Gillespie, C. C., *The Edge of Objectivity*. Princeton, 1960. Especially Chs. III, IV, and X, on physical theory from Galileo to field physics.

Hesse, Mary B., *Forces and Fields*. London, 1961. Action at a distance and field theory in the history of physics, with commentary on philosophical issues.

Jammer, M., *Concepts of Force*. Cambridge, Mass., 1957.

Papers on Philosophic Issues

Hutten, E. H., "On the Principle of Action by Contact." *The British Journal for the Philosophy of Science*, Vol. 2 (1951), 45–51.

McCrea, W. H., "Action at a Distance." *Philosophy*, Vol. 27 (1952), 70–76.

There is also a considerable literature on the problem of action at a distance within the Aristotelian and Thomist traditions. No account of this has been attempted in the body of the article, but for a survey and discussion, see:

Tallarico, J., "Action at a Distance." *The Thomist*, Vol. 25 (1962), 252–292.

Van Laer, P. H., *Philosophico-Scientific Problems*, translated by H. J. Koren. Pittsburgh, 1953.

The Problem in Greek Philosophy

Aristotle, *Physics*.

Bailey, C., *The Greek Atomists and Epicurus*. Oxford, 1928. A standard history of atomism.

Cornford, F. M., *Laws of Motion in Ancient Thought*. Cambridge, 1931. Describes the anthropomorphic, nonmechanistic theories of interaction in early Greek thought.

Heidel, W. A., *The Heroic Age of Greek Science*. Washington, 1933.

Heidel, W. A., *Hippocratic Medicine*. New York, 1941. Describes the mechanistic physiology of the Hippocratic schools.

Jaeger, W., *Theology of the Early Greek Philosophers*. Oxford, 1947. Ch. 9 on mechanistic theories.

Plato, *Timaeus*.

Sambursky, S., *The Physical World of the Greeks*. London, 1956.

The Mechanization of Physics

SOURCES

Alexander, H. G., ed., *The Leibniz-Clarke Correspondence*. Manchester, 1956.

Bacon, F., *Sylva Sylvarum* (1623) Secs. 904 ff., in R. L. Ellis and J. Spedding, eds., *Works*, Vol. II. London, 1857–1874. A catalogue of phenomena involving different types of interaction and showing the transition to mechanism.

Berkeley, G., *De Motu* (1721), in A. A. Luce and T. E. Jessop, eds., *Works*, Vol. IV. London, 1948–1957. Attraction interpreted as a mathematical hypothesis.

Boscovich, R., *Theoria Philosophiae Naturalis* (1758), translated by J. M. Child. Chicago, 1922. Influential for the introduction of field theory in nineteenth-century physics.

Boyle, R., "The Excellency and Grounds of the Mechanical Hypothesis" (1674), in T. Birch, ed., *Works*, 2d ed., Vol. IV. London, 1772. A manifesto of mechanism.

Descartes, R., *Les Principes de la philosophie*, in C. Adam and P. Tannery, eds., *Oeuvres*, Vol. IX. Paris, 1897–1913.

Gilbert, W., *De Magnete* (1600), translated by P. F. Mottelay. New York, 1893. One of the first works of "experimental philosophy," with detailed discussions of modes of physical interaction.

Kant, I., *Metaphysische Anfangsgrunde der Naturwissenschaft*. Riga, 1786. A theory of matter in terms of attractive and repulsive forces. There is no reliable English translation.

Newton, I., *Principia Mathematica Philosophiae Naturalis* (1687), translated by B. Motte, F. Cajori, ed. Berkeley, 1947.

Newton, I., *Optics*. London, 1718; subsequent editions. Especially the Queries to the 2d.

Thayer, H. S., ed., *Newton's Philosophy of Nature*. New York, 1953. Contains useful extracts from the foregoing and other works of Newton.

HISTORIES

There are many general histories of science in this period. Some of the most useful for this topic are:

Burtt, E. A., *The Metaphysical Foundations of Modern Physical Science*. London, 1932.

Dijksterhuis, E. J., *The Mechanization of the World Picture*, translated by C. Dikshoorn. Oxford, 1961. Part 4, Chs. 2 and 3.

Koyré, A., *From the Closed World to the Infinite Universe*. Baltimore, 1957.

Whyte, L. L., ed., *Roger Joseph Boscovich*. London, 1961. Especially Chs. 2–5.

Field Theories

SOURCES

Faraday, M., "A Speculation Touching Electric Conduction and the Nature of Matter." *Experimental Researches in Electricity*, Vol. 2 (1844).

Faraday, M., "On the Physical Character of the Lines of Magnetic Force." *Ibid*, Vol. 3 (1855), 407–437.

Helmholtz, H. von, "On the Conservation of Force" (1847), in J. Tyndall and W. Francis, eds., *Scientific Memoirs*. London, 1853. The classic paper on conservation of energy.

Hertz, H., *Electric Waves*, translated by D. E. Jones. London, 1893. Especially Ch. 1 on the alternative interpretations of field action consistent with Maxwell's equations.

Maxwell, J. C., "On Faraday's Lines of Force" (1856); "On Physical Lines of Force" (1861); "A Dynamical Theory of the Electromagnetic Field" (1864), in W. D. Niven, ed., *Scientific Papers*. Vol. I. Cambridge, 1890. The classic papers on the electromagnetic theory of light.

Maxwell, J. C., "On Action at a Distance," *Ibid*. Vol. II, pp. 311–323.

Maxwell, J. C., *Treatise on Electricity and Magnetism*, Vol. II. Oxford, 1873. Chs. 2 and 23, on the Continental action-at-a-distance theories.

HISTORIES

Hesse, Mary B., "Action at a Distance in Classical Physics." *Isis*, Vol. 46 (1955), 337–353.

Whittaker, E. T., *History of the Theories of Aether and Electricity*, Vol. I, *The Classical Theories*. London, 1951. Vol. II, *The Modern Theories*. London, 1953. A standard technical history that is more useful for reference than for a general view of the philosophical implications of the development of concepts.

Woodruff, A., "Action at a Distance in Nineteenth Century Electrodynamics." *Isis*, Vol. 53 (1962), 439–459.

Interaction in Modern Physics

Einstein, A., "On the Electrodynamics of Moving Bodies" (1905), translated by W. Perrett and G. B. Jeffrey. London, 1923. Einstein's first paper on special relativity theory. Reprinted in *The Principle of Relativity, A Collection of Original Memoirs*. New York, 1952.

Heitler, W., *Quantum Theory of Radiation*. Oxford, 1944. A standard account of early quantum field theory.

Reichenbach, H., *Philosophic Foundations of Quantum Mechanics*. Berkeley and Los Angeles, 1944. Part I, on the restrictive interpretation of quantum mechanics.

Schilpp, P. A., ed., *Albert Einstein, Philosopher–Scientist*. Evanston, Ill., 1949. Many of the essays in this volume contain relevant material.

Wheeler, J. A., and Feynman, R. P., "Interaction with the Absorber as the Mechanism of Radiation." *Review of Modern Physics*, Vol. 17 (1945), 157–181.

Wheeler, J. A., and Feynman, R. P., "Classical Electrodynamics in Terms of Direct Particle Interaction." *Ibid*., Vol. 21 (1949), 425–433. An attempt to reintroduce action at a distance in physical theory.

MARY HESSE

ADLER, ALFRED (1870–1937), medical psychologist and founder of Individual Psychology, was born in Vienna of Hungarian–Jewish parents. He received his M.D. from the University of Vienna in 1895 and practiced general medicine before turning to psychiatry. His soundest scientific works were written before World War I and largely prepared during his ambivalent association with the early Freudian group. After serving in the Austrian army he became concerned with child guidance as a method of preventive medical psychology, and gaining favor with the new Austrian government, opened child-guidance centers in Vienna, Berlin, and Munich schools. Family-guidance interviews in public, with general discussion periods, disseminated his methods and theories, particularly among educators. He became an international lecturer in Europe and the United States and was America's first professor of medical psychology, at Long Island

Medical School. In the 1930s his efforts to spread his doctrine of "social interest" in the face of Europe's totalitarian nationalisms marked him as preacher rather than scientist, and his later published work served to promulgate a faith rather than to report scientific work. He died in Aberdeen, Scotland, during a lecture tour.

Adler's first psychologically important work, the *Study in Organ Inferiority and Its Psychical Compensation* (1907), was "a contribution to clinical medicine" in constitutional pathology. In it Adler explored constitutional defects of structure and function and their physiopathological compensation and also described "psychical" compensatory changes in disposition and way of life; overcompensation could produce not only "genius," like the deaf Beethoven, but also neurotic or psychotic responses, like hysteria or paranoia. Adler gave a causal-deterministic exposition of development as dependent upon constitutional endowments, innate biological drives, and environmental pressures. His papers of 1908 described as innate an "aggression drive" (to subdue the environment) and a "need for affection." Both concepts were then rejected by Freud's group but reappeared in later psychoanalytic theories.

Adler himself modified both concepts and reformulated his whole psychology in *The Neurotic Constitution* (1912). He repudiated drive psychology and causal determinism. He viewed inferiority (vis-à-vis adults) and consequent "inferiority feeling" as experiences common to every child. The child responds as a whole individual with a "striving for superiority" (the former "aggression drive") directed toward a "fictive goal" of manly strength and dominance, which is pursued through a "guiding fiction," or life plan, modified by the "antifiction" of social demands. Goal and fiction are subjective creations of the individual's making, but unrealistic, rigid, neurotic patterns may be favored by organ inferiority, pampering, or neglect in childhood, or the child's age-ranking in the family. To Adler the Nietzschean "will to power" was this kind of neurotic pattern, not a universal human trait. He also described an opposite but equally effective response to increased insecurity:

> It is one of the triumphs of human wit to put through the guiding fiction by adapting it to the anti-fiction, . . . to conquer by humility and submissiveness . . . to cause pain to others by one's own suffering, to strive to attain the goal of manly force by effeminate means, to make oneself small in order to appear great. Of such sort . . . are often the expedients of neurotics.

In contrast to the neurotic, the psychotic character attempts to shape reality to the fiction, while the normal character adapts itself to the environment.

Adler's later works reiterated, renamed, elaborated, and finally, simplified and broadened the concepts on which he had founded Individual Psychology in 1912 after breaking with Freud. The basis of character was the response of the whole individual to a universal infantile inferiority feeling. Accentuated inferiority feeling became the celebrated "inferiority complex," and a pathological striving for superiority was a "superiority complex." The guiding fiction was renamed the "life style," usually unconscious or "not understood," which Adlerian analysis endeavored to illuminate with insight. The antifiction and the early "need for affection" fused in the important concept of social interest. Adler first diverged from psychoanalysis over Freud's emphasis on sexual instincts. Ultimately, where Freud saw animal instincts humanized through repression, Adler described inborn trends—social interest and striving for superiority—whose full development perfected the personality. In summary, "Heredity only endows [the individual] with certain abilities. Environment only gives him certain impressions. . . . it is his individual way of using these bricks, . . . his attitude toward life, which determines [his] relationship to the outside world."

Despite their differences, Adler always acknowledged his debt to Freud's psychogenetic theory of neurosis. He acknowledged Pierre Janet's *sentiment d'incomplétitude*, a predecessor of the inferiority feeling. Adler's formulation of personality somewhat resembled the "psychic structure" and "attitudes" of Wilhelm Dilthey's psychology, but direct influence is unlikely: Adler never mentioned Dilthey, although he did cite a work of Dilthey's contemporary Hans Vaihinger, the *Philosophy of "As If"* (New York, 1924), for the theory of fictions. Individual psychology had a brush-fire success in continental Europe and the United States, rather less in Britain; everywhere it found more acceptance among educators, psychologists, even writers than among physicians and psychiatrists. Adler's work has been largely absorbed into practice and thought without retaining a separate identity despite the familiar phrases—"overcompensation," "inferiority complex," "organ jargon"—which enrich a conversational rather than a psychological vocabulary. Individual Psychology still has its own centers, schools, and work groups, but Adler's influence has permeated other psychologies. His "aggression drive" reappeared in the ego psychology of orthodox psychoanalysis; other Adlerian echoes are found in Karen Horney, Harry Stack Sullivan, and Franz Alexander, and in Ian Suttie's mother-relationship theories, which surely influenced the contemporary mother-need ethological school. Child-guidance practice is non-Adlerian, and his name is not now invoked in progressive pedagogy, but those who try to see the backward child, the delinquent, the psychopath, or the psychiatric patient as a whole person are sharing Adler's viewpoint.

Adler's approach to psychology, normal and abnormal, was speculative rather than scientific. From 1912 on, he sought the elegantly economical theory rather than the proven fact. At first he recognized his theory as a fiction in Vaihinger's nonpejorative sense; a person behaves "as if" compensating for inferiority feeling. Later this step was omitted—these things *were* so. Adler often illustrated his theory with case material, but this was invariably anecdotal and in excerpts, never statistically organized. He openly despised statistics. It is uncertain how many patients Adler treated in continuity, apart from single consultations to advise physicians or teachers. The same case histories appear as examples through many books over many years, with no systematic follow-up. He made no use of normal "controls," an omission he justified by his insistence upon the uniqueness of the individual, but this left unsolved the problem of why one creative self chose neurosis, another not. Adler never experimented, never firmly predicted, never attempted systematically to verify a hypothesis. He had great intuitive insight, the greater, perhaps, for having grown up as a second son and a sickly rachitic child of a Hungarian–Jewish family in the Austrian imperial capital. His intuitions and their formulations, if not so close to reality as he believed, remain as valuable guiding fictions.

Works by Adler

Studie über die Minderwertigkeit von Organen. Berlin and Vienna, 1907. Translated by Smith Ely Jelliffe as *Inferiority and Its Psychical Compensation.* New York, 1917.

Über den nervösen Charakter. Wiesbaden, 1912. Translated by Bernard Glueck and John E. Lind as *The Neurotic Constitution.* New York, 1926.

Praxis und Theorie der Individualpsychologie. Munich, 1920. Translated by P. Radin as *Practice and Theory of Individual Psychology.* New York and London, 1927.

Menschenkenntnis. Leipzig, 1927. Translated by W. Béran Wolfe as *Understanding Human Nature.* London, 1927.

Der Sinn des Lebens. Vienna and Leipzig, 1933. Translated by John Winton and Richard Vaughan as *Social Interest; a Challenge to Mankind.* London, 1938.

Superiority and Social Interest, Heinz and Rowena Ansbacher, eds. Evanston, Ill., 1965. Adler's later papers edited and annotated.

Works on Adler

Ansbacher, Heinz and Rowena, eds., *The Individual Psychology of Alfred Adler.* New York, 1956. Extracts, full bibliography, and critical annotations, including evaluation of Adler's proclaimed finalistic subjectivism as approximating William James's "soft determinism."

Orgler, Hertha, *Alfred Adler, the Man and His Work.* London, 1939; 3d ed., London, 1963.

J. D. Uytman

AEGIDIUS COLONNA ROMANUS. *See* Giles of Rome.

AENESIDEMUS, the most important dialectician of the Greek Skeptics, was probably born in Cnossus, Crete. Almost nothing is known of his life, but scholars agree that he lived sometime between the death of Pyrrho in 270 B.C. and the death of Sextus Empiricus in 210 A.D. Most scholars place him in the first century A.D. It is known that he taught in Alexandria for a while.

We have none of his writings, but we know more about his philosophy, by way of Sextus' detailed descriptions, than we do about any other Greek Skeptic, except Sextus Empiricus himself. In general we know that he rejected the Academic Skeptics because, on the one hand, they attacked dogmatism but, on the other, dogmatically defended a sharp distinction between the probable and the improbable. Moreover, though he agreed with all other Skeptics that *ataraxia* or unperturbedness was a central need of man, he seems to have had little to say positively about living well. In this respect, though he was a defender of the old Pyrrhonism, he was not, like Pyrrho, primarily a practical moralist; rather, he seems to have been mainly a dialectician or theorist.

His most important contribution to Greek Skepticism was his ten *tropoi,* or modes of conducting skeptical argumentation, which first were presented in his work called *Pyrrhonian Discourses.* These came to be accepted by Skeptics as a logical model and a heuristic tool, and Sextus Empiricus put them at the foundations of Greek Skepticism. There are ten ways, which Sophists and Skeptics before Aenesidemus had apparently been using in some form or other, to suspend judgment on the objects that purportedly stimulate our organs and cause our sense perceptions. They guide us to set up mutually contradictory, but equally plausible, claims about the same causal or unperceived external object. In summarizing them, Sextus' numbering will be used, but the *tropoi* will be considered in three broad groups in order to see more plainly their over-all rationale.

The first group, the first four *tropoi,* is concerned with finding contradictions that arise from the nature of the perceiving subject. The first mode refers to the variety of sense perception to be found in various animals. Differently shaped eyeballs, skin covered with shells, feathers, or hair, different temperatures of blood, etc., all attest to the different ways that animals sense objects. Since we are only one kind of animal, and since we cannot be a judge at our own trial without prejudice, we cannot conclusively ascertain which, if any, animal's perceptions reveal the object as it is, independently of the senses. The second mode in this group is based upon differences in men's perceptions. The same object affects different men differently, and only the dogmatist will say that we ought to prefer the perceptions of the Ethiopian, who happily eats scorpions and snakes, to the perceptions of the European, who is repulsed and harmed by eating them (to use an example Sextus offers). The third mode is based upon differences between the senses themselves. For example, to the eye a painting may have projections and recesses, but not to the touch. Again, only the dogmatist will beg the question in favor of one of these mutually contradictory senses. Finally, the fourth mode is based upon different circumstances, such as waking or sleeping, hatred or love, drunkenness or sobriety. How are we to choose conclusively between these states?

The second group has less to do with the perceiver than with what is perceived, and it contains the seventh and tenth modes. The seventh mode is based upon different manners of composition of a given stuff. For example, silver filings appear black when scattered but look bright when united in a mass. How do we conclusively determine the color of silver? The tenth mode touches on ethical considerations and attacks the dogmatic claim that in human actions we can perceive a natural moral law. Habits, customs, and laws differ from people to people, so that the Good Life is as difficult to defend without question-begging or prejudice as is any claim about the essential nature of any nonhuman object.

The last group has more to do with the relationship between subject and object than it has to do with either taken separately, and it includes the fifth, sixth, eighth, and ninth modes as given by Sextus. The fifth mode, based upon locations, positions, and distances, indicates that the same object can appear small and stationary from a great distance, but large and in motion when seen from close up. A painting's surface may look flat when seen from one angle and rough when seen from another. How can one choose with finality one of these positions over the others? The sixth mode is based upon admixtures of our sense organs and the intervening air with the object perceived. Only the dogmatist will claim to have determined the nature of the external object apart from all such admixtures with other things like air, liquids in the eye, passages in the ear, etc. The eighth mode is a summary of all of the others, since it is concerned with the relativity of perceptions to both the person who judges and to the aspect of the thing he is perceiving. This mode emphasizes the skeptical claim that our knowledge is not absolute, not independent of the relationship between object and subject. The ninth mode states that since rarely seen things (like earthquakes) are perceived as amazing, and ordinary things (like the sun) are perceived as unexciting, it is difficult to determine objectively what is amazing or unexciting, apart from accidents of perceptual rarity or frequency.

Another of his major contributions (again we do not know whether it originated with him) is the distinction between signs that are *ypomnestika* (commemorative) and signs that are *endeiktika* (indicative). A scar reminds us of the bleeding wound we previously saw and is a sign of that wound—a commemorative sign of it. Another person's bodily movement indicates a soul residing in that body, but we can never observe a soul—the bodily movement is an indicative sign of that soul. According to Aenesidemus and the Skeptics who followed him, philosophy falls into contradictions when it deals with indicative signs that purportedly refer to hidden things (*adela*); phenomena and the commemorative sign relationships that obtain between them are the province of consistent, fruitful philosophizing. In short, doubt applies to indicative signs, not commemorative ones.

Another of his contributions is the aetiological *tropoi*, a group of eight *tropoi* pointing out ways of reasoning badly about causal relationships. In them, for instance, he criticizes the tendency to stop arbitrarily at one causal generalization when there are other equally plausible ones available; and he points out the tendency to account for phenomena by imagined elements instead of by way of phenomena commonly accepted by mankind as the origin of these things.

But despite all his strictures, if we are to believe Sextus, Aenesidemus himself wrote dogmatically about hidden things. For instance, he held with Heraclitus that reason was outside the human body, common (*koine*) to men, and he shared other Heraclitean convictions. Scholars have tried to reconcile these metaphysical doctrines with his contributions to Skepticism, but on the whole their efforts remind us that the philosophy of Aenesidemus is not fully understandable to us now, though its influence upon subsequent Skepticism is obviously great.

Bibliography

CLASSICAL WORKS

Photius, *Bibliotheca*. I. Bekker, ed. Berlin, 1824. Our only analysis of the *Pyrrhonian Discourses of Aenesidemus*.

Sextus Empiricus, *Philosophical Works*, R. G. Bury, ed., 4 vols. Loeb Classical Library. Cambridge, Mass., and London. 1955–1961. Our most detailed source of knowledge on Aenesidemus.

Sextus Empiricus, *Scepticism, Man, and God*, P. P. Hallie, ed. Middletown, Conn., 1964. A one-volume annotated edition containing all *tropoi* of Aenesidemus.

MODERN WORKS

Bréhier, E., "Les Tropes d'Enésidème contre la logique inductive." *Revue des études anciennes*, Vol. 20 (1918), 69–76.

Brochard, V., *Les Sceptiques grecs*. Paris, 1923. A full, clear account of the controversies over the thought and life of Aenesidemus.

Goedeckemeyer, A., *Die Geschichte des Griechischen Skeptizismus*. Leipzig, 1905. Reliable but not detailed.

Maccoll, N., *The Greek Sceptics from Pyrrho to Sextus*. London, 1869. Brief, but easily the fullest treatment of Aenesidemus available in English.

Ogden, G. K., and Richards, I. A., *The Meaning of Meaning*, Appendix C. New York, 1930.

PHILIP P. HALLIE

AESTHETICS. The Encyclopedia features two very detailed survey articles, AESTHETICS, HISTORY OF and AESTHETICS, PROBLEMS OF, as well as the following articles: BEAUTY; HUMOR; METAPHOR; TRAGEDY; and UGLINESS.

AESTHETICS, HISTORY OF. In the West, the history of systematic philosophizing about the arts begins with Plato. But his great achievement was preceded, and prepared for, by certain developments in the preceding two hundred years, of which we know or can guess only a little. Thus, the famous aesthetic judgment—if such it was—of the picture on Achilles' shield, "That was a marvellous piece of work" (*Iliad* XVIII 548), hints at the beginning of wonder about imitation, i.e., the relation between representation and object, or appearance and reality. Plato shows the aesthetic consequences of the thinking on this problem by Democritus and Parmenides. Further, the elevation of Homer and Hesiod to the status of wise men and seers, and moral and religious teachers, led to a dispute over the truthfulness of poetry when they were attacked by Xenophanes and Heraclitus for their philosophical ignorance and misrepresentation of the gods. Homer and Hesiod themselves raised the question of the source of the artist's inspiration, which they attributed to divine power (*Odyssey* VIII; *Theogony* 22 ff.). Pindar traced this gift to the gods but allowed that the poet's skill can be developed by his own effort. Pythagoras and his Order discovered the dependence of musical intervals on the ratios of the lengths of stretched strings, generalized this discovery into a theory about the elements of the material world (that they either are, or depend upon, numbers), and developed an elaborate ethical and therapeutic theory of music, which, according to them, is capable of strengthening or restoring the harmony of the individual soul—*harmonia* being the term for the primary interval, the octave.

PLATO

Nearly all of the fundamental aesthetic problems were broached, and some were deeply considered, by Plato. The questions he raised and the arguments he framed are astonishingly varied and deep. They are scattered throughout his dialogues, but the principal discussions are in (*a*) the *Ion*, *Symposium*, and *Republic*, belonging to Plato's early, pre-Academy period (roughly 399–387 B.C.);

(*b*) the *Sophist* and *Laws*, written at the end of his life (roughly 367–348/347 B.C.); and (*c*) the *Phaedrus*, which lies between these periods. Though perhaps not Plato's, the *Greater Hippias* is very Platonic and may be drawn upon. (In this article, no distinction will be attempted between Plato's views and those of Socrates.)

Art and craft. When today we speak of Plato's aesthetics, we mean his philosophical views about those fine arts that he discusses: visual arts (painting, sculpture, architecture), literary arts (epic, lyric, and dramatic poetry), and mixed musical arts (dance and song). Plato does not himself assign them a special name; for him they belong in the more general class of "craft" (*technē*), which includes all skills in making or doing, from woodcraft to statecraft. In the *Sophist* (265–266), crafts are divided into "acquisitive" and "productive," the latter being subdivided into (1) production of actual objects, which may be either human or divine (plants and elements by god, houses and knives by men), and (2) production of "images" (*idola*), which may also be human or divine (reflections and dreams by god; pictures by men). Images, which imitate their originals but cannot fulfill their function, are further subdivided; the imitator may produce (1) a genuine likeness (*eikon*), with the same properties as his model, or (2) an apparent likeness, or semblance (*phantasma*), which merely *looks* like the original (as when the architect makes his columns swell at the top so that they will not appear to diminish). There is thus false imitation, the making of deceptive semblances. Yet Plato finds this distinction troublesome to maintain, for it is essential to any imitation that in some way it falls short of its original; if it were perfect, it would not be an image (*eidolon*), but another example of the same thing, another bed or knife (*Cratylus* 432). So all imitation is in a sense both true and untrue, has both being and nonbeing (*Sophist* 240C).

Imitation. The term "imitation" (*mimesis*) is one of the most troublesome in Plato's aesthetics, for its denotation constantly expands and contracts with the movement of the dialectic, along with that of its substitutes and near synonyms, *methexis* (participation), *homoiosis* (likeness), and *paraplesia* (resemblance).

If, in one sense, all created things are imitations of their eternal archetypes, or "forms," Plato seems also to regard paintings, dramatic poems, and songs as imitations in a narrower sense: they are images. It is this that places the arts at the second remove from the reality of the forms, on the lowest of the four levels of cognition, *eikasia* (imagining) (*Republic* 509–511). Some works of art, however—and Plato sometimes speaks as though he meant all of them—are imitative in the more pejorative sense, as deceptive semblances. In Book X of the *Republic*, the painter is said to represent the bed, not as it is but as it appears. It is this that puts him in the "tribe of imitators" (*Timaeus* 19D) and allies him with those pseudo craftsmen of the *Gorgias* (463–465) who do not possess a genuine craft, like medicine, but a pseudo craft, or knack (*tribē*), like cosmetics, which gives us the bloom of health rather than health itself.

Beauty. By this route, Plato approaches the question that is of great importance to him as a metaphysician: Do the arts contain, or convey, knowledge? Before coming to this question, there is another to be considered. If the architect, as a maker of semblances, changes reality to make it look better, why does he do this? He seeks those images that will appear beautiful (*Sophist* 236A). This is another basic fact about the arts, in Plato's view; they can embody in various degrees the quality of beauty (*to kalon*—a term that can branch out into more general senses of appropriateness or fitness to function but that often appears in a more strictly aesthetic sense). The beauty of concrete things may change or disappear, may appear to some but not to others (*Republic* 479A); but behind these temporal embodiments there is an eternal and absolute form of beauty. Its existence can be demonstrated dialectically, like that of the other forms; but direct acquaintance with it is to be sought, Plato says, via the partial and dimmer beauties open to the senses—and it is easier of access than the other forms (*Phaedrus* 249B–C).

The path to beauty is described most fully in the *Symposium:* A man possessed by love (*eros*) of beauty is to progress from bodily beauty to beauty of mind, to beauty of institutions and laws and the sciences themselves, and finally to beauty in itself. It is noteworthy that Diotima of Mantineia, who presents this picture, does not assign to the arts any role in assisting this progress; that step was taken by Plato's successors.

It is also important to ask what beauty is, or, if that cannot be stated abstractly, what the conditions are under which beauty will be embodied in an object. The argument in the *Greater Hippias* takes up several possibilities, especially the possibility that the beautiful either is, or depends upon, what is beneficial or what pleases through the senses of hearing and sight. But in the *Philebus*, a careful discussion leads to the conclusion that beautiful things are made with care in the due proportion of part to part, by mathematical measurement (cf. *Timaeus* 87C–D; *Statesman* 284A). "The qualities of measure (*metron*) and proportion (*symmetron*) invariably . . . constitute beauty and excellence" (*Philebus* 64E, Hackforth translation). And because it is, or depends upon, measure, beauty is assigned a high place in the final list of goods (*Philebus* 66A–B; cf. *Sophist* 228B).

Art and knowledge. Knowledge (*episteme*), as distinct from mere opinion (*doxa*), is a grasp of the eternal forms; and Plato clearly denies it to the arts, as imitations of imitations (*Republic* 598–601). So the poet is placed on the sixth level of knowledge in the *Phaedrus* (248D), and Ion is said to interpret Homer not by "art or knowledge" (532C) but in an irrational way (cf. *Apology* 22), for he does not know what he is saying or why he might be right or wrong. On the other hand, a work of art that embodies beauty has some direct relation to one form. And if the artist inspired by the Muses is like a diviner in not knowing what he is doing (*Meno* 99C; *Timaeus* 71E–72A), he may have a kind of insight that goes beyond ordinary knowledge (cf. *Laws* 682A). His madness (*mania*) may be possession by a divinity that inspires him to truth (*Phaedrus* 245A; *Ion* 533E, 536B). Moreover, since the arts can give us genuine likenesses, not only of appearances but of actualities, and even imitate the ethical character of the human soul (*Republic* 400–401B; cf. Xenophon, *Memorabilia* III viii), it is possible, and indeed obligatory, to judge them by their truth, or their resemblance to actuality. The competent judge, especially of dance and song, must have "first, a knowledge of the nature of the original; next, a knowledge of the correctness of the copy; and thirdly, a knowledge of the excellence with which the copy is executed" (*Laws* 669A–B, Bury translation).

Art and morality. The supreme craft, for Plato, is the art of the legislator and educator, who must have the final say about the arts, for his task is to insure that they play their proper role in the life of the entire social order. The first problem is to discover what effects the arts have on people, and this problem has two aspects. First, there is the enjoyability of art. On the one hand, just insofar as it has beauty, the pleasures art gives are pure, unalloyed, and harmless (*Phaedrus* 51B–C), unlike the pleasure of scratching an itch, which is preceded and followed by discomfort. But, on the other hand, dramatic poetry involves the representation of unworthy characters behaving in undesirable ways (ranting and wailing) and tempts the audience into immoderate laughter or weeping. Therefore its pleasures are to be condemned for their unworthy effect on character. Second, when we consider this tendency of the arts to influence character and conduct, there are again two sides to the matter. In his *Republic* and *Laws*, Plato makes it quite clear that he thinks the literary imitation of evil conduct is an implicit invitation to imitate the conduct in one's life (*Laws* 665B). Thus the stories of gods and heroes who behave immorally have to be excluded from the education of the young guardians in the *Republic*, and stories in which the gods and heroes behave as they should must either be found or written (*Republic* 376E–411; cf. *Laws* 800–802, 664A). Music composed in enervating modes must also be replaced by a suitable kind (*Republic* 398E, 411A).

But this does not mean that the arts have no role to play in the cultural life and education of the citizens. Indeed, the fear of their power that underlies Plato's severe censorship and regulation is accompanied by an equally great respect. The measure that is so closely allied to beauty is, after all, closely allied to goodness and virtue too (*Laws* 655A; *Protagoras* 326A–B; *Republic* 432). Music and poetry and dancing are, at their best, indispensable means of character education, able to make men better and more virtuous (*Laws* 653–654, 664). The problem, as Plato in his role of legislator sees it, is to ensure the social responsibility of the creative artist by insisting that his own good, like that of every citizen, be subordinated and made conducive to the good of all.

ARISTOTLE

Our knowledge of Aristotle's aesthetic theory comes chiefly from the little collection of lecture notes that has come down to us as the *Poetics*, composed probably about 347–342 B.C. and later added to. The text is corrupt, the argument condensed and puzzling. No work in the history of aesthetics has given rise to such vexatious problems of interpretation; no work has had so great an influence on the theory and practice of literary criticism.

The art of poetry. Aristotle's first task is to define the art of poetry (*poietike*), which is his subject. He assumes a distinction between three kinds of "thought," knowing (*theoria*), doing (*praxis*), and making (*poiesis*) (see *Metaphysics* E 1; *Topics* VI 6); but in the *Poetics*, "poiesis" is taken in a narrower sense. One kind of making is imitation, which Aristotle seems to take fairly straightforwardly as representation of objects or events. The imitative art divides into (1) the art of imitating visual appearances by means of color and drawing and (2) the art of poetry, the imitation of a human action (*praxis*) through verse, song, and dance (*Poetics*, Ch. 1). Thus the art of poetry is distinguished from painting by its medium (words, melody, rhythm) and from versified history or philosophy (the poem of Empedocles) by virtue of the object it imitates. Two of the species of the poetic art are of primary concern to Aristotle: drama (either tragic or comic) and epic poetry, distinguished from comedy by the gravity of the actions imitated (Chs. 2, 6).

What is of the first importance in Aristotle's treatise is his method of inquiry, for he aims to present a systematic theory of a particular literary genre. He asks: What is the nature of the tragic art? And this leads him to inquire not only into its material, formal, and efficient causes (many of his observations under these headings are of permanent value to literary theory) but also into its final cause or end (*telos*). What is a good tragedy, and what makes it good; what are "the causes of artistic excellence and the opposite" (Ch. 26, G. F. Else translation)? This function of tragedy, he thinks, must be to provide a certain kind of enjoyable experience—the "proper pleasure" (*oikeia hedone*) of tragedy (Chs. 14, 23, 26)—and if the nature of this pleasure can be determined it will then be possible to justify the criteria by means of which one can say that one tragedy is better than another.

The pleasure of imitation. Aristotle suggests briefly (Ch. 4) two motives that give rise to tragedy. The first is that imitation is natural; and the recognizing of imitation is naturally pleasurable to man because man finds learning pleasant, and recognizing, say, a picture of a dog, is a form of learning (cf. *Rhetoric* I xi). Since tragedy is an imitation of a special sort of object, namely fearful and pitiable events, its proper pleasure "is the pleasure that comes from pity and fear by means of imitation" (Ch. 4, Else translation). The problem that evidently arises is how we can derive pleasure from feeling emotions that are painful (cf. the definitions of "fear" and "pity" in *Rhetoric* II v, viii). Aristotle's nearest answer seems to be that though the object imitated may be in itself unpleasant to contemplate, the pleasure of seeing the imitation may overcome our distaste—as with skilled drawings of cadavers (see *De Partibus Animalium* I v; *Rhetoric* I xi). Here Aristotle is offering a partial answer to one of Plato's grounds for skepticism about art; he takes the basic aesthetic pleasure as a cognitive one, of the same genus as the philosopher's (though no doubt of a lower level).

The pleasure of beauty. Tragedy also grows, Aristotle says (Ch. 4), out of our natural disposition to "melody and rhythm." He does not develop this point and may be postulating a kind of decorative impulse. But if we may think here of Plato's *Philebus*, our pleasure in melody and rhythm may be taken as pleasure in beauty in general. "A beautiful (*kalliste*) thing, either a living creature or any structure made of parts, must have not only an orderly arrangement of those parts, but a size which is not accidental" (Ch. 7). Thus a tragedy, or its plot, may be "beautiful," i.e., artistically excellent (Chs. 1, 13). And the "proper pleasure" of the epic, for example, depends on its unity, on being "like a single whole creature" (*zoon*) with a beginning, middle, and end (Ch. 23). This analogy echoes Plato's *Phaedrus* 264C. For the fineness of the object sensed or contemplated produces the highest degree of that pleasure that is proper to the organ sensing or mind contemplating (*Nicomachean Ethics* X iv).

The universal. If the function of tragic poetry is to provide a certain species of enjoyment, we can then inquire into the features of a particular work that will promote or inhibit this enjoyment. Its concentration and coherence depend in large part upon the plot and the sense of inevitability in its development (Ch. 10). This is evidently achieved most fully when the characters act in accordance with their natures, when they do the "kinds of thing a certain kind of person will say or do in accordance with probability or necessity, which is what poetic composition aims at" (Ch. 9, Else translation). These sorts of behavior, i.e., behavior that is motivated in accordance with psychological laws, Aristotle calls "universal," contrasting them with the events in a historical chronicle, which he thinks of as a causally unconnected string of particular incidents ("what Alcibiades did or had done to him").

This famous passage has inspired many later theories about art imitating universals or essences, but the gist of it (for Aristotle) is that the poet must make his plot plausible by relying on general psychological truths. This important point adds another level to Aristotle's defense (against Plato) of the cognitive status of poetry, for the poet must at least understand human nature or he cannot even produce a good plot.

The catharsis. In Aristotle's definition of tragedy (Ch. 6) there is one phrase that has given rise to an enormous amount of interpretation: *di eleou kai phobou perainousa ten ton toiouton pathematon katharsin* (translated in the traditional way by Butcher: "through pity and fear effecting the proper purgation of these emotions"). Thus Aristotle is interpreted as having a further theory, not about the immediate pleasure of tragedy but about its deeper psychological effects. This phrase is the only basis for such an interpretation in the *Poetics;* but in the *Politics* (VIII 7), Aristotle clearly does propose a cathartic theory of music and even says he will explain catharsis further "when hereafter we speak of poetry"—a remark that possibly refers to the presumed lost parts of the *Poetics.* If tragedy produces a catharsis of the emotions, there are still other problems in deciding what Aristotle had in mind—whether, for example, he meant it in a medical sense (a purgation of the emotions, their elimination by mental physic) or in a religious and lustratory sense (a purification of emotions, their transformation into a less harmful form). Both senses had precedents. There is also the question whether Aristotle believed in a catharsis of pity and fear alone, or, through them, of all destructive emotions.

In any case, on this interpretation, Aristotle would be answering Plato's second objection to poetry in Book X of the *Republic,* by saying that poetry helps men to be rational. The traditional interpretation has been interestingly challenged in recent years by Professor Gerald F. Else, who argues that the catharsis is not an effect on the audience or reader but something accomplished in the play itself, a purification of the hero, a release from the "blood pollution" of his crime, through his recognition of it, his horror at it, and the discovery that it was due to a "serious mistake" (*hamartia*) on his part. This reading does not seem to fit some of the tragedies. If it is correct, Aristotle has no therapeutic theory of tragedy at all, but he may still be replying to Plato that the immoral effects of tragedy are not to be feared, since the finest ones, at least, will have to show a kind of moral progress if they are to be structurally capable of moving the spectator tragically.

THE LATER CLASSICAL PHILOSOPHERS

Aristotle's *Poetics* does not seem to have been available to his successors. His ideas had some influence via the works (now largely lost) of his favorite pupil, Theophrastus; and the *Tractatus Coislinianus* (Greek, probably first century B.C.) shows an acquaintance with his work, for its definition of comedy parallels remarkably Aristotle's definition of tragedy. During the later classical period, Stoicism, Epicureanism, skepticism, and Neoplatonism flourished competitively, and each of these schools of thought had some contribution to make to the history of aesthetics.

Stoicism. The Stoics were much interested in poetry and in problems of semantics and logic. Zeno, Cleanthes, and Chrysippus wrote treatises on poetry, no longer extant. From Philodemus we know of a work on music by the Stoic Diogenes of Babylon, and from Cicero's *De Officiis* of a work on beauty by Panaetius. Both seem to have held that beauty depends on the arrangement of parts (*convenientia partium,* in Cicero's phrase). The delight in beauty was connected with the virtue that expresses itself in an ordered life, with decorum (*to prepon*). Thus not only irrational pleasure (*hedone*), but a rational elevation of the soul (*chara*), in keeping with the Stoic goal of tranquillity, was thought to be obtainable from poetry of the right sort. The Stoics emphasized the moral benefit of poetry as its chief justification and held that it might allegorize true philosophy (see Strabo, *Geography* I, i, 10; I, ii, 3).

Epicureanism. The Epicureans are said (by Sextus Empiricus, *Against the Professors* VI, 27) to have disapproved of music and its pleasure, but it appears that this is partly based on a misunderstanding of Epicurus' aversion to music *criticism* (see Plutarch, *That It Is Not Possible to Live Pleasurably According to the Doctrine of Epicurus* 13). Two important works by Philodemus of Gadara (first century B.C.), parts of which have been unearthed at Herculaneum, give further evidence of Epicurean thinking about the arts. In his work *On Music* (*Peri Mousikes*), Philodemus strikes the earliest known blow for what later was called "formalism," by arguing (against the Pythagoreans, Plato, and Aristotle) that music by itself—apart from the words, whose effects are often confused with the music itself—is incapable either of arousing emotions or of effecting ethical transformations of the soul. And in his work *On Poems (Peri Poematon)* he argued that specifically poetic goodness (*to poietikon agathon*) is not determined either by the moral-didactic aim (*didaskalia*), by the pleasure of technique and form (*psychagogia*), or by a mere addition of the two, but by a unity of form and content—his conception of which we do not now know.

The main lines of reflection about literature during the Roman period seem to have been practical and pedagogical. Two works were outstandingly influential (the second, however, not until its rediscovery in the modern period): the *Ars Poetica*, or *Epistle to the Pisos*, of Horace, which discusses many questions of style and form, and the work *On Elevation in Poetry (Peri Hypsous*, or *On the Sublime)*, probably written during the first century A.D., perhaps by a Greek named "Longinus." This lively and brilliant work defines the quality of great writing in affective terms, as that which transports the soul; and it investigates the stylistic and formal conditions of this effect.

Plotinus. The philosophical reflection that continued in the Platonic schools until the Academy at Athens was closed by Justinian I in A.D. 529, culminated in the Neoplatonic system of Plotinus. Three of his fifty-four tractates, which make up the six *Enneads*, deal especially with aesthetic matters: "On Beauty" (I, vi); "On the Intellectual Beauty" (V, viii); and "How the Multiplicity of the Ideal-Forms Came into Being; and on the Good" (VI, vii).

Behind the visible world, in this view, stands "the one" (*to hen*), or "the first," which is ultimate reality in its first "hypostasis," or role, beyond all conception and knowledge. In its second hypostasis, reality is "intellect," or "mind" (*nous*), but also the Platonic forms that are known by mind. In its third hypostasis it is the "all-soul" (*psyche*), or principle of creativity and life. Within his scheme—infinite gradations of being "emanating" from the central "light"—Plotinus develops a theory of beauty that is highly original, though inspired by the *Symposium* and other Platonic dialogues. The tractate "On Beauty" (MacKenna and Page translation) begins by noting that beauty lies in things seen and heard, and also in good character and conduct (I, vi, 1); and the question is, "What . . . is it that gives comeliness to all these things?"

The first answer considered, and rejected, is that of the Stoics. Beauty is, or depends on, symmetry. Plotinus argues that simple sense qualities (colors and tones), and also moral qualities, can have beauty though they cannot be symmetrical; moreover, an object can lose some of its beauty (as when a person dies) without losing any symmetry (VI, vii, 22). Therefore, symmetry is neither a necessary nor sufficient condition of beauty. It is not beauty but participation in ideal-form, that is, embodiment of Platonic ideas, that marks the difference in a stone before and after the sculptor carves it; for he gives it form. Where ideal-form enters, he says, confusion has been "rallied . . . into co-operation" (I, vi, 2): when an object becomes unified, "Beauty enthrones itself." A homogeneous thing, like a patch of color, is already unified by similarity throughout; a heterogeneous thing, like a house or ship, is unified by the dominance of the form, which is a divine thought (I, vi, 2). In the experience of beauty, the soul finds joy in recognizing in the object an "affinity" to itself; for in this affinity it becomes aware of its own participation in ideal-form and its divinity. Here is the historical source of mysticism and romanticism in aesthetics.

Love, in Plotinus' system, is always the love of beauty (III, v, 1) and of absolute and ultimate beauty through its lesser and dimmer manifestations in nature or in the work of the artist-craftsman (I, vi, 7; VI, ii, 18; V, viii, 8–10). Something of Plato's ambivalence toward art reappears in Plotinus' account at this point, though muted and closer to being overcome in the basic monism of the system. We ascend from the contemplation of sensuous beauty to delight in beautiful deeds, to moral beauty and the beauty of institutions, and thence to absolute beauty (I, vi, 8–9; II, ix, 16). Plotinus distinguishes three ways to truth, that of the musician, the lover, and the metaphysician (I, iii, 1–2); and he speaks of nature as offering a loveliness that cannot help but lead the admiring contemplator to thought of the higher beauties that are reflected there (II, ix, 7; V, viii, 2–3). Nor are the arts to be neglected, on the ground that they are mere imitations (here he comes closest to correcting the *Republic*, Book X), for both the painting and the object it copies are, after all, both imitations of the ideal-form; moreover, the painter may be able to imitate form all the more truly, to "add where nature is lacking" (V, viii, 1; cf. V, ix, 11). Yet, in his more religious mood, Plotinus reminds us that earthly and visible beauty may distract us from the infinite (V, v, 12), that "authentic beauty," or "beyond-beauty," is invisible (VI, vii, 33); and he who has *become* beautiful, and hence divine, no longer sees or needs it (V, vii, 11). The ladder, to use once more a too-familiar similitude, is kicked away by the philosophic mystic once he reaches home.

THE MIDDLE AGES

The early church Fathers were somewhat doubtful of beauty and the arts: they feared that a keen interest in earthly things might endanger the soul, whose true vocation lies elsewhere—especially since the literature, drama, and visual art they were acquainted with was closely associated with the pagan cultures of Greece and Rome. But despite the danger of idolatry, sculpture and painting became accepted as legitimate aids to piety, and literature became accepted as part of education in the liberal arts. Concern with aesthetic problems was not a prominent part of medieval philosophy, but some important lines of thought can be observed in the works of the two greatest thinkers.

St. Augustine. In his *Confessions* (IV, xiii), Augustine tells a little of his lost early work, *De Pulchro et Apto* ("On the Beautiful and Fitting"), in which he distinguished a beauty that belongs to things in virtue of their forming a whole and a beauty that belongs to things in virtue of their fitting in with something else or being part of a whole. It is not possible to be sure, from his brief description, of the exact nature of this distinction. His later thoughts on beauty are scattered throughout his works, and especially in *De Ordine* ("Concerning Order," A.D. 386), *De Vera Religione* ("Concerning True Religion," A.D. 390), and *De Musica* (A.D. 388–391), a treatise on meter.

The key concepts in Augustine's theory are unity, number, equality, proportion, and order; and unity is the basic notion, not only in art (*De Ordine* II, xv, 42) but in reality. The existence of individual things as units, and the possibility of comparing them with respect to equality or likeness, gives rise to proportion, measure, and number (*De Musica* VI, xiv, 44; xvii, 56; *De Libero Arbitrio* II, viii, 22). Number, he emphasizes in various places, is fundamental both to being and to beauty—"Examine the beauty of bodily form, and you will find that everything is in its place by number" (*De Libero Arbitrio* II, xvi, 42, Burleigh translation). Number gives rise to order, the arrangement of equal and unequal parts into an integrated complex in accordance with an end. And from order comes a second-level kind of unity, the emergent unity of heterogeneous wholes, harmonized or made symmetrical through internal relations of likeness between the parts (*De Vera Religione* xxx, 55; xxxii, 59; *De Musica* VI, xvii, 58).

An important feature of Augustine's theory is that the perception of beauty involves a normative judgment. We perceive the ordered object as being what it ought to be, the disordered object as falling short; hence the painter can correct as he goes along and the critic can judge (*De Vera Religione* xxxii, 60). But this rightness or wrongness cannot be merely sensed (*De Musica* VI, xii, 34); the spectator must bring with him a concept of ideal order, given to him by a "divine illumination." It follows that judgment of beauty is objectively valid; there can be no relativity in it (*De Trinitate* IX, vi, 10; *De Libero Arbitrio* II, xvi, 41).

Augustine also wrestled with the problem of literary truth, and in his *Soliloquies* (A.D. 387) he proposed a rather sophisticated distinction between different sorts of lying or deception. In the perceptual illusion, the straight oar pretends to be bent, and could be bent, but the statue could not be a man and therefore is not "mendacious." So, too, the fictional character could not be real and does not pretend to be real by his own will, but only follows the will of the poet (II, ix, 16; x, 18; cf. *Confessions* III, vi).

St. Thomas Aquinas. Thomas' account of beauty is given tersely, almost casually, in a few key passages that have become justly famous for their rich implications. Goodness is one of the "transcendentals" in his metaphysics, being predicable of every being and cutting across the Aristotelian categories; it is Being considered in relation to desire (*Summa Theologica* 1, q. 5, art. 1). The pleasant, or delightful, is one of the divisions of goodness—"that which terminates the movement of appetite in the form of rest in the thing desired, is called the *pleasant*" (*S.T.* I, q. 5, art. 6, Dominican Fathers translation). And beauty is what pleases on being seen (*Pulchra enim dicuntur quae visa placent, S.T.* I, q. 5, art. 4).

Here, of course, "seeing" extends to all cognitive grasp; the perception of beauty is a kind of knowing (this explains why it does not occur in the lower senses of smell and taste, *S.T.* I–II, q. 27, art. 1). Since cognition consists in abstracting the form that makes an object what it is, beauty depends on the form. Thomas' best-known statement about beauty occurs in the course of a discussion of Augustine's attempt to identify the persons of the Trinity with some of his key concepts, the Father with unity, etc. Beauty, he says, "includes three conditions" (*S.T.* I, q. 39, art. 8). First, there is "integrity or perfection" (***integritas sive perfectio***)—broken or injured objects, incomplete objects, are ugly. Second, there is "due proportion or harmony" (***debita proportio sive consonantia***), which may refer partly to the relations between parts of the object itself but mainly refers to a relation between the object and the perceiver: that the eminently visible object, for example, is proportioned to the sight. Third, there is "brightness or clarity" (*claritas*), or brilliance (see also *S.T.* II–II, q. 145, art 2; q. 180, art. 2). The third condition has been variously explicated; it is connected with the medieval Neoplatonic tradition in which light is a symbol of divine beauty and truth (see the pseudo-Dionysius on the *Divine Names*, Ch. 4; Robert Grosseteste, *De Luce*, and his commentary on the *Hexaëmeron*). Clarity is that "splendor of form [*resplendentia formae*] shining on the proportioned parts of matter" in the opusculum *De Pulchro et Bono* (I, vi, 2), written either by the young Thomas or his teacher Albertus Magnus. The conditions of beauty can be stated univocally, but beauty, being a part of goodness, is an analogical term (that is, has different senses when applied to different sorts of things). It signifies a whole family of qualities, for each thing is beautiful in its own way (Aquinas, *Commentary on the Psalms*, Psalm xliv, 2; cf. *Commentary on the Divine Names* iv, 5).

The theory of interpretation. The consuming tasks of the early Fathers, clarifying, reconciling, and systematizing Biblical texts in order to defend Christianity against external enemies and heretical deviations, required a method of exegetical interpretation. The Greek tradition of allegorizing Homer and Hesiod and the Rabbinical tradition of allegorical exposition of Jewish scriptures had been brought together and elaborately refined by Philo of Alexandria. His methods were adopted by Origen, who distinguished three levels of meaning in scripture: the literal, the moral, and the spiritual or mystical (see *De Principiis* IV, i, 16, 18, 20). This method was taken into the West by Hilary of Poitiers and Ambrose, bishop of Milan, and further developed by John Cassian, whose formulation and examples became standard throughout the medieval period up to the time of Dante (see Dante's letter to Can Grande, 1319, the Preface to the *Paradiso*).

In Cassian's example (*Collationes* xiv, 8), Jerusalem, in the Old Testament, is, "literally" or "historically," the city of the Jews; on the "allegorical," or what came to be called the "typical," level, it refers prophetically to the later church of Christ; on the "tropological," or moral, level, to the individual soul; on the "anagogical" level, to the heavenly City of God. The last three levels together are sometimes called the "allegorical," or (as by St. Thomas) the "spiritual," meaning. As Thomas also indicates (*Summa Theologica* I, q. 1, art 10), the "literal" meaning also includes metaphorical statements.

Origen insisted that all Biblical texts must have the highest level of meaning, the "spiritual," though they may lack a moral sense and may even fail to make sense on the literal level, if too great an absurdity would be entailed by taking them that way. In this he was followed by St. Augustine (*De Doctrina Christiana* III, x, 14; xv, 23) but not by Hugh of St. Victor (*De Scripturis*, v; *Eruditiones Didascalicon* VI, iv, viii–xi), who held that the second-level meanings are a function of the first level, and a first-level meaning can always be found if metaphor is included in it.

Because Christianity taught that the world was created *ex nihilo* by God, rather than generated or molded out of something else, Christian thinkers tended, in the Middle

Ages, to hold that nature itself must carry the marks or signs of its origin and be a symbolic embodiment of the Word; in this respect, like Holy Scripture, God's other creation, it can be subjected to interpretation. Thus, nature becomes an allegory, and every natural object a symbol of something beyond. This view reaches its fullest development in John Scotus Erigena (*De Divisione Naturae* I, iii) and St. Bonaventure (*Collationes in Hexaëmeron* II, 27).

Though these reflections were primarily theological, rather than aesthetic, they were of great significance to the later history of aesthetics: they raised important questions about the nature of metaphor and symbol, in literature as well as in theology; they initiated reflection on the general problem of interpreting works of art; and they showed the possibility of a broad philosophy of symbolic forms, in which all art might be understood as a kind of symbolism.

THE RENAISSANCE

The most interesting philosophical development in the fifteenth and sixteenth centuries was the revival, by a number of thinkers, of Platonism and the creation of a vigorous Neoplatonism. Of these thinkers, Marsilio Ficino, translator of Plato and Plotinus and founder of the new Academy (1462), was the greatest. In *De Amore* (his commentary on the *Symposium*, written 1474–1475) and in his principal work, the *Theologia Platonica*, Ficino took over a number of the leading aesthetic notions of the Greeks and of St. Augustine, and to them he added one of his most original ideas, a theory of contemplation based on Plato's *Phaedo*. In contemplation, he held, the soul withdraws to some extent from the body into a purely rational consciousness of the Platonic forms. This inward concentration is required for artistic creation, which involves detachment from the real, to anticipate what does not yet exist, and also is required for the experience of beauty (this explains why beauty can be grasped only by the intellectual faculties—sight, hearing, and thinking—and not by the lower senses).

More significant for the future, however, were the changes taking place in basic assumptions about the arts and in attitudes toward them.

The most significant works on the fine arts were the three books on painting, sculpture, and architecture by Leon Battista Alberti, the large collection of notes toward a systematic treatise on painting by Leonardo da Vinci, and surviving memoranda and the two books, on geometry and perspective and on human proportions by Albrecht Dürer. One of the most serious endeavors of these artists and others was to establish a status for painting within the liberal arts, separating it from the other manual crafts among which it had been classified throughout the medieval period. The painter, Alberti argued (in his *Della pittura*, 1436), requires a special talent and skill; he needs a liberal education and a knowledge of human affairs and human nature; he must be a scientist, in order to follow the laws of nature and produce accurate representations of natural events and human actions. His scientific knowledge, indeed, must be basically mathematical, for the theory of proportions and the theory of linear perspective (which preoccupied Renaissance theorists, and especially Dürer) are mathematical studies; and they provide the principles in terms of which paintings can be unified and made beautiful, but at the same time made to depict correctly. Leonardo's argument for the superiority of painting to poetry and music (and also, in some degree, to sculpture) followed similar lines (see the first part of the *Treatise on Painting*).

The concern for faithfulness of representation that is fundamental to Renaissance fine arts theory is also found in the developing theory of music. The music theorists, aiming to secure the place of music as a humanistic discipline, sought for a vocal music that would attain the powerful emotional and ethical effects attributed to Greek music. They stressed the importance of making the music follow the text, to intensify the meanings of the words. These ideas were defended, for example, by Gioseffe Zarlino, in his *Istitutioni Armoniche* (1558) and by Vincenzo Galilei, in his *Dialogo della musica antica e della moderna* (1581).

Renaissance poetics was dominated by Aristotle (especially the concept of poetry as imitation of human action) and Horace (the thesis that poetry aims to delight and instruct—though this dualism was rejected by one of the major theorists, Lodovico Castelvetro, in his commentary on Aristotle's *Poetics*, 1570). The concept of imitation was variously interpreted and criticized by the Italian theorists. Among the chief points of disagreement and contention was the question whether poetry must belong to fixed genres and obey rigid rules, such as the dramatic "unities" adopted so adamantly by Julius Caesar Scaliger in his *Poetics* (1561), and the question (as discussed, for example, in Sidney's *Defense of Poesie*, 1595) whether the poet is guilty of telling lies and of leading his readers into immorality. In these discussions, the Aristotelian *katharsis* and Plato's condemnation of the poets were central and recurrent topics.

THE ENLIGHTENMENT: CARTESIAN RATIONALISM

Though Descartes had no aesthetic theory, and indeed wrote nothing about the arts apart from his early *Compendium Musicae* (1618), his epistemological method and conclusions were decisive in the development of neoclassical aesthetics. As in other areas, the search for clarity of concept, rigor of deduction, and intuitive certainty of basic principles penetrated the realm of critical theory, and its effects can be traced in numerous works, for example, in Nicolas Boileau-Despréaux's *L'Art poétique* (1674); in Alexander Pope's *Essay on Criticism* (1711); in Charles Du Fresnoy's *De Arte Graphica* (translated into French by Roger de Piles, 1668, into English by Dryden, 1695); and in Jean Philippe Rameau's *Traité de l'harmonie réduite à ses principes naturels* (1722). Cartesian and Aristotelian elements combined in the richly polysemous concepts of reason and nature, which became central to all theories of the arts. To follow nature and to follow rules of reason were identified in counsel to the creative artist as well as in critical judgment.

In the sixteenth century, the rules for making and for judging works of art were generally (but not always) supported by authority, either the supposed authority of Aristotle or the models provided by classical writers. The new rationalism in aesthetics was the hope that these rules could be given a more solid, a priori, foundation by deduction from a basic self-evident axiom, such as the principle that art is imitation of nature—where nature comprised the universal, the normal, the essential, the characteristic, the ideal. So, in Samuel Johnson (*Preface to Shakespeare*, 1765), "just representations of general Nature" become the end of art; the painter "is to examine, not the individual, but the species" (*Rasselas*, 1759, Ch. 10). And in the *Discourses* (1778) of Sir Joshua Reynolds, the painter is advised to "consider nature in the abstract, and represent in every one of his figures the character of its species" (III).

The problem of the rules. The controversy over the authority and infallibility of the rules reflected a conflict between reason and experience, between less and more empirical approaches to art. For example, Corneille, in his three *Discourses* (1660), admitted the necessity of observing unity of space, time, and action in dramatic construction but confessed also that he was by no means their "slave" and sometimes had to break or modify them for the sake of dramatic effect or the audience's enjoyment. Molière, in his *Critique de l'école des femmes* (1663), was even more outspoken in making experiment the test. However, other theorists held the line in France, for example, George de Scudéry and Charles de Saint-Évremond. Dryden, in his *Defense of an Essay of Dramatic Poesy* (1668), suggested that if drama has a function or end, there must be rules, but the rules themselves are only probable and rest in part upon experience. In this spirit, Johnson criticized the pseudo-Aristotelian rules of time and place.

In music, the conflict between reason and experience appeared in controversies over harmony and consonance, as well as over the absoluteness of rules, such as the avoidance of parallel fifths. The followers of Zarlino insisted on a mathematical basis for acceptable chords; the followers of Vincenzo Galilei were more willing to let the ear be the judge. A kind of reconciliation of these views appears in Leibniz' theory (*Principles of Nature and of Grace*, 1714, § 17) that, like all sensations, musical tones are confused mélanges of infinite sets of *petites perceptions* that at every moment are in pre-established harmony with the perceptions of all other monads; in hearing a chord, the soul unconsciously counts the beats and compares the mathematical ratio which, when simple, produces concord.

Toward a unified aesthetics. The Cartesian theory of knowledge led to a more systematic attempt at a metaphysics of art in the *Meditationes Philosophicae de Nonnullis ad Poema Pertinentibus* (1735) of Alexander Gottlieb Baumgarten. Baumgarten, who coined the term "aesthetics," aimed to provide an account of poetry (and indirectly of all art) as involving a particular form, or level, of cognition—"sensory cognition." He began with Descartes's distinctions (*Principles of Philosophy* I, xlv–xlvi), elaborated by Leibniz (*Discourse on Metaphysics*, xxiv), between clear and obscure ideas, and between distinct and confused ideas. Sense data are clear but confused, and poetry is "sensate discourse," that is, discourse in which such clear-confused ideas are linked together into a structure. The "extensive clarity" of a poem consists in the number of clear ideas combined in it, and the rules for making or judging poetry have to do with ways in which the extensive clarity of a poem may be increased or diminished.

Baumgarten's book is remarkably concise, and its formalized deductive manner, with definitions and derivations, goes out of its way to declare the possibility of dealing in an acceptably rigorous Cartesian way with matters apparently so little suited for rigorous treatment. Though he did not finish his *Aesthetics*, which would have generalized his study of poetry, the makings of a general theory are present in the *Meditations*. Its basic principle is still the imitation of nature—the principle that is also fundamental to the influential work of the Abbé Charles Batteux, *Les Beaux Arts réduits à un même principe* (1746), and to the important classification of the fine arts in d'Alembert's *Discours préliminaire* to the *Encyclopédie* (1751).

The importance of Lessing's *Laokoon oder über die Grenzen der Malerei und Poesie* (1766) is that, though he did not reject the possibility of a system that will relate all the arts, he attacked superficial and deadening analogies (many of them based on the Horatian formula, *ut pictura poesis*, torn from its context). He looked for the specific individual potentialities and values of painting and poetry in their own distinctive mediums. The medium of an art is, he says, the "signs" (*Zeichen*) it uses for imitation; and painting and poetry, when carefully examined for their capacities to imitate, turn out to be radically different. Consisting of shapes and colors, side by side, painting is best at picturing objects and visible properties, and can only indirectly suggest actions; poetry is just the opposite. When a secondary power of an art is made primary, it cannot do its best work. By the clarity and vigor of his argument and his sharp criticism of prevailing assumptions, Lessing gave a new turn to aesthetics.

THE ENLIGHTENMENT: EMPIRICISM

Contemporaneous with the development of neoclassical critical theory was the divergent line of aesthetic inquiry pursued principally, though not exclusively, by British theorists in the Baconian tradition of empiricism. They were greatly interested in the psychology of art (though they were not merely psychologists), especially the creative process and the effects of art upon the beholder.

The imagination. That the imagination (or "fancy") plays a central, if mysterious, role in artistic creation had long been acknowledged. Its mode of operation—the secret of inventiveness and originality—was not systematically investigated before the empiricists of the seventeenth century. Among the rationalists, the imagination, considered as an image-registering faculty or as an image-combining faculty, played little or no role in knowledge. (See Descartes's Rule III of the *Regulae* ["the blundering constructions of imagination"]; *Principles* I, lxxi–lxxiii; and *Meditation* VI.) But Bacon's *Advancement of Learning* (1605) placed the imagination as a faculty alongside memory and reason and assigned poetry to it, as history and philosophy (including, of course, both moral and natural philosophy) were assigned to the other faculties.

Thomas Hobbes, in the first chapters of his *Leviathan* (1651), undertook to give the first analysis of imagination, which he defined as "decaying sense" (I, ii), the phantasms, or images, that remain when the physiological motions of sensation cease. But besides this "simple imagination," which is passive, there is also "compound imagination," which creates novel images by rearranging old ones. Hobbes stated that the mind's "trains" of thought are guided by a general principle of association (I, iii), but he did not work it out very fully. Nor did Locke develop this idea very far in the famous chapter "Of the Association of Ideas" (II, xxxiii) that he added to the fourth edition (1700) of his *Essay Concerning Human Understanding* (1690). The tendency of ideas that have accompanied each other to stick together and pull each other into the mind was noted by Locke as a pathological feature of the understanding: it explains various sorts of error and the difficulty of eradicating them (cf. *Conduct of the Understanding*, §41). The work of fancy is best seen, according to Locke, in the tendency of poetic language to become figurative. As long as we are interested in pleasure, we cannot be troubled by such ornaments of style; but metaphors and similes are "perfect cheats" when we are interested in truth (III, x, 34; cf. *Conduct of Understanding*, §§32–42). Locke here reflects a widespread distrust of imagination in the later seventeenth century. It is shown in a famous passage from Sprat's *History of the Royal Society* (1702), in which Sprat describes the "close, naked, natural way of speaking," in clearly defined words, required for scientific discourse, and contrasts it with the "specious tropes and figures" of poetry.

The theory of the association of ideas was developed into a systematic psychology by Hume, in his *Treatise of Human Nature* (1739–1740), and Hartley, in his *Observations on Man* (1749). In Hume, the tendency of ideas to consort with one another because of similarity, propinquity, or causal connection became a powerful principle for explaining many mental operations; and Hartley carried the method further. Despite attacks upon it, associationism played a crucial role in several eighteenth-century attempts to explain the pleasures of art.

The problem of taste. The investigation of the psychological effects of art and of the aesthetic experience (in modern terms) developed along two distinct, but occasionally intersecting, paths: (1) the search for an adequate analysis and explanation of certain basic aesthetic qualities (the beautiful, the sublime) or (2) an inquiry into the nature and justification of critical judgment, the problem of "taste." Without trying to keep these completely separate, let us first consider those philosophers in the early part of the eighteenth century in whose thinking the second problem was uppermost.

One phase of aesthetic thinking was launched by the very influential writings of the third earl of Shaftesbury (see especially his *Moralists*, 1709, III; *Inquiry Concerning Virtue or Merit*, 1699, I; and *Characteristics*, 1711). Shaftesbury's philosophy was basically Neoplatonic, but to emphasize the immediacy of our impression of beauty, and also to underline his view that the harmony perceived as beauty is also perceived as virtue, Shaftesbury gave the name "moral sense" to that "inward eye" that grasps harmony in both its aesthetic and ethical forms. The concept of a special faculty of aesthetic apprehension was one form of the theory of taste. Shaftesbury's other contributions to the development of aesthetics are his description of disinterestedness as a characteristic of the aesthetic attitude (*Moralists* III) and his appreciation (along with his contemporaries John Dennis and Thomas Burnet) of wild, fearful, and irregular forms of nature—a taste that helped bring into prominence, in the eighteenth century, the concept of the sublime as an aesthetic quality distinct from beauty.

Joseph Addison's *Spectator* papers on aesthetic enjoyment (1712, Nos. 409, 411–421) conceived taste as simply the capacity to discern those three qualities that give rise to "the pleasures of the imagination," greatness (that is, sublimity), uncommonness (novelty), and beauty. Addison made some attempt to explain why it is that the perception of these qualities is attended by so much pleasure of so special a sort, but he did not go far; his service (earning the appreciation he received from succeeding thinkers) was the lively and provocative way in which he raised many of the basic questions.

The first real treatise on aesthetics in the modern world was Francis Hutcheson's *Inquiry Concerning Beauty, Order, Harmony, and Design*, the first part of *An Inquiry Into the Original of our Ideas of Beauty and Virtue* (1725). From Shaftesbury, Hutcheson took the idea of an inner sense; the "sense of beauty" is the power to frame the idea of beauty when confronted with those qualities of objects suited to raise it. The sense of beauty does not depend on judgment or reflection; it does not respond to intellectual or utilitarian features of the world, nor does it depend on association of ideas. His analysis showed that we sense beauty in an object when it presents "a compound ratio of uniformity and variety" (2d ed., p. 17), so that beauty varies with either of these, if the other is held constant. A basis is thus laid for a nonrelativistic standard of judgment, and variations in actual preference are explained away as due to different expectations with which the beautiful object, in art or nature, is approached.

The question of a standard of taste was the chief concern of David Hume's thinking on aesthetic matters. In his *Treatise* (II, i, 8), he suggested that "beauty is such an order and construction of parts, as either by the *primary constitution* of our nature, by *custom*, or by *caprice*, is fitted to give a pleasure and satisfaction to the soul," thus allowing, like Hutcheson, who influenced him considerably, an immediate delight in beauty, but allowing also for a transfer of this delight by association. For example, the appearance (not necessarily the actuality) of convenience or utility explains why many objects are esteemed beautiful (III, iii, 1). Some types of beauty, then, are simply seen or missed; judgments of them cannot be corrected. But in other cases, especially in art, argument and reflection can correct judgment (see *Enquiry Concerning the Principles of Morals*, 1751, Sec. 1). This problem is discussed most carefully in the essay "Of the Standard of Taste" (in *Four Dissertations*, 1757). Hume argued that it is natural to seek for a standard of taste, by which aesthetic preferences can be called correct or incorrect, especially as there are clear cases of error ("Bunyan is a better writer than Addison"). The rules, or criteria, of judgment are to be established by inductive inquiry into those features of works of art that enable them to please most highly a qualified perceiver, that is, one who is experienced, calm, unprejudiced. But there will always be areas within which preference is due to temperament, age, culture, and similar factors unchangeable by argument; there is no objective standard by which such differences can be rationally resolved.

The aesthetic qualities. The search for necessary and sufficient conditions of beauty and other aesthetic qualities (the concept of the "picturesque" was added late in the century) was continued enthusiastically in the latter half of the eighteenth century. In this debate, an important part was played by Edmund Burke's youthful work, *A Philosophical Enquiry into the Origin of Our Ideas of the Sublime and Beautiful* (1757). Its argument develops on two levels, phenomenological and physiological. The first task is to explain by what qualities objects excite in us the feelings of beauty ("love" without desire) and sublimity ("astonishment" without actual danger). The feeling of the sublime, to begin with, involves a degree of horror—controlled horror—the mind being held and filled by what it contemplates (II, 1). Thus, any object that can excite the ideas of pain and danger, or is associated with such objects, or has qualities that can operate in a similar way, can be sublime (I, 7). Burke then goes on to argue that obscurity, power, privation and emptiness, vastness approaching infinity, etc. contribute to sublimity (II, 3–8). Beauty is analogously treated: the paradigm emotion is response to female beauty, minus lust; and objects that are small, smooth, gently varying, delicate, etc. can give the feeling of beauty (III, 1–16). The same scene can be both beautiful and sublime, but because of the opposition in several of their conditions it cannot be very intensely either if it is both.

Burke then moves to his second level of explanation (IV, 1, 5). He asks what enables the perceptual qualities to evoke the feelings of beauty and sublimity, and he answers that they do so by producing physiological effects like those of actual love and terror. "Beauty acts by relaxing the solids of the whole system" (IV, 19)—this is one of Burke's celebrated hypotheses, a pioneering attempt at physiological aesthetics.

In this very fertile period of aesthetic investigation, many other writers, of various degrees of sophistication, contributed to the theory of beauty and sublimity and to the foundations of taste. Among the most important works, still worth reading for some of their suggestions, are Alexander Gerard's *Essay on Taste* (written by 1756, published 1759; see also his *Essay on Genius*, 1774), which made much use of association in explaining our pleasure in beauty, novelty, sublimity, imitation, harmony, ridicule, and virtue; Henry Home's (Lord Kames) *Elements of Criticism* (1762); Hugh Blair's *Lectures on Rhetoric and Belles Lettres* (given from 1759 on, published 1783); Thomas Reid's essay on Taste in his *Essays on the Intellectual Powers of Man* (1785). On the Continent, the question whether there is a special aesthetic sense was discussed, along with many other problems, by Jean-Pierre de Crousaz, *Traité du beau* (1714), and the Abbé Dubos, *Réflexions critiques sur la poésie et sur la peinture* (1719). Noteworthy also are Voltaire's *Temple du goût* (1733), Yves-Marie André's *Essai sur le beau* (1741), and especially the article on beauty that Diderot wrote for the *Encyclopédie* (1751), in which the experience of beauty is analyzed as the perception of "relationships" (*rapports*).

In general, the later development of empiricist aesthetics involved increasingly ambitious attempts to explain aesthetic phenomena by means of association; a further broadening of the acknowledged aesthetic qualities, away from a limited concept of beauty; further reflection on the nature of "genius," the capacity to "snatch a grace beyond the reach of art"; and a growing conviction that critical principles have to be justified, if they can be justified at all, in terms of empirical knowledge of the characteristic effects of art. The achievements and the high level of discussion reached by the empiricist movement can be seen very well in a later treatise by Archibald Alison, his *Essays on the Nature and Principles of Taste* (1790; rev. ed., which became highly influential, 1811). Alison abandoned the hope for simple formulas of beauty and resolved the pleasure of taste into the enjoyment of following a train of imaginations, in which some of the ideas produce emotions and in which the entire train is connected by a dominant emotion. No special sense is required; the principles of association explain everything. And the arguments by which Alison supported his main theses, the careful inductions at all points, are models of one kind of aesthetics. For example, he showed, by experimental comparisons, that particular qualities of objects, or of Hogarth's "line of beauty" (II, iv, 1, Part II), do not produce aesthetic pleasure unless they become "expressive," or take on the character of signs, by being able to initiate a train of associations; and it is the same, he said, with colors: "Purple, for instance, has acquired a character of Dignity, from its accidental connection with the Dress of Kings" (II, iii, 1).

GERMAN IDEALISM

By assigning to the problems of aesthetic judgment the major part of his third *Critique* (*The Critique of Judgment*, 1790), Kant became the first modern philosopher to make his aesthetic theory an integral part of a philosophic system. For in this volume he aimed to link the worlds of nature and freedom, which the first two *Critiques* had distinguished and separated.

Kant's analysis of judgments of taste. Kant recast the problems of eighteenth-century aesthetic thought, with which he was thoroughly familiar, in the characteristic form of the critical philosophy: How are judgments of the beautiful and the sublime possible? That is, in view of their evident subjectivity, how is their implicit claim to general validity to be vindicated? That such judgments claim general validity and yet are also subjective is argued by Kant, in careful detail, in the "Analytic of the Beautiful" and the "Analytic of the Sublime."

Judgments of beauty (also called "judgments of taste") are analyzed in terms of the four "moments" of the table of categories: relation, quantity, quality, and modality. First, the judgment of taste does not (like ordinary judgments) subsume a representation under a concept, but states a relation between the representation and a special disinterested satisfaction, that is, a satisfaction independent of desire and interest (§5). Second, the judgment of taste, though singular in logical form ("This rose is beautiful"), lays title to universal acceptance, unlike a report of mere sensuous pleasure, which imposes no obligation to agree. Yet, paradoxically, it does not claim to be supportable by reasons, for no arguments can constrain anyone to agree with a judgment of taste (§9; cf. §33). Third, aesthetic satisfaction is evoked by an object that is purposive in its form, though in fact it has no purpose or function: because of a certain wholeness, it looks as though it were somehow made to be understood (§10; cf. §65 and Introduction): it has "purposiveness without purpose" (*Zweckmässigkeit ohne Zweck*). Fourth, the beautiful is claimed by the judgment of taste to have a necessary reference to aesthetic satisfaction (§18): not that when we find ourselves moved in this way by an object we can guarantee that all others will be similarly moved, but that they *ought* to take the same satisfaction we do in it.

The problem of validation. It is the above four aspects of the judgment of beauty that give rise to the philosophical problem of validation, which Kant formulates as he had the parallel problems in the earlier *Critiques:* How can their claim to necessity (and subjective universality) be legitimized? This can only be done, he argues, if it can be shown that the conditions presupposed in such a judgment are not confined to the individual who makes it, but may reasonably be ascribed to all rational beings. A minor clue is offered by the disinterestedness of aesthetic satisfaction; for if our satisfaction is in no way dependent on individual interests, it takes on a kind of intersubjectivity (§6). But the validation of the synthetic a priori judgment of taste requires something more searching, namely, a transcendental deduction.

The gist of this argument is as follows: Empirical knowledge is possible because the faculty of judgment can bring together general concepts and particular sense-intuitions prepared for it in the imagination. These cases of *determinate* judgment presuppose, however, a general harmony between the imagination, in its freedom as synthesizer of representations, and the understanding, in its a priori lawfulness. The formal purposiveness of an object as experienced can induce what Kant calls "a free play of the imagination," an intense disinterested pleasure that depends not on any particular knowledge but just on consciousness of the harmony of the two cognitive powers, imagination and understanding (§9). This is the pleasure we affirm in the judgment of taste. Since the general possibility of sharing knowledge with each other, which may be taken for granted, presupposes that in each of us there *is* a cooperation of imagination and understanding, it follows that every rational being has the *capacity* to feel, under appropriate perceptual conditions, this harmony of the cognitive powers. Therefore a true judgment of taste can legitimately claim to be true for all (§9; cf. §§35–39).

Kant's system requires that there be a dialectic of taste with an antinomy to be dissolved on the principles of critical philosophy. This is a paradox about the role of concepts in the judgment of taste: If the judgment involves concepts, it must be rationally disputable, and provable by reasons (which it is not); if it does not involve concepts, it cannot even be the subject of disagreement (which it is). The solution is that no determinate concept is involved in such judgments, but only the indeterminate concept of the supersensible, or thing-in-itself that underlies the object as well as the judging subject (§§56–57).

Kant on the sublime. Kant's analysis of the sublime proceeds on quite different grounds. Essentially, he explains this species of satisfaction as a feeling of the grandeur of reason itself and of man's moral destiny, which arises in two ways: (1) When we are confronted in nature with the extremely vast (the mathematical sublime), our imagination falters in the task of comprehending it and we become aware of the supremacy of reason, whose ideas reach toward infinite totality. (2) When we are confronted with the overwhelmingly powerful (the dynamical sublime), the weakness of our empirical selves makes us aware (again by contrast) of our worth as moral beings (see the "Analytic of the Sublime"). In this analysis, and again in his final remarks on beauty in nature, Kant goes some way toward re-establishing on one level a connection between realms whose autonomy he has fought for on a different level. As he had done earlier with the a priori concepts of the understanding and the sphere of morality, he has here tried to show that the aesthetic stands on its own feet, independent of desire and interest, of knowledge or morality. Yet because the experience of beauty depends upon seeing natural objects as though they were somehow the artifacts of a cosmic reason bent on being intelligible to us, and because the experience of the sublime makes use of natural formlessness and fearfulness to celebrate reason itself, these aesthetic values in the last analysis serve a moral purpose and a moral need, exalting and ennobling the human spirit.

Schiller. Kant's aesthetic theories were first made use of by the dramatic poet Friedrich Schiller, who found in them the key to a number of profound problems about culture and freedom that he had been meditating. In several essays and poems, and principally in the remarkable *Briefe über die ästhetische Erzieung des Menschen* ("Letters on the Aesthetic Education of Man," 1793–1795), he developed a neo-Kantian view of art and beauty as the medium through which humanity (and the human individual) advances from a sensuous to a rational, and therefore fully human, stage of existence. Schiller distinguishes (Letters 12–13) two basic drives in man, the sensuous impulse (*Stofftrieb*) and the formal impulse (*Formtrieb*), and argues that they are synthesized and lifted to a higher plane in what he calls the play impulse (*Spieltrieb*), which responds to the living shape (*Lebensform*) or beauty of the world (Letter 15). Play, in his sense, is a more concrete version of Kant's harmony of imagination and understanding; it involves that special combination of freedom and necessity that comes in voluntary submission to rules for the sake of the game. By appealing to the play impulse, and freeing man's higher self from dominance by his sensuous nature, art renders man human and gives him a social character (Letters 26–27); it is therefore the necessary condition of any social order that is based not upon totalitarian compulsion but upon rational freedom.

Schelling. Friedrich Wilhelm von Schelling was the first philosopher to claim to have discovered an "absolute standpoint" from which the dualisms and dichotomies of Kant's epistemology could be overcome, or overridden; and he was the first since Plotinus to make art and beauty the capstone of a system. In his *System of Transcendental Idealism* (1800), he attempted a reconciliation of all oppositions between the self and nature through the idea of art. In the artistic intuition, he says, the self is both conscious and unconscious at once; there is both deliberation, *Kunst*, and inspiration, *Poesie.* This harmony of freedom and necessity crystallizes and makes manifest the underlying harmony that exists between the self and nature. There is at work an unseen creative drive that is, on the unconsciousness level, the same as conscious artistic activity. In Schelling's lectures on the *Philosophy of Art* (given 1802–1803, but not published until 1859), transcendental idealism becomes "absolute idealism" and art becomes the medium through which the infinite "ideas," which are the expressions of the various "potencies" involved in the ultimate absolute self-identity, become embodied in finite form, and therefore the medium through which the absolute is most fully revealed. This same general position underlies the famous work *Über das Verhältniss der bildenden Künste zu der Natur* (*On the Relation Between the Plastic Arts and Nature,* 1807).

Hegel. The most fully articulated idealistic system of aesthetics was that of George Friedrich Wilhelm Hegel, in his lectures between 1820 and 1829, the notes for which were published (1835) as his *Philosophy of Fine Art.* In art, he says, the "idea" (the notion at its highest stage of dialectical development) becomes embodied in sensuous form. This is beauty. Man thereby renders explicit to himself what he is and can be (see *Philosophy of Fine Art,* Osmaston translation, I, 41). When the sensuous is spiritualized in art (I, 53), there is both a cognitive revelation of truth, and also a reinvigoration of the beholder. Natural beauty is capable of embodying the idea to some degree, but in human art the highest embodiment takes place (see I, 39, 10–11, 208–214).

Hegel also worked out, in great detail, a theory of the dialectical development of art in the history of human culture, from Oriental "symbolic" art, in which the idea is overwhelmed by the medium; through its antithesis, classical art, in which the idea and the medium are in perfect equilibrium; to the synthesis, romantic art, in which the idea dominates the medium and spiritualization is complete (see Vols. III, IV). These categories were to prove very influential in nineteenth-century German aesthetic thought, in which the Hegelian tradition was dominant, despite attacks by the "formalists" (such as J. F. Herbart), who rejected the analysis of beauty in terms of ideas as an overintellectualization of the aesthetic and a slighting of the formal conditions of beauty.

ROMANTICISM

Without attempting to trace its roots and early stages, we may say that the romantic revolution in feeling and taste was fully under way in Schelling's philosophy of nature and in the new forms of literary creation explored by the German and English poets from about 1890 to 1910. From the start, these developments were accompanied by reflection on the nature of the arts themselves, and they led in time to fundamental changes in prevailing views about the arts.

Emotional expression. The romantics generally conceived of art as essentially the expression of the artist's personal emotions. This view is central to such basic documents as Wordsworth's 1800 Preface to *Lyrical Ballads,* Shelley's *Defense of Poetry* (written 1819) Mill's "What is Poetry?" (1833), and the writings of the German and French romantics. The poet himself, his personality as seen through the "window" of the poem (Carlyle's term in "The Hero as Poet," 1841), becomes the center of interest, and sincerity (in Wordsworth, Carlyle, Arnold) becomes one of the leading criteria of criticism.

Imagination. A new version of the cognitive view of art becomes dominant in the concept of the imagination as a faculty of immediate insight into truth, distinct from, and perhaps superior to, reason and understanding—the artist's special gift. The imagination is both creator and revealer of nature and what lies behind it—a romanticized version of Kant's transcendental idealism, ascribing the form of experience to the shaping power of the mind, and of Fichte's Ego "positing" the non-Ego. A. W. Schlegel, Blake, Shelley, Hazlitt, Baudelaire, and many others spoke of the imagination in these terms. Coleridge, with his famous distinction between imagination and fancy, provided one of the fullest formulations: The fancy is a "mode of memory," operating associatively to recombine the elementary data of sense; the imagination is the "coadunating faculty" that dissolves and transforms the data and creates novelty and emergent quality. The distinction (based on Schelling) between the "primary" and "secondary" imagination is between the unconscious creativity involved both in natural processes and in all perception and the conscious and deliberate expression of this in the artist's creating (see Chs. 13 and 14 of Coleridge's *Biographia Literaria,* 1817). Through most of Coleridge's work there runs his unfinished task of supplying a new theory of mind and of artistic creation that would replace the current associationism, which he had at first enthusiastically adopted and then, under the influence of Plotinus and the German idealists, came to reject.

Organism. Another important, and related, aspect of Coleridge's critical theory was his distinction (derived essentially from A. W. Schlegel's Vienna *Lectures on Dramatic Art,* 1809–1811) between mechanical and organic form and his conception of a work of art as an organic whole, bound together by deeper and more subtle unity than that explicated in the neoclassic rules and having a vitality that grows from within (see his Shakespearean criticism for examples). The concept of nature as organic, and of art as growing out of nature like a living being, had already been developed by Johann Gottfried Herder (see, for example, his *Vom Erkennen und Empfinden der Menschlichen Seele,* 1778), and by Goethe, in some of his essays (e.g., "Vom Deutscher Baukunst," 1772; "Über Wahrheit und Wahrscheinlichkeit der Kunstwerke," 1797).

Symbolism. The idea of the work of art as being, in some sense (in some one of many possible senses), a symbol, a sensuous embodiment of a spiritual meaning, though old in essence, as we have seen, came into a new prominence in the romantic period. Goethe distinguished allegory, a mechanical combination of universal and particular, and symbol, as a concrete unity (see "Über die Gegenstände der bildenden Kunst," 1797); and Friedrich and August Wilhelm Schlegel followed with a new interest in myth and metaphor in poetry. The English Romantic poets (notably Wordsworth) evolved a new lyric poetry in which the visible landscape took on the attributes of human experience. And in France, later in the century, the symbolist movement, launched by Jean Moréas in 1885, and the practice of such poets as Baudelaire, Rimbaud, and Mallarmé emphasized concrete symbolic objects as the heart of poetry.

Schopenhauer. Though first written in the climate of post-Kantian idealism, and, in that context, largely ignored, Arthur Schopenhauer's *Die Welt als Wille und Vorstellung* ("World as Will and Idea," 1819; 2d ed. enlarged, 1844) came into its deserved fame in the second half of the century. Its romantic pessimism and intuitionism and, more particularly, the central position it assigned to the arts (especially music) made it one of the most important aesthetic documents of the century. Schopenhauer's solution of the basic Kantian dualism was to interpret the thing in itself, or noumenal world, as the "Will to Live" and the phenomenal world as the objectification, or expression, of that primal will. The objects of the phenomenal world fall into a hierarchy of types, or grades, that embody, according to Schopenhauer, certain universals or Platonic ideas, and it is these ideas that are presented to us for contemplation by works of art. Since the idea is timeless, the contemplation of it (as, for example, some general character of human nature in a poem or painting) frees us from subjection to the "principle of sufficient reason," which dominates our ordinary practical and cognitive consciousness, and hence from the constant pressure of the will. In this "pure will-less state," we lose individuality and pain. Schopenhauer has much to say about the various arts and the forms of ideas suited to them; the uniqueness of music in this scheme is that it embodies not ideas but the will itself in its striving and urging and enables us to contemplate its awfulness directly, without involvement. Schopenhauer's theory of music was one of his most important contributions to aesthetic theory and influenced not only those theorists, such as Richard Wagner (see his essay on Beethoven, 1870), who emphasized the representative character of music, but also those critical of this view, such as Eduard Hanslick in *Vom Musikalisch-Schönen* ("The Beautiful in Music," 1854).

Nietzsche. Friedrich Nietzsche repudiated romantic art as escapist, but his own aesthetic views, briefly sketched in the notes published posthumously as *The Will to Power* (1901), are best understood in relation to those of Schopenhauer. Nietzsche's early work, *The Birth of Tragedy from the Spirit of Music* (1872), presented a theory of tragedy as arising from the conjunction of two fundamental impulses, which Nietzsche called the Dionysian and Apollonian spirits: the one a joyful acceptance of experience, the other a need for order and proportion. In Nietzsche's later thinking about art, it is the former that becomes dominant; he insists, for example, as opposed to Schopenhauer, that tragedy exists not to inculcate resignation and a Buddhist negation of life, by showing the inevitability of suffering, but to affirm life in all its pain, to express the artist's overabundance of will to power. Art, he says, is a "tonic," a great "yea-sayer" to life.

THE ARTIST AND SOCIETY

Political, economic, and social changes in the nineteenth century, in the wake of the French Revolution and the rise of modern industry, raised in a new form the Platonic problem of the artist's relation to his society, his possibly conflicting obligations to his craft and to his fellow men. In the nineteenth century, an important part of aesthetic thinking was concerned with this problem.

Art for art's sake. One solution to the problem was to think of the artist as a person with a calling of his own, whose whole, or at least primary, obligation is to perfect his work, especially its formal beauty, whatever society may expect. Perhaps the artist, because of his superiority, or higher sensitivity, or the demands of his art, must be alienated from society, and, though perhaps doomed to be destroyed by it, can carry his curse as a pride. This notion stems from the German romantics, from Wilhelm Wackenroder, Johann Ludwig Tieck, and others. From 1820–1830 it became the doctrine of "art for art's sake," the center of continuing controversy in France and, later, in England. In its extreme forms, as reflected, for example, in Oscar Wilde (*Intentions*, 1891) and J. A. M. Whistler ("Ten O'Clock" lecture, 1885), it was sometimes a claim that art is more important than anything else and sometimes a flaunting of the artist's freedom from responsibility. More thoughtfully and fundamentally, as in Théophile Gautier (Preface to *Mademoiselle de Maupin*, 1835) and throughout Flaubert's correspondence with Louise Colet and others, *l'art pour l'art* was a declaration of artistic independence and a kind of professional code of dedication. In that respect, it owed much to the work of Kant in carving out an autonomous domain for art.

Realism. The theory of realism (or, in Zola's sense, naturalism) arose as a broadened conviction of the cognitive duty of literature, a desire to give it an empirical, and even experimental status (in Zola's essay on "The Experimental Novel," 1880), as exhibitor of human nature and social conditions. In Flaubert and Zola, realism called for the cool, analytical eye of the novelist, treating virtue and vice, in Hippolyte Taine's words, as "products like vitriol and sugar"; see the Introduction to his *History of English Literature* (1863), in which Taine set forth his program for explaining art deterministically in terms of race, context, and epoch (*race, milieu, moment*). Among the Russian literary theorists, Vissarion G. Belinsky, Nikolai G. Chernyshevski ("The Aesthetic Relation of Art to Reality," 1855), and Dmitri I. Pisarev ("The Destruction of Aesthetics," 1865), all art was given a similar treatment—as a reproduction of factual reality (sometimes an aid in explaining it, which may have value as a substitute, like a photograph, says Chernyshevski) or as the bearer of social ideas (Pisarev).

Social responsibility. The theory that art is primarily a social force and that the artist has a social responsibility was first fully worked out by the French socialist sociologists. Claude Saint-Simon (*Du Système industriel*, 1821), Auguste Comte (*Discours sur l'ensemble du positivisme*, 1848, Ch. 5), Charles Fourier (*Cités ouvrières*, 1849), and Pierre Joseph Proudhon (*Du Principe de l'art et de sa destination sociale*, 1865) attacked the idea that art can be an end in itself and projected visions of future social orders free of violence and exploitation, in which beauty and use would be fruitfully combined and for which art will help prepare. In England, John Ruskin and William Morris were the great critics of Victorian society from an aesthetic point of view. They pointed to the degradation of the worker into a machine, unfree to express himself, the loss of good taste, the destruction of natural beauty, and the trivialization of art. Ruskin's essay on "The Nature of Gothic" (*Stones of Venice,* 1851) and many other lectures (for example those in *The Two Paths,* 1859; *Lectures on Art,* 1870) insisted on the social conditions and effects of art. Morris, in his lectures and pamphlets (see, for example, "Art under Plutocracy," 1883; "The Aims of Art," 1887; "Art and Socialism," 1884), argued that radical changes were needed in the social and economic order to make art what it should be: ". . . the expression of man's happiness in his labor . . . made by the people, and for the people, as a happiness to the maker and the user" ("The Art of the People," 1879).

The functionalist tendencies of Ruskin and Morris also turned up, even earlier, in the United States, in the trenchant views of Horatio Greenough ("American Architecture," 1843) and in some essays of Ralph Waldo Emerson ("Thoughts on Art," 1841; "Beauty," *Conduct of Life,* 1860; "Art," *Essays, First Series,* 1841).

Tolstoy. It was, however, Leo Tolstoy who drove the social view of art to its farthest point in the nineteenth century and issued the most fundamental challenge to art's right to exist. In *What Is Art?* (first uncensored edition, 1898, in English), he asked whether all the social costs of art could be rationally justified. If, as he argued, art is essentially a form of communication—the transmission of emotion—then certain consequences can be deduced. Unless the emotion is one that can actually be shared by men in general—is simple and human—there is either bad art or pseudo art: this criterion rules out most of the supposedly great works of music and literature, including Tolstoy's own major novels. A work must be judged, in the end, by the highest religious criteria of the age; and in Tolstoy's age that meant, he said, its contribution to the sense of human brotherhood. Great art is that which transmits either simple feelings, drawing men together, or the feeling of brotherhood itself (*Uncle Tom's Cabin*). In no other way can it claim genuine social value (apart from the adventitious value of jewelry, etc.); and where it falls short of this high task (as it usually does), it can only be a social evil, dividing men into cliques by catering to sensuality, pride, and patriotism.

CONTEMPORARY DEVELOPMENTS

Aesthetics has never been so actively and diversely cultivated as in the twentieth century. Certain major figures and certain lines of work stand out.

Metaphysical theories. Though he later proposed two important changes in his central doctrine of intuition, the early aesthetic theory of Benedetto Croce has remained the most pervasively influential aesthetics of the twentieth century. The fullest exposition was given in the *Estetica come scienza dell'espressione e linguistica generale* ("Aesthetic as Science of Expression and General Linguistic," 1902), which is part of his *Filosofia dello spirito.* Aesthetics, in this context, is the "science" of images, or intuitive knowledge, as logic is knowledge of concepts—both being distinguished from "practical knowledge." At the lower limit of consciousness, says Croce, are raw sense data, or "impressions," which, when they clarify themselves, are intuitions, are also said to be "expressed." To express, in this subjective sense, apart from any external physical activity, is to create art. Hence, his celebrated formula, "intuition = expression," on which many principles of his aesthetics are based. For example, he argued that in artistic failure, or "unsuccessful expression," the trouble is not that a fully formed intuition has not been fully expressed but that an impression has not been fully intuited. R. G. Collingwood, in his *Principles of Art* (1938), has extended and clarified Croce's basic point of view.

The theory of intuition presented by Henri Bergson is quite different but has also been eagerly accepted by many aestheticians. In his view, it is intuition (or instinct become self-conscious) that enables us to penetrate to the *durée,* or *élan vital*—the ultimate reality which our "spatializing" intellects inevitably distort. The general view is explained in his "Introduction à la métaphysique" (1903) and in *L'évolution créatrice* (1907) and applied with great ingenuity and subtlety to the problem of the comic in *Le Rire* (1900).

Naturalism. Philosophers working within the tradition of American naturalism, or contextualism, have emphasized the continuity of the aesthetic with the rest of life and culture. George Santayana, for example, in his *Reason in Art* (1903; Vol. IV of *The Life of Reason*), argues against a sharp separation of "fine" from "useful" arts and gives a strong justification of fine art as both a model and an essential constituent of the life of reason. His earlier book, *The Sense of Beauty* (1896), was an essay in introspective psychology that did much to restimulate an empirical approach to art through its famous doctrine that beauty is "objectified pleasure."

The fullest and most vigorous expression of naturalistic aesthetics is *Art as Experience* (1934), by John Dewey. In *Experience and Nature* (1925), Dewey had already begun to reflect upon the "consummatory" aspect of experience (as well as the instrumental aspects, which had previously occupied most of his attention) and had treated art as the "culmination of nature," to which scientific discovery is a handmaiden (see Ch. 9). *Art as Experience,* a book that has had incalculable influence on contemporary aesthetic thinking, develops this basic point of view. When experience rounds itself off into more or less complete and coherent strands of doing and undergoing, we have, he says, "*an* experience"; and such an experience is aesthetic to the degree in which attention is fixed on pervasive quality. Art is expression, in the sense that in expressive objects there is a "fusion" of "meaning" in the present quality; ends and means, separated for practical purposes, are reunited, to produce not only experience enjoyable in itself but, at its best, a celebration and commemoration of qualities ideal to the culture or society in which the art plays its part.

A number of other writers have worked with valuable results along similar lines, for example, D. W. Prall, *Aesthetic Judgment* (1929) and *Aesthetic Analysis* (1936); C. I. Lewis, *An Analysis of Knowledge and Valuation* (1946, Chs. 14, 15); and Stephen C. Pepper, *Aesthetic Quality*

(1937), *The Basis of Criticism in the Arts* (1945), *The Work of Art* (1955).

Semiotic approaches. Since semiotics in a broad sense has undoubtedly been one of the central preoccupations of contemporary philosophy, as well as many other fields of thought, it is to be expected that philosophers working along this line would consider applying their results to the problems of aesthetics. The pioneering work of C. K. Ogden and I. A. Richards, *The Meaning of Meaning* (1923), stressed the authors' distinction between the "referential" and the "emotive" function of language. And they suggested two aesthetic implications that were widely followed: first, that the long-sought distinction between poetic and scientific discourse was to be found here, poetry being considered essentially emotive language; second, that judgments of beauty and other judgments of aesthetic value could be construed as purely emotive. This work, and later books of Richards, have been joined by a number of aesthetic studies in the general theory of (artistic) interpretation, for example, John Hospers, *Meaning and Truth in the Arts* (1946); Charles L. Stevenson, "Interpretation and Evaluation in Aesthetics" (1950); Morris Weitz, *Philosophy of the Arts* (1950); and Isabel C. Hungerland, *Poetic Discourse* (1958).

Meanwhile, anthropological interest in classical and primitive mythology, which became scientific in the nineteenth century, led to another semiotical way of looking at art, particularly literature. Under the influence of Sir James G. Frazer's *The Golden Bough* (1890–1915), a group of British classical scholars developed new theories about the relations between Greek tragedy, Greek mythology, and religious rite. Jane Ellen Harrison's *Themis: A Study of the Social Origins of Greek Religion* (1912) argued that Greek myth and drama grew out of ritual. This field of inquiry was further opened up, or out, by C. G. Jung, in his paper "On the Relation of Analytical Psychology to Poetic Art" (1922; see *Contributions to Analytical Psychology*, 1928) and in other works. Jung suggested that the basic symbolic elements of all literature are "primordial images" or "archetypes" that emerge from the "collective unconscious" of man. In recent years the search for "archetypal patterns" in all literature, to help explain its power, has been carried on by many critics and has become an accepted part of literary criticism.

The most ambitious attempt to bring together these and other lines of inquiry to make a general theory of human culture ("philosophical anthropology") is that of Ernst Cassirer. In his *Philosophie der Symbolischen Formen* (3 vols., 1923, 1925, 1929), the central doctrines of which are also explained in *Sprache und Mythos* (1925) and in *An Essay on Man* (1944), he put forward a neo-Kantian theory of the great "symbolic forms" of culture—language, myth, art, religion, and science. In this view, man's world is determined, in fundamental ways, by the very symbolic forms in which he represents it to himself; so, for example, the primitive world of myth is necessarily different from that of science or art. Cassirer's philosophy exerted a strong influence upon two American philosophers especially: Wilbur Marshall Urban (*Language and Reality*, 1939) argued that "aesthetic symbols" are "insight symbols" of a specially revelatory sort; and Susanne K. Langer has developed in detail a theory of art as a "presentational symbol," or "semblance." In *Philosophy in a New Key* (1942), she argued that music is not self-expression or evocation but symbolizes the morphology of human sentience and hence articulates the emotional life of man. In *Feeling and Form* (1953) and in various essays (*Problems of Art*, 1957), she applied the theory to various basic arts.

Charles W. Morris presented a closely parallel view in 1939, in two articles that (like Mrs. Langer's books) have been much discussed: "Esthetics and the Theory of Signs" (*Journal of Unified Science* [*Erkenntnis*], VIII, 1939–1940) and "Science, Art and Technology" (*Kenyon Review*, I, 1939; see also *Signs, Language and Behavior*, 1946). Taking a term from Charles Peirce, he treats works of art as "iconic signs" (i.e., signs that signify a property in virtue of exhibiting it) of "value properties" (e.g., regional properties like the menacing, the sublime, the gay).

Marxism–Leninism. The philosophy of dialectical materialism formulated by Karl Marx and Friedrich Engels contained, at the start, only the basic principle of an aesthetics, whose implications have been drawn out and developed by Marxist theoreticians over more than half a century. This principle is that art, like all higher activities, belongs to the cultural "superstructure" and is determined by sociohistorical conditions, especially economic conditions. From this it is argued that a connection can always be traced—and must be traced, for full understanding—between a work of art and its sociohistorical matrix. In some sense, art is a "reflection of social reality," but the exact nature and limits of this sense has remained one of the fundamental and persistent problems of Marxist aesthetics. Marx himself, in his *Contribution to the Critique of Political Economy* (1859), pointed out that there is no simple one-to-one correspondence between the character of a society and its art.

In the period before the October Revolution of 1917, Georgi V. Plekhanov (*Art and Social Life*, 1912) developed dialectical materialist aesthetics through attacks on the doctrine of art for art and the separation of artist from society, either in theory or in practice. After the Revolution, there ensued a period of vigorous and free debate in Russia among various groups of Marxists and others (e.g., the formalists, see below). It was questioned whether art can be understood entirely in sociohistorical terms or has its own "peculiar laws" (as Trotsky remarked in *Literature and Revolution*, 1924) and whether art is primarily a weapon in the class struggle or a resultant whose reformation awaits the full realization of a socialist society. The debate was closed in Russia by official fiat, when the party established control over the arts at the First All-Union Congress of Soviet Writers (1934). Socialist realism, as a theory of what art ought to be and as a guide to practice, was given a stricter definition by Andrei Zhdanov, who along with Gorki became the official theoretician of art. But the central idea had already been stated by Engels (letter to Margaret Harkness, April 1888): the artist is to reveal the moving social forces and portray his characters as expressions of these forces (this is what the Marxist means by a "typical" character), and in so doing he is to forward the revolutionary developments themselves. (See also Ralph Fox, *The Novel and the People*, 1937; Christopher Caudwell, *Illusion and Reality*, 1937, and other works.)

Indications of recent growth in dialectical materialist aesthetics, and of a resumption of the dialogue with other systems, can be seen in the important work of the Hungarian Marxist Georg Lukács (see, for example, *The Meaning of Contemporary Realism*, translated, 1962, from *Wider den missverstandenen Realismus*, 1958) and in the writings of the Polish Marxist, Stefan Morawski (see "Vicissitudes in the Theory of Socialist Realism," *Diogenes*, 1962).

Phenomenology and existentialism. Among many critics and critical theorists, there has been, in the twentieth century, a strong emphasis on the autonomy of the work of art, its objective qualities as an object in itself, independent of both its creator and its perceivers. This attitude was forcefully stated by Eduard Hanslick in *The Beautiful in Music* (1854); it was reflected in the work of Clive Bell (*Art*, 1914) and Roger Fry (*Vision and Design*, 1920); and it appeared especially in two literary movements. The first, Russian "formalism" (also present in Poland and Czechoslovakia), flourished from 1915 until suppressed about 1930. Its leaders were Roman Jakobson, Victor Shklovsky, Boris Eichenbaum, and Boris Tomashevsky (*Theory of Literature*, 1925). The second, American and British "New Criticism," was inaugurated by I. A. Richards (*Practical Criticism*, 1929), William Empson (*Seven Types of Ambiguity*, 1930), and others (see René Wellek and Austin Warren, *Theory of Literature*, 1949).

This emphasis on the autonomy of the work of art has been supported by Gestalt psychology, with its emphasis on the phenomenal objectivity of Gestalt qualities, and also phenomenology, the philosophical movement first developed by Edmund Husserl. Two outstanding works in phenomenological aesthetics have appeared. Working on Husserl's foundations, Roman Ingarden (*Das Literarische Kunstwerk*, 1930) has studied the mode of existence of the literary work as an intentional object and has distinguished four "strata" in literature: sound, meaning, the "world of the work," and its "schematized aspects," or implicit perspectives. Mikel Dufrenne (*Phenomenologie de l'expérience esthétique*, 2 vols., 1953), closer to the phenomenology of Maurice Merleau-Ponty and Jean-Paul Sartre, has analyzed the differences between aesthetic objects and other things in the world. He finds that the basic difference lies in the "expressed world" of each aesthetic object, its own personality, which combines the "being in itself" (*en-soi*) of a presentation with the "being for itself" (*pour-soi*) of consciousness and contains measureless depths that speak to the depths of ourselves as persons.

The "existential phenomenalism" of Heidegger and Sartre suggests possibilities for an existentialist philosophy of art, in the central concept of "authentic existence," which art might be said to further. These possibilities have only begun to be worked out, for example, in Heidegger's paper "Der Ursprung des Kunstwerkes" (in *Holzwege*, 1950) and in a recent book by Arturo B. Fallico, *Art and Existentialism* (1962).

Empiricism. The contemporary empiricist makes a cardinal point of attacking the traditional problems of philosophy by resolving them into two distinct types of questions: questions about matters of fact, to be answered by empirical science (and, in the case of aesthetics, psychology in particular), and questions about concepts and methods, to be answered by philosophical analysis.

Some empiricists emphasize the first type of question and have called for a "scientific aesthetics" to state aesthetic problems in such a way that the results of psychological inquiry can be brought to bear upon them. Max Dessoir, Charles Lalo, Étienne Souriau, and (in America) Thomas Munro have formulated this program (see, especially, Munro's *Scientific Method in Philosophy*, 1928, and later essays). The actual results of work in psychology, over the period since Fechner inaugurated experimental aesthetics (*Vorschule der Ästhetik*, 1876) to replace "aesthetics from above" by an "aesthetics from below," are too varied to summarize easily (see Bibliography). But two lines of inquiry have had an important effect on the way in which twentieth-century philosophers think about art. The first is Gestalt psychology, whose studies of perceptual phenomena and the laws of Gestalt perception have illuminated the nature and value of form in art (see, for example, Kurt Koffka's "Problems in the Psychology of Art," in *Art: A Bryn Mawr Symposium*, 1940; Rudolf Arnheim, *Art and Visual Perception*, 1954; Leonard Meyer, *Emotion and Meaning in Music*, 1956). The second is Freudian psychology, beginning with Freud's interpretation of Hamlet (*Interpretation of Dreams*, 1900) and his studies of Leonardo (1910) and Dostoyevsky (1928), which have illuminated the nature of art creation and appreciation. Description of aesthetic experience, in terms of concepts like "empathy" (Theodor Lipps), "psychical distance" (Edward Bullough), and "synaesthesis" (I. A. Richards), has also been investigated by introspective methods.

Analytical aesthetics, in both its "reconstructionist" and "ordinary language" forms, is more recent. This school considers the task of philosophical aesthetics to consist in the analysis of the language and reasoning of critics (including all talk about art), to clarify language, to resolve puzzles due to misapprehensions about language, and to understand its special functions, methods, and justifications (see M. C. Beardsley, *Aesthetics: Problems in the Philosophy of Criticism*, 1958; Jerome Stolnitz, *Aesthetics and Philosophy of Art Criticism*, 1960; William Elton, ed., *Aesthetics and Language*, 1954; Joseph Margolis, ed., *Philosophy Looks at the Arts*, 1962).

Classical Greek Philosophers

See J. W. H. Atkins, *Literary Criticism in Antiquity*, Vol. 1 (Cambridge, 1934), Chs. 1, 2; G. F. Else, "'Imitation' in the Fifth Century," in *Classical Philology*, Vol. 53, No. 2 (1958), 73–90; T. B. L. Webster, "Greek Theories of Art and Literature down to 400 B.C." in *Classical Quarterly*, Vol. 33, Nos. 3, 4 (1939), 166–179; Alice Sperduti, "The Divine Nature of Poetry in Antiquity," in *Transactions and Proceedings, American Philological Association*, Vol. 81 (1950), 209–240.

PLATO

See Raphael Demos, *The Philosophy of Plato* (New York, 1939), Chs. 11–13; Rupert C. Lodge, *Plato's Theory of Art* (London, 1953), G. M. A. Grube, "Plato's Theory of Beauty," in *Monist*, Vol. 37, No. 2 (1927), 269–288; J. Tate, "Plato and 'Imitation,'" in *Classical Quarterly*, Vol. 26, Nos. 3, 4 (1932), 161–169.

ARISTOTLE

See G. F. Else, *Aristotle's Poetics: The Argument* (Cambridge, 1957); S. H. Butcher, *Aristotle's Theory of Poetry and Fine Art*, 4th ed. (London, 1923); Ingram Bywater, *Aristotle on the Art of Poetry* (Oxford, 1909); G. F. Else, "Aristotle on the Beauty of Tragedy," in *Harvard Studies in Classical Philology*, Vol. 49 (1938); Roman Ingarden, "A Marginal Commentary on Aristotle's Poetics," in *Journal of Aesthetics and Art Criticism*, Vol. 20, No. 2 (Winter, 1961), 163–173; *Ibid.*, No. 3 (Spring, 1962), 273–285; Richard McKeon, "Literary Criticism and the Concept of Imitation in Antiquity," in R. S. Crane, ed., *Critics and Criticism* (Chicago, 1952).

Later Classical Philosophers

See Phillip De Lacy, "Stoic Views of Poetry," in *American Journal of Philology*, Vol. 49, No. 275 (1948), 241–271; L. P. Wilkinson, "Philodemus and Poetry," in *Greece and Rome*, Vol. 2, No. 6 (1932–1933), 144–151; L. P. Wilkinson, "Philodemus on *Ethos* in Music," in *Classical Quarterly*, Vol. 32, Nos. 3, 4 (1938), 174–181; Craig La Drière, "Horace and the Theory of Imitation," in *American Journal of Philology*, Vol. 60, No. 239 (1939), 288–300; Philippus V. Pistorius, *Plotinus and Neoplatonism* (Cambridge, England, 1952), Ch. 7.

The Middle Ages

See Edgar de Bruyne, *Etudes d'esthétique médiévale*, 3 vols. (Brugge, 1946); Edgar de Bruyne, "Esthétique païenne, esthétique chrétienne," in *Revue Internationale de Philosophie*, No. 31 (1955), 130–144; Emmanuel Chapman, *Saint Augustine's Philosophy of Beauty* (New York, 1939); K. Svoboda, *L'esthétique de Saint Augustin et ses sources* (Brno, 1933); Jacques Maritain, *Art and Scholasticism*, translated by J. F. Scanlan (London, 1930), esp. Ch. 5; Maurice de Wulf, *Études historiques sur l'esthétique de S. Thomas d'Aquin* (Louvain, 1896); Leonard Callahan, *A Theory of Esthetic According to the Principles of St. Thomas Aquinas* (Washington, 1927); Bernard F. Huppé, *Doctrine and Poetry* (Albany, N.Y., 1959), Chs. 1, 2; H. Flanders Dunbar, *Symbolism in Medieval Thought* (New Haven, 1929); Murray Wright Bundy, *The Theory of Imagination in Classical and Medieval Thought*, in University of Illinois Studies in Language and Literature (Urbana, 1927), Chs. 8–12.

The Renaissance

See Nesca A. Robb, *Neoplatonism of the Italian Renaissance* (London, 1935), Ch. 7; Erwin Panofsky, *Idea*, 2d ed. (Berlin, 1960); Erwin Panofsky, *The Codex Huygens and Leonardo da Vinci's Art Theory* (London, 1940); Erwin Panofsky, *The Life and Art of Albrecht Dürer*, 4th ed. (Princeton, 1955), Ch. 8; Rensselaer W. Lee, "*Ut Pictura Poesis:* The Humanistic Theory of Painting," in *Art Bulletin*, Vol. 22, No. 4 (1940), 197–269; Anthony Blunt, *Artistic Theory in Italy, 1450–1600* (Oxford, 1940); Edward E. Lowinsky, "Music in the Culture of the Renaissance," in *Journal of the History of Ideas*, Vol. 15, No. 4 (1954), 509–553; D. P. Walker, "Musical Humanism in the 16th and Early 17th Centuries," in *Music Review*, Vol. 2, No. 1 (1941), 1–13; *Ibid.*, No. 2, 111–121; *Ibid.*, No. 3, 220–227; *Ibid.*, No. 4, 288–308; Vol. 3, No. 1 (1942), 55–71; Bernard Weinberg, *A History of Literary Criticism in the Italian Renaissance*, 2 vols. (Chicago, 1961); Baxter Hathaway, *The Age of Criticism: The Late Renaissance in Italy* (Ithaca, 1962).

The Enlightenment

CARTESIAN RATIONALISM

See Émile Krantz, *Essai sur l'esthétique de Descartes* (Paris, 1882); Brewster Rogerson, "The Art of Painting the Passions," in *Journal of the History of Ideas*, Vol. 14, No. 1 (1953), 68–94; Scott Elledge, "The Background and Development in English Criticism of the Theories of Generality and Particularity," in *PMLA*, Vol. 62, No. 1 (1947), 147–182; A. O. Lovejoy, "'Nature' as Aesthetic Norm," in *Modern Language Notes*, Vol. 42, No. 7 (1927), 444–450; Hoyt Trowbridge, "The Place of Rules in Dryden's Criticism," in *Modern Philology*, Vol. 44, No. 2 (1946–1947), 84–96; Meyer H. Abrams, *The Mirror and the Lamp* (Oxford, 1953), Chs. 1, 2; Samuel H. Monk, *The Sublime*, rev. ed. (Ann Arbor, 1960), Ch. 9; Claude V. Palisca, "Scientific Empiricism in Musical Thought," in H. H. Rhys, ed., *Seventeenth Century Science and the Arts* (Princeton, 1961); Louis I. Bredvold, "The Tendency toward Platonism in Neo-classical Esthetics," in *ELH: A Journal of English Literary History*, Vol. 1, No. 2 (1934), 91–119; Cicely Davis, "Ut pictura poesis," *Modern Language Review*, Vol. 30, No. 2 (1935), 159–169; P. O. Kristeller, "The Modern System of the Arts," in *Journal of the History of Ideas*, Vol. 12, No. 4 (1951), 496–527; *Ibid.*, Vol. 13, No. 1 (1952), 17–46; Ernst Cassirer, *The Philosophy of the Enlightenment*, translated by Koelln and Pettegrove (Princeton, 1951), Ch. 7.

EMPIRICISM

See Clarence DeWitt Thorpe, *The Aesthetic Theory of Thomas Hobbes* (Ann Arbor, 1940); Donald F. Bond, "The Neo-classical Psychology of the Imagination," in *ELH: A Journal of English Literary History*, Vol. 4, No. 4 (1937), 245–264; Martin Kallich, "The Association of Ideas and Critical Theory: Hobbes, Locke, and Addison," in *ELH: A Journal of English Literary History*, Vol. 12, No. 4 (1945), 290–315; R. L. Brett, *The Third Earl of Shaftesbury* (London, 1951); Jerome Stolnitz, "On the Significance of Lord Shaftesbury in Modern Aesthetic Theory," in *Philosophical Quarterly*, Vol. 11, No. 43 (1961), 97–113; Clarence D. Thorpe, "Addison and Hutcheson on the Imagination," in *ELH: A Journal of English Literary History*, Vol. 2, No. 3 (1935), 215–234; Martin Kallich, "The Argument against the Association of Ideas in Eighteenth-Century Aesthetics," in *Modern Language Quarterly*, Vol. 15, No. 2 (1954), 125–136; Margaret Gilman, *The Idea of Poetry in France from Houdar de la Motte to Baudelaire* (Cambridge, Mass., 1958), Ch. 2; Wladyslaw Folkierski, *Entre le classicisme et le romantisme* (Krakow and Paris, 1925); Walter Jackson Bate, *From Classic to Romantic* (Cambridge, Mass., 1946); Ernest Lee Tuveson, *The Imagination as a Means to Grace* (Berkeley, 1960); Jerome Stolnitz, "'Beauty': Some Stages in the History of an Idea," in *Journal of the History of Ideas*, Vol. 22, No. 2 (1961) 185–204; Walter John Hipple, Jr., *The Beautiful, The Sublime, and the Picturesque in Eighteenth-Century British Aesthetic Theory* (Carbondale, Ill., 1957); Samuel H. Monk, *The Sublime*, rev. ed. (Ann Arbor, 1960).

German Idealism

See H. W. Cassirer, *A Commentary on Kant's Critique of Judgment* (London, 1938); James C. Meredith, *Kant's Critique of Aesthetic Judgement* (Oxford, 1911); Hermann Cohen, *Kant's Begründung der Ästhetik* (Berlin, 1889); Victor Basch, *Essai critique sur l'esthétique de Kant*, 2d ed. (Paris, 1927); Humayun Kabir, *Immanuel Kant on Philosophy in General*, essays on the first Introduction to the *Critique of Judgment* (Calcutta, 1935); G. T. Whitney and D. F. Bowers, eds., *The Heritage of Kant* (Princeton, 1939); Robert L. Zimmerman, "Kant: The Aesthetic Judgment," in *Journal of Aesthetics and Art Criticism*, Vol. 21, No. 3 (Spring, 1963), 333–344; Frederic Will, *Intelligible Beauty in Aesthetic Thought from Winckelmann to Victor Cousin* (Tubingen, 1958); S. S. Kerry, "The Artist's Intuition in Schiller's Aesthetic Philosophy," in *Publications of the English Goethe Society*, New Series 28 (Leeds, 1959); Elizabeth E. Bohning, "Goethe's and Schiller's Interpretation of Beauty," in *German Quarterly*, Vol. 22, No. 4 1949), 185–194; Jean Gibelin, *L'Esthétique de Schelling d'après la philosophie de l'art* (Paris, 1934); E. L. Fackenheim, "Schelling's Philosophy of the Literary Arts," in *Philosophical Quarterly*, Vol. 4, No. 17 (1954), 310–326; H. M. Schueller, "Schelling's Theory of the Metaphysics of Music," *Journal of Aesthetics and Art Criticism*, Vol. 15, No. 4 (June, 1957), 461–476; W. T. Stace, *The Philosophy of Hegel* (London, 1924), Part IV, Third Div., Ch. l; Israel Knox, *The Aesthetic Theories of Kant, Hegel, and Schopenhauer* (New York, 1936).

Romanticism

See René Wellek, *A History of Modern Criticism: 1750–1950,* Vol. 2 (New Haven, 1955); M. H. Abrams, *The Mirror and the Lamp: Romantic Theory and the Critical Tradition* (Oxford 1953); W. J. Bate, *From Classic to Romantic* (Cambridge, Mass., 1949), Chs. 5, 6; Paul Reiff, *Die Ästhetik der deutschen Frühromantik* in University of Illinois Studies in Language and Literature, Vol. 31 (Urbana, 1946); M. Z. Shroder, *Icarus: The Image of the Artist in French Romanticism* (Cambridge, Mass., 1961); A. G. Lehmann, *The Symbolist Movement in France, 1885–1895* (Oxford, 1950); Joseph Ciari, *Symbolism from Poe to Mallarmé: The Growth of a Myth* (London, 1956); John M. Bullitt, "Hazlitt and the Romantic Conception of the Imagination," in *Philological Quarterly,* Vol. 24, No. 4 (1945), 343–361; J. B. Baker, *The Sacred River: Coleridge's Theory of the Imagination* (Baton Rouge, La., 1957); James Benziger, "Organic Unity: Leibniz to Coleridge," in *PMLA,* Vol. 66, No. 2 (1951), 24–48; John Stokes Adams, *The Aesthetics of Pessimism* (Philadelphia, 1940); J. M. Stein, *Richard Wagner and the Synthesis of the Arts* (Detroit, 1960); E. A. Lippman, "The Esthetic Theories of Richard Wagner," in *Musical Quarterly,* Vol. 44 (1958), 209–220.

The Artist and Society

See R. F. Egan, "The Genesis of the Theory of 'Art for Art's Sake' in Germany and in England," in *Smith College Studies in Modern Languages,* Vols. 2, 5; Albert Cassagne, *La Théorie de l'art pour l'art en France* (Paris, 1906); Irving Singer, "The Aesthetics of 'Art for Art's Sake,'" *Journal of Aesthetics and Art Criticism,* Vol. 12, No. 3 (March, 1954), 343–359; H. A. Needham, *La Développement de l'esthétique sociologique en France et en Angleterre au XIXe siècle* (Paris, 1926); Bernard Weinberg, *French Realism: The Critical Reaction 1830–1870* (New York, 1937); H. M. Kallen, *Art and Freedom,* 2 vols. (New York, 1942); René Wellek, "Social and Aesthetic Values in Russian Nineteenth-Century Literary Criticism," in E. J. Simmons, ed., *Continuity and Change in Russian and Soviet Thought* (Cambridge, Mass., 1955); F. D. Curtin, "Aesthetics in English Social Reform: Ruskin and his Followers," in Herbert Davis et al., eds., *Nineteenth-Century Studies* (Ithaca, 1940).

Contemporary Developments

METAPHYSICAL THEORIES

See G. N. G. Orsini, *Benedetto Croce: Philosopher of Art and Literary Critic* (Carbondale, Ill., 1961); John Hospers, "The Croce–Collingwood Theory of Art," in *Philosophy,* Vol. 31, No. 119 (1956), 291–308; Alan Donegan, "The Croce–Collingwood Theory of Art," in *Philosophy,* Vol. 33, No. 125 (1958), 162–167; T. E. Hulme, "Bergson's Theory of Art," in Herbert Read, ed., *Speculations* (New York and London, 1924); Arthur Szathmary, *The Aesthetic Theory of Bergson* (Cambridge, Mass., 1937).

NATURALISM

See W. E. Arnett, *Santayana and the Sense of Beauty* (Bloomington, Ind., 1955); Jack Kaminsky, "Dewey's Concept of *An Experience,*" in *Philosophy and Phenomenological Research,* Vol. 17, No. 3 (March, 1957), 316–330; E. A. Shearer, "Dewey's Aesthetic Theory," *Journal of Philosophy,* Vol. 32, Nos. 23, 24 (1935), 617–627, 650–664; Sidney Zink, "The Concept of Continuity in Dewey's Theory of Esthetics," *Philosophical Review,* Vol. 52, No. 4 (1943), 392–400; S. C. Pepper, "The Concept of Fusion in Dewey's Aesthetic Theory," in *Journal of Aesthetics and Art Criticism,* Vol. 12, No. 2 (December, 1953), 169–176.

SEMIOTICS

See Richard Rudner, "On Semiotic Aesthetics," in *Journal of Aesthetics and Art Criticism,* Vol. 10, No. 1 (September, 1951), 67–77; E. G. Ballard, "In Defense of Semiotic Aesthetics," in *Journal of Aesthetics and Art Criticism,* Vol. 12, No.1 (September, 1953), 38–43; Max Rieser, "The Semantic Theory of Art in America," *Journal of Aesthetics and Art Criticism,* Vol. 15, No. 1 (September, 1956), 12–26.

MARXISM–LENINISM

See Karl Marx and Friedrich Engels, *Literature and Art: Selections from Their Writings* (New York, 1947); Victor Erlich, "Social and Aesthetic Criteria in Soviet Russian Criticism," R. M. Hankin, "Main Premises of the Communist Party in the Theory of Soviet Literary Controls," and E. J. Simmons, "Review," in Simmons, ed., *Continuity and Change in Russian and Soviet Thought* (Cambridge, Mass., 1955); Max Rieser, "The Aesthetic Theory of Socialist Realism," in *Journal of Aesthetics and Art Criticism,* Vol. 16, No. 2 (December, 1957), 237–248; Ernst Fischer, *Von der Notwendigkeit der Kunst* (Dresden, 1959). Translated by Anna Bostock as *The Necessity of Art, A Marxist Approach* (Baltimore, 1963).

PHENOMENOLOGY AND EXISTENTIALISM

See Herbert Spiegelberg, *The Phenomenological Movement: A Historical Introduction,* 2 vols. (The Hague, 1960); Fritz Kaufmann, "Art and Phenomenology," in Marvin Farber, ed., *Philosophical Essays in Memory of Edmund Husserl* (Cambridge, Mass., 1940); Anna-Teresa Tymieniecka, *Phenomenology and Science in Contemporary European Thought* (New York, 1961); J.-Claude Piguet, "Esthétique et Phénomenologie" (discussion review of Dufrenne), in *Kantstudien* (1955–1956), 192–208; E. F. Kaelin, *An Existentialist Aesthetic: The Theories of Sartre and Merleau-Ponty* (Madison, Wis., 1962).

EMPIRICISM

See Douglas Morgan, "Psychology and Art: a Summary and Critique," in *Journal of Aesthetics and Art Criticism,* Vol. 9, No. 2 (December, 1950), 81–96; Douglas Morgan, "Creativity Today," in *Journal of Aesthetics and Art Criticism,* Vol. 12, No. 1 (September, 1953), 1–24; A. R. Chandler, *Beauty and Human Nature* (New York, 1934); C. W. Valentine, *The Experimental Psychology of Beauty* (London, 1962); Edward Bullough, in Elizabeth Wilkinson, ed., *Aesthetics: Lectures and Essays* (London, 1957); William Phillips, ed., *Art and Psychoanalysis* (New York, 1957); D. E. Schneider, *The Psychoanalyst and the Artist* (New York, 1950).

BIBLIOGRAPHIES

For further bibliographies on contemporary aesthetics, see M. C. Beardsley, *Aesthetics* (New York, 1958); Guido Morpurgo-Tagliabue, *L'Esthétique contemporaine* (Milan, 1960).

General Histories

See the following general histories of aesthetics: Katherine Gilbert and Helmut Kuhn, *A History of Aesthetics* (New York, 1939; Bloomington, Ind., 1954); M. C. Beardsley, *Aesthetics from Ancient Greece to the Present* (New York, 1965); Bernard Bosanquet, *A History of Aesthetic* (London, 1892; New York, 1957).

MONROE C. BEARDSLEY

AESTHETICS, PROBLEMS OF. Aesthetics is the branch of philosophy that is concerned with the analysis of concepts and the solution of problems that arise when one contemplates aesthetic objects. Aesthetic objects, in turn, comprise all the objects of aesthetic experience; thus, it is only after aesthetic experience has been sufficiently characterized that one is able to delimit the class of aesthetic objects. Although there are those who deny the existence of any distinctively aesthetic type of experience, they do not deny the possibility of making aesthetic judgments or of giving reasons in support of such judgments; and the term "aesthetic objects" would then include those objects concerning which such judgments and reasons are given.

Aesthetics asks the typically philosophical questions "What do you mean?" and "How do you know?" in the aesthetic domain, just as philosophy of science asks these questions in the scientific domain. Thus, the concepts of aesthetic value, aesthetic experience, as well as the entire battery of concepts occurring specifically in the philosophy of art, are examined in the discipline known as aesthetics, and questions such as "What features make objects beautiful?" and "Are there aesthetic standards?" and "What is the relation of works of art to nature?"—as well as all questions occurring specifically in the philosophy of art—are aesthetic questions.

The philosophy of art covers a somewhat narrower area than does aesthetics, since it is concerned only with the concepts and problems that arise in connection with works of art and excludes, for example, the aesthetic experience of nature. Nevertheless, most of the interesting and perplexing aesthetic questions through the ages have been concerned specifically with art: "What is artistic expression? Is there truth in works of art? What is an artistic symbol? What do works of art mean? Is there a general definition of art? What makes a work of art good?" Although all these questions are questions of aesthetics, they have their locus in art and do not arise in the consideration of aesthetic objects other than works of art.

The philosophy of art should be distinguished carefully from art criticism, which is concerned with the critical analysis and evaluation of works of art themselves, as opposed to an elucidation of the concepts involved in such critical judgments, which is the task of aesthetics. Art criticism is directed toward specific works of art or classes of works of art (for example, those in the same style or genre), and its aim is the enhanced appreciation and greater understanding of these works. The task of the critic presupposes that of the aesthetician, for in discussing and evaluating works of art, the critic employs the concepts that are analyzed and clarified by the philosopher of art. The critic, for example, says that a given work of art is expressive or beautiful; the philosopher of art asks what one means when one says that a work of art has these characteristics and whether and how such statements may be supported. In speaking and writing about art, the art critic presupposes the clarification of the terms he uses, as set forth by the philosopher of art: consequently, the writing of the critic who is not aware of this is liable to lack clarity. If a critic calls a work of art expressive, without being clear about what it means to say this, the result is great conceptual confusion.

THE AESTHETIC

Before considering the aesthetic questions that occur in the philosophy of art, we should consider the question, What is it to view (listen to, etc.) an object aesthetically?, since in the absence of the experience of aesthetic objects, none of the other questions would arise. Is there an aesthetic way of looking at things, and if so, what distinguishes it from other ways of experiencing these things? On this question there have been many different views, usually overlapping but still distinguishable.

Aesthetic and nonaesthetic attitudes. The aesthetic attitude, or the "aesthetic way of looking at the world," is most commonly opposed to the *practical* attitude, which is concerned only with the utility of the object in question. The real estate agent who views a landscape only with an eye to its possible monetary value is not viewing the landscape aesthetically. To view a landscape aesthetically one must "perceive for perceiving's sake," not for the sake of some ulterior purpose. One must savor the experience of perceiving the landscape itself, dwelling on its perceptual details, rather than using the perceptual object as a means to some further end.

> The needs of our actual life are so imperative, that the sense of vision becomes highly specialized in their service. With an admirable economy we learn to see only so much as is needful for our purposes; but this is in fact very little, just enough to recognize and identify each object or person; that done, they go into an entry in our mental catalogue and are no more really seen. In actual life the normal person really only reads the labels as it were on the objects around him and troubles no further. Almost all the things which are useful in any way put on more or less this cap of invisibility. It is only when an object exists in our lives for no other purpose than to be seen that we really look at it, as for instance at a China ornament or a precious stone, and towards such even the most normal person adopts to some extent the artistic attitude of pure vision abstracted from necessity. (Roger Fry, *Vision and Design*, pp. 24–25)

One might object, of course, that even in aesthetic contemplation we are regarding something not "for its own sake" but for the sake of something else, namely, enjoyment. We would not continue to attend to the perceptual object if doing so were not enjoyable; hence, is not enjoyment the end in the aesthetic case? One may indeed so describe it, and perhaps the terminology of "perceiving for its own sake" is a misleading one. Still, there is a difference between savoring the perceptual experience itself and merely using it for purposes of identification, classification, or further action, as we commonly do in daily life when we do not really look at the tree but perceive it only clearly enough to identify it as a tree and then walk around it if it is in our path. The distinction remains, and only the mode of describing it is subject to clarification.

The aesthetic attitude is also distinguished from the cognitive. Students who are familiar with the history of architecture are able to identify quickly a building or a ruin, in regard to its time and place of construction, by means of its style and other visual aspects. They look at the building primarily to increase their knowledge and not to enrich their perceptual experience. This kind of ability may be important and helpful (in passing examinations, for example), but it is not necessarily correlated with the ability to enjoy the experience of simply viewing the building itself. The analytical ability may eventually enhance the aesthetic experience, but it may also stifle it. People who are interested in the arts from a professional or technical aspect are particularly liable to be diverted from the aesthetic way of looking to the cognitive. This leads us directly into a further distinction.

The aesthetic way of looking is also antipathetic to the personal, in which the viewer, instead of regarding the aesthetic object so as to absorb what it has to offer him, considers its relation to himself. Those who do not listen to music but use it as a springboard for their own personal reveries provide an example of this nonaesthetic hearing that often passes for listening. In Edward Bullough's famous example, the man who goes to see a performance of *Othello* and instead of concentrating on the play thinks only of the similarity of Othello's situation to his own real life situation with his wife, is not viewing the play aesthetically. His attitude is one of personal involvement; it is a personalized attitude, and the personalization inhibits whatever aesthetic response the viewer may otherwise have had. In viewing something aesthetically we respond to the aesthetic object and what it has to offer us, not to its relation to our own lives. (The latter often occurs, and it is not necessarily undesirable, but it should be sharply distinguished from the aesthetic response.)

The formula "we should not get personally involved" is sometimes used to describe this criterion, but this too is misleading. It does not mean that a playgoer may not identify with the characters in the play or be vitally interested in what happens to them; it only means that he must not make any personal involvement he may have with the characters or the problems in the play substitute for a careful viewing of the play itself. We can see the difference clearly if we contrast the situation of being involved in a shipwreck with viewing a newsreel of it or a movie about it. In the first case we would do what we could to save our own lives and assist others. In the second case, however, we know that whatever disastrous events occurred have already happened and there is nothing we can do about it now, and realizing this, our tendency to respond to the situation with action is automatically cut off. However much we may identify with the sufferers, we are not personally involved in any sense that is geared to action.

It is evident from the above criteria that many types of responses to objects, including to works of art, are excluded from the realm of the aesthetic. For example, pride of ownership may interfere with the aesthetic response. The person who responds enthusiastically to the playing of a symphony before guests on his own stereo set, but fails to respond to the playing of the same symphony on an identical recording set in his neighbor's house, is not responding aesthetically. The antiquarian or the museum directors who, in choosing a work of art, must attend to historical value, prestige, age, and so on, may be partly influenced by an estimate of its aesthetic value, but his attention is necessarily diverted to nonaesthetic factors. Similarly, if a person values a play or novel because he can glean from it items of information concerning the time and place about which it was written, he is substituting an interest in acquiring knowledge for an interest in aesthetic experience. If a person favors a work of art because it offers moral edification or "supports the right cause," he is confusing a moral attitude with the aesthetic, which is also true if he condemns it on moral grounds and fails to separate this condemnation from his aesthetic evaluation of it. (This is particularly likely to occur with persons who never really view an object aesthetically at all, but simply as a vehicle for propaganda, whether moral, political, or otherwise.)

Other criteria of the aesthetic attitude. Still other terms have been employed to define the aesthetic attitude. "Detachment," for example, is an attitude which is said to distinguish the aesthetic from the nonaesthetic way of looking at things, but this term seems to be more misleading than useful. Like the phrase "not being personally involved," it sounds as though the viewer is not supposed to care greatly about what goes on in the drama or the symphony, whereas there is a sense (as we have seen) in which we are very much involved with the fate of Oedipus when we witness *Oedipus Rex*. We are detached only in the sense in which we know that it is a drama and not real life (although it may be a drama about real life), and that what is on the other side of the footlights is a different world, to which we are not supposed to respond as we do to the practical world around us. In this sense we *are* "detached," but not in the sense of failure to identify with the characters or to be totally absorbed in the drama.

The term "disinterested" is also widely employed to describe the aesthetic attitude. Disinterestedness is a quality of a good judge and occurs when he is impartial. The judge may be personally involved in the sense that he cares deeply about the disposition of a case (for example, who will get custody of the children in a divorce case), but in deciding the case, he must not be personally involved in the sense of letting his personal feelings and sympathies sway him or prejudice him one way or the other. Impartiality in moral and legal matters certainly characterizes what has been called "the moral point of view," but it is far from clear in what way we are supposed to be disinterested (that is, impartial) when we look at a painting or listen to a concert. Impartial as between what conflicting parties? "Judging impartially" makes sense, but what of looking or listening impartially? "Impartial" is a term geared to situations in which there is a conflict between opposing parties in a dispute, but it does not appear to be a very useful term when one is attempting to describe the aesthetic way of looking at things.

Internal and external relations. A somewhat less misleading way of describing the aesthetic experience is in terms of internal versus external relations. When we are viewing a work of art or nature aesthetically, we concentrate on internal relations only, that is, on the aesthetic object and its properties, and not on its relation to ourselves or even its relation to the artist who created it or to our knowledge of the culture from which it sprang. Most works of art are quite complex and require our full attention. The aesthetic state is one of close and complete concentration. Intense perceptual awareness is required, and the aesthetic object and the various relations within it (that is, internal to it) must be the sole focus of our attention. The student who is not accustomed to viewing a nude human figure may be so distracted by seeing nude goddesses in a painting that he cannot view the painting aesthetically. Because of his own impulses, he is bothered by external relations (that is, relations external to the work of art) so that he cannot properly focus his attention upon the object and the perceptual relations internal to it. Sometimes the freedom from awareness of external relations is labeled "aesthetic distance" or "psychical distance," but again, this term may be more misleading than helpful because of the metaphorical use of the term "distance," which implies that we should somehow keep the aesthetic object at arm's length. Moreover, while it may be said that the spectator who identifies with Othello is suffering from lack of distance, the person who is just feeling his way in the appreciation of an art form that is new to him (such as a symphony, when he is not accustomed to hearing more than one melody at a time) may be said to be suffering from too much distance. The meaning of the metaphor "distance" has shifted: in the first case, it refers to the nonpractical way of viewing and in the second case, to lack of familiarity, which is a different matter entirely. (Ambiguities of this type run through Edward Bullough's famous paper "Psychical Distance" and render the use of the term "distance" more confusing than helpful, because the same word is used to cover several different types of attitude which must be carefully distinguished.)

The phenomenal object. Several other attempts to distinguish the aesthetic way of looking at the world from all others have been suggested, either by reference to the attitude itself or by restricting the kind of objects toward which the attitude should be taken.

Aesthetic attention is always to the phenomenal object, not to the physical object (Monroe C. Beardsley, *Aesthetics*, Ch. 1). Without the presence of a physical object, such as paint on canvas, we would not of course perceive any painting, but the attention must be focused on the perceived characteristics, not on the physical characteristics which make the perceived ones possible. Thus, we should concentrate on the color combinations in the painting, but not on the way the paints had to be mixed in order to produce this color, nor anything else involving the chemistry of paints. The latter has to do with the physical basis of the perceptual (i.e., phenomenal) object, rather than with the visual percept itself. Similarly, we may be disturbed because we cannot hear all the instruments in the orchestra from a certain spot in the auditorium, and this is relevant to aesthetic perception because it involves what we hear (or fail to hear). But the investigation of the physical cause of this failure is strictly a physical enterprise, involving a technical knowledge of acoustics; and acoustics is a branch of physics, not of music.

This distinction is surely an important one and serves at least the useful negative function of eliminating certain kinds of attention as being nonaesthetic (such as that of the engineer when he is attempting to remedy the acoustics of an auditorium). That which cannot be perceived (seen, heard, etc.) is not relevant to aesthetic perception because it makes no difference to the nature of the "sensuous presentation" before us. The fact that the painter had to use a very difficult method to get his painting to look "shimmering" is not a relevant aesthetic consideration; it may lead us to admire the painter for undertaking a difficult task, but not to admire the painting itself any more than we did before. However, the fact that the completed painting, as perceived by us, has a "shimmering" look, is aesthetically relevant, for this is a part of what we perceive. But it is still not entirely clear what precisely the criterion includes or excludes. When I focus attention on the color combinations in a painting, or on the harmony of the shapes, I am clearly attending to perceptual phenomena; but what if I also enjoy the painting because of its prevailing mood? or music, not because it is fast or slow, but because it is sad? or dislike a poem because it is sentimental, maudlin, or "phony"? Are these, or is the apprehension of these, aesthetic? Although they are not characteristics of the physical object, are they to be classified as phenomenal?

Indeed, there has been considerable controversy over whether aesthetic attention is limited to the perceptual at all. In the case of perceiving the color combination or the formal arrangement of parts in a painting, it is certainly so; we are concentrating on the perceived (or at any rate perceivable) qualities of the aesthetic object. But must there be, in every case, a perceptual object at all in order for aesthetic attention to be possible? Granted that if we savor the intense color, shape, contour, and even the apparent delicacy and grace of a rose, this is perceptual, while if we attend to its hardiness or disease-resistant qualities, this is not; so far the distinction seems clear. But when we say that a symphony is heroic, that a play is melodramatic, and that a painting is suffused with *joie de vivre*, is not the kind of attention that results in this description aesthetic also? Yet it is difficult to see how the "heroic quality" is perceptual. To be sure, we apprehend it, if at all, by means of noting the music's perceived qualities, but it is also through perception that we are aware of an object's physical qualities, which are not supposed to be relevant to aesthetic attention.

When we enjoy or appreciate the elegance of a mathematical proof, it would surely seem that our enjoyment is aesthetic, although the object of that enjoyment is not perceptual at all: it is the complex relation among abstract ideas or propositions, not the marks on paper or the blackboard, that we are apprehending aesthetically. It would seem that the appreciation of neatness, elegance, or economy of means is aesthetic whether it occurs in a perceptual object (such as a sonata) or in an abstract entity (such as a logical proof), and if this is so, the range of the aesthetic cannot be limited to the perceptual.

Moreover, what of the art of literature? No one would wish to say that our appreciation of literature is nonaesthetic, and yet the "aesthetic object" in the case of literature does not consist of visual or auditory percepts. It is not sounds or marks on paper, but their *meanings* that constitute the medium of literature, and meanings are not concrete objects or percepts. In this respect, the distinction between literature and all the other arts is a very great one, so much so that the auditory and visual arts have been called sensory arts (consisting of sensuous presentations to the eye or ear), as distinguished from literature, which is an ideo-sensory art (T. E. Jessop, "The Definition of Beauty," *PAS*, Vol. 33, 1932–1933, 170–171). Because the reading of the words evokes sensuous images in the minds of readers, so that there are percepts after all (imagined ones, but still sensuous, as in dreams), it has been suggested that literature *is* actually sensory. This suggestion, however, is hardly plausible, for many readers can read appreciatively and intelligently without having any visual or other images evoked in their minds. Is the attention of such readers therefore to be dismissed as being non-aesthetic? It would appear that the reader of literature must, at the very least, focus attention upon words and their meanings (some would say, on words only as vehicles for their meanings), but these are not percepts in the way that colors, shapes, sounds, tastes, and smells are. The inclusion of literature in the category of the perceptual by means of some image evocation theory constitutes a desperate attempt to make the facts fit a theory. However, the dismissal of literature as not being the object of aesthetic attention because of its nonperceptual character would seem to be a prime case of throwing the baby out with the bath water.

Sense modality. Within the sense domain, attempts have been made to restrict the area of aesthetic attention by means of sense modality—specifically, to include vision and hearing as acceptable and to dismiss smell, taste, and touch (the "lower" senses) as unacceptable for aesthetic attention. But this suggestion also seems doomed to failure. What reason could be offered for denying that the enjoyment of smell, taste, and touch is aesthetic? Is not the savoring of the smell of a rose or the taste of a wine aesthetic? We can enjoy tastes and smells just as we enjoy sights and sounds—for their own sakes alone, or, if one prefers, for the sake of enjoyment only. It is true that works of art have not, on the whole, been produced in sensuous media other than the visual and auditory; for example, we do not have "smell symphonies." There are various reasons for this: (1) It is more difficult in this instance to separate the practical from the nonpractical—for example, to separate the enjoyment of food because we are hungry from the enjoyment of it because it tastes good. The "lower" senses are so closely connected with the fulfillment of bodily needs that it is difficult to isolate the strictly aesthetic enjoyment derived from them. (In the case of a wine, however, it may be argued that we do not ordinarily drink it because we are thirsty, but simply because we enjoy it for its own sake.) (2) Perceptually, even if not physically, the data of the "lower" senses are less complex, so that the perceived elements do not lend themselves to the complex formal arrangement that is so characteristic of works of art. In a series of smells and tastes, there is a "before" and "after," but not much beside this strictly serial order—that is, there is no "harmony" or "counterpoint." Colors and sounds, however, fall into a complex order, enabling us to make fine distinctions between countless visual and auditory sensations. This type of distinction makes possible the apprehension of a great formal complexity in works of visual and auditory art which it is impossible for human perceivers to apprehend in the other sense modalities. In this instance, we refer to a phenomenal rather than to a physical order, for there are exact physical correlates for experienced smells just as there are for sounds (pitch, volume, timbre) and colors (hue, saturation, brightness). But if precise distinctions among these sensory data cannot be made in the case of smell and taste, they are unavailable for the use of human perceivers, even though an exact order of physical correlates exists equally for all of them.

Denials of distinct aesthetic attitude. Some writers have despaired of finding any criteria at all for distinguishing an aesthetic attitude from other kinds of attitudes. For example, some aestheticians have denied that there is any distinctively aesthetic attitude at all (J. O. Urmson, "What Makes a Situation Aesthetic?" *PAS*, Suppl. Vol. 31, 1957). They find the distinguishing characteristic of the aesthetic not in any attitude, experience, or mode of attention that observers may have, but in the reasons they give to support their judgments—that is, aesthetic reasons, moral reasons, economic reasons, and so forth. Although most aestheticians agree that there are distinctively aesthetic reasons, they go further and hold that these reasons presuppose a type of attitude or attention that is given to objects (that is, a way of perceiving) which, although difficult to identify precisely and even more difficult to explain verbally without being misleading, does exist and distinguishes this one mode of attention from all others. It has also been held that there is no such thing as a distinctively aesthetic attitude, unless one simply defines it as "paying close attention" to the work of art (or nature) in question (George Dickie, "The Myth of the Aesthetic Attitude," *American Philosophical Quarterly*, Vol. 1, No. 1, 1964, 56–65). There is no special kind of attention to objects that can be called aesthetic; there is only "paying close attention to the qualities of the object" as against failure to do so. According to this view, we may come to a work of art with various motives that can be distinguished from one another, but there is no special type of attention in the witnessing of a play that distinguishes, for example, the spectator from the play producer or the playwright in search of ideas: the type of attention is the same in all cases, that is, all should concentrate carefully upon the aesthetic object. The distinction between viewing aesthetically and nonaesthetically becomes strictly a motivational distinction, not a perceptual one.

PHILOSOPHY OF ART

We speak of the philosophy of art, but what is art? In its broadest sense, art includes everything that is made by man, as opposed to the workings of nature. In this sense, paintings, houses, atomic reactors, cities, matchboxes, ships, and piles of garbage are art, whereas trees, animals, stars, and ocean waves are not. It was in this sense that André Gide said, "The only unnatural thing in the world is a work of art," and it is in this sense that his statement is a tautology. (A borderline case is the work of animals, such as beaver dams, which would be included under art if "man-made" were extended to mean "made by sentient beings," but otherwise not.)

The quality of being man-made constitutes one necessary condition for an object's being called a work of art. If what we thought was a piece of sculpture turns out to be a piece of driftwood, we would continue to regard it as an aesthetic object, and it would still be as beautiful (or ugly) as before, but it would not be a work of art. Other restricting conditions, however, are much more controversial: there have been endless definitions of "art" in the history of aesthetic theory, and of most of them it can be said that we are more certain that a given work is or is not a work of art than we are that the proffered definition is satisfactory. As with so many other terms (for example, "romanticism"), we are surer of the term's denotation (i.e., what instances it covers) than we are of its designation (i.e., the criterion by which certain works would be included and others excluded). Moreover, as we shall shortly see, many definitions of art are stated in terms of some specific theory of art and, accordingly, depend on the correctness of that theory. Most such theories are best regarded as generalizations *about* art, of the form "Everything that is a work of art *also* has such-and-such characteristics," rather than as definitions with which we should begin. Any such generalization, in fact, when it uses the term "art," presupposes some already existing meaning for the term, rather than assigning a meaning to the term in the first place. Those who thus "define" art must presuppose some rough working definition of the term, at any rate, or their readers will not know what the generalization is about.

In any case, in aesthetic theory we are concerned with a far narrower range of objects than the total array of man-made things, or, perhaps more precisely, with a far narrower function of objects. We are concerned with man-made things only to the extent that they can be regarded aesthetically. Now it may be that all objects can be so regarded, but it is quite certain that they do not all (or at least not all equally) repay aesthetic scrutiny. It is also quite certain that there are many ways in which to regard the objects of man's making other than the aesthetic way. The field must be narrowed, then, to exclude, if not the vast majority of man-made objects, at least the vast majority of ways of regarding them.

We are primarily concerned with what has been called (somewhat unfortunately, perhaps) *fine* art. Fine art might be distinguished from art in the broad sense by saying that the objects of fine art are those which were created in order to be viewed, read, or heard aesthetically. The painting was intended to be viewed, studied, enjoyed, savored—not to be used as a washboard or table top. Nevertheless, to distinguish a class of objects solely on the basis of the intention of the creators of those objects is always dangerous: it is often difficult to say what the intention was, and it sometimes happens that the intention was very different from what one would have inferred from viewing the object. Some art—indeed, perhaps some of the greatest art—was created in order to convert men to Christianity or to communism or to edify and ennoble their characters, rather than to be viewed aesthetically (or, possibly, to do both simultaneously). The fact that certain Egyptian temples were built in order to honor the god Isis does not prevent us from viewing them as works of art; we view them today in a way that is probably greatly at variance with the original intention of the designers and builders.

The most plausible distinguishing mark of fine art is not what it was intended to do, but how it actually does function in our experience. What can one do with symphonies but hear and enjoy them? What else are they good for? They function by producing aesthetic responses in listeners, and not in any other distinctive way. Works of fine art may be defined, accordingly, as those man-made objects that function either entirely or primarily *aesthetically* in human experience.

As opposed to fine art, we may distinguish what has historically been called "useful" art. All objects of useful art serve some purpose in the life of man other than that of being viewed aesthetically, though as a secondary function they can also be viewed aesthetically. Automobiles, glass tumblers, baskets, vases, handicraft of all kinds, and countless other items are examples of useful art. Many of them are rewarding to the aesthetically sensitive eye, but they all serve some nonaesthetic purpose, and when one contemplates them their practical function should not be forgotten.

There are, to be sure, "straddling" cases, of which architecture is perhaps the principal one. Some have held that architecture is first and foremost a fine art, that buildings are primarily aesthetic objects and are only incidentally to be lived in or worshiped in; others have held that buildings are primarily objects of utility and that their aesthetic function is incidental. This has long been a subject of controversy among architects themselves: the department of architecture in some universities is placed in the school of liberal arts, and in others, in the school of engineering.

When an aesthetic object is also a useful object, the relation of its practical function to its aesthetic character becomes an important one. The controversy about functionalism in art has to do with the relation of the practical function to the aesthetic. The question is, should form always follow function, or should the form of the object be regarded relatively independently of the practical function that it serves. In regard to works of fine art, upon which philosophers of art have focused most of their attention, this problem does not occur, for it is in this area that the aesthetic character of objects, whatever it is, exists without admixture.

Classification of the arts. The fine arts may be classified in a variety of ways, but the nature of the medium in which they are created is perhaps the safest guide.

Auditory arts include all the arts of sound, which, for all practical purposes, means music. Music consists of musical tones—that is, sounds of a definite pitch—together with rests, presented in a temporally successive order.

Visual arts include all those arts that consist, phenomenally, of visual percepts. Their appeal is primarily to the eye, although not exclusively, because some may also appeal to the sense of touch. The visual arts include a wide variety of genres—painting, sculpture, architecture, as well as virtually all of the useful arts.

Literature is much more difficult to classify. It is certainly not a visual art: indeed, a poem need not be written down at all. Neither is literature an auditory art. It is often true that a poem's effect is enhanced when it is read aloud, but its value is not decreased when it is not read aloud, nor need it be read aloud to function as a poem. If literature were an auditory art it would belong with the art of music; and for sheer auditory delight poetry can hardly compare with musical compositions. Musically, the English language for example, is a rather poor thing, and one who heard the sounds of an English poem without knowing the meaning of the words would soon experience boredom. Virtually all of the effect of poetry, which we might at first attribute to the sounds themselves (the auditory element), is actually due to the meaning of the words. As I. A. Richards has pointed out, "deep within a gloomy grot" sounds not very different from "peep within a roomy cot." If the word "sea" is a poetic word, it is not because the sound of this monosyllable strikes us as beautiful, but because we know what the word means, and it serves to evoke thoughts and images of the tropical sea, the stormy sea, the sunset sea, and so on. It is the meaning—both the literal meanings of the words and the associations that surround the word in the minds of those who are acquainted with the language in which the poem is written—that distinguishes literature from all the other arts. Literature has been called a symbolic art; it derives its distinctive mediumistic character from the fact that all of its elements are words, and words are not mere noises or pen marks, but noises with meanings that have to be known before the poem can be understood or appreciated.

Mixed arts include all those arts which combine one or more of the above media. Thus, opera includes music, words, and visual designs, although the music is predominant. Stage plays combine the art of literature with stagecraft and visual design. In the dance, visual patterns normally take precedence, while the music is an accompaniment. In motion pictures all the elements are present.

The kind of job that each art can perform depends primarily upon the nature of the medium. Thus, visual arts in general are arts of space and can depict the visual appearance or "look" of objects far better than any description can. On the other hand, they cannot depict motion, or sequences of events, in time; this can be done in literature, in which the order of the elements in the medium is temporally sequential. In a painting our attention is sequential, since we can concentrate now on one portion and now on another. However, the entire painting is before us all the time, and there is no prescribed order, such as left to right, in which we must view it; indeed, if we attend to its parts sequentially at first, this is only in order that we may later apprehend it as a whole. The effect of viewing a work of sculpture often depends on the direction in which we go round it, and since we cannot view the entire three-dimensional object at once, the temporal aspect is more important than it is in a painting. Music is as inextricably committed to a temporal order of tones as literature is to a temporal order of words; we could no more reverse the order of two tones in a melody than we could reverse two words in a sentence.

Although mixed arts combine more than one kind of medium, they have distinctive functions which are not duplicated by any of the other arts. Motion pictures possess an enormous mediumistic advantage in that they can depict spatial relations and temporal sequences of events at the same time. Drama can do the same. Yet that which is appropriate to the medium of drama may be most inappropriate to the medium of cinema. An excellent stage play, if transcribed directly to the screen, will usually result in a mediocre motion picture; the principal advantage of drama—living contact with living actors—is totally lost in the more impersonal medium of cinema, which can, however, make up for this disadvantage by countless devices not available on the stage.

Students of the arts have drawn different conclusions from these facts about the nature of the artistic media. The aesthetic "purists," following the lead of the essay *Laokoon* by the eighteenth-century German dramatist and critic Gottfried Lessing, view with revulsion any attempt to make a work of art transcend the limits of its own distinctive medium. Thus, they contend, poems should not attempt to depict the exact visual appearances of things, a function reserved for the visual arts; nor should visual arts attempt to render motion, which is reserved for literature; neither should music attempt to have a program and tell stories, which is also for literature; nor should movies forsake their distinctive capacity to render motion in favor of conversation among the characters. Opponents of this view argue that such rules may be broken to advantage, and that while each art medium admittedly has its own distinctive capacities, there is no reason why one art medium should not adopt devices that another art would admittedly be able to accomplish better. Lessing's advice, according to this view, is a counsel of perfection that would eliminate many great works of art and many interesting experiments as well. Wagner, for example, was convinced (although in this he was undoubtedly mistaken) that in his musical dramas he was creating a super-art in which the auditory, the visual, and the literary were all of equal importance.

Concepts and media. Because of the differences among the media of the various arts, there are concepts which apply in a straightforward manner to one or more of the arts but not at all, or in a different sense, to other arts. Some of the most important examples follow.

Subject matter. The subject matter of a work of art is what it is about. A person who read a work of literature without attempting to interpret it could still state its subject matter: for example, the *Odyssey* is about the wanderings of Odysseus. Any work of fiction has some subject matter; it may or may not have in addition a theme, or underlying idea, which is either explicitly stated or implicitly present in the work. Whether the *Odyssey* has a theme as well as subject matter is a matter of conjecture, but often the issue is clear: for example, the subject matter of Bunyan's *Pilgrim's Progress* is a series of events in the life of a man named Christian, while the theme of the work is man's salvation. In addition, a work of literature may also have a thesis, that is, a proposition or set of propositions which it presents, attacks, or defends. A thesis, too, may be implicit as well as explicit: the thesis of *Pilgrim's Progress* is repeatedly stated, whereas the thesis of many of Hardy's novels—that man is caught in the toils of a hostile "fate" which controls his life and from which he cannot escape—is seldom or never stated explicitly.

Not all works of art have subject matter: poems, plays, and novels are always about something, but most musical works are not: Beethoven's Symphony No. 5 is not about man's fate, heroism, or any of the things that have sometimes been suggested as its subject matter. Some paintings, especially nonrepresentational paintings consisting of colors and shapes, are not about anything, but others do have subject matter (for example, the Crucifixion). The term "theme" is often used in music, but in this instance it has an entirely different meaning; when we speak of a composition's "thematic material" we are speaking not of any underlying idea nor of anything beyond it presented through the medium, but of a series of tones within the medium itself.

Representation. Visual art can quite literally be said to represent objects in the world. Strictly speaking, painting presents a series of colors and shapes which we then interpret or construe as representations of various objects from life. Not all paintings, to be sure, are representational. But many works of painting, sculpture, and other visual arts do clearly represent objects in nature. The sense in which they do this, however, is not always the same: there is a difference between depicting an object and portraying it. A painting, let us say, depicts a dark-haired man clad in a toga. But the same painting may also be said to represent Julius Caesar—that is, it may be said to portray Julius Caesar. Portrayal is a trickier concept: the painter may change the title of a painting without changing the painting itself, so that what is said to be portrayed changes (for example, a man dressed up to look like Julius Caesar). What is depicted can be inferred from looking at the painting, plus a certain amount of knowledge of the world; what is portrayed can usually be inferred only from the title. If the title were changed, the portrayal subject would be different, but that which was depicted would remain the same.

In regard to music, it is doubtful whether we should speak of representation at all. Nature does not produce musical sounds: these are produced only by man-made instruments (a clarinet sounds like nothing except a clarinet). Nature does indeed present us with sounds, but these are primarily noises rather than musical tones, and it is of the latter that music is composed. Music, then, presents us with a wide variety of musical sounds which do not, however, represent.

There is, to be sure, program music—that is, music with a title that indicates some subject. But what exactly is the connection between a work of music and its "program"? Only that in the music we hear a variety of tones, which, with the help of the title (and almost never without it), may remind us of, or evoke in us the impression of, the subject indicated in the title. The same music with a different title might remind us of something else and channel our mental associations in an entirely different direction. Perhaps the closest resemblance between musical tones and things in nature lies in certain rhythms: the galloping of horses' hoofs may be paralleled by certain rhythmic patterns in a musical composition. The musical value of such representation, however, is highly questionable.

The case of literature is still different, for it can only be called representational in a more indirect way. Literature cannot present visual representations as painting and sculpture do; anything that may be said to be represented must be represented by means of verbal symbols. In this sense, however, it is convenient, and perhaps not too misleading, to say that one of Fielding's novels represents the adventures of its hero, Tom Jones, and many other characters, or, more precisely, that it depicts a set of people of such-and-such descriptions involved in such-and-such adventures, and that it portrays Tom Jones and a number of other characters. But there is no particular point in distinguishing between depiction and portrayal in literature, since the reference to Tom Jones occurs in the medium (i.e., words), whereas in the visual arts the portrayal subject is known only from the title, which is not a part of the visual medium itself. In a work of literature the portrayal subject could not be changed without changing the words in the novel itself.

Meaning. "What does a work of art mean?" is a question full of traps for the unwary. In the straightforward sense of conventional reference, the only art in which meanings occur is literature. The elements which constitute literature have meanings in a sense that does not apply to any of the other arts. The word "cat" has a meaning, but the musical tone of middle C and a jagged line do not: they may evoke various responses, but they have no conventional reference.

But when we ask what a work of art means as a whole, we are not talking about conventional symbols. In asking this question about a work of art, we may intend any of the following: (1) We may be asking "What is it about?"—a question which can be answered by stating the work's subject matter, in those cases in which it has one; (2) We may be asking "What is its theme?"—for example, whether the motion picture *He Who Must Die* is really about Christ; (3) We may be asking for the thesis, or central proposition(s) stated or implied in the work—for example, whether the thesis of a particular poem is that childhood is the happiest time of life; (4) We may be asking, "What kind of effect does (or should) the work have on the audience?"—a sense in which all works of art have meaning, since they all have effects, but one which cannot be stated in words. If one wants to know what a symphony "means" in this sense, one can only listen carefully to it while it is played. However, this is an extremely misleading use of the word "meaning." Doubtless, each work of art has unique and induplicable effects, but if this is what the critic wishes to say, why does he not say it in so many words? Many persons who wish to attribute "meanings" to even the most abstract musical composition seem to assume that a work of art is not quite worthwhile and has not really earned its right to our attention unless they can read into it, or attribute to it, a particular "meaning."

Aspects of works of art. There are several distinguishable ways in which we can attend to works of art, or, stated otherwise, there are several different kinds of values which art has to render us, which are worth distinguishing in aesthetic analysis. The following, at any rate, can be fruitfully distinguished.

Sensuous values. Sensuous values in a work of art (or in nature) are apprehended by an aesthetic observer when he enjoys or takes satisfaction in the purely sensuous (not sensual) characteristics of the phenomenal object. In the appreciation of sensuous values, the complex formal relationships within the work of art are not the object of attention, nor are any ideas or emotions which the work of art may embody. We find sensuous values in a work of art when we delight in texture, color, and tone: the sheen of jade, the rough-hewn quality of wood, the deep blue of the sky, the visual and tactile qualities of ivory or marble, or the timbre of a violin. It is not the physical object per se that delights us; it is the sensuous presentation (that is, the phenomenal object, rather than the physical object).

Formal values. The appreciation of sensuous values quickly becomes involved in the appreciation of formal values. We do not long remain enraptured by the quality of single tones or colors, but soon notice the relations among these elements. A melody consists of tone relations and is radically altered the moment any tone in the system of tone relations is changed to even a small degree. On the other hand, a melody survives many changes of key, in which the individual tones are all different from the ones in the original key, and yet is readily recognizable as the same melody—that is, as the same series of tone relations.

The term "form" has a somewhat different meaning in connection with works of art from its meaning in nonaesthetic contexts. Thus, "form" does not mean the same as "shape," not even in the visual arts. The form has to do with the total interrelations of parts, the over-all *organization* of the work, of which the shapes—even in visual art—are only one aspect. If the form in a painting were defined as its shape, or even the totality of shapes in it, this would not account for the colors whose boundaries constitute the shapes and which are as important to the formal organization of the painting as are the shapes. Nor does form refer to structural form, as it does in logic and mathematics, when we speak of different arguments or different formulas in the same form. It is true that many works of art do have certain structural properties in common, and in this sense we do speak of "forms of art," such as musical compositions in the sonata form. But when we speak of the particular form of an individual work of art, we refer to its own unique mode of organization and not to the type of organization that it shares with other works of art.

It is useful, in this connection, to distinguish "form-in-the-large" (structure) from "form-in-the-small" (texture). When we speak of the structure of a work of art, we mean the over-all organization that results from the interrelations of the basic elements of which it is composed. Thus, a melody is but one item in the structure of a symphony, although a melody too is composed of related parts and constitutes "form-in-the-small." What is considered but one element in the structure is considered as a whole in the texture—a whole which in turn can be broken up and analyzed, as a melody or a phrase in a poem is analyzed.

The distinction between structure and texture is admittedly relative, for one could question how large a part must be before it constitutes a single element in the structure—whether it must be a single melody, a single stanza, or one-eighth of a painting. Nevertheless, the distinction is useful: we may often wish to distinguish, for example, the work of those composers who are masters of structure and less adept at texture from the work of those composers of whom the opposite is true. Beethoven was a master of musical structure, although often the melodic material which constitutes his building blocks is extremely unpromising and is unrewarding to listen to by itself. On the other hand, Schubert and Schumann were masters of texture and melodic material, but often failed to unify these elements in an aesthetically satisfying over-all structure.

We cannot grasp the important concept of form in art without mentioning some of the principal critera that critics and aestheticians have employed in analyzing aesthetic form. What, then, are the principles of form by which a work of art is to be judged, at least in its formal aspect? Many writers have offered various suggestions on this matter, but the central criterion, and the one most universally recognized, is unity (sometimes called organic unity). Unity is the opposite of chaos, confusion, disharmony: when an object is unified, it can be said to hang together, be of one piece, contain nothing superfluous. However, this condition must be specified further: a blank white wall or an undifferentiated blue sky has unity in the sense that there is nothing to disrupt it. But this is hardly what is desired in works of art, which usually have great formal complexity. Accordingly, the usual formula is "variety in unity." The unified object should contain within itself a large number of diverse elements, each of which in some way contributes to the total integration of the unified whole, so that there is no confusion despite the disparate elements within the object. In the unified object, everything that is necessary is there, and nothing that is not necessary is there.

Usually the adjective "organic" is prefixed to the noun "unity." Since a work of art is not an organism, the term is clearly metaphorical. The fact on which the analogy is based is that in living organisms, the interaction of the various parts is interdependent, not independent. No part functions in isolation; each part or element interacts with every other part in such a way that a change in one of them makes a difference to all, or in other words, the parts are internally, not externally, related. The functioning of the stomach depends on the functioning of the heart, the liver, and other organs of the body, and the malfunction of one of these involves the malfunctioning of the others as well. Similarly, in a work of art, if a certain yellow patch were not in a painting, its entire character would be altered, and so would a play if a particular scene were not in it, in just the place where it is.

It is quickly apparent that no organism is a perfect organic unity; some parts are clearly more important than others. The same is true of works of art: some lines in a poem are less important than others (the catalogue of ships in the *Iliad*, for example), and their alteration or removal would not destroy the aesthetic effect of the poem, or even, on occasion, damage it at all. In works of art there are high spots and low spots, more integrated and less integrated parts; but this is only to say that works of art, like organisms, are not examples of perfect organic unity. Whether they ever should be is a moot question (see Catherine Lord, "Organic Unity Reconsidered," *Journal of Aesthetics and Art Criticism*, Vol. 22 [1964], 263–268); perhaps the ideal is not only impossible but undesirable. Most works of art, at any rate, subsist on something much less than complete organic unity, although some seem to approach the ideal very closely.

Still, unity is an important formal property of works of art; a work is never praised simply for being disunified or disorganized. If a less unified work is considered better than a more unified one, it is in spite of the former's lack of unity, not because of it; the presence of factors other than unity is held to outweigh the lesser degree of unity that exists in the former case.

Clearly, unity is a value concept. It means, for example, that in a good melody, or painting, or poem, one could not change a part without damaging (not merely changing) the whole, for of course any whole, even a collection of disparate parts, would be changed somewhat if any part of it were to be changed.

Although unity is important as a formal criterion, it is not the only one that critics employ in assessing works of art. As to others, there is no unanimity among the critics themselves. DeWitt Parker, in a well-known essay on aesthetic form in his book *The Analysis of Art*, holds that the other principles are subsidiary to the one main principle of organic unity. These other principles include: (1) theme—a theme or dominant motif which stands out in a work of art; (2) thematic variation—variation (rather than mere repetition) which introduces novelty, and which should be based on the theme in order to retain unity; (3) balance—the arrangement of the various parts in an aesthetically pleasing order (for example, not all the interesting things in a painting are on one side); (4) development or evolution—each part of a temporal work of art is necessary to the succeeding parts, so that if any earlier portion were altered or deleted, all later portions would have to be altered in consequence. Everything that occurs before is an indispensable prerequisite for what occurs later.

Formal criteria have also been discussed by Stephen Pepper in his book *Principles of Art Appreciation*. Employing a psychological approach, Pepper holds that the two enemies of aesthetic experience are monotony and confusion; the way to avoid monotony is variety, and the way to avoid confusion is unity. A delicate balance between these two qualities must be maintained: interest cannot be sustained by mere repetition, and for this reason the thematic material must be varied; yet the variations must be integrally related to the theme, for an anchor of unity must be present in order to keep the work from "flying to the four winds." Pepper invokes four main principles. To avoid both monotony and confusion, the artist must employ (1) contrast among the parts and (2) gradation—transitions from one sense quality to another (for example, red to pink in a painting) that introduce change within a basic unity. He must also employ (3) theme and variation—theme, to retain a unified base, and variation, also to avoid monotony; and (4) restraint—economy in expenditure of interest so that it will be adequately distributed over the whole duration and extent of the work of art and the "store of interest" of the spectator will not be used up too quickly.

Much more could be said about form in art, and we shall return to the subject when we discuss formalism as a theory of art. Meanwhile, a third type of value to be found in works of art should be mentioned.

Life values. Sensuous and formal values are both mediumistic: they are concerned with what the work of art contains in its very medium—that is, colors and shapes, tones and rests, the words in a poem and their arrangement. But there are other values imported from the life outside art, and these are not contained in the medium but are conveyed through the medium. For example, works of art that are representative (such as a painting of the Crucifixion) cannot be fully appreciated unless we have a certain amount of knowledge of the life outside art. Also, concepts and ideas may be presented, particularly in works of literature. Further, art may "contain" (in a sense to be explored later) feelings: music may be sad, playful, melancholy, vivacious, sprightly; the mood of a painting may be prevailingly playful or somber, and so may that of a poem. In regard to all of these values, a certain amount of acquaintance with the life outside art is required, and therefore the values here presented are called life values. (Sometimes they are called associational values, because they are said to be associated in the mind of the observer with items in the medium rather than being directly contained in the medium; but this term is somewhat unfortunate, since it prejudges the question of whether they do arise through a process of association—for example, whether the sadness is associated with the music rather than being in some sense contained or embodied in it.) More will be said about these values when we discuss theories of art.

Contextualism versus isolationism. With what things outside the work of art must be we acquainted in order to appreciate a work of art? The issue is not whether the work of art should be the focus of our attention: if we are viewing the work aesthetically, presumably it should. If the work of art is used merely as a vehicle for acquiring historical knowledge about the period or facts about the author's life or his unconscious motives, then the work is not being apprehended aesthetically at all. (Of course, it can be apprehended aesthetically and *also* as a source of historical or biographical information.)

Isolationism is the view that in order to appreciate a work of art, we need do nothing but look at it, hear it, or read it—sometimes again and again, with the most concentrated attention—and that we need not go outside it to consult the facts of history, biography, or anything else. (If it is necessary to do this, the work of art is not self-sufficient and hence it is artistically defective.) The English art critic Clive Bell, for example, held that to appreciate a work of art (and in this instance he was speaking primarily of the visual arts, and deliberately excluding literature) we need bring with us nothing whatever from the world and our store of the world's knowledge, except, in the case of some paintings, an acquaintance with three-dimensional space (he held that some paintings require a knowledge that the two-dimensional presentation on canvas is a representation of spatial depth not given on the canvas itself). A work of visual art should be approached as an exercise in pure form, and if one brings a knowledge of the world to a work of art, this knowledge will fill the observer's mind with irrelevancies that distract him from the contemplation of the formal relations in the painting.

In contrast to this view, contextualism holds that a work of art should be apprehended in its total context or setting, and that much historical and other knowledge "feeds into" the work of art, making the total experience of it richer than if it were approached without such knowledge. All appreciation of works of art should be in context, even the appreciation of pure music and nonrepresentational painting.

It is not necessary for a critic to hold either position in

its pure or undiluted form: one may be an isolationist about some works of art, or types of works of art, and a contextualist about others. Let us be more specific, however, about the kinds of factors (other than a careful perusal of the work of art itself) which, according to the contextualist, may be necessary, or at the very least helpful, in the appreciation of works of art.

(1) Other works of art by the same artist. If the same artist has created other works, particularly in the same genre, according to the contextualist it may enhance our appreciation to compare or contrast them with one another, even while we are attending to just one of them. Sheer quantity of works has, of course, no merit in itself; yet when one is listening to any one of Mozart's piano concertos, one may (more unconsciously than consciously) compare its general mood, its thematic material, its mode of development and resolution, with some of the 26 other concertos that Mozart composed: In this case, knowledge of the complete body of works may heighten one's enjoyment of the individual work.

(2) Other works of art in the same medium by other artists, especially in the same style or the same tradition. Our appreciation of Milton's "Lycidas" is enhanced by a study of the pastorals of Vergil, and indeed by a study of the entire pastoral tradition in poetry. According to contextualists, to study "Lycidas" in isolation from this tradition would needlessly deprive us of much of the richness in the poem and, indeed, would make some of the references in it unintelligible.

Thus far, the extensions, from our original attention to the work of art only, have been to other works of art, not to the background of works of art. At this point, however, we come to items which are not works of art at all.

(3) A study of what one might call "external facts about the artistic medium"—for example, a study of the instrumental limitations or advantages of pipe organs in Bach's time or knowledge of the dramatic conventions of the Elizabethan theater as a background for reading or viewing Shakespeare's plays. An acquaintance with the artistic conventions, limitations, or idioms in which the artist operated often leads to a better understanding of the work and puts one in a better position to appreciate it, rather than merely to have extraneous knowledge about it; and negatively, knowledge of facts of this kind will often help to avoid misunderstanding or misinterpreting it.

(4) A study of the age in which the artist lived—the spirit of the times, the ideas then current, the complex influences that molded the artist. The contextualist would say that a knowledge of these factors may often be helpful. Is it not important for us to know that Milton was aware of the new Copernican astronomy, but deliberately chose to make his cosmos in *Paradise Lost* Ptolemaic? The isolationist would say that this is merely "background material," interesting enough in its own right as history or biography but not relevant to the aesthetic experience of the work of art, whereas the contextualist would say that our aesthetic experience of the work of art is richer because we have this background knowledge.

(5) A study of the artist's life. Anthologists of literature constantly assume that this is an important consideration, since they append detailed biographies to the selected samples of poetry and prose by each author. It is true (as isolationists repeatedly emphasize) that knowledge of the artist's life can distract our attention from the work of art. Yet it may also be true that such knowledge (for instance, of Milton's ideals and struggles) may heighten our experience of the created work. In this case, the aesthetic relevance of such knowledge is the point of dispute, although the contextualist will say that even in the case of music, which is the most autonomous of the arts, a knowledge of Beethoven's life will enhance our appreciation of his music. The knowledge, of course, must be a means, and the enhanced appreciation the end, and not the other way round, as it is when an artist's work is simply used—for example, to establish some thesis in psychoanalytic theory. The facts about the artist's life should be used to "illuminate" the work.

(6) A study of the artist's intentions. Especially important among the facts about the artist's life is a knowledge of what the artist intended his work to be, to do, or to achieve. Hence, critics have paid special attention to records, left to us by the artist or his contemporaries, of what the artist intended to convey in his work, especially if the work itself is obscure or difficult.

Isolationists held that if one must look outside the work of art in order to understand what it should achieve, this constitutes an artistic defect: the work of art is not "standing on its own." The person who feels that he needs such knowledge is committing "the intentional fallacy"—the fallacy of requiring a knowledge of what the artist intended before one is in a position to appreciate his work. In this instance, the isolationist has a plausible case; many critics, at any rate, would hold it to be a defect in a work of art if one cannot infer its meaning, message, or general import from a careful perusal of the work itself. A work of art, they would say, should be a self-contained and self-sufficient entity. On the other hand, the contextualist will argue that even though ideally the artist's intentions should be manifest in his work, still we should not condemn or dismiss a work of art because of a failure in this respect, if it proves to be much worth appreciating once we have learned the artist's intentions. If we are told that Prokofiev intended his "Classical Symphony" to be a parody of classical symphonies, we may enjoy it ever so much more; the hint is helpful regardless of the source from which we obtain it. The contextualist would say that it is simply self-limiting to reject information that might heighten an aesthetic experience, whether or not we fall into an "intentional fallacy."

The contextualist is not, of course, comitted to subscribe to any particular set of evaluative criteria, such as the one set forth by the poet Goethe: (1) What was the artist trying (intending) to do? (2) Did he do it? and (3) Was it worth doing? What the artist intended is in and of itself of no consequence at all: he might have intended one thing and achieved something quite different, or he might have intended to create a banal popular work and succeeded brilliantly. But as long as knowledge of intention is used, not as a sacred key to true interpretation (regardless of what other evidence indicates), but as one key among many which may be used, then it is difficult to maintain that such knowledge is never helpful.

Theories of art. The position that one takes on the issue of contextualism versus isolationism will depend to a large extent upon one's view of the essential nature and function of art. The first of these views that we shall consider is the theory of art as pure form. Even those philosophers of art who have written most about the formal properties of art have not usually held that form is the only criterion by which aesthetic value is to be judged, but some have gone on to make this claim and are called "formalists" in art.

Formalist theory. Clive Bell, who was a critic of visual art, held a formalist view with regard to visual art and music, though not to literature. He argued that formal excellence is the one timeless feature of art through the ages; it can be recognized by observers of different periods and cultures, despite varying subject matter, topical references, and accidental associations of all sorts. He called this property of works of art "significant form," although the name seems somewhat inappropriate because the property in question is distinguished precisely by the fact that it signifies, and hence is significant of, nothing whatever.

The formalist theory considers representation, emotion, ideas, and all other "life values" to be irrelevant to aesthetic appreciation. It admits only the "mediumistic" values, which in visual art means colors, lines, and combinations of these into planes and surfaces. A painting is none the worse for being representational, but the representation is aesthetically irrelevant: a painting is never good simply because it represents something from the real world, however well or movingly this may be done. Nor is it better or worse because it evokes emotions. Any form of anecdote (storytelling, historical narration, etc.) is similarly excluded as being "literary"—a quality that is perfectly appropriate to literature (which, according to formalism, is an art of a very different order, and only minimally aesthetic), but irrelevant to visual and musical art.

Formal properties alone are relevant to aesthetic value, and other writers have discussed in detail such formal properties as organic unity, thematic variation, and development. Bell, however, speaks in a somewhat mystical manner of "significant form" without offering any criteria for detecting its presence. Significant form is that to which aesthetic emotion is the response. When we ask what the aesthetic emotion is, however, we find that it is the emotion evoked by significant form. This circular definition is, of course, quite unhelpful. Nevertheless, it is clear that the aesthetic emotion has nothing to do with the emotions of life, such as joy and sadness. It is a response to formal properties only—in a painting, the complex interrelations of shapes and colors organized into an aesthetic unity. Most people who claim to enjoy paintings do not respond greatly to this aspect and therefore miss the distinctive pleasure that works of art can give them.

> [They] read into the forms of the work these facts and ideas for which they are capable of feeling emotion, and feel for them the emotions that they can feel—the ordinary emotions of life. When confronted by a picture, instinctively they refer back its forms to the world from which they came. They treat created form as though it were imitated form, a picture as though it were a photograph. Instead of going out on the stream of art into a new world of aesthetic experience, they turn a sharp corner and come straight home to the world of human interests. For them the significance of a work of art depends on what they bring to it; no new thing is added to their lives, only the old material is stirred. A good work of visual art carries a person who is capable of appreciating it out of life into ecstasy; to use art as a means to the emotions of life is to use a telescope for reading the news. (Clive Bell, *Art*, pp. 28–29)

Space permits neither the further elucidation of the formalists' fundamental thesis by means of specific examples (such as are to be found in abundance in the various books of art criticism by Clive Bell and Roger Fry), nor the systematic criticisms that the theory has received from its opponents. The direction of these criticisms can perhaps best be indicated by explaining another well-known theory of art, that of art as expression.

Art as expression. Most philosophers and critics of art have not been formalists, although many of them agree that the emphasis on formalism has been a healthy one, in that it has served the useful purpose of directing our attention toward the work of art itself—that is, on what it presents, rather than what it represents. These critics hold that art has other values to offer us, but that these must emerge through the form and cannot be apprehended without close attention to the form. In this respect they have agreed with the emphasis on form, but have not agreed that the form deserves exclusive emphasis. Specifically, many critics have held that in addition to satisfying formal requirements, a work of art must in some way be expressive, especially of human feeling. This view is chiefly exemplified in the expression theory of art.

"Art is an expression of human feeling" is a stock formula, and most students of art respond to it at once. However, philosophers must ask what it means to say this. Like many terms that can refer both to a process and to the product resulting from that process, the term "expression" (and the related term "expressive") can refer both to a process engaged in by the artist and to a feature of the product of that process.

Traditionally, the expression theory of art has been a theory concerning what the artist experiences and undergoes when he creates a work of art. Eugène Véron, Tolstoy, Benedetto Croce, R. G. Collingwood, and a host of other writers have in one way or another promulgated this formula, and the general public still responds to the formula "art is expression" more favorably than to any other. A typical statement of the view, which is to be found in Collingwood's *The Principles of Art*, describes the artist as being stimulated by an emotional excitement whose nature and source he does not know until he can find some form of expressing it, which involves bringing it before his conscious mind. This process is accompanied by feelings of release and new understanding. The main question is whether this process is relevant to aesthetic theory, or whether it is concerned rather with psychology—the psychology of artistic creation.

Has anything been said about the work of art itself, as opposed to the conditions under which it was created? Even if we are considering not the art product but rather the process of its creation, the question arises, What is the connection between the expression theory's description of the creative process and the creation of works of art? One would have thought that the creation of works of art implies at least that the artist is working with materials *in a medium*—that is, he is exploring new combinations of elements in a given medium. Indeed, this constitutes his creative activity as an artist. Where is the transition from the emotions which animate or inspire the artist, and which in some way he is supposed to "express," and the medium in which he is working? Suppose we agree that a certain musical composition is a great one and learn subsequently that the composer felt no emotions whatever while he was composing it (Richard Strauss, for example, said, "I work very coldly, without agitation, without emotion even; one must be completely master of oneself to organize that changing, moving, flowing chessboard, orchestration"). Must we then conclude that the work of art was not as good as we thought it was when we heard it without having this knowledge?

Whether or not the artist has in some sense expressed his own feelings in creating the work of art is, it would seem, irrelevant to the question of what, if anything, the work of art is expressive *of.* "The music expresses sadness" does not mean the same as "The composer expressed his own feelings of sadness when he wrote his music." If the music is sad, it is so regardless of how the composer felt when he wrote it.

But what does it mean to say that the music is sad or expresses sadness? Clearly it is a metaphor, for in the literal sense only sentient beings capable of emotion can be sad. How can music be sad, or have or contain any other feeling quality?

One answer to this question—an extremely simple one, but quite surely mistaken—is that "The music is sad" means "The music makes me (or other listeners, or most listeners, or a selected group of listeners) feel sad when they hear it." But if this is what is meant, we already have a perfectly satisfactory word for it, namely, *evocation*—"The music evokes sadness in me (or in most listeners)." But this is a most unsatisfactory analysis. A person can recognize certain melodies as being sad without feeling sad himself. If hearing the music really made him feel sad, as a person does when he feels sad at the loss of a dear one, he would probably not wish to repeat the experience. In any case, the recognition of the quality of the melody is quite distinct from the emotions a person feels when he hears it. One may hear happy music and be bored by it. What a person feels and what quality he attributes to the music are two different things. The sadness of the music is phenomenally objective (that is, felt as being "in the music"), whereas a person's sadness when he hears it (if such sadness occurs) is quite distinguishable from the sadness of the music; it is felt as being "phenomenally subjective," belonging to him and not to the music, and only evoked by the music. There is no reason why the two phenomena should even accompany each another. To say, then, that the music expresses sadness, or simply that it is sad, is to say something about a felt quality of the music itself, rather than about how it makes listeners feel.

But what is this quality which inheres in, is embodied in, or is in some way contained in or a property of the music? It is difficult to explicate what it means to say that a work of art contains emotional properties. The andante is not sad in the same sense in which it is so many notes long or has certain rising and falling rhythms. If a disagreement arises concerning its expressive quality, how is one to defend one's position?

Perhaps the most satisfactory approach is to analyze the most basic sense of the term "expression," namely, that of outer behavior manifesting or reflecting inner states. When people feel sad they exhibit certain types of behavior: they move slowly, they tend to talk in hushed tones, their movements are not jerky and abrupt or their tones strident and piercing. Now music can be said to be sad when it exhibits these same properties: sad music is normally slow, the intervals between the tones are small, the tones are not strident but hushed and soft. In short, the work of art may be said to have a specific feeling property when it has features that human beings have when they feel the same or similar emotion, mood, etc. This is the bridge between musical qualities and human qualities, which explains how music can possess properties that are literally possessed only by sentient beings.

The same considerations apply to the other arts. We can claim that a line in a painting is graceful because it possesses similarities to the contour of the limbs of human and animal bodies when they are said to be graceful. The horizontal line is restful (as opposed to vertical or jagged lines) because the human being in a horizontal position is in a situation of rest and sleep and is in a secure position from which he cannot fall. The horizontal line is not intrinsically restful and secure, but is so for creatures subject to gravitation, for whom the natural position of rest is horizontal. For human beings, at any rate, the connection is a universal one, not subject to individual variation or even to cultural relativity. If a horizontal line had one effect on one individual and an entirely different effect on another, how could the creative artist rely on the effect of his work upon other human beings? Moreover, such claims can be put to a test. If someone were to insist that a fast sprightly waltz was really sad or melancholy, we would refer him to the behavioral features of sad people and show him that when people are in that state they do exhibit the qualities in question (i.e., the qualities of sad music), rather than speed or sprightliness.

Works of art, then can be expressive of human qualities: one of the most characteristic and pervasive features of art is that percepts (lines, colors, progressions of musical tones) can be and are suffused with affect. Hence, this claim of the expression theory seems quite certainly to be true. The work of art can properly be said to contain or embody feeling qualities. A piece of music is sad; it does not merely evoke sadness. The formalists' objections to seeking emotional effects from works of art is, at least in part, based upon the mistaken belief that the only sense in which a work of art can "be emotional" is for it to evoke emotions, whereas in fact (in the sense just explained) the feeling quality is a genuine quality of the work of art.

In conclusion, we may note that in presenting and defending its claim, the expression theory has in a sense made itself unnecessary. It is no longer necessary to say that the work of art is expressive of feeling qualities; it is only necessary to say that is has them—that it is sad or embodies sadness as a property.

Art as symbol. Some philosophers of art have gone beyond the expression theory to another view, the signification theory, according to which art is more properly described as a symbol of human feeling than as an expression of it.

To avoid the lengthy debate over the distinction between sign and symbol, we shall simply speak of signs, leaving others to choose which kinds of signs they prefer to regard as symbols. In the broadest sense, *A* is a sign of *B* when *A* stands for *B* in some way or other. The verb "to signify" means "to be a sign of": thus, clouds signify rain, the musical note (mark on paper) signifies the tone that is to be played, the word signifies the thing it stands for, the bell signifies that someone is at the door. Most signs do not resemble the things that they signify. Some signs, however, are called iconic signs, in that they resemble, or have a considerable similarity to, that which they signify. The word "stop" on a road sign is not an iconic sign, but a curve bending leftward (to indicate that there is a left turn ahead) is. According to the signification theory, works of art are iconic signs of psychological processes taking place in human beings, specifically, signs of human feeling. Music is the clearest example, since here the representational element is not present. Music is essentially kinetic, being a temporal art, it flows in time—surging, bounding, wavering, driving, soaring, hesitating, always moving. The rhythmic patterns in music parallel those of life: in other words, they are iconic with those of life (i.e., the life of sentient beings). Thus, to take an obvious example, the patterns of rising and falling, crescendo and diminuendo, rising gradually to a climax and then concluding (such as are to be found in the "Liebestod" of Wagner's *Tristan und Isolde*) possess a considerable structural similarity to, or isomorphism with, the rhythm of the sexual climax. The pattern of the slow movement of Beethoven's Quartet No. 16, Op. 135, is similar to the voice inflection of a person asking questions and then answering them.

A degree of iconicity is surely present in many cases, but whether all musical passages are iconic with psychological processes is another question—not to mention the question of whether their value as music depends on this iconicity. There is an enormous variety of rhythmic patterns and variations in Bach's preludes and fugues, for example, and it would seem impossible to point out corresponding psychological processes for each separate case. One may say that the musical passages are iconic with psychological processes but that the distinctions are too subtle to be named, and that, indeed, language contains no names for the vast variety of unique feeling states. This last point is surely true, but it does not show that every musical passage is iconic with some such feeling state; in fact, there seems to be no way to show this.

Moreover, many musical passages appear to be iconic with more than one psychological process, so that there is no one-to-one correlation between them: "A long crescendo, as in Ravel's *Bolero*, might signify bursting with joy or blowing your top" (Monroe C. Beardsley, *Aesthetics*, p. 336).

We may now raise the still more fundamental question of whether the admitted iconicity ever proves that music is a sign of psychological processes, even if there were no ambiguity in the signification. Is the *Tristan* passage that is iconic with the rhythm of the sexual process therefore a sign of that process? The similarity of two things to each another—say, that of one tree to another tree—does not make one a sign of the other. What more is required in order for it to become a sign?

In conventional signs, *A* is a sign of *B* because human beings have made it so: A word signifies a thing, a bell signifies the end of class, and so on. In each case we could have employed a different sign to stand for the same thing. In natural signs, on the other hand, there is a causal relation of some kind between *A* and *B*: clouds are a sign of rain, a fever is a sign of illness, and so on. There is no resemblance in this case between the *A* and *B* terms, but they occur together in a causal order, and when we know what that order is we can discover (not invent or devise) that *A* is a sign of *B*.

The relation between *A* and *B* in our examples from art is neither conventional nor causal. There is a relation of iconicity (in the musical examples given, the resemblance was one of a structural relation between processes). But do we want to say that this is sufficient to make *A* a sign of *B*? Is similarity alone sufficient? The similarity of the curve in the road sign to the curve in the road ahead is not sufficient: there is a rule, or convention, to the effect that when a curve of that shape appears, it signifies a curve of similar (though not exactly similar) kind in the road ahead. And similarly in music, without some conventional indication that a certain passage is a sign of a certain process, there is no way of establishing this relationship, for the structural similarity could extend to any number of processes.

Art and truth. Space does not permit any further treatment of current theories of art. Before we leave the philosophy of art, however, it is important to consider the relation of art to two other concepts: truth and goodness (i.e., morality).

An aesthetic judgment is not a judgment about the goodness or badness of something in any moral sense, nor is it a judgment about the truth or falsity of statements. A work of literature is not considered better or worse aesthetically because it is based upon historical events, or because it contains true descriptions of geological or astronomical matters, or even because the view of life presented in it is true (assuming that it is correct to describe a view of life as "true"). Opposed views of the world are presented in the poems of Dante and Lucretius, but as aesthetic observers we do not have to choose between them; we can appreciate each view of life as it is presented without having to commit ourselves to either. Nevertheless, works of art—particularly works of literature—do have some connection with truth, one which should be briefly described.

Stated and implied propositions. There are many explicitly stated propositions in works of literature, and only in literature, since only literature has words as its medium. Since every proposition is either true or false, and since literature contains many true propositions, the art of literature does contain truth in this obvious sense. For example, a novel about the life of Napoleon doubtlessly contains many true propositions about his life.

But more interesting and important are those propositions (many of which may also be true) which are implicit, rather than explicitly stated. The over-all *Weltanschauung* of a work of literature is usually implicit and must be inferred from a careful reading of the work.

This at once raises the question, What is the sense of "imply" in which works of literature may contain implicit propositions? It is not the usual logical sense. Rather, the sense of "imply" in question is probably the same one that we constantly employ in daily life when we say, for example, "He didn't say that she had rejected him, but he implied it," The explicit statement did not logically imply the proposition, but it contextually implied it. This means that the utterance of that statement (not the statement per se), on that particular occasion, accompanied (in speech, at any rate) by those particular gestures and tones of voice, implied a proposition in the sense that it provided us with an inference ticket: it entitled us to infer certain propositions that were not stated outright. In a more complex manner, although no differently in principle, many views about human life, death, and love, and about the cosmic setting of human life, are implied in countless works of literary art.

From reading works of literature, one may sometimes also infer propositions about the author—his intentions, his conscious and unconscious motives, his general state of mind, his desires and sympathies. Such inferences are often dangerous (notoriously, in the case of Shakespeare), but sometimes the inference is a valid one: in a novel one can infer what type of human being is most favorably regarded by the author from which characters are sympathetically treated, or which subjects preyed most upon his mind from the frequency with which certain themes are treated. Inferences concerning the author's motives, particularly his unconscious ones, are far less secure, but with increasing psychiatric knowledge there is no reason (in principle, at least) why they cannot be made.

Truth to human nature. In works of literature, and to some extent in works of visual art, human beings are depicted and their actions are described. Even when there are no historical counterparts to the characters in a work of fiction, critics quite universally apply a criterion of "fidelity to human nature" in evaluating novels and dramas. Aristotle's test of "how a person of that kind probably or necessarily would behave" (in the given circumstances) has been applied to art, at least to literary art, throughout many centuries of criticism. The test is roughly as follows: Would a person, such as has been described thus far in the novel, act, think, feel, or be motivated in the way that the author describes in the circumstances presented? It is often very difficult to decide this question, either because our knowledge of human nature is insufficient or because the novelist has not given us enough clues. But once a critic is convinced that the character in question would not behave in the way that the author describes him as behaving, he will condemn the characterization (at least with respect to that action or motivation) as implausible, and his negative judgment on the truth of the characterization will count against a favorable judgment of the work. The aesthetic relevance of truth-to-human-nature has scarcely been questioned, at least in the case of literature.

This test of "truth to human nature," however, is a tricky one which may easily become question-begging. One may say, for example, "If the character of type *T* does not, in circumstances *C*, perform act *A*, then this shows only that he is not after all a character of type *T*," and thus the test could never have a negative result. The way to get around this is to make sure that his being a character of type *T* is determined quite independently of his doing act *A*; and thus, if he is a character of type *T*, as shown by the previous incidents in the story, and still he does not perform act *A* under circumstances *C*, then his characterization (at least with respect to act *A*) is untrue to human nature. For example, if a character is described as spending his life attempting to achieve a certain goal, and suddenly without explanation he deserts this goal when he is within sight of its attainment, we would say, following Aristotle, that he did not act as a person of the kind described would "probably or necessarily" act. It is true that there are people who do things of just this kind, but the novelist must have made clear through prior characterization that this particular character is of this type. If he has not made this clear to us, we condemn his characterization (or at any rate this part of it) as implausible and unconvincing—and it is of the truth of his characterization that the novelist must convince us. It would seem, then, that the merit of a work of art—at least a work that contains characterization, as is usually the case in literature—does depend on truth—not the truth of an astronomical system (as in the Ptolemaic astronomy employed by Milton), nor the truth of geography (as in Lilliput and the other geographical falsehoods in *Gulliver's Travels*), nor of his delineation of the facts of history (even a historical drama can be false to many facts of history when formal considerations such as development and climax demand it, as in the case of Shakespeare's *Henry IV*), nor even the truth of his philosophical system (as in Dante versus Lucretius, for example), but on the truthfulness of the portrait of human beings.

Assuming that the requirement of "truth to human nature" is accepted, how does it harmonize with our earlier characterization of the aesthetic attitude? If we are to concentrate solely on the work of art itself, on internal relations rather than external relations, how can this be made consistent with any requirement of truth, which after all is a relation of what is contained in the work of art to something outside it (i.e., the behavior of human beings in the world outside art)? It is precisely at this point that formalistically minded critics like Bell would say that literature differs importantly from the other arts, that the appreciation of literature does involve "life values," whereas that of the other arts does not, and that the appreciation of literature is not primarily aesthetic at all. (Formalists would admit that there are elements of characterization in some works of visual art—for example, self-portraits by Rembrandt—but they would not admit that such characterization plays the slightest role in our aesthetic appreciation of such works. But other critics would reply that the appreciation of literature, although of a different nature, is still aesthetic and does not violate the requirements for aesthetic appreciation as long as it is not necessary to turn from the work of art to a conscious comparison of the character that is being presented with actual people in the world outside. Knowledge of human nature, they would say, is something we bring with us to the work of art, just as we have the ability to recognize such objects as trees and houses in representational paintings; and this recognition is no more inimical to aesthetic appreciation in the one case than in the other.

Art and morality. An aesthetic judgment is not a moral judgment, and the value of a work of art as an aesthetic object is not at all the same thing as its value in edifying readers or improving their moral character, which may be effects of the reading of works of art but not what we are judging when we judge a work of art to be good. Nevertheless, as in the case of truth, there may be a relation between art and morality that is worth pursuing. At any rate, there have been several distinguishable historical positions on the relation between aesthetic and moral values, which we would do well to consider.

The moralistic conception of art dates back to Plato's *Republic* and has its most vigorous modern defense in Tolstoy's *What Is Art?*; it is the official view of the Soviet government and is the view held consciously or unconsciously by most laymen. According to this view, art is the handmaiden of morality—acceptable and even desirable when it promotes morality (presumably the "true" or "acceptable" morality), but unacceptable and undesirable when it does not. Art may give people unorthodox ideas; it may disturb and disquiet them, and since it emphasizes individuality and deviation rather than conformity, it may be dangerous in undermining beliefs on which (it is thought) our society rests. Consequently, art is (and should be, according to this view) always viewed with suspicion by the guardians of the established order. When art does not affect people greatly, it is considered a harmless pleasure, a luxury, and an escape; but when it does, it becomes insidious and even subversive, damaging the substructure of our most socially desirable beliefs and attitudes.

A view of art exactly opposite to this one is that of aestheticism, according to which morality is the handmaiden of art rather than the other way round. According to this view, the experience of art is the greatest experience available to mankind, and nothing should interfere with it. If it conflicts with morality, so much the worse for morality; and if the masses fail to appreciate it or to receive the experience it has to offer, so much the worse for the masses. When Mussolini's son-in-law waxed lyrical in his description of the beauty of a bomb exploding among a crowd of unarmed Ethiopians, he was carrying to its fullest extreme the aestheticist's view of art. The vital intensity of the aesthetic experience is the paramount goal in life; above all, in Walter Pater's famous words, one should aspire to "burn with a hard gemlike flame." Therefore, if there are any morally undesirable side effects of art, they do not really matter in comparison to this all-important experience which art alone can give us.

Very few persons would wish to go so far. Even the most ardent and enthusiastic art lovers would stop short of saying that the value of art is exclusive or that it holds a monopoly over all other ones. It may well be that the experience of works of art is the greatest experience available to human beings, but it is not the only one available, and we do have to consider the others. Aesthetic values, although far greater than most people realize, are still just a few among many. This being the case, we can hardly behave as if the other values did not exist. We must therefore consider the relation of aesthetic values to the others that life has to offer us.

This leads us to a third position, surely more plausible than either of the two extremes mentioned above, which for lack of a better word we may term "interactionism." This is the view that aesthetic and moral values have distinctive roles to play in the world, but that neither operates independently of the other: indeed, art and morality are intimately related, and neither functions fully without the other. On this assumption, let us see what some of these interrelations are. It will be most convenient to consider first the relation of the art of literature to morality, since in this case the relation is more obvious.

Literature sometimes does teach a lesson, point a moral, or convey a message that it is important for us to learn, and thus it can enter directly into the service of morality. Even great art can sometimes be didactic (for example, Dante's *Divine Comedy* and Milton's *Paradise Lost*). Those who praise art for its moral lessons are not always in error, but if this is their only ground for praise, they are deriving from art much less than it is able to give. To use a comparison that Clive Bell employed in another connection, didacticists in art are cutting blocks with a razor or using a telescope to read the news. A telescope can, with some difficulty, be used for this purpose, but this is not what a telescope is built for, and if someone uses it for this purpose alone, he is using it to do a job that a far less valuable object could do much better. Art may indeed teach, but usually not by explicit preachment. As John Dewey put it in his *Art as Experience*, art teaches as friends and life teach—not by preaching but simply by being. The variety of situations presented, the human characterizations, the crises and struggles through which these characters pass—these alone, when set before us in all their vividness and complexity, are sufficient to produce moral effects. If this were not so, the author might have done better to write an essay or a tract.

But how then does art achieve a moral effect, if no moral is specifically stated? It does so by presenting us with characters in situations (usually of conflict and crisis) that generally have a greater complexity than our own everyday experiences. By deliberating on the problems and conflicts of these characters, we can enrich our own moral perspectives; we can learn from them without having to undergo in our personal lives these same conflicts or having to make the same decisions, for in art we can view their situations with a detachment that we can seldom achieve in daily life, when we are immersed in the stream of action. Literature is often a potent stimulus to moral reflection, for it presents the moral situation in its total context, with nothing relevant omitted—and nothing less than this is required in making one's own moral decisions.

We have already expanded our concept of the moral relevance of literature considerably beyond crude didacticism, but we can go still further. The chief moral effect of literature doubtless lies in its unique power to stimulate the imagination. Shelley's defense of this position in his essay "A Defense of Poetry" stands virtually unchallenged to this day. "The imagination," wrote Shelley, "is the great instrument of moral good, and poetry administers to the effect by acting upon the causes." Through great literature we are carried beyond the confines of our daily life into a world of thought and feeling more profound and varied than our own, and in which we can enter directly the experiences, thoughts, and feelings of people far removed from us in space and time. Through the exercise of the sympathetic imagination, art, more than preachment or moralizing, tends to reveal the common human nature that exists in all men behind the façade of divisive doctrines, and thus to unite mankind more effectively than the doctrines themselves could ever do. This is (to use Dewey's term) the "leavening" influence of art.

In order for a work of art to have moral effects, then, it is not necessary that it present us with a system of morality. It need not present us with any system at all; indeed, its moral potency is likely to be greatest when it presents us, not with systems, but with characters and situations convincingly drawn and vividly described, so that through the use of imagination we can see their views and live through their experiences.

Finally, what of the effects on the audience of reading, hearing, or seeing works of art? Aristotle's theory of catharsis was the first in a long succession of views attributing moral value to the consumption of works of art, although his theory was limited to dramatic tragedy only. According to him art acts as an emotional cathartic, a purgative of the emotions. During the course of our daily lives, certain emotions (which need not be limited to Aristotle's pity and fear) are generated which we would be better off without and which we should try to expel; and art is the agency that helps us to do this. By witnessing a powerful drama or hearing a choral concert, we can "work off" these emotions, instead of letting them fester inside of us or inflicting them on our fellow men.

Undoubtedly this view is somewhat crude in the light of modern psychology. Moreover, it regards the effect of art as that of getting rid of that which is undesirable, rather than the positive production of anything desirable. Yet it can hardly be denied that the experience of reading, viewing, or listening to a work of art does give a peculiar relief and release, a freedom from inner turbulence. It is not merely that for a few hours we can forget our troubles: any form of diversion, including intoxication, may also achieve this end. Great art does not merely provide people with a break or interruption in the course of their worried lives, at the end of which they are just what they were before: in the very act of concentrating our energies upon an aesthetic object, our spiritual state is improved; there is a release from tension and a kind of inner clarification that was not present before. The effect includes a heightening of our sensibilities ("heightened consciousness" was Edith Sitwell's phrase for the effect of poetry), a refining of our capacities for perceptual and emotional discrimination, and a capacity to respond more sensitively to the world around us.

All these may be called moral effects of art and tend to show that art and morality, far from being enemies, are supplementary. Yet there may be occasions on which they clash—when, as has often been claimed, a work of art has a deleterious moral effect, and one must choose between aesthetic and moral values, since both cannot be preserved. Thus arises the problem of censorship of the arts.

The question of what the actual effects of works of art are is a complex one on account of the diversity of response among viewers and readers. Some persons are so affected by the nudity of a statue that they cannot view it aesthetically, while others are not distracted at all. At any rate, it is difficult to conceive of any great work of art as being morally objectionable if one approaches it aesthetically; this task requires such full attention that it dispels any allegedly undesirable side effects. If one contemplates James Joyce's *Ulysses* as the complex whole that it is, the passages that some readers find indelicate shade into insignificance; they are absorbed into the total unity of the work of art, and that the severest critic of the novel could hardly say that taken as a whole the work is morally objectionable. The aesthetic power of a work of art tends to paralyze any incipient "immoral" tendencies. The aesthetic way of approaching a work of art is incompatible with any wholesale practical effects it might have, such as impelling the reader or viewer to commit crimes or set out to change the world. One usually finds that those who criticize works of art on moral grounds are approaching it neither as the artist intended nor in the way that it can most fruitfully be approached.

Even in the case of works of art that are less than great, and of audiences that are something less than aesthetically sensitive, the "immoral" effects of art have been greatly overstated (see Jerome Frank, "Obscenity and the Law," in Marvin Levich, ed., *Aesthetics and the Philosophy of Criticism*, p. 418). There is no evidence that readers of novels of crime and detection tend to commit the crimes they read about. Indeed, this may operate the other way round: such reading sometimes helps the individual to discharge innocently, through the experience of the novel itself, any tendencies which, if unreleased, might have become uncomfortable or dangerous. Nor is there any evidence that criminals who read a certain book commit crimes because they have read that book, the roots of crime are much deeper than this. A criminal tendency, if already present, may possibly be reinforced by reading a book, but it may also be satisfied (as a substitute gratification) by reading the book. Accordingly, if the book were banned, all actual and potential readers would be deprived of it, and the alleged good moral effects would not occur any more than before—surely a bad bargain.

Such empirical considerations about the effects of works of art could be multiplied indefinitely. But even if it were granted that certain works of art do have bad moral effects, the question would still remain, Should they on that account be banned or censored? On this point the very principle of censorship is in question. Does one body of human beings have the right to sit in judgment upon another, and larger, body of human beings and tell them what they may and may not read or see? A strong case can be made for replying in the negative. First, by what right do the censors rule? They are as finite and as fallible as those who are censored, and there is no guarantee that they are better moral guardians than the people they are allegedly guarding. Second, does it really improve the moral stature of adult individuals to be prevented from making a choice, even a poor choice? Is not the freedom to acquaint oneself with a variety of ideas and opinions essential to the preservation of a free society? But this choice is denied him when a book or film is banned. Third, any approval of censorship is likely to boomerang on the person who approves it. Censors, once established, tend to act according to their individual prejudices without respect to the wishes of those who originally established them. The person who wants certain works of art banned, only to find that other things are banned instead (including some to which he would like to have access), has in effect asked for the treatment that he is receiving by admitting the principle of censorship in the first place.

The definition of art. A concluding word should be said about the concept of art itself. The word "art" and the phrase "work of art" have been used many times in the above discussion, and yet they have not been precisely defined. One negative condition has been given, namely, that what is not man-made (or at any rate made by sentient beings) may be an aesthetic object but is not to be classified as art; and a more positive stricture has also been mentioned, namely, that in the case of fine art (as opposed to useful art), the primary function is aesthetic. These criteria, to be sure, offer little basis for distinguishing good art from bad art, but it is doubtful whether a definition of art should do this (the definition should be neutral with respect to value), any more than a definition of "road" should distinguish good roads from bad roads. Much confusion has arisen from a failure to distinguish neutral definitions from value definitions—(for example, from a failure to distinguish between definitions of art and the writer's opinions as to what constitutes good art).

It would be comparatively easy to define the terms "music," "painting," "sculpture," and other terms referring to the specific arts by the nature of the various media in which these arts are cast. (There may, of course, be many other arts in the future, of which we have no conception at present.) But in the case of art as a general concept, it is doubtful whether any definition more stringent than the one given above will be satisfactory. Most proffered definitions, at any rate, exclude some things we would want to call art (at least as that term is used in ordinary discourse) or include some which we would not. "Art is an expression of feeling through a medium"—but is art an expression of feeling at all (as we asked in discussing the expression theory of art)? Is it always "feeling" that is "expressed"? And is every medium an art medium (for example, when a child expresses his anger by stamping in the sand, is the sand a medium)? "Art is an exploration of reality through a sensuous presentation"—but in what sense is it an exploration? Is it always concerned with reality, and if so, in what sense? And in what way are the words in a poem sensuous presentations? "Art is a re-creation of reality"—but is all art a re-creation of something, even music? (One would have thought that it was the creation of something, that is, a series of tonal relationships that never existed in that order before the composer created them.) And in what sense does music deal with reality? Such definitions prejudge the answers to many difficult questions and raise far more problems than they solve.

Even more elaborate definitions, such as that of DeWitt Parker in his essay "The Definition of Art," are subject to similar criticisms. According to Parker, there is a set of conditions, each of which is necessary and all of which are together sufficient, which must be satisfied by something that is called a work of art. First, it must provide a source of satisfaction through the imagination. In daily life, desire is occupied with real objects and is satisfied through a course of action leading to a goal that involves interaction with the environment, but in the case of art the desire is appeased in present given experience. Second, the object must be social: it must involve a real publicly available physical object that can be a source of satisfaction to many people on repeated occasions—it cannot be a dream, an illusion, a lock of hair, or a victory medal that is satisfying only to the owner or someone dear to him. The satisfaction we derive from the work stems partly from knowing that others enjoy it also—that the experience of it is shared. Third, all art must have aesthetically satisfying form—harmony, pattern, design. On this point of course, many questions can be raised, such as, Is it a definition of art or an attempt to describe good works of art? (The reference to being "satisfying" would seem to indicate that the latter is the case.) Is it necessary that the artist's creative faculty be embodied in some publicly available object? Croce and the idealists think otherwise: they hold that the "real" work of art is present only to the mind of the artist, even before he has put pen to paper or paint to canvas, provided that his vision of the work of art is conceived entirely in the artistic medium. There are also difficulties about the sense in which music, for example, is a "publicly available object." Does it exist even when it is not being played? As long as the musical score (which is not the music) exists, the music can always be performed again, but the second performance may sound very different from the first, and how different can it be without ceasing to be the same "publicly available object"? And does the satisfaction one takes in a work of art really depend on the knowledge that others take satisfaction in it also? If works of art had been available to Robinson Crusoe, he might have enjoyed them more rather than less because of his solitude. In Parker's definition it seems that we have a statement of the author's ideal of what art should be, rather than a definition of what actually constitutes art.

Once the question "What is art?" has been carefully distinguished from the question "What is good art?," it is the latter question that seems to be the more interesting one. It is, at any rate, the subject of many age-old controversies in such areas as, What is beauty? Are there standards of aesthetic value? How can one distinguish a good work of art from a bad one? We turn, then, to the problem of aesthetic value, and since this includes all aesthetic objects, in nature as well as in art, the problem is not restricted to the domain of philosophy of art.

AESTHETIC VALUE

"Truth, goodness, and beauty" constitute the principal triad of concepts with which philosophy was traditionally supposed to deal. Whatever may be said of the others, beauty was traditionally the province of aesthetic theory, although truth was also, since it was the truth about beauty that aesthetics was supposed to provide. To ask the question "What is beauty?" in the sense that the word "beauty" is used today, however, would be to ask too narrow a question, for we want to ask questions of value with regard to all objects of aesthetic experience. The word "beauty" tends to carry with it the connotation of something that is pleasing to the eye or ear, and since works of literature are (as we observed earlier) ideo-sensory rather than sensory arts, they do not fall easily into that classification. ("A beautiful painting" sounds natural enough, but not "a beautiful novel.") Even in visual and auditory art, not all works to which we would attribute aesthetic value would be considered beautiful. We may, for example, consider Picasso's *Guernica* a work of great aesthetic value, but some of its admirers may find that it does not please the eye, and the word "beautiful" is too pallid for it. Works of art may move us deeply, reorient our vision or our feeling, shock or stun us, but we need not find them pleasing; and yet it is this hedonic quality that is ordinarily connoted when we call something "beautiful." In the forthcoming discussion we may occasionally use the word "beautiful" when it seems appropriate to do so; when we do, however, it will be used as a synonym for "aesthetic value," not in the narrower sense associated with the quality of being pleasing. The term "aesthetic value" refers to the more general concept, and accordingly our question is "What is aesthetic value?" What is involved in attributing aesthetic value to an object? on what grounds? and how is the claim that something has aesthetic value to be defended?

The traditional classification into subjectivist and objectivist theories of aesthetic value is a natural one. A theory of aesthetic value is objectivistic if it maintains that the properties which constitute aesthetic value, or make an object aesthetically valuable, are (in some fairly straightforward sense) properties of the aesthetic object itself. A theory is subjectivistic if it holds that what makes something aesthetically valuable is not its own properties but its relation to aesthetic consumers (such as liking it, enjoying it, having aesthetic experiences in response to it, and so forth).

Subjectivist theories. Statements such as "When I say something is beautiful I just mean that I like it," and "Beauty is a subjective thing—it's beautiful for you if you enjoy it, and it's not beautiful for me if I don't" are frankly subjectivistic. Subjectivism in aesthetic theory, although it may become considerably more sophisticated than these statements suggest, holds throughout that there are no beauty-making properties of aesthetic objects, but only various responses to these objects, and that the attribution of aesthetic value can be made validly only when the viewer responds to the object in a certain way. To put it differently, beauty is always a "to you" or a "to me" characteristic. "It's beautiful to me" would make no sense if beauty were an objective characteristic of objects like squareness, just as "It's square to me" makes no sense, unless one merely means by this, "It looks square to me." But "It's interesting to me" and "This is strange to me" make sense, because interestingness and strangeness are not objective characteristics. When the critic calls a painting beautiful, he is referring to some relation between himself and the aesthetic object—usually the relation of liking or aesthetically enjoying.

The simplest subjectivistic theory, which has a superficial attractiveness but is quite certainly mistaken, is the view that when someone says "*X* has aesthetic value," he is saying only "I aesthetically enjoy *X*" or "I have an aesthetic experience in response to *X*." All such judgments are, of course, merely autobiographical; they tell us something about the aesthetic observer and report his mental state. Most aestheticians, indeed, would say that they are statements of personal liking or preference and not aesthetic judgments at all. "I like it" is quite different from "I think it is (aesthetically) good." A person may like a painting without considering it good, and he may also consider it good without actually liking it: he may have some blind spot with regard to the appreciation of that kind of painting and may be perfectly aware of his own deficiency in this regard. "I like it" and "I think it's good" are not synonymous expressions, even in common parlance.

There are many other objections to the subjectivist view, the principal one perhaps being that it makes disagreement on aesthetic matters impossible. If one person says "*X* is good" and another replies "*X* is not good," and if the first one is merely saying "I enjoy *X*" and the second is merely saying "I do not enjoy *X*," there is no disagreement whatever between them. Both of their statements are probably true; neither of them is lying about his likes and dislikes. There is no statement that one of them holds to be true and the other holds to be false, and this situation at least must occur if the term "disagreement" is to retain any distinctive meaning. If the suggested analysis were correct, the proper reply to "*X* is good" would be "No, you're lying—you *don't* really enjoy it!" This would, certainly be an appropriate reply if one were questioning the other's autobiographical report, but not if he were questioning the other's aesthetic judgment.

Perhaps the main reason why this autobiographical analysis of "*X* is good" is so often accepted without further reflection is that the person confuses the meaning of a sentence with the conditions of its utterance. A person would not usually (though, as we have just seen, he sometimes might) say that a work of art is good unless he also enjoys it or likes it in some way, or thinks that he could if certain conditions were different. But this does not entail the implication that when he says it is good he means only that he enjoys it. What a person means by a statement and the conditions under which he utters it are two different things.

In order to overcome some of these difficulties, one might adopt the "sociological" view that "*X* is (aesthetically) good" means not that the speaker aesthetically enjoys *X*, but that the majority of people do. On this question there could indeed be disagreement, which could be resolved by taking a poll to discover what works of art the majority of the population prefers. Such a poll would settle a genuine disagreement, but unfortunately for the theory, it would be disagreement about the wrong thing. It is one thing to dispute about what the majority of people prefer and quite another to dispute about what works of art are good ones. A person who enthusiastically favored a certain work of art would not be deterred in his enthusiasm by knowing that the majority of people were against him. The fact that the majority prefers *A* to *B* tells us nothing about *A* or *B*; it only tells us that more people like *A* than *B*. May not a majority be mistaken, as they may be about anything else?

One might try to remedy this defect by specifying that only the responses of a certain class of people are to be counted in the poll. Thus, "*X* is good" means "The majority of the best critics enjoy *X*." But who are the best critics?

One could amend this view by eliminating the word "best" and specifying instead the precise qualifications of the critic whose vote is to be counted. Thus, one could say that the critic in question must have a long experience with the art medium which he is judging, that he must be knowledgeable about the history of the art in question, that he must be trained in the handling of the medium, that at the time of judging he must not be worried or otherwise distracted but must be "in a calm frame of mind," that he must (in addition to his training in the field) be a person of "aesthetic sensitivity," and so on. But these requirements are difficult to define, and each of them can easily be questioned. Any number of critics have demonstrated an excellent capacity for evaluating the aesthetic worth of an art work without being expert historians or having more than a minimal acquaintance with such technical problems as the chemistry of paints or the casting of bronze. Moreover, interest in factual and technical detail very often only follows upon enjoyment of aesthetic objects. Some people find themselves more perceptive in an excited rather than a calm frame of mind; and there seems to be no way to determine just who possesses the elusive quality of "aesthetic sensitivity."

It would seem that all such requirements tell us more about the art critic than about the work of art. If we know that the majority of critics, even of those who pass certain tests (which, as we have just seen, would be very difficult to specify), favor a certain work of art, does it necessarily follow that the work of art is a good one? The majority of art critics in El Greco's time did not value his paintings above those of his contemporaries, although today we are all sure that El Greco's work is greater than that of his contemporaries. What does this prove about El Greco's work, except that it was not highly valued in his own time?

We could, of course, further extend the classification by saying that *X* is good if the majority of critics (who pass certain tests) of all ages enjoy it or would enjoy it if they were to scrutinize it carefully over a period of time. This would take care of unduly hasty or superficial judgments and (by means of the contrary-to-fact conditional) would also take care of works of art of different times and places that some critics were never able to observe. But even in this amended form, it is still the critic's responses that we are describing and not the work of art. It would seem that the two assertions "*X* is a good work of art" and "The majority of critics who pass qualifications *A*, *B*, and *C* enjoy *X*, or would do so if they had a chance to see it and scrutinized it carefully over a period of time" are logically distinct. Even if, with regard to a given work of art, the two statements were always true together or always false together, it would not follow that they mean the same; it would be a case of logical equivalence without identity of meaning. There always seems to be a difference in meaning between a statement about the merit of a work of art and a statement about the verdict of those judging it.

Objectivist theories. Unlike subjectivist theories, objectivist theories claim, as we all tend to assume in any case, that when we attribute aesthetic value to a work of art we are attributing value to the work itself. We are saying that it has aesthetic value and that this value is grounded in the nature of the object itself, not in the fact that most observers (or observers of a certain kind) favor it or enjoy it. If observers favor it, this would be a consequence of the fact that it has aesthetic value, but the attribution of value does not consist in the fact that any observers or critics favor it. What a work of art demands from the observer is his considered judgment of its merit, and this judgment is based upon the work's properties alone, not on the properties of any observers or their relation to it.

Is there any property or set of properties that constitutes aesthetic value? Is there any finite set of properties *A*, *B*, *C* . . . which if present will ensure that the aesthetic object is a good one, and if absent will insure that it is not?

One view on this issue is that there is a property of all aesthetic objects which may be present in varying degrees (for example, brightness or intensity), but which to the degree that it is present confers upon the work its aesthetic value. This property is usually called "beauty."

But still one must ask, What constitutes beauty, and how does one recognize its presence? At this point it is often said that beauty is a simple, unanalyzable property whose presence can only be intuited but not determined by any empirical tests: "Beauty is directly apprehended by the mind in just the same way that shape is directly apprehended" (C. E. M. Joad). But this only raises further questions. We usually agree on what an object's shape is, and if we do not we can subject our conceptions to empirical tests; however, we do not as often agree on whether an object is beautiful, and if we do not, what then is the next step? We can say, to be sure, that one of the parties to the dispute is mistaken, but there is no way to discover which one is in error, since the property in question is not empirically verifiable but can only be intuited—and it is a notorious fact that people have conflicting intuitions. At this point all we seem to be able to say is, "Now ends the argument and begins the fight."

Unless we are given some clue as to how to resolve controversies about aesthetic value, it remains a useless concept. But it is difficult indeed to arrive at a criterion that is useful and true, for the properties that critics cite as "good-making" properties of aesthetic objects are extremely varied and differ considerably from one art medium to another. The use of colors for which a critic may praise a painting and the use of certain kinds of orchestration and tonal color in a work of music must be limited to those art media only and cannot be general criteria for evaluating all art, much less all aesthetic objects. Even the use of rich imagery, which is considered grounds for praise in one poem, is not considered so in another poem; whether the imagery is praiseworthy depends on the type of poem and the total context of the passage. In regard to aesthetic judgment, so much depends upon the context that it is difficult if not impossible to isolate any one feature of a work of art and say that whenever that feature is present the work of art is a good one, or even that it is better than it would have been without it.

Nevertheless, there have been attempts to devise a set of criteria for judging aesthetic value, perhaps the clearest and most plausible of which has been set forth by Monroe Beardsley. According to his view, there are "specific canons" of aesthetic criticism as well as "general canons":

the specific canons are applicable to certain art media or even to certain kinds of work (for example, tragedy versus comedy) within a given art medium. They differ from medium to medium as well as from genre to genre within the medium, and no attempt is made to set forth in detail what these canons are. The general canons, however, are applicable to all aesthetic objects, no matter what the kind. There are three general canons: (1) unity, (2) complexity, and (3) intensity. Unity and complexity have already been discussed in our earlier section on form (the "unity in variety" or "variety in unity" criterion), but a word should be added about intensity. It is a requirement that the work of art have certain pervasive (i.e., regional) qualities. "A good aesthetic object must have *some* marked quality, and not be a sheer nonentity or a zero. The quality does not matter—it can be sad or cheerful, graceful or rugged, soft or stern, provided it be *something*" (Beardsley, *Aesthetics*, p. 463). Thus, to praise a painting because "it has such a sense of eternal calm and stillness about it" is to praise it for the intensity of a certain pervasive (regional) quality; to praise it for being developed on a large scale, or being subtle or rich in contrasts, is to praise it for complexity; and to praise it for being well organized, or formally perfect, is to praise it for unity. These three attributes together constitute the general "good-making" properties of aesthetic objects. A work of art may be better than another and at the same time possess less of one of these properties, provided that it has more of the others. The evaluation of a work of art, as far as the general canons of aesthetics are concerned, is a function of these three properties together, and any ground of praise of a general sort (that is, applicable to all aesthetic objects) falls under one or another of these three criteria. (This view is defended at length in Chapter 10 of Beardsley's *Aesthetics*.)

But within an objectivist framework there is still another way of analyzing the concept of aesthetic value. One need not mention any specific properties of an aesthetic object, only its capacity to produce an aesthetic response. (Roughly speaking, this is the view of John Dewey in his *Art as Experience*, but in Chapter 11 of his *Aesthetics*, Beardsley presents it with greater sharpness and precision.) According to this view, man-made objects, and some natural objects as well, fall into what is called "function-classes," depending on what function they best fulfill. A chair is primarily for sitting on, a wrench is primarily for tightening nuts, and so on. This is not because the makers of these objects intended them to do this, for their intentions may have misfired, but because this is actually what they do best. Paintings, poems, and symphonies primarily fulfill the function of rewarding the aesthetic attention of the reader, viewer, or listener. To say "This is a good *X*" is the same as to say "This is an *X*, and there is a function of *X*'s that it successfully fulfills." A good work of art is one that successfully evokes an aesthetic experience in an audience and is therefore a good instrument toward the achievement of aesthetic experience as an end in itself. It should be noted, however, that the work of art itself possesses instrumental value, for it and other members of its function-class fulfill the end of evoking aesthetic experience; but the experience of works of art is an intrinsic value, worth having for its own sake alone and not as a means toward any further end. To say that an object, *X*, has aesthetic value is therefore to say roughly that "*X* has the capacity to produce an aesthetic experience of a fairly great magnitude (such an experience having value)," and to say that "*X* has greater aesthetic value than *Y*" means "*X* has the capacity to produce an aesthetic experience of greater magnitude (such an experience having more value) than that produced by *Y*."

"Capacity" is, of course, a dispositional term like the term "nutritious." A capacity statement can be true (but not verified) even though the capacity is never actualized. An object's capacity to produce aesthetic response, and hence its aesthetic value, is not determined by counting the number of people who are aesthetically moved by it. Greater concentration and familiarity is required for the appreciation of some works of art than for others. All that the formula tells us is that if the consumer of the work of art is in a position to realize the capacity of the work, then if *X* is better than *Y* he will respond more to *X* than to *Y*. "The object with the greater capacity may not have its capacity actualized as often as the object with less—the heavier the sledge, the greater its force, but the fewer who can use it well. If, therefore, the aesthetic value of Tschaikovsky is more often had and enjoyed than that of Bach, it still may be true that the value of the latter is greater" (Beardsley, *Aesthetics*, p. 532).

It is debatable whether this view should be called objectivistic in the same sense as the earlier ones. No properties of the work of art, such as unity, are mentioned. On this point the instrumentalist theory is noncommittal and leaves open the possibility that a set of criteria other than unity, intensity, and complexity could be devised which might be more satisfactory. Nevertheless, in a broad sense the theory may be called objectivistic, for the capacity of an object to produce a given type of response is indeed a property of the object—a property of a different sort, perhaps, but a property nonetheless. Redness is a property of objects, although, in the opinion of many philosophers at any rate, all it consists in is the capacity of the object that is called red to produce in viewers a certain type of visual experience. In the same way, the aesthetic value of an object, whether one of nature or of art, is equally a property, although the property is described only in capacity terms—that is, the capacity of the object, under appropriate conditions, to produce in observers a certain type of response, namely, the aesthetic.

Bibliography

READINGS IN THE HISTORY OF AESTHETICS

Aschenbrenner, Karl, and Isenberg, Arnold, *Aesthetic Theories*. Englewood Cliffs, N.J., 1965. Long selections from selected philosophers.

Caritt, E. F., *Philosophies of Beauty from Socrates to Robert Bridges*, 3d ed. London, 1928. Numerous short excerpts.

Sesonske, Alexander, *What is Art? Aesthetic Theory from Plato to Tolstoy*. New York, 1965.

READINGS IN CONTEMPORARY AESTHETICS

The following anthologies contain many of the most important papers on aesthetics written during the twentieth century, taken largely from philosophical journals. Since most of the important papers are included in the anthologies listed below, they are not separately listed as journal articles. Many excellent articles, however, have not been anthologized and appear in various philosophical periodicals, particularly the *Journal of Aesthetics and Art Criticism* and the *British Journal of Aesthetics*, both of which should be consulted for further bibliography.

Kennick, W. E., *Art and Philosophy: Readings in Aesthetics.* New York, 1964.

Levich, Marvin, *Aesthetics and the Philosophy of Criticism.* New York, 1963.

Margolis, Joseph, *Philosophy Looks at the Arts.* New York, 1962.

Rader, Melvin M., *A Modern Book of Aesthetics*, 3d ed. New York, 1961.

Stolnitz, Jerome, *Aesthetics.* New York, 1965. Brief paperback anthology.

Weitz, Morris, *Problems in Aesthetics.* New York, 1958.

SURVEYS OF THE PROBLEMS OF AESTHETICS

Aldrich, Virgil C., *Philosophy of Art.* Englewood Cliffs, N.J., 1963. A brief but readable introduction to the problems of the field.

Beardsley, Monroe C., *Aesthetics: Problems in the Philosophy of Criticism.* New York, 1958. An excellent and thorough systematic introduction to all the major problems of aesthetics. Contains detailed topical bibliographies.

Mead, Hunter, *Aesthetics.* New York, 1950. A brief general introduction.

Stolnitz, Jerome, *Aesthetics.* Boston, 1958. A lucid and systematic introduction to the problems in the field.

GENERAL WORKS ON AESTHETICS

Collingwood, Robin G., *The Principles of Art.* London, 1938. Clear and systematic presentation of a Crocean theory of art. Opinionated, clear, stimulating, and eminently readable.

Croce, Benedetto, *Aesthetic.* New York, 1953. Important and influential, but badly translated and difficult reading.

Dewey, John, *Art as Experience.* New York, 1934. Although often vague and difficult to summarize, this book is one of the few modern classics in the field and is perhaps Dewey's greatest book. It displays great insight into the problems of aesthetics as seen by the artist as well as by the philosopher.

Ducasse, Curt J., *The Philosophy of Art.* New York, 1929. Lucid and systematic presentation of an expressionist theory of art.

Greene, Theodore M., *The Arts and the Art of Criticism.* Princeton, N.J., 1941. Germanic in its style and in the multiplicity of distinctions, but systematic and thorough in coverage.

Langer, Susanne K., *Feeling and Form.* New York, 1952. Systematic presentation of a theory of art as symbolic of human feeling.

Osborne, Harold, *Aesthetics and Criticism.* An unusually clear presentation of aesthetic problems, with incisive criticism of most aesthetic theories.

Parker, DeWitt, *The Analysis of Art.* New Haven, 1926. An insightful discussion of many of the major problems of the philosophy of art.

Pepper, Stephen, *The Basis of Criticism in the Arts.* Cambridge, Mass., 1949. A survey of the major theories of aesthetic criticism.

Pepper, Stephen, *Principles of Art Appreciation.* New York, 1949. A stimulating introduction to the aesthetics of the visual arts, with a psychological orientation.

Reid, Louis A., *A Study in Aesthetics.* New York, 1920. Although dated, it contains many insightful discussions of aesthetic problems and distinctions.

Santayana, George, *The Sense of Beauty.* New York, 1896. A classic work on the problems of form, expression, and beauty.

Tolstoy, Leo, *What is Art?*, translated by Aylmer Maude. New York, 1898. Presents with unparalleled clarity and vigor a moralistic view of art.

Weitz, Morris, *Philosophy of the Arts.* Cambridge, Mass., 1950. Lucid commentary on some of the major contemporary positions in aesthetics.

SPECIAL PROBLEMS IN AESTHETICS

Abell, Walter, *Representation and Form.* New York, 1946. Detailed criticism of formalist theories of art, particularly visual art.

Alexander, Samuel, *Beauty and Some Other Forms of Value.* London, 1933. Having written primarily in other areas of philosophy, the author offers interesting views on the nature of beauty.

Arnheim, Rudolf, *Art and Visual Perception.* Berkeley, 1954. A noted psychologist of art discusses form and expressiveness in the visual arts.

Barnes, Albert C., *The Art in Painting.* New York, 1937. A clear and brilliant analysis of the aesthetics of painting, followed by concise critical comments (with illustrations) on specific paintings.

Bell, Clive, *Art.* London, 1914. Vigorous presentation of a formalist theory of visual art.

Bernheimer, Richard, Carpenter, Rhys, Koffka, Kurt, and Nahm, Milton, *Art: a Bryn Mawr Symposium.* Bryn Mawr, Pa., 1940. Four excellent papers on selected problems in aesthetics.

Carritt, E. F., *What is Beauty?* Oxford, 1932. A clear and concise introduction to the theory of beauty, with Crocean orientation. More systematic and readable than his *The Theory of Beauty* and *Introduction to Aesthetics.*

Elton, William, ed., *Aesthetics and Language.* Oxford, 1953. Essays illustrating linguistic analyses in aesthetics—some fruitful, some sterile.

Forster, E. M., *Aspects of the Novel.* New York, 1927. Remains the classic introduction to the aesthetics of the novel.

Fry, Roger, *Vision and Design.* London, 1920. Clear and provocative essays presenting a formalist theory of visual art. Fry's *Transformations* presents his viewpoint in the context of analyses of specific paintings.

Gurney, Edmund, *The Power of Sound.* London, 1880. Classic introduction to the aesthetics of music.

Hanslick, Eduard, *The Beautiful in Music.* New York, 1957. Brief presentation of a formalist theory of music.

Hartshorne, Charles, *The Philosophy and Psychology of Sensation.* Chicago, 1934. Excellent study of the perceptual aspects of the arts.

Heyl, Bernard C., *New Bearings in Aesthetics and Art Criticism.* New Haven, 1943. Brief survey and assessment of objectivism, subjectivism, and relativism in aesthetics.

Hospers, John, *Meaning and Truth in the Arts.* Chapel Hill, N.C., 1946. Discussion of the concepts of meaning and truth in the context of the arts.

Hungerland, Isabel, *Poetic Discourse.* Berkeley, 1957. Unexcelled analyses of the aesthetic problems of literature, particularly poetry.

Osborne, Harold, *Theory of Beauty.* London, 1952. Theories of beauty, including the author's own, thoroughly and lucidly presented.

Prall, D. W., *Aesthetic Judgment.* New York, 1929. Particularly detailed discussions of the sensory media of the arts.

Pratt, Carroll C., *The Meaning of Music.* New York, 1931. Written by a psychologist, this book gives detailed criticism of "emotionalist" theories of music and presents an alternative theory.

Richards, I. A., *Principles of Literary Criticism.* New York, 1925. Together with Richards' *Practical Criticism*, this remains the classic introduction to the subject.

Richards, I. A., *Science and Poetry.* London, 1926. Brief and provocative discussion.

Santayana, George, *Reason in Art.* New York, 1905. Reflections on the relation of art to human life; one of the author's four-volume series *The Life of Reason.*

Stace, W. T., *The Meaning of Beauty.* New York, 1937. Clear presentation of a distinctive theory of the nature of beauty.

JOHN HOSPERS

AETHER. *See* ETHER.

AGAPE. *See* LOVE.

AGNOSTICISM. In the most general use of the term, agnosticism is the view that we do not know whether there is a God or not. Although the history of agnosticism, in this general sense, is continuous with that of skepticism (thus reaching back to the ancients), the term itself was coined by T. H. Huxley and its distinctive philosophical bearings emerged in the course of the nineteenth-century debate on religious belief. Participants in that debate often used the word in a strong and specific sense: to be an agnostic was to hold that knowledge of God is impossible because of the inherent, insuperable limitations of the human mind. To assert confidently either the existence or the nonexistence of a deity with definite and intelligible attributes was to transgress these limits.

This consciousness of limitation is classically expressed in the "Transcendental Dialectic" of Kant's *Critique of Pure Reason* (1781). There is a continual temptation, Kant stated, to raise questions about the totality of things; but these questions, he argued, are demonstrably unanswerable. Contradictions are encountered, for instance, whether it is assumed that the world is finite in space and time or infinite in space and time. Or, in another instance, one event may properly be called the cause of another event, but such a concept cannot be used to assert that something (a First Cause) is the cause of the universe as a whole. Of this "whole" one has, and can have, no experience. The main line of agnostic argument in the nineteenth century followed Kant closely in his criticism of cosmological reasoning, although many agnostic writers were not thoroughgoing Kantians. Nor did they have to be Humeans to have their metaphysical assurance called in question by Hume's famous (or notorious) criticism of speculation in *An Enquiry Concerning Human Understanding* (1748): "If we take in our hand any volume; of divinity or school metaphysics, for instance; let us ask, *Does it contain any abstract reasoning concerning quantity or number?* No. *Does it contain any experimental reasoning concerning matter of fact and existence?* No. Commit it then to the flames: for it can contain nothing but sophistry and illusion."

A person who calls himself agnostic commonly judges that he cannot have both agnosticism and, say, Christian belief. Yet the main positions of nineteenth-century agnosticism were in fact worked out and held by "religious agnostics," writers who argued that a very high degree of ignorance concerning the deity was nonetheless compatible with a religious commitment of some kind. In fact, if not in name, this view is also found in the twentieth century; it is essentially the view of those who disclaim metaphysical knowledge of God, but yet stake all upon "faith," "authority," or Christianity as a practical way of life. Kant may again provide the archetypal model: having denied that theoretical reasoning could furnish arguments for the existence of God, he nevertheless claimed that God had to be "postulated" in order to make sense of moral experience.

In his most influential article, "Philosophy of the Unconditioned" (*The Edinburgh Review,* 1829), Sir William Hamilton tersely introduced themes that were to be developed, refined, and repudiated by writer after writer to the end of the century and well beyond. "The mind," he wrote, "can . . . know only the *limited, and the conditionally limited.*" To attempt to think the unconditioned or absolute is to think away "those very conditions under which thought itself is realized." "Loath to admit that our science is at best the reflection of a reality we cannot know, we strive to penetrate to existence in itself; . . . But, like Ixion, we embrace a cloud for a divinity. . . ."

H. L. Mansel, in his Bampton lectures, *The Limits of Religious Thought* (1858), tried to show in detail that alleged knowledge of the Absolute is self-contradictory at many points. One attributes personal qualities to God, for instance, and yet one cannot think through the notion of personality without the idea of limitation; thought must be distinguished from thinker, and so on. But limitation is incompatible with infinite and absolute deity. The conclusion, however, is not a total religious skepticism. For although speculation about the divine nature is a vain attempt to escape the inescapable conditions of human thought, yet through the "feeling of dependence" and in moral conviction faith may still operate where speculative reason cannot.

Herbert Spencer in his *First Principles* (1862) accepted this picture of a limited human reason, aware of its limits and yet (in his view) aware also that those limits are decidedly not the limits of the real. Science and religion could, in fact, be reconciled by realizing that each of them testifies to a mystery, to an inscrutable Absolute, quite beyond the frontiers of knowledge or conception but yet not mere negation or nothingness.

The sources of nineteenth-century agnosticism—particularly the agnosticism of those who abandoned organized religion—were, however, more numerous and complex than has been indicated so far. It is rare indeed that a single line of philosophical argument produces by itself either religious conviction or disillusionment. At least three additional sources should be mentioned.

First, a growing mass of data and theory supplied by the physical sciences was *prima facie* at variance with Biblical history and cosmology. There was the new time scale of geology, the impersonal and amoral Darwinian evolutionary theory, and the radical textual, historical criticism of the Bible itself.

Second, once the strong initial resistance to systematic and searching criticism of Christian teaching had been overcome, it was possible to express openly a good many moral misgivings about the Christian conception of God and his governance of the world. J. S. Mill declared it was impossible for a thoughtful person to ascribe "absolute perfection to the author and ruler of so clumsily made and capriciously governed a creation as this planet" (*Three Essays on Religion,* 1874). He found "moral difficulties" also in "the recognition . . . of the object of highest worship, in a being who could make a Hell" and create creatures whom he foreknew to be destined to suffer in it eternally. No less morally repugnant to many writers was the insistence of the orthodox that their dogmas required sheer unswerving acceptance, and that breakdowns in argument or intelligibility were simply occasions for the exercise of an intensified faith. T. H. Huxley was forthright. In "Agnosticism and Christianity" (1889) he wrote, "I, and many other Agnostics, believe that faith, in this sense, is an abomination." In "Agnosticism" (1889) he said, "I verily believe that the great good which has been effected . . . by Christianity has been largely counteracted by the pestilent doctrine . . . that honest disbelief in their more or less astonishing creeds is a moral offence, indeed a sin of the deepest dye. . . ."

Third, the same authors were vehemently critical of the standards of evidence and reasoning normal in theology, and contrasted them with the severe, rigorous, and dispassionate criteria of the sciences. To Mill, "The whole of the prevalent metaphysics of the present century is one tissue of suborned evidence in favour of religion." If one considers the nature of the world as one actually observes it, the very most one could dare to hazard is the existence of a good but finite deity; and Mill put forward even this possibility with a characteristically agnostic tentativeness. For Huxley agnosticism was "not a creed but a method, the essence of which lies in the rigorous application of a single principle": reason should be followed "as far as it can take you," but undemonstrable conclusions should not be treated as if they were certain. "One may suspect," he said, "that a little more critical discrimination would have enlarged the Apocrypha not inconsiderably." In a similar vein, Leslie Stephen protested against theologians who ventured to define "the nature of God Almighty with an accuracy from which modest naturalists would shrink in describing the genesis of a black beetle" (*An Agnostic's Apology*, 1893).

It is not the purpose here to estimate how far theologians remedied, or could ever remedy, the deficiencies in their arguments that offended their agnostic critics. Some permanently valuable lessons can be learned, however, from the course of the controversies. An obvious one is the odd instability or ambiguity of certain agnostic positions. Let us suppose—as did many of the writers just quoted—that one ceases to find convincing the arguments for the existence of a deity. Experience, one now judges, is limited to the observable world; and reason, although it may lay bare the conditions and presuppositions of that experience, cannot extend our experience of what is. A religiously minded person, in this situation, is tempted to divide reality into the knowable and the unknowable and to attribute to the latter many of the lineaments of deity. Thus, "negative theology" and a religiously toned agnosticism can be the closest of relatives. No sweeping philosophical criticism can demonstrate that all such positions are untenable or involve a cryptotheism; each case must be scrutinized individually. Certain religious attitudes toward the unknown or unknowable—attitudes, for example, of wonderment and awe—can be perfectly appropriate and invulnerable to criticism, whereas others—such as the expectation of personal encounter with the unknown—are obviously most vulnerable. One can turn to history for some examples.

In 1896 James Ward delivered his Gifford lectures, *Naturalism and Agnosticism* (published in 1899), at Aberdeen University. These contained a vigorous attack on the basic presuppositions of the Hamilton–Mansel–Spencer approach. The sciences, Ward said, do not form a whole that floats in a surrounding "nescience." The world we know does not consist of "appearance" concealing an "ultimate reality" that lies behind or beyond it. In any case, nescience is nescience. "Where nescience is absolute, nothing can be said; neither that there is more to know nor that there is not." Spencer and like-minded writers had, however, said a good many mysterious things about their Absolute, things that, by their own account, were strictly unsayable.

R. Flint (*Agnosticism*, Croall lectures, 1887–1888, published in 1903) also denounced the equivocations (as he saw them) of a religious agnosticism. "All that the mind can do on the side of the Unknowable is to play at make-believe, to feign faith, to worship nothingness." "Call your doubts mysteries," said Leslie Stephen, satirizing the complacent, "and they won't disturb you any longer."

Is it possible for a reflective person to be an agnostic in the present time? Logical positivists have answered "No." In *Language, Truth and Logic* (1936), A. J. Ayer claimed that since "all utterances about the nature of God are nonsensical," the agnostic's statements about God are no less nonsensical than the theist's. Both assume, wrongly, that "the question whether a transcendent God exists is a genuine question." According to positivism and postpositivist logical analysis, the theological problem is not a problem of evidence and argument, but a problem of meaningfulness. If "God" is a meaningless word, the sentence "Perhaps God does not exist" is also meaningless.

In stating the situation thus, positivism was dramatically drawing attention to what it believed to be distinctive in its approach, but it simultaneously obscured some important lines of continuity with the earlier debate on agnosticism. Before the nineteenth century had ended, Flint had written, in criticism of Hamilton, "*Credo quia absurdum* can be the only appropriate motto of a philosopher who holds that we may believe in a God the very idea of whom we can perceive to be self-contradictory." The possibility of internal illogicality in the very notion of deity, the risk of the absurd and nonsensical, were well enough recognized. Spencer, wrestling with the problems of the world's origin and beginning, said that the questions here are not questions of credibility but of *conceivability*. Notions such as self-existence and creation by an external agency "involve symbolic conceptions of the illegitimate and illusive kind." The logical positivist tethered his theory of meaning to the demands for observational verification and falsification of our claims about existents. Compare Spencer once more, writing in 1899: "Intellect being framed simply by and for converse with phenomena, involves us in nonsense when we try to use it for anything beyond phenomena." It must, of course, be added that the positivists and later analysts carried out their austere program with far greater thoroughness and consistency than did their predecessors. But the lines of continuity are there; and they are—once more—those same lines that reach back to Kant's "Transcendental Dialectic" and to David Hume. They justify the use of "atheist" to describe one who rejects the performances and attitudes of religion on the grounds that talk about God is unverifiable talk, or that the concept *God* contains inner illogicalities.

But is there still room for agnosticism as undogmatic dubiety or ignorance about the existence of God? A case for saying that there is still room can be made on the following lines. Where one gives an account of an expression in our language, and where that expression is one that refers to an existent of some kind, one needs to provide not only a set of rules for the use of the expression, but also an indication of how the referring is to be done—through direct pointing, perhaps, or through giving instructions for an indirect method of identifying the entity. Can this be done in the case of God? Pointing, clearly, is inappropriate, God being no finite object in the world. The theologian may suggest a number of options at this point. He may say: God can be identified as that being upon whom the world can be felt as utterly dependent, who is the completion of its incompletenesses, whose presence is faintly adumbrated in experience of the awesome and the numinous. Clear direction-giving has here broken down; the theologian may well admit that his language is less descriptive or argumentative than obliquely evocative. Does this language succeed in establishing that statements about God have a reference? To persons susceptible to religious experience but at the same time logically and critically alert, it may seem just barely to succeed, or it may seem just barely to fail. Some may even oscillate uneasily between these alternatives without finding a definite procedure of decision to help them discriminate once for all. A person in this last category is surely an agnostic. His agnosticism takes full account of current linguistic criticisms of religion; it is in the course of his reflections upon meaning that he sees the necessity of relating the linguistic to the extralinguistic, and his answers to this problem, the problem of reference, plunge him into the deepest uncertainty.

The temper of mind just outlined, with all its inner turbulence and anxiety, is probably the most creatively fruitful of the many varieties of agnosticism. Where there is no temptation to believe, there can be little philosophical interest in not believing. Where there has been little or no religious experience, no sense of the haunting strangeness that makes the believer wittingly violate language and logic to express it, there can be little incentive to explore minutely the possible interpretations—theistic, pantheistic, naturalistic—of that experience. As a matter of history, agnostics of this temper are to be found far more rarely today than at the height of the agnosticism controversy a century ago. For the great writers of that controversy were in most cases brought up within the Christian faith, had identified themselves with it, and subsequently suffered a bewildering disorientation. Yet, if one is to take seriously today the problems of philosophical theology, there must be some suspension of disbelief, at least an imaginative venture, in order to see why the believer feels compelled to use the extraordinary language he does use. He knows well enough that it is extraordinary; but he deems that it is ordinary language that is found wanting, and not his experiences and the interpretations he puts upon them. The agnostic knows that sometimes ordinary language needs to be violated, as a poet often violates it. He knows also that to disturb our linguistic apparatus in so radical a way can obscure some movements of thought of a very questionable (or downright invalid) logic. Has this happened in the particular case of theism? Searching in this obscurity, the agnostic reports that he cannot tell. For the health of philosophy and theology, it is well that he should continue to search.

Bibliography

HUME AND KANT

Hume, David, *Enquiry concerning Human Understanding.* London, 1748. Especially sections X and XI.

Hume, David, *Dialogues concerning Natural Religion.* London, 1779.

Kant, Immanuel, *Kritik der reinen Vernunft* (1781), in Berlin Academy, *Complete Works.* Berlin, 1902–1955.

See also SKEPTICISM and EMPIRICISM.

NINETEENTH-CENTURY DOCUMENTS

Flint, R., *Agnosticism.* Edinburgh and London, 1903.

Hamilton, Sir William, "Philosophy of the Unconditioned." *The Edinburgh Review* (1829).

Huxley, T. H., "Agnosticism and Christianity" (1889), in his *Collected Essays,* Vol. V. London, 1894. Entire volume is relevant.

Mansel, H. L., *The Limits of Religious Thought.* London, 1858.

Mill, J. S., *Three Essays on Religion.* London, 1874.

Spencer, Herbert, *First Principles.* London, 1862.

Stephen, Leslie, *An Agnostic's Apology.* London, 1893. First published as an essay in 1876.

Ward, James, *Naturalism and Agnosticism.* London, 1899; 2d ed., with alterations, 1903.

SECONDARY SOURCES

Armstrong, R. A., *Agnosticism and Theism in the Nineteenth Century.* London, 1905.

Britton, K., *John Stuart Mill.* London, 1953.

Burtt, E. A., *Types of Religious Philosophy.* New York, 1951.

Collins, J., *God in Modern Philosophy.* London, 1960.

Garrigou-Lagrange, R., *Dieu, son existence et sa nature; solution thomiste des antinomies agnostiques.* Paris, 1915.

Packe, M. St. John, *John Stuart Mill.* London, 1954. Biography.

Passmore, J., *A Hundred Years of Philosophy.* London, 1957. Especially Ch. 2.

Stephen, Leslie, *English Thought in the Eighteenth Century.* London, 1876.

Willey, Basil, *Nineteenth Century Studies.* London, 1950.

RONALD W. HEPBURN

AGRIPPA is one of the many important ancient Skeptics whose lives are almost entirely unknown to us. All that we can say with any certainty about his life is that he was a Greek, that he lived before the middle of the third century A.D., and that he was famous enough in his day to have a book (by Apellas) named after him. The only extant ancient writing in which his name appears is the *Lives* of Diogenes Laërtius.

The only contribution that we can attribute to Agrippa with any certainty is five *tropoi,* or ways of achieving doubt. They are more general than the famous tropes of Aenesidemus, since they cast doubt not only on the senses but on the understanding too; the tropes of Aenesidemus more modestly point out ten special types of conflict, primarily with respect to sense experience. The five tropes of Agrippa are closer to the radical, sweeping Skepticism of the Academy (Arcesilaus and Carneades) than they are to the more cautious doubt to be found elsewhere in Greek Skepticism. But they are even more severe than the arguments of the members of the New Academy: the latter distinguished phenomena from "nonevident" or "hidden" (*adela*) things and cast doubt only upon claims made about hidden things; Agrippa's tropes do not make this distinction and cast doubt upon phenomenal and transphenomenal claims.

The first trope is that of conflict or discrepancy. It is plainly the case that ordinary people as well as philosophers are involved in conflicts over the nature of external objects and over the way we can know them. Some people assert that only the senses give us true knowledge; others assert that only pure reason gives us such knowledge; and still others assert that both the senses and reason give us knowledge. But since there is no criterion for concluding who is right, the conflict continues. If we face the plain fact that this conflict exists and persists, we must suspend judgment on these matters.

The second trope is that of infinite regress. If we want to prove a given conclusion, we need premises to do so; but these premises themselves require proof, and these proofs in turn require proof, and so on ad infinitum. We can decide or prove nothing in any final way, and we must suspend judgment. Moreover, if we claim that a given premise is self-evident, we must demonstrate that this is the case, and we are again caught in a regress.

The third trope is that of relativity. In order to know something, we must know it by way of its relationship to the perceiving subject and to our perceptions of other things. And so we cannot know a thing in itself and must suspend judgment about what it is in itself.

The fourth trope is that of hypothesis. In order to avoid an infinite regress, we adopt some premise as true without proving it to be true. For instance, we adopt as true a statement usually more general than our conclusion (this we call a "hypothesis"), and we "prove" our conclusion by pointing to our hypothesis and then logically deducing that conclusion from this hypothesis. But the hypothesis itself has not been established by argument and is undemonstrated; therefore we must suspend our judgment concerning both it and the conclusion to be proved.

The fifth and last trope, similar to the fourth and the second, is that of circularity. When a given premise that is supposed to prove our conclusion derives its plausibility from that conclusion itself, the premise cannot establish that conclusion because we cannot assume the premise to be true without assuming, not proving, that the conclusion is true.

The tropes of Agrippa may not have been invented by him; in fact, we have some reason to think that he, as a later Skeptic, was formulating the practice of his predecessors and contemporaries. But the formula he gives in the five tropes is the most concise statement of the Skeptical method for achieving doubt to be found in the history of Greek Skepticism. Moreover, it represents the most destructive type of Skepticism to emerge in the course of that history.

Bibliography

ANCIENT SOURCES

Diogenes Laërtius, *Lives of Eminent Philosophers*, translated by R. D. Hicks, 2 vols. Loeb Classical Library. Cambridge, Mass., and London, 1925.

Sextus Empiricus, *Philosophical Works*, translated by R. G. Bury, 4 vols. Loeb Classical Library. Cambridge, Mass., and London, 1955–1961. See *Outlines of Pyrrhonism*.

MODERN SOURCE

Brochard, Victor, *Les Sceptiques grecs*. Paris, 1923.

PHILIP P. HALLIE

AGRIPPA VON NETTESHEIM, HENRICUS CORNELIUS (1486–1535), a colorful Renaissance figure—a diplomat, a military adventurer, a cabalist, an expert on occult science, a medical doctor, a lawyer, a theologian, an early Reformer, as well as a troublesome and troubled intellectual—was born of minor nobility in or near Cologne. His first official position was that of a court secretary of the Holy Roman emperor. He was sent to Paris in 1506 and there joined a secret group of theosophists. He next became involved in a revolutionary plot in Catalonia. In 1509 he gave lectures at the University of Dôle, on Reuchlin's cabalistic *De Verbo Mirifico*. He learned Hebrew and immersed himself in cabalistic, Gnostic, and hermeneutic writings. This research culminated in three volumes on occult science, *De Occulta Philosophia*, written in 1509–1510 but not published until 1531–1533 in Cologne (trans. by J. F., London, 1651). At Dôle he also wrote on the superiority and nobility of women and entered into his first marriage. These early unpublished writings touched off a fight between Agrippa and certain conservative monks, who accused him, along with Reuchlin, Erasmus, and the French humanist–Reformer Lefèvre d'Etaples, of being Judaizers and heretics.

In 1510 Agrippa was sent to London, where he lived with Erasmus' friend John Colet, who interested Agrippa in St. Paul's epistles. Next, Agrippa lectured on theology in Cologne. From 1511 to 1513 he fought in various Italian campaigns and engaged in theological battles, even with the pope. In 1515 he taught occult science at the University of Pavia. Three years later Agrippa became public advocate and orator of Metz and was soon embroiled again in theological battles and in defending a peasant woman accused cf sorcery. The opposition of the inquisitor of Metz forced him to leave. Agrippa's wife died soon after, and he retired to Geneva. In 1522 he remarried and became a medical practitioner. He was appointed physician to the queen mother of France and became involved in a demoralizing struggle to collect his salary and to fulfill his duties. At the queen mother's orders he was stranded in Lyons from 1524 to 1526 without funds and without permission to leave. Agrippa wrote many bellicose letters to the court, antagonizing numerous people but settling nothing. His only official duty was the drawing up of horoscopes (which he knew were useless and fraudulent). In this period Agrippa wrote his major work, *De Incertitudine et Vanitate de Scientiarum et Artium* (Antwerp, 1530; trans. by James Sandford as *Of the Vanitie and uncertaintie of artes and sciences*, London, 1569), attacking every type of intellectual endeavor and art, as well as courtiers, princes, and monks. Even cabalistic and occult researches were disowned as superstitious rhapsodies. Only pious Bible study remained worthwhile.

Agrippa abandoned hope of regaining court favor or receiving his salary and in 1528 went to Antwerp, where he had a brief flurry of success. He was appointed historiographer to Charles V, achieved success as a medical doctor, and finally published his works. This happy phase was soon followed by catastrophes. His second wife died of the plague. The publication of his *Vanity of the Sciences* outraged Charles V. Agrippa was jailed and branded a heretic. A disastrous marriage left him financially ruined and miserable. He returned to Germany, battled with the inquisitor of Cologne, and was banished in 1535. Having fled to France, he was arrested for having criticized the queen mother, was released, and died in Grenoble.

Agrippa was notorious as a magician and as a stormy opponent of the monks and the "establishment." He made his main intellectual contributions as an expositor of cabalism and occult science, as a critic of all intellectual activities, and as a Reformer within Catholicism. His *De Occulta Philosophia* tried to explain the universe in terms of cabalistic analyses of Hebrew letters and their relations to natural phenomena and divine understanding; in terms of the Pythagorean numerological symbols; and of the Christian interpretation of cabalism and Pythagoreanism. *De Occulta Philosophia* played a major role in Renaissance magical and cabalistic studies.

Agrippa's *Vanity of the Sciences* was one of the first contributions to the Renaissance revival of skepticism, but its weapons were denunciation and ridicule, not philosophical analysis. It is more a bitter version of Erasmus' *In Praise of Folly* than a serious epistemological examination of whether knowledge can be gained by human means. Its final appeal is to a type of fundamentalistic anti-intellectualism. The work represents a stage in Agrippa's journey from occult studies to a simple Biblical faith opposed to late medieval Scholasticism. Agrippa, although he did not revolt against Catholicism, lacked Erasmus' patience and calm and became almost a Catholic Luther, violently denouncing monks, Scholastic theologians, and others. In the end he rejected occult studies—and all others—as a way of penetrating the divine mysteries, and he proclaimed: "It is better therefore and more profitable to be idiots and know nothing, to believe by Faith and Charity, and to become next unto God, than being lofty and proud through the subtilties of sciences to fall into the possession of the Serpent."

Works by Agrippa

Opera. Lyons, n.d.

Die Eitelkeit und Unsicherheit der Wissenschaften und die Verteidigungschrift, Fritz Mauthner, ed. Munich, 1913.

Works on Agrippa

Bayle, Pierre, "Agrippa," in *Dictionnaire historique et critique*, 2 vols. Rotterdam, 1695–1697.

Blau, Joseph, *The Christian Interpretation of the Cabala in the Renaissance*. New York, 1944.

Morley, Henry, *The Life of Henry Cornelius von Nettesheim*, 2 vols. London, 1856.

Nauert, Charles G., "Magic and Skepticism in Agrippa's Thought," *Journal of the History of Ideas*, Vol. 18 (1957), 161–182.

Popkin, R. H., *History of Scepticism from Erasmus to Descartes*. Assen, 1960; New York, 1964.

Prost, Auguste, *Les Sciences et les arts occultes au XVIe siècle: Corneille Agrippa, sa vie et ses oeuvres*, 2 vols. Paris, 1881–1882.

Walker, D. P., *Spiritual and Demonic Magic from Ficino to Campanella*. London, 1958.

Yates, Frances A., *Giordano Bruno and the Hermetic Tradition*. London, 1964.

RICHARD H. POPKIN

AILLY, PIERRE D' (1350–1421), Ockhamist philosopher. D'Ailly was born at Compiègne in France and studied at the Navarre College in Paris in 1372, receiving his doctoral degree in 1380 and becoming chancellor of the university in 1389. He was made bishop of Puy in 1395 and bishop of Cambrai in 1396 and cardinal in 1411. He took a leading part in the Council of Constance (1414–1418), where he asserted the superiority of a general council of the church over the pope. He died as papal legate at Avignon.

D'Ailly's literary output was vast and wide-ranging. It comprehended philosophy, theology, scientific theory, political theory, canon law, and ecclesiastical politics and touched on mysticism. Among his more important writings were the treatise *De Anima*, commentaries on Boethius' *Consolation of Philosophy* and the four books of the *Sentences*, two studies of mysticism and asceticism, three works on different aspects of church government, and a series of works on logic, astronomy, and geography.

In his philosophical outlook d'Ailly seems to have been sympathetic to Ockhamism. Like so many fourteenth-century thinkers he postulated different degrees of certainty. The main distinction d'Ailly made was between what he called "natural light" and reason. Natural light corresponded to knowledge which was indubitable—namely, that which could be reduced to the principle of contradiction or immediate intuition of the existence of the self, in the manner of John of Mirecourt. Reason, on the other hand, was only relative in its certainty and was confined to the natural order. Included within it were the traditional arguments for God's existence, which d'Ailly treated as merely probable. The influence of Ockham is also apparent in d'Ailly's treatment of God's omnipotence; since it was independent of the natural order, God was in no way bound to follow nature's laws. Accordingly, God could create the illusion that something existed when in fact it did not; this was one of the most insistent Ockhamist arguments against the infallibility of experiential knowledge. At the same time d'Ailly was careful to distinguish the realm of God's absolute power (*potentia absoluta*) from the realm subject to his ordained power (*potentia ordinata*). Whereas the first realm referred to God's omnipotence as such, the latter constituted the specific application of his omnipotence to this world; it provided the laws by which creation was regulated, and among them d'Ailly included the laws of physics. They therefore operated constantly and with certainty.

D'Ailly's debt to Ockham and John of Mirecourt is also to be seen in his views on essences. There was no inherent reason why hot was hot or cold cold other than God's willing it. The same applied to the moral order, where good and bad were such because of God's voluntary decree: "Nothing is good or bad of itself such that God must love or hate it." Similarly, a man was just not from possessing the intrinsic property of justice but because God accepted him as just. Here was the same absence of a constant scale of values which had proved so destructive of the traditional teachings in the time of Ockham and the first generation of his followers, who included Robert Holkot, Adam of Woodham, and John of Mirecourt. D'Ailly further emphasized the uncertain nature of natural experience by his acceptance of the so-called *complexe significabile*, by which an expression such as "sin" did not denote a specific object but was a description or statement which referred to an action. As employed by Nicholas of Autrecourt, it had denied the reality of a wide range of expressions. Thus the word "God" stood not for a specific being but for a verbal expression: supreme or highest being. As such it lacked correspondence to anything but a grouping of words. At the same time, in keeping at the natural level, d'Ailly granted a correspondingly wider area of jurisdiction to faith. Thus evidence for God's existence could be held only as a matter of belief.

Works by d'Ailly

Tractatus Exponibilium Magistri Petri de Allyaco. Paris, 1494.

Quaestiones Super Primum, Tertium et Quartum Sententiarum. Venice, 1500.

De Anima. Paris, 1501.

Tractatus et Sermones. Douai, France, 1639. Includes *De Anima.*

Destructiones Modorum Significandi. Conceptus et Insolubilia Secondum Viam Nominalium Magistri Petri de Allyaco. (No date.)

Works on d'Ailly

Dictionnaire de théologie catholique, Vol. I. Paris, 1903–1951. Pp. 642–654.

Gandillac, M. P. de, "Usage et valeur des arguments probables chez Pierre d'Ailly." *Archives d'histoire doctrinale et littéraire*, Vol. 8 (1933), 43–91.

GORDON LEFF

AJDUKIEWICZ, KAZIMIERZ (1890–1963), logician and semanticist, was educated at the University of Lwów where he studied philosophy, physics, and mathematics. Having obtained his doctorate he visited Göttingen (the seat of David Hilbert's formalism), where he stayed one year. His teachers at Lwów included Kazimierz Twardowski, Jan Łukasiewicz, and Wacław Sierpiński. He became a lecturer in philosophy in 1921 and taught at the universities of Lwów, Poznań, and Warsaw until his retirement in 1961. He was a member of the Polish Academy of Science, held an honorary doctor's degree from the University of Clermont-Ferrand, and took an active role in the work of Polish and international philosophical organizations (Polish Institute of Philosophy and Sociology, International Institute of Philosophy, International Union for History and Philosophy of Science). He was an influential teacher and one of the leaders of the Warsaw school of philosophy and logic, whose members, such as Stanislaw Leśniewski, Jan Łukasiewicz, and Tadeusz Kotarbiński, made important contributions to the advancement of knowledge and exercised a profound influence upon the intellectual life of their country.

Ajdukiewicz was interested in a wide range of subjects. He gave perhaps the earliest formulation of the deduction theorem for elementary logic (1920), which enabled him to define the concept of logical consequence in purely syntactical terms. He devised a neat notation for Stanisław Leśniewski's theory of semantical categories and formulated the necessary and sufficient conditions for a linguistic expression compounded of simple meaningful expressions to be itself meaningful and syntactically connected. Thus he was able, by means of purely structural criteria, to show that such expressions as "$p \vee p. \supset .p$" and "lilacs smell sweet" are syntactically connected, while "$F(\varphi): \equiv :\sim\varphi(\varphi)$" and "the horse if then" are not. While analyzing the Marxist belief that internal contradictions are inherent in all things and in all phenomena of nature (in the course of which he persuaded his opponents in Poland of the need to respect the laws of logic), Ajdukiewicz discovered some serious errors of inference in Zeno's paradox of the flying arrow. In particular, he showed that Zeno's conclusions result from the application of an invalid rule of transformation that given a premise of the form $(x)(\exists y)\varphi xy$ (for all x, there is at least one y such that x bears the relation φ to y), we can establish a conclusion of the form $(\exists y)(x)\varphi xy$ (there is at least one y such that for all x, x bears the relation φ to y). He made an effective use of semantical concepts in the examination of the idealistic language in the theory of knowledge and produced vigorous and persuasive arguments in favor of the freedom of science.

The logical analysis of language and of the relationship of language to knowledge were, however, the dominating interest of Ajdukiewicz' entire life. He was one of the philosophers who contributed to the appreciation of the profound influence of language upon knowledge. While he did not share the hope of Bertrand Russell that language may help us understand the structure of the world, he felt sure that our conception of language is largely responsible for what we recognize as valid knowledge. Since he believed that our scientific views about the world are determined both by experience and the language used in their formulations, he was a conventionalist in his conception of science. In the closing period of his life, Ajdukiewicz began moving, however, toward the position of radical empiricism, that is, the view that only empirical sentences are scientific, in an important sense of this expression. Since the test of experience is the only satisfactory criterion of truth, only sentences based directly on experience are true.

Ajdukiewicz maintained that to mean is neither to denote nor to connote. He rejected the associationist and the syntactical theory of meaning, because he thought that the sense of an expression must be distinguished from the associated image and that the vocabulary and the rules of syntax are not sufficient to define a language, L, univocally. The expressions of L also have a meaning dependent on the rules that determine the correct use of the expressions of L. To use L is to follow the meaning rules of L and to follow the meaning rules of L is to assert or to reject certain definite sentences of L in certain corresponding situations, either linguistically or extralinguistically defined. The existence of the universe of meanings is an undeniable fact, since mankind possesses a vast and ever-increasing number of concepts transmitted from generation to generation.

Three kinds of meaning rules can be distinguished: (1) the axiomatic rules of meaning that require an unconditional acceptance of certain sentences, for example, the sentence "Every square has four sides"; (2) the deductive rules of meaning that, given a sentence or sentences, such as "Some birds are predatory," prohibit the rejection of another sentence, "Some predatory animals are birds"; (3) the empirical rules of meaning that preclude the rejection of certain sentences, without violating their meaning, in the presence of certain data of experience. For instance, should a dentist touch the open nerve of a patient and the patient assert, "It is soothing," he would be using this expression in a way other than that prescribed in the English language. Ajdukiewicz regarded the invariance of the meaning rules of *L* as the necessary and sufficient condition for the synonymity of two or more expressions of *L* (a view later revised, for the invariance in question is only a necessary condition of synonymity). Because of this and because synonymity is a reflexive, symmetric, and transitive relation, he defined the meaning of an expression, *E*, in *L* by the principle of abstraction as the class of all expressions in *L* synonymous with *E*. The class of all meanings assigned to the expressions in *L* is called the *conceptual apparatus of L*, and the class of all sentences determined by the meaning rules of *L* together with certain data of experience is called the *world-perspective of L*.

The rules of meaning can be univocally specified only for artificial languages. Natural languages are actually families of languages in which the combinations of meaning rules vary from one group of users to another. Consequently, natural languages cannot be made logically perfect, and their conceptual apparatuses may overlap or be incompatible. This does not invalidate the significance of a theory of meaning based on the rules of language. The philosopher is concerned with relations of meaning, and he can analyze the meaning assigned to expressions of *L* if he can establish the inference relations among these expressions.

If language is a system of connected and meaningful expressions, and there is no scientific knowledge unless it is expressed in some language, knowledge is bound to include a priori elements. Moreover, empirical knowledge is not entirely independent of choice of language, for deductive meaning rules are determined by language. Empirical knowledge consists of hypotheses, whose validity depends on the confirmation of empirical consequences derived from the hypotheses by means of the deductive rules of meaning.

In a language in which there are no axiomatic rules of meaning, no analytic sentences could occur; it is not possible to obtain analytic sentences by means of the deductive rules alone. To eliminate the remaining a priori elements (from our knowledge), the deductive rules would have to be retained but as mere rules of inference. Since rejecting them would no longer constitute a violation of the meanings of language, the rules of inference could be accepted provisionally and, therefore, be changed just as much as the asserted hypotheses. In cases where consequences derived from a set of scientific hypotheses, by means of some provisionally accepted inference rules, are falsified in direct experience, the treatment of the rules of inference and scientific hypotheses on the same footing offers the choice of rejecting either the hypotheses or the rules of inference. For instance, some physicists and philosophers maintain that within quantum mechanics we are faced with the choice of retaining the logical principle of bivalence and regarding some statements about unobserved entities as meaningless or of considering all such statements as meaningful and rejecting the logical principle of bivalence. In the latter case, the rule derived from the assumption that every *p* is either true or false or indeterminate would take the place of the familiar rule based on the principle that every *p* is either true or false. The reduction of the rules of inference to the status of hypotheses requires, however, the abandonment of the whole conception of language as a system fully determined by its vocabulary, its syntax, and its meaning rules and its replacement by another theory compatible with the thesis of radical empiricism.

Major Works by Ajdukiewicz

Z Metodologii Nauk Dedukcyjnych ("On the Methodology of the Deductive Sciences"). Lvov, 1921.

Jezyk i Poznanie ("Language and Knowledge"), Vols. I–II. Warsaw, 1960–1965. These two volumes include all important articles published in the years 1920–1939 and 1946–1964 respectively.

"Sprache und Sinn." *Erkenntnis*, Vol. 4 (1934), 100–138.

"Das Weltbild und die Begriffsapparatur." *Erkenntnis*, Vol. 4 (1934), 259–287.

"Die syntaktische Konnexität." *Studia Philosophica*, Vol. 1 (1935), 1–27.

"Die wissenschaftliche Weltperspektive." *Erkenntnis*, Vol. 5 (1935–1936), 22–30. Translated by W. Sellars as "The Scientific World-perspective," in H. Feigl and W. Sellars, *Readings in Philosophical Analysis*. New York, 1949. Pp. 182–188.

"Zmiana i Sprzeczność" ("Change and Contradiction"). *Mysl Współczesna*, No. 8–9 (1948), 35–52.

"Epistemology and Semiotic." *Proceedings of the Tenth International Congress of Philosophy*, Vol. 1 (Amsterdam, 1949), 607–609.

"Logic and Experience." *Synthese*, Vol. 8 (1950), 289–299.

"On the Freedom of Science." *Review of the Polish Academy of Science*, Vol. 2 (1957), 1–19.

"Le Problème du fondement des propositions analytiques." *Studia Logica*, Vol. 8 (1958), 259–272.

"Three Concepts of Definition." *Logique et analyse*, No. 3–4 (1958), 115–126.

"La Notion de rationalité dans les méthodes d'inférence faillible." *Logique et analyse*, No. 5 (1959), 3–18.

"The Axiomatic Systems From the Methodological Point of View." *Studia Logica*, Vol. 9 (1960), 205–216.

Works on Ajdukiewicz

Beth, E. W., *The Foundations of Mathematics*. Amsterdam, 1959. Pp. 619–621.

Bocheński, J. M., "On the Syntactical Categories." *New Scholasticism*, Vol. 23 (1949), 257–280.

Jordan, Z. A., *The Development of Mathematical Logic and Logical Positivism in Poland Between the Two Wars*. London, 1945.

Jordan, Z. A., *Philosophy and Ideology: The Development of Philosophy and Marxism-Leninism in Poland Since the Second World War*. Dordrecht, Netherlands, 1963. Pp. 38–41, 95–96, 200–217.

Nagel, E., *Logic Without Metaphysics*. Glencoe, Ill., 1956. Pp. 241–246.

Z. A. JORDAN

ALBERT OF SAXONY, or Helmstadt or Rickmersdorf (c. 1316–1390), had a prominent career at the University of Paris, becoming rector in 1357. He was appointed the first rector of the University of Vienna in 1365. In the following year he was made bishop of Halberstadt, in which office he remained until his death. Albert used to be considered one of the great original scientific thinkers of the Middle Ages because of the influence his writings exerted upon subsequent scientific thought. It has recently been recognized, however, that most of his ideas were not his own but were derived primarily from John Buridan and Nicholas of Oresme and in particular that he was neither an originator nor an exponent of a new method of mathematical calculation.

Albert's name is particularly associated with the theory of impetus, his doctrine being a combination of the views of Buridan and Oresme. With Buridan he defined impetus as an innate quality of movement; from both Buridan and Oresme he took the notion of a greater mass generating greater impetus and thus giving increased acceleration (for that reason a stone will travel faster and longer than a feather). Albert also followed Oresme in holding that impetus was acquired naturally in the course of movement and was destroyed by the absence of a force to conserve it and by the natural inclination of a body to rest; it ended when movement ceased. With Marsilius of Inghen, Albert was responsible for the opinion, which continued to prevail, that impetus was the cause of a constant speed in movement, that it was a disposition facilitating movement.

Albert also treated many other scientific questions, including the structure of a material substance (mixtum) and gravitation. On the first he answered the problem of whether and how the four elements—air, fire, earth, and water—remained distinct in a material substance by positing their development into two new qualities. These were a mean between heat and cold and damp and dryness. Hence, since they were displaced for Albert, the original elements no longer inhered in a material substance, such as wood, either formally or merely as accidents. Further combinations of the new qualities were the product of the substantial form and as such constituted certain tendencies within the material substance. Albert, like many others, offered no judgment of Buridan's radical solution that the *mixtum* and the elements were numerically the same.

On gravitation Albert held that the cause of a falling body is found within the body itself as an intrinsic principle. He adopted the commonly expressed formula that it is moved by its form *substantialiter* and by its weight *instrumentaliter.* He agreed with Buridan that a simple body possessed no inner resistance to movement but went further than Buridan in locating a body's center of gravity in the center of the earth. Nicholas of Oresme had already put forward the view that the earth's center of gravity should be identical with the center of the earth, and from this Albert inferred that a body falls in its effort to be united with its center of gravity in the center of the earth. This idea was to have widespread currency until the seventeenth century, as was Albert's uniting of impetus with speed, so that once a moving body had acquired impetus, speed, in turn, gained increased velocity.

Works by Albert

Sophismata. Paris, 1489.
Tractatus Obligationum. Paris, 1490.
Insolubilia. Paris, 1495.
Questions on Ockham's Logic, in William of Ockham, *Expositio Aurea.* Bologna, 1496.
Quaestiones Super Libros Posteriorum. Venice, 1497.
Questions on De Generatione. Venice, 1504.
Questions on Physics. Venice, 1504.
Questions on De Caelo et Mundo. Venice, 1520.
Logica. Venice, 1522.

Works on Albert

Heidingsfelder, G., *Albert von Sachsen: Sein Lebensgang und sein Kommentar zur Nikomachischen Ethik.* Münster in Westfalen, Germany, 1928.
Maier, A., *Die Vorlaüfer Galileis im 14 Jahrhundert.* Rome, 1949.
Maier, A., *Zwei Grundprobleme der scholastischen Naturphilosophie.* Rome, 1951.
Maier, A., *An der Grenze von Scholastik und Naturwissenschaft.* Rome, 1952.
Maier, A., *Metaphysische Hintergründer der spätscholastischen Philosophie.* Rome, 1955.
Maier, A., *Zwischen Philosophie und Mechanik.* Rome, 1955.

GORDON LEFF

ALBERT THE GREAT (d. 1280), bishop of Ratisbon, saint, and Doctor (*Doctor Universalis*) of the Roman Catholic church, was born at Lauingen, Bavaria, sometime between 1193 and 1206. In 1223 he entered the Dominican order, studying at Padua and Bologna. He spent the years 1228–1240 lecturing on theology in various convents in Germany; this "lecturing" probably included preliminary commentaries on the Sentences of Peter Lombard, accounting, in part, for the difficulty modern historians have in dating the oft-revised copy now possessed. In 1240 Albert took his baccalaureate at the University of Paris, where he also taught as master (that is, with the degree Doctor of Theology) from 1245 to 1248; at this time, Thomas Aquinas was his pupil and assistant. In 1248 Albert was sent to Cologne to organize a new course of studies for his order. In 1260 he was consecrated bishop of Ratisbon and administered the diocese for two years, after which time he returned to a life of writing, teaching, and controversy until his death at Cologne.

Albert's more important works include *Summa de Creaturis* ("Handbook of Doctrine Concerning Creatures"), 1240–1243; *Commentarium in IV Libros Sententiarum* ("Commentary on the Four Books of Lombard's Sentences"), 1240–1249; a number of Biblical commentaries dating from his early lecturing and teaching at the University of Paris; commentaries on the whole of the writings of the Pseudo-Dionysius (1248–1254); paraphrases of nearly all of Aristotle, Boethius, pseudo-Aristotelian works, and works that he considered Aristotelian, notably, the *Liber de Causis et Processu Universitatis* ("Book of the Causes and Procession of the Universe"), 1254–1270; and finally there is the *Summa Theologiae* ("Handbook of Theology"), 1270–1280.

Albert's lifetime nearly coincides with the thirteenth century, the "Golden Age of Scholasticism"; his literary production covers at least forty years. He was undoubtedly the dominant figure of his time, the most prolific writer of the century, the most influential teacher, an experienced traveler, a keen observer of nature; the one learned man of the "Golden Age" to be called "the Great," he was cited by name even before his death—a most unusual occurrence in medieval authorship. In describing Albert's accomplishments, however, we face a number of textual problems. First, there are problems of authenticity; doubtful works include a number of fair importance, for example, *Speculum Astronomiae* ("The Mirror of Astronomy"). Second, there are problems of critical editions of texts and even of publication, for example, the commentaries on Pseudo-Dionysius which exist only in manuscripts; the process of collating and editing manuscripts has only just begun, and a final verdict on Albert's thought must await completion of this task. The third, and perhaps most difficult, is that of interpretation. For example, in the *Liber de Causis et Processu Universitatis*, a metaphysical work describing the basic structure of the whole of reality, what is to be thought of passages proclaiming that the author is merely responding to the requests of his associates to explain the teachings of the "Peripatetics" and that the doctrine is "not necessarily" to be taken as his own? And, indeed, the first impression of Albert's encyclopedic production is its aspect of compilation and syncretism. We find Christian Father and pagan philosopher, Aristotelian and Neoplatonic sources: Augustine, Boethius, the Pseudo-Dionysius, Aristotle, Avicenna, Averroës, al-Farabi, and, through the anonymous *Liber de Causis*, Proclus and Plotinus head the cast of contributors to Albert's writings. The influence, if any, that Thomas Aquinas had upon his teacher has not yet been determined precisely; this influence, at present, appears to have been small. Albert may be described as scientist and philosopher, as well as theologian; he is considered here under the first two titles.

Scientist. In general, Albert's works in science and natural philosophy follow the plan of Aristotle's treatises, representing each area of the study of nature: physics, psychology (including the interpretation of dreams), astronomy (and astrology), geography, zoology, botany, mineralogy, as well as discussions of the universe and life-processes in general. Albert, however, does not follow the usual procedure of the Aristotelian commentator, explicating the text line by line, phrase by phrase; rather, his discussion is in the form of a paraphrase, a continuous exposition to which he adds abundant "digressions" expressing his own observations and experiments. Of course, the term "experiment" cannot be understood in the modern sense of a clearly defined and purposeful laboratory enterprise. More often than not, the term indicates a careful, scrutinizing process of observing, describing, and classifying; Albert's works on botany and zoology contain many passages in which he recognizes "experience" as a criterion of truth, noting that experience alone is reliable concerning the individual existent. We find such expressions as: "I have tested this"; "I and my associates have experienced"; "I have not experienced this"; "We pass over what the ancients have written on this topic because their statements do not agree with experience"; "But it is not sufficient to know something as included in a universal; but we strive to know each thing as it is in its own individual kind of being, for this is the best and perfect kind of knowing." This attitude, Albert notes, is not contrary to a religious outlook. Some men, for example, would attribute the deluge simply to the divine will, not seeking other causes. Albert, however, while also ascribing the event ultimately to the divine will, maintains that God acts through natural causes in natural phenomena; while he does not attempt to investigate the divine will, he does feel free to seek those natural causes that were divine instruments.

Further, in Albert's books on animals we find some attempts at crude experiments in the more modern sense. For example, he and his associates showed that a cicada goes on singing in its breast for some time after its head has been cut off; that, contrary to the then current story, ostriches to whom he offered iron did not eat and digest the metal, although they would eat stones and bones broken into small bits. Even more technical procedure and methodology are described in *Liber de Alchima* ("Book on Alchemy") ascribed to Albert. When dealing with a subject he considered closer to "natural magic" than to physics or physical science, Albert displays some notion of "laboratory technique" by describing both the general conditions under which the alchemist should work as well as the precise order of carrying out the various stages in his experimentation. The allusion to "natural magic" recalls that one of the titles popularly given Albert was *magnus in magia*. In general, "magic" appears to designate an area of common ground between the ruling science of astronomy (and astrology) together with the subordinate sciences of the natural forces of stones and plants on the one hand, and the evil of necromancy on the other; the concern of all these areas is the *virtutes* (powers) of nature and the universe. The *Speculum Astronomiae*, ascribed to Albert, seems to have been written to safeguard astronomy (good magic) by separating it from necromancy (evil magic).

The idea that the primary causes of, and influences upon, earthly events are in some way bound up with celestial phenomena is present in Albert's thought as a part of the Aristotelian–Ptolemaic view of an earth-centered universe that he accepted without question. The theory of four terrestrial elements is completed by the idea of a causal nexus to the heavens and the heavenly bodies composed of a fifth distinct element. The astronomical view of a universe of causally related entities thus gives rise to an astrological attempt to understand these relationships. The largest problem that Albert has to face is reconciling the natural causality of the stars, planets, and earthly bodies with the voluntary, free causality of man. In a universe where natural, physical causality means movement and contact, the universe is a plenum, a series of concentric material spheres whose original existence and movement is created and conserved by God. This accounts for the observable change, generation, destruction, and alteration that takes place on earth through the instrumentality of the immutable heavenly bodies whose only alteration is local movement. While even the body of man is subject to this causal influence, his soul is from God alone; thus, human reason and will are free. Yet, man may consult heavenly movements to discover when natural events are most propitious for his free initiation of some action. Astrology concerns, then, the conditions for human action, not its causes. As is evident, Albert's astronomical views imply and are bound up with a metaphysical view of the universe as a whole and with its causes, the discussion of which is properly philosophical rather than scientific.

Philosopher. Albert's primary philosophical importance rests upon his accomplishments as a scholar rather than as an original thinker. The problem Albert faced was that common to the Latin world of the time: how to cope, in a Christian way, with the pagan Greek and Arabian learning just being discovered, translated, and introduced into Western thought. Rather than simply criticizing the new doctrines, Albert, along with such men as Robert Grosseteste and Roger Bacon, led the movement to synthesize this learning with Christian doctrine. But while Albert's ultimate aim was synthesis, his writings teach that secular learning must first be acquired in order to be used, that scientific knowledge and philosophy are good in themselves, and that Christian men could never acquire too much of such knowledge. Albert contrasts, however, the acquisition of philosophical knowledge with the acquisition of scientific knowledge; while the latter is learned from the experience and observation of nature, the former is learned from books. Albert achieved, then, a systematic ordering and interpretation of the ideas expressed by the philosophers; his writings, consequently, represent a huge source book of Greek and Arabian thought, blended with the world view of his Christian heritage.

Thus we find a view of the structure of reality that parallels the order of thought: being is the "first created" and the "first known." Being (*ens*) is "first created" in the sense that it is the proper effect of divine causality, an effect that, in the concrete, is determined by distinct intrinsic principles forming a composition in all created entities. Albert calls upon Boethius to explain this composition: that which is (*id quod est*) is other than its essence (*esse quo est*), which is other than those principles that limit and determine it further (*aliquid esse*). Being (*ens*) is "first known" in the sense of the simplest concept from which no further abstraction can be made. The analyzing intellect (*intellectus resolvens*) stops at the notion of being because a notion of being only, not of this or that being, represents the limit of abstraction. But this abstraction, because it concerns created being, still involves a twofold composition: (*a*) being plus relation to creator; (*b*) being plus relations of further determination to particular beings. Hence the only truly and purely simple notion of being lies beyond this abstracted being as its cause: the First Being, God. In God there is no composition, and that which is, essence, and whatever else may be said of God is identified within Him.

In his discussion of abstraction Albert associates Aristotle, through his Arabian commentators, with Augustine. Albert retains the distinction of agent and possible intellectual powers; decides, against Averroës, that these powers are not one for all men, but each has his own as powers of his own soul; modifies Avicenna's separated agent intellect by invoking Augustine to the effect that the only true separate agent intellect is God, whose light of understanding fortifies the human agent intellect. A qualified Avicennian notion of "common nature" helps Albert to complete his doctrine: natures have existence (1) as Divine Ideas (*ante rem*), (2) as the species of things where they are individualized by matter (*in re*), (3) as abstracted and recognized as universal because applicable to many (*post rem*). Thus, intelligible species are the species of things that are the effects of Divine Ideas.

The whole universe represents an ordered and hierarchical procession from God. Although in his commentary on the Neoplatonically inspired *Liber de Causis,* Albert uses such terms as *emanatio* (emanation) and *fluxus* (flowing forth), whose connotations involve necessity and the hint of pantheism, he gives these terms a definitely Christian significance. The *Liber de Causis* also describes being as "the first of created things," and Albert, both here and in his later *Summa Theologiae,* did not hesitate to espouse a doctrine of free creation *ex nihilo.* That the world is not eternal cannot be proven but is accepted as revealed by God in *Genesis.* Aristotle thought that he had established the eternity of the world, but the best he did, having no notion of a creation from nothingness, was to show that the world could not come to be from any pre-existing matter.

Although the human body owes its production, ultimately, to the same universal causes operative in the whole of the universe, the human soul is directly created by God. Albert attempts to explain the human composite and to reconcile Plato's description of the soul with that of Aristotle by calling upon a formula of Avicenna: in itself, essentially, the soul is an incorporeal substance; operationally, however, the soul functions as the vivifying form of the body. Thus, the name "soul" (*anima*) is derived not from its essence, but from its operation as form of the body, which is "accidental" to that essence. Since the soul is a substance in itself, it is immortal, surviving the body because it is not dependent upon it. Rather than saying that the soul is in the body, we should say that the body is in (that is, participates in the existence of) the soul.

Bibliography

Albert's *Opera Omnia* are edited by August Borgnet (Paris, 1890–1899), 38 vols. A modern critical edition is still in process by Bernard Geyer (Westphalia, 1951—).

For bibliographical information see G. G. Meersseman, *Introductio in Opera Omnia B. Alberti Magni* (Bruges, Belgium, 1931); Francis J. Catania, "A Bibliography of St. Albert the Great," *The Modern Schoolman,* Vol. 37 (1959), 11–28.

For biography see Franz Pelster, *Kritische Studien zum Leben und zu den Schriften Alberts des Grossen* (Freiburg, 1920); C. H. Scheeban, *Albertus Magnus* (Köln, 1955); T. M. Schwertner, *St. Albert the Great* (New York, 1932).

For information on Albert as a scientist, see L. Thorndike, *A History of Magic and Experimental Science,* Vol. II (New York, 1923), pp. 517–592; H. Balss, *Albertus Magnus als Biolege* (Stuttgart, 1947); "Serta Albertina," *Angelicum,* Vol. 21 (1944).

For information on Albert as a philosopher, see E. Gilson, *A History of Christian Philosophy in the Middle Ages* (New York, 1955) pp. 277–294, 666–673; "Studia Albertina," in *Beiträge zur Geschichte der Philosophie des Mittelalters,* Suppl. 4 (Münster, 1952); L. de Raeymaeker, "Albert le Grand, philosophe. Les Lignes fondamentales de son système métaphysique," *Revue néoscolastique de philosophie,* 35 (1933), 5–36.

FRANCIS J. CATANIA

ALBO, JOSEPH (c. 1380–c. 1444), Spanish-Jewish preacher and philosopher, was the last major figure of the philosophical surge in medieval Jewry. Little is known about his early life; he was probably born at Monreal, in the kingdom of Aragon, and he asserted that Hasdai Crescas was his teacher. Albo was one of the principal apologists for the Jews at the Colloquium of Tortosa (February 7, 1413–November 3, 1414); his activities as apologist and preacher are reflected in the style of his philosophic classic, *Sefer ha-'Ikkarim (The Book of Roots).*

Albo's acknowledged and unacknowledged borrowings from other writers are so extensive that he was accused of plagiarism in his own age, as well as in more recent and more sensitive times. We must recognize, however, that Albo's purpose was to systematize and thus to defend the dogmas of Judaism rather than to produce an original philosophic work. Clarity and lucidity, systematic and easily remembered organization of materials, and simple and uninvolved style of presentation have made Albo's *The Book of Roots* one of the most popular works of medieval Hebrew literature. Indeed, it was one of the earliest printed Hebrew books, the first edition having been issued at Soncino, Italy, in 1485. Albo's occasional use of medical materials to illustrate his thought has suggested to critics that he may have been trained as a physician. He was well trained in Jewish philosophy, and in addition he knew, probably at second hand, the works of the Arabic Aristotelians.

Albo asserted that there are three essential dogmas ("roots") of Judaism: the existence of God, revelation, and reward and punishment. Seven secondary principles were derived from these three. The existence of God yields four: his unity, his incorporeality, his timelessness, and his perfection. From the dogma of revelation Albo derived two secondary principles: the prophets were the medium of revelation, and the Mosaic law will have binding force until another law is proclaimed with equal publicity; that is, before 600,000 men. God's providential knowledge in the matter of retribution was, for Albo, the sole secondary derivative from the doctrine of reward and punishment. Beyond these primary and secondary roots are other logically derived "branches" that every professing Jew must believe or be guilty of heresy, among them the doctrine of the Messiah.

It may be presumed that Albo removed the doctrine of the Messiah from the center of the Jewish faith as an important part of his polemic against Christianity, a recurrent feature of *The Book of Roots.* As an aspect of this polemic, Book III, Chapter 25 contains an actual summary of a disputation between a Jew and a non-Jew (omitted in some editions).

Bibliography

BILINGUAL EDITION

Husik, Isaac, *Sefer ha-'Ikkarim,* 5 vols. Philadelphia, 1929–1930. Critical edition of the Hebrew text, with facing English translation.

DISCUSSIONS

Agus, Jacob B., *The Evolution of Jewish Thought.* London and New York, 1959.

Blau, Joseph L., *The Story of Jewish Philosophy.* New York, 1962.

Guttmann, Julius, *Philosophies of Judaism,* translated by D. W. Silverman. New York, 1964.

Husik, Isaac, *History of Medieval Jewish Philosophy.* New York, 1916.

J. L. BLAU

ALCMAEON OF CROTON, physician and speculative philosopher of the first half of the fifth century B.C. Aristotle compares Alcmaeon's theory of opposites as first principles with that of Pythagoras and the early Pythagoreans, and later commentators, misled by similarities between Alcmaeon's doctrines and those of earlier philosophers, regarded him as a Pythagorean. It is more likely that he was born during Pythagoras' old age, was a contemporary of Empedocles and Anaxagoras, and was older than Democritus. Aristotle and Theophrastus are the first to report on him. The following interpretation is based on their reports and on the amplifications of their reports supplied by the doxographic tradition.

Alcmaeon was a brilliant physician who lived during a transitional period in the history of medicine. He was engaged in research when medical ideas had not been separated from philosophical generalities. A uniform approach to medical studies was nonexistent, the strict empiricism of the Hippocratics was unknown, the concepts of therapy and diagnosis were confused. At this time doctors persistently asked, "What is health?" In the same spirit the question "How do the different senses function?" was also raised. Alcmaeon attempted to answer both.

His doctrine of physical equilibrium (*isonomia*) was introduced to define and explain the state of health. His detailed physiological investigations of the different senses explored the causes of sensation. The ingenious combination of old physical theories (for example, the doctrine of opposites) with new scientific approaches (dissection and observation) suddenly proved revealing.

Alcmaeon noted that understanding differed from sensation, and he thought it could be compared only with the eternal rotatory motions of the stars. Because of this motion he held the soul to be immortal. Although each sense had its own sense organ, sense awareness was possible because a coordinating brain synthesized different sense reports; sense organs like the eye and the ear communicated directly with the brain through special passages. Sleep was caused by the retirement of the blood to large blood vessels; awakening, by the blood's redistribution. Finally, he held that although health was the equilibrium between the opposites in the body, such a balance could not be preserved forever. Hence, the inevitability of death.

Observations of such originality were bound to affect later philosophy and medicine. Plato's and Aristotle's psychologies show the effects of the new ideas. Revised epistemologies of sense perception reflect Alcmaeon's attention to detail. The empirically oriented physiologies of the Hippocratic school learned much from the new approach. With Alcmaeon the emancipation of medicine from philosophy had begun.

Bibliography

Beare, J. I., *Greek Theories of Elementary Cognition.* Oxford, 1906.

Burnet, John, *Early Greek Philosophy,* 4th ed. London, 1930. Pp. 193–196.

Diels, H., and Kranz, W., eds., *Fragmente der Vorsokratiker,* 5th ed., Vol. I. Berlin, 1934. Pp. 210–216.

Guthrie, W. K. C., *A History of Greek Philosophy,* Vol. I. Cambridge, 1962. Pp. 341–359.

Heidel, W. A., *Hippocratic Medicine.* New York, 1941.

Pauly, A., and Wissowa, G., eds., *Real-Encyclopädie der classischen Altertumswissenschaft.* Vol. I, Col. 1556. Stuttgart, 1893.
Vlastos, Gregory, "Isonomia." *American Journal of Philosophy,* Vol. 74 (1953), 337–366.
Wachtler, J., *De Alcmaeone Crotoniata.* Leipzig, 1896.

P. DIAMANDOPOULOS

ALEMBERT, JEAN LE ROND D' (1717–1783), French mathematician and Encyclopedist, was the illegitimate son of Madame de Tencin and the artillery general Destouches-Canon. He was abandoned by his mother on the steps of the baptistry of Saint-Jean-Le-Rond in Paris, from which he received his name. Shortly afterward his father returned from the provinces, claimed the child, and placed him with Madame Rousseau, a glazier's wife, with whom d'Alembert remained until a severe illness in 1765 forced him to seek new quarters. Through the Destouches family, Jean Le Rond was placed in the exclusive Jansenist Collège de Mazarin and given the name of d'Aremberg, which he later changed to d'Alembert, no doubt for phonetic reasons. At the college an effort was made to win him over to the Jansenist cause, and he went so far as to write a commentary on St. Paul. The intense Jesuit–Jansenist controversy served only to disgust him with both sides, however, and he left the college with the degree of bachelor of arts and a profound distrust of, and aversion to, metaphysical disputes.

After attending law school for two years he changed to the study of medicine, which he soon abandoned for mathematics. His talent and fascination for mathematics were such that at an early age he had independently discovered many mathematical principles, only to find later that they were already known. In 1739 he submitted a *mémoire* on integral calculus to the Académie des Sciences, but it was his *Traité de dynamique* in 1743 that won him acclaim and paved the way for his entry into the academy that same year. The introduction to his treatise is significant as the first enunciation of d'Alembert's philosophy of science. He accepted the reality of truths rationally deduced from instinctive principles insofar as they are verifiable experimentally and therefore are not simply aprioristic deductions. Although admitting unproved axioms at the base of his principles of mechanics, thus revealing his debt to Descartes, d'Alembert rejected metaphysical affirmations and the search for universals and expressed admiration for Bacon's experimental and inductive method.

The decade of the 1740s may be considered d'Alembert's mathematical period during which he made his most outstanding and fruitful contributions to that discipline. In addition to the *Traité de dynamique* he wrote *Mémoire sur la réfraction des corps solides* (1741); *Théorie de l'équilibre du mouvement des fluides* (1744 and 1751); *Réflexions sur la cause générale des vents,* which won him the prize of the Berlin Academy in 1746 as well as membership in that body; a *mémoire* on vibrating strings (*Recherches sur les cordes vibrantes*), written in 1747 for the Berlin Academy; *Recherches sur la précession des équinoxes et sur la nutation* (1749); *Réflexions sur la théorie de la résistance des fluides* (1752); *Recherches sur differents points importants du systéme du monde* (1754–1756), plus eight volumes of *Opuscules mathématiques* (1761–1780).

D'Alembert's first philosophical work, the *Discours préliminaire* to the *Encyclopédie,* appeared in 1751. As early as 1746 he, with Diderot, had been on the publisher's payroll as translator, in connection with the projected French version of Chambers' *Cyclopaedia.* We may suppose that, like Diderot, he had already worked for the publishers as a translator of English works for French consumption, thus exposing himself to the writings of the English empiricists and supplementing the meager pension left him by his father. In any event, d'Alembert had read Bacon as early as 1741; and his *Discours préliminaire* revealed not only his debt to the Descartes of the *Regulae,* shorn of metaphysics, but his admiration for, and indebtedness to, Bacon for his experimental method; Newton, whom he admired for proving gravitational force without trying to explain its first cause; and Locke, whose metaphysical method he adopted. While paying lip service to the traditional religious concepts of his time, d'Alembert utilized Lockian sensationalist theory to arrive at a naturalistic interpretation of nature. It is not through vague and arbitrary hypotheses that nature can be known, he asserted, but through a careful study of physical phenomena. He discounted metaphysical truths as inaccessible through reason. In the *Discours,* d'Alembert began by affirming his faith in the reliability of the evidence for an external world derived from the senses and dismissed the Berkeleian objections as metaphysical subtleties that are contrary to good sense. Asserting that all knowledge is derived from the senses, he traced the development of knowledge from the sense impressions of primitive man to their elaboration into more complex forms of expression. Language, music, and the arts communicate emotions and concepts derived from the senses and, as such, are imitations of nature. For example, d'Alembert believed that music that is not descriptive is simply noise. Since all knowledge can be reduced to its origin in sensations, and since these are approximately the same in all men, it follows that even the most limited mind can be taught any art or science. This was the basis for d'Alembert's great faith in the power of education to spread the principles of the Enlightenment.

In his desire to examine all domains of the human intellect, d'Alembert was representative of the encyclopedic eighteenth-century mind. He believed not only that man's physical needs are the basis of scientific and aesthetic pursuits, but also that morality too is pragmatically evolved from social necessity. This would seem to anticipate the thought of Auguste Comte, who also placed morality on a sociological basis, but it would be a mistake to regard d'Alembert as a Positivist in the manner of Comte. If d'Alembert was a Positivist, he was so through temporary necessity, based on his conviction that since ultimate principles cannot be readily attained, one must reluctantly be limited to fragmentary truths attained through observation and experimentation. He was a rationalist, however, in that he did not doubt that these ultimate principles exist. In the *Discours préliminaire* he expressed the belief that everything could be reduced to one first principle, the universe being "one great truth" if we could only see it in a broader perspective. Similarly, in the realm of morality and aesthetics, he sought to reduce moral and aesthetic norms to dogmatic absolutes, and this would seem to be in conflict with the pragmatic approach of pure sensationalist theories. He was forced, in such cases, to appeal to a sort of intuition or good sense that was more Cartesian than Lockian, but he did not attempt to reconcile his inconsistencies and rather sought to remain within the basic premises of sensationalism. D'Alembert's tendency to go beyond the tenets of his own theories, as he did, for example, in admitting that mathematical realities are a creation of man's intellect and do not correspond to physical reality, has led Ernst Cassirer to conclude that d'Alembert, despite his commitment to sensationalist theory, had an insight into its limitations.

During the early 1750s d'Alembert engaged actively in the polemics of the time, particularly in the defense of the *Encyclopédie* and the party it represented. Many of the articles he wrote for that publication, as well as his preface to Volume III (1753), were aimed at the enemies of the *Encyclopédie*, notably the Jesuits, who were among the first to attack it for its antireligious and republican orientation. In addition, he took part in the controversy over French versus Italian music, which was inflamed by Rousseau's attack on French music in "Lettre sur la musique française" (1753). D'Alembert had already published his *Éléments de musique* (1752), based on Rameau's theories on harmonics, and in 1754 he published anonymously his *Réflexions sur la musique en général et la musique française en particulier.*

However, d'Alembert's chief preoccupation at this period was with philosophy and literature. His *Mélanges de littérature et de philosophie* appeared in 1753 in two volumes (expanded to four volumes in 1759, with a fifth volume added in 1767), and it is here that his skepticism concerning metaphysical problems is delineated. Proceeding on the premise that certainty in this field cannot be reached through reason alone, he considered the arguments for and against the existence of God and cautiously concluded in the affirmative, on the grounds that intelligence cannot be the product of brute matter. Like Newton, d'Alembert viewed the universe as a clock, which necessarily implies a clockmaker, but his final attitude is that expressed by Montaigne's *"Que sais-je?"* Man's uncertainty before this enigmatic universe is the basis of d'Alembert's plea for religious tolerance. He maintained his skeptical deism as an official, public position throughout his life, but there is evidence for believing that in the late 1760s, under the influence of Diderot (whose *Rêve de d'Alembert* appeared in 1769), d'Alembert was converted to Diderot's materialism. In private correspondence with intimate friends, d'Alembert revealed his commitment to an atheistic interpretation of the universe. He accepted intelligence as simply the result of a complex development of matter and not as evidence for a divine intelligence.

Aside from the publication of a polemical brochure, *Histoire de la destruction des Jésuites*, in 1765 (with two additional *Lettres* on the subject in 1767), d'Alembert spent the last two decades of his life in furthering the cause of the *philosophes* in the Académie Française—by writing his *Éloges*, which were read in the Académie (and published in 1779), and by fostering the election of candidates of his own choice. Mademoiselle de Lespinasse's salon, where d'Alembert presided, became, in the words of Frédéric Masson, the "obligatory antechamber of the Académie." In this period he became influential with young aspiring men of letters, whom he recruited for his party and whose careers he fostered. The most notable of his disciples was Condorcet. After years of ill health, d'Alembert died of a bladder ailment and was buried as an unbeliever in a common, unmarked grave.

Works by d'Alembert

Oeuvres philosophiques et littéraires, J. F. Bastien, ed., 18 vols. Paris, 1805. Not so complete as the Belin edition but contains letters to d'Alembert not included elsewhere. *Nouvelle édition augmentée*, Belin, ed., 5 vols. Paris, 1821. The most complete edition to date.

Oeuvres et correspondance inédites de d'Alembert, Charles Henry, ed. Paris, 1887. Contains important supplements to above editions in the fields of philosophy, literature, and music, as well as additional correspondence.

Discours préliminaire de l'Encyclopédie, P. Picavet, ed. Paris, 1912. Standard critical edition.

For a fuller listing, see *A Critical Bibliography of French Literature*, D. C. Cabeen, ed. New York, 1947–1951. Vol. IV, pp. 136–138.

Works on d'Alembert

Bertrand, Joseph, *D'Alembert*. Paris, 1889. Despite shortcomings and reliance on Condorcet's *Eloge de d'Alembert*, the most complete biography to date.

Grimsley, Ronald, *Jean d'Alembert*. Oxford, 1963. A good, comprehensive treatment of d'Alembert's philosophy and ideas. Less concerned with biography.

Kunz, Ludwig, "Die Erkenntnistheorie d'Alemberts." *Archiv für Geschichte der Philosophie*, Vol. 20 (1907), 96–126. Considers relation between d'Alembert's metaphysics and English empiricists. Presents him as a link between empiricists and Comte.

Misch, Georg, *Zur Entstehung des französischen Positivismus*. Berlin, 1900. Influence of d'Alembert's empiricism and materialistic viewpoint on Comte's Positivism.

Muller, Maurice, *Essai sur la philosophie de Jean d'Alembert*. Paris, 1926. Most important and complete study of d'Alembert's general philosophy.

Pappas, John N., *Voltaire and d'Alembert*. Bloomington, Ind., 1962. Considers d'Alembert's position and method in spreading the ideals of the Enlightenment and his influence on Voltaire.

JOHN N. PAPPAS

ALEXANDER, SAMUEL (1859–1938), British realist metaphysician, was born in Sydney, New South Wales, and was educated at Wesley College, Melbourne. He came to England in 1877 on a scholarship to Balliol College, Oxford, where he read mathematics, classics, and philosophy (*literae humaniores*). In 1882 he was elected to a fellowship at Lincoln College, Oxford, becoming the first Jew to be a fellow of an Oxford or Cambridge college. His earliest work, the Green Prize essay in moral philosophy, subsequently published as *Moral Order and Progress* (1889), shows the influence of the idealist ethics dominant in Oxford at the time. But he soon began moving toward an approach to philosophy that could be more closely related to the development of the empirical sciences, particularly biology and psychology. He gave up his fellowship and spent a year in Hugo Münsterberg's psychological laboratory at Freiburg, Germany, continuing in private study until his election to the chair of philosophy at Owens College (later the Victoria University of Manchester) in 1893. He held the chair until his retirement in 1924 and lived in Manchester until his death in 1938, a beloved, influential, and, indeed, legendary figure in both city and university.

Empirical metaphysics. Alexander wrote occasional papers and a small book on John Locke, but it was not until 1920 that he published his major work, *Space, Time and Deity* (delivered as the Gifford Lectures in Glasgow in 1915). This was a comprehensive and constructive system, which he claimed was metaphysics following an "empirical method." By this he meant that he understood metaphysics to be a very inclusive kind of science, differing from the special sciences "not in its spirit, but only in its boundaries, dealing with certain comprehensive features of experience which lie outside the purview of the special sciences." Alexander called these features "categorial" and "a priori" but said that this must not be taken to mean that they are imposed or constructed by thought; they are discerned by reflective inspection as pervasive features of the world. As such he called them "nonempirical," reserving the term "empirical" for the variable features of the world. But the *study* of both, as a study of what is found in experience, he called "empirical." This could be considered an empirical way of thinking only in a much broader and more speculative sense than subsequent forms of empiricism, with their stricter notions of what constitutes tests in observation and experiment. Nevertheless, Alexander insisted that his system not only was a speculative world view but also took account of certain ways of thinking he believed were suggested by work in contemporary experimental science. Here his starting point was probably his interest in physiological psychology (he had introduced this study into the University of Manchester at a time when British universities were still slow to recognize it).

Mind. In contrast to idealistic or dualistic views, Alexander regarded mind as, in one sense, identical with an organized structure of physiological and neural processes, there being no animistic or purely "mental" factor over and above these. But in another sense, mind could be looked on as a new "emergent"—when neural processes are organized in a certain way, they manifest a new quality, consciousness, or awareness.

Emergents. By "emergents" (a term generally ascribed to C. Lloyd Morgan, though its first use can be found in G. H. Lewes) Alexander designated certain organized patterns which, he held, produce new qualitative syntheses that could not have been predicted from knowledge of the constituent elements of the pattern before they were so organized. Emergents are thus what others have called gestalt properties of organized systems; Alexander thought of them particularly as characteristics of those syntheses where some strikingly new quality can be discerned. He generalized the idea that new qualities emerge from patterns of subvening elements of certain degrees of complexity, so as to look on the world as a hierarchy of qualities, a hierarchy in which those higher in the scale depend on the lower but manifest something genuinely new.

Space-time. At the basis of nature Alexander set *space-time* as a continuum of interrelated complexes of motion. These can be analyzed into relations between "point-instants," a point-instant being the limiting case of a motion. Sometimes he spoke of point-instants as if they were real elements, the smallest instances of spatiotemporal motions, sometimes as if they were ideal concepts, the bare notion of time at a point or space at an instant, while any actual motion has a spatiotemporal spread.

Space-time was also distinguished into "perspectives." A perspective defines how space-time can be ordered with reference to particular point-instants. It is a line of advance, or phase of a spatiotemporal process, seen in relation to some point-instant as its center of reference. Alexander used the illustration of a tree sawn across. For the carpenter the concentric rings are simultaneous, but this is to look on it as an artificial section. For the botanist they are of different dates, carrying with them the history of the tree. Thus, a perspective is a historical phase of the process of nature, ordered with reference to some event, *e*, as center and integrating other events related to the event from which the perspective is developed. These may be integrated as observably contemporaneous or as earlier and later stages in motions of which *e* is a stage.

The definition of a perspective thus depends on the notion of motions and their interrelation, and even on their causal relations. It is difficult to see how these notions can be derived purely from that of structures within space-time. Indeed, the notion of space-time itself as the fundamental stuff or matrix out of which things arise is certainly not one that it is natural to see as an "empirical" description of the most general features of the world as it discloses itself to an observing mind.

Categories. It might be more plausible if Alexander could be taken to have meant that the basic universal feature of all experience is its spatiotemporal character. He did indeed claim to follow Kant in holding that the world is apprehended first and foremost as a spatiotemporal manifold, under categories. Apart from the union of space and time in a four-dimensional continuum, his categories follow closely the Kantian ones of substance, cause, number, and relation. But Alexander insisted that these categories are discovered or discerned in the world and are not a conceptual framework imposed by the mind. Indeed, according to his realist theory of knowledge, thought does not construct or impose conceptual schemes. Knowledge is "contemplation" of an object where there is a relation of "compresence" between a mind and an object (except in the special case of a mind's knowledge of itself, for a mind cannot be compresent as an object to itself but is aware of itself as knowing and perceiving; Alexander calls this kind of knowing "enjoyment"). But it is surely difficult to understand why any mind compresent with the world of nature would see in it just these particular all-pervasive categorial features.

Empirical features of regions of space-time. Beside the categorial features, which Alexander called "nonempirical," meaning by this that they are invariable and all-pervasive, we discover "empirical" features, defined as variable qualities characterizing particular regions of space-time. "Universals" are discerned *in rebus*, as plans of configurations of motions in space-time showing persistent identities; Alexander called them "habits" of space-time. Within space-time arises the hierarchy of emergent qualities. The patterns of motions that differentiate it are in the first place bearers of the properties of extension and inertia that characterize "matter." These organized patterns of matter are bearers of the qualities found in physical structures and chemical syntheses. Some of these syntheses, in turn, are bearers of the quality of "life," and some living structures are bearers of mind or consciousness, which is the highest empirical quality known to us. There is no reason, however, to assume that this is the highest possible emergent quality. Alexander held that the structures that are bearers of "mind" may in their turn become productive of a new emergent quality, which he called "deity."

Deity. The term deity does not here stand for a God who precedes the universe as its cause or creator. Alexander did not try to find in such terms an "explanation" of why the universe should exist. Existence, he held, should be accepted with "natural piety" (borrowing a phrase of Wordsworth's), and its general character should then be described. This general character is first and foremost spatiotemporal. In addition, Alexander held that it exhibits a *nisus,* or creative tendency, toward the production of new qualitative syntheses. So in one sense God can be thought of as *Deus sive Natura,* the universe of space-time "pregnant" with emergent qualities. In another sense deity is "the next highest emergent quality which the universe is engaged in bringing to birth." This quality, Alexander suggested, may emerge in beings—we do not yet know what they would be like—who would be bearers of deity as we are of mind, and these in their turn might prepare the basis for a yet further emergent quality. Alexander held that the existence of religious sentiments and aspirations witnesses to an experience of the *nisus* toward the higher quality of deity in some of those who are already bearers of mind. Such religious feelings, he thought, are incipient aspirations toward a new level of development. It is toward this further stage of development, not toward an already existent object, that the religious sentiment is directed. Alexander claimed that he started from the empirical fact of this sentiment, rather than from a theory of its object, and asked what it suggests; the religious sentiment can be interpreted as the feelings of beings caught up in the *nisus* of a universe "pregnant" with the quality of deity.

Time as mind. Is there any reason in the nature of space-time itself why there should be this *nisus*? Alexander sometimes spoke as though the mere fact of conjoining time with space in itself produces the possibility not only of a dynamic but even of a creative process. He summed this up in the saying "Time is the Mind of Space"—surely one of the most astonishing remarks ever made by a metaphysician. But it was not intended merely to shock. It should be read in connection with Alexander's interest in physiological psychology and the view of the body–mind relation that he derived from this and that he here extended in a daring analogy. Alexander reported that he reached his notion of perspectives in space-time by considering the unity of the self. There is no such thing as awareness of the self at an instant. The least moment of conscious experience is a "specious present" with a durational aspect and, as embodied, a spatialized aspect. Our consciousness of what we are thinking at any moment is linked with the memory of what we were thinking, for example, a fraction of a second ago, and it is directed in anticipation toward what we are going to think a fraction of a second from now. What we are, at any given stage, is partly constituted by memories of the past and anticipation of the future.

Hence, the unity of the self depends on events of different dates being brought into a perspective with reference to the self of "present" experience. Similarly, a physical perspective consists of all events that can be shown to be earlier or later stages in lines of development in which a given event, taken as center of reference, is a phase. A perspective thus describes a historical line of advance. The temporal aspect of this is said to be the analogue of its "mind" and the spatial aspect the analogue of its "body." This is because mental experience is partly constituted by memory of the past and anticipation of the future and, more specifically, because the "mind" aspect of anything is looked on as the *new* quality it may exhibit at its latest point of development, whereas the organized structure that is the bearer of this property and could be described beforehand as accomplished fact is looked on as its body. Time is not mind in the sense of consciousness or thought, which is the distinctive quality characteristic of the level we call mind proper. It is "mind" in an analogical sense, as whatever is the new property characteristic of a new qualitative synthesis. Thus, for example, to Alexander the defining qualities of matter are the primary qualities, such as extension and inertia. Secondary qualities, such as color, are emergents from organized complexes of matter and may, as such, be called their "mind." This is not to give them some rudimentary degree of consciousness; it is to say that on each level there is an element that can be called the analogue of mind, as introducing something new. But what is new appears sometimes to be not describable as an *element,* but rather as a new way of *functioning* released in some particular kind of ordered structure. When this happens, the new way of functioning dominates the lower levels that support it but does not transform them into something different. Physicochemical processes continue to be physicochemical processes, and neural processes to be a form of physicochemical processes. But where there is conscious thinking, although no separate animistic or mental factor may be present, the whole ordered structure becomes a vehicle for this new activity, and we say we are confronted by an "embodied mind."

Time as an attribute of reality. Alexander's view of a hierarchy of syntheses with new emergent qualities may be significant, but can time, as the pure notion of irreversible succession, be sufficient to account for their possibility? To say that there is a general tendency for complexes of one order to combine and form complexes of what will become a new order must surely presuppose some fundamental property or properties in the world besides those of space and time; Alexander, in fact, admits this when he speaks of a *nisus,* or creative tendency, in space-time. But is this a necessary property of an infinite four-dimensional continuum, unless one can assume that the mere fact of succession entails creative advance? Alexander may have been near enough to nineteenth-century ideas of inevitable evolutionary progress to be able implicitly to assume this. In agreement with these ideas, he insisted that philosophers must "take Time seriously"; that is to say, they must incorporate a conception of time as an essential attribute of reality and not only as describing a way of experiencing or measuring a reality that is ultimately nontemporal. Alexander said that if Spinoza could be rewritten with time as well as extension as an attribute of substance, this would represent the type of past philosophy most congenial to him; indeed, if someone were to write on his funerary urn *"Erravit cum Spinoza,"* he would be content.

Reality as process. Alexander's view of space-time as the final reality seems, however, open to two interpretations. On the one (perhaps the more Spinozistic) interpretation, space and time are the two necessary attributes of an infinite substance, distinguishable, it is true, into perspectives defined by reference to point-instants, but where "motions" (analogous to Spinoza's "modes") are simply the redistribution of spatiotemporal coefficients within the whole already existent space-time. In this view space-time is looked on as that out of which things come, and we can ask whether, as with the materialist's conception of matter, this is not to treat an abstraction as though it were a reality. In another sense Alexander was giving a view of reality as essentially a process, and as historical. There is an irreversible direction in it, defined by "time's arrow" (to use Eddington's expression). In this, nature is focused in lines of development whose "history" describes the successive levels of ordered structures they exhibit. At each stage in time, where there is a new emergent quality, this quality is the spearhead of a genuine creative advance. Yet if this new emergent quality at each stage is said to be analogous to mind, is it satisfactory to equate this with saying that it is analogous to time? It might be more plausible to say that it was Alexander's notion of the *nisus* in space-time that corresponds to the "mind" factor in those complexes whose extended patterns can be regarded as the analogue of the body. Or one might say that the "body" of anything is the external view of nature as unified in that particular perspective, while its "mind" is the "idea" of the distinctive internal quality of that particular perspective; this indeed suggests comparison with Spinoza's view of the body–mind relation.

Values. Alexander wrote no large work besides *Space, Time and Deity*. The volume *Beauty and the Other Forms of Value* (1933) is a collection of occasional papers and lectures on themes relating to aesthetics and ethics. The general notion underlying these is that of values as related to the satisfaction of impulses. Values are "tertiary qualities" (supervening on the primary and secondary qualities), characterizing complexes where one component is a mind capable of interest or appreciation. The higher values —beauty, truth, and goodness—are qualities that arise in the satisfaction of certain impulses where these have become contemplative and disengaged from their immediate practical ends. Thus aesthetic creation and enjoyment grow out of the impulse to construct things, which Alexander traced down to the animals ("impulse," he thought, was a less question-begging term than "instinct"). The impulse to construct something out of physical materials, including sounds, becomes a contemplative delight in the form so imposed on the material. Truth is a value analogous to beauty, as that which satisfies the impulse of curiosity when this too becomes contemplative rather than practical. Moral value is a quality created out of natural impulses by the introduction of another natural impulse that can bring form and harmony into the impulses that are its materials. This impulse Alexander called "gregariousness." His interpretation of this was close to Adam Smith's view of "sympathy" as fellow feeling with the feelings of others. Gregariousness, like Smith's sympathy, becomes disinterested and so is able to act as a harmonizing agent both among a person's other impulses and in producing "sociality." The impulse of "sociality" was also invoked in support of Alexander's view that we are directly aware of other minds in such experiences as friendly conversation or quarrels, which are completed as experiences through reciprocated responses. These are not, in Alexander's view, adequately described as merely responses to behavior; they are responses to behavior as expressing the mind of the other person.

A collection of occasional papers and addresses, *Philosophical and Literary Pieces* (1939), was published posthumously by John Laird, prefaced by a memoir that gives a sympathetic account of Alexander the man, including a number of the stories, true or apocryphal, that were told about him. Some of the pieces on nontechnical themes —on Dr. Johnson, for instance, or Jane Austen, or Pascal— show Alexander in his happiest vein.

Alexander was awarded the Order of Merit in 1930. His appearance was impressive; a bust by Jacob Epstein in the entrance hall of the Arts Building of the University of Manchester gives a good impression of his massive head and beard but misses his kindliness. The library of the University of Manchester contains a large collection of letters written to him by his contemporaries, including the philosophers F. H. Bradley, G. F. Stout, and T. Percy Nunn, the physiologists C. Lloyd Morgan and Sir Charles Scott Sherrington, and the Jewish leaders Chaim Weizmann and Claude Montefiore.

Works by Alexander

BOOKS

Moral Order and Progress. London, 1889.

Locke. London, 1908.

Space, Time and Deity. 2 vols. London, 1920.

Beauty and the Other Forms of Value. London, 1933.

Philosophical and Literary Pieces, J. Laird, ed. London, 1939. The papers of particular philosophical interest appearing in this volume are "Art and Instinct," Herbert Spencer Lecture (1927); "Artistic Creation and Cosmic Creation," Annual Philosophical Lecture of the British Academy (1927); and "Spinoza and Time," Arthur Davis Memorial Lecture (1921). The book also contains a list of Alexander's published works, including reviews and contributions to journals.

PERIODICALS

"The Method of Metaphysics; and the Categories." *Mind*, n.s., Vol. 21 (1912), 1–20.

"On Relations" and, in particular, "The Cognitive Relation." *Mind*, n.s., Vol. 21 (1912), 305–328.

"Collective Willing and Truth." *Mind*, n.s., Vol. 22 (1913), 14–47 and 161–189.

"The Basis of Realism," in *Proceedings of the British Academy*,

1914. Republished in *Realism and the Basis of Phenomenology*, Roderick M. Chisholm, ed. Glencoe, Ill., 1960. This lecture relates Alexander's views on the theory of knowledge to those of other philosophers of the time and presents his theory that mind and object are both empirically within nature, their relation being a particular form of a more general relation of "compresence."

"Sense-Perception: A Reply to Mr. Stout." *Mind*, n.s., Vol. 32 (1923), 1–11. Written in answer to criticisms by G. F. Stout, in *Mind*, n.s., Vol. 31 (1922), 385–412.

Works on Alexander

Broad, C. D., *The Mind and Its Place in Nature*, pp. 646–650. London, 1925. Discusses Alexander's "emergence" theory of mind. See also two reviews by Broad of *Space, Time and Deity*, in *Mind*, n.s., Vol. 30 (1921), 25–39 and 129–150.

Devaux, P., *Le Système d'Alexander*. Paris, 1929.

McCarthy, J. W., *The Naturalism of Samuel Alexander*. New York, 1948.

DOROTHY M. EMMET

ALEXANDER OF APHRODISIAS, who was teaching at Athens in A.D. 200, was recognized for centuries as the most authoritative exponent of Aristotle. His influence has probably been most far-reaching in the development of the theory of universals because he emphasized certain elements in Aristotle's not always unambiguous account. These were the unqualified priority of the particular substance and the existence of universals only as concepts, or "acts of intellect." The form was what made "this" matter (that is, an identifiable piece) what it was, but it was contingent whether the form was universal in the sense of generic. (Alexander does not notice that a class with only one member, like his case of the sun, is still a class.) What the form is as a subject remains unclear.

More famous is his doctrine about soul and intellect. A human being's intellectual faculty can exist in three conditions, described as three intellects: (1) the "material" intellect (*intellectus possibilis*), which is nothing actual but the bare potentiality (so Aristotelian matter) of the body to develop reason—the condition of babies; (2) the intellect (*intellectus in habitu*) that is the possession of—in fact, is identical with—concepts, or universals gained from sense experience—the condition of adults; (3) the "active" intellect (*intellectus agens*), which is exercising the thoughts that form the *intellectus in habitu* and is thus equivalent to the intellect as aware of itself. What is distinctively Alexandrist is the identification he made, or seemingly made, of the "active" intellect both with the intellect that Aristotle said entered the body "from outside" and with the intellect eternally thinking of itself that Aristotle said was God. Intellect was, of course, the highest part or function of the soul, but since only the "active" intellect, as a "separate form," could exist without matter, it followed that there was no individual immortality for human beings. The exact relation of the "active" intellect to the individual soul or intellect is obscure in Alexander. He does not describe an active intellect acting directly like an efficient or even formal cause on a passive intellect but suggests rather the quasi-logical relationship which was fundamental to Neoplatonism and which made the less perfect instance of a kind entail the existence of the perfect. Thus, it is not at all certain that he meant thinking itself to go the way of immortality.

In the fifteenth century Italian philosophers known as Alexandristi defended this interpretation of Aristotle's psychology against both Averroës' version and the theologically orthodox version of Themistius and Aquinas.

In other subjects we see Alexander less original but often attacking Stoic doctrine, notably in his tracts *On Fate* and *On Mixture*. But the exact understanding of him is colored always by the difficulty of knowing how far we can trust the writings attributed to him. The commentary on Books E (VI) to N (XIV) of Aristotle's *Metaphysics* and parts of Book II of his own *De Anima* are probably not his. The latter includes the section *On Intellect* which greatly influenced later Greek, Arab, and medieval philosophers. But both may well depend on and be closer to his thought than is allowed by a modern tradition which underestimates Neoplatonizing features of Aristotle as well as of Alexander.

Bibliography

Alexander's works, including dubious ones, are in *Commentaria in Aristotelem Graeca*, Vols. I–III, and *Supplementum Aristotelicum*, Vol. II (Berlin, 1883–1901). P. Moraux, *Alexandre d'Aphrodise, exégète de la noétique d'Aristote* (Paris, 1942), includes a French translation of *On Intellect*. See also F. E. Cranz, in *Catalogus Translationum et Commentariorum: Mediaeval and Renaissance Latin Translations and Commentaries*, Vol. I (Washington, D.C., 1960), pp. 77–135; Ernst Cassirer, *Das Erkenntnisproblem*, 3d ed., Part I, "Die Reform der aristotelischen Psychologie" (Berlin, 1922); and J. H. Randall, Jr., *The School of Padua and the Emergence of Modern Science* (Padua, 1961).

A. C. LLOYD

ALEXANDER OF HALES (c. 1185–1245), "Doctor Irrefragabilis," friar minor, was an English Scholastic at the University of Paris. He was born in Hales Owen, Shropshire and died in Paris.

Alexander was a student at Paris about 1200 and received his M. A. before 1210. He joined the faculty of theology, becoming a master regent about 1220. After 1222 Alexander made an innovation in the university by using the *Book of Sentences* of Peter Lombard as the basic text for theological courses. His newly published *Glossa* (identified only in 1945) was the result of this work. At the height of his career, about 1236, he became a Franciscan, "edifying the world and giving new status to the Order" (in the words of Roger Bacon). After he was put in charge of the school at the Paris friary, he continued his teaching, especially through his *Disputed Questions*, and had some part to play in the "great Summa weighing more than a horse, which the friars out of reverence ascribed to him and called 'the Summa of Friar Alexander'" (R. Bacon). At the same time, he participated in the affairs of the order, attending the chapter that deposed Brother Elias in 1239, and was a coauthor of an *Exposition of the Rule of St. Francis;* he was also active in the affairs of the church, both in the university and in the First Council of Lyon (1244–1245). His sudden death after his return from Lyon apparently resulted from an epidemic current in Paris. An epitaph in the convent church saluted him as *Gloria doctorum, decus et flos philosophorum* (Glory of learned men, the honor and pride of philosophers).

Teachings. Alexander's own doctrines are found in his *Glossa* and *Disputed Questions* (which are divided in the

British Museum manuscript *Royal 9. E. 14.* into two series: those written before and those written after he became a friar); the *Summa* ascribed to him does not necessarily represent his opinions. Both the *Gloss* and the *Questions* labor under the disadvantage of being students' reportations (although some copies seem to have had a kind of official approval); both, however, justify the encomium of Bernard of Bessa: *maximus in theologia et philosophia magister* (greatest master in theology and philosophy). Alexander is both theologian and philosopher, masterfully handling a wide range of questions. Undoubtedly a traditionalist whose prime sources are Augustine, John of Damascus, and Pseudo-Dionysius, and whose thought is close to the scholastic traditions of his predecessors, Alexander nonetheless surpasses his contemporaries in the breadth and profundity of his questions and in the new problems and tracts he introduced into theology. To this extent he was an innovator who helped open the way for the scholastic renaissance of the mid-thirteenth century. In particular, as head of the friars' studium at Paris, he initiated a certain approach that came to characterize such representatives of the Franciscan school as Odo Rigaldus, Bonaventure, and Matthew of Aquasparta.

The problems of the distinction between philosophy and theology, and the nature of theology as a science, much discussed after 1240, are not treated explicitly (though it is possible that Alexander authored a question on the subject; see below). These problems are implicitly considered in scattered remarks on the kinds of human knowledge and the validity of arguments, in the general organization of material into specific questions and problems, and in the principles used in the solution of the problems. For example, our knowledge of God arises both from authority and from reason; that is, either from faith, which "depends on hearing" (Romans 10.17), or from knowledge drawn from the things God has made. Proofs of God's existence are suggested rather than developed at length: one is derived from the transcendental attributes of truth, goodness, and unity found in things; others are argued from the changing to the Unchanged, from dependent being to the Highest Being, from participated and partial good to the *summum bonum* (*Glossa* I, pp. 39–41). In the tradition of Augustine, Alexander finds analogies of the triune God in all creatures, thus setting the pattern for the Franciscan school, which, with St. Francis, delights to make of creation a "ladder" to the Creator. At the same time, Alexander shows the simplicity of the divine being to be in marked contrast to the composite character of all created being (*Glossa* I, p. 254; *Quaestiones*, pp. 14, 19). The doctrine here, that of *quod est* (the substance) and *quo est* (essence), is derived ultimately from Boethius, not from Avicenna, who seems to have been unknown to Alexander. In contrast to the *Summa Fratris Alexandri* and to Bonaventure, Alexander vehemently rejects any composition of matter and form either in angels or in the human soul (*Glossa* II, p. 28; other texts are in V. Doucet, *Prolegomena*, pp. 237, 268, n. 2). Apart from a lengthy question on immortality (*Quaestiones*, pp. 556–565), only passing remarks embody his notion of the soul. His attention is drawn more to the problem of free will (*Ibid.*, pp. 566–608, plus an unedited question). Here, Alexander teaches that man by his nature is free and that freedom of choice resides both in the intellect and in the will. The primary purpose for which man has been given this freedom is to choose that which is morally good. Alexander considers the moral life of man in such *Disputed Questions* as "On Ignorance," "On Scandal," "Love of Neighbor," "Fraternal Correction," "On Impediments to Reason," "On Lying," and "Conscience" (the last two as yet unpublished). To the last question must be joined his study of synderesis (*Glossa* II, pp. 380–385), which seems to make Alexander, not Philip the Chancellor, the creator of such a tract in Scholasticism.

Literary problems of the "Summa Fratris Alexandri." Since the *Summa* attributed to Alexander was unfinished at his death, William of Militona, who became master regent in 1248, seems to have undertaken its completion, for in 1255 Pope Alexander IV charged the provincial of Paris to supply Militona with capable assistants who without delay would bring the work to a finish. The text as it now stands consists of four parts. Book I deals with the nature of theology, the existence and nature of God, the divine names, and the Trinity. Book II is divided into two sections: II–1, creation in general, the angels, the six days of creation, the soul, the body, and the human composite, and II–2, a lengthy study of moral theology—the nature of evil, definition and classification of sins, and original and actual sins. Book III considers the Incarnation and mysteries of Christ's life, law (eternal, natural, positive, the commandments), grace, and faith (tome IV). Book IV treats of man's reparation through the sacraments, the mass, prayer, fasting, and almsgiving; quite evidently a section on "Last Things" was to be included as the climax of the work. Except in a few manuscripts and in the protest of Roger Bacon, however, the compilatory nature of the *Summa* was forgotten. All four books came to be attributed to Alexander, despite the manifest contradictions and conflicting opinions in the various parts. Only since the end of the nineteenth century, with the renewal of interest in medieval Scholasticism, has the question of authorship attracted attention. A few writers, it is true, have gone to an extreme in claiming that the whole *Summa* was a compilation of the last half of the thirteenth century, in basic dependence on Thomas Aquinas, Albert the Great, and Bonaventure. But more mature and solid scholarship has established that, if by and large the *Summa* is a compilation, it existed as a whole by 1257. The first three books were in existence before the death of Alexander, with three notable exceptions: the last tract of Book I was added between 1250 and 1253, while in Book II–1 the two sections "On the Human Body" and "The Human Composite" were composed after Bonaventure, almost certainly in 1255–1257, as was the last book. On the other hand, modern research is forced to agree with Roger Bacon that Alexander was not the author, in the strict sense, of the pre-1245 *Summa*. At most, it appears that he planned and organized the work, while the details were left to others. Internal criticism of style, language, and doctrine would show essentially two authors at work, neither of whom, by reason of doctrinal positions, can be Alexander. Books I and III were almost certainly the work of John of La Rochelle, although the presence of other collaborators may be detected. Both parts of Book II, on the other hand, were written or compiled by some unknown friar who possessed a keen philosophical mind and a greater spirit of independence.

Doctrines of the pre-1245 "Summa." The work of the "Summists" was largely one of compilation, yet not without a certain new and fresh viewpoint. If they drew on earlier material, they did not hesitate to insert their own views or add fresh tracts written specifically for the *Summa*. Relatively new was the opening inquisition on the nature of theology, based on the tract in manuscript *Vatican Latin 782*, folio 184d–186d (which may be by Alexander himself); it bears witness to the growing influence of Aristotle's ideal of a science. This inquisition is followed by an original tract on natural theology, remarkable for its metaphysical doctrine of God and creatures. This doctrine holds that the very conditions of finite being demand the existence of a First Being, even as the positive perfections of finite things reflect and lead to the infinite. The unknown author of Book II does not hesitate to repeat some of this material in an interesting and well-balanced dissertation on Creator and creature; he examines in detail the meaning of the act of creation, the properties of created being that reflect the divine cause, and those properties peculiar to creatures: composition, changeableness, time and space, and the beauty and order of the universe. Several questions seem to have bearing on problems that arose in the early thirteenth century under the influence of the newly known Arabian philosophers.

The importance of the *Summa* lies chiefly, perhaps, in its presentation and defense of the so-called Augustinian traditions in theology and philosophy without neglecting whatever was solid in the new philosophical literature. It may rightly be called the *Summa Minorum*, embodying the fundamental doctrines of the Franciscan school of the early thirteenth century.

Bibliography

For texts of Alexander, see *Glossa in Quattuor Libros Sententiarum Petri*, 4 vols. (Quaracchi, 1951–1957); *Quaestiones Disputatae "Antequam Esset Frater,"* 3 vols. (Quaracchi, 1960)—the series "after he became a friar" awaits publication at Quaracchi; *Expositio Quattuor Magistrorum Super Regulam Fratrum Minorum*, L. Oliger, ed. (Rome, 1950). The text of the *Summa* is *Doctoris Irrefragabilis Alexandri de Hales Summa Theologica*, 4 vols. (Quaracchi, 1924–1948), books I–III; Book IV is found in several early editions, such as Nuremberg, 1482, and Cologne, 1622.

With regard to studies of Alexander's works, writings previous to 1948 that are concerned with doctrinal problems rather than literary ones must be interpreted in the light of new discoveries. For literary and historical aspects, see V. Doucet, *Prolegomena in Librum III Necnon in Libros I et II Summa Fratris Alexandri* (Quaracchi, 1948), partially translated in *Franciscan Studies*, Vol. 7 (1947), 26–41, 274–312; *Ibid.*, Vol. 6 (1946), 403–417; and Doucet's introductions to the authentic *Glossa* and *Quaestiones*.

Doctrinal studies on the authentic Alexander are just beginning to appear: A. Fuerst, *A Historical Study of the Doctrine of the Omnipresence of God* (Washington, D. C., 1951); E. Lio, *Determinatio "Superflui" in Doctrina Alexandri Halensis* (Rome, 1953); A. Hufnagel, "Die Wesensbestimmung der Person bei Alexander von Hales," in *Freiburger ZPT*, Vol. 4 (1957), 148–174; E. Bettoni, *Il problema della cognoscibilità di Dio nella scuola francescana* (Padua, 1950); see also *Franciscan Studies*, Vol. 10 (1950), 164–185, 286–312; Vol. 19 (1959), 334–383; Vol. 20 (1960), 96–148; Vol. 22 (1962), 32–149.

For earlier and somewhat outdated studies on Alexander as author of the *Summa*, see I. Herscher, "A Bibliography of Alexander of Hales," in *Franciscan Studies*, Vol. 5 (1945), 434–454; and P. Boehner, "The System of Metaphysics of Alexander of Hales," in *Ibid.*, 366–414.

IGNATIUS BRADY, O.F.M.

ALEXANDRIAN SCHOOL is the name applied to Platonism as taught in Alexandria from about the middle of the fourth century to the capture of the city by the Arabs in 642. It was in close contact with the School of Athens as long as the latter existed; and many of its members, such as Hierocles, Hermeias, and Ammonius Hermeion, were students of Athenians. Some, like Ammonius, were also teachers of Athenians. However, each school represents a different kind of Platonism. In Athens the speculative, mystical, theurgic, and religious elements predominated; and that school remained to the end a stronghold of paganism. In Alexandria scholarly interests and a noncommittal exegesis of texts prevailed. The Platonism that the Alexandrian School professed was in some respects closer than that of the Athenian School to the pre-Plotinian version; thus, the doctrine of the ineffable One and the mystic union with it had no prominent place. Finally, a number of its members presented Plato in a manner at times acceptable to Christians; and others actually professed Christianity, though some might have done so only in form.

Thus, the "baptizing" of Greek philosophy—including the stress on those parts of the Aristotelian philosophy that were metaphysically neutral—so often considered characteristic of the medieval period, was to a certain extent anticipated in Alexandria; after the Arab conquest it was perhaps replaced by "Islamizing." One of the last members of the school, Stephanus, accepted an invitation—probably just before the Arab invasion—to teach philosophy at the University of Constantinople, thus transplanting Alexandrian Platonism to the Byzantine Empire.

It is usual to consider Hierocles (c. 420) the first representative of the Alexandrian School. His doctrine that the Demiurge who created the cosmos is the supreme deity (that is, has no One above him) is opposed to that of Plotinus and may have been that of Origen the Pagan, since the latter seems to have been the author of a writing directed against Plotinus on this very score. Hierocles' thesis that Plato and Aristotle agree in fundamentals could hark back to Plotinus' teacher Ammonius Saccas. Thus, the School of Alexandria may have been the heir of pre-Plotinian Platonism; some scholars are inclined to trace the school back to Eudorus (first century) or even to Antiochus (first century B.C.). Several doctrines of Hierocles have a Christian flavor, such as that the Demiurge needs no pre-existing matter and creates by an act of will out of nothing and that, as far as reasonable creatures are concerned, he exercises providence over them through subordinate deities and spirits (angels); they are not subject to fate. On the other hand, Hermeias, when interpreting Plato's *Phaedrus*, made full use of lectures by Syrianus and applied the method of Iamblichus, which permitted multiple senses (physical, mathematical, theologico-metaphysical) to be found in any passage of that work. A different kind of exegesis was practiced by his son Ammonius (435/445–517/526), Ammonius' pupil Olympiodorus (still a professing pagan), and

Olympiodorus' pupils Elias and David (whose very names indicate that they were not pagans).

The tension between Athens and Alexandria is best represented by the polemic against Proclus by another pupil of Ammonius, Johannes Philoponus (from his surname probably a member of a Christian brotherhood calling itself "lovers of work" and probably also a Christian from birth rather than a convert). Proclus, in turn, was defended by Simplicius. The point of disagreement was whether the creation of the cosmos, as presented in Plato's *Timaeus*, should be taken as a temporal event or a timeless one. Philoponus asserted the former; Proclus, the latter. This controversy went back to the Old Academy. Philoponus also wrote a commentary on Genesis and was one of those who asserted that Plato was familiar with it. As a Christian theologian, Philoponus originated an interpretation of the Trinity known as tritheism. Of the relations between the School of Alexandria and the catechetical school (Clement and Origen), we know nothing.

One of the most dramatic incidents in the history of the school was the lynching in 415 of its famous member Hypatia by a Christian mob that accused her of preventing a reconciliation between the Christian prefect of Alexandria and Archbishop Cyril. Among Hypatia's admiring disciples was Bishop Synesius, in whose writings Christian and Platonic doctrines appear side by side.

Bibliography

Courcelle, P., *Les Lettres grecques en Occident*. Paris, 1948.

Enciclopedia filosofica. Venice, 1957. Articles on Hierocles, Hermeias, Ammonius, Olympiodorus, Johannes Philoponus, Hypatia, and Synesius.

Evrard, E., "Les Convictions religieuses de Jean Philopon . . . ." *Bulletin de l'Academie royale belgique (lettres)*, (Brussels, 1953), 299–357. On Johannes Philoponus.

Geffcken, J., *Ausgang des griechisch-römischen Heidentums*. Heidelberg, 1926–1929.

Kremer, K., *Der Metaphysikbegriff in den Aristoteles-Kommentaren der Ammonios-Schüler*. Münster, 1961. On Ammonius and his followers.

Pauly-Wissowa, *Realenzyklopädie*. Stuttgart, 1893 ff. Articles on Hierocles, Hermeias, Ammonius, Olympiodorus, Johannes Philoponus, Hypatia, and Synesius.

Saffrey, H.-D., "Le Chrétien Jean Philopon et la survivance de l'École d'Alexandrie au VIe siècle." *Revue des études grecques*, Vol. 67 (1954), 396–410. On Johannes Philoponus.

Vancourt, R., *Les Derniers Commentateurs alexandrins d'Aristote*. Lille, 1941. On the end of the Alexandrian School.

Vogel, C. J. de, *Greek Philosophy*, Vol. III. Leiden, 1959. Collection of texts with annotated bibliography.

Westerink, L. G., *Anonymous Prolegomena to Platonic Philosophy*. Amsterdam, 1962. On Ammonius and his followers.

Zeller, E., and Mondolfo, R., *La filosofia dei Greci nel suo sviluppo storico*, Vol. III, Part 6, G. Martano, ed. Florence, 1961.

PHILIP MERLAN

AL-FARABI. *See* FARABI, AL-.

ALGAZEL OR AL-GHAZZALI. *See* GHAZALI, AL-.

ALGEBRA OF LOGIC. *See* BOOLE, GEORGE; LOGIC, HISTORY OF.

ALIENATION. The term "alienation" (estrangement) has many different meanings in everyday life, in science, and in philosophy; most of them can be regarded as modifications of one broad meaning which is suggested by the etymology and the morphology of the word—the meaning in which alienation (or estrangement) is the act, or result of the act, through which something, or somebody, becomes (or has become) alien (or strange) to something, or somebody, else.

In everyday usage alienation often means turning away or keeping away from former friends or associates. In law it usually refers to the transfer of property from one person to another, either by sale or as a gift. In psychiatry alienation usually means deviation from normality; that is, insanity. In contemporary psychology and sociology it is often used to name an individual's feeling of alienness toward society, nature, other people, or himself. For many sociologists and philosophers, alienation is the same as reification: the act (or result of the act) of transforming human properties, relations, and actions into properties and actions of things which are independent of man and which govern his life. For other philosophers, "alienation" means "self-alienation" (self-estrangement): the process, or result of the process, by which a "self" (God or man) through itself (through its own action) becomes alien (strange) to itself (to its own nature).

HISTORY OF THE CONCEPT

The concept of alienation was first philosophically elaborated by Hegel. Some writers have maintained that the Christian doctrine of original sin and redemption can be regarded as a first version of Hegel's doctrine of alienation and dealienation. According to others, the concept of alienation found its first expression in Western thought in the Old Testament concept of idolatry. Still others have maintained that the source for Hegel's view of nature as a self-alienated form of Absolute Mind can be found in Plato's view of the natural world as an imperfect picture of the sublime world of Ideas. As investigation continues, probably more forerunners of Hegel will be discovered. But it seems established that G. W. F. Hegel, Ludwig Feuerbach, and Karl Marx were the three thinkers who first gave an explicit elaboration of alienation and whose interpretation is the starting point for all discussions of alienation in present-day philosophy, sociology, and psychology.

Hegel. It is a basic idea of Hegel's philosophy that whatever is, is, in the last analysis, Absolute Idea (Absolute Mind, Absolute Spirit, or, in popular language, God) and that Absolute Idea is neither a set of fixed things nor a sum of static properties but a dynamic Self, engaged in a circular process of alienation and dealienation. Nature is only a self-alienated (self-estranged) form of Absolute Mind, and man is the Absolute in the process of dealienation. The whole of human history is the constant growth of man's knowledge of the Absolute and, at the same time, the development of self-knowledge of the Absolute, who through finite mind becomes self-aware and "returns" to himself from his self-alienation in nature. However, finite mind also becomes alienated. It is an essential characteristic of finite mind (man) to produce things, to express itself in objects, to objectify itself in physical things, social institutions, and cultural products; and every objectification is, of necessity, an instance of alienation: the produced objects become alien to the producer. Alienation in this sense can be overcome only in the sense of being adequately known. Again, it is the vocation of man as man to serve as the organon of the self-knowledge of the Absolute. To the extent that he does not perform this function, he does not fulfill his human essence and is merely a self-alienated man.

Feuerbach. Feuerbach accepted Hegel's view that man can be alienated from himself, but he rejected both the view that nature is a self-alienated form of Absolute Mind and the view that man is Absolute Mind in the process of dealienation. Man is not self-alienated God. On the contrary, God is self-alienated man; he is man's essence absolutized and estranged from man. And man is not alienated from himself when he refuses to recognize nature as a self-alienated form of God; man is alienated from himself when he creates and puts above himself an imagined alien higher being and bows before that being as a slave. The dealienation of man consists in the abolition of that estranged picture of man which is God.

Marx. Marx praised Hegel for having grasped that the self-creation of man is a process of alienation and dealienation. But he criticized Hegel for, among other things, having identified objectification with alienation and the suppression of alienation with the abolition of objectivity, for having regarded man as self-consciousness and the alienation of man as the alienation of his self-consciousness, and for having assumed that the suppression of objectification and alienation is possible only and merely in the medium of pure thought. Marx agreed with Feuerbach's criticism of religious alienation, but he stressed that the religious alienation of man is only one among many forms of man's self-alienation. Man not only alienates a part of himself in the form of God; he also alienates other products of his spiritual activity in the form of philosophy, common sense, art, morals, and so on. He alienates products of his economic activity in the form of commodities, money, capital, etc.; he alienates products of his social activity in the form of the state, law, and social institutions. Thus, there are many forms in which man alienates from himself the products of his own activity and makes of them a separate, independent, and powerful world of objects toward which he is related as a slave, powerless and dependent. However, man not only alienates his own products from himself; he also alienates himself from the very activity through which these products are produced, from the natural world in which he lives, and from other men. All these kinds of alienation are, in the last analysis, one; they are only different aspects of man's self-alienation, different forms of the alienation of man from his human "essence" or "nature," from his humanity. The self-alienated man is a man who is really not a man, a man who does not realize his historically created human possibilities. A nonalienated man would be a man who really is a man, a man who fulfills himself as a free, creative being of praxis.

The concepts of alienation and dealienation were elaborated by Marx in his early writings, especially in his *Economic and Philosophical Manuscripts*, written in 1844 and first published in 1932. In his later works the two concepts were basic, but they were used implicitly rather than explicitly. Their importance was therefore overlooked. In no exposition or interpretation of Marx's views written in the nineteenth century or in the first three decades of the twentieth did the concepts of alienation and dealienation play any important role. But since the publication of the *Manuscripts* and especially since World War II, they have become the object of passionate discussions, not only among Marxists but also among non-Marxists (especially existentialists and personalists), and not only among philosophers but also among psychologists (especially psychoanalysts), sociologists, literary critics, and writers.

CONTEMPORARY INTERPRETATIONS AND DEFINITIONS

Present-day writers who use the term "alienation" differ very much in the ways in which they understand and define it. Some authors think that the concept can be applied both to man and to nonhuman entities (to God, world, and nature, for instance); but most writers insist that it is applicable only to man. Some of those who apply it only to man insist that it can refer only to individuals and not to society as a whole. According to a number of such authors, the nonadjustment of the individual to the society in which he lives is a sign of his alienation. Others maintain that a society also can be alienated, or "sick," so that an individual who cannot adapt to the existing society is not, of necessity, alienated.

Many of those who regard alienation as applicable merely to individuals conceive it as a purely psychological concept referring to a feeling, or a state of mind. Others insist that alienation is not only a feeling but that it is also an objective fact, a way of being. Some of the writers who characterize alienation as a state of mind regard it as a fact or concept of psychopathology; others insist that although alienation is not good or desirable, it is not strictly pathological. They often add that one should distinguish alienation (a psychological state of the individual characterized by feelings of estrangement) both from anomie (relative normlessness in a social system) and from personal disorganization (disordered behavior arising from conflict within the individual).

Those who oppose characterizing alienation as a psychological concept usually say that it is also (or primarily) an economic, or political, or sociological, or ethical concept. Some insist that it is basically a concept of general philosophy, or a concept of ontology and philosophical anthropology.

According to Gwynn Nettler, alienation is a certain psychological state of a normal person, and an alienated person is "one who has been estranged from, made unfriendly toward, his society and the culture it carries" ("A Measure of Alienation," p. 672). For Murray Levin, "the essential characteristic of the alienated man is his belief that he is not able to fulfill what he believes is his rightful role in society" (*Man Alone*, p. 227). According to Eric and Mary Josephson, alienation is "an individual feeling or state of dissociation from self, from others, and from the world at large" (Introduction to *Man Alone*, p. 13). For Stanley Moore, the terms "alienation" and "estrangement" "refer to the characteristics of individual consciousness and social structure typical in societies whose members are controlled by, instead of controlling, the consequences of their collective activity" (*The Critique of Capitalist*

Democracy, p. 125). According to Jean-Yves Calvez, alienation is "a general type of the situations of the absolutized subject who has given a world to himself, a formal world, refusing in this way the true concrete and its requirements" (*La Pensée de Karl Marx*, p. 51); and according to Erich Fromm, "Alienation (or 'estrangement') means, for Marx, that man does *not* experience himself as the acting agent in his grasp of the world, but that the world (nature, others and he himself) remain alien to him. They stand above and against him as objects, even though they may be objects of his own creation. Alienation is essentially experiencing the world and oneself passively, receptively, as the subject separated from the object" (*Marx's Concept of Man*, p. 44).

With such a variety of definitions, it is difficult to say which is the best one. One may reserve the term for a specific phenomenon in which one is interested and, consequently, define it in such a narrow way as to make the majority of existing uses of "alienation" entirely inadmissible; or one may define it so broadly as to make as many as possible of the existing uses at least partly admissible and then distinguish between different forms of alienation in order to account for the variety of phenomena and to prevent possible confusions. The latter course seems more promising.

FORMS OF ALIENATION

All authors who have used the concept of alienation have distinguished between different forms of alienation; but not all of them have done so explicitly. Hegel attempted no explicit classification of the forms of alienation; but since, for him, the essence of all development was a process of alienation and dealienation, different stages in the development of the Absolute could be regarded as so many forms of alienation. It would be much more difficult to develop a similar classification for Feuerbach's works because the essence of his philosophy was negation of systematic philosophy. "Alienated Labor," a well-known fragment in Marx's *Economic and Philosophic Manuscripts*, seems to suggest that we should distinguish between four forms of man's alienation: the alienation of man from the products of his own activity, the alienation of man from his productive activity itself, the alienation of man from his human essence, and the alienation of man from other men. But in other places Marx talked about other forms and subforms of alienation not mentioned in this fragment. The enumeration seems to be defective also in that it puts on the same level forms of alienation that should not be at the same level.

Twentieth-century writers differ greatly in their enumeration of the basic forms of alienation. Frederick A. Weiss has distinguished three basic forms (self-anesthesia, self-elimination, and self-idealization); Ernest Schachtel has distinguished four (the alienation of men from nature, from their fellow men, from the work of their hands and minds, and from themselves); Melvin Seeman, five (powerlessness, meaninglessness, social isolation, normlessness, and self-estrangement); and Lewis Feuer, six (the alienation of class society, of competitive society, of industrial society, of mass society, of race, and of generations).

In listing five different forms of alienation, Seeman tried to define them strictly. According to him, powerlessness is "the expectancy or probability held by the individual that his own behavior cannot determine the occurrence of the outcomes, or reinforcements, he seeks"; meaninglessness results "when the individual is unclear as to what he ought to believe—when the individual's minimal standards for clarity in decision-making are not met"; normlessness is the characteristic of a situation "in which there is a high expectancy that socially unapproved behaviors are required to achieve given goals"; isolation is characteristic of those who "assign low reward value to goals or beliefs that are typically highly valued in the given society"; and self-estrangement is "the degree of dependence of the given behavior upon anticipated future rewards, that is upon rewards that lie outside the acitivity itself" ("On the Meaning of Alienation," pp. 786, 788, 789, 790).

Instead of trying to enumerate all classifications of the forms of alienation that have been made so far, we shall only mention a few of the basic criteria according to which such classifications could be made and actually have been made.

(1) According to the nature of that which is alienated, we may distinguish between alienation of things and alienation of selves. And if we distinguish different types of things or selves, we may add further subdivisions. To those for whom the only self is man, alienation of self is only another name for the alienation of man. But they may distinguish between individual alienation and social alienation. We may classify as types of social alienation the alienation of societies as a whole (such as feudal societies and capitalist societies), the alienation of social groups (capitalists, workers, intellectuals, bureaucrats, producers, consumers, etc.), and the alienation of social institutions (such as the state, the church, and cultural institutions).

(2) According to the question, we can distinguish between alienation from something else or somebody else and alienation from oneself. The distinction is applicable only to alienation of selves; a thing cannot be alienated from itself. A self can be alienated either from something or somebody or from itself. According to the different kinds of "others" and according to the different aspects or sides of the self, further subdivisions can be added (for example, alienation from nature, alienation from fellow men, or alienation of the self from its body, its feelings, its needs, or its creative possibilities).

(3) According to whether that which is alienated is alienated through its own activity or through the activity of another, we could distinguish between alienation through others and alienation through oneself. Alienation of a thing can obviously be only an alienation through others. There can be different kinds of alienation of things (stealing, giving, and buying and selling). Alienation of self can be either alienation through others or an alienation through oneself.

SELF-ALIENATION

The concept of self-alienation, found in Hegel and Marx and of the greatest interest for philosophy, is a result of applying a combination of the above three basic criteria. What Hegel and Marx called self-alienation is alienation *of* a self *from* itself *through* itself. They differ in that Marx recognized only one self-alienated self (man), while Hegel recognized two (man and God, or Absolute). Some writers hold that one could also speak about self-alienation of nature or of the world. In religious myths we find self-alienated angels (for example, Lucifer), and in children's stories and fables we find self-alienated animals (the cowardly lion, the naive fox) and even plants (a humpy fir tree, a stinking rose). But the concept of a self-alienated man is basic.

In what sense is it possible for a self (either an individual man or a society) to be alienated from itself? It seems plausible to say that to be self-alienated means to be internally divided, split into at least two parts that have become alien to each other. But in that case, why talk of self-alienation; why not, instead, simply refer to an internal division or split? The term "self-alienation" seems to suggest some or all of the following points. (1) The division of the self into two conflicting parts was not carried out from the outside but is the result of an action of the self. (2) The division into conflicting parts does not annihilate the unity of the self; despite the split, the self-alienated self is nevertheless a self. (3) Self-alienation is not simply a split into two parts that are equally related to the self as a whole; the implication is that one part of the self has more right to represent the self as a whole, so that by becoming alien to it, the other part becomes alien to the self as a whole.

One way to specify and clarify the inequality of the two parts into which a self-alienated self is split is to describe the self-alienation as a split between man's real "nature," or "essence," and his factual " properties," or " existence." The self-alienated man in such a case is a man who is not in fact what he is in essence: a man whose actual existence does not correspond to his human essence. Similarly a self-alienated society would be a society whose factual existence does not correspond to the real essence of human society.

How can the actual existence of man deviate from his real essence or nature? If one were to conceive man's essence as something shared by all men, then somebody alienated from man's essence could not be a man in fact. Accordingly, if alienation of man from his essence is possible, his essence must not be conceived as something that all men have in common.

One possible interpretation would be the conception of man's essence as an eternal or nontemporal idea of man toward which the real man ought to strive. This interpretation is full of difficulties and leads to unanswerable questions, such as Where and in what way does such an idea of man exist? What is the way or method to achieve an adequate knowledge of it? Why should a real man strive toward it?

Another interpretation would consist in conceiving man's essence as something actually belonging to men—not to all, but only to some men; for example, to the majority of all so-far-existing men or to the majority of future men. Whichever interpretation one chooses, new difficulties arise. Why should a majority be more representative of the nature of man than a minority? If we already allow the split into essence and existence, why should we not also allow the possibility of the split being present in the majority? And why should a future actuality have any advantage over the past and the present one?

The third, and perhaps the most promising, interpretation consists in saying that man's essence is neither an eternal idea nor a part of actuality, but the sum of historically created human possibilities. To say that a man alienates himself from his human essence would then mean that a man alienates himself from the realization of his historically created human possibilities. To say that a man is not alienated from himself would mean that a man stands on the level of his possibilities and that in realizing his possibilities he permanently creates new and higher ones. The third interpretation seems more plausible than the first two, but it too leads to difficulties. In what way do the possibilities exist, and how do we discover them? On what basis do we divide man's real possibilities into human and inhuman possibilities?

SELF-ALIENATION AND HISTORY

Another much-discussed question asks whether self-alienation is an essential, imperishable property of man as man or whether it is characteristic only of one historical stage in man's development. Some philosophers, especially existentialists, have maintained that alienation is a permanent structural moment of man's existence. Man as man is necessarily self-alienated; in addition to his authentic existence he leads a nonauthentic one, and it is an error to expect that he will one day live only authentically.

Opposed to this view is the view that the originally nonself-alienated man, in the course of development, alienated himself from himself, but that he will return to himself in the future. This view was held by Engels and is accepted by many contemporary Marxists; Marx himself seems to have been inclined to think that man had always been self-alienated, but that in spite of this, he can and ought to overcome his self-alienation in the future. In this sense, Marx, in *Economic and Philosophical Manuscripts*, wrote about communism as the positive supersession of all alienation and the return of man from religion, family, state, etc., to his human (that is, social) existence. Such a conception of communism as a dealienation of human community formed the basis of all of Marx's other works.

Alienation in past and present. If we assume that the whole of history up to now has been a history of man's self-alienation, then it may be asked whether history has been characterized by the gradual elimination of alienation or by its permanent deepening. Those who believe in constant progress have maintained that alienation has always been diminishing. But many contemporary philosophers and sociologists have found that alienation has constantly increased, so that it is much deeper and more pervasive than ever before in contemporary capitalism and bureaucratic socialism. A third group of authors have maintained that alienation has diminished in some respects and increased in others. Some have insisted that the question cannot be answered simply in terms of more or less, that we should investigate different types of self-alienated men typical of different periods in human history. An interesting attempt in this direction was made by Erich Fromm, who distinguished four basic types of "nonproductive" (self-alienated) character orientations (the receptive, hoarding, exploitative, and marketing orientations), each typical of a successive stage of historical development. According to Fromm, all four are found in contemporary self-alienated society, but whereas the first three were inherited from earlier periods, the marketing orientation is "definitely a modern product," typical of twentieth-century capitalism (*Man for Himself*, pp. 62–81).

Alienation in the future. For those who regard alienation as a historical phenomenon, the question about a possible end of alienation (dealienation or disalienation) naturally arises. Two main answers have been given.

According to one group of thinkers, absolute dealienation is possible; all alienation, both social and individual, can be once and for all abolished. The most radical among this group have even maintained that all alienation has already in principle been eliminated in socialist countries, that it exists there only as a case of individual insanity or as an insignificant remnant of capitalism. More realistic representatives of this view have not denied facts showing that in countries considering themselves socialist, many old forms and even some new forms of alienation exist. But they have insisted that in more mature stages of socialism all these forms of alienation are destined to disappear.

According to a second group, only a relative dealienation is possible. It is impossible to eliminate alienation completely and finally because human nature is not something given and unchangeable that can be fulfilled once and for all. It is possible, however, to create a basically nonalienated society that would stimulate the development of nonalienated, really human individuals.

Overcoming alienation. The means recommended for overcoming self-alienation differ according to one's view of the essence of self-alienation.

Those who regard self-alienation as a psychological fact, as a fact of the life of the individual human self, dispute the importance or even the relevance of any external changes in circumstances and suggest the individual's own moral effort, a revolution within the self, as the only cure. Those who regard self-alienation as a result of the neurotic process are quite consistent in offering a psychoanalytical medical treatment; they regard the new creative experience of acceptance and meeting in a warm, truly mutual and trusting doctor–patient relationship as the main therapeutic factor.

Diametrically opposed to this view are those philosophers and sociologists who, basing their ideas on a degenerate variant of Marxism called economic determinism, hold that individuals are the passive products of the social organization, that the whole of social organization is determined by the organization of economic life, and that all economic life is dependent on the question of whether the means of production are or are not private property. For economic determinists, the problem of dealienation is reduced to the problem of social transformation, and the problem of social transformation is reduced to the abolition of private property.

In criticizing "the materialist doctrine that men are products of circumstances and upbringing," Marx stressed that "it is men that change circumstances," so that "the coincidence of the changing of circumstances and of human activity can be conceived and rationally understood only as *revolutionizing practice* (Praxis)" (*Basic Writings on Politics and Philosophy*, with Friedrich Engels, New York, 1959, p. 244).

Those who have tried to elaborate such a conception have insisted that dealienation of the society and dealienation of individuals are closely connected: one cannot be carried out without the other or reduced to the other. It is possible to create a social system that would enable and even stimulate the development of dealienated individuals, but it is impossible to organize a society that would automatically produce such individuals. A nonalienated individual is an individual who fulfills himself as a free and creative being of praxis, and free creativity is not something that can be given as a gift or forced upon anyone from outside. An individual can become free only through his own activity.

It is not simply that dealienation of individuals cannot be reduced to dealienation of society; the dealienation of society, in turn, cannot be conceived as a change in economic organization that will automatically be followed by change in all other fields and aspects of social life. Far from being an eternal fact of social life, the split of society into mutually independent and conflicting spheres and the predominance of the economic sphere is, according to Marx, a characteristic of a self-alienated society. Therefore, the dealienation of society is impossible without abolishing the alienation of the different human activities from each other.

Finally, the problem of dealienation of economic life cannot be solved by the abolition of private property. The transformation of private property into state property does not introduce an essential change in the situation of the working man, the producer. The dealienation of economic life also requires the abolition of state property, that is, its transformation into real social property; and this can be achieved only by organizing the whole of social life on the basis of the self-management of immediate producers.

Bibliography

ANTHOLOGIES

Josephson, Eric, and Josephson, Mary, eds., *Man Alone: Alienation in Modern Society*. New York, 1962.

Sykes, Gerald, ed., *Alienation: The Cultural Climate of Our Time*, 2 vols. New York, 1964.

CLASSICAL WORKS

Feuerbach, Ludwig, *Das Wesen des Christentums*. Leipzig, 1841. Translated by Marian Evans as *The Essence of Christianity*, 2d ed. London, 1882.

Hegel, G. W. F., *Die Phänomenologie des Geistes*. Bamberg and Würzburg, 1807. Translated by J. B. Baillie as *Phenomenology of Mind*. London and New York, 1910; 2d ed., 1931.

Hegel, G. W. F., *Encyclopädie der philosophischen Wissenschaften im Grundrisse*. Heidelberg, 1817.

Hegel, G. W. F., *Theologische Jugendschriften*, H. Nohl, ed. Tübingen, 1907.

Marx, Karl, *Die oekonomisch-philosophischen Manuskripte aus dem Jahre 1844*, in Karl Marx and Friedrich Engels, *Historisch-kritische Gesamtausgabe*. Berlin, 1932. Div. I, Vol. III. Translated by Martin Milligan as *Economic and Philosophical Manuscripts of 1844*. London, 1959.

Marx, Karl, *Grundrisse der Kritik der politischen Ökonomie (Rohentwurf) 1857–1858*, 2 vols. Moscow, 1939–1941; 2nd ed., Berlin, 1953.

Marx, Karl, *Das Kapital*, 3 vols. Hamburg, 1867–1894. Translated by S. Moore, E. Aveling, and E. Untermann as *Capital*, 4 vols. London, 1887–1909. Especially Vol. I, Ch. 1, Sec. 4.

Marx, Karl, and Engels, Friedrich, *Die deutsche Ideologie* (1844–1845), in their *Historisch-kritische Gesamtausgabe*. Berlin, 1932. Div. I, Vol. III. Translated as *The German Ideology*, R. Pascal, ed. London, 1939.

Works on Hegel, Marx, and Engels

Calvez, Jean-Yves, *La Pensée de Karl Marx*. Paris, 1956.

Fromm, Erich, *Marx's Concept of Man*. New York, 1961.

Hyppolite, Jean, *Études sur Marx et Hegel*. Paris, 1955.

Kangrga, Milan, *Eticki Problem u Djelu Karla Marxa*. Zagreb, 1963.

Lukács, Georg, *Der junge Hegel und die Probleme der kapitalistischen Gesellschaft*. Zurich and Vienna, 1948.

Marcuse, Herbert, *Reason and Revolution*. New York, 1941.

Oizerman, T. I., *Formirovanie Filosofii Marksizma*. Moscow, 1962.

Popitz, Heinrich, *Der entfremdete Mensch. Zeitkritik und Geschichtsphilosophie des jungen Marx*. Basel, 1953.

Tucker, Robert, *Philosophy and Myth in Karl Marx*. Cambridge, 1961.

RECENT STUDIES

Arendt, Hannah, *The Human Condition*. Garden City, N.Y., 1958.

Fromm, Erich, *Escape from Freedom*. New York, 1941.

Fromm, Erich, *Man for Himself*. New York, 1947.

Fromm, Erich, *Sane Society*. New York, 1955.

Goldmann, Lucien, *Recherches dialectiques*, 3d ed. Paris, 1959.

Lefebvre, Henri, *Le Matérialisme dialectique*. Paris, 1939.

Lefebvre, Henri, *Critique de la vie quotidienne*. Paris, 1947; 2d ed., 1958.

Levin, Murray B., *The Alienated Voter*. New York, 1960.

Lukács, Georg, *Geschichte und Klassenbewusstsein*. Berlin, 1923.

Mills, C. Wright, *White Collar*. New York, 1951.

Moore, Stanley, *The Critique of Capitalist Democracy*. New York, 1957.

Naville, Pierre, *De l'Aliénation à la jouissance*. Paris, 1957.

Pappenheim, Fritz, *The Alienation of Modern Man. An Interpretation Based on Marx and Tönnies*. New York, 1959.

Riesman, David, *The Lonely Crowd*. New Haven, 1950. Written with Nathan Glazer and Reuel Denney.

Whyte, William H., Jr., *The Organization Man*. New York, 1956.

ARTICLES

Bell, Daniel, "The 'Rediscovery' of Alienation: Some Notes Along the Quest for the Historical Marx." *The Journal of Philosophy*, Vol. 56 (1959), 933–957.

Braybrooke, David, "Diagnosis and Remedy in Marx's Doctrine of Alienation." *Social Research*, Vol. 25 (1958), 325–345.

Cornu, Auguste, "L'Idée d'aliénation chez Hegel, Feuerbach et K. Marx." *La Pensée*, No. 2 (1948), 65–75.

Dean, Dwight, "Alienation and Political Apathy." *Social Forces*, Vol. 38 (1960).

Dean, Dwight, "Meaning and Measurement of Alienation." *American Sociological Review*, Vol. 26 (1961), 753–758.

Duhrsen, Alfred, "Philosophic Alienation and the Problem of Other Minds." *Philosophic Review*, Vol. 69 (1960), 211–220.

Easton, Loyd D., "Alienation and History in the Early Marx." *Philosophy and Phenomenological Research*, Vol. 22 (1961), 193–205.

Feuer, Lewis, "What is Alienation? The Career of a Concept." *New Politics*, Vol. 1, No. 3 (1962), 116–134.

Garaudy, Roger, "O Ponjatii Otčuždenie." *Voprosi Filosofii*, No. 8 (1959), 68–81.

Glazer, Nathan, "The Alienation of Modern Man." *Commentary*, Vol. 3 (April 1947).

Kraft, Julius, "Die Selbstentfremdung des Menschen." *Geist und Tat* (March 1956).

Löwith, Karl, "Man's Self-Alienation in the Early Writings of Marx." *Social Research*, Vol. 21 (1954), 204–230.

Nettler, Gwynn, "A Measure of Alienation." *American Sociological Review*, Vol. 22 (1957), 670–677.

Petrović, Gajo, "Man as Economic Animal and Man as Praxis." *Inquiry*, Vol. 6 (1963), 35–56.

Petrović, Gajo, "Marx's Theory of Alienation." *Philosophy and Phenomenological Research*, Vol. 23 (1963), 419–426.

Rose, Arnold M., "Alienation and Participation: A Comparison of Group Leaders and the 'Mass.'" *American Sociological Review*, Vol. 27, No. 6 (1962), 834–838.

Seeman, Melvin, "On the Meaning of Alienation." *American Sociological Review*, Vol. 24 (1959), 783–791.

Sommer, Robert, and Hall, Robert, "Alienation and Mental Illness." *American Sociological Review*, Vol. 23 (1958), 418–420.

Vignaud, P., "L'Aliénation selon Karl Marx." *La Vie intellectuelle* (February 1937).

"Symposium on Alienation and the Search for Identity." *American Journal of Psychoanalysis*, Vol. 21, No. 2 (1961).

G. PETROVIĆ

ALIOTTA, ANTONIO (1881–1964), Italian philosopher, was born in Palermo and taught at the universities of Padua and Naples. Moving from studies in experimental psychology, *La misura in psicologia sperimentale* (1905), Aliotta published in 1912 a vast critical analysis of contemporary philosophy entitled *La reazione idealistica contro la scienza* (English translation, London, 1914) in which he defended a monadological spiritualism with a theistic tendency. When the shadow of the neo-Hegelianism of Croce and Gentile began to loom over Italy, Aliotta took sides with the opponents of this idealism and in his teaching and writings spread the news of other philosophical movements going on outside Italy, especially the philosophy of science, realism, and pragmatism. From 1917 to 1936, in the mature phase of his thought, Aliotta's sympathies were above all with pragmatism, and his experimentalism suggests many points of similarity with the philosophies of James and Mead. Experimentation is the only means of establishing the truth of any knowledge whatever, even metaphysical and religious. By "experimentation," Aliotta does not mean simply the techniques of the laboratory but any kind of trial-and-error procedure in any field of human activity. History is a kind of grand laboratory in which men seek, through conflict, to attain more harmonious forms of life. The success of the experiment, according to Aliotta, consists in the elimination of conflict and in the realization of a certain degree of harmony. "The quest for truth," he says in *Relativismo e idealismo*, "is the quest for a superior harmony of active human and non-human forces, operating in the universe of our experience." Obviously, the presupposition is that experience is not a single and continuous process, but is composed of a plurality of individual centers that meet and limit each other by stages and, through conflicts, try to realize a growing coordination. Common sense, science, and philosophy are the steps, or phases, of this coordination. The "thing" of common sense makes possible a certain degree of coordination between individual intuitions. The syntheses of science represent a superior degree of coordination, since they eliminate the disparity between the perspectives of common sense; and philosophical inquiry seeks to collect the remaining dissident elements, to correct the restricted vision of the particular sciences, and to achieve a more comprehensive view. The concept limit toward which this process tends is the coordination of all activities and their convergence to a single end, which is, in other terms, the Leibnizian monad of monads, or God.

Aliotta insists, however, on the social character, in Mead's sense, of all degrees of knowledge. He denies the absoluteness of truth and defends philosophical relativism, of which he sees implicit proof in the physics of Einstein; and he holds that the measure of truth is in every case determined by the degree of coordination that is experimentally realized between the intuitions, the perspectives, and the individual points of view that constitute the rough fabric of experience.

In later writings, for example, *Il sacrificio come significato del mondo* (1943), Aliotta sought to extend this point of view to ethics with an inquiry into what he calls "the fundamental postulates of action." The indeterminacy of the world and its relative uniformity, the value of the human person and the transcendence of reality, and the plurality of persons and their tendency toward unity are among these postulates, but *the* fundamental postulate is that of the "perennial character of human-values" and of the existence of God, which guarantees this character. The spiritualistic and fideistic aspect prevails over the pragmatic and methodological aspect in this final phase of Aliotta's thought.

Works by Aliotta

La misura in psicologia sperimentale. Florence, 1905.

La reazione idealistica contro la scienza. Palermo, 1912. Translated by Agnes McCaskill as *The Idealistic Reaction Against Science*. London, 1914.

La guerra eterna e il dramma dell'esistenza. Naples, 1917.

Relativismo e idealismo. Naples, 1922.

La teoria di Einstein. Palermo, 1922.

L'esperimento nella scienza, nella filosofia, e nella religione. Naples, 1936.

Il sacrificio come significato del mondo. Rome, 1947.

Evoluzionismo e spiritualismo. Naples, 1948.

Le origini dell'irrazionalismo contemporaneo. Naples, 1950.

Pensatori tedeschi della fine dell'800. Naples, 1950.

Opere complete (complete works), 7 vols. Rome, 1942–1954.

Works on Aliotta

Carbonara, Cleto, et al., *Lo sperimentalismo di Antonio Aliotta*. Naples, 1951. Essays on the occasion of Aliotta's 80th birthday.

Sciacca, M. F., *Il secolo XX*, 2d ed., Vol 1 (Milan, 1947), pp. 470–490.

NICOLA ABBAGNANO
Translated by *Nino Langiulli*

AL-KINDI. *See* KINDI, AL-.

ALL. *See* ANY AND ALL.

AL-MUKAMMAS, DAVID BEN MERWAN. *See* MUKAMMAS, DAVID BEN MERWAN AL-.

ALTHUSIUS, JOHANNES (1557–1638), German legal and political philosopher, was born at Diedenshausen, a village of the county of Wittgenstein-Berleburg in the Westphalian Circle. He is thought to have been the son of a farmer, although all data of his early youth are quite unknown. By 1581 he was studying Aristotle in Cologne, and he later studied Roman law at Basel. His experience of the Swiss way of life gave him a predilection for municipal freedom and self-government and for republican constitutionalism. Although deeply influenced by Calvinist piety, he was eager to become a learned classical scholar. The forces of Christian faith, humanistic learning, and democratic feeling formed his character. He was both a man of strong will with a tendency to stubbornness and an austere moralist. It is, therefore, not surprising that he was a rigorous logical thinker and a systematic teacher as well as a realistic positivist with a desire to describe the empirical realities of social life.

Althusius passed his examination for the doctorate of civil and ecclesiastical law at Basel in 1586 with theses on the right of succession. In the same year he published a booklet, *Iurisprudentia Romana, vel Potius Iuris Romani Ars, 2 Libri, Comprehensa, et ad Leges Methodi Rameae Conformata* (Basel, 1586), that discussed fundamental questions of Roman law and that is also of philosophical interest. Through this work Althusius introduced into political science the systematic method of the French philosopher Petrus Ramus that contrasted with the prevailing humanistic method based on philological concerns. But although Ramus opposed the traditional Scholastic method of instruction, he had nevertheless retained the formalism of his predecessors insofar as he used the "method of dichotomy." This specific "ramistic" method divided every logical concept into two others, and each of them into two new concepts. This method of an endless, progressing, systematic presentation was applied by Althusius to all his later writings.

Soon after receiving his doctorate, Althusius became a lecturer in Roman law and in philosophy at Herborn, a newly established Calvinist college attended by students from many countries. In 1594 he became professor of law, and he was appointed rector of the college in 1597 and again in 1602. He also served as an advocate in the chancellery at Dillenburg. In this capacity he defended the rights of the college against the ambitions of the noblemen of the county. He was also involved in controversies with his colleague, the law professor Anton Matthäus (1564–1637), and with some of the Herborn theologians. In spite of these activities, he found time to write his most famous work, *Politica Methodice Digesta et Exemplis Sacris et Profanis Illustrata* ("Politics Methodically Arranged and Illustrated by Holy and Profane Examples," Herborn, 1603; 2d enlarged ed., Groningen, 1610; 3d enlarged ed., Herborn, 1614). This work was, as C. J. Friedrich wrote, "the culminating point of his life." The book clearly showed Althusius' systematic strength. He undertook to coordinate the diverse views of the Bible, Roman law, and the advocacy of the right to resist an unjust monarch of George Buchanan and the monarchomachs, and, on this basis, to write a compendium of political science.

The book was a natural and rational system of sociology, involving all the contemporary discussions of the problematical questions of theology, ethics, and jurisprudence. Althusius' fundamental view was that "politics is the science of linking human beings to each other for a social life." The whole of mankind, living in natural cooperative groups, builds up a universal community of civil and private corporations. The members join each corporation by the force of their sympathetic emotions. In this respect Althusius resembled both Grotius and Rousseau. However, he was a strong opponent of Bodin's doctrine of royal absolutism, believing that the constituent power belongs to the community and that sovereignty is an attribute of the organized people, not of the king. The people decide all fundamental political questions through the representative assembly, and the chief of state is only a commissioner of the people and may be deposed if he acts contrary to the contract between him and the community. The representative assembly must obey the commandments of God and observe the natural laws. The necessities of human nature are as much a source of social order as is God's will.

Thus, Althusius held a threefold conception of social order: as a biopsychological social phenomenon, as a historically conditioned reality, and as a divinely limited work of man.

The principal sources of Althusius' thought were faith, reason, and experience. A major work composed somewhat later, *Dicaiologicae Libri Tres Totum et Universum Ius, Quo Utimur, Methodice Complectentes* ("Digest of Jurisprudence," Herborn, 1617), is based on these three elements. In this work Althusius discussed the fundamental principles, institutions, and concepts of public and private law as they were found in the Roman jurisprudence of his day. By presenting the law as the realization of the concept of law and of its component legal categories, Althusius became one of the most important forerunners of modern Continental "legal conceptualism."

Meanwhile, in 1604 Althusius had been called as a syndic to Emden, a Calvinist city in eastern Frisia. He was soon appointed to the council, and he played an important part in the struggles of the city with the count of Frisia. He also became a dominant figure in the consistory of the Reformed church in Emden.

Additional Works by Althusius

"Politica Methodice Digesta" of Johannes Althusius (Althaus), Carl J. Friedrich, ed. Cambridge, Mass., 1932.

The Politics of Johannes Althusius, abridged and translated by Frederick S. Carney. Boston, 1964. With a preface by Carl J. Friedrich.

Works on Althusius

Gierke, Otto von, *Johannes Althusius und die Entwicklung der naturrechtlichen Staatstheorien.* Breslau, 1913; 5th ed., Aalen, 1958. Translated by Bernard Freyd as *The Development of Political Theory.* New York, 1939.

Wolf, Erik, *Grosse Rechtsdenker der deutsche Geistesgeschichte,* 4th ed. Tübingen, 1963. Pp. 177–219. Has a full bibliography.

ERIK WOLF

ALTRUISM. *See* EGOISM AND ALTRUISM.

AMERICAN PHILOSOPHY. It may be appropriate to consider first whether American philosophical thought is distinguished by any special characteristics. Has American philosophy made any unique contribution to world philosophy? An examination of American thought of the past and present shows that it has been pluralistic and that no single generalization can describe it accurately. The United States has been receptive to a variety of intellectual themes and movements, from Puritanism and idealism to naturalism and positivism. Any formula designed to reduce these diverse elements to a uniform tradition is bound to involve oversimplification.

Nevertheless, one tendency does appear to be constant in the American tradition: ideas are evaluated pragmatically, and their importance is generally determined by reference to their practical applications. In America, prior to the late nineteenth century, technical philosophy was not fully developed; hence, American ideas of this period must be considered primarily (although not exclusively) in terms of their institutional setting. This is not to say that these ideas were without philosophical significance, but they were inherent in the mode of life and in the language of the people. Indeed, in 1835, Alexis de Tocqueville commented that although the inhabitants of the United States paid little attention to the various European philosophical schools, they nevertheless possessed a common philosophical method and directed their minds according to a common set of rules—albeit undefined rules.

Pragmatism, as a doctrine, was not explicitly formulated until the end of the nineteenth century, but the history of American thought indicates that the roots of the pragmatic method lay deep within the American experience. Pragmatism was hailed as the unique American contribution to philosophy, but many foreign critics argued that it was simply a rationalization of the existing way of life, a philosophical expression of the American tendency to evaluate ideas according to their purposes and consequences.

It is true that Americans have made extensive use of foreign ideas, but these have been transformed to meet American needs. The successive waves of immigration and the divergent philosophies and ideas that accompanied them were a continuing challenge to American intellectual development but only in recent times can it be said that America has made a contribution to philosophy proper.

THE COLONIAL PERIOD

Puritanism. The British, more than any other people, influenced the formation of American institutions; and the New England colonists, especially the Puritans of the Massachusetts Bay area, appear to have left an indelible mark on the American character.

The Puritans agreed with many of the principles of Calvinism. They believed that God is absolutely sovereign and that man, beset with original sin, is totally dependent upon him. Salvation cannot be earned by virtuous works; God has foreordained who shall be elected to the "Society of Saints," although presumably the performance of good works predisposes man's soul to receive God's grace.

The Puritans, therefore, were deeply involved in the conflict between the doctrines of free will and determinism. But in general it was agreed that life was a moral process, and certain moral virtues such as discipline, devotion, honesty, moderation, temperance, frugality, industry, and simplicity were typically praised. The Puritan ethic was one of serious work and practical achievement. But the dynamic activism of these early settlers may perhaps be better accounted for in terms of the necessities imposed upon them by their primitive environment than in terms of their religious philosophy.

It has often been pointed out that the Puritans' rejection of the authority of the church and their stress on the privacy of man's relation to God manifested a certain individualism. Lest too much be inferred from this tendency, however, it should be mentioned that the Puritan community did not tolerate heresy, and in practice the covenant with God seems to have been more in the nature of a corporate arrangement than an individual affair.

Colonial immaterialism and materialism. In general, seventeenth-century America was so oriented toward practical accomplishment and religious devotion that there was little attention given to theoretical inquiry. Philosophical and scientific pursuits were not directly encouraged until the eighteenth century.

Jonathan Edwards was undoubtedly the outstanding philosophical mind of colonial America. His aim was to use philosophical idealism to defend the Calvinistic system against its critics. In *Freedom of the Will* (1754), Edwards defended determinism, arguing that every event has a cause, but that Divine Predestination, Omnipotence, Foreknowledge, and Efficacious Grace are consonant with moral responsibility. Elsewhere, Edwards defended the conception of "true virtue" as "beauty of heart" and a religious love of "being in general," that is, a love of God. Edwards claimed that man, being sinful and corrupt, is naturally incapable of true virtue; yet there is the grace of God that is given to those who are elected for salvation. A sign of having received this grace is an individual's religious affection and sense of beauty. Belief in God has its source in the affections of religious love and joy, but these are not to be comprehended by the natural senses and are transmitted from a supernatural source. Edwards' philosophy is grounded in a metaphysical defense of idealistic immaterialism, the doctrine that mind and spirit, rather than corporeal matter, are fundamentally real.

Samuel Johnson, the founder of Kings College (Columbia), also wished to use philosophical immaterialism to reinterpret and combat Newtonian materialism. Johnson, however, was deeply influenced by Berkeley, who had visited the Americas, and with him he maintained that *esse* is *percipi*, that spiritual, not material, being is real, and that the human mind receives what the Divine Mind impresses upon it. Unlike Berkeley, however, he introduced the existence of abstract "archetypes."

Although there were intermittent periods of religious revival, the influence of new ideas prevailed over the religious philosophy of Edwards and Johnson. At this time the modern tendencies in philosophy and science were perhaps most strongly represented by Cadwallader Colden and Benjamin Franklin. Colden was an able student of Newtonian philosophy, although he accepted a form of dualistic occasionalism. He also attempted to go beyond Newton by suggesting an explanation for gravitation, attributing it to the joint action of the various powers of matter. Although material substance was unknowable, he wrote, we could know the motions of bodies—their resisting, moving, and elastic properties (*The Principles of Action in Matter*, 1751).

In Europe, Franklin was considered to be America's "first philosopher." His electrical experiments were thoroughly consonant with Newtonianism; indeed, they constituted an application of its general principles, and they helped to illustrate both the Newtonian natural philosophy and the experimental possibility of a completely mechanical explanation of the universe.

THE AGE OF REASON AND REVOLUTION

The ideals of the Age of Reason had their greatest influence on American life at the time of the onset of the American Revolution. Many of the colonists were directly inspired by the liberal, deistic, and empirical ideas of French and British philosophers. As a result, there was a further development of materialism in philosophy, a greater emphasis on humanistic, naturalistic, and secular morality, and most important, there was a strong movement toward realizing the ideals of republicanism and revolution.

Materialism. During the latter part of the eighteenth century, the interest in Newtonian materialism came to full maturity. Many of its supporters were members of the medical profession. These included Benjamin Rush; Joseph Priestley, the famous chemist and clergyman who fled to America in 1784; Thomas Cooper, Southern leader of liberal thought; and Joseph Buchanan, who promoted a remarkable renaissance in secular naturalism at Transylvania University in Kentucky. The materialists were enthusiastic students of science, and some attempted to extend their doctrine to all aspects of the cosmos, including man. Rush, for example, applied physical and mechanistic explanations to mind and morality.

Deism. Closely linked with the interest in materialism was a growing acceptance of deism as a religious philosophy. It was espoused by many American political leaders, notably Thomas Jefferson, and was most vigorously defended by Thomas Paine (*The Age of Reason*, 1794–1796), Ethan Allen (*Reason the Only Oracle of Man*, 1784), and Elihu Palmer. These deists upheld the supremacy of reason and rejected the authority of such supernatural phenomena as scriptural revelation, prophecies, and miracles. In opposition to the established church, the deists supported the principles of religious freedom and the separation of church and state. This extreme position was perhaps not entirely approved by the community, but there was widespread sympathy for deistic views. It should be pointed out that deism was totally incompatible with the Calvinist notion of the essential sinfulness of man. Paine and Allen, for instance, argued that God, as first cause, designed the order of the universe, and that all events are determined by natural laws. Therefore, nature (including man) is a manifestation of the goodness of God.

Humanism. The deists held that man, as a rational being, was capable of achieving the good life on earth and did not need to wait for the heavenly kingdom to come. Thus, their moral philosophy was humanistic and relative to human aims and goals; happiness, not faith, provided the standard of choice. The Enlightenment manifested an optimistic faith in science, reason, and education as the instruments of human progress. Following the advent of Lockean empiricism, all knowledge was held to have had its origin in sensations, and man was seen as the product of conditioning forces in his environment. There was a general conviction that if one improved the social environment, one might improve man and thereby achieve social justice.

Political ideals. During the colonial period, the most striking American achievement was the practical development of contemporary social and political ideals. Like many Europeans, the colonists were inspired by the writings of Locke and Montesquieu, but the effort to realize the aims of liberalism in an actual state involved unprecedented problems. In the revolutionary situation there was general support for the polemics of Jefferson, Paine, Joel Barlow, and others who argued that "natural rights" (life, liberty, and the pursuit of happiness) constitute the foundation of social justice. Governments are artificial contracts designed to protect these inalienable rights: if they fail to fulfill their original purpose, their claim to rightful authority is void, and they may justly be altered or dissolved. There was not, however, unanimity concerning the form of the new government to be established. *The Federalist* papers (1787–1788), written by Alexander Hamilton, James Madison, and John Jay, bear witness to the problem that the colonists faced in attempting to balance the claims of the federal government against the claims of the various social classes and the individual states under its jurisdiction. But Americans, unencumbered by tradition, succeeded in creating a workable government based on Enlightenment principles.

PHILOSOPHY BEFORE THE CIVIL WAR

No sooner had the American republic been established than a conservative reaction set in. Indeed, this seems to be a recurrent phenomenon in American history: liberal advances have been periodically suppressed by a resurgence of religious and/or political conservatism. However, it may well be argued that despite these periods of reaction, American society manifests a dominant tendency to incorporate changing (and progressive) social values.

In the years between the Revolution and the Civil War, Americans were concerned with consolidating the gains of the Revolution and resolving threatening social problems, such as the existence of slavery. There was little interest in philosophizing, and in fact this period is in general without intellectual distinction.

Conservatism. In political thought, fear of the "mob" and the excesses of the French Revolution led to a reaction against the liberal principles of the Declaration of Independence. The South rejected the Jeffersonian doctrine of natural rights, liberty, and human equality. John C. Calhoun held that man was by nature social, that government was an organic outgrowth of human instincts, and that inequality was essential to human progress. Calhoun feared the tyranny of the majority, which he proposed to check by utilizing a concurrent rather than a numerical majority, based on both the state and federal governments (*A Disquisition on Government*, 1851). There were times, of course, when the liberal point of view was expressed, as during the Jacksonian period (1829–1837), when frontier individualism and egalitarianism returned. But these political differences represented a fundamental division that was only to be resolved by force.

A similar reaction in religion took place during the first part of the nineteenth century. Optimistic faith in the potency of human intelligence and reason was displaced by a renewed feeling of human frailty and dependence. The interests of science were subordinated to the interests of orthodox religion. New national religious denominations were organized, and while many liberal arts colleges were founded under religious leadership, an independent philosophy did not have a conspicuous place in their curriculums. The radical deistic spirit was no longer in evidence, and philosophy was now approached as an "edifying" subject and was frequently taught by the college president, who often was also a clergyman. Philosophy was considered under three headings—natural, mental, and moral. It was assumed that the purpose of philosophy was to demonstrate the divine order of the universe and to justify the existing order of society. Noah Porter commented that philosophy was approached chiefly as an "applied science" relating to theology, morality, and politics. Typically, Francis Wayland's widely read philosophical work, *Elements of Moral Science* (1835), was primarily devoted to "practical ethics."

Scottish realism. Two schools of philosophy did, however, have a significant influence during this period—namely, Scottish realism and an eventually dominant philosophical idealism. John Witherspoon and Samuel Stanhope of Princeton first introduced Scottish realism, and this doctrine was later supported, in one form or another, by Francis Bowen, Joseph Haven, Samuel Miller, Frederick Beasley, Noah Porter, and others. James McCosh, who immigrated to America in 1868, was struck by the Yankee aptitude for practical observation and invention and concluded that realism based on common sense might very well become the distinctive American philosophy.

The realists, who were dissatisfied with transcendental idealism, materialistic psychology, and Humean skepticism, held that by intuitions of the mind one has simple and immediate perceptions of the real and objective order. The mind seizes its objects directly, whether these objects are sensory, relational, or abstract. We have truth only when our ideas conform to things, which means that we must employ the inductive method and pay close attention to "the facts." Among the perceived facts are real objects that exist independently of man. But the realists thought that self-evident intuitions might also establish other "first and fundamental truths," such as basic scientific universals, the principle of causality, the uniformity of nature, mathematical forms, standards of right and wrong, God's existence, and the immortality of the soul. Thus, what at first appeared as a solution to besetting philosophical problems was extended to embrace a whole set of orthodox ideas and values.

Transcendentalism. Many critics and historians consider Transcendentalism to be the most distinctive American intellectual movement of the nineteenth century. Emanating chiefly from Boston, the influence of Transcendentalism was strongest in the years before the Civil War. Among its advocates were Ralph Waldo Emerson, Henry David Thoreau, William Ellery Channing, and Theodore

Parker (Henry James, Sr., who was a Swedenborgian mystic, may also be included).

It is easier to define Transcendentalism in terms of the ideas it opposed than by the ideas it supported. The movement represented no single system of thought and was initially inspired by a Unitarian reaction against the pessimism and morbidity of Calvinist religion. The Unitarian Transcendentalists, led chiefly by Channing, Parker, and Emerson, were liberal in sentiment and inclined toward religious optimism. They maintained that God is loving and just and that man, through his own efforts, is able to attain moral virtue. On the other hand, the Unitarians rejected the rational religion of the deists as well as the concept of a mechanistic universe. Like the deists, the Unitarians wished to apply reason to the interpretation of Scripture, but many Unitarians (for example, Channing) were willing to accept the validity of revelation.

In general, however, the Transcendentalists, many of whom rejected Biblical religion, wished to go beyond the limits of rational Unitarianism to extend what they considered the too narrow boundaries of the Lockean concept of experience and to expand the Enlightenment vision of human existence. The Unitarians held that in religion man may transcend ordinary experience and understanding and that his soul may attain direct union with God. Following this line of reasoning, and further influenced by the romantic idealists Coleridge, Kant, Friedrich von Schelling, and Victor Cousin) and by Platonism and Indian mysticism, the Transcendentalists claimed that the universe was far richer and deeper than empirical philosophy would allow. Writers such as Parker argued that empirical and scientific investigations could yield no more than probable evidence and that dependence upon such evidence could only result in skepticism. Unlike most Transcendentalists, however, Parker did believe that "Reason" could grasp the "ultimate truth" from which the bases of metaphysics, ethics, and politics could be derived. But the majority of Transcendentalists were not interested in such rational demonstration: they were poets and mystics who believed that truth is attained through subjective intuition.

In the area of metaphysics, the Transcendentalists were idealists. Emerson's early essay *Nature* (1836) presents their general position. The world is divided into two realms. On the one hand, there is the unreal world of appearances and sensations that is the object of empirical science. Ultimate reality, however, is founded upon the unseen transcendental world in which mind, spirit, and the oversoul prevail, and this world can be discovered only through poetry and philosophy.

As a movement, Transcendentalism was inspired less by speculative philosophy than by moral idealism. The Transcendentalists wished to free the individual from a blind adherence to convention and custom. Thoreau, for example, maintained that the individual must be at liberty to consult and follow the dictates of his personal insight and conscience. He even went so far as to maintain that if civil society interferes with the individual's personal moral convictions, then civil disobedience becomes the individual's highest obligation. The Transcendentalists strove for social and political progress; many of them defended natural rights and equality and worked for the abolition of slavery.

THE LATE NINETEENTH CENTURY

Speculative and absolute idealism. After the Civil War there was a resurgence of interest in philosophical idealism, and speculative technical philosophy became the dominant academic tradition. The most influential force in this revival of speculative idealism was generated by a group called the St. Louis Hegelians. Among its members were William T. Harris, Henry C. Brockmeyer, Thomas Davidson, George H. Howison, and Denton J. Snider; many were German immigrants who fled to America after the revolution of 1848 and who were interested in sponsoring the translation and study of the writings of German absolute idealists. This work was begun with the foundation of the Kant Club and developed under the auspices of *The Journal of Speculative Philosophy* (1867–1893), the first philosophical journal of its kind in America.

William T. Harris, the influential editor of this journal, thought it essential that Americans be acquainted with the great masters of philosophy, especially Hegel, and he and his colleagues argued intensely for the claims of "abstract philosophy" and the speculative method against the claims of empiricism, positivism, and agnosticism. They believed that through reason one may attain knowledge of ultimate reality, and they thought that Hegelianism proffered a comprehensive and consistent world view that could be applied to ethics, religion, art, politics, law, and education.

This doctrine spread rapidly throughout the Midwest and eventually to New England. Among the many noteworthy defenders of idealism in the nineteenth century were Laurens P. Hickok, George T. Ladd, Paul Carus, and Borden P. Bowne. (Idealism was carried over into the twentieth century by Frank Thilly, George Fullerton, Mary W. Calkins, Hugo Münsterberg, George H. Palmer, and others.) Perhaps the high point in the progress of idealism was reached with the founding of the *Philosophical Review* in 1892 at Cornell University by J. Gould Schurman. At this time Howison maintained, "We are all agreed . . . in one great tenet . . . that the only thing absolutely real is mind; [and] that all material and all temporal existences take their being from Consciousness" (quoted by A. O. Lovejoy in "A Temporalistic Realism," *Contemporary American Philosophy*, New York, 1930, Vol. II, p. 85).

Almost the last, and probably the greatest, defender of idealism in America was Josiah Royce. In all of his writings, from *The Religious Aspect of Philosophy* (1885) to *Lectures in Modern Idealism* (1919), Royce was dominated by one aim: to discover the Absolute in the universe. Beginning with fragmentary experience, he was led to "the larger self": from the possibility of error he argued to a standard of Absolute Truth, and from individual value to a universal standard of value. For Royce, mind is the ultimate reality, but reality is not to be identified with subjective consciousness; absolute mind, which is the true reality, is greater than the individual mind and comprises the total intelligible structure of the universe. It is only in terms of Absolute experience, in which all things are present and understood, that any finite experience can be comprehended.

Darwinism and evolution. The introduction of Darwin's theory of evolution marks a turning point in American philosophy. Darwin's theory conflicted with traditional religion, metaphysics, and morality and led to a fundamental challenge of the dominant idealism of the age. Thus, it provided a daring stimulus to philosophical inquiry. In England, Herbert Spencer and T. H. Huxley defended Darwinism, and in the United States it was defended by John Fiske, Francis E. Abbot, Chauncey Wright, and the pragmatists Charles S. Peirce, William James, and John Dewey.

Fiske, a disciple of Spencer, attempted to construct a theory of the cosmos based on the findings of the sciences (*Outlines of Cosmic Philosophy*, 1874). He elaborated a form of "cosmic theism" which, he claimed, went beyond Spencer's agnosticism and at the same time avoided anthropomorphism. Although Wright was equally pro-Darwin, he criticized attempts to convert the theory of evolution into a grandiose metaphysical scheme. Although Wright did not write much, he anticipated many of the ideas that were later to become focal in philosophy, including the verifiability principle, the pragmatic criterion, and naturalism.

A major effect of Darwinism on philosophy in America was that it transformed the idea of nature from a fixed system of eternal reality into one of dynamic change and replaced the category of substance and essence with that of process and event. Darwinism stimulated the extension of scientific explanations beyond the physical sciences to the psychological and social sciences. It helped to break down the dualism between man and nature and between mind and body, and it encouraged the study of consciousness and language in objective terms. It also contributed to the naturalization of morality and to the application of science to ethics and politics. Most importantly, perhaps, Darwinism undermined the established authority of idealism and made possible the development of an experimental approach to philosophy.

GOLDEN AGE OF AMERICAN PHILOSOPHY

Toward the end of the nineteenth century, there emerged in America a creative, vital, and profound interest in philosophy that has continued down to the present. The period from 1880 to 1940 has sometimes been called the "golden age" of American philosophy because of the emergence of a number of original thinkers and fresh movements. The most important figures of the "golden age" were Peirce, James, Dewey, Royce, George Santayana, and Alfred North Whitehead, and the most significant movements were pragmatism, realism, and naturalism.

Pragmatism. During the 1870s in Cambridge, the members of the Metaphysical Society (including Peirce, James, Wright, and Fiske) first discussed the philosophical ideas that were later to be developed as pragmatism. Of them all, however, Charles Peirce, probably America's most profound philosopher, is usually considered the originator of pragmatism.

Peirce. For Peirce, pragmatism was primarily a formal method of clarifying confusions in conceptual statements. In a series of articles, and especially in the essay "How to Make Our Ideas Clear" (1878), he outlined the essentials of pragmatism. "Consider what effects, that might conceivably have practical bearings, we conceive the object of our conception to have," wrote Peirce, "then, our conception of these effects is the whole of our conception of the object." Peirce made it clear that the pragmatic method was to be used chiefly to ascertain the meaning of "hard words" and "abstract concepts," and that he was not concerned with all ideas but only with "intellectual concepts." The meaning of ideas is properly stated in hypothetical form; the experimental consequences of ideas *are* their meaning. To say that something is "brittle" means that "if we were to strike it it would shatter." One does not actually have to perform such an experiment in order to understand the meaning of an idea, but unless the idea represents some conceivable experimental procedure and consequence it is without meaning.

James. Peirce's work went almost completely unrecognized until William James discussed Peirce's ideas in a famous lecture at the University of California in 1898. However, by "pragmatism" James meant not only Peirce's method of determining meaning but also a new theory of truth which James thought was implicit in Peirce's method. In Lecture VII of *Pragmatism* (1907), James wrote, "'The true' is only the expedient in the way of our thinking, just as 'the right' is only the expedient in the way of our behaving. Expedient in almost any fashion; and expedient in the long run and on the whole of course." At another time James said that the quality that characterizes both beliefs and true statements is that they both "pay." Following this line of thought, he also commented that the statements "It is useful because it is true" and "It is true because it is useful" have exactly the same meaning. Many of James's critics, including Bertrand Russell and A. O. Lovejoy, objected that James used the words "expedient," "pay," and "useful" in an ambiguous way. These critics claim that there is a difference in saying that a scientific theory is useful in the sense that it enables one to derive certain predictions and saying that a belief is useful in the sense that it gives emotional satisfaction. However, it is clear that James himself did not accept this difference. In justification of religious belief he wrote, "On pragmatic principles we can not reject any hypothesis if concepts useful to life flow from it. . . . If the hypothesis of God works satisfactorily in the widest sense of the word, it is true. Now . . . experience shows that it certainly does work" (*Pragmatism*, Lecture VIII).

This theory of truth was not shared by other American pragmatists, and Peirce naturally was hostile to its subjectivistic element. His criterion was based upon public tests of laboratory science. He too was interested in a theory of truth, but he defended the "method of science" as the most effective way of resolving doubt and fixing belief. Nevertheless he maintained that there were limitations to the use of the pragmatic criterion, and in order to dissociate himself from James's position he renamed his theory "pragmaticism"—a word, he said, which was so ugly that it would be safe from kidnapers.

Dewey. Among the pragmatists, John Dewey was the most influential in public life. Philosophically he differed from both James and Peirce. Like James he opposed the traditional correspondence and coherence theories of truth, but he was unwilling to accept the subjectivism of James's interpretation of pragmatism, and he had no desire to justify religious belief. On the other hand, he differed from Peirce in that he wished to apply the pragmatic criterion to a wider area of experience. According to Dewey, the word "pragmatic" refers simply to "the rule of referring all thinking, all reflective considerations, to *consequences* for final meaning and test" (*Essays in Experimental Logic*, Chicago, 1916, p. 330). He maintained that language is an instrument that transforms raw experience in accordance with human purposes: the meaning of an idea is "a set of operations" to be performed or the "consequences" of a thing or an event. It should be noted that Dewey named his theory "instrumentalism," in order to distinguish it from the earlier pragmatism.

In the development of Dewey's philosophy, the concept of the "situation" came to be central, especially to his theory of inquiry. Within immediate experience ("primary experience") arise conflicts that initiate inquiry: reflective thinking ("secondary thinking") serves to resolve the problematic situation. Inquiry, then, "is the controlled or directed transformation of an indeterminate situation into one that is so determinate in its constituent distinction and relations as to convert the elements of the original situation into a unified whole" (*Logic: The Theory of Inquiry*, 1938, pp. 104–105). Ideas that are arrived at in the process of inquiry are said to be hypotheses—in other words, plans of action that are tested by experimental consequences. "That which satisfactorily terminates inquiry is, by definition, knowledge" (*ibid.*, p. 8). (Dewey frequently referred to true knowledge as "warranted assertability.")

Another crucial element in Dewey's pragmatism was his development of a biological and behavioristic theory of experience. (A similar theory was implicit in some chapters of James's *The Principles of Psychology*, 1890.) Dewey argued that thinking was a mode of adapting to the challenges of the environment. He considered conscious processes to be transactions of the living organism.

Pragmatism also presupposed a social theory of experience. George H. Mead, who influenced Dewey to a certain degree, held that "mind" and "self" developed out of the process of social communication and that the individual could not be considered in isolation from the community (*Mind, Self, and Society*, 1934).

Influence of Pragmatism. One of the most significant effects of pragmatism was that it contributed to the downfall of traditional concepts in metaphysics. Peirce, James, and Dewey were hostile to traditional metaphysics and rejected all notions of absolute being or ultimate certainty such as the idealists espoused. They thought that any defensible metaphysics would have to be empirical and tentative in character. Peirce formulated a number of ingenious metaphysical ideas, although at times they seem to bear only a remote relation to the pragmatic criterion. He suggested roles for chance, love, habit, and continuity in the universe, and he questioned the postulate of determinism. Peirce frequently described his position as a form of "scholastic realism," and he also suggested a phenomenology of the given, a categorial scheme of "Firstness," "Secondness," and "Thirdness." James likewise outlined several generative ideas in metaphysics: "radical empiricism" (relations as well as particulars are given as real); "pure experience" (reality is not made of one stuff, but of neutral experience out of which different relations are composed); and "pluralism" (the universe may not be a block universe but may exist in distributive, plural, and indeterminate form).

The influence of pragmatism was not restricted to academic philosophy; its effect soon began to be felt in the behavioral sciences, law, history, politics, and education. But in these areas the pragmatists were only applying their basic principle that ideas must be related to practical consequences and be responsive to the broader problems of civilization.

Realism. The realistic revolt against idealism in the early decades of the twentieth century was not confined to the United States, but it was perhaps more widespread there than elsewhere. Peirce, James, and even Whitehead were sympathetic to aspects of realism, but most important to its development were two schools, known as "New" Realism and "Critical" Realism.

New Realism. During the first decade of the twentieth century, the New Realists published numerous articles and books, including Ralph Barton Perry's influential article, "The Ego-Centric Predicament" (1910). The New Realists established themselves as an organized movement when R. B. Perry, W. P. Montague, R. B. Holt, E. G. Spaulding, W. T. Marvin, and W. B. Pitkin wrote "The Program and First Platform of Six Realists" (1910) that appeared in *The Journal of Philosophy*. The same authors later published an influential book, *The New Realism* (1912). Among other philosophers who were sympathetic to the New Realist outlook were F. J. E. Woodbridge, E. B. McGilvary, M. R. Cohen, J. Lowenberg, and J. E. Boodin.

The New Realists rejected the epistemological subjectivism of the idealists (and some pragmatists) and defended instead the doctrine of the real independence of the thing known. This required a commitment to naive realism (the view that particulars persist independently of our consciousness of them); to Platonic realism (the view that universals subsist); and to a form of epistemological monism (the view, as interpreted by Montague, that particulars and universals that are reals are apprehended directly rather than indirectly through copies or mental images). New Realism did not deny knowledge through intermediaries, but maintained that it was subordinate to direct or presentative knowledge.

The New Realists, however, did not long remain united. They agreed in general that external physical objects exist, but they differed on many other issues, especially on the nature of error, and on how to distinguish between veridical and false perceptions. Holt and Perry were led to the view that since percepts in consciousness are identical with their immediate objects, then illusion and hallucination exist objectively, and false percepts, like true percepts, are "real." Montague agreed that false percepts subsist, although he denied that they have causal force. This line of argument seemed to lead to contradictory conclusions—for example, that a staff in water is both straight and bent at the same time.

Critical Realism. The Critical Realists were no less concerned than the New Realists to vindicate the ordinary man's belief in the independent reality of material objects. However, they were convinced that what is directly given in perception is not the physical object itself, but rather a datum that may provide the perceiver with evidence for the existence of the object but is not in any way a part or characteristic of the object. In other words, physical objects are known by inference and not directly. In upholding this distinction between the datum and the object, Critical Realists espoused a form of epistemological dualism. This theory, it was thought, had the advantage of enabling us to explain error by attributing it to the psychological state of the perceiver.

Some of the leading Critical Realists—George Santayana, A. O. Lovejoy, Roy Wood Sellars, C. A. Strong, J. B. Pratt, Durant Drake, and A. K. Rogers—contributed to the volume *Essays in Critical Realism* that was published in 1920. Even here they disagreed among themselves concerning the status of the data given in perception, and eventually the Critical Realists divided into two camps. Drake, Rogers, Strong, and Santayana held that what is given in consciousness are "essences." As the logical characteristics of the object, these essences are independent of both the object and of the mental states which entertain them. In knowing an object, we assign a certain essence to an independently existing reality. Santayana, like Plato, maintained that essences are eternal. Lovejoy, Sellars, and Pratt, however, denied the doctrine of essences and held that the given in perception is the character complex of the mental existent of the moment—a particular sense datum, not an independent entity.

This naturally involved them in a difficulty that has haunted dualists since the time of Locke and Descartes: If the object is never given in experience, how do we know that there is an object, and even if it is granted that there is one, how can we know what characteristics it has? In *Skepticism and Animal Faith* (1923) Santayana tried to meet the problem by replying that although it is not possible to establish the nature of the external object by rational means, we can still bridge the gap by means of "animal faith" and instinct: man (as an actor in the environment) has a dynamic relation to objects, and he is not restricted to a simple passive, knowing, or perceiving relationship. Lovejoy, in *The Revolt Against Dualism* (1930), argued that belief in a real physical world entails a dualism because the datum is never identical with the object known. He admitted that one cannot "prove" the existence of physical objects. Nonetheless, he maintained that one may affirm their existence; this assumption is made by all men of common sense, and no man can deny it.

After the mid-1930s, realism ceased to be an important movement in American philosophy. Very few philosophers had any inclination to doubt the independent reality of physical objects, and most of the younger philosophers turned to other issues that they considered to be more fundamental.

Naturalism. In the wide sense of the word, "naturalism" may refer to any philosophical theory which maintains that in principle all phenomena can be explained in terms of natural causes or principles. By this definition several philosophies of the past (including most forms of materialism and certain aspects of Hume's thought) may be considered naturalistic. The naturalism that became influential in philosophy during the twentieth century, however, is somewhat different from earlier varieties. Undoubtedly Dewey was a crucial influence in this development, but the new naturalism should not be confused with pragmatism or instrumentalism; in fact, many of the outstanding naturalists were not at all sympathetic to pragmatism. Several of the philosophers mentioned above were naturalists as well as realists. Santayana's early book, *The Life of Reason* (1905–1906), was generally naturalistic in outlook. Other realists who also may be considered naturalists are Sellars, Woodbridge, Cohen, Montague, Perry, and Drake. *Naturalism and the Human Spirit* (1944), an important collection of essays, included papers by Dewey, Ernest Nagel, Sidney Hook, H. W. Schneider, J. H. Randall, Jr., Abraham Edel, Harold Larrabee, H. T. Costello, and George Boas. Naturalism is often considered as a movement belonging to the "golden age" because of its association with Dewey and Santayana. But unlike pragmatism and realism, naturalism is still one of the most vital influences in American philosophy.

American naturalism, like the traditional naturalistic systems, maintains that cognitive claims can be established only by the logico-empirical method of science. The scientific method is not regarded as an arcane procedure but as continuous with the operations of thought used in ordinary life; it is considered adequate to the study of everything there is, including consciousness and social phenomena. By contrast, neither intuition nor mystical insight is thought to be capable of arriving at any sort of truth, whatever their emotional, moral, or aesthetic value. Naturalism clearly precludes not only transcendent metaphysics but also the need for any special method to deal with uniquely human phenomena.

Unlike earlier forms of naturalism, American naturalism has been characterized by a vigorous antireductionism. According to Nagel, for instance, there are at least as many qualitatively distinct features in the world as are present in human experience, and it is misleading to attempt any sort of "nothing but" reduction of nature to elementary constituents ("Naturalism Reconsidered," *Proceedings and Addresses of the American Philosophical Association*, Vol. 28, 1954–1955). Closely connected to this is the principle of contextualism. Many American naturalists reject the distinction between appearance and some reality that is supposed to be behind appearances. Such a distinction, it is argued, only makes sense in a given context in terms of the aims of a given inquiry. Nagel has also said that there is no absolutely privileged context. Every quality and event is a genuine occurrence and possesses ascertainable relations and functions in some complex process or context. A quality, like sweetness, is no less a constituent of nature than the qualities with which physical science concerns itself.

The American naturalists have always insisted that they do not deny the occurrence of novel features in the world or the uniqueness of the human race. While the conditions of man's life are continuous with the rest of nature, man possesses an inquiring mind which enables him to master many of the forces in his environment. However, this inquiring mind is not beyond the scope of scientific investigation. Most American naturalists have opposed a mind–body dualism, and many have favored some form of nonreductive materialism. Although consciousness cannot be simply identified with its physical conditions, it is causally dependent upon them. There is no place for the operation of disembodied forces, immaterial spirits, or immortal souls.

Many naturalists have been outspoken critics of the claims of traditional religion. However, naturalists have not been unanimously antireligious. Some (such as Santayana and J. H. Randall, Jr.) have held that religious experiences may be of inestimable value and have important moral and aesthetic functions, although it is a mistake to regard this as evidence for the existence of a supernatural reality. Dewey distinguished "religion" from the "religious" quality of experience, and he claimed that it is the latter which is significant—a religious experience is a consummatory experience in which we become aware of our highest ideals and aspirations. Indeed, "God" for Dewey may refer to "the ideal ends" and values to which one is "supremely devoted." Most naturalists are "humanists" in the sense that man and the things he needs and desires are considered the bases of value.

Naturalists have written extensively on moral questions. However, they have generally been interested in the wider problem of value and valuation rather than simply in the question of moral value alone. In his *General Theory of Value* (1926), Perry defined value as "the object of any interest." C. I. Lewis, in *An Analysis of Knowledge and Valuation* (1946), argued that value judgments are in principle confirmable in the same way as other empirical judgments. Dewey and his followers argued that value judgments cannot be understood or assessed except in the framework of the concrete problems and situations that they are designed to resolve. Moral problems usually concern the adjustment of competing needs and preferences, and any attempt to refer them to some transcendent realm of values is completely misguided.

American naturalists have found themselves faced with the challenge of G. E. Moore's *Principia Ethica*, which presents an acute criticism of the "naturalistic fallacy." They have in general agreed with Moore that there is no *one* constant meaning of moral statements, if only because such statements are plural and always specific; there can therefore be no simple or unique analysis or definition of moral judgments. However, they do not admit that this entails that in concrete situations there can be no empirical resolution of value judgments. Naturalists claim that in many moral disputes certain facts are relevant to their settlement, and it makes good sense to speak of some judgments as being well supported and others as being unsupported by the evidence. Thus, American naturalists have emphasized the role of scientific knowledge in matters of value and valuation.

Recent idealism and rationalism. Although idealism holds a minority position in the mid-twentieth century, it does not lack some respected champions, such as James E. Creighton, William E. Hocking, and Wilbur Urban. One of the most influential idealists of recent years was Edgar S. Brightman, the leader of a school known as personalism, which is still active. Personalism makes personality the key to all philosophical problems and has an affinity with idealism because all being is defined as personal consciousness.

Brand Blanshard does not speak of himself as an idealist, but in the *Nature of Thought* (1939) he defended the coherence theory of truth and the idea that all phenomena in the world are connected by logical necessity; both of these views are also strongly upheld by idealists and rationalists. Two other rationalists who are prominent in twentieth-century thought are Morris R. Cohen (*Reason and Nature*, 1931) and Alfred North Whitehead, neither of whom was an idealist.

In his later years, Whitehead, utilizing elements of idealism, naturalism, and realism, attempted to develop a comprehensive cosmic system. He criticized the Newtonian mechanical world view, and what he called the principles of "misplaced concretion" and "simple location," whereby bits of isolated matter and absolute space and time are abstracted and reified. But he also attempted to modify aspects of Einstein's theory of relativity and to place it on more empirical foundations. Nature for Whitehead is a domain of multiple occasions or events in process: each event is an indivisible stretch of time, and each appropriates to itself, in a creative act, all else in the universe. Organic life, he said, is as fundamental as material entities to any metaphysical account of reality (*Process and Reality*, 1929). Whitehead was perhaps the chief proponent of speculative philosophy during the "golden age."

THE CONTEMPORARY PHILOSOPHICAL SCENE

It would be difficult to try to fix a precise date for the end of the "golden age" of American philosophy, for some of the theories widely discussed in the early years of the twentieth century are still being vigorously debated at the present time. Nevertheless, certain significant differences have arisen recently that relate both to the kinds of problems usually discussed and the kinds of answers that are receiving serious attention. Few observers would deny that philosophical analysis—logical positivism and linguistic philosophy—has become the dominant philosophical tendency in America.

Logical positivism. Logical positivism, which was first developed by the Vienna circle in the 1920s, began to be influential in the United States in the 1930s. Perhaps the chief factor in its growth in America was the fact that many of the leaders of the movement fled the Nazis and settled in the United States. Among these should be mentioned Rudolf Carnap, Hans Reichenbach, Philip Frank, Richard von Mises, Herbert Feigl, Carl Hempel, and Alfred Tarski. Their continued presence has significantly affected the American philosophical scene.

The positivists were interested in a fundamental reform of philosophy. They considered philosophy to be the analysis and clarification of meaning, and they looked to logic and to the sciences as their models for constructing formally perfect languages. Probably the most controversial of the new ideas was the "verifiability principle" and the resulting condemnation of metaphysics as "nonsense." The verifiability principle maintains that a sentence is cognitively or descriptively meaningful if and only if it is empirically verifiable. Another important doctrine of logical positivism is that all sentences of pure mathematics and logic and all sentences expressing necessary propositions are tautological. In conjunction with the verifiability principle, this doctrine leads to the conclusion that statements of metaphysics are literally without sense. They are not empirically verifiable, and they can hardly be regarded as purely formal sentences; but even if they were, this would not render them meaningful, since tautologies "say nothing," being compatible with anything whatsoever. Indeed, it was claimed that metaphysical questions were "pseudo-questions."

The philosophical journals of the late 1930s and 1940s were filled with vigorous discussions and criticisms of the positivistic thesis on metaphysics. The views of the logical positivists were not really much different from the view implicit in the pragmatic theory of meaning as proposed by Peirce and James, although the positivist's expression was considerably more violent. It should also be mentioned that in *Mind and the World Order* (1929), C. I. Lewis almost entirely independently proposed a pragmatic theory concerning the nature of logic and mathematics that was similar to the ideas of Wittgenstein and Moritz Schlick; and the physicist P. W. Bridgman developed an operational theory that bore a strong resemblance to the verifiability principle.

American naturalism and logical positivism have much in common. For one thing, both are critical of the claims of traditional speculative metaphysics. For another, both deny that there is any radical difference between the natural sciences and the sciences that study man. This position was forcefully defended by Hempel in his famous article "The Function of General Laws in History" (1942), and was wholeheartedly endorsed by naturalists such as Nagel (in *The Structure of Science*, 1961) and Hook.

The position that many positivists took in regard to moral judgments seemed far too extreme to many American philosophers. The point of the controversy was the "emotive theory," according to which ethical statements serve simply to express the speaker's attitude and to evoke a similar attitude in the hearer; therefore, moral judgments are not descriptive and cannot properly be called true or false. On this theory both naturalists and intuitionists have overlooked the most distinctive feature of moral judgments, namely, their "dynamic" character.

Although the emotive theory was first proposed by Carnap and Ayer, C. L. Stevenson was responsible for defending it in America (*Ethics and Language*, 1944). However, he added a number of important qualifications to this theory, and in its later version it is much closer to naturalism. The emotive theory has nevertheless been severely attacked by naturalists, otherwise sympathetic to positivism, who claim that it fails to do justice to the cognitive character of moral judgments and that it ultimately implies some kind of nihilism. Philosophers of other schools also very generally disapprove of what they take to be the unduly restrictive attitude of the logical positivists in their insistence that the philosopher must confine himself to metaethics and not make moral recommendations. They claim that logical postivism has trivialized ethical philosophy and neglected its chief function.

Linguistic analysis. Representatives of what is called the school of linguistic analysis are the ones most frequently accused of trivializing philosophy in general and of indulging in pointless verbal exercises. These charges are leveled at a somewhat heterogeneous group of philosophers that includes G. E. Moore, the later Wittgenstein, and several influential Oxford philosophers, particularly Gilbert Ryle and John Austin. Among American philosophers, Max Black, Norman Malcolm, Alice Ambrose, Morris Lazerowitz, and O. K. Bouwsma are usually considered linguistic analysts rather than logical positivists, although the boundary line is not always clear. Logical positivists and linguistic analysts can perhaps be most easily distinguished by their differing attitudes toward metaphysics. Although the followers of the later Wittgenstein do not generally engage in metaphysics or encourage its practice, they do not call it nonsense or reject it entirely. While they may say that there is something "queer" about most metaphysical theories, many of them also claim that there is something to be learned from metaphysics, at least about the way language functions in certain areas.

There seems to be little in the way of common doctrine among linguistic analysts. Some uphold determinism and some oppose it; some favor a behavioristic interpretation of psychological statements, while others maintain that psychological statements do imply something other than the manifestations in behavior; a minority even support religious belief. But the linguistic analysts do seem to share a common approach; they are all motivated by a special interest in ordinary language and the belief that by studying its use, we shall more easily understand philosophical problems and therefore avoid the pseudo problems. For instance, the majority of these philosophers feel that the traditional problem of induction is a pseudo problem, and that if one is clear about the various uses of such words as "reason" or "evidence," one would not be tempted to raise the issue at all. "Problems" of this kind have no solution, but they can be "dissolved" in the sense that once certain confusions are brought into the open, any temptation to ask the question disappears.

The linguistic analysts have little enthusiasm for the use of symbolic logic as a means of clarifying philosophical questions, and they are entirely opposed to the idea that language is a kind of calculus. They maintain, for example, that any attempt to provide a simple definition of the meaning of "cause" can at best only point out one of the many uses of the word. They are equally unsympathetic toward the application of formal systems to ethical and psychological problems in philosophy.

Although this "informal" approach is apparently the most popular among young American philosophers, two of the most important and influential contemporary Americans, W. V. Quine and Nelson Goodman, represent the more "formal" approach associated with the thought of Russell and Carnap. (Quine is also sympathetic to pragmatism.) It may be noted that the logical positivists tend to work more in the area of philosophy of science than do the linguistic analysts.

The similarities in purpose between the logical positivists and the linguistic analysts, however, may be more important than their differences. All would probably agree with Wittgenstein's statement in the *Tractatus* that "the object of philosophy is the logical clarification of thoughts," and all tend to reject metaphysical, mystical, and obscure systems of thought. Many contemporary American philosophers are loath to label themselves by schools, but there are many similarities and convergences between the pragmatists, positivists, and linguistic analysts. The problems that tend to dominate their interest are in the areas of logic, language, and the philosophy of science.

Existentialism. Since the end of World War II, existentialism has been the philosophical movement that has attracted the greatest public attention. It has not, however, been very influential in academic philosophy. Many American philosophers object to what they consider an irrationalist element inherent in existentialist doctrines. In particular, they oppose the attitude embodied in Kierkegaard's dictum, "Truth is subjectivity." They feel that statements about "Being" and "Nothingness" revive obscurities that were exposed years ago.

Nevertheless, existentialism has appealed to some philosophers who believe that it restores to philosophy a concern for basic human problems and avoids a current tendency toward triviality. Many nonexistentialists feel that existentialist writings have made worthwhile comments on modern experience—on the "alienation" of modern man, on his anxieties, and on the "inauthenticity" of his mode of life. Moreover, the humanism of Sartre, Camus, and other writers bears some similarity to the ethical views of most naturalists and positivists. Some Anglo-Saxon writers, such as C. A. Campbell, have proposed theories that are quite close to Sartre's doctrine of the freedom of the will, which is also compatible with the contention of some analytic philosophers that rational action is in principle unpredictable and that motive explanations differ from causal explanations. However, few American philosophers would endorse Sartre's earlier extreme form of indeterminism; nor would they endorse his view that man has no "essence" or his defense of "philosophical anthropology."

The most influential existentialist in the United States has undoubtedly been the theologian Paul Tillich. In fact, Protestant philosophy in general has been very strongly influenced by existentialist thought. Closely following Kierkegaard and Heidegger, Tillich is opposed to efforts to "prove" theological claims such as the existence of God or to reduce theology to anthropomorphism. But Tillich insists that although the existence of God cannot be demonstrated, it does not follow that there is no God in the true, nonanthropomorphic sense. Tillich has also proposed a redefinition of what it is to be religious. In his new sense, a person is religious as long as he has some object of "ultimate concern," and this definition of religiosity might even apply to a humanist or atheist.

Phenomenology and metaphysics. Another philosophical movement that is considered very important in Europe, but which until recently has had little influence in America, is phenomenology. Since 1939, however, when Marvin Farber founded the journal *Philosophy and Phenomenological Research*, there has at least been a forum in America for phenomenological views. And phenomenology's association with existentialism has also served to attract attention to its doctrines.

Husserl's view that philosophy is not a factual science and that it cannot use the methods and findings of the sciences, as well as his attack on "psychologism" and on the attempt to reduce the basic laws of logic and mathematics of psychological generalizations now find some support among linguistic philosophers. The phenomenological emphasis on the "intentional" nature of conscious states also has had a certain influence on American philosophers. Many writers who use the phenomenological method, such as John Wild, accept it broadly as an exploration of the *Lebenswelt* (life-world), a kind of introspective study in depth of all phases of the conscious world of lived experience—aesthetic, moral, religious, and so forth. And there are some parallels here with the study of language by analytic philosophers and of immediate experience by pragmatists. Although many phenomenologists do not actually describe themselves as dealing in metaphysics, the remaining metaphysicians on the American philosophical scene nevertheless tend to regard them, along with the existentialists, as allies in the battle against philosophical analysis.

Metaphysics in the sense of speculation about some transcendent reality is no longer fashionable, but the work of a number of contemporary philosophers can properly be referred to as "metaphysics." Some naturalists and linguistic analysts of the mid-twentieth century are even quite willing to be described as "metaphysicians," but what they mean by "metaphysics" is not at all the sort of thing that the positivists would want to banish. *The Review of Metaphysics*, founded by Paul Weiss, has attempted to keep alive the spirit of metaphysical inquiry and is an exception to the above.

Minor movements. Some minor movements in American philosophy deserve brief comment.

Neo-Thomism has had some influence among Roman Catholic philosophers, especially through the writings of Jacques Maritain and Étienne Gilson. Most non-Catholic philosophers have found little that is new or inspiring in this revival of Thomas Aquinas, and there is a wide gulf between Neo-Thomists and most other American philosophers.

Marxism has attracted some thinkers in the United States (for example, Sidney Hook), reaching its high point in the 1930s. The impact of Marxism, however, was political and moral rather than dialectical and metaphysical, although recently some attention has been given to the concept of "alienation" in the early philosophical papers of Marx.

Zen Buddhism and other Asian philosophies and religions have also attracted some attention. The journal *Philosophy East and West* is devoted to efforts at a *rapprochement* between the Eastern and Western cultures. Some writers even claim that Zen Buddhism has some affinities with Western humanism, psychoanalysis, and James's ideas on pure experience.

If any single generalization can be made about present-day philosophy in America, it is that its predominant characteristic is its pluralism. In spite of an apparently dominant naturalistic trend, which includes logical positivism, linguistic analysis and pragmatism, there is nevertheless a receptiveness in the United States to various points of view, and virtually every contemporary approach to philosophy has found some supporters there.

(See also CRITICAL REALISM; NEW ENGLAND TRAN-

SCENDENTALISM; NEW REALISM; PERSONALISM; AND PRAGMATISM. See American Philosophy in Index for articles on American philosophers and other figures important to American philosophy.)

Bibliography

SOURCES

Anderson, P. R., and Fisch, M. H., eds., *Philosophy in America From the Puritans to James.* New York, 1939.

Blau, Joseph, ed., *American Philosophical Addresses, 1700–1900.* New York, 1946.

Fisch, M. H., ed., *Classic American Philosophers: Peirce, James, Royce, Santayana, Dewey, Whitehead.* New York, 1951.

Frankel, Charles, ed., *The Golden Age of American Philosophy.* New York, 1960.

Kurtz, Paul, ed., *The American Philosophers,* 2 vols. New York, 1965. Vol. I, *American Thought Before 1900: A Sourcebook From Puritanism to Darwinism.* Vol. II, *American Philosophy in the Twentieth Century: A Sourcebook From Pragmatism to Philosophical Analysis.*

Muelder, W. G., Sears, Laurence, and Schlabach, A. V., eds., *The Development of American Philosophy,* 2d ed. New York, 1960.

COMMENTARIES

Blau, Joseph, *Men and Movements in American Philosophy.* New York, 1952. A very readable history of American philosophy written from a naturalistic point of view.

Cohen, Morris R., *American Thought, A Critical Sketch.* Glencoe, Ill., 1954. Cryptic critical study, not only of American philosophy but also of thought in general, and full of Cohen's reflective evaluations.

Mayer, Frederick, *A History of American Thought.* Dubuque, Iowa, 1950. Informative study.

Perry, R. B., *Characteristically American.* New York, 1949. Perry presents his own judgments of some distinctive "American" traits.

Reck, A. J., *Recent American Philosophy.* New York, 1964. Biographical and philosophical sketches of ten recent representative American thinkers.

Riley, I. W., *American Philosophy, the Early Schools.* New York, 1907. One of the first and most valuable source books in the history of American philosophical thought, particularly of the colonial period.

Riley, I. W., *American Thought: From Puritanism to Pragmatism and Beyond.* New York, 1915. Very useful but dated study up to World War I.

Schneider, H. W., *A History of American Philosophy,* rev. ed. New York, 1963. Considered to be the standard reference work in the field. Contains excellent bibliographies.

Smith, J. E., *The Spirit of American Philosophy.* New York, 1963. Brief attempt to delineate what the author believes to be the key characteristics of American philosophy.

Townsend, H. G., *Philosophical Ideas in the United States.* New York, 1934. An earlier history of American philosophy.

Werkmeister, W. H., *A History of Philosophical Ideas in America.* New York, 1949. Contains little on the pre-Civil War period, but concentrates on idealism, pragmatism, and realism.

White, M. G., *Social Thought in America,* 2d ed. Boston, 1957. Useful analysis of social and political thought as it developed in America, especially the impact of liberalism.

PAUL KURTZ

AMPÈRE, ANDRÉ MARIE (1775–1836), French physicist and philosopher, whose main achievement in physics was the foundation of electrodynamics. He correctly recognized that Oersted's discovery, in 1819, of the effect of electric current on a magnetic needle was merely a special case of the general correlation of electricity in motion with the rise of a magnetic field. His explanation of magnetism in terms of molecular electric currents was a bold anticipation of one feature of the later electron theory.

Shortly after Ampère's death his *Essai sur la philosophie des sciences* appeared with a biographical note by Sainte-Beuve and a warm appraisal by Émile Littré. Its subtitle, *Exposition analytique de toutes les connaissances humaines,* indicated that the main topic was the classification of sciences, in which Ampère was as much interested as his contemporary Auguste Comte. Ampère's main division of sciences into "cosmological" and "noological" was inspired by Cartesian dualism. The details of the classification, which also included "applied sciences" —medicine, agriculture, etc.—are now of only historical interest.

Far more interesting is *La Philosophie des deux Ampères,* edited by J. Barthelémy Saint-Hilaire. The title is misleading because the only contribution of Ampère's son Jean Jacques is an introduction to the philosophy of his father. Besides this, the book contains some unfinished philosophical manuscripts as well as Ampère's letters to Maine de Biran, with whom he remained in personal contact and in correspondence until Maine de Biran's death in 1824. Ampère accepted the central idea of Maine de Biran's voluntaristic idealism that the true nature of the self is revealed in the introspective experience of effort. But unlike Maine de Biran, Ampère more cautiously differentiated what he called *emesthèse* (that is, consciousness of personal activity) from the sensation of muscular effort that can be induced by some external agency.

This was not the only instance of Ampère's remarkable gift for introspective analysis. In dealing with the association of ideas he distinguished two cases. The first is *commémoration,* or ordinary recall, when two associated ideas remain unaffected by their contiguity. The second is *concrétion,* when two ideas merge, for example, when the present perception of an object seen before blends with the recollection of its previous perception. But the main difference between Ampère and Maine de Biran concerned the problem of knowledge of the external world. Maine de Biran, under the influence of Kant, denied any possibility of knowing things-in-themselves, Ampère, under the influence of Newton, Locke, and his own scientific interests, believed in the possibility of knowing inferentially the relations between things-in-themselves. These "noumenal relations" are similar to Locke's primary qualities; they can be known when the general spatial, temporal, and numerical relations are divorced from the qualitative content (Locke's secondary qualities) of sensory experience. But unlike Locke, Ampère interpreted the impenetrability of matter dynamically, as being a result of inextensive resistances (*résistances inétendues*) of which there is an indefinite number in each body. This view of matter as being a product of inextensive dynamic centers is thus closer to the dynamism of Leibniz, Boscovich, and Faraday than to the traditional atomism of Newton. On the other hand, Ampère remained a Newtonian in his insistence on the reality of absolute space and time, which he interpreted theologically, again like Newton, as attributes of God. Equally Newtonian was his rejection of the Cartesian plenum.

Works by Ampère

Théorie mathématique des phénomènes électrodynamiques, uniquement déduite de l'expérience. Paris, 1827. Ampère's account of electrodynamics.

Essai sur la philosophie des sciences, 2 vols. Paris, 1834–1843.

La Philosophie des deux Ampères, J. Barthelémy Saint-Hilaire, ed. Paris, 1866. 2d ed., 1870.

Works on Ampère

Broglie, Louis de, *Continu et discontinu en physique moderne.* Paris, 1941. Pp. 241–266.

Cantor, Georg, "Über verschiedene Theoreme aus der Theorie der Punktmengen." *Acta Mathematica,* Vol. 7 (1885), 105–124.

"Lettres de Maine de Biran à A.-M. Ampère." *Revue de metaphysique et de morale,* Vol. 1 (1893), especially 553.

Lorentz, Borislav, *Die Philosophie André-Marie Ampère.* Berlin, 1908. Inaugural dissertation.

MILIČ ČAPEK

ANALOGY IN SCIENCE. *See* MODELS AND ANALOGY IN SCIENCE.

ANALOGY IN THEOLOGY. Christian theology inherits, from its Scripture and from Hellenistic philosophy, traits generating a perplexity that some have thought can be solved only by appeal to analogy. As derived from Scripture, this perplexity is based on the prima facie conflict between repeated Biblical warnings that God is wholly incommensurable with his creation and vivid Biblical imagery depicting things divine combined with fairly explicit statements on the Deity's purposes, emotions, and characteristic modes of behavior. On Hellenistic assumptions, the Highest Being is taken to be entirely simple, immutable, and thus essentially beyond our fragmentary concepts but, at the same time, to be the supreme source of all intelligibility and, consequently, the one supremely knowable reality.

Christian theology thus finds itself committed, from both sides of its heritage, to apparently incompatible axioms. On the one hand God, to be the God of the Bible or of the philosophers, must be so utterly different from all finite created beings that no statement with God as referent can mean what it would mean if it had any other referent. Theologians must deny that their statements attributing properties to God can properly be understood univocally; the predicate terms themselves, if this is so, cannot have the same use or carry the same meaning appropriate in other contexts; and any claim to knowledge of God would seem profoundly threatened. On the other hand, however, genuine knowledge of God—of some kind—must be insisted upon if God has somehow been revealed to men. Statements about God must not be totally unintelligible; the terms attributed to him must continue to mean something; the loss of univocality in regard to God must not be allowed to drive theological talk into sheer equivocation.

Thus we may properly consider the "middle way" of analogy as a second-order attempt to escape from a first-order collision between basic theological premises. The statements incorporating man's knowledge of God, we are told, are not wholly univocal, nor are they entirely equivocal. Instead, it is claimed, such statements are analogical.

DEVELOPMENT OF THE WAY OF ANALOGY

Specification of this claim is mandatory in light of the background of the word "analogy" itself and its varied uses at the hands of the Greeks, who invented it. Αναλογια was originally a term developed within mathematics to indicate a proportionality—that is, a common or reciprocal (ἀνα) relation, such as "double" or "triple"—between two direct proportions (λόγοι). However, this original employment of ἀναλογία did not long remain its only one, either in ordinary Greek usage or in philosophic discourse. "Analogy" came soon to have the now more familiar sense of a direct comparison between somehow similar *terms,* as well as its older sense of a likeness between *relations.*

TWO KINDS OF ANALOGY

Postponing consideration of the nest of metaphysical assumptions that may lie behind doctrines of analogical knowledge of God, let us begin by examining the two primary theological appeals to ἀναλογία, in terms of the logical adequacy of these theories to solve the epistemological problem posed above.

The analogy of proportionality. One theological analogy is based on the earlier sense of ἀναλογία, namely, a similarity between two proportions. As such, it seems to offer a means of retaining the requisite literal incomparability between God and creation by refraining from asserting or implying any direct likeness between the particular terms involved, while simultaneously preserving some kind of knowledge by maintaining that a relational likeness holds between the manner in which the attributes of God are directly proportioned to his nature and the manner in which some of the attributes of creatures are directly proportioned to their natures. Hinting at the roots of this analogy in Greek mathematics, the analogy of proportionality is sometimes symbolized:

$$\frac{\text{God's qualities}}{\text{God's nature}} = \frac{\text{creature's qualities}}{\text{creature's nature}}$$

Such a proportionality seems not to violate the axiom of God's otherness because it does not support any claim that God's "goodness" (for example) is in any way merely like man's goodness; but it appears to support the axiom that some knowledge of God must remain, since it does permit the assertion that as, for example, goodness stands to man in his finite and created way, so something stands to God in his infinite and creative way. The irreducible disparity *between* infinite and finite remains; but *within* each, in a way appropriate to each, a similar proportion may be thought to obtain.

Serious objections may be raised, however, against the adequacy of the analogy of proportionality.

1. This analogy is powerless by itself to originate any knowledge of God's properties. The terms being fitted into its formal structure must be independently explained. If "God's nature" is given as "infinite," and if "goodness" is given as an appropriate attribute to replace the quality-variable in the formula, then the analogy may be stated. But it cannot move a step toward explaining the "givens" of its own formulation, nor can it explain the possibility of the

independent, nonanalogical knowledge on which they depend.

2. A dilemma rises out of attempts to specify the exact character of the relation between the two direct proportions composing the proportionality. Either the two proportions are to be linked (as in mathematics) by an equality sign, or they are not. If the first alternative is chosen, then the relation between the proportions is identity, and God's goodness is to God *exactly* as man's goodness is to man. Identity in the relation leads to univocation and a threat to God's uniqueness. If, on the other hand, the equality sign is replaced by some other link between the proportions, then the analogy loses its precision and its usefulness. To be able to say no more than that God's qualities relate to his infinite being in some entirely unspecified way "like" the way in which man's qualities relate to his finite being is, in its emptiness, the death of knowledge.

3. Still worse, any talk of comparing relations in creatures with "relations" in God must pose a serious difficulty for many theologians. God, we recall, is traditionally held to be absolutely simple; and relations within a perfectly simple or indivisible reality are an absurdity. The alleged analogy here must, therefore, accomplish the impossible task of finding some meaningful likeness between (on creation's side) relations and (on God's side) no relations.

4. Keeping the analogy of proportionality exclusively relevant to likenesses between relations, as distinct from the terms composing the relations, has seldom proved feasible. If knowledge of God is what is wanted, discussing likenesses between proportions while carefully avoiding reference to the Deity's nature or attributes seems jejune. Hence, attention is often directed toward those qualities, such as "goodness" or "wisdom," that are supposed on this analogy to bear a similar proportion in God to his nature and in creatures to their natures. At this point, however, a choice must be made. The analogy of proportionality may be taken as affirming only that whatever characterizes something must be said to do so in a way appropriate to the thing characterized. Thus interpreted, it is uninformative (because tautological) to announce that any of God's attributes will be of a kind appropriate to God's nature. This analogy may, however, be interpreted as a formula for gaining fresh knowledge about God's qualities. Such an interpretation would then lead to a direct comparison between, say, "goodness in God" and "goodness in creatures." But the analogy of proportionality has vanished when this happens, and has been replaced by an analogy of *direct proportion*.

5. It may be doubted, further, that such "fresh knowledge" can in principle be provided by an analogy of proportionality. Before any such attribute can be provided a meaning on this analogy, "the nature of God" must first be specified. God's nature, however, cannot be specified apart from a knowledge of God's essential attributes. If both God's qualities and God's nature are unknown, this analogy can never advance us toward understanding.

6. Finally, what is the basis for the fundamental ontological claim implicitly assumed by the analogy of proportionality, namely, that there *is* a similarity of relation between creature and Creator? Undergirding this claim must lie an even more basic supposition: that the creature, simply because it is an effect of the Creator, shares certain fundamental likenesses with the source of its being. Only some such metaphysical position could support the view that effects necessarily have some likeness to their causes. And on no other ground would it be possible to argue that a similar proportion links creatures with their creaturely properties and the Creator with his divine properties. This assumption of a likeness between cause and effect, however, serves as the fundamental and explicit basis for the analogy of attribution, on which the analogy of proportionality may thus be seen to depend.

The analogy of attribution. The analogy of attribution (or proportion) is rooted in the second sense of *ἀναλογία*, now designating a direct linking of two terms (the analogates) that are compared with respect to one property attributed in some nonunivocal way to both analogates. In this form of analogy one of the terms must always be the "prime analogate," of which the analogous property is predicated "formally" or intrinsically, while the other term or terms receive their attribution in a secondary sense by virtue of some relevant, real relation to the prime analogate. The standard illustration, used from classical times, is of the property "healthy" as attributed to man, to medicine, and to urine. "Man" is the prime analogate, to whom alone "healthy" pertains intrinsically and properly; but because medicine contributes as a *cause* to the state of health of the prime analogate, we may attribute the word "healthy" to it; and because the urine of a healthy man is related to the prime analogate as a *sign* of his health, we are entitled to speak of "healthy" urine as well.

With respect to the analogy between God and the world, God is sometimes taken as the prime analogate (as, on the "order of being," he must be), to whom alone such qualities as "goodness" and "wisdom" pertain in the full sense; thus these words, when attributed to finite creation, are taken as merely analogous uses based on God's causal act. Considering God the prime analogate is irrelevant to the present problem, however, inasmuch as every such approach presupposes prior nonanalogical knowledge of God; for without such knowledge human virtues could not be known to be merely imperfect approximations of the divine.

If any analogy of attribution is to avoid *petitio principii*, then, it must begin frankly with the "order of knowing" and consider creation, not God, the prime analogate. Thus God may be termed "good" or "wise" in an analogous sense based on human goodness and wisdom, just as sunlight and pure water may be spoken of as "healthy" by an analogy grounded in organic health. In both cases a presumed real relation of cause and effect undergirds the direct comparisons between widely dissimilar analogates.

However, problems surround the analogy of attribution no less than the analogy of proportionality.

1. It is not always clear whether or not theologians employing this analogy intend to attribute properties to God in a wholly extrinsic (or virtual) sense; i.e., using quality-words of him only to affirm that he is the cause of these qualities. Some do insist on an extrinsic interpretation of the analogy; but then knowledge of God is not advanced. A wholly extrinsic attribution of qualities to God says nothing at all about the intrinsic or proper attributes

of God. We are left with no more idea of God's own characteristics than that he is responsible for the various characteristics of creation—a premise, however, that was assumed prior to the use of this analogy.

2. If all attributions of properties of God are understood as merely extrinsic, one is puzzled by the practice of theologians of selecting certain properties and rejecting others for such attribution. Why should God not be described (extrinsically) equally well by *any* quality drawn from the creation for which he is assumed to be causally responsible? Any cognitive principle of selection must tacitly presuppose knowledge of what is "appropriate" to God. But what status has this knowledge? It can hardly be univocal, or there would, after all, be no need for a way of analogy. But if it is supposed to be analogical, identical questions must be raised concerning its own principles of selection, and we enter an infinite regress from which knowledge can never emerge.

3. We may perhaps suppose, with other interpreters, that the analogy of attribution supports intrinsic predication of properties in the secondary analogate. There must be some real likeness between a cause and its effect, it may be argued, to account for the effect's having been produced. Theologically speaking, the likeness would be strained if the analogous quality (on God's side) were more and better beyond all comprehension; but the attribution of this quality remains intrinsic; it is only the mode of signification of this quality (qua finite created things) that can have nothing to do with the mode of the existence of these attributes in the thing signified (qua infinite creator God). This answer, however, seems unable to solve any problems relative to human knowledge of God, since the meaning of attribute-words when completely disengaged from their standard modes of signification would become entirely vacuous.

4. We may now note the metaphysical assumption on which this analogy, when interpreted as warranting intrinsic attribution, rests: namely, that some significant likeness must exist between all causes and their effects. Is there adequate evidence to support such a principle? Can the conception of causality that this principle presupposes sustain modern criticisms? Keen debate must be expected here.

5. Even if it could be demonstrated—perhaps through some "chain of being" conception of ontology—that causes universally "resemble" their effects in some important way, one must still refrain from attributing the properties of a "cause" to God in any univocal sense. The analogy of attribution, on either of its interpretations, depends upon bridging the prima facie logical gulf between finite, conditioned, and contingent relations of cause and effect—however they are analyzed—and the wholly unique links of "creation from nothing" and of "unconditioned and necessary" ontological support alleged to hold between God and everything else. If God is to be spoken of as "first cause" of the world, that attribution must be proposed in some nonunivocal sense. Thus, even if an analogy of attribution can be shown to hold informatively among objects in the world, it appears to flounder helplessly in an infinite regress of equivocations on its key word, "cause," when applied in hopes of gaining knowledge of God.

6. Similarly, the appeal to an ontological assumption of structural similarities among all beings, which we now find to be an essential prop for any theory of analogical knowledge of the Supreme Being, is itself challenged to examine its logical status. Is any such ontology itself univocally expressible? Only an affirmative reply here would seem able to support the weight of theory erected upon it and at the same time save the theologian from entering yet another endless regress into equivocation; but in view of current inquiries into the logical status of the language of metaphysics, such a claim might be difficult to defend.

EVALUATION OF THE WAY OF ANALOGY

Analogy, developed to satisfy certain systematic demands within Christian theology, seems powerless to supply either fresh knowledge of God or an independent "middle way" interpretation of the meaning of statements traditionally made about him. Only if certain metaphysical claims can be upheld against vigorous modern challenges, a question clearly beyond settlement within the purview of this article, may standard uses of analogy be justified.

It remains possible even aside from these issues, however, that the fairly precise rules worked out for the application of theological analogies may serve a useful function within the theological enterprise at the systematic level that originally provoked the need for an analogical way. Rather than looking to these analogies for the establishment of meaningful connections *between* theological systems and general knowledge, philosophers might consider investigating their functions in maintaining syntactical connections and embodying standards for the construction of well-formed formulae *within* such systems. This approach might reveal much about how doctrines of analogy have actually functioned as statemental rules, and much about the logic of theological thinking in general. With respect to the latter, the study of analogy with attention to the internal systematic requirements that demand analogy lays bare a basic epistemological dynamic in Judeo-Christian thought: the constant tension between affirmation and negation, anthropomorphism and agnosticism, the provision of vivid images and their abrupt withdrawal.

This being the case, it may be thought that the main weakness of traditional theories of analogy is located not in the recognition of the deeply figurative logic of the entire theological enterprise, but in the premature attempt to "cash" individual concepts and statements. It may be that the elements of a theological system are too intimately interdependent to permit their analogical explication in isolation from the entire (nonliteral) system. In any event, it is evident that since any adequate philosophical understanding of theological knowledge-claims must recognize and account for both sides of the inner dynamic we have noticed, continued attention to theories of analogy may safely be expected.

Bibliography

Aquinas, Thomas, *Summa Theologica* I, q. 13. The primary source for much Christian theological discussion of analogy. This is only one of many discussions by St. Thomas, but it is central and accessible. For detailed bibliography on analogy in the writings of St. Thomas, see Klubertanz (below); for bibliography on his commentators, see Lyttkens (below).

Bocheński, I. M., "On Analogy." *The Thomist*, Vol. II, No. 4 (October 1948), 424–447; reprinted in A. Menne, ed., *Logical-Philosophical Studies*. Dordrecht, Holland, 1962. An attempt to apply modern logical techniques to problems in the traditional theory of analogy as presented by the Thomist school.

Emmet, Dorothy, *The Nature of Metaphysical Thinking*. London, 1945. Chapters 8 and 9 give a clear presentation and criticism of traditional theories of analogy, followed by constructive suggestions for the cognitively fruitful use of analogy within modern metaphysical thought.

Ferré, Frederick, *Language, Logic and God*. New York, 1961. Chapter 6 contains a concise critical discussion of theological analogies in the light of contemporary problems arising from philosophies of language.

Klubertanz, George P., *St. Thomas Aquinas on Analogy: A Textual Analysis and Systematic Synthesis*. Chicago, 1960. A sympathetic study of Thomistic doctrines of analogy, frankly indebted to Lyttkens and unusually free from forced exegesis in traditional patterns. Appendix offers complete collection of passages (in Latin) on analogy by St. Thomas.

Lyttkens, Hampus, *The Analogy Between God and the World: An Investigation of Its Background and Interpretation of Its Use by Thomas of Aquino*. Uppsala, Sweden, 1953. A published doctoral dissertation presenting a monumental study of its subject, including original investigation of historical background and a fresh look at primary sources.

Mascall, E. L., *Existence and Analogy*. New York, 1949. A Neo-Thomist discussion of theological analogy, arguing for continued reliance on traditional analogies but interpreting their usefulness in somewhat nontraditional ways.

FREDERICK FERRÉ

ANALYSIS, PHILOSOPHICAL. In the history of philosophy idealism contrasts with materialism, rationalism with empiricism, monism with pluralism. But what does analysis contrast with? Although analyses of concepts or complexes are present in philosophy from the pre-Socratics on, it is only in philosophy of recent years that the contrast between analysis and other methods is sharply drawn and the precise nature and the role of philosophical analysis are clearly stated. In contemporary philosophy Bertrand Russell was the first to articulate, employ, and justify analysis as the proper method of philosophy. G. E. Moore, Ludwig Wittgenstein, C. D. Broad, Gilbert Ryle, John Wisdom, Susan Stebbing, Rudolf Carnap, and A. J. Ayer, among others, have been important in practicing, clarifying, or defending analysis as the proper method of philosophy.

BERTRAND RUSSELL

Russell was not only the first to articulate the method of analysis in contemporary philosophy but also the foremost practitioner of that method. Indeed, it is no exaggeration to say that every major doctrine of contemporary analysis is present in his writings or derived from them by others.

Defense of external relations. After a brief excursion into absolute idealism, which lasted until 1898, Russell formulated a dualistic theory of reality: a dualism of mind and matter and of universals and particulars that—despite modifications, especially toward neutral monism—he retained throughout his work. Taking reality as one great analyzable complex, he persistently asked, What are its ultimate constituents? Analysis reveals that these constituents are the mental and the physical, the universal and the particular. Arguments against this theory rest at least in part on the absolute idealist doctrine that pluralism (of which dualism, of course, is a species) and its accompanying method of analysis entail a view the idealists hold to be self-contradictory, namely, that the world consists of independently existing terms, qualities, and relations. In particular, F. H. Bradley (*Appearance and Reality*, 1893) castigated "analytical thinking" as a falsification of reality because it inevitably reduces the immediately felt unity of the world to an unintelligible series of mere assemblages of unrelated terms. In this historic dispute between pluralism and monism, the most important issue was the reality of external relations. Indeed, Russell's reply to Bradley and his (and G. E. Moore's) arguments for external relations started "Cambridge analysis" in the twentieth century.

Without a defensible theory of external relations the independence of matter and of mathematics from mind can not be justified, nor can analysis as a method of thought and discourse about the world be vindicated. Russell's early concern for science and mathematics made it imperative that he refute the denial of external relations. Absolute idealism or monism assumes that relations are never ultimate, that a relation is always reducible to a fact about the nature of each of the related terms; hence, each of the related terms is internal to the nature of the others. Russell rejected that assumption on the grounds that it render unintelligible asymmetrical relations, such as "greater than"; it self-contradictorily distinguishes between the nature of a term and its qualities and then identifies them; and it reduces identity in difference to absolute identity so that even the fundamental thesis of absolute idealism and monism, that there is one subject and its predicate, becomes meaningless.

Relations, Russell countered, are real in the precise sense that they are irreducible to qualities of subjects or of the whole. They are external not because they are independently existing terms along with subjects and their qualities, but because they are irreducible. Pluralism, then, is the doctrine that there are analyzable unities or facts, consisting of individuals and their qualities in relation, not—as Bradley supposed—of individuals, qualities, and relations as three never-to-be related sets of terms. A necessary metaphysical condition of analysis—which Russell defined as "the discovery of the constituents of a complex"—is that there be independently existing unities whose constituents are terms and qualities in their external relations. Analysis as "relational thinking" can render experience intelligible, as well as the commonsensical and scientific categories of physical object, space, time, causality, and motion. Dialectical argument, of the Bradley variety, that is designed to destroy the efficacy of analysis fails: pure feeling of immediacy is not a satisfactory alternative to the method of analysis for an understanding of the world.

Having disposed of the arguments of absolute idealism against dualism, Russell employed analysis to refute Berkeley's subjective idealism. Borrowing from Moore's "The Refutation of Idealism" (1903), Russell pointed out that analysis of our awareness of sense data discloses the irreducible distinction between consciousness and its object; qualities, such as a particular color or sound, need not and, in most cases, do not depend for their existence upon any consciousness. He also used analysis, especially the doctrine of external relations, to refute nominalism by showing that the reduction of universals to names rests upon the affirmation of the one universal of resemblance, which is itself an irreducible relation among certain qualities. (For Russell's application of analysis to mathematics and his derivation of the fundamental propositions of mathematics from logic, see articles on RUSSELL, BERTRAND, and LOGIC, HISTORY OF.)

By 1912, in *The Problems of Philosophy*, Russell's dualism of mind and matter, universals and particulars, was fully formed. Although Russell was led to resolve mind and matter into simpler entities, such as sensibilia or events, he never repudiated the basic pluralism of his philosophy or his continuing attempts to discover and state the ultimate constituents of reality or of some of its analyzable complexes.

Formal analysis and logical atomism. Formal analysis, as Russell conceived it, is the examination of the world from a purely logical point of view. Its primary concern is with the various modes of organization which are revealed by language and reality; formal analysis is abstract cosmology, dealing with the ultimate structures of language and the world. It was developed by Russell at the very beginning of his philosophical career, but it reached its climax after the publication of *Principia Mathematica* (1910–1913), in a series of articles, "Philosophy of Logical Atomism."

Form may be defined either linguistically or nonlinguistically. Russell defined it linguistically and then interpreted his findings as a clue in the analysis of nonlinguistic form. Propositional form, the "way in which the constituents of the proposition . . . are put together," is that which one gets when one substitutes variables for the constituents of a proposition.

A proper name is a simple symbol that designates a particular which is the meaning of the name. It stands for a particular with which the speaker is acquainted, for one cannot name anything one is not acquainted with. "This" and "that"—not ordinary proper names like "Socrates"—are examples of real proper names. Particulars are self-subsistent entities, much like traditional substances, except that, at least so far as our experience of them is concerned, they persist only "through a very short time."

A proposition is an indicative sentence that asserts or denies something. It differs from a name in that it has two possible relations to a fact, being true or being false, whereas a name has only the one relation to a particular, that of naming it. A fact is a complex of a particular or particulars, qualities, and relations. It makes a proposition true or false. It, too, exists independently of our thinking about it.

An atomic proposition is one which asserts that a certain thing has a certain quality, or that certain things have a certain relation. Examples are: "This is white," "This is below that." Atomic facts correspond to atomic propositions. They are the simplest kinds of facts and consist in the possession of a quality or relation by some particular(s). There is a perfect isomorphism between atomic propositions and atomic facts: subjects (proper names) correspond to terms (particulars), adjectives, to qualities, and verbs, to relations. A molecular proposition is one that contains other propositions as its components. In it occur truth-function words, such as "or," "if," "and." An example is, "If you come, so will your friend." Russell at first denied the existence of molecular facts but when he discussed general facts, of which they are a species, he accepted their existence.

An existence proposition asserts the truth of at least one value of a propositional function, for example, "Some men are interesting." That there are existence facts as distinct from atomic facts Russell regarded as obvious. A general proposition asserts (or denies) the truth of all values of a propositional function. A general fact is one that corresponds to a general proposition. One cannot deny the existence of general facts or reduce them to other facts. A completely general proposition is one that occurs in logic, either as an axiom or a theorem. It contains only variables and truth-functions. It is analytic and a priori.

Besides positive and negative propositions and positive facts, Russell held that negative facts also are ultimate.

> Otherwise you will find it so difficult to say what it is that corresponds to a proposition. When, e.g., you have a false positive proposition, say, "Socrates is alive," it is false because of a fact in the real world. A thing cannot be false except because of a fact, so that you will find it extremely difficult to say what exactly happens . . . unless you are going to admit negative facts. ("Philosophy of Logical Atomism," Lecture 3, p. 46)

Theory of descriptions. In his *Principles of Mathematics* (1903) Russell retained as a fundamental doctrine the realist view that any object of thought or discourse "has being, i.e., *is* in some sense" (p. 43). But Russell saw immediately after the publication of the *Principles* that this doctrine leads to contradiction. Consider, for instance, the proposition "The round square does not exist." This is a significant and true proposition; yet, as Russell later put it, "if there were such an object, it would exist: we cannot first assume that there is a certain object, and then proceed to deny that there is such an object." In abandoning that doctrine, Russell set as his problem the analysis of propositions containing symbols of unreal or self-contradictory objects, an analysis which would both preserve our robust sense of reality and still allow us to talk about these "pseudo-objects" intelligibly. This problem he solved in his famous theory of descriptions. Basic to the theory is a fundamental distinction between two kinds of symbols: proper names and descriptions. A proper name, taken in an extended sense, is a simple symbol, such as "Scott." It designates an individual directly; that individual is its meaning, and it has this meaning in isolation, that is, independently of all other words. A description is a complex symbol, such as "the author of *Waverley*." It does not designate an individual directly, hence, is an "incomplete symbol," that is, a symbol which has no meaning in isolation, but which can be given a meaning in a context with other symbols.

"The author of *Waverley*" is an incomplete symbol, first, because it is not a proper name for three reasons: (*a*) It is not a simple symbol that designates a particular or an individual treated as a particular, but is a complex symbol. (*b*) Its meaning is determinate as soon as we know the meanings of the separate words, whereas the meaning of a proper name is not determined by words but by our knowing to whom the name is applied. (*c*) If it were a proper name, then "Scott is the author of *Waverley*" would be either a trivial tautology or a truth independent of any and all facts about the world (equivalent to "Scott is Scott") or a falsehood (if "the author of *Waverley*" stood for anything other than Scott). But the proposition is informative (i.e., nontautological) and true, disclosing a fact of literary history. It cannot therefore be treated as a proper name.

Descriptions are incomplete symbols for a second reason: what they are supposed to refer to are not really "constituents of propositions." By this Russell meant that there is no actual entity which we can call its denotation; when a description occurs in a proposition, there is no constituent of that proposition corresponding to that description as a whole. This is a consequence of the fact that we may utter significant and true propositions that deny the existence of something, for example, "The golden mountain of Virginia does not exist."

How are descriptions to be resolved? By putting them into propositional contexts and analyzing the whole context in such a manner that the grammatical subject disappears and is replaced by other symbols. We analyze, for example, "Scott is the author of *Waverley*," not "the author of *Waverley*."

"Scott is the author of *Waverley*" is false if (1) *Waverley* had never been written; (2) several people had written *Waverley;* or (3) the person who wrote *Waverley* was not Scott. Consequently, in order to obtain the correct analysis of this proposition, we need only negate these three conditions of falsity. Then (1) becomes " 'X wrote *Waverley*' is not always false, that is, at least one person wrote *Waverley*"; (2) becomes "If X and Y wrote *Waverley*, then X and Y are identical, that is, at most one person wrote *Waverley*"; and (3) becomes " 'If X wrote *Waverley*, then X was Scott,' is always true." Together, these three propositions state that " 'X wrote *Waverley*' is always equivalent to 'X was Scott.' "

This analysis of propositions containing descriptions enables us to talk intelligibly about unreal and self-contradictory objects, such as "the present king of France" or the "round square," because propositions about them also can now be interpreted as ones involving propositional functions and variables, not objects which are somehow not real.

The theory of descriptions became extremely important after its development in "On Denoting" (1905) and *Principia Mathematica* (1910–1913), because it served as a model to Russell in his treatment of other problematic symbols and putative entities. Classes, numbers, relations (in extension), points, instants, particles of matter, even ordinary objects, such as tables or persons, were dealt with in the same way as descriptions: the symbol for each of these was treated as an incomplete symbol analyzable in terms of propositional functions and variables or values of variables. In many influential essays and books, from 1914 to 1927, especially *Our Knowledge of the External World* (1914), "The Relation of Sense-Data to Physics" (1914), "Philosophy of Logical Atomism" (1918–1919), *The Analysis of Mind* (1921), and *The Analysis of Matter* (1927), Russell applied analysis as resolution of incomplete symbols to the symbols or concepts of the natural sciences.

It was the status of the entities which the symbols of natural science apparently designate that led Russell to treat these symbols as incomplete. For example, physics talks about points in space, instants of time, and particles of matter. It also claims to be an empirical science; hence, its points, instants, and electrons ought to be observable, which they are not. Only immediate data of sense, with certain spatiotemporal relations, are observable. Consequently, if physics is to justify itself as an empirical science, it must be defined in terms of these sense data. The entities of physics are no longer the denotata of names or descriptions, but become unnecessary inferential entities, for everything in physics can now be stated in terms of sense data. "Points," "instants," "particles," etc., because they have no meaning in isolation—that is, *name nothing*—Russell interpreted as incomplete symbols, and the propositions in which these entities are supposedly designated he interpreted in such a manner that the symbols for these unnecessary entities were resolved into others, whose denotata are empirical. Instead of inferring the existence of scientific entities, we construct them out of empirical materials.

This process involves (1) determining what are the ultimate empirical entities and (2) defining the symbols of science in terms of these empirical entities. The definitions of these symbols in their appropriate propositional contexts, along with the construction of unreal, self-contradictory, and described objects in their appropriate propositional contexts, then, constitute analysis as resolution of incomplete symbols in Russell's philosophy.

What Russell means by analysis. Although Russell, unlike Moore and others, has never stated what he means by analysis, it is quite clear from his uses of the term that he conceives it as a form of definition—either real or contextual, nonlinguistic or linguistic. If real definition is separated from its Aristotelian setting and interpreted as an attempt to enumerate the various constituents of factual, independently existing complexes, Russell has certainly practiced real definition. "What are the ultimate constituents of reality, or of certain aspects of it?" has been a perennial philosophical problem for Russell.

However, real and contextual definitions (i.e., definitions of symbols in use—the substitution of one set of symbols for another) sometimes proceed together in Russell's philosophy. In *The Analysis of Mind*, for example, there is a persistent attempt to arrive at contextual definitions of psychological terms. But much real definition is involved in the process of formulating contextual definitions. Russell's analysis of memory, for instance, not only contains such phrases as "true analysis," "complete analysis," and "faulty analysis," phrases which make sense only on a view of analysis as real definition but is also primarily the enumeration of the empirical constituents of the given complex that psychology or common sense calls "memory." Such analysis assumes that the term "memory," or its equivalents, is not a legitimate constituent of the propositions in whose verbal expressions it occurs, but must be replaced by other symbols, in certain propositional contexts, which refer to sensations and images together with their characteristics and relations.

Russell follows the same practice in his philosophy of physics. A model example is his analysis of "time" and "instant." It begins with the recognition that these terms do not refer to simple entities, at least so far as our experience is concerned. It then proceeds to an enumeration of the constituents, which are certain events, their characteristics, and their relations. Finally, on the basis of this enumeration or real definition, contextual definitions are offered. The proposition, "Time consists of instants," is contextually defined as: "Given any event *x*, every event which is wholly later than some contemporary of *x* is wholly later than some initial contemporary of *x*."

G. E. MOORE

After almost fifty years of doing philosophical analysis Moore, in his "Reply to My Critics" (*The Philosophy of G. E. Moore*, 1942), articulated what he had persistently meant or intended to mean by "analysis." Analysis, he stated, is a form of definition, not of words, but of concepts or propositions. One starts with a particular concept or proposition—the *analysandum*—and attempts to provide another set of concepts or propositions—the *analysans*—which is logically equivalent to the original concept or proposition. Although Moore confessed that he was unable to formulate the necessary and sufficient conditions of a correct analysis and, consequently, could not give an analysis or definition of the concept of analysis, he did affirm at least three necessary conditions of a correct analysis:

> If you are to "give an analysis" of a given *concept*, which is the *analysandum*, you must mention, as your *analysans*, a *concept* such that (*a*) nobody can know that the *analysandum* applies to an object without knowing that the *analysans* applies to it, (*b*) nobody can verify that the *analysandum* applies without verifying that the *analysans* applies, (*c*) any expression which expresses the *analysandum* must be synonymous with any expression which expresses the *analysans*. (p. 663)

Now, according to (*c*), analysis, even though it is not linguistic, does involve the use of language. What, then, Moore asked, is the proper way of expressing an analysis? Employing as his favorite example the concept of a brother, he suggested four such ways: "The concept 'being a brother' is identical with the concept 'being a male sibling.'" "The propositional function 'X is a brother' is identical with the propositional function 'X is a male sibling.'" "To say that a person is a brother is the same thing as to say that that person is a male sibling." "To be a brother is the same thing as to be a male sibling."

Each of these ways of expressing the analysis of the concept of brother satisfies the three requirements. But it also engenders "the paradox of analysis." Take, for example, "To be a brother is the same thing as to be a male sibling." If this statement is true, it seems identical with the statement, "To be a brother is to be a brother"; yet it is obvious that these are not the same and that the latter, unlike the former, is not an analysis of the concept of brother. Moore admitted he could not solve this paradox. But he did insist that any purported solution must "hold fast" to the facts that the *analysandum* and *analysans* of a correct analysis are the same concepts and that the expression used for the *analysandum* must differ from that used for the *analysans* in that the latter expression must explicitly mention concepts not explicitly mentioned by the former, along with the way in which the concepts are combined.

Analysis, then, according to Moore, presupposes a distinction between words and concepts, or sentences and propositions. Analysis is confined to clarification and definition of concepts or propositions; and the verbal expression of an analysis must follow a standard pattern of paraphrase in which what is analyzed is equivalent to a larger, more explicit, and synonymous expression. The central point of doing analysis is the clarification of concepts, not the discovery of new facts about the world.

Is analysis identical with philosophy? Moore denied that it is. Analysis is but one task, among many, of philosophy. Philosophy, he claimed, has also, as a legitimate goal, to "give a general description of the *whole* of the Universe" (*Some Main Problems of Philosophy*, p. 1). In "A Defence of Common Sense" (1925) Moore distinguished sharply between philosophical statement of common-sense truisms, which all of us understand and know to be true, and philosophical analysis of these truisms. So, too, in "Proof of an External World" (1939) Moore distinguished between giving a proof of a philosophical proposition and giving an analysis of the premises and conclusion of that proof. After carefully clarifying the notion of an external world, which he equates with "things outside us," such as dogs, trees, planets, and hands, he offers a proof that there are things that exist outside us by holding up his hands and stating, "Here is one hand; here is another; therefore, at least two things outside us exist." The premises, he contends, are true and known to be true, and the conclusion follows from the premises; hence, the proof is conclusive. The analyses of the premises and the conclusion, however, remain in doubt.

Is analysis as Moore conceived it, compatible with his own practice of it? It is certainly true that many of Moore's specific analyses of ethical and perceptual concepts and propositions are attempts—whether complete or not, successful or not—at conceptual definitions which satisfy his criteria of a correct analysis. But Moore's practice also reveals another use of analysis that is not definition of concepts and does not result in linguistic paraphrase. This use is identical with Russell's notion of analysis as the discovery of the constituents of certain nonlinguistic, nonconceptual complexes. An example of this use of analysis as real definition is contained in Moore's "Refutation of Idealism" (1903). In that essay, after much clarification of the principle that *esse* is *percipi*, which Moore regarded as central in the argument for idealism, he not only attempted to refute this doctrine by exposing its self-contradictory nature but he also stated his own view about sensation.

In his analysis, for example, of the nonlinguistic, nonconceptual sensation of blue, Moore discovered blue, awareness, and a unique relation of awareness and blue. Indeed, the conception of analysis he employed there was identical with his actual statement of analysis as real definition in the opening chapter of *Principia Ethica* (1903). Much of Moore's philosophy, especially his analyses of the good and of sense data, and perhaps even of relational properties (as presented in "External and Internal Relations," 1919), is intelligible only on the basis of this conception of analysis as real definition.

Analysis, either as conceptual or as real definition, occupies an important place in Moore's philosophy, but it is not central, as it is in Russell's philosophy. It is even doubtful that Moore's contributions to analysis are his most important contributions to philosophy. For, as many recent admirers of Moore have noted, it is Moore's persistent concern for absolute clarity of expression, linguistic propriety, and common sense, and, perhaps above all, his incipient recognition that analysis of concepts must ultimately give way to their elucidation that constitute his great achievement and explain his contemporary influence.

SOME FOLLOWERS OF RUSSELL AND MOORE

For Russell, analysis is either real or contextual definition, either ontological or linguistic. For Moore, analysis is either conceptual or real definition, always ontological, never purely linguistic. During the 1920s and 1930s exponents of analysis, such as C. D. Broad, Ludwig Wittgenstein (of the *Tractatus*), Susan Stebbing, John Wisdom, and Gilbert Ryle, emphasized or refined one or another of the analytic conceptions of Russell and Moore.

Wittgenstein. Although Wittgenstein's *Tractatus Logico-Philosophicus* is universally acknowledged as a classic of twentieth-century analytic philosophy, there is vast disagreement on the nature of its fundamental doctrines concerning language, logic, mathematics, and scientific laws, as well as the relation between language and the world and the proper function of philosophy.

Although the work contains little of or about analysis, what seems clear in the *Tractatus* is the *role* Wittgenstein assigns to analysis. The function of analysis is to resolve all descriptive, complex propositions into their elementary ones and these into their ultimate units of unanalyzable names and their combinations, which represent and mean the ultimate simples of the world. The task of analysis is to make every statement an adequate picture of the reality it describes. As such, analysis is rooted in the "thesis of extensionality," that is, the claim that every statement is either a logically simple statement (an elementary proposition) or a truth-function of such statements.

Analysis, then, is a form of linguistic transformation—the reduction of complex propositions, no matter what their grammatical form, into their atomic constituents and connections, which *show* their correct logical form. It is neither ontological nor conceptual definition. Like Russell's theory of descriptions, it is a resolution of grammatically misleading propositions into their correct logical expression. Since it clarifies rather than confuses logical as distinct from grammatical forms and since it does not transgress the limits of language by trying to *describe* the relation between language and the world (which can only be shown), analysis is presumably a legitimate procedure. But it is not identical with philosophy, which has as its proper assignment the making clear of what can and what cannot be said. Once this job is completed, analysis can aid in the actual clarification. But philosophy itself is ultimately nonsensical (in trying to say what language can only show), and because analysis rests upon philosophy, it is not immediately apparent that analysis is not also ultimately nonsensical.

Wisdom. In 1929, F. P. Ramsey characterized Russell's theory of descriptions as a paradigm of philosophy. Russell's notion that one task of philosophy is the translation of grammatically misleading or defective expressions into their logically correct form was certainly one of the dominant themes of analytic philosophy during the 1930s. Indeed, the preoccupation of a number of analytic philosophers seems to have been with the analysis of analysis.

John Wisdom, in his article "Is Analysis a Useful Method in Philosophy?" (1934), distinguished among three sorts of analysis: material, formal, and philosophical. Ordinary definitions of the natural sciences are examples of the first, and Russell's theory of descriptions, of the second; both are "same-level" analysis. Philosophical analysis is "new-level" and is characterized by the fact that more ultimate terms replace less ultimate ones. That is, individuals, for example, are more ultimate than nations, and sense data and mental states are more ultimate than individuals. Analysis, then, consists in reducing statements about minds to statements about mental states, and statements about material objects to statements about sense data.

Ryle. Gilbert Ryle, in his article "Systematically Misleading Expressions" (1931–1932) stated that the primary (perhaps the whole) job of philosophy is the analysis of certain expressions which systematically mislead philosophers into thinking that these expressions record one kind of fact when they actually record another. The logical form of these expressions, as against their grammatical form, can be elicited only by correct logical paraphrases of the original expressions. The major result of such analysis is that it reveals the persistent confusions of grammatical with logical form as the sources of traditional philosophical theories and disputes. With Russell's theory of descriptions as a model of logical paraphrase of certain expressions, Ryle classified and analyzed a number of expressions which mislead.

Among systematically misleading expressions are: (1) quasi-ontological statements, such as "God exists," "Mr. Pickwick is a fiction," "Carnivorous cows do not exist"; (2) quasi-Platonic statements, such as "Virtue is its own reward," "Unpunctuality is reprehensible"; (3) certain descriptive statements, such as "whoever is vice-chancellor of Oxford University is overworked," "The present king of France is wise"; and (4) quasi-descriptive statements, such as "I saw the top of the tree." Each of these is misleading in that its grammatical form is inappropriate to the fact recorded; each must be paraphrased so that the logical form of the fact recorded is brought out. Thus, "Carnivorous cows do not exist" is true, significant, and looks grammatically like an ordinary subject–predicate statement. But when compared to the fact recorded, "carnivorous cows" does not denote and "does not exist" does not predicate. So the grammatical clue of subject—predicate must be rejected, and the logical form of the fact must dictate the restatement. The fact recorded by the original statement is better expressed by "Nothing is both a cow and carnivorous," since this latter statement does not imply that anything is either. Philosophical analysis—to generalize from this one example—can say, consequently, that one expression really means another and that that other is a better expression than the original because it exhibits better the logical form of the fact it records.

LOGICAL POSITIVISM

Logical positivism, which lasted roughly from the beginnings of the Vienna circle (1922) to C. G. Hempel's "Problems and Changes in the Empiricist Criterion of Meaning" (*Revue Internationale de Philosophie*, 1950; reprinted in A. J. Ayer, ed., *Logical Positivism*) was characterized by a number of interrelated, radical doctrines. Among these were the verifiability theory of meaning, the rejection of metaphysics, the unity of science, the conception of language as a calculus, the conventionalist interpretation of logic and mathematics, and the view that legitimate philosophy is identical with logical analysis of a special kind. Most of these doctrines, it is generally agreed, stem from or were wrongly attributed to Wittgenstein's *Tractatus*. The basic doctrine was the theory of meaning, according to which the cognitive meaning of a sentence is its method of verification: if a sentence is not verifiable and is not a tautology, it is cognitively meaningless. On the basis of this criterion, which sinned against itself and thereby vitiated logical positivism from the beginning, all of traditional philosophy was ruled out as meaningless because it was unverifiable. What remained respectable in the domain of knowledge were logic and mathematics, as tautologies, and the sciences, as verifiable sentences.

Logic, mathematics, and the sciences, however, are calculi, consisting of variables or constants and certain formation and transformation rules from which certain sentences can be constructed or derived. One question that seemed neither meaningless nor scientific strongly suggested itself: What is the syntax of these calculi? The attempt to provide an answer to this question reconstituted itself as philosophical analysis. Philosophy was reconceived as the systematic presentation of the logical syntax of the language of science.

This conception of philosophy as the logical analysis of the language of science had two important formulations—Rudolf Carnap's, in *The Logical Syntax of Language* (1934) and in *Philosophy and Logical Syntax* (1935), and A. J. Ayer's, in *Language, Truth and Logic* (1936).

Carnap. In Carnap's version, philosophy became the logic of science—the logical analysis "of its sentences, terms, concepts, theories, etc." Such an analysis constitutes the logical syntax of science. Generalizing from Hilbert's metamathematics, Carnap characterized the logical syntax of language as a purely formal theory of language. Philosophy or analysis, thus, has no proper concern whatever with the meanings of the words and sentences of language, that is, with the semantical relations between language and the world.

Analysis, however, can do more than state the rules of the language of science. It can also expose the quasi-syntactical, hence misleading, nature of many traditional philosophical sentences and disputes. Consider, for example, these three sentences: (1) "The rose is red." (2) "The rose is a thing." (3) "The word 'rose' is a thing-word." Sentence (1) is clearly an empirical sentence about an extralinguistic object; it is a "real object-sentence." Sentence (3) is clearly a sentence about a word; it is a "syntactical sentence." Sentence (2), however, is ambiguous, for it is like (1) in its form and like (3) in its content; it is, therefore, a "pseudo object-sentence" and, because it is really syntactical, should be translated into (3).

Syntactical sentences, Carnap says, are in the formal mode of speech; pseudo object-sentences in the material. Many pseudo-philosophical problems and disputes are engendered by the use of the material mode of speech; all of these can be solved or avoided by "translating" the relevant sentences into the formal mode. The dispute, for example, between phenomenalism and realism can be clarified and solved by such translations. Every meaningful sentence is either a real object-sentence, which, as such, belongs to one of the natural sciences, or a syntactical sentence in logic or mathematics; and philosophy, as logical analysis, is identical with the sum total of the true syntactical sentences concerning the language of the sciences.

Ayer. A. J. Ayer's *Language, Truth and Logic* was historically more important for its immediate impact on English philosophers and continuing influence on them than for its intrinsic novelty of doctrines, Ayer's view of analysis not excepted. Most of his doctrines derived directly from members of the Vienna circle, especially Carnap. In this work, Ayer identified philosophy with analysis and analysis with contextual definition of the sort that Russell provided in his theory of descriptions, which Ayer took as the paradigm of philosophy. Philosophy, for Ayer, is an activity that makes no factual claims in competition with the sciences; it exhausts itself in formulating certain definitions of symbols in use "by showing how the sentences in which it [a symbol in use] significantly occurs can be translated into equivalent sentences, which contain neither the *definiendum* itself, nor any of its synonyms" (p. 68). The whole purpose of these contextual definitions is to provide understanding of the logical structure of certain sentences, hence of language, and through this understanding to gain insight into the logical sources of the mistakes of much traditional philosophy. "A complete philosophical elucidation of any language," Ayer concluded, "would consist, first, in enumerating the types of sentence that were significant in that language, and then in displaying the relations of equivalence that held between sentences of various types"(p. 71).

Both Carnap and Ayer in their later work repudiated their views about analysis. As early as 1935, in "Truth and Confirmation" (reprinted in H. Feigl and W. Sellars, eds., *Readings in Philosophical Analysis*), Carnap allowed that analysis can encompass semantical as well as syntactical questions; and Ayer, in the "Introduction" (1946) to the second edition of *Language, Truth and Logic,* admitted that analysis, especially some analyses of Moore, is more than, and, in some cases, other than, contextual definition. Nevertheless, both Ayer and Carnap identified philosophy with analysis and analysis with linguistic concerns, as did the logical positivists in general; analysis for them is purely linguistic and can have no legitimate truck with conceptual or ontological definitions.

THE REJECTION OF ANALYSIS

Contemporary philosophical analysis began with Russell and ended with logical positivism. Although analysis, in any of its many contemporary forms—as real, conceptual, or contextual definition, as reduction and translation of linguistic complexes into more simple or ultimate units of discourse, or as logical syntax—persists among philosophers even today, it seems to have lost its great hold on serious contemporary philosophy. Three of the great analysts themselves, Wisdom, Ryle, and especially Wittgenstein, have repudiated or replaced analysis as the proper method of philosophy. Some writers, anxious to retain the term "analysis"—perhaps because of its laudatory associations with clarification—characterize the later work of these three philosophers, as well as that of others, such as John Austin and P. F. Strawson, as "linguistic analysis" or "ordinary language analysis." But this extension of the term is misleading, since an essential part of the recent work of these philosophers involves the explicit rejection of analysis in any of its contemporary modes as primary in philosophy. Their concern shifted from definition, reduction, or translation to description, from analysis to elucidation. Indeed, we can now answer the question with which we started: What does contemporary philosophical analysis contrast with? It started by contrasting itself to the intuitionism of Bradley (and later of Bergson); and it ended by being contrasted with the conception of philosophy as the elucidation of difficult and basic concepts. When Wittgenstein, even as early as the 1930s, admonished, "Don't ask for the meaning, ask for the use," he signaled the decline of analysis (which was, after all, basically the search for the meaning) as an effective moment in the history of contemporary philosophy.

Analysis as real definition—as the discovery of the constituents of nonlinguistic complexes—was first called into question by Wittgenstein himself in the *Tractatus.* His claim that philosophy is an activity, not a body of propositions about the world, implied the rejection of ontological discovery as a legitimate philosophical pursuit. According to Wittgenstein's *Philosophical Investigations* (1953), Russell, Moore, and even "the author of the *Tractatus,*" when they engage in ontological analysis, are actually describing the use of certain fundamental concepts but, because of certain false preconceptions about these concepts, are in effect misdescribing their use. In the *Investigations,* all ontological discourse is interpreted as inadequate elucidation of the logical grammar of certain fundamental concepts.

The view that analysis is contextual definition or resolution of incomplete symbols has been rejected, as well as the view of Russell's theory of descriptions as the paradigm of philosophy. Basic to Russell's theory are the concept of a logically proper name and the denotational theory of meaning. Russell's claim that, for instance, "the present king of France" is an incomplete symbol because it names nothing and, hence, has no meaning by itself has been repudiated primarily on the ground that the claim confuses the meaning or analysis with the use of a descriptive expression. Strawson, in "On Referring" (1950), brings to a climax certain disaffections with Russell's theory of descriptions, already present in the early Wisdom, and presents his counterviews on descriptions and other referring expressions. Indeed, there is no other essay that illustrates as well as Strawson's the fundamental and irreconcilable differences between philosophical analysis and philosophical elucidation of expressions or concepts.

Doubts about analysis as reduction or translation also take many forms. Basic to doubts about analysis as reduction is the paucity of successful reductive analyses. Wisdom and, later, Stebbing ("Moore's Influence," 1942) raised serious questions about the feasibility of reducing, for example, statements about physical objects to statements about sense data. Doubts about analysis as translation are based on the question whether there are real forms of facts which can serve as the corresponding models of the real as against the grammatical forms of propositions. Wittgenstein brought these doubts to a head when he pointed out in the *Investigations* that the whole notion of the real forms of fact and language is an illusion imposed upon language and thought by a fundamental misconception of language itself.

Finally, doubts about analysis as logical syntax of the language of science mainly take the form of calling into question the view of language as a rigid calculus with its implicit denotational theory of meaning and its explicit doctrine that the only legitimate uses of language are to state facts and logical equivalences.

But central to the rejection of analysis, at least historically, was the refutation of the whole theory of language implicit in or attributed to it. After the *Tractatus,* Wittgenstein and others began seriously to question all the fundamental doctrines of this theory. The view was repudiated that language is essentially a picture or isomorphic structure of the world, whose meanings are the objects named by the fundamental units of language and whose sole use is to state facts. In the *Investigations* the repudiation is total and complete; indeed, the whole theory is now seen as an illusion imposed upon language by the bewitchment of language itself. If we turn the whole examination around and "look and see" how language actually functions, if we remind ourselves of all the various things language does and how it does it, we find that language does not function merely as a picture, mirror, or corresponding isomorphic structure of reality, but as an enormous toolbox, replete with the most diversified sorts of tools, practically none of which resembles at all those things in the world they may be applied to. We also discover that words and sentences by themselves, that is, independently of their use, do not refer to or name anything; rather, it is in the context of their employment that some words are used to name something, others, to classify, still others, to prescribe, and that sentences are used variously to refer, describe, emote, etc. Meaning, too, we realize, must be reconstrued; it can no longer be conceived as a relation between words and objects, but is to be interpreted as the rules, regulations, conventions, and habits which govern the actual uses of expressions.

Without the notion of an ideal language the need to analyze disappeared. The philosopher's task, among other tasks, became instead to assemble the reminders regarding the roles of certain expressions, to describe all the various jobs assigned these expressions and the conditions under which they function; the aim of philosophy became the elucidation of the logical grammar of certain expressions. Although certain recent philosophers, such as Ryle, Austin, or Strawson, have disagreed with Wittgenstein that these reminders should be assembled for the sole purpose of relieving puzzlement or mental cramp, they have concurred with Wittgenstein (and Wisdom) that an essential feature of proper philosophical activity is to describe fully the actual workings of language, rather than to resolve these workings into some sort of unworkable schema of an ideal language. The need to analyze vanishes with the illusion that produced it.

Russell on Analysis

A Critical Exposition of the Philosophy of Leibniz. Cambridge, 1900.

The Principles of Mathematics. Cambridge, 1903.

"On Denoting." *Mind*, Vol. 16 (1905), 479–493.

Principia Mathematica, 3 vols. Cambridge, 1910–1913. Written with A. N. Whitehead.

Philosophical Essays. London, 1910. Especially "The Monistic Theory of Truth."

"Some Explanations in Reply to Mr. Bradley." *Mind*, Vol. 19 (1910), 373–378. The best summary statement of his arguments against internal relations.

The Problems of Philosophy. London, 1912.

Our Knowledge of the External World. London, 1914.

Mysticism and Logic. London, 1918. Especially "The Relation of Sense Data to Physics."

"Philosophy of Logical Atomism." *Monist*, Nos. 28–29 (1918–1919).

Introduction to Mathematical Philosophy. London, 1919.

The Analysis of Mind. London, 1921.

"Introduction," in Ludwig Wittgenstein, *Tractatus Logico-Philosophicus*. London, 1922.

"Logical Atomism," in J. H. Muirhead, ed., *Contemporary British Philosophy* (First Series). London, 1924.

The Analysis of Matter. London, 1927.

An Inquiry into Meaning and Truth. New York, 1940.

Logic and Knowledge: Essays 1901–1950, R. C. Marsh, ed. London, 1956. Includes "On Denoting," "Philosophy of Logical Atomism," and "Logical Atomism."

ON RUSSELL'S THEORY OF ANALYSIS

Weitz, M., "Analysis and the Unity of Russell's Philosophy," in P. Schilpp, ed., *The Philosophy of Bertrand Russell*. Evanston, Ill., 1944.

Moore on Analysis

"The Nature of Judgment." *Mind*, Vol. 8 (1899), 176–193.

"Necessity." *Mind*, Vol. 9 (1900), 289–304.

Principia Ethica. Cambridge, 1903.

Philosophical Studies. London, 1922. Especially "The Refutation of Idealism" and "External and Internal Relations."

"A Defence of Common Sense," in *Contemporary British Philosophy*, Second Series. London, 1925.

"Proof of an External World." *Proceedings of the British Academy*, Vol. 25 (1939), 273–300.

"Reply to My Critics," in P. Schilpp, ed., *The Philosophy of G. E. Moore*. Evanston, Ill., 1942.

"Russell's 'Theory of Descriptions,'" in P. Schilpp, ed., *The Philosophy of Bertrand Russell*. Evanston, Ill., 1944.

Some Main Problems of Philosophy. London, 1953. Lectures given in 1910 and 1911.

On Moore's theory of analysis, see:

Langford, C. H., "Moore's Notion of Analysis," in P. Schilpp, ed., *The Philosophy of G. E. Moore*. Evanston, Ill., 1942.

White, A. R., *G. E. Moore: A Critical Exposition*. Oxford, 1958.

Some Followers of Russell and Moore

C. D. BROAD

"Critical and Speculative Philosophy," in J. H. Muirhead, ed., *Contemporary British Philosophy* (First Series). London, 1924.

LUDWIG WITTGENSTEIN

"Logisch-Philosophische Abhandlung." *Annalen der Naturphilosophie*, 1921. Translated by C. K. Ogden as *Tractatus Logico-Philosophicus*. London, 1922. New and revised translation by D. F. Pears and B. F. McGuinness. London, 1961.

"Some Remarks on Logical Form." *PAS*, supplementary volume (1929), 162–171.

ON WITTGENSTEIN'S "TRACTATUS"

Anscombe, G. E. M., *An Introduction to Wittgenstein's Tractatus*. London, 1959.

Stenius, Erik, *Wittgenstein's Tractatus*. Oxford, 1960.

F. P. RAMSEY

The Foundations of Mathematics and Other Essays. London, 1931.

L. SUSAN STEBBING

"The Method of Analysis in Metaphysics." *PAS*, Vol. 33 (1932–1933), 65–94.

"Logical Positivism and Analysis." *Proceedings of the British Academy*, 1933.

"Moore's influence," in P. Schilpp, ed., *The Philosophy of G.E. Moore*. Evanston, Ill., 1942.

JOHN WISDOM

"Logical Constructions." *Mind*, Vol. 40 (1931), 188–216, 460–475; Vol. 41 (1932), 441–464; Vol. 42 (1933), 43–66, 186–202.

Problems of Mind and Matter. Cambridge, 1934.

"Is Analysis a Useful Method in Philosophy?" *PAS*, supplementary volume 13 (1934), 65–89.

GILBERT RYLE

"Systematically Misleading Expressions." *PAS*, Vol. 32 (1931–1932), 139–170.

Logical Positivism

RUDOLF CARNAP

Logische Syntax der Sprache. Vienna, 1934. Translated by A. Smeaton as *The Logical Syntax of Language*. London, 1937.

Philosophy and Logical Syntax. London, 1935.

A. J. AYER

Language, Truth and Logic. London, 1936 and 1946.

The Rejection of Analysis

JOHN WISDOM

Philosophy and Psycho-analysis. Oxford, 1953. See especially the papers "Philosophical Perplexity" and "Metaphysics and Verification."

GILBERT RYLE

The Concept of Mind. London, 1949.
"The Theory of Meaning," in C. A. Mace, ed., *British Philosophy in the Mid-Century*. London, 1957.

LUDWIG WITTGENSTEIN

Philosophische Untersuchungen. Translated by G. E. M. Anscombe as *Philosophical Investigations*. Oxford, 1953.

ON WITTGENSTEIN'S "INVESTIGATIONS"

Malcolm, N., "Wittgenstein's *Philosophical Investigations*." *Philosophical Review*, Vol. 63 (1954), 530–559.
Strawson, P. F., "*Philosophical Investigations*." *Mind*, Vol. 63 (1954), 70–99.

JOHN AUSTIN

Philosophical Papers. Oxford, 1961. Especially "Other Minds," "A Plea for Excuses," "Ifs and Cans," and "Performative Utterances," all important essays in the new style.
Sense and Sensibilia. Oxford, 1962. A meticulous elucidation of basic perceptual concepts contrasted with traditional misdescriptions of them.

P. F. STRAWSON

"On Referring." *Mind*, Vol. 59 (1950), 320–344.

General Works on Analysis

Ayer, A. J., ed., *Logical Positivism*. Glencoe, Ill., 1959. An anthology of analytic philosophy which contains essays by philosophers who reject both positivism and analysis as well as by philosophers who accept analysis. Contains a superb bibliography of everyone remotely connected with contemporary analytic phi losophy.
Black, M., ed., *Philosophical Analysis*. Ithaca, N.Y., 1950. An anthology of papers in and on analysis, plus some essays in elucidation.
Feigl, H., and Sellars, W., eds., *Readings in Philosophical Analysis*. New York, 1949.
Urmson, J. O., *Philosophical Analysis*. Oxford, 1956.
Warnock, G., *English Philosophy Since 1900*. London, 1958.

General Anthologies on Elucidation

Flew, A., ed., *Logic and Language* (First Series). Oxford, 1952.
Flew, A., ed., *Logic and Language* (Second Series). Oxford, 1953.
Flew, A., ed., *Essays in Conceptual Analysis*. London, 1956.

MORRIS WEITZ

ANALYTIC AND SYNTHETIC STATEMENTS.

The distinction between analytic and synthetic judgments was first made by Kant in the Introduction to his *Critique of Pure Reason*. According to him, all judgments could be exhaustively divided into these two kinds. The subject of both kinds of judgment was taken to be some thing or things, not concepts. Synthetic judgments are informative; they tell us something about the subject by connecting or synthesizing two different concepts under which the subject is subsumed. Analytic judgments are uninformative; they serve merely to elucidate or analyze the concept under which the subject falls. There is a prima facie difficulty as to how a judgment can be simultaneously about an object, uninformative in relation to it, and explicative of the concepts involved, but this question will be examined later.

Kant associated this distinction with the distinction between a priori and a posteriori judgments. The one distinction was taken to cut across the other, except that there are no analytic a posteriori judgments. The remaining three classifications were, in Kant's opinion, filled; there are analytic a priori judgments, synthetic a posteriori judgments, and synthetic a priori judgments. Since Kant there has been little argument concerning the first two of these, but considerable argument and opposition, chiefly from empiricists, about the last (see A PRIORI AND A POSTERIORI). Analytic a priori and synthetic a posteriori judgments correspond roughly to logically and empirically true or false judgments. In distinguishing them, Kant was following in the steps of Leibniz and Hume, both of whom had made a similar distinction, although in different terms. Leibniz had distinguished between truths of fact, guaranteed by the principle of sufficient reason, and truths of reason, guaranteed by the principle of contradiction. The latter were such that their denial involved a contradiction; they could indeed be reduced to identical propositions via chains of definitions of their terms. Hume had likewise distinguished between matters of fact and relations of ideas. The former were merely contingent, while the latter were necessary and such that their denial involved a contradiction. Kant's innovation was to connect this distinction with the two further distinctions between the analytic and the synthetic and the a priori and the a posteriori.

It should be noted that Kant's distinction between the analytic and the synthetic was made in terms of judgments and concepts. This gave it a psychological flavor for which it has been criticized by many modern philosophers. The notion of judgment is ambiguous between the act of judging and what is judged. One problem is how to extend what Kant said so that it applies only to what is judged or to propositions. Furthermore, an implication of Kant's formal account of the distinction was that it is limited in its application to subject–predicate judgments (although it was also one of Kant's doctrines that existential judgments are always synthetic).

KANT'S CRITERIA AND USE OF THE ANALYTIC/SYNTHETIC DISTINCTION

Criteria. Apart from the general distinction, Kant offered two criteria for it. According to the first criterion, an analytic judgment is one in which the concept of the predicate is contained (although covertly) in the concept of the subject, while in a synthetic judgment the concept of the predicate stands outside the concept of the subject. According to the second criterion, analytic judgments are such that their denial involves a contradiction, while this is not true of synthetic judgments of any kind. Kant was here following his predecessors, although, with Leibniz, he did not suggest that analytic truths can be reduced to simple identities. This criterion can scarcely be said to suffice as a definition of an analytic statement, although it may provide grounds for saying whether a judgment is analytic or not. It will do the latter if it can be assumed that all analytic judgments are logically necessary, since reference to the principle of contradiction may provide the basis of logical necessity.

The first criterion seems on firmer ground in this respect, since it offers what seems to be a formal characteristic of all analytic judgments. It specifies what we must be doing in making an analytic judgment, in terms of the relations between the concepts involved. It has been objected that the idea of one concept being contained in another is also a psychological one, but this was certainly not Kant's intention. The point may perhaps be expressed in terms of meaning. When we make an analytic judgment, what we mean when we invoke the predicate concept is already included in what we mean by the subject concept. Just as the notion of a judgment is ambiguous, so a concept can mean either the act of conceiving or what is conceived, and it is the latter which is relevant here. By this criterion, therefore, a judgment is analytic when, in judging about something, what we judge about it is already included in what is meant by the term under which we subsume the subject. Kant assumed that all judgments of this kind are a priori, presumably on the grounds that their truth can be ascertained merely by considering the concepts involved, without further reference to the facts of experience.

Characteristics of analytic statements. Kant's criterion could be applied only to statements of subject–predicate form, and could not, therefore, be used to make an exhaustive distinction between all statements. However, if Kant's distinction is to be of use, it must be extended to cover propositions or statements and, moreover, statements of any form, not just those of subject–predicate form. If an analytic judgment is of an object, an analytic statement must similarly be about the object or objects referred to by the subject expression. Analytic statements cannot, therefore, be equated with definitions, for the latter are surely about words, not things. It has sometimes been said (for instance, by A. J. Ayer in his *Language, Truth and Logic*) that analytic statements make clear our determination to use words in a certain way. Apart from the fact that the use of words cannot be a simple matter of choice, what Ayer says cannot be the main function of analytic statements, since this would be to identify them with (possibly prescriptive) definitions. If we learn something about the use of words from analytic statements, this must at most be indirect.

Analyticity, a property of statements. We have seen that Kant's point of view might be represented as saying that only the meaning of the terms involved, the nature of the corresponding concepts, makes the judgment true. It might, therefore, seem feasible that an analytic statement could be characterized as a statement about something which says nothing about the thing but is such that the meanings of the words involved make it true. To be more exact, it would be the meanings of the words involved in a sentence—*any* sentence that expresses the statement—that make that statement true. It is important to stress the words "any sentence," for analytic truth can be a feature only of *statements*. It cannot be a feature of sentences per se, nor can it be limited to sentences in a given language (as Rudolf Carnap in effect supposes). Truth is a property of statements, not sentences, and the same must be the case with analytic truth. No account of analyticity which explains it in terms of what is the case with regard to sentences in any one language will do. If someone who says "All bodies are extended" makes an analytic statement, so will anyone who says the same thing in any other language.

Analyticity as a function of the meanings of words. What is meant by saying that the meanings of the terms involved *make a statement true*? Are analytic truths those which follow from the meanings of the words involved; that is, from their definitions? This cannot be so, since all that can follow from a definition is another definition, and how, in any case, can a statement about things follow directly from one about words? If analyticity is connected with meaning, it must be more indirectly. Friedrich Waismann has suggested that an analytic truth is one which is so *in virtue of* the meanings of the words involved. But the words "in virtue of" are themselves vague. It has been held by certain empiricists that "All bodies are extended" is analytic if and only if we use "body" in exactly the same way we use "extended thing"; that is, if we attach the same meaning to each expression. However, the truth of "All bodies are extended" does not follow simply from the fact that the expressions "body" and "extended thing" have the same meaning, for the substitution of expressions equivalent in meaning leaves one with a statement corresponding in form to the law of identity. Hence, the original statement will be true only if the law of identity holds. In other words, an analytic statement will be one whose truth depends not only on the meanings of the words involved but also on the laws of logic. This raises the question of the status of these laws themselves. It is sometimes claimed that they, too, are analytic; but this cannot be so if a definition of analyticity involves reference to the laws of logic (see CONTINGENT AND NECESSARY STATEMENTS).

Analyticity as a function of the laws of logic. The necessity of referring to the laws of logic in any account of analyticity has been noted in modern times by many philosophers. Waismann, for example, eventually defines an analytic statement as one which reduces to a logical truism when substitution of definitional equivalents is carried out. Frege had much earlier defined an analytic truth as one in whose *proof* one finds only "general logical laws and definitions," and he had sought to show that arithmetical propositions are analytic in this sense. Both of these accounts make reference to logical truisms or logical laws. Whatever the status of these, it certainly seems that analytic statements must depend for their validity not only on the meanings of the terms involved but also on the validity of the laws of logic; and these laws cannot themselves be analytic.

OBJECTIONS TO THE DISTINCTION

The problem of synonymy. However, objections to the notion of analyticity have been made, particularly by Willard Quine, on the basis of supposed difficulties about meaning itself, and not merely on those about the status of the truths of logic—although here, too, Quine has found difficulties. He distinguishes between two classes of analytic statements. There are, first, those which are logically true, such as "No unmarried man is married"; these are statements which are true and which remain true under all reinterpretations of their components other than the logical particles. Second, there are those, such as "No bachelor is married," which can be turned into logical truths by substituting synonyms for synonyms. It is the second kind of analytic statement which raises problems here, and these problems arise from the notion of synonymy or, to be precise, cognitive synonymy; that is, synonymy that depends on words having the same meaning for thought, as opposed to merely applying to the same things. The notion of definition which other philosophers have invoked in this connection rests, Quine maintains, on that of synonymy. How is this to be explained?

Quine's difficulties here are associated with general difficulties about synonymy raised by himself and Nelson Goodman in the effort to embrace a nominalism which does not involve the postulation of so-called meanings, and to push as far as possible the thesis that language is extensional; that is, such that it can be built up from variables and an indefinite set of one and many-place predicates, so that complex sentences are related to atomic sentences by truth-functional relationships and by quantification. In such a language, sameness of meaning might be equivalent to extensional equivalence, such that any two extensionally equivalent expressions are interchangeable *salva veritate;* that is, leaving unchanged the truth value of the statements in which they occur, wherever the expressions occur. The outcome of Goodman's argument in this connection is that since there may always be some occurrence in which the two expressions are not interchangeable *salva veritate*, no two expressions are identical in meaning. Quine himself recognizes something of this and has explored the restrictions which must be put upon the general thesis.

In the present connection, Quine explores the possibility that synonymity might be explained by interchangeability *salva veritate* except within words. But the interchangeability of, say, "bachelor" and "unmarried man" in this way may be due to accidental factors, as is the case with "creature with a heart" and "creature with kidneys." If it is the case that all—and only—creatures with a heart are creatures with kidneys, this is due simply to the fact that, as it happens, the two expressions always apply to the same things and not to any sameness of meaning. How do we know that the situation is not the same with "bachelor" and "unmarried man"? It is impossible to reply that it is because of the truth of "Necessarily, all—and only—bachelors are unmarried men," for the use of "necessarily" presupposes a nonextensional language. Furthermore, a sense has already been given to the kind of necessity involved here: analyticity. Hence, while cognitive synonymy might be explained in terms of analyticity, to try to explain analyticity in terms of cognitive synonymy would involve something like circularity.

Quine argues that similar considerations apply to attempts, such as Carnap's, to deal with the matter in terms of a semantic rule. Quine then considers the further possibility that, given that the truth of statements in general rests upon a linguistic component and a factual component, an analytic statement might be one in which the factual component is null. This, while apparently reasonable, has not, he objects, been explained; and the attempt by positivists to do so by reference to the verification theory of meaning (with its assumption that there are basic propositions in which the factual component is all that matters and, on the other hand, that there are analytic propositions in which the linguistic component is all that matters) involves reductionism, an unjustified dogma.

Synonymy and meaning. A possible objection to Quine—one in effect made by H. P. Grice and P. F. Strawson—is that his difficulty over synonymy involves a refusal to understand. There is a family of terms which includes analyticity, necessity, and cognitive synonymy, and Quine will not accept, as explanations of any one of them, accounts which involve reference to other members of the family. On the other hand, to go outside the family in one's explanations, as is involved in having recourse to extensional equivalence, is necessarily an inadequate explanation. This is a situation which frequently occurs in philosophy, wherever one is confronted with families of terms between which and any other family there is a radical or categorial distinction. This is perhaps an oversimplification of the situation, true though it is. It must be remembered that Quine's basic urge is to do without meanings, so as not to introduce unnecessary entities into our ontology. However, the failure of this particular enterprise of defining synonymy is, in fact, a demonstration of its futility. Meaning is a notion which must be presupposed rather than explained away in this connection.

The boundary between analytic and synthetic statements. Quine also has a second thesis in connection with analyticity, a thesis which has been echoed in different forms by other philosophers. It is a quite general thesis, in the sense that it does not depend on considerations about synonymy and is not, therefore, restricted to statements whose truth turns on synonymy. This thesis states that even if a distinction could be drawn between analytic and synthetic statements or between logical and factual truth, it is impossible to draw a sharp boundary between them. The contrary supposal rests on the dogma of reductionism already referred to. On that thesis, there is clearly an absolute distinction to be made. The denial of the dogma entails that there can be, at the most, a relative distinction. Within any particular system it is possible to distinguish those statements, those of logic and mathematics, which we should be extremely reluctant to give up and those, on the other hand, which we should be ready to give up if required to do so. The former are entrenched because of their close connections with other elements of the system. It has often been pointed out that the giving up of some high-grade scientific statements would involve the giving up with them of whole scientific systems. On Quine's view, the situation is worse, but not intrinsically different, with logical statements. There are no statements that depend for their truth on a direct confrontation with experience. The best that can be produced in the way of a distinction between different kinds of statements is a relative distinction between those which are more or less entrenched. No absolute and sharp distinction between analytic and synthetic statements can be drawn. Quine's conventionalism here reflects pragmatist tendencies.

One possible reply to this thesis is that the rejection of the dogma of reductionism does not by itself dispose of an absolute distinction of this kind. Even if it is accepted that there are no statements in which the factual component is everything, it does not follow that there are no statements in which the linguistic component is everything. Despite what Quine says, the thesis that there is a distinction between analytic and synthetic statements is independent of that of reductionism. Grice and Strawson have also attempted to deal with the issue by making a distinction in terms of the responses to attempts to falsify a statement. Analytic statements are those which, in a falsifying situation, demand a revision in our concepts; synthetic statements are those which demand a revision in our view of the facts. It has frequently been pointed out that it is possible to preserve a scientific statement against falsifying circumstances by making it logically true and thus immune to falsification. In doing this, we revise our concepts but not our view of the facts. It is clear that Quine could not accept this suggestion as such, since it presupposes that an answer has been given to the first of his problems—the definition of analyticity—in terms of notions like those of a concept or meaning. But, given that Quine's thesis is untenable in this first respect, there is no reason for denying its untenability in the second.

Statements that are neither analytic nor synthetic. Other reasons for dissatisfaction with a sharp distinction between analytic and synthetic statements have been offered by other philosophers. Waismann, for example, has maintained that there are some statements which do not admit of a clear classification; for instance, "I see with my eyes." In this case there are reasons for saying that it is analytic, since whatever I see with might be called "eyes"; on the other hand, it might be said that it is a matter of fact that it is with my eyes that I see. Hence, Waismann maintains, such statements are neither analytic nor synthetic, properly speaking. The objection to this, as has been pointed out by W. H. Walsh, is that Waismann has failed to consider the contexts in which such statements are made. The sentence "I see with my eyes" may be used in one context to express an analytic statement and in another to express a synthetic one. The fact that the same sentence may have different uses and that the analyticity or syntheticity of a statement is a function of those uses (a statement is just the use of a sentence) shows nothing about the necessity of abandoning the analytic–synthetic distinction.

Are there any analytic statements? Emphasis of the point that analyticity is a function of use prompts the question of whether sentences which purport to express analytic statements have a use at all and whether, in consequence, there *are* any analytic statements. It has been emphasized from Kant onward that analytic statements are trivial, and similar things were said even before Kant—by Locke, for instance. The truth of an analytic statement makes no difference to the world. It is, therefore, difficult to see why anyone should ever make an analytic statement. A possible reply is that such a statement might be made in order to clarify something about the concepts involved. However, if the statements in question are about concepts, rather than about the thing or things referred to by the subject expression, why are they not simply definitions? Definitions are not in themselves analytic statements, whatever their exact status. It could thus be argued that any statement which has a use either provides information about things or about the meanings of words, and in either case the statement would be synthetic, or at least not analytic. The only viable function remaining for the term "analytic" would be as a term of logical appraisal, not as a classificatory expression. That is to say, the use of the words "That is analytic" would not be to classify the statement in question, but to say, in effect, "You have not said anything."

Whether or not this is plausible in itself, the crucial question remains: How is it possible for a statement both to be about something and to elucidate the concepts involved? (The question is probably more crucial for judgments than for statements, since it might seem obvious what a judgment must be about, while the criteria of "aboutness" are less obvious in the case of statements.) The issues are simple. A statement is one use of a sentence, and an analytic statement is such a use which conforms to certain conditions—two of which are that it says nothing about its subject and that its truth depends at least in part on the meanings of the words involved. If this is so, it cannot be used to make clear those meanings. If an analytic statement does serve to make clear those meanings to someone, this must be an incidental and unintended consequence of its use, not an essential part of that use. On the other hand, if the triviality of analytic statements is accepted, there can be no argument to show that their use is impossible, for there is no reason why a statement, if it is to be about something, should also *say* something about that thing. The use of such statements would simply lack point.

A POSSIBLE WAY OF MAKING THE DISTINCTION

Wittgenstein pointed out in the *Tractatus Logico-Philosophicus* (4.4611) that tautologies are senseless but not nonsense. By "senseless" he meant that they do not pick out any determinate state of affairs which makes a difference to our view of the world. They are, in effect, trivial. However, they are not nonsense, because they are part of our symbolism, just as "0" is part of the symbolism of arithmetic, although it is useless for counting. Given a system of symbolism, or a language, it must always be possible to construct sentences which could be used to assert analytic truths or falsehoods (contradictions), whether or not there would be any point in doing so. This possibility is a necessary consequence of the nature of language. However, a language is not just a system of symbols; it is something whose function is, among other things, to state and communicate facts. Hence, it is possible to say that, given that these sentences have a use, the truth of their uses (or, in the case of contradictions, their falsity)—that is, the truth of the relevant statements—is a necessary condition of the employment of the language from which the corresponding sentences are drawn, or of any language in which there are sentences with the same meaning. More briefly, analytic statements will be those whose truth is necessary to the employment, as expressed in language, of the system of concepts on which they depend. Any statement of which this is not true will be synthetic. Of these other statements, many will be such that their truth is not necessary in any way, but there may be others whose truth is necessary in some way other than that of analytic statements—as Kant maintained about the synthetic a priori.

Bibliography

BOOKS

Ayer, A. J., *Language, Truth and Logic,* 2d ed. London, 1947. Ch. 4.

Carnap, Rudolf, *Introduction to Semantics.* Cambridge, Mass., 1942.

Frege, Gottlob, *Foundations of Arithmetic,* translated by J. L. Austin. Oxford, 1950.

Hume, David, *Treatise of Human Nature.* I.iii.1.

Kant, Immanuel, *Critique of Pure Reason,* translated by Norman Kemp-Smith. London, 1953. Especially the Introduction.

Leibniz, G. W., throughout his works. Especially *Monadology,* 31 ff.

Pap, Arthur, *Semantics and Necessary Truth.* New Haven, 1958. Useful discussions of general issues.

Quine, W. V., *From a Logical Point of View.* Cambridge, Mass., 1953. Ch. 2.

ARTICLES

Goodman, Nelson, "On Likeness of Meaning." *Analysis,* Vol. 10, No. 1 (October 1949), 1–7.

Grice, H. P., and Strawson, P. F., "On Defence of a Dogma." *Philosophical Review,* Vol. 65 (March 1956), 141–158.

Hamlyn, D. W., "Analytic Truths." *Mind,* Vol. 65, N.S. No. 259 (1956), 359–367.

Hamlyn, D. W., "On Necessary Truth." *Mind,* Vol. 70, N.S. No. 280 (1961), 514–525.

Putnam, Hilary, "The Analytic and the Synthetic," in *Minnesota Studies in the Philosophy of Science.* Minneapolis, 1962. Vol. III, pp. 358–397.

Waismann, Friedrich, "Analytic and Synthetic." *Analysis,* Vols. 10, 11, and 13 (1949–1952). A series of articles.

Walsh, W. H., "Analytic and Synthetic." *PAS,* Vol. 54 (1953/54), 77–96.

White, M., "Analytic-Synthetic: An Untenable Dualism," in Sydney Hook, ed., *John Dewey: Philosopher of Science and Freedom.* New York, 1950. Pp. 316–330.

D. W. HAMLYN

ANALYTIC JURISPRUDENCE. "Analytic jurisprudence" is a term used to distinguish an important school of legal thought and the characteristic doctrines associated with this school, and also to designate a branch of inquiry in which legal concepts are analyzed by techniques associated with or derived from the Analytic school. This article will first describe the school and its main doctrines and then attempt to characterize the main groups of problems that generally form the subject matter of analytic jurisprudence and the analytical methods employed in this discipline.

The school and its doctrine. The Analytic school of jurisprudence flourished in England and the United States especially during the second half of the nineteenth and the early years of the twentieth centuries, and on the continent of Europe during the period between the two world wars. Its most important writer was John Austin (1790–1859), whose *Lectures on Jurisprudence* (1863) remain the *locus classicus* of the analytic doctrines. Austin's influence was so great that the Analytic school is often characterized without qualification as the Austinian school and analytical jurisprudence identified with Austinian jurisprudence. Apt as this identification is for some purposes, it is likely to be on the whole seriously misleading, for many of the doctrines for which Austin is most famous, such as the command theory of law and the theory of undivided sovereignty, were not shared by all, or even most, of the Analytic school. The leading analytic jurists are Austinians only in the sense that they all share Austin's general conception of law as "established fact" subject to "scientific" treatment and orderly classification. The particular nature of the established fact called law, and the identification of the fundamental terms of its "science," however, were questions that divided analytical jurists from one another, and most of them from Austin himself.

Positive law. There was enough agreement on some matters, however, for a commentator to speak of central doctrines or defining tenets of the school. All agreed with Austin that the proper "province" of jurisprudence, insofar as it can have any claim to an exact and "scientific" methodology, is the positive law, that set of rules established in a political community by political authority and enforced by the power of the state. The primary, or strict and literal, sense of law, they claimed, is politically sanctioned law; and larger, vaguer kinds of law—such as, international law, moral law, customary law—are law only by courtesy of metaphor or analogical extension of meaning. Positive law, so conceived, is a "pure" fact; that is, a body of data that can be isolated from data of all other kinds and studied on its own terms, quite apart from any consideration of its causes, purpose, history, or value.

Such a study Austin called "general jurisprudence" or "the philosophy of positive law." It is a science only in the very general sense of a discipline or rational mode of inquiry, not in the narrower sense in which physics and biology are sciences. It is comparative in that it seeks to find the concepts and principles common to all legal systems, or at least to all advanced systems, that are necessary, or as Austin put it, such that "we cannot imagine coherently a system of law without conceiving them as constituent parts of it." Such a science is analytic in that it attempts to reduce the large number of legal concepts to a basic few that are not themselves further analyzable, and in terms of which the others must be defined. The science of jurisprudence so conceived invites comparison with twentieth-century analytic ethics in respect to the moral neutrality the science's practitioners claimed for it; for a study of what law *is,* they claimed, can be undertaken quite independently of any inquiry into the question of what its content *ought* to be. The former they held to be a formal or conceptual study that can be pursued with a rigor rivaled only by mathematics; the latter, on the other hand, must draw on the empirical sciences and particularly on an account of divergent human interests and purposes as they may conflict in a legislative arena.

Legal positivism. The negative side of the Analytic school's conception of law is the doctrine, often called "legal positivism," that no reference need be made to morality or natural justice in either the definition of "law properly so called" or a determination of whether or not a given rule is a "valid" rule of law. In this sense of positivism, all analytical jurists have been positivists; but not all positivists have been regarded as members of the Analytic school. In particular, those writers who, under the influence of Henry Maine and O. W. Holmes, Jr., insisted on the importance of history to jurisprudence, are usually contrasted with the analytic jurists, although both groups are equally "positivistic." To the analytic jurist his own conceptual inquiries and the historian's account of the origin and growth of law are designed to answer different, and logically distinct, questions about law. To the historical positivist, on the other hand, the two questions cannot be separated: to understand what the law is, it is necessary to know what it has been and how it has evolved.

Use of the deductive method. Some critics find in the classic analytic writings, either explicitly or implicitly, an unbounded confidence in the power of the deductive method to derive from a handful of "necessary" principles a certain, consistent, and complete body of law. Roscoe Pound has argued, in his book *Law and Morals,* that the Analytic school was strongly influenced by the dogmas of the separation of powers and of the complete separation of law from morals, and by an expectation of ever greater certainty in the application of law by the courts following from those dogmas. Only the more extreme analytic jurists ever maintained, however, that courts, even in principle, could grind out decisions "mechanically" by a simple subsumption of fact under rule, or that extralegal standards (e.g., "the reasonable man," "good faith," "fairness") can be wholly eliminated from the formulation of legal rules. The problem of statutory interpretation, though, was an especially difficult one for this school; and there are passages in Austin's writings, especially in his celebrated eulogy of Roman law, where he suggests that any advanced system of law can be reconstructed as a coherent deductive system, however close its first appearance to "an assemblage of arbitrary and unconnected rules."

Rival schools. The leading rivals of the Analytic school in the nineteenth century were the Hegelian and the Ethical (Natural Law) schools. The former, although often called the Historical school, had little in common with Maine or Holmes. The Hegelian school identified law with the customs of a community, existing quite independently of political enactment and sanction and evolving inexorably according to its own inner logic. Judges and legislators, from this view, discover the law in the customs of their people, but no more make positive law than they make the laws of physics. The analytic jurists found this conception obscurantist in theory and anarchical in practice. Custom might well be an important source of law, they granted, but it is no part of the law itself. Similarly, as against the natural law theory's identification of law and (true) morality, the analytic jurist argued that, for that clarity and practical certainty required for legal order, a separation of law from morals was as necessary as the separation of law from history and custom.

Problems of analytic jurisprudence. Of the many different kinds of theoretical questions that can be raised about law, only some are called "the problems of analytical jurisprudence." Excluded from this category are questions requiring exposition of the actual contents of a particular legal system, questions of legal history, both particular and general, and questions calling for ethical judgments of the sort Austin and his followers delegated to the "science of legislation." The great miscellany of problems remaining for analytical jurisprudence are all questions of conceptual analysis, and these can be divided into four groups.

Analysis of the concept of "law" itself. Efforts to clarify the concept of law generally lead into systematic treatises that overlap works on the basic principles of political theory insofar as both must examine such terms as "state" and "sovereignty." Systematic efforts to analyze the concept "law" must disentangle and come to terms with at least the following questions: (*a*) Under what conditions can we say that a legal system exists? (*b*) What general criteria must a rule satisfy to be a valid law in a given system? (*c*) How does law differ from other modes of social control? (*d*) How can law be distinguished from the sources of law (e.g., precedents, legislation, custom)? (*e*) How are statutes, legal rules, and precedents related to particular judicial decisions? (*f*) How is the body of law best divided into its various departments?

Definition of basic terms. Many legal concepts are complex and derivative; that is, capable of reduction to the simpler notions of which they are composed. Soon, however, this process of reduction must come to an end, as we discover those fundamental terms whose meaning cannot be elucidated by other legal terms without a vitiating circularity, and that are therefore capable of theoretically enlightening definition only, if at all, in terms from outside the law. Austin gave, as examples of such terms, "duty," "right," "liberty," "injury," "punishment," "redress"; others have suggested "person," "property," "possession," "corporation." H. L. A. Hart, in his article "Definition and Theory in Jurisprudence," has pointed out that efforts to define such terms have generated a "familiar triad" of theories. (The same is true of ethical theories that purport to define such terms as "ought" and "good.") Some writers (such as the Legal Realists) argue that the basic legal terms stand for some familiar kind of empirical fact, the behavior of judges, for example. These definitions have the effect of reducing the whole subject matter of law to the social sciences. Other theorists find that basic legal terms stand for irreducibly legal (nonempirical) entities. The Scandinavian school (Axel Hägerström, Karl Olivecrona, Alf Ross) holds that basic legal terms stand for no kind of entities, empirical or nonempirical; rather, they are "fictions" or "imaginary ideas."

Interdefinition of basic terms: Jural relations. A great part of the technical vocabulary of law consists of words for legal relations between persons, e.g., "master–servant," "principal–agent," "offeror–offeree"; or for complex clusters of legal relations, e.g., "contract," "property," "marriage." One of the perennial aims of analytical jurisprudence has been to locate the basic "building-block" legal relations out of which all the others can be constructed, to specify the logical relations between them, and to purge the terms that express them of ambiguity and vagueness. The most influential efforts to provide such a coherent body of definitions have been those of Wesley

Hohfeld (1879–1918) and his followers. Common to the various forms of Hohfeldian analysis is the assumption that all legal relations are between two persons, "no more, no less," and hence there can be no basic legal relations between a person and a thing. Basic legal relations are of four kinds, and for each kind there are two legal terms ("correlatives"), one describing the relation from the point of view of one person, and one from that of the other. Moreover, for each term there is another standing for its "opposite," or contradictory. The four basic relations can be illustrated as follows:

	Person *A*		Person *B*
I.	Right (or Claim)	⟷	Duty
	OPPOSITE: No–Right		
II.	Privilege	⟷	No–Right
	OPPOSITE: Duty		
III.	Power	⟷	Liability
	OPPOSITE: Disability		
IV.	Immunity	⟷	Disability (No–Right)
	OPPOSITE: Liability		

If *B* owes *A* a hundred dollars, it is *B*'s *duty* to pay the money to *A*, which is to say that *A* has a legally enforceable *claim* against *B*. *A* is under a legal duty not to strike *B*, i.e., *B* can claim that forebearance from *A*; but if *B* first strikes *A*, then *A* has the (restricted) legal *privilege* of striking back, and *B* has *no claim* on *A*'s forebearance. A privilege to do *x* is simply the absence of a duty to forebear from doing *x*, and thus does not imply a claim of noninterference against another person. *A* has a legal *power* in respect to *B* if *A* has the ability to create by his voluntary behavior new legal relations involving *B*. Thus, if *B* has made *A* an offer, *A* has the power of creating a claim–duty contractual relation by accepting; and *B* made himself *liable* to that new relation by offering. Finally, *A* has an *immunity* with respect to *B* insofar as his legal relations are not subject to alteration by *B*.

Analysis of other concepts and distinctions. A treatise of analytical jurisprudence is likely also to attempt to clarify and render precise such distinctions as those between person and thing, rule and fact, possession and property. Some of the terms of concern to analytical jurisprudence also have important uses outside of the law—"motive," "intention," "act," "cause," "fault," and "promise," for example. Insofar as the law makes use of the familiar, common-sense notions expressed by these words, they mark an important point of intersection between the subject matters of analytical jurisprudence and analytical philosophy.

Works on the Analytic School

Austin, John, *The Province of Jurisprudence Determined*. London, 1832.

Austin, John, *Lectures on Jurisprudence*, 5th ed. London, 1911.

Gray, John C., *The Nature and Sources of the Law*. New York, 1909. Severely analytic, but departs completely from Austin. Law defined as the rules laid down by courts.

Kocourek, Albert, "The Century of Analytic Jurisprudence Since John Austin," in A. Reppy, ed., *Law, a Century of Progress*. New York, 1937. Vol. II.

Pound, Roscoe, *Law and Morals*. London, 1926. Discusses critically the three leading nineteenth-century schools—the Historical, the Analytical, and the Philosophical.

Pound, Roscoe, "The Progress of the Law: Analytical Jurisprudence, 1914–1927." *Harvard Law Review*, Vol. 41 (1927–1928), 174–199. An excellent account of French and German analytic jurists, notably Solmó, Roguin, Lévy-Üllmann, and Kelsen.

Salmond, John T., *Jurisprudence*, 11th ed. London, 1957. Perhaps the clearest and most balanced of all the classic works on analytic jurisprudence.

Schuman, Samuel I., *Legal Positivism*. Detroit, 1963. Ch. 1 contains a somewhat different account from the above of the difference between analytic jurisprudence and legal positivism.

Works on Problems of Analytic Jurisprudence

THE CONCEPT OF LAW

Fuller, Lon, *The Morality of Law*. New Haven, 1964.

Hart, H. L. A., *The Concept of Law*. Oxford, 1961.

DEFINITION OF BASIC TERMS

Hart, H. L. A., "Definition and Theory in Jurisprudence." *Law Quarterly Review*, Vol. 70 (1954) 37–60. Contains an important critique of standard theories and references to leading books and articles.

JURAL RELATIONS

Corbin, Arthur L., "Legal Analysis and Terminology." *Yale Law Journal*, Vol. 29 (1919), 163–173. An early adaptation and very clear explanation of the Hohfeldian analysis.

Goble, George W., "A Redefinition of Basic Legal Terms." *Columbia Law Review*, Vol. 35 (1935), 535–547. Attempts to reduce Hohfeld's four relations to one: the power–liability relation.

Hoebel, E. A., *The Law of Primitive Man*. Cambridge, Mass., 1954. Application by an anthropologist of the Hohfeldian analysis to the study of primitive law.

Hohfeld, Wesley N., *Fundamental Legal Conceptions as Applied in Judicial Reasoning, and Other Essays*. New Haven, 1923.

Kocourek, Albert, *An Introduction to the Science of Law*. Boston, 1930. Ch. 4. Kocourek rests his system on only two basic relations: claim–duty and power–liability.

Stone, Julius, *The Province and Function of Law*. Cambridge, Mass., 1950. Ch. 5.

COMMON-SENSE CONCEPTS IN LAW

Morris, Herbert, *Freedom and Responsibility, Readings in Philosophy and Law*. Stanford, 1961.

JOEL FEINBERG

ANANKE. *See* MOIRA/TYCHE/ANANKE.

ANARCHISM, a social philosophy that rejects authoritarian government and maintains that voluntary institutions are best suited to express man's natural social tendencies. Historically the word "anarchist," which derives from the Greek *an archos*, meaning "no government," appears first to have been used pejoratively to indicate one who denies all law and wishes to promote chaos. It was used in this sense against the Levelers during the English Civil War and during the French Revolution by most parties in criticizing those who stood to the left of them along the political spectrum. The first use of the word as an approbatory description of a positive philosophy appears to have been by Pierre Joseph Proudhon when, in his *Qu'est-ce-que la propriété?* (*What Is Property?*, Paris, 1840), he described himself as an anarchist because he believed that political organization based on authority should be replaced by social and economic organization based on voluntary contractual agreement.

Nevertheless, the two uses of the word have survived together and have caused confusion in discussing anarchism, which to some has appeared a doctrine of destruction and to others a benevolent doctrine based on a faith in the innate goodness of man. There has been further confusion through the association of anarchism with nihilism and terrorism. In fact, anarchism, which is based on faith in natural law and justice, stands at the opposite pole to nihilism, which denies all moral laws. Similarly, there is no necessary connection between anarchism, which is a social philosophy, and terrorism, which is a political means occasionally used by individual anarchists but also by actionists belonging to a wide variety of movements that have nothing in common with anarchism.

Anarchism aims at the utmost possible freedom compatible with social life, in the belief that voluntary cooperation by responsible individuals is not merely more just and equitable but is also, in the long run, more harmonious and ordered in its effects than authoritarian government. Anarchist philosophy has taken many forms, none of which can be defined as an orthodoxy, and its exponents have deliberately cultivated the idea that it is an open and mutable doctrine. However, all its variants combine a criticism of existing governmental societies, a vision of a future libertarian society that might replace them, and a projected way of attaining this society by means outside normal political practice. Anarchism in general rejects the state. It denies the value of democratic procedures because they are based on majority rule and on the delegation of the responsibility that the individual should retain. It criticizes utopian philosophies because they aim at a static "ideal" society. It inclines toward internationalism and federalism, and, while the views of anarchists on questions of economic organization vary greatly, it may be said that all of them reject what William Godwin called accumulated property.

Attempts have been made by anarchist apologists to trace the origins of their point of view in primitive nongovernmental societies. There has also been a tendency to detect anarchist pioneers among a wide variety of teachers and writers who, for various religious or philosophical reasons, have criticized the institution of government, have rejected political activity, or have placed a great value on individual freedom. In this way such varied ancestors have been found as Lao-Tse, Zeno, Spartacus, Etienne de La Boétie, Thomas Münzer, Rabelais, Fénelon, Diderot, and Swift; anarchist trends have also been detected in many religious groups aiming at a communalistic order, such as the Essenes, the early Christian apostles, the Anabaptists, and the Doukhobors. However, while it is true that some of the central libertarian ideas are to be found in varying degrees among these men and movements, the first forms of anarchism as a developed social philosophy appeared at the beginning of the modern era, when the medieval order had disintegrated, the Reformation had reached its radical, sectarian phase, and the rudimentary forms of modern political and economic organization had begun to appear. In other words, the emergence of the modern state and of capitalism is paralleled by the emergence of the philosophy that, in various forms, has opposed them most fundamentally.

Winstanley. Although Proudhon was the first writer to call himself an anarchist, at least two predecessors outlined systems that contain all the basic elements of anarchism. The first was Gerrard Winstanley (1609–c. 1660), a linen draper who led the small movement of the Diggers during the Commonwealth. Winstanley and his followers protested in the name of a radical Christianity against the economic distress that followed the Civil War and against the inequality that the grandees of the New Model Army seemed intent on preserving. In 1649–1650 the Diggers squatted on stretches of common land in southern England and attempted to set up communities based on work on the land and the sharing of goods. The communities failed, but a series of pamphlets by Winstanley survived, of which *The New Law of Righteousness* (1649) was the most important. Advocating a rational Christianity, Winstanley equated Christ with "the universal liberty" and declared the universally corrupting nature of authority. He saw "an equal privilege to share in the blessing of liberty" and detected an intimate link between the institution of property and the lack of freedom. In the society he sketched, work would be done in common and the products shared equally through a system of open storehouses, without commerce.

Like later libertarian philosophers, Winstanley saw crime as a product of economic inequality and maintained that the people should not put trust in rulers. Rather, they should act for themselves in order to end social injustice, so that the land should become a "common treasury" where free men could live in plenty. Winstanley died in obscurity and, outside the small and ephemeral group of Diggers, he appears to have wielded no influence, except possibly over the early Quakers.

Godwin. A more elaborate sketch of anarchism, although still without the name, was provided by William Godwin in his *Enquiry Concerning Political Justice* (1793). Godwin differed from most later anarchists in preferring to revolutionary action the gradual and, as it seemed to him, more natural process of discussion among men of good will, by which he hoped truth would eventually triumph through its own power. Godwin, who was influenced by the English tradition of Dissent and the French philosophy of the Enlightenment, put forward in a developed form the basic anarchist criticisms of the state, of accumulated property, and of the delegation of authority through democratic procedure. He believed in a "fixed and immutable morality," manifesting itself through "universal benevolence"; man, he thought, had no right "to act anything but virtue and to utter anything but truth," and his duty, therefore, was to act toward his fellow men in accordance with natural justice. Justice itself was based on immutable truths; human laws were fallible, and men should use their understandings to determine what is just and should act according to their own reasons rather than in obedience to the authority of "positive institutions," which always form barriers to enlightened progress. Godwin rejected all established institutions and all social relations that suggested inequality or the power of one man over another, including marriage and even the role of an orchestra conductor. For the present he put his faith in small groups of men seeking truth and justice; for the future, in a society of free individuals organized locally in parishes and linked loosely in a society without frontiers and with the minimum of organization. Every man should take part in the production of necessities and should share his produce with all in need, on the basis of free distribution. Godwin distrusted an excess of political or economic cooperation; on the other hand, he looked forward to a freer intercourse of individuals through the progressive breaking down of social and economic barriers. Here, conceived in the primitive form of a society of free landworkers and artisans, was the first sketch of an anarchist world. The logical completeness of *Political Justice,* and its astonishing anticipation of later libertarian arguments, make it, as Sir Alexander Gray said, "the sum and substance of anarchism."

NINETEENTH-CENTURY EUROPEAN ANARCHISM

However, despite their similarities to later libertarian philosophies, the systems of Winstanley and Godwin had no perceptible influence on nineteenth-century European anarchism, which was an independent development and which derived mainly from the peculiar fusion of early French socialist thought and German Neo-Hegelianism in the mind of Pierre Joseph Proudhon, the Besancon printer who has been called the father of anarchism. This tradition centered largely on a developing social revolutionary movement that attained mass dimensions in France, Italy, and Spain (where anarchism remained strong until the triumph of Franco in 1939), and to a lesser extent in French-speaking Switzerland, the Ukraine and Latin America. Apart from Proudhon, its main advocates were Michael Bakunin, Prince Peter Kropotkin, Errico Malatesta, Sebastien Faure, Gustav Landauer, Elisée Reclus, and Rudolf Rocker, with Max Stirner and Leo Tolstoy on the individualist and pacifist fringes respectively. Also, there arose among nineteenth-century anarchists a mystique that action and even theory should emerge from the people. Libertarian attitudes, particularly in connection with the anarchosyndicalism of France and Spain, were influenced by the rationalization and even romanticization of the experience of social struggle; the writings of Fernand Pelloutier and Georges Sorel in particular emanate from this aspect of the anarchist movement. Nineteenth-century anarchism assumed a number of forms, and the points of variation between them lie in three main areas: the use of violence, the degree of cooperation compatible with individual liberty, and the form of economic organization appropriate to a libertarian society.

Individualist anarchism. Individualist anarchism lies on the extreme and sometimes dubious fringe of the libertarian philosophies since, in seeking to assure the absolute independence of the person, it often seems to negate the social basis of true anarchism. This is particularly the case with Max Stirner, who specifically rejected society as well as the state and reduced organization to a union of egoists based on the mutual respect of "unique" individuals, each standing upon his "might." French anarchism during the 1890s was particularly inclined toward individualism, which expressed itself partly in a distrust of organization and partly in the actions of terrorists like "Ravachol" and Emile Henry, who alone or in tiny groups carried out assassinations of people over whom they had appointed themselves both judges and executioners. A milder form of individualist anarchism was that advocated by the American libertarian writer Benjamin Tucker (1854–1939), who rejected violence in favor of refusal to obey and who, like all individualists, opposed any form of economic communism. What he asked was that property should be distributed and equalized so that every man should have control over the product of his labor.

Mutualism. Mutualism, developed by Proudhon, differed from individualist anarchism in its stress on the social element in human behavior. It rejected both political action and revolutionary violence—some of Proudhon's disciples even objected to strikes as a form of coercion—in favor of the reform of society by the peaceful spread of workers' associations, devoted particularly to mutual credit between producers. A recurrent mutualist plan, never fulfilled, was that of the people's bank, which would arrange the exchange of goods on the basis of labor notes. The mutualists recognized that workers' syndicates might be necessary for the functioning of industry and public utilities, but they rejected large-scale collectivization as a danger to liberty and based their economic approach as far as possible on individual possession of the means of production by peasants and small craftsmen united in a framework of exchange and credit arrangements. The mutualists laid great stress on federalist organization from the local commune upward as a substitute for the national state. Mutualism had a wide following among French artisans during the 1860s. Its exponents were fervently internationalist and played a great part in the formation of the International Workingmen's Association in 1864; their influence diminished, however, with the rise of collectivism as an alternative libertarian philosophy.

Collectivism. Collectivism is the form of anarchism associated with Michael Bakunin. The collectivist philosophy was developed by Bakunin from 1864 onward, when he was forming the first international organizations of anarchists, the International Brotherhood and the International Alliance of Social Democracy. It was collectivist anarchism that formed the principal opposition to Marxism in the International Workingmen's Association and thus began the historic rivalry between libertarian and authoritarian views of socialism. Bakunin and the other collectivists agreed with the mutualists in their rejection of the state and of political methods, in their stress on federalism, and in their view that the worker should be rewarded according to his labor. On the other hand, they differed in stressing the need for revolutionary means to bring about the downfall of the state and the establishment of a libertarian society. Most important, they advocated the public ownership and the exploitation through workers' associations of the land and all services and means of production. While in mutualism the individual worker had been the basic unit, in collectivism it was the group of workers; Bakunin specifically rejected individualism of any kind and maintained that anarchism was a social doctrine and must be based on the acceptance of collective responsibilities.

Anarchist communism. Collectivism survived as the dominant anarchist philosophy in Spain until the 1930s;

elsewhere it was replaced during the 1870s by the anarchist communism that was associated particularly with Peter Kropotkin, although it seems likely that Kropotkin was merely the most articulate exponent of a trend that grew out of discussions among anarchist intellectuals in Geneva during the years immediately after the Paris Commune of 1871. Through Kropotkin's literary efforts anarchist communism was much more elaborately worked out than either mutualism or collectivism; in books like *La Conquête du pain (The Conquest of Bread,* 1892) and *Fields, Factories and Workshops* (1899) Kropotkin elaborated the scheme of a semiutopian decentralized society based on an integration of agriculture and industry, of town life and country life, of education and apprenticeship. Kropotkin also linked his theories closely with current evolutionary theories in the fields of anthropology and biology; anarchism, he suggested in *Mutual Aid* (1902), was the final stage in the development of cooperation as a factor in evolution.

Anarchist communism differed from collectivism on only one fundamental point—the way in which the product of labor should be shared. In place of the collectivist and mutualist idea of remuneration according to hours of labor, the anarchist communists proclaimed the slogan "From each according to his means, to each according to his needs" and envisaged open warehouses from which any man could have what he wanted. They reasoned, first, that work was a natural need that men could be expected to fulfill without the threat of want and, second, that where no restriction was placed on available goods, there would be no temptation for any man to take more than he could use. The anarchist communists laid great stress on local communal organization and even on local economic self-sufficiency as a guarantee of independence.

Anarchosyndicalism. Anarchosyndicalism began to develop in the late 1880s, when many anarchists entered the French trade unions, or syndicates, which were just beginning to re-emerge after the period of suppression that followed the Paris Commune. Later, anarchist militants moved into key positions in the Confédération Générale du Travail, founded in 1895, and worked out the theories of anarchosyndicalism. They shifted the basis of anarchism to the syndicates, which they saw as organizations that united the producers in common struggle as well as in common work. The common struggle should take the form of "direct action," primarily in industry, since there the workers could strike most sharply at their closest enemies, the capitalists; the highest form of direct action, the general strike, could end by paralyzing not merely capitalism but also the state.

When the state was paralyzed, the syndicates, which had been the organs of revolt, could be transformed into the basic units of the free society; the workers would take over the factories where they had been employees and would federate by industries. Anarchosyndicalism created a mystique of the working masses that ran counter to individualist trends; and the stress on the producers, as distinct from the consumers, disturbed the anarchist communists, who were haunted by the vision of massive trade unions ossifying into monolithic institutions. However, in France, Italy, and Spain it was the syndicalist variant that brought anarchism its first and only mass following. The men who elaborated the philosophy of anarchosyndicalism included militants, such as Fernand Pelloutier, Georges Yvetot, and Emile Pouget, who among them created the vision of a movement arising from the genius of the working people. There were also intellectuals outside the movement who drew theoretical conclusions from anarchosyndicalist practice; the most important was Georges Sorel, the author of *Réflexions sur la violence* (*Reflections on Violence,* 1908), who saw the general strike as a saving "social myth" that would maintain society in a state of struggle and, therefore, of health.

Pacifist anarchism. Pacifist anarchism has taken two forms. That of Leo Tolstoy attempted to give rational and concrete form to Christian ethics. Tolstoy rejected all violence; he advocated a moral revolution, its great tactic the refusal to obey. There was much, however, in Tolstoy's criticisms of contemporary society and his suggestions for the future that paralleled other forms of anarchism. He denounced the state, law, and property; he foresaw cooperative production and distribution according to need.

Later a pacifist trend appeared in the anarchist movement in western Europe; its chief exponent was the Dutch ex-socialist, Domela Nieuwenhuis. It differed from strict Tolstoyism by accepting syndicalist forms of struggle that stopped short of violence, particularly the millenarian general strike for the abolition of war.

Despite their differences, all these forms of anarchism were united not merely in their rejection of the state, of politics, and of accumulated property, but also in certain more elusive attitudes. In its avoidance of partisan organization and political practices, anarchism retained more of the moral element than did other movements of protest. This aspect was shown with particular sharpness in the desire of its exponents for the simplification of life, not merely in the sense of removing the complications of authority, but also in eschewing the perils of wealth and establishing a frugal sufficiency as the basis for life. Progress, in the sense of bringing to all men a steadily rising supply of material goods, has never appealed to the anarchists; indeed, it is doubtful if their philosophy is at all progressive in the ordinary sense. They reject the present, but they reject it in the name of a future of austere liberty that will resurrect the lost virtues of a more natural past, a future in which struggle will not be ended, but merely transformed within the dynamic equilibrium of a society that rejects utopia and knows neither absolutes nor perfections.

The main difference between the anarchists and the socialists, including the Marxists, lies in the fact that while the socialists maintain that the state must be taken over as the first step toward its dissolution, the anarchists argue that, since power corrupts, any seizure of the existing structure of authority can only lead to its perpetuation. However, anarchosyndicalists regard their unions as the skeleton of a new society growing up within the old.

The problem of reconciling social harmony with complete individual freedom is a recurrent one in anarchist thought. It has been argued that an authoritarian society produces antisocial reactions, which would vanish in freedom. It has also been suggested, by Godwin and Kropotkin particularly, that public opinion will suffice to deter those who abuse their liberty. However, George Orwell has pointed out that the reliance on public opinion as a force replacing overt coercion might lead to a moral tyranny which, having no codified bounds, could in the end prove more oppressive than any system of laws.

Bibliography

George Woodcock, *Anarchism: A History of Libertarian Ideas and Movements* (Cleveland, 1962) is a complete history. The most recent study is James Joll, *The Anarchists* (London, 1964).

Earlier and less complete works include Paul Elzbacher, *Anarchism* (New York, 1908); E. V. Zenker, *Anarchism* (London, 1898); and Rudolf Rocker, *Anarcho-Syndicalism* (London, 1938). Much valuable material is contained in Max Nettlau's three volumes, *Der Anarchismus von Proudhon zu Kropotkin* (Berlin, 1927); *Anarchisten und Social-Revolutionäre* (Berlin, 1931); and *Der Vorfrühling der Anarchie* (Berlin, 1925).

Alexander Gray, *The Socialist Tradition* (London, 1946) contains provocative critical studies of Godwin, Proudhon, and Bakunin; Bertrand Russell, *Proposed Roads to Freedom* (New York, 1919) has a chapter (2) entitled "Bakunin and Anarchism."

GEORGE WOODCOCK

ANAXAGORAS OF CLAZOMENAE, the pre-Socratic who first advanced Mind as initiator of the physical world, spent much of his active life at Athens, where he was intimately associated with Pericles and exercised a considerable influence on Euripides. Unfortunately, in antiquity there were two (or more probably three) differing chronologies for his life, and the actual span of his life is a matter of considerable controversy. The scheme most commonly adopted puts his birth at about 500 B.C., his arrival in Athens either in 480 B.C. or 456 B.C., and his death in exile in 428 B.C. His exile followed his prosecution for impiety; and while some put this shortly before his death, others place it in 450 B.C. or earlier.

Anaxagoras appears to have written only one work. It may have occupied more than one roll, but it was probably fairly short; copies were on sale in Athens for one drachma in 399 B.C., according to Plato (*Apology* 26D). The work was concerned primarily with problems of cosmology, and the quite considerable number of fragments quoted by Simplicius in the sixth century seems to show that he was still able to find a copy in Athens at that date.

Everything in the interpretation of Anaxagoras has been the subject of controversy, and some would say that the real nature of his thought cannot now be recovered. A more optimistic view is suggested in what follows. We must first distinguish three types of evidence: (1) the fragments of Anaxagoras' own writings, whether in his own words or direct summaries; (2) the way in which his doctrines were understood in antiquity by Aristotle, Theophrastus, and Simplicius; (3) general considerations, primarily of a logical nature, that have caused many modern scholars to reject much in (2) and to substitute other interpretations regarded as intellectually more plausible.

The fragments show that Anaxagoras began with a doctrine of a mixture (fr. 1), which he placed at the beginning of his book. This mixture occurred at some past time. In it all things were present, infinite in number and infinitesimal in size, not revealed because of their smallness. Air and ether, being themselves infinite, held them all down. This mixture contained an infinite number of seeds in no way like one another, together with the traditional opposites and earth; and the mixture was colorless (fr. 4). *Nous* (Mind) caused a rotation of the mixture, resulting in a separation of objects (fr. 13). However, the objects so separated still have a share of everything else in them —only Mind is an exception—and they are what they are because there is in them most (i.e., a majority) of what they are (fr. 12). According to this last statement, Mind is not mixed with anything; but according to another view, it is present in some things (fr. 11), presumably those that are alive.

It is clear that in these fragments Anaxagoras envisages two points in time—an earlier mixture, virtually complete, with only air and ether separately perceptible, and a later stage, at which we now are. The rotation that produced the present stage will in the future cover a still wider area (fr. 12). The separation, while it does not produce pure substances (fr. 12), does involve a process of aggregation of some sort (frs. 15 and 16); however, we are told quite clearly that the present state is like the earlier state—there is still a mixture of all things together, as there was originally (fr. 6). We are to suppose that matter is infinitely divisible at both stages (frs. 3 and 1).

All of these fragments come to us from Simplicius, who quotes them to elucidate statements of Aristotle. He presents an interpretation based on what Aristotle and Theophrastus had said, which in all essentials appears to represent correctly what may be called the Aristotelian interpretation of Anaxagoras' doctrine. According to this interpretation, Anaxagoras' starting point was the contention of Parmenides that nothing comes into being out of nothing (so fr. 17). But since the number of things that appear to come into existence is very large, and since they arise in all sorts of circumstances and on all sorts of occasions, we must say that everything that appears to come into existence is in fact already present in that out of which it arises: since hair, for example, can come only out of hair, there must be hair present, even though concealed, in bread and apparently, according to Aristotle, in every other substance as well. Hence, in everything there is a portion of everything else. But hair will none the less be hair because hair predominates in some way. Hair, like everything else, will be infinitely divisible; at every level it will contain a mixture of everything else and yet will be what it is in virtue of a predominance of itself. According to both Simplicius and Theophrastus (*Aëtius* I.3.5), Anaxagoras called these sources of things *homoiomereiai* ("things with like parts") clearly because, according to this theory, everything comes into existence out of something like itself. Anaxagoras' use of this term has often been denied; but the attribution comes from those who had used the original text of Anaxagoras, and it may be correct.

This "Aristotelian" interpretation has been under sustained attack in modern times, primarily because of the supposed absurdity of such an account of the nature of substances. These attacks have led to a whole series of substitute interpretations that differ radically from each other. But first we must consider the objections to the Aristotelian interpretation. This interpretation rests upon four principles: (1) the infinite divisibility of matter; (2) the Principle of Homoeomereity, according to which gold, for instance, consists of gold and nothing else; (3) the Principle of Universal Mixture, according to which gold contains a portion of everything else; (4) the Principle of Predominance, according to which gold is gold by virtue of the predominance of gold in it.

F. M. Cornford claimed that there was a flat contradiction between the principle of homoeomereity and the principle of universal mixture of such a kind that Anaxagoras could not have held both principles in their unmodified form. But to this there are two possible answers: (*a*) the principle of homoeomereity as stated in ancient discussions of Anaxogoras merely stipulates that gold consists of gold without adding "and nothing else." This weaker version of the principle is not in contradiction to the Principle of Universal Mixture (*cf.* Mathewson, 1958), and it might be all that Anaxagoras intended to maintain. (*b*) Provided gold is taken to be the name of the predominant ingredient in a mixture and not the name of the mixture itself, then it would be possible to hold that the predominant element at a given level of mixture consists exclusively of the predominant element at the next level downward in the process of division and so on to infinity, even though at each level the Universal Mixture is present through the presence of nonpredominant or minority constituents. This would avoid contradiction between the strong form of the homoeomereity principle and the principle of universal mixture.

It has further been claimed that the principle of predominance breaks down when combined with the principle of homoeomereity, and still more when we add in universal mixture. Two main objections seem to be involved here. First, it is claimed that if we suppose that gold consists of a predominance of gold, which in turn consists of a predominance of gold at the next level of subdivision, which in turn consists of a predominance of gold . . . we are led into a vicious infinite regress in that we would never be able to state what is physically distinctive about gold (Strang, 1963). But it may be that Anaxagoras was not concerned with stating what gold is, or indeed with making any other statement about gold that would require the elimination of the term from the predicate of his statement. In this case such a regress need not be vicious. Indeed, on the principle enunciated in fragment 17, Anaxagoras probably could not eliminate "gold" from the predicate of such a statement without introducing the coming into being of gold out of not-gold. Suppose that he was concerned with reiterating that, at all levels, gold comes into being only out of gold; then the regress ceases to be vicious.

The second objection involves the principle of universal mixture, as well as the principles of homoeomereity and predominance. If gold is the predominant constituent in a mixture, and at the second level of subdivision this predominant constituent itself consists of a predominant constituent, and again at the third level of subdivision, then we shall quite soon in the process of division arrive at a situation where gold is in a minority in the mixture as a whole. This need not be inconsistent with the principle of homoeomereity, provided the principle is applied to the predominant ingredient in a mixture and never to the mixture as a whole. However, it would mean that in the process of subdivision we would pass from a mixture dominated by gold to a mixture that as a whole was not so dominated. This may have been what Anaxagoras had in mind in fragments 1 and 4, where there are apparently no predominant qualities that can be perceived.

The above discussion suggests either that there are no inherent contradictions in the Aristotelian interpretation or that, if there are, they are sufficiently subtle and concealed to have quite possibly escaped the notice of Anaxagoras. Those who are not prepared to take this view attempt to develop alternative interpretations, usually on the basis of some hint in the fragments themselves. One group of theories argues for a special place for "seeds," which are mentioned in fragment 4, or for the pre-Socratic opposites, which are certainly referred to in fragments 4, 8, 12, and 15. All such theories involve a "two-stage" analysis of matter. Most commonly, homoeomereity is confined to one of these stages, and frequently the range of universal mixture is very much limited, applying, for example, to a mixture of the opposites only and not of all substances. The "homoeomeries," since Zeller usually regarded as an Aristotelian term not actually used by Anaxagoras, are sometimes identified with seeds, qualities, the opposites, or two or more of these. G. Vlastos (1950) sought to save universal mixture by introducing the idea of "powers" that are potentially everything that can come into existence from a given substance.

Many of these interpretations are of considerable ingenuity and elegance. The difficulty in all of them, which is usually admitted to a greater or lesser degree by those who put them forward, is that they involve either complete rejection of, or at the very least radical surgery upon, the interpretation provided by Aristotle, Theophrastus, and Simplicius; positive evidence for their support either in the fragments or elsewhere is almost completely lacking. It is for these reasons that the Aristotelian interpretation is here regarded as more likely to be correct.

In addition to his general view of the structure of matter, Anaxagoras is credited with a number of special doctrines of considerable interest. The process of separation was begun by Mind (fr. 13). While Mind is not mixed in all things by universal mixture, it is somehow in contact with, if not present in, all things (fr. 14). It is itself material, although it is extremely fine and pure; it has knowledge of everything and controls all things that have life (fr. 12). It was responsible for the initial rotation of the mixture and its progressive acceleration. And yet, once initiated, the rotation acts mechanically. In a famous passage in the *Phaedo* (97C ff.) Plato makes Socrates express his disappointment that Anaxagoras made no direct use of Mind as an explanation of motion in the phenomenal world. Fragment 4 refers to other civilizations "just as we have here," and Simplicius saw that Anaxagoras is hinting at some world other than ours. Simplicius was satisfied that this was not in the past. He may have had in mind a perishing of our world, to be followed by a subsequent world according to a cyclical pattern. But more probably he is referring to the present, and to other parts of our one world, although it is possible that he envisaged a plurality of contemporary worlds. Anaxagoras thought of the earth as flat and supported by air. The moon derives its light from the sun; yet sun, moon, and stars alike are red-hot stones, and the sun is larger than the Peloponnese. He may have been converted to this view by the fall of a meteorite at Aegospotamos in 468 B.C. It was clearly this view of the heavenly bodies that played a large part in his condemnation for impiety. Sensation, he supposed, contrary to Empedocles' view, took place by opposites, since like is not affected by like. Everything is in us already (no doubt by the basic constitution of the matter in us). We know cold, for example, by the warm in us, whereas we do not feel a temperature identical to our own.

Bibliography

Testimonia and fragments are found in H. Diels and W. Kranz, *Fragmente der Vorsokratiker*, 10th ed. (Berlin, 1961), Vol. II.

The more important modern discussions are P. Tannery, *Pour l'Histoire de la science hellene* (Paris, 1887; 2d ed., Paris, 1930); A. L. Peck, "Anaxagoras: Predication as a Problem in Physics," in *Classical Quarterly*, Vol. 25 (1931), 27–37 and 112–120; A. L. Peck, "Anaxagoras and the Parts," in *Classical Quarterly*, Vol. 20 (1926), 57–71; F. M. Cornford, "Anaxagoras' Theory of Matter," in *Classical Quarterly*, Vol. 24 (1930), 14–30 and 83–95; G. Vlastos, "The Physical Theory of Anaxagoras," in *Philosophical Review*, Vol. 59 (1950), 31–57; J. E. Raven, "The Basis of Anaxagoras' Cosmology," in *Classical Quarterly*, Vol. 48 (1954), 123–137; G. S. Kirk and J. E. Raven, *The Presocratic Philosophers* (Cambridge, 1957), Ch. 15; R. Mathewson, "Aristotle and Anaxagoras," in *Classical Quarterly*, Vol. 52 (1958), 67–81; and C. Strang, "The Physical Theory of Anaxagoras," in *Archiv für Geschichte der Philosophie*, Vol. 45 (1963), 101–118.

G. B. KERFERD

ANAXIMANDER is the first Greek scientist and philosopher whose thought is known to us in any detail. He was born in Miletus c. 610 B.C. and died shortly after 546 B.C. He was thus in his twenties in 585 B.C., the year of the famous solar eclipse that Thales is said to have predicted. According to the ancient tradition, Anaximander was the "pupil and successor of Thales"; but in view of our ignorance of Thales' real achievements, it is perhaps Anaximander who should be considered the founder of Greek astronomy and natural philosophy. Nothing is known of his life except an unverifiable report that he led a Milesian colony to Apollonia, on the Black Sea. His lifetime corresponds with the great age of Miletus, when it was the richest and most powerful Greek city in Asia Minor.

His scientific achievements are said to include the first Greek world map, the first Greek star map or celestial globe, and the invention, or rather adaptation, of the gnomon (the vertical pointer of a sundial) for use in measuring the hours of the day and annual variations in the course of the sun. According to Pliny, he also traced the sun's annual path in the ecliptic and noted its inclination with regard to the celestial axis. This last discovery may really belong to a later age, but there is no doubt that Anaximander conceived (and almost certainly constructed) a spherical model for the heavens, in the center of which was placed the earth, as a disk or cylinder whose height was one-third its diameter. The ratio 1:3 seems also to have been used in the spacing of the celestial circles or rings assigned to stars, moon, and sun: the conjectural sizes for these rings are 9, 18, and 27 earth diameters, respectively. (His strange error in assigning the lowest circle to the stars is unexplained. There is, unfortunately, no evidence to support Burnet's attractive suggestion that this circle corresponds not to the fixed stars but to bright planets such as Venus. If we could accept this, the fixed stars might then be assigned to their natural place at the periphery of the celestial sphere.)

Anaximander is thus the author of the first geometrical model of the universe, a model characterized not by vagueness and mystery but by visual clarity and rational proportion, and hence radically different in kind from all known "cosmologies" of earlier literature and myth. The highly rational character of the scheme (despite its factual errors) is best indicated by Anaximander's explanation of the earth's stable position in the center: it remains at rest because of its equal distance from all points of the celestial circumference, having no reason to move in one direction rather than in another. This argument from symmetry contrasts not only with all mythic views but also with the doctrine ascribed to Thales: that the earth floats on water. Here Anaximander is clearly the precursor of the mathematical approach to astronomy developed later by the Pythagoreans, Eudoxus, and Aristarchus.

The book of Anaximander, quoted later under the standard title *On the Nature of Things* (*peri physeôs*), seems to have contained a description of his map and celestial model, as well as an account of how the natural world functions and how it reached its present form. Beginning from a first principle called the Boundless or Infinite (*to apeiron:* see below), he describes how "something capable of generating Hot and Cold was separated off . . . and a sphere of fire from this source grew around the air in the region of earth like bark around a tree. When this sphere was torn off and enclosed in certain rings, the sun and moon and stars came into existence" (Diels-Kranz, 12 A 10). These heavenly bodies are "wheel-like, compressed masses of air filled with fire, which exhale flames from an orifice at one point" (Diels-Kranz, 12 A 17a). Eclipses and lunar phases are explained by obstruction of the orifices. The sea is what remains of the primeval moisture, the rest having been evaporated as air or dried up by the celestial fire to form the earth. Land, sea, air, and heavens are thus all explained by a continual process of separating off from the primeval pair of Hot (dry) and Cold (wet). Wind, rain, lightning, thunder, and related phenomena are explained by the interaction of these elemental principles (water, air, fire) and opposite powers (hot, cold; dry, moist; thick, thin; light, dark). The origin of living things is explained as part of the same process: they arose as aquatic beings in moisture and later transferred to dry land. The first examples of each species developed to maturity within a protective membrane. In an interesting anticipation of modern ideas, Anaximander remarked that the first human beings could never have survived as helpless infants, but must have been born "from living things of another kind, since the other animals are quickly able to look for their own food, while only man requires prolonged nursing" (Diels-Kranz, 12 A 10).

The one quotation from Anaximander's book that seems to have been preserved in very nearly the original wording is his famous statement on cosmic justice: "Out of those things whence is the generation of existing things, into them also does their destruction take place, as is right and due; for they make retribution and pay the penalty to one another for their offense [or "injustice," *adikia*], according to the ordering of time." The interpretation of this oldest surviving philosophic text has been a subject of much controversy. The earlier commentators (including Nietzsche) interpreted the "injustice" as the separation of individual things from their infinite source and saw the eventual reabsorption of all things back into the *apeiron* as their only fitting atonement. This fails to explain how the things that perish can pay the penalty *to one another*, or why the source of generation is referred to in the plural. It is now generally agreed that offense and compensation must both refer to the strife of opposing principles (such as the hot and cold), and that the "ordering of time" stands primarily for periodic regularity in the daily and seasonal variation of heat, moisture, daylight, and the like. Whether there is also a reference here to a larger cycle in which the cosmos itself would perish into its source is more doubtful.

Anaximander's fame rests chiefly on his doctrine of the Boundless as the *arche*, the starting point and origin of the cosmic process. For him, the term *apeiron* meant "untraversable" or "limitless" rather than "infinite" in any precise mathematical sense. He described this principle with the Homeric epithets for divinity, calling it "ageless and immortal," and probably even "the divine" (*to theion*). This *apeiron* surrounds and embraces all things and apparently "steers" or governs them as well. It seems to have been conceived as ungenerated as well as imperishable, and thus contrasts in every respect with the limited, perishable world it engenders. Our sources refer to "worlds" (*kosmoi*) in the plural; a succession rather than a simultaneous plurality of worlds seems to be meant. The Boundless transcends this process of world creation, circumscribing each individual world in space, outlasting all of them in time, and providing the inexhaustible material source, the eternal motive power, the vital energy, and (presumably) the geometrical form and cyclical regularity for the cosmic process as a whole. In its archaic complexity, the *apeiron* is thus both a physical and a metaphysical or theological concept, and points the way not only to the infinite void of the atomists but also to the cosmic deity of Xenophanes, Aristotle, and the Stoics.

Bibliography

ANCIENT EVIDENCE

Diels, H., and Kranz, W., *Die Fragmente der Vorsokratiker*, 6th ed. Berlin, 1951. Vol. I, Ch. 12.

FULL-LENGTH DISCUSSIONS

Burnet, J., *Early Greek Philosophy*, 3d ed. London, 1920.

Guthrie, W. K. C., *A History of Greek Philosophy*. Cambridge, 1962. Vol. I.

Kahn, C. H., *Anaximander and the Origins of Greek Cosmology*. New York, 1960.

Kirk, G. S. and Raven, J. E., *The Presocratic Philosophers*. Cambridge, 1957.

Seligman, P., *The "Apeiron" of Anaximander*. London, 1962.

Zeller, E., *Die Philosophie der Griechen*. Vol. I. Latest German edition by W. Nestle, ed. Leipzig, 1923. Revised Italian edition by R. Mundolfo, Florence, 1932. Translated by S. F. Alleyne as *A History of Greek Philosophy From the Earliest Period to the Time of Socrates*. London, 1881.

IMPORTANT SPECIAL STUDIES

Jaeger, W., *The Theology of the Early Greek Philosophers*. Oxford, 1947. Ch. 2.

Vlastos, G., "Equality and Justice in the Early Greek Cosmogonies." *Classical Philology*, Vol. 42 (1947), 156–178.

CHARLES H. KAHN

ANAXIMENES, the third and last member (the others were Thales and Anaximander) of what is traditionally called the Milesian school of natural philosophers (*physiologoi*). The date of his death is estimated 528/526 B.C.; it is probable that he "flourished" about 545 B.C. Although we know little about his life and work, fragments of ancient testimony credit him with studies under his older contemporary, Anaximander; with the writing of a book in "simple Ionic"; and with the doctrine that air is the underlying principle of the universe, changes in physical state being the result of its condensation and rarefaction. It is likely that Aristotle read Anaximenes' book and that Theophrastus had access to it. Several of the doxographers (Aëtius, Hippolytus, Diogenes Laërtius) may have read later Hellenistic versions of the work.

On the strength of ancient testimony, historians of philosophy after Aristotle regarded Anaximenes' doctrine as a contribution to the Milesian debates on Nature. They assumed that from Thales to Anaximenes there was a continuous development in physical thought, and they insisted that this development was intelligible only in terms of the supposedly unique problem of the period: the birth and structure of the physical world. On this interpretation, Anaximenes' air was taken to be an *arche*, and his condensation–rarefaction doctrine was construed as a theory about physical transformations. The physical system reconstructed along these lines was then usually shown to be, in comparison with that of Anaximander, not as cogent; and whatever could not be accommodated within such a reconstruction was relegated to Anaximenes' "retrogressive astronomy."

Recent studies in mythical and early cosmogonic discourse (Hesiod) perhaps call for some revision of the traditional estimate. At a time when mechanical change and biological growth had not yet been distinguished from each other, when physical permanence was regarded as incomprehensible apart from "justice" between the warring Opposites, when inanimate continuity was mistaken for animal kinship, when experience was permitted only to illustrate but never to refute supposed insight, when meteorology served as the foundation for astrophysics—several of Anaximenes' ideas were pioneering. A schematic reconstruction of some of these ideas follows.

The fundamental and most pervasive thing in the world is air (*aer*), according to Anaximenes. Air is infinitely vast in extent but perfectly determinate in character: It is ordinary atmospheric air, invisible where most even in consistency, visible through the Hot and Cold and Damp and motion. It is from air that all the things that exist, have existed, or will exist come into being. This applies to gods and divine things and also to the rest of the world, inasmuch as the world is compounded out of the offspring of air. On this account, Anaximenes suggests, the primordial air is continually in motion, and this motion is the cause of alternating physical states. Condensation and rarefaction are the key manifestations of changing air: rarefied air generates fire; condensed air creates winds; condensed winds, clouds; condensed clouds, water; condensed water, earth; earth, stones and the rest of the world.

Throughout the process of cosmic change, the Hot and the Cold are dominant states of physical activity, but in no way are they forces distinct from air. They never come out of air by "separating off" (*ekkrisis*); rather, they are "attributes" of air when it condenses through "felting" or is rarefied through "loosening up."

From the genesis of the universe at large, Anaximenes moves to the description of the shape of the Earth and of the visible sky. The Earth, according to him, is broad, flat, and shallow—tablelike. All the heavenly bodies are fires in the sky, caused by the moist exhalations of the Earth. The heavenly bodies are nailed on a hemispherical diaphanous membrane and move around the Earth like a cap that can be turned around one's head, and not under the Earth. The stars do not produce any sensible heat because of their distance. When the sun, moon, and stars disappear, they are hidden by the distant elevations of the Earth. The stars may also be likened to fiery leaves floating on the air.

Clouds, rain, hail, and snow—all these phenomena, too, are caused by condensed air. And the same is true of the violent breaks of the clouds that produce lightning and thunder.

With the elements of his cosmology worked out, Anaximenes seems to need a general natural law guaranteeing the regularity of the world. He observes that as our souls, being air (according to an ancient tradition), hold us together, so does the cosmic Air hold the world together by enclosing it. Presumably what Anaximenes meant by this was that the regularity of an animated world is reliable and intelligible, as is the regularity of an animated body, a body that is organically self-regulative and autonomous—a microcosm. For Anaximenes, lawlike regularities were inconceivable without access to the idea of cause. The notion of physical constraint was accordingly effected through containment. The divine Air, by encasing the world, successfully regulates it.

Bibliography

Burnet, J., *Early Greek Philosophy*, 4th ed. London, 1930. Pp. 72–79.

Coxon, A. H., "Anaximenes," in *Oxford Classical Dictionary*. London, 1949. P. 51.

Diels, H., and Kranz, W., eds., *Fragmente der Vorsokratiker*, 5th ed. Berlin, 1954. Vol. I, pp. 90–96.

Guthrie, W. K. C., "Anaximenes and τὸκρυσταλλοειδές." *Classical Quarterly* (1956), 40–44.

Guthrie, W. K. C., *A History of Greek Philosophy*. Cambridge, 1962. Vol. I, pp. 115–150.

Heidel, W. A., "The δίνη in Anaximenes and Anaximander." *Classical Philology* (1906), 279–282.

Kerferd, G. B., "The Date of Anaximenes." *Museum Helveticum* (1954), 117–121.

Kirk, G. S., and Raven, J. E., *The Presocratic Philosophers*. Cambridge, 1957. Pp. 143–162.

Tannery, P., "Un Fragment d'Anaximene." *Memoires scientifiques*, Vol. 8 (1925).

"Anaximenes," in Pauly-Wissowa, *Realenzyklopädie der altertums Wissenschaft*, Vol. I. Stuttgart, 1893. P. 2086.

P. DIAMANDOPOULOS

ANCIENT PHILOSOPHY. The following articles contain discussions of ancient schools and movements: ALEXANDRIAN SCHOOL; ARISTOTELIANISM; ATHENIAN SCHOOL; CYNICS; CYRENAICS; EPICUREANISM AND THE EPICUREAN SCHOOL; GNOSTICISM; GREEK ACADEMY; HELLENISTIC THOUGHT; HERMETICISM; MEGARIANS; NEOPLATONISM; ORPHISM; PERIPATETICS; PLATONISM AND THE PLATONIC TRADITION; PRESOCRATIC PHILOSOPHY; SKEPTICISM; SOPHISTS; and STOICISM.

The Encyclopedia also has separate articles discussing the following terms which played an important role in Greek philosophy: APEIRON/PERAS; ARCHE; ARETE/AGATHON/KAKON; CHAOS AND COSMOS; DEMIURGE; HEN/POLLA; KATHARSIS; LOGOS; MIMESIS; MOIRA/TYCHE/ANANKE; NEMESIS; NOUS; PHYSIS AND NOMOS; PNEUMA; and PSYCHE.

Particular aspects of ancient thought are surveyed in the Encyclopedia's general articles, including the following: AESTHETICS, HISTORY OF; EPISTEMOLOGY, HISTORY OF; ETHICS, HISTORY OF; LOGIC, HISTORY OF; METAPHYSICS, HISTORY OF; SEMANTICS, HISTORY OF. See also articles on CATEGORIES; EMANATIONISM; GREEK DRAMA; UNIVERSALS, PROBLEMS OF.

See Ancient Philosophy in Index for articles on figures important to ancient philosophy.

ANDERSON, JOHN (1893–1962), Scottish-born Australian philosopher, was the son of a politically radical headmaster. Born at Stonehouse, Lanarkshire, and educated at Hamilton Academy and at the University of Glasgow, which he entered in 1911, he was at first principally interested in mathematics and physics; he turned to philosophy partly under the influence of his brother William, then a lecturer at Glasgow and later professor of philosophy at Auckland University College, New Zealand. Anderson graduated M.A. in 1917, with first-class honors both in the school of philosophy and in the school of mathematics and natural philosophy (physics). He lectured at Cardiff (1918–1919), Glasgow (1919–1920), and Edinburgh (1920–1927) before accepting an appointment in 1927 as professor of philosophy at the University of Sydney, Australia. He remained there, except for a visit to Scotland and the United States in 1938, until his retirement in 1958. He had almost no personal contact with philosophers in England, a country he regarded with the suspicion characteristic of a Scottish radical.

Anderson's career as a professor was an unusually stormy one. He attacked whatever he took to encourage an attitude of servility—and this included such diversified enemies as Christianity, social welfare work, professional patriotism, censorship, educational reform of a utilitarian sort, and communism. For a time he was closely associated with the Communist party, seeing in it the party of independence and enterprise, but he broke with it in the early 1930s. His passionate concern for independence and his rejection of any theory of "natural subordination" were characteristic of his whole outlook—political, logical, metaphysical, ethical, and scientific. Attempts were made to silence him and even to remove him from his professorship; he was subjected to legislative censure and clerical condemnation. In the debates that these attacks provoked, he spoke out forcibly and fearlessly in defense of free speech and university autonomy.

Metaphysics and epistemology. Anderson was trained at Glasgow as an Absolute Idealist. However, he soon abandoned Idealism, influenced by William James, whom he studied very closely, G. E. Moore, Bertrand Russell, the American "new realists," and, most significantly, Samuel Alexander, whose Gifford lectures on *Space, Time and Deity* he attended in Glasgow in 1916–1918. James and Alexander taught him that it was possible to reject absolute idealism without, like Russell, reverting to a modified version of traditional British empiricism. Anderson set out to show that continuity, stressed by absolute idealists, and distinction, stressed by empiricists, are equally real and equally involved in every experience. In experience, he argued, we encounter neither an undifferentiated continuum nor isolated sense data; our experience is of complex states of affairs, or "propositions," understood not as sentences, but as what true utterances assert to be the case. These propositions do not mediate between ourselves and reality; to take that view, Anderson argued, is to leave us in a state of invincible ignorance about this supposed "reality." To be real simply is to be "propositional," that is, to be a thing of a certain description, or, in Anderson's view, a complex of activities in a spatiotemporal region.

Unlike many of his British contemporaries, Anderson was by no means opposed to the use of philosophical labels; he was prepared to describe himself as an empiricist, a realist, a pluralist, a determinist, a materialist, or a positivist—but always in a somewhat individual sense. For example, although he insisted that he was an empiricist, he rejected what is usually taken to be the most characteristic doctrine of empiricism—that our experience is of "impressions" or "sense data." For Anderson, empiricism consisted in the rejection of the view that there is anything "higher" or "lower" than complex states of affairs as we encounter them in everyday experience; he rejected ultimates of every sort, whether in the form of ultimate wholes, like Bradley's Absolute, or ultimate units, such as "sense data" or "atomic propositions."

Similarly, although he agreed with positivists in their opposition to metaphysics, when it is understood as the revelation of realities "beyond facts," he shared neither the positivist hostility to traditional philosophy as such, nor its conception of experience as consisting in "having sensations," nor its interpretation of logic and mathematics as calculi. He was a realist, insofar as he argued that what we perceive exists independently of our perceiving it; but he forcibly criticized the phenomenalism characteristic of so many twentieth-century realists. He described himself as a pluralist, but whereas classical pluralism had defended the thesis that there is a plurality of ultimate simples, everything, for Anderson, is complex. No state of affairs is analyzable into just so many ingredients—whether in the form of sense data or of abstract qualities. Pluralities, in his view, consist of pluralities, not of simples. For the same reason he was not a determinist in the classical sense, because for him no description of a situation was ever complete; his determinism consisted only in his holding that there are sufficient and necessary conditions for the occurrence of any state of affairs. Finally, his materialism did not incorporate the classical conception of matter; what is essential to his view is the idea that every state of affairs is describable in terms of physical laws—which does not exclude its also being describable in terms of biological, psychological, or sociological laws.

The arguments by which Anderson attempted to establish his philosophical conclusions were manifold and diverse. What was perhaps his fundamental argument can be put thus: As soon as we try to describe "ultimate" entities or offer any account of their relation to those "contingent" entities whose existence and behavior they are supposed to explain, we find ourselves obliged, by the very nature of the case, to treat the alleged "ultimates" as possessing such-and-such properties as a "mere matter-of-fact." The metaphysician either sees his ultimate entities vanish into emptiness—like Locke's "substance"—or else he is forced to admit that they exhibit precisely the logical characteristics which were supposed to indicate that a thing is not ultimate.

The emptiness of ultimates, Anderson thought, is often disguised by the fact that they are defined in wholly relational terms—as when, for example, substance is defined as "that which underlies qualities," or a sense datum as "that which is an object of immediate perception." Anderson attacked this procedure as "relativism," that is, as the attempt to think of an entity or a quality as being wholly constituted by its relation to something else. To be related, Anderson argued, an entity must be qualitatively describable; relational definitions, it follows, cannot be used to avoid the conclusion that the "ultimate," if it exists at all, must itself be a thing of a certain description. According to Anderson, every state of affairs is "ultimate," in the sense that it is something we have to take account of; but it is contingent, too, in the sense that there are circumstances in which it might not have come about. There is nothing whose nature is such that it must exist, but there is nothing, either, whose nature is exhausted by its relation to other states of affairs.

Particularly in Anderson's lectures, through which his influence has been mainly exerted, such general considerations were supported by detailed analyses of specific philosophical theories. Although he was not, in a professional sense, a scholar, it was his habit both to develop his own views by way of a criticism of his predecessors and also to ascribe to those predecessors—especially perhaps to Heraclitus and to the Plato of the later dialogues—the views that he took to be correct.

Logic and mathematics. Anderson's approach to philosophy was in some respects formal. He agreed with the Russell of *Our Knowledge of the External World* that logic is the essence of philosophy—if by this is meant that philosophical problems are to be settled by an analysis of propositions. But despite strong mathematical interests, he was only to a very limited degree influenced by Russell's mathematical logic. He worked out, and defended against Russell's criticisms, a reformulated version of the traditional formal logic, which he tried to show had a much greater range and power than its critics would allow to it.

He related logic very closely to discussion: the conception of an "issue," of what is before a group for consideration, bulks very large in his logic. The issue, he thought, is always whether some kind of thing is of a certain description, and discussion consists in drawing attention to connections between such descriptions. Unless these connections actually hold, discussion falsifies unless it is actually the case, for example, that what one person brings forward as an objection is logically inconsistent with what another person has said. To point to logical relations, Anderson concluded, is to assert that something is the case, just as much as to draw attention to any other sort of relation.

He took a similar stand concerning mathematics, which, he argued, can be applied to the world only in virtue of the fact that it describes that world. "Application," in Anderson's view, consists in drawing conclusions from what is being applied. If mathematics offered no description of the world, no application of it could describe the world.

He did not, however, agree with John Stuart Mill that mathematical propositions are "inductions from experience." He was a vigorous critic of induction. If, as traditional empiricists had assumed, all our experience is of "pure particulars," then, according to Anderson we would not have the slightest ground for believing in—we could not even conceive the possibility of—general connections. But, in fact, the least we can be acquainted with is not a bare particular but a particular state of affairs; from the very beginning, generality is an ingredient of our experience. We can recognize directly that, say, fire burns, although we can be mistaken in this as in any other of our beliefs; for to "recognize" is nothing more or less than to hold a belief.

Aesthetics, ethics, and political philosophy. Although even in his aesthetic, ethical, and political writings, Anderson was constantly concerned to make formal points—as, for example, that the definition of good as "that whose nature it is to be an end" exhibits the vice of "relativism"—yet he was also a good deal influenced by, and deeply concerned with, the issues raised by economists like Marshall, social theorists like Marx and Georges Sorel, critics like Matthew Arnold, psychologists like Freud, novelists like Joyce and Dostoevsky. His aesthetic, ethical, and political writings conjoin the logical and the concrete; in virtue of this fact he has influenced many Australian intellectuals who would not accept his formal analyses.

In his aesthetics, Anderson argued that the beauty of works of art is independent of the observer; and similarly in ethics, that acts are good or bad in themselves. He was influenced by Moore's *Principia Ethica* but critical of Moore's attempt to treat "good" as being a simple and indefinable quality and at the same time to define it as "that which ought to be," and thus a quality. Anderson took "good" to be a predicate of certain forms of mental activity—the spirit of inquiry, love, courage, artistic creation, and appreciation—and tried to work out a theory of the connection and distinction between these different forms of activity.

In his political theory, Anderson attacked, on the one hand, the view that human society has a single "good" to which all activity ought to be subordinated, and, on the other hand, the doctrine that it is a set of contractual relations between individuals. Society, as he saw it, is a complex of complex institutions, of which the state is only one. A community flourishes when this fact is fully realized, when no attempt is made to enforce uniformity upon these diverse competing and cooperating types of institutions. The attempt to achieve absolute security by social planning, Anderson held, is doomed to failure and is stultifying in its effects in society.

Influence. Anderson's ideas were presented in a series of articles, mainly in the *Australasian Journal of Philosophy*, and in his influential lectures at the University of Sydney, where he founded what has been described as "the only indigenous school of philosophy in Australia." Among those philosophers who have, in varying degrees, felt his influence, the best known are D. M. Armstrong, A. J. Baker, Eugene Kamenka, J. L. Mackie, P. H. Partridge, and J. A. Passmore.

Bibliography

Anderson's principal contributions to periodicals, together with two previously unpublished papers, have been brought together as *Studies in Empirical Philosophy* (Sydney, 1962), with an introduction by J. A. Passmore, which contains a full bibliography. For further information, see Gilbert Ryle, "Logic and Professor Anderson," in *Australian Journal of Philosophy*, Vol. 28, No. 3 (1950), 137–153; J. L. Mackie, "The Philosophy of John Anderson," in *Australian Journal of Philosophy*, Vol. 40, No. 3 (1962), 264–281; J. A. Passmore, "Philosophy in Australia," in *Australian Culture* (Ithaca, 1963).

JOHN PASSMORE

ANDŌ SHŌEKI, a critical thinker in the Tokugawa period of Japan. All that is known of his life is that he was born in Akita toward the end of the seventeenth century and died in the second half of the eighteenth century, that his profession was medicine, and that he went to Nagasaki, the first Japanese port to receive Western trade, where he learned about conditions in foreign countries. He is described as a man of stern character who in his teaching never quoted, except to criticize, the Chinese classical books, meaning that he followed only his own ideas, a very unorthodox way of teaching for Tokugawa Confucianists. Very fond of the peasant class, he insisted that his pupils, and he had very few, should do manual work to be in contact with nature, the greatest master of all. Until recently he was virtually unknown, because of his nonconformist ideas, although nowadays he is overpraised. His manuscripts were found only in 1889, and only in part. They were published with difficulty. The better-known are *Shizen shin-eidō* ("The Way and Activity of Nature," written in 1755) and *Tōdō shinden* ("A True Account of the Ruling of the Way"). They are the most devastating critique ever made of Tokugawa society and of every kind of Japanese ideology.

Andō's iconoclasm was directed first of all against Shintoism and Buddhism. He sharply attacked Shinto mythology and Prince Shōtoku (574–622) for his role in spreading Buddhism. Other rulers, too, and priests of all sects came under his critical scrutiny, which is too negative. Nor had he a better appreciation of the different schools of Confucianism, for he accused them of perverting the teaching of the old sages in their interpretation of nature.

Nature for Andō is an eternal *ki*, or material energy, in perpetual motion. Nature is not to be conquered but to be known; and in following nature man attains the ideal. More positive were his ideas about society; he was the only genuine equalitarian of Tokugawa Japan, arguing against the evils of a system which oppressed the peasant. He cannot be considered completely iconoclastic, since he was not against authority as such, nor was he an atheist, and even his alleged materialism has to be qualified.

Bibliography

For a guide to primary sources, see bibliography of JAPANESE PHILOSOPHY. See also E. H. Norman, "Andō Shōeki and the Anatomy of Japanese Feudalism," *Transactions of the Asiatic Society of Japan*, 3d series, Vol. 2 (1949), 1–340; and Y. B. Radul-Zatulovskij, *Andō Shōeki, Filosof Materialist XVIII Veka* (Moscow, 1961).

GINO K. PIOVESANA, S.J.

ANIMAL SOUL. The debates which have surrounded the animal soul or mind have been sensitive indicators of a number of fundamental issues in modern philosophy and science: the immateriality of the human mind, the immortality of the soul, the existence of other minds, and the basis of free will and responsibility. These debates have also been persistent symptoms of dissatisfaction with the mechanistic paradigm of explanation of seventeenth-century science as applied to biological and psychological phenomena. The theory of evolution, the methods of modern psychology, and the emergence of cybernetics have forced us to look again at the metaphysical foundations of modern science and to assess their adequacy for understanding adaptive systems, whether they be machines, animals, men, or all three at once.

The concept of the animal soul did not give rise to any serious problems until the seventeenth century, when Cartesian dualism brought out distinctions which had been latent in the dominant Aristotelian tradition. Aristotle had postulated gradations from inert, inanimate matter to plants, which had the additional functions of nourishment and reproduction, to animals, which were also endowed with sensation, motion, and all degrees of mental functions except reason: he reserved reason for man. Aristotle's general analysis of causation, which included final causes along with material, efficient, and formal causes, precluded a sharp discontinuity between physical and mental functions.

DESCARTES AND THE ANIMAL-MACHINE

Descartes's doctrine that animals are pure machines, while men are machines with minds, was in part a compromise between his scientific aims and his voluntaristic, Christian view of man. If biological phenomena could be included in the domain of his universal physics, then the boundary would no longer lie between inanimate and animate beings; physics would include all of nature except the mind of man. Harvey's discovery of the circulation of the blood encouraged Descartes to attempt a general mechanistic physiology in hydraulic terms. Descartes argued that most human motions do not depend on the mind and gave examples of physiological functions (such as digestion), reactions (such as blinking), and feelings (such as passions) which occur independently of the will. In man, however, the mind could also direct the course of the fluid ("animal spirits") which controls movements.

However, to attribute minds to animals would threaten traditional religious beliefs, since the psychological concept of mind was conflated with the theological concept of soul. Descartes argued that it would be impious to imagine that animals have souls of the same order as men and that man has nothing more to hope for in the afterlife than flies and ants have. Similarly, God could not allow sinless creatures to suffer; without souls, animals would not suffer, and man would be absolved from guilt for exploiting, killing and eating them. But he considered the most important reason for denying souls to animals to be their failure "to indicate either by voice or signs that which could be accounted for solely by thought and not by natural impulse" (letter to Henry More, February 1649). Thus, the use of language became the criterion of thought—"the true difference between man and beast." This argument has been accepted in much of the subsequent debate, and discussion has centered on the characteristics of a "true language."

It has often been suggested that Descartes was not consistent because occasionally he did ascribe mental functions to animals—sensation, imagination, passions, memory. Although some passages support this view, it seems clear that he attempted to maintain a rigid dualism by granting these functions to animals yet insisting that they were purely corporeal, while in man alone they had a mental counterpart; for instance, man had *both* corporeal and mental perceptions, and the dualism of mind and matter extended *into* his account of feelings. If attention is confined to the animal-machine hypothesis, it might therefore appear that there is little to choose between the Cartesian account and the views of his opponents, who did attribute mental functions to animals. The very extensive literature on the animal soul controversy lends support to this contention. However, the debate was not primarily about what animals could do but about the implications for man of various interpretations of their behavior. More generally, it concerned the adequacy of mechanistic explanation to account for biological and psychological phenomena.

Descartes excluded explanation by purpose (the "final causes" of the Aristotelian tradition) from physics and from biology. Yet mechanistic explantion was remarkably unsuccessful in accounting for biological phenomena without making some implicit or explicit appeal to concepts derived from mental intention or without postulating some intermediate substance or special vital force. The discontinuity in Cartesian metaphysics represented, then, a highly unstable compromise. The application of mechanism to animals and to the human body had considerable utility as an alternative to animistic explanation in physiology, but the demands of functional explanation in biology made it ultimately untenable. Science, the analogy between animals and men, and common sense called for a continuity which metaphysics and theology denied.

Reactions to Descartes. Descartes's analysis put the issues so starkly that there has been no peace since. Adherence to the animal-machine doctrine became the crucial test of loyalty to Cartesianism, and no anti-Cartesian held it. As the subsequent debate showed, Descartes was in grave danger of proving too much. If one could not infer the existence of minds in animals from their behavior, then how could the possession of minds by other men be inferred from *their* behavior? The analogy could just as well be extended to man's mind as to his body, God being capable of contriving both human and animal automata. Conversely, to ascribe thought to animals involved granting them immortal souls, since Descartes considered mental substances to be indivisible. The extremes of universal mechanism and universal spiritualism were the obvious alternatives to a radical distinction between man and animals, and both were theologically unacceptable.

Descartes's most formidable opponents in the seventeenth century were the Peripatetics, who explained animal behavior by reverting to a version of the Aristotelian view and postulated a third substance intermediate between matter and mind. Animals were said to possess a "substantial form," a sensitive soul endowed with all mental attributes except reflection, reason, and will. The Peripatetics were more successful in criticizing Descartes than in gaining general acceptance for their own doctrine. A simpler solution was to accord sensation and an inferior degree of reason to animals but to deny them an immortal soul. This approach was favored by naturalists, who were most struck by the capacities of animals and less concerned with the subtleties of metaphysics. If one combined an appreciation of the complicated behavioral capacities of animals with a belief in the principle of the continuity of nature ("Nature makes no leaps"), different degrees of mentality could be ascribed to creatures at different levels of the "scale of beings."

Late in that century, Leibniz elaborated a philosophy based on the principle of continuity, but he retained distinct levels of mentality in his classification of monads. Animals were denied self-consciousness and the power to recognize eternal truths, which were defining attributes of the souls of men. In the eighteenth century the principle of continuity was applied much more rigorously. If *all* possible gradations in the scale of beings were realized, *no* qualitative distinctions could be upheld, and no sharp demarcation would be tenable. Indeed, some extended mental continuity below animals and concerned themselves with the sensations, wishes, and loves of plants; matter alone was held to be completely insensitive.

Throughout the debate, continuity was opposed by explicit or implicit appeal to separate mental faculties or powers. The issue became one of deciding which faculties belonged to man alone. The less sure man felt about his dignity and the power of his reason, the more he accepted the continuity between man and animals; and the more seriously one took biological continuity, the less one could appeal to the clear demarcations on which a "faculty psychology" depends. It followed that man differed only in degree from the nearest subhuman species, and a heightened interest in apes and savage tribes reflected this implication. All that was left in doubt was the amount of difference and the means of determining it.

In the early eighteenth century the Cartesian doctrine of the animal-machine was waning, and by 1730 most participants in the debate granted some measure of mentality to animals, although their reasons varied. The whole controversy was reduced to absurdity in 1739, when a Jesuit, Father Bougeant, wrote a very telling criticism of the Cartesian doctrine and the prevailing alternatives. He concluded that the only solution which would not threaten religion was to grant souls to animals but to consider these the souls of demons or fallen angels inhabiting animal bodies as a punishment. His position allowed him to concede reason and a true language to beasts and neatly to justify their suffering. His order rewarded his ironical wit by applying stern disciplinary measures.

SENSATIONALISM AND THE MAN-MACHINE

The most influential alternatives to the Cartesian view in the emergence of modern animal psychology arose from the philosophy of Locke and the associationist psychology of Hartley and Condillac. Sensationalist psychology did not reject dualism, but it fragmented the Cartesian indivisible thinking substance, thereby allowing continuous degrees of intelligence at various levels of the scale of beings. Locke's psychological remarks were incidental to his preoccupation with epistemology; in his partial rejection of the Cartesian theory of knowledge he postulated two sources of ideas: sensation and reflection. However, his influence has derived primarily from his sensationalism and his division of knowledge into sensory units, as conceived by analogy from the atoms or corpuscles of the mechanical philosophy: complex ideas are built up from simple ones. By distinguishing ideas of sensation and ideas of reflection, Locke was able to demarcate man from animals: animals had particular sensory ideas and a degree of reason but no general ideas or powers of abstraction and consequently no language for their expression. Condillac developed Locke's psychology and made it consistently sensationalist by rejecting ideas of reflection and concluding that all faculties and contents of the mind arise from sensations and their transformations. Although this eliminated the basis for a clear demarcation between the minds of men and those of animals, Condillac attributed the inferior minds of animals to inferior sense organs.

Hartley's systematic physiological psychology was based on the two principles of *mental association* (derived from Locke) and parallel *physical vibrations* in the brains and nerves of men and animals (suggested by speculations of Newton). This was the effective beginning of the "association psychology," according to which all complex mental and behavioral phenomena are analyzable into sensations, and the larger elements are built up by habit or repetition. The effect of Hartley's argument was to distinguish men from animals only by degrees: the laws of vibration and association applied to both, but animals had comparatively restricted experiences; because their brains were smaller and less organized, they lacked language and symbols and relied more heavily on instincts. Hartley argued that what was learned through studying man could be applied analogically to animals, and conversely.

The complete correlation of mind with material corpuscles implied mental determinism, and Hartley accepted this consequence: "the mechanism or necessity of human actions, in opposition to what is generally termed free-will" (*Observations on Man, His Frame, His Duty, and His*

Expectations, London, 1749, Vol. I, p. 500), and, in so doing, abandoned one historically important support for Cartesian dualism. The end of the century saw Hartley's theory extended in two directions. First, Joseph Priestley abandoned dualism entirely and considered perception and other mental powers to be properties of matter, although he retained immortality by holding that the covenant between God and man promised the resurrection of the *body*. His materialist hypothesis led him to argue that not only animals but also plants differed from men only in degree. Second, there was the evolutionism of Erasmus Darwin, Priestley's friend and grandfather of Charles Darwin. Erasmus Darwin placed Hartley's sensationalism and the principle of continuity on a temporal basis and put forward a speculative theory of evolution from a single irritable filament through all plants and animals to man. The association of pleasures and pains with rewards and punishments and the inheritance of acquired habits and structural changes provided the requisite evolutionary mechanism. Unlike Priestley's views, Erasmus Darwin's were influential, and they form an important part of the background to modern theories of evolution and learning; the theories attributed to Lamarck and developed by Herbert Spencer in the nineteenth century were very similar and extended the principles of sensation and association from the *tabula rasa* of the individual to that of the race and beyond that to the origin of species.

La Mettrie's "L'Homme machine." The materialism of Cartesian animal automatism was, in keeping with its orgin in physics, purely mechanistic; Priestley's materialism involved assimilating the attributes of mind to matter as a natural extension of Hartley's close correlation of mental associations with vibrations in the brain. The notorious "man-machine" hypothesis, developed independently by La Mettrie, was a biological recasting of these two approaches at the expense of dualist metaphysics. When La Mettrie said, "Let us boldly conclude that man is a machine," he was not denying the existence of mental functions but of mental substances: ". . . there is nothing in all the universe but a single substance diversely modified." The polemical title of his best-known work, *L'Homme machine* (1748), along with some of its more provocative passages, implied the extension of the animal-machine doctrine to man that Descartes's critics had feared a century earlier, and the outcry of La Mettrie's contemporaries was based on this reading of his book. However, this interpretation obscures the originality of his approach. The thesis of another of his works was that animals are *more than* machines. This apparent inconsistency is resolved if one appreciates that he was attempting to dispense with the traditional alternatives of materialism and spiritualism and to emphasize the evident properties of certain states of living matter.

His first attempt at interpreting the problem of mind and body was cast in Aristotelian terms, but his approach was later altered by two considerations from general biology. First, it had been found that a species of polyp had a remarkable ability to regenerate a complete organism from each of the tiny parts into which it might be divided. This implied that its soul or "vital principle" was indefinitely divisible along with its body. The controversies surrounding this discovery originated in the fear that the soul might be indistinguishable from the body and that this argument could easily be extended to man. Second, La Mettrie was impressed by early versions of the concept of irritability (the general property of living matter to respond to stimuli) and combined this with the implications of the polyp's regenerative powers to provide a rationale for the doctrine that matter is capable of activity, regeneration, sensation, motion, and all other properties usually explained by appeal to a vital principle or soul.

Although La Mettrie openly proclaimed his debt to Descartes, his views did great violence to dualism, which he dismissed as a ruse employed by Descartes to trick the theologians into swallowing the "poison" hidden in the analogy between man and the animal-machine. Animals were endowed with reason and conscience, and an ape might be taught to employ language. The result was a monistic version of the chain of being, with no break in the continuum from crude matter through plants and animals to man. "It thus appears that there is but one type of organization in the universe, and that man is the most perfect example" (*Man a Machine,* translated by Gertrude Bussey, La Salle, Ill., 1953, p. 140; cf. Vartanian ed., p. 190). The Cartesian concept of matter was thus enriched by utilizing the principle of continuity and the properties of living organisms, while the ethical and theological aspects of the Cartesian concept of mind were sacrificed. La Mettrie saw this reformulation as the obvious consequence of the demonstrated dependence of the mind on the brain and of the findings of biologists. His hypothesis put the problem squarely: prospects of advance in biology and psychology were dim unless Cartesian dualism could be transcended *without* embracing the ostensible alternative of Descartes's mechanism.

EVOLUTION, COMPARATIVE PSYCHOLOGY, AND BEHAVIORISM

The formulation and general acceptance of the theory of evolution has been the most important single factor in the debate on the mind since Descartes. The principle of continuity ceased to be merely a way of viewing the scale of beings and became a necessary consequence of the fundamental law of life. Whatever was said of men could differ only in degree from what was said of other animals. Mind ceased to be viewed primarily as an instrument for knowing and was progressively seen as an adaptive function of the organism. Psychology ceased to lie in a limbo between metaphysics, natural history, and physiology and became a biological science. Debates on the "animal soul" became irrelevant as investigators began to study the evolution of mind.

Given the general influence of evolution on the development of the comparative and functional viewpoints in psychology in the last half of the nineteenth century, the specific contribution to psychology made by Darwin's writings is curiously disappointing. With the notable exception of his incisive work in *The Expression of the Emotions in Man and Animals*, his comparative observations were more often about structures than about functions. His most extensive discussion of mental evolution is in *The Descent of Man*, where he argues forcefully that although there is an immense difference between the minds of the lowest men and the highest animals, it is still a difference of degree, not of kind. Where philosophers and theologians had artificially broadened the gap, Darwin attempted to minimize it by showing that in varying degrees animals use tools, form abstract concepts, employ language, and experience beauty and reverence. It is man's possession of a highly developed moral sense, or conscience, that constitutes his most important difference from the lower animals.

Most of Darwin's psychological remarks reveal an uncharacteristic naïvete in their use of anecdotal evidence, of excessive anthropomorphism, and of categories of analysis adopted uncritically from the association psychology. He usually referred to mental and bodily evolution as parallel processes and made no considered effort to account for the origin of mind or its physiological basis. His early notebooks contain a passage on the plausibility of considering thought as a secretion of the brain, just as gravity is a property of matter, as well as other remarks on the metaphysical bearings of evolution, but he never developed these ideas. A letter written two years before he died contains speculations on the origin of mind through the emergence of pleasure and pain as properties of certain nervous excitations, but he did not publish this account. His works contain little reference to the evolution of the organ of mind, and it was left to Huxley to provide the only extensive discussion, in an appendix to *The Descent of Man.*

The theory of evolution made the conflict between dualism and the principle of continuity perfectly explicit. T. H. Huxley faced this issue in his essay "On the Hypothesis That Animals Are Automata and Its History." His solution was to accept automatism but to argue for the continuous evolution of consciousness. The comparison of the brains of men with those of animals supported a belief in the proportional development of their functions; animal consciousness arose with the evolution of nervous structures corresponding to the human cerebrum. The development from the simplest protoplasm to reflexes, instincts, and then reason involved no demarcations, except that animals have no language or symbols. The crucial point, however, was his assertion that both animals and men are "conscious automata" of differing degrees of complexity. But what of the efficacy of mind? He argued that mind is an epiphenomenon, like the whistle on a locomotive, with no causal role in the operation of the machine; mechanical forces form a closed, causal system. Thus, Huxley rejects the theological and ethical aspects of the Cartesian doctrine, while granting the existence of consciousness.

Darwin fulfilled his claim "Much light will be thrown on the origin of man and his history," but when he turned to psychology, he was deferential: "Psychology will be securely based on the foundation already well laid by Mr. Herbert Spencer, that of the necessary acquirement of each mental power and capacity by gradation." Similarly, Darwin gave his extensive notes on instinct to George Romanes, who used them as the nucleus for his pioneer work in modern comparative psychology. Spencer spelled out the implications of uniting evolution with associationism and the study of the nervous system, and he constantly emphasized that learning is the continuous adjustment or adaptation of internal relations to external relations. Mind is a concomitant of nervous action and arose when life's adjustments reached a certain level of complexity.

Comparative psychology. Between 1890 and 1910, comparative psychologists became increasingly critical of the sentimental way in which anecdotal evidence about animal behavior had been employed to demonstrate mental continuity in evolution. There were three salutary reactions: (1) C. Lloyd Morgan attempted to restrain speculative anthropomorphism with his "canon of parsimony"— "In no case may we interpret an action as the outcome of the exercise of a higher psychical faculty, if it can be interpreted as the outcome of the exercise of one which stands lower on the psychological scale." (2) E. L. Thorndike introduced controlled, quantified experimental tests into the study of animal learning and brought comparative psychology into the laboratory. (3) Jacques Loeb attempted to extend the mechanistic principle of forced movements, or "tropisms," in plants, to account for as much animal behavior as possible. He concluded that consciousness appeared at the stage in evolution when animals began to learn from experience; "associative memory" became a widely accepted criterion for consciousness. Experiments conducted on the assumption that consciousness can be identified with trial and error learning led to the conclusion that all animals, including the amoeba, have some degree of mental life, however simple.

Although evolution, the canon of parsimony, and the development of experimental methods increased the confidence and (in most cases) the rigor of comparative psychologists, the fundamental issues had not changed since Descartes's opponents insisted that animals have minds; all that remained at stake was deciding the point on the scale where mind first appeared, and this decision reflected more about the attitudes of various psychologists than about their experimental findings. It seemed almost an elective matter whether one applied mechanism as far up the scale as possible or extended mind as far downward as was consistent with some observation or other. The context of the debate remained dualistic, and the attempt was made to infer mental states from behavior.

It soon became clear that the interpretation of the animal mind depended on an inescapable anthropomorphism— that the analogy to human experience is necessary for inferring psychic functions. Clearly, the problem with animals differs in no essential way from that of attempting to find a basis for knowing the mental processes of other men. From 1910 to 1930 two sorts of answers were proposed. First, the subjectivists saw that in order to find criteria for the ascription of mental states to other species, it would first be necessary to find a reliable index for ascribing ideas to other men. This index could then be modified and used in animal experiments. Whereas this approach begins with the concept of mind and sets out to derive methods for making the study of mind objective, the alternative—behaviorism—calls for objective methods and attempts to achieve them by abrogating the concept of mind.

Behaviorism. Behaviorism began as a methodological reform which was closely linked with a growing interest in the study of animal behavior and a growing frustration with the methods being employed in human psychology. J. B. Watson claimed that introspection in human psychology and anthropomorphism in animal psychology could never produce objective results. He proposed that the subject matter of psychology should be confined to observable behavior—movements and the stimuli which evoke them—and that psychologists should stop trying to infer mental states from the behavior of animals and men. (Later behaviorists stressed the relationship between behavior, brain function, and endocrine secretions.) Watson coupled these claims with a polemic against dualism and the concept of mind and in favor of mechanistic reduction, using the neurological concept of conditioned reflex as the paradigm for learning. The principle of the association of ideas was recast in objective form as the association of stimuli and responses. Thought was reduced to subvocal speech; language and speech remained parts of behavior but provided no basis for inference to unobservable mental events. In the hands of Watson, K. S. Lashley, and B. F. Skinner, methodological behaviorism became metaphysical behaviorism—the assertion that there are no minds and that the phenomena of behavior are reducible, without remainder, to the quantitative variables of physics and chemistry. Whereas La Mettrie and Huxley had retained consciousness as a function of matter, the behaviorists were the true heirs of Cartesian animal mechanism and extended it to man.

MECHANISM AND TELEOLOGICAL EXPLANATION

Most experimental psychologists have accepted methodological behaviorism, determinism, and epiphenomenalism, but there are a number who have insisted that metaphysical behaviorism cannot account for the purposive aspects of behavior and that stimulus-response psychology cannot completely replace the phenomena of experience. Consequently, familiar controversies have reappeared in a new guise. It has been suggested that animal behavior can be wholly explained by reflexes but that human behavior requires reference to thought or rationality. In animal psychology it has sometimes appeared that American (behaviorist) rats learn by trial and error, while European (Gestalt) rats learn by insight. In both of these cases the question is whether "getting the point" in solving a problem consists of something more than a combination of movements and rewards leading to the establishment of a habit. Do such issues involve a simple choice of explanatory paradigms, or do they point to a fundamental shortcoming of mechanistic explanation?

Throughout the debates on the animal soul or mind and its implications for man, two issues have constantly recurred: the problem of other minds and the problem of reduction of mental events to physical events. Recent developments have provided new perspectives on both issues. First, it has been shown that the solipsist position is probably not amenable to coherent statement. The ascription of consciousness to oneself presupposes ascribing it to others, and conversely. Such ascriptions require criteria (whatever they may be), which must be public. Hence, we cannot consider ourselves to be conscious unless we consider others to be so, and the argument by analogy leads both from and to our own mental states. This does not solve the further problem of finding precise criteria for ascribing consciousness, intentions, or actions to other persons or to nonlanguage-users, but it does eliminate the most serious philosophic barrier. The problem of language, moreover, remains crucial: on the one hand, evolutionary continuity means that the analogy from and to our own consciousness must extend down the evolutionary scale; on the other hand, it has been argued that the possession of a public language is a prerequisite for calling an organism rational, since the public criterion of rationality is the ability to make general statements and statements about the past. Thus, we confidently believe in continuity but cannot demonstrate it scientifically. However, this is an empirical issue, depending on advances in the study of the evolution of language in animals and our ability to translate from animal languages or protolanguages into our own.

The second issue is whether or not one wants to ascribe mental states to *any* organisms: a metaphysical behaviorist would not. Critics of the reductionist program have attempted to show that the task of specifying the elements of behavior entirely in terms of physical variables is endless unless the behaviorist assumes that the animal is seeing the stimuli and his own responses in terms of the same class concepts as the experimenter himself does. This is a prerequisite for deciding what behavior shall count as a valid test for identifying a given response or class of responses. Thus, the control techniques of behavioral experiments can produce or shape a desired response, and the experimenter can specify the contingencies of reinforcement necessary to do this. However, it is objected that in order to specify the *sufficient* conditions, the behaviorist must make an implicit or explicit appeal to congruence between the animal's behavior and concepts derived from both the experimenter's *and the animal's* consciousness. It is further argued that this analogy to subjective human psychology employs teleological and intentional concepts. Thus, some aspects of the concept of mind in animal and human psychology have not yet been shown to be entirely reducible to the units of physics and chemistry.

Cybernetics. Cybernetics (the study of communication and control in machines and living organisms) and its technological applications have helped immensely in clarifying the problem of reduction. There can be no doubt that computers and artificial automata are mechanical systems which are also adaptive; their self-regulatory features are apparently purposive, and they perform numerous operations which have traditionally been cited as evidence for mind. It is becoming increasingly clear that the problems encountered in discussing the behavior of artificial automata are strictly analogous to those involved in the traditional mind–body debate and that if minds are to be ascribed to men and animals, they must also be ascribed to some types of machines. The modern issue is thus an inversion of the traditional one. Instead of asking if animals and men have minds or are machines, we now ask if we can account for the mindlike behavior of machines in purely mechanistic terms. In this context there can be no appeal to special vital forces or separate mental substances. Yet, as with behaviorism, discussions of the self-regulating and other mindlike features of machines invariably mention some conception drawn from the analogy to human intention.

This fact points to an important inconsistency in the conceptual scheme of modern science that has plagued biology and psychology since the paradigm of materialist explanation was laid down in the seventeenth century. We are convinced that material objects are fundamental to scientific explanation and that matter and force are sufficient to produce all phenomena. However, our discussions of the adaptive features of mechanical systems (including biological ones, among which are animals and men) have invariably made reference to purposive and intentional variables which the Cartesian system restricted to the mental realm. The reaction against Cartesian animal automatism and the subsequent debate can be seen as persistent symptoms of this problem; behaviorism and cybernetics have made it necessary to face it squarely: material forces and objects are basic to both the causal and the explanatory schemes of modern science; nevertheless, materialistic explanation has so far been unable to account for all the features of adaptive systems. Mentalism cannot satisfy the requirements of the causal scheme or the objective methods of science, while Cartesian mechanism has not adequately accounted for purposive functions. At present this is a historical, rather than a philosophical, conclusion: explicit paradigms of explanation notwithstanding, the employment of the language of purpose and intention has not yet been eliminated from discussions of the functions and adaptations of certain material objects, such as nails, thermostats, computers, homeostatic systems, amoebas, monkeys, and men. Teleology has not yet been avoided; it remains to be shown that it is, in principle, unavoidable.

Whatever the outcome of this debate, we may decide that seventeenth-century mechanism involves a system of abstractions which has ceased to serve us well in investigating certain features of nature. If so, a new metaphysic will be required which selects its primitive concepts from among the following: organism, intention, adaptation, function, utility. It may be convenient to make the concept of person primitive in human psychology and the social sciences, while recognizing that it is ultimately derivative from that of organism by virtue of evolutionary continuity. To commit the pathetic fallacy with caution would thereby become a responsible scientific activity.

Bibliography

The extensive primary literature can best be approached by means of the following works, bearing in mind that the debate from Descartes through La Mettrie has been much more carefully studied than other periods: Jean A. Guer, *Histoire critique de l'âme des bêtes* (Amsterdam, 1749); Albert G. A. Balz, *Cartesian Studies* (New York, 1951); Leonora C. Rosenfield, *From Beast-Machine to Man-Machine* (New York, 1941), which is valuable as an outline and contains a bibliography; Aram Vartanian, *Diderot and Descartes* (Princeton, N.J., 1953), and his edition (with introductory monograph) of La Mettrie's *L'Homme machine* (Princeton, N.J., 1960), both of which contain excellent analyses and history of ideas; Carl J. Warden, "The Historical Development of Comparative Psychology," in *Psychological Review*, Vol. 34 (1927), 57–85 and 135–168, an introductory survey which has a bibliography from the Greeks to behaviorism; Harvey Carr, "The Interpretation of the Animal Mind," in *Psychological Review*, Vol. 34 (1927), 87–106; Gustav Bergmann, "The Contribution of John B. Watson," in *Psychological Review*, Vol. 63 (1956), 265–276; and Keith Gunderson, "Descartes, La Mettrie, Language, and Machines," in *Philosophy*, Vol. 39 (1964), 193–222, which relates animal soul to cybernetics.

The best critical histories of the philosophical issues involved in continuity and seventeenth-century mechanism as applied to biology and psychology are Arthur O. Lovejoy, *The Great Chain of Being* (Cambridge, Mass., 1936), which covers the Greeks to the eighteenth century; Edwin A. Burtt, *The Metaphysical Foundations of Modern Physical Science*, 2d ed. (London, 1932); and Alfred N. Whitehead, *Science and the Modern World* (Cambridge, 1925).

Recent philosophical discussions of mind, teleology, and cybernetics are P. F. Strawson, *Individuals* (London, 1959); Charles Taylor, *The Explanation of Behaviour* (London, 1964); and Alan R. Anderson, ed., *Minds and Machines* (Englewood Cliffs, N.J., 1964).

On the philosophical significance of symbols and language, see Ernst Cassirer, *An Essay on Man* (New Haven, 1944), and Jonathan Bennett, *Rationality* (London, 1964).

ROBERT M. YOUNG

ANIMISM. *See* MACROCOSM AND MICROCOSM; PANPSYCHISM.

ANNET, PETER (1693–1769), English freethinker and deist. By profession a schoolmaster, Annet lost his employment in 1744 because of his outspoken attacks on certain Christian apologists. A debater at the Robin Hood Society (named after a public house where the meetings were held), he soon became a popular lecturer. The first published result was a pamphlet of 1739, entitled *Judging for Ourselves: Or Free-Thinking, the Great Duty of Religion. Display'd in Two Lectures, deliver'd at Plaisterers-Hall,* "By P. A. Minister of the Gospel. With A Serious Poem address'd to the Reverend Mr. Whitefield." The tone of the work is indicated by the statement: "If the Scriptures are Truth, they will bear Examination; if they are not, let 'em go." This was followed by several tracts directly attacking Thomas Sherlock, bishop of London: *The Resurrection of Jesus Considered: In Answer To the Tryal of the Witnesses* "By a Moral Philosopher," which ran through three editions in 1744; *The Resurrection Reconsidered* (1744); *The Sequel of the Resurrection of Jesus considered* (1745); and *The Resurrection Defenders stript of all Defence* (1745).

In *Social Bliss Considered* (1749) Annet, like Milton before him, advocated the liberty of divorce. He answered Gilbert West's *Observations on the Resurrection of Jesus Christ* (1747) in *Supernaturals Examined* (1747) and George Lyttleton's *Observations on the Conversion and Apostleship of St. Paul in a Letter to Gilbert West* (1747) in *The History and Character of St. Paul examined* (1748). Arguing that all miracles are incredible, Annet proceeded to attack Old Testament history in his journal, *The Free Enquirer* (9 numbers, October 17, 1761–December 12, 1761). For this work he was accused of blasphemous libel before Lord Mansfield in the Court of King's Bench in the Michaelmas term of 1762. There is some evidence that Lord Mansfield, urged on by Bishop Warburton and others, used Annet as a scapegoat after a fruitless attempt had been made to suppress the publication of David Hume's *Four Dissertations* of 1757.

Annet pleaded guilty to the charge. "In consideration of which, and of his poverty, of his having confessed his errors in an affidavit, and of his being seventy years old, and some symptoms of wildness that appeared on his inspection in Court; the Court declared they had mitigated their intended sentence to the following, viz., to be imprisoned in Newgate for a month; to stand twice in the pillory [Charing Cross and the Royal Exchange] with a paper on his forehead, inscribed Blasphemy; to be sent to the house of correction [Bridewell] to hard labour for a year; to pay a fine of 6s.8d.; and to find security, himself to 100 £ and two sureties in 50 £. each, for his good behaviour during life." Having survived this "mitigated," charitable, and humane punishment based on the iniquitous Blasphemy Act of 1698, Annet returned to schoolmastering. Archbishop Secker is said to have so far relented as to afford aid to the culprit until his death in 1769. In 1766 Annet issued *A Collection of Tracts of a Certain Free Enquirer noted by his sufferings for his opinions*, a work containing all of the tracts mentioned above.

Annet was long thought to have been the author of *The History of the Man after God's own Heart* (1761), in which the writer took exception to a parallel drawn by a divine between George II and King David. The anonymous writer argued that such a comparison was an insult to the late king. Recent scholarship has proved that the real author was John Noorthouck, a respected member of the Stationers' Company.

Among his accomplishments, Annet was the inventor of a system of shorthand. Unlike most of the leading English deists, Annet had relatively little formal education and spoke and wrote plainly and forcefully directly to the masses. He was the last to suffer physical punishment for his heterodox religious opinions.

Bibliography

There is no collected edition of Annet's works, and the texts mentioned in the article are extremely rare. However, a useful article regarding the authorship of *The History of the Man after God's own Heart* is the anonymous "John Noorthouck, 'The Man after God's own Heart,'" in *Times Literary Supplement*, (August 25, 1945), 408.

See also *The English Reports*, Vol. 96, King's Bench Division, XXV (Edinburgh and London), 1909; and E. C. Mossner, "Hume's *Four Dissertations:* An Essay in Biography and Bibliography," in *Modern Philology*, Vol. 48 (1950), 37–57.

Ernest Campbell Mossner

ANSELM, ST., of Canterbury (1033–1109), originator of the Ontological Argument for the existence of God and one of the foremost figures of medieval theology. Anselm was born of noble family at Aosta, in Piedmont. After study in the north, he entered the Benedictine order and became prior, later abbot, of Bec. He succeeded his teacher Lanfranc as archbishop of Canterbury in 1093; his primacy was marked by a vigorous defense of the rights of the church against the king.

An Augustinian in theology, Anselm stood firmly against the anti-intellectualism of his day, holding that rational analysis of the Christian faith is not an intrinsic source of doubt and religious skepticism, but, rather, is essential to the understanding of faith and is a religious duty. This claim, and Anselm's application of it in theology, helped to initiate the high Scholasticism of the twelfth and thirteenth centuries. Anselm's own view of the relation of reason to faith is that faith provides conclusions which reason, assured of their truth, can often prove necessary—*credo ut intelligam* ("I believe in order that I may understand") in a very strong sense indeed. Anselm's arguments, therefore, are meant as compelling to any rational mind. To judge them on purely intellectual grounds is to judge them as Anselm would have had them judged.

ANSELM'S PROOFS

Among philosophers, Anselm is chiefly known for his *Monologion* and *Proslogion*, a soliloquy and a discourse, respectively, on the nature and attributes of God. It is on the *Proslogion* that his fame mainly rests, for it contains the Ontological Proof (the term is Kant's) for the existence of God. That proof has often been treated as a gem—or paste—whose worth can be judged apart from its setting; in fact, it must be understood through the *Monologion*, which provides an account of two concepts vital to it, the concepts of existence and of goodness. (For discussion of the *Proslogion*, see Ontological Argument for the Existence of God.)

The *Monologion* undertakes to prove the existence of "one Nature which is the highest of existing things . . . and which confers upon and effects in all other beings, through its unlimited goodness, the very fact of their existence is good." Two major arguments are offered.

Proof from goodness. The first proof is one from goodness, Anselm's version of an argument of the ancient Academy, that "wherever there is a better, there must be a best." (1) Certain attributes are comparative, that is, admit of degree. Goodness is such an attribute, for one thing may be as good as, better than, or less good than, another. (2) Where an attribute admits of degree, there is some element common throughout its variation; to say that a is good and that b is good is to use "good" in exactly the same sense, even though a may be better than b. This argument is restricted: it is not meant to apply to every common term of discourse, but only to comparatives. (3) That through which good things are good is a cause of their goodness; if it did not exist, good things, as good, would not exist. Anselm is offering a theory of universals and a realistic, as opposed to a nominalistic or conceptualistic, theory. (4) That which causes other things to be good must itself be good, and furthermore, supremely good; for since other things are good through it, while it is good only through itself, it can neither be equaled nor excelled by any other good thing. The universal proved to exist, then, is an exemplar: it is the cause of goodness in those things which, in Anselm's phrase, participate in it, and, as cause, itself exemplifies goodness superlatively.

Argument from existence. The second main argument of the *Monologion* is from existence. Everything that exists, exists through something. (To exist through x is to derive existence from x.) Now, it is self-evidently false to suppose that things can exist through each other—Anselm had not heard of Hegel or of "internal relations." Nor can a plurality of things exist independently, through themselves; for then each of them would have the *power* of existing through itself, and therefore all of them would exist in virtue of that power, which is one and the same. Thus there is one and only one thing such that it exists through itself, and all other things must exist through it, for to say of a thing that it exists through nothing is to say that it does not exist.

That through which other things exist is the pre-eminent existent, and exists through itself. Further, it is identical with the supreme Good. Anselm's argument of this point assumes that a thing is better if it exists through itself than if it exists through something else; since Goodness is supremely good, it must exist through itself; but what exists through itself is Existence. Therefore, Existence and Goodness are one. Anselm goes on to prove that this Supreme Being must be living, wise, powerful, true, just, blessed, and eternal, since, as the Supreme Good, it must be whatever it is absolutely better to be than not to be.

The Divine Nature, however, does not *have* these characteristics, for that would imply that it has them through something other than, and therefore higher than, itself. The Divine Nature *is* these characteristics. It is the same thing to say of God that he exists and that he is Existence, to say of him that he is good and that he is Goodness. "God is good" and "Socrates is good" are very different statements: in one, the "is" means identity; in the other, roughly, predication. Were this not true, an infinite regress, Plato's Third Man, would arise (*cf. Monologion* VI) And as there is a difference in the meaning of the copula, so there is also a difference in the meaning of the predicate; the difference is indicated by the fact that "God is good" is equivalent in sense to "God is Goodness," whereas no such equivalence holds for "Socrates is good." "Good" has a primary and a derivative use: primarily, it designates Goodness; derivatively, it designates anything that participates in Goodness. Assertions about God, then, are analogical, and the ground of the analogy lies in the fact that God is the source or cause of such absolutely good characteristics as he imparts to things. Anselm's analysis of God's nature adapted Platonic exemplarism to the needs of the Christian church.

ANSELM'S THEOLOGY

Anselm's intellectual interests were essentially theological, and his philosophical speculation was the work of a believer seeking to understand his faith. His view of the theologian's task, however, was anything but narrow. On the one hand, unlike many monastic teachers, he believed that, for all who were capable of it, rigorous reasoning must be an integral part of the quest for closer communion with God. On the other hand, he was a sensitive apologist, concerned to make dissenters and unbelievers appreciate the inherent reasonableness of Catholic Christianity.

Anselm's theology can fairly be described as a rethinking of the Augustinian tradition in the context of the Benedictine life and with a contemporary apologetic aim. While his work was obviously inspired by Augustine's synthesis of Biblical faith and Plotinian philosophy, it bears the stamp of his own original genius and contains few direct references to earlier authorities.

Method. Anselm's originality is most apparent in his characteristic use of dialectic—prompted, no doubt, by the philosophical awakening of his time but unparalleled in the theological work of his contemporaries. Augustine and other Church Fathers had already made use of metaphysical, logical, and ethical notions, borrowed or adapted from Greek philosophy, to defend and expound Christian doctrine. Anselm, however, developed a distinctive systematic method, characterized by a subtle analysis of Christian doctrines and their metaphysical presuppositions (such as truth and rectitude, necessity and liberty, possibility and impossibility), and designed to demonstrate the logical coherence of the Christian faith. An elementary example of his analytic technique, uncomplicated by theological considerations, can be seen in the dialogue *De Grammatico*, in which he introduced the Aristotelian categories in the course of his discussion of a contemporary dialectical question: whether words that occur both as concrete nouns and as adjectives (for instance, the Latin *grammaticus*, which can mean either "grammarian" or "grammatical") signify substances or qualities. Rejecting the initially appealing claim that *grammaticus* sometimes signifies a substance and sometimes a quality, he contrasted the term's direct signification of the quality with its indirect signification of a person. But there is no *thing* signified by the word when the quality is meant; it signifies only being in possession of the quality (see SEMANTICS, HISTORY OF).

Anselm's analysis of ideas sometimes derived its premises from universal human experience, as in the *Monologion*, which has its starting point in our common awareness of innumerable goods, perceived by the senses or discerned by reason. At other times he drew his conclusion from distinctively Christian premises. Thus the *Cur Deus Homo*, in which faith in Christ is put to a rational test, bases its argument on the dogmatic principles of creation, eternal life, and original sin. Taken as a whole, Anselm's work can be said to move from what we should readily identify as philosophical to more specifically Christian and theological themes. (His *Epistola de Incarnatione Verbi*, in which he defends the dogma of the Trinity against the nominalism of Roscelin, and his *De Processione Spiritus Sancti*, written in response to Greek criticisms of Latin theology, fall to some extent outside the natural line of development of his thought.) It would be misleading, however, to describe some of Anselm's writings as essentially philosophical and others as theological. From start to finish, his speculative thought is an analysis of the logical structure of Christian faith, rather than an attempt to discover religious truth by philosophical argument.

God as supreme Good. The central theme of Anselm's theology is the relation of creatures in general, and of mankind in particular, to God. From the *Monologion* and *Proslogion* and the three metaphysical dialogues (*De Veritate, De Libertate Arbitrii, De Casu Diaboli*) to the great Christological works of his later years, the same interest is unmistakable: Anselm wants to explain how the nature of creatures is related to the divine nature and what that relationship involves for human thought and behavior.

The fundamental principle of Anselm's theology is the doctrine of God as the supreme Good and the primordial Truth, self-existent and eternal. The universe is totally dependent on God's creative power, and its nature and purpose are determined by his nature and reason. The essential reality of every creature is measured by its conformity to God, the supreme and creative Truth. Insofar as creatures reflect the divine reason and will, they realize the authentic order of creaturely existence, which Anselm calls truth or rightness (*rectitudo*).

Anselm is most deeply interested in the particular forms that rightness takes in rational creatures—in angels and men. The rational creature is capable of thought, of choice, and of action, and all three capacities are subject to the same ultimate standard. The criterion of the sound mind, the good will, and the right action is its truth, its intelligible rightness, its order grounded in the divine Being itself.

The fundamental form of spiritual order is truth, the rightness of intelligence. Unless the mind is informed by the inherent rational order of God's world, right choice and action are impossible. Furthermore, it is evident that for Anselm a rational understanding of the real order of things is in itself a spiritual good.

The quality of personal life is decisively determined, however, by will and action, rather than by thought. The rational creature, whose mind can apprehend the order of God's truth and whose will can accept that order for its own decisions and actions, is obligated to maintain moral rightness or righteousness (*iustitia*) in the exercise of its freedom, which was bestowed on it for that very purpose. When it freely conforms will, word, and deed to the order of righteousness, the rational creature is right and just.

Hierarchy of goods. The actual requirements of the moral order are primarily determined by the structure of the Anselmian universe. The fundamental distinction between moral order and disorder presupposes a hierarchy of finite goods ranged beneath the supreme Good. This hierarchy is most clearly depicted in the *Monologion*, in successive affirmations of the supreme Truth and Good which is God, of the complete and adequate expression of that Truth in the divine Word, of the truth of creatures as reflecting the creative Word, and of the possession of the supreme Truth as the end of the rational creature. To live righteously is to subordinate all creaturely loves and relationships to love for God and the quest for communion with him. It is because righteousness is essentially an orientation to the supreme and transcendent Good that Anselm can see in it the supreme value of creaturely life, to be cherished for its own sake, and the gift of God, rather than a human achievement.

Anselm's major Christological works must be read in the light of this doctrine of moral order. In the *De Conceptu Virginali* Anselm presents man's actual state of subjection to sin and death as the result of the Fall, in which Adam lost for all men God's primeval gift of righteousness. In the *Cur Deus Homo* he interprets Christ's satisfaction for sin as God's reversal of the Fall; by Christ's death man is restored to that righteousness which he had lost by his own fault, yet no violence is done to the justice and order of God's treatment of his creatures. It can fairly be claimed that Anselm's analyses of the Christian gospel in the light of his reasoned theory of God and creation constitute his greatest and most influential theological achievement.

Bibliography

S. Anselmi Opera Omnia, F. S. Schmitt, ed., 6 vols. (Edinburgh, 1946–1961), is the standard edition of the Latin text.

Translations are *St. Anselm*, translated by S. N. Deane (La Salle, Ill., 1903), which includes English translations of the *Proslogion, Monologion*, Gaunilo's reply and Anselm's answer, and *Cur Deus Homo; St. Anselm's 'Proslogion,' With 'A Reply on Behalf of the Fool' by Gaunilo and 'The Author's Reply to Gaunilo,'* translated with an introduction and philosophical commentary by M. J. Charlesworth (Oxford, 1965); *The De Grammatico of Saint Anselm: The Theory of Paronymy*, Latin and English text with discussion by D. P. Henry (Notre Dame, Ind., 1964); and E. R. Fairweather, ed., *A Scholastic Miscellany: Anselm to Ockham* (Philadelphia, 1956), which contains translations of *Proslogion, Cur Deus Homo, De Conceptu Virginali* (in part), some shorter items, and an excerpt from Eadmer's memoir of Anselm.

On Anselm's theology, see J. McIntyre, *St. Anselm and His Critics* (Edinburgh, 1954).

See also R. W. Southern, *St. Anselm and His Biographer* (Cambridge, 1963).

Anselm's Life and the Proofs: R. E. ALLEN
Anselm's Theology: EUGENE R. FAIRWEATHER

ANTHROPOLOGY. *See the article on* PHILOSOPHICAL ANTHROPOLOGY.

ANTISTHENES (*ante* 443 B.C.–*post* 366 B.C.), son of an Athenian father and Thracian mother, was a pupil of the rhetorician Gorgias and an intimate and admirer of Socrates. He taught professionally at Athens, maintaining his own interpretation of Socrates against other Socratics like Plato and Aristippus. There is, however, only one reference in classical literature to Antistheneans (Aristotle, *Metaphysics* 1043b24); later antiquity saw him as a founder of Cynicism, a view that may have gained support through later historical systematization or from Stoics attempting to trace their philosophical pedigree to Socrates. Nevertheless, while the historical relationship between Antisthenes and Diogenes remains obscure, there were elements in Antisthenes' thought that heralded and may have given some impulse to Diogenes. His numerous works have not survived (a list of titles is found in Diogenes Laërtius' *Lives*, 6.15–18); but he is characterized in Xenophon, and Diogenes preserves a doxographical and anecdotal account. Antisthenes had rhetorical and sophistic interests and was famed for his style and his myths as well as for his Socratic dialogues.

The influence of Socrates shaped Antisthenes' overriding interest in practical ethics. He held happiness to be dependent solely on moral virtue, which involved practical intelligence and so could be taught, partly from a study of the names of things and definitions. But the good man also required strength of mind and character; for by contrasting external goods with the inviolability of the "wealth of the soul," Antisthenes came to stress the importance of self-control by a hostility to luxury and sensual pleasure that went some way toward Cynic asceticism. Thus, the achievement of virtue necessitated a mental and physical effort to toil through opposing difficulties, suffering, and pain. Antisthenes glorified this struggle in the myths of Heracles; and for Cynics "toil" (*ponos*) became a technical good and Heracles a saint.

Antisthenes combined a moral interest in politics with a wariness of the dangers of participation, and attacked the rules of convention when they were in opposition to the laws of virtue. He denounced famous statesmen of previous generations and outlined his own ideal king, whose pre-eminence was due to his own moral self-mastery.

Most tantalizing is the brief glimpse Aristotle affords of Antisthenes' interest in the logic of predication and definition. He denied the possibility of contradiction (*Topics* 104b21), apparently because he believed (*Metaphysics* 1024b27 ff.) that each object could be spoken of only by its own peculiar verbal designation that said what it was; i.e., words corresponded directly with reality, and since predication was confined to assigning names to things, or limited to formulae determining their real structure, any other predicative account must then refer to something different or to nothing at all, and contradiction did not arise. There was a similar difficulty with falsity. Elsewhere (*Metaphysics* 1043b23 ff.) the Antistheneans are said to have denied the possibility of defining what a thing (like silver) was; one could only explain what sort of thing it was (for instance, "like tin"). Aristotle's context referred to simple substances that could not be analyzed but only named or described. Similar problems to these occur in Plato (as in *Sophist* 251A f.; *Theaetetus* 201C ff.; *Euthydemus* 283E ff.; *Cratylus* 429B ff.). It has been argued that in one or more of these passages Plato had Antisthenes in mind, but this is not at all certain. The problems were common to the period. Interesting similarities have been pointed out between Antisthenes' logic and the nominalism of Hobbes.

Bibliography

CLASSICAL

Antisthenis Fragmenta, A. W. Winkelmann, ed. Zurich, 1842.
Diogenes Laërtius, *Lives*. 6.1–19.
Xenophon, *Symposium* and *Memorabilia*.

MODERN

Dudley, D. R., *A History of Greek Cynicism*. London, 1937.
Dümmler, F., *Antisthenica*. Halle, 1882.
Field, G. C., *Plato and His Contemporaries*. London, 1930; 2d ed., 1948.
Fritz, K. v., "Zur Antisthenischen Erkenntnistheorie und Logik." *Hermes*, Vol. 62 (1927), 453–484.
Fritz, K. v., "Antisthenes und Sokrates in Xenophons Symposium." *Rheinisches Museum*, n. F. 84 (1935), 19–45.
Gillespie, C. M., "The Logic of Antisthenes." *Archiv für Geschichte der Philosophie*, Vol. 26 (1913), 479–500; Vol. 27 (1914), 17–38.
Höistad, R., *Cynic Hero and Cynic King*. Uppsala, Sweden, 1949.
Sayre, F., *The Greek Cynics*. Baltimore, 1948.

I. G. KIDD

ANY AND ALL. The universal quantifier, commonly represented as $(x)(\cdot \cdot \cdot x \cdot \cdot \cdot)$, is used in symbolic logic to express general propositions. Ordinary language has many devices to the same purpose; to mention only affirmative forms:

(1) A tiger is an animal.
(2) The viper is a poisonous snake.
(3) Cats love mice.
(4) All men are mortal.
(5) Every paper I read ran the story.
(6) Each letter I sent was intercepted.
(7) Any doctor will tell you what to do.

These devices are not freely interchangeable. Sentences like "Any letter I sent was intercepted" and "Each cat loves mice" are ungrammatical or odd; the sentences "A paper I read ran the story" and "The letter I sent was intercepted" lack the generality of (5) and (6). No wonder, then, that in face of such linguistic complexities logicians hail the simplicity of technical notation. "Quantification cuts across the vernacular use of 'all,' 'every,' 'any' and also 'some,' 'a certain' etc., . . . in such a fashion as to clear away the baffling tangle of ambiguities and obscurities. . . . The device of quantification subjects this level of discourse for the first time, to a clear and general algorithm" (W. V. Quine, *Mathematical Logic*, pp. 70–71).

Unfortunately, the theory of quantification not only gets rid of the stylistic and linguistic ballast but leaves a good deal of the logical burden behind as well. Even if we confine our attention to the explicitly quantifying particles "each," "every," "all," and "any," we still encounter important logical differences that cannot be handled by a simple application of the theory of quantification.

"Each," "every," and "all." Let us first contrast "each" and "every" with "all." With respect to nonrelational predicates no logical difference emerges. The proposition "All these blocks are red" is true if and only if the proposition "Each (every one) of these blocks is red" is true. This is not so with relational predicates:

(8) All these blocks are similar.
(9) All these blocks fit together.

These sentences are by no means equivalent to

(10) Each (every one) of these blocks is similar to every other.
(11) Each (every one) of these blocks fits every other.

Sentence (10) does not imply (8) if, say, three blocks have the following characteristics: *ab*, *bc*, *ac*. In that case any two will be similar owing to a shared property, which makes (10) true, but there will be no property shared by all, which makes (8) false. As to (9) and (11), a jigsaw puzzle satisfies (9) but not (11), and L-shaped blocks, of which any two fit together to make a cube, satisfy (11) but not (9).

Thus, it is clear that although the generality of "each" and "every" is always distributive, that of "all" may be collective. To the same point, although "All these items cost $5" is ambiguous (do they cost $5 each or $5 together?), "Each (every one) of these items costs $5" is not. The conclusion can be supported on purely linguistic grounds, too; "All these people are similar," "All these blocks fit together," and "All these divisions make up the army" are correct sentences, but "Each (every one) of these people is similar," "Each (every one) of these blocks fits together," and "Each (every one) of these divisions makes up the army" are not. This is, of course, connected with the fact that "all" normally requires the plural form of the noun but that "each" and "every" must be followed by the singular.

Now, the theory of quantification does not discriminate between these two kinds of generality. The import of the universal quantifier is always distributive; thus, we have to look for other means to express the collective sense of "all."

"Any." Turning to "any," the first thing that strikes us is the impossibility of using it in simple indicative sentences in the present or past tense. "Any tiger lives in Asia," "I saw any tigers," and "Any doctor told me what to do" are all deviant sentences. The appropriate contexts are modal, interrogative, negative, or imperative:

(12) I can beat any one of you.
(13) Take any apples.
(14) Any doctor will tell you what to do.
(15) Did you see any birds in the cage?
(16) I did not see any birds in the cage.

Now, compare (12) with

(17) I can beat one of you.

It is clear that "any" adds some sort of generality to the indefinite "one." Sentence (17) tolerates the question "Which one?"; sentence (12) does not. Yet "any" does not amount to "every" and still less to the collective "all." I may be prepared to fight any one of you without committing myself to fight every one of you. The same holds with respect to the apples. Permitting you to take any one does not mean that you are allowed to take all or every one. The generality of "any," therefore, is neither collective nor distributive; it is the generality of indifference. Contrast the following sentences:

(18) Ask Dr. Jones, and he will tell you what to do.
(19) Ask any doctor, and he will tell you what to do.

"He" in (18) refers to Dr. Jones; "he" in (19) refers to the doctor you choose, and you are free to select any one. Thus, it is you who name the referent. Sentence (19) is something like a carte blanche warranty; you fill in the name. The same thing is true with respect to (12) and (13). "Any" offers you a choice, but after the choice is made, "any" loses its point. This explains the impossibility of using "any" in statements of fact. "I have beaten any one of you," "He took any apple," and "Any doctor told me what to do" are all ungrammatical. Facts are not free, and the function of "any" in affirmative contexts is to grant freedom of choice.

This choice need not be a singular one; "any" is compatible with more than one. Sentence (13), in fact, permits you to take more than one apple. How many? Again, this is up to you. If I ask you, "Did you take any?" you will answer in the affirmative regardless of the number you took. Had I asked, "Did you take two?" and, say, you had taken three, you would have to answer, "No, I took three." Of course, I can specify how many you may take: "Take any two (three, etc.) apples." Yet even here "any" cannot amount to "all." Suppose there are only three apples in the basket. I cannot then say, "Take any three," for to do so would preclude free selection, which, once again, is the essential presupposition in the use of "any."

Existential neutrality. Sentences (15) and (16) lead to another interesting difference between "any" and the other particles. It is obvious that (15) and (16) do not assume the existence of any birds in the cage. "Each" and "every" do. "Did you see every (each) bird in the cage?" and "I did not see every (each) bird in the cage" imply that there are some birds in the cage. This existential neutrality of "any" is put to good use in explicit questions of existence—"Are there any birds in the cage?"—and, more importantly, in contexts where the existence of appropriate subjects is problematic—"Any persons found on the premises will be prosecuted"—and in contexts that exclude such subjects—"Any letters you might have sent would have been intercepted."

Note that "all" (but not "each" or "every") can supplant "any" in the last two cases—"All persons found on the premises will be prosecuted" and "All letters you might have sent would have been intercepted."

It appears, then, that both "any" and "all" are by themselves (that is, without additional referential apparatus like "all the," "any one of these," and so on) existentially neutral; "each" and "every," on the other hand, have existential import by themselves. The affinity of "each" and "every" and of "any" and "all" is shown by the possibility of combined forms—"each and every" versus "any and all." Although "Each and every letter has been returned" has existential import "Any and all letters will be returned" does not. And the combined quantifiers cannot be exchanged.

Declarative contexts. As mentioned above, "any" does not occur in straight declarative contexts. A sentence like "Any raven is black" is somewhat odd. We can correct the situation by introducing a restrictive clause: "Any raven you may select will be black."

Now, "all" is more liberal in this respect. We do not need clauses or modalities to form the correct sentence "All ravens are black." Yet the import of the nonreferential "all" is similar to that of the nonreferential "any." First, it is existentially neutral. "All bodies not acted upon by external forces . . ."; there are no such bodies. The law is important and fertile, however. For one thing, it warrants counterfactual inferences like "If this body were not acted upon by external forces . . . ." Second, as I can *claim* that any doctor will tell you what to do but not *state* that any doctor told you what to do, so I can also *claim* that all ravens are black but cannot *state* that all ravens were black. The best I can do is "All the ravens we inspected were black," which is the same as "Each (every) raven we inspected was black."

Thus, the nonreferential "all" statement, much the same way as the nonreferential "any" statement, cannot be found true as a result of enumerative induction. Such statements always remain open, whereas statements of evidence, statements of fact, are necessarily closed. Laws are not statements of fact, and statements of facts are not laws. Consequently, "all" jumps into the breach to carry the logical import of "any" in simple declarative contexts where "any," owing to its linguistic constraints, would be out of place. And the result is the standard form of a scientific law.

Laws of science. We just saw that scientific laws cannot be verified in a straightforward sense; this, however, does not mean that they cannot be confirmed. And it is exactly in view of their confirmation that the affinity of "all" to "any" rather than to "every" becomes crucial.

The following finite model shows this. A bag contains a hundred marbles. We inspect ten at random, and all ten are red. Thus, the probability that any marble we care to pick out of the hundred will be red is very high. Yet the probability of every marble's being red remains low. If the bag contains a thousand marbles, then, given the same evidence, the probability of the latter proposition becomes much lower while that of the former will hardly change. And, obviously, if the number of marbles approaches infinity, the probability of the "every" proposition approaches zero while the probability of the "any" proposition remains substantially the same. Now, let us suppose that our evidence is mixed; we found nine red marbles and one black marble. The "any" proposition still retains a fair probability, but the probability of the "every" proposition will be zero. Any acceptable theory of probability would agree with these intuitive conclusions.

It follows that if the law

(20) All ravens are black

is taken in the sense of

(21) Every raven in the universe is black

then, no matter how large our evidence is, the law's probability will stay close to zero in view of the near infinity of ravens past, present, and future. If, however, (20) is interpreted as

(22) Any raven we may select will be black

then, given the actual evidence, its probability will be high regardless of the size of the universe and the number of ravens in it. Moreover, although an albino raven makes (21) plainly false, the probability of (22) will be only slightly affected. The scope of (22) can be extended—any two, three, and so on—as far as we care to go. Ample evidence will support us in taking larger risks.

Considering the actual practice of science, it is clear that its "all" statements are interpreted in the sense of "any" rather than that of "every." Carnap recognizes this in proposing "qualified-instance-confirmation" as the true measure of confirmation for inductive laws (*Logical Foundations of Probability*, Sec. 110 G).

Thus, the logical aspects of "any" may help us in handling problems concerning the recognition, existential import, and confirmation of lawlike propositions.

Bibliography

A more detailed treatment of the same topic can be found in Zeno Vendler, "Each and Every, Any and All," *Mind*, Vol. 71 (April, 1962), 145–160. Some other relevant passages are in W. V. Quine, *Mathematical Logic*, rev. ed. (Cambridge, Mass., 1951), Sec. 12, and *Word and Object* (New York and London, 1960), Sec. 29; Gilbert Ryle, *The Concept of Mind* (New York, 1949), Ch. 5, Sec. 2; E. S. Klima, "Negation in English," in J. A. Fodor and J. J Katz, eds., *The Structure of Language* (Englewood Cliffs, N.J., 1964); J. Nicod, *Foundations of Geometry and Induction* (London, 1930), p. 211; and Rudolf Carnap, *Logical Foundations of Probability* (London, 1950), Sec. 110 G.

ZENO VENDLER

APEIRON/PERAS. The Greek term *Apeiron*, meaning originally "boundless" rather than "infinite," was used by Anaximander for the ultimate source of his universe. He probably meant by it something spatially unbounded, but since out of it arose the primary opposite substances (such as the hot and the cold, the dry and the wet) it may have been regarded also as qualitatively indeterminate. Aristotle, summarizing the views of certain early Pythagoreans (*Metaphysics* A, 5), puts the pair *Peras* ("Limit") and *Apeiron* ("Unlimited") at the head of a list of ten opposites. *Peras* is equated with (numerical) oddness, unity, rest, goodness, and so on; *Apeiron* is equated with evenness, plurality, motion, badness. The two principles *Peras* and *Apeiron* constituted an ultimate dualism, being not merely attributes but also themselves the substance of the things of which they are predicated. From the Pythagoreans on, the opposition of *Peras* and *Apeiron* was a standard theme in Greek philosophy.

Parmenides (fr. 8, 42 ff.) seems to have accepted Limit and rejected the Unlimited for his One Being. The later Pythagoreans removed unity from the list of identities with *Peras* and argued that unity was the product of the imposition of the *Peras* upon the *Apeiron*, or else it was the source of both of them. Plato in the *Philebus* regards *Peras* and *Apeiron* as contained in all things, and supposes that it is through limit that intelligibility and beauty are manifested in the realm of Becoming. Exactly how the Ideas fit into this scheme is controversial, but in the doctrine of ideal numbers which Aristotle attributes to him Plato seems finally to have identified a material principle with the *Apeiron* and a formal principle with the *Peras*. Both principles apply to the ideal as well as to the sensible world. This leads in due course to the doctrine in Proclus (*Elementa* 89–90) that true being is composed of *Peras* and *Apeiron*, and beyond being there is a first *Peras* and a first *Apeiron*. The Christian writer known as Dionysius the Areopagite identified this doubled First Principle with God.

Infinity. The concept of infinity, for long wrongly regarded as contrary to the whole tenor of Greek classicism, was in fact a Greek discovery, and by the fifth century B.C. the normal meaning of *Apeiron* was "infinite." Infinite spatial extension was implied in the doctrines of Anaximander, Anaximenes, and Xenophanes and was made explicit by the Pythagoreans (see Aristotle, *Physics* IV, 6). Denied by Parmenides, it was reasserted for the Eleatics by Melissus (frs. 3–4) and adopted by the Atomists. Plato however (in the *Timaeus*) and Aristotle (*Physics* III) insisted upon a finite universe, and in this they were followed by the Stoics and most subsequent thinkers until the Renaissance. Aristotle had, however, admitted that infinity could occur in counting and he stated the concept clearly for the first time. He also accepted infinite divisibility (*Physics* VI), which had been "discovered" by Zeno and adopted wholeheartedly by Anaxagoras. It was rejected by the Atomists. Plato rejected it in the *Timaeus*, although he seems to have admitted it at the precosmic stage in *Parmenides* 158B–D, 164C–165C. Aristotle accepted infinite divisibility for movements, for magnitudes in space, and for time. The concept of a continuum so reached has been a basic concept in physical theory ever since. The mathematical concept of infinitesimal numbers associated with infinite divisibility and also with the doctrine of incommensurables remained important until the development of calculus in modern times.

Bibliography

Mondolfo, R., *L'infinito nel pensiero dell'antichita*, 2d ed. Florence, 1956.

Solmsen, F., *Aristotle's System of the Physical World*. Ithaca, N.Y., 1960. Ch. 8.

G. B. KERFERD

APOLOGISTS is the term used historically in reference to Christian teachers from the second century to the fourth who wrote treatises defending their religion against charges of godlessness and immorality and usually ascribing these traits to their opponents. The way had been prepared for such writings in Hellenistic Judaism when Philo of Alexandria wrote an apologetic *Hypothetica* (now lost). All his extant writings can be regarded as attempts to set forth the nature of Judaism in a way comprehensible to a Greek audience. Josephus had explained away the revolt against Rome (*History of the Jewish War*), had rewritten the history of Israel (*Antiquities of the Jews*), and had provided an explicitly apologetic defense of Judaism (*Against Apion*). In addition, fragments of apologetic sermons are preserved in the New Testament book of Acts (14.15–17; 17.22–31), and perhaps may be reflected in I Thessalonians 1.9, I Corinthians 12.2, and Romans 1.18–32. The earliest known Christian apologists, however, wrote early in the second century.

Quadratus apparently wrote at Athens in the reign of Hadrian (117–138), and the one extant fragment of his work contrasts "our Savior" with some other savior. He argues that Jesus' healings and revivifications were authentic because some of the beneficiaries survived until Quadratus' own time. The *Apology* of Aristides (second century) begins with a semi-Stoic definition of God and goes on to show that all the gods of popular cult and legend cannot be gods because their deeds or sufferings are not in harmony with the definition. Finally, Aristides provides rather faint praise of Jews and high commendation for Christians. These writings cannot have won much, if any, favor with the pagans who read them.

The principal Christian apologist of the second century was Justin (c.100–c.165), born in Samaria of Greek parents and converted to Christianity (c.130) after a fruitless quest for truth that had led him to religious-minded Middle Platonism. His education, he says, had not included many of the liberal arts; and from his account of his conversion, it is evident that he knew little about philosophy. A Christian whom he met by chance used Peripatetic arguments to indicate inconsistencies in Platonism. Justin, seeking new authority, was given the Old Testament prophecies. He had already admired the constancy of Christian martyrs; he soon became a Christian himself and instructed others, first in Asia Minor, later at Rome. He was martyred there between 163 and 167. Three of his works have survived: his *Apology*, written about 150 to show that Christians are not immoral and that Christ's life was foretold in the Old Testament; the *Dialogue With Trypho*, written about 160, developing this argument from the Old Testament; and an appendix to the *Apology*, also written about 160. His writings reflect a combination of Middle Platonism with Stoic terminology; he speaks of the divine Logos ("Word" for earlier Christians, "Reason" for Philo and the apologists), which was seminally present in some Greek philosophers but was incarnate in Christ. By working out some of the implications of this identification, Justin produced the first semiphilosophical Christian theology. It is possible that he knew something about Philo, but he cannot have understood his writings.

Justin's disciple Tatian (born c.120), who later left the church, knew little about philosophy except for odd details from philosophers' biographies, although like Justin he discussed the Logos as God's agent in creation and criticized the Stoic doctrine of fate. From Alexandria, perhaps, came the *Plea for the Christians* by Athenagoras (second century). He is the first Christian writer to reflect knowledge of the compendium of philosophical opinions apparently used in school teaching, especially by Skeptics. On the basis of earlier arguments in the schools, Athenagoras constructed a defense of the unity of God; and his later work *On Resurrection* contains a similar rearrangement of arguments from the schools to prove that God is able and willing to raise corpses, and will do so because man is a unity of soul and body. The last Greek apologist of the second century was Theophilus, bishop of Antioch, whose work in three books, *To Antolycus*, is concerned with the works of the invisible God (Philonic–Platonic arguments), God's revelation to the prophets and his six-day work of creation, and Christian ethics and the antiquity of the Jewish–Christian revelation. Theophilus used handbooks for much of his information about philosophy, but he may have read some works by Plato.

Generally speaking, the second-century apologists knew something about Platonism (that is, Middle Platonism) and Stoicism (largely the older Stoics) and made use of philosophy at points where it supported—or could be made to support—their own ideas of revelation, creation, providence, free will, divine punishment, and resurrection. They reinterpreted the Johannine "Word" as the divine Reason, instrumental in creation and revelation alike; Justin, unlike the others, used this Reason to explain how it was that some Greeks possessed inklings of the truth. The apologists also stressed the disputes among various schools in order to show how wrong the Greek philosophers usually were and how subjective their knowledge was.

At the very end of the second century an ex-lawyer named Tertullian produced two apologies in Latin. The first, *Ad Nationes*, is not very original, since much of it is derived from Varro's critique of Roman religion; the second, the *Apologeticum*, is a completely rewritten, and much more brilliant, revision of the first. Either before or after these works were published, another Latin apology, the *Octavius* of Minucius Felix, appropriated much of Cicero's treatise *De Natura Deorum* to Christian use. Both Tertullian and Minucius also made use of their Greek predecessors' writings.

Greek apologetic continued to be produced in the third century; examples include the anonymous booklet *To Diognetus*, the *Protrepticus* by Clement of Alexandria, and the highly important work *Against Celsus* by Origen, in which the author often makes use of philosophical *topoi* (commonplaces) in his argument (for instance, Platonic discussions of the divine nature; Stoic arguments in favor of providence) and reveals that he shares many presuppositions with Celsus himself. Apparently some of the writings later ascribed to Justin, such as the *Cohortatio* and the *Oration*, also come from the third century. In them we find extensive use of handbooks and a little firsthand knowledge of philosophical writings.

Stimulus for the production of further apologies was provided about 260, when the Neoplatonist Porphyry produced a work in 15 books, *Against the Christians*. Now lost because it was later proscribed, this work criticized the Old and New Testament, the apostles, and the life and thought of the church. The *Praeparatio Evangelica* of Eusebius is primarily a reply to it and to the similar work by Hierocles. In the fourth century the emperor Julian composed a work in three books, *Against the Galileans;* this was answered by Theodoret and Cyril of Alexandria, among others. Among the later Latin apologists we should mention Arnobius (died c. 330, vaguely acquainted with Neoplatonism), Lactantius (c.240–c.320, who relied extensively on Cicero), and—above all—Augustine, whose *City of God* contains much from Varro and sets forth a Christian philosophy of history in response to Porphyry and other critics.

The significance of the apologists lies not so much in what they actually wrote (their works seem to have been read chiefly within the church) but in the influence their effort had on one another's thought and on the thought of later theologians. Their criticisms of Greco–Roman philosophy compelled them not only to learn something about it but also to employ its modes of discourse and some of its axioms in expounding the nature of Christianity. It was through the apologists that philosophical theology entered, and to some measure shaped, Christian thought. To be sure, later theologians could not accept the apologists' rather naive theologies (Irenaeus, for example, learned from the apologists but also corrected some of their statements); but impetus for philosophical study was given in the apologists' works and by the school of Alexandria, whose members were more at home in philosophy, especially Platonism.

All the early apologists, and most of the later ones, admired Plato and were influenced by Middle Platonism; the work they valued most highly was the *Timaeus*, in which they found intimations of Christianity (sometimes explained as derived from the Old Testament). They usually employed traditional Stoic arguments in defense of providence and anti-Stoic arguments in opposition to fate. When they dealt with pagan mythology, they often employed the arguments of Skeptics. Their approach, then, was eclectic; and the famous statement of Justin, "Whatever has been well spoken by anyone belongs to us," had been made by eclectic philosophers. At the same time, the apologists were aware of the difference between all philosophies and their own cardinal doctrines of God (*Creator ex ouk ontōn*, "wrathful against sin"), the Incarnation, and the future corporeal resurrection. Even those apologists who were most eager to express their doctrines in philosophical modes of discourse were usually aware that the basic beliefs could not be so expressed. Theophilus, for example, defines *pistis* (faith) in a manner strongly reminiscent of the probabilism of Carneades and then provides analogies to the resurrection of the body that are based on Stoic arguments for the cosmic cycle. He admits, however, that only faith is ultimately convincing.

Bibliography

Amand, David, *Fatalisme et liberté*. Louvain, 1945.
Becker, Carl, *Tertullians Apologeticum*. Munich, 1954.
Canivet, Pierre, *Histoire d'une enterprise apologétique au Ve siècle*. Paris, 1958.
Daniélou, Jean, *Message évangélique et culture hellénistique*. Tournai, 1961.
Geffcken, Johannes, *Zwei griechisch Apologeten*. Leipzig, 1907.
Pellegrino, Michele, *Gli apologeti*. Rome, 1947.
Puech, Aimé, *Les Apologistes grecs*. Paris, 1912.

ROBERT M. GRANT

APPEARANCE AND REALITY. In *The Problems of Philosophy* Bertrand Russell referred to the distinction between appearance and reality as "one of the distinctions that cause most trouble in philosophy." Why it should cause trouble in philosophy, however, when it causes little or no trouble outside of philosophy, Russell did not say. The distinction has played an important part in the thinking of many philosophers, and some of them, including Russell, have employed it in curious ways to support odd and seemingly paradoxical claims. It may be this last fact that Russell had in mind when he spoke of trouble.

Before turning to some of its troublesome uses in philosophy, let us consider some of its relatively untroublesome uses in everyday discourse.

LOOKS AND APPEARANCES

There is a potentially troublemaking ambiguity in the term "to appear" and its cognates. (This ambiguity is not peculiar to English but is also to be found, for example, in the Greek verb *phainesthai* and its cognates.) Contrary to Russell's suggestion, the distinction between appearance and reality is not simply the distinction "between what things seem to be and what they are", more precisely, the distinction between what things seem to be and what they are is not a simple distinction. There are at least two groups of appearance idioms—what might be called "seeming idioms" and "looking idioms." The first group typically includes such expressions as "appears to be," "seems to be," "gives the appearance of being"; the second, such expressions as "appears," "looks," "feels," "tastes," "sounds."

The two groups are not always as obviously distinct as these examples make them appear to be. The same expression, particularly one from the second group (notoriously, "appears," but also such expressions as "looks as if"), may be used either as a seeming expression or as a looking expression. For example, "The oar appears bent" may mean either "The oar looks bent" or "The oar appears to be bent." These are by no means the same. I may say that the oar appears to be bent *because* it looks bent, and this is not to say that the oar appears to be bent because it appears to be bent or that it looks bent because it looks bent. Nor is there any necessary connection between the two statements—or, generally, between statements employing seeming idioms and those employing looking idioms. "The oar looks bent" does not imply or entail "The oar appears to be bent"; for the oar may look bent—immersed in water, it naturally does—without appearing to be bent. As St. Augustine put it in a striking passage in *Contra Academicos* (III, xi, 26): "'Is that true, then, which the eyes see in the case of the oar in water?' 'Quite true. For since there is a special reason for the oar's looking (*videretur*) that way, I should rather accuse my eyes of playing me false if the oar looked straight (*rectus appareret*) when dipped in water; for in that case my eyes would not be seeing what, under the circumstances, ought to be seen.'" (Compare J. L. Austin, *Sense and Sensibilia*, p. 26.) The oar's looking bent in water is not an illusion, something that appears to be the case but isn't; but this does not mean that the oar does not look bent. Conversely, "The oar appears to be bent" does not imply "The oar looks bent"; for the oar may appear to be bent without its looking bent; there may be reasons for saying that it appears to be bent (evidence that suggests that it is bent) other than its looking bent. (On this distinction, compare C. D. Broad, *Scientific Thought*, pp. 236–237.)

An example of the troublemaking neglect—or at least apparent neglect—of this distinction is to be found in Russell (*op. cit.*): "Although I believe that the table is 'really' of the same colour all over, the parts that reflect the light look much brighter than the other parts, and some parts look white because of reflected light. I know that, if I move, the parts that reflect the light will be different, so that the apparent distribution of colours on the table will change." But further on he wrote: "To return to the table. It is evident from what we have found, that there is no colour which pre-eminently appears to be *the* colour of the table, or even of any one particular part of the table—it appears to be of different colours from different points of view, and there is no reason for regarding some of these as more really its colour than others." But if all we have found is that the parts of the table that reflect the light *look* brighter than the others, it is by no means "evident" that there is no color which *appears to be* the color of the table.

Seeming idioms. Seeming idioms have nothing strictly to do with the senses; looking idioms characteristically do. From the evidence at hand, it may *appear*, or *look as if*, there will be an economic recession within the year. The characteristic uses of seeming idioms are to express what one believes is probably the case, to refrain from committing oneself, or to express hesitancy about what *is* the case. (Compare G. J. Warnock, *Berkeley*, p. 186: "The essential function of the language of 'seeming' is that it is noncommittal as to the actual facts.") Hence, "I know that *X* is *Y*, but it appears (to me) that it is not *Y*" is odd or paradoxical in much the same way as is "I know that *X* is *Y*, but it may not be the case that it is." From "*X* appears to be *Y*" (though *not* "merely appears to be *Y*"), I cannot validly infer either "*X* is *Y*" or "*X* is not *Y*." But "*X* appears to be *Y*" entails that it is possible that *X* is *Y* and possible that *X* is not *Y*.

The same is not true of looking idioms, except in so far as they double as seeming idioms. No oddity or paradox is involved in saying such things as "I know that the two lines in Müller-Lyer's drawing *are* the same length, but one of them still *looks* longer than the other."

Looking idioms. Looking idioms have a number of uses or senses which must be kept distinct.

Noticing resemblances. To notice that an inkblot has the appearance of (looks like) a face or that Alfredo's voice sounds like Caruso's is to note a visible resemblance between the inkblot and a face or an audible resemblance between Alfredo's voice and Caruso's. Here appearance does not normally contrast with what is possibly reality; rather it is a reality. "Alfredo's voice sounds like Caruso's" does not mean either "Alfredo's voice appears to be Caruso's" or "Alfredo's voice (merely) sounds like Caruso's, but it isn't Caruso's voice." To be sure, in certain circumstances one might be misled by appearances. For instance, by the audible resemblance between Alfredo's voice and Caruso's one might suppose that he was hearing Caruso's voice. Compare, however, "At a distance (in this light, at a quick glance) that looks like blood (a dollar bill), but it's really just red paint (a soap coupon)."

Describing. To describe something's appearance may merely be to describe its perceptible (visible, audible, tactile) features, and as such it is to describe how something *is*, not how it looks or appears as possibly *opposed* to how it is. Here the *apparent* qualities of something are the *real* perceptible qualities of it. To describe a man's appearance, as opposed, say, to his character, is to describe those features of him (his "looks") that he can be seen to possess. Appearances in this sense are what are most often referred to as phenomena in the nonphilosophical use of the latter term, in such phrases as "biological phenomena."

"Looks" and "merely looks." The phrase "mere appearance" ("merely looks, sounds") shows that there is a sense of "appears" as a looking idiom which is neutral with respect to how things are. "*X* merely looks red (to me, or under such-and-such conditions)" implies that *X* is not (really) red. But simply from "*X* looks red (to me, or under such-and-such conditions)" I cannot validly infer either that *X* (really) is red or that *X* (really) is not red. If it is possible, however, for *X* to look (sound, feel, taste) *Y*, it must at least be possible for *X* (really) to be *Y*. This logical feature of looking idioms, which—in this sense—they share with seeming idioms, may be the source of some confusion between them.

PROTAGOREAN RELATIVISM

According to Plato (*Theaetetus*, 152; Cornford trans.), Protagoras held that "man is the measure of all things—alike of the being of things that are and of the non-being of things that are not." And by this he meant that "any given thing is to me such as it appears to me, and is to you such as it appears to you." This statement can be read in two different ways, depending on whether "appears" is construed as a seeming idiom or a looking idiom. In either interpretation, however, it is a paradox or else a tautology.

Expressions such as "is for me" and "is for you" are distinctly odd, and one is puzzled to know what to make of them. If they are construed to mean the same as "is," Protagoras' statement then becomes manifestly paradoxical. For if "*X* appears to me to be *Y* (or looks *Y* to me)" and "*X* appears to you to be *Z* (or looks *Z* to you)" are equivalent respectively to "*X* is *Y*" and "*X* is *Z*," where *Y* and *Z* represent logically incompatible predicates, then the joint affirmation of two (possibly) true propositions, "*X* looks *Y* to me" and "*X* looks *Z* to you," would be equivalent to the necessarily false proposition that *X* is both *Y* and *Z*.

On the other hand, if we interpret "is for me" to mean the same as "appears to me" and "is for you" as "appears to you," Protagoras' dictum reduces to a tautology. For if

"*X* appears to me to be *Y*" and "*X* appears to you to be *Z*" are equivalent respectively to "*X* is *Y* for me" and "*X* is Z for you," then, even if *Y* and *Z* represent logically incompatible predicates, the equivalent statements can be substituted for one another. In that case, Protagoras' dictum, generalized, reduces to either "Everything is for any given person such as it is for that person" or "Everything appears to any given person such as it appears to that person." But since the two statements are themselves equivalent, the effect of Protagoras' dictum is to obliterate any possible distinction between appearance and reality, or to claim what is clearly false, that there is no such distinction.

Protagoras' statement can be read in yet another way, but read in that way it is also a truism. The Greek verb *phainesthai*, especially with the participle, was used to state, not that something (merely) appears to be so, but that something manifestly is so. Read in this way, Protagoras' claim that appearance is reality is simply the claim that what is manifestly the case is the case. This innocent truism may have been intended to remind those of Protagoras' contemporaries who contemned the common run of men for living by appearances, which they equated with error, that what is reliably observed to be the case is justifiably said to be the case.

THE ARGUMENT FROM ILLUSION

What has been called the "argument from illusion" has been used by many philosophers (for example, Berkeley in *Three Dialogues, I*, and A. J. Ayer in *Foundations of Empirical Knowledge*, pp. 3–5) to justify some form of phenomenalism or subjective idealism. The argument rests on the fact that things sometimes appear (for example, look) different to different observers or to the same observer in different circumstances. This fact is supposed to show that sensible qualities, such as colors or odors, are not really "in" things. For if things can, say, look one color when they are (supposedly) really another, then we can never say what color they really are, what color really "inheres" in them. For all sensible qualities, as Berkeley put it, "are equally apparent"; he seems to have meant that for every putatively veridical perception there is a possible corresponding illusory one (or wherever it is possible that "*X* is *Y*" is true, it is equally possible that "*X* merely looks *Y*" is true). Hence, given any perception, *P*, it is possible that *P* is veridical and possible that *P* is illusory. But since there is no apparent or observable difference between a veridical *P* and an illusory *P*, we cannot in principle tell which it is. We cannot, for example, say what colors things *are;* we can only say what colors they *look*.

The consequence of this argument is the same as that of Protagoras' dictum, namely, to obliterate in principle any distinction between "is" and "(merely) looks or sounds." But this is a distinction on which the argument itself rests: if the distinction cannot, in principle, be made, then the argument cannot get off the ground; but if the distinction can, in principle, be made, the conclusion of the argument cannot be true. (For more on this argument, see ILLUSION.)

"Is Y" as a function of "appears Y." Many philosophers who have used the argument from illusion have attempted to resist the consequence that there is then no distinction between "is" and "(merely) looks." Berkeley, for example, protested that "the distinction between realities and chimeras retains its full force" (*Principles of Human Knowledge,* §34). He was able to suppose that it does because he supposed that "*X* is *Y*" is a logical function of "*X* appears (appears to be *or*, for example, looks) *Y*": when the appearances of *X* are not only "lively" but "steady," "orderly," and "coherent," we say that *X is* (really) *Y* and not that it merely *appears* *Y*. Being is orderly and coherent appearing (*Principles,* §29).

But if this is so, the distinction between realities and chimeras does not retain its full force. "*X* appears *Y* consistently (steadily, in an orderly and coherent way)" neither is equivalent to, nor does it entail, "*X* is *Y*"; for it is possible that the former is true while the latter is false. The truth of the former may be *evidence for* the truth of the latter, but the latter is not a logical function of the former. (Compare Warnock, *op. cit.*, pp. 180–182.) The same holds for such claims as that of G. E. Moore (*Commonplace Book*, p. 145) that "'This book is blue' = This book looks (or *would* look) blue to normal people . . . who look at it by *good* daylight at *normal distances,* i.e. not too far off or too near."

PHENOMENA AND THINGS-IN-THEMSELVES

One of the foundation stones of Kant's philosophy is the claim that "we can know objects only as they *appear* to us (to our senses), not as they may be in themselves" (*Prolegomena*, §10.) Read in one way, Kant's claim is tautologous. If by "an appearance" we mean a possible object of knowledge and by "a thing-in-itself" something that can be "thought" but cannot be known, the claim reduces to "What we can know, we can know; and what we cannot know, we cannot know." As such, this tells us nothing about the limits of knowledge, about what we can know, any more than "God can do everything that it is possible for God to do" tells us anything about the extent of God's powers.

Kant may, however, have meant the following: I can know that *X* is *Y* only if *X* can appear (to be) *Y*; if, in principle, *X* cannot appear (to be) *Y*, then I cannot know that *X* is *Y*. This, too, is a truism. But it does not follow from this that "the things we intuit are not in themselves what we intuit them as being. . . . As appearances, they cannot exist in themselves, but only in us" (*Critique of Pure Reason*, A42; Kemp Smith trans.). That is, it does not follow that *X* as it appears is not what it is apart from how it appears; nor does it follow that what *X* is apart from how it appears is different from how it appears. To allow Kant's inference is implicitly to endorse a paradox or to adopt a new use of "appears" to which no sense has been given. For if something appears (to be) so, it must be *possible* for it to *be* so "in itself"; and this is precisely the possibility which Kant does not allow.

Appearances of the impossible. Closely related to Kant's distinction between appearances and things-in-themselves is the notion of appearances of the impossible. According to Parmenides and Zeno, multiplicity and motion, empty space and time, are impossible; yet things appear to be many, some of them appear to move, and so on. Similarly, for Leibniz bodies with their qualities, such as colors, are well-founded appearances (*phaenomena bene fundata*), mere appearances "grounded" in monads and their perceptions; in reality there can be no such things as colored bodies. And according to F. H. Bradley in *Appearance and Reality*, space, time, motion and change, causation, things, and the self are "unreal as such" because they "contradict themselves"; hence, they are "mere appearances" or "contradictory appearances."

Taken at face value, this view is blatantly paradoxical: if for something to appear (to be) the case it must be *possible* for it "really" to be the case, then if it is *impossible* for it to be the case, it is impossible for it to appear (to be) the case. (Compare Morris Lazerowitz, *The Structure of Metaphysics*, pp. 208–209.) The metaphysician of "contradictory appearances," however, may mean that for certain kinds of things, *t*, it is *never* permissible to say "There are *t*'s," but only "There appear to be *t*'s." But this, as Lazerowitz has pointed out (*op. cit.*, esp. p. 225), has the consequence of obliterating the distinction between "is" and "appears" and hence of depriving "appears" of its meaning. For if "There are *t*'s" is in principle disallowed, "There appear to be *t*'s" loses its sense.

Bibliography

Augustine, St., *Contra Academicos*. Translated by John J. O'Meara as *Against the Academics*. Westminster, Md., 1951.

Austin, J. L., *Sense and Sensibilia*. Oxford, 1962.

Ayer, A. J., *The Foundations of Empirical Knowledge*. London, 1940.

Berkeley, George, *A Treatise concerning the Principles of Human Knowledge*. Dublin, 1710.

Berkeley, George, *Three Dialogues Between Hylas and Philonous*. London, 1713.

Bradley, F. H., *Appearance and Reality*, 2d ed. Oxford, 1897.

Bradley, F. H., *Essays on Truth and Reality*. Oxford, 1914. Ch. 9.

Broad, C. D., *Perception, Physics and Reality*. Cambridge, 1914. Ch. 2.

Broad, C. D., *Scientific Thought*. London, 1923. Part 2.

Chisholm, R. M., *Perceiving: A Philosophical Study*. Ithaca, N.Y., 1957.

Chisholm, R. M., "The Theory of Appearing," in *Philosophical Analysis*, Max Black ed. Ithaca, N.Y., 1950. Pp. 102–118.

Chisholm, R. M., "Theory of Knowledge," in his *Philosophy*. Humanistic Scholarship in America, The Princeton Studies. Englewood Cliffs, N.J., 1964. Pp. 233–344.

Kant, Immanuel, *Critique of Pure Reason*. Translated by Norman Kemp Smith. London, 1919.

Lazerowitz, Morris, "Appearance and Reality," in his *The Structure of Metaphysiçs*. London, 1955. Ch. 10.

Lean, Martin, *Sense-Perception and Matter*. London, 1953.

Moore, G. E., "The Conception of Reality," in his *Philosophical Studies*. London, 1922. Ch. 6.

Moore, G. E., *The Commonplace Book 1919–1953*. London, 1962. Passim.

Plato, *Theaetetus*. Translated by F. M. Cornford as *Plato's Theory of Knowledge*. London, 1935.

Price, H. H., "Appearing and Appearances." *American Philosophical Quarterly*, Vol. 1 (1964), 3–19.

Price, H. H., *Perception*. London, 1932.

Prichard, H. A., "Appearances and Reality." *Mind*, Vol. 15 (1906), 223–229.

Russell, Bertrand, *The Problems of Philosophy*. London, 1912. Ch. 1.

Ryle, Gilbert, *The Concept of Mind*. London, 1949. Ch. 7.

Sibley, Frank, "Aesthetics and the Looks of Things." *The Journal of Philosophy*, Vol. 16 (1959), 905–915.

Taylor, A. E., *Elements of Metaphysics*. London, 1903. Bk. 2, Ch. 3.

Warnock, G. J., *Berkeley*. London, 1953. Ch. 9.

Wollheim, Richard, *F. H. Bradley*. London, 1959. Ch. 5.

W. E. KENNICK

APPERCEPTION is usually defined as the mental process which raises subconscious or indistinct impressions to the level of attention and at the same time arranges them into a coherent intellectual order. However, the term "apperception" has been used ambiguously, sometimes to mean merely consciousness or awareness, at other times to mean the acts of concentration and assimilation. Inevitably, a process of such significance has implicitly and explicitly been dealt with by philosophers ever since they first concerned themselves with the cognitive process. Aristotle, the Church Fathers, and the Scholastics all distinguished between vague notions and feelings on the one hand, and conceptions brought about by an act of intellectual willing on the other.

Descartes. The concept of apperception (in the form of the verb *apercevoir*) appears in Descartes's *Traité des passions*.

Later writers generally use the term "perception" for denoting a state of dim awareness. So Locke believes that perception is "the first step and degree towards knowledge, and the inlet of all materials of it. . . ." It "is in some degree in all sorts of animals" (*Essay Concerning Human Understanding*, Book II, Ch. 9). On the other hand, apperception denotes a state of conscious or reflecting awareness.

In contrast, Descartes makes no distinction between the two. But he stresses the volitional element (which he calls passion) in the cognitive process: "For it is certain that we would not even know how to will something, unless we had apperceived it by the same medium by which we will. And just as one can say with regard to our soul that willing is a form of action, so one can also say that there is in the soul an element ["passion"] by which it apperceives that which it wills" (*Traité des passions*).

Leibniz. It was Leibniz who introduced the concept of apperception into the more technical philosophical tradition. In his *Principes de la nature fondés en raison et de la grâce* he says: "One should distinguish between *perception*, which is an inner state of the monad reflecting the outer world, and *apperception*, which is our conscious reflection of the inner state of the monad."

For the understanding of Leibniz' ideas about perception and apperception, one should also refer to his *Nouveaux Essais sur l'entendement humain*, which contain a discussion of Locke's *Essay Concerning Human Understanding*. There Leibniz objects to Locke's *tabula rasa* theory, according to which "there are no innate principles in the mind" (Book I, Ch. 2). Leibniz' insistence on innate mental powers had a decisive influence on the idealism of Kant and Herbart.

Kant. The concept of apperception was taken up by Kant in his *Critique of Pure Reason*. There he distinguished between empirical apperception, the person's awareness of himself which depends on the changing conditions of his consciousness, and transcendental apperception, or "pure reason," the inner, unchangeable fundamental, and therefore "transcendental" unity of consciousness. This transcendental unity of consciousness precedes all data of perception and makes possible their inner order and meaning ("Transcendental Logic," Para. 12). It consists of the ideas of space and time, which are not objects of perception but modes of perceiving, and a number of categories which Kant orders under the headings of quantity, quality, relation, and modality. Kant's attempt to organize these categories and their subcategories according to a symmetrical scheme has been generally rejected as artificial. However, Kant's rejection of the opinion that our conscious reasoning about the world reflects the world as it really is remains as one of the great epistemological problems in his concept of apperception.

Idealists. The self-critical quality in Kant's philosophy was not heeded by romantic idealists impatient to achieve a complete insight into the essence of all existence. Thus Fichte turned Kant's self-critical concept of apperception into the absolute self; Hegel developed logical idealism; and Schelling maintained in his philosophy of identity that the evolution of mind or consciousness is nothing but the evolution of ultimate reality from its prerational and groping state of willing toward self-consciousness and self-direction, toward the discovery of its inherent and universal laws. Whatever we think about Schelling's lofty speculation, it led its author to the understanding of myth. For in myth, so Schelling concluded, the human mind in its prerational state creates its first perceptions of reality in the form of artistic intuition and imagery. Myth, so we could say with Schelling, is not untruth but pretruth. About half a century later, following Schelling's lead, Wilhelm Wundt became one of the foremost interpreters of prerational or mythical thinking.

Herbart. In contrast with the romanticists, Kant's successor, Johann Friedrich Herbart, insisted on a less romantic and more empirical interpretation of the transcendentalist position. However, in the second part of his *Psychologie als Wissenschaft*, Herbart characterizes the gift of apperception as one—though not the only one—of the qualities that distinguish man from animal because it gives him the power of reflection. In the human soul, so Herbart says, there are operating series of presentations, combinations, and whole masses of perceptions which are sometimes completely and sometimes incompletely interwoven, in part conforming and in part opposed to each other. It is the function of apperception to assimilate the various and often divergent ideas. In this process the older apperceptive mass, consisting of concepts, judgments, and maxims, will tend to assimilate more recent and less settled impressions. No one, however, can measure how strong the older apperceptive mass must be in order to fulfill effectively the function of assimilation.

Obviously, the power of apperception as conceived by Herbart is closely related to a person's inner stability, self-consciousness, and self-identity. Apperception requires will and attention in order to function adequately. A mentally sick person will be unable to perform it.

Inevitably, the concept of apperception plays a decisive role in Herbart's pedagogical theory. In his *Allgemeine Pädagogik aus dem Zweck der Erziehung Abgeleitet*, Herbart emphasizes the obligation of the teacher to arrange the course of instruction in such a way that the new material can be properly integrated with the already available store of knowledge. If the two fall apart, the learner cannot assimilate the new experience and will feel frustrated.

Wundt. The qualities of will and attention, which from Descartes to Herbart were emphasized as inherent in the apperceptive process, are still more accentuated by Wilhelm Wundt. In his *Grundriss der Psychologie*, Wundt distinguishes between passive apperception, in which the consciousness simply accepts impressions, and active apperception, in which the new impression is met by an emotional state of tension followed by a sense of satisfaction. Furthermore, in all apperception a personifying element is at work in that the apperceived objects are colored by the mode of the apperceiving subject. This is the reason why we tend to identify apperceived objects with our own form of existence. The most obvious historical example of this tendency is myth, in which, for example, animals, the forces of nature, and the gods appear in anthropomorphic transfiguration.

Entirely in the spirit of Wilhelm Wundt is the following (freely translated) passage from the well-known *Grundriss der Geschichte der Philosophie seit Beginn des neunzehnten Jahrhunderts:*

> There is nothing inside and outside of man which he could call totally his own but his will . . . . Hence, looking for the terminus of individual psychological regression, we discover the *inner will* or the *pure apperception*, which is not in a state of quiet, but in a state of never resting activity. The apperceptive will is not an a-posteriori conception, but an a-priori, postulated by reason, a transcendental quality of the soul, postulated by empirical psychology as the ultimate source of all mental processes, yet at the same time beyond the competence of the empirical psychologist.

The deeper unity. In quoting the foregoing passage (omitted in later editions of Ueberweg-Heinze) we have already indicated the deeper unity that in spite of all differences underlies the apperception theories of Leibniz, Kant, Herbart, and Wundt. They predicate a transcendental element, or an inherent logos, in the human process of cognition because they are convinced that there is no other explanation for its uniting and ordering capacity. They belong, in the wide sense of the term, to the "idealistic" tradition of the *philosophia perennis*, although they are in no way opposed to painstaking empirical and statistical inquiry, as the examples of Herbart and Wundt prove.

However, in postulating a transempirical factor as the condition of experience, they expose themselves to the reproach of mysticism by the empiricist. And there can be no doubt that the modern experimental, associationist, and behaviorist schools have made us more critical of psychological concept. However, it still seems to many contemporary philosophers and psychologists that a purely empirical account of knowledge is inadequate and that in order to achieve a defensible position it is necessary to have recourse to nonempirical factors such as apperception.

Bibliography

In addition to the works cited in the text, the following may be consulted: Benno Erdmann, "Zur Theorie der Apperzeption," in *Vierteljahrsschrift für wissenschaftliche Philosophie,* Vol. 10 (1886), 307 ff.; Karl Lange, *Ueber Apperception,* 6th rev. ed. (Leipzig, 1899), translated by E. E. Brown (Boston, 1893); L. H. Lüdtke, "Kritische Geschichte der Apperzeptionsbegriffs," in *Zeitschrift für Philosophie* (1911); Hugo Münsterberg, *Grundzüge der Psychologie* (Leipzig, 1900), pp. 436–457; G. F. Stout, "Apperception and the Movement of Attention," in *Mind,* Vol. 16 (1891), 23–53, and *Analytic Psychology* (London, 1896); and Friedrich Ueberweg, *Grundriss der Geschichte der Philosophie seit Beginn des neunzehnten Jahrhunderts,* Max Heinze, ed., 10th ed. (Berlin, 1902).

ROBERT ULICH

A PRIORI, LINGUISTIC THEORY OF THE. *See* LINGUISTIC THEORY OF THE A PRIORI.

A PRIORI AND A POSTERIORI. The distinction between the a priori and the a posteriori has always been an epistemological one; that is to say, it has always had something to do with knowledge. The terms "a priori" and "a posteriori" are Scholastic terms which have their origin in certain ideas of Aristotle; but their use has been considerably extended in the course of history, and their present use stems from the meaning given to them by Kant. The terms literally mean "from what is prior" and "from what is posterior." According to Aristotle, *A* is prior to *B* in nature if and only if *B* could not exist without *A; A* is prior to *B* in knowledge if and only if we cannot know *B* without knowing *A*. It is possible for these two senses of "prior" to have an application in common; substance, for example, is prior to other things in both of these senses and in others. It follows that to know something from what is prior is to know what is, in some sense, its cause. Aristotle believed that it is possible to demonstrate a causal relationship by means of a syllogism in which the term for the cause is the middle term. Hence, to know something in terms of what is prior is to know it in terms of a demonstrable causal relationship. To know something from what is posterior, on the other hand, can involve no such demonstration, since the knowledge will be inductive in form.

The transition to Kant's conception of the matter is evident in Leibniz. According to the latter, to know reality a posteriori is to know it from what is actually found in the world, that is, by the senses, by the effects of reality in experience; to know reality a priori is to know it "by exposing the cause or the possible generation of the definite thing" (*Nouveaux Essais*, Bk. III, Ch. 3). It is also possible to speak of a priori proofs. As a general consequence of this, Leibniz could distinguish between "truths a posteriori, or of fact," and "truths a priori, or of reason" (*Ibid.*, Bk. IV, Ch. 9); for a priori truths can be demonstrated in terms of their being based on identical propositions, while a posteriori truths can be seen to be true only from experience. Thus the distinction between the a posteriori and the a priori comes to be a distinction between what is derived from experience and what is not, whether or not the notion of the a priori also has the notion of demonstration in terms of cause or reason associated with it. Such is the distinction in Kant, and it has remained roughly the same ever since. Since in Kant there is no simple opposition between sense experience and reason (there being also the understanding), it is not possible to express the distinction he laid down as one between what is derived from experience and what is derived from reason.

The distinction, then, is roughly equivalent to that between the empirical and the nonempirical. Kant also connected it with the distinction between the necessary and the contingent, a priori truths being necessary and a posteriori truths contingent. But to assume without further argument that the two distinctions coincide in their application is to assume too much. The same is true of the distinction between the analytic and the synthetic; this too cannot be assimilated without argument to that between the a priori and a posteriori. Whether or not these distinctions coincide in their applications, they certainly cannot have the same meaning. The distinction between the a priori and a posteriori is an epistemological one; it is certainly not evident that the others are.

THE DISTINCTION APPLIED TO CONCEPTS

The distinction between the a priori and the a posteriori has been drawn not only in connection with truths or propositions but also in connection with concepts. Indeed, some truths are doubly a priori; not only is their truth knowable independently of experience but the concepts which they involve are similarly independent of experience. The distinction between a posteriori and a priori concepts may seem a perspicuous one; for it may be thought to be a distinction between concepts which we derive from experience by building them up therefrom and concepts which we have independently of experience. It has sometimes been said also that the latter concepts are innate ideas, with which we are born, so that we have no need to acquire them. But the question whether ideas are innate or acquired seems to be one of psychology, as is the question of how we acquire ideas if we do. The distinction under consideration, being an epistemological one, has no direct connection with psychology. A concept which is independent of experience may or may not be innate; and although it cannot be acquired directly from experience, it may still be that experience is in some way a necessary condition of our having the concept. What then does it mean to say that a concept is independent of experience? The answer must be in terms of the validation of the concept.

It may be assumed for present purposes that a concept is what is meant by the corresponding term (although this may not be a fully adequate view and bypasses the question whether concepts are independent of words). To have a concept will thus at least be to understand the corresponding term. Perhaps, then, an a posteriori concept is one expressed by a term understandable purely in terms of experience, and an a priori concept one which does not satisfy this condition. The point has sometimes been made by saying that an a posteriori, or empirical, concept or term is one which is cashable in terms of sense experience. This is of course a metaphor, and what it means is that the meaning of empirical terms can be given by definitions which must ultimately depend on ostensive definitions only. Ostensive definitions are those which provide the definition of a term by a direct confrontation with experience. To define a term ostensively it is necessary only to repeat the expression together with some form of pointing to the object or phenomenon in question. It is highly questionable, however, whether any performance of this kind could ever constitute definition as such. For the meaning of a word to be taught in this way there would have to be (as Wittgenstein in effect pointed out at the beginning of his *Philosophical Investigations*) a previous understanding that the noise made was a word in a language and in a language of a definite sort. Furthermore, it would have to be understood what sort of term was being defined—whether it was descriptive and, if so, what range of phenomena it was being used to describe. If all this must be understood, it can scarcely be said that the term in question is defined purely by reference to sense experience.

Nevertheless, there is some distinction to be made here. Even if terms like "red" cannot be defined purely by reference to experience, they could not be understood fully without experience, for example, by someone who does not possess and never has possessed sight. There is a sense in which the blind *can*, up to a point, understand terms like "red," in that they can know that red is a color and even a color of a certain sort related to other colors in certain ways. But since they cannot know when to apply the term in fact, there is an obvious sense in which they do not have a full understanding of it—and the same applies to the notion of color itself. A posteriori terms and concepts may thus be defined as those that directly require our having experience in order for us to apply them or those that can only be fully understood by reference to terms that directly require our having experience to apply them. Whether or not a creature without experience could ever come to have a concept such as, for example, validity, it is clear that being able to apply the concept does not directly require experience. This may afford the basis of a distinction between a posteriori and a priori concepts. There may be various views about a priori concepts, concerning, for example, whether they are to be restricted to concepts of, or concepts involved in, mental operations on a posteriori concepts. Empiricists have in general held that the only a priori concepts are those which express relations of ideas. The field is thus restricted to the concepts of logic and mathematics.

THE DISTINCTION APPLIED TO PROPOSITIONS

In a sense, the distinction between concepts presupposes the distinction between propositions, since concepts can be applied only in propositions. According to the rough criteria already mentioned, an a priori proposition will be one whose truth is knowable independently of experience. It may be questioned, however, whether there are any truths which can be known if the subject has no experiences whatever. Hence, the matter is better put in terms of the validation of the proposition in question, in terms of its verification or falsification. It has sometimes been suggested that a proposition is a priori if its truth is ascertainable by examination of it alone or if it is deducible from such propositions. An a priori proposition would thus be one which provides its own verification; it is true in itself. This account is too restrictive, since there may be propositions whose truth is ascertainable by argument that makes no reference to empirical matters of fact, but which may not be deducible from any propositions of the kind previously mentioned. That is to say, there may be circumstances in which it is possible to validate propositions by argument that makes no reference to matters of fact discoverable by experience. Empiricists have generally denied this, but the possibility of what Kant called "transcendental arguments" cannot be so lightly dismissed. Aristotle's argument for the truth of the principle of contradiction would be a case in point, namely, that a denial of it already presupposes it.

On the other hand, to say simply that a priori propositions are those whose truth can be discovered without reference to experience is too wide a definition. For, it may be argued that the terms in which many such propositions are expressed could only be fully understood by reference to experience. A proposition may be a priori without its involving terms which are without exception a priori. It was for this reason that Kant distinguished between a priori and *pure* a priori judgments; only in the latter are all the terms a priori. In view of this, an a priori proposition may be defined as one whose truth, given an understanding of the terms involved, is ascertainable by a procedure which makes no reference to experience. The validation of a posteriori truths, on the other hand, necessitates a procedure that does make reference to experience.

Can analytic propositions be a posteriori? It has already been mentioned that Kant superimposed upon the a priori–a posteriori distinction the distinction between the analytic and the synthetic. There are difficulties involved in defining this latter distinction, but for present purposes it is necessary to note that Kant assumed it impossible for analytic judgments to be a posteriori. He does this presumably on the grounds that the truth of an analytic judgment depends upon the relations between the concepts involved and is ascertainable by determining whether the denial of the judgment gives rise to a contradiction. This latter procedure is surely one which makes no reference to experience. Kant is clearly right in this. As already seen, it is not relevant to object that since analytic judgments, propositions, or statements need not involve purely a priori terms, evaluation of the truth of some analytic propositions will involve reference to experience; for in determining whether a proposition is a priori, it is necessary to take as already determined the status of the terms involved. It is similarly irrelevant to maintain that it is sometimes possible to come to see the truth of an analytic proposition through empirical means. It may be possible, for example, for a man to realize the truth of "All bachelors are unmarried men" as an analytic proposition as a consequence of direct experience with bachelors. But this consequence will be an extrinsic one. That is to say that while the man may attain this insight in this way, it will be quite accidental; the validity of the insight does not depend upon the method by which it is acquired. That is why the definition of an a priori proposition or statement involves the idea that its truth must be ascertainable without reference to experience. As long as a nonempirical procedure of validation exists, the proposition in question will be a priori, whether or not its truth is always ascertained by this procedure. It is quite impossible, on the other hand, for an a posteriori proposition to be validated by pure argument alone.

Must a posteriori propositions be contingent? Given that all analytic propositions are a priori, it is a further question whether all synthetic propositions must be a posteriori. This is a hotly debated question, with empiricists maintaining that they must be. But first it is necessary to consider the relation between the a priori–a posteriori dichotomy and the necessary–contingent one.

Kant certainly associated the a priori with the necessary, and there is a prima facie case for the view that if a proposition is known a posteriori, its truth must be contingent. For how can experience alone tell us that something must be so? On the other hand, it might be maintained that we can learn inductively that a connection between characteristics of things holds as a matter of necessity. Some philosophers maintain that natural laws represent necessary truths, and they do not all think this incompatible with the view that natural laws can be arrived at through experience. What is sometimes called intuitive induction—a notion originating in Aristotle—is also something of this kind; we see by experience that something is essentially so and so. An even greater number of philosophers would be willing to assert that, in *some* sense of the word "must," experience can show us that something must be the case. Certainly the "must" in question is not a logical "must," and empiricists have tended to maintain that all necessity is logical necessity. This, however, is just a dogma. It seems plausible to assert that an unsupported body must in normal circumstances fall to the ground.

Yet it must be admitted that the normal philosophical conception of necessity is more refined than this, and to say that an unsupported body must in normal circumstances fall to the ground need not be taken as incompatible with saying that this is a contingent matter. Similarly, there is an important sense in which natural laws are contingent; they are about matters of fact. If we also think of them as necessary, the necessity in question stems from the conceptual framework into which we fit them. It is possible to conceive of empirical connections in such a way that, within the framework of concepts in which we place them, they are treated as holding necessarily. It is still a contingent matter whether the whole conceptual framework has an application. If propositions expressing such connections are a priori, it is only in a relative sense.

Must a priori propositions be necessary? It seems at first sight that there is no necessity for nonempirical propositions to be necessary, or rather that it is possible to construct propositions which, if true, must be true a priori, while they apparently remain contingent. These are propositions which are doubly general. They may be formalized in such a way as to contain both a universal and an existential quantifier, for example, $(x) \cdot \exists y \cdot \phi xy$. Such propositions have been called by J. W. N. Watkins (following Karl Popper) "all and some propositions." Because they have this kind of double generality, they are both unverifiable and unfalsifiable. The element corresponding to the universal quantifier makes them unverifiable; that corresponding to the existential quantifier makes them unfalsifiable. Under the circumstances they can hardly be said to be empirical. An example of this kind of proposition is the principle of universal causality, "Every event has a cause," which is equivalent to "For every event there is some other event with which it is causally connected." It has been claimed by some philosophers, for instance, G. J. Warnock, that this proposition is vacuous, since no state of affairs will falsify it. But the most that can be claimed in this respect is that no *particular* state of affairs *which can be observed* will falsify it. It is clearly not compatible with any state of affairs whatever, since it is incompatible with the state of affairs in which there is an event with no cause. It remains true that it is impossible to verify that an event has no cause.

Watkins does not claim that the proposition is necessary, although the principle of causality has been held by many, for instance, Kant, to be an example of a necessary truth, and it could no doubt be viewed as such. But it is also possible to treat it as a contingent truth, one which holds only in the contingency of every event being causally determined. How we could know that such a contingency held is a further question. It is clear that nothing that we could observe would provide such knowledge. Such propositions certainly could not be *known* a posteriori; if true, they must be known a priori if they are to be known at all. The difficulty is just this—how *are* they to be known at all? Thus, it may be better to distinguish between a priori propositions and nonempirical propositions of this kind. A priori propositions are those which can be known to be true and whose truth is ascertainable by a procedure that makes no reference to experience; nonempirical propositions of the kind in question are not like this, for their truth is, strictly speaking, not ascertainable at all. If we accept them, it must be as mere postulates or as principles whose force is regulative in some sense.

This does not exclude the possibility that there are other propositions whose truth can be ascertained by a nonempirical procedure but which are less than necessary. It has been argued by J. N. Findlay that there are certain propositions asserting connections between concepts that are only probable, as opposed to the commonly held view that all connections existing among concepts are necessary. He maintains that our conceptual systems may be such that there are connections between their members which are by no means analytic; the connections do not amount to entailments. Perhaps something like the Hegelian dialectic is the prototype of this. Findlay argues, for example, that if one has likings, there is the presumption that one will like likings of this sort; on this sort of basis one could move toward the notion of a community of ends. It is difficult to speak more than tentatively here. Given, however, that the propositions stating these conceptual connections are, if true, then true a priori (as they surely must be), it is not clear that it is necessary to claim only that what one knows in relation to them is probable. Certainly the connections do not constitute entailments; but this of itself does not mean that what one knows is only probable. The fact that the argument for a certain position is not a strictly deductive one does not mean that the position cannot be expressed by truths which are necessary and can be known to be so. For the argument may justify the claim to such knowledge in spite of the fact that the argument is not deductively valid in the strict sense. If such a necessary proposition does not seem to have universal application, this may be due to the fact that it holds under certain conditions and that its necessity is relative to these conditions. This was Kant's position over the principle of universal causality. He held that the principle that every event has a cause is necessary only in relation to experience. If propositions of this sort lack absolute necessity, they need not lack necessity altogether. The tentative conclusion of this section is that while some propositions may in a certain sense be both nonempirical and contingent, it nevertheless remains true that if a proposition is known a priori, it must be necessarily true in some sense or other.

Must a priori propositions be analytic? It has been suggested in the previous section that there may be a priori propositions that are not analytic. They depend for their validation on a priori argument but cannot be given a deductive proof from logical truths. The question of the synthetic a priori is one of the most hotly debated topics in philosophy and has, indeed, been so ever since Kant first stated the issues explicitly. Empiricists have always vehemently denied the possibility of such truths and have even tried to show that a proposition that is a priori must be analytic by definition. Most attempts of this sort rest on misconceptions of what is meant by these terms.

Kant's synthetic a priori. Kant claimed that synthetic a priori truths were to be found in two fields—mathematics and the presuppositions of experience or science—although he denied that there was a place for them in dogmatic metaphysics. He maintained that although mathematics did contain some analytic truths (since there were propositions which summed up purely deductive steps), the main bulk of mathematical truths were synthetic a priori; they were informative, nonempirical, and necessary, but not such that their denial gave rise to a contradiction. These characteristics were in large part due to the fact that mathematical knowledge involved intuitions of time (in the case of arithmetic) and space (in the case of geometry). Kant's conception of arithmetic has not found much support, and his view of geometry has often been considered to have been undermined by the discovery of non-Euclidean geometries. It is doubtful, however, whether the situation is quite so simple as this, for what Kant maintained was that an intuition of space corresponding to Euclidean geometry was necessary at any rate *for creatures with sensibility like ours*. That is to say, what we perceive of the world must conform to Euclidean geometry, whether or not it can be conceived differently in abstraction from the conditions of perception. Whether or not this is true, it is not obviously false.

The main attack on the Kantian view of arithmetic, and thereafter on that view of other branches of mathematics, came from Frege and from Russell and Whitehead. Frege defined an analytic proposition as one in the proof of which one comes to general logical laws and definitions only; and he attempted to show that arithmetical propositions are analytic in this sense. The crucial step in this program is Frege's definition of "number" roughly in terms of what Russell called one-to-one relations. (Russell himself gave a parallel definition in terms of similarity of classes.) Given Frege's definition of number, arithmetical operations had to be expressed in terms of the original definition. It is at least an open question whether this attempt was successful. The definition has been accused of being circular and/or insufficient. This being so, the most that can be claimed is that arithmetic, while not reducible to logic, has a similar structure. However, Gödel's proof that it is impossible to produce a system of the whole of formal arithmetic that is both consistent and complete may be taken to cast doubt even on this claim. At all events, the exact status of arithmetical truths remains arguable.

Other synthetic a priori truths claimed by Kant were the presuppositions of objective experience. He tried to demonstrate that the truth of such propositions as "Every event has a cause" is necessary to objective experience. These propositions indeed express the necessary conditions of possible experience and of empirical science. As such, their validity is limited to experience, and they can have no application to anything outside experience, to what Kant called "things-in-themselves." According to Kant, these principles—which are of two kinds, constitutive or regulative in relation to experience—are ultimately derived from a list of a priori concepts or categories, which he claims to derive in turn from the traditional logical classification of judgments. These principles, in a form directly applicable to empirical phenomena, are also established by transcendental arguments. In the "Second Analogy" of the *Critique of Pure Reason*, for example, Kant sought to show that unless objective phenomena were irreversible in time, and therefore subject to rule, and therefore due to causes, it would be impossible to distinguish them from merely subjective phenomena. Causality is therefore a condition of distinguishing phenomena as objective at all. The cogency of this position depends upon the acceptability of the arguments, and it is impossible to examine them here. It is to be noted, however, that what the arguments seek to show is that certain necessary connections between concepts must be accepted if we are to give those concepts any application. The connection between the concepts of "objective event" and "cause" is not an analytic one, but it is a connection which must be taken as obtaining if the concepts are to have any application to empirical phenomena.

Another instance of this kind of situation, perhaps more trivial, can be seen in such a proposition as "Nothing can be red and green all over at the same time in the same respect." This proposition has sometimes been classified as empirical, sometimes analytic; but it has been thought by empiricists a more plausible candidate for synthetic a priori truth than any of Kant's examples. There is clearly some kind of necessity about this proposition. It may be possible for something to *appear* red and green all over, but to suggest that something might *be* red and green all over or that one might produce examples of such a thing has little plausibility; for in some sense red excludes green. The question is, In what sense? Since "red" does not mean "not-green" and cannot be reduced to this (for terms like "red" and "green" do not seem capable of analysis), the proposition under consideration cannot, strictly speaking, be analytic. How can red and green exclude each other without this being a logical or analytic exclusion? It is not merely a contingent exclusion, since it is clearly impossible to produce something which is red and green all over (shot silk, for example, although it appears so, does not conform to the conditions of being two-colored all over), and we cannot imagine what such a thing would be like.

It may be suggested that red and green are different determinates of the same determinable—color. We distinguish colors and use different terms in order to do so. To allow, then, that something might be described by two such terms at the same time would be to frustrate the purposes for which our system of color classification was devised. However, this may sound too arbitrary. After all, given two colors that do in fact shade into each other, we might be less reluctant to allow that something might be both of them at once. It is no accident that we distinguish colors as we do. For creatures of our kind of sensibility, as Kant would put it, colors have a definite structure; it is natural to see them in certain ways and to conceive of them accordingly. We then fit them to a conceptual scheme which reflects those distinctions. If we will not allow that something may be red and green all over, it is because the mutual exclusion of red and green is a necessary feature of our scheme of color concepts. Yet the whole scheme has application to the world only because we see colors as we do.

The relative and absolute a priori. Because of the empirical preconditions for our scheme of color concepts, if we maintain that we can know a priori that something cannot be red and green all over, it cannot be absolutely a priori. For the truth that something which is red cannot also be green at the same time and in the same respect can scarcely be said to be ascertainable without any reference whatever to experience. The same is true of the principle of universal causality discussed earlier. It might be maintained that the truth that every event has a cause is necessary because "cause" and "event" are so definable that there is an analytic connection between them (implausible as this may be in fact). In that case the proposition in question would be true in all possible worlds (to use a Leibnizian phrase), since its truth would not depend on what is. In a world in which no events occurred, it would be true, in this view, that every event (if there were any) would have a cause. We can know the truth of this proposition absolutely a priori. However, if the principle is not analytic (and it is clearly not, in its ordinary interpretation) but is still thought to be necessary, this can be so only because the connection between cause and event is necessary to our conception of the world as we see it. Similarly, the mutual exclusion of red and green is necessary to our conception of colors as we see them. These propositions are not true in all possible worlds, and while their truth can be known a priori, it is not known absolutely a priori.

On the other hand, the so-called laws of thought, such as the principle of contradiction, while not analytic, must again be known absolutely a priori, whatever the kind of necessity they possess. The truth of the principle of contradiction is necessary to the possibility of thought in general, including the thought of the principle itself. It is not possible even to deny the principle without presupposing it. It cannot be maintained that its truth is in any way ascertainable by a procedure that makes reference to experience. Its truth is a necessity of thought, not of experience, and is not relative to experience. Hence it may be said to be known absolutely a priori.

Of those propositions which are absolutely a priori there are two kinds—analytic truths and the principles of logic themselves. (It is perhaps not surprising that these have sometimes been classified together, even if wrongly so.) On the other hand, there are some truths which are necessary but known only relatively a priori—truths such as the principle of causality and the principle of the incompatibility of colors. Finally, of course, there is that large class of truths which can only be known a posteriori. But for philosophers these are naturally much less interesting than truths of the first two kinds—those which are a priori in some sense or other. And over these there is still much argument.

Bibliography

For Kant's distinction between a priori and a posteriori, see the Norman Kemp Smith translation of the *Critique of Pure Reason* (London, 1953), especially the introduction but also the chapters on the aesthetic and the analytic of principles. For the precedents to Kant's distinction, see Aristotle, *Posterior Analytics*, especially Bk. I.2; Gottfried Leibniz, *Nouveaux Essais*, translated by A. G. Langley as *New Essays Concerning Human Understanding* (Chicago, 1916), especially III.3 and IV.9. See also Arthur Pap, *Semantics and Necessary Truth* (New Haven, 1958), Pt. 1.

For the application of the distinction to concepts or terms, see H. H. Price, *Thinking and Experience* (London, 1953); for criticisms of the notion of ostensive definition, see the opening sections of Ludwig Wittgenstein, *Philosophical Investigations* (Oxford, 1953); and Peter Geach, *Mental Acts* (London, 1957), especially sections 6–11; and for discussion of the a priori in relation to analyticity, see G. H. Bird, "Analytic and Synthetic," *Philosophical Quarterly*, Vol. 11 (1961), 227–237; L. J. Cohen, *The Diversity of Meaning* (London, 1962), Chs. 6 and 10; and Ch. 5 of the work by Arthur Pap cited above.

For discussion of nonempirical propositions which are not necessary, see J. N. Findlay, *Values and Intentions* (London, 1961); two articles by J. W. N. Watkins: "Between Analytic and Empirical," *Philosophy*, Vol. 32 (1957), 112–131, and "Confirmable and Influential Metaphysics," *Mind*, Vol. 67 (1958), 344–365; and compare G. J. Warnock, "Every Event Has a Cause," in *Logic and Language* (Oxford, 1953), Vol. II.

For Kant's views on the possibility of the synthetic a priori, see the Kemp Smith translation cited above. For discussions of examples, see: D. W. Hamlyn, "On Necessary Truth," *Mind*, Vol. 70 (1961), 514–525; S. N. Hampshire, "Identification and Existence," in *Contemporary British Philosophers* (3d Series) (London, 1956); D. J. O'Connor, "Incompatible Properties," *Analysis*, Vol. 15 (1955), 109–117; D. F. Pears, "Incompatibility of Colours," in *Logic and Language* (Oxford, 1953), Vol. II; and compare Aristotle's discussion of the principle of contradiction in *Metaphysics* IV.4.

D. W. HAMLYN

A PRIORI KNOWLEDGE. *See* A PRIORI AND A POSTERIORI; INNATE IDEAS; RATIONALISM.

AQUINAS, ST. THOMAS. *See* THOMAS AQUINAS, ST.

ARABIC PHILOSOPHY. *See* ISLAMIC PHILOSOPHY.

ARCESILAUS, founder of the Middle, or New, Academy of Athens, was born around 315 B.C. in Pitane in Aeolia, and died around 240 B.C. He took over the headship of the Athenian Academy when Crates died. In his prime he was a handsome man, with fiery eyes and a splendid voice, a gifted orator whose dialectical skills were enormous.

We have none of his writings. From the accounts of Cicero and Sextus Empiricus it is hard to tell whether the philosophy of his Academy descended directly from the interrogatory methods of the Platonic Socrates, or whether it got most of its skepticism from Pyrrho and Timon of Phlius. We do know that his break with the Old Academy was profound; he rejected the dogmatic Platonic metaphysics being taught there by his predecessors. But his main opponents were the Stoics. In his attacks upon them he employed for the first time, if we can believe Cicero, the notion of *epoche*, or suspension of judgment. His main attack upon them had to do with their doctrine of the *phantasia kataleptike*, their belief that there were certain perceptions so distinct from all others and so prima facie true that no doubt was possible concerning them. Upon this doctrine the Stoics built their philosophy, saying that the sage was one who, having such perceptions, assented to them and built a conclusive science upon them. Arcesilaus said that when a wise man claims that he has such a perception, we call it the truth; and when a fool thinks he has one, we call it falsity. However, this begs the whole question, since we have no criterion for deciding who is a sage and who is a fool. Lacking this criterion, we must withhold our assent to the very foundations of dogmatic Stoical epistemology.

But the Stoics had one important card to play. They accused the Skeptics of paralyzing men with their *epoche* and thereby making impossible the main thing philosophy sought to obtain, a happy, vigorous life. In response to this very important counterattack, Arcesilaus produced his famous doctrine of the *eulogon*. The "reasonable" or "probable" is that which one can justify by displaying good reasons agreeing with and supporting each other. Though these reasons are not conclusive for all men, if they support the conclusion, they may help us to live well and to defend our way of life with plausibility.

Bibliography

ANCIENT SOURCES

Cicero, Marcus Tullius, *De Natura Deorum* and *Academica*, translated by H. Rackham. New York, 1933.

Sextus Empiricus, Vol. I, *Outlines of Pyrrhonism*, translated by R. G. Bury. Loeb Classical Library. Cambridge, Mass., 1955; Vol. III, *Against the Physicists*, translated by R. G. Bury. Loeb Classical Library. Cambridge, Mass., 1960.

MODERN SOURCES

Brochard, V., *Les Sceptiques grecs*. Paris, 1923. A careful analysis asserting that the approach of Arcesilaus comes not from Pyrrho, but from the dialectic of Socrates and Plato.

Goedeckemeyer, A., *Die Geschichte des griechischen Skeptizismus*. Leipzig, 1905. Defends the thesis that Arcesilaus got his skeptical method indirectly from Pyrrho and dressed it up to make it look Socratic and Platonic.

Hallie, Philip P., ed., *Scepticism, Man, and God*. Middletown, Conn., 1964. Introduction.

PHILIP P. HALLIE

ARCHE, a Greek term signifying beginning, or origin. In its earliest technical use the term referred to the primordial stuff out of which the world, according to the Ionian philosophers, was generated. But questions about origin raised issues about foundations; these issues, in turn, posed problems about principles, and principles led to controversies about knowledge or cause of being. As a result, there was a corresponding pressure on *arche* to accommodate these ideas. In practical usage, the meaning of *arche* increasingly changed from "first power" to "method of government," "sovereignty," "realm," or "political authority." In philosophical discussions, it ceased to designate the primordial stuff and became instead a word for "principle of knowledge," "basis of being," "cause of motion," or "source of action."

Anaximander was the first to use *arche* in a restricted sense and to identify it with his peculiar idea of *apeiron*. He appears to have asserted, through the use of this word, the existence of something that antedated the cosmos—something that had no beginning; was the source and origin of everything as well as the controlling influence over everything; and was eternal (*aidion*), undying (*athanaton*), and divine (*theion*). By virtue of these associations, the beginning of the world acquired a sense other than temporal; it seemed to imply extratemporal priority and physical ultimacy. Change and permanence in the created world were envisaged, respectively, as evidence of the dynamism and of the sustaining power of the *arche;* all observable regularities were viewed as reflections of the beginning's pervasive presence in the cosmos.

While Anaximander's versatile use of *arche* proved an economical way of explaining natural phenomena, philosophical criticism subsequently detected its weaknesses. First, Anaximenes was compelled to identify *arche* with something within the range of human experience (air) in order to make its pervasiveness clearer. In doing so, he was forced to introduce rarefaction and condensation to account for the *arche*'s relation to the actual world, thereby compromising conceptual economy. Similarly, Heraclitus, by sidestepping the whole issue, was constrained to argue paradoxically for both universal change and the permanence of Logos. Later on, the Pythagoreans tried to dissociate the notion of *arche* from anything physical; they restricted it to the origin of number series, thus marking the abandonment of old-style physics. Parmenides was led to replace the idea of cosmic Beginning with that of permanent Being. This amounted to an exposé of the inconsistencies inherent in all purely genetic interpretations of *arche*. When the post-Eleatic pluralists (Empedocles, Anaxagoras, and the atomists) tackled the same problem of nature, they recognized that the only way to preserve the idea of originating material was to regard it as something inert. They saw it as generative of the world, but only through the introduction of a cause of motion (*philia, neikos, nous*). Finally, for reasons too complicated even to outline here, Plato found no use in his cosmology for an *arche* in any technical sense.

From Anaximenes to the atomists, the process of critical discrimination created an awareness in philosophical thought of the nature and conditions of successful physical theorizing; of the implications of general explanatory principles; of the presuppositions for a comprehensive doctrine of Being; and of the character of rules regulating human action. The term *arche* could be used in each of these instances, but its meaning could no longer be deduced from the idea of a precosmic mysterious Beginning. The new sense of the term would have to be dissociated from all crudely referential uses, and would have to become associated with newly evolved systematic concepts. Words and phrases such as matter, cause, demonstrative principle, ground of being, motive force, and spring of action were recognized as apter synonyms of *arche*.

The critical appreciation of the revolution that brought about these changes in *arche*'s meaning is the exclusive accomplishment of Aristotle's genius. The reasons he offered to account for these changes represent the heart of his philosophy.

Bibliography

Cornford, F. M., "Innumerable Worlds in Presocratic Cosmogony." *Classical Quarterly* (1934), 1–16.

Guthrie, W. K. C.,*A History of Greek Philosophy*. Cambridge, 1962. Vol. I.

Heidel, W. A., "On Anaximander." *Classical Philology* (1912), 212–234.

Jaeger, W., *The Theology of the Early Greek Philosophers*. Oxford, 1947. Pp. 24–28.

Kirk, G. S., and Raven, J. E., *The Presocratic Philosophers*. Cambridge, 1957. Pp. 105–108.

Vlastos, G., "Presocratic Theology and Philosophy." *Philosophical Quarterly* (1952), 97–123.

P. DIAMANDOPOULOS

ARCHYTAS OF TARENTUM, a celebrated figure of the second-generation Pythagoreans, lived in southern Italy during the first half of the fourth century B.C. He studied under Philolaus and was known in antiquity as a brilliant mathematician, distinguished physicist, and astute and humane ruler of his native city where he held the office of *strategos* for seven consecutive one-year terms—a tribute to his popularity. He was a close friend of Plato and was influential in the development of Platonic thought. Reconstructions of Archytas' thought usually stress his indebtedness to Pythagoras and his originality in advancing the special sciences. The old Pythagorean number metaphysics was transformed by Archytas into a principle for generalizing special mathematical discoveries. His specific contributions to technical issues remain his clear accomplishments.

Archytas was the first to restrict mathematics exclusively to the technical disciplines of geometry, arithmetic (theory of numbers), sphaerics (descriptive astronomy), and music (theory of sound and harmonics). Confident in the power of number to account for everything, he held that the whole of nature, and each particular thing in it, is mathematically explainable (he was said to have been the first to apply mathematics to mechanics). He also applied this theory to human relations and to the organization of society. His genius in geometry is attested to by his three-dimensional construction for finding two mean proportionals in continued proportion between two given straight lines. This construction marked the definitive solution of the problem of doubling the cube, as simplified by Hippocratus of Chios.

Archytas regarded finding the "natures of numbers" (*eide*) as essential to the understanding of the foundations of mathematics. He specified the characteristics of arithmetical, geometrical, and harmonic progressions, and he proved the impossibility of finding a number which is a geometrical mean between two numbers in the *superparticularis* ratio [(n + 1) : N]—a most telling anticipation of later Euclidean contributions to arithmetic.

Archytas reaffirmed the Pythagorean belief in infinite extension beyond the cosmos by the use of an ingenious argument based on the conceptual possibility of imagining ourselves at the rim of the world—thus supporting Melissus' thesis of the infinity of the One.

He explained the nature of sound by tracing its physical source to vibrations but related its quality or pitch, mistakenly, to the speed of propagation; its audibility he attributed to man's physiological possibilities. He also explained the musical ratios of the intervals between the notes of a tetrachord for the enharmonic, chromatic, and diatonic scales.

His contributions reflect the attempts of a comprehensive mind to adjust old Pythagorean ideals to the new insights gained from the advancement of the various sciences.

Bibliography

Cornford, F. M., "Mysticism and Science in the Pythagorean Tradition." *Classical Quarterly* (1922), 137–150; (1923), 1–12.

Diels, H., *Fragmente der Vorsokratiker*, 5th ed., Vol. 1. Berlin, 1934. Pp. 421–439. Edited with additions by W. Kranz.

Frank, E., *Plato und die sogenannten Pythagoreer*. Halle, 1923.

Freeman, K., *The Pre-Socratic Philosophers*. Oxford, 1953. Pp. 233–239.

Guthrie, W. K. C., *A History of Greek Philosophy*. Cambridge, 1962. Vol. I, pp. 333–336.

Heath, T. L., *A History of Greek Mathematics*. Oxford, 1921.

Heath, T. L., *A Manual of Greek Mathematics*. Oxford, 1931. Pp. 134–138.

Heidel, W. A., "The Pythagoreans and Greek Mathematics." *American Journal of Philology* (1940), 1–33.

Van der Waerden, B. L., "Die Arithmetik der Pythagoreer." *Mathematische Annalen*, Vol. I (1948), 127–153; Vol. II (1948), 676–700.

P. DIAMANDOPOULOS

ARDIGÒ, ROBERTO (1828–1920), the principal figure in Italian positivism, was born in Casteldidone in Cremona. He became a Catholic priest, but left the priesthood when, at the age of 43, he found it no longer compatible with his beliefs, particularly his conviction that human knowledge originates in sensation—a conviction that came to him suddenly, as he recounted it, while staring at the red color of a rose (*Opere*, Vol. III, p. 368). From 1881 to 1909 he taught history of philosophy at the University of Padua. He spent the last years of his life defending and illustrating his fundamental ideas and debating with the prevailing idealism, which had supplanted positivism as the dominant viewpoint within and without the Italian universities during the last three decades of the nineteenth century. He died in Padua after two attempts at suicide.

The basic interests of Ardigò's positivism were not historical and social, as were Comte's, but scientific and naturalistic, like Spencer's. From Comte, Ardigò accepted the principle that facts are the only reality and that the only knowledge possible is the knowledge of facts, which consists in placing one fact in relation to others either immediately or by means of those mental formations that constitute ideas, categories, and principles. When these relations are established, the fact is "explained." Science, therefore, is the only kind of knowledge possible; and philosophy itself is a science that, like all other sciences, uses induction and does not have at its disposal privileged principles or procedures. Metaphysics, which claims to start from principles independent of facts and to use deduction, is a fictitious science. Yet philosophy is not just a "synthetic" discipline in Spencer's sense of the unifier of the general results of the individual sciences. On the one hand, it is a complex of special disciplines that is left after the natural sciences have gone their way. As such, it encompasses the disciplines that are concerned with the "phenomena of thought" and finds articulation in two spheres: psychology, which includes logic, "gnosis" (epistemology), and aesthetics; and sociology, which includes ethics, *dikeika* (doctrine of justice or of law), and economics. On the other hand, to philosophy belongs the field of the *indistinct*, which lies outside the realm of the distinct, which constitutes the object of the individual sciences (matter, for physics; life, for biology; society, for sociology; mind, for psychology, etc.). This realm of the indistinct constitutes the unique and common origin of all the realms of the distinct, and it is the object of philosophy as *peratology* (*Opere*, Vol. X, p. 10).

The indistinct in the philosophy of Ardigò had the same function as the unknowable in Spencer. Ardigò distinguished it from the unknowable in that the indistinct is not that which is not known but that which is not yet known distinctly. It is a relative concept, because the distinct that emerges from some knowledge is in its turn indistinct with respect to further knowledge insofar as it is that which produces, solicits, and explains that knowledge (*Opere*, Vol. II, p. 350). The indistinct–distinct relationship was, moreover, used by Ardigò—in a manner analogous to the way Spencer used the homogeneous–heterogeneous relation—to explain "the natural formation" of every known reality. Every natural formation, in the solar system as well as in the human spirit, is a passage from the indistinct to the distinct. This passage occurs necessarily and incessantly, regulated by a constant rhythm, that is, by an immutable order. But the distinct never exhausts the indistinct, which both underlies and transcends it; and since the distinct is the finite, then we must admit that, beyond the finite, lies the infinite as indistinct. Ardigò conceived the infinite as a progressive development without beginning or end (the analogue to Spencer's evolution), denying that such a development leads to a transcendent cause or principle (*Opere*, Vol. II, p. 129; Vol. III, p. 293; Vol. X, p. 519). All natural formations, including thought, which is a kind of "meteor" in the life of the universe, emerge from and return to this infinite (*Opere*, Vol. II, p. 189).

In the domain of psychology, Ardigò held that the I (self) and natural things are constituted by neutral elements, that is, sensations. The self and things differ, therefore, only by the nature of the synthesis, that is, by the connections that are established among the sensations. Those sensations that refer to an internal organ and have the character of continuity are associated in the "autosynthesis," or the self. Those sensations that refer to an external organ and are discontinuous are associated in the "heterosynthesis" that gives rise to things (*Opere*, Vol. IV, p. 529 ff.). This doctrine, propounded by Ardigò in his very first work, *La psicologia come scienza positiva* (Mantua, 1870), is similar to that later propounded by Ernst Mach in *Die Analyse der Empfindungen* (Jena, 1886).

In the moral domain Ardigò carried on a polemic against every kind of religious and rationalistic ethic. It is a fact, according to Ardigò, that man is capable of disinterested or altruistic actions, but such actions can be explained by recourse to natural and social factors. The ideals and the prescriptive maxims that determine them derive from the reactions of society to acts that either preserve or damage it—reactions that impress the individual and become fixed in his conscience as norms or moral imperatives. That which is called "conscience," therefore, is the progressive interiorization accomplished by the repeated and constant experience of the external sanctions that the antisocial act encounters in society (*Opere*, Vol. III, p. 425; Vol. X, p. 279).

Finally, Ardigò tried to mitigate the rigorous determinism found in all forms of positivism by giving some emphasis to the notion of chance. Chance consists in the intersecting of various causal series that, taken together, constitute the order of the universe. These intersections are unpredictable, though the events that constitute every individual series are not unpredictable. So-called human "freedom" is an effect of the plurality of the psychical series, that is, of the multiplicity of the possible combinations of various causal orderings that constitute man's psychical life (*Opere*, Vol. III, p. 122).

Works by Ardigò

Opere, 12 vols. Padua, 1882–1918.

La scienza dell'educazione. Padua, 1893; 2d ed., 1903. Not included in the *Opere.*

Works on Ardigò

Amerio, F., *Ardigò.* Milan, 1957. With bibliography.

Bluwstein, J., *Die Weltanschauung Roberto Ardigòs.* Leipzig, 1911.

Marchesiani, G., and Groppali, A., eds., *Nel 70o anniversario di Roberto Ardigò.* Turin, 1898.

Marchesiani, G., *La vita e il pensiero di Roberto Ardigò.* Milan, 1907.

Marchesiani, G., *Lo spirito evangelico di Roberto Ardigò.* Bologna, 1919.

Marchesiani, G., *Roberto Ardigò, l'uomo e l'umanista.* Florence, 1922.

NICOLA ABBAGNANO
Translated by *Nino F. Langiulli*

ARETĒ/AGATHON/KAKON. *Aretē,* traditionally translated as "virtue," is a key word in Greek ethical thought. Its central meaning was excellence of any kind, but from the beginning it was also associated with the idea of fulfillment of function: excellence, whether in animate or inanimate objects, consists in the fullest performance of the object's function or its power to achieve the fullest performance. From the time of the Homeric poems onward, *aretē*, with its associated adjective *agathos* ("good") and various synonyms, was the strongest word of commendation that could be used. The negative of *agathos* was *kakos*, and the neuter forms, *agathon* and *kakon*, mean what is good and what is bad. Differences between Greeks about *agathon* and *kakon* did not normally concern the meaning of the words, but only the question of what actions and what sort of behavior were manifestations of *aretē* and hence what kind of behavior was entitled to be described by the adjectives *agathos* and *kakos*.

In the *Iliad* and the *Odyssey*, *aretē* is most commonly found in the nobleman and the hero, applying above all to courage and strength, especially when exhibited in competition. Although certain restraints were regarded as necessary, the "quiet" virtues on the whole played little part in the composition of a man's *aretē*. The situation was different for women: Penelope, for example, in contrast to Clytemnestra, is praised by Agamemnon (*Odyssey* XXIV, 193) for her possession of the cooperative excellences, not for those appropriate to a Homeric male hero. By the fifth and fourth centuries B.C., the changes in Greek society from the Homeric pattern were such that there was a strong need to commend the quieter virtues, like *dikaiosyne* ("justice") and *sophrosyne* ("self-restraint"), as appropriate and necessary in the adult male citizen. The natural way to do this was to apply to such virtues the highest terms of commendation available by treating these virtues as *agathos* and as constituents of *aretē*. But the accepted denotations of the terms made this application seem strange and even paradoxical. Plato tackled the problem by appealing to the connotation of the words; he also attempted to show that justice, self-restraint, and control by reason were ways in which men could fulfill their functions as men and that without them they could not adequately do so. This approach culminated in the system of thought presented by Aristotle in the *Nicomachean Ethics*. According to Aristotle, man has a function which it is his nature to try to fulfill. The fulfillment of this function constitutes *aretē*, and for man the *agathon* is a life that involves such fulfillment.

This approach to ethics remained the dominant one throughout antiquity. But Plato's doctrine of the Form of the Good in the *Republic* raised the possibility of a transcendent source of obligation and thus of a source of *aretē* that lay outside and beyond the nature of man.

Bibliography

Adkins, A. W. H., *Merit and Responsibility, A Study in Greek Values*. Oxford, 1960.

Jaeger, Werner, *Paideia*, 2d ed., 3 vols. Translated into English by Gilbert Highet, Vol. I., Oxford, 1939. Chs. 1 ff.

G. B. KERFERD

ARISTIPPUS OF CYRENE, close friend and follower of Socrates and traditional founder of the Cyrenaic school of hedonism, earned his living by teaching and writing at the court of Dionysius of Syracuse and elsewhere during the first half of the fourth century B.C. Of his works only lists of titles survive (including dialogues like other Socratics; see Diogenes Laërtius, *Lives*, Book II, 83 ff.), but some of the apothegms ascribed to him may have occurred in his books. Our knowledge of Aristippus is also limited by a doxographic practice that groups him with general Cyrenaic doctrine; the formulation of this doctrine, however, is more probably the work of his grandson Aristippus, whose epithet was "Mother-taught." But the personal anecdotes indicate that the elder Aristippus' teaching, which, incidentally, earned high fees, was the matrix of the later system.

Like Socrates, Aristippus was interested almost exclusively in practical ethics, the end of which he believed to be the enjoyment of present pleasure. His hedonism was distinguished by a Socratic element of self-control, which he interpreted not as self-denial but as rational control over pleasure as opposed to slavery to it (as illustrated by his remark on his expensive mistress: "I have Lais, not she me"). Since all acts were indifferent except in their capacity to provide immediate pleasure, the science of life was displayed in a calculated adaptation of self to circumstances, combined with the ability to use people and situations for self-gratification. The key to this philosophy was the character of Aristippus himself, which superimposed on a Socratic freedom from desires an uninhibited capacity for enjoyment. Anecdotes tell how he could revel in luxury or be content with the simplest needs, choosing each as he saw fit and as the circumstances demanded. His successors, however, found it more difficult to reconcile the two main elements of his teaching.

Bibliography

Giannantoni, G., *I cirenaici*. Florence, 1958.

Mannebach, E., *Aristippi et Cyrenaicorum Fragmenta*. Leiden and Cologne, 1961.

I. G. KIDD

ARISTOTELIANISM. What is called Aristotelianism is not the philosophy of Aristotle himself but of those who have more or less consciously used his doctrines, his conceptual apparatus, or his methods in their own thinking. These men include the Arabian Aristotelians, from al-Kindi and ibn-Sina (Avicenna) at Baghdad in the ninth and tenth centuries to ibn-Bajjah (Avempace) and ibn-Rushd (Averroës) in Spain in the twelfth, the various Christian Aristotelians, and the authors of the traditional "Aristotelian" logic of the textbooks. Aristotle was no Aristotelian.

The legacies of great philosophers usually become diversified as they are transmitted to later ages. Doctrinal formulas may be preserved while their fundamental concepts are altered by reinterpretation in the light of new circumstances or by use in the service of new interests or methods. On the other hand, the methods and aims of an earlier thinker may be revived without explicit use of his terms and propositions. In the case of Aristotle, whose stature has been acknowledged in nearly every age, the proliferation of Aristotelianisms has been as active during periods when his philosophy was little understood and his writings all but unknown as during more informed ages.

Moreover, the influence of Aristotle has evoked the most contrary judgments, and he has been regarded as both the friend and the enemy of progress. The intellectual renaissance of the thirteenth century in western Europe, stimulated by the new availability of the Aristotelian corpus in Latin, looked to him as The Philosopher, "the master of them that know," in Dante's words, the ally of innovation and expanded horizons. But to the scientific revolution of the sixteenth and seventeenth centuries Aristotelianism was the straitjacket that had kept learning in confinement for two thousand years. The latter opinion has achieved a certain academic orthodoxy, occasionally enlivened by such remarks as Bertrand Russell's, in his *History of Western Philosophy* (1945), that "Aristotle's present-day influence is so inimical to clear thinking that it is hard to remember how great an advance he made upon all his predecessors." Even so, recent Anglo-American analytic philosophers have turned to such works as the *Nicomachean Ethics* for distinctions to help them clarify the concepts of mind and of intentional action, if not for moral insights.

There is a broad sense in which we are all Aristotelians, for in founding the first institute for specialized scientific and scholarly research, Aristotle gave us a surprising number of our names for university departments and for the studies we pursue in them: logic, rhetoric, ethics, physics, metaphysics, political science, economics, meteorology, and psychology. He also invented many technical terms that scientists and scholars have used ever since in Greek derivatives or their Latinized equivalents: substance, attribute, essence, property, accident, category, topic, proposition, universal, induction, demonstration, energy, and dynamic. But to give the learned world much of its vocabulary is not to control the meaning one's successors give it, nor is it to determine the nature of the inquiries carried on in departments one has helped name. The inevitable ambiguities and shifts in meaning have been such that our bondage to Aristotle has been more nominal than real.

Writings. A sketch of Aristotelianism may well begin with an account of what Aristotle would call its material cause, the documentary materials that have been available to stimulate philosophical comment and speculation since he retired from the Lyceum. During his lifetime, Aristotle published a number of dialogues in the Platonic manner. Although they seem to have been widely circulated and were generally praised—Cicero spoke of their "golden" style—they have all been lost, except for a few fragments cited at second or third hand by later scholars. In contrast with these "exoteric" published works on comparatively popular and edifying themes, the terse and intricate didactic treatises that we know remained the "esoteric" property of the Lyceum until someone, presumably Andronicus of Rhodes, eleventh head of the school, edited and published them about 70 B.C. Cicero mentioned some of them, and their influence in his time appears to have been chiefly in rhetoric and logic, for by then few Greeks or Romans were interested in either the natural or the social sciences as Aristotle understood them. By the third century, Porphyry's commentary on the *Categories* at once distorted Aristotle's logical theory, began the "Aristotelian" logical tradition, and set the stage for subsequent centuries of controversy about universals. By the sixth century, when knowledge of Greek was declining rapidly in the West, Boethius planned to translate all of Plato and Aristotle into Latin. Unfortunately, he was executed for treason before he could execute his plan; but he did manage to translate and comment on the *Categories* and *On Interpretation*, logical works that became the only Aristotle known at first hand in Europe before the twelfth century.

Meanwhile, the treatises had found their way to Syria, where the Arabs of the caliphate encountered them in Syriac versions and translated them into Arabic. The writings first reached the West in the twelfth century, in Arabic and sometimes in Hebrew versions, through Spain and Sicily; it was another hundred years before reliable Greek texts reached Paris and Oxford from Constantinople. Good Latin translations were soon made of all but the *Poetics*, which was discovered during the Renaissance, and the *Constitution of Athens*, which turned up among some papyri in 1890.

Since the thirteenth century, then, Aristotle's writings have been accessible to readers of Greek and Latin, so that familiarity with them has been limited less by necessity than by fluctuations of interest and fashion. Critically sound texts were established with the publication of the Berlin edition at intervals between 1831 and 1870; and with the Oxford English translations dating from the 1920s, and similar ventures in other countries, the whole range of Aristotle's thought is available to more readers than ever before.

In sum, the works we know were not published by Aristotle but were edited, perhaps with rearrangements, omissions, and embellishments, 250 years later. Many were subsequently lost and recovered; and the "known" works have sometimes been known only in translations of yet other translations or even in paraphrases by commentators. Thus, if Aristotle was a dominant influence in philosophy before the thirteenth century, it was by reputation or through imaginative extrapolations from a fraction of the writings we possess.

All this helps to explain why Aristotle has been credited with a variety of dubiously Aristotelian opinions, and why the traditional Aristotelian corpus includes both a core of unquestionably authentic works and a more doubtful fringe that has fluctuated according to the credulity and the philosophical predilections of many generations of scholars. This fringe has included not only writings now attributed to Aristotle's successors in the Peripatetic School but also such obviously foreign intrusions as a Neoplatonic work by Proclus and even a section of the *Enneads* of Plotinus that once passed as "the theology of Aristotle."

Problems of interpretation. Such unsteadiness in judgments about what Aristotle wrote is inseparable from changing views about what he thought, for anyone who could accept the words of Plotinus or Proclus as those of Aristotle would read him as a Neoplatonist, and vice versa. And despite developments in higher textual criticism, the decisive factors in judgment about Aristotle's authorship have been and remain philosophical in several senses.

First among such considerations would naturally be some prior conception of what is essential in Aristotle's philosophy; this would affect what he might be expected to say and therefore whether a particular work or passage should be accepted as genuine. Such a criterion is indispensable, notwithstanding advances in the attribution of authorship on the basis of vocabulary and style; and it is still employed in deciding whether admittedly authentic parts of the corpus should be assigned to his early "Platonic" years or to his "Aristotelian" maturity. Second, the philosophy of the interpreter tends to influence his conception of the essence of Aristotle's philosophy. To a Platonist—and Aristotle's interpreters have most often been Platonists of some sort—Aristotle will be a Platonist too, although usually a literal-minded one with a knack for the special sciences: as Coleridge put it, "the sovereign lord of the understanding—the faculty of judging by the senses," but incapable of raising himself to the comprehensive perspective of reason, "that higher state which was natural to Plato."

One of the most subtly decisive forms of philosophical reinterpretation arises from implicit commitments about the aims of philosophy, its "final cause." For example, Aristotle was a systematic thinker, and his multiple analytic distinctions were oriented toward the precise formula tion of problems (*aporiai*) for inquiry. His most characteristic scientific treatises, from the *Metaphysics* to *The Parts of Animals*, were carefully organized presentations of problems, with extensive and meticulous discussions of the methods most appropriate to a particular inquiry. But most of Aristotle's interpreters, from the beginning down through the great Scholastics, assumed that his systematic efforts were directed, as theirs were, toward an encyclopedic synthesis of doctrines rather than toward an analytical classification and clarification of unambiguous questions. Such an inversion of priorities as that between the advancement of inquiry and the conservation and transmission of truth makes a great difference, for it amounts to an alteration of principles.

A second preoccupation of most ancient and medieval commentators may be summed up under the ambiguous heading of personal "salvation," which covers objectives as diverse as Stoic equanimity, retreat to an Epicurean garden, and the more radical redemption sought by Gnostics, Neoplatonists, Muslims, and Christians. But no such conception of man's vocation can be found in Aristotle, for whom philosophic activity was, to be sure, the most precious element of a good life and that in which man most nearly approaches the blessedness of divinity, but hardly a refuge from this world or a means of access to another. And so in this respect also, later ages saw Aristotle's philosophy in an altered perspective. Thus, Boethius not only wrote *The Consolations of Philosophy* but also sought to render Plato and Aristotle into Latin so that he could reconcile the insights of each with those of the other and those of both with the goodness of God. With the rise of Christianity and Islam it became one of the offices of philosophy to "justify God's ways to man" in a sense quite unknown to Aristotle, who had no conception of an authoritative theology or of the use of his logical apparatus for theology's dialectical defense.

Traditional "Aristotelianism." Gradually, from varied textual materials and guided by un-Aristotelian aims, the philosophers of the Middle Ages fashioned an "Aristotelian" view of the world and of philosophy with a cosmological framework derived from Aristotle himself. Once fixed by tradition, it was the intellectual support for a generally shared conception of a finite, hierarchically and purposefully ordered universe in which everything had its proper place between the center of the earth and the outermost heaven of fixed stars. It was this, as an essentially complete and dogmatically defended obstruction to inquiry, that Bruno, Copernicus, and Galileo gladly helped destroy; it was its eventual collapse that John Donne and many since have lamented because they felt "all coherence gone"; and it is to the memory of many of its features that the nostalgic hearken when they seek to revivify "the perennial philosophy." Let us trace its genesis.

Acquainted only with the two introductory treatises of Aristotle's logic, scholars of the Dark Ages were disposed to employ their considerable talents upon the little that they knew of Aristotle in the spirit of the Platonism that they also knew. In consequence, the logic that developed in the *trivium* beside the grammar of Donatus and Priscian and the rhetoric of Cicero and Quintilian was without the means of observing Aristotle's fine distinctions between scientific demonstration, which the *Posterior Analytics* restricted to specific subject matters, and the free-ranging but less than demonstrative dialectic of the *Topics*. This logic favored the treatment of all kinds of problems by a common method in which the dialectical reconciliation and refutation of opinions took precedence, and which reached its fruition in the method of Scholasticism.

Meanwhile the Arabs, sharing the apologetic and Neoplatonic biases of their European counterparts, amplified Aristotle's cryptic remarks about the "active intellect" (*On the Soul*) to a full-blown teaching about a superpersonal world soul that was heavily indebted to Plato and Plotinus. This was to implicate Aristotelianism in charges of heresy when Christians reflected on its consequences for personal immortality; but it is of interest now primarily as an illustration of how, under Platonizing influences, the functions and activities typical of Aristotle's scientific analyses became entities that gave rise to "metaphysical" speculation, much as had happened in logic when Porphyry asked his fateful question about the independent existence of genera and species.

Aquinas. In the thirteenth century's enthusiastic response to the breadth of Aristotle's inquiries, Aquinas fully appreciated the range and complexity of the recovered logical and scientific works. Indeed, he was an extraordinarily accurate and illuminating interpreter of the texts on which he commented. But he nevertheless saw them in the light of theological ideas that, after centuries of Augustinian and Platonic habituation, had acquired the inevitability of second nature. For a rough indication of these ideas and the nature of their influence, consider the Arabs' world soul as the third person of the Trinity; conceive God as like the demiurge of Plato's *Timaeus*, but as the Creator instead of a "workman" wrestling with intractable materials; and finally, restore the Platonic Ideas as exemplars that, being at once the objects of the divine intellect and the patterns of creation, are the measures of "God's truth."

Teleology. Truth, according to Aquinas' famous discussion of the subject, is "the adequation of thing (*res*) and understanding"; but it varies in application according to what is taken to conform to what. Truth for man is properly attributed to our understanding insofar as it is adequate to the natures of the things which are its objects and its measures. But truth is also attributable to things insofar as they are adequate to their exemplars in God's understanding. In brief, man's thoughts are true to the degree that they conform to things; but things are true to the degree that they conform to God's thoughts. In everyday terms, nature embodies God's plan, so that final causes in nature will reflect "purposes" in an anthropocentric (or at least theocentric) sense quite foreign to Aristotle's understanding of natural teleology. The latter was much more in keeping with modern biology: If one proposes to understand, say, the liver, one needs to know its functions, such as its handling of glucose, and how, without its contribution, the organism would be crippled. Given the functions "for the sake of which" we have a liver, one also needs to understand that organ's physiology and the chemical reactions by which it does its work. So considered, "final causes" are innocent, unmysterious, and perhaps indispensable; and it does not follow that the liver "has a purpose" which it tries vitalistically to achieve, or that it "has a purpose" as a hacksaw does, having been made to serve a purpose of its maker. But for the Aristotelianism considered here, these clean distinctions were muddied: Everything had a hacksawlike purpose in the divine plan, although some things were more purposive than others.

Natural law. Similarly, the laws of nature were considered to reflect divine legislation in a manner that blurred the difference between laws describing necessary regularities and laws prescribing obligations that were necessary in quite a different sense; and this undermined Aristotle's efforts to discriminate theoretic problems from practical ones. The laws of the new Aristotelian cosmos, whose principle of order was the natural subordination of things in a scale of perfection, were a paradigm for the moral order, where rational agents and their "natural" ends were ordered by analogously natural laws. Aristotle had spoken cryptically of a natural justice that is everywhere the same despite variations in local law and custom, but not the same in the sense that fire burns in Persia exactly as it does in Hellas. Such qualifications were superseded by metaphysical and theological analogies: The once autonomous criteria of rational deliberation and choice became subject to prior criteria of knowledge and proof more authoritative than the natural scientist's knowledge. Theology, the Angelic Doctor explained, is based upon revealed premises and is both a practical and a theoretic science. It does not conflict with natural knowledge, as the Averroists had implied, but supplements and completes it.

Reaction to the tradition. Associated with Scholasticism and especially Thomism, traditional Aristotelianism has shared their fortunes. Although they won official endorsement by Pope Leo XIII in the 1870s, they have generally been in eclipse since the Renaissance, when scholastic logic-chopping was as despised by humanists as its final causes and substantial forms were by astronomers and physicists. On the whole, association with such a comprehensive and institutionalized ideology has been an obstacle to the use of Aristotle's work so as to be relevant to the problems of the day.

However, from time to time philosophers and scientists have employed Aristotelian concepts and criticisms with strategic effect apart from the larger synthesis of the tradition. Among them are William of Ockham in logic, William Harvey in his work on the circulation of the blood, Leibniz in his pointed but premature criticism of the Newtonian concepts of space, time, and motion, and the biology of D'Arcy Thompson, who also translated *The History of Animals* for the Oxford edition, that has made it easier for us to know the analytical, problem-oriented Aristotle as well as a synthetic Aristotelianism.

Bibliography

WORKS BY ARISTOTLE

The Works of Aristotle Translated Into English Under the Editorship of W. D. Ross. Oxford, 1928.

The Basic Works of Aristotle, Richard McKeon, ed. New York, 1941. Introduction by McKeon. A selection of the most important works, using the Oxford translations.

GENERAL WORKS

Case, Thomas, "Aristotle," in *Encyclopaedia Britannica*, 11th ed. London, 1910. Vol. II, pp. 501–522.

Randall, John Herman, Jr., *Aristotle.* New York, 1960.

Ross, W. D., *Aristotle.* London, 1923.

STUDIES

Gilson Étienne, *History of Christian Philosophy in the Middle Ages.* New York, 1955.

Koyré, Alexandre. *From the Closed World to the Infinite Universe.* Baltimore, 1957.

Lovejoy, Arthur O., *The Great Chain of Being: A Study of the History of an Idea.* Cambridge, Mass., 1936.

McKeon, Richard, "Aristotelianism in Western Christianity," in J. T. McNeill, Matthew Spinka, and Harold Willoughby, eds., *Environmental Factors in Christian History.* Chicago, 1939.

Moody, Ernest A., *The Logic of William of Ockham.* New York, 1935.

Shute, Richard, *On the History of the Process by Which the Aristotelian Writings Arrived at Their Present Form.* Oxford, 1888.

Stocks, John Leofric. *Aristotelianism.* New York, 1927.

WARNER WICK

ARISTOTLE (384–322 B.C.), son of Nicomachus, the court physician to Amyntas II, king of Macedon, was born in the Ionian city of Stagira in Chalcidice. His father died when he was still a boy and he was brought up by a guardian, Proxenus, who sent him to Athens, where he entered Plato's Academy, about 367 B.C. He remained at the Academy until Plato's death in 347 B.C. Plato was succeeded as head of the Academy by his nephew and heir Speusippus, and Aristotle, together with Xenocrates, joined a circle of Platonists living at Assos in the Troad under the protection of the tyrant Hermias of Atarneus. The story that there had earlier been a quarrel and a break in relations between Plato and Aristotle belongs to a later tradition hostile to Aristotle and is contradicted by contemporary evidence.

But the departure of Aristotle and Xenocrates from Athens did involve the secession of a group of those associated with Plato, and it was probably related to the choice of Speusippus as Plato's successor. After three years in Assos, Aristotle moved in 345 B.C. to Mytilene on the island of Lesbos. A number of details in his biological treatises make it clear that many of his zoological investigations belong to this period. Then in 342 B.C. he accepted an invitation to supervise the education of the thirteen-year-old son of Philip II of Macedon, the future Alexander the Great, at the Macedonian court at Pella. This lasted for some three years. The following five years Aristotle spent at Stagira; and about 335 B.C. he returned to Athens to open a new school in a gymnasium called the Lyceum, a short distance northeast of the city. On the death of Alexander the Great in 323 B.C., the school was in danger of attack from the anti-Macedonian party at Athens, and Aristotle himself took refuge in Chalcis on the island of Euboea, leaving Theophrastus in charge of the school. He died in Chalcis the following year, at the age of 62.

WRITINGS

It is convenient to consider Aristotle's writings under three headings: popular writings, memoranda and collections of material, and scientific and philosophical treatises.

Popular writings. Among Aristotle's popular writings may be included some poems, of which three fragments survive, and also the fragments of certain letters, not all of which are genuine. But far more important are the dialogues and certain other philosophical works constituting what Aristotle refers to in the treatises as "exoteric writings." (The term "exoteric" thus applied is now understood to mean simply "written for those outside the school," and it is opposed to "esoteric," applicable to the treatises and meaning "for those inside the school" without conveying any idea of secrecy or mystery.) Of these exoteric writings the most important are the *Eudemus*, the *Protrepticus, On Philosophy, On the Good*, and *On the Ideas.* None of these survive, but in some cases we have substantial extracts or summaries; and overall there are more than one hundred direct quotations and references in later writers to these works. The dialogues were on the Platonic model, and the high opinion of Aristotle's prose style several times expressed in antiquity clearly refers to them and not to the treatises or memoranda.

Memoranda and collections of material. Over two hundred titles are preserved in the three ancient catalogues of Aristotle's works. Here belong the 158 constitutions of Greek states, of which the *Constitution of the Athenians,* rediscovered in a papyrus in 1890, alone survives; a record of dramatic festivals, called the *Didascaliae*, no longer extant; and perhaps also the surviving *Problems* and *Historia Animalium.* Clearly, Aristotle commissioned others within the school to prepare collections of research materials, and this work continued after his death. Later writers drew extensively on such works as Theophrastus' *Opinions of the Physical Philosophers* and his writings on botany, Eudemus' histories of various branches of mathematics and of theology, and other similar works which may well have been begun during Aristotle's lifetime.

Scientific and philosophical treatises. The scientific and philosophical treatises constitute the surviving corpus of Aristotle's writings and, excluding certain spurious works, they may be listed as follows:

(1) Logical works (the *Organon*)
- *Categories*
- *On Interpretation* (*De Interpretatione*)
- *Prior and Posterior Analytics*
- *Topics*
- *On Sophistical Refutations* (*De Sophisticis Elenchis*)

(2) Physical works
- *Physics*
- *On the Heavens* (*De Caelo*)
- *On Coming-to-be and Passing-away* (*De Generatione et Corruptione*)
- *Meteorologics*

(3) Psychological works
- *On the Soul* (*De Anima*)
- *Parva Naturalia*: short treatises including *On Memory and Reminiscence, On Dreams, and On Prophesying by Dreams*

(4) Works on natural history
- *On the Parts of Animals* (*De Partibus Animalium*)
- *On the Movement of Animals* (*De Motu Animalium*)
- *On the Progression of Animals* (*De Incessu Animalium*)
- *On the Generation of Animals* (*De Generatione Animalium*)
- *Minor treatises*

(5) Philosophical works
- *Metaphysics*
- *Nicomachean Ethics*
- *Eudemian Ethics*
- *Magna Moralia*
- *Politics*
- *Rhetoric*
- *Art of Poetry*

The nature of these surviving Aristotelian treatises has been much discussed. Some have supposed that they represent lecture notes, either Aristotle's own or those taken by pupils, while others regard them as essentially textbooks or working notes prepared for the use of students in the Aristotelian School. However they first came to be written down, they seem to have continued in use in the school for a considerable period. Some were edited by members of the School, and it is probable that at least until the death of Theophrastus they remained subject to additions and amplifications. Some of the works now judged spurious may be later revisions of original material going back to Aristotle's own day.

History of the writings. Before discussing Aristotle's thought in relation to his writings, it is necessary to know something of the external history of them. The treatises passed to Theophrastus on Aristotle's death, and Theophrastus in turn bequeathed them to Neleus of Scepsis in the Troad. According to the story, they remained in the hands of Neleus' family until they were sold, together with the works of Theophrastus, to Apellicon of Teos, who died about 86 B.C. Apellicon published them, but they had been damaged by damp and vermin, and he filled in the gaps incorrectly. Upon the death of Apellicon, Sulla carried off the books from Athens to Rome. There the elder Tyrannion got possession of them, and together with Andronicus of Rhodes, the eleventh president of the Peripatetic school, he published them sometime between 43 and 20 B.C. The story is told by Strabo, a pupil of Tyrannion, and probably is true in its essentials. There is certainly every reason to believe that all subsequent versions of the treatises stem from this recension by Andronicus of Rhodes.

But the implications of the story have been much discussed. Taken literally, it implies that the Aristotelian treatises were lost to the Peripatetic school during the period from Strato (the successor of Theophrastus) to Andronicus of Rhodes. It is both true and important to note that the vast majority of references to Aristotle's doctrines in the Hellenistic period before Andronicus are to the dialogues and not to the treatises. This has led to the doctrine of the "lost Aristotle," expounded especially by Ettore Bignone in *L'Aristotele perduto* (2 vols., Florence, 1936). Nonetheless, it is unlikely that the treatises were altogether lost. It is hard to believe that no copies of them were retained in the school at Athens.

The oldest catalogue of Aristotle's writings probably goes back to Ariston of Ceos, head of the school at Athens about 200 B.C. His catalogue lists works known to him at that time, including most but not all of the treatises. The library at Alexandria housed books sought with anxious care from all over the world and is said to have contained forty copies or versions of the *Analytics*—it probably held the rest of the treatises as well as the dialogues. There are some references to the treatises, especially to the biological works, during the earlier Hellenistic period (see Ingmar Düring, "Notes on the Transmission of Aristotle's Writings," in *Göteborgs Högskolas Årsskrift,* Vol. 56, No. 3 (1950), 37–70).

Andronicus' edition undoubtedly gave a fresh stimulus to Aristotelian studies and concentrated attention once again on the treatises. Comparison of the dialogues with the treatises revealed considerable differences in doctrine. In the second century A.D. the successors of Andronicus began the series of great commentaries on the treatises culminating in the work of Alexander of Aphrodisias, who explained that in the treatises Aristotle gave his own opinions and the truth, while in the dialogues he gave the opinions of others, which were false. Other commentators supposed that he preached a doctrine to those inside the school (in the treatises) different from that offered (in the dialogues) to those outside. From Andronicus onward, for over nineteen centuries, it was assumed that Aristotle gave his real doctrines in the treatises. The logical extension of this approach came in 1863, when Valentin Rose concluded that all the dialogues must have been spurious works not written by Aristotle at all (*Aristoteles Pseudepigraphus,* Leipzig, 1863).

DEVELOPMENT OF ARISTOTLE'S THOUGHT

The belief that the Aristotelian corpus gave a systematic statement of Aristotle's thought written mostly in the period after 335 B.C. dominated Aristotelian studies until it was challenged by Werner Jaeger, first in *Studien zur Enstehungsgeschichte der Metaphysik des Aristoteles* (Berlin, 1912), and then in his definitive *Aristoteles, Grundlegung einer Geschichte seiner Entwicklung* (Berlin, 1923), which has had a profound effect on all subsequent discussions. Jaeger maintained that Aristotle's thought went through a gradual development that lasted most of his life. He distinguished three periods. In the first, down to 347 B.C., Aristotle was an emphatic and enthusiastic defender of Platonism. Here belong the dialogues, with the exception of *On Philosophy,* and in them Aristotle holds fast both to the Platonic view of the soul as given in the *Phaedo* and *Republic* and to the doctrine of the Forms. In the second period, from 347 to 335 B.C., Aristotle became increasingly critical of Platonism, above all of the doctrine of Forms. In this period he wrote *On Philosophy.* Finally, in the period after 335 B.C., Aristotle was feeling his way toward a type of thinking based on a wholly new principle, that of empirical science; and by the end of his life he had come to reject all the essential features of Platonic otherworldly metaphysics. In many of the treatises it was, Jaeger held, possible to distinguish quite clearly parts written at different periods and reflecting different and inconsistent stages in Aristotle's thought, ranging all the way from the full-blooded Platonism of the first period, typified by the dialogues, through the period of increasing criticism to the final period, when metaphysics in the old sense was virtually abandoned.

Jaeger's radical genetic approach inevitably provoked differing reactions from scholars. Apart from die-hard opposition, the initial tendency was to acknowledge that a new era had dawned in Aristotelian studies. Some adopted Jaeger's scheme wholeheartedly and attempted to apply it in detail to treatises that had not been subject to such analysis in Jaeger's book. But some from the beginning, and an increasing number as time went on, while accepting the genetic approach, were doubtful whether Jaeger had correctly identified the actual stages of Aristotle's development. In particular, Jaeger had argued that Book Λ of the *Metaphysics* belonged to Aristotle's middle period while admitting that Chapter 8 must have been written toward the end of Aristotle's life. But further study has suggested that Chapter 8 cannot be separated from the rest of the book in this way. It would follow that the whole of Book Λ must belong to the later period, and this means that Aristotle never abandoned interest in metaphysical problems.

This continued interest in metaphysical problems was suggested also by a fuller investigation into Aristotle's discussion of soul. The biological treatises rest largely on studies made in the Aegean area around Lesbos in Aristotle's second period and may well have been partly written in that period. Aristotle, on this view, began with a Platonist conception of the soul as a separate substance, moved to a view of the body as instrument of the soul in the second or biological period, and in the final period developed the doctrine of the soul as form of the body in the light of his developed theory of substance as expressed in his *Metaphysics* (see F. Nuyens, *L'Evolution de la psychologie d'Aristote*). This comes close to inverting the order of Jaeger's middle and later periods in terms of Aristotle's dominant interests at each stage. This reversal of Jaeger's scheme has been carried a step further, not without an element of deliberate paradox, by Ingmar Düring's apothegm that it would be truer to say that Aristotle began as an empiricist and spent the rest of his life in striving to become a Platonist.

More recently the whole genetic approach has come under fresh attack. It is pointed out that there are many passages in the treatises which imply a systematic order of exposition. In all probability the treatises as we have them represent lecture courses given in the later years of Aristotle's life. The attempt to dissolve them into a series of doctrines classified as earlier or later according to whether they are closer to or more remote from positions adopted by Plato is inherently vicious, in that it assumes at the start what should only be a conclusion, namely, that "nearer to Plato" means "earlier in date." Inconsistencies there certainly are, and no doubt different treatises or parts of treatises were written at different times. But the over-all intention, it is argued, was to produce an organized system of thought. This was no doubt subject to continuous revision, and the process of revision was never completed. Nonetheless, we miss the whole point of Aristotle's undertaking if we reverse his intention in order to dissolve his thought into a series of stages. Even the doctrinal chaos within some of the treatises has been exaggerated, it is claimed, and in the crucial case of the *Metaphysics* it is possible to discern a logical progression from book to book which suggests unitary composition.

So some would say that the break with Platonism was for all practical purposes complete by the time Aristotle went to Assos—all that happened after that was a prolonged and sustained attempt to work out the consequences of the rejection of Plato's metaphysics. Others would attack even the contrast between the treatises and the dialogues, interpreting the dialogues as Aristotelian rather than Platonic in outlook. Above all, it is now quite widely held that there is no evidence anywhere in the dialogues that Aristotle there accepted Plato's theory of the Forms as transcendent, and if this be the case, then Jaeger's thesis is indeed in ruins.

This is a discussion which will long continue. In the present article the view is taken that in most of the dialogues Aristotle accepts a number of Platonic positions which he later abandoned, that a movement away from Platonism occupied most of his life but that he never abandoned or rejected metaphysical interests although he recognized that the rejection of earlier views required modifications in his metaphysical doctrine. On the view assumed here, he was engaged from the start in attempts to present a systematic view of the whole field of knowledge and reality, and he remained throughout a determined and unrepentent systematizer without ever succeeding in producing a fully coordinated system that could satisfy his own high standards of criticism; finally, the right way to present his doctrines, on this account, is not to begin by attempting to distinguish any general stages or layers in his thinking at different periods but to discuss separately the main positions to which he gives expression when discussing different topics, problems, or branches of philosophy, in the expectation that sometimes inconsistencies can be explained along geneticist lines but that at other times Aristotle may have been confronted with difficulties for which he had no solution. Indeed, much of his thinking is what he himself calls aporetic, that is, raising difficulties without solving them; and it may be that the aporetic element is more fundamental than has usually been recognized.

The problem of knowledge. In what follows, no account will be offered of Aristotle's important biological studies, and only some of his basic philosophical ideas will be discussed—and then only in the most general terms. But before embarking upon this extremely hazardous undertaking, it may be worth attempting to state some of the guidelines which Aristotle follows in his thinking, above all with reference to the problem of knowledge.

For Plato, knowledge, if it is to be knowledge, must be clear, certain, and not subject to change. It can have these characteristics only if they are found also in the objects known. The objects of knowledge must consequently be definite, real, and unchanging, and so they must be nonsensible and universal—in other words, the Forms. (It may be noted that even if the view is taken that this misrepresents Plato, it is unquestionably what Aristotle attributed to him.) Aristotle came to reject the transcendence of the Platonic Forms, but he retained the Platonic view of knowledge as knowledge of the universal and of the real. His problem, then, was to find a way of giving reality and permanence to the universal without reintroducing the Platonic Forms. Second, Plato had regarded the Forms as the causes of things being or becoming what they are or become. The change in the status of the Forms required of Aristotle a new doctrine of causation and a new source or sources of change and of motion. Third, when Aristotle attempted to systematize the various branches of knowledge on the basis of his changed or changing conceptions of universals and of causes, he was led step by step to make profound changes in the general pictures implied by Plato and by Plato's predecessors, the pre-Socratics. These changes were so vast that we are fully justified in regarding Aristotelianism as a philosophical innovation of the first importance.

So much has, indeed, been generally recognized. But the interpretation of Aristotle has itself been a part of the subsequent history both of European philosophy and of Christian theology and at many points has provided the terrain for subsequent battles. A sound historical approach to Aristotle must to some extent discard considerations of this kind, and the attempt must be made to see Aristotle against the background of Plato and the pre-Socratics rather than in the light of the subsequent history of philosophy. But not completely. Aristotle was a thinker of great philosophical subtlety and persistence and has much to offer those concerned with the discussion of similar problems today. Ideally, what is wanted is a critical historical approach accompanied by a sympathetic philosophical interest in the many problems which occupied Aristotle's thoughts for a lifetime.

CLASSIFICATION OF THE SCIENCES

In *Topics* (I, 14) Aristotle divides propositions into ethical, physical, and logical, thus suggesting the standard Hellenistic division of philosophy into logic, physics, and ethics, a division which Sextus Empiricus tells us (*Against the Logicians* I, 16) originated with Plato but was first made explicit by Xenocrates. However, in *Topics* (VI, 6) Aristotle gives his own famous tripartite division of knowledge into theoretical, practical, and poetic (or, rather, productive). Elsewhere he subdivides theoretical knowledge into first philosophy, physics, and mathematics, and practical knowledge into ethics, politics, and a number of other activities. The bases of these divisions and subdivisions are stated differently on different occasions, but the primary division seems usually to be based on the purpose involved—knowledge pursued for its own sake is theoretical; pursued for the sake of actions, practical; and pursued for the sake of making or producing something, productive. The subdivisions of theoretical knowledge, on the other hand, are usually related to differences in the objects studied. Things that cannot be other than what they are, but can exist separately, are the subject of first philosophy; things that cannot change and cannot exist separately are the subject of mathematics; and things that can change and can exist separately are the subject of physics.

Clearly, this second principle of division leads to an inconsistency with the primary division, since physics, for example, could be pursued either as a part of theoretical or productive or (as in psychology) practical science. A twofold division between theoretical and productive science is found in *Protrepticus* (*Aristotelis Dialogorum Fragmenta*, R. Walzer, ed., Fr. 6), but the primary threefold division may well go back to the dialogue *On Justice.* The problem that results is typical. While all inconsistencies could be removed by positing a series of stages in the development of Aristotle's thought, all stages seem to be combined in *Nicomachean Ethics* (VI, 3–4). It seems probable that Aristotle had not completely systematized his thought on the classification of the sciences, or at the least that he did not intend a single classification to be used for all purposes. His classification was in fact ignored in the Hellenistic period, and its very considerable influence on subsequent thought, down to the present day, probably goes far beyond anything which Aristotle had in mind.

LOGIC

Whether logic was to be a separate part or merely an instrument of philosophy was a standard subject of debate between the Stoics and the Peripatetics. Aristotle's preferred view did not include logic in his classification of the sciences at all, but treated it as a preliminary to the study of each and every branch of knowledge. Hence, for him it was an instrument (*organon*) of study, and the name *Organon* came later to be applied to the collection of Aristotle's logical treatises. Aristotle's own name for logic was "analytics," and the term "logic" only subsequently came to have its full modern sense. This sense is sometimes said to have occurred first in Alexander of Aphrodisias about A.D. 200. But the term is found in a somewhat restricted sense in Aristotle's own writings (for example, *Topics* I, 14); and there is evidence that it was beginning to be used as the equivalent of dialectic or analytics almost immediately after Aristotle's death, so that it may have been the Stoics who first consciously gave it its modern application.

For Aristotle, the heart of logic was the syllogism. His treatment of syllogistic argument, with some restatements and embroideries, provided the basis of the teaching of traditional formal logic until the beginning of the twentieth century. While it is becoming clear that the traditional formal logic in some ways distorted Aristotle's teaching on particular points, the main lines of his treatment of the syllogism are too well known and also too detailed to justify exposition in this present article (see LOGIC, HISTORY OF). The *Organon* has two preliminary treatises, the *Categories* and *On Interpretation*, dealing respectively with terms and with propositions. Then come the *Prior Analytics*, dealing with the syllogism, and the *Posterior Analytics*, dealing with the conditions of scientific knowledge, including what extra requirements besides consistency are necessary for the attainment of truth. The *Topics*, to which *On Sophistical Refutations* forms an appendix, deals with syllogistically correct kinds of reasoning which fall short of the conditions of scientific accuracy. Genetic studies, without achieving any unanimity, have tended to place the *Topics*, or the greater part of it, earliest in date of composition, on the strong ground that at least part of it was written before the development of the doctrine of the syllogism. An attempt to date the *Posterior Analytics* before the *Prior Analytics* has met with more criticism—while it owes more to Plato than the *Prior Analytics* does, this in itself is not surprising, since the doctrine of the syllogism is not Platonic anyway. The *Categories* and *On Interpretation* are also generally regarded now as early works, but the importance of the *Categories* justifies a fuller discussion.

The "Categories." Since it deals with terms in isolation, it is natural that the *Categories* should be placed first in the *Organon*. It is probable that the second part of the treatise, usually known as the *Post-Predicaments*, is as genuine as the earlier part, although its authenticity was generally doubted until quite recently. According to Aristotle, isolated expressions signify either substance, quantity, quality, relation, place, time, position, condition, action, or passivity. These "categories" were referred to quite frequently elsewhere, but neither the order nor the number was precisely fixed. Most expressions properly signify one category only, but (in *Metaphysics* Δ 10) certain pervasive terms are recognized as able to run through all the categories, terms such as "one," "being," "same," and "other," a fact which is reminiscent of the doctrine of "greatest kinds" in Plato's *Sophist* (254B ff.).

The term "category" properly means "predicate," but it is clear that for Aristotle the expressions with which he is dealing can occur either in the subject or in the predicate position in a sentence. It follows that Aristotle is not simply giving a theory of predication. What is he doing? According to one view, he is classifying terms upon the basis of grammatical distinctions as to their use—noun, adjective, and so on. A second view argues that he is not classifying linguistic symbols but what they symbolize, in other words, things. On this "ontological" interpretation, Aristotle is attempting to classify the main aspects of reality. Others suppose that he is already dealing with strictly "logical" entities. The answer probably is that Aristotle would not have regarded these three views as mutually exclusive—in the words of Porphyry's commentary on the *Categories* (in *Commentaria in Aristotelem Graeca*,

A. Busse, ed., Vol. IV, Part I, Berlin, 1887, p. 71, l. 13): "As things are, so are the expressions which primarily indicate them."

It is certainly as part of a theory of reality that Aristotle later uses the categories to criticize Plato's theory of Forms. For Aristotle, Plato was involved in a confusion between the category of substance and the other categories when, for example, he attributed substantiality to predications of quantity, such as "being tall." However, in Chapter 5 of the *Categories* Aristotle distinguishes within the category of substance between "primary substance" and "secondary substance." Primary substances are particular men, horses, and so on, and "secondary substances" are the species and genera to which the individuals belong. It is noteworthy that Aristotle does not, as we tend to do, treat all simple nonrelational predicates as qualities—for him the genus and species to which a thing belongs are substances and not qualities and so belong in the first category. In the *Metaphysics* this treatment of species and genera as involving substantiality seems to have been abandoned, and we have a more simple opposition between substance and the universal. If, then, Aristotle did in fact gradually move farther and farther away from Platonism, this movement would help to support an early date for the *Categories*.

PHYSICS

The Eleatic doctrine of being initiated by Parmenides seemed to make predication impossible by treating identity and being as the same and by arguing that being excludes diversity, so that a thing cannot have any predicate attached to it which is different from itself. To this, Aristotle replied with the doctrine of the *Categories*, distinguishing a number of different senses of being and so making possible a series of different subject–predicate relations. The same Eleatic doctrine of being also seemed to make change and movement impossible by arguing that that which is, always is, and that being cannot come into existence out of nonbeing. The pre-Socratics after Parmenides endeavored to keep change and movement by positing unchanging elements which combine or emerge or separate on varying principles. Plato in the *Phaedo* struck a death blow at such elements and principles as sources of change by arguing that a thing can never change into its opposite without being itself destroyed. Thereafter there were two predictable courses for physical theory to follow. The first was to seek reality in a substrate behind the elements, a substrate to which varying qualities could attach. This was the course taken by Aristotle. The other alternative was to seek reality in unchanging permanent qualities, the Platonic Forms, with a minimal "location" in which varying temporary projections and combinations of Forms could occur and so constitute the phenomenal world. This second view is the "Platonic" view, and it was the view toward which Plato himself usually tended.

Matter, privation, and form. Aristotle's three basic ingredients for the explanation of change are discussed at the beginning of his treatise *Physics* (I, 5–7)—they are the substrate (that which persists through change), the absence of (a particular) form, and the form which appears in the process of change. Change consists in a substrate (matter) acquiring a form which it did not previously possess. Hence we can speak of three principles, matter, privation, and form. Not-being is associated with privation, and the substrate, since it is always in existence, is in itself free of not-being. But since form follows privation, there is a sense in which we do have "genesis out of not-being." The mention of the doctrine of potentiality as an *alternative* explanation of change (191b27 ff.), whether a later insertion or not, is good evidence for the early date of the discussion in the *Physics*, and the first seven books are dated by Jaeger, for example, as belonging originally to the early or Academic period in Aristotle's development. Nonetheless, the doctrine of privation provides a wholly new approach to the problem of change on the part of Aristotle. The doctrine of the substrate clearly has affinities with that of the receptacle in Plato's *Timaeus*. But it inverts Plato's hierarchy of reality between form and substrate, and the doctrine of privation has its roots in the doctrine of the opposites in Plato's *Phaedo*.

Substance. In the *Categories* substance is characterized above all by its power to be the recipient of contrary qualifications (4a10), but it alone among the categories has no opposite. In the *Physics* change is from opposite to opposite, and this would seem to exclude the genesis of substances from substances. The logical answer might seem to be to treat only the substrate as a substance, and this is indeed what is implied in the *Physics*. But in *On Coming-to-be and Passing-away* Aristotle has to deal explicitly with the genesis of substance. Once again potential being is considered, but only to be dismissed as a possible source for substance (317b19–33), and an unhappy attempt is made to distinguish certain elements, such as earth, as "not-being" so that another element can come into being out of not-being. In the *Metaphysics* the question is taken up again, and from two points of view. First, the question of substance is much more thoroughly discussed (see below under the heading "Metaphysics"), and second, the doctrine of potential being is used to provide a more nearly adequate solution (*Metaphysics* Z 7–9 and Θ). In the strict sense, substance does not come into existence or pass out of existence either as matter or as form. What comes into existence is a "this-such," or concrete object combining matter and form. Both the matter and the form were already in existence, but in relation to each other their previous existence was only potential. The genesis of a new substance involves the passage from potential to actual existence for both matter and form in a new "this-such" or concrete object.

Efficient and final causes. The cause of a genesis or of any other change requires for Aristotle a twofold analysis—first, a correct analysis of the process of change itself, and second, the identification of the source or sources of the change. Virtually the same account of the doctrine of "the four causes" is found in the *Physics* and the *Metaphysics* (Δ 2), but there is reason to suppose that the account was first given in the *Physics*. Two "causes" have already been identified in the account of substrate and privation. These are matter and form. Two more must be added, the efficient cause and the final cause. All four can be separately identified in Plato's writings, but they do not form a system as they do for Aristotle. Thus Aristotle can actually criticize Plato for operating only with the formal and material causes, just as he criticized most of the pre-Socratics for employing only the material cause, although he recognized the emergence of efficient causes in Empedocles' Love and Strife.

For Aristotle, to know is to know by means of causes, and it is clear that the four Aristotelian causes are necessary elements in things, which must be known or understood if full understanding is to be reached, rather than causes in the modern sense. Viewed in this way, the material cause deals with the substrate, such as the bronze of a statue, while the formal cause is concerned with the shape of the statue. The final cause is the end or purpose for the sake of which the process of making the statue was commenced, and the efficient cause is that which initiates the process of change and so is its primary source. In some cases this might be a person acting as agent. It might seem at first that two of the causes, matter and form, are sited within the object to be explained, and two outside, the efficient and the final causes. This would misrepresent Aristotle's views in two ways. First, it is, strictly speaking, not the object, but the process of change by which it comes into existence, that the doctrine of the four causes is intended to explain. Second, Aristotle tells us (*Physics* 198a24) that in many cases the formal, final, and efficient causes all coincide. In the case of living creatures, the form of an object may also be that at which nature was aiming when the object was produced, and in the case of an artifact the final cause may be the form as known by the artist or manufacturer. In this last case the formal cause may be the efficient cause as well, in that the form as present in the artist's mind and desired by him in the object is the true source of the process of change that results. When applied to objects of different kinds, the doctrine of the four causes is capable of considerable elaboration and subtlety. For example, in the case of a city one might say that the matter is the people, the form is its organization, the final cause is living or living well, and the efficient cause is the realization or acceptance of the final cause as desirable by some or all of the people.

The ultimate source of motion. The distinction between external and internal causes raises in an acute way the question of the ultimate source or sources of motion and change in the universe. For the earlier pre-Socratics, *Physis* (Nature) as the object of study by physical philosophers was assumed, rather than consciously concluded, to have its own quasi-living source of motion within itself. Thinkers after Parmenides made increasing use of external agents acting upon the primary elements in order to initiate or maintain change. Plato in the *Laws* (894c ff.) supposed that the primary cause of movement must be that which can move both itself and other things, and this he identified as soul. Soul carries round the sun, moon, and stars, but he leaves it doubtful whether this is because soul is present in the sun as it is in man or because soul pushes the sun from outside or because the sun is moved from outside by soul in some other way. But for Plato the real world itself is not in motion. He supposes that things in the phenomenal world are imitations or reflections of the Forms, and on occasion he can speak of them as endeavoring to reproduce the Forms. When this happens, the Forms and the "love" they inspire are causes of change in the phenomenal world. Aristotle takes over from the pre-Socratics the concept of nature as possessing a source of motion within itself. In *On Philosophy* three causes of motion are distinguished—nature, force, and free will—and the motion of the stars is attributed to free will. This seems to represent the first stage of Aristotle's thinking, and there seems to be no evidence yet for any single transcendent mover of the heavens.

In *On the Heavens* the doctrine of natural movement is carried a step further. Of the four elements, air and fire naturally move upward and earth and water downward, a doctrine already implied in *On Philosophy*. A fifth element, *aether*, now appears (the later "quintessence"), with a natural circular movement which explains the movements of the stars, since these are composed of aether. We now seem to have only two sources of motion, nature and force, and we are probably justified in concluding that here too Aristotle is not envisaging any transcendent mover, certain passages to the contrary being best explained as later insertions.

Both in *On the Heavens* and in *On Philosophy* it is to be understood that living creatures move themselves and also are moved (on occasion) by forces from without. But what *makes* a living creature move itself? This question is tackled in *Physics* VIII, where it is argued that even a self-moved mover requires a cause outside itself to initiate its movement. If we are to avoid an infinite regress, we must suppose that this leads us to one or more prime movers that are themselves unmoved and that have the power to move by acting as objects of desire. Aristotle actually supposes that the prime mover is one, eternal, and nonmaterial and that there is one first-moved object, namely, the outermost heaven. The introduction of this transcendent mover is sometimes interpreted as the fulfillment rather than the negation of the view found in *On the Heavens* because it is possible to identify what is first moved with the aether. The identification is no doubt correct, but the loss of aether's natural movement is a major change. The unmoved mover is necessarily at rest, and this doctrine clearly is in some danger of introducing a conflict with the doctrine that nature is that which has a source of movement within itself. This would fit in well with an analysis of the *Physics* which would make the first six books represent an earlier stage in Aristotle's thought than Books VII–VIII. But it should be pointed out that if this is correct, the doctrine of the unmoved mover in the later books is nonetheless more Platonic in character than the doctrine of nature in the earlier books.

The final stage comes in *Metaphysics* Λ, the lateness of which is now generally regarded as established by the reference in Chapter 8 to the astronomical theories of Callippus, which can hardly be earlier than 330 B.C. In this chapter Aristotle puts forward the theory that there are 47 or 55 celestial spheres, each eternal, and for each of them there is a separate unmoved mover. The preceding chapter speaks of an unmoved mover in the singular, and the relation between the two chapters is a considerable problem. But there is a single unmoved mover clearly referred to within Chapter 8, and it is probable that there is no rejection of a single unmoved mover—it should, rather, be regarded as standing on a higher plane than the "departmental" movers assigned to individual planets.

Teleological physics. Nature for Aristotle makes nothing without a purpose (*On the Heavens* 271a33), and a word must be said about the teleological character of Aristotle's physical theories, which has brought so much censure upon his head. It has tended in modern times to seem a natural but dangerous doctrine in biological studies and wholly wrong in the study of inanimate nature. Its usefulness is clearly a matter for scientists to decide for themselves, but two points seem worth making. Normally Aristotle's teleology is not a doctrine of any over-all pattern of purpose in the universe, nor is it even intended to show how natural objects may serve purposes outside themselves. It is, rather, a doctrine of internal finality, that is, a doctrine that the end of each object is to be itself. Second, his teleology is rooted in his equation of final cause with formal cause. The study of the end or purpose of a thing is the study of its form, and to the extent that a modern scientist is concerned with the formal and universal elements in nature, he is, paradoxically enough, following Aristotle's approach. He would differ in supposing that the achievement of form in inanimate objects cannot profitably be described as their end.

PSYCHOLOGY

For Aristotle, the study of soul and of life is a part of the study of the physical world. In the *Eudemus* he had argued for the pre-existence of the soul, and in refuting the view that the soul was a harmony, he was clearly enough defending the full Platonic doctrine of the soul, even including the doctrine of recollection of knowledge acquired by the soul before birth, and maintaining that the life of the soul in the body is "contrary to nature." In the *Protrepticus*, while the importance of the soul and its superiority to the body are emphatically proclaimed, we have not enough information to say whether there is any change from the view expressed in the *Eudemus*. But in Fragment 60 (*Aristotelis Fragmenta*, Valentin Rose, ed.) the implication that the soul is fitted "part to part" throughout the body clearly involves a view of the soul as a separate substance. In the dialogue *On Philosophy*, while apparently disagreeing with Plato on some points, Aristotle puts forward a series of Platonic-type views of the soul, including the attribution of divinity to mind (Fr. 26, Rose).

The two-substance view of soul and body is found both in the biological treatises and throughout the *Parva Naturalia*, where the soul is frequently given a physical basis in heat and located or at least concentrated in a central governing place in the body, the heart. This has been called the second stage in the history of Aristotle's view of the soul. If we were dealing with human beings, this conclusion could be accepted with confidence. But since the reference is to animals and plants, we cannot be certain that Aristotle had abandoned his earlier view of the human soul at this stage, and at least one passage suggests that he had not (*On the Generation of Animals* 736b28). In the treatise *On the Soul*, however, we do find a sharply contrasting doctrine, according to which the soul and body constitute a single substance, standing to each other in the relation of form to matter. While it is true that in the *Eudemus* at one point the soul is rather vaguely referred to as a sort of form (Fr. 46, Rose), it is also in the same passage described as "receiving the Forms," implying that it is itself a separate substance. Apart from this there do not seem to be any anticipations of the doctrine presented in *On the Soul*.

Active and passive reason. The analysis of the functions of the soul in *On the Soul* is elaborate and detailed. After the usual survey of earlier theories, the soul is defined in technical language and its functions treated one by one. In the third and final book we come to the doctrine of Intelligence (*Nous*). The main functions of the soul have earlier been distinguished as the nutritive, the perceptive, the power of initiating movement, and the intelligence. They form a hierarchy, with the intelligence found only in man, so that living creatures can be arranged in a series according to the number of faculties possessed. Thinking is treated by Aristotle as analogous to perceiving. The mind is related to intelligible objects in the same way that sense is related to sensible objects. It is thus impassive and is itself nothing but potentiality (namely, the potentiality of receiving forms), and it has no form of its own.

Generally Aristotle speaks of *Nous* as one, but in the famous fifth chapter of Book III of *On the Soul* he distinguishes two, of which one *Nous* becomes all things like matter and the other makes all things, just as light makes potential colors actual. This latter *Nous* is separable, impassive, and unmixed, and only when it is separated does it have its true nature, immortal and eternal. What Aristotle means by this doctrine of an active and a passive reason is not explained elsewhere and has given rise to a famous controversy lasting over the centuries. Some suppose that we have really only one intellect functioning in two ways. One tradition interprets the active reason as a transcendent entity, identical with the prime mover and in effect God himself, thinking in us. This view began with Alexander of Aphrodisias in the second century A.D. and was developed further by Averroës, who regarded the active reason as a unique separate substance, inferior, however, to God. But Aristotle says that the distinction arises "within the soul," and Themistius cited these words against Alexander in the fourth century A.D. when arguing for a wholly immanent view of the active reason (in this he was followed by Thomas Aquinas).

It could be that we have here a vestige of an earlier Platonic view of the soul (see *Protrepticus* Fr. 61, Rose), but the doctrine seems to arise out of the discussion in earlier chapters in Book III of *On the Soul*, and, obscure though it is, it probably belongs to the latest stage of Aristotle's thought, when he was concerned with the consequences of analyzing the soul–body relationship in terms of form and matter. The question of a divine element in the human soul was possibly related in Aristotle's mind to the doctrine of God as actuality (which will be discussed under the heading "Theology"). His theory of knowledge likewise belongs as much to metaphysics as to psychology. (Another important aspect of Aristotle's psychology, his account of movement and desire, will be discussed under the heading "Ethics.")

METAPHYSICS

The title *Metaphysics* is of uncertain origin, but it seems clearly to have arisen only after Aristotle's death. The traditional explanation supposes that it refers to the order of the treatises in the Aristotelian corpus as organized by Andronicus of Rhodes, in which the *Metaphysics* comes after the *Physics* (*meta ta physika*). But there is some evidence that the title may be earlier than Andronicus. However, if its origin was a matter of chance, the meaning of the term was not interpreted as a matter of chance by the Greek commentators. Simplicius, speaking in a Platonizing vein, interpreted *meta* as meaning "beyond" and supposed that the reference was to a hierarchic order in the objects studied—metaphysics was concerned with objects which were beyond or outside the world of nature. The majority supposed that *meta* meant "after" and referred to an order of succession in knowledge, according to which metaphysical knowledge comes *after* physical knowledge. Aristotle himself uses the term "first philosophy," which he says deals with things that exist separately and are not subject to change or movement (*Metaphysics* 1026a16). Whether for Aristotle first philosophy covered the whole subject matter of the *Metaphysics* or only a part of it depends mainly on what view we take of the ultimate subject of study in the treatise.

The starting point for Aristotle's thought here, as so often, was his reaction to Plato's two-world doctrine, and in particular to the doctrine of the Forms. On Jaeger's view, Aristotle began by accepting the essentials of Plato's doctrine of the Forms, which Jaeger found clearly implied by *Eudemus* (Fr. 41, Rose). At this stage of Aristotle's thought, metaphysics, it is claimed, was identical with theology. The concept of metaphysics as the science of being-as-such belonged to the second stage, and in the third stage metaphysics either comprised or at least was based on the subject matter of physics. Jaeger's interpretation of the *Eudemus* fragment has since been denied by some, but probably without good reason. A similar controversy, which is currently unresolved, concerns the *Protrepticus* (Fr. 13, Walzer and Ross), which uses highly Platonic language to describe the objects of the theoretical knowledge that is the concern of the true philosopher. There is clearly a reference to the Forms as distinct from phenomena, and while it may be conceded that the fragment does not *say* that the Forms have separate transcendent existence, it does not say they have not; and the conclusion that it is the transcendent Forms to which Aristotle is referring seems the more natural one.

Whether or not Aristotle accepted transcendent Forms in the *Eudemus* and *Protrepticus*, it is clear that he had come to reject them in *On the Ideas*. There (Fr. 187, Rose) he took the view that, while there must be things other than sensible particulars and that these are universals, it does not follow that universals are Ideas or Forms in the Platonic sense; and he brought against the Ideas a number of the objections later elaborated in the *Metaphysics*. In *On Philosophy*, which Jaeger placed in the period after Aristotle left Athens for Assos, we have an attack on the Platonic doctrine of ideal numbers (Fr. 9, Rose). Proclus and Plutarch, apparently independently (Fr. 8, Rose), state that Aristotle rejected the doctrine of Ideas completely in the dialogues as well as elsewhere. But there is no evidence that these statements refer to the *On Philosophy*, so that they cannot be used to argue that that dialogue represents a later stage in Aristotle's thought than, say, *On the Ideas* or any other dialogue. All that we know is that in some of the dialogues Aristotle did criticize the theory of Forms, but this could very well be in the period before he left Athens, when, for all we know, *On Philosophy* itself was composed.

What is substance? The key to Aristotle's considered rejection of the Platonic Forms lies in his doctrine of substance, which was always for him the basic question in philosophy, as he himself says in the famous sentence in the *Metaphysics* (Z, 1028b2): "The question that was asked long ago, is asked now, and always is a matter of difficulty, 'What is being?' is the question 'What is substance?' " Rightly or wrongly Aristotle interpreted the Platonic Forms as universals and asked from the *Categories* onward how universals stand in relation to substance. He began by distinguishing between primary substance and secondary substance. Primary substance is always the individual concrete thing, and as such it is the subject of attributes in all the categories. The genera and species to which the individual thing belongs are secondary to it and would not exist without some primary substance to which they may apply (*Categories* 2b5). But every genus and species can be the subject of the same attributes as the primary substance of which they are genus and species (apart, of course, from that of coming under the genus and species which they themselves are). Accordingly genus and species, as subjects, can still claim to be substances. In this way the Platonic Forms, as species and genera, retain a kind of secondary existence.

The search for substance is for Aristotle the search for what *is*, as distinct from what "is something," since if a thing does not exist, it cannot be anything. In the *Categories* the Form as genus can still "be something," and so it retains its claim to substance. But Aristotle had already had the basic intuition which was to destroy Platonic transcendence—the substance of the genus or species is not a different substance from the substance of all or any members of the genus or species. In the statement "Socrates is a man," the substantiality of "man" *is* the substantiality of Socrates and not an independent substantiality. So while "man" stands for an entity, this entity *is* the subject of which it is predicated and not some other entity. In *Metaphysics* Z the priority of substance among the categories rests on three grounds. (1) It can exist alone, while what is signified by the other categories cannot. Of course a substance will have qualities, but it does not depend on them for its existence, while they do depend on it. (2) Substance is prior in definition, since a definition of the substance of a thing must be present in any definition. (3) Substance is prior for knowledge, since we need to know *what* a thing is before we know its quantity, quality, and so on.

There are four objects to which the term "substance" is applied: the essence, the universal, the genus, and the substrate. But substrate in the sense of matter, which in itself is not a particular thing, cannot be substance because both separability and "thisness" are lacking. The same objections are sufficient to show that the universal cannot be a substance, although the opportunity is taken to bring a whole range of other objections against the Platonic Forms; and the objections to the universal as substance apply also to the genus. However, substrate in the sense of subject to which predicates attach may properly be called substance. But we want further information as to what such subjects are. Essence is the traditional rendering of Aristotle's curious coinage of which even the syntax is not altogether clear, but which perhaps should be literally rendered "the what it was to be (something)." (For a discussion of other views, see Joseph Owens, *The Doctrine of Being in the Aristotelian Metaphysics*, 2d ed., pp. 353–354). But the meaning is clear enough in general—the essence is what a thing is by its very nature, what gives it its identity and makes it what it is. Consequently we may say that the essence of a thing is the thing in its truest sense, and so the essence can be identified with substance.

Essence. A fuller account is needed of the essence of a thing than identifying it with substance. In what does a thing's essence consist? Aristotle's answer is given in terms of the doctrine of causes, which was intended to answer the questions of how and why a thing comes to be what it is. Normally the essence of a thing will be its final cause, which in turn will tend to be the same as its formal cause. We may say, then, that essence consists in form. But here an important distinction must be made. The essence of a thing consists in the form which it has achieved, not in any form which it does not have but might acquire. Achieved form is form actually realized in a concrete thing, and Aristotle uses two virtually interchangeable technical terms for it, "entelechy" and "actuality." (Strictly speaking, "actuality" refers primarily to the process which reaches its termination in the "entelechy.") These are opposed to potentiality. Form without matter exists potentially but not actually, and matter without form would also exist only potentially. Thus the concrete individual object is the essence, which is substance for Aristotle.

The nature of metaphysics. The discussion of potentiality and actuality provides a bridge to Aristotle's theology. But it also uncovers a major problem as to the nature of metaphysics as Aristotle saw it. Side by side in the *Metaphysics* there appear to be two conceptions. On one view, there is a separate subject of study, the study of being-as-such, distinct from the study of particular kinds of being which form the subject matter of separate sciences. On the other view, the subject matter of metaphysics is separate but unchanging being, in other words, transcendent supersensible being of which God is the outstanding case. The former view is the antecedent of the scholastic general metaphysics, and the latter, which Aristotle tended to call first philosophy or theology, is the later special metaphysics. According to Jaeger, Aristotle's progression was from metaphysics as theology to metaphysics as the science of being-as-such. But Aristotle's fullest discussion of theology comes in *Metaphysics* Λ, which is probably one of the latest parts of the treatise as a whole. The transition to theology begins in the discussion of potentiality and actuality in Book Θ, and the doctrine of actuality, which seems to be a later addition in the *Physics*, looks very like the latest formulation of Aristotle's thinking on the problem of being-as-such. So it could be that Jaeger's order of progression should be inverted—in this case, Aristotle would proceed from being-as-such to theology. A unitarian interpretation of the *Metaphysics* would argue that such a progression is indeed there but that it is a logical progression, a progression in argument, rather than a reflection of any chronological sequence in the stages of Aristotle's thought.

THEOLOGY

The relation of the divine world to the physical world was one of the main themes in the dialogue *On Philosophy*. It seems clear that Aristotle had already rejected much of Plato's cosmology as expressed in the *Timaeus*, above all the view (which he thought he found there) that the world had a beginning. But he deployed a whole series of arguments to establish the existence and importance of divine beings. The divinity of the heavenly bodies seems to have been accepted together with the souls in them, which were the sources of their movements. This does not, as has sometimes been claimed, exclude a transcendent mover as well; but there is no positive reference anywhere to such a mover, and Jaeger was not justified in claiming such a mover for this dialogue. The position concerning the unmoved mover is probably the same in the treatise *On the Heavens*, where there are indeed positive references—but these are probably later additions. The general impression here also is that the outermost heaven is the primary source of movement and that it initiates movement by moving itself.

The Unmoved Mover. By the time he wrote the last two books of the *Physics*, Aristotle had come to believe in the necessity of an unmoved mover, and the doctrine is developed fully in the *Metaphysics*. In Book Θ, Chapter 8 he develops the contrast between actuality and potentiality. The potential is actualized only by some actually existing thing acting as cause. Consequently the prime mover must exist actually because it actualizes potential movements throughout the universe, and this is supported by additional arguments. In Book Λ we have a separate treatise on theology which begins with a fresh rehearsal of the doctrines of substance, form, privation, matter, actuality, and potentiality. It is then argued that change must be eternal because the nature of time excludes the possibility of time without change, whether in the past or the future. If change is eternal, then the actuality which causes it must be eternal. Therefore the prime mover must be eternal; and if it is eternal, it must be immaterial, since matter involves potentiality of change and consequently militates against eternal existence. The prime mover, then, as actuality must be pure actuality without matter—a concept of actuality which it is difficult indeed to bring into accord with Aristotle's doctrine of actuality as matter + form. Being immaterial, the prime mover is not extended in space. It moves other objects as the object of their desire and their thought. This is the source of the principle of movement *within* nature which continues to lie at the root of Aristotle's conception of physics. As object of desire it is good, and as actuality it must be substantial because it moves substances. Its freedom from change is explained by identifying it with thought, an identification made the easier for Aristotle because of his normal equation of form without matter and thought. The prime mover turns out to be eternal and thus divine thought or mind, and Aristotle now no longer hesitates to call it God.

But what is this divine thought about? In his famous sentence (*Metaphysics* 1072b19) Aristotle says, "Thought thinks itself as object in virtue of its participation in what is thought." The plain meaning of this is that God is the object of his own thinking. A long tradition going back to Alexander of Aphrodisias and given further currency by Aquinas, maintains that in thinking himself as object, God thinks all the things that are in the world. But this cannot have been Aristotle's meaning. Knowledge of the visible world would involve knowledge of material and so of changeable being, and since the quality of thought depends, for Aristotle as for Plato, on the nature of its objects, to think changeable objects would make the thought itself subject to change, and so God would no longer be immutable. The objects of God's thought must be limited to what is unchangeable and so to himself. This does not mean, however, that Aristotle has produced thought with no object of thought. We should, rather, suppose that God *is* those truths which are free from change and that it is these which he thinks.

This is the theology which there is good reason to suppose represents the latest stage of Aristotle's thinking. While completely un-Platonic in its details, it can not unfairly be characterized as a fresh affirmation of the basic Platonic position that the world of the senses is a derivative world dependent for its continued activity upon a reality outside itself. Metaphysical inquiry understood in this way was clearly something which Aristotle never abandoned. On the other hand, his doctrine of the substantiality of the concrete individual remained with him also, and this marks a decisive break with Platonism.

ETHICS AND POLITICS

Of the three major ethical treatises in the Aristotelian corpus—the *Nicomachean Ethics*, the *Eudemian Ethics*, and the *Magna Moralia*—only the first was generally accepted as genuine in the pre-Jaeger period of Aristotelian studies, the *Eudemian Ethics* being attributed to Aristotle's pupil Eudemus of Rhodes and the *Magna Moralia* regarded as a later Peripatetic compilation. Since Jaeger, the *Eudemian Ethics* is usually accepted as also genuine and as representing an earlier stage in Aristotle's ethical thinking. A minority of scholars would regard the *Magna Moralia* as a still earlier work by Aristotle, but most would still regard it as a later Peripatetic compilation based on the *Eudemian Ethics* rather than on the *Nicomachean Ethics*. The relationship between the two works is complicated by the apparent absence of three books in the manuscripts of the *Eudemian Ethics* and the statement made at the end of Book III that the three missing books are identical with Books V, VI, and VII of the *Nicomachean Ethics*. The older view that these three books should be transferred to the *Eudemian Ethics* is now better abandoned in favor of the view that they represent the latest stage in Aristotle's thinking about the topics dealt with and so are correctly placed in the *Nicomachean Ethics*, the original books of the *Eudemian Ethics* being replaced by them.

The earliest Aristotelian treatment of ethical themes of which we have any knowledge is the *Protrepticus*. There philosophy in a highly Platonic sense is the key to the grasping of the norms of right conduct. No distinction is made between practical and theoretical wisdom, both being called *phronesis*, and ethics is treated as an exact science. *Eudemian Ethics* I, 6 admits an empirical part of ethics but still does not divide *phronesis*. In *Nicomachean Ethics* VI, however, *phronesis* as practical wisdom is contrasted with *sophia* (theoretical wisdom), and both are necessary for achieving "intellectual virtue." All this is most simply explained by the hypothesis that we are witnessing a progressive development of Aristotle's ideas and that the culmination (in the *Nicomachean Ethics*) of this development is the product of his attempt to apply his later metaphysical and psychological doctrines in the sphere of ethics.

It is difficult for a modern philosopher not to either misconstrue or wholly condemn Aristotle's ethical thought. This is because Aristotle begins by implicitly rejecting the basic modern contention that value judgments either are not judgments of fact at all or, if they are, are judgments of a kind of fact altogether different from the facts involved in judgments about the physical world. The good for Aristotle is whatever is in fact aimed at. So the good for man is what man by nature *is* seeking. His seeking is not identical with what he wishes, since his seeking is rooted in his nature in a way in which his wishing need not be. What man is seeking may be given the formal name *eudaimonia*, which we misleadingly translate as "happiness," but if we have to be more explicit as to what *eudaimonia* involves, we will say that the good for man is the fulfillment of his function. This, in terms of Aristotle's metaphysical thought, is expressed as "the actuality of a soul with respect to its function" (1098a16). The soul has a rational part and a nonrational part. The rational part has one aspect which is completely rational and another which is also an aspect of the irrational part, namely, the seat of the appetites and of desire. Insofar as desires conform to reason, the part is rational, and insofar as they do not, it is irrational. The rational control of desires is the province of what Aristotle calls moral virtue. This is confined to cases where a choice is possible. Moral virtue is promoted by regular practice, which induces habits; and it involves following a mean course between extremes, which are vices—as courage is a mean between rashness and cowardice. But action is not virtuous because it follows a mean course—it is virtuous because it is in conformity with reason, and as a result it will in fact involve a mean.

The wholly rational part of the soul is the province of "intellectual virtue," and it is itself twofold inasmuch as one part of it is concerned with the contemplation of unchangeable truths and the other with truths and objects which are subject to change. The virtue of the first part is *sophia*, or theoretical wisdom, and that of the second is *phronesis*, or practical wisdom. It is *phronesis* which discovers what is right in action and so makes it possible for desires to conform to reason by discovering ends and then relating means to ends. But the ultimate end for man, which is living well (*eudaimonia*), is not a matter of deliberation or choice—it is, rather, something given in the nature of man. This is something which could vary, although it is clear that Aristotle does not suppose that in fact it does vary. The highest of the virtues is, however, theoretical wisdom, and this is an activity of which man is capable because of something divine in his nature—in its exercise he approximates to the life of God; and for man, as for God, his highest function is thought. This thought will be about objects which cannot be other than what they are and so never change.

For Aristotle, politics is a branch of practical knowledge, being that part of ethics which deals with men in groups. Some groups have limited purposes, but a polis, or "political" group, is one whose ends are coterminous with the ends of human life. Man is a "political animal," by which Aristotle means that it is his nature to form groups of this kind. These principles are established at the beginning of the *Politics*. Critical and descriptive surveys of various types of constitutions occupy most of Books II–VI, and in Books VII–VIII Aristotle discusses the best form of the polis without actually saying what it is, although earlier he had expressed his approval of rule by the best men, whether a group or an individual. It is possible that the treatise as we have it is unfinished. Attempts to rearrange the books in a more "logical" order must fail, for the present order is that laid down at the end of the *Nicomachean Ethics*. Nor is it plausible any longer to distinguish an empirical trend as representing a later stage in Aristotle's thought than the search for the ideal or best constitution. On this question, as elsewhere, the search for the ideal Form is for Aristotle a search for actuality, and this involves consideration of concrete individual cases.

Bibliography

The complete works of Aristotle in Greek may be found in *Aristotelis Opera*, I. Bekker and others, eds., 5 vols. (Berlin, 1831–1870); there is a new edition of Vols. I, II, IV, and V, edited by Otto Gigon (Berlin, 1960–1961). The fragments may be found in *Aristotelis Fragmenta*, Valentin Rose, ed. (Leipzig, 1886); *Aristotelis Dialogorum Fragmenta*, R. Walzer, ed. (Florence, 1934); and *Aristotelis Fragmenta Selecta*, W. D. Ross, ed. (Oxford, 1955). There are improved Greek texts for most of the treatises by various editors in the Teubner Series (Leipzig, 1868–1961) and the Oxford Classical Texts (Oxford, 1894–1965); with French translations in the Budé Series (Paris, 1926–1964); and with English translations in the Loeb Series (London, 1926–1965).

The complete works of Aristotle in English may be found in *The Works of Aristotle Translated Into English*, W. D. Ross, ed., 12 vols. (Oxford, 1908–1952).

Medieval Latin translations are *Aristoteles Latinus* (Bruges, 1939—), which is to be in some 34 vols., and *Opera cum Averrois Commentariis*, 12 vols. in 14 (Venice, 1562–1574; reprinted Frankfurt, 1961).

Works of the Greek commentators may be found in *Commentaria in Aristotelem Graeca*, together with *Supplementum Aristotelicum*, 26 vols. (Berlin, 1882–1909).

Major modern editions and commentaries on individual works include the following: *Prior and Posterior Analytics*, W. D. Ross, ed. (Oxford, 1949); *Aristotle's Categories and De Interpretatione Translated With Notes*, translated by J. L. Ackrill (Oxford, 1963); *De Anima*, W. D. Ross, ed. (Oxford, 1961); *De Generatione et Corruptione*, H. H. Joachim, ed. (Oxford, 1922); *L'Éthique à Nicomaque*, R. A. Gauthier and J. Y. Jolif, eds., 3 vols. (Louvain, 1958); *Metaphysics*, W. D. Ross, ed., 2 vols. (Oxford, 1924); *Parva Naturalia*, W. D. Ross, ed. (Oxford, 1955); *Physics*, W. D. Ross, ed. (Oxford, 1936); G. F. Else, *Aristotle's Poetics, the Argument* (Cambridge, Mass., 1957); *Politics*, W. L. Newman, ed., 4 vols. (Oxford, 1887–1902); *Politics*, translated by Ernest Barker (Oxford, 1946); and Ingmar Düring, *Protrepticus, an Attempt at Reconstruction* (Göteborg, Sweden, 1961).

Works on Aristotle's life and writings include Ingmar Düring, *Aristotle in the Ancient Biographical Tradition* (Göteborg, Sweden, 1957), and P. Moraux, *Les Listes anciennes des ouvrages d'Aristote* (Louvain, 1951).

General accounts, including the question of development, are Werner Jaeger, *Aristoteles, Grundlegung einer Geschichte seiner Entwicklung* (Berlin, 1923), translated by Richard Robinson as *Aristotle, Fundamentals of the History of His Development* (Oxford, 1934; 2d ed., 1948); W. D. Ross, *Aristotle* (London, 1923; 6th ed., 1955); P. Wilpert, *Zwei Aristotelische Frühschriften über die Ideenlehre* (Regensburg, 1949); D. J. Allan, *The Philosophy of Aristotle* (London, 1952); J. Moreau, *Aristote et son école* (Paris, 1962); Harold Cherniss, *Aristotle's Criticism of Plato and the Academy* (Baltimore, 1944); and G. E. M. Anscombe, "Aristotle," which is Ch. 1 in G. E. M. Anscombe and P. T. Geach, *Three Philosophers* (Ithaca, N.Y., 1961).

Works on Aristotle's logic are Friedrich Solmsen, *Die Entwicklung der Aristotelischen Logik und Rhetorik* (Berlin, 1929); E. Kapp, *Greek Foundations for Traditional Logic* (New York, 1942); Jan Łukasiewicz, *Aristotle's Syllogistic From the Standpoint of Modern Formal Logic* (Oxford, 1951; 2d ed., 1957); S. McCall, *Aristotle's Modal Syllogisms* (Amsterdam, 1963); G. Patzig, *Die Aristotelische Syllogistik*, 2d ed. (Göttingen, 1963); and J. M. Le Blond, *Logique et méthode chez Aristote* (Paris, 1939).

Aristotle's physics is discussed in A. Mansion, *Introduction à la physique aristotelicienne* (Paris, 1913; 2d ed., Louvain, 1946); Friedrich Solmsen, *Aristotle's System of the Physical World* (Ithaca, N.Y., 1960); and W. Wieland, *Die Aristotelische Physik* (Göttingen, 1962).

For discussions of Aristotle's psychology, see F. Nuyens, *Ontwikkelingsmomenten in de Zielkunde van Aristoteles* (Nijmegen, the Netherlands, 1939), translated by Theo Schillings and others as *L'Évolution de la psychologie d'Aristote* (Louvain, 1948).

For Aristotle's metaphysics, see Joseph Owens, *The Doctrine of Being in the Aristotelian Metaphysics* (Toronto, 1951; 2d ed., 1957), and P. Aubenque, *Le Problème de l'être chez Aristote* (Paris, 1962).

Aristotle's theology is discussed in H. von Arnim, *Die Entstehung der Gotteslehre des Aristoteles* (Vienna, 1931), and W. K. C. Guthrie, "Development of Aristotle's Theology," in *Classical Quarterly*, Vol. 27 (1933), 162–171.

Discussions of Aristotle's ethics may be found in H. von Arnim, *Die drei Aristotelischen Ethiken* (Vienna, 1924); R. Walzer, *Magna Moralia und Aristotelische Ethik* (Vienna, 1929); and J. Léonard, *Le Bonheur chez Aristote* (Brussels, 1948).

Aristotle's mathematics is discussed in T. L. Heath, *Mathematics in Aristotle* (Oxford, 1949).

For Aristotle as a biologist, see M. Manquat, *Aristote naturaliste* (Paris, 1932), and D'Arcy W. Thompson, "Aristotle the Naturalist," in R. W. Livingstone, ed., *The Legacy of Greece* (Oxford, 1922), reprinted in Thompson's *Science and the Classics* (Oxford, 1940).

An invaluable index of Greek words is provided by Hermann Bonitz, *Index Aristotelicus*, which was originally in Vol. V of I. Bekker's edition of *Aristotelis Opera* (Berlin, 1870) and was reprinted separately (Graz, 1955). Of more limited range is Troy Wilson Organ, *An Index to Aristotle in English Translation* (Princeton, N.J., 1949), which is based on the first 11 volumes of W. D. Ross, ed., *The Works of Aristotle Translated Into English*.

G. B. KERFERD

ARITHMETIC. *See* MATHEMATICS, FOUNDATIONS OF; NUMBER.

ARIUS AND ARIANISM. Arius, the heresiarch (died A.D. 335), was concerned to maintain consistently the unity of God. God, he held, is one, the monad, completely indivisible and without parts. Therefore, he could not separate part of himself by emanation to make a second divine being. The son, or logos, of God is called the dyad, separate from and inferior to the monad. Arius represented a strain of Platonic tradition within the early church, a tradition which included Justin, Clement, Origen, and the theologians of the Greek Church who came after them. From Libya he went to Alexandria; then, theologically unsatisfied, he went to Antioch and became a pupil of Lucian. Here the continuing influence of Origen's transcendent monotheism helped to stress the ultimacy of God: God alone is unbegotten and this is God's distinctive quality. Arius spoke and wrote against the teaching of his bishop, Alexander, who maintained a plurality within the unity of the Godhead and spoke of the monad as existing in the triad, the son and the Father being inseparable realities, both eternal and without beginning. Arius, in his insistence on the solitary perfection of God, was unable to assign the son, or logos, the place which the faith of the church considered he should have. The result of the conflict was the council of Nicaea in 325, at which Arius and his doctrine were condemned. Fifty years of controversy followed, with Athanasius as the chief opponent of Arianism. The controversy culminated in the council of Constantinople in 381.

Arius begins a statement of his beliefs, "We confess one God, who alone is unbegotten, alone eternal, alone without beginning, alone true, alone possessing immortality, alone wise and good." God is alone or unique (*monos*). This was a theme of Platonic philosophy and early Christian thought. There can be only one unbegotten. The presence of this last term has led some to call Arius an Aristotelian, but the term was also used by Platonists and by Christians like Justin nearly two centuries earlier. (In the fourth century Aristotelianism existed only as part of Platonism.) There can be only one being who has no beginning, Arius held, and his wisdom and goodness must be different from the wisdom and goodness of those who are inferior to him. But God is not merely unique in transcendent isolation. He is also unique because his relationship to the world is that of complete sovereignty. He is the only ruler, judge, and disposer of all things. There are no other beings to rival his sovereignty and power. He does not change and does not vary. He is the God of the law and the prophets as well as the God of the new covenant. Arius maintained consistently that there is one God, unique in his power and unique in his relationship to all other things.

The son of God cannot possess the unique qualities of the Father. He is begotten and had a beginning. There was a time when he did not exist. He is a creature and belongs to the realm of becoming. His creation came through the will of God. "By the will and wish of the Father he arose before time and before the ages." God made him so that, through him, God might create the world and men. The existence of the logos, or son, is derived from God's will to create, and he is the first step in God's creating act. The logos is the first of all creatures but belongs with them and not with the transcendent Father.

The relationship of the logos to God is one of difference or contrast. The Father is foreign in substance to the son as he is foreign in substance to, and unlike, all things. The logos is unlike the Father in every respect. The triad of the three persons of the godhead are distinct entities and are not mixed up with one another in any way. There is an infinite difference of glory between one and the other. Arius explained the attribution of divinity to the son through the Platonic doctrine of participation. By participation the son has become divine. Sharing in the divine nature is possible to all creatures, but he alone has achieved it and has received the name of God. Like all creatures he is changeable, but by his own free will he remains good. Arius' system was one of uncompromising dualism. All things other than God are created by the will of God out of nothing.

Athanasius and others reacted strongly to the teaching of Arius; after many maneuvers the council of Nicaea adopted a statement which was incompatible with Arius' views. It insisted that Jesus Christ is the son of God, begotten of the Father in a unique way, "only begotten, that is, of the substance of the Father, God of God, light of light, true God of true God, begotten not made, of one substance with the Father." A statement was added in condemnation of those who claimed that "there was a time when he did not exist, and before he was begotten he was not, and that he came into being out of nothing or from another substance, or that the son of God is created or changeable or subject to alteration." These were the distinctive points of Arianism. Arius was banished by the emperor Constantine.

However, Arianism was far from finished, for the statement of Nicaea was not a true expression of the belief of the church at that time. There was a reaction in favor of Arius against the creed of Nicaea. Arian leaders who had been exiled were brought back, and after the death of Constantine in 337 they were dominant in the East. From 350 to 361 Constantius made every effort to destroy the doctrines put forward at Nicaea. Nevertheless, between 361 and 381 Arianism was gradually discredited, and at Constantinople in 381 the creed of Nicaea was reaffirmed and Arianism permanently rejected. It lingered on among the Goths but ended with their conversion to orthodoxy at the end of the sixth century.

In the controversy the three main terms were *homoousios* (of the same substance), *homoiousios* (of like substance), and *anomoios* (unlike). The extreme Arians insisted that the logos was of different substance from God and unlike him. The Nicene account and Athanasius insisted that the son was of the same substance as God. A version of the doctrine of like substance was a key to a solution, because it avoided a division within the Godhead and conveyed the basic meaning of Nicaea without pluralistic overtones. Once it became clear that Athanasius was prepared to accept a doctrine of *homoousios* interpreted in the generic sense, agreement became possible. It is difficult to give an exact account of *homoousios* as a logical term in the thought of Athanasius. For him it meant the essential unity of God, Father, Son, and Holy Spirit, interpreted in conjunction with such Biblical metaphors as father and son, light, image, spring, and river. In this way Athanasius understood plurality within the divine unity and avoided the literalistic dualism of Arius. Arians objected still more strongly to the idea that the Holy Spirit was of the same substance with the Father and the Son, for this in their view implied that the Father had two sons. Athanasius insisted that Father, Son, and Holy Spirit were of the same substance. The Cappadocian fathers (Gregory of Nazianzus, Gregory of Nyssa, and Basil) developed the notion that the Godhead is one *ousia* and three *hypostaseis*. *Ousia* is essential being, while *hypostasis* is objective individuality. While in all other cases a *hypostasis* is the realization of a particular *ousia*, in the case of God the one *ousia* is realized in three *hypostaseis*, or *prosopa*. The Latin *tres personae in una substantia* has led to the English rendering, "three persons in one substance."

Texts on Arius and Arianism

Migne, J. P., ed., *Patrologia Graeca*. Paris, 1857. Vols. 25–28.

Opitz, H. G., ed., *Athanasius Werke*. Berlin, 1934. Vol. III, Pt. I: "Urkunden zur Geschichte des Arianischen Streites."

Stevenson, J., ed., *A New Eusebius*. London, 1957.

Works on Arius and Arianism

Gwatkin, H. M., *Studies of Arianism*. Cambridge, 1882; 2d ed., 1900.

Kelly, J. N. D., *Early Christian Doctrines*. London, 1958.

Prestige, G. L., *God in Patristic Thought*, 2d ed. London, 1952.

Stead, G. C., "The Platonism of Arius." *Journal of Theological Studies*, Vol. 15 (1964), 16–31.

Stead, G. C., "The Significance of the *Homoousious*." *Texte und Untersuchungen*, Vol. 78 (1961), 397–412.

E. F. OSBORN

ARMINIUS AND ARMINIANISM. Jacobus Arminius (Jacob Harmanszoon, 1560–1609), who gave his name to a variant of Reformed belief, was born in Oudewater, Holland. After his father's early death, the boy was protected in turn by a minister, who converted him to Protestantism; by Rudolphus Snel van Rooijen the mathematician; and by Pieter Bertius of Rotterdam. With Pieter Bertius, Jr., later important in the great Arminian disputes, Arminius studied at Leiden under the French Protestant Lambertus Danaeus. Later Arminius studied under Theodorus Beza in Geneva, where he met Johannes Uytenbogaert (Wtenbogaert), the chief proponent of Arminian doctrines after the death of Arminius.

Soon after his ordination (1588), Arminius was called upon by the ecclesiastical court of Amsterdam to refute the arguments of the Dutch "libertine" theologian Dirck Volckertszoon Coornhert, an exercise that undermined Arminius' orthodox Calvinism. He came to doubt the deterministic doctrine of damnation, and believed that election, dependent in part on man's free will, was not arbitrary but arose from God's pity for fallen men. Arminius was consistently attacked by orthodox clergymen (notably Petrus Plancius and Franciscus Gomarus) for his alleged Pelagianism; in spite of all opposition, however, he was made professor of theology at Leiden in 1603 and thereafter exercised great influence upon the next generation of divines. He died just prior to the national schism brought about by his beliefs.

Arminianism. In 1610 the Arminian clergy published their Great Remonstrance, a codification of Arminius' creed. This work dealt with five doctrinal points: it rejected the doctrine of election and predestination, both supralapsarian and sublapsarian. It rejected the idea that Christ died for the elect alone and belief in irresistible grace. It asserted belief in the sufficient power of saints, rejecting the idea that saints could fall from grace.

To the orthodox, these were Romish heresies; for eight years the battle of the pulpits raged, with Uytenbogaert, Bertius, and Hugo Grotius the great defenders of the Remonstrance. A theological question of this magnitude necessarily involved political theory and practice: the Remonstrants developed several versions of a theory by which, to protect consciences, the magistrate, rather than the Dutch Reformed church, was given final say in matters of religion. Naturally, since such a theory favored republican administration, Arminianism gained support in the town governments and in the States-General, particularly in the figure of the pensionary of Holland, Jan van Olden Barneveldt.

In 1618 a synod was called to rule on Remonstrant doctrine, with the open support of the stadholder, Prince Maurice of Orange, who realized that the theological controversy might be used to curb the power of the States-General. For the hearing at Dordrecht (Dort), Arminian tenets were slightly modified by Uytenbogaert. Election was interpreted as God's grace to true believers; but this grace was not irresistible, and salvation still depended on the cooperation of the human will, which was sufficiently strong to overcome the temptations of evil. By the time the sessions began, the leading Arminian laymen had been arrested for treason: Olden Barneveldt was sentenced to be beheaded in The Hague; Grotius and Rombout Hogerbeets were imprisoned in Loevestein Castle.

The Synod was international: representatives from Germany, Geneva, and England took part in the hearings, but the Remonstrants were barely allowed to be heard. Their five tenets were declared inadmissible, or heretical, and orthodox Calvinism was upheld. Remonstrants were given the choice of recantation or exile.

Most chose exile—in France, Geneva, or England. Until the death of Prince Maurice in 1625, Arminianism was persecuted in Holland; but with the accession to the stadholderate of the tolerant Frederick Henry, Arminians began to return, particularly to the great cities of Amsterdam and Rotterdam. In 1630 a church was organized in Amsterdam, to which in 1632 an academy was attached, to train Remonstrant clergymen and the sons of Remonstrants barred from studying at the universities.

Dutch Arminianism was closely allied with advanced secular learning, both philosophical and scientific. The Remonstrant "Illustre School" (later the nucleus of the University of Amsterdam) was distinguished for its mathematical and medical, as well as its theological and philosophical, faculties. Whatever the philosophical implications of Arminius' humanistic doctrine, in the seventeenth century it was coupled with broad learning: an Arminian professor translated Descartes' *Discourse upon Method* into Latin for the general use of the learned world; Arminian professors contributed to the periodicals of the republic of letters; and John Locke found a home among the Arminians during his exile from England.

Bibliography

PRIMARY SOURCES

Arminius, Jacobus, *Disputationes XXIV*. Leiden, 1609.

Arminius, Jacobus, *The Works*, translated and edited by James Nichols, 3 vols. London, 1825–1875.

Brandt, Gerard, *The History of the Reformation and Other Ecclesiastical Transactions in the Low Countries*, 4 vols. London, 1720–1723.

Limborch, Philippus van, and Hartsoeker, Christiaan, *Praestantium ac Eruditorum Virorum Epistolae Ecclesiasticae et Theologicae*. Amsterdam, 1684. Letters of Uytenbogaert, Arminius, Grotius, et al.

Triglandius, Jacobus, *Kerckelycke Geschiedenissen, Begrypende de Swaere Ende Bekommerlijke Geschillen, in de Vereenigde Nederlanden Voor-gevallen, met Derselver Beslissinge*. Leiden, 1650.

Uytenbogaert, Johannes van, *Kerckelycke Historie*. Rotterdam, 1647.

SECONDARY SOURCES

Colie, R. L., *Light and Enlightenment: A Study of the Cambridge Platonists and the Dutch Arminians*. Cambridge, 1957.

Davies, Godfrey, "Arminian versus Puritan in England, c. 1620–1650." *Huntington Library Bulletin*, Vol. 5 (1934).

Harrison, A. W., *The Beginnings of Arminianism*. London, 1926.

Harrison, A. W., *Arminianism*. London, 1937.

Itterzoon, G. P. van, "Koning Jacobus I en de Synode van Dordrecht." *Nederlandsch Archief voor Kerkgeschiedenis*, Vol. 24 (1932).

Nobbs, Douglas, *Theocracy and Toleration. A Study in the Disputes in Dutch Calvinism from 1600 to 1650*. Cambridge, 1938.

Rogge, H. C., *Johannes Wtenbogaert en Zijn Tijd*, 2 vols. Amsterdam, 1874–1876.

Tideman, Johannes, *De Remonstrantie en het Remonstrantisme*. Amsterdam, 1851.

R. L. Colie

ARNAULD, ANTOINE (1612–1694), Jansenist theologian and philosopher, was one of the most brilliant thinkers of the seventeenth century. He was born in Paris into a large and distinguished family that was to be long associated with Jansenism. His sister Angélique was the abbess of Port-Royal and reformed it along Jansenist lines. Ordained a priest and awarded a doctorate in theology in 1641, Antoine entered the Sorbonne in 1643 after the death of Cardinal Richelieu, who had opposed his admittance. Twelve years later he was expelled from the Sorbonne, and for the balance of his life, like most members of the Jansenist faction, he was subjected to almost continual persecution by the Jesuits. However brilliant the members of the Jansenist, or for that matter of the Cartesian, parties may have been, they proved to be no match for the political machinations of the Jesuits. Arnauld died in exile in Brussels.

Criticisms of Descartes. Arnauld's works have not been printed since the eighteenth century. A major portion of his writing was devoted to purely theological topics, to the Jansenist controversy (in which he was aided by his friends Blaise Pascal and Pierre Nicole), and to polemics with Calvinists. Nevertheless, his philosophical contribution was both large and significant. Descartes expressed pleasure at having Arnauld, a doctor of the Sorbonne, present objections to his *Méditations*. One of Arnauld's criticisms has become a standard item in the Cartesian literature—the question of the circularity of Descartes's argument: "The only secure reason we have for believing that what we clearly and distinctly perceive is true, is the fact that God exists. But we can be sure that God exists only because we clearly and evidently perceive that; therefore prior to being certain that God exists, we should be certain that whatever we clearly and evidently perceive is true" (*Quatrièmes Objections*, 1641).

He pressed Descartes on at least two other issues. First, he challenged Descartes's account of the nature of the human mind—specifically, on the adequacy of Descartes's radical distinction between mind and body. Arnauld argued that since Descartes seemed to distinguish between his own ideas and the perfect ones in God's Mind, there is a problem (which demands further clarification) involved in showing that from a belief that the mind is not corporeal it follows that the mind truly is not corporeal. Second, he queried Descartes on whether an account of the Eucharist can be given on Cartesian grounds, since the position of Descartes with reference to sense qualities would seem to create theological difficulties. As Descartes subsequently discovered, Arnauld's suspicions proved correct.

The "Port-Royal Logic." Arnauld's second major philosophical contribution was the logic text, that he wrote with Pierre Nicole, *La Logique, ou l'art de penser* (1662), best known as the *Port-Royal Logic*. A handbook on method rather than a study of formal logic in the strict sense, it was strongly and consciously Cartesian—roughly, a development from Descartes's *Regulae* rather than Aristotle's *Prior Analytics*. By greatly elaborating the theory of clear and distinct ideas, Arnauld sought to provide a way to science that would escape Pyrrhonism.

Controversy with Malebranche. Arnauld's third and most important contribution is to be found in his extended dispute with his onetime friend, Nicolas Malebranche, priest of the oratory, who although not a disciple of Descartes, was nevertheless a philosopher in the Cartesian tradition. Malebranche's *Recherche de la vérité* appeared in 1674. Arnauld had objections to the *Recherche*, but did not initiate his dispute until after the publication of Malebranche's *Traité de la nature et de la grâce* (1680). Profoundly disturbed by the theological views expressed in the *Traité*, Arnauld sought to show the fallacies in the theological account by undermining the philosophical aspects of it. Thus, in 1683, Arnauld published *Des Vraies et des Fausses Idées contre ce qu'enseigne l'auteur de la recherche de la vérité*, and he published almost a dozen more works against Malebranche before his own death. He was primarily concerned over what he took to be the theological consequences of Malebranche's thesis that "we see all things in God," in reference to such issues as grace, God's will, faith versus reason, and so forth. Thus, his first attack on Malebranche was an attempt to disprove Malebranche's account of representative ideas as being "in" God and to return to what he took to be the more purely Cartesian account of such ideas—that is, as being ontologically "in" us.

Accordingly, the Arnauld–Malebranche dispute has generally been classified as being over a representative theory of perception. This is an oversimplification, however, because Arnauld, and not just Malebranche, accepted some sort of representative component in perception. The crucial factor in their disagreement was the question of the ontological status of that component. Despite the considerable heat generated by this dispute (Arnauld argued that the church should condemn the *Traité*, Malebranche was charged with Spinozism, and Arnauld was criticized for defending Jansenism), it nevertheless contains a great deal of philosophical material on such topics as intentionality, the correct analysis of mental acts, and the ontological status of conceptual entities. Arnauld had been sensitive to Descartes's discussion of our ideas in relation to God's. According to Malebranche's view, we apprehend these ideas in God's mind without any mediation. These ideas, or Platonic essences, are the eternal archetypes of all possible worlds, and their content is primarily mathematical. They "represent" the created world in that they "make it known" to us. This realm of Ideas, or as Malebranche later called it, Intelligible Extension, comprehends the essence of extended objects but not their existence (which depends on God's will rather than his intellect). Malebranche held that we can believe that material objects exist but not know it, and that while such objects may be the causal occasion of certain sensations in us, the proper objects of knowledge are the eternal Ideas.

Redundancy of ideas. Arnauld pressed Malebranche on several points. First, he argued that Ideas (*êtres représentatifs*) are redundant, since our perceptions are already representative of objects. Thus, if anything, Arnauld appears as the defender of a representative theory of perception, while Malebranche seems to be the defender of direct realism with regard to our knowledge of the Ideas in God's mind.

For his part, Malebranche saw a grave source of Pyrrhonism in Arnauld's attempt to make perception representative. Arnauld's account seemed subject to the traditional problem of how one can ever be said to *know* a thing that one "grasps" only mediately, and also the more peculiarly Cartesian problem (which Arnauld himself had originally formulated) of whether one's set of internal ideas relate to anything external at all. Sometimes they argued about these ideas by arguing about the correct interpretation of Descartes's own discussions. Each was willing to grant that "perception" covered both the mental act proper (e.g., seeing, knowing) and the conceptual element whereby perceptions (e.g., seeing a cube, seeing a sphere) differed from one another. Arnauld argued that this conceptual element (i.e., the idea of a cube or a sphere) was mental, both in Descartes's philosophy and in truth. Malebranche argued that this conceptual element was to be distinguished sharply from the mental substance to which it might be related in perception, and that this was required both by Descartes and by the truth, if the ontological independence of the object known was to be preserved. Malebranche felt it was clear that Descartes's frequent use of mathematical examples was ample evidence for saying that Descartes never held that the triangle "objectively in the mind" was mental in the sense of being ontologically part of the mind. Since Malebranche had discussed both the infinite and the eternal, and since he did not think the human mind was either, it seemed clear to him that Descartes had given special status to these "ideas"—and of course Descartes had, having ranked them among the innate ideas. This classification also gave Arnauld some good Cartesian reasons for treating these "ideas" as mental modes—that is, dependent for their being on minds.

Arnauld and Malebranche were attempting to offer accounts of the nature of concepts just as their scholastic predecessors had done—but with one crucial difference: the mind–matter relation had became problematic, and with it the status of the concept. The concept could no longer merely be assumed to function as that *by which* I know an independent thing, since the relation between concept and thing known was precisely what the Cartesian revolution required to be rethought.

Descartes rested his case on innate ideas, whereas Malebranche placed them in God, a move in which Arnauld saw nothing but philosophical confusion and religious heresy. Arnauld obviously knew the problem of getting "outside" our ideas, and the hopeless Pyrrhonism that followed from successfully challenging the existence of a relation between mind and object known; indeed, he had raised such a question against Descartes. He started from the position that our clear and distinct ideas *must* refer beyond themselves and sought to show that, with all its difficulties, such a position was both closer to Descartes's and preferable to Malebranche's.

Perception and pleasure. The lengthy dispute between Arnauld and Malebranche was chronicled in Pierre Bayle's *Nouvelles de la république des lettres.* Arnauld accused Bayle of being a partisan of Malebranche and drew him into the conflict. One of the topics raised in the Arnauld–Malebranche discussions also appears in the side controversy with Bayle—that is, the general question of extending analyses of knowing and perceiving to the sensible feeling of pleasure. Briefly, Bayle argued that Arnauld had been misled in claiming a logical analogy between perceptions and pleasures. Bayle claimed that while the former necessarily have objects, the latter need not. (A reference to this dispute is to be found in Bayle's *Dictionnaire*, "Epicure," Remark H.) This served to bring out a second point probed by Arnauld, namely, the sort of relation to be found between the mental act per se (for example, knowing, feeling, etc.) and the concept that might qualify it.

Mind's relation to ideas. The third point on which Arnauld pressed Malebranche was closely linked to the first two. How did Malebranche propose to explain the relation between an individual mind and eternal Intelligible Extension (the realm of Ideas)? Arnauld fully appreciated the dialectical motivations (for example, the anti-Pyrrhonism and the traditional Platonic attempt to guarantee the reality of the object known) behind Malebranche's appeal to "intimate union," but he felt that such metaphors merely served to obscure the question. When Arnauld argued that Malebranche's *êtres représentatifs* were redundant, he showed that another question, fully as problematic, had been added to the question of how mind and matter were related—namely, How are minds related to Intelligible Extension? Despite the fact that many harsh words passed between the disputants, the texts of the Arnauld–

Malebranche dispute constitute what is perhaps the most careful, historically well-informed, and extended philosophical analysis of the cluster of problems usually ranged under "mental acts."

Although Thomas Reid, writing in the second half of the eighteenth century, discussed Arnauld at length in his analysis of modern philosophy and of its basic mistake (i.e., the "way of ideas"), Arnauld is now probably best known as the author of the Fourth set of Objections (in which the problem of "Arnauld's Circle" was proposed), and of a correspondence with Leibniz on the topic of the latter's philosophical system.

Works by Arnauld

A complete edition of Arnauld's work is *Oeuvres*, 43 vols. (Paris, 1775 ff.). His Objections to Descartes and his correspondence with Leibniz are available in many forms, as is the *Art de penser.* A new English version of the *Art de penser,* translated by James Dickoff and Patricia James, is *The Art of Thinking* (Indianapolis, Ind., and New York, 1964). The first contribution to the discussion with Malebranche, *Des Vraies et des Fausses Idées,* is also to be found in a volume which includes Malebranche's first *Réponse* and is inaccurately entitled *Oeuvres philosophiques de Antoine Arnauld,* edited by Jules Simon (Paris, 1843).

Works on Arnauld

For secondary material, see especially Gregor Sebba, *Bibliographia Cartesiana: A Critical Guide to the Descartes Literature 1800–1960* (The Hague, 1964) and *Nicholas Malebranche: A Preliminary Bibliography* (Athens, Ga., 1959). See also A. O. Lovejoy, "'Representative Ideas' in Malebranche and Arnauld," in *Mind,* Vol. 32 (1923), 449–461; Ginette Dreyfus, *Commentaire* on Malebranche's *Traité de la Nature et de la Grâce* (Paris, 1958); and André Robinet, ed., *Oeuvres complètes de Malebranche,* currently being published.

The Jansenist literature is not primarily philosophical, and in any case it is too large to be surveyed here, but for some indication of Arnauld's role in the Port-Royal issue, see the recent studies in Jean Laporte, *Le Morale de Port-Royal,* 2 vols. (Paris, 1951–1952). See also D. C. Cabeen and J. Brody, eds., *A Critical Bibliography of French Literature* (Syracuse, 1961), Vol. III.

HARRY M. BRACKEN

ARNOLD, MATTHEW (1822–1888), English poet and social and literary critic, was the son of Dr. Thomas Arnold, headmaster of Rugby. He was educated at Winchester and Rugby and entered Balliol College, Oxford, in 1841. In 1847 he became private secretary to Lord Lansdowne, who in 1851 appointed Arnold inspector of schools, a position he held until 1886. In 1857 he was elected professor of poetry at Oxford.

As a critic, Arnold ranged over a broad spectrum from literary criticism through educational theory to politics, social thought, and religion.

Arnold's most important contribution to nineteenth-century thought was his discussion of the significance of culture as a social ideal. His related discussion of the function of criticism has been widely influential. He also contributed to the dispute over the relation between the Christian Scriptures and belief.

In *Culture and Anarchy* (London, 1869), Arnold defined "culture" as "a pursuit of our total perfection by means of getting to know, on all the matters which most concern us, the best which has been thought and said in the world; and, through this knowledge, turning a stream of fresh and free thought upon our stock notions and habits." Culture is thus a process of learning, which can refine individuals and reform societies. Arnold often attacked the kind of reforming or progressive spirit that is not governed by this humane reference. At the same time, he made it clear that the object of the learning and refining process was indeed reform. He laid great stress on the development of the individual through the right use of literature and knowledge, but the pursuit of total perfection was still the ultimate objective. He argued that culture taught men "to conceive of true human perfection as a *harmonious* process, developing all sides of our humanity; and as a *general* perfection, developing all parts of our society." Perfection, although an "*internal* condition," is nevertheless "not possible while the individual remains isolated. The individual is required, under pain of being stunted and enfeebled in his own development if he disobeys, to carry others along with him in his march towards perfection, to be continually doing all he can to enlarge and increase the volume of the human stream sweeping thitherwards."

This position illuminates some of the apparent paradoxes of Arnold's thinking. In one sense, he was clearly a liberal thinker, stressing the criticism of institutions and beliefs by thought and knowledge and placing central emphasis on the development of the individual toward a possible perfection. In other respects Arnold was a notable critic of much of the liberal thought of his time. He criticized the "stock notions" of nineteenth-century liberalism and was a particularly firm advocate of increased social intervention by the state. He criticized the common liberal conception that progress is merely mechanical and the liberals' preoccupation with material and external improvement, which not only ignored the human results of its materialist emphasis, but also failed to advance any conception of humanity toward the realization of which material progress might be a means. His criticism of the "stock notions" of industry and production as major social ends is of this character. He similarly criticized the standard conception of freedom—"a very good horse to ride, but to ride somewhere." It is the way men use freedom, not merely their abstract possession of it, that for Arnold is really important. Most liberal thought in his time opposed the state in the name of just this kind of abstract freedom. Arnold argued that the state was simply "the representative acting-power of the nation." To deny its right to act was to deny the possibility of any general action on behalf of the nation as a whole and to reserve the power of action to particular interests and classes. In the England of his time, he distinguished three classes—the aristocracy ("Barbarians"), the middle classes ("Philistines"), and the working class (the "Populace"). Social action by any one of these interests alone merely led to the clash of men's "worst selves." This disorder, or the resultant breakdown of effective government, would be "anarchy." But there existed, within each of these classes, "persons who are mainly led, not by their class spirit, but by a general *humane* spirit, by the love of human perfection." Each member of this human "remnant," maintaining his own "best self" by the process of culture and seeking to awake in others the "best self" now obscured by the "stock notions" and habits of the group, represented the "best self" of society as a whole. It was this "best self" that the state must represent and express.

Arnold never translated these ideas into a coherent political philosophy, but his liberal critique of liberalism was of considerable historical importance. The state, he felt, had to become a "centre of authority and light"; yet it must do this through the existing struggle, or deadlock, between limited interests and classes. Arnold's arguments, at this point, were sometimes vague. In line with his definition of culture as a learning process and with his career as inspector of schools, he stressed, not politics, but education. It was in education that the state most needed to intervene, and Arnold acted as a tireless propagandist for a new system of humane state education.

Arnold saw the study of literature as a principal agency of the learning process, that is, of culture. At times, his definitions of criticism and of culture were virtually identical. Criticism was the central way of learning "the *best* that is known and thought in the world." Poetry in particular offered standards for the development of the best life of man.

In the same vein, in *Literature and Dogma* (London, 1873) Arnold offered to "reassure those who feel attachment to Christianity, to the Bible, but who recognise the growing discredit befalling miracles and the supernatural." For any adequate reading of the Bible, after the effects of the Higher Criticism and the scientific controversies, the spirit of culture was indispensable. Only by this approach could the Christian ethic, and its intense expression in the Scriptures as read undogmatically, be preserved in a time of inevitable change. In particular, it was necessary to understand that "the language of the Bible is fluid, passing and literary, not rigid, fixed, and scientific"; its truth had to be verified through reading, rather than merely assumed. The Christian ethic so verified would be stronger than the dogmatic theology that had made the Bible into what it evidently was not.

Works by Arnold

Poetical Works, C. B. Tinker and H. F. Lowry, eds. Oxford, 1950.

Essays in Criticism. London, 1865.

God and the Bible. London, 1875.

Mixed Essays. London, 1879.

Passages from the Prose Writings of Matthew Arnold, Selected by the Author. London, 1880. Ed. by W. E. Buckler. New York, 1963.

Discourses in America. London, 1885.

Essays in Criticism, Second Series. London, 1888.

Works on Arnold

Bonnerot, Louis, *Matthew Arnold, Poète*. Paris, 1947.

Brown, E. K., *Matthew Arnold*. Toronto, 1948.

Eliot, T. S., "Matthew Arnold," in *The Use of Poetry and the Use of Criticism*. Cambridge, Mass., 1932.

Trilling, Lionel, *Matthew Arnold*. New York, 1939.

RAYMOND WILLIAMS

AROUET, FRANÇOIS-MARIE. *See* VOLTAIRE, FRANÇOIS-MARIE AROUET DE.

ARTIFICIAL AND NATURAL LANGUAGES. The distinction between artificial and natural languages has been of special importance in twentieth-century philosophy, although its beginning can be traced to antiquity (see SEMANTICS, HISTORY OF). The contrast is between languages ordinarily called the natural languages—English, French, and so on—and the artificial languages—various symbolisms constructed or contemplated by philosophers for special purposes. Artificial languages, in the sense occurring in contemporary philosophical thought, are to be distinguished from artificial languages like Esperanto and Ido—that is, from invented languages intended to be full-blown substitutes for natural languages. Artificial languages in the philosophical sense are also sometimes called formal, formalized, symbolic, or ideal languages.

An artificial language may be characterized more explicitly as an interpreted formal system. A formal (or logistic) system in the sense involved here is a symbolism whose structure and manipulation are strictly specified by rules giving the vocabulary and syntax of the system. In addition, this formal system is interpreted; that is, certain rules, the semantical rules, specify what meaning or denotation is to be attached to certain elements of the vocabulary. At least in this century artificial languages have always contained a logic (at least a propositional, and usually a functional, calculus); thus, their vocabulary ordinarily contains variables of one or more sorts—perhaps punctuation symbols and two sorts of constants, logical and descriptive, both sorts being symbols with definite meanings specified by the semantical rules (including rules of definition, if any). The syntactical rules of the artificial language specify which strings of these symbols are to count as well-formed formulas and as sentences (if these two differ) and which formulas or sentences are regarded as asserted in the system (the axioms and theorems).

There are two distinct and essentially quite different uses to which artificial languages have been put in twentieth-century philosophy: (1) for the formalization of particular theories and (2) as what are usually termed ideal languages.

Formalization of particular theories. In the formalization of particular theories, the vocabulary will contain, in addition to the symbols required for the strictly logical part of the system, one or more descriptive or theoretical constants whose logic and semantics are being formalized, along with the theory stated in terms of them. To take examples from twentieth-century empirical science, where the added constants are unquestionably descriptive, there are the artificial languages created for cell theory (Woodger), learning theory (Hull and others), quantum theory (Reichenbach), classical mechanics (Suppes and others), phonemics (Bloch), and kinship relationships (Greenberg). The same use of artificial languages is also found in mathematics—for instance, in proof theory (Gödel), mathematical semantics (Tarski, Chwistek), probability theory (Carnap), modal logic and entailment (C. I. Lewis), classical mathematics generally (Peano). This is essentially the same use, since one or more constants and one or more axioms are added to an already given formal logic (extensional).

These artificial languages are intended to deal only with particular topics, which means that the person constructing the artificial language intends to formalize a particular theory, usually one that existed beforehand in one or more unformalized versions. The artificial language is not intended to formulate all of science or everything factual or cognitive but at most only some particular field or theory. Most, though not all, efforts of this kind have been motivated by philosophical considerations and usually have involved philosophers, most frequently logical positivists. This use, however, is one which need not, and frequently does not, involve anything more than a desire to clarify and systematize whatever theory is in question.

Ideal languages. The use of artificial languages as ideal languages differs from that for the formalization of particular theories in that an artificial language is intended to have the power of expressing, besides the basic logic, more than just a single theory. Now, as has been said, artificial languages in the philosophical sense are not, at least any longer, intended to provide substitutes for natural languages. Thus, no recent ideal language has been intended to have the full expressive power of a natural language; none was intended to express imperatives or questions, for example. (Some artificial languages contemplated by earlier thinkers were apparently so intended.) Rather, ideal languages are conceived of as being capable, in principle, of expressing any proposition, any fact, or anything cognitively meaningful; that is, they are intended to be capable of expressing only the fact-stating part of what a natural language can express. (This set of things has sometimes been identified with the statements involved in science and its applications.) Philosophers who have used the notion of such an ideal language in their philosophizing include Leibniz, Frege, Russell, the early Wittgenstein, the logical atomists (including C. A. Mace and L. S. Stebbing), the logical positivists, W. V. Quine, Nelson Goodman, and Gustav Bergmann—a large, historically important, and influential collection. It should also be noted that these philosophers in no sense constitute a school or movement, unless merely using the notion of an ideal language makes them one. They differ in epistemology, metaphysics, philosophy of science, philosophy of language, and even methodology. In some cases—for instance, with Russell and Bergmann—the use of ideal languages has survived what seem to be significant changes in viewpoint.

Case for artificial languages. The case in favor of using artificial languages in the two ways described is, on the face of it, very strong; moreover, in some areas definite results in the form of new discoveries and even new and profitable fields of inquiry—for example, mathematical semantics—may be cited. The reasons for using an ideal language in philosophy may be regarded simply as a generalization, to all propositions, facts, and so forth, of the reasons for using artificial languages for the elucidation of a particular area or theory, a generalization it was natural to make after special artificial languages had been applied to logic. This is not to say that their use as ideal languages is just the sum of their uses for particular theories. Clearly, one could not even pretend to accomplish the exclusion of metaphysics from philosophy (as the logical positivists did) by simply adding up uses of the second kind; one also needs the contention that nothing of interest is left out. Apart from this, however, the arguments for using artificial languages appear to be the same for the two uses described.

The reasons commonly cited by proponents of the use of artificial languages in philosophy involve, of course, various alleged contrasts between artificial and natural languages. It has been said that the expressions of natural languages are ambiguous, vague, and otherwise imprecise, whereas in an artificial language with precise semantical and logical rules these defects can be avoided; that in an artificial language it can be precisely determined that certain things are logical consequences of a given proposition and, as a corollary, in favorable cases, whether paradox or contradiction results from certain assumptions; that artificial languages can be so contrived as to avoid certain known kinds of paradox or inconsistency which allegedly arise in any natural language (such as the liar and the Grelling paradoxes) or in unformalized mathematics and logic (the Russell and Richard paradoxes).

These reasons carry over to the ideal-language conception of artificial languages and are generalized to all facts or propositions, not just those of some particular theory. In order to justify the contention involved in this that nothing is left out in the way of facts that might be stated, some independent criterion of what these are is necessarily involved. At first, common-sense intuitions appear to have furnished the criterion for Frege, Russell, and the logical atomists; the verifiability principle of meaning (that is, of cognitive meaning) did so for the logical positivists, so that the propositions admitted were those of the empirical sciences and mathematics; and a behaviorist account of meaning does so for Quine, with the same result. Now, when some such criterion is added and the generalization is made to all facts or propositions, there derive other advantages that have commonly been claimed for artificial languages. Thus, Russell thought that in an artificial language one could give logical constructions of certain kinds of thing out of other kinds of thing or, in other words, show that statements about the former could be eliminated by definitions in favor of statements about the latter, thereby minimizing one's ontological assumptions. This view of Russell's has been modified by Quine, who offers as an ideal-language criterion of ontological commitment that to be is to be the value of a variable, that those things to whose existence one is committed are precisely those things which in one's ideal language one is committed to saying there are.

Earlier—and perhaps this cannot be consistently combined with Quine's logical pragmatism—Russell, Wittgenstein, and the logical atomists and, more recently, Bergmann and his followers have held that consideration of the nature of the ideal language would reveal or exhibit more clearly and closely the structure of reality. In this connection it should be kept in mind that ideal languages have only rarely been intended to be a medium of actual communication (though Leibniz and others apparently had this in mind); rather, the contention has been that what an ideal language is, would be, can be, or must be like is philosophically revealing. (In connection with the use of artificial languages, for particular theories, it may be mentioned that the mathematician Peano and his associates did intend to formulate the entire content of mathematics in an ideal language, with improved communication among mathematicians as one of their aims.)

Case against artificial languages. In Wittgenstein's later work and in John Wisdom, J. L. Austin, Gilbert Ryle, and their followers (the ordinary-language philosophers), there has been serious questioning of the philosophical utility of an ideal or, indeed, any artificial language. Much criticism of philosophers who have used artificial languages as ideal languages has, of course, been directed at other aspects of their philosophies; thus, for example, a criticism of early logical positivism directed at its phenomenalism is not necessarily a criticism of its use of an ideal language. However, criticism has been aimed directly at the use of artificial languages as ideal languages and, in connection with some philosophical applications, at their use as formalizations of particular theories. Ryle and Strawson criticize ideal language because they believe that philosophical problems arise concerning ordinary concepts rather than technical analogues of them, so that studying technical analogues will not, or will not necessarily, solve the problems engendered by ordinary concepts. Closely related to this is the argument that formalizing an everyday concept is certain to distort it (rather than simply render it precise, unambiguous, and so forth), since everyday concepts are, by nature, fluid and open to unforeseen possibilities of vagueness (Waismann's "open texture") and even in their regular use stand for sets of things having no single set of common properties (Wittgenstein's "family resemblance"). In connection with the generalization to ideal languages, it has been further held that the meaning or force of an ordinary expression is not determined and cannot be characterized merely by consideration of its ability to state facts but involves the role it plays in language as a whole (Wittgenstein); it has also been held that the primary, fundamental use of certain expressions, such as "I promise," from which their other uses derive, is not to state facts or make assertions but to perform other "illocutionary," or speech, acts, like promising, greeting, agreeing, commending (Austin and ordinary-language philosophers in general). The relevant point here would be that formalization entails confining oneself to stating facts or making assertions, just one of numerous things done in speaking. (Some beginnings of a formal logic of imperatives and questions have been made. For these see LOGIC, DEONTIC, and QUESTIONS.)

There are strong arguments on both sides of this essentially methodological question, which is of considerable import for contemporary philosophy. At this time it is at least clear that the issue between those philosophers who attempt to survey natural language (primarily English) and those who confine themselves to artificial languages (usually a tidied up *Principia Mathematica*) is, though often disputed, not yet settled.

Bibliography

HISTORICAL WORKS

Ayer, A. J., et al., *The Revolution in Philosophy*. London, 1956.
Kretzmann, Norman, *Semiotic and Language Analysis in the Philosophies of the Enlightenment*. Doctoral dissertation, Johns Hopkins University, 1953.
Quinton, A. M., "Linguistic Analysis," in Raymond Klibansky, ed., *Philosophy in the Mid-Century*, Vol. II. Florence, 1958. See pp. 146–202 for a survey, with good bibliographies, of twentieth-century developments.
Urmson, J. O., *Philosophical Analysis*. Oxford, 1956. A historical exposition, primarily of logical atomism and logical positivism.
Urmson, J. O., "L'Histoire de l'analyse," in *La Philosophie analytique*. Paris, 1962.
Warnock, G. J., *English Philosophy Since 1900*. London, 1958.
Weinberg, J. R., *An Examination of Logical Positivism*. London, 1936.

FORMALIZATION OF PARTICULAR THEORIES

Bloch, Bernard, "A Set of Postulates for Phonemic Analysis." *Language*, Vol. 24, No. 1 (1948), 3–46.
Carnap, Rudolf, *Foundations of Logic and Mathematics*. Chicago, 1939. An introduction.
Carnap, Rudolf, *Introduction to Symbolic Logic and Its Applications*. New York, 1958. See Part 2 for formalizations of various mathematical and scientific theories.
Carnap, Rudolf, *Logical Foundations of Probability*, 2d ed. Chicago, 1962. Ch. 1 discusses the nature and purpose of formalization.
Carnap, Rudolf, "P. F. Strawson on Linguistic Naturalism," in P. A. Schilpp, ed., *The Philosophy of Rudolf Carnap*. La Salle, Ill., 1963.
Church, Alonzo, "The Need for Abstract Entities in Semantic Analysis." *Proceedings of the American Academy of Arts and Sciences*, Vol. 80, No. 1 (1951), 100–112.
Greenberg, J. H., "The Logical Analysis of Kinship." *Philosophy of Science*, Vol. 16, No. 1 (1949), 58–64.
Hempel, C. G., and Oppenheim, Paul, *Der Typusbegriff im Lichte der neuen Logik*. Leiden, the Netherlands, 1936.
Hull, C. L., et al., *Mathematico-deductive Theory of Rote Learning*. New Haven, 1940.
Lewis, C. I., and Langford, C. H., *Symbolic Logic*. New York, 1932. Formalizations of strict implication (entailment).
Martin, R. M., *Truth and Denotation*. London, 1958. See Ch. 1 for arguments for formalizing concepts.
Peano, Giuseppe, *Notations de logique mathématique*. Turin, Italy, 1894.
Reichenbach, Hans, *Philosophic Foundations of Quantum Mechanics*. Los Angeles, 1944.
Strawson, P. F., "Carnap's Views on Constructed Systems Versus Natural Languages in Analytic Philosophy," in P. A. Schilpp, ed., *The Philosophy of Rudolf Carnap*. La Salle, Ill., 1963.
Suppes, Patrick, et al., "Axiomatic Foundations of Classical Particle Mechanics." *Journal of Rational Mechanics and Analysis*, Vol. 2 (1953), 253–272.
Tarski, Alfred, "The Semantic Conception of Truth." *Philosophy and Phenomenological Research*, Vol. 4, No. 3 (1944), 341–376.
Woodger, J. H., *The Axiomatic Method in Biology*. Cambridge, 1937.
Woodger, J. H., *The Technique of Theory Construction*. Chicago, 1939. An elementary account of the formalization of theories.

IDEAL LANGUAGES

Austin, J. L., "A Plea for Excuses." *PAS*, Vol. 57 (1956), 1–30.
Bergmann, Gustav, *Meaning and Existence*. Madison, Wis., 1960. His later work.
Bergmann, Gustav, *The Metaphysics of Logical Positivism*. New York, 1954.
Carnap, Rudolf, *Der logische Aufbau der Welt*. Berlin, 1928. Exposition of an ideal-language theory.
Carnap, Rudolf, *The Unity of Science*. London, 1934.
Carnap, Rudolf, *Philosophy and Logical Syntax*. London, 1935.
Carnap, Rudolf, *The Logical Syntax of Language*. London, 1937.
Carnap, Rudolf, "Empiricism, Semantics, and Ontology." *Revue internationale de philosophie*, Vol. 4, No. 11 (1950), 20–40.
Frege, Gottlob, *Begriffsschrift*. Halle, Germany, 1879.
Frege, Gottlob, *Grundgesetze der Arithmetik*, 2 vols. Jena,

Germany, 1893–1903. Part I, Vol. I, translated by Montgomery Furth as *The Basic Laws of Arithmetic: An Exposition of the System*. Berkeley, 1965.

Goodman, Nelson, *The Structure of Appearance*. Cambridge, Mass., 1951. Detailed working out of the ideal-language approach.

Goodman, Nelson, and Quine, W. V., "Steps Toward a Constructive Nominalism." *Journal of Symbolic Logic*, Vol. 12, No. 4 (1947), 105–122.

Quine, W. V., *Word and Object*. Cambridge, Mass., 1960. Ideal-language theory with a behaviorist theory of meaning.

Quine, W. V., *From a Logical Point of View*, 2d ed. Cambridge, Mass., 1961.

Russell, Bertrand, "Logical Atomism," in J. Muirhead, ed., *Contemporary British Philosophy, First Series*. London, 1924.

Russell, Bertrand, "The Philosophy of Logical Atomism," in Robert Marsh, ed., *Logic and Knowledge*. London, 1956. This essay was originally published in 1918.

Russell, Bertrand, and Whitehead, A. N., *Principia Mathematica*, 2d ed., 3 vols. Cambridge, 1925–1927.

Ryle, Gilbert, *Dilemmas*. Cambridge, 1954. See Ch. 8.

Ryle, Gilbert, "Ordinary Language." *Philosophical Review*, Vol. 62, No. 2 (1953), 167–186.

Strawson, P. F., "Analyse, science, et métaphysique," in *La Philosophie analytique*. Paris, 1962. Contains arguments against formalization.

Waismann, Friedrich, "Verifiability," in A. G. N. Flew, ed., *Logic and Language, First Series*. Oxford, 1951.

Weitz, Morris, "Oxford Philosophy." *Philosophical Review*, Vol. 62. No. 2 (1953), 187–233. An expository survey of ordinary-language philosophy.

Wittgenstein, Ludwig, *Tractatus Logico-philosophicus*. London, 1922. His early, ideal-language work.

Wittgenstein, Ludwig, *Philosophical Investigations*. Oxford, 1953. His later thought.

CHARLES E. CATON

ASCETICISM. There is a morbid fascination in any survey of the ascetic practices of man. Fasting, the virgin priestess, and the mutilation of the body are common features of ancient religions. In monastic Christianity the austere ideals of celibacy, obedience, and poverty have been both practiced and admired. Even today there are many who observe Lent and those for whom fasting and penance are seldom out of season. The most accomplished ascetics have been the wanderers (*sunnyasins*) of ancient India and the anchorites of fourth-century Egypt. One *sunnyasin* held his arms above his head with fists clenched until the muscles in his arms atrophied and the nails grew through his palms. It is said that the anchorite St. Simeon Stylites tied a rope tightly around himself until it ate into his body and his flesh became infested with worms. As the worms fell from his body he replaced them in his putrefied flesh, saying, "Eat what God has given you."

Behind such ascetic practices usually lies the philosophical theory of asceticism, a theory that demands and justifies this unnatural way of life. Although the term "ascetic" was originally applied to any sort of moral discipline, it has since acquired a narrower and more negative meaning. Asceticism may now be defined as the theory that one ought on principle to deny one's desires. Asceticism may be partial or complete. Partial asceticism is the theory that one ought to deny one's "lower desires," which are usually identified as sensuous, bodily, or worldly and are contrasted with more virtuous or spiritual desires. Complete asceticism is the theory that one ought to deny all desires without exception. Asceticism may also be moderate or extreme. Moderate asceticism is the theory that one ought to repress one's desires as far as is compatible with the necessities of this life. Extreme asceticism is the theory that one ought to annihilate one's desires totally.

History. The belief that austerities (*tapas*) burn away sin was a product of the non-Aryan tradition of ancient India. This belief persisted, and austerities were recommended by the yogis and the Jains. All orthodox systems of Indian philosophy agreed that the goal of life is liberation (*moksa*) from this world of suffering, and most maintained that the renunciation of worldly desires is necessary for liberation. Although the Buddha tried and rejected austerities, his principle that the cause of suffering is craving led later Buddhists to advocate renunciation and even to practice austerities. The Jains held that liberation is possible only when one has annihilated all passion, because passion attracts karma, believed by this sect to be a subtle form of matter that holds the soul in bondage.

Asceticism seems to have entered Western philosophy from the mystery religions that influenced Pythagoreanism about the end of the sixth century B.C. Although Greek ethics was predominantly naturalistic, Plato sometimes argued that one ought to repress the bodily desires in order to free the soul in its search for knowledge. Some Cynics renounced worldly desires in order to pursue virtue in independence. The early Stoics defined emotion as irrational desire and held up the ideal of the apathetic man in whom all emotions had been annihilated. Plotinus emphasized the ascetic side of Plato's philosophy and claimed that matter is the source of all evil.

This undercurrent of asceticism rose to the surface in medieval philosophy with its emphasis on religious otherworldliness. The foundations of this asceticism were laid by such theologians as St. Athanasius, St. Gregory of Nyssa, St. Ambrose, and even St. Augustine. They believed that the desires of the flesh should be repressed in order to achieve moral virtue and the contemplation of God. Their view molded the monastic institutions that were established in the fourth century. Virtually unchallenged, this asceticism remained a potent influence on religious life until the Renaissance.

Of modern philosophers, only Schopenhauer has been an important advocate of asceticism; he would have one completely annihilate the will to live in all its manifestations. Bentham and Nietzsche have each criticized asceticism from very different standpoints.

Arguments for asceticism. The arguments for asceticism fall into three main classes. First, there are those that attempt a direct justification of self-denial. Although some of these arguments might justify a complete asceticism, they have traditionally been used to support only a partial asceticism. (1) We know by some authority that one ought to deny one's lower desires. One authority is the Bible, in which we find both express ascetic commandments and examples like those of the Virgin Mary and the celibate Christ. (2) The sacrament of penance requires the denial of worldly desires. Although one is cleansed of original sin by baptism, subsequent sins must be expiated by penance; the best way to make penance more than a formal ritual is to express repentance in a life of self-denial. (3) By undergoing the suffering of self-denial, one is taking up the cross of Christ. Since Jesus came into this world as a model for all men, all men ought to share in his redemptive suffering. (4) Man ought to deny his lower desires to prove his virtue, for the ascetic life is a test of devotion to God, and those who pass the test will win a heavenly reward. (5) The suffering of self-denial is required by our guilt. Since all men have sinned, the retributive theory of punishment requires that all men suffer. By inflicting pain upon oneself, one balances the scales of justice and lifts the guilt from one's soul. (6) Self-denial is valuable because it develops in man certain character traits like persistence and self-discipline, which are essential to living well.

The second class of arguments attempts to justify denial indirectly through a criticism of the lower desires. Since these criticisms are aimed only at certain desires, they can support only a partial asceticism. (1) The lower desires cost too much to satisfy. Gratification must be purchased with great effort, and perhaps these desires are insatiable, so that no expenditure of effort will gratify them. (2) The lower desires are misguided, for their objects are really evils or, at best, indifferent things. In either case, no genuine value is realized by fulfilling one's desires. (3) Although the objects of the lower desires are good, they are much less good than higher values like virtue, knowledge, or heaven. Since an individual's time and energy are limited, one ought not to allow these lower desires to distract from the pursuit of what really matters. (4) The lower desires are intrinsically evil. Since they turn man away from God and his commands toward earthly objects, they are infected with the sin of pride. (5) Although not sinful in themselves, the lower desires do motivate one to sinful actions. Thus greed may tempt a person to steal, and lust can lead him to adultery. (6) These lower desires interfere with the pursuit of knowledge, which is essential for the good life. They interfere either by causing an agitation that destroys one's power of reasoning or by fixing one's attention on sensory objects that distract from the transcendent reality.

The third class of arguments also attempts to justify asceticism indirectly through a criticism of desire per se. Since these arguments are aimed at all desires, they support a complete asceticism. (1) Schopenhauer argued that desire, by its very nature, can yield nothing but suffering. Desire springs from a lack and consists in a dissatisfaction. When it meets with hindrances, it produces nothing but frustration, because it cannot attain its object; when it does attain its object, it produces nothing but boredom, because desire ceases with fulfillment and leaves one with an undesired object. Since desire necessarily involves dissatisfaction, frustration, and boredom, the only escape is by the annihilation of all desire. (2) The Buddhists and the Jains maintain that one ought to annihilate desire in order to achieve liberation from this world of pain. A person must destroy all desire because desire is the cause of rebirth into this world. For the Buddhist, desire causes rebirth because, being selfish, it causes selfish actions; these, by the moral law of karma, cause rebirth in painful forms. For the Jain, desire magnetizes the soul so that it attracts karmic matter which, by the physical laws of mechanics, weighs down the soul and causes it to be reborn into this lower world of pain.

Arguments against asceticism. It is much harder to classify the traditional arguments against asceticism. Many of them attack some presupposition of the doctrine. (1) Many, but not all, forms of asceticism require a dualism of mind and body. The various philosophical difficulties with metaphysical dualism therefore tend to undercut asceticism. (2) Ascetic practices are often recommended as a means of freeing the soul from the body so that it can contemplate the truth. Actually these practices make knowledge in all its forms impossible because self-denial produces frustration, uneasiness, and pain, which make clear thinking difficult, and self-mutilation destroys the bodily health that is the physiological basis of thought. (3) Asceticism usually assumes that desires are like little animals inside the self that grow when they are fed and wither when they are starved. Freudian psychology, however, reveals that one does not destroy a desire by suppressing it but that the desire continues to exist and to exert itself in new and usually devious ways. Hence ascetic practices may not be an effective means of annihilating or even of controlling desire. (4) Ascetic practices are often thought to be a means to, and even a guarantee of, moral goodness, but in fact they are no protection against vice. The ascetic may become complacent in his confidence in his ascetic practices; he may become proud of his ascetic achievements; and he may even despise fellow men who are less accomplished in asceticism. (5) The religious arguments for asceticism frequently assume that God requires one to renounce available goods and even to inflict harm upon himself, but this is inconsistent with the benevolence of God. (6) There is also a religious argument against the view that bodily desires or worldly objects are essentially evil. Both this world and human nature must be good, because they are creatures of a Creator who is perfectly good.

Another group of arguments is pragmatic in nature. (1) As Bentham pointed out, asceticism cannot be consistently practiced because it runs counter to the basic motives in human nature. Since the function of morality is to guide conduct, asceticism is incapable of becoming a genuine moral standard. (2) To the limited extent that asceticism can be put into practice, its effects are harmful. It obviously increases the amount of suffering in the world. If Freudian psychology is correct, its attempt to suppress natural desires will result in various neuroses. Finally, it stultifies vitality, produces emotional excesses, and fosters the weakling at the expense of the strong man.

Then there are those arguments that attempt to refute asceticism by showing that it has unacceptable implications. (1) Asceticism condemns worldly concerns and natural impulses. This implies that one ought to abandon all social ties and mortify all family affection, which would be immoral. (2) If it is good for one to suffer, it should be better for everyone to suffer. This implies that a person has a duty to inflict pain on others, but not even the hardened ascetic will accept this. (3) If pleasure is really bad, it would seem that pain must be good. This implies the absurd conclusion that the best of all possible worlds would be the one with the least pleasure and the most pain.

Finally, there is Nietzsche's *ad hominem* argument. Those who are incapable of living well disguise their impotence and fear by inverting morality in order to excuse their own moral sickness and to restrain the strong men who appear dangerous. Although the ascetic priest condemns the will to power, he uses ascetic ideals as a means of maintaining his own power over the sick herd. Thus an analysis of the psychological origin of asceticism reveals that it is far from a worthy ideal.

Asceticism is the doctrine that one ought to deny his desires. In practice, denial means refraining from the fulfillment of desires and sometimes mortifying the desire by inflicting upon oneself the very opposite of what is desired. This involves abstinence from genuine goods, the frustration of unfulfilled desires, and even self-inflicted pain. Unless one is prepared to accept the view that abstinence, frustration, and pain are intrinsically good, the ascetic life can hardly be defended as an end in itself.

If ascetic practices are to be recommended, they must be a necessary evil, a means to something better. One might regard the ascetic life as a means to liberation from this world of suffering. It would be unrealistic to deny that we all suffer from time to time and that there are those for whom life is mostly suffering. It would be equally unrealistic, however, to deny that for most of us the evils we experience are more than balanced by the genuine values we enjoy. Granted the existence of evil, the obvious expedient is to improve our world rather than to make it even worse by adding the sufferings involved in ascetic practices. If escape were desirable, there is no guarantee that the ascetic life would actually lead to freedom.

One might advocate the ascetic life as a means of pleasing God and winning the eternal bliss of heaven. Asceticism seems most plausible within a religious context. But are its theological presuppositions themselves plausible? Is there really an immortal soul to be rewarded or a God to do the rewarding? Even the believer may reject asceticism on religious grounds. A benevolent deity would hardly have created us with natural desires and then commanded us to deny these very desires and to suffer the consequent evils of frustration and pain.

The ascetic life might be urged as a means to that knowledge which in turn brings the good life. Ascetic practices are supposed to help by freeing the soul from the body. Still, no empiricist would admit that the body, which is the source of all experience, is a hindrance to knowledge, and even a rationalist like Plato concedes that experience reminds reason of the truth. Unless reason is thought of as a disembodied spirit—in which case it is hard to see how the body hinders reason in the first place—it would seem that ascetic practices make one less, rather than more, capable of the clear and sustained reasoning that is required for attaining knowledge.

Finally, the ascetic life might be advanced as a means to virtue. It must be admitted that some desires sometimes cause one to act wickedly, but these same desires also cause one to act virtuously. The sexual desire that can lead to adultery more often leads to conjugal fidelity. Hence there is a double error in regarding sexual desire as evil. It does not always, or even usually, express itself in sinful action; and if adultery is a sin, that is because it does violence to the institution of marriage, which is itself an expression of sex. As this example shows, natural desires are in themselves morally neutral, and to deny desire is to forbid the virtuous act as well as the sin. Instead of being a means to virtue, self-denial is actually a vice. Virtue requires at least prudence and benevolence, but the ascetic is imprudent in abstaining from available goods and in even inflicting harm upon himself. By concentrating on the cultivation of his own soul through suffering, the ascetic tends to become callous toward the suffering of others and to ignore his obligation to work for their welfare.

The ascetic life is not good in itself, nor is it a means to liberation, divine reward, knowledge, or virtue. It does not follow that one must accept the advice of Callicles to attempt gratification of every desire without regard for temperance or justice. Self-discipline is a genuine virtue, but it denies desire only when this is necessary to achieve an inclusive and harmonious satisfaction. Asceticism goes beyond this point to advocate an unnecessary and pointless denial. The logical conclusion is that asceticism should be rejected.

Bibliography

Ambrose, St., "Concerning Virgins" and "Letter LXIII," in *Nicene and Post-Nicene Fathers*, 2d series, Vol. X. New York, 1896. A justification of asceticism on primarily scriptural grounds.

Athanasius, St., "Life of Antony," in *Nicene and Post-Nicene Fathers*, 2d series, Vol. IV. New York, 1892. The biography of a model ascetic.

Augustine, St., *De Civitate Dei*, translated by Marcus Dods as *The City of God*. Edinburgh, 1872. Books 14 and 19. An attack on the life of the flesh.

Bentham, Jeremy, *An Introduction to the Principles of Morals and Legislation*. London, 1789. Ch. 2. A brief, incisive criticism.

Blanshard, Brand, *Reason and Goodness*. New York, 1961.

Davids, T. W. Rhys, and Davids, C. A. F. Rhys, translators, *Dialogues of the Buddha*. London, 1957. See *Udumbarika-Sihanada Suttanta* for a criticism of austerities.

Diogenes Laërtius, "Diogenes" and "Zeno," in *Lives and Opinions of Eminent Philosophers*, translated by R. D. Hicks. London, 1925. Limited but helpful information.

Gregory of Nyssa, St., "On Virginity," in *Nicene and Post-Nicene Fathers*, 2d series, Vol. V. New York, 1893. A defense of the ascetic life as a means to virtue.

Lecky, William Edward Hartpole, *History of European Morals*. London, 1869. Vol. II, pp. 107–148, 164–194. A critical history of the rise of Christian asceticism.

Nietzsche, Friedrich, *Zur Genealogie der Moral*. Leipzig, 1887. Translated by Horace B. Samuel as *The Genealogy of Morals*. Edinburgh, 1910. Third essay. Nietzsche's most sustained criticism of ascetic ideals.

Pantanjali, *Yoga Sutra*, translated by James Haughton Woods as *The Yoga System of Pantanjali*. Cambridge, Mass., 1914. Ch. 2, Sutras 32 and 43. An injunction to practice austerities.

Plato, *Phaedo*, translated by R. Hackforth. Cambridge, 1955. An important argument for freeing the soul from the body.

Plotinus, *Enneads*, edited and translated by Stephen Mackenna as *The Enneads of Plotinus*. London, 1917. Bk. VIII, 1st Ennead. An influential condemnation of matter.

Reid, J. S., "Asceticism," in *Encyclopedia of Religion and Ethics*. Edinburgh, 1908–1926. Vol. II, pp. 106–111. An informative survey.

Schopenhauer, Arthur, *Die Welt als Wille und Vorstellung*. Leipzig, 1819. Translated by R. B. Haldane and J. Kemp as *The World as Will and Idea*. London, 1883. Bk. IV. A wordy but interesting argument for the annihilation of the will.

Umasvati, *Tattvarthadhigama Sutra*, A. S. Sastri, ed. Mysore, 1944. The basic document of the Jains.

Warren, H. C., *Buddhism in Translations*. Cambridge, Mass.,

1947. See *Visuddhi-Magga,* Ch. 17, for a brief statement of the view that liberation requires the annihilation of desire.

CARL WELLMAN

ASSOCIATIONISM. *See* PSYCHOLOGY, HISTORY OF.

ATHEISM. The terms "atheist" and "godless" are still frequently used as terms of abuse. Nevertheless, there are relatively few people nowadays in whom the thought of atheism and atheists arouses unspeakable horror. It seems to be agreed that an atheist can be a good man and that his oaths and promises are no less trustworthy than those of other people, and in most civilized lands atheists have the same or nearly the same rights as anybody else. What is more, it appears to be generally realized that some of the world's foremost philosophers, scientists, and artists have been avowed atheists and that the increase in atheism has gone hand in hand with the spread of education. Even spokesmen of the most conservative religious groups have in recent years conceded that atheism may well be a philosophical position that is adopted for the noblest of reasons. Thus, in "The Contemporary Status of Atheism" (1965), Jean-Marie Le Blond appealed to his fellow believers for a "truly human and mutually respectful dialogue" with atheists, insisting that a "life without God need not be . . . bestial, unintelligent, or immoral" and that atheism can be "serene and deeply human." In the previous year Pope Paul VI, in his encyclical *Ecclesiam Suam,* had observed that some atheists were undoubtedly inspired by "greathearted dreams of justice and progress" as well as by "impatience with the mediocrity and self-seeking of so many contemporary social settings."

HOSTILITY TO ATHEISM

It was otherwise in earlier ages. One could fill many volumes with the abuse and calumny contained in the writings of Christian apologists, learned no less than popular. The tenor of these writings is not simply that atheism is mistaken but also that only a depraved person could adopt so hideous a position and that the spread of atheism would be a horrifying catastrophe for the human race. "No atheist as such," wrote Richard Bentley in *Eight Sermons* (Cambridge, 1724), "can be a true friend, an affectionate relation, or a loyal subject." In the preface to his *The True Intellectual System of the Universe* (1678), Ralph Cudworth made it clear that he was addressing himself not to "downright and professed atheists" but to "weak, staggering and sceptical theists." Downright atheists were beyond the pale, for they had "sunk into so great a degree of sottishness" that they evidently could not be reached. Writing almost exactly two centuries later, the Protestant theologian Robert Flint, who readily admitted that he had met atheists of great courage and integrity, nevertheless expressed his extreme concern over the "strenuous propagation" of atheism, especially in the "periodical press." "The prevalence of atheism in any land," he wrote, "must bring with it national decay and disaster." The triumph of atheism in England would "bring with it hopeless national ruin." If once the workers of the large cities became atheists, "utter anarchy would be inevitable" (*Anti-Theistic Theories,* pp. 36–37). All these quotations are from British Protestants. Very similar and frequently more virulent remarks could be quoted from German, French, Italian, and American believers of the same periods.

In France until the Revolution and in most other countries until some time later, it was illegal to publish works in defense of atheism, and in fact real or alleged atheists were subject to dire persecution throughout the times of Christian domination. Some of the world's greatest philosophers were among those who advocated and in some instances actively promoted this persecution. The story antedates Christianity, and persecution of atheists was already advocated in Plato's *Laws.* Plato divided atheists into several groups, all of which must be punished; but whereas the members of some groups required no more than "admonition and imprisonment," those belonging to others deserved punishment exceeding "one death . . . or two." Aquinas (*Summa Theologica,* II, 11, 3 and 4) had no doubt that unbelievers should be "shut off from the world by death." Such a course, he argued, is justified since it surely is "a much more serious matter to corrupt faith, through which comes the soul's life," than it is "to forge money, through which temporal life is afforded." If, as is just, forgers of money and other malefactors are straightaway put to death, it is all the more just that "heretics . . . be not only excommunicated but also put to death."

John Locke, one of the great pioneers of religious toleration, explicitly exempted Roman Catholics and atheists from the application of the principles he advocated. "Promises, covenants, and oaths, which are the bonds of human society," he wrote, "can have no hold upon an atheist." Moreover, since atheism is not a religion but, on the contrary, a position which is out to "undermine and destroy all religion," it cannot come under the privilege of the toleration that is justly claimed by bona fide religions (*A Letter Concerning Toleration*). It may be assumed that Locke did not advocate that atheists be shut off from the world, but that he was merely opposed to the free advocacy of atheism in writing and speech.

After Locke's time, the "shutting off" approach became infrequent, but atheists continued to be the victims of persecution and discrimination in various forms. To give some interesting and far from untypical illustrations: Baron d'Holbach's *The System of Nature* was falsely attributed in its first edition to Mirabaud, a former secretary of the French Academy who had been dead for ten years. Very shortly after its publication in 1770, it was condemned to be burned by the public hangman after a trial in which the public prosecutor expressed his regret that he could not lay his hands on the unknown real author, adding that the corruption of morals evident in almost all sections of society was very probably due to the spread of ideas like those contained in the condemned book. When the poet Shelley was an undergraduate at Oxford, he published a short and very temperate pamphlet entitled *The Necessity of Atheism.* This at once aroused a violent protest which resulted in the burning of all undistributed copies and in the expulsion of Shelley and his friend Thomas Hogg from the university. Some years later Shelley was judicially deprived of the custody of his children on the ground that he was "likely to inculcate the same [atheistic] principles upon them." As late as 1877 Annie Besant, the noted social reformer, was judged to be unfit to take care of her children on the same ground, although the judge admitted that she had been a careful and affectionate mother. Until the passing of the Evidence Amendment Act of 1869, unbelievers in Great Britain were considered incompetent to give evidence in a court of law. Atheists were thus in effect unable to sue when they were the victims of fraud or slander. Charles Bradlaugh, whose efforts were largely responsible for the Act of 1869, was also the main figure in a prolonged battle to secure the right of avowed atheists to sit in the House of Commons. After Bradlaugh was elected, he was found unfit to take his seat. He won the resulting by-election and was again declared unfit to sit in the House, and this merry-go-round continued for several years, until a Conservative speaker found a legal way of securing Bradlaugh's admission. In the United States there has not been similar legal discrimination against atheists, but there is perhaps to this day more *de facto* discrimination and prejudice than in any other Western country.

A comprehensive article on atheism would, among other things, trace the history of the persecution of real and alleged atheists, of the changes in public attitudes, and of the gradual repeal of discriminatory legislation. It would also inquire into the psychological sources of the hatred of atheists that is sometimes found in otherwise apparently kindly and sensible men. Because of space limitations, the present article will, however, be largely confined to what is undoubtedly the most interesting question for philosophers: is atheism a logically tenable position? What are the arguments for it, what are the arguments against it, and how strong are these, respectively? It will not be possible to deal exhaustively even with these questions, but an attempt will be made to sketch the position of a philosophically sophisticated atheist and to explain why a view of this kind has appealed to many important thinkers in recent times.

DEFINITION OF "ATHEISM"

No definition of "atheism" could hope to be in accord with all uses of this term. However, it would be most confusing to adopt any of several definitions which can only be regarded as eccentric. These would result in classifying as believers many people who would not regard themselves as such (and who would not commonly be so regarded) and in classifying as atheists many people who have not usually been thought of in this way. Thus, Fichte, in denying the charge of atheism, wrote in "Über den Grund unseres Glaubens an eine Göttliche Weltregierung" that the "true atheist" is the person who, instead of following the voice of conscience, always calculates consequences before acting in a moral situation. Friedrich Jodl, who was himself a positivist and an unbeliever, similarly remarked that "only the man without ideals is truly an atheist," implying, no doubt, that, although he did not believe in God, he was not a "true" atheist (*Vom Lebenswege*, 2 vols., Stuttgart and Berlin, 1916–1917, Vol. II, p. 370.). In our own day Paul Tillich has defined "atheism" as the view that "life has no depth, that it is shallow." Anybody who says this "in complete seriousness is an atheist"; otherwise, he is not (*Shaking of the Foundations*, New York, 1948, p. 63). Recently, Stephen Toulmin, in an article ("On Remaining an Agnostic," *The Listener*, Oct. 17, 1957) in which he champions agnosticism as he understands it, distinguishes his own position from that of both believers and atheists in that, unlike them, he does not "find personal attitudes of any sort in Nature-at-large." The believer, according to Toulmin, regards the Cosmic Powers as friendly to man, while the atheist regards the cosmos as indifferent or as "positively callous."

Whatever the point of the definitions just quoted, their paradoxical consequences make them useless in the present context. For our purposes, definitions of "atheism" and corresponding definitions of "God" will be serviceable only if they preserve, at least roughly, the traditional battle lines. Whatever their differences, Augustine, Aquinas, Locke, Berkeley, William Paley, H. L. Mansel, J. S. Mill, William James, Paul Tillich, and John Hick should continue to be classified as believers; T. H. Huxley, Leslie Stephen, and Clarence Darrow as agnostics; and Holbach, Büchner, Feuerbach, Marx, Schopenhauer, Nietzsche, and Sartre as atheists. The definition proposed in the present article will, in taking account of certain complexities of the situation, depart in a significant respect from the one that is most popular, but it will not involve reclassification of any of the great philosophers of the past. According to the most usual definition, an "atheist" is a person who maintains that there is no God, that is, that the sentence "God exists" expresses a *false* proposition. In contrast, an agnostic maintains that it is not known or cannot be known whether there is a God, that is, whether the sentence "God exists" expresses a true proposition. On our definition, an "atheist" is a person who *rejects* belief in God, regardless of whether or not his reason for the rejection is the claim that "God exists" expresses a false proposition. People frequently adopt an attitude of rejection toward a position for reasons other than that it is a false proposition. It is common among contemporary philosophers, and indeed it was not uncommon in earlier centuries, to reject positions on the ground that they are meaningless. Sometimes, too, a theory is rejected on such grounds as that it is sterile or redundant or capricious, and there are many other considerations which in certain contexts are generally agreed to constitute good grounds for rejecting an assertion. An atheist in the narrower, more popular sense, is *ipso facto* an atheist in our broader sense, but the converse does not hold.

Theistic positions. Before exploring the implications of our definition any further, something should be said about the different uses of the word "God" and the correspondingly different positions, all of which have been referred to as "belief in God." For our purposes, it will be sufficient to distinguish three of these. All the believers in question have characterized God as a supreme personal being who is the creator or the ground of the universe and who, whatever his other attributes may be, is at the very least immensely powerful, highly intelligent and very good, loving, and just. While some of them would maintain that the predicates just mentioned—"powerful," "good," and the rest—are used in a literal sense when applied to God, other believers insist that when applied to God, these, and indeed all or almost all, predicates must be employed in "metaphorical," "symbolic," or "analogical" senses. Let us, without implying anything derogatory, refer to the belief that predicates can be applied literally to God as the "anthropomorphic" conception of God and to the belief that predicates can only be applied analogically to God as the "metaphysical" conception of God.

Among professional philosophers, belief in the metaphysical God has been much more common than belief in the anthropomorphic God. This metaphysical position is at least as old as Aquinas (and, it may be plausibly argued, as old as Plato). In the early eighteenth century it was championed by Peter Browne, bishop of Cork, who was trying to answer difficulties raised by the infidel John Toland. In the nineteenth century this position was defended by Dean Mansel in his Bampton lectures, and in our own day it has been a key feature of Tillich's philosophy. God, on Tillich's view, "infinitely transcends every finite being"; between the finite and the infinite there is "an absolute break, an 'infinite jump' "; there is here "no proportion and gradation." When we say, for example, "God is Love," or "God is Life," the words "love" and "life" are used symbolically, not literally. They were originally introduced in connection with "segments of finite experience," and when applied to God, they cannot have the same meaning that they have in ordinary human situations.

The anthropomorphic position is by no means confined to unsophisticated believers. It has commanded the support of several eminent philosophers, especially believers who were also empiricists or otherwise opposed to rationalism. Thus, Berkeley emphatically defended the anthropomorphic position against Bishop Browne. In *Alciphron* Berkeley attacked Browne's procedure on the ground that unless "wise" and "good" are used in the same sense for God and man, "it is evident that every syllogism brought to prove those attributes, or (which is the same thing) to prove the being of a God, will be found to consist of four terms, and consequently can conclude nothing." In the nineteenth century J. S. Mill championed anthropomorphic belief as opposed to the metaphysical theology of Hamilton and Mansel; more recently, Unamuno, who is perhaps best classified as a fideist, indicted the metaphysical God as a "Nothing-God" and a "dead thing." In *The Tragic Sense of Life in Men and in Peoples* he wrote that such a fleshless abstraction cannot be the answer to the cravings of the human heart. Only the anthropomorphic God can ever be "the loving God," the God to whom we come "by the way of love and of suffering."

Among those who believe in an anthropomorphic God, there are two positions to be distinguished. First, there is the more traditional position which allows no limitations upon the extent to which God possesses the various admirable characteristics—on this view, God is all-powerful, all-loving, infinitely good, perfectly just, and so on. Second, there is the somewhat heretical position of those who, while maintaining that God possesses these characteristics to a high degree, allow that he is limited at least in his power or in his goodness. Mill, who believed in such a finite anthropomorphic deity, claimed that regardless of the official pronouncements of the various religions, in actual practice most Western believers adhered to a theory like his own.

Creation. A few words must be said about the possible meanings of "creation" when God is referred to as the creator (or ground) of the universe. Aquinas, in his *On the Eternity of the World* and elsewhere, makes a distinction between the temporal sense in which God is supposed to have made the universe at a certain moment in time, prior to which it did not exist, and the more sophisticated sense in which it is asserted that the universe is absolutely dependent on God so that it would cease to exist if God were not sustaining it. Aquinas himself believed in God's creation of the universe in both senses, but it was only in the second sense that he regarded the theory of divine creation as susceptible of logical proof. Both these senses must be distinguished from the creative activity ascribed to the demiurge of Plato's *Timaeus* or to Mill's God. Here the deity is not, strictly, a creator but merely an arranger of pre-existing material. For the purposes of this article, a person will count as a believer in the creation of the universe by God if he makes any of three claims just distinguished.

The broader sense of atheism. Let us now return to our definition of "atheism." A person is an atheist in our sense if he adopts an attitude of rejection toward all three theistic positions previously stated—belief in a metaphysical God, in an infinite anthropomorphic God, and in a finite anthropomorphic God. He will count as a believer in God if he maintains that "God exists" expresses a true proposition, where "God" is employed in one of the three ways described. A person will be an agnostic if he does not accept any of these three claims but at the same time suspends judgment concerning at least one of them. It will be observed that on our way of drawing the lines, agnosticism and atheism remain distinct positions, since suspension of judgment and rejection are different attitudes.

The broader definition here adopted enables us to classify together philosophers whose attitudes toward belief in God are exceedingly similar, although their detailed reasons may not always coincide. Rudolf Carnap, for example, regards metaphysical theology as meaningless, while treating belief in an infinite as well as a finite anthropomorphic God as "mythology," implying that both are false or probably false. In our sense, he can be classified as an atheist without further ado, and it is doubtful that believers would consider him less hostile than atheists in the narrower sense. It is also worth observing that our broader definition receives a good deal of backing from the actual writings of philosophers and others who regarded themselves as atheists. Many of them were by no means unaware of the fact that the word "God" has a number of uses and that what may be a plausible justification for rejecting one kind of belief in God may be quite inappropriate in the case of another. Charles Bradlaugh, for example, made it very clear that in calling himself an atheist he did not simply maintain that there is no God. In his "Plea for Atheism," he wrote:

> The atheist does not say "there is no God," but he says "I know not what you mean by God; I am without idea of God; the word 'God' is to me a sound conveying no

> clear or distinct affirmation. . . . The Bible God I deny; the Christian God I disbelieve in; but I am not rash enough to say there is no God as long as you tell me you are unprepared to define God to me."

The writings of Jean Meslier, Holbach, and other eighteenth-century and nineteenth-century atheists, while certainly containing remarks to the effect that the sentence "God exists" expresses a false proposition, are also full of claims that once we critically examine the talk about a "pure spirit" which supposedly exists timelessly and without a body, we find that words have been used without any meaning. In any event, by using the word "atheism" in the broader sense, it will be possible to discuss certain antitheological considerations of great interest which would otherwise have to be excluded.

TRADITIONAL ATHEISTIC ARGUMENTS

In this section we shall discuss two of the arguments popular among atheistic writers of the eighteenth and nineteenth centuries. In later sections we shall present considerations commonly urged by Anglo-Saxon writers in recent years. However, in a rudimentary form these more recent reflections are already present in the writings of earlier atheists, just as the older arguments continue to be pressed in current literature.

The eternity of matter. The first of the two older atheistic arguments is based on the doctrine of the eternity of matter, or, to bring it more in accord with recent physical theory, the eternity of mass-energy. (As far as the basic issues here are concerned, it is not of any moment whether what is said to be eternal is matter or energy or mass-energy, and for the sake of convenience we shall speak only of the eternity of "matter.") There are two steps in this argument. It is claimed, first, either as something self-evident or as a proposition proved by science, that matter is eternal; second, it is asserted that this claim rules out a God conceived as the creator of the material universe. If the physical universe had been created by God, it would follow that there was a time when the quantity of matter was less than it is now, when it was in fact zero. But physics proves or presupposes that the quantity of matter has always been the same.

Since most ordinary people include "creator of the material universe" in their concept of God, and since they mean by "creation" a temporal act of making something out of nothing, the appeal to the eternity of matter is effective as a popular argument for atheism. A little reflection shows, however, that by itself the argument is of very limited significance. To begin with, regardless of any scientific evidence, the doctrine of the eternity of matter, in all its forms, would be challenged by anybody who accepts any of the causal varieties of the Cosmological Argument (see COSMOLOGICAL ARGUMENT FOR THE EXISTENCE OF GOD). Such a person would presumably argue that while conservation principles may accurately describe a certain feature of the material universe *ever since it began existing*, the material universe itself requires a nonmaterial cause. Hence, any atheistic conclusion in the present context would have to be accompanied by a refutation of the causal forms of the Cosmological Argument. But granting for the moment that the eternity of matter is fully established, this is not incompatible with the theory of divine creation in the sense in which it has been put forward by its philosophically more sophisticated adherents. The eternity of matter is no doubt incompatible with the existence of a God who made the material universe out of nothing and with the kind of activity in which the demiurge is supposed to engage (since bringing order into previously chaotic materials requires the addition of energy); but it is not incompatible with creation in the second of the two senses distinguished by Aquinas, in which "creation" means "absolute dependence" and does not refer to any datable act. There may indeed be some difficulty in the notion of a nonphysical entity nonphysically sustaining the universe, and it is tempting to think that this is an intelligible doctrine simply because the words "sustain" and "depend" immediately call up certain pictures in one's mind; but these difficulties raise rather different questions. Finally, in this connection it should be pointed out that the eternity of matter in all its forms is compatible with a belief in God or gods, like those of the Epicureans and Hobbes (if Hobbes was serious), who are physical beings, or in gods of any kind, as long as it is not claimed that these have created the universe or any aspect of it.

A few words should perhaps be added here about the claim of some writers that the doctrine of the eternity of matter in all its forms has now been refuted by physics and that physics even somehow proves the existence of God. In this connection it should be mentioned, first, that the great majority of scientifically informed philosophers agree that the findings of recent physics do not affect the issues dividing believers and unbelievers, and, second, that even if the doctrine of the eternity of matter were now untenable in all its forms, this would undermine one of the arguments for atheism, but not atheism itself. If there was a time when matter did not exist (assuming this to be a meaningful assertion), it does not automatically follow that matter was created by God. To show that matter was created by God, an appeal to the Cosmological Argument (and not to physics) would be as necessary as ever. As for the theory of continuous creation, advocated by some cosmologists, it does indeed imply that the principle of the conservation of mass-energy is false. However, the basic assumption behind the theory of continuous creation is the so-called "perfect cosmological principle," which is in effect an endorsement of the eternity of matter. This principle asserts that the large-scale aspects of the universe are the same at all times and in all places; and this, more specifically, means that the stars and galaxies have *always* been about as evenly distributed as they are at the present time.

Evil and other imperfections. Among the traditional atheistic arguments a second type has generally been regarded as more formidable and still enjoys an undiminished popularity. This type of argument points to some imperfection or defect in the universe and argues that the defect is incompatible with the existence of God insofar as God is defined as a perfect being.

Among the imperfections or alleged imperfections,

emphasis has frequently been placed on the enormous waste in nature, especially in matters of reproduction, and on the trial-and-error "method" of evolution. Referring to the process of evolution, G. H. Lewes remarked that "nothing could be more unworthy of a supreme intelligence than this inability to construct an organism at once, without making several tentative efforts, undoing today what was so carefully done yesterday, and repeating for centuries the same tentatives and the same corrections in the same succession." And if the end of this entire process is man, it has been questioned whether it was worth all the pain and tribulations that preceded it. "If I were granted omnipotence, and millions of years to experiment in," writes Bertrand Russell, "I should not think Man much to boast of as the final result of my efforts" (*Religion and Science*, p. 222). Again, it has been suggested by several writers, and not at all facetiously, that if there were a God, then surely he would have provided human beings with clearer evidence of his own existence. If an omniscient and omnipotent God did not take care that his intentions should be understood by his creatures, asked Nietzsche, "could he be a God of goodness?" Would he not, rather, be a cruel god if, "being himself in possession of the truth, he could calmly contemplate mankind, in a state of miserable torment, worrying its mind as to what was truth?" (*Morgenröte*, Aphorism 91). If a God exists, then, in the words of Charles Bradlaugh, "he could have so convinced all men of the fact of his existence that doubt, disagreement, or disbelief would be impossible."

The most widely discussed of all these arguments from the imperfections of the universe is the argument from evil, and it may be best to restrict our discussion to it. The following is a recent statement by Brand Blanshard:

> We are told that with God all things are possible. If so, it was possible for him to create a world in which the vast mass of suffering that is morally pointless—the pain and misery of animals, the cancer and blindness of little children, the humiliations of senility and insanity—were avoided. These are . . . apparently . . . inflictions of the Creator himself. If you admit that, you deny his goodness; if you say he could not have done otherwise, you deny that with him all things are possible. ("Irrationalism in Theology," in John Hick, ed., *Faith and the Philosophers*, London, 1964, p. 172)

It should be emphasized that the argument from evil, as here stated, is directed against the *conclusion* of the believer in an infinite anthropomorphic God and is not merely a criticism of his *evidence*. On occasions, for example in Hume's *Dialogues Concerning Natural Religion*, the argument has been used for the milder purpose of showing that the Design Argument cannot succeed in establishing a maker of the universe who is both omnipotent and perfectly good. It argues from the nature of the world to the nature of its cause, and since the world is a mixture of good and evil, it cannot be established in this way that its creator is perfectly good. The form in which we are concerned with the argument from evil—what we may call its stronger sense—maintains that the evil in the world shows the theological claim to be false. The argument may be construed as comparing the theological assertion to a falsified scientific hypothesis: If the theory that the universe is the work of an all-powerful and all-good being were true, then the universe would not exhibit certain features; experience shows that it does exhibit these features, and hence the theory is false.

The argument from evil has no logical force against belief in a finite God. The evil in the world is perfectly compatible with the existence of a God who is lacking either omnipotence or perfect goodness, or both. In fact, E. S. Brightman and the American personalists and other well-known champions of belief in a finite anthropomorphic God adopted their position precisely in order to reconcile belief in God with the existence of evil. There is also no obvious incompatibility between the existence of the metaphysical God and the evil in the world, since it is not claimed for the metaphysical God either that he is all-powerful or that he is perfectly good in the ordinary senses of these words. Mansel, for example, in *Limits of Religious Thought* openly acknowledged that in the light of the injustice and suffering we find in the world, the moral character of God cannot be represented "after the model of the highest human morality which we are capable of conceiving." His position, Mansel insisted, unlike the position of anthropomorphic believers, to whom Mansel referred as "vulgar Rationalists" in this context, was immune from difficulties like the problem of evil Substantially similar remarks are to be found in the writings of many other members of this tradition.

The most basic objections to metaphysical theology will be discussed in the next section, but perhaps it should be mentioned in passing that according to some critics, philosophers like Mansel have a tendency to revert to the view that God is good in the very same sense in which human beings are sometimes good and, more generally, to anthropomorphic theology. This is not at all surprising since, like other believers, they derive or wish to derive comfort and reassurance from their theology. Such comfort may be derivable from the view that the ultimate reality is good and just in the sense or one of the senses in which we use these terms when we praise good and just human beings. No comfort at all, on the other hand, seems derivable from the statement that God is good and just but that "the true nature and manner of all the divine operation of goodness," in the words of Bishop Browne, "is utterly incomprehensible" or that they differ from human justice and goodness, as Mansel put it, "in kind," not only in degree.

There is a long history of attempts by believers to show that the argument from evil does not really refute the assertion that an infinite anthropomorphic God exists. It has been maintained by some that evil is unreal; by others that, although real, it is of a "privative" rather than a "positive" character; that it is real and positive but that it is the consequence of man's abuse of his gift of free will and that a universe without evil and without free will would be worse than one with both; that the argument is based on a narrow hedonistic conception of good and evil and that, in any event, the theological position cannot be adequately judged unless it is viewed in conjunction with belief in an afterlife in which the wrongs of the present life will somehow be righted; and many more (see EVIL, PROBLEM OF).

Critics have come up with various answers to these rejoinders, and the discussion has been going on with unabated vigor in recent years. There would be little point in reviewing this debate here, but something should perhaps be said about two retorts by believers which have not been adequately discussed by the proponents of the argument from evil.

A Christian rejoinder. One rejoinder to the argument from evil seems to be of considerable value in showing that this argument does not *by itself* justify rejection of belief in an infinite anthropomorphic God. It has been argued (for example, by Arnold Lunn in his exchange of letters with C. E. M. Joad published in *Is Christianity True?*, London and Philadelphia, 1933) that although the existence of evil cannot be reconciled with the existence of an infinite anthropomorphic God, this is not too serious a problem in view of the powerful affirmative evidence for this position. In other areas too, Lunn reminds us, we do not abandon a well-supported theory just because we meet with some counterevidence. He is not in the least disturbed by "the fact that divine science, like natural science, brings us face to face with apparently insoluble contradictions." This hardly disposes of the argument from evil, as Lunn seems to think. The comparison between the difficulty that a believer faces from the facts of evil and the difficulties besetting a scientific theory for which there is otherwise strong evidence is somewhat tenuous. There are indeed cases answering to this description in science, but they are invariably resolved by further inquiry. Either we come to see that the difficulty or exception was merely apparent or else the original theory is modified or abandoned. In the theological case, several millennia of experience and debate do not seem to have brought us any nearer a resolution. But, assuming that Lunn's comparison fails as a defense of belief in an infinite anthropomorphic God, there can be no question that he would have made out a strong case in favor of agnosticism as opposed to atheism if there were in fact good evidence for the existence of the God in question. If, for example, the Cosmological Argument were, as far as we can judge, free from fallacious transitions, we would have a situation similar to the kind we frequently face in which there is significant and roughly equally impressive evidence both ways (for example, some apparently trustworthy witnesses implicating the defendant in a court case, and other equally trustworthy witnesses exonerating him) and in which suspense of judgment is the most rational attitude. The moral for our discussion is that an atheist cannot afford to neglect the arguments for the existence of God. Unless he can demolish them, the argument from evil will not by itself establish the atheist's case, even if none of the answers mentioned earlier are in fact successful.

A fideistic rejoinder. Another rejoinder to the argument from evil has become extremely popular in recent years among existentialist believers and all who maintain that arguments for or against the existence of God are, as it is put, radically beside the point. We are told that one simply either has faith or one has not, one is either "open" to the presence of God or one is not. If one has faith, proofs and reasoning are not needed; if one lacks faith, they are of no avail. A person who has faith is not shaken by absence of evidence or by counterevidence; a person who has no faith will never become a true believer even if he is intellectually convinced by the arguments of rationalistic theology.

Systematic defenses by those who adopt such a position are exceedingly rare, but recently an article appeared by an existentialist philosopher who seems familiar with contemporary analytic philosophy and whose answer to the argument from evil is representative of this entire approach. In his "On the Eclipse of God" (*Commentary*, June 1964, pp. 55–60), Emil Fackenheim insists that the essential mark of the faith of a person who is "primordially open to God" is certainty, or, specifically, "*the believer's certainty of standing in relation to an unprovable and irrefutable God*" (Fackenheim's italics). It is this "irrefutability" of his faith that, Fackenheim believes, enables him to circumvent the problem of evil. No conceivable experience, he insists, can possibly upset the true Biblical faith. If there is good fortune, it "reveals the hand of God." If the fortune is bad and if this cannot be explained as just punishment, the conclusion is that "God's ways are unintelligible, not that there *are* no ways of God." To put it "radically": "*Religious faith can be, and is, empirically verifiable; but nothing empirical can possibly refute it*" (Fackenheim's italics). Fackenheim cites the examples of Jeremiah, Job, and the Psalmist, all of whom encountered tragedy and disaster without losing their faith in the existence of God. Biblical faith, he observes in this connection, "is never destroyed by tragedy but only tested by it," and in the course of such a test, it "conquers" tragedy. To underline the invulnerability of this position, Fackenheim adds that no amount of scientific evidence can "affect" Biblical belief any more than "historical tragedy" or "an empty heart" can.

What is to be said in reply to all this, especially to the remarkable claim, made in all seriousness, that although faith is empirically verifiable, nothing can possibly refute it? The answer is surely that there is a confusion here between logical and psychological issues. Fackenheim may well have given an accurate account of faith as a psychological phenomenon, but this is totally irrelevant to the question at issue between believers, agnostics, and atheists—namely, which position is favored by the evidence or lack of evidence. All the words—"destroy," "test," "conquer," "affect," and "refute"—are used ambiguously in this as in countless similar discussions. They refer on the one hand to certain psychological effects (or their absence) and they also refer on the other hand to the relation between facts and a proposition for or against which these facts are (or fail to be) evidence. If the question at issue were whether tragedy and injustice can *produce loss of belief* in a person who has the "Biblical faith," the answer may well be in the negative, and Fackenheim's examples support such an answer. They have not the slightest bearing, however, on the question of whether the tragedies and the injustices in the world *disprove* or *make improbable* or are any kind of evidence against the statement that the world is the work of an all-powerful and all-good God—the statement *in* which the believers have faith. The first question may be of great psychological and human interest, and if Fackenheim is right, then a person interested in dissuading "Biblical" believers would be foolish even to try. It is the second question alone, however, that is of interest to philosophers, and it alone is at issue between believers and unbelievers. By telling his Biblical stories, Fackenheim has done nothing whatsoever to circumvent the problem of evil or to show that what the believer has faith in is immune to criticism.

Before leaving this topic, a few words are in order about a certain concession, occasionally made by unbelievers, which does not appear to be warranted. Some atheists are willing to concede that whereas they can come to grips with rationalistic believers, they are powerless when faced with a fideist like Fackenheim. Thus, Ernest Nagel, in his "Defense of Atheism," remarks that such a position is "impregnable to rational argument." Now, if a proposition, *p*, is endorsed on the basis of faith and not on the basis of logical arguments, then indeed a critic cannot undermine any *arguments* supporting *p*, but he may well be in a position to test (and falsify) *p* itself. If a fideist were to maintain, admitting from the outset that he has no evidence for this proposition and that it is based on faith alone, that the *New York Times* sells for 50 cents on weekdays, there is of course no evidence for his proposition that can be attacked, but this would not prevent us from disproving his assertion. Any plea by the fideist that he gave no evidence or that no evidence can ever move him will not have the slightest bearing on the soundness of the refutation. A proponent of the argument from evil would similarly maintain that the assertion of the existence of an infinite anthropomorphic deity has certain publicly testable consequences—that there is no evil in the world or at least not certain kinds of evil—and that experience shows these to be false. It would be to the point to argue either that the assertion of the existence of such a deity does not really have the consequences in question or that experience does not really falsify them; but it is totally beside the point to maintain either that faith in an infinite anthropomorphic God is not, in the case of a particular believer, based on any evidence or that the believer will not abandon his position, come what may.

REJECTION OF METAPHYSICAL THEOLOGY

In presenting the case against metaphysical theology, we shall concentrate on the views of Tillich and his disciple, Bishop J. A. T. Robinson, whose *Honest to God* created such a stir among theologians when it was published in 1963. No defender of this position has had as much influence in recent years as Tillich. Moreover, his statement of the position is radical and uncompromising and is thus easier to discuss than more qualified versions. At the same time it may well be the case that some of these more qualified versions are not open to quite the same objections. In particular, it might be claimed that the Thomistic doctrine of analogy enables its proponents to escape both the difficulties of straightforward anthropomorphic theology and those besetting Tillich's position (see ANALOGY IN THEOLOGY).

Tillich and Robinson entirely agree with atheists that belief in any anthropomorphic deity should be rejected. Traditional theism, Tillich writes, "has made God a heavenly, completely perfect person who resides above the world and mankind" (*Systematic Theology*, Vol. I, p. 271). Against such a highest person, he goes on, "the protest of atheism is correct." Elsewhere Tillich repeatedly pours scorn on what he terms "monarchic monotheism" and the theology of the "cosmic policeman." Following Tillich, Bishop Robinson tells us that we must now give up belief in God as somebody "out there," just as Copernican astronomy made people abandon "the old man in the sky." Most believers, he writes, are inclined to think of God as a kind of "visitor from outer space" (*Honest to God*, p. 50). Unlike the "old man in the sky" or the "visitor from outer space," the God of Tillich and Robinson is not another individual entity besides the familiar entities of experience, not even the "most powerful" or the "most perfect" one. He is "being-itself." As such, God is not contingent but necessary, and arguments for his existence are not required. The idea of God, writes Tillich, is not the idea of "something or someone who might or might not exist" (*Systematic Theology*, Vol. I, p. 205). "In making God an object besides other objects, the existence and nature of which are matters of argument, theology supports the escape to atheism. . . . The first step to atheism is always a theology which drags God down to the level of doubtful things" (*Shaking of the Foundations*, p. 52).

It should be mentioned in passing that to some readers of Tillich and Robinson there appears to be a radical ambiguity in their entire position, specifically in the reasons they give for rejecting the anthropomorphic theory of the God "out there." At times we are told that the old-fashioned believers are mistaken because God is really inside us—insofar as our lives have "depth," insofar as we live "agapeistically." This is what we may call the Feuerbachian tendency in Tillich and his followers. At other times anthropomorphic theology is denounced because God so radically transcends anything we ever experience that the picture of a glorified man cannot possibly do justice to the reality. In the former context, God must not be said to be "out there" because he is really "in here deep down," in the latter context, because he is too removed to be *even* out there. In the former context, theological sentences become a species of very special psychological statements, and in the latter they are clearly items of transcendent metaphysics. There seems to be a constant oscillation between these two positions, so that at times traditional theology is denounced for not being sufficiently this-worldly, while at other times it is condemned for being too close to the world. The former position is of no interest to us, since it may rightly be dismissed as not being in any accepted sense a theological position at all—it is clearly quite compatible with the most thoroughgoing positivism and atheism. Our discussion will therefore be confined to the latter position exclusively.

As already explained in a previous section, Tillich (that is, Tillich the transcendent metaphysician) regards God as so vastly transcending any finite, familiar entity that predicates taken from ordinary experience cannot be employed in their literal senses when applied to God but must be used symbolically or metaphorically in that connection. There is just one statement that we can make about God in which all words are used "directly and properly," namely, that "God as being-itself is the ground of the ontological structure of being without being subject to the structure himself." Tillich expands this statement as follows: "God *is* that structure; that is, he has the power of determining the structure of everything that has being" (*Systematic Theology*, Vol. I, p. 239). If anything is said beyond this "bare assertion," Tillich insists it cannot be regarded any longer as a "direct and proper statement." Although all other predicates must be used symbolically when applied to God, certain symbols are justified or appropriate, while others are unjustified or inappropriate, since the former "point" to aspects of the ultimate reality, while the latter do not. Thus, we are justified in speaking of God, symbolically, as "King," "father," and "healing." These are "pointers" to the "divine life."

Unintelligibility of metaphysical theology. A philosophically sophisticated atheist would object to Tillich's theology not on the ground that it is false or not proven but on the very different ground that it is unintelligible—that it consists of sentences which may be rich in pictorial associations and in expressive meaning but which fail to make any genuine assertions. Tillich's position may indeed be immune to the difficulties of an anthropomorphic theology, but only at the expense of not saying anything about the world. This criticism would almost certainly be offered by anybody who accepts an empiricist criterion of meaning, but it is worth pointing out that it is an objection that has been endorsed, in substance if not in precisely these words, by numerous believers in an anthropomorphic God. Voltaire on occasion objected on such grounds to the theologians who claimed that we must not use words in their familiar senses when applying them to God, and it has already been mentioned that Unamuno dismissed the metaphysical God as a "Nothing" and a "dead thing." Similarly, William James objected to the emptiness of the "universalistic" theology of the Hegelians of his day, preferring what he called a particularistic belief.

Untranslatable metaphors. This criticism might be backed up in the following way. While recognizing that he constantly uses words symbolically or metaphorically, Tillich does not appreciate the difference between translatable and untranslatable metaphors, and he does not see that *his* metaphors are untranslatable. Very frequently indeed, especially in ordinary life, when words are used metaphorically, the context or certain special conventions make it clear what is asserted. Thus, the editor of an encyclopedia, when asked why he looks so troubled, may reply, "Too many cares are weighing down on me—the pressure is too great." He is obviously using the words "weighing down" and "pressure" metaphorically, yet we all understand what he is saying. Why? Because the metaphorical expressions are translatable—because we can eliminate them, because we can specify in nonmetaphorical terms what the sentence is used to assert. If the metaphors could not be eliminated, we would not have succeeded in making any assertion.

A critic would proceed to argue that Tillich's metaphors are of the untranslatable variety and that when he has offered what seem to him translations, he has really only substituted one metaphor for another. Tillich believed that in his basic statement, quoted earlier, all words are used literally, or "properly." But this is open to question. The word "ground," for example, is surely not used in any of its literal senses when being-itself is said to be the ground of the ontological structure of being. It can hardly be used in the physical sense in which the floor or the grass underneath our feet could be regarded as a "ground," or in the logical sense in which the premises of an argument may be the ground for endorsing the conclusion. Similar remarks apply to the use of "structure," "power," and "determine." Hence, when we are told that "God is personal" (which is acknowledged to be metaphorical) means "God is the ground of everything personal" or that "God lives" (which is also acknowledged to be metaphorical) means "God is the ground of life," one set of metaphors is exchanged for another, and literal significance is not achieved. Tillich's God, it should be remembered, is so transcendent that not even mystical experience acquaints us with him. "The idea of God," he writes, "transcends both mysticism and the person-to-person encounter" (*The Courage To Be*, p. 178). Consequently, he does not have at his disposal any statements in which God is literally characterized and which could serve as the translations of the metaphorical utterances. The absence of such statements literally characterizing being-itself equally prevent Tillich from justifying the employment of his set of "symbols" as appropriate and the rejection of other symbols as inappropriate.

Unfalsifiability of metaphysical theology. We noted earlier that a metaphysical theology like Tillich's avoids the troublesome problem of evil because it does not maintain that God is perfectly good or, indeed, omnipotent in any of the ordinary or literal senses of these words. This very immunity would, however, be invoked by some critics as a decisive objection and they would, by a somewhat different route, reach the same conclusion—namely, that Tillich's theological sentences do not amount to genuine assertions. The point in question may perhaps be most forcefully presented by contrasting Tillich's position with that of anthropomorphic believers like John Hick or A. C. Ewing. Hick and Ewing are (theoretically) very much concerned with the problem of evil. They argue that given the nature of man and a world with dependable sequences (or causal laws), evil of certain kinds is unavoidable and, furthermore, that (though they do not, of course, claim to be able to prove this) in the next life there will be appropriate rewards and compensations. They admit or imply that *their* belief would be logically weakened, perhaps fatally so, it if could be shown that there is no afterlife or that in the afterlife injustice and misery, far from vanishing, will be even more oppressive than in the present life, or that the evils which, given the nature of man and a world of dependable sequences, they thought to be unavoidable, could in fact have been prevented by an omnipotent Creator. Tillich, however, need not be (theoretically) concerned about any such contingencies. Even if things in this life became vastly more horrible than they already are, or even if we had conclusive evidence that in the afterlife things are so bad that by comparison, Auschwitz and Belsen were kingdoms of joy and justice, Tillich's theology would be totally unaffected. Being-itself, as Tillich put it, would still be "actual": it is not "something or someone who might or might not exist." God, as Bishop Robinson puts it, is not a "problematic" entity, which might conceivably not have been there." This is true of the anthropomorphic deity, but not of what Tillich in one place terms "the God above God" (*The Listener*, August 1961, pp. 169 ff.).

In other words, unlike the position of Hick and Ewing, Tillich's theology is compatible with anything whatsoever in this life as well as in the next one; and it is the opinion of many contemporary philosophers, believers as well as unbelievers, that if a putative statement is compatible with anything whatsoever, if it excludes no conceivable state of affairs, then it is not a genuine assertion (it should be noted that "state of affairs" is not used in a narrow way so that much that positivists exclude, for example, happiness or suffering in the next world, could count as conceivable states of affairs). This criterion may, of course, be questioned, but if it is accepted, then Tillich's theology, unlike that of anthropomorphic believers, would have to be condemned as devoid of any assertive force.

We have not here considered other variants of metaphysical theology but those opposed to Tillich's system for the reasons here outlined would maintain that other forms of this general outlook are bound to be open to some of the same objections: In every case, words would have to be used in a metaphorical way in crucial places, and these metaphors would turn out to be untranslatable; in every case it would be impossible to justify the employment of one set of metaphors or symbols in preference to another; and in every case the author of the system would be unable to specify what conceivable state of affairs is excluded by his sentences or, if he did do so, the exclusion could be shown to be arbitrary in a way that would not be true of the statements of anthropomorphic believers.

ATHEISM OR AGNOSTICISM?

It is time to discuss a very common challenge to atheists. The challenge is usually issued by agnostics, but it would in general also be endorsed by fideistic believers. "It is admittedly impossible," the critic would reason, "to prove the existence of God, but it is equally impossible to disprove his existence; hence, we must either suspend judgment or, if we embrace some position, we must do so on the basis of faith alone." To avoid misleading associations of the words "prove" and "disprove," the same point may be expressed by saying that we have no evidence either for or against God's existence. Sometimes the reminder is added that the mere failure of the arguments for the existence of God does not show that there is no God. Anybody who supposed this would plainly be guilty of the fallacy of *argumentum ad ignorantiam.*

If certain of the considerations advanced by atheists which were discussed in previous sections are sound, this agnostic charge would be quite beside the point as far as belief in an infinite anthropomorphic or a metaphysical God is concerned. For in that event, the first theory can be shown to be false (with certain qualifications explained earlier), and the second can be rejected on the ground that it is unintelligible. In the case of an infinite anthropomorphic God, there is evidence against the position; in the case of a metaphysical God, we do not have a coherent position. However, when we turn to the question of a finite anthropomorphic God, the challenge does at first sight seem very plausible. As already pointed out, the argument from evil does not affect this position, and we may, at least provisionally, grant that belief in a finite anthropomorphic God is intelligible because the predicates which are used in expressing it are applied to this deity in their familiar senses. We shall see, before long, that there are difficulties in regard to the intelligibility of even this position, but waiving all considerations of this kind for the moment, let us inquire how an atheist could reply to this challenge. It is admitted by the challenger that there is no evidence for the existence of such a deity; where, he asks, is the evidence against its existence? If there is none, why should one be an atheist rather than an agnostic? Why is atheism justified if we cannot be sure that there is no God in the sense under discussion?

Grounds for the rejection of theories. In justifying his position, an atheist should perhaps begin by calling attention to the fact that the agnostics who suspend judgment concerning God are not also agnostics in relation to the gods of the Greeks or in relation to the devil and witches. Like the majority of other educated people, most agnostics reject and do not suspend judgment concerning the Olympian gods or the devil or witches. Assuming that rejection is the appropriate attitude in these cases, what justifies this rejection?

It will be instructive to look at a concrete example of such a belief which is rejected by agnostics and atheists alike and, incidentally, by most believers in God. Billy Graham is one of the few Protestant ministers who still believe in the devil. The devil is introduced by Dr. Graham as the only plausible explanatory principle of a great many phenomena. He is brought in to explain the constant defeat of the efforts of constructive and well-meaning people, the perverse choices of men who so commonly prefer what is degrading to what is "rich and beautiful and ennobling," the speed with which lies and slander spread in all directions, and also the failure of the world's diplomats. "Could men of education, intelligence, and honest intent," asks Dr. Graham, "gather around a world conference table and fail so completely to understand each other's needs and goals if their thinking was not being deliberately clouded and corrupted?" All such failures are "the works of the devil" and they show that he "is a creature of vastly superior intelligence, a mighty and gifted spirit of infinite resourcefulness." The devil is no "bungling creature" but "a prince of lofty stature, of unlimited craft and cunning, able to take advantage of every opportunity that presents itself" (*Peace With God*, New York, 1954, pp. 59–63).

What reasons could or would be given for rejecting this explanation of diplomatic failures in terms of the devil's cunning ways? Aside from possibly questioning some of Dr. Graham's descriptions of what goes on in the world, that is, of the "facts" to be explained, our reasons would probably reduce to the following: first, we do not need to bring in the devil to explain the failure of diplomats to reach agreement on important international issues. We are confident, on the basis of past experience, that explanations of these failures in terms of human motives, in terms of human ignorance and miscalculation, are quite adequate, although in any particular case we may not be in the possession of such an explanation; and, second, the devil hypothesis, granting it to be intelligible, is too vague to be of any use. It is hinted that the devil has a body, but what that body is like or where it lives and exactly how it operates, we are not told. If "devil" is construed on the analogy of the theoretical terms of the natural sciences, our complaint would be that no, or none but totally arbitrary, correspondence rules have been assigned to it.

It should be observed that the devil theory is rejected although it has not been tested and, hence, has not been falsified in the way in which certain exploded medical theories have been tested and falsified. There are, in other words, theories which we reject (and which agnostics, like others, believe they have good reason to reject), although they have not been falsified. It is important to distinguish here two very different reasons why a theory may not have been tested and, hence, why it cannot have been falsified. The theory may be sufficiently precise for us to know what would have to be done to test it, but we may be chronically or temporarily unable to carry out any of the relevant tests. This is to be sharply contrasted with the situation in which a theory is so vague that we do not know what we must do to subject it to a test. In the former case, suspension of judgment may well be the appropriate attitude; it does not follow that the same is true in the latter case, and in fact most of us regard rejection as the appropriate attitude in such a situation until and unless the theory is stated with more precision.

An atheist would maintain that we have just as good grounds for rejecting belief in a finite anthropomorphic deity of any sort as we have for rejecting belief in Zeus or in the devil or in witches. It should be noted that the believers in the finite anthropomorphic God usually advance their theory as a hypothesis which is the best available explanation of certain facts. Mill, for example, thought that the Design Argument, in the form in which he advocated it, affords "a large balance of probability in favor of creation by intelligence," although he conceded that new evidence for the Darwinian theory would alter this balance of probability (*Three Essays on Religion*, New York, 1874, p. 174). An atheist would argue that we do not need a finite God to account for any facts any more than we need the devil theory; and, more important, that the theory is too vague to be of any explanatory value. Mill, for example, talks of "creation by intelligence," but he does not tell us in any detail what the "Author of Nature" is like, where he can be found, how he works, and so on. Furthermore, because of its vagueness the theory is totally sterile. It does not lead to subsidiary hypotheses about celestial laboratories or factories in which eyes and ears and other organs are produced. Nor does it help us to interpret fossils or other remains here on earth. It is tempting, but it would be misleading, to say that the accumulation of evidence for the Darwinian theory (or some modified version of it) since Mill wrote on the subject has put the design theory "out of court." This would suggest that the theological explanation was at some time "in court," in the way in which a falsified scientific explanation may once have been a serious contender. It is true, of course, as a matter of history, that informed people cease to bring in God as an explanation for a given set of phenomena once a satisfactory scientific or naturalistic explanation is available. In a more important sense, however, the theological explanations were never serious rivals, just as the devil explanation of diplomatic failures is not a serious rival to psychological explanations. The theological explanations never were serious rivals because of their excessive vagueness and their consequent sterility. We do not at present have anything like a satisfactory scientific explanation of cancer, but no theological theory would be treated as a genuine alternative by a cancer researcher, even if he were a devoutly religious man.

It should be added to all this that believers who, unlike Mill, do not treat their theology as a kind of hypothesis, are not affected by the above objections. Indeed, quite a number of them have strenuously opposed any kind of "God of the gaps." However, some of the very writers who insist that their theology must not be regarded as a scientific hypothesis elsewhere make statements which imply the opposite. They also frequently maintain that certain phenomena—for example, the universal hunger for God or the origin of life—can be explained only, or can be explained best, on the assumption that there is a God, and a God of a certain kind. Whatever they may say on other occasions, insofar as they propose their theology as the only possible, or as the best available, explanation of such phenomena, they are committed to the position that has been criticized in this section.

THE DEMAND FOR A COSMIC BRAIN

There was a good deal of discussion in the late nineteenth century of an antitheological argument which ought to be briefly mentioned here. To many persons, including unbelievers, the argument will seem to be merely grotesque; but in view of the revival in recent years of several forms of extreme materialism, it deserves some discussion. Moreover, even if it is granted that the argument fails to prove its conclusion, the very grotesqueness of some of its formulations enables a more sophisticated contemporary atheist to state his challenge in a particularly forceful way.

The two writers chiefly associated with this argument were the German physiologist Emil Du Bois-Reymond and the English mathematician W. K. Clifford, both of whom wrote extensively on philosophical subjects. However, the argument is really much older, and versions of it are found in Meslier and Holbach. The remark attributed to Laplace that "in scanning the heavens with a telescope he found no God" may be regarded as an argument belonging to the same family. "Can we regard the universe," asked Clifford in his essay "Body and Mind," "or that part of it which immediately surrounds us, as a vast brain, and therefore the reality which underlies it as a conscious mind? This question has been considered by the great naturalist, Du Bois-Reymond, and has received from him that negative answer which I think we also must give." The student of nature, Du Bois-Reymond had written, before he can "allow a psychical principle to the universe," will demand to be shown "somewhere within it, embedded in neurine and fed with warm arterial blood under proper pressure, a convolution of ganglionic globules and nerve-tubes proportioned in size to the faculties of such a mind" (*Über die*

Grenzen des Naturerkennens, p. 37). But, in fact, no such gigantic ganglionic globules or nerve-tubes are discoverable, and, hence, we should not allow a "psychical principle" to the universe. The following would be a more systematic statement of the argument: experience shows that thinking, volition, and other psychological phenomena do not and cannot occur without a certain physiological basis—more specifically, without a brain and nervous system. Our observations appear to indicate, although this is not a matter of which one can be certain, that no cosmic brain or nervous system exists. Hence, it is probable that no cosmic consciousness exists either.

This argument has been criticized on the ground that it assumes a certain view (or a certain group of views) about the relationship between body and mind which is not self-evidently true and which many believers would deny. It assumes that consciousness can exist only in conjunction with a nervous system and a brain. However, the objector would maintain, the actual evidence on the subject does not warrant such a claim. It is true that within our experience, conscious processes are found only in connection with a highly developed brain, but this does not prove that consciousness may not occur in conjunction with other physical structures or without any physical "attachments" whatsoever. This is a big question about which nothing very useful can be said in a few words. Perhaps all we can do here is point out that if materialism of some kind is true, then the demand to be shown the bodily foundation or aspect of the divine consciousness is not misplaced, while if the opposite view that consciousness can exist independently of a physical structure is correct, the Du Bois-Reymond argument would have no force.

Quite aside from this objection, the argument probably seems to many people, believers and unbelievers alike, to rest on a total, one is almost inclined to say a willful, misunderstanding of the theological position. James Martineau, who replied at some length to Du Bois-Reymond, protested that the "demand for organic centralization" was "strangely inappropriate," indeed quite irrelevant to the question at issue between the believer and the unbeliever. If Du Bois-Reymond himself, wrote Martineau, were "ever to alight on the portentous cerebrum which he imagines, I greatly doubt whether he would fulfill his promise and turn theist at the sight: that he had found the Cause of causes would be the last inference it would occur to him to draw: rather would he look round for some monstrous *creature*, some cosmic megatherium, born to float and pasture on the fields of space" (*Modern Materialism and Its Relation to Religion and Theology*, p. 184). Martineau then likened the argument to Laplace's remark, mentioned earlier, that in looking at the heavens with his telescope, he could nowhere see God and to statements by certain physiologists that in opening the brain, they could not discover a soul. All such pronouncements Martineau regarded as absurd. Although the physiologist finds no soul when he opens up the brain, "we positively know" (by introspection) the existence of conscious thought. Similarly, that "the telescope misses all but the bodies of the universe and their light" has no tendency to prove "the absence of a Living Mind through all." If you take the "wrong instruments" you will not find what you are looking for. "The test tube will not detect an insincerity," nor will "the microscope analyse a grief"; but insincerity and grief are real for all that. The organism of nature, Martineau concludes, "like that of the brain, lies open, in its external features, to the scrutiny of science; but, on the inner side, the life of both is reserved for other modes of apprehension, of which the base is self-consciousness and the crown is religion."

One is strongly inclined to agree with Martineau that there is something absurd in scanning the heavens for God. Étienne Borne, a French Catholic whose discussions are distinguished by fairness and sympathy for the opposition, refers to this approach as "a tritely positivist atheism" which "misses the point of the problem altogether" (*Modern Atheism*, p. 145). One must not expect to find God or God's body in the heavens because God is not a huge man with huge arms, legs, arteries, nervous system, and brain. Only children think of God as a "king" sitting on his throne in Heaven. Educated grownups do not think of God in any such crude fashion. Du Bois-Reymond, Clifford, and Laplace are all guilty of an enormous *ignoratio elenchi*.

Is anthropomorphic theology intelligible? Let us grant the force of Borne's objection. A critic may nevertheless raise the following questions: What is God like if he is not a grand consciousness tied to a grand body, if he is so completely nonphysical as to make any results of telescopic exploration antecedently irrelevant? If the telescope, as Martineau put it, is the "wrong instrument," what is the right instrument? More specifically, what does it mean to speak of a pure spirit, a disembodied mind, as infinitely (or finitely) powerful, wise, good, just, and all the rest? We can understand these words when they are applied to human beings who have bodies and whose behavior is publicly observable; we could undoubtedly understand these words when they are applied to some hypothetical superhuman beings who also have bodies and whose behavior is in principle observable; but what do they mean when they are applied to a pure spirit? Do they then mean anything at all? In recent years it has come to be widely questioned whether it makes *any* sense to talk about a disembodied consciousness. It is widely believed, in other words, that psychological predicates are *logically* tied to the behavior of organisms. This view, it should be pointed out, is not identical with reductive materialism. It does not, or at least does not necessarily, imply that the person is just his body, that there are no private experiences, or that feelings are simply ways of behaving. It makes the milder claim that however much more than a body a human being may be, one cannot sensibly talk about this "more" without presupposing (as part of what one means, and not as a mere contingent fact) that he is a living organism. Anybody who has studied and felt the force of this thesis is not likely to dismiss as facetious or as "trite positivism" the question as to what words like "wise," "just," and "powerful" can mean when they are applied to an entity that is supposedly devoid of a body. What would it be like to be, for example, just, without a body? To be just, a person has to *act* justly—he has to behave in certain ways. But how is it possible to perform these acts, to behave in the required ways, without a body? Similar remarks apply to the other divine attributes.

One may term this the "semantic" challenge to anthropomorphic theology, as distinct, for example, from arguments like the one from evil or from the eternity of matter, which assume the meaningfulness of the position attacked. A proponent of this challenge does not flatly maintain that anthropomorphic theology is unintelligible. For his point—that the predicates in question lose their meaning when applied to a supposedly disembodied entity—would be accompanied by the observation that in fact most anthropomorphic believers do, in an important sense of the word, believe in a god with a body, whatever they may say or agree to in certain "theoretical" moments. If we judge the content of their belief not by what they *say* during these "theoretical" moments but by the images in terms of which their thinking is conducted, then it seems clear that in this sense or to this extent they believe in a god with a body. It is true that the images of most Western adults are not those of a big king on his heavenly throne, but it nevertheless seems to be the case that, when they think about God *unself-consciously* (and this is, incidentally, true of most unbelievers also), they vaguely think of him as possessing some kind of rather large body. The moment they assert or deny or question such statements as "God created the universe" or "God will be a just judge when we come before him," they introduce a body into the background, if not into the foreground, of their mental pictures. The difference between children and adults, according to this account, is that children have more vivid and definite images than adults.

This entire point may perhaps be brought out more clearly by comparing it with a similar "semantic" criticism of belief in human survival after death. The semantic critic would maintain that while a believer in reincarnation or the resurrection of the body may be immune from this objection, those who claim that human beings will continue to exist as disembodied minds are really using words without meaning. They do not see this because of the mental pictures accompanying or (partly) constituting their thoughts on the subject. Or, alternatively, they do not see this because, in spite of what they say in certain "theoretical" contexts, in practice they believe in the survival of the familiar *em*bodied minds whom they know in this life. When they wonder whether their friends, enemies, certain historical personages, or, for that matter, anybody did or will go on existing after death, they think of them automatically in their familiar bodily "guises" or else in some ghostly "disguises," but still as bodily beings of some kind. If these images are eliminated on the ground that they are irrelevant or inappropriate because the subject of survival is a disembodied mind, it is not clear that an intelligible statement remains. What, for example, do words like "love" and "hate" or "happiness" and "misery" mean when they are predicated of a disembodied mind? (See IMMORTALITY.)

It will be seen from all this that the argument of Du Bois-Reymond and Clifford is not without some point. One may incorporate what is of value in their discussion into the following challenge to anthropomorphic theology: Insofar as the believer believes in a god with a body, what he says is intelligible; but in that case the available evidence indicates that there is no such body, and the remarks of Du Bois-Reymond and Clifford are to the point; if or insofar as God is declared to be a purely spiritual entity, the observations of Du Bois-Reymond and Clifford become irrelevant, but in that case the predicates applied to God have lost their meaning, and, hence, we no longer have an intelligible assertion.

Summary of the atheist's position. Let us summarize the atheist's case as it has here been presented. A philosophically sophisticated atheist would begin by distinguishing three types of belief in God—what we have called the metaphysical God, the infinite anthropomorphic God, and the finite anthropomorphic God. He will then claim that he can give grounds for rejecting all three, although he does not claim that he can prove all of them to be false. He will try to show that metaphysical theology is incoherent or unintelligible, and, if he can do this, he will certainly have given a good ground for rejecting it. He will also question the intelligibility of anthropomorphic theology insofar as God is here said to be a purely spiritual entity. If and insofar as belief in an infinite anthropomorphic God is intelligible, he will maintain that it is shown to be false by the existence of evil. In the sense in which he will allow the existence of a finite anthropomorphic God to be an intelligible hypothesis, he will argue that it should be rejected because it is not needed to account for any phenomena and, further, because it is too vague to be of any explanatory value. We saw that some of these justifications, even if sound as far as they go, would not establish the atheist's case unless they are accompanied by a demolition of the arguments for the existence of God.

SOME OBJECTIONS TO ATHEISM

If there were reason to believe that any of the arguments for the existence of God are sound or have at least some tendency to establish their conclusions, then they would of course constitute objections to atheism. Since these arguments are fully discussed elsewhere in this encyclopedia, we shall here confine ourselves to objections which are logically independent of them. Some of these objections have been put forward by writers who explicitly reject all the traditional proofs but nevertheless regard atheism as an untenable position.

The mystery of the universe. It has been argued by several writers that whatever the objections to the different forms of theology may be, atheism is also unacceptable since it has no answer to the "ultimate question" about the origin of the universe. Thus, the nineteenth-century physicist John Tyndall, after endorsing a thoroughgoing naturalism, proceeded to reject atheism in favor of an agnostic position. In a paper entitled "Force and Matter," he tells the story of how Napoleon turned to the unbelieving scientists who had accompanied him to Egypt and asked them, pointing to the stars, "Who, gentlemen, made all these?" "That question," Tyndall comments, "still remains unanswered, and science makes no attempt to answer it." Later he adds that "the real mystery of this universe lies unsolved, and, as far as we are concerned, is incapable of solution" (*Fragments of Science*, pp. 92–93). In much the same vein, the celebrated American freethinker and social reformer, Clarence Darrow, after pointing out the weaknesses of the First Cause Argument, observed that the position of the atheist is just as vulnerable. If, he wrote, the atheist answers the question "What is the origin of it all?" by saying that the universe always existed, he has the same difficulty to contend with as the believer has when he is asked the question "Who made God?" To say that "the universe was here last year, or millions of years ago, does not explain its origin. This is still a mystery. As to the question of the origin of things, man can only wonder and doubt and guess" (*Verdicts out of Court*, pp. 430–431).

A philosophically acute atheist could offer a twofold answer to arguments of this kind. First, he would maintain that the question about the "origin of the universe" or the "origin of it all" is improper and rests on the mistaken or doubtful assumption that there is a thing called "the universe." It is tempting to suppose that there is such a thing because we have a tendency to think of the universe as a large container in which all things are located and, perhaps more important, because grammatically the expression functions analogously to expressions like "this dog" or "the Cathedral of Notre Dame," which do denote certain things. Upon reflection, however, it becomes clear, the rejoinder would continue, that "the universe" is not a thing-denoting expression or, putting the point differently, that there is not a universe over and above the different things within the universe. While it makes sense to ask for the origin of any particular thing, there is not a further thing left over, called "the universe" or "it all," into whose origin one can sensibly inquire. The origin of a great many things is of course unknown to us, but this is something very different from "the ultimate mystery" that figures in the argument under discussion; and there is no reason to suppose that questions about the origin of any individual thing fall in principle outside the domain of scientific investigation.

Furthermore, even if it is granted both that the question concerning the origin of the universe is proper and that we do not and cannot discover the true answer, this is not by itself an argument against atheism. It may well be possible to know that a certain suggested answer to a question is false (or meaningless) without knowing the true answer. All kinds of crimes have never been solved, but this does not prevent us from knowing that certain people did not commit them. An atheist can quite consistently maintain "I have no idea how the origin of the universe is to be explained, but the theological theory cannot be the right answer in view of such facts as the existence of evil." To support his position, the atheist must be able to justify his rejection of theological answers to the question "What is the origin of the universe?" He does not have to be able to answer that question.

Atheism presupposes omniscience. In the popular apologetic pronouncements of liberal believers, it is customary to contrast the agnostic, who is praised for his circumspection, with the atheist, who is accused of arrogant dogmatism and who, like the orthodox or conservative believer, claims to know what, from the nature of the case, no mere human being can possibly know. "The atheist," in the words of Dr. W. D. Kring, a contemporary Unitarian, "can be just as closed-minded as the man who knows everything. The atheist just knows everything in a negative direction" (*New York Times*, March 22, 1965).

Reasoning of this kind figured prominently in several influential works by nineteenth-century Protestant theologians. Their favorite argument was the following *reductio ad absurdum:* Atheism could be known to be true only if the atheist knew everything; but this is of course impossible; hence, atheism cannot be known to be true. For a man to deny God, wrote Thomas Chalmers, "he must be a God himself. He must arrogate the ubiquity and omniscience of the Godhead." Chalmers insists that the believer has a great initial polemical advantage over the atheist. For, he argues, some very limited segment of the universe may provide the believer with strong or even decisive evidence, with an "unequivocal token" of God's existence. The atheist, on the other hand, would have to "walk the whole expanse of infinity" to make out his case (*On Natural Theology*, Vol. I, Book I, Ch. 2). By what miracle, asks John Foster, can an atheist acquire the "immense intelligence" required for this task? Unless he is "omnipresent—unless he is at this moment at every place in the universe—he cannot know but there may be in some place manifestations of a Deity by which even *he* would be overpowered." And what is true of space equally applies to "the immeasurable ages that are past" (*Essays*, 18th ed., p. 35). The atheist could not know that there is no God unless he had examined every part of the universe at every past moment to make sure that at no time was there a trace of divine activity.

According to Robert Flint, who endorsed and elaborated the arguments of Chalmers and Foster, the situation should be clear to anybody who reflects on the difficulty of "proving a negative." If a man landed on an unknown island, any number of traces in almost any spot would be sufficient to show that a living creature *had* been there, but he would have to "traverse the whole island, examine every nook and corner, every object and every inch of space in it, before he was entitled to affirm that *no* living creature had been there" (*Anti-Theistic Theories*, pp. 9–11). The larger the territory in question, the more difficult it would become to show that it had not a single animal inhabitant. If, then, it is "proverbially difficult to prove a negative," there can surely "be no negative so difficult to prove as that there is no God." This is plain if we reflect that "before we can be sure that nothing testifies to His existence, we must know all things." The territory in this case is "the universe in all its length and breadth." To know that there is no trace of God anywhere in eternal time and boundless space, a man would have had to examine and to comprehend every object that ever existed. This would indeed require omnipresence and omniscience, and Chalmers was there perfectly right when he maintained that the atheist's claim implies that "he is himself God" (*ibid.*).

Whatever its rhetorical force, this argument is so patently invalid that it can be disposed of in just a few words. We have in preceding sections of this article presented several of the most widely used arguments and considerations that have been advanced in support of atheism. These may or may not be logically compelling, but none of them in any way imply that the atheist must be omniscient if he is right. To establish that the existence of evil is incompatible with the view that the universe is the work of an all-powerful and all-good creator, to show that a given theory is too vague to be of any explanatory value, or to call attention to the fact that certain words have in a certain context lost their meaning—none of these require omniscience.

Writers like Chalmers, Foster, and Flint seem to labor under the impression that as far as its refutability is concerned, "God exists" is on par with a statement like "A hippogriff exists, existed, or will exist in some place at some time." It may be plausible to maintain that our not having found any hippogriffs on earth is no conclusive evidence that such an animal does not exist in some other part of the universe to which we have no access. The same does not at all apply to the question of whether one is or can be entitled to reject the claims of believers in God. For, unlike the hippogriff, God is by some declared to be the all-powerful and all-good creator of the universe; he is said by most believers to be a mind without a body; and it is asserted by some that predicates taken from ordinary experience can never be applied to God in their literal senses. These features of theological claims may make it possible to justify their rejection although one has not explored every "nook and cranny" of the universe.

ATHEISM, ZEAL, AND GLOOM

In the opening section of this article we referred to the view, common in previous centuries, that atheism is bound or, at any rate, very likely to lead to immorality, to national ruin, and to other disasters. This warning is no longer taken very seriously among reputable thinkers, but certain other statements about the baleful consequences of unbelief in general and atheism in particular continue to be widely discussed. Thus, it is frequently maintained that if atheism were true or justified, life would be deprived of all meaning and purpose. Again, it has been held that without God the universe becomes "terrifying" and man's life a lonely and gloomy affair. "Old age," wrote William James in his *Varieties of Religious Experience* (New York and London, 1902), "has the last word: a purely naturalistic look at life, however enthusiastically it may begin, is sure to end in sadness." Pascal, who was particularly concerned about the terror of a "silent universe" without God, observed in a similar vein that "the last act" is always tragic—"a little earth is thrown upon our head, and that is the end forever."

James and Pascal were believers, but very similar statements have frequently come from unbelievers themselves. "I am not ashamed to confess," wrote G. J. Romanes, a nineteenth-century biologist, at the end of his *A Candid Examination of Theism* (a work which was published anonymously in London in 1878 and which caused a commotion at the time), "that with this virtual denial of God, the universe has lost to me its soul of loveliness."

Much more recently, the anthropologist Bronislaw Malinowski spoke of the state of mind of an unbeliever like himself as "tragic and shattering." Not only does the absence of God, in the opinion of these writers, make the universe "lonely," "soulless," and "tragic," but it also deprives it of love. Only when we have become accustomed to a "loveless" as well as a "Godless universe," in the words of Joseph Wood Krutch, shall "we realize what atheism really means."

Finally, it has been claimed that atheism is fatal to what William James called the capacity of the strenuous mood. James himself had no doubt that the unbeliever is prevented from "getting out of the game of existence its keenest possibilities of zest." Our attitude toward concrete evils, he asserted, "is entirely different in a world where we believe there are none but finite demanders, from what it is in one where we joyously face tragedy for an infinite demander's sake." Religious faith sets free every kind of energy, endurance, and courage in the believer and "on the battlefield of human history," religion will for this reason always "drive irreligion to the wall" (*The Will to Believe*, pp. 213 ff.)

Some of these claims seem a great deal more impressive than others. It is not easy to deal with the charge that atheism deprives life of its meaning, chiefly because the word "meaning" in this connection is both ambiguous and extremely vague. However, if what is meant is that an atheist cannot be attached to certain goals which give direction to his life, then the charge is quite plainly false. If what is meant is that although the atheist may, like other men, pursue certain goals, he will not be able to *justify* any of his activities, then it should be pointed out that most human beings, even believers in God, do not justify the great majority of their acts by reference to God's will. Hence, the justification of these actions, if they ever are justified, could not be affected by the soundness of atheism. It is difficult to see how such activities as engaging in scientific research, assisting people who are in trouble, singing or dancing or making love or eating superb meals, if they ever were worthwhile, would cease to be so once belief in God is rejected. If what is meant by the charge is that the unbeliever will eventually have to fall back, in his justification, on one or more value judgments which he cannot justify by reference to anything more fundamental, this may be true, but it is not necessarily baleful, and it is not a consequence of atheism. Anybody who engages in the process of justifying anything will eventually reach a stage at which some proposition, principle, or judgment will simply have to be accepted and not referred back to anything else. The unbeliever may, in justifying his acts, regard as fundamental such judgments as "happiness is intrinsically worthwhile" or "the increase of knowledge is good for its own sake," whereas some believers may say that only service of God is intrinsically valuable. If it is a sign of irrationality, which in any normal sense of the word it is not, to accept a value judgment that is not based on another one, then the atheist is not one whit more irrational than the believer.

On the question of zest, it should be observed that neither James nor anybody else has ever offered empirical evidence for the assertion that unbelievers lead less active or strenuous lives than believers. What we know about human temperament suggests that the acceptance or rejection of a metaphysical position has, in the case of the vast majority of men, exceedingly little to do with whether they lead active or inactive lives. The Soviet astronauts, who are atheists (to take one recent illustration), appear to display the same courage and endurance as their American counterparts, who are believers. In general terms, a survey of the contributions of atheists and other unbelievers to science and social progress, often in conditions requiring unusual stamina and fortitude, would seem to indicate that James was in error. The a priori character of James's views on this subject remind one of Locke's conviction, mentioned earlier in this article, that atheists, since they do not fear divine punishment, cannot be trusted to keep oaths and promises.

As for the "loveless universe" presented by atheism, it must of course be admitted that if there is no God who loves his creatures, there would be that much less love in the world. But this is perhaps all that an atheist would have to concede in this connection. Aside from certain mystics and their raptures, it may be questioned whether a biologically normal human being is capable of feeling any real or deep love for an unseen power; and it hardly seems credible to suppose that a person will cease to love other human beings and animals (if he ever loved them) just because he does not believe them to be the work of God. Perhaps one may hazard a guess that if more human beings grow up in an environment that is free from irrational taboos and repressions (and these, one may add, have not been altogether unconnected with religious belief in the past), there will be more, not less, love in the world—people will be more lovable and will also be more capable of giving love. As far as love is concerned, the record of theistic religions has not been particularly impressive.

The writers whose views we are discussing have probably been on stronger ground when they maintain that atheism is a gloomy or tragic philosophy, but here too some qualifications are in order. To begin with, if atheism implies that life is gloomy, it does so not by itself but in conjunction with the rejection of the belief in life after death. There have been atheists, of whom J. E. McTaggart is probably the most famous, who believed in immortality, and they would deny that *their* atheism had any gloomy implications. However, since the great majority of atheists undoubtedly reject any belief in survival, this does not go to the root of the matter. It cannot be denied that the thought of annihilation can be quite unendurable; but it may be questioned whether believers, whatever they may be expected to feel, do in fact find the thought of death any less distressing. In the opinion of some observers, this is due to the fact that regardless of his profession, the believer frequently does not really believe that death is the gate to an eternal life in the presence of God. "Almost inevitably some part of him," in the words of Bertrand Russell, is aware that beliefs of this kind are "myths and that he believes them only because they are comforting" (*Human Society in Ethics and Politics*, p. 207). Russell and Freud regard belief in God and immortality as illusions which usually do not work, but they are quick to add that anybody who refuses to be the victim of unworthy fears would dispense with such illusions even if they did work. "There is something feeble and a little contemptible," in Russell's words, "about a man who cannot face the perils of life without the help of comfortable myths" (*ibid.*). Some years earlier, in an essay entitled "What I Believe," Russell had put the point very bluntly:

> I believe that when I die I shall rot, and nothing of my ego will survive. I am not young, and I love life. But I should scorn to shiver with terror at the thought of annihilation. Happiness is nonetheless true happiness because it must come to an end, nor do thought and love lose their value because they are not everlasting. . . . Even if the open windows of science at first make us shiver after the cozy indoor warmth of traditional humanizing myths, in the end the fresh air brings vigor, and the great spaces have a splendor of their own.

Bibliography

The only full-length history of atheism in existence is Fritz Mauthner's four-volume work, *Der Atheismus und seine Geschichte im Abendlande* (Stuttgart, 1920–1923). Although this work contains much interesting information that cannot easily be obtained elsewhere, it is marred by extreme repetitiousness and by a curiously broad use of the word "atheism," which allows Mauthner to speak of agnostic and even deistic atheists. Probably of greater value are the various works on the history of free thought by J. M. Robertson, chiefly his *A Short History of Free Thought* (New York, 1957). Accounts of the struggles of atheists in England in the nineteenth century will be found in H. Bradlaugh Bonner, *Charles Bradlaugh: A Record of His Life and Work* (London, 1894); G. J. Holyoake's two-volume *Sixty Years of an Agitator's Life* (London, 1892); and A. H. Nethercot, *The First Five Lives of Annie Besant* (London, 1961).

An early defense of atheism is found in Vol. II of Holbach's two-volume *The System of Nature*, translated by H. D. Robinson (Boston, 1853) and in his briefer work *Common Sense*, translated by A. Knoop (New York, 1920). Shelley defended atheism in his essays *The Necessity of Atheism* and *A Refutation of Deism*, and in one of the Notes to Canto VII of *Queen Mab*, entitled "There is no God." All of these are included in D. L. Clark, ed., *Shelley's Prose* (Albuquerque, N.M., 1954). Charles Bradlaugh's "A Plea for Atheism" was first published in 1864 and reprinted in the Centenary Volume, *Charles Bradlaugh: Champion of Liberty* (London, 1933). Although he rarely used the term "atheism," Schopenhauer is usually and quite properly classified as an atheist. His fullest discussion of the reasons for rejecting belief in God are found in his "The Christian System" and in his "Religion: A Dialogue." Both of these are available in a translation by T. B. Saunders in *Complete Essays of Schopenhauer* (New York, 1942). Another nineteenth-century work defending atheism is Ludwig Feuerbach, *The Essence of Christianity* (1841), translated by George Eliot, with an introduction by Karl Barth (New York, 1953). Of early critical works, special mention should be made of Ralph Cudworth's two-volume *The True Intellectual System of the World* (London, 1678), which is an enormously detailed onslaught on all forms of atheism known to the author, and of Voltaire's article "Atheism" in his *Philosophical Dictionary*, translated by Peter Gay (New York, 1962). Part II of Voltaire's article is an extended critique of *The System of Nature*.

In more recent years, atheism has been championed in R. Robinson, *An Atheist's Values* (Oxford, 1964); in Ernest Nagel, "A Defence of Atheism," which is available in Paul Edwards and Arthur Pap, eds., *A Modern Introduction to Philosophy* (New York, 1965), and in Michael Scriven, *Primary Philosophy* (New York, 1966). Rudolf Carnap's position, which is briefly mentioned in the present article, is presented in his "The Elimination of Metaphysics Through Logical Analysis of Language," which is available in a translation by Arthur Pap in A. J. Ayer, ed., *Logical Positivism* (Glencoe, Ill, 1959). A somewhat similar position is defended by Antony Flew in "Theology and Falsification." This paper is available in various anthologies, perhaps most conveniently in John Hick, ed., *The Existence of God* (New York, 1964). An interesting and unusual defense of theology against contemporary criticisms like those of Carnap and Flew is found in I. M. Crombie's "The Possibility of Theological Statements," in Basil Mitchell, ed., *Faith and Logic* (London, 1957). The comments in the present article about the attempts of fideists to circumvent the argument from evil and other difficulties are elaborated in Paul Edwards, "Is Fideistic Theology Irrefutable?" in *The Rationalist Annual* (1966).

There is a kind of "ontological" argument for atheism proposed by J. N. Findlay in "Can God's Existence Be Disproved?"; this, together with various rejoinders, is reprinted in Antony Flew and Alasdair MacIntyre, eds., *New Essays in Philosophical Theology* (London and New York, 1955). The view that belief in God is not false but self-contradictory and that, hence, atheism is necessarily true is advocated by Jean-Paul Sartre in his *Being and Nothingness*, translated by Hazel Barnes (New York, 1956). Bertrand Russell wavers between calling himself an atheist and an agnostic. Many of his publications may plausibly be regarded as defenses of atheism. In this connection special mention should be made of *The Scientific Outlook* (London and New York, 1931), *Religion and Science* (London and New York, 1935), and *Why I Am Not a Christian and Other Essays on Related Subjects* (London and New York, 1957), which includes "What I Believe."

What we have been calling metaphysical theology is defended by H. L. Mansel in *The Limits of Religious Thought* (London, 1858). Mansel's views were vigorously attacked by John Stuart Mill in his *An Examination of Sir William Hamilton's Philosophy* (4th ed., London, 1872); and Mill in turn was answered by Mansel in *The Philosophy of the Conditioned* (London, 1866). The version of metaphysical theology on which we concentrated in the present article is expounded by Paul Tillich in Vol. I of his three-volume *Systematic Theology* (Chicago, 1951–1963), in his *The Courage to Be* (New Haven, 1952), and in J. A. T. Robinson, *Honest to God* (London, 1963). This position is criticized in great detail in Paul Edwards, "Professor Tillich's Confusions," in *Mind*, Vol. 74 (1965), 192–214, and in Dorothy Emmet, " 'The Ground of Being,' " in *The Journal of Theological Studies*, Vol. 15 (1964), 280–292. Various reactions to the views of Robinson are collected in D. L. Edwards, ed., *The Honest to God Debate* (London, 1963). The Thomistic doctrine of "analogical predication," which was not discussed in the present article, is expounded in the *Summa Theologica*, I, 13, 5, and in the work by Thomas Cajetan available in *On the Analogy of Names and the Concept of Being*, translated by E. A. Bushinski and H. J. Koren (Pittsburgh, 1953). Contemporary expositions of it may be found in G. H. Joyce, *The Principles of Natural Theology* (London, 1923), and in E. L. Mascall, *Existence and Analogy* (London, 1949). The theory is criticized in Frederick Ferré, *Language, Logic and God* (New York, 1961), and in W. T. Blackstone, *The Problem of Religious Knowledge* (Englewood Cliffs, N.J., 1963). There is an interesting attempt to state the doctrine with great precision by using the tools of contemporary logic in I. M. Bochenski, "On Analogy," in *The Thomist*, Vol. 11 (1948), 474–497. Tillich's theory, as well as the Thomistic theory, is criticized in Sidney Hook, *The Quest for Being* (New York, 1960).

Aquinas' views on the nature of creation and the possibility of proving that the material universe has not always existed are given in *On the Eternity of the World*, translated by Cyril Vollert (Milwaukee, 1964), which also contains relevant extracts from the *Summa Theologica* and the *Summa Contra Gentiles*. The argument for atheism based on the eternity of matter is stated in Ludwig Büchner, *Force and Matter* (4th English ed., London 1884; reprinted New York, 1950). The question of whether contemporary theories in physical cosmology have any bearing on the question of the existence of God is discussed in William Bonnor, *The Mystery of the Expanding Universe* (New York, 1964); M. K. Munitz, *Space, Time and Creation* (Glencoe, Ill., 1957); E. L. Mascall, *Christian Theology and Natural Science* (London, 1956); and Antony Flew, "Cosmology and Creation," in *The Humanist* Vol. 76 (May 1961) 34–35. All the writers just mentioned incline to the view that physical cosmology has no bearing on the question of the existence of God. The opposite position is supported by E. A. Milne in *Modern Cosmology and the Christian Idea of God* (London, 1952).

The argument for atheism based on the premise that there is no "cosmic brain" is expounded in Emil Du Bois-Reymond, *Über die Grenzen des Naturerkennens* (Berlin, 1873), and by W. K. Clifford in an essay entitled "Body and Mind," which is available in Vol. II of Clifford's two-volume *Lectures and Essays*, F. Pollock, ed. (London and New York, 1879). It is criticized in James Martineau, *Modern Materialism and Its Relation to Religion and Theology* (London, 1876; New York, 1877). According to Mauthner, *op. cit.*, Vol. III, pp. 439 ff., the remark that "in scanning the heavens with a telescope he found no God" has been falsely attributed to Laplace and occurs in fact in one of the writings of another distinguished astronomer of the same period, Joseph Jérôme de Lalande. Arguments by Indian philosophers, similar to those of Du Bois-Reymond and Clifford, are found in *Slovavartika*, Sec. I, verses 43–59, reprinted in Sarvepalli Radhakrishnan and C. A. Moore, eds., *A Source Book in Indian Philosophy* (Princeton, N.J., 1957).

The essay by Tyndall in which he defends agnosticism in contrast to atheism is contained in his *Fragments of Science* (New York, 1871). A similar argument by Clarence Darrow occurs in his lecture "Why I Am an Agnostic," which was first delivered in 1929 and is now available in A. Weinberg and L. Weinberg, eds., *Clarence Darrow—Verdicts out of Court* (Chicago, 1963). Agnosticism is criticized from an atheistic viewpoint in several of the writings of Friedrich Engels. There is a useful collection of all the main discussions of religion by Marx and Engels in Karl Marx and Friedrich Engels, *On Religion* (Moscow, 1957; New York, 1964).

The argument that atheism must be untenable since, if it were true, the atheist himself would have to be omniscient, is advanced in Thomas Chalmers' two-volume *On Natural Theology* (New York, 1836); in J. Foster, *Essays* (London, 1844); and in Robert Flint, *Anti-Theistic Theories* (London, 1878). There is a reply to Chalmers and Foster in G. J. Holyoake, *Trial of Theism* (London, 1858). A somewhat similar argument is contained in Paul Ziff, "About 'God,' " in Sidney Hook, ed., *Religious Experience and Truth* (New York, 1961). There is a reply to this in Paul Edwards, "Some Notes on Anthropomorphic Theology," in *Religious Experience and Truth*.

Pascal's horror of a universe without God is expressed in numerous passages in his *Pensées*, translated by W. E. Trotter, with an introduction by T. S. Eliot (New York, 1958). William James's claims that unbelief is fatal to "the strenuous mood" is contained in his essay "The Moral Philosopher and the Moral Life," which is reprinted in his *The Will to Believe* (New York, 1897). The view that atheism makes the universe "loveless" is defended by J. W. Krutch in his *The Modern Temper* (paperback ed., New York, 1956). Malinowski's remarks about the "tragic" nature of life without God are found in his contribution to the B.B.C. symposium *Science and Religion* (New York, 1931). The very different view that there is something liberating in the rejection of belief in God is advocated in J. M. Guyau, *The Non-Religion of the Future*, with an introduction from N. M. Glatzer (New York, 1962); in Friedrich Nietzsche, *Die Fröhliche Wissenschaft*, in Vol. II of his three-volume *Werke*, Karl Schlechta, ed. (Munich, 1954–1956); and in Sigmund Freud, *The Future of an Illusion*, translated by W. D. Robson-Scott (New York, 1927).

In recent years there have been numerous books and articles by religious thinkers in which the atheist's position is treated with a certain amount of sympathy. The following writings are especially worth mentioning in this connection: James Collins, *God in Modern Philosophy* (Chicago, 1959); Henri de Lubac, *The Drama of Atheist Humanism*, translated by E. M. Riley (New York, 1950); Étienne Borne, *Atheism*, translated by S. J. Tester (New York, 1961); Ignace Lepp, *Atheism in Our Time*, translated by Bernard Murchlord (New York, 1963); W. A. Luijpen, *Phenomenology and Atheism*, translated by W. van de Putte (Pittsburgh, 1965); Jacques Maritain, "The Meaning of Contemporary Atheism," in *The Listener* (March 1950), 427–432; Gabriel Marcel, "Philosophical Atheism," in *International Philosophical Quarterly*, Vol. 2 (1962), 501–514; and Jean-Marie Le Blond, "The Contemporary Status of Atheism," in *International Philosophical Quarterly*, Vol. 5 (1965) 37–55.

PAUL EDWARDS

ATHEISMUSSTREIT, a famous controversy in Germany during the closing years of the eighteenth century concerning the allegedly subversive philosophical views of Johann G. Fichte (1762–1814) and of the much less well known Friedrich C. Forberg (1770–1848).

Fichte, who died as a pillar of respectability, had advanced various radical views in his earlier years, and on the nature and reality of God he never became fully orthodox. In 1793, while living as a private tutor in Zurich, Fichte published two political pamphlets entitled "Reclamation of the Freedom of Thought from the Princes of Europe" and "Contributions Designed To Correct the Judgment of the Public on the French Revolution" in which he enthusiastically supported the basic principles of the French Revolution, arguing for free expression of opinion as an inalienable human right and subjecting the privileges of the nobility and the church to trenchant criticism. Fichte was at that time already famous, largely as a result of his Kantian work, *Versuch einer Kritik aller Offenbarung* ("Essay Toward a Critique of All Revelation"), which had been published anonymously in Königsberg in 1792. Some reviewers attributed the essay to Kant, who thereupon revealed Fichte as the true author, at the same time bestowing high praise on his gifts. In spite of Fichte's reputation as a political radical, he was appointed professor of philosophy at Jena in 1794.

For some time things went fairly smoothly at Jena. Fichte, who was a dynamic lecturer, made numerous converts among both his colleagues and the students, although there were some acrimonious exchanges with the psychologist C. C. E. Schmid and others distrustful of Fichte's speculative bent. There were two violent controversies before the *Atheismusstreit* broke out. One of these concerned a series of public lectures which Fichte had scheduled on Sundays from ten to eleven o'clock in the morning. Local clergymen were outraged, and the Over-Consistory (of which no less a man than Herder was a member) appealed to the government at Weimar to intervene. One local journal called attention to Fichte's revolutionary politics and asserted that he and his democratic followers were engaging in a deliberate attempt to substitute the worship of reason for the worship of God. The senate of the university and the government of Weimar decided in Fichte's favor, but it was agreed to give the lectures at three in the afternoon. The other controversy involved the university fraternities, which Fichte regarded as unethical and corrupt and whose abolition he publicly recommended. On New Year's Eve of 1795 students belonging to the fraternities attacked Fichte's house, breaking windows and heaping insults upon him and his wife. In the early months of 1795 Fichte felt his life to be in danger and found it necessary to reside outside of Jena until the tempers of the fraternity members had calmed down.

The offending articles. The *Atheismusstreit* itself began in 1798 with the publication in the *Philosophisches Journal*, a periodical of which Fichte was coeditor, of an essay by Forberg entitled "The Evolution of the Nature of Religion." Fichte's conservative English biographer, Robert Adamson, dismisses Forberg's position as an "exaggeration of the dismal rationalism into which the weaker Kantians had drifted." In fact, however, Forberg's paper shows a powerful and independent thinker at work and does not seem dated even now. (Interestingly enough, Hans Vaihinger called attention to the philosophical merits of Forberg's work after almost total neglect for a century, citing him as an early positivistic fictionalist and praising his unusually fine appreciation of the more radical aspects of Kant's philosophy of religion.)

What, Forberg asks, is the foundation of the belief in a moral world order? There are three possible sources—experience, speculation, and conscience. Experience certainly lends no support to such a belief; if anything, it shows an evil deity in conflict with, and more often than not triumphing over, a good one. As for speculation, Forberg briefly and very clearly repeats Kant's objections to the ontological, cosmological, and teleological arguments, adding some critical observations of his own. Accordingly, the foundation of religion must be sought in our conscience. Religion is "purely and solely the fruit of a morally good heart . . . ; it originates entirely from the wish of the good heart that the good in the world should triumph over the evil." To have "genuine religion" is not to have a belief in God; it is to be a partisan of the good, to act as if the kingdom of God, which for Forberg simply means a just and moral world, were attainable. Forberg himself evidently did not believe that such a world was attainable. This belief, however, is no more essential to true religion than is the belief in God. What is essential is the striving in the direction of a moral world whether or not one believes in its attainability. Forberg most emphatically insists that an atheist can be a religious person in his sense of religion. "Practical belief and theoretical unbelief on the one hand and theoretical belief and practical unbelief on the other may very well coexist."

At first sight this position may appear to be a kind of voluntaristic defense of traditional religion and an endorsement of Kant's moral argument, as this has frequently been interpreted. In fact, Forberg is very far removed from any such point of view. He is not saying that since there is no evidence either way, it is as well to believe in a just God or the attainability of a moral world. We are not, according to him, required to believe any such thing, and it does not really matter whether we do. We *are* required to *act as if we believed this.* Forberg was highly critical of the common interpretation of Kant's moral argument as providing cognitive support for belief in God. In his later defense of himself, *Friedrich Carl Forbergs Apologie seines angeblichen Atheismus* (Gotha, 1799), he castigates the "usual, far too theoretical presentation of the notion of a practical belief," adding that it is "an unphilosophical conception which allows people to reintroduce through a back door every kind of nonsense of which theoretical philosophy has rid us with much effort."

In the same issue of the *Philosophisches Journal*, Fichte published an essay, "Concerning the Foundation of Our Belief in Divine Government of the World," which was intended to complement Forberg's paper. In a somewhat patronizing opening Fichte informs the reader that although he agrees with much in Forberg's piece, there are some important questions on which Forberg has not "quite reached" his, Fichte's, position and that since he had not previously had an opportunity to explain himself on these issues, he would do so now. Attempts to infer the existence of God from the world of sense objects, he proceeds, must inevitably fail. From the point of view of common sense and science, the world of sense objects is "absolute" and self-existing, and any attempt to go beyond it is "total nonsense." The assumption of a cosmic intelligence, moreover, would not explain anything, since it is quite unintelligible to talk about the creation of material things out of ideas. Considered from the transcendental viewpoint, the world of the senses is a "mere reflection of our own activity," and as a "nothing" it can hardly require an explanation outside itself.

Our belief in God can be grounded only in the supersensible world, which for Fichte is the only ultimately real world. This is the world of free moral agents, and unlike Forberg, Fichte teaches that the universe is, in fact, moral and just, that "every truly good act must succeed, that every evil one must surely fail, that for those who really love the good all things must turn out for the best." This does not mean that the good necessarily receive rewards in terms of pleasure but the world in which we experience pleasure is not the real world. The world of sense objects exists only as a "stage" on which free agents perform or fail to perform their duty. It has not "the slightest influence on morality or immorality, not the slightest power over our free nature." It is, in fact, nothing more than the "material objectification of our duty; our duty is what is ultimately real, what is the fundamental stuff of all phenomena."

God is identical with the moral world order. A person believes in God insofar as he does his duty "gaily and without concern," without doubts or fears about consequences. The "true atheist" is he who calculates the consequences instead of following the voice of his conscience; he "raises his own counsel above the counsel of God and thus raises himself to God's position." He who does evil in order to produce good is godless. "You must not lie," Fichte adds by way of illustration, "even if the world were to go to pieces as a consequence"; a moral agent knows, however, that the world could not go to pieces, since "the plan of its preservation could not possibly be based on a lie." Both here and elsewhere Fichte argued that all cognition is based on the existence of the moral world order. The existence of God, which here, of course, simply means the moral world order, is therefore more certain than anything else. It is presupposed in any piece of valid reasoning, and hence it cannot be, nor does it need to be, proved. "It is the ground of all other certainty and the only absolutely valid objective reality."

The anonymous pamphlets. Attention was drawn to these essays and their alleged subversion in a pamphlet published late in 1798 under the title "Letters From a Father to His Student-Son Concerning the Atheism of Fichte and Forberg." The pamphlet was signed *G* and was at first attributed to D. Gabler, a respectable theologian teaching at Altdorf. Gabler vehemently denied any connection with the pamphlet, however, and publicly expressed his high regard for Fichte. Fichte himself attributed it to one of his enemies at Jena, Gruner, but the authorship remains uncertain. The main argument of the pamphlet followed a simple, popular line: Belief in an ever present "witness and judge" is essential to the moral behavior of human beings; if men were not afraid of punishment in the next world, they would be certain to do evil whenever they expected to escape the secular penalties. As a high school teacher, Forberg in particular is regarded as a most dangerous man. How could such a rector give a "thorough religious education" to the students under his charge? "To sow the seeds of immorality among young people and make belief in God suspect is not a permissible game." When compared to the protector of morality who hunted Bertrand Russell in New York City 150 years later, the attack was conducted with decorum and refinement; however, several later anonymous pamphlets were somewhat less refined. As usually happens in such cases, they contained slanderous comments about Fichte's private life and "sexual philosophy."

Fichte's dismissal. The rest of the story does little credit to any of the parties except Fichte and Forberg. Moved by the "Father's Letter," the Saxon government, on November 19, 1798, published a Rescript ordering the universities of Leipzig and Wittenberg to confiscate all copies of the *Philosophisches Journal* because of the atheistic articles contained in it. This was followed by a request to the neighboring German governments to take similar steps. The dukes of Saxe-Weimar were informed that Saxon students would not be allowed to enroll in Jena unless there was an immediate investigation into the conduct of the two offenders. The grand duke of Weimar, a ruler with a genuine respect for scholarship, was free from any trace of religious fanaticism; however, any attempt he might have made to hush up the case was prevented by Fichte's public defenses of himself. In January 1799, Fichte wrote his "Appeal to the Public Concerning the Accusation of the Expression of Atheistic Opinions," a copy of which was promptly sent to the grand duke. In March 1799 he wrote the "Juridical Defense Against the Accusation of Atheism," which was primarily addressed to the university authorities but a copy of which was also forwarded to the grand duke. In these "defenses" Fichte contended, first, that his philosophical position, although far removed from the anthropomorphic popular religion, could not fairly be regarded as a form of atheism and was, in fact, "true Christianity" and, second, that any punishment inflicted on Forberg or himself would be a gross violation of academic freedom. The case, Fichte insisted, was one of great importance; since the accusation had been public, the verdict should also be public. Fichte's friends regarded this as a most imprudent demand, and rumors were soon current that the Weimar government was about to impose a public censure on Fichte. In the hope of preventing this, Fichte wrote a letter to Privy Councilor Voigt in which he declared that he would under no circumstances submit to censure. In such an event, he said, he would instantly resign. He added that several distinguished members of the Jena faculty shared his opinion that censure would constitute infringement of their academic rights and that they would resign with him. Voigt was told that he was free to show the letter to others, including, presumably, the Weimar authorities, who were about to reach their verdict.

This letter turned out to be Fichte's undoing at Jena. The Weimar government quite improperly treated it as a formal document. It avoided any censure of Fichte (or of his coeditor Niethammer) on the charge of atheism. Instead, both were rebuked in the mildest possible language for their "indiscretion" and advised to exercise greater caution in their selection of articles for the *Philosophisches*

Journal. The journal itself was not proscribed, nor was there any mention of what teachers should or should not say in their classrooms. In a postscript, however, reference was made to Fichte's letter to Voigt, and his threatened resignation in case of censure was noted and accepted. In effect, this amounted to Fichte's dismissal, and two petitions on his behalf by the Jena student body to the duke were of no avail. Goethe, who a few years earlier had been largely instrumental in securing the Jena chair for Fichte, was one of those in the Weimar council who demanded Fichte's ouster. Fichte's support of the French Revolution was apparently a minor thing, but the language used in the letter to Voigt was unforgivable. "For my own part," Goethe wrote in a letter a few months later, "I declare that I would have voted against my own son if he had permitted himself such language against a government." Forberg was mildly censured by his superiors and did not return to any writings on religion until shortly before his death, when he published his autobiography, in which there is a very full account of the entire episode and a reaffirmation of all his earlier convictions.

The charge of atheism. In his "Appeal to the Public," Fichte had vehemently denied the charge of atheism. Using language which is very similar to that employed today by Paul Tillich and Bishop J. A. T. Robinson, he inveighed against the popular "idol-worship" of God as a "substance," as another entity *in* the world, and against the vulgar "eudaemonistic" morality which makes God a giver of "sensuous" rewards for good deeds and "sensuous" punishments for evil deeds. Such a conception—or, indeed, any attribution of personal characteristics to God—constitutes a lowering and limiting of the deity and has to be opposed in the interests of true religion. There is no need to question Fichte's sincerity, and in more senses than one it may be granted that he was a religious man.

At the same time the charge of atheism does not appear to have been totally unjustified. People do not usually mean by God simply the moral world order, and the denial of God as an entity over and above the more familiar objects of experience (including moral human agents) is precisely what is ordinarily meant by atheism. On all these points Fichte had been very explicit in the original essay. "There can be no doubt," he had written, "that the notion of God as a separate substance is impossible and contradictory, and it is permitted to say this plainly." Again, "We need no other god [than the moral world order], and we cannot comprehend another one. There is no rational justification for going beyond the moral world order to a separate entity as its cause."

Granting that there was some basis for the charge of atheism against Fichte, this in no way excuses the behavior of the Weimar authorities or of Fichte's and Forberg's other detractors. Not one distinguished voice was raised anywhere in Germany in defense of the accused men. Kant himself, who was still alive, was moved to a statement in the *Allgemeine Literaturzeitung* (1799, No. 109) in which he emphatically dissociated his philosophy from Fichte's system. "When I compare the state of the German republic of letters of this period with the Enlightenment literature of France a generation earlier, I am overcome with the deepest shame," was the apt comment of the historian Fritz Mauthner.

Bibliography

The main documents of the *Atheismusstreit* have been collected in F. Medicus, ed., *Fichte und Forberg. Die philosophischen Schriften zum Atheismusstreit* (Leipzig, 1910), and H. Lindau, ed., *Die Schriften zu J. G. Fichte's Atheismusstreit* (Munich, 1912).

Critical appraisals of the actions and writings of the participants are found in Vol. IV of Fritz Mauthner's *Der Atheismus und seine Geschichte im Abendlande* (Stuttgart, 1923); F. Paulsen's "G. J. Fichte im Kampf um die Freiheit des philosophischen Denkens," in *Deutsche Rundschau*, Vol. 99 (1899), 66–76; and H. Rickert's "Fichte's Atheismusstreit und die kantische Philosophie," in *Kant Studien*, Vol. 4 (1899), 137–166.

There is a discussion of the originality of Forberg as well as of the evidence favoring a "left-wing" interpretation of Kant's moral argument for the existence of God in Appendix A and Appendix B of Hans Vaihinger, *Die Philosophie des Als Ob* (Berlin, 1911), translated by C. K. Ogden as *The Philosophy of "As If"* (New York, 1924).

PAUL EDWARDS

ATHENIAN SCHOOL, the name given to Plato's Academy in its post-Plotinian period, was strongly influenced by Plotinus himself, by Porphyry, and by Iamblichus. Its first representative known to us is Plutarch of Athens (d. 431/432). Following Plotinus, he found his five realms of reality (One, Intelligence, Soul, Nature, Matter) in the hypotheses of Plato's *Parmenides.* He tried to connect Aristotle's noetic with Plato's anamnesis theory; contradicting Alexander of Aphrodisias, he asserted that by Active Intelligence Aristotle meant not the divinity but an actual, although divine, part of our soul. Plutarch's successor, Syrianus, declared the study of Aristotle to be preliminary and ancillary to that of Plato, but did not try to harmonize the two; rather, he defended Plato from Aristotle's criticism. But his interpretation of Plato made full use of Aristotle's report, according to which Plato recognized the One and the Indefinite Dyad as supreme principles, deriving from them ideas, ideal mathematicals, and sensibles. In his probable successor Domninus, who was of Jewish origin, mathematical interests seem to have been predominant.

It is different with Proclus, for, in addition to mathematical, astronomical, physical, astrological, and philological works, he also wrote on philosophic and religious topics (including theurgy, which he practiced), besides composing hymns to various gods—a remarkable example of Neoplatonic piety. In presenting what he conceived to be Plato's theology, he made full use of the system of Plotinus. But in all his philosophical works (among them a number of commentaries on Plato's dialogues) he gave to Plotinus' system a great rigor. Particularly remarkable was his description of the emanative process; the lower in one aspect remains in the higher, in another leaves it, in a third returns to it. By splitting the Plotinian hypostases vertically and horizontally, he created many entities, which he identified on one hand with philosophic concepts (taken from various contexts), on the other with deities of Greek and non-Greek religions. Like Plotinus he assumed the One (whose transcendence and ineffability he described by a wealth of terms, only to negate them) to be the source of the emanative process, but whereas according to Plotinus the first emanative step produces Intelligence (*nous*), Proclus, probably inspired by the doctrine of ideal numbers that Aristotle attributed to Plato, interposed between the One and Intelligence a very peculiar kind of number, which he called henads and identified with highest deities. The emanative process is, as in Plotinus, a descent; but matter, in which the descent terminates, was not considered evil by Proclus, as it was by Plotinus; Proclus often made the soul responsible for the origin of evil. Like Plotinus, Proclus taught the mystical union with the One as man's ultimate goal but described with greater clarity than Plotinus the part of the soul making such a union possible as superior to Intelligence. He called it the flower of Intelligence, borrowing the term from the *Chaldaean Oracles* (a forgery of the second century, on which Proclus wrote a commentary, as did Syrianus before him, and which he considered one of the only two works unconditionally worth preserving—the other was Plato's *Timaeus*). The influence of Proclus' philosophy on both the scholastic and mystical philosophy of the Middle Ages was extraordinary, although Proclus—and with him the entire School of Athens—was opposed to Christianity and was a fervent polytheist. This paradoxical influence is partly explained by the fact that a man whose identity is still unknown, pretending and believed to be Dionysius the Areopagite, disciple of the Apostle Paul (*Acts* 17.34), and therefore enjoying unlimited authority, presented Christianity in terms of Proclus in a number of works (or, as could also be said, presented Neoplatonism, disguising it as Christianity).

Proclus' successor was Marinus, a Jew, which lends support to the hypothesis that the fountainhead of Jewish mysticism, the *Sefer Yezirah* ("Book of Creation"), in its doctrine that the first entities after God were ten Sephirot (a peculiar kind of numbers) was inspired by Proclus. The last scholarch was Damascius (born c. 458), with whom the school came, perhaps, to its apt conclusion. According to him, it is not only the One that is ineffable and therefore above any rational knowledge. To no moment, or result of the emanative process can concepts such as sameness or difference, cause or effect, remaining, stepping forward, or turning be applied. All these concepts are only our modes of thinking. The One is and remains one and indeterminate and has never become many or determinate. Among Damascius' fellow scholars were Priscianus and Simplicius. The latter personally and in spirit represented a link between the School of Athens and the School of Alexandria. He was a scholar and a commentator rather than a systematic thinker. According to him, the differences between Plato and Aristotle were merely verbal; and where Aristotle seemed to contradict Plato, he actually criticized only erroneous interpretations of Plato. In 529, as part of his antipagan campaign, Justinian made it unlawful for any pagan to teach, and as a result the School of Athens was closed. A number of its members left for Persia (Priscianus wrote a philosophic manual for the Persian King Chosroes), but after some two years in that country they returned to the Roman Empire.

Bibliography

On Plutarch of Athens, Syrianus, Domninus, Proclus, Marinus, Damascius, Priscianus, and Simplicius, see articles in Pauly-Wissowa, *Realenzyklopädie* (Stuttgart, 1893 ff.) and in *Enciclopedia filosofica* (Venice, 1957).

On Pseudo-Dionysius, see H. F. Müller, *Dionysios, Proklos, Plotinos*, 2d ed. (Münster, 1926).

On the *Sefer Yezirah*, see L. Baeck, "Zum Sepher Jezira," in *Monatsschrift für Geschichte und Wissenschaft des Judentums*, Vol. 70 (1926), 371–376; Vol. 78 (1934), 448–455.

PHILIP MERLAN

ATOMISM is a doctrine that has a long history in both philosophy and science. For this reason it is not easy to define its content in such a way as to comprehend all the historical variations and especially the historical development of the doctrine. In a very general sense, however, atomism may be defined as the doctrine that material reality is composed of simple and unchangeable minute particles, called atoms. It holds that all observable changes must be reduced to changes in the configuration of these particles. The multiplicity of visible forms in nature must likewise be based upon differences of configuration. The best way to discuss the variations of this general idea of atomism is to follow the historical development, which shows a gradual shift of emphasis from philosophical to scientific considerations. Consequently, the first part of this article, covering the period from the sixth century B.C. to the seventeenth century, will be of a philosophical nature because in this period atomism was considered preponderantly from a philosophic point of view. The second part is concerned primarily with science, for it was in the period after the seventeenth century that atomism evolved in a scientific theory.

THE PHILOSOPHICAL PERIOD

In Greek philosophy we are already confronted with several types of atomism. Atomism in the strict sense, propounded by Leucippus and Democritus (fifth century B.C.), should be looked upon as an attempt to reconcile the data of sense experience with Parmenides' thesis that matter is unchangeable. Parmenides rejected the possibility of change on rational grounds; change seemed to be unintelligible. He was convinced that reality must be one, that it must possess unity, and that, being *one* reality, it could not change. It may be remarked that this thesis of Parmenides is a presupposition for all rational science. Without fundamental unity, no universal laws are possible; without fundamental immutability, no laws covering past, present, and future can be valid. Yet, it is clear that Parmenides' approach is one-sided. Science may presuppose unity and immutability, but it also presupposes change. Only by studying changes is science able to discover the immutable laws of nature.

Democritus agreed with Parmenides on the unintelligibility and impossibility of qualitative change. He did not agree on the unintelligibility and impossibility of quantitative change. This type of change is subject to mathematical reasoning and therefore is possible. By the same token, Democritus denied qualitative multiplicity, but accepted multiplicity based on purely quantitative differences. Consequently, he accepted a numeric multitude of original beings, the atoms. These atoms did not differ qualitatively; only their sizes and figures differed. The infinite variety of observable things could be explained by the different shapes and sizes of the atoms that constituted them and by the different ways in which the atoms were combined. Observable changes were based upon a change in combinations of the atoms. During such changes, however, the atoms themselves remained intrinsically unchanged. They did not change their nature, or even their size or figure; they were indivisible (hence their name ἄτομος, or indivisible).

Other forms of Greek atomism differed from that conceived by Democritus mainly in two points. First, they did not restrict the differences between the atoms to purely quantitative ones, but also accepted differences in quality. There was even a system that assumed as many qualitatively different atoms as there are different observable substances (Anaxagoras, fifth century B.C.). Usually, however, only a few kinds of atoms were assumed, based upon the famous doctrine of the four elements: earth, water, air, and fire (Empedocles, fifth century B.C.).

The second point of difference concerned the indivisibility of atoms. It is evident that a system that does not accept the indivisibility of atoms cannot properly be called atomism, but since such systems have played an important role in the history of atomism, we must mention them. For Democritus, the indivisibility of atoms was an absolute indivisibility, being the consequence of an absolute immutability. There were systems, however, that considered the indivisibility and immutability as only relative. The "atoms" could be divided, but they then became "atoms" of another substance; they changed their nature. (Here again an exception must be made for atoms as conceived of by Anaxagoras. These could be divided, but remained of the same kind. Hence they received the name of *homoiomerics*, possessing similar parts.) From the historical viewpoint, the most important system with qualitatively different atoms is that developed by the commentators on Aristotle—Alexander of Aphrodisias (second century A.D.), Themistius (fourth century) and John Philoponus (sixth century). In their system the atoms are called *elachista* (very small or smallest), the Greek equivalent of the Latin *minima*, which in medieval Latin writings indicates the smallest particles.

That these commentators on Aristotle combined the existence of "atoms" with the possibility of their changing their nature is not surprising. Aristotle was not satisfied by Democritus' atomism and was of the opinion that Democritus went only halfway. Atomism certainly opened up the possibility of explaining some changes that occur in nature, but not all. Nor did it account for all variety. Thus, the first task imposed upon Aristotle was a careful and critical re-examination of Parmenides' thesis. The result was his matter–form doctrine, stating that every material being is composed of *primary matter* and *form of being*. This composition, however, is not chemical or physical; it goes deeper. The possibility of change presupposes a certain fundamental nonsimplicity, for otherwise it is not possible to account for both aspects that are present in change: the aspect of a certain permanence (matter) and the aspect of something that is really new (form). Matter in the Aristotelian sense is not a substance, but the capacity to receive "forms."

To a certain extent, Democritus followed the same line of thought. Democritus, however, "substantialized" the permanent aspect (the atoms), thus narrowing the possibility of change. For Aristotle the "atoms" too should be subject to change and therefore "composed." However, Aristotle did not propound a corpuscular theory of his own. Only a few remarks that could have been the starting point are found in a passus (*Physics* I 4, 187B18–34) in which he criticizes Anaxagoras' theory about the infinite divisibility of material things. Somewhere there must be a limit to divisibility. This limit depends on the specific nature of a thing. It was left to Aristotle's Hellenistic, Arabian, and medieval commentators to develop the casual remarks of their master into the *minima naturalia* theory, stating that each kind of substance has its specific *minima naturalia*.

In Greek philosophy there were also transitional theories between qualitative and quantitative forms of atomism. Plato (427–347 B.C.), for example, adhered to the doctrine of the four elements; but the differences between the atoms of the respective elements were quantitative. An atom of fire had the form of a tetrahedron; that of air, an octahedron; that of water, an icosahedron; and that of earth, a cube.

When evaluating the importance of Greek atomism in the light of modern atomic theories, it should be borne in mind that in Greek thought philosophy and science still formed a unity. Greek atomism, therefore, was as much inspired by the desire to find a solution to the problem of mutability and plurality in general as by the desire to provide scientific explanations for specific phenomena. Although we meet with some ideas that can rightly be considered as precursors of classical physics and chemistry, the main importance of the old atomistic doctrines to modern science does not lie in these rather primitive scientific anticipations. The greatest achievement of Greek atomism was its general view of nature. The multitude of phenomena must be based upon some unity, and the ever-changing aspects of the phenomena are nevertheless aspects of a fundamentally unchanging world. To this view both the quantitative and the qualitative atomism have contributed—the latter by drawing attention to empirical aspects; the former, to the mathematical.

The history of the two forms of philosophical atomism until the birth of a scientific atomic theory has been rather different. This can easily be explained. Owing to the influence of Plato and Aristotle, Democritus' atomism did not gain pre-eminence in Greek, Arabian, and medieval thought. Yet that is not the only reason. Much more important is the fact that Democritus' atomism was more or less complete; and his followers, such as Epicurus (341–270 B.C.) and the Latin poet Lucretius Carus (96–55

B.C.), could confine themselves simply to taking over Democritus' doctrine.

The Aristotelian minima theory, however, existed only in an embryonic state. To Aristotle and his Hellenistic commentators the *minima naturalia* did not mean much more than a theoretical limit of divisibility; they were potentialities rather than actualities. With Averroës, however, we find an important development. According to him, the minima play an important role during chemical reactions. The Latin Averroists followed up this line of thought. Whereas most of the Latin commentators on Aristotle restricted themselves to a more or less systematic treatment of the minima as theoretical limits of divisibility, such Averroists as Agostino Nifo (1473–1538) attributed to the minima a kind of independent actual existence. The minima were considered as actual building stones of reality. The increase or decrease of a quantity of a substance amounts to the addition or subtraction of a certain number of minima. A chemical reaction takes place among the minima.

The fundamental importance of this view to science will be clear. Because the minima had acquired more physical reality, it became necessary to examine how their properties could be reconciled with the specific sensible properties of different substances. A first attempt to do so is found in Julius Caesar Scaliger (1484–1558). Some properties of matter, such as fineness and coarseness, depend on the minima themselves, while others depend on the manner in which the *minima* configurated. Rain, snow, and hail are composed of the same minima; but their densities are different because the minima of these three substances are at smaller or greater distances from one another. As to the chemical reaction, Scaliger remarked: "Chemical composition is the motion of the minima towards mutual contact so that union is effected" (*Exercitationes,* p. 345). Like Aristotle, he was convinced that Democritus was wrong. In a chemical compound the particles are not just lying close together; they form a real unity. However, Scaliger was also convinced that the minima play a role in effecting the composition; and for that reason he was not satisfied with the Aristotelian definition of chemical composition as "the union of the reagents," in which the minima are not mentioned.

To sum up our survey of the development of the minima doctrine, and to prove that the opinions of Nifo and Scaliger were no exceptions, we may quote Francis Toletus (1532–1596), one of the best-known sixteenth-century commentators on Aristotle: "Concerning the manner of chemical composition, the opinions of authors vary, but they all agree in this: the reagent substances are divided into minima. In this division the separated minima of one substance come alongside the minima of the other and act upon each other till a third substance, having the substantial form of the compound is generated." (*De Generatione et corruptione* I, 10, 19).

THE SCIENTIFIC PERIOD

The seventeenth century is an important period in the history of atomism. Not only did atomism come to occupy a central position in philosophical discussion, but it also became an inspiring idea for the spiritual fathers of modern science. The philosophic differences between the atomic systems were soon pushed into the background, while the more scientific aspects that were held in common came to the foreground. Daniel Sennert (1572–1657) offers a clear example of this tendency. Basically, his corpuscular theories were derived from the doctrine of *minima naturalia,* but they also contain typically Democritean ideas. In a sense the same could be said of Scaliger; but the difference is that Scaliger discussed the philosophical controversies between Aristotle and Democritus, whereas Sennert showed a pronounced eclectic tendency. He was interested mainly in a chemical theory, and he found that from a chemical point of view the two theories really amount to the same thing. In order to support this opinion, Sennert refused to accept the interpretation that Democritus meant to deny the qualitative differences of atoms. As a chemist, Sennert was convinced that elementary atoms differ qualitatively. His main contribution to the corpuscular theory lies in the clear distinction that he made between elementary atoms and atoms of compounds (*prima mista*). This distinction forced itself upon Sennert through chemical experience. Each chemical substance, elementary or compound, must have its own atoms.

Contrary to Sennert, Pierre Gassendi (1592–1655) faithfully copied Epicurus and therefore Democritus as well. His own contribution consisted of a number of annotations designed to make the original atomic doctrine acceptable to his contemporaries. In order to effect this purpose, two things were necessary. First of all, the atomic system had to be divested of the materialistic interpretation with which it was hereditarily connected. Second, Gassendi had to "adapt" the original atomic theory to the science of his time. Science had reached the stage at which certain definite physical and chemical properties were attributed to the atoms—i.e., the atoms must possess definite natures; they could not be qualitatively equal. For this reason Gassendi stated that from the original atoms certain molecules were formed first; these differed from each other and were the seeds of different things.

While Gassendi's system is basically without any trace of originality, the corpuscular theory of Descartes (1596–1650) is original in outline and execution. According to Descartes, matter and extension are identical. This thesis of course excludes the idea of indivisible atoms, but not of smallest particles. To the question of how such particles are separate and distinct from each other, Descartes answered that when a quantity of matter moves together, that quantity forms a unit, distinct from other units that have different motions. Along these lines, Descartes succeeded in devising a corpuscular theory in which the corpuscles were characterized by differences in mass, in amount of motion, and other properties that could be expressed in physical terms and treated mathematically. Descartes's corpuscles were endowed with exactly those properties that could be used in contemporaneous mechanics. As we have seen with Sennert, the seventeenth century was less interested in philosophical considerations than in scientifically fruitful ideas. Therefore, a corpuscular theory was judged, first of all, by this standard; and underlying philosophical discrepancies did not much interest the scientist. This explains why, to their contemporaries, Gassendi and Descartes could stand fraternally united as the renovators of the atomic theory.

Robert Boyle (1627–1691), for example, repeatedly confessed how much both Descartes and Gassendi had inspired him. On the other hand, Boyle was too much a chemist to be satisfied with a general idea of atoms or even with atoms endowed only with mechanical properties. Boyle looked for specific chemical properties. In contrast with mechanics, however, chemistry was not yet sufficiently developed to provide the theoretical framework necessary for a satisfactory chemical atomic theory. Boyle was keenly aware of this situation, as his *The Sceptical Chymist* (Oxford, 1661) proves. Neither the traditional theory of four elements nor the three-principle theory current among chemists could be of any use to him. Yet he was convinced that the distinction between elements and compounds was a sound one. This distinction therefore governed his own atomic theory. Theoretically, he adhered to the atoms of Democritus; practically, he did not use them. He was convinced that atoms were associated into so-called primary concretions, "which were not easily dissipable into such particles as composed them." Thus the primary concretions were corpuscles with definite qualities; they corresponded to the smallest particles of elements, and consequently Boyle treated them as such. The primary concretions could combine to form compounds of a higher order that may be compared with Sennert's *prima mista*. Although Sennert's corpuscular theory was based more on the minima theory and Boyle's theory more on the ideas of Gassendi and Descartes, in practice their theories were not very different. Both theories recognized atoms of compounds that are composed of atoms of elements. For Sennert the latter were elements, both theoretically and practically. For Boyle, theoretically they were not elements, but practically they were, because in chemical and physical processes primary concretions are not dissolved.

By combining the relative merits of the minima theory (qualitative atoms) and of Democritus' atomism (open to quantitative treatment), the seventeenth century laid the foundations for the scientific atomic theory of the nineteenth century. However, the further development of the seventeenth-century atomic theory required better chemical insights, and especially a method of distinguishing elementary from compound substances. This method was found by Antoine Lavoisier (1743–1794), who postulated the conservation of weight as the guiding principle in chemical analysis. For the first time in history, a list of chemical elements could be given, based upon the results of chemical analysis.

The outstanding achievement of John Dalton (1766–1844) was that he connected these chemical results with the atomic theory. His atoms were no longer smallest particles with some general and rather vague physical properties, but atoms endowed with the properties of chemical elements. Dalton himself in *A New System of Chemical Philosophy* stressed the great importance of "ascertaining the relative weights of the ultimate particles, both of simple and compound bodies, the number of simple elementary particles which constitute one compound particle, and the number of less compound particles which enter into the formation of one more compound particle." (2d ed., p. 213).

The fact that Dalton's theory is primarily a chemical theory does not mean that it has no philosophical implications. It is interesting to note that Dalton conceived the union of atoms in a compound as their simple juxtaposition without their undergoing any internal change. On this point the founder of the chemical atomic theory did not differ from the Democritean tradition. On another point, however, he followed the minima tradition. Dalton's atoms were specifically different for every kind of substance. He did not even think of building these atoms from particles without qualities, as Gassendi and Boyle had done.

After Dalton, the development of the atomic theory was very rapid. Jöns Jakob Berzelius (1779–1848) determined the relative atomic weights with surprising accuracy, guided by the hypothesis that under the same pressure and at the same temperature the number of atoms in all gaseous substances is the same. Since hydrogen and oxygen combine in the constant volume proportion of two to one, Berzelius concluded correctly that two atoms of hydrogen combine with one atom of oxygen. Berzelius also gave to chemistry its modern symbols. Amedeo Avogadro (1776–1856) completed the atomic theory by assuming that compound atoms, or molecules, do not necessarily have to be formed out of atoms of different elements; molecules of elements (H_2; O_2) also exist. According to Avogadro, the law that postulated an equal number of atoms in equal volumes of gas had to be understood as applying to an equal number of molecules. In a short time, the framework for classical chemistry was completed on the basis of Dalton's atomic theory. Chemical reactions were conceived of as a reshuffling of atoms and described by such chemical equations as $2\ H_2 + O_2 \rightarrow 2\ H_2O$.

An important contribution to the development of the atomic–molecular theory came from physics in the form of the kinetic theory of gases. With the aid of the calculus of probability, James Maxwell and Ludwig Boltzmann succeeded in deriving the behavior of gases, as described in the empirical laws of Boyle and Gay-Lussac, from the motions of the molecules.

The discovery of the electron, the electric atom, paved the way for a new theory about the nature of chemical compounds and chemical reactions. According to the new theory, a molecule such as NaCl did not consist of an Na atom and a Cl atom, but of an Na ion and a Cl ion; the Na ion was an Na atom minus an electron, and the Cl ion was a Cl atom plus an electron. Thus the so-called ionic theory revealed the nature of the forces of attraction between the various atoms of a molecule. The Na ion with its positive electric charge was attracted by the Cl ion with its negative charge. As a result of the connection that the theory of electricity established between physics and chemistry, theoretical and experimental materials were available at the beginning of the twentieth century. They led to a new development of the atomic theory that would endeavor to penetrate into the interior of Dalton's atoms.

The atomic model of Niels Bohr (1913) considered every

atom as built of a positively charged nucleus around which circled, in fixed orbits as many electrons as were indicated by the charge of the nucleus. This charge corresponded to the place of the element in the periodic system. Bohr's model could explain not only the fundamental chemical properties of the elements, but also such physical properties as the spectrum that is characteristic of each element when it is emitting or absorbing light. However, there were also serious difficulties with this model. According to electrodynamics, the moving electrons would ceaselessly emit electromagnetic waves. The atom would not be stable, but would always be losing energy. Hence, the motion of the electrons would gradually decrease and finally cease entirely. In order to save his model, Bohr postulated that emission of energy occurs only when an electron "jumps" from one orbit to another. In other words, the emission of energy is discontinuous. The emitted energy could be only a whole multiple of an elementary quantity of energy.

Thus, following the work of Max Planck, the idea of minima of energy was added to the idea of minima of matter, the traditional basis of atomism. Even light seemed to show an atomistic structure (photon theory). This would have meant a complete victory for the atomistic view if there had not been a complication. This complication was that the reasons which had formerly settled the dispute about the nature of light in favor of Christian Huygens' wave theory against Newton's corpuscular theory still retained their value. Light showed a dual character. In 1924, it occurred to Louis de Broglie that the same dualism might very well apply to the particles of matter. On the basis of this hypothesis, he could readily explain Bohr's postulate. This resulted in quantum mechanics, a new theory propounded by Erwin Schrödinger and Werner C. Heisenberg, which showed that both the atomic theory and the wave theory were only approximate models and not adequate representations of material reality.

The evolution of the atomic theory in the twentieth century was not limited to these rather startling new theoretical developments; it also gave rise to a new branch of physical science, nuclear physics, which studies the changes that the atomic nucleus is subject to. The first work in this area was in connection with the study of natural radioactivity. It had been observed that through radiation the nucleus of one element changes in charge and mass and thus becomes the nucleus of another element. In 1919 Ernest Rutherford succeeded in effecting an "artificial" transmutation; many others followed. The atoms of chemical elements appeared to be composed like the molecules of chemical compounds. Through nuclear processes a confusingly great number of new elementary particles has been discovered, all of which are subject to transformation under certain conditions. Particles can be changed into other particles and even into radiation. With such transmutations enormous amounts of energy are released.

Thus, twentieth-century science has revolutionized many fundamental ideas of the nineteenth century; the atom is not only much more complex than Dalton thought; it is also much more dynamic. Yet Dalton is far from antiquated. Modern chemistry still works along the lines drawn by Dalton and his contemporaries. Can the same be said in relation to his forerunners in the philosophical period of atomism? The answer to this question can be found in the fact that the main mistake of Dalton and other advocates of essentially mechanistic theories lay in the conviction that atoms did not undergo any internal change. Science showed that this assumption was erroneous, but this should not be a *de facto* statement only. For if we think of the nature of science as experimental, then it is clear that unchangeable atoms would not offer any possibility of being investigated by experimental means. Without change, matter could not respond to experimental questions. Classical science could overlook this simple truth by assuming that it already knew all the relevant features of atoms. This assumption followed from the mechanistic doctrine that, from the seventeenth century onward, formed the philosophical background of the atomic theory and of classical science in general. The mechanistic doctrine points up the fact that classical science originated in a rationalistic climate. The idea of an unchangeable atom endowed with mechanical properties seemed to be in accordance with what an element should be. It satisfied both the imagination and the intellect. The program of science seemed to consist in explaining the forms of nature on the basis of component elements that were already known.

With the development of science, however, increasing knowledge of chemical compounds affected our understanding of elements. The elements, too, became the object of experimental investigation. From this it may be concluded that the mechanistic doctrine was not a real presupposition of the scientific method. In using the experimental method, science presupposed a much more fundamental mutability in nature than traditional mechanism could account for, and the scientific method implied a much more refined view of material reality than the mechanistic interpretations of science suggested. For this reason, the less orthodox forms of atomism were as important to the origin of the scientific atomic theory as were the orthodox. From the point of view of twentieth-century science, the Greek philosophical discussions about the nature of change remain amazingly modern.

Bibliography

Dalton, John, *A New System of Chemical Philosophy*. London, 1808; 2d ed., 1842.

Dijksterhuis, E. J., *The Mechanization of the World Picture*. Oxford, 1960. Excellent history of science from antiquity to the seventeenth century.

Hooykaas, R., "Elementenlehre und Atomistik im 17. Jahrhundert," in his *Die Entfaltung der Wissenschaft*. Hamburg, 1957. Pp. 47–65.

Lasswitz, K., *Geschichte der Atomistik vom Mittelalter bis Newton*, 2 vols. 2d ed., Leipzig, 1926. A nineteenth-century classic.

Melsen, A. G. M. van, *From Atomos to Atom, the History of the Concept Atom*. 2d ed., New York, 1960. Includes references for the primary sources.

Nash, Leonard K., *The Atomic-Molecular Theory*. Cambridge, Mass., 1950. Discusses the classical chemical theories.

Scaliger, J. C., *Exotericarum Exercitationum Libri XV de Subtilitate ad Hier*. Frankfurt, 1557; 2d ed., 1607.

Whittaker, E., *History of the Theories of Aether and Electricity*, 2 vols. New York, 1951 and 1954. For readers with a good background in science.

Whyte, L. L., *Essay on Atomism: From Democritus to 1960*.

London and New York, 1961. A brief introduction to the idea of atomism and its history.

Yang, Chen Ning, *Elementary Particles, a Short History of Some Discoveries in Atomic Physics*. Princeton, 1962. Gives a general outline of the research done since 1900.

ANDREW G. M. VAN MELSEN

ATOMISM, LOGICAL. *See* ANALYSIS, PHILOSOPHICAL; RUSSELL, BERTRAND; WITTGENSTEIN, LUDWIG.

ATTRIBUTE. *See* SUBJECT AND PREDICATE; SUBSTANCE AND ATTRIBUTE; UNIVERSALS, PROBLEMS OF.

AUGUSTINE, ST. (354–430), also known as Aurelius Augustinus, was one of the key figures in the transition from classical antiquity to the Middle Ages. He was born at Thagaste, in north Africa, and died as the invading Vandals were closing in on his episcopal city, Hippo. He lived through nearly eighty years of the social transformation, political upheavals, and military disasters that are often referred to as the "decline of the Roman Empire." His life also spanned one of the most important phases in the transition from Roman paganism to Christianity. The old Roman pagan tradition was by no means dead, although the Roman emperors had been Christians since Constantine's conversion some forty years before Augustine was born. Augustine's youth saw the brief rule of Julian the Apostate as well as the last great pagan reaction in the empire, which broke out in the 390s. Nevertheless, it was during this period that the Roman state adopted Christianity as the official state religion. Medieval Europe began to take shape within the framework of the Roman Empire.

Augustine belonged to the world of late Roman antiquity, and its cultural and educational system had a decisive and lasting role in shaping his mind. His education, following the standard pattern of the time, was almost entirely literary, with great stress on rhetoric. Its aim was to enable its recipients to imitate the great literary masterpieces of the past. It tended, inevitably, to encourage a conservative literary antiquarianism. The culture it produced rarely rose above the level of the sterile cult of "polite letters" and generally had little contact with the deeper forces at work in contemporary society. There were many creative minds still at work; but even at their best, their thought was largely derivative. This is especially true of the philosophy of the period. Its stock of learning was in large part contained in compendia, though works of Cicero were still widely read, and those of the Neoplatonist thinkers gave inspiration to both pagans and Christians.

This culture and its educational system were the two sources that supplied the initial impulse for Augustine's thinking. His search for truth and wisdom began with his reading at the age of 18 of a now lost dialogue by Cicero, the *Hortensius*. The work made an impact that Augustine could not forget and that he often mentions in his later writings. When he recounts the experience in the *Confessions* (III, 4, 7), written in his forties, he tells us that it was this work that changed his interests and gave his life a new direction and purpose: the search for wisdom. The search led him far afield; but looking back on it, Augustine could interpret its start as the beginning of the journey that was finally to bring him back to God.

Philosophy and Christianity. It was not until 386 that Augustine was converted to Christianity; he was baptized the following year. Meanwhile, his career as a teacher of rhetoric took him from his native Africa to Italy, first to Rome and then to Milan. During this period he was under the spell of the Manichaean religion. Its teachings appeared for a time to offer Augustine the wisdom for which he had been searching, but he became increasingly dissatisfied with it and finally broke with the sect through the influence of his new friends in Milan, Bishop Ambrose and the circle of Christian Neoplatonists around him. In Milan he learned the answers to the questions that had worried him about Manichaean doctrine, and there he encountered a more satisfying interpretation of Christianity than he had previously found in the simple, unintellectual faith of his mother, Monica. There was no deep gulf between the Christianity of these men and the atmosphere of Neoplatonic thought of the time. At this stage of his life Augustine saw no need to disentangle exactly what belonged to Christian and what to Neoplatonic teaching: what struck him most forcibly was how much the two bodies of thought had in common. The blend of Neoplatonism and Christian belief won his adherence, and the moral conflict recounted in his *Confessions* (Books VI–VIII) ended with his baptism.

Even in 400, when he wrote his *Confessions*, he spoke of the teachings of the "Platonists" as preparing his way to Christianity. In a famous passage (VIII, 9, 13–14) he describes Neoplatonism as containing the distinctive Christian doctrines about God and his Word, the creation of the world, and the presence of the divine light; all these he had encountered in the books of "the Platonists" before reading of them in the Scriptures. What he had failed to find anticipated in Neoplatonism were the beliefs in the Incarnation and the Gospel account of the life and death of Jesus Christ. Later in life Augustine came gradually to see a deeper cleavage between philosophy and Christian faith; but he never ceased to regard much of philosophy, especially that of the Neoplatonists, as containing a large measure of truth and hence as capable of serving as a preparation for Christianity.

From Milan he returned to north Africa and retired to live a kind of monastic life with like-minded friends until he was ordained, under popular pressure, to assist the aged bishop of Hippo as a priest. Within four years, in 395, he became bishop of Hippo. From the 390s onward, all of Augustine's work was devoted to the service of his church. Preaching, administration, travel, and an extensive correspondence took much of his time. He continued to lead a quasi-monastic life with his clergy, however, and the doctrinal conflicts with Manichaeans, Donatists, Pelagians, and even with paganism provoked an extensive literary output. Despite this multifarious activity, Augustine never ceased to be a thinker and scholar, but his gifts and accomplishments were turned increasingly to pastoral uses and to the service of his people. The Scriptures took a deeper hold on his mind, eclipsing the strong philosophical interests of the years immediately preceding and following his conversion.

Augustine did not, however, renounce his philosophical

interests. He shared with all his contemporaries the belief that it was the business of philosophy to discover the way to wisdom and thereby to show men the way to happiness or blessedness (*beatitudo*). The chief difference between Christianity and the pagan philosophies was that Christianity considered this way as having been provided for men in Jesus Christ. Christianity could still be thought of as a philosophy, however, in that its aim was the same as that of other philosophic schools. The ultimate source of the saving truths taught by Christianity was the Scriptures, which for Augustine had supplanted the teachings of the philosophers as the gateway to truth. Hence, authority rather than reasoning, faith rather than understanding, came to be the emphasis of "Christian philosophy." For although the pagan philosophers had discovered much of the truth proclaimed by the Christian Gospel, what their abstract speculation had not, and could not have, reached was the kernel of the Christian faith: the belief in the contingent historical facts that constitute the history of salvation—the Gospel narrative of the earthly life, death, and resurrection of Jesus.

Belief and understanding. Belief in the above facts was the essential first step along the way to saving truth and blessedness, but it was only a first step. Faith, while required of a Christian, was not in itself sufficient for a full realization of the potential rationality of man. For Augustine, an act of faith, or belief, was an act of rational thinking, but of an imperfect and rudimentary kind. In a late work he defined "to believe" as "to think with assent" (*De Praedest. Sanct.* 2, 5). The act of believing is, therefore, itself an act of thinking and part of a context of thought. What distinguishes it from understanding or knowledge is best brought out by Augustine in passages where he contrasts believing with "seeing." By "seeing" Augustine meant either vision, literally, or, metaphorically, the kind of knowledge to which its object is clear and transparent. This kind of knowledge could be acquired only through direct experience or through logical demonstration, such as is possible in mathematics and other forms of rigorous reasoning. Believing, though a necessary and ubiquitous state of mind without which everyday life would be impossible, is therefore a form of knowledge inferior to understanding. Its object remains distant and obscure to the mind, and it is not intellectually satisfying. Faith demands completion in understanding.

In this emphasis on the priority of belief and its incompleteness without understanding, we may see a reflection of Augustine's own intellectual pilgrimage. His tortuous quest for wisdom, with its false trails, had ultimately led him to consider the Christian faith as the object of his search. But this faith offered no resting place, for Augustine never lost his passion for further intellectual inquiry. His faith was only the first step on the way to understanding. He never ceased to regard mere faith as only a beginning; he often returned to one of his most characteristic exhortations: "Believe in order that you may understand; Unless you shall believe, you shall not understand." The understanding he had in mind could be fully achieved only in the vision of God face to face in the life of blessedness; but even in this life, faith could be—and had to be—intensified in the mind by seeking a deeper insight into it. Progress in understanding, founded on faith and proceeding within its framework, was part of the growth of faith itself. After his conversion, then, reasoning and understanding were for Augustine no longer an independent, alternative route to faith. They still had their work, but now within a new setting and on a new foundation.

Some things, like contingent historical truths, could be the objects only of belief; others could be the objects of either belief or understanding (understanding means having an awareness of grounds and logical necessity). For instance, a mathematical theorem can be believed before it is understood. With understanding, however, belief inevitably follows. God, Augustine thought, belongs among the objects that are first believed and subsequently understood. In the process of gaining this understanding, the ordinary human endowments of rational thought, culture, and philosophy have a part to play. They form the equipment of which a Christian may avail himself in the work of seeking deeper insight into the meaning of his faith.

In his *De Doctrina Christiana* Augustine discusses the ways in which the various intellectual disciplines may serve to assist the Christian in understanding the faith he derives from scriptural sources. Philosophy, along with the other branches of learning, is here seen as subordinated to the service of a purpose outside it, that of nourishing and deepening faith; it is no longer to be pursued for its own sake, as an independent avenue to truth. It is also in *De Doctrina Christiana* that Augustine uses the image of the children of Israel, on their way to the Promised Land, spoiling the Egyptians of their treasures at God's bidding: in the same way, Christians are bidden to take from the pagans whatever is serviceable in understanding and preaching the Gospel. Again, we may see here a reflection of Augustine's narrowing of interests and the growing dominance of pastoral concerns in his mind. The theoretical statement of his subordination of secular learning and culture and their consecration to the service of preaching the Gospel (in its widest sense) is contained in the program laid down in the *De Doctrina Christiana.*

Therefore, Augustine is not interested in philosophy, in the modern sense of the word. Philosophical concepts and arguments play a subordinate role in his work; and where they occur, they are usually employed to help in the elucidation of some aspect of Christian doctrine. Typical examples are his use of Aristotle's *Categories* in an attempt to elucidate the notions of substance and relation in the context of Trinitarian theology, especially in his great work *De Trinitate;* his subtle inquiries into human knowledge and emotions, in the second half of the same work, with a view to discovering in man's mind an image of God's three-in-oneness; and his analysis of the temporal relations "before" and "after," undertaken to elucidate the nature of time in order to solve some of the puzzles presented by the scriptural doctrine of the creation of the world. In all these cases and many more, his purpose would be described today as theological. In Augustine's day the distinction between theology and philosophy did not exist, and "philosophy" could be—and often was—used in a sense so wide as to include what we should call theology.

To study Augustine's thought *as philosophy* is in a sense, to do violence to it: it is to isolate from their purpose and context what he would have regarded as mere techniques and instruments. To focus attention on what Augustine would have regarded as belonging to the sphere of means, however, allows us to see something more than a mere agglomeration of philosophical commonplaces derived, in large measure, from Neoplatonism. Augustine's originality lies not only in his determination to use his inherited philosophical equipment but also in the often slight, but sometimes profound, modification it underwent at his hands. And in the service of Augustine's purpose, many old ideas received new coherence and new power to move. Through his "spoiling of the Egyptians" much of the heritage of late antiquity received a new life in the European Middle Ages.

The mind and knowledge. At an early stage of Augustine's intellectual development, the skepticism of the Academic tradition of philosophy appears to have presented him with a serious challenge. His early philosophical dialogues, written in the period immediately after his conversion, are full of attempts to satisfy himself that there are at least some inescapable certainties in human knowledge on which we may absolutely rely. The basic facts of being alive, of thinking, or of simply existing are disclosed in one's immediate awareness of oneself. But Augustine did not limit the range of what was indubitably reliable in one's experience; nor did he seek to build an entire structure of indubitable knowledge on the basis of the absolute certainties of immediate awareness and its strict logical consequences, as Descartes was to do. He tried instead to vindicate the whole range of human knowledge as being capable of arriving at truth, though also liable to err.

His vindication proceeds on two fronts, according to the fundamental duality of knowledge and of the objects corresponding to it. This duality, like much in his theory of knowledge, is of Platonic origin. Plato is the source of his belief that "there are two worlds, an intelligible world where truth itself dwells, and this sensible world which we perceive by sight and touch" (*C. Acad.* III, 17, 37); and of its corollary, that things can be divided into those "which the mind knows through the bodily senses" and those "which it perceives through itself" (*De Trin.* XV, 12, 21). Although he never departed from this dualistic theory of knowledge, Augustine also always insisted that all knowledge, of either kind, is a function of the mind, or the soul.

He defines the soul as "a substance endowed with reason and fitted to rule a body" (*De Quant. Anim.* 13, 22). Augustine's use of the conceptual framework of the Platonic tradition made it difficult for him to treat man as a single, substantial whole. He did, nevertheless, attempt to stress the unity of body and soul in man as far as his inherited conceptual framework allowed. In a characteristically Platonic formula he defines man as "a rational soul using a mortal and material body" (*De Mor. Eccles.* I, 27, 52). The soul is one of two elements in the composite, but it is clearly the dominant partner: the relation between it and its body is conceived on the model of ruler and ruled, or of user and tool. This conception gave Augustine considerable trouble in his attempt to work out a theory of sense knowledge.

Sense and imagination. It was a basic axiom of Augustine's view of soul and body that while the soul can act on the body, the body cannot act on the soul. This is a consequence of the user–tool model in terms of which he understood their relation. The tool cannot wield its user; the inferior in nature has no power to effect or induce any modification in the higher. Augustine could not, therefore, elaborate a theory of sense knowledge in which the bodily affections would in any way cause or give rise to modifications in the soul; nevertheless, he insisted that even sense perception was a function of the soul, one that it carried out through the bodily sense organs. The mere modification of a sense organ is not in itself sense experience, unless it is in some way noticed by the mind. Augustine's problem was to explain this correlation between the mind's awareness and the modification of the organ without allowing the latter to cause or to give rise to the former.

In an early discussion of this problem, Augustine tried to explain the process of seeing as a kind of manipulation by the mind of its sense organs, much like a blind man's manipulation of a stick to explore the surface of an object (*De Quant. Anim.* 23, 41–32, 69). This is very much in line with his general conception of the relation of the body to the mind as that of an instrument to its user, but its inadequacy as an explanation of sense perception may have been apparent to Augustine. At any rate, he later came to prefer an account constructed in quite different terms. This account (elaborated in *De Genesi ad Litteram*, Book XII and generally underlying his later views, for instance, those stated in *De Trinitate*) is based on a distinction between "corporeal" and "spiritual" sight. "Corporeal sight" is the modification undergone by the eyes in the process of seeing and is the result of their encounter with the object seen. "Spiritual sight" is the mental process that accompanies corporeal sight, in the absence of which the physical process cannot be reckoned as sense experience (since all experience is a function of mind). Spiritual seeing is not, however, caused by corporeal seeing, since the body cannot affect the mind. Indeed, spiritual sight is a separate process that may take place in the mind spontaneously, in the absence of its corporeal counterpart—for instance, in dreaming or imagining. The mental processes involved in sight and in dreaming and imagination are identical; what is before the mind is, in all these cases, of the same nature. What the mind sees in each case is not the object outside it, but the image within it. The difference between sensation and imagination is that in sensation a process of corporeal seeing accompanies the mental process; this is absent in imagination.

Augustine never quite answers the question of how we may know the difference between perception and imagination. The part, however, which he attributes to attention in the process of sense perception is important and gives a clue: it is attention that directs the mind's gaze, and it appears that it is attention that checks the free play of imagery in the mind. Thus, perception and imagination can be distinguished in experience by adverting to the presence of attention; its presence immobilizes the creative imagaination and insures that the content of the mind has some sort of rapport with the bodily senses and their world. It is difficult to escape the impression that under the guise of "attention" Augustine has introduced what he had begun by excluding—mental process as responsive to bodily change. This is the peculiar difficulty that his two-level theory of man never quite allowed him to escape.

Augustine also speaks of a third kind of sight, one that he calls intellectual. This, the highest kind of sight, is the work of the mind whereby it interprets, judges, or corrects "messages" from the lower kinds of sight. The type of activity Augustine has in mind here is exemplified by any act of judgment on the content of sense perception; for instance, the judgment that an oar partly submerged in water is not actually bent, even though it looks bent. This activity of interpretation and judgment brings us to the second kind of knowledge, that which the mind has independently of sense experience.

Reason and illumination. In his account of sense knowledge, Augustine's Platonic inheritance was a source of difficulty. In the elaboration of his views on reason and intelligence, the reverse is the case: Augustine's account of these is largely an adaptation of the fundamental tenets of the Platonic tradition. Typical instances of knowledge that the mind has independently of sense experience are the truths of mathematics. Here Augustine discovered the universality, necessity, and immutability that he saw as the hallmarks of truth. Although he did not believe that knowledge obtained through the senses possessed these characteristics, Augustine widened the scope of truth considerably beyond the necessary truths of mathematics and logic. He thought that our moral judgments and judgments of value, at least of the more fundamental kind, also shared the character of truth. He did not, however, trace this universality and necessity of such propositions to their logical form or to the nature of the definitions and logical operations involved in them. (He wrote 14 centuries before Kant's distinction between analytic and synthetic judgments.)

Like all his predecessors and contemporaries, Augustine thought that this kind of knowledge was just as empirical as sense experience, and that it differed from the latter only in having objects that were themselves superior to the physical objects of sense experience by being immutable and eternal, and therefore capable of being known with superior clarity and certainty. The knowledge open to the mind without the mediation of the senses was conceived as analogous to sight; indeed, Augustine often speaks of it as sight, sometimes qualifying it as "intellectual sight." Its objects are public, "out there," and independent of the mind that knows them, just as are those of physical sight. In its knowing, the mind discovers the objects; it does not create them any more than the eyes create the physical objects seen by them. Together, the truths accessible to this kind of knowledge form a realm that Augustine, following the whole Platonic tradition of thought, often calls the intelligible world. This he identifies with the "Divine Mind" containing the archetypal ideas of all things. He was not, however, the first to take this step; this identification was the key to all forms of Christian Platonism.

Before Augustine, Plato had already used the analogy between sight and understanding. Its details are worked out in the analogy of the sun in the *Republic*. Here the intellectual "light" that belongs to the world of intelligible forms is analogous to the visible light of the material world. Like the latter, it renders "visible" the objects seen by illuminating both them and the organ of perception—in this case, the mind. All understanding is a function of illumination by this light. The intellectual light that illuminates the mind and thus brings about understanding is spoken of in various ways by Augustine. Since it is a part of the intelligible world, it is naturally conceived as a kind of emanation from the divine mind or as an illumination of the human mind by the divine. Augustine also refers to it as the human mind's participation in the Word of God, as God's interior presence to the mind, or even as Christ dwelling in the mind and teaching it from within.

Plato had tried to account for the mind's knowledge of the forms in the theory, expressed in the language of myth, that this knowledge was left behind in the mind as a memory of its life among the forms before it was enclosed in an earthly body. After some early flirtation with this theory of reminiscence, Augustine came to reject it; to hold that the mind's knowledge derived from a premundane existence would have raised serious theological difficulties. Therefore, instead of tracing this knowledge to a residue of a past experience, he accounted for it in terms of present experience; it was the result of continual discovery in the divine light always present to the mind. For this reason, too, his conception of *memoria* became so widened as to lose the reference to past experience that *memory* necessarily implies in English. Augustine's *memoria* included what we should call memory; in it, he thought, were preserved traces of past experience, as in a kind of storehouse or a stomach. But *memoria* included very much more than this. He speaks of our a priori mathematical ideas, numbers and their relations, as being contained in it; and in the course of the tenth book of the *Confessions*, in which he devotes a long discussion to the subject, the scope is so widened as to extend to our knowledge of moral and other values, of all truths of reason, of ourselves, and of God. It is, in effect, identified with all the latent potentialities of the mind for knowledge. *Memoria* and divine illumination are alternative ways of expressing the basis of Augustine's theory of knowledge. The theory is, in its essence, the belief that God is always intimately present to the mind, whether this presence is acknowledged or not. His presence pervades everything and is operative in everything that happens. To this metaphysical principle the human mind is no exception. The only difference between the human mind, in respect to the divine presence within it, and other things is that unlike these other things, the human mind is able to turn freely toward the light and to acknowledge its presence, or to turn away from it and to "forget" it. Whether the mind is present to the divine light or not, however, the light is present to the mind; on this presence is founded all the mind's ability to know.

The manner of operation of this illumination in the mind and what exactly it produces in the mind have been the subject of much debate. This uncertainty is due partly to the enormous variety of expressions used by Augustine to describe the divine light, but it is also partly the result of approaching Augustine's views with questions formulated in terms of concepts between which he would not have made a distinction. It is clear, at any rate, that Augustine did not think that the divine light in the mind gave the mind any kind of direct access to an immediate knowledge of God. This kind of knowledge was, to him, the result of understanding, a goal to be reached only at the end of a long process—and not this side of the grave. If, however, we ask further what exactly he thought illumination did reveal to the mind, the answer is more difficult. In particular, if we ask whether he conceived illumination primarily as a source of ideas in the mind or, alternatively, as providing the mind with its rules for judgment, the answer is not at all clear. He did not distinguish as sharply as one might wish between the making of judgments and the formation of concepts; he often speaks of both activities in the same breath or in similar contexts, or passes without the least hesitation from one to the other in the course of discussion. Sometimes he speaks of illumination as implanting in the mind an "impressed notion" (*notio impressa*), whether it be of number, unity, wisdom, blessedness, or goodness. Such passages suggest that Augustine thought of illumination primarily as a source of ideas, as providing "impressed notions." It is clear, however, that such "impressed notions" were also to serve as the yardsticks for judging all imperfect participations in individual instances of these notions. And in other passages, again, illumination is spoken of not as supplying any ideas or notions but simply as providing a criterion of the truth or falsity of our judgments.

It was very easy to pass from ideas to judgments in Augustine's way of speaking of illumination. In addition, Augustine's language when he speaks of the mind's judgment made in the light of divine illumination often has further overtones; the judgment he speaks of appears as a kind of foreshadowing of the ultimate divine judgment on all human life and action. The basic reason why Augustine had found Platonic metaphysics so congenial was that it harmonized so easily with the moral bearings of his own views; and its theories, especially in some of their more imaginative and dramatic expressions, allowed themselves to be exploited to serve Augustine's interests as a moralist. In his discussion of knowledge, as in his discussion of the relation of mind and body, ethical considerations very often play the major part. The central theories of Platonic thought buttressed views held by Augustine primarily on account of their moral bearings.

Will, action, and virtue. Morality lies at the center of Augustine's thought. There are many reasons for this, the most noteworthy being his conception of philosophy. As we have seen, philosophy was for Augustine far from being an exclusively theoretical study; and morality itself belonged to its substance more intimately than the discussion and analysis of moral concepts and judgments. Philosophy was a quest for wisdom, its aim being to achieve man's happiness; and this depended on right living as much as on true thinking. Hence the practical orientation of Augustine's thought—an orientation that it shared with most contemporary forms of thinking.

On human conduct and human destiny Augustine's thinking was, of course, molded very largely by the New Testament and by the Christian church's tradition in understanding its conceptions of divine law and commandment, of grace, of God's will, of sin, and of love. Much of this, being specifically theological in interest, lies outside the scope of this presentation of Augustine's thought. What is remarkable is the extent to which Augustine was prepared to read back the characteristic teaching of the Christian church into the works of the philosophers, Plato in particular. Thus he held that Plato had asserted that the supreme good, possession of which alone gives man blessedness, is God. "And therefore," Augustine concluded, Plato "thought that to be a philosopher is to be a lover of God" (*De Civ. Dei* VIII, 8). *Rapprochements* of this kind helped to reconcile the Christian and the Platonic teachings to each other; in Augustine's treatment of ethical topics the characteristically Christian themes and distinctively Platonic concepts are so closely interwoven that they are often inseparable.

Augustine is able, therefore, to define blessedness itself in terms that make no reference to any distinctively Christian teaching, for instance, when he says that man is blessed when all his actions are in harmony with reason and truth (*cum omnes motus eius rationi veritatique consentiunt—De Gen. C. Man.* I, 20, 31). Blessedness, according to this view, does not consist simply in the total satisfaction of all desires. In another discussion Augustine makes this more explicit: while blessedness is incompatible with unsatisfied desires, the satisfaction of evil or perverse desires gives no ultimate happiness; hence blessedness cannot be identified simply with total satisfaction. "No one is happy unless he has all he wants and wants nothing that is evil" (*De Trin.* XIII, 5, 8; for the entire discussion, see *ibid.* XIII, 3, 6–9, 12). The only element in all this that is specifically Christian is the insistence that this happiness cannot be attained by man except with the aid of the way revealed by Christ and of God's grace given to men to enable them to follow it.

The dramatic account, given in his *Confessions*, of his own turning to God, though steeped in the language of the Bible and throbbing with the intensity of Augustine's feelings, is, at the same time, an illustration of a central theme in Greek metaphysics. The book opens with a powerful evocation of his coming to rest in God; it ends with a prayer for this rest, peace, and fulfillment. This central theme of longing and satisfaction is a commonplace of Greek thought from Plato's *Symposium* onward. Man, according to the cosmology implicit in this picture, illustrates in his being the forces that are at work in nature in general. Man, like everything else, is conceived as part of a vast nexus of interrelated things within an ordered hierarchy of beings which together form the cosmos. But it is an order in which the components are not stationary but are in dynamic rapport; they are all pursuing their own ends and come to rest only in attaining these ends. Their striving for rest, for completion or satisfaction, is the motive power that drives all things toward their purposes, just as weight, according to this image, causes things to move to the places proper to them in the cosmos—the heavy things downward, the light upward. Augustine thought of the forces that move men as analogous to weight and called them, collectively, love or loves. In a famous passage he wrote, "My weight is my love; by it am I carried wheresoever I am carried" (. . . *eo feror quocumque feror—Conf.* XIII, 9, 10).

Love, law, and the moral order. Man, however, differs from other things in nature in that the forces which move him, his "loves," are very much more complex. Within him there are a great many desires and drives, impulses and inclinations—some of them conscious, others not. The satisfaction of some often involves the frustration of others, and the harmonious satisfaction that forms the goal of human activity appears to be a very distant and scarcely realizable purpose. The reason for this is not only the multiplicity of elements that go into the making of human nature; a further reason is the fact that these elements have been disordered and deprived of their original state of harmony. Augustine interpreted this aspect of the human condition as a consequence of the sin of Adam and the fall of man.

There is, however, a further respect in which man differs from other things in the way his activity is determined. This lies in the fact that even with his disordered impulses, he is not—at least not entirely—at the mercy of the conflicting forces within him. His activity is not, so to speak, a resultant of them: he is, in some degree, capable of selecting among them, deciding which to resist, which to follow. In this capacity for choice Augustine saw the possibility of what he called voluntary action as distinguished from natural or necessary behavior. He called this human capacity "will." It is a source of some confusion that he used the term "love," or its plural, "loves," to designate the sum total of forces that determine a man's actions, whether they are "natural" or "voluntary." As a collective name for natural impulses, "love" is therefore morally neutral; only insofar as the will endorses or approves love of this kind is love morally praiseworthy or blameworthy. Augustine expresses this graphically by distinguishing between loves that ought to be loved and loves that ought not to be loved; and he defines man's moral task in terms of sorting out these commendable and reprehensible loves in himself and putting his loves in their right order.

Augustine's favorite definition of virtue is "rightly ordered love" (as in *De Civ. Dei* XV, 22). This consists in setting things in their right order of priority, valuing them according to their true worth, and in following this right order of value in one's inclinations and actions. The idea of order is central to Augustine's reflections on morals. Before becoming a Christian, he had believed with the Manichaeans that the existence of good and of evil in the world was accounted for by their different origins, respectively from a good and an evil deity. The Neoplatonism of his Christian friends in Milan helped Augustine find an alternative explanation, one that was more in keeping with the Christian doctrine of one world created by one God. According to this theory, evil had no independent, substantial existence in its own right; it existed as a privation, as a distortion or damage within the good. All evil was thus in some sense a breach of the right relation of parts within a whole, a breach of order of some kind. Hence the great emphasis on order in Augustine's thought, from the time of his conversion to the writing of his last works.

Augustine calls the pattern to which human activity must conform "law." Law is, in the first place, the archetypal order according to which men are required to shape their actions and by which their actions are to be judged. Augustine makes it clear that by "law" he means very much more than the actual legal enactments of public authorities. These "human laws" deal only with a part, greater or lesser, of human conduct; they vary from place to place and from time to time; they depend on the vagaries of individual legislators. The true "eternal law" by which all human behavior is judged leaves no aspect of man's life out of its purview; it is the same everywhere and at all times. It is not quite clear how Augustine conceived the relation between divine and human, eternal and temporal, law. His terminology is variable, and although he thought that human law ought to seek to approach the divine, or at least not to contradict it, he does not appear to have denied its claim to being law even when it failed to reflect the eternal law. Also, as we shall see, he appears to have changed his views on this matter in the course of his life.

The "eternal," or "divine," law is in effect the intelligible world or the divine mind (see discussion of reason and illumination above) insofar as it is considered as the pattern that should regulate activity. The language in which Augustine speaks about the divine law is the same as that which he uses in speaking of the eternal truth, and he believed that the achievement of wisdom consisted in pursuing this truth by understanding and then embodying in oneself the order understood. It is clear that there is no significant difference between "eternal law" and "eternal truth"; the two are identical: eternal law is eternal truth considered under its aspect as a standard of moral judgment. Thus, the problem of how the eternal law is known to men is the same as the problem discussed above of how the eternal truth is known. Here, too, he speaks of the eternal law as being "transcribed" into the human mind or of its "notion" as being impressed on the mind. The deliverance of conscience or reason as manifested in moral judgment is thus no less and no more than the human mind's illumination by the eternal law, or its participation in it; Augustine describes conscience as "an interior law, written in the heart itself" (. . . *lex intima, in ipso . . . corde conscripta—En. in Ps.* 57, 1). He refers to this law, inscribed in man's heart or known to him by reason, as "natural." He can thus speak of law (eternal or natural), reason, and order interchangeably when discussing the ordering of human action to bring about its virtuous disposition.

In defining this order of priority in value, the following of which constitutes virtue, Augustine makes a fundamental distinction between "use" and "enjoyment." These two forms of behavior correspond to the twofold classification of things according to whether they are valuable for their own sake or as means, for the sake of something else. Things valued for themselves are to be "enjoyed," things valued as means are to be "used"; the inversion of the relation between use and enjoyment is the fundamental perversion of the order of virtue. To seek to use what is to be enjoyed or to enjoy what is to be used is to confuse means with ends. The only object fit for enjoyment, in this sense, is God; he alone is to be loved for his own sake, and all other things are to be referred to this love. In elaborating this theory, Augustine was expressing the traditional view that it behooves men to journey through their lives on earth as pilgrims and not to regard any earthly goal as a fit resting place. This did not, of course, imply, to Augustine's mind, that nothing but God was a fit object of love; on the contrary, it was a way of stressing the need to put loves in their right order and to love each thing with the kind and degree of love appropriate to it. Although he clearly conceived of love as capable of an endless series of gradations, Augustine is usually content to speak of two kinds of love, which he contrasts: charity (*caritas*) and cupidity (*cupiditas*). The basic distinction is between upright, well-ordered, and God-centered love and perverse, disordered, and self-centered love. A great deal of Augustine's thinking and writing hinges on this distinction.

The individual virtues interested Augustine less than the concept of love. He was content to take over the classical enumeration of the four cardinal virtues. But his own characteristic thoughts on the moral life are always developed in terms of love rather than of any of the virtues. Indeed, as we have seen, he defined virtue in terms of love; similarly, he liked to define the individual cardinal virtues as different aspects of the love of God. This tendency is one of the most important links between what we would distinguish as the theological and philosophical sides of his thought.

The world and God. Order is a key idea in Augustine's reflections on the morality of human behavior. It also plays a large part in his reflection on the physical universe in its relation to God. The world of nature was not in itself an object of particular interest to Augustine. In cosmological thinking of the kind to be found in Aristotle's *Physics*, for instance, he had little interest. The physical world concerned him only insofar as it was related either to man or to God. Order, then, for Augustine was the expression of rationality. In human action this was something that men should seek to embody in their conduct; in the world of physical and animate nature, which did not share the freedom of human activity, order expressed the divine rationality at work in all natural happenings. To human eyes, however, this order was often glimpsed only in isolated instances, while a great deal of disorder was manifest in the misery, disease, and suffering with which the world is shot through. In part these frustrations of order were held to be due, ultimately, to the initiative of human sin; in part they were held to be merely apparent and capable of being resolved within a perspective larger than that of finite human vision.

Behind the world order stands its author and sovereign ruler, God. All things testify to his presence; the world is full of his "traces" (*vestigia*). God's presence in and behind his creation was, for Augustine, not so much something to be established by argument as it was the premise, taken for granted, of a further argument. This argument, to which Augustine returned on a number of occasions, is particularly well expressed in a chapter of his *Confessions* (X, 6, 9 and 10). He there speaks of putting things to the question in order to allow them to reveal themselves as dependent on their creator. It is clear that what primarily interested Augustine was the questioner's moral attitude: the point of his argument is not so much that the order and beauty of things imply the existence of God, but rather that since God had created them, we must so discipline ourselves as to see things for what they are—his handiwork—and to value them at their true worth and worship only him, their creator—not his handiwork. Again, the moral concern is uppermost in Augustine's mind.

This is not the case with the discussion of the problem of time, in Book XI of the *Confessions*. The problem was forced on Augustine's attention by the scriptural doctrine of creation, but it is clear that it fascinated him and that he pursued it simply because he was interested in it. Manichaean objectors to the Christian doctrine of creation from nothing had raised difficulties about speaking of an absolute beginning. These critics had pointed out that in our ordinary language there is no room for an absolute beginning of the kind envisaged by adherents of the doctrine; we can always ask what happened before something else, even if this was the first of all happenings. Questions of this kind revealed the arbitrariness and absurdity of the belief that God made the world out of nothing: What was God doing before the creation? Why did he create the world when he did and not sooner, or later?

In answer to these difficulties Augustine in effect undertook a critique of the conception of time that underlay them. Such difficulties arise from the fact that time is thought of as having the same kind of being as the events and happenings going on in time; the question "What happened before time?" was thought to be of the same logical form as questions about what happened before any particular events. Augustine denied this assumed logical similarity behind the grammatical similarity of the questions. He pointed out that whereas it makes sense to ask what happened before any particular event, it does not make sense to ask what happened before all events, because time is the field of the relationships of temporal events, and there could *ex hypothesi* be nothing before the first temporal event. In this argument Augustine in effect rejected the conception of time according to which time has a substantial reality of its own, and he adopted a theory according to which time is the field of temporal relations between temporal events.

He did, however, go further in his reflections on time. Neoplatonic thought had always treated time in close relation to the soul, and Augustine could scarcely avoid discussing this topic. The reality of the past and of the future puzzled him: Can what is not yet but will be, and what is no longer but has been, be said to *be*? If not, then only the present has any reality. But if only the present is real, then reality shrinks to a dimensionless point at which the future is becoming the past. Augustine resolved the whole problem by locating time in the mind and adopting at the end of his discussion, though with hesitation, a definition of time as "extension [*distentio*], I am not sure of what, probably of the mind itself" (*Confessions* XI, 26, 33).

Another question that the doctrine of creation raised for Augustine concerns the natural activity, functioning, and development of creatures. This problem arose from the need to harmonize the story of the creation of the world in seven days or, according to an alternative version, at once, with the fact that some things came into existence only after the creation took place. Augustine's solution of this problem lay essentially in asserting that God created different things in different conditions; some left his hands complete and ready-made, others in a potential or latent state, awaiting the right conditions and environment for their full development. The latter are analogous to seeds, which are thought of as containing in themselves the fully developed plant in potency; and on this analogy, and using the traditional vocabulary, Augustine called these potentialities for later development "seminal reasons" (*rationes seminales*, or *causales*).

Apart from helping him to resolve the apparent contradiction between the belief in a primordial creation and the concept of continued development as a process of natural causality, this theory of "seminal reasons" also prompted Augustine at least to begin to feel his way toward some conception of nature and natural causality. At times, he comes very close to the later medieval distinction between the "First Cause" and the whole range of "second causes," the distinction according to which things depend in different senses both on God (the First Cause) and on their own immediate or distant created causes. Augustine, too, tried to endow the world of created causes with a specific reality of its own, one distinct from the causal activity of God in the world. In this he did not quite succeed. His failure becomes apparent in his treatment of miracles. He did not treat these—as the Scholastics later did as effects of the First Cause (God) produced without the instrumentality of second causes. He allowed the distinction between the two orders of causality (which he had never clearly formulated and which is hinted at, rather than stated, in his writings) to disintegrate during his discussion of miracles. In this context the very idea of "nature" is so widened as to include the miraculous within its scope. Miracles do not contradict the order of nature; they contradict only our idea of this order, an idea based on our restricted view and limited experience. They are not against nature, since nature is God's will; they are only against nature as it is known to us. The distinction between nature and miracle vanishes here, and in his well-known chapter in *The City of God* (X, 12) they become synonymous to the extent that nature itself and man, its crown, become the greatest miracles of all.

Man in society. Society was not one of the subjects that loomed large in Augustine's earlier thought. Such hints as he gives us of his conception of society in his earlier works (those written before the mid-390s) suggest that he thought that organized human society and the state were part of the worldly dispensation whereby man is assisted to fulfill his destiny. A properly ordered society, like a properly ordered moral life, is a stage on the way to man's ultimate destination in eternity; and as far as Augustine's hints enable us to tell, he expected a properly ordered society to reflect, particularly by means of its legal institutions, the perfection of the eternal, intelligible world.

In step with his theological development, however, his views on human society underwent profound changes, and by the time that society became an important theme in his reflection, especially in his great work *The City of God* (written 413–427), these views had been radically transformed. An important factor in the course of this transformation was the increasing stress Augustine had come to lay on the power of sin in human life and in all earthly institutions, on man's need for redemption through Christ, and on his need for grace. In the most general terms Augustine came to see man's destiny and his realization of it more in terms of the scriptural pattern of a redemption-history and less in terms of the Neoplatonic theme of the ascent of the soul. Accordingly, human society came to be understood more in terms of its horizontal, historical relationships within the divine plan for men's salvation and less in terms of what we might call its vertical relationship to the intelligible world.

The first event in the course of the Biblical redemption-history, man's fall from grace through Adam's sin, is of decisive importance for Augustine's changed attitude to organized human society. To live in society, according to Augustine, was natural to men; without society they would not be able to realize fully their human potentialities, and the company of their fellow human beings was necessary to them. This, he held, was as true before man's fall as after; even in his state of primal innocence, in full possession of his nature prior to its distortion by sin, man was a social animal by nature; even the life of the blessed in heaven is a social life. But although Augustine believed that man's nature is social, he did not agree with Aristotle that it is also political. Politically organized society—the machinery of authority, government, and coercion—is, in Augustine's view, not natural to man. It was a useful and necessary arrangement for man in his fallen condition, and indeed the purpose of political society was to remedy at least some of the evils attendant upon man's fallen state. Its function was to check the social disorder and disintegration that followed from the general loss of order at the Fall. The institutions of government, the subjection of governed to government, and the coercive power of political authority over its subjects are thus but one instance of the subjection of man to man, and this was something that, Augustine held, did not exist in man's primal state of innocence. No slavery, servitude, or subjection could exist in that state of natural integrity; these things make sense only if understood as God's punishment for the sin that incurred the loss of integrity and, at the same time, as his dispensation for coping with the needs of man's condition in his new, fallen state.

Augustine used the traditional language of Christian theology to state his view of political society. For reasons to be considered below, he never drew out, at least not explicitly, the full implications of this view. In this view of society, however, the legitimate functions of the state are very much more restricted in scope than in theories according to which man is by nature a political animal. In Augustine's view, the state's sphere is confined to the requirements of social order and welfare; the individual's ultimate welfare and eternal destiny lie outside its realm of competence, whereas they are very much a part of the state's interest if the state is thought of as an ordinance of nature, as an indispensable means of man's realizing his ultimate destiny. In Augustine's estimate, the task of the state in the economy of salvation would be rather to establish the conditions in which men may work out their own salvation in relative peace and security than actively to promote their individual salvation through legislation and coercion.

The state was, for Augustine, synonymous with the Roman Empire; and having revised his ideas on the state in terms of the large categories of the scriptural redemption-history, he had inevitably to take the measure of the state he knew in this same perspective. Here his ideas make sense only if seen as a rejection of views of the empire generally current among Christians during the fourth century, after the adoption of Christianity by the emperors. The empire, represented as eternal ever since Vergil's day, was now widely regarded among Christians as an essential instrument of divine purpose in history, bound up with the possibility of salvation and destined to last until the end of time. It had been taken up into the dimension of the Biblical redemption-history. The sack of Rome by the Visigoths in 410 gave a profound shock to this mentality. It led Augustine, whose mind had already moved a long way from the popular picture, to devote his greatest work, *The City of God*, to a reappraisal of the Empire's place in the divine providential plan. The upshot was that the empire was no longer allowed an eternal destiny and was removed from the dimension of the redemption-history; the possibility of salvation was not necessarily bound up with it as a means of God's grace. It was simply one of a series of empirical, historic societies. The eternal categories of sin and holiness, of salvation and reprobation, did not apply to it or, indeed, to any other human assembly; they were embodied only in what Augustine called the earthly city and the heavenly city.

The two "cities" consist, respectively, of those predestined to eternal glory and those predestined to eternal torment or, as Augustine also defined them (clearly intending the various definitions to be equivalent), of those who live according to God and those who live according to man, of the altruistic and the selfish, of those whose love is upright and those whose love is perverse, and so forth. In none of these senses, however, have the two "cities" any discernible reality as communities until their final separation at the Last Judgment. In all discernible human communities they are inextricably intertwined. Here again we may see Augustine's modest estimate of the state's function, for when he discusses it in this context, the realm of the state is identified with the sphere in which the concerns of the two cities overlap. Its task is to secure the temporal peace: the order, security, and material welfare that both the wicked and the righteous cities require during their earthly careers. Its concern is with specifically communal, public matters affecting all its members. Citizens of the heavenly city will not, of course, be content with the welfare and peace thus secured: they will use these things but refer their use to the ultimate enjoyment of a peace beyond the terrestrial.

The general tendency of these views of Augustine's was to undermine the extremely close links that had come to exist between the empire and the Christian church, especially during his own lifetime. He was clearly ill at ease with the current representations of this relationship; but there were considerable pressures working on the minds of his contemporaries to keep them active, and Augustine himself was not exempt from their operation. In the course of the struggle with the Donatist movement in north Africa, a dissenting movement increasingly repressed by the imperial authorities, he came gradually and reluctantly to give his consent to the coercive measures that were being brought into use against the movement. His endorsement of these means of repression ran counter to the most fundamental direction of his thought. Although his endorsement must be regarded as a development in his practical, pastoral, and political attitudes rather than as a reversal of his basic views on the nature of political society, it left deep marks on those views. In later centuries his use of the Gospel phrase "Compel them to come in" (*Coge intrare*—Luke 19.23) and its consecration of repression, persecution, and coercion paved the way to much tragedy. It also helped to obscure the most profound and most original of his contributions to Christian political thinking.

Bibliography

The most complete and generally reliable Latin edition of Augustine's works is the edition by the Benedictines of Saint-Maur (1679–1700). It supersedes all earlier editions and was reprinted in J. P. Migne's *Patrologia Latina,* Vols. 32–46 (Paris, 1841–1842), with some unfortunate variants and errors. It is also the basis of the texts of the works now being published in *Bibliothèque augustinienne* (with French translation and useful notes). Modern critical editions of many works exist, mainly in *Corpus Scriptorum Ecclesiasticorum Latinorum* (Vienna) and *Corpus Christianorum.* Details are in E. Dekkers, "Clavis Patrum Latinorum," in *Sacris Erudiri,* Vol. 3 (1962).

English translations of many works appear in various series, such as Loeb Classical Library, Library of the Fathers, Select Library of Nicene and Post-Nicene Fathers of the Christian Church, Library of Christian Classics, The Fathers of the Church, Ancient Christian Writers, and the Catholic University of America Patristic Studies. A detailed, convenient, and fairly up-to-date list of translations is included in the bibliography by J. J. O'Meara appended to Marrou's *Saint Augustine.*

Of short introductory works, the best is H. I. Marrou, *Saint Augustine* (London, 1958), translated from the French in the series Men of Wisdom. It contains a brief biography and a discerning characterization of Augustine's thought by a great scholar, as well as a selection of illustrative texts in translation. R. W. Battenhouse and others, *A Companion to the Study of Saint Augustine* (New York, 1955), has now been superseded by G. Bonner, *St. Augustine—Life and Controversies* (London, 1963), as a survey and guide to Augustine's career and literary output. An essential to understanding Augustine in the setting of contemporary education and culture is H. I. Marrou, *Saint Augustine et la fin de la culture antique* (Paris, 1938), completed by his, *Retractatio* (Paris, 1949). On Augustine as a bishop, see F. van der Meer, *Augustine the Bishop* (London, 1962).

Among the many books on Augustine's intellectual development and his conversion, P. Alfaric, *L'Évolution intellectuelle de saint Augustin* (Paris, 1918), stands behind much of the subsequent controversy; C. Boyer, *Christianisme et néo-Platonisme dans la formation de saint Augustin* (Paris, 1920), is one of the best-balanced replies provoked by it. P. Courcelle, *Recherches sur les Confessions de Saint Augustin* (Paris, 1950), has put the problem on new footing altogether; it is further pursued, with qualifications, by J. J. O'Meara, *The Young Augustine* (London, 1954).

Of the philosophical aspects of Augustine's thought, the best general account is E. Gilson, *The Christian Philosophy of Saint Augustine,* translated by L. E. M. Lynch (London, 1961). See also the survey by R. A. Markus in *Critical History of Western Philosophy,* D. J. O'Connor, ed. (New York, 1964).

On particular aspects, see C. Boyer, *L'Idée de vérité dans la philosophie de saint Augustin* (Paris, 1941); J. Guitton, *Le Temps et l'éternité chez Plotin et saint Augustin,* 2d ed. (Paris, 1955); and E. Dinkler, *Die Anthropologie Augustins* (Stuttgart, 1934), on the topics named in their titles. M. Schmaus, *Die psychologische Trinitätslehre des heiligen Augustinus* (Münster, 1907), is the classic work on Augustine's theory of mind and the Trinitarian speculations based on it. Also valuable on his theory of knowledge are J. Hessen, *Augustins Metaphysik der Erkenntnis*, 2d. printing (Berlin, 1960), and R. Jolivet, *Dieu soleil des esprits* (Paris, 1934).

On ethical topics, see J. Mausbach, *Die Ethik des heiligen Augustins* (Freiburg, 1909); T. Deman, *Le Traitement scientifique de la morale chrétienne selon saint Augustin* (Paris, 1957); J. Burnaby, *Amor Dei* (London, 1938); and R. Holte, *Béatitude et sagesse: Saint Augustin et le problème de la fin de l'homme dans la philosophie ancienne* (Paris, 1962). On the state and society the least unsatisfactory accounts are R. A. Deane, *The Political and Social Ideas of Saint Augustine* (New York, 1963) and the short treatment by N. H. Baynes, *The Political Ideas of Saint Augustine's De Civitate Dei* (London, 1936).

Many of the most important recent articles on Augustine are to be found in one of the following collections: *Augustinus Magister: Communications et actes du Congrès international augustinien* (Paris, 1954); *Recherches augustiniennes*, Vols. I and II (Paris, 1958–1963); *Studia Patristica*, Vol. VI, F. L. Cross, ed.; *Texte und Untersuchungen zur Geschichte der altchristlichen Literatur*, Vol. 81 (1962); and in the quarterly journal *Revue des études augustiniennes*.

The most up-to-date and best-selected bibliography is *Bibliographia Augustiniana*, appended to C. Andresen, ed., *Zum Augustin-Gespräch der Gegenwart* (Darmstadt, 1962), which is Vol. V in the series *Wege der Forschung*. Gilson's book (see above), in which the classified selection of the original is replaced by an alphabetical list in the English translation; B. Altaner, *Patrologie*, 5th printing (1958); and O. Bardenhewer, *Geschichte der altchristlichen Literatur*, Vol. IV (Freiburg, 1924; reprinted 1962), also have good bibliographies. Current literature is surveyed in the bibliographical supplements to *Revue des études augustiniennes*.

R. A. MARKUS

AUGUSTINIANISM may be described as that complex of philosophical ideas which reflected to a greater or lesser degree the philosophy of Augustine. Many of the philosophers who came after Augustine not only restated his leading ideas but also frequently modified them with their own interpretations. Such interpretations were often the result of the impact of other schools of thought, notably the Avicennian and the Aristotelian. Occasionally doctrines that were only implicit in Augustine—for instance, the plurality of forms and universal hylomorphism—were made explicit and assumed considerable importance. Thus there originated in the medieval period what has been termed the Augustinian tradition, which in the later years of its development was closely identified with the Franciscan order. Such a tradition dominated medieval thought to the time of Aquinas. After Aquinas it gradually disintegrated owing to the impact of Thomism and a resurgent Aristotelianism, and no longer represented a distinctive school or tradition. However, it continued to be influential to the extent that it inspired or characterized in varying degrees later medieval and modern philosophers. The principal theses of Augustinianism will be discussed under seven headings.

Faith and understanding. The relationship between faith and understanding (or reason), with the implications of such a relationship for philosophy and theology, and the conception of Christian wisdom and Christian mysticism are central in the structure of Augustinian philosophy. One of the most influential and significant expressions of the relation between faith and understanding in Augustinian thought is summarized in the famous maxim of Anselm: *Credo ut intelligam* (I believe in order to understand). Abelard similarly expressed the idea of the primacy of faith over understanding in his comments on the function of philosophy: "I do not want to be a philosopher if it is necessary to deny Paul. I do not want to be Aristotle if it is necessary to be separated from Christ. 'For there is no other name under heaven given to men, whereby we must be saved.'" With Roger Bacon the relationship of philosophy and theology is profoundly Augustinian. A conservative theologian despite his enthusiasm for scientific method and experimentation, he was convinced that the highest wisdom is found in Scripture and that philosophy exists only to explicate that wisdom. A similar theme is developed by Bonaventura in his *De Reductione Artium ad Theologiam.* He declared that all the sciences and philosophy should be subordinated to theology, which in turn must be subordinated to faith and the love of God; for faith alone enables man to avoid error and attain a union with God. Other philosophers of the Middle Ages who accepted this primacy of faith over reason and the complete subordination of philosophy to theology were Alexander of Hales, John of La Rochelle, Matthew of Aquasparta, and Roger Marston.

Psychology. The Augustinian psychology is characterized by the definition of man as a soul using a body and the implication of this definition for the relation of soul and body. The soul is regarded as an image of the Trinity and is said to have a direct knowledge of itself. Hugh of St. Victor is notably Augustinian, not only in his mysticism but also in his identification of the soul with man and his belief that we have a direct knowledge of the soul and its spirituality. The union of soul and body he described as one of "apposition" rather than composition. Similarly, William of Auvergne is Augustinian in his account of man as a soul using the body, his affirmation of the presence of the soul in all parts of the body, and his statement that: "No knowledge is more natural to the soul than the knowledge of its own self." The mysticism of Bonaventura is characterized by the notion of the journey of the soul to God, the presence of the Trinity in the soul of man, and the direct knowledge the soul has of itself. This principle that the soul has a direct knowledge of itself is characteristic of both the Augustinian psychology and the Augustinian theory of knowledge. It has been termed the "principle of interiorization." Augustine expressed it: "For what is so present to knowledge as that which is present to mind? Or what is so present to the mind as the mind itself?" In modern philosophy the principle of interiority was to have significant influence upon writers like Descartes, Pascal, Tommaso Campanella, and Maurice Blondel.

Epistemology. The Augustinian theory of knowledge had an extensive influence upon medieval philosophers, but it was frequently compromised with Aristotelianism. This was particularly true with respect to the Augustinian theory that sensation is essentially an act of the soul. However, the theory of the divine illumination, in conjunction with the doctrine of exemplary ideas, and the concept of truth as identified with God and present to, but superior to, all minds had a much stronger influence; but it, too, was often qualified with an Aristotelian theory of knowledge. Anselm held that truth is based on the Divine Ideas that are one with God. William of Auvergne accepted the doctrine of divine illumination but interpreted it as giving us an intuitive knowledge of the intelligible forms. Robert Grosseteste combined the Augustinian theory of the divine illumination with an empirical approach in science; he regarded truth as the conformity of a thing with its divine exemplar. Roger Bacon considered divine illumination as an inspiration, and he compared the divine action in illumination to that of the active intellect. Alexander of Hales combined the theory of divine illumination with an Aristotelian theory of abstraction. John of La Rochelle also combined the two theories of knowledge, especially the notion of the active intellect and the divine illumination. Bonaventura and Matthew of Aquasparta also modified the Augustinian theory of knowledge. The former accepted an Aristotelian account of sense knowledge and abstraction, of the existence of a possible and an active intellect, as well as the Augustinian concept of the necessity of the divine illumination for the attainment of truth. Aquasparta modified the Augustinian theory of sensation. On the other hand, Roger Marston and Peter Olivi followed closely Augustine's theory of knowledge. Among modern philosophers, the Augustinian doctrine of divine illumination was particularly influential with such philosophers as Nicolas de Malebranche, Antonio Rosmini, and Vincenzo Gioberti.

Rationes seminales. The conception of the *rationes seminales* (physical powers or "seeds") that Augustine postulated as potentially present in matter in order to explain the origin of creatures after the creation of the six days reappeared most markedly in the philosophical systems of the Augustinians of the thirteenth century.

Hylomorphism and plurality of forms. Hylomorphism and plurality of forms were doctrines that were developed from the thought of Augustine. The latter is said to have appeared first in Robert Grosseteste's metaphysics of light and his analysis of bodies as possessing a number of different forms—for instance, the forms of elements, plants, animals. The highest form possessed by any body he held to be light, which was designated as the "form of corporeity." This notion of a plurality of forms was widely accepted by Augustinians after Grosseteste and is particularly prominent in the philosophies of Bonaventura, Raymond Lull, and Duns Scotus. Generally it appears with its corollary universal hylomorphism, which states that all creatures are composed of matter and form. Thus angelic beings and human souls were said to be composed of a form and a spiritual matter. These doctrines enabled philosophers like Bonaventura and Scotus to maintain more effectively their conception of the completeness of the substantial character of the human soul apart from the body. The Franciscan school strongly supported both doctrines. Robert Kilwardby and John Peckham in particular appealed to the plurality of forms in their vigorous opposition to the Thomistic doctrine of the oneness of man's substantial form.

The meaning of history. Augustine rejected emphatically the cyclical conception of history as expressed in the Christian revelation and the doctrines of the Incarnation and salvation. History is a part of the divine plan and providence, and reflects the presence of the divine reason. The divine dispensation of grace gives hope to man and makes it possible for him to attain his eternal beatitude in the City of God after his pilgrimage in the earthly city. Few medieval philosophers escaped the influence of this Augustinian conception. It is particularly noticeable in the work of Dante and in Roger Bacon's idea of a Christian republic. It influenced such later philosophers as Campanella, Jacques Bossuet, and Leibniz. And it is indirectly represented in modern secularized versions of the idea of progress and social utopias.

Ethics of charity and superiority of the will. The ethics of charity and the principle of the superiority of the will over the intellect in man as formulated by Augustine were important in the development of religious thought. The former, with its correlative doctrines of grace, election, and predestination, is essentially a religious ethic. It found universal acceptance within the Franciscan school and exerted considerable influence on all medieval theology and ethics. It affected such later thinkers as Luther and Calvin. The principle of the primacy of the will is reflected in Bonaventura's insistence upon the need for moral as well as intellectual illumination. Richard of Middleton held that the will is a faculty that determines itself without being determined by any other faculty. Duns Scotus asserted that the will is free, whereas the intellect is determined by that which is known. The will is the nobler of the two faculties and commands the intellect.

Bibliography

Cayré, F., "Augustinisme (développement de l')," *Note complémentaire, "Tables générales," Dictionnaire de théologie catholique,* Vol. 2. Paris, 1953. Cols. 317–324.

Congrès international augustinien, *Augustinus Magister,* 3 vols. Paris, 1954.

Copleston, F., *History of Philosophy.* London, 1950. Vols. 2 and 3.

Gilson, E., *The Christian Philosophy of St. Augustine.* New York, 1950.

Gilson, E., *History of Christian Philosophy in the Middle Ages.* New York, 1955.

Marrou, Henri, *St. Augustine and His Influence Through the Ages.* New York, 1958.

Miscellanea agostiniana: testi e studii. Rome, 1930.

Portalié, E., *A Guide to the Thought of St. Augustine.* Chicago, 1960.

Rondet, H., *Saint Augustine parmi nous.* Paris, 1954.

Rottmanner, O., *Der Augustinismus.* Munich, 1892.

JOHN A. MOURANT

AUREOL, PETER. *See* PETER AUREOL.

AUROBINDO GHOSE (1872–1950), commonly referred to as Sri Aurobindo, was an Indian metaphysician and founder of a new religious movement with headquarters in Pondicherry, in former French India. Aurobindo was educated mainly in England, at St. Paul's School, London, and at King's College, Cambridge, where he was an outstanding undergraduate student in classics. After his return to India in 1893 and a few years of college and university teaching, he became involved in nationalist politics, which led to his imprisonment in 1908. While under detention, he had a powerful religious experience, and in 1910, shortly after his release, he settled in Pondicherry, where his Ashram (religious community) was established. He remained there until his death. The religious movement associated with him has increased its following in India, and has made some converts in the West.

Aurobindo's writings constitute a reinterpretation of the Indian heritage in the light of his own Western education. He modified traditional accounts of the relation between the world and the Divine Being, or Brahman (see HINDUISM), by introducing the concept of evolution. Further, he rejected what he called the supracosmicism of much influential Hindu theology—namely, the doctrine that the cosmos is in some sense illusory, Brahman being the sole reality (this doctrine was held by Śankara). Thus Aurobindo formulated a set of doctrines which retained the contemplative ideal but rejected the world negation often accompanying it, and delineated the evolutionary process as centering on the progressive manifestation of the spirit. The chief expression of these doctrines is found in his massive work *The Life Divine*.

According to Aurobindo, the emergence of consciousness is not satisfactorily explained either as the consequence of the increased complexity of material organisms or as the work of an extracosmic deity. Nevertheless, on the basis of contemplative intuition and the Indian religious tradition, he believed in a Divine Being. He concluded that consciousness is somehow already concealed in living matter before its evolutionary emergence, and that the Divine Being is in some way immanent in the process. Aurobindo therefore argued that Brahman by a transformation (or "involution," as he called it), manifests itself as matter and then progressively brings about an unfolding of its powers through evolution. There is a hierarchy of substances appearing successively, but in such a way that each higher stage includes its predecessor, although transformed. For instance, rational beings are also material organisms, but the animal characteristics of man are transformed because of the presence of his mental powers. Aurobindo inferred that evolution is not completed by the emergence of *Homo sapiens*. The stage is set for the arrival of "superman"; this appearance will change the character of social, cultural, and individual life.

The concept of Brahman and associated ideas gives this metaphysical scheme a religious dimension. In one respect the Divine Being is in repose: the Absolute is a timeless and nonspatial being. But in its creative energy the Absolute manifests itself as the Supermind (Aurobindo regards this as corresponding roughly to the God of theism), which is, so to say, an intermediary between the world as we observe it and the Absolute. Thus, the next stage of spiritual progress is to attain Godhood or the life divine. For this, two things are necessary. First, men must prepare themselves through a new form of yoga ("integral yoga," implying that spiritual insight should accompany and permeate physical, social, and cultural life). Second, God must "descend" into human experience. This illumination of individuals will lead to the emergence of a divinized community. In accordance with the principle that each higher stage transforms, or should transform, what it transcends, Aurobindo produced a synthesis between older Indian religious ideals and the world-affirming attitudes of Christian theism. Thus, religious mysticism should give a new character to ordinary life, not negate it. Since the process is divine, the human possibilities released by the descent of God will be limitless.

In accord with his "integralism," Aurobindo had much to say about physical and cultural pursuits and was the author, among other things, of a considerable body of poetry in English. The Pondicherry Ashram, which is an efficiently organized community, emphasizes physical and educational activities—an unusual feature in comparison with other Indian religious communities.

Bibliography

Most of Aurobindo's works are published by the Sri Aurobindo Ashram in Pondicherry. For a list, see *The Integral Philosophy of Sri Aurobindo*, Haridas Chaudhuri and Frederic Spiegelberg, eds. (London, 1960), which also includes discussions of Aurobindo's philosophy.

The Life Divine is reprinted in various editions, including New York, 1949.

NINIAN SMART

AUSTIN, JOHN (1790–1859), the most influential English legal philosopher of the analytical school. He was born in London; at the age of 16 he enlisted in the army and served five years, resigning his commission to study law. He was called to the bar in 1818. The following year he married Sarah Taylor, a woman of great intelligence and beauty, to whom many distinguished men of the age were deeply devoted.

The Austins became neighbors of Bentham and the Millses and for twelve years remained closely associated with individuals in the Benthamite circle. The practice of law held little appeal for Austin, whose interests were primarily scholarly and theoretical; and after seven years he gave it up. In 1826, on the founding of the University of London by the Benthamites with whom he had been closely associated for years, he was offered its chair in jurisprudence. He accepted with enthusiasm and immediately began to prepare himself by establishing his family in Bonn, where he taught himself German and studied the newly discovered *Institutes* of Gaius; the *Pandects*; and the works of Gustav Hugo, Thibaut, and Savigny. Some of the finest young minds in England—John Stuart Mill, George Cornewall Lewis, Sir John Romilly, and Sir William Erle among them—attended the first series of lectures at London. *The Province of Jurisprudence Determined*, published in 1832, is an expanded version of the first part of these lectures. Apart from this work, Austin published in his lifetime only two articles and a pamphlet attacking reform, *A Plea for the Constitution*. Austin, who once remarked, "I was born out of my time and place—I ought to have been a schoolman of the twelfth century—or a German professor," never again reached the high point of his first year at London. Student interest declined, and the chair, which had been supported by student fees, was given up by Austin in 1832 for financial reasons. His wife tells us that this was "the real and irremediable calamity of his life—the blow from which he never recovered." Plagued by illness and self-distrust, he served a brief and frustrating period, beginning in 1833, on the Criminal Law Commission; and later, with more satisfaction, he served as royal commissioner of Malta. During his remaining twenty years Austin spent some time on the Continent and a final period in Weybridge, not far from London, which proved to be the quietest and most contented part of his life. The second edition of the *The Province* was published in 1861, two years after his death. The first complete edition of *The Lectures on Jurisprudence or The Philosophy of*

Positive Law, reconstructed from his notes by his wife, was published in 1863.

Both the nature and the results of Austin's inquiry deserve attention. What are the characteristics of his inquiry? First, his aim was to keep rigorously separate two questions that had formerly been confused, with much practical harm resulting: what is law? and what ought the law to be? Austin wished to lay a solid foundation for answering the second question by clarifying the first. His answer to the second question was along strictly utilitarian lines. Second, his inquiry was analytical rather than empirical. He was concerned with the analysis of concepts, not, for example, with historical or sociological questions. Finally, connected with the preceding analysis, he hoped to provide a general theory of law—"General jurisprudence"—whose concepts would permit us to grasp the essential features of any legal system without describing any particular system; this task of description was reserved for "particular jurisprudence."

What were the results of Austin's inquiry into the nature of law? The province of jurisprudence, the subject matter selected for study, is law "strictly so-called," or positive law, as contrasted, for example, with divine law (related to it by analogy) or physical laws of nature (related to it by metaphor). Positive law is a rule set for subjects by a sovereign in a politically independent society. A major part of *The Province* consists of analyses of the concepts in this explanatory definition. A rule is a species of command; it is a command that obliges the performance of a class of actions. A command is an expression or intimation of a wish that another do or forbear from doing some act, coupled with the ability and intention to inflict harm in case of noncompliance. The command concept, the key to the science of jurisprudence for Austin, encompasses the concept of a sanction (the evil that will probably be incurred in case of noncompliance), the concept of superiority (the power of forcing compliance with one's wishes), and the concept of obligation or duty (sometimes, for Austin, one is "obliged" because one fears the sanction, sometimes when one is "liable" to the sanction). A sovereign is that person or group of persons receiving habitual obedience from most members of a given society but not in turn having a like habit of obedience to a superior. An independent political society is one in which most members of the society have a habit of obedience to some person or group of persons who have no such habit of obedience to another.

Austin addressed his first class at London in these words: "Frankness is the highest compliment . . . I therefore entreat you, as the greatest favour you can do me, to demand explanation and ply me with objections—turn me inside out." Legal philosophers have paid him this compliment. His method and his results have come in for severe and often valid criticism. The inadequacies of Austin's theory result mainly from his selecting as basic tools of analysis the concepts of a command and habitual obedience. The former cannot account for certain commonly accepted features of law. It fails, first, to explain the varied content of laws, for if we view all law as an order or command backed by threats, we neglect those many laws that do not impose duties but, rather, function in a variety of ways. It also fails to account for the range of persons to whom laws are normally applicable, for orders are addressed to others, whereas most laws bind those who have enacted them as well as those who have not. Next, orders are deliberate datable events; only with much stretching of meaning and introduction of fictions (the sovereign commands what he permits) can they account for the legal status of customary law and the decisions of the courts. Finally, the concept of a command leads Austin to the erroneous claim that one has a legal obligation because one fears the sanction.

The peculiar deficiency of a concept that links the law to habitual obedience is that serious difficulties are encountered in accounting for either the continuity of legal authority or the persistence of law. With the concept of habitual obedience alone, we should be unable to explain the common legal phenomena of one person's succeeding another in the authority to legislate or of laws that remain obligatory long after the legislator and those who habitually obeyed him are dead. Finally, focusing on coercion as the essence of law prevented Austin from developing sufficiently the connections that law has with morality, connections that make understandable one's moral obligation to obey the law.

In addition to these criticisms, Austin has been charged with lack of originality, even in his fundamental mistakes, for identical views may be found in Hobbes and Bentham. Bryce commented, "Bentham . . . drops plenty of good things as he goes along. Austin is barren." It is understandable that we should wonder at Austin's great influence, and his reputation as a great legal philosopher.

First, Austin's positivism, his insistence on separating questions of fact and value, has made legal philosophers sensitive to how easily these questions may be confused and how we may, as a result, delude ourselves into thinking we have answered one of these questions when we have, in fact, answered the other. Even more important, Austin's failures, all associated in some way with his imperativism, have been helpful. He was not alone in feeling the grip of a certain idea, the idea that law is simply the impressing of the will of the stronger upon the weaker. Austin's chief virtue was that he systematically developed, defended, and refined this idea, stripping it of excess philosophical baggage. In doing this he enabled us to focus with greater precision on those features of law that connect it with coercion. More than this, his model presses us to remark upon its limitations, the respects in which viewing law as coercion obscures its complicated role in our lives. After Austin, we understand better what there is in law that connects it with coercion and what there is in law that does not. This is his principal legacy. He provides one more instance in philosophy of our gaining something from a false statement that we might not have gained from a true one.

Works by Austin

Lectures on Jurisprudence, 5th ed., 2 vols. London, 1885.

The Province of Jurisprudence Determined, introduction by H. L. A. Hart. London, 1954.

Works on Austin

Brown, Jethro, *The Austinian Theory of Law*. London, 1906.

Bryce, James, *Studies in History and Jurisprudence*, Vol II. London, 1901.

Hart, H. L. A., *The Concept of Law*. Oxford, 1961.
Maine, Henry, *Early History of Institutions*. London, 1875, Chs. XII and XIII.
Mill, J. S., *Dissertations and Discussions*, Vol. III. London, 1867.
Morison, W. L., "Some Myths About Positivism." *Yale Law Journal*, Vol. 68 (1958), 212–233.
Morris, Herbert, "Verbal Disputes and the Legal Philosophy of John Austin." *UCLA Law Review*, Vol. 7 (1960), 27–56.

HERBERT MORRIS

AUSTIN, JOHN LANGSHAW, born in 1911, was White's professor of moral philosophy at Oxford from 1952 until his death in 1960. Educated at Shrewsbury School and Balliol College, Oxford, he became a fellow of All Souls College in 1933; in 1935 he moved to Magdalen College, where he taught with conspicuous success until elected to the White's chair. During World War II he served with distinction in the British Intelligence Corps; he attained the rank of lieutenant-colonel and was awarded the O.B.E. and the Croix de Guerre, as well as being made an officer of the Legion of Merit.

In the years before the war Austin devoted a great deal of his time and energy to philosophical scholarship. He made himself an expert in the philosophy of Leibniz and also did much work on Greek philosophy, especially Aristotle's ethical works. At this period his own thought, although notably acute and already distinctive in style, was largely critical and altogether lacked the positive approach that distinguished his postwar work. His one published paper belonging to this early period, "Are There *A Priori* Concepts?" very fairly represents the astringent style and outlook that gave him the reputation of being a rather terrifying person. According to Austin's own statements, it was not until the beginning of the war that he began to develop the outlook on philosophy and method of philosophizing that marked his mature work, and it is of this work alone that an account will be given.

AIMS AND METHODS

The practical exigencies of lecturing and the traditions of paper reading (especially in symposia, to which some of his important papers were contributions) prevented some of the most characteristic features of Austin's preferred methods and aims from being clearly and fully exemplified in his written work. Lecturing is essentially a solo effort, whereas Austin believed that the best way of doing philosophy was in a group, and papers, especially in symposia, are almost inevitably on topics of traditional philosophical interest, whereas Austin preferred to keep the traditional problems of philosophy in the background. We shall therefore start by giving some account of the method and aims that Austin always advocated and practiced, most notably in meetings held regularly on Saturday mornings in the Oxford term with a group of like-minded Oxford philosophers.

Language. Austin did not present his aims and methods as the only proper ones for a philosopher; whatever one or two uncautious remarks in his British Academy lecture "Ifs and Cans" may suggest to the contrary, he did not claim more than that his procedures led to definite results and were a necessary preliminary for anyone who wished to undertake other kinds of philosophical investigation. But he certainly considered them so valuable and interesting in their results, and so suited to his own linguistically trained capabilities and tastes, that he never felt it necessary to investigate for himself what else a philosopher might usefully do. What he conceived of as the central task, the careful elucidation of the forms and concepts of ordinary language (as opposed to the language of philosophers, not to that of poets, scientists, or preachers) was, as Austin himself was well aware, not new but characteristic of countless philosophers from Socrates to G. E. Moore. Nor were the grounds for this activity especially novel. First, he claimed, it was only common prudence for anyone embarking on any kind of philosophical investigation, even one that might eventually involve the creation of a special technical vocabulary, to begin with an examination of the resources of the terminology already at his disposal; clarification of ordinary language was thus the "begin-all," if not the "end-all," of any philosophical investigation.. Second, he thought that the institution of language was in itself of sufficient interest to make it worthy of the closest study. Third, he believed that in general a clear insight into the many subtle distinctions that are enshrined in ordinary language and have survived in a lengthy struggle for existence with competing distinctions could hardly fail to be also an insight into important distinctions to be observed in the world around us—distinctions of an interest unlikely to be shared by any we might think up on our own unaided initiative in our professional armchairs.

It is not too soon to remove at this stage some common misconceptions about Austin's aims and methods. First, although he was not concerned with studying the technical terminology of philosophers, he had no objection in principle to such terms; he thought that many such technical terms had been introduced inappropriately and uncritically, as is clear from his discussion, in *Sense and Sensibilia*, of the sense-datum terminology, but he used much of the traditional technical vocabulary of philosophy and added many technical terms of his own invention—as almost any page of *How to Do Things With Words* will bear witness. Second, Austin did not think that ordinary language was sacrosanct; he certainly thought it unlikely that hopelessly muddled uses of languages would survive very long and felt that they were more likely to occur in rather specialized and infrequently used areas of our vocabulary, but there was never any suggestion that language as we found it was incapable of improvement; all he asked was that we be clear about what it is like before we try to improve it.

Technique. We have seen that there was nothing essentially novel in Austin's philosophical aims; what was new was the skill, the rigor, and the patience with which he pursued these aims. Here we are dealing with Austin's own personal gifts, which cannot be philosophically dissected. Nor did Austin have any theory of philosophical method; what he had was a systematic way of setting to work, something on a par with a laboratory technique rather than with a scientific methodology. This technique, unlike the skill with which he followed it, was quite public and one that he was willing and eager to employ in joint investigations with others, so we can easily give an account of it.

A philosopher or, preferably, a group of philosophers using this technique begins by choosing an area of discourse in which it is interested, often one germane to some great philosophical issue. The vocabulary of this area of discourse is then collected, first by thinking of and listing all the words belonging to it that one can—not just the most discussed words or those that at first sight seem most important—then by looking up synonyms and synonyms of synonyms in dictionaries, by reading the nonphilosophical literature of the field, and so on. Alongside the activity of collecting the vocabulary one notes expressions within which the vocabulary can legitimately occur and, still more important, expressions including the vocabulary that seem to be a priori plausible but that can nonetheless be recognized as unusable. The next stage is to make up "stories" in which the legitimate words and phrases occur; in particular, one makes up stories in which it is clear that one can appropriately use one dictionary "synonym" but not another; such stories can also be found ready made in documents. In the light of these data one can then proceed to attempt to give some account of the meaning of the terms and their interrelationships that will explain the data. A particularly crucial point, which is a touchstone of success, is whether one's account of the matter will adequately explain why we cannot say the things that we have noted as "plausible" yet that in fact we would not say. At this stage, but not earlier, it becomes profitable to examine what other philosophers and grammarians have said about the same region of discourse. Throughout (and this is why Austin so much preferred to work in a group) the test to be employed of what can and what cannot be said is a reasonable consensus among the participants that this is so. Such a consensus, Austin found, could be obtained in an open-minded group most of the time; where such agreement cannot be obtained the fact should be noted as of possible significance. Austin regarded this method as empirical and scientific, one that could lead to definitely established results, but he admitted that "like most sciences, it is an art," and that a suitably fertile imagination was all important for success.

It was the lack of thoroughness, of sufficient research before generalization, in previous investigations of language, whether by those who called themselves grammarians or by those who called themselves philosophers, that Austin most deplored. He seriously hoped that a new science might emerge from the kind of investigations he undertook, a new kind of linguistics incorporating workers from both the existing linguistic and the philosophical fields. He pointed to other "new" sciences, such as logic and psychology, both formerly parts of philosophy, as analogues and was indifferent about whether what he was doing "was really philosophy."

So much must suffice as an account of the method of work that Austin advocated. It has been based on a set of notes for an informal talk, characteristically entitled "Something About One Way of Possibly Doing One Part of Philosophy." As Austin admitted in those notes, he had said most of this in his papers "A Plea for Excuses" and "Ifs and Cans," and to all who worked with him it was familiar from his practice. Although inevitably, as we have noted, this method could not be followed in writings (it is in any case a method of discovery and not of presentation), its use underlies and can be discerned in his published work. Thus, before writing "Words and Deeds" or *How to Do Things With Words* he went right through the dictionary making a list, which still survives, of all verbs that might be classed as "performative" in his terminology. The art of telling "your story" is amusingly illustrated over and over again in his paper "Pretending" and, indeed, in all his other published writings. His insistence that it is a mistake to dwell only on a few well-examined notions in a field of discourse is illustrated by his concentration on such notions as "mistake," "accident," and "inadvertence" (in "A Plea for Excuses") and on the use of "I can if I choose" (in "Ifs and Cans"), rather than on "responsibility" and "freedom," in his papers that have a bearing on the free-will problem. Similarly, when his Saturday morning group turned its attention to aesthetics Austin betrayed far more interest in the notions of dainty and dumpy milk jugs than in that of a beautiful picture.

WORK

It is not possible to give a systematic account of Austin's "philosophy," for he had none. His technique lent itself rather to a set of quite independent inquiries, the conclusions of none of which could serve as premises for a further inquiry; his discussions of the language of perception (in *Sense and Sensibilia*), the concept of pretending, the notion of truth, and the terminology of excuses were all based on the study of speech in those fields and not on any general principles or theories. Nor would it serve any useful purpose to attempt to summarize his various investigations one by one, since they depend so much for their interest and force on the detailed observations about language that they contain. It will be more useful to discuss, first, what he thought of as his main constructive work—the doctrine of illocutionary forces that arose out of his earlier distinction of performative and constative utterances, contained in *How to Do Things With Words*—and, second, the application of his technique to the criticism of some traditional theories about perception as found in his *Sense and Sensibilia.*

Theory of illocutionary forces. Austin's theory of illocutionary forces arose from his observation that a considerable number of utterances, even those in the indicative mood, were such that in at least some contexts it would be impossible to characterize them as being true or false. Examples are "I name this ship the Saucy Sue" (which is part of the christening of a ship, and not a statement about the christening of a ship), "I promise to meet you at two o'clock" (which is the making of a promise and not the report of a promise or a statement about what will happen), and "I guarantee these eggs to be new-laid" (which is the giving of a guarantee and not a report of a guarantee). These utterances Austin called "performative," to indicate that they are the performance of some act and not the report of its performance; he did not speak as some do who purport to discuss his views, of "performative *verbs*," for the verb "promise" can well occur in reports—for example, "I promised to meet him." To provide the necessary contrast, Austin coined the technical term "constative" to apply to all those utterances that are naturally called true or false; he thought that "statement" and similar words often used by philosophers roughly as he used "constative" had in ordinary use too narrow a meaning to serve the purpose.

For a time Austin appears to have been fairly satisfied with this distinction, which he gave in print in his "Other Minds" article in 1946, using it to illuminate some features of utterances beginning "I know. . . ." But although the distinction is clearly useful at a certain level, Austin began to doubt whether it was ultimately satisfactory. He found it impossible to give satisfactory criteria for distinguishing the performative from other utterances. The first person of the present indicative, which occurs in the three examples given above, is clearly not a necessary feature; "Passengers are warned to cross the tracks only by the bridge" is an act of warning as much as "I warn you to cross. . . ." Further, in a suitable context "Don't cross the tracks except by the bridge" may also be an act of warning (as in another context it might be an act of commanding); this makes it necessary to distinguish the *primative* performative from the *explicit* performative, the latter, but not the former, making clear what act was being performed in its formulation.

Still more important, the constative seemed to collapse into the performative. Let us consider the four utterances "I warn you that a train is coming," "I guess that a train is coming," "I state that a train is coming," and "A train is coming." The first of these is an act of warning, the second is surely one of guessing, the third apparently one of stating, while the fourth may be any of these as determined by context. Thus, the various forms of constatives—stating, reporting, asserting, and the rest—seem to be merely a subgroup of performatives. It might seem that still one crucial difference remains, that while performative utterances may be in various ways unhappy (I may say "I promise to give you my watch" when I have not got a watch, or am speaking to an animal, or have no intention of handing the watch over), the characteristic and distinctive happiness or unhappiness of constatives is truth and falsehood, to which the other performatives are not liable.

In a brilliant, if not always immediately convincing, discussion (Lecture XI of *How to Do Things With Words*) Austin tried to break down even this distinction. First, we cannot contrast doing with saying, since (in addition to the trivial point that in stating one is performing the act of uttering words or the like) in constative utterances one is stating, describing, affirming, etc., and these acts are on a par with warning, promising, etc. Second, all constatives are liable to all those kinds of infelicity that have been taken to be characteristic of performatives. Just as I should not promise to do something if I do not intend to do it, so I should not state that something is the case unless I believe it to be so; just as my act of selling an object is null and void if I do not possess it, so my act of stating that the king of France is bald is null and void if there is no king of France; just as I cannot order you to do something unless I am in a position to do so, so I cannot state what I am not in a position to state (I cannot *state*, though I can hazard a guess about, what you will do next year). Further, even if we grant that "true" and "false" are assessments specific to constatives, is not their truth and falsity closely parallel to the rightness and wrongness of estimates, the correctness and incorrectness of findings, etc.? Is the rightness of a verdict very different from the truth of a statement? Further, to speak of inferring *validly*, arguing *soundly*, or judging *fairly*, is to make an assessment belonging to the same class as truth and falsehood. Moreover, it is only a legend that "true" and "false" can always be appropriately predicated of constatives; "France is hexagonal" is a rough description of France, not a true or false one, and "Lord Raglan won the battle of Alma" (since Alma was a soldiers' battle in which Lord Raglan's orders were not properly transmitted) is exaggerated—it is pointless to ask whether it is true or false. It was on the basis of such considerations as these that Austin felt himself obliged to abandon the distinction between the performative and the constative.

To replace the unsatisfactory distinction of performatives and constatives Austin introduced the theory of illocutionary forces. Whenever someone says anything he performs a number of distinguishable acts, for example, the *phonetic* act of making certain noises and the *phatic* act of uttering words in conformity with grammar. Austin went on to distinguish three other kinds of acts that we may perform when we say something: first, the *locutionary* act of using an utterance with a more or less definite sense and reference, for example, saying "The door is open" as an English sentence with reference to a particular door; second, the *illocutionary* act, which is the act I may perform *in* performing the locutionary act; third, the *perlocutionary* act, which is the act I may succeed in performing by means of my illocutionary act. Thus, in performing the locutionary act of saying that a door is open I may be performing an illocutionary act of stating, or hinting, or exclaiming; by performing the illocutionary act of hinting I may succeed in performing the perlocutionary act of getting you to shut it. In the same way, by performing the locutionary act of saying "Down with the monarchy" I may succeed in the perlocutionary act of bringing about a revolution, whereas in performing the locutionary act I would be inciting to revolution (successfully or unsuccessfully).

We now see that the constatives, along with performatives, can be construed as members of one particular subclass of illocutionary forces. Thus, in his provisional classification of illocutionary forces Austin had a subclass of *expositives*, which included the "constative" acts. In performing a locutionary act we may be affirming, denying, stating, describing, reporting, agreeing, testifying, rejoining, etc., but in performing a locutionary act we may also perform an act with *commissive* force, as when we promise, bet, vow, adopt, or consent; with *verdictive* force, as when we acquit, assess, or diagnose; with *exercitive* force, as when we appoint, demote, sentence, or veto; or with *behabitive* force, as when we apologize, thank, or curse.

Such is the crude outline of Austin's theory of illocutionary forces. Though his own exposition is of course much more full and rewarding, he said of it (*How to Do Things With Words*, p. 163): "I have purposely not embroiled the general theory with philosophical problems (some of which are complex enough almost to merit their celebrity); this should not be taken to mean that I am unaware of them." We may be permitted to illustrate the philosophical importance of bearing in mind the distinctions Austin made with one example of our own. Very often in recent years philosophers have set out to explain the meaning of the word "good" or of sentences containing the word "good." Some of them have done so by saying that in such sentences the speaker expresses his own feelings (attitudes) and evokes similar feelings (attitudes in others). It might well seem that here they have set out to give an account relevant to locutionary force and that they have instead given one possible illocutionary force ("In saying that it was good I was expressing my favorable attitude toward it") and, alongside it, one possible perlocutionary force ("By saying that it was good I evoked in him a favorable attitude"). It should be clear in the light of Austin's work that such an account will not do. But Austin said very little about locutionary force in detail, and one of the most pressing general questions that arise from his work is that of the relationship between illocutionary force and locutionary force; while recognizing that they are different, and that locutionary force is in some way prior, can we, for example, conclude that the locutionary force of utterances containing the word "promise" can be explained without reference to the typical illocutionary force of "I promise"? This is far from clear.

Criticism of traditional philosophy. We have examined in outline an example of Austin's work on a piece of clarification of language without any reference, save incidental, to the traditional problems of philosophy. We shall now turn to *Sense and Sensibilia*, which is emphatically a polemical discussion of one of the central problems of epistemology. But we shall find the essential features of Austin's method still present, the presentation only being different. Austin had recommended that when the method is used as one of inquiry the vocabulary and phrases, natural and odd, that occur to us should be studied and conclusions drawn *before* the conclusions of traditional philosophy are compared with them. Here, however, when he presents results he at each stage presents first the traditional philosophical theses and then shows their errors by confronting them with the actual facts, linguistic and otherwise.

In *Sense and Sensibilia*, Austin examines the doctrine that we never directly perceive material things but only sense data (or ideas, or sense contents, etc.), insofar as that doctrine is based upon the so-called argument from illusion. He maintains that it is largely based on an obsession with a few words "the uses of which are oversimplified, not really understood or carefully studied or correctly described" (*Sense and Sensibilia*, p. 3). With special reference to Ayer and Price, he shows how illusions are traditionally confused with delusions, are defined in terms of belief that one sees a material thing when in fact one does not (whereas some illusions, such as one hatched line appearing to be longer than another of equal length, involve nothing of the sort), and are taken to include such phenomena as sticks looking bent in water, which are not illusions at all. A portion of the argument that clearly exhibits his method at work is where he contrasts the actual complexities and differences in our use of "looks," "appears," and "seems" with the traditional confusion of these terms in traditional philosophy. Especially interesting is the discussion of the traditional accounts of "reality"; these he contrasts with the multifarious uses of the word "real," which takes its significance only from the implied contrast in context with "artificial," "fake," "bogus," "toy," "synthetic," etc., as well as with "illusory" and "apparent."

But it is perhaps more important now for us to notice another element in the argument that is very characteristic but that we have as yet given little notice, which is Austin's care to avoid oversimplification and hasty generalization of nonlinguistic, as well as linguistic, fact. The ordinary man does not, as is so often stated or implied in accounts of the argument from illusion, believe that he always sees material things; he knows perfectly well that he sees shadows, mirror images, rainbows, and the like. The number of kinds of things that we see is large and to be settled by scientific investigation, not by philosophy; the question whether the invariable object of perception is a material thing or a sense datum is thus absurd. Again, it is not true that a straight stick in water normally looks like a bent stick out of water, for we can see the water; an afterimage does not look like a colored patch on a wall; a dream is distinguished by the dreamlike quality that occasionally, but only occasionally, we attribute to some waking experience. Again, he points out that situations in which our perception is queer may arise because of defects in sense organs or peculiarities of the medium or because we put a wrong construction on what we (quite normally) see, and it is a mistake to attempt to give a single account of all perceptual error. None of these are linguistic points, and Austin had no purist, theoretical notion that he was prohibited as a philosopher from any attention to nonconceptual issues; he thought that philosophical error did arise from empirical error.

Once again, it would be pointless to attempt to reconstruct the whole argument of *Sense and Sensibilia* here; we must be content with noticing the few points made that perhaps have some bearing on a general understanding of his general position. But it should perhaps be stressed that Austin in these lectures discussed only one theory of perception as based on one particular kind of argument; although one may expect to get help from it in study of other problems in the field of perception, it would be a mistake to suppose that the book contains a full study of all problems of perception or to criticize it because it leaves many difficult problems unanswered.

It is hardly imaginable that anyone would ever deny that Austin displayed a very great talent in the kind of work he chose to do. Some have criticized him on the ground that there are more important things for philosophers to do than this; on that point Austin always refused to argue, simply saying that those who preferred to work otherwise should do so and asking only that they not do what he did in the traditional slipshod way. To those who said that philosophers should work with an improved scientific language he replied flatly that the distinctions of ordinary language were of interest in their own right and that one should not modify what one does not fully understand, but he offered no theoretical objections to such projects. He was content to work in a way which he felt he understood and found rewarding. As for the assertion sometimes made, that Austin's kind of work is private to his own peculiar gifts and that it was therefore a mistake for him to recommend the method to others, time alone can decide.

A final word should be said about Austin's relation to other philosophers. He greatly admired G. E. Moore, but it is a mistake to view his work as an offshoot of Cambridge philosophy. Moore, like Austin and unlike most Cambridge philosophers, had a linguistic and classical background rather than a scientific one. Austin owed no special debt to Russell and was far more unlike Wittgenstein than is sometimes recognized. For Wittgenstein an understanding of ordinary language was important because he believed that the traditional problems of philosophy arose from misunderstandings of it, but Wittgenstein had in mind gross category mistakes, and he wished to study ordinary language only so far as was essential for eliminating these. Austin was interested in fine distinctions for their own sake and saw the application of his results to the traditional problems of philosophy as only a by-product. He was uninterested in the party conflicts of philosophy, following always his individual bent.

Works by Austin

For brevity, first publication of individual papers (collected in *Philosophical Papers*) is omitted.

Foundations of Arithmetic. Oxford, 1950. Translation of Frege's *Grundlagen der Arithmetik*.

Critical notice of J. Łukasiewicz' *Aristotle's Syllogistic: From the Standpoint of Modern Formal Logic*. *Mind*, Vol. 61 (1952).

Philosophical Papers. Oxford, 1961.

Sense and Sensibilia. Oxford, 1962.

How to Do Things With Words. Oxford, 1962. The William James lectures delivered at Harvard.

"Performatif-constatif" and contributions to discussion in *La Philosophie analytique*. Paris, 1962.

J. O. Urmson

AUTHORITY. "Authority" is often defined as "legitimate power." Nevertheless, many writers insist, with de Jouvenel, that "power is something very different from authority. The distinguishing mark of the latter is that it is exercised only over those who voluntarily accept it" (*Sovereignty*, p. 32). This disagreement is partly due to the vagueness and ambiguity of "power." One sense of the word suggests the coercion of unwilling subjects who, far from acknowledging a ruler's authority, submit to his power as to a gunman's, for fear of what he might do to them. But in a broader sense, to have power is to be able to get what one wants by affecting the behavior of others. This sense of "power" covers a wide range of relations between actor and subject and includes that of authority, at any rate in one sense of "authority." If, however, "authority" does signify a kind of power, it is evidently not the kind manifest in the exercise of naked or coercive power.

The relations between power and authority are complicated, however, not only by the vagueness of "power," but also by the varying shades of meaning of "authority." Authority cannot always be understood as a capacity to affect other men's behavior. A man who has authority to act may yet be unable to make his will effective, like a policeman vainly trying to quell a riot. Again, an authority on Etruscan ceramics may command respectful attention and may influence beliefs but have no effect on men's behavior.

Nor is authority necessarily *legitimate*, if by that one means that it derives from some recognized set of institutionalized rules or traditions. Max Weber distinguished three ideal types of authority, according to the type of their legitimacy: traditional, legal–rational, and charismatic. The sense in which the first two are legitimate is reasonably clear, but the last is more elusive. "Charisma" is a theological term meaning "a gift or talent specially vouchsafed by God." Weber used it to cover the kind of relation that exists characteristically between the prophet or the insurgent leader and his followers. It is an eminently personal relation, and may often imply a repudiation of institutionalized authority, whether of law or custom. "It is written . . . but I say unto you . . . ," says Weber, expresses the characteristic authority of the innovating leader; he impresses his will by the appeal of his personality, by generating a faith in his mission, or by the belief that he can save his followers from their doubts and perplexities.

Though there seems at first sight very little in common between the last type of authority and the policeman's authority to detain on suspicion, or the savant's to pronounce on the age of a vase, they are, nevertheless, related. One must distinguish, however, between *de facto* and *de jure* uses of the word "authority."

De jure authority. "Authority" is used in a strictly *de jure* sense when one says, for instance, that a subordinate official has exceeded his authority. This presumes a set of rules, according to which certain persons are competent (authorized) to do certain things, but not to do other things. In this instance, there may be no question of securing the obedience or compliance of others—the extent of the official's authority depends not on whether he can get others to act, but rather on what actions are open to him within the rules. But, of course, governmental authority is very often authority, under rules, to issue instructions to others. This is the aspect of authority that writers such as Hannah Arendt and C. J. Friedrich have in mind. They want to distinguish it from power, and particularly from despotic or tyrannical power. The latter, they say, is subject to no limits, whereas true authority, because it is always derived from rules, must, therefore, be limited and restrained by rules. This is dubious because the rules may confer, as in the case of a sovereign legislature, an unlimited authority, even to change the rules at will. So long as it makes sense to say that a person has a right to command, there seems no good reason to deny that he has true authority, however much one dislikes it.

Closely related to the concept of rule-conferred authority is the authority that a person gives another to act on his behalf. Hobbes treated this, indeed, as the standard use, defining the expression "done by authority" as "done by commission, or licence from him whose right it is" (*Leviathan*, ch. 16), the latter being the "author" of the act, as opposed to the "actor." The authority of the ruler, as actor, was an unconditional commission from his subjects, the authors, to represent them, that is, to act on their behalf. From this, Hobbes concluded that "every particular man is author of all the sovereign doth" (*Ibid.*, ch. 18). Hobbes wanted to treat this initial authorization as the source of all rule-making authority and, therefore, of all rules. But this cannot be the case. The concept of action on behalf of another does not describe a natural fact. It presupposes a normative category defined by a rule, namely, that whatever the effects of A's actions, they shall, if done with B's authority, carry the same normative consequences as if done by B himself. But in that case, "authority" and "authorization" are meaningless without a pre-existing system of rules. So the sense of authority (*de jure*) as a rule-created competence must logically precede that sense in which authority is granted by one person to another.

De facto authority. Authority in a *de facto* sense exists whenever a man *recognizes* another as *entitled* to command him. That is not quite the same as saying, as some writers do, that all compliance with authority is willing compliance; for, on a given occasion, one may comply very reluctantly, or not at all, yet still recognize that one ought to comply. The real difference between this case and that of the man who disobeys someone who simply is powerful (i.e., whom he does not recognize as in authority) is that the former would see his disobedience as a lapse or a failure, while the latter's only anxiety would be to avoid reprisals.

To have *de facto* authority is to stand in such a relation to other people that one can, as a matter of fact, induce them to do (or, equally, to believe) what one tells them, because, for whatever reason, they are convinced that they ought to do so. Of course, the relationship of *de facto* authority most commonly arises from *de jure* authority—where some principle of legitimacy, of law, custom, religion, and so on, gives an official or ruler a right to command or to make pronouncements for others to accept. Providing the subject respects the legitimating principle, the official will also enjoy *de facto* authority. This, in turn, can be a source of power, in the narrow sense of coercion, over those who reject the person in authority, since those who accept it can be used to coerce those who do not.

A person may fall in with another's suggestions, however, not precisely because he feels that he has a duty to obey, but because the other person is an *authority*, meaning that he is believed to possess expert knowledge and therefore the right to be listened to because "he knows what he is talking about." This is the borderline case between authority and influence. If A has influence with B, B is predisposed, perhaps because of ties of friendship or of loyalty, to consider A's suggestions favorably, but not because he considers that he ought to defer to A's judgment or thinks it presumptuous or impudent to ask him for his reasons. The authority of the expert, on the other hand, involves the notion of someone qualified to speak. It presumes standards by which expertise is assessed and recognized, for example, degrees or professional reputation. Evidence of this kind serve as reasons why laymen should take the expert's word without understanding *his* reasons, even without asking for them.

"Authority," "competence," and "recognition" are thus all very closely related concepts; and this is true even of the cases that come closest to Weber's pure charisma—the prophet with the mark of grace, the Napoleon, the Lenin, or the de Gaulle, whom men follow even though, at first, their claim to obedience derives from no established rules. It is misleading to talk of authority as if it were a kind of natural force emanating from some individuals and attracting followers as a magnet attracts iron filings. The qualities that sustain leadership and authority vary with the group and its traditions and standards. Among some peoples, epilepsy is a mark of divine inspiration; among others, soldiers are highly regarded and readily qualify as charismatic, particularly in emergencies. Again, the authority a man enjoys in a special field may spill over if that field has high prestige in the society, into fields where he has no special competence, as when soldiers are greeted as political oracles and scientists as prophets.

But while the qualities that characterize authority may vary with the society, it is a fair generalization that the less a leader's authority is firmly rooted *de jure* in an established tradition or in accepted institutions, the more it will depend on continuing success, on his faith in his own mission or destiny and on his ability to communicate this faith to others. Conversely, de Jouvenel argues that institutionalized authority, by its very nature, must have a built-in tendency to exclude the dynamic and thrusting innovator. The kind of leader who relies on personal ascendancy rather than on the authority of office is liable to disrupt the limiting structure of legitimate authority, if once he gets a foot inside. The tension between those in *de jure* authority and what de Jouvenel calls "emergent authority, the active force in politics" is, he maintains, a natural feature of every political system.

Justifying authority. The question, "What, in general, can justify authority?" became pressing in political philosophy only after the Reformation. The Greeks and the Romans, taking the need for authority for granted, were mainly concerned about who should exercise it, under what conditions, and within what limits. Christianity taught that all authority was of God, as a remedy for sin, and men owed obedience to earthly authorities because they were divinely commissioned. Only with the growth of early liberalism, out of the wreck of the universal church, and under the influence of Protestant doctrine of the equal priesthood of all believers and the doctrine of the Inner Light, did the problem of justifying human authority in secular terms become urgent.

The liberal tradition in political philosophy can be regarded as a prolonged exploration of the relations between three concepts: authority, reason, and freedom. On the face of it, there would seem to be a fundamental conflict between the liberal ideal of the free, rational individual, choosing his own course in the light of reason or conscience, and the plain necessity that members of a society must forgo acting on their own judgment and making their own choices and must submit instead to the instructions of another man, not because they recognize them as wiser or better, but because they are *his*. According to Locke, tutelage is a natural condition for children; but when man grows to be a reasonable being, he achieves freedom and equality with other reasonable men. If men are born free, asked Rousseau, what can justify their chains?

Rousseau's answer was a variant of Hobbes's. To be justified, authority must be self-imposed. It must derive from a compact, or covenant, whereby each member of the society agrees with all the rest to submit to one or a few of their number (Hobbes), or to the General Will of the whole people (Rousseau). This solution had the merit, at least, of taking into account recognition and acceptance as necessary conditions for *de facto* authority. But it conceded too much: the subject was committed, by a free act of will, to a total submission, no matter what he might think of the actual purposes to which authority was put. Hobbes, it is true, took it for granted that the point of the compact was the welfare of the subject; and Rousseau believed that, at its highest, this was identical with that of the whole community. The liberal, rationalist tradition in politics, however, has been reluctant to grant that there could *never* be a right to disobey a government. Even Hobbes admitted that a man's duty to submit ended if the sovereign threatened his life or failed to protect him. Locke went much further, making political obligation depend on good government and the safeguarding of natural rights. But confronted with the dilemma that it would be incompatible with order to give every individual the right to withhold obedience whenever he judged himself aggrieved, Locke faltered and seemed to reserve the right to judge to the people, deciding by majorities. Thus, Locke threatened in the end to subordinate individual judgment to majority decisions as absolutely as Hobbes subordinated it to the sovereign, or Rousseau to the General Will.

Applied consistently, consent theory presents two major difficulties. If consent is taken as a necessary condition for authority, it seems to deny a government any rightful authority over anyone who dissented from it, or, at least, from the basic principles of the constitution (considered as the terms of the contract), from which the government's authority derived. The only possible relation between the government and the dissenter would then be naked power. But this would not meet the liberal democrat's usual requirement. He wants to say that precisely because the form and principles of democracy are more just than its rivals, a democratic government is *morally justified* in preventing subversion and coercing dangerous dissenters. If the dissenters mistakenly fail to recognize this moral superiority, that error does not invalidate a democratic government's right to exact obedience, provided it has majority support. Consent theory in this form, therefore, will not provide the justification for political authority that is generally required of it.

If, however, consent is taken as a *sufficient* condition for authority, one may be committed to too much, for instance, to defending anyone who condoned and submitted to immoral abuses of authority on the grounds that he once voted for it. If one consents for self-interested, even immoral, reasons to authorities to which one ought not to consent, is one therefore morally committed to cooperating with them in their immoral policies? Or should one rather say that since one ought not to have given consent in the first place, the authority is illegitimate and the duty void?

Consent theory is an attempt to define the conditions under which there can be a *moral* duty to accept authority, without giving up that conception of morality that stresses rationality and personal judgment. It tries to find a way out of the difficulty characterized by the fact that whereas, in *political* terms, we speak of a *right* to act according to one's own best judgment or conscience, in *moral* terms we speak of a *duty* to do so. Whatever its weaknesses, consent theory suggests an important principle, namely, that a moral theory of authority can never be a theory of *absolute* authority. Recognizing that authority is essential to social survival, a rational man would concede that he could not insist on a right or a duty to disregard authority, whenever he disagreed with it, and to act instead on his own judgment. Nevertheless, he need surrender only his right to act, not to judge. It is consistent with submission to political (though not perhaps to religious) authority to obey while believing the injunction to be wrong. Nor is this irrational, if disobedience or revolt would be more disastrous than obedience. A democrat might properly submit to a corrupt oligarchy, if the alternative were tyranny or total disruption of society.

Even so, submission even in this spirit can be neither absolute nor final. If authority is justified by its general consequences, consistently evil consequences would condemn it. The duty to submit, which is the reverse side of the right to command, must always depend, therefore, on whether the authority tends in general to realize the ends that are held to justify it. One cannot be rationally committed to refrain from judging for oneself whether the authority has that tendency, nor to continue to recognize it as an authority once one concludes that it has not. Of course, anyone who still believes that the proper ends of authority are being served will continue to support it, and he will be quite consistent if he holds that the recalcitrants must be restrained by force if necessary. From his point of view, they are simply wrong in judging that the conditions for obedience are not being fulfilled, and therefore wrong to reject the authority. Nevertheless, he cannot rationally deny them the right to judge or, given their judgment, the right to act on it; he can complain only that they have judged wrongly, and that their rebellion is not therefore justified in reality.

In short, a moral duty to submit to authority may involve, in a sense, suspending the moral duty to act on one's own immediate judgment; but that can only arise from, and be conditional upon, one's own continuing judgment of the broader issues involved. The idea that one could give up this fundamental duty, or suffer its extinction, would be incompatible with the idea of a morally responsible and rational person.

Bibliography

For general symposia, see C. J. Friedrich, ed., *Nomos I—Authority* (Cambridge, Mass., 1958), with essays by Friedrich, Hannah Arendt, Bertrand de Jouvenel, Talcott Parsons, David Easton, and others. R. McKeon et al., *Le Pouvoir (Annales de Philosophie Politique, 1 & 2)* (Paris, 1956; 1957), although concerned primarily with power, deals also with authority; esp. article by Jacques Maritain "Démocratie et autorité."

For analytical discussion of the concept, see R. S. Peters, P. G. Winch, A. E. Duncan-Jones, "Symposium: Authority," in *Proceedings of the Aristotelian Society*, Supplementary Vol. 32 (1958), 207–260; R. S. Peters, *Authority, Responsibility and Education* (London, 1959); S. I. Benn and R. S. Peters, *Social Principles and the Democratic State* (London, 1959); T. D. Weldon, *The Vocabulary of Politics* (London, 1953); C. W. Cassinelli, "Political Authority: Its Exercise and Possession," in *Western Political Quarterly*, Vol. 14 (September, 1961), 635–646; S. de Grazia, "What Authority

Is Not," in *American Political Science Review*, Vol. 53 (June 1959), 321–331.

For an extensive examination of the relations between authority and rules, see H. L. A. Hart, *The Concept of Law* (Oxford, 1961).

For a consideration of the role of authority in political society, see Bertrand de Jouvenel, *Sovereignty: an inquiry into the political good*, translated by J. F. Huntington (Cambridge, 1957), and *Pure Theory of Politics* (Cambridge, 1963); H. D. Lasswell and Abraham Kaplan, *Power and Society*, (New Haven, Conn., 1950). For Max Weber's account of the types of authority, see M. Weber, *Wirtschaft und Gesellschaft* (Tübingen, 1925), Part I, edited and translated by Talcott Parsons and H. M. Henderson, with an introduction by T. Parsons, published as *Theory of Social and Economic Organization* (New York, 1947); *From Max Weber—Essays in Sociology*, edited and translated by H. H. Gerth and C. Wright Mills (London, 1947).

For the history of theories of authority, see G. H. Sabine, *History of Political Theory*, 3rd ed. (New York, 1951); Otto von Gierke, *Political Theories of the Middle Age* (Cambridge, 1900) translated by F. W. Maitland; W. Ullmann, *Principles of Government and Politics in the Middle Ages* (London, 1961); John Plamenatz, *Man and Society* (London, 1963). For social contract theories, see J. W. Gough, *The Social Contract*, 2d ed. (Oxford, 1957).

STANLEY I. BENN

AVEMPACE. *See* IBN BAJJA.

AVENARIUS, RICHARD (1843–1896), German positivist philosopher, was born in Paris. He studied at the University of Leipzig, where he became a *Privatdozent* in philosophy in 1876. The following year he was appointed professor of philosophy at Zurich, where he taught until his death. His most influential work was the two-volume *Kritik der reinen Erfahrung* (1888–1890), which won him such followers as Joseph Petzoldt and such opponents as Lenin.

Avenarius was the founder of empiriocriticism, an epistemological theory according to which the task of philosophy is to develop a "natural concept of the world" based on "pure experience." To obtain such a coherent, consistent view of the world requires a positivistic restriction to that which is directly given by pure perception, together with the elimination of all metaphysical ingredients which man, through introjection, imports into experience in the act of knowing.

There is a close kinship between the ideas of Avenarius and those of Ernst Mach, especially as set forth in Mach's *Analyse der Empfindungen*. The two men never became personally acquainted, and they developed their points of view quite independently of one another; hence, it was only gradually that they became convinced of the profound agreement of their basic conceptions. They held the same fundamental view on the relationship between physical and mental phenomena, as well as on the significance of the principle of the "economy of thought." Above all, both were persuaded that pure experience must be recognized as the sole admissible—and thoroughly adequate—source of knowledge. Thus, the elimination of introjection by Avenarius is only a special form of that total elimination of the metaphysical which Mach sought.

In addition to Petzoldt and Lenin, others who dealt at length with the philosophy of Avenarius were Wilhelm Schuppe and Wilhelm Wundt. While Schuppe, the philosopher of immanence, agreed with Avenarius on essential points, Wundt criticized the scholastic character of Avenarius' expositions and sought to point out internal contradictions in his doctrines.

Cognition. The two presuppositions of empiriocriticism are the empiriocritical axiom of the contents of cognition and the axiom of the forms of cognition. The first axiom states that the cognitive contents of all philosophical views of the world are merely modifications of the original assumption that every human being initially assumes himself to be confronted with an environment and with other human beings who make assertions and are dependent on the environment. The second axiom holds that scientific knowledge does not possess any forms and means essentially different from those of prescientific knowledge and that all the forms and means of knowledge in the special sciences are extensions of the prescientific (*Kritik der reinen Erfahrung*, Vol. I, Preface).

Especially characteristic of Avenarius' theory of human cognition was his biological approach. From this biological point of view, every process of knowledge is to be interpreted as a vital function, and only as such can it be understood. Avenarius' interest was directed chiefly to the pervasive relations of dependency between individuals and their surroundings, and he described these relations in an original terminology involving many symbols.

The point of departure for his investigations was the "natural" assumption of a "principal coordination" between self and environment, in consequence of which each individual finds himself facing both an environment with various component parts and other individuals who make assertions about this environment which also express a "finding." The initial principal coordination thus consists in the existence of a "central term" (the individual) and "opposite terms" about which he makes assertions. The encountering individual is represented and centralized in system *C* (the central nervous system, the cerebrum), the basic biological processes of which are nourishment and work.

System *C* is exposed to change in two ways; changes in it are dependent on two "partial-systematic factors": variations in the environment (*R*) or stimuli from the external world (whatever can, as a stimulus, excite a nerve), and fluctuations in metabolism (*S*), or absorption of food (whatever in the environment of system *C* conditions and constitutes its metabolism). System *C* constantly strives for a vital maximum conservation of its strength (*V*), a state of rest in which the mutually opposed processes $f(R)$ and $f(S)$—that is, the variations of system *C* as functions of *R* and *S*—cancel each other out, and the two variations maintain an equilibrium ($f(R) + f(S) = 0$, or $\Sigma f(R) + \Sigma f(S) = 0$). If $f(R) + f(S) > 0$, then there arises in the state of rest or equilibrium state of system *C* a disturbance, a relationship of tension, "a vital difference." The system strives to diminish or cancel out and equalize this disturbance by passing over spontaneously to secondary reactions in order to re-establish its original state (the conservation maximum, or *V*). These secondary reactions to deviations from *V* or to physiological fluctuations in system *C* are the so-called independent vital sequences (the vital functions in system *C*, the physiological processes in the brain), which run their course in three phases: the initial segment (appearance of the vital difference), the middle segment, and the final segment (reappearance of the earlier state). The canceling out of a vital difference is possible, of course, only in the manner and to the extent that system *C* exhibits a readiness for it. Among the changes preparatory to achieving readiness are hereditary dispositions, developmental factors, pathological variations, practice or exercise, and the like. The "dependent vital sequences" (experiences, or *E*-values) are functionally conditioned by the independent vital sequences. The dependent vital sequences, which, like the independent, proceed in three stages (pressure, work, release), are the conscious processes and cognitions ("assertions about contents"). For example, an instance of knowledge is present if in the initial segment the characterization reads "unknown" and in the final segment it reads "known."

Avenarius sought to explain the rise and disappearance of problems in general as follows. A disparity can arise between the stimulation from the environment and the energy at the disposal of the individual either (*a*) because the stimulation is strengthened as a result of the individual's having found anomalies, exceptions, or contradictions in the given, or (*b*) because an excess of energy is present. In the first case, problems arise that can, under favorable circumstances, be solved by knowledge; in the second case, practical—idealist goals arise. The latter are the positing of ideals and values (for example, ethical or aesthetic ideals and values), the testing of them (that is, the forming of new ones), and through them the alteration of the given.

The *E*-values, which depend on the fluctuations in the energy of system *C*, fall into two classes. The first are "elements," or simple contents of assertions—contents of sensation, such as green, hot, and sour, which depend on the objects of sensation or stimuli (whereby the "things" of experience are understood as nothing more than "complexes of elements"). The second are "characters," the subjective reactions to sensations, or the feelinglike modes of apprehension. Three groups of basic characters (kinds of awareness) are distinguished: the "affective," the "adaptive," and the "prevailing." Among the affective characters are the feelings proper (the "affectional," pleasure and aversion) and the feelings in a figurative sense (the "coaffectional," such as anxiety and relief, and the "virtual," such as feelings of movement). The adaptive characters include the "identical" (sameness or "tautote," difference or "heterote"); that is, the "fidential," the "existential" (being, appearance, nonbeing), the "secural" (certainty, uncertainty), and the "notal" (the being known, the being unknown), together with many modifications of these. For example, modifications of the "idential" include, among others, generality, law, whole, and part.

Pure experience and the world. Avenarius constructed the concept of pure experience and related it to his theory of the natural concept of the world on the basis of his views on the biology and psychology of knowledge. The ideal of a natural concept of the world of pure experience is fulfilled in the complete elimination of metaphysical categories and of dualistic interpretations of reality, by means of his exclusion of introjection. The basic prerequisite for this is first to acknowledge the fundamental equivalence of everything that is encountered and that can be grasped, regardless of whether it is given through external or internal experience. As a consequence of the empiriocritical principal coordination between self and environment, individuals and environment are encountered in the same fashion, without distinction. "With respect to givenness, I and the environment are on completely the same footing. I come to know the environment in exactly the same sense that I come to know myself—as members of a single experience; and in every experience that is realized the two experience-values, the self and the environment, are in principle coordinated to each other and equivalent" (*Der menschliche Weltbegriff*).

Likewise, the difference between *R*-values and *E*-values is conditional upon the mode of apprehension. Both values are equally accessible to description. They differ only in that the former are interpreted as constituents of the environment, while the latter are conceived of as the content of an assertion of another human individual. In the same way, there is no ontological distinction between the mental and the physical; rather, there is a logical functional relation between them. A process is mental insofar as it is dependent on a change in system *C* and has more than mechanical significance, that is, insofar as it signifies an experience. Psychology has no separate subject matter at its disposal; it is nothing other than the study of experience insofar as experience is dependent on system *C*. Avenarius rejected the usual interpretation of and distinction between mind and body. He recognized neither the mental nor the physical but only a single kind of being.

Economy of thought. Of particular importance for the realization of the cognitive ideal of pure experience and for the notion of the natural concept of the world is the principle of the economy of thought. In the same way that thinking in conformity with the principle of least exertion is the root of the theoretical process of abstraction, so knowledge generally orients itself by the degree of exertion required to fulfill experience. Hence, one should exclude all elements of the mental image that are not contained in the given, in order to think about that which is encountered in experience with the least possible expenditure of energy, and thus to arrive at a pure experience. Experience, "cleansed of all adulterating additions," contains nothing but constituents of experience that presuppose constituents of the environment only. Whatever is not pure experience, and thus is not the content of an assertion (an *E*-value) subject to the environment itself, is to be eliminated. What we term "experience" (or "existing things") stands in a certain relationship of dependence to system *C* and to the environment; and experience is pure when it is cleansed of all those contents of assertions that do not depend on the environment.

A world concept relates to the "sum total of the constituents of the environment" and is dependent on the final character of the *C*-system. It is natural if it avoids the error of introjection and is not falsified by animistic "insertions." Introjection transfers the perceptual object into the perceiving man. It splits our natural world into inner and outer, subject and object, mind and matter. This is the origin of metaphysical problems (like immortality and the mind–body problem) and metaphysical categories (like substance). All of these must therefore be eliminated.

Introjection, with its unwarranted duplication of reality, must be replaced by the empiriocritical principal coordination and the natural concept of the world that rests on it. Thus, at the end of its development the world concept returns to that natural form with which it began: a purely descriptive comprehension of the world, with the least expenditure of energy.

Works by Avenarius

Philosophie als Denken der Welt gemäss dem Prinzip des kleinsten Kraftmasses. Prolegomena zu einer Kritik der reinen Erfahrung ("Philosophy as Thinking of the World in Accordance With the Principle of the Least Amount of Energy. Prolegomena to a Critique of Pure Experience"). Leipzig, 1876.

Kritik der reinen Erfahrung ("Critique of Pure Experience"), 2 vols. Leipzig, 1888–1890.

Der menschliche Weltbegriff ("The Human Concept of the World"). Leipzig, 1891.

Works on Avenarius

Ewald, Oskar, *Richard Avenarius als Begründer des Empiriokritizimus.* Berlin, 1905.

Lenin, V. I., *Materializm i Empiriokritizism.* Moscow, 1909. Translated as *Materialism and Empiriocriticism.* New York, 1927.

Raab, Friedrich, *Die Philosophie von Richard Avenarius.* Leipzig, 1912.

Schuppe, Wilhelm, "Die Bestätigung des naiven Realismus." *Vierteljahrsschrift für wissenschaftliche Philosophie,* Vol. 17 (1893), 364–388.

Suter, Jules, *Die Philosophie von Richard Avenarius.* Zurich, 1910.

Wundt, Wilhelm, "Über naiven und kritischen Realismus." *Philosophische Studien,* Vol. 12 (1896), 307–408, and Vol. 13 (1897), 1–105 and 323–433.

FRANZ AUSTEDA
Translated by *Albert E. Blumberg*

AVERROËS, or ibn-Rushd (c. 1126–c. 1198), was the foremost figure in Islamic philosophy's period of highest development (700–1200). His pre-eminence is due to his own immense philosophical acuity and power and to his enormous influence in certain phases of Latin thought from 1200 to 1650.

Averroës ("ibn-Rushd" is a more exact transliteration of the Arabic, while "Averroës" is the medieval Latin version) was born in Córdoba into a family of prominent judges and lawyers; his grandfather, bearing the same name, served as the chief *qādī* (judge) of Córdoba, and there is a tradition that his father carried out the same duties. (In Muslim society a *qādī*'s professional concepts and practical duties were simultaneously civil and religious. Thus, a "lawyer" had expert knowledge of divine law.)

There are, however, few other specific details about his life and career. Ernest Renan and Salomon Munk mention that he studied under the most learned teachers in theology and law (in the Muslim world the two disciplines are effectively the same). It has been suggested that he studied with such scientists and philosophers as ibn-Tufail (d. 1185) and ibn-Bajja (or Avempace, d. 1138), but the tenuous evidence would indicate that he became acquainted with the former only when he was past forty and that the death of the latter occurred when Averroës was only 11 or 12 years of age. Thus, significant pedagogical influence by these personalities upon Averroës is doubtful..

There remain, nevertheless, scattered pieces of evidence and suggestions of dates delineating his career. Averroës himself mentions that he was in Marrakesh in 1153, on which occasion he observed the star Canope, not visible in Spain at that time. This sighting confirmed for him the truth of Aristotle's claim that the world was round. Some years later he seems to have been associated with the family of the Ibn Zuhr, traditionally physicians and scholars of medicine. He is reported to have been well acquainted with Abū Marwān ibn-Zuhr, perhaps the most outstanding member of the family, and when Averroës composed his medical handbook entitled *Kulliyat* (literally, "generalities," which became latinized to *Colliget*), he encouraged Abū Marwān to write a companion text concerned with the details of specific ailments.

Tradition next reports that Averroës came into the favor of the sultan of Marrakesh, a notable patron of scholarship and research, through the personal recommendation of his friend and presumed mentor, ibn-Tufail. His ready intelligence seems to have pleased the *cālīf*, who, according to a student of Averroës, subsequently encouraged the vast series of commentaries on Aristotle which became known in the West around 1200. It is generally conjectured that the association among ibn-Tufail, the *cālīf*, and Averroës can be dated between 1153 and 1169.

Through the *cālīf*'s offices, Averroës was appointed *qādī* of Seville in 1169, and he began his array of commentaries on Aristotle about that time. In 1171 he returned to Córdoba, probably as *qādī*, and eventually became chief *qādī*. He was, however, continually traveling to Seville and to Marrakesh, as the colophons of various of his writings attest. In 1182 he became physician to the *cālīf* of Marrakesh, continuing as a court favorite until about 1195. At that time he is supposed to have retired, possibly under a cloud as the result of religious controversy, or perhaps to be protected from conservative theologians, to a village outside Seville; details are not available. In any case, he soon returned to Marrakesh, where he died.

His death coincided with the virtual disappearance of the dynamic speculative tradition evidenced in Arabic thinking for the several centuries after 700. Interestingly, it also coincided with the bursting forth of a similarly active tradition in the Latin West, which was greatly stimulated by the translations of Aristotle and Greek science from Arabic and Hebrew manuscripts. All these events—the death of Averroës, the abrupt decline of Arab intellectual dynamism, the translation into Latin of Aristotle (notably the *Metaphysics* and *De Anima* about 1200), and the exponential acceleration of Western philosophizing—occurred virtually within two decades. These are perhaps neither radically causative nor dependent events, but their close association is historically remarkable.

Writings. During the course of his active professional life as *qādī*, physician, scientist, and philosopher, Averroës found time to compose an impressive number of scientific, philosophical, and religious writings. It is possible that some of his appointments may have been, in part, preferments for the purpose of sustaining scholarship. Certainly in the medieval Latin West, many a Sorbonne scholar formally designated "canon of Rheims," for example, could rarely be found at Rheims fulfilling his canonic responsibilities.

Most of Averroës' writings that can be dated fall between 1159 and 1195. There is the medical encyclopedia *Kulliyat* (composed before 1162), along with expositions of and commentaries on such medical writers as the Greek Galen and the Eastern Islamic ibn-Sīna (normally latinized as Avicenna). There are writings on astronomy. In religious philosophy there is the famous reply to the philosopher al-Ghazzali's attack on the pretensions of rationalism in matters of divine law (*The Incoherence of the Philosophers*); Averroës' response is titled *The Incoherence of the Incoherence*, in which he strongly affirms the solid adequacy of natural reason in all domains of intellectual investigation. There are many lesser writings, on problems of divine law, on logic, on natural philosophy, and on medicine. Finally, there is the massive set of commentaries on the Aristotelian corpus, which profoundly affected medieval Latin thought—sometimes with official ecclesiastical approbation, sometimes not.

Commentaries on Aristotle. The commentaries on Aristotle are of three kinds: short, often called paraphrases or epitomes; intermediate; and long, usually meticulous and detailed explications. These different versions may well correspond to stages in the educational curriculum.

The commentaries survive in many forms. For some writings of Aristotle, all three commentaries are available, for some two, and for some only one. Since Aristotle's *Politics* was not accessible to him, Averroës wrote a commentary on Plato's *Republic*, under the assumption that Greek thought constituted a coherent philosophical whole. He believed that the *Republic* contributed to this total philosophical construction. In still a further attempt to complete the presumed integrity of all Greek natural philosophy, Averroës supplemented Aristotle's *Physics* and *De Caelo* with a treatise of his own entitled *De Substantia Orbis*.

In supplementing Aristotle in this fashion, Averroës did violence to the original methodology of the Stagirite. For Aristotle the *Physics* and *De Caelo* investigated motions and processes according to two different perspectives—*Physics*, motion as such; *De Caelo*, motion in the particular context of the activities of the heavenly bodies. These investigations were not conceived as standing in any hierarchical order, reflecting any vertical order of being or reality; they were simply different investigations and must not be taken, as did many ancient and medieval commentators, in terms of category and subcategory. Averroës, with methodological dispositions akin to the Platonic, did take them in this way, and thus eventually he found it necessary to provide an all-comprehensive celestial physics—hence, the *De Substantia Orbis*.

Textual tradition. The actual textual tradition of Averroës' works is extremely complex. Some of the commentaries remain in Arabic versions, some in Hebrew translations from the Arabic, some in Arabic texts recorded in Hebrew script, and many in Latin translations. These categories are not mutually exclusive. Beginning in 1472 there appeared numerous printed editions of some, but by no means all, of the commentaries; the format usually consists of a paragraph of Aristotelian text followed immediately by Averroës' comments on and interpretation of that text. This was no doubt an apparatus designed for the practical needs of the teaching of natural philosophy in the Western Latin universities, for it is clear that Averroës' analyses had become influential by the first quarter of the thirteenth century, accompanying as they did the translations of Aristotle, and they remained influential in the traditions of the universities well into the seventeenth century.

AVERROËS' PHILOSOPHY

Averroës' own philosophical position can best be characterized as Aristotle warped onto a Platonic frame. He inherited Greek thought as a literary corpus and, like his Islamic philosophical predecessors, viewed this corpus as an intellectually integrated totality. Aristotle, his commentators (such as Alexander of Aphrodisias and Simplicius) and such thinkers as Plotinus and Proclus were all understood as parts dovetailing into a single coherent philosophical system. Al-Fārābi (died c. 950) is an eminent example of this syncretism: he composed a work entitled *The Harmony between Plato and Aristotle*, and Averroës himself, lacking Aristotle's *Politics*, found little difficulty in incorporating Plato's *Republic* within his compass of speculation.

Reliance on Neoplatonism. The doctrinal positions of Greek and Alexandrian thinkers were, in fact, often quite divergent and even incompatible, and to complete the final union of their philosophies into a single intellectual system the Arab philosophers made use of a writing called the *Theology*. Late ancient tradition attributed this treatise to Aristotle, but modern scholarship has established that the *Theology* is fundamentally a compendium based on Plotinus' writings. This work was taken uncritically by Arabic philosophers as the capstone of all Greek speculative thought and, as such, was employed by them to effect the unity of ancient philosophy.

"Mystical" knowledge. There were at least two reasons for the eager Islamic approval of the *Theology*. First, it strongly reflected the Neoplatonic emphasis especially evident in Plotinus' *Enneads*, on the culminating "mystical" experience at the apex of human knowledge. This experience involved a passing from a condition of ordinary logical ratiocination over into a condition of nondiscursive (although quasi-rational) grasp of ultimate reality. Such an attitude is strongly sympathetic to the Islamic conception of ultimate religious experience, in which there is an analogous passing from individuality into an impersonal fusion with a Whole or Divine Essence.

Hierarchy of reality. Correlative to its reflection of Neoplatonic "mystical" knowledge, the *Theology* reflected the Neoplatonic methodological conception that is ordered in an organic hierarchy, with interlocking levels indicating superordinate and subordinate dependency. Such relationships involve levels of being and, concomitantly, sources and receivers of being. Such an intellectual structure might be visualized as a series of pyramids successively superimposed, with the pre-eminent pyramid pointing to an ultimate One which simultaneously comprehends being as such and is the culmination of human reflective experience. This structure is, moreover, dynamic and not static, with a continuing flow of creativity downward and a continuing activity of noetic discovery upward.

Analysis of the soul. The general methodology described above is evident in many specific places in Averroës' philosophy. In his analysis of the soul, for example, Aristotle's original doctrine undergoes a transformation. Whereas Aristotle's insistence on the physical principle that every form separate from matter is one in species leads to a presumption against the possibility of individual immortality, Averroës takes the obverse: separate forms or substances can subsist in the general hierarchy of being, and thus immortality, in a purely impersonal sense, is possible.

Scientific knowledge. The case in natural science is similar to that of the soul. In Aristotle the various sciences are diverse and not necessarily reducible to one another in any formal sense: the *Physics* views natural behavior from one perspective and in accordance with one set of working principles, while the *De Caelo*, in contrast, uses another perspective and another set of principles. Aristotle's natural sciences are irrefragably diversified. In the *Metaphysics* he goes so far as to say that similar terminology is employed in the several sciences; however, this apparent unity of the sciences is qualified by his insistence that the use of the most general metaphysical language is, in disparate domains, only analogous and not semantically equivalent. The particular subject matter that a science encompasses controls the precise significance of the terms and logic used in the analysis and description of that science; the term "being" as it is used in the *Physics* does not possess the same meaning as "being" used in *De Anima*.

For Averroës, however, such differentiations among the sciences were not the case. "Being" had a univocal significance, not equivocal, as it had for Aristotle; and Averroës viewed nature and reality as exhibiting a single coordinated and coherent structure, proceeding in orderly hierarchical fashion from levels that are lesser (both metaphysically and noetically) to greater and richer levels of being. Aristotle's horizontal and discrete conglomeration of sciences became a harmonious order of vertically structured science with dependent and causative relationships.

Active and passive intellects. From Aristotle, Averroës understood that the knowing process in man comprised a passive aspect—adumbrant concepts capable of being fully activated—and an active aspect—a power of dynamically activating such concepts. This power, termed during the medieval period the "active intellect," was taken to operate against a "passive intellect" to actualize concepts and thus constituted the thinking activity; and the resulting fusion of function was termed the "acquired intellect." This terminology applicable to the noetic process was based on Aristotle's *De Anima*, and appears, with minor variations, in Greek and Arabic thought down to the time of Averroës. God, as the First Intelligence, provides through the next subordinate level of intelligences—the celestial bodies, upon which he exercises immediate control—activating power for the active intellect controlling man's thought.

However, the active intellect is not personalized because it is Aristotelian form, and each such form is a species and never an individual. Nor is the passive intellect, in its nonnoetic status apart from participation in the acquired intellect—a further pressing of Aristotle impelled by Platonic dispositions. In Averroës' philosophy, consonant with Muslim theology, it is thus a domain of reality which looks upward to God for its sustaining power and with which individual souls strive to fuse impersonally, in knowledge and ultimately in immortality. Thus Averroës, and certainly his medieval interpreters, believed in the unlikelihood of individual immortality—the active intellect with which man hopes to unite at death being a single undifferentiated form—and the soul, as individuated in this life, cannot subsist without the body.

Metaphysics, natural philosophy, science. Averroës' metaphysics, natural philosophy, and science can be classified as a moderate Platonism, tempered with a profound appreciation of Aristotle. Unlike many of his Islamic predecessors, Averroës accepted Aristotle's rigorous rationalism wholeheartedly, although at various crucial points his renderings of Aristotle's laconic texts are governed by his own Platonic methodological predispositions. Against the latter, he held the principle of the univocality of being, flowing downward from a Supreme Principle. God's existence is established from the *Physics*, in that the eternity of motion demands an unmoved mover, which is in itself pure form. In addition to being the source of motion, such pure form is also Intelligence as such, operating not only as the source of the celestial bodies and all subordinate motions but also as the creative originator and sustaining force behind all lesser intelligences.

Theology and natural philosophy. In the Christian intellectual environment of the thirteenth century, apparent conflicts between argumentation in natural philosophy and argumentation in matters of theological doctrine became exceptionally acute. The newly introduced writings from the ancients—Greek philosophy and science, accompanied by Arabic and Hebrew commentary—rigorously set forth propositions alien to fundamental dicta of Christian faith: for example, the eternity of the world, the impossibility of individual immortality, and the radical noncontingency of existence as such. Averroës' rendering of the Aristotelian writings contributed heavily to these conflicts. Aristotle was read in the medieval faculties of arts as the staple of natural philosophy and science, and Averroës was read as his primary interpretive adjunct. In fact, in later medieval writings Averroës is merely referred to as "the Commentator." Thus, since he put forward analyses understanding Aristotle to deny the creation of the world in time, personal immortality, and the contingency of existence, such views attained wide currency among masters of arts.

The response from the theological side was early and direct. "Arabic" commentary was forbidden to be read in 1210 and 1215, and permitted only with censoring in 1231, at the University of Paris. Albert the Great published a treatise, *Contra Averroistas*, and Thomas Aquinas wrote about 1269, at a time of great intellectual controversy at Paris, a *Tractatus de Unitate Intellectus Contra Averroistas*.

"Double-truth" doctrine. The replies to Averroës were reasoned and moderate, but they seem to have been accompanied by many contemporary declarations that the

"Averroists" were actually maintaining a doctrine of "double truth," according to which conclusions in natural philosophy were said to be true, while simultaneously conclusions affirming the contrary in theological argument were held true—presumably an intolerable intellectual situation. Thus there were official condemnations of "unorthodox" doctrines at the University of Paris in 1270 and 1277, including specific injunctions against two standards of truth. It is not, however, clear that any philosophers in the thirteenth century explicitly held such a theory of "double truth"; in the writings that survive, philosophers faced with these conflicts take great pains to concede truth itself to the declarations of faith and say of Aristotelian writings only that they have been properly arrived at according to Aristotle's methods.

Averroës himself composed the short treatise *On the Harmony Between Religion and Philosophy;* his main effort in this work was to establish that there is but one truth to which there are several modes of access—the rhetorical, open to any man through the persuasions of teachers; the dialectical, available for some to explore the probability of truths of divine law; and the philosophical, to be used only by those few capable of exercising pure ratiocination with the fullest competence. Such a variety of methods insures for each man, depending on his individual capability, the possibility of grasping ultimate realities. The fact that in this work Averroës distinguishes between such modes of access to truth has, by many historians, been taken to adumbrate the theory of the "double truth," as attributed to many thinkers in the thirteenth century, but this is not probable. First, this work of Averroës was not available to medieval Latin scholars and thus obviously cannot have been directly influential; second, the doctrine of alternative modes of access to truth is hardly the same as that of maintaining incompatible truths in disparate domains.

Thus, the attribution of a doctrine of "double truth" to medievals cannot be sustained by any writings of Aristotle accompanied by Averroistic commentaries, nor can it be justified explicitly from any Christian medieval master. The oppositions between Aristotelian–Averroist argument and basic Christian doctrine constituted a fundamental intellectual dilemma within Christian speculation—one never resolved by the masters of arts in an explicit proclamation of a logical contradiction between two domains of reflection but always by an absolute accession of truth to faith. Averroës did not contribute specifically to the discussion arising from this dilemma, except insofar as his rigorous analysis of Aristotle made necessary certain conclusions in natural philosophy.

Averroës stands as a philosopher in his own right, but his influence was felt essentially in Western Latin philosophy from 1200 to 1650. His commentaries on Aristotle, an integral part of the educational curriculum in the faculties of arts of western European universities, shaped several centuries of Latin philosophy and science. Despite institutional criticism and even formal condemnation, his powerful statements of Aristotelian doctrine were sustained among Latin scholars and thinkers well into the mid-seventeenth century.

Bibliography

The most important general references are Ernest Renan, *Averroès et l'averroisme* (Paris, 1852; modern ed., Paris, 1949); Salomon Munk, *Mélanges de philosophie juive et arabe* (Paris, 1859), pp. 418–458; Léon Gauthier, *Ibn Rochd* (Paris, 1948); and G. Quadri, *La Philosophie arabe dans l'Europe médiévale* (Paris, 1947), pp. 198–340. The last two of these studies depend heavily on the first two, which are the unsuperseded (except in occasional detail) classics in the literature on Averroës, although Gauthier properly views some of the indirect traditions with caution. For Averroës' predecessors, mentors, and contemporaries, see George Sarton, *Introduction to the History of Science,* Vol. I (Baltimore, 1927) and Vol. II (Baltimore, 1931), *passim.* Significant recent interpretations, with varying emphases, can be found in Étienne Gilson, *History of Christian Philosophy in the Middle Ages* (New York, 1955); A. A. Maurer, *Medieval Philosophy* (New York, 1962); and D. Knowles, *Evolution of Medieval Thought* (Baltimore, 1962).

For a detailed catalogue of Averroës' writings, see George Sarton, *Introduction to the History of Science,* Vol. II, Part 2, pp. 356–360. Also see Léon Gauthier, *Ibn Rochd,* pp. 12–16, and M. Bouyges, *Notes sur les philosophes arabes connus de Latins au moyen âge,* Vol. IV, *Inventaires des textes arabes d'Averroès* (Beirut, 1922). The latter, a monograph, is in the *Mélanges de l'Université Saint-Joseph* (Beirut, 1922), Vol. VIII, Fascicle 1. H. A. Wolfson has meticulously stated the ambitious program for preparing and publishing modern editions of the Aristotelian commentaries in "Plan for the Publication of a Corpus Commentariorum Averrois in Aristotelem," in *Speculum,* Vol. 6 (1931), 412–427, and "Revised Plan for the Publication of a Corpus Commentariorum Averrois in Aristotelem," in *Speculum,* Vol. 38 (1963), 88–104. The latter article provides the most reliable listing of the surviving writings. There are other modern editions and translations of some works: for instance, E. I. J. Rosenthal, *Averroës' Commentary on Plato's Republic* (Cambridge, 1956); G. F. Hourani, *Averroës on the Harmony of Religion and Philosophy* (London, 1961); and S. Van den Bergh's translation of *The Incoherence of the Incoherence* (Oxford, 1954).

STUART MACCLINTOCK

AVERROISM. As a designation applicable to a tradition or mode of philosophizing, Averroism cannot be used in any account of Arabic thought after the death of Averroës (1198). After that, in a most unusual intellectual situation, Averroës' influence is to be found not in Muslim thought but in Western Latin philosophy between 1200 and 1650, for the dynamic speculative activity vital for five centuries in the Arabic tradition, which was founded in large part on Greek writings in philosophy and science (Aristotle's in particular), disappears after 1200, reappearing almost immediately in Western Latin thought. Throughout the century 1150–1250 a vast number of translations of most of Greek and Alexandrian philosophy and science were made from Arabic and Hebrew into Latin. This literary corpus, which had made its way around the Mediterranean littoral translated from Greek into Syriac and thence into Arabic and Hebrew, caught the attention of Latin scholars and such patrons of scholarship as King Frederick II of Sicily and Archbishop Raymond of Toledo. As a consequence, by about 1200 the indefatigable efforts of many translators working in many locations had made Greek thought, especially that of Aristotle, available to Latin thinkers. The impact of this solid and integrated corpus of natural science on the Western intellectual world was enormous, coming as it did into a climate where for centuries scholars eager for knowledge had had to content themselves with third-hand encyclopedic compilations of inadequately developed science and scientific methodology.

Averroës' commentaries. The translations of the Greek writings were normally accompanied by many Greek and Arabic commentaries. Commentaries by Alexander of Aphrodisias and by Simplicius were frequent, but those by the Arab Averroës on the Aristotelian works were ultimately the most influential. During a long and varied career as judge, teacher, philosophical and medical adviser to several Muslim rulers, Averroës found time to compose a series of glosses and commentaries on Aristotle's works. These fall into three categories—short (often called epitomes), intermediate or middle, and long, a differentiation which probably corresponds to stages in the academic curriculum. The particular argumentation of certain passages of Aristotle presented by Averroës in the mass of commentary had strong appeal for many Western Latin thinkers, and the reflection of his interpretations in their own philosophical analyses gave rise to attitudes which were first termed (by Christian scholars suspicious of their novelties) Arabic and later more specifically called Averroist.

Initial impact in the West. Upon translation the Greek writings, with their attendant commentaries, were rather quickly absorbed into Western Latin scholarship, but not without some formal opposition. These writings were banned at the University of Paris in 1210 and 1215, deemed usable only if corrected in 1231, and not officially introduced into the curriculum until 1255. This literature was nevertheless being intensively read during these years; the philosophical writings of Albertus Magnus (active at least as early as 1230), William of Auvergne (died 1249), and Alexander of Hales (died 1245), to name only three prominent examples, reveal an intimate acquaintance with the recently acquired corpus of Greek science. Similarly, in England the philosophy of Robert Grosseteste (bishop of Lincoln, died 1253) shows strong influences derived directly from the newly inherited Greek literature. In Italy, too, the Greek tradition was rapidly assimilated into the scholarly milieu, but the Italian intellectual atmosphere was either medical, as it had been at the University of Salerno for several centuries, or else legal, as at Bologna. There do not appear proscriptions by Italian ecclesiastical authorities as stringent as those made at the University of Paris throughout the thirteenth century, and the possible intellectual conflicts raised by the introduction of these writings into a context of Christian philosophy do not seem to have been seriously felt.

Intellectual conflicts became extremely explicit, however, when the Aristotelian writings were conceived to be in direct confrontation with doctrines of Christian faith. Aristotle asserted, for example, the eternity of the world, the unlikelihood of individual immortality, the possibility of man's attaining ethical perfection in this life, and other theses incompatible with tenets of Christian belief. The appearance of such philosophical conclusions, apparently well reasoned and buttressed by Arabic commentary, occasioned some severe crises for Western Christian philosophy.

The chief agents presenting these, as well as other, renderings of Aristotle were the commentaries of Averroës. For centuries he was called simply the "Commentator" in Latin writings, and his expositions of the Aristotelian corpus were read into the seventeenth century. Cesare Cremonini (died 1631), the last of the self-proclaimed Averroists, used these commentaries, and even at that late date he was considered unorthodox enough to be included in an array of formal proceedings along with Galileo himself. Unorthodoxy makes strange bedfellows when the resolute claimant of Aristotelianism and the architect of a scientific rupture with Aristotelian Scholasticism are included in the same condemnatory document.

Latin Averroism. Historically, Averroism is a designation applied to certain interpretations of Aristotelian doctrine by Western Latin thinkers. (There are medieval Jewish philosophers holding positions close to these, but the epithet itself does not seem to have been applied to them.) It was originally a term of opprobrium; no one called himself Averroist until possibly John of Jandun (died 1328), who was followed by Urban of Bologna (fl. 1334) and Paul of Venice (died 1429). During the thirteenth century Averroists were the object of violent philosophical attack and severe authoritarian action.

Averroës insisted upon, and many scholars in the Western faculties of arts concurred in, the reliable logic of Aristotle's argumentation. Thus, there was clearly the necessity of the purely rational acceptance, given Aristotle's premises, of such "unorthodox" conclusions as have been mentioned. Acceptance is, however, intolerable for serious Christian thinkers, and so such conclusions were taken to be erroneous and thus subversive when pronounced in the schools. When thirteenth-century arts masters taught Aristotle in this fashion, they were awarded (by their opponents) the pejorative title Averroist, and official action often resulted. Siger of Brabant, Boethius of Dacia, and Bernier of Nivelles, masters in the faculty of arts at Paris, were all named in condemnations of the 1270s. This special mention seems to have had limited effectiveness; although these particular masters disappeared from the intellectual scene, countless commentaries on Aristotle dating from the last quarter of the thirteenth century offer similar interpretations and similar caveats as to the logical validity, if not truth, of these interpretations. No recorded disapprovals have been found.

Incidentally, this represents another aspect of the history of intellectual conflict. Explicit authoritarian condemnations were more often the result of a refusal to accept organizational discipline than of a genuine philosophical error or ideological heresy. This can be illustrated in the careers of Gottschalk (died c. 868), Peter Abelard (died 1142), and Roger Bacon (died c. 1290), all of whom were subjected to ecclesiastical punishment although little of their thinking was drastically at variance with established or recommended philosophical systems.

The "double truth" problem. Every exposition of Averroism must examine the problem, arising in the thirteenth century, of the "double truth." The masters of arts, reading Aristotle and following his rigorous logic to conclusions incompatible with certain propositions held by faith, tried to resolve apparent contradictions by including in their commentaries reservations of this nature: "Although this conclusion has been reached according to the method of

Aristotle and the Commentator, nevertheless faith and truth declare otherwise." While proclaiming logical rigor and precise validity for Aristotelian arguments, they conceded the final determination of truth itself to the Christian faith.

In this historical context it has often been maintained, both in the thirteenth century and in contemporary scholarship, that such thinkers were actually practicing a system of "double truth," in which a proposition can be true in natural philosophy but contradict a proposition true in theology and conversely. But, as Étienne Gilson and other scholars have convincingly pointed out, no master of arts has yet been found explicitly holding such a radical position. Regardless of the apparent persuasiveness of Aristotelian argument, the truth itself was always the dominant prerogative of Christian faith. In the face of such overwhelming requirements, the limitations and inadequacies of natural reason were recognized by the arts masters.

Attempted solutions. Thus, an intellectual crisis of the first magnitude appeared in Western scholarship in the early thirteenth century. The attempts to deal with this conflict between important arguments in Greco-Arab philosophies and Christian-oriented intellectual systems fall into several main categories.

Reason not apodictic. First, the masters of arts, whose primary professional obligation was teaching natural philosophy, the core of which was Aristotle and his commentators, resorted to the attitude that although such science was orderly and rigorous, the unreliability of reason and the merely probable nature of its results suggested that conclusions based on such unaided reason must always yield, with respect to truth, to the apodictic proclamations of the faith. Such masters never claimed "truth" for a proposition of natural philosophy in conflict with a proposition of faith; they insisted on its logical validity, however, and conceded the determination of truth-value to faith. In this manner they endeavored to handle an intractable intellectual dilemma and at the same time to avoid subjecting themselves to overt charges of intellectual and ideological inconsistency.

Augustinians. Second, masters of theology—for example, Bonaventure, Peter John Olivi, and, in the first decade of the fourteenth century, John Duns Scotus—employed a methodology often termed Augustinian. Their attempt to resolve the difficulties entailed, essentially, an assimilation of Aristotelian natural philosophy into a hierarchical scheme of knowledge. Such a resolution provided a coherent and orderly vertical relation among the several sciences, proceeding from the less perfect to the more perfect, from the less well known to the more surely known, from the less exact to the more exact. Such a structure, culminating in God himself, the ultimate source of perfection, knowledge, and precision, could be coherent and consistent and could accommodate both Christian doctrine and a qualified, because essentially incomplete, natural philosophy. But the achievement of this coherence was purchased at the cost of Aristotle himself, for his scheme of the sciences does not envisage a vertical, or hierarchical, ordering, whereby lesser sciences derive their logic, meaning, and reality from superior sciences. His sciences are basically ordered horizontally, diversified methodologically, and irreducible to any single set of common and univocally meaningful fundamental principles.

Aquinas. Third, the pre-eminent theologian Thomas Aquinas (died 1274) attempted a massive resolution maintaining the logical integrity and autonomy of Aristotelian natural philosophy while setting forth a supplementary and compatible structure of Christian theology. The two disciplines run in parallel courses, with differences based on distinctive premises and arguments, but there are many points where the propositions in each discipline are the same and are concluded to be true in both domains. These points were taken by Aquinas to ensure the compatibility of Aristotelian natural philosophy and Christian theology, and by this means St. Thomas sought to sustain a consistent intellectual whole comprehending Greek philosophy and Christian truth.

The carefully poised system of Aquinas was not, however, influential in his own time, and most of his immediate successors in the theological faculties preferred to continue in the Augustinian methodology. By the early fourteenth century, moreover, both approaches—the Augustinian assimilative technique and Aquinas' sophisticated and delicately poised structure of complementary systems—were abandoned. This becomes explicit in the philosophy of William of Ockham, in whose thought natural science and systematic theology are totally independent domains.

Insofar, then, as the masters of arts, reading Averroës in close conjunction with Aristotle, tended to bring forward the incompatibilities between the two systems, it is possible to affirm the judgment of Étienne Gilson that "the rupture of Christianity is from this moment an accomplished fact."

Italian Averroism. As a designation Averroism disappeared in the intellectual history of the University of Paris after the first quarter of the fourteenth century, although there are many manuscripts making explicit these crucial difficulties; however, their overt dependence on and acknowledgment of Averroës' commentaries diminish. From about 1300 to 1650 the term Averroism—assumed favorably by some thinkers and in a derogatory fashion by others—is found associated with philosophical activity in the Italian universities—Bologna and especially Padua.

Renan wished to establish a dichotomy between Averroist and Alexandrist Aristotelianism in Italy at this time. This distinction was based on alternative interpretations of Aristotle's *De Anima.* The Averroist view emphasized that personal, individual immortality could not be established in Aristotle's writings. In this interpretation the soul, when separated from the body, loses all individuality—a conception congenial to the Muslim doctrine of complete impersonal fusion at the apex of noetic experience. In purely Aristotelian terminology this is known as the theory of the unity of the active intellect—that is, that any form distinct from matter is one in species and never individuated.

The Alexandrist analysis likewise denied the possibility of individual immortality but argued against the separate subsistence of the soul under any conditions whatsoever; when the soul-body composite dissolves, nothing remains.

This distinction is an oversimplification of the complexities of Italian Aristotelianism between 1300 and 1650, but it was employed by the scholars themselves and may thus be used with appropriate reservations. However, whether or not these thinkers were designated Averroist or Alexandrist, they all did agree in affirming the logical integrity of Aristotelian natural philosophy, even though some conclusions reached in this philosophy appeared in radical contradiction to dicta of Christian faith.

Although it would be misleading to speak crudely of an Alexandrist tradition in the later Middle Ages, there were eminent philosophers who, though thoroughly convinced of the logical autonomy of Aristotelian thought as such, did not adhere to the letter of Averroës' rather Platonic or Augustinian interpretation. Jean Buridan (died c. 1358) at Paris and Pietro Pomponazzi (died 1525) and Jacopo Zabarella (died 1589), both at Padua, can be taken to fall within the non-Averroist but still naturalistic method of Aristotelian natural philosophy.

Averroism as a term designating a tradition, type, or method of philosophizing is difficult to make precise. Thinkers of varied methodological persuasions—for instance, Siger of Brabant and John of Jandun—have been called Averroist. Averroism can, however, be solidly connected with Latin Aristotelianism where Latin Aristotelianism is taken to include philosophies that agree on the logical rigor and systematic autonomy of natural philosophy as exemplified in Aristotle's writings. Since such arguments appear to lead to conclusions inconsistent with truths of Christian faith, Averroism in its earliest usage was pejoratively employed. But the demands of reason, working with the Aristotelian corpus, were insistent, and by the middle of the fourteenth century philosophers began to proclaim themselves openly Averroist. Gilson has suggested that Averroism was essentially conservative and sterile, but it is clear that it was an integral part of the tradition of Aristotelian scholasticism and that its disappearance in the seventeenth century coincided with the demise of medieval Scholasticism itself.

Bibliography

The fundamental work on Averroism is by Ernest Renan, *Averroès et l'averroïsme*, rev. ed. by H. Psichari (Paris, 1949), originally published in Paris, 1852. Renan's basic argument has yet to be superseded, although manuscript research has recommended minor modifications and amplifications in his account. See also Hastings Rashdall, *The Universities of Europe in the Middle Ages*, rev. ed. (Oxford, 1936); Étienne Gilson, *History of Christian Philosophy in the Middle Ages* (New York, 1955); F. Van Steenberghen, *Siger de Brabant d'après ses oeuvres inédites*, 2 vols. (Louvain, Belgium, 1931–1942); J. H. Randall, Jr., *The School of Padua and the Emergence of Modern Science* (Padua, 1961); and C. J. Ermatinger, "Averroism in Early Fourteenth Century Bologna," *Medieval Studies*, Vol. 16 (1954), 35–56.

ARABIC ARISTOTELIANISM

The major figures of Arabic Aristotelianism are al-Kindi (died 873), al-Farabi (died 950), ibn-Sīnā (Latinized Avicenna, died 1037), and Ibn-Bajja (Latinized Avempace, died 1138). See George Sarton, *Introduction to the History of Science*, Vol. II (Baltimore, 1931), Parts 1–2, and Vol. III (Baltimore, 1947–1948), Parts 1–2; also DeLacy O'Leary, *How Greek Science Passed to the Arabs* (London, 1948). These important works provide references to many other equally valuable and supplementary studies. On the other hand, al-Ghazzali (died 1111) set himself strongly against the philosophical trends derived from the Greeks. His *Incoherence of the Philosophers* was replied to by Averroës in his own *Incoherence of the Incoherence*. In this debate the term "philosophers" is a translation of the Arabic *falasifa*, which is in turn a transliteration of the Greek *philosophoi*. *Falasifa* thus has the special meaning of "thinkers following the Greek tradition" and not the general sense of philosophers as such.

TRANSMISSION OF GREEK PHILOSOPHY

See Sarton, *op. cit.* Important additional works are G. H. Haskins, *Studies in the History of Mediaeval Science*, 2d ed. (Cambridge, Mass., 1927), and O'Leary, *op. cit.*

STUART MACCLINTOCK

AVICEBRON. *See* IBN-GABIROL, SOLOMON BEN JUDAH.

AVICENNA (980–1037), whose full name was Abū 'Alī al-Husayn ibn 'Abd-Allāh ibn Sīnā, was the most renowned and influential philosopher of medieval Islam. He was a Persian, born near Bukhara, then the capital of the Persian Samānid dynasty. His father was a partisan of the heterodox Ismā'īlī sect, whose theology drew on current popularized Neoplatonism. As a boy, Avicenna was exposed to Ismā'īlī doctrine but found it intellectually lacking. He received some of the basic Islamic religious education, then studied logic, mathematics, the natural sciences, philosophy, and medicine, mastering these subjects by the age of 18. A certain al-Nātilī introduced him to logic, geometry, and astronomy, but Avicenna was largely self-taught. He records that he was able to fathom Aristotle's *Metaphysics* only after a chance discovery of a commentary on it by Alfarabi (al-Fārābī). Appointed physician at the Samānid court, he intensified his studies at its excellent library. Thereafter, he states, he added little to his stock of learning but deepened his understanding of what he had acquired.

In 999 Samānid rule disintegrated with the onslaught of the Turkish Ghaznawid dynasty. Avicenna left Bukhara to roam the cities of Transoxania and Iran, serving local warring princes. Between 1015 and 1022 he acted as both vizier and physician to the ruler of Hamadan; after the latter's death he was imprisoned but was released four months later when 'Alā al-Dawla, the ruler of Isfahan, temporarily occupied the city. Soon afterward, disguised as a dervish, Avicenna left Hamadan for Isfahan, where he spent the rest of his life as physician to 'Alā' al-Dawla. This was a relatively peaceful period of his life, during which he undertook astronomical investigations. A serious interruption occurred in 1030, when the Ghaznawids sacked Isfahan and some of Avicenna's works were pillaged and lost. He died in Hamadan while accompanying his patron on a campaign against that city.

Over a hundred of Avicenna's works have survived, ranging from encyclopedic treatments to short treatises and covering, apart from philosophy and science, religious, linguistic, and literary matters. He wrote some works in Persian, of which the *Dānishnāma-yi 'Alā'ī* ("The Book of Science Dedicated to 'Alā al-Dawla") is the most important. Most of his works, however, are in Arabic. His chief medical work is *al-Qanūn fī al-Tibb* ("The Canon of

Medicine"), a synthesis of Greek and Arabic medicine which also includes his own clinical observations and views on scientific method. The most detailed philosophical work is the voluminous *al-Shifā'* ("The Healing"). *Al-Najāt* ("The Deliverance") is largely a summary of *al-Shifā'*, although there are some deviations. *Al-Ishārāt wa al-Tanbīhāt* ("The Directives and Remarks") gives the quintessence of Avicenna's philosophy, sometimes in an aphoristic style, and concludes with an expression of his mystical esoteric views, a part that relates to certain symbolic narratives which he also wrote.

PHILOSOPHY

Avicenna forged a comprehensive philosophical system that owed a great deal to Aristotle, but his system cannot be strictly called Aristotelian. In both his epistemology and his metaphysics he adopted Neoplatonic doctrines but formulated them in his own special way. There were other Greek influences: Plato on his political philosophy; Galen on his psychology; the Stoics on his logic. Nearer home was the influence of Islamic theology and philosophy. The theologians had stressed the contingent nature of things, subjecting Aristotelian causal theory to severe logical and empirical criticism. Avicenna undertook to meet this criticism and attacked the theologians' formulation of the notion of contingency, but he nonetheless was influenced by it. The Islamic philosopher who influenced him most was Alfarabi; Avicenna adopted Alfarabi's concept of the identity of divine essence and existence, and developed his dyadic emanative system into a triadic scheme. As both metaphysician and political thinker, Avicenna interpreted the Islamic religion in terms of his own system. Whether this religion remains "Islamic" when so interpreted is a debatable point, but it conditioned the way Avicenna formulated his philosophy.

Metaphysics. Although Avicenna's system rests on his conception of the Necessary Existent, God, he held that the subject matter of metaphysics is broader than theology. As distinct from physics, which considers moving things "inasmuch as they move," metaphysics is concerned with the existent "inasmuch as it exists." We arrive at the Necessary Existent by first examining the attributes of the existents. Avicenna undertook such examination in detail, drawing those distinctions which greatly influenced Latin scholastic thought. One such distinction is that between a universal like "horse," by definition predicable of many instances, and a universal like "horseness," in itself outside the category of such predication; considered in itself, horseness is simply horseness, neither one nor many. Related to this is the fundamental distinction between essence and existence.

If we examine any existing species, we find nothing in its essence to account for its existence. In itself, such an existent is only possible: it can exist or not exist. From *what* it is, we cannot infer *that* it exists, although in fact it exists. Something has "specified" it with existence; and this something, argued Avicenna, must be its necessitating cause. If it were not—if it were a cause that may or may not produce its effect—we would have to suppose another cause; and if this cause were not necessitating, yet another; and so on ad infinitum. But an infinity of such causes—even if allowed—would not specify the possible with existence. Hence, such an existent must be necessitated by another, by which Avicenna meant that its existence is the consequence of the essence of another existent. The theory involved here is that of essential causality, where causal action is a necessary attribute of a thing's essential nature and where cause and effect coexist. Existents form a chain of such essential causes; and since these coexist, the chain must be finite. Otherwise it would constitute an actual infinite, which Avicenna deemed impossible. The chain must proceed from an existing essence that does not derive its existence externally. This is God, the Necessary Existent, who, Avicenna attempted to demonstrate, must be eternal, one, and simple, devoid of all multiplicity. Since God, the necessitating cause of all the existents, is eternal, his effect, the world, is necessarily eternal.

The world emanates from God as the consequence of his self-knowledge. Self-knowledge, however, does not imply multiplicity in the knower; nor does multiplicity proceed from God directly. God's act of self-knowledge necessitates the existence of one intellect. Multiplicity proceeds from this intellect which undergoes three acts of awareness, corresponding to the three facts of existence it encounters: (1) God's existence as necessary in itself; (2) the intellect's own existence as necessitated; (3) the intellect's own existence as only possible in itself. These three acts of awareness necessitate the existence of three things—another intellect, a soul, and the first heaven, respectively. The second intellect, in turn, undergoes a similar cognitive process, necessitating another triad; the third intellect, yet another; and so on down to the sphere of the moon. The last intellect thus generated is the Active Intelligence, whose acts of cognition necessitate the world of generation and corruption.

Avicenna's cosmology was oriented toward the Ptolemaic system as modified by some of the Islamic astronomers, who, in order to explain the precession of the equinoxes, added another heavenly sphere beyond that of the fixed stars, and Avicenna inclined toward regarding the number of intellects as ten. He was not dogmatic on this point, however, leaving the question of the number of intellects adjustable to changes in astronomical and cosmological theory. What he insisted on was that the number of intellects should be at least equal to the number of heavens.

In this scheme Avicenna attempted to make precise the relation of the celestial intellects to God, something left uncertain in Aristotle. According to Avicenna, the intellects derive their existence from God and are arranged in an ontological and normative hierarchy corresponding to their proximity to God. God, for him, is not only the prime mover but also the cause of existence. The celestial intellects, in turn, although deriving their existence from God, cause other existents and act as teleological causes. Thus, in each of the triads the heavenly body is moved by its soul through the soul's desire for the intellect. The souls differ from the intellects in that they have a material aspect enabling them to have direct influence over the particulars in the sublunar world and to know them in their particularity. Neither God nor the celestial intellects have this direct influence and know these particulars only "in a universal way."

The human soul. According to Avicenna, both the human soul and the rational knowledge it acquires are emanations from the Active Intelligence. As such, the body "receives" the soul and the soul "receives" rational knowledge. Certain combinations of formed matter induce the reception from the Active Intelligence of the vegetative soul. Other combinations induce, in addition to this, the reception of the animal soul; and others, in addition to these two, induce the reception of the rational soul, with its practical and theoretical aspects. The human rational soul is an individual, indivisible, and immaterial substance that does not exist as an individual prior to the body—Avicenna denied the theory of transmigration. Further, it is created *with* the body, not "imprinted" on it. The body is no more than the soul's instrument, which the soul must use for perfecting itself through the attainment of theoretical knowledge; this involves complete control of the animal passions. Souls inherently incapable of attaining theoretical knowledge can still control the body and live pure lives by adhering to the commands of the revealed law. With the body's corruption (death), the soul separates to exist eternally as an individual. Souls that have led pure lives and have actualized their potentialities continue in eternal bliss, contemplating the celestial principles. The imperfect souls, tarnished by the body, continue in eternal torment, vainly seeking their bodies, which once were the instruments of their perfection.

Avicenna denied bodily resurrection but insisted on the Soul's individual immortality. To begin with, he held that the immaterial is incorruptible. Moreover, he was convinced not only of the soul's immateriality but also of its individuality. He argued for both these points simultaneously: When one refers to himself as "I," this cannot be a reference to his body. If a man were to come into being fully mature and rational but suspended in space so that he was totally unaware of his physical circumstances, he would still be certain of one thing—his own existence as an individual self.

Theoretical knowledge consists in the reception of the intelligibles from the Active Intelligence. The primary intelligibles, the self-evident logical truths, are received by men directly, without the need of the soul's preparatory activities on the sensory level. The secondary intelligibles, concepts and logical inferences, whose reception is limited to people capable of demonstrative knowledge, normally require preparatory activities involving the external and internal senses—sensation, memory, imagination, estimation, and cogitation, or imaged thinking. Avicenna assigned special faculties and physiological places to these activities. The human intellect undergoes various stages in its acquisition of the intelligibles. At first it is a material intellect, a pure potentiality analogous to prime matter, ready for the reception of the intelligibles. With the reception of the first intelligibles it becomes the intellect with positive disposition. When it is *in the act* of receiving the secondary intelligibles, it becomes the acquired intellect. When an intellect that receives the secondary intelligibles is not engaged in the act of reception, it is termed "the actual intellect."

Political and religious philosophy. Avicenna followed Alfarabi in holding that revealed religion gives the same truths as philosophy but in the symbolic, particular, imaged language which the masses can understand. According to Avicenna, some prophets receive this particular symbolic knowledge directly from the celestial souls. Such reception involves the prophet's imaginative faculty. In a higher form of prophecy that is intellectual, the prophet receives from the celestial intellects not only the first intelligibles, without the need of the soul's preparatory activities, but also the second. Prophetic reception of knowledge thus differs from the philosophical "in manner." It also differs "in quantity." Avicenna suggested that the prophet receives all or most of the intelligibles from the Active Intelligence "all at once." This intellectual revelation is then translated into the language of imagery and divulged to the public. It includes the basic commands of the revealed law, without which man as a political animal cannot survive. Hence, divine goodness must reveal the law at certain moments of discussion through prophets. Prophecy is thus necessary in the sense that it is required for the survival of civilized society and in the sense that it is necessitated by the divine nature. Having argued for the necessity of prophecy, Avicenna proceeded to accommodate Islamic institutions within his philosophical framework.

The high point of Avicenna's religious philosophy is his discussion of mysticism in the *Ishārāt*. In this work he adopted the language of Islamic mysticism (*ṣufism*) to describe the mystic's spiritual journey to God: Beginning with faith and motivated by desire and love, the mystic undertakes spiritual exercises that first bring him to interrupted glimmerings "of the light of the Truth." These experiences become progressively more frequent and durable until the stage of "arrival" is reached, in which the mystic has a direct and an uninterrupted vision of God. According to Avicenna, there are further stages beyond this, but he declined to discuss them. He also ascribed some of the prophetic qualities to mystics, without implying that all mystics are law-revealing prophets. On the other hand, his language suggests that he held that all prophets are mystics.

Logic and demonstrative method. Avicenna inherited the Aristotelian and Stoic logical tradition as expounded by Alfarabi and the Baghdadi school of logicians but treated his subject more independently. He found the then current classification of syllogisms into "attributive" (categorical) and "conditional" too narrow. Instead, he classified them as "connective" and "exceptive." Connective syllogisms have the *form* of the categorical, but their premises may consist of combinations of attributive and conditional statements. Similarly, exceptive syllogisms have the form of one of the two types of conditional syllogisms—the conjunctive, corresponding to the *modus ponens* and the *modus tollens*, and the disjunctive in which the logical relation is exclusive—but their premises may consist of attributive statements conditionally related, or combinations of conditional and attributive statements. He attempted the quantification of both conjunctive and disjunctive premises, discussed the temporal aspects of quantification in general, and treated the modality of premises and arguments at length.

Although Avicenna held logic to be merely a tool of knowledge and strove to treat it as distinct from philosophy, his discussion of the epistemic status of premises (which carried him considerably beyond anything in Aristotle) rendered his logic philosophically committed; his discussion of demonstrative premises was committed to his epistemology and metaphysics of causality. He followed Aristotle in his treatment of demonstrative inference, distinguishing between demonstrations that give the reasoned fact and those that give the fact. The former involve inference from cause to effect; the latter, inference from effect to cause. He also included in the latter class inferences from one effect to another. This is possible when it has been established that a single cause necessitates two effects; Avicenna gave a medical example of a disease that has two symptoms.

Avicenna's endorsement of the *Posterior Analytics* extended to much of the *Physics*. He rejected, however, Aristotle's account of falling bodies, substituting for it a theory of acquired force that was a forerunner of the theory of momentum.

Although some Jewish and Islamic philosophers (Maimonides, Avempace, Averroës) showed a preference for Alfarabi, Avicenna's influence overshadowed the latter's in the Islamic world. The mystical side of his philosophy was elaborated in the illuminationist thought of the philosophers of Persia. The orthodox Ash'arite theologians who condemned his metaphysics adopted his logic, and his medical works continued to dominate the Islamic world until the emergence of the modern university.

In the Latin West his emanative metaphysics and epistemology blended with the Augustinianism of the Franciscan schools as a basic ingredient of their thought. His influence on Thomas Aquinas was considerable, notwithstanding Aquinas' rejection of many Avicennian doctrines. He also greatly influenced the development of logic and science, his *Canon of Medicine* remaining an authoritative medical text into the seventeenth century.

Bibliography

There is no collected edition of Avicenna's works in the original. The closest thing to a collection of Persian works consists of Volumes X–XXV of the series *Silsila-i Intishārāt-i Anjuman-i Āthāri Millī* (Publications of the Society of National Monuments). These volumes, published by the University of Teheran, appeared in 1951 on the occasion of Avicenna's millenary.

Critical editions of parts of the *al-Shifā'*, in the original Arabic have been appearing in a series sponsored by the Egyptian ministry of education and supervised by Dr. Ibrahīm Madkūr. The following volumes have appeared: *Al-Madkhal* ("Isagoge," Cairo, 1952); *Al-Khaṭaba* ("Rhetoric," Cairo, 1954); *Al-Burhān* ("Demonstration," Cairo, 1955); *Jawami 'ilm al-Mūsīqā* ("Music," Cairo, 1956); *Al-Safsaṭa* ("Sophistic," Cairo, 1958); *Al-Maqūlāt* ("Categories," Cairo, 1959); *Al-Ilāhīyāt* ("Metaphysics," 2 vols., Cairo, 1960); and *Al-Qiyās* ("Syllogism," Cairo, 1964).

Translations of Avicenna's works include *Avicenna on Theology*, translated by A. J. Arberry (London, 1951); *A Treatise on the Canon of Medicine*, translated by O. C. Gruner (London, 1930); *Avicennae de Congelatione et Conglutinatione Lapidum*, translated by E. J. Holmyard and D. C. Mandeville (Paris, 1927); *Die Metaphysik Avicennas*, translated by Max Horten (Halle, 1907); *La Métaphysique du Shifā'*, translated by M. M. Anawati, mimeographed ed. (Quebec, 1952); *Le Livre de science*, translated by Mohammad Achena and Henri Massé, 2 vols. (Paris, 1955); *Le Livre des directives et remarques*, translated by A. M. Goichon (Paris, 1955); *Psychologie d'Ibn Sīnā (Avicenne) d'après son oeuvre Aš-šifa'*, edited and translated by Jan Bakoš (Prague, 1956); Ralph Lerner and Muhsin Mahdi, eds., *Medieval Political Philosophy: A Source Book* (New York, 1963), pp. 95–121; and *Avicenna's Psychology*, translated by Fazlur Rahman (London, 1952).

Studies include S. M. Afnan, *Avicenna, His Life and Works* (London, 1958); M.-T. d'Alverny, "Anniya-Anitas," in *Mélanges offerts à Étienne Gilson* (Paris and Toronto, 1959), pp. 59–91; E. G. Browne, *Arabian Medicine* (Cambridge, 1921); Henri Corbin, *Avicenna and the Visionary Recital*, translated by W. R. Trask (New York, 1960); M. Cruz Hernandes, *La metafísica de Avicena* (Granada, 1949); Louis Gardet, *La Penséd religieuse d'Avicenne (Ibn Sīnā)* (Paris, 1951); Étienne Gilson, "Les Sources gréco-arabes de l'augustinism avicennisant," in *Archives d'histoire doctrinale et littéraire du moyen âge*, Vol. 4 (1929), 5–149; A. M. Goichon, *La Distinction de l'essence et de l'existence d'après Ibn Sīnā (Avicenne)* (Paris, 1937), *Lexique de la langue philosophique d'Ibn Sīnā (Avicenne)* (Paris, 1938), *La philosophie d'Avicenne et son influence en Europe médiévale* (Paris, 1944), and *Vocabulaires comparés d'Aristote et d'Ibn Sīnā* (Paris, 1939).

See also M. E. Marmura, "Avicenna's Theory of Prophecy in the Light of ash 'arite Theology," in W. S. McCullough, ed., *The Seed of Wisdom* (Toronto, 1964), pp. 159–178, and "Some Aspects of Avicenna's Theory of God's Knowledge of Particulars," in *American Journal of Oriental Studies*, Vol. 82, No. 3 (1962), 299–312; S. H. Nasr, *Islamic Cosmological Doctrines* (Cambridge, Mass., 1964), pp. 177–281; Shlomo Pines, "La 'Philosophie orientale' d'Avicenne et sa polémique contre les Bagdadiens," in *Archives d'histoire doctrinale et littéraire du moyen âge*, Vol. 27 (1952), 5–37; Nicholas Rescher, *Studies in Arabic Logic* (Pittsburgh, 1963), pp. 76–86 and 91–105; Djamil Saliba, *Étude sur la métaphysique d'Avicenne* (Paris, 1926); and G. M. Wickens, ed., *Avicenna Scientist and Philosopher: A Millenary Symposium* (London, 1952).

Bibliographies include G. C. Anawati, *Essai de bibliographie avicennienne* (Cairo, 1950), and Yahya Mehdawi, *Bibliographie d'Ibn Sīnā* (Teheran, 1954).

MICHAEL E. MARMURA

AXIOLOGY. *See* VALUE AND VALUATION.

AXIOM AND AXIOMATIC METHOD. *See* LOGICAL TERMS, GLOSSARY OF.

AYER, ALFRED JULES, contemporary British philosopher. Ayer was born in 1910. He received his education at Eton, where he was a king's scholar, and at Christ Church, Oxford. After graduating in 1932, he spent some time at the University of Vienna familiarizing himself with the logical positivist movement, then little known among English-speaking philosophers. He returned to Oxford in 1933 as a lecturer in philosophy at Christ Church and in 1935 became a research fellow of the college. Army service in World War II kept him from philosophy until 1945, when he went back to university teaching as fellow and dean of Wadham College, Oxford. In the following year he became Grote professor of the philosophy of mind and logic at University College, London, where he remained until his return to Oxford as Wykeham professor of logic in 1959.

Ayer's first book, *Language, Truth and Logic*, was published in 1936. Its combination of lucidity, elegance, and vigor with an uncompromisingly revolutionary position has made it one of the most influential philosophical books of the century. As Ayer explains in the preface, the views he advocates derive from Russell and Wittgenstein among modern philosophers and from the earlier empiricism of Berkeley and Hume and have much in common with the logical positivism of the Vienna circle. But he accepts none of these influences uncritically and clearly puts his own stamp on the position he outlines. He adopts Hume's division of genuine statements into logical and empirical, together with a principle of verification which requires that an empirical statement shall not be counted as meaningful unless some observation is relevant to its truth or falsity. This starting point has drastic and far-reaching results. Metaphysical statements, since they purport to express neither logical truths nor empirical hypotheses, must accordingly be reckoned to be without meaning. Theology is a special case of metaphysics; affirmations of divine existence are not even false, they are without sense. For the same reason, value statements in ethics or aesthetics fail to attain the status of genuine statements and are exposed as expressions of emotion with imperative overtones. The a priori statements of logic and mathematics are empty of factual content and are true in virtue of the conventions that govern the use of the words that compose them. The tasks left for philosophy after this withdrawal from its traditional boundaries are those of solving by clarification the problems left untouched by the advance of the sciences. Philosophy is an activity of analysis and is seen, in the end, to be identical with the logic of science.

The second edition of the book (1946) contains an introduction which modifies, though it does not retract, the main theses of the first edition. Ayer's attention here is directed chiefly to giving a precise formulation of the principle of verification. His original version is replaced by a much more elaborate and carefully worded formula. Both versions have, however, been shown to be faulty in admitting as meaningful metaphysical statements of precisely the kind that the principle is designed to outlaw. Indeed, there seems to be a weakness of the principle in that it appears plausible only when its expression is left uncomfortably vague.

The Foundations of Empirical Knowledge (1940) is concerned with two groups of problems, those of perception and those of "the ego-centric predicament" (privacy and publicity in language and in sense experience and the problem of other minds). The most interesting and original feature of the book is Ayer's treatment of the terminology of sense data as a language in which the problems of perception can be most appropriately dealt with rather than as a thesis embodying a discovery about the facts of sense experience. *Thinking and Meaning* (1947) was Ayer's inaugural lecture in the University of London. It is a trenchant application of Ockham's razor to the problems of intentionality and the relations between minds, thinking objects, words, and meaning. This short, powerful essay has so far received less than its due of critical attention. *Philosophical Essays* (1954) is a collection of papers ranging over philosophical logic, the theory of knowledge, and moral philosophy. Half the papers are carefully argued treatments of problems raised in Ayer's first two books; in particular, "The Analysis of Moral Judgements" is a moderate and persuasive restatement of the hints on ethics thrown out in *Language, Truth and Logic.*

In 1956 Ayer published *The Problem of Knowledge*, his most important book since 1936. It is a sympathetic and constructive treatment of the various problems of philosophical skepticism. After a short discussion of philosophical method and the nature of knowledge, he discusses at length the pattern of skeptical arguments. He then examines three problems familiar from his earlier work —perception, memory, and other minds—as instances of skepticism at work. It may be that no statement is immune from doubt, but this does not entail that no statement can be known to be true. Where statements cannot, even in principle, be justified, we may conclude not that they are to be rejected but rather that no justification is called for.

The Concept of a Person (1963) is a collection of essays. The most striking, the one that gives the book its title, is a notable survey of some aspects of the problems of body, mind, and personal identity. The outcome can be roughly summarized as follows: to say that I own a mental state *M* is to say that there is a physical body *B* by which I am identified and that a state of *B* causes *M*.

Ayer's most recent work, embodied in his Shearman lectures at the University of London in 1964 and so far unpublished, is on induction and probability. This is a new field of interest for Ayer, although it was foreshadowed in two papers in *The Concept of a Person.*

Ayer's work is very much of a piece, both in style and attitude. He is now more catholic in interest and more cautious and temperate in expression than in his earlier writings. But his arguments are informed by the same principles and set out with the same grace and clarity. He leans perhaps too heavily on Hume's dichotomy of statements into logical and factual, and he has not so far set himself seriously to meet contemporary criticisms (particularly those of W. V. O. Quine) that have been made of this famous distinction. This is at once a weakness of his present position and, perhaps, a presage of its future development.

Works by Ayer

BOOKS

Language, Truth and Logic. London, 1936; 2d ed., 1946.
The Foundations of Empirical Knowledge. London, 1940.
Thinking and Meaning. London, 1947.
Philosophical Essays. London, 1954.
The Problem of Knowledge. London, 1956.
The Concept of a Person. London, 1963.

ARTICLES AND SYMPOSIUM PIECES

"Jean-Paul Sartre." *Horizon* (1945).
"Albert Camus." *Horizon* (1945).
"Some Aspects of Existentialism." *Rationalist Annual* (1948).
"Logical Positivism—A Debate," delivered on the BBC June 13, 1949. The participants were Ayer and F. C. Copleston. Published in Edwards, P., and Pap, A., eds., *A Modern Introduction to Philosophy* (New York, 1957).
"Professor Malcom on Dreaming." *Journal of Philosophy* (1960), 517–535. Malcolm's reply, with Ayer's rejoinder, *ibid.* (1961), 294–299.

WORKS ON AYER

For critical discussion of Ayer, see John Wisdom, "Note on the New Edition of Professor Ayer's *Language, Truth and Logic,*" *Mind*, Vol. 57, No. 228 (1948), 401–419, reprinted in Wisdom's

Philosophy and Psycho-analysis (Oxford, 1953); H. H. Price, "Critical Notice of A. J. Ayer's *The Foundations of Empirical Knowledge*," *Mind*, Vol. 50, No. 199 (1941), 280–293; H. H. Price, "Discussion: Professor Ayer's Essays," *Philosophical Quarterly* (1955); D. J. O'Connor, "Some Consequences of Professor A. J. Ayer's Verification Principle," *Analysis* (1949–1950); W. V. O. Quine, "Two Dogmas of Empiricism," in *From a Logical Point of View* (Cambridge, Mass., 1953); M. Lazerowitz, "Strong and Weak Verification I," *Mind* (1939) and "Strong and Weak Verification II," *Mind* (1950), reprinted in Lazerowitz' *The Structure of Metaphysics* (London, 1955).

D. J. O'CONNOR

B

BAADER, FRANZ XAVIER VON (1765–1841), German philosopher and theologian, was born in Munich. He studied medicine at Ingolstadt and Vienna and practiced for a short time, but soon abandoned this career. While he was in England from 1792 to 1796 studying mineralogy and engineering, he became interested in philosophy and theology. On his return to Germany he formed friendships with Jacobi and Schelling. Although Baader later broke with Schelling, the three philosophers continued to exert strong influence on one another. Baader was appointed superintendent of the Bavarian mines and won a prize from the Austrian government for inventing a new method of glass manufacture. He retired in 1820 to devote himself to philosophy.

Baader's two major works were *Fermenta Cognitionis* (Vols. I–IV, Berlin, 1822–1824; Vol. V, Munich, 1825) and *Spekulative Dogmatik* (5 fascicles, Munich, 1827–1828). He was appointed professor of philosophy and speculative theology at the new University of Munich in 1826. He stopped lecturing on theology in 1838, when the Catholic bishop banned the public discussion of theology by laymen, but he continued to lecture on philosophy until his death.

Baader's philosophy is couched in aphorisms, symbols, and analogies, and it is therefore difficult to summarize. He detested Hume's empiricism, Godwin's radicalism, and Kant's rationalism. He turned the critical method he had learned from Kant against criticism itself, calling for a return to the mystical tradition of Boehme, Paracelsus, Eckhart, the Cabala, the Neoplatonists, and the Gnostics. He believed that since God is in all things, all knowledge is partly knowledge of God. God is not an abstract being but an eternal process, eternally becoming. As God creates himself, he comes to know himself. The relation between his will and his self-consciousness is the Holy Spirit. The Trinity is an eternal possibility in God and only becomes actual in nature, which is the principle of selfhood eternally produced by God. Nature is God alienated from himself—his shadow, his desire, his want. The purpose of the existence of nature is to afford an opportunity for the redemption of man.

Morality is not a matter of inner law, as Kant believed, but apprehension of, and obedience to, God's will. Salvation depends on prayer, faith, and the sacraments as well as on morality and good works. Man is a social being under the law of the state, and the subject owes total subservience to his ruler. But the state is under the law of the church. Any departure from this divinely ordained order leads to the twin modern evils of despotism and liberalism.

Baader sought a theistic, Catholic philosophy reconciling nature and spirit, science and religion, the individual and society. He believed that philosophy had to go back to its sources, from which it had been separated since the time of Descartes. Baader was thus a precursor of the neoscholastic revival, but his own teachings, close to heresy, have no important place in the movement.

Bibliography

The collected works of Franz von Baader were published as *Sämmtliche Werke*, 16 vols. (Leipzig, 1851–1860). Vol. XV contains a biography; Vol. XVI, a systematic exposition of Baader's ideas.

Works on Baader are D. Baumgardt, *Franz von Baader und die philosophische Romantik* (Halle, 1927); J. Claasen, *Franz von Baaders Leben und theosophische Werke*, 2 vols. (Stuttgart, 1886–1887), and *Franz von Baaders Gedanken über Staat und Gesellschaft* (Gütersloh, 1890); and Kuno Fischer, *Zur hundertjährigen Geburstagsfeier Baaders* (Erlangen, 1865).

ADAM MARGOSHES

BACHELARD, GASTON (1884–1962), French epistemologist and philosopher of science. Bachelard was born at Bar-sur-Aube. He was a postal employee until 1913, when he gained his *licence* in mathematics and science and became a teacher of physics and chemistry at the Collège of Bar-sur-Aube. In 1927 he received his doctorate of letters and in 1930 became professor of philosophy at the University of Dijon. From 1940 to 1954 he held the chair of history and philosophy of science at the University of Paris.

Bachelard expounded a dialectical rationalism, or "dialogue" between reason and experience. His philosophy was a departure from the view of rational discovery as a process whereby new knowledge is assimilated into a system that changes only insofar as it grows. He rejected the Cartesian conception of scientific truths as immutable elements of a total truth that is in process of being put together like a jigsaw puzzle.

According to Bachelard, experiment and mathematical

formulation are mutually complementary. Mathematics is not merely a means of expressing physical laws, nor is it a static realm of ideas; it is "committed." In this context Bachelard talked of "applied rationalism." Bachelard held that the empirical world is not utterly discontinuous and absurd; the confrontation of an isolated, rational human mind with an indifferent and meaningless world postulated by some existentialists is naive. Scientific hypotheses, and even scientific facts, do not present themselves passively to the patient investigator but are created by him. The investigator's reasoning and the natural world on which it operates together constitute a second nature over and above the crudely empirical one.

Bachelard described his conception of this two-way process in which rational organization and experiment are in constant cooperation as a "philosophy of saying no" (*philosophie du non*). It involves negation because the scientific attitude is necessarily "open" or "available" (*disponible*), and the scientist may be obliged at any time to recast his formulation of reality by facts which fail to fit into the old formulation. Since it is frequently mathematical, the reformulation may not necessarily involve the adoption of a new model, but it will often be analogous to a change of structure. At the same time, there will be no jettisoning of truths: The *philosophie du non* destroys nothing, Bachelard held; it consolidates what it supersedes. The framework may be recast and the picture of reality transformed, but only in such a way that the new phenomenon might have been foreseen.

Bachelard did not confine himself to an exclusively rationalist philosophy of science. He saw both technological and imaginative thinking as issuing from reverie and emotion into practical expression. His works on the psychological significance of the four elements, earth, air, fire, and water, illustrate this. He rejected, for example, the common account of the discovery of fire in the rubbing together of two sticks, seeing it rather as the outcome of a kind of symbolical representation of sexual intercourse. Thus passion is no more metaphorical fire than fire is metaphorical passion. Our science and our poetry have a common origin accessible only to psychoanalysis. There is a unity in Bachelard's studies on reason and imagination. In both cases he stressed the projective or creative role of the mind; in art "the subject projects his dream upon things," and in modern science, "above the *subject*, beyond the immediate object . . . is the *project*."

Works by Bachelard

L'Intuition de l'instant. Paris, 1932.
Le Pluralisme cohérent de la chimie moderne. Paris, 1932.
La Dialectique de la durée. Paris, 1933.
Le Nouvel Esprit scientifique. Paris, 1934.
La Psychanalyse du feu. Paris, 1938.
La Formation de l'esprit scientifique. Paris, 1938.
Lautréamont. Paris, 1939.
L'Eau et les rêves. Paris, 1942.
La Philosophie du non. Paris, 1940.
L'Air et les songes. Paris, 1942.
La Terre et les rêveries de la volonté. Paris, 1945.
La Terre et les rêveries du repos. Paris, 1945.
Le Rationalisme appliqué. Paris, 1949.
La Poétique de l'espace. Paris, 1957.
La Poétique de la rêverie. Paris, 1960.
La Flamme d'une chandelle. Paris, 1961.

Works on Bachelard

For a complete bibliography of Bachelard's works and for articles on him, see the "Bachelard" issue of the *Revue internationale de philosophie*, Vol. 19 (1964). See also Jean Hyppolite's article, "Gaston Bachelard ou le romantisme de l'intelligence," *Revue philosophique de la France et de l'étranger,* Vol. 144 (1954), 85–96.

COLIN SMITH

BACHOFEN, JOHANN JAKOB (1815–1887), Swiss jurist, cultural anthropologist, and philosopher of history, studied philology, history and law at the universities of Basel, Berlin (under Savigny), and Göttingen. After taking his doctorate in 1839 in Roman law, he spent two years at the universities of Oxford, Cambridge, and Paris. In 1841, Bachofen was offered the chair in Roman law at the University of Basel, and a year later he was appointed a judge of the criminal court at Basel. In 1844 he resigned his professorship to devote himself to legal and anthropological research. In 1866 he also gave up his position as a judge. He traveled widely and lived for long periods in Greece, Italy, and Spain.

Bachofen's major works were in the fields of ancient Roman law and Greek antiquity. The work for which he is best known is *Das Mutterrecht. Eine Untersuchung über die Gynaikokratie der alten Welt nach ihrer religiösen und rechtlichen Natur* (Stuttgart, 1861). Following up Herodotus' description of a matriarchal system among the Lycians, Bachofen investigated diverse ancient myths and concluded that both matrilineal descent and matriarchal rule developed out of a state of unregulated promiscuity (*Hetärismus*) by virtue of the difficulty of ascertaining paternity under such conditions. He maintained that the dominant role of the mother in both the economic and political spheres was a phenomenon common to all primitive societies and that this role was inseparably linked to religious beliefs that established the secular primacy of woman on the basis of the cult of a female deity.

There is no element of evolution in Bachofen's theory. His main interest lay in tracing the transmission of social cultures, not in the biological characteristics attending heredity. Bachofen likewise rejected interpretations of myths in terms of individual psychology. The elements that constituted for him the essential ingredients of historical traditions—myths, cults and rituals, customs, law, and folklore—were *shared* characteristics and hence, in his view, objective factors. They embodied a people's collective "spirit," or *Volksgeist,* which, though a persistent continuum in social development, nonetheless operated at a nonrational and subconscious level. According to Bachofen it was the function of the woman and mother to preserve and uphold these nonrational historical forces and thus to exercise a uniting influence, whereas man, representing the progressive and rational forces, exercised a dividing influence over the development of mankind. The historical process consisted in a continuous striving for reconciliation between these opposing tendencies.

Das Mutterrecht encountered considerable skepticism, if not hostility, among contemporary anthropologists. Bachofen was charged with introducing rather fanciful and value-loaded notions into his theory and with confusing matrilineal descent with a matriarchate. But even though some of his theses have been disproved and others continue to be challenged, many of his suggestions have led to fruitful further research into the family customs of primitive peoples. Increasingly, too, Bachofen's works have been appraised as a major contribution to the philosophy of history.

Bachofen stressed the continuity of historical sequences and, above all, the close interpenetration of myth and history. In opposition to Hegel, Bachofen attached decisive importance to myths and symbols in the shaping of human history, since he accorded to them a far greater and more lasting emotive power than he did to rational concepts. In his stress on the irrational elements in history, as also in his insistence on regarding history as a continuous organic growth, Bachofen shared some of the basic premises of romantic thought. Yet, like Herder, the great precursor of romanticism, he never regarded himself as a romantic. Indeed, he explicitly repudiated the nostalgic sentimentality with which a number of romantics approached the study of the past.

Bachofen's political views show an undeniable affinity for the conservatism of the political romantics, but here also he was more directly influenced by Burke, whom he had assiduously studied during his stay in England. Paradoxically enough, Bachofen has often been associated with L. H. Morgan as one of the founders of a socialist philosophy of history. Bachofen did stipulate a "communist" origin of mankind in that he denied the existence of private property among primitive communities. He also prophesied an ultimate return to communism, understood in this sense. But he viewed such a return as a regression, not as "progress." Bachofen saw in socialism and democracy portents of social and political decay, for he held them to be inherently inimical to harmonious community life. Social and political harmony presupposed, in his view, the willing acceptance of the principle of subordination, for he regarded this principle as the prime source of a naturally and divinely ordered historical process.

Bachofen may have gone too far in the political application of his tradition-centered historicism, just as he probably overstated the role of woman in the development of religion, morals, law, and customs. But he did advance a functional conception of social development, in which social structures are seen as elements of a historical continuum and as constituents of an "idea-system" of nonrational and nonlogical beliefs and symbols, and in so doing he substantially contributed to the understanding of both ancient communities and societies of the modern world.

Works by Bachofen

COLLECTIONS

J. J. Bachofens gesammelte Werke, Karl Meuli, ed., 10 vols. Basel, 1943——.

Der Mythus von Orient und Occident, Manfred Schroeter, ed., 2d ed. Munich, 1956. Contains a selection of Bachofen's works, with an introduction by Alfred Baeumler and a bibliography of Bachofen's published works.

INDIVIDUAL WORKS

Das Naturrecht und das geschichtliche Recht in ihren Gegensätzen. Basel, 1841.

Das römische Pfandrecht. Basel, 1847.

Ausgewählte Lehren des römischen Civilrechts. Bonn, 1848.

Versuch über die Gräbersymbolik der Alten. Basel, 1859; 2d ed., 1925.

Das Mutterrecht. Stuttgart, 1861.

Die Unsterblichkeitslehre der orphischen Theologie. Basel, 1867.

Die Sage von Tanaquil. Heidelberg, 1870.

Antiquarische Briefe, 2 vols. Strassburg, 1880, 1886.

Römische Grablampen. Basel, 1890.

Works on Bachofen

Bernoulli, C. A., *J. J. Bachofen als Religionsforscher.* Leipzig, 1924.

Bernoulli, C. A., *J. J. Bachofen und das Natursymbol.* Basel, 1924.

Burckhardt, Max, *J. J. Bachofen und die Politik.* Basel, 1943.

Kerenyi, K., *Bachofen und die Zukunft des Humanismus.* Zurich, 1945.

Klages, Ludwig, *Der Kosmogonischen Eros.* Munich, 1922.

Wolf, Erik, article on Bachofen, in *Neue Deutsche Biographie,* Vol. 1, 502–503. Berlin, 1953. Also contains a detailed bibliography of secondary literature.

FREDERICK M. BARNARD

BACON, FRANCIS, Baron Verulam, Viscount St. Albans (1561–1626), English statesman and philosopher of science. Francis Bacon was a versatile man, if not the *uomo universale* so beloved of Renaissance historians. He was distinguished in politics, law, literature, philosophy, and science; he achieved the highest political office in the kingdom of James I; and at a time when the religious fanaticism of the Counter Reformation had driven modern science from its birthplace in Italy, Bacon became the founding father of modern science in England. He was not, strictly speaking, a scientist himself; he had no laboratory and he made no new discoveries. However, he was both the philosopher and, in an important sense, the prophet of modern science; he gave it its method and its inspiration. The French Encylopedist Diderot once said that the genius of Bacon lay in the fact that "when it was impossible to write a history of what men knew, he drew up the map of what they had to learn."

Life. The personality of Bacon is a puzzling one. His nobility of purpose and great powers of intellect seem occasionally to have been mixed with base unscrupulousness and sheer folly. But while admitting that he lived by his wits, he claimed that ill luck had obliged him to do so. He was born into the privileged family of Sir Nicholas Bacon, lord keeper of the great seal under Elizabeth I. His mother, Lady Bacon, was a woman of unusual learning and strong religious sentiments: she was a zealous Puritan. Francis, the youngest child, was frail and solemn. He entered Trinity College, Cambridge, at the age of 12 and later attracted the interest of the queen because of his intellectual precocity. His mother encouraged his earnestness and piety; his father, who hoped to see him become a diplomatist, taught him the worldly ways of a courtier. It was a contradictory upbringing.

When Francis Bacon was 18, his father died; and since he was the youngest son, he found himself at once virtually penniless. He therefore turned to the career that seemed to offer most to a poor man with rich connections—the law. He qualified quickly, and at the age of 23 he had already found a seat for himself in the House of Commons. But Bacon's influential relations did not bestir themselves on his behalf as much as he had hoped, and the progress he made was through his own efforts. Then, when he seemed on the point of being made attorney general to Queen Elizabeth, Bacon criticized her taxation policy in Parliament, thus ruining his prospects for office. He drew from this experience the conclusion that sincerity in politics is unprofitable.

Bacon's friends did better for him than did his relations; his best friend was the earl of Essex, the queen's favorite, who pressed Bacon's claims to office with unflagging devotion. But Elizabeth shilly-shallied because she mistrusted Bacon. When Essex finally realized that she was not going to appoint Bacon, he personally settled a handsome estate on his friend. A few years later, Essex himself fell from the queen's favor, and when Essex was accused of treason, Bacon was called in by the queen to prepare the legal prosecution of his friend and patron. After some attempt to reconcile the queen and the earl, Bacon did as he was ordered; and the same Essex who had done so much for Bacon was brought to trial—and then to the scaffold—by Bacon's efforts. Bacon defended his conduct in a pamphlet entitled *An Apology in Certain Imputations Concerning the late Earl of Essex.* His argument, against charges of perfidy, was that he had put duty to his queen above personal affection and that he had been morally right to do so.

The death of Elizabeth and the succession of James I improved Bacon's fortunes still further. He was made solicitor general, then attorney general, and soon afterward lord keeper of the great seal (the office his father had held). When the king, for reasons of prestige, wanted a certain prisoner tortured to obtain a confession and then pronounced guilty, Bacon obliged him while the other chief law officer, Sir Edward Coke, resisted. Coke was duly humbled, and Bacon rose to greater heights. Bacon was named lord chancellor at the age of 57, ennobled as a baron, then advanced to a viscountcy.

The rivalry between Bacon and Coke was more than a personal struggle for advancement. The two men were the spokesmen of competing philosophies of law; and it was Bacon's theory—an absolutist one—that the king preferred. All seemed to be going wonderfully well for Bacon when suddenly, at the age of sixty, he was ruined. He was indicted for accepting a bribe from a litigant, found guilty, and removed in disgrace from all his offices under the Crown. He did not deny the accusations but regarded his dismissal as a misfortune rather than a punishment; he admitted he was "frail" and "did partake of the abuse of the times." He spent the few years that remained to him writing books and working out schemes for the advancement of science.

Bacon published books at intervals throughout his life, and his interest in philosophy and science was never entirely separate from his activities as a lawyer and statesman. There was a good reason for this. Bacon believed that science, if it was to be effectively promoted, must be organized on a large scale and lavishly financed. Indeed, he was the first to see the amount of planning and money that modern science was to need. His aim was to persuade the king, as head of the state, to subsidize the new scientific institutions he proposed to establish; and he hoped that by proving himself to be a wise and successful statesman, he might be able to win the king's assent to his schemes. Bacon's general political theory was in accord with this ambition. He believed in a large, modern, centralized nation-state and in a powerful, dominant monarchy. Bacon was against medieval ideas of feudalism and the division of power just as much as he was against medieval notions in metaphysics.

All this underlay Bacon's disagreement with Coke. Coke believed that sovereignty resided not in the king alone, but in the king and Parliament; he also believed that neither the king nor the Parliament was at liberty to legislate as they pleased. The law itself—by which Coke meant the traditional common law—was supreme. Any enactment of the king and Parliament would be void if it were contrary to common law. Bacon rejected Coke's theory of the supremacy of the common law, preferring to ascribe supremacy to natural law, or to what he went so far as to call reason. He pointed out that legal theorists tended to be either philosophers, who knew nothing of reality, or lawyers, who could not see beyond the bounds of existing legal institutions. What was needed was the vision of the statesman, and this Bacon himself volunteered to contribute. The statesman was ready to agree that the judges should be honored as lions, but the lions should be "under the throne." Bacon argued that the throne should be above the law, not the law above the throne. It was this opinion that recommended him to James I, who believed that his right to make law came not from Parliament but from God himself. Although Bacon did not accept the divine right of kings in James's own terms, he did believe in the absolute sovereignty of kings, which came, in practice, to much the same thing.

Despite the fact that Bacon and his monarch saw eye to eye about the need to exalt kingly power, Bacon did not succeed in winning James's sympathy, even when he was closest to him, for any of his scientific projects. James was by nature a reactionary man; and his imagination was not in the least fired, as Bacon's was, by progressive dreams of human betterment.

To Bacon himself, such improvement was a crucial factor. The new science, as Bacon envisaged it, was not just an academic or intellectual enterprise to increase man's knowledge of nature; its purpose was to give man mastery over nature, a mastery that would enable man to transform the quality of his life on earth. Once again, Bacon spoke as no one had spoken before, as the champion of science, on the grounds that science could be *useful.*

Bacon's manner of death was much in character. He went out one winter's day to stuff a chicken with snow to see how long the cold would preserve the flesh. He caught a cold but retired to a damp bed in the best room of a nobleman's house in preference to a dry bed in a more modest room. This led to his death from bronchitis. The debts he left were colossal. He had always lived on a grand scale, excusing his extravagance, as well as his ambition and his corruption, by saying that he needed to live splendidly to hold power and that he needed power to do good in the world.

PHILOSOPHY

Bacon wrote of himself in the Preface to *De Interpretatione Naturae:*

> Believing that I was born for the service of mankind, I set myself to consider what service I was myself best fitted to perform. Now if a man should succeed, not in striking out some new invention, but in kindling a light in nature—a light that should eventually disclose and bring into sight all that is most hidden and secret in the universe—that man (I thought) would be benefactor indeed of the human race. . . . For myself I found that I was fitted for nothing so well as the study of truth, as having a mind nimble and versatile enough to catch the resemblances of things (which is the chief point) and at the same time steady enough to fix and distinguish their subtler differences; as being gifted by nature with desire to seek, patience to doubt, fondness to meditate, slowness to assert, readiness to reconsider, carefulness to dispose and set in order; and as being a man that neither affects what is new nor admires what is old, and hates every kind of imposture. So I thought that my mind had a kind of familiarity and relationship with truth.

These words might serve as his epitaph. His celebrated *Essays*, largely on moral themes, were published in 1597, when Bacon was 36. His philosophical works were all published after he had achieved high office under James I. They include the *Advancement of Learning* (1605), *Cogitata et Visa* (1607), *De Sapienta Veterum* (1609), the *Novum Organum* (1620), *De Augmentis Scientiarum* (1623), and the *New Atlantis* (1624). In the pages of these various works Bacon argued that "natural philosophy" had made no progress since ancient times; in many respects, modern philosophers knew even less than the Greeks did. Though he had a minimal regard for Plato and Aristotle, Bacon greatly admired some of the more materialist Greek philosophers, including Democritus. He saw no merit whatever in the speculative philosophers of his own time, whose work was barren while knowledge in other fields had made swift, and in some cases revolutionary, advances. Bacon mentioned the geographical discoveries of Marco Polo and the other explorers, the technical innovations of the men who had introduced the use of gunpowder and printing, and the great discoveries in astronomy by Copernicus and Galileo, who had taught men for the first time what the universe was really like. These, said Bacon, were the makers of a new world, and a new world needed a new philosophy. The traditional debased philosophy had nothing more to offer and had contributed nothing to the new advances that had been made in knowledge.

The traditional metaphysical philosophers, Bacon argued, were like spiders; they spun webs of marvelous ingenuity and formal perfection out of their own bodies, but they had no contact with reality. They existed side by side with alchemists and other such crude empirics, who collected a certain amount of random and recondite knowledge but could not put it into any coherent intellectual framework. Such people were like ants, who gather raw materials without selectiveness and store them up without modification. Spiders and ants were both bad models; a true scientific philosopher should model himself on the bee—he should work together with other men in the systematic accumulation of knowledge. Men should amass data, interpret them judiciously, conduct experiments, and thus learn the secrets of nature by planned and organized observation of its regularities.

The Great Instauration. Bacon himself called the method described above the Great Instauration, because he saw it as a technique of restoring man to his lost mastery over the natural world. The theory of the Great Instauration was presented in six parts: a complete classification of the existing sciences; the principles of the new art of interpreting nature, a new inductive logic, to provide a reliable guide to the invention of new arts and sciences; the collection of empirical data and the conducting of experiments; a series of examples illustrating the successful working of the new method; a list of the generalizations that could be derived inductively from the study of natural history; and the new philosophy set forth as a complete science of nature.

Such was the outline of knowledge that Bacon drew up. Needless to say, he did not complete the project. It was, as Diderot said, more a history of what had to be learned than a résumé of what Bacon had himself fully worked out. Bacon said, with a certain self-satisfaction, "I hold it enough to have constructed the machine, though I may not succeed in setting it to work." He saw himself, above all, as a pioneer, the one whose destiny was to make the decisive break with the past.

Respect for antiquity was a habit of mind that Bacon had, he felt, to oppose most vigorously. He set himself against both the Schoolmen—that is, against the medieval tradition in philosophy—and the new Renaissance cult of the rediscovered classics. The Schoolmen, with their love of disputation, only passed from one question to another, without ever reaching knowledge. The Renaissance humanists were so much in love with the style of the classical writers that they had come to cultivate eloquence for the sake of eloquence and thus to "hunt after words more than matter." Looking at scholars in general, Bacon declared that many of them sought in knowledge "a couch whereon to rest a searching and restless spirit" instead of a "rich storehouse for the glory of the Creator and the relief of man's estate."

The "Idols." Beyond the defects of current learning, Bacon discerned certain general tendencies of the human mind that needed to be corrected if knowledge was to be advanced. He called these false notions Idols, and he divided them into four types. The first are the "Idols of the Tribe," so called because they are "inherent in human nature and the very tribe or race of men." It is natural for men, said Bacon, to suppose that their senses give direct and veridical knowledge of reality. They forget that their sense perceptions are at least partially dependent on their own minds and that thus all sensory knowledge is relative. Our faculties of perception often act like "false mirrors," distorting what is received from outside. Our understanding imposes on the external world an order and regularity that comes from us and does not belong to reality itself.

Furthermore, said Bacon, our judgments are colored by our feelings—we tend to believe what we want to believe. For example, if we have a dream that comes true, we jump to the conclusion that our dreams are prophetic, forgetting the numerous instances of dreams that have not come true. The only way to correct this tendency, Bacon argued, is to give as much attention to negative as to positive instances of such seemingly connected sequences.

Such are the ways in which all men tend to be deceived,

and because they are common to the generality of men, they are the "Idols of the Tribe." But there are also defects that are peculiar to each individual; these are the "Idols of the Den." By "den" Bacon referred to the Platonic myth of people living in a cave, or den, and mistaking the shadows that pass before them for reality. Each person, said Bacon, "has his own private den or cavern, which intercepts and discolours the light of nature." Each of us is prone to interpret what he learns in the light either of his "peculiar and singular disposition" or of his favorite theories. Each of us tends to see the whole in the light of a particular part with which he is specially acquainted. Bacon had a rule that he thought might serve as a corrective to this tendency: whatever one's mind "seizes and dwells upon with peculiar satisfaction is to be held in suspicion."

Bacon called the third class of false notions the "Idols of the Market Place." Here he was thinking of the errors that arise from commerce and intercourse between men. Men converse with one another in language, by means of words, and words have two dangers: they are often ambiguous and they are apt to be taken for things. Two men use the same word with a different meaning and do not realize what they are doing; they think they are agreed when they are not agreed, and that they disagree when they do not disagree. Likewise, men treat those words which serve to name fictions as if they were the names of real entities.

Last come the "Idols of the Theater," the errors "which have crept into men s minds from the various dogmas of systems of philosophy." These systems, Bacon argued, are really inventions, like stage plays; they do not give a picture of the universe as it actually is. One type of philosophy is defective because it "leads experience like a captive in a procession"; another is worse because it has "abandoned experience altogether." Yet another type passes hastily from a few obscure experiments to create a complete natural philosophy. Then there is the type that confuses philosophy with theology: this was Plato's mistake. Bacon wrote sternly: "Not only fantastical philosophy but heretical religion springs from an absurd mixture of matters divine and human."

Views on religion. The above reference to "heretical religion" is a reminder that Bacon, for all his devotion to science, was no enemy of the church. Some of Bacon's progressive admirers—such as Diderot—as well as some of his reactionary critics—such as Joseph de Maistre—regarded him as an atheist who paid only lip service to religion; nevertheless, the category of the supernatural plays a prominent part in the outline of knowledge that Bacon gives in the Great Instauration, however little part the worship of God may have played in Bacon's personal life. Bacon's attitude toward religion was perhaps closest to that of the more worldly Anglican Latitudinarians of the eighteenth century, who believed that a national church was needed to provide for the spiritual needs of the people and to act as a firm prop for the state, while avoiding the fanaticism of both the Catholic and the Calvinistic teachings. Once, in speaking of metaphysics, Bacon said, "The research into final causes, like a virgin dedicated to God, is barren and produces nothing." Although this may sound like an attack on both metaphysics and religion, Bacon had no objection to either, providing that each was kept in its place. What he wished most to bring about was the separation of metaphysics and science.

However, in speaking of theology, Bacon certainly said things that skeptics like Diderot could regard as anticipations of their own ironical attitude toward Christianity. For example, Bacon said there was no reason to expect God's nature to conform to our own wishes or fancies, and that the more preposterous a religious doctrine, the more merit there was in believing it—just as in the realm of morals, the more painful the duty, the more virtuous the execution of it. Again, what Bacon seems to have been most concerned to say was that whereas it did not matter much what people believed in theology, the realm of faith, it was very important that they should not be deceived in science, the realm of knowledge.

Natural philosophy. Bacon divided philosophy into natural theology and natural philosophy. The latter branch he further separated into the theoretical, which seeks the causes of effects, and the practical, which tries to produce effects by applying knowledge of causes. The theoretical part of natural philosophy is, in turn, divided into metaphysics and physics; metaphysics is concerned with first and formal causes, whereas physics concerns itself with material and efficient causes.

In working toward what he intended to be a comprehensive account of man's actual and possible knowledge, Bacon suggested that part of our knowledge is supernatural in origin (it comes from God), while other parts of what we know are obtained through our own endeavors. Bacon further divided knowledge into reason, memory (in which he included knowledge derived from the senses), and imagination. Memory and imagination are concerned with things, events, facts; memory with what is real, imagination with what is feigned. Reason is concerned with general laws and ideas. In Baconian psychology, a man has two souls: one that is peculiar to human beings alone; the other, shared with all animals. The study of man's animal soul is part of science, but the higher soul is immaterial and cannot be investigated by the same techniques.

Bacon said that we can enter the kingdom of nature, as we can the kingdom of heaven, only by becoming as little children. But what does this mean? Bacon's argument is that to know anything is to have understood its antecedents or causes, and that knowledge of causal relationships is the greater part of science. To know is to be able to interpret an event as an instance of a general law, or to be able to put a particular fact into the context of a wider system, which would hardly seem to require a childlike mind. However, what Bacon was thinking of when he invoked the image of the child was a mind that was both humble and uncorrupted by false notions. These virtues are, so to speak, the entrance qualifications; the actual work of the scientist, as Bacon envisaged it, is by no means unsophisticated.

Scientific method. Bacon began the outline of his scientific method with what he called the three Tables of Investigation. The first of these was the Table of Affirmation, or "the rule of presence." This was to be the assembling of all known instances of a phenomenon that agreed in having the same characteristic. For example, if the subject was heat—a subject, incidentally, in which

Bacon was especially interested—then the scientific investigator would have to study all known instances of warm "bodies": the sun, flames, human blood, and so forth. However, such a study of affirmative instances alone would suffice to instruct only God and the angels, but not men. Men must therefore add to the study of affirmative instances the study of negative instances. This, in the case of the problem of heat, would mean the investigation of such entities as the moon's rays and the blood of dead animals, which do not give forth heat. Bacon's Tables of Affirmation and Negation are reproduced in John Stuart Mill's "Joint Method of Agreement and Difference."

Bacon's third table is the Table of Comparison, or "the rule of differing degrees." This enjoins the study of variations in different phenomena to see if there is any correlation between the various changes observed. When Mill adopted this method, he called it the Method of Concomitant Variations. To these three Tables of Presentation, as he also called them, Bacon added some further "helps of the understanding in the interpretation of nature." Such are his "prerogative instances." These are the cases in which certain events by their very singularity force themselves on our attention. Bacon divided these into no fewer than 27 types, of which the most important are the following; "solitary instances," where bodies, otherwise the same, differ with respect to only one characteristic; "traveling instances," where one characteristic is seen to change, as when water freezes and becomes hard; "glaring instances," where one feature is particularly conspicuous, such as the weight of quicksilver; "analogous instances," as when one natural phenomenon seems at once to throw light on another; and "crucial instances," which are the decisive ones when the mind is "at the crossroads" or divided between two equally compelling theories.

Although Bacon's scientific method is richer than any brief summary can indicate, it is undoubtedly defective in parts and in several ways outmoded. However, it would be an error to underestimate either its originality or its value. Some crude anticipation of Bacon's inductivism can be found in Greek philosophy, notably in that of the pre-Socratics, but these are fragmentary, whereas Bacon offers a complete theory, so complete that even J. S. Mill in the nineteenth century could really add very little to what he had said.

Some parts of Bacon's theory remain obscure, and critics are divided as to how they should be interpreted. This is especially true of Bacon's theory of forms. Bacon agreed with Plato that forms were the "true object of knowledge," but it is clear that Bacon did not understand forms, as Plato did, as ideas existing in some metaphysical realm. Bacon's forms were in nature itself; forms belonged to the empirical, not the metaphysical, universe. Sometimes Bacon speaks of forms as the *ipsissima res* (the real thing), sometimes as "the source from which a thing emanates," sometimes as "those laws of absolute actuality which govern and constitute any simple nature." It seems most plausible that what Bacon had in mind when he spoke thus of forms was something that later theorists—Locke, for example—called primary, as opposed to secondary, qualities. Secondary qualities for Locke were those properties of a material object whose existence depended at least in part on their being perceived by a knowing mind; primary qualities belonged to the objects themselves. Primary qualities included extension, figure, number, and impenetrability. Bacon did not give the same account of his forms, but it is fairly clear that when he spoke of forms, he was thinking of those properties of which an object cannot be stripped (even in imagination) without its ceasing to be an object.

Bacon was led from these reflections on forms—as was many another philosopher—into a flirtation with the ambition of all alchemists: to make gold. Bacon argued that the congeries known as gold has a certain schematism, a way in which its properties—density, softness, color, and so forth—are arranged. Find that schematism and the forms, and gold can be made. In a short essay on natural history, entitled *Sylva Sylvarum*, Bacon writes: "if a man can make a metal that has all these properties, dispute whether it be gold or no." Failing to find these simple natures, Bacon necessarily left his scheme unfinished.

Bacon was not a disappointed man, for he never expected that he would be able to do much alone, or that any man could do much alone in the field of science. Science must be a collective enterprise, and one of Bacon's just boasts was that he "rang the bell which brought the wits together." In Bacon's imaginary society, described in his *New Atlantis*, there is a college of science called Solomon's House, which is "dedicated to the study of the works and creatures of God." Bacon did not think such schemes utopian or impossible to realize. He was continually pressing on James I the idea of founding a great college where men could pursue experimental science; he proposed to set up learned societies for research and to create professorships of science at Oxford and Cambridge. None of these proposals were adopted in Bacon's lifetime, but several of them were taken up soon after his death: the Royal Society, for example, of which the grandson of James I—Charles II—was the enthusiastic patron, was an essentially Baconian institution; so were the various learned societies that grew up in France, where the influence of Bacon's writings was quite as great as it was in England.

The twentieth century, with its more sophisticated theories of scientific method, has become somewhat impatient with Bacon, and one seldom hears modern scientists speak, as Newton and Darwin spoke, of their debt to him. This may be because men have forgotten what the world was like before the lessons of Bacon were learned. There were one or two great scientists before Bacon's time, but they were men who worked alone and by largely haphazard methods. It was Bacon who introduced the notion of science as a *systematic* study. He was by far the most "modern" of Renaissance thinkers. In the words of one of his biographers, Thomas Fowler, "He stood like a prophet on the verge of the promised land, bidding men to leave without regret the desert that was behind them, and enter with joyfulness and hopefulness on the rich inheritance that was spread before them."

Works by Bacon

The Works of Francis Bacon, J. Spedding, R. L. Ellis, and D. D. Heath, eds., 14 vols. London, 1857–1874.

The Letters and Life of Francis Bacon, Including All His Occa-

sional Works, J. Spedding, ed., 7 vols. London, 1861–1874. Includes literary writings.

Novum Organum, Thomas Fowler, ed. Oxford, 1889.

The Advancement of Learning, W. A. Wright, ed. London, 1900.

The Philosophical Works of Francis Bacon, John M. Robertson, ed. London and New York, 1905.

New Atlantis, A. B. Gough, ed. Oxford, 1915.

Essays, F. Storr and C. H. Gibson, eds. London, 1918.

The New Organon and Related Writings, F. H. Anderson, ed. New York, 1960.

Works on Bacon

Abbott, A. E., *Francis Bacon: An Account of His Life and Works*. London, 1885. A sound Victorian exposition.

Anderson, F. H., *The Philosophy of Francis Bacon*. Chicago, 1948. The most up-to-date study available.

Broad, C. D., *The Philosophy of Francis Bacon*. Cambridge, 1926. A short, sophisticated essay.

Church, R. W., *Bacon*. London, 1909. A clear, scholarly exposition.

Fischer, Kuno, *Francis Bacon of Verulam, Realistic Philosophy and Its Age*, translated by John Oxenford. London, 1857. An influential nineteenth-century German reading of Bacon.

Fowler, Thomas, *Bacon*. London and New York, 1881. A reliable guide to the simpler branches of Bacon's thought.

Levine, I., *Francis Bacon, Viscount of St. Albans*. London, 1925. A useful introduction.

Nichol, John, *Francis Bacon, His Life and Philosophy*, 2 vols. Edinburgh and London, 1901. Chiefly of biographical interest.

Rémusat, C. de, *Bacon, sa vie, son temps, sa philosophie, et son influence jusqu'à nos jours*. Paris, 1857. Depicts Bacon from the French point of view.

Taylor, A. E., "Francis Bacon." *Proceedings of the British Academy*, Vol. 12 (1927). A little-known but valuable essay.

MAURICE CRANSTON

BACON, ROGER, English philosopher and scientist, known as *Doctor Mirabilis*, was probably born between 1214 and 1220 and died in 1292, probably at Oxford. Bacon wrote in 1267 that he had learned the alphabet some forty years before and that his once wealthy brother had been ruined by his support of King Henry III during the barons' revolt. He studied arts at Oxford and then at Paris, where as regent master (c. 1237) he was among the first to lecture on the forbidden books of Aristotle when the ban was lifted. Here he wrote his *Summa Grammatica, Summulae Dialectices, Summa de Sophismatibus et Distinctionibus*, his *Quaestiones* on Aristotle's *Physics, Metaphysics*, and *De Sensu et Sensibili*, and on the pseudo-Aristotelian *De Plantis* and *Liber de Causis;* he also wrote commentaries, now lost, on *De Anima, De Generatione et Corruptione, De Caelo et Mundo*, and *De Animalibus*.

These early lectures reveal a philosopher, immature but of unusual ability, conversant with the new literature of Aristotle and his Arabic commentators. They are of some historical interest, since Bacon was representative of the new breed of masters at Paris who prided themselves on being pure Aristotelians. In fact, however, like Avicenna and Gundissalinus before them, they were still strongly influenced by other traditions (especially Neoplatonism) that dominated such apocryphal works as the *Liber de Causis* and, in Bacon's case, the popular *Secret of Secrets*. This latter work, thought to be Aristotle's esoteric instructions to Alexander the Great, is a study in kingcraft which, in addition to advocating a sound, practical philosophy, gives much astrological advice and hints at the magical virtues of herbs and gems and the occult properties of numbers. From his glosses on the book, it seems that Bacon was most impressed by its vision of a universal science of great practical import which included all the secrets of nature. This unified science, revealed by God to the Hebrews, who passed it on through the Chaldeans and Egyptians to Aristotle, was concealed in figurative and enigmatic language but might be rediscovered by one morally worthy and mentally qualified to receive it. Where the pagans failed, Bacon held, a Christian might succeed. Therefore, around 1247 he left Paris, where he had been pursuing a mastership in theology, and returned to Oxford, where Adam Marsh, Robert Grosseteste's Franciscan associate, introduced him to that great man's work. For two decades, Bacon writes, he studied languages and the sciences, training assistants, cultivating the fellowship of savants, and spending more than £2,000 on "secret books," instruments, and tables.

Sometime during the latter half of this period he must have joined the Franciscans, to whom Grosseteste bequeathed his library. Neither his impoverished brother nor the mendicant friars could provide the experimental equipment Bacon longed to have; nor did the majority of the friars share his views on the importance of his work. Resenting the preference shown to the more orthodox theologians, Bacon became embittered and vented his spite in cutting and often unjust criticisms of some of the best minds of the age. Worse, his childlike credulity with regard to the apocalyptic literature of the times led him to side with the extremist followers of Joachim of Floris. This made his views suspect; he was sent to Paris and forbidden to circulate his writings outside the order. But Pope Clement IV, learning of Bacon's proposed encyclopedia of unified science in the service of theology and unaware that the work was largely in the planning stage, wrote for a secret copy on June 22, 1266. Hoping for papal aid to complete the project, Bacon, in the short space of 18 months, composed as a preliminary draft his *Opus Maius* (synopsized and implemented by the *Opus Minus* and *Opus Tertium*, the latter rich in biographical detail). With the *Opus Maius*, Bacon sent the pope a copy of his *Multiplicatio Specierum*, a concave lens "made at great expense," and "a precious map of the world." Unfortunately, Clement died in November 1268, before the last of the *opera* arrived.

Bacon probably returned to Oxford; he completed his *Communia Mathematica* and *Communia Naturalium* (two of his most mature works) and wrote Greek and Hebrew grammars and his *Compendium Studii Philosophiae*. The last, intended as a general introduction to his principal writings, degenerated into an emotional diatribe against the evils of the age; these were, according to Bacon, especially manifest in the universities where the two teaching orders (Dominicans and Franciscans) were neglecting his favorite subjects. It also revealed a revival of Joachite interests (Bacon referred to the ridicule his "logical proof" of the imminence of Antichrist provoked among the friars).

According to the *Chronicle of the Twenty-four Generals*, written in 1370, the Franciscan minister general, Jerome of Ascoli (later Pope Nicholas IV), imprisoned him for "suspected novelties." This account has been questioned, primarily because nothing could be found in Bacon's scientific or astrological views that had not been endorsed by many reputable theologians of the day, such as Albertus Magnus. More likely, it was a political move to silence the irascible friar, whose caustic views on the morals of the secular masters would do little to ease the strained relations between them and the friars (whose orthodoxy had been seriously compromised by the fanatical Joachite fringe). At any rate, Bacon's confinement could hardly have been rigorous or long enough to inhibit his penchant for frank expression; in 1292 he was writing in the *Compendium Studii Theologiae* on his favorite topics with all his old verve and biting invective. He died, however, before this work was completed.

Thought. The strength and the weakness of Bacon's erratic genius are nowhere more apparent than in the *Opus Maius*, his most characteristic and distinctive work. Both a plea and a plan for educational reform along the study lines pursued by Bacon himself, it is divided into seven parts—the causes of error, philosophy, the study of languages, mathematics, optics, experimental science, and moral philosophy. The first part descries four barriers blocking the road to truth: submission to unworthy authority (for example, crediting living theologians with a prestige due only to the Church Fathers or the Scriptures), the influence of custom, popular prejudice, and concealment of one's ignorance with a technical show of wisdom. Although by far the greatest portion of the book is devoted to mathematics, optics, and moral philosophy (to which, Bacon claimed, all speculative science should be ordered), Bacon's fame until recently rested on this first part and the relatively short section on experimental science. The belief that experimental science was the keystone of Bacon's reform was in part based on the misleading evidence of Samuel Jebb's 1733 edition of the *Opus Maius*, which omitted Part VII. By *scientia experimentalis*, however, Bacon meant any knowledge through experience as opposed to inferential or reasoned knowledge. When he said that nothing can be known with certainty without experience, his use of the term "experience" was twofold. One aspect of experience is based on sense perception and is called human or philosophical; the other aspect is interior and is derived from an illumination of the mind by God (whom Bacon identified with Aristotle's agent intellect). Thus, although sense perception is necessary to knowledge, certainty cannot be attained without divine illumination. Interior experience admits of seven degrees, beginning with that required for certitude in mathematics or the natural sciences and culminating in such mystical or ecstatic states as St. Paul's vision of heaven.

Bacon devoted the most attention, however, to what man can know about the wonders of nature by sense perception and the first degree of illumination. From the examples cited in Part VI and throughout the work, Bacon seems to have been less an original experimenter and more a propagandist for scientists such as Peter of Maricourt. His contributions to scientific theory, like his empirical research, were confined largely to optics. With the aid of new source material from Alhazen and Alkindi, he was able to develop significantly many of Grosseteste's views concerning the tides, heat, and double refraction and to give the most mature expression to Grosseteste's theory that light (and all physical force generally) is transmitted in pulses like sound waves. Since this "multiplication of species" requires a medium, Bacon argued, the transmission cannot be instantaneous, even though the time interval is imperceptible. His application of the theory to vision and the working of the eye was one of the most important studies done on this subject during the Middle Ages and became the point of departure for developments in the seventeenth century. Bacon seems to have surpassed his teachers both in his knowledge of convex lenses and parabolic mirrors and in his ability to foresee such applications of science as automobiles, motorboats, and aircraft.

If, by continuing the Oxford tradition begun by Grosseteste, Bacon was in advance of his contemporaries, he was also incredibly naive in some of his other views. His uncritical acceptance of what others claimed to have observed is often in violation of his own canons for avoiding error. Much of his stress on the importance of language studies came from his conviction that all knowledge can be found in the Scriptures and "secret books," whose full meaning God reveals by interior illumination only to those whose lives are pure. He held that because of men's sins, God's scientific revelations were obscured by errors—which is one reason for testing empirically what the ancient sages say. Bacon seems to have had little use for abstract reasoning or speculation for its own sake. His interest in mathematics and logic, like his interest in astrology and alchemy, was purely practical. If all physical force, like light, is propagated rectilinearly, it is subject to geometric analysis. This, together with his conviction that the movement of the planets influences all terrestrial events except free will itself, was his reason for thinking that mathematics is the key to all natural sciences.

Not only was his faith in astrology unwarranted, but his ideas of theology belonged to a bygone age. Even prior to 1250, the Paris Franciscans, impressed by the Euclidean-Aristotelian ideal of a deductive science, were exploring how far the concepts of theology might be analyzed with greater logical rigor and theological propositions formalized in terms of axioms (first principles of reason and philosophy), postulates (the articles of faith), and theses (theological conclusions). Despite his sporadic attendance at theological lectures, Bacon seems to have had no comprehension of what the avant-garde theologians were doing. Perhaps this, more than any insistence on scientific values or the need for experimentation, brought him into conflict with his educated confreres, who apparently considered him, for all his flashes of brilliance and his scientific lore, something of a crank.

Bibliography

Fr. Rogeri Bacon Opera Quaedam Hactenus Inedita, J. S. Brewer, ed. (London, 1859) contains *Opus Tertium, Opus Minus, Compendium Studii Philosophiae*, and *Epistola de Secretis Operibus et de Nullitate Magiae*. For supplements to *Opus Tertium*, see Pierre Duhem, *Un Fragment inédit de l'Opus tertium de R. Bacon* (Quaracchi, 1909), and A. G. Little, *Part of the Opus Tertium of Roger Bacon* (Aberdeen, 1912). Also see J. H. Bridges, ed., *Opus Majus*, 3 vols. (Oxford, 1897–1900; reprinted Frankfurt am Main, 1964), Vol. II of which contains *Multiplicatio Specierum* as an appendix. For the complete text of Part VII, which is incomplete in Bridges, see F. Delorme and E. Massa, *Rogeri Baconis Moralis Philosophia* (Zurich, 1953).

Other writings by Bacon may be found in F. A. Gasquet, "An Unpublished Fragment of a Work by Roger Bacon," in *English Historical Review*, Vol. 12 (1897), 494–517, a prefatory letter to the *Opus Maius* or *Opus Minus* or both; E. Nolan and S. A. Hirsch, *The Greek Grammar of Roger Bacon and a Fragment of his Hebrew Grammar* (Cambridge, 1902); and H. Rashdall, ed., *Fr. Rogeri Bacon Compendium Studii Theologiae* (Aberdeen, 1911). Most of Bacon's remaining works have been published by R. Steele (with individual volumes by F. M. Delorme, A. G. Little, and E. Withington) in *Opera Hactenus Inedita Fratris Rogeri Baconis*, 16 fascicles (Oxford, 1905 – 1940). The *Compotus* (Fasc. 6), ascribed to Bacon, is, however, the work of Giles of Lessines. See also S. H. Thomson, "An Unnoticed Treatise by Roger Bacon on Time and Motion," in *Isis*, Vol. 27 (1937), 219–224, and F. M. Delorme, "Le Prologue de R. Bacon à son traité De influentiis agentium," in *Antonianum*, Vol. 18 (1943), 81–90.

English translations of Bacon's work are R. B. Burke, *The "Opus Majus" of Roger Bacon*, 2 vols. (Philadelphia, 1928; reprinted New York, 1962), and T. L. Davis, *Roger Bacon's Letter Concerning the Marvelous Power of Art and Nature and Concerning the Nullity of Magic* (Easton, Pa., 1923). For a bibliography of Bacon's works, see F. Alessio, "Un seculo di studi su Ruggero Bacone (1848–1957)," in *Rivista critica di storia della filosofia*, Vol. 14 (1959), 81–108.

A discussion of the life and works of Roger Bacon appears in the introduction and appendix of A. G. Little, *Roger Bacon Essays Contributed by Various Authors on the Occasion of the Commemoration of the Seventh Centenary of His Birth* (Oxford, 1914). Also see S. C. Easton, *Roger Bacon and His Search for a Universal Science* (Oxford and New York, 1952), which contains an extensive and annotated bibliography. For a discussion of Bacon's philosophy, see T. Crowley, *Roger Bacon, the Problem of the Soul in His Philosophical Commentaries* (Louvain and Dublin, 1950), a good account of hylomorphic theory; D. Sharp, *Franciscan Philosophy at Oxford* (Oxford, 1930); and E. Heck, *Roger Bacon. Ein mittelalterlicher Versuch einer historischen und systematischen Religionswissenschaft* (Bonn, 1957). For Bacon's contributions to science, see L. Thorndike, *A History of Magic and Experimental Science* (New York, 1929), Vol. II, pp. 616–691, which minimizes Bacon's contributions—a reaction to earlier exaggerations; and A. C. Crombie, *Robert Grosseteste and the Origins of Experimental Science 1100–1700* (Oxford, 1953), pp. 139–162, a more balanced account.

ALLAN B. WOLTER, O.F.M.

BAHRDT, CARL FRIEDRICH, probably the most widely read German theologian except for Luther, was born in 1740 or 1741 in Bischofswerda in the electorate of Saxony. He held professorships and lectureships of theology, Biblical studies, Christian ethics, classical languages, and many other subjects at the universities of Leipzig, Erfurt, Giessen, and Halle. He was the headmaster of a boys school, or *Philanthropinum*, in Marschlins in Switzerland and established his own *Philanthropinum* in Heidesheim while he was at the same time *Superintendent* (the highest ecclesiastical official) in the domains of Count Carl of Leiningen-Dachsburg. In his last years, he was an innkeeper near Halle. He died at Halle in 1792.

Bahrdt was always at the center of a controversy. In his early days he wrote in a fiery orthodox vein, but very soon he seems to have been started on the road to "enlightenment" by suddenly learning that the language of I John 5:7, did not, when subjected to philological scrutiny, constitute proof of the doctrine of the Trinity. He was still further dismayed to learn that the passage was considered by some excellent scholars to be an interpolation. Bahrdt then set out to find undoubted philological support for the orthodox Lutheran system of theology, and instead found that his doubts continued to increase, until by the end of his life he had arrived at a fully rationalistic concept of natural religion.

The high points in Bahrdt's "Rationalist's Progress" are his four-volume paraphrase of the New Testament, *Neueste Offenbarungen Gottes* (Riga, 1773–1774), his confession of faith, *Glaubensbekenntnis, veranlasst durch ein Kaiserliches Reichshofratsconclusum* (1779), and his fictionalized life of Jesus, *Briefe über die Bibel im Volkston* (Halle, 1782–1783) and *Ausführung des Plans und Zweckes Jesu* (Berlin, 1783–1785). Bahrdt's New Testament paraphrase was up-to-date, intelligible, fluent, and coherent, but it was also a propagandistic vehicle for his heretical views. His enemies were thus enabled to secure, in 1778, a decree barring him from all ecclesiastical offices in the Holy Roman Empire and adjuring him to recant. Bahrdt immediately published his confession of faith, stating in clear and succinct language what he did and did not believe. Through discarding beliefs that he felt could not endure the acid test of rational examination, Bahrdt was left with a Jesus who was a mere product of his life and time. In this almost completely naturalistic view, the teasing question was, "In what way did Jesus obtain his amazing wisdom?" In order to give a hypothetical answer to this question, Bahrdt produced his fictional life of Jesus, the culmination of his development and the first work of its kind. It took the form of a series of weekly letters about the Bible, written in a popular vein, and tried to demonstrate how Jesus might have learned and built up his teachings from the writings of Greek sages, which Providence could have put into his hands through his association with Hellenistic Jews. These first letters were continued in a series on the execution of Jesus' plan and purpose, in which Bahrdt advanced the theory that Jesus founded a kind of Freemasonry to aid him in his purpose to destroy superstition, eliminate all positive religion, restore reason to its rightful rule, and unite people in a rational faith in God, Providence, and Immortality.

Bibliography

Bahrdt, C. F., *Dr. Carl Friedrich Bahrdts Geschichte seines Lebens, seiner Meinungen und Schicksale.* Berlin, 1790–1791.

Brewer, John T., *"Gesunde Vernunft" and the New Testament: A Study of C. F. Bahrdt's* Die neuesten Offenbarungen Gottes. Austin, Texas, 1962.

Flygt, S. G., *The Notorious Dr. Bahrdt.* Nashville, Tenn. 1963.

Schweitzer, Albert, *Geschichte der Leben-Jesu-Forschung.* Tübingen, 1913.

STEN G. FLYGT

BAHYA BEN JOSEPH IBN PAQUDA (fl. 11th century), Jewish Neoplatonist, was the author of the first systematic philosophic work on ethics in the Jewish tradition. Beyond the fact that he served as a judge (*dayyan*) of the rabbinical court in Saragossa, details of his life are unknown. About 1040 he wrote in Arabic *Al-Hidaja ila Faraid al-Qulub* ("Guide to the Duties of the Heart"). This work, as translated into Hebrew about 1160 by Judah ibn Tibbon, under the title *Hoboth Ha-Lebaboth (Duties of the Heart)*, has achieved great popularity, both in full text and in abridged versions.

Bahya's work cites Arabic as well as Jewish philosophers and contains many fine quotations from Arabic literature. There are considerable similarities between his general philosophic orientation and that of the Arabic school of encyclopedists known as the Brothers of Purity. If this relationship is accepted, there is no need to search further for the sources of the somewhat mystical, somewhat ascetic Neoplatonism that moderates the generally Aristotelian character of his position. It has also been suggested that Bahya fell under the influence of the Sufi mystics of Islam, chiefly because of his emphasis on the cultivation of self-renunciation and indifference to the goods of the world in the last three books of *Duties of the Heart*.

The distinction between outward and inward obligation, "duties of the limbs" and "duties of the heart," which accounts for the title of the treatise, is a familiar distinction in both Arabic and Hindu religious literature. Bahya used the theme to suggest that the rabbis, the leaders of the Jewish community, were overly concerned with the external obligations of men, rather than with the duties of the heart, and that, because of the rabbis' insistence on the duties of the limbs, the masses of the Jewish people remained totally unconcerned about all religious obligations. He tried to correct this deficiency by presenting Judaism as a message of great spiritual vitality and force, directed to the human heart and resting on the threefold base of reason, revelation, and tradition. The fundamental principle upon which the whole structure of Bahya's work is based is the wholehearted conviction of God's existence and unity, the subject of the first book of *Duties of the Heart*. From this, he moves to the necessity for apprehending the wisdom, power, and goodness of God by careful study of the larger world in which we live and the smaller world of our own human nature. In this latter study there emerge the duties of the heart: service of God, trust in God, wholehearted devotion to God, humility in God's presence, repentance, self-communion, and renunciation. In this way, man reaches the height of the religious life, the love of God. Despite the superficially rational structure of the book, Bahya was not truly a rationalist; rather, he used the techniques of reason to subserve the ends of a contemplative view of life whose method was moral intuition, and whose goal was piety.

An Arabic treatise, *Ma'ani al-Nafs* ("The Attributes of the Soul"), known only in manuscript until its publication in the early twentieth century, bears the name of Bahya on its title page, but this is now generally conceded not to be his work. No other works of Bahya are known.

Bibliography

For Bahya's work, see *Torath Hoboth Ha-Lebaboth*, 5 vols. (New York, 1925–1947). This contains Judah ibn Tibbon's Hebrew translation plus a facing English translation and an introduction by Moses Hyamson.

For discussions of Bahya, see Isaac Husik, *A History of Mediaeval Jewish Philosophy* (New York and Philadelphia, 1916); Jacob B. Agus, *The Evolution of Jewish Thought* (London and New York, 1959); and Joseph L. Blau, *The Story of Jewish Philosophy* (New York, 1962). See G. Vajda, *La Théologie ascétique de Bahja ibn Paquda* (Paris, 1947), for a comparison of Bahya's doctrines with Islamic ascetic literature.

J. L. BLAU

BAIN, ALEXANDER (1818–1903), Scottish philosopher and psychologist, was the son of a weaver. He was mainly self-educated but managed to attend Marischal College, in his native city of Aberdeen. After graduating he assisted the philosophy professor there from 1841 to 1844. A confirmed radical, Bain established close contacts with utilitarian circles in London, helping John Stuart Mill in the revisions of his unpublished *System of Logic* in 1842 and helping Edwin Chadwick with his sanitation reforms from 1848 to 1850. During the next decade, supporting himself by journalism, he produced his magnum opus in two installments, entitled *The Senses and the Intellect* (London, 1855) and *The Emotions and the Will* (London, 1859). Appointed professor of logic and rhetoric at Aberdeen in 1860, he published his *Manual of Rhetoric* (London, 1864) and his *Logic, Deductive and Inductive* (London and New York, 1870). On the proceeds of these and other textbooks he founded *Mind* in 1876, choosing his disciple George Croome Robertson as editor. After Bain's death his *Autobiography* (London, 1904), which gives his personal background and a useful criticism of his own books, was published.

Criticisms of associationism. Bain was not simply a pedestrian disciple of the two Mills. Fundamentally loyal to associationism, he was as discontented as J. S. Mill with its tenets but more systematic in his criticisms of them. What apparently made Bain uneasy was the narrow combination of introspection and emphasis on facts that characterized the associationistic science of mind. He was attracted by the physiologists' contemporary program of studying mind by a method uniting emphasis on facts with observation rather than introspection. At the same time Bain was interested in the recent efforts of the epistemologists to found a science that, while still introspective, was concerned not with empirical facts but with necessary truths. He had contacts with William Sharpey among the physiologists and James Ferrier among the epistemologists. Physiology and epistemology were interests alien to Mill.

The will. The fusion of diverse tendencies in Bain's philosophy is best seen in the final section of his chief work—the discussion of the will—and especially its last hundred pages, which contain Bain's spirited defense of determinism, his justly famous theory of belief, and his equally interesting, though less known, analysis of consciousness. For Bain the central problem of the will apparently is the question of how I exercise voluntary control over my limbs. From the traditionalist standpoint it seemed an insoluble mystery how the mind knows just what motor nerves to activate when, for instance, expecting a blinding light to be switched on, it causes the eyes to close in advance. Bain's theory swept aside the traditional analogy with the case of first getting information about what is ahead and then operating a lever. The limbs are not inert like levers but possess an inherent spontaneity, and this spontaneity means that the expectation of the painful glare is inseparably associated with preparations to close the eye. The idea is that theory and practice are one. This doctrine of spontaneity, a direct ancestor of pragmatism, Bain rightly considered to be his most original contribution to philosophy, and he both discussed it effectively at the animal level and struggled honestly, in his discussion of effort, with the difficulty of applying it at the human level.

Belief. Bain's doctrine of belief arose in the context of his view of will. When he spoke of belief as being inseparable from "a preparation to act," he was envisaging as basic a situation in which one seriously expects alleviation of a present pain from something that is visible but out of reach. In the ensuing action of trying to grasp this thing, the belief is inevitably put to the test: "We believe first and prove or disprove afterwards." The essence of the human situation was thus for Bain a kind of circle of activity in which we inevitably acquire new nonrational beliefs as a direct consequence of practically and experimentally testing those we start with. The point is apparently that our actions have unforeseen consequences.

Consciousness. By an ingenious turn Bain used the pragmatist analysis of belief as a basis for a theory of consciousness inspired by William Hamilton's doctrine of the inverse ratio of sensation and perception. In Bain's version of the theory, a sharp contrast is drawn between the emotive pole of consciousness, where absorption in one's pains or pleasures prevents the objective assessment of one's situation, and the cognitive pole, where pleasures and pains are forgotten in the business of mapping one's world and where emotion appears only in the shock of scientific discovery, as a feeling that, like boredom, is outside the pleasure–pain sphere. The movement from feeling to knowledge in consciousness is linked with the same facts that give human life the character of a passage from belief to self-criticism.

But what, then, is this consciousness that underlies both the emotional side and the intellectual? Inspired by Hamilton and Ferrier, Bain made two points. First, we are unconscious of the undifferentiated. "A constant impression is to the mind a blank"—if temperature were unvarying we would not notice it. Second, we are conscious of the constant only in the midst of variety and difference. The essence of consciousness is thus to be discriminative, and Bain pointed out that of the discriminations involved in consciousness, the most liable to be misunderstood is that implicit in the problem of the external world. Bain argued that although Berkeley was right in denouncing as meaningless the notion of material objects independent of experience, he overlooked an important point—that a distinction can be drawn within experience between the person sensing and the sensation sensed. Thus Bain, unlike J. S. Mill, conveyed a profound sense of the complexity of the problem of the external world.

Bain was aware that his philosophy was far removed from ordinary associationism. Above all, in the important Note F to the third edition of *The Senses and the Intellect*, he made it clear that for him association presupposed dissociation.

Bain progressively broke away from the heritage of the Mills, in logic as well as in psychology (he ultimately gave up Mill's view of logic for De Morgan's). At the same time there always survived in him certain tracts of unredeemed associationism. Thus, he retained to the last Mill's peculiar doctrine about the dependence of sight on muscular sense. So, too, his discussions of sympathy and of our knowledge of other minds are very crude examples of associationism.

These weaknesses in Bain have been too much stressed by his critics to the neglect of his merits. Thus, in dealing with the emotions the important role he gave to pure malice, or sadism, as a human motive contrasts refreshingly with the more commonplace views of such critics as Bradley. However, the only part of Bain's work that has been justly appreciated in our time is not his philosophy but his contribution to rhetoric.

Bibliography

Mental and Moral Science (London, 1868) is an abridgment of *The Senses and the Intellect* and *The Emotions and the Will.*

For works on Bain, see W. L. Davidson, "Professor Bain's Philosophy," in *Mind*, N.S. Vol. 13 (1904), 161–179; and Howard C. Warren, *A History of the Association Psychology* (New York, 1921), pp. 104–117. For Bain's contributions to rhetoric, see Stephen Potter, *The Muse in Chains* (London, 1937).

GEORGE E. DAVIE

BAKUNIN, MICHAEL (1814–1876), anarchist writer and revolutionary leader, was born on the estate of Premukhino in the Russian province of Tver. His family were hereditary noblemen of liberal political inclinations. His father had been in Paris during the French Revolution and had taken his doctorate of philosophy at Padua. His mother was a member of the Muraviëv family; three of her cousins were involved in the earliest Russian revolution, the December rising of constitutionalists in 1825. Bakunin was carefully educated under the supervision of his father, who regarded himself as a disciple of Rousseau; later he was sent to the Artillery School in St. Petersburg. He received his commission and went on garrison duty in Lithuania. An awakening taste for literature made him discontent with military life, and in 1835 he obtained his discharge from the army and went to Moscow to study philosophy. There he joined the discussion circle centered on Nicholas Stankevich, which concentrated on contemporary German philosophy.

Hegelianism and revolution. Bakunin was first influenced by Fichte; his earliest literary task was the translation of that philosopher's writings for Vissarion Belinsky's periodical, *The Telescope*. Later he transferred his allegiance to Hegel, and he advocated the Hegelian doctrine in its most conservative form with such enthusiasm that when Stankevich left for western Europe, Bakunin became the leader of the Hegelian school in Moscow and challenged the liberalism of the rival group associated with Alexander Herzen, who propagated the ideas of Charles Fourier, Saint-Simon, and Pierre-Joseph Proudhon.

Bakunin left Russia in 1840 to study German philosophy in Berlin. He still wished to become a professor of philosophy, and assiduously attended the lectures for some time; in his leisure hours he frequented the literary salons in the company of Ivan Turgenev, who used him as a model for the hero of his first novel, *Rudin*.

In 1842 Bakunin moved to Dresden, an intellectual as well as a physical journey. He had made the acquaintance of Arnold Ruge, leader of the Young Hegelians, whose contention that Hegel's dialectical method could be used more convincingly to support revolution than reaction was to influence almost every school of socialist philosophy in mid-nineteenth-century Europe. Bakunin's meeting with Ruge, combined with his reading of Lorenz von Stein's writings on Fourier and Proudhon, effected a change of his viewpoint that had all the strength of religious conversion.

The first manifestation of this change was the essay "Reaction in Germany—A Fragment by a Frenchman," which Bakunin published under the nom de plume of Jules Elysard in Arnold Ruge's *Deutsche Jahrbücher für Wissenschaft und Kunst* (October, 1842). It puts forward a Young Hegelian view of revolution; before it succeeds, revolution is a negative force, but when it triumphs, it will, by a dialectical miracle, immediately become positive. However, the most striking feature of the essay is the apocalyptic tone in which Bakunin introduces the theme —recurrent in his writings—of destruction as a necessary element in the process of social transformation. "Let us put our trust in the eternal spirit which destroys and annihilates only because it is the unsearchable and eternally creative source of all life. The urge to destroy is also a creative urge."

"Reaction in Germany," with its glorification of the idea of perpetual revolt, was the first step toward Bakunin's later anarchism, but he went through many stages before he reached that destination. At first, in Switzerland, he associated with the German revolutionary communist, Wilhelm Weitling. This drew the attention of the Russian authorities to Bakunin's awakening radicalism, and he was condemned *in absentia* to indefinite exile with hard labor in Siberia.

Pan-Slavism. Meanwhile, Bakunin moved to Paris, where he associated with Marx, Robert de Lamennais, George Sand, and, most important, Proudhon. Only in later years did these discussions bear fruit, when Bakunin became Marx's great enemy and Proudhon's great disciple; for the time being, he was concerned with the liberation of the Poles and other Slav peoples. For his speeches against the Russian government he was expelled to Belgium; he returned to Paris with the February Revolution of 1848. The years of the revolutions in Europe—1848–1849 —were the most dramatic period of Bakunin's life. He was an enthusiastic partisan of the uprising in France; later in 1848 he fought on the barricades of Prague, and in March 1849, he took a leading part, with Richard Wagner, in the Dresden revolution. He was captured there and, after periods in Saxon and Austrian prisons and twice being sentenced to death and reprieved, he was handed over to the Russian authorities, who imprisoned him in the Peter and Paul Fortress. Six years there ruined his health. In 1857 he was sent to exile in Siberia, and in 1861 he escaped, via Japan and the United States, to western Europe.

During the years of action and imprisonment Bakunin produced two important works, the *Appeal to the Slavs*, written in the interval between the Prague and Dresden revolutions, and the *Confession*, which he wrote in prison at the request of Tsar Nicholas II and which was published after the Russian Revolution. The *Appeal to the Slavs* is much more than a statement of Bakunin's Pan-Slavism; in many ways it anticipates his later anarchist attitudes. The social revolution, he declares, must take precedence over the political revolution and, on moral grounds, he claims that the social revolution must be total. "We must first of all purify our atmosphere and transform completely the surroundings in which we live, for they corrupt our instincts and our wills. . . . Therefore the social question appears first of all as the overthrow of society," by which Bakunin evidently means the overthrow of the contemporary social order. Bakunin further maintains that liberty is indivisible and thus implies the rejection of individualism in favor of the collectivism that becomes explicit in the later development of his anarchist doctrine. The *Confession* is important principally for its account of the early development of Bakunin's revolutionary philosophy.

After his escape to western Europe in 1861, Bakunin resumed the course of Pan-Slavism he had been forced to abandon in 1849 but, after taking part in an abortive Polish attempt to invade Lithuania in 1863, he went to Italy.

Anarchism. In 1865 Bakunin founded the International Brotherhood in Naples. Its program—embodied in Bakunin's *Revolutionary Catechism*—was anarchism without the name; it rejected the state and organized religion, advocated communal autonomy within a federal structure, and maintained that labor "must be the sole base of human right and of the economic organization of the state." In keeping with the cult of violence that was part of the romantic revolutionary tradition, Bakunin insisted that the social revolution could not be achieved by peaceful means.

The International Brotherhood was a conspiratorial organization, for Bakunin never outlived his taste for the dark and the secret. Nevertheless, in 1867 he emerged into public life as a figurehead of the short-lived League for Peace and Freedom. This was mainly a body of pacifistic liberals, within which Bakunin led the left wing.

Bakunin was not a systematic writer. He admitted that he had no sense of "literary architecture" and saw himself primarily as a man of action, although his action was rarely successful and his life was punctuated by abortive revolutions. His writings were intended to provoke action; they were topical in inspiration, if not always in content, and it is in pamphlets on current events and in reports written for congresses and organizations that his opinions are scattered. One such report, prepared for the benefit of the central committee of the League for Peace and Freedom, was eventually published as *Federalism, Socialism and Anti-Theologism*. More than any other work, it contains the gist of Bakunin's anarchism.

Bakunin was not a great theoretical originator. The influences in his writings are obvious—Hegel, Comte, Proudhon, Ruge, Darwin, and even Marx. Original in Bakunin are his insight into contemporary events (he prophesied with uncanny exactitude the way in which a Marxist state would operate) and his power to create a synthesis of borrowed ideas around which the early anarchist movement could crystallize. In *Federalism, Socialism and Anti-Theologism* the view of the structure of a desirable society is almost completely derived from Proudhon's federalism. In one vital respect, however, Bakunin's view differs from Proudhon's: while he follows Proudhon in measuring the consumer's right to goods by the quantity of his labor, he also advocates the collectivization of the means of production under public ownership; Proudhon and his mutualist followers wished to retain individual possession of land and tools by peasants and artisans as far as possible, in order to create a guarantee of personal independence. This difference was regarded as so important that Bakunin's followers were actually described as "collectivists" and did not assume the name of "anarchists" until the 1870s.

In 1868 Bakunin left the League for Peace and Freedom to found the International Alliance of Social Democracy, which was dissolved when he and his followers entered the International Workingmen's Association in 1869. Within the International, Bakunin and the southern European federations challenged the power of Karl Marx. The dispute centered on disagreement over political methods. Marx and his followers held that socialists must seize the state and usher in a transitional dictatorship of the proletariat. Bakunin argued that power seized by workers was no less evil than power in other hands, and a communist state would magnify the evil of other states; he called for the earliest possible destruction of the state and the avoidance of political means toward that end. The workers must win their own liberation by economic and insurrectional means. The dispute came to a head at The Hague Congress of the International in 1872, when Bakunin was expelled. The southern federations and those of the Low Countries seceded to form their own federation, and Marx's remnant faded away.

Meanwhile, Bakunin's health declined rapidly. He took part in the Lyons rebellion of 1870 and in the abortive Bologna uprising of 1874. He died, exhausted, two years later at Bern. After his death, the anarchist communism of Kropotkin superseded his collectivist anarchism, except in Spain, where the large anarchist movement held his ideas in their purity until 1939.

Bibliography

After his death, most of Bakunin's works were collected in J. Guillaume, ed. *Oeuvres*, 6 vols. (Paris, 1896–1914). Other editions of his selected works have been published in Russian, German, and Spanish, and in 1961 the International Institute of Social History announced that it would undertake the publication of his unpublished works; Vol. I is A. Lehning, A. J. C. Ruter, and P. Scheibert, eds., *Michel Bakounine et l'Italie 1871–1872* (Leiden, 1961).

English translations are scanty; they include *God and the State*, translated by Benjamin Tucker (Boston, 1893); *Marxism, Freedom and the State*, translated by K. J. Kenafick (London, 1950); and G. P. Maximoff, ed., *The Political Philosophy of Bakunin* (Glencoe, Ill., 1953).

The only English biography is E. H. Carr, *Bakunin* (London, 1937). H. E. Kaminski, *Bakounine, la vie d'un révolutionnaire* (Paris, 1938), is a useful study. In Bertrand Russell, *Proposed Roads to Freedom* (New York, 1919), Ch. 2 is a discussion of Bakunin and anarchism.

GEORGE WOODCOCK

BALFOUR, ARTHUR JAMES (1848–1930), first earl of Balfour. Born at Whittingehame, Haddington, East Lothian, he was the son of a Scottish landowning family and was connected, through his mother, with the aristocratic house of Cecil. After an education at Eton and Trinity College, Cambridge, where he came under the influence of Henry Sidgwick (later his brother-in-law), he became a Conservative M.P. in 1874 and, despite an early reputation for indolence and frivolity, soon rose, by a combination of influence and ability, to ministerial rank. Having made his name as a courageous and enlightened chief secretary for Ireland during the turbulent period from 1887 to 1891, he became leader of the House of Commons in 1891 and in 1902 succeeded his uncle, Lord Salisbury, as prime minister. Beset by dissensions over tariff reform, his administration fell in 1905; but he remained leader of the Opposition until 1911. He resumed office in the wartime coalition as first lord of the admiralty, later becoming foreign secretary and lord president of the council. In these capacities he played a major part in the postwar negotiations at Versailles and Washington and, by the Balfour Declaration of 1917, in the eventual establishment of the state of Israel. He received the Order of Merit in 1916 and a Garter knighthood, followed by an earldom, in 1922. Among many other distinctions, he was chancellor of both Cambridge and Edinburgh universities, fellow of the Royal Society, president of the British Academy, the British Association, and the Aristotelian Society, and one of the founders of the Scots Philosophical Club. As an elder statesman whose disinterested sagacity was equally valued by both parties, Balfour in his later years enjoyed a unique position in British political life. He died, unmarried, at Woking.

Balfour's intelligence, versatility, and charm were at the service of many causes besides politics. Science and education were among his keenest interests; with his sister, Mrs. Sidgwick, he was a leading figure in the Society for Psychical Research. His leisure was divided equally between the arts and society, on the one hand, and tennis and golf on the other. Philosophy, however, was his main pursuit in private life, and in this sphere also—like his fellow statesman Haldane—he made a definite, if temporary, mark. Aside from having considerable literary merits, his writings are chiefly notable as a vigorous and independent contribution to the literature of the perennial conflict between science and religion.

Balfour had a strong distaste for the evolutionary naturalism of his younger days, and made repeated attempts to expose its pretensions as a prelude to stating the case for a "higher Reason" and the acceptance of Christian belief. To this end he employs skeptical weapons of a type forged by Berkeley and Hume and subsequently wielded by Mansel, while his own defenses owe more than a little to Burke. If the would-be scientific answers to the problems of knowledge and human existence turn out, on examination, to be at once ungrounded and inconsistent, they supersede neither the time-honored beliefs of common sense nor the equally cherished, albeit unprovable, convictions of religion. Balfour's first book, *A Defence of Philosophic Doubt* (London, 1879), argues derisively against the claims of any prevailing system of thought to justify, let alone criticize, the natural and "inevitable" beliefs in the external world, in the uniformity of nature and, to a lesser extent, in theism. His second book, the widely read *Foundations of Belief* (London, 1895), renews the polemic against Mill and Spencer, dwelling on their inability to account either for the facts of perception or for the appearance of natural law, and still less for the data of ethical and aesthetic experience. So far from being rational, they degrade reason to the status of an evolutionary by-product and ignore the importance of belief. The latter, it is argued in a famous chapter, is founded, not on induction, but on the more enduring basis of "authority"—the climate of traditional opinion, by which all reasonable men live. Where nothing is certain and everything rests on belief, science not only cannot dictate to religion, but even presupposes theism as the basis for its own claims to rationality.

If Balfour's strictures on naturalism were not infrequently mistaken by his opponents for a tory attack upon science, his defense of the faith tended equally to unnerve the faithful who distrusted its appearances of skepticism. So far as these misunderstandings resulted from his own rather casual employment of such terms as "naturalism," "rationalism," "theism," "reason," "authority," and the like, they were clarified, in part, by his two sets of Gifford Lectures, *Theism and Humanism* (London, 1915) and *Theism and Thought* (London, 1923). These works, however, though readable enough as a restatement of his position, are essentially products of a bygone phase of controversy and have little to add that is new.

Bibliography

Balfour's minor writings are represented in *Essays and Addresses* (London, 1905) and *Essays, Speculative and Political* (London, 1920). See also an anthology by his secretary, W. M. Short, *A. J. Balfour as Philosopher and Thinker* (London, 1912).

The leading biographies are Mrs. Dugdale (his niece), *Arthur James Balfour*, 2 vols. (London, 1937), and K. Young, *Arthur James Balfour* (London, 1963). The former has an appraisal of his philosophy by A. Seth Pringle-Pattison, an old friend, whose *Man's Place in the Cosmos* (London, 1897) also contains a useful appreciation of Balfour's earlier point of view.

P. L. HEATH

BALGUY, JOHN (1686–1748), English theologian and moral philosopher, was born in Sheffield and educated at the Sheffield grammar school and at St. John's College, Cambridge. He was admitted to the B.A. in 1706, ordained in the established church in 1710, and granted the living of Lamesley and Tanfield in Durham in 1711. Later he was made a prebendary of Salisbury (1727), and finally vicar of Northallerton, York (1729). He was an associate of Bishop Benjamin Hoadley and was the bishop's defender in the Bangorian controversy. Hoadley was the close friend of Samuel Clarke.

Balguy's first piece of moral philosophy was an attack on the philosophy of Shaftesbury, entitled *A Letter to a Deist Concerning the Beauty and Excellency of Moral Virtue, and the Support Which It Receives from the Christian Religion* (London, 1726). His most important work was *The Foundation of Moral Goodness* (Part I first published in London in 1728, Part II in 1729). Part I is a criticism of the moral philosophy of Francis Hutcheson and an exposition of Balguy's own views, much influenced by Samuel Clarke. Part II is a set of critical queries with Balguy's answers. A Lord Darcy, an admirer of Hutcheson's philosophy, is said to have proposed the queries.

Hutcheson claimed that we distinguish between virtue and vice by means of the perceptions of a moral sense. These perceptions are kinds of pleasure and uneasiness, and they are invoked to account for our approval of virtue and our abhorrence of vice, as well as our obligation to behave virtuously and to avoid viciousness. Hutcheson believed that our moral sense has been determined by God to operate as it does and that we are naturally endowed with a benevolence toward our fellow creatures.

Balguy agreed that God has endowed our minds with benevolent affections toward others, but these affections are only helps or incentives to virtue and not the true ground or foundation of it. By making virtuous behavior flow from divinely founded instincts, Hutcheson had made virtue arbitrary. It is compatible with Hutcheson's view that God might have made us different from what we are, even inverting virtue and vice if he pleased. What is more, if God had not given us an instinct for benevolence, it appears that we should be altogether incapable of virtue; and this would be so even if we were possessed of reason and liberty.

Balguy argued that there is something in actions absolutely good (or bad) that is antecedent to both affections and laws. If this were not so, no reason could be given for God's preferring us to act benevolently and disposing us accordingly. For an action to be virtuous, there must be a perception or a consciousness of its reasonableness, or we would have to admit that beasts can be virtuous. Genuine goodness consists in our being determined to do a good action merely by the reason and the right of the thing. This is the purest and most perfect virtue of which any agent is capable. The obligation to perform a virtuous act is to be found in its reasonableness, and for a rational creature to refuse to be reasonable is unthinkable.

Balguy's elucidation of "reasonable" is found in his account of our knowledge of virtue. He argued that our understanding is altogether sufficient for the perception of virtue. Virtue is the conformity of our moral actions to the reasons of things; vice is the contrary. Moral actions are actions directed toward some intelligent being, and Balguy called them moral to distinguish them from other kinds of action. By a moral action's conformity to reason, Balguy meant the agreeableness of the action to the nature and circumstances of the persons concerned and the relations existing between them. Gratitude is an example of what he meant by conformity to reason: "We find . . . that some actions are agreeable, others disagreeable, to the nature and circumstances of the agent and the object, and the relations interceding between them. Thus, for instance, we find an agreement between the gratitude of A and the kindness of B; and a disagreement between the ingratitude of C and the bounty of D. These agreements and disagreements are visible to every intelligent observer, who attends to the several ideas" (*The Foundation of Moral Goodness*). He likens our perception of such an agreement to our perception of the agreement between the three angles of a triangle and two right ones, or our perception of the agreement between twice three and six. Since we do not require an intellectual sense superadded to our understanding in order to perceive these mathematical agreements, then clearly we do not require a moral sense to perceive the agreement of A's gratitude and B's kindness.

There are difficulties in Balguy's account of virtue as conformity to reason. The agreement between twice three and six is an equality, which is logically necessary. But the agreement of A's gratitude and B's kindness is not a defined equality. How, then, does the agreement come about? One of Balguy's synonyms for "agreement" is "fitting," and it appears to let the proponents of the moral sense in at the back door. For why is gratitude a fitting response to kindness and a lack of gratitude unfitting? What can we say but that we feel gratitude to be fitting and the lack of gratitude unfitting? "Fitting" and "unfitting" are normative terms, and while one can learn such a rule as "Gratitude is the fitting response to kindness," the rule must originally have been given life by someone's feeling that gratitude is the fitting response to kindness. Balguy would treat the rule as an end in itself, because he believed it exhibits some inherent self-consistency. The proponents of the moral sense would argue that the consistency of gratitude and kindness lies not in them but in us who find them to be consistent.

Balguy would agree, of course, that it is we who find gratitude to be the fitting response to kindness. The dispute is only over how we find it to be fitting, and we find it so not by a moral sense as by using our reason or understanding. The final defense for this contention is Balguy's assessment of reason as the noblest of our faculties, superior to any sense. Therefore, reason must be the arbiter of virtue and vice. The question of what faculty assesses the relative superiority of our faculties is never asked.

Balguy also wrote *Divine Rectitude: or a Brief Inquiry Concerning the Moral Perfections of the Deity, Particularly in Respect of Creation and Providence* (London, 1730). He argued that God's goodness follows from a regard for a real and absolute order, beauty, and harmony.

Bibliography

L. A. Selby-Bigge, ed., *The British Moralists* (Oxford, 1897), Vol. II, reproduces Part I of *The Foundation of Moral Goodness* and representative selections from Part II.

For critical discussion, see B. Peach, "John Balguy," in V. Ferm, ed., *Encyclopedia of Morals* (New York, 1956).

ELMER SPRAGUE

BÁÑEZ, DOMINIC (1528–1604), Spanish theologian, was born at Valladolid and died at Medina del Campo. He studied at the University of Salamanca, where he entered the Dominican order. He first taught courses in philosophy and theology in various houses of study of his order in Spain (Salamanca, Ávila, Alcalá de Henares, Valladolid) and then became a professor at the University of Salamanca, teaching philosophy from 1577 and theology from 1581. He was noted for his role as the spiritual director of St. Teresa of Ávila and for his bitter controversy with the Jesuit Luis de Molina concerning divine grace. Báñez' view on grace and human liberty is called "physical predetermination," which means that man's will is unable to act unless empowered and applied to action by an ultimate principal cause, which is God. Apart from a commentary on Aristotle's treatise *On Generation and Corruption* (1585), Báñez' philosophy is found in his theological work *Scholastica Commentaria in Primam Partem Angelici Doctoris* ("Commentary on the First Part of the Summa of Theology," 2 vols., Salamanca, 1584–1588). As a philosopher, Báñez was at his best in interpreting the metaphysics of St. Thomas. Unlike most of his contemporaries, he saw the importance of the act of being (*esse*) as constituting every nature in existence (see L. Urbano, ed., *Scholastica Commentaria*, I, p. 141). In this he anticipated the existential view of Thomistic metaphysics now favored by such thinkers as Jacques Maritain and Étienne Gilson. On the other hand, Báñez interpreted the real distinction of essence and existence as the difference between two individual things (*res*) and then rejected this notion. Moreover, he regarded the limitation of the act of existing by the essence that receives it as an indication that essence may, in this sense, be more noble than existence.

Bibliography

Works by Báñez include *Scholastica Commentaria*, new edition, edited by L. Urbano (Madrid and Valencia, 1934). A later section of the same *Commentary* has also been published as *Commentaria in Primam Secundae*, edited by B. de Heredia, 2 vols. (Madrid, 1942–1944).

For works on Báñez see W. R. O'Connor, "Molina and Báñez as Interpreters of Thomas Aquinas," in *New Scholasticism*, Vol. 21 (1947), 243–259; and L. Gutiérrez-Vega, "Báñez filósofo existencial," in *Estudios Filosóficos*, Vol. 3 (1954), 83–114.

VERNON J. BOURKE

BANFI, ANTONIO (1886–1957), Italian philosopher. Banfi was born in Milan and studied at the Academy of Science and Letters there and at the University of Berlin. Banfi enjoyed a long acquaintance with Edmund Husserl, who influenced Banfi's thought along with the Marburg Neo-Kantians. Banfi taught at the universities of Florence, Genoa, and Milan. In 1940 he founded the review *Studi filosofici*, which played an important part in the Italian revolt against idealism. Banfi participated actively in political life. In 1925 he adhered to the manifesto of the antifascist intellectuals prepared by Benedetto Croce. After World War II he sat in the Italian Senate as a Communist.

German rather than Italian influences are apparent in Banfi's major work, *Principi di una teoria della ragione* ("Principles of a Theory of Reason," Milan, 1926). According to Banfi philosophical inquiry does not spring from an immediate spontaneity of thought but arises as critical reflection on the cultural heritage of the speculative tradition. By studying the structures of knowledge, reflection grasps the function of reason. Reason is to be understood neither in a psychological sense nor in the metaphysical sense of Hegelianism. Reason, according to Banfi, is the indefinite law of the process of organization or of coordination of experience.

The task of science, Banfi held, is to study experience and resolve it into functional relations or laws. Philosophy continues the work of science in its own manner. It clarifies experience in terms of dialectical antitheses (reality and appearance, matter and form, necessity and liberty, and so on); it resolves the opposition of the antitheses in the unity of an idea; and in the phenomenological conclusion it discloses the rational structure progressively attained in the ordering of experience.

In subsequent works Banfi sought to emphasize the problematic nature of reason as an open system and as the self-ordering of experience. He saw in dialectical materialism the elimination of the mythical moment of knowledge, the affirmation of the unending development of reason, and the liberative function of reason.

Bibliography

Banfi's *L'uomo copernicano* was published in Milan in 1950. His two-volume *La ricerca della realtà* was published in Florence in 1959.

For literature on Banfi, see Giovanni Maria Bertin, *L'idea pedagogica e il principio di ragione in Antonio Banfi* (Rome, 1961); and Fulvio Papi, *Il pensiero di Antonio Banfi* (Florence, 1961).

EUGENIO GARIN

Translated by *Robert M. Connolly*

BARTH, KARL, Swiss theologian, was born in Basel, in 1886, and has held professorships at Göttingen, Münster, Bonn, and Basel. His impact on the theological world dates from 1921, with the substantially revised second edition of his *Der Römerbrief* (the first edition was published in 1919). Herein he attacked the prevalent "subjectivism" of Protestant theology, in which he perceived the attempt to fit the Christian revelation into the mold of human preconceptions. Since then, though Barth has changed and developed many of his ideas, a single main concern has run through all his writings: namely, how to prevent theology from becoming an ideology, that is, a creation of human culture. This was the reason for his early violent attacks on the then fashionable liberal theology, as expounded, for instance, by Adolf von Harnack. According to Barth, the danger of such attempts to formulate a "reasonable" Christianity is threefold: intellectual, ethical, and soteriological. First, there is the danger of identifying human conclusions with the Word of God and thus of destroying the validity of the concept of revelation, which is God's self-manifestation and owes nothing to human initiatives. Second, there is the danger that the church will simply reflect the social and cultural situation, thus losing its power of criticism and its prophetic function. Barth was deeply disturbed by the support given to the kaiser by a number of his liberal theologian teachers in 1914. It is notable that, while at Bonn, he threw his support behind the Confessing church in its opposition to the Nazis, an action that cost him his chair. Third, salvation comes from God alone, and the attempt to identify a human *Weltanschauung* with God's Word is an instance of the refusal to accept that the only justification is by grace. As Barth wrote: "This secret identification of ourselves with God carries with it our isolation from him."

The principle that theological exposition should be basically independent of human speculations (except insofar as historical and linguistic investigations, etc. are a necessary part of understanding Scripture) was reinforced by Barth's interpretation of the Fall. Not only is the human will vitiated by the Fall, but reason also, in such a way that it is impossible for men to discover the truth about God through their own efforts. Only if God manifests himself can there be any revelation. Thus Barth rejected the whole of natural theology as expounded by, for instance, Aquinas, and in particular its basis in the doctrine of the analogy of being (*analogia entis*), on the ground that it implies some similarity between creatures and God. A strong motif in Barth's theology, therefore, is the transcendence of God (in the sense of his distance from creatures—"the great Calvinist distance between heaven and earth"). Methodologically, all this implies that interpretation of the Bible should not betray the genuine meaning of the text by explaining away or avoiding those hard sayings that are supposedly scandals to modern thought. Nevertheless, Barth is no fundamentalist: the Word of God is not to be identified with the witness to it found in the Bible, and there is no question of using the latter as a "paper pope."

Der Römerbrief was critical rather than constructive, and during the 1920s Barth's theology had the character of being dialectical (to use a term that he later came to reject), that is, it called in question human preconceptions about God, often by denying them in the sharpest terms; but since theology is designed to proclaim what is God-given, it is always necessary to reach out beyond such denials. In this way, there is a constant dialectic between grace and man's religion. The concept that religion itself is under divine judgment, and is a human rather than strictly a divine phenomenon, has had great influence, culminating in Dietrich Bonhoeffer's idea of a "religionless Christianity."

In the late 1920s Barth started on the second main phase of his theological writing, and after what he called his "well-known false start," with the *Prolegomena to a Christian Dogmatics (Christliche Dogmatik im Entwurf,* 1927), he began on his many-volumed *Church Dogmatics* (*Die kirkliche Dogmatik,* 1932 and onwards). Herein he was influenced by his study of Anselm (expressed in *Fides Quaerens Intellectum,* 1931). The heart of the Ontological Argument is the recognition that theology does not need any metaphysical substructure; it contains within itself its own rationale, namely the unfolding of the inner form of God's Word. Thus dogmatics is systematic in that it presents the material in an orderly way and in that it aims exhaustively to touch on all areas of human concern, but it is not a deduction from some principle or set of principles.

The *Church Dogmatics* is a rich work, though not altogether a consistent one, since Barth's thought has been developing in the course of his writing. Its main emphasis is Christocentric. God's revelation is essentially seen in the Christ-event, and Christ is God's Word. However, the God so revealed is trinitarian: ". . . the work of the Son of God includes the work of the Father as its presupposition and the work of the Holy Spirit as its consequence." The first article, the work of the Father, is "to a certain extent the source, the third article, the work of the Holy Spirit, the goal of our path. But the second article, the work of the Son, is the Way upon which we find ourselves in faith. From that vantage we may review the entire fullness of the acts of God." Consequently, such doctrines as creation must be seen from this perspective. The Bible presents no cosmology, but it does contain an anthropology; and thus God's relation to the natural world can only be understood by analogy with his saving revelation to human beings. Notions of a First Cause and Necessary Being, as explaining the existence of the cosmos, are thus beside the point, for they make no use of the concepts of grace and personality as ascribed to God. By contrast, the biblical saga of creation makes it continuous with God's covenant relationship with Israel.

Barth's exposition is controlled throughout by two considerations. First, dogmatics is necessarily church dogmatics, i.e., it is an activity that must be carried on within the church, as the place where the preaching or proclamation of the Word occurs. Thus the theologian's continuous concern is to test the doctrine and preaching of the church, which, because it is carried on through human beings, is liable to go astray. Second, the standpoint from which the proclamation is tested is that of Scripture, which is "the document of the manifestation of the Word in Jesus Christ." Dogmatics would become irrelevant if it sacrificed this standard.

The implications of Barth's thesis for the relationship between philosophy and theology are clear. Insofar as philosophy is metaphysical, in the sense of saying something about God or some such substitute as the Absolute, it collides with theology; and it is the theologian's proper task to show how metaphysics has here gone beyond its legitimate limits. Philosophy, as logic, philosophy of science, etc., is a proper inquiry, but one which is quite separate from theology. Barth does, however, allow (in his *Fides Quaerens Intellectum* and elsewhere) that philosophical concepts may be used in exegesis, so long as they are kept strictly subordinate to the Word of God. But Barth remains insistent that theologians should not make concessions to secular thought; indeed, he holds that such concessions are a principal reason for the contempt that many philosophers have had for "philosophical" theologians. Thus traditional forms of apologetic are ruled out.

Two issues arising from Barth's whole approach are crucial. First, how is one to know that the revelation in Christ is the true one? Or more particularly, how is one to know that the whole doctrine of God as expounded by Barth is true? Second, how can these propositions about God be meaningful if the similarity or analogy between God and human persons is denied? For Barth, the first question is one that virtually does not arise. The Bible, for instance, does not set out to prove God's existence or attributes, rather, it witnesses to his acts. The task of the preacher or theologian is to proclaim this revelation. Theology must be a rational inquiry that is appropriate to its subject matter, namely God's gracious self-revelation; and any attempt to establish the truth of doctrine upon grounds that are extraneous to its subject matter is both irrelevant and dangerous. Thus the Christian message is not to be seen as a religious teaching amid rival teachings, for all religious and metaphysical revelations and conclusions are projections of human wishes (here the influence of Ludwig Feuerbach is apparent). It by no means follows, however, that any particular statement of theology that is consistent with these presuppositions as to the nature of theological inquiry is correct. Barth holds that dogmatics is a continuing process within the church, and it is, of course, a human activity suffering from the defects of human reason. It is therefore necessary to consider the criteria of the worth of a system of dogmatics. These criteria are necessarily derived internally from God's self-revelation (by the former arguments). Barth singles out two. First, theological thinking must be humble: this is a practical test of whether it is refraining from establishing its own claim to truth, i.e., its being in effect an ideology. Second, it must express the doctrine of predestination, which encapsulates the whole of the revelational approach—what man "achieves" in relation to God is due to God. Because of the element of paradox in the first criterion (for the Thomist can be humble in his approach), Barth is at times inclined to speak in a syncretistic way. Imagining a conversation in heaven, he says: "Yes, dear Schleiermacher, I understand you now. You were right, except on some points!" (*Karl Barth's Table Talk*). Further, the notion that theology is dialectical, so that a statement can be balanced by affirming its apparent contradictory, has rendered Barth less rigid than many of the Barthians.

As to the problem of the meaning of theological utterances, Barth holds that revelation is a relational concept, and thus God does not, so to say, reveal himself independently of the human apprehension of his self-manifestation. Consequently, the knowledge of God is itself given by God, through grace. Thus, the *analogia entis* is replaced by the *analogia fidei* (the analogy of faith); faith gives us understanding of the nature of God and is God-given. Thus God is the cause of true theological assertions, as well as their ground.

Barth's influence has been great. This is partly because he has provided the outline of a theology that is powerfully biblical without being fundamentalist and, therefore, can escape the charge of being irrational by being nonrational. The most eminent Europeans who stand close to Barth are Emil Brunner and Oscar Cullmann. The former entered into controversy with Barth in the early 1930s over the question of the fallen character of human reason. Brunner held that in some areas this thesis was obviously false, for example, in the natural sciences; but, nevertheless, in relation to knowledge of God, men are capable of only the most shadowy awareness on their own. One of the most important attempts to apply Barth's theology has been Hendrik Kraemer's *The Christian Message in a Non-Christian World* (1938), which aims to show that all religions, including empirical Christianity, are under the judgment of the revelation in Christ. Thus there is no need to argue for Christianity as an empirical phenomenon as against other religions. But the question remains: If there is no correspondence between the Gospel and empirical Christianity, the church is a sham; and if there is, then the comparison and contrast between empirical Christianity and other faiths is possible, and apologetics unavoidable. This is one illustration of the central problem posed by Barth's theology.

Bibliography

There is a useful bibliography of Barth's works in T. F. Torrance's *Karl Barth, an Introduction to His Early Theology, 1910–1931* (London, 1962). The main works translated into English are *The Epistle to the Romans* (London, 1933); *Church Dogmatics,* edited by G. W. Bromiley and T. F. Torrance (London, 1936; Edinburgh, 1956 onward), 4 vols., comprising 11 separately published sections, one of which is *Church Dogmatics, A Selection with Introduction,* edited by H. Gollwitzer and translated by G. W. Bromiley (New York, 1961). An outline, by Barth himself, of the thought in this work is *Dogmatics in Outline* (London, 1949). Later works include *The Humanity of God* (Richmond, Va., 1960); and *Anselm: Fides Quaerens Intellectum* (London, 1960); and

Evangelical Theology: an Introduction (London, 1963). See also *Karl Barth's Table Talk*, recorded and edited by John D. Godsey (Edinburgh, 1963).

Works expressing related thought are E. Brunner, *Dogmatics*, 2 vols. (London, 1949; 1952); O. Cullmann, *Christ and Time* (London, 1951); and H. Kraemer, *The Christian Message in a Non-Christian World* (London, 1938). Philosophical criticisms of Barth's position can be found in H. D. Lewis, *Morals and Revelation* (London, 1951) and R. W. Hepburn, *Christianity and Paradox* (London, 1958), Ch. 5.

NINIAN SMART

BASEDOW, JOHANN BERNHARD (1724–1790), German philosopher, theologian, and educational theorist, was born in Hamburg into the family of a poor wigmaker, whose name, more properly, was Bassedau. A benefactor financed his studies, first at Hamburg under H. S. Reimarus. In 1746 he entered the faculty of theology at Leipzig University, where he studied philosophy under the Pietist philosopher C. A. Crusius. In 1749 he became a private tutor in the family of Herr von Quaalen in Holstein. His experiences as a tutor turned his attention to educational problems, which were the subject of his master's thesis at Kiel University in 1752. On Klopstock's recommendation, he was appointed professor of philosophy and rhetoric at the Knightly Academy at Soro, Denmark. A heterodox work, *Praktische Philosophie für alle Stände* ("Practical Philosophy for all States," Copenhagen, 1758), led to his dismissal. In 1761 he moved to the gymnasium at Altona, but again lost his position, and his writings were prohibited. He left theology and, supported by his benefactor, published his *Vorstellung an Menschenfreunde für Schulen, nebst dem Plan eines Elementarbuchs der menschlichen Erkenntnisse* ("Appeal to the Friends of Mankind about Schools, with a Plan for an Elementary Book on Human Knowledge," Hamburg, 1768"), his first significant work on education, which met with a tremendous response. With financial help from several influential people, he published during the following years several textbooks, the most important being his *Methodenbuch für Väter und Mütter der Familien und Völker* ("Methodology for Fathers and Mothers of Families and Nations," Leipzig, 1770; edited by T. Fritzsch, Leipzig, 1913). Prince Franz Leopold Friedrich of Dessau invited him to organize an experimental school in Dessau. Basedow accepted, and the school, called the *Philanthropin*, opened in 1774. It was soon imitated by a number of similar institutions in Germany and Switzerland.

By 1776 Basedow had returned to theology, living in Dessau, Leipzig, Halle, and Magdeburg. During this period he published his *Examen in der alten natürlichsten Religion* ("Examination of the Old Most Natural Religion"), which he considered his masterpiece. Basedow's theological ideas, inspired by the English and French deists, aimed at a natural religion, rational and practical, refraining from dogmas and rejecting every kind of orthodox Christianity.

Basedow was one of the "popular philosophers" (*Popularphilosophen*), but his importance as a theoretical philosopher has been underrated by modern historians. His work on theory of knowledge and metaphysics, *Philalethie* (Lübeck, 1764), inspired by Crusius, Hume, and the French *philosophes*, was one of the most significant books on methodology of its time and influenced Kant, Tetens, and others. He supported a moderate skepticism based on common sense and denied the possibility of reaching absolute demonstrative truth in natural philosophy (out of skepticism concerning causation), in rational psychology, or in theology.

Basedow's chief importance lies in his educational theories, which are based on Comenius, Locke, and Rousseau. He claimed that education should be cosmopolitan, free from any confessional imprint, equal for all classes, and aimed at enabling men to live useful and happy lives as good citizens. Instruction should appeal to the child's sensibility rather than to his understanding and should be encouraged by games and colloquial intercourse. Images (*Zeichen*) are more effective than words.

Works by Basedow

Ausgewählte Schriften, Hugo Göring, ed. Langensalza, 1880.

Works on Basedow

Basedow, Armin, "Johann Bernhard Basedow." *Friedrich Manns pädagogisches Magazin*, Vol. 995 (1924).

Diestelmann, Richard, *Johann Bernhard Basedow*. Leipzig, 1897.

Meyer, J. C., *Leben, Charakter und Schriften Basedows*, 2 vols. Hamburg, 1791–1792.

Rammelt, Johannes, *J. B. Basedow, der Philanthropinismus und das Dessauer Philanthropin*. Dessau, 1929.

Rathmann, H., *Beiträge zur Lebensgeschichte Basedows*. Magdeburg, 1791.

Surakoff, K. D., *Der Einfluss der zeitgenössischen Philosophie auf Basedows Pädagogik*. Giessen, 1898.

Zimmermann, Hans, *Die Pädagogik Basedows vom Standpunkte moderner Geschichtsauffassung*. Langensalza, 1912.

GIORGIO TONELLI

BASIC STATEMENTS. Any statement of fact is true or false in virtue of some existing state of affairs in the world. In many cases the truth-value of a statement is determined by appealing to the truth-values of certain other statements, but this process must terminate somewhere if the truth-value of any statement of fact is to be assessed at all. An epistemological view according to which the process of verification or falsification terminates with statements of a logically distinct kind is a view to the effect that there is a distinct class of *basic statements*. The principal questions that have been considered are (1) Is there such a class of statements? (2) If there is, what is the relation between these statements and certain nonverbal occurrences called experiences? (3) Are basic statements descriptions of the private experiences of the speaker or of publicly observable events? (4) Are these statements either incorrigible (that is, of such a character that they cannot be false, or cannot be shown to be false) or indubitable (that is, such that they cannot rationally be doubted)? These questions have been much discussed by modern empiricists, especially in connection with the verifiability criterion of meaning. The problems concerning basic statements are not, however, essentially confined to empiricist theories of meaning and truth; they are fundamental in any theory of knowledge.

Wittgenstein. The thesis that there is a class of basic or elementary propositions is powerfully presented in Wittgenstein's *Tractatus Logico-philosophicus* (1921; first English translation, 1922). Wittgenstein argues that if a proposition contains expressions standing for complexes, the sense of the proposition will depend upon the truth of other propositions describing those complexes. This will again be the case if any one of those other propositions contains expressions standing for complexes. Thus, the determinateness of the sense of the original proposition requires that its analysis should terminate in elementary propositions consisting only of names of simple things (see 2.0211–2.0212, 3.23). An elementary proposition is an arrangement of names which represents a possible arrangement of simple things; it is a logical picture of an elementary state of affairs. Wittgenstein gave no explicit interpretation of "simple things," "names," or "elementary propositions." He is reported as saying that at the time he wrote the *Tractatus* he thought it was not his business, as a logician, to give examples of simple things, this being a purely empirical matter; the *Tractatus* view is that the application of logic decides what elementary propositions there are (5.557).

Schlick. Moritz Schlick and some other members of the Vienna circle gave an empiricist interpretation to Wittgenstein's theory. In "Über das Fundament der Erkenntnis" (1934) and other articles, Schlick inquired whether there is a class of statements which provide an "unshakeable, indubitable foundation" of all knowledge. This kind of incorrigibility, he argued (against Neurath and Carnap), cannot depend simply upon the coherence of a statement with the existing system of science, nor simply upon someone's decision to accept a statement as true. It is possessed only by the statements a person makes about his own experiences. Schlick called such statements *Konstatierungen* ("confirmations") and contrasted these with the "protocol sentences" described by Neurath and Carnap. *Konstatierungen* have the following characteristics: (1) They have the form "here, now, so and so"; examples are "here two black points coincide," "Here yellow borders on blue," "Here now pain." (2) In the case of other synthetic statements, understanding their meaning is quite distinct from the actual process of verifying them, and their meaning does not determine their truth-value; but in the case of a *Konstatierung* (since "'this here' has meaning only in connection with a gesture . . . one must somehow point to reality"), the occasion of understanding it is the same as that of verifying it. Therefore a (significant) *Konstatierung* cannot be false. (3) Unlike "protocol sentences," these statements cannot be written down or recorded at all because of the fleeting reference of the demonstratives that occur in them; but they provide the occasions for the formation of protocol sentences. (4) They are the only empirical statements which are not hypotheses. (5) They are not the starting points of science in either a temporal or a logical sense, but simply the momentary consummations of the scientific process; they are the means by which all scientific hypotheses are confirmed.

The first and most obvious objection to the view that there are *Konstatierungen* (in Schlick's sense) is that it results immediately in a radical form of solipsism. It may also be objected that *Konstatierungen* are either genuine contingent statements, in which case they cannot be of such a nature that they cannot be false, or they are purely demonstrative, in which case they are not statements. Following Wittgenstein's later work, many philosophers would deny the possibility of the essentially private use of demonstratives and descriptions which are supposed to occur in *Konstatierungen*. Further, no adequate account is given of the relation between these private statements and the public protocol sentences to which they give rise. Moreover, if the *Konstatierungen* are meaningful only at the moment at which they are verified, they cannot occur in predictions, and hence it cannot be through them that scientific hypotheses are confirmed.

Carnap. Rudolf Carnap, in "Die physikalische Sprache als Universalsprache der Wissenschaft" (1931; translated as *The Unity of Science*, 1934) and elsewhere, had at first held that science is a system of statements based upon sentences describing the experiences of scientific observers. These "primitive protocol sentences," Carnap supposed, contain no inferential or theoretical additions; they describe only what is directly given, and hence they stand in no need of any further justification. At this time Carnap left it an open question whether protocol sentences describe the simplest sensations and feelings of the observer (for example, "here now red," "joy now"), or partial or complete gestalts of single sensory fields (for example, "red circle now"), or the total experience of the observer during an instant, or macroscopic material things (for example, "A red cube is on the table"). Later, however, in *Logische Syntax der Sprache* (1934) and other publications, due mainly to the criticisms of Neurath, Carnap held that the question of what protocol sentences describe is not a factual but a linguistic question and that we are free to choose whatever form of language is most convenient for reporting observations in science.

Neurath. Otto Neurath, in "Soziologie im Physikalismus" (1931/1932; English translation, 1959) and other articles, had argued that sentences cannot be compared with the private experiences of the observer, nor with public material things, but only with other sentences. Some sentences are reports of acts of observation, in the sense of being behavioral responses to those acts, and such protocol sentences may have whatever form we find most convenient. In "Protokollsätze" (1932/1933), Neurath maintained that for the purposes of science it must be possible to incorporate the protocol sentences expressed at one time in those expressed at another time, and that comparison of protocols, even with one's own past protocols, requires an intersubjective language. Neurath remarks, "*every* language *as such* is inter-subjective." Carnap later agreed that if protocol sentences were regarded as describing the observer's private experiences, they could be understood, if at all, only solipsistically. Neurath suggested that a convenient form for protocol sentences would be one which contained a name or description of an observer and some words recording an act of observation; he gives as an example "Otto's protocol at 3:17 o'clock [Otto's word-thought at 3:16: (In the room at 3:15 was a table perceived by Otto)]." In this example, it is supposed that the entire sentence is written down by Otto at 3:17, simply as an overt verbal response; the sentence in brackets is Otto's response at 3:16, and the sentence in parentheses is his response at 3:15. The word "Otto" is repeated, instead of using "my" and "me," in order that the components of the protocol may be independently tested, for example, by being found in the protocols of other observers. The protocols of different observers or of the same observer may conflict, and when this happens, one or more of them is to be rejected. According to Neurath, Carnap, and also Hempel in "On The Logical Positivists' Theory of Truth" (1934/1935) it is a matter of convenience and decision which of the conflicting protocols should be rejected; hence, no protocol is incorrigible. The aim of science is to build up a coherent system of sentences, but no sentence at any level is sacrosanct; every sentence in science is in the end accepted or rejected by a decision made in the interests of coherence and utility. This view was strenuously opposed—by Schlick, Russell, and Ayer, among others, who argued that (1) on this account protocol sentences are distinguished from others only in respect of their syntactical form; (2) a purely syntactical criterion of truth cannot do the work required of it; and (3) the Neurath–Carnap doctrine is a complete abandonment of empiricism.

Russell. According to Bertrand Russell's early doctrine of knowledge by acquaintance and knowledge by description, "every proposition we can understand must be composed wholly of constituents with which we are acquainted." A person is acquainted with those objects that are directly presented to his mind, and Russell held that sense data and universals are so presented. Later, in *The Analysis of Mind* (1921), Russell maintained that it is not possible to make a distinction between sensation and sense datum and that a sensation is not itself a cognition, although it is a cause of cognitions. This view led to the account of basic propositions that Russell gives in *An Inquiry into Meaning and Truth* (1940). In epistemology, he says, we can arrange our propositions about matters of fact in a certain order such that those that come later are known, if they are known, because of those that come earlier. At the beginning of such an ordering there will be "basic propositions"—those which "on reflection appear credible independently of any argument in their favour." A basic proposition is one whose utterance is caused as immediately as possible by a perceptual experience. It is known independently of inference but not independently of evidence, since the perceptual experience which causes it to be expressed also gives the reason for believing it. The perceptual experience in question provides the strongest possible evidence for the basic proposition; no previous or subsequent occurrence and no experiences of others can prove that the proposition is false. Nevertheless, according to Russell, a basic proposition is not incorrigible; it cannot be disproved, but it may be false. Since one of the aims of epistemology is to show that all empirical knowledge is based upon these propositions, it is desirable that they should be given a logical form which makes contradiction between them impossible. Russell therefore defines a basic proposition as one "which arises on the occasion of a perception, which is the evidence for its truth, and . . . has a form such that no two propositions having this form can be mutually inconsistent if derived from different percepts" (*Inquiry Into Meaning and Truth*, p. 139). Examples are "there is a canoid (shaped) patch of color," "I am hot," "that is red." Alternatively, "we can consider the whole body of empirical knowledge and define 'basic propositions' as those of its logically indemonstrable propositions which are themselves empirical" (*ibid.*). Russell believes that this logical definition is extensionally equivalent to his epistemological definition.

Ayer. Whether basic propositions are incorrigible or indubitable, and if so in what sense, has been considered at length by A. J. Ayer. In "Basic Propositions" (1950) he defends the view that if a sentence is a direct description of a private experience, it may be verbally incorrect, but it cannot express a proposition about which the speaker can be factually mistaken. He explains this in the following way. Many descriptive sentences, for example, "That is a table," may be used correctly (that is, in accordance with the rules of the language and on occasions generally agreed to be appropriate for their use), and yet the propositions they express may turn out to be false. But in the case of a sentence which directly describes a present experience, if the sentence is used correctly (that is, in accordance with the speaker's rules), the proposition it expresses cannot turn out to be false. Thus, "the sense in which statements like 'This is green,' 'I feel a headache,' 'I seem to remember______' can be said to be indubitable is that, when they are understood to refer only to some immediate experience, their truth or falsehood is conclusively determined by a meaning rule of the language in which they are expressed" ("Basic Propositions," p. 72).

Later, in *The Problem of Knowledge* (1956) and elsewhere, Ayer argues that language rules may be essentially private and that basic statements may be expressed in a sense-datum terminology, provided that this terminology is translatable into a terminology of seeming. Incorrigibility is not a property belonging to statements as such; "the sentences 'He has a headache,' when used by someone else to refer to me, 'I shall have a headache,' used by me in the past with reference to this moment, and 'I have a headache' all express the same statement; but the third of these sentences alone is used in such conditions as make it reasonable for me to claim that the statement is incorrigibly known" (*The Problem of Knowledge*, p. 58). But Ayer here allows that if he were asked, regarding two lines in his visual field, which looked to him to be the longer, he might very well be uncertain how to answer; and this uncertainty would not be about the meaning of the expression "looks longer than" but about a matter of fact. If anyone can have doubt about such matters of fact, he can presumably come to the wrong decision, that is, he can judge that one of the lines looks to him longer than the other when in fact it does not. No direct test of such a mistake is possible, but there may be various kinds of indirect evidence to show that it has occurred; hence, Ayer concludes, there is no class of descriptive statements which are incorrigible.

Popper. The requirements made upon basic statements are very often governed by the general nature of the theory of knowledge held by a philosopher. Thus, according to Karl Popper, our experiences cannot justify or establish the truth of any statement; the question for epistemology is not ". . . on what does our *knowledge* rest? . . . or more exactly, how can I, having had the *experience* S, justify my description of it and defend it against doubt," but rather "how do we test scientific statements by their deductive consequences . . . *what kind* of consequences can we select for this purpose if they in their turn are to be intersubjectively testable?" (*The Logic of Scientific Discovery*, p. 98). Popper requires a class of basic statements by reference to which it can be decided whether a theory or hypothesis in science is falsifiable. Evidently a theory can be falsified by a basic statement only if the negation of the latter is derivable from the theory. Popper finds that his requirements are met by taking singular existential statements of the form "There is a so-and-so in space-time region *k*" as basic. It follows that the negation of a basic statement is not itself a basic statement (Popper allows some simple exceptions to this in *Conjectures and Refutations*, Addenda, p. 386); it also follows that any conjunction of basic statements which is not a logical contradiction is a basic statement and that the conjunction of a nonbasic and a basic statement may be a basic statement (for example, the conjunction of "There is no pointer in motion at *k*" with "There is a pointer at *k*," which is equivalent to "There is a pointer at rest at *k*"). Given a theory *t* conjoined with a statement of initial conditions *r*, from which a prediction *p* can be derived, it follows that $r \cdot \sim p$ will be a falsifier of *t* and a basic statement—since if $(t \cdot r) \rightarrow p$, then $t \rightarrow (r \rightarrow p)$, that is, $t \rightarrow \sim(r \cdot \sim p)$.

Popper also stipulates that the event referred to in a basic statement should be observable, that is, a basic statement must be intersubjectively testable by observation. He claims that the concept of an observable event can be elucidated either in terms of the experiences of an observer or in terms of macroscopic physical bodies, and hence that his account is neutral regarding the issue between psychologism and physicalism. In Popper's theory, the expression "observable event" is introduced "as an undefined term which becomes sufficiently precise in use: as a primitive concept whose use the epistemologist has to learn. . . ." According to Popper, "a science needs points of view and theoretical problems"; hence, in the practice of science we should not accept stray basic statements but only those which occur in the course of testing theories. Every test of a theory must terminate with some basic statement, but every basic statement can itself be subjected to further tests. There are no logical grounds for stopping at any particular basic statement. It is a matter for agreement and decision among those engaged in testing a theory; the process of corroboration or falsification terminates at the point at which they are satisfied for the time being.

From the preceding selection of views, held by recent and contemporary philosophers, it will be seen that there is no consensus concerning basic statements. The questions listed at the beginning of this article can be answered only in relation to a more general semantic and epistemological theory. Many such theories allow that there is a distinct class of basic statements. It seems that the relation between these statements and certain "experiences" of the speakers who express them must be partly semantic, and perhaps also partly causal, but the correct analysis of this relation is a matter of great difficulty. Many philosophers at the present time deny that there can be a class of statements that describe the *private* experiences of the speaker, on the grounds that there cannot be a language that is essentially private; but this latter view is also strongly contested. Finally, although on some views basic statements are indubitable, it seems that these statements cannot be incorrigible, at least in any sense that implies that they cannot be false. For if basic statements are to play the role assigned to them—namely, of being the terminating points of empirical verification—they must be genuine contingent statements; and a contingent statement is one whose negation is significant and could, as far as logic is concerned, be true.

Bibliography

Wittgenstein's view in the *Tractatus Logico-philosophicus* (London, 1922) is the object of his own criticism in *Philosophical Investigations* (Oxford, 1953), especially in Part I, Secs. 1–64.

Schlick's "Über das Fundament der Erkenntnis," in *Erkenntnis*, Vol. 4 (1934), has been translated by David Rynin in A. J. Ayer, ed., *Logical Positivism* (Glencoe, Ill., 1959), pp. 209–227. The same volume also contains English translations by Morton Magnus and Ralph Raico of Otto Neurath's "Soziologie im Physikalismus" (which originally appeared in *Erkenntnis*, Vol. 2, 1931/1932) on pp. 282–317, and by Frederic Schlick of Neurath's "Protokollsätze" (which originally appeared in *Erkenntnis*, Vol. 3, 1932/1933) on pp. 199–208.

For Carnap's views, see "Die physikalische Sprache als Universalsprache der Wissenschaft," in *Erkenntnis*, Vol. 2 (1931/1932), translated by Max Black as *The Unity of Science* (London, 1934), and *Logische Syntax der Sprache* (Vienna, 1934), translated by Amethe Smeaton as *The Logical Syntax of Language* (London, 1937).

The views of Hempel may be found in "On the Logical Positivists' Theory of Truth," in *Analysis*, Vol. 2, No. 4 (1934/1935).

Russell's views on basic statements can be found in *The Analysis of Mind* (London, 1921) and *An Inquiry Into Meaning and Truth* (London, 1940).

Ayer's contributions to this topic include the following: *Language, Truth and Logic* (London, 1936; 2d ed., 1946), Ch. 5 and Sec. 1 of Introduction to 2d ed.; "Verification and Experience," in *PAS*, Vol. 37; *Foundations of Empirical Knowledge* (London, 1940), Ch. 2; "Basic Propositions," in Max Black, ed., *Philosophical Analysis* (Ithaca, N.Y., 1950), reprinted in *Philosophical Essays* (London, 1954); and *The Problem of Knowledge* (London, 1956).

Relevant works by Karl Popper are *The Logic of Scientific Discovery* (London, 1959), especially Ch. 5, and *Conjectures and Refutations* (London and New York, 1963).

Further discussion of Quine's views may be found in "Two Dogmas of Empiricism," in *Philosophical Review* (1951), reprinted in *From a Logical Point of View* (Cambridge, Mass., 1953); *Methods of Logic* (London, 1952), Introduction; and *Word and Object* (New York, 1960), Secs. 8–10.

R. W. ASHBY

BAUER, BRUNO (1809–1882), German theologian and historian, studied theology under P. H. Marheineke in Berlin, at the height of Hegel's influence there. When Bauer became a docent at the University of Berlin in 1834, he joined Marheineke on the Hegelian right wing. However, when he transferred to the University of Bonn in 1839, he was already reacting theologically against right-wing Hegelianism. D. F. Strauss' *Life of Jesus* (1835–1836) rocked the theological world, but it seemed to Bauer not sufficiently critical, and helped to spur him on to his own investigations of the Gospels.

Bauer began with literary criticism of the Gospel texts themselves, without making any assumptions about the historical life of Jesus or the early church. The fourth Gospel was simply a work of reflective Christian art dominated by Philo's logos concept, impressive as such, but without historical basis (*Kritik der evangelischen Geschichte des Johannes,* Bremen, 1840). The situation was the same with regard to the Synoptic Gospels, except that they were based on the conception of the Messiah (*Kritik der evangelischen Geschichte der Synoptiker,* 3 vols. Leipzig, 1841–1842.) Bauer adopted the conclusion of C. H. Weisse and C. Wilke that only Mark's Gospel was original, but argued further that there was no reason to assume any historical tradition behind this single literary source. Incongruities in Mark's text suggested that Mark had invented the events he related. Mark's story was accepted because it answered the spiritual needs of his age. Jesus was the man in whose consciousness the antitheses between heaven and earth, God and man, were reconciled. His character evoked the Messiah concept, into which his life was absorbed by Mark. Bauer's view seemed to undercut the historical basis of Christianity so sharply that the theological faculties of the Prussian universities were polled (with mixed results) as to whether Bauer should be dismissed from Bonn. Bauer sealed his fate with the article "Theological Shamelessness" (1814), in which he denounced the Christian faith as the source of lies and servile hypocrisy; he was dismissed in March 1842. Ultimately, Bauer denied the historicity of Jesus altogether, holding that Christianity was an amalgam of Stoic and Gnostic ideas in Jewish dress.

Meanwhile, Bauer had written his anonymous *Die Posaune des jüngsten Gerichts über Hegel den Atheisten und Antichristen* ("Trumpet of the Last Judgment on Hegel the Atheist and Anti-Christ," Leipzig, 1841), ostensibly from the standpoint of faith, attempting to show that the real result of Hegelian philosophy was neither the pantheism of Strauss nor the humanism of Feuerbach—much less a defense of the Gospel—but Bauer's own out-and-out atheism.

At that time living on a small estate in Rixdorf, near Berlin, Bauer gathered around himself a circle of "free spirits" (including his brother Edgar) who frequented Berlin cafes. Bauer wrote brilliantly ironical "critiques" of recent historical developments in which he announced the downfall of Western philosophy and culture. For a time he collaborated with Arnold Ruge and with other left-wing Hegelians. But Bauer was as contemptuous of their revolutionary programs as he was of the bourgeois establishment. He attacked the inconsistencies and misconceptions of both groups; special class interests, he argued, are blindly one-sided, and the masses are so much dead matter, and inimical to the spirit. Only criticism, without presupposition, reservation, or special pleading, can be pure, can replace blindness with true conceptions, and can bring about the fundamental change in human consciousness that would really be liberating. History will, by its own "logic," bring about the transformation which no deliberate program can institute: what criticism has destroyed in thought today, history will destroy in fact tomorrow. Bauer justified these views by means of a metaphysic of consciousness, according to which the world is the projection of the ego. Matter is the as yet unclarified aspect of the world; evil social conditions are the product of uncritical and self-alienated principles. Christianity, for example, freed the ego from its thralldom to the material world, but only through an alienation of spirit from matter that had in its turn created a new burden. But Bauer held that once Christianity's historical roots are exposed, its self-alienating power is broken; hence the importance of criticism. The same must be done with other forms of human bondage: revolutionary programs which do not reach to the roots of consciousness are futile.

Accordingly, Bauer attacked various reform movements as insufficiently radical. Jewish agitation for political rights, for example, was based on the separate religious identity of the Jew, and could never be defended on those grounds against those whose religious prejudices took a different form; the Jew could become free only by ceasing to be religious. Marx answered this argument in his essay "On the Jewish Problem" (1844), and attacked Bauer as "St. Bruno" in *The Holy Family: Critique of the Critical Critic, Against Bruno Bauer and Consorts* (1845). The real problem, according to Marx, was economic class behavior, and not the religious projections of that behavior. Bauer's view that social conditions could be changed by changing men's minds was a vestige of idealist–theological error, and the practical result of Bauer's theoretical radicalism would be political reactionism.

Bauer did in fact become a defender of Prussian conservatism, on the radical grounds, that limited reform movements seemed to him to do more harm than good. But after 1850 his influence waned; though he continued to write prodigiously, his views were generally too eccentric to be relevant.

Additional Works by Bauer

Vollständige Geschichte der Parteikämpfe in Deutschland während der Jahre 1842–1846, 3 vols. Berlin, 1847.

Die bürgerliche Revolution in Deutschland seit dem Anfang der deutsche-katholischen Bewegung bis zur Gegenwart. Berlin, 1849.

Russland und das Germanentum. Berlin, 1853.

Die Hegelsche Linke, Karl Löwith, ed. Stuttgart and Bad Cannstatt, 1962. Includes *Die Posaune* and selections from *Russland und das Germanentum.*

Christus und die Cäsaren, der Ursprung des Christentums aus dem römischen Griechentum. Berlin, 1877.

Works on Bauer

Hertz-Eichenrode, Dieter, *Der Junghegelianer Bruno Bauer im Vormärz.* Berlin, 1959.

Hook, Sidney, *From Hegel to Marx.* New York, 1936. pp. 89–125.

Löwith, Karl, *Von Hegel zu Nietzsche,* 4th ed. Stuttgart, 1958. pp. 120–125; 322–324; 366–374. For an extensive bibliography see pp. 432–433.

Schweitzer, Albert, *Geschichte des Leben-Jesu-Forschung.* Tübingen, 1926. pp. 141–161. Translated from the first German edition, *Von Reimarus zu Wrede* (1906), by W. Montgomery under the title *The Quest of the Historical Jesus.* London, 1910. pp. 137–160. Reprinted New York, 1950.

STEPHEN D. CRITES

BAUMGARTEN, ALEXANDER GOTTLIEB (1714–1762), German Wolffian philosopher and aesthetician, was born in Berlin, the son of an assistant to the Pietist theologian and pedagogue August Hermann Francke; his brother was the famous divine and church historian Sigmund Jakob. Baumgarten studied philosophy and theology at Halle. After receiving a master's degree in 1735, he was appointed a teacher at Halle and in 1738 became extraordinary professor. While teaching there, Baumgarten, in reaction against the Pietism dominant at Halle after the expulsion of Christian Wolff in 1723, reintroduced Wolffian philosophy. In 1740 he was appointed full professor at Frankfurt an der Oder, where he remained until his death.

Baumgarten's Latin handbooks on metaphysics, ethics, and practical philosophy were widely used in German universities both in his time and after his death, and his influence was extraordinary. Kant considered him to be one of the greatest metaphysicians of his time and adopted his *Metaphysics* and *Practical Philosophy* as textbooks for his own lectures at Königsberg. With the exception of his works on aesthetics, Baumgarten in general kept very close to Wolff's teachings, although he dissented from Wolff on several special points. For instance, he adopted a middle position in the controversy over the problem of the interaction of substances by reconciling Wolff's theory of the "pre-established harmony" of the soul and body with the theory of physical influence supported by the Pietists. Baumgarten, as a supporter of Leibnizian panpsychism, applied his solution to the connections among all substances. Wolff, to the contrary, distinguished very sharply between spiritual and material substances. Baumgarten was thus less Leibnizian than Wolff in accepting physical influence and more Leibnizian in his panpsychism.

Baumgarten made his most important contributions in the field of aesthetics, expanding a subject which had been summarily treated by Wolff and going far beyond Wolff in developing it. In this field he collaborated so closely with his pupil G. F. Meier (1718–1777) that it is difficult to establish the real authorship of many doctrines. There is a very close connection between Baumgarten's *Meditationes Philosophicae de Nonnullis ad Poema Pertinentibus* and his unfinished *Aesthetica* and Meier's *Anfangsgründe aller schönen Künste und Wissenschaften,* (3 vols, Halle, 1748–1750). Baumgarten introduced the term "aesthetics" to designate that section of empirical psychology which treats of the inferior faculty, that is, the faculty of sensible knowledge. The problem of beauty was only one part of this subject. Even in Kant, "aesthetics" referred both to sensible knowledge in general and to knowledge of beauty and the sublime in particular. Only later was it restricted to the field of beauty and sublimity. Aesthetics and logic together composed, in Baumgarten's view, a science which he called "gnoseology," or theory of knowledge.

According to Baumgarten, the foundations of poetry and the fine arts are "sensitive (*sensitivae*) representations," which are not simply "sensual" (*sensuales*), but are connected with feeling (and therefore are pertinent both to the faculty of knowledge and to that of will). A beautiful poem is a "perfect sensitive discourse," that is, a discourse which awakens a lively feeling. This requires a high degree of "extensive clarity," which is different from "intensive (or intellectual) clarity." This means that an aesthetic representation must have many "characteristics," that is, it must be characterized by many different traits or particular elements, rather than by a few well-differentiated characters. Beauty must be "confused" and, therefore, excludes "distinctness," the main property of intellectual representations. Distinctness is reached by rendering clearly each of the characteristics of the characteristics of a representation. Establishing these characteristics presupposes intensive clarity and leads to a further abstraction of the concept of representations. This abstraction is obnoxious to aesthetic liveliness and leads to pedantry.

The artist is not an imitator of nature in the sense that he copies it: he must add feeling to reality, and thereby he imitates nature in the process of creating a world or a whole. This whole is unified by the artist through a coherent "theme," which is the focus of the representation.

This does not mean that the artist should prefer fiction to truth; on the contrary, knowledge of the beautiful is, at its best, sensible knowledge of truth made perfectly lively. This is a main point of divergence between Wolff and Baumgarten. Baumgarten held that, since rational knowledge of several orders of facts or of many facts in general is impossible, it must be replaced or supplemented by "beautiful knowledge," i.e., reliable sensible knowledge of things that cannot be known rationally; such knowledge is as reliable as rational knowledge; typical aesthetic elements of the cognitive process are inductions and examples. By stressing the importance and relative independence of the inferior faculty (which Wolff held to be only an imperfect stage of knowledge, to be superseded by intellect and reason), Baumgarten foreshadowed Kant's doctrine of the peculiar and independent function of sensibility in knowledge.

Works by Baumgarten

Meditationes Philosophicae de Nonnullis ad Poema Pertinentibus. Halle, 1735. Translated by K. Aschenbrunner and W. B. Hoelther, eds., as *Reflections on Poetry*. Berkeley, Calif., 1954.

Metaphysica. Halle, 1739.

Ethica Philosophica. Halle, 1740.

Aesthetica, 2 vols. Frankfurt an der Oder, 1750–1758.

Initia Philosophiae Practicae Primae. Halle, 1760.

Acroasis Logica. Halle, 1761.

Ius Naturae. Halle, 1765.

Sciagraphia Encyclopaediae Philosophicae, J. C. Förster, ed. Halle, 1769.

Philosophia Generalis, J. C. Förster, ed. Halle, 1769.

Works on Baumgarten

Abbt, Thomas, *A. G. Baumgartens Leben und Charakter.* Halle, 1765.

Bergmann, Ernst, *Die Begründung der deutschen Aesthetik durch A. G. Baumgarten und G. F. Meier.* Leipzig, 1911.

Cassirer, Ernst, *Die Philosophie der Aufklärung.* Tübingen, 1932. Translated by F. C. A. Koelln and J. D. Pettegrove as *The*

Philosophy of the Enlightenment. Princeton, N.J., 1954. Pp. 338–357.

Meier, G. F., *A. G. Baumgartens Leben und Schriften.* Halle, 1763.

Poppe, B., *A. G. Baumgarten, seine Bedeutung und seine Stellung in der Leibniz–Wolffschen Philosophie und seine Beziehung zu Kant.* Münster, 1907.

Riemann, A., *Die Ästhetik A. G. Baumgartens.* Halle, 1928.

ON BAUMGARTEN'S RELATION TO KANT

Bäumler, A., *Kants Kritik der Urteilskraft.* Halle, 1923.

Tonelli, Giorgio, "Kant, dall'estetica metafisica all'estetica psicoempirica." *Memorie della Accademia delle Scienze di Torino,* Series 3, Vol. 3, Pt. 2.

GIORGIO TONELLI

BAUTAIN, LOUIS EUGENE MARIE (1796–1867), French cleric and philosopher, was born in Paris. After studying at the École Normale under Victor Cousin, he taught philosophy at Strasbourg. A breakdown and sudden conversion led to his taking orders in 1828, and he was appointed professor of moral theology in the theological faculty in 1853.

Bautain's main contribution to philosophy lay in his defense of faith as superior to reason. Reason, he believed, varies from man to man and from group to group, as is proved by the conflicts in the conclusions of the rationalistic schools. But above the reasoning processes of individuals there is a divine reason, one and eternal, revealed in Scripture, whence all true reasoning proceeds. One must always start with unproved premises, regardless of one's problem, and it is wiser to use those that come from God than those that are invented *ad hoc.* These premises must be accepted on faith, for from their very nature as premises they cannot be proved. Once accepted, the reason can deduce their consequences. In his *Philosophie du christianisme* (Paris, 1833), Bautain attributed this idea to the influence of Kant's antinomies, which leave man in a state of doubt about those truths of which he has the greatest need. But he also introduced a pragmatic element into his argument in maintaining that the moral consequences of this procedure are more satisfactory than those that follow from a purely rationalistic technique.

Bautain's *fidéisme* was condemned by Pope Gregory XVI, and in 1840 Bautain recanted and signed the following six theses: (1) reason can prove the existence of God with certainty; and faith, a divine gift, is posterior to revelation and cannot be asked of an atheist in proving God's existence; (2) the divinity of the Mosaic revelation is proved by the oral and written tradition of synagogue and church; (3) the proof of the miracles of Jesus Christ is contained in the testimony of eyewitnesses; (4) the skeptic cannot be asked to accept the Resurrection until he has been given rational arguments; (5) in certain questions, faith surpasses reason and ought to lead us to it; (6) however weak reason may have become because of original sin, it retains enough clarity and power to lead us to recognize the existence of God, the revelation made to the Jews through Moses, and that made to Christians through "our adorable Man-God." Bautain's signing ended *fidéisme* within the church.

Bautain's affiliation with traditionalism lay not only in his emphasis on the Christian tradition itself but also in his acceptance of the thesis that language is identical with truth once its meaning is reflected upon because language has a divine origin in the Logos.

Works by Bautain

La philosophie du christianisme, 2 vols. Paris, 1833.

Psychologie expérimentale, 2 vols. Strasbourg, 1839. Revised ed. *L'Esprit humain et ses facultés,* 2 vols. Paris, 1859.

Philosophie morale, 2 vols. Paris, 1842.

Religion et liberté. Paris, 1848.

Works on Bautain

Boas, George, *French Philosophies of the Romantic Period.* Baltimore, 1926, pp. 233–239.

Denzinger, H., *Enchiridion Symbolorum et Definitionum,* 13th ed. Freiburg, 1921, nos. 1622–1627 inc. The theses to which Bautain subscribed.

Ferraz, M., *Histoire de la philosophie en France au XIXe siècle, traditionalisme et ultramontanisme.* Paris, 1880, Ch. 6.

GEORGE BOAS

BAYLE, PIERRE (1647–1706), the most important and most influential skeptic of the late seventeenth century, was born in Carla, a French village near the Spanish frontier, where his father was the Protestant pastor. He grew up during the religious persecutions under Louis XIV that culminated in the revocation of the Edict of Nantes (1685) and the outlawing of Protestantism in France. Bayle was sent first to a Calvinist school and then to the Jesuit college at Toulouse, where after studying the controversial literature and hearing the dialectical arguments of some of the professors, he converted to Catholicism. The intellectual considerations that led him to Catholicism, after further examination, soon led him back to Calvinism. He became technically a *relaps,* a person who has returned to heresy after having abjured it, and under French law he was therefore subject to severe penalties. He left France for Geneva, where he completed his philosophical and theological studies. In 1674 he returned to France incognito and became a tutor in Paris and Rouen. The next year he obtained the philosophy professorship at the Protestant academy of Sedan as the protégé of Pierre Jurieu, a superorthodox theologian who was to become Bayle's greatest enemy. Bayle taught at Sedan until the school was closed in 1681. He and Jurieu went to Holland; they became members of the *École illustre* of Rotterdam and of the French Reformed church there. Bayle brought with him his first work, a letter concerning the comet of 1680, which he published under a pseudonym. This volume, like many of those to follow, attacked superstition, intolerance, and poor philosophy and history. The work was immediately successful and was soon followed by others, including an answer to Father Maimbourg's history of Calvinism and a collection of defenses of Cartesianism.

During these early years in Rotterdam, Bayle apparently made some fundamental personal decisions that affected the rest of his life. The first was not to marry but to devote himself to the solitary life of the dedicated scholar seeking truth. The second was to refuse any important professorship in order to carry on his work in Rotterdam (where he lived almost continuously for the rest of his life). Lastly, after his father and his brothers died in France as a result of the religious persecutions, Bayle apparently committed himself both to the cause of Calvinism and the cause of toleration.

From 1684 until 1687 Bayle edited the *Nouvelles de la république des lettres,* one of the first learned journals of modern times, in which he reviewed works in many fields. His critical appraisals soon made him a major figure in the learned world and brought him in contact with the leading lights of his day, among them, Antoine Arnauld, Robert Boyle, Leibniz, Locke, and Malebranche.

Toleration. In 1686 Bayle published in Amsterdam his *Commentaire philosophique sur ces paroles de Jésus-Christ "Constrains-les d'entrer"* ("Philosophical Commentary on the Words of Jesus 'Constrain Them to Come in'"), a brilliant argument for complete religious toleration. Starting with the problem raised by Louis XIV's persecutions, Bayle developed a defense of toleration for Jews, Moslems, Socinians (Unitarians), Catholics, and even atheists, extending its scope far beyond Locke's not yet published *Essay on Toleration.*

Enmity had begun to develop between Bayle and Jurieu, who conceived of himself as the chief spokesman for Calvinist orthodoxy, opposed all kinds of deviation as heresy and atheism, and advocated political victory over Louis XIV. As Jurieu became a violent political radical and religious bigot, Bayle drifted away from the views and company of his erstwhile mentor. According to Jurieu, the disaffection reached the breaking point with the publication of Bayle's "Philosophical Commentary." Bayle had tried to hide his authorship, but Jurieu soon guessed the truth and realized that they disagreed completely about almost everything. He saw his colleague as a menace to true religion and a secret atheist. Bayle intensified the quarrel by ridiculing Jurieu, attacking his intolerance and his political plans. Bayle, throughout the quarrel, insisted that he, Bayle, was a true follower of Calvin and that he had imbibed his orthodoxy from Jurieu's antirational theology.

When Bayle began to publish his views, the Protestant liberals thought that he was on their side. But Bayle quickly employed his dialectical and critical skill to decimate their contentions and to show that there was no way of making the rational and scientific world compatible with the basic claims of Christianity, as they in part believed it to be. As a result, various liberal Protestants spent years defending themselves against Bayle's sharp criticisms, while Bayle alternately joined them in attacking Jurieu and Jurieu in attacking them.

Between 1690 and 1692 the argument between Bayle and Jurieu reached fever pitch, especially concerning whether or not Bayle was the author of the notorious "Advice to the French Refugees," a work criticizing the romantic optimism and hopes of the Protestant exiles. (Bayle so confused the evidence that even present-day scholars are unwilling to state positively that he did write it.) These controversies with Jurieu led in 1693 to Bayle's dismissal from his teaching post, an event which allowed him time to carry on his many controversies and to complete his great *Dictionnaire historique et critique* (first published in two volumes in Rotterdam in 1695 and 1697), a work in which Jurieu is constantly attacked.

History and composition of the "Dictionary." Bayle had conceived the basic idea of the *Dictionary* long before its composition. For many years he had been assembling collections of errors uncovered in various historical works. As early as 1675, Bayle's letters show, he was actively interested in skeptical thought. In the lectures Bayle gave at Rotterdam he criticized every possible theory. The *Dictionary* brought his critical and skeptical sides together. Originally Bayle planned only to write a dictionary that would list the mistakes in all other dictionaries and in particular the one by Louis Moréri. A sample portion of this project was printed in 1692 to test public interest. The negative reaction led to a change of plan; the dictionary became a historical and critical one, dealing principally with persons and mainly with those who were not treated fully or at all (usually because of their obscurity or insignificance) in Moréri's opus. The result was two folio volumes full of articles on very little known or totally unknown figures, omitting very significant figures like Plato, Montaigne, and Cardinal Richelieu.

The *Dictionary* was composed in Talmudic style. Relatively brief biographical articles appeared at the top of the page, while all sorts of digressive notes on factual, philosophical, religious, or other matters appeared below, with notes on notes appearing in the margins. The biography of some extremely little-known personage, like Rorarius, would provide the stage for profound discussions of the nature of man and beasts, the mind–body problem, and the new metaphysical theory of Leibniz. Other subjects would provide forums for discussing the problem of evil; the immorality of great figures, especially Old Testament ones; the irrationality of Christianity; the problems of Locke's, Newton's, Malebranche's, Aristotle's, or anyone else's philosophy; or for some salacious tale about a famous theologian, Catholic or Protestant, or a famous political figure of almost any age. There was little relation between the official subject of an article and its real content. But there were several major themes and threads that ran through many or most of the articles, themes that amounted to a massive onslaught against almost any religious, philosophical, moral, scientific, or historical view that anyone held. (Once Bayle explained that he was a Protestant in the true sense of the term, that he opposed everything that was said and everything that was done.)

The *Dictionary* was an instant success and immediately led to criticism and condemnation, both by the French Reformed church of Rotterdam and by the French Catholic church. The latter group banned the work, while the former demanded that the author revise or explain his views about the good moral character of atheists, the inability of Christians to answer the Manichaean views about the nature of evil, the strength of Pyrrhonian skepticism, the immoral character of King David, and to explain why so many obscenities appeared in the work. Bayle promised the congregation of the French Reformed church that he would revise the article "David" and would offer explanations of the other matters. Almost as soon as the first edition of the *Dictionary* appeared, Bayle began work on the second, revising the article "David" and adding many additional articles, plus a set of clarifications. This final edition appeared in Rotterdam in 1702 and consisted of seven to eight million words. After this monumental effort, the rest of Bayle's career was devoted to carrying on various controversies, defending some of the claims in the *Dictionary* and fighting a growing list of opponents. He died on Dec. 28, 1706 while completing his *Entretiens de Maxime et de Thémiste* ("Conversations between Maxime and Themiste," Rotterdam, 1707), a final reply to the liberal Protestants.

Replies to Bayle kept appearing, written by such figures as Leibniz, Bishop William King, and Jean-Pierre Crousaz; and the avant-garde spirits of the Enlightenment found much ammunition in Bayle's folio columns with which to attack the ideological and theological *ancien regime*. Voltaire, Hume, Gibbon, Diderot, and many others found intellectual nutrition in Bayle's skeptical and critical efforts. Thomas Jefferson recommended the *Dictionary* as one of the hundred basic books with which to start the Congressional Library. Poets and writers of fiction like Alexander Pope, Henry Fielding, and Herman Melville found inspiration and plots in some of Bayle's spicy tales. Ludwig Feuerbach, in the nineteenth century, saw Bayle as a major figure in the rise of modern thought and devoted a whole volume to him.

The *Dictionary* was enormously influential during the eighteenth century, both for its spirit and for its wealth of information. Though it was written in the form of a reference work, its lopsided contents, overloaded with lives of obscure theologians and figures of French political history, made it difficult for the *Dictionary* to maintain its character as a guide to research and scholarship. Efforts to improve it by adding and updating articles were only temporarily successful. The editors of the 1734–1741 English edition put in hundreds of articles on English and Arabic figures, plus some "correctives" to what they regarded as outlandish in Bayle's original. Jacques-Georges Chaufepié in 1740 translated many of the English articles into French, adding a great many more on Bayle's opponents, and put out a four-volume folio supplement. However, the type of critical and careful research Bayle had fostered gave birth to projects that would forever make his *Dictionary* obsolete as a reference work. *La Grande Encyclopédie* and the *Encyclopaedia Britannica*, which replaced it, were continuing team efforts, rather than one man's appraisal of the whole intellectual world. Thus Bayle's work became a victim of its own offspring. It gradually disappeared as an important element in the intellectual world and was superseded by the works of leaders of the Enlightenment who had imbibed at least part of Bayle's spirit.

Philosophical aspects of the "Dictionary." The discussions in the *Dictionary* that had the greatest philosophical impact were those dealing with the problem of evil, with the independence of morality from religion, and with the unintelligible nature of the physical and mental world, especially when analyzed in terms of the categories of the "new science" and the "new philosophy." With a dialectical skill unknown to earlier skeptics Bayle dissected every theory and showed that it was unsatisfactory. Instead of merely utilizing the classical epistemological arguments of Sextus Empiricus, slightly modernized by the Montaignians, Bayle employed primarily the method of one of his heroes, the "subtle Arriaga" (Roderigo Arriaga, the last of the Spanish scholastics, who died in 1667), a method that Bayle had probably learned from the Jesuits at Toulouse. The technique consisted in exposing the weakness of every rational attempt to make sense of some aspect of human experience. Bayle, like Arriaga before him, repeatedly exhibited man's sorry intellectual plight. All human rational efforts are always their own undoing and terminate in theories that are "big with contradiction and absurdity." Bayle concentrated on a few shocking illustrations of this thesis. In a series of articles, "Manichaeans," "Marcionites," "Paulicians," and "Rufinus," he contended that the Manichaean or dualistic theory of two gods, one good and one evil, could not be refuted by orthodox Christian theology, that it was a better explanation of human experience of evil, but that it was ultimately repugnant to sound reasoning. (Leibniz' *Theodicy* was largely an attempt to refute Bayle on Manichaeanism and the problem of evil.)

Religion and morality. Throughout his writings, from his letter on the comet to the *Dictionary* and its various defenses, Bayle argued the then scandalous thesis that a society of atheists could be moral and a society of Christians immoral. He tried to show that people's moral behavior is not a consequence of their beliefs but is rather the result of many irrational factors, such as education, custom, passion, ignorance, and the grace of God. In the article "Jupiter" Bayle pointed out that Greek mythology was absurd and immoral, but the Greeks lived moral lives nonetheless. In his "Clarification on Atheism" he stated that he could find no case of a classical atheist, or a modern one like Spinoza, who lived a wretched, morally degenerate life. Instead, the cases he found all seemed to be ones of highly moral people, who also happened to be atheists. On the other hand, Bayle knew of myriad cases—from Biblical ones to leading Catholic and Protestant clergy of his day—of religious heroes who were quite immoral and whose behavior seemed to have been influenced by the most irreligious factors. Among many articles dealing with the sexual aberrations of different religious fanatics, early reformers, and Renaissance popes, the very long one on "David" brought this point out most forcefully. David was introduced as the most holy figure in the Old Testament, and a series of notes outlined and analyzed his immoral conduct.

This massive assault on any alleged rational or necessary connection between religious belief and moral behavior greatly influenced the earl of Shaftesbury (who lived and argued with Bayle for awhile), and Bernard Mandeville (who was apparently one of Bayle's students at Rotterdam), and through them many of the eighteenth-century British moralists.

Metaphysics. In metaphysics Bayle employed his dialectical skill to show that theories about the nature of matter, space, time, motion, mind, and mind–body relationships, when thoroughly analyzed, are contradictory, inadequate, and absurd. Starting with Zeno's paradoxes and the sections in Sextus against metaphysics, Bayle attacked all sorts of ancient and modern forms of atomism, Platonism, and Aristotelianism, as well as the modern substitutes offered by Descartes, Hobbes, Spinoza, Malebranche, Leibniz, Locke, Newton, and many others. He showed the weird, incredible conclusions that would follow from each of these theories. (Bayle's article "Rorarius" was the first public examination of, and attack on, Leibniz' theories of pre-established harmony and of monads.) In the articles "Pyrrho" and "Zeno of Elea" (which greatly influenced Berkeley and Hume) Bayle brilliantly challenged the distinction between primary and secondary qualities, so fundamental in the theories about reality of all of the "new philosophers."

Skepticism. Bayle repeatedly showed that the many attempts by human beings to explain or understand their world were all just "highroads to Pyrrhonism," since they only made every supposition more perplexing, absurd, and dubious. Rational activity, no matter what problem it is directed at, leads to complete skepticism, since reason invariably leads us astray. In the article "Acosta" Bayle compared reason to a corrosive powder that first eats up errors, but then goes on to eat up truths. "When it is left on its own, it goes so far that it no longer knows where it is, and can find no stopping place."

Faith. Each time Bayle reached this point he would proclaim that in view of the inability of reason to arrive at any complete and adequate conclusion about anything, man should abandon the rational world and seek a different guide—faith. (This claim was forcefully stated in the articles "Bunel," "Charron," "Manichaeans," "Pomponazzi," "Pyrrho," and the "Clarification on the Pyrrhonians." Bayle's dwelling on the theme that reason makes men perplexed and so requires that they look for another guide suggests, perhaps, that his purpose was something like that of Maimonides in *The Guide of the Perplexed*, one of Bayle's favorite works.

Revelation. In various discussions (such as the articles "Pyrrho," "Simonides," and the "Clarification on the Pyrrhonians"), Bayle insisted that the rational and the revealed worlds are in complete conflict, because the latter is based on claims that are in direct opposition to the principles that appear most evident to reason. Starting with the first line of Genesis, the world of faith contains claims that are rationally unintelligible and unacceptable. According to Bayle, the principle that reason finds the most evident and certain is that nothing comes from nothing, whereas faith reveals that God created the world *ex nihilo*. Similarly, the most acceptable rational moral principles are at complete variance with the accounts revealed to us of the behavior of the heroes of the faith, the leading figures of the Old Testament. In this total opposition between reason and revelation, faith is man's only refuge. Bayle insisted that his irrational fideism was the traditional orthodox position from St. Paul and Tertullian down to Calvin and Jurieu. (In fact, some passages of Bayle sound like Kierkegaard and other more recent fideistic theologians.)

Bayle's religious position. No matter how often Bayle claimed that he was advocating the faith and was merely restating what orthodox Christians had always said, his opponents, especially Jurieu and some of the liberals, insisted that Bayle was actually an unbeliever trying to destroy the faith by making it sound as ridiculous and irrational as possible. Certainly some of Bayle's passages have such a ring. And none of his statements of the fideistic message have the anguish of Pascal or Kierkegaard, or even the despair of the truth seeker unable to find satisfaction in either the rational world or in revealed truths.

However, this may not necessarily be a sign that Bayle was insincere. Bayle himself offered an alternative possibility in a discussion in the longest article in the *Dictionary*, that on Spinoza. In note *M*, Bayle described two kinds of people, those who have religion in their minds, but not in their hearts, and those who have religion in their hearts, but not in their minds. The first kind are convinced of the truth of religion, but their consciences are not affected by the love of God. The second kind lose sight of religion when they seek it by rational means and are lost in the wilderness of the pros and cons; but when they listen only to their feelings, conscience, or education, they find that they are convinced of religion and regulate their lives accordingly, within the limits of human frailities. If Bayle had religion in the heart in this sense (rather than Pascal's), it was an emotionless religion, which became confused and perplexing whenever he tried to explain or comprehend it. When he abandoned the attempt to be rational about it, then it became a calm guide for a life of pious study.

In the article "Bunel, Pierre" Bayle presented this fervorless religion as almost a testimonial of faith. Bunel, an obscure Renaissance pedant from Toulouse (who accidentally had an enormous influence on the development of modern skepticism by giving Raimond Sebond's *Natural Theology* to Montaigne's father) is one of the very few genuine heroes of Bayle's *Dictionary*. He was pictured as a perfect Christian, in contrast to myriad imperfect ones (including Jurieu), because he rejected all worldly goals and devoted himself solely to the life of the pure scholar, harming no one and seeking truth. Bayle's own life was very much like Bunel's. Beyond this Bayle's religion seems to have had little or no content, though he always claimed to be a Calvinist Christian.

The lack of content in Bayle's religion may account for his important doctrine of toleration of the rights of the erring conscience. In many works Bayle insisted that man's ultimate appeal for justification of his beliefs and actions was his own conscience and that man had no further ultimate standard to employ in order to determine if his conscience was correct. Therefore, each man could act only as he saw fit, and no one was justified in trying to compel another to act contrary to the dictates of his conscience, erring or otherwise.

Though Bayle continually presented his appeal to faith, and his own faith, in tranquil and colorless terms, a fundamental problem remains of determining what Bayle did in fact believe and what his arsenal of doubts was intended to achieve. Shaftesbury, who knew Bayle well, called him "one of the best of Christians." Jurieu was sure he was an atheist. The Enlightenment leaders saw him as one of them, perhaps a deist, but definitely a scoffer at all historical religions. The biographical data would suggest that, barring some strange private joke, Bayle was committed to some aspects of the French Reformed church. He persisted in belonging to it, attending it, and proclaiming his sincere adherence to it, no matter how much he was abused by Jurieu and others. He could have lived and prospered in Holland either in a more liberal church or as a complete independent. In tolerant Holland it was extremely unlikely that he would have been punished or have had his works censored, no matter what he said or believed. Coming from a family that suffered inordinately from persecution for its Calvinism, he may have felt a need and desire to maintain his original tradition. His last message to a friend as he knew his life was ending was, "I am dying as a Christian philosopher, convinced of and pierced by the bounties and mercy of God, and I wish you a perfect happiness." Madame Labrousse has pointed out that this is a most minimal Christian testament, since Jesus is not mentioned, nor any Christian doctrine, nor anything about Bayle's church. In his writings Bayle rarely discussed religion without making Manichaeanism or Judaism seem either more plausible or more significant than Christianity; and he occasionally (as in the article "Takiddim") even called Judaism the true religion. Bayle may have been either a Christian in his own sense or actually a Manichaean or Judaizer or both, working out an enormous defense of his cause by undermining the rational or moral foundations of other possibilities.

Until it is possible to ascertain Bayle's actual beliefs, it will remain extremely difficult to determine his aims and whether the impact he had was the intended one. Bayle undermined all the philosophical positions of the great seventeenth-century metaphysicians, and posed basic problems that Berkeley, Hume, Voltaire, and others were to use to establish other approaches and alternatives. He provided an enormous amount of argument and ridicule for the Enlightenment to use in destroying the intellectual *ancien régime* and in launching the Age of Reason. But even Voltaire and Hume were aware that Bayle was much more given to doubt and destructive criticism than they considered themselves to be. At times they believed they had found new ways of overcoming Bayle's doubts. Perhaps they were both too far removed from Bayle's calm religious haven to be able to entertain his complete doubt about everything without utter dismay and horror. Bayle seems to have lived in a different world from that of the Enlightenment that he helped produce. Though he may not have been "the greatest master of the art of reasoning," as Voltaire called him, he was one of the best. He was a genius at seeing how to attack and destroy theories about almost anything and a master at determining what the facts in the case were. Bayle would turn his attacks against everyone and everything, modern, ancient, scientific, rationalistic, or religious. He did not, apparently, see a new and better world emerging from his critique, nor see the need for one. The havoc he was wreaking seemed to leave him completely tranquil. It was for subsequent generations to discover the problem of living in a world in which all is in doubt and in which the solution proffered by Bayle seems meaningless or unattainable.

Works by Bayle

Oeuvres diverses, 4 vols. The Hague, 1727. Collection of Bayle's writings other than the *Dictionary*. A photoreproduction edition is being issued from Hildesheim, Germany.

Dictionnaire historique et critique, 5th ed. Amsterdam, 1740. Translated by J. P. Bernard, T. Birch, and J. Lockman as *A General Dictionary, Historical and Critical,* 10 vols. London, 1734–1741.

Historical and Critical Dictionary (Selections). Indianapolis, 1965. Newly translated and with an introduction by Richard H. Popkin, this work contains selections from forty articles, plus Bayle's clarifications.

Works on Bayle

Barber, W. H., "Bayle: Faith and Reason," in W. G. Moore, R. Sutherland, and E. Starkie, eds., *The French Mind: Studies in Honour of Gustav Rudler.* Oxford, 1952. Pp. 109–125. Suggests that Bayle was sincerely religious.

Bracken, Harry M., "Bayle Not a Sceptic?" *Journal of the History of Ideas,* Vol. 25 (1964), 169–180. Attempts to clarify the sense in which Bayle was a skeptic and a fideist.

Courtines, Leo, *Bayle's Relation with England and the English.* New York, 1938. Deals with Bayle's contacts with and influence on English philosophers, theologians, and writers, including Berkeley and Hume.

Delvolvé, Jean, *Religion, critique, et philosophie positive chez Pierre Bayle.* Paris, 1906. A major French study that began the modern reconsideration and re-evalution of Bayle.

Dibon, Paul, ed., *Pierre Bayle, le philosophe de Rotterdam.* Amsterdam, 1959. An important collection of articles in French and English re-evaluating Bayle's views.

Feuerbach, Ludwig, *Pierre Bayle. Ein Beitrag zur Geschichte der Philosophie und Menschheit.* Leipzig, 1848. Bayle seen as caught between rationalism and the irrationality of Christianity.

Hasse, Erich, *Einführung in die Literatur des Refuge.* Berlin, 1959. A monumental study of the French Protestant refugees. Places Bayle in the context of this group.

Hazard, Paul, *La Crise de la conscience européenne, 1680–1715.* Paris, 1935. Translated by J. Lewis May as *The European Mind, 1680–1715.* London, 1953. The intellectual climate of Bayle's time.

James, E. D., "Scepticism and Fideism in Bayle's Dictionnaire." *French Studies,* Vol. 16 (1962), 307–324. Challenges the views of Popkin and others regarding Bayle's religious views.

Kemp Smith, Norman, *Hume's Dialogues Concerning Natural Religion.* Edinburgh, 1947. Introduction discusses what Hume drew from Bayle for the *Dialogues.*

Kemp Smith, Norman, *The Philosophy of David Hume.* London, 1941. Contains analyses of sections in Bayle that influenced Hume, especially in the *Treatise.*

Labrousse, Elisabeth, *Pierre Bayle. Tome 1, du pays de foix à la cité d'Erasme.* The Hague, 1963. First life of Bayle in recent times, based on monumental researches.

Labrousse, Elisabeth, *Pierre Bayle. Tome 2, hétérodoxie et rigorisme.* The Hague, 1964. A study of Bayle's theology by the leading authority today. Contains a massive bibliography.

Mason, H. T., "Pierre Bayle's Religious Views." *French Studies,* Vol. 17 (1963), 205–217. Defends interpretation of Bayle as an irreligious thinker.

Mason, H. T., *Pierre Bayle and Voltaire.* London, 1963. A comparison, with an attempt to assess what Voltaire borrowed from Bayle.

Norton, David, "Leibniz and Bayle: Manicheism and Dialectic." *Journal of the History of Philosophy,* Vol. 2 (1964), 23–36. An attempt to see how Bayle might have dealt with Leibniz' *Theodicy* and a new analysis of Bayle's dialectic.

Popkin, Richard H., "The Sceptical Precursors of David Hume." *Philosophy and Phenomenological Research,* Vol. 16 (1955), 61–71. A study of the skeptical tradition up to Hume, including Bayle.

Popkin, Richard H., "Berkeley and Pyrrhonism." *Review of Metaphysics,* Vol. 5 (1951/1952), 223–246. Includes an examination of Bayle's influence on Berkeley.

Popkin, Richard H., "The High Road to Pyrrhonism." *American Philosophical Quarterly.* Vol. 2 (1965) 1–15. Places Bayle in relation to other skeptics of the late seventeenth century.

Popkin, Richard H., "Bayle and Hume." *Transactions of the XIIIth International Congress of Philosophy, Mexico City, 1963.* Forthcoming. A discussion of the similarities and differences in these two skeptics.

Rex, Walter, "Pierre Bayle: The Theology and Politics of the Article on David." *Bibliothèque d'Humanisme et Renaissance,* Vol. 25 (1963), 168–189 and 366–403. A study of the seventeenth-century background of Bayle's views in article "David."

Robinson, Howard, *Bayle the Skeptic*. New York, 1931. The only book-length study of Bayle in English, offering the view that Bayle was an irreligious skeptic and a precursor of the Enlightenment.

Sandberg, K. C., "Pierre Bayle's Sincerity in His Views on Faith and Reason." *Studies in Philology*, Vol. 61 (1964), 74–84. Interprets Bayle as a sincere Calvinist. Shows Bayle had no need to fear censorship.

RICHARD H. POPKIN

BAZAROV, VLADIMIR ALEKSANDROVICH (1874–1939), Russian Marxist economist and philosopher; his real name was Rudnev. Bazarov was educated at Moscow University. His first publication was a study in economic theory. After 1922 he worked as an economist in the Soviet State Planning Commission, publishing technical papers throughout the 1920s. He was arrested in 1930 and died, presumably in a forced-labor camp, in 1939.

Bazarov was a prolific translator, producing Russian versions of Émile Boutroux, Harald Höffding, Karl Kautsky, Karl Pearson (with P. Yushkevich), and Marx's *Das Kapital* (with I. I. Skvortsov-Stepanov, 3 vols., 1907–1909). He was less involved in politics than either Bogdanov or Lunacharski but was prominent in the Bolshevik faction from 1904 to 1907.

Most of Bazarov's philosophic writings are polemical; all of them are forceful, some brilliant. His first critical studies (1904) were aimed at the Kantian revision of Marxism by Nicholai Berdyaev, Sergey Bulgakov, and P. B. Struve. Bazarov also published a critique of Kropotkin's anarcho-socialism (1906) and of Plekhanov's realistic epistemology and materialistic ontology (1908). In 1910 a volume of his essays appeared at St. Petersburg under the title *Na Dva Fronta* ("On Two Fronts"). It was directed on the one hand against such philosophical idealists as Vladimir Solovyov, Leo Shestov, Nicholas Lossky, and Berdyaev, and on the other against such "orthodox" materialists as Plekhanov and Lenin. Bazarov's last philosophical publication was an article on relativity theory, "Prostranstvo i Vremya v Svete Printsipa Otnositelnosti" ("Space and Time in the Light of Relativity Theory"), in *Teoriya Otnositelnosti i Marksizm* ("Relativity Theory and Marxism," Moscow, 1923).

Bazarov was harshly critical of normative ethics. With Nietzschean *élan* he assailed "sodden, dull, self-satisfied moral systems," urging a "revolt against norms as such" (*Na Dva Fronta*, p. 105). His own "amoralistic hedonism" involved a Machian "least-action" principle for harmonizing pleasures. It did not preclude suffering, but only the "suffering which degrades" (*ibid.*, p. xiv).

Bazarov scorned the Kantian dictum, defended by Berdyaev and Struve, that the individual person must always be treated as an end, never as only a means. "The recognition of the 'individual person' as an absolute principle," he declared, "has always been, and will always be, alien to the proletariat" (*ibid.*, p. 141). Bazarov's social ideal was collectivistic. In "objective social creativity," he wrote, "the very notion of 'the individual' and his interests will be extinguished." The intimacy of lovers offers only a "faint hint of that fusion of all human souls which will be the inevitable result of the communist order (*ibid.*, pp. 140–141).

Bibliography

In addition to the works mentioned in the text, Bazarov wrote "Avtoritarnaya Metafizika i Avtonomnaya Lichnost" ("Authoritarian Metaphysics and the Autonomous Individual"), in S. Dorovatovski and A. Charushnikov, eds., *Ocherki Realisticheskovo Mirovozzreniya* ("Studies in the Realist World View," St. Petersburg, 1904), pp. 183–275.

See also the article on Bazarov in *Bolshaya Sovetskaya Entsiklopediya* ("Great Soviet Encyclopedia," Moscow, 1926), Vol. IV, cols. 334–336.

GEORGE L. KLINE

BEATTIE, JAMES (1735–1803), common-sense philosopher, was born at Laurencekirk, Kincardine, Scotland. He was educated at the parish school in Laurencekirk and at Marischal College, Aberdeen. He taught school in Fordoun and Aberdeen, and became professor of moral philosophy and logic at Marischal College in 1760. Thomas Reid was his colleague. Beattie was famous both as a poet and as the refuter of the philosophies of Berkeley and Hume. For his efforts in this latter direction, George III honored him with a pension of £200 a year in 1773, and Dr. Benjamin Rush secured his election to the American Philosophical Society.

Beattie's philosophical reputation rests on his *Essay on the Nature and Immutability of Truth, in Opposition to Sophistry and Scepticism* (Edinburgh, 1770). Following Reid, Beattie argued that mankind is possessed of a faculty called common sense, which perceives truth by an instantaneous, instinctive, and irresistible impulse. It is natural, and it acts independently of our will. By attending to this faculty, we may provide ourselves with a set of incontrovertible first principles, safe from skeptical doubts. We may also turn this faculty on the skeptical philosophers and expose the lack of truth in their sophistical doctrines. It is this latter enterprise that was Beattie's chief interest. Without tying his conclusions too closely to the operations of the common sense, Beattie fired away at Descartes, Malebranche, and, occasionally, Locke. But his principal targets were Berkeley and Hume. He construed Berkeley's denial of substance as a denial of the real existence of such things as tables and chairs, and joked repeatedly about Berkeley's followers' breaking their necks because they cannot distinguish between real precipices and imagined ones. However, he also saw that the world is not changed for those who take Berkeley seriously but is only talked about differently.

Hume received by far the largest part of Beattie's attention; and from time to time the strictures on Hume's philosophy give way to outright attacks on Hume's character. When Beattie's *Essay* was published, Hume was living less than a hundred miles away in Edinburgh, surrounded by his friends. They thought that Beattie was rude, but the battalions of the faithful who had too long felt the sting of Hume's sarcasm thought Beattie a brave man. Hume never replied to the *Essay*, perhaps because much of it was directed against *A Treatise of Human Nature*, a work that he disavowed in the Advertisement prefixed to his own *Essays* (posthumous ed., 1777).

While the *Essay* was extravagantly received by the general public in Beattie's lifetime, it is now largely neglected. Despite his partisan motives, however, Beattie made certain telling criticisms of Hume. He challenged the doctrine that ideas are distinguished from impressions only by their weakness or faintness. He found the meanings of "copy" and "resemble" unclear in the doctrine that ideas copy or resemble impressions. He found Hume's denial of the distinction between objects and perceptions untenable, because ordinary discourse tells against it. He was dubious of the scope to be allowed the doctrine that the meaning of words must be accounted for as ideas, which in Hume's system can only be derived from impressions. Finally, he pointed out that by defining the self as a bundle of perceptions, Hume is at a loss to account for a percipient being to perceive these perceptions.

Bibliography

Beattie is also the author of *Elements of Moral Sciences*, 2 vols. (Edinburgh, 1790–1793). These books are the syllabus of his college course, comprising his lectures on psychology, natural theology, moral philosophy, economics, politics, and logic. Since he did not believe that professors should be innovators in their lectures, his are largely expositions of Locke, Clarke, and Butler. Beattie's poetic reputation rests on *The Minstrel.* The Aldine edition of *The Poetical Works of James Beattie* (London, 1831) is edited and contains a memoir by the Rev. Alexander Dyce.

Works on Beattie are Sir William Forbes, *An Account of the Life and Writings of James Beattie*, 2 vols. (Edinburgh, 1807) and Margaret Forbes, *Beattie and His Friends* (London, 1904). For criticism, see Joseph Priestley, "Remarks on Dr. Beattie's Essay," in his *Theological and Miscellaneous Works*, J. T. Rutt, ed., 25 vols. (London, 1817–1832), Vol. III.

ELMER SPRAGUE

BEAUTY. Until the eighteenth century, beauty was the single most important idea in the history of aesthetics. One of the earliest works in the literature of aesthetics, the *Hippias Major* (probably by Plato), was addressed to the question, "What is beauty?" Around this question most of later thought revolves. The treatment of the other major concept, *art*, when it is not ancillary to that of beauty, lacks comparable generality, for it is often restricted to a single artistic form or genre, or its theoretical status is equivocal, because art is taken as identical with craft or skill. The modern notion of the *fine arts* did not appear until the eighteenth century and, more important, it was then too that the concept of *aesthetic experience* was first formulated systematically. As a consequence, beauty lost its traditional centrality in aesthetic theory and has never since regained it.

Our survey of these historical developments will be selective. Specific theories will be singled out because they are paradigms of the major *kinds* of theory of beauty. Thus, where beauty is taken to be a property, we will be less concerned with what, on some particular proposal, this property is, more with the logical relations of beauty, so construed, to the other properties of beautiful things and to the conditions of its apprehension. Where it is not so construed, the chief alternative meanings for beauty will be illustrated. *Beautiful* is used to esteem or commend and therefore to make a claim that is honored in the processes of criticism. Throughout this article, accordingly, the implications of the major kinds of theory for evaluation of the object will be traced.

CLASSICAL AESTHETICS

The concluding section of Plato's *Philebus* is the prototype of the dominant ways of thinking about beauty prior to the eighteenth century. This will be shown by unpacking its major theses, which, whether they were taken over or whether they became the focuses of dispute, made up the framework of classical theory and defined its preoccupations.

The discussion of beauty in the *Philebus*, as in other dialogues, arises in the course of discussion of a larger question not itself aesthetic, namely, whether pleasure or knowledge is the supreme good for man. Socrates wished to distinguish "pure" from "mixed" pleasures, and among the examples that he gives of the former are the pleasures evoked by objects that are "beautiful intrinsically." He cited simple geometrical shapes, single colors, and musical notes (50E–52B).

The first thing to see is that Plato took beauty to be a property ingredient in things. It is nonrelational twice over, for its existence is not dependent upon, or affected by, perceiving it; and whereas "relative" beauty exists only by virtue of comparison with things that are of a lesser degree of beauty or simply ugly, "intrinsic" beauty does not. This view can be specified in two different ways, both of which appear to be suggested by Plato: Either the property of beauty is identified with, and defined by, certain properties of the object, here the determinate ordering or "measure" of the whole (64E), or beauty is itself indefinable, but supervenes upon a further, distinct property, the internal unity of the parts, which is the condition of its existence (66B).

On the former theory, whether a thing is beautiful is decided just by finding whether it does or does not possess the salient property. In the *Philebus*, the success of such inquiry, even on Plato's rigorous conception of knowledge, is assured by the markedly intellectualist character of measure. It is a formal or structural property and therefore cognate with the nature of intelligence (59B–C, 65D), unlike matter which is opaque to mind. It is no accident that, having illustrated intrinsic beauty by objects produced by the "carpenter's rule and square," Socrates later eulogized carpentering for its cognitive exactness (55D–56E). This insistence on the clarity and knowability of beauty (shared by Aristotle in *Metaphysics* 1078b) is also reflected in the choice of sight and hearing, the senses most appropriate to rational cognition, as the sole avenues of the perception of beauty (cf. *Phaedrus* 250D).

The nondefinist theory is, for the reasons to be cited in later philosophers, more plausible but considerably more complicated. This theory is that, given unity in variety in a thing, beauty is also necessarily present. It will still be true that whether a thing is beautiful can be decided by showing that it possesses internal unity *if*—but this proviso is crucial—we can be certain that the two properties do, in all instances, exist together. Hence we must be able to apprehend beauty in its own right. Yet to say that beauty is indefinable is to say that what it is cannot be identified conceptually and therefore in commonly understandable terms. The cognitive assurance and stability of definist theory may be lost as a result. Plato was amply aware of the possibility of uncertainty and disagreement among judgments of beauty (*Laws* Bk. II). The account of intrinsic beauty in the *Philebus* guards against these dangers. Things are beautiful intrinsically precisely because they are "always beautiful in their very nature" (51C–D). Though the objects cited by Socrates are empirical—"the surfaces and solids which a lathe, or a carpenter's rule and square, produces from the straight and the round"—they nevertheless enjoy the self-identity, unaffected by adventitious or contextual factors, that is also characteristic of the Platonic Ideas. Unlike objects of relative beauty, they resemble the ideal beauty described in the *Symposium* (211–212), which cannot be "fair in one point of view and foul in another" (cf. *Republic* 479). Socrates held that they will necessarily arouse in the beholder a kind of pleasure that is peculiar to intrinsic beauty (51D). That the apprehension of such beauty will be veridical is further assured in the *Philebus* by the notion of "pure" pleasures, i.e., those unmixed with pain. Pain warps or falsifies judgment (36C et. seq.), but it is never present in the appreciation of intrinsic beauty. The related concepts of the *intrinsic* and the *pure* are used to guarantee the stability of the experience of beauty. They lead, however, to a severe delimitation of the class of beautiful objects. Paintings and living creatures are excluded as relative, tragedy and comedy (50A–B) because they are impure. Human significances are hostile to beauty because they encourage error and diversity in our responses to it.

In its analysis of the concrete phenomena of beauty, the *Philebus* is distinguished from the mythic and metaphysical approaches of the *Phaedrus* and *Symposium* and the social moralism of the *Republic* and *Laws*. Even here, however, the beautiful does not constitute a distinct and autonomous subject matter. It is treated as a "form" or mode of goodness in general, and the term *beautiful* is used, as it was by the Greeks generally, interchangeably with *excellent*, *perfect*, and *satisfying*. It is also worthy of note that the concept of art enters in hardly at all. Painting and literature are mentioned only so that they may be excluded. By contrast, Aristotle's *Poetics* devotes itself to a single art form, tragedy, making only a casual reference to beauty —measure is a necessary condition (VII). Later treatments of beauty and art are even less congenial to our modern conception of aesthetics, which led the historian Bosanquet to speak of a centuries-long "intermission" in aesthetics between the Graeco-Roman and the modern eras. The metaphysic of Plotinus, which derived from Plato, is spiritualist and Idealist; and here, as in later philosophy, the bias of such thought is to encourage regard for, and insight into, the experience of beauty. The soul is said to strive toward beauty, which is a manifestation of the spiritual force that animates all of reality. It is just because of the vitality and moving appeal of beauty that Plotinus rejected the identification of beauty with a merely formal property. The living face and the dead face are equally symmetrical, but only the former stirs us. Hence "beauty is that which irradiates symmetry rather than symmetry itself" (*Enneads* VI; VII, 22). Further, some simple, sensory objects lacking internal structure are beautiful, and, finally, symmetry is present in some ugly things as well (I; VI, 1). Plotinus' critique of formalism effectively made the larger point that beauty cannot be identified with any single element of the object, form or any other. It is the total object, the whole of form and expressiveness and what the form is of, that possesses beauty. If, on the other hand, beauty is thought to be a global quality that "irradiates" this object and moves us, it is difficult or impossible, in a definition, to specify conceptually the nature of this quality. Moreover, Plotinus' argument cast doubt on the possibility of finding even the conditions of beauty. A formal property such as symmetry is the most likely candidate, because it can be shared by objects that are otherwise highly diverse, artistic or natural, abstract or representational, sensory or mathematical. Yet if the negative instances cited by Plotinus show that this property is not even a universal concomitant of beauty, then a fortiori it cannot be the necessitating ground of beauty.

Still, the effort to enunciate a set of conditions for beauty is persistent in Western thought, because it answers to the desire for a criticism whose verdicts will be certifiable and authoritative. The high noon of such criticism was the neoclassical period, particularly the sixteenth and seventeenth centuries, when the conditions were detailed and formalized, and endowed with the institutional sanctions of the new "Academies." A multiplicity of treatises were devoted to particular arts or genres, each of which was taken to be subject to "rules," inherent in its specific nature and function, which can be rationally known (e.g., Castelvetro, Palladio). The treatises borrowed heavily from their Greek and Roman antecedents—Aristotle, Horace, Vitruvius. The "lawmakers of Parnassus" thereby invested their claims to speak on behalf of "reason" and "nature" with the authority of antiquity. Given that beauty is an objective property, attainable artistically and knowable critically, by reference to the rules, the question of the percipient's response to it was scanted. As in the *Philebus*, beauty can be expected to arouse the appropriate response, which was referred to briefly and loosely as "pleasure," or "delight."

THE EIGHTEENTH CENTURY

The rebellion against the rules, in the name of the spectator's felt response—"the taste is not to conform to the art, but the art to the taste" (Addison)—intimates, in art criticism, the larger and more profound reconstruction of thought that took place in aesthetic theory. In the eighteenth century, indeed, aesthetics first established itself as an autonomous philosophical discipline. It defined a subject matter that is not explicable in terms of any of the other disciplines and is therefore taken out of the metaphysical and moral context of much traditional aesthetics, to be studied in its own right. The pioneer work is to be found in the prolific and assiduous writings of the British who, throughout the century, carried out the inquiry that Addison, at its beginning, justly described as "entirely new."

The century was a Copernican revolution, for instead of looking outward to the properties of beauty or the art object, it first examined the experience of the percipient, to determine the conditions under which beauty and art are appreciated. The decisive condition is disinterestedness, i.e., perception directed upon an object without, as in practical or cognitive activity, any purpose ulterior to the act of perception itself. In aesthetic theory so conceived, beauty is no longer the central concept. It now stands for just one kind of aesthetic experience among others, and it can be defined and analyzed only by reference to the logically more basic concept of *aesthetic perception*.

The introspective examination of our "ideas," stimulated by Locke's *Essay*, discloses experiences that differ significantly, in their felt quality, from that of beauty. This century distinguished a great many other "species" of aesthetic response, but the most important was that of sublimity. Sublimity is profoundly unlike beauty, for whereas the latter arouses "joy" and "cheerfulness," the feeling of the sublime is "amazement" and awe. Still, most of the British hold that the two can coexist and that the experience of both is pleasurable. The most drastic distinction was drawn by Edmund Burke (1757), who argued that beauty and sublimity are, conceptually, mutually exclusive and, existentially, antithetical. He at the same time limited the range of beauty severely and pushed back the boundaries of the aesthetic to include a radically different kind of experience, that cannot be accommodated in the traditional category. Indeed Burke clearly considered the experience of sublimity to be the more valuable of the two. Both Moses Mendelssohn and Kant read Burke and were greatly affected by him, and through their influence Burke's critique of beauty made a lasting impression on Continental thought.

Burke granted that a beautiful object arouses pleasure, but he argued that a sublime object, that is, one that is "terrible," even though it is apprehended disinterestedly, arouses "some degree of horror." Beauty "relaxes," but the experience of sublimity is of great emotional intensity. The two experiences are therefore incompatible with each other. Moreover, the properties that Burke attributed to sublime objects are just the opposites of those that the *Philebus* had enshrined in the classical conception of aesthetic value. Against clarity and lucidity, Burke urged that we are moved most greatly by what is "dark, uncertain, confused." In place of formal ordering, Burke eulogized what is "vast" and "infinite." The sublime therefore renders beauty "dead and unoperative." When beauty had been taken as the sole value category, ugliness, its contradictory, had necessarily been excluded from aesthetic value. Burke went so far as to suggest that even the ugly can be an object of aesthetic appreciation. In all this, he is pointing the way to the nineteenth-century and twentieth-century concept of *expression*, which, more catholic by far than classical beauty, admits a limitless diversity of subject matter, treatment, and form, if only the work of art be moving and powerful.

A comparable challenge to the classical values of order and serenity came from another direction. The historical study of art, pioneered by Winckelmann (1764), disclosed that these values are found only in relatively limited epochs and styles, even, indeed, of Greek art itself. Later research emboldened the protest against the once unchallenged arbiters of classical and neoclassical criticism that they had identified selected stylistic properties of Greek and High Renaissance art with what is beautiful "naturally" and universally.

In the eighteenth century, also, the "logic" of beauty underwent a profound sea change. Francis Hutcheson (1725) announced a new locus for beauty: "Let it be observed, that in the following papers, the word *beauty* is taken for *the idea raised in us*." It follows that any object whatever that does in fact excite this idea must be judged to be beautiful. But this invites the possibility of diverse and conflicting judgments that, if subjective response is the sole and decisive test, must all be accepted as equally valid. Are there, however, any properties peculiar to beautiful objects, which can be pointed to, to legitimate certain judgments and whose absence will show others to be mistaken? Hutcheson thought that there was—the classical property of "uniformity in variety." Yet to be consistent with the definition of beauty with which he began, he had to guarantee that things possessing this property would uniquely and universally arouse the appropriate idea. It can be said summarily that he failed to do so, and his failure is instructive. It points up the tension between the old and the new ways of thinking, between taking beauty to be an inherent, nonrelational property and using *beauty* to refer to the capacity of things to evoke a certain experience. A capacity is not, however, an observable property in things like uniformity. It must be interpreted as either a very different sort of property or else it is not a property at all. Hume drew out the radical implications of Hutcheson's initial meaning for beauty with the acute remark that Euclid described all of the properties of a circle, but beauty is not among them ("The Sceptic").

In general, the later British aestheticians did not take *beautiful* to denote a property. Necessarily, therefore, the logical status of the properties that they attribute to beautiful objects—proportion, utility, etc.—is correspondingly altered. Such properties are no longer, as in the *Philebus*, either identical with, or the conditions of, a property of beauty. They are, rather, causes of the experience of beauty. Even so considered, however, the traditional formulas of beauty were brought under fire throughout the eighteenth century. Since the attribution of causes can be justified only by the evidence of their effects in experience, the British, arguing from the things that people do in fact find beautiful, showed that none of these properties are shared by all these things. There was also the more subtle and damning criticism that the traditional formula of "unity in variety" is simply devoid of meaning, because it applies indiscriminately to any object whatever. By the close of the century, Alison (1790) concluded that any attempt to find properties common and peculiar to beautiful objects is "altogether impossible." Finally it was suggested that "beautiful" is just "a general term of approbation" (Payne Knight, 1805).

The British thereby generated the problem that is central to Kant's *Critique of Judgment* (1790): How, if the aesthetic judgment arises from subjective feeling and predicates nothing of the object, can it claim to be more than an autobiographical report and can, indeed, claim to be universally binding?

THE NINETEENTH AND TWENTIETH CENTURIES

The most novel development in this period has been the attempt at a scientific approach to aesthetics. This has taken two forms, generally, and the status of beauty in each is worth noting. Psychological aesthetics applies experimental methods to aesthetic experience in an effort to work out "laws" of appreciation. These are to be derived from the consensus of pleasure and displeasure reported by the laboratory subject in the face of various objects. When beauty is used at all in speaking of these objects, as it was by Fechner (1876), it is a loose, omnium-gatherum term. The objectivist–formalist connotations of the word have made it increasingly unsatisfactory to later psychologists. Either they have stipulated that it refers to certain psychological responses (e.g., O. Külpe, 1921), or they have abandoned it in favor of the more apt "liberal and comprehensive" (E. Bullough, 1907) concept of "aesthetic value." The last decades of the nineteenth century also saw the rise of *Kunstwissenschaft*, which may be rendered as "the sciences of art," for it comprises historical, anthropological, and other empirical studies of art as a cultural product. One of the impulses to the development of this field was a pervasive dissatisfaction with beauty, either because it is too limited, if interpreted on the classical model, and cannot therefore encompass, for example, primitive art, or too vague, if it is not. Art, by contrast, is a concrete, institutional phenomenon that is tractable to science. Thus *Kunstwissenschaft*, which is at present one of the most thriving and fruitful branches of aesthetics, defines itself by opposition to the concept of beauty.

The distinction between the meaning of beauty when it is synonymous with aesthetic value generally and when it stands for one class or kind of such value has been commonly remarked in recent aesthetics. In the former sense, it is often used to signalize the characteristic excellence of a work of art or an aesthetic object. Thus *beautiful* does not denote a property such as symmetry but also it is more than just a "term of approbation." It makes a claim on behalf of the object, which must be supported by appealing to the relevant value criteria. These criteria need not, however, be the same for two different artistic media or even for two works in the same medium. They are, perhaps indefinitely, plural; they are of different weight in different cases, and no one of them can be said to be a necessary condition for the use of *beautiful*. Their relevance is determined by the unique character of each work. In its second meaning, *beauty* generally connotes a relatively high degree of value, in contrast to, for example, the *pretty*, a fairly orthodox style or genre, pleasure unmixed with pain and the absence of bizarre or discordant elements. But this is just why so much of recent aesthetics and ordinary discourse finds the word awkward or even irrelevant for evaluation. It will do for Mozart, but not the later Beethoven, for Raphael, but not Goya. In the *Philebus*, Socrates had, for his own purposes, narrowed the range of beauty severely, but it was just this narrowness that made it impossible for later thought to preserve *beauty* as the sole, or perhaps even the major, concept of aesthetic value.

Bibliography

Bosanquet, Bernard, *A History of Aesthetic*. New York, 1957. Fairly difficult but thoughtful and acute; sees the history of aesthetics as a movement from the concept of "unity in variety" to "significance, expressiveness."

Bullough, Edward, "The Modern Conception of Aesthetics," in E. Wilkinson, ed., *Aesthetics*. Palo Alto, Cal., 1957. A vigorous polemic, by an able psychologist-philosopher, against the "sterile" effort to find a definition of "beauty"; the "modern conception" is the "study of aesthetic consciousness."

Carritt, E. F., *The Theory of Beauty*. London, 1931. A readable account, by a leading Crocean, of many of the major historical theories.

Kainz, Friedrich, *Vorlesungen über Ästhetik*. Vienna, 1948. Translated by Herbert Schueller as *Aesthetics the Science*. Detroit, 1962. A valuable conspectus of the major tendencies in recent Continental aesthetics; examines the relation between beauty and the aesthetic attitude.

Morpurgo-Tagliabue, Guido, *L'Esthétique contemporaine*. Milan, 1960. An extremely comprehensive and well-documented study of aesthetics since 1800, weighted heavily on the twentieth century. Stresses the distinction between the theories of art and beauty.

Osborne, H., *Theory of Beauty*. New York, 1953. Lucid and informed criticism of some of the major historical theories.

Stolnitz, Jerome, "'Beauty': Some Stages in the History of an Idea." *Journal of the History of Ideas*, Vol. 22, No. 2 (April–June, 1961), 185–204. An analysis of the history of the concept in eighteenth-century British aesthetics. An extensive bibliography includes works by authors referred to above.

JEROME STOLNITZ

BECCARIA, CESARE BONESANA (1738–1794), Italian criminologist and economist, was born in Milan of aristocratic parents. His formal education began at the Jesuit college in Parma and ended with his graduation from the University of Pavia in 1758. After graduation Beccaria came under the intellectual influence of two brothers, Pietro and Alessandro Verri, who had gathered around themselves the young Milanese intelligentsia to form a society known as the "academy of fists," committed to promoting reforms in political, economic, and administrative affairs.

Beccaria was prompted by Pietro Verri to read the then prominent philosophies of Montesquieu, Helvétius, Diderot, Hume, and Buffon. At the suggestion of his friends, Beccaria wrote and published his first treatise, *Del disordine e de' rimedi delle monete nello Stato di Milano nell'anno 1762* (Lucca, 1762). It was also through the encouragement of the Verri brothers that Beccaria composed his most important work, *Dei delitti e delle pene* (trans. by H. Paolucci as *On Crimes and Punishments*, New York, 1963). Through Alessandro Verri, who was an official of the prison in Milan, Beccaria visited that institution and saw the conditions that furnished information and moral stimulus for his writing. Pietro, who had already begun writing a history of torture, in many conversations on the errors of criminal law and administration provided Beccaria with new arguments and insights for the treatise. In the end, the work was almost a collaboration by the three men, for Beccaria until that time had been relatively uninformed about crime and punishment. Begun in March 1763 and completed in January 1764, the book was published anonymously at Livorno out of fear of reprisals because of its devastating attack on the legal and judicial system then in operation. But anonymity was soon dropped when it became clear that the Milanese authorities were receptive and when the essay drew the attention and respect of the Parisian intelligentsia.

Beccaria held a chair in political economy in the Palatine School of Milan from 1768 to 1770, and his lectures during this period were published posthumously in 1804 under the title, *Elementi di economia pubblica*. His economic ideas on the division of labor and the determination of wages have been compared to those of Adam Smith (who wrote the *Wealth of Nations* seven years after publication of Beccaria's economic views). In economics Beccaria espoused a form of mercantilism based on some of the ideas of the physiocrats, expressed the belief that agriculture was the most productive enterprise, advocated commercial freedom within a nation and the abolition of guilds, and displayed a Malthusian concern with the relation of population growth to the means of subsistence. He also held a series of minor public offices through which he aided his friends in securing reforms in taxation, currency, and the corn trade.

On Crimes and Punishments was a protest against the use of torture to obtain confessions, secret accusations, the arbitrary discretionary power of judges, the inconsistency and inequality of sentencing, the influence of power and status in obtaining leniency, the lack of distinction in treatment of the accused and the convicted, and the use of capital punishment for serious and even minor offenses.

The concepts that Beccaria employed—rationalism, the social contract, utility, and hedonism—were current among the intellectuals of his time. The application of these ideas to crime and punishment, and the style of writing, were his own. Building upon Rousseau's social-contract philosophy, he argued that each person willingly sacrifices to the political community only so much of his liberty as "suffices to induce others to defend it." Laws are only the necessary conditions of this contract, and punishments under the law should have no other purpose than to defend the sum of these sacrificed shares of liberty "against private usurpations by individuals." Punishments for any other reason are unnecessary and unjust.

Beccaria declared that the law should be clear in defining crimes and that judges should not interpret the law but simply ascertain whether a person has or has not violated the law. He also held that punishment should be adjusted in severity to the seriousness of the crime. The primary purpose of punishment, Beccaria argued, is to insure the existence of society, and the seriousness of the crime, therefore, varies according to the degree to which the transgressor's act endangers that existence. Treason and other acts against the state are most harmful, followed by injuries to the security of person and property and finally, by acts which are disruptive of public harmony and peace, such as rioting or inciting to disorder.

To insure the continuance of society, punishment should aim at deterrence, that is, at preventing offenders from doing additional harm and others from committing crimes. To be effective as a deterrent to crime, punishment should be swift and certain; it is the certainty rather than the severity of punishment that deters. Life imprisonment is sufficient to deter: the death penalty is not necessary, nor is it legitimate, for individuals did not under the social contract relinquish the right to their lives. Corporal punishment is bad, and torture as part of a criminal investigation makes the suffering of pain rather than evidence the test of truth. Crimes against property should be punished by fines or, when fines cannot be paid, by imprisonment.

Beccaria's classic conclusion—the principles of which were adopted almost in their entirety by the revolutionary National Assembly of France in 1789 as Article VIII of the "Declaration of the Rights of Man and of the Citizen" —read in part as follows: "In order for punishment not to be, in every instance, an act of violence of one or of many against a private citizen, it must be essentially public, prompt, necessary, the least possible in the given circumstances, proportionate to the crimes, dictated by the laws."

Beccaria's essay became famous almost overnight. It was translated into French in 1766 by the Abbé Morellet, passed through six editions within 18 months, one of which was embellished by a laudatory comment by Voltaire, and was thereafter translated into every important language. The Church of Rome placed the treatise on the Index in 1766, but the Austrian government, which controlled Milan, defended and honored Beccaria. Maria Theresa of Austria, Leopold II, grand duke of Tuscany, and Catherine the Great of Russia announced their intentions to be guided by Beccaria's principle in the reformation of their laws. The essay both paved the way for, and was the guiding force in, the major penal reforms that took place for two centuries afterwards.

Works by Beccaria

Opere, Pasquale Villari, ed. Florence, 1854. A recent edition was edited by S. Romagnoli, 2 vols. (Florence, 1958), with a bibliography, Vol. 2, pp. 917–918.

Scritti e lettere inediti raccolti ed illustrati da Eugenio Landry, Eugenio Landry, ed. Milan, 1910.

Works on Beccaria

Cantù, C., *Beccaria e il diretto penale*. Florence, 1862.

Monachesi, E., "Cesare Beccaria," in H. Mannheim, ed., *Pioneers in Criminology*, pp. 36–50. London, 1960.

Paolucci, Henry, "Introduction" to his translation of Beccaria, Cesare, *On Crimes and Punishments*. New York, 1963. Pp. ix–xxiii.

Phillipson, Coleman, *Three Criminal Law Reformers: Beccaria, Bentham, Romilly*. London, 1923.

Schumpeter, J. A., *History of Economic Analysis*. New York, 1954.

MARVIN E. WOLFGANG

BECK, JAKOB SIGISMUND (1761–1840), German Kantian philosopher, was born in Marienburg. He studied mathematics and philosophy in Königsberg with P. Krause and Kant, completing his studies in 1783. In 1791 he became a teacher at the gymnasium in Halle and, in 1796, extraordinary professor of philosophy at Halle University. He was called to Rostock as professor of metaphysics in 1799 and remained there until his death.

Purporting to defend the "true" Kantian position against "dogmatic" misinterpretations, Beck called attention to problems concerning the role of the thing-in-itself in Kant's theory of perception. Beck rejected any positive role for the thing-in-itself and argued that the object affecting our senses must be phenomenal. Kant's theory of affection is to be understood not in the transcendent sense, as the working of an unknowable thing-in-itself on an unobservable "I"-in-itself, but only in the empirical sense: a phenomenal body in phenomenal space affects the "I" of inner sense.

But this "I" and this body, according to Beck, are themselves the products of an original activity of the understanding. The synthetic activity of "representing" (*vorstellen*) is presupposed by our viewing sense data as given *by* something objectively outside ourselves. Beck therefore objected to Kant's definition of sensibility as an immediate relation to an affecting object. The intuitions of sense say nothing about their own objectivity or source. Not until they are subjected to the categories of the understanding do they become objective, for only then can we invoke the notion of external objects and speak of intuitions as given to our senses by such objects. The order of exposition of the *Critique of Pure Reason* is therefore misleading. One ought not to begin with sensibility, but with the synthetic unity or "original activity" (*ursprüngliche Beilegung*) of the understanding, the unique a priori act of combination (*Zusammensetzung*).

In philosophy of religion, Beck held that God is a symbol created by man, a symbol of man's ethical conscience. Piety consists simply in obedience to the commands of conscience.

In letters to Beck (1792) Kant complimented him for investigating "what is just the hardest thing in the *Critique*," approved Beck's reorganization of the Critical Philosophy, and said that he himself planned to write a work on metaphysics that would utilize the order of exposition that Beck had suggested. Kant's *Opus Postumum* shows the extent of Beck's influence, particularly in Kant's manuscript on the progress of metaphysics since Leibniz and Wolff.

Some of Kant's followers classed Beck with Fichte and accused Beck of making the understanding the creator of objects. Beck did write: "Reality is itself the original act of representing, from which the concept of objects subsequently derives." But although he spoke of the original act as object-generating, he told Kant that he did not mean that the understanding *creates* objects. Beck granted the existence and importance of the given in knowledge while he attempted to bridge the dualism of sense and intellect and to insist that neither the given nor the notion of "things" could be taken as epistemologically primary.

Works by Beck

Erlaüternder Auszug aus den kritischen Schriften des Herrn Prof. Kant, auf Anrathen desselben. Riga, 1793–1796. Volume III of this work, *Einzig möglicher Standpunkt aus welchem die kritische Philosophie beurteilt werden muss* ("Only Possible Standpoint from Which the Critical Philosophy Must Be Judged"), contains Beck's most important ideas.

Grundriss der kritischen Philosophie. Halle, 1796.

Kommentar über Kants Metaphysik der Sitten. Halle, 1798.

Lehrbuch der Logik. Rostock, 1820.

Lehrbuch des Naturrechts. Jena, 1820.

Works on Beck

Dilthey, Wilhelm, "Die Rostocker Kanthandschriften." *Archiv für Geschichte der Philosophie*, Vol. II (1889), 592–650. Discusses Beck's place among Kant's disciples and critics.

Durante, G., *Gli epigoni di Kant.* Florence, 1943.

Potschel, W., *J. S. Beck und Kant.* Breslau, 1910.

Vleeschauwer, H. J. de, *L'Evolution de la pensée kantienne.* Paris, 1939. Translated by A. R. C. Duncan as *The Development of Kantian Thought.* London, 1962. Discusses Beck's influence on Kant's last reworking of the *Critique of Pure Reason.*

ARNULF ZWEIG

BECOMING. See CHANGE.

BEHAVIORISM, as philosophical theory, is as old as reductive materialism. In his *De Corpore* Hobbes attempted to interpret all mental states in terms of matter in motion; his is probably the most celebrated theory of this sort. Contemporary discussion of behaviorism, however, starts with the work of J. B. Watson.

Watson aimed to establish psychology as a science, protesting against what he viewed as the subjectivism of introspectionist psychology. Holding that a truly scientific enterprise seeks prediction and control, Watson maintained that only "objective" methods will enable achievement of these goals. He believed that objectivity in turn requires that different scientists be able to observe the same objects and events. States of consciousness being private, observation of behavior alone is able to provide the necessary data for a scientific psychology. The behaviorism Watson espoused received powerful support from the dramatic experimental work of Ivan Pavlov.

Watson believed that psychology could be reduced to physics—that psychological phenomena were ultimately nothing more than molecular motions. But the reduction could be achieved only through physiological investigation. Hence, sound physiological theory was, for Watson, the door to the promised land. Other behaviorists, for example, B. F. Skinner, are content to adopt as their unit of analysis molar behavior—that is, such behavior as bar-pressing, running, and blinking—not molecular behavior, that is, the simplest behaviors that constitute molar behavior. However, behaviorists who favor molar units have in common with those who favor molecular units a deep desire to establish psychology as a science as rigorous in its methods and reliable in its results as the physical sciences. They also share the conviction that experimentation with animals is of inestimable importance in the pursuit of their goal.

Although philosophers have been influenced by scientific behaviorists, they have more distinctively philosophical motives as well. In particular, many have viewed the two-substance metaphysical doctrine that derives principally from Descartes's work as a myth which must be demolished.

The fact that behaviorism is historically rooted in different concerns and traditions has led to the following situation: If behaviorists are broadly viewed as sharing the conviction that what is termed "behavior" is in some way the matter of central importance in the study of human beings, two behaviorists may yet not agree about anything of importance.

For one thing, their interests may be very different. A philosophical behaviorist may be primarily concerned to analyze ordinary psychological language; a behaviorist in psychology, more concerned to provide scientific explanations of psychological phenomena. For another thing, the term "behavior" may not have a single meaning. Finally, behaviorists disagree about the role that behavior is supposed to play. Some psychologists insist that every term of the science of psychology must be behaviorally *defined.* Others require only that behavioral *criteria* for the application of all or some of the terms of psychology must be provided. Similarly, certain philosophers are behaviorists in the strict sense that they maintain that behavior alone exists or is real and that all so-called nonbehavioral mental states are merely the mythological constructions of excessively fertile philosophical imagination. Others more modestly contend that bits of behavior, while not constituting mental phenomena, are the indispensable conditions for proper application of all or most psychological terms.

Because these variations exist, it is impossible to give a single account that covers all forms of behaviorism. Instead, the different kinds of behaviorism must be explored.

Because the view that behavior alone is real is generally defended on grounds either of the analysis of our ordinary use of psychological expressions or on the basis of scientific utility of behavioral definitions of concepts, it will be necessary to deal only with these two forms of the doctrine. Before discussing them, however, preliminary remarks about the meaning of the term "behavior" are required.

DEFINITIONS OF "BEHAVIOR"

A behaviorist believes that behavior is in some way central to the study of human beings. But what is meant by "behavior"? The question is not as simple as it seems.

Suppose "behavior" is defined, following common sense, as any movement of an organism. This definition encounters a number of difficulties. First, there are certain behaviorists who wish to restrict the range of movements to which the term "behavior" applies so as to exclude physiological processes. (Is the heart's pulsation a form of behavior?) Although Watson's classical formulation of behaviorism embraces such movements, B. F. Skinner prefers a more restrictive conception: In *The Behavior of Organisms* Skinner first defines "behavior" as "the action of the organism upon the outside world." His aim was to eliminate physiological processes from the range of phenomena with which the psychologist is properly concerned. Watson and Skinner agree, however, that by "behavior" is meant some sort of movement of the organism.

A second difficulty immediately arises. Skinner, like most psychologists, discusses "verbal behavior." By this he means not such behavior as an organism's movements but rather sounds produced by those movements. To accommodate this extension Skinner adds that "it is often desirable to deal with an effect rather than with the movement itself, as in the production of sounds."

But this modified conception encounters still another difficulty. The movement of one's arm would clearly seem to be an instance of behavior, but suppose that the arm's motion was the result of a hurricane's effect on that limb. Would a movement produced in this way be behavior? Or must the movement be involved in something the organism is *doing,* some *action it performs?* This qualification seems to throw the net too wide, for among the things a human organism *does* are dreaming, reflecting, observing, inferring, and so on. These do not seem to be behavior in any obvious sense. They seem to be precisely the sorts of processes behaviorism was originally designed to exclude. (Nonetheless, there are those who regard these states as forms of behavior.) For behaviorism of any variety seeks to restrict the scope of the term "behavior" to those things which are *overt,* are *observable.* Perhaps, then, "behavior" may be defined as "whatever an organism does, provided it acts upon the outside world," the necessary and sufficient test of whether the movement does "act upon the outside world" being its observability. For if the thing done acts upon the outside world, then it is presumably the sort of thing that can be observed. "Behavior" in its secondary sense indicates those effects produced by such movements when it happens to be convenient so to regard such effects.

But even this definition encounters difficulties—which a few illustrations will make clear: Among the things human organisms *do* and which are observable are moving one's arm, throwing rocks at windows, and writhing in pain. The following locutions are perfectly common: "I saw him move his arm"; "I noticed him throwing a rock at the window"; "As soon as I saw that he was writhing in pain, I called the doctor." (That is, these are actions we are able to observe.) Although such reports are frequently made, they may be false. Although his arm moved, he may not have moved it. Although the rock he threw did go through the window, he may not have intended that it should. Although he did lie on the ground, twisting, grunting and groaning, he may have been play acting; he may not have been in pain at all. In all three cases the error may depend on the nonoccurrence of something that is, in an obvious sense, not observable: that is, whatever distinguishes his moving his arm from his arm moving, an *intention* to throw the rock through the window, or a pain. We are left with the paradoxical situation that, for example, although one can observe a person writhing in pain, one cannot observe the pain without which the report would be false. It seems clear that if behaviorism is not to be made trivial, at least in relation to the concerns that originally generated the position, the criterion of observability must be modified so that it pertains only to those aspects of something *done* which can be observed. One can observe the movements that are described as "writhing," but not the pain. One can observe the motions of the arm and rock but not the intention with which the rock was thrown. One can observe the moving but not the elusive something which makes it a case of his moving his arm. But if this restriction is imposed, behaviorism collapses into what might be called the *motionism* previously rejected. Some behaviorists (for example, Paul Ziff) welcome the extended sense implicit in the view that writhing in pain is behavior in the intended sense. Others (for example, B. F. Skinner) try to get round the problem by defining such things as "intentions" and "pains" in terms of functional relations that refer exclusively to antecedent stimulus conditions and motions of bodies. The differences between behaviorism construed in these different ways quite significantly influence what philosophers and psychologists take to be their proper object of inquiry.

PHILOSOPHICAL BEHAVIORISM

Current philosophical defenses of behaviorism have a common point of origin: the conviction that our ordinary psychological language cannot be correctly analyzed in a way consistent with the defining tenets of Cartesian dualism. That is, what we actually mean when we say things like "He is in pain" cannot be explained in Cartesian terms. By Cartesian dualism is meant the view that (1) there are two causally unrelated substances, mental and physical; (2) whatever is mental is private; and (3) therefore, the only way a person can know that he is in a certain mental state is through observation of his own internal states. It is important to note that behaviorism is only one of many alternatives to Cartesian dualism. For example, one might deny that mental states are the sorts of things that one *observes* about oneself but accept the two-substance view. Behaviorism results only if one denies that there are two substances and maintains that all mental terms can be analyzed in terms of behavior. Normally, those who are behaviorists in this sense understand the position as implying that all so-called mental states are simply behavior and are therefore overt and publicly observable. Seemingly private events, such as talking silently to oneself, are reinterpreted as verbal behavior which it may be difficult but not, in principle, impossible for others to observe (for example, via laryngeal movements).

Ryle. Gilbert Ryle's *The Concept of Mind* contains the most sustained contemporary attack on the Cartesian view—a view which he labels "the dogma of the ghost in the machine." His central claim is that the Cartesian doctrine involves a "category-mistake." Asking whether ordinary psychological concepts logically signify mental episodes or physical movements is like asking whether someone came home in a bus or in a flood of tears. There is only the illusion of mutually exclusive alternatives, and failure to see that this is so is due to conceptual confusion. In developing an array of arguments against the Cartesian position, Ryle attempts to reduce to absurdity specific Cartesian theses about particular aspects of our mental life. For example, Ryle considers the Cartesian claim that when someone performs an action *carefully*, there is a private inner event that accompanies the overt behavior which corresponds to the *care* involved. There is the *attending*, and there is the *doing*. He argues that this two-occurrence account is comparable to claiming that when a bird migrates south there is behavior which constitutes its flying south and an inner event which constitutes the migratory aspect of that flight. But such a supposition, he argues, is absurd. Another example would be the claim that there is some private thought that is the counterpart mental act which accompanies the physical movements that occur when someone does something *intelligently*. But if this were so, then we could ask whether the mental act presumed to occur was done intelligently or not. If it were, we would have to postulate another mental act which is the intelligent aspect of that first mental act, and so on *ad infinitum*, which is absurd. Although Ryle is willing to have his views labeled "behaviorism," some of the concessions he makes imply that he does not believe that straightforward behavioral analyses can be provided for all our mental terms—particularly not for sensation terms like "pain."

Although Ludwig Wittgenstein cannot be called a behaviorist, some of the arguments and suggestions that appear in his *Philosophical Investigations* have heavily influenced and reinforced behaviorism. This influence derives from his conception of a criterion, specifically, of a criterion covering third-person psychological statements, such as "He is in pain." But no such criterion covers analogous first-person utterances like "I am in pain"; therefore, whatever validity a behavioral analysis might have in the case of third-person statements, the behavioral elucidation of first-person psychological statements surely presents a most formidable difficulty for philosophical behaviorism (see CRITERION and OTHER MINDS).

The behaviorist has unexpected dialectical resources. This can be shown by examining three important criticisms made by A. O. Lovejoy and C. D. Broad. At first glance their objections seem crushing.

Lovejoy's criticism. A. O. Lovejoy, in "Paradox of the Thinking Behaviorist," sought to prove that "behaviorism . . . belongs to that class of theories which become absurd as soon as they become articulate." In his argument, directed principally against J. B. Watson's views, Lovejoy tried to show that the behaviorist does make cognitive claims; for example, he may claim to be aware of objects external to himself. But the moment the behaviorist makes such claims he involves himself in contradiction from which he can extricate himself only by denying that he knows anything—which is an absurd alternative from the behaviorist's own point of view. Hence, the behaviorist must either contradict himself or lapse into absurdity. The alleged contradiction consists in this: Awareness of things distant in time and space cannot be identical with movements of certain muscles (Watson maintained that they are identical) or with bodily movements of any sort. For no such description of internal bodily events can account for the reference made to external objects.

In reply to this kind of argument, Ryle argues that what it is to be aware of something has to be understood dispositionally. An analysis of "*A* is aware of (or observes) the chair" will take the following form: "If a chair is present, and given such and such other conditions, *A* will behave in such and such ways." This dispositional statement makes the required reference to external objects. But the only things not external to the body to which the dispositional statement refers are behavioral processes.

Broad's criticism. C. D. Broad advances two arguments against behaviorism. One of his criticisms is that "however completely the behavior of an external body answers to the behavioristic test for intelligence, it always remains a perfectly sensible question to ask: 'Has it really got a mind, or is it merely an automaton?'" Here it is assumed that "having a mind" or attributing similar psychological predicates to an object cannot have the same meaning as any terms referring to actual and possible behavior. But to this the behaviorist can reply that living organisms are in fact automata, although of very complicated sorts. That is, the behaviorist can claim that Broad begs the underlying question which is at issue—whether human animals are not, after all, merely very complex automata, and whether living organisms in general are not more or less complicated automata. On this view, minds would simply be understood to be properties of relatively complicated, self-directing automata.

Alternatively, the behaviorist can admit the distinction between automata and living organisms but can insist that Broad is wrong in supposing that his question makes sense once certain behavior is observed. That is, the occurrence of certain behavior is a logically sufficient ground for denying that what is observed is an automaton. For example, if you saw an object making martinis, passing them to other objects, uttering sounds in an animated fashion while pouring some of the liquid through an orifice in the round thing on top of the object, you might take this as conclusive evidence that the object is, after all, a living human being.

The third response open to a behaviorist is that the essential difference between an automaton and a living organism has nothing to do with behavior but is instead a matter of mode of origin or chemical composition. For example, a living being is born of woman and has calcium compounds constituting its bones, in contrast to the metal automata manufactured by an affiliate of the International Business Machines Corporation.

Broad's second criticism is that perception necessarily involves sensations and that this sensational element cannot be analyzed behaviorally. He supposes, for purposes of argument, that certain molecular changes accompany particular sensations. It is nevertheless true that the sensation and the molecular changes are distinct. For, Broad maintains, we can ask questions about the molecular changes—for example, are they slow, circular, etc.?—which are nonsensical in the case of a sensation like the awareness of a red patch. But the behaviorist can reply to this that of course sensations are distinct from molecular changes, but that this is so because sensations are dispositional properties. Broad considers the possibility and argues that the sort of behavior that will occur depends on the intentions or wants of the person who perceives. But again the behaviorist has a ready reply. Intentions and wants, he can maintain, are themselves nothing but dispositional properties of organisms.

At this point the critic of behaviorism might argue that it is absurd to suppose that sensations such as pain can be analyzed dispositionally. After all, he might claim, if pain were a behavioral disposition, it would be necessary for a person who is in pain to discover the fact by observing his own behavior. But the supposition is absurd, as pain is something one is directly aware of. To this, however, the behaviorist can reply as Paul Ziff does, that events which are undoubtedly behavioral, such as moving one's arm, are events of which the actor is directly aware. It is not necessary for a person to observe that he is moving his arm in order to know that he is. There is no essential difference between behavior and sensations in precisely that respect to which the critic appeals.

However, as was observed earlier, this defense of behaviorism seems to purchase life for the doctrine by so construing "behavior" as to reintroduce precisely those elements the elimination of which generated behaviorism in the first place—that is, states of consciousness or other mental states not accessible to direct observation. Although I can observe someone moving his arm, I cannot observe the aspect of things that is involved in *his moving* it, rather than its moving without his moving it (see VOLITION).

To summarize, philosophical behaviorists seem to be able to draw on unsuspected dialectical resources in meeting criticism. But in so doing they seem to purchase impregnability at the expense of those very features of the behaviorist outlook that attracted theorists to the position in the first place.

SCIENTIFIC BEHAVIORISM

Attention will be restricted in this section to the case that is made for a behaviorist psychology and to the importantly different methodological doctrines embraced by that expression.

The argument for behaviorism in psychology may be stated in the following way (this is not meant to express any particular person's argument; but it does make explicit much that underlies commitment to behaviorism in any of its scientific variants):

(1) The criterion of the fruitfulness of any scientific result or process is the extent to which it facilitates prediction (and, some would add, "control") of human behavior. (This presupposes that investigation of animal behavior is generally regarded as ancillary to the study of human behavior.)

(2) In order to establish that a predicted event has occurred, it is necessary that the investigator observe some publicly observable property or event.

(3) The only human properties or events that are publicly observable are *behavioral* in character.

(4) Hence, in the case of human beings the only prediction which can be established is one that enables us to foresee behavioral properties or events. (This ties things down to behavior at one end.)

(5) The predictive power of the human scientist is maximized to the extent that he discovers *laws* that relate publicly observable circumstances (independent variables) to behavioral properties or events. (These may be statistical laws.)

(6) Insofar as these independent variables are human properties, they must be behavioral. (This ties things down to behavior at the other end.)

(7) Therefore, the central aim of a scientific study of human beings should be to discover laws relating behavior and other publicly observable circumstances to subsequent behavior.

All behaviorists accept some form of this argument as a basis for their behaviorism. But there are disagreements among behaviorists that are not brought out by an examination of this argument. More specifically, behaviorists disagree about what it is scientifically permissible to say about processes that intervene between the terminal behaviors predicted and the antecedent behavior used as the basis for prediction.

Some behaviorists (for example, B. F. Skinner) claim that whether or not such processes occur, nothing scientifically useful can be said about them. The argument for their view can best be expressed in terms of what Carl Hempel has called the theoretician's dilemma. The dilemma can be stated in the following way. A proposed theory either facilitates prediction (and control) of behavior or it does not. If it does not, then it is scientifically superfluous. If it does, then it succeeds only by relating certain antecedent, nontheoretical conditions to specified behaviors. But if theories do this, then they can be eliminated in favor of empirical laws that relate antecedent conditions to behavior without reference to intervening theoretical processes. Hence, in either case theoretical notions and statements are scientifically superfluous. But it is generally recognized that the fact that a scientific theory can be eliminated does not render it irrelevant. In particular, it may be scientifically fruitful because it provides a means of simplifying complex relationships without which limited human intelligence could not function effectively. Hence, *radical* behaviorists like Skinner are forced to supplement the theoretician's dilemma with some other argument by which they purport to show that theories are, from the point of view of prediction (and control), either *absolutely* pernicious or *relatively* unfruitful. One of the ironies of this position is that although part of the inspiration for behaviorism is the enormous success of the physical sciences, it tends to ignore the undoubted fruitfulness of theorizing in those sciences. Radical behaviorists are willing to use terms that are ordinarily thought to denote mental states or processes—for example, such terms as "motive" and "purpose." But to the extent that they are willing to use such expressions, they require that the expressions be behaviorally *defined* in terms of functional relationships.

It would be unfortunate if readers were to infer that most behaviorists are *radical* behaviorists. We have dwelt on this form of behaviorism at length only because it is convenient to formulate the family of views under consideration by complicating the radical position. In fact, most other behaviorists reject radical behaviorism either on the grounds that intervening variables for which behavioral (or physiological) criteria (not necessarily *defining* criteria) can be given are permissible, or on the grounds that the radical behaviorists' skepticism about the unfruitfulness of theories is unjustified. The second group understand by "theory" a set of statements that contain constructs for which it is not even possible to provide behavioral criteria of application. As Hempel puts it:

> A scientific theory might therefore be likened to a complex spatial network: Its terms are represented by the knots, while the threads connecting the latter correspond, in part, to the definitions and, in part, to the fundamental and derivative hypotheses included in the theory. The whole system floats, as it were, above the plane of observation and is anchored to it by rules of interpretation. (*Fundamentals of Concept Formation in Empirical Science*, Chicago, 1952, p. 36)

Hempel goes on to explain that these rules of interpretation (or, as they have variously been called, coordinating rules, operational definitions, or rules of correspondence) function as threads which permit ascent to the theory and descent back down to the observational plane. The point is that not every "knot" in the floating network *requires* a rule of interpretation.

Among the permissible theoretical constructs one might find terms that denote "unobservable" mental states and processes. It seems clear that anyone who accepts a behaviorism of this kind is participating in a methodological milieu far removed from radical behaviorism.

The psychologist Clark Hull, although he often expresses himself in ways which suggest his commitment to *theories*, actually embraces the first, more limited departure from radical behaviorism. That is, he does require that criteria of application for every concept of psychology be provided—although not necessarily *defining* criteria.

Those who reject behaviorism altogether usually also reject the very first assumption of the original argument. They view the scientific investigation of human beings as aiming essentially at *understanding* and only incidentally at prediction and control. And they hold that understanding cannot be achieved when one adopts the constraining methodological maxims of behaviorism in any of its forms.

Bibliography

Classical statements of psychological behaviorism are J. B. Watson, *Behaviorism* (New York, 1924), and *Psychology From the Standpoint of a Behaviorist* (Philadelphia, 1919); Ivan Pavlov, *Conditioned Reflexes* (London, 1927); B. F. Skinner, *The Behavior of Organisms* (New York, 1938), Chs. 1 and 2; and Clark L. Hull, *Principles of Behavior* (New York, 1943).

Some important discussions of philosophical behaviorism are to be found in two excellent anthologies: V. C. Chappell, ed., *The Philosophy of Mind* (Englewood Cliffs, N.J., 1962), which contains articles by D. W. Hamlyn, Norman Malcolm, U. T. Place, J. J. C. Smart, and Paul Ziff; and D. F. Gustafson, ed., *Essays in Philosophical Psychology* (Garden City, N.Y., 1964), which includes a number of articles that criticize Gilbert Ryle's *Concept of Mind* (London and New York, 1949). C. D. Broad, *The Mind and Its Place in Nature* (London, 1925), especially pp. 612–624, and A. O. Lovejoy's article, "Paradox of the Thinking Behaviorist," in *Philosophical Review* (1922), 135–147, contain influential criticisms of behaviorism. Michael Polanyi, *Personal Knowledge* (Chicago, 1958), attacks the idea that science is principally concerned with facilitating prediction and control—a view that underlies much behaviorist thought. T. W. Wann, ed., *Behaviorism and Phenomenology* (Chicago, 1964), contains several important and interesting articles, including an exchange between B. F. Skinner (pp. 79–96) and Norman Malcolm (pp. 141–155).

Besides the books already mentioned, the following books and articles contain especially interesting discussions of behaviorism from a scientific point of view: B. F. Skinner, *Science and Human Behavior* (New York, 1953), and *Verbal Behavior* (New York, 1957), apply his radical behaviorism to the full range of human phenomena. A collection of his essays, *Cumulative Record* (New York, 1959 and 1961), contains his main methodological discussions. Two articles contain especially penetrating criticisms of Skinner's views: Noam Chomsky's review of *Verbal Behavior* in *Language*, Vol. 35 (1959) 26–58, is especially vigorous. The other essay is Michael Scriven, "A Study of Radical Behaviorism," in Herbert Feigl and Michael Scriven, eds., *Minnesota Studies in the Philosophy of Science*, Vol. I (Minneapolis, 1956). Carl Hempel's "The Theoretician's Dilemma" appears in H. Feigl and G. Maxwell, eds., Vol. II of the *Minnesota Studies* (Minneapolis, 1958). An interesting study of Skinner by William S. Verplanck and of C.L. Hull by Sigmund Koch are included in William K. Estes, et al., *Modern Learning Theory* (New York, 1954). A number of methodological articles are reprinted in Melvin Marx, ed., *Psychological Theory* (New York, 1951). This book has been revised by Marx and published under the title *Theories in Contemporary Psychology*

(New York, 1963). Articles by K. Spence, G. Bergman, C. L. Hull, E. C. Tolman, and K. S. Lashley appear in the first edition and are of special interest.

An excellent bibliography of both philosophical and psychological works is contained in the revised edition of Paul Edwards and Arthur Pap, eds., *A Modern Introduction to Philosophy* (New York, 1965), pp. 268–271.

ARNOLD S. KAUFMAN

BEHAVIORISM, PSYCHOLOGICAL. See PSYCHOLOGICAL BEHAVIORISM.

BEING. Philosophy proceeds in part by the asking of large, imprecise, and overgeneral questions. In the attempt to answer them, the questions themselves come to be reformulated with greater clarity, and one large question often comes to be replaced by several smaller ones. The history of pre-Socratic philosophy is the best example of this process, and Being first appeared on the philosophical scene as part of it. To the question "What is Being?" the Parmenidean answer that there is Being and nothing else besides Being appears to have the merit of truth, even if it is tautological truth. What is, is; and what is not, is not. But what Parmenides' question in fact contains is a nontautological demand for the characteristics of what is, to which the answer that Being is one, unchanging, and eternal is appropriate. Since the objects we perceive are many, changing, and transient, they do not belong to the realm of Being. Parmenides thus fathered in broad outline a doctrine of Being from which philosophers as diverse as Aristotle, Hegel, and John Dewey have tried to rescue us. This is the doctrine that Being is a name.

"Being" as a name. "Being" may be thought to name a property possessed by everything that is. Or it may be thought to name an object or a realm beyond, above, or behind the objects of the physical world; in this case, physical objects somehow exist by virtue of their relationship to "Being." Or again, "Being" may be the name of the genus to which everything that is, belongs in virtue of the possession of the property of Being or of standing in relation to Being. The doctrine that "Being" is a name implies some kind of dualism, according to which the realm of Being is contrasted with that of the merely phenomenal. Variations on this doctrine are general enough to be put to a number of different uses in the attempt to solve quite different problems. Nevertheless, the basic doctrine is founded on a false assumption, for it obscures the facts that the verb "to be" has a number of different uses and that in its central and commonest use it does not ascribe a property, a relation, or class membership in any way. "Being" is normally a participle, not a noun. To break with normal usage without special justification is to be gratuitously liable to confusion. We can investigate the type of confusion generated by the acceptance of "Being" as a name, and also the type of clarification that came to be needed, by considering what Plato and Aristotle make of Being.

Plato and Aristotle. Plato was anxious to mark the distinction between properties and objects that possess properties. He located the former in the realm of Being and the latter in the realm of the transient. One reason for this distinction was that Plato accepted the identification of Being with the unchanging (in this case, the unchanging meanings of predicate, the Forms). As a consequence, he was forced to deny that physical objects "are"—they belong to a stage intermediate between Being and Not-Being, that of becoming. This is not the only paradox in Plato's analysis of the subject: The Form of the Good, which exists at a higher level than that of the other Forms, cannot just "be," either; it must exist "beyond being."

Thus, we can see in Plato one of the characteristic results of treating Being as either a special kind of object or a special kind of attribute, namely, that all sorts of ordinary uses of the verb "to be" must be qualified or rewritten. The outcome of the attempt to make what is mystifying clear is to make what was clear mystifying. The author who first attacked this kind of mystification was, of course, Plato himself. In the *Sophist*, the problem of negative judgment is handled in such a way that it is no longer possible to make Parmenides' mistake of supposing that when one speaks of what is not, one is speaking of what does not exist. Moreover, it is scarcely proper to speak casually of confusion and mistake at this stage in the development of philosophy. The first steps toward producing a logical grammar of the verb "to be" perhaps necessarily involved assimilating the different senses and uses of the words, and of consequently becoming caught up in paradox and learning how to free oneself. When Aristotle, in Book I of the *Metaphysics*, clarified earlier errors, he was able to do so only because he had learned from the efforts and missteps of Parmenides and Plato.

Aristotle made three crucial points about the study of Being as Being. The first is that the special sciences may make use of the concept of Being and of other similar fundamental concepts, but these concepts are not the objects of their inquiries—only philosophy has such fundamental concepts as the proper object of its studies. The second point is that to inquire about Being as Being is to attempt to isolate the unifying strand of meaning in the multifarious senses in which the word "is" is used. The third point is that this inquiry can be carried on only as an inquiry into a whole range of closely related fundamental concepts, in which the different species of cause and the notions of unity and plurality are foremost.

Aristotle recognized that we use "is" to deny as well as to affirm, and to ascribe properties as well as to ascribe existence; and in various passages he makes use of these distinctions to clarify conceptual points. He recognized, as did the Scholastics, that in ascribing properties to a subject we sometimes imply the existence of that subject and we sometimes do not (see EXISTENCE). But in his willingness to recognize the diversity of uses of "is," Aristotle almost too easily accepted the view that we can speak of abstract entities as well as of physical objects without allowing the former "separate" existence. Aristotle said very little, in fact, about the common thread that binds together the various uses of "is."

Scholastic philosophers. The non-Aristotelian medieval writers who insisted on a single meaning for "is" unintentionally provided a *reductio ad absurdum* proof of the correctness of the Aristotelian approach. Both nominalists and realists, at least in their extreme and consistent versions, asserted that properties and objects exist in the same way: properties for the nominalists were merely collections of objects, and objects for the realists were merely properties of properties. For the nominalist Eric of Auxerre, "Being" was simply the collective name of all the individuals that exist taken together and was logically equivalent to "this and this and this . . .," while for the realist Odo of Tournai, individuals were accidents of properties that are substances, and the realm of Being was a realm only of properties.

Abelard to some extent reasserted the Aristotelian distinctions (and Anselm suggested some new ones of his own), but it was Aquinas who returned to the pure Aristotelian tradition. Aquinas refuted once again the view that Being can be either a genus or a property.

In his Commentary on Aristotle's *Metaphysics*, Aquinas diagnosed Parmenides' mistake and applied his conceptual insights to related problems, notably in his refutation of Anselm's Ontological Argument. But Aquinas' position necessarily has a complexity lacking in some other writers who have been equally careful, for although he could not accept Anselm's view that to know what God is, is to know that he is, he also could not reject the identification of God's Being with his essence. According to Aquinas, with all finite creatures it is the case that what they are—their essence—is one thing, and that they are—their existence—is another. But God simply is Being—*Esse Ipsum Subsistens*. Because this is so, Aquinas was obliged to agree with Anselm that *if* God exists, he exists necessarily. But from this it does not follow that God does exist. That there is such a being, who *is* Being, is shown, according to Aquinas, by a posteriori proofs. And of course in Thomist terms it is improper to think of God as just *a* being, one entity among others. The difficulty here, however, is derived from difficulties that are implicit in the notion of the God of monotheism and not from difficulties in the notion of Being itself.

Central questions. We are now in a position to discriminate different kinds of questions about Being raised by the Greeks and the Scholastics.

Is existence a predicate? How should we characterize the difference between ascribing existence to a subject and ascribing a property to a subject? Is "is" ever a predicate? If it is, what sort of predicate? Later writers who have discussed this problem include Descartes, in his version of the Ontological Proof; Gottlob Frege, with his clarification of the nature of predicates; G. E. Moore, with his argument that "existence" is not a predicate because we cannot, for example, significantly replace "growl" with "exist" in all the quantified and negated forms of "Tame tigers growl"; and W. V. Quine, with his analysis of Being as "to be is to be the value of a variable." This list of names points up the fact that these questions are susceptible of solution only within the philosophy of logic, and the solution depends upon an adequate characterization of names, predicates, variables, functions, and so on. It is also clear that it is of primary importance to discriminate the metaphysically noncommittal "is," formalizable by means of the existential quantifier, from other uses of the verb "to be" that are far more committed in their implications. Noncommittal uses of the verb appear in ordinary language in such expressions as "There is a prime number between six and eight," "There are three basic colors," "There is a mountain more than 29,000 feet high." Other uses of the verb "to be," however, are far more committed. For example, in the statement "Rachel wept for her children because they were not," "to be" is equivalent to "to be alive." Clearly, however, if I say "There is such-and-such a prime number," there is no such implication; hence, this sense of "there is" must be different.

One finds that all analyses of existential assertions that treat them as predicative are generally unsatisfactory. Briefly, the reason for this is that predicates refer to properties, and properties are what discriminate individuals from each other and enable us to pick out similarities and dissimilarities, and hence to classify. But Being cannot be a property in this sense, for it is not something that it is logically possible for two objects either to have or not to have in common. Two objects cannot be said to resemble each other in virtue of their both being, and since existence is not a shared property, it cannot characterize a class of objects. For this reason, Being can be neither a property nor a genus.

Of course some philosophers—Leibniz, for example—have talked as though Being were a property shared by actual objects but not possessed by *possibilia*. There is no objection to talking like this, provided that it is noticed that the word "property" is not now being used to refer to distinguishable characteristics of real things. Hence, the assertion by such philosophers that Being is a property is not compatible with the Aquinas–Moore view that it is not, given the two different senses in which the word is used.

Abstract entities. How do we characterize the status of abstract entities, numbers, possibilities, fictions? These are all different problems, each of them complex. They are envisaged as part of the problem of Being, partly because of our ordinary use of "There is/are" in, for example, "There are two possibilities," "There is a prime number between six and eight," and partly because of a misunderstanding involved in describing certain possibilities by such terms as "real." When we apply the adjective "real" both to possible states of affairs and to actual states, we suggest that there is a realm of reality wider than the merely existent. This is one source of the belief that there is a genus Being, of which the existent and the nonexistent (such as the possible) are species. Everything called real belongs to the realm of Being. The mistake lies in not seeing the difference between the way in which "real" functions as an adjective and the way in which "reality" functions as a noun. If I call a dollar bill real, I contrast "real" with "counterfeit." If I call a painting "a real Vermeer," I contrast it with a copy. But I do not ascribe to dollar bill and painting the common property of "being real," in virtue of which they belong to the same realm, that of "reality." To say that there is a kind of Being in which both what exists and what does not exist can share is obviously to commit the same mistake. But at this point we have returned to the question of whether Existence and Being can be properties, which belongs to our first group of questions.

The characterization of Being-as-such. Can we find any characteristic that belongs to everything that is and that may therefore be said to characterize Being-as-such, rather than individual objects? Here again, one must distinguish two kinds of questions. Aristotle pointed out that of any object whose existence I affirm, I shall also be able to say that it is *one*, that it is *an* object. That is, by picking out something for the purpose of saying that it is, or that it is such and such, I pick it out as an individual. But just because this is so, individuality or unity is not something that it is logically possible for a given object to possess or not to possess any more than existence is; hence, they are not properties any more than existence is. The Aristotelian question of what concepts must be applicable to anything that exists must not, therefore, be identified with the question of whether there are any properties that belong to everything that exists.

There might, of course, have been some property that belonged to everything that existed just as a matter of contingent fact. The world might have been such that everything was green or cubic, or made of blancmange. But this would be philosophically uninteresting (quite apart from the fact that in most such worlds there would be no philosophers). It has been held, however, that it is necessary on, for example, metaphysically epistemological grounds that everything which is, shall be of a certain character. Hence, Plato's view in his middle period that only Forms exist, and hence Leibniz' view that there are only monads, and Berkeley's view that to be is always either to be percipient or to be perceived.

Absolute Being. Is there a being who exists without the limitations of finite beings and who may therefore just be said to be? This is the question of God's existence.

Realm of Being-as-such. Is there—beyond, over, and above the being of individual objects—a realm of Being-as-such? If so, what is its character? The belief that there is such a realm has always haunted metaphysics. The notion that Aristotle held such a belief has pervaded the history of metaphysics. This misinterpretation of Aristotle has similarly been foisted upon Aquinas, and a Neo-Thomist myth of the history of philosophy has been constructed in which the four questions that have already been distinguished, all of which are genuine questions, are merged into this fifth question, whose character is much more dubious. It then becomes possible to suggest that there is a single problem: "What is Being?" to which different philosophers have given rival answers. The kind of metaphysics to which reference is being made can be found in Jacques Maritain's *Preface to Metaphysics*, where Maritain is ostensibly expounding Aquinas. However, in order to treat Being as a subject matter, Maritain invokes what he calls the intuition of Being, a notion that cannot be found anywhere in Aquinas. Aquinas, as we have already seen, never treated "Being" as the name of an independent subject matter and thus had no reason to suggest any means of becoming aware of the existence of such a subject matter.

The kind of history of metaphysics to which reference is being made can be found in D. A. Drennan's *A Modern Introduction to Metaphysics*, which asserts that to the question "What is Being?" Parmenides replied that it was One; Plato, that it was One and Many; Aristotle, that it was Substance; Descartes, that it was Substance in the modes of thought and extension; and so on. However, an awareness of the nonexistence of the single question of Being rids us of the misleading idea that we have here a set of competing answers to a single question.

The temptation to see the history of metaphysics in this light seems often to be provoked by an espousal of the metaphysics that makes "Being" a name. We can illustrate this point by considering two sequences in the history of modern philosophy. Hegel argued that Being is the most fundamental of concepts because the most elementary forms of judgment must involve some assertion of existence, no matter how bare. But, he continued, the notion of Being by itself is the emptiest of all notions. Merely to say of something that it is, is to say nothing at all about it; hence, the notion of Being merges into that of its apparent opposite, Nothing. It is not necessary to follow through the Hegelian scheme of categories to see that Hegel is, in fact, extremely cautious at this point. His extreme antidualism always led him to assert that there is nothing else beyond what we confront in experience. The Hegelian Absolute is the rational culmination of historical experience, not a power beyond and outside it. Similarly, for Hegel, Being is a concept expressed in our judgments of experience at a certain level, not the name of a realm beyond all judgments about experience.

In Nicolai Hartmann's philosophy, however, we find a misreading of Hegel parallel to the Neo-Scholastic misreading of Aquinas and Aristotle. In *Grundzüge einer Metaphysik der Erkenntnis*, Hartmann begins by stating a set of antinomies between, for example, the nature of consciousness as consciousness of what is other than itself and the nature of consciousness as self-contained, so that whatever consciousness is aware of is part of consciousness. That is, Hartmann describes consciousness in two ways that appear incompatible and then inquires how he may reconcile these two descriptions. However, instead of asking whether the incompatibility is perhaps only apparent, he suggests that the problem arises, and is soluble, because both the knowing, conscious subject and the known object exemplify modes of Being, although different modes. Clearly, it is true that both knower and known *are*, but equally clearly—for reasons given earlier—this is not a property that is open to further study and that has strange characteristics which enable us to resolve antinomies. This, however, was Hartmann's conclusion, and he attributed it to Hegel. He merged Hegel's classification of different subject matters and his scheme of concepts in order to read him as a metaphysician who understood Being as having different grades and modes.

Just as Maritain misreads Aquinas and Hartmann misreads Hegel, so Heidegger has misread the pre-Socratics. Heidegger's own views have a mixed ancestry. Kierkegaard, one of the important influences on him, in the *Concept of Dread* writes of dread as an experience whose object is Nothing. Usually in Kierkegaard this sort of statement appears to be a dramatically effective and logically innocent way of characterizing dread as objectless, but at times it seems as if Kierkegaard is no longer saying that dread has no object. Rather, he gives it a particular object whose name is "Nothing," thus making—but not as a joke—the mistake of the Red King in *Through the Looking-Glass*, who thought that if Nobody had passed the messenger on the road, Nobody should have arrived first. To treat "Nothing" as a name is like treating "Something" as a name and easily becomes a counterpart to treating "Being" as a name, as it does with Heidegger. Heidegger takes up Leibniz' question, "Why is there something rather than nothing?" He objects that this question does not take seriously the fact that Being and Nothing necessarily exist together as contrasted and opposed powers. Heidegger allows that he is using "Being" and "Nothing" as names and is therefore involved in treating "Nothing" as if it were the name of something. He even allows that this is "unscientific," but he concludes that this is so much the worse for science and so much the better for philosophy and poetry. Being and Nothing are not objects, and Being is indeed sharply contrasted with beings. Logic presupposes Being and Nothing, but they lie beyond the grasp of logic. Heidegger treats what others have written of the indeterminateness of the concepts as evidence of the elusiveness of Being and Nothing.

Heidegger extends his metaphysics into the history of philosophy by finding his views anticipated in the thought of Heraclitus and Parmenides. The evidence for this claim depends partly on a set of unreliable etymologies that Heidegger thinks he has found for key Greek words, but even when Heidegger is plausible in his interpretation at the linguistic level, he is at the least anachronistic in his view of the kind of problem the pre-Socratics confronted. They progressively recognized as paradoxical, and therefore as needing reformulation, those very forms of utterance that to Heidegger are and remain fundamental.

If the philosophy of Being has bred not merely rival doctrines but rival views of the history of philosophy, it has also bred rival diagnoses of the errors involved in treating "Being" as a noun. A. J. Ayer has suggested that a misuse of the verb "to be" is the root of the error. This would imply, however, that standard forms of grammar embodied in ordinary usage are somehow philosophically normative—and this appears to get matters upside down. Linguistic distortion is certainly liable to breed confusion, but there is, in fact, nothing grammatically wrong with forming a verbal noun such as "Being" as an analogy with, for example, "riding." "Riding" is used as the name of an activity; why, then, should "Being" not be made into a name? It is surely because of the logical and metaphysical confusion involved that we want to criticize the linguistic construction and not because the linguistic construction itself is an error.

John Dewey diagnosed a twofold root of errors about Being. They are partly a survival from religious modes of thought, the retention of belief in a realm free from change and decay and separate from the realm of sense perception. This is explained by the fact that although mythological thought has been discredited, the impulses behind it still need satisfaction. Also, belief in changeless Being is a consequence of man's habit of abstracting truths from the contexts of practice and activity in which they were acquired (and where alone they have meaning) and treating them instead as belonging to a timeless realm in which they wait upon our apprehension. Dewey's diagnosis, however, while it may explain how we come to hold and retain confused views of Being, does not embody an explanation of why the views are confused, except perhaps to those who are already convinced in general of the truth of Dewey's pragmatism.

In order to clarify the issue, we must, in fact, make the sort of analysis of concepts that Aristotle used in the *Metaphysics*. We may expect any analysis of the concept of Being to vary with the general framework of concepts within which it is considered. Aristotelians, Hegelians, Quineans (see ONTOLOGY) will not all agree, but any analysis that fails to discriminate the different questions involved, and that fails to identify the confusion that results from merging them into a single question, will be doomed to conceptual error and very likely to a misreading of the history of philosophy as well.

Bibliography

TEXTS

Aquinas, Thomas, *De Ente et Essentia*, M.-D. Roland-Gosselin, ed. Le Saulchoir, 1926. Translated by Armand Maurer as *On Being and Essence*. Toronto, 1949.

Aquinas, Thomas, *In Metaphysicorum Aristotelis Commentaria*, M. R. Cathala, ed. Turin, 1935.

Aquinas, Thomas, *Summa Theologica*. Ottawa, 1941–1945. Translated by the Dominican Fathers of the English Province, 3 vols. New York, 1947.

Aristotle, *Metaphysics*, translated by H. Tredennick. Cambridge, Mass., 1945.

Aristotle, *Metaphysics*, W. D. Ross, ed., Oxford translation. Oxford, 1948.

Cajetan, *Commentaria in De Ente et Essentia*, M. H. Laurent, ed. Turin, 1934.

Cornford, F. M., *Plato and Parmenides*. London, 1935; New York, 1957. A translation of the *Parmenides*.

Dewey, John, *The Quest for Certainty*. New York, 1929.

Duns Scotus, *Opera Omnia*, 12 vols. Paris, 1891–1895. Vol III, *Quaestiones Subtillissimae Super Libros Metaphysicorum Aristotelis*.

Hartmann, Nicolai, *Grundzüge einer Metaphysik der Erkenntnis*. Berlin, 1921.

Hegel, G. W. F., *The Science of Logic*, translated by W. H. Johnston and L. G. Struthers. New York, 1929.

Heidegger, Martin, *Existence and Being*, translated by D. Scott, R. Hall, and A. Crick. Chicago, 1949. Includes various works.

Kant, Immanuel, *Critique of Pure Reason*, translated by Norman Kemp Smith. London, 1933.

Kirk, G. S., and Raven, J. E., eds., *The Presocratic Philosophers*. Cambridge, 1960. Ch. 10, Parmenides texts. Also contains translation and commentary.

Plato, *Platonis Opera*, J. Burnet, ed. Oxford, 1899–1906. The *Theaetetus* and the *Sophist*. Translated by F. M. Cornford as *Plato's Theory of Knowledge*. London, 1935; New York, 1957.

Quine, W. V., *From a Logical Point of View*. Cambridge, Mass., 1953.

Wolff, Christian von, *Philosophia Prima Sive Ontologia*. Frankfurt and Leipzig, 1730.

DISCUSSIONS OF TEXTS

Gilson, Étienne, *L'Être et l'essence*. Paris, 1948.

Gilson, Étienne, *Being and Some Philosophers*. Toronto, 1949.

Martin, Gottfried, *Immanual Kant: Ontologie und Wissenschaftstheorie*. Cologne, 1951. Translated by P. G. Lucas as *Kant's Metaphysics and Theory of Science*. Manchester, 1955.

Owens, Joseph, *The Doctrine of Being in the Aristotelian Metaphysics*. Toronto, 1951.

ARTICLES

Geach, P. T., "Form and Existence." *PAS*, Vol. 55 (1954/55), 251–272.

Geach, P. T., Ayer, A. J., and Quine, W. V., "Symposium: On What There Is." *Aristotelian Society Supplement*, Vol. 25 (1951), 125–160.
Moore, G. E., "Is Existence a Predicate?" *Aristotelian Society Supplement*, Vol. 15 (1936), 175–188.
Quine, W. V., "On What There Is." *Review of Metaphysics*, Vol. 2 (1948–1949), 21–38.
Weiss, P., "Being, Essence and Existence." *Review of Metaphysics*, Vol. 1 (1947–1948), 69–92.

ALASDAIR MACINTYRE

BELIEF. See KNOWLEDGE AND BELIEF.

BELIEF SENTENCES. See INTENTIONALITY; PROPOSITIONS, JUDGMENTS, SENTENCES, AND STATEMENTS.

BELINSKI, VISSARION GRIGORYEVICH (1811–1848), Russian literary critic, was an early leader of the Russian intelligentsia and a major representative of German Absolute Idealism, as well as of the subsequent reaction against it, in nineteenth-century Russian philosophy.

Belinski was born in Sveaborg, Russia (now Finland), the son of a provincial physician. He entered the University of Moscow in 1829 but was expelled after three years, perhaps for the radical criticism of serfdom in a romantic drama he wrote; his subsequent education was self-acquired. He began a journalistic career in 1833 and soon became the chief critic for a succession of literary journals in Moscow and (after 1839) in St. Petersburg, principally *Otechestvennyye Zapiski* ("Annals of the Fatherland"). His brilliant, philosophically oriented critical essays, including perceptive early appreciations of Gogol, Lermontov, and Dostoyevsky, won him great renown but little material reward; he died in St. Petersburg after a short life filled with poverty and illness.

Belinski's intellectual development typifies that of the early Russian "Westernizers," or admirers of Western progressive ideas and institutions, whose leader he became: he passed from the romantic extremes of German Absolute Idealism through Hegel to a mature position representing the influence of the French socialists and Feuerbach. In Belinski's case, the doctrinal changes were magnified and accelerated by a mercurial personality, while their expression was often clouded by the pressures of journalistic writing under tsarist censorship. Belinski published no systematic theoretical works, and his voluminous critical essays and private correspondence leave room for divergent interpretations of his views.

Belinski's earliest writings (1831–1836) show the clear influence of Schiller and Schelling. Basing his views on Schelling's nature philosophy and philosophy of art, Belinski glorified art and the creative process, and emphasized man's inner aesthetic and moral experience in rising above empirical reality to the "eternal Idea."

In 1837, after a brief enthusiasm for Fichte, Belinski was introduced by his friend and mentor, Michael Bakunin, to the thought of Hegel. Belinski found in the Hegelian formula "all that is real is rational" a summons to a "reconciliation with reality" that turned his attention from man's subjective world to the objective reality around him and led him to praise Russian autocracy, to view the state as sacred, and to regard society as metaphysically and ethically superior to the individual. He expressed a Hegelian conception of art as "thinking in images" and as reproducing rational reality.

Belinski's Hegelianism, however, could not extinguish the regard for human individuality that in some degree had always marked his thinking and had been manifested most explicitly during his brief Fichtean period. By 1841 he repudiated Hegel's subordination of the individual and thenceforth turned from Absolute Idealism to an ethical personalism that emphasized the supreme value of the individual personality. At the same time, he abandoned the attempt to show the rationality of the tsarist order: he became acquainted with the writings of Saint-Simon and other French socialists, and called increasingly for radical social reforms in the direction of democracy and socialism. His mature view of art stressed art's moral and political functions in expressing socially progressive ideas, for which reason he is generally regarded as the founder of the dominant tradition of social or "civic" criticism in Russia.

Belinski's socialism remained individualistic in inspiration, and there is evidence that toward the end of his life he moved to a more moderate liberal position, advocating the development of a middle class in Russia. His reformist enthusiasm and generally enlightened outlook were well expressed in a famous "Letter to Gogol" (1847), which set a moral tone for the Russian intelligentsia for generations. The "Letter" illustrates the antiecclesiasticism and positivist leanings of Belinski's final period, if not the outright atheism and materialism attributed to him by Soviet interpreters.

Works by Belinski

Polnoye Sobraniye Sochineni ("Complete Works"), 13 vols. Moscow, 1953–1959.
Izbrannyye Filosofskiye Sochineniya ("Selected Philosophical Works"), 2 vols. Moscow, 1948.
Selected Philosophical Works. Moscow, 1956.

Works on Belinski

Bowman, Herbert E., *Vissarion Belinsky, 1811–1848: A Study in the Origins of Social Criticism in Russia*. Cambridge, Mass., 1954.
Masaryk, T. G., *Russland und Europa*, 2 vols. Jena, 1913. Translated by Eden and Cedar Paul as *The Spirit of Russia*, 2 vols. London, 1919; 2d ed., London, 1955.
Zenkovsky, V. V., *Istoriya Russkoy Filosofii*, 2 vols. Paris, 1948–1950. Translated by George L. Kline as *A History of Russian Philosophy*, 2 vols. New York and London, 1953.

JAMES P. SCANLAN

BELLARMINE, ST. ROBERT (1542–1621), an Italian cardinal and controversialist, was born at Montepulciano in Tuscany and died at Rome. Educated in the Jesuit order, of which he became a member, he taught philosophy and theology at the University of Louvain (1570–1576), then at the Roman (Jesuit) College, where he later served as rector. After Bellarmine was created a cardinal in 1599, much of his time was devoted to the administrative and diplomatic affairs of the Roman Catholic church, in which he is now venerated as a saint. His chief published work is the *Disputations on Controversial Matters (Disputationes de Controversiis)*, in which Book

III (*De Laicis*) treats questions of political and social philosophy. Another treatise in political philosophy is the *Defense of His Reply to King James I of England* (*Apologia Bellarmini pro Responsione Sua ad Librum Jacobi Magnae Britanniae Regis*, reprinted in Giacon's *Scritti politici*), concerning the theory of the divine right of kings.

In general, Bellarmine's philosophic thought is Thomistic. His lectures at Louvain covered all of Aquinas' *Summa Theologiae* and are now preserved in the Vatican Archives, though they have not been printed. As a result, little is known of his metaphysical and psychological views, except for occasional explanations given in his more practical writings. It is assumed that he had a very sound understanding of the speculative thought of Thomas Aquinas, however, and the publication of the Louvaine lectures is a desideratum. In ethics and philosophy of law, Bellarmine is a strong opponent of the view that the source of justice is the will of God; instead, he argues that man's awareness of moral law derives from his understanding of the nature of man and his environment, and that ultimately the command (*imperium*) of God's law is intellectual, stemming from the divine wisdom. Thus, he is opposed to voluntarism and defends intellectualism in morals and jurisprudence.

Bellarmine's political theories developed in part from opposition to King James's claim that both spiritual and temporal power belong to the civil monarch. In defending the autonomy of ecclesiastical authority, Bellarmine strongly supported the distinction and separation of the powers of church and state. In chapter 13 of the *Apologia*, he argued that, though the ultimate source of both powers is divine, the civil power is conferred on rulers, *mediately*, through the people as a medium. Thus, with Francisco Suárez, Bellarmine is one of the most prominent Catholic advocates of the "translation theory" of political sovereignty.

Bellarmine was firmly convinced of the importance of the individual citizen and the dignity of every man. His social and political thinking is reminiscent of the fourteenth-century views of Marsilius of Padua. There is a possibility that Bellarmine's arguments influenced British antimonarchist thinking and, through John Locke, the founders of American democracy. He also recognized something of the investment value of money and helped to modify the older Catholic theory that all taking of interest on loans was to be condemned as usury. In a treatise on the power of the pope (*De Summo Pontifice*, I, 9), Bellarmine favored the idea of a world state but admitted that a plurality of national states regulated by international law might be more practical.

About Bellarmine's role in the prosecution of Galileo it is hard to be precise; in 1616 he seems to have warned Galileo to discuss the Copernican theory merely as a "mathematical supposition," but he almost certainly did not enjoin him from "teaching or discussing Copernicanism in any way," as was charged after Bellarmine's death. Galileo's publication of the *Dialogue of the Two Chief World Systems*, in 1632, caused him to be prosecuted for heresy on the grounds that he had thereby violated the supposed stricter warning.

Works by Bellarmine

Disputationes de Controversiis Christianae Fidei Adversus Huius Temporis Haereticos, 3 vols. Ingolstadt, 1586–1593. Venice, 1596 (4 vols.). The Venice edition is the definitive Latin text.

Opera Omnia, J. Fèvre, ed., 12 vols. Paris, 1870–1874.

De Laicis or the Treatise on Civil Government, translated by K. E. Murphy, New York, 1928.

Scritti politici, C. Giacon, ed. Bologna, 1950. Selected politico-social writings in Latin.

Works on Bellarmine

Brodrick, J., *Robert Bellarmine: Saint and Scholar*. Westminster, Md., 1961.

Davitt, T., *The Nature of Law*. St. Louis, 1951. Pp. 195–218.

Riedl, J., "Bellarmine and the Dignity of Man," in G. Smith, ed., *Jesuit Thinkers of the Renaissance*. Milwaukee, 1939. Pp. 193–226.

VERNON J. BOURKE

BENEKE, FRIEDRICH EDUARD (1798–1854), German philosopher and psychologist. He was born in Berlin and after his gymnasium education studied theology and philosophy, first at Halle and then at Berlin. He became university lecturer (*Privatdozent*) at the University of Berlin in 1820 and, despite Hegel's power and official connections, managed to have a considerable number of students.

His first books were *Erkenntnisslehre nach dem Bewusstsein der reinen Vernunft* (Theory of Knowledge According to the Consciousness of Pure Reason) and *Erfahrungsseelenlehre als Grundlage alles Wissens* (Experiential Theory of the Soul as Foundation of All Knowledge). Both were published in Jena in 1820. Two years later, he published in Berlin *Grundlegung zur Physik der Sitten* ("Foundations of the Physics of Morals"), a work which found disfavor among the entrenched Absolute Idealists and resulted in his being forbidden to lecture. Beneke was accused of Epicureanism, although the objections given by Minister von Altenstein, a Hegelian who opposed Beneke's attempted application of science to ethics, were that the book was not so much wrong on particular points as that it was *unphilosophisch* in its totality because it did not attempt to derive everything from the Absolute. Beneke's anti-Hegelian position led to further difficulties. An offer of a position at the University of Jena was overruled by the authorities in Berlin, who managed to find a state law to support this move. Beneke moved to Göttingen, where his reception was more cordial, and remained there until 1827, when he received permission to resume his lectures in Berlin. After Hegel's death, Beneke managed to advance to the rank of "extraordinary professor." Although he was active in teaching and writing, his later years were plagued by illness. In 1854, under unexplained circumstances, his body was found in a Berlin canal.

Along with Herbart and some others, Beneke represented a reaction against the Fichte-Schelling-Hegel phase of German philosophy. He insisted that psychology, which ought to be established inductively, is the necessary presupposition of all disciplines in philosophy. Logic, ethics, metaphysics, and especially the philosophy of religion should be based on it. Beneke's psychology is a form of associationism, and shows the influence of both Kant and the British empiricists, especially Locke, whose disciple Beneke claimed to be. The senses give us only a mediated knowledge of the external world and of ourselves. However, we can obtain an immediate, fully adequate knowledge of our own mental acts by means of inner perception. Starting from this perception, we infer the inner nature of other beings by analogy with our own. The result of this inference is a picture of reality as containing an uninterrupted series of minds or "faculties of representation" (*Vorstellungsfähigkeit*), extending downward from man. The soul consists of a system of powers or forces; it is a "bundle" but, contrary to Hume, not a bundle of perceptions.

Beneke used the language of faculty psychology, although he did not intend "powers" or "faculties" to be viewed as hypostatized concepts. All psychological processes, he claimed, can be traced back to four basic ones: (1) the process of stimulus appropriation (*Reizaneignung*), in which the mind creates sensations and perceptions out of externally caused impressions; (2) the process of formation of new "elementary faculties" (*Urvermögen*) by means of the assimilation of received stimuli; (3) the process of transmission (*Übertragung*) and equalization (*Ausgleichung*) of stimuli and powers, whereby a systematic connection is formed between our becoming conscious of one idea and our becoming unconscious of another idea; (4) the process of mutual attraction and "blending" (*Verschmelzung*) of ideas of the same sort.

Beneke's attempt to explain the mind's activities in terms of their genesis is reminiscent of Herbart. Unlike the latter, however, he assumed that philosophy must proceed from what is immediately given in consciousness. We have no alternative to this starting with inner experience, he believed, because our own soul is the only thing that we know as it is in itself. We recognize it as a nonspatial and therefore an immaterial entity. At least we have no reason to suppose it to be material, since it is not perceived through outer sense. However, the soul cannot be simple, as Herbart had maintained. It has, as we have noted, specific powers or capacities for receiving and organizing stimuli; these powers must be underivative, since stimuli of different kinds can be received even at the outset of our experience. Each of our senses is supposed to include several of these *Urvermögen*. But the soul must also be capable of forming new *Urvermögen*, in order to be receptive to new sorts of stimuli.

Beneke thus conceived the mental life as compounded of active impulses (*Triebe*) that are activated by external stimuli. The seemingly substantial unity of mind is explained by the persistence of traces (*Spuren*) of ideas that have become unconscious and by the mutual adjustment of faculties that produce new impulses.

Additional Works by Beneke

Neue Grundlegung zur Metaphysik. Berlin, 1822.
Psychologische Skizzen, 2 vols. Göttingen, 1825–1827.
Das Verhältniss von Seele und Leib. Göttingen, 1826.
Kant und die Philosophische Aufgabe unserer Zeit. Berlin, 1832.
Lehrbuch der Psychologie als Naturwissenschaft. Berlin, 1833.
Die Philosophie in ihrem Verhältnisse zur Erfahrung zur Spekulation und zum Leben. Berlin, 1833.
Grundlinien des näturlichen Systems der praktischen Philosophie. Berlin, 1837. Beneke regarded the last part of the *Grundlinien*, which contains his theory of morals, as his best work.
Metaphysik und Philosophie der Religion. Berlin, 1840.

Works on Beneke

Benner, H., *Benekes Erkenntnistheorie*. Leipzig, 1902.
Gargano, V., *L'Etica di Beneke*. Catania, Sicily, 1912.
Gramzow, O., *Benekes Leben und Philosophie*. Bern, 1899.
Murtfeld, R., "Vergeblischer Kampf gegen den Idealismus: Friedrich Eduard Beneke," in *Zeitschrift für Geschichte der Erziehung und des Unterrichts* (Berlin, 1923), 1–48.
Samuel, E., *Die Realität des Psychischen bei Beneke*. Berlin, 1907.
Wandschneider, A., *Die Metaphysik Benekes*. Berlin, 1903.

ARNULF ZWEIG

BEN GERSHON, LEVI. See GERSONIDES.

BENN, GOTTFRIED (1886–1956), German poet and critic, was born in Mansfeld in Westprignitz, of mixed Prussian and Swiss–French parentage. After studying philosophy and philology at the universities of Marburg and Berlin, he received a military scholarship to the Kaiser Wilhelm Academy of Berlin, from which he graduated as doctor of medicine in 1912. Commissioned as a medical officer in the German Imperial Army, he served briefly in 1912 and then again after the outbreak of the war in 1914. A close friendship with the poet Else Lasker-Schüler ended in 1913, and in July 1914 he married the actress Eva Brandt. From 1917 to 1935 he practiced in Berlin as a specialist in venereal and skin diseases. After his wife's sudden death in 1922, he befriended Ellen Overgaard, a Danish woman, who adopted his daughter.

Benn collaborated with Paul Hindemith on the oratorio *Das Unaufhörliche*, which was performed in 1931. Extensive contact with representative writers of the Weimar Republic led to his election, in 1932, into the German Academy of Arts (whose president, Heinrich Mann, the brother of Thomas, Benn eulogized in an essay in 1931). A somewhat sordid period of jockeying for positions in the new Reich ended in 1935 with Benn's losing the post of municipal medical specialist, and in 1938 all his writings were banned. He rejoined the army in 1935, coining for this move the much-publicized term *innere Emigration*, in contrast to the actual emigration of his former friends. In 1938 he married his secretary, Herte von Wedemeyer; she committed suicide in 1945, when the Russian armies were approaching the village to which she had been evacuated. After the war Benn's writings were banned, but the publication of *Statische Gedichte* in Switzerland (1948) marked the beginning of a new creative phase. In 1946 he married Ilse Kaul, a young dentist. Benn gave up his medical practice in 1953. Through his decision to remain in Berlin, he became something of a spokesman for the intelligentsia of the city. At his death he was hailed as the greatest German poet since Rilke; his influence on the styles and themes of contemporary German poetry, certainly, is second to none.

Benn always insisted on the hermetic nature of his poetry and prose; nevertheless, his work faithfully reflects both the historical events and the intellectual turmoil of his age. His first collection of poems, *Morgue* (1912), achieved notoriety and success because of its ruthless exploitation of the phenomena of physical decay and disease. The stark naturalism of such a poem as "Man and Woman Walking Through a Cancer Ward" lies both in its rhythmically weak form and in the direction of its argument, typical of much of Benn's later work: the poem attempts to designate some bedrock of "reality" that will withstand contemporary skepticism. The "reality" that emerges from behind the clinical details is a representation of life as impersonal, merely physical or biological, and bereft of all spirit.

The major German poets of the twentieth century have expressed an acute consciousness of their historical situation, a consciousness that derives from Nietzsche's critique of the historical imagination and from Spengler's *Decline of the West.* Benn, in the wake of these works, described the age after the defeat of 1918 as "postnihilistic." In the face of national collapse he set out to formulate an "absolute aesthetic," the aim of which was to "transcend" the actual situation by means of the idea of a "pure poem," the poem of "absolute expressiveness" (as opposed to the poem of communication or opinion with didactic intent). In Benn's poetry, however, there are elements of self-disclosure that seem not to be consistent with his concept of the "pure poem." And his doctrine that art should be exclusively concerned with "style, not truth," raises more questions than it answers.

Benn's ideas on the role of art in life varied. He was able to speak of art as "historically ineffective, without practical consequences," but also to define it (in the wake of Nietzsche) as "the only valid vindiction of life." The "biologism" of Benn's earlier poetry had been morally indifferent, and he had nothing but contempt for every form of social organization and democratic politics, especially those of the Weimar Republic. It is therefore not surprising that after March 1933 he emerged as the most important of those German poets who convinced themselves that national socialism offered an answer to their search for a valid artistic ideology—or, rather, for valid poetic symbols. Benn discerned in Hitler's regime the rule of "a new biological type . . . [and] the victory of the national idea, the victory of genuine human values, in perfect harmony with the logic of history." His courtship with national socialism was brief, yet even in 1950 (in his embarrassing autobiographical apologia, *Doppelleben*) his main criticism of the Hitler regime was that it "lacked style." "Style" was for Benn the product and the justification of an image-making faculty that conforms to certain "absolute" laws; these laws are "autonomous" in the sense of being indifferent to the demands of personal experience and social reality alike. Questions of personal expediency apart, Benn's astonishing expectations for Hitler's regime seem to have sprung from that contemptuous disregard of political realities that had been characteristic of an important section of the German cultural scene for many years. He saw no contradiction in asserting the hermetic nature of poetry while claiming that the heroic virtues of the new regime would be more propitious for its creation. The historicism he cultivated served Benn (as it did Heidegger in 1933) as justification for his collaboration, but it did not lead him to a clear understanding of the total claim of Hitler's dictatorship.

Benn is the only major German poet who felt, albeit briefly, that his vision was realized in the National Socialist ideology, even though his poems soon proved to be incompatible with the party line in art. The elements that form his best poems derive from the cosmopolitan expressionist school that flourished in Germany in the 1920s as much as from French and Italian imagism; even his invocation of chthonic and instinctual values (in his praise of "Quaternary man" and his values) has its parallels in Ezra Pound, T. E. Hulme, and Julian Benda. His poetic style is clipped, paratactic, full of laconic allusions to the natural sciences. Memories are imaged by means of strong and complex sense perceptions; striking physical details are selected, often for their sound values; all mention of "you" and "we" is rhetorical, the solipsistic circle hardly ever being breached; and the situations invoked are almost always related to a self whose isolation is, if anything, underlined by an appeal to primordial memories.

Works by Benn

Gesammelte Werke. Wiesbaden, 1958–1961. The most important aesthetic statements are to be found in "Züchtung I" and "Züchtung II," Vol. I; "Roman des Phänotyps," and "Der Ptolemäer," Vol. II; "Doppelleben" and "Ausdruckswelt," Vol. III; and "Autobiographische und vermischte Schriften," Vol. IV.

Statische Gedichte. Zurich, 1948. These two volumes contain representative selections of Benn's poetry.

Trunkene Flut, 2d ed. Wiesbaden, 1952.

Works on Benn

Hamburger, M., *Reason and Energy.* London, 1957.

Holthusen, H. E., *Das Schöne und das Wahre.* Munich, 1958.

Jens, W., *Statt einer Literaturgeschichte.* Tübingen, 1958.

Lohner, E., *Gottfried Benn.* Wiesbaden, 1956. Bibliography.

Loose, G., *Die Ästhetik Gottfried Benns.* Frankfurt, 1961.

Wellershoff, D., *Gottfried Benn: Phänotyp dieser Stunde.* Cologne, 1958.

Wodtke, F. W., *Gottfried Benn.* Stuttgart, 1962. Biography.

J. P. STERN

BENTHAM, JEREMY (1748–1832), English Utilitarian and leader of the Philosophical Radicals, was born in Houndsditch, in London. He entered Queen's College, Oxford, at the age of 12, graduated in 1763, and immediately entered Lincoln's Inn to study law, his father's profession. He was called to the bar in 1767 but, although the law was his major preoccupation throughout his long life, he never practiced it. Instead, he set himself to work out a system of jurisprudence and to codify and reform both civil and penal law. His motive was a profound dissatisfaction both with what he witnessed in the courts as a student, and with its theoretical justification by such expositors as Blackstone. The theory did not seem to Bentham either coherent in itself or in accordance with the practice; the practice was brutal, cumbersome, costly, and wrapped in unnecessary obscurity. Bentham's life work was the advocacy of a clear, coherent, humane, and simplified legal system.

In pursuit of this aim, Bentham wrote many thousands of pages, but in a curiously desultory way. Before finishing one work, he would start on another; many were left unfinished, and those that he did finish he often did not bother to publish; some were made known to the world only through the French translations of his Swiss follower, Étienne Dumont.

Bentham began his writings on legal reform with a rationale of punishment and an elaborate *Comment* on Blackstone's *Commentaries.* It was about 35 years before the first was published (in Paris by Dumont, in 1811, together with some later material, as *Théorie des peines et des récompenses);* the second escaped publication for nearly 150 years, until 1928. Bentham did, however, publish an extract from it, in which he attacked Blackstone's eulogy of the English constitution, under the title *A Fragment on Government* (London, 1776). The only major theoretical work he published himself was the *Introduction to the Principles of Morals and Legislation* (Oxford, 1789). He did publish a large number of pamphlets on topical issues, attacking the law of libel, the packing of juries, the oath, the extortions of the legal profession, the established church, and much else; or defending the lending of money at interest, reforms in education, and his elaborate scheme for a model prison, on which he spent much time and money. His more theoretical works—such as *The Book of Fallacies* (London, 1824), prepared and edited at Bentham's direction from unfinished manuscripts by Peregrine Bingham; the *Rationale of Judicial Evidence* (London, 1827), similarly edited by J. S. Mill after the publication of a shorter version by Dumont; *Traité des preuves judiciares* (Paris, 1823), edited by Dumont; and the posthumous *Deontology* (London and Edinburgh, 1834), edited by Bowring—were mostly left in an unfinished state by Bentham. The book that did most to make him known was Dumont's *Traités de législation civile et pénale* (Paris, 1802), which was in part an exposition of Bentham's ideas and in part a translation of some of Bentham's published and unpublished works. There are several translations of Dumont's work, the first by John Neal (Boston, 1840).

Bentham tried to interest Catherine of Russia and other European rulers in his *Constitutional Code* (Vol. I first published London, 1830; the complete work first published in the *Works.*) He was made a citizen of the infant French republic in 1792, and had some influence there and in other European countries, as well as in that other infant republic, the United States of America. His most abiding influence was, however, in England, where the Benthamites became a powerful political force that attracted men of the caliber of James Mill and his son John Stuart Mill, continued long after Bentham's death, and eventually accomplished at least some of the political and legal reforms Bentham had hoped for. By the time Bentham died, he was already the revered sage of a strong movement. It had a journal, the *Westminster Review,* which Bentham had established in 1824, at his own expense, as an organ of radical opinion to counter the Whig *Edinburgh* and the Tory *Quarterly.* The movement had even succeeded in founding a university—University College, London—in which one of Bentham's most notable disciples, John Austin, became the first professor of jurisprudence. There Bentham's embalmed body, surmounted by a wax model of his head, and dressed in his accustomed clothes, is still to be seen.

Moral theory. It is as the exponent of utilitarianism and as the acknowledged leader of the philosophical radicals, whose program of social reform was firmly based on utilitarian theory, that Bentham is chiefly remembered. He thought of the principle of utility as primarily a guide for legislators. Through it he hoped to impart some order into the chaos and illogic of the law.

Attack on intuitionism. This chaos was, it seemed to him, partly the result of intuitionism (or the belief in intuitively apprehended absolute principles), which he called "the principle of sympathy and antipathy," or "ipsedixitism." The legislator happened to be revolted by some actions, so he punished them heavily, even though they caused suffering to no one. Bentham cited sexual offenses as one example of this. On the other hand, other types of action that caused great public suffering were either left unpunished or were punished very leniently. This was the inevitable result of basing a penal code on immutable "moral laws" that stigmatized actions as bad in themselves, without regard to their consequences. Nor was it merely penal law that suffered from this error in moral theory. Civil law was traditionally based on contract: the appeal was to an absolute principle, "promises must be kept." But it sometimes happened that the law was unwilling to enforce a contract, perhaps because it was against public policy. Instead of drawing the conclusion that the rule about keeping promises was not absolute, but subordinate to a more binding rule about the public interest, the lawyers said that in this case the contract was null and void, that there never had been a contract. In other words, they saved their moral theory by deliberately falsifying the facts. On the other hand, when the law wished to enforce an obligation that patently did not rest on a contract, since none had been made, it pretended that one had been made, and spoke of a quasi-contract.

Legal fictions. Bentham put these cases forward as typical examples of the "fictions" by which, he claimed, the law was constantly bedeviled. (Bentham's more general, and more positive, doctrine of "fictions" is discussed below.) These cases also made clear the role that the principle of utility would play in a more rational system. Once legislators were forced to recognize that legal obligations rested, not on arbitrary absolute moral principles but on the single aim of increasing happiness and reducing suffering, it would be possible to lay down much more rational and consistent principles as to which obligations should be waived and which enforced.

Hedonic calculus. Bentham was, then, the theorist of the philosophical radicals, in that he laid down general principles from which programs of legislative and social reform might follow immediately. But he was much less concerned with the more abstract and metaphysical questions involved. His most characteristic contribution to utilitarian theory was his elaboration of the "hedonic calculus." According to this doctrine, the way to judge between alternative courses of action is to consider the consequences of each, in terms of the pleasure and pain of all the people affected. Let us suppose, for example, that a Benthamite is trying to decide whether to take his small nephew to the circus or to spend his evening at home with a book. He knows that the circus will bore him: he may estimate this boredom at, let us say, 5 units of pain; i.e. −5 units of pleasure. He will, on the other hand, gain some sympathetic pleasure from watching the small boy's pleased excitement, though not enough, certainly, to compensate for his boredom. He may put this at +2 units of pleasure. But the boy may be expected to gain great pleasure from the outing: perhaps 10 units. Taking the child to the circus, then, may be expected to yield (10+2)−5 units of pleasure; i.e., 7 units. Now consider the alternative. A quiet evening at home, though pleasurable, does not transport an adult as much as an evening out does a child: perhaps we may evaluate it at 6 units. His pleasure will be spoiled a little, too, by the sympathetic pain that knowledge of his nephew's disappointment will cause: say −2 units. Then there is that disappointment itself: since both the pains and pleasures of childhood are intense, we may put it at −8 units. To stay at home, then, will cause 6−2−8 units of pleasure; i.e., 4 units of pain. The choice, then, is between a course of action that will cause, on balance, 7 units of pleasure, and one that will cause 4 units of pain. The first is clearly the one that will contribute most to the sum of human happiness. It is, then, the right action in these circumstances. Its rightness is not an intrinsic characteristic, but depends entirely on its consequences in any given case: if the uncle found circuses more boring, or the nephew found them less pleasant, staying at home might become the right action.

This is, of course, a comparatively crude example. Bentham devoted great ingenuity to refining the calculus and working out its implications for legal reform. Punishment, for example, must be just harsh enough to deter, and no harsher. Any more pain than is necessary for this purpose is unjustifiable. On the other hand, too lenient a punishment is a worse evil, since the pain inflicted on the criminal, being insufficient to deter, will not be counterbalanced by the pain spared future victims of similar crimes.

Greatest happiness principle. Utilitarianism presupposes one overriding moral principle: that one ought to aim at the greatest happiness of the greatest number. Bentham could not entirely avoid the question of the ontological status of this principle. He did say that it could not be proved, since "it is used to prove everything else," and "a chain of proofs must have their commencement somewhere." This might be taken to mean that it is a self-evident principle known by reason, rather like the principle of the syllogism. But Bentham could hardly insist on this, since he maintained that the appeal to self-evident principles was an appeal to one's own prejudices. He might perhaps have meant that a careful analysis of men's moral judgments would show that the greatest happiness principle always did underlie them, so far as they were consistent: the principle itself could then be accepted just as an aim that men did have, as a matter of fact. In part, this does seem to be Bentham's argument. He could not quite let the matter rest there, however. A prejudice universally held is still a prejudice. He needed an indisputable fact of human nature on which to base his ethics. That men seek their own pleasure would seem to be such a fact. "Why bother about the pleasure and pain of others?" is not a silly question in the sense that "Why bother about one's own pain and pleasure?" is. Bentham's dictum "Nature has placed mankind under the governance of two sovereign masters, pain and pleasure" has all the air of an obvious psychological fact; but only if the pain and pleasure in question are our own.

Psychological hedonism. The word "pleasure" is notoriously ambiguous. Bentham was not entirely guiltless of using it ambiguously; but J. H. Burton, in his introduction to Bentham's *Works,* took him to mean that "what it pleases a man to do is simply what he wills to do"; and this was perhaps his most consistent meaning. Among his catalogue of pleasures Bentham listed the pleasures of sympathy; and he did not think it necessary, as Hobbes did, to reduce these to self-interest in the narrower sense. If this was his meaning, Bentham's psychological hedonism cannot be dismissed as simply false. But is it, then, just a trivial tautology? What Bentham was saying is that the central fact of human psychology is that men have desires and seek to gratify them. It follows, he thought, that the only rational way to judge between alternative courses of action is to choose the one that gratifies most desires. This is scarcely trivial, since many moralists have held that the gratification of desire is sinful, and that virtue consists in repressing desires. Bentham's central contention was that gratification as such is always good, and that, while it may often be necessary to repress some desires, this is only in order that other desires may be gratified. The opposition between duty and inclination is a false one: the real contest is between conflicting inclinations, and is to be settled by considering which inclinations lead to the greatest pleasure; i.e., the most intense and lasting satisfaction.

There remains a further charge. Is egoism, so interpreted, compatible with utilitarianism? If "pleasure" means "whatever a man wills," he may well take pleasure in the happiness of others. But it certainly does not follow that he must. Moreover, while we can now understand why "Why bother about your own pleasure?" is a silly question (since it means "Why bother about whatever you bother about?"), it is clearer than ever that "Why bother about the desires of others?" is not at all silly. Again, the hedonic calculus implies that men's desires conflict, that the action that will bring pleasure to one man will bring pain to another. Why, then, should either of them worry about the other's pleasure?

Bentham did not give any very explicit answer to this question. He was certainly influenced by the quite elaborate theory of David Hartley, according to which the most satisfying pleasures were those that did not interfere with the cultivation of sympathy. This version of the natural harmony of interests is compatible with the artificial harmony of interests that, according to Bentham, it is the business of the legislator to bring about through an elaborate apparatus of punishments and rewards. For, even granted that the course of action that brings most pleasure to the individual in the long run will be the one that also brings most pleasure to others, it may still be necessary for the legislator to intervene. Men are easily seduced by the temptation of the immediate pleasure. The criminal, for example, might eventually find himself, in his old age, looking back on his misspent years with regret; but this prospect is much less likely to deter him in his youth than the threat of imprisonment in the very near future. On the other hand, though Bentham certainly made some use of Hartley's associationism, the presupposition behind the hedonic calculus would seem to be that individual interests may really, and not just apparently, conflict.

The units of pleasure. Some of the other stock criticisms of Bentham are easier to answer. One obvious objection to the hedonic calculus is that the units of pleasure and pain of which Bentham spoke are quite fictitious. It is not merely that accurate calculation is difficult, but that the question "how many times greater?" is, in this context, meaningless. There is no homogeneous stuff called "pleasure" that can be weighed and measured; there are many different kinds of pleasurable experience, each yielding its own kind of satisfaction. This is, of course, true, and was quite apparent to Bentham. But it is also true that we cannot avoid, in some quasi-metaphorical sense, weighing pleasures against each other. It is not nonsensical to say that the uncle in our example asks himself whether his nephew's pleasure does or does not outweigh his own boredom, though it is nonsensical to take "outweigh" literally. Yet the notion of quantity is not entirely absent, since it makes a difference if the uncle is very, instead of slightly, bored, and the nephew only slightly, instead of very, pleased.

No doubt Bentham went too far when he tried to specify a unit of pleasure: the minimum state of sensibility that can be distinguished from indifference. But elsewhere he made it clear that there are no real units of pleasure and that reference to them is merely a convenient device for making our calculations as accurate as the nature of the case allows. He did insist that the calculations themselves are indispensable. For example, when fines are imposed in the courts, some alternative punishment must be found for those who cannot, or will not, pay the fine. Clearly we cannot strictly say that the pain of losing five pounds is precisely equivalent to the pain endured during seven days in prison. Yet it is necessary to find some such equivalent, and the job of finding equivalents can be better or worse done. So understood, the weighing of pleasures and pains against each other is not at all absurd. That the process is not mathematically exact can hardly count against it as an analysis of moral evaluation, since moral evaluation is not mathematically exact either.

Quality of pleasures. It may still be objected, however, that Bentham's hedonic calculus ignores the quality, as distinct from the quantity, of pleasure. This comes out clearly in his famous aphorism that "quantity of pleasure being equal, pushpin is as good as poetry." Quite apart from the difficulty of deciding how many games of pushpin (one million? two million?) are worth one Shakespearean sonnet, it is objected that poetry has a kind of value that is completely absent from pushpin. That is to say, it would be contended that there are "higher" pleasures, such as poetry, that are intrinsically more valuable than "lower" pleasures, such as pushpin. Lower pleasures may sometimes please us more than higher pleasures; but even then the higher pleasures are to be preferred. If this is admitted, the utilitarian contention that pleasure is the sole good would seem to collapse, since the higher pleasures apparently have an element of value, other than the mere quantity of pleasure, that the lower pleasures lack.

Unlike John Stuart Mill, Bentham did not admit this distinction between higher and lower pleasures. But there are two points here that need to be carefully distinguished. As we have seen, Bentham did not deny that pleasures differ in quality as well as in quantity. He gave, indeed, quite an elaborate classification of the different kinds of pleasure. But this is, after all, also true of the lower pleasures. The point about the quality of pleasures, then, is quite distinct from the point about higher and lower pleasures. What Bentham did deny is that the higher pleasure may be better, even though less pleasant, than the lower pleasure. It is true that the lower pleasure may be more intense; but more is involved in quantity of pleasure than just intensity. Bentham distinguished other "dimensions" of pleasure: apart from intensity, these are duration, certainty, propinquity, fecundity, and purity. Now it is arguable that the so-called "higher" pleasures are just those that afford a more lasting satisfaction than the "lower" pleasures (duration), that enlarge our horizons and so open up new possibilities of pleasure (fecundity), and that are less likely to be followed eventually by the pain of satiety and boredom (purity). These are the characteristics that distinguish intellectual activity, for example, from purely physical pleasure. Once these dimensions are taken into account, it is by no means certain that the difference between higher and lower pleasures is not, after all, a quantitative one. The higher pleasures, it may be argued, are those which men have found, through long experience, to be productive of most pleasure when all these factors are taken into account.

Justice. Perhaps the crucial question for a utilitarian ethic intended mainly for lawyers and legislators is whether it can account adequately for justice. It may be argued that justice requires the equalization as well as the maximization of pleasure. It is not unjust to require me to endure five units of pain on Monday for the sake of ten units of pleasure on Tuesday. But is it just to require Smith to endure five units of pain for the sake of ten units of pleasure for Jones? It is doubtful whether Bentham can meet this objection. He does, however, argue that the maximization of pleasure will itself involve an equalizing tendency. This is because the economist's law of diminishing utility applies to pleasure. The minor amenities of life afford much pleasure to someone whose other pleasures are few, but comparatively little to someone whose pleasures are many. Consequently, while it is true that a utilitarian, forced to choose between a course of action that gives X and Y 10 units of pleasure each and one that gives X 31 units of pleasure and Y 10 units of pain, will prefer the second, it is also true that such choices are most likely to arise when X's life is as a general rule more painful than Y's.

In Bentham's view, our conviction that it is unjust to punish an innocent man is based on nothing but the empirical consideration that punishing the innocent is not likely to deter others from crime. This is, however, not always true: the innocent man may be a hostage, or he may be generally thought to be guilty. Bentham met this kind of criticism by distinguishing between first-order evil, or pain caused to assignable individuals, and second-order evil, or pain caused to the community in general. Insecurity is a very great second-order evil. The point is a general one, of central importance. Utilitarians need to invoke Bentham's distinction between first-order and second-order evil in order to explain the common belief that general rules should be kept even in those cases where some slight increase in the general happiness might seem to result from breaking them. This slight increase in first-order good, it is argued, is outweighed by the second-order evil, which usually consists in the lessening of public confidence. (A *large* increase in first-order good, it is conceded, may justify breaking the rule.)

The argument is plausible, though of course there is no way of proving that the precise point at which we feel justified in breaking the rule is the point at which the first-order good begins to outweigh the second-order evil. It is, however, open to the objection that, while it may be true as a matter of fact that punishing the innocent or breaking a promise will in general cause more pain than pleasure, most of us feel that these actions would be wrong even if this were not the case. The utilitarian can only reply that this is a mistake. Moral rules, he will say, embody human experience about what kinds of action make for the general happiness—human nature and the world in which we live both being what they are. If either were different, morality would be different; it is a mistake, though a natural one, to believe otherwise.

Political and legal theory. If the central question of political philosophy is taken to be: "Why, if at all, should the citizen obey the state?" the utilitarian answer is quite clear. The citizen should obey just so far as obedience will contribute more to the general happiness than disobedience. If the central question is taken to be the nature and ontological status of the state, the answer is equally clear: the state is not a super-entity with purposes and a will of its own, but a human contrivance to enable men to realize as many of their desires as possible. The "general happiness," or "the interest of the community in general," is always, in Bentham, to be understood as the resultant of the hedonic calculus, the sum of the pleasures and pains of individuals.

Accordingly Bentham opposed, on the one hand, those individualist theories of the state that invoke the concepts of "the social contract" and of "natural rights," and, on the other, all "natural law" and "organic" theories of the state.

Criticism of social contract theories. Bentham repeated Hume's arguments against the social contract. His suspicion of it was increased by its being one of those legal fictions in which he saw the root of so much evil. It was not asserted that every citizen had in fact contracted to obey the law, but only that he should be deemed to have so contracted. But this is mischievous unless obeying the laws does in fact make for the general happiness. The principle of utility, then, is the real basis of obedience. To suppose anything else is misleading, since it suggests that the individual need not obey any law to which he has not personally assented—a principle that, if taken seriously, could lead only to anarchy.

Criticism of natural rights doctrines. Bentham attacked natural rights in his *Anarchical Fallacies; being an Examination of the Declaration of Rights issued during the French Revolution* (written about 1791 and first published in French by Dumont as *Sophismes politiques*, Paris, 1816), and declared the whole concept to be "nonsense on stilts." The basic confusion, in Bentham's view, is the failure to distinguish between what is and what ought to be. To say that men have inalienable rights is clearly false, when the assertion is made by way of protest against a government that has in fact alienated rights. There would be no need for revolutions if men were in fact equal, as they are asserted to be: what is meant is that they ought to be treated as equal but are not. On the other hand, if we take the doctrine of natural rights as a statement of what governments ought to do, it will be found untenable. No government could continue to govern if it abstained from ever depriving any of its citizens of life, liberty, or property (still less of happiness), since taxation and punishment would then be impossible. So indeed would law itself, since any law is a restriction on liberty. The only principle that can be justified to the extent that it is backed by coercion, is that the law should not impose restrictions on any individual unless this is necessary to avoid greater pain, on balance, to other individuals: in short, the principle of utility.

Denial of natural law. Bentham opposed natural law on much the same grounds. It is a confusion to think of natural law as being literally law, so that an enactment that contravenes it is null and void. This would mean that the "supreme governors," who make the laws, have a *legal* duty not to make certain kinds of law. But "that is my *duty* to do, which I am liable to be *punished*, according to law, if I do not do. . . . Have these supreme governors any such duty? No: for if they are at all liable to punishment, according to law, . . . then they are not, what they are supposed to be, supreme governors" (*A Fragment on Government*, ch. 5, §7). What is meant, doubtless, is that they have either a religious duty or a moral duty. In accordance with Bentham's definition of "duty," a religious duty is one whose neglect renders one liable to punishment by God, and a moral duty is one whose neglect renders one liable, not to punishment in a strict sense, but to various unorganized "mortifications and inconveniences" at the hands of one's fellow men. This is in line with his classification of "sanctions": the "moral sanction" is fear of public opinion. In this sense, moral duties are certainly political realities: Bentham agreed that the ruler is limited by what public opinion will tolerate. But he insisted on distinguishing this from a legal limitation, and both from a nebulous natural law.

It may be objected that Bentham himself was clearly postulating a moral duty in a different sense from the one he allowed. For his main theme is that the legislator ought to make those laws that promote the greatest happiness of the greatest number. He did make some attempt to assimilate this to his "moral sanction," but it is clear that a law that, on balance, causes more suffering than it prevents is not necessarily one so unpopular that it provokes the citizens to active resistance. A similar objection may be made about natural rights: Bentham does seem to have postulated at least one moral right: the right to have one's happiness considered equally with that of other men. This is clearly not the same as the fact that men will seek their own happiness, nor does it follow from the further fact that the legislator, seeking *his* own happiness, will see to it, if he is wise, that he does not provoke his subjects too far. It is here, indeed, that the weakness of Bentham's attempt to base utilitarianism upon egoism shows itself.

Sovereignty. Bentham's theory of sovereignty is the one that he had inherited from Hobbes and that was later to be elaborated by Austin. A man has political authority when other men habitually obey him. The laws are the commands of such men, when enforced by punishment or the threat of punishment. Bentham anticipated some of the objections that were to be made to Austin. It is, he said, quite possible for the same man to be alternately governor and subject: "to-day concurring in the business of issuing a *general* command for the observance of the whole society, amongst the rest of another man in quality of *Judge:* tomorrow, perhaps, punished by a *particular* command of that same Judge for not obeying the general command which he himself (in character of governor) had issued . . ." His recognition of the moral sanction enabled him to say that the sovereign would find himself compelled to pay attention to those customary ways of behavior that embody the experience of the community about what makes for the general happiness, and so to allow for the part played in law by custom and tradition. He insisted, however, that it is through the command of the sovereign that custom has the force of law.

Theory of meaning. Although his main interest was in moral and political philosophy and jurisprudence, Bentham's numerous if fragmentary writings include an *Essay on Logic* and many passing references to the theory of meaning. An uncompromising nominalist, Bentham drew the conclusion that most of our words refer to fictitious entities and not to real ones. To consider any part or aspect of a real entity in abstraction is to create a fictitious entity. Hence qualities, relations, and classes are all fictions: so are the abstract notions of time, place, motion, and substance. A fiction, Bentham said, is nothing; and a quality of a fiction is equally nothing. Thus most of our talk is strictly nonsense, though it can be given meaning by translating it into terms referring to real entities. The possibility of making such translations gives rise to what he called "definition by paraphrasis." Some words, he said, are best defined by translating the sentences in which they occur into other sentences in which all the words refer to real entities. Examples are "duty," "right," "power," and "title," which can be understood only by reference to such concrete situations as one man being punished by another. Legal and political fictions and the mental confusion that results from them are, Bentham thought, largely due to the failure to make such translations; men are caught in what he called "the shackles of ordinary language." "Metaphysical speculations," he said, have as their object "understanding clearly what one is speaking of."

In this Bentham was anticipating both the "definition in use" of the logical atomists and much of their underlying theory. In other ways, too, he anticipated some of the views that became influential early in the twentieth century. Since he regarded mathematics as concerned purely with fictitious entities and as being essentially "a species of short-hand," he was not far from the concept of a postulate set in which the rules of the system itself must be sharply distinguished from the rules governing the application of the system. In a rather different area, he insisted on the distinction between the "eulogistic" and the "dyslogistic" use of words, maintaining that the eulogistic and the corresponding dyslogistic term refer to the same real entity. What is the difference, Bentham asked, between "that *luxury* which all the world condemns, and that *prosperity* which all the world admires"?

To give another example, he claimed that "vanity," "ambition," and "honor" were different names for the same motive. In each case the motive (what moves us) is the love of reputation, which is in itself neither good nor bad. Let us suppose that one father slaves day and night to pay off his son's gambling debts and so clear the family name, while another devotes his energies to marrying his daughter into a titled family. In saying that the former is moved by a sense of honor and the latter by ambition we are expressing a difference in our attitudes to the two men that is, on utilitarian principles, thoroughly justified, since the one course of action is more likely than the other to increase the general happiness. We are not, however, referring to any difference in motive; for both men act from precisely the same motive, the desire that his family shall stand well in the general esteem.

Bibliography

Bentham's published works and his voluminous unpublished manuscripts were collected by J. Bowring in *The Works of Jeremy Bentham,* 11 vols. (Edinburgh, 1838–1843). This is not complete. Volumes 10 and 11 contain a not very accurate life of Bentham, written by Bowring from Bentham's reminiscences in his old age.

Other biographies include C. M. Atkinson, *Jeremy Bentham* (London, 1905); C. W. Everett, *The Education of Jeremy Bentham* (New York, 1931); Leslie Stephen, *The English Utilitarians,* Vol. 1 (London, 1900).

For critical works, see J. S. Mill, "Bentham," in *London and Westminster Review* (1838), reprinted in Mill's *Dissertations and Discussions* (London, 1859–1875) and in F. R. Leavis, ed., *Mill on Bentham and Coleridge* (London, 1950); Elie Halévy, *La Formation du radicalisme philosophique,* 3 vols. (Paris, 1904), translated by Mary Morris as *The Growth of Philosophical Radicalism* (London, 1928); John Wisdom, *Interpretation and Analysis in Relation to Bentham's Theory of Definition* (London, 1931); C. K. Ogden, *Bentham's Theory of Fictions* (London, 1932), which republishes Bentham's writings on theory of meaning, with a long introductory essay by Ogden; David Baumgardt, *Bentham and the Ethics of Today* (Princeton, 1952); Mary P. Mack, *Jeremy Bentham,* 2 vols. (London, 1962–).

D. H. MONRO

BERDYAEV, NIKOLAI (1874–1948), Russian religious philosopher, was born near the city of Kiev. Like many of his contemporaries in the nobility, he became associated with populism and Marxism during his university days—an association which resulted in a three-year exile to Vologda at the turn of the century. These same socialist tendencies gained him official favor early in the Revolution, and in 1920 he was appointed professor of philosophy at the University of Moscow, only to be exiled in 1922 after it had become apparent that he would never become an orthodox Marxist. With the aid of fellow exiles and representatives of the Young Men's Christian Association, he established the Academy of Philosophy and Religion in Berlin, which he moved to Paris in 1924. He also founded a Russian review, *Put* ("The Way"), in Paris, where he remained active in philosophical research and discussion until his death.

Metaphysics. Berdyaev's thought is primarily a "religious metaphysics," influenced not only by philosophers like Kant, Hegel, Schopenhauer, Vladimir Solovyev, and Nietzsche, but also by religious thinkers such as Meister Eckhart, Angelus Silesius, Franz von Baader, Jakob Böhme, and Dostoevsky. The unique position Berdyaev wove from these influences was presented in a rambling, sometimes aphoristic, style in over twenty books and numerous articles. This unsystematic form was the result of Berdyaev's continuous effort to relate his theoretical interpretations to concrete, existential concerns. He never made a clear separation between his metaphysics and his more specific interests in religion, society, and history.

The most basic notion of this religious metaphysics is that of the *Ungrund* (the term comes from Böhme). The *Ungrund* is analogous to Aristotle's prime matter or Plato's receptacle. It might best be defined as pure potentiality; but actually it is indefinable, and Berdyaev called it a "myth," thereby signifying that it is an ultimate presupposition whose value is ascertained not by demonstration, but through its success in the interpretation of actual experience. A synonymous term is "meonic freedom" (from Greek *μή*, not; *'όν*, being), intended to designate ultimate reality as dynamic, nonobjective, and indeterminate. The essence of every existent is process; and meonic freedom is nothing but the creative energy underlying the forms and directions of all processes. The *Ungrund* does not exist, but precedes being in the sense that it is the possibility of being, the negative ground essential for the realization of the novel, creative aspects of existence.

Since actual existence, as distinct from the merely possible, is not an indeterminate, anarchic chaos, there must also be an initial creative, purposeful act, determining the pure possibility; this is God. Through God, possibility becomes identified with potentiality; and one may speak of the tendency of freedom to become, or of freedom "linked with cosmic aim." Insofar as this aim achieves existential embodiment, God is the "Creator" bringing value into being *ex nihilo;* that is, out of freedom. This activity, which on the phenomenal level is identical with the production and pursuit of the various forms of order and value, is termed the "theogonic process" (from Greek Θεός, God; *γένω*, to become, be born). Since all existents (but especially man) participate in the determination of value, God and creatures are mutually related in the pursuit of the common goal of realizing maximum value. Due to this fundamental correlation, all positive value experience may be interpreted as the immanence of God. Contrariwise, all evil and frustration, as instances of unrealized potentiality, involve a separation between the divine purpose and the creatures' actuality that may be described as the transcendence of God. Berdyaev appropriately termed his theory "monopluralism" or "theo-pantheism," and the nature of actuality as interpreted by this theory he called "theandric existence" (from Greek Θεός, God; *ἀνήρ*, man).

The term for creative process is "Spirit"; and since God and all the other lesser universal existents (which constitute the world) are such processes, only spirit exists. Every existent, as a creative activity realizing value, is free subjectivity; that is, a unique, individual, self-determining process. Objectivity arises solely through "objectification," which is the apprehension or hypostatization within some spirit of the past qualitative states of other spirits.

All spirit is individual; no general being exists. However, spirit is also universal, for its activity is the realization of values (which cannot be particular). Moreover, each entity is internally related to other entities, for spirit is "concretely universal," existing only as individuals whose fullest potentialities are realizable only in communion (Russian, *sobornost*) with and dependence upon the others, especially God. Berdyaev calls this highest realization of a spirit's essence "personality," the primary meaning of which is unification of purposeful self-determination and creative activity throughout changing experiences. God is the only complete personality, and the relationship of men to God is not the objective aim of worship but the subjective one of identity of purpose in every creative act. It is through personality that the totality of existence is unified, not as a completed organic or hierarchical whole but as a meaningful unity in process of realization in and through the many individual centers of activity.

Philosophical anthropology. Berdyaev's major concern was always man, as understood in terms of his metaphysical theory. Whenever spirit takes the special form of human existence, it constitutes an ego; but in accordance with the form of relation between spirit and personality, not all egos are actually persons. Only when the ego freely acts to realize its own concrete essence, rather than abstract or arbitrary goals, is it a person. A society that furthers the goal of the development of egos into persons is a true community, and the relationship existing among its members is "communality" (*sobornost*).

Communality is opposed by the processes of individualization and socialization. Socialization is the tendency of an ego to assume the characteristics of objectified, abstract society, thereby sacrificing its true nature for the false role of a "theatrical ego." Individualization is the tendency of the ego to become solitary, to lead a "hermetic existence." However, since the deepest solitude stems from the awareness of existing in a world of socialized abstractions, these two processes are more complementary than opposed. The fateful element in both tendencies is their implicit preference for the objective; they are types of objectification.

The ideal of Berdyaev's own theory, "personalist socialism," was the replacement of social objectification with the inherent developmental tendencies of human nature. Society should be founded upon the existence and maintenance of the creatively free individual; and the individual should recognize and develop his nature as it truly is; namely, in its organic unity with the universal. Personalist socialism is not collectivist (Marxist) socialism, for the latter is merely one of the more vicious forms of social objectification. The goal of personalist socialism is *soborny* (communal) society; and *sobornost* finds its expression, not in economic forces, but in love, for only "love transforms the Ego into a personality."

The realization of communality has many facets. Three

of the most important can be highlighted by taking, in succession, the perspectives of government, ethics, and history. From the first perspective, the process would appear as the replacement of nationalistic ideals by the "personalist principle," according to which "every personality ought to be situated in a condition of human existence corresponding to its human dignity" (*Solitude and Society*, p. 149). Implementation of this principle would produce an "aristocracy of freedom," and would avoid the leveling tendency of democracy as well as communism's antipersonal myth of a classless society. The state would cease to have any intrinsic value and would be reduced to the purely instrumental level of a tool employed for the implementation of various humanitarian goals.

Berdyaev's ethical theory emphasized freedom and creativity and rejected all utilitarian moralities with their fixed ends in favor of an "immanently spiritual" morality, for which the distinction between ends and means is a false abstraction. Man is free not only to act morally or immorally but also to decide for himself what is moral or immoral. It must be remembered that man is concretely involved with others, so this radical freedom is not at all a license to dominate. No truly human act can use a person as a means; the ethics of freedom and creativity must also be the ethics of compassion. The moral ideal is complete, harmonious being, manifesting beauty in the form of creative energy guiding and unifying the entire world in the project of value realization.

If such a goal seems overly optimistic, the historical perspective tends to promote a realistic balance. Significant approximation to ideal existence would seem to require a creative epoch—a "New Middle Ages" in which immanent values would be substituted for the wholly transcendent values of the first Middle Ages. However, even this could not result in complete perfection, for the very structure of our existence forbids the realization of any utopia, not only because some actions fail to achieve their intended results but also because some goods are mutually exclusive. Moreover, since the goal is the fullest development of spirit, and since spirit has unlimited freedom, the end of history can only be a limiting ideal to guide future action rather than an actual event in future history. Therefore, history is tragic in that it proposes a goal that is never completely attained.

However, a tragedy is always meaningful; and history possesses significance to the extent that those spirits whose lives constitute history achieve their divine purpose. Consequently, even if history involves failure and suffering, its failure is a "profound failure" and its suffering is justified to the degree that historical beings actualize that nonhistorical community of personal values that is Berdyaev's equivalent of the Kingdom of God.

Bibliography

Further information on Berdyaev's life and intellectual development may be obtained from his autobiography, *Samopoznaniye* (Paris, 1949), translated by Katherine Lampert as *Dream and Reality* (London, 1950). The most important of his philosophical works are *Smysl Istorii* (Berlin, 1923), translated by George Reavey as *The Meaning of History* (London, 1923); *O Naznachenii Chelovyeka* (Paris, 1931), translated by Natalie Duddington as *The Destiny of Man* (London, 1937); *Ya i Mir Obyektov* (Paris, 1934), translated by George Reavey as *Solitude and Society* (New York, 1939); and *Opyt Eskhatologicheskoi Metafiziki* (Paris, 1947), translated by R. M. French as *The Beginning and the End* (London, 1952).

For other literature on Berdyaev, see Oliver Fielding Clarke, *Introduction to Berdyaev* (London, 1950); P. B. Schulze, S. J., *Die Schau der Kirchl bei Berdiajew* (Rome, 1938); George Seaver, *Nicolas Berdyaev* (London, 1950); and Matthew Spinka, *N. Berdyaev, Captive of Freedom* (Philadelphia, 1950).

JAMES W. DYE

BERGERAC, CYRANO DE. See CYRANO DE BERGERAC, SAVINIEN DE.

BERGSON, HENRI (1859–1941), French philosopher of evolution, was born in Paris of Anglo-Polish parentage. During a lifetime of teaching, lecturing, and writing, he gained an international reputation as the author of a new and distinctive philosophical outlook presented in a succession of books whose fluent, nontechnical style gave them a wide appeal. In 1900 Bergson became professor of philosophy at the Collège de France, a post he held until 1921, when ill health obliged him to retire. He received many honors, including election to the French Academy and in 1927 the Nobel Prize for literature. After World War I, Bergson devoted much attention to international affairs, in the hope of promoting peace and cooperation among nations. But World War II had begun and France had been occupied by the armies of Nazi Germany at the time of his death.

Despite the novelty of his outlook, Bergson owed much to his predecessors in the European, and especially in the French, philosophical tradition, primarily to thinkers whose ideas supported his opposition to materialism and mechanism; he was convinced that neither of these doctrines is philosophically tenable. Thus, he was influenced by the idea of Maine de Biran that we sense the "flow" of life as a primary inner experience; by the contentions of Felix Ravaisson that philosophic thought should be focused on the directly intuited, concrete individual, and that mechanism is the external form of an inner spiritual activity; by the contention of Alfred Fouillée that there is an intrinsic freedom in human action; and by the teaching of Émile Boutroux that there exists a radical contingency in nature. His obligation to ancient thought was chiefly to Plotinus, whose mysticism became increasingly congenial to Bergson in the later years of his life. The theory of biological evolution, in both Darwin's scientific formulation and Spencer's speculative formulation deeply influenced him. He was once "very much attached to the philosophy of Spencer" (*The Creative Mind*, p. 93), but broke away because of its unsatisfactory treatment of evolution and of time.

TWO KINDS OF TIME

Of central importance in Bergson's outlook is his distinction between the time that occurs in the theories of natural science and the time that we directly experience. Scientific time is a mathematical conception, symbolized in physical theory by the letter t and measured by clocks and chronometers. Because these measuring instruments are spatial bodies, scientific time is represented as an extended, homogeneous medium, composed of standard units (years, hours, seconds). Most of man's practical life in society is dominated by these units. But time thus represented neither "flows" nor "acts." It exists passively, like a line drawn on a surface. When we turn to our direct experience, Bergson urged, we find nothing that corresponds to this mathematical conception. What we find, on the contrary, is a flowing, irreversible succession of states that melt into each other to form an indivisible process. This process is not homogeneous but heterogeneous. It is not abstract but concrete. In short, it is "pure time" or "real duration" (*durée reelle*), something immediately experienced as active and ongoing. If we try to represent it by a spatial image, such as a line, we only generate abstract, mathematical time, which is at bottom an illusion. The great weakness of mechanistic modes of thought is that they consider this illusion to be a reality.

DETERMINISM AND FREEDOM

In *Time and Free Will* Bergson undertook to show that the recognition of real duration provides a basis for vindicating human freedom and disposing of determinism. The determinist, according to Bergson, holds that freedom of choice does not exist. He supports his view by picturing the situation in which one confronts an ostensible choice as being like arriving at a point on a line where a branching occurs, and taking one of the branches. The determinist then contends that the particular branch taken could not *not* have been taken. He further holds that, given full knowledge of the antecedent states of mind of the agent, the branch taken could have been predicted beforehand.

The force of this argument, according to Bergson, derives from misrepresenting the situation of choice by using an abstract, spatialized conception of time. At best the determinist's image of the line symbolizes the choice already made, not the choice in the making. In acting we do not move along a path through time. Deliberating about a choice is not like being at a point on a line and oscillating in space between various courses confronting us. Deliberation and choice are temporal, not spatial, acts. Moreover, the determinist makes the associationist's mistake of supposing that the mind of the agent consists of a succession of atomic states that determine how he will act. The associationist's mechanistic interpretation of the mind produced a fallacious picture upon which determinism was superimposed.

Freedom of action, according to Bergson, is something directly experienced. Man feels himself to be free as he acts, even though he may be unable to explain the nature of his freedom. However, we are free only when our act springs spontaneously from our *whole* personality as it has evolved up to the moment of action. If this spontaneity is absent, our actions will be simply stereotyped or mechanical responses. In such cases we behave like automata. Hence, freedom is far from being absolute. Indeed, for most people free acts are the exception, not the rule. To this extent the determinists are right.

BODY AND MIND

Direct experience not only establishes the reality of time and of freedom; it also testifies that each of us is a body, subject to the same laws as all other bits of matter. Bergson's dualism emerges clearly in *Matter and Memory*. Bodies are there interpreted as "images"; that is, objects perceived in space. Among these images is one that I know from the outside by perception and from the inside by sensation or affection. This is my own body, which I also know to be a center of action.

What is the relation between the body and the mind? Materialism holds that mind, or consciousness, is either identical with brain activity or existentially dependent on brain activity. Bergson rejected both positions because, he claimed, there is vastly more in a given occasion of consciousness than in the corresponding brain state. The attempt to substantiate this claim led him to reject the doctrine that a parallelism exists between the series of conscious states and the series of brain states. The considerations to which he appealed came mainly from an examination of memory.

TWO KINDS OF MEMORY

Living organisms, unlike nonliving objects, retain their past in the present. This phenomenon is manifested, according to Bergson, in two kinds of memory. One kind consists of sensory–motor mechanisms or "habits" fixed in the body of the organism and designed to ensure adaptation to a present situation. When an appropriate stimulus arises, one of these mechanisms "unwinds" as a response. The other kind of memory, which man alone possesses, records in the form of memory images all the events of daily life as they occur in time. These images provide the content of occasions of recalling. This is "pure" memory, which is wholly spiritual. "Consciousness signifies, before everything, memory."

To defend his view of pure memory, Bergson argued against any correlation of memory images with hypothetical memory traces stored in the brain. Physiologically, the brain consists of a vast number of neurons, synapsing with each other and with afferent and efferent nerves. It resembles a telephone exchange, not a storage device. There is no evidence that memories are located spatially within it. Moreover, if a visual recollection of an object were dependent on a brain trace, there would have to be thousands of traces, corresponding to all the variations due to different points of view from which the object has been perceived. But what we actually have in each case is one practically invariable memory image of an object, not a large class of different images. This, Bergson thought, constitutes proof that something quite distinct from mechanical registration is involved. Finally, there are facts associated with loss of word memory and its restoration which point to the conclusion that the recollective process is independent of brain traces. It follows that materialism and psychoneural parallelism are untenable doctrines.

How, then, is pure memory related to the brain? Bergson's answer is derived from his contention that pure memory retains the whole of our past. If this is the case, something must prevent all our memories from being simultaneously present to consciousness, since we do in fact recall only one or two things at a time. The brain must therefore act as a filter for our memories, allowing only those that are practically useful to emerge on a given occasion. In other words, the brain is a mechanism invented by nature to canalize and direct our attention toward what is about to happen, in order to assist our actions. It is designed not so much to promote remembering as to promote forgetting. By bringing pure memory into contact with practical actions, it also establishes a link with habit memory, since most of our everyday actions tend to be habitual and routine. In this way the two kinds of memory are united.

Although he would not countenance the idea that memory traces are stored in the brain, Bergson allowed for the storage of images in pure memory. He asserted that pure memory retains all our conscious states "in the order in which they occur." This view led him to accept the conclusion that part of the mind is unconscious or subconscious. It is erroneous to suppose that the existence of psychical states depends on their apprehension by consciousness. To suppose this is to vitiate the concept of mind by casting an artificial obscurity over the idea of the unconscious. The significance of pure memory can be understood only by supposing that past psychological states have a real, though unconscious, existence.

It is now possible to explain the relation between the body and the mind. Here, as elsewhere, there has been a strong temptation to think in spatial terms, envisaging two separate substances that have to be connected. But the relation between body and mind must be understood in temporal, not spatial, terms. The point becomes clear when we unite the insight derived from our consciousness of real duration with the recognition that the body is a center of action, for on an occasion of action, body and mind are related by a convergence in time. No spatial representation of this convergence can be adequate. It can be grasped only by noting what takes place whenever we act. A familiar example is our perception of the external world.

PERCEPTION AND THE EXTERNAL WORLD

The discussion of this question forms an integral part of *Matter and Memory*. In considering perception, traditional realism and idealism have, according to Bergson, made two unjustified assumptions. First, they have assumed that perception is a kind of photographic process that yields a picture of what is perceived. The mind is envisaged as a *camera obscura* inside which images are generated. Second, they have regarded perception as a cognitive function whose aim is to provide pure knowledge. Bergson contended that perception cannot possibly be a photographic process, for images are not inside the mind but are part of the spatially extended world. Moreover, perception does not generate images, but selects those images that have a possible bearing on actions. Nothing remotely akin to pure knowledge is involved at the perceptual level. Once these assumptions are discarded, the dispute between realism and idealism can be resolved.

In supporting this idea Bergson used biological considerations. Biologists are agreed that there has been an evolution of the structure and the functions of the central nervous system in living organisms. This evolution has proceeded from relatively simple types of organization toward greater and greater complexity, through a series of minute, adaptively significant changes. In simple organisms the rudiments of perception are to be found in mechanical responses to external stimulation. Direct contact with bodies, such as we experience in tactile perception, belongs to this stage. The role of the rudimentary nervous system is to facilitate action. What occurs is a reflex activity, not a "representation" of things. The sole difference between this stage and much later ones is that voluntary action became possible as a result of the evolution of the higher brain centers. But the difference is not one of kind, but only one of complication. Accordingly, since the nervous system is constructed from one end of the evolutionary scale to the other as a utilitarian device, we must conclude that perception, whose evolution is regulated by the evolution of the nervous system, is also directed toward action, not toward knowledge.

If that is so, why is human perception a conscious process, and why does everything happen as if consciousness were a product of brain activity? The reason is that human perception is normally "impregnated with memory images." It is possible to form a metaphysical concept of "pure perception" free from any admixture of memory. It is even possible, Bergson thought, to have such a pure perception, which he spoke of as an "intuition." But most of the time our perceptions are interlaced with memories; conversely, a memory becomes actual by being embodied in some perception. The convergence that takes place accounts for the fact that perceptual images (objects perceived) have a "subjectivity." We become conscious of them. This phenomenon has a biological significance, for in man, and in higher organisms generally, perception is predominantly directed toward distant objects spread over a wide field. These objects have a great many potential effects on action. One way an organism has of adapting to this situation is to anticipate the effects by "reflecting" possible lines of action from its body to the distant objects. This gives the organism a biological advantage by putting it in a position where it can select a course of action that will serve its needs. Thus the world is consciously perceived by us; but it is not a different world from the one that antedated our perception. It is the same world related to our needs and intentions.

Body and mind, then, are united in the selective act of perception. The body contributes perceptive centers that respond to the influences of environing bodies. The mind contributes appropriate memory images that give to what is perceived a completed, meaningful form. There is no "constructing" of the external world out of subjective impressions; no "inferring" of the existence of that world from ideas in the mind; no positing of things in themselves that are beyond the limits of possible experience. By interpreting physical things as images, Bergson was able to regard the material world as directly perceivable. Traditional idealism was therefore repudiated. Yet a partial concession to idealism was made by calling things "images." This term implies a rejection of the realist's view that things consist only of material particles, or of primary qualities, or of some hidden substance. Things have all the qualities they are perceived to have. A partial concession to realism was made by admitting that the totality of perceived things, past, present and future, must always be a small fragment of material reality. The upshot is a doctrine, intermediate between idealism and realism, that combines, Bergson contends, what is sound in each and discards what is unsound.

Body and mind are above all united in real duration, for perception is an event in the concrete present, and the present is no geometrical point or "knife edge" separating past from future. It is a continuous flowing, an "invisible progress of the past gnawing into the future." Perceptual acts are intrinsically temporal and dynamic. Yet the world we come to know by means of them is not a flux. It has a relative stability. Our concepts often refer to things that remain much the same for long periods. These things may have fixed position, sharp outlines, and clearly marked qualities. In view of what has been said about perception, how are such facts accounted for? The reply involves Bergson's conception of the intellect and its functioning.

THE INTELLECT AND THINGS

The evolution of the human species gave rise to the capacity for conceptual or rational thought. This capacity is traditionally referred to as the intellect. Its origin, Bergson contended, was conditioned by several circumstances. First, man is one of the social animals, and effective action in human societies requires some use of rational thought. Second, man is a tool-using and tool-making animal. These activities could not advance far without fostering conceptualization. Third, man is an animal who invents and uses language. This powerful instrument of communication stimulated the development of intellect, and was in turn profoundly influenced by it. Here again the aim was to promote community of action. Thus, both in origin and in function, the intellect is a practical capacity. It is no more speculative than is perception.

By using his intellect, civilized man has produced a vast body of knowledge about the world. Is not much of this knowledge speculative, in the sense of being a cognitive reflection of the world as it really is? Bergson held that this is not so. Since the intellect is practical, its products must be instrumental to action, not mirror-like reflections. Concepts, even when they belong to advanced theories in the sciences, are still pragmatic devices. For scientific knowledge is directed toward prediction and control of events, being in this respect an extension of common-sense knowledge. The technological triumphs of modern man provide the clue to the proper understanding of his intellectual powers.

Because of its practical orientation, the intellect functions in a characteristic way. It treats whatever it deals with in spatial terms, as if the latter were a three-dimensional body. Ordinary language is pervaded by spatial metaphors; and scientific theories, especially those of physics, make great use of geometrical models. The operations of our intellect, especially in science, "tend to geometry, as to the goal where they find their perfect fulfilment" (*Creative Mind*, Introduction II). Again, the intellect has an inherent tendency to break up whatever it deals with into homogeneous units. A whole can be understood only by analyzing it in terms of uniform parts. This tendency is reflected in the predominance of measuring operations and instruments, such as clocks, scales, and yardsticks, in civilized societies. Furthermore, the intellect is at home only when dealing with what is static, fixed, immobile. Hence, in seeking to understand the phenomenon of motion, the intellect has recourse to immobile units, such as points of space or instants of time, out of which motion is reconstructed. Bergson spoke of "the cinematographical method" of the intellect, likening it to a movie camera that translates motion into a series of static "frames." An important consequence of this is that the intellect is committed to the use of formal logic and mathematics, both of which supply unchanging structures for thought. Finally, when something comes into existence or ceases to exist, the intellect interprets what happens as a rearranging of constituent elements. This means that the arising of something absolutely new, the creation of novelty, cannot be admitted by rational thought. Even growth and evolution must be understood as new arrangements of old parts.

It is now possible to explain why the world external to us consists of relatively stable, discrete things. The intellect, functioning in its characteristic way, is responsible. It "breaks up," "cuts up," or "carves up" matter into distinct and separate objects so as to promote the interests of action. Presumably, the operation requires the collaboration of perception, although Bergson did not make the point clear. He also failed to make clear whether the intellect is perfectly free in carving out individual things, or whether it has to follow certain lines of cleavage in the intrinsic structure of matter. Sometimes he talked as if the external world of things had been "fabricated" by the intellect's imposing form on a featureless, material flux. At other times, he implied that the intellect "carves nature at the joints," following "the lines which mark out the boundaries of real bodies or of their real elements." In one place he even stated that "matter is primarily what brings division and precision" into things; but this can hardly be construed as an acceptance of the doctrine that matter is the principle of individuation. Despite these obscurities, Bergson's position entails that the intellect is necessary, if not sufficient, for the "individuating" of things in space.

This requirement is relevant, of course, only to things of which we have conceptual knowledge. What is its bearing on the knowledge each of us has of his own body? Here a further obscurity arises. Bergson declared that we know our body in two ways, externally by perception and internally by affection. But since at the level of affection the intellect is not involved, it would appear to follow that the object known cannot be a separate, individual thing. Nevertheless, Bergson did speak of the central image, "distinct from all others," that each of us identifies as his body. What determines its distinct individuality? In *Matter and Memory* he remarked that "our needs . . . carve out, within this continuity [of the perceptible world], a body which is to be their own." This is a puzzling remark, because often the body is what has the needs, and hence it can scarcely be "carved out" by them. It may be that the living human body, unlike inanimate bodies, has an individuality that does not depend on the functioning of the intellect. Or it may be that the obscurity here originates in Bergson's doctrine about what the intellect knows and what can be known only by intuition.

INTUITION AND INTELLECT

Alongside the capacity for conceptual thought, there exists in man a capacity that Bergson called "intuition." Both capacities are the result of evolution, but the second is derived from instinct, the type of biological activity most elaborately manifested in the social insects. Instinctive activity has consciousness "slumbering" within it, and evolution has awakened the consciousness in man. Intuition for Bergson is "instinct that has become disinterested, self-conscious, capable of reflecting upon its object and of enlarging it indefinitely." Since it is disinterested, the capacity is detached from the demands of action and of social life. It is like a painter's power of seeing the world just as it is presented to him in pure perception. But instead of yielding an aesthetic experience, intuition yields knowledge. Hence, it is of profound importance for the philosopher.

In his *Introduction to Metaphysics*, Bergson emphasized the immediate, nonconceptual character of intuition, envisaging it as a direct participation in, or identification with, what is intuited. In the case of the external world, intuition is an act "by which one is transported into the interior of an object in order to coincide with what there is unique and consequently inexpressible about it." In the case of the self, intuition is an immersion in the indivisible flow of consciousness, a grasping of pure becoming and real duration. The result is "knowledge which is contact and even coincidence." Unlike the intellect, which remains outside what it knows, requires symbols, and produces knowledge that is always relative to some viewpoint, intuition enters into what it knows, dispenses with symbols, and produces knowledge that is absolute.

Bergson subsequently modified this doctrine in certain respects. He came to emphasize the cogitative character of intuition instead of its immediacy, and even spoke of it as a mode of thinking. As such, it is not a spontaneous flash of insight but an act that is engendered by mental effort. To achieve an intuition, we must turn our attention away from its natural concern with action. This act demands concentration of thought. Even when we are successful, the results are impermanent. Yet the intellect can effect a partial communication of the results by using "concrete ideas," supplemented by images. "Comparisons and metaphors will here suggest what cannot be expressed." Consequently, the knowledge attained by intuition is not altogether ineffable. Nor is it, in the strict sense, absolute, for intuition is a progressive activity that can widen and deepen its scope indefinitely. Its limits cannot be fixed a priori. These modifications were related to changes in Bergson's conception of the roles of metaphysics and the natural sciences.

THE NATURAL SCIENCES AND METAPHYSICS

The natural sciences are for Bergson a typical achievement of the intellect, and they therefore reflect a limitation in the intellect's functioning. This limitation emerges when the sciences form their conceptions of time and motion. In each case a static abstraction is produced. Time is conceived as what clocks measure in spatially discrete units. Motion is conceived as a succession of fixed positions on a linear path. Both abstractions are practically useful, but they falsify the nature of time and motion as concretely experienced by ignoring the crucial element of becoming. This falsification is inherent in the intellect's way of working. By its very nature, the intellect is equipped to handle only what is repetitive and routine; real becoming baffles it. Hence the sciences have a severe disability built into them. Moreover, as the ancient philosopher Zeno of Elea first pointed out, conceptual thought runs into contradictions or "paradoxes" whenever it tries to give a thorough analysis of motion. These paradoxes, although designed by Zeno for a different purpose, show, according to Bergson, that the scientific concept of motion is basically incoherent. The conclusion must be that the sciences can never provide a complete and adequate account of the universe. They need to be supplemented by some other discipline.

An obvious choice would seem to be metaphysics, but classical metaphysics is equally a creation of the intellect and suffers from the same disability as the sciences. Metaphysicians, with a few exceptions like Heraclitus, have misconstrued change and failed to give it the priority it actually has in the world. They have regarded being as ultimate, and becoming as derivative. Accordingly, metaphysical theories have been based on such concepts as the indestructible atoms of Democritus, the eternal forms of Plato, or the fixed categories of Kant. These concepts illustrate the intellect's addiction to unchanging units that are mechanically combined or separated according to the rules of logic. Neither time nor change can be understood when so approached. The constructions of metaphysics are as inadequate here as those of science, without the latter's usefulness.

Classical metaphysics has also mistakenly supposed that an all-embracing "system" can be constructed, bringing within its scope not only what is actual but also what is possible. This idea rests on a fallacious assumption that there is a "realm of possibility" over and above the realm of actuality. The belief in possibles that would be realized by acquiring existence is an illusion of the intellect, designed to exclude the notion of absolute novelty. "Let us have done," Bergson urged, "with great metaphysical systems embracing all the possible and sometimes even the impossible!"

By following this course, we shall automatically get rid of a number of pseudo problems that classical metaphysicians have generated. They have asked, for instance, why something exists rather than nothing. This has seemed a sensible question because they could always add, "There could be nothing." Bergson replied that the sentence "There could be nothing" has no meaning. " 'Nothing' is a term in ordinary language which can only have meaning in the sphere proper to man, of action and fabrication." The term designates the absence of what we are seeking in the world around us. It can be properly used only because many things already exist. To oppose "nothing" in an absolute sense to existence is to embrace a pseudo idea and engender pseudo problems.

These criticisms do not imply that metaphysics is to be rejected, for Bergson proposed to redefine metaphysics and provide it with a new method. Instead of employing the intellect, it is to employ intuition. This is the theme of the *Introduction to Metaphysics*. In elaborating it, Bergson sometimes seemed to be saying that since intuition alone provides knowledge of the real, the intellect is restricted to knowledge of appearances. It would follow from this that metaphysics is a discipline superior to the natural sciences. Indeed, from a philosophical standpoint the sciences are cognitively worthless because they can say nothing about reality. The impression was thus created that Bergson's outlook was "anti-scientific." In later writings he endeavored to correct this impression by urging that metaphysics and the sciences must be coordinate and equal in value. Both are concerned with the real, the sciences with the domain of matter, metaphysics with the domain of spirit. Moreover, the knowledge that each gains is capable of indefinite expansion, and can approach completeness as an ideal limit. It was in this connection that Bergson seems to have revised his doctrine of intuition, closing the gap between it and the intellect without obliterating the distinction between the two. His objective was to formulate a philosophy that would submit to the control of science and that could in turn enable science to progress. The disciplines would then have a common frontier. In adopting the method of intuition, metaphysics is able to supplement the sciences by giving a true account of duration, of becoming, and even of evolution.

MECHANISTIC AND CREATIVE EVOLUTION

Bergson was born in the same year that *The Origin of Species* was published, and the revolutionary implications of this work permanently affected his thought. He accepted the historical reality of evolution, but rejected attempts to explain it in mechanistic or materialistic terms. Hence he criticized Darwin's explanation, and also the less influential explanations of Lamarck, Theodor Eimer, and Spencer. In place of them he advanced a doctrine that owed much to the tradition of European and especially French vitalism, and at the same time drew inspiration from Plotinus. The result was a vision of the cosmos going far beyond the facts of biology, though purportedly based on them. These matters were presented in *Creative Evolution*, Bergson's most famous book.

Darwin explained the evolutionary process by supposing that in every population of organisms there occur random variations that have different degrees of adaptive value. The variations having maximum value for the survival and reproduction of the organisms are "naturally selected"; that is, they are preserved and transmitted to subsequent generations, while the other variations are eliminated.

Bergson argued that this explanation failed to account for a number of facts. A multicellular animal, or an organ like the vertebrate eye, is a functional whole made up of coordinated parts. If just one or a few of the parts happened to vary independently of the rest, the functioning of the whole would be impaired. Since evolution has occurred, we must suppose that at each stage all the parts of an animal and of its complex organs have varied contemporaneously so that effective functioning was preserved. But it is utterly implausible to suppose, as Darwin did, that such coadapted variations could have been random, for then their coadaptation would remain a mystery. Some agency other than natural selection must have been at work to maintain continuity of functioning through successive alterations of form.

Another fact that Darwinism failed to explain is why living things have evolved in the direction of greater and greater complexity. The earliest living things were simple in character and well adapted to their environments. Why did the evolutionary process not stop at this stage? Why did life continue to complicate itself "more and more dangerously"? To appeal to the mechanism of selection for an answer was, Bergson thought, insufficient. Something must have driven life on to higher and higher levels of organization, despite the risks involved.

Darwin's predecessor Lamarck avoided the idea of random variations by supposing that variations were caused by the "effort" exerted by individuals in adapting to the environment. Bergson considered this a more adequate explanation than the Darwinian. Yet it involved accepting the principle that acquired characteristics are transmitted from one generation to the next, and empirical evidence is heavily against this. Furthermore, the Lamarckian notion of a conscious "effort" is too limited to serve as an explanatory device. It could perhaps operate in the case of animals but hardly in the case of plants or microorganisms. To make the notion work, it must be broadened and deepened. Similarly, Eimer's appeal to orthogenesis; that is, to an inner principle that directs the course of evolution, has merit if interpreted nonmechanistically, but not if interpreted, as Eimer did, in physico-chemical terms. The synthetic philosophy of Spencer also had merit in so far as it sought to extend the evolutionary conception to the universe at large. Yet because Spencer relied exclusively on the intellect, and because he subscribed to the false idea that philosophy can be a super science, Spencer failed to do justice to real duration and to the creation of novelty. He held that evolution is due to combinations of matter and motion. This makes his philosophy a thinly disguised version of mechanical materialism, which reconstructs evolution "with fragments of the evolved."

To obtain a true understanding of the evolutionary process, the findings of biology must be supplemented, Bergson thought, by the findings of metaphysics. The chief clue is found in what intuition reveals of our own inner nature as living beings; we are typical constituents of the universe, and the forces that work in us also work in all things. When we focus upon what intuition discloses of ourselves, we find not only continuous becoming and real duration, but also a consciousness of a vital impetus (*élan vital*), of our own evolution in time. We are thus led to the idea of "an *original impetus* of life" (*un élan original de la vie*) that pervades the whole evolutionary process and accounts for its dominant features. Accordingly, the history of life is to be understood in creative, not mechanistic, terms.

THE VITAL IMPETUS AND EVOLUTION

Bergson's doctrine of the vital impetus is speculative, although often formulated as if it were a report of an established fact. The impetus is declared to be "a current of consciousness" that has penetrated matter, given rise to living bodies, and determined the course of their evolution. The current passes from one generation to the next by way of reproduction—in bisexual organisms, by way of the reproductive cells. The vital impetus is the cause of variations that accumulate and produce new species. It coordinates the appearance of variations so as to preserve continuity of functioning in evolving structures. And it carries life toward ever higher complexity of organization. Strictly speaking, the impetus does not generate energy of its own, over and above that already present in matter. What it does is "to engraft on to the necessity of physical forces the largest possible amount of indetermination." This indetermination is evident in the contingency and creativity that have characterized the history of life. At every stage the impetus has been limited by recalcitrant matter. Hence, it is always seeking to transcend the stage it has reached and always remains inadequate to what it tries to produce.

The earliest living things were physico-chemical systems into which the vital impetus "insinuated itself." Its potentialities could be realized only minimally in these systems. Consequently, it divided so that life moved forward in several quite different directions. One direction was taken by the plants, another by the insects, and a third by the vertebrates. The three directions illustrate respectively the predominance of stability, instinct, and intelligence. No predetermined plan or purpose was involved in all this. Bergson expressed as much opposition to the doctrine of radical finalism as he did to mechanism. Both doctrines deny that there has been an unforeseeable creation of forms, that these forms involve discontinuous "leaps," and that real duration is a cumulative, irreversible flow. Yet although the vital impetus is not finalistic, it does engender progress. A perfecting of functions has occurred through successive stages. An increasing realization of consciousness has also occurred.

This last contention made it difficult for Bergson to maintain an opposition to finalism, for it is in man that consciousness has been most fully realized. Here the vital impetus has found its most adequate expression as intelligence. It has likewise achieved genuine freedom by at last making matter its instrument. There was in fact "a sudden leap from the animal to man." Hence in *Creative Evolution* Bergson said that man might be considered the reason for the existence of the entire organization of life on our planet. He immediately qualified this statement by adding that it is "only a manner of speaking." We should not think that humanity was "prefigured" in the evolutionary process from the beginning.

By the time he wrote the essay that became the "Second Introduction" to *The Creative Mind,* Bergson was more forthright. He there stated categorically that the appearance of man is the *raison d'être* of life on the earth. In *The Two Sources of Morality and Religion* he also contended that it is man, "or some other being of like significance, which is the purpose of the entire process of evolution." This contention seems very close to finalism. However, Bergson continued to insist that the appearance of man was in no sense predetermined, though "it was not accidental, either." Terrestrial evolution might have produced some other being "of the same essence." Such beings have doubtless arisen elsewhere, for Bergson thought that the vital impetus animates innumerable planets in the universe. The impetus is thus not limited to the earth; creative evolution is a cosmic process.

This contention is not argued for in any detail. As so often in his writings, Bergson tried to make the contention acceptable by means of analogies. He likened the vital impetus to steam escaping at high pressure through the cracks in a container. Jets gush out unceasingly, the steam condenses into drops of water, and the drops fall back to the source. Each jet and its drops represent a world of matter animated by life. A small part of the jet remains uncondensed for an instant, and makes an effort to raise the drops that are falling. But it succeeds at most in retarding their fall. So the vital impetus achieves a moment of freedom at its highest point, in man. It might be inferred from this analogy that matter is not something *sui generis,* but is rather the lowest form assumed by the outpouring of spirit. However, matter and spirit were repeatedly described by Bergson as coexistent and interdependent.

GOD AND THE MYSTICS

The religious aspect of Bergson's outlook became increasingly pronounced toward the close of his life. Even in *Creative Evolution* he had spoken of the vital impetus as a "supra-consciousness" to which the name "God" might be attached. But this is very different from the conception of traditional Western theology. For if God is identical with the vital impetus, then he is pure activity, limited by the material world in which he is struggling to manifest himself. He is neither omnipotent nor omniscient. God "has nothing of the already made," but is ceaselessly changing. In *The Two Sources of Morality and Religion,* Bergson moved somewhat closer to the Christian position; he affirmed that God is love and the object of love. There is also a divine purpose in the evolutionary process. Evolution is nothing less than God's "undertaking to create creators, that He may have, besides Himself, beings worthy of His love."

The discovery of this purpose and of the reality of God cannot be made by the intellect. It can be made only by the sort of intuition that is the mystical experience. For the vital impetus, Bergson contended, is communicated "in its entirety" to exceptional persons. These are the mystics who achieve contact and partial coincidence with the creative effort that "is of God, if it is not God Himself." This experience does not terminate in passivity, but leads to intense activity. The mystics participate in God's love for mankind. They are therefore impelled to advance the divine purpose by helping to complete the development of man. They want to make of humanity what it would straightway have become if humanity had been able to reach its final form without the aid of man himself. The spirit of the mystics must become universal in order to ensure man's future evolution.

Bergson acknowledged that the biggest obstacle to the spread of the mystical spirit is the ceaseless struggle that most men must wage against the material conditions of life. Yet he did not believe that these conditions could be ameliorated by programs of political and economic reform devised by the intellect. Consequently, the most we can hope for at present is that the spirit of the mystics will be kept alive by small groups of privileged souls, "until such time as a profound change in the material conditions imposed on humanity by nature should permit, in spiritual matters, of a profound transformation." The mystics, through their experience of love, will keep open a trail along which the whole of humanity can eventually pass.

CLOSED AND OPEN SOCIETIES

Since man is a social animal, his future evolution will be accelerated or retarded by the sort of group in which he lives. Bergson discussed this question in *The Two Sources of Morality and Religion,* where he drew a distinction between a society that is "closed" and one that is "open," describing in each case corresponding types of religion and of morality.

A closed society is one dominated by the routine and mechanical. It is resistant to change, conservative, and authoritarian. Its stability is achieved by increasing its self-centeredness. Hence, conflict with other self-centered groups, often involving war, is a condition of its preservation. Internal cohesiveness is secured by a closed morality and a closed religion. Bergson's analysis was influenced by the sociological doctrines of Durkheim. Closed morality is static and absolutistic; closed religion is ritualistic and dogmatic. Both institutions exert pressure on individuals to accept the standard practices of the community. Spontaneity and freedom are reduced to a minimum. Conformity becomes the prime duty of the citizen. There is an obvious analogy between such a society and the repetitive mechanisms dealt with by the intellect. Indeed, Bergson regarded closed societies as in large measure the intellect's products.

The existence of a multiplicity of closed societies on the earth is an obstacle to human evolution. Accordingly, the next development in man requires the establishment of an open society. Instead of being limited, it will embrace all mankind; instead of being static, it will be progressive; instead of demanding conformity, it will encourage the maximum diversity among individuals. Its moral and religious beliefs will be equally flexible and subject to growth. Religion will replace the stereotyped dogmas elaborated by the intellect with the intuition and illumination now achieved by the mystics. The spread of the mystical spirit must ultimately create an open society whose freedom and spontaneity will express the divine *élan* which pervades the universe.

Bergson's outlook had a marked influence on the thought and literature of Europe. His gifts as a writer, his ingenuity in constructing vivid analogies, and his flair for describing the subtleties of immediate experience—"true empiricism," as he called it—contributed to the popularity of his work, as did the impressive use that he made of the biological and psychological ideas of his time. On the other hand, critics have contended that many of his doctrines are vague and ill-supported by arguments. Too often, it is said, rhapsodic formulations are offered where there ought to be sustained logical analysis. There is, for instance, no clear statement of how real duration, the flow of consciousness, and the vital impetus are related. Are these separate processes, or just distinguishable aspects of one process? Does matter have an independent status, or is it simply a "devitalized" form of the *élan vital*? Such questions are difficult, if not impossible, to answer. Many critics have also deplored the encouragement that Bergson's doctrine of the intellect gave to the advocates of irrationalism and the cruder versions of pragmatism. Yet when all these criticisms have been made, the Bergsonian heritage remains an important element in twentieth-century philosophy.

Works by Bergson

Quid Aristoteles de Loco Senserit. Paris, 1889. Bergson's doctoral thesis. Translated by Robert Mossé-Bastide as "L'Idée de lieu chez Aristote," in *Les Études bergsoniennes.* Paris, 1949. Vol. II.

Essai sur les donnés immédiates de la conscience. Paris, 1889. Translated by F. L. Pogson as *Time and Free Will: An Essay on the Immediate Data of Consciousness.* New York, 1910.

Matière et mémoire. Paris, 1896. Translated by Nancy Margaret Paul and W. Scott Palmer [pseud.] as *Matter and Memory.* New York, 1911.

Le Rire. Paris, 1900. Translated by Cloudesley Brereton and Fred Rothwell as *Laughter. An Essay on the Meaning of the Comic.* New York, 1910.

"Introduction à la métaphysique." *Revue de la métaphysique et de morale,* Vol. 11 (Jan. 1903), 1–36. Translated by T. E. Hulme as *Introduction to Metaphysics.* New York, 1913 and 1949.

L'Évolution créatrice. Paris, 1907. Translated by Arthur Mitchell as *Creative Evolution.* New York, 1911.

L'Énergie spirituelle. Paris, 1919. Translated by H. Wildon Carr as *Mind-Energy.* New York, 1920. A collection of essays.

Durée et simultanéité. Paris, 1922; 2d ed. with 3 appendices, 1923. On aspects of the theory of relativity; not included in centenary edition of Bergson's works.

Les Deux Sources de la morale et de la religion. Paris, 1932. Translated by R. A. Audra and Cloudesley Brereton as *The Two Sources of Morality and Religion.* London, 1935.

La Pensée et le mouvant. Paris, 1934. Translated by Mabelle L. Andison as *The Creative Mind.* New York, 1946. A collection of essays.

Écrits et paroles, R. M. Mossé-Bastide, ed., 3 vols. Paris, 1957–1959. Preface by Édouard LeRoy.

Oeuvres. Édition du centenaire. Paris, 1959. Annotated by André Robinet, introduction by Henri Gouhier.

Works on Bergson

ENGLISH

Carr, H. W., *The Philosophy of Change.* New York, 1912.

Chevalier, Jacques, *Henri Bergson.* London, 1928.

Hanna, Thomas, ed., *The Bergsonian Heritage.* New York and London, 1962. Articles on Bergson's thought by various scholars.

Höffding, Harald, *Henri Bergson's Filosofi.. Karacteristik ag Kritik.* Copenhagen, 1914. Translated by Alfred C. Mason in *Modern Philosophers and Lectures on Bergson.* London, 1915.

Huxley, Julian, *Essays in Popular Science.* New York, 1927. Claims that Bergson's vitalism was based on dubious factual material.

LeRoy, Édouard, *Une Philosophie nouvelle: Henri Bergson.* Paris, 1912. Translated by Vincent Benson as *The New Philosophy of Henri Bergson.* New York, 1913.

Lindsay, A. D., *The Philosophy of Henri Bergson.* London, 1911.

Ruhe, A., *Henri Bergson.* London, 1914.

Russell, Bertrand, *The Philosophy of Bergson.* London, 1914. Highly critical.

Russell, Bertrand, *Our Knowledge of the External World.* London, 1914. Ch. 1. Highly critical.

Santayana, George, *Winds of Doctrine.* New York, 1913. Highly critical.

Scharfstein, Ben-Ami, *Roots of Bergson's Philosophy.* New York, 1943.

Stephen, Karin, *The Misuse of Mind.* London, 1922.

Stewart, J. McK., *A Critical Exposition of Bergson's Philosophy.* London, 1912.

FRENCH

Delhomme, Jeanne, *Vie et conscience de la vie: Essai sur Bergson.* Paris, 1954.

Les Études bergsoniennes. Paris, 1948–1959. Vols. I–V.

Husson, Léon, *L'Intellectualisme de Bergson.* Paris, 1947.

Jankélévitch, Vladimir, *Henri Bergson.* Paris, 1959.

Marietti, Angèle, *Les Formes du mouvement chez Bergson.* Paris, 1957.

Maritain, Jacques, *La Philosophie bergsonienne.* Paris, 1930.

T. A. GOUDGE

BERKELEY, GEORGE (1685–1753), Irish philosopher of English ancestry, and Anglican bishop of Cloyne, was born at Kilkenny, Ireland. He entered Trinity College, Dublin in 1700 and became a fellow in 1707. In 1709 he published his first important book, *An Essay Towards a New Theory of Vision.* This was well received, and a second edition appeared in the same year. The following year *A Treatise Concerning the Principles of Human Knowledge,* Part 1, was published. This is the work in which Berkeley first published his immaterialist philosophy, and although it made him known to some of the foremost writers of the day, its conclusions were not taken very seriously by them. In 1713 Berkeley went to London and there published the *Three Dialogues Between Hylas and Philonous,* a more popular statement of the doctrines of the *Principles.* While in London, Berkeley became acquainted with Addison, Swift, Pope, and Steele and contributed articles to Steele's *Guardian,* attacking the theories of the freethinkers. He traveled on the Continent in 1713–1714 (when he probably met and conversed with Malebranche) and again from 1716 to 1720. During this tour he lost the manuscript of the second part of the *Principles,* which he never rewrote. Toward the end of the tour, he wrote a short essay, in Latin, entitled *De Motu,* published in London in 1721, criticizing Newton's philosophy of nature and Leibniz' theory of force. In 1724 Berkeley was made dean of Derry.

About this time, Berkeley began to prepare a project for establishing a college in Bermuda, at which not only the sons of American colonists but also Indians and Negroes were to receive a thorough education and be trained for the Christian ministry. Having obtained promises of subscriptions from many prominent people, Berkeley promoted a bill, which was passed by Parliament, providing for considerable financial help from the government. In 1728, before the money was forthcoming, Berkeley, who had just married, left for Rhode Island, where he intended to establish farms for supplying food for the college. He settled in Newport, but the grant never came; and in 1731, when it was clear that the government was diverting the money for other purposes, Berkeley had to return home. While in Newport, however, Berkeley had met and corresponded with the Samuel Johnson who later became the first president of King's College, New York (now Columbia University). Johnson was one of the few philosophers of the time to give close attention to Berkeley's philosophical views, and the correspondence between him and Berkeley is of considerable philosophical interest. While he was in Newport, Berkeley also wrote *Alciphron,* a series of dialogues in part developed from the articles he had written for the *Guardian,* directed against the "minute philosophers," or freethinkers. This was published in 1732.

Berkeley was in London from 1732 to 1734 and there wrote *The Analyst* (1734), a criticism of Newton's doctrine of fluxions and addressed to "an infidel mathematician." This and *A Defence of Free-Thinking in Mathematics* (1735) aimed at showing that the mathematicians so admired by freethinkers worked with concepts that could not withstand close scrutiny, so that the confidence given to them by "the philomathematical infidels of these times" was unjustified. It is not surprising that Berkeley was made bishop of Cloyne, Ireland, in 1734.

Berkeley carried out his episcopal duties with vigor and humanity. His diocese was in a remote and poor part of the country, and the problems he encountered there led him to reflect on economic problems. The result was *The Querist* (1735–1737), in which he made proposals for dealing with the prevailing idleness and poverty by means of public works and education. He also concerned himself with the health of the people and became convinced of the medicinal value of tar water. In 1744 he published *A Chain of Philosophical Reflexions and Inquiries concerning the Virtues of Tar-Water, and divers other Subjects connected together and arising from one another.* When the second edition appeared in the same year, the title *Siris,* by which the book is now known, was added. Much of the book is concerned with the merits of tar water, but Berkeley passed from this subject to the causes of physical phenomena, which, he held, cannot be discovered in the phenomena themselves but must be sought for in the Divine activity. This is in line with his earlier views, but some readers, on the basis of his admiring references to Plato and the Neoplatonists, have considered that by this time he had considerably modified his original system. The *Siris* was Berkeley's last philosophical work. He died suddenly in Oxford nine years later.

An account of Berkeley's life and writings would be inadequate without some reference to his *Philosophical Commentaries.* A. C. Fraser discovered a series of notes by Berkeley on all the main topics of Berkeley's philosophy and published them in 1871 in his edition of Berkeley's works, under the title of *Commonplace Book of Occasional Metaphysical Thoughts.* It was later noticed that these notes had been bound together in the wrong order, and it has now been shown that they were written by Berkeley, probably in 1707–1708, while he was thinking out his *New Theory of Vision* and *Principles.* This work makes it clear that Berkeley was already convinced of the truth of immaterialism before he published the *New Theory of Vision,* in which that view is not mentioned. The *Philosophical Commentaries* throw valuable light upon Berkeley's sources, bugbears, prejudices, and arguments.

MAIN THEMES OF BERKELEY'S PHILOSOPHY

Since the word *idealism* came into use in the eighteenth century, Berkeley has been known as a leading exponent of idealism, and even as its founder. He himself referred to his main view as "the immaterialist hypothesis," meaning by this that he denied the very possibility of inert, mindless, material substance. This description has some advantage over idealism in that it brings out Berkeley's radical opposition to materialism; whereas the opposite of idealism is realism, and there are grounds for doubting whether Berkeley intended to deny the realist contention that in perception men become directly aware of objects that persist unchanged when they cease to be perceived. Berkeley's fundamental view was that for something to exist it must either be perceived or else be the active being that does the perceiving. Things that are perceived he called "sensible things" or "sensible qualities," or, in the terminology he had borrowed from Locke, "ideas." Sensible things or ideas, he held, cannot exist except as the passive objects of minds or spirits, active beings that perceive and will. As he put it in the *Philosophical Commentaries,* "Existence is *percipi* or *percipere,*" and he added "or *velle* i.e. *agere*"—existence is to be perceived or to perceive or to will, that is, to be active. Thus there can be nothing except active spirits on the one hand and passive sensible things on the other, and the latter cannot exist except as perceived by the former. This is Berkeley's idealism or immaterialism.

Criticism of contemporary science. The above account of Berkeley's writings emphasizes their apologetic intent, an intent that can be seen in the subtitles of his major writings—that of the *Principles* is typical: *Wherein the chief causes of error and difficulty in the sciences, with the grounds of scepticism, atheism and irreligion, are inquired into.* It will be seen that "the chief causes of difficulty in the sciences" are also prominent. Berkeley considered that in the mathematics and natural sciences of his day insufficient attention was given to what experience reveals to us. Apart from Newton, the mathematicians were, he wrote in the *Philosophical Commentaries,* "mere triflers, mere Nihilarians." For example, they conceived of lines as infinitely divisible, but this is not only absurd, it could be maintained only by men who "despised sense." Thus Berkeley regarded himself as protesting against the excesses of uncontrolled rationalism. Hence he put forward a most antirationalistic view of geometry, although he never developed its implications very far. Similarly he thought that the natural philosophers deluded themselves with words when they tried to explain the physical world in terms of attractions, forces, and powers. Natural science, as he understood it, was descriptive rather than explanatory and was concerned with correlations rather than with causes. He thus sketched out a view of science that was revived and developed by nineteenth-century and twentieth-century positivists.

Sensible qualities are the signs of God's purpose. Berkeley's positivism, however, was confined to his account of natural science. The order of phenomena, he held, was willed by God for the good of created spirits. In deciphering the conjunctions and sequences of our sense experience we are learning what God has decreed. Thus sensible qualities are the language in which God speaks to us. In the third and fourth editions (1732) of the *New Theory of Vision* Berkeley said that the objects of sight are a divine visual language by which God teaches us what things are good for us and what things are harmful to us. In the *Alciphron,* published that same year, he argued that "the great Mover and Author of Nature constantly explaineth Himself to the eyes of men by the sensible intervention of arbitrary signs, which have no similitude or connexion with the things signified." We learn that certain visual ideas are signs of certain tactual ones, certain smells signs of certain colors, and so on. There is no necessity about this, any more than things necessarily have the names that convention assigns to them. Just as some sensible qualities are signs of others, so sensible qualities as a whole are signs of the purposes of God who "daily speaks to our senses in a manifest and clear dialect."

Thus, taken as a whole, Berkeley's philosophy is a form of immaterialism combined with an extreme antirationalist theory of science. The regularities between phenomena are regarded as evidence for, and as signs of, God's purposes. Just as a man's words reveal his thoughts and intentions by means of the conventional signs of language, so the sensible order reveals God's will in phenomena that could have been ordered quite differently if he had so decided.

THE NEW THEORY OF VISION

Although Berkeley did not mention his immaterialism in *An Essay Towards a New Theory of Vision,* this work throws important light upon his quarrel with the mathematicians and his rejection of the rationalist point of view. It contains, too, an interesting statement of what Berkeley then thought about geometry. Furthermore, the *Essay* helps us to see, from what Berkeley said about the objects of vision, how he came to the view that sensible qualities cannot exist "without the mind." Among the main contentions of the book is the claim that distance or "outness" is not immediately perceived by sight; it is "suggested" in part by the sensations we get in moving our eyes but mainly by association with the ideas of touch. According to Berkeley, we see the distance (and size) of things only in the sense in which we see a man's shame and anger. We see his face, and the expression on it suggests to us how he is feeling. In themselves, shame and anger are invisible. Similarly, we see shapes and colors, which are signs of what we would touch if we were to stretch out our hands, but distance itself is no more seen than anger is. In expounding this view, Berkeley developed the thesis that the objects of sight and touch are utterly disparate, so that no feature of the one can have more than a contingent connection with any feature of the other.

Descartes' theory of the perception of distance. Consideration should first be given to Berkeley's criticisms of an important geometrical account of how distance is perceived and assessed, the account given by Descartes in his *Dioptrics* (1637). In this work Descartes referred to six "qualities we perceive in the objects of sight," namely, light, color, shape, distance, magnitude, and situation. Descartes argued that one of the ways in which men ascertain the distance of objects is by means of the angles formed by straight lines running from each of their eyes and converging at the object seen. He illustrated this by reference to a blind man with a stick (the length of which he does not know) held in each hand. When he brings the points of the sticks together at the object, he forms a triangle with one hand at each end of the base, and if he knows how far apart his hands are, and what angles the sticks make with his body, he can, "by a kind of geometry innate in all men" know how far away the object is. The same geometry would apply, Descartes argued, if the observer's eyes are regarded as ends of the base of a triangle, and straight lines from them are regarded as converging at the object. The more obtuse the base angles formed by the lines running from this base and converging at the object, the farther away the object must be; the more acute these angles, the nearer the object must be. Berkeley put the matter somewhat differently from Descartes, pointing out that according to the latter's view the more acute the angle formed at the object by the lines converging from the eyes, the farther away it must be; the more obtuse this angle, the nearer the object must be. It is important to notice that this "must" is the "must" of mathematical necessity. From what Descartes said, it is necessarily the case that the more acute this angle is, the farther away the object is; the more obtuse the angle, the nearer the object. "Nearer" and "farther" logically depend upon the obtuseness or acuteness of the angle. In criticizing this view, therefore, Berkeley was criticizing the view that distance is known a priori by the principles of an innate geometry according to which we know that the distance of the object must vary in accordance with the angle made at the object by straight lines converging there from the eyes of the observer.

Berkeley's criticism of Descartes. Against Descartes's view Berkeley brought a complex argument that for purposes of exposition, is here broken up into three parts. The first is that people who know nothing of the geometry of the matter can nevertheless notice the relative distance of things from them. This is not very convincing, for Descartes obviously thought that the geometry he regarded as "innate in all men" might be employed by them without their having reflected on it. The second argument used by Berkeley is that the lines and angles referred to by Descartes "have no real existence in nature, being only an hypothesis framed by the mathematicians. . . ." This argument is of interest in showing how Berkeley thought that mathematicians were inclined to deal in fictitious entities, but it is unlikely that Descartes was deceived by them in this way.

Berkeley's third and main argument was based upon a theory that he expressed in the words, "distance, of itself and immediately, cannot be seen." William Molyneux, from whose *Dioptrics* (1692) Berkeley borrowed this theory, had supported it by the argument that since distance is a line or length directed endwise from the object seen to the eye, it can reach the eye at only one point, which must necessarily remain the same however near or far away the object is. If this argument is accepted, then distance could not possibly be seen, and could only be judged or, as Berkeley believed, "suggested."

Distance is suggested by what is seen. What, then, according to Berkeley, is seen? The answer is not altogether clear, but it would seem that he thought that the immediate object of vision is two-dimensional, containing relations of above and below and of one side and the other, with no necessary connection with a third dimension. Hence the relation between what is immediately seen on the one hand and the distance of objects on the other must be contingent and cannot be necessary. Distance, then, must be ascertained by means of something that has only a contingent relationship with what is seen. Berkeley mentioned the sensations we have when we adjust our eyes, the greater confusedness of objects as they come very close to the eyes, and the sensations of strain as we try to see what is very near. But he mainly relied on the associations between what a man has touched and what he now sees. For example, when a man now sees something faint and dim, he may, from past experience, expect that if he approaches and touches it he will find it bright and hard. When he sees something at a distance, he is really seeing certain shapes and colors, which *suggest* to him what tangible ideas he would have if he were near enough to touch it. Just as one does not hear a man's thoughts, which are suggested by the sounds he makes, so one does not directly see distance, which is suggested by what is seen.

Sight and touch. Berkeley's view that distance is not immediately perceived by sight is rejected by some writers, for instance by H. H. Price, in his *Perception* (1932), on the ground that it is plainly contradicted by experience. We just do see visual depth, it is held, so that it is idle to deny this fact on the basis of an argument purporting to prove that we cannot. Again, some critics, such as T. K. Abbott in *Sight and Touch* (1864) have argued not only that we do get our idea of distance from sight, but also that touch is vague and uninformative by comparison with sight, and hence less effective in giving knowledge of the material world. This discussion need not be developed, however, since, although he said in the *Essay* that by touch we get knowledge of objects that exist "without the mind" (§55), Berkeley's real view was that no sensible thing could so exist. It cannot be denied that on occasion Berkeley's language was imprecise. A crucial example of this occurs in his discussion of the question of whether a man born blind would, on receiving his sight, see things at a distance from him. According to Berkeley, of course, he would not; but to such a man, the most distant objects " . . . would all seem to be in his eye, or rather in his mind" and would appear "(as in truth they are) no other than a new set of thoughts or sensations, each whereof is as near to him as the perceptions of pain or pleasure, or the most inward passions of his soul" (*Essay*, §41). It will be noticed how readily Berkeley passed from "in his eye" to "in his mind," and how he assimilated such very different things as sensations and thoughts. Indeed it is hard not to conclude that he thought that whatever was not seen at a distance must appear to be in the mind. If this is true, then one of the objects of the *Essay* was to show that the immediate objects of vision must be in the mind because they are not seen at a distance. (For further discussion of points raised in this paragraph, see TOUCH.)

Geometries of sight and of touch. As already seen, an extremely important thesis of the *Essay* is that the objects of sight and the objects of touch are radically different from one another. We see visible objects and we touch tangible objects, and it is absurd to suppose that we can touch what we see or see what we touch. According to Berkeley, it follows from this that tangible shape and visible shape have no necessary connection with one another. Geometers certainly supposed themselves to be concerned with shapes in abstraction from their being seen or touched, but Berkeley did not allow that this is possible. A purely visual geometry would necessarily be confined to two dimensions, so that the three-dimensional geometry that we have must be fundamentally a geometry of touch. He reinforced this strangely pragmatic view with the observation that a sighted but disembodied being that could not touch or manipulate things would be unable to understand even plane geometry, since without a body it would not understand the handling of rulers and compasses and the drawing of lines and the placing of shapes against one another.

ARGUMENTS FOR IMMATERIALISM

The arguments now to be considered are set out in the *Principles* and in the *Three Dialogues*. They are largely concerned with what Berkeley called "ideas," "ideas or sensations," "sensible things," or "sensible qualities." The very use of the word *idea* itself and, even more, its use in apposition with *sensation* had the purpose of indicating something that does not exist apart from the perception of it. Pains and itches are typical sensations, and no one supposes that they could exist apart from a being that experiences them. Rocks do not suffer, and water does not itch. When, therefore, sensible things such as colors, sounds, tangible shapes, tastes, and smells are called ideas, they are assimilated with sensations and hence relate to the perceiving beings that have them. It is now necessary, therefore, to examine the arguments with which Berkeley justified this.

Seventeenth-century materialism. Berkeley's arguments for immaterialism can be understood only if we first consider the sort of view it was intended to refute. When Berkeley was forming his views, the natural sciences had been so far advanced by the work of such men as Galileo, Vesalius, Harvey, Boyle, and Newton as to have given rise to a scientific view of the world. Such a view had been elaborated, in its philosophical aspects, by Locke in his *Essay concerning Human Understanding* (1690). Space and time were, so to say, the containers within which material things were situated. The movements and relations of material things could be explored by experiments and characterized in mathematical formulae.

Explanation in terms of particles in motion. The features of the world, thus revealed as fundamental, were those of place, shape, size, movement, weight, and the like; and it was in terms of these that heat and cold and color and sound found their explanation. Heat was thought to be due to the rapid movement of atomic particles, color to the transmission of particles or to the spreading of waves, and sound to the movement of the air between the emitting object and the ear. Whereas solid, shaped, moving objects, and the air and space within which they existed, were regarded as basic features of nature, the colors we see, the heat we feel, and the sounds we hear were held to be the effects that substances possessing only the basic characteristics produced in creatures with sense organs. If all creatures with sense organs and consciousness were removed from the world, there would no longer be any experienced sounds, but only pulsations in the air; particles would increase or decrease their speed of movement, but no one would feel hot or cold; light would be radiated, but there would be no colors as we know them. In such a world colors and sounds, heat and cold, would exist, as Boyle put it, in his *Origins of Forms and Qualities* (Oxford, 1666), only "dispositively," i.e., those primary things would be there that would have given rise to the secondary ones if creatures with the requisite sense organs and minds had been there too.

Primary and secondary qualities. In this way a distinction was made between the primary qualities of things, which are essential and absolute, and their secondary qualities, which are those among the primary ones that give or would give rise to heard sounds, seen colors, and felt heat. It was an important element of this view that nothing could be perceived unless it acted upon the sense organs of the percipient and produced in his mind an idea. What was immediately perceived was not the external object but an idea representative of it. Locke had made people familiar with this theory, and had maintained that whereas the ideas we have of heat and cold and of color and sound correspond to nothing *like* themselves in the external world; for all that exists in the external world are solid bodies at rest or in movement, the ideas we have of the solid, shaped, moving bodies, i.e., our ideas of primary qualities are like their sources or archetypes outside us. According to the view, then, that Berkeley was considering, material objects are perceived mediately or indirectly by means of ideas, some of which, the ideas of primary qualities, are like their originals; others, the ideas of secondary qualities, are relative to percipients and are unlike anything that exists in the external world.

Materialism leads to skepticism. Berkeley had two objections to the view that material objects are perceived mediately by means of ideas. One is that since it is held that we never perceive material things directly, but only through the medium of ideas, then we can never know whether any of our ideas are like the qualities of material substances since we can never compare our ideas with them; for to do so we should require direct or immediate acquaintance with them (*Principles*, §18). Indeed, if we accept Locke's position, then the very existence of material substances is in doubt, and we are constantly under the threat of skepticism (*Principles*, §86). Thus Berkeley argued that Locke's theory was in fact, although not by intention, skeptical, and that it could be remedied only by the elimination of material substances that could never be directly apprehended.

Distinction between primary and secondary qualities untenable. Berkeley's second objection is that there can be no distinction between ideas of primary qualities and ideas of secondary qualities such as to make secondary qualities relative to the mind in a way in which primary qualities are not. In the *Three Dialogues* Berkeley elaborated the arguments, already used by Locke, to show that the ideas we have of secondary qualities are relative to the percipient and are what they are by reason of his condition and constitution. Things have no color in the dark; the same water can feel hot or cold to different hands, one of which has been in cold water and the other in hot; heat and cold are inseparably bound up with pain and pleasure, which can only exist in perceiving beings; and so on. But Berkeley then went on to argue that just as heat, for example, is inseparably bound up with pleasure and pain, and can therefore, no more than they can, exist "without the mind," so extension is bound up with color, speed of movement with a standard of estimation, solidity with touch, and size and shape with position and point of view (*Principles*, §§10–15). Thus Berkeley's argument is that nothing can have the primary qualities without having the secondary qualities, so that if the latter cannot exist "without the mind," the former cannot so exist either.

All sensible qualities must be either perceived or perceptible. The preceding argument, however, is only a hypothetical one to the effect that if secondary qualities cannot exist "without the mind," primary qualities are in like case. What must now be considered are the reasons for holding that secondary qualities and, indeed, all sensible qualities can exist only in the mind so that their being is to be perceived. Berkeley, as already indicated, stated and elaborated well-known arguments to show that heat and cold, tastes, sounds, and the rest are relative to the percipient. Perhaps the most persuasive of these are those that purport to establish an indissoluble connection between heat, taste, and smell on the one hand, and pain or pleasure or displeasure on the other. Since no one denies that pain and pleasure can exist only if felt, then this applies to heat so intense as to be painful and to lesser degrees of heat as well. But in the *Principles*, his systematic treatise on the subject, Berkeley did not make use of these arguments, but said that "an intuitive knowledge may be obtained of this, by any one that shall attend to what is meant by the term *exist* when applied to sensible things" (§3). His view here is that "sensible things" are by their very nature perceived or perceivable. He supported this by asserting that to say there was an odor is to say that it was smelled, to say that there was a sound is to say that it was heard, to say that there was a color or shape is to say that it was seen or touched. According to Berkeley, unsmelled odors, sounds unheard, colors unseen, and shapes unseen or untouched are absurdities or impossibilities; brown leaves could not rustle on a withered tree in a world where life was extinct and God was dead. The very notion is absurd or impossible. Can more light be shed on the matter than is provided by the assertion that we have "intuitive knowledge" of it?

It must be remembered, in the first place, that Berkeley was contrasting the sounds we hear, for example, with the movements in the air, which men of science sometimes call sounds. Sounds in the latter sense, he said, "may possibly be *seen* or *felt*, but never *heard*" (*Three Dialogues*, 1). From this it may be seen that Berkeley looked upon sensible qualities as each the object of its own mode of perception, so that sounds are heard but not seen or touched, colors seen but not heard, heat felt but not seen, and so on. Hence colors require a viewer, sounds a hearer, and heat someone who feels it; and this is one reason why the being of sensible things is held to be their being perceived. The various modalities of sense are distinguished from one another by the mode of perception peculiar to each one, and in making these distinctions it is implied that perception is essential to them all. It is well known, of course, that Berkeley's critics accuse him of failing to distinguish between the object perceived and the perceiving of it. The perceiving of it, they say, can only be an act of a percipient without whom it could not exist, but the perceived object, whether it be a sound or a color or a shape, is distinct from the perceiving and could conceivably exist apart from it. Whatever may be thought of this argument, it should not be used against Berkeley as if he had not thought of it. In fact he put it into the mouth of Hylas in the first of the *Three Dialogues* and rejected it on the ground that in perception we are passive and so are not exerting an act or activity of any kind. It should also be noticed that when Berkeley discussed sensation in detail he stated that sensible things or sensible qualities are perceived *immediately*, i.e., without suggestion, association, or inference. We say that we hear vehicles and that we hear sounds. According to Berkeley, we hear sounds immediately, but vehicles, if they are out of sight, are suggested by or inferred from what we do hear, and so are heard only mediately or by means of the sounds immediately heard. Thus the sound we hear immediately is neither suggested nor inferred, but is heard just as it is. For this to be so, it must be before the mind; for if it were not before the mind, it would have to be inferred or suggested. Thus sensible qualities, as immediately perceived, must be objects of perception; their being is to be perceived.

Inconceivability of a sensible object existing unperceived. A very famous argument is now to be considered: It is inconceivable that anything should exist apart from, or independent of, mind. This argument was put forward by Berkeley in similar terms both in the *Principles* (§§22, 23) and in the *Three Dialogues* (1) and takes the form of a challenge to the reader to conceive of something—e.g., a book or a tree—existing absolutely unperceived. Berkeley argued that the attempt is impossible of fulfillment, since in order to conceive of a tree existing unperceived we who conceive of it, by the very fact of doing so, bring it into relation to our conception and hence to ourselves. As Hylas admits, in recognizing the failure of his attempt, "It is a pleasant mistake enough. As I was thinking of a tree in a solitary place, where no one was present to see it, methought that was to conceive a tree as existing unperceived or unthought of, not considering that I myself conceived it all the while." This is an argument that was later accepted as fundamental by idealists of such different persuasions as Fichte and Bradley, who held that it shows that mind or experience is essential to the universe.

Sensible objects are complex ideas. Berkeley's example of a tree makes it necessary to consider how trees and other things in nature are related to ideas, sensible qualities, sounds, colors, shapes, etc. According to Berkeley, such things as trees, books, and mountains are groups of ideas or sensible qualities and are hence as much within the mind as the latter are. Indeed, in his view, books, trees, and mountains *are* ideas, though complex ones. He admitted (*Principles*, §38) that this use of the word *idea* for what is ordinarily called a *thing* is somewhat odd, but held that, the facts being as they are, *idea* is better than *thing*. A tree is a group of ideas touched, seen, and smelled; a cherry, a group of ideas touched, seen, smelled, and tasted. The sensible qualities or ideas, without which we should have no conception of a tree or cherry, do not belong to some unseen, untouched, untasted substance or substratum, for the very conception of such a "something I know not what" (as Locke had called it) is incoherent, and rests upon the false view that we can conceive something in complete abstraction from ideas of sense.

Sensible objects, as ideas, are perceived directly. Berkeley therefore concluded that it is his theory that conforms with common sense, not that of the materialists or the dualists. For according to Berkeley we perceive trees and cherries directly by seeing, touching, and tasting them, just as the plain man thinks we do, whereas his opponents regard them as perpetually hidden from us by a screen of intermediaries that may be always deceiving us. Berkeley considered that by this view he had refuted skepticism of the senses, for, according to his theory, the objects of the senses are the things in the world: the trees, houses, and mountains we live among. But trees, houses, and mountains, as compounded of sensible qualities or ideas, cannot exist "without the mind."

Sensible objects not copies of material archetypes. Berkeley's arguments showing that all sensible qualities or ideas exist only as perceived and that, therefore, things in nature, being groups of such ideas, cannot exist "without the mind" have now been expounded. It is now necessary to complete this account of Berkeley's arguments for immaterialism with his argument to show that not only must sensible qualities or ideas exist in the mind, but also that nothing *like* them can exist outside it. For anyone reluctant to accept immaterialism is likely to fall back on the view that our ideas, although in our minds, are copies of material archetypes. Berkeley's objection to this in the *Principles* (§8) is that "an idea can be like nothing but an idea," which he illustrated by saying that a color or shape can only be like another color or shape. In the *Three Dialogues* (1) he expanded the argument in two ways. Ideas, he said, are regarded by some as the perceived representatives of imperceptible originals, but "Can a real thing in itself *invisible* be like a color; or a real thing which is not *audible*, be like a *sound*?" His other reason for holding that ideas cannot be like any supposed external originals is that ideas are "perpetually fleeting and variable," and "continually changing upon every alteration in the distance, medium or instruments of sensation," while their supposed originals are thought to remain fixed and constant throughout all changes in the percipient's organs and position. But something that is fleeting and relative cannot be like what is stable and absolute, any more than what is incapable of being perceived can be like what is essentially perceptible.

Summary. The following are Berkeley's central arguments in favor of immaterialism. They arose out of his exposure of the weaknesses and inconsistencies in the then current scientific view of the world, with its distinction between primary and secondary qualities and its theory of representative perception. According to Berkeley, since primary qualities cannot exist apart from secondary qualities, and since secondary qualities, and indeed all sensible qualities, cannot exist "without the mind," the independent material world of the then current scientific view was a conceptual absurdity. This was supported by the argument that our ideas cannot be likenesses of an external material world, since there is nothing conceivable they could be likenesses of except mind-dependent existences of their own type. The theory of representative perception was held to be essentially skeptical, and Berkeley claimed that his own theory, according to which we directly perceive ideas and groups of ideas that exist only as perceived, eliminates skepticism and accords with common sense.

METAPHYSICS AND THEOLOGY

In section 3 of the *Principles*, where Berkeley stated that we have intuitive knowledge of the fact that for sensible qualities to exist they must be perceived, he also stated that when we say that the table is in the room that we have left we mean that if we were to return there we could perceive it "or that some other spirit actually does perceive it." This shows that Berkeley was concerned with the problem of giving an account, within the terms of his immaterialism, of the continued existence of things that are not being perceived by any human being. It also shows that he considered two ways of dealing with this problem. One way was to extend the doctrine that the existence of sensible things is their being perceived into the doctrine that the existence of sensible things is their being *perceptible*. The other way was to argue that when sensible things are not being perceived by human beings they must be perceived by "some other spirit."

Berkeley not a phenomenalist. The first way points in the direction of the modern theory of phenomenalism, the theory according to which, in John Stuart Mill's happily chosen words, material objects are "permanent possibilities of sensation." But might not anything, even material substances possessing only primary qualities, be perceptible, even if not actually being perceived? Some twentieth-century upholders of phenomenalism have argued that the world was perceptible before there was any life or mind, in the sense that if there had been gods or human beings they would have perceived it. This could not be possible on Berkeley's theory, however, since, as we have seen, he held that only ideas or sensible things can be *like* ideas or sensible things, so that what is perceptible is limited by what is perceived.

Perceptible objects perceived by God. The perceptible, therefore, is limited to the mind-dependent, and, for Berkeley, the very notion of something that might be perceived, but is not, is unacceptable. Thus it seems that Berkeley was forced to supplement his phenomenalist account of unperceived objects with the view that whatever is not being actually perceived by human beings, but is only perceptible by them, must be an object of perception by "some other spirit." He used this same expression in section 48 of the *Principles*, where he denied that "bodies are annihilated and created every moment, or exist not at all during the intervals between our perception of them." In the *Three Dialogues* (2) he argued that since sensible things do not depend on the thought of human beings and exist independently of them *"there must be some other mind wherein they exist."* This other mind is God; and thus, according to Berkeley, the existence of sensible things when not being perceived by finite spirits is a proof of the existence of an infinite spirit who perceives them always. Indeed, Berkeley considered it a merit of immaterialism that it enables this brief and, as he thought, conclusive proof to be formulated.

Our ideas come from God. In the *Principles* Berkeley put forward another proof of the existence of God, this time a proof based upon God as the cause of our ideas. As has been shown, Berkeley held that ideas are passive and that the only active beings are minds or spirits. Now some of our ideas, namely, ideas of imagination, we ourselves produce, but others, the ideas of sense, come to us without our willing them. "There is therefore some other will or spirit that produces them" (*Principles*, §29). That this is God may be concluded from the regular order in which these ideas come to us. The knowledge we have of God is analogous to the knowledge we have of other men. Since men are active spirits, we do not have ideas of them, but only of their expressions, words, and bodily movements. Through these we recognize them as possessors of minds and wills like those we know ourselves to have. Similarly, God reveals himself to us in the order of nature: "every thing we see, hear, feel, or in any wise perceive by sense, being a sign or effect of the Power of God."

Active spirits and passive ideas. These, then, are the elements of Berkeley's metaphysics. There are active spirits on the one hand and passive ideas on the other. The latter could not exist apart from the former, but the ideas in the minds of human beings are caused in them by God and sustained by him when they are not perceiving them. Regularly recurring groups of ideas are called bodies, and the ideas that form them are arbitrarily connected together and might have been connected quite differently. Thus there is no natural necessity or internal reason about the laws of nature, but the regular sequences of ideas reveal to us a single infinite being who orders things for our benefit. Active spirits and passive ideas are of different natures. The mind is not blue because the idea of blue is in it, nor is the mind extended because it has an idea of extension. Ideas are neither parts nor properties of minds. Berkeley seems to have thought that the relationship is *sui generis*, for he said that sensible qualities are in the mind "only as they are perceived by it, that is, not by way of *mode* or *attribute, but only by way of idea*" (*Principles*, §49).

God's ideas and our ideas. As already seen, Berkeley held that God was both the cause of the ideas in the minds of embodied finite spirits and also the Mind in which these ideas continued to exist when embodied finite spirits were not perceiving them. Berkeley was thus faced with the problem of how the ideas in finite minds are related to the ideas in God's mind. If we recall Berkeley's claim that he was on the side of common sense against the skeptics, then we should expect the ideas that continue to exist in God's mind to be identical with those that had been in the minds of the embodied finite spirits who had formerly perceived them.

However, he found that there were difficulties in this view. Men perceive ideas of sense by means of sense organs, and their ideas vary in accordance with their position and condition, but God does not have sense organs. Furthermore, some ideas—for example, those of heat and cold, and sensations of smell and taste—are inseparable from sensations of pain and pleasure, but God is impassible, i.e., not subject to feeling or emotion; hence he cannot be supposed to perceive ideas of this nature. In the *Three Dialogues* (3), therefore, Berkeley concluded that "God knows or hath ideas; but his ideas are not conveyed to Him by sense, as ours are." From this it is natural to conclude that the ideas that God perceives are not identical with the ideas that embodied finite spirits perceive. Berkeley was obviously thinking along these lines when, in the same *Dialogue*, he said that the things that one perceives, "they or their archetypes," must, since one does not cause them, have an existence outside one's mind. Elsewhere in this *Dialogue* he distinguished between what is "ectypal or natural" and what is "archetypal and eternal." Thus Berkeley's arguments and the language he used combine to suggest that the ideas in God's mind are not the same ideas as those in the minds of embodied percipients.

This point was taken up by the Samuel Johnson referred to earlier, in his correspondence with Berkeley. Johnson suggested that Berkeley's view is that "the real original and permanent existence of things is archetypal, being ideas *in mente Divina*, and that our ideas are copies of them." Johnson was too polite to press the point, but it follows that what we directly perceive are copies or representatives of divine originals, so that Berkeley's claim to have reinstated the direct, unmediated perception of common sense, in place of the representative and skeptical theory of the philosophers and scientists, cannot be substantiated. In his reply, Berkeley hardly met this point when he stated that material substance is an impossibility because it is held to exist apart from mind, whereas the archetypes in the divine mind are obviously inseparable from God's knowledge of them.

PHILOSOPHY OF NATURE

Berkeley carried on a persistent battle against the tendency to suppose that mere abstractions are real things. In the *New Theory of Vision* he denied the possibility of "extension in abstract," saying "A line or surface which is neither black, nor white, nor blue, nor yellow, etc., nor long, nor short, nor rough, nor smooth, nor square, nor round, etc., is perfectly incomprehensible" (§ 123). In the

Introduction to the *Principles*, his most explicit discussion of the matter, he quoted Locke's account of the abstract idea of a triangle "which is neither oblique nor rectangle, neither equilateral, equicrural, nor scalenon, but all and none of these at once," and pointed out that any actual triangle must be one of these types and cannot possibly be "all and none" of them. What makes any idea general, he held, is not any abstract feature that may be alleged to belong to it, but rather its being used to represent all other ideas that are like it in the relevant respects. Thus if something that is true of a triangle of one of these types is not true of it because it is of that one type, then it is true of all triangles whatever. Nothing exists but what is particular, and particular ideas become general by being used as representatives of others like them. Generality, we might say, is a symbolic device, not a metaphysical status. Thus Berkeley's attack on abstractions is based on two principles: (1) that nothing exists but what is particular, and (2) that nothing can exist on its own except what can be sensed or imagined on its own. If we accept the first principle, then abstract objects and Platonic forms are rejected, and if we accept the second, then possibility is limited to the sensible or imaginable.

Space, time, and motion. We have already seen how Berkeley applied the above two principles to the abstract conception of unperceived existence, and to the abstract conception of bodies with only the primary qualities. It must now be shown how he applied them to some of the other elements in the scientific world view he was so intent on discrediting. Chief among these were the current conceptions of absolute space, absolute time, and absolute motion. According to Berkeley, all these are abstractions, not realities. It is impossible, he held, to form an idea of pure space apart from the bodies in it. We find that we are hindered from moving our bodies in some directions and can move them freely in others. Where there are hindrances to our movement there are other bodies to obstruct us, and where we can move unrestrictedly we say there is space. It follows that our idea of space is inseparable from our ideas of movement and of body (*Principles*, §116).

So too our conception of time is inseparable from the succession of ideas in our minds and from the "particular actions and ideas that diversify the day"; hence Newton's conception of absolute time flowing uniformly must be rejected (*Principles*, §§97, 98).

Newton had also upheld absolute motion, but this too, according to Berkeley, is a hypostatized abstraction. If there were only one body in existence there could be no idea of motion, for motion is the change of position of two bodies relative to one another. Thus sensible qualities, without which there could be no bodies, are essential to the very conception of movement. Furthermore, since sensible qualities are passive existences, and hence bodies are too, movement cannot have its source in body; and as we know what it is to move our own bodies, we know that the source of motion must be found in mind. Created spirits are responsible for only a small part of the movement in the world, and therefore God, the infinite spirit, must be its prime source. "And so natural philosophy either presupposes the knowledge of God or borrows it from some superior science" (*De Motu*, §34).

Causation and explanation. The thesis that God is the ultimate source of motion is a special case of the principle that the only real causes are spirits. This principle has the general consequence, of course, that inanimate bodies cannot act causally upon one another. Berkeley concluded from this that what are called natural causes are really signs of what follows them. Fire does not cause heat, but is so regularly followed by it that it is a reliable sign of it as long as "the Author of Nature always operates uniformly" (*Principles*, §107). Thus Berkeley held that natural laws describe but do not explain, for real explanations must be by reference to the aims and purposes of spirits, that is, in terms of final causes. For this reason, he maintained that mechanical explanations of movements in terms of attraction were misleading, unless it was recognized that they merely recorded the rates at which bodies in fact approach one another (*Principles*, §103). Similar arguments apply to gravity or to force when these are regarded as explanations of the movements of bodies (*De Motu*, §6). This is not to deny the importance of Newton's laws, for Newton did not regard gravity "as a true physical quality, but only as a mathematical hypothesis" (*De Motu*, §17). In general, explanations in terms of forces or attractions are mathematical hypotheses having no stable being in the nature of things but depending upon the definitions given to them (*De Motu*, §67). Their acceptability depends upon the extent to which they enable calculations to be made, resulting in conclusions that are borne out by what in fact occurs. According to Berkeley, forces and attractions are not found in nature but are useful constructions in the formulation of theories from which deductions can be made about what is found in nature, that is, sensible qualities or ideas (*De Motu*, §§34–41).

PHILOSOPHY OF MATHEMATICS

We have already seen that when he wrote the *New Theory of Vision*, Berkeley thought that geometry was primarily concerned with tangible extension, since visual extension does not have three dimensions, and visible shapes must be formed by hands that grasp and instruments that move. He later modified this view, an important feature of which has already been referred to in the account of Berkeley's discussion of Locke's account of the abstract idea of a triangle. A particular triangle, imagined or drawn, is regarded as representative of all other triangles, so that what is proved of it is proved of all others like it in the relevant respects. This, he pointed out later in the *Principles* (§126), applies particularly to size. If the length of the line is irrelevant to the proof, what is true of a line one inch long is true of a line one mile long. The line we use in our proof is a representative sign of all other lines. But it must have a finite number of parts, for if it is a visible line it must be divisible into visible parts, and these must be finite in length. A line one inch long cannot be divided into 10,000 parts because no such part could possibly be seen. But since a line one mile long can be divided into 10,000 parts, we imagine that the short line could be divided likewise. "After this manner the properties of the lines signified are (by a very usual figure) transferred to the sign, and thence through mistake thought to appertain to it considered in its own nature." Thus it was Berkeley's view that infinitesimals should be "pared off" from mathematics (*Principles*, §131). In the *Analyst* (1734), he brought these and other considerations to bear in refuting Newton's theory of fluxions. In this book Berkeley seemed to suggest that the object of geometry is "to measure finite assignable extension" (§50, Q.2).

Berkeley's account of arithmetic was even more revolutionary than his account of geometry. In geometry, he held, one particular shape is regarded as representative of all those like it, but in arithmetic we are concerned with purely arbitrary signs invented by men to help them in their operations of counting. Number, he said, is "entirely the creature of the mind" (*Principles*, §12). He argued, furthermore, that there are no units and no numbers in nature apart from the devices that men have invented to count and measure. The same length, for example, may be regarded as one yard, if it is measured in that unit, or three feet or thirty-six inches, if it is measured in those units. Arithmetic, he went on, is a language in which the names for the numbers from zero to nine play a part analogous to that of nouns in ordinary speech (*Principles*, §121). Berkeley did not develop this part of his theory. However, later in the eighteenth century, in various works, Condillac argued in detail for the thesis that mathematics is a language, and this view is, of course, widely held today.

CONCLUDING COMMENTS

Berkeley's immaterialism is a strange and unstable combination of theses that most other philosophers have thought do not belong together. Thus he upheld both extreme empiricism and idealism, both immaterialism and common sense, and both subjectivism (as it would seem) and epistemological realism (as it would also seem). Are these mere skillful polemical devices in the war against the freethinkers, or can they be regarded as elements in a distinctive and reasonably coherent metaphysics?

It is odd that Berkeley had so much to say about the relativity of each particular sense and so little to say about our perception of the physical world. He referred to perspectival distortions and the like in the course of defending his view that the existence of sensible qualities is their being perceived, but he did not seem to realize the difficulties they made for his view that perception is direct. Indeed, when, in the *Three Dialogues* (3) he mentioned the case of the oar that looks bent in the water when in fact it is straight, he said that we go wrong only if we mistakenly infer that it will look bent when out of the water. There is something seen to be straight, something else seen to be crooked, and something else again felt to be straight. We go wrong only when we expect that when we see something crooked we shall feel something crooked. But this implies that our perceptions of such things as oars, as distinct from our perceptions of colors and pressures, are not direct as common sense supposes. This reinforces the criticism we have already mentioned, that the ideas perceived by finite spirits with sense organs are different from, and representative of, the ideas in the mind of God. Berkeley was farther from common sense and closer to the views that he was criticizing than he was ready to admit.

It is obvious enough that Berkeley's immaterialism is not in accord with common sense. What place, then, must be given to his empiricism? He certainly rejected the Cartesian conception of a natural world that deceives the senses and is apprehended by the reason. He denied that mathematics reveals the ultimate necessities of things and anticipated to some extent the linguistic theory of mathematics. In arguing that causes are not to be found in nature, and in maintaining that the sciences of nature are primarily concerned with predicting human experiences, he formulated views that Ernst Mach and his twentieth-century followers have advocated. Furthermore, although he did not himself adopt it, he briefly formulated the theory of the physical world known as phenomenalism, the theory that consistent empiricists have adopted in order to avoid postulating objects that transcend sense experience. But, in spite of all this, Berkeley was an idealist rather than an empiricist. He held that sensible qualities or ideas are not independent or substantial existences and that minds or spirits are. On this most important matter, he was in agreement with his great contemporary, Leibniz. Furthermore, Berkeley's antiabstractionism, as we may call it, was constantly leading him towards the conclusion that the universe is a concrete unity in which an infinite mind is manifesting itself. If we look at his writings as a continuing and developing critique of abstraction, then we shall see that the *Siris* is not an aberration or a recantation but, as Bergson said in his lectures on Berkeley, 1908–1909, a natural continuation of Berkeley's earlier views (*Écrits et paroles*, 2, p. 309).

Bibliography

LIFE AND PRINCIPAL EDITIONS OF WORKS

Luce, A. A., *The Life of George Berkeley, Bishop of Cloyne.* London, 1949.

Rand, Benjamin, *Berkeley and Percival.* Cambridge, 1914.

Fraser, A. C., *The Works of George Berkeley*, 4 Vols. London, 1871. New (first complete) edition, 1901.

Luce, A. A., and Jessop, T. E., eds., *The Works of George Berkeley, Bishop of Cloyne*, 9 Vols. London and New York, 1948–1957. The Introduction and Notes in this definitive edition are of great value.

MAIN THEMES OF BERKELEY'S PHILOSOPHY

Hicks, G. Dawes, *Berkeley.* London, 1932.

Wild, J., *George Berkeley. A Study of His Life and Philosophy.* New York, 1936, 1962.

Warnock, G. J., *Berkeley.* London, 1953.

Leroy, A.-L., *George Berkeley.* Paris, 1959.

THE NEW THEORY OF VISION

Bailey, S., *A Review of Berkeley's Theory of Vision.* London, 1842.

Abbot, T. K., *Sight and Touch.* London, 1864.

Turbayne, C. M., "Berkeley and Molyneux on Retinal Images." *Journal of the History of Ideas*, Vol. 16 (1955).

Armstrong, D. M., *Berkeley's Theory of Vision.* Melbourne, 1960.

Vesey, G. N. A., "Berkeley and the Man Born Blind." *PAS*, Vol. 61 (1960–1961).

ARGUMENTS FOR IMMATERIALISM

Moore, G. E., "Refutation of Idealism," in *Philosophical Studies.* London, 1922.

Laird, J., "Berkeley's Realism." *Mind,* N. S. Vol. 25 (1916), pp. 308 ff.
Luce, A. A., "Berkeley's Existence in the Mind." *Mind,* N. S., Vol. 50 (1941), pp. 258 ff.
Luce, A. A., "The Berkeleyan Idea of Sense." *PAS,* Supplementary Vol. 27 (1953).
Broad, C. D., "Berkeley's Denial of Material Substance." *Philosophical Review,* Vol. 43 (1954).
Mates, Benson, "Berkeley Was Right," in *George Berkeley, Lectures Delivered Before the University of California.* Berkeley and Los Angeles, 1957.
Sullivan, Celestine J., "Berkeley's Attack on Matter," *Ibid.*
Bracken, H. M., "Berkeley's Realism." *The Philosophical Quarterly,* Vol. 8 (1958).

METAPHYSICS AND THEOLOGY

Luce, A. A., *Berkeley and Malebranche.* London, 1934.
Fritz, Anita D., "Berkeley and the Immaterialism of Malebranche." *Review of Metaphysics,* Vol. 3 (1949–1950).
Gueroult, M., *Berkeley. Quatre études sur la perception et sur Dieu.* Paris, 1956.
Sillem, E. A., *George Berkeley and the Proofs for the Existence of God.* London and New York, 1957.
Bracken, H. M., "Berkeley on the Immortality of the Soul." *The Modern Schoolman,* Vol. 38 (1960–1961).
Myerscough, Angelita, "Berkeley and the Proofs for the Existence of God," in J. K. Ryan, ed., *Philosophy and the History of Philosophy,* Vol 1. Washington, 1961.
Davis, J. W., "Berkeley and Phenomenalism." *Dialogue. Canadian Philosophical Review,* Vol. 1 (1962–1963), 67–80.

PHILOSOPHY OF NATURE
AND PHILOSOPHY OF MATHEMATICS

Mach, Ernst, *The Analysis of Sensations.* Chicago, 1914.
Whitrow, G. J., "Berkeley's Critique of the Newtonian Analysis of Motion." *Hermathena,* Vol. 82 (1953).
Wisdom, J. O., "Berkeley's Criticism of the Infinitesimal." *British Journal for the Philosophy of Science,* Vol. 3 (1953–1954).
Whitrow, G. J., "Berkeley's Philosophy of Motion." *Ibid.*
Popper, K. R., "A Note on Berkeley as Precursor of Mach." *Ibid.*
Myhill, John, "Berkeley's *De Motu*—An Anticipation of Mach," in *George Berkeley, Lectures Delivered Before the University of California.* Berkeley and Los Angeles, 1957.
Strong, Edward W., "Mathematical Reasoning and Its Object," *Ibid.*

H. B. ACTON

BERNARD, CLAUDE (1813–1878), French physiologist, was born in Saint-Julien (Rhône). He received his M.D. in 1843 and became a professor at the Sorbonne in 1852, taking the new chair in physiology in 1854. The following year he was appointed professor of experimental medicine at the Collège de France and in 1868 professor of general physiology at the Museum of Natural History in Paris. He was elected a member of the Academy of Sciences in 1854 and of the Académie Française in 1868; in 1869 he became a senator.

Bernard early gave up any idea of clinical practice in favor of experimental physiology. He made a number of important contributions in this field (on the chemistry of digestion, the production of sugar in animals, the nervous system, poisons, and anesthetics), many of which were awarded scientific prizes. After a period of ill health, while not ceasing laboratory work, he turned to more general and programmatic questions of scientific method and published, in particular, his famous *Introduction à l'étude de la médecine expérimentale* (Paris, 1865; translated by H. C. Green as *An Introduction to the Study of Experimental Medicine,* New York, 1927).

In the *Introduction,* Bernard based his conclusions as much as possible on his own scientific experiences, since he believed that proper procedure cannot be legislated for scientists from without but must be developed from the nature and needs of science itself. He distinguished the mature experimental method from empiricism, which is merely its first step. Bernard identified crude empiricism, which observes and experiments at random, not only with his own teacher, François Magendie, but also, mistakenly, with Francis Bacon, regarding himself rather in the tradition of Descartes, despite the fact that he insisted on constant laboratory experimentation and criticism and had a low opinion of the application of mathematics to biological problems. His hostility to the use of statistical methods in biology derived from the one article of faith he regarded as necessary to any scientist: belief in the operation of a determinism without exceptions, such that a set of conditions (a cause) will invariably produce the same phenomenon (an effect). This determinism he called an absolute principle, in contrast to theories and hypotheses, which are always provisional and subject to revision or abandonment because of the discovery of incompatible facts. But theories and hypotheses, the products of human reason, are on the other hand the necessary guides for rational experimentation.

Bernard saw no difference in principle between scientific method as applied to living beings and to inorganic matter, although results were more difficult to achieve in physiology because of the far greater complexity of the phenomena. He believed in a fundamental unity among all forms of life, the higher forms being distinguished by their greater independence of the external environment and a correspondingly greater dependence on their "internal environment" (above all, the blood). He also held that the phenomena taking place in living beings are ultimately reducible to physicochemical processes. Efforts to enlist Bernard in the cause of vitalism are wide of the mark. Equally mistaken is the attempt to affix a positivist label. He strenuously advocated scientific doubt and self-criticism, and was opposed to all philosophical systems, including the positivist, while not denying the usefulness of the work of philosophers in their own sphere. Bernard's critical method was closer to twentieth-century methods based on the principle of falsifiability, used by Karl Popper and others, than to those of many of his contemporaries.

Bibliography

Bernard's general works also include *La Science expérimentale* (Paris, 1878) and *Principes de médecine expérimentale* (Paris, 1947).

For works on Bernard, consult J. M. D. Olmsted and E. H. Olmsted, *Claude Bernard and the Experimental Method in Medicine* (New York, 1952); Robert Clarke, *Claude Bernard et la médecine expérimentale* (Paris, 1961); and Paul Foulquié, *Claude Bernard* (Paris, n.d.).

W. M. SIMON

BERNARD OF CHARTRES (died c. 1124–1130), a Breton and elder brother of Theodoric of Chartres, was a master at Chartres at periods during the second and third decades of the twelfth century and became chancellor at least by 1119. He is no longer to be confused with Bernard Silvestris of Tours. To Bernard of Chartres belongs much of the credit for bringing the intellectual life of Chartres to its apogee, and his pupils included Gilbert of Poitiers, William of Conches, and Richard the Bishop. No complete writing by Bernard has survived, although he is known to have written philosophical verse and to have expounded Porphyry's *Isagoge*. However, John of Salisbury learned of the character of Bernard's literary and philosophical teaching through William and Richard, and in John's writings we find a sympathetic portrait of Bernard as a real lover of learning and a leading grammarian, the most abounding spring of letters and the most finished Platonist of those days. John eulogizes the "old Chartrain" as an excellent teacher of Latin language and literature, whose aim was to produce well-lettered and well-spoken students by means of an unhurried, cultured, humanist education, firmly based upon a groundwork of grammar. Bernard's love of the ancients was expressed in a famous simile of the moderns as dwarfs who can see farther than the ancients because they are perched upon the shoulders of giants.

Bernard was a philosopher with a taste for speculative grammar and for Platonism. He held opinions which the more Aristotelian John did not entirely share. We know only one of Bernard's grammatical speculations, namely, that the relationship of a quality-word (e.g., whiteness) to its derivatives (e.g., to whiten, white) resembles the relationship of the Platonic Ideas to the things in which they participate. As a Platonist, Bernard held that true reality is found in the eternal Ideas, which are the models of all perishable things. Particular sensible things, being unstable and ephemeral, cannot properly be said to be. Bernard's contribution to the disputes of his time over the nature of universals was to equate universals with Ideas; hence universals, in his view, were real beings. Guided by Boethius, Bernard and his school also labored to reconcile the differences between Plato and Aristotle.

Under the influence of the ninth-century thinker John Scotus Erigena, Bernard also sought to reconcile the teaching of Plato's *Timaeus* with that of the Bible by reexamining the relationships between the three categories of true being: God, matter, and the Ideas. He adhered to patristic teaching in accepting the view that matter was created by God. He also held that the eternal Ideas are in some way posterior to God. The Ideas are assimilated with God's mind or the divine providence; but although they are immanent in the mind of God, they are also a created effect. They are eternal, but not, in Bernard's view, coeternal with God. Only the three persons of the Trinity are both coequal and coeternal.

On the other hand, Bernard also attempted to show that the Ideas were not directly mixed with sensible objects. He distinguished between Ideas which subsist in the mind of God and the copies of these Ideas which are concreated with matter. To the latter Ideas he gave, under Boethian influence, the name of native forms (*formae nativae*).

Essentially, Bernard sought to affirm the transcendence of God over the Ideas and to avoid pantheism by the theory of native forms, which allowed no confusion of God with creation. Insofar as we can judge his motives, Bernard was adapting the Platonism that he knew to Christianity, just as he modified this Platonism in the light of Aristotelianism. His teaching was promoted by other Chartrains, especially by Gilbert of Poitiers.

Bibliography

PRIMARY SOURCES

John of Salisbury, *Metalogicon*, C. Webb, ed. Oxford, 1929. I, v, xi, xxiv; II, xvii; III, ii; IV, xxv. Translated under the same title by D. D. McGarry, Berkeley, 1955.

John of Salisbury, *Policraticus*, C. Webb, ed. Oxford, 1909. VII, 13.

Otto of Freising, *Gesta Friderici*, G. Waitz, ed., 3d ed. Hanover, 1912. I, xlvii; lii.

SECONDARY SOURCES

Clerval, A., *Les Écoles de Chartres au moyen âge*. Paris, 1895. Pp. 158–163.

Gilson, É., "Le Platonisme de Bernard de Chartres." *Revue néo-scolastique de philosophie*, Vol. 25 (1923), 5–19.

Gilson, É., *History of Christian Philosophy in the Middle Ages*. London, 1955, Pp. 619–620.

Gregory, T., *Anima Mundi. La filosofia di Guglielmo di Conches*. Florence, 1955. Pp. 76–79.

Parent, J., *La Doctrine de la création dans l'école de Chartres*. Paris and Ottawa, 1938. Pp. 45–48, 84–85.

Poole, R. L., *Illustrations of the History of Medieval Thought*, 2d ed. London, 1920. Pp. 100–107.

(See also CHARTRES, SCHOOL OF.)

DAVID LUSCOMBE

BERNARD OF CLAIRVAUX, ST. (1090–1153), monastic reformer and theologian, was born of a noble family at Fontaine, France, near Dijon. He became a Cistercian at Cîteaux in 1112 and founding abbot of Clairvaux in 1115. Throughout his life he was a tireless founder, reformer, preacher, and writer who, as friend or opponent, made contact with almost every notable in western Europe. His influence as a simple abbot on high ecclesiastical affairs is without parallel in the history of the Western church, and his spiritual teaching has been a living force to the present day. Though he was a professed enemy of secular culture (he "raided" the schools of Paris on a celebrated occasion in 1140) and was lacking in scholastic training, Bernard was a literary genius of the first order, and no mean theologian. His treatises *De Diligendo Deo* ("On the Love of God," 1126) and *De Gratia et Libero Arbitrio* ("On Grace and Free Will," 1127), though based on St. Augustine, also show the influence of Origen, Gregory of Nyssa and the pseudo-Dionysius, as do also some of his longer letters. In the history of thought he is remembered for his controversies with Abelard and Gilbert de La Porrée. He distrusted contemporary dialectic, partly because of a justified apprehension of the dangers in the formulas of both his opponents, but most of all because his approach to theological truth was by way of meditation and intuitive penetration, whereas theirs was by way of logical expression and analysis. His influence restrained theological improvisation and methodical virtuosity, and left the field clear for the great scholastics of the next century.

His most valuable contribution to thought was in the realm of mystical theology. He was a medieval pioneer of the analysis and explanation of mystical experience. His teaching, ostensibly based on St. Augustine, was in many respects new, and was followed by that of the Victorines and others, though later rivaled and eclipsed by the Dionysian–Thomist school of Rhineland Dominicans. Bernard's mysticism was one of love. Man, by recognizing his own nothingness, turns to God with humility and love, and man's will, with divine help, can reach perfect accord with the divine will. The divine Word can then teach him (infused knowledge) and move him (infused love) in an intimate union sometimes momentarily experienced as ecstasy. Thus Bernard differs, in expression at least, from the intellectual mysticism of Neoplatonism reflected in both Augustine and Dionysius. In his *Sermons on the Canticle*, Bernard was also a pioneer in the clear description of his own mystical experience, which in many ways resembled that of St. Teresa of Ávila.

Bibliography

Works by Bernard are to be found in *Patrologiae Cursus Completus, Series Latina*, J. P. Migne, ed., Vols. 182–185 (Paris, 1844–1864).

For biography, see E. Vacandard, *Vie de saint Bernard*, 2 vols. (Paris, 1895), often reprinted. Also useful are articles on Bernard by E. Vacandard in *Dictionnaire de théologie catholique* (Paris, 1910) and by J. Canivez in *Dictionnaire d'histoire et de géographie écclesiastique* (Paris, 1935).

For Bernard's contribution to mystical theology, see Étienne Gilson, *Théologie mystique de saint Bernard* (Paris, 1934), translated by A. H. C. Downes as *The Mystical Theology of Saint Bernard* (London, 1940); C. Butler, *Western Mysticism: The Teaching of SS. Augustine, Gregory and Bernard on Contemplation and the Contemplative Life*, 2d. ed. (London, 1951). Dom J. Leclercq is preparing a critical edition of St. Bernard's works.

David Knowles

BERNARD OF TOURS (d. after 1167), was a humanist who taught at Tours and was known as Bernardus Silvestris. He is uncertainly identified with Bernard, chancellor of Chartres circa 1156 and bishop of Quimper from 1159 to 1167. Very little else is known of his life except that he taught the art of writing and wrote an *Ars Versificatoria*, which has not been found. He also wrote a moralizing allegorical commentary on part of Vergil's *Aeneid* which displays leanings toward a naturalistic ethic. He translated into Latin an Arabic treatise on geomancy, the *Experimentarius*, and, inspired by Quintilian, composed the *Mathematicus*, a poem about an astrological prediction.

His most famous work, dedicated to Theodoric of Chartres in about 1150, is the *De Mundi Universitate*, an allegory in prose and verse on the origin of the world and man. The theme is Nature's appeal to Nous (mind), the providence of God, to end the chaos of *hylē* (matter), the primordial matter of the megacosmos. In Nous exist the exemplary forms of creation. Nous separates four elements out of *hylē* and informs the world with a soul ("entelechy," the Aristotelian εντελεχια). Nous next sends Nature to find Urania and Physis. Urania, queen of the stars, and Physis, in the lower world, use the remains of the four elements, in collaboration with Nature, to form man (the microcosmos). The sources of Bernard's inspiration were the Latin version of Plato's *Timaeus* with the commentary of Chalcidius, and also Ovid, Claudian, Macrobius, Boethius, and Augustine. There is, in addition, a marked Biblical and a Hermetic influence.

The humanism of this work is more profane than Christian; the world is that of the *Timaeus* rather than that of *Genesis*. But the paganism, even unorthodoxy, of Bernard should not be exaggerated. Thus, Bernard was silent about a divine creation of matter, but his concern was to depict the organization of matter into the universe. There is no consistent dualism of God and matter; *hylē* is pre-existent to the ordering work of Nous, but the problem of its eternity is not broached. One should not conclude from the emanation of a world soul from Nous that Bernard was a pantheist. We cannot, in fact, extract from this often nebulous work a unified view of Bernard's thought. Bernard's purpose was imaginative rather than strictly philosophical. Nonetheless, Bernard reflects the speculative interests of his time, particularly those of the Chartrains; he reflects their desire for a more rational explanation of the universe and of Biblical cosmology with the aid of Greek ideas.

Works by Bernard of Tours

Commentum Super Sex Libros Eneidos, G. Riedel, ed. Greifswald, 1924.

De Mundi Universitate, C. S. Barach and J. Wrobel, eds. Innsbruck, 1876.

"Experimentarius," M. B. Savorelli, ed. *Rivista critica di storia di filosofia*, Vol. 14 (1959), 283–342.

Mathematicus, B. Hauréau, ed. Paris, 1895.

Works on Bernard of Tours

Curtius, E. R., *European Literature and the Latin Middle Ages*. London, 1953. Pp. 108–113. Translated from the German edition of 1948 by W. R. Trask.

Faral, E., "Le Manuscrit 511 du Hunterian Museum." *Studi medioevali*, n. s. Vol. 9 (1936), 69–88.

Gilson, E., "La Cosmogonie de Bernardus Silvestris." *Archives d'histoire doctrinale et littéraire du moyen âge*, Vol. 3 (1928), 5–24.

Gregory, T., *Anima Mundi. La filosofia di Guglielmo di Conches*, Florence, 1955. Pp. 64–67.

Silverstein, T., "The Fabulous Cosmogony of Bernardus Silvestris." *Modern Philology*, Vol. 46 (1948/1949), 92–116.

Thorndike, L., *A History of Magic and Experimental Science*. New York, 1929. Vol. II, pp. 99–123.

(See also Chartres, School of.)

David Luscombe

BERTALANFFY, LUDWIG VON, one of the chief exponents of the "organismic" standpoint in theoretical biology, was born in Austria in 1901 and educated at the universities of Innsbruck and Vienna. Until 1948 he taught at the University of Vienna, first as an instructor and later as professor of biology in the medical school. He emigrated to Canada in 1949 and held academic posts at the University of Ottawa and the University of Alberta, where he was appointed professor of theoretical biology in 1962. Von

Bertalanffy's writings are voluminous, amounting to more than two hundred items. These include scientific papers in such fields as animal growth, cell physiology, experimental embryology, and cancer research. His two best-known books on philosophical biology are *Kritische Theorie der Formbildung* (Berlin, 1928; translated by J. H. Woodger as *Modern Theories of Development*, London, 1933) and *Das biologische Weltbild* (Bern, 1949; translated by the author as *Problems of Life*, New York, 1960). Since 1950 he has been active in promoting an interdisciplinary field called "General System Theory." The society associated with this enterprise has issued several yearbooks.

Von Bertalanffy contends that neither classical mechanism nor vitalism provides an adequate model for understanding organic phenomena. Vitalism is intellectually sterile because it appeals to a mysterious *élan vital*, entelechy, or psychoid to account for the properties of living things. Mechanism, von Bertalanffy declares, involves three mistaken conceptions: (1) the "analytical and summative" conception, according to which the goal of biological inquiry is the analysis of organisms into fundamental units and the explaining of organic properties by a simple adding up of these units; (2) the "machine-theoretical" conception, which regards the basis of vital order as a set of pre-established structures or "mechanisms" of a physicochemical kind; and (3) the "reaction-theoretical" conception, according to which organisms are automata, reacting only when subjected to stimulation and otherwise quiescent. These conceptions, von Bertalanffy argues, cannot yield a well-grounded explanatory theory of life.

In place of them he proposes an organismic model on which such a theory can be built. The model represents organisms as wholes or systems that have unique system properties and conform to irreducible system laws. Organic structures result from a continuous flow of processes combining to produce patterns of immense intricacy. Far from being passive automata, living things are centers of activity with a high degree of autonomy. Biological systems are stratified. There is a hierarchy of levels of organization from living molecules to multicellular individuals and supraindividual aggregates. The whole of nature is "a tremendous architecture in which subordinate systems are united at successive levels into ever higher and larger systems."

Von Bertalanffy seeks to show that this conception illuminates such matters as embryonic development, genetic processes, growth, self-regulation, metabolism, and evolution. Thus, in embryology it is no longer necessary to take sides in the old contest between preformationism and epigenesis, if we adopt the hypothesis that a fertilized ovum is a system whose development is determined by internal system conditions. Similarly, the ostensible purposefulness manifested by this development is an illustration of the unique property of "equifinality," which marks the behavior of organisms as "open" systems. These systems differ in important respects from the closed systems dealt with by physics. The thermodynamic principles that apply to the two cases are by no means the same. However, von Bertalanffy believes that "there are general principles holding for all systems, irrespective of their component elements and of the relations or forces between them." These principles, he thinks, can be studied through General System Theory, whose function is to bring about the unity of science.

The organismic conception of life is presented by its author as an intellectual breakthrough that "may well be set beside the great revolutions in human thought." Critics have found this claim extravagant in view of the sketchy and programmatic character of von Bertalanffy's presentation. They contend that the organismic conception has no right to be called "revolutionary" until its merits have been shown in detailed and extensive biological analysis. Nevertheless, von Bertalanffy has called attention to issues of major importance for the future of theoretical biology.

Additional Works by Bertalanffy

"An Outline of General System Theory." *British Journal for the Philosophy of Science*, Vol. 1 (1950), 134-165.

"Problems of General System Theory," *Human Biology*, Vol. 23 (1951), 302-311.

Bertalanffy, Ludwig von, and Rapoport, A., eds., *General Systems Yearbook*. Published yearly since 1956.

Works on Bertalanffy

Buck, R. C., "On the Logic of General Behavior Systems Theory," in *Minnesota Studies in the Philosophy of Science*, H. Feigl and M. Scriven, eds. Minneapolis, 1956. Vol. I, pp. 223-238.

Hempel, Carl G., "General System Theory and the Unity of Science." *Human Biology*, Vol. 23 (1951), 313-327.

Jonas, Hans, "Comment on General System Theory." *Human Biology*, Vol. 23 (1951), 328-335.

Medawar, P. B., review of *Problems of Life*. *Mind*, Vol. 43 (1954), 105-108.

T. A. GOUDGE

BIBLIOGRAPHIES OF PHILOSOPHY. See PHILOSOPHICAL BIBLIOGRAPHIES.

BIEL, GABRIEL (c.1410-1495), Ockhamist philosopher and theologian, was born at Speyer, Germany, and died at Einsiedel (Schönbuch). He studied philosophy and theology at Heidelberg and Erfurt, joined the Brethren of the Common Life, and became a professor of theology (1484) at the newly founded University of Tübingen, where he taught the "modern way," that is, according to the nominalist position of William of Ockham. Biel's "Commentary on the Sentences" (*Epithoma Pariter et Collectorium Circa IV Sententiarum Libros*, Tübingen, 1495) is a skillful summary of Ockham and a collection of the views of other medieval thinkers from Anselm to Duns Scotus. Widely read in the German universities, Biel exerted a strong influence on Martin Luther (see P. Vignaux, *Luther, Commentateur des Sentences*, Paris, 1935).

As a philosopher, Biel was quite ready to criticize and to offer his own developments of Ockham's nominalism. Basically a theory of knowledge, his thought had some influence in ethics and political philosophy. For Biel formal logic displaced metaphysics because he considered universals to be but names (*nomina*) arbitrarily applied to classes; he considered all existents to be completely individual in character. Essence and existence are not really distinct principles in things but are merely distinguished in thought.

Biel's psychology was, like Ockham's, close to Augustinianism: the powers of the soul are not distinct faculties; intellect is the soul understanding, will is the soul desiring and loving. Biel was a psychological voluntarist; for him the most important psychic activity of man was willing. He taught that all man's conscious activities entailed some use of will. Man was viewed as a volitional rather than as a rational animal.

In practical philosophy, he considered moral goodness to consist in volitional conformity to God's will. The obligatory force of law has no basis in the nature of created things but is solely due to the fact that God has willed a certain action to be right. This is moral and legal voluntarism. "God could command that a man deceive another through a lie," wrote Biel, "and he would not sin" (*Epithoma*, II, 38, q. 1, G).

Bibliography

Bonke, E., *Doctrina Nominalistica de Fundamento Ordinis Moralis apud Guillelmum de Ockham et Gabriel Biel*. Rome, 1944. Pp. 57–83.

Davitt, T., *The Nature of Law*. St. Louis, 1951. Pp. 55–68.

Feckes, C., *Die Rechtfertigungslehre des Gabriel Biel und ihre Stellung innerhalb der nominalistischen Schule*. Münster, 1925.

VERNON J. BOURKE

BILFINGER, GEORG BERNHARD (1693–1750), German philosopher who coined the expression Leibniz–Wolffian philosophy for the view he expounded. Bilfinger, whose family name was also spelled Buelffinger, was born in Kannstadt, Württemberg. He studied theology at Tübingen, and mathematics and philosophy at Halle under Christian Wolff. He was appointed extraordinary professor of philosophy at Tübingen in 1721, but after Wolff's expulsion from Halle in 1723, Bilfinger was accused of atheism and deprived of his positions. On Wolff's recommendation he was appointed professor of philosophy and academician in St. Petersburg. His growing reputation as a natural philosopher caused Duke Eberhard Ludwig of Württemberg to recall him to Tübingen as professor of theology. In 1735 the new Duke Karl Alexander of Württemberg called Bilfinger to his capital, Stuttgart, as a member of the privy council. Bilfinger became president of the Consistorium, a council for ecclesiastical and educational affairs, and in this capacity permitted Pietism to be taught in Württemberg.

Although Bilfinger's doctrines are quite close to Wolff's, he showed a certain originality, discussing Wolff's doctrines critically and frequently accepting them only with reservations. In an early work he held, against Locke, the view that there are innate ideas in the human mind, identifying them with axioms. In psychology he did not accept the distinction, introduced by Wolff, between empirical and rational psychology, but proceeded in a more traditional manner. In his later writings, Bilfinger referred less frequently to Wolff.

The most independent part of Bilfinger's system was his theory of possibility, expounded in his main work, *Dilucidationes Philosophicae de Deo, Anima Humana, Mundo et Generabilis Rerum Affectionibus* (Tübingen, 1725). He asserted that the notion of possibility is more fundamental than the principles of identity and contradiction. Possible things are not absolute beings in an independent realm of ideas, but they depend for their existence on God's understanding (not on his will). It is a part of God's essence to think possible things as they are, but they are, only insofar as God thinks them.

Additional Works by Bilfinger

De Harmonia Animi et Corporis Humani Maxime Praestabilita ex Mente Illustris Leibnitii, Commentario Hypothetica. Frankfurt and Leipzig, 1723.

"De Viribus Corpori Moto Insitis et Illarum Mensura." *Commentarii Academiae Petropolitanae*, Vol. 1 (1728). A famous essay on the measurement of forces.

Praecepta Logica, C. F. Vellnagel, ed. Jena, 1739.

Varia in Fasciculos Collecta, 3 vols. Stuttgart, 1743.

Works on Bilfinger

Kapff, P., "G. B. Bilfinger als Philosoph." *Württembergischen Vierteljahrshefte für Landesgeschichte*, N. F. (1905).

Liebing, H., *Zwischen Orthodoxie und Aufklärung. Das philosophische und theologische Denken G. B. Bilfingers*. Tübingen, 1961.

Wahl, Richard, "Professor Bilfingers Monadologie und prästabilirte Harmonie in ihrem Verhältniss zu Leibnitz und Wolff." *Zeitschrift für Philosophie und philosophische Kritik*, Vol. 85 (1884), 66–92 and 202–231.

GIORGIO TONELLI

BINET, ALFRED (1857–1911), French psychologist, was born at Nice. The son of a doctor and an artist, Binet studied at the Sorbonne, qualifying in 1878 in both law and science. He embarked immediately on a doctorate under Edouard Balbiani, embryologist and professor at the Collège de France, whose daughter Binet married in 1884. In the same year he submitted an article on the fusion of images to *La Revue philosophique*. The editor, Théodule Ribot, persuaded him in due course to devote his energies to psychology. Through Charles Féré, Binet came to work with Jean Charcot at the Salpêtrière hospital.

Binet is known mainly for his work, with his younger colleague Théodore Simon, in devising tests for assessing children's intelligence. The Binet–Simon scale, published in 1905 and revised in 1908 and 1911, constituted the first systematic, effective, and widely accepted attempt to devise sets of simple verbal and nonverbal tasks, performance on which could be quantified with a fair degree of objectivity, and on which norms for different age groups in the school population were carefully worked out. The principal American versions were produced, revised, and restandardized by L. M. Terman and his colleagues at Stanford University in 1916 and 1937. It was, however, Binet's and Simon's careful studies that showed the necessity of valid data to ascertain the intellectual skills and concepts normally to be expected of children at each age before any assessment of a child's retardation can fairly be made. The revised tests are still employed for research and clinical purposes, although increasing use is now being made of the Wechsler tests.

Binet himself was well aware that cultural factors have a bearing on test performance and that interestingly different patterns of results on various subtests might be shown by children achieving similar over-all scores. Hence, the conception of an intelligence quotient (IQ) as

$$\frac{\text{mental age}}{\text{chronological age}} \times 100$$

although popularly linked with Binet's name, in fact runs counter to his stress on studying and appreciating individual differences.

The practical utility of the Binet–Simon scale has overshadowed to a large extent the rich background of inquiries from which the tests were developed. A man of wide theoretical and practical interests, Binet wrote in lucid and lively French a dozen books and some 250 articles, many of which appeared in *La Revue philosophique* and in *L'Année psychologique*, of which he was the editor. Seven of his books and a few articles appeared in English, which Binet wrote and spoke fluently. The *Psychologie des grands calculateurs et joueurs d'échec* (Paris, 1894), and *L'Étude expérimentale de l'intelligence* (Paris, 1903), the latter reporting studies of his own children, remain neglected classics of French psychology. Both works provided evidence of individual differences in imagery and evidence that images could be less important in thinking than the associationists supposed. Furthermore, these studies, especially the former, showed that the subsequent line of thought was affected by the nature and presentation of the problem a thinker was asked to solve, by the mental set induced by that problem, and by his attitudes in other respects. The studies of his young daughters illustrate Binet's patient, systematic mode of inquiry into children's thought processes, and they enhance understanding of the developmental approach to psychology to which Piaget was the heir.

Chronological scrutiny of his writing shows Binet's work on intelligence to have been the practical outcome of prolonged theoretical and experimental study of the nature of thought processes—subnormal, normal, outstanding, and abnormal. These investigations were carried out in hospitals, notably the Salpêtrière, in schools, and in the psychological laboratory at the Sorbonne, of which Binet became director. Influenced by Hippolyte Taine in France and by the British empirical tradition (including J. S. Mill, Alexander Bain, and Francis Galton), Binet had started as a narrowly orthodox associationist. His evidence for conceptual processes not involving visual imagery anticipated some of the Würzburg experimental findings on "imageless thought." This evidence and that found by Binet and his collaborators for central factors, for unconscious processes, and for attitudes influencing a train of thought led Binet slowly to change his standpoint. In doing so, he moved from treating thinking by analogy with visual inspection to emphasizing the affinities of thought and action and to stressing the importance of developmental studies. Such an approach has proved more acceptable in the 1960s than when Binet died, unfortunately leaving his own research and theory incomplete.

Works by Binet

"Mental Imagery." *The Fortnightly Review*, Vol. 52 (1892), 95–104.

"The Mechanism of Thought." *The Fortnightly Review*, Vol. 55 (1894), 785–799. Except for this and the preceding reference, all of Binet's works are listed in the Varon monograph (see below).

"L'Intelligence des imbéciles." *L'Année psychologique*, Vol. 15 (1909), 1–147. Written with Théodore Simon. This and the following article are of salient importance for understanding Binet's later treatment of thinking.

"Qu'est ce qu'une émotion? Qu'est ce qu'un acte intellectuel?" *L'Année psychologique*, Vol. 17 (1911), 1–47.

Works on Binet

Bertrand, F. L., *Alfred Binet et son oeuvre*. Paris, 1930.

Groot, A. D. de, *Thought and Choice in Chess*. The Hague, 1965.

Reeves, Joan Wynn, *Thinking about Thinking*. London, 1965. Ch. 7.

Varon, Edith J., *The Development of Alfred Binet's Psychology*. *Psychological Monographs*, 1934–1935, Vol. 46 (No. 207). Includes a full bibliography of Binet's works except for the first two cited above.

Wolf, Theta A., "An Individual Who Made a Difference." *American Psychologist*, Vol. 16, No. 5 (1961), 245–248.

JOAN WYNN REEVES

BINSWANGER, LUDWIG, Swiss psychiatrist whose school of *Daseinsanalyse*, or existential analysis, is the most extensive attempt to relate the philosophies of Edmund Husserl and Martin Heidegger to the field of psychiatry. He was born in Kreuzlingen, Thurgau, Switzerland, in 1881 into a family line of eminent physicians and psychiatrists. After attending the universities of Lausanne, Heidelberg, and Zurich, he received his medical degree from Zurich in 1907. In 1910 he succeeded his father, Dr. Robert Binswanger, as chief medical director of the Sanitorium Bellevue, an institution founded by his grandfather at Kreuzlingen. He relinquished his directorship in 1956.

Daseinsanalyse is an original amalgam of phenomenology, Heideggerean existentialism, and psychoanalysis, the goal of which is to counter the tendency of scientific psychology to view man's being as solely that of a natural object. However, the school does not seek spheres of human existence that argue against the explanatory power of psychoanalysis. Binswanger complained of the overreductionism of natural science as applied to man, but in doing so he was not questioning science's ability to explain; he was, rather, urging that that which is being explained be kept in mind in its full phenomenal reality. Binswanger is a phenomenologist in that he demands a presuppositionless discipline in which the investigator can apprehend the world of the patient as it is experienced by the patient. To this end he limits his analysis to that which is actually present (or immanent) in the patient's consciousness. He seeks the essential structure of these phenomena without relying on reductive theory, his aim being to allow the phenomena to speak for themselves. As an existentialist he views the essential structures that the phenomena reveal on their own terms as "universals with power." That is, he sees them as the matrix within which the individual's world and self—his essence—are determined. He seeks in each patient a general context of meaning within which the patient exists. He calls this meaning-context the transcendental category of that patient's world design.

This notion of a general existential meaning-context must be understood as that which expresses with equal validity all aspects of the patient's life and world. The criterion of a complete expression is based on Heidegger's ontology of man and includes his orientation in space, his mode of being in time, his relation to his bodily life and to his fellow man, his way of thinking, and his fears and anxieties. For example, a universal such as continuity is equally understandable and expressive in reference to time (continuity of events versus the sudden and unexpected), space (contiguity), relationships with others (for example, oedipal ties or bonds), and the individual's own world ("inner" continuity, continuity of feelings or of affections). But such explanatory categories as aggression or libidinal energy emphasize one aspect of man's being as most real and are therefore rooted in a one-sided ontology of human existence.

What psychoanalysis takes as conditioning factors—such as instinct or childhood sensations—are regarded by Binswanger as already being representations of a basic world design. It is not that Binswanger wants to push back the causal chain beyond instincts or childhood sensations, but rather that the causal chain itself, as described in scientific depth analysis, must be viewed as a whole, without any a priori privileged reference point in terms of which all else is to be explained. Explanation in terms of a privileged reference point presupposes a theory, and a theory assumes a world outlook—in this case the world outlook of natural science. Binswanger does not, therefore, use the past to account for the present. He sees the past of a patient as existing in the present in that the entire world design—within which a particular event in the past "conditioned" a present neurosis—*is* the patient. Therefore, the present, or the conscious, or the manifest content of dreams and the manifest verbal expressions, all point to a unity or category(ies) that is the basis of the patient's world. In other words, because the self cannot experience a "pure" event outside of a meaning-context, even if the self be that of a child, it is that source meaning-context which Binswanger seeks to apprehend.

Binswanger does not offer his approach as a substitute for psychoanalysis; insofar as the goal of psychiatry is intervention in the patient's life—manipulation of or change in it—only a scientific approach, such as psychoanalysis or clinical psychiatry, is adequate. For Binswanger, phenomenology and reductive explanation are two complementary aspects of the *Geisteswissenschaften*, including psychology. Phenomenology can provide us with an essential description of the data, and phenomenological existentialism can provide a full dynamic understanding of the individual's life on his own terms. But if we are willing and find it necessary to transform and control phenomena, natural science is at present our major tool. However, whereas in the natural sciences we confer meanings, in the *Geisteswissenschaften* the phenomena under investigation are themselves meanings to a self, and it becomes necessary phenomenologically to receive these meanings on their own terms.

Bibliography

PRINCIPAL WORKS BY BINSWANGER

Wandlung in der Auffassung und Deutung des Traumes von der Griechen bis zur Gegenwart ("Changes in Understanding and Interpretation of the Dream From the Greeks to the Present"). Berlin, 1928.

Über Ideenflucht ("On the Flight of Ideas"). Zurich, 1933.

Einführung in die Probleme der allgemeinen Psychologie ("Introduction to the Problems of General Psychology"). Berlin, 1942.

Grundformen und Erkenntnis menschlichen Daseins ("Basic Forms and Cognition of Human Existence"). Zurich, 1942; 2d rev. ed., Zurich, 1953.

Ausgewählte Vorträge und Aufsätze ("Selected Lectures and Essays"), 2 vols. Bern, 1947–1955.

Drei Formen Missglückten Daseins ("Three Forms of Unsuccessful Dasein"). Tübingen, 1956.

Schizophrenie. Pfullingen, 1957. Contains Binswanger's well-known clinical studies of Ilse, Ellen West, Jürg Zünd, Lola Voss, and Suzanne Urban.

Melancholie und Manie. Pfullingen, 1960.

ENGLISH TRANSLATIONS

May, Rollo; Angel, Ernest; and Ellenberger, Henri F., eds., *Existence.* New York, 1958. This and the following work contain some of Binswanger's works in translation.

Needleman, Jacob, *Being-in-the-World.* New York, 1963.

WORKS ON BINSWANGER

Needleman, Jacob, *Being-in-the-World.* New York, 1963. A philosophical critique of Freud and Binswanger, taking account of the background of Kant and Heidegger.

Sonnemann, Ulrich, *Existence and Therapy.* New York, 1954. Brilliant and unreadable.

Van Den Berg, J. H., *The Phenomenological Approach to Psychiatry.* Springfield, Ill., and Oxford, 1955. Simple and clear.

JACOB NEEDLEMAN

BIOLOGY in the largest sense refers to any systematic study of living organisms, including their history, structure, functions, manner of life, heredity, reproduction, and development. In this sense paleontology, histology, physiology, and embryology are counted as branches of biology. In a narrower sense, the term is restricted to the manner of life of organisms and to its study. It is customary to refer to the biology of a group, in contrast to its evolutionary history, genetics, comparative morphology, and so on. In this sense the study of biology is the study of ecology, together with whatever facts concerning structure and physiology that have an immediate bearing on ecology.

There is no general agreement on the precise boundaries of the science of biology in either sense. This is due, in part, to the fact that there is no agreement on what is a living organism. The various criteria that have been suggested for distinguishing the living from the nonliving—for example, the powers of self-replication, self-regulation, and self-repair—have been eroded by the construction, either actually or theoretically, of evidently nonliving machines that possess these properties and by the discovery of natural systems—various viruses, cellular structures, and macromolecules—that possess some of these properties but otherwise seem to be nonliving. However, biologists are not disturbed by the lack of a definition of "living"; and it is difficult to discern much philosophical interest in the question.

The border line of biology is obscured by other factors, the relevance to biology of the physical sciences and the relevance of biology to psychology. When the physical aspects of an ostensibly biological question are so large as virtually to absorb it, there is no conventional way to decide whether the question belongs to the physical or biological sciences. An example would be the way in which the genetic code is embodied in the chromosome—a problem that only a chemist could handle. A similar indeterminacy as to biology or psychology concerns such questions as the operation of animal instinct.

We may distinguish three ways in which philosophy and biology bear upon each other. First, biology, like all the sciences, has in the past been heavily influenced by metaphysical, theological, and methodological theories. This influence is perhaps easier to see in the case of biology than in the physical sciences. Any biological treatise written prior to the nineteenth century is saturated with philosophical thought—not merely as incidental philosophizing, but as an influential factor in the choice, formulation, and treatment of problems. No doubt the reason why later works seem to us less influenced by philosophy lies in the greater difficulty in discerning the operation of our own philosophical views.

Second, biology, again like all the sciences, has influenced philosophy, especially metaphysics and the theory of knowledge: It has been maintained that Aristotle's metaphysics is an ontological embryology. In the nineteenth and twentieth centuries biology has inspired and informed a number of political philosophies (such as social Darwinism and the fascism of Mussolini's philosophical apologists) and metaphysical systems (such as those of Bergson, Whitehead, and, to a lesser degree, Dewey).

Finally, biology presents to philosophy a number of special issues that call for philosophical treatment. The remainder of this article will be concerned with the analysis of some of these issues.

THE AUTONOMY OF BIOLOGY

Most (although not all) of the questions raised by philosophers of science, insofar as they are questions about biology in particular rather than about science in general, are related directly to the issue of autonomy.

It arose historically in the controversies between mechanists on the one hand, and vitalists and organismic biologists on the other, concerning the relations of such organic activities as growth, regulation, and reproduction to the complex physical and chemical processes that undoubtedly go on in living systems. Roughly speaking, the mechanists think that all organic activities are exemplifications of laws, *all* of which are also exemplified in nonliving systems; the vitalists and organismic biologists deny this, although they differ from each other in the accounts they give of characteristically organic systems. The answer to this question has an important implication for methodology. If the mechanists are wrong, then biological theory must be regarded as autonomous with respect to the physical sciences. If, however, the mechanists are right, and if biological activities are reducible to nonbiological ones (an additional assumption), then there seems to be no reason why biology should not ultimately become a branch of the physical sciences.

Among the questions that pertain both to the nature of biology and to the issue of autonomy are the following: (1) Can biological concepts and laws be "reduced," in some sense, to the concepts and laws of physics and chemistry? (2) Does the biologist employ patterns of explanation (for instance, historical or teleological explanation) that are inappropriate in the physical sciences? (3) Do some of the phenomena exhibited by organic systems involve modes of causation (such as final or mnemic causation) not exhibited by inorganic systems? (4) Is the relation of part to whole in organic systems a sort of relation significantly different from any shown by inorganic systems? In assessing the issue of autonomy, it will be necessary to say something about each of these questions. We shall venture to answer "no" to each of them, but at the same time try to do justice to the prima-facie case for the affirmative.

Attitude of biologists. J. H. Woodger's formulation of the issue of autonomy is representative. There is, he argues, a "characteristically biological way of thinking." However, the prestige of the physical sciences, and the tendency of philosophers to regard them as paradigms of scientific reason, have tended to divert the biologist from considering the purely biological features of organic systems and to turn his efforts toward applying to biology the concepts, theories, and explanatory patterns of the physical sciences. Biology has suffered from this tendency. The biologist can, and for some purposes must, consider biological phenomena as exhibiting types of organization not present in inorganic systems; and he must be led by these phenomena, without bias, in developing the intellectual tools for their analysis—an autonomous biology with concepts and laws of its own.

There is no doubt that Woodger is correct in his contention that biologists tend to stand in awe of the physical sciences. Probably most biologists think that the facts of physiology, genetics, morphogenesis, and such are, in an obvious sense, nothing more than complex physicochemical facts. After all, it is argued, there is not the slightest evidence to suppose that there are any components other than the physicochemical ones in an organic system. To suppose otherwise is to step back into vitalist superstition. And—so it seems to follow—since we have only physicochemical components to deal with, physicochemical methods and theories ought, in principle, to be sufficient.

This is only a slight caricature of the prevailing view among biologists—and the exaggerations of the caricature are corrected if we note that most biologists also are sympathetic to the thesis that biology does possess at least a measure of autonomy. None would deny that it is valuable to possess principles—for example, of genetics or ecology—that are not derived from physics or chemistry.

The situation is this: Biologists admit that their science is, in practice, to some extent autonomous; but they are also inclined to believe that any autonomous principles, such as Mendel's laws, are only provisionally autonomous and that, if we only knew enough, they could be shown to be consequences of nonbiological theory. Woodger's view, then, is that too much effort goes into research and theorizing directed toward such possible reduction.

We have been describing in rough fashion a discernible attitude among biologists. We must now conduct a more careful investigation of the autonomy thesis and of the arguments that have been offered for and against it. The concept of autonomy is itself unclear, to say nothing of such concepts as "biological," "reduction," and "teleology," and requires some preliminary clarification.

Kinds of autonomy. It is necessary to draw a distinction between what we may term doctrinal autonomy and ontological autonomy. Suppose that there are two bodies of theory, T_1 and T_2; and let P_1 and P_2 be the phenomena that are described and explained with the help of T_1 and T_2, respectively. The issue of autonomy is raised in biology because, if we construe T_1 as any branch or all of biology, and T_2 as any branch or all of physical theory, the following conditions seem to be satisfied: (1) If T_1 is applicable to any system, S, so also is T_2 (but not vice versa; there are many types of systems to which physical, but not biological, theory is applicable). (2) Even when T_1 is applicable to system S, S may be analyzed into subsystems S'_1, S'_2, etc., to which T_2, but *not* T_1, is applicable.

Doctrinal autonomy. Doctrinal autonomy consists in asserting one or more of the following: (1) T_1 contains concepts not definable in terms of concepts that belong to T_2 (conceptual autonomy); (2) T_1 contains laws not derivable from the laws of T_2, even with the help of principles that coordinate P_1 and P_2 (nomic autonomy); (3) the explanation or analysis of some types of P_1 consists of patterns of propositions that are inapplicable to P_2 (methodological autonomy).

Ontological autonomy. Ontological autonomy is the view that P_2 consists, in part, in a mode of activity that is radically different from any activity shown in P_1. This statement is vague, but the thesis of ontological autonomy is intrinsically a vague one (of course it might, for all that, still be true). What differences can be counted as "radical"? The following suggestions have been made.

(1) Even though T_2 is applicable to system S when T_1 is, nevertheless S cannot be analyzed exhaustively into subsystems that show only P_2. Any such analysis—for instance, the analysis of living organisms into chemical systems—overlooks some system that is causally relevant to the activities of S. This is the doctrine of vitalism.

(2) Even though S can be exhaustively analyzed into subsystems that are definable by means of concepts drawn solely from T_2, these subsystems, in virtue of their place as parts of S, show P_1 as well as P_2 activities. This is the thesis of organismic biology, often expressed in the catch formula "the whole is more than the sum of its parts." This doctrine, which is rather more subtle than its detractors allow, is not merely that a "whole" S shows activities P_1 that are not shown by any of its physical parts. It is a truism, for instance, that a lion courts a lioness, but that no part of a lion, such as his liver, can court a lioness. Rather, when physical parts are so organized into a system, S, that is capable of P_1 activity, the physical parts show activities that are no longer physical—that is, that are no longer instances of the operation of the physical laws of T_2.

(3) Organic systems show goal-directed activities unlike any exhibited by inorganic systems.

Defenders of the doctrine of ontological autonomy are fond of the term "emergence." For our purposes, it is sufficient to note that if any of the above three conditions are satisfied, then the emergence of properties P of a system S, which could not be predicted on the basis of a theory of the subsystems of S, is a reality.

Philosophical concern. From the point of view of philosophical investigation, the thesis of doctrinal autonomy is the more fundamental, for it is clear that ontological autonomy is of no great interest unless it involves some measure of doctrinal autonomy. Some writers have passed, for example, without argument from the assumption of a subject matter that is irreducible to the physical sciences to the conclusion that biology requires methods that are irreducible to the methods of the physical sciences. This inference, without further support, cannot pass muster. A special problem, although it requires a special solution, does not necessarily require a special *method* of solution. For instance, even if organisms were unique in showing goal-directed activity, it would not follow that biology requires a special pattern of teleological explanation.

Moreover, it is difficult—some philosophers would say impossible—to give an intelligible account of ontological autonomy except in terms of doctrinal autonomy. Indeed, most contemporary discussions of autonomy define a strict relation of reducibility and then specify the meaning of "emergence" or "organic whole," for example, as failure to satisfy this relation. Accordingly, we shall direct primary attention to the theses distinguished under the head of doctrinal autonomy.

DOCTRINAL AUTONOMY

Conceptual autonomy. Are there specifically biological concepts? In an uninteresting sense there certainly are. There are many concepts that apply only to biological systems and that are defined in terms of other such concepts, such as "chromosome," "cell," and "predation." It is perhaps worthwhile just to point out that they exist and are legitimate and ubiquitous. Are they definable in terms of nonbiological concepts? There is a difficulty in principle about answering this question one way or the other, since the concept of the nonbiological is just as vague as the concept of the biological; and proof or disproof of possibility is, in general, notoriously subject to pitfalls. However, it is feasible to examine the logic of concepts that are thought to be specifically biological, in order to gain a closer understanding of what would be involved in such definability.

Polytypic concepts. All taxonomists are agreed that no single criterion can allow us to decide whether or not a group of organisms constitutes a species. If one encounters in nature—on an island, let us say—a group of sexually reproducing insects that resemble each other closely, that are quite unlike any other insects in their order, that interbreed freely with others of the group, are infertile when crossed with nonmembers of the group, and are all descendants of a relatively recent homogeneous population that is indistinguishable from them in appearance, then a taxonomist would regard the group as a species. In nature, however, things are not so clear-cut: A group suspected of being a species may be geographically dispersed, asexual or hermaphroditic, intersterile with other members of the group, or fertile in crosses with obviously distinct species. It is clear that each of the conditions for the ideal case is relevant, and that they are representative of the sorts of properties that the biologist actually investigates in determining the applicability of the term "species." However, it is also clear that none of these properties (logically) must be satisfied; that no small subset of them is (logically) sufficient; and that any large subset that is sufficient would seldom or never be encountered. The term "species" is actually applied on the basis of a group's possession of a sufficiently large number of these (and similar) properties. All of the objects to which the term applies will, in Wittgenstein's well-known phrase, bear a "family resemblance" to each other.

Let *K* be the class of all objects to which concept *C* correctly applies. Then we can say that both *K* and *C* are polytypic with respect to a set of properties, *G*, if the following conditions are satisfied: (1) Possession or lack of the properties in *G* constitutes the basis on which *C* is applied. (2) Every member of *K* possesses a significant proportion of the properties in *G*. (3) Every property in *G* is possessed by a significant proportion of the members of *K*. (4) No property in *G* is regarded as logically necessary for membership in *K* (even though it may be an empirical fact that some property in *G* is possessed by all the members of *K*).

For example, we may say that the class of all species, or the concept "species," is polytypic with respect to the set of characteristics that constitutes relevant grounds for regarding a group as a species. Indeed, it seems that such concepts as "life," "animal," "male," "insect," "stomach," and "leaf" are polytypic with respect to the features that we ordinarily regard as defining them. This contention —which, incidentally, would not pass unchallenged by some philosophers—is supported by a logical peculiarity of concepts like "life" and "species": if any single property is suggested as logically necessary, it is easy to construct a real or imaginary case that lacks the property but that nevertheless would be universally regarded as a genuine case. The possibility of this line of argument is indicative of polytypic character.

Now suppose that the species concept, as well as many others, is polytypic with respect to its diagnostic features. How would this be connected with the thesis of conceptual autonomy? It may be noted that when a biologist decides to apply a polytypic concept, he cannot simply consult a textbook definition and compare its specifications with the single object—specimen, group, organ—that he is examining. He must consider the broad pattern of distribution shown by the relevant specifications in an incompletely determined class, and he must make the judgment as to whether or not the object in question possesses a significant proportion of the relevant properties. Moreover, his judgment as to what constitutes a significant proportion is not just a matter of deciding how many of the properties ought to be represented, for in practice some of the properties will admit of degrees and some will carry more weight than others. For example, in the set, *G*, that determines the application of the concept "species," we may count the properties of fertility in crosses within the group, sterility in crosses outside it, and geographical continuity. All of these evidently admit of degrees. The members of a species at one border of its geographical range may be infertile or show reduced fertility when crossed with members at a distant opposite border. Large proportions of a species may be completely sterile (for example, the worker bees). Moreover, fertility and sterility relations carry greater weight than does geographical continuity, the relative weights being suggested, although not rigidly determined, by the reigning theories of species dynamics—especially, in this case, the theory of evolution. Within this theory, fertility plays a relatively essential, and geographical distribution a relatively fortuitous, role.

Finally, we must note that when biological concept *C* is polytypic with respect to *G*, some or all of the properties in *G* may be specified with the help of concepts that are themselves polytypic. And these also in turn may be specified with the help of polytypic concepts, and so on. This state of affairs may appear scandalous to lovers of rigor and exactitude; but we are simply describing, not judging, the conceptual structure of biology. One point relevant in making a judgment should, perhaps, be made now—very exact descriptions may be given with the help of concepts whose meanings can be specified only vaguely.

Polytypic concepts are designed to cover a wide range of cases; for example, the concept of a stomach applies to the stomachs of men, worms, starfishes, and rotifers—stomachs that may differ in virtually every morphological respect. The decision as to how wide a range of dissimilar structures should be regarded as stomachs is dependent upon the use that the biologist intends to make of the concept, and this use depends upon the current state of biological theory.

The meaning of polytypic concepts, we may conclude, is determined by a complex network of relations with other concepts, some polytypic and some not—the whole system being influenced both by the unformalized judgment of biologists and by the state of biological theory. We may, accordingly, make the following points:

(1) If a biological concept, *C*, is polytypic with respect to every set of *physical* properties, *G*, there is a sense in which a thesis of conceptual autonomy is satisfied. If by "definition of *C* in terms of the properties in *G*" one means "specification of a function of the properties in *G* as a logically necessary and sufficient condition for applying *C*," then *C* is not definable in terms drawn from the physical sciences.

(2) A concept that is polytypic with respect to every set of physical properties may nevertheless possess a biological definition. Such a concept clearly warrants the title of "specifically biological."

(3) Concepts that are specifically biological in this sense are controlled in their application by biological, and not physical, theory. They could not (logically) have their meaning specified—in some weaker manner than "definition" in the sense of (1) above—in physical terms unless relevant portions of biological theory were reduced to physical theory.

Functional and historical concepts. Another aspect of some biological concepts is brought to light when we consider the examples "gamete" and "hybrid." These may be termed, respectively, "functional" and "historical" concepts. When we consider the enormous variety of objects that are counted as gametes (reproductive cells), from ostrich eggs to pollen grains, and the variety of organisms that could be hybrids, it is reasonable to conclude that both concepts are polytypic with respect to any set of physical properties. Each concept has a further peculiarity. An object cannot be a gamete unless it performs a particular function in the process of reproduction, and an organism cannot be a hybrid unless it has a certain ancestry. Let us call any concept, *C*, "functional" whenever it is logically necessary that, for the correct application of *C* to object *S*—organ, event, process—there exist a distinct process, *F*, in a distinct object, *S'*, and a set of conditions under which *F* will not occur in the absence of an *S*. When this condition is met, we may say that the function of *S* is to contribute to the performance of *F*. Thus, "gamete" is a functional concept because it is logically impossible for anything to be a gamete unless it so functions in the process of reproduction. Terms with functional definitions are common, both in biology and in everyday speech. Biological examples are "stomach," "connective tissue," "gene," "predator," and "antibody"; everyday examples are "lawyer," "philosopher," "charity," "umpire," and "balance wheel."

By a "historical concept" we shall understand any concept, *C*, that is so defined that it is logically impossible to apply it correctly to an object, *S*, unless *S* has a specified history. Thus, "hybrid" is historical because no organism can (logically) be a hybrid unless the history of its generation meets certain specifications. Such concepts as "mutant," "homology," "hypertely," "convert," "graduate," "retired," and "veteran" are also historical.

We cannot here investigate the uses of functional and historical concepts, but their existence in biology has a number of implications for the thesis of conceptual autonomy:

(1) Functional and historical concepts are extrinsic. They are applied to an object, *S*, not on the basis of characteristics in *S* itself but on the basis of the relation of *S* to other objects and processes or to historical antecedents. Moreover, these external relations are significant only within biology proper—physical theory indeed contains functional and historical concepts, but it has no need of those introduced by the biologist. In this minimal sense they are "specifically biological."

(2) Functional and historical concepts are ordinarily polytypic with respect to any set of intrinsic or physical properties, and they are themselves often employed in the polytypic specification of the meaning of other biological concepts. Their existence therefore reinforces the conclusions drawn about polytypic concepts.

(3) Can we regard functional or historical definition as definition in terms of physical properties? There is probably no solid answer to this question, but it should be noted that the physical sciences are likely to be regarded as defective insofar as they employ either functional or historical concepts. If, then, the definability of biological concepts in physical terms is secured by the expedient of regarding historical and functional concepts as physical, it is only at the cost of admitting as "physical" concepts that would be judged inappropriate for physical theory.

Nomic autonomy. Biology can possess specifically biological laws if, and only if, there are specifically biological concepts. If there is a law that employs only the concepts of some branch of physical theory, it would surely be regarded as an instance of physical law; and a law that employs only the concepts that are clearly biological would be regarded as biological.

There is an ambiguity in the question of whether biological concepts and laws are reducible to physical theory. Given an existing biological theory, T_1, we can ask whether the concepts and principles of T_1 are reducible to a physical theory, T_2. Or we can ask whether the phenomena, P_1, that T_1 describes can be given an alternative description in a physical theory, T_2, equal to or surpassing T_1 in explanatory power. Any arguments that center about existing biological theory, such as the above arguments in favor of conceptual autonomy, can at the very best support irreducibility in the first sense. It is difficult to see how irreducibility in the second sense could be given support, at least by the conceptual analysis of existing sciences.

Methodological autonomy. Are there logical patterns of analysis or explanation appropriate in biology but not appropriate in the physical sciences? The leading contenders for this honor are teleological and historical explanations. (It is granted that historical explanation has some place in the physical sciences, but only a marginal one.)

It is impossible to say anything useful on this vexed topic without some rather lengthy preliminaries. In the first place, the meaning of the thesis that there are patterns of explanation peculiar to biology needs some examination. If, for example, there are teleological explanations in biology, they will share some features in common with explanations in the physical sciences—those features in virtue of which they are all explanations. On the other hand, there must be some prima-facie differences, those that lead us to identify some explanations as teleological. Are these differences great enough, or of such a type, that we may reasonably describe them as formal, or as differences in logical pattern; or are they merely superficial differences in subject matter or vocabulary? We need, evidently, a clear account of the formal pattern of all explanations—if, indeed, one exists. In the second place, in examining the logical pattern of explanation, it becomes necessary to investigate the nature of implication.

There is general agreement that any explanation possesses the form of an argument $P/\therefore C$, where *C* is a proposition that describes the state of affairs—event, law, or whatever—to be explained and *P* is a set of propositions that offer premises in explanation of *C*. Moreover, both *P* and *C* must be true: *C* cannot be false, for explanation consists in showing why something is the case and it is senseless to suppose that a falsehood can be explained; and *P* must be true, for falsehoods cannot explain why something is the case. Finally, it is agreed that *P* must in some sense be more general than *C*.

There is less agreement among philosophers on the logical relation of *P* to *C*. The commonest assumption is that *C* must be deducible from *P*, or from *P* together with other truths that may be taken for granted in the context. This requirement yields the so-called deductive model of explanation. One motivation behind the deductive model consists in construing explanation in such a way that prediction and explanation are logically parallel. Thus, any suppressed premises needed, in conjunction with *P*, for the deducibility of *C* must concern factors that are, in principle, just as available for investigation as those explicitly mentioned in *P*. If this condition is satisfied, then *C* is explained by *P* when, and only when, *C* could have been predicted by deduction from premises whose truth could be known without knowing the truth of *P*.

It is precisely on the requirement of a parallel between prediction and explanation that teleological and historical explanations seem to differ from explanations that conform to the deductive model. Consider, for example, a typical historical explanation. An animal geographer raises the question of why a particular species of fish is found in a lake far outside its normal range. Suppose that historical research uncovers the fact that fifty years ago several breeding pairs of the species were artificially introduced. This might very well be the explanation of why they are there at the present time, but it seems certain that an investigator observing the past event could not have deduced, from any truths available to him at that time, that fish of this species would be present fifty years later. He would not be in a position to rule out accidental extinction by disease, the presence of an efficient osprey, and similar possibilities.

Or consider a typical teleological explanation. Why do animals in colder climates have shorter appendages than do their close relatives in warmer climates? Because shorter appendages are less subject to freezing and are less efficient radiators of body heat. It seems that such explanations conform to the requirements of the deductive model even less than do historical explanations. It would be incredible to suppose that the shortness of appendages could be deduced from any set of known biological and thermodynamic truths. So incredible, indeed, that it is often suggested that so-called teleological explanations are not explanations at all.

What, then, is the pattern of historical and teleological explanations? It will now be argued that it is quite possible to construe the deductive model in such a way that fully predictive historical and teleological explanations turn out to have the same logical form. The differences concern only the nature of the set of premises, *P*. Consequently, it will be necessary for us to judge the thesis of methodological autonomy as unsound insofar as it rests on the supposition that teleological and historical explanations do not conform to the logical pattern formulated in the deductive model.

The requirement in the deductive model that *C* be deducible from *P* is defended by the correct observation that *P* must lay down a sufficient condition for *C*. We should not say that *P* explains *C* unless the truth of *P* also commits us to the truth of *C*. However, deducibility of *C* from *P* is not the only logical relation that guarantees that *P* is a sufficient condition of *C*; this is equally guaranteed if *P* merely implies *C*. We propose that no stronger relation than implication be required for the soundness of an explanation; and we propose to define "implication" in a way that does justice to the letter, if not the spirit, of the deductive model.

Moreover, we need a definition of implication that will aid us in rectifying a certain weakness of the deductive model. Suppose—*per impossibile*—that we could deduce that there would now be fish of species *X* in a lake from information that the lake had been seeded. We should still not regard the seeding as the explanation of their presence if the seeding, although sufficient, was redundant. If a few breeding pairs are thrown into a lake already teeming with fish of the same species, we should have to look elsewhere for an explanation of their presence. In short, not only must *P* lay down a sufficient condition of *C*; it must also lay down a necessary condition.

Any number of distinct occurrences could be sufficient for the presence of fish in a lake, and if any one of a number is sufficient, it would appear that not one of them is necessary. In order to resolve this paradox, we shall introduce the concept of a context-dependent implication, and the concept will be employed in formulating the requirement that *P* imply *C*.

Logicians have defined a number of relations that may plausibly be interpreted as implication relations—for example, "material," "intuitionistic," "strict," and "rigorous" implications. For reasons that we cannot discuss in detail here, none of these relations represent the concept we need for dealing with explanations. They are either too narrow or admit versions of the paradoxes of implication. Instead, we propose to define a concept of entailment and employ it in specifying the relation of implication that we require.

G. H. von Wright in *Logical Studies* (London, 1957, p. 181) defines entailment as follows: *A* entails *B* if, and only if, it is possible to demonstrate by logical (formal) methods that "$\sim A$ or *B*" ("not *A* or *B*") is true, without at the same time demonstrating either *A* or *B*. This definition is an informal description of a relation that, if satisfied by a formal theory, would have the property that if *A* entails *B*, then *A* would be relevant to *B*, thus avoiding the paradoxes of strict implication. We shall add the proviso that *A* does not entail *B* if the truth of *both* "$\sim A$ or *B*" and "$\sim A$ or $\sim B$" are demonstrable; or if *both* "$\sim A$ or *B*" and "*A* or *B*" are demonstrable.

For our purposes, then, we define entailment as follows: *A* entails *B* if both von Wright's definition and our proviso are satisfied. And we shall say that *A implies B* (symbolically: $A \rightarrow B$) if, and only if, either *A* entails *B*; or *G* and *A* together entail *B*, where *G* (the "ground" of the implication) is true and neither *G* nor *A* entails, or is entailed by, *B*.

This concept of implications is designed to have the following effect: If it is true to say that $A \rightarrow B$, then it would always make sense to offer *A* in support or explanation of *B*. "$A \rightarrow B$" cannot be shown to be true merely by showing that *A* is false or *B* true. If "$A \rightarrow B$" is not certifiable by formal methods alone, then the implication must have a true ground, *G*, that engages logically with both *A* and *B*. Thus, if *A* is true, then (*G* being true), *B* must also be true. Implication, in short, is to be regarded as either direct or enthymematic entailment. It can be argued that this is the way implication is regularly regarded outside of logical theory, but that is a story we cannot pursue here.

The question of whether an implication (that is not an entailment) is true, therefore, is to be settled partly by logical and partly by empirical procedures. To demonstrate its truth we must find a logically appropriate true ground.

For example, if we ask whether "If Socrates is a man, then he is mortal" is a true implication, we can answer that it is, because there is a true statement—"All men are mortal"—that, together with the antecedent, entails the consequent.

Can we make any general remarks about the sort of statement that we ordinarily take as grounding implications? Suppose that a physician says, "If you have fever, sniffles, and a sore throat, then you have an infection." Is his statement true or false? If the statement "Everyone who has these symptoms has an infection" were true, it could serve as a suitable ground. But it is possible to have these symptoms and lack the infection: The patient may have taken a fever-producing drug, his sniffles may be due to allergy, and he may have rubbed his throat with a wire brush. Of course this concatenation of possibilities is extremely unlikely, but it is sufficient to require us to regard the proposed ground as false.

Nevertheless, something very much like the proposed ground is in fact the ground of the physician's inference from symptoms to diagnosis. He recognizes that the general rule has exceptions, but he satisfies himself that the patient in question is not one of the exceptions. We may accordingly formalize his grounds in a pair of statements, G_1 and G_2, the former stating the rule, but so hedged as to guarantee its truth, and the latter stating that the case in question is not one of the acknowledged exceptions:

G_1: "Everyone with fever, sniffles, and a sore throat has an infection, except cases of kind *A, B, C* . . . ."

G_2: "The present patient is not a case of kind *A, B, C* . . . ."

G_1 and G_2, together with the antecedent of the conditional, do entail the consequent "The present patient has an infection"; therefore, the conditional is true if both G_1 and G_2 are. G_1 obviously has a very good chance of being true, even if we specify *A, B,* and *C*, since the list of possible exceptions is left open. G_1, we might say, is a medical truism. The burden of the question concerning the truth of the conditional rests on G_2; that is, the implication holds only if G_2, the most dubious premise in the entailment *P* and G_1 and G_2 $\therefore$ *C*, is true. The truth of the conditional is assessed by reference to the particular case.

We shall call any implication that is grounded by means of a universal statement with an open-ended hedging clause a "context-dependent" implication, since the hedging clause can be disarmed only by close attention to the context in which the implication is asserted.

We are now in a position to reformulate the logical pattern of the deductive model in order to admit context-dependent implications between *P* and *C* and to make clear what is involved in holding that *P* must lay down a necessary condition of *C*. In place of the requirement that *C* be deducible from *P* together with true suppressed premises, we introduce the stricter requirements that *P* imply (in the above-defined sense) *C* and that *P* entail some *P'* such that *C* implies *P'*; that is, we require that *P* either is, or entails, a necessary condition of *C*, but we admit that the implication of *P'* by *C* may be context-dependent. The fully explicit pattern of explanation may therefore be specified as follows:

If "$P / \therefore C$" is a sound explanation, then:

(1) "(G_1 and G_2 and *P*) $\rightarrow$ ($P' \leftrightarrow C$)" is a logical truth;

(2) "$P \rightarrow P'$" is a logical truth;

(3) G_1, G_2, and *P* are true.

G_1 is the ground of the implication from *P* to *C*; and G_2, of the implication from *C* to *P'*. Notice that *C* need not imply the whole of *P*, but only something "involved" in *P*. Both G_1 and G_2 *may* be conjunctions of hedged statements and statements that discount the hedging. It is a further important feature of this pattern, not relevant to our present concern with biological explanation that if "$P \rightarrow C$" is true, either *P* or G_1 must be more general than *C*.

Let us call this full pattern the implicational model of explanation in order to distinguish it from the usual formulations of the deductive model. It is easy to see that if any explanation satisfies the deductive model, it also satisfies the implicational model.

It must be admitted that lovers of rigor and exactitude will be just as unhappy with this doctrine of hedged explanation as with the doctrine of polytypic classes. Indeed, the two doctrines are not unconnected. On the one hand, one motivation for introducing polytypic concepts is to reduce hedging to a minimum. For instance, the statement "Hybrid crosses of closely inbred strains exhibit hybrid vigor" can be made without much hedging; but if we were restricted to the employment of concepts that are not polytypic with respect to physical properties, any equivalent statement would be closely hedged. On the other hand, inferences that culminate in the application of concepts polytypic with respect to some set, *G*, and that are based on an investigation of the properties in *G*, are necessarily hedged: "The specimen is a six-legged arthropod with three body segments. Therefore it is an insect." This inference is not tautological, but any specimen that has these properties would be a biological anomaly if it were not an insect. The implication is guarded, and the guarding is bypassed in the specific judgment that the specimen before us is not such a strange anomaly.

Consider our example of a historical explanation. The implication from the past seeding of a lake to the present population is grounded on the general truth that such seedings are effective in the absence (here we hedge) of such contingencies as pestilence and efficient ospreys. What right have we to discount the hedging? In the case of historical explanations, we have the best piece of evidence that *could* be available, the presence of the population itself. If this seems to be cheating (and it would seem to be to the lover of rigor), we can reply that the explanation is sound; that everyone admits it is not predictive; that this is, in fact, the way that historical explanations are justified; that there are very few unguarded rules available for historical explanations; and that we might as well admit that historical explanations answer to the letter, if not to the spirit, of the deductive model.

An analogous heavily guarded implication is needed to establish the seeding as necessary for the presence of a population. The ground of this implication is a statement to the effect that there would be no population in the absence of seeding, unless the lake is within the normal range of the species, or unless . . . . These "unlesses" must be discounted if the explanation is to be regarded as sound.

In teleological explanations a function is ascribed to a process, structure, or property. For example, in the teleological explanation of the relatively shorter appendages of animals in cold climates as compared with their close relatives (other subspecies of the same species) in warm climates, the shorter appendages are assigned the functions of reducing the probability of damage by freezing and of helping in temperature regulation. Normally an object or state of affairs, S, that contributes to the performance of a biological function, *F*, cannot be regarded without qualification as either necessary or sufficient for *F*. Obviously, short appendages are not sufficient for proper temperature regulation—in fact, not all of the necessary factors are known. And short appendages are not generally necessary, since an animal can have long appendages so long as other mechanisms insure proper temperature regulation. However, it is possible to make the judgment that in the concrete circumstances under consideration, short appendages are both necessary and sufficient for temperature regulation, although the grounds of both implications will be heavily guarded. A teleological explanation is precisely such a judgment.

We may now summarize the bearings of these analyses of concept formation and explanation on the general question of autonomy in biological theory.

(1) There is no case for supposing that biology employs *sui generis* modes of explanation. On the other hand, it was necessary to reformulate the deductive model, allowing context-dependent implications, in order to exhibit the unity of explanatory pattern. It can be shown that explanations in the physical sciences also involve context-dependent explanations, so even their use cannot count as a peculiar feature of biology. It must be admitted, however, that in historical and teleological explanations there is a certain feedback from conclusion (the *explanandum*) to premises (the *explanans*). In historical explanations, the fact to be explained is taken as evidence for the ground of an implication; in teleological explanations, a fully functioning biological economy is taken as conclusive evidence that necessary functions are being performed.

(2) As long as polytypic concepts are admitted into biology, it is trivial to say that there are biological concepts not definable in physicochemical terms, since such concepts are not definable at all.

(3) Finally, and most important, existing biological theory is irreducibly autonomous in the sense that is most important for the biologist. This autonomy is insured by the necessity of what has been called the "unformalized skill" of the biologist. Whatever the stage of development and articulations of a system of biological concepts and laws, the meaning of the concepts and the scope of application of the laws is determined in part by purely biological considerations. For example, the application of a term such as "vertebrate" is decided by reference to the history of evolution, to large regions of the taxonomic system, and to evolution theory—the theory that indicates what weight is to be assigned to the presence or absence of the conventional diagnostic features of the vertebrates. These considerations are brought to bear within biological thinking through the agency of the biologist, who has achieved his skill, judgment, and flair in the course of an apprenticeship with biological materials. He is familiar with, or once studied and has forgotten, a range of paradigms, collections of similar and dissimilar cases, rules together with typical sorts of exceptions, abnormal and pathological specimens, and so forth. We are not merely making the uninteresting point that a biologist can learn his trade, or that there is such a thing as skill and flair. We are saying that skill and flair are the necessary prerequisites for attaching to biological theories whatever sense they do in fact possess. The analysis of polytypy and of the hedging of principles exhibits just where the "book" components end and the "unformalized" components begin. Autonomy thus consists in the existence of essentially open-ended concepts and principles whose use is regulated by biological considerations alone.

ONTOLOGICAL AUTONOMY

Even if the case for the doctrinal autonomy of existing biological theory were proved, it might still be argued that a biology is possible in which no specifically biological concepts appear. It is relevant to point out that this possibility is purely logical, no more—there is not the slightest reason to think that it will ever be realized. But if we should wish to refute the possibility, we should have to defend a doctrine of ontological autonomy. We shall now examine briefly the three commonest attempts to locate an ontological gulf between the organic and the inorganic—vitalism, holism, and purposiveness.

Vitalism. The vitalist argues that the activities of an organic system are controlled in part by a nonphysical entity that is present in them. Most vitalists have supposed that the control of the vital entity is best exhibited in the phenomena of regulation during morphogenesis and in purposive activities, arguing that the details of these activities are inexplicable on any possible materialistic hypothesis. It is acknowledged that organic systems are just as subject to physical laws as are inorganic ones, but it is held that organic systems are continually in a physical state that is open with respect to the future—the state may change in a number of alternative ways, each of which is compatible with, but not determined by, the laws of physical nature. The activities of the vital entity are exercised in choosing these alternatives.

Vitalism is worth an extensive examination, but we must content ourselves with a few observations:

(*a*) The vitalist thesis was a favorite target for application of the verifiability principle in the heyday of Positivism. Studies such as M. Schlick's *Philosophy of Nature* (New York, 1949) demonstrate to the satisfaction of most philosophers that no evidence can be shown to bear unambiguously on the thesis.

(*b*) The vital entity, if it exists, must be so remarkable, and so mysterious in its mode of exercising control, that it should be regarded as supernatural. As C. D. Broad remarks in *The Mind and Its Place in Nature* (New York,

1925, p. 86), if we are going to admit an entelechy with the power of making its own organism, we might as well postulate God without further ado.

(c) Some phenomena that have been cited in favor of vitalism have proved to be ephemeral—for example, the alleged inability to carry out an organic synthesis in the test tube; other phenomena have been offered as alternative, nonvitalistic explanations, such as the development of polarity in fertilized eggs.

Holism. A favorite thesis of organismic biology is that the parts of organic wholes exhibit patterns of behavior that they do not show outside these wholes. Unfortunately, the thesis is fatally ambiguous. If it means that parts of organic wholes violate the laws they exhibit outside the wholes, then the evidence is all against it. If it means that the parts have properties within the whole that they lack outside it, then it is true but hardly supports the doctrine of an unbridgeable gulf. A description of a part's relation to a whole *is* the specification of a property of the part. Thus, holism in this sense is true of any whole whatever. Indeed, organismic biologists sometimes give an exact description of a physical field when describing the features of an organic whole.

Finally, the thesis may mean that even if we possess a comprehensive theory of the behavior of the parts outside organic wholes, we still could not derive from that theory an account of the parts' behavior within an organic whole. This is a restatement of the thesis of nomic autonomy.

Teleology. Vitalists, organismic biologists, and others have placed great weight on the argument that organic systems show purposive or goal-directed behavior, and that this indicates the presence of a special mode of causation in such systems. The contention is commonly rebutted—and the rebuttal seems to be sound—by arguing that purposive behavior is not the result of a special sort of teleological causation, but is the result of a special sort of organization among ordinary causal processes. There have been many descriptions of this pattern of organization, all variations on a common theme. It is shown that a process may be regarded as directed toward a specified goal if chance variations away from the goal are compensated for by other, partially independent, processes. Thus, partially independent occurrences can be so related that their joint occurrence is the achievement of a specified goal. No appeal need be made to any special sort of process or occurrence. Indeed, the recent analyses of simulated purposive activity in machines have largely silenced appeals to teleology as a *sui generis* biological phenomenon.

(See also DARWINISM; EMERGENT EVOLUTIONISM; LIFE, ORIGIN OF; MECHANISM IN BIOLOGY; ORGANISMIC BIOLOGY; TELEOLOGY; and VITALISM. See Biology in Index for articles on biologists and thinkers who developed philosophical theories arising from biological concepts.)

Bibliography

Beckner, Morton, *The Biological Way of Thought*. New York, 1959. An examination of the special features of biological concepts and explanations, including a consideration of models, taxonomic systems, genetic and functional analysis, and teleological explanation.

Bertalanffy, Ludwig von, *Problems of Life*. New York, 1952. An extensive defense of doctrinal autonomy from the organismic biologist's standpoint.

Braithwaite, Richard Bevan, *Scientific Explanation*. Cambridge, 1953. This standard work on explanation includes discussions of models and of teleology.

Haldane, J. S., *The Philosophical Basis of Biology*. London, 1931.

Lillie, Ralph Stayner, *General Biology and Philosophy of Organism*. Chicago, 1945.

Nagel, Ernest, *The Structure of Science*. New York, 1961. A thorough and careful treatment of a large range of problems in the philosophy of science; the discussions of reduction, historical analysis, and teleological systems are especially valuable.

Russell, Edward Stuart, *The Directiveness of Organic Activities*. Cambridge, 1945.

Schubert-Soldern, Rainer, *Mechanism and Vitalism: Philosophical Aspects of Biology*. Notre Dame, Indiana, 1962.

Sommerhoff, George, *Analytical Biology*. London, 1950. A pioneering attempt to show that goal-directed activity can be described without reference to special modes of causation.

Woodger, J. H., *Biological Principles*. London, 1948. An influential and classical source of subsequent work in the philosophy of biology, partially Whiteheadian.

MORTON O. BECKNER

BIOLOGY, MECHANISTIC. See MECHANISM IN BIOLOGY.

BIOLOGY, ORGANISMIC. See ORGANISMIC BIOLOGY.

BLACK, MAX, American analytical philosopher, was born in Baku, Russia, in 1909. He read mathematics at Cambridge and, following his B.A., received a fellowship for research at Göttingen, where he wrote *The Nature of Mathematics* (London, 1933). He then returned to the University of London for further study and was awarded a doctorate for his dissertation *Theories of Logical Positivism* (1939, unpublished). He took up his first academic position, as a lecturer and tutor in the Institute of Education of the University of London, in 1936 and held it until he left England.

Black came to the United States in 1940 and was naturalized in 1948. His first appointment was at the University of Illinois. In 1946 he went to Cornell University, where he became Susan Linn Sage professor of philosophy in 1954. He was president of the eastern division of the American Philosophical Association in 1958, and gave special lectures on contemporary American philosophy in Japan in 1957 and in India in 1962.

The influence of Black's early years in Cambridge is evident. In addition to an analytic orientation, Black still retains a wide range of scientific interests and a careful regard for common sense, such as characterized C. D. Broad and Frank Ramsey on the one hand and G. E. Moore on the other; but the impact of Ludwig Wittgenstein was most profound. Black's first work, an exposition of the logistic, formalist, and intuitionist conceptions of mathematics, led him naturally to Wittgenstein, and his subsequent study of logical positivism required coming directly to grips with Wittgenstein's *Tractatus*. Continuing interest in that work culminated many years later in *A Companion to Wittgenstein's Tractatus* (Cambridge and Ithaca, N.Y., 1964), a massive work that contains critical expository essays on the principal topics and extensive information about Wittgenstein's sources, as well as exegesis.

Many of Black's essays also take up problems or themes that are prominent in Wittgenstein's later work, although Black invariably comments on the problems rather than expounding Wittgenstein. Problems about meaning are of great importance. Black's conception of philosophy emphasizes linguistic method: "philosophical clarification of meaning is . . . as practical as slum clearance and as empirical as medicine." However, we need not fret about what meanings are: he examines what is involved when we explain the meaning of an utterance, and concludes that it is a mistake to suppose that there are "such things as meanings to be categorized." A similar conclusion led Wittgenstein and others to focus on rules rather than on meanings; Black takes up the challenge by analyzing what a rule is, how a rule is related to a statement formulating it or a practice exemplifying it, and how so-called necessary statements, which depend only on the meaning of the terms involved, may be seen as "surrogates" for certain rules. Black is aware that a certain vagueness or "looseness" is an important aspect of these rules governing ordinary usage, and two essays explore what vagueness is and how we can reason with loose concepts. He finds that the underlying factor is our presupposition, in particular cases where such reasoning is possible, that the looseness does not matter. This calling attention to the presuppositions of a linguistic act is characteristic of Black; in other essays he emphasizes that definitions and assertions have presuppositions, and he gives a detailed comparison of presupposition and implication, with special reference to the controversy about denoting phrases.

Black's respect for the claims of common sense is evident in his remark that "the use of language made by the critic of induction deviates in a misleading manner from some ordinary usage." Behind this remark lies an important principle: "To say that a word is correctly used, in accordance with a normal usage, in certain circumstances, is to say that a certain sentence containing the word is, in those circumstances, true." This principle sanctions arguing from paradigm cases, and in another essay Black insists that a paradigm case of a man raising a glass shows that "it is perfectly certain that persons do sometimes make something happen." Such arguments are controversial, some philosophers maintaining that paradigm cases prove nothing at all. Black's later essay, "Reasoning With Loose Concepts," provides a kind of justification for his procedure by showing that we can be sure of clear cases even though we do not know at what point cases cease to be clear. Nevertheless, paradigm cases do not constitute a road from language to metaphysics, for "the conception of language as a mirror of reality is radically mistaken."

The topics of Black's analytical essays range from formal logic to education; in science he has commented on both cosmology and sociology; and he has kept his early interest in the foundations of mathematics. His work in the philosophy of language has included reviews of many contemporaries, including Frege, Russell, Dewey, Korzybski, Carnap, Whorf, and Tarski. His writing is markedly free from special terminology and wholly free from reliance on inherited terminology or jargon.

Bibliography

In addition to his own contributions to philosophical analysis and philosophy of language, Black has published translations from the German works of Carnap and Frege; he has edited two volumes of philosophical essays, *Philosophical Analysis* (Englewood Cliffs, N.J., 1950) and *Philosophy in America* (London, 1964), and a volume of general essays on language, *The Importance of Language* (Englewood Cliffs, N.J., 1962); he has been an editor of *The Philosophical Review* since 1946, and is general editor of the Contemporary Philosophy series published by the Cornell University Press; he has organized seminars for social scientists, one series of which resulted in a collection of contributed essays, *The Social Theories of Talcott Parsons* (Englewood Cliffs, N.J., 1961).

Other principal writings include a logic text, *Critical Thinking* (New York, 1946), and three volumes of philosophical essays, *Language and Philosophy* (Ithaca, N.Y., 1949), *Problems of Analysis* (Ithaca, N.Y., 1954), and *Models and Metaphors* (Ithaca, N.Y., 1962).

NEWTON GARVER

BLAKE, WILLIAM (1757–1827), English poet, painter, and engraver. Blake was born in London, the second of five children in the family of a retail hosier. His social status precluded university education, and he was apprenticed to an engraver. Apart from that training and a few months at the Royal Academy, Blake was self-educated. Most of his pictorial work took the form of illustrations for books, Biblical subjects forming the largest group. His painting and engraving were thus primarily related to literature, and the interdependence of poetry and painting is a central principle of all his work. He lived in London nearly all his life, very frugally, sometimes in poverty, and constantly dependent on patrons. He met Wordsworth, Coleridge, and Lamb, and was admired by the last two; but he died practically unknown as a poet, although he had been writing poetry since the age of twelve. After one volume of juvenile verse (*Poetical Sketches*, 1783) was published through the efforts of friends, Blake determined to produce his poetry by engraving the text himself and accompanying it with illustrations. Practically all his later poetry, except what was left in manuscript, took the form of a text and designs etched on copper, stamped on paper, and then colored by hand. Most of his lyrics are in two collections: *Songs of Innocence* (first engraved in 1789) and *Songs of Experience* (1794). Others are longer poems, generally called prophecies, which are sequences of plates. The "prophecies" include *The Book of Thel* (1789), *The Marriage of Heaven and Hell* (1793), *America* (1793), *Europe* (1794), *Milton* (about 1808, in 50 plates) and *Jerusalem* (about 1818, in 100 plates).

Thought. The prophecies are symbolic poems in which the characters are states or attitudes of human life. This means that these poems embody religious and philosophical concepts as well as poetic imagery. These concepts are mainly concerned with Blake's sense of the relevance and importance of the arts and of the creative faculty of man, and seem to have been derived mainly from a negative reaction to the British empirical tradition of thought. He tells us that he had read Locke and Bacon in his youth and had decided that they mocked inspiration and vision. Blake's attitude would be better understood if it were thought of as anti-Cartesian, although he is unlikely to have read Descartes, and his attitude embodies many elements that would now be called existential.

Imagination. According to Blake, man is a working or constructing imagination—the creative artist is normative man. In this context there is no difference between human essence and human existence, for the imagination is the human existence itself and is also essential human nature. Works of art are neither intellectual nor emotional, motivated neither by desire nor by reason, neither free nor compelled: all such antitheses become unities in them. Even more important, the imagination destroys the antithesis of subject and object. Man starts out as an isolated intelligence in an alien nature, but the imagination creates a world in its own image, the world of cities and gardens and human communities and domesticated animals.

Interpretation of the Bible. For Blake, the Bible is a definitive parable of human existence, as it tells how man finds himself in an unsatisfactory world and tries to build a better one—one which eventually takes the form of a splendid golden city, the symbol of the imaginative and creative human community. God in Blake's work is the creative power in man (here Blake shows the influence of Swedenborg, with his emphasis on the unity of divine and human natures in Jesus), and human power is divine because it is infinite and eternal. These two words do not mean endless in time and spaces; they mean the genuine experience of the central points of time and space, the now and the here. Many features of Blake's anti-Lockean position remind us of Berkeley, especially his insistence that "mental things are alone real"; but this doctrine of God takes Blake far beyond the subjective idealism and nominalism of Berkeley.

In Blake's reading of the Bible, "the creation"—the alien and stupid nature that man now lives in—is part of "the fall" and is the world man struggles to transcend. The objective world is the anticreation, the enemy to be destroyed. Blake says that man has no body distinct from his soul. He does oppose mind and body, but as contrasting attitudes to nature, not as separate essential principles. The "corporeal understanding," or perverted human activity, contemplates nature as it is (as a vast, objective, subhuman body) and tries to overcome the alienation of the subject by identifying the subject with nature as it sees nature. Nature is controlled, apparently, by automatic laws like the law of gravitation and by a struggle to survive in which force and cunning are more important than love or intelligence. Perverted human life imitates nature by continually waging war and by maintaining a parasitic class. Perverted religion, or natural religion, as Blake calls it, invents harsh and tyrannical gods on the analogy of nature. Perverted thought exposes itself passively to impressions from the external world and then evolves abstract principles out of these impressions which attempt to formulate the general laws of nature. These are the operations known as sensation and reflection in Locke. The abstracting tendency is perverted because it is not a genuine effort to understand nature, but is a step toward imitating the automatism of nature by imposing a conforming morality on human life. The principle of this conformity is the acceptance of injustice and exploitation as inescapable elements of existence. The end of this perverted process is hatred and contempt of life, as expressed in the deliberate efforts at self-annihilation which Blake saw as beginning with the Napoleonic wars in his own time.

Prophetic books. The action in Blake's prophecies is concerned with the conflict of these creative and perverted states in human life. The sense of conservatism, of accepting things as they are, is symbolized by Urizen, who is associated with old age and the sky. When conservatism deepens into hatred of life itself, Urizen is replaced by Satan. The force that struggles against Urizen is the revolutionary impulse in man, called Orc or Luvah, who is associated with youth and sexual desire. Orc cannot achieve a permanent deliverance from Urizen; that is possible only for the creative power itself, called Los. The central theme of the prophecies is the effort of humanity, called Albion, to achieve through Los the kind of civilization which is symbolized in the Bible as Jerusalem and thus to reach the integration of human and divine powers represented in Christianity by Jesus.

Bibliography

The most convenient edition of Blake's literary work is the one-volume *The Poetry and Prose of William Blake*, Geoffrey Keynes, ed. (London and New York, 1927).

Works on Blake include Bernard Blackstone, *English Blake* (London, 1949); Foster S. Damon, *William Blake: His Philosophy and Symbols* (Boston and New York, 1924); David V. Erdman, *Blake: Prophet Against Empire* (Princeton, 1954); Northrop Frye, *Fearful Symmetry: A Study of William Blake* (Princeton, 1947); and Mark Schorer, *William Blake: The Politics of Vision* (New York, 1946).

NORTHROP FRYE

BLANSHARD, BRAND, American philosopher whose task is best described in his own words as the "vindication of reason against recent philosophical attacks." Blanshard has thus been a critic—a critic of all those who, he alleges, reject rationality—but at the same time he has tried to exhibit the credentials that reason can show in its own right.

Blanshard was born in 1892 and educated at the University of Michigan, Columbia, Oxford, and Harvard—where he received his Ph.D. He taught at the University of Michigan, at Swarthmore College, and at Yale—where he was Sterling professor of philosophy and chairman of the department. The multitude of honors he has received during his career precludes their enumeration here.

Blanshard's first major work was *The Nature of Thought* (London, 1939), in two volumes, each divided into two books. The first volume is largely concerned with a subject matter common to both philosophy and psychology. The stated goal is to discover a theory of perception (Book I) and a theory of ideas (Book II) that will simultaneously satisfy the psychologist, who views percepts and ideas as contents of the mind, and the philosopher, who views them as potential items of knowledge. Various theories are examined and rejected—most notably the traditional empiricist approach—and it is finally argued that only a theory along the lines developed by Bradley, Bosanquet, and Royce is able to meet this double demand. The universal,

Blanshard maintained, is present in all thought, even in the most rudimentary forms of perception; and it is the presence of the universal that is the most important feature of thought. This conclusion exhibits a theme that recurs throughout both volumes: the use of doctrines drawn from the idealist tradition in dealing with contemporary problems.

In the second volume of *The Nature of Thought*, the subject matter becomes more specifically philosophical. The main task of Book III (entitled "The Movement of Reflection") is to answer the epistemological problem: what is the test and the nature of truth? Once more, after examining and rejecting alternatives, Blanshard turns to the idealist tradition for his answer, adopting a version of the coherence theory of truth. His exposition of the coherence theory has a number of distinctive features. Foremost is the clarity, rigor, and persuasiveness of the presentation; in this respect Blanshard has only Royce as a rival. Furthermore, he develops the theory independently of metaphysical doctrines that are for the most part now repudiated. Finally, he develops the theory in full cognizance of contemporary criticisms and attempts to offer direct answer to them.

In Book IV (entitled "The Goal of Thought") Blanshard moves from epistemology into metaphysics. Still operating within the framework of idealism, he accepts the connected notions of internal relations, concrete universality, and concrete necessity. But he does not, as do most idealists, give these doctrines a gratuitous theological turn, nor does he attempt to secure the foundation of the entire system through an a priori proof that the completed, fully articulated system must exist. He does introduce the conception of a transcendent end for thought, which he considers a necessary postulate for knowledge, but he admits that it is possible (though unlikely) that this postulate is mistaken.

Some two decades after the publication of *The Nature of Thought*, and upon retirement from Yale, Blanshard began a projected three-volume sequence which would bring together material originally presented in his Carus and Gifford lectures. *Reason and Analysis* (London, 1962), the second of the three volumes, is his most polemical work. It is in large measure a systematic and unremitting attack upon the analytic tradition as it has emerged in various forms during the twentieth century. Some of the arguments presented are refinements of those used in *The Nature of Thought*, but *Reason and Analysis* is not a mere echo of the earlier work. On the constructive side, many of the earlier idealistic doctrines, although not silenced, seem decidedly muted. If philosophies are to bear labels, this later position might better be called rationalism than idealism.

The first work in the sequence, *Reason and Goodness* (London, 1961), introduces another aspect of Blanshard's thought. In this work he traces out the dialectical interplay between the demands of reason and the demands of feeling throughout the history of ethical theory. Not surprisingly, Blanshard rejects any theory that will not provide a place for reason in the account of human values, and he thus offers elaborate critiques of subjectivism, emotivism, and related theories.

In developing his own ethical position Blanshard does not turn, at least primarily, to the idealist tradition but rather to the works of Henry Sidgwick, G. E. Moore, H. A. Prichard, and W. D. Ross. Throughout his career Blanshard has favored teleology in ethics, and for a time he was attracted by Moore's ideal utilitarianism. He came to reject this position largely because of the difficulties associated with Moore's conception of nonnatural properties. In *Reason and Goodness* Blanshard rejects Moore's critique of naturalism and argues that goodness is characterized by the joint properties of satisfaction and fulfillment. The idea of fulfillment is associated with the idealist tradition, but as Blanshard uses it, it carries no suggestion of loss of individuality and is thus quite different from the idea of fulfillment as employed by Bradley and most other idealists. By including both satisfaction and fulfillment in the definition of goodness, Blanshard hopes to provide for feeling on one hand and reason on the other and, in this way, to resolve the dialectical tension outlined earlier in the work.

Reason and Belief is not yet published, but from Blanshard's lectures it may be assumed that in this work he will challenge the religious irrationalism that is currently fashionable in some quarters. What positive doctrines he will espouse is more a matter of speculation.

Bibliography

Additional works by Blanshard are "Current Strictures on Reason," in *Philosophical Review*, Vol. 54 (1945), 345–368, and *On Philosophical Style* (Bloomington, Ind., 1954).

A work on Blanshard is Ernest Nagel, "Sovereign Reason," in his *Sovereign Reason* (Glencoe, Ill., 1954), pp. 266–295.

ROBERT J. FOGELIN

BLOCH, ERNST, German Marxist philosopher, was born at Ludwigshafen in 1885. Influenced by late German expressionism and by the atmosphere of Munich after World War I, Bloch's style and thought reveal contradictory and uncertain trends. He began his career at the University of Leipzig by publishing *Von Geist der Utopie* in 1918. This work was followed in 1922 by a study of Thomas Münzer in which mystical and eschatological ideas blend with dialectic elements of Marxist–Hegelian origin. *Spuren* followed in 1930 and *Erbschaft dieser Zeit* in 1933. In the latter work the various elements of Bloch's thoughts are for the first time clearly placed within a Marxist framework showing revisionist tendencies.

In 1933 Bloch left Germany, eventually reaching the United States, where he created his major work, *Das Prinzip Hoffnung*, a huge work that has been called "a monstrous essence of his thoughts."

After World War II Bloch, like Bertolt Brecht, went to East Germany, where from 1948 until his retirement in 1957 he was professor at the University of Leipzig. At first, Bloch's political and intellectual influence in East Germany was limited, but nevertheless, he was never fully appreciated by party authorities. His winning the *Nationalpreis* of the German Democratic Republic in 1955 stirred controversy, and Bloch's views had changed considerably during his sojourn there. His ideas, which were carefully watched by party authorities, became the center of many discussions. In 1953, after the publication of *Subjekt-Objekt, Erläuterung zur Hegel* and *Avicenna und die Aristo-*

telische Linke, Bloch became editor of the *Deutsche Zeitschrift für Philosophie*. But the journal's comparative independence led to a series of arrests and trials of its collaborators and editors. Wolfgang Harich, Günther Zehm, and Manfred Hertwig were sentenced to prison, and Richard Lorenz and Gerhard Zwerenz fled to the Federal Republic. Although Bloch was only slightly involved, he was forbidden to publish, and in 1957 his works were officially condemned. When Bloch tardily made a declaration of loyalty, it was vague and noncommittal.

Although he was finally permitted to publish the third volume of his *Das Prinzip Hoffnung* in 1959, Bloch asked for political asylum during a visit to the Federal Republic in 1961, where he is now a visiting professor at the University of Tübingen.

Although Bloch is generally known in the West as a major Marxist philosopher, he has drawn on a far wider heritage which includes classical German thought, Christian and Jewish mysticism, Neoplatonism, and even the esoteric speculation of the *Zohar*. His major work, *Das Prinzip Hoffnung*, gives the impression that Bloch, although claiming that the economic element is fundamental, relegates it to a secondary level and focuses his attention on what Marxist theory regards as only a superstructure, the problem of intellectual culture.

According to Bloch, all reality is "mediation," or the subject–object relation, a dynamic relation that tends ultimately toward the final goal (*Endziel*) of the reunion of subject and object. The *Urgrund*, the primordial stuff prior to the distinction between subject and object, matter and spirit, is moved by an obscure immediate cosmic impulse, which Bloch terms "hunger" and contrasts with Freud's libido. After subject and object have been distinguished, Bloch claims, this hunger remains essential to both subject and object. Thus the reality of both subject and object is in the future, and the category of possibility comes to play a central role in his thought.

Subject. In man, the primordial hunger becomes desire, or hope. Hope presents itself as utopia, as a vision of a possibility that might be realized. Hope is tension toward the future, toward the new. It moves from a mere state of mind (*Stimmung*) to a representation, and then to knowledge. Although hope is founded on the will, in order to be hope that understands (*begriffene Hoffnung, docta spes*), it must draw strength from something real that will survive even when hope itself is completely satisfied. This residue makes hope something more than a project of reason and puts it in relation to what is objectively possible. The future possibility is not just a dream, even if it is heralded in dreams.

Possibility. The relations between subject, object, reality, and possibility are complex. The nature of the real is a tendency toward, or anticipation of, the future, and thus its reality is the reality of something in the future. But the future is already real as objective possibility. Bloch distinguishes between objective possibility, which (because the object as object is not real) is merely theoretical, and real possibility, which is practically connected with the future. What is really possible is concretely connected with utopia. Reality always contains elements of possible change, possibilities not yet actually existing. Utopias are concerned with these possibilities and thus have an essential function in man's consciousness. On the other hand, these possibilities must have a foundation in the object because thought can represent in imagination infinitely many possible objects in infinitely many relationships.

If an event were completely conditioned, it would be "unconditionally certain." Therefore, what can possibly come into existence is possible only insofar as it is not conditioned. What is objectively possible, therefore, is so only insofar as it is not constrained by predetermined conditions. Bloch distinguishes between two senses of objective possibility. One sense concerns the thing and is the thing's "behavior," or the appearance of the thing as an object of knowledge. The other sense concerns our knowledge of the thing. The objectivity (*Sachlichkeit*) of the thing concerns only our knowledge of it, while its factuality (*Sachhaftigkeit*) concerns only the object of knowledge.

Matter. The distinction between objectivity and factuality leads Bloch to claim that Marxism is only a partial outlook on reality and needs completion, even though the reconciliation of the real and the possible is achieved in historical materialism, which retains, in its complete immanentism, an element akin to the doctrine of salvation of the great religions. According to Marxism, historical changes arise out of precise historical socioeconomic conditions, and physical movement arises out of contradiction, the clash of opposites. But just as Bloch supplements the claims of historical materialism with his concept of hope, so he supplements the claims of dialectical materialism. In the object, or matter, the primordial hunger becomes a motive force (*agens*). But even though Bloch affirms that this force is completely immanent in matter, it is doubtful whether his view is still materialistic. His hostility toward all forms of mechanism and his inclination toward organic solutions weaken the materialistic features of Marxism to the point of nonexistence. The innate drive that he ascribes to matter has meaning only from the point of view of the final goal. Matter is not predetermined, since it has the capacity not only to express itself in existence but also to do so in forms that are always new. Nevertheless, the teleological doctrine of a final goal for the entire world process is not an extension of a psychological category or historical principle to nature. Rather, it is the cosmic unity of the subject process and object process when being finally becomes thinking and thinking finally becomes being. The historical process of society is thus related to the world process and ultimately to matter. Thus Bloch identifies dialectical matter with real possibility, but its being in process is not material and contradicts the fundamental Marxist tenet that matter is an independent reality that cannot enter into a relation with anything. Several critics have remarked that Bloch's conception of matter has its sources in the romantic *Naturphilosophie* of Hegel and Schelling; on this view, Bloch belongs among the idealist critics of natural science.

Utopia. The reconciliation of subject and object comes through utopia. In utopia, romantic *Sehnsucht*—the nostalgic regret that our dream of rationally conquering the world is blocked by a limit that we try unceasingly but perhaps vainly to overcome—is united with messianic expectancy. Utopia foresees the "kingdom of the children of God" of Thomas Münzer, the kingdom of freedom in which the exploitation of man by man ceases. At this time will come that unification, the identification of subject and object, which Bloch claims Marx foresaw when he spoke of the future historicization of nature and naturalization of man. It is thus from man that the world expects its realization, and the realization of the world process coincides with the self-realization of man. The Marxist epistemological theory of reflection will no longer be needed, since knowledge itself will be overcome by hope and the object as object will disappear; it will no longer be the having-become (*Gewordenes*) but rather pure process, the becoming (*Werdendes*), the not-yet (*noch nicht*).

Block's thought is very far from Marx's historical outlook and perhaps not too far from the early views of Georg Lukács. In his conflict with the schematicism and dogmatism of orthodox Marxism, Bloch belongs with such idealist and existentialist revisionists as Lukács, Antonio Gramsci, and Jean-Paul Sartre. Bloch's attempt to save Marxist theory from ossifying has wider implications than their attempts, however, for it is related to the problem of how Marxism is to make use of a cultural heritage, especially the heritage of classical German philosophy and, at least for Bloch, the heritage of the great religions of salvation. Bloch's solution has been to develop one vast comprehensive vision of reality, combining the original intuitions of the Old Testament and apocalyptic literature with the dynamic and messianic elements in Marxism. Bloch's very language reveals this mixture of ancient and modern. Difficult and intense, it echoes both recent expressionism and the language of the Bible and of mystical literature. The past is for Bloch not something fixed in an unreachable dimension, its cultural wealth to be discarded in order to start anew, but a dynamic field of research still of use to man.

Works by Bloch

Gesamtausgabe, 6 vols. Frankfurt, 1959—.

Vom Geist der Utopie, 1918.

Thomas Münzer als Theologe der Revolution. Munich, 1921.

Spuren. 1930.

Erbschaft dieser Zeit. Zurich, 1935.

Freiheit und Ordnung, Abriss der Sozial-Utopien. New York, 1946.

Subjekt-Objekt: Erläuterung zur Hegel. Berlin, 1951.

Avicenna und die Aristotelische Linke. Berlin, 1951.

Das Prinzip Hoffnung, 3 vols. Berlin, 1954–1959.

Naturrecht und menschliche Würde. Frankfurt, 1960. Vol. VI of *Gesamtausgabe*.

Philosophische Grundfragen, zur Ontologie des Noch-Nicht-Seins. Frankfurt, 1961. Vol. I of *Gesamtausgabe*.

Fromm, Erich, ed., *Socialist Humanism: An International Symposium*. New York, 1965. Contains an essay by Bloch.

Works on Bloch

Baumgart, J., "E. Bloch, Erbschaft dieser Zeit," in *Neue Rundschau*, Vol. 2 (1963).

Buhr, M., "Der religiöse Ursprung und Charakter der Hoffnungsphilosophie," in *Deutsche Zeitschrift für Philosophie*, Vol. 6 (1958), 576–598.

Bütow, H. G. *Philosophie und Gesellschaft im Denken Ernst Blochs*. Wiesbaden, 1963.

Eucken-Erdsiek, E., "Prinzip ohne Hoffnung. Kritische Betrachtungen zum Hauptwerk von E. Bloch," in *Philosophische Jahrbuch*, Vol. 70 (1962), 147–156.

Holz, H. H., "Der Philosoph E. Bloch und sein Werk 'Das Prinzip Hoffnung,'" in *Sinn und Form*, Vol. 3 (1955).

Kurella, A. "Zur Theorie der Moral. Eine alte Polemik mit E. Bloch," in *Deutsche Zeitschrift für Philosophie*, Vol. 6 (1958), 599–621.

Ley, H., "Ernst Bloch und das Hegelsche System," in *Einheit*, Vol. 3 (1957).

Lorenz, K., "Hoffnung als Wissenschaft. Die Philosophie Ernst Blochs," in *Deutsche Universitätszeitung*, Vol. 22 (1957), 9–11.

Rühle, Jürgen, "Philosopher of Hope: Ernst Bloch," in Leopold Labedz, ed., *Revisionism*. New York, 1962. Pp. 166–178.

Strolz, W., "Der Marxist und die Hoffnung. Einige Überlegungen zu dem Werke Ernst Blochs," in *Wort und Wahrheit* (1960).

Tjaden, K. M., "Zur Naturrechts Interpretation Ernst Blochs," in *Archiv für Rechts-und Sozialphilosophie*, Vol. 56 (1962), 573–584.

Zehm, G. A., "Ernst Bloch," in *Der Monat*, Vol. 158 (1961).

See also *Ernst Bloch: Festschrift zum 70. Geburtstage* (Frankfurt, 1956); and *Ernst Blochs Revision des Marxismus* (Berlin, 1957), an anthology with an introduction by J. H. Horn.

Franco Lombardi

BLONDEL, MAURICE (1861–1949), is considered one of the foremost French Catholic philosophers of the twentieth century. Blondel was born at Dijon. He studied at the local *lycée*, and in 1881 entered the École Normale Supérieure, where he was taught by Léon Ollé-Laprune. Because of pragmatic tendencies in his thought, Blondel's name was associated for a time with the modernist movement. He was, however, essentially orthodox, and his work has been increasingly influential among those Catholic thinkers who look for an alternative to Thomism.

Through Ollé-Laprune, Blondel was influenced by Newman's theory that belief is a matter of will as well as of logical demonstration. Blondel was far from being a thoroughgoing pragmatist or vitalist and showed none of the naturalism of thinkers like Bergson and James, yet he held that truth is to be reached not only through the intellect but through the whole range of experience, and to this extent he departed from the emphasis on rational demonstration found in traditional Catholic philosophy. Most of Blondel's teaching was done at the University of Aix-en-Provence, where he taught from 1896 until his death.

Thought. An extended statement of Blondel's philosophy is found in the book *L'Action,* first published in 1893 and revised near the end of his life. This book should not be confused with another of the same title, published in 1937.

The claim of Blondel's early work is that philosophy must take its impetus from action rather than from pure thought. The expression "action" is used in a wide sense to refer to the whole of our life, thinking, feeling, willing. Blondel tells us that it is to the whole man in his concreteness that philosophy must look in its quest for truth. One must turn from abstract thought to actual experience in all its fullness and richness. It is indeed this experience itself that motivates the philosophical quest, for man by his nature must act, and then he cannot help questioning the meaning of his action. Blondel anticipated the ideas later developed in existentialism when he pointed out that although we have not chosen to live and know neither whence we come nor even who we are, we are continually taking action and engaging ourselves in chosen policies.

Blondel rejected any nihilistic attempt to set aside the question of the meaning of action, and he had an ingenious argument to show that we cannot be content to say that action has no meaning. He claimed that to affirm nothing is really to affirm being. The very idea of nothing can be formed only by conceiving something positive and then denying it. There is something positive and affirmative underlying the denials of the nihilist, and even from his pessimistic view of life he derives a certain satisfaction. Blondel argued that the nihilist's nothing is his all. The very extent of what he denies reveals the greatness of what he wishes, for he cannot prevent affirmative ideas and aspirations from asserting themselves in the midst of his denials. Therefore, Blondel claimed, the problem of action and of its meaning must have a positive solution.

This solution is to be sought by means of a kind of phenomenology of action, though a phenomenology that is meant to show that we must pass beyond the phenomena to the discovery of the "supraphenomenal." We are impelled to this solution by reason of an immanent dialectic in action itself, made clear by a phenomenological description.

The basis of the dialectic is the gap between action and its realization. Man cannot in his action equal what he himself demands, and so there is in life a permanent dissatisfaction set up by the contrast between action and the realization at which it aims. This impels man to further action, and in the effort to close the gap, Blondel visualized the expansion of action in terms of an ever wider outreach. Self-regarding action passes over into various forms of social action, and these in turn come to their limit in the highest type of moral action—that which aims at the good of all mankind.

But although this process partially overcomes the contrast between action and its realization, it never does so completely, and the gap reappears at each stage. There is no immanent solution to the problem of action. But we have seen already that an affirmative solution is demanded, and Blondel claimed that the demands of action itself point us from the immanent to the transcendent or supraphenomenal. The Catholic dimensions of Blondel's philosophy become fully apparent at this point, for it is essentially a philosophy of grace. God is immanent within man, in the sense that human action is already directed beyond the phenomenal order. To will all that we do will is already to have the action of God within us. Yet this quest for realization would be a frustrating one were it not that God in turn moves toward us in his transcendence, and human action is supported and supplemented by divine grace.

Since action is concrete, the beliefs that arise out of action and the experience of acting are not abstract formulations. It is in action that we apprehend God, but if we try to imprison him in a proposition or prove his existence by a logical demonstration, he escapes us.

In *La Pensée* and subsequent writings, Blondel gave a more prominent place to thought and modified some of the anti-intellectualist tendencies that characterized his earlier period. At the same time, he reduced the differences that had separated him from traditional Catholic philosophy. But it must not be supposed that he departed in any essential respect from his philosophy of action. Thought and action were never rival principles for Blondel, but were at all times to be taken together. Action is no blind drive, but always includes thought; thought can attain its philosophical goals only as it remains closely associated with action. Thus, in his later phase, when he reconsidered the rational proofs of theism, he claimed that these proofs are possible only on the basis of a prior affirmation of God that has arisen out of our experience as active beings.

Works by Blondel

L'Action: Essai d'une critique de la vie et d'une science de la pratique. Paris, 1893; rev. ed., 1950.

La Pensée, 2 vols. Paris, 1934.

L'Être et les êtres. Paris, 1935.

L'Action, 2 vols. Paris, 1937.

La Philosophie et l'esprit chrétien, 2 vols. Paris, 1944–1946.

Exigences philosophique du christianisme. Paris, 1950.

Works on Blondel

Dumery, H., *Blondel et la religion.* Paris, 1954.

Dumery, H., *La Philosophie de l'action.* Paris, 1948.

Lefèvre, F., *L'Itinéraire philosophique de Maurice Blondel.* Paris, 1928.

Taymans d'Eypernon, F., *Le Blondélisme.* Louvain, 1935.

Tresmontant, Claude, *Introduction à la métaphysique de Maurice Blondel.* Paris, 1963.

John Macquarrie

BLOUNT, CHARLES (1654–1693) was an English deist, freethinker, and controversial writer on religion and politics. He was born at Upper Holloway, and was educated under the supervision of his father, Sir Henry Blount, traveler and author of *Voyage to the Levant* (1636). A disciple of Lord Herbert of Cherbury ("father of English deism") and of Hobbes, Blount is commonly regarded as the second English deist. Although not particularly original, he was the first popularizer of deistic thought. By artful writing—associating himself not only with Lord Herbert and Hobbes but also with John Dryden, Dr. Thomas Sydenham, Bishop Thomas Burnet, and Sir Thomas Browne—and by family influence, Blount was able to steer clear of prosecution under the Licensing Act and the blasphemy laws.

In 1679 Blount began a career of publication with *Anima Mundi: or an Historical Narration of The Opinions of the Ancients Concerning Man's Soul After this Life: According to Unenlightened Nature*, a collection from pagan writers concerning disbelief in immortality. This was shortly followed by *The Last Sayings, or Dying Legacy of Mr. Thomas Hobbs of Malmsbury, who departed this Life on Thursday, December 4th, 1679* (1680). This work is a compilation of some of Hobbes's rationalistic (deistic) passages on religion: for example, "To say he [man] speaks by supernatural inspiration, is to say he finds an ardent desire to speak, or some strong opinion of himself, for the which he can alledge no natural reason"; "He that believes a thing only because it may be so, may as well doubt of it, because it may be otherwise."

Also in 1680 Blount published an oblique attack on priestcraft in *Great is Diana of the Ephesians, or the Original of Idolatry, Together with the Politick Institution of the Gentiles Sacrifices.* In the same year there appeared his ironic survey of a sham pagan miracle-maker in *The Two First Books of Philostratus Concerning the Life of Apollonius Tyaneus, written originally in Greek, with philological notes upon each chapter.* In 1683 Blount published *Religio Laici*, "Written in a Letter to John Dryden, Esq.," whose poem of the same name had appeared the previous year. Blount's work, long supposed to have been derived from Lord Herbert's prose tract of 1645 also entitled *Religio Laici*, is now known to be much more closely related to a similarly entitled manuscript of Lord Herbert's, unpublished until 1933. In his tract, Blount, under the guise of defending universal or natural religion, attacked by indirection the whole concept of a particular revelation. Attributed to Blount (by Antony a Wood) was the free translation (1683) of Chapter VI of Spinoza's *Tractatus Theologico-Politicus* (in Latin, 1670; in English, 1689), under the title of *Miracles No Violations of the Laws of Nature*, which emphasized the Spinozistic interpretation of Biblical miracles as natural phenomena or metaphorical or exaggerated language.

The appearance of Bishop Thomas Burnet's *Archaeologiae Philosophicae* (Latin and English versions in 1692) gave Blount the welcome opportunity to "vindicate" the pseudoscientific and allegorical attempts of the writer to explain certain delicate problems in the early chapters of Genesis. Writing in the form of a letter to Charles Gildon, Blount cited the authority of Sir Thomas Browne that "there are in Scripture stories that do exceed the Fables of Poets" and proceeded to ridicule Burnet's amiable rendition of the conversation between Eve and the Serpent, and his handling of such questions as "how out of only one rib a woman's whole body could be built" and "what language Adam spoke in the first hour of his nativity in naming the animals." This work, edited by Gildon, appeared in 1693, the year of Blount's death, in *The Oracles of Reason*. Another letter in the same collection from Blount to Dr. Thomas Sydenham is prefixed to *A Summary Account of the Deist's Religion*, wherein the worship of God by means of images and sacrifices or through a mediator is impugned and worship by imitation of God's perfections is upheld.

Blount, a Whig, was also active on the political front. Derived from Milton's *Areopagitica*, his *A Just Vindication of Learning, And the Liberty of the Press*, and *Reasons humbly offered for the Liberty of Unlicensed Printing* were published in 1693. A third work of the same year, written under the pseudonym "Junius Brutus," was a master stroke demonstrating the futility of licensing. It was titled *King William and Queen Mary Conquerors: Or, A Discourse Endeavouring to prove that their Majesties have on Their Side, against the Late King, the Principal Reasons that make Conquest a Good Title*, and Blount duped the Tory licenser, Edmund Bohun, into granting permission to publish. By order of the House of Commons the work was burnt by the common hangman, and Bohun was dismissed in disgrace (Macaulay makes much of the incident in Chapter 19 of his *History of England).*

In this year of triumph Blount let emotionalism get the better of rationalism and committed suicide over hopeless love for his deceased wife's sister, who would not agree to a marriage deemed illegal by the Church of England.

Bibliography

The nearest approach to a collection of Blount's works is *Miscellaneous Works* (London, 1695), edited by Charles Gildon with a life of Blount and a justification of his suicide. But see J. S. L. Gilmour, "Some Uncollected Authors XVII: Charles Blount," in *Book Collector*, Vol. VII (1958), 182–187.

Modern studies of Blount include Harold R. Hutcheson, "Lord Herbert and the Deists," in *Journal of Philosophy*, Vol. 43 (1946), 219–221; Eugene R. Purpus, "Some Notes on a Deistical Essay Attributed to Dryden," in *Philological Quarterly*, Vol. 30 (1950) 342–349; George F. Sensabaugh, "Adaptations of *Areopagitica*," in *Huntington Library Quarterly*, Vol. XIII (1950), 201–205.

(See also the general bibliography under DEISM.)

ERNEST CAMPBELL MOSSNER

BODIN, JEAN (1530–1596), French philosopher, statesman, and early writer on economics, is known chiefly for four major systematic works: *Method for the Easy Comprehension of History* (*Methodus ad Facilem Historiarum Cognitionem*, Paris, 1566); *Six Books of the Republic* (*Six Livres de la république*, Paris, 1576); "The Theater of Nature" (*Universae Naturae Theatrum*, Lyons, 1596); and "Dialogue of Seven Wise Men (*Heptaplomeres Sive Colloquium de Abditus Rerum Sublimium Arcanus*, Schwerin, 1857).

Although Bodin's life is only imperfectly known, he was probably born in Anjou into a Catholic family who sought social promotion through service to the king and in clerical charges. Through the help of his bishop, Bodin was admitted at an early age to the Carmelite friars of Angers, who sent him to their school in Paris. While in Paris he probably later studied under the *lecteurs royaux* instituted by Francis I, who personified for Bodin the ideal sovereign. Bodin was probably imprisoned for some time, but later released, on charges of professing Lutheran views. He later studied in Toulouse and was an assistant in the faculty of law there. He participated enthusiastically in the Renaissance ferment at Toulouse, which at that time was a great center of international learning, in close contact with Germany, Switzerland, Italy, Spain, and the papacy at Avignon. Bodin kept in touch with all foreign publications on religion and history, which benefited his lectures on the *Pandects*. He envisaged for a short time the career of a humanist historian in the capacity of headmaster of the Collège de l'Esquille, to which idea we owe a superb discourse of 1559, *Oratio de Institutenda in Republica Juventate*. In addition to a panoramic picture of the French Renaissance inspired by Francis I, the discourse presents a complete humanist pedagogical system.

The failure of his local ambitions and the expectation that the approaching religious wars would engulf Toulouse induced Bodin to leave for Paris, where he found a position as advocate of the Parliament of Paris, a favorable post for receiving any nomination of significance in the king's service. In his work in parliament, Bodin found a type of practical law far superior to the exegesis of ancient texts. He broke with the writers of such exegeses in the preface to his first systematic work, the *Method of History*. The history of the title is the history of knowledge and is similar in conception to that which Descartes later presented in the preface to his *Principles*. For Bodin the three main branches of knowledge are human history, or anthropology; natural history, or physics; and divine history—theology or religion. The *Method* is a general outline of Bodin's whole system; his other three major works are each devoted to one of the three branches. The *Method* itself, though it outlines the entire system, covers in detail only Bodin's anthropology and discusses nearly all of the topics of the later *Republic*.

Social theory. The *Republic* itself, though it partly owes its genesis to Bodin's entire scheme, is also an outcome of a serious French political crisis of the period, which engaged Bodin's attention for many years. The book is a defense of the theory of the French monarchy, as Bodin conceived it, against Machiavellians in the Court and against various rebellious groups. The book seeks to demonstrate that monarchy, and the French monarchy in particular, is the best of all possible regimes.

The state, the republic, is a lawful government of the several households composing it. The state arises when each head of a household, each *pater familias,* acts in concert with the others. These men are the citizens of the republic. Private property is an inalienable right of the family. At the head of this group of households is the sovereign, the administrator of the republic, whose task is the proper government of the households composing the state.

Sovereignty. Bodin's whole political philosophy rests on the doctrine of sovereignty. Sovereignty is defined in the *Republic* as ". . . the absolute and perpetual power of a Republic, that is to say the active form and personification of the great body of a modern State."

In Bodin's conception of sovereignty two different traditions, that of Roman law and that of French monarchy, converge. The former brought with it the notion of *majestas,* which gave supreme authority established above all magistrates, however important they might be, to an absolute power of which they were but a reflection. The tradition of French monarchy, in order to demonstrate the autonomy of the French king in relation to the emperor, had been concerned chiefly with cataloguing the privileges acknowledged as the king's by the pope; these were regarded as so many proofs of the king's sovereign authority. Of these *insignia pecularia,* one list contains no fewer than 208 items.

Bodin reinterprets this twofold juridical trend and attempts to synthesize it. In the *Method* he therefore retains only five marks of sovereignty: the power of appointing higher magistrates and delineating their offices, the power of promulgating or repealing laws, the power of declaring war and concluding peace, the power of judicial review, and the power of life or death even when the law requires death.

When he wrote the *Republic,* Bodin had realized that the essential mark of sovereignty was that of making and repealing laws and that the others were dependent on this right. This right of the sovereign cannot be restricted by custom; the sovereign sanctions customary law by allowing it to continue in force. "Thus, all the force of civil laws and custom lies in the power of the Sovereign Prince." All legislative and judicial power is concentrated in the sovereign, but the sovereign is conceived as the incarnation of a principle and cannot be regarded as having a personal will at variance with the interests of the state. Against the medieval theory, reaffirmed in France in Bodin's day, of the *Politie*—a state in which supreme authority was shared among the prince, an aristocracy based on birth and office, and the representatives of the people—Bodin contends that, if sovereignty is absolute, it is therefore indivisible, wherever it resides. There can be monarchies, aristocracies, or democracies, but never a mixed state.

In a given system of government, different modes of rule are possible. An aristocracy may be governed monarchically, as in Germany, or more or less democratically, as in Venice. But a monarchy, in which the king guarantees all liberty, is the best of regimes.

The state that Bodin depicts—a complex of families and of corporations, classes, and heterogeneous provinces—is enriched by the differences and interactions of its components. They all obey the sovereign, their sole arbiter and the personification of a public weal that is also the weal of its parts. Thus the absolute power of the sovereign transcends that of the *pater familias,* but is conceived in the latter's image. Though the authority of the sovereign is absolute with respect to the other elements of the state, the source of this authority lies in social law, as is clear from the long history of the French state, with its hereditary monarchy subject to a higher law. Though sovereignty is not limited by custom, it is limited by the requirements of justice: Authority is acknowledged as belonging only to a just government—a regime that gives every person, even the wicked, his chance. Sovereignty is also limited externally through the recognition of the legitimacy of other sovereignties, even of conflicting types. The sovereign is further obliged to collaborate with neighboring countries, so that M. J. Basdevant was enabled to see in Bodin one of the founders of modern international law. Bodin's thought is very close to the concept of peaceful coexistence that today forms one of the norms of international law.

The theory of climates. Besides outlining the structure of his ideal republic, a monarchy, Bodin also examines the diversity of states offered by experience. On the one hand he follows the pattern of the Greek philosophers, tracing historically the degradation of this ideal prototype and the manner in which are successively engendered the various forms, sound and pathological, of political organization—tyranny, democracy, aristocracy, and so on. But Bodin also studies the modes of a state's adaptation to its territory. In this investigation, which is known as the theory of climates from a later similar exposition by Montesquieu, Bodin seeks to define more precisely the ways through which geography influences human societies: ". . . the nature of Northern and Southern peoples as well as that of the Eastern and Western ones, then, the influence of the various places, either mountainous, marshy, windswept or sheltered" (*Method of History,* Ch. 5). He gives a rather circumstantial account agreeing in many respects with modern human geography and ethnic psychology. He describes northerners as unequaled in wars and industry and southerners as unequaled in the contemplative sciences, but the inhabitants of the median region are in a particularly fit position for the blossoming of arts and laws.

In the *Method,* Bodin uses anthropogeography as a critical weapon to detect errors committed by outstanding historians in their assessment of facts, and to build a solid framework relating human history to natural history. In the *Republic* his point of view becomes more dogmatic, though his individual observations are more perspicacious. And he makes the important observation that, whatever the ontological superiority of monarchy over other forms of government may be, for a given state the most appropriate regime is the one that answers best to the people and the geography of the place. "One of the greatest and perhaps the chief foundation of Republics is to adapt the state to the citizens' nature, and the edicts and ordinances to the character of places, persons, and times."

Bodin's defense of the French monarchy in the *Method* and his vast culture and philosophical wisdom won him the confidence of the royal family, and in 1571 he entered the service of the duke of Alençon, the brother of the future Henri III, who, after his coronation in 1574, befriended Bodin. But in 1576, at a meeting of the States-General, Bodin delivered a speech in which he succeeded in defeating the king's request for the financial means necessary to suppress the French Protestants. By this speech Bodin temporarily diverted the civil war, but lost the king's favor and was relegated to a humble post in Laon, where he took advantage of the relative calm to write in 1578 the Latin version of the *Republic* (published Paris, 1586) and the *Demonomanie des sorciers* (Paris, 1580). The latter work, which went through some ten editions, advocates the repression of witchcraft and contains as well a complete demonology, in great part taken from the Bible.

Natural history. Upon his return to Laon from trips to the Court of Queen Elizabeth I and to Belgium on missions with the duke of Alencon, Bodin returned to work on the second part of his system, his physics. The *Amphiteatrum Naturae* is in the form of a dialogue in which a "mystagogue" expounds to a "theoretician" a complex and obscure philosophy that attempts to reconcile Neoplatonic idealism with Aristotelian naturalism and also with important religious attitudes derived from the Hebrew tradition. Living beings are explained in terms of Platonic forms, but the nature of the explanation and of the forms remains obscure. The soul is corporeal and is the form of the body. It is separable from the body both in life and at death. It possesses unity, and its function is to vivify the extended matter of the body. The powers of the soul, including sensation and appetite, are seen as modeled on the will: they act directly upon the body with no need of an intermediary. Angels, too, are material, and the human soul is inhabited not only by a good angel and a bad angel, but also by a large number of spirits, each in charge of a special gift. But Bodin is constrained from scrutinizing too closely the mysteries of nature by his awareness of the abyss that separates the Creator from the world of creatures. The *Amphiteatrum Naturae* thus fails, in the end, on a level where Bodin's contemporaries could not question its failure, the religious level.

Theology. A similar failure is evident in the *Dialogue of Seven Wise Men,* a work composed during the last years of Bodin's life and published in part in 1841 and completely in 1857. This work is on the third of Bodin's three branches of knowledge, theology. The seven sages of the title represent three branches of Christianity, Judaism, Islam, natural religion, and skeptical materialism. Despite fertile discussion and a generous courtesy to one another, they cannot arrive at a common foundation for religious matters. In the progress of the discussion, it becomes apparent that in almost every instance the majority agrees with the doctrine of the Jews and that all might accept the decalogue, looked upon as a spiritualization of the natural law and as embodying such fundamental principles. (Bodin had in an earlier work made a comparative study of the institutions of the most diverse countries, from the ancient empires to the recently discovered nations of Africa and America. From this study he had conceived the idea of replacing Roman law with a synthetic and universal law that allowed for different modes of application depending on the place, the era, and the geographic or economic conditions.) But from the historical standpoint, which is so significant for Bodin, only the Christian faiths can contend for victory. Among these, the discussion goes badly for the Protestants, who cannot rationally justify their conservatism, their innovations, or their contradictions. The Catholic church, since it possesses the most elaborate body of doctrine, is subjected to the most criticism; but the fact that the Catholic church remains the religion of the state, and is relatively stable in the midst of uncertainty, is for Bodin to some degree a vindication of the faith of its partisans. The book proposes, therefore, that the church is to be believed, as the Catholic prelate has held successfully throughout the dialogue.

This justification of the Catholic church is in line with Bodin's support of the Catholic League during his last years, a support that was not dictated simply by the instinct of self-preservation. But Bodin was not fully trusted by the members of the League and was more or less confined to his house, where he spent most of his time in contemplation and the education of children, for whom he wrote a catechism in the spirit of the *Amphiteatrum Naturae.* Bodin died as a Christian and was buried in the choir of a church.

Bodin's work enjoyed outstanding renown until the middle of the seventeenth century but was totally disregarded in the eighteenth, and without a famous article in Bayle's *Dictionary,* it would never have recovered from this neglect. Bodin's work was restored to favor in 1853 through Henri Baudrillart's *Jean Bodin et son temps,* and in the twentieth century he has resumed his place among the acknowledged great political philosophers of all time. Bodin also merits consideration as one of the most representative spirits of the Renaissance, and one of the first to formulate historical laws in each of the three realms—divine, natural, and human—that he considered.

Works by Bodin

Le Théâtre de la nature, translated by François de Fougerolles. Lyons, 1597.

The Six Books of a Commonweale, translated by Richard Knolles. London, 1606. Modern edition, K. D. McRae, ed. Cambridge, Mass., 1962.

Johannis Bodini Colloquium Heptaplomeres, L. Noack, ed. Paris and London, 1857.

La Réponse à M. de Malestroict, Henri Hauser, ed. Paris, 1932. One of Bodin's economic works.

La Méthode de l'histoire, translated by Pierre Mesnard. Algiers, 1941.

Method for the Easy Comprehension of History, translated by Beatrice Reynolds. New York, 1945.

Oeuvres philosophiques, Pierre Mesnard, ed. Paris, 1951. Vol. I.

Works on Bodin

Brown, L. S., *The Methodus ad Facilem Historiarum Cognitionem.* Washington, 1939.

Chauvire, R., *Jean Bodin l'auteur de la République.* Paris, 1914.

Garosci, A., *Jean Bodin.* Milan, 1934.

Mesnard, Pierre, *L'Essor de la philosophie politique au XVIième siècle,* 2d ed. Paris, 1952.

Mesnard, Pierre, *Jean Bodin en la historia del pensamiento,* translated by José Antonio Maravall. Madrid, 1962.

Mesnard, Pierre, "The Psychology and Pneumatology of Jean Bodin." *International Philosophical Quarterly,* Vol. 2 (May 1962).

PIERRE MESNARD

BODY – MIND PROBLEM. See MIND – BODY PROBLEM.

BOEHME, JAKOB (1575 – 1624), the Lutheran contemplative, was born at Alt Seidelberg near Görlitz in Silesia and lived there nearly all his life, working chiefly as a cobbler. Among his mystical experiences, the seminal one occurred in 1600, when he glanced at a pewter dish that reflected the sunlight and in a rapt state saw "the Being of Beings, the Byss and the Abyss, the eternal generation of the Trinity, the origin and descent of this world, and of all creatures through the Divine Wisdom" (*Second Epistle,* §6). Though not formally educated, Boehme read rather widely and was influenced by, among others, Paracelsus (1493 – 1541) and Valentin Weigel (1538 – 1588), the Lutheran mystic. The above quotation, however, hints at most of the main features of Boehme's *Weltanschauung,* which he first expressed in his *Aurora, oder die Morgenröte im Aufgang* (1612) and then in other works (from 1618 onward—he did not write in the intervening period because of ecclesiastical pressure). The "Abyss" is God considered as the *Ungrund*—the undifferentiated Absolute that is ineffable and neither light nor darkness, neither love nor wrath. The "eternal generation of the Trinity" occurs because the *Ungrund* contains a will to self-intuition. This will (identified with the Father) finds itself as the "heart" (the Son). Emanating from these is the "moving life" (the Spirit). This eternal process toward self-knowledge and outgoing dynamic activity generates the inner spiritual world, which is the prototype of the visible universe. With differentiation, conflict of wills becomes possible; and Satan, in severing himself from the "heart," falls. Sometimes Boehme writes as if evil were necessary, at others as though it were a contingent spoiling of the cosmic harmony. Indeed, Boehme in general shifted his position, and no single metaphysical theory fits all his writings.

This was partly because, in addition to his doctrine of the Trinity considered in itself, Boehme also enunciated a theory of seven qualities or energies in nature; and the fluidity of his metaphysics results from different ways of coordinating these two main aspects of his thought. The seven qualities divide into two triads, a higher and a lower, between which there is the crucial energy he called "the flash" (*Blitz*). The lower triad is (1) contraction (whereby substances become individuated), (2) diffusion (whereby things gravitate to one another), and (3) rotation or oscillation (the tension produced by the interplay of the forces of contraction and diffusion). The higher triad is in effect the lower triad transformed: it is (1) love, (2) expression, and (3) eternal nature or the Kingdom of God, through which there is achieved a harmony between the material and spiritual worlds.

The meaning of this evolutionary scheme is that the Trinity considered in itself is merely formal or ideal. The abysmal will needs a real object to arouse self-knowledge. Thus the Father differentiates himself through the first (lower) triad into material nature. An obstacle is thereby created to the abysmal will, which can be overcome, not by abolition, but only by transformation. The flash is the collision, as it were, between the absolute will and nature. Herein the Spirit reveals in its light the higher triad, identified with the Son as the incarnation of spirit in matter. This is the goal of the divine operation, whereby the opposition is overcome and made into a harmony.

Psychologically, the flash reveals to man his choices. He can remain at the level of anguish implicit in the welter of sensation represented by the oscillation of nature; or he can "die" unto self, and identify himself with the abysmal will—which also has to negate itself in order to achieve victory. Thus the mystical life is an imitation of Christ's suffering and triumph.

Boehme's doctrines brought him into conflict with church authorities. He was critical of the bibliolatry he detected in contemporary Protestantism, of a formalistic doctrine of election, and of crude notions of heaven (for Boehme, heaven is not a place). In England, William Law and the Behmenists (Boehme's disciples), who merged with the Quakers, were strongly influenced by him. And German Romanticism owed something to him—especially F. W. J. von Schelling, notably in his later writings.

Works by Boehme

The German edition of Boehme is *Jakob Böhmes sämmtliche werke,* 7 vols. (Leipzig, 1832 – 1860); translated by J. Ellistone and J. Sparrow as *The Works of Jacob Behmen,* 4 vols. (London, 1644 – 1662; re-edited, 1764 – 1781; reprinted, 1909 – 1924). *The Signature of All Things* and two other works are to be found in the Everyman edition, Emert Rhys, ed.; introduction by Clifford Bax (London, 1912). See also W. S. Palmer, ed., *The Confessions of Jacob Boehme* (London, 1920).

Works on Boehme

A good introduction is Rufus M. Jones, *Spiritual Reformers in the 16th and 17th Centuries* (London, 1914), Chs. 9 – 11. See also H. H. Brinton, *The Mystic Will* (New York, 1930) and H. L. Martensen, *Jacob Boehme: His Life and Teaching,* translated by T. Rhys Evans (London, 1885).

NINIAN SMART

BOETHIUS, ANICIUS MANLIUS SEVERINUS (c. 480 – 524), late Roman statesman and philosopher, was born into the ancient Anician family in Rome, the son of a distinguished father who was consul in 487 and twice prefect of the city. Carefully educated in the liberal arts and philosophy—possibly in Athens—and precocious in genius, he entered public life at an early age under Theodoric the Ostrogoth, the Arian king of Italy from 493 to 526, who made use of Romans and the traditional administrative methods in his government.

Boethius became consul in 510 and for many years was Theodoric's principal minister (*magister officiorum*). In 522 his two sons became consuls; shortly thereafter Boethius was arrested on a charge of treason that cannot now be defined but that he denounced as a calumny. It has been suggested that Boethius wished to exalt the Roman senate and to negotiate with Byzantium; it is also possible that as a Catholic he was distasteful to Theodoric. Condemned to exile and then to death, he was imprisoned for a year at Pavia and executed in 524. His father-in-law Symmachus and Pope John II were similarly put to death in 525 and 526.

Boethius' cult at Pavia, apparently resting on a confusion with Severinus of Cologne, won him popular canonization as a martyr. In recent centuries, however, his Christian allegiance has been questioned because of the absence of religious themes in his *De Consolatione* and the doubtful authenticity of his theological writings. The question was settled when definite proof of his authorship of these pieces was provided by H. Usener in 1877. Many readers have felt it strange that Boethius, faced with death, should have found his principal stay in Stoic and Neoplatonist philosophy, but such an attitude is not without parallels in the cultured circles of late Roman society. We may note that the readers of Boethius in the ages of faith seem to have felt no uneasiness on this count.

Writings. The literary fecundity of Boethius is astonishing, especially in view of his family life and exacting official duties. He wrote on education, science, philosophy, and theology, but he was above all a logician, a translator, and a commentator. His *Elements of Arithmetic*, *Elements of Music*, and *Elements of Geometry* (written 500–510) all summarize existing works by Nicomachus of Gerasa and by Euclid. Of theological works attributed to him, four are now recognized as authentic: *On the Trinity* and *On the Person and Two Natures in Christ, Against Eutyches and Nestorius*, and two smaller tracts. The treatise *On the Catholic Faith* is of doubtful authenticity.

In philosophy Boethius set himself the task of translating and commenting upon all the works of Plato and Aristotle, with a view to a final harmonization of their teachings.

Translations. As part of his ambitious program, Boethius produced the following translations: the *Introduction* (*Isagoge*) of Porphyry and the *Categories* of Aristotle (the so-called old logic); the *Prior Analytics* and *Posterior Analytics*, the *Sophistic Arguments* and the *Topics* of Aristotle (the so-called new logic). It is questionable whether the Boethian translations are still extant among the various primitive translations that were supplanted by versions by Gerald of Cremona and others.

Commentaries. Boethius produced two commentaries on the *Introduction* of Porphyry, one for beginners and the other, his chief philosophical work, for advanced students (composed 507–509); one on the *Categories* (510); on Victorinus' translation of the *Introduction* (before 505); and on the *Topics* of Cicero. In addition, he wrote several short treatises on logic.

Finally, there is Boethius' masterpiece, *On the Consolation of Philosophy*, written while he was in prison at Pavia, a dialogue in prose and verse between the writer and Philosophy personified, in which the just man unjustly suffering is confirmed in his conviction that happiness and fortitude may be found in adversity. The arguments used are in part Stoic and in part Neoplatonic, but the sentiment throughout is religious, though not explicitly Christian.

Boethius lived during a period of considerable intellectual activity in Rome. Cassiodorus was his colleague, and among his elder contemporaries were the great popes Gelasius I and Hormisdas, and the canonist and chronologist Denis the Little. By his early death he escaped the disasters that befell Italy during Justinian's attempt to recapture the peninsula for the Byzantine Empire and the ravages of the Goths.

The sack and evacuation of Rome in 546 may with some assurance be taken as the dividing line in Italy between the ancient and the medieval cultures. Standing thus at the very end of a civilization, Boethius may rightly be called an eminent founder of the Middle Ages and a figure of supreme importance in the history of Western thought. Himself one of the "last of the Romans," he was also the last Western thinker to whom the works of Plato and Aristotle were familiar in Greek and to whom ancient thought in all its fullness was still comprehensible. His translations and commentaries, though neglected for centuries, stimulated and fed the minds of those who brought about the revival of dialectic in the eleventh century, and gave to medieval speculation the dialectical bent and the Aristotelian color that it never lost. Moreover, his approach to theological issues, though consciously reflecting the procedure of Augustine, was in fact more technical and dialectical in method than that of any of his predecessors. He professedly used the human power of reasoning to penetrate and explain the dogmas of Christianity and regarded the effort of reason (*ratio*) to support and discuss authority (*auctoritas*) as a principal means in the elucidation of revealed truth. On the technical level of a translator he had a genius second only to that of Cicero for exact reproduction of terms of art in his native language. Many of these terms became current coin in the Middle Ages, and a number of his definitions—those of nature, substance, person, eternity, providence, and beatitude—were accepted and stereotyped by Aquinas and others.

Boethius' influence upon the thinkers of the early scholastic period (1000–1150) can scarcely be exaggerated. It was the Boethian age as surely as the next age was Aristotelian. It was his commentary on Porphyry, in which he gave the answers of Plato and Aristotle to the "problem of universals" that initiated the great controversy on universals in the eleventh century. The early Scholastics' concentration of interest upon logic gave to the whole fabric of medieval thought from Roscelin to William of Ockham, and to the form and content of academic teaching, that preoccupation with method rather than with matter which characterized scholastic thought, giving it accuracy and subtlety but also tending to divorce it from life and to substitute logic for discovery.

The "Consolation." In another realm, the *Consolation of Philosophy* was one of the two or three books of universal appeal throughout the Middle Ages. Philosophically it is notable for containing a long discussion of the eternity of God, defined as the full and perfect possession of endless life always present in its entirety, and the "aeviternity" of the created universe, without beginning or end but existing in the ever-changing succession of time. On the basis of this definition, Boethius tried to solve the problem raised by God's prevision of free human acts. God in eternity has a simultaneous *vision* of all temporal reality, and he sees free acts as free. Here Boethius also made the valuable and influential distinction between that which is (*id quod est*)—for instance, the totality of parts of an individual compound substance—and that by which a substance is what it is, its being (*quo est, esse*). He identified the latter with the "form" of the whole, an important metaphysical declaration rendered classical by Aquinas. Boethius, who was engaged in distinguishing God from all other things, went on to remark that in creatures the form (*esse*) is mentally separable from the substance (*id quod est*), whereas in God his being is identical with "that which is." This is not, as has sometimes been stated, a first enunciation of the celebrated Thomist distinction between essence and existence—it is, rather, the distinction between a substance and its metaphysical cause—but it was a step on the journey, inviting further progress. The mingled melancholy, resignation to divine providence, and sense of the supreme value of the good in life in the *Consolation* appealed powerfully to the experience of those confronting the risks and disasters of medieval life, and it was to them, rather than to monks or theologians, that the work of Boethius brought comfort. It was translated into Anglo-Saxon by King Alfred the Great (c. 890), into German by Notker (c. 1000), and into French by Jean de Meung (c. 1300). It was favorite reading of Dante, Boccaccio, and Chaucer, and inspired numerous imitators.

Works by Boethius

Patrologia Latina, J. P. Migne, ed. Vols. 63 and 64. Complete works, presented uncritically.

In Isagogen Porphyrii Commenta ("Commentaries on Porphyry"), G. Schepss and S. Brandt, eds. Corpus Scriptorum Ecclesiasticorum Latinorum. Vienna, 1906.

Theological Tractates, translated and edited by H. F. Stewart and E. K. Rand. Loeb Classical Library. New York, 1918.

De Consolatione Philosophiae, A. Forti Scuto (Adrian Fortescue), ed. London, 1925. Translated into English by H. R. James. New Universal Library. London and New York, 1906. Another Latin version edited by Weinberger. Corpus Scriptorum Ecclesiasticorum Latinorum. Vienna, 1934.

Works on Boethius

Cappuyns, M., "Boèce," in *Dictionnaire d'histoire et de géographie ecclésiastique*. Paris, 1936. Pp. 348–380. Good and full, with ample bibliography to date of publication.

Cooper, Lane, *A Concordance of Boethius*. Cambridge, Mass., 1928.

Courcelle, P., "Études critiques sur les Commentaires de Boèce." *Archives d'histoire doctrinale et littéraire du moyen âge*, Vol. 13 (1939), 5–140.

Courcelle, P., *Les Lettres grecques en occident de Macrobe à Cassiodore*. Paris, 1943. Pp. 257–312.

Geyer, B., *Die patristische und scholastische Philosophie*. Berlin, 1928; Basel, 1951.

Grabmann, M., *Die Geschichte der scholastischen Methode*, Vol. I. Freiburg im Breisgau, 1909. Pp. 149–160.

Patch, H. R., *The Tradition of Boethius. A Study of His Importance in Medieval Culture*. New York, 1935.

Rand, E. K., *Founders of the Middle Ages*. Cambridge, Mass., 1928.

Usener, H., *Anecdoton Holderi: Ein Beitrag zur Geschichte Roms in Ostgotischer Zeit (Festschrift)*. Bonn, 1877. Usener publishes an unknown text of Cassiodorus referring to four of Boethius' theological writings, hence authenticating them.

David Knowles

BOETIUS OF DACIA

BOETIUS OF DACIA was an Aristotelian and Averroist philosopher of the thirteenth century, sometimes called Boetius of Sweden, after the country of his birth. Born during the first half of the century, he was probably a secular cleric and canon of the diocese of Linkoping. He was an associate of Siger of Brabant as a teacher of philosophy in the faculty of arts at Paris and, as a leader of the Averroist movement, condemned in 1277 by Stephen Tempier, bishop of Paris. With Siger, Boetius fled the city after the condemnation and appealed to the pope. After detention at the pontifical curia at Orvieto, Boetius joined the Dominican order as a member of the province of Dacia. The date of his death is unknown.

Boetius wrote works on logic, natural philosophy, metaphysics, and ethics. Some of these are lost; only a few have been edited. A complete edition of his extant works is now in progress.

Boetius philosophized in a rationalistic spirit, defending his right as a philosopher to discuss any subject falling within the competence of reason and to come to whatever conclusions reason dictated, even though they might contradict Christian faith. He taught, for example, that philosophizing is the most excellent human activity, that philosophers alone are the wise men of this world, that creation *ex nihilo* is impossible, that the world and the human species are eternal, and that there can be no resurrection of the dead. His treatise *On the Highest Good, or On the Life of the Philosopher* contains one of the most glowing and optimistic descriptions of the life of pure reason written in the Middle Ages. Setting aside the teachings of faith, Boetius inquires what reason tells us about the ultimate purpose of human life. Following Aristotle, he defines man's supreme good as the philosophical contemplation of truth and virtuous living according to the norms of nature. The philosopher alone, he concludes, lives rightly and achieves the ultimate end of human life.

Despite his rationalism, Boetius did not abandon his Christian faith but sought an ultimate reconciliation with it. Philosophy, in his view, is the work of human reason investigating the natural causes and principles of the universe, whereas the Christian religion rests on supernatural revelation and miracles of God. Because the teachings of faith have a higher source than those of philosophy, in cases of conflict the latter must give way to the former. Human reason is fallible and often comes to only probable conclusions. Even when its conclusions seem necessary, if they are contrary to revealed doctrine they are not true. In these cases truth is on the side of revelation and not on the side of reason. For example, the philosophical conclusion that the world is eternal must give way to the revealed truth that the world was created in time.

Boetius was condemned for speaking as though there were a double truth, one of faith and another of philosophy. But he carefully avoided calling true a philosophical conclusion contrary to faith.

Bibliography

Doncoeur, P., "Notes sur les averroistes latins. Boèce le Dace." *Revue des sciences philosophiques et théologiques,* Vol. 4 (1910), 500–511.

Gilson, E., *History of Christian Philosophy in the Middle Ages.* New York, 1955.

Grabmann, M., "Die Opuscula De Summo Bono sive De Vita Philosophi und De Sompniis des Boetius von Dacien." *Archives d'histoire doctrinale et littéraire du moyen âge,* Vol. 6 (1931), 287–317.

Grabmann, M., *Mittelalterliches Geistesleben,* 2d ed. Munich, 1936. Vol. II.

Grabmann, M., *Neuaufgefundene Werke des Siger von Brabant und Boetius von Dacien.* Munich, 1924.

Mandonnet, P., "Note complémentaire sur Boèce de Dacie." *Revue des sciences philosophiques et théologiques,* Vol. 22 (1933), 246–250.

Maurer, A., *Medieval Philosophy.* New York, 1962.

Sajó, G.,"Boèce de Dacie et les commentaires anonymes inédits de Munich sur la physique et sur la génération attribués à Siger de Brabant." *Archives d'histoire doctrinale et littéraire du moyen âge,* Vol. 33 (1958), 21–58.

Sajó, G., "Boetius de Dacia und seine philosophische Bedeutung," in *Miscellania Mediaevalia,* Vol. II, *Die Metaphysik im Mittelalter.* Berlin, 1963.

Sajó, G., *Tractatus de Aeternitate Mundi.* Berlin, 1964.

Armand A. Maurer

BOGDANOV, ALEXANDER ALEKSANDROVICH (1873–1928), Russian Marxist economist and philosopher. Bogdanov, whose real name was Malinovski, was trained in psychiatry at the medical school of Kharkov University, served as an army surgeon during World War I, and was one of the founders (in 1926) of the Moscow Institute for Blood Transfusion. (He died as the result of a transfusion experiment which he performed on himself.) However, most of his mature energies were devoted either to politics or to the elaboration and popularization of Marxist economic, sociological, and philosophic theory.

Bogdanov sided with Mach and Avenarius against Plekhanov and Lenin on the question of whether there is a material substance or thing-in-itself that causes our sense experience. As an empiriomonist, he modified empiriocriticism by defining the psychic as experience individually organized and the physical as experience collectively organized. For Bogdanov there was nothing more real than experience, but experience that is collective and stable was more real than that which is individual and transient. In this sense, the objective physical world is more real than the subjective psychic world. Intermediate in reality are space, time, and causality as "organizing forms" of collective experience. Bogdanov's epistemology is thus half Kantian and half realist. His ontology, as Lenin complained, is closer to Berkeley's idealism than to Engels' materialism.

Bogdanov reinterpreted Marxist "objective dialectical contradiction" in the empiriomonist terms of "organization," "energy transfer," and "equilibrium." Tensions develop—not within, but among, entities and processes—when a dynamic equilibrium is disturbed. The tensions are resolved when the equilibrium is restored. Like Hegel (and unlike Lenin), Bogdanov saw synthesis and harmony as more permanent and productive than opposition and conflict.

In ethics and social philosophy Bogdanov distinguished between "coercive norms" (*normy prinuzhdeniya*) and "expediency norms" (*normy tselesoobraznosti*). In Kantian terms, the former are categorical imperatives; the latter, hypothetical imperatives. (They might better be called sanctioning and instrumental norms.) Socialism, according to Bogdanov, will tear down the "great fetishism" of coercive norms, admitting only expediency norms, whose form is "If you want *x*, you must do *y*." The *x* that free men will want is vaguely characterized as a "maximum of life." The social ideal is a collective "integration of man," beyond both coercive obligation and functional specialization.

Historically, in Bogdanov's view, ruling classes have been "organizers of production." The capitalist monopoly of managerial experience will be broken not by abolishing private ownership of the means of production but by disseminating managerial experience and knowledge among the noncapitalists. Emphasis was thus shifted from violent political and economic "expropriation" à la Lenin to mass education and "proletarian culture." (Beginning in 1913 Bogdanov attempted to develop a generalized methodology and theory of modes of organization under the name "tectology.") Such education in the principles of production management was a chief aim of the short-lived *Proletkult* movement of the early 1920s, in which Bogdanov was prominent.

Bibliography

Works by Bogdanov are "Matter as Thing-in-Itself," translated by G. L. Kline, in James M. Edie, James P. Scanlan, Mary-Barbara Zeldin, and George L. Kline, eds., *Russian Philosophy* (Chicago, 1965) *Empiriomonism: Stati po Filosofii* ("Empiriomonism: Articles on Philosophy"), 3 parts (Moscow, 1904–1906); and *Filosofiya Zhivovo Opyta* ("A Philosophy of Living Experience," St. Petersburg, 1912).

See also Gustav Wetter, *Der Dialektische Materialismus* (Vienna, 1956), translated by Peter Heath as *Dialectical Materialism* (New York, 1959), pp. 92–100.

George L. Kline

BÖHME, JAKOB. See Boehme, Jakob.

BOLINGBROKE, HENRY ST. JOHN (1678–1751), English Tory statesman, orator, man of letters, friend of the Augustan wits, libertine, and deist, was born at Battersea, the son of Sir Henry St. John and Lady Mary Rich, daughter of the second earl of Warwick. After early schooling by his paternal grandmother, he was educated at Eton and, putatively, at Christ Church, Oxford, for in 1702 he was made an honorary doctor of Oxford. He had made the customary dissipated grand tour, 1698–1699, but he also mastered several languages and studied the history and customs of the lands he visited. In 1701 he became M.P. for the family borough of Wootton Bassett in Wiltshire. His eloquence and brilliance soon made him a leader of the Tory party. With the help of Robert Harley, he became secretary at war in 1704, but resigned in protest over the dismissal of Harley in 1708. The growing unpopularity of the "Whiggish" War of the Spanish Succession brought Harley back into power in 1710, and Bolingbroke joined the new Tory ministry as secretary of state. Two years later he was created Viscount Bolingbroke and was one of the negotiators of the Treaty of Utrecht signed in 1713. Following the accession of George I in 1714, Bolingbroke and the other Tory ministers were dismissed from office. In 1715 he fled to France to take political asylum for alleged Jacobitism. In 1723 he was pardoned and spent the remainder of his life living variously in England and in France.

Works. Some of Bolingbroke's political writings appeared in the Tory periodical *The Craftsman* between 1726 and 1736; but most others, including the philosophical, were published posthumously in 1754 by David Mallet in an edition of five quarto volumes. This publication elicited Dr. Johnson's famous attack on this "blunderbuss against religion and morality." Hume's reaction is less well known but more pertinent:

> Lord Bolingbroke's posthumous Productions have at last convinc'd the whole World, that he ow'd his Character chiefly to his being a man of Quality, & to the Prevalence of Faction. Never were so many Volumes, containing so little Variety & Instruction: so much Arrogance & Declamation. The Clergy are all enrag'd against him; but they have no Reason. Were they never attack'd by more forcible Weapons than his, they might for ever keep Possession of their Authority.

Political and historical works. Bolingbroke's contributions to *The Craftsman* exhibit much vigorous political writing, including *Remarks on the History of England* and *Dissertation on Parties*. Other tracts, political and historical, are *On the True Use of Retirement and Study*, *On the Spirit of Patriotism*, and *Letters on the Study and Use of History*, the last of which made famous the maxim, "History is philosophy teaching by examples." *The Idea of a Patriot King* also became famous because of its use in the education of the future George III. Matthew Arnold was to lament that Bolingbroke's historical writings were unduly neglected. Unfortunately, the neglect of his philosophical writings is less to be regretted.

Philosophical writings. Bolingbroke made much of the antithesis between nature and art; that is, the alleged superiority of a pure state of nature over the evils of civil society. Edmund Burke, who wrote his *Vindication of Natural Society* (1756) as an imitation of Bolingbroke's style and as an ironic refutation of this antithesis, asked rhetorically in *Reflections on the Revolution in France* (1790): "Who now reads Bolingbroke? Who ever read him through?" The long-held myth of Voltaire's great indebtedness to Bolingbroke has been completely disproved by N. L. Torrey. A similar claim of Pope's great indebtedness has been vigorously challenged by Maynard Mack, who presents evidence that Bolingbroke's *Fragments or Minutes of Essays* were composed later than the *Essay on Man*. There is, however, no question that Pope discussed many matters with his "Guide, Philosopher, and Friend." With the single exception of Peter Annet, Bolingbroke was the last of the distinguished group of English deists beginning with Lord Herbert of Cherbury; but he proves somewhat of a disappointment to students of the history of ideas. Scrappy and unsystematic in his presentations, he is replete with contradictions. Despite recent attempts, especially by D. G. James and W. McMerrill, to take Bolingbroke's philosophy more seriously than has been customary, candor demands the conclusion that, although his style is more eloquent than that of most other deists, he contributed little or nothing original to the movement. This is not, however, to accuse him of plagiarism; for his ideas were part and parcel of the Augustan climate of opinion.

Despite frequent use of the name of Locke (a device used by many deists), Bolingbroke was an unmitigated but curiously inconsistent rationalist. At one moment he asserts that the existence of Deity can and must be proved empirically, and at the next he asserts that only Right Reason can demonstrate the existence of Deity. He wrote *Reflections Concerning Innate Moral Principles* to prove that compassion or benevolence is founded on reason alone. Unlike many of the deists, he was a metaphysical optimist, explaining away the evils of the universe and arguing that it is for man the best of all possible worlds despite the sufferings of individuals. He did not, however, believe that immortality and a future state of rewards and punishments can be proved by reason; and, although he accepted God as spirit, he was a materialist insofar as man is concerned.

He believed that there is no separation between soul and body and that at death man is annihilated; even in life, there is no communication between divine spirit and human matter.

Bolingbroke's concept of Natural Religion was essentially the same as the Common Notions of Lord Herbert of Cherbury. Yet with all his insistence on a priori reason, he lamented time and again that reason is fallible and must be corrected by a return to the primitive religions, particularly those of China and Egypt. Like all the deists, he was contemptuous of priestcraft and, despite his rationalism, of metaphysics. His criticism of Christian revelation is much like Matthew Tindal's, and the insinuation is that any revelation that is not universal is unnecessary.

In sum, Bolingbroke was more the orator than the philosopher. There is, however, considerable truth in his statement that "There is no reason . . . to banish eloquence out of philosophy; and truth and reason are no enemies to the purity, nor to the ornaments of language." He considered Plato, Malebranche, and Berkeley as poets, not philosophers, and his own best defense is the eloquence he admired.

Bibliography

After Mallet's edition (London, 1754) there were three editions of Bolingbroke's collected works (London, 1777 and 1809; Philadelphia, 1841). His *Letters* appeared toward the end of the eighteenth century (London, 1798).

Modern studies include: Sir Douglas Harkness, *Bolingbroke:*

The Man and His Career (London, 1957); D. G. James, *The Life of Reason: Hobbes, Locke, Bolingbroke* (London, 1949); Walter McMerrill, *From Statesman to Philosopher: A Study in Bolingbroke's Deism* (New York, 1949); Sir Charles Petrie, *Bolingbroke* (London, 1937); Alexander Pope, *An Essay on Man*, Maynard Mack, ed., Twickenham edition (London, 1950), Vol. III, I; George H. Nadel, "New Light on Bolingbroke's *Letters on History*," in *Journal of the History of Ideas*, Vol. 23 (1962), 550–557; Walter Sichel, *Bolingbroke and His Times*, 2 vols. (London, 1901–1902); Norman L. Torrey, *Voltaire and the English Deists* (New Haven, 1930), Ch. 6, "Chubb and Bolingbroke: Minor Influences."

ERNEST CAMPBELL MOSSNER

BOLLAND, GERARD J. P. J. (1854–1922), Dutch philosopher, disciple of Hegel, was born in Groningen, the Netherlands, and died in Leiden. Although he was self-taught, Bolland became a teacher, first in grade school, then in high school, in the Dutch East Indies. From 1896 to 1922 he was professor of philosophy at Leiden. Bolland entered into many disputes by reason of his confident comprehension in the most different fields of science and letters. He struggled passionately against materialism, democracy, socialism, and Catholicism, preferring an autocratic royal government. His philosophical influence did not reach beyond the Dutch frontier, and passed with the generation of his immediate students.

At first Bolland was a follower of the transcendental realism of E. von Hartmann, but later he became a Hegelian, editing and commenting on Hegel's *History of Philosophy* and *Phenomenology*, and producing Hegelian studies of his own. Bolland regarded Hegel's philosophy as the highest stage of the emergent self-consciousness of the Absolute Spirit. He was aware, however, of the danger that this process might end in a fixed canon of philosophical theories. Bolland held that self-conscious reasoning proceeds by means of the dialectical method, which resolves the contradictions that conceptual thought opposes one to another by uniting them in a synthesis or higher unity without annulling their differences. The logical principle of noncontradiction loses its validity in this formulation: rational thought must proceed by the highest rational unit, the Idea or the Absolute Spirit, and by use of deduction discover the sense of reality and explain the connection of appearances.

Works by Bolland

Die Lebenserscheinungen und der Erklärungswahn in der Physiologie der Gegenwart. Batavia, Java, 1890.
Het Wereldraadsel. Leiden, 1896.
Hegel's kleine Logik. Leiden, 1899.
Alte Vernunft und neuer Verstand. Leiden, 1902.
Het Verstand en Zijne Verlegenheden. Leiden, 1903.
Zuivere Rede. Leiden, 1904.
Collegium Logicum. Leiden, 1905.
Hegel's Encyclopädie der philosophischen Wissenschaften. Leiden, 1906.
De Natur. Leiden, 1908.
De Logica. Leiden, 1911.

Works on Bolland

Clay, J., "Bolland en Zijn *Invloed*." *Pallas Leidensis* (1925).
De Idee (1927). Bolland number.
Van den Bergh van Eysinga, G. A., *Bolland Herdacht*. Amsterdam, 1932.

F. L. R. SASSEN

BOLLNOW, OTTO FRIEDRICH, German philosopher and educational theorist, was born in 1903 at Stettin. He first studied mathematics and physics, obtaining his doctorate at Göttingen in 1925. Later he studied philosophy and pedagogy at Göttingen and Freiburg. After qualifying as an instructor at Göttingen in 1931, he was appointed professor of philosophy and pedagogy at Giessen in 1939. Subsequently he served at Mainz (1946), and since 1953 he has taught at Tübingen.

Bollnow's writings center on the problem of a philosophical anthropology. As the hermeneutics of human life, philosophical anthropology interprets every individual phenomenon within the context of the whole of life, taken as a fundamentally "open" unit of significance. There is no such thing as an invariable, a priori structure of essences, capable of being formally isolated. But every historically and culturally defined manifestation of life enters into the constitution of the human essence and has the same title to being interpreted.

This forthright formulation of the question has far-reaching, objective consequences, among them an airing of differences with Heidegger. Bollnow disputes the preeminence given selected phenomena (such as anxiety or dread) as guidelines for an ontological analytic of human existence (*Dasein*); he rejects the existentialist view which ties man down to a quite specific form of existence. Essential and indispensable as they are, the categories of anxiety, decision, authenticity, and the like are one-sided and must be corrected by the different experiences of reality obtained in happy moods. What is involved here is not merely supplementation of the categories recognized by existentialists, but the central insight that without a positive reference to a sustaining reality, without confidence and hope, life would be utterly impossible.

Poetry points the direction to a "restored or healed world" (*Bergengruen*), but it is above all revealed in the educational experience that a child can develop and mature only in an atmosphere of security (*Geborgenheit*). Existentialism overlooks its own assumptions. Freedom of decision is possible only on a sustaining subsoil of security; only on this basis can one endure the constant threat to which human reality is subject. It follows that security does not signify a naive safety or certainty. Rather, it designates that condition—which itself is to be fulfilled and guaranteed—under which the tension of life can be endured. A philosophical anthropology cannot omit the ethical aspect, and this leads in the case of Bollnow to the long-misunderstood virtues of a "simple morality."

Whereas existentialism conceives of man in terms of temporality, the problem raised by Bollnow of a "new security" results in a philosophy of the "space lived in" (*gelebter Raum*): the characteristic manner in which man is in the world is that he dwells in it. The term "space lived in" designates a nonobjective relationship to reality that is captured only approximately by such concepts as familiarity, intimacy, and identification, and that corresponds most closely to the way in which a man may be said to have his body. Here for the first time the existentialist problem of man's becoming himself is given a deeper foundation. For if confidence, hope, security, and dwelling are indispensable conditions for the possibility of human life, then the concerns of the philosophy of existence can be retained and validated anew only in a philosophical anthropology of the kind undertaken by Bollnow.

Bibliography

Bollnow's works include the following: *Dilthey* (Stuttgart, 1936); *Das Wesen der Stimmungen* (Frankfurt, 1941); *Existenzphilosophie* (Stuttgart, 1943); *Einfache Sittlichkeit* (Göttingen, 1947); *Rilke* (Stuttgart, 1951); *Die Pädagogik der deutschen Romantik* (Stuttgart, 1952); *Neue Geborgenheit. Das Problem einer Überwindung des Existentialismus* (Stuttgart, 1955); *Die Lebensphilosophie* (Berlin, 1958); *Existenzphilosophie und Pädagogik* (Stuttgart, 1959); *Mass und Vermessenheit des Menschen* (Göttingen, 1961); and *Mensch und Raum* (Stuttgart, 1963).

FRIEDRICH KÜMMEL
Translated by *Albert E. Blumberg*

BOLTZMANN, LUDWIG (1844–1906), Austrian physicist and philosopher of science, was born in Vienna and received his Ph.D. in physics from the University of Vienna in 1866. He held chairs of mathematics, mathematical physics, and experimental physics at Graz, Munich, and Vienna. In addition, he taught courses on the methodology and general theory of science.

Boltzmann combined a strong and unerring philosophical instinct with a sharp intellect, a great sense of humor, a somewhat violent temperament, and an exceptional mastery of presentation. His lectures in theoretical physics were attended by many nonphysicists, who could understand the problems which Boltzmann took care to state independently of the mathematical arguments. "The true theoretician," he wrote, "makes only sparing use of formulae. It is in the books of the allegedly practical thinkers that one finds formulae only too frequently, and used for mere adornment." His lectures on experimental physics were exquisite performances which he prepared with care and presented with flamboyance. Boltzmann often invited his academic opponents, such as Friedrich Jodl, to his philosophical lectures and debated with them in front of the students. Music was a special interest: he had studied with the composer Anton Bruckner and played the pianoforte; and he periodically arranged evenings of chamber music and more lighthearted parties at his home.

The effect of his teaching upon the younger generation of natural scientists can hardly be exaggerated. "All of us younger mathematicians were then on Boltzmann's side," Arnold Summerfeld wrote about the Lübeck discussions on energetics in 1895, where the "bull" Boltzmann, supported by the mathematician Felix Klein, defeated the "torero Ostwald despite the latter's expert fencing." Svante Arrhenius and Walther Nernst studied with Boltzmann in Graz, Paul Ehrenfest attended his Vienna lectures, and Einstein—not inclined to listen to lectures—read his published work and was strongly influenced both by the physics and by the philosophy it contained. Wilhelm Ostwald called Boltzmann "a man who was superior to us all in intelligence, and in the clarity of his science." On the occasion of Boltzmann's sixtieth birthday, thinkers from many different countries—among them A. Chwolson, Pierre Duhem, Gottlob Frege, Max Planck, and Ernst Mach—contributed to an impressive *Festschrift* (Leipzig, 1904). Two years later Boltzmann, who was subject to severe depression, committed suicide.

PHILOSOPHY OF SCIENCE

Physics and philosophy are inseparably connected in Boltzmann's work. He was one of those rare thinkers who are content neither with general ideas nor with simple collections of facts, but who try to combine the general and the particular in a single coherent point of view. He felt scorn and even hatred for the "philosophers of the schools" (he mentions Berkeley's "crazy theories," Kant, Schopenhauer, Hegel, and Herbart), who, according to him, offer but a few "vague and absurd ideas." He admitted that they had "eliminated theories of a still more primitive nature," but he criticized them for not going further and for believing that the final truth had already been obtained (see *Populäre Schriften*, Chs. 18 and 22). The same criticism was applied to those contemporary physicists—and especially to their philosophical leaders, Ernst Mach and Wilhelm Ostwald—who thought that they had achieved a purely phenomenological physics which did not transcend physical experience and which could therefore be retained in all future developments.

Hypothetical character of knowledge. The reasons Boltzmann gave for his dissatisfaction with dogmatic systems of thought were partly biological, partly logical. Boltzmann's biological argument took the following lines: Our ideas are the result of a process of adaptation by trial and error (Boltzmann was an enthusiastic follower of Darwin, whose theory he extended both to the origin of life—thus anticipating Aleksander Oparin—and to the development of thought). Some of these ideas, such as that of the Euclidean character of space, may be "inborn" in the sense that the individual is endowed with them through the development of the species. Such an origin explains their force, the impression of incorrigibility, but "it would be a fallacy to assume, as did Kant, that they are therefore absolutely correct" (*ibid.*, Ch. 17). The future development of the species, aided by scientific research, may lead to further modifications and to further improvement.

The logical argument (*ibid.*, Chs. 10, 14, 19) was as follows: It is to be admitted that one can try to adhere as closely as possible to experience and that one might in this way obtain a physics that is free from hypotheses. But, first of all, such a physics has not yet been achieved—"the phenomenological physics only apparently contains less arbitrary assumptions. Both [that is, atomism and the phenomenological theory] proceed . . . from experimental laws which are valid for macroscopic objects. Both derive from them the laws which are supposed to be valid on the microlevel. Pending further examination, the latter laws are therefore equally hypothetical." Second, it is very doubtful whether a physics without hypotheses would be desirable—"the bolder one is in transcending experience, the greater the chance to make really surprising discoveries . . . the phenomenological account of physics therefore really has no reason to be so proud for sticking so closely to the facts!" Boltzmann's conclusion was that "the edifice of our theories does not consist of . . . irrefutable truths. . . . It consists of largely arbitrary elements . . . so-called hypotheses" (*ibid.*, Ch. 8).

In his realization of the hypothetical character of all our knowledge, Boltzmann was far ahead of his time and perhaps even ahead of our own time. Apriorists and empiricists both claimed to have shown the existence of incorrigible principles, the former supporting their claims by reference to "laws of thought," the latter by reference to "experience" and "induction"; and the majority of thinkers supported either one group or the other. Therefore, the particular consequences that Boltzmann drew from his views were recognized only slowly and rather reluctantly. These consequences are the following.

Scientific theories. Theories transcend experience in two ways. They express more than is contained in our experimental results, and they represent even the latter in an idealized manner. They are therefore only partly determined by the facts. The rest, which is usually almost the whole theory, must be regarded as "an *arbitrary* invention of the human mind" and can be judged only by its simplicity and by its future success. This being the case, it is "quite conceivable that there are two theories, both equally simple, and equally in agreement with experiment, although they are both completely different, and both correct. The assertion that one of them gives a true account can in this case be only the expression of our subjective conviction" (see *ibid.*, Chs. 1, 5, 9, 10, 14, 16, 19). Einstein wrote in *On the Method of Theoretical Physics* (Oxford, 1933), concerning the idea that theories are "free inventions of the human mind," that a clear recognition of the correctness of this notion really only came with the general theory of relativity which showed that we can point to two essentially different principles, both of them corresponding to experience to a large extent.

Deductive and inductive methods. The method of presentation which is best suited to such a situation is the deductive method. Boltzmann discussed both the deductive method and the inductive method in the introductory chapter of his treatise on mechanics (1897).

The deductive method begins with a formulation of basic ideas and establishes contact with experience only later, by specific deductions. It emphasizes the arbitrariness of the basic ideas, clarifies their content, and exhibits the inner consistency of the theory. Its disadvantage is that it gives no account of the arguments that led to the theory in the first place.

The inductive method only apparently removes this disadvantage. It tries to demonstrate how theoretical ideas are obtained from experience, but its proofs cannot stand up under closer examination. Despite considerable effort the gaps in the derivation have not been closed. The inductive method's peculiar way of mixing theoretical ideas and experimental notions leads to a loss in clarity and makes it impossible to judge the consistency of the edifice. "The lack of clarity in the principles of mechanics seems to be connected with the fact that one did not at once start with hypothetical pictures, framed by our minds, but tried to start from experience. The transition to hypotheses was then more or less covered up and it was even attempted artificially to construct some kind of proof to the effect that the whole edifice was free from hypotheses. This is one of the main reasons for the lack of clarity."

The historical development of a physics consisting entirely of hypotheses would be "by leaps and bounds," by cataclysmic changes which would wipe out almost all that is believed at a certain time without regard for even the most fundamental principles; it would not be a gradual process of growth which adds to, but never takes away from, an already existing body of facts and theories.

Criticism. Finally, the hypothetical character of our knowledge makes criticism the most important method of investigation. Boltzmann developed important elements of the point of view which is today connected with the name of K. R. Popper. In his obituary for Josef Loschmidt, Boltzmann suggested, half jokingly, half seriously, a journal dealing only with experiments that had failed (note that the Michelson—Morley experiment, for example, was long regarded as a dismal failure). Criticism can be by comparison with facts, but it can also be by comparison with other theories. "To attack problems from different sides furthers science and [I welcome] each original, enthusiastic piece of scientific research." Boltzmann even encouraged the defenders of the inductive mode of presentation to attempt to reveal the errors in his description so that both sides might profit from the controversy.

PHYSICS

Boltzmann maintained the critical attitude even in actual research. Almost all of his better-known investigations were based upon classical mechanics and on the idea of localizable mass points in Euclidean space. Yet he was fully aware that these notions were not final and tried to formulate them as clearly as possible in order to make future criticism easier. He speculated on the possibility of an electromagnetic explanation of mass, force, and inertia; he doubted the continuity of time, even the notion of continuity itself, and he suggested that the laws of mechanics and perhaps all laws of nature "might be approximate expressions for average values, and not differentiable in the strict sense"; he pointed out that mass points need not be individually distinguishable; he regarded the concept of Euclidean space as a matter in need of further examination. These were striking anticipations of later developments. But Boltzmann did not elaborate them further. He was convinced that the resources of the existent mechanics and of the existent atomic theory were not yet exhausted, and his work in physics was guided by this conviction. He was largely responsible for the central position which the atomic theory and statistical considerations have assumed in contemporary thought.

Toward the end of the last century, the atomic theory was all but abandoned. Boltzmann was regarded as a brilliant defender of a lost cause. The reasons given by most French and German scientists for opposing atomic theory were in part methodological. The idea of small and invisible particles seemed metaphysical in comparison with the theories of thermodynamics that postulated measurable

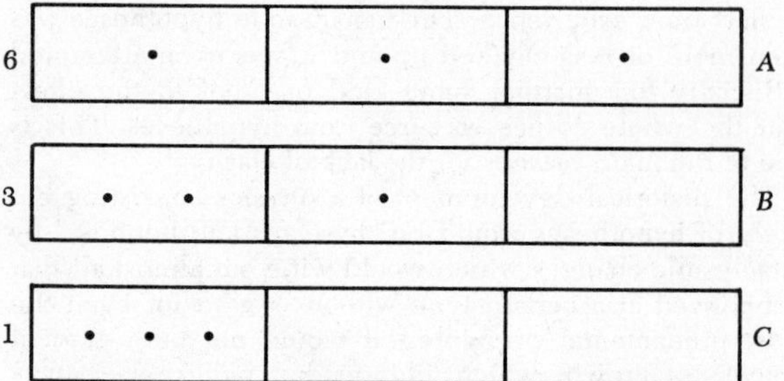

quantities only. In part these reasons were based on real physical difficulties: the Second Law of thermodynamics asserts the existence of irreversible processes which apparently cannot be explained by the atomic theory. However, for any motion that is in accordance with the laws of mechanics, the reverse motion is equally in accordance with the same laws. Now Boltzmann pointed out that while this argument correctly describes the properties of the laws of mechanics, it has not considered the initial conditions or "microstates" the distribution of which will certainly play an important role in systems containing a great number of constituents. It may well be that initial conditions leading to a reversal in motion are almost never realized in nature. In order to explain this, consider, first, a container with three molecules (1, 2, and 3) and assume that our macroscopic measurements (on which the phenomenological account is based) allow us only to determine density differences in volumes of the indicated size (see diagram). Situation A will then be described as a gas having equal density α all over the container. Situation B is a gas with density 2α on the left, α in the middle, 0 on the right. Situation C has density 3α on the left and 0 everywhere else. Now A may be realized in six different ways, by the following six different arrangements of the individual molecules: 123, 132, 213, 231, 312, 321. Situation B can be realized in three ways only: [12]3, [32]1, [13]2. And there is only one way to realize C. Hence, if all arrangements are equally likely, it is more likely to find equal density than unequal density. For three molecules the probabilities are 6:3:1 for A, B, and C. For N molecules, the relation between A and B will be about 2^N, a tremendous number for real gases. Therefore, while the Second Law of thermodynamics correctly represents the statistically most probable distribution, the possibility of minor fluctuations in the microstates is still open.

We must realize, however, that so far we have allowed the molecules to move freely and to take their positions according to the laws of chance. In actual fact, the molecules obey the laws of mechanics, which means that there exist relations of dependence between their positions at different times and —via collisions—between the positions of different molecules. The assertion that all arrangements are equally likely and that A is therefore vastly more probable than B is no longer guaranteed. Boltzmann's so-called H-theorem (which he had to reformulate various times as the result of criticism) solves this problem to some extent by showing that the laws of mechanics, combined with certain probabilistic assumptions about collisions, would lead to the very same result we have just obtained: whatever the initial conditions, there is an overwhelming probability that the magnitude H will decrease until the case of maximum probability according to the above reckoning is realized.

Entropy. In connection with the above investigations, Boltzmann also established a relation between the number of arrangements W leading to a certain macroscopic situation and the entropy S of that situation:

$$S = k \cdot \log W$$

This equation provides a definition of entropy that is more general than the thermodynamic definition (which is applicable only to systems in a state of equilibrium). It is also seen that the newly defined entropy does not satisfy the strict Second Law but admits fluctuations between the situation of maximum probability and other, less probable but by no means impossible, situations of a lower entropy. "As soon as one considers bodies which are so small that they contain only a few molecules the [second] law must cease to be valid." (This was written in 1878, in the *Vorlesungen über Gastheorie*, and was severely criticized. The existence of the predicted fluctuations of 1905 had been confirmed by Jean Perrin and Theodor Svedberg.) The problem of irreversibility is not yet completely solved by this account, however, for the probability that a state of low entropy is followed by a state of higher entropy is identical with the probability that a state of high entropy is followed by a state of lower entropy. In order to solve this difficulty, Boltzmann, in *Vorlesungen über Gastheorie*, compared local developments to the over-all development of large regions of the universe. The large-scale development provides a reference point for small-scale fluctuations and in this way determines a local direction of time in a "timeless" universe.

> Considering the universe as a whole both directions of time are still indistinguishable just as space knows no above and below. Yet at a specific point of the surface of the earth we call the direction towards the center the "downward" direction; in the same way a living being dwelling in a certain time-phase of such a local world will distinguish the direction towards the more improbable state from the opposite direction, calling the former the past, and the latter the future. This seems to be the only method which will allow us to conceive the second law, the unidirected development of each partial world without postulating an unidirected development of the whole universe.

All the above ideas have led to further developments. The statistical physics of today, quantum statistics included, is inconceivable without the work of Boltzmann, who provided a framework that could be retained despite the need to change some more specific assumptions. The same is true of the highly technical developments in connection with the H-theorem and the ergodic hypothesis. It is unfortunate that Boltzmann's general philosophy, which is intimately connected with his physics, is practically unknown, for his ideas are still relevant to contemporary discussions and present a promising field for further study.

Bibliography

Boltzmann's research papers were collected in three volumes by F. Hasenöhrl and published as *Wissenschaftliche Abhandlungen* (Leipzig, 1909). His larger works are *Vorlesungen über die Prinzipien der Mechanik*, 2 vols. (Leipzig, 1897–1904); *Vorlesungen über Maxwells Theorie der Electrizität und des Lichtes*, 2 vols. (Leipzig, 1891–1893); and *Vorlesungen über Gastheorie*, 2 vols. (Leipzig, 1896–1898). Boltzmann's more general writings have been collected in *Populäre Schriften* (Leipzig, 1905).

The biography by E. Broda, *Ludwig Boltzmann* (Vienna, 1955), contains an excellent account of Boltzmann's physics and his philosophy. For a more technical discussion of the *H*-theorem and of related questions, see Paul and Tatiana Ehrenfest, *The Conceptual Foundations of the Statistical Approach in Mechanics* (Ithaca, N.Y., 1959); Hans Reichenbach, *The Direction of Time* (Berkeley, 1956); and Dirk ter Haar, "Foundations of Statistical Mechanics," in *Reviews of Modern Physics* (July 1955).

PAUL K. FEYERABEND

BOLZANO, BERNARD (1781–1848), philosopher, theologian, logician, and mathematician. Bolzano was born in Prague, where his father, an Italian art dealer, had settled; his mother was a German merchant's daughter. Bolzano studied mathematics, philosophy, and theology in Prague and defended his doctor's thesis in mathematics in 1804; he was ordained a Roman Catholic priest the following year. Shortly thereafter he was appointed to a temporary professorship in the science of religion at Karlova University in Prague and two years later was given a newly established chair in this field. Some time later he was accused of religious and political heresy and was removed from his teaching position in December 1819. Bolzano spent much of his time thereafter with the family of his friend and benefactor, A. Hoffmann, at their estate in southern Bohemia. He had difficulty getting his later publications through the Metternich censorship. Some of his books were put on the Index, and many appeared only posthumously. Some manuscripts are yet to be published; the most important of these are in the National Museum and the University Library in Prague, others are in the Österreichische Nationalbibliothek in Vienna. In December 1848, Bolzano died of a respiratory disease from which he had suffered for most of his life.

Mathematics. Bolzano's mathematical teachings were not quite understood by his contemporaries, and most of his deep insights into the foundations of mathematical analysis long remained unrecognized. A famous theorem in the early stages of a modern presentation of the calculus is known as the Bolzano–Weierstrass theorem, but another masterful anticipation (by more than forty years) of Weierstrass' discovery that there exist functions that are everywhere continuous but nowhere differentiable remained buried in manuscripts until the 1920s. But perhaps more important than Bolzano's actual discoveries of new theorems was the meticulousness with which he endeavored to lay new foundations for the *Grössenlehre*, the science of quantity—which was how Bolzano, using a very broad interpretation of "quantity," designated mathematics. In particular, his insistence that no appeal to any intuition of space and time should be acknowledged for this purpose and that only "purely analytical" methods were to be recognized put him in opposition to the then current Kantian ways of thinking and back into the Leibnizian tradition.

Bolzano's most famous posthumously published work is *Paradoxien des Unendlichen* (F. Prihonsky, ed., Leipzig, 1851; translated by D. A. Steele as *The Paradoxes of the Infinite*, London, 1950), in which he anticipated certain basic ideas of set theory, developed only a generation later by Georg Cantor, who fully acknowledged his indebtedness to Bolzano in this respect. This anticipation should, however, not be overrated. Bolzano was not quite able to rid himself of all the prejudices of his time and was, therefore, unable to reach a clear and fruitful conception of equivalence between infinite sets.

Ethics and philosophy of religion. Bolzano was, in his time, much more influential as a theologian and social moralist than as a mathematician. An advocate of the Bohemian Catholic enlightenment, he lectured on religion and moral philosophy with strong pacifistic and socialistic overtones. He used the pulpit to proclaim before hundreds of impressed students a kind of utopian socialism. In his sermons he tried to prove the essential equality of all human beings, attacked private property obtained without work, and exhorted his listeners to sacrifice everything in their struggle for human rights. These sermons served him as a preparation for what he regarded as his most important book, *Von dem besten Staate*, which he finished in 1837 but was unable to publish. It first appeared in Prague in 1932.

Bolzano's philosophy of religion is presented in the books *Athanasia oder Gründe für die Unsterblichkeit der Seele* (Sulzbach, 1827) and *Lehrbuch der Religionswissenschaft* (4 vols., Sulzbach, 1834), the latter being a revised version of his lectures at the Prague university. He tried to prove that Catholicism is in full harmony with common sense. To this end he either disregarded or interpreted allegorically all mystical elements of Catholicism.

Bolzano derived his utilitarian ethics from a "highest ethical principle": "Of all actions possible to you, choose always the one which, weighing all consequences, will most further the good of the totality, in all its parts" (*Lehrbuch der Religionswissenschaft*, Vol. I, Sec. 87). This reminds one, of course, of Bentham. "The most important idea of mankind" Bolzano took to be the "essential" equality of all human beings, which he tried to prove from historical, rational, and ethical considerations.

Logic and epistemology. It is as logician, methodologist, and epistemologist that Bolzano, after a long period of neglect, has regained philosophical attention in the twentieth century. Mainly in order to combat radical skepticism, he found it necessary to base his teachings in these fields on certain ontological conceptions. He was convinced that there exist truths-in-themselves *(Wahrheiten an sich)* prior to and independent of language and man. These truths he carefully distinguished from truths expressed in words and conceived truths. The set of truths-in-themselves is a subset of the set of propositions (in-themselves) *(Sätze an sich)*, again to be distinguished from propositions expressed in words and conceived propositions. Propositions consist of terms (ideas-in-themselves, *Vorstellungen an sich*). These are likewise to be distinguished, on the one hand, from the words or word sequences by which they are denoted and, on the other, from subjective ideas that occur in our mind. Although linguistic entities and conceived entities exist concretely, terms, propositions, and truths do not. Terms were equally carefully distinguished from their objects, whether or not these objects themselves existed concretely. Though Bolzano was a Platonist (in the modern sense), his ontology was rather remote from that of Plato or, for that matter, from that of Kant, in spite of the common *an sich* terminology.

Beyond these negative determinations, Bolzano had little positive to say on the ontological status of terms and propositions except that they are the matter (*Stoff*) or sense (*Sinn*) of their correlates in language and thought.

Terms can be either simple or complex and either empty (*gegenstandslos*) or nonempty (*gegenständlich*); if nonempty, they are either singular or general. Examples of empty terms are −1, 0, Nothing, Round Square, Green Virtue, and Golden Mountain; absolutely simple terms are Not, Some, Have, Be, and Ought, but Bolzano was uncertain about others. Simple, singular terms he called intuitions (*Anschauungen*).

Propositions are composed of terms and are perhaps best regarded as ordered sequences of terms, while the content (*Inhalt*) of a proposition is the (unordered) set of the simple terms out of which the terms constituting the proposition are composed. The content of a complex term is similarly defined. The terms 3^5 and 5^3 are different, though they have the same content. The terms 2^4 and 4^2 are different, though they have not only the same content but even the same object. With this conception of content, the traditional doctrine of the reciprocity between the extension of a term (the set of objects falling under it) and the content of a term can easily be seen to be invalid.

Among Bolzano's many idiosyncratic convictions, perhaps the most interesting, but also the most strange to the modern mind, was his belief that each branch of science has a unique, strictly scientific presentation, which for him meant not only a unique finite axiom system (a belief he shared with many) but also an essentially unique entailment (*Abfolge*) of each theorem of this science by the axioms, a belief which might well be unique to Bolzano.

This relationship of entailment, as presented by Bolzano, is very peculiar and obscure. Bolzano was never quite sure that he understood it himself, though he was convinced that there objectively must exist some such relationship, that each science must have its basic truths (*Grundwahrheiten*) to which all other truths of that science stand in the peculiar relation of consequence (*Folge*) to ground (*Grund*). Bolzano was constantly struggling to differentiate this relation of entailment from the relation of derivability (*Ableitbarkeit*), which was the basic relation of his logic (see LOGIC, HISTORY OF, section on Bolzano). Though he did not succeed in putting his theory of entailment into consistent and fruitful shape—and could not possibly have done so, in view of the chimerical character of his goal—his acumen, mastery of the contemporary logical and methodological literature, intellectual honesty, and lifelong self-criticism more than made up for his numerous shortcomings. Bolzano remains a towering figure in the epistemology, logic, and methodology of the first half of the nineteenth century.

Additional Works by Bolzano

Bolzano's masterwork is his *Wissenschaftslehre*, 4 vols. (Sulzbach, 1837; W. Schulz, ed., Leipzig, 1929–1931). *Grundlegung der Logik* (Hamburg, 1964) is a very useful selection by Friedrich Kambartel from the first two volumes of the *Wissenschaftslehre*, with summaries of omitted portions, an excellent introduction, and a good index.

Works on Bolzano

Bolzano's philosophical work was virtually disregarded until Edmund Husserl called attention to it at the turn of the century. Hugo Bergmann's monograph, *Das philosophische Werk Bernard Bolzanos* (Halle, 1909), increased the revived interest in Bolzano's ideas. Heinrich Scholz's articles, especially "Die Wissenschaftslehre Bolzanos," in *Abhandlungen des Fries'schen Schule*, new series, Vol. 6 (1937), 399–472, reprinted in *Mathesis Universalis*, pp. 219–267 (Basel, 1961), presented Bolzano's contributions to logic, semantics, and the methodology of the deductive sciences in a modernized form. The best recent study in English of Bolzano as a logician is J. Berg's *Bolzano's Logic* (Stockholm, 1962). D. A. Steele's historical introduction to his translation of Bolzano's *Paradoxien des Unendlichen* is useful. Among other secondary works the most important are Eduard Winter's *Bernard Bolzano und sein Kreis* (Leipzig, 1933), G. Buhl's *Ableitbarkeit und Abfolge in der Wissenschaftstheorie Bolzanos* (Cologne, 1961), and (from a Marxist viewpoint) A. Kolman's *Bernard Bolzano* (in Russian, Moscow, 1955; in Czech, Prague, 1957; and in German, Berlin, 1963).

YEHOSHUA BAR-HILLEL

BONALD, LOUIS GABRIEL AMBROISE, VICOMTE DE, French publicist and philosopher, was born in the château of Le Monna, near Millau (Aveyron) in 1754 and died in 1840. He emigrated in 1791, during the Revolution, to Heidelberg, moving later to Constance, and joined the circle of royalist writers who in 1796 published a number of books attacking the Revolutionary party and defending the monarchy. His own contribution to the propaganda was his famous *Théorie du pouvoir politique et religieux* (3 vols., Constance, 1796), the first of a long series of volumes expressing the ultramontane position, the political supremacy of the papacy, absolute monarchy, and traditionalism.

The basic premise of Bonald, as far as his philosophy was concerned, was the identity of thought and language. Against the usual eighteenth-century idea that language was a human invention, he revived Rousseau's argument that since an invention requires thought and thought is internal speech, language could not have been invented. Consequently, he argued, it must have been put into the soul of man at creation. By means of certain philological investigations, Bonald was able to convince himself that there was a basic identity in all languages, as indeed there is in the Indo-European.

But language is a social, not an individual, phenomenon. It binds men together into groups and expresses an interpersonal set of ideas. These ideas are tradition. The unity of tradition may be disrupted, as it was during the Revolution, but nevertheless mankind will have to return to it if they have any hope of regaining social health. When this return occurs, men will cooperate in a single political system and a single set of religious beliefs. The former will be absolute monarchy, the latter Roman Catholicism, both having single and omnicompetent heads. Thus, just as the universe is created and governed by one God, so both the church and state must preserve administrative unity. But since the church is the direct channel of communication between God and his creatures, the state and its subjects must be governed in moral affairs by the church.

The ultramontanism of Bonald was as extreme as logically possible. He maintained that the arts, for instance, flourished only in an absolute monarchy, and hence saw nothing to praise in Greek art. In fact, he had nothing good to say about anything Greek, since Greece was given to democracy, though he made an exception of the Spartans. He was opposed to the legalization of divorce and to equal rights for women. He accepted capital punishment, since God would see to it that the innocent would not suffer in the afterlife. He supported general censorship and denounced freedom of the press. And since he was a man of Stoic morals, he did not worry much about human dissatisfaction or unhappiness.

Bonald was a philosopher who never changed his views. In each of his numerous works he repeated the same fundamental theses. His influence was restricted to men of the extreme right, in spite of his ingenuity in argument and logical rigor. His ideas survived in France in *l'Action française* and even in the nonpolitical writings of Charles Maurras, through whom they passed in diluted form to T. S. Eliot.

Bibliography

The collected works of Bonald appeared as *Oeuvres complètes*, Abbé Migne, ed. (Paris, 1859).

For works on Bonald, see G. Boas, *French Philosophies of the Romantic Period* (Baltimore, 1925), ch. 3; Harold Laski, *Authority in the Modern State* (New Haven, 1919), which follows Moulinié; H. Moulinié, *De Bonald* (Paris, 1915); C. Sainte-Beuve, *Causeries du lundi* (Paris, 1851–1862), Vol. IV, 426; Émile Faguet, *Politiques et moralistes du dix-neuvième siècle*, 1ère série (Paris, 1890).

GEORGE BOAS

BONATELLI, FRANCESCO (1830–1911), an Italian spiritualist philosopher, was born in Iseo, Brescia. He studied at the University of Vienna and taught philosophy at the universities of Bologna (1861–1867) and Padua (1867–1911). Bonatelli belonged to the tradition of Catholic spiritualism. He was one of the principal editors of *Filosofia delle scuole italiane*, a review founded in 1870 by Terenzio Mamiani to defend a Platonizing position, but he resigned in 1874 when the Platonist Giovanni Maria Bertini published criticisms of Catholicism which Bonatelli considered too bold. Bonatelli introduced the analytic method of German psychological research into Italy.

Bonatelli attempted to distinguish consistently between the unity of the ego and the multiplicity of psychic events. In his first work, *Pensiero e conoscenza* ("Thought and Consciousness," Bologna, 1864), Bonatelli distinguished two ways of life for the soul, one which is subject to the laws of fate and another which, although it recognizes these laws, is able to rise above them and use them as tools.

The conscious subject can be aware of other things only if it is capable at one and the same time of being modified and of remaining identical with itself, or inalterable. The solution of this apparent contradiction might lie in distinguishing between consciousness, understood as thought or pure mentality, and sensibility. In his most important work, *La coscienza e il meccanismo interiore* ("Consciousness and the Internal Mechanism," Padua, 1872), Bonatelli insisted that consciousness neither is changed by the object nor changes it. The act of consciousness detaches the psychic event from its matrix in reality and thinks its possible essence or its "possibility or quiddity or whatever you wish to call it." Bonatelli investigated both consciousness itself and the relation between the psychic mechanism external to consciousness and consciousness, between the existing object and the object thought in its "quiddity."

He regarded consciousness as thought turned back upon itself and almost creating itself, but also as freely accepting the "yoke of logic." If consciousness were not of this nature, it would be reduced to a "logical machine," whereas it is free reflection on itself, grasping itself by directing itself toward objects. However, although the distinctive essence of consciousness is its infinite turning back upon itself (*la riflexione infinita degli atti*, "the infinite reflection of acts"), this reflection is not an infinite succession in which consciousness would lose itself in an endless postponement but rather is a completed penetration of self, the fullness and richness of the activity of thought.

Additional Works by Bonatelli

La filosofia dell'inconscio di Edoardo von Hartmann. Rome, 1876.

Elementi di psicologia e logica. Padua, 1892.

Works on Bonatelli

Alliney, Giulio, *Francesco Bonatelli.* Brescia, 1947.

Gentile, Giovanni, *Le origini della filosofia contemporanea in Italia.* Messina, 1917. Vol. I, pp. 220–227.

Scatturin, Umberto, "Francesco Bonatelli." *Filosofia*, Vol. 3 (1952), 433–439.

Varisco, Bernardino, *Francesco Bonatelli.* Chieri, 1912.

See also "In onore di Francesco Bonatelli," by various authors. *La cultura filosofica*, Vol. 4, No. 2 (1910). Contains a bibliography.

EUGENIO GARIN

Translated by *Tessa Byck*

BONAVENTURE, ST. (c. 1217–1274), Italian Scholastic philosopher, was known as the Seraphic Doctor. Bonaventure, whose real name was John of Fidanza, was born in Bagnorea, in Tuscany. After obtaining a Master of Arts degree at Paris, Bonaventure joined the Franciscan friars (probably in 1243) and studied theology under their masters, Alexander of Hales and John of La Rochelle. After their deaths in 1245, he continued his studies under Eudes Rigaud and William of Meliton. He also came under the influence of the Dominican Guerric of Saint-

Quentin and the secular master Guiard of Laon. In 1248 as a bachelor of Scripture he began lecturing on the Gospel of St. Luke and then on other books of Scripture (not all of these commentaries have survived). His monumental "Commentary on the *Sentences* of Peter Lombard," perhaps the most perfect example of this form of medieval literature, was composed between 1250 and 1252.

In 1253 he was licensed by the chancellor of the University of Paris and functioned as regent master of theology until 1257. During this time he composed four sets of *Quaestiones Disputatae,* of which the *De Scientia Christi* ("On Christ's Knowledge") is important for his theory of illumination; *De Mysterio Trinitatis* ("On the Mystery of the Trinity") contains the best exposition of his proofs of God's existence; and *De Caritate et de Novissimis* ("On Charity and the Last Things") contains sections taken over literally by Thomas Aquinas.

Bonaventure's formal reception into the masters' guild was delayed until October 1257 by the controversy between the mendicant friars and the secular masters. By that time, however, he was no longer actively teaching; in February 1257 he had been elected minster general of the Franciscan order and had resigned his chair at the university to devote himself to the administration of that post. Although often absent on business for the order or church, he continued to make Paris his general headquarters and was largely responsible for the friars' being so active in academic pursuits. He himself preached frequently at the university, touching on many of the religious and philosophical troubles that disturbed faculty and students.

It was during these years that he composed the *Breviloquium* (1257), or brief compendium of speculative theology, which was a departure from the usual scholastic method of presentation; *De Reductione Artium ad Theologiam* ("On the Reduction of the Arts to Theology"), whose exact date of composition is unknown; and *Itinerarium Mentis in Deum* ("The Journey of the Mind to God," 1259). All of these are important for understanding his general system of thought and the particular role of philosophy in it. Even more important in this connection are the three sets of *Collationes*—a series of informal evening conferences given during Lent to the faculty members and students in the Paris friary—including *De Decem Praeceptis* ("On the Ten Commandments," 1267), *De Septem Donis Spiritus Sancti* ("On the Seven Gifts of the Holy Spirit," 1268), and *In Hexaemeron Sive Illuminationes Ecclesiae* ("On the Six Days of Creation or Enlightenments of the Church," 1273). All of these reflect the Averroistic tendencies in the arts faculty and Bonaventure's reaction to them. The last of these *Collationes* was left unfinished when Bonaventure was called from Paris and made cardinal bishop of Albano by Pope Gregory X, with whom he worked in organizing the Second Ecumenical Council of Lyons. He died shortly before the council closed and was buried there in the presence of the pope.

Spirit of Bonaventure's philosophy. Bonaventure's fame rests primarily on his reputation as a theologian rather than as a philosopher. In both Dante's *Paradiso* and Raphael's "Disputà" he appears as the equal of Aquinas, and in the field of mystical theology he has been considered without peer. It is more difficult, however, to isolate the philosophical components of his system. This is partly due to the fact that all Bonaventure's extant works postdate his entrance into the Franciscan order and the beginning of his career as a theologian and ascetical writer. The chief reason, however, for the prevalence of theological interests in all of his writings was his understandable reaction against the rationalism rampant in the arts faculty at Paris that threatened the very *raison d'être* of speculative theology and led to the condemnations of 1270 and 1277 by Stephen Tempier, bishop of Paris. Among the 219 items listed as theological errors in the second of these condemnations, for example, are such statements as

(*a*) The most exalted of all vocations is that of the philosopher.

(*b*) There is no subject he is not competent to discuss and settle.

(*c*) One gains nothing in the way of knowledge by knowing theology.

(*d*) Only the philosophers deserve to be called wise; the speech of the theologian is founded on fables.

In the face of such views, it is understandable why Bonaventure, who believed in the validity of Christian revelation, should have stressed the inability of philosophers in general and of Aristotle in particular to learn the full truth about man's existential situation. Conversely, Bonaventure tried to show the continuity between the aims of philosophy and those of theology. He maintained that philosophy has a genuine, albeit limited, autonomy; the knowledge it yields is a stage in the over-all ascent of the human mind to true wisdom, the culmination of which in this life is found in quasi-experiential knowledge of God, achieved by such mystics as Francis of Assisi.

Part of the great literary charm of Bonaventure's style is his ability to play upon words. Throughout his later works, particularly his sermons and *Collationes,* he continually gives a deliberately theological twist to technical philosophic terms, with the result that he has frequently been unjustly accused of confusing theology with philosophy either in principle or in practice. The truth of the matter is that while he was eminently able to conduct a purely philosophical discussion and often did so in his university lectures, he preferred to limit himself to particular topics. He never formed a complete system from his philosophical analyses, but he put them into the service of his over-all theological synthesis.

BONAVENTURE'S METAPHYSICS

Bonaventure's linguistic sophistication and his idea of the continuity between philosophy and theology are perhaps best represented in his discussion of metaphysics in the *In Hexaemeron.* Christ, the Son of God, not Aristotle, is the "metaphysician" par excellence.

> As the Son said: "I came forth from the Father and have come into the world; again I leave the world and go to the Father" [John 16.28], so anyone may say: "Lord, I came forth from you, the All High; I go to you, the All High, and by means of you, the All High." Here is the metaphysical medium leading us back. And this is the whole of our metaphysics: it concerns emanation, exemplarity, and consummation [that is,

being illumined by spiritual rays and led back to the All High]. It is in this way you become a true metaphysician. (*Collatio* I, No. 17; in *Opera*, Vol. V, p. 332)

Emanation. Bonaventure uses the term "emanation" to designate the general theory of how creation proceeds from God. With its Plotinian overtones, however, "emanation" suggested more specifically the thesis of al-Farabi, Avicenna, and Averroës that all creatures, by an inevitable and eternal process, spring from the creative mind of God through a chain of intermediary causes of continually diminishing perfection. This thesis was designed to reconcile Aristotle's eternal world with the creation concept of the Koran. Bonaventure, however, wished to reconcile "emanation" with Christian theology. His counterthesis is summarized in the *Breviloquium:* "The whole of the cosmic machine was produced in time and from nothing, by one principle only who is supreme and whose power, though immense, still arranges all according to a certain weight, number and measure" (Book II, Part 1, in *Opera*, Vol. V, p. 219). It is to be noted that he rejects the concepts of the eternity of the world, of the eternity of matter, of a dual principle of good and evil, and of the existence of intermediary causes.

His description of the supreme principle implies that a perfect power must be free to create varying degrees of perfection, in contrast with the Arab belief that direct creation by a perfect power could only result in perfect effects. Also, the use of Augustine's triad of weight, number, and measure suggests the seal of the Blessed Trinity stamped on every creature. This becomes clearer if we consider the next and most characteristic feature of Bonaventure's metaphysics.

Exemplarism. Emanation concerns natural philosophy as much as metaphysics. God, as final cause and ultimate goal of man's quest for happiness, is the concern of the moral philosopher as well as the metaphysician. But only the metaphysician can understand God as exemplar cause. And it is in analyzing this aspect of the science of causes and first principles that man is most truly a metaphysician.

Though this metaphysical pursuit begins with reason, it can be successfully terminated only by a man with faith. Comparing the two greatest pagan philosophers, Aristotle and Plato, Bonaventure maintained that Plato, the master of wisdom, erred in looking only upward to the realm of eternal values, of the immutable ideas, while Aristotle, the master of natural science, looked only earthward to the everyday sensible world that Plato neglected. But Aristotle's was the greater sin, for in rejecting the Platonic ideas *in toto*, he closed the door to a full understanding of the universe in terms of its causes. Bonaventure saw Augustine as the model of Christian wisdom because he combined the science of Aristotle with Plato's wisdom (*Christus Unus Omnium Magister*, Nos. 18–19, in *Opera*, Vol. V, p. 572). As a Christian he could complete what Plato could only begin. Not only did he demonstrate that Plato's archetypal Ideas are the exemplar causes or models that God used in creating the universe, a point that a philosopher alone could establish, but he also showed further that these Ideas are associated in a special way with the second person of the Trinity, an insight only divine revelation could help one discover. Bonaventure, following Augustine, explained that since the Father begets the Son by an eternal act of self-knowledge, the Son may also be called the wisdom of the Father and expresses in his person all of God's creative possibilities. As such, the Son is the Word or Logos adumbrated in the writings of the philosophers but fully revealed only at the beginning of the Gospel of John, where he appears as the one through whom all things are made (that is, as exemplar cause) and who "enlightens every man who comes into the world" (an allusion to Augustine's theory that only some illumination by divine ideas can account for man's knowing immutable truths). "From his [magisterial] chair in heaven Christ teaches us interiorly," wrote Bonaventure. "If as the Philosopher [Aristotle] says, the knowable qua knowable is eternal, nothing can be known except through that Truth which is unshaken, immutable and without limit" (*In Hexaemeron, Collatio* I, No. 13; in *Opera*, Vol. V, p. 331).

Averröes had written of Aristotle: "I believe this man to be nature's model, the exemplar which nature found to reveal the ultimate in human perfection" (*De Anima* III, 2). Bonaventure maintained that Christ, not Aristotle, is God's model for humanity. The Word is not only God but also a perfect man. He gives us "the power of becoming the sons of God," and he is the "one master of all the sciences" (*Sermo IV;* in *Opera*, Vol. V, p. 567); to know him fully is to know all that can be known.

Bonaventure held that Plato's theory of Ideas was a first philosophical approximation to this theological insight, and Aristotle's rejection of this view led to his errors about God. For if God lacked the exemplar ideas, he would know only himself and nothing of the world. He would be, as Aristotle claimed, related to the world only as final cause and not as creator. Moreover, in Aristotle's world, since chance clearly does not explain the cyclic changes of the cosmos, the universe must be ruled by determinism, as the Arabic commentators claim. But then man would no longer be a responsible agent; he would deserve neither reward nor punishment, and divine providence would be a myth.

With the recognition of exemplarism, on the other hand, the whole of creation takes on a sacramental character—that is, it becomes a material means of bringing the soul to God. Nature becomes the "mirror of God," reflecting his perfections in varying degrees. Although we see only a shadowy likeness (*umbra*) or trace (*vestigium*) of the creator in inorganic substances and the lower forms of life, the soul of man is God's image (*imago*) and the angel his similitude (*similitudo*).

The recognition of God in nature begins in philosophy, but it is continued and perfected in theology. In *De Mysterio Trinitatis* Bonaventure argued that philosophers know that secondary beings imply a first; dependent beings imply an independent being; contingent things imply some necessary being; the relative implies an absolute; the imperfect, something perfect; Plato's participated beings imply one unparticipated being; if there are potential beings, then pure act must also exist; composite things imply the existence of something simple; the changeable can only coexist with the unchangeable. Pagan philosophers, knowing that these ten self-evident conditionals have their antecedents verified in the corporeal world, learned much about God (*De Mysterio Trinitatis* I, 1; in *Opera*, Vol. V, pp. 46–47).

More can be learned, however, by the soul reflecting upon itself. In his other works Bonaventure went on to suggest that the soul, possessed of memory, intelligence, and will, is an image of God, not only mirroring his spiritual nature but adumbrating the Trinity itself. Memory, which creates its own thought objects, resembles the Father who begets the Son or Logos (intelligence) as an intellectual reflection of himself, and the two through their mutual love (will—the active principle of "spiration") breathe forth the Holy Spirit. But although a philosopher can discover a spiritual God as the ultimate object of the soul's search for truth and happiness, only a man of faith like Augustine can find the Trinity manifest throughout creation.

Consummation or enlightened return. The third aspect of Bonaventure's metaphysics concerns a creature's fulfillment of its destiny by returning to God. This return (called technically a *reductio*) in the case of the lower creation is achieved in and through man (who praises God for and through subhuman creation). Man's return is made possible in turn by Christ. For man returns to God by living an upright life—that is, by being rightly aligned with God—and this can be accomplished only through the grace of Christ. Man's mind is right (*rectus*) when it has found truth, and above all, eternal truth. His will is right when it loves what is really good, his exercise of power is right when it is a continuation of God's ruling power. Through original sin or the Fall, man lost this triple righteousness. His intellect, lured by vain curiosity, has enmeshed itself in interminable doubts and futile controversies; his will is ruled by greed and concupiscence; in his exercise of power he seeks autonomy. But although man lost the state of original justice, he still hungers for it. This longing for the infinite good is revealed in his ceaseless quest for pleasures. Through faith and love (grace), man can find his way back. Since knowledge is involved at every stage of the return, *reductio* is also a quest for wisdom and hence, in an extended theological sense, it is metaphysical. It is an enlightened return, because every branch of learning is a gift from above, from the "Father of lights" (Epistle of St. James, 1. 17), and can be put into the service of theology (this is the theme of Bonaventure's *De Reductione Artium*). Although man's return begins with the natural light of reason reflecting first on the external world and then turning inward in an analysis of the soul, it is perfected initially by a natural illumination of the divine ideas and then by varying additional degrees of supernatural illumination which culminate in the experiential cognition of God through mystical union (the theme of the *Itinerarium*). This experience is not the same as the clear vision of the blessed in heaven but is the "learned ignorance" referred to by the mystical writers—a union of the soul with God in darkness, granted to saints like Francis before death.

OTHER DOCTRINES

The elements of Bonaventure's philosophy are woven into his religiously oriented system. Like all the Parisian thinkers of this period, Bonaventure developed a basically Aristotelian philosophy, but he included a larger admixture of Neoplatonic and Augustinian elements than we find in St. Thomas, for instance, who studied Aristotle somewhat later and more thoroughly under Albert the Great.

Theory of knowledge. Bonaventure believed that the mind has no innate ideas, not even in the sense postulated by the authors of the *Summa Theologica* (ascribed to Alexander of Hales), who argued that ideas are latent in the agent intellect but are actually acquired only when the light of the agent intellect illumines the possible intellect. Bonaventure rejected this, holding with Aristotle that the mind at birth is a *tabula rasa*. It needs sensory stimulation before it can acquire any notions about the external world of objects. However, Bonaventure did use the Augustinian theory of illumination to explain how the mind passes judgment on sensible things in terms of their values. For when the mind judges something to be, for example, good or beautiful, there must be an implicit awareness of what beauty and goodness are in themselves; and this requires that the human mind have some knowledge of the divine ideas. Obviously this is not a clear or intuitive knowledge of God such as the angels or the blessed in paradise possess. Yet just as one can see by sunlight without looking into the sun itself, so one can have knowledge of the divine ideas. On the other hand, Bonaventure rejected the interpretation (also found in the *Summa* of Alexander) that we attain these ideas only in terms of the residual effects of the divine action—effects which remain in the soul like habitual or buried memories. Bonaventure claimed that in some mysterious way (which he called *contuition* but which he never fully explained), when we know a created object, our mind is simultaneously enlightened so that it is moved to judge correctly about the object and is hence in accord with God's own mind on the subject.

Although Bonaventure agreed with Aristotle that our knowledge of the external world is sense-dependent, he did not fully subscribe to Aristotle's principle that "nothing is in the intellect that was not first in the senses." He held that the intellect can turn inward, reflecting on the soul and its tendencies. In analyzing the precise nature of the object of these tendencies, the mind discovers God and itself as his image. The reasoning process involved is neither deductive nor inductive in the usual meaning of these terms, but is called technically a "reduction" and seems to resemble in some respects the "abduction" of C. S. Peirce. Reasoning proceeds by progressively deepening insights into what the desire for truth and perfect happiness involve. If the reduction remains imperfect and does not go on to completion, God is not discovered and one may err about his nature or even his existence. Although at times Bonaventure, following the authority of John of Damascus, Boethius, or Augustine, spoke of the existence of God as a truth implanted by nature in the human mind, he meant this to be interpreted as referring immediately to man's natural desire for knowledge, truth, happiness, or goodness—all of which need explication before man realizes they have God as their ultimate object (*De Mysterio Trinitatis*, I, 1; in *Opera*, Vol. V, p. 49).

Cosmology. In his analysis of material creation, Bonaventure introduced extraneous elements into Aristotle's theory of matter and form. Thus, for instance, he adopted Avicebrón's theory of the hylomorphic composition of spiritual as well as corporeal creatures. The argument here is that since creatures have some measure of potentiality (only God is pure actuality), they must have some kind of matter, for according to Aristotle matter is the principle and source of potentiality. This spiritual matter, found both in the angel and in the human soul, is never separable from its spiritual form; hence, such spiritual substances are not subject to change—they cannot die or disintegrate like terrestrial bodies, nor can they be perfected by a hierarchy of forms, as can corporeal matter.

In *Breviloquium*, Book II, Bonaventure, in explaining the visible universe, made use of the theories of light developed by Robert Grosseteste and the Oxford school. He distinguished light (*lux*), luminosity (*lumen*), and color. The first is the most basic of substantial forms; it enables both terrestrial and celestial bodies to subsist and is the root source of whatever internal dynamism they possess. *Lumen* is the invisible radiation which has its origin especially in celestial bodies like the sun but exists in the intervening transparent medium. It is described by Bonaventure as being both an active power (*virtus activa*) and something substantial in itself but only accidentally related to the transmitting medium through which it flows continually and instantaneously by a self-generative process called multiplication. Being neither an accidental nor a substantial form properly speaking, it is not educed from the potentialities of matter as are other corporeal forms, with the exception of *lux*. Yet it requires some material medium or body and coexists with such without changing it substantially. Not only does it penetrate the bowels of the earth, where it governs the formation of minerals, but in virtue of its purity and similarity to the spiritual, this substantial radiation disposes bodies to receive the life form and acts as a sort of intermediary between soul and body. It is active in the reproduction of animals, functioning as one of the external agents that educes the higher forms from the matter where they exist as "seminal reasons."

This theory of seminal reasons was adopted on the authority of Augustine, but Bonaventure interpreted it within the framework of the general Aristotelian formula that forms are educed from the potency of matter. Unlike Aquinas, Bonaventure interpreted these "potencies" as active powers rather than passive potentialities. They are really latent forms existing in matter in an inchoate or germinal state. External agents only cooperate with these powers, in much the way that a gardener cultivates a rosebush or a seedbed so that it bears flowers or germinates (*Commentarium in Librum II Sententiarum*, Dist. 7, in *Opera*, Vol. II, p. 198). All forms, except the primary light form and the human soul, which are directly created by God, arise through the cooperation of seminal powers and external agents, under the influence of light.

Bonaventure, unlike Aquinas, believed that creation in time (in contrast with Aristotle's belief in the eternity of the world) is demonstrable from reason, using Aristotle's own principles (*Commentarium in Librum I Sententiarum*, Dist. 1, in *Opera*, Vol. II, pp. 20–22). His arguments, although interesting, are based on a medieval concept of number and infinity and on the presupposition that the immortality of the human soul is a purely rational truth.

As his name implies, Bonaventure's character seems to have represented all that the medieval Christian regarded as ideal. Born at a critical period in the history of his church, his order, and of speculative theology, he saw himself cast in a mediating role. As a bachelor of theology, trained in the arts, he sought to put the new philosophy into the service of theology. As a master of theology he tried not only to defend the new mendicant orders against the attacks of the secular masters but also to heal their differences. As minister general he took a middle position between the extreme factions of the Franciscan order, who differed on the subjects of evangelical poverty and the pursuit of studies. Bonaventure's works, such as *De Reductione Artium ad Theologiam* and *Itinerarium Mentis in Deum* were not only theoretical expressions of his gift for synthesis but also served the practical purpose of silencing the anti-intellectual friars who claimed that the academic life was incompatible with the ascetical aims of a follower of St. Francis. As cardinal, Bonaventure played a major role at the Council of Lyons in healing the rift between Greek and Latin Christendom. Under the aegis of Augustine, he consolidated theological opposition to the cult of Aristotle and Averroistic rationalism. Although this led eventually to the Parisian condemnations of 1270 and 1277, in which even theses of St. Thomas were included, it also bore fruit in a renewed interest in Augustine's contributions to philosophy by Matthew of Acquasparta, Roger Marston, Peckham, and others of the Augustinian school.

Bibliography

The collected Latin works of St. Bonaventure were published as *S. Bonaventurae Opera Omnia*, 10 vols. (Quaracchi, 1882–1902). The two works not contained in that collection are *Questions disputées "De Caritate," "De Novissimis,"* P. Glorieux, ed. (Paris, 1950), and a second redaction of *Collationes in Hexaemeron*, F. Delorme, ed. (Quaracchi, 1934). *Commentary on the Sentences* has been reprinted in 4 vols. (Quaracchi, 1934–1949) without the critical notes. Also see *Tria Opuscula*, 5th ed. (Quaracchi, 1938), which includes *Breviloquium, Itinerarium Mentis in Deum*, and *De Reductione Artium ad Theologiam*.

English translations of Bonaventure's work include *St. Bonaventure's De Reductione Artium ad Theologiam*, translated by E. T. Healy (St. Bonaventure, N.Y., 1955), in Latin and English; *St. Bonaventure's Itinerarium Mentis in Deum*, translated by Philotheus Boehner (St. Bonaventure, N.Y., 1956), in Latin and English; *Breviloquium by St. Bonaventure*, translated by E. E. Nemmers (St. Louis and London, 1946); J. de Vinck, *The Works of St. Bonaventure* (Paterson, N.J., 1960—); and four questions from the "Commentary on the Sentences" in Richard McKeon, ed., *Selections From Medieval Philosophers* (New York, 1930), Vol. II, pp. 118–148.

A Latin and Spanish translation is L. Amoros, B. Aperribay, M. Oromi, and M. Oltra, eds., *Obras de S. Buenaventura*, 6 vols. (Madrid, 1945–1949), Vol. I of which contains an extensive bibliography and new data on authentic works not in *Opera Omnia.*

General bibliographies for Bonaventure can be found in F. Ueberweg and B. Geyer, *Grundriss der Geschichte der Philosophie*, 12th ed. reprint (Basel, 1951), Vol. II, pp. 735–738, and Étienne Gilson, *History of Christian Philosophy in the Middle Ages* (New York, 1955), pp. 685–686. For studies after 1953, see the annotated *Bibliographia Franciscana* (Rome, 1962—), Vol. XI ff. The classic introduction to Bonaventure's thought is Étienne Gilson, *La Philosophie de saint Bonaventure*, 2d ed. (Paris, 1953;

English translation of 1st ed., London, 1938). Critical evaluations of this and alternate views are B. A. Gendreau, "The Quest for Certainty in St. Bonaventure," in *Franciscan Studies*, Vol. 21 (1961), 104–227, and J. G. Bugerol, *Introduction à l'étude de S. Bonaventure* (Paris, 1961). Bonaventurean themes in Raphael are discussed in H. B. Gutman, "The Medieval Content of Raphael's 'School of Athens,'" in *Journal of the History of Ideas*, Vol. 2 (1941), 420–429, and "Raphael's 'Disputà,'" in *Franciscan Studies*, Vol. 2 (1942), 35–48. For Bonaventure's own theory of art, see E. J. M. Spargo, *The Category of the Aesthetic in the Philosophy of St. Bonaventure* (St. Bonaventure, N.Y., 1953). Also see R. P. Prentice, *The Psychology of Love According to St. Bonaventure*, 2d ed. (St. Bonaventure, N.Y., 1957), which is a comparison of Bonaventure and Max Scheler, and A. Schaefer, "The Position and Function of Man in the Created World According to St. Bonaventure," in *Franciscan Studies*, Vol. 20 (1960), 261–316 and Vol. 21 (1961), 233–382.

ALLAN B. WOLTER, O.F.M.

BONHOEFFER, DIETRICH (1906–1945), German theologian and religious leader during the period of national socialism. Bonhoeffer was active in the resistance to Hitler; and his anti-Nazi activities led to his death in a concentration camp. The heroism of his end served to call attention to his life and character, but by itself the drama of his life does not account for the continuing interest he has aroused in postwar Christian theological circles. He has been read eagerly, particularly by younger churchmen, both for the substance of his thought and for his provocative portrayal of the secular setting in which Christianity now exists. The Nazi milieu prevented him from making a sustained impact on the academic world during his lifetime. He was known chiefly for his involvement in the nascent ecumenical movement and for his leadership of a clandestine seminary at Finkenwalde, near Stettin.

Philosophy and theology. Only one of Bonhoeffer's works, *Akt und Sein*, is wholly devoted to formal questions concerning the relation of philosophy to theology. *Akt und Sein* was his inaugural dissertation, and it is marked by a certain pretentiousness and heavy-handed systematic concern. At times its jargon obscures the author's line of thought. It is doubtful whether the work possesses any great worth in isolation from Bonhoeffer's life. However, since it anticipates many of the themes that he later elaborated without explicit philosophical reference, it is of some interest.

In *Akt und Sein* Bonhoeffer carried on a veiled polemic, on the one hand, against those who wished to reduce Christianity either to a philosophy of transcendence (*Akt*) or of being (*Sein*), and on the other hand against those who believed that Christian theology could be expressed independently of philosophical concerns. His own interests were in many ways synthetic. Critical of philosophical attempts to account for or exhaust the meaning of Christian revelation, he admitted the general necessity of philosophy. He appreciated the Kantian *Akt*-philosophy, which stresses the thinker or the knower "in relation to" the known, but he criticized its lack of interest in the problem of the known. He turned with some interest to the *Sein* philosophies, which focus on God as the known but which lack a due interest in the concrete historical events in which God is revealed. These philosophies Bonhoeffer categorized repeatedly throughout his career as "theologies of glory" that seek to explicate the nature of the Divine on a philosophical basis. He advocated mainly what in his Lutheran theological lineage has always been called "a theology of the Cross" because it accented act and event in history, specifically in the crucifixion of Jesus Christ.

If Bonhoeffer's most important literary work is to be related to philosophy it must be categorized as a philosophy of history. In all his writings there is an active and positive interest in the concrete character of Divine revelation. Bonhoeffer often voiced an agnostic position on the possibility of making meaningful statements about God apart from revelation in Jesus Christ. In lectures on Christology delivered in 1932 and available today in the form of classroom notes, he concentrated consistently on the historical, concrete, and conditioned character of revelation in Jesus Christ and the church over against philosophies of transcendence.

Ethics. Bonhoeffer's *Ethics* is his most systematic work (although it survives only in fragments from the concentration camp years). While it profits from philosophical debate, it is largely a rejection of philosophical ethics. In it Bonhoeffer takes a negative view of Roman Catholic ontological ethics, which moves from general abstract ethical statements to specific Christian principles; he was closer to modern existentialism, but it too he saw as an abstraction from revelatory events in Jesus Christ. Bonhoeffer has been accused along with his teacher Karl Barth of presenting an obsessively Christological philosophy and ethic.

However, one strand of thought developed in *Akt und Sein* kept Bonhoeffer from losing interest in and appreciation for philosophical thought. In that work he developed what has been called a theory of "a complementarity of languages," by which is meant a realization that no single language (ontological philosophy, Biblical theology) suffices for all the church's needs. His personality also was catholic in its openness to what might be learned from many sources, including philosophers.

Later thought. In his last two years, according to letters and rescued papers written during his imprisonment, Bonhoeffer's thought underwent some apparently radical changes. He has come to be best remembered for his interpretation of modern history, developed at this time. He saw the general process of secularization in extremely radical and liberating terms. From the Christian point of view he regarded it as largely positive. In a celebrated historical analysis he saw the "god of explanation" as gradually disappearing from Western history; disappearing with it was "the religious *a priori*." By this term he referred to the idea that a person must adopt a specific metaphysics, a specific view of transcendence, a specific form of piety and churchly existence before he can become a Christian. All this, Bonhoeffer claimed, belonged to man's spiritual adolescence. Recent man was reckoning less and less with a transcendent and hypothetical deity located outside the circle of the empirical. Bonhoeffer cherished those Biblical texts and those aspects of theological tradition that spoke of transcendence in the center of human affairs, particularly in the history of Jesus Christ.

In this historical context, Bonhoeffer pointed out, the role of philosophy has become increasingly secularized and increasingly points to the autonomy of man. Descartes saw the world as a mechanism. Spinoza was a pantheist. Kant, in Bonhoeffer's view, was close to the deists in his reluctance to deal philosophically with God as the known. Fichte and Hegel developed special brands of pantheism. All of these developments reveal the "growing tendency to assert the autonomy of man and the world" (*Prisoner for God*, p. 163). Bonhoeffer has been seen as a forerunner of recent antimetaphysical theologians who insist that Christian life and language are most free when they are not based on a philosophy of being or the expression of transcendence. Elements of Bonhoeffer's thought were influential, for instance, in the controversial *Honest to God* (London, 1963) by Bishop John A. T. Robinson and in a radical volume whose title relates to a thesis of Bonhoeffer's, Paul van Buren's *The Secular Meaning of the Gospel* (New York, 1963).

Works by Bonhoeffer

Sanctorum Communio. Munich, 1930. Translated by Ronald Gregor Smith and others as *The Communion of Saints* (London and New York, 1963).

Akt und Sein. Gütersloh, 1931. Translated by Bernard Noble as *Act and Being* (London and New York, 1962).

Nachfolge. Munich, 1937. Translated by Reginald H. Fuller as *The Cost of Discipleship* (London and New York, 1948).

Ethik. Munich, 1949. Translated by Neville Horton Smith as *Ethics* (London and New York, 1955).

Widerstand und Ergebung. Munich, 1951. Translated by Reginald H. Fuller as *Letters and Papers from Prison* (London, 1953) and as *Prisoner for God* (New York, 1954).

Gesammelte Schriften, 4 vols. Munich, 1958–1961.

Works on Bonhoeffer

Bethge, Eberhard, "The Challenge of Dietrich Bonhoeffer's Life and Theology." *The Chicago Theological Seminary Register*, Vol. 51 (Feb., 1961), 1–38.

Godsey, John D., *The Theology of Dietrich Bonhoeffer*. Philadelphia, 1960.

Marty, Martin E., ed., *The Place of Bonhoeffer*. New York, 1962.

MARTIN E. MARTY

BONNET, CHARLES (1720–1793), Swiss naturalist, "religious cosmologist," and philosopher, was born and died in Geneva. An original if eccentric thinker, Bonnet was widely read and influential. He was early attracted to natural history, and especially to entomology, by René Réaumur's work and by the Abbé Pluche's apologetic, *Spectacle de la nature* (1732). At the age of twenty, he discovered that the aphis can reproduce for several generations without mating, and that animals other than the "polyp" (hydra) can regenerate themselves. He treated these and other matters in his *Traité d'insectologie* (1745). When his eyesight became severely weakened from microscopic work, he turned to botany and philosophy. In *Recherches sur l'usage des feuilles dans les plantes* (1754), he outlined a vitalistic concept of plant behavior in relation to physical environment. In the *Essai de psychologie* (1754) and the *Essai analytique sur les facultés de l'âme* (1760), he followed Condillac by using the device of the imaginary statue to illustrate the genetic method of explaining the development of the personality. The personality arises from memory, which grows out of sensations. Especially concerned with the body–mind relation, Bonnet accepted David Hartley's theory of association of ideas. He defined freedom as the power of the soul to follow necessary motives; but in granting man a substantial mind, he denied mechanical determinism. He held that the relation between mind and body indicates that the mind must operate in a physical organism, but survives it—an idea that was to be developed in his cosmic speculations.

With the *Considérations sur les corps organisés* (1762) and the popular *Contemplation de la nature* (1764–1765), Bonnet approached the general problems that were crucial in the biology of his time. In the *Considérations* he espoused the preformation theory (which he also needed for his cosmological speculations), utilizing the work of Albrecht von Haller and Lazzaro Spallanzani. In the *Contemplation,* he developed the traditional idea of the chain of beings, temporalizing it as a process rather than as a static creation. Bonnet's cosmic philosophy received full development in his *Palingénésie philosophique, ou Idées sur l'état passé et sur l'état futur des êtres vivants* (1770), a work that Arthur O. Lovejoy termed "one of the most extraordinary speculative compounds to be found in the history of either science or philosophy." Bonnet looked to biology as a support for his religious beliefs, and used both biology and religion to build a view of cosmic evolution.

Bonnet's theory held, essentially, that the immortal soul ("the ethereal machine") is a "subtle matter" (as distinguished from "gross matter") in the pineal gland. The ethereal machine is the germ of the resurrected body. All possible beings, all individuals, were created at once, according to the principle of plenitude. They exist in germ until released by the death of other individual organisms. The lower souls of animals are perfectible, and the universe is one in which all things tend to perfection. The principal changes occur as the result of catastrophes. The earth has passed through a series of epochs, each terminated by a cataclysm that destroyed all organic life except the immortal germs, allowing the germs to take on different forms, all foreseen in the original creation and all ascending to higher levels. Ontogenesis is a proof of this. Thus, every germ will reappear in a succession of higher embodiments, the soul of each waiting until the proper state of the earth evokes its next and higher incarnation. The entire creation is moving upward; man will become angel, and apes and elephants will take man's place. There is also life on other worlds, more or less advanced in perfection than on earth.

This theory cannot be called one of organic evolution (as is sometimes erroneously affirmed), since species, according to Bonnet, have no natural history within a single world epoch. Species do not evolve from lower forms in the way modern biology conceives this process; their history is predetermined and fully inscribed in the germ at the moment of the original creation. The germ bears the form of all it will ever be. Nevertheless, Bonnet's universe is self-differentiating and progressive.

Bonnet considered finalism in organisms an incontrovertible argument against atheism. An optimist, he maintained there is greater good than evil in the universe, and that created things necessarily have a lesser degree of perfection than their creator. Man is superior to animals in his sensual apparatus, brain, and speech organs; but he is part of the general, unfolding order of nature. Man knows a Natural Law that is virtual in him but develops by experience; however, he is moved by self-love and by passions, which may be beneficent or may be destructive and cruel. In considering the inherited organization more determining than education (experience), Bonnet was closer to the "man-machine" school of La Mettrie than to the sensationist theories of Helvétius.

Bibliography

The best work on Bonnet is Max Offner, *Die Psychologie Charles Bonnets* (Leipzig, 1893). See also Georges Bonnet, *Charles Bonnet* (Lac, 1929); Edouard Claparède, *La Psychologie animale de Charles Bonnet* (Geneva, 1909); Jacques Roger, *Les Sciences de la vie dans la pensée française du XVIII siècle* (Paris, 1963). For further bibliographical information, see D. C. Cabeen, *A Critical Bibliography of Eighteenth Century French Literature* (Syracuse, N.Y., 1951), pp. 294–296.

L. G. CROCKER

BOODIN, JOHN ELOF (1869–1950), Swedish-American philosopher, sought to base his system of idealism on science. Born in Sweden, he immigrated to the United States in 1887. He received his B.A. from Brown University and then attended Harvard University, where he studied under Josiah Royce and received his Ph.D. in 1899. He subsequently taught philosophy at Grinnell College, the University of Kansas, Carleton College, and the University of California in Los Angeles. His first major publication, *Time and Reality* (New York, 1905), propounded a theory of time as dynamic nonbeing—as that aspect of reality that is experienced as passage and change. This theory of time as a negative factor in the universe offers a counterpoint to the timeless Absolute posited by Royce.

Truth and Reality (New York, 1911) presents Boodin's epistemology of pragmatic realism. As a realist Boodin held that there is an objective reality. As a pragmatist he insisted that the meaning of reality consists in the difference it makes to our reflective purposes. Boodin emphasized the formal factors in the knowledge process. *Truth and Reality* contains a table of 15 a priori categories as well as four unchanging formal postulates of thought; a metaphysical treatise on the categories, unfinished at the time of his death, was published in 1957 (Berkeley and Los Angeles) as *The Posthumous Papers of John Elof Boodin.*

In *A Realistic Universe* (New York, 1916; 2d ed. rev., New York, 1931) Boodin constructed a metaphysics upon pragmatic epistemology and scientific procedures and results; his purpose was to secure a place in the cosmos for human life and values. Boodin equated the category of substance with the epistemological postulate of totality; he held that the world is a whole in which every fact, under certain conditions, can make a difference to all other facts. Further, he distinguished five ultimate attributes of substance: being (stuff or energy), time, space, consciousness, and form. Reality is a temporal flux of energetic centers spread out in space and characterized by sensitivity or awareness. Form as part of the executive constitution of nature imparts direction and validity to the flux. The ideals of human life (truth, beauty, virtue) are expressions of the metaphysical attribute of form.

Cosmic Evolution (New York, 1925) spells out Boodin's cosmology as "empirical realism and cosmic idealism." Empirical realism demands strict adherence to the methods and results of the sciences, while cosmic idealism maintains that in the flux of matter, Form (here interpreted to be Spirit or God) exercises control and direction, guaranteeing the final victory of the ideals to which man aspires. Boodin's theory of evolution is "cosmic interaction." The universe *as a whole* does not evolve; rather, all its levels—matter, mind, and God—coexist. Evolution in one part of the universe is due to the responsiveness of this part to communication of form from a higher level.

Boodin elaborated the implications of his metaphysics and cosmology for religion and social philosophy. In *The Social Mind* (New York, 1939) Boodin posited "social minds" as syntheses of individual minds into wholes with new properties. These minds may overlap in a hierarchy of increasing complexity until hopefully the highest social mind, embracing and reconciling the values of all lower orders, is evolved. In *God and Creation* (4 vols., New York, 1934), and *The Religion of Tomorrow* (New York, 1943), Boodin defined God as the form that guides the creative process of evolution within the cosmos and as the presence that urges each part to respond by further creation.

Boodin's philosophy never won a wide audience in its own time, and after World War II it receded from attention. Relativity theory in physics had raised difficulties with regard to Boodin's categories of space and time, and the retreat from holistic concepts in the life sciences had weakened the plausibility of his system. When contrasted with more recent forms of scientific philosophy, Boodin's thought seems to be vague and unwarranted, but also imaginative and speculative.

Bibliography

Discussions of Boodin's philosophy are to be found in E. C. Holmes, *Social Philosophy and the Social Mind* (New York, 1942); A. J. Reck, *Recent American Philosophy* (New York, 1964), pp. 123–153; and W. H. Werkmeister, *A History of Philosophical Ideas in America* (New York, 1949), pp. 512–518.

ANDREW J. RECK

BOOLE, GEORGE (1815–1864), English mathematician and logician, was born in humble circumstances at Lincoln, where his father was a shoemaker, a mathematical amateur, and a pillar of the Mechanics Institute. Locally educated, and largely self-taught, Boole became a schoolmaster at 16 and at 23 published his first mathematical paper, on analytical transformations. In 1844 his paper "On a General Method in Analysis" was awarded a Royal Society medal and brought him to the notice of D. F. Gregory and other Cambridge mathematicians. Three years later the public altercation between Sir William Hamilton and Augustus De Morgan over the quantification of the predicate led Boole to publish his celebrated pamphlet *The Mathematical Analysis of Logic* (Cambridge, 1847), which marks the first successful application of algebraical methods to logic and is the foundation of all subsequent developments in this field. A fuller elaboration of the same ideas, with applications to probability theory, was given in

An Investigation of the Laws of Thought (London, 1854). Boole, in the meantime—and despite his lack of a degree—had been rescued from schoolmastering by his appointment, in 1849, as first professor of mathematics at Queen's College, Cork, where he taught successfully for 15 years until his unexpected death, due to lecturing in clothes wet from the rain. Besides two mathematical treatises, *On Differential Equations* (Cambridge, 1859) and *On the Calculus of Finite Differences* (Cambridge, 1860), he left some fifty published papers on mathematics and the theory of probabilities, the latter of which have been collected, with his logical remains, by Rush Rhees in *Studies in Logic and Probability* (London, 1952).

Guided though he was by then-recent work in the calculus of operators, Boole's great and almost single-handed achievement was to perceive a far-reaching, if not quite perfect, analogy between the operations of logic—in particular, of a logic of classes in extension—and those of ordinary algebra. Having adopted suitable symbols for the universe class (1) and null class (0) and for a class (x) and its complement ($1 - x$), he was able to operate freely with these symbols by purely algebraic methods (chiefly addition and multiplication) to produce results not only valid in themselves but also vastly more extensive than those obtained by traditional means. (See LOGIC, HISTORY OF, section on Boole.) It is important, however, to note (what Boole himself realized) that the intervening manipulations of his symbolism frequently bear no resemblance to any recognizable process of logic, and that the system is essentially a technique for the solution of problems, rather than an axiomatic development. The first of these defects was largely remedied by his successors and codifiers, W. S. Jevons, John Venn, C. S. Peirce, and Ernst Schröder, while the necessary postulates were first established by E. V. Huntington in 1904. The name "Boolean algebra" is currently applied to a variety of abstract systems whose axiomatic basis is similar to that of the classic Boole–Schröder algebra of logic in that they admit variables but not quantifiers, employ the operations of union and intersection, make use of complements (in effect, negative terms), and satisfy in one way or another the Boole–Schröder laws. Such algebras have interpretations in fields other than logic (such as computer design and switching theory) and may extend either to finite or to infinite numbers of elements. They are commonly studied nowadays as a branch of lattice theory.

Boole believed that the parallels between his class calculus and ordinary algebra were due to their common subservience to a "higher logic," which he identified with the "laws of thought." He was thereby led to seek other applications of the same principles in propositional logic and the calculus of probabilities. In their propositional interpretation, his symbols are restricted to the values 1 and 0, representing truth and falsity; in the calculus of probabilities, they take on fractional values between the limits of certainty and impossibility and measure the degree of rational expectation attributable to future events in virtue of their known relative frequency of occurrence in the past. Boole thereby parts company with both the subjective and the frequency interpretations of probability, and is also an effective critic of the more dubious uses of the principle of indifference by speculations of the Laplacean school. His own method is to "translate" the data into terms of an idealized set of "free, simple" events, whose independent probabilities are then combined or disjoined in accordance with his calculus to yield the desired result. Where the initial data can already be assumed independent, the translation is straightforward; where not, they can still be so formalized, provided they satisfy "the conditions of possible experience"—for instance, that the combined probabilities of two such events shall not exceed that of either taken alone.

Boole's conceptions of independence have not gone unquestioned; and here, as elsewhere in his system, his methods of working have been found cumbersome and abstruse. The details of that system have accordingly fallen into neglect, though its consistency has not, in general, been disputed and its influence remains profound.

Bibliography

No life of Boole exists, though there are biographical sketches of merit by Robert Harley, in *British Quarterly Review*, Vol. 44 (1866), 141–181, reprinted in Boole's *Studies in Logic and Probability*, and by William Kneale, "Boole and the Revival of Logic," in *Mind*, Vol. 57 (1948), 149–175; there is a more domestic portrait by his wife, M. E. Boole, "The Home Side of a Scientific Mind," in *The University Magazine*, n.s., Vol. 1 (1878), reprinted in her *Collected Works*, Vol. I (London, 1931), pp. 1–53.

Boole's logic is discussed in W. S. Jevons, *Pure Logic, With Remarks on Boole's System* (London, 1864); Alexander MacFarlane, *Algebra of Logic* (Edinburgh, 1879); John Venn, *Symbolic Logic*, 2d ed. (London, 1894); A. T. Shearman, *Development of Symbolic Logic* (London, 1906); C. I. Lewis, *Survey of Symbolic Logic* (Los Angeles, 1918); J. M. Keynes, *Treatise on Probability* (London, 1921); Jørgen Jørgensen, *Treatise of Formal Logic*, Vol. I (Copenhagen, 1931); *Proceedings of the Royal Irish Academy*, Vol. 57, No. 6 (1955); J. A. Passmore, *A Hundred Years of Philosophy* (London, 1957); and William and Martha Kneale, *Development of Logic* (Oxford, 1962).

P. L. HEATH

BOSANQUET, BERNARD (1848–1923), English philosopher, was born at Altwick and educated at Harrow and at Balliol College, Oxford. He taught ancient history and some philosophy at Oxford from 1871 to 1881, when he left Oxford for London. In London he edited translations of Lotze's *Logic* and *Metaphysics*, played an active part in the London Ethical Society, worked with the Charity Organisation Society, and did some teaching in the adult education movement. In 1895 he married Helen Dendy, who had been employed by the Charity Organisation Society and who later wrote much on social problems and became a member of the important Royal Commission on the Poor Law of 1909. From 1903 to 1908 he held the chair of moral philosophy at St. Andrews. He died in London.

Bosanquet's first important philosophical work is an essay entitled "Logic as the Science of Knowledge" in *Essays in Philosophical Criticism* (A. Seth and R. B. Haldane, eds., London, 1883), a collection of papers in memory of T. H. Green. In *Knowledge and Reality* (London, 1885) he criticized F. H. Bradley's *Principles of Logic* for divergences from the central and, as Bosanquet thought, correct course charted in that book. In 1888 Bosanquet's *Logic or the Morphology of Knowledge* (2 vols., London) was published. Bosanquet had earlier translated the introduction to Hegel's *Philosophy of Fine Art* (London, 1886), and his own *History of Aesthetics* appeared in London and New York in 1892. His Gifford lectures were published as *The Principle of Individuality and Value* (London, 1912) and *The Value and Destiny of the Individual* (London, 1913). Bosanquet was a prolific writer who contributed to discussion in all branches of philosophy and also took part in some social controversy. He was two years younger than Bradley and, like him, came to the Idealist point of view partly through the influence of T. H. Green and partly through reading Hegel. Bradley's *Ethical Studies* influenced him, but Bradley, in his turn, learned from Bosanquet's writings, especially from those on logic. Although both were Idealists, and both were called Absolutists, Bosanquet was more Hegelian and less of a skeptic than Bradley.

Logic. In the essay "Logic as the Science of Knowledge," which appeared in the same year as Bradley's *Logic* and seems to be independent of it, Bosanquet set out the main lines of his 1888 *Logic.* In this preliminary essay he argued that truth is comprehensible only within systems of knowledge, and that although truth is correspondence with fact, such correspondence is conceivable only within systems because "the facts by which we test conclusions are not simply given from without," and they are not available for judgment until they are "organised into knowledge." He also argued that judgment and inference are not fundamentally distinct, but that judgment is inference not yet made explicit and inference is explicit judgment. A further feature of this striking essay is that in it the forms of judgment are not regarded as fixed and rigid but as "elastic" in their application, so that a form of sentence best suited to express one form of judgment can in fact be used to express many others. In *Knowledge and Reality* Bosanquet suggested that Bradley had, in spite of his "essential and original conceptions" as to the general nature of judgment and inference and their connection with each other, fallen into some of the errors of "reactionary logic." Bradley said, for example, that categorical judgments state facts, whereas hypothetical judgments (and with them universal ones) do not. By an ingenious choice of examples, Bosanquet shows that such a contrast cannot be sustained and that there is no contrast between being a fact and being a universal. Bosanquet's method is to cite intermediate cases that make impossible the acceptance of sharp distinctions between forms of judgment. He thinks that Bradley was inclined to isolate his examples from their contexts and to lose sight of the subtleties and complexities of language. An instance of this part of Bosanquet's argument is his discussion of Bradley's example "the sea-serpent exists." Bosanquet points out that it is far from clear what this means in the abstract and that "'exist' is a formal predicate which receives material interpretation from context."

In *Logic or the Morphology of Knowledge* these views are worked out in systematic form. The first volume is concerned with judgment and the second with inference, but the two parts are very closely linked. Bosanquet did not think that, in actual and advancing thought, form and subject matter could be separated. Thus he regarded formal logic not as the standard of thought but as a highly specialized and idealized, and somewhat subsidiary, type of thinking. The forms of judgment and inference with which he concerns himself, therefore, are those that he regards as operative in the actual advancement of knowledge. Judgment is concerned with truth, and mere interjections do not claim to be true; but there are rudimentary judgments of quasi-interjectional type, such as "How ugly!" or "Oh, horrible!" Such impersonal judgments as "It rains" take us still further along the road of developing thought, and demonstratives take us still further. "This" is always so by relation to "that," so that demonstratives lead on to comparison; and as comparison is made more exact, it leads on to proportion and measurement.

At this point, according to Bosanquet, the series diverges, one route being that taken by what he calls "the concrete or categorical series" and the other by what he calls "the abstract or hypothetical series." Along the first route there are singular judgments and those he calls generic judgments, in which a kind is regarded as real, as when we say "Man is mortal" or "Water boils at 212 degrees Fahrenheit." Along the second line of development there are the various types of abstract judgment, such as "Heat is a mode of motion" or "$7+5=12$," in which the emphasis is on necessary connection rather than on concreteness. The two series converge again in the hypothetical judgment, and the whole culminates in the disjunctive judgment, which Bosanquet regards as the most adequate form. His reason for this is that it combines the concreteness of the categorical series with the necessity of the hypothetical series. The various disjuncts, in this view, reveal a system in which every member has its distinct place. Bosanquet illustrates this by such examples as "The triangle is either scalene, isosceles, or equilateral." In the *Essentials of Logic* (London and New York, 1895), he refers to functions within a social order of the sort which, if an individual exercises one of them he does not and cannot exercise any of the others: if a person is king, he is not subject; if he is judge, he is not prosecutor. In his account of inference, Bosanquet also lays great stress on intermediate and transitional forms. Furthermore, just as he minimizes the difference between judgment and inference, so he minimizes the difference between deduction and induction. He holds that knowledge advances neither by generalization from particulars nor by the elimination of hypotheses. Inference, in his view, depends upon the existence of systematic connections, and neither mere counting nor mere discarding can reveal these to us. What is needed is "depth and complexity of insight into a sub-system of the world," and the word "induction" is used when our points of contact with the real world are "isolated perceptions, occurrences or qualities." But the aim of all inquiry is to break down this isolation and to show how the elements of a system must be what they are. Thus, as knowledge advances, the aspect of contingency is less prominent, mere facts or mere observations play a vanishing part, and we come to see that things must be as they are.

Metaphysics. For Bosanquet, as for Hegel, there is no sharp division between logic on the one hand and epistemology and metaphysics on the other. Indeed, although logic is concerned with the forms of judgment and inference, the study of these forms leads to the conclusion that reality is systematic. If facts were distinct and isolated, it would be impossible to infer from one to another. Since inferences can be made, facts are not isolated but are "implicated" with one another and "transcend" themselves. The possibility of inference points to the metaphysical fact of "self-transcendence."

Bosanquet's metaphysical system is outlined in his *Principles of Individuality and Value* and given more detailed application in *The Value and Destiny of the Individual.* These titles indicate Bosanquet's concern with individuality and individuals. His view is that individuals are concrete universals. He contrasts (as Bradley had done) abstract universals, such as redness, with concrete universals, such as Julius Caesar. Abstract universality is the repetition of an identical quality in many instances, whereas concrete universality is the realization of the same individual in its various interrelated acts or manifestations. The many red things are extremely diverse, whereas the actions of an individual are more or less systematically connected with one another. According to Bosanquet, "there can be only one individual, and that, *the* individual, the Absolute." When men are called individuals, it is in a "secondary sense," insofar as they are regarded as relatively independent, stable, and unique. But this uniqueness is not some internal, private, inaccessible feature of them. The "inwardness" of persons is not something private, not "the banishment of all that seems outward, but the solution of the outward in the circulation of the total life."

McTaggart complained that everything Bosanquet says about mind and body "might have been written by a complete materialist," and Bosanquet himself in *Knowledge and Reality* had written that "a consistent materialist and a thorough idealist hold positions that are distinguishable only in name." Bosanquet rejects both psychophysical interactionism and the view that mind is an effect of matter. He holds that mind is a perfection of the organism and that an organism possesses more or less of it as the organism selects from, and adapts itself to, the circumstances of its world. He rejects the possibility of a mind independent of matter, and draws ethical conclusions from this. Without things, he says, there would be no problems for men. If there were nothing but disembodied persons, there would be nothing to do.

In bringing these general principles to bear upon aspects of experience, Bosanquet comes to some surprising conclusions. His view of individuals as concrete universals might have been expected to lead to a respect for historical knowledge, as it has done with other Idealists. But, according to Bosanquet, history is "a hybrid form of experience," "the doubtful story of successive events." His view is that the spatiotemporal contingencies of human life must, as knowledge grows, become absorbed into a fuller understanding of society, art, philosophy, and religion. These, he says, are "concrete and necessary living worlds." Bosanquet also rejects the view, advocated by Carlyle, Froude, and Bradley, that human conduct and discovery cannot be predicted. He argues that this thesis depends upon the false assumption that individuals cannot overlap, and he holds that such facts as "anticipatory" inventions that have to be "re-invented" are evidence to the contrary. Thus, in *The Value and Destiny of the Individual* he concluded that "intelligences must overlap" and stigmatized as "the pathos and bathos of sentimentalism" the view that selves are essentially withdrawn and alone.

Social philosophy. From what has already been said about Bosanquet's metaphysics, it follows that societies are individuals to a fuller degree than individuals can be. In the *Philosophical Theory of the State,* he treats the relation between the individual and the state as that of microcosm to macrocosm. The individual world and the social world are held to be correlated with one another in such a way that for every element in the one there is some corresponding element in the other. Like Aristotle and Rousseau, he emphasizes the civilizing influence of the state on the individual. He rejects the common-sense, pluralistic metaphysics that he thinks misdirects the social philosophy of Bentham and Mill. "All individuals," he writes, "are continually reinforced and carried on, beyond their average immediate consciousness, by the knowledge, resources, and energy which surround them in the social order." "The common self or moral person of society," he holds, "is more real than the apparent individual." Hence, like Rousseau, he regards coercion by the state as coercion exercised by the social aspect of the individual upon the recalcitrant and less real aspects of his being. According to classical liberalism, the individual is free when he is left alone to do what he wants. According to Bosanquet, this is a metaphysical as well as a practical impossibility, so he develops the conception of freedom as self-mastery. But since selves are not exclusive atoms, self-mastery, social control, and freedom are held to coincide. Bosanquet accepts T. H. Green's view that action under compulsion has less value than action freely willed, thus recognizing that state enforcement can lead to mere external conformity. But just as he regarded nature as the necessary complement of mind, so he regarded force, habit, and tradition as the necessary complements of creative choice. Thus, although punishment acts on the "lower self" by means of threats, it can also stimulate the "higher self" by producing a shock that forces attention to legitimate social demands. Still, the function of the state is forcibly to "hinder hindrances to the best life or common good," and the very notion of promoting morality by force is "an absolute self-contradiction." Thus, although Bosanquet minimizes and even denies the reality of individual men, he does not advocate totalitarian or even socialistic measures. Indeed, just as Bastiat, the publicist of laissez-faire, considered that society as a whole was moved by an impersonal reason, so Bosanquet believed that intelligence is manifested in society to a greater degree than it ever could be in any particular person. He has been criticized for failing to distinguish between society and the state and for suggesting that the state can do no wrong. There is justice in the former criticism, even though we may agree that force is inevitable if developed societies are to continue in existence. As to the second, Bosanquet's main philosophical point was that theft, murder, and such are concepts that apply to men within a society, and that war, conquest, confiscation, and such are concepts of a different type, applying to beings of a different type.

Bosanquet's account of what makes them different types is very complex. He points out that many crimes committed on behalf of the state result from the desire of some individual agent of the state to take a short cut or to save trouble and hence are not imputable to it. Furthermore, the state cannot commit wrongs of the sort that are the consequences of individual selfishness or sensuality. On the other hand, a state that ordered the killing of a hostile statesman would rightly be criticized, not on the ground of murder but "by the degree of its failure to cope with the duties of a state." Bosanquet seems to mean that when a state is rightly criticized, it is compared with more adequate specimens of its own type but is not blamed or punished as are individual men who break the law. Bosanquet holds that states are morally responsible beings, but that they cannot do wrong in the way that individual men can and do. States fall short rather than do wrong. Furthermore, he repudiates the idea that individuals are guilty of murder when a state wages war or of theft when it annexes or confiscates; any moral criticism, he holds, should be directed against the morally responsible agent, the state itself, and such criticism must relate to the general level of life it sustains and promotes. At the end of World War I Bosanquet opposed such popular appeals as "Hang the Kaiser" and "Punish the Germans," and although he said that the League of Nations was "the hope and refuge of mankind," he believed that individual members should no more submit themselves unreservedly to this organization than individual men should submit themselves unreservedly to their own governments.

Bibliography

On Bosanquet's life, see Helen Bosanquet, *Bernard Bosanquet* (London, 1924) and J. H. Muirhead, ed., *Bernard Bosanquet and His Friends. Letters Illustrating the Sources and Development of His Philosophical Opinions* (London, 1935).

Apart from the works mentioned in the text, Bosanquet's books include: *A Companion to Plato's Republic* (London and New York, 1895); *The Psychology of the Moral Self* (London and New York, 1897); *Three Lectures on Aesthetics* (London, 1915); *Some Suggestions in Ethics* (London, 1918); *Implication and Linear Inference* (London, 1920); *What Religion Is* (London, 1920); *The Meeting of Extremes in Contemporary Philosophy* (London, 1921); and other shorter works.

There are also the following collections of essays and lectures: *Essays and Addresses* (London, 1889); *The Civilisation of Christendom* (London, 1893); *Social and International Ideals* (London, 1917); *Science and Philosophy and Other Essays* (London, 1927).

For discussions of Bosanquet's views, see: J. M. E. McTaggart's critical notice of *The Principle of Individuality and Value* in *Mind* n.s. Vol. 21 (1912), 416–427; H. B. Acton, "The Theory of Concrete Universals," in *Mind* n.s. Vol. 45 (1936), 417–431 and n.s. Vol. 46 (1937), 1–13; and F. Houang, *Le Néo-Hégélianisme en Angleterre: la philosophie de Bernard Bosanquet* (Paris, 1954).

On Bosanquet's social philosophy, see: L. T. Hobhouse, *The Metaphysical Theory of the State* (London, 1918) and A. J. M. Milne, *The Social Philosophy of English Idealism* (London, 1962), Ch. VII.

H. B. ACTON

BOSCOVICH, ROGER JOSEPH, or Rudjer Josip Bošković (1711–1787), was a Jesuit scientist whose originality and advanced views have only recently been appreciated. A natural philosopher, mathematician, physicist, astronomer, geodesist, engineer, and poet, Boscovich was, in the words of the physicist John Henry Poynting, "amongst the boldest minds humanity has produced." Boscovich published about one hundred books and papers, most of them in Latin. These works display an unusual combination of enthusiasm and logic as well as a passionate conviction that simple fundamental assumptions and precise reasoning can lead to the understanding of natural phenomena. The French astronomer Joseph Jérôme Le Français de Lalande said that in each of these works there are ideas worthy of a man of genius.

Boscovich was born at Ragusa (now Dubrovnik, Yugoslavia) of Serb and Italian parentage. He entered the novitiate of the Society of Jesus in Rome in 1725 and the Collegium Romanum in 1727. At the Collegium stress was laid on clear logical thought and on the development of a way of thinking which combined religious convictions with the results of science. Boscovich devoted himself chiefly to mathematics and physics and published his first scientific paper in 1736. He became professor of mathematics at the Collegium in 1740, and in 1744 he took his vows as a priest. Since his gifts were scientific, Boscovich was left free to apply himself to teaching, research, and tasks designated by the religious authorities. In 1734 Pope Benedict XIV appointed him, with others, as a technical adviser concerned with cracks in the dome of St. Peter's, and in 1750 commissioned him with Christopher Maire, an English Jesuit, to measure an arc of the meridian through Rome. Later, Boscovich was designated to arbitrate a dispute between the Republic of Lucca and Austrian Tuscany over the drainage of a lake. This task took him to Vienna, where he already enjoyed a high reputation as a scholar and a diplomat. From 1759 on, Boscovich was engaged in extensive travels as far away as Constantinople. In 1760 he met Benjamin Franklin and many other leading personalities in London and Cambridge, and he was elected a fellow of the Royal Society in 1761. He became professor of mathematics at Pavia in 1765, but his health was failing and he grew restless. A chair was created for him at Milan in 1769, and he pursued studies at the Brera observatory. In 1775 Boscovich was appointed director of naval optics for the French navy and went to Paris, where he was made a subject of France by Louis XV. He returned to Italy in 1783. During his last years he suffered from melancholia.

Despite these activities Boscovich continued to publish. Each of his numerous works in pure and applied mathematics presented either a new method for or a survey of some branch of mathematical inquiry. Among the topics he discussed were spherical trigonometry, the cycloid, conic sections, infinitely great and infinitely small quantities, the accuracy of astronomical observations, the telescope, sunspots, eclipses, the determination of the sun's rotation and of the orbits of planets and comets, the aurora borealis, the transit of Mercury, the shape of the earth, the variation of gravity, the center of gravity, and optical problems. His last major publication was a five-volume work on optics and astronomy, *Opera Pertinentia ad Opticam et Astronomiam*, published at Venice in 1785.

Boscovich's masterpiece, and his work of greatest interest to philosophers, is *Philosophiae Naturalis Theoria Redacta ad Unicam Legem Virium in Natura Existentium* ("A Theory of Natural Philosophy Reduced to a Single Law of the Actions Existing in Nature"), published in Vienna in 1758 and, in an improved edition, at Venice in 1763. In this work Boscovich presented an atomic theory on which he had been working for 15 years. The importance of this theory was widely recognized, especially in Britain, where the Encyclopaedia Britannica devoted 14 pages to it in 1801. Boscovich had been the first supporter in Italy of Newton's theory of gravitation, and the *Theoria* was looked upon in Britain as an interesting speculative extension of the Newtonian system.

Boscovich's atomic theory arose, as he himself stated, from an attempt to build a comprehensive physics based on the ideas of Newton and Leibniz but going beyond both to obtain new results. Boscovich developed the idea that all phenomena arise from the spatial patterns of identical point particles (*puncta*) interacting in pairs according to an oscillatory law which determines their relative acceleration. This view of matter is akin to that of recent physics in that it is relational, structural, and kinematic. It contains three original features:

(1) Material permanence without spatial extension: Quasi-material point-centers of action are substituted for the rigid finite units of matter of earlier atomists.

(2) Spatial relations without absolute space: Internal spatial coordinates (the distances between the two members of pairs of *puncta*) are used instead of external coordinates.

(3) Kinematic action without Newtonian forces: In modern dimensional terms, Boscovich's theory is kinematic rather than dynamical. It uses only two dimensional quantities (length and time) rather than the three (mass, length, and time) used by Newton. Since all particles are identical, the number of particles in a system, which is an integral pure number obtained by counting, is employed in place of Newtonian mass.

Although all of these features are of interest, the first is most important, for by it Boscovich helped emancipate physics from naive atomism's uncritical assumption that the ultimate units of matter are small, individual, rigid pieces possessing shape, size, weight, and other properties. The alternative point atomism assumes that the ultimate units are persistent quasi-material points, all identical, which form stable patterns or interact to produce changes of pattern and relative motion. Between 1710 and 1760 such other thinkers as Giambattista Vico, Leibniz (whose theory of monads and relational conception of space influenced Boscovich), Emanuel Swedenborg, John Michell, and Kant had produced atomic theories based on points, but Boscovich was the first scientist to develop a general physical theory using point particles.

Boscovich preferred the concept of *puncta* to that of rigid pieces of matter because they were simpler and, since they avoided the awkward discontinuity at the surface of a piece of matter, were better adapted to mathematical treatment. His law of oscillatory change from attraction to repulsion enabled him to posit points of stable equilibrium at finite distances and thus to account for the finite extension of gross matter, as Kant did also. The complexity of the world, according to Boscovich, arises from two factors: the varied arrangement of different numbers of particles, and the parameters determining the law of oscillation.

To a modern reader, the impressive feature of the *Theoria* is Boscovich's interpretation of the universe as a three-dimensional structure of patterns in equilibrium or change determined by points and their mutual distances. There is no distinction between occupied and empty space, for space is only the relation between *puncta*. Space, time, and motion are all relative; the *puncta* form a vast variety of stable patterns; the laws of the universe are simple, but their consequences are complex; the laws contain several natural units of length, as do the laws of modern physics since the introduction of Planck's constant; there is a pervasive continuity in nature permitting inference from the macroworld to the microworld; geometry is in part a creation of the human mind and can to some extent be chosen at will; the ability of atomism to account for the forms and processes of the natural universe is unlimited, and even organic forms are easy to understand, because complex patterns of particles will adhere to one another in figures of certain shapes.

As a speculative vision of a universe of changing structure supported by an appropriate philosophy of physics, Boscovich's system is brilliant, but as a scientific theory it is incorrect because it does not allow for the highly complex properties of the wave-particles of present-day physics. No data concerning the atomic world were available to provide a quantitative basis for Boscovich's theory, and he was able to give only a qualitative description of simple mechanical and physical properties. The physical world is more complex than the world Boscovich created from his imagination. Nevertheless, his philosophy of physics was in some respects near the truth, for he predicted—a century and a half before the facts were known—that matter is penetrable by high-speed particles and that relative motion affects the measurement of space and time. Moreover, these predictions were necessary consequences of his mathematical conception of three-dimensional structure. Boscovich's standard of simplicity remains a challenge to physics, and only a future, fully unified, particle theory will be able to show precisely where his assumptions were mistaken. Boscovich postulated that there is only one fundamental particle; we do not yet know how many must be assumed. Modern conceptions of molecular structure have much in common with Boscovich's ideas, but since the development of the physical concept of a field, it can be seen that the Boscovichian particle is inadequate even to account for electromagnetic processes.

It is not certain how far the *Theoria* influenced the development of atomic theory. It was widely studied, and Michael Faraday, Sir William Hamilton, James Clerk Maxwell, and Lord Kelvin (to mention only English scientists) stressed the theoretical advantages of the Boscovichian atom over rigid atoms. In any case, Boscovich's work marked an important stage in the history of our ideas about the universe, and his system will remain the paradigm of the theory of point particles.

Bibliography

The second edition of the *Theoria* was republished in a Latin–English edition, with the English translation by J. M. Child, as *Theory of Natural Philosophy* (Chicago and London, 1922).

For literature on Boscovich, see L. L. Whyte, ed., *Roger Joseph Boscovich, S. J., F.R.S., 1711–1787: Studies of His Life and Work on the 250th Anniversary of His Birth* (London, 1961; New York, 1964), which contains a biographical essay by Hill and eight papers on aspects of Boscovich's work by English, American, and Yugoslav scholars. Its extensive bibliography of works by and about Boscovich does not, however, cover Yugoslav studies. See also H. V. Gill, *Roger Joseph Boscovich, S.J., 1711–1787: Forerunner of Modern Physical Theories* (Dublin, 1941), and L. Pearce Williams, *Michael Faraday* (London and New York, 1965).

LANCELOT LAW WHYTE

BOSSUET, JACQUES BÉNIGNE (1627–1704), was born in Dijon, the son of a lawyer. At the age of thirteen he was a boy canon of Metz. After a period in Paris, where he became known in the salons and distinguished himself as a theologian, he was ordained priest in 1652 (having been prepared by Vincent de Paul) and began his ministry at Metz. Friends in high places secured his recall to Paris in 1659, and he soon established a reputation as preacher and spiritual director. Contemporaries agree that he had the ability, and presumably the desire, to please everyone; and his early reputation for moderation may reflect tactics more than convictions. Winning favor at Court, he was rewarded in 1669 with the see of Condom and was appointed tutor to the dauphin, Louis XIV's son, in 1670. He is most famous for the series of funeral orations he delivered as Court preacher (1666–1687), of which the last and finest commemorates the great Condé. Besides these set (and published) pieces, he preached numerous sermons for all occasions, often using the feast of a particular saint for an exposition of his own views on a contemporary question, such as the relations between church and state, lucidly discussed in the panegyric of St. Thomas of Canterbury (Becket). Some two hundred sermons survive, mostly as notes on which he usually improvised, and it is easier to establish his main ideas than to reconstruct his mastery of the spoken word.

On completion of the tutorial task, he was transferred in 1681 to Meaux, conveniently near Paris, where he remained until his death. His influence at Court gave him more effective power than his hierarchical superiors, and in 1682 he composed and presented the Gallican Articles as spokesman for the whole French church. His last years were marred by quarrels, especially with his former protégé François Fénelon, whose condemnation for quietism he secured only by resorting to methods so ignoble that formal victory was bought at the cost of moral defeat. Despised at Court and broken in health, he ended his life among relatives of notoriously unedifying character.

All Bossuet's thinking was deeply influenced by St. Augustine and characterized by a peculiar emphasis on authority. In his eyes, obedience and discipline are the highest virtues. The supreme authority of the church and the divine right of kings are inseparable and constantly recurrent themes in his work. In the *Politique tirée de l'ecriture sainte* ("Politics Drawn from Scripture"), written for the dauphin, he is heavily in favor of the absolute monarch, chosen by God and responsible to him alone (distinguished, however, from the arbitrary monarch, a tyrant who merely gratifies his own whims). The *Traité de la connaissance de Dieu et de soi-même* ("Treatise Concerning the Knowledge of God and Oneself") combines Thomist and other standard teaching with a marked sympathy for the reassuringly authoritarian side of Cartesianism, with its insistence on order and certainty, although Bossuet elsewhere denounced the dangers of encouraging individual reason and inquiry. The unfinished *Discours sur l'histoire universelle* ("Discourse on Universal History") was intended to teach the dauphin not so much what had happened as why. Though later editions made some concessions to currently changing views on the chronology of ancient times, history was primarily interpreted as showing the ways of God to man, especially as revealed in the Bible. In tracing the fortunes of empires down to Charlemagne (and to Louis XIV, if he had completed his plan) Bossuet emphasized moral and religious development, regarding freedom as a prime cause of decadence.

Similarly, the *Histoire des variations des églises protestantes* ("History of the Variations of the Protestant Churches") attributes to Protestant reliance on individual liberty of conscience a disunity amounting to near anarchy. Bossuet naturally regarded heresy and sedition as twinned evils; and in his orations on Henrietta Maria and Henrietta Anne (widow and daughter of Charles I), he adduces the recent revolution in England to prove his contention that social equality is an impious chimera. He was curiously ambivalent in his relations with Protestants, converting many individuals (including the vicomte de Turenne) and courteously corresponding with Leibniz in an attempt to effect a reconciliation, while greeting the revocation of the Edict of Nantes, followed as it was by brutal persecution, with an embarrassingly effusive eulogy of Louis' piety.

Bossuet earns his place in history above all as a public figure, "the eagle of Meaux." In the *grand siècle* Bossuet was the church, just as Louis was the state.

Works by Bossuet

Oeuvres complètes, F. Lachat, ed., 31 vols. Paris, 1862–1866.

Works on Bossuet

Adam, A., *Histoire de la littérature française au XVIIe siècle* Paris, 1956, Vol. V, Ch. 4.

Calvet, J., *Bossuet, l'homme et l'oeuvre*. Paris, 1941.

Hazard, P., *La Crise de la conscience européenne*, 2d ed. Paris, 1961. Translated by J. L. May as *The European Mind*. London, 1953.

Lebarcq, J., *Histoire critique de la prédication de Bossuet*. Lille, 1888.

Rebelliau, A., *Bossuet*. Paris, 1900.

A. J. KRAILSHEIMER

BOSTRÖM, CHRISTOPHER JACOB (1797–1866), Swedish Idealist philosopher. Boström studied and also taught at Uppsala University, where he was assistant professor of "practical philosophy" (the philosophy of morals, law, and religion) from 1828 to 1833. After an interlude as tutor to the royal princes in Stockholm from 1833 to 1837, he resumed his academic teaching, and from 1842 to 1863 he held the chair in practical philosophy. His "rational idealism" is a spiritualistic metaphysics, combining traits from Plato's theory of ideas, Leibniz' monadology, and Berkeley's immaterialism. With arguments, some of which are reminiscent of Berkeley's, he tried to show that nothing but minds and their perceptions exist.

Two of his more original, though hardly very convincing, arguments were these: (1) Truth means agreement between the perception and the perceived object. Perfect truth, therefore, is perfect agreement; and perfect agreement is the same as identity. Hence, the object of any perfectly true perception is identical with that perception; in other words, any object, when perceived with perfect truth, is itself a perception. (2) "Outside" has a meaning only when it refers to space. Since a mind is not in space, nothing can be outside a mind. Hence, everything exists inside a mind.

Particular minds and particular perceptions are forms of "self-consciousness," which can be likened to "a substance or stuff of which everything ultimately consists." With this spiritualistic position Boström combined the Leibnizian–Kantian distinction between a thing as it is in itself (essence) and a thing as it appears to us (phenomenon). The spatiotemporal world of experience is merely phenomenal. Or, more correctly, the spatiotemporal world of a person's experience is merely the way in which the things-in-themselves appear to that person because of the imperfection of his particular perceptive faculty. The things-in-themselves, which underlie the appearances, are purely rational minds whose existence is nonspatial and nontemporal. Boström usually called them "ideas," the word being borrowed from Plato rather than from British empiricism. These ideas form a series that, according to him, is similar to the series of natural numbers—except that it contains a maximal idea, God. In this series each idea contains and perceives all the preceding, but none of the succeeding, ones. On this point, however, he was apparently not quite consistent. Simultaneously he asserted that every idea perceives the entire system of ideas but with varying perfection and clarity. God alone has a perfect perception of the whole system. Because every idea that is not God perceives the system imperfectly, the system presents a phenomenal appearance to that idea.

Boström's system contains several other apparent inconsistencies. Although each mind is a purely rational, nonspatial, and nontemporal idea, Boström also taught that each mind other than God has a double existence. Besides existing as a rational idea, it also exists as a temporal mind with a mixed rational and sensual nature. Each mind even has a whole (temporal?) sequence of such mixed and temporal manifestations. (Boström himself points to the analogy between this doctrine and the Hindu belief in reincarnation.) He was thinking primarily of human beings in this context, but the doctrine of double existence is also supposed to apply to such "moral personalities" as the state, the "people," and each one of the four estates.

Boström was aware of the nonintellectual motives that attracted him to this view of the world and once asserted that no philosopher would ever embrace a system that was repugnant to his feelings. Simultaneously, however, he made excessive claims concerning the provability of his own doctrine, to which he attributed the same kind of certainty that has traditionally been ascribed to mathematics.

From the vantage point of his rather fantastic metaphysics, Boström took an active part in public debate in Sweden. In religious questions he was, on the whole, a liberal, vigorously attacking many of the dogmas of Lutheran orthodoxy, especially the dogma of eternal damnation. On political questions, on the other hand, he took an ultraconservative stand. He was one of the staunchest opponents of the parliamentary reform that took place in 1866, soon after his death, and that replaced the four estates by a two-chamber system. His metaphysics might seem to indicate a mystical strain, but his very systematic, precise, and dry mode of writing does not corroborate this impression. The dominant traits in his philosophic temperament would seem to be a strong, puritanical, moral pathos, an unorthodox but firm religious belief, a love of neat systematics, and a rather naïve private dogmatism. Boström's philosophy represents the culmination of the idealistic tradition that dominated Swedish philosophy through the entire nineteenth century. In the 1860s, 1870s, and 1880s, Boströmianism and Hegelianism reigned supreme in Swedish academic philosophy. At the turn of the century a strong Neo-Kantian current set in.

Works by Boström

Skrifter av Christopher Jacob Boström, H. Edfeldte and J. G. Keijser, eds. Vols. I and II, Uppsala, Sweden, 1883; Vol. III, Norrköping, Sweden, 1901. Collected works.

C. J. Boströms Förëlasningar i Religionsfilosofi, S. Ribbing, ed. Stockholm, 1885. Lectures on philosophy of religion.

Prof. C. J. Boströms Förëlasningar i Etiken, S. Ribbing, ed. Uppsala, Sweden, 1897. Lectures in ethics.

C. J. Boströms Förëlasningar i Religionsfilosofi II, G. J. Keijser, ed. Vol. I, Stockholm, 1906; Vol. II, Stockholm, 1910; Vol. III, Stockholm, 1913. Second series of lectures in the philosophy of religion.

Prof. C. J. Boströms Förëlasningar i Etik Vårterminen 1861, G. Klingberg, ed. Uppsala, Sweden, 1916. Boström's lectures in ethics of the spring term of 1861.

TRANSLATIONS

Grundlinien eines philosophischen Systems, translated by R. Geijer and H. Gerloff. Leipzig, 1923. German translation of various writings.

Philosophy of Religion, translated by V. E. and R. N. Beck. New Haven, 1963.

Works on Boström

Larsson, H., *Minnesteckning över C. J. Boström.* Stockholm 1931. Memorial oration.

Morin, H., *Om Dualismen i Boströms Definitiva Filosofi.* Uppsala, Sweden, 1940. On the dualism in Boström's definitive philosophy.

Nyblaeus, A., *Den Filosofiska Forskningen i Sverige,* 4 vols. Lund, Sweden, 1873–1897.

Rodhe, S. E., *Boströms Religionsfilosofiska Åskådning.* Goteborg, Sweden, 1950. Boström's views in the philosophy of religion.

Wedburg, A., *Den Logiska Strukturen hos Boströms Filosofi.* Uppsala, Sweden, 1937. Logical structure of Boström's philosophy.

GENERAL BACKGROUND

Ueberweg, F., and Heinze, M., *Grundriss der Geschichte der Philosophie,* 12th ed. Berlin, 1928. Vol. 5. Excellent survey of Swedish philosophy up to the beginning of the twentieth century.

A. WEDBURG

BOULAINVILLIERS, HENRI, COMTE DE (1658–1722), or Henry, comte de Boulainviller, as he preferred to spell his name, historian, philosopher, astrologer and savant, was born at Saint-Saire, Normandy. From 1669 to 1674 he was educated at the Oratorian school at the College of Juilly, where Richard Simon taught rhetoric and philosophy. Boulainvilliers took up military service, as befitted a member of an old aristocratic family, proud of his lineage. After leaving the army, he developed an interest in history, first studying his own family tree and then the social and political institutions of the Middle Ages. He approved of feudalism, which he envisaged as a kind of federal republic governed by distant and independent aristocratic families, whom he considered to be the inheritors of the Franks who had conquered the Gauls. He deplored the increase in the power of the central authority—the king—and in the liberties of the people as encroachments on the rights of the nobles. He favored a patriarchal society. Many of his reforms, submitted to the regent, recommended the fostering of trade, proportional taxation, the suppression of tax collectors, and the calling of the États Généraux. The count had access to Court circles; he was connected with d'Argenson, president of the council of finance, to whom it is thought he passed on a number of clandestine philosophical tracts. He also frequented the home of the maréchal, duc de Noailles, where he met César Dumarsais, a disciple of Fontenelle, future author of articles for the *Encyclopédie* and probable author of *La Religion chrétienne analysée* and *Examen de la religion;* Nicolas Fréret, a devotee of Pierre Bayle; and Jean-Baptiste de Mirabaud, the *secrétaire perpétuel* of the *Académie Française.*

For a time Boulainvilliers was the center of much intellectual activity, and in the history of free thought his coterie antedates by fifty years the better-known *côterie holbachique.* Voltaire in his *Dîner du comte de Boulainvilliers* (1767) has given us an insight into this milieu, which certainly disseminated a surprisingly large number of clandestine manuscripts and seems to have provided the only organized center for the compiling, copying, and distribution of philosophical tracts. Boulainvilliers is best known as the probable author of parts of the *Essai de métaphysique,* which was published in 1731 under the title *Réfutation des erreurs de Benoît de Spinoza.* He became interested in Spinoza through reading the *Tractatus Theologico-politicus,* which he annotated copiously, and also the *Ethics,* which he read in 1704. The first part, or *Vie de Spinoza,* of the *Essai de métaphysique* has been attributed to J. M. Lucas. The second part, or *Esprit de Spinoza,* has been attributed by I. O. Wade and others to Boulainvilliers. Both parts are commonly coupled together in the manuscripts and in the editions under the title *La Vie et l'esprit de Spinoza.* Boulainvilliers correctly presents Spinoza's doctrine that God and the universality of things are one and the same, then proceeds to argue that Spinoza's "attributes" are in fact "modes"; i.e., "modes" of something he terms existence.

In this work, he has evolved an original philosophy. Starting from the Cartesian principle that he knows himself to be a thinking being, he infers that other beings exist, some endowed with thought, others only with feeling, and others without feeling or thought. All beings, whether living or nonliving, thinking, feeling, or merely extended, have one property in common: existence. From such premises, he proceeds to a universal Idea or Being more all-embracing than matter. He stresses the degrees of being, and claims that sensations are the source of all experience. He concludes by asserting that at death the body returns to universal matter while the soul remains as an idea in the infinite mind and is, therefore, capable of being restored to the body. It is clear that Boulainvilliers' exposition of Spinoza is curiously based on the Cartesian assertions and incorporates ideas borrowed from Locke.

He strove to harmonize the notion of a single substance with a sensationalist psychology and a naturalistic ethics. He believed in a "chain of being," in the capacity of animals to think, and in evidence (as opposed to judgment) as the only criterion of truth; he also helped to discredit Christian revelation. In an *Abrégé d'histoire ancienne* he expressed his belief in the primacy of natural laws, denying the possibility of miracles. These points were later taken up by Diderot in the article "Certitude" of the *Encyclopédie.*

"The Three Imposters." Figuring as part of the *Essai de métaphysique,* sometimes entitled *L'Esprit de Spinoza,* is to be found a treatise commonly known as the *Traité des trois imposteurs,* under which title it was published in 1719 (2d ed., 1721; numerous others throughout the century). Since printed copies were commonly impounded and consequently hard to find, manuscript copies continued to circulate both before and after publication. Polemic and concise, it provided freethinkers with valuable ammunition. Its aggressive title helped to ensure its success and may have been chosen by the Dutch printers as the last and profitable stage of an elaborate hoax. It is an allusion to a lost treatise, *De Tribus Impostoribus* (1230), supposedly written by Frederick II for the edification of his friend Othon. Interest in this Latin work, evidenced in *Theophrastus Redivivus* (1659), had been revived at the close of the seventeenth century and the beginning of the eighteenth.

The author of the *Traité des trois imposteurs,* believed by Voltaire to be Boulainvilliers, launched a virulent attack on the prophets and apostles; he expressed his disbelief in heaven or hell, rewards or punishments, his faith in natural law as enshrined in the hearts of men, and in the soul as the expression of the principle of life. The system of religion is, according to him, the work of false legislators, among whom are Moses, Christ, and Muhammad. Moses was nothing more than a magician and a charlatan; Christ, who may be likened to Genghis Khan, was a casuist in his discussions with the Philistines and in claiming to be the son of a god; his religion owes much to Greek mythology and his ethics compare unfavorably with those of Epictetus and Epicurus. Muhammad differs from the other two impostors in having recourse to violence in the establishment of his kingdom. Voltaire, among others, seized on these points to bolster his polemics against the church. He, too, saw the advantage of an oblique attack on the church by an onslaught against Islamic fanaticism, coupled with the claim that all religions are equal. The treatise marks an early, if crude, attempt to consider religion from the comparative standpoint.

Boulainvilliers is best remembered as a confirmed "spinoziste," and his views on the subject of nature and matter, the relationship of matter and thought, and the origin and nature of government won him a place as a forerunner of the philosophes.

(See also CLANDESTINE PHILOSOPHICAL LITERATURE.)

Works by Boulainvilliers

État de la France, etc., avec des mémoires historiques sur l'ancien gouvernement de cette monarchie jusqu'à Hugues Capet . . ., 3 vols. London, 1727.

Histoire de l'ancien gouvernement de la France, avec 14 lettres historiques sur les parlements ou états généraux, 3 vols. The Hague and Amsterdam, 1727.

Mémoires présentés au duc d'Orléans, régent de France, contenant les moyens de rendre ce royaume très puissant et d'augmenter considérablement les revenus du roi et du peuple, 2 vols. The Hague, 1727.

La Vie de Mahomed. London, 1730. Unfinished.

Essai de métaphysique dans les principes de Spinoza. Brussels, 1731. Published under the title *Réfutation des erreurs de Benoît de Spinosa*, par M. de Fenelon, par le P. Lami et par M. le Comte de Boullainvilliers, avec *La Vie de Spinosa* écrite par M. Jean Colerus. . . .

Histoire des Arabes, 2 vols. Amsterdam, 1731.

Mémoire pour la construction d'un nobiliaire général and *Mémoire sur la noblesse* (1753). Both unpublished; Mss. at Angoulême.

Works on Boulainvilliers

Buranelli, V., "The Historical and Political Thought of Boulainvilliers." *Journal of the History of Ideas*, Vol. 18, No. 4 (1957).

Gargallo di Castel Lentini, Gioacchino, *Boulainvilliers e la storiografia dell'Illuminismo francese.* Giannini-Naples, 1954.

Simon, R., *Henry de Boulainviller, historien, politique, philosophe, astrologue.* Paris, 1939.

Spink, J. S., *French Free-Thought from Gassendi to Voltaire.* London, 1960.

Torrey, N. L., "Boulainvilliers: The Man and the Mask." *Travaux sur Voltaire et le XVIIIe siècle*, Vol. I (1955), 159–173.

Wade, I. O., *The Clandestine Organization and Diffusion of Philosophic Ideas in France from 1700 to 1750.* Princeton, 1938.

ROBERT NIKLAUS

BOUTROUX, ÉMILE

BOUTROUX, ÉMILE (1845–1921), French philosopher of science, was born at Montrouge, near Paris. In 1865 he entered the École Normale Supérieure; there he was a pupil of Jules Lachelier, who exerted great influence on Boutroux and induced him to make a close study of Kant. When Boutroux turned his attention to science and to the principles underlying it, Lachelier pointed out to him that mechanistic causes are never adequate explanations. There is ample evidence that Boutroux took this remark to heart. Two student essays of this period, one on the nature of mathematical proof and the other on final causes, both show a recognition of the limited validity of explanations of change in terms of analytical relations. They also show that Boutroux's thought was already differently oriented from that of Hamelin. In 1868 he was successful in the *agrégation*, and spent 1869 studying in Germany, mainly at Heidelberg. He was appointed as a teacher in the *lycée* of Caen in 1871, and began to work on his thesis on determinism in its relation to the physical and moral sciences, which earned him his doctorate in 1874. Thereupon he was appointed to the University of Montpellier, followed by a year in Nancy (1876–1877). From 1877 to 1886 he taught at the École Normale Supérieure, from which he went on to the University of Paris. He was elected to the French Academy in 1914, and in that year he undertook an extensive lecture tour abroad, visiting Britain, America, Belgium, and Germany. His health was at no time good, and the strain of the war years and the loss in 1919 of his wife, to whom he had been devoted since their marriage in 1877, told on him. He died two years later.

From the time of Kant, the problem of freedom and determinism has been uppermost in French philosophy, expressed as a conflict between science and consciousness; the problem lives on in the mid-twentieth century. French philosophy since 1800 has produced various versions of a reaction against the empiricism and sensationalism of the followers of Condillac, and later Comte. Maine de Biran had made the self, conscious of its action in opposition to a resistant world, the basis of knowledge. Félix Ravaisson, Jules Lachelier, and Octave Hamelin were even more anxious to discount, or even eliminate, the non-ego, so that along one line of development neocriticism ended in uncompromising idealism. It may appear that Boutroux's philosophy is little different in its conclusions. Nevertheless, Boutroux's first concern was to meditate upon the science of the scientist, and to leave it intact while putting it into a wider metaphysical framework.

Boutroux's ideas on the nature of necessity and contingency were contained in his doctoral thesis, *De la Contingence des lois de la nature*, and developed in a course of lectures delivered at the Sorbonne and published in 1895 as *De l'Idée de loi naturelle dans la science et dans la philosophie contemporaine*. These works stressed that there is a basic discontinuity separating different levels of being—material, instinctive, thinking—each of which displays an element not present in its predecessor and not deducible from it, and that consequently it is impossible to reduce the science of any one level to that of the others. Higher forms of life, despite their physical and chemical characteristics, are not wholly explicable in terms of the mechanical laws that govern matter. The large-scale concentration of energy presented by the universe as a whole runs counter to the entropy to which the universe is subject, and suggests the possibility of a contingent and creative initial act. The course of biological evolution produces constant novelty. Thus the order of nature is not one of permanence and identity, but one of change.

Boutroux examined the principle of this change by first analyzing the notion of necessity and showing the distinction between this notion and determinism. Pure necessity is identity, and is expressed by $A=A$. But empirical equivalencies, such as $A=a+b+c$, are not tautological, and everything connected with empirical reality is therefore synthetic. Boutroux accepts Kant's synthetic a priori judgments such as "Every change has a cause." Even empirical a posteriori syntheses provide a sort of "necessity," in that they display constant relationships. Thus Boutroux holds that though all of these classes of statements are in some sense "necessary," all but tautologies are contingent. His arguments are, first, that the reality that we experience is not necessary, because its constituent data are not deducible from anything outside themselves. He then shows that, although we can discover a certain quantitative identity underlying physical change, we cannot ignore the manifestly new phenomena that prompted inquiry in the first place. This restriction is even more striking when we pass from the physical sciences to the biological ones, where it is precisely qualitative changes that are significant. Emphasis is thus shifted in Boutroux's philosophy from the search for substantial identity to the examination of the *history* of things.

Boutroux also questions whether we can in fact be absolutely sure, with our fallible means of observation and measurement, that strict quantitative identity does run through purely physical change. The search for an underlying quantitative identity does not seem particularly fruitful in any case, since it is the qualitative change that is really of interest. If there were not a fair measure of some kind of continuity observable between phenomena, change would never present itself as problematical and our minds would never find an anchorage in reality at all. Thus Boutroux's dilemma—Do we have necessity without determinism, or determinism without necessity?—becomes: How do we account for the discontinuity that is apparent in both phenomena and our thinking about them? Boutroux's answer to the second part of the question has been more influential upon subsequent French philosophy than his answer to the first part. He holds that our thought itself is pluralistic, the pluralism being governed by basically pragmatic considerations. Our scientific laws are "the least defective compromises" that allow us to deal with a shifting reality. (This view anticipates, among other things, the dynamic conception of reason developed by Gaston Bachelard.) These compromises are defective in that they are never definitive, but must be modified or discarded in response to the demands of a developing reality. There is thus what André Lalande was later to call a "constituted reason," in the shape of established scientific laws, and a "constituting reason," which makes and breaks molds of thought and hypothesis as it gropes its way toward knowledge. Thus reason itself is discontinuous; but reasoning is not random, and it would seem that the constraints to which reason conforms have much in common with the unique constraints that govern artistic creation and moral pioneering. In his *Science and Religion* Boutroux states that guiding and informing reason is "what is called religion." Boutroux's normative conception of reason has found an important place in more recent French philosophy.

As a solution of the problem of the discontinuity of the material reality with which our minds deal, Boutroux offered something of a metaphysical system. The primacy of mind is such that all reality is seen as strung out in a hierarchy from spiritual perfection in God down to inanimate matter. Man is endowed with pure spontaneity and freedom, but these can degenerate into habit, or the mere repetition of behavior patterns. May it not be, Boutroux asked, that the laws of nature reflect such degradations of the mental? Here he echoed Ravaisson's *De l'Habitude*, and to some extent anticipated Bergson's preoccupations. The invasion of the whole of reality by varying degrees of mentality clears Boutroux of the charge of being a pure pragmatist, or the charge of being a subjective idealist, implied by the late Susan Stebbing when she protested that there must be an underlying necessity that we *find* in things, and not merely an order that we *impose* on them. For Boutroux there was no essential difference between the vital and the inanimate; material objects already have something in common with us—a sort of tendency toward spirituality, embryonic and incarcerated in matter, progressively free and creative in the higher forms of life. Thus, in place of mechanistic causality there stands a teleological one.

Works by Boutroux

De la Contingence des lois de la nature. Paris, 1874. Translated by F. Rothwell as *The Contingency of the Laws of Nature.* Chicago and London, 1916.

De Veritatibus Aeternis apud Cartesium. Paris, 1874.

De l'Idée de loi naturelle dans la science et la philosophie contemporaines. Paris, 1895. Translated by F. Rothwell as *Natural Law in Science and Philosophy.* London, 1914.

Science et religion dans la philosophie contemporaine. Paris, 1908. Translated by J. Nield as *Science and Religion in Contemporary Philosophy.* London, 1909.

Works on Boutroux

Crawford, Lucy S., *The Philosophy of Émile Boutroux.* New York, 1924.

Gaultier, P., *Les Maîtres de la pensée française.* Paris, 1921.

La Fontaine, A. P., *La Philosophie d'Émile Boutroux.* Paris, 1921.

Parodi, D., *La Philosophie contemporaine en France,* 3d ed. Paris, 1925.

COLIN SMITH

BOWNE, BORDEN PARKER (1847–1910), American Personalist philosopher, spent his scholarly life, that is, from 1876 to 1910, at Boston University, where he taught in the liberal arts college and the school of theology, and where he became the first dean of the graduate school. In many articles and in seventeen books, Bowne expounded his Personalism, or Personalistic Idealism, which held that the Creator–Person, God, and created persons constitute the real.

Bowne was constantly concerned with taking full account of every dimension of human experience, be it the logical, the emotional, the moral, or the religious. Each dimension should be given full value and not be arbitrarily explained away by pontifical claims made in the name of such doctrines as Christian supernaturalism, psychological associationism and materialism, or ethical utilitarianism. For Bowne, reason is the criterion of truth. This means that for him reasoning discovers the real by interweaving and interpreting the different dimensions of experience.

The presupposition of thought and action is a unified, thinking self, or person. Were the person unable to will freely (granted limitations) and to choose in accordance with moral and intellectual ideals, there could be no trustworthy science or philosophy and no significance to moral and religious living. It is in the nature and experience of this self-identical, thinking, willing, and feeling person, who may not be reduced either to a mode of matter or to a mode of divinity, that Bowne finds his clue to, and his model of, reality.

Persons, however, do not create themselves, or each other. They could not communicate with each other were they not bound by the same laws of reason and subject to a common world. Each knower is bombarded by a flux of discontinuous sense impressions to which he responds as constructively as he can in accordance with his own dynamic categories, such as time, space, quality, quantity, cause, substance, and purpose. Thus the "common world" is the phenomenal world as organized by knowers who interact with, and ultimately depend upon, the structure of the real world independent of them. The phenomenal world is not a mask of the real world; it is the real world as related to the cognitive nature and purposes of finite knowers.

Bowne argues that the real world is neither nonmental nor independent of persons. For in knowing, and in interacting with an order other than itself, the mind must meet not only the conditions of its own nature but those of some agency or agencies independent of it. Since knowledge exists, and yet is not imported into a passive mind, the realist's contention that the real is unaffected by knowing is unintelligible. The fact must stand that minds, in following their own natures, can know with reasonable assurance the reality in which they live and can construct a common world of thought and action, even though they are not identical with the real in knowing.

Furthermore, minds in their theoretical and practical action are clearly neither alien to each other nor to the reality that is the source of their experiences. The world as known is the world persons construct, following the nature of their own theoretical interests, on the basis of the reality beyond their thought. Why, then, hold that any reality beyond finite things is nonmental if such cooperative interaction is possible?

Bowne granted that the case against nonmental "material being" is not proved beyond a shadow of a doubt. But he argued that what we do know about the relation of mind to nature is more economically explained if we think of nature as the energizing of a cosmic Person. Nature is God willing in accordance with rational principles, hence nature dependably supports the orderly common world our finite reasons construct in response to it. God, however, is not identical with the natural world. He is transcendent as well as immanent in relation to it. He is the unified, dynamic ground of nature, and he uses it for his purposes, inclusive of his interaction with finite persons.

How, then, are finite persons related to God? Finite persons are created by God and have relative, delegated autonomy. The real world, whose structure maintains and guides the constructive cognitive adjustments of persons, does not force their moral and appreciative responses. But when persons do not treat each other as persons in a realm that is morally purposeful, they fall short of what their own natures in God's world can be. God created man free, to work out the content of his freedom in a world order that at once limits and gives him opportunity for fulfillment. Human freedom could effect nothing in a world without order, for persons do not create the rational or moral principles by which they guide their thought and action in the given ultimate order.

For Bowne, then, the natural world as known by persons is the objectification of the orderly interaction between finite wills and cosmic Will. The ethical world is the objectification of the orderly, chosen, interaction among free, finite persons in the natural world God makes possible. Bowne's universe is not (like Spinoza's) a unity with many fiinite modes. It is a realm of persons united both by God's purposive action in nature and by the further moral unity created as persons freely respond to the reason, will, and love of the cosmic Person.

Bibliography

Among the most interesting philosophical works by Borden Parker Bowne are *The Theory of Thought and Knowledge* (New York, 1897); *Metaphysics* (New York, 1898); *Theism* (New York, 1902); and *Personalism* (Boston, 1908).

Works about Bowne include E. S. Brightman, "Personalism and the Influence of Bowne," in E. S. Brightman, ed., *Proceedings of the Sixth International Institute of Philosophy* (New York, 1927); A. C. Knudson, *The Philosophy of Personalism* (New York, 1927).

For bibliography, see F. J. McConnell, *Borden Parker Bowne* (New York, 1929).

PETER A. BERTOCCI

BOYLE, ROBERT (1627–1691), English natural philosopher, was the fourteenth child of Richard Boyle, the first earl of Cork, who by judicious marriages and land purchases had made himself the most influential man in Ireland and the richest in England. The political and financial fortunes of the earl of Cork fluctuated considerably during his son's lifetime, but ultimately Robert Boyle inherited a considerable income, which greatly facilitated his scientific researches.

In October 1635, Boyle entered Eton, which with Sir Henry Wotton as provost was a notable center of culture and learning. As a result of a change of teachers, Boyle left Eton in 1638 to be privately tutored. In 1639 he went to Geneva, where he studied mathematics; his devotion to religion, so he tells us in his fragment of an autobiography, *An Account of Philaretus during his Minority,* dates from this same period. A visit to Florence in 1641/1642 introduced him to Galileo's ideas and confirmed him in his hostility to Roman Catholicism. His return to England was delayed by a crisis in his father's affairs. When Boyle was free to return to England in 1644, his father was dead and he had inherited the manor of Stalbridge in Dorsetshire.

Boyle stayed at first in London with his favorite sister, Lady Ranelagh, whose house was a center of intellectual life. There he met Samuel Hartlib (d. 1670?), enthusiastic educator and intellectual middleman, through whom Boyle was brought in touch with the burgeoning scientific activities of London. In Boyle's correspondence with Hartlib there are several references to their membership in an "Invisible College"; this has generally been identified by biographers with the Gresham's College group out of which the Royal Society was to develop. The "Invisible College" Boyle referred to, however, would seem rather to have been an independent group centering on Hartlib and having an interest in social and educational reform as well as in science.

From 1645 until 1652 Boyle lived in retirement at Stalbridge, remote from the political upheavals of the times. He was still essentially a dilettante, interesting himself—but not too seriously—in chemistry, writing theological tracts of a highly moral character, and composing what was perhaps the first religious novel, *Seraphic Love* (1648). In 1652/1653 he visited his Irish estates; unable to obtain materials for chemical experiments, he studied anatomy under William Petty. The interest in biological processes thus engendered remained with him. In bad health from early manhood, he was particularly interested in the application of chemical methods to the cure of disease and was a diligent collector of prescriptions.

The Commonwealth had appointed a number of London scientists to posts at Oxford; in 1654 Boyle accepted an invitation from John Wilkins to make his home there. Now his serious career as a scientist began. He built a laboratory and employed a number of research assistants, in particular Robert Hooke (1635–1703), later to be curator of experiments at the Royal Society. With Hooke's help, Boyle constructed a greatly improved air pump, experiments with which provided the groundwork for Boyle's first and most important scientific work: *New Experiments Physico-Mechanical touching the Spring of the Air and its Effects* (1660). Following up the work of Galileo and Torricelli, Boyle demonstrated that air has both weight and elasticity and that the phenomena that had traditionally been ascribed to an anthropomorphically conceived "horror of a vacuum" were, in fact, a product of the air's elasticity.

His conclusions created an immediate stir but were not universally accepted. Boyle was criticized on philosophical grounds by Thomas Hobbes, Henry More, and the Jesuit Franciscus Linus (1595–1675), to all of whom he replied in detail. In the course of his reply to Linus, Boyle formulated what is known as Boyle's Law. (On the Continent it is called Mariotte's Law, Mariotte having confirmed it in 1676.) In the years that followed, Boyle took part in the meetings of the embryonic Royal Society at Oxford, conducted and published a great many experiments, corresponded voluminously with most of the leading thinkers of Europe, studied Oriental languages, actively supported the distribution of the Bible in foreign parts—becoming for that purpose a governor of the Corporation for the Spread of the Gospel to New England and a director of the East India Company—and wrote a considerable number of scientific, philosophic, and theological treatises. After the Restoration most of his scientific friends returned to London; Boyle left Oxford for London in 1668 and lived in Lady Ranelagh's household until her death. He died a week later.

Science and philosophy. Boyle was profoundly influenced by Francis Bacon's conception of science; much of his published work consists of what Bacon called "histories"—systematic accounts of such qualities as color, firmness, and coldness as they appear under a variety of circumstances. His *Spring of the Air* was the first scientific paper of the modern type. He encouraged scientists to write relatively brief experimental "essays" rather than general treatises. His *Animadversions upon Mr. Hobbes' Problemata de Vacuo* (published in Boyle's *Tracts,* 1674) emphasized the fruitlessness of a priori philosophical reasoning—what Boyle called "book philosophy"—about issues that could be settled only by experiment.

But it is wrong to suppose that Boyle was an opponent of theorizing. He discusses the place of theory in science in his proemial essay to *Certain Physiological Essays and other Tracts* (1661). Scientists, he says, should "set themselves diligently to make experiments and collect observations, without being over forward to establish principles and axioms." Theories ought never to be taken as final; they should be thought of as "the best we have but capable of improvement." Nevertheless, it is the scientist's task to develop theories that are as clear, as simple, and as comprehensive as possible—a point that particularly emerges in Boyle's essay "About the Grounds of the Mechanical Hypothesis" (published in *The Excellency of Theology,* 1674).

Indeed, it was Boyle's main object "to beget a good understanding between the chemists and the mechanical philosophers, who have hitherto been too little acquainted with each other's learning." The corpuscular theory, which Gassendi had revived, suffered, Boyle thought, in the eyes of practical chemical experimentalists because so little had been done to test it. Theorists had been accustomed to illustrate their theories rather than to test them. On the other side, the work of the chemists had been ignored by physical theorists, largely because it had been associated with theories of a totally inadequate kind.

Doctrine of matter. Boyle's *The Sceptical Chemist* (1661) is mainly concerned with demonstrating the unsatisfactory character of the standard chemical theories. It is written in the form of a dialogue in which the main speaker, Carneades, attacks not only the traditional theory of elements but also the alchemical theories that had been proposed by Paracelsus and van Helmont. None of these theories, Boyle argued, can be reconciled with experiment, unless they are interpreted in so vague and symbolic a manner as to make them scientifically worthless. As an alternative, he set up the corpuscular theory. It is sometimes said that he also so redefined "elements" as to prepare the way for the modern doctrine of elements; but that is a mistaken interpretation. Indeed, what his chemistry lacked was precisely this modern conception of elements. That is why he was still able to believe in the possibility of alchemical transmutations. In 1689 he secured the repeal of Henry IV's statute against "multiplying gold."

In a sense, however, Boyle's work was too advanced theoretically. Not enough was known about chemical substances to enable the corpuscular theory to be effectively applied in chemistry. Although, by trying to bring together physics and chemistry and chemistry and biology, Boyle anticipated the long-range development of science, the program that he laid down for chemistry was one that for the moment no one knew how to fulfill; the immediate effect may well have been to hold back the development of chemistry. Boyle conceded, it is true, that explanations referring to perceptible properties rather than to the behavior of corpuscles are, at a certain level, perfectly satisfactory; but the general effect of his work was to discourage explanations of the only sort that chemists were actually in a position to offer. His own writings abound in interesting theoretical suggestions—in his *General History of the Air* (1692), for example, he anticipated the kinetic theory of gases—but for a very long time they had to remain no more than suggestions. Although Boyle's actual contributions to science are very few in number, the range of his anticipations is remarkable. He had set out to make chemistry respectable; he had succeeded, many chemists thought, only at the cost of turning it into physics.

Primary and secondary qualities. Boyle exerted an important influence on philosophy by lending the authority of a practicing scientist to the corpuscular theory of matter and the associated doctrine of primary and secondary qualities. In *The Experimental History of Colours* (1663), Boyle sets out to demonstrate that color is a "secondary quality" (his own terminology). Objects give rise to sensations of color, he tries to show, not because they are themselves colored but because the structure of their corpuscles modifies light in a special way. The word "color" is most properly applied, he argues, to the modified light that "strikes upon the organ of sight and so causes that sensation we call colour"; if we say that bodies themselves are colored, this can mean no more than that, by virtue of "a certain disposition of the superficial particles," they are capable of refracting or reflecting light.

This thesis is generalized in *The Origin of Forms and Qualities according to the Corpuscular Philosophy* (1666), in which the theory of qualities, which John Locke was to rely upon in his *Essay Concerning the Human Understanding,* is set forth in detail and contrasted with the scholastic doctrine of substantial forms. The qualities of a material object, Boyle argues, consist of "the size, shape and motion or rest of its component particles, together with that texture of the whole which results from their being so contrived as they are." These primary qualities of objects, operating upon the "peculiar texture" of a sensory organ, "occasion ideas in us."

Science and religion. The corpuscular philosophy had generally been associated with atheism. Boyle sets out to show that "by being addicted to experimental philosophy a man is rather assisted than indisposed to be a good Christian" (*The Christian Virtuoso,* 1690). His views about the relation between God and Nature, however, are by no means clear. In "An Hydrostatical Discourse occasioned by some Objections of Dr. Henry More," included in *Tracts* (1672), Boyle strongly opposes More's view that mechanical principles cannot explain the phenomena of pressure or any other physical phenomena. We do not need, he says, to have recourse to More's "incorporeal creatures"; mechanism is enough. Yet, at the same time, in *Forms and Qualities* he argues against Descartes that we cannot account for the behavior of living organisms by supposing that they consist of particles on which God bestowed motion. We have to suppose, Boyle says, that the Creator not only set the world moving but also introduced into it "seminal seeds" that are responsible for the growth and propagation of animal organisms.

Again, in *A Disquisition about the Final Causes of Natural Things* (1688), he expresses his disagreement with those who would reject final causes completely, although he also argues that the scientist, in his day-to-day work, need pay no attention to anything except the size, shape, texture, and motion of particles. At times, indeed, as in *The Excellency of Theology, or the Pre-eminence of the Study of Divinity above that of Natural Philosophy,* Boyle's anxiety about the contemporary tendency to abandon theology in favor of scientific inquiries leads him into a skepticism about science. If theology has its obscurities, he argues, they are as nothing to the obscurities inherent in the scientific account of continuity or of the relation between mind and body. Revelation can tell us far more about the place of man in nature than can science. But the example of Boyle the scientist was more influential than the precepts of Boyle the theologian. His last gesture in favor of Christianity was to leave in his will a sum sufficient to endow lectures for the defense of Christianity against its opponents; his intellectual legacy, however, was that mechanical interpretation of the world which deism took as its starting point.

Bibliography

For a bibliography of Boyle's voluminous works, see John Farquhar Fulton, *A Bibliography of the Honourable Robert Boyle,* rev. 2d ed. (Oxford, 1961). The only complete collected edition of Boyle's *Works,* edited by Thomas Birch, and with a still useful life by Birch that incorporates Boyle's *Account of Philaretus,* was published in London in five volumes in 1744 and in six volumes in 1772. *The Sceptical Chemist* is in the Everyman Library (London, 1911), and *The Weight and Spring of the Air* is in Vol. I of *Harvard Case Histories in Experimental Science* (Cambridge, Mass., 1957), an anthology edited by James B. Conant.

For works on Boyle, see Edwin A. Burtt, *The Metaphysical Foundations of Modern Physical Science* (London, 1925; rev. ed., 1932), Ch. 6, "Gilbert and Boyle"; Louis T. More, *The Life and Works of the Hon. Robert Boyle* (New York and London, 1944); Mitchell S. Fisher, *Robert Boyle, Devout Naturalist* (Philadelphia, 1945); Marie Boas, *Robert Boyle and Seventeenth Century Chemistry* (Cambridge, 1958)—an excellent book; Richard S. Westfall, "Unpublished Boyle Papers relating to Scientific Method," in *Annals of Science,* Vol. 12, No. 1 (March 1956), 63–73 and Vol. 12, No. 2 (June 1956), 103–117.

JOHN PASSMORE

BRADLEY, FRANCIS HERBERT (1846–1924), English idealist philosopher. He was born in Clapham and educated at University College, Oxford; in 1870 he was elected to a fellowship at Merton College, Oxford, terminable on marriage. Since he never married and the terms of the fellowship did not require him to teach, he was able to devote himself entirely to philosophical writing. His first published work was a pamphlet entitled *The Presuppositions of Critical History* (Oxford, 1874). There followed *Ethical Studies* (London, 1876), *Principles of Logic* (London, 1883), and *Appearance and Reality* (London, 1893), as well as many articles in philosophical journals, some of which were published in *Essays on Truth and Reality* (Oxford, 1914) and others in *Collected Essays* (Oxford, 1935).

Like Bosanquet, Bradley was influenced by T. H. Green. Like Bosanquet, too, he read and admired Hegel, but was less in sympathy with Hegelianism than Bosanquet was. Bosanquet was active in social reform, as Green had been, whereas Bradley was a Tory who hated liberalism and sometimes thought along the lines of Carlyle's later writings. Bradley was, and intended to be, a highly polemical writer. His *Ethical Studies* and *Principles of Logic* are a sustained attack on the utilitarianism and empiricism of John Stuart Mill and his followers and upon the positivist outlook of the times. Later in his career, Bradley crossed swords with William James (who, however, greatly influenced Bradley's views on existence and reality) and with Bertrand Russell. His views were at their maximum influence during the first decade of the twentieth century, and the philosophical analysis of Russell and G. E. Moore arose largely in the attempt to refute them. Bradley's literary style has been much admired, notably by T. S. Eliot, who, as a graduate student at Harvard, studied Bradley in detail and wrote a thesis about him. Few if any other works on logic have been written with the verve, eloquence, and exuberant clarity of Bradley's *Principles*, but *Appearance and Reality* is less varied, and, from a stylistic point of view, much less successful.

ETHICS

Bradley's *Ethical Studies* is the most Hegelian of his writings. There is much criticism in it of Mill and some criticism of Kant. There are amusing skirmishes with Matthew Arnold and with Frederick Harrison, the English positivist. Running through the book is the idea that it is not for the moral philosopher to tell people what to do, but rather to dispel false views of the nature of morality and to provide an analysis of morality that can stand up to philosophical criticism. Thus he starts with an analysis of the moral concepts of the plain man, which, he holds, are not consistent with utilitarian views on punishment and responsibility. He goes on to criticize hedonism, largely on the ground that since pleasure is an "infinite perishing series," it cannot be the object of a rational pursuit. (The influence of Hegel's doctrine of the False Infinite is apparent here.) As to utilitarianism, Bradley holds that in the light of the Greatest Happiness Principle *any* course of conduct *might* conceivably be right, and "this is to make possible, to justify, and even to encourage, an incessant practical casuistry; and that, it need scarcely be added, is the death of morality." Like Hegel, Bradley considered Kantian ethics to be formal and abstract, and, again like Hegel, he endeavored to supplement Kant's theories by a more concretely social view of ethics. In the study "My Station and its Duties" he developed the concept that Hegel had called "social morality" (*Sittlichkeit*). According to this view, duties are determined by the agent's place and functions in society. Bradley argued, furthermore, that men themselves are what they are because the society in which they are born and bred is what it is. The "individuals" of liberal and utilitarian social theory do not exist. The community is not, as the liberals assumed, a mere collection of individuals who are logically prior to it, but is a real being "and can be regarded (if we mean to keep to facts) only as the one in the many." This language shows that Bradley regarded communities as both real and as concrete universals, and individual men as factually and logically dependent upon them, a view that was to achieve logical status in the *Principles of Logic*. Bradley wrote of morality as "self-realization," and some writers have therefore classed him as an ethical egoist. But the self that realizes itself is, according to Bradley, a socialized self that expresses and develops itself in making its contribution to the whole. It should be noted (and here again he is following Hegel) that Bradley did not regard "my station and its duties" as the culmination of morality. He held that on the basis of social morality other forms are developed. In pursuing science or in producing works of art, men are not confined to any particular station, and they also set themselves ideals that go beyond what mere duty would require of them. Perhaps mankind is the beneficiary in such cases, but mankind is not a being or community (this is in criticism of the positivists) in the way that a state or a nation is. Thus, on the basis of "the objective world of my station and its duties" ideals of social and of nonsocial perfection are constituted. These various spheres and duties often clash with one another, but the moral philosopher cannot formulate rules (as the utilitarians thought they could) that would enable the clashes to be avoided or settled. Conflict and failure are inseparable from morality, which could not exist without them.

The *Ethical Studies* are impressive today by virtue of the anticipations in them of twentieth-century views on socialization and the formation of conscience. But Bradley's position is different from that of present-day sociologists in that he thought that the plain man's views on responsibility are superior to any utilitarian reformulation of them and that they presuppose a nonatomistic metaphysics. The facts of moral judgment and of moral action, he held, force the philosopher to a monistic view of social life and to a metaphysics of the self as a being that can be itself only by transcending itself.

LOGIC

In his *Principles of Logic*, Bradley endeavored to refute false views of the subject without going thoroughly into questions of epistemology and metaphysics. The main objects of his attack were: the traditional subject–predicate, syllogistic, formal logic; the inductive logic with which, since the appearance of Mill's *Logic*, this traditional logic had been supplemented; and the confusion he claimed to see in the current empiricist logic between logical and psychological problems.

Bradley thought that the traditional logic was inadequate and incomplete. For example, in treating all judgments as of the subject–predicate form it omitted relational judgments, and the doctrine of the syllogism failed to take account of relational arguments. He maintained, too, that universal affirmative judgments are not categorical but hypothetical, since they do not necessarily assert that there are members of the subject class. These are theses that subsequent logicians have accepted.

Bradley denied that the advance of knowledge was from particulars to universals, or from particulars to particulars as Mill had suggested. Hence he denied the existence of induction as understood by Mill and the writers of textbooks who followed him. The great mistake of the empiricists, Bradley argued, was to suppose that thought could possibly get started with knowledge of separate and independent particulars. Such particulars, in his view, could be known only after a preceding condition of vagueness, ambiguity, and generality. This, however, is a historical, not a logical, consideration. Bradley's main argument is that inference is possible only on the basis of universals and hence cannot be a procession from particulars to particulars or from particulars to universal. Inference presupposes judgments and ideal contents, and these, in their turn, presuppose generality and universality. It is only legitimate to argue from some to all if it is known or surmised that the particulars share some universal character. Bradley supported this by a detailed examination of Mill's inductive methods, an examination that owes something, as Bradley acknowledged, to Whewell's criticism of them in his *Philosophy of Discovery*. The main point is that the facts or particulars from which the induction is alleged to start must already be ordered and defined in terms of some sort of theory, and hence in terms of a universal, if they are to give rise to an advance in knowledge. Both premises and conclusion must be organized around the central concept in a system of related concepts.

The empiricists subordinated logic to psychology. Hume's account of thought was in terms of ideas that, by the very fact of being described as "fainter" than impressions, were regarded as a sort of mental image. Based on Hume's views, there had grown up a theory that knowledge advanced by the association of ideas. Bradley set out to refute this view, which today is known as psychologism. He argued that logicians are not concerned with ideas as psychical facts, but with ideas as meanings. As meanings, ideas do not have dates and histories, but are "ideal contents" and hence abstract. The real distinction between subject and predicate, he argued, is not to be found in the relation of one ideal content to another but in the relation of a complex ideal content to the reality to which it is referred. In judgment, therefore, an ideal content is referred to a reality existing beyond the act of judgment. The real subject of a judgment is thus often quite different from the grammatical subject of the sentence, as can be seen in such an example as "A four-cornered circle is an impossibility," where the real subject is not a four-cornered circle, for there could be no such reality, but the nature of space. (This distinction between the grammatical form and the logical form was later to play an important part in analytic and linguistic philosophy.) If this view is accepted, then psychological accounts of inference fare no better than psychological accounts of judgment, since it is meanings, not psychical occurrences, that are relevant. There could not be any association between particular mental occurrences since they perish as they pass, and past ones would have somehow to be revived or re-created if they were to be associated with those existing in the present. Thus similarity and reproduction presuppose universals, just as inference itself does.

We have said that in his *Logic* Bradley tried to avoid being drawn into epistemological and metaphysical discussions. It is not surprising that he failed in this. Part of his attack on the "School of Experience" consisted in his bringing to light the untenable atomistic metaphysics that he regarded as basic to it. This is a parallel operation to his assault on utilitarianism. The claim that scientific knowledge is based on a prior knowledge of facts or particulars he rejected on the ground that from atomistic particulars no inference could be made. No inference could be valid apart from identities or universals linking one fact with another. It is clear, therefore, that Bradley thought that the fact of inference invalidated metaphysical pluralism, as the facts of morality went against it too. At this point Bradley has some important things to say about universals. He takes the view that what is essential to universality is identity in difference. Identity in difference can take two main forms. It can be abstract, as with such adjectives as "red" or "hard," which require substances in which to inhere. Or it can be concrete, as with an individual man, who is identical throughout his many actions, or a community, which persists through many generations of men. Abstract universals, therefore, are dependent, insubstantial, unreal, whereas concrete universals are (relatively) independent, substantial, and real. If what is real is individual, then concrete universals are individuals. Bradley ends this part of the discussion with the words: "It might be urged that if you press the enquiry, you will be left alone with but a single individual. An individual which is finite or relative turns out to be no individual; individual and infinite are inseparable characters." He does not pursue this in the *Logic*, but says that such a "revision" (an interesting choice of words) "must be left to metaphysics." So it is to his metaphysics that we now turn.

METAPHYSICS

Bradley's metaphysics, apart from the glimpses of it given in the *Ethical Studies* and the *Logic*, is set out in *Appearance and Reality* and in *Essays on Truth and Reality*. The main argument of *Appearance and Reality* is quite simple. It is divided into two books. The first and shorter one is entitled "Appearance" and is about the contradictory character of mere appearances. Book II is entitled "Reality" and is about the Absolute.

In Book I, certain common-sense concepts, such as relation, cause, space, time, thing, and self, and certain philosophical concepts, such as the thing-in-itself and the distinction between primary and secondary qualities, are declared to be self-contradictory and are in consequence "degraded to the rank of mere appearances." In Chapters 2 and 3 of Book I, entitled respectively "Substantive and Adjective" and "Relation and Quality," Bradley argues that the very notion of a relation is self-contradictory and that this inconsistency is alone sufficient to condemn "the great mass of phenomena," since space, time, causation, the self, all imply relations. In Chapter 2, in considering the suggestion that all things are groups of related attributes, Bradley argues that if *A* and *B* stand in relation to *C*, then *C* must be related to *A* and *B* by another relation *D*, and this by a third relation *E*, and so on indefinitely. In Chapter 3 he argues that if simple qualities are to be conceived, they must be conceived as related to one another; but if *A* is related to *B*, then there must be the independent aspect of *A* and the aspect in which it is related to *B*, and hence it cannot be simple; but if *A* is not simple, then the independent aspect and the aspect in which it is related to *B* must be related to one another, so that there is set up in each of them a further plurality of aspects generating what Bradley calls "a principle of fission which conducts us to no end."

In Book II, it is argued that if it is being self-contradictory that degrades mere appearances, then reality must at least be not self-contradictory, but consistent and harmonious. Furthermore, reality must also be of the nature of experience, for what is not experience cannot be conceived of without self-contradiction. Finally, it is clear that reality must be comprehensive and include all that is. If reality is a consistent and harmonious and all-inclusive experience, then it cannot be a plurality of independent reals, for whatever is related to anything else must be to some extent dependent on it. "Plurality and relatedness are but features and aspects of a unity." Furthermore, the sort of unity that reality or the Absolute must have may be understood by analogy with feeling or immediate experience, for here there is diversity without relatedness. According to Bradley, our experience of related things arises out of a prior immediate experience in which there are felt differences but no distinct qualities, and therefore no conception of things with different qualities in relation with one another. In passing from the primitive harmonious vagueness to a knowledge of related things, we pass from what might be called the state of precognitive innocence to the flawed world of contradiction. Wherever there is thought, there is the distinction between the what and the that, between ideal content and reality, between adjective and substantive; and hence wherever there is thought, there is contradiction. Thus reality, or the Absolute, must transcend thought, and thought always points beyond itself to something in which "mere thinking is absorbed." The Absolute must be conceived as analogous to immediate experience but transcending thought rather than falling short of it.

It is clear that contradiction, error, and evil are not harmonious and hence are not real, but it is equally clear that they are not nothing. How then must they be considered in the light of the Absolute? To this question Bradley gives a very interesting answer. He says that although error and evil are discordant and hence not real, it is possible that they contribute to the harmony of the whole, and if this is possible then we must conclude that it is so even though we do not know how it is possible. "For what is *possible*," he says, "and what a general principle compels us to say *must be*, that certainly *is*" (*Appearance and Reality*, Ch. 16). In this way, he protects himself against demands to show exactly how appearances are self-contradictory, unreal, not nothing, and yet are elements in the total harmony. Even so, he does make some attempts to show how all this is possible. In Book I, for example, time is condemned as self-contradictory, but in Book II Bradley says that although it is not real it nevertheless exists.

In explaining what he means by existence, he says it consists in being an event in time, in being a fact, in being directly perceived. In a later essay he says that what exists is what is continuous with our waking body. Existence, therefore, is the mode of being of the phenomenal world. But this would seem to bring us back to the point from which we started. Bradley also says that the real, the Absolute, must appear in what exists, that it cannot remain unmanifested. But he also attempts to mitigate the dualism between harmonious reality and self-contradictory appearance–existence by sketching a scheme in which reality permits of degrees. At the bottom of the scale, there are sheer contradictions and the abstract being of lifeless matter. Organic matter has more reality and is higher in the scale, and mind is higher still, for in mind the whole is immanent in its manifestations and the manifestations express the whole.

It is in mind that we see how the real must appear. But insofar as mind is thought, it suffers the disruption into the what and the that, which we have already considered. Perhaps, then, reality is to be found in mind as practical. This is rejected on the ground that practice essentially contains the distinction between reality as it is and reality as it will be when altered. Reality cannot be found in aesthetic experience either, for art entails pleasure, pleasure is an experience of selves, and selves, Bradley has argued, cannot be ultimately real. "The Absolute," Bradley concludes, "is not personal, nor is it moral, nor is it beautiful or true." Yet in spite of all this he ends *Appearance and Reality* with the words: ". . . the more that anything is spiritual, the more is it veritably real."

The weakest part of *Appearance and Reality* is Book I. The amount of space and care given in it to the task of discrediting the whole of common sense and much of the philosophy of the past is trifling compared with the magnitude of the desired result. Bradley seems almost to take the reader's agreement for granted and to hasten on to the more congenial, yet only slightly more constructive, task of showing what the Absolute must be. A good part of the argument of Book I assumes that predication is identity, in accordance with "the old puzzle how to justify the attributing to a subject something other than itself." After all, Bradley had refuted this view of predication in his *Logic*. Perhaps then he is arguing dialectically, in order to bring out the unhappy consequences of working with this "logic of identity." But if this were so, then relation, space, time, the self, etc. would only be self-contradictory if looked at in the light of a false logic, and might be reinstated if the true logic were brought to bear on them. The doctrine of degrees of reality goes some way towards meeting this difficulty. But in Book I there is no indication that the self is more real or less self-contradictory than space and time. As A. S. Pringle-Pattison put it in his review of *Appearance and Reality:* "Mr. Bradley has the air of swallowing at a gulp in Book II what he had choked over in the successive chapters of Book I." As to Book II, there are two main defects. One is that the Absolute described in it seems to be without any definite features but is an amorphous refuge into which appearances are "fused," "transformed," "transmuted," or "dissolved." The other is that in the course of developing the doctrine of degrees of reality Bradley unwittingly reverts on occasion to the arguments of Book I, as when he says that aesthetic experience cannot be or reveal the Absolute since it involves pleasure and selves and selves are self-contradictory. Bradley here seems to be reverting to the logic of identity that in Book II he had been moderating. On the other hand, there is much excellent discussion of details. The account of time is particularly good. Bradley holds that we should not think in terms of one time series only, but in terms of several or many. Just as the events of one fiction are not temporally related to the events in another fiction, so there may be various time series in which what is past in one may be yet to come in another. What Bradley said about time and about existence and reality greatly exercised G. E. Moore who, in various writings, notably "The Conception of Reality" (1917–1918), endeavored to make clear what it is to say that something exists. Moore argued that Bradley's view that time, although unreal, must exist, depended upon his assuming that whatever can be thought of must somehow exist in order to be thought of. But Moore rejected this assumption. Bradley, he thought, was deceived into making it because he did not notice that although "unicorns are objects of thought" is of the same *grammatical* form as "lions are objects of the chase," it is of quite a different *logical* form. Moore's reason for this was that if lions are to be hunted there must be lions, whereas unicorns can be thought of although there are no unicorns. Thus Moore used against Bradley the distinction between logical and grammatical form that Bradley had formulated in 1883. A weapon that Bradley had himself devised was employed against him by a philosopher who had improved its range and sophistication.

Bibliography

Bradley's main writings and the dates of publication have been indicated in the body of the article. A second edition of *Ethical Studies* (Oxford, 1927) contains corrections and additional notes that Bradley left at his death. A second edition of *Principles of Logic* (Oxford, 1922) contains the original unaltered text with an extensive commentary, which owes much to Bosanquet, at the end of each chapter and a set of "Terminal Essays" at the end of the book. The second edition of *Appearance and Reality* (London, 1897) contains an Appendix occasioned by criticisms of the first edition. See also *Aphorisms* (Oxford, 1930), a few of which appeared in the Preface to *Appearance and Reality*.

For a detailed critical study of Bradley's philosophy, see Richard Wollheim, *F. H. Bradley* (London, 1959). This contains further bibliographical references. See also C. A. Campbell, *Scepticism and Construction* (London, 1931); R. W. Church, *Bradley's Dialectic* (London, 1942); and T. S. Eliot, *Knowledge and Experience in the Philosophy of F. H. Bradley* (London and New York, 1964), the thesis mentioned above.

A. S. Pringle-Pattison, "A New Theory of the Absolute," reprinted in *Man's Place in the Cosmos* (Edinburgh and London, 1897, 1902), is probably the best criticism of Bradley's metaphysics. G. E. Moore, *Some Main Problems of Philosophy* (London, 1953), Chs. 11, 12, 16, contains a detailed discussion of parts of Bradley's metaphysics.

Criticism of Bradley's view that the notion of relation is self-contradictory is contained in J. Cook Wilson, *Statement and Inference* (Oxford, 1926), Vol. I, p. 255, Vol. II, pp. 692–695. See also W. H. Walsh, "F. H. Bradley," in *A Critical History of Western Philosophy*, edited by D. J. O'Connor (London and New York, 1964).

H. B. ACTON

BRADWARDINE, THOMAS (c. 1290–1349), theologian and mathematician, was born in Sussex, England. He studied at Oxford, where he was a member of Merton College and from 1325 to 1327 was proctor of the university. After 1335, when he joined Richard de Bury's circle in London, most of his career was spent close to the court of Edward III. In 1339 he became the king's chaplain, accompanying him on his French wars. He was elected archbishop of Canterbury in 1349; a previous attempt to appoint him had failed. Four months after his appointment he died of the "Black Death."

Although he wrote several scientific treatises, he made no attempt to combine philosophical and scientific concepts as many of his contemporaries did. Indeed, Bradwardine's thought is distinguished by its almost complete divorcement from the main outlooks of his day. His only point of contact with his epoch came from his outright denunciation of the doctrines associated with Ockhamism—in particular, those concerning grace and free will. Bradwardine constructed his main work, *De Causa Dei*, around these two doctrines. Originally given as a course of lectures, the work appeared in 1344. Its aim was avowedly polemical—to reassert "the grace of God as it is prevenient both in time and nature to all good works" (Preface). He countered the emphasis upon free will of the "modern Pelagians" (as he called his opponents) by asserting the primacy of God's will. Where they destroyed any inherent order between grace and glory, sin and free will, Bradwardine reasserted dogmatic first principles. But—and this is what distinguished him—he did so in speculative, not dogmatic, terms. Starting from the Thomist conception of God as first cause, he reached a point where God was more immediately the author of an action than the creature who acted. By this means he was able to show that there could be no such thing as an act of free will, let alone merit, other than by God first willing it. Similarly with future contingents, God not only foresaw future actions, he willed them; contingency, far from being outside his knowledge, was the product of his willing. God was so actively involved in his creatures, as the senior partner in all that they did, that creation was virtually an extension of his will.

Although the antecedents of Bradwardine's thought in Augustine, Thomas Aquinas, and Duns Scotus are all discernible, the use to which he put them can hardly be regarded as traditional. In the first place, while his framework was the contrast between man's infirmities and God's omnipotence as established by authority, he relied upon speculation rather than dogma to assert it. The Fall played no part in his outlook, as it did in St. Augustine's: man was weak by definition and therefore dependent upon God. In the second place, it would be hard to deny that Bradwardine took the Thomist relation between first and second causes to an extreme that allowed the latter no independent standing. This is particularly apparent in his treatment of sin in which, because God is so implicated in a man's actions, his role is not clearly delimited from that of the sinner. For these reasons Bradwardine had little in common with his own age and also overstepped the bounds of tradition.

Works by Bradwardine

De Geometria Speculativa. Paris, 1516.

De Causa Dei Adversus Pelagium et de Virtute Causarum. H. Saville, ed. London, 1618.

Tractatus de Proportionibus; Its Significance for the Development of Mathematical Physics, translated and edited by H. L. Crosby. Madison, Wis., 1955.

Works on Bradwardine

Hahn, S., *Thomas Bradwardinus und seine Lehre von der menschlichen Willensfreiheit.* Munster in Westfalen, 1905.

Leff, Gordon, "Thomas Bradwardine's *De Causa Dei.*" *Journal of Ecclesiastical History*, Vol. 7 (Apr. 1956).
Leff, Gordon, *Bradwardine and the Pelagians; a Study of His "De Causa Dei" and Its Opponents.* London, 1957.
Oberman, H., *Thomas Bradwardine.* Utrecht, 1957.

GORDON LEFF

BRAITHWAITE, RICHARD BEVAN, English philosopher, was born in 1900 in Banbury. He was educated at King's College, Cambridge (M. A. 1926), where he studied physics and mathematics before turning to philosophy. Braithwaite is Knightbridge professor of moral philosophy at Cambridge University. He has served as president of the Mind Association (1946) and the Aristotelian Society (1946–1947). In the philosophy of science, Braithwaite has made important contributions on the nature of scientific theories and explanation, theoretical terms, models, foundations of probability and statistics, the justification of induction, and teleological explanations. He also has written on subjects in moral and religious philosophy.

Scientific theories. Braithwaite defends the view that a scientific theory consists of a set of initial hypotheses, together with empirically testable generalizations that follow deductively. To explain a generalization is to show that it is implied by higher-level generalizations in the theory. Often, especially in the physical sciences, the initial postulates will contain so-called theoretical terms, such as "electron" or "field," that refer to items not directly observable. To understand the meaning of such terms, as well as the logical structure of the theory, one must begin by considering the theory as a formal calculus; that is, as a set of uninterpreted formulas. A calculus designed to represent a specific theory will have to be interpreted, but not all at once and not completely: meanings are directly given only to those formulas representing the lower-order empirical generalizations, rather than to initial formulas containing theoretical terms. The latter are indirectly and partially interpreted by the former.

Braithwaite's major contribution here consists in the detailed attention he has devoted to the nature of the initial or "theoretical" postulates. He divides these postulates into "Campbellian hypotheses," which contain only theoretical terms, and "dictionary axioms," which relate theoretical terms to observational ones. The latter include "identificatory axioms," which identify single observational terms with theoretical terms—for example, a color word with expressions referring to wavelengths of light. Braithwaite argues that the advantage of systems containing theoretical terms over those whose initial postulates are entirely observational is that the former can more readily be extended to new situations than can the latter. However, Braithwaite holds, there is no special advantage to Campbellian hypotheses, because, at least for certain systems, the same testable consequences can be derived from identificatory axioms.

Scientific models are to be construed as alternative interpretations of a theory's calculus where the theoretical concepts in the original theory (such as molecules) are interpreted as designating more familiar and intelligible items (such as billiard balls). Accordingly, the theory and the model are to be distinguished; and while a model is not essential, it can sometimes be of help in extending a theory and clarifying its concepts.

Probability and induction. Braithwaite proposes a novel finite-frequency theory of probability. Consider the statement (*P*), "The probability of a child being born a boy is 51/100," and the observed data that among 1,000 children 503 are boys. Such a situation is to be understood by imagining 1,000 sets of children, each containing 100 children of whom 51 are boys, and a selection of one child from each of the 1,000 sets, of whom 503 are boys. Since *P* is logically consistent with any observed data, the problem is to decide when to reject *P*. For this purpose it is necessary to have a rule specifying that a probability statement is to be rejected if the observed relative frequency differs from the probability postulated by more than a specified amount. This amount is determined by extralogical considerations involving the purpose for which the hypothesis is to be used and the value attached to possible consequences of its adoption. Such a rejection rule, Braithwaite claims, is what gives empirical meaning to probability statements considered as constituents of theoretical systems. But suppose there are alternative probability hypotheses not rejected by the evidence in accordance with this rule. How is one to choose among them? Here again considerations of value must be invoked, and Braithwaite outlines a "prudential policy" of choosing the probability hypothesis that maximizes the minimum mathematical expectation of value.

Braithwaite has also provided an original defense of C. S. Peirce's solution to the problem of justifying induction. The problem is formulated by Braithwaite as follows: What warrant do we have for adopting the policy of accepting a hypothesis on the basis of numerous positive instances (the policy of "induction by simple enumeration")? The answer proposed consists of the following argument (where π is the principle of induction by simple enumeration): the policy of using π has been effective in numerous instances in the past; therefore (using π as the rule of inference) π will continue to be effective. Such an argument has traditionally been dismissed as viciously circular, and Braithwaite undertakes to prove this charge unjustified. The argument can be deemed valid and hence free from circularity, he claims, because it enables one to pass from a mere belief in the general effectiveness of using π as a rule of inference, together with a reasonable belief in π's past effectiveness, to a *reasonable* belief in π's general effectiveness. It would be viciously circular only if one were required to have an initial reasonable belief in π's general effectiveness. Since this requirement is unnecessary, the argument is not invalidated.

Moral and religious philosophy. Many of the conclusions and techniques of the philosophy of science are applied by Braithwaite in areas of moral and religious philosophy. Thus, just as one can defend the adoption of a particular scientific hypothesis by appeal to an inductive policy, so one can justify a particular action, such as returning a book, by reference to a moral policy, such as promise-keeping. Both sorts of policies are in turn justified by reference to the ends they subserve. Braithwaite shows how the mathematical theory of games, which he invokes in his discussion of hypothesis selection, can also be used to shed light upon such notions as prudence and justice in situations involving human choices and cooperation between individuals. Finally, just as a moral assertion is to be construed as an expression of an intention to act in accordance with a certain policy, so a religious assertion must be understood, according to Braithwaite, as a declaration of adherence to a system of moral principles governing "inner life" as well as external behavior. The major difference between religious and moral assertions consists in the fact that the former, being associated with empirical narratives, have a propositional element lacking in the latter.

Works by Braithwaite

BOOKS

Scientific Explanation. Cambridge, 1953.

An Empiricist's View of the Nature of Religious Belief. Cambridge, 1955.

Theory of Games as a Tool for the Moral Philosopher. Cambridge, 1955.

ARTICLES

"Propositions About Material Objects." *PAS*, Vol. 38 (1937–1938), 269–290.

"Teleological Explanation." *PAS*, Vol. 47 (1946–1947), 1–20.

"Moral Principles and Inductive Policies." *Proceedings of the British Academy*, Vol. 36 (1950), 51–68.

"Probability and Induction," in C. Mace, ed., *British Philosophy in the Mid-Century.* New York, 1957.

"Axiomatizing a Scientific System by Axioms in the Form of Identifications," in L. Henkin, P. Suppes, and A. Tarski, eds., *The Axiomatic Method.* Amsterdam, 1959. Pp. 429–442.

"Models in Empirical Science," in E. Nagel, P. Suppes, and A. Tarski, eds., *Logic, Methodology, and Philosophy of Science.* Stanford, 1962. Pp. 224–231.

Works on Braithwaite

Black, Max, review of *Theory of Games as a Tool for the Moral Philosopher. Philosophical Review*, Vol. 66 (1957), 121–124.

Coburn, Robert C., "Braithwaite's Inductive Justification of Induction." *Philosophy of Science*, Vol. 28 (1961), 65–71.

Hirst, R. J., review of *Scientific Explanation. Philosophical Quarterly*, Vol. 4 (1954), 351–355.

Nagel, Ernest, "A Budget of Problems in the Philosophy of Science." *Philosophical Review*, Vol. 66 (1957), 205–225.

Russell, L. J., review of *Scientific Explanation. Philosophy*, Vol. 20 (1954), 353–356.

PETER ACHINSTEIN

BRENTANO, FRANZ (1838–1917), German philosopher and psychologist, nephew of the poet Clemens Brentano and of the author Bettina von Arnim, taught at Würzburg and at the University of Vienna. As a teacher he exerted extraordinary influence upon his students, among whom were Alexius Meinong, Edmund Husserl, Kasimierz Twardowski, Carl Stumpf, Tomas Masaryk, Anton Marty, Christian Ehrenfels, and Franz Hillebrand. Brentano became a Roman Catholic priest in 1864, was involved in the controversy over the doctrine of papal infallibility, and left the church in 1873. At his death he left behind voluminous writings and dictation (he was blind during the last years of his life) on almost every philosophical subject. Some of this material has since been published.

The most important of Brentano's works published during his lifetime is *Psychologie vom empirischen Standpunkt* (Leipzig, 1874). The two-volume second edition (Leipzig, 1911) includes revisions and supplementary material; the third edition, edited by Oskar Kraus, was published in Leipzig in 1925. The second edition includes *Von der Klassifikation der psychischen Phänomene*, which had also been published separately (Leipzig, 1911). The posthumously published *Vom sinnlichen und noetischen Bewusstsein*, also edited by Kraus (Leipzig, 1928), is referred to as Volume III of the *Psychologie.*

Objects of mental phenomena. Brentano took the mental to comprise such phenomena as hearing, seeing, sensing, thinking, judging, inferring, loving, and hating. He held that what is common to mental phenomena and what distinguishes them from the physical is "intentional inexistence," which he also described as "reference to a content" and "direction upon an object." Mental phenomena, he said, may be defined as phenomena that "include an object intentionally within themselves." He did not mean to imply, however, that when, for example, a person thinks of a horse, there is a duplicate of the horse, a mental simulacrum, existing within the mind. The essential point, as he later emphasized, is that a person could think of a horse even if there were no horse. In the second edition of the *Psychologie*, he contrasted strict relations with mental relations. *A* and *B* cannot be related in the strict sense of the term "relation" unless *A* and *B* exist; if one tree is to the left of another, then both trees exist. "But in the case of psychical relations the situation is entirely different. If someone thinks of something, then, although there must be a thinker, the thing that he thinks about need not exist."

Reference or "direction upon something" (*Gerichtetsein*) thus is common and peculiar to what is mental, and Brentano classified mental phenomena in terms of the different ways in which they may refer to, or be directed upon, their objects. There are three ways in which one may be "intentionally" related to any object *A*. (1) One may think of *A*, or, as we sometimes say, have it "before the mind" or "present to consciousness." (2) One may take an intellectual stand with respect to *A*; this stand will consist either of accepting *A* or of rejecting *A*. (3) One may take an emotional stand with respect to *A*: this is a matter of loving or hating *A*, in a very broad sense of these terms. It is a matter of pursuit or avoidance, or, as one might now say, a matter of having a "pro-emotion" or an "anti-emotion" with respect to *A*. Brentano identified these three types of phenomena with (1) *Vorstellungen* (ideas, thoughts, or presentations); (2) judgments; (3) "emotive phenomena," or "phenomena of love and hate," a category including both emotions and volitions.

Ideas, or thoughts, are basic in that the other two types of mental phenomena presuppose them. In judging that there is food, or in wanting it, one has *ipso facto* the thought of food. However, judging is not simply a matter of "combining ideas"; if we combine the idea of gold and the idea of a mountain, we obtain not a judgment but another idea—that of a golden mountain. The members of the third class of mental phenomena, the "phenomena of love and hate," are like judging—and unlike the mere having of an idea—in that they involve an "opposition of intentional relation." We adopt toward the object of our idea an attitude of liking or disliking, love or hate.

There is still another respect in which the third class of phenomena is like the second and unlike the first. This is stated in Brentano's *Ursprung sittlicher Erkenntnis* ("The Origin of Our Knowledge of Right and Wrong," 1889).

> Concerning acts of the first class, none can be called either correct [*richtig*] or incorrect. In the case of the second class, on the other hand, one of the two opposed modes of relation, affirmation and rejection, is correct and the other incorrect. The same naturally holds good of the third class. Of the two opposed modes of relation, love and hate, being pleased and being displeased, one of them in every case is correct and the other incorrect.

This significant thesis is basic to Brentano's theory of knowledge and to his moral philosophy.

To judge, then, is to take an intellectual stand with respect to an object, and the object of the judgment is the same as the object of the idea that the judgment presupposes. If one judges that there are horses, the object of one's judgment is simply the object *horse*, which one thereby accepts, affirms, or acknowledges (*erkennt*); if one denies that there are horses, the object of one's judgment is again the object *horse,* which this time one denies or rejects (*leugnet*). In neither case does the judgment take as its object either a proposition or state of affairs or the type of entity that other philosophers have attempted to designate by such phrases as "the being of horses," "the nonbeing of horses," and "that there are horses."

This nonpropositional theory of judgment, which is fundamental to Brentano's theory of truth and his theory of categories, may be put schematically, in slightly oversimplified form, as follows. To judge that there are *A*'s is to accept (or affirm) *A*'s. To judge that there are no *A*'s is to reject (or deny) *A*'s. To judge that some *A*'s are *B*'s is to accept *AB*'s (*A*'s that are *B*'s), and to judge that no *A*'s are *B*'s is to reject *AB*'s. To judge that some *A*'s are not *B*'s, therefore, is to accept *A*'s that are non-*B*'s, and to judge that all *A*'s are *B*'s is to reject them. (Brentano noted, however, that the sentence "All *A*'s are *B*'s" is normally used to express a twofold judgment: the acceptance of *A*'s that are *B*'s and the rejection of *A*'s that are non-*B*'s.)

Brentano attempted to extend his theory to apply to so-called compound judgments. "He judges that there are *A*'s and *B*'s" presents no difficulty, since, according to Brentano's theory of categories, if *A* is a concrete object and *B* is a concrete object, then the collective consisting of just *A* and *B* is also a concrete object. The object of this conjunctive judgment is simply *A*-and-*B*, which the judger is said to accept. Brentano suggests two interpretations of "He judges that if there are *A*'s, then there are *B*'s."According to the first interpretation, the judger is said simply to reject *A*'s-without-*B*'s. The second interpretation is more complex, making use of the terms "true" and "apodictic." (The latter term designates a mode of judgment. To reject *A* "apodictically" is, in effect, to reject the possibility of *A*; but Brentano explicated "possibility" in terms of "apodictic rejection," and not conversely.) If by "a correct *A*-acceptor" we mean a man who accepts *A* truly, or correctly, then the hypothetical judgment becomes: "He apodictically rejects judgers who are both correct *A*-acceptors and correct *B*-rejectors." The disjunctive judgment "He judges that either there are *A*'s or there are *B*'s" could then become "He apodictically rejects judgers who are both correct *A*-rejectors and correct *B*-rejectors."

The philosophical consequences of this nonpropositional theory of judgment are far-reaching. One consequence is an interpretation of Kant's dictum that "existence" is not a predicate. According to Brentano, when we say that *A* exists, "it is not the conjunction of an attribute of 'existence' with '*A*,' but '*A*' itself which we affirm." The word "exists" is a synsemantic term that is used to express the act of judgment.

All of the doctrines set forth above fall within the province of what Brentano called descriptive psychology. Unlike experimental psychology—including genetic and physiological psychology—descriptive psychology, according to Brentano, is an exact science, capable of arriving at laws that hold true universally and not merely "for the most part." It is the basis for all philosophy and is even capable of providing a *characteristica universalis* of the sort that Leibniz had conceived. Descriptive psychology is closely related to what Husserl was to call phenomenology. Husserl had studied with Brentano in Vienna from 1884 to 1886, when Brentano used the expression *beschreibende Phänomenologie* ("descriptive phenomenology") as an alternative name for descriptive psychology. (Husserl later wrote that without Brentano's doctrine of intentionality, "phenomenology could not have come into being at all.") Brentano's conception of psychology has led some of his critics to accuse him of what Frege and Husserl called psychologism. However, this accusation does not take into account Brentano's theory of evidence and his moral philosophy, both of which he took to be branches of descriptive psychology.

Moral philosophy. Brentano's ethical views are set forth in *Ursprung sittlicher Erkenntnis* (Leipzig, 1889; 3d ed., Oskar Kraus, ed., 1934), translated by Cecil Hague as *The Origin of Our Knowledge of Right and Wrong* (London, 1902), and in *Grundlegung und Aufbau der Ethik* ("The Basis and Structure of Ethics," F. Mayer-Hillebrand, ed., Bern, 1952). Brentano based his ethics upon the assumption that the members of the third class of mental phenomena, loving and hating, may be said to be correct or incorrect, just as judgments may be said to be correct or incorrect. To say that something, *A*, is good is to say that it is impossible to love *A* incorrectly; that is, it is apodictically to reject incorrect lovers of *A*. Analogously, to say that *A* is bad is apodictically to reject incorrect haters of *A*.

The only way to grasp the concept of correct emotion, according to Brentano, is to contrast actual cases of emotions that are "qualified as correct" with cases of emotions that are not. This is analogous to the way in which we understand, for example, what it is to be red and what it is to be colored. Thus we learn that knowledge is good, joy is good (unless it is joy in what is bad), every enrichment within the realm of ideas is good, love of the good is good, love of the bad is bad, and the right end in life is to choose the best among all attainable ends.

The correctness of loving and hating, like that of judging, is objective in that it is impossible for anyone to love correctly what anyone else hates correctly or to love incorrectly what anyone else hates incorrectly.

Ethics must make use of the comparative concept *better than*, for which there is no analogue in the theory of knowledge. "*A* is better than *B*," according to Brentano, means that it is correct to prefer *A*, as an end, to *B*.

Evidence and truth. Brentano's views on evidence and truth may be found in the posthumously published *Wahrheit und Evidenz* (Oskar Kraus, ed., Leipzig, 1930). The distinction between judging on the basis of evidence and judging "blindly" is not to be described in terms of instinct, feelings, degree of conviction, or impulse to believe. We arrive at the general concept of being evident, according to Brentano, in the same way we arrive at the concept of a correct emotion: by contemplating actual instances of the concept, in this case actual instances of evident judgments and of blind judgments.

Every evident judgment is either directly or indirectly evident; if a judgment is indirectly evident, its evidence is conferred, ultimately, by judgments that are directly evident. Directly evident judgments are of two kinds. First, there are the judgments of "inner perception," such as the judgments that I am now judging in a certain way, that I seem to see such-and-such, that I think I remember so-and-so. Second, there are judgments of reason or insights (*Einsichten*), such as the judgments that two things are more than one thing; that that which is red is, as such, other than that which is green; that there cannot be a triangle with four sides; or that a whole cannot exist if its parts do not exist.

Every judgment that is evident is true, but not every judgment that is true is evident. Most judgments of "outer perception" (of the external world), Brentano believed, are true, but all of them are "blind"; they are not evident. He argued, however, that the hypothesis of a three-dimensional external world, with its familiar details concerning physical bodies, has an "infinitely greater probability" than any of its alternatives. Judgments based on memory, too, are "blind"; but many of them confirm each other, and they are worthy of our confidence.

In *Wahrheit und Evidenz* Brentano characterized truth by reference to evidence: "Truth pertains to the judgment of the person who judges correctly . . . hence it pertains to the judgment of one who asserts what the person who judges with evidence would assert" (p. 139). In addition, to say that *A* exists is to say that anyone who judged about *A* with evidence would accept *A*, and to say that *A* does not exist is to say that anyone who judged about *A* with evidence would reject *A*. The "measure of all things," then, is the man who judges with evidence.

However, these statements, relating truth to evidence, do not give us the whole of Brentano's theory of truth. "Evident" is said to be predicate in the strict sense of the term, but "true" and "exists" are not, being only synsemantic. This brings us to Brentano's theory of categories.

Theory of categories. The basic theses of Brentano's theory of categories may be stated as (1) there is nothing other than concrete particular things, and (2) every judgment is either the acceptance or the rejection of some concrete particular thing. "Concrete" must be taken as the opposite of "abstract" and not as a synonym for "physical." Human souls and God, according to Brentano, are concrete things but not physical things.

Our language seems to make reference to a great variety of *irrealia*—entities that are not concrete things. In fact, however, "the objects of our thought are never anything other than concrete things," and therefore for every sentence that is true and that seems to mention some nonconcrete thing, "one can form an equivalent in which the subject and predicate are replaced by something referring to a real thing" (*Psychologie*, Vol. II, p. 163). For example, "There is a lack of gold" becomes "There is no gold" (a rejection of gold); "He believes that there are horses" becomes "He accepts (affirms) horses"; and "Red is a color" becomes "A red thing is, as such, a colored thing." This latter translation is more effective in German—*Das Rotes ist als solches ein Farbiges*—where adjectives are readily transformed into nouns.

Many philosophically troublesome words, such as "exists," "good," "impossible," and "true," are synsemantic; their linguistic function is not that of referring to concrete things. "Exists" in "God exists," as we have noted, is used to express acceptance of God; "does not exist," analogously, is used to express rejection. "*A* is good" expresses an apodictic rejection of incorrect lovers of *A*. "*A* is impossible" expresses an apodictic rejection of evident acceptors of *A*—of judgers who accept *A* with evidence.

A true judgment, according to Brentano, is a judgment that cannot contradict an evident judgment. Thus "true," in "It is true that God exists," may be used to express apodictic rejection of evident rejectors of God. "It is not both true and false that God exists" may express apodictic rejection of collectives consisting of evident acceptors and evident rejectors of God. (He also noted that "true" may be used to express agreement and that, at times, it is simply redundant.) Brentano could thus be said to have an expressive theory of truth, but one that involves an objective—and not merely expressive—theory of evidence. His theories of existence and of the nature of goodness may be similarly described.

Brentano's theory of categories contains important material on substance and accident, wholes and parts, the theory of relations, causation, and time and space that cannot be summarized here.

Logic. Brentano proposed the following revision of the theory of the syllogism on the basis of his theory of judgment. He wrote "All *S* are *P*" (A) as "There is no *S* which is a non-*P*"; "No *S* are *P*" (E) as "There is no *S* which is a *P*"; "Some *S* are *P*" (I) as "There is an *S* which is a *P*"; and Some *S* are not *P*" (O) as "There is an *S* which is a non-*P*." Since in this account both A and E are denials, and both I and O affirmations, Brentano was able to say that no affirmative judgment is universal and no negative judgment is particular. Barbara is written as "There is no *M* which is a non-*P*; there is no *S* which is a non-*M*; hence there is no *S* which is a non-*P*." And Ferio is written as "There is no *M* which is a *P*; there is an *S* which is an *M*; hence there is an *S* which is a non-*P*." Brentano was then able to formulate the doctrine of the syllogism in three rules, which may be confirmed by the two examples just cited.

(1) Every categorical syllogism contains *four* terms, two of which are opposed to each other and the other two of which occur twice. (2) If the conclusion is negative, then each premise is negative and has a term in common with the conclusion. (3) If the conclusion is affirmative, then one premise will share its quality and contain one of its terms, and the other premise will have the opposite quality and contain the opposite of one of its terms. (*Psychologie*, Vol. II, p. 78)

The so-called weakened and strengthened moods, according to this account, are invalid. The subaltern inferences from A to I and from E to O fail, but all four propositions, if written in Brentano's notation, may be simply converted. (See LOGICAL TERMS, GLOSSARY OF for explanation of technical terms and symbols.)

Other writings. *Vom Dasein Gottes* ("On the Existence of God," Alfred Kastil, ed., Leipzig, 1929), is a systematic theodicy in which Brentano appealed to the fact of contingency and the principle of sufficient reason, a principle that he believed to be logically necessary, in order to prove that there is a Necessary Being. He appealed to the evidence of design in order to prove that this Being is intelligent and good. Here, and in *Religion und Philosophie* (F. Mayer-Hillebrand, ed., Bern, 1954), he attempted to show that the soul is both spiritual and immortal. The subject of consciousness is said to be a nonspatial substance, forming no part of the physical body but capable of acting upon and being affected by the brain; it is created *ex nihilo* at the time of the conception of the body. Brentano defended the concept of creation *ex nihilo* by noting that whenever one calls an image to mind, one creates *ex nihilo*.

In *Versuch über die Erkenntnis* ("Inquiry into the Nature of Knowledge," Alfred Kastil, ed., Leipzig, 1925) and *Grundlegung und Aufbau der Ethik*, Brentano argued that the assumption that there can be absolute chance is self-contradictory and that the thesis of indeterminism is incompatible with the existence of human responsibility. But we have "freedom of the will" in that we are able to bring about some of the things we desire to bring about and are able to deliberate and then to decide accordingly. Moreover, we can "will to will" in that, at any given time, there are things we can do that will affect our volitions at some later time.

According to *Die vier Phasen der Philosophie* (Oskar Kraus, ed., Leipzig, 1926), those periods in which philosophy flourishes tend to be followed by three phases of decline: the first phase is characterized by a transfer of interest from the theoretical to the practical, the second by a tendency toward skepticism, and the third by a relapse into mysticism. This was the pattern of Greek philosophy; in modern philosophy the period of Locke, Descartes, and Leibniz was followed by the Enlightenment, then by the skepticism of Hume, and finally, according to Brentano, by the obscurities of Kant and the idealists who followed him.

Bibliography

Brentano's historical writings include the following works on Aristotle: *Von der mannigfachen Bedeutung des Seienden nach Aristoteles* (Freiburg, 1862; republished Darmstadt, 1960), an important work that is the source of much of Brentano's later thought; *Die Psychologie des Aristoteles* (Mainz, 1867); *Aristoteles Lehre vom Ursprung des menschlichen Geistes* (Leipzig, 1911); and *Aristoteles und seine Weltanschauung* (Leipzig, 1911). His *Geschichte der griechischen Philosophie*, F. Mayer-Hillebrand, ed. (Bern, 1963), is compiled from the notes for his university lectures.

Brentano's other writings include *Untersuchungen zur Sinnespsychologie* (Leipzig, 1907); *Die Lehre Jesu und ihre bleibende Bedeutung*, Alfred Kastil, ed. (Leipzig, 1922); *Grundzüge der Ästhetik*, F. Mayer-Hillebrand, ed. (Bern, 1959); and *Aenigmatias*, 5th ed. (Bern, 1962).

Certain portions of the *Psychologie* are translated in R. M. Chisholm, ed., *Realism and the Background of Phenomenology* (Glencoe, Ill., 1960); other translations are being prepared.

The most informative works on Brentano are Alfred Kastil, *Die Philosophie Franz Brentanos: Eine Einführung in seine Lehre* (Bern, 1951) and Oskar Kraus, *Franz Brentano: Zur Kenntnis seines Lebens und seiner Lehre* (Munich, 1919). The latter contains "Erinnerungen an Franz Brentano," by Carl Stumpf and Edmund Husserl. See also G. E. Moore, "Review of Franz Brentano, *The Origin of the Knowledge of Right and Wrong*," in *International Journal of Ethics*, Vol. 14 (1903), 115–123.

RODERICK M. CHISHOLM

BRIDGMAN, PERCY WILLIAM (1882–1962), American physicist and professor of mathematics and natural philosophy at Harvard, was awarded the Nobel Prize for physics in 1946 for his work on the properties of matter under extremely high pressures. He wrote at length on the philosophical implications of the discoveries of modern physics, particularly Einstein's revolutionary special theory of relativity, and on the analysis of scientific concepts. To Bridgman it seemed that Einstein's theory arose chiefly from the application of sound conceptual analysis based on what Bridgman called the "operational point of view." In his opinion, Einstein had not shown "something new about nature"—he was "merely bringing to light implications already contained in the physical operations used in measuring time." Bridgman held that analysis shows that there exists no answer to the question of what we should do, what operations we could perform, in order to determine whether or not two distant events occurred simultaneously. Therefore, it is meaningless to speak of the two events as having or not having occurred simultaneously.

According to Bridgman, then, Einstein's work dramatically highlighted an important feature of scientific methodology, the determination to link all scientific concepts to experimental procedures. From the operationalist views implicit in the practices of working scientists, we should learn to undertake a rigorous analysis of all scientific concepts, cleansing science of operationally undefinable elements.

Bridgman disclaimed all intention of founding a new philosophical school, yet his name has become linked inseparably with operationalism. Many scientists have hailed Bridgman's ideas as indispensable to the correct understanding of modern science, and some, particularly psychologists, have urged the inauguration of an extensive program of analysis of scientific concepts along the lines laid down by Bridgman. Others have regarded Bridgman's philosophy as not only wrong, but also harmful—if it were imposed on science, it could stifle creative inquiry. Bridgman later claimed that each concept need not be completely definable in terms of performable instrumental operations, but that it is sufficient that a concept should be one "indirectly making connection with instrumental operations."

The controversy over operationalism diverted attention from Bridgman's numerous other ideas, many of which are original and provocative. Perhaps the most interesting is Bridgman's view that discoveries in physics may help us to deal with problems in quite different domains. In his opinion, the great achievements in physics are discoveries of new ways in which our minds can master problems, discoveries about our conceptual make-up.

Through relativity physics, we have learned how apparent contradictions may arise through inadvertently admitting into science meaningless propositions that cannot stand up to operational analysis. Similarly, in human affairs seemingly irreconcilable demands of different groups may be eliminated by showing that some of the basic tenets on which the demands rest are meaningless. The methodology of the social sciences no doubt can learn much from the methodology of physics, but Bridgman's suggestion as to how human conflicts may be resolved will strike many as overly optimistic and somewhat naive. (See OPERATIONALISM.)

Bibliography

WORKS BY BRIDGMAN

The Logic of Modern Physics. New York, 1927.
The Nature of Physical Theory. Princeton, N.J., 1936.
Reflections of a Physicist. New York, 1950.
The Nature of Some of Our Physical Concepts. New York, 1952.

SECONDARY SOURCES

Cornelius, B. A., *Operationalism.* Springfield, Ill., 1955.
Frank, Philipp, *The Validation of Scientific Theories.* Boston, 1957.

G. SCHLESINGER

BRIGHTMAN, EDGAR SHEFFIELD (1884–1953), leading American advocate of personalism. At Boston University he studied under Borden Parker Bowne, the first philosopher in America to develop the personalistic position. Brightman taught at Nebraska Wesleyan University (1912–1915), Wesleyan University (1915–1919), and from 1919 on at Boston University, occupying the chair of Borden Parker Bowne professor of philosophy from 1925 until his death. He was president of the Eastern Division of the American Philosophical Association in 1936.

Brightman conceived of personalism as a mediating position in philosophy. As such, for him it superseded James's pragmatism and Royce's absolute idealism, to each of which, in turn, he had been attracted early in his career. Brightman also held that personalism could resolve the impasse between supernaturalism and naturalism. Furthermore, although he criticized positivism for being too restricted an empiricism and although he eschewed much in existentialism, Brightman's personalism can be understood as an attempt to combine the surface experience (sense) of positivism and the depth dimension (value) of existentialism in a concept of the total person.

Epistemology. Brightman held firmly to an epistemic dualism of the "shining present" (immediate experience) and "the illuminating absent" (the referent). Constantly emphasizing that all primary data were present experiences, he advocated a radically empirical method; that is, a method which considers whatever is, at any time, present in consciousness. Since knowledge involves reference, it is always hypothetical and tentative. Brightman accepted this as a healthy probabilism (and not a destructive skepticism), because he found in the principle of coherence an adequate test of reference (or criterion of truth). Deeply influenced by Hegelian dialectic, he viewed coherence not as formal consistency but as a principle for interpreting experience: a statement or a set of statements is true to the extent that it organizes and orders experience.

Ontology. The metaphysical perspective which emerges is a pluralistic idealism. Reality is a society of persons: the ultimate (uncreated) Person and finite (created) persons. Reality is thus not nature but history. The natural order does not have ontological identity "outside" the ultimate Person; rather, this order is his "behavior." The laws of logic do not have privileged priority; they are constitutive of the supreme mind. In philosophy of religion, this position is idealistic theism (not theological dualism). God is a conscious Person who creates finite persons and cooperates with them in the cosmic endeavor. A human person is a context of experience capable of self-consciousness, reason, and ideal values.

Evil. Brightman is probably most widely known for his controversial treatment of the problem of evil. He argued that the power of God is limited by nonrational conditions (the Given) within the divine nature which God's will neither created nor approves. God maintains constant and growing, though never complete, control of the Given.

Bibliography

Brightman's chief works are *Introduction to Philosophy* (New York, 1925; revised editions, 1951 and 1963, the latter edited by Robert N. Beck); *The Problem of God* (New York, 1930); *The Finding of God* (New York, 1931); *Moral Laws* (New York, 1933); *A Philosophy of Religion* (New York, 1940); *Nature and Values* (New York, 1945); *Person and Reality* (edited by Peter A. Bertocci in collaboration with Jannette E. Newhall and Robert S. Brightman, New York, 1958). A selected bibliography of his philosophical writings, including some 200 monographs and articles in addition to books, may be found in *Person and Reality*, pp. 367–370, or in the Brightman Memorial issue of *The Philosophical Forum*, Vol. 12 (1954), 22–28.

For references to discussions of Brightman's influence, see Peter A. Bertocci, "Edgar S. Brightman—Ten Years Later," in *The Philosophical Forum*, Vol. 20 (1962/1963), 3–10.

JOHN H. LAVELY

BRITISH PHILOSOPHY. There is a widely accepted and largely correct view that British philosophy has a greater unity than could be conferred on it simply by its place of origin. The point is well expressed by C. S. Peirce.

> From very early times, it has been the chief intellectual characteristic of the English to wish to effect everything by the plainest and directest means, without unnecessary contrivance. . . . In philosophy this national tendency appears as a strong preference for the simplest theories, and a resistance to any complication

of the theory as long as there is the least possibility that the facts can be explained in the simpler way. And, accordingly, British philosophers have always desired to weed out of philosophy all conceptions which could not be made perfectly definite and easily intelligible, and have shown strong nominalistic tendencies since the time of Edward I, or even earlier. (Review of A. C. Fraser's edition of the *Works of Berkeley* in *North American Review*, Vol. 93 (October, 1871), 449–472)

Nominalism and empiricism are both prominent in the thought of William of Ockham. The two trends are respectively continued in the philosophies of Hobbes and Bacon and are brought firmly together in the work of Locke and his successors. This way of thinking shows a certain suspicion of the apparent intimations of language about the nature of things. The English language is unique in the degree of its etymological impurity and, perhaps in consequence, of its grammatical simplicity. There are few rules but a wealth of particular idioms. At any rate, since the time of Ockham, English philosophers have been conscious of the mutable and conventional character of language and at no time since the fourteenth century more than at present. The English language had to fight its way to acceptance against the Norman French of England's medieval rulers and the Latin of its medieval thinkers. Its humble social and intellectual beginnings have ensured that English philosophers have never lost sight of its instrumental nature. At the same time they have been of unparalleled excellence as users of language. Most German philosophy is abominably written, and although no one made a greater contribution than Descartes and Pascal to the establishment of the modern French language, French philosophers bulk much smaller in the history of their national literature than do Bacon, Hobbes, Berkeley, and Hume in theirs, not to speak of such marginal philosophers, English Pascals as it were, as Burke, Coleridge, and Newman.

But at most periods of English history there has been an effective rationalist opposition to the ruling current of thought. Erigena, Duns Scotus, Wyclyf, the Cambridge Platonists, the Scottish philosophers, and the absolute idealists constitute something like what J. H. Muirhead called the "Platonic tradition in Anglo-Saxon philosophy" in his book of the same name. Neither this tradition nor the empiricist one opposed to it has been continuous. There have been three great ages of philosophy in Britain: the first, from about 1200 to 1350, from Grosseteste to Ockham; the second, from 1600 to 1750, from Bacon to Hume; and the third, from about 1870 to the present. But only in the fifteenth and sixteenth centuries is the subject wholly inert and lifeless. Certainly in the period from 1750 to 1850 such interesting philosophy as there was must be called British rather than English, since its exponents were all Scotsmen.

THE MIDDLE AGES

The idea that there is such a thing as English philosophy, strictly so called, in the Middle Ages should not be taken too seriously. The linguistic unity of educated Christendom made all English philosophers of the age part of a single community. As David Knowles remarks:

For three hundred years, from 1050 to 1350, and above all in the century between 1070 and 1170, the whole of educated Western Europe formed a single undifferentiated cultural unit. In the lands between Edinburgh and Palermo, Mainz or Lund and Toledo, a man of any city or village might go for education to any school, and become a prelate or an official in any church, court or university [when these existed] from north to south, from east to west. . . . In [their] writings . . . there is not a single characteristic of language, style or thought to tell us whence they sprang. (*Evolution of Medieval Thought*, New York, 1962, pp. 80–81)

Thinkers born in one country would study in a second and teach in a third. In the biographies of most English-born philosophers of the period there is constant travel between the great intellectual centers of Oxford and Paris and between the universities and the seats of papal power, whether in Rome or Avignon. The national as well as the personal characteristics of thought were muted by its expression in a common learned language, Latin.

All the same, there is a real point to saying that Erigena, Duns Scotus, and William of Ockham were British philosophers, whereas St. Anselm, although he became archbishop of Canterbury, was not. All three, as well as being born in the British Isles, studied and wrote there during the full maturity of their minds even if all three spent much of their adult lives abroad.

Erigena and after. John Scotus Erigena (c. 810–c. 877) stands in lonely and magnificent prominence at the beginning of British philosophy. The gap in time that separates him from the beginning of a continuous philosophical tradition in the twelfth century is no greater in its way than the difference in outlook between him, as a speculative, mystical Neoplatonist, and the dominant figures in British thought. Born, presumably, in Ireland, he was called in 847 to head the palace school of Charles the Bald. He translated the writings of the sixth-century Pseudo-Dionysius, mistakenly accepting the prevailing belief that he was Dionysius, the disciple of St. Paul, and developed the Neoplatonic ideas of Pseudo-Dionysius into a massive pantheistic system.

In his *De Divisione Naturae,* Erigena divided reality into four parts: that which creates and is not created (God conceived of as the efficient cause of the world); that which creates and is created (the divine ideas that are the archetypes of the contents of the natural world); that which does not create and is created (the concrete order of sensible things); and that which neither creates nor is created (God conceived of as the final cause of everything, the "nothingness" out of which everything is created and toward which it progresses). From God as the efficient cause the rest of reality emanates in a freely overflowing manner—first the highest Platonic Idea of the Good, then, successively, genera and species, and, finally, matter as a coming together of insensible qualities.

Erigena held that God can be known only by the way of negation and, fortified by the belief that his Neoplatonic ideas had the endorsement of St. Paul, took extensive liberties with Christian orthodoxy. He regarded creation as timeless, seeing the Biblical account of it as an allegory and the Eucharist as a symbol. His theory of knowledge was essentially the Augustinian doctrine of divine illumination, which was the persisting defense of medieval English philosophers against the more empirical Aristotelian naturalism of St. Thomas.

Erigena was concerned with the problem of evil in a way that anticipates the difficulties of the absolute idealists of the nineteenth century. Negation and finitude are part of the nature of things in a created world, so that although evil is unreal, God is the cause of it. Again, God creates the world freely although at the same time it is a necessity of his nature. As in other pantheistic systems the human soul, as an integral center of free action, tends to be absorbed into the deity, unification with which is its highest perfection. Erigena knew Greek and the writings of the Church Fathers. For all its mystical quality his great system was worked out in a wholly rational, and, indeed, rationalistic, way. In its scope, articulation, and splendid indifference to humdrum fact, it was the herald of many series of Gifford lectures to be delivered a millennium later.

After two hundred years the first great age of British philosophy begins, following the primacy of St. Anselm, which began in 1093, when he was about sixty, and lasted until his death in 1109. Adelard of Bath (c. 1080–c. 1145) is perhaps the first strictly English philosopher, not on account of the scientific work under Arabian influence for which he is most renowned—his translation of Euclid and his treatises on the astrolabe, the abacus, and astronomy—but for his treatment of the problem of universals in *De Eodem et Diverso*. In this work he attempted to reconcile the views of Plato and Aristotle: Universals are immanent in things and have to be abstracted by us, but they are also ideas in the mind of God. This view can be regarded, according to choice, as evidence either of the English talent for compromise or of the limits of English speculative power. A more shadowy figure is that of Robert Pullen, who was possibly not an Englishman at all. His importance lies in the fact that he lectured in Oxford in 1133, the earliest reliable record of any activities of higher education in that city.

John of Salisbury and Christian apologetic. The most impressive figure in English intellectual life in the early twelfth century was John of Salisbury (1115–1180), the most learned and civilized man of his age. He was a pupil of Pullen and Abelard and wrote excellent Ciceronian Latin. He was the chief ornament of the distinguished group of scholars at Canterbury under the patronage of Archbishop Theobald and became the friend and supporter of Becket. He died as bishop of Chartres. He was something of a gentleman-amateur of philosophy, defending Aristotle's logic in his *Metalogicon* as the proper instrument for philosophy and theology but deploring the tendency of its exponents toward excessive technical and sophistic refinement. A critic of the nominalism of Roscelin, he attempted to combine Augustine's version of Platonic realism about universals, which sees them as ideas in the mind of God, with the newly discovered doctrines of Aristotle on the subject. We cannot, he said, know the nature of universals in themselves; such awareness as we have of them we must acquire from observation of natural resemblances. He is more valuable as a source of accurate accounts of the prevailing opinions of his age than as a direct contributor to them.

In John of Salisbury is to be seen the main concern of the philosophers of the high Middle Ages, the reconciliation of philosophical rationality as represented by Aristotle, "the Philosopher," with the revealed foundations of Christian belief. The work of the Fathers, culminating in Augustine, had clothed Christian dogma in essentially Platonic and Neoplatonic garments. The discovery of the whole encyclopedic range of Aristotle's works introduced ideas that clashed with the received doctrine at a number of points. Aristotle's view that the world had no beginning in time conflicted with the literal reading of the doctrine of creation. Aristotle's conception of the soul as the form of the body opposed the dualist conception of soul and body as distinct substances. This was the most urgent and persistent focus of controversy. The hylomorphist conviction that every substance has both matter and form led orthodox thinkers, such as Bonaventure, to accept spiritual matter as part of the composition of the soul-substance and to ascribe a plurality of forms to the human individual as against Aquinas' theory of a single substantial form with its seemingly negative implications for human survival of bodily death. Aristotelians, such as Aquinas, had to do the best they could with the concept of the active intellect, possibly identical in all men, to incorporate the dogma of immortality. Aristotle's theory that knowledge is the result of sensory interaction with the world was incompatible with the attribution of knowledge to the grace of divine illumination. Aristotle's idea of matter as merely passive and potential ruled out the Augustinian, rather than strictly Christian, theory that seminal principles are contained in matter and are responsible for the development of things.

There were three main stages to this conflict. During the first period, in which the great medieval universities were established and the mendicant orders acquired their near monopoly on philosophical scholarship, the works of Aristotle were appropriated, and their bearing on Christian belief worked out. In the second the major systematizations of the opposing doctrines were produced—more or less Augustinian orthodoxy by the Franciscan Bonaventure, devout but rational Aristotelianism by Thomas Aquinas. The third stage began in 1277, three years after the death of Aquinas, with the official, though, as it proved, ineffective, condemnation of Thomism by the decrees of Étienne Tempier, bishop of Paris. The condemnation neither restored Augustinian orthodoxy nor destroyed Thomism. Official hostility gave the firmness of an embattled creed to Thomism, and the intellectual opposition to it took an altogether new form in the original and sophisticated philosophy of Duns Scotus. This new development led in the end to a sharp division between the supernatural realm of theology, where knowledge comes from revelation, and the natural realm of philosophy, where knowledge is acquired in the broadly empirical fashion described by Aristotle. This division, orginally proposed by the Islamic philosopher Averroës, became explicit in the work of Ockham and his followers.

English philosophers were active in all three stages, in the first as translators and interpreters of Aristotle, then as the leaders of the conservative Augustinian resistance to

Thomism, and, finally, with Duns Scotus and Ockham, as the initiators of wholly new forms of Christian philosophy. Until the time of Duns Scotus conservative Augustinianism was almost wholly dominant in England. Étienne Gilson said of Augustine, "Nothing seems to have been able to dislodge [him] from Oxford until toward the last few years of the thirteenth century" (*History of Christian Philosophy in the Middle Ages,* New York, 1955, p. 360). For the next 250 years Duns Scotus took his place, until Thomas Cromwell's Protestant commissioners sent the leaves of his works flying about the quadrangle of New College.

Alexander of Hales. Alexander of Hales (c. 1178–1245) was one of the most assiduous compilers of Aristotle and was perhaps the first to know his work in its entirety even if he did not understand it very well. He was the teacher of Bonaventure, whose systematization of the main Augustinian ideas became almost the official philosophy of the Franciscan order. Alexander argued for divine illumination and seminal principles and developed Augustine's suggestion that light was the primary constituent of the sensible world, a parallel to the intellectual light shone by grace into the human mind. He followed Augustine in thinking that Platonic Ideas are contained in the mind of God, not in a realm of essence of their own, and he held that the creation of the world is a free act of God for which no cause can be given.

Grosseteste and his contemporaries. Robert Grosseteste (1168 or 1175–1253) helped to make Aristotle accessible by producing the first European translation of the *Ethics* into Latin, but his chief intellectual work was in natural philosophy, where he showed great learning and some originality in mathematics, optics, and astronomy. His main historical significance lies in his administrative work as the first great chancellor of Oxford and as the introducer and patron there of the Franciscan order, from which Oxford's chief medieval philosophers were to come.

Grosseteste accepted the divine illumination theory of knowledge and thought that the mind needs the senses as an aid only to the extent that it is rendered dull and imperceptive by the body in which it is contained. In a parallel manner he thought that light is the ultimate stuff of the physical world. He regarded soul and body as distinct substances and argued against the Aristotelian view that the world has no beginning in time.

Four of his lesser contemporaries deserve a brief mention. The Dominican Richard Fishacre (died 1245) wrote the first English commentary on the *Sentences* of Peter Lombard. He knew Aristotle well but argued against him in support of the idea of a plurality of forms, and he had an influence on St. Bonaventure. John Blund (died 1248) introduced Aristotle's *De Anima,* the crucial text in the controversy about the soul, into Oxford, perhaps in the period 1202–1208, with Avicenna's influential commentary on it, the original source of the doctrine of a plurality of forms. Here the Aristotelian active intellect is treated as a unity outside individual human beings and thus in a way that must exclude it from a Christian philosophy. Adam Marsh (1200–1258) was the pupil and friend of Grosseteste and the master of Roger Bacon. The first Franciscan doctor of Oxford, he left no works that have yet been identified. Thomas of York (died 1260), also a Franciscan, went further toward Aristotle than his Oxford contemporaries but denied that substance is individuated by matter and propounded a dualistic theory of soul and body that contains both the plurality of forms and the conception of spiritual matter.

Roger Bacon and after. Roger Bacon (1214 or 1220–1292) was a pupil of Grosseteste and shared his interest in natural philosophy. Commentators hostile to the metaphysical interests of the Middle Ages formed exaggerated estimates of Bacon's scientific originality, and a wider circle exaggerated his necromantic leanings. He was certainly uncharacteristic of his age both in the interest he showed in mathematics and physics and in following the life of a researcher rather than a teacher. He adopted the broadly Augustinian light-metaphysics of Grosseteste, identifying Aristotle's active intellect with the divine light but equally insisting on the importance of observation and mathematical reasoning for natural knowledge. This measure of naturalism emerges in his support of a causal proof of God's existence as opposed to the purely dialectical proof of Anselm. He argued that mathematical knowledge possesses a pre-eminent degree of certainty on the ground that it is derived from definitions alone and involved no reasoning from effect to cause. His *Opus Majus* is in large part an appeal for the reform of inquiry by greater reliance on mathematics and experiment. This anticipation of Francis Bacon extends to matters of comparative detail. The later Bacon's Idols, which obstruct the advancement of learning, are much like the obstacles pointed out by the earlier one—authority, custom, popular prejudice, and spurious pretenses to knowledge.

Roger Bacon was a lonely and offensively combative figure. One of the few men of his time to receive his praise was William Shireswood (died c. 1267), who wrote a sophisticated treatise on logic which was widely used in Oxford and Paris. The most energetic defenders of the conservative Augustinian position against the questionably orthodox Aristotelian innovations of St. Thomas were Robert Kilwardby (died 1279), who succeeded Fishacre as head of the Dominicans in England and became archbishop of Canterbury, and the Franciscan John Peckham (1225–1292), also archbishop of Canterbury, a disciple of Bonaventure. Kilwardby was supported by Richard of Mediavilla, or Richard of Middleton (died 1300), another Franciscan follower of Bonaventure, who held that a plurality of worlds is possible. Roger Marston (died 1303) was a follower of Roger Bacon. Kilwardby and Peckham were not original thinkers, but they authoritatively set out the conservative position and made effective use of their powerful administrative positions to bring it to bear on the Thomists, requiring assent from them to the plurality of forms and to seminal principles. The English Thomists were few and obscure. Thomas of Sutton (c. 1310) was perhaps the most notable of them. Nicholas Trivet (1258–1328) had his academic rigor immortalized by the idiom "right as a trivet."

Duns Scotus and Scotism. It was John Duns Scotus (c. 1266–1308), the first major British philosopher since Erigena and perhaps the most powerful philosophical intellect of the Middle Ages, who initiated a new system of ideas which led English thought in a fresh direction, away from the conflict of Aristotle and Augustine. He was born in Roxburghshire, Scotland, was brought up at Oxford in the Augustinian orthodoxy of Bonaventure and Peckham and the scientific concerns of Grosseteste, and taught thereafter in Oxford and Paris. Scotus died comparatively young, before his ideas were fully ordered and worked out. The state of his writings, whose precise identification has led to controversy, together with the novelty of his ideas and language, for he was a fertile terminological innovator, has led to conflicting interpretations. The pronounced partisan interests of most of his commentators have compounded the difficulties.

What is clear is that although animated by the same kind of general rationalistic intent as Aquinas, Scotus took the first effective steps toward that firm demarcation between the domains of revealed faith and philosophical reason that was the fundamental principle of Ockham's philosophy and that tended to eliminate rational discussion of religious truth altogether. Scotus held that the concept of being is univocal as applied to God and sensible things but that only the existence of God, and not his attributes, can be demonstrated. Similarly, the immortality of the soul cannot be proved but must rest on revelation for its acceptance. He favored conceptual and a priori proofs of God's existence. He argued that the notion of an uncaused cause is possible and that any being not in fact an uncaused cause cannot be one, which meant for Scotus that if it is possible for something to be an uncaused cause, then it is one. Thus, he concluded that the possibility of such a being entails its actuality. There is a resemblance between this argument and Leibniz' variant of the Ontological Proof of Anselm, which states that God must exist if the concept of God is possible rather than that existence is part of the concept of God.

Scotus rejected the view of Aristotle and Aquinas that it is matter that individuates substance, claiming that each individual thing has a unique singular form, or haecceity, by which the common nature is contracted to individuals. This doctrine that an individual has both shared and proprietary forms, together with the Augustinian theory of plurality of forms in general, led Scotus to the concept of a formal distinction, which, like the real distinction between things that can exist without one another, lies in the nature of things and is not a product of our way of looking at them but does not involve the independence of the things formally distinguished. The distinction between essence and existence is a formal one. Scotus was, then, a realist, but his theory of natural knowledge is Aristotelian rather than Augustinian. He rejected divine illumination and innate ideas, saying that our knowledge of material things comes from sensation. Although we can conceive what is not sensible, we do not, in our earthly careers, have any intuition of nonsensible things. He also rejected seminal principles but against the Aristotelian view maintained that matter is actual and has a nature of its own, is not a mere potentiality. He regarded knowledge of the self in much the same way as he regarded knowledge of God. I know *that* I exist, but I have no natural or rational knowledge of the nature of my soul. In his ideas about God and the soul Scotus stopped just short of the Ockhamist view that we have no natural knowledge of any sort about either. Another respect in which his views resemble Ockham's is in the priority he accords to will over intellect. Things are good because God wills them and not vice versa, so moral truth is not accessible to the natural reason. Similarly, God's creation of the world is a free act of will. All possible ideas of created things are present in God's mind, and man's philosophy can explore these possibilities but cannot anticipate the free act of will by which God selects some of them for creation.

Scotus remained the authoritative philosopher in the universities for the next 250 years. Bradwardine and Wyclyf, the leading figures of the middle and later fourteenth century, drew on him to confute the adherents of Ockham, and his authoritative position survived the condemnation of Wyclyf, which was prompted by Wyclyf's anticlerical rejection of pope, priests, and miraculous ideas of the Eucharist but extended to the abstract philosophy on which these rejections were founded. One of his immediate followers was Henry of Harclay (c. 1270–1317), who tended toward nominalism in his theory that the notion of a common nature, shared by a plurality of things, is arrived at by confusedly running together their several haecceities. Another Scotist, Walter Burleigh (1275–1343), the tutor of Edward the Black Prince, was the most resolute opponent of Ockham's new logic in Oxford.

Ockham. William of Ockham (c. 1285–1349) carried Scotus' various initiatives away from the rationalism of the high Middle Ages to their logical completion. For him the division between philosophy, now reduced in its scope from being in general to the natural order, and theology is absolute. Directly against Scotus he held that we can have no knowledge whatsoever of the abstract and universal. Everything that we can intuit as existing outside us is singular; generality is a function of the mind and attaches only to the images that are the natural signs with which we think and to the terms which we attach to these natural signs by convention. Abstract universals are impossible; if they were Platonic essences, they would be individuals, and if they were Aristotelian forms, they would be pluralities, collections of individuals. Natural knowledge is in the first instance an intuitive awareness through the senses of singular individuals. Ockham admitted that God could, in his absolute power, produce an experience of such an intuition in our minds even if there were no corresponding existent outside us but did not himself draw skeptical implications about our knowledge of the external world from this variant of the argument from illusion. What his skepticism applies to is not the common objects of empirical knowledge but the nonsensible objects of theology and metaphysics. Demonstrative proofs of God and the soul are invalid and at best confer probability on their conclusions. In self-awareness all we encounter is our mental states; for any knowledge about the nature of their possessor we must have recourse to revelation. Scotus had held that even if the concepts we abstract from the things we perceive are inadequate, we can have certain knowledge of their relations. In Ockham's terminism no question can arise about the correspondence between our conceptions and the essences or quiddities they represent, for according to the theory of terminism, only terms, not things, are general.

Thus, logical or necessary truths susceptible of demonstration are only truths of the second order; they are verbal propositions about the analysis of terms. In this, Ockham anticipated Hume and the analytic philosophers of the twentieth century. Another anticipation is Ockham's theory that causation is regular succession as far as our natural knowledge of it is concerned.

The main theological implication of Ockham's philosophy, besides the view that God's existence and nature cannot be proved and must be revealed, is that no limit but that of noncontradiction can be set to God's absolute power and freedom of action. Ockham's followers were often to revel in the speculative freedom that this doctrine gave them. There is no contradiction in God's commanding men to hate him or in his making murder an obligation; anything consistently conceivable is within his absolute power. In practice this attitude led to the abandonment of all guidance from reason and tradition as to God's actions and purposes. The vacuum thus created came to be filled by authority, whether of the pope, the Scriptures, or inner personal conviction.

Ockham's denial of the demonstrability of God or the soul was emphasized by his followers Adam Wodham (died 1358) and Robert Holkot (died 1349), who was singular in being both a Dominican and a Cambridge man. Holkot argued that there is need for a special logic of faith since what is false in philosophy can nevertheless be true in theology, a further step forward from Ockham's view that the theologically true can be philosophically unknowable. At Merton College, Oxford, there was an able group of logicians and mathematicians, including Richard Swineshead and William Heytesbury, who developed the terminist logic and the antimetaphysical theory of knowledge associated with it.

Bradwardine. The most impressive and respected of Mertonians in Ockham's time was the learned Thomas Bradwardine (c. 1290–1349), an Augustinian and Scotist who was passionately opposed to Ockham and all his works. In his *De Causa Dei* (1344) he argued that the divine will is the cause of everything that is and happens, including sin and evil, and that man is wholly impotent in himself, dependent in all respects on God's grace. The two alternative views against which Bradwardine's theological determinism was directed were the more or less Aristotelian view that the world is a natural causal system and, of more immediate interest, the Pelagian doctrine of many followers of Ockham that man is the free and primary cause of his actions. What was objectionable in the Pelagian view was its implication that merit accrues to man by reason of his autonomous activity and, thus, that salvation is earned rather than bestowed as a gift by God. The Pelagian view was derived from Ockham's skepticism about the knowability of the supernatural. God as unknowable is wholly indeterminate; his absolute power and freedom leave the field of action open to natural man. Bradwardine agreed with Ockham that there can be no rational theology, but he held that our revealed knowledge of God is just one aspect of the workings of all-inclusive grace. His Pelagian opponents had exploited the idea of God's absolute power to form a conception of man left to his own devices in the world. He used it for the directly opposite purpose, to conceive God as working in every detail of the created world.

Pelagians. In Bradwardine's polemic the new center of interest in English philosophy emerged clearly. Before Ockham the goal of philosophy had been an understanding of the nature of God and of the immortal human soul. Once this had been ruled out as a topic of rational inquiry, interest moved to the place of man in the natural world. The crucial problem was that of future contingents. If God both causes and foresees everything that is going to happen, how can men affect it or be responsible for it? The Pelagian followers of Ockham—for example, Holkot and Wodham—contended that either God does not know at all what is going to happen or that he has only a contingent and fallible knowledge of the future.

Thomas of Buckingham (1300–1356) argued that sin and grace are not mutually exclusive. Where neither is present, the absence of sin must be ascribed to man's natural and autonomous propensity to right action. The will of God is free, and so it must be contingent and not determinative of everything that happens. In later life Thomas receded from this Pelagian position, no doubt under the influence of Bradwardine, to a somewhat watery mediating standpoint. Stopping short of the full rigor of Bradwardine's determinism, he held that we are free despite God's foreknowledge of our acts since it is our freedom rather than our actions that he causes. He permits our sins but does not will them.

Uthred of Boldon (born 1320) was an independent-minded Pelagian whose innovations brought censure down upon him in 1368. He held that at the moment of death man has a clear vision of God, a crucial opportunity for earning salvation. Not only did Uthred uncompromisingly reject the orthodox doctrine of grace, but he also held that every event has an assignable cause which made reference to God's will vacuous, and his doctrine of the clear vision in effect denied that the Christian sacraments are necessary for salvation and even that they can contribute to it.

Wyclyf and after. After the middle of the fourteenth century, English philosophy began to contract. In his visitation of 1411, Arundel, archbishop of Canterbury, extended the condemnation of Wyclyf's religious views to include his philosophy, marking the end of a process of decline which must be ascribed to the Black Death of 1348–1349, the isolation imposed on England by the Hundred Years' War, and the Great Schism of 1378. John Wyclyf (c. 1320–1384), although most famous as the chief English precursor of Protestantism, was an academic philosopher until about 1371, the most powerful influence of his time at Oxford before he turned to ecclesiastical reform in his later years. He is the last English medieval philosopher of importance. Two and a half centuries of comparative philosophical torpor were to intervene between Wyclyf's abandonment of philosophy and a completely new start with the publication of Bacon's *Advancement of Learning* in 1605. Wyclyf's *Summa de Ente* is a significant work in its own right, quite apart from the support it provided for his innovating and essentially Protestant ideas in religion. Wyclyf approached the problems of his age from a body of new and extreme opinions about the problems of his predecessors. Like them he was a confident rationalist who believed that metaphysics can yield certain and positive knowledge and not just the possibilities to which the Ockhamists limited it. He was flatly opposed as well to their terminism, the theory that since only terms, not things, are general, abstract knowledge must relate to conventional terms and not reality. Wyclyf was a more uncompromising realist even than Scotus. For him the real objects of knowledge are objective and eternal universals, not perishing singulars. A loyal Oxonian, he traced his Platonism back to Grosseteste. These real universals are substances, eternal and unannihilable, whether as exemplars in God's mind or as accidents in things. Wyclyf concluded that everything in passing time is predestinately known by God. It is God's knowledge rather than his will that is unlimited. He cannot annihilate substance, but this is a limitation he has freely imposed on himself.

From these abstract contentions Wyclyf's main reforming principles follow. Scripture is the word of God, an emanation from him and thus eternally and literally true. Since substance cannot be annihilated, there can be no transubstantiation in the Eucharist, and with this goes the claim of the priesthood to be the indispensable intermediary between God and man. These deductions lead directly to Wyclyf's support for clerical disendowment and to the theory of dominion, in which he contended that earthly authority can be forfeited by sin, in particular papal authority by the corruptions of the church.

In the politically disturbed fifteenth century philosophy stagnated. Humphrey, duke of Gloucester, helped to introduce Italian humanism to England but in literary rather than philosophical form. English humanism was basically an educational movement, not a revolution in fundamental ideas. Humphrey was also the patron of the one original voice of the century that had something philosophical to say, Reginald Pecock (1395?–1460?). Pecock resembled Wyclyf in his rationalism and in the fact that he wrote much in the vernacular, but Wyclyf's followers, called Lollards, were the prime objects of his criticism. A kind of self-made Thomist, Pecock exalted the "doom of reason" above Scripture, the Fathers, and the authority of the church and sought to win back heretics by syllogisms. For the next century and a half the universities slumbered, and the lively concerns of the English mind were outside philosophy, in politics with Thomas More and church organization with Richard Hooker.

THE RENAISSANCE

The Tudor period in England was philosophically negligible; the universities were little touched by the immense intellectual vitality of the age. The great efflorescence of imaginative literature owed something to humanism, while religious thought at the concrete level of liturgical and ecclesiastical reform was inspired by the Reformation. But the religious turbulence of the age did more harm than good to the universities, which were paralyzed by a bewildering sequence of changes—the breach with Rome under Henry VIII, extreme Protestantism under Edward VI, Roman Catholic reaction under Mary, an uneasy settlement between the two extremes under Elizabeth. With the dissolution of the monasteries the universities lost a leading provider of men and money. As a result, the number of students was reduced, and the social composition of the university was altered; poor scholars gave way to gentlemen in search of polish. A lively and expert interest in classical literature grew up at Oxford under the influence of humanism, but this had no effect on the dominance of Aristotle in the realm of fundamental ideas. The logic and metaphysics of the Scholastics held on to their increasingly unwelcome authority until well into the seventeenth century. Bacon, Hobbes, and Locke all vigorously repudiated the philosophy they had been taught, and with them philosophy passed from the hands of academics to free, private individuals, where it remained until well on in the nineteenth century. Oxford's medieval pre-eminence became a heavy burden of tradition, impeding adjustment to the new currents of thought. Cambridge at least showed some interest in the logical innovations of Peter Ramus, the French critic of Aristotelianism, and the Cambridge Platonists of the mid-seventeenth century were the last group of original academic philosophers in England until the rise of the absolute idealists at Oxford in the 1870s, two centuries later.

The logic of Aristotle continued as the basic undergraduate instruction. It was expounded in Latin by John Sanderson (died 1602) and Richard Crakanthorpe (1567–1624) and also, a new development, in English by Thomas Wilson (c. 1525–1581) in his *The Rule of Reason* (1551) and by Ralph Lever (died 1585) in his *Arte of Reason Rightly Termed Witcraft* (1573), in which neologisms of impeccably Saxon origin were introduced instead of the customary Latinate expressions. At Cambridge, Sir William Temple (1555–1627) defended the logic of Ramus against the leading exponent of orthodoxy, Everard Digby (1550–1592), whose lectures were attended by Bacon. Ramus' differences with Aristotle were of little theoretical interest. His aim was to simplify logic by removing its heavy scholastic encumbrances so that it would be a more effective instrument for practical purposes. His superficiality was appropriate to the worldliness of the age. A more serious worldliness and practicality are evident in the more thorough condemnation of scholastic logic by Francis Bacon in the interests of a logic of discovery that would, by unlocking the secrets of nature, give man mastery over it.

Although Digby was logically orthodox, his metaphysics (*Theoria Analytica,* 1579) was more forward-looking. Eclectically composed of borrowings from Scholasticism, Neoplatonism, and occult, Hermetic philosophy, it was the first of a series of only mildly influential writings in which some of the new philosophical material provided by such Italian Platonists as Ficino and Pico della Mirandola was incorporated into English thought. The visit to England of Giordano Bruno in 1582 gave some impetus to this concern with the prescientific Renaissance philosophy of nature. The copious Robert Fludd (1574–1637) wrote of magic, alchemy, and astrology in close adherence to the visionary Neoplatonism of Paracelsus. Robert Greville, Lord Brooke (1608–1643), in *The Nature of Truth* (1640) also argued for the Neoplatonist view that the world is an emanation from God but in a manner less encumbered with fantastic and occult detail than Fludd. There is a hint of later and more developed idealisms in his view that the natural world with all its diversities is merely appearance. In Sir Kenelm Digby (1603–1665), whose *Two Treatises* (on bodies and on the immortality of the soul) appeared in 1644, traces of all the intellectual interests of the time, mystical and naturalistic, are to be found, the corpuscularian view of matter among others, along with traditional ideas.

Thomas More. Neither of the two most powerful English minds of the sixteenth century, More and Hooker, was primarily philosophical. Thomas More (1478–1535) was an admirer of Pico della Mirandola, but he died as a martyr to the old faith and his *Utopia* (1516) was neither a philosophical work nor, in its support for religious toleration, in conformity with his real allegiances. His ideal society is interesting as the first expression of a persistent English distaste for the urbanized, commercial social order. An organic community, it embodies a large measure of equality, rests on an agricultural base, and has as its highest aim the fostering of free, cultivated individuals, bearing their share of common labor but detached from material interests.

Hooker. Richard Hooker (1553–1600) was the theorist of the Elizabethan church settlement. His *The Laws of Ecclesiastical Polity* (Books I–IV, 1593 or 1594; Book V, 1597; Book VI, 1648; Book VIII, 1651; Book VII, 1662) begins with an abstract consideration of natural law, which governs both physical and social phenomena. Whether it governs the behavior of material bodies or sets the ends of human conduct, natural law is an expression of the divine order of the world. It can be discovered through reason and is not an outcome of God's arbitrary will. Hooker's position is opposed to the voluntarism of Ockham and Hobbes; it has affinities with the rationalism of Aquinas and played an important part in Locke's theory of government. Hooker did not see contract as the essential ground of political obligation, though he accepted it as a possible ground, but regarded some sort of consent as indispensable for the justification of government. His ideas, mediated through Locke, are continuous with a native tradition of ethical rationalism as well as with the specifically political employment of the conception of natural law.

Francis Bacon. With Francis Bacon (1561–1626) the conventional beginning of English philosophy was reached. Certainly, Bacon was the first to write a philosophical work of major importance in the English language, *The Advancement of Learning* (1605), and he was a strikingly original thinker, owing little or nothing to his immediate predecessors or contemporaries. But it is no derogation of his originality to detect earlier English lines of thought in his work—an insistence on the separation of philosophy from theology as great as Ockham's and a preoccupation with the study of the natural world that recalls Grosseteste and Roger Bacon. But even if he was not the first English philosopher, he was the first *modern* English philosopher.

No one before Bacon had so uncompromisingly held natural knowledge to be the prime and central concern of philosophy. The negative side of this principle is his firm distinction between the natural, which can be rationally known by induction from experience, and the divine, for knowledge of which we must depend wholly on revelation. A pronounced suspicion of irony is aroused by his emphatic assertion that the less amenable to reason the content of revelation, the better, since it is thus a greater testimony to faith. He approached natural knowledge in strictly secular terms. It is to be acquired not as a witness to the glory of God or as a source of evidence about God's existence and nature but for practical use, for the relief of man's estate. The goal of Bacon's investigations is a fruitful method, and the first step in this direction is a criticism of the sterile procedures that have thus far obstructed the achievement of natural knowledge. He distinguished three defective methods—the disputatious learning of Aristotelian Scholasticism, an obsession with a priori deduction which leads to empty verbalism; the delicate learning of the individual scholar, which merely preserves the falsely authoritative errors of the past; and the fantastic learning of the occultists and Hermetic philosophers, who accumulate dubious records of isolated marvels. Against them he urged the claims, respectively, of observation, cooperative research, and a systematic method.

In his doctrine of Idols the battle against error is conducted on a wider front. There are certain general propensities of the human intellect which lead to unjustified beliefs, such as an excessive expectation of order; these are the Idols of the Tribe. Man must also guard against individual peculiarities and prejudices, the Idols of the Cave. The Idols of the Market Place are those features of language which we wrongly suppose to correspond to distinctions in reality. Finally, there are the Idols of the Theater, those received systems of ideas which prevent us from seeing the world as it really is.

In the *Novum Organum* (1620), Bacon proposed an inductive method that has properties that will, he believed, protect us from all these dangers; it is cautious, uniform, observational, and untouched by the influence of previous speculation. Its first phase is the compilation of a natural history, a collection of carefully observed instances. These are then arranged for comparison in various tables which will clearly reveal the connections and independences of the observable properties of things. From the tables laws are derived, and from them yet more general and inclusive laws by a process of gradual ascent. Comprehensive theory is to be approached step by step. A general account of the natural world, for which Bacon reserved the term metaphysics, must be attained by way of a prior knowledge of its detailed constitution, the task of physics. The laws that induction yields are laws of efficient causality; final causes are remitted to the sphere of revelation.

However, a traditional note is sounded in Bacon's view that metaphysics is a knowledge of forms, an understanding of the limited alphabet of ultimate, underlying properties in terms of which the empirical variety of the world can be explained. Bacon's theory of forms expresses an unsupported if not unjustifiable confidence in the ultimate simplicity of nature which led him to ignore the essential tentativeness and corrigibility of inductive reasoning and kept him unaware of the need for a justification of induction pointed out by Hume.

In Bacon's first work he had expounded a classification of the sciences. In a wealth of other works he wrote with perception and originality about politics, where he favored an efficient absolute monarchy, and recent history, where he gave a critical appreciation of the achievements of Henry VII. He had original ideas about education, which influenced Comenius; both men were hostile to exclusive verbal or linguistic education and favored techniques involving the perception of objects. About literature, too, he had original ideas, holding that excellence is not determined by conformity to abstract canons; "beauty," he said, "lies in the strangeness of the proportions." Given the all-inclusive scope of his interests, the vast magnitude of his main task, and the fact that he had an active career in public life until the few years before his death, it is not surprising that his "great instauration," a total system of natural knowledge, should be only a fragment and that the methodological studies he did complete should be defective in many respects. There is justice in the conventional opinion that Bacon was blind to two essential aspects of scientific thinking, mathematics and imaginative hypothesis. It was a recognition of the place of mathematics in physical science that underlay the doctrine of primary qualities, the Democritean theory, supported by Galileo, Descartes, and Locke, that the sole intrinsic qualities of natural objects are measurable quantities. Bacon's idea that science should be cooperatively produced by a mechanical method and put to practical use underestimates the role of individual creativeness in science. In fact, Bacon was too much ahead of his time. His method was less apt for physics, the dominant scientific interest of the immediately succeeding age, than for biology. It was not to come into its own until the nineteenth century.

Boyle. Although Bacon had no disciples in the doctrinal sense, one aspect of his work had an immediate effect. A feature of the ideal society sketched in his *New Atlantis* is Salomon's house, a scientific research institute, realizing his view that the study of nature should be a social, cooperative undertaking. Within twenty years of Bacon's death a discussion circle, which was the nucleus of the Royal Society, had been formed in Oxford. A leading member was the brilliantly productive Robert Boyle (1627–1691), in whom converged all the fruitful lines of scientific thinking of the age.

Accepting Bacon's inductive and experimental method, Boyle added to it, first, an informed appreciation, derived from study of Galileo and Descartes, of the place of mathematics in physical science and, second, Gassendi's doctrine of atomism. In his compound of Bacon, Descartes, and Gassendi is first evident that bifurcation of nature, as Whitehead called it, which divided the world into an objective order of particles with measurable qualities, the topic of physical science, and a subjective order of images and feelings. Boyle gave its familiar name to the distinction between primary and secondary qualities and laid down the main lines of the English philosophy par excellence, the conception of the natural world brought to completion by Locke and Newton. For good measure Boyle anticipated the main direction of the rational theology of the succeeding age, much of it presented in the lectures, endowed in his will, that are named after him. Rejecting Bacon's politic revelationism, he held that natural science supports religious belief by displaying the evidences of intelligent design in the universe.

Hobbes. Nothing showed more brutally the danger to religion of the scientific way of thinking than the philosophy of Thomas Hobbes (1588–1679), the greatest systematizer of the major British philosophers. Hobbes came to philosophy comparatively late in life and was led to it not by a period spent as Bacon's secretary but by a sudden infatuation with the intellectual beauty of Euclid's geometry. Hobbes's theory of knowledge is an idiosyncratic compound of empirical nominalism and rationalism. He held that concepts, and, thus, generality in thought, are the results of the conventional attachment of terms to empirically perceived resemblances. His theory that ideas are "decaying sense" constitutes a stringently empirical theory of meaning that he applied with robust vigor to scholastic abstractions. But although the raw materials of knowledge are empirical, knowledge itself is not. The propositions of science are necessary truths, ascertained by reason; empirical belief is mere prudence, something men share with animals. Reason is not an awareness of eternal verities; it is a matter of reckoning conducted with conventionally regulated terms. Hobbes, rightly seeing the importance of Galileo's physics, was misled by its deductive form into overidentifying it with Euclid's geometry.

On the basis of his theory of knowledge Hobbes conceived an all-inclusive philosophical system that, beginning with geometry, which he regarded as the abstract science of motion, should proceed to cover the actual motion of bodies or physics and the minute motions of the human body in terms of which men's thoughts and actions are to receive their mechanical explanation. A final extension of the same principles yields the most notorious part of the whole construction, his theory of society. In *De Corpore* (1655) the total program is outlined, and its first two parts, his logic or theory of knowledge and his physics, are expounded. Reality consists of corporeal substance, all of whose properties can be deduced from motion. Immaterial substance is a plain contradiction. A Galilean technique of analysis is invoked to explain the perceived variety of the physical world in terms of the elementary motions discussed in geometry. All causation is efficient.

The most disturbing novelty in Hobbes was the extension of his mechanical materialism to man, carried out in a series of works and most notably summarized in *Leviathan* (1651). Perception and will, the two seemingly proprietary attributes of mankind, are brought within the scope of the theory of motion. Sensation is a physical response to a physical stimulus. The small motions within men that it sets up interact with the vital motions of the body. If this interaction is harmonious, pleasure is experienced; if discordant, pain. Pleasure leads man toward the source of harmony; pain leads him away from the source of discord. The fundamental law of human behavior is self-preservation, the maintenance and protection of vital motion on which continued existence depends. Hobbes saw the mental life of man as a multiplicity of minute motions within the body, of "endeavors" toward or away from the environment as determined by its propitiousness or hostility to self-preservation.

Hobbes's view of man is deterministic as well as materialistic. Furthermore, it is taken by him to imply an egoistic theory of value as well as of behavior. For man considered outside society the sole meaning that "good" can have is "pleasing" or "desired" or, more fundamentally, "self-preservative." But this is an interim position, since man outside society has little chance of preserving himself for long. It is a rational deduction from the fundamental law of self-preservation that we should seek whatever means are necessary to protect ourselves from the dangers created by the self-preservative activities of others. The only sure protection is submission to a common sovereign, remitting to him all our natural liberties of action except that of preserving our lives. Hobbes used the conventional moral terminology of political thought—law, covenant, obligation, right—but in a wholly secular and naturalistic sense. We ought to do what is rationally prudent, not what is autonomously morally binding. His egalitarianism has a characteristic basis. We all have an equally good reason to seek the protection of the sovereign because any man can be killed by any man. Hobbes's bleak secularism was repellent to both parties in the Civil War, to the Royalists because he defended monarchy as useful and not as divinely authorized, to the Parliamentarians because he allowed the rejection of sovereigns on the ground of their impotence rather than of their moral and religious offenses.

The most unattractive of all Hobbes's uncompromising views was his apparent atheism. In his rational society the church is wholly subject to the state and matters of doctrine are to be settled by the sovereign. God is not an immaterial spirit but a large, invisible, corporeal substance. In *Leviathan* Hobbes attacked Christianity in the guise of Roman Catholicism; his defense of the Church of England largely turns on its subordination to the sovereign.

Hobbes was not anxious to please, and his marvelously caustic style enabled him to give the maximum of offense. It is not surprising that his work evoked no support and a violent frenzy of refutation. He conducted an extended controversy with Bishop Bramhall about free will and determinism and a much less successful one with the mathematician John Wallis on the subject of his geometrical idiosyncrasies. His political views, however, produced the most criticism. Little of this is of more than historical interest apart from the *Oceana* (1656) of James Harrington, for most of Hobbes's critics were too preoccupied with the shocking details of his opinions to penetrate to their foundations. Pointing out the dependence of power on property, Harrington reasonably drew attention to the social and economic unreality of Hobbes's theory of power, which in effect admits only naked power at one end and fear of death at the other.

Hobbes's materialism has had little influence in English philosophy; only David Hartley and Joseph Priestley were able to shake themselves free of the Cartesian assumptions of Locke's "way of ideas" sufficiently to adopt something like it. But the empiricism of Locke and Hume owes something to Hobbes's resolutely scientific approach to man as a part of nature, and if Hume was the father, Hobbes was certainly the grandfather, of utilitarianism.

Herbert and the Cambridge Platonists. The most serious and fundamental of more or less contemporary responses to the philosophy of Hobbes is to be found in the work of Henry More and, especially, Ralph Cudworth, the leading theoreticians of the Cambridge Platonist school. In a time of intense religious conflict the Cambridge Platonists argued for tolerance and rationality in matters of religious belief, seeing right conduct as more important than liturgical exactitude. Although of Puritan background for the most part, they deplored enthusiasm. They are the English philosophical equivalents of the Politiques of the French wars of religion. As philosophers strictly so called, their main object was to establish the reality and pre-eminence of spirit against various adversaries, in particular against Hobbes, who would have subjected it to matter, and Descartes, who would have expelled it from the natural world into an autonomous realm of its own.

Herbert of Cherbury. There is a marked strain of Augustinianism to the Cambridge Platonists' underlying theory of knowledge, an acceptance of the mind's capacity to obtain intuitive knowledge of eternal and necessary truths. In this respect they followed the lead of the curious Lord Herbert of Cherbury (1583–1648), who endeavored with comic extravagance and very limited success to live up to the Renaissance ideal of the complete man. In his *De Veritate* (1624) he defined truth in terms of the correspondence between the faculties of the human mind and their proper objects. Distinguishing a great host of faculties, he grouped them under four main heads—outer and inner senses, the discursive or logical faculty, and, his particular contribution, "natural instinct." Natural instinct, in his view, is our capacity for apprehending substantial rather than merely analytic necessary truths. These Stoic common notions are the foundations of our knowledge; without them perception, introspection, and logic can give us little worth having. This conception of rational insight into fundamental principles has a continuing history in subsequent British philosophy. Outliving the particular theses of the Cambridge Platonists, it comes to be the cornerstone of the Scottish philosophers' answer to Hume and is also present in the thought of a long line of ethical rationalists from Cudworth to Richard Price and beyond. In the twentieth century it can be discerned in the generous readiness of philosophers of the school of John Cook Wilson to ascribe self-evidence to large and controversial propositions.

A particular group of common notions assigned by Herbert to natural instinct is that composed of five first principles of natural religion—that God exists, that he should be worshiped, that piety is shown in right conduct, that sin should be repented, and that God will distribute rewards and punishments in an afterlife. This minimal basis of essential religion was to constitute the starting point of deism. Religious belief detached from any particular revelation and thus from any particular church and cult was objectionable to the orthodox. Herbert took universal assent to be the main criterion for discerning the real deliverances of natural instinct, and to show that his religious common notions passed this test, he entered the field of comparative religion in his *De Religione Gentilium* (1663).

Cudworth. Although properly described as latitudinarians, the Cambridge Platonists did not follow Herbert this far. However, they drew on his theory of natural instinct to give body to the slogan of Benjamin Whichcote, their spiritual leader, that reason is the candle of the Lord. Ralph Cudworth (1617–1688) was the most learned, circumspect, and philosophically important member of the school. In his copious *The True Intellectual System of the Universe* (1678) he drew on a wide knowledge of the history of philosophy to confute all possible forms of materialism, whether deliberate, as with Hobbes, or inadvertent, as with Descartes. He insisted that there could be no mechanical explanation or reduction of the immediate fact of consciousness, the central position of all subsequent resistance to the materialism of Hobbes. Mind, he held, is "senior to the world" both in the sense that there must be an infinite self-existent spirit and that intellectual, nonempirical concepts must play a part in our perception of things. Mind is essentially active. There must be a spiritual mover behind the evident motion of the natural world, and on the human level knowledge is not passive sensation; in knowledge mind is actively involved with its environment. In *Eternal and Immutable Morality* (1731) the theory of first principles is applied to morals. Cudworth endorsed the Augustinian argument from eternal truths to God, but his position was by no means entirely backward-looking. He accepted atomism as an account of the physical world and, indeed, the main lines of the new mechanical philosophy, but he was anxious to circumscribe its claims. He firmly denied the associated view that the physical world is causally self-contained. Fastening on the classical Greek idea that motion indicates life and mind, Cudworth concluded, with the Greeks, that since the most material-seeming bodies move, they are not wholly nonmental and on this ground resisted the Cartesian view that the worlds of matter and spirit are strictly divided from each other.

Henry More. Henry More (1614–1687) had a more enthusiastic and mercurial mind; his love of the new and the strange was expressed in a large accumulation of somewhat precipitate works. An early admiration for Descartes gave way to hostility. The Cartesian doctrine he took most exception to was "nullibism," the view that spirit is not extended or in space. Impenetrability and divisibility, not extension, constitute the essence of matter. For spirit, which is to say God's activity, is present everywhere. More resurrected the Augustinian concept of seminal principles in his theory of "plastic nature." Cudworth had embraced the concept of seminal principles to account for the self-determining character of organic life. In More it came to take the form of the theory of a world soul or anima mundi. His detachment of the concept of space from the concept of matter led him to consider space as more or less spiritual in nature, as, indeed, an attribute of God. This idea was taken up by Newton in his contention that space is God's sensorium, a contention criticized by Leibniz in his correspondence with Samuel Clarke. More's strong propensity to find the workings of spirit throughout the natural world induced him to take a rather credulous interest in such occult topics as ghostly apparitions and witchcraft.

Glanvill. Joseph Glanvill (1636–1680), a highly eclectic thinker of broadly similar tendency, devoted his *Sadducismus Triumphatus* (1681) to a defense of the belief in witches. In his *Vanity of Dogmatizing* (1661) he drew on all the new philosophical initiatives of the age to attack the still official academic scholasticism. But his elevation of Democritus and Epicurus above Aristotle by no means led him into materialism. He derived from More a belief in the soul's pre-existence, and it has been reasonably said of him that he recommended skepticism only with regard to traditional thought. More's and Glanvill's interest in the paranormal is the first appearance of a characteristic peculiarity of English philosophy, recurring in the nineteenth century with Sidgwick and in the twentieth century with Broad and Price, all of whom were interested in psychical research.

Moralists. The ethical rationalism of the Cambridge Platonists was expressed in the *Light of Nature* (1652) of Nathanael Culverwel (c. 1618–c. 1651), who asserted the harmony of reason and faith and the accessibility of moral truth to the natural light of reason. In the *De Legibus Naturae* (1672) of Richard Cumberland (1631–1718) Cudworth's style of argument against Hobbes was rejected as altogether too facile. Cumberland anticipated the utilitarians in taking the common good as the supreme moral end and sought to justify it, in something like the manner of Bishop Butler, by a teleological consideration of the place of man in the world.

EMPIRICISM FROM LOCKE TO MILL

We have reached a point in time when all the raw materials exist for the construction of the most pervasively influential of all English philosophies, the empiricism of Locke and his successors. Bacon's inductive conception of natural knowledge, Descartes's dualism, Hobbes's naturalistic view of man—each made positive contributions to Locke's system of ideas; the Cambridge Platonists would seem to be the object of Locke's preliminary assault on innate knowledge. But Locke's repudiation of rationalism, as will appear, is less thoroughgoing than he intended it to be.

Locke. John Locke (1632–1704) is at once the most representative and the most influential of English philosophers. Every familiar generalization about English philosophy is confirmed by his work—its distrust of rational insight by his critique of innate knowledge; its nominalism by his doctrine that generality is not encountered by the mind but is, rather, a by-product of its abstracting power; its empiricism by his tracing all ideas and knowledge to sensation and reflection; its critical attitude to language by his account of nominal essence; its pedestrian fidelity to common sense by his often inconsistent rejection of such counterintuitive Cartesian principles as that the mind is always active or that there is no such thing as empty space. Locke's *Essay Concerning Human Understanding* (1690) soon became the main instrument of academic instruction in England and has retained this pre-eminence ever since, except during the Hegelian interlude at the end of the nineteenth century. Imported into France by Voltaire, Locke's ideas became, together with Newton's picture of the physical world, the theoretical foundation of the thinking of the Enlightenment. Locke was quite sincere in describing himself as "an under-labourer to the incomparable Mr. Newton," and the relationship thus exemplified between philosophy and science has persisted throughout most of the subsequent course of philosophy in Britain.

Locke owed a great deal—much more than he recognized—to Descartes, but the main burden of the *Essay* is to reject a polemically simplified version of rationalism and to provide as a positive alternative to it, first, an account of the workings of the mind which allows it only native capacities, not native knowledge, and, second, an account of natural ideas or knowledge which makes a firm distinction in principle between mathematics and physics. Locke's attack on rationalism has no clearly identified target; it is muddled in execution, and its apparent lessons—for example, that there are no innate ideas—were frequently ignored by him. But he adhered firmly to the main point. Intuition and demonstration, the mind's capacities for the acquisition of a pirori and necessary truth, are kept strictly distinct from the more or less conjectural knowledge of "real existence," which constitutes natural science. Ostensibly refuting the view that there are innate ideas, Locke argued against the possibility of literally innate knowledge, giving special attention to the refutation of Herbert of Cherbury's criterion of universal consent.

There are three significant limitations to Locke's empiricism. He insisted that in the concept of substance we have an idea that is essential to knowledge and yet is not derived from, but brought to, experience. Second, he admitted that there is much a priori knowledge—intuitive knowledge of one's own existence, demonstrative knowledge of mathematical and moral truth. Finally, his account of perception requires the admission of two substantial nonempirical principles, that everything, in particular sensation, is caused and that some of our sensations resemble their causes.

Ideas are the raw material of all thought and knowledge, and all ideas (except substance) are acquired from sensation and reflection, or inner sense. The complex fabric of knowledge is assembled from these elementary empirical data by the combining activity of the mind. We combine simple, qualitative ideas into complex ideas of objects and relations. We run similar ideas together to form abstract ideas that serve as the inner criterion for the application of the words with which they are conventionally associated. Locke took an uncritical attitude toward the concept of causation, which he interpreted as a more or less perceptible property, a "power," of the things related by it. The crucial element of his philosophy is his representative theory of perception. Sensation yields us simple ideas of many kinds. These are all caused by qualities of objects, and in the case of primary, measurable qualities there is a resemblance between the ideas and the qualities that cause them. Ideas of secondary qualities like color and texture are caused by the primary qualities of the minute parts of external things. We find qualities going together in persistent groups, and this leads us to conceive a substantial support, a substratum, for these assemblages. It follows that the physical world consists of material substrata endowed only with primary qualities, gross and minute. Only the vocabulary of Newtonian physics is literally descriptive of the external world. Locke's sense of the gap between our empirical data and our beliefs about physical things led him to admit that these beliefs are probable opinions rather than knowledge strictly so called.

In Locke's theory of the mind there are three distinct lines of thought at work. First, there is the Cartesian view that we have a direct and intuitive awareness of our own existence. Second, there is the view that the mind as something persisting through time must be conceived as a sequence of ideas related by memory, the concept of mental substance being wholly inadequate for the explanation of personal identity. Finally, Locke made the parenthetical suggestion that God might have annexed consciousness to a material substance, a somewhat scandalous supposition that was taken up by Priestley and others.

Locke's theory of knowledge established the agenda for philosophy in Britain for a century and a half, during which external influences from Europe were of negligible importance. Leibniz' great critique of the *Essay* had little effect, and it was not until the closing decades of the nineteenth century that Kant and Hegel secured the attention of philosophers rather than imaginative writers. The most immediately influential aspects of Locke's thought were in the fields of politics and theology, to which his general principles were applied in *Two Treatises of Civil Government* (1690) and *The Reasonableness of Christianity* (1695). Locke's political theory was an answer to Hobbes, even if the overt adversary was Robert Filmer, whose absolutism was based on divine right rather than self-preservation and whose not unreasonable analogy between the monarch and the father of a family was smothered by an antiquated legalism. But although Locke insisted against Hobbes that a justified government must be limited in its authority, that it must earn its title to rule by the protection of a large range of individual natural rights, he accepted the whole formal apparatus of Hobbes's political doctrine. For him, as for Hobbes, the state is a means to an end, set up purposively by men to remedy the inconveniences of the state of nature, its authority being contingent upon the adequacy of its performance of its intended function.

If Locke's conception of natural rights is rationalistic, in line with his theory that moral truths are demonstrable, his notion of the state is earth-bound and pragmatic. The neglect of economic factors noted in Hobbes by Harrington was remedied in Locke by his derivation of the right of property from the mixture of a man's labor with land and other natural goods. Locke's theory of government became the theoretical basis of the Whig party's domination of eighteenth-century political life as the most articulate expression of the "principles of 1689" celebrated in Thomas Macaulay's *History of England.* Although Locke was an individualist in his hostility to the extension of state power, he was neither a radical nor a democrat. He combined a strong attachment to personal freedom with the view that those should have the most say in government who have the most to lose from its operations.

Locke's religious ideas were equally timely though their effect was different. His politics seemed to make political speculation superfluous until the French Revolution and the controversy between Edmund Burke and the radicals. But his theology had a large share in bringing about the deist movement. Like the deists Locke was persuaded that there is a God, the indispensable cause of the perfections to be found in the world, and he shared both their view that morality is the essence of religion and that attention should be diverted from the mysteries that produce dogmatic controversy. There can be no doubt of the sincerity of Locke's Christian faith although he reduced its content to the belief in Christ's divinity and an earnest acceptance of Christian morality. In particular, he anticipated the deists in holding that the revelations of the incarnate God are not indispensable for the acquisition of correct moral and religious opinions. Those who lived before Christ were not in complete darkness. The purpose of revelation is not the diffusion of new truths but the corroboration of old ones.

Deists. The deists were, for the most part, modestly equipped thinkers of much less capacity and distinction than their chief adversaries. But despite local defeats they came out of the conflict better than the orthodox did. Some of their opponents, such as Clarke, really shared all their main assumptions, and they had the advantage of moving in the direction of the general tendency of their age; they were only doing for religion, it could be said, what Newton had done for physical nature and Locke for the human mind. The Newtonian picure of the world was a most unfavorable background for the traditional idea of revelation. In Newton's vast and broadly intelligible universe there was no place for a mysterious tribal deity, arbitrary in his actions and revealing himself only for a short time to a small, geographically confined group of men.

Toland. The *Christianity Not Mysterious* of John Toland (1670–1722), the first important strictly deist work, appeared in Locke's lifetime (1696) and was disowned by him, but there is a clear correspondence between its teaching and Locke's. Toland's main point is that revelation must be clearly intelligible and that it must rest on the support of rational principles of natural religion like those propounded by Herbert of Cherbury. Historical Christianity, in Toland's view, is heavily encrusted with nonsense. He cited the dogma of transubstantiation as an example, but his readers took him to have the Trinity in mind. In fact, Toland was a pantheist, so Locke's disquiet was justified.

Tindal. The most solid and influential of deist writings was the *Christianity as Old as the Creation* (1730) of Matthew Tindal (c. 1656–1733). Since God is good, Tindal argued, he cannot have concealed his essential message from those who lived before Christ. It follows that the vital content of revelation is accessible to all through natural reason and, therefore, that revelation is superfluous. Human nature is always the same, and so is God's law for man. It is in the moral demands of this law that the essence of religion is contained. Tindal rejected the orthodox idea that the Fall of Adam had made revelation necessary, holding that men had not perceptibly improved since Christ's incarnation. The real corruption was to be found in what the positive religion of the church had done to the natural religion of reason. Tindal is typical of his age in his choice of the Chinese as symbols of dispassionate reasonableness and in his hostility to the dramatic emotionalism and ascetical excesses of the Jews.

Wollaston. William Wollaston (1660–1724) took a position of extreme intellectualism in his *Religion of Nature Delineated* (1722). He maintained that all sin is of the nature of lying and deduced the immortality of the soul from the fact of human suffering on earth and the principle that God is perfectly and exactly just.

Collins. While most Deists addressed themselves to issues of general principle, Anthony Collins (1676–1729), in a number of works, considered the more concrete evidences of Christianity. A none too well contrived assault on the supposed fulfillment in the New Testament of Old Testament prophecies brought down on his head the elaborate scholarly wrath of the great classicist Richard Bentley. Collins was the leading representative of a numerous array of more or less amateur Biblical investigators.

Bolingbroke. Henry St. John, Viscount Bolingbroke (1678–1751), employed his enforced retirement from politics with speculations of a more or less deistic character. His ideas figure in Pope's *Essay on Man* (1733), and the posthumous publication of Bolingbroke's philosophical works in 1754 drew a memorable observation from Dr. Johnson, who described him as "a scoundrel, for charging a blunderbuss against religion and morality; [and] a coward, because he had not resolution to fire it off himself, but left half a crown to a beggarly Scotchman [the publisher], to draw the trigger after his death!" Bolingbroke drew on Bacon and Locke to attack the "metaphysical delirium" of Plato, Cudworth, and Clarke, arguing that although we can infer the existence of a designer-God from the fact that the world had a beginning, we can know nothing of his moral attributes. In his view the sole office of revealed religion is to serve as a device for pacifying the lower orders.

Opponents of deism. In his will Robert Boyle endowed a lectureship for the defense of Christianity against "notorious infidels," which led to the composition of some of the more notable attacks on deism. There is some justice in the remark of the inevitably partial Collins that "nobody doubted the existence of the Deity until the Boyle lecturers undertook to prove it."

Bentley. The first Boyle lecturer was Richard Bentley (1662–1742), who in his *Matter and Motion Cannot Think* (1692) supported Boyle's favorite argument from design with considerations drawn from the structure of organisms and of the Newtonian heavens. Bentley had a taste for flimsy physical speculations. He exploited Newton's unwillingness to offer a hypothesis to explain gravitation by asserting that since gravity is immaterial, it must be interpreted as a direct expression of God's will for the natural order. He also discerned divine intervention in the irregular distribution of matter, holding that if materialism were true, matter would be concentrated in a single lump or else evenly diffused throughout space.

Clarke. The most admired and learned defender of orthodoxy was Samuel Clarke (1675–1729). In his first Boyle lectures, *Demonstration of the Being and Attributes of God* (1704), he set out the foundations of religious belief in a rigorously deductive manner that won wide applause. He argued that there must be an eternal and self-existent being on the ground that an infinite series of dependent beings is impossible. Since this being is necessary, it cannot be material, for the nonexistence of matter, total or partial, is never contradictory. Among the provable attributes of the self-existent being are unity, infinity, intelligence, freedom, and goodness. Man's freedom is safeguarded from obliteration, a familiar result of this kind of abstract reasoning, by the verbal maneuver of describing man as a dependent first cause. One of Clarke's novel conceptions is that space and time are properties of God and therefore real, the thesis that led to his illuminating controversy with Leibniz, who maintained that space is merely a system of relations and therefore ideal, or "semi-mental."

In his second series of Boyle lectures (1705), Clarke put forward a correspondingly rationalistic ethical theory in which moral truth is conceived in close analogy to mathematics as concerned with the eternal and intuitable fitnesses of actions to situations. Moreover, morality is prior to God's will; an action is not good because God commands it but is commanded by God because it is good. So far, Clarke's ideas are entirely harmonious with those of the deists even if they are developed in a more academic and sophisticated way. His heavy commitment to rationalism left little room for revelation in his scheme of things. He saw it, in fact, as having only the secondary function of making moral truth clear to corrupt men and of bringing the sanctions of morality firmly before their attention. It is also required to give us assurance of immortality.

Warburton. The most copious and energetic opponent of deism was William Warburton (1698–1779), whose oxlike imperceptiveness led him to suppose that invective is a sufficient answer to the critics of orthodoxy. That his blustering confidence was an anachronism is shown by the anxious caution and tentativeness of his great contemporary Joseph Butler.

Butler. In his labored *Analogy of Religion* (1736), Joseph Butler (1692–1752) could return no better answer to deism than *tu quoque.* Certainly, there are difficulties and mysteries for revealed religion to contend with, but there also are for natural religion. Against the deists' cheerful inferences from the orderliness of nature, Butler, with a Johnsonian sense of the darker aspects of the world and human life, drew attention to the imperfections of the natural order. Although he accepted the conventional demonstrations of God's existence, he held that we must rely on a great accumulation of probabilities to understand God's purposes and activities in the world. There is injustice on earth, but, broadly speaking, the natural outcome of virtue is happiness and of vice suffering. No natural fact can exclude the immortality of the soul and a just rectification of the balance in an afterlife. Butler's apologetic might disconcert the adherents of natural religion, but it was little calculated to discourage complete unbelief.

Locke's critics. Not all of the philosophers of Locke's age were as preoccupied with theology as the deists and their opponents. Richard Burthogge (c. 1638–c. 1694) in his *Essay on Reason and the Nature of Spirits* (1694) countered Locke with a version of Neoplatonic rationalism. Peter Browne (1665–1735) also criticized Locke in his *Procedure, Extent and Limits of the Human Understanding* (1728), seeking to defend religion by emphasizing the confinement of the human mind to the empirical order unless it has the assistance of revelation. Browne held that reason can operate only on the materials of sense and cannot pronounce on supernatural matters.

A less obviously edifying intention lies behind *An Essay Towards the Theory of the Ideal and Intelligible World* (1701–1704) of John Norris (1657–1711), another opponent of Locke. Norris was the principal English adherent of Malebranche and against Locke's account of perception as a response to external nature affirmed Malebranche's doctrine that "we see all things in God," that the ideas in our minds are the direct results of divine activity. Norris was an acute critic of Toland and emphasized the distinction between things above reason and things contrary to reason.

The same kind of idealist theory is to be found in the *Clavis Universalis* (1713) of Arthur Collier (1680–1732), who argued, in a manner that anticipates Kant, for the Berkeleian thesis that the notion of an external world as the cause of our ideas is superfluous. Collier attempted to demolish the hypothesis of an external world by showing that it is strictly self-contradictory, deriving from it antinomies of infinite and finite extent, duration and divisibility.

Berkeley. The most brilliant and historically influential criticism of the materialistic element in the philosophy of Locke was one that started from Locke's own premises, that of George Berkeley (1685–1753). Berkeley agreed with Locke that the mind's only objects are its own ideas, but where Locke had smuggled in this presupposition under cover of his definition of the word "idea," Berkeley gave a number of excellent arguments for it. He then powerfully criticized the fragile reasoning that turns on primary qualities and material substance by whose aid Locke had endeavored to establish contact for the mind with anything outside it. No perceptible feature of our ideas can justify the inference that there is something unperceived that resembles them, nor can unperceived matter be the cause of our ideas. Matter is by nature "inert"; its lack of active efficacy is just what distinguishes it from mind.

Berkeley was, however, a causal theorist of perception. Our ideas of sensation must have a cause, and this we can infer, by way of a profoundly questionable analogy with our own activities of imagination, to be a mind which is other than our own, that of God. God is not only the cause of our sensations; he is also both cause and perceiver of those sensible ideas (making up the unperceived parts of what we usually call "objects") not present to any finite mind but which we believe exist nevertheless on the grounds of continuity.

For Berkeley it was inconceivable that there should be ideas that are not present to some mind or spirit. It was equally inconceivable that minds are not always occupied with ideas; the two sides of the relation of perception are essential to each other.

If Berkeley's introduction of God is boldly unplausible, his theory of mind is furtive and unconvincing. He admitted that we can have no idea of spirit but allowed that we have something called a notion of it, a retreat from his initial empiricism which prompts the question of why we should not have a notion of matter. While maintaining that unperceived existence is a self-contradictory idea, he asserted that mind in general and God in particular exist and are unperceivable.

Berkeley's positive theological metaphysics is a flimsy tour de force. His empiricist first principles and his negative criticisms of Locke's representative theory of knowledge are the aspects of his philosophy that have had an influence on the history of thought. For him a material thing is an orderly system of ideas of sensation. Ordinary material objects and the theoretical entities of science are not substantive things but intellectual constructions. Furthermore, the causal relationships studied by science are merely regular correlations; true causal efficacy is only to be found in the relation between a mind and the ideas it produces. Berkeley used his empiricist principles for the detection and analysis of abstractions. Their application is partial, however. They are brought in full force against the abstractions of physical science but are withheld from God and the soul, the abstractions of theology. Berkeley maintained that the concepts of physics are devices for summarizing and predicting the course of sensation and thus referred to patterns of sensation, not to substantive things. He degraded matter and force to protect God and the soul. But Hume applying Berkeley's principles in a less partial spirit, treated all abstractions in the same way and turned the destructive instrument Berkeley had forged on the things it had been designed to protect.

In the introduction to his chief work, *A Treatise Concerning the Principles of Human Knowledge* (1710), Berkeley set out a somewhat rhetorical criticism of Locke's theory of abstract ideas, arguing that there can be no such things as the indeterminate mental constructions which constituted conceptual thinking for Locke. The apparent point of this theory was to provide a framework for the subsequent rejection of matter, but in fact it is not the generality of the concept of matter that he subsequently argued against but its inapplicability to what is observed. Here, as in his theory of perception, Berkeley was closer to Locke than he imagined. Just as he rejected one causal account of perception only to accept another, rather than rejecting causal theories of perception altogether, so he had to introduce something like Locke's activity of abstracting to explain how the particular, wholly determinate ideas with which we think stand for some particular things that resemble them rather than for other things.

Berkeley was regarded by his contemporaries as an ingenious propounder of paradoxes. The "immaterialist" hypothesis attracted attention but led to the exclusion of the theology it was designed to support and evoked a great deal of piteously uncomprehending refutation, of which Dr. Johnson's is typical. Later philosophers, if they have understood Berkeley better, have been equally selective in their approach to his ideas. His own protestations that he was simply vindicating common sense and disentangling it from Locke's accretions of metaphysical materialism went unregarded. By the mid-nineteenth century the two sides of his philosophy had come to stand in direct opposition to each other. J. S. Mill's account of material objects as permanent possibilities of sensation directly descended from Berkeley, as did the central thesis of T. H. Green, Mill's most categorical opponent, that nature cannot be intelligibly conceived except as the object of an eternal consciousness.

Moral philosophers. In the century that followed Berkeley's first writings metaphysical speculation in the grand manner was completely abandoned in England. Until Coleridge came to respond in his intellectually light-fingered way to the speculations of Schelling, the sole exponent of this type of philosophy was the curious and isolated figure of James Burnett, Lord Monboddo (1714–1799). Best known for his view that the human race had evolved from monkeys, as witnessed by the appearance and capacities of the orangutan, Monboddo sought to revive in his *Antient Metaphysics* (1779) the whole range of classic metaphysical notions, such as the anima mundi and the various souls of Aristotle.

Man himself, rather than the universe, came, appropriately, to occupy the attention of thinkers of the politest century in English history. The ultimate stimulus to these thinkers was Hobbes, in particular his egoistic account of human motives, just as Hobbes's apparent atheism had led to the revival of philosophical theology by the Cambridge Platonists.

Shaftesbury. The tone and direction of the tradition of largely autonomous moral inquiry was set by Lord Shaftesbury (1671–1713), the grandson of Locke's patron. In his *Characteristics of Men, Manners, Opinions, Times* (1711) he proclaimed, in a style of relaxed and fulsome gentility, the essentially social nature of man while disdaining the emotional and intellectual excesses of enthusiasm. Shaftesbury took an optimistic view of human nature, which he saw as containing, though not exhausted by, social impulses of benevolence. Following classical models, he defined the proper end of conduct as the development of natural potentialities, but his defense of virtuosity lacked Renaissance strenuousness. He contended that men have a moral sense, which is more a matter of taste and feeling than of intellectual insight, by means of which they respond to the beauties and deformities of human character. He held that individual happiness and fulfillment are best achieved by the establishment of a proper balance between private and social impulses.

Hutcheson. Shaftesbury's somewhat desultory moral aestheticism was expounded in a more systematic form by Francis Hutcheson (1694–1746) in his *System of Moral Philosophy* (1755) and other works. For Hutcheson virtue and benevolence are one and the same, whereas he regarded self-love as morally indifferent. The utilitarian formula of the greatest good of the greatest number makes an incidental appearance in his writings, but perhaps his chief significance is to be found in the effect his doctrine of instinctive or natural beliefs—that there are certain things we cannot help believing and that are therefore senseless to doubt—had on Hume.

Butler. The notion of virtue as the outcome of a correct balance of the elements of human nature reappears in the rather different context of the ethics of Joseph Butler (*Fifteen Sermons*, 1726). While agreeing with Shaftesbury and Hutcheson that virtue is natural to man and while accepting and developing their critique of Hobbes's egoism by pointing out that neither cool and calculating self-love nor particular passions are either selfish or, in general, compatible, he rejected the Hutchesonian equation of virtue with benevolence, on the ground that we can have no reliable knowledge of the consequences of our acts, and accorded supreme moral authority to the conscience, which he conceived as both a source of intuitive moral knowledge and the basic spring of moral action. In Butler's ethics all the competing doctrines of the age are held in an uneasy suspension.

Mandeville. A lone voice spoke in the accents of Hobbes, that of Bernard Mandeville (1670–1733). In his *The Fable of the Bees* (Part I, 1714; Part II, 1729) he argued that the welfare of society resulted from individual selfishnesses, starkly presenting in moral terms the fundamental thesis of classical economics that the most satisfying results for all would follow from each man's rational pursuit of his own advantage. Without the stimulus of self-interest, Mandeville held, society will stagnate; luxury requires effort, and effort can be evoked only by selfishness or, as he sentimentally put it, "vice."

Smith. Adam Smith (1723–1790) put Mandeville's notion, divested of its satirical trappings, to work in developing the first systematic presentation of economic theory. But having the sense to see that not all the values of life are monetary, Smith explained in the ethical doctrine of his *Theory of Moral Sentiments* (1759) our capacity to take a disinterested view of our own and others' conduct by the presence of sympathy as an original constituent in human nature. Useful consequences confirm our sympathetic judgments of approval but are not their ultimate basis. Considering the problem of moral judgment by a man of his own actions, Smith advanced the criterion of the impartial spectator to characterize the distinctive standpoint of morality.

Price. The kind of ethical rationalism supported by Clarke was defended in an age of moralities of sentiment and benevolence by Richard Price (1723–1791). In his *Review of the Principal Questions in Morals* (1757) he argued that "morality is a branch of necessary truth." We are endowed with a capacity for the intellectual intuition of self-evident moral principles. On this simpler foundation he built up a theory which, like Kant's, sees value as intrinsic to actions and independent of their consequences, and he insisted that the morality of an agent is determined by whether his action is motivated by a sense of the rightness of his acts.

Burke. Price, although an ethical rationalist, was a political radical and was a victim of the wrath of the conservative traditionalist Edmund Burke (1729–1797). In a large number of eloquent discussions of current political issues Burke more or less inadvertently laid the foundations of modern conservative theory.

In a way Burke is the Berkeley of politics. His distrust of abstract political speculation had an empiricist basis. Political knowledge and skill can be acquired only by experience, not by reflection. A society's traditional institutions are a vast, interlocking structure brought into being by a great number of small adjustments made over a long period of time by politically experienced men. It is too dense and complex an affair to be reduced to a tidy mental diagram. But superimposed on this essentially skeptical foundation is a more or less mystical reverence for the established results of the historical process which Burke saw as revealing divine guidance.

The empiricism of Burke's aesthetics in his treatise *On the Sublime and Beautiful* (1756) is more blunt and pedestrian. He derived the two kinds of aesthetic interest by association from the self-regarding and social or affectionate impulses respectively. The sublime is that which by its size and roughness inspires a terror in use that is pleasant because fictitious; the beautiful is that which attracts a more or less sexual affection by reason of its smallness, smoothness, and delicacy.

Hume. David Hume (1711–1776) was a part, and to some extent a product, of the tradition of ethical inquiry, as well as the continuer of the epistemological reflections of Locke and Berkeley. He described his masterpiece, the *Treatise of Human Nature* (1739–1740) as an attempt to introduce the experimental method of reasoning into moral subjects, and he was clearly animated by the characteristic amibition of his age to do for human nature what Newton had done for the physical world, to explain it by a single, all-inclusive system of laws. It has been suggested that the real point of his skepticism about knowledge of the external world was to show that knowledge of man is no more ill-founded than knowledge of nature. He certainly maintained that the very general and dialectical kind of psychology that he practiced was the indispensable foundation of all other disciplines. His skepticism has always puzzled his readers. At times he suggested that philosophy shows all our claims to knowledge to be unfounded, the sole remedy he could propose for this depressing result being the frivolous one of carelessness and inattention. On the other hand, his description of our instinctive propensity to ascribe persistent identity and causal connection to things as "natural belief," as well as his distinction between the fixed and regular principles of science and the wavering and arbitrary principles of superstition, suggests a less despondent view. Ultimate principles cannot be rationally demonstrated; however, they can be psychologically explained, and the fact that they are universal and compulsive is all the justification they require.

Hume formulated empiricism in terms of a distinction between impressions, which are given in sensation and reflection, and ideas, the less vivid copies of previous impressions. All simple and unanalyzable ideas must be derived from previous impressions. He developed Berkeley's rejection of abstract ideas, accounting for our understanding of general terms by way of their association with a disposition to bring before the mind any one of a collection of similar ideas. We can have certain knowledge of the relations of ideas, as in geometry, and of the immediate character of our impressions, but most of our beliefs about matters of fact go beyond our current impressions to what is causally connected to them or identical with them but existing at another time.

Causation is the subject of the most extended application of Hume's methods. It is, he claimed, a complex idea. Two of its elements, priority and contiguity, are accessible to the senses, but we can have no sense impression of the third, necessary connection. Hume concluded that it is an internal impression of reflection from which this elusive idea is derived, a kind of compulsive expectation which leads us from a present impression to the idea of its usual associate. If in our experience two kinds of event have constantly accompanied each other, association will lead us to expect an event of the second kind when we have an impression of an event of the first kind. There can be no proof of the proposition that every event has a cause, though Hume thought it true as a matter of fact, and there is no logical necessity in any particular relation between a cause and its effect. There is never a contradiction in conceiving one to occur without the other.

Our conceptions of material bodies and of minds both involve the dubious notion of identity through time. What we perceive is in fact discontinuous and dependent on the fact of our perceiving it, yet we ascribe continued and distinct existence to the objects of perception. Hume explained this unjustifiable but irresistible maneuver as the outcome of the constancy and coherence of our impressions. Using the imagination to fill in any gaps in the sequence of impressions, we "feign" an identity between what is actually distinct because it is easy and tidy. Hume had more trouble with the idea of the self. He insisted that we have no impression of it but only of particular mental states. He rejected Locke's account of personal identity, as Butler had done, on grounds of circularity, but he was no better pleased with his own proposal of resemblance and causation as the relations that unite a plurality of mental states into a continuous personality.

The general formula of Hume's theory of human nature is to trace the production of complex mental constructions from their elementary components by the undirected workings of custom and association. Applied to the understanding, this technique explains the ideas of cause, body, and mind; applied to the passions, it explains the complexities of our desires and emotions. Hume's ethics consist primarily in the application of this technique to the sentiment of moral approval, which he defined as the favorable emotion evoked by the disinterested contemplation of actions. The actions that produce the favorable emotion are those which are useful or agreeable to the agent or to others, and such actions please the contemplator because of sympathy.

It is a short step from Hume's view that general utility is the cause of approval to the position of utilitarianism proper that general utility is its justification. In effect, Hume took this step in his account of the artificial virtues of promise keeping, respect for property, and obedience to government. Toward these, unlike the natural virtue of benevolence, we have no instinctive promptings; we have to reason causally to see that they are necessary means to the end of general utility that we desire. Hume understood his theory of artificial virtue to be a refutation of the contract theory since it puts promise keeping and political obedience on the same level. Despite his doubts about the concept of causation, Hume was convinced of the empirical truth of the causal principle, especially as applied to human actions, arguing that moral praise and blame of conduct presuppose rather than exclude their causal determination.

Hume did not exert himself to conceal his religious skepticism, though he had the restraint to leave his fatal analysis of the Argument from Design, the *Dialogues Concerning Natural Religion* (1779), to be published after his death. In his notorious essay on miracles he argued that testimony of events counter to natural law can hardly be strong enough to upset the laws in question, especially since the lawfulness of nature is assumed in accepting some present record as testimony in the first place. Hume also treated the phenomenon of religion comparatively, in his essay the *Natural History of Religion* (1755), arguing that its earliest form was polytheistic and that it was inspired by fears and hopes directed toward nature.

For all his hostility to religion, Hume was not in the least a materialist. As much an infidel as Hobbes, he completely reversed Hobbes's view of the reducibility of mind to body. However, the two English philosophers of Hume's time who were materialists, Hartley and Priestley, were both enthusiastically devout religious believers.

Hartley. David Hartley (1705–1757) in his *Observations on Man* (1749) carried out an associationist investigation of the mind that was much more detailed and systematic than Hume's since its purpose was more straightforwardly descriptive. From some remarks of Newton he derived the hypothesis that every mental event is accompanied by vibrations in the brain and nervous system, and he believed that the associative workings of the mind could be related to corresponding processes in the mind's physical basis. But he maintained the distinction between mind and brain, even if he regarded the brain as cause and mind as effect. Hartley was a resolute determinist and sought to continue Locke's attack on innate ideas by showing that the individual's moral impulses are not instinctive but acquired through the mechanism of association.

Priestley. Joseph Priestley (1733–1804) abandoned Hartley's reserve and firmly asserted that there is no immaterial substance underlying thought, which he saw as an activity of the brain. At the same time he somewhat qualified the bruteness of matter, in the light of the speculations of Boscovich, by contending that it is neither inert nor impenetrable, its apparent impenetrability being attributable to repellent forces exerted by it. To combine the materialism of his *Disquisitions on Matter and Spirit* (1777) with his lively religious faith, he had to give the doctrine of the resurrection of the body an extremely literal interpretation. A determinist, he carefully dissociated his position from the fatalism of the followers of Calvin. With regard to the institutions of society, Priestley was a notably humane liberal. He regarded human happiness as the measure of value and the institution of government as the servant of public welfare. He opposed state education as a danger to liberty.

Tucker and Godwin. Abraham Tucker (1705–1774) in his extensive *Light of Nature Pursued* (1768–1778) continued Hartley's interests, sharing his view that altruism is not instinctive. He developed a more or less utilitarian ethics in which pleasures are seen as only quantitatively distinguishable.

Priestley's moral and social doctrines were carried further, without Priestley's humanity, in the *Enquiry Concerning the Principles of Political Justice* (1793) of William Godwin (1756–1836). Godwin was an anarchist who regarded all institutions as corrupting, property and marriage as much as government. He carried the environmental views of Hartley to an extreme, holding that men's characters and capacities are wholly acquired, and called for an unearthly disinterestedness, recognizing no prior responsibilities of affection, in morals.

Paley. William Paley (1743–1805) was the last philosopher of an epoch in the sense that he cheerfully carried on with a natural religion based on the Argument from Design long after Hume had written. It was not necessary to agree with Hume, but he should have been taken into account. Paley in his *View of the Evidences of Christianity* (1794) and *Natural Theology* (1802) emphasized anatomy rather than the order of the heavens as a proof of God's existence. Paley's perfect lucidity of exposition was combined with, and no doubt partly caused by, his complete confidence in the sufficiency of his mechanical argumentation as a support for the essentials of religious faith. His procedure was not one to conceal a certain crudity of mind, as in his ethical theory, which he memorably summarized in the formula "Virtue is doing good to mankind, in obedience to the will of God, and for the sake of everlasting happiness." Paley's combination of exemplary clarity with a wholly respectable point of view made his work suitable for teaching purposes. However, the philosophers who were to dominate the first half of the nineteenth century were either answering Hume, like Reid and the Scottish school of common sense, or applying his principles in new fields, like the utilitarians.

THE NINETEENTH CENTURY

Scottish school of common sense. The Scottish philosophers have had to pay for the respectable applause they received for attacking Hume by undergoing almost total neglect since Hamilton was fatally examined by Mill in 1865. Yet in the century after the publication of Reid's *Inquiry* in 1764 their moderate, reasonable, and readily intelligible position became the official academic philosophy in Britain and the United States and exercised thanks to Victor Cousin, a considerable influence in France. It is desirable to distinguish Reid and his direct followers, who had, and were equipped to have, a serious interest in philosophy, from more or less scurrilous pamphleteers of the stamp of James Beattie (1735–1803), who earned a royal pension and other rewards from his assault on Hume in the *Essay on Truth* (1770). The confusion stems, perhaps, from the fact that Kant, who knew no more of the common-sense school than what he found in an answer by Priestley to Hume's early critics, regarded it as having missed the point of Hume's philosophy.

Reid. Thomas Reid (1710–1796) treated Hume as an important philosopher, not a dangerous infidel. In his *Inquiry into the Human Mind on the Principles of Common Sense* (1764) he praised Hume for clear-sightedly arriving at the skeptical *reductio ad absurdum* of Locke's way of ideas. Agreeing with Hume's criticisms of his predecessors but finding his conclusions incredible, Reid argued that the first principle of empiricism, that ideas are the immediate objects of perception, must be false. He distinguished between the perception of external things and the mere having of sensations and criticized Locke for his veiled assumption that the mind can only operate where it, or, rather, where the body of its possessor, is. But Reid's direct realism is somewhat tentative. His view that sensations give rise to the perception of external things by "suggestion" is too close to Locke's position for comfort. Perception, Reid held, involves judgment and relates to objects; it is not a simple apprehension of ideas in the perceiver's mind. His other main thesis was directed against Hume's interpretation of the generally accepted principles of explanation, especially those of causation and identity, as expressions of passive habits of imaginative supplementation. He asserted that there are many self-evident principles, much more firmly based than any arguments that might be invoked to cast doubt upon them, such as that qualities must inhere in substance, that every event has a cause, and that the senses, memory, and induction are generally reliable.

Stewart. Dugald Stewart (1753–1828), the most admired philosophical teacher of his age, gave elegant literary expression to Reid's ideas in his *Elements of the Philosophy of the Human Mind* (1792), adding, as his own contribution, a carefully worked-out version of Hobbes's nominalism about general ideas. Stewart renamed Reid's principles of common sense, calling them the fundamental laws of human belief, and proposed as criteria for them universal consent, the absence of any propositions for or against them that are more certain than they and their acceptance in practice by those who claim to reject them.

Brown. Thomas Brown (1778–1820), a gifted introspective psychologist, came very close to Hume in his *Inquiry Into the Relation of Cause and Effect* (1804). He adopted a strict regularity view of causation as invariable association but hoped to escape Hume's inductive skepticism by asserting the intuitive self-evidence of the principle that every event has a cause.

Hamilton. The most grandiose of the Scottish philosophers was Sir William Hamilton (1788–1856). The massive learning that so awed his contemporaries has come to appear a jumble of often trivial and generally uninterpreted detail, and his trumpeted logical innovations, most notably the "quantification of the predicate," can at best be seen as some sort of crude anticipation of the algebraic treatment of logic propounded in the 1840s by George Boole and Augustus De Morgan. His main ideas were set out in three articles of the period 1829–1833 (reprinted in his *Discussions on Philosophy, Literature and Education* of 1852), covering his logical novelties, his metaphysical agnosticism, and his natural realist theory of perception. In rough and ready correspondence to Kant, he maintained that all knowledge is relative and concerns only what is conditioned by the fact that we know it. Absolute or unconditioned reality is unknowable. We can conceive it and even have faith that it exists, but at best we can have only negative knowledge of it. This doctrine consorts uneasily with the main theme of his theory of perception, which is that in the most elementary perceptual experiences we have an immediate consciousness of the self being confronted by the not-self. The two positions can be reconciled, however, if the unknowableness of reality is attributed to its being infinite rather than to its being objective and not just private appearance. Hamilton himself was none too clear about this distinction and further undermined the reconciliation of his two views in his development of the principle of the relativity of knowledge. In maintaining that knowledge is relative, he reverted to something very like the "ideal theory" of Hume and the empiricists that the objects of perception are in the mind, a theory which he, like Reid, wished to reject.

Mansel. H. L. Mansel (1820–1871) gave a clear and articulate form to Hamilton's ideas in his *Metaphysics* (1860) and applied them to theology in his celebrated lectures *The Limits of Religious Thought* (1858). There are echoes of William of Ockham in Mansel's view that positive religious knowledge can come only from revelation and that God cannot be submitted to humanly rational standards of morality. Mansel's Hamiltonian philosophy was the official academic doctrine of the mid-nineteenth century. It was the teaching of the "school of intuition" against which J. S. Mill set himself, and its influence persisted in the evolutionary philosophies of Herbert Spencer and G. H. Lewes, who both incorporated its agnostic doctrine of the unknowable into their thought. Its irrationalistic defense of the proprieties of morals and religion was discarded by the idealists, but there is an affinity between its reliance on self-evident intuitions and the realism of Moore and Cook Wilson in the Edwardian period.

Utilitarianism. Utilitarianism, the most influential trend of thought in the first part of the nineteenth century developed outside the universities.

Bentham. Jeremy Bentham (1748–1832) and his followers took over the more usable and less skeptical aspects of Hume's philosophy, in particular his view that association is the indispensable instrument for any inquiry into the nature of the mind and his identification of value with utility. Bentham's philosophy proper is minimal and dogmatic, a handful of simple-minded convictions about value and human motivation on which to base his project of a thoroughgoing simplification and rationalization of law and morality, of public and private principles of conduct. In his *Fragment on Government* (1776) Bentham forcefully criticized the Lockean social philosophy of William Blackstone, the authoritative commentator on English law, with its apparatus of natural rights and a social contract. In his *Introduction to the Principles of Morals and Legislation* (1789) only brief preliminary attention is given to the foundations of the utilitarian framework: the theses that the general welfare is the only rational measure of value and that men are wholly moved to act by considerations of pleasure and pain.

Bentham's ambition was to construct a wholly rational and systematic code of law to replace the untidy traditional mass of custom and precedent that made up the English law of his time. The utilitarian measure of value showed what kinds of conduct should be prohibited; the associated theory of human motivation showed what sanctions are needed to make the prohibition effective. For Bentham the legislator's task is to bring about an artificial harmony of interests by attaching just sufficient dissuasive penalties to antisocial forms of conduct. He regarded pleasure as homogeneous in quality and, thus, as an extensive magnitude which can be numerically measured. The principles used to arrive at a rational system of law can equally well be applied to establish the content of a rational code of morals. At first, Bentham paid no attention to politics, and he had little interest in the ordinary liberal ideals of personal freedom and democatic government. But the neglect of his proposals by the ruling power led him to accept the thesis of his energetic follower James Mill (1773–1836) that since only the public at large has an interest in a rational system of law, only a government directly accountable to that public would be disposed to introduce such a system. Bentham's first commitment was to rational efficiency. The liberal convictions of his school were adopted consequentially, as means to his primary end.

James Mill. James Mill's chief work was the construction of a general theory of the mind in which the doctrine of association is applied with unexampled thoroughness to support the assumptions of Bentham's social philosophy. In his *Analysis of the Phenomena of the Human Mind* (1829), where inspiration from Hartley is recognized, the complex architecture of human mental life is rigorously deduced from the application of elementary laws of association to the raw materials of sense. Mill followed Hartley and Godwin in attributing the forms and excellences of human character to environmental circumstances, and like Godwin, he had great faith in the power of a reformed environment to contribute to the perfection of man.

J. S. Mill. The open-mindedness and flexibility of John Stuart Mill (1806–1873) stand out with particular clarity when he is set beside his father and Bentham. Although he preserved an ultimate loyalty to the associationism of the one and the utilitarianism of the other, he considerably qualified and extended the stock of common doctrines he had inherited to include a logic and a theory of knowledge. His *System of Logic* (1843) was in essence a restatement of Bacon's philosophy of scientific method with special reference to Hume's project of a science of human nature and human affairs. Mill had little use for deduction. He limited its scope by arguing that the propositions of mathematics are very large-scale empirical generalizations, and he depreciated deductive reasoning as a source of knowledge by holding it to be merely explicative verbal inference. All real inference, in his view, is inductive. In its primitive and unreflective form induction is enumerative, a matter of arriving at generalizations from accumulations of like instances. The main importance of enumeration is that it establishes, in a manner that does not stand up well to examination, the law of universal causation. Given this law, we can confidently go on to use Mill's celebrated "methods," which are directly transcribed from Bacon's tables.

Mill's *Logic* was the sacred methodological text of Victorian scientific naturalism, triumphantly vindicated by Darwin's *Origin of Species* (1859). Mill's theory of induction had more direct influence than Bacon's two centuries before because it could be more easily applied to the great work of biological discovery which followed it than could Bacon's theory to the mathematical physics of the seventeenth century. But for all its influence it was soon powerfully assailed from two different directions. The idealism that began to flourish at the time of Mill's death repudiated its whole conception of the mind's nature and activities in the pursuit of truth. A more immediate and, in the end, substantial challenge came from the reforming defenders of deductive logic. Richard Whately (1787–1863), with the curiously inappropriate assistance of Newman, had expounded the traditional theory of deduction in a refreshingly lucid and unencumbered way in his *Elements of Logic* (1826). Recognizably modern treatment of deduction begins with George Boole (1815–1864) and Augustus De Morgan (1806–1871). In 1847 each of them published a treatise in which deductive logic was presented as a kind of algebra. Both gave formal, mathematical accounts of arguments involving probability, and De Morgan enlarged the scope of deduction to include inferences containing relational as well as attributive propositions. This line of thought, enriched by German and American contributions, reached its highest point with the *Principia Mathematica* (1910–1913) of Whitehead and Russell.

Mill's theory of knowledge was put forward in a negatively critical fashion in his *Examination of Sir William Hamilton's Philosophy* (1865). In essentials it is the empiricist epistemology of Berkeley and Hume without Berkeley's theism or Hume's skepticism. Mill defined matter as the "permanent possibility of sensation" and only narrowly held himself back from a corresponding phenomenalism about the nature of the mind, being reluctant to define the mind as simply a series of experiences on the somewhat flimsy ground that he could not see how such a series could be conscious of being so.

His principal revisions of his intellectual inheritance are to be found in his famous essays *On Liberty* (1859) and *Utilitarianism* (1863). In *On Liberty* he voiced his suspicions of democracy as a possible danger to individual variety and excellence, and in his concern to protect it from the pressures of institutions and conformist public opinion, Mill paid little attention to whether there is a utilitarian justification of individual self-determination as a supreme value. Bentham had treated the first principles of utilitarianism as self-evident, but Mill endeavored, with an educationally useful lack of success, to prove them. His unsuccessful attempt embodies mistakes that every student of philosophy must learn to identify but shows, nevertheless, the direction any justification of utilitarianism must take. He also rejected Bentham's doctrine that pleasure and pain are qualitatively homogeneous, sensitive to Thomas Carlyle's attack on Benthamite ethics as a pig philosophy. There is a final display of broad-mindedness in Mill's posthumous *Three Essays on Religion* (1874), in which he conceded a faint probability to the hypothesis of a limited God.

Bain and Sidgwick. Two of Mill's numerous followers deserve mention. Alexander Bain (1818–1903) greatly enlarged the thoroughness and accuracy of the associationist theory of mind in *The Senses and the Intellect* (1855) and *Emotions and the Will* (1859). He restored Hartley's physiological dimension to the empirical study of the mind and anticipated behaviorism in his theory that belief consisted in a readiness to act. Henry Sidgwick (1838–1900) followed out Mill's ethical intimations in his *Methods of Ethics* (1874), arguing that utilitarianism must be supplemented by the admission of intuited and self-evident principles of benevolence and justice.

Evolutionary theories. Darwin's theory of evolution, by scientifically establishing that man is a part of nature, as opposed to the religious idea of his uniqueness as the possessor of an immortal soul, was the most important event in British intellectual history in the nineteenth century, and a chorus of philosophically unprofessional voices was soon raised to proclaim the wider significance of Darwin's discoveries.

Spencer. The most sustained and penetrating of the voices was that of the indefatigably prolix Herbert Spencer (1820–1903). In his *First Principles* (1862) a large selection of unrelated philosophical notions is assembled to flesh out the central evolutionary dogma that absolutely everything moves from a state of indefinite, incoherent homogeneity to one of definite, coherent heterogeneity. The aim of his system of "synthetic philosophy" is to articulate the whole of scientific knowledge into a single structure, and the evolutionary principle is employed to interpret the entire range of biological, mental, and social phenomena. For science can consider only phenomena. As with Hume, phenomena are either vivid impressions or faint ideas, evincing, as with Hamilton, the not-self and the self, respectively. These clear data were seen by Spencer as manifestations of an inapprehensible, transempirical something, the Unknowable, toward which he shared the religious emotions of Hamilton and Mansel. Spencer applied evolutionary ideas to the theory of knowledge in his view that a priori truths are beliefs that men inherit from the ancestors who discovered them and to ethics, where the view that quantity of life is the supreme value is uneasily qualified by admissions of the importance of a "surplus of agreeable feeling."

Huxley. T. H. Huxley (1825–1895), a great biologist and a brilliant expositor and controversialist, is a more appealing figure than Spencer. But his philosophical ideas revealed their incoherence all the more plainly because of the clarity with which they were expressed. On the one hand, Huxley argued that mind is an epiphenomenon, a by-product of the workings of the body; yet on the other, in his *Hume* (1879), he held that our knowledge is confined to the impressions of the senses, that the only certainty we have is of our own mental states. Similarly, in his ethics he wavered between the view that the course of evolution is the criterion of moral progress and the doctrine of his *Evolution and Ethics* (1893) that the task of morality is to counteract the cruel injustices of the natural order of things.

Lewes and Stephen. George Henry Lewes (1817–1878), best known as the lover of George Eliot, presented a view of mind as the product of social evolution in his rambling *The Problems of Life and Mind* (1874–1879). Leslie Stephen (1832–1904), the great historian of literature and ideas, propounded a characteristically hearty version of evolutionary morality in his *Science of Ethics* (1882), laying much stress on the analogy between the moral well-being of society and the health of the physical organism.

Clifford and Pearson. Much the most interesting philosophically of these Victorian naturalists, with their evolutionary theories of morality and their half-materialist, half-skeptical view of natural knowledge, were W. K.

Clifford (1845–1879) and the statistician Karl Pearson (1857–1936), who both arrived at a position very close to the phenomenalism of Ernst Mach. Clifford attempted to circumvent the solipsistic consequences of the traditional empiricist theory of perception by attaching to it the assumption that the mind is social in nature. The "social object," the public, material thing, is a compound of my impressions and of "ejects," the impressions I attribute to other minds whose existence is a primary datum. There is an anticipation of the neutral monism of William James and Bertrand Russell in Clifford's doctrine of "mind-stuff" as the ultimate raw material of reality, conceivable as either mind or matter in accordance with the manner of its arrangement. A persistent theme in Clifford's *Lectures and Essays* (1879) is Mach's principle of the economy of thought, which interprets the theoretical concepts of natural science as conceptual constructions, referring not to substantive things but to patterns in the course of sense experience. This point of view was developed in Pearson's influential *The Grammar of Science* (1892), in which the aim was to eliminate all metaphysical residues from the vocabulary and theories of science and to present scientific knowledge in a purified and radically empirical form. Clifford's ethics turn on the conception of the "tribal self," seen as an evolutionarily developed system of impulses mitigating the demands of private interest for the sake of the welfare of the group in the struggle for existence. Clifford was a passionate opponent of ordinary religious belief but was prepared to endorse some kind of religion of humanity inspired by cosmic emotion.

The Victorian naturalists, rather like the deists, were philosophers only *per accidens,* and it might be held that their chief contribution to the subject is to be found in the criticism their work provoked. The traditional British answer to radical empiricism, the Scottish philosophy, was an inadequate protection for orthodox religion and morality. The naturalists had incorporated some of the doctrines of Scottish philosophy into their own thought; Mill had subjected its last authoritative exponent to a thorough and demolishing criticism; it was itself in the last resort a version of empiricism. An altogether more far-reaching critique of the assumptions of Locke and Hume was needed, and it was provided by the long-delayed importation of the German idealism of Kant and Hegel in the last third of the nineteenth century.

Idealism. Kant and his more speculative successors had had a minimal impact on the insular course of British intellectual life. Samuel Taylor Coleridge (1772–1834) had plunged into their work with characteristic depth and irregularity and had mastered the central idea of the distinction between reason, understood as a grasp of things in their interrelated wholeness, and understanding, the useful but ultimately falsifying analytic mode of thought employed in natural science. He applied this distinction effectively in his aesthetic doctrine of the nature of the difference between imagination and fancy, and it lies behind his traditionalist political theory and his philosophy of religion. But neither he nor anyone else before T. H. Green apprehended the fundamental notions of post-Kantian idealism in such a way as to be able to give them effective expression. There had, however, been some considerable defenses of religion and some interesting intimations of the idealist point of view before Green called on his contemporaries to close their Mill and Spencer and to open their Kant and Hegel.

Newman and his contemporaries. First place among the dissenters from the prevailing naturalist enthusiasm must be given to J. H. Newman (1801–1890) by reason of his personal distinction, his literary excellence, the prophetic nature of his ideas, and the astounding tour de force in which he made use of traditional British philosophical principles, derived from Locke, Butler, and Hume, to construct, in his *Grammar of Assent* (1870), a coherent and articulate answer to the religious skepticism of his age.

Newman's starting point was a distinction between real assent, which we give to what is directly present to us, and conceptual assent, the tentative acceptance we give to the results of inference. Now although God's existence is not given to us, we can have more than only the weak degree of belief that formal demonstration yields. We have, he said, an "illative sense," which draws conclusions, in a nonmechanical fashion, from a huge mass of supporting evidence and whose working is to be seen in many of our common beliefs which are neither directly given nor the consequences of any clearly formulable deduction from a small number of clearly specified premises. The illative sense sustains a real assent to the existence of God on the basis of the deliverances of conscience. Newman's distinction of formal demonstration from the illative sense corresponds to that of understanding from reason, and his account of its raw material recalls the moral theology of Kant. Another idealist notion, that of the dialectical unfolding of the nature of things, is suggested in his *Essay on the Development of Christian Doctrine* (1845), where he argued that the content of the Christian revelation is to be found in the totality of what successive generations have made of it, in its full development in time and not in its primitive origins.

James Martineau (1805–1900) advanced idealist views that show the influence of Kant in his *Study of Religion* (1888) and an intuitionist moral philosophy, which stresses motive as the determinant of the moral character of action, in his *Types of Ethical Theory* (1885). F. D. Maurice (1805–1872), much influenced by Coleridge, expressed idealist sympathies in his *Moral and Metaphysical Philosophy* (first published as an article in *Encyclopaedia Metropolitana,* 1848).

Of more narrowly philosophical interest is J. F. Ferrier (1808–1864). In his *Institutes of Metaphysics* (1854) he put forward more or less Berkeleian ideas in the rigorously demonstrative sytle of Spinoza. He tackled the main weakness in Berkeley's philosophy in his bold first principle that with everything that the mind knows it must also know itself. Confident in the speculative reliability of the pure deductive reason, he was sharply critical of common sense and of the Scottish philosophers' supine reliance on its seemingly self-evident intimations.

John Grote (1813–1866) was a careful critic of the prevailing empiricist assumptions of the time. In a way that later idealists were to follow much further, he held that scientific thinking interferes with its objects by abstractly averting attention from the fact that they are, after all, the objects of a knowing mind. Natural science, it follows, speaks only of a partial and incomplete reality; furthermore, it is not applicable, as Mill had supposed, to the mind itself (*Exploratio Philosophica*, Vol. I, 1865).

Green. With T. H. Green (1836–1882) the idealist movement in Britain reaches its full stride. Green was a man of noble character and a most influential teacher despite his cumbrous and ungainly style. That he founded a school is in part due to the thoroughness of his criticism of British empiricism, in part to the extent of his knowledge and philosophical interests, and in part, perhaps, because his concern was less to defend orthodox religion than to reaffirm the moral and social responsibilities of philosophy at a moment when the harshness of evolutionary social doctrine seemed to serve as an apology for the barbarism and rapacity of Victorian capitalism. Green was always animated more by concern for the improvement of man's life in society than by a desire to protect habitual objects of pious feeling, and he put a conservative philosophy to the service of a progressive social ideal.

Green's starting point was an unprecedentedly thorough criticism of the first principles of empiricism in the introduction to his edition of the works of Hume (1874). Against the conception of knowledge as the outcome of passively accepted atoms of sense experience he insisted on the broadly Kantian view that knowledge is a system of relations and that relations are the work of the active mind. Reality, since it can be known only as an interrelated system, requires an active individual consciousness to know it. We can conceive the reality we know only as part of a wider reality, or system of relations, that contains it and anything we may come to know. Such a system must be the object of an eternal consciousness, just as the limited reality we know must be conceived as the object of a finite consciousness. Green intended his slogan, "The understanding makes nature," in a double sense, as establishing the existence of both the soul and God, the Soul being regarded by him as a developing part, not a detached creation of God.

In his *Prolegomena to Ethics* (1883) Green first set forth his positive metaphysical views and then formulated their main practical result, the anti-Darwinian thesis that mind is prior to nature, not a part or product of it, which he used in the interpretation of the active life of man. Green's distinction between natural wants and self-conscious motives parallels that between mere successions of feelings and experiences of related objects. He concluded that the will is no more part of nature than is the understanding and, consistently enough, that it is not subject to causal law. Green's positive ethics are teleological, the end of self-realization being austerely interpreted as virtue or moral perfection and as something permanent and social, unlike the momentary and private character of the utilitarian end, pleasure. In *Principles of Political Obligation* (in his *Works*, 1885–1888) the political implications of this moral philosophy are drawn out. Green saw the state as an agent of moral improvement, not as a mere protector of private rights, but he did not follow Hegel in setting it above individual conscience. While rejecting pure natural rights, he still subordinated the state to the moral consensus of the community.

Bradley. Although Green died young, with his work unfinished, he left a large body of energetic disciples imbued with a consciousness of their responsibility for the Platonic education of a ruling class in the ideals of public service. Anglicized Hegelianism had much of its ultimate inspirer's breadth of interests. Green's school developed a modernistic philosophy of religion, which saw dogma as the imaginative expression of metaphysical and moral truth, an organicist political theory, and an idealist aesthetics. The most important member of the group was the least orthodox, F. H. Bradley (1846–1924), who was for a generation the most admired, if not the most closely followed, of British philosophers. In his early *Ethical Studies* (1876) the skeptical tendency and the lordly indifference to common sense and respectability of Bradley's remorselessly speculative mind are already evident. The work begins, acceptably enough, with a rejection of the two abstract extremes of hedonism and of Kant's rigorous doctrine of duty for duty's sake in the interests of an acceptance by the individual of his functional place in the community. But it goes on to assert the existence of duties that transcend the demands of society and again to assert the transcendence of morality by religion. In his final metaphysics Bradley was to go further still, denying both the personal nature of absolute reality and the freedom and immortality of the finite human soul.

In *The Principles of Logic* (1883) Bradley undermined the associationist theory of thought, asserting a radical distinction between logic and psychology. All thinking is judgment; it is all categorical in form and has reality as a whole as its ultimate subject. In affirming general predicates of the real, it inevitably falsifies it by abstract selection from what is an interrelated whole. This skeptical thesis that all discursive thought necessarily falsifies its subject matter is argued in detail and further developed in Bradley's main work, *Appearance and Reality* (1893). In the first part of this book Bradley purported to demonstrate, by arguments of very varying value which are least convincing when they are of his own invention, that all the strategically central organizing conceptions of discursive thought—substance, quality, relation, change, cause, space, time, the soul—are riddled with self-contradiction. The common world of discursive thought is, then, a world of appearance. Below it lies inarticulate experience, which at least has the unity that discursive thought illusively destroys. Above it is the level of absolute experience, which has the unity of primitive feeling but also the completeness that mere feeling lacks. The absolute is a harmonious whole, neither personal nor moral, in which all the conflicts of discursive thought are somehow reconciled and in which all the broken variety of appearance is somehow absorbed. Bradley admitted that his own philosophy, as a product of discursive thought, is ultimately abstract and erroneous but maintained that it is at least intellectually incorrigible. The closest approach to reality, it would seem, is a self-identifying mystic contemplation of its all-inclusive harmony.

Bosanquet. Bradley's leading disciple, Bernard Bosanquet (1848–1923), was a fertile and conciliatory thinker who sought to mitigate the scornful extremism of his master's doctrines. His persistent theme is that systematic unity or coherence is the criterion of truth and reality, that beliefs are more true and things more real to the extent that they approximate the harmonious unity of Bradley's absolute. In his *Logic* (1888) Bosanquet attacked the conception of thinking as a step-by-step movement in a single direction, proposing in its place a view of thought as the total development of an idea in all its aspects and relations. In his chief metaphysical book, *The Principle of Individuality and Value* (1912), he used Bradley's notion of the absolute as the one true concrete individual not, as Bradley had, to depreciate the reality of everything that fell short of it but, rather, to assert the reality of all those more or less systematic wholes—minds, societies, works of art, and scientific theories—that to some extent approximated it. Particularly influential was his *Philosophical Theory of the State* (1899), in which Green's circumspect modifications of traditional liberalism are abandoned for an enthusiastic endorsement of the Hegelian theory of the total subordination of the individual to the state.

Personal idealism. The feature of Bradley's metaphysics which attracted most critical attention from those broadly sympathetic to the assumptions of idealism was, not surprisingly, its religious skepticism, since much of the original appeal of this philosophy was its apparent power to give sophisticated protection to an orthodoxy under heavy attack from biology, geology, and the textual criticism of the Bible. A. S. Pringle-Pattison (1856–1931) expressed this discontent with the impersonal absolute and the doctrine of the ultimate unreality and dependence of the human soul in his *Hegelianism and Personality* (1887).

McTaggart. By far the most impressive of the dissident "personal idealists" was J. M. E. McTaggart (1866–1925), a writer of incomparable grace and clarity. In *The Nature of Existence* (1921–1927) he produced the most finished and rigorous metaphysical system of any British philosophical writer. From a very small number of trivially obvious premises (for example, that something exists) and with the aid of some rather less obvious principles of inference he deduced that reality is a society of immortal souls related by love and that time and matter are unreal. In contrast to most of Green's successors, McTaggart had a very pronounced taste and capacity for precise dialectical argument, and this has given many of the details of his work an interest for those who have no use for its general style and purposes. There is no finer example in British philosophy of the exercise of speculative reasoning for its own sake. Although avowedly religious in spirit (he defended metaphysics for the emotional comfort it could yield), McTaggart saw no adequate reason for belief in God.

Ward. James Ward (1843–1925) approached the conclusions of personal idealism by a very different route. He began from a critique of the atomistic associationism of the empiricist theory of mind, urging against it that experience takes the form of a "presentational continuum," an undifferentiated flux, not a partitioned series. In all experience, he further held, the self is immediately present as an agent. The idea of a passive nature, over against an active mind, is the product of abstractive attention; in the real world mentality is present everywhere, even if in a low-grade form in what we call matter. Like McTaggart, Ward saw the universe as a plurality of minds, but he was prepared to recognize many levels of mind below the human soul. Although willing to assert the existence of a transcendent God, limiting himself by his own activity, he did not regard it as philosophically demonstrable.

Rashdall. Hastings Rashdall (1858–1924) based his more confident theism on Berkeleian arguments, arriving at the somewhat heterodox conclusion that God is finite and limited. In his ethical treatise, *The Theory of Good and Evil* (1907), he put forward an ideal utilitarianism which judges the rightness of acts by their contribution to a range of intuitably good ends, a more sensible but less challenging version of the ethics of G. E. Moore.

Schiller. *Personal Idealism* (1902) was the joint manifesto of a group, most of whom were to make up the English pragmatist movement. F. C. S. Schiller (1864–1937) was the most notable and the most copious of them. Agreeing with the idealists that the world is somehow a construction of the mind, he interpreted the mind not as an all-inclusive absolute but as concrete, practically active human personality. Putting man's will above his reason, Schiller was a lively, if diffuse, critic of all forms of intellectualism. Against the formal logic of deduction, in his view a sterile and mechanical affair, Schiller argued for a psychological logic of discovery that would recognize the practical impulses behind the pursuit of knowledge.

By the end of the nineteenth century, idealism in one form or another was the undisputedly dominant philosophy in Britain. The main empiricist tradition was almost extinct outside Sidgwick's ethics, and the philosophy of John Stuart Mill was recalled only as a dreadful example. However, idealism was soon to fall before the new realism, in which Moore's revival of certain doctrines of Reid was fortified by Russell's fatal criticism of idealist logic.

THE TWENTIETH CENTURY

Development of realism. The latest phase of British philosophy can be said, with more precision than is usual in the history of thought, to have begun in the year 1903. It was the year of the first major work of Bertrand Russell (born 1872), his *Principles of Mathematics*, and of the two most influentical writings of G. E. Moore (1873–1958), his *Principia Ethica* and his essay "Refutation of Idealism." In the years before 1914, Russell and Moore developed their fatal criticisms of idealism, propounded an alternative to it that others were to develop further while Moore and Russell moved off in fresh directions, and succeeded in laying down both the analytic method and the epistemological focus of interest that were to be accepted by the great majority of philosophers in Britain ever since.

Russell and Moore rejected the idealism in which they had been brought up as being in plain conflict with something they held more certain than philosophy, in Russell's case the findings of mathematics and natural science, in Moore's case common sense. Russell, convinced of the absolute truth of mathematical propositions, discarded the coherence theory with its implication that truth is a matter of degree. By distinguishing between the act of perception, which is unquestionably mental in nature, and its objects, which are not, Moore sought to undermine the principle that the mind can be aware only of its own ideas. Both assailed the fundamental doctrine underlying the whole structure of idealism, the theory of internal relations which holds that everything in the world is essentially constituted by its relations to other things. From the internal relations point of view all analysis is falsification; the world can be understood only as an interrelated whole. Russell's work in formal logic, culminating in his attempt to show that mathematics is a deductive continuation of the richer and more rigorous logic in his and Alfred North Whitehead's *Principia Mathematica* (1910–1913), shows that analysis is indispensable for the interpretation of the most solid and indubitable part of human knowledge. Analysis for Russell was a matter of resolving a complex body of beliefs into elementary concepts in terms of which all others can be clearly defined and elementary propositions from which all others can be clearly inferred. For Moore it was something rather different, a matter of establishing, by the closest possible attention to the actual meaning of words, what is really involved in the familiar beliefs about which idealist metaphysicians say such surprising things.

Despite their differences of approach, Moore and Russell arrived, for the time at any rate, at a common realism in which all the distinctions that had been confounded by the school of Green and Bradley are lucidly redrawn. They held that the world consists of a vast plurality of logically distinct and independent things of radically different kinds. Some are minds; some, material objects; and some, abstract universals and propositions. In perception the mind is aware of material things quite different in nature from it; in thought, of equally different abstract entities. Necessary knowledge concerns the relations of timeless universals to one another, as in the Platonic theory of mathematical truth; contingent knowledge is of material things by perception or of the mind by introspection. To this realism about universals and the material world Moore added a realistic account of our knowledge of value. Goodness, he held, is a unique property, not part of the order of nature and irreducible to any properties met with in perception or introspection. Truth for Moore and Russell consists in the correspondence of propositions and facts; certainty is to be found only in necessary truth and in the deliverances of the senses. They soon gave up the view that the senses provide direct acquaintance with material things and came to adopt a causal theory of perception much like Locke's, Russell arguing in *The Problems of Philosophy* (1912) that the hypothesis of an independent external world is the simplest theory to account for the order of our sense experience.

This body of ideas, with its perceptible infusion of rationalism about necessary truth, the uniformity of nature, and the objectivity of value, came to be pretty much the official academic philosophy in Britain between the wars of 1914 and 1939. At its first home, Cambridge, it was continued and extended by C. D. Broad (born 1887) and A. C. Ewing (born 1899). Broad gave the fullest defense of the representative theory of perception, and in *The Mind and Its Place in Nature* (1925) accommodated the mind–body dualism to new scientific discoveries and to the speculations of psychoanalysts and psychical researchers. Ewing in his *Idealism* (1934) systematically brought together all the realist criticisms of the preceding orthodoxy.

In the heyday of idealism at Oxford, realism had never been totally extinguished there; the lonely, lucid, and combative voice of Thomas Case (1844–1925) had been raised on behalf of the view that the immediate objects of perception are the physical responses of the nervous system to the world of mathematically characterized objects outside it (*Physical Realism*, 1888).

Cook Wilson school. Much more influential was the movement, parallel to that of Russell and Moore, initiated by John Cook Wilson (1849–1915) and carried on by his ablest follower, H. A. Prichard (1871–1947). In Cook Wilson's *Statement and Inference* (1926) the idealist logic is cumbrously criticized, and the concept of knowledge is held to be simple and indefinable in the way Moore claimed the property of goodness to be. This conception of knowledge lay behind the extensive attributions of self-evidence made by the school of Cook Wilson to philosophically important propositions—most notably, perhaps, that the known is independent of our knowledge of it.

Prichard, who resembled Moore in his predilection for plain language and rigorous argument, was most influential as a moral philosopher. He insisted that the rightness of actions is intrinsic to them and in no way derivable from their consequences; any such derivation turns morality into mere expediency. W. D. Ross (born 1877), the Aristotelian scholar, developed these ideas with greater fullness and sophistication.

Collingwood. The only effective defender of idealism left in its spiritual home was the brilliant but intellectually irresponsible R. G. Collingwood (1889–1943). Closely similar in outlook to Croce, he maintained the traditional Hegelian interest in the higher activities of the human mind at a time when most philosophers were preoccupied with the most elementary forms of thought. In *The Idea of History* (1946) he argued that human action can be understood only by sympathetic insight, by reliving the thoughts of others, and not by the methods of inductive science. In *Principles of Art* (1938) he elaborated a theory of imagination to sustain the Crocean view of art as expression.

Metaphysical systems. Modern analytic philosophy is generally thought of as antimetaphysical, but there was no hostility in principle to metaphysics in the first realistic phase of the movement. Although Russell and Moore provided a general picture of the world only by implication, the task of constructing such a picture on a realistic basis was undertaken by others.

Alexander and Anderson. Samuel Alexander (1859–1938) started his *Space, Time and Deity* (1920) from the premise that in knowledge independent objects are directly present to the mind and that the mind itself is not contemplated but "enjoyed." He saw the world as a process of emergent evolution in which new, higher levels of being successively develop; from the raw material of undifferentiated space time came the world of mathematical physics, from that the perceived order of sensible qualities, then life, then mind, and, finally, in a time yet to come, God, conceived as the ideal goal of the whole evolutionary process. The materialistic implications of Alexander's philosophy were drawn by the Scottish-born Australian philosopher John Anderson (1893–1962), who held that everything real is in space and time, that there are no different kinds or levels of being and that all knowledge, including its philosophical and ethical forms, is essentially scientific.

Whitehead. Alfred North Whitehead (1861–1947) was the most ambitious of modern British metaphysicians. His aim was to overthrow the whole mechanical system of ideas associated with the name of Newton, in particular its atomistic view of clearly demarcated substances, its theory that our awareness of nature is indirect, and the underlying "bifurcation of nature" which sharply marks off the world of physics from the world of experience. For Whitehead perception was more a matter of responding to the heavy causal impact of nature than of contemplating lively visual impressions of it. In his *Process and Reality* (1929) he gave an account of the nature of the world as a continuous stream of "actual entities," short-lived pulses of feeling connected to one another and to the Platonic "eternal objects," from which they derived their characteristics, by an all-comprehending relation of "prehension." Between actual entities prehension is a kind of perception in one direction and causation in the other. The process of the world is driven onward into novelty by a creative urge, and God is invoked as a principle to limit and order the process. Whitehead's emphasis on the interconnectedness of things brought him, as he realized, back to something like the internal relations doctrine of the idealists. In the period just after 1920, when his thought was taking this turn, the ideas of Russell, his great logical collaborator, were moving further than ever from this side of idealism.

Wittgenstein's logical atomism. It was in the years just preceding World War I that Ludwig Wittgenstein (1889–1951), the most powerfully original influence in modern British philosophy, arrived in Cambridge and began the work with Russell that was to determine the course of philosophy in Britain up to the present time. Wittgenstein's *Tractatus Logico-philosophicus* (1922) is the most authoritative, though by reason of its sibylline concision by no means the most readily intelligible, exposition of the logical atomism that Russell and he arrived at. Its central idea is an account of the conditions under which the elements of language have meaning and can aspire to truth. For Wittgenstein the ultimately meaningful kind of sentence is a picture of a state of affairs or possible fact. If the state of affairs depicted obtains, the proposition expressed by the sentence is true. The world is wholly composed of an array of logically independent facts of the sort that would verify elementary propositions. Any proposition that cannot be analyzed into an assemblage of elementary propositions is devoid of meaning. To understand a complex proposition is to know with what collection of elementary propositions it is equivalent in meaning, and the technique of reductive analysis that became the methodological ideal of many philosophers in the 1930s is a technique for the formal expression of such equivalences.

Wittgenstein held that the complex propositional forms of Russell's logic were all "truth-functions" of their components, meaning by this that the truth or falsity of the complex was wholly determined by the truth or falsity of its components. Two limiting cases of truth-functions are of special importance, tautologies, which are true, and contradictions, which are false, whatever the truth-value of their components. A tautology, because it is true in any conceivable state of affairs, in effect says nothing about the world; its significance lies in the fact that it is the scheme of a possible deductive inference. In every valid inference of this kind the conclusion does no more than repeat some or all of what was asserted in the premises; the inference is simply a repetition. Tautologies and the contradictions that are their negations are senseless.

Three other kinds of sentence Wittgenstein brands as positively nonsensical. The utterances of traditional metaphysicians and theologians are the first of these. Second, there are mystical utterances, which are at least important nonsense. Finally, there are Wittgenstein's own utterances about the relation between language and thought, on the one hand, and the world they concern, on the other. What Wittgenstein tried to say about meaning can only be shown. The right way to do philosophy would be to respond to nonsensical utterances with significant propositions and not to produce more nonsense. "Philosophy," Wittgenstein said, "is not a theory but an activity."

Russell's logical atomism. The stark and uncompromising doctrine of the *Tractatus* is purely formal; it is intended to state the conditions which must be satisfied by any language capable of meaningful application to the world. Wittgenstein did not specify what elementary propositions must be like, nor did he say what, if any, propositions of our actual language are elementary. Russell in *Our Knowledge of the External World as a Field for Scientific Method in Philosophy* (1914) and "Philosophy of Logical Atomism" (*Monist*, 1918–1919) supplied this deficiency by identifying the elementary propositions of logical atomism with the reports of immediate experience of Hume's radical empiricism. Following William James, he held that the ultimate elements of thought and knowledge are neither mental nor physical but neutral; he saw minds and material things as differently arranged complexes of neutral elements. He was less confident of the reducibility of all kinds of complex propositions than was Wittgenstein; in particular, he doubted the interpretation of general laws as indefinitely long conjunctions of singular propositions and found it hard to reduce propositions about such attitudes as belief and hope, whose direct objects are themselves propositional, to elementary terms. In his *Analysis of Mind* (1921), however, he resolutely attempted a reduction of all mental phenomena to sensations and images. With *The Analysis of Matter* (1927), though, he returned to something very like his original causal theory of perception, abandoning the phenomenalist identification of material things with their actual and possible appearances he had worked out in his first period of association with Wittgenstein.

Logical positivism. Wittgenstein's most talented English adherent, F. P. Ramsey (1903–1930), died too young to have much influence, though the essays collected in his *Foundations of Mathematics* (1931) are of a quality to justify the respect that Wittgenstein paid him. The direct continuation of Wittgenstein's early thought was carried out by the logical positivists of the Vienna circle. Their highly selective use of the *Tractatus* was inspired by an aim less grandiose than Wittgenstein's. They sought to interpret the concepts and theories of mathematics and empirical science and disentangle them from the confusing influence of metaphysical and moral considerations. This aim made itself felt in Britain through the work of a number of younger philosophers, most notably A. J. Ayer (born 1910), whose *Language, Truth and Logic* (1936) is the most concise and effective formulation of the logical positivist doctrine in English.

Ayer and the positivists rejected Wittgenstein's account of the conditions of linguistic significance and the ontology of atomic facts that is associated with it. They held that a sentence is meaningful only to the extent that it is capable of being verified in sense experience or by reflection on the meaning of the words it contains. Every genuine proposition is either analytic or empirical. All genuine philosophy, as well as logic and mathematics, is analytic. Its task is to exhibit the meaningless of metaphysics, theology, and ethics and to provide reductive analyses of the significant remainder of discourse. Much in the manner of Russell's neutral monism, minds and material objects are interpreted as logical constructions out of sensory elements. Judgments of value are not true or false statements at all but expressions of feeling, and to the extent that the utterances of metaphysicians and theologians are anything more than verbal confusions, they must be understood as a kind of tortured academic poetry.

Throughout the 1930s the main topics of philosophical controversy in Britain were determined by the direction of the interests of positivism. In particular, the analytic nature of necessary truth, the phenomenalist theory of perception, the emotive theory of value, and the identification of philosophy with reductive analysis occupied the center of attention. Moore remained a potent force. He objected to the implication of phenomenalism that all beliefs about material things are less than certain, arguing that some beliefs of this kind are the very paradigms of certainty, and he wrestled with the problem of the nature of analysis. Wittgenstein returned to Cambridge in 1929, but the radically new style his thinking began to take on at that time did not make itself widely felt until the end of the war, in 1945. The main preoccupations of philosophers of the period are well indicated in Russell's *An Inquiry Into Meaning and Truth* (1940), accurately described by its author as a combination of Hume's premises with the methods of the positivists, and in the masterly *Perception* (1932) of H. H. Price (born 1899), a thorough Russellian treatment of the main problem of knowledge.

The suspension of philosophical activity in the years from 1939 to 1945 was followed by a sharp move away, led by Wittgenstein himself, from his earlier ideas in the form they had been given by Ayer and Russell. The formalistic type of analytic philosophy, which reposes unlimited confidence in the logic of *Principia Mathematica* as both instrument and ideal model of analytic procedure, gave way to a quite different kind of philosophical concern with language, one that sought to understand it as it actually is rather than to criticize it for failure to conform to the mode of expression of mathematically formulated natural science. Ayer remained faithful to the main principles of his earlier position, while defending them in a qualified form, in *The Problem of Knowledge* (1956) and various essays.

Popper. Besides Ayer the main recent exponent in Britain of the formalistic tradition of analysis has been Karl Popper (born 1902), who was associated with the Vienna circle at the time his *Logik der Forschung* was first published in 1935 (translated as *Logic of Scientific Discovery,* 1959). In this influential book Popper argued that falsifiability, not, as the other positivists had contended, verifiability, is the essential criterion for the scientific character of discourse. Furthermore, falsifiability does not distinguish the meaningful from the meaningless but, rather, empirical science from equally meaningful, and often historically important, metaphysics.

Popper maintained that scientific knowledge does not grow by any sort of mechanical, inductive process. It begins with the imaginative conjecturing of hypotheses, something that cannot be subjected to rules, and proceeds by the determined exposure of the consequences of these hypotheses to the risk of empirical falsification. Theories cannot be positively established; they can be made only provisionally acceptable by successful submission to empirical tests. Popper came to England soon after his application of these ideas about method to history and the social sciences in *The Open Society and Its Enemies* (1945), in which he attacked Plato, Hegel, and Marx for their historicism, their belief in inevitable laws of historical development.

Linguistic analysis. Between 1945 and 1959 two related but nevertheless distinct kinds of linguistic philosophy were dominant in Britain. The first of these is the pure doctrine of the later Wittgenstein, as expressed in his *Philosophical Investigations* (1953). The second is the Oxford philosophy of ordinary language, whose most prominent exponents have been Gibert Ryle (born 1900) and J. L. Austin (1911–1960).

The two forms of linguistic philosophy share a conception of the nature of philosophy and a predominating interest in questions about meaning and about the nature of mind. For both the characteristic mark of wrong, traditional, metaphysical philosophy is its collision with obvious common-sense certainties. Another link with Moore is the explanation both give of philosophical paradox; they attribute it to .the misuse of ordinary words, inspired by treacherous analogies. Where they differ is that Wittgenstein and his followers were chiefly concerned to dispel confusion and paradox by any means that come to hand; they strenuously repudiated any desire to assert a contrary philosophical position. For the philosophers of ordinary language, however, metaphysical paradox is not simply a conceptual disorder to be cured; it is, rather, a convenient point of entry into the task of setting out the complex and informal logic of the philosophically crucial terms of ordinary speech, a task that Ryle has called "logical geography" and Austin "rational grammar."

Wittgenstein. Much of Wittgenstein's *Investigations* takes the form of a polemic against his own earlier work. Language is not, as the *Tractatus* had suggested, something whose essence can be displayed as a formal, logical calculus. It is, rather, a bewildering variety of complex human activities, undertaken with multifarious purposes. To discover the meaning of words, we must consider them in use, and the right way for philosophy to proceed is by assembling reminders of the actual common employment of words to show up, by contrast, the metaphysical distortions they have been subjected to. Language has many more uses than that of bare, neutral description, and even where it is descriptive, it does not function in any simple pictorial fashion.

Wittgenstein's prime application of these principles is in his account of the language in which we speak of the mental. He mounted a complicated and resourceful attack on the view that the words we use to talk of mental acts and states refer to the inner, private experiences of their owners. He argued that the notion of a private language is an impossible one and showed with a wealth of detail that "inner processes stand in need of outward criteria," that we tell, for example, what another man understands by considering what he can do, not by guessing hopelessly at what must be going on within him.

An analogue to the self-destructive conclusion of the *Tractatus,* that the sentences of which it is composed are nonsensical, survives in Wittgenstein's later work. Philosophical error cannot be corrected by the explicit assertion of philosophical truth, for there is no such thing. It must be annihilated by a purely descriptive assemblage of the common linguistic practices and conventions in whose defiance philosophical error consists.

Ryle. In Ryle's *The Concept of Mind* (1949) the positive theory about the nature of mind that is suggested in Wittgenstein's *Investigations* is forthrightly stated. For Ryle, to talk about the mind, whether one's own or another's, is to talk about propensities to behave in certain ways. There is no special problem about our knowledge of the minds of others since we have the same sort of access to their minds as to our own. Knowledge, for example, is not some sort of infallibly accurate vision; it is an ability to do someting like answer questions or, more generally, carry out some sort of nonverbal task with skill. Thinking, again, is not a silent, interior accompaniment to our speech; it is a matter of using words in an intelligent way, being ready to parry objections to them, and so forth. Ryle made his case against the "Cartesian myth" of the mental and the physical as two utterly distinct worlds by pointing out the absurdity of the ways of speaking about the mind that we should have to follow if it were true; for example, if influences or acts of will are inner mental events, we would have to suppose that there are definite answers to the question of how many of them we have had in a given period of time. At all points his discussion is enforced with concrete reminders about ordinary speech.

Austin. The most refined investigations of ordinary discourse are to be found in the writings of Austin. In his *Sense and Sensibilia* (1962) he subjected to the most minutely discriminating attention the crucial first steps in the arguments of philosophers like Price and Ayer, who have contended that the immediate objects of perception are not public material things but private sense impressions. In an influential early essay Austin maintained that to claim knowledge is not simply to describe one's state of mind but is, more importantly, to perform an action in the way one makes a promise. In his *How to Do Things With Words* (1962) he endeavored to develop his initial distinction between the descriptive and performative uses of language into a system wholly free from the simple-minded assumptions about meaning of the earlier type of analytic philosophy.

Strawson and Hampshire. Wittgenstein's rigid avoidance of philosophical conclusions and Austin's unswervingly detailed analytic practice encouraged a widespread criticism that linguistic philosophy had degenerated into trivial lexicography. In contrast to this detailed analysis, however, in 1959 two books of an avowedly general and systematic nature were published—*Individuals,* by P. F. Strawson (born 1919), and *Thought and Action,* by Stuart Hampshire (born 1914). In these books many of the detailed conclusions of previous linguistic investigation are assembled into a comprehensive theory.

Both start from the premises that thought depends upon language and that language is an essentially social institution. On this foundation Strawson built a general account of the conceptual devices with which we refer to the world, arguing that if discourse is to be possible at all, a primary place in it must be accorded to material bodies and a particular species of such bodies—namely, persons. And just as bodies of these two kinds must be identified if we are to be in a position to refer to any other kinds of particular things, so reference to particulars must be prior to any reference to universals. The idea that language is essential is seen here to have as its consequence a rejection of the Cartesian view of the detached contemplative thinker, certain only of his inner life, who finds the existence of the outside world and his own body a problem.

The same derivation of broadly realistic conclusions from an account of the nature of thought is to be found in Hampshire and is reinforced by the consideration, which has some distant affinity with existentialism, that man is an essentially active being, perceiving the world more through bodily interaction with it than through disengaged aesthetic contemplation, and conscious of his continuing identity and the passage of time by way of the flow of his intentions.

Both Strawson and Hampshire are practitioners of what Strawson has called "descriptive metaphysics," which they see as an extrication of those features of our conceptual scheme which are necessary to our having a language and, thus, to the capacity for any but the most elementary kind of thinking. Such a project is similar in general form to that of the *Tractatus,* but the execution of it is very different from the early Wittgenstein's, not least because it owes so much to Wittgenstein's later work, with its emphasis on linguistic practices as social institutions or "ways of life." More remotely, there is a connection between this procedure and Kant's idea of a critical philosophy.

Current interests. A good indication of the prevailing philosophical atmosphere of a period is the problems that are most insistently discussed, the issues in which all philosophical controversy has a tendency to terminate. In the 1930s the cardinal topics were the view of all necessity as tautological and the phenomenalist account of material objects. In the 1950s philosophers in Britain were preoccupied with the varieties of meaning and our knowledge of other minds.

In the mid-1960s, at the time of the writing of this article, the main interests are the concept of identity that underlies the reference to things and persons, without which discourse cannot begin, and the problem of the nature of action. According to Wittgenstein and others, human actions are quite different in character from natural happenings in the physical world and cannot be explained in the same causal way. Opposed to this view is a revived materialism that identifies mental events, including the mental causes of bodily behavior, with occurrences in the brain. At this moment the sort of psychologistic empiricism which is often thought of as the British philosophy par excellence is at a low ebb; the intellectual descendants of Kant confront those of Hobbes. But it should be remembered that Hobbes was the greatest progenitor of empiricism, just as Kant was its greatest apostatizing critic. The themes of classical epistemology are still central to philosophy in Britain.

(See also ANALYSIS, PHILOSOPHICAL; CAMBRIDGE PLATONISTS; COMMON SENSE; DARWINISM; DEISM; EMPIRICISM; MORAL SENSE; OCKHAMISM; PELAGIUS AND PELAGIANISM; PHYSICOTHEOLOGY; SCOTISM; and UTILITARIANISM. See British Philosophy in Index for articles on British philosophers and other figures important to British philosophy.)

Bibliography

Benn, A. W., *History of English Rationalism in the Nineteenth Century*, 2 vols. London, 1906. A very detailed survey of the Victorian controversy between religion and science, strongly biased toward the latter combatant.

Carré, M. H., *Phases of Thought in England.* Oxford, 1949. An excellent general survey of the whole field.

Cassirer, Ernst, *The Platonic Renaissance in England,* translated by James P. Pettegrove. Austin, Tex., Edinburgh, and London, 1954. A learned, somewhat amorphous work.

McCosh, J., *Scottish Philosophy From Hutcheson to Hamilton.* London, 1875. A detailed catalogue.

Metz, Rudolf, *A Hundred Years of British Philosophy,* translated by J. W. Harvey, T. E. Jessop, and Henry Sturt, London, 1938. Despite some quaint Teutonisms, an admirably thorough and reliable study.

Muirhead, J. H., *The Platonic Tradition in Anglo-Saxon Philosophy.* London, 1931.

Passmore, John A., *A Hundred Years of Philosophy.* London, 1957. First-rate, both in detail and in proportion.

Seth, J., *English Philosophers and Schools of Philosophy.* London, 1912. A reasonable account of the main figures.

Sharp, Dorothea Elizabeth, *Franciscan Philosophy at Oxford in the Thirteenth Century.* Oxford, 1930. A technical study of a neglected field.

Sorley, W. R., *A History of English Philosophy.* Cambridge, 1920. A standard work; reasonable, judicious, and comprehensive.

Stephen, Leslie, *History of English Thought in the Eighteenth Century,* 2 vols. London, 1876; 3d rev. ed., New York, 1963. A marvelous and most readable book, though often unreliable in interpretation.

Taylor, H. O., *Thought and Expression in the Sixteenth Century,* 2 vols. New York, 1920. See Vol. II for the intellectual life of the philosophically sterile period between Ockham and Francis Bacon.

Tulloch, J., *Rational Theology and Christian Philosophy in England in the Seventeenth Century.* Edinburgh and London, 1872. A good account of the Cambridge Platonists.

Urmson, J. O., *Philosophical Analysis: Its Development Between the Two World Wars.* Oxford, 1956.

Warnock, G. J., *English Philosophy Since 1900.* London, 1958.

ANTHONY QUINTON

BROAD, CHARLIE DUNBAR, English epistemologist, historian of philosophy, moral philosopher, philosopher of science, and writer on the philosophical aspects of psychical research, was born at Harlesden, now a suburb of London, in 1887. The only child of middle-class parents in comfortable circumstances, he received a good education at Dulwich College. With his special interest and ability in science and mathematics he won, in 1905, a science scholarship to Trinity College, Cambridge, with which Broad's philosophical career was to be chiefly associated. Despite success in his work at Cambridge, he became convinced that he would never be outstanding as a scientist and turned to philosophy, in which he took first-class honors with special distinction in 1910. A year later he was elected to a fellowship at Trinity because of a dissertation that became his first book, *Perception, Physics, and Reality* (Cambridge 1914).

From 1911 to 1920 Broad was at the University of St. Andrews, first as assistant to G. F. Stout, the professor of logic and metaphysics, then as a lecturer at Dundee. During World War I, he combined his lecturing duties with work for the Ministry of Munitions in a chemical laboratory. He followed C. Lloyd Morgan in the chair of philosophy at the University of Bristol in 1920, but after a few years he returned to Trinity College to succeed J. M. E. McTaggart as lecturer in moral science. In 1933 Broad somewhat reluctantly became Knightbridge professor of moral philosophy. Until his retirement in 1953, Broad had not traveled outside Great Britain except for periodic visits to Scandinavia, in particular to Sweden, a country whose people, life, and language had long attracted him. Broad's encouragement of Swedish philosophers and philosophy led to his being generously honored by the academicians of that country. In Britain his services to philosophy were recognized by bestowal of most of the honors available to a don so secluded from public activity.

At Cambridge, Broad was most influenced by his teachers, McTaggart and W. E. Johnson, and by Russell and Moore. These four men, with the important additions of G. F. Stout and A. E. Taylor at St. Andrews, represent in the diversity of their thought something of the extraordinary range of Broad's own interests. Among British philosophers of this century, no one, including Russell, published so much on so many different philosophical topics. The largest part of Broad's writing falls within the theory of knowledge and the philosophy of science—provided that we assign some of the problems of traditional metaphysics to these two fields—although he also wrote extensively, if less systematically, on ethics and on the life and thought of such scattered figures as Bacon, Newton, Butler, and Kant. The ample scope and scale of Broad's work were displayed early in his career. Within his first three years of serious publication, he had produced almost two dozen reviews of widely different books, essays on "The Doctrine of Consequences in Ethics" (*International Journal of Ethics*, vol. 24, April 1914, 293–320) and "Lord Hugh Cecil's 'Conservatism'" (*Ibid.*, vol. 23, July 1913, 396–418), a critical notice of Meinong's *Über Annahmen* (*Mind*, N.S., vol. 22, January 1913, 90–102), and his own first volume, which discussed the relation between causation and perception. This catholicity of interest remained apparent for the next fifty years, despite Broad's confession in the autobiographical chapter of *The Philosophy of C. D. Broad* that some time after his acceptance of the Knightbridge chair he gave up philosophy in all but title and routine: "I no longer believed in the importance of philosophy, I took little interest in its later developments, and I knew very well that I at least had shot my bolt and had nothing further of value to contribute." The most curious feature of this confession is that it makes the development of ennui coincide with a period of considerable publication by Broad. The eight hundred pages of the second volume of his *Examination of McTaggart's Philosophy* (Cambridge 1933–1938) were written at this time, as were his essays on Locke (*Hibbert Journal*, vol. 31, January 1933, 249–267) and Sidgwick (*Ibid.*, vol. 37, October 1938, 25–43), his inaugural lecture on determinism, a number of papers given to the Aristotelian Society, and a spate of notes on psychical phenomena. Broad's changed attitudes and feelings toward his chosen field had little substantial effect on the work he contributed to it.

Theory of knowledge. Broad's writings on perception and knowledge, like the rest of his work, form neither a system nor a set of unequivocal answers to a group of related questions. For every philosophical position there were always reasons pro and con; and on any given issue Broad often found it difficult to decide where the weightier reasons lay.

Sense data. Thus, following Stout, and ultimately Locke, in distinguishing between the odors, noises, and colored patches that we sense and the physical objects like coins and books that we perceive, Broad gave rather cautious support to a version of the causal theory of perception. There are, he thought, two kinds of particulars involved in perception—persistent substances (bodies) with properties like shape, size, inertial mass, and spatial position; and the "sense-qualified occurrents" of which we are immediately aware in sensing, as when we see the upper surface of a dinner plate. Broad argued that visual sense data, or *sensa* as he called them, at least are never, in fact, identical with, or parts of, the surface of the physical object that is seen. If we recall that the sense data obtained by a given person in looking at the same surface from different positions and angles form a continuous series, and that the velocity of light is finite, it is reasonable to believe that at least some of the properties of sense data must be different from those of their correlated bodies, that a penny, for example, retains the same size and shape while our sense data of it change in these respects as we alter position. The greater the distance between our eyes and the body seen, the more obvious it is that the properties of the body and of our sense data must differ. It is likewise reasonable that if this difference sometimes holds, it must always hold; for there is no gap in the continuity of conditions in which we obtain sense data of a particular surface that would allow us to identify only some of the sense data with that surface. As underpinning for this sharp distinction, Broad tried to establish that a sense datum must have all the properties that it is sensed as having, although it may also have unnoticed properties; that unsensed sense data can exist; and that the word "sensation" refers both to bodily feelings and to "genuine sensations," the former of which are not, although the latter are, analyzable into an act of sensing and its object, the sense datum.

In general, Broad treated these claims about the existence and properties of sense data as being empirical ones, and so was led to a similar treatment of such questions as: Are sensa qualitatively mind-dependent? Can two people sense the same sensum? How long can a sensum last? Do we infer from the properties of our sensa to the properties of physical objects? How much resemblance is there between the properties of sensa and the properties of physical objects? In his "Reply to Critics," written late in his career, Broad indicated that he did not feel the force of the view, made familiar by G. A. Paul and A. J. Ayer, that these questions can be answered only by decisions in particular cases or else are misconceived, since the sense-data theory is simply an elaborate terminological proposal for dealing with the argument from illusion. Nor did he recognize the radical criticism that this view offered of his own attempts to deal with sense data as private objects interposed between human observers and the unobservable physical world. The latter is the "remote causal ancestor" of our sensations, he thought, and the kind of isomorphism one must postulate between the properties of sense data and the properties of "the hypothetical system of physical things and events" he was "willing to leave to experts to decide."

The mind–body problem. In his discussion of the mind–body problem, Broad set out to produce a theory that would account for the apparent fact that brain events are a necessary condition of mental events, and also leave open the possibility that some mental events occur after the death of their associated bodies. He suggested that minds are the result of two components—a nervous system, and a "psychogenic factor," which is modified by experience and capable of persisting after bodily death. Since no other properties are assigned to the psychogenic factor, nor is its relation to the brain described, the factor remains unobservable, either directly or indirectly; and the parent theory is obviously *ad hoc.* Broad would have welcomed a theory that was more open to experimental testing; although he distinguished metaphysical from scientific theories by the latter's susceptibility to such testing. He was thus in the position of answering the philosophical question, How are bodies related to minds? with what was, by his own criteria, an inadequate scientific theory. Just as he took sense data to be private objects whose properties could be investigated by introspection, so he took the mind–body relation as being similar to the relation between a visible body and an invisible one—a relation open in theory, if not in practice, to empirical investigation.

General explanatory principles. Closely related to this treatment of philosophical problems was Broad's attempt, throughout his writings, to isolate a set of very general principles that would be both necessarily true and genuinely explanatory of the most pervasive and important features of the world. Broad was not convinced either that every necessarily true statement is analytic or that every synthetic statement is testable by means of perceptual experience. He thought that there might well be propositions, such as "The cause of any change contains a change as an essential factor," which are synthetic—informative about the world—but necessarily true. The denial of this proposition is not self-contradictory, so the proposition cannot be analytic; yet a counterexample is impossible to imagine, so the proposition, rather than being an ordinary empirical one, is self-evidently true. Propositions as general as this, Broad half suggested, are the appropriate axioms of metaphysical theories, theories whose results he compared unfavorably to the "beautiful and surprising consequences" deduced from the premises of geometry and such physical premises as the "entropy principle." Broad's pessimism about the utility of deductive metaphysics seems to have been the outcome of a desire to treat speculative philosophy as a suprascience, one that accounted for our most general concepts, such as cause, substance, potentiality, and actuality, in much the same way that physics accounted for such less general concepts as velocity, mass, simultaneity, and the atom.

A priori concepts. This distinction between the concepts dealt with by the sciences and those more general ones dealt with by philosophy has its parallel, and perhaps its source, in the distinction drawn by Broad between empirical and a priori (nonempirical) concepts. He believed that the simplest empirical concepts, for example, the ideas of red or yellow, are formed by our contrasting and comparing many different red or yellow objects. Eventually, we abstract the required quality from all other qualities and from any particular substance in such a way that we are able to think of the quality in the absence of any instance or image of it. In thus accepting the traditional story of the genesis of empirical concepts, Broad hesitated between the two equally ancient views of how we form a priori concepts. The first view is that we have innate dispositions to form specific ideas like those of cause, substance, and rightness as the result of having certain kinds of experiences. The second is that we have "a general power of non-perceptual intuition," distinct from our ability to have sense perceptions and to introspect, which allows us to intuit such relations as causation and rightness whenever we have the appropriate kinds of experiences to stimulate the power.

A standard criticism of these theories of concept formation is that the story about abstraction is logically circular; and that the accounts of a priori concepts apply equally well or little to empirical ones, so that Broad's distinction between the two cannot be drawn. The abstraction story is circular because in order to compare and contrast one color with another we must already have the ability to recognize and distinguish those colors. Yellow objects that are to be compared must be seen as yellow before the suggested procedure can begin. Hence, we can rightly claim that innate ideas or nonempirical intuitions are needed for the concept of yellow as they are for concepts like that of substance.

However, thinking of an absent quality yellow is not the intellectual analogue of sensing a yellow patch, for thinking of yellow is not a matter of "contemplating the characteristic" yellow, as Broad once assumed it was. Noting the logically necessary relations between concepts, for example, that all yellow things must be colored, is not like having a sense datum and noting that in it a red patch borders on a yellow patch. Granting these two points, as Broad did in his "Reply to Critics," would make it less plausible to hold that some synthetic propositions may be necessarily true. For once we abandon the sense-datum picture of logical necessity, there is little temptation to appeal to self-evidence (the intellectual sensing of universal connections) in support of metaphysical principles.

Psychical research. Broad often urged philosophers to take something of his own keen interest in psychical research. He claimed that no one could answer the question as to whether any person actually has the power of paranormal precognition without having made a careful study of the available evidence; but most philosophers obviously considered this to be a scientific task for psychologists. In the absence of any encouragement from scientists, few philosophers would join Broad in discussing the further question, which chiefly interested him, How does the existence of supernormal precognition affect such philosophical topics as causation, the mind–body problem, immortality, and sense perception? Suppose we took seriously the suggestion that each person has an extended but intangible and invisible body as well as his ordinary body and that the invisible body puts forth pseudopods which touch and affect external objects. The existence of such a body would certainly alter a number of our views on topics like causation and the mind–body problem. But exactly how they were altered would depend on such factors as the degree of control we could exert over our invisible bodies, whether they survived our corporeal bodies, and what sort of knowledge we could have of our intangible bodies. Thus until there is scientific agreement on what has been established concerning paranormal cognition, it is difficult to say how its existence would affect philosophical discussion. What can undoubtedly be done is to consider whether the notion of supernormal precognition is logically coherent. Broad thought that it is and tried to rebut arguments that it is self-contradictory to speak of precognizing something that does not yet exist as well as arguments that paranormal precognition makes an effect precede its cause—correctly guessing a card symbol would be influenced by what is to be known later about the card. However, showing that paranormality is logically possible does nothing to advance its claims over alternative hypotheses in the explanation of unlikely experimental data, data that may be unlikely because of selective sampling alone.

Probability and induction. Although Broad's two papers entitled "Induction and Probability" gave what will probably be a definitive expression to their point of view, they were overshadowed by the simultaneous appearance of J. M. Keynes's *A Treatise on Probability.* In much the same way, Broad's *Scientific Thought* (London, 1923)—perhaps his best book—was neglected after the publication, a few years later, of Russell's *The Analysis of Matter.*

Broad argued that the degree of belief we give to well-established inductions cannot be justified "by any known principle of probability unless some further premise about the physical world be assumed." Yet this premise is notoriously difficult to state. If induction is to be a rational procedure, nature must consist of a few kinds of substances that combine in various lawlike ways and thus produce variety in a finite world. In brief, we need Keynes's Principle of Limitation of Independent Variety. Without such a principle we cannot make use of inductive analogies, for they assume that future cases will resemble past cases, or in other words, that no one object has an infinite number of independent qualities or is producible by an infinite number of different causes. In "The Principles of Problematic Induction" (*PAS*, N.S., vol. 28, 1927–1928, 1–46), Broad went on to consider, and answer affirmatively, the question whether we can know that nature has this desirable structure.

Thus, Broad held that the problem of justifying inductive inferences is a genuine one. He thought that the two questions, What is meant by calling this inductive belief well-supported? and What makes induction a valid procedure? have similar answers. Each question requires us to state the criteria by which we can distinguish sound from unsound inferences, and these criteria will enable us to provide the necessary and sufficient conditions for well-grounded inferences. Such conditions must in turn be based on fundamental principles that will serve as general premises in every sound inductive inference. This last step of Broad's claim has been much criticized as confusing two quite different issues. The first concerns the empirical statement, for which there is ample evidence, that nature is so organized that in the future at least some of our inductive beliefs will be correct. The second concerns the logically necessary truth that induction is a rational procedure; for we could not have an inductive policy that was both successful and irrational, that is, not supported by good evidence. What we mean by "rational inductive procedure" is one that is well supported by evidence. It is this support that "justifies" the policy in the only permissible sense of "justify." The structure of nature is known inductively and so cannot itself be referred to for support of the inductive procedure; nor is there any need to do so. The only justification we require is the success of the policy, and that we already have.

Ethics. On the problems of ethics, Broad showed a cautious hesitancy to commit himself. Two of his late papers, "Some Reflections on Moral-Sense Theories in Ethics" (*PAS*, N.S., vol. 45, 1944–1945, 131–166) and "Some of the Main Problems of Ethics" (*Philosophy*, vol. 21, July 1946, 99–117), have been widely read; but they provide only hints as to Broad's own views. As in the early chapters of *Five Types of Ethical Theory* (London 1920), on such writers as Spinoza and Hume, Broad classified types of ethical theories, exposed their assumptions, and drew out their logical implications, without committing himself. For example, in his paper on moral-sense theories he distinguished three analyses of "That act is right": the sentence does not express the speaker's judgment, but his emotions or desires or commands; what is expressed is a judgment about "certain human experiences, certain sensations or emotions or desires," that is, a "moral feeling"; and a judgment is made that ascribes a property like "what it is fitting to approve" or "conducive to social stability," properties independent of the speaker's opinions, desires, or feelings.

In his "Reply to Critics" Broad said that theories of the second and third types must admit the existence both of nonempirical concepts of moral attributes and of synthetic a priori propositions like "any act of promise-breaking tends as such to be wrong." Since he was not convinced that there were no such concepts and propositions, he was able to sympathize with theories of these types, as well as with theories of the first type. But to the question, does "That act is right" express a judgment, a feeling, or a command? Broad could only reply, "I have no definite opinion." He was similarly undecided on the question whether ethical terms like "wrong" and "duty" stand for properties, and if so, exactly what sort of properties these might be. His attitude here, as to many other philosophical problems, resembled that of a prudent scientist awaiting further evidence before coming to a decision.

Broad had no "philosophy" in the sense of a deeply original way of interpreting and dealing with the issues of his field. He was a scientist manqué who took up philosophical problems much as he found them, leaving them classified and more manageable but not transformed. His impressive ability to understand and recast the most difficult arguments, the elegance of his writing, his unrivaled thoroughness and lucidity, were placed at the service of other people's questions rather than his own.

Bibliography

Broad's other books include *The Mind and Its Place in Nature* (London, 1925), his most characteristic work, and *Lectures on Psychical Research* (London, 1963). Some of his essays have been collected in two volumes, *Ethics and the History of Philosophy* (London, 1952) and *Religion, Philosophy, and Scientific Research* (London, 1953). His two papers entitled "Induction and Probability" appeared in *Mind*, Vol. 27 (1918), 389–404 and Vol. 29 (1920), 11–45. There is a complete bibliography up to 1959 in *The Philosophy of C. D. Broad*, edited by P. A. Schilpp (New York, 1959), which also contains 21 essays on his work by various philosophers, Broad's "Reply to Critics," and his "Autobiography." A critical examination of Broad's theory of perception is given in Martin Lean, *Sense Perception and Matter* (London, 1953).

ROBERT BROWN

BROUWER, LUITZEN EGBERTUS JAN, the founder of mathematical intuitionism, was born in 1881 in Overschie, near Rotterdam, the Netherlands. After attending schools in Medemblik, Hoorn, and Haarlem, he studied mathematics at the Municipal University of Amsterdam. He obtained his doctorate in 1907 for his thesis, *Over de Grondslagen der Wiskunde* (Amsterdam and Leipzig, 1907). He became *privaat-docent* at Amsterdam in 1909 and served as professor there from 1912 until his retirement in 1955. In the year that he became a professor he was elected to the Royal Dutch Academy of Sciences.

Besides contributions to the foundations of mathematics, Brouwer has made major contributions to other areas of mathematics, in particular to topology, in which his most important publications date from the period 1909/1913.

Combinatorial or algebraic topology came into being through discoveries of Henri Poincaré in the 1890s. A fundamental technique of Poincaré was to analyze figures into combinations of simple figures and to represent the topological structure of the figures by algebraic properties of the combination. Brouwer extended and deepened this technique, particularly in relation to questions of the existence of mappings and fixed points. He proved such classic results as the topological invariance of dimension, which implies that there is no bicontinuous one-to-one mapping of Euclidean m-dimensional space onto Euclidean n-dimensional space, for $m \neq n$.

Although he is primarily a mathematician, Brouwer has always been preoccupied with general philosophy and has elaborated a highly individual philosophical vision. Indeed, the most remarkable feature of Brouwer's work in the foundations of mathematics is the boldness and consistency with which, starting from his own philosophical position, he has questioned the principles on which the mathematics he inherited was based, down to so elementary a principle as the law of excluded middle, and then has proceeded to criticize these principles in detail and to begin to reconstruct mathematics on a basis which he regards as sound.

Although he later presented them more systematically, the essentials of Brouwer's philosophy were already present in his thesis of 1907 and, in certain respects, in *Leven, Kunst, en Mystiek* (Delft, 1905). These works antedate the decisive steps in the development of mathematical intuitionism. In effect, Brouwer argued in his thesis that logic is derivative from mathematics and dependent for its evidence on an essentially mathematical intuition that rests on a basis close to Kant's notion of time as the "form of inner sense." Intellectual life begins with "temporal perception," in which the self separates experiences from each other and distinguishes itself from them. Brouwer describes this temporal perception as "the falling apart of a life moment into two qualitatively different things, of which the one withdraws before the other and nonetheless is held onto by memory" ("Weten, Willen, Spreken," 1933). This perception, however, belongs to an attitude (which Brouwer earlier termed "mathematical consideration") which the self adopts to preserve itself; the adoption of this attitude is an act of free will, in a broad sense which Brouwer probably derived from Schopenhauer. The fundamental intuition of mathematics is this structure of temporal perception "divested of all content"; in mathematics one sees that the process of division and synthesis can be iterated indefinitely, giving rise to the series of natural numbers. In the temporal order thus revealed, one can always imagine new elements inserted between the given ones, so that Brouwer could say that the theories of the natural numbers and of the continuum come from one intuition, an idea that, from his point of view, was made fuller and more precise by his theory of free choice sequences, but one might argue that it was made superfluous by that theory.

Brouwer's constructivism was developed in this context. His constructivism was probably motivated less by an insistence on absolute evidence and a rejection of hypotheses (which might have led to "finitism" in David Hilbert's sense of the term or even to a still narrower thesis) than by Brouwer's subjectivism and his insistence on the primacy of will over intellect. On these grounds, mathematics should consist in a constructive mental activity, and a mathematical statement should be an indication or report of such activity. Brouwer credited this way of looking at mathematics to the inspiration of his teacher, Gerrit Mannoury.

In his thesis Brouwer limited himself to criticizing alternative theories of the foundations mathematics and to criticizing Cantorian set theory, but in "De Onbetrouwbaarheid der Logische Principes" (1908), perhaps urged on by Mannoury, Brouwer raised doubts about the validity of the law of excluded middle, although he still regarded the question as open. In *Intuitionisme en Formalisme* (1912) Brouwer did not say flatly that the law of excluded middle is false, but he gave an instance of his standard argument, an example like that presented in the section on Intuitionism in MATHEMATICS, FOUNDATIONS OF, which also gives a fuller exposition of constructivism.

In a number of publications beginning in 1918 and extending through the 1920s, Brouwer developed intuitionist mathematics and worked out in detail his critique of classical mathematics, determining for different branches of mathematics which of their theorems are intuitionistically true. In "Begründung der Mengenlehre unabhängig vom logischen Satz vom ausgeschlossenen Dritten," Brouwer undertook to develop an intuitionist set theory, on which a theory of the continuum could be based. In this work Brouwer introduced his concept of set (*Menge;* later, in "Points and Spaces," 1954, he called it "spread") and therefore the idea of an arbitrary infinite sequence as generated by successive free choices. He also introduced the notion of species, which led to his own version of a predicative hierarchy of classes. The principle that the value of a function everywhere defined on a spread must, for a given sequence as argument, be determined by a sufficiently large finite number of its terms is already present in "Begründung der Mengenlehre." This "continuity axiom" is the first of the two distinctive principles of intuitionist analysis.

In "Beweis, dass jede volle Funktion gleichmässig stetig ist" (1924), Brouwer announced a proof that a function everywhere defined on the closed unit interval is uniformly continuous. In this proof Brouwer used two fundamental assertions about spreads, later called the bar and fan theorems. The bar theorem, or an equivalent assertion, constitutes the other distinctive principle of intuitionist analysis. Brouwer's proof was presented in full in "Über Definitionsbereiche von Funktionen" (1927) and reworked, in a more general setting, in "Points and Spaces."

Since World War II Brouwer has published a long series of short papers in which he developed a new type of counterexample to classical theorems, based on another new principle.

Brouwer's philosophy is not limited to what is relevant to the foundations of mathematics. Mathematical consideration has a second phase, which he calls causal attention. In this phase " . . . one identifies in imagination certain series of phenomena with one another," an operation by which one can pick out objects and postulate causal rules. (The relation between temporal perception and causal attention is analogous to that between Kant's mathematical and dynamical categories.) The whole point of mathematical consideration lies in the fact that it makes possible the use of means: one produces a phenomenon which will be followed in a certain repeatable series by a desired phenomenon which cannot be directly reproduced. This makes the pursuit of instinctual satisfaction more efficient.

Especially in *Leven, Kunst, en Mystiek* and in "Consciousness, Philosophy, and Mathematics" (1948), Brouwer regards this "mathematical action" as a kind of fall from grace, whose results are uncertain and ultimately disappointing. With this view Brouwer couples a pessimism about society. Society is based on communication, which is itself a form of mathematical action. What is ordinarily called communicating one's thoughts actually amounts to influencing the actions of another, although sometimes a deeper communication of souls is approached. However, Brouwer was not always aloof from all efforts at social reform, as is shown by his participation, immediately after World War I, with the poet Frederik van Eeden, Mannoury, and others, in the Signific Circle, whose original goal, inspired by the abuses of propaganda during the war, was a far-reaching reform of language.

Additional Works by Brouwer

"De Onbetrouwbaarheid der Logische Principes." *Tijdschrift Voor Wijsbegeerte,* Vol. 2 (1908), 152–158. Reprinted in *Wiskunde, Waarheid, Werkelijkheid.*

"Die Theorie der endlichen kontinuerlichen Gruppen." *Mathematische Annalen,* Vol. 69 (1910), 181–202.

"Beweis der Invarianz der Dimensionenzahl." *Mathematische Annalen,* Vol. 70 (1911), 161–165.

"Über Abbildung von Mannigfaltigkeiten." *Mathematische Annalen,* Vol. 71 (1912), 97–115.

Intuitionisme en Formalisme. Amsterdam, 1912. Reprinted in *Wiskunde, Waarheid, Werkelijkheid.* Translated by A. Dresden as "Intuitionism and Formalism." *Bulletin of the American Mathematical Society,* Vol. 20 (1913), 81–96. Reprinted, with other writings by Brouwer, in Paul Benacerraf and Hilary Putnam, eds., *Philosophy of Mathematics: Selected Readings.* Englewood Cliffs, N.J., 1964.

"Über den naturlichen Dimensionsbegriff." *Journal für die reine und angewandte Mathematik,* Vol. 142 (1913), 146–152.

"Begründung der Mengenlehre unabhängig vom logischen Satz vom ausgeschlossenen Dritten." *Verhandelingen der Koninklijke Nederlandse Akademie van Wetenschappen,* Series A, Vol. 12 (1918–1919), Nos. 5 and 7.

Wiskunde, Waarheid, Werkelijkheid. Groningen, 1919.

"Besetzt jede reele Zahl eine Dezimalbruchentwicklung?" *Mathematische Annalen,* Vol. 83 (1921), 201–210.

"Begründung der Funktionenlehre unabhängig vom logischen Satz ausgeschlossenen Dritten." *Verhandelingen der Koninklijke Nederlandse Akademie van Wetenschappen,* Series A, Vol. 13 (1923), No. 2.

"Über die Bedeutung des Satzes vom ausgeschlossenen Dritten in der Mathematik, insbesondere in der Funktionentheorie." *Journal für die reine und angewandte Mathematik,* Vol. 154 (1924), 1–7. Translated in John van Heijenoort, ed., *From Frege to Gödel: A Source Book in Mathematical Logic, 1879–1931.* Cambridge, Mass., 1965.

"Beweis, dass jede volle Funktion gleichmässig stetig ist." *Koninklijke Nederlandse Akademie van Wetenschappen, Proceedings.* Series A, Vol. 27 (1924), 189–194 (cf. the remarks in *ibid.,* 644–646).

"Zur Begründung der intuitionistischen Mathematik." *Mathematische Annalen,* Vol. 93 (1924), 244–257; Vol. 95 (1926), 453–473; Vol. 96 (1927), 451–489.

"Über definitionsbereiche von Funktionen." *Mathematische Annalen,* Vol. 97 (1927), 60–75. Translated in van Heijenoort.

"Weten, Willen, Spreken." *Euclides,* Vol. 9 (1933), 177–193.

"Synopsis of the Signific Movement in the Netherlands." *Synthese,* Vol. 5 (1946), 201–208.

"Address to Prof. G. Mannoury." *Synthese,* Vol. 6 (1947), 190–194.

"Consciousness, Philosophy, and Mathematics," in *Proceedings of the Tenth International Congress of Philosophy.* Amsterdam, 1949. Vol. II, pp. 1235–1249. Last section of this paper reprinted in Benacerraf and Putnam.

"Historical Background, Principles, and Methods of Intuitionism." *South African Journal of Science,* Vol. 49 (1952), 139–146.

"Points and Spaces." *Canadian Journal of Mathematics,* Vol. 6 (1954), 1–17.

Works on Brouwer and Intuitionism

Heyting, Arend, *Les Fondements des mathématiques. Intuitionnisme. Théorie de la démonstration.* Paris, 1955. Expanded version of German original, *Mathematische Grundlagenforschung. Intuitionismus. Beweistheorie.* Berlin, 1934.

Heyting, Arend, *Intuitionism: An Introduction.* Amsterdam, 1956. This work by Heyting, and the one above, contain the most comprehensive bibliographies on intuitionism.

CHARLES PARSONS

BROWN, THOMAS (1778–1820), philosopher on the periphery of the common-sense school, was born at Kirkmabreck in Scotland. Radically opposed eighteenth-century traditions met in him. He shared with the common-sense school, which derived from Thomas Reid, a number of its metaphysical doctrines and its appeal to intuitive truths; and he was also Reid's tireless critic. Philosophy, for Brown, was very largely "analysis": analysis of what he regarded as darkened notions, designed to exhibit their character free from spurious mystery and complication; analysis of the genuinely complex into its elementary constituents and of the deceptively simple into its real complexity. He saw Reid as a great resister of analysis. In the procedure of analysis Brown was influenced by French empiricism in the line of descent from Condillac.

During the course of his studies at the University of Edinburgh, Brown attended the lectures given by Dugald Stewart, Reid's close adherent. He subsequently graduated in medicine. In 1798 he published a criticism of the *Zoonomia* of Erasmus Darwin and in 1804 a defense of Hume's account of causal relations (enlarged in 1806 and again in 1818, when it appeared under the title *Inquiry Into the Relation of Cause and Effect*). Brown was among the first of the contributors to the *Edinburgh Review* (he attacked Kant in the second number of the *Review*). In 1810 he was appointed conjoint professor of moral philosophy with Stewart and took over the teaching duties of the chair. His lectures were a dazzling success; they were published after his death and went through many editions in a few years.

Cause and effect. Brown's views on causation typically combined an empiricist analysis with what he called a principle of intuitive belief. He defined a cause as "that which immediately precedes any change, and which, existing at any time in similar circumstances, has been always, and will be always, immediately followed by a similar change" (*Cause and Effect*, p. 13). Brown thought that if we reflect with sufficient patience and imagination, we can see that this definition exhausts the notion of a cause. To suppose that a cause is something more than the antecedent of an invariable consequent is to suppose that we might know all the unfailing regularities of nature and yet have no conception of a causal connection. Material and volitional agents, Brown argued in detail, do not differ in agency; all agency is the same. The omnipotence of God resides simply in the fact that whenever he wills anything, his will is "immediately and invariably *followed* by the existence of its object" (*ibid.*, p. 103).

In tracing the sources of the complex illusion which, he thought, hangs over the relation of cause and effect, Brown emphasized the power of metaphor to mislead. Thus, things which are connected or bound together dependably go together; from this circumstance various figurative expressions enter the language and their figurative character is unnoticed. No bond or connection between causally connected events ever presents itself; yet unless we shift our attention from words to things, we shall easily suppose that it must be insensibly present. Experience (coupled with a kind of negative insight) enables us to see that the causal relation is merely one of sequence; but on what authority do we import the notion of invariableness into this sequence? Brown maintained that we are intuitively certain that the same antecedents will always be followed by the same consequents.

The will. Under Brown's analysis, mystery vanished from the will: will is an amalgam of desire and the belief that one has it in one's power to realize the desire; there is no further, indefinable operator in our voluntary actions. Brown was not impressed by denials of the identity of will and desire on the ground that there can be opposition between them—Reid had said, "We may desire what we do not will, and will what we do not desire." When the types of situation referred to are looked at more carefully, Brown said, the opposition is seen to lie between desire and desire, and to be terminated by the desire upon which action immediately depends.

Consciousness. The examination of consciousness which provides data for the philosophy of mind is not, in Brown's opinion, conducted by consciousness. Once again, he saw entities as having been multiplied beyond necessity and, in this case, beyond possibility. He maintained that consciousness is not, as some philosophers have supposed, a surveyor of the mind's various states as they occur; rather, it is constituted by them. To suppose that "the same indivisible mind" could exist at the same time in two different states, one of them an object to the other, is "a manifest absurdity" (*Philosophy of the Human Mind*, Lectures XI and XII). What is thought of as an introspective examination of mental phenomena is therefore, strictly speaking, retrospective.

Below the phenomena of the mind, analysis encounters metaphysical bedrock. Let us imagine, Brown said, a man born with fully matured powers and a completely blank mind. Let him now be allowed a single sensation. This will be his total consciousness. Let a second sensation be added and let him be made to recall the first. He will then come to a recognition of something different from either—of himself as their common subject. The conviction that we exist with an "absolute" identity through time is intuitive and irresistible; only the circumstances in which it arises afford matter for inquiry. This identity is the prerogative of our minds; "some sort of identity of the body" is associated with it in our ordinary ideas about "sameness of person" (*ibid.*, Lecture XII).

Perception. Brown's most subtle analyses occur in his theory of perception. His general problems were to explain how we come to know of the existence of an external, physical world and to specify the precise content of this knowledge. He was very conscious of the danger of question-begging assumptions; he maintained that at every turn we take externality for granted, and that all our language implies it. ("There is no distinct vocabulary of scepticism." *Ibid.*, Lecture XXII). Brown considered that our original awareness of things in their externality—their independence of our perception—is brought about by means of sensations commonly but inaccurately ascribed to touch. The sensations belonging to other senses acquire an external reference by association with these.

Brown proceeded first to reductive simplification: the various tangible qualities were maintained to be various modifications of either extension or resistance. He then went on to disclose and systematize the complexity of sensations involved in our tactual relations with things. He argued that sensations of mere touch do not primitively inform us of extension and externality. We derive the notion of spatial extension from our repeated experience of the temporal succession of muscular feelings in the movements of arms and fingers. When a familiar series of these feelings is interrupted by feelings of resistance to muscular effort—as, for example, our fingers closed around an object—we become aware for the first time of something separate from ourselves and learn something of its dimensions. Physical objects were, for Brown, essentially extended, resisting objects; but before his argument has ended, extension and resistance seem to have become merely phenomenal and, in their unperceived existence, to have disappeared into their unknown causes.

Moral theory. Brown's zeal for simplification is nowhere more conspicuous than in his moral theory. The distinctions, for example, between the obligatoriness, rectitude, and merit of an action are simply a matter of tense: contemplated before performance, the action is "obligatory"; in performance, it is "right"; and it is "meritorious" afterward. And what makes it so is the "emotion" of approval it arouses in us when we are in a fit state of mind to form a moral judgment—an emotion in no way arbitrary, for as morally definitive it proceeds from constitution of human nature. The strength and elevation of Brown's moral sentiments assisted his great, brief reputation.

Bibliography

Principal works by Thomas Brown are *Inquiry into the Relation of Cause and Effect* (Edinburgh, 1818); and *Lectures on the Philosophy of the Human Mind* (Edinburgh, 1820). Selections from Brown appear in Daniel Sommer Robinson, *The Story of Scottish Philosophy* (New York, 1961).

For literature on Brown, see David Welsh, *Account of the Life and Writings of Thomas Brown* (Edinburgh, 1825), and François Réthoré, *Critique de la philosophie de Thomas Brown* (Paris, 1863). Sir William Hamilton, *Discussions on Philosophy and Literature*, 2d ed. (Edinburgh, 1853), pp. 39–99, attacks Brown in defense of Reid. Brown is defended against Hamilton by John Stuart Mill in *An Examination of Sir William Hamilton's Philosophy* (London, 1865), Ch. 10.

There are chapters on Brown in James McCosh, *The Scottish*

Philosophy (London, 1875), and in Henry Laurie, *Scottish Philosophy in Its National Development* (Glasgow, 1902). An indication of Brown's influence in America can be found in Terence Martin, *The Instructed Vision* (Bloomington, Ind., 1961).

S. A. Grave

BROWNSON, ORESTES AUGUSTUS (1803–1876), Transcendentalist philosopher and journalist, was born in Stockbridge, Vermont. He had little formal education. Until 1822 he belonged to the Congregationalist church; he then joined the Presbyterians but was quickly repelled by their depreciation of human reason and by the Calvinist doctrine of predestination. In 1824 he became a Universalist, being ordained a minister in 1826. Three years later he abandoned Christianity and joined the socialist sect of Robert Dale Owen and Fanny Wright; at this time he wrote in behalf of the Workingmen's party. He was reconverted to the Christian religion in 1832, when he joined the Unitarians.

Brownson was introduced to philosophy in 1833, through the works of Victor Cousin, whose disciple he remained for ten years. Cousin was warm in his praise of Brownson as a philosopher. Though Brownson later criticized Cousin's philosophy for its eclecticism and psychologism, he always remained under its influence. His reading of Kant and the Italian idealist Gioberti were major factors in shaping his mature philosophy. For a while he was a member of the Transcendentalist group that met in Boston and at Brook Farm, but he considered their thinking poorly grounded and undisciplined.

In 1838 he founded the *Boston Quarterly Review*, which in 1842 was merged with *The U.S. Magazine and Democratic Review of New York.* In 1844, he was received into the Catholic church. The same year he founded *Brownson's Quarterly Review*, which he published, except for the years 1865–1872, until 1875. Most of Brownson's numerous articles and reviews appeared in this publication. His most important book was *The American Republic: Its Constitution, Tendencies, and Destiny.*

Although Brownson was a deeply religious thinker, he insisted that philosophy should begin not with authority or faith, but with data of reason. He criticized the notion of Christian philosophy proposed by the *Annales de philosophie chrétienne* for failing to do justice to the rational nature of philosophy.

Like Cousin, he made the starting point of philosophy the analysis of thought, stressing, in opposition to Cousin, its objective, rather than its subjective, side. All thought, he maintained, presupposes the presence of an object that can be analyzed into three elements: the ideal, the empirical, and the relationship between them. The ideal is the a priori element in all thought; it is that which makes any experience intelligible. The ideal is not a Kantian category, which Brownson interpreted to be a subjective form, but a necessary aspect of the object of knowledge. Since the object must be real in order to present itself to thought, its ideal, or content, must also be real. Further analysis revealed that this content includes both necessary and contingent "being," which Brownson identified respectively with God and creatures. God is a necessary and independent being; creatures are dependent existences, so called because they stand outside (*exstare*) their cause. Hence Brownson adopted the "ideal formula" of Gioberti: "Being creates existences" (*Ens creat existentias*). Accordingly, creative being is present to the mind in all its thinking; it alone makes thought possible.

Brownson defended himself against the charge of ontologism, which was condemned by Rome in 1861, on the ground that he did not teach that we have an immediate intuition of God, but only of being. Though being is God himself, we discover this only by rational analysis.

In his early days, Brownson believed in the divinity of humanity and the infallibility of the popular will. Political experience in later life convinced him of the absurdity of these notions. He rejected the idea that government and law have a purely human origin. Only in a qualified sense did he admit that governments derive their powers from the assent of the governed. All power ultimately comes from God; he alone has absolute sovereignty. Brownson thought the American Constitution more nearly perfect than others because it recognizes the existence of the Creator and of God-given rights of individuals, which the government is bound to respect and protect.

Works by Brownson

The Works of Orestes A. Brownson, 20 vols. Detroit, 1822–1907. Edited by H. F. Brownson.

Works on Brownson

Brownson, H. F., *Orestes A. Brownson's Early, Middle, and Latter Life,* 3 vols. Detroit, 1898–1900.

Cook, T. I., and Leavelle, A. B., "Orestes A. Brownson's *The American Republic.*" *Review of Politics,* Vol. 4, No. 1 (January 1942), 77–90; Vol. 4, No. 2 (April 1942), 173–193.

Farrell, B., *Orestes Brownson's Approach to the Problem of God.* Washington, 1950.

Fitzsimons, M. A., "Brownson's Search for the Kingdom of God: The Social Thought of an American Radical." *Review of Politics,* Vol. 16, No. 1 (January 1954), 22–36.

McMahon, F. E., "Orestes Brownson on Church and State." *Theological Studies,* Vol. 15 (1954), 175–228.

Maynard, T., *Orestes Brownson, Yankee, Radical, Catholic.* New York, 1943.

Parry, S. J., "The Premises of Brownson's Political Theory." *Review of Politics,* Vol. 16, No. 2 (April 1954), 194–211.

Raemer, S. A., *America's Foremost Philosopher.* Washington, 1931.

Schlesinger, A. M., Jr., *Orestes A. Brownson, A Pilgrim's Progress.* Boston, 1939.

Armand A. Maurer

BRUNNER, EMIL (1899–1966), was a Swiss theologian. He was educated in Switzerland and served in the Swiss army in 1914. Later he became a pastor and then professor of theology at Zurich. He participated extensively in the work of the World Council of Churches and also for a time in the Moral Re-Armament movement. He lectured on theology in many countries, notably in the United States, Japan, and Scotland.

Brunner's earliest theological positions were typical of Swiss and German Protestantism before 1914. He accepted the liberal theological emphasis on the social and ethical aspects of the gospel, as well as its stress upon the rational alliance between philosophy and theology. Even in his earliest theological writings he exhibited his personal interest in philosophy in a well-informed discussion of Husserl, *Das Symbolische in der religiösen Erkenntnis* (Tübingen, 1914). But after World War I he embarked upon a critique of liberalism that at first seemed to make him the natural ally of Karl Barth. His *Die Mystik und das Wort* (Tübingen, 1924) is a hostile discussion of Friedrich Schleiermacher's attempt to find a basis for Christianity in the general form of religious experience. Against this, Brunner poses the distinctive claims of Christian revelation, a revelation that cannot be discovered or appropriated through the use of criteria derived from natural theology or private experience.

The adjective much used of Brunner's (and also Barth's) concept of revelation was "dialectical." Theology is dialectical in that its attempts to grasp revelation necessarily involve the use of concepts that in purely philosophical discourse would cancel each other out. So the contradictions that arise, for example, in combining belief in divine goodness and omnipotence with an acknowledgment of the occurrence of physical evil are taken by the dialectical theologian to be simply manifestations of the necessarily paradoxical character of theological concepts. Contradiction is not a sign of intellectual failure, but of the inadequacy of our intellects before the splendor of divine revelation. Thus, if we try to use our ordinary criteria of consistency, we shall fail to grasp revelation at all. The major reason for this is that we shall be at fault if we try to understand revelation as consisting in a set of propositions. When God reveals himself, he does so as a person. Revelation is the act of a person, not the setting out of a doctrine.

It is for this reason that philosophy must necessarily limit its aspirations. The god of whom philosophy speaks is not the God of Christian revelation for at least two reasons. First, he is an inferred entity; and second, he is an object. It is not always clear whether Brunner believes that what philosophy says about God is false or simply inadequate. At times it seems clear that it is the former, yet Brunner is unlike Barth in the stress he puts upon the positive contribution that philosophy can make to theological thinking. Philosophy's role is to be critical, in the Kantian sense. It is to exhibit the limitations of human reason, and so to prevent speculative reason from attempting to occupy territory that belongs by right to revelation.

In revelation, God encounters man as person to person; man cannot argue his way to God by philosophy or discover God apart from the Biblical revelation, yet when God calls, man at least can answer. Even this minimal concession to human powers brought Brunner into conflict with Barth. Barth's position, which he outlined in the short, bitter pamphlet *Nein! Antwort an Emil Brunner* (1934), is that man, totally corrupted by the Fall, cannot advance an inch toward God by means of his natural powers. Grace has to supply even the capacity of responding to God's initiative. Brunner, who always feared the depiction of men as mere puppets, laid great stress on the natural man's capacity for speech and for elementary rationality as a precondition of any response to God.

The contrast between Brunner's theology and both liberalism on the one hand and Barthianism on the other is most marked in Brunner's ethics and social philosophy. Unlike Barth, Brunner believes that the basis for a natural ethics, even if a very limited one, exists. He revives the idea, which is found in Luther, of orders of creation. An order of creation is a social institution or practice of ordinary human origin, not derived from revelation, but shown by Biblical evidence to have divine authorization. So Christ blessed monogamy in his appearance at the wedding at Cana and in his utterances about marriage; so he expressed the divine source of the state's authority when he said, "Render unto Caesar. . . ." These orders supply human beings with norms to whose validity revelation itself testifies, but for knowledge of which revelation is not necessary. Such norms have the negative function of restraining sin, rather than any positive role. Brunner differs from liberal theology in his belief that no secular morality can hope to provide a satisfactory way of life, but is bound to founder on the sinfulness of human nature.

The key way in which sin manifests itself in human life is in the failure of men, both in theory and in practice, to understand themselves as persons. (It should be noted that it is not clear how far Brunner uses the word "person" in the same sense when he speaks of God as a person and men as persons. He speaks of God as the "original" person and of men as "derivative" persons, and says that before the Fall men were persons as God is a person. Some analogy is intended, but we are not told how strong the analogy is.) Brunner makes the position of philosophy in respect to human beings parallel to that which he gives it in respect to the knowledge of God. Philosophy as philosophy cannot grasp men as persons, but only as objects and inferred entities. The ghost of the view of both God and the self as Kantian noumena haunts his thought at this point. But it is not only in philosophy that the secular view of man is inadequate. In practice, too, men continually reject their status as persons.

They do this by seeking to be autonomous. The will, as the center of man's rebellion against God, seeks continually to be its own master. The ideal of the self-sufficient individual is one human ideal that must be rejected. Its counterpart, the concept of man in the mass—collective man—is equally subhuman. But secular thought provides us with no adequate basis for rejecting these alternatives. Only revelation can do this, for it is only in revelation that we discover not only God as a person but also ourselves as persons. This is where Brunner's doctrine of atonement finds its place. What Jesus Christ showed us in his life, death, and resurrection was a love that alone can break our rebellious self-will and that alone can provide us with a model for goodness. Secular ethics can at best exhibit the kind of goodness that can defeat depersonalization as a hypothetical possibility. The revelation of Christ alone makes it actual. Revelation, however, does not provide us with a code that we can then detach from its origin and live by. We must return continually to revelation for renewal. This is in part because of the character of human sin, but it is also in part because we must reassert the personal character of social life in new contexts.

According to Brunner, the depersonalization that is a consequence of technology is distinctive of the contemporary context. Men are degraded to the status of tools and means. The social incarnation of this process is the totalitarian state. For Brunner, totalitarianism is the category ultimately opposed to that of true community, and both Nazism and communism are forms of it. This political judgment took Brunner into further public argument with Karl Barth, on the grounds that Barth's theological views obliterate the moral differences between rival political systems by insisting on the sinfulness of human nature as such.

Additional Works by Brunner

"Religionsphilosophie evangelischer Theologie," in *Handbuch der Philosophie* (Munich, 1927). Translated by A. J. D. Farrer and B. L. Woolf as *Philosophy of Religion from the Point of View of Protestant Theology*. Edinburgh, 1937.

Der Mittler. Tübingen, 1927. Translated by Olive Wyon as *The Mediator*. London, 1934.

Das Gebot und die Ordnungen. Tübingen, 1932. Translated by Olive Wyon as *The Divine Imperative*. London, 1937.

Der Mensch im Widerspruch. Zurich, 1937. Translated by Olive Wyon as *Man in Revolt*. London, 1939.

Christianity and Civilisation. London, 1948–1949. Parts I and II.

Critical Study

Kegley, C. W., ed., *The Living Theology of Emil Brunner*. New York, 1962.

ALASDAIR MACINTYRE

BRUNO, GIORDANO (1548–1600), the most famous of the Italian philosophers of the Renaissance, was born at Nola, near Naples. At an early age he entered the Dominican order and became an inmate of the Dominican convent in Naples. In 1576 he was accused of heresy and fled, abandoning the Dominican habit. Thereafter he wandered through Europe. After visiting Geneva, and lecturing on the *Tractatus de Sphaera Mundi* of Sacrobosco at Toulouse, Bruno reached Paris in 1581. Here he gave public lectures which attracted the attention of King Henri III, and published two books on the art of memory which reveal him as greatly influenced by that textbook of Renaissance magic, the *De Occulta Philosophia* of Henry Cornelius Agrippa, from which he quotes lists of magic images of the stars, incantations, and other occult procedures. Bruno as a Renaissance magus, in line of descent from the learned philosophical magic inaugurated by Marsilio Ficino, is already present in these books. The title of one of them, *De Umbris Idearum* ("Shadows of Ideas"), is taken from the necromantic commentary on the *Sphere* of Sacrobosco by Cecco d'Ascoli, whom Bruno mentions admiringly in other works. It may be inferred that the lectures at Toulouse were probably based on this commentary.

Early in 1583 Bruno went to England with letters of recommendation from Henri III to the French ambassador in London. He lived in the French embassy during the two years he spent in England, and the ambassador protected him from the tumults aroused by his writings, which were clandestinely printed in London. These included the *Triginta Sigilli* ("Thirty Seals"), an extremely obscure work on his magic art of memory; those who manage to reach the end of it find an advocacy of a new religion based on love, art, magic, and mathesis. It is dedicated to the vice-chancellor and doctors of the University of Oxford in high-sounding terms in which Bruno announces himself as "the waker of sleeping souls, tamer of presumptuous and recalcitrant ignorance, proclaimer of a general philanthropy."

In June 1583 the Polish prince Albert Alasco (Laski) visited Oxford and was entertained with public disputations. Bruno was in his train, and, according to a recently discovered account by George Abbot, afterward archbishop of Canterbury, Bruno returned to Oxford after the party had left and delivered, uninvited, lectures which were largely a repetition of Marsilio Ficino's work on astral magic, the *De Vita Coelitus Comparanda* ("On Drawing Down the Life of Heaven"), although he also maintained Copernicus' opinion "that the earth did go round and the heavens did stand still." Abbot says that Bruno was induced to discontinue the lectures when the plagiarism from Ficino was pointed out to him.

While in England, Bruno published five dialogues in Italian. In *La cena de le ceneri* ("The Ash Wednesday Supper," 1584) he defends his version of the Copernican theory against Oxford "pedants," a reflection of his visit to Oxford. In *De la causa, principio e uno* (1584) he apologizes for the storms aroused by his attack on Oxford, but makes matters worse by defending the friars of pre-Reformation Oxford, whom he prefers to their Protestant successors. The *De l'infinito, universo e mondi* (1584) is an exposition of his vision of an infinite universe and innumerable worlds. The *Spaccio de la bestia trionfante* ("The Expulsion of the Triumphant Beast," 1584) envisages a universal moral and religious reform and is dedicated to Sir Philip Sidney. The *Cabala del cavallo pegaseo* ("Cabal of the Horse Pegasus," 1585) indicates Bruno's adaptation of the Jewish cabala. The *De gli eroici furori* ("On Heroic Enthusiasms," 1585) also dedicated to Sidney, is in the form of a sonnet sequence with commentaries expounding the philosophical and mystical meanings of the poems. It is upon this series of most striking and brilliant works, in which Bruno appears as the propagator of a new philosophy and cosmology, a new ethic and religion, that his fame largely rests. They are all full of Hermetic influences and are bound up with a complex religious, or politico-religious, mission for which Bruno believed he had the support of Henri III, and which cannot have been uncongenial to the French ambassador, Michel de Castelnau de Mauvissière, to whom three of the books are dedicated. Sidney's reactions to Bruno are unknown.

Late in 1585 Bruno returned to Paris, where he delivered an address on his philosophy in the Collège de Cambrai, arousing strong opposition, and where he had a curious controversy with Fabrizio Mordente about the compass which Mordente had invented. Paris was in a disturbed state, on the eve of the wars of the League, and Bruno's activities added to the "tumults," from which he fled in 1586 and began his travels through Germany. He was favorably received at the University of Wittenberg, and during his stay there he wrote a number of works, particularly on the art of Ramón Lull, to which he attached great importance and which he believed he understood better than Lull himself. From Wittenberg he went to Prague, where he tried to obtain the favor of Emperor

Rudolph II with his *Articuli Adversus Mathematicos* (1588), in which he states that he is strongly against mathematics, which he regarded as a "pedantry" lacking in deep magical insight into nature. His objection to Copernicus as a "mere mathematician" had been on similar lines. The work is illustrated with magical diagrams, representing what he called his mathesis, and its preface outlines a movement of tolerance and general philanthropy which is to replace sectarian bitterness. He next spent some time at Helmstedt, where he enjoyed the favor of the reigning duke, Henry Julius of Brunswick-Wolfenbüttel, and made a speech in praise of the late duke in which he outlined his program of moral reform in language similar to that used in the *Spaccio de la bestia trionfante.* It was probably while at Helmstedt that Bruno wrote the *De Magia* and other works on magic unpublished in his lifetime.

With the money Henry Julius gave him for the oration, Bruno went to Frankfurt to have printed the Latin poems he had written during his wanderings. These were the *De Innumerabilibus, Immenso et Infigurabili,* the *De Triplici Minimo et Mensura,* and the *De Monade Numero et Figura,* all of which were printed by John Wechel in 1591. In these Latin poems, written in a style imitating Lucretius, Bruno expresses his philosophical and cosmological speculations in their final form. Like the Italian dialogues on these themes, the Latin poems are full of Hermetic influences, particularly of the mathesis, or magical numerology, which Bruno had been further developing during his travels. He also published the last of his books on his magical arts of memory at Frankfurt.

Trial and death. In August 1591, Bruno returned to Italy at the invitation of a Venetian nobleman who wished to learn the secrets of his art of memory. There can be little doubt that Bruno was encouraged to take this step by the hopes of greater religious toleration aroused by the conversion of Henri IV of France. Bruno had in his baggage the manuscript of a book he intended to dedicate to Pope Clement VIII. It is strange that one who had stated in his published works that Christ was a magus and that the magical religion of the Egyptians was better than Christianity should have felt that he could place himself with impunity within reach of the Inquisition. Bruno seems, however, always to have sincerely believed that his religious and moral reform could take place within a Catholic framework. He was arrested in Venice and thrown into the prisons of the Inquisition. At the end of the Venetian trial he recanted his heresies, but was sent to Rome for another trial. Here he remained in prison for eight years, at the end of which he was sentenced as a heretic (having refused, this time, to recant) and was burned alive on the Campo de' Fiori.

Although the actual *processo* stating on what grounds he was condemned is not extant, it seems most probable that Bruno was burned as a magician, as an "Egyptian" who had been propagating throughout Europe some movement the nature of which remains mysterious, although it may well be connected with the origins of Rosicrucianism and of Freemasonry. His philosophical views in themselves can have had little to do with the condemnation, unless insofar as they, too, were associated with the movement.

Later interpretation. In the seventeenth century there was a conspiracy of silence about Bruno and his reputation. Where the silence was broken, he usually appeared in the character of a diabolical magician. It was rumored that he had made a speech in praise of the devil at Wittenberg (Bayle and Leibniz heard this story). In the eighteenth century he was interpreted by Toland as a deist. The nineteenth century rediscovered Bruno and read its own beliefs and attitudes into his works. It was then that he appeared as the martyr for modern science and the Copernican theory, and statues were erected in his honor by anticlericals in Italy. The crudity of this approach was modified in later philosophical studies of Bruno, but the attempt to isolate a philosophy or a metaphysics from his works and to discuss his thought in a context of straight history of philosophy meant that large areas in his writings must be disregarded as unimportant or unintelligible. Moreover, no coherent philosophical system could be extracted in this way, as Olschki saw when he criticized Bruno as a confused thinker. But when Bruno is placed in the context of the Renaissance Hermetic tradition, his philosophy, his magic, and his religion can all be seen as forming part of an outlook on nature and on man which, however strange, is nevertheless perfectly coherent within its own premises (see HERMETICISM).

Hermetic philosophy. The extraordinary prestige of the Hermetica in the Renaissance was encouraged by the belief that they were the writings of Hermes Trismegistus, an Egyptian sage who foretold Christianity and whose wisdom had inspired Plato and the Platonists. The Hermetic core in Renaissance Neoplatonism was an important factor in the revival of magic. Christian magi, like Ficino and Pico della Mirandola, used some caution in their approach to the magical passages in the Hermetic *Asclepius,* which is the basis of the astral magic described by Ficino in his *De Vita Coelitus Comparanda.* These safeguards were largely abandoned by the magician Cornelius Agrippa and totally abandoned by Bruno, who adopted the position that the Hermetic magical religion was the true religion, the religion of nature in contact with its powers. The cure for the wars, persecutions, and miseries of contemporary Europe was a return to the magical religion of the Egyptians—hence the long quotations in the *Spaccio de la bestia trionfante* from the passages in the *Asclepius* describing the religious practices of the Hermetic pseudo Egyptians, ecstatically interpreted by Bruno as their worship of "God in things," and as a "profound magic" by which they were able to draw down cosmic powers into the statues of their gods. The lament for the Egyptian religion in the *Asclepius* was interpreted by Bruno as a lament for a better religion, destroyed by Christianity. Since Augustine had condemned these passages as referring to the wicked demon worship of the Egyptians, it is easy to see how Bruno's "demonic" reputation arose. Bruno's "Egyptian" religion included belief in metempsychosis, which he also derived from the Hermetic writings.

Bruno's views on religion are organically related to his philosophy, for the philosophy of the living earth moving around the divine sun and of the innumerable worlds, moving like great animals with a life of their own in the infinite universe, is the animist philosophy of a magus who believes he can establish contact with the divine life of nature. The sun is frequently mentioned in the Hermetic writings as a god, and it is the chief of the astral gods worshiped in the religion described in the *Asclepius*. Ficino's use of the astral magic of the *Asclepius* was chiefly directed toward the sun, whose beneficent influences he sought to draw down through solar talismans and incantations.

Bruno's Copernicanism. That Bruno thought of the Copernican sun in the context of the magic of Ficino's *De Vita Coelitus Comparanda* is indicated in the report of his lectures at Oxford, in which he is said to have repeated the Ficinian text while also maintaining the opinion of Copernicus. This report fits in with passages in Bruno's works in which the sun appears in a magical context, and particularly with his defense of the Copernican opinion against the Oxford doctors in *La cena de le ceneri*, where he describes Copernicus as "only a mathematician" who has not seen the true meaning of his discovery as he, Bruno, has seen it. When a speaker in these dialogues asks what is the cause of the earth's movement around the sun, the reply is an almost verbatim quotation from *Corpus Hermeticum* XII, in which Hermes Trismegistus explains that the energy of life is movement and that therefore nothing in the living universe is immobile, not even the earth. Bruno applied these words as an explanation of the cause of the earth's movement around the sun. The Copernican opinion had, for him, confirmed the "Egyptian" philosophy of universal animation. He also repeated from the same Hermetic treatise one of his most characteristic doctrines: that there is no death in nature, only change.

Thus Bruno's acceptance of Copernican heliocentricity did not rest on Copernicus' mathematical arguments. On the contrary, Copernicus as a mere mathematician was despised by him as a superficial person who had not understood the true meaning of his discovery. Bruno was always "against" mathematics. Although he had some acquaintance with the scientific basis of the Copernican theory, it was not on mathematical grounds that Bruno defended Copernicanism from reactionary Aristotelians, but on animist and magical grounds. In fact, when the passages on the sun in the different works are compared, it becomes apparent that Copernican heliocentricity was for Bruno a kind of celestial portent of the approaching return of "Egyptian" philosophy and religion. "Aristotelianism" was for Bruno a symbol of all that is dead and dry—or, as he would say, "pedantic"—in philosophy and religion (the two were for him inseparable), compared with his own philosophy and religion—in contact, so he believed, with living, divine nature.

New vision of the universe. The essence of the Hermetic writings is that they give a religious impulse toward the world. It is within the setting of the universe, not through any divine mediator, that the Hermetic gnostic achieves his religious experience. The closest parallel to Bruno's imaginative leap upward through the spheres is the description in the Hermetic *Pimander* of how man "leant across the armature of the spheres, having broken through their envelopes." So did Bruno break through the spheres in his ecstatic ascent to his new vision of the universe. The immediate source of his vision of infinite space and innumerable inhabited worlds was Lucretius' poem *De Rerum Natura*, But Bruno transformed the Epicurean and Lucretian notions by imparting animation to the innumerable worlds—a feature totally absent from Lucretius' universe—and by imparting the function of being an image of the infinite divinity to the infinite. The godless universe of Lucretius turns in the Brunian vision into a vast extension of Hermetic gnosis; in order to receive this within himself, man, that "great miracle," as he is defined in the *Asclepius*, must expand himself infinitely. The *magnum miraculum est homo* passage is quoted from Trismegistus near the beginning of the *De Immenso* as a preliminary to the new vision of the world to be revealed in the poem.

This infinitely extended All was nevertheless One. The unity of the All in the One is a basic theme of the Hermetic writings and also of Bruno's. The unity of the All in the One is for Bruno "a most solid foundation for the truths and secrets of nature. For you must know that it is by one and the same ladder that nature descends to the production of things and the intellect ascends to the knowledge of them; and that the one and the other proceeds from unity and returns to unity . . ." (*De la causa, principio e uno*, in Giovanni Aquilecchia, ed., *Dialoghi italiani*, p. 329).

This is the philosophy conducive to magic—that the magus can depend on the ladders of occult sympathies running through all nature. When this philosophy is not only a magic but also a religion, it becomes the religion of the Hermetic pseudo Egyptians who, as Bruno says in the *Spaccio de la bestia triofante*, "with magic and divine rites . . . ascended to the height of the divinity by that same scale of nature by which the divinity descends to the smallest things by the communication of itself" (*Dialoghi italiani*, p. 777). Bruno's philosophy and religion are one and the same, and both are Hermetic. This accounts for the main aspects of his philosophy, his panpsychism and his monism, and also for the magic and the references to magical practices with which his books are filled.

Like all Renaissance magi, Bruno was a syncretist and drew from his vast reading many philosophies which had accreted to the Hermetic core The pre-Socratics, Plato and the Platonists, the Scholastics (Bruno revered Thomas Aquinas as a great magus), Nicholas of Cusa—all were incorporated into the central theme. Bruno's chief textbook of magic was Agrippa's *De Occulta Philosophia;* he also used the conjuring books of Trithemius and admired, and perhaps practiced, the Paracelsian medicine.

Art of memory. The side of Bruno's work which he regarded as the most important was the intensive training of the imagination in his occult arts of memory. In this he was continuing a Renaissance tradition which also had its roots in the Hermetic revival, for the religious experience of the Hermetic gnostic consisted in reflecting the universe within his own mind or memory. The Hermeticist believed himself capable of this achievement because he believed that man's *mens* is in itself divine and therefore able to reflect the divine mind behind the universe. In Bruno, the cultivation of world-reflecting magic memory becomes the technique for achieving the personality of a magus, and of one who believes himself to be the leader of a religious movement. Strange though these beliefs and practices are, Bruno had some profound things to say in his books on memory concerning the imagination, which he made the sole cognitive power (sweeping away the divisions of the Aristotelian faculty psychology by a kind of inner anti-Aristotelianism), and on the mental image in relation to the psychology of the "inspired" personality. When the magical aspect (which includes such practices as the use of talismans or images of the stars as mental images) is discounted or allowed for, Bruno's bold explorations of the inner world may become important to the historian of psychology.

Significance and influence. The emphasis on the Hermetic and magical side of Bruno's thinking does not discredit his significant contribution to the history of thought. He exemplifies the Hermetic religious impulse as a motive force behind the imaginative formulation of new cosmologies. From within his own frame of reference, this highly gifted man made guesses which may have given hints to seventeenth-century thinkers. A notable example is his transformation of the Democritean atoms, of which he read in Lucretius, into magically animated monads; this may well have been a stage leading to Leibniz' monadology, and there are other curious links between Bruno and Leibniz. Although Bruno was obviously not in the line leading to the mathematical advances, his extraordinary vision of an immensely expanded universe, ruled by the laws of magical animism, may be said to prefigure, on the Hermetic plane, the new cosmology of the seventeenth century. Drained of its animism, with the laws of inertia and gravity substituted for the psychic life of nature as the principle of movement, Bruno's universe would turn into something like the universe of Isaac Newton, moving under laws placed in it by a God who is not a magician but a mathematician and a mechanic. In the Hermetic phase of European thought, which was the immediate prelude to the seventeenth-century revolution, Bruno is an outstanding figure. Regarding him in this light, the old legend of the martyrdom of the advanced thinker becomes almost true again, although not in the old sense.

Bibliography

Additional works by Bruno in Italian are *Dialoghi italiani*, edited by Giovanni Gentile and revised by Giovanni Aquilecchia (Florence, 1957), which contains all the Italian dialogues in one volume, and *Il candelaio*, a comedy, edited by Vincenzo Spampanato (Bari, 1923). In Latin, see *Opera Latine*, edited by Francisco Fiorentino, Vittorio Imbriani, C. M. Tallarigo, Felice Tocco, and Girolamo Vitelli, 3 vols. (Naples and Florence, 1879–1891), issued in eight parts; there is also a facsimile reprint (Naples and Florence, 1962).

Translations include *The Heroic Enthusiasts*, translated by L. Williams (London, 1887); *Des Fureurs héroïques*, translated by P.-H. Michel (Paris, 1954); *Giordano Bruno's The Heroic Frenzies*, translated by P. E. Memmo, Jr. (Chapel Hill, N.C., 1964); *The Expulsion of the Triumphant Beast*, translated by A. D. Imerti (New Brunswick, N.J., 1964); "On the Infinite Universe and Worlds," in D. W. Singer, *Giordano Bruno, His Life and Thought* (New York, 1950), pp. 227 ff.; and "Concerning the Cause, Principle and One," translated by D. W. Singer in S. Thomas Greenberg, *The Infinite in Giordano Bruno* (New York, 1950), pp. 77 ff.

Documentary sources on Bruno's life are Vincenzo Spampanato, ed., *Documenti della vita di Giordano Bruno* (Florence, 1933), and Angelo Mercati, ed., *Il sommario del processo di Giordano Bruno* (Vatican City, 1942). A biography is Vincenzo Spampanato, *Vita di Giordano Bruno* (Messina, 1921). On his trial, see Luigi Firpo, "Il processo di Giordano Bruno," in *Rivista storica italiana*, Vol. 60 (1948), 542–597 and Vol. 61 (1949), 5–59.

For a bibliography of Bruno's works and of books and articles on him up to and including 1950, see Virgilio Salvestrini and Luigi Firpo, *Bibliografia di Giordano Bruno 1582–1950* (Florence, 1958).

Studies of Bruno include Felice Tocco, *Le opere latine di Giordano Bruno* (Florence, 1889), and *Le fonti più recenti del Bruno* (Rome, 1892); J. L. McIntyre, *Giordano Bruno* (London, 1903); Giovanni Gentile, *Giordano Bruno e il pensiero del Rinascimento* (Florence, 1920); Leonardo Olschki, *Giordano Bruno* (Halle, 1924), which has also been translated into Italian (Bari, 1927); Ernst Cassirer, *Individuum und Kosmos in der Philosophie der Renaissance* (Berlin and Leipzig, 1927), translated by Mario Domandi as *The Individual and the Cosmos in Renaissance Philosophy* (New York, 1963); Antonio Corsano, *Il pensiero di Giordano Bruno* (Florence, 1940); Eugenio Garin, *La filosofia* (Milan, 1947); Alexandre Koyré, *From the Closed World to the Infinite Universe* (Baltimore, 1957); Paolo Rossi, *Clavis Universalis* (Milan, 1960); P.-H. Michel, *La Cosmologie de G. Bruno* (Paris, 1962); and Paul O. Kristeller, *Eight Philosophers of the Italian Renaissance* (Stanford, 1964). Also see F. A. Yates, *Giordano Bruno and the Hermetic Tradition* (Chicago, 1964) and *The Art of Memory* (Chicago, 1966).

FRANCES A. YATES

BRUNSCHVICG, LÉON (1869–1944), French idealist philosopher, was born in Paris and educated at the Lycée Condorcet, where he won awards in science as well as in classics and philosophy. He received both the *licence ès lettres* and the *licence ès sciences* from l'École Normale Supérieure in 1891. During the following nine years he taught philosophy at lycées in Lorient, Tours, and Rouen. His doctoral thesis, *La Modalité du jugement*, was presented to the Sorbonne in 1897, and published in Paris the same year. In 1900 he returned to Paris to teach at his old lycée, later moving to the Lycée Henri IV and l'École Normale de Sèvres. In 1909 he was named professor of general philosophy at the Sorbonne. Except for the period 1914–1918, when he served in the armed forces auxiliary and as adviser to the government on educational reform, Brunschvicg held various chairs at the Sorbonne until the German occupation of Paris in 1940. He then settled in Aix-en-Provence and finally in Aix-les-Bains until his death.

Brunschvicg was one of the founders of the *Revue de Métaphysique et de Morale* (1893) and of the Société française de Philosophie (1901). In 1919 he was elected to the Académie des Sciences morales et politiques, serving as president in 1932. A prolific writer, editor of Pascal, and well known for his studies of Descartes and Spinoza, Brunschvicg was a major figure in French intellectual life for nearly half a century.

The "critical idealism" of Brunschvicg primarily recalls Kant's analysis of the conditions of knowledge, but Brunschvicg's method was historical rather than deductive: he wished to grasp the mind's activity as it has revealed itself in the history of mathematics, science, and philosophy. In general perspective, Brunschvicg may be seen as heir to two currents in nineteenth-century French philosophy: the tradition of epistemological idealism descending through Charles Renouvier from Kant and Antoine Cournot, and the metaphysical idealism of Maine de Biran, Félix Ravaisson, Jules Lachelier, and Jules Lagneau.

For Brunschvicg, the goal of philosophical reflection was to disclose intellectual activity tending toward self-consciousness as it progressively constitutes knowledge. He therefore frequently characterized history as "the progress of consciousness" (*le progrès de la conscience*). The double meaning of this expression—the progress of conscience as well as of consciousness—also suggests the moral dimension of Brunschvicg's monistic idealism. Viewed subjectively, the process is a conversion from naive acceptance of reality as external to an affirmation of the primacy of the mind as it provides intelligibility. Brunschvicg equated this with recognition of the supremacy of intelligence in a moral sense, which is to say that self-knowledge progresses toward refinement of conscience and moral autonomy. According to Brunschvicg, personal conversion reflects an absolute historical development undetermined in form but immanently oriented toward spiritual values (of which Unity is highest) and self-knowledge on the part of humanity as a whole.

The critique of this process, Brunschvicg insisted, cannot depend on a priori assumptions, nor can it hope to specify categories or functions of thought; such analysis would only falsify the mind's essential freedom and inventiveness. The emphasis on creative spontaneity suggests a relationship with Bergson that Brunschvicg was proud to acknowledge, but not to the extent that he wished to embrace Bergson's intuitionism. Although Brunschvicg preferred the general terms "mind" and "intelligence" to "thought" and "reason," this does not imply a commitment to nonintellectual modes of understanding. At the heart of his work lay studies in the history of science and of mathematics. Brunschvicg regarded scientific progress not only as a triumph of intellect but also as an exemplification of mankind's growing self-understanding. In this way, he defended a moral or "spiritual" conception of science as opposed to positivistic and conventionalistic theories. In his view, the truth of a theory essentially depends on the creative vitality of the mind as it assimilates what is given as nonmental, and as it judges, in turn, the adequacy of this synthesis.

In *La Modalité du jugement*, Brunschvicg attempted to delineate the mind's developing accord with being or the real in a theory that classifies judgments according to the forms of "internality" and "externality." Brunschvicg took judgment, rather than the concept or category, as fundamental because he saw it as a synthesizing or unifying act, combining form and content. The form of "externality" was interpreted (evidently following Fichte) as a restraining activity that the mind imposes dialectically on its own creative freedom or "internality."

In *Les Étapes de la philosophie mathématique* (Paris, 1912), Brunschvicg examined the highest expression of "internality," mathematical judgment, which he regarded as uniquely appropriate to science because it is at once a free creation—not to be justified through physical interpretation—yet inseparable from experience in its origin and in its "collaborative" task of assimilating being to the understanding. Brunschvicg substantiated this theme in *L'Expérience humaine et la causalité physique* (Paris, 1922), which further revealed an implicit dualism and a reluctance to employ categories or principles of analysis, however provisional.

Brunschvicg's last decade was marked by works of a religious nature, following a comprehensive history of philosophy, *Le Progrès de la conscience dans la philosophie occidentale* (Paris, 1927), intended to bear witness to humanity's spiritual unification. "Our destiny is to tend toward unity." Religious value apparently attaches to a particular dimension of the "progress of consciousness": the assimilation of being to consciousness insofar as the process is regarded as immanently guided by the value of unity. In this assimilation, mankind moves toward self-identification through the communion of shared intelligence.

Although it appears likely that Brunschvicg felt a moral or spiritual ideal to be predominant in his career, he will perhaps be best remembered as an interpreter of the French philosophical tradition and as a leading spokesman for the life of reason and the value of science.

Additional Works by Brunschvicg

Les Âges de l'intelligence. Paris, 1934.
Écrits philosophiques, 3 Vols. Paris, 1951, 1954, 1958.
Introduction à la vie de l'esprit. Paris, 1920.
La Raison et la religion. Paris, 1939.
Spinoza et ses contemporains. Paris, 1923.

Works on Brunschvicg

Cochet, M. A., *Commentaire sur la conversion spirituelle dans la philosophie de Léon Brunschvicg.* Brussels, 1937.

Deschoux, Marcel, *La Philosophie de Léon Brunschvicg.* Paris, 1949. Contains a complete bibliography.

Messaut, J., *La Philosophie de Léon Brunschvicg.* Paris, 1938.

BERNARD ELEVITCH

BUBER, MARTIN, religious existentialist, was born in 1878 in Vienna and spent his childhood in Lvov, Galicia, at the home of his grandfather Solomon Buber, a businessman and well-known scholar of rabbinic literature. From 1896 to 1900 he studied philosophy and art history at the universities of Vienna, Leipzig, Berlin, and Zurich. He was early active in the Zionist movement, especially in its cultural and religious aspects, and in 1901 he was appointed editor of the Zionist journal *Die Welt.* Instrumental in the founding of the publishing house Jüdischer Verlag in 1902, in 1916 he founded the German Jewish monthly *Der Jude,* which, until it ceased publication in 1924, was the most respected and literate voice of German Jewry. From 1924 until 1933 Buber was professor of the philosophy of Jewish religion and ethics at Frankfurt-am-Main University, the only chair in Jewish religion at any German university. In 1920 he and Franz Rosenzweig founded the Freies Jüdisches Lehrhaus, an institute for adult Jewish education, and with Hitler's coming to power Buber devoted his energy to strengthening the religious and spiritual resources of German Jewry in the face of the unprecedented challenge posed to it. Buber continued in the institute until 1938, when he left for Palestine, where he was appointed professor of sociology of religion at the Hebrew University. With Y. L. Magnes he led the Yihud movement, devoted to Arab–Jewish understanding and to the creation of a binational state. In 1952 and 1957 he traveled widely in the United States, lecturing at many universities and to diverse student groups. While his acceptance of various German awards in the postwar period led to criticism from some Jewish quarters, Buber remained steadfast in his encouragement of those German circles that realize the magnitude of the Nazi crimes against the Jews and seem genuinely repentant. He died in Jerusalem in 1965.

Buber's basic insight, an insight that runs through all of his work and that determines his approach to everything he touches, is the realization that there is a basic difference between relating to a thing or to an object which I observe, and to a person or a "Thou" that addresses me and to whose address I respond. In its simplest form, this is the difference between the way people usually relate to inanimate things on the one hand and to living persons on the other. Inanimate objects are watched, while persons are spoken to. However, the distinction cannot be drawn simply on this basis. A person as well as an inanimate thing can be viewed as a thing, or, in Buber's terminology, an "It." Whenever we take an "objective" attitude toward a person, whenever we view him as part of the world and caught in its causal chain, we are in an "I–It" relationship, even though the object happens to be a person. The "I–It" relationship is characterized by the fact that it is not a genuine relationship because it does not take place *between* the I and the It. When another person is an It to me, I am, first of all, perfectly alone. I gaze at him and view him from every possible direction, I observe his place in the scheme of things, and I find elements that he has in common with other persons and things and elements that distinguish him from them. All of this, however, takes place within me; *I* am judging and *I* am observing, and the external world is relevant only to the extent that it enters my being.

It is otherwise in the "I–Thou" relationship. Here the relationship is genuine because it is between me and the Thou that addresses me. This Thou is no longer one thing among other things of the universe; the whole universe is seen in the light of the Thou, and not the Thou in the light of the universe. In fact, it is not only the object in the "I–Thou" relationship that is different from that in the "I–It" situation; the very "I" is different in the two situations. There is no "I" that sometimes relates to a Thou and sometimes to an It. If that were the case, both the It and the Thou would be objects that float into the I's field of vision and then out of it, leaving the I essentially unaffected. Instead, Buber argues, the I of the I–It is a different I from that of the I–Thou because it is not the I as such that has pre-eminent reality, but the relations I–It and I–Thou. The I appears and is shaped only in the context of some relationship with either an It or a Thou and can never be viewed independently of such a relationship.

Buber further states that the I–It relationship is maintained with only part of ourselves in it. There is always a part of us that remains outside the relationship and views it from some vantage point. In the I–Thou relationship, on the other hand, our whole being must be involved. Should I attempt to hold back any part of myself, I will find myself in an I–It situation because there will be a part of me that is not participant but spectator, a sure sign of the I–It. This means that the I–Thou relationship carries with it much greater risk than the I–It, since there is no withholding of the self possible, as in the I–It. In the I–It situation the part of the self that remains outside the relationship cannot be injured by the other party because he cannot reach it. In the I–Thou relationship there is no such security because the Thou of the I is addressed with the whole of the I, and any response elicited necessarily pertains to this total I. In the I–Thou relationship, therefore, everything possible is risked without any defensive position being left to which the I can withdraw in case of need. However, this is not the only risk involved in the I–Thou situation. The Thou who is addressed cannot be viewed in the context of any causal, deterministic framework. He must be encountered in the full freedom of his otherness, an otherness that is addressed and that responds in the total unpredictability of human freedom. The moment the responses of the Thou are calculated, the moment the I asks itself what impression its speech and being will make on the Thou, it is relating to an It instead of to a Thou.

Because of this, Buber tells us, there is never a present for the I–It relationship, only a past. This is so because all objective knowledge about a human being is knowledge about his past, of what he has been rather than of what he is. If the present moment is to have genuine novelty, if it is not perfectly determined by the events of the past, then it must be possible for the present to produce a break with the past in the form of a response that could not have been calculated from a knowledge of the past. In the I–Thou relationship we are therefore genuinely living in the present because we are prepared for any and every response to our address, the expected as well as the unexpected—and it is this that constitutes genuine listening. The difference between a pseudo listening and a genuine listening is that while in the pseudo listening situation the listener pretends to listen, what he hears is determined by his past knowledge of the person he is listening to or by his theories concerning the nature of man. Genuine listening does not know ahead of time what it will hear; in the full uniqueness of the present it listens to the speech of the other without filtering what it hears through the screen of its own prejudgments. The purpose of genuine listening is therefore really to hear what the other is saying, constantly being aware that he is saying something that is new and not just a revelation of his nature, which the hearer has already identified and which is fixed as the other's "psychology."

It is in the religious context that the significance of Buber's distinctions emerges most clearly. In contrast to much of mysticism that aims at the obliteration of the abyss between the self and the Absolute in the ecstasy of mystical union, the essence of Biblical religion, as conceived by Buber, is the dialogue between man and God in which each is the other's Thou. "The extended lines of relations meet in the eternal Thou," writes Buber in the opening sentence of the final portion of *I and Thou*. Life is an endless transition from the Thou to the It and back to the Thou. Sooner or later, the time comes when even the most cherished Thou recedes, when a spiritual tiredness overtakes the most authentic I–Thou relationship and turns it into the I–It. There is one Thou, argues Buber, who by his very nature cannot become an It. A man may hate God and curse him, he may turn away from him when the suffering of human destiny becomes unbearable; but no man can reduce God to the status of a thing who no longer addresses him and who becomes one object among others in the world for him. Much of traditional theology, for Buber, errs in dealing with God as if he could be turned into an It. Time and again, however, man turns from thinking about God to addressing him, and it is then that he communicates with the living God, as distinct from merely giving intellectual assent to the God of the philosophers. This is true even when the Absolute Thou addressed is not called God. "But when he, too, who abhors the name, and believes himself to be godless, gives his whole being to addressing the Thou of his life as a Thou that cannot be limited by another, he addresses God."

In the course of his long career Buber applied these basic ideas to a diversity of fields. In a number of works devoted to Biblical interpretation, he developed in detail his view of the Bible as the record of Israel's dialogue with God. He wrote a definitive work on the relation between Christian and Jewish faith. In this work he distinguishes between the Jewish *emunah* and the Greek *pistis*, the former of which, according to Buber, is faith in the sense of trust while the latter is faith in the sense of belief in the truth of propositions. Jewish faith, as found in the Hebrew Bible, is Israel's trust in the faithfulness of God's word as that word is spoken in dialogue. The faith of the New Testament, particularly in its Pauline version, is heavily influenced by Greek philosophical elements that are reflected in the emphasis on salvation as resulting from belief in the truth of propositions concerning the divinity and resurrection of Jesus. In Paul, Buber thus sees a profound departure from the Hebrew Biblical spirit, a departure that is no more than partial and implicit in the Gospels.

In his later years Buber's interest to some extent turned to psychotherapy, in which he emphasized the necessity for the therapist not to hide behind the teachings of his school and not to forget that psychotherapy is above all dialogue in which therapist and patient speak to each other. When seen in this light, the therapist encounters the patient for the individual he is and is ready for the unexpected that the theoretical categories of his discipline do not prepare him for. Similarly, in the field of social philosophy Buber contrasted Marxist socialism, with its centralized control and allegiance to impersonal and inevitable historical forces, with the socialism of the community in which the authenticity of the I–Thou relationship is the foundation on which the living community is built and to which it must return, again and again, for renewal. In the Israeli *kibbutz* Buber saw an exemplification of the communal or "Utopian" socialism for which he stands.

Bibliography

Publication of the collected works of Buber in German, *Werke*, was begun in 1962 by Kosel Verlag in Munich. The first three volumes appeared by 1964.

Buber's most important work is *Ich und Du* (Berlin, 1922), translated by R. G. Smith as *I and Thou* (New York, 1958). *Die Frage an den Einzelnen* (Berlin, 1936), translated by R. G. Smith in *Between Man and Man* (Boston, 1955), develops the basic themes in some detail. *Der Glaube der Propheten* (Zurich, 1950), translated from the Hebrew by C. Witton-Davies as *The Prophetic Faith* (New York, 1960), is one of Buber's best Biblical studies. *Paths in Utopia*, translated by R. F. C. Hull (London, 1949), is Buber's study of social philosophy; *Two Types of Faith*, translated by N. P. Goldhawk (New York, 1961) is his study of Judaism and Christianity.

Other writings that have been translated into English are *Eclipse of God; Studies in the Relation Between Religion and Philosophy*, translated by Maurice Friedman et al. (New York, 1952) and *Bilder von Gut und Bose* (Cologne, 1952), translated by R. G. Smith and M. Bullock as *Good and Evil; Two Interpretations* (New York, 1953); *Pointing the Way; Collected Essays*, translated and edited by Maurice Friedman (New York, 1957); and *Martin Buber, Writings*, a selection edited and introduced by Will Herberg (New York, 1956).

Maurice Friedman's *Martin Buber: The Life of Dialogue* (Chicago, 1955; New York, 1960) is a thorough secondary work with an extensive bibliography.

MICHAEL WYSCHOGROD

BÜCHNER, LUDWIG (1824–1899), German physician, philosopher, and popularizer of science, was born in Darmstadt. He wrote his famous *Kraft und Stoff* (*Force and Matter*, Frankfurt, 1855) while lecturing in medicine at Tübingen. This volume, which went through numerous editions and became a best seller in many languages, was so controversial that he was forced to resign his post. On his return to Darmstadt he practiced medicine, did research, and published. Enlightenment of the general public was an urgent interest of his, and he was concerned with the social and political implications of science. Büchner frequently criticized professional philosophers for attempting to determine the nature of reality by thinking rather than by observation. The obscurity and incomprehensibility of some German metaphysicians drew his special scorn: "Philosophers are wonderful people. The less they understand of a thing, the more words they make over it" (*Force and Matter*, p. 257).

Doctrine of monism. Büchner found the basic materialism of the ancient philosophers confirmed by scientific developments of the nineteenth century. In the preface to the fifteenth German edition of *Force and Matter* (1884), Büchner was enthusiastic over the progress of science in the 28 years since the first edition. Among other developments, he mentioned the discovery of spectral analysis, Darwinian evolution, cellular anatomy, brain physiology, a clearer understanding of heredity, and chemical synthesis as supporting his basic theory. Büchner was so convinced that his theory had been strikingly confirmed that he changed the subtitle of *Force and Matter* from *Empirical Studies on Natural Philosophy* to *Principles of the Natural Order of the Universe*.

The central theme of *Force and Matter* is "Force and matter are fundamentally the same thing, contemplated from different standpoints." Büchner distinguished three phases in the development of theories about force and matter. In the first phase, force and matter were regarded as entirely distinct entities resulting from the activities of supernatural beings. In the second phase, the two notions were only incompletely separated; imponderable force, although fundamentally different from ponderable matter, was yet somehow united to it. In the third and modern phase, he maintained, the two are unified and inseparable, both empirically and conceptually.

Force was defined by Büchner as an activity or motion of

matter or of the smallest particles of matter, or, "more precisely, as an *expression for the reason of a possible or actual movement*—differences which in reality alter nothing in the matter itself" (*ibid.*, p. 7). He went on to say that force can no more exist independently of matter than seeing can exist without an organ of sight. He further held that the "universe or matter with its properties, conditions or movements" is eternal and cannot have been created. From this point of view, he rejected all theories of an independent or supernatural force creating the universe.

Büchner regarded motion as a necessary condition, and an eternal and inseparable property, of matter. Motion "is the very essence" of force. He argued against any notion of matter as "dead" or motionless, and approvingly quoted Engels' view that motion is matter's mode of existence.

Although often regarded as a materialist both by his supporters and by his enemies, Büchner took pains to differentiate his monism from materialism. He defended the materialists in their battles against spiritualists and idealists, especially against the accusation that they were gross and immoral, yet he insisted that the traditional battles between materialism and idealism were "futile and groundless." He held that there can be no matter without force, no mind without matter, no arrangement without nature, no earth without heaven, no time without eternity—and vice versa.

Büchner was interested in the status of scientific laws, for he held that considerable confusion has resulted from the ambiguity of "law." The assumed analogy between man-made laws and scientific laws resulted in a widespread belief that some lawgiver outside or above nature prescribed scientific laws. Human laws necessarily presuppose some controlling will or lawgiver, but laws of nature do not. In no sense are natural laws imposed upon matter or upon nature; rather, they express the interaction of physical forces.

Scientific laws are mechanical and immutable, and describe all possible behavior. Nothing can happen in any aspect of nature that violates natural laws, and no outside influence can change them. Human behavior is, of course, no exception. In short, all nature is unified, including the unexplored parts of the universe, and the same laws hold everywhere and at all times.

Theory of mind. Büchner's views on mind were carefully elaborated. He rejected the approach of Karl Vogt and Pierre Cabanis, which compared thinking to the secretions of bodily organs. Although thinking is a brain process, Büchner argued that thought is not comparable to urine, bile, or other such secretions. "Thinking can and must be regarded as a special mode of general natural motion," and is characteristic of the central nervous elements in the same way that contraction is characteristic of muscles. All intellectual activity stems from sensations and the responses to sensations. The words "mind," "spirit," "thought," "sensibility," "volition," and "life" do not designate any entities; rather, they designate properties, capacities, or actions of living substances. "Mind," for example, is only a collective word that comprehensively includes all of the activities of the brain and its parts. Consciousness, according to Büchner, is an activity of certain parts of the brain, but it is not known precisely how matter brings forth consciousness. The detailed explanation of consciousness must wait until more is known about matter.

According to Büchner, natural laws "cannot but be reflected or reproduced in some measure" in human knowing, since that knowing is derived from sensation. Human intellectual behavior, although dependent to a considerable extent on the size and weight of the brain, is also dependent on other factors. In addition to morphological, histological, and chemicophysical circumstances within the brain, exercise, training, and environmental factors are important. The Eskimo, Büchner held, are unlikely to develop their intellectual potentialities because of their geographical environment; day laborers compelled to live in constant drudgery likewise will not be likely to realize their capacities.

Ethics and religion. There were strong relativistic strands in Büchner. Arguing against things-in-themselves, he insisted that all things exist only for each other and derive significance only from their mutual relations. He also held that theological notions are relative to culture and often to individuals. Somewhat uncritical in accepting the evidence of travelers' tales, he emphasized the relativity to culture of ethical and aesthetic preferences and cited many striking examples. Despite this relativistic note, he maintained that the black "race" was innately inferior to the white.

Although Büchner typically took a stand for "hard" determinism in ethics, insisting that not only what man is, but also what he wants, does, thinks, and feels, depends on the necessities of nature, he sometimes seemed to hint that there might be a minute scope for free volition. However, the main emphasis of his writings in this area was on the factors causally accounting for human decisions. The acceptance of determinism, he held, would lead to a change in many attitudes, especially in regard to criminals. The vast majority of criminals should be looked upon as unfortunates rather than as objects of execration.

Morality, Büchner said, could be defined "as the law of an equal mutual respect for general as well as private human rights, which law itself has for its object to provide the largest amount of human happiness" (*ibid.*, p. 387). That which promotes such happiness is good; that which disturbs or undermines it is evil. Self-love is the most powerful motive of all human actions. A proper social organization will assume that the welfare of one person is not detrimental to the welfare of others and that the promotion of the individual's happiness will promote the general welfare. Büchner admitted that, given the way men often behave, the adoption of his ethical theory might lead some people to strive only for their own transitory pleasure. He maintained, however, that even if this should happen, such egoistic hedonists will do no more damage than that done by those supposedly following a theological morality.

Büchner had both intellectual and practical objections to religion. He was convinced that all scientific evidence to date indicated the absence of any force outside the natural order of the universe. However, he found unorthodox deities as offensive as he found the traditional God. He compared pantheism to an attempt "to season old dishes with new sauces." The "Unknowable" of the agnostics "is nothing more than the good old God of the theologians." In short, Büchner admitted nothing behind, outside, or above the natural order—and he saw no reason to worship that order.

Büchner regarded the doctrines of teleology and vital forces as major errors stemming from supernaturalism. He attempted to show how alleged design can be explained in entirely natural terms, and also argued that much of the alleged design is bad. For example, he said of the human eye: "If a human optician were to supply an instrument made in the same way, it would, as *Helmholtz* remarked, be at once rejected as a bad piece of workmanship" (*ibid.*, p. 175).

Although Büchner was sometimes dogmatic (holding, for example, that the existence of the planet Vulcan was proved), although much of his science is no longer accepted, and although he occasionally was inconsistent, most of what he had to say can still be read with profit. His clarity of style, his fervor for enlightening man, and his enthusiasm for science make him an interesting author. His courage in maintaining his views despite extreme opposition and pressure deserve notice. Numerous critics complained of what they considered immoral consequences of Büchner's theories. He argued, in reply, that superstition and ignorance are two of the most dangerous enemies of humanity. Büchner emphasized that the truth is often unpleasant, and inveighed against a "fictitious happiness" based on emotionally consoling falsehoods.

Additional Works by Büchner

Natur und Geist. Frankfurt, 1857.

Aus Natur und Wissenschaft. Leipzig, 1862.

Die Stellung des Menschen in der Natur. Leipzig, 1869.

Fremdes und Eignes aus dem geistigen Leben der Gegenwart. Leipzig, 1890.

Darwinismus und Sozialismus. Leipzig, 1894.

Last Words on Materialism and Kindred Subjects, translated by Joseph McCabe. London, 1901. Contains a biographical sketch by Buchner's son.

Force and Matter. New York, 1950. Reprint of the fourth English edition (London, 1884) translated from the fifteenth German edition.

Works on Büchner

Frauenstädt, Julius, *Der Materialismus. Eine Erwiderung auf Dr. Ludwig Büchners "Kraft und Stoff."* Leipzig, 1856.

Lange, Frederick A., *Geschichte des Materialismus,* 2 vols. Iserlohn and Leipzig, 1866. Translated by E. C. Thomas as *The History of Materialism,* 3 vols. London, 1877–1879. Contains much helpful information on Büchner.

Merz, John T., *A History of European Thought in the Nineteenth Century.* Edinburgh, 1903. Vols. III and IV.

ROLLO HANDY

BUCKLE, HENRY THOMAS (1821–1862), English historian, was the son of a prosperous businessman who left him sufficient money to devote his life to private study and writing. In common with a number of other dominant thinkers of the Victorian age—such as J. S. Mill, Spencer, and T. H. Huxley—he was largely self-educated. As he was a delicate child, it was thought unwise for him to undertake work involving much intellectual effort or strain, with the consequence that he was (as he put it) "never much tormented with what is called Education, but allowed to pursue my own way undisturbed . . . whatever I may be supposed to know I taught myself." Thus he was taken from school, at his own request, at the age of fourteen, never went to a university, and conducted his subsequent reading and research (which by any standards were vast) in the absence of all external supervision or direction. Buckle expressed no regret at not having gone to Oxford or Cambridge, considering both universities to be in a contemptible condition and believing himself in any case to be equipped with natural aptitudes and talents that more than compensated for the lack of a rigorous academic training. Certainly his gifts were far from negligible. He had an excellent memory, he could express himself both in writing and in conversation with great fluency and eloquence, and he was a first-class linguist (by the age of 30 he could read 18 foreign languages and speak six); he possessed, moreover, an immense capacity for methodical work, together with an intense intellectual curiosity and a meticulous eye for detail.

Buckle led a comparatively uneventful life, his energies being to a large extent absorbed by the ambitious project of writing a history of civilization, to which, from his early twenties, he had decided to dedicate his career. But though the preparation of this enormous enterprise always remained his chief concern, he was not without other interests. He was, for example, a brilliant chess player, achieving an international reputation; he traveled widely, in Europe and beyond; and by the end of his life he had established a wide circle of acquaintances, including Thackeray, Kingsley, Darwin, and John Stuart Mill. For Mill in particular he had the highest admiration, and in 1859 he wrote a long review in *Fraser's Magazine* praising Mill's essay "On Liberty"—a review that created considerable stir at the time, since in it Buckle drew public attention to the fantastic sentence of 21 months' imprisonment recently passed upon a man for inscribing on a gate words offensive to Christianity. Although Buckle never married, he liked feminine society and secretly kept a mistress; when, after his death, the truth ultimately leaked out, it caused consternation and dismay among some of his close friends and relatives.

Significance of the "History." Buckle died at the age of forty while touring the Middle East. Only two volumes of his *History of Civilisation in England* had appeared, and these represented no more than an introduction to the vast work he had envisaged writing. Yet they had been sufficient to achieve for their author sensational fame, not merely in his own country but also throughout Europe and in the United States; Charles Darwin applauded the work's brilliance and originality; and an influential American writer, Theodore Parker, attributed to it an importance in the history of thought comparable to that of Bacon's *Novum Organum.* Buckle's reputation has since suffered a heavy decline, and many of the claims made on behalf of his work at the time of its publication seem grotesquely exaggerated today. Even so, what he wrote represents (as Sidgwick pointed out) the first major attempt on the part of a thinker versed in the tradition of British empiricism and inductivism to enter the treacherous field of historical speculation, and to offer a comprehensive and detailed theory of historical development of the type that previously only Continental philosophers had ventured to provide. For this reason alone it preserves a certain interest and is still worth studying.

Buckle's intentions. Buckle was fully aware of what had been done by some of his predecessors in Germany and France; and references to their works, particularly those of Herder and Comte, are to be found scattered among the footnotes that abound throughout his own volumes. Like Herder, he was anxious to connect the facts of human history with the conditions imposed by different forms of natural and geographical environment; like Comte, he wished to present the course of history as exemplifying a fundamental pattern of progress and improvement. But he rejected the tendency to revere past ages and to exalt imagination at the expense of rational and scientific modes of thinking that often manifested itself in Herder's writings; and he equally distrusted the strain of aprioristic dogmatism and respect for authoritarian methods of social control that he detected in Comte's historical system, calling the latter's theory of government "monstrously and obviously impracticable." Buckle's allegiance lay chiefly with the ideals set out by English radicals and Utilitarians early in the nineteenth century, and it was these that finally determined the valuations embodied in his conception of social and historical progress.

Human actions subject to laws. Early in his book Buckle raised the question, "Are the actions of men, and therefore of societies, governed by fixed laws, or are they the result either of chance or of supernatural interference?" He supposed these possibilities to represent exhaustive alternatives, and argued that either variety of the latter hypothesis was plainly unacceptable.

So far as the theory of supernatural interference was concerned, this, together with the associated theological doctrine of predestination, must remain a "barren hypothesis," since no conceivable experience could count for or against its truth. On the other hand, the view that what occurs in the realm of human affairs is the product of chance was demonstrably false; it had, however, been given an aura of spurious respectability by metaphysical philosophers who had carried the principle in question over into the sphere of individual human psychology. There it emerged as the famous doctrine of free will, according to which a mysterious, undetermined power of free choice is held to be directly vouched for by the evidence of the introspective consciousness. But in Buckle's opinion it is precisely such blind reliance upon the findings of individual introspection that has been the besetting sin of "metaphysicians," leading them to construct their impressive-looking, though nonetheless mutually incompatible, systems in accordance with a radically mistaken procedure.

By contrast, in order to achieve a realistic conception of the nature and workings of the human psyche it is necessary to adopt an external and general view of human behavior analogous to that taken by natural scientists in the investigation of nonhuman phenomena: from this altered standpoint it can indeed be seen that the actions of men are subject to regularities as strict and mathematically exact as those that operate in other spheres of scientific inquiry. As a conclusive demonstration of his thesis, Buckle cited the evidence afforded by large-scale statistical surveys concerning the numbers of marriages contracted, and of murders and suicides committed, in particular countries and towns during successive years; the relative uniformity of the results obtained would, he held, be unintelligible on any other assumption than that there are certain social laws capable of keeping the level constant.

When discussing this topic, Buckle on occasions fell into confusions; he did not, for example, always distinguish between the necessary and the sufficient conditions of an occurrence, and was prone to disregard the difference between causal laws and statistical frequencies. In consequence he sometimes interpreted the statistical data in a misleading way, suggesting that the sole effective determinant individual actions was what he called "the general condition of society." He also spoke as if the mere existence of a proportional average, observed to hold over a period of time, necessitated, with a kind of irresistible momentum, the commission of a particular number of crimes in any given year. As a result, a picture is presented wherein human beings appear as the helpless victims of social forces over which they can exert no effective influence or control—a conclusion in no way entailed by the premises from which Buckle initially proceeded.

Origin and development of civilization. Be this as it may, it is noticeable that when Buckle approached his principal theme—the genesis and development of civilization—he made little further reference to precise numerical regularities or frequencies; although he still spoke of "laws," it was the broad, indeterminate, and sometimes very doubtful generalizations concerning the factors influencing the evolution of human societies that he chiefly appealed to in providing his explanations. Thus, the fundamental agents of social growth were deemed to be material or, to use his term, "physical," and were listed as being "Climate, Food, Soil, and the General Aspect of Nature." These—and not, as some previous theorists had alleged, innate racial characteristics or mysterious "national spirits" —originally determine the divergent forms of organization and progress achieved by different historical cultures.

Food supply and civilization. Buckle believed that the degree of civilization attained by a society depended upon its wealth and upon the manner in which this wealth was distributed; such factors were in turn dependent upon the population of the country concerned, and the size of the population was determined by its food supply. In countries where cheap food was plentiful, the population increased in a fashion that led to the labor market's becoming overstocked; as a consequence there was unemployment and also poverty, since there is an inevitable tendency in societies where there is a surplus of labor for laborers to be underpaid and for immense economic inequalities to develop. He cited such examples as Egypt, Peru, Mexico, and India, where riches were concentrated in a very few hands and where the vast majority of the inhabitants lived in a miserable and depressed condition: "Among nations subjected to these conditions, the people have counted for nothing, they have had no voice in the management of the state, no control over the wealth their own industry created."

European conditions ideal. Buckle, in fact, considered that the ideal conditions for the development of civilization were to be found in Europe. Here the food supply was not so abundant as to lead to overpopulation, nor was it so scanty as to make the accumulation of wealth and the enjoyment of leisure (on which intellectual progress depends) impossible. Here, also, the temperate climate was favorable to enterprise and the energetic exploitation of natural resources; moreover, the aspect that nature presented to human beings was of a less extreme and unpredictable character than in other parts of the world. Thus, men did not regard it with superstitious awe as a terrifying and insuperable power, but saw it instead as something that obeys regular laws and is therefore capable of being tamed and utilized for their purposes. It followed (he thought) that Europe could be distinguished from all other centers of human society by the circumstance that it was human rather than natural or physical factors that had determined the course taken by its history and progress. Man was here the master of nature, and consequently the key to the development of European culture lay in the influence exercised by "the laws of the human mind."

Knowledge determined direction of culture. It might be expected that Buckle would go on to state what these laws of the human mind were, using them to explain patterns of social change in European history in a fashion comparable to that suggested by Mill in Book VI of his *System of Logic* when he spoke of the possibility of deriving principles governing historical development from the "ultimate" laws of human psychology. Buckle can scarcely be said, however, to have adopted this procedure, perhaps because he believed that the psychological and historical data available at his time were insufficient to make it practicable. Instead, he contented himself mainly with trying to show that it was the advance and diffusion of knowledge, and particularly of scientific knowledge, that had in the last analysis given European history its characteristic over-all direction—" . . . the progress Europe has made from barbarism to civilization is entirely due to its intellectual activity."

Other factors were considered, but only to be ruled out. Thus Buckle claimed—as if (rather surprisingly) it were a self-evident truth—that men's moral opinions had remained essentially unaltered for thousands of years: how then could these have been responsible for the far-reaching transformations that had overtaken European nations like England and France in the course of their historical evolution? Likewise, he rejected the claims of religion, literature, and government to be "prime movers of human affairs." Acceptance of a particular religious creed is a symptom rather than a cause of the condition in which a given society finds itself. The literature of a country merely reflects and serves to fix the degree of civilization already attained; it does not initiate further achievement. So far as the influence of government is concerned, Buckle maintained that the rulers of a nation were only "creatures of the age, never its creators." Enlightened legislation occurs only as a consequence of the pressure exerted by changes in the climate of opinion, these being due in the first instance to the efforts of "bold and able thinkers" who belong to the intellectual, and not the governing, classes; nor will such legislation be effective unless the ground has been prepared for it and "the age is ripe."

Political thought. Writing very much as an exponent of the principles of laissez-faire radicalism, Buckle displayed an intense distrust of governmental interference and "protectionism," which tended to be identified in his mind with the suppression of free opinion and free trade. Accordingly, he argued that most beneficial legislation is negative in character, taking the form of repealing the bad enactments passed by earlier generations; and, generally speaking, he restricted the legitimate functions of government to such things as the maintenance of order and the preservation of public health. The moral drawn is that the ineluctable laws of historical development should be permitted to take their course freely and without impediment; unlike many other philosophers of history, Buckle did not try to combine a doctrine of historical inevitability with a comprehensive positive program of political action and social reconstruction.

Buckle's significance. There is much that is intellectually naive in Buckle's theory of history, and it is easy to find inconsistencies and *non sequiturs* among his arguments; Leslie Stephen's gibe that Buckle's "mental fibre was always rather soft" is not wholly beside the mark. His uncritical use of vague abstractions like "intellectual progress" and the "spirit of a time" often led him into treating vacuous truisms as significant discoveries, and the collectivist conception of historical change that pervades much of his work contrasts oddly with the influence he ascribes to individual scientists and economists in promoting social advance. Nevertheless, the impact of his ideas upon his age was undeniably great, and his criticisms of previous and current historiography were not without important long-term effects. Like Marx, though with far less insight and imagination, he helped to turn the eyes of historians away from the political surface of events, making them look more closely at the technological and economic realities of human life that lie beneath; at the same time, through his determinism, he provided a corrective to the tendency toward excessive moralizing that his contemporaries exhibited in their treatment of the past. And, by enlarging the perspective of historical study to include cultures and societies remote in time or space from his own, he made a definite, if limited, contribution to widening the horizons and counteracting the provincialism of future students of human affairs.

Bibliography

PRIMARY SOURCES

Buckle, H. T., *The History of Civilisation in England,* 2 vols. London, 1857–1861.

Taylor, Helen, ed., *Miscellaneous and Posthumous Works of Henry Thomas Buckle,* 3 vols. London, 1872.

STUDIES AND COMMENTARIES

Huth, A. H., *Life and Writings of H. T. Buckle,* 2 vols. London, 1880.

Robertson, J. M., *Buckle and His Critics.* London, 1897.

St. Aubyn, G., *A Victorian Eminence.* London, 1958.

Stephen, Leslie, *The English Utilitarians,* Vol. III. London, 1900.

PATRICK GARDINER

BUDDE, JOHANN FRANZ (1667–1729), or Buddeus, German philosopher, theologian, and historian. Budde was born in Anklam, Pomerania. He entered the University of Wittenberg in 1685 and became an assistant there in 1689. Budde was appointed professor of moral philosophy at Halle in 1693, full professor of theology at Jena in 1705, and church councilor at Gotha in 1715. Although he insisted on his independence from all schools and considered himself an eclectic, he was close to Pietist thought and to the philosophy of Christian Thomasius, his colleague at Halle.

Budde's most significant work in theoretical philosophy was his *Institutiones Philosophiae Eclecticae* (2 Teile, Halle, 1703). In the first section, in which he expounded his logical doctrines and the intent was chiefly methodological, the influences of Locke and Thomasius are apparent. Budde derived error from original sin and prescribed means for restoring the "good health" of the mind. He regarded ontology as a part of logic and as consisting in a simple explanation of basic metaphysical terms. According to Budde, these terms had a purely instrumental value because he refused to confer upon metaphysics the rank of independent and universal science. Rather, he interpreted it as the science of the most general nouns used in theology and philosophy.

In the second section of the *Institutiones*, Budde first discussed natural philosophy in a phenomenalistic manner, holding that we cannot know the real nature of things, but only their appearances and effects. He attempted to reconcile the physical animism or spiritualism typical of Pietist natural philosophy with mechanism. He frequently appealed to the Bible and gave an important place to final causes. At the end of this section he discussed spirits and God, whose existence he demonstrated by rational proofs.

In practical philosophy (*Elementae Philosophiae Practicae*, Halle, 1697) Budde followed Grotius, Pufendorf, and Thomasius. He completely denied human freedom, referring the possibility of good actions to God's grace and restricting accountability to a narrow and extrinsic sphere of material liberty. He devoted much space to discussions of practical psychology and prudence, for he believed that such practical psychology was a better means than abstract instruction of healing the human will from sin. However, revelation is essential to this healing process.

As with the Pietists, practical philosophy is central to Budde's thought. He also agreed with the Pietists in stressing the will's independence of the intellect, in his emphasis on psychology in practical philosophy and on spiritualism in cosmology, and in the importance he placed on revelation. However, Budde was much more systematic than Thomasius, who was likewise very much influenced by Pietism. Budde joined the Pietists in their fight against Wolff, and in 1723 he wrote a pamphlet attacking Wolff.

Although in practical philosophy Budde agreed with the Pietists, in theology he tried to reconcile the views of orthodoxy and Pietism. Because he held that man has an original religious impulse, he gave an important position to natural religion. He presented cosmological, physicotheological, and historical proofs of God's existence, and tried to refute atheism by argument.

Budde was one of the most learned men of his time. His writings on the history of Jewish philosophy (*Introductio ad Philosophiam Ebraeorum*, Halle, 1707), on general history of philosophy, and on the history of theology (*Historia Theologiae Dogmaticae et Moralis*, Frankfurt, 1725) were excellent in their time and are still valuable for the information they contain.

Additional Works by Budde

Selecta Iuris Naturae et Gentium. Halle, 1704.
Institutiones Theologiae Moralis. Leipzig, 1711.
Institutiones Theologiae Dogmaticae. Leipzig, 1723.

Works on Budde

Hirsch, E., *Geschichte der neuren evangelischen Theologie*. Gütersloh, 1960. Vol. II, pp. 319–340.

Stolzenburg, A. F., *Die Theologie des Joh. Fr. Buddeus und des Chr. Pfaff*. Berlin, 1926.

Wundt, Max, *Die deutsche Schulphilosophie im Zeitalter der Aufklärung*. Tübingen, 1945. Pp. 63–75, 242–243.

GIORGIO TONELLI

BUDDHISM is so called because of its allegiance to the Buddha, or Enlightened One, a title given to Gautama, who lived in north India in the latter part of the sixth and early fifth centuries B.C. (probably 563–483 B.C.). The religion has evolved into three main schools: the Theravāda (Doctrine of the Elders), which is the surviving form of the so-called Hīnayāna, or Lesser Vehicle; the Mahāyāna, or Great Vehicle; and the Vajrayāna, or Diamond Vehicle, which has Mahāyāna affinities. The Theravāda is found in Ceylon, Burma, and southeast Asia; the Mahāyāna, in China, Korea, and Japan; and the Vajrayāna in Tibet and its environs. In India, Buddhism was at one time widespread, but it now exists there only marginally. It is hard to determine the number of Buddhists in the world today, partly because of the overlap and fluidity of allegiances in China. Excluding China, there are probably some 150 million adherents.

THE BUDDHA'S LIFE

The Buddha's family name was Gautama (in Pāli, Gotama); his personal name was Siddhārtha. He is also referred to as Śākyamuni ("sage of the Sakya clan"); as the Tathāgata (obscure, but probably meaning "Thus-gone"—that is, one whose career can be indicated but not described); and as the Jina (literally, "Victor," the same title given to the main teacher of Jainism). His life has been overlaid by legend, but the following facts emerge. Born at Kapilavastu, just inside modern Nepal, he was the son of a chieftain or petty king, Suddhodana, of the *Kṣatriya*, or noble, caste (the Buddha was not a Brahman and so was not one of the traditional holders of sacred knowledge), and was brought up in relative luxury.

At the age of 29 he abandoned this life, his wife, and young son, and set off to discover the cause of human suffering and its spiritual cure. He became a wandering recluse and sat at the feet of various ascetics and teachers. After six years—including a period of extreme self-mortification, which he found to be damaging and not conducive to insight—he eventually attained Enlightenment (*bodhi*) while seated beneath a tree (the bo or bodhi tree) at Buddh Gaya. Thereafter he repaired to the holy city of Banaras, and he preached his first sermon at Sārnāth, just outside the city. The rest of his long life was spent in meditation, preaching, and the guidance of his followers. He founded an order (Sangha), at first only of monks (nuns were later admitted). He died at the age of 80 at Kusinagara (Kasia), not far from his birthplace, thus attaining final nirvana. His remains were cremated and the relics distributed.

THE BUDDHA'S TEACHINGS

The doctrine or *dharma* (in Pāli, *dhamma*) taught by the Buddha was summed up in the Four Noble Truths, corresponding to the traditional form in which a physician expressed his conclusions about a patient. They affirm that (1) life is permeated by suffering or dissatisfaction (*dukkha*); (2) the origin of suffering lies in craving or grasping (*taṇhā*); (3) the cessation of suffering is possible, through the cessation of craving; and (4) the way to the latter is the Noble Eightfold Path (*ariya aṭṭhangika magga*). This path has the following "stages," or constituents: right views, right aspiration, right speech, right conduct, right livelihood, right effort, right mindfulness, and right contemplation. The first two concern the preliminary frame of mind of the aspirant; the next three are the ethical requirements; and the final three concern the meditative training needed for contemplative or mystical knowledge of the ultimate truth and for the serenity that goes with it. This attainment of peace and insight is called *nirvāṇa* In Pāli, *nibbāna*), and implies that the saint (*arhat*) will upon death be no more reborn. (For a fuller discussion of the doctrine of rebirth, see REINCARNATION.)

Individuals are described by the Buddha as having three characteristics—suffering (*dukkha*), *anattā*, or absence of an eternal self; and *anicca*, or impermanence. The no self doctrine (*anattā*) implies both that living beings have no eternal souls and that there is no cosmic Self. The Buddha, indeed, did not believe in a Creator and seems to have found the existence of evil and suffering to be an insuperable obstacle to such a belief. Also, he deemed questions as to the finitude of the cosmos in space and time, and certain other cosmological and metaphysical questions, as "undetermined"—intrinsically unanswerable. In regard to persons, the Buddha analyzed them as series of mental and physical states. The concept of an underlying self is superfluous and erroneous. This is in line with the doctrine of impermanence, which implies that all entities whatsoever can be analyzed as series of transitory states. Under suitable circumstances the individual can attain nirvana, and then the series conventionally known as "John Smith," for example, ceases, so that the question "Does the saint continue to exist after final nirvana?" is unanswerable or wrongly put. Briefly, then, the Buddha's teaching amounts to a recasting of the atheistic tradition in early Indian thought, as exemplified contemporaneously in Jainism and later in classical Sāṃkhya, an Indian philosophical system. The plurality of transmigrating eternal selves controlled by karma is replaced by a plurality of impermanent individuals; and a metaphysically minimal description of nirvana is given as a transcendent, permanent state. The contrast of substances (soul and matter) is replaced by a contrast of states (permanent and impermanent).

Morals and meditation. Buddhism early involved a marked separation of monks (and nuns) and laity. The monastic life was conceived as necessary to the attainment of nirvana; the laity would have to wait their turn in some future existence. Consequently, the moral rules are laxer for them than for monks. Their duties are summed up in the Five Precepts (*pañcasīla*), which ban the taking of life (including animal life); stealing; wrong sexual relations; wrong use of speech (not just lying; malicious gossip, for instance, even though true, is forbidden); and the consumption of drugs and alcohol. The requirements for monks and nuns are designed to promote a moderate austerity: they enjoin, in addition to the rules listed above, such practices as strict celibacy and the repudiation of property (except for a few simple specified objects—such as begging bowl and robe). The laity have a special duty to support and revere the Sangha (monastic orders), and pious works, such as the attendance at and contribution to temples are encouraged. The monks and nuns are supposed to teach the doctrine (*dhamma*) to the faithful and to improve themselves through self-control and meditation. (More attention is given to these practices in MYSTICISM, HISTORY OF and YOGA.) A special feature of this training is mindfulness (*sati*), through which the aspirant attempts at all times to be clear about his own motives. This emphasis on self-awareness is one reason lying behind the ban on intoxicants, since it is held that these cloud such awareness.

EVOLUTION OF THE MAHĀYĀNA SCHOOL

The Theravāda (Doctrine of the Elders) school most probably represents the basic original teachings of the Buddha, although with a good deal of scholastic elaboration. In it there is no belief in God, nor even in a divine Absolute; nirvana is not a substance underlying or embracing phenomena; and the Buddha is not regarded as a god (thus temple "worship" is, strictly speaking, the paying of respects to the memory of a vanished teacher). These relatively austere teachings, however, became transformed in the development of the Mahāyāna (Greater Vehicle), from about the first century B.C. onward. This development had both religious and associated metaphysical roots.

Religiously, two strands of sentiment brought about a divinization of the Buddha (and of other Buddhas). First, it was increasingly felt that the path of the *arhat* (saint) was essentially selfish—seeking his own nirvana. This did not harmonize well with the Buddha's emphasis upon compassion; and it made the separation of monks and laity too sharp. Hence, there came to be new importance attached to the ideal of the Bodhisattva, or Buddha-to-be, who sacrifices himself on behalf of others and puts off his own release. Scriptural justification of this concept was found in the story of the Buddha's temptation by Māra (the Buddhist Satan) at the time of his Enlightenment: it was suggested to him that on attaining Enlightenment he might disappear at once into nirvana; instead, he remained on earth to teach the saving doctrine. Thus there arose the cult of numerous Buddhas-to-be who help others toward liberation—a cult much reinforced by the concept of *pariṇāmanā*, or transfer of merit, whereby the heroic moral deeds of the Bodhisattva in the course of innumerable lives create such a store of merit that he can freely transfer merit to otherwise unworthy adherents. Consequently, followers of the Bodhisattva can gain, through faith, rebirth in a paradise where the conditions for attaining nirvana are especially favorable. Important among these mythological paradises is the Pure Land of the West, created by the celestial Buddha Amitābha. All this went with an intensification of the spirit of *bhakti*, or loving adoration, within Buddhism: this became attached to the Buddhas and helped to elevate them to divine status.

Metaphysically, there was during this period (second century B.C.–third century A.D.) a development of absolutistic and idealistic views. These are represented by the Mādhyamika and Yogācāra schools of philosophy respectively. According to the Mādhyamika, all views about ultimate reality involve contradictions, and the only thing that can be said is that reality is void (*śūnya*). This indescribable Absolute that, as it were, embraces or underlies empirical phenomena (which are thus also essentially void), is conceived, in effect, as a shadowy substance and is identified with nirvana. Thus, the concept of nirvana is transformed: it is no longer just a *state*. This also allows the paradoxical identification of nirvana with *samsāra*,—the flow of empirical existence, including the cycle of rebirth—for ultimate reality can be conceived as the inner essence of the observable world. The Yogācāra school is an extension and transformation of these ideas, holding that phenomena are the product of the mind. Thus, the existence of matter is denied and things are analyzed as complexes of perception. But although the external world is independently unreal, the existence of the mental phenomena that we mistake for reality requires some explanation. Here the Yogācāra invokes the notion of their evolution out of the Absolute Mind. Under one aspect, this is spoken of as the Store Consciousness (*ālayavijñāna*), which contains the seeds of mental states. The goal of the adept is to realize the unreality of the world through contemplative experience. Thereby he sheds his illusions and cannot be considered distinct from the Absolute. As the name of the school implies, it concentrated on the practical side of this goal through the use of yoga and *dhyāna* (contemplation). Here the emphasis was different from that of the Mādhyamika, which was considered too intellectualist in its approach to liberation.

These religious and metaphysical developments were brought together in the formulation of the Three-body (*trikāya*) Doctrine. According to this, Buddhahood can be considered under three aspects. At one level the Buddha appears in his "Transformation Body" (*nirmāṇakāya*), as the historical Buddha and as earlier earthly Buddhas. At another level there is the "Enjoyment Body" (*sambhogakāya*), in which the Buddhas appear celestially to the eye of faith and have virtually the status of heavenly gods. Finally, and most importantly, there is the "Truth Body" (*dharmakāya*), where Buddhahood is identified with the Absolute; it also symbolizes the inner unity of all the Buddha manifestations. The *trikāya* notion not only tidied up doctrinally the various tendencies of the Mahāyāna at the popular and metaphysical levels but also expressed the status attached to the religion of worship and *bhakti*. This was focused especially upon the celestial Buddhas and Bodhisattvas, but in the last resort it was subordinate to the contemplative or mystical attainment of identity with the Absolute. This in turn implied that the final goal was Buddhahood itself. Thus, all men contain the potentiality for Buddhahood, the Buddha nature, within them. Consequently, the Buddhas are indefinitely multiplied and are as "numerous as the sands of the Ganges." Moreover, the worshiper who reveres a heavenly Buddha is essentially revering his own (very distantly, no doubt) future state. All this tied in with the Bodhisattva ideal. The good life is seen as the imitation of the Bodhisattva, and in entering upon this compassionate and self-sacrificing career the devotee is following his own destiny of being himself a Buddha-to-be. The whole structure of Mahāyāna religious absolutism has affinities to the teachings of Śankara and influenced his thought.

Buddhism in India and southeast Asia. Before and while the above developments were taking place, Buddhism was widely established in India. It was patronized by the Emperor Aśoka (third century B.C.), who sent a mission to Ceylon (c. 246 B.C.), where Buddhism took root. The present form of Ceylonese Buddhism is the Theravāda, partly because in the twelfth century the Ceylonese king, Parākrama Bāhu I, ordered all the Sangha to adopt it, and accompanying it there was a revival of the Hīnayāna there. In India itself, however, after centuries of prosperity, Buddhism virtually died away by the twelfth century. Three main causes contributed to this. First, Mahāyāna Buddhism became too assimilated with Hindu ideas and practices, so that its separate identity was undermined. Moreover, the fading of the *arhat* ideal weakened the status of the Sangha. Second, there was the revival of Hinduism under the leadership of Śankara, Rāmānuja and Madhva. Third, the Muslim invasions, from the eleventh century on, involved the destruction of the monasteries in north and central India. Except on the borders of Tibet, Buddhism is therefore virtually nonexistent in India and Pakistan.

The Ceylon mission, however, proved to be very important. Buddhism spread by various routes into Burma, Thailand, Laos, Cambodia and Vietnam, and the medieval Theravādin renaissance that was centered in the Ceylonese Sangha spread into these countries, which therefore are now Theravādin. In Indonesia, Buddhism flourished over a long period but is now replaced by other faiths, mainly Islam.

Buddhism in China and Japan. Under the patronage of the Indian King Kanishka (first century A.D.), Buddhism became well established throughout the area of the Kushan Empire and thereby penetrated north into central Asia. From there it spread along the trade routes into western China. The Emperor Ming of the Han Dynasty (who reigned from 58 to 75 A.D.), is reported to have had a dream of the Buddha, which led to his bringing in Indian missionaries. Whether this legendary story is true or not, certainly by the middle of the second century Buddhist texts were being translated into Chinese. However, there was firm resistance by Confucian orthodoxy, and not until the disturbed period between 184 (the end of the Han Dynasty) and the restoration of imperial unity in 589 was Buddhism able to make real headway. Under the Sui and T'ang dynasties (589–907) it flourished, although persecution toward the end of that period reduced its power and influence. From the fourth century on, Buddhism also penetrated Korea and was thence taken to Japan in 550, as part of the importation of Chinese culture.

The doctrines of karma and rebirth were new to China, and consequently the type of Mahāyāna doctrine that played down these teachings, through the idea of personal salvation by the grace of the Buddha, proved more easily assimilable. Hence, the Pure Land sect, whose devotions were aimed principally at the Buddha Amitābha, became firmly established. At the same time, Taoist teachings and meditative practices were a basis upon which Buddhism could build, and this gave rise to the Ch'ān (in Japanese, *Zen*) school, which had in turn a considerable effect upon Chinese art and literature. Although the Hīnayāna was introduced into China, it never had the success of the Mahāyāna. One other Chinese school, the T'ien-t'ai (in Japanese, *Tendai*) is worth separate mention, since it attempted to coordinate the various scriptures and teachings of the different Greater Vehicle sects by arranging them in an order of priority, culminating in the *Lotus Sūtra* (*Saddharmapuṇḍarīka*).

In Japan various Chinese schools were introduced in the early period, and there was a tendency to syncretize Buddhism and Shinto. The Shingon school (dating from the ninth century) flowed from a sacramental understanding of Buddhism analogous to that of Lamaism in Tibet and Mongolia (for instance, the use of sacred formulae as a means of material and spiritual advancement), and represented one main form of this syncretism; it remains one of the leading Japanese sects today. The Tendai (ninth century) and Zen (eleventh and twelfth centuries) also took firm hold in Japan. The teacher Hōnen (1133–1212), in the tradition of the Pure Land school, emphasized very strongly the need for calling on the name of the Buddha Amitābha (in Japanese, Amida) as a way of gaining grace, and his disciple Shinran (1173–1262), founder of the True Pure Land school (*Jōdo Shinshu*), carried this further in preaching salvation by faith alone. Nichiren (1222–1282), partly in line with these tendencies, started a more radical school, known as Hokkes, unique in Buddhism in being militant and intolerant of other forms of the Buddhist faith. His prophetic zeal and messianism are reflected in some of the new religions that have sprung up in Japan in recent times.

Buddhism in Tibet and environs. Buddhism infiltrated into Tibet from India and China during the seventh century and after. Despite resistance from the indigenous Bön religion, it became well established in its Indian form by the eleventh century. The type of religion was Tantric, a form of religion found also in India that involved esoteric sacramental practices, some of which centered on breaking taboos as a means of spiritual enlightenment. For instance, sexual intercourse was used as a controlled way of symbolizing the attainment of nondual mystical experience (in which the distinction between the mystic and the object of his experience is held to disappear). The most famous Tantric teacher was Milarepa (twelfth century).

Tibetan Buddhism has come to be divided into two main wings, the Nyingmapa, known as the "Red Hats" from their style of dress, and the Gelugpa, known as the "Yellow Hats." The Nyingmapa has a strong admixture of Bön ideas and practices. Perhaps the most interesting document of this school is the *Bardo Thödol*, or *Book of the Dead*, which describes the experiences of the self during the 49 days that are supposed to intervene between death and rebirth. The Gelugpa represents a reformed Tantrism and has as its chief spiritual head the Dalai Lama. Tibetan Buddhism is sometimes known as Lamaism, from the title of its monks. From Tibet, it spread into Mongolia from the thirteenth century on, and a separate Mongolian canon was established. A similar form of Buddhism is found in Nepal, Bhutan, and in general along the Himalayan foothills.

THE BUDDHIST SCRIPTURES

The Theravādin scriptures are written in Pāli, a Middle Indic dialect related to Sanskrit. They are divided into three sections, or "baskets" (*Tipitaka;* in Sanskrit, *Tripiṭaka*): "Sutta ("Discourses"), "Vinaya" ("Rules of Conduct"), and "Abhidhamma" ("Analysis of Doctrine"). The first comprises the discourses and conversations, together with incidents in the life of the Buddha. The second contains rules for the discipline of the Sangha. The third contains analyses and expositions of doctrines. These scriptures were first committed to writing in the latter part of the first century B.C. in Ceylon and therefore depend on quite a long prior oral tradition.

The Mahāyāna canons comprise Sanskrit documents that overlap in content with the Pāli writings, together with various later scriptures, notably the collection of metaphysical and religious works known as the *Prajñāpāramitā Sūtras*. The most famous "high Mahāyāna" document is the *Saddharmapuṇḍarīka* ("Lotus of the Good Law," often known simply as the "Lotus Sūtra"). The Sanskrit works were translated into Chinese and Japanese and added to in the process. A similar process occurred in the Vajrayāna, Diamond Vehicle. The Tibetan canon, known as the *Kanjur*, contains the "Vinaya," the *Prajñāpāramitā Sūtras*, and other works, including Tantric texts. Thus there are in Buddhism a series of overlapping canons.

Attitudes to the scriptures vary. In the Theravāda they simply represent an account, both historical and analytical, of the Buddha's and early Buddhist teachings and precepts, while there is a tendency in the Mahāyāna to ascribe sacred properties to the texts. This is in part the result of the phenomenon that can be called "identification with the reference"; that is, regarding the essential meaning of the scriptures as being what they refer to—ultimate reality or the experience thereof. A distinction is also drawn between word and reference, and it is the latter that is important. The doctrinal and scriptural words are, as it is said, like "fingers pointing at the moon," and it is wrong to confine one's gaze to the "fingers." This is in line with the developing conception of the teaching (*dharma*) of the

Buddha. Whereas the scriptures are thought of as propositional knowledge in the Theravāda, the Mahāyāna came to consider the essence of the teaching as being "Truth Body" of the Buddha, as identified with what the contemplative perceives in the highest nondual mystical experience. This "identification with the reference" had two divergent consequences. On the one hand, the sacredness of Buddhahood is transferred to the scriptures, so that salvation can be assured by uttering with faith a single sentence of the *Lotus Sūtra*. On the other, the words must be transcended, as illustrated by the famous Zen picture of the holy man tearing up the scriptures.

MODERN BUDDHISM

In recent times there has been both a revival and a decline of Buddhism. The work of both Western and Eastern scholars in editing and translating Buddhist texts since the middle of the nineteenth century has stimulated interest in the faith. A partial consequence has been the conversion of quite a number of Westerners and the foundation of Buddhist societies in the Occident (for example, England, 1906; France, 1929). At the same time, in Eastern countries an increasing awareness of their heritage, together with political advances, has brought about a revival of Buddhism there. This trend culminated in the Sixth Great Council in Rangoon (1954–1956), which marked the 2,000th anniversary of the Buddha's final nirvana and expressed a deepening cooperation between the different branches of Buddhism. On the other hand, in China, Marxist ideology is liable to submerge Buddhism; and Lamaism in Tibet has been so severely hit by the policy of the Chinese Communists that in 1959 the Dalai Lama felt forced to flee to India.

Bibliography

INTRODUCTIONS

Erik Zürcher, *Buddhism: Its Origin and Spread in Words, Maps and Pictures* (London, 1962) is useful. Edward Conze, *Buddhism, Its Essence and Development* (London, 1951), and F. H. Smith, *The Buddhist Way of Life* (London, 1934), are clear introductions. Christmas Humphreys, *Buddhism* (London, 1951), is a somewhat unscholarly best seller.

THE BUDDHA'S LIFE

E. J. Thomas, *The Life of the Buddha in Legend and History* (London, 1927), is the classic treatment of the sources then available.

THE BUDDHA'S TEACHINGS

Edward Conze, *Buddhist Thought in India* (London, 1962), is an important attempt toward a history of early Buddhist teachings. See also S. N. Dasgupta, *A History of Indian Philosophy* (London, 1922), Vol. I, Ch. 5; and E. J. Thomas, *History of Buddhist Thought* (London, 1933).

MORALS AND MEDITATION

Edward Conze, *Buddhist Meditation* (London, 1956); and Ninian Smart, *Reasons and Faiths* (London, 1958), Ch. 3, indicate some of the main practices of meditation. E. G. Parrinder, *Worship in the World's Religions* (London, 1961), pp. 95–137, usefully describes popular religion.

EVOLUTION OF MAHĀYĀNA

See bibliography to INDIAN PHILOSOPHY. On the Theravāda, T. W. Rhys Davids, *Buddhism: Its History and Literature* (New York, 1927), remains good; T. O. Ling, *Buddhism and the Mythology of Evil* (London, 1962), shows clearly the relation between doctrine and mythology. On the Mahāyāna, D. T. Suzuki, *Outlines of Mahāyāna Buddhism* (London, 1907), is introductory. T. R. V. Murti, *The Central Philosophy of Buddhism* (London, 1955), is excellent. See also Har Dayal, *The Bodhisattva Doctrine in Buddhist Sanskrit Literature* (London, 1932).

INDIA AND SOUTHEAST ASIA

R. C. Mitra, *The Decline of Buddhism in India* (Visvabharati, 1954); and J. B. Pratt, *The Pilgrimage of Buddhism* (New York, 1928), deal with Buddhism in India and southeast Asia.

CHINA AND JAPAN

Erik Zürcher, *The Buddhist Conquest of China*, 2 vols. (Leiden, 1959), is the best scholarly account. Charles Eliot, *Hinduism and Buddhism* (London, 1921), Vol. II, is lively if incomplete. A recent, full survey is Kenneth Ch'en, *Buddhism in China: A Historical Survey* (Princeton, 1964). See also Wing-tsit Chan, *Religious Trends in Modern China* (New York, 1953).

On Japan, see Charles Eliot, *Japanese Buddhism* (London, 1935), which is unsympathetic to Zen. See also the bibliography to ZEN. Masaharu Anesaki, *History of Japanese Religion* (London, 1930), is good. See also his *Nichiren, the Buddhist Prophet* (Cambridge, Mass., 1916).

TIBET AND ENVIRONS

Charles Bell, *The Religion of Tibet* (London, 1931); and W. Y. Evans-Wentz, *Tibet's Great Yogi Milarepa* (London, 1929), deal with Tibet. David Snellgrove, *Buddhist Himālaya* (London, 1959), mainly concerns Nepal.

BUDDHIST SCRIPTURES

Useful selections from the Buddhist scriptures are E. J. Thomas, *Early Buddhist Scriptures* (London, 1935); H. C. Warren, *Buddhism in Translation* (Cambridge, Mass., 1906); and (the most comprehensive in scope) Edward Conze et al., *Buddhist Texts Through the Ages* (Oxford, 1954). The series Sacred Books of the Buddhists (Oxford, 1899—) and Pali Text Society Translations (London, 1909—) have covered most Pāli texts. The series Sacred Books of the East. Max Muller, ed. (London, 1879—), contains both Theravādin and Mahāyāna writings. See also Edward Conze, *The Buddhist Wisdom Books* (London, 1959); D. T. Suzuki, *The Lankāvatāra Sūtra* (London, 1932); and W. E. Soothill, *The Lotus of the Wonderful Law* (Oxford, 1930).

MODERN BUDDHISM

For Western attitudes, see John Blofeld, *The Jewel in the Lotus* (London, 1948); and M. O'C. Walshe, *Buddhism for Today* (London, 1962). See also Kenneth Morgan, ed., *The Path of the Buddha* (New York, 1956). For an outstanding philosophical interpretation of the Buddha's teaching, see K. N. Jayatilleke, *Early Buddhist Theory of Knowledge* (London, 1963).

NINIAN SMART

BUFFON, GEORGES-LOUIS LECLERC, COMTE DE (1707–1788), French naturalist and author, enjoyed international acclaim for the artistic expression of his own grandiose, often brilliant theories and for presenting in similar fashion the discoveries of leading contemporaries, particularly in the field of natural science.

Life. Born at Montbard, son of an upper middle-class magistrate, Buffon was first educated by the Jesuits of

Dijon. Details about his personal life are sparse and uncertain. It is generally believed that, after studying law and despite a marked proclivity for mathematics, he went to Angers at the age of 22 to study medicine while indulging in botany and horsemanship. His stay ended abruptly when, presumably having killed an opponent in a duel for no verifiable reason, he set out on travels through France and Italy with the irresponsible young duke of Kingston. His mother's death in 1731 recalled him to Montbard where, as heir to her wealth, he turned the family manor into a château. Assuming the name of de Buffon, he adroitly enlarged his estates, which, in due course, were raised to an earldom.

The rest of his long life was divided between Montbard and Paris; no evidence has yet appeared supporting the belief that he also spent a year in England. When only 26, he was, through influence in high places, elected to the Academy of Science after having presented a paper on mathematical probability. He was soon engaged in silviculture and publishing experiments on the means of preserving and strengthening wood, and his reputation as a scientist was further enhanced by a translation in 1735 of Hales's *Vegetable Staticks* and, five years later, of Newton's *Method of Fluxions*, for which he wrote a much admired preface on the history of calculus.

From 1739 until his death he was curator of the Jardin du Roi in Paris, which, under his direction, expanded greatly and became an important scientific center. By 1740 he had begun work on his monumental 44-volume *Histoire naturelle*, the most ambitious and comprehensive history of natural science until recent times. Buffon was aided in this enormous task by reports from correspondents scattered throughout the world and by a team of highly specialized collaborators at home.

The first three volumes of the *Natural History*, including *Theory of the Earth* and *History of Man*, appeared in 1749. Published by the royal press, they were exempt from censorship. Almost immediately, however, they incurred the wrath of the Sorbonne for the bold views that ran counter to the book of Genesis. Out of deference to religious authority, Buffon penned an act of submission, only to proceed serenely in the same audacious manner.

Along with the volumes on quadrupeds (1753–1767), birds (1770–1783), and minerals (1783–1788) were the so-called *Supplements* (1774–1779), which included his justly famous work on the earth's geological periods, *The Epochs of Nature* (1778). After Buffon's death the vast project was brought to a close by B. G. E. Lacépède, with eight volumes on oviparous quadrupeds, snakes, fishes, and whales.

Buffon's *Discourse on Style*, delivered upon the occasion of his admission to the French Academy in 1753, remains the best known of his shorter pieces. It contains the celebrated dictum: "The style is the man himself," the meaning of which has often been simplified to the point of misinterpretation.

Thought. Buffon's death in Paris shortly before the French Revolution was mourned by the leading journals of Europe as the passing of one of the great figures of the century. His place in the history of ideas has since been undergoing a gradual reassessment still far from settled; certain areas of agreement have, nevertheless, been established. It is generally accepted that while he often engaged in scientific investigation, either through personal observation or through wide reading, his true inclination was for generalization. Influenced especially by Bacon, Newton, Leibniz, and Locke, he held seminal views that frequently inspired others to push his inquiries to fruitful conclusions. He rejected the popular conception of God as the Great Clockmaker and, instead of final causes, he looked for natural causes to explain the world about him. He insisted, and the stand was unusual for the day, that religion and science should be strictly separated. Thus, he evolved the theory that our planetary system had resulted from the glancing blow of a comet against the sun's molten surface. Perhaps the most original contribution of Buffon's cosmogony to science was to have introduced a new concept of the vast expanses of geological time. His published calculation of the earth's age as some 80,000 years, rather than the traditional estimate of 6,000, was in itself a generous concession to the prevailing spirit of the day; in his unpublished manuscripts he deals with figures that run into the millions.

Not an evolutionist in the modern sense, he nevertheless persistently stressed change at least in varieties, if not in species, of animal life. This and similar propositions or speculations led Charles Darwin to acclaim Buffon as the first author in modern times to have treated transformism in a scientific spirit. Moreover, in biology he rightly opposed epigenesis to the more widely accepted preformation theory of generation, though his ideas on "inner molds," "organic molecules" and spontaneous generation have long since fallen into disrepute. "He may be said to have asked all the questions which were to be answered in the course of the succeeding century," the oft-quoted comment of Henry Fairchild Osborn, perhaps remains the best generalization to date on Buffon's contribution to posterity.

Works by Buffon

Oeuvres complètes de Buffon, J.-L. Lanessan, ed., Vols. 13 and 14, *Correspondance inédite*. Paris, 1885.

Histoire naturelle, générale et particulière, 44 vols. Paris, 1749–1804. Translated and edited by William Smellie as *Natural History, General and Particular*, 20 vols. London, 1812. More recent edition edited by Jean Piveteau. Paris, 1954.

Works on Buffon

Fellows, Otis, "Buffon's Place in the Enlightenment." *Studies on Voltaire and the Eighteenth Century*, Vol. 25 (1963), 603–629.

Flourens, Pierre, *Des Manuscrits de Buffon*. Paris, 1860.

Heim, Roger, et al., *Buffon*. Paris, 1952.

Wilkie, J. B., "The Idea of Evolution in the Writings of Buffon." *Annals of Science*, Vol. 12, No. 1 (1956), 45–62; Vol. 12, No. 3 (1956), 212–227; Vol. 12, No. 4 (1956), 255–266.

Wohl, Robert, "Buffon and His Project for a New Science." *Isis*, Vol. 51, No. 2 (1960), 186–199.

OTIS FELLOWS

BULGAKOV, SERGEY NIKOLAYEVICH (1871–1944), Russian economist, philosopher, and theologian, was a leading twentieth-century religious philosopher in the tradition of Vladimir Solovyov.

Bulgakov was born in Livny, Russia, the son of a priest.

He attended a church school in Livny and spent four years in a theological seminary before enrolling in the faculty of law at the University of Moscow in 1890. He graduated in 1894 and began teaching political economy at the Moscow Technical School in 1895. From 1898 to 1900 he traveled in western Europe and Great Britain, gathering material for his master's dissertation, *Kapitalizm i Zemledeliye* ("Capitalism and Agriculture," 2 vols., St. Petersburg, 1900). Through this and other writings on economic and social questions he soon acquired a national reputation. After teaching in Kiev for five years, he returned to Moscow in 1906 to become professor of political economy at the Moscow Institute of Commerce; in the same year he was elected to the second state Duma as a Constitutional Democrat. In 1912 he received a doctorate from the University of Moscow, and in 1917 he was named professor of political economy at that institution.

Although Bulgakov was a leading "legal Marxist" in the 1890s, he even then acknowledged the philosophical supremacy of Kant and soon began to depart from orthodox Marxism on socioeconomic issues as well. In his master's dissertation he argued that Marx's theory of the centralization of production is inapplicable to agriculture, where small-scale production is more stable and viable than large-scale. When, in the early years of the twentieth century, Bulgakov underwent a religious crisis, he abandoned Marxism completely, first for the idealistic position represented in his book of essays, *Ot Marksizma k Idealizmu* ("From Marxism to Idealism," St. Petersburg, 1903), and subsequently for a mystical, "Sophiological" interpretation of the Russian Orthodox faith showing the direct and extensive influence of Solovyov and Paul Florensky and the ultimate influence of Plato and Schelling. In 1909 Bulgakov contributed to the celebrated miscellany, *Vekhi* ("Landmarks"), in which ex-Marxist Russian intellectuals, including Nicolas Berdyaev and Peter Struve, criticized the radical intelligentsia. Bulgakov first outlined his positive religious philosophy in his doctoral dissertation, *Filosofiya Khozyaystva* ("The Philosophy of Economics," Moscow, 1912) and over the years 1911–1916 he composed the work in which this philosophy received its fullest expression, *Svet Nevecherni* ("The Unfading Light," Moscow, 1917).

During the same period Bulgakov studied for holy orders, and in 1918 he was ordained a priest in the Russian Orthodox church. He moved to the Crimea, where he became professor of political economy and theology at the University of Simferopol, but in 1921 he lost this position because he was a member of the clergy. At the end of 1922 he was expelled from Russia along with many other non-Marxist scholars and writers. He settled first in Prague and lived from 1925 in Paris, where he took part in founding the Orthodox Theological Institute, serving as its dean and professor of dogmatic theology until his death. During these years Bulgakov wrote extensively on theological subjects and took an active part in ecclesiastical conferences in many countries, becoming an internationally known church figure. Some of his later theological works, particularly *Agnets Bozhi* ("The Lamb of God," Paris, 1933) and *Nevesta Agntsa* ("The Bride of the Lamb," Paris, 1945) also carried further the development of his distinctive philosophical outlook.

Basic to this outlook is a cosmology that, although marked in its expression by obscurities and progressive modifications, centered consistently on the following themes: (1) The world, or cosmos, is an organic whole animated by a "world soul" or entelechy that is revealed in the structure, function, and connection of its parts. (2) God, or the Absolute, in creating the cosmos "out of nothing," created it not as something external or alien to him (for then it would limit the Absolute, which is impossible), but as an emanation of his own nature; the world is God as becoming, the divine nature fused with nothingness. (3) Mediating between the Absolute and the cosmos, uniting them both within itself, is a "third being"—Sophia, the principle of divine wisdom. As the world of Platonic Ideas, Sophia is the ideal basis of the cosmos; as the object of divine love, purely receptive and conceiving everything within herself as the womb of being, Sophia is "eternal femininity"; as the principle of the Divine within the created, she is the "world soul," or entelechy; as a participant with the Trinity in the generation of the cosmos, she is a kind of "fourth hypostasis" in God. In his later works Bulgakov distinguished between the "divine Sophia" in God and the "created Sophia" in the cosmos, but he still emphasized their ultimate metaphysical identity and thus the consubstantiality of God and the cosmos.

Bulgakov resisted the pantheistic implications of his position, preferring to call it a form of panentheism, and strove to provide solutions to the chief philosophical problems it raised, such as the problems of evil and human freedom. He attributed evil to the nothingness or nonbeing that is the substratum of the cosmos: through the willfulness of created beings, nothingness is actualized as a chaotic force erupting into the created world, which in itself is not evil but simply incomplete. He provided for human freedom through a doctrine of self-creation: man is free even in the act by which he comes into existence, for God allows man to collaborate in his own creation; at the same time, however, Bulgakov also asserted that Sophia guides history by a kind of necessity.

Like Florensky, Bulgakov laid great stress on the antinomic character of rationality and looked to divine revelation through religious experience for knowledge of the highest truths, but his epistemological views in general received no thorough, original development or synthesis; the same is true of his scattered treatments of ethical questions and of his aesthetic reflections—the latter appearing principally in *Tikhiye Dumy* ("Quiet Meditations," Moscow, 1918). The work Bulgakov himself regarded as his most strictly philosophical product—*Filosofiya Imeni* ("Philosophy of the Name")—was written in 1919 but first published posthumously in Paris in 1953. It is an exhaustive study of language, with particular application to theology, in which Bulgakov argued that words are not mere outward signs of meanings but are internally related to them as animate symbols.

Bulgakov's later works abounded in imaginative theological conceptions, including a doctrine of universal salvation and original treatments of the Incarnation and of the theological differences between Roman Catholicism and Orthodoxy. Some of his theological views, particularly his Sophiology, were severely censured in the early 1930s by the Moscow patriarchate, which affirmed that the doctrine of Sophia is incompatible with the Trinitarian nature of God and that it falsely introduces a distinction between masculine and feminine principles into the divine essence.

Additional Works by Bulgakov

Dva Grada, 2 vols. Moscow, 1911.
Die Tragödie der Philosophie. Darmstadt, 1927.
The Orthodox Church, translated by Elizabeth Cram. London, 1935.
The Wisdom of God: A Brief Summary of Sophiology. New York, 1937.
Avtobiograficheskiye Zametki. Paris, 1946.

Works on Bulgakov

Kindersley, R., *The First Russian Revisionists: A study of Legal Marxism in Russia*. Oxford, 1962.
Lossky, N. O., *History of Russian Philosophy*. New York, 1951, Ch. 15.
Zander, L. A., *Bog i Mir: Mirosozertsaniye Ottsa Sergiya Bulgakova*, 2 vols. Paris, 1948.
Zenkovsky, V. V., *Istoriya Russkoi Filosofii*, 2 vols. Paris, 1948–1950. Translated by George L. Kline as *A History of Russian Philosophy*, 2 vols. New York and London, 1953, pp. 892–916.

JAMES P. SCANLAN

BULGARIAN PHILOSOPHY. Three main eras may be distinguished in the history of the Bulgarian people. The aim of this article is to indicate briefly some principal philosophical expressions of the three periods in Bulgarian history.

Medieval period. During the medieval period, the conversion of the Bulgarian people to Christianity in the ninth century was marked also by heretical movements resistant to ecclesiastical orthodoxy. The first important upsurge of theological and cosmological radicalism was that of the Bogomile movement. Its religious philosophy shared the dualistic tendencies of earlier sectarian doctrines—Gnostic, Manichaean, Paulician. It proclaimed the strictly spiritual nature of God and Christ and stigmatized all material existence as the work of the devil. The Bogomiles rejected the doctrine of the Incarnation and of the bodily life of Christ as well as every material aspect of religious thought and practice—sacraments, the cross, church edifices, ecclesiastical ceremonies. They advocated asceticism and simple spiritual devotion. Despite severe official restrictions, this movement spread not only in Bulgaria but westward into Bosnia and across the Adriatic. In the land of their origin the Bogomiles stood their ground against persecution, then were gradually repressed and eventually swept away by the invasion and conquest of the Balkans by the Turks who, beginning in the fourteenth century, dominated Bulgaria for five hundred years.

Revival of Bulgarian culture. The end of Turkish domination in 1878 was signalized by nation wide cultural activity in all directions. Bulgarian students by the hundreds and thousands pursued advanced studies in the universities of Russia and western Europe, especially in Germany, and on their return stirred in Bulgarian minds a ferment of modern ideas and doctrines. The publication of numerous translations of philosophical classics reflected the spreading interest in the historical development of thought. At the University of Sofia the study of the history of philosophy was cultivated by Ivan Georgoff (1862–1936). Beyond strict professional philosophy, the influence of philosophical ideas and problems could be noted in the thought of literary critics like Krusto Krustev (1866–1919). An ironical poet, Stoyan Michailovsky (1856–1927), grappled with the problem of evil, and another epic and lyric poet of outstanding power, Pencho Slaveykov (1866–1912), manifested the influence of Nietzschean and other philosophical ideas.

Among other philosophical minds, Dimiter Michaltchev was outstanding. As professor at the University of Sofia, as a very productive philosophical writer, and as editor of a journal of philosophy, he was for a whole generation the animating power in Bulgarian philosophy. His three most important works are *Philosophische Studien* (Leipzig, 1909), *Forma y Otnoshenie* ("Form and Relation," Sofia, 1914) and *Filosofiata Kato Nauka* ("Philosophy as a Science," Sofia, 1946). In his philosophical position Michaltchev was from the outset an acknowledged disciple and advocate of Johannes Rehmke's theory of philosophy as fundamental science (*Grundwissenschaft*). With his master, he held that we perceive objects and their qualities directly, that the reality of the mind and its perceived world does not point to any other transcendent metaphysical reality, that relations and development are likewise objective and immediately known to us.

Similarly Rehmkean is his approach to the problems of time and motion. Time is not the mind's form of comprehending the events it perceives. The very succession of changes in which one event follows another is time itself. And likewise with motion: as spatial location is itself a quality of things, so motion from place to place is an objective fact. All these views, according to Michaltchev, are essential to philosophy considered as the fundamental science.

In the field of practical philosophy Michaltchev, following Rehmke, criticized the ethics of dutiful conduct and proposed instead the principle of purely disinterested will and action as alone truly virtuous. Moral disinterestedness springs from love, in advocating which Michaltchev recognized the significance of the New Testament teaching but revised its theological exposition. Michaltchev's vigorous advocacy of Rehmke's theory, against much better known philosophical alternatives, gained few disciples; but it stirred in Bulgarian circles fresh discussion of philosophical problems and contributed to the vitalization of fundamental thinking.

Communist period. In Bulgaria as well as in other eastern European countries communist "scientific socialism" has included not only political and economic partisan propaganda but also an ideology expounded in many fields of cultural life—in education, in literary and artistic criticism, in religion (or, rather, irreligion), and in the basic tenets of dialectical materialism. Among the many Bulgarian writers who have pursued socialism, Dimitri Blagoev (1855–1924) was especially active during the generation prior to the establishment of the communist regime after World War II. The more recent period of Bulgarian philosophy has been marked by the increasing suppression of non-Marxist ideas.

The most vigorous representative of the communist strain in Bulgarian thought has been Todor Pavlov, president of the Bulgarian Academy of Sciences. His main philosophical work has been in the field of aesthetics, especially in literary criticism, but he has also presented more general expositions of dialectical materialism. The main conclusions of his work, *Osnovny Vuprosy na Estetikata* ("Fundamental Problems of Aesthetics," Sofia, 1949) should indicate Pavlov's basic position, which he has defined as "socialist realism." The purpose of art and of the artist should be to become, in Stalin's words, "engineers of men's souls," to contribute to the aesthetic realization of the proletarian-communist program. Dialectical materialism should be not only the fundamental view of nature and human life but also the basis of all art. Pavlov's unwavering party view has involved him in continual controversies, especially with Michaltchev, in which the latter has defended his position very effectively. These polemics have concerned philosophical issues; but they have also reflected the conflicting ideologies that have divided, and still divide, Bulgarian thought.

Bibliography

Groseff, G., *Istoriya na Bulgarskata Filosofiya*. Sofia, 1959.

Obolensky, D., *Bogomils: A Study in Balkan Neo-Manichaeism*. Cambridge, 1948.

Sharenkoff, V. N., *A Study of Manicheanism in Bulgaria*. New York, 1927.

RADOSLAV A. TSANOFF

BULTMANN, RUDOLF, Biblical historian and theologian, was born in 1884 at Wiefelsted, Oldenburg, Germany. He studied at Marburg, Tübingen, and Berlin and taught first at Marburg and then at Breslau and Giessen. In 1921 he became professor of New Testament studies at Marburg, where he remained until 1951. He has since been in retirement.

Bultmann's work and the controversies it has generated are of undoubted importance for the philosophy of religion. His ventures in "demythologizing" the New Testament and in reinterpreting its content "existentially" have raised (and have tried to answer) crucial questions about the logical status of religious language and the nature of Christian belief.

CHRISTIAN FAITH

Bultmann's thought has been inspired by his keen sense of the remoteness and unacceptability of the thought forms of New Testament Christianity to most people of the twentieth century. We do not and cannot see our world as a theater of conflict between supernatural powers, the demonic seeking to possess and destroy us, and God intervening to secure our salvation. Moreover, miracle stories lie at the very heart of New Testament belief: "If Christ be not raised, your faith is vain" (I Corinthians 15.17). Thus, the critical question is: must a man, in order to be a Christian, commit himself simultaneously to two mutually incompatible world pictures—that of twentieth-century science and that of first-century prescientific speculation? According to Bultmann, to attempt this is to make Christian belief *unnecessarily* difficult. It is equally unrewarding to view Christianity as a strictly and objectively "historical" religion and anxiously to sift all the evidence for and against the recorded events of the life of Jesus. The evidence is substantial enough to show that Jesus indeed lived and that he made a quite extraordinary impact upon certain contemporaries. But if religious faith is to stand or fall with the historicity of, say, the birth stories or the Easter narratives, if its degree of assurance must rationally be tempered with the historical probabilities, the assurance will be pitifully uncertain, and faith will almost certainly fall.

To these perplexities Bultmann offers a bold remedy. The Christian may properly grant that a very large part of the New Testament message is couched in mythical language and does not record objective history. This mythical material is not, however, an embarrassment, and it need not be discarded. It can be interpreted as indirect description not of the cosmos but of the conditions and possibilities of human existence. Historical studies derive their real seriousness not from sheer factuality but from what they discover about viable ways of life and viable options for human decision. Among such options, the Christian gives pre-eminence to that displayed in the accounts of the cross and the resurrection. For it is through these that God makes available a distinctively "authentic" and free mode of existence to all humanity.

INFLUENCE OF HEIDEGGER

"Authentic" is Martin Heidegger's term. It is only one of Bultmann's many borrowings from *Sein und Zeit*. There is a prima-facie oddness here—a Christian theologian reinterpreting the New Testament teachings in terms of concepts drawn from atheist existentialism. Nevertheless, the concepts are undeniably relevant and, within limits, illuminating. There are clear and suggestive analogies between Heidegger's general picture of inauthenticity and the New Testament's accounts of life "in" and "after" the flesh, the life of the "natural man" who is alienated from God. In both views men are uneasy, anxious, and guilty over their condition. If to Heidegger *Angst* reveals that man is "not at home" in the world, the New Testament affirms that here we have no continuing city but seek one to come. To both we are strangers and pilgrims.

On the "authentic" type of existence, there are both marked similarities and differences in the views of Heidegger and Bultmann. Heidegger's account centers upon a total acceptance of the fundamental conditions of our life. This involves, for any man, a realization of his own death, not as some vague, unpleasant, but indefinite future event, but as something whose constant presence, in possibility, should modify his sense of his own existence at every moment. Christianity, too, speaks of renouncing the world and a life entangled with the world, of "dying" to the life of self. It has, however—or ought to have—some very different things to say about life eternal.

Heidegger's authentic man sees and accepts the limitations on his freedom imposed by the given circumstances of his life as so far lived ("facticity"); he sees the present moment as the locus of decision, and it is in the future that he will work out those authentic possibilities of existence for which he decides. The Judaeo-Christian tradition also has a dualism of facticity and freedom: it claims both that man was created "out of the dust of the ground," stressing the given factuality of human existence, and that God "breathed into his nostrils the breath of life," endowing him with freedom to pursue his diverse possibilities.

How can we discover our authentic possibilities? In answering this question both Heidegger and Bultmann point to the thoroughly temporal, historical nature of human life. History discloses human possibility. For Bultmann the Christian is he who, in R. G. Collingwood's term, "incorporates" the essentials of the New Testament story in his present thought and action.

Bultmann's account of the human situation is, therefore, an "existential" analysis, and to call it that is to contrast it both with the findings of empirical psychology and with a philosophical analysis of nonpersonal structures. Far from being based on empirical investigations, existential analysis tries to uncover the concepts that are, and have to be, employed in any such researches—the fundamental concepts of personal existence.

But there are complexities to be noted here. Although to Bultmann the New Testament has much to say about the general human predicament, we must not analyze its discourse exhaustively as delineating permanent and universal human possibilities. The authentic life, crucially, is available to a man only by virtue of divine grace and through his appropriating the Word revealed in Christ.

DEMYTHOLOGIZING

There is, however, an uneasy duality in Bultmann's thought. Almost everything in the New Testament is to be understood as describing modes of personal existence, but not so the central claim of the kerygma itself, the claim that God decisively acted in Christ. This contains a reference to God that cannot be eliminated. Yet it must be noted that although Bultmann refuses to "dekerygmatize," others (Fritz Buri, for instance) have tried to do just that. They have been unable to stop at what looks to them like a halfway house and have taken the kerygma too as material for existential analysis.

Other theologians have offered various arguments to show that Bultmann's position is too extreme. They claim that he has underestimated the importance of objective history, that he has made too many concessions to twentieth-century skepticism, that his existentialist concepts cannot express the full meaning, the nuances, the complex mesh of associations of the Biblical writings, that the myth must be kept intact.

It is not surprising, therefore, that the controversy over demythologizing has been intense and involved. I shall single out for brief discussion only a few of the most crucial issues, beginning with the question of Bultmann's existentialism.

Crucial issues. (1) Without doubt, Heidegger's existential analysis has provided Bultmann with a valuable nonmythical vocabulary, able to express an important part of the New Testament message. However, there are certainly some points at which his analyses appear to clarify the Christian position but in fact tempt a theologian to distort it seriously. For example, if Christianity were no more than a philosophy of life, then matters of objective history would not be crucial to it. So long as we knew that someone had lived roughly the sort of life Jesus allegedly lived, we could at least take the "imitation of Christ" as an ideal for human living. "Possibility," in this rather weak sense, would be enough. But if we want to go beyond that (as Bultmann certainly does) and claim that God was actually imparting himself in a quite distinctive and decisive way in the events of Jesus' life, then it is a matter of immense seriousness to learn what these events were. We cannot have a historical religion, in that strong sense, without historical vulnerability. For all its subtlety (most likely because of its subtlety), the existential analysis of historicity deflects attention from this uncomfortable fact.

One should not conclude, however, that Bultmann has never stated a coherent and clear position on historicity and Christian belief. In *History and Eschatology* (1957) he expressed himself much more lucidly in alternative terms derived from R. G. Collingwood. But the link between his position in this book and traditional Christian theology has become very tenuous indeed. Whatever the impression we receive from other writings of Bultmann, in *History and Eschatology* the Gospel seems to be about human self-understanding from first to last; dependence on objective historicity has receded to the vanishing point.

(2) Several important and difficult New Testament concepts seem to yield very readily to existential analysis; yet these concepts remain philosophically problematic. The concept of "body" has clear existential meaning—related to Heidegger's concept of what it is to "exist-in-a-world." Likewise, "eternal life," in the New Testament, characterizes a manner, or quality, of living. Yet even if much of the meaning of these expressions is translatable into existentialist language, there surely remains a vital part that is not. The existential analysis by itself cannot answer such a question as "Does our existence end with our bodily death?" Nor does it help solve the problems of meaning and logic (particularly problems of personal identity) that arise over concepts like life after death and the resurrection of the dead.

(3) Because the life and personality of Jesus play so muted a part in this theology, and because the summons to authentic existence tends to be rather individualistic in its emphasis, it is very difficult to build up an adequate account of Christian discipleship and Christian love on Bultmann's foundations. The quality of the Christian ethical life has always been determined by the believer's response not simply to the bare proclamation that a new life has been made available to him, but to the concrete particularities of the life and teaching of Jesus. One guesses that a theology like Bultmann's can succeed in expressing this quality only through implicit dependence on a more conservative view of the New Testament that is still secretly operative in the religious imagination.

(4) From the philosopher's point of view, perhaps the most urgent need is for Bultmannian theology to construct a much more precise logical map of its key concepts, myth, mythology, and analogy. "Mythology," Bultmann wrote, "is the use of imagery to express the other worldly in terms of this world and the divine in terms of human life, the other side in terms of this side." But Bultmann does not want to conclude that discourse about God is always, and

necessarily, mythological. To speak mythologically is to represent God as a kind of superentity, observably acting upon and interacting with natural entities. However, Bultmann has claimed (in *Kerygma and Myth*) that it is possible to speak of God's "acts" analogically, and to do so with the help of concepts borrowed once again from the field of human personal existence.

Bultmann is here in pursuit of what may well be a valuable distinction, but it has not been at all clearly articulated. The different modes of discourse about God are not rigorously defined, and thus a good deal of uncertainty is left about appropriate tests for sense and nonsense, truth and falsity, in claims about God. It is by no means obvious, for instance, whether one can really think through those existential, "analogical" utterances about God without implicitly relying upon a mythological picture of God as a superperson and superentity. Further, since both mythological discourse and analogical discourse are indirect or oblique, we need to ask whether any direct, literal talk about God is possible, or whether it is necessarily all oblique. If it must all be oblique, the problem of how we can refer to God and relate the myths and analogies to him surely becomes unmanageable. If it is not all oblique, then we still need to discover what, and how much, can be affirmed directly and literally about God. The temptation is to resort to theological makeshifts—to analyze virtually all talk about God in terms of human self-understanding, but to rely, devotionally and pastorally, upon an unanalyzed transcendent remainder, of which, however, no clear account is given in a systematic theology.

All these puzzling instabilities in Bultmann's thought are not careless or stupid blunders of reasoning. They are illuminating, disturbing indications of how immensely hard it is to steer between, on the one hand, a wholly secularized Christianity, a humanism, and, on the other, a religion of the supernatural and the miraculous.

Works by Bultmann

Existence and Faith: Shorter Writings of Rudolf Bultmann, selected, translated, and introduced by Schubert M. Ogden. London, 1961.

Die Frage des Entmythologisierung. Munich, 1954. Written with Karl Jaspers.

Glauben und Verstehen, 2 vols. Tübingen, Vol. I, 1933; Vol. II, 1952. Vol. II has been translated as *Essays: Philosophical and Theological*. London, 1955.

History and Eschatology. Edinburgh, 1957. For a pungent critique, see A. MacIntyre's review in *The Philosophical Quarterly*, Vol. 10 (1960), 92.

Jesus. Berlin, 1926. Translated as *Jesus and the Word*. New York and London, 1934.

Jesus Christ and Mythology. New York, 1958; London, 1960.

"Neues Testament und Mythologie" (written 1941), in H. W. Bartsch, ed., *Kerygma und Mythos*, Vol. I. Translation in Bartsch, ed., *Kerygma and Myth*, Vol. I.

Theologie des Neuen Testaments. Tübingen, 1948–1953. Translated as *Theology of the New Testament*, 2 vols. New York and London, Vol. I, 1952; Vol. II, 1955.

Related Works

Barth, Karl, *Rudolf Bultmann—Ein Versuch, ihn zu verstehen*. Zollikon, Zurich, 1952. Translation in Bartsch, ed., *Kerygma and Myth*, Vol. II.

Bartsch, H. W., ed., *Kerygma und Mythos*, 5 vols. Hamburg and Volksdorf, 1948–1955. A collection of essays by Bultmann and others. Translations from these essays in *Kerygma and Myth*. Vol. I, London and Naperville, Ill., 1953; Vol. II, New York and London, 1962.

Braaten, C. E., and Harrisville, R. A., eds., *Kerygma and History*. Nashville, Tenn., 1962. A symposium on Bultmann's theology.

Braithwaite, R. B., *An Empiricist's View of the Nature of Religious Belief*. Cambridge, 1955.

Buri, Fritz, "Entmythologisierung oder Entkerygmatisierung der Theologie," in Bartsch, ed., *Kerygma und Mythos*, Vol. II. See also Vol. III, p. 81.

Cairns, David, *A Gospel Without Myth?* London, 1960.

Collingwood, R. G., *The Idea of History*. New York and Oxford, 1946.

Gogarten, Friedrich, *Entmythologisierung und Kirche*. Stuttgart, 1953. Translated as *Demythologizing and History*. London, 1955.

Heidegger, Martin, *Sein und Zeit*. Halle, 1927. Translated as *Being and Time*. London, 1962.

Hepburn, R. W., *Christianity and Paradox*. London, 1958.

Hepburn, R. W., "Demythologizing and the Problem of Validity," in A. G. N. Flew and A. MacIntyre, eds., *New Essays in Philosophical Theology*. London, 1955. Also in G. L. Abernethy and T. A. Langford, eds., *Philosophy of Religion: A Book of Readings*. New York, 1962.

MacKinnon, D. M., "Our Contemporary Christ," broadcast talk (BBC). Reprinted in *The Listener*, Vol. 67, No. 1732 (June 7, 1962), 9908.

Macquarrie, John, *An Existentialist Theology*. New York and London, 1955.

Macquarrie, John, *The Scope of Demythologizing*. London, 1960.

Malevez, Leopold, *Le Message chrétien et le mythe*. Brussels, Bruges, and Paris, 1954. Translated as *The Christian Message and Myth*. London, 1958; Westminster, Md., 1960.

Miegge, G., *L'evangelo e il mytho nel pensiero di Rudolf Bultmann*. Milan, 1956. Translated as *Gospel and Myth in the Thought of Rudolf Bultmann*. London, 1960.

Owen, H. P., *Revelation and Existence*. Cardiff, 1957.

Wingren, G., *Theology in Conflict*. Philadelphia, 1958.

For bibliographies of Bultmann's writings and of works on his thought, see the books by Miegge and Cairns listed above; also *Kerygma and Myth*, Vols. I and II.

RONALD W. HEPBURN

BURCKHARDT, JAKOB (1818–1897), Swiss cultural historian, was born in Basel, the son of a Protestant minister. He began his university education as a theology student, but lost his faith in orthodox Christianity comparatively early and turned instead to history. He spent part of his formative years in liberal and freethinking circles in Germany; it was in Germany, too, that he discovered and worked under Leopold von Ranke, probably the most potent and lasting influence upon his future career as a historian. On his return to Switzerland in the 1840s, Burckhardt was at first attracted to the political and religious dissensions that he found there. The violence to which they subsequently led, however, was repulsive to his temperament; and he retired to Italy, having, in his own words, "given up political activity forever." Some time later he finally settled in Basel, dedicating himself, as professor of history and history of art, to the routine of teaching and lecturing that was to occupy him continuously up to the last years of his life.

Burckhardt's chief writings were all published before he was fifty: *The Age of Constantine the Great* (1852), *Cicerone* (1855), *The Renaissance in Italy* (1860), and *The*

History of the Renaissance (1867). In addition to these major works, he also gave a number of lectures between 1868 and 1871 on the general study of history, the notes for which were preserved and eventually published posthumously under the title of *Weltgeschichtliche Betrachtungen* ("Reflections on World History"). These are remarkable, not only for the prophetic insight they display in their analysis of contemporary trends, but also for the many subtle and individual observations they contain concerning the purposes of historiography and the theoretical problems it poses. They were attended by Nietzsche, who at the time was professor of classics at Basel and whose later essay, *The Use and Abuse of History*, bears the impress of some of Burckhardt's ideas.

Burckhardt did not regard his lectures as representing a contribution to "philosophy of history" in the then current sense. Indeed, he made it clear at the outset that he was profoundly suspicious of fashionable schemes and systems that attempted to exhibit the course of historical development as conforming to a rationally ordered pattern, and referred with especial scorn to the Hegelian conception of history as the "inevitable march of the world spirit." For him such projects were the manifestation of a crude and vulgar "optimism"; they sprang from the arrogant and egotistical assumption that "our time is the consummation of all time" and tended to "justify" the crimes and disasters of previous ages as necessary to the promotion of what came afterward. Burckhardt thought that the role of moral judgment in history could not be spirited away in this complacent manner; but neither, on the other hand, should the historian allow his view of the past to be distorted by moral predilections peculiar to his own time and society. What was above all requisite for true historical understanding was a contemplative, disinterested sense of the abiding and tragic aspects of human existence. Only through such detachment from prevailing concerns and preoccupations could the historian transcend the barriers that separate the mental life of one age from that of another.

Burckhardt admired Schopenhauer, and he tended to extend to the historian a position in some ways similar to that which the German philosopher had reserved for the artist. It was not merely that works of art and culture provided the historian with his most fertile material for the interpretation of previous phases of human experience; history itself was (or should be) a form of art. The mechanical piling up of the results of specialized research, dear to so-called "scientific" historians, was not enough; there must also be "intuition," an imaginative ability to re-create the vision of life underlying the relics left by former times. To see the past in these terms was to see it as the expression of the inexhaustible creative power of the human mind—great individuals, great artistic achievements, great moments of civilization, all exemplified in different ways its potentialities. Scholarship, painstaking investigation, were indeed essential, but they must be properly used and directed. Only thus could a particular source or authority throw light on the character of a person, the significance of a style, the pervasive atmosphere of a period.

Ultimately, Burckhardt claimed, the subject of historical study was man himself, not the hypostatized abstractions of the philosophers of history. These philosophers, by implying that the historical process followed a fixed and predetermined course, betrayed a fundamental blindness to its most striking feature, the revelation of individual originality and creativity. Likewise, their "astrological impatience" to set limits to its future by talk of world plans and metaphysical goals was not only unwarranted; it failed to respect the very conditions of uncertainty and suspense that make human achievement possible. From this point of view, and insofar as the development of mankind is concerned, "a future known in advance is an absurdity."

Toward the close of the nineteenth century the tide of historical speculation began to recede. Philosophers, rather than continuing to offer sweeping interpretations of the human past, turned their attention toward examining the distinctive characteristics of historical thought and inquiry. In retrospect, Burckhardt can be seen to occupy an interesting position in this development. Though not a philosopher himself, he nonetheless anticipated in his own reflections on historical procedure some of the ideas that later found philosophical expression in the writings of Dilthey and Croce.

Works by Burckhardt

Gesammelte Werke, 7 vols. Basel, 1957.

Die Zeit Constantins des Grossens. Basel, 1852. Translated by Moses Hadas as *The Age of Constantine the Great.* New York, 1949.

Der Cicerone. Basel, 1855. Translated by Mrs. A. H. Clough as *Cicerone*, rev. ed. London, 1879.

Die Cultur der Renaissance in Italien. Basel, 1860. Translated by S. G. C. Middlemore from 15th German ed. as *The Civilization of the Renaissance in Italy*, 2d ed. London, 1890.

Geschichte der Renaissance in Italien. Stuttgart, 1867.

Weltgeschichtliche Betrachtungen, J. Deri, ed., 2d ed. Berlin, 1910. Translated by J. H. Nichols as *Force and Freedom: Reflections on History.* New York, 1955.

Works on Burckhardt

Duerr, E., *Freiheit und Macht bei Jacob Burckhardt.* Basel, 1918.

Heller, E., "Burckhardt and Nietzsche," in *The Disinherited Mind.* Cambridge, 1952, Ch. 3.

Joel, K., *Jacob Burckhardt als Geschichtsphilosoph.* Basel, 1910.

Martin, A. W. O. von, *Burckhardt und Nietzsche philosophieren über Geschichte.* Krefeld, 1948.

Meinecke, F., "Ranke and Burckhardt," in H. Kohn, ed., *German History: Some New German Views.* London, 1954.

Trevor-Roper, H. R., "The Faustian Historian: Jacob Burckhardt," in *Men and Events.* New York, 1957, Ch. 40.

PATRICK GARDINER

BURIDAN, JEAN, or Joannes Buridanus (c. 1295–1356), French philosopher and scientist, was probably born at Béthune in Artois. He studied philosophy at Paris with Ockham and remained there as a very successful professor of philosophy and a highly influential member of the faculty, serving as rector in 1328 and again in 1340. In 1345 Buridan was deputed to defend the interests of the University of Paris before Philip of Valois at Rome. Now-discredited traditions made Buridan founder of the University of Vienna and lover of a queen of France, a legend immortalized by François Villon in verses beginning:

> *L'histoire dit que Buridan*
> *Fut jeté en un sac en Seine*

In science Buridan's contributions fall into the areas of physics mainly cultivated by the Paris school, optics and mechanics. His optical concepts were in the tradition of John Philoponus, Alpetragius (al-Bitruji), Peter John Olivi, and Francis of Marchia; he advanced ideas relating to the succession and sequence of optical images that anticipated concepts basic to modern cinematics. In mechanics Buridan again followed the tradition of Philoponus (whose influence upon medieval and Renaissance science has yet to be fully fathomed) and his followers. Opposing Aristotle's concept that a projectile is kept moving by the motion-supporting agency of the medium (*antiperistasis*), Buridan endorsed the theory of impetus: The moving object imparts to the moved a "power" proportional to the moving object's speed and mass; this transmitted force keeps the projectile in motion after loss of contact with its launching mover until the resistance of the air (or other medium) progressively reduces the impetus.

In philosophy Buridan was a conservative nominalist, supporting the condemnation of radical Ockhamism during his rectorship in 1340. (His own works were prohibited from 1474 to 1481 because of nominalist tendencies but received wide circulation during the next generation, with extensive printings between 1487 and 1520.) Buridan supported a moderate Aristotelianism against the more extreme tendencies of Arabic provenance; for instance, he attacked Nicholas of Autrecourt's atomization of time and causation and defended the traditional principle of causality.

In logic Buridan commented extensively on Aristotle, with reference to the views of Peter of Spain and of Ockham. He interested himself particularly in the logical theory of modal propositions and modal syllogisms, a sector of medieval logic that remains largely unexplored. In logic the work of Buridan's that is now most widely acclaimed is his *Consequentiae*, which, in the words of E. A. Moody, "is one of the most interesting works of medieval logic because it undertakes an axiomatic derivation of the laws of valid deduction" and thus "is apparently the first attempt in the history of logic to give a deductive derivation of the laws of deduction" (*Truth and Consequence in Medieval Logic*, p. 8). A study of Buridan's *Sophismata* from a modern point of view would be certain to yield interesting results, some of which have already been cited by P. T. Geach. For example, *A*, *B*, *C*, and *D* make statements on a certain occasion, *A* and *B* uttering some palpable truth, *C* a palpable falsehood, and *D* saying that just as many truths as falsehoods have been uttered on this occasion. *D*'s statement can then be classed neither as false nor as true.

"Buridan's ass." Buridan's theory of the relationship of will and reason merits special notice. He advanced a qualified moral determinism—a man must will that which presents itself to his reason as the greater good, but the will is free to delay choice until reason has made a more extensive examination of the values involved. This led to the celebrated problem of "Buridan's ass," starving in indecision between two equal bales of hay. The example is not found in Buridan's extant writings but is based on an illustrative analogy in Aristotle's *De Caelo* (295b32) that became a standard item in the Aristotelian tradition, and occurs in the form of a dog starving between equally attractive portions of food in Buridan's commentary (*Expositio Textus*) on this passage of *De Caelo*.

The example was first found in its essentially ultimate form in the Arabic philosopher Ghazali (1058–1111):

> Suppose two similar dates in front of a man who has a strong desire for them, but who is unable to take them both. Surely he will take one of them through a quality in him the nature of which is to differentiate between two similar things. All the distinguishing qualities you have mentioned, like beauty or nearness or facility in taking, we can assume to be absent, but still the possibility of the taking remains. You can choose between two answers: either you merely say that an equivalence in respect to his desire cannot be imagined—but this is a silly answer, for to assume it is indeed possible—or you say that if an equivalence is assumed, the man will remain for ever hungry and perplexed, looking at the dates without taking one of them, and without a power to choose or to will, distinct from his desire. And this again is one of those absurdities which are recognized by the necessity of thought. Everyone, therefore, who studies, in the human and the divine, the real working of the act of choice, must necessarily admit a quality the nature of which is to differentiate between two similar things. (Averroës, *Tahafut al-Tahafut*, translated by Simon van den Bergh, London, 1954, Vol. I, p. 21.)

It seems probable that the traditional example of "Buridan's ass" arose as a refutation of Buridan's theory of will: Reason can find no preference, so that the will is (according to Buridan's theory) incapable of any immediate selection, yet delay is dangerous as well as pointless.

There is almost no discussion in modern literature of the logical issues involved in resolving the problem of "Buridan's ass"; that is, of reasoned choice in the absence of preference. However, a defensible resolution is not difficult to establish. The leading idea of the solution lies in noting the logical kinship between a choice in the case of a symmetry of *knowledge* on the one hand, and a choice in the case of a symmetry of *preference* on the other.

A person is offered a choice between two apparently similar boxes. He is told that one box contains a prize and that the other is empty, but he is not told which is which. Here there is no problem of absence of preference: the person has a clear preference for the treasure box. The only lack is one of information—the choice is to be made in the absence of any clue to the identity of the treasure box. With regard to the crucial question—"Which box is empty and which one holds the prize?"—the information about the boxes is completely symmetrical. Thus, there is no item of information at the disposal of the chooser that could be taken by him as reason for selecting one box rather than the other. He therefore cannot reasonably incline toward one box vis à vis the other. This fact of itself must characterize the manner of his choice: if he is to be reasonable, he must make his selection in a manner that does not favor one box over the other; he must make his selection in a random manner.

This is a matter susceptible of reasoned demonstration. Assume that the boxes are labeled *A* and *B*. Three courses of action are open, and they are mutually exclusive and exhaustive: (1) to make the choice in some manner that favors selection of box *A* rather than box *B*; (2) to make the choice in some manner that favors selection of box *B* rather than box *A*; (3) to make the choice by means of a selection process that is wholly impartial between box *A* and box *B*; that is, to choose randomly.

Here probabilistic considerations as to expected gain do not enter in at all—on the basis of the available information it is *equally probable* that box *A* holds the treasure as that box *B* does, so that the expected gain with any of the three procedures is precisely the same—half the value of the treasure. Thus, solely on the grounds of expected gain there is no difference among these alternatives. However, from the standpoint of reasonableness there is a very significant difference among the selection procedures. For by the defining hypothesis of the problem, there is no known reason for favoring box *A* over box *B*, or the converse. This very fact renders it rationally indefensible to adopt (1) or (2). On the contrary, this symmetry of knowledge of itself constitutes an entirely valid reason for adopting (3). This line of reasoning establishes the thesis that *in the case of symmetrical knowledge, random choice is the reasonable policy.*

Let us now return from the discussion of choice in the face of symmetrical knowledge to the problem of symmetrical preference. It is at once clear upon careful consideration that the matter of choice without preference—that is, under conditions of symmetrical preference—can actually be subsumed as a special case under the topic of symmetrical knowledge. For in a case of strictly symmetrical preference (two essentially similar dates, two glasses of water, two bales of hay), the knowledge or information at our disposal constrains us to regard the objects of choice as equally desirable because each reason for valuing one applies, *mutato nomine*, to the other(s). So far as the factor of their value or desirability for us is concerned, our knowledge regarding each object is precisely the same. Problems of choice with symmetrical valuation can therefore be regarded as merely a species within the symmetrical knowledge genus, so that here too a random selection rather than any proper "choice" is the rationally justified procedure.

Bibliography

Buridan's printed works are *Summulae de Dialectica*, alternatively entitled *Compendium Logicae* (Paris, 1487; Lyons, 1490; Venice, 1499; Oxford, 1637; London, 1740); *Consequentiae* (Paris, 1493); *Sophismata* (Paris, 1489); and *Quaestiones* on the following treatises of Aristotle: *Physics* (Paris, 1509), *De Caelo*, E. A. Moody, ed. (Cambridge, Mass., 1942), *De Anima* and *Parva Naturalia* (Paris, 1516), *Metaphysics* (Paris, 1518), *Ethics* (Paris, 1489; Oxford, 1637), and *Politics* (Paris, 1530; Oxford, 1640).

Regrettably, only one of Buridan's many extant writings (including many unpublished books, such as his Commentaries on Aristotle's *Organon*, *Metaphysics*, and *Economics*) exists in a usable modern edition. One opuscule has recently appeared: M. E. Reina, "Giovanni Buridano: Tractatus de Suppositionibus," in *Rivista critica di storia della filosofia*, Vol. 12 (1957), 175–208, 323–352.

Secondary sources include Pierre Bayle, "Buridan," in *Dictionnaire*, 5th ed. (Amsterdam, 1740); H. Bascour, "Buridan," in *Dictionnaire d'histoire et de géographie ecclésiastique* (Paris, 1939); E. Faral, "Jean Buridan," in *Histoire littéraire de la France*, Vol. 38 (Paris, 1949) and in *Archives d'histoire doctrinale et littéraire du moyen âge*, Vol. 15 (1946), 1–53; Friedrich Ueberweg, *Geschichte der Philosophie*, B. Geyer, ed. (Berlin, 1928), Vol. II; A. Maier, *Die Impetustheorie* (Rome, 1940), re-edited in *Zwei Grundprobleme* (Rome, 1951); Marshall Clagett, *The Science of Mechanics in the Middle Ages* (Madison, Wis., 1959); M. Zalba, "El valor económico en los escolásticos," in *Estudios eclesiásticos*, Vol. XVIII (Madrid, 1944), pp. 5–35, 145–163; Pierre Duhem, *Études sur Léonard de Vinci*, Vols. II and III (Paris, 1909 and 1913; reprinted Paris, 1955); H. Siebeck, "Die Willenslehre bei Duns Scotus und seine Nachfolgern," in *Zeitschrift für Philosophie und philosophische Kritik*, Vol. 112 (1898), 179–216; K. Michalski, "Les Courants philosophiques à Paris pendant le XIV siècle," in *Bulletin international de l'académie polonaise des sciences et des lettres* (Classe d'histoire et de philosophie), Vol. I (1919–1921; printed 1922), pp. 63–68; Nicholas Rescher, "Choice Without Preference: A Study of the Logic and of the History of the Problem of 'Buridan's Ass,'" in *Kant-Studien*, Vol. 21 (1959/1960), 142–175; K. Prantl, *Geschichte der Logik . . .*, Vol. IV (Leipzig, 1870, reprinted Leipzig, 1955); I. M. Bochenski, *History of Formal Logic*, translated and edited by I. Thomas (Notre Dame, Ind., 1961); A. N. Prior, "Problems of Self-Reference in John Buridan," in *Proceedings of the British Academy*, Vol. 48 (1962), 281–296; and P. T. Geach, *Reference and Generality* (Ithaca, N. Y., 1962). E. A. Moody, *Truth and Consequence in Medieval Logic* (Amsterdam, 1953), draws extensively on Buridan's work and is highly informative.

NICHOLAS RESCHER

BURKE, EDMUND (1729–1797), British statesman and political philosopher, was born in Ireland to a family of modest means. His mother's family was Catholic, his father's Protestant. He was raised a Protestant and educated at a Quaker school and at Trinity College, Dublin, where he took the equivalent of a first-class honors degree in classics. He went to London to read law but was never called to the bar. He devoted most of his time to authorship and literary journalism. Robert Dodsley, leading London bookseller of the time loyally backed him; by 1757, Dodsley had published two books by Burke, *A Vindication of Natural Society* (1756) and *Philosophical Inquiry into the Origin of Our Ideas on the Sublime and the Beautiful* (1756), had given him employment as editor of *The Annual Register*, and had contracted to pay him £300 for an *Abridgment of the History of England*.

A Vindication of Natural Society is a satire on the views of Bolingbroke. It claimed to be a recently discovered work by Bolingbroke and was designed to ridicule the idea that the rise of civilized society is attended by misery and suffering. The parody was written with such conviction, however, that many assumed it was in fact the work of Bolingbroke, and even when it was known that Burke was the author, some critics still thought it was a sincere expression of his true opinion.

Burke's book *On The Sublime and the Beautiful* is more important; indeed, it might well be said to signalize the point at which aesthetic taste in England changed from the classical formalism of the earlier years of the eighteenth century to the romanticism of the later years. Burke attacked the rationalist, classicist notion that clarity is an essential quality in great art. He argued, on the contrary, that what is greatest and noblest is the infinite, and that the infinite, having no bounds, cannot be clear and distinct. He argued that the imagination, moreover, is most strongly affected by what is suggested or hinted at and not by what is plainly stated. Burke also maintained that fear plays a large part in our enjoyment of the sublime. Such fear is diminished by knowledge, but sharpened by veiled intimations. Obscurity, not clarity, is the property of the most powerfully moving art; and, Burke added, "It is our ignorance of things that causes all our admiration and chiefly excites our passions."

Both of Burke's first two works were well received, but neither set him on the road to any further achievement. The *Annual Register* was a success, although Burke regarded it as mere hack work. He never finished the projected *History of England.* Burke's growing interest in questions of ethics and politics provided him, in time, with an escape from the frustrations of Grub Street. He entered the House of Commons at the age of 37, and this new life brought him satisfactions he had never known in his earlier career. He became an outstanding parliamentarian; what distinguished him and made him a philosopher among politicians, however, was his capacity to look beyond the matters of the day and to articulate general principles in terms of which he believed the problems of the day should be judged.

A diligent study of Burke's letters and manuscripts brings home the extent to which Burke's approach to politics was a religious one. What is often spoken of as his "empiricism" appears in this light to be better described as Christian pessimism. As a Christian, Burke believed that the world is imperfect; he regarded his "enlightened" contemporaries' faith in the perfectibility of man as atheistical as well as erroneous. Thus, whereas the fashionable intellectuals of his time looked for the progressive betterment of the world through the beneficent influence of Reason and Nature, Burke maintained that the moral order of the universe is unchanging. The first duty of rulers and legislators, he argued, is to the present, not to the future; their energies should be devoted to the correction of real ills, not to the promotion of an ideal order that exists only in the imagination.

Burke put great faith in the inherited wisdom of tradition. He held that the moral order of the temporal world must necessarily include some evil, by reason of original sin. Men ought not to reject what is good in tradition merely because there is some admixture of evil in it. In man's confused situation, advantages may often lie in balances and compromises between good and evil, even between one evil and another. It is an important part of wisdom to know how much evil should be tolerated. To search for too great a purity is only to produce fresh corruption. Burke was especially critical of revolutionary movements with noble humanitarian ends because he believed that people are simply not at liberty to destroy the state and its institutions in the hope of some contingent improvement. On the other hand, he insisted that people have a paramount duty to prevent the world from getting worse—a duty to guard and preserve their inherited liberties and privileges.

These considerations explain the so-called inconsistencies often attributed to Burke, who supported the movement for the independence of Ireland and the rebellion of the American colonists against the English government, but bitterly opposed the French Revolution. The reason for this seeming inconsistency was that Burke regarded the Irish movement and the American rebellion as actions on behalf of traditional rights and liberties which the English government had infringed on. The French Revolution was quite different, he argued, because it was designed to introduce a wholly new order based on a false rationalistic philosophy. Burke did not object to a resort to force as such; it was the aims of the French revolutionists to which he objected. Similarly, Burke approved of the English Revolution of 1688 because he saw it as designed to restore the rights of Englishmen and to secure the hereditary succession to the throne. The French Revolution, on the contrary, was intended to establish the so-called rights of man and the republican ideals of liberty, equality, and fraternity at the expense of personal property, religion, and the traditional class structure of a Christian kingdom.

In one of his most celebrated works, *Reflections on the Revolution in France* (1790), Burke attacked those of his contemporaries who made an abstraction of liberty, and who invited people to seek liberty without any real knowledge of what they meant by it. He claimed that he himself loved "a manly, moral, regulated liberty as well as any gentleman in France," but he would not "stand forward and give praise" to an "object stripped of all concrete relations" and standing "in all the solitude of a metaphysical idea." As for equality, Burke insisted that it was contrary to nature and therefore impossible to achieve; its advocates, moreover, did "great social harm," for by pretending that real differences were unreal, they inspired "false hopes and vain expectations in those destined to travel in the obscure walk of laborious life." Burke dismissed talk of fraternity as so much "cant and gibberish"; such splendid words were simply the pretexts of the French revolutionists; the causes of the French revolution, however, were "men's vices—pride, ambition, avarice, lust, sedition."

Burke's view of the *ancien régime* in France was in many ways a romantic one; he was certainly no less a "man of feeling" than was Rousseau, whom he detested. But Burke was essentially a religious man living in a rationalistic age. Although he often spoke the language understood by that age—the language of calculation, expediency, utility, and political rights—he had a mind which his contemporaries, and many others, could not readily comprehend. Burke was conscious, above all things, of the reality and unavoidability of evil, and was thus led to claim that the only hope for mankind was to cling to safeguards which had stood the test of time. His hopes for bliss lay in heaven; on earth, his policy was to defend the tolerable, and sometimes the bad, against the immeasurably worse.

Until recently Burke was considered too unsystematic, too empirical, too "unphilosophical," and too much of a theorist to deserve serious attention. His conservative views were uncongenial to left-wing historians, such as

Harold J. Laski and Richard Wollheim, who found him inconsistent. In 1948, however, the Sheffield Public Library (Yorkshire, England) acquired the Wentworth Woodhouse manuscripts, and the largest known collection of Burke's private papers became available to scholars for the first time since the writer's death. The study of these papers did much to enhance Burke's reputation as a political philosopher of signal importance and originality.

Works by Burke

Works, F. Lawrence and W. King, eds., 16 vols. London, 1803–1827.

Correspondence of Edmund Burke, E. Fitzwilliam and R. Bourke, eds., 4 vols. London, 1844.

Correspondence of Edmund Burke, T. W. Copeland, ed., 8 vols. Chicago, 1958——.

Works on Burke

Cobban, A., *Edmund Burke and the Revolt Against the Eighteenth Century.* London and New York, 1929. Throws new light on the resemblances between Burke's thought and that of Rousseau.

Cone, C. B., *Burke and the Nature of Politics.* Lexington, Ky., 1957. A valuable introductory study, from a modern standpoint.

Copeland, T. W., *Our Eminent Friend, Edmund Burke: Six Essays.* New Haven, 1949. Essays by a literary historian who is a leading Burke scholar of the present generation.

MacCunn, J., *The Political Philosophy of Burke.* London and New York, 1913. A useful traditional reading of Burke's philosophy.

Magnus, P., *Edmund Burke.* London, 1939. A reliable short biography.

Parkin, C., *The Moral Basis of Burke's Political Thought.* London and New York, 1956. Stresses the importance of religion in Burke's political philosophy.

MAURICE CRANSTON

BURLEY, WALTER (also spelled Burleigh), English Franciscan philosopher, was born in 1275 and died after 1343. His lifetime thus spanned the change in intellectual climate which followed the Paris condemnation of Aristotelianism of 1277 and culminated in Ockham's teachings. Burley's output was vast, and he is among the most important later medieval thinkers still awaiting thorough examination. So far, isolated studies all point to his having been a conservative both in the more traditional subjects like logic and in science. He is also considered to have been a leading opponent of Ockham; certainly his writings are full of references to the *moderni,* whom he opposed. During his career Burley seems to have taught at both Oxford and Paris. He wrote numerous commentaries on Aristotle, including the *Peri Hermeneias,* the *Posterior Analytics,* the *Logica Vetus,* the *Physics,* the *Ethics,* the *Politics, De Caelo et Mundo* as well as a *Summa Totius Logicae,* and a series of treatises on form and matter, the intensification and remission of forms, and on forms.

As far as is known, Burley adopted a traditionalist attitude toward most of the topics he treated. On universals, for long regarded as the main area of Ockham's radicalism Burley held to the older logic, rejecting the *suppositio simplex* by which Ockham had relegated all general concepts to purely mental phenomena; Burley held that universals were in all things and referred to real things, not simply to words and concepts. Accordingly, in opposition to the moderns, Burley explicitly affirmed two propositions: that universals existed independently of the mind and that propositions were composed of things existing outside the mind. The intellect directly grasped the individual, only reaching the universal by reflection. This it did by means of the active intellect, which directed the imaginative faculty to a true understanding of the object encountered.

The same assumption of the reality of universal categories is apparent in much of Burley's many-sided scientific activity. It is still too early to form a just estimate of his thinking here, as elsewhere, but it is already clear that Burley was as fertile as he was traditional. He broached the full range of scientific topics then coming to the fore, and in at least one respect he seems to have introduced a new notion. This was his view that the intensification and remission of forms took place by means of a *latitudo,* or "variation," in the species of the existing forms; that is, although an already existing form (heat, cold) could not itself be modified, the subject in which it inhered (water, for example) could take on new forms of the same species which were more or less perfect. According to the degree of this variation, intensification or remission followed. This was not an isolated hypothesis; Burley derived it from analogy with movement. Here, in adherence to his traditional mode of thinking, he rejected the doctrine of *impetus* which located the source of movement in that which was moving and instead held that in each movement, a new place (*ubi*), a new terminus, and a new form were engendered, each displacing the previous one.

The same attitude is to be seen in Burley's consideration of time and quantity, where once again he opposed Ockham. He treated both as independent categories which existed outside the mind, the one as succession, the other as extension. Neither was therefore to be identified with other cognate qualities. Time was not movement, as he took a comparison of them to show. Movement can be past or present but only in virtue of time; time can be fast or slow only as the measure of movement, not of itself. Quantity, likewise, remained separate from substance. In fact, Burley's entire world was peopled with self-subsisting entities—not only points, lines, and surfaces but also the absence (*privatio*) of beings. However, there were also matters on which Burley showed himself in agreement with Ockham and Buridan, as, for example, on gravitation, and this must make us hesitate to pass final judgement.

Works by Burley

Commentary on *Logica Vetus.* Venice, 1485.

De Materia et Forma. Oxford, 1500.

Commentary on *Ethics.* Venice, 1500, 1521.

Summa Totius Logicae. Venice, 1508.

Commentary on *Physics.* Venice, 1509, 1524.

De Intentione et Remissione Formarum. Venice, 1519.

Commentary on *Posterior Analytics.* Venice, 1537, 1559.

De Puritate Artis Logicae, P. Boehner, ed. New York, 1951.

Works on Burley

Baudrey, L., "Les Rapports de Guillaume d'Occam et de Walter Burleigh." *Archives d'histoire doctrinale et littéraire du moyen âge,* Vol. 9 (1934), 55–73.

Maier, A., *Die Vorlaüfer Galileis*. Rome, 1949.
Maier, A., *An der Grenze zwischen Scholastik und Naturwissenschaft im 14. Jahrhundert*. Rome, 1951.
Maier, A., *Zwei Grundprobleme der scholastischen Naturphilosophie*. Rome, 1951.
Maier, A., *Metaphysische Hintergründe der spätscholastischen Naturphilosophie*. Rome, 1956.
Maier, A., *Zwischen Philosophie und Mechanik*. Rome, 1958.
Thomson, S. H., "Walter Burley's Commentary on the Politics of Aristotle," in *Mélanges A. Pelzer*. Louvain, 1947. Pp. 557–578.

GORDON LEFF

BURTHOGGE, RICHARD, English physician and idealist philosopher, was born in Plymouth about 1638 and died about 1698. After taking an arts degree at Lincoln College, Oxford, he studied medicine at the University of Leiden and returned to his native country to practice near Totnes in Devonshire. Of pacific and conciliatory disposition, he seems to have wavered in the religious controversy between Catholicism and Puritanism, and in philosophy, between Lockean sensationalism and Cambridge Platonism. He distinguished between heresy and error, maintaining that the former "must be eradicated," but the latter tolerated for humanity's sake. His life is obscure, and little is known of it beyond that information revealed in his writings, which have a certain importance as anticipations of Kant.

We know the world, according to Burthogge, only through our own ideas, and these do not give us its real nature. On the contrary, our ideas transform the nature of things into qualities which are purely subjective. Similarly, our values are our own; and such relative judgments as those involving categories of cause and effect, or whole and part, are arrived at through the constitution of our minds, not discovered embedded *in rerum natura*. The things themselves, though remaining unknowable, nevertheless cause ideas to arise in our minds. Here Burthogge foreshadowed Kant's paradox of the relation between *noumena* and *phenomena*. Burthogge's view that the human mind projects relations into the external world exemplifies his Neoplatonic streak. However, this strain was accompanied by a Lockean one which led him to assert that no confidence could be placed in an idea contradicted by sensation. Burthogge thus seems to have accepted Locke's theory of two kinds of ideas, those of sensation and those of reflection.

For Burthogge, there were also two kinds of truth—metaphysical and logical. Metaphysical truth is found in the conformity between our ideas and those in the mind of God; logical truth, in the conformity between our ideas and the things of which they are ideas. We cannot apprehend the former kind of truth; but since the latter involves knowing the unknowable, logical truth is reduced to consistency. Burthogge would not accept the doctrine of innate ideas, because if we had such ideas, we would be able to discover truth through introspection alone. He asserted dogmatically that there is a coherent system of ideas, duplicating the system of things, even though no individual possesses it. This system, he maintained, exemplifies God's ideas.

In his treatise on the soul of the world, Burthogge supported the Neoplatonic concept of a plastic nature permeating the universe and accounting for its "harmony." This is breathed into things by God himself but is not to be identified with God. If nothing else, this treatise is valuable as an example of the philosophy of nature which was acceptable to learned men of the time.

Burthogge, in sum, is one of the anomalies of the history of philosophy. He advanced startlingly "modern" ideas, side by side with fantasies no longer taken seriously.

Works by Burthogge

Organum Vetus et Novum. London, 1678.
An essay upon Reason, and the Nature of Spirits. London, 1694.
Of the Soul of the World, and of Particular Souls. London, 1699.
Landes, Margaret W., ed., *The Philosophical Writings of Richard Burthogge*. Chicago and London, 1921. Contains reprints of the three above works by Burthogge as well as a valuable introduction, notes, and bibliography.

Works on Burthogge

Boas, George, *Dominant Themes of Modern Philosophy*, pp. 253–259. New York, 1957.
Cassirer, Ernst, *Das Erkenntnisproblem in der Philosophie und Wissenschaft der neueren Zeit*, Vol. 1, pp. 464–73. Berlin, 1906.
Grünbaum, Jacob, *Die Philosophie Richard Burthogges*. Unpublished Ph. D. dissertation, Bern, 1939.
L[ee], S. L., "Burthogge, Richard," in *Dictionary of National Biography*, Vol. 7, p. 453. London, 1885–1900.
Lovejoy, A. O., "Kant and the English Platonists," in *Essays Philosophical and Psychological in Honor of William James*, pp. 265–302. New York, 1908.

GEORGE BOAS

BUTLER, JOSEPH (1692–1752), moral philosopher and natural theologian, was born at Wantage, Berkshire, to a Presbyterian family. His father, a retired draper, could afford to send Butler to the dissenting academy kept by Mr. Samuel Jones, first at Gloucester and later at Tewkesbury. For reasons now unknown, Butler, when a young man, left Presbyterianism for the Church of England. He entered Oriel College, Oxford, as a commoner. After taking his degree he was ordained a priest in the established church in 1718. Throughout his life Butler held a series of church offices. In 1738 he was made bishop of Bristol, and in 1751 he became bishop of Durham. He also served as clerk of the closet, first to Queen Caroline, and later to George II. When one considers Butler's writings, with their judicious but nonetheless optimistic analysis of human nature, it is well to remember that he was a man of affairs, with ample opportunity to become acquainted with the ways of the world. Butler died at Bath, where he had gone for his health. He was buried in Bristol Cathedral.

Moral philosophy. Since Butler writes as a Christian and a priest, his philosophical interests, moral philosophy, and natural theology are inseparable from his vocation. His moral philosophy must be gleaned from all his writings, the most systematic statement being found in the "Three Sermons on Human Nature."

Butler's writings are a part of the seventeenth- and eighteenth-century effort to find a foundation for morals in something other than appeals to the divine will. Because he believes that nature and revelation are complementary, Butler is willing to eschew appeals to revelation, and search in nature for the basis of morality. But where in nature are the foundations of morality to be discovered? Butler sees two possible ways of proceeding. The first is to inquire into the abstract relations of things; the second is to argue from a matter of fact (the nature of man) to conclusions about the course of life which is fitting for the nature of man. The method of exploring the abstract relations of things had already been used by Butler's older contemporary, Samuel Clarke; and while Butler is not unsympathetic to Clarke's efforts, he finds the method of analyzing the nature of man more appropriate to the limitations of a sermon.

In the task of accounting for morals by appeals to the nature of man, Butler had a set of vigorous and impressive predecessors. On the one hand, he had Thomas Hobbes and his contemporary, Bernard Mandeville, the partisans of self-love; and on the other hand, Shaftesbury, the partisan of an instinct for benevolence. Butler, however, regards his predecessors as having offered only partial analyses of human nature. His method is to show that both self-love and benevolence are part of a larger whole.

Butler claims to have made his observations from the bulk of mankind; and he urges his readers not to be misled about human nature, either by judging only from their own natures or by giving too much weight to exceptions from the general run of men. Butler finds that men are neither exceptionally self-regarding to the exclusion of benevolence nor exceptionally benevolent to the exclusion of self-interest. What is more, he finds that these affections are not necessarily incompatible and may even reinforce one another. The satisfaction of performing a benevolent action will certainly encourage acts of benevolence in someone who desires the advantages of society.

Butler also argues that self-love and benevolence are but two affections among many; that neither has any priority over the rest; and that neither is such that all other affections can be reduced to it. He points out that self-love is a complex affection, in that its object is not simply the self, but rather the gain of all things pleasing to the self. Butler also claims that there are no affections directly contradictory to self-love and benevolence, namely self-hatred and ill will toward others. Rather, he finds that when self-love or benevolence is opposed, it is by passions for particular things; and it is in the pursuit of these objects that we may harm ourselves or injure others. It must be remembered, here, that Butler means to describe the generality of mankind, and not exceptions.

Thus far, Butler's moral philosophy is a synthesis, with corrections, of the doctrines of his immediate predecessors in the analysis of human nature. But man is something more than a bundle of affections. Butler finds that his predecessors have overlooked the fact that man possesses a faculty superior to affections, which judges both them and the actions which flow from them. This faculty is reflection, or conscience. In his strongest characterization of this "superior principle," he speaks of it as pronouncing "determinately some actions to be in themselves just, right, good; others to be in themselves evil, wrong, unjust." Conscience "without being consulted, without being advised with, magisterially exerts itself, and approves or condemns him the doer of them accordingly . . ." ("Second Sermon Upon Human Nature"). It is conscience (the capacity to reflect on his affections) which distinguishes man from the beasts, by rescuing him from subjection to whatever passion is uppermost at the moment. It is conscience which makes man a moral agent, by enabling him to be a law unto himself—a law which he is obliged to obey, because it is the law of his nature.

Butler might have been clearer about the way conscience works. To characterize it as operating "without being consulted, without being advised with" makes conscience too much of a mechanism in a too mechanical theory of human nature. Here, Butler appears to be caught in the unexamined assumptions of a faulty psychology borrowed from his contemporaries. Nor is Butler as clear as one might wish about the standards in accordance with which conscience makes its judgments. Conscience approves of whatever contributes to the good of the whole man and condemns whatever disproportionately favors some part of the whole. But how does conscience learn to assess these matters? It would seem that this question did not weigh too heavily on Butler, perhaps because of his theology. No questions about how conscience does its job need be asked, since it has been designed by God for its appointed end. As he says, conscience, "if not forcibly stopped, naturally and always of course goes on to anticipate a higher and more effectual sentence, which shall hereafter second and affirm its own" ("Second Sermon Upon Human Nature"). Of course, Butler believes man to be naturally fitted for life in society, and of course, he approves of the social virtues; but in his philosophy society and the social virtues are never reckoned to be inherently valuable.

Something has already been said about Butler's immediate predecessors, but an additional word must be said about the classical springs of his moral philosophy. Oxford tutors think of Butler's sermons as a painless way of conveying Aristotle's *Ethics* to Greekless undergraduates. Canon J. N. D. Kelly, who became the principal of St. Edmund Hall in 1951, has spoken of Butler as "Aristotle, clad in a diaphanous mantle of Christianity." For the distinctive feature of his moral philosophy, the doctrine of conscience, Butler himself cites Arrian's *Discourses of Epictetus*, Book I, Chapter 1, as the source.

Natural theology. Butler's natural theology is contained in *The Analogy of Religion, Natural and Revealed, to the Constitution and Course of Nature* (London, 1736). The title might lead one to believe that Butler is going to compare religious doctrines with what may be learned by studying nature. But this expectation is not quite right, for Butler does not regard nature as a religiously neutral system. Rather, nature is a product of providential design; by studying nature, one will find confirmation there for the revealed doctrines of Christianity. Appealing to our experience of the conduct of nature with respect to intelligent creatures, Butler states the terms of his analogy in two presumably synonymous ways. He will compare "the known constitution and course of things" with "what is said to be the moral system of nature"; or again, he will compare "the acknowledged dispensations of Providence," that is, "the (natural) government which we find ourselves under," with "what religion teaches us to believe and expect." Through such comparisons we may see whether the terms of these analogies are not "analogous and of a piece."

On an abbreviated scale, the following may be taken as an example of Butler's style of argument. If we begin by assuming that the existence of nature implies an operating agent, then the good and bad consequences of our actions occur by his appointment. Any foresight we have of the consequences of our actions is a warning given by him on how we are to act. The satisfaction we feel at certain consequences, and the pain we suffer at others, are ordained by God and are signs that we are already under his government. Thus, a consideration of nature alone shows that we must acknowledge the place of God in our lives. Hence, if Christian doctrines really are revealed truths (and Butler considers this difficulty with great care), our discoveries in nature have already prepared us to accept the main claims of revelation about God as a creator and judge. Butler does not suppose that his sort of study can do much more than establish the plausibility of the main lines of revelation. We must treat the details with patience and respect, as not being absolutely ruled out by a study of nature.

From the assumption that nature implies an operating agent, it seems clear that Butler did not intend his arguments to appeal to the religious skeptic. At best, he may have hoped to convince deists, who already acknowledged the existence of a god, that their convictions might reasonably lead them to accept Christianity. At the very least, he must have expected to make deists acknowledge Christianity's right to be treated as a subject worthy of serious discussion. Followers of Shaftesbury are then his special target.

In the *Analogy*, Butler treated probability (in the Introduction), habit (in Part I, Chapter 5), and body, mind, and death (in Part I, Chapter 1, "Of a Future Life"). He makes a clear distinction between demonstrative reasoning and probable reasoning by pointing out that probability admits of degrees, while demonstration does not. A slight presumption in favor of a thing does not make it probably true. Yet, Butler argues, the slightest possible presumption is, nonetheless, of the nature of probability, for ". . . such low presumption, often repeated, will amount even to moral certainty. Thus a man's having observed the ebb and flow of the tide today, affords some sort of presumption, though the lowest imaginable, that it may happen again tomorrow: but the observation of this even for so many days, and months and ages together, as it has been observed by mankind, gives us a full assurance that it will." While an infinite intelligence must see everything as certainly true or certainly false, for us, with our limited capacities, "probability is the very guide of life."

Habit is examined in Butler's consideration of the acquisition and practice of moral virtues. In the course of the discussion, he includes certain remarks about knowledge and habit which are of the greatest interest. He claims, first, that neither the perception of ideas nor knowledge of any sort is a habit. However, contrary to this, he goes on to observe "that perceptions come into our minds readily and of course, by means of their having been there before"; and this reappearance of perceptions "seems a thing of the same sort as readiness in any particular kind of action, proceeding from being accustomed to it." He then cites, as one of our habits of perception, ". . . our constant and even involuntary readiness in correcting the impressions of our sight concerning magnitude and distances, so as to substitute judgment in the room of sensation imperceptibly to ourselves." And he adds immediately ". . . it seems as if all other associations of ideas not naturally connected might be called *passive habits*." (A natural connection of ideas would be, for example, flame and fire.)

In his discussion of a future life, Butler argues for the probability that the mind may be separable from the body. Hence, death may have no effect on the mind. The programs of Butler and Descartes coincide here, but the statement of Butler's case gains greatly through the force and conciseness of his style.

Personal identity. The *Analogy* is followed by two short dissertations. Dissertation II, "Of the Nature of Virtue," should be read with the sermons as a supplement to his moral philosophy as stated in them. Dissertation I, "Of Personal Identity," is in part a criticism of Locke. Butler endeavors to clarify the role of consciousness in personal identity. He argues against those whose reason for rejecting consciousness as a source of personal identity is that no two acts of consciousness are identical. Such an argument, Butler says, overlooks what we are really interested in: not an identity of acts of consciousness, but an identity of the object of which we are conscious—ourselves. Of this identity we can be as certain as we are of the identity of any other thing. Anyone who asks for a greater certainty of personal identity than this wishes for something which the subject will not admit.

Works by Butler

Butler's *Fifteen Sermons*, including the "Three Sermons Upon Human Nature," were first published in London in 1726. *The Works of Joseph Butler*, The Rt. Hon. W. E. Gladstone, ed., 2 vols. (Oxford, 1897) contains the above, along with the *Analogy*, "Six Sermons Preached Upon Public Occasions" and Butler's "Charge to the Clergy of the Diocese of Durham," a moving commentary on the tasks of the clergyman in eighteenth-century England.

Works on Butler

For critical discussions, see A. E. Duncan-Jones, *Butler's Moral Philosophy* (Harmondsworth, Middlesex, 1952); E. C. Mossner, *Bishop Butler and the Age of Reason* (New York, 1936); "Butler," in C. D. Broad, *Five Types of Ethical Theory* (London, 1930), Ch. 3; Leonard G. Miller, "Joseph Butler," in *Encyclopedia of Morals*, V. Ferm, ed. (New York, 1956).

ELMER SPRAGUE

BUTLER, SAMUEL (1835–1902), English writer and critic, author of the satirical novels *The Way of All Flesh*, *Erewhon*, and *Erewhon Revisited*, as well as several discussions of philosophical biology and the theory of evolution. He was the son of the Reverend Thomas Butler, whom he depicted as a domestic tyrant in *The Way of All Flesh*. Butler was sent to Cambridge by his father in the hope that he would become a clergyman, but after graduating he refused to take orders because of doubts about the Christian creed. In 1859 he emigrated to New Zealand, where he became a successful sheep farmer and for a time a convert to Darwinism. Returning to England in 1864 with enough money to live on, he began a career as an author, painter, and musician. The subject of evolution continued to occupy his mind for many years. It forms the substance of several essays and four books: *Life and Habit* (London, 1878), *Evolution, Old and New* (London, 1879), *Unconscious Memory* (London, 1880), and *Luck or Cunning?* (London, 1887). These works reflect a mounting hostility to the ideas of Charles Darwin and a desire to champion those of Erasmus Darwin and Lamarck. This hostility first made its appearance in *Erewhon* (London, 1872).

Evolution. Butler was neither a scientist nor a philosopher. His discussions of evolution are the work of a literary man with strong intellectual interests but little capacity for exact thought. He was at his best when giving scientific and philosophical ideas an original twist that often put them in quite a new light. To many fellow Victorians he seemed an irreverent skeptic or even an atheist; but in fact, he wanted to retain religion while discarding the Christian creed and to discard Darwin while retaining evolution. This outlook pervades all his major writings.

The central weakness of Darwinism, according to Butler, was its failure to identify the cause of the variations on which selection was said to operate. They were described as random or accidental, which would mean that the course of evolution has been a matter of luck. The older evolutionists, such as Erasmus Darwin and Lamarck, were far sounder in their views, for they attributed the cause of variations to the activity of organisms and to the inherited effects of the use or disuse of their various functions. Not luck, they claimed, but cunning displayed by organisms in coping with their environment lies at the basis of evolution. Hence, the activity of organisms is profoundly purposive. The great mistake of Charles Darwin was to dismiss teleology from the domain of living things, for they then become indistinguishable from machines.

In an essay of 1865 Butler toyed with the idea that machines are adjuncts to organisms, like extra, though inferior, limbs, by means of which organisms have become more highly evolved. Hence, "a leg is only a much better wooden leg than anyone can manufacture." This led Butler to consider the problem of how living things have come to produce their natural organs and to equip themselves with adaptive habits. The answer, he asserted is that the individual plant or animal must "know" at the start what to do. A fertilized ovum possesses the knowledge it needs to make itself into an embryo and subsequently into an adult organism. This knowledge is really a remembering of what its ancestors did in the past. Hence, we must postulate an "unconscious memory" at work in all living things, binding successive generations and providing the basis for the transmission of acquired characteristics.

Butler then leaped to two sweeping conclusions. First, consciousness and intelligence exist throughout the whole organic world. "For the embryo of the chicken, we claim exactly the same kind of reasoning power and contrivance which we claim for the amoeba, or for our own intelligent performances in later life." Second, since evolution involves a continuous process of derivation, there must be an "identity" between parents and offspring: the latter are not different individuals but *are* the parents at a later evolutionary stage. "Birth has been made too much of." A newborn infant is simply part of an unbroken biological process, not an utterly separate individual. Accordingly, there is a deep unity of all life, so that it constitutes "in reality, nothing but one single creature, of which the component members are but, as it were, blood corpuscles or individual cells."

With the aid of these conclusions, Butler sought to justify an idealistic and religious interpretation of evolution. In *Unconscious Memory* he contended that his earlier separation of the organic from the inorganic was unwarranted. "What we call the inorganic world must be regarded as up to a certain point living, and instinct with consciousness." Hence, "all space is at all times full of a stuff endowed with a mind," and "both stuff and mind are immaterial and imperceptible, so long as they are undisturbed, but the moment they are disturbed, the stuff becomes material and the mind perceptible." Evolution is therefore the life history of this primordial world stuff, "to which no name can be so fittingly applied as 'God.' "

Many of Butler's criticisms of Darwinism have been made irrelevant by the rise of the science of genetics. Yet he was justified in urging those criticisms at the time and in calling attention to vacillations in Darwin's thought on basic issues. If Butler had been more scrupulous in his own thinking and less facile with his pen, his works on philosophical biology might have had greater survival value.

Theology. Butler's rather unusual theology is set forth in three essays, posthumously published as *God the Known and God the Unknown* (London, 1909). He there contended that an adequate concept of God requires him to be a living person with a material body. To regard God as *merely* a spirit is tantamount to atheism. At first Butler held that the divine body is just the totality of life, the "one single creature" whose unconscious memory is part of the divine mind. When he rejected the distinction between the organic and the inorganic, his view shifted from a "panzoistic" conception of God to pantheism. He intended to rewrite his theology in the light of this shift, but never managed to do so. One odd belief he expressed was that the grand design of the cosmos points to the existence of "some vaster Person who looms out behind our God, and who stands in the same relation to him as he to us. And behind this vaster and more unknown God there may be yet another, and another, and another." This pyramiding of deities was one of the many items with which Butler enlivened the Victorian scene.

Social thought. Despite the barbs which he directed at the institutions of his day, Butler's social outlook was conservative. He took the position that those who are rich and successful are the highest types thus far produced in the evolutionary process. Poor men are biological misfits; hence, the sooner they disappear and leave room for those better able to take care of themselves, the better. In the imaginary society of Erewhon, "if a man has made a fortune of over £20,000, they exempt him from all taxation, considering him a work of art and too precious to be meddled with." Butler's account of this society is not so much a blueprint of utopia as a device for satirizing the beliefs and practices of middle-class Englishmen by inverting accepted values. Thus, in Erewhon bodily illness was considered a punishable crime, whereas moral failings deserved sympathy and were given therapeutic treatment. Instead of fostering machinery, the Erewhonians, after a long struggle, destroyed it when they realized that machines, like organisms, were evolving and would soon acquire a mastery over men. In *Erewhon Revisited* (London, 1901), Butler depicted a community showing signs of degeneration, as if to underline the conclusion that a social order is an impermanent evolutionary product and inevitably alters. Yet here again no consistent point of view was worked out.

Bibliography

Furbank, P. N., *Samuel Butler*. Cambridge and New York, 1948.

Jones, H. Festing, *Samuel Butler, a Memoir*, 2 vols. London, 1919. The standard biography.

Kingsmill, Hugh, *After Puritanism*. London, 1929.

Muggeridge, Malcolm, *The Earnest Atheist, A Study of Samuel Butler*. London, 1936.

Willey, Basil, *Darwin and Butler, Two Versions of Evolution*. London and New York, 1960.

T. A. GOUDGE

BYZANTINE PHILOSOPHY. The Byzantines (that is, the Greeks of the Middle Ages, 284–1453) were, for the most part, scholars and exegetes rather than creative thinkers, and none of them, not even those who, like John of Damascus (died c. 751), Michael Psellus (1018–c. 1096), John Italus (fl. 1082), and Georgius Gemistus Pletho (c. 1355–1452), made systematic presentations of their views of the universe, ever seriously attempted to propound what we should regard as a new or original system of philosophy. They were all traditionalists in one way or another and usually were satisfied to make use of the ideas they inherited from their predecessors.

Except for the few genuine pagans among them (the Neoplatonists, for example, and Pletho) and some of the commentators on Plato and Aristotle, they did not usually deal with philosophy separately from theology. In their treatment of cosmology, for example, the starting point was the account of creation as it was to be found in Genesis, and this led to cosmological treatises like the *On the Hexaemeron* (that is, on the six days of creation) by Basil of Caesarea in Cappodocia (d. 379) and the similar work by Severianus of Gabala (died c. 408). Basil was receptive to the results of ancient philosophy and science, on which he drew extensively, Severianus was hostile to pagan learning and thus proved to be a congenial source for Cosmas Indicopleustes (see below). Moreover, apart from a few writers like Basil of Caesarea, Nemesius of Emesa in Syria (fl. c. 400), John Chrysostom, the fiery archbishop of Constantinople (d. 407), Archbishop Eustathius of Thessalonica (fl. 1175), and the pagan Pletho, the Byzantines ignored ethics almost entirely.

Nevertheless, they have a place of importance in the history of philosophy for two reasons. First, they preserved the extant works of the Greek philosophers and transcribed all of them by hand. They not only literally saved these texts, as well as the whole of ancient Greek literature (including the writings of the mathematicians, astronomers, and physicians), from destruction but also, in typically Byzantine fashion, produced a huge corpus of commentaries on Plato (notably those by Proclus) and on Aristotle (the *Commentaria in Aristotelem Graeca*, in 23 volumes), and thus laid the foundation for the critical analysis and interpretation of Greek philosophy, which still forms one of the major topics of philosophical discussion. If it had not been for the Byzantine interest in Plato, Aristotle, and their successors, these philosophers would have been virtually unknown today, and the whole history of philosophy would have taken a very different turn.

Second, it must not be forgotten that one of the major contributions of Byzantium to modern civilization was the formulation of the Christian dogmas of the Trinity and the Incarnation at the seven ecumenical councils (325–787), all of which were convoked and presided over by the Byzantine emperors or their legates. Rome was represented at all of these except the first and second councils of Constantinople and has given its sanction to the dogmatic decisions of all the councils. But the creeds and formulas were originally drafted in Greek and were essentially Byzantine productions. Strictly speaking, this subject falls into the domain of dogmatic theology and cannot be discussed in this article. Since, however, the doctrine of the Creator, of God, and of the divine (or the avoidance of these absolutes) looms large in every system of cosmology and metaphysics, theology cannot be altogether excluded from consideration. Because of the enormous influence of theology on the whole of Western civilization, the medieval Greeks made a contribution which merits favorable comparison with that of the ancient Greek philosophers themselves.

Although the great philosophical tradition of ancient Greece always remained a living force in Byzantium, there were religious obscurantists and bigots in every age who repudiated Greek philosophy and even forbade the reading of all pagan books. Eusebius of Caesarea (*Praeparatio Evangelica*, 11, 10, 14) is one of many who quoted with approval the pagan philosopher Numenius (second century of the Christian era) to the effect that Plato was nothing but Moses speaking Attic Greek. Some theologians took comfort in thus deriving Greek philosophy from a Mosaic source. But the Byzantines did not value Greek philosophy any the less on this account, and the great majority agreed with the ecclesiastical historian Theodoret of Cyrrhus (died c. 466) and the polymath Psellus (see below) that Greek philosophy and the ancient classics in general were a valuable adjunct to Biblical and patristic studies.

Neoplatonism. One important ingredient in much of Byzantine philosophy was the revised Platonism of the so-called Neoplatonists, as set forth by Plotinus (205–270), the founder of the movement, and by his principal followers. Offensive as Neoplatonism was to them because of its pagan outlook, Christian theologians were fascinated by it as a metaphysical system, purged it of its polytheistic elements, and adapted it to their own purposes.

Like the Latin West, the Byzantines made extensive use of Porphyry's *Isagoge*. But, most of all, they were enthralled by the Neoplatonic triads (that is, the analysis of all orders of being into three forms or groups, such as the One, mind, and soul), which the Neoplatonists traced back to Plato, who, however, used them far less extensively than his successors did. In Christianity the triad becomes a central theological concept; and the godhead itself is conceived of as a Trinity, the Greek word for which is τριάς, the very term the Neoplatonists used for their triad.

Moreover, the orthodox Christian notion of the consubstantiality of the Trinity (the doctrine according to which the Father, the Son, and the Holy Spirit are of the same essence [ὁμοούσιοι], all equally divine and eternal) is also Neoplatonic in origin, or at least arose out of the same philosophical milieu that produced Neoplatonism. This is especially true of the insistence of the orthodox theologians, against the Arians (the principal opponents of the "orthodox" in Trinitarian doctrine), that the Father in begetting the Son suffered no loss or diminution of his essence (Proclus, *The Elements of Theology,* E. R. Dodds, ed., 2d ed., Oxford, 1963, Prop. 26; cf. 30 and 35 and Dodds's notes) and that the Son and the Holy Spirit are eternal, just as the Father is (*ibid.,* Prop. 34, Corollary).

On the other hand, the Christian dogma that the Son and the Holy Spirit are not only coeternal and consubstantial with the Father but also coequal with him and in no way inferior conflicted with Neoplatonism. For the Neoplatonists, followed in essentials by the Arians, held that the highest forms of being, although resembling the One (the first cause) in varying degree (according to their proximity to it) and eternal like it, were inevitably inferior to it (Dodds, *op. cit.,* Props. 7, 18, 20, 24, 34, 36 ff.). Thus, it is of interest to note that both the orthodox and the heretics were indebted to Neoplatonism, as also, it should be added, they were both somewhat similarly influenced by Origen (185–254), the greatest and most original of the Christian philosophers, whose writings were drawn on by theologians of every school.

No less striking is the obligation of Christian mysticism to the Neoplatonism which permeates the works of the pseudo-Dionysius (fl. 500), whose account of the means by which the initiate seeks, or attains, union with God is derived directly from Proclus (409/412–485), the greatest of the Athenian philosophers of the medieval period. Through the numerous Latin translators of the pseudo-Dionysius, Neoplatonism even penetrated into the theology of the Latin West and into the works of Thomas Aquinas.

Athens and Alexandria. Under philosophers like Proclus and his successors, Athens became a flourishing center of pagan thought and learning. For this reason, in 529 the Emperor Justinian I (ruled 527–565), who made a determined and ruthless attack on heathenism in all forms, issued an edict which closed the Athenian schools of law and philosophy. This put a final end to the intellectual supremacy of Athens, which had been enjoying a brief revival in the fourth and fifth centuries after suffering an eclipse during the Hellenistic period. Cultural primacy then passed to Constantinople, the imperial capital, and, until about the middle of the sixth century, to Alexandria.

The great philosophical academy of Alexandria reached its acme during the sixth century and apparently suffered no evil consequences as a result of Justinian's antipagan legislation. Its success in so doing is probably to be explained by the fact that one of its most distinguished members, John Philoponus, despite monophysite tendencies, was militantly hostile to paganism.

Indeed, it is not improbable that Philoponus published his antipagan polemic, the *De Aeternitate Mundi Contra Proclum,* in 529 (he gives the date clearly and unambiguously), the year of crisis for philosophical studies in Athens, precisely in order to show by his attack on Proclus, the major pagan authority of the day, that the Alexandrian School, notwithstanding its preoccupation with Aristotelianism, was free of heathen pollution. The head of the Alexandrian School at this time was Ammonius Hermeion, a pagan. But Philoponus, his "research assistant," demonstrated the Christian orientation of the Alexandrian School by vigorously espousing the Christian doctrine of the creation (and eventual dissolution) of the universe by God against the pagan notion of its eternity and indestructibility as set forth by Proclus.

After 529 it seems that Philoponus himself shifted his emphasis from Aristotle, on whose works he had written numerous commentaries, to Christian theology. Nevertheless, he never abandoned the classics and frequently cited pagan texts in support of the dogma of creation, even when they did not fit his scheme without some distortion. Nevertheless, his great classical erudition did not prevent him from concluding in his *De Opificio Mundi* that the Mosaic conception of the universe accords better with nature than Aristotle's. This conclusion illustrates his independence from Aristotle, from whom he occasionally dissented, as, for example, in his treatment of the void, in which he discusses the speed of descent of objects of varying weight in a manner that anticipates Galileo's experiment with falling weights.

Less sensible than Philoponus but only slightly less learned was his contemporary, Cosmas Indicopleustes, who was acquainted with but rejected ancient science and philosophy in favor of the Mosaic system, according to which, he informs us in his *Christian Topography,* the universe resembles a two-story house resting on a flat earth.

As a result of the closing of the School of Athens, seven erudite philosophers, praised by the historian Agathias (536–582) as the most distinguished men in their field, felt compelled by Justinian's edict to exile themselves to Persia, where, they had been led to believe, they would find a kind of Platonic utopia and a monarch who conformed to the Platonic ideal of the philosopher-king. These scholars, Damascius (the last head of the School of Athens), Simplicius of Cilicia, Eulamius of Phrygia, Priscian of Lydia, Hermeias and Diogenes of Phoenicia, and Isidore of Gaza (the first, second, and fourth of whom were authors of celebrated philosophical treatises) were soon disillusioned and longed to return to the Byzantine Empire, to which, as a result of a treaty the Persian king Chosroes concluded with Byzantium in 532, they were restored under a guarantee of freedom from interference with their religious beliefs.

After 529, also, the Aristotelian School of Alexandria was Christianized, as can be seen in the names of its leaders, Elijah and David in the sixth century and Stephen of the early seventh, who was apparently the last Greek representative of the school (which did not survive the Arab conquest of Alexandria in 641), and ended his career in Constantinople, to which he had been invited by the Emperor Heraclius (ruled 610–641).

John of Damascus and Photius. There was no official or standard Byzantine philosophy. Some medieval Greeks took Plato as their principal guide, others preferred Aristotle, and most of them made use also of Neoplatonism. The only system of philosophy which could be termed "orthodox" was a theological one like that set forth by John of Damascus in his three-part theological encyclopedia (*Fountain of Knowledge*), which was based primarily on the Bible, the dogmatic definitions of the seven ecumenical councils (325–787), and the works of the orthodox fathers. As a preface to his exposition of theology, John gives an outline of what he takes to be the basic principles of philosophy, including the "five universals" (*quinque voces*, from Porphyry's *Isagoge*) and the ten categories of Aristotle, all fifteen of which he meticulously defines and illustrates. The second section of his encyclopedia is devoted primarily to a sketch of the history of heresy. In the third part (known to the Latins as the *De Fide Orthodoxa*), which contains John's systematic exposition of Christian dogma, John found room for a survey of popular science (the sky, the stars, the planets, the signs of the zodiac, the comets, the seas, etc.), based largely upon patristic sources, many of which were themselves derived from the pagan philosophical tradition.

The following century produced Photius (patriarch of Constantinople from 858 to 867 and from 877 to 886), who is deemed by many to have been the greatest scholar of the Middle Ages. In his *Bibliotheke* ("Library"), a vast anthology of ancient Greek literature, Photius devoted only two sections to philosophy, but he was learned in this subject and refers frequently to the ancient philosophers in his other works. He favored Aristotle over Plato. But Archbishop Arethas of Caesarea in Cappadocia (fl. 900), who is usually supposed to have been his disciple, is celebrated for having commissioned (in 895) the transcription of the famous Bodleian (Clarkianus) codex, which is one of the two major sources of the text of Plato.

Psellus to Pachymeres. The tenth century, during which historical studies flourished under the direction of the Emperor Constantine VII Porphyrogenitus (ruled 912–959), was not especially memorable in the history of philosophy. In the eleventh century, however, the reestablishment of the University of Constantinople (in 1045) led to a new burst of activity on the part of the philosophers. The most distinguished of these was Michael Psellus, who was much indebted to Neoplatonism and, like the Neoplatonists, interested in demonology and magic. He used his knowledge of these subjects to combat paganism, he said, and managed to defend himself successfully against the attacks of clerical obscurantists. He wrote commentaries on Aristotle and on the *Timaeus* of Plato, as well as an encyclopedia, *On Universal Knowledge* (*Didaskalia Pantodape*), which is much like that of John of Damascus, except that it is shorter and more dependent on the Neoplatonists than John's was.

Psellus was a Platonist, but his contemporaries Michael of Ephesus and John Italus were Aristotelians. John Italus was a popular teacher but less able than Psellus to cope with the narrow-minded clergy of his day, who succeeded in having him condemned (1082). Another philosopher of the age, Eustratius (fl. 1100), commented on Aristotle and at the same time defended the Platonic theory of ideas. But he, too, fell victim to the monks, who objected to the use he made of Aristotelian logic in the analysis of theological problems.

About a generation after Eustratius' condemnation, Bishop Nicholas (died c. 1165) of Methone (in the Peloponnesus), who took an active part in the polemic against the Latins, wrote a lengthy refutation of Proclus' *Elements of Theology*, which summarized the basic principles of Neoplatonism, the most subversive form of medieval paganism and therefore a choice target for attack.

In the thirteenth century, philosophical studies were represented by Nicephorus Blemmydes (c. 1197–1272), who wrote a treatise on physics and logic that was largely dependent upon Aristotle, and by the leading scholar of his day, George Pachymeres (1242–1310), from whom we have an outline of the philosophy of Aristotle.

The humanists. Of the humanists of the fourteenth century, the leading philosophers were Theodore Metochites (d. 1332), whose commentaries on Aristotle have not yet been published in the original Greek; Nicephorus Chumnus (c. 1250/1255–1327), the author of a number of treatises on philosophical subjects, including a refutation of Plotinus' theory of the soul; and the polymath Nicephorus Gregoras, who did not write treatises on philosophy as such but dealt extensively in his writings with philosophical subjects.

Byzantine scholars had been eclectic in their use of Plato and Aristotle. In the fifteenth century, however, largely as the result of Georgius Gemistus Pletho's passion for Platonism, the conflict between the Platonists and the Aristotelians waxed hot. Pletho, who visited Italy from 1438 to 1439 and was widely hailed as the most learned man of his time, wrote, among other things, a treatise called the *Laws*, which contained an elaborate scheme for a neopagan utopia based primarily upon Plato and the Neoplatonists. This work is known to us only from the fragments preserved by Patriarch Georgios Scholarios (who, when he became patriarch of Constantinople, took the name of Gennadius, 1453–1459) to prove that it was blatantly pagan and therefore deserved to be consigned to the flames.

The humanistic debate over the relative merits of Plato and Aristotle began with Pletho's essay "On How Aristotle Differs From Plato," in which Pletho championed Plato against Aristotle with such fervor that he provoked angry rebuttals from the Aristotelians. The most violent of his opponents, George of Trebizond, was so vituperative in his reply that he, in turn, called forth the *In Calumniatorem Platonis* of Cardinal Bessarion (1402–1472), who had studied under Pletho. Bessarion was deeply opposed to paganism in all forms. But he was a close student of Greek philosophy, and, overriding his personal preference for Aristotle, he gave a sympathetic summary of the Platonic philosophy, which he deemed reconcilable with Aristotelianism.

Despite Bessarion's best efforts (he issued his *In Calumniatorem Platonis* in both Greek and Latin), most of the

Greeks and the Latins preferred Aristotle to Plato, who, in the eyes of the majority, was compromised because of what seemed to be the exclusively pagan implications of his thought. Nevertheless, the Latins never ceased to hold Pletho in awe, and Cosimo de' Medici gave him the credit for having inspired the foundation of the Platonic Academy of Florence, which, however, was not established until many years after Pletho's visit to Italy. Pletho left his mark on the West in other ways also, and in introducing the geography of Strabo (one of Columbus' chief sources) he even played an indirect role in the discovery of America in 1492, which ushered in the modern era.

Bibliography

The major collection of Byzantine commentators on Aristotle is the *Commentaria in Aristotelem Graeca* in 23 volumes, edited by Michael Hayduck, Hermann Diels, Hugo Rabe, et al. (Berlin, 1883–1907), which was reviewed and summarized in Karl Praechter, "Die griechischen Aristoteleskommentare," in *Byzantinische Zeitschrift*, Vol. 18 (1909), 516–538.

Other important texts are L. G. Westerink, ed., *Damascius, Letters on the Philebus Wrongly Attributed to Olympiodorus* (Amsterdam, 1959), which contains a bibliography of other texts; Perikles Joannou, ed., *Ioannes Italos, Quaestiones Quodlibetales*, Vol. IV of *Studia Patristica et Byzantina* (Ettal, Germany, 1956); Philippe Chevallier et al., eds., *Dionysiaca*, 2 vols. (Bruges, 1937), which contains 18 texts, among them the original Greek of the works of the pseudo-Dionysius, the six Latin medieval translations, and those of the Renaissance; C. Alexandre and A. Pellisier, *Pléthon, Traité des lois*, which contains an introduction and French translation (Paris, 1858); L. G. Westerink, ed., *Michael Psellus, De Omnifaria Doctrina* (Nijmegen, the Netherlands, 1948); and L. Petit, X. A. Sidéridès, M. Jugie, eds., *Oeuvres complètes de Gennade Scholarios*, 8 vols. (Paris, 1932–1936).

Valuable for the influence of Byzantine scholarship on Western philosophy are (1) the *Corpus Philosophorum Medii Aevi*, divided into *(a) Aristoteles Latinus*, G. Lacombe, A. Birkenmajer, M. Dulong, A. Franceschini, A. Mansion, L. Minio-Paluello, P. Michaud-Quantin, et al., eds. (Paris, Bruges, Rome, and Cambridge, 1939—), 9 scattered volumes already published out of a projected 33 volumes, and *(b)* the *Corpus Platonicum Medii Aevi, Plato Latinus*, R. Klibansky, C. Labowsky, V. Kordeuter, L. Minio-Paluello, H. J. D. Lulofs, J. H. Waszink, P. J. Jensen, eds. (London, 1940—), 4 vols. already published; and (2) the *Corpus Latinum Commentatorium in Aristotelem Graecorum*, Vols. I–II, commentaries of Themistius and Ammonius, translated into Latin from the Greek by William of Moerbeke, G. Verbeke, ed. (Louvain and Paris, 1957–1961).

For a more detailed treatment of Byzantine philosophy in general, see M. V. Anastos, *The Mind of Byzantium* (New York, 1966); Hans-G. Beck, *Kirche und theologische Literatur im byzantinischen Reich*, Pt. 2, Vol. I of *Byzantinisches Handbuch* (Munich, 1959), which has much useful data, bibliography, etc.; Louis Bréhier, *La Civilisation byzantine*, Vol. III of *Le Monde byzantine* (Paris, 1950), often valuable for philosophy; W. Buchwald, A. Hohlweg, and O. Prinz, *Tusculum-Lexikon griechischer und lateinischer Autoren des Altertums und des Mittelalters*, 2d ed. (Munich, 1963), which has a valuable compendious list of all authors, Greek and Latin, ancient and medieval, with vital dates, bibliography, etc., occasionally defective but extremely useful; Bernard Geyer, *Die patristische und scholastische Philosophie*, Vol. II of Friedrich Ueberweg's *Grundriss der Geschichte der Philosophie*, 11th ed. (Berlin, 1928), new ed. in preparation by Max Heinze and Paul Wilpert, which has lists of names, texts, bibliography; Endre von Ivánka, *Plato Christianus* (Einseideln, 1964), a collection of valuable articles on this subject; Karl Krumbacher, *Geschichte der byzantinischen Litteratur von Justinian bis zum Ende des oströmischen Reiches*, 2d ed. (Munich, 1897), a standard treatment with lists of names, texts, etc.; Klaus Oehler, "Aristotle in Byzantium," in *Greek, Roman, and Byzantine Studies*, Vol. 5 (1964), 133–146, with valuable recent bibliography; Basile Tatakis, *La Philosophie byzantine*, a volume of Émile Bréhier, *Histoire de la philosophie*, fascicle suppl. 2 (Paris, 1959), the only full treatment of the subject; Harry A. Wolfson, *The Philosophy of the Church Fathers*, 2d ed., Vol. I (Cambridge, Mass., 1964), an indispensable work; and Maurice de Wulf, *Histoire de la philosophie médiévale* (Louvain, 1924), *passim*.

For the Church Fathers, see Johannes Quasten, *Patrology*, 3 vols. (Westminster, Md., Antwerp, and Utrecht, 1950–1960), to be completed in 5 volumes; Berthold Altaner, *Patrologie*, 5th ed. (Freiburg im Breisgau, 1958), translated by Hilda C. Graef as *Patrology*, 2d ed. (Freiburg im Breisgau and New York, 1960).

MILTON V. ANASTOS

The Encyclopedia of Philosophy

The ENCYCLOPEDIA *of* PHILOSOPHY

PAUL EDWARDS, *Editor in Chief*

VOLUME TWO

Macmillan Publishing Co., Inc. & The Free Press
NEW YORK
COLLIER MACMILLAN PUBLISHERS
LONDON

MACMILLAN PUBLISHING CO., INC.
COLLIER-MACMILLAN CANADA LTD.

MANUFACTURED IN THE UNITED STATES OF AMERICA

REPRINT EDITION 1972

The Encyclopedia of Philosophy

C

CABALA (literally "tradition") is used both as a general name for Jewish mysticism and as the specific designation for its major medieval variety. Mystical awareness is to be found in the Biblical and rabbinic tradition and had literary expression in some of the prophetic writings, psalms, and apocalypses. More characteristically, however, what is referred to as Cabala is a type of occult theosophical formulation of the doctrines of the Jewish religion, particularly those concerned with creation, revelation, and redemption. This occult system structures and, in part, fossilizes individual intuitions of divine reality in terms of the culture in which it arose. Typically, the purpose of the complicated structuring of these formulated intuitions is to supply a focus in contemplation by which the Cabalist can recover the untarnished brightness of direct mystical awareness.

Besides the sources of Cabala in the doctrines and literature of the Jewish tradition, a wide variety of other sources has been noted, which have introduced elements from the various cultures with which the Jewish people have come in contact in their dispersion. Among these influences should be included some Persian elements, both Parsi and Zoroastrian, and Neo-Platonic and Neo-Pythagorean elements which entered during the Hellenistic period; Christian influences and Gnostic themes added at a somewhat later time; and borrowings from Muslim sectarianism after the emergence of Islam. This mixture of elements explains the difficulty that scholars have found in disentangling the sources of Cabala. It should be said, however, that the pursuit of sources has less relevance here than it may have for other subjects, because what is essential is not the materials out of which the Cabalistic theosophical system was created, but rather the use that was made of the materials.

MAJOR DOCTRINES

Creation. All Jewish mysticism has seen the need for reinterpretation of the literal account of creation given in the book of Genesis. As it stands, the account does not sufficiently emphasize the transcendence of God. God is too close to man and the world to be the Supreme Mystery that the mystical temper insists He must be. The reinterpretation has generally taken form as a demiurgic theory. In such a theory, God Himself, the Boundless, the Infinite, the Transcendent, did not perform the material act of creating the world. This was the work of a lesser spirit, or demiurge, who was brought into existence by God in order to do this specific job. As the conception of God's transcendence developed, one demiurge seemed insufficient to express the sense of awesome distance between divinity and the material world. The remoteness of God from the world was heightened, therefore, by adding other intermediaries and thus forming a chain from God to matter whose links were of increasing materiality.

A second problem in the Biblical account of creation concerns matter. If we accept God as infinite, all must be contained in Him. Where, then, is there a place for matter outside of God? This issue was finally resolved by a theory that combined the idea of God's voluntary self-contraction with the concept of emanation. In this account, God, prior to creation, was actually infinite. To make room for creation, however, He voluntarily contracted or limited Himself. Some excess of spiritual substance overflowed into the space from which God had removed Himself, and this excess, or emanation, provided both the demiurgic intermediaries described above and the matter out of which the world was created. Because all substance is thus ultimately an overflowing of God's substance, Cabala is a pantheistic doctrine. The completed series of emanations served the additional purpose of providing the road by which man's aspiring spirit might reach the heights of divinity; thus, it served both as the mechanism of creation and as the "itinerary of the mind to God" (to borrow an expression from St. Bonaventure).

Revelation. After the first destruction of the Temple at Jerusalem, and even more after its second destruction, the Scriptures served as a focus for the religious devotion of the Jews. Their state was no more; their cultus was no more; all that was left to them was their belief in God and His Word. For the continuance of the Jewish religion, it came to seem necessary that not only the content of revelation, but even its physical form, should be considered sacrosanct and unchangeable. In all types of Judaism this regard for the letter of Scripture made necessary the development of exegetic techniques for raising the level of significance of much that is trivial in the Scriptures. For the mystics the problem was particularly difficult, because the level on which they had to interpret revelation to make it serve their purpose was highly symbolical. To make this reinterpretation possible, the Cabalists developed letter and number symbolisms of great variety and complexity.

Redemption. The Cabalists maintained and even intensified the traditional Jewish view of redemption. In the Cabalistic view salvation of the individual was little considered; it entered only as a means to the greater end of the salvation of mankind. This would come about through the agency of a Messiah of the Davidic line, who would lead the Jews in triumph to the Holy Land and inaugurate a reign of truth, justice, and mercy. The ideal of salvation is thus the establishment of an earthly paradise of human life, raised to its highest humanity. Other elements clouded this doctrine at various times in the history of mystical Messianism. For example, in the sixteenth century Isaac Luria introduced the idea that this regeneration could not take place until all pre-existing souls had satisfactorily completed their earthly existence and that, since some souls were too weak to go unaided through life to perfection, other superior souls might coexist with them in one body to insure their success. Although Luria's doctrine of transmigration found followers, it was exceptional rather than typical; in general, the Cabalistic view of redemption was an extreme form of traditional Messianism. Attempts to calculate the exact date of the coming of the Messiah were widespread; the coincidence of various calculations in fixing on dates close to each other was sufficient to start a wave of Messianic movements and even to touch off a major explosion like the widespread impassioned support of Sabbatai Zevi, the so-called Messiah of Ismir (1626–1676).

HISTORICAL EXPRESSIONS

While a number of smaller groups, such as the Essenes of Palestine, the Therapeutae of whom Philo wrote, and the eighth-century Persian "Men of the Caves" whom the tenth-century Karaite historian Joseph ben Jacob al-Kirkisani described, maintained views similar in part to those that have been presented, these groups do not lie in the mainstream of Jewish mysticism. The main development is rather to be traced from the Jewish Gnosticism of the first millennium of the Common Era, with its concentration on the glory of God as manifested in His throne, supposedly located in the innermost of seven heavenly mansions, into the parallel forms of the medieval European developments of the Cabala—the practical, ethical, and sometimes magical mysticism of the German Jews and the speculative mysticism of the French and Spanish Jews. Thence the movement became enmeshed in the morbidity of seventeenth-century Messianism, before the two strains of mystical speculation and socioethical piety were reunited, in eastern Europe, in the still-flourishing movement of Hasidism.

The German pietist movement developed during the century between 1150 and 1250. Its chief formulators were Samuel the Hasid (fl. 1150), his son Judah the Hasid (d. 1217), and a relative, Eleazar of Worms (fl. 1220). The chief literary expression of the movement is the *Book of the Pious* (Hebrew, *Sefer Hasidim*), a collection of the literary remains of the three founders, with special emphasis on Judah the Hasid, whose character and influence recall those of his Christian contemporary, St. Francis of Assisi, and, perhaps, remind one also of Paracelsus, who lived in the sixteenth century and who also combined genuine piety with magic. In addition to its concern with the doctrinal elements that have already been discussed as characteristic of all forms of Jewish mysticism, German Hasidism defined an ideal human type and a way of life—devoutness, rather than learning or traditionalism. The three chief elements in this devoutness were mental serenity, ascetic renunciation, and extreme altruism, leading to heights of devotion in which true fear of God and love of God became one. At these heights, the Hasid was thought to achieve a creative power of a magical nature.

In southern France, at the beginning of the thirteenth century, a more speculative Cabalistic development began, under the sponsorship of Isaac the Blind (fl. 1200) and his disciples Ezra and Azariel. Their chief concern was the elaboration of emanation theory; they also suggested a doctrine of metempsychosis, although they did not develop it fully. In Spain, Abraham ben Samuel Abulafia (1240–c. 1292) combined this speculation with the development of number and letter symbolism and thus became one of the central figures in the development of Cabala. His disciple, Joseph ben Abraham Gikatilia (c. 1247–1305), presented both the techniques for symbolic interpretation and the doctrine of the ten emanations (Hebrew, *sephiroth*) in systematically interrelated form. About 1290 the Spanish Cabalist Moses ben Shemtob de Leon (d. 1305) produced the work that, for many, represents the Cabala in its entirety: the lush compendium of esoteric doctrines in the form of a commentary on the Pentateuch known as *The Book of Splendor* (Hebrew, *Sefer Ha-Zohar*). From the time of its composition, this work has been the chief source of inspiration for later Jewish mystics and for Jewish mysticism. Of later Cabalistic leaders, two in particular should be mentioned: Moses ben Jacob Cordovero (1522–1570), whose book, *A Garden of Pomegranates* (Hebrew, *Pardes Rimmonim*), is the most systematic and philosophical exposition of the doctrines of the Cabala up to his time; and his pupil, Isaac Luria (1534–1572), who left no written legacy, but whose disciples have made it clear that he developed the theosophic doctrines of creation and redemption far beyond his predecessors.

There are still Cabalistic groups in existence, chiefly in Israel, but they are for the most part outgrowths of eighteenth-century Polish Hasidism, a movement akin to, though by no means identical with, earlier German pietism. Among major Jewish thinkers of the twentieth century, the late chief rabbi of Jerusalem, Abraham Isaac Kook (1865–1935), approached most closely the spirit of the Cabala in his mystical awareness of the Messianic role of the Jewish people and in his Lurianic and Hasidic stress on the spark of holiness that is veiled by the material shell of things perceived by the senses. Martin Buber, whose reinterpretations of the Hasidic view of life are profound and suggestive, may also be named here and, among younger thinkers, Abraham Joshua Heschel, whose thought has clear kinship with Hasidic social ethics.

Bibliography

TEXTS

Of the primary Cabalistic literature, only the chief sections of *The Zohar* are available, in an English translation by H. Sperling, Maurice Simon, and P. P. Levertoff, 5 vols. (London, 1931–1934). Other segments of *The Zohar* in inferior translations are included in S. L. MacGregor Mathers, *The Kabbalah Unveiled* (London, 1887). A theosophized version of *Sefer Yetzirah* is Knut Stenring, *The Book of Formation* (London, 1923). The Hebrew texts have not been critically edited.

Among recent writers of a mystical bent, the works of Martin Buber are readily available in English translations. None of Abraham Isaac Kook's works have been translated; however, there are good discussions of his life and thought in Jacob Agus, *Banner of Jerusalem* (New York, 1946) and Isidore Epstein, *Abraham Kook, His Life and Works* (London, 1951). A. J. Heschel is best represented by *God in Search of Man. A Philosophy of Judaism.* (New York, 1955).

HISTORY OF CABALA

See Joshua Abelson, *Jewish Mysticism* (London, 1913); Christian D. Ginsburg, *The Kabbalah: Its Doctrine, Development, and Literature* (London, 1920); Adolph Franck, *The Kabbalah: or, the Religious Philosophy of the Hebrews* (New York, 1926); Abba Hillel Silver, *A History of Messianic Speculation in Israel from the First through the Seventeenth Centuries* (New York, 1959); Gershom G. Scholem, *Major Trends in Jewish Mysticism* (New York, 1946; and Joseph L. Blau, *The Story of Jewish Philosophy* (New York, 1962).

J. L. Blau

CABANIS, PIERRE-JEAN GEORGES

CABANIS, PIERRE-JEAN GEORGES (1757–1808), was, with Destutt de Tracy, the leader of the Idéologues. A precocious student of philosophy and of the classics, he chose medicine as a career, but he never practiced. As a protégé of Helvétius' widow, he frequented the company of Condillac, Holbach, Benjamin Franklin, and Thomas Jefferson. When Voltaire disparaged his poetry in 1778, Cabanis turned to physiology and philosophy. During the Revolution, he collaborated with Mirabeau on public education and was an intimate of Condorcet. Later, he backed the Directory and Napoleon's *coup d'état* of 18 Brumaire. Although Napoleon made him a senator, Cabanis opposed his tyrannical policies. Bitter and scornful, Napoleon dubbed Cabanis' group "Idéologues." Cabanis wrote on medical practice and teaching, but his fame and influence derive from one book, *Rapports du physique et du moral de l'homme* (12 memoirs written between 1796 and 1802, published in 1802).

The Idéologues (who also included Constantin Volney, Marie Jean Condorcet, Antoine L. Lavoisier, and Pierre S. de Laplace) were often scorned in their time, and later, as belated *philosophes* and purveyors of visionary speculations. In the rising tide of metaphysical idealism, their positivistic approach was held in disfavor. They suffered from the influence of the religious revival and the spell exercised by Chateaubriand's *Le Génie du Christianisme*, as well as from the popularity of "Illuminist" fads derived from Masonic practices. Their political activity during the Revolution also worked against them, and Napoleon's suppression of their movement left them without an outlet for publication.

Cabanis, like the others, sought a mechanistic explanation of the universe, nature, and human behavior—an approach later continued by Comte and Taine. Matter alone is real and eternal in its many transitory forms. As Lavoisier had applied analysis to chemistry, so—Cabanis declared—it could be applied to ideas, which could thereby be reduced to the original sensations whence they spring. Self-interest, the pursuit of happiness and pleasure, and self-preservation are the only motives of action. These notions, already advanced by the eighteenth-century materialists, were systematically developed by Cabanis and Destutt de Tracy. The study of man, they held, must be reduced to physics and physiology. Man must be observed and analyzed like any mineral or vegetable. The medical expert, said Cabanis, should play the part formerly taken by the moralist (an idea that harks back to Descartes and Julien O. La Mettrie). "Physiology, analysis of ideas, and morals are three branches of one science which may be called the science of man." Consequently, Cabanis and his fellow theorists refused to recognize notions not based on phenomena or sensations, that is, not susceptible of exact knowledge and (ultimately, at least) of mathematical notation. An understanding of the "mechanism of language" was considered essential to the understanding of the "mechanism of the intellect" and to the meaning of ideas. Language itself, however, had to be illumined by analysis of the sensations which constitute an idea an by the functioning of the intellect.

In his preface to the *Rapports du physique et du moral de l'homme*, Cabanis insisted that both the moralist and the physician are interested in the whole man; that is, in the physical and the moral, which are inseparable, and incomprehensible taken separately. The moral sciences must be placed on a physical basis. The union of mind and body is the theme of the first "Mémoire." Sensation is the necessary cause of our ideas, feelings, needs, and will. Since sensitivity is the connection between biological life and mind, the mental is only the physical considered from a certain point of view. Cabanis makes a famous comparison between the brain and the stomach: as the latter is a machine for digesting food, so the former is a machine for digesting impressions, by "the secretion of thought." He then develops a genetic analysis of sensations and ideas. There are no causes except those which can act on our senses, no truths except in relation to "the general way of feeling" of human nature, which varies with such positive factors as age, sex, disposition, health, climate, and so on. Thus the state of the abdominal viscera may influence the formation of ideas.

The second "Mémoire" is a "physiological history of sensations." Cabanis defines life as feeling and, following the work of Albrecht von Haller and La Mettrie, discusses the difference between sensitivity and irritability. The latter, he maintains, is only a result of the former, which is the basic biological phenomenon; since both depend on the nerves, they are essentially the same. Voluntary movements come from perceptions, which arise from sensations. Involuntary movements are caused by the organs' sensitivity, which produces the unconscious (autonomic) impressions that determine many of our ideas and decisions. The action of the nervous system, moreover, is only a specialized application of the laws of physical motion, which are the source of all phenomena. The third "Mémoire" develops a theory of the unconscious. The nervous system is affected by internal changes, that is, by memory and imagination; thus within man exists "another internal man" in constant action, the effects of which are noticeable in dreams. The fourth "Mémoire" explores the influence of age on ideas and "moral affections." The organs, like all else in nature, are in constant motion, and are therefore involved in decomposition and recomposition. Consequently, variations in the cellular tissue produce physical and psychic changes due to chemical action. The fifth "Mémoire" takes up sexual differences. The generative organs are essentially glandular, and their secretions influence the brain and the whole body. Unknown primitive "dispositions" (structures), which cause the embryo to be male or female, are also the cause of sexual differences, both physical and psychic. The fact that women can be forced to reproduction and men only excited to it produces vast differences in habits and mental outlook. What the sexes have in common constitutes human nature.

The sixth "Mémoire" treats the influence of "temperament," that is, the determining effects of the inherited physical constitution. Thus a large heart and lungs produce an energetic character, small ones an intellectual character. Because of heredity, the human race could be improved by hygienic methods. Believing in the inheritance of acquired characteristics and in improvement of species through crossbreeding, Cabanis pleads for a program of eugenics that will do for the human species what human beings have done for dogs and horses. In the seventh "Mémoire" Cabanis explores emotional and mental perturbations caused by diseases. For instance, weakness and irritability of the stomach produce muscular enervation and rapid alternations between excitement and depression. The eighth "Mémoire" discusses such effects of diet, air pressure, humidity and temperature, as excitation and sedation. Cabanis analyzes the effects of different foods and drinks, but his information and conclusions are rather fantastic. Climate is the subject of the ninth "Mémoire." Man, the most modifiable animal, responds to heat and cold with differences in sexual and physical activity, and consequently in mental and moral habits. The tenth "Mémoire" is the longest. It explores the phenomena of animal life, including sensitivity, instinct, sympathy, sleep, dreams, and delirium. The forces that cause matter to organize (a natural tendency) are unknown, and will always remain so. Nevertheless these forces are only physical, and life is only organization. Cabanis believed in spontaneous generation. Species have evolved through chance mutations ("fortuitous changes") and planned mutation ("man's experimental attempts"), which change the structures of heredity. Cabanis does not, however, develop a general theory of evolution. The eleventh "Mémoire" concerns the influence of the "moral" (mental) on the physical, which is merely the action of the brain on the body. The last "Mémoire," on "acquired dispositions," treats the influence of habituation and experience in general.

As a positivist, Cabanis was willing to renounce ultimate explanations. He was interested only in cause and effect on the level of phenomena. Unlike the other Idéologues, he was much influenced by La Mettrie and the man–machine school. He opposed the psychological method of Condillac and the sensationists, which was limited to external sensations. He preferred the physiological approach, which emphasized hereditary dispositions, the state of the organs, dreams, and automatic or unconscious impulses. These factors were more significant for him than experience (sensation) in determining the individual's behavior; for the *tabula rasa* concept ignored what the child or adult brings to experience. For the same reason, Condillac's statue is only an unreal abstraction from the reality of the unified, total, active organism. Cabanis was interested in the moral and social improvement of mankind, which he considered possible through an understanding of physiology—a science that he thought would eventually influence even positive law.

Cabanis and the Idéologues were one moment of a tradition that extends from Epicurus to the contemporary logical positivists (whose interest in linguistic analysis was prefigured by the Idéologues). Cabanis, like the others, has frequently been accused of impoverishing human experience by reducing it to the physical and mechanical level, and by denying the possibility of transcending internal and external sensations. On the other hand, the Idéologues considered man to be his own justification and the master of his own destiny. They had faith in his capacity to progress indefinitely by means of his own resources.

Works by Cabanis

The *Oeuvres complètes* (Paris, 1823–1825) of Cabanis was edited by P. J. G. Thurot.

Works on Cabanis

The best study of the Idéologues (although it ignores Cabanis' connection with La Mettrie and the man–machine outlook) is Emile Cailliet, *La Tradition littéraire des Idéologues* (Philadelphia, 1943). See also Charles H. Van Duzer, *The Contribution of the Idéologues to French Revolutionary Thought* (Baltimore, 1935), and the more apologetic F. Picavet, *Les Idéologues* (Paris, 1890).

L. G. CROCKER

CAIRD, EDWARD (1835–1908), a leading Scottish Hegelian, was born in Greenock, the fifth of seven boys. His eldest brother, John Caird, became well known as a preacher and theologian, and exercised considerable influence on the young Edward. Educated at Greenock Academy and Glasgow University (with a brief interlude at St. Andrews), Edward Caird went to Balliol College, Oxford, gaining first class honors in Classical Moderations and in "Greats." From 1864 to 1866 he was a fellow and tutor of Merton, leaving to take the chair of moral philosophy at Glasgow, which he held until 1893. He then returned to Oxford to succeed Benjamin Jowett as master of Balliol. He resigned because of ill health in 1907, and died the year after.

Caird had a profound influence on his students, who regarded themselves as his disciples and included such distinguished philosophers as Henry Jones, J. H. Muirhead, J. S. Mackenzie, and John Watson. "The greatest theme of modern philosophy," Caird held, "is the problem of the relation of the human to the divine" (*The Evolution of*

Theology in the Greek Philosophers, 1904). Many of his Glasgow students were destined for the church, and his liberalizing influence on religion was widely transmitted through them beyond the classroom.

Caird's philosophy was a form of speculative idealism, based on Kant but going beyond him. It was essentially a philosophy of reconciliation. The need for philosophy, he held, arises from the apparently irreconcilable opposition between different elements in our spiritual life—between subject and object, religion and science, freedom and determination, reason and desire. Unless we reconcile these antagonisms in a higher unity, we cannot achieve the spiritual harmony without which the highest achievements of man are impossible.

Kant, he was convinced, had found the key to the problem, but had failed to grasp the implications of his own doctrine. Caird had first to clear away what he thought was a common misinterpretation of Kant and then to go further along the Kantian road, with Hegel as his guide. Kant had been held, according to Caird, to teach that the material of knowledge is given in sense perception and that the mind then goes to work on it, ordering it by concepts supplied by itself. But, in fact, for Kant there *are* no objects until thought has done its work. Thought enters into the very constitution of experience. And further, the process of knowing is dominated by an "idea of the Reason," which drives the mind to seek a form of experience in which all differences are seen as elements in a single system.

But instead of insisting that the larger the part played in knowledge by the mind's synthetic activity, the more adequate that knowledge is, Kant took the view that this activity confines us to appearances and bars us from things-in-themselves. He should have shown, Caird argued, that our knowledge of objects will be imperfect insofar as we fail to recognize that they are only partial aspects of the ideal whole toward which reason points.

Caird's ethical theory had close affiliations with that of his lifelong friend, T. H. Green. His main problem centered on the opposition of inclination and duty, and his solution lay in establishing the power of human beings to determine their conduct by reference to the self, as a permanent center, as distinct from its relatively isolated and transient desires. A self-conscious being seeks *self*-satisfaction, not just the satisfaction of this or that desire. And in this power of determining conduct by reference to the self lies human freedom.

The principle of evolution, Caird recognized, was of great value in reconciling differences, and in his Gifford Lectures, *The Evolution of Religion* (1891–1892), he traced the development of a single religious principle through its varied manifestations in the main religions of the world.

Works by Caird

A Critical Account of the Philosophy of Kant. Glasgow, 1877.
Hegel. Edinburgh, 1883.
The Social Philosophy and Religion of Comte. Glasgow, 1885.
The Critical Philosophy of Immanuel Kant. Glasgow, 1889.
Essays in Literature and Philosophy. Glasgow, 1892.
The Evolution of Religion. Glasgow, 1893.
The Evolution of Theology in the Greek Philosophers. Glasgow, 1904.

Works on Caird

Jones, Sir Henry, and Muirhead, J. H., *The Life and Philosophy of Edward Caird*. Glasgow, 1921.
Mackenzie, J. S., "Edward Caird as a Philosophical Teacher." *Mind*, Vol. 18 (1909), 509–537.
Watson, John, "The Idealism of Edward Caird." *Philosophical Review*, Vol. 18 (1909), 147–163, 259–280.

A. K. STOUT

CAJETAN, CARDINAL (Thomas de Vio), theologian and philosopher of the Renaissance scholastic revival, was born at Gaeta, Italy, in 1468 and died in 1534. He entered the Order of Preachers at the age of 16 and studied philosophy and theology at Naples, Bologna, and Padua. From 1493 to 1496 Cajetan ("the man from Gaeta") taught philosophy at Padua, where he engaged in controversy with representatives of Scotism, including Trombetta, and with several Italian Averroists, Vernia, Pomponazzi, and Nifo. He taught at Pavia from 1497 to 1499.

From 1500 on, Cajetan served in various administrative posts in the Dominican order and also taught both philosophy and theology in Rome. He became master general of his order in 1508 and was raised to the cardinalate in 1517. As cardinal legate to Germany (1518–1519) he was involved in controversy with Martin Luther. The last years of his life were devoted to study and writing.

Commentaries constitute a good part of Cajetan's writings. His most influential work is the *Commentary on St. Thomas' Summa of Theology*, which contains much of his speculative thought. Cajetan was one of the most famous interpreters of the thought of Thomas Aquinas, although his own philosophy is closer to Aristotle's than is that of Aquinas. Because he spent much of his time in controversy with Scotists and Averroists, Cajetan adopted some of their terminology and faced questions that had been unknown in the thirteenth century. He became less confident than Aquinas had been of the capacity of human reason to handle ultimate problems, such as the immortality of the human soul and the existence of divine providence.

Cajetan's logic was the standard Aristotelian syllogistic, but he developed a special theory of analogy. Following a famous text from Aquinas' commentary on the *Sentences* of Peter Lombard (*In I Sententiarum*, d. 19, q. 5, 2, ad 1), Cajetan, in his *De Nominum Analogia*, described: (1) The analogy of inequality, according to which, for example, sensitive life is more perfectly present in men than in beasts, a shifting signification with a genus (here, animal). This type was eventually rejected by Cajetan as not analogy in the proper sense. (2) The analogy of attribution, for example, of "healthy" as applied to an animal, urine, and medicine. In this type of analogy (much stressed by his contemporary Sylvester of Ferrara) the primary analogate is found in one item (animal) and is merely attributed to the others. Cajetan did not favor this meaning of analogy. (3) The analogy of proportionality (e.g., seeing is related to the sense of vision as intellectual vision is to the power of understanding). This is the basic type of analogy, according to Cajetan (in this he was followed by John of St. Thomas and many recent Thomists—R. Garrigou-Lagrange, J. Gredt, G. M. Manser, A. Forest, and A. Marc). Cajetan tried to use this type of analogy to show how knowledge of God is possible and to demonstrate that argument by analogy from creatures to God does not necessarily commit the fallacy of equivocation.

In explaining the psychic activities and powers of man, Cajetan was very close to Aquinas. He viewed intellectual abstraction as an act of "objective" illumination. The first principles of reasoning (e.g., that the same predicate is not to be at once both affirmed and denied of the same subject) are known by virtue of sense experience; not only the meaning of the terms of such principles but also the nexus of the judgment enunciating them originates in sense perception (*In Summa Theologiae*, I, q. 16, 2). Thus, the usual Thomistic dictum, that all our knowledge comes from the senses, was vigorously stressed by Cajetan.

Concerning man's soul, he at first (c. 1503) offered a proof for its immortality based on the immateriality of the operations of understanding and willing, concluding to the spirituality and simplicity of the soul and, consequently, to its incorruptibility and immortality. However, in commenting on the treatise *De Anima*, in 1509, he asserted that Aristotle had denied the immortality of the understanding of the individual man. In 1527, in a commentary on Matthew (Ch. 22), Cajetan said that the immortality of the soul is not rationally demonstrable, and the next year, commenting on Paul, he put it among the mysteries of faith. In 1534, in a commentary on Ecclesiastes (Ch. 3), he stated that no philosopher had proved the immortality of man's soul.

In metaphysics Cajetan explained the constitution of personality by using the notion of subsistence, a formal perfection added to the basic being of an individual to make it complete as an existing substance and uncommunicated to any other (*In Summa Theologiae*, III, q. 4, 2). The principle of individuation, he said, is matter quantified but without the notion of indefinite dimensions. Analogous to his position on the immortality of the soul, Cajetan held that God's existence could not be proved. Aquinas' five proofs for the existence of God (*Summa Theologiae*, I, 2, 3) validly conclude to the existence of an Absolute Being but not to a Creator.

Works by Cajetan

COMMENTARIES

In Praedicamenta Aristotelis, M. H. Laurent, ed. Rome, 1939. On Aristotle's *Posterior Analytics* and *Categories*.

Super Libros Aristotelis De Anima, I. Coquelle, ed. Rome, 1938–1939. On Aristotle's psychology.

Commentaria in De Ente et Essentia, M. H. Laurent, ed. Turin, 1934. On Aquinas treatise *On Being and Essence*.

In Summa Theologiae Divi Thomae Aquinatis. Venice, 1508, 1514, 1518; Bologna, 1528. This commentary on Aquinas' *Summa of Theology* is now printed in the Leonine edition of the works of Aquinas, *Opera Omnia*, Vols. IV–XII. Rome, 1888–1906.

In Porphyrii Isagogen, I. M. Marega, ed. Rome, 1934. On Porphyry's *Introduction to Logic*.

PERSONAL PHILOSOPHICAL WRITINGS

De Nominum Analogia et de Conceptu Entis, N. Zammit, ed. Rome, 1934. Translated by E. A. Bushinski and H. J. Koren as *On the Analogy of Names and the Concept of Being*. Pittsburgh, 1953.

Essays in practical philosophy, especially one, "De Cambiis," on the exchange value of money, in *Scripta Philosophica: Opuscula Oeconomica-socialia*, P. Ammit, ed. Rome, 1934.

Works on Cajetan

Gilson, E., "Cajétan et l'existence," in *Tijdschrift voor Philosophie*, Vol. 15 (1953), 267–286.

Grabmann, M., "Die Stellung des Kardinal Cajetan in der Geschichte des Thomismus," in *Angelicum*, Vol. 11 (1934), 547–560.

Schwarz, H. T., "Analogy in St. Thomas and Cajetan," in *New Scholasticism*, Vol. 28 (1954), 127–144.

A more extensive bibliography appears in the Cajetan number of *Revue Thomiste*, Vol. 17 (1934–1935), 3–49.

VERNON J. BOURKE

CALDERONI, MARIO (1879–1914), ranks next to his teacher Giovanni Vailati as an Italian "Peircean pragmatist." He graduated in law from the University of Pisa in 1901, and later lectured on the theory of values at the universities of Bologna and Florence.

Calderoni engaged in analyses of human behavior. These began with the interpretation of voluntary acts, which he regarded as the only nonmetaphysical problem of free will. In everyday life we all possess as good a criterion as is necessary to distinguish between voluntary and involuntary acts. To find out whether an act is to be called voluntary or not, we must modify the circumstances in which it usually occurs. If it still occurs in any case, we call it "involuntary"; if not, we call it "voluntary." The difference rests on the "plasticity" of voluntary acts, on their liability to modification by certain influences. A voluntary act "is liable not to be performed if the actor . . . is given some new information on its consequences." What determines his acting is some expectation, which we can modify "either by changing one of the actor's beliefs by means of persuasion or reasoning, or, so to say artificially, by adding to the consequences the act would bring about if it were performed." (*Scritti*, vol. 2, pp. 25–26.) This criterion would hold good even if it were proved that all our acts are subject to the principle of causality. In Calderoni's hands, it became an empirical, perfectible tool applied to the analysis of moral and legal responsibility.

In *Disarmonie economiche e disarmonie morali* (Florence, 1906) Calderoni viewed moral life as a "wide market where some men . . . make determinate demands on other men who oppose such demands with more or less resistance and claim in their turn . . . some sort of reward." Moral acts are judged not according to their total value, but according to their marginal or comparative value. We tend to confer the highest moral value not on common acts but on acts so rare that we would be obliged to repress them if their normal production increased. The moral value of actions is therefore related to their supply.

Additional Works by Calderoni

I postulati della scienza positiva ed il diritto penale ("The Postulates of Positive Science and Penal Law"). Florence, 1901. His doctoral dissertation, containing his main ideas in brief.

Scritti, O. Campa, ed., 2 vols. Florence, 1924. Preface by G. Papini.

For joint papers by Calderoni and Vailati, see VAILATI.

Works on Calderoni

Bozzi, Paolo, "Il pragmatismo italiano: Mario Calderoni." *Rivista critica di storia della filosofia*, Vol. 12, No. 3 (1957), 293–322.

Renauld, J.-F., "L'Oeuvre inachevée de Mario Calderoni." *Revue de Métaphysique et de Morale*, Vol. 23 (1918), 207–231.

Santucci, Antonio, *Il pragmatismo in Italia*. Bologna, 1963. Ch. 5, 216–262.

FERRUCCIO ROSSI-LANDI

CALVIN, JOHN (1509–1564), Protestant reformer and theologian, was born at Noyon, France. The son of middle-class parents of considerable local importance, Calvin was early directed toward an ecclesiastical career. From 1523 to 1528 he studied theology in Paris, there becoming acquainted with both the scholastic and humanist trends of his day. When he had achieved the master of arts degree, Calvin, in response to his father's wishes, left Paris to study law at Orléans, finishing his doctorate there by early 1532.

By 1534 Calvin had decisively broken with his Catholic heritage and had joined the Protestant reform movement in France. From this time on, all his efforts were devoted to the cause of the Reformation, and most of the remainder of his life was spent preaching, teaching, and writing in Geneva. He carried on a voluminous correspondence with thinkers and reformers all over Europe, and he had a powerful voice in the political and educational, as well as the ecclesiastical, institutions of Geneva.

Calvin's major work was the *Institutes of the Christian Religion*, first published in 1536 and originally addressed to King Francis I of France in defense of the French Protestants. It was extensively revised several times, and the last edition, published in 1559, provides a systematic presentation of virtually all the lines of thought found in Calvin's other mature works.

Knowledge of God and self. "Nearly all the wisdom we possess," wrote Calvin in the opening of the *Institutes*, "consists of two parts: the knowledge of God and of ourselves." The overarching question in the *Institutes* is how we acquire this twofold knowledge, and the answers to this question have proved to be the most influential part of Calvin's thought.

Thomas Aquinas had taught that the theologian should start with God and then consider creatures insofar as they relate to God as their beginning and end. Calvin broke decisively with this approach in claiming that knowledge of God is so interrelated with knowledge of ourselves that the one cannot be had without the other. He taught that when we accurately reflect on ourselves, we realize the excellence of our natural gifts; but we also realize that our exercise of these gifts yields "miserable ruin" and unhappiness, and that "our very being is nothing but subsistence in the one God." Without this realization of our misery and dependence—especially of our misery—none of us comes, or even tries to come, to a knowledge of God. On the other hand, there is also no knowledge of self without a knowledge of God. Without a standard by which to measure ourselves, we invariably yield to pride, overestimating the worth of our natural gifts and overlooking the corruption that has resulted from the exercise of those gifts. Calvin readily allowed that "the philosophers," without knowing God, can give us much accurate and worthwhile information concerning man's faculties and constitution (I, XV). However, philosophy cannot yield a true estimate of our worth and condition.

In any discussion of Calvin's views on how we can come to know ourselves and God, it is very important to understand what he meant by knowing God, for his views on this point are both original and subtle. The Scholastics tended to equate knowing God with knowing truths about God. Calvin invariably regarded this as inadequate. He did not deny, indeed he insisted, that knowing God presupposes knowing *about* God. But in addition to this he always maintained that an essential aspect of our knowledge of God is our acknowledgment of his attitude toward us, especially his attitude of benevolence and love. Again, Calvin never equated acknowledging God's benevolence toward us with believing *that* God is benevolent toward us. Rather, acknowledging God's benevolence presupposes worshiping and obeying him. Thus, as Calvin uses the concept "knowing God," there is no knowledge of God apart from worship of, and obedience to, him. For this reason E. A. Dowey has recently said that Calvin conceived of knowledge of God as existential. It may be added that Calvin held, as did many of the Scholastics, that what can be known about God is never his nature (*quid est*), but only what he is like (*qualis est*); and more specifically, what he is like toward us.

How is knowledge of God to be achieved? Calvin always held that knowledge of God can, in principle, be achieved by nourishing one's subjective awareness of deity and its will, with reflection on the structure of the objective world.

"There is," he said, "within the human mind, and indeed by natural instinct, an awareness of divinity [*sensus divinitatis*]" (I, iii, 1). Although this concept of a sense of divinity played a significant role in Calvin's thought, he spent little time elucidating it. Apparently he thought of it as yielding a rudimentary conviction of dependence on some Maker, as well as a numinous awareness of the glory and majesty of the Creator. In support of his conviction that this sense is universal in mankind, Calvin frequently quoted Cicero. It is this universally innate sense of divinity in mankind that, according to Calvin, accounts for the universality of religion in human society. It is a seed of religion (*semen religionis*). Religion is intrinsic to human life; it was not "invented by the subtlety and craft of a few to hold the simple folk in thrall" (I, iii, 2).

In Calvin's thought, conscience (*conscientia*), as a subjective mode of revelation, was closely related to the sense of divinity. Conscience too, he said, is part of the native endowment of all men, written "upon the hearts of all." Typically he spoke of it as a sort of knowledge whose object is God's will; or, equivalently, the difference between good and evil, the law of God, or the law of nature. Thus it is by virtue of conscience that man is aware of his responsibility—aware of the moral demands to which he is subject with respect to God and man. Calvin did not state with any exactitude the actual principles that all men know by virtue of conscience. He did say, however, that "that inward law . . . written, even engraved, upon the hearts of all, in a sense asserts the very same things that are to be learned from the [Decalogue]" (II, viii, 1); and he said that what the Decalogue requires is perfect love of God and of our neighbor.

The subjective awareness of divinity and of its will can be supplemented, Calvin taught, by reflecting on the structure of the external world and the pattern of history. "[God has] not only sowed in men's minds that seed of religion of which we have spoken but revealed himself and daily discloses himself in the whole workmanship of the universe. As a consequence, men cannot open their eyes without being compelled to see him" (I, v, 1). At various times Calvin called the universe at large a book, a mirror, and a theater for the display of God's attributes—preeminently for the display of his goodness to us but also of his glory, wisdom, power, and justice. In the course of expounding his view that God can be known through his works, Calvin explicitly opposed the view that God can be known by speculation concerning his essence. It is by nourishing his sense of divinity and his conscience, with the contemplation of God's works, that man can in principle arrive at a knowledge of God.

Sin. It was Calvin's persistent teaching, however, that in fact no one does come to know God in the manner described above. The positive demands placed on all men by God's internal and external revelation are rejected, and this rejection results in an endless series of spurious religions. This resistance to God's demands is what Calvin identified as sin. Thus sin is not primarily ignorance about God; although such ignorance, or blindness, as Calvin often called it, will always be a consequence. Rather, Calvin viewed sin as an active willful opposition to God, as a positive refusal to acknowledge his demands of worship and obedience and as a deliberate alienation from him. Its prime characteristic is perversity, and its root is ordinarily pride and self-love.

Thus, being in sin is just the opposite of knowing God. Calvin, however, was quite willing to allow that a person who does not know God because he refuses to worship and obey him can still know or believe a variety of propositions about God that happen to be true. This explains what has, to so many readers, proved to be such an infuriating feature of Calvin's thought—his insistence, sometimes in adjacent sentences, that the pagans do not at all know God but are not wholly ignorant of him. For example, Calvin, speaking of man's natural ability to know God, said, ". . . the greatest geniuses are blinder than moles." In the very next sentence he said, "Certainly I do not deny that one can read competent and apt statements about God here and there in the philosophers" (II, ii, 18).

Not only was Calvin insistent that knowing or believing "competent and apt" propositions about God was not sufficient for knowing God; he was also profoundly convinced that man's proud refusal to worship and obey God leads him to resist acknowledging the truth about God. Sin, although primarily a matter of the will, infects man's reason as well. Perversity leads to blindness and distortion. Immediately after saying that the philosophers make competent and apt statements about God, Calvin added, "but these always show a certain giddy imagination. . . . They [the philosophers] saw things in such a way that their seeing did not direct them to the truth, much less enable them to attain it." Thus the consequence of man's willful alienation from God is not merely that he does not know God but also that his views about God are now so incomplete and distorted that nothing at all can be built on them. This is Calvin's judgment on natural theology.

It must be added that Calvin regarded the effects of sin as far more pervasive than have yet been indicated. Not only does sin disrupt man's relation to God; it thereby spreads corruption throughout the whole of human life. Of course, it does not impair our natural faculties as such. Calvin typically spoke of reason and will as man's chief faculties, and he held that the man in sin may be as intelligent and as capable of making decisions as the man who knows God. The corruption is to be found, rather, in the *use* we make of our native capacities.

Calvin maintained that if we are to state accurately what sin does to man's use of his native talents, we must distinguish between man's supernatural gifts, his abilities concerning heavenly things, and his natural gifts, his abilities concerning earthly things (II, ii, 12–13). The supernatural gifts comprise man's ability to know God, to worship him properly, and to obey him inwardly as well as outwardly. However, we have been stripped of these gifts. The natural gifts pertain to matters of the present life, such as government, household management, all mechanical skills, and the liberal arts. Concerning these, said Calvin, our abilities have certainly not been destroyed. Not only are ancient law, medicine, and natural philosophy worthy of the highest admiration (II, ii, 15); but man, even in his estrangement from God, retains some sense of the laws that must be obeyed if human society is to be preserved. Man "tends through natural instinct to foster and preserve society. Consequently, we observe that there exist in all men's minds universal impressions of a certain civic fair dealing and order. . . . And this is ample proof that in the arrangement of this life no man is without the light of reason" (II, ii, 13). Calvin immediately added, however, that although man's abilities concerning earthly things have not been destroyed, they have been profoundly corrupted. In opposition to what he understood as the teaching of the Greek philosophers, he held that both reason and will have been gravely wounded; the mind "is both weak and plunged into deep darkness. And depravity of the will is all too well known" (II, ii, 12).

If man's natural gifts are to be healed and his supernatural gifts restored, his sin must be overcome; he must come to know God. We have already seen that for this purpose man's conscience, his sense of divinity, and his awareness of God's revelation in the objective world are all inadequate. Thus, if human life was to be renewed, it was necessary that God should choose some special means. This he did by revealing himself with special clarity in the history of the Jewish people, culminating in the life and words of Christ. When God leads man to respond to this revelation with faith, then man again knows God. Indeed, faith, consisting as it does in a clear knowledge about God coupled with proper worship and true obedience, is a certain sort of knowledge of God—that sort which focuses on Christ as interpreted in the Scriptures. Thus, in Calvin's thought there is never a contrast between faith in God and knowledge of God; rather, given man's prior perversity, faith is the only kind of knowledge of God available to men. Also, faith, in Calvin's teaching, is never understood in scholastic fashion as an assent to divinely revealed propositions. Rather, the object of faith is God as revealed in Christ.

Social and political teachings. Calvin's social and political theory has also proved most influential. Man, according to Calvin, is a creature of fellowship, created with tendencies that find their fulfillment in a variety of natural groupings, each concerned with a certain facet of man's life in society. One of these groupings is the church, another the state. Church and state are differentiated primarily by reference to their different tasks. The concern of the church is the spiritual realm, the life of the inner man; the concern of the state is the temporal realm, the regulation of external conduct. In regulating external conduct, the general aim of the state, in Calvin's view, is to insure justice or equity in society at large. This equity has two facets. Obviously the state must enforce restrictive justice, but Calvin also believed that the state should secure distributive justice, doing its best to eliminate gross inequalities in the material status of its members.

It is the duty of the church to seek the welfare of the state, but equally it is the duty of the state to seek the welfare of the church. Thus, part of the state's duty is to promote piety; and Calvin, along with most of his contemporaries, regarded blasphemy as a civil crime. However, it was Calvin's view that church and state ought to be structurally independent of each other. Church officials are not, by virtue of their office, to have any official voice in the state; and state officials are not, by virtue of their office, to have any official voice in the church.

Although he thought that the best form of government would vary with circumstances, Calvin quite firmly believed that the ideal government would be a republic in which those of the aristocracy who are competent to rule are elected by the citizenry, and in which power is balanced and diffused among a number of different magistrates. The magistrate has his authority from God. In a sense his authority is God's authority; for magistrates, Calvin said, are ministers of Divine justice, vicegerents of God. Thus the duty of the magistrate is to apply the law of God, implanted on the hearts of all and clarified in the Scriptures, to the affairs of civil society. To what extent and under what circumstances Calvin regarded civil disobedience as justified is a matter of debate. What is clear is that Calvin regarded the law of nature as in some sense a standard by which the decisions of the magistrate are to be judged, and at the same time he regarded revolutions which rip apart the entire fabric of human society as not to be condoned.

Influence. Both the theological and social views of Calvin have had an enormous influence throughout history. The Reformed churches of the Continent and the Presbyterian churches of England adhered fundamentally to his thought, and the dominant theological thought of the American colonies was Calvinistic. In the eighteenth and nineteenth centuries the impact of Calvinism on society and theological thought suffered a decline, but the twentieth century has seen a resurgence in Calvin's influence. In the early part of the century in the Netherlands, Abraham Kuyper led a revival of Calvinism in politics and education as well as in theology. And the so-called neo-orthodox theology, represented by such figures as Karl Barth and Emil Brunner, has not only been accompanied by a renewed interest in the writings of Calvin but also in large measure marks a return to the main patterns of Calvin's theological thought.

Bibliography

The standard edition of Calvin's works is that by J. W. Baum, E. Cunitz, E. Reuss, et al., in the *Corpus Reformatorum*, 59 vols. (Brunswick, Germany, 1863–1900). Most of these were translated by the Calvin Translation Society as *Works*, 48 vols. (Edinburgh, 1843–1855). An especially fine annotated translation is J. T. McNeill, ed., *Calvin: Institutes of the Christian Religion*, translated by F. L. Battles, 2 vols. (Philadelphia, 1959). The classic study of Calvin's life is Émile Doumergue, *Jean Calvin; les hommes et les choses de son temps*, 7 vols. (Lausanne, 1899–1927).

For discussions of the sources of Calvin's thought, see François Wendel, *Calvin: Sources et évolution de sa pensée religieuse* (Paris, 1950), translated by Philip Mairet as *Calvin* (New York, 1963); and Josef Bohatec, *Budé und Calvin* (Graz, Austria, 1940). A good discussion of Calvin's theology as a whole is Wilhelm Niesel, *Die Theologie Calvins* (Munich, 1938), translated by Harold Knight as *The Theology of Calvin* (Philadelphia, 1956). The most adequate discussion of Calvin's views on the knowledge of God is E. A. Dowey, *The Knowledge of God in Calvin's Theology* (New York, 1952). Calvin's doctrine of man is treated in T. F. Torrance, *Calvin's Doctrine of Man* (London, 1949). Calvin's social and political thought is well discussed in André Biéler, *La Pensée économique et sociale de Calvin* (Geneva, 1959); and Josef Bohatec, *Calvins Lehre von Staat und Kirche* (Breslau, 1937). The finest survey of the history of Calvinism is J. T. McNeill, *The History and Character of Calvinism* (New York, 1954).

NICHOLAS WOLTERSTORFF

CAMBRIDGE PLATONISTS, a group of seventeenth-century English moralists, divines, and philosophers. Their moral and religious attitudes derive from Benjamin Whichcote, whose hostility to fanaticism, enthusiasm for Plato, and confidence in reason they all shared.

Whichcote himself published nothing; his role was that of teacher with a gift for pregnant utterance rather than systematic exposition. Ralph Cudworth and Henry More were the most prolific and systematic of the Cambridge Platonists. John Smith devoted himself to the defense of Whichcote's version of Christianity; Gilbert Burnet is best known for his *History of His Own Time* (1724–1734), which includes a sympathetic account of the Platonists; George Rust, John Worthington, and Simon Patrick made their reputations as practical churchmen rather than as philosophers. Rust's *A Discourse of Truth* (1677) is a brief, enthusiastic summary of Cudworth's moral philosophy. Worthington is remembered as the editor of John Smith's sermons and as the author of a diary which throws a certain amount of light on the personal relations of the Platonists, rather than for his *Miscellanies* (1704) and *Discourses* (1725). Patrick probably wrote—it is published with S. P. as the author—*A Brief Account of the New Sect of Latitude-Men* (1662), one of the few contemporary accounts of the Cambridge Platonists; it is particularly interesting because it emphasizes their allegiance to the "mechanical philosophy" of Descartes.

Nathanael Culverwel, Richard Cumberland, and Peter Sterry were influenced by Whichcote without being wholly persuaded by him. Sterry at one time stood very close to Whichcote; he is said to have been the first to "make a public profession of Platonism in the University of Cambridge." He came to feel, however, that the Platonists placed too much emphasis on reason. In direct opposition to Whichcote, Sterry exalted the claims of spirituality above rationality. His writings, indeed, are poetical rather than argumentative in structure, although many a phrase recalls Whichcote's teachings.

These were all Cambridge men. At Oxford, Joseph Glanvill was strongly influenced by More, and John Norris was sympathetically inclined toward the Platonists. Insofar as John Locke was an empiricist, he represented the philosophical tendency to which the Platonists were most opposed, but he was a close friend of Damaris Cudworth, later Lady Masham, Cudworth's daughter; he at least shared the Platonists' religious and moral outlook. Edward Fowler, after taking his first degree at Oxford, studied at Cambridge from 1653 to 1655; in his *The Principles and Practices of Certain Moderate Divines in the Church of England* (1670), he defended the general outlook of Cambridge Platonism. Fowler was violently attacked by John Bunyan for placing undue stress upon a merely human morality, in opposition to the doctrine of "justification by faith"; this is a typical orthodox Puritan reaction to the teachings of the Platonists.

Opposition to Calvinism. The Cambridge members of the Platonic group, except More, were educated at Emmanuel College, Cambridge, which from its foundation in 1583 had been the intellectual center of the Puritan, more particularly of the Calvinist, wing of the Church of England. Whichcote's tutor, Dr. Anthony Tuckney, was a firm adherent of Calvinism. Cambridge Platonism, however, was primarily a rejection of Calvinism as being dogmatic, irrational, and therefore opposed to the true interests of both religion and morality. The Calvinists had conceived of God as operating in an arbitrary manner. For the Cambridge Platonists, in the sharpest possible contrast, God was essentially rational. To be a good Christian was to share in God's rationality, as distinct from blindly obeying an omnipotent will. God, being rational, will ordain what is good, but what he ordains is good in its own nature, not because he ordains it. "To go against Reason," wrote Whichcote, "is to go against God; it is the self same thing, to do that which the Reason of the case doth require; and that which God Himself doth appoint: Reason is the Divine Governor of Man's Life; it is the very Voice of God" (Aphorism 76). Not surprisingly, the orthodox Tuckney complained that in Whichcote's teachings "Reason hath too much given to it."

The Platonists criticized not only the Calvinist doctrine of the relation between God and morality but even more strongly the attempt by the Calvinist party to establish that doctrine as a binding creed. Milton moved in the same intellectual atmosphere as the Platonists and shared many of their beliefs; his "New Presbyter is but old Priest writ large" sums up their attitude. The Platonists had joined with the Calvinists in opposition to Archbishop Laud's attempt to impose high church Anglicanism on the Church of England, but they were no less opposed to the attempt to force Calvinism upon it. They were also quite out of sympathy with the fanatic "enthusiastic" sects which flourished among the non-Calvinistic Puritans. "There is no genuine and proper effect of religion," wrote Whichcote, "where the mind of man is not composed, sedate, and calm" (Discourse LI); the Platonist distrust of "enthusiasm" could scarcely be more succinctly formulated. The Platonists stood for the idea of a single church to which everybody could belong who was neither an atheist nor a papist; this church was conceived of as a broad Christian society within which men could seek salvation in their own way rather than as a sect with a dogmatic creed. Christianity, in the eyes of the Platonists, was a way of life; rituals and creeds could be aids to godliness but nothing more. The nickname "latitude men" or "latitudinarian" which their enemies fastened upon them is an admirable description of their religious attitude.

Philosophical orientation. It is less clear that the name "Cambridge Platonists" suits them. Whichcote, it is true, recommended Plato to his pupils, but what he found in Plato is not what a modern scholar would find there. He was interested in what he took to be the general moral atmosphere of Platonism, its "tranquillity of soul, contempt for worldliness, love of truth, concern for rectitude and justice," rather than its specific doctrines. Also, Plato's insistence that goodness is eternal and immutable provided an intellectual stiffening for Whichcote's opposition to Calvinism.

Cudworth and More, especially, the former were Platonists in a rather more precise sense. But although they read Plato closely, they read him through the eyes of the Neoplatonists and the Florentine Academy. Coleridge thought they ought to be renamed the "Cambridge Plotinists."

Among his philosophical contemporaries Whichcote was most conscious and critical of Francis Bacon. Bacon drew a sharp distinction between reason and faith; religion was a matter of faith, not of reason. Whichcote rejected any such contrast. "What has not reason in it, or for it," he wrote, ". . . is man's superstition: it is not religion of God's making" (Aphorism 102). Cudworth and More were no less hostile to Bacon, but their main philosophical enemy was Hobbes. In certain respects Hobbes and the Calvinists could be merged into a single enemy, for both made morality dependent upon the will, even if in one case it was the will of the sovereign and in the other the will of God. Hobbes's doctrine of experience and knowledge also presented an obvious challenge to any Platonist.

The relation of the Platonists to Descartes is less straightforward. They first welcomed his teachings. More engaged in a long correspondence with him; Cudworth's epistemology and metaphysics owe much to him; Smith drew upon his physiology. They saw in Descartes an ally against empiricism, a reviver of the Platonic conception of knowledge, a defender of Christianity; they welcomed "the new science" insofar as it helped to destroy scholasticism. In the end, however, they came to fear Descartes as a threat to religion. By carrying mechanical explanation too far—into the realm of the living as distinct from the inanimate—he threatened, they thought, the spiritual interpretation of the universe.

Evaluation. For all their emphasis on rationality, there are many points at which the Platonists looked backward rather than forward. Both More and Joseph Glanvill defended the belief in witchcraft, which Puritanism had revived and strengthened; to deny witches and apparitions, they argued, would lead straight to atheism. At times they displayed a degree of credulity which is somewhat startling even by seventeenth-century standards. Careful reasoning, exact argumentation, and liberality of spirit were joined with uncritical speculation, unscholarly interpretation, and fanciful legends to a degree which bewilders and confuses the modern reader. These characteristics do not apply to Whichcote himself, who scarcely ventured into metaphysics or scholarship, but they make the study of More and Cudworth, interesting and important though many of their ideas are, difficult and often very tedious. To ignore the Platonists, however, is to run the risk of misunderstanding and grossly oversimplifying the history of British speculative ideas and moral attitudes, which are too often taken to be wholly dominated by empiricist and utilitarian concepts. Undoubtedly, too, for all the vagaries of More and Glanvill, the general effect of Cambridge Platonism was to increase men's confidence in rationality and their willingness to tolerate beliefs with which they disagreed.

Of those who felt their influence, the third earl of Shaftesbury and Richard Price both derived their leading ideas from Cambridge Platonist sources. Outside professional philosophy they have won the admiration of men as different as John Wesley, Samuel Taylor Coleridge, and Matthew Arnold. They have never been fashionable, even in their own age their appeal was restricted to a relatively narrow circle. Unlike most of their philosophical-theological contemporaries, however, they have never been entirely forgotten or uninfluential.

Bibliography

See WHICHCOTE, MORE, CUDWORTH, SMITH, CULVERWEL, NORRIS, and GLANVILL for their writings. There are selections from Whichcote, Smith, and Culverwel in Ernest Trafford Campagnac, *The Cambridge Platonists* (Oxford, 1901). The diary and correspondence of John Worthington have been published in *Remains Historical and Literary* of the Chetham Society, Manchester, Vol. 13 (1847), Vol. 36 (1855), Vol. 114 (1886). The 1826 edition of Worthington's *Select Discourses* (London) also includes a number of his minor writings. George Rust's *A Discourse of Truth* and Joseph Glanvill's *Lux Orientalis* were printed as *Two Choice and Useful Treatises,* edited with notes by Henry More (London, 1677). Rust's *A Discourse of the Use of Reason in Matters of Religion, Shewing that Christianity Contains Nothing Repugnant to Right Reason, Against Enthusiasts and Deists* was translated from the Latin and annotated by H. Hallywell (London, 1683). Vivian de Sola Pinto (the Elder), *Peter Sterry, Platonist and Puritan* (Cambridge, 1934), contains selections from Sterry and a bibliography.

The best study of the Cambridge Platonists is still John Tulloch, *Rational Theology and Christian Philosophy in England in the Seventeenth Century,* 2 vols. (London and Edinburgh, 1872). See also John Alexander Stewart, "The Cambridge Platonists," in *Encyclopedia of Religion and Ethics* (London, 1911), Vol. III; Edwin Arthur Burtt, *The Metaphysical Foundations of Modern Physical Science* (London, 1925); Frederick James Powicke, *The Cambridge Platonists* (London, 1926), especially good for Sterry; Marjorie Nicolson, "Christ's College and the Latitude-men," in *Modern Philology,* Vol. 27, No. 1 (1929), 35–53; Geoffrey Philip Henry Pawson, *The Cambridge Platonists* (London, 1930); John Henry Muirhead, *The Platonic Tradition in Anglo-Saxon Philosophy* (London, 1931); Ernst Cassirer, *The Platonic Renaissance in England,* translated by J. P. Pettegrove (Edinburgh, 1953); William Fraser Mitchell, *English Pulpit Oratory* (London, New York, and Toronto, 1932); Basil Willey, *The Seventeenth Century Background* (London, 1934); Wilbur Kitchener Jordon, *The Development of Religious Toleration in England* (London, 1940), Vol. IV; Gerald Robertson Cragg, *From Puritanism to the Age of Reason* (Cambridge, 1950); Charles Earle Raven, *Natural Religion and Christian Theology* (Cambridge, 1953); Rosalie Littell Colie, *Light and Enlightenment: A Study of the Cambridge Platonists and the Dutch Arminians* (Cambridge, 1957); and J. E. Saveson, "Differing Reactions to Descartes among the Cambridge Platonists," in *Journal of the History of Ideas,* Vol. 21, No. 4 (1960), 560–567. For a fuller bibliography see John Arthur Passmore, *Ralph Cudworth* (Cambridge, 1951).

JOHN PASSMORE

CAMPANELLA, TOMMASO (1568–1639), a Renaissance philosopher and scholar, was born at Stilo, in Calabria, Italy. At an early age he entered the Dominican order and devoted himself to the study of philosophy. In 1599 he was arrested by order of the Spanish government on charges of heresy and conspiracy. Although he never confessed to either charge, he was considered to be a dangerous subject and was kept in prison at Naples for 27 years. Released in 1626, he was arrested again and arraigned before the Holy Office in Rome to stand trial for certain suspect propositions found in his works. After regaining his freedom, he spent some time at the Dominican monastery of Minerva in that city. In 1634, fearing further persecution, because of the suspicion that he might be involved in a new conspiracy, he followed the advice of Pope Urban VIII and fled to France, where he was befriended by Cardinal Richelieu and King Louis XIII. He died in the quiet of the Dominican monastery of Rue St. Honoré in Paris.

Campanella wrote a great number of books dealing with subjects ranging from grammar and rhetoric to philosophy and theology, from apologetics to politics, and from medicine to magic and astrology. He conceived of philosophy as an all-embracing science to which all other sciences must be referred as their ultimate source and foundation. No subsidiary science deals with all things as they are, but only as they appear, whereas philosophy, and especially metaphysics, deals with all things as they are and insofar as they are. Philosophy is an inquiry after the truth of both human and divine things, based on the testimony of God, who reveals himself either through the world of created things or by direct teaching. Consequently, nature and the Scriptures are the two codes on which philosophy must be built.

Epistemology. In his actual approach to philosophy, Campanella discussed first the possibility and reality of knowledge, thus anticipating a common trend among later thinkers. He was the first philosopher (antedating Descartes) to assert the need of positing a universal doubt at the beginning of his system and to state the principle of self-consciousness as the basis of knowledge and certitude. He distinguished between innate and acquired knowledge. Innate knowledge (*notitia innata*) is cognition through self-presence and belongs to the very essence of the soul; acquired knowledge (*notitia illata*) is the soul's cognition of external things. Innate knowledge is superior to, and more certain than, acquired knowledge; for the soul cannot be mistaken about what belongs to its nature. Knowledge of the external world can be obtained either by intuition or by abstraction. By intuition one grasps a thing immediately in its concrete reality, so that nothing of the object escapes the penetrating and all-embracing act of the intellect. By abstraction, one obtains only an indistinct and confused image of a thing. This image is what Campanella called the Aristotelian universal and is the object of both sense and intellect. The Platonic universal, on the contrary, is the idea as the formal cause of a thing and can be grasped exclusively by the intellect.

As to the essence and process of knowledge, Campanella gave a twofold explanation. A first explanation is contained in his early works and developed along the general lines of Bernardino Telesio's system. It represents his empirical approach to knowledge, which he reduced mainly to sensation and explained in terms of partial assimilation of the object known. This assimilation is made by contact between the knower and the sensible species of the object known. These species are neither the intentional species of the Aristotelians nor the corporeal images of Democritus. Although they may assume as many different forms as there are sensations, they are always something material that impinges on the senses and represents to a certain extent the external object.

A second and more advanced explanation of knowledge is what may be called the metaphysical approach from the standpoint of the soul as an essentially knowing nature. Here we meet Campanella's characteristic doctrine that to know is to be (*cognoscere est esse*). In this new approach, knowledge is still called sensation and assimilation, but the assimilation is carried so far as to mean a real transformation of the knower into the object known. This doctrine that to know is "being" or "to be" must not be understood in the idealistic sense of the absolute identity of object and subject. Campanella introduced a distinction between knowledge that a person has of himself in virtue of his own nature and knowledge that a person acquires from outside himself. Campanella called this the distinction between "innate" and "illate" knowledge. Both types of knowledge are said to belong to "being": but the former refers to knowledge of the original being of the knower, and the latter refers to the knowledge of being that is inferred by reasoning and is formally distinct from the being of the knower. In the first case, knowledge *is* the *esse;* in the second case, it becomes intentionally the *esse* in the possession of the extramental reality.

Metaphysics. For Campanella the object of metaphysics is "being," namely, whatever exists either within or outside our mind. He denied a real distinction between essence and existence in creatures, but admitted a real distinction between essence and extrinsic existence, or that type of existence that corresponds to the particular circumstances and environment wherein an essence happens to be in the physical world. All things, whether spiritual or material, consist ultimately, although in different degrees, of power, knowledge, and love as their transcendental principles. These are called "primalities" and are found in creatures as well as in God, of whom creatures are faint imitations. Whereas God is pure and infinite being, creatures are composites of finite being and infinite nonbeing. Being and nonbeing concur in making up finite things, not as physical components but as metaphysical principles. Just as a creature is essentially and necessarily a particular and limited entity, so it also is essentially and necessarily the nonbeing of all other things and of God himself.

Psychology. In psychology Campanella accepted the trichotomic theory, according to which man is a composite of three substances, body, spirit, and mind or *mens*. The spirit or sensitive soul is the corporeal principle that animates the body and serves as a link between body and mind. The mind or intellective soul is created and infused by God into the body already organized by the spirit; it is a spiritual substance and the form of the whole man. With the Platonists, Campanella defended the doctrine of a world soul, and developed the theory of universal animation by endowing all things with some kind of sensation.

Philosophy of nature. Campanella was greatly influenced by Telesio's *De Rerum Natura*, which he defended against the attacks of G. A. Marta (1559–1628). He conceived of space as a primary and incorporeal substance having the capacity to receive all bodies. Space is the substratum of all things. In this space God placed matter, a body that is formless and inactive but capable of being molded into many forms, just as wax is acted upon by a seal. Matter is not pure potency, as Aristotle taught, but has a reality of its own distinct from the form. This, in turn, is not a substantial principle of material beings and is only improperly called an act. In short, Campanella dismissed the Aristotelian hylomorphic theory and substituted for it Telesio's naturalistic doctrine of heat and cold as the active principles and matter as the passive principle of all material beings. He also rejected Aristotle's notion of time as measure of movement and claimed that time is not something ideal and subjective, but something real. Time is the successive duration of things having a beginning and an end. Or, more concretely, time is the thing itself considered in its successive duration through change.

Ethics. Following Telesio, Campanella taught that man's supreme good consists in self-preservation. However, this must not be understood in a purely egoistic sense, but rather as the conservation of one's existence in God in the next life. Whereas God is his own supreme good and does not look to another being outside himself for his preservation, so that to be and to be happy are for him one and the same thing, man depends entirely on God for his own preservation. God is therefore the supreme good toward which man must direct all his acts and operations.

Political theory. Campanella advocated a universal monarchy with the pope as its supreme temporal and spiritual ruler. This ambitious but hardly realistic plan is described in the *Monarchia Messiae* ("The Messiah's Monarchy") and represented the dream of his entire life. *Civitas Solis* (*The City of the Sun*), on the other hand, contains the scheme of a state modeled after Plato's *Republic* and Sir Thomas More's *Utopia*, where people, who live in the pure order of nature, organize themselves into an ideal society ruled by philosophers and share everything. Many of the ideas expressed in this work have some practical value, inasmuch as they contain the germs of social, political, and educational reforms that would be beneficial to the state. In this respect, Campanella may be considered as an original thinker and a forerunner of various modern theories and practices.

Principal Works by Campanella

Philosophia Sensibus Demonstrata, in defense of Telesio. Naples, 1591.

Monarchia Messiae. Jesi, 1633.

Atheismus Triumphatus. Paris, 1636.

Disputationum in Quatuor Partes Suae Philosophiae Reales Libri Quatuor. Paris, 1637.

Philosophiae Rationalis Partes Quinque. Paris, 1638.

Universalis Philosophiae, seu Metaphysicarum Rerum Iuxta Propria Dogmata Partes Tres, Libri 18. Paris, 1638.

Del senso delle cose e della magia, A. Bruers, ed. Bari, 1925.

Epilogo Magno, C. Ottaviano, ed. Rome, 1939.

Theologicorum Libri XXX, R. Amerio, ed. Florence and Rome, 1949——.

Civitas Solis. Frankfurt, 1623. Translated by W. J. Gilstrap as *The City of the Sun*. New York, 1952.

Works on Campanella

Amerio, Romano, *Campanella*. Brescia, 1947.

Bonansea, Bernardine M., "Campanella as Forerunner of Descartes." *Franciscan Studies*, Vol. 16, Nos. 1 and 2 (1956), 37–59.

Bonansea, Bernardine M., "The Concept of Being and Nonbeing in the Philosophy of Tommaso Campanella." *The New Scholasticism*, Vol. 31, No. 1 (1957), 34–67.

Bonansea, Bernardine M., "Knowledge of the Extramental World in the System of Tommaso Campanella." *Franciscan Studies*, Vol. 17, Nos. 2 and 3 (1957), 188–212.

Bonansea, Bernardine M., "The Political Thought of Tommaso Campanella," in John K. Ryan, ed., *Studies in Philosophy and the History of Philosophy*. Washington, D.C., 1963. Vol. II, pp. 211–248.

Corsano, Antonio, *Tommaso Campanella*. Bari, 1961.

Di Napoli, Giovanni, *Tommaso Campanella, filosofo della restaurazione cattolica*. Padua, 1947.

BERNARDINE M. BONANSEA, O.F.M.

CAMPBELL, NORMAN ROBERT (1880–1949), English physicist and philosopher of science, was educated at Eton. From Eton he went as a scholar to Trinity College, Cambridge, and became a fellow there in 1904. From 1903 to 1910 he also worked as a research assistant at the Cavendish Laboratory, whose director, the celebrated J. J. Thomson, became the most important inspiration of his scientific work. In 1913 he became an honorary fellow for research in physics at Leeds University, but he left this post after the war and from 1919 to 1944 was a member of the research staff of the General Electric Company.

The writers who seem to have influenced him most are Ernst Mach and Henri Poincaré, apart from classical authors like Whewell, Mill, and W. S. Jevons. On the other hand, philosophers like Russell and Whitehead came too late to have much effect on him; the main outlines of his thought developed during the first decade of the century, and there are only occasional references to their writings.

Campbell exhibited the very rare combination of competence in both physics and philosophy, but while he preferred to think of himself primarily as an experimental physicist, it is as a philosopher of science that he made his mark. This point is brought out in the writings of F. P. Ramsey, R. B. Braithwaite, and Ernest Nagel, although these concentrate largely on the formal parts of Campbell's doctrines and pay scant attention to the more valuable contributions that he made to certain methodological ideas, particularly that of analogy. These philosophical views, shaped by Campbell's actual experiences and ideas as a physicist and expositor of physical theories, were meant to be construed as answers to intellectual pressures and problems that confronted him in the years that saw the rise of the twentieth-century atomic theory on the one hand and relativity and quantum mechanics on the other. In philosophy of science, his most important contributions were in the fields of the logic of theory construction and (to a lesser extent) the principles of physical measurement.

Philosophy of theory construction. Campbell's views were stated in systematic form for the first time in a popular book, *The Principles of Electricity*. Thereafter they were developed, with minor changes of emphasis and greater attention to the nature of "mathematical theories," in *Physics: The Elements*. In contrast with the usual textbook approach, his views were deeply interwoven with, and at times even explicitly discussed in, his more formal scientific treatises.

Concepts and ideas. Campbell distinguishes sharply between the laws and theories of a science. In the case of laws, the constituent terms (Campbell calls them concepts) designate entities whose magnitudes may be determined more or less directly by instrumental means; they are not unlike what later came to be called operational concepts. The explanatory part of theories, the hypotheses, involve terms that Campbell calls ideas. These lack the instrumental relations of concepts, for a variety of reasons that Campbell does not always clearly distinguish.

Sometimes the ideas refer to the unobservable infrastructure of a physical system, as in the case of the atoms and electrons of modern electrical theory or, more properly (as Campbell points out), to their adjectival aspects, such as their mass, velocity, and momentum. At other times, the ideas pertain to such interstructural devices as Faraday's lines of force, or the carriers of the transfer of electrical and optical phenomena, such as light waves, light corpuscles (photons) or even the "aether," considered the substantival carrier of electromagnetic energy. (Infrastructural entities are unobservable in a sense different from interstructural ones, but the question is controversial.) A third case in which theories are said to involve unobservables is that of geological and evolutionary theories. And there is yet another case, for Campbell denominates certain notions "ideas" because they involve an amount of idealization and abstraction to which no physical entities could correspond. The most frequent and important cases are those ideas which involve infinitesimals, such as the differential coefficients in Maxwell's equations or Fourier's theory of heat.

It follows from the nature of ideas that the hypotheses in which they occur are not directly testable. Their function consists merely in systematically relating a set of corresponding laws, and, through extensions of the theory, in foreshadowing further laws and experiments. This foreshadowing is sometimes negative, for when the ideas are too narrowly framed, they demand not only extension but also the formulation of additional concepts and theories.

"Dictionary" of a theory. Since the ideas of the hypotheses lack operational meaning, and since their deductive development can, in the first place, yield only statement forms containing either ideas or combinations of them, it is necessary to add certain rules (a kind of "dictionary") that will coordinate the ideas with those operational concepts which occur in the laws to be explained. Of course, not all ideas need dictionary entries. In the beta-ray theory, for instance, the velocity, v, of the hypothetical electrons *means* "the quantity that is defined by the relation $F=e[X+(v \cdot H)]$." However, this expression is a hypothesis in Campbell's sense because v never occurs either alone or in combination in the testable derivations at all.

"Mathematical" theories. All this provided Campbell with a means of distinguishing so-called mathematical theories from nonmathematical ones. In the former, each and every idea is separately coordinated with a corresponding concept by means of a dictionary entry. It follows that whether a theory is of the mathematical type depends partly on historical accidents: Maxwell's theory *became* a mathematical theory only *after* Hertz's experiment had demonstrated the existence of the displacement current.

Nonetheless, ideas so far have no meaning apart from their use in hypotheses and their coordination with concepts. In the mathematical cases this is often forgotten, but in the nonmathematical cases this fact is more difficult to overlook. Because of the lack of independent significance of ideas, Campbell held that a theory is not a real explanation unless certain additional requirements are satisfied. One of his reasons for this view was that it is always possible to construct an indefinite number of hypotheses that would account for a set of laws. In the case of mathematical theories, the additional element of consolidation that Campbell suggests is the regulative feature of simplicity and aesthetic elegance—for instance, through symmetrical arrangements of the parts of a theory. (Thus, it was the introduction of Maxwell's displacement current into the original equations of Ampère and Faraday that produced a symmetrical set of equations regarding the relations between the electrical and magnetic phenomena for the case of open circuits.) Furthermore, the hypotheses are not entirely arbitrary because their ideas mirror the corresponding concepts of the laws. There is, according to Campbell, a sort of analogy between ideas and concepts (*Physics: The Elements*, p. 141).

Analogy. Analogy plays a more central role in the case of the nonmathematical theories. As we have seen, their ideas frequently cannot be clarified at all by the concepts that occur in the laws. According to Campbell, it is an analogy of the hypotheses and their ideas with corresponding laws and concepts of some testable field of science that imparts the missing element of significance and logical strength to the theory. It follows that analogies are not merely aids to the establishment of theories; "they are an utterly essential part of theories, without which theories would be completely valueless and unworthy of the name" (*ibid.*, p. 129).

Campbell's point is that "a theory is not a law" (*ibid.*, p. 130); that hypotheses are, from the nature of the case, never directly testable; and, hence, that their addition to the corpus of scientific knowledge would make no difference to science at all if it were not for some additional features that make the hypotheses significant. He dismisses the fact that they supply a systematic relation between the laws of the theory on the grounds that an infinity of such hypotheses can be constructed.

Campbell's positive grounds for the necessity of analogies are of various kinds. The fundamental reason is that since hypotheses are not directly testable but are only instruments for deductive development, possessing a purely formal content, they lack the sort of meaning required for genuine explanatory power: only analogy can supply this. Another ground of a more heuristic nature is that analogies aid in the extension of theories, especially when a new field is grafted onto the dictionary of an existing theory (as when optical conceptions were added to Maxwell's generalization of the electrical theories of Ampère and Faraday).

However, as mentioned, analogy must be supplemented by additional criteria, which are clearly needed for dealing with mathematical theories. These criteria are largely derived from Campbell's actual experience with the theories with which he had been dealing in his physical textbooks. In addition to simplicity and aesthetic elegance, there is "simplification in our physical conceptions," such as was produced by the early theories of Faraday, Thomson, and Lorentz. Campbell insists on the importance of such regulative conceptions precisely because "scientific propositions are [not] capable of direct and irrefutable proof." An additional criterion is the "anticipative force" of a theory—for instance, the suggestiveness of Faraday's lines in the direction of the existence of electromagnetic radiation, of a motion that is displaced in time, with a given velocity, in empty space.

Finally, another regulative criterion is that of importance, or depth, of the ideas involved. This is invoked particularly in those cases where analogy is barely a relevant consideration, as in such mathematical theories as Maxwell's, or Einstein's special theory of relativity.

Methodological contributions. Campbell's clear account of the logical structure of a theory, with its hypotheses, laws, and dictionary, offers an elegant means of formalizing the place of ideas (theoretical concepts) within theories. He emphasizes also the logical gap between hypotheses and laws even in cases where its existence had previously been practically overlooked—the mathematical theories. He uses this fact to question Mach's preference for such theories (called phenomenological by Mach), on the grounds that they employ hypotheses and hypothetical ideas just like any other theory. (Whether this does sufficient justice to the difference between the two types of theories must be left an open question.) The theoretical nature of such substantival entities as atoms and electrons seems to differ from that of lines of force on the one hand and, say, from the entropy functions on the other, in deeper ways not caught by Campbell's criteria of ideas.

The fact that the systematizing power of hypotheses is an insufficient criterion of their truth or explanatory power introduces the remaining feature of Campbell's doctrine—such regulative notions as the existence of a strong analogy, of simplicity, symmetry, anticipative force, and, finally, of importance. The most interesting of these is analogy, which in the end emerges as a metaphysical device in terms of which to formulate the special aspect of those theories that involve unobservables. The "absolute necessity" for an analogy is the result of the emasculation of the semantic power of hypotheses, coupled with the consideration that this emasculation entails the introduction of a special constraint that prevents such hypotheses from being mere arbitrary formulas.

Theory of measurement. The second part of *Physics: The Elements* is a detailed discussion of the principles of physical measurement; this, like most of Campbell's ideas, was already contained in embryo in *The Principles of Electricity* (Ch. 2). His interest in measurement is not altogether removed from his main philosophical preoccupations mentioned so far. Just as he was concerned with a clear delineation of laws from theories, he was equally firm in stating the differences as well as the relations between laws and definitions. In *Measurement and Calculation* Campbell defines measurement "as the assignment of numerals to present properties in accordance with . . . laws. Thus, every measurable property must have a definite order; the systems to be measured must be capable of "addition," but what operation is considered "addition" must be carefully specified in a given situation; and whether the resultant quantities yield consistent measurements is a matter for lawlike experience. Campbell points out that the specification in question is usually tacitly adopted *ab initio* and is, indeed, often suggested by theory and the relevant analogy. Hence, he believes that "no new measurable quantity has ever been introduced into physics exept as the result of the suggestion of some theory" (*The Principles of Electricity,* p. 41).

Bibliography

Campbell's works include *Modern Electrical Theory* (Cambridge, 1907; 2d ed., 1913); *The Principles of Electricity* (London, 1912); *Physics: The Elements* (Cambridge, 1920), which was reprinted as *Foundations of Science* (New York, 1957); *Measurement and Calculation* (London, 1928); and *Photoelectric Cells,* written with Dorothy Ritchie (London, 1929; 3d ed., 1934).

As supplementary chapters of *Modern Electrical Theory,* the following monographs by Campbell were published in the Cambridge Physical Series: *Series Spectra,* Suppl. Ch. 15 (Cambridge, 1921); *Relativity,* Suppl. Ch. 16 (Cambridge, 1923); and *The Structure of the Atom,* Suppl. Ch. 17 (Cambridge, 1923).

For works with detailed references to Campbell, see Brian D. Ellis, *Basic Concepts of Measurement* (Cambridge, 1965), Chs. 4, 5, and 8; Mary B. Hesse, *Models and Analogies in Science* (London, 1963), Ch. 1; and George Schlesinger, *Method in the Physical Sciences* (London, 1963), Ch. 3, Sec. 5.

GERD BUCHDAHL

CAMUS, ALBERT (1913–1960), French novelist and essayist, was born in Mondovi, Algeria, and was educated at the University of Algiers. From 1934 to 1939 he was active writing and producing plays for a theater group he had founded in Algiers. About the same time he began his career as a journalist, and in 1940 he moved to Paris. During the German occupation of France, Camus was active in the resistance movement, and after the liberation of Paris he became the editor of the previously clandestine newspaper *Combat.* His literary fame dates from the publication in 1942 of his first novel, *L'Étranger* (*The Stranger*), and an essay entitled *Le Mythe de Sisyphe* (*The Myth of Sisyphus*). During the immediate postwar period Camus was deeply involved in political activity, and his name was for a time closely associated with that of Jean-Paul Sartre and with the existentialist movement. In 1947 he published a second major novel, *La Peste* (*The Plague*), and, in 1951, *L'Homme revolté* (*The Rebel*), an essay on the idea of revolt. The latter book provoked a bitter controversy between Camus and Sartre, which ended with a severance of relations between them. In 1957 Camus was awarded the Nobel Prize for literature. His last major work was *La Chute* (*The Fall*), a novel that appeared in 1956. In 1960 Camus was killed in an automobile accident.

Although Camus studied philosophy for a number of years at the University of Algiers, he was not a philosopher in any technical or academic sense. Nevertheless, virtually all his literary work was deeply influenced by philosophical ideas, and in two major essays, *The Myth of Sisyphus* and *The Rebel,* he undertook a more or less systematic exposition and defense of the moral attitudes that had in each case found expression in his novels and plays. *The Myth of Sisyphus* can thus be regarded as in some sense a philosophical commentary on *The Stranger,* and *The Rebel* has clear affinities with *The Plague.* There can be no doubt that there are profound differences between the views set forth in these two essays. Camus's philosophical career was essentially a movement away from the nihilism of *The Myth of Sisyphus* toward the humanism of *The Rebel.* Ideas that had been present in his work from the beginning, in one form or another, were to retain their place there; but he progressively revised his views of their relative importance within the moral life.

Although Camus's name is often associated with contemporary European phenomenology and existentialism, there is no evidence that he was ever deeply influenced by, or very much interested in, the doctrines of Husserl or Heidegger or even Sartre; and on occasion he expressed himself as having distinct reservations with respect to existentialism as a philosophy. In fact, his philosophical thought was formed on much more traditional models. His deepest interest was in those great figures in the Western philosophical tradition—among them Socrates, Pascal, Spinoza, and Nietzsche—whose lives and personalities were all reflected in their philosophizing. If he came, as he did, to reject the exaggerated claims that philosophers have made for human reason and subscribed to many of the criticisms that contemporary existentialists have made of the classical tradition, he continued to regard the striving of the great thinkers of the past to achieve a total conception of reality and of man's relation to the world as reflecting one of the deepest human aspirations and to view its inevitable failure as marking a crisis in man's relation to himself. On the other hand, Camus does not appear to have had any theoretical interest in the analysis of philosophical problems. His interest in philosophy was almost exclusively moral in character; when he had come to the conclusion that none of the speculative systems of the past could provide any positive guidance for human life or any guarantee of the validity of human values, he found himself in the situation that he describes in *The Myth of Sisyphus.* This essay is ostensibly a consideration of the problem of suicide, which Camus describes as the only serious philosophical problem. The question he asks is whether it makes any sense to go on living once the meaninglessness of human life is fully understood and assimilated. Camus gives a number of somewhat different formulations of what this meaninglessness or "absurdity" comprises. At bottom, it is the failure of the world to satisfy the human demand that it provide a basis for human values—for our personal ideals and for our judgments of right and wrong.

It is very important for an understanding of Camus's point of view to see how closely he thought ordinary moral attitudes are dependent upon metaphysical belief in some kind of congruence between human values and the nature of reality. The external supports on which the validity of moral distinctions rested in the past were, of course, primarily religious in character; but Camus held, as do many others, that with the decline of religious belief in the modern period a number of secular religions—in particular, Hegelian and Marxist historicism—have attempted to tie values to reality by means of a postulated schedule of historical development that guarantees their eventual realization. In *The Myth of Sisyphus*, Camus presupposes, without very much argument, that none of these interpretations of reality as value-supporting can survive critical scrutiny; the tenability of any purposive or evaluative attitude on the part of human beings—the only moral beings—is thus called into question. It is this isolation of man as an evaluative and purposive being in a world that affords no support to such attitudes that Camus calls the absurdity of the human condition.

Camus maintained that suicide cannot be regarded as an adequate response to the experience of absurdity. The reason he gives is that suicide deals with absurdity simply by suppressing one of the two poles—the human being and the "world"—that together produce the tension described above. Suicide is thus an admission of incapacity, and such an admission is inconsistent with that human pride to which Camus openly appeals. Indeed, he goes so far as to say that "there is nothing equal to the spectacle of human pride." Only by going on living in the face of their own absurdity can human beings achieve their full stature. For Camus, as for Nietzsche, whose influence at this stage of Camus's thought is very marked, the conscious espousal of the metaphysical arbitrariness of human purpose and action transforms nihilism from a passive despair into a way of revolting against and transcending the world's indifference to man.

It is evident that in *The Myth of Sisyphus* Camus believed that absurdity, in the sense of recognition and acceptance of the fact that there are no metaphysically guaranteed directives for conduct, could by itself generate a positive ethic. In particular, the ideal of human fraternity was connected with Camus's heroic nihilism on the grounds that to accept oneself as the sole guarantor of one's own values would necessarily involve accepting a principle of respect for other human beings. It is here, however, that Camus encountered a very serious difficulty. He found it necessary to show by means of examples just what the specific implications for conduct of his doctrine of absurdity are and also make it plausible that these implications are consistent with the humanistic ideal to which he as an individual is clearly devoted. In *The Myth of Sisyphus*, however, the specimens that are offered of the mode of life appropriate to the "absurd" man bear only a rather remote affinity to that ideal or, for that matter, to any general social ethic. Camus did not demonstrate satisfactorily either that the kind of life that followed from an acceptance of nihilism bore any clear relation to his own moral ideals or that a life dedicated to these ideals could be adequately motivated by an acceptance of absurdity.

What is clear is that Camus, from the beginning, regarded certain responses to absurdity as morally unacceptable. In his "Letters to a German Friend" (1943–1944), he interpreted Nazism as one reaction to the very nihilistic vision of the world that he himself had come to accept. He then went on to condemn it in the severest terms for its denial of human fraternity. Even at this stage in the development of his thought, Camus insisted that an authentic revolt against the human condition had to be a revolt in the name of the solidarity of man with man.

In the character of Meursault, the "hero" of *The Stranger*, this tension between Camus's nihilistic vision and his ethical demands becomes particularly clear. Meursault is presented as a man characterized by the moral equivalent of achromatic vision. Although he is not at all given to philosophical reflection, he views the whole conventional human apparatus of moral distinctions, of justice and of guilt, as a kind of senseless rigmarole with no basis in reality. He stands, in fact, outside the whole moral world in a peculiar state that Camus describes as "innocence," apparently because in a world that affords no transcendental sanction for human judgments of right and wrong there can be no real guilt. His relationship to his mother and to his mistress are devoid of feeling, and he eventually kills an Arab for no particular reason. But at the very end of the novel, after Meursault, facing execution, has burst into a rage against a priest who tries to persuade him to accept the reality of his guilt and the possibility of redemption, there is a long semipoetic passage in which he declares his love of the world and its sensuous immediacy and speaks tenderly and almost lovingly of his fellow men and of their common fate, which he shares. As a number of critics have noted, there is nothing in the novel that prepares one for this passage. Camus, however, clearly wishes to persuade us that these two aspects of Meursault's character are not just consistent but intimately related to one another; but again he experienced difficulty in showing how a positive ethic of human fraternity can be generated by a nihilistic attitude toward all values.

There can be little doubt that in the years immediately following the publication of *The Stranger* and *The Myth of Sisyphus* Camus substantially revised his view of the moral significance of value-nihilism. Increasingly, it was the injustice and cruelty of man to man that aroused Camus to action; by comparison with the hideous but remediable evils of human society, the cosmic injustice of the human condition seems to have lost some of its obsessive hold on his mind. Like many of the existentialists, Camus still tried to present these two revolts—the revolt against the human condition and the revolt against human injustice—as essentially continuous with one another. Nevertheless, he came to feel that the relationship between these two revolts had been misconceived and that this misconception was at the heart of twentieth-century totalitarianism, to which he was as resolutely opposed in its communistic as in its Nazi version. Camus gradually came to believe that the reason for the extraordinary miscarriage of the Soviet revolution was that the revolutionary tradition had its roots in a revolt against the human condition as such, and that such a revolt can never lead to human fraternity but leads instead to a new enslavement of man by man. This radical revision of his earlier views found its full expression in Camus's second main philosophical essay, *The Rebel.*

The Rebel begins with a consideration of the problem of murder or, more exactly, with the problem of political justification for the killing of human beings. For Camus, political action is essentially violent revolt, and it thus inescapably raises the question of whether one has the right to take the life of another human being. Camus's answer is that taking a human life is inconsistent with true revolt since, as he now makes clear, that revolt involves the implicit assertion of a supraindividual value, the value of human life. It is not altogether clear how this rejection of violence is to be interpreted, but it is interesting to note the approval that Camus expresses in his play *The Just* (1950) of the Russian terrorist Kaliaev who murders the Grand Duke Serge but insists that he himself pay for his act with his life in order to affirm the moral inadmissibility of murder. In any case, the revolt that Camus still advocates in *The Rebel* is presented there as ethically inspired from its inception. He rejects, however, what he now calls "metaphysical revolt," which he sees as a radical refusal of the human condition as such, resulting either in suicide or in a demonic attempt to depose God and remake the world in the image of man. Its deepest motive is not a love for mankind but a desire to destroy the world as it is. The order it attempts to impose on the new world it constructs is informed by no ethically creative principle because, as Camus now declares, nihilism can yield no such principle. A nightmare state of power for power's sake is the ultimate fruit of metaphysical revolt.

In order to substantiate this thesis, Camus reviews the intellectual history of the past two hundred years and discusses in detail a number of poets, philosophers, and practicing revolutionaries whom he regards as the chief fomentors of metaphysical revolt. Among them are the Marquis de Sade, Max Stirner, Nietzsche, Lautréamont, Saint-Just, and Nechaiev, to mention only a few. Hegel and Marx are assigned a central role in the construction of a view of history and of the state that exempts man from all moral controls and that proposes as the only valid ideal man's total mastery of his own fate. The two political revolutions that Camus thinks were inspired by the ethos of metaphysical revolt are the French and the Russian, although the Nazi "revolution" represents some of the same tendencies in even purer form. Camus considers none of the modern revolutions that did not eventuate in political terrorism, and he makes no attempt to evaluate or even consider other kinds of explanation of the revolutions that he does discuss. As many critics have remarked, the apocalyptic character of the historical tableau that he presents is in good part due to a principle of selection that seems to reflect a personal predilection for extreme or crisis situations rather than any objective assessment of the real influence that the representatives of metaphysical revolt may have had on the course of events.

Camus's novel *The Plague*, which appeared four years before *The Rebel*, gives clear indications of his re-evaluation of nihilism. The plague that descends on Oran symbolizes not just the Nazi occupation of France or even totalitarianism as a political system but all of the many forms that injustice and inhumanity can assume. A variety of reactions to this "plague" is presented; but it is Dr. Rieux, the organizer of the "sanitation squads" that fight the plague, who represents Camus's ideal of moral action. Rieux is not inspired by any dream of a total conquest of evil. Instead, his conception of himself is modest and limited; throughout the struggle he retains his sense of humanity and his capacity for love and for happiness. The doctor is in fact what many have said Camus aspired to be, a kind of "saint without a God."

If *The Rebel* and *The Plague* represent—as they seem to do—Camus's mature position, it would appear that this position differs from traditional nonreligious humanism mainly by virtue of the terminology of revolt that Camus retained even after he had so thoroughly moralized his conception of revolt as to make most of the normal connotations of that term inapposite. As he himself says in *The Rebel*, the true significance of nihilism is negative; it clears the ground for new construction but by itself provides no principle of action. As such it survives in Camus's view of the moral world mainly as a prophylactic against the kind of mystification, religious or metaphysical, by which a man tries to rid himself of his radical contingency and confer upon himself a cosmic status that makes it easier for him to be a human being. Camus was a pitiless critic of all such forms of shamming, and he was convinced that their general tendency was to enable their practitioners to evade the responsibility that goes with moral self-ownership and to confirm them in their inhumanity to their fellow men. Nihilism would seem, in Camus's final view, to be a kind of immunizing experience, although one with very considerable dangers of its own, by virtue of which one is enabled to grasp the ideal of human fraternity in its pure form without the entanglements of ideology and doctrine by which it has so often been disfigured. Camus's attitude toward life is thus, at bottom, simply a stubborn moral integrity and a deep sympathy with his fellow men, to which the somewhat meretricious rhetoric of revolt adds very little. At the same time, however, it must be conceded that the absence or unavailability of absolute values, whatever these might be, remains for Camus anything but trivial, and it pervades the atmosphere of the humanistic ethic that he erected in their place.

The work of Camus's last years reinforces one's impression that an essentially nonmetaphysical and strongly moralistic humanism was his final view of life. He drew away more and more from direct political action; his refusal to side unambiguously with the Algerian rebels brought him the bitter reproaches of many former associates, among them Sartre. In 1960 in *Réflexions sur la peine capitale* ("Reflections on the Guillotine"), Camus argued that society does not have the right to put its criminals to death, and one wonders in what circumstances Camus would have regarded war as morally defensible. Finally, in *The Fall*, he seems to have abandoned political and social action entirely in favor of a conception of evil that no longer situates it in unjust social institutions or in the terms on which man is permitted to exist but in the very heart of man himself. The protagonist, Clamence, is a man whose interior corruptness is concealed from the world—and for a long time from himself—by a life of philanthropy and active sympathy for his fellow men. He is, in fact, a sort of monster whose ultimate self-knowledge leads him to create a sense of guilt and unworthiness in others by advertising his own corruption. In this way he again feeds his obsessive need for superiority, which was the real motive of his earlier philanthropy. It is not justifiable to impute the unrelieved pessimism of this novel to Camus personally, or to suggest, as some have, that he had accepted the doctrine of original sin; but there can be little doubt that his treatment of the character of Clamence is indicative of a further shift in the locus of the struggle between good and evil. The shift, broadly speaking, is one that emphasizes our inner complicity with evil and our lack of the kind of innocence that Camus had always claimed for man. Whether this strain would have been developed further in Camus's thought if he had lived longer is a question to which there can be no answer.

Works by Camus

L'Etranger. Paris, 1942. Translated by S. Gilbert as *The Stranger.* New York, 1946.

Le Mythe de Sisyphe. Paris, 1942. Translated by J. O'Brien as *The Myth of Sisyphus.* New York, 1955.

Lettres à un ami allemand. Paris, 1945. Translated by J. O'Brien as "Letters to a German Friend," in *Resistance, Rebellion and Death.* New York, 1961.

La Peste. Paris, 1947. Translated by S. Gilbert as *The Plague.* New York, 1948.

Les Justes. Paris. 1950. Translated by S. Gilbert as "The Just," in *Caligula and Three Other Plays.* New York, 1958.

L'Homme revolté. Paris 1951. Translated by A. Bower as *The Rebel.* New York, 1954.

La Chute. Paris, 1956. Translated by J. O'Brien as *The Fall.* New York, 1957.

Réflexions sur la peine capitale. Paris, 1960. Translated by J. O'Brien as "Reflections on the Guillotine," in *Resistance, Rebellion and Death.* New York, 1961.

Carnets. Paris, 1962. Translated by P. Thody as *Notebooks 1935–42.* New York, 1963.

Critical Studies of Camus

Brée, G., *Camus.* New Brunswick, N.J., 1959.

Cruickshank, J., *Albert Camus and the Literature of Revolt.* London, 1959. Contains a detailed bibliography.

Thody, P., *Albert Camus: A Study of His Work.* London, 1957.

FREDERICK A. OLAFSON

CAN. What can be true or can be done varies with the meaning of "can." As far as philosophy is concerned, the important senses of this word ("could," past indicative) fall into five major groups. For convenience these groups, most of which are distinguished in *Webster's Third New International Dictionary,* may be singled out as the "can" of ability, of right, of inclination or probability, of opportunity, and of possibility.

"Can" of ability. The "can" of ability has at least three subsenses: (1) to have the skill—"He can speak five languages or paint lifelike portraits"; (2) to have the requisite mental or physical power—"He can solve difficult problems, invent remarkable machines, or foretell the future" or "He can swim a mile or do one hundred push-ups"; (3) to have the requisite strength of character—"He can resist anything but pleasure, pass up a free drink, or bear criticism of his books."

"Can" of right. The "can" of right, which is often used interchangeably with "may," has at least four subsenses: (1) logically or axiologically can—"Equivalent formulas can be interchanged, *salva veritate,* in any extensional context" or "From this we can reasonably infer . . ."; (2) can in virtue of custom, agreement, law, and so on—"One can be prosecuted for saying that" or "An ambulance can disregard traffic lights"; (3) permission-giving "can"—"You can borrow my car if you'd like"; (4) be permitted by conscience or feeling—"I can condone no willful act of destruction" or "I can accept electrocution but not hanging."

"Can" of inclination or probability. Examples of the "can" of inclination or probability are "I was so angry that I could have killed him" and "That car could hardly have made a trip across the desert."

"Can" of opportunity. "He could have played chess had he known how," "Come in here where we can talk," and "The traffic was so heavy that I could not cross" illustrate the "can" of opportunity.

"Can" of possibility. The "can" of possibility has at least five subsenses: (1) consistency with knowledge—"For all that I know, Jones could have been the one"; (2) whether it is possible for someone (compare with the "can" of opportunity)—"Can you get away for lunch?" (3) the "can" of physical possibility—"If such-and-such has to happen, then it cannot fail to happen" or "A man, properly equipped, can survive indefinitely in outer space"; (4) the "can" of logical possibility (compare with the logical or axiological use of the "can" of right)—"Nothing can be red all over and green all over at the same time"; (5) conditional possibility (logical or physical)—"If the conclusion of a valid argument is false, not all of the premises can be true" or "In a deterministic system everything that can occur is necessitated by something else."

Can and free will. Because the field of philosophical perplexity is virtually limitless, any one of the "cans" listed above is a possible source of trouble to the philosopher. However, several of them (especially the "cans" of ability, opportunity, and possibility), have proved exceptionally potent in bewitching the philosophical imagination, mainly in connection with the age-old problem of free will. This problem is partly generated by the conviction that a man can be said to perform an action freely only if he did not have to perform it but he could have done something else instead. A conviction of this kind tends to generate a problem because if the metaphysical thesis of determinism is intelligible, tenable, and applicable to human actions, it becomes doubtful whether it is ever true that a man can do anything other than what he does do, at least in one of these three basic senses of "can."

"Can" of ability. How the ability senses of "can" bear on the free will issue has received perhaps the largest share of attention in the recent literature, possibly because questions about a man's abilities are often so crucially relevant in moral contexts. Yet the decisive points about abilities in this connection are easily stated. In all of the subsenses of the "can" of ability, there is an essential distinction between the possession of an ability and the exercise of that ability. To show that a person lacks an ability is more complicated than to show that he does not exercise it. A failure to perform a certain action implies that a man lacks the corresponding ability only if both he wants, wills, intends, or chooses to perform that action and his failure to perform it occurs in relevantly normal conditions. This fact has tempted philosophers (for instance, Nowell-Smith) to analyze "He can" (in the sense of ability) as meaning "He will if . . . ." Important difficulties with such hypothetical analyses have been pointed out by Austin and others, but it has not been shown that there is anything wrong with the line of thought that prompted these analyses—namely, that our use of "can" in this sense is built on the idea that a man need not do what he can do and that in order to find out what he can do, we must find out what he will do if, in relevantly normal conditions, he wants, wills, intends, and so forth to do certain things. This line of thought is not, moreover, inconsistent with determinism, since determinism does not imply that if, under appropriate conditions, I wanted and were to try to perform an alternative action, I should certainly fail. On the contrary, it is presumably only because a measure of determinism does hold that my trying, in certain circumstances, to perform a particular action is likely to meet with consistent success.

"Can" of opportunity. Although the truth of determinism does not imply that if a man performs a certain action, he could not (in the sense of the "can" of ability) have done otherwise, it might still be claimed that he would not, under these conditions, have the opportunity to do otherwise and, thus, that he could not do otherwise in the sense of the "can" of opportunity. But this claim is simply false, since in the ordinary sense of "opportunity" one can be said to have the opportunity to do many things that one is not presently doing, whether or not determinism holds. As the examples of the "can" of opportunity indicate, "having the opportunity to do X" does not mean anything like "being in a situation in which nothing physically essential for one's performance of X is lacking," which the claim in question seems to suppose (for more on this point see Taylor, *Metaphysics*). On the contrary, to have the opportunity to do something requires only that one be in a situation such that if, roughly speaking, one wanted to do it, it would be reasonable to expect that one would be successful in doing it if one were able to do it (that is, could do it in the sense of ability). And such a situation would normally be lacking in many things essential, in the required sense, to one's performing that action. Not only might it lack the essential interest or even ability on one's own part, but it might also fail to involve the means that one would have to take in order to accomplish that action if it were at all complex—for instance, walking across the room in order to grasp the vase that one "has the opportunity" to break, throwing it toward the floor with sufficient force, and so on.

"Can" of possibility. In spite of all this, it still seems possible to argue that, given determinism, a man cannot do other than what he does do in the sense that any alternative action on his part is physically impossible. A claim of this sort is, however, false if taken literally, since what is physically possible *simpliciter* need be consistent only with the laws of nature, not consistent with the laws of nature *and* certain initial conditions. If, however, the claim is to be taken in a slightly different way—namely, that it is *conditionally* physically impossible for the man to perform some other action—then it is entirely unexceptionable if the thesis of determinism is tenable and applicable to human actions. The reason for this is simply that the notion of conditional possibility is a technical one, definable by reference to determinism: Roughly, "A is conditionally physically possible" is by definition equivalent to "Nothing has happened that physically determines non-A."

Because one is to make sense of "conditional physical possibility" by reference to determinism or something like it, it is clear that the hard-fought question whether determinism rules out human freedom is not the question whether determinism rules out the conditional possibility of a man's doing other than what he does do. There is, in fact, little that is controversial about the last question; it gets an analytic "Yes." What is controversial is the question whether the sense of "can" involved in the morally relevant query "Can he do otherwise?" is to be understood as the "can" of conditional possibility. For if, as both libertarians and sophisticated fatalists seem to think, this "can" *is* of basic moral significance, then free actions are possible only if determinism is false, untenable, or inapplicable to human actions. If, on the other hand, this sense of "can" is *not* the one that does concern us or should concern us when in a moral context we wonder whether a man can do other than what he does do—the opinion of the "reconcilers" of the empiricist tradition—then there is, perhaps, no incompatibility between determinism and human freedom after all.

Normative "can." How is this basic question about the "can" in the morally crucial use of "He can do otherwise" to be resolved? Only a few, admittedly feeble, hints can be given here. First, the idea that this "can" is that of conditional possibility seems extremely dubious, since this sense of the word is pretty clearly a contrived one, not mentioned even in unabridged dictionaries and thus hardly one that, like the "can" of ability and opportunity, is likely to be used in the familiar, everyday, morally compelling assessment of free, responsible actions. Second, the less heavy-handed and therefore far more tempting claim—that it is at any rate naive or unreasonable to describe an action as free if it is conditionally impossible for the agent to have done otherwise—seems very unsatisfactory when it is carefully pressed. For one thing, to think of free actions as differing from unfree ones in being conditionally undetermined is to make the very notion of a free action practically useless, since any question that might arise about the freedom of a given act would presumably then have to be settled by a fairly hopeless hunt for causes in the jungles of neurology. For another thing, to conceive of free actions in this way is to sever their ties with those complex principles of personal responsibility that incline us to excuse, rather than emphatically condemn, the kindly old parson who (we might imagine) suddenly, spontaneously, and without cause wills to, and does, brain the infant he is baptizing. The last point really seems to go to the heart of the matter: To conceive of free actions as conditionally physically indeterminate actions is to conceive of them in too naturalistic a way. After all, the very identity of an action—think of promising or murdering—is determined not just by the physical movements involved but also by a complex system of rules, laws, and so forth. Since it is the application of such rule concepts that distinguishes actions involving the same physical movements—murder and defensive or punitive acts—the basic vocabulary of action descriptions is essentially normative to a very large extent. (Actually, the vocabulary of action description is "intentional" in a way in which "scientific" language presumably is not.) Because the "can" in the morally crucial claim "He can do otherwise" plainly belongs to the family of words specifically used in connection with human actions, there is an inescapable force to the claim, made by many contemporary philosophers, that to identify this sense of the word with "conditional physical possibility" is to confuse a practical, largely normative "can" with an aseptic, scientific, theoretical one and thus to misconceive drastically the purpose, point, and import of the familiar, nontechnical statement "His action was done freely."

Bibliography

Aune, Bruce, "Abilities, Modalities, and Free Will." *Philosophy and Phenomenological Research*, Vol. 23 (1963), 397–413.

Austin, J. L., "Ifs and Cans," in J. O. Urmson and G. J. Warnock, eds., *Philosophical Papers.* Oxford, 1961.

Baier, Kurt, "Could and Would." *Analysis*, Supp. Vol. (1963), 20–29.

Edwards, Paul, and Pap, Arthur, eds., *A Modern Introduction to Philosophy.* Glencoe, Ill., 1957. See Ch. 1; this book should also be consulted for more detailed bibliographical information.

Hook, Sidney, ed., *Determinism and Freedom in the Age of Modern Science.* New York, 1958.

Melden, A. I., *Free Action.* London, 1961.

Morgenbesser, Sidney, and Walsh, James, eds., *Free Will: A Book of Readings.* Englewood Cliffs, N.J., 1962.

Nowell-Smith, P. H., *Ethics.* Harmondsworth, England, 1954.

Pears, D. F., ed., *Freedom and the Will.* London, 1963.

Raab, F. V., "Free Will and the Ambiguity of 'Could.'" *Philosophical Review*, Vol. 64 (1955), 60–77.

Taylor, Richard, *Metaphysics.* Englewood Cliffs, N.J., 1963. See Chs. 4–5.

BRUCE AUNE

CANTOR, GEORG (1845–1918), mathematician and logician who created set theory, which now constitutes one of the principal branches of mathematics. Cantor was born in St. Petersburg, Russia. He went to Germany with his parents in 1856 and attended various schools, although he was primarily educated by his father. Even when he was quite young he longed to become a mathematician, but not until 1862 did he overcome his father's opposition. From 1862 to 1867 he studied mathematics, for the most part at Berlin University, where he came under the influence of Karl Weierstrass. Both his Berlin doctoral thesis (1867) and his inaugural dissertation at Halle (1869) dealt with conventional problems of number theory. Cantor remained at the University of Halle, where he became associate professor of mathematics in 1872 and full professor in 1879. His hope of receiving a chair at Berlin was never realized.

Cantor was at the zenith of his productivity from 1874 to 1884. A serious breakdown of his health, from which he never completely recovered, occurred in 1884; later, normal periods alternated with attacks of mental illness. His collapse is sometimes attributed to the antagonism to his work shown by almost all his mathematical contemporaries, headed by Leopold Kronecker, as well as to his desperate efforts, in the early 1880s, to solve the continuum problem—a problem not solved until 1963, by Paul J. Cohen. About 1897 Cantor ceased his scientific work, just as his achievements were beginning to be widely acknowledged, especially in England and France, and honors bestowed upon him. From 1913 on his health deteriorated rapidly, and he died five years later in Halle.

About 1870 the Halle mathematician Eduard Heine suggested to Cantor some research on trigonometric series. In the course of the work, Cantor soon became interested in the influence of "exceptional" points of other analytical expressions and upon the behavior of series. To investigate these problems he felt the need to develop ideas "which serve to illuminate situations that result whenever finitely or infinitely many numbers are given." This rather cryptic program refers to the introduction of accumulation-points and derivatives of sets of points (real numbers). To this end Cantor developed his arithmetical theory of irrational numbers based on fundamental series of rationals. This was in 1872, simultaneous with but independent of Richard Dedekind's quite different theory. Next to set theory, this foundation of the concept of real number constituted Cantor's most important contribution to mathematics. Only subsequently was it discovered that materially, if not formally, the theory of Eudoxos, which appears in Books V and X of Euclid's *Elements*, coincides with the modern arithmetical theories.

Cantor was led by his program to differentiate between diverse sets of numbers or points. This yielded his first and fundamentally his most important paper on set theory, "Über eine Eigenschaft des Inbegriffes aller reellen algebraischen Zahlen" (1874), which demonstrates the existence of two nonequivalent infinite sets: denumerable and nondenumerable sets. Not only is the terminology of this paper unspecific (even the term *abzählbar*—"denumerable"—does not yet appear), but the paper's title suggests that Cantor was unaware of his major achievement. In the first section, the only one to which the title alludes, it is proved that the set *A* of all algebraic (real) numbers is denumerable, which is almost trivial. Yet in the second section Cantor shows that the continuum of all real numbers is not equivalent to *A;* therefore "almost all" real numbers are transcendental (not algebraic). This is proved by the diagonal method, one of the most powerful procedures of mathematics, used here for the first time (although in complicated form). The method was later simplified by Cantor (1892) and given a form that lends itself to far-reaching generalizations.

This first discovery constitutes the base of set theory, for the concept of transfinite magnitude—in the present case, cardinal number—is insignificant so long as only one such magnitude was known to exist. The demonstration that *A* and the continuum have different cardinals was a challenge to further progress.

From 1874 on Cantor tried to determine a set of a higher cardinality than the linear continuum *L*. In particular, he tried to prove that the two-dimensional continuum (square, plane) cannot be mapped onto *L*. The effort itself was remarkable, for leading mathematicians told him that this impossibility was evident and needed no proof, since "two independent variables cannot be reduced to a single one." For three years Cantor devoted his energies to this problem, until in 1877 he discovered that his conjecture was false and that mappings do exist between continua of different dimensions. This greatly surprised him, and he wrote to Dedekind, *"Je le vois, mais je ne le crois pas."* In the 1878 paper presenting his discovery, Cantor introduced the concepts of equivalence and of power (cardinal). In it he formulated for the first time the continuum hypothesis, which maintains that the power of the continuum is the next power to that of denumerable sets (see SET THEORY). He still considered it evident that any two powers are comparable, and this he later tried in vain to prove. As is well known, only Ernst Zermelo's 1904 proof of the well-ordering theorem (Cantor had conjectured it to be valid and "postulated" it earlier) yields comparability.

Cantor's 1877 proof of the existence of mappings between continua of different dimensions seemed to destroy the concept of dimension. Although his own treatment of the subject was unsuccessful, others, from Bernard Bolzano, Dedekind, and Jacob Lüroth to L. E. J. Brouwer, analyzed the concept and disclosed its dependence on the continuity of the mapping.

The years 1879 to 1884 were the most fertile in Cantor's life, in which he produced the six parts of the comprehensive essay, "Über unendliche lineare Punktmannichfaltigkeiten" ("On Infinite Linear Manifolds of Points"), as well as some shorter papers. Although most of this work is of a mathematico-technical character, bearing upon sets of points rather than upon abstract sets, a few subjects and results (primarily from the fifth part of the "Über unendliche") are especially important. These are the introduction of the transfinite ordinal numbers, including arithmetical operations, and the use of these numbers to show the existence of infinitely many different cardinal numbers; the idea of the second number-class; the rejection of infinitely small magnitudes (infinitesimals) which supposedly would correspond to transfinite cardinals or ordinals; a detailed critique of finitist philosophers—from the Greeks and the scholastic theologians to Spinoza, Leibniz, and Kant—who reject actual infinity; a survey of the two thousand years of unsuccessful attempts to define and explain the concept of continuum, with Cantor's first precise definition of the linear continuum given solely in terms of order; a new exposition of his theory of irrational numbers, including a comparison with other theories.

The fifth part of "Über unendliche," which was published individually in 1883, is noteworthy not only as mathematics and as philosophy but also for history of science. Cantor revealed himself as conscious of the importance of set theory for the theory of functions on the one hand and for logic and epistemology on the other. Two quotations (both translated from the German) will serve to point out decisive developments in Cantor's thought.

Opening the fifth part of "Über unendliche," Cantor said:

> The previous exposition of my investigations in the theory of manifolds [that is, sets] has arrived at a stage where the continuation becomes dependent on a generalization of the concept of real integer beyond the usual limits, a generalization that takes a direction which, as far as I know, nobody has as yet looked for. I depend on this generalization . . . to such an extent that without it I should hardly be able to take freely even the least step forward in the theory of sets; may this serve as a justification or, if necessary, an apology for my introducing seemingly strange ideas into my considerations. In point of fact the venture is to generalize or to continue the series of real integers beyond the infinite. Daring as this may appear, I express not only the hope but the firm conviction that in due time this generalization will be received as a quite simple, suitable, and natural step. Still I am well aware that by taking this step I put myself in a certain opposition to wide-spread views of the infinite in mathematics and to current opinions regarding the nature of number.

In an 1885 letter to Gustav Enerström, Cantor wrote:

> All supposed proofs against the possibility of actually transfinite numbers . . . are faulty in this respect—and here lies their πρῶτονψεῦδος—that from the first they impute to, or rather enforce upon, the numbers in question all properties of finite numbers, whereas the actually transfinite numbers . . . must, by their contrast with finite number, constitute an entirely new kind of number the nature of which depends completely on the situation and should be the object of our investigations but not of our discretion or prejudice.

After 1884 Cantor produced few new original ideas. Some of his papers are philosophical and partly polemical. His inclination to Platonic realism and his deep religious interests become conspicuous. Cantor even asked the Prussian ministry of education to change his chair from mathematics to philosophy. The comprehensive paper, "Beiträge zur Begründung der transfiniten Mengenlehre" (1895–1897) gives a lucid systematization of most of his set-theoretical work, together with an extension of the theory of well-ordered sets. It begins with Cantor's famous "definition" of set as "a collection into a whole of definite distinct objects of our intuition or our thought." At precisely this time, however, Cantor became aware that the generality of the definition implies contradictions, and this induced him to distinguish between sets and "inconsistent" systems, notably in his correspondence with Dedekind of 1899. As early as 1895 he discovered Cesare Burali-Forti's antinomy.

Stimulated by his own experience of the suppression of original ideas by predominant individual authorities, Cantor became a founder (1890) and the first president of the

Deutsche Mathematiker-Vereinigung. He also labored to institute international congresses of mathematicians; the first one took place in Zurich in 1897 and proved a great personal success for Cantor.

Works by Cantor

Gesammelte Abhandlungen ("Collected Papers"). E. Zermelo, ed. Berlin, 1932; reprinted Hildesheim, 1962. Contains a biography by A. Fraenkel.

"Beiträge zur Begründung der transfiniten Mengenlehre," in *Mathematische Annalen*, Vol. 46 (1895), 481–512; Vol. 49 (1897), 207–248. Translated by P. E. B. Jourdain (who also wrote an introduction) as *Contributions to the Founding of the Theory of Transfinite Numbers* (Chicago, 1915).

Briefwechsel Cantor–Dedekind, E. Noether and J. Cavaillès, eds. Paris, 1937.

Works on Cantor

Fraenkel, A., "Georg Cantor." *Jahresbericht der Deutschen Mathematiker Vereinigung*, Vol. 39 (1930), 189–266.

Schoenflies, A., "Die Krisis in Cantors mathematischen Schaffen," with remarks by G. Mittag-Leffler. *Acta Mathematica*, Vol. 50 (1928), 1–26.

ABRAHAM A. FRAENKEL

CAPPADOCIAN FATHERS. *See* GREGORY OF NAZIANZUS; GREGORY OF NYSSA.

CAPREOLUS, JOHN (c.1380–1444), French Dominican theologian, was born in Rodez. He studied at the University of Paris, receiving the magistrate in theology in 1411. Later he taught in Dominican houses of study at Toulouse and Rodez and came to be recognized as the "Leader of the Thomists" (*Princeps Thomistarum*). His chief work is *Defensiones Theologiae D. Thomae* ("Defenses of the Theology of St. Thomas"). This is the first commentary that considers the *Summa Theologiae* more important than Aquinas' *Commentary on the Sentences*, a view which has persisted in later Thomism. The *Defensiones* is historically useful for its information on scholastic philosophical controversies of the fourteenth century and the views of Duns Scotus, John of Ripa, Peter Aureolus, and Durand de Saint-Pourçain. Capreolus' contributions to philosophy are in the field of metaphysics. On the then central question of the relation between essence and existence, he taught that they are distinguished as two different beings (an extreme real distinction) and used the terminology of Giles of Rome (*esse essentiae* and *esse existentiae*) to express his position. Capreolus regarded essences as eternal and uncreated entities, not efficiently produced by God but subject only to divine formal causality. On the other hand, he stressed the importance of existence in treating personality (divine and human), teaching that personality is the very subsistence of the act of existing (*esse actualis existentiae*, see *Defensiones*, Vol. V, pp. 105–107). Where other thinkers required some sort of formal or modal constituent of the person, Capreolus demanded nothing more than the act of existing as an intelligent individual nature. He taught that the intrinsic principle that individuates bodies is matter marked by quantity (*materia signata*), as did Aquinas, but Capreolus insisted that the quantification must be actual (under definite dimensions) and not indeterminate (*Defensiones*, Vol. III, pp. 200–241).

Works by Capreolus

Defensiones Theologiae D. Thomae, Paban-Pègues, ed., 7 vols. Turin, 1900–1908. There are no known English translations of Capreolus' work.

Works on Capreolus

Grabmann, M., "J. Capreolus, O.P., der Princeps Thomistarum und seine Stellung in der Geschichte der Thomistenschule." *Divus Thomas* (Freiburg), Vol. 22 (1944), 85–109, 145–170.

Wells, N. J., "Capreolus on Essence and Existence." *Modern Schoolman*, Vol. 38 (1960), 1–24.

VERNON J. BOURKE

CARABELLESE, PANTALEO (1877–1948), Italian philosopher, was professor of philosophy at Palermo from 1923 to 1929 and at Rome from 1929 to 1948. A pupil of Bernadino Varisco, he was early influenced by the spiritual realism of Rosmini, but he was also impressed by the subjective idealism of Croce and Gentile. To overcome this tension between realism and idealism he returned to the origins of the idealist tradition in Kant and Fichte.

Carabellese called his theory "Critical Ontologism" because his central aim was to establish a concept of ontology and an interpretation of the Ontological Argument that could be defended within the context of a philosophy that was critical in the Kantian sense. He sought a positive and not merely a negative conception of the thing-in-itself; and for this purpose, a critique not of reason but of consciousness was needed. This "critique of the concrete" would make it clear that human experience is not the self-consciousness of an Absolute Subject, as Kant's successors thought; rather, it is the inadequate consciousness of an Absolute Object by a plurality of subjects. The subjects must be a plurality because to exist—to be conscious—is to be reciprocally related to an "other"; and an "other," to be truly other to the subject, must be like the subject. Reciprocity is possible only because each individual is conscious of an Absolute Object that is the ground of his likeness to the other, and the ground also of mutual otherness. The objectivity of consciousness is manifested empirically in the fact that we inhabit one common world; but this empirical community is a posteriori and always remains problematical. That the world of different observers is one world must be taken on faith; and this faith is justified only when the observers actually succeed in reaching agreement. The "real world" is the result, not the condition, of this agreement.

The a priori principle, in which our experience of a common world is grounded, Carabellese called "God." Thus, concrete consciousness is the immanence of God, the absolutely unique Object, in a plurality of reciprocally related subjects. But Carabellese's Absolute Object does not *exist:* it is not a person but a principle. What his Ontological Argument proves is not that God exists but that *Being is.* If the Absolute Being existed, it would necessarily be in relation with its own other; but if it has an "other," it is not Absolute.

In his early book, *Critica del concreto*, Carabellese

distinguished three moments within the Object. Viewed as past, the Object is knowable as Truth; as present, it is sensible as Beauty; and as future, it can be willed as Good. Thus, we might describe the Object in secular terms as real time. Real time differs from Kant's pure form of succession in that its moments are not successive but mutually immanent: no experience is absolutely past or present or future; whatever can be cognized can also be appreciated or willed, and vice versa. During his last years Carabellese developed this theory in detail in a series of systematic treatises, some of which were privately printed for students but never formally published.

Principal Works by Carabellese

La coscienza morale. La Spezia, 1915. Rewritten as *Critica del concreto.* Pistoia, 1921; 3d ed., Florence, 1948.

Il problema teologico come filosofia. Rome, 1931.

La Conscience concrète. Selections translated by Luigi Aurigemma and Giovanni Bufo. Paris, 1955. Provides a useful introduction and a full bibliography as well as selections from later works.

H. S. Harris

CARLINI, ARMANDO (1878–1959), the founder and leading exponent of Italian Christian spiritualism, succeeded Gentile in the chair of theoretical philosophy at Pisa in 1922.

He was at first very sensitive to the tension between the two then dominant philosophies in Italy, the "worldly" historicism of Benedetto Croce and the "theologizing" actualism of Giovanni Gentile. Finding it impossible to accept the claims of either in unmitigated form, he sought to retain the value of each, within a "higher synthesis" that would transcend both, a goal he announced in his introductory lecture on succeeding to Gentile's chair ("Genesi dei problemi della filosofia," 1922). Carlini's final position is incomprehensible without reference to this process.

In order to overcome any metaphysical or quasi-naturalistic interpretation of spirit in man, Carlini preferred to speak of "spirituality," by which he meant an interior and valuative activity of the human existent, not a category of being. The essential activity of spirituality is to initiate a process of self-distinction by which the constitutive act of existence is reduced from its initial abstract self-identification to a concrete unity in difference. This leads to the postulation of an "exterior world," for without such a "world" the identity of the subject must remain abstract.

Values can be realized, communicated, and related only within the diverse dimensions consequent to the process of self-distinction. In this way Carlini retained contact with Croce's historicism, for Croce made history, a realm of incarnate ideality, the sole locus of value. This incarnation of spirituality gives point to Gentile's theologizing, for the world, while it makes possible the realization of values, disperses rather than integrates them. A principle of the integration of value is needed. This principle cannot lie in spiritual activity itself, for in that case it would become the norm of those values and hence could not establish their transcendentality. God is this transcendent and transcendental principle of the integrity of values. The first manifestation of this integrity is to be found in the concrete unity of the incarnate human person. The world and God become the twin poles between which the human person mediates and, in the process of mediation, creates both its own selfhood and the concrete locus of the integrity of all values.

Principal Works by Carlini

La vita dello spirito. Florence, 1921.

Mito del realismo. Florence, 1936.

Lineamenti di una concezione realistica dello spirito umano. Rome, 1942.

Alla ricerca di me stesso. Florence, 1951. Carlini's moving philosophical autobiography.

Works on Carlini

Alberghi, S., "Sul pensiero di Armando Carlini." *Rivista rosminiana,* Vol. 48 (1950), 86–106.

Delle Volpe, G., *Lo spiritualismo italiano contemporaneo,* Vol. I, *La filosofia di Armando Carlini.* Messina, 1949.

Giornale di metafisica, Vol. 5 (1950). Carlini commemorative issue containing essays by M. Antonelli, M. F. Sciacca, V. A. Sainati, and others.

Pareyson, L., "Pre-esistenzialismo di Armando Carlini," in his *Studi sull'esistenzialismo.* Florence, 1943.

Sciacca, M. F., "Problemi dello spiritualismo di Armando Carlini." *Logos* (1937), 104–120.

A. Robert Caponigri

CARLYLE, THOMAS (1795–1881), essayist, historian, and philosopher of culture, was born in Ecclefechan, Scotland, the eldest son of a stern, puritanical stonemason. There can be little doubt that the often hysterical extravagances of Carlyle's later social doctrines had a direct emotional origin in the Calvinism of his childhood. In 1809 he became a divinity student at Edinburgh University, but he soon stopped attending the university courses and read widely on his own in modern literature. After leaving Edinburgh in 1814, he taught school, at the same time broadening his already impressive span of reading. In addition to imaginative literature and German philosophy, Carlyle's serious interests at this time extended to Voltaire and François Fénelon, as well as to the scientific works of Newton and Benjamin Franklin. A reading of Gibbon in 1817 immediately precipitated Carlyle's rejection of the Bible as a historical record and gave impetus to his growing interest in history and social institutions. Convinced that he could never become a minister, he returned to Edinburgh in 1819 and began his literary career as a free-lance journalist. The next three years were the most miserable in a generally agonized life. He was unknown; he was socially, ideologically, even stylistically antipathetic to the fashionable literary world. He was also very poor, desperately lonely, and because of his irregular eating habits, almost permanently dyspeptic. Religious doubts quickly darkened into unbelief, and in 1822 he experienced the spiritual crisis later hieroglyphically recorded in *Sartor Resartus* (1833–1834). Like the hero of *Sartor*, Diogenes Teufelsdröckh, Carlyle found a new (if decidedly secular) faith in the moral efficacy of work: "Doubt of any sort cannot be removed except by Action," extolls Teufelsdröckh. Conviction is worthless until it is converted into activity, mere speculation being "endless, formless, a vortex amid vortices." Therefore, one must

"Do the Duty which lies nearest thee . . . Work while it is called To-day; for the Night cometh wherein no man can work." Here, in a language persuasively familiar to his readers, Carlyle expressed the chief psychotherapeutic discovery of his youth—one which was more widely disseminated in the writings of Thomas Arnold, Ruskin, Newman, and particularly the later prophetic Carlyle himself, and was to become a leitmotiv of mid-Victorian culture. Soon Carlyle found a role in which his genuine talents could emerge. His translation of Goethe's *Wilhelm Meister* in 1824 and his *Life of Schiller*, which was published as a book in 1825, established him as the first interpreter of German literature to the British public.

Carlyle's marriage in 1826 to Jane Baillie Welsh, an attractive, high-strung, and unusually intellectual 25-year-old girl, ended his loneliness without in any way soothing the more creative ontological anxieties upon which his work depended. Carlyle's long years of isolated reading now bore fruit in a series of remarkable articles published in the Great Reviews.

Literary criticism. Carlyle's early essays, especially "Jean Paul Friedrich Richter" (1827), "The State of German Literature," "Goethe," "Burns" (1828), "Voltaire," and "Novalis" (1829), are masterpieces of literary and ideological exegesis. However, his critical method, which was uncompromisingly didactic even for its day, was much more a criticism of life than any technical analysis of words on a page; in effect, it was essentially romantic criticism. Carlyle viewed literature as a form of self-revelation and literary criticism as a heightened confrontation of personalities engaged in the quest for moral truth. He stressed the primary need for the "transposition of the critic into the author's point of vision," which is the prerequisite of all historical and biographical as well as literary studies. Like Coleridge before him, Carlyle recognized Germany as the great contemporary source of spirituality and inwardness. For Carlyle, however, Goethe rather than Kant was Germany's spiritual leader. More than any other writer, Goethe triumphed over all doubts and denials and manifested the freedom of belief and activity. In this respect Carlyle believed that there was a significant contrast to be made between Goethe and Voltaire. In the essay "Voltaire," Carlyle argued that despite Voltaire's intellectual adroitness, his power of rapid, perspicuous arrangement of scientific and historical data, his humanity, and his universal susceptibility of mind, his real claim to greatness was that he "gave the death-stab to modern superstition." Such an achievement was, however, too negative: for Carlyle, Voltaire remained essentially a mocker, "the greatest of all Persifleurs," his chief fault being a terrible lack of earnestness.

This contrast between Voltaire and Goethe—between the pragmatic values of the eighteenth century and those of a new age of belief which was, if not actually beginning, at least imminent—ran through Carlyle's works in ever-widening applications. Moreover, it is symptomatic of the type of thinker Carlyle was that most of his later ideas were already contained embryonically in his very earliest writings (for example, in his first original publication in 1822 in the *New Edinburgh Review*, which was significantly a critique of Goethe's *Faust*). Had he stuck to literature and written more about the English classics, Carlyle would today no doubt be placed between Coleridge and Matthew Arnold as one of the major British literary critics of his age. But his interest in literature was only a steppingstone to a more vital concern with history and social diagnosis. He never really methodologically distinguished between criticism, biography, and historical and philosophical analysis. They were all used as media through which the current *crise de conscience* was to be more clearly seen and diagnosed. In this respect Carlyle may be thought of, in his early works, as an amateurish practitioner of *Geisteswissenschaften* (or "human studies"), in roughly the sense given to that term by Wilhelm Dilthey.

Early social criticism. "Signs of the Times" (1829), "On History" (1830), and particularly "Characteristics" (1831) were Carlyle's earliest communications in the self-assumed role of Victorian prophet. The early nineteenth century, he claimed, was a mechanical age, both externally and internally, its chief symptom being an excessive self-consciousness. With its inheritance of the largely negative contributions of the Enlightenment, it was an age of inquiry and doubt rather than of meditation and faith. Outwardly, social mechanization was more prized than individual vitality. Inwardly, morality no longer sprang from belief in a transcendental authority but arose out of prudential feeling grounded on mere calculation of consequences. The most grievous mistake of bourgeois liberalism was its doctrine that social welfare can be promoted solely through external politico-economic legislation, whereas, in truth, all human progress that is genuine ("dynamical") must emerge from the moral culture of individual men. According to Carlyle, although the present time is thus out of joint, there is nevertheless strong hope for the future. History is a cyclical but progressive (perhaps spiral) unfolding of human capabilities, and borrowing freely from Herder and the Saint-Simonians, he affirmed that the modern period is the end of a critical phase. Even as the darkest hour heralds the dawn, so the springtime of organic rebirth is now at hand.

As it happened, Carlyle was not the only British subscriber to this philosophy of history in the early 1830s. J. S. Mill's papers on "The Spirit of the Age," which appeared in the *Examiner* for 1831, propounded very similar views. These papers, which immensely impressed Carlyle, led to the formation of his somewhat precarious friendship with Mill. Doubtless the chief obstacle for Mill was Carlyle's blatantly authoritarian concept of morality and his notorious views on liberty and democracy, three notions that were soon to be dramatically embodied in Carlyle's theory of the hero.

The hero and history. In the *French Revolution* (1837), Carlyle stereoscopically visualized the events between the death of Louis XV and the appointment of Napoleon as commander in chief of the Army of the Interior in 1795 as the accumulated result not so much of economic or social, but of moral and, in the last analysis, theological causes. The French Revolution, he sometimes seemed to suggest, was an upheaval ordained by the Creator to punish the sins of the world. Yet at the same time, and importantly for Carlyle's anthropomorphic imagination, it was an exhibition of individual personalities (of Mirabeau, Danton, Robespierre, etc.) in their most intense form. "History," he had written in 1830, "is the essence of innumerable Biographies." Biography, which is based on insight into human personality, is the foundation of all historical inquiry; hence, the true history of an age is the biography of its great men. Carlyle's main interest in history (as in literature) was in the moral psychology of specific individuals who seemed to him endowed with certain admirable traits of character that he felt to be chronically lacking in the contemporary *Zeitgeist*.

The lectures he delivered in 1840, *On Heroes, Hero Worship, and the Heroic in History*, blended mythology with metaphysics to produce an image of the ideal type of individual needed as the savior of mankind. The hero can take many forms: he can be a god (Odin), a prophet (Muhammad), poet (Dante and Shakespeare), priest (Luther and Knox), a man of letters (Johnson, Rousseau, Burns), or a political ruler (Cromwell and Napoleon). In fact the hero can be "what you will, according to the kind of world he finds himself born into": his ever-varying persona results from the deeper needs of society. He is directed not by the "mechanical" needs of men, but by their "dynamical," unseen, mystical needs. Thus, all heroes have discerned "truly what the time wanted" and have led it "on the right road thither." In this sense, the hero is a gift from heaven, or as Carlyle otherwise puts it, a force of nature; his essential quality is "Original Insight" into the "primal reality of things." Because of the hero's firm contact with the "great Fact of Existence," he cannot lie. "He is heartily in *earnest*"; an unconscious sincerity emanates from him turning his acts or utterances into "a kind of 'revelation'" which the ordinary, unheroic man is morally obliged to recognize and obey. For "all that is *right* includes itself in this of co-operating with the real tendency of the World." Indeed, the proper feelings of ordinary men toward the heroes of their age are loyalty (which is "akin to religious Faith"), reverence, admiration, and "an obedience which knows no bounds." Hero worship, Carlyle significantly concludes, is a basic and indestructible tendency of human nature: it is "the one fixed point in modern revolutionary history, otherwise as if bottomless and shoreless."

As with Nietzsche's *Übermensch*, there has been a tendency in the twentieth century to view Carlyle's theory of the hero far too much in terms of recent political experience—that is, to think of the hero as a direct ancestor of fascism. But Carlyle, like Nietzsche, was essentially a philosopher of culture, not a political theorist. The hero concept is best understood as a rather curious and obsessional example of a spiritual phenomenon that reached something of a climax in the nineteenth century, most notably in the thought of Ludwig Feuerbach, Auguste Comte, Marx, and Nietzsche—namely, the uneasy substitution of purely secular objects of veneration for the traditional transcendental one. Worship of God gave way to worship of man and human society.

After 1840. Beginning with *Chartism* (1839), and more disastrously in *Past and Present* (1843) and the *Latterday Pamphlets* (1850), Carlyle explicitly incorporated the hero concept within the central tenets of his early social criticism to produce not only a renewed attack upon the materialistic spirit of industrial society but also an indictment of political liberty and democracy. Once more he protested against laissez-faire, the irresponsible pursuit of wealth in which "cash payment" has become the "sole nexus" between men, thus displacing the traditional ties of obligation. But social justice, he now paradoxically asserted, can be achieved only through the enforcement of social inequality. Members of the aristocracy and those heroes of the business world, the "Captains of Industry," must assume their responsibilities as rulers of the masses: freedom consists in "the right of the ignorant man to be guided by the wiser." In this instance, as in nearly all of Carlyle's writing after about 1840, it seems that genuine social criticism was lost sight of in an increasingly pathological obsession with power: nothing could have been further from the spirit of Mill's *On Liberty* (1859) and *Representative Government* (1861). In *Oliver Cromwell's Letters and Speeches, with Elucidations* (1845) and the *History of Frederick the Great* (1858–1865), Carlyle tried to give some historical backing to his by now hopeless moral aberrations for which he ultimately received the Prussian Order of Merit in 1874.

It is impossible to exaggerate Carlyle's impact, for better and worse, upon all aspects of Victorian culture, ranging from the development of the novel (particularly as evidenced in the work of Dickens), to the formation of social policy. Nietzsche described him as a man constantly misled by a craving for a strong faith which he lacked the necessary capacity to experience. But it was hardly the capacity Carlyle lacked; rather, like Nietzsche himself, he needed something to have faith in. In the absence of his father's God, he chose what seemed to him the best substitute—the hero.

Works by Carlyle

The Centenary Edition, edited by H. D. Trail, 30 vols. (London, 1896–1899; New York, 1896–1901) is the most complete edition of Carlyle's *Works*. Carlyle's correspondence, most notably with Goethe, Emerson, Mill, and John Stirling, is essential reading for anyone interested in Carlyle's thought or, indeed, in nineteenth-century intellectual history in general. See also *Correspondence of Emerson and Carlyle*, J. Slater, ed. (Oxford and New York, 1965).

Works on Carlyle

To date there exists no full-scale analysis of the whole range of Carlyle's thought. The best short account is given by Ernst Cassirer in *The Myth of the State* (New Haven, 1946), Chs. 15–16. J. A. Froude, *Thomas Carlyle 1795–1835*, 2 vols. (London, 1882) and *Thomas Carlyle 1834–1881*, 2 vols. (London, 1884) are still indispensable. Among the many important specialized studies are B. H. Lehmann, *Carlyle's Theory of the Hero* (Durham, N.C., 1928); C. F. Harrold, *Carlyle and German Thought: 1819–1834* (New Haven, 1934); René Wellek, "Carlyle and the Philosophy of History," *Philological Quarterly*, Vol. 23 (1944), 55–76; and G. Holloway, *The Victorian Sage* (London, 1953), Chs. 1–3.

MICHAEL MORAN

CARNAP, RUDOLF, is the most prominent representative of the logical empiricist, or logical positivist, school in the philosophy of science and logic. He was born in 1891 at Ronsdorf, near Barmen, Germany. After attending the Gymnasium at Barmen, he studied at the universities of Freiburg and Jena from 1910 to 1914, specializing in physics, mathematics, and philosophy. One of his teachers at Jena was Gottlob Frege, who, with Bertrand Russell, exerted the greatest influence on Carnap's thinking.

After service in World War I, Carnap resumed his studies and in 1921 obtained his doctorate in philosophy at Jena, with a thesis entitled *Der Raum: Ein Beitrag zur Wissenschaftslehre* ("Space: A Contribution to the Theory of Science"), which was published the following year as a monograph in *Kantstudien.* The thesis analyzed the differences in logical character among the mathematical, physical, and intuitive (or psychological) concepts of space and sought to trace differences of opinion concerning "space" to the fact that the term had a different meaning for mathematicians, for physicists, and for philosophers. Although the monograph cannot, of course, be regarded as a developed formulation of logical positivism, it already contained many of the chief elements of Carnap's philosophical thought—in particular, a tendency to look on philosophical disputes as being largely due to failure to analyze logically the concepts employed, and a commitment to a basic empiricism supplemented by the methods of modern logic and mathematics.

In 1926, at the invitation of Moritz Schlick, Carnap went to the University of Vienna as *Privatdozent.* He participated actively in the discussions of the Vienna circle, of which he soon became a leading figure. In 1928 he published his first major systematic work, *Der logische Aufbau der Welt* ("The Logical Construction of the World"), based on an early version completed in 1925. During his first years in Vienna, Carnap, with other members of the circle, made an intensive study of Ludwig Wittgenstein's *Tractatus Logico-philosophicus.* Despite major differences between them, Wittgenstein exercised an influence on Carnap probably second only to that of Russell and Frege. With Hans Reichenbach (then in Berlin), Carnap founded a new journal, *Erkenntnis* (1930–1940), as a forum for scientific philosophy. A year later he accepted the chair of natural philosophy in the division of natural sciences at the German University in Prague. Continuing his relationship with the Vienna circle, Carnap turned his attention increasingly to problems of logic, language, and the foundations of mathematics. One result was the appearance, in 1934, of his second major work, *Logische Syntax der Sprache* (*Logical Syntax of Language*).

Because of the spread of Nazism, Carnap found it impossible to remain at the German University. In December 1935 he came to America and within a few months had received a permanent appointment as professor of philosophy at the University of Chicago. He taught there until 1952, a tenure broken only by visiting professorships at Harvard and Illinois and leaves of absence for research. While in Chicago he assumed, with Otto Neurath and Charles W. Morris, editorship of the *International Encyclopedia of Unified Science* (which gave primary emphasis to the unification of scientific terms rather than of laws). Supplementing and modifying his *Logische Syntax,* Carnap devoted himself to studies in semantics, publishing in succession *Introduction to Semantics* (1942), *Formalization of Logic* (1943), and *Meaning and Necessity* (1947). From about 1941 his interest gradually shifted to problems of probability and induction. This research culminated in the publication of his monumental *Logical Foundations of Probability* (1950).

After his departure from the University of Chicago, Carnap spent two years at the Institute for Advanced Study, in Princeton, working on induction, probability, and other topics. In 1954 he accepted the chair in philosophy at the University of California at Los Angeles made vacant by the untimely death of his friend Reichenbach. He retired from active teaching in 1961.

Throughout a long and productive career Carnap has displayed traits of high intellectual and moral integrity. There have been many changes in his views over the years, chiefly in the direction of greater flexibility. Always attentive to responsible criticism, he has not feared to abandon positions once convinced of their error or inadequacy. Nevertheless, he has adhered to a logically oriented empiricism and a view of the task of philosophy as the analysis, by means of the methods of modern logic, of empirical—particularly scientific—discourse. He has explored the world of abstract logic and theoretical science as few have before him. But he has also found time for a deeply humanistic involvement in daily life and social concerns.

Carnap's contributions to philosophy are most conveniently surveyed in terms of successive, and often overlapping, major periods and interests, beginning with the *Aufbau,* followed by his views on the elimination of metaphysics and on physicalism and the unity of science and his studies in logical syntax, the empiricist philosophy of science, semantics, probability, and ontology and scientific theory.

"AUFBAU"

The *Logische Aufbau* can be viewed as involving three complementary aspects: a somewhat novel methodological approach, the use of this approach to construct in outline a technical system, and the application of the method to the solution of philosophical problems.

Methodology. The methodology of the *Aufbau* Carnap calls constitution (or construction) theory (*Konstitutionstheorie*). This may be regarded as a continuation and refinement of methods previously used by Ernst Mach (especially in *The Analysis of Sensations*), Russell (especially in *Our Knowledge of the External World*) and perhaps, to a degree, Wittgenstein. The principal concept is that of reducibility (*Zurückführbarkeit*). A concept x is said to be reducible to a set of concepts Y if every sentence concerning x can be transformed into sentences concerning concepts belonging to Y (with preservation of the truth-value). This transformation is carried out by means of a rule, or constitutional definition. Although such a rule is formally a definition, it need not be a definition in the sense of a purely verbal transformation; that is, it need not be the case that the objects indicated by the definition are the same objects as those indicated by the definiendum. In fact, the method of constitution derives its basic character from the fact that this is typically not so.

These constitutional definitions are to be arranged in a

structure that reduces a field to a much more limited set of concepts called the basis, the resulting complex being referred to as a constitution system (*Konstitutionssystem*). In this process Carnap made use of the methods of modern logic. A constitution system is a structure of exact definitions and theorems and in its purest form is best expressible in the language of modern logic, with the addition of special undefined terms. Accordingly, the *Principia Mathematica* of Whitehead and Russell may be regarded as an example of a constitution system; in fact, it seems clear that the *Principia* inspired Carnap's idea of constitution.

Construction of a system. The field that Carnap sought to put into a constitution system was the field of all known (or knowable) objects, so the system he presented may be regarded as a constitution system for epistemology. He considered known objects to be of four main types: sociocultural (*geistige*) objects, other minds (*fremdpsychische*), physical (*physische*) objects, and one's own experiences, or private-psychical (*eigenpsychische*) objects.

In terms of epistemological priority, Carnap concluded, the order is the inverse of that stated just above. And since he sought an epistemological system, he chose the experiences of one's own mind as the basis ("solipsistic basis"). Within the *eigenpsychische* he selected a single primitive asymmetrical relation, remembrance of similarity (*Ähnlichkeitserinnerung*), abbreviated "Er." Thus, Er(x,y) holds between two objects (experiences) x and y if x is remembered as being similar to y. With the aid of this concept we can define elementary experiences as the field of the relation Er, partial similarity as the relation that exists if the experiences are the same or if Er holds in either direction, and similarity regions (*Ähnlichkeitskreise*) as the abstraction classes of partial similarity. Through the use of analogous, but more complex definitions Carnap constructed "class of qualities," "similarity of qualities," "sense class," "sensation," "neighboring colors," and the similar concepts of temporal ordering. At this point he stopped his exact formal development and proceeded in a more common informal, but careful, manner reminiscent of that used by Russell in *Our Knowledge of the External World.* Carnap constructed the space-time world and indicated the assignment of sense qualities to its points. He was then able to define "visual objects" and "my own body." This done, he went on to the world of perception and the biological world and thence to human beings and their cultural objects.

In discussing these matters Carnap often used—sometimes alone, sometimes supplemented by other formulations—what he termed the realistic language customary in natural science. But he insisted, initially and at various places in the construction, that this is merely a matter of convenience in formulation and that everything essential can be translated into the formal symbolism (which, however, he did not provide, except for the initial section). Further, he insisted that the choice of a "solipsistic" basis is a matter of methodology, not metaphysics. Other bases are possible, if we drop the requirement that the order of constitution follow the epistemological order—for example, a physicalistic basis or a basis lying in the whole psychical realm, not in the *eigenpsychische* alone. Finally, he stated explicitly that what he was attempting was not a description of the actual process of concept formation but rather its logical reconstruction.

Practical bearings. In the concluding portion of the *Aufbau* (Part V), Carnap examined the bearing of constitution theory on philosophy and science, epistemology and metaphysics, primarily through an inquiry into the problems of psychophysical parallelism and reality. With respect to the first problem, Carnap distinguished the empirical noting of a certain parallelism between two different series of experiences (namely, between observations of events in one's own brain and experiences of one's own mind) from the interpretation placed on this phenomenon. Only the former, he held, is a scientific question; the latter is a purely metaphysical one. Similarly, he distinguished between the constitutional or empirical problem of reality (for example, "Is the Trojan War a real event or merely a product of poetic imagination?") and the metaphysical problem of reality (for example, "Are perceived physical things real or merely contents of consciousness?"). The former has to do with whether (and how) an object can be incorporated into a comprehensive system of regularities and what its position is in the time ordering. The metaphysical problem, on the other hand, cannot even be expressed in constitutional terms.

Thus, the view of the *Aufbau* is that metaphysical problems have nothing to do with science. Hence, constitution theory, according to Carnap, is neither idealistic nor realistic but metaphysically neutral.

ELIMINATION OF METAPHYSICS

With a short monograph that appeared the same year as the *Aufbau* (1928), Carnap, largely influenced by Wittgenstein, moved from skeptical neutrality regarding metaphysics to radical opposition. The publication, entitled *Scheinprobleme in der Philosophie: Das Fremdpsychische und der Realismusstreit* ("Pseudo Problems in Philosophy: Other Minds and the Realism Controversy"), argued that metaphysical problems in general, and the problem of realism and idealism in particular, must be characterized as pseudo problems. This view soon came to prevail in the Vienna circle; Carnap persuaded even Schlick to abandon (perhaps not altogether) his realism.

Meaning and verification. The notion of pseudo problem in philosophy is important both because of its influence on other writers and because of its recurrence in one form or another throughout Carnap's writings, although it is never central to Carnap's systematic thought. This notion is best understood in the context of empiricist theories of meaning. In its original version it is based directly on what Carnap refers to as Wittgenstein's principle of verifiability. This asserts that the meaning of a statement is given by the conditions of its verification and that a statement is meaningful if and only if it is in principle verifiable. The verifiability requirement was later replaced by the weaker one of confirmability.

More generally, an empiricist theory of meaning holds that words derive their meaning from satisfying certain conditions, these conditions being identified with some kind of direct or indirect empirical reference. Carnap and other logical empiricists also regard certain linguistic and mathematical expressions and statements as meaningful (although without factual content) in that they concern the structure of languages in which empirical statements are made. But all statements other than those with empirical reference and the linguistic ones just mentioned are to be discarded as meaningless. The rejected statements include most, if not all, of the statements generally dealt with under the heading of metaphysics and many of those dealt with in ethics and aesthetics. Carnap holds that problems in these areas, as usually formulated, admit as "answers" only such meaningless statements. Accordingly, they are not real problems at all. They are merely formulations that have the appearance of being statements of problems, whereas in reality they violate empirical (and syntactical) criteria of meaningfulness.

Pseudo statements. The notion of pseudo problem is at the base of the Vienna circle program against metaphysics. A vigorous defense of the program is found in Carnap's essay "Überwindung der Metaphysik durch logische Analyse der Sprache" ("The Elimination of Metaphysics Through Logical Analysis of Language," 1932). In this essay Carnap distinguished two kinds of pseudo statements, those that contain a word erroneously thought to have empirical meaning and those whose constituents, although meaningful, are put together in a countersyntactical way. Arguing that both varieties occur in abundance in metaphysics, he cited as illustrations certain sentences from Martin Heidegger's *Was ist Metaphysik?* (*What Is Metaphysics?*). The last of these is the famous *Das Nichts selbst nichtet* ("The nothing itself nothings"), which, according to Carnap, sins doubly. It contains both an utterly meaningless word, the verb *nichtet*, and a countersyntactical use of the word "nothing" as a noun (instead of as the verbal rendering of the negation of an existential quantifier, as in "$\sim(\exists x)Px$" or "Nothing is *P*").

PHYSICALISM AND THE UNITY OF SCIENCE

In the *Aufbau*, Carnap chose a phenomenalistic or sense-data basis for his construction, influenced by the neopositivist epistemology of Mach and Russell. He encountered strong opposition on this point from another active participant in the Vienna circle, Otto Neurath. Raised in a materialist tradition, Neurath favored a "physicalistic" basis or language and succeeded in persuading Carnap to adopt this attitude.

Protocol sentences. The issue between phenomenalism and physicalism, already foreshadowed in the *Aufbau*, was the choice not of a metaphysics but of a language. The central problem was the nature and preferred form of the so-called protocol, or report, sentences—the sentences that form the confirmation basis of science. So long as the aim of philosophy, as in the *Aufbau*, was to reduce all knowledge to a basis of certainty in terms of a neopositivist "immediately given," the preference was for the phenomenalistic language. But Carnap's abandonment of the preferred epistemological status of phenomenal reports reopened the question of the relative merits, for construction, of the phenomenalistic as against the physical report language.

Physicalism. In agreement with Neurath, Carnap adopted the position of physicalism that the protocol sentences of science can be expressed as quantitative descriptions of definite space-time points. In this view all of science (biological and psychological, as well as physical) consists of sentences equivalent to sentences of the physical protocol language.

The physical language was to be preferred because it was intersensual (common to various senses), intersubjective, and universal—in that all sentences in all sciences were asserted to be translatable into protocol sentences. The translation, as in the *Aufbau*, is a kind of reduction; the condition for reducibility is that the sentence being reduced be equivalent in a prescribed sense to the proposed reduction. This procedure, as will be shown, was later to raise certain problems and to lead to a reconsideration both of the problem of reduction and of the verifiability theory of meaning.

Unity of science. Along with physicalism Neurath advocated the principle of the unity of science, that all empirical sciences are fundamentally one and that the division into branches is purely practical in nature. This principle was directed chiefly against the prevailing sharp distinction between natural science and the *Geisteswissenschaften* (the social sciences and the humanities). Such a distinction, Neurath believed, hindered the application of scientific methods to the social sciences.

Carnap adopted this principle in the form of the thesis that the total language of science can be constructed on a physicalistic basis. This position and its application to psychology were presented in two articles published in 1932, "Die physikalische Sprache als Universalsprache der Wissenschaft" (*The Unity of Science*) and "Psychologie in physikalischer Sprache" ("Psychology in Physical Language").

LOGICAL SYNTAX OF LANGUAGE

Carnap's attention in the period following the *Aufbau* was focused mainly on the foundations of logic and mathematics. His underlying aim was to create a theory of linguistic expressions as a means of bringing greater clarity into the formulation of philosophical problems.

Foundations of mathematics. In disputes on the foundations of mathematics Carnap, following Frege, took the logicist view, publishing a number of papers in its defense. But he also found common ground with aspects of David Hilbert's formalism and L. E. J. Brouwer's intuitionism. In particular, the formalist investigations led him to stress the distinction between what he called "object language" (the language that is the object of a study) and "metalanguage" (the language in which the theory of the object language is formulated). In these terms Carnap's goal became the construction of a suitable metalanguage in which to conduct philosophy or the logical analysis of language. The first major fruit was *Logische Syntax der Sprache* (*Logical Syntax of Language*), published in 1934.

From a technical logical viewpoint, the *Logische Syntax* represents a clarification and systematization, with further development, of methods that had been devised by Hilbert and the Polish logicians (and at the time Carnap was preparing the *Syntax* had proved their immense value in connection with Gödel's famous proof). In the book Carnap developed two model languages. The first of these (Language I) is definite; the second (Language II) is not—"definite" meaning that either all constants and closed expressions are undefined or their defining expressions contain no unlimited quantifiers. Language I has many of the features that Brouwer and his followers regard as requirements; Carnap looked upon it as more or less representative of their constructivist or finitist intentions (although Brouwer and Arend Heyting never accepted this partial identification). Language II was offered as representative of classical mathematics. In clarifying his attitude with regard to these languages, Carnap enunciated his principle of tolerance (or "principle of the conventionality of language forms"): "*It is not our business to set up prohibitions.* . . . In logic there are no morals. Everone is at liberty to build up his own, i.e. his own form of language, as he wishes" (pp. 51–52).

Syntactic structure. The systematic portion of the *Syntax* outlined a general structure for characterizing the syntax of any language whatsoever. This consists of the formation rules (which, typically, specify the admissible symbols and sentences) and transformation rules of the language, together with a number of concepts that can be used in characterizing the language. Among these latter are the d-terms (terms relating to the concept of derivation, such as "derivable," "proof," "demonstrable," "refutable," and "resoluble") and the c-terms (terms relating to the concept of consequence, such as "consequence," "consequence class," "valid," "contravalid," and "indeterminate"). The transformation rules always include at least some of a logico-mathematical character. These Carnap called the L-rules; the others (if any) he called the physical, or P-, rules. In any language there is a sublanguage (possibly the whole) containing all of the L-rules and no P-rules. This is the L-sublanguage. It, in turn, can be characterized in the same way as the whole language, and this gives rise to L-c- and L-d-terms which correspond one-to-one with c- and d-terms. For example, "analytic" can be regarded as L-valid, "synthetic" as L-indeterminate, and so on. The result is the following classification of sentences: (1) demonstrable, (2) analytic but not demonstrable, (3) P-valid, (4) P-indeterminate, (5) P-contravalid, (6) contradictory but not refutable, and (7) refutable. In terms of the d-classification the members of classes 2 to 6 can be called irresoluble. For the L-classification 1 and 2 are analytic, 3, 4, and 5 synthetic, and 6 and 7 contradictory. For the c-classification 1, 2, and 3 are valid and 5, 6, and 7 contravalid.

Translation and interpretation. With the aid of the outlined structure Carnap characterized the translation and interpretation of languages. In view of the later development of his thought, it is important to note that in the *Syntax* he treated "consequence" as a syntactical relation, one, therefore, that does not involve the meanings of the sentences in question.

Philosophical relevance. In the last part of the *Logische Syntax*, as in all his major works, Carnap discussed the philosophical relevance of his findings. (The same ground was covered in popular form in his *Philosophy and Logical Syntax* of 1935, based on lectures delivered at the University of London in October 1934.) Two main points deserve mention. First, he identified the logic of science (which, for the Vienna circle, was to replace traditional philosophy) with the logical syntax of the language of science. Second, he located a prime source of philosophical pseudo problems in the use—in talk about syntax—of what he termed the "material mode of speech."

The latter notion was a kind of by-product of Frege's distinction between use and mention. The normal, or object, use of a word (or expression) is to designate the object to which it refers. But words and sets of words can also be used—and in syntactical discourse are used—to designate words (or expressions). Certain sentences, however, which seem at first glance to be object sentences turn out on closer inspection to be about words. Such sentences are said by Carnap to be in the "material mode." An example is "Five is not a thing but a number." For Carnap this is merely an alternative way of saying "'Five' is not a thing-word but a number-word." As the illustration shows, the material mode is used because it yields simpler, less complicated sentences.

However, an element of danger arises from the fact that such sentences appear to be in the object language. Where these are translatable into the formal (syntactical) mode and the context makes the translation reasonably unambiguous, Carnap does not object to the material mode. He does believe, however, that its use is the source of much confusion in philosophy. For one thing, in most cases the syntactical assertion intended depends on the context; freed from a sufficiently delimited context, sentences in the material mode may create a false impression of generality, so that disputes about which language should be, or is being, used take on the aspect and heat of factual disputes. For another, because such sentences appear to be object sentences, there is a standing temptation to ask questions and provide "answers" (formed by analogy with object sentences) that end up either in being untranslatable into the formal mode or in yielding absurd results when so translated. This situation, according to Carnap, is largely responsible for the development of metaphysical and other pseudo problems.

EMPIRICIST PHILOSOPHY OF SCIENCE

While still in Prague, Carnap had been made aware of some grave defects in the logical positivist view of scientific knowledge. Logical positivists had demanded that all sentences of empirical science be reducible to, or translatable into, basic or protocol sentences, which express our knowledge of the "immediately given." This requirement of reducibility, together with the verifiability theory of meaning, entailed that all meaningful sentences admit of complete, definite verification or refutation. The result, whether expressed in phenomenalist or physicalist terms, was a semiclosed system of knowledge whose rigidity was in sharp contrast with the real situation in science. Stimulated by such critics as Karl Popper, as well as by his own misgivings and those of other Vienna circle members, Carnap initiated some radical changes designed to bring the circle's views more into accord with the open character of scientific knowledge. The changes centered on the reducibility thesis and the principle of verification.

Reducibility. Refinements in the notion of reduction were reported on by Carnap in a paper, "Über die Einheitssprache der Wissenschaft" ("The Unity Language of Science"), presented to the International Congress of Scientific Philosophy in Paris in 1935 (*Actes du Congrès international de philosophie scientifique*, Fasc. II, Paris, 1936). The paper considered reductions (such as those of disposition terms) in which what can be asserted is not that a new symbol is equivalent to certain other symbols but only that it is equivalent under certain appropriate circumstances. Take, for instance, the reduction sentence for "soluble (in water)." This might read either (1) "A substance is soluble if and only if when it is placed in water it dissolves" or (2) "If a substance is placed in water it is soluble if and only if it dissolves." Carnap showed that (2), not (1), captures the ordinary sense of "soluble (in water)." He proposed henceforth to call sentences of form (1) definitions and to reserve the term "reduction" for sentences of form (2).

The difference between the two forms is more important than appears at first sight. Definitions permit the uniform elimination of a newly introduced symbol, such as "soluble (in water)," through the use of the equivalent symbols; reductions do not. And since many scientific terms, Carnap argued, are reducible but not definable, sentence-by-sentence reducibility (in the original sense of explicit definability) can no longer be made a general requirement. We must therefore distinguish two forms of positivism and physicalism, one that claims that all scientific concepts are definable in terms of protocols in the phenomenalistic or physicalistic language and one that makes the weaker claim of reducibility to such protocols. The definability thesis is obviously wrong, as is the corollary that all sentences of science are translatable into the sense-data and physical languages. There is a logical relation between the sentences of science and the languages in question, but it is more complicated than had been thought.

Verification and confirmation. The problems posed by the verification principle were dealt with in Carnap's important paper "Testability and Meaning" (1936–1937). Accepting Popper's criticism, Carnap agreed that scientific hypotheses can never be completely verified by observational evidence. He therefore replaced the concept of verification with that of confirmation. He proposed to say that hypotheses are more or less confirmed or disconfirmed by the evidence (leaving open the question of a possible quantitative account of confirmation). In addition, he distinguished between confirmability and the stronger notion of testability. A sentence is confirmable if observation sentences can contribute to its confirmation or disconfirmation. A confirmable sentence, moreover, is testable if we can define and produce at will experiments that would lead to a confirmation. Thus, a sentence may be confirmable without being testable—as when we know that the observation of a certain course of events would confirm the sentence but are unable to set up the experiments required for such an observation.

After a careful logical analysis of these concepts Carnap concluded that there are four different ways of stating the principle of empiricism: we may require that every synthetic sentence be (1) completely testable, (2) testable (3) completely confirmable, or (4) confirmable. Formulations (2) and (4) would admit, and (1) and (3) exclude, universal scientific statements. Carnap holds that all four come within the general point of view represented by empiricism. His own preference is for the more liberal requirement of (mere) confirmability.

Thus, the demand that all scientific concepts be explicitly definable in terms of observables is replaced by the weaker requirement of reducibility. The demand that all scientific sentences be translatable into sentences about observables gives way to the weaker requirement of confirmability.

STUDIES IN SEMANTICS

In the *Logische Syntax*, Carnap held that philosophical problems are really problems of syntax. But Alfred Tarski's pioneering researches in semantics soon persuaded Carnap to broaden his view. The logical analysis of language, he concluded, must go beyond syntax, the study of the forms of expressions without regard to meaning. It must also embrace semantics, the theory of the concepts of meaning and truth. This new field now became his major interest, and once settled in America, he published a monograph for the *International Encyclopedia of Unified Science* entitled *Foundations of Logic and Mathematics* (1939) and then a series of works entitled *Studies in Semantics*.

Mechanism of semantics. The first study in Carnap's series, *Introduction to Semantics* (1942), undertook to construct the mechanism of semantics in a way similar to the construction in the *Syntax*. As before, Carnap paid special attention to the L-concepts, those that are applicable on logical grounds alone, such as "logically true" or "logically deducible." These are readily defined for particular semantical systems. But the task of defining "absolute" correlates of the L-concepts, applicable to semantical systems in general, presents special difficulties. It can be achieved, Carnap believes, but only with an intensional logic, and in the *Semantics* he restricted discussion to extensional logics. He then went on to reformulate syntax and to consider the relations between syntax and semantics.

Syntax and semantics. An interesting appendix to the *Introduction to Semantics* (Paragraph 39) outlined changes in Carnap's views since publication of the *Syntax*. In the main these were of two types. First, he now believed that certain concepts hitherto regarded as syntactical are basically semantical. These include "range," "extensionality," "analytic," "synthetic," "contradictory" (applied to sentences), "implication," and "equivalence." In many instances the concepts have syntactical correlates—and it is these that had been dealt with in the *Syntax*. Carnap concluded that usage in science and, to a degree, in ordinary discourse makes the semantical accounts more reasonable. Second, he introduced a corresponding change with respect to the task of philosophy: instead of rejecting the logic of meaning, Carnap now regarded it as being "fulfilled by semantics." The translations of philosophical sentences into syntactical terms, presented in the final part of the *Syntax*, he replaced with less strained translations into semantical terms. He still endorsed, in general, his strictures on the material mode of speech. But the chief thesis of the *Syntax* was amended to read: "The task of philosophy is semantic analysis."

Propositional calculus. The second study in semantics, actually completed before the first, was *Formalization of Logic* (1943). In it Carnap showed that the conventional formalizations of the propositional calculus constitute a formalization of propositional logic as a semantic system; that is, the relations of c-implication (the converse of "derivable") and L-implication hold in the same cases. It is not a full formalization, however, since nonnormal interpretations of the calculus are possible. By means of the new concept of "junctives" he was able to set up fully formalized propositional, as well as functional, calculi.

Nonextensional logic. The third volume on semantics, *Meaning and Necessity* (1947), and the article "Modalities and Quantification" (1946) were devoted to the question of nonextensional logic. Carnap first gave plausible explications, in terms of equivalence and L-equivalence, respectively, of the old concepts of extension and intension. He used this pair of concepts as the basis for a new method of semantical analysis which he offered in place of the usual method of the name relation, which had dominated discussions of meaning since Frege. In discussing nonextensional contexts Carnap cited certain kinds (belief sentences, for example) for which intension in his sense fails to provide an adequate explanation; he suggested a stronger concept, "intensional isomorphism," which he believed would be satisfactory. He also considered the question of the possibility of an extensional metalanguage adequate for semantics and concluded that this question, though not yet solved, is solvable. Finally, having formulated semantical rules for modal concepts, he was able to construct a modal functional logic (in "Modalities and Quantification") the propositional part of which proved to be equivalent to C. I. Lewis' system S5.

FOUNDATIONS OF PROBABILITY

The key to an empiricist theory of meaning, Carnap had argued in "Testability and Meaning," lay in the concept of degree of confirmation. Accordingly, once his work in semantics was well advanced he turned his attention to this concept. In an appendix to the *Introduction to Semantics* he had already criticized the identification of confirmation with probability, which he then interpreted as relative frequency.

Degree of confirmation. In an article called "The Two Concepts of Probability" (1945), Carnap pointed out the need to distinguish between two logically different meanings of the word "probability." The first, which he termed probability$_1$ or "degree of confirmation," is a relation between two sentences, a hypothesis *h* and a sentence *e* reporting, say, a series of relevant observations. This relation is a logical one, weaker than, but generally similar to, those holding in deductive logic. Elementary statements of probability$_{(1)}$ are L-determinate (analytic or contradictory). The second, termed probability$_{(2)}$ or "relative frequency," is the statistical concept used, for example, by Richard von Mises and Hans Reichenbach. It is a relation between properties or classes of events. Elementary statements of probability$_{(2)}$ are factual, not logical, although the general theorems, of course, express mathematical relations and hence are L-true. Thus, the two meanings are basically dissimilar concepts, not two explications of one concept. Carnap later suggested that probability$_{(1)}$ was the initial meaning and that probability$_{(2)}$ originated in a confusion between an estimate and a predicted value.

Inductive and deductive logic. The field of probability was treated systematically and in detail in Carnap's major treatise, *Logical Foundations of Probability* (1950). His guiding thought was that a parallel exists between deductive logic and inductive logic. In deductive logic if we assert, say, a relation of L-implication between two sentences, we state something that (at least in principle) can be established by a logical analysis of the meanings of the sentences, provided a definition of "L-implication" is given. Our assertion is a complete statement and does not need to be supplemented by reference to specific rules. And, of course, the truth of the statement implies consequences with respect to the rationality of decisions: if *A* L-implies *B* and we accept *A*, then a decision based on *B* is justified. Similarly, in inductive logic if we assert that the degree of confirmation of *A* on the basis of *B* is some number *k*, we are also stating something that follows from the logical analysis of the meanings of the sentences and from the definition of "degree of confirmation." This assertion is likewise a complete sentence, requiring no reference to specific inductive rules, although it does depend on the definition of "degree of confirmation." Its truth, too, implies consequences about the rationality of decisions. In view of these similarities Carnap feels justified in claiming that basically the same relations exist between his inductive logic and the inductive processes as between deductive logic and the process of deduction.

Confirmation functions. The construction in *Probability* is based primarily on the concepts of state description and range, which Carnap had already used in *Semantics*. Essentially the technique consists in defining a measure function $m(p)$ on the ranges of sentences p and then defining $c(h,e)$, the degree of confirmation of a hypothesis h on evidence e, as $m(e \cdot h)/m(e)$. In order for the definition to agree with standard usage it is necessary to restrict m to positive values such that their sum over the state descriptions is 1. If these conditions are satisfied Carnap calls the resulting measure and confirmation functions, m and c, regular. A considerable number of standard probability theorems (for instance, Bayes' theorem) can be proved for all regular c-functions. A further condition which Carnap believes should be imposed is the invariance of the values over variation of individual constants. The c-functions that satisfy this condition he calls symmetrical. Among theorems provable for symmetrical c-functions are those of direct inductive inference (that is, the inference from the frequency of a property in a population to its frequency in a sample), such as Bernoulli's theorem.

Among the symmetrical c-functions Carnap, mostly on grounds of plausibility, prefers one that assigns the same value to all structure descriptions (sets of isomorphic state descriptions). This function he calls c^*. Although c^* gives plausible values for many standard cases, a problem arises, for where h is a scientific law, $c^*(h,e)=0$ for Carnap's language with an infinite number of individuals. This seems at first sight to make c^* implausible, for example, the individual constants are to be interpreted as space-time points. Even for this case, however, we get nontrivial values for the instances, and Carnap believes that instance confirmation provides a suitable explication of what is usually meant by the confirmation of a law.

In discussing his system Carnap insists that inductive logic is to be useful, in two senses. First, he believes that if this type of system were extended to the whole of the language of science—as distinguished from the very simple language on which his actual system is based—it would serve as a logical foundation for statistical inference. Second, the system can serve as a justification for practical decisions, especially in cases where knowledge of relative frequency is incomplete so that decisions must be based on estimates of relative frequencies. In such instances recourse must be had to probability$_{(1)}$.

Some problems in Carnap's system. In *Probability*, Carnap chose to operate with languages of relatively simple structure. Primitive predicates were required to be logically independent. Relational predicates were not considered. However, a problem was pointed out independently by John G. Kemeny ("Carnap on Probability," in *Review of Metaphysics*, Vol. 5, 1951, 145–156) and Yehoshua Bar-Hillel ("A Note on State-descriptions," in *Philosophical Studies*, Vol. 2, 1951, 72–75). As they showed, Carnap's independence requirement would exclude any primitive predicate that by virtue of its meaning has logical structure. The predicate "warmer than" is by its meaning asymmetric; hence, the sentences "*a* is warmer than *b*" and "*b* is warmer than *a*" are incompatible rather than independent. No state description containing both could represent a possible case. The difficulty can be overcome in two ways. One is to maintain the independence requirement but to avoid primitive predicates with logical structure. The other, first proposed by Kemeny and endorsed by Carnap in his preface to the second edition of *Probability* (1962), admits primitive relational (and one-place) predicates with logical structure but restricts the concept of state description to the possible cases by means of meaning postulates. There are interesting analogies between this result and Carnap's conclusions about reducibility in "Testability and Meaning."

ONTOLOGY AND SCIENTIFIC THEORY

Existence. Although most of his recent work centers on induction and probability, Carnap has continued to write on other problems related to empiricism and scientific theory. Particular interest was aroused by his paper "Empiricism, Semantics, and Ontology" (1950). In this paper Carnap sought to clarify issues raised by the use of abstract entities (for example, properties as designated by predicates) in semantics and to dispel the fear that such use is incompatible with empiricism. His chief point was that we must distinguish two kinds of questions about the existence or reality of entities. The first ("internal questions") concern the existence of entities within a given theoretical or linguistic framework. These are genuine questions and are settled by empirical or purely logical means, depending on whether the framework is factual or logical. The second ("external questions") concern the ontological status of the systems of entities as a whole. Carnap's contention was that "acceptance of a framework" carries no commitment with respect to these "external questions" of existence. Indeed, such questions (exemplified in the realism–idealism and Platonism–nominalism controversies) were once again affirmed to be pseudo questions. The only real issue involved is the purely practical one of the choice of linguistic forms—and concerning this, as in the *Syntax* years before, Carnap counseled tolerance.

Theory and observation. The relation between scientific theory and observation is discussed in two recent papers, "The Methodological Character of Theoretical Concepts" (1956) and "Beobachtungssprache und theoretische Sprache" ("Observation Language and Theoretical Language," 1958). In these Carnap extended the process, begun in "Testability and Meaning," of liberalizing the empiricist criterion of significance for the theoretical language of science. He specifically rejected not only the requirement of translatability but also that of reducibility—in the sense that every term must either refer to something directly observable or be explicitly involved in the correspondence rules connecting the theoretical language to the observation language. He now offered instead a tentative minimum criterion that goes somewhat as follows: A theoretical term t is significant if there exists a sentence S using t such that from S and the remainder of the theory it is possible to derive an observation sentence that would not follow without S. Sentences are then regarded as significant if all their terms are.

Although this formulation, too, is within the empiricist tradition, it is substantially more liberal than any Carnap had previously proposed. It constitutes a still further recognition of the open character of scientific concepts. In a sense, perhaps, Carnap has moved to meet his pragmatist critics, such as W. V. Quine. But he has not joined them, for he still holds the view that one can do full justice to the open character of science and yet retain a sharp distinction between those terms and sentences that have cognitive meaning and those that do not.

Works by Carnap

P. A. Schilpp, ed., *The Philosophy of Rudolf Carnap*, Vol. XI in the Library of Living Philosophers (La Salle, Ill., 1963), is indispensable. This 1,100-page volume contains Carnap's illuminating intellectual autobiography, 26 critical essays on various aspects of his philosophy, his replies to the critics, and an exhaustive bibliography.

Carnap's major works include *Der Logische Aufbau der Welt* (Berlin, 1928); *Scheinprobleme in der Philosophie: Das Fremdpsychische und der Realismusstreit* (Berlin, 1928); *Logische Syntax der Sprache* (Vienna, 1934), translated by Amethe Smeaton as *Logical Syntax of Language* (London, 1937); *Philosophy and Logical Syntax* (London, 1935); "Testability and Meaning," in *Philosophy of Science*, Vol. 3 (1936), 419–471, and Vol. 4 (1937), 1–40; *Foundations of Logic and Mathematics*, Vol. I, No. 3, of *International Encyclopedia of Unified Science* (Chicago, 1939); *Introduction to Semantics* (Cambridge, Mass., 1942); *Formalization of Logic* (Cambridge, Mass., 1943); *Meaning and Necessity: A*

Study in Semantics and Modal Logic (Chicago, 1947; 2d enl. ed., 1956); *Logical Foundations of Probability* (Chicago, 1950; 2d ed., 1962); *The Continuum of Inductive Methods* (Chicago, 1952); and "The Methodological Character of Theoretical Concepts," in Herbert Feigl et al., eds., *Minnesota Studies in the Philosophy of Science,* Vol. I (Minneapolis, 1956), pp. 38–76.

Other important writings of Carnap are *Der Raum. Ein Beitrag zur Wissenschaftslehre* (Berlin, 1922); *Physikalische Begriffsbildung* (Karlsruhe, 1926); *Abriss der Logistik* (Vienna, 1929); "Die Mathematik als Zweig der Logik," in *Blätter für Deutsche Philosophie,* Vol. 4 (1930), 298–310; "Überwindung der Metaphysik durch die logische Analyse der Sprache," in *Erkenntnis,* Vol. 2 (1931–1932), 219–241, translated by Arthur Pap as "The Elimination of Metaphysics Through Logical Analysis of Language," in A. J. Ayer, ed., *Logical Positivism* (Glencoe, Ill., 1959), pp. 60–81; "Die physikalische Sprache als Universalsprache der Wissenschaft," in *Erkenntnis,* Vol. 2 (1931–1932), 432–465, translated by Max Black as *The Unity of Science* (London, 1934); "Psychologie in physikalischer Sprache," in *Erkenntnis,* Vol. 3 (1932–1933), 107–142, translated by George (i.e., Frederic) Schick as "Psychology in Physical Language," in Ayer, *op. cit.,* pp. 165–198; *Die Aufgabe der Wissenschaftslogik* (Vienna, 1934); "Über Extremalaxiome," written with F. Bachmann, in *Erkenntnis,* Vol. 6 (1936–1937), 166–188; "Logical Foundations of the Unity of Science," in Vol. I, No. 1, of *International Encyclopedia of Unified Science* (Chicago, 1938), pp. 42–62; "The Two Concepts of Probability," in *Philosophy and Phenomenological Research,* Vol. 5 (1945), 513–532, reprinted in Herbert Feigl and W. S. Sellars, eds., *Readings in Philosophical Analysis* (New York, 1949), pp. 330–348; "Remarks on Induction and Truth," in *Philosophy and Phenomenological Research,* Vol. 6 (1946), 590–602; "Modalities and Quantification," in *Journal of Symbolic Logic,* Vol. 11 (1946), 33–64; "Probability as a Guide in Life," in *Journal of Philosophy,* Vol. 44 (1947), 141–148; "Empiricism, Semantics, and Ontology," in *Revue internationale de philosophie,* 4th year (1950), 20–40, reprinted in *Meaning and Necessity,* 2d ed., *op. cit.,* pp. 205–221; *An Outline of the Theory of Semantic Information,* written with Yehoshua Bar-Hillel (Cambridge, Mass., 1952); "Meaning Postulates," in *Philosophical Studies,* Vol. 3 (1952), 65–73, reprinted in *Meaning and Necessity,* 2d ed., *op. cit.,* pp. 222–229; *Einführung in die symbolische Logik, mit besonderer Berücksichtigung ihrer Anwendungen* (Vienna, 1954), translated by W. H. Meyer and John Wilkinson as *Introduction to Symbolic Logic* (New York, 1958); "Meaning and Synonymy in Natural Languages," in *Philosophical Studies,* Vol. 6 (1955), 33–47, reprinted in *Meaning and Necessity,* 2d ed., *op. cit.,* pp. 233–247; "Beobachtungssprache und theoretische Sprache," in *Dialectica,* Vol. 12 (1958–1959), 236–248 (with English abstract); "The Aim of Inductive Logic," in Ernest Nagel, Patrick Suppes, and Alfred Tarski, eds., *Logic, Methodology, and Philosophy of Science* (Stanford, Calif., 1962), pp. 303–318.

Works on Carnap

A detailed analysis of *Der logische Aufbau* is in Nelson Goodman, *The Structure of Appearance* (Cambridge, Mass., 1951). The views of the Vienna circle of the 1930s are presented and summarized, with special reference to Carnap, in Victor Kraft, *Der Wiener Kreis* (Vienna, 1950), translated by Arthur Pap as *The Vienna Circle* (New York, 1953), Joergen Joergensen, *The Development of Logical Empiricism* (Chicago, 1951); and Julius Weinberg, *An Examination of Logical Positivism* (London, 1936). Important reviews of *Logische Syntax* include one by Ernest Nagel in *Journal of Philosophy,* Vol. 32 (1935), 49–52, and one by L. Susan Stebbing in *Philosophy,* Vol. 13 (1938), 485–486. *Meaning and Necessity* was given a very hostile review by Gilbert Ryle in *Philosophy,* Vol. 24 (1949), 69–76. See also Max Black, "Carnap on Logic and Semantics," in *Problems of Analysis* (London, 1954), reprinted from *Philosophical Studies—Essays in Memory of L. Susan Stebbing* (London, 1948). Wolfgang Stegmüller, *Die Wahrheitsidee und die Idee der Semantik* ("The Idea of Truth and the Idea of Semantics," Vienna, 1957), gives a detailed analysis of Carnap's work in semantics.

Several valuable discussions of various aspects of Carnap's thought are contained in B. H. Kazemeir and D. Vuysje, eds., *Logic and Language* (Dordrecht, Netherlands, 1962), a collection of studies dedicated to Carnap on the occasion of his seventieth birthday.

NORMAN M. MARTIN

CARNEADES (c. 213–c. 128 B.C.), a leader of the Academic Skeptics who as head of Plato's Academy developed its antidogmatism far beyond the point to which Arcesilaus had brought it. As in the case of Arcesilaus, we have nothing written by Carneades. His philosophy as we know it is a set of criticisms of the Epicureans and the Stoics, especially of the Stoic Chrysippus.

Carneades was born in Cyrene, Cyrenaica (now in Libya), and lived to be about 85 years old, becoming blind in his old age. He dressed negligently and never accepted an invitation to dinner, so that he could keep at his work. It is said that while eating he would become so absorbed in his thoughts that friends had to move his hands for him. But he was unbeatable in argument and had great oratorical powers. About 156 B.C. he went on a mission to Rome with some other Athenian notables in order to convince Rome to exempt Athens from a fine that had been imposed. At this time he illustrated the logic of Skepticism by delivering his two famous orations, one praising justice and proving that its foundations are in natural law, the other, with equal persuasiveness, praising injustice and reducing the notion of justice to utility.

Epistemology. All philosophers of this era held that knowledge came by way of *phantasia* (representations), not by way of pure, intuitive *theoria* (knowledge of intelligible forms). The Stoics, in particular, believed that the mind in certain cases receives sense representations that irresistibly make the mind assent to them (*phantasia kataleptike*). Such true representations are the foundations upon which the Stoics built their whole dogmatic epistemology and metaphysics. But, said Carneades, all representations involve an affection or action of the mind considering them—if there is no action, there is no apprehension of the representation—so a representation is not received like a stamp upon wax but is mixed in with subjective or affective elements of various sorts. This we plainly see in those cases where representations that pass for true are in fact false (for example, Hercules' mistaking his sons for enemies and killing them by mistake; oars appearing crooked in water).

Indeed, Carneades asserted, there is no one intrinsic mark that sets off the *phantasia kataleptike* from only apparently true ones; there is no criterion that can be used for distinguishing them, so must suspend judgment upon the objective truth of each given representation.

But a representation is not only *of* something purportedly objective; it is also a representation *to* or *for* some subject, some person. Furthermore, the great strength of the Stoics lay in the practicality, the direct relevance of their philosophy to expediential and moral action. They attacked the New Academy for undermining human action by trying to put into *epoche,* or suspension, the reasonable grounds of human action. From Zeno to Chrysippus they claimed that the Skeptics paralyzed men in the process of rendering them skeptical. To meet this claim, so important to philosophers at the time, Carneades developed his doctrine of the probable, *to pithanon*. In action we do not need dogmatic, objective truth; all we need is probable understanding. The probable is that which, to some extent, appears true, induces our assent. There are three degrees of probability. The first and lowest is that which involves belief but has no support from other representations. A higher kind excites belief but is also consistent with, and supported by, other representations. The highest degree of probability occurs when a given belief not only is plausible in itself, and related to other representations, but is such that an investigation of these other, supporting representations reveals each of them to be as vivacious and distinct as our first representation.

The highest degree of probability is possessed by the *tested* representation. In practical life we must, in various circumstances, be satisfied with varying degrees of probability (an unarmed man confronting a lion in a jungle acts upon a lower level of probability than does a physician confronting a disease). But we must never forget that this is probability *for us* and not necessarily *the* objective truth concerning the external cause or the origin of that representation. In this awareness we remain skeptics and are at the same time capable of practical and moral action.

Theology. The Stoics' doctrines concerning the existence and nature of God were put into *epoche* by Carneades in various ways. He cast doubt upon their *consensus gentium* argument for God's existence by simply pointing out that there are atheists and that there are nations we know nothing about—how then can we defend the claim that all men believe in God? Besides, that a belief is *universal* is one thing; that it is *true* is another, different thing. Chrysippus had used an argument from design: given that there is something man cannot build, the one who builds it is superior to man; the world is such a structure; and so God, who is superior to man, exists. Carneades attacked this argument by pointing out that the "superior" force need not be God; it can be nature, or the forces of nature. Moreover, why use the question-begging word "build" in the argument? "Form" will do just as well to describe the processes we find in nature, and nature could have formed the things we see without a personal God being involved at all. In addition to such refutations, Carneades pointed out inevitable contradictions that the notion of God leads to. For instance, he is infinite, but the infinite, having no place to move, is limited, restricted, unable to move. So an infinite God is limited. He is supposed to be virtuous and perfect, but virtue involves overcoming pains and dangers, and only for a being who can suffer or be destroyed are there pains and dangers. Neither suffering nor destructibility is consistent with perfection, so God cannot be both virtuous and perfect.

Regarding the Stoics' doctrine of a rational, providential universe informed by the *logos*, Carneades agreed that there is regularity in the world, but this involves fogs, diseases, deadly animals, and death for all. What sort of providence is this? And if each individual animal is fated to have all things turn out for its own good, is it for its own good that the pig is killed? As for man, how can God's providence permit him to allow so many men to use their reason faultily, in a way injurious to themselves and to others? Moreover, if he allows weaknesses and misery in the universe—whether intentionally or unintentionally—he is at fault, since intentional neglect and unintentional neglect are both faults. And these evils cannot be dismissed as "minor"; they are of great importance to the creatures who suffer from them.

Morality. Chrysippus and the other Stoics asserted that virtue, conformity to nature, is the sole good; vice, deviation from nature, the sole evil; and the rest of human actions *adiaphora*, morally indifferent. But, said Carneades, the Sage of the Stoics wants certain things in nature other than virtue, and therefore these things are not indifferent; they are in fact good, along with virtue. He caused Antipater the Stoic to admit that a good reputation is good too, even though Chrysippus, in the traditional manner, had put it among the *adiaphora*. All that it is necessary to talk about is what men in fact pursue. The art of effectively pursuing what we want was designated the "art of living" by Carneades. This art uses common sense and probability, *to pithanon*, to attain the fullest satisfaction of one's *orge*, or natural impulse, and eschews all arrogant, dogmatic claims to the Truth.

Stoicism, Epicureanism, and Skepticism all grappled with one of the basic problems of morality, the freedom of man to do good and evil. Carneades found that the Stoics had excluded this freedom from their tight, providential causal chain, despite their efforts to fit it in. He defended human freedom by asserting the following: (1) The will is caused, but it is caused by itself and moves by virtue of its own nature (like the Epicurean atoms, with their clinamen). (2) There are successions of events, human actions preceded by certain events and conditions, but a succession is not the same as an efficacious, causal relationship. Events precede a man's action but do not force him to act; a man's will always has the last move. (3) Even if there were a rigid causal chain predetermined from all eternity, *we* could not predict with certainty particular effects, given the many fortuitous causes that are always entering the picture; so for all practical human purposes there is no such chain, only successions of events.

Works on Carneades

ANCIENT SOURCES

Cicero, Marcus Tullius, *De Natura Deorum; Academica*, translated by H. Rackham. New York, 1933.

Diogenes Laertius, *Lives of Eminent Philosophers*, translated by R. G. Bury, Vol. I, Book IV, ch. 9. Loeb Classical Library. London, 1955.

Sextus Empiricus, translated by R. G. Bury. Loeb Classical Library. Vol. I, *Outlines of Pyrrhonism*. Cambridge, Mass., 1955. Vol. III, *Against the Physicists*. Cambridge, Mass., 1960.

MODERN REFERENCES

Brochard, V., *Les Sceptiques grecs*. Paris, 1923.

Croissant, J., "La Morale de Carnéade." *Revue internationale de la philosophie*, Vol. 1 (1938–1939), 545–570. A profoundly informative article.

Hallie, P. P., ed., *Scepticism, Man, and God*, Introduction. Middletown, Conn., 1964.

Maccoll, N., *The Greek Sceptics from Pyrrho to Sextus.* London, 1869.

Zeller, E., *The Stoics, Epicureans and Sceptics.* London, 1870. Zeller has done a masterful job of collating Cicero's remarks concerning Carneades.

PHILIP P. HALLIE

CAROLINGIAN RENAISSANCE. The reign of Charlemagne (768–814) ended the long period of cultural decay and intellectual stagnation which had begun over three centuries before with the barbarian invasions of Western Europe. Despite the disintegration of the Carolingian Empire under Charlemagne's successors, the cultural revival which he inspired continued until the Vikings put an end to it, and even then something of the achievement of the eighth and ninth centuries survived to foster the renaissance of the eleventh and twelfth centuries.

The Carolingian Renaissance was dominated by two practical interests, ecclesiastical reform and social progress. Since Charlemagne depended on churchmen to implement his educational policy, the religious motives and ecclesiastical achievements—liturgical reform, monastic renewal, advancement of clerical education—inevitably predominated. Literary sensibility and intellectual curiosity were not, however, wholly lacking in the churchmen of the age, and some charming poems and substantial doctrinal treatises remain to testify to their intellectual versatility.

The chief agent, though not the finest mind, of the Carolingian Renaissance was the Englishman Alcuin (735–804). The Irishman John Scotus Erigena (died c. 877), the Lombard Paul Warnefrid (died c. 800), the Spaniard Theodulf of Orleans (died 821), the Frenchman Remigius of Auxerre (died c. 908), and the German Rabanus Maurus (died 856) exemplify the cosmopolitan character of the movement.

The centers of the revival were cathedral and monastic schools established by legislation throughout the Frankish dominions. In addition to a theology consisting mainly of traditional Biblical exegesis, their curriculum included the seven liberal arts—the trivium of grammar, rhetoric, and logic and the quadrivium of arithmetic, geometry, astronomy, and music. The assimilation of ancient learning was stressed, and little original work was done; the chief forms of academic literature were commentaries and handbooks.

In philosophy the arts curriculum did not go beyond logic. Several scholars are known to have touched on the question of universal ideas, but the issue does not seem to have been widely debated. The Carolingian Renaissance produced very little speculative philosophy; the great exception, the work of Erigena, stands alone both in its systematic character and in its Neoplatonic inspiration. The few philosophically interesting ideas of the age emerged more or less incidentally in the course of theological reflection and debate.

Perhaps the most important single fragment of philosophical theology to survive from the ninth century is the *Dicta Candidi de Imagine Dei*, attributed to the monk Candidus, schoolmaster at Fulda in 822, which includes the earliest known dialectical demonstration of God's existence by a medieval author. The principle of the proof is the idea of the scale of perfection. Moving from that which simply exists through that which exists and lives and that which exists, lives, and possesses intelligence, the writer argues that the scale would be incomplete without the omnipotent intelligence which is God.

Another small work of some philosophical interest was obviously inspired by consideration of the problem of universals. Fredegisus of Tours (died 834), in his *Epistola de Nihilo et Tenebris*, assumes that every term has some real entity corresponding to it. He concludes that the "nothing" (*nihil*) of the orthodox Christian doctrine of creation "out of nothing" must be conceived as a preexistent, undifferentiated stuff out of which God created everything, including human souls and bodies. Fredegisus was evidently an early instance of a theological dialectician who found difficulty in reconciling the results of his logical analysis of the meaning of terms with doctrinal orthodoxy; the problem was not widely recognized as urgent until the eleventh century.

The outstanding intellectual issue of the Carolingian Renaissance was unquestionably the problem of predestination. The German monk Gottschalk (died c. 868) was accused of teaching that from eternity God has infallibly predestined some men to salvation and others to damnation; that God therefore does not in any sense will the salvation of all men; that Christ's atoning sacrifice was offered only for the elect; and that each man's will is irresistibly determined either to good or to evil. The authority of Augustine and of his great disciples Fulgentius of Ruspe and Prosper of Aquitaine was invoked by Gottschalk and others in favor of these ideas. In opposition to this intransigent Augustinianism, Erigena expounded a libertarian doctrine, inspired by Greek thought; others sought a middle way within the Augustinian tradition. The controversy was long and heated, and its terms were not always clearly defined, but it is obvious that the crucial issue was the relation between divine immutability and omnipotence, on the one hand, and human freedom and moral responsibility, on the other. After a series of conflicting synodical decisions, the moderate Augustinians were officially vindicated, but the debate was to be repeatedly renewed in the later Middle Ages and the Reformation and Counter Reformation.

A second vigorous controversy of the period had to do with the presence of Christ in the Eucharist. Paschasius Radbertus (died c. 860), in his *De Corpore et Sanguine Domini*, the first technical elaboration of Eucharistic doctrine in theological history, asserted the identity of the sacramental elements with the historical body of Jesus crucified and glorified. Although he insisted at the same time on the spiritual and mystical manner of Christ's presence, some of his statements could be interpreted in a crudely materialistic sense, and Ratramnus (died 868), in his *De Corpore et Sanguine Domini*, opposed an ostensibly symbolist doctrine to the realism of Radbertus; owing to vagueness of definition, however, it remains uncertain how far and in precisely what way the two doctrines were incompatible. The debate is significant primarily because it eventually issued in the definition of the dogma of transubstantiation by the Fourth Lateran Council (1215) and in the subtle metaphysical elaboration of that dogma in the theology of Thomas Aquinas.

Bibliography

LATIN TEXTS

Dicta Candidi de Imagine Dei, in B. Hauréau, *Histoire de la philosophie scolastique*, Vol. I. Paris, 1872. See pp. 134–137.

Fredegisus, *Epistola de Nihilo et Tenebris*, in J. P. Migne, *Patrologia Latina*, 221 vols. Paris, 1844–1864. Vol. CV, Cols. 751–756.

Paschasius Radbertus, works, *ibid.* Vol. CXX.

Ratramnus, works, *ibid.* Vol. CXXI.

WORKS ON CAROLINGIAN RENAISSANCE

Laistner, M. L. W., *Thought and Letters in Western Europe, A.D. 500–900.* London, 1931.

McCracken, G. E., ed., *Early Medieval Theology.* Philadelphia, 1957.

Waddell, Helen, *The Wandering Scholars*, 6th ed. London, 1932.

EUGENE R. FAIRWEATHER

CARROLL, LEWIS, is the pen name of Charles Lutwidge Dodgson (1832–1898). The eldest son of a large clerical family, he was born at Daresbury, Cheshire, was educated at Rugby School, and entered Christ Church, Oxford, in 1850. On obtaining first-class honors in mathematics in 1854, he was appointed student and mathematical lecturer of the college, and remained on its foundation until his death. In many ways an archetype of the pernickety bachelor don, Dodgson had a wholly uneventful academic career. Hampered by a stammer, he shone neither as lecturer nor as preacher (he took deacon's orders in 1861). He embroiled himself—often amusingly, although usually without effect—in academic politics, was for a time curator of the college common room, and visited Russia in 1867. His leisure was spent in gallery-going and theatergoing; in photography, at which he was an expert; in the writing of light verse; and in the patronage of an interminable succession of small girls. The last peculiarity has endeared him to psychoanalytical biographers, who would seem, however, to have enriched the literature of nonsense on the subject more often than they have been able to explain it.

Dodgson the mathematician published a number of books and pamphlets, none of any lasting importance. The best known is *Euclid and His Modern Rivals* (London, 1879); the most useful, probably his edition of *Euclid I & II* (London, 1882); and the most original, his contributions to the mathematical theory of voting, to which attention was drawn by D. Black in his *Theory of Committees* (Cambridge, 1958). Dodgson's mathematical outlook was, in general, conservative and provincial, aiming no higher than the improvement of elementary teaching or routine calculation. His talent found greater scope in the construction of puzzles contained in *A Tangled Tale* (London, 1885) and *Pillow Problems* (London, 1893), which at times show depth as well as ingenuity. The same can be said of his dabblings in symbolic logic, which otherwise make little advance on the work of De Morgan and Venn. His *Game of Logic* (London, 1887) and *Symbolic Logic, Part I* (London, 1893) present logic merely as a mental recreation devoted to the solution of syllogistic problems by means of a square diagram and colored counters. His logical output (see LOGIC, HISTORY OF) was completed by nine papers on elementary logic and by two short pieces in *Mind* (N.S. Vol. 3, 1894 and N.S. Vol. 4, 1895). His influence is to be seen mainly in the attempts of later logicians to imitate the elegant absurdity of his examples. Their failure merely emphasizes the rarity of his own peculiar gift.

Needless to say, that gift finds its happiest exercise in his writings for children. *Alice in Wonderland* (London, 1865), *Through the Looking-Glass* (London, 1871), and *The Hunting of the Snark* (London, 1876) and, to a lesser extent, the two parts of *Sylvie and Bruno* (London, 1889 and 1893), are the only works that keep his name alive—or deserve to do so. Apart from *Pickwick*, and perhaps *Waverley*, they seem also to be the only works of fiction generally known to philosophers, and have been constantly pillaged for quotations. All five are dream narratives or have episodes depicting dreams, whose aberrant logic is responsible for much of their philosophic interest and fun. *Alice in Wonderland* exploits the idea of sudden variations in the size of the heroine; its sequel, the conception of a world in which time, space, and causality are liable to operate in reverse. The characters—a bizarre medley of nursery and proverbial figures, animals (fabulous or otherwise), plants, playing cards, and chessmen—are all much addicted to argument; and their humor, where it does not rely upon puns, is largely a matter of pursuing logical principles to the point of sophistry or absurdity. The frog, who supposes that an unanswered door must have been asking something, is a simple case in point. The King of Hearts and the White King, who both take "nobody" for a person, are victims of the same error and have often been cited as a warning to less venial, because less nonexistent, hypostatizers of the null class.

These books are further remarkable for their echoes—and pre-echoes—of philosophic controversy. Tweedledum and Tweedledee are Berkeleian metaphysicians, and the latter has notions of logic that bespeak the influence of Leibniz. Alice herself, on the road to their house, is a step ahead of Frege in discovering the difference between *Sinn* and *Bedeutung*. Humpty Dumpty has been taken, on anatomical grounds, for a Hegelian; but his ascription of fixed meaning to proper names and denial of it to general terms, plus his confident philology and shaky mathematics, proclaim him beyond doubt an early, if eccentric, linguistic analyst. The White Knight's reactionary views on the mind–body question give no hint of the metalinguistic virtuosity he later displays in the announcement of his song. The distinctions there enunciated have been formalized by Ernest Nagel in "Haddocks' Eyes" (in J. R. Newman, *The World of Mathematics*, New York, 1956, Vol. III, pp. 1886–1890). They would not have troubled the Duchess, another adroit logician, although her primary interest is in morals. Her cat, on the other hand, although adept enough at defying the principle that an attribute must inhere in a substance, offers a regrettably invalid proof of its own madness, as does the pigeon of Alice's serpentinity. The Hatter, March Hare, and Dormouse are sounder reasoners; whatever their troubles with time, they know a fallacy of conversion when they see one, and it is no great wonder that Messrs. Russell, Moore, and McTaggart, who were supposed to resemble them, should have been known at one time as the "Mad Tea Party of Trinity."

Not even Nobody, in his senses, would venture to identify that other and more formidable trio, the Queen of Hearts and her chessboard cousins. The former's principle of government by decapitation scarcely ranks as a political theory; but the White Queen is respected by philosophers both for her abilities in believing the impossible and for her success in proving, for the special case of jam at least, that the future *will* resemble the past, if not the present. The Red Queen is no less celebrated, among physicists, for her anticipations of the theory of relativity. In this, however, she meets competition from the Bellman in the *Snark*, who has been acclaimed, on the strength of his map, as the first general relativist and is, in any case, the undisputed inventor of an interesting three-ply version of the semantic theory of truth (⊢p. ⊢p. ⊢p ≡ "p" is true). Of his crew members, the Baker, with his lost identity and Heideggerian premonitions of impending *Vernichtung*, has been plausibly represented as a protoexistentialist; but the other protagonists still abide the conjecture of commentators, as do the quest and the quarry itself. The Snark has been taken for everything from the Tichborne inheritance to the North Pole, and from a business depression to the atom bomb. F. C. S. Schiller's interpretation of it in *Mind!* (1901, pp. 87–101) as the Absolute is elaborately argued, and doubtless finds an echo in the *Oxford Dictionary*'s definition of the creature as a "chimerical animal of ill-defined characteristics and potentialities"; but its fondness for bathing machines is not really explained thereby, and the theory founders completely on the Bellman's explicit assertion, confirmed by the Baker's uncle, that Snarks are Many and not One. Nobody, it is true, has been more successful than Schiller on this point, and his views have been generally accepted; but the opinions of nonentities have no place in a grave work of learning such as the present, so neither use nor mention of them is appropriate here.

Bibliography

Apart from the standard *Life and Letters* by his nephew, S. D. Collingwood (London, 1898), the soberest accounts of Carroll's life are D. Hudson, *Lewis Carroll* (London, 1954), and R. L. Green, *Story of Lewis Carroll* (New York, 1951) and *Lewis Carroll* (New York, 1961).

The least incomplete version of Lewis Carroll's works is *The Complete Works of Lewis Carroll* (London and New York, 1939). The most philosophical editions are *The Annotated Alice* and *The Annotated Snark*, M. Gardner, ed. (New York, 1960 and 1962).

The pioneer work of logical investigation in this field is P. E. B. Jourdain, *The Philosophy of Mr B°rtr°nd R°ss°ll* (Chicago, 1918). Further light on the subject may be obtained, *inter alia*, from R. B. Braithwaite, "Lewis Carroll as Logician," in *Mathematical Gazette*, Vol. 16 (1932), 174–178; P. Alexander, "Logic and the Humour of Lewis Carroll," in *Proceedings of the Leeds Philosophical and Literary Society*, Vol. 6, Part 8 (1951), 551–566; and, despite some inaccuracies, from W. Weaver, "Lewis Carroll, Mathematician," in *Scientific American*, Vol. 194, No. 4 (1956), 116–128; and R. W. Holmes, "The Philosopher's *Alice in Wonderland*," in *Antioch Review*, Vol. 19, No. 2 (1959), 133–149.

P. L. HEATH

CARTESIANISM. According to one panoramic view of modern philosophy, Descartes is the father and Cartesianism an inherited characteristic or family trait. With no disparagement intended of this assessment of Descartes's influence, the term "Cartesianism" will be used here in a less contentious way to refer to the multifarious, more or less self-conscious efforts on the part of his contemporaries and immediate successors to supply what they found lacking in his ambitious attempt to reconstitute human knowledge. Three directions of their activities can be distinguished and, corresponding to them, three particular applications of the term "Cartesianism."

(1) It was evident that Descartes's project of a universal and all-encompassing science of nature was not fully realized. His intended *summa philosophiae*, *Principia Philosophiae* (*Principles of Philosophy*, Amsterdam, 1644), lacked the proposed parts on plants and animals and man; and his posthumously published and widely read *Traité de l'homme* (*Treatise on Man*, Paris, 1664) ended abruptly. Moreover, in his *Discours de la méthode* (*Discourse on Method*, Leiden, 1637) and in the letter prefacing the French translation of the *Principles* (Paris, 1647), he asked for assistance in carrying out his program for the sciences, suggesting that cooperative endeavor in the acquisition of *expériences* would be necessary to decide among equally possible explanations of the more particular facets of nature. His early admirers, attracted as much—and often far more—by his physics than by his metaphysics, accepted the invitation, and, working within the framework of his methodological prescriptions and cosmologic theory, distinguished themselves not only from their scholastic opponents of the academic establishment but also from other non-Aristotelian scientists of the time whose work went against views they had inherited. In the seventeenth century, *les cartésiens* were predominantly Descartes's followers in physics; and the term "Cartesianism" has acquired some of its less favorable associations from its application to this maligned movement in the history of science.

(2) A second line of development can be traced from Descartes's novel use of the term *idea* in presenting what has sometimes been considered the characteristically Cartesian view that knowledge is attained by way of ideas. These "as it were images of things" (*tanquam rerum imagines, veluti quasdam imagines*), as they were introduced in the *Third Meditation*, were variously described in his works, and a host of questions arose about their origin and nature. "Orthodox" Cartesians differed in their interpretations of Descartes's answers to these questions, while the more independently minded, accepting the thesis that knowledge is attained by way of ideas, produced deviant answers of great subtlety and originality. Since Locke and his followers accepted Descartes's general thesis although they disagreed on the subject of innate ideas, Cartesianism, in a second application of the term, has been taken to cover a considerable domain, including family squabbles

among rationalists and empiricists as well as more recent disputes, such as that about the genesis and status of sense data. (It should be noted that this use of "Cartesianism" to refer to the "way of ideas" differs from another use, in which "Cartesianism" and "rationalism" are roughly coextensive and connote a view or views about innate ideas or principles.

(3) When Descartes was presented with objections to his metaphysics framed in terms of traditional categories and distinctions, a number of thorny problems became apparent; notably, concerning the substantiality and causal efficacy of his seemingly formless and inert corporeal things and concerning the union in man of a body and a soul, or mind, that is alleged to be really distinct from the body. In these sensitive areas, Descartes's teachings were interpreted and developed in various ways; and those who chose to follow the natural light rather than Descartes came to conclusions far removed from, and incompatible with, his. Yet, because of a common view concerning the distinction of mind and matter, Malebranche and Spinoza, as well as some less celebrated metaphysicians, have been called Cartesians; and Cartesianism, in a third acceptation of the term, comprises various monist, pluralist, and occasionalist variations on a common metaphysical theme. Within the limits of this general survey of Descartes's influence, Cartesianism will be mapped in each of the three general areas to which the term has been applied.

PHYSICS AND DERIVATIVE SCIENCES

Like Descartes, the Cartesians attracted to his program for the sciences thought of themselves as possessing a powerful method for investigating nature; and, though they disagreed with him and among themselves on particular applications, they accepted a general theory in physics, salient features of which were the laws of motion in Part II of the *Principles;* the theory of vortices in Part III; and the doctrine of subtle matter which underlies explanations of various phenomena, both celestial and terrestrial, in Parts III and IV of the *Principles.* Although Descartes's laws of motion became increasingly troublesome—Nicolas Malebranche accepted them at first but was later forced to modify them beyond recognition—the cosmogonic picture of which they were part was altered but not effaced. It was an integral feature of the picture that the earth, like the other planets, was transported in a whirlpool that centered about the sun; and, while Descartes took pains in the *Principles* to distinguish his view from that of Copernicus and to point out that, in his view and according to his definitions, the earth, though indeed a planet, was, strictly speaking, at rest, his followers were less concerned to establish a difference. They, too, rejected the possibility of unoccupied space or a vacuum, and claimed that apparently empty spaces—the heavens, the "pores" of bodies, and experimentally produced vacuums—were actually filled with subtle matter. Like Descartes, they made free use of the adaptable particles of subtle matter in their jigsaw-puzzle explanations of the workings of nature. There was some question as to what they conceived the vaunted "true" method to be, as evidenced by Leibniz' skeptical queries. Nonetheless, some general characteristics of their practice were apparent.

Following the rule of evidence in the *Discourse,* they understood Descartes's injunctions against preconception and precipitancy as condemnations of merely accepted opinion and of idle speculation; and contrary to a popular conception of their apriorism, they were keenly interested in the detailed observation of nature and in experiments, thinking of themselves as countering the bookish physics of the Scholastics and the wanton practices of alchemists, astrologers, and the like. Lenses, Torricellian tubes, and sundry apparatus were much in evidence; and, like Descartes, many of them took pleasure in anatomical and physiological investigations. To what use they put their observations and experiments is one thing; their cult of *expériences,* another—and an indisputable fact. The requirement of clear and distinct ideas was met in the doctrine that matter is extension and the corollary that change is local motion, or *translatio.* The methodological implications of these complex views were manifold. Negatively, they ruled out explanations involving qualitative entities or "real" qualities, such as light, heat, and weight, in physics, and substantial forms, such as vegetative and sensitive souls, in biology. Also banished were final causes, including natural place, gravitation, and attraction; faculties, virtues, and powers as causes of change; and sensible qualities supposed to inhere in bodies and to be mysteriously purveyed to us by intentional species. Distinctly conceived, bodies were geometrical solids occupying parts of space and were subject to alteration by the crowding, or impact and pressure, of their neighbors. A vacuum, or void, was thought impossible, as were, at least for the "orthodox" Cartesians, indivisible particles or atoms. Sharing corpuscular and mechanistic assumptions with other nonscholastic scientists, they showed the mark of the master in their geometrical notions of—or, as some would have it, their lack of concepts of—mass and force. Quantity of matter was volume; weight was a centripetal reaction in a vortex of bodies of a certain size. Force, as effort or action on the part of bodies, was as suspect as were the powers and virtues of the Scholastics. Distinctly conceived, it was derived from a principle of inertia, and the force of a body in motion was reckoned as the product of mass (volume) and velocity.

Holland: Regius and Clauberg. During Descartes's long expatriation in Holland, he made a number of converts to his program for the sciences; and despite outbreaks of official opposition, Cartesianism made an impression on academic life that it did not make in France.

Regius. Of special note is Descartes's sometime friend and disciple Henri de Roy, or Regius (1598–1679), professor of medicine at the University of Utrecht, who typified Cartesian scientists in following the master more or less closely in physics and the derivative sciences while departing from his views in metaphysics. His *Fundamenta Physices* (Amsterdam, 1646), which appeared two years after the *Principles,* recapitulated the physics of Parts II, III, and IV, to which were added views from the earlier *Meteors* and *Dioptric* and also from unpublished work. Regius' physics, unlike Descartes's in the *Principles,* was not represented as derived from metaphysical principles.

Moreover, in the concluding chapter on man, adverting to issues concerning the soul, he presented views to which Descartes could only take exception. In the preface to the French translation of the *Principles* (1647), Descartes disowned both the physics and the metaphysics of his disciple; and Regius in turn circulated a defense of his metaphysical theses, arguing for an empiricist view of the origin of ideas and against the necessity of a real distinction of mind and body. Descartes's reply to Regius, his *Notae in Programma* (1648), contained the prototype of later defenses of innate ideas against empiricist incursions. Innate ideas, he maintained, need not be *actually* present in the mind. Moreover, certain ideas—for example, of God—differ in kind from "adventitious" ideas; and even the latter do not, strictly speaking, come to us from the senses, that is, the sense organs.

Clauberg. From Holland, Cartesianism was taken to Germany by Johann Clauberg, who attempted to explain and defend both Descartes's physics and his metaphysics. Working out apparent implications of the metaphysics in *De Cognitione Dei et Nostri . . .* (Duisberg, 1656), he too came to hold a deviant view of the relation of mind and body (though not Regius'), a view linking him with the occasionalists. Clauberg also faced the problem of the relation of traditional logic and Cartesian methodology, and his work in logic anticipated the more famous *Logique, ou L'Art de penser* (*Port-Royal Logic,* 1662) of Antoine Arnauld and Pierre Nicole, which was the chief contribution of the Cartesians (Leibniz, of course, excluded) to logic.

France: Rohault and Régis. In France, Cartesianism, though it was not received in the universities and was, in effect, interdicted in 1671, flourished in extra-academic circles. Dissemination of Descartes's unpublished works and letters was in the hands of his devoted admirer Claude Clerselier (1614–1684), while leadership of his scientific enterprise devolved upon Jacques Rohault.

Rohault. The most gifted of the Cartesian scientists, Rohault devised ingenious experiments for his popular weekly meetings and presented the results of his work in his influential *Traité de physique* (Paris, 1671; translated by John Clarke as *System of Natural Philosophy*, London, 1723). Like Regius, he was inclined to separate Descartes's physics from his metaphysics; and, in line with this, he developed Descartes's notion of hypothesis or *supposition*, eliminating, however, any qualification to the effect that hypotheses were to be accepted for lack of something better.

Régis. Pierre-Sylvain Régis succeeded Rohault as leader of the Cartesian school. In his *Système de philosophie . . .* (Paris, 1690), a comprehensive work containing sections on logic, metaphysics, and moral philosophy as well as his extensive physics, he assimilated work that had been done since Descartes's death. The apogee of the Cartesian movement in physics has been set at about the time of Régis's *Système* and of Fontenelle's imaginative exploration of the vortices in his *Entretiens sur la pluralité des mondes* (Paris, 1686).

Critical reception. While receiving acclamation, the Cartesians were simultaneously threatened—and eventually discredited—by discoveries, such as that of the finite velocity of light, that contravened crucial parts of their system and by the objections and strictures of Leibniz and of Newton and his followers. These adverse judgments have been generally accepted. It is commonplace (and true) that Newton showed beyond the shadow of a doubt the incompatibility of the theory of vortices and Kepler's laws, while Leibniz neatly proved the inconsistency of Descartes's laws of motion with Galileo's. Citing Leibniz' derogatory characterization of the Cartesians, the not unsympathetic historian Charles Adam has reiterated comments on the paucity of equations in their work and on the uncontrolled play of their imagination in assigning jobs to the ubiquitous particles of subtle matter. His verdict was that Descartes's physics threatened to become as harmful to the progress of science as Aristotle's had been.

Yet, more recently, some less disparaging comments have been made. The picture is considerably brightened when Malebranche and especially Christiaan Huygens (1629–1695) are, by virtue of obvious influences, included among the Cartesians (as in Paul Mouy's account.) It has also been suggested that the attempted geometrization of physics was premature rather than perverse (Mouy; Max Jammer, *Concepts of Force*, Cambridge, 1957) and that the unstable and indeterminate particles of the Cartesians, not the billiard-ball atoms of the opposition, were in line with things to come (Geneviève [Rodis-] Lewis, *L'Individualité selon Descartes*, Paris, 1950). Nonetheless, Descartes's followers in physics and the derivative sciences, Malebranche and Huygens aside, have not, on the whole, enhanced his reputation.

THEORY OF KNOWLEDGE

Proposing, in the *Third Meditation*, the term *idea* for those of his thoughts that are the "as it were images of things," Descartes proceeded to classify ideas according to their apparent origin—as innate or adventitious or made by him. He introduced distinctions bearing on their nature—between formal and material truth or falsity, and between objective and formal reality. Discussions generated by these passages concerned both Descartes's intent and the tenability of the views attributed to him. Four main problems can be distinguished, two relating to the tentative classification of ideas according to origin and two having to do with the distinctions bearing on their nature.

Innate ideas. The contratraditional notion of innate ideas—that is, of ideas not derived in some way from the senses but instead having their source in the mind itself—presented an obvious difficulty; namely, how could such an idea, taken to be the form of a thought, exist or pre-exist in a person's mind if he did not in fact have the thought or indeed never had it? It seemed that Descartes's metaphor of a treasure house in which these ideas were stored needed to be cashed—a process that he attempted and that was carried out in various ways, in the face of some formidable difficulties, by supporters of his doctrine of innate ideas.

Adventitious ideas. It was evident that ideas provisionally classified as adventitious—for instance, of a sound, the sun, or a fire—could not, strictly speaking, come to us from external objects; for, in Descartes's view, there was nothing in the objects or in the sense organs exactly like these ideas, or at least like many of them. Although these ideas could, in some sense, be said to be caused by external objects, they could not, strictly speaking, originate there; and some other cause or source more in keeping with their nature seemed to be necessary. Descartes suggested that the mind had the faculty or power of forming these ideas on the occasion of motions in the brain and that ideas seeming to come to us from without were in fact innate. Both suggestions were explored by his successors.

Materially false ideas. Noting that falsity (formal falsity) was to be found in judgments and not in ideas, Descartes added that nonetheless certain ideas—for instance, the idea of cold—might be materially false; that is, if cold were a privation, then the idea of cold, representing a privation or what is not a thing, as if it were a thing would be materially false. The implications to be drawn from this remark were that, in his view, ideas of sensible qualities—of heat as well as cold, of sounds, colors, and the like—were materially false; and questions arose as to whether the notion of a materially false idea (literally, an idea misrepresenting what is not a thing) made sense, and whether sensations of heat, cold, and the like were, in a strict sense of the term, ideas. Two models seemed to be at work in Descartes's account of sense perception, and a problem bequeathed to his followers was that of specifying the latent distinction between the nonrepresentational and the representational elements—sensations and ideas properly so called—that were supposed to be ingredients of sense experience.

Ideas of extended things. There was also a problem concerning ideas of extended things derived from the dual reality—objective and formal—accorded them. As representations, it seemed that they must have something in common with, or be in some respect like, the extended things they represented. However, it was taken to follow from their formal reality as modes of thought that they were totally unlike extended things. A dilemma presented itself: either ideas of extended things were totally unlike extended things, in which case they could not represent them; or, if they were in some respect like extended things, then they could not be accommodated in the mind.

Malebranche. Malebranche, among others, addressed himself to these problems; and, in his elaborate discussions of the nature and origin of ideas and in the numerous polemics to which they gave rise, various answers were surveyed and the major lines of development of Descartes's theory of knowledge were represented. Regarding the problem of materially false ideas and the difficulty concerning ideas of extended things, Malebranche, in the numerous editions of *De la Recherche de la vérité* (first published 1674–1675) and in the *Éclaircissements* added to them, drew a sharp distinction between the perception of heat, color, and the like and the perception of objects as extended. The former consisted in sensations or feelings (*sentiments*), nonrepresentational modifications of the mind conceived on the analogy of feelings of pain, and did not, in his precise use of the term, involve ideas (*idées*). The latter required ideas, which were distinguished from the mind's awareness of them and were not, in his view, modifications of the soul. Approaching the problem of the location or status of these ideas, Malebranche investigated a number of possibilities suggested by Descartes's tripartite classification (adventitious, made by the mind, and innate). Finding difficulties in the suggested sources, he concluded that ideas of extended things were neither adventitious nor made by the mind nor innate. (For an account of his ingenious arguments, see MALEBRANCHE.) The arguments against these possibilities served as indirect evidence for his own thesis: that these ideas were (as in a medieval use of the term) archetypes of created things in the Divine Understanding and that the human mind, intimately united with God, perceived created, extended things by way of ideas in him. Since, in this theory, ideas of extended things were not modifications of the human mind, the problem of their existence in an unextended mind did not arise, though, as became evident in the ensuing controversies, there was a related problem about the possibility of their existence in God.

Foucher. Two of the polemics were especially revealing. In his *Critique de la recherche de la vérité* . . . (Paris, 1675) and subsequent writings, Simon Foucher, though he misunderstood parts of Malebranche's tortuous theory, raised problems worthy of serious consideration. First, he urged that, if ideas of extended things had to have something in common with what they represented, they could not be, as he at first wrongly interpreted Malebranche, modifications of the mind or—as Malebranche in fact believed—inhabitants of the divine understanding. Second, granted that ideas of extended things were not modifications of the human mind but were divinely situated, could they be immediately perceived? The basis of the question was that, if immediate perception were tied to Descartes's views about indubitability and the *cogito*, then we could not be immediately aware of anything outside or apart from the mind. Third, he also questioned the distinction (to use Locke's terms) of primary and secondary qualities along lines that were continued by Bayle and Berkeley, noting what, in Malebranche's distinction of sensation and idea, seemed to require explanation: that, when we perceive an object, we are aware of one uniform appearance of something having both shape and color. Unfortunately, Malebranche was inclined to dismiss Foucher's criticisms on the ground of misinterpretation, but Dom Robert Desgabets (d. 1678), in his *Critique de la Critique de la recherche de la vérité* . . . (Paris, 1675), attempted to defend Cartesian views (though not Malebranche's peculiar versions of them) against this attack.

Arnauld. The most interesting controversy was with Arnauld, who, in *Des Vrayes et des Fausses Idées* (Cologne, 1683), attacked Malebranche's view of ideas as entities distinct from the mind's perception of them by tracing the source of this view to a misconceived analogy with ocular vision and a confusion of presence in the mind with local presence. For Arnauld, as for Descartes, ideas were modes of thought; and, as Descartes was content to explain the objective presence of objects in the mind as the way they were wont to be there, so Arnauld took it to be the nature of thought or mind, requiring no explanation of the kind Malebranche proffered, to represent objects—near or at a distance, present or absent, real or imaginary. Though Malebranche was not moved by this attempt to impugn his theory as the answer to a pseudo problem, in the course of the controversy he was forced to articulate his view that we perceive extended things in God, not by way of individual archetypes but by way of infinite, intelligible extension, which is the common archetype of all extended things, actual or possible.

Locke and Leibniz. A significant event in the annals of the Cartesian theory of knowledge was the publication of Locke's *An Essay Concerning Human Understanding* (London, 1690). Locke's attack on innate ideas and principles and Leibniz' defense in his *Nouveaux Essais sur l'entendement* (published posthumously, Amsterdam and Leipzig, 1765) are a long story, that cannot be told here. Suffice it to say that, in this division of Cartesianism into empiricism and rationalism, Leibniz used arguments like Descartes's in the *Notae in Programma* and, on this question, represented the orthodox Cartesian point of view.

METAPHYSICS

The occasionalist, monist, and pluralist developments included in the third application of the term "Cartesianism" were foreshadowed in Descartes's views about corporeal substance.

Occasionalism. In the *Principles* (II, 36), maintaining that God was the primary and universal cause of motion, Descartes explained that, when God created matter or extension, he created it with motion and rest; and Descartes implied that, but for God's imparting motion to matter, it would have been motionless and undifferentiated, and that motion and rest, and the resulting differentiation of matter, did not follow necessarily from its nature or essence. He further explained that, in conserving matter from moment to moment, God preserved the same quantity of motion that He originally introduced; and it seemed to follow that God's continuing to impart motion to matter was a necessary condition of the continued existence of motion and that bodies of themselves did not have the power of remaining in motion or of producing motion in other bodies. The conclusion toward which Descartes was drawn was that, although motion (*translatio*) was a characteristic or mode of bodies, the moving force of bodies was not in bodies themselves but in God. However, he did not draw this conclusion. In a letter to Henry More, he noted that he was reluctant to discuss the question of the moving force (*vis movens*) of bodies in his published works, for fear that his view might be confused with that of God as *anima mundi;* and the view that he apparently wished to maintain was that, though the moving force of bodies was from God and in a sense was in God, it was also a characteristic or mode of bodies.

The occasionalists, taking the views that matter was inert and that the motion ascribed to bodies was simply change of position, did not hesitate before the conclusion that the force required to move bodies was not in bodies themselves but in the primary and universal Cause of motion, God. According to their conclusion, when a billiard ball that was in motion came in contact with a second ball that was at rest, there was no power or force in the first ball capable of moving the second, and the movement of the second ball required the action of God, who, on the occasion of impact, moved the second ball in accordance with rules that he had established for the motion of bodies. By virtue of the uniformity of God's action, the first ball could be called the cause—the particular or occasional cause—of the second ball's moving; but, without God's action, it was inefficacious, and the primary and universal cause of motion, that is, God, was the effectual cause of the second ball's moving. The occasionalists took it to be true a fortiori that bodies of themselves lacked the power of producing, as in sense perception, changes in the mind; and they offered a number of arguments to show that the mind in turn lacked the power, as in volition, of moving the body. The true cause of both sensations and voluntary movements was God, who instituted laws for the union of mind and body and acted accordingly in particular instances.

The originators of the occasionalist movement were Louis de La Forge and Géraud de Cordemoy.

De La Forge. In the *Traité de l'esprit de l'Homme* (Paris, 1666), de La Forge represented himself as continuing work that Descartes had left unfinished in his *Treatise on Man* and undertook to explain and develop the notion of a mind or soul distinct from, yet united to, the body. Facing problems concerning the possibility of the body acting on the mind and vice versa, he noted that these problems were not isolated and that there was a related problem concerning the possibility of one body acting on another. In his discussion of these problems, de La Forge did not deny that bodies acted on one another or on the mind, or that the mind acted on the body; on the contrary, he insisted that God in his omnipotence could delegate the power of acting to created things. Yet, distinguishing two senses of "cause," he denied that created things were unambiguously the causes of the effects attributed to them and called them the "occasional" or "equivocal" causes.

Cordemoy. In *Le Discernement du corps et de l'âme* (Paris, 1666), Cordemoy, unlike de La Forge, was not concerned with presenting views necessarily in harmony with Descartes's, and he denied outright the action of bodies on one another or on the mind and the action of the human mind on the body. In his formally presented proof that God was the true cause of the movement of bodies, he made use of principles that Descartes would have accepted but drew conclusions from them that it would be safe to say would have greatly disturbed Descartes. Descartes had written of a motion in the brain as giving occasion (*donnera occasion*) to the soul to have a certain sensation or thought, and Cordemoy may have had these passages in mind in employing the expression *cause occasionelle* to refer to what, as in the case of a motion in the brain, might be thought to be the true cause of an event. But, unlike Descartes, he denied that the occasion or occasional cause was, strictly speaking, the cause of the event and maintained that the true cause was God.

Geulincx. Arnold Geulincx apparently developed his version of occasionalism independently of de La Forge and Cordemoy. Illustrating the lack of causal relation between mind and body, he used the analogy of synchronized clocks, which was later taken up by Leibniz; and, to prove a lack of genuine causation, he made use of the principle that nothing can be done unless there is knowledge on the part of the putative agent or cause of how it is done.

Malebranche. Malebranche, the most celebrated of the occasionalists, was familiar with the work of Cordemoy and adapted, for his own purposes and with great originality, the theory of causation he found in Cordemoy. He added powerful arguments, extended the view to cover volitions not pertaining to bodily movements (such as the volition to form an idea), and presented it as an integral part of his theocentric vision of the universe. (See GEULINCX and MALEBRANCHE for fuller accounts of their versions of occasionalism.)

Monism and pluralism. It has been argued that the dualisms and pluralism found in Descartes's statements about substance—of uncreated and created substance, corporeal and spiritual substance, and individual substances—contradicted his own definitions and principles and that Spinoza's doctrine of the unity of substance was the consistent and pure form of Cartesianism. It has also been maintained that Spinoza's monism and Leibniz' pluralism were the opposite poles to which philosophers accepting a notion of substance like that of Descartes were inescapably driven. Discussions of these views and of Spinoza's and Leibniz' metaphysics of substance is beyond the limits of this article, though it need hardly be added that the historical and logical relations of Descartes's assertions about substance and those of Spinoza and Leibniz have figured importantly in discussions of Cartesianism and that the essence of Cartesianism has sometimes been located in a common notion of, or presupposition about, substantiality.

It may be noted, however, that Descartes's assertions about corporeal substance also gave rise to conflicting theories among less renowned students of his metaphysics. On the one side, Geulincx, following Descartes's inclination to think of particular bodies as portions of a common stuff or substance, contended that "body itself" (*corpus ipsum*) was primary and substantial and that particular bodies were limitations or modes of corporeal substance. On the other side, Cordemoy, sharing Descartes's inclination to think of particular bodies as objects really distinct from one another, came to the unorthodox conclusion that body in general, or matter, was an aggregate and that the parts of which it was composed were indivisible extended substances, or atoms.

Bibliography

Balz, Albert G. A., *Cartesian Studies.* New York, 1951.

Belaval, Yvon, *Leibniz critique de Descartes.* Paris, 1960.

Berthé de Besaucèle, Louis, *Les Cartésiens d'Italie.* Paris, 1920.

Bohatek, Josef, *Die cartesianische Scholastik in der Philosophie und reformierte Dogmatik des 17. Jahrhunderts.* Leipzig, 1912.

Bordas-Demoulin, Jean Baptiste, *Le Cartésianisme*, 2d ed. Paris, 1874.

Bouillier, Francisque, *Histoire de la philosophie cartésienne*, 3d ed. Paris, 1868. A standard work, to be used with caution.

Cousin, Victor, *Fragments philosophiques*, 5th ed. Paris, 1866.

Damiron, Jean Philibert, *Essai sur l'histoire de la philosophie en France au XVIIe siècle.* Paris, 1846.

Dibon, Paul, *La Philosophie néerlandaise au siècle d'or.* Amsterdam, 1954.

Dijksterhuis, E. J., and others, *Descartes et le cartésianisme hollandais.* Paris, 1950.

Lemaire, Paul, *Le Cartésianisme chez les bénédictins; Dom Robert Desgabets, son système, son influence et son école.* Paris, 1901.

Monchamp, Georges, *Histoire du cartésianisme en Belgique.* Brussels, 1886.

Mouy, Paul, *Le Développement de la physique cartésienne, 1646–1712.* Paris, 1934. An invaluable account—intelligent, informed, and judicious—of Cartesianism in physics.

Prost, Joseph, *Essai sur l'atomisme et l'occasionalisme dans la philosophie cartésienne.* Paris, 1907.

Sortais, Gaston, *Le Cartésianisme chez les jésuites français au XVIIe et au XVIIIe siècle.* Paris, 1929.

Thijssen-Schoute, Caroline Louise, *Nederlands cartesianisme.* Amsterdam, 1954.

Vartanian, Aram, *Diderot and Descartes.* Princeton, N.J., 1953.

WILLIS DONEY

CARUS, CARL GUSTAV (1789–1869), German physician, biologist, and philosopher. Carus was born in Leipzig and studied chemistry and then medicine at the University of Leipzig. In 1811 he became the first person to lecture there on comparative anatomy. Two years later he became director of the military hospital at Pfaffendorf and, in 1814, professor of medicine at the medical college of the University of Dresden, where he remained to the end of his life. He was appointed royal physician in 1827 and privy councilor in 1862.

Carus was widely known for his work in physiology, psychology, and philosophy, and was one of the first to do experimental work in comparative osteology, insect anatomy, and zootomy. He is also remembered as a landscape painter and art critic. He was influenced by Aristotle, Plato, Schelling, and Goethe, about whom Carus wrote several works, the most important of which is *Goethe dessen seine Bedeutung für unsere und die kommende Zeit* (Vienna, 1863). Carus' philosophical writings were more or less forgotten until the German philosopher and psychologist, Ludwig Klages, resurrected them.

Carus' philosophy was essentially Aristotelian in that it followed the unfolding or elaboration of an idea in experience from an unorganized multiplicity to an organized unity. This universal, unfolding unity or developing multiplicity within unity Carus called God. God, or the Divine, is not a being analogous to human intelligence; rather, it is the ground of being revealed through becoming, through the infinitely numerous and infinitely varying beings or organisms that come into being through the Divine in space and time.

Carus called his theory of a divine or creative force "entheism." The unknown Divine is revealed in nature through organization, structure, and organic unity. As the ground of being, it is outside space and time, unchanging, and eternal. As thought or insight, it is the God-idea of religion, found everywhere in life and the cosmos. As life, it is the sphere, the basic form taken by living cells and the heavenly stars. As matter, it is the ether exfoliating in infinitely varied things.

According to Carus, the body cannot be separated from the soul. Both are soul, but we speak of "body" when some unknown part of the soul affects the known part; and we speak of "soul" when the known part affects the unknown part.

Carus' metaphysics, and his important contribution to

psychology, is a theory of movement from unconsciousness to consciousness and back again. Whatever understanding we can have of life and the human spirit hinges upon observation of how universal unconsciousness, the unknown Divine, becomes conscious. Universal unconsciousness is not teleological in itself; it achieves purpose only as it becomes conscious through conscious individuals like men. Consciousness is not more permanent than things; it is a moment between past and future. As a moment, it can maintain itself only through sleep or a return to the unknown.

Principal Works by Carus

Psyche: zur Entwicklungsgeschichte der Seele. Pforzheim, 1846; 3d ed., Stuttgart, 1860.

Physis: zur Geschichte des leiblichen Lebens. Stuttgart, 1851.

Symbolik der menschlichen Gestalt. Leipzig, 1853.

Natur und Idee. Vienna, 1861.

Lebenserinnerungen und Denkwürdigkeiten, 4 vols. Leipzig, 1865–1866.

Vergleichende Psychologie. Vienna, 1866.

Works on Carus

Bernouilli, Christoph, *Die Psychologie von Carl Gustav Carus.* Jena, 1925.

Kern, Hans, *Carus: Personlichkeit und Werk.* Berlin, 1942.

RUBIN GOTESKY

CARUS, PAUL (1852–1919), philosopher and monist, was born at Ilsenburg, Germany, and died in La Salle, Illinois. After receiving his Ph.D. at Tübingen, in 1876, and completing his military service, he taught in Dresden. Censure of religious views he had expressed in pamphlets led him to leave Germany for England. He then went to New York, where in 1885 he published *Monism and Meliorism.* This book aroused the interest of a German chemist in La Salle, Illinois, Edward Carl Hegeler, who had started a periodical, *The Open Court.* He invited Carus to take over the editorship. In 1888 another and more technical journal, *The Monist,* was founded, and Carus became its editor. Carus also published a series of philosophical classics, edited by leading professors of philosophy, which are still widely used in classrooms. The Carus family has continued to operate the Open Court Publishing Company, and through it they publish the volumes of the Carus Lectures, which are given at meetings of the American Philosophical Association. *The Monist* was revived in 1962 under the editorship of Eugene Freeman.

For *The Monist,* Carus chose articles on the history and philosophy of religion, archeology, Biblical criticism, and especially the philosophy of science, both philosophy for the scientifically minded and philosophy about the sciences. He invited contributions from France and Germany and arranged for their translation. Important articles by Russell, Mach, Hilbert, Poincaré, Dewey, and Peirce appeared in *The Monist.* Carus frequently published articles of his own in criticism of his contributors, but the debates seem not so much to have modified his own monistic philosophy as to have led him to explain in detail how it differed from other monisms, such as Ernst Haeckel's.

Monism, for Carus, was the doctrine that all the things that are—however varied, diverse, and independent of each other they may appear to be—are somehow one. What makes them one are certain eternal laws that reside in things and are discovered, not created, by the investigator. These laws of nature are asserted to be dependent on a single law, which Carus identified with God.

Carus viewed his metaphysics as a speculative generalization from the view of mathematics that he had learned from Hermann Grassmann, his teacher at the Stettin Gymnasium. Whitehead, too, acknowledged the influence of Grassmann, in his *Universal Algebra.* Some of the similarities between the metaphysics of Carus and Whitehead may have resulted from this common influence.

Carus can be called a realist inasmuch as he rejected the notion that the laws of nature depend on the mind of the investigator. In this he found himself in opposition to the Kantians. Nor did he hold to a materialism. Rather, he insisted that every part of the world is both material (acting in accord with the laws of matter) and spiritual (acting in accord with the laws of mind). The characteristic of mind, or spirit, is the ability to mirror the world. Thus Carus was also a realist in his account of knowing. In ethics he held that the worth of any part of the world depends on the degree to which it knows—that is, mirrors—the whole. This is achieved through greater and greater knowledge of the laws of nature. Hence, devotion to knowledge is the way to greater goodness. Prayer is recommended as a means of changing the will of the man who prays so that he can mirror the one law in his actions.

Bibliography

Hay, William H., "Paul Carus: A Case-Study of Philosophy on the Frontier." *Journal of the History of Ideas,* Vol. 17 (1956), 498–510.

Meyer, Donald Harvey, "Paul Carus and the Religion of Science." *American Quarterly,* Vol. 14 (1962), 597–607.

Sheridan, James Francis, *Paul Carus: A Study of the Thought and Work of the Editor of the Open Court Publishing Company.* Ann Arbor, Mich., 1957.

WILLIAM H. HAY

CASO, ANTONIO, Mexican philosopher and diplomat, was born in Mexico City in 1883 and died there in 1946. He was a professor of philosophy at the National University of Mexico, rector of that institution, lecturer at the Colegio Nacional, and ambassador to several South American nations. He wrote voluminously over a period of three decades and had great influence as a teacher. For his sources he turned especially to Bergson but also to Kant, Schopenhauer, and Husserl.

The metaphysics of Caso emphasizes process, freedom, life, and spirit. He conceived of reality as a fluent dynamism whose operations and forms are unified organically. The subject–predicate bias of traditional logic distorts reality by its apparatus of static terms related as in a closed machine. Modern science has more insight with its realization that even the physical world eludes a rigorous determinism. The individual particle has a factor of spontaneity; law is only statistical, applying to groups by virtue of the mutual compensation of individual irregularities. By the same token, living process has a unique character that cannot be reduced to the terms of physics and chemistry but stimulates and directs the material vehicle. A conscious living being discovers its own freedom in the simple act of willing a bodily movement: freedom coincides with causation from within. Consciousness is not passively derived from more primitive conditions by laws of association and evolution. On the contrary, the pure ego projects its own structures upon the data of raw feeling, thus supplying the objects of mature experience and the principles underlying those of association and evolution.

The ethics of Caso is concerned with two triads: that of things, individuals, and persons, and that of economy, disinterest, and love. Things are merely physical, are deficient in unity, are divisible, and are not subjects of value. Individuals are living beings that are indivisible but can be substituted for each other. The value of the merely biological is economy, found in egocentricity and utility and illustrated in nutrition, growth, reproduction, toolmaking, and death. Beyond individuals are persons, which add the character of spirit to life. Persons are capable of both disinterest and love. Disinterest suspends the mechanisms of selfishness and usefulness in the act of contemplation; love identifies the self with another in sympathy and service and is at its noblest in self-sacrifice. Persons are unique; they play a role as creators of values in society, and in them freedom is most advanced and responsible. Their interplay defines human culture, the enemies of which are individualism and totalitarianism; both are forms of egoism and of economic value. The error of totalitarian philosophy is to transfer the notion of the absolute from a universal principle of existence, where it is justified, to the state, where it does not exist. This philosophy has its source in Hobbes; it should not be imputed to Hegel, who placed art, religion, and philosophy above the state.

Caso's aesthetics begins with the concept of a surplus of energy, or vital excess, that is the basis of play, art, and the spirit of sacrifice. Art is distinguished from play and from the spirit of sacrifice by disinterest. In addition to the suspension of selfishness and usefulness, disinterest implies abstraction from questions of reality and goodness of the object contemplated. Disinterest preserves art from any possibility of immorality, which requires an interested attitude. It is associated with the intuitive nature of the aesthetic experience, since absorption in the object as an end favors appreciation of its full individuality. The nonconceptual nature of the experience is reconciled with the claim of universality, after the manner of Kant. However, the experience does not terminate with an image within the mind. The conative tendency of psychic states leads to empathy, or projection of the state upon the outer world. Aesthetic empathy differs from the projection mentioned earlier in that it is emotional and concrete rather than logical and formal, and from that empathy and religious empathy in that it is disinterested. But natural objects do not readily satisfy the aesthetic need. Aesthetic empathy therefore leads to expression, or the creation of works of art, in which are consummated the empathic tendency and disinterested intuition. In his account of intuition and expression, Caso claimed to follow Croce, but he did not do so without wavering.

Main Works by Caso

La filosofía de la intuición ("The Philosophy of Intuition"). Mexico City, 1914.

La existencia como economía, como desinterés y como caridad ("Existence as Economy, as Disinterest, and as Love"). Mexico City, 1919.

Discursos á la nación mexicana ("Discourses to the Mexican Nation"). Mexico City, 1922.

El concepto de la historia universal ("The Concept of Universal History"). Mexico City, 1923.

Principios de estética ("Principles of Aesthetics"). Mexico City, 1925.

La Persona humana y el estado totalitario ("The Human Person and the Totalitarian State"). Mexico City, 1941.

Works on Caso

Berndtson, Arthur, "Mexican Philosophy: The Aesthetics of Antonio Caso." *Journal of Aesthetics and Art Criticism*, Vol. 9, No. 4 (June 1951), 323–329.

Romanell, Patrick, *Making of the Mexican Mind.* Lincoln, Neb., 1952. Ch. 3.

ARTHUR BERNDTSON

CASSIRER, ERNST (1874–1945), German Neo-Kantian philosopher, was born in Breslau, Silesia. He studied at the universities of Berlin, Leipzig, Heidelberg, and Marburg and taught first at Berlin. From 1919 to 1933 he was professor of philosophy at Hamburg University; and he served as rector from 1930 to 1933. Cassirer, who was Jewish, resigned his post in 1933 and left Germany. He taught at Oxford from 1933 to 1935, at Göteborg, Sweden from 1935 to 1941, and at Yale from 1941 to 1944. He died in New York City while a visiting professor at Columbia University.

Cassirer was both a prolific historian of philosophy and an original philosopher. His philosophy is in many important respects a development and modification of Kant's critical philosophy, idealistic in outlook and transcendental in method. Like Kant, he holds that the objective world results from the application of a priori principles to a manifold that can be apprehended only as differentiated and ordered by them. His method is transcendental in the sense that he investigates not so much the objects of knowledge and belief as the manner in which these objects come to be known or are constituted in consciousness. His work has to some extent also been influenced by Hegel and, of his own contemporaries, by his teacher Hermann Cohen and by Edmund Husserl.

Cassirer differs from Kant mainly in holding that the principles by which the manifold of experience receives its structure are not static, but developing; and that their field of application is wider than Kant supposed. Kant, according to Cassirer, assumed that the science and mathematics of his day admitted of no philosophically relevant alternatives, and therefore he conceived the synthetic a priori principles of the understanding to be unchangeable. He could not foresee the development of non-Euclidean geometry, of the modern axiomatic method, of the theory of relativity, or of quantum mechanics. Also, in Kant's day many areas of human culture had not yet been subjected to scientific investigation: there existed in particular no developed science of language and no scientific treatment of religion and myth. The idea of the humanities or moral sciences (*Geisteswissenschaften*) arose only in the nineteenth century. Cassirer's professed aim was to extend Kant's static critique of reason, i.e., his critique of the organizing principles of natural science and morality, into a dynamic critique of culture, i.e., of the organizing principles of the human mind in all its aspects. This aim is apparent in all his works, especially in his *magnum opus, Die Philosophie der symbolischen Formen.*

The nature of symbolic representation. A fundamental problem for the Kantian philosophy had been to understand the conceptualization of experience, in particular the relation between concepts and that to which they apply. For Cassirer, conceptualization, i.e., the apprehension of the manifold of experience as instantiating general notions or as perceptual matter exhibiting a conceptual structure, is merely a special case of what he calls "symbolization," "symbolic representation," or simply "representation." Symbolic representation, according to Cassirer, is the essential function of human consciousness and is cardinal to our understanding not only of the structure of science, but also of myth and religion, of language, of art, and of history. Man is a symbolizing animal.

Symbolization creates, and exhibits within our consciousness, connections between perceptual signs and their significance or meaning. It is the nature of symbolic representation in general to constitute, or bring into being, a totality that both transcends the perceptual sign and provides a context for it. The unity of sign and signified allows for distinction in thought, but not in fact—just as color and extension are separable in thought but not in fact. The given always shows itself as a totality, one part of which functions as a representative of the rest. This basic self-differentiation of every content of consciousness is given a more enduring structure by the use of artificial signs that, as it were, articulate the stream of consciousness and impose patterns on it. The artificial signs or symbols, like the Kantian concepts and categories, do not mirror an objective world, but are constitutive of it. Scientific symbols constitute, or bring about, only one kind of objective world—the world of science. Mythical pictures constitute the reality of myths and religion; the words of ordinary language constitute the reality of common sense.

To the three symbolic systems that articulate three types of reality under different "symbolic forms" there correspond three modes of the one function of symbolic representation. The first and most primitive of these modes Cassirer calls the "expression function" (*Ausdrucksfunktion*). In the world it constitutes, the primitive world of myth, the sign and its significance merge into each other. The difference between them exists, but is not consciously noted. The thunder by which a primitive god shows his anger is not merely an external sign that the god is angry. It *is* the god's anger. In the same way, in ordinary perception we often not merely associate a smile with a kind intention, but also perceive a kindly smile.

The second mode of symbolic representation is "intuition function" (*Anschauungsfunktion*), which by the use of ordinary natural languages constitutes the world of common sense. The intuition function differentiates our perceptual world into spatially and temporally related material objects or substances that become the bearers of properties, the more permanent properties being apprehended as distinctive of the various kinds of substance, the less permanent being apprehended as accidental. Aristotle's philosophy represents, according to Cassirer, a prescientific stage of thinking about objects, based on the predominance of symbolic representation in the mode of the intuition function.

The third mode of symbolic representation, the "conceptual function" (*reine Bedeutungsfunktion*) constitutes the world of science, which is a system of relations as opposed to a system of substances with attributes. The particular, in this mode, is not subsumed under a universal but rather under a principle of ordering, which relates particulars to each other in ordered structures that, Cassirer seems to hold, are always serial in nature. He finds the prototype of this kind of symbolization in the works of Dedekind, Peano, Frege, and their successors.

The transcendental inquiry into the nature and function of symbolic representation is supported by a wealth of illustrations taken from the history of philosophy, the natural sciences, general linguistics, anthropology, and the humanities. Symbolic representation as a fundamental and logically primitive function must be seen at work in order to be understood. The philosophical analysis of symbolic representation can hardly do more than point out that in any symbolic representation two moments, the symbol and the symbolized, are united into an essential unity yet stand in polar relationship to each other. It has been objected that this analysis, by identifying a unity with an opposition of two different moments, results in a contradiction. Cassirer's answer to this objection, and to accusations that his professedly Kantian position is really Hegelian, is that his philosophy is not intended as a logic or a metaphysics, but as a phenomenology of consciousness.

Philosophy of culture. The highly general character of Cassirer's analysis of symbolic representation gives flexibility to a philosophy of culture. It does not force the variety of the ever-changing contents and structure of culture into rigid and artificial molds. But the very generality of Cassirer's conception makes it, perhaps, too easy to fit it to any situation and comparably difficult to test. It also makes it difficult to place the conclusions of Cassirer's special investigations in order of importance. The order here followed is in the main that of the summary given at the end of his *Essay on Man*, itself a synopsis of his *Philosophie der symbolischen Formen.*

Cassirer holds that the polarity that he finds in the relation between symbol and significance or meaning continually expresses itself in two opposing tendencies, a tendency toward stabilization and a tendency toward the breaking up of permanent symbolic patterns. In myth and the primitive religions the conservative tendency is stronger. Mythological explanation explains patterns of the present in terms of origins in a remote past—a type of explanation still regarded in the Platonic dialogues as containing important elements of truth. The more advanced religions exhibit the opposing evolutionary tendency at work. This is mainly the result of conceiving forces in nature as individuals and persons, and of the consequent emergence of the notion of morality as being rooted in personal responsibility.

In natural languages, through which the common-sense world of substances in public space and time is constituted, the conservative tendency shows itself in the rules to which a language must conform if communication is to be possible. The evolutionary tendency, which is equally essential, works through phonetic and semantic change. The psychology of the processes by which children acquire their language shows important similarities to the development of a language through succeeding generations in a community.

In the arts, the tendency toward new patterns, which has its source in the originality of the individual artist, predominates over the tendency to preserve a tradition. Yet traditional forms can never be entirely discarded, since this would imply the breakdown of communication, making art, which is a cultural and social phenomenon, impossible. The polarity in artistic creation is mirrored in the history of aesthetic theories. Theories of art as based on imitation and as based on inspiration have in one way or another continuously arisen in opposition to each other. Cassirer's own view of the nature of art is largely influenced by Kant's *Critique of Judgment,* in which the essence of artistic creation and aesthetic experience is held to lie in the interplay of the understanding, which imposes rules, and of the free imagination, which can never be completely subsumed under determinate concepts.

In science the stabilizing and objective tendency predominates over that toward change and subjective innovation. Cassirer's philosophy of science is recognizably Kantian, although Kant's absolute a priori is replaced in it by a relative a priori. Scientific theories contain, apart from empirical concepts and propositions, concepts that are a priori and propositions that are synthetic a priori with respect to a given theoretical system. This idea has proved both fruitful and influential and has been further developed by, among others, Arthur Pap, at one time a pupil of Cassirer. Relative a priori concepts and propositions are hardly distinguishable from the theoretical concepts and propositions admitted by logical positivist philosophers of science when it appeared that their original positions were not wholly tenable.

Cassirer regards language, art, religion, and science as aspects in a continuous development that although it is not predictable in advance, does show an organic unity. Every aspect expresses the fundamental function of symbolic representation in human consciousness and the power of man to build an "ideal" or symbolic world of his own, which is human culture. Cassirer's work depends to a very great extent on the illustrative power of his detailed analyses. For this reason it is difficult to do it justice in a brief survey, especially since philosophical disagreement with his critical idealism is quite compatible with a deep appreciation of his informed scholarship and his sensitive judgment as to what is and what is not important in the various symbolic and conceptual systems that he has investigated.

Selected Works by Cassirer

THEORETICAL

Substanzbegriff und Funktionsbegriff. Berlin, 1910.

Zur Einsteinschen Relativitätstheorie. Berlin, 1921. These two works have been translated in one volume as *Substance and Function and Einstein's Theory of Relativity.* Chicago, 1923; reprinted New York, 1953.

Philosophie der Symbolischen Formen, 3 vols. Berlin, 1923, 1925, 1929. *Index,* Berlin, 1931. Translated by Ralph Manheim as *Philosophy of Symbolic Forms,* 3 vols. New Haven, 1953, 1955, 1957.

An Essay on Man. New Haven, 1944.

HISTORICAL

Leibniz' System in seinen wissenschaftlichen Grundlagen. Marburg, 1902.

Das Erkenntnisproblem in der Philosophie und Wissenschaft der neueren Zeit, 3 vols. Berlin, 1906, 1907, 1920. Vol. 4 translated by W. H. Woglom and C. W. Hendel as *The Problem of Knowledge.* New Haven, 1950.

Freiheit und Form, Studien zur deutschen Geistesgeschichte. Berlin, 1916.

Kants Leben und Lehre, Vol. XI of *Immanuel Kant's Werke,* Cassirer, Ernst, and Cohen, Hermann, eds. Berlin, 1918.

Individuum und Kosmos in der Philosophie der Renaissance. Leipzig and Berlin, 1927. Translated by Mario Domandi as *The Individual and the Cosmos in Renaissance Philosophy.* New York, 1964.

Die Platonische Renaissance in England und die Schule von Cambridge. Leipzig and Berlin, 1932. Translated by F.C.A. Koelln and James P. Pettegrove as *The Platonic Renaissance in England.* Austin, Texas, 1953.

Die Philosophie der Aufklärung. Tübingen, 1932. Translated by F. C. A. Koelln and James P. Pettegrove as *The Philosophy of the Enlightenment.* Princeton, 1951.

Works on Cassirer

Schilpp, P. A., ed., *The Philosophy of Ernst Cassirer.* New York, 1949. Critical studies and full bibliography to 1949. For bibliography to 1964, see H. J. Paton and Raymond Klibansky, eds., *Philosophy and History, Essays Presented to Ernst Cassirer* (new ed., New York, 1964).

S. KÖRNER

CASTRO, ISAAC OROBIO DE. *See* OROBIO DE CASTRO, ISAAC.

CATEGORIES. Philosophical categories are classes, genera, or types supposed to mark necessary divisions within our conceptual scheme, divisions that we must recognize if we are to make literal sense in our discourse about the world. To say that two entities belong to different categories is to say that they have literally nothing in common, that we cannot apply the same descriptive terms to both unless we speak metaphorically or equivocally.

ARISTOTELIAN THEORY

The word "category" was first used as a technical term in philosophy by Aristotle. In his short treatise called *Categories,* he held that every uncombined expression signifies (denotes, refers to) one or more things falling in at least one of the following ten classes: substance, quantity, quality, relation, place, time, posture, state, action, and passion. By "uncombined expression" Aristotle meant an expression considered apart from its combination with other expressions in a sentence, and he intended his account to apply only to those expressions we now call "descriptive" and "nonlogical." Logical expressions, such as "not," "or," "some," and "every," are excluded; these were called by medieval philosophers "syncategorematic," to distinguish them from the categorematic expressions covered by Aristotle's account of categories.

Each of the ten classes of entities signified constitutes a category, or genus, of entities, and each categorematic expression is said to be an expression in the category constituted by the class of entities it signifies. The nouns "plant" and "animal," for example, signify kinds of substances and are said to be expressions in the category of substance; the nouns "color" and "justice" signify kinds of qualities and are said to be expressions in the category of quality. On the other hand, the adjectives "colored" and "just" signify, respectively, colored and just things (substances) and also connote (consignify) the qualities color and justice. Aristotle labeled such expressions "derivative terms" or "paronyms" and held that instead of signifying substances simply, as expressions in the category of substance do, they signify substances derivatively by connoting accidents of substances.

Although Aristotle implied that his ten categories constitute the ten highest genera of entities and hence the only true genera—the only genera that cannot be taken as species of higher genera—he also implied that it is not essential to his theory that the categories be exactly ten in number or even that they be mutually exclusive and exhaustive. Categories are listed in various of Aristotle's writings, but the list usually stops short of ten without indication that categories have been omitted. He explicitly stated that no absurdity would result if the same items were included in both the category of quality and that of relation. He remarked that the expressions "rare," "dense," "rough," and "smooth" do not signify qualities, since they apply to a substance with reference to a quality it possesses, yet he did not specify in which category or categories these expressions are included. Despite these indications that his theory of categories is not entirely complete, medieval philosophers generally wrote as though Aristotle's list of ten provided a final, exhaustive enumeration of the highest genera of being.

What is essential to Aristotle's theory of categories is that substances be properly distinguished from accidents and essential predication from accidental predication. Any entity, regardless of the category in which it is included, can be an entity referred to by the subject term of an essential predication. "Man is an animal." "Red is a color." "Four is a number." "A year is twelve months." The subject terms denote entities that fall, respectively, in the categories of substance, quality, quantity, and time, and the predication in each case is essential. On the other hand, only entities in the category of substance can be entities referred to by subject terms of accidental predication. There is no such thing as an accident of an accident; accidents happen to substances and not to other accidents. "Red is darker than orange" does not assert something that happens to be, but need not be, true of red; it asserts what is essentially true of red, something that red must always be if it is to remain the color red. "Red is John's favorite color" does not assert anything that may happen to be true of red; rather, it asserts something that may happen to be true of John. To undergo change through time while remaining numerically one and the same thing is what principally distinguishes substances from entities in other categories. If John ceases to regard red as his favorite color, we say not that red has changed while remaining the same color but that John has changed while remaining the same person.

Categorematic expressions, for Aristotle, are technically "predicates," but they are not "predicates" in a sense that keeps them from serving as subject terms in essential predication. The minor term of an Aristotelian "scientific syllogism" occurs only as a subject, though Aristotle gave no examples in which it is a proper name. He regarded the ultimate subject terms in demonstration as common names marking species that are not further divided. Such expressions are still "predicates" in that like more generic terms they are applied to individuals in answer to the question What is it? But proper names are in a class by themselves; they are applied only in answer to the question Who? or Which? and are not "predicates" at all. Yet if proper names are thus not categorematic expressions, they are still fundamental to Aristotle's theory of categories. Without proper names there are no names for the subjects of accidental as distinct from essential predication. Man as such is an animal—"man" names every man indifferently if it names any, and the question of naming which one (or ones) does not arise. But only some man (or men) is (are) snub-nosed, and until the question Which? is answered by a proper name the subject of the accidental predication remains unnamed.

Category-mistakes. If we ask what, according to Aristotle's theory, would be the sort of thing often called today a "category-mistake," we must distinguish a mistake that violates what is essential to the theory from a mistake that violates a particular category-difference marked by the theory. Only a mistake of the first kind is strictly a category-mistake. Mistakes of the second kind form a subclass of equivocations. In his *Topics* (107a3–17), Aristotle listed as one example of equivocation the sentence "The musical note and knife are sharp." That "sharp" is here used equivocally is shown by the fact that a musical note and a knife belong to different categories. A musical note is a kind of sound, and sounds are qualities. (Aristotle argued in *On the Soul*, 420a25–28, that we speak of the sound of a body as we speak of the color of a body.) A knife is a kind of substance, and one who believes that "sharp" applies in the same sense to musical notes and to knives may be said to have made the category-mistake of confusing a quality and a substance. Yet an appeal to category-differences is not necessary to expose the equivocation, and many equivocations cannot be exposed in this way because there is no violation of a category-difference. Aristotle claimed that the equivocal use of "sharp" in the example is also exposed by the fact (among others) that musical notes and knives are not compared with respect to their sharpness. Two notes may be equally sharp, or two knives, but not a note and a knife. Again, two flavors are equally sharp, but not a flavor and a note or a flavor and a knife. The equivocation in "The flavor and note are sharp" is exposed, although since flavors and sounds are both qualities there is no violation of a category-difference.

The appearance of absurdity produced by an equivocation can always be removed and literal meaning restored by distinction between the different senses of the crucial words. But with a genuine category-mistake there is no literal meaning to restore. In a passage in his *Posterior Analytics* (83a30–33), where he was discussing features of essential and accidental predication, Aristotle remarked that Plato's forms can be dismissed as mere sound without sense. The point is illustrated by a sentence like "The color white is white." The sentence may seem to make sense if one claims that since the color white is the standard by which we judge things to be white, it is itself white. But the sense is only apparent, because whatever is white remains numerically one and the same object even if its color changes. Such an object cannot be the quality, that is, the color white itself, as we then have the absurdity that the color white changes its color. Plato's theory of forms, as Aristotle interpreted it, makes the mistake of confusing accidental with essential predication. "The color white is the color white" is not an accidental but a trivially true essential predication; it is clearly not what is intended by the Platonic assertion that the color white is white. But the latter is just as absurd as the assertion that sitting sits.

Except in the passage in the *Posterior Analytics*, Aristotle did not refer to Plato's forms as mere sound without sense. Plato's theory has certain affinities with Aristotle's metaphysical account of substance as a composite of form and matter, and in his *Metaphysics*, Aristotle criticized Plato's forms, not as sound without sense, but as entities that fail to do the job they should, since they cannot be formal causes (991a11; 1033b26) and lead to an infinite regress (the third-man argument: 990b17). His criticism of the theory of forms receives attention in the history of philosophy mainly in this context of form, matter, and substance, and the passage in the *Posterior Analytics* that dismisses the forms as sound without sense is generally passed over or dismissed as a result of more than usual hostility toward Platonists. Yet apart from hostility, Aristotle was required by his theory to regard a sentence like "The color white is white" strictly as a category-mistake.

KANTIAN THEORY

Aristotle's theory dominated discussion of categories until the work of Kant, where we find a radically new conception of a category. Kant professed in his theory of categories to have achieved what Aristotle had tried but failed to achieve in such a theory. Instead of beginning with uncombined expressions, Aristotle should have started with expressions of statements or judgments. Every statement is universal, particular, or singular in quantity; affirmative, negative, or infinite in quality; categorical, hypothetical, or disjunctive in the relation of its parts; and problematic, assertoric, or apodictic in modality (*Critique of Pure Reason*, "Transcendental Analytic," I, 2–3). Each of these 12 ways in which judgments are classified in logic corresponds to a function of the understanding indispensable to the formation of judgments, and each such function yields a category, or pure concept of the understanding, in one of the 4 major divisions of categories: quantity, quality, relation, and modality. The function, for example, of relating subject to predicate in a categorical judgment yields the relational category of substance and accident, and the function of relating antecedent to consequent in a hypothetical judgment yields the relational category of cause and effect.

Kant's conception of substance leads to important departures from Aristotle in the treatment of common names and paronyms. Whether an expression serves as a common name or as a paronym depends on its function in a given statement and not on its signification as an uncombined expression. "Stone," for example, serves as a common name of the substance in which a change occurs in "The stone grows warm," but it serves to specify a kind of change that occurs in a substance in "The sand becomes stone." In the second case "stone" serves as a paronym; it connotes certain properties, such as hardness and solidity, and denotes any substance, such as a certain amount of sand, that acquires these properties. For Aristotle the change from sand to stone is substantial change, or coming to be, rather than alteration; for Kant substantial change is impossible because substance is related to accident as that which undergoes alteration is related to that which becomes and ceases to be. A substance is altered when one of its accidents ceases to be and is followed by another accident, so accidents, not substances, become and cease to be.

With Kant's theory there are no ordinary equivocations that can be exposed as category-mistakes, since categories are pure (formal), as opposed to empirical, concepts. "Substance" and "quality," in Aristotle's theory, are the highest generic terms that apply, respectively, to knives and sounds, so the equivocation in "The knife and musical note are sharp" can be exposed as a confusion of a substance and a quality. In Kant's theory, by contrast, generic terms represent empirical concepts, and an equivocation that confuses genera, as "The knife and musical note are sharp" confuses bodies and sounds, is not a category-mistake but a confusion of empirical concepts. One makes a category-mistake—violates what is essential to Kant's theory—by misapplying a category rather than by mistaking the category in which an entity belongs. The important point is that Kant's categories apply only to phenomena or appearances, not to entities or things in themselves. Every appearance can be judged according to every category and cannot be said to belong properly in one category rather than another. An appearance of red, for example, has extensive magnitude equal to a spatial area and is hence a quantity; it has intensive magnitude as a sensation with a certain degree of intensity and is hence a quality; it is related to further appearances as accident is to substance and effect to cause; and in relation to other appearances it is possible, actual, or necessary.

In Aristotle's theory, on the contrary, a redness is properly an accident in the category of quality; it exists in a substance from which it may be separated in thought but not in being. The extensive magnitude comprising a spatial area is a quantity of the substance and not of the redness; the intensity of the sensation of redness is a quality of the perceiving subject. Questions concerning the cause or the possibility, actuality, and necessity of the redness can be answered only by references to the substance that is said to be red. When the color is separated in thought from the substance the resulting abstract entity, the color red, can be characterized essentially (red, for example, is darker than orange), but to take it as an entity that itself has accidents is to make the category-mistake of confusing a quality with a substance.

To say that the color red is red is, for Kant, to misapply the relational category of substance and accident. Categories can be applied correctly only to phenomena, and in the case of a relational category both terms of the relation must be phenomena. The phrase "the color red" stands for the concept under which appearances of red are subsumed and not for an appearance that may be related to an appearance of red as substance to accident. This sort of category-mistake needs little attention since with Kant's theory there is no compelling tendency of the human mind to confuse a concept with its instances. But there is a natural tendency to make the mistake of applying categories to what are technically, for Kant, ideas and ideals; the former give rise to antinomies of pure reason and the latter to fallacious proofs of God's existence. Platonism in the form that gains a hold on men's minds is the mistake of applying the category of existence to ideals, not the mistake of confusing a concept with its instances. Along with antinomies and fallacious proofs of God, Kant argued for a third kind of category-mistake, a mistake that occurs when categories are misapplied in judgments about a thinking substance; the result is a set of equivocations giving rise to what Kant called "paralogisms of pure reason." These three kinds of category-mistakes are to be exposed not as sound without sense but as illusions to which the human mind is naturally prone.

POST-KANTIAN THEORIES

Although Kant's theory of categories marks the single most important development in the subject since Aristotle, his list of 12 categories never acquired anything like the dominant role once held by Aristotle's list of 10. Kant's influence has been to change the conception of how a list of categories should be formed, rather than to provide the list itself. Instead of looking for the highest genera of being, the most universal kinds of entities, one should look for the most universal forms of understanding presupposed in the formation of judgments. The strong influence of Kant is evident in the theories of categories of such philosophers as Hegel, Husserl, and Peirce.

Peirce's theory is closely connected with his contributions to logic, but his conception of what constitutes a category is sufficiently Kantian to distinguish his theory radically from the theory usually associated with the development of modern logic.

Theory of types. Russell originally devised his theory of types as a means of avoiding a contradiction he had discovered in Frege's logic, but the theory has profound implications for philosophy in general, and under its influence "category" has come to be used frequently as a synonym for "logical type."

As the theory of types is presented in *Principia Mathematica*, its cardinal principle (called by Russell the "vicious-circle principle") is that whatever involves all of a collection must not be one of the collection. The class of white objects, for example, includes (and hence involves) all white objects, and to say that this class is itself a white object is to violate the principle and to utter nonsense. The set of entities consisting of all white objects and the class of white objects is for Russell an "illegitimate totality," a set that "has no total" in the sense that no significant statement can be made about all its members. The purpose of the theory of types is to provide a theoretical basis for breaking up such a set into legitimate totalities. A totality is legitimate when and only when all its members belong to the same logical type, and two entities are of different logical types when and only when their inclusion in the same class yields an illegitimate totality. Whenever an entity involves all the members of a given class its logical type is said to be higher than the type of the members of this class. Logical types thus form an infinite hierarchy with individuals at the lowest level, or zero type, classes of individuals at the next level, then classes of classes, and so on. Since to every class there corresponds a defining property of that class, there is an equivalent hierarchy of logical types with individuals again at the lowest level, but with properties of individuals next, then properties of properties of individuals, and so on. "*X* is a member of the class of white objects" is equivalent to "*X* is white," and the two sentences "The class of white objects is a white object" and "The color white is white" are equally expressions of a type-mistake or category-mistake and are equally nonsensical.

The theory of types, if true, gets rid of the contradiction Russell wanted to avoid. This contradiction arises when the class of all classes that are not members of themselves is said to be or not to be a member of itself. According to the theory of types the attempt to make either assertion violates the vicious-circle principle and results in nonsense. But if this way of avoiding the contradiction is to be satisfactory, there must be reasons for accepting the theory of types other than the fact that if it is accepted the contradiction it was designed to avoid is avoided. Efforts to find such reasons have carried investigations concerning the theory of types from the sphere of technical issues in mathematical logic into the sphere of philosophical issues in a theory of categories. Developments in both spheres have often proceeded independently, and even though technical work in mathematical logic has developed alternatives to the theory of types (especially to the theory as first stated by Russell), the fact that the theory is not needed to avoid the original contradiction is not in itself conclusive evidence that the theory has nothing to be said for it as a theory of categories.

Russell offered in support of the theory of types the fact that it outlaws not only conditions giving rise to the paradox concerning class membership but also those giving rise to an indefinite number of other paradoxes of self-reference, including the ancient paradox of the liar. But alternative ways of avoiding these other paradoxes have been developed. More serious than its nonuniqueness as a consistent solution to the problems it was designed to avoid is a difficulty intrinsic to the theory itself. Even if the theory is true, there seems to be no way to state it without contradiction. The word "type" illustrates the point. In stating the theory one uses this word, which is itself a particular entity, with reference to all entities, so one entity is made to involve the collection of all entities. Russell tried to cope with the difficulty by proposing that a difference in logical type be taken as a difference in syntactical function rather than a difference in the totalities to which two entities may be legitimately assigned. Instead of saying that the color white and a table are of different logical types because the latter but not the former can be included in the class of all white objects without forming an illegitimate totality, we may say that the phrases "the color white" and "a table" belong to different logical types because the latter but not the former yields a significant statement when it replaces X in the sentence-form "X is white."

Reference to linguistic expressions rather than entities avoids a vicious-circle fallacy because the hierarchy of types asserted by the theory then includes only the totality of expressions within a given language, not the totality of all entities. But any given statement of the theory must be in a metalanguage whose expressions are not included in the totality of expressions covered by the statement. While the theory can thus never be applied to the language in which it is itself stated, it can always in principle be restated in a further language (a meta-metalanguage) so that it applies to the language in which it was originally stated as well as the language to which it originally applied. Universal application of the theory is thus possible in principle by proceeding up an infinite hierarchy of languages, while the application of the theory to each particular language asserts the existence of an infinite hierarchy of types of syntactical functions within that language. But in neither case is there the simple assertion that the class of all entities comprises an infinite hierarchy of logical types.

The conception of logical type as syntactical function is much easier to maintain when the expressions typed are those of an artificial language, such as a logical calculus, rather than those of a natural language, such as English. Generalization about the totality of expressions in an artificial language is easy because this totality is generated by the rules one must lay down if one is to construct an artificial language in a clear and definite sense. But such relativity to the rules of an artificial language makes it impossible to maintain all that was originally claimed for the theory of types. Russell was originally understood as claiming to have *discovered* that what appears to be stated by sentences like "The color white is white" and "The class of white objects is a white object" is simply nonsense. But then it seems that the most one can say is that Russell *constructed* an artificial language (a calculus or formalism) in which the translations of these English sentences are not well-formed formulas. The mere construction of such a language is clearly not the same as the discovery that in point of logic certain apparent statements are really nonsense. The case against Russell's original claim is all the more damaging in view of the fact that formalisms have since been constructed in which translations of certain sentences that are nonsense according to the theory of types are well-formed formulas, and the contradiction the theory of types was designed to avoid does not appear. Enlarging the notion of logical type to include semantic as well as syntactical function does not change the picture. Semantic rules for an artificial language are necessary if one is to do certain things with the language, but these rules, like syntactical rules, are stipulated in the construction of the formalism; addition of such rules in no way furthers the claim to having discovered that certain sentences are nonsense rather than having constructed a language in which they become nonsense.

CATEGORIES AS DISCOVERED IN A NATURAL LANGUAGE

The claim to discovery is essential to a theory of categories, and the claim may still be made if types are found among the expressions of a natural language rather than imposed on the expressions of an artificial language. Instead of beginning with the vicious-circle principle as defining a condition we must impose on any language if we want to make sense, we may begin with expressions in the natural language we ordinarily use—expressions with which we assume we make sense, if we make sense at all—and try to determine what differences in type our making sense requires us to recognize in these expressions. This sort of approach is taken by Ryle in *The Concept of Mind*, where he considers expressions we use in talking about mental powers and operations and argues that certain of these expressions cannot belong to the same type or category as others. Ryle's test for a category-difference is a case where one of two expressions cannot replace the other without turning the literal meaning of a sentence into an absurdity. To begin with an obvious case, when "the man" in "The man is in bed" is replaced by "Saturday" the result is clearly an absurd sentence if taken literally. Less obvious cases often go undetected by philosophers and remain a source of philosophical confusion. "He scanned the hedgerow carefully" becomes absurd when "saw" replaces "scanned," although the absurdity disappears when the adverb is omitted. Failure to note that "to see" belongs in the category of "achievement" verbs while "to scan" is a "task" or "search" verb has misled philosophers to posit a mental activity corresponding to seeing that is analogous to the genuine activity of scanning.

For Ryle categories are indefinitely numerous and unordered. The totality of categories is not in principle an infinite hierarchy of types; categories provide no architectonic such as Kant's fourfold division of triads; and there is no distinction setting off one category from all the others as basic regardless of their number, as Aristotle's distinction between substance and accident. There are thus no mistakes that are strictly category-mistakes rather than ordinary equivocations or absurdities. Ryle explains in his article "Categories" that he uses "absurdity" rather than "nonsense" because he wants to distinguish a category-mistake from mere sound without sense. According to Ryle, a category-mistake is not a meaningless noise but a remark that is somehow out of place when its literal meaning is taken seriously; many jokes, he observes, are in fact "type-pranks."

WHAT IS A THEORY OF CATEGORIES?

The above observations suggest that Ryle has no *theory* of categories at all—no principles by which categories can be determined and ordered. Yet he seems unwilling to give up all claims to a theory of categories. He is especially concerned with countering the impression that category-differences are on a par with differences created by a particular set of linguistic rules. In his article "Categories" he considers briefly the question What are types of? He suggests that instead of saying absurdities result from an improper coupling of linguistic expressions, it is more correct to say that they result from an improper coupling of what the expressions signify. But one must be wary of saying that types are types of the *significata* of expressions. A phrase like "*significata* of expressions"can never be used univocally, because such use presupposes that all *significata* are of the same type. Ryle claims we can get along without an expression that purports to specify what types are types of, since the functions of such an expression are "purely stenographic"; if we want an expression performing these functions, he suggests "proposition-factor" but cautions that to ask what proposition-factors are like is ridiculous since the phrase "proposition-factor" has all possible type-ambiguities.

Ryle seems hardly to have advanced the question of the status of a theory of categories beyond the point where Russell left it. It appears to be just as difficult to establish category-differences by appeal solely to ordinary language as to establish them by appeal solely to an artificial language. J. J. C. Smart points out, in "A Note on Categories," that with Ryle's test of a category-difference we are led to make very implausible (if not absurd) claims about category-differences. When, for example, "table" replaces "chair" in "The seat of the chair is hard," the result seems clearly an absurd sentence. Yet if "table" and "chair" do not belong in the same category, what words do? If the phrase "category-difference" is to have anything like the force it has had from Aristotle to Russell, the claim to having discovered that "table" and "chair" are expressions in different categories is itself absurd. Though Ryle may not want to make the claim, he cannot avoid it and maintain his test of a category-difference.

Yet Ryle, whatever his intentions, may be said to have established the negative point that absurdity alone is never a sufficient test of a category-mistake. Aristotle, Kant, and Russell each began with metaphysical or logical principles that purport to set limits of literal sense; a violation of these principles results either in sound without sense or in intellectual illusion, and in both cases in more than simple absurdity. Ryle appears to want the advantages of a theory of categories and at the same time to avoid the embarrassment of having to defend its principles. Such a theory promises to rid philosophy of many fallacious arguments and contradictions, but the promise is worthless if the principles of the theory are no more tenable than the arguments and contradictions it sweeps away. Aristotle's metaphysics of substance and accident, Kant's transcendental logic, and Russell's elevation of the vicious-circle principle have proved as philosophically debatable as Platonic forms, proofs for the existence of God, and paradoxes of self-reference. It is comforting to believe that such debatable principles can be discarded and that the forms, proofs, and paradoxes can be exposed as category-mistakes by appeal to nothing more than what a man of common sense will recognize as an absurdity in his own ordinary language. But unfortunately our common use of "absurdity" covers too much. One can hardly hope to rid philosophy of Platonic forms with no more argument than the claim that saying the color white is white is like saying the seat of a table is hard.

Ryle also calls attention to another negative point about a theory of categories. The theory cannot have a subject matter in the usual sense. We cannot generalize about all proposition-factors, all entities, or all of whatever it is types are said to be types of as we generalize about, for example, all bodies or all biological organisms. We may say that every proposition-factor is of some type, but we cannot say what it is like regardless of its type as we can say what every body or biological organism is like regardless of its type. Since everything we can talk about is a proposition-factor, we have nothing with which they can be contrasted; we do, however, have things with which to contrast bodies and biological organisms. Ryle sees this point as forcing us to accept a phrase like "proposition-factor" as merely a kind of dummy expression we may use to preserve the ordinary grammar of "type" and "category," although the important thing is not to preserve the grammar but to avoid the error of thinking we can preserve it with other than a dummy expression. If we take "proposition-factor" as a metalinguistic expression applying to factors in a particular language, we succeed in preserving the grammar without a dummy expression, but only at the price of making categories relative to a particular set of linguistic rules. The use of a dummy expression is at least consistent with the claim (which Ryle seems to want to make) that a recognition of absurdity is not relative to the rules of a particular language. We may be said to recognize, regardless of our language, the absurdity of saying that the seat of a table is hard or that the color white is white, although we are unable to give criteria of absurdity.

Aristotle tried to cope with the subject-matter problem by holding that while we cannot generalize about all entities as we can about all bodies or all biological organisms ("being is not a genus," as he put it), we can have a science of being because there is one primary type of being—substance—and every other type exists by being an accident of substance. Although we have, then, nothing with which to contrast all beings, we can contrast substances with accidents, and the science of substance is the science of being *qua* being in that conditions for the being of substance are conditions for the being of everything else. A theory of categories may thus be founded on the principle that substances alone can have accidents and all categories other than substance are categories of accidents. For Kant categories do not distinguish beings or entities but a priori forms of understanding, and, unlike Aristotle's beings or Ryle's proposition-factors, these forms comprise not everything we can talk about but only necessary conditions for judgments about objects of experience. The forms stand in sharp contrast with other objects of discourse and constitute a single subject matter belonging to the science of transcendental logic.

Neither Aristotle's nor Kant's theory of categories seems immune to the objection that its subject matter is created rather than discovered. Aristotle's pronouncements about substance and accident and Kant's about forms of understanding each provide principles that yield a scheme of categories, but one may ask whether the pronouncements are anything more than rules for the construction of a certain kind of language—whether the construction of an Aristotelian metaphysics or that of a Kantian transcendental logic provides a theory of categories with anything more than an artificial language within which certain category-differences are established. An answer to this question is proposed by P. F. Strawson in his *Individuals.* Strawson suggests that theories of metaphysics have tended to be either descriptive or revisionary. A metaphysics is descriptive insofar as it yields a scheme of categories that describes the conceptual scheme we actually presuppose in ordinary language. A theory becomes revisionary to the extent that it leads to a departure from our ordinary scheme. Strawson cites the metaphysical theories of Aristotle and Kant as descriptive, those of Descartes, Leibniz, and Berkeley as revisionary. While all five philosophers construct special languages, only Aristotle and Kant do so in a way that results in a scheme of categories that describes the conceptual scheme of our ordinary language.

But if in this sense Aristotle and Kant in their theories of categories describe rather than create a subject matter, what they describe is not what they claim as their subject matter. Strawson professes in his own theory of categories to describe the conceptual scheme of our ordinary language, but he does not profess to give principles of being *qua* being or a transcendental deduction of pure concepts of the understanding. If Aristotle and Kant to some extent describe the scheme Strawson sets out to describe, this achievement was certainly not their primary objective, and since they differ radically at crucial points, as in their views of alteration and substantial change, they can hardly be said in any case to describe the same scheme. One must say, rather, that each offers metaphysical or transcendental hypotheses that purport to account for and establish the necessity of the conceptual scheme underlying common sense. One may of course accept much of what they say in description of their schemes as true of what one takes to be our common-sense scheme and yet reject their hypotheses. With the rejection there is no need to defend the hypotheses' claims to a metaphysical or transcendental subject matter, but one then needs to explain how our common-sense scheme is subject matter for description. A description of common features in the grammars of Indo-European languages is not exactly what Strawson means by a description of the conceptual scheme of our ordinary language. But it can hardly be said that his efforts to distinguish the two descriptions are entirely successful. In some of his arguments he seems to appeal to metaphysical hypotheses of his own and hence to have a theory accounting for, and not simply a description of, the conceptual scheme he claims as his subject matter. In other arguments he seems, like Ryle, to make an ultimate appeal to our common-sense recognition of absurdity.

The construction of a theory of categories as descriptive metaphysics differs, according to Strawson, from what is called today philosophical, or logical, or conceptual analysis. But the difference is not "in kind of intention, but only in scope and generality." Strawson describes philosophical analysis as relying on "a close examination of the acutal use of words," and while this is "the best, and indeed the only sure, way in philosophy," what it can yield is not of sufficient scope and generality "to meet the full metaphysical demand for understanding." But Strawson does not elaborate the demand and gives no criterion for deciding when philosophical analysis must give way to descriptive metaphysics. He sometimes implies that we may pass imperceptibly from one to the other, and this may be the case if to do descriptive metaphysics is simply to articulate what is presupposed in a given philosophical analysis. But it can hardly be the case if descriptive metaphysics, unlike philosophical analysis, has its own peculiar subject matter—being *qua* being, pure concepts of the understanding, our common-sense conceptual scheme, or whatever. Philosophical analysis is clarification of thought about a given subject matter, and to articulate the presuppositions of a given analysis is not to analyze a new subject matter but only to push the original analysis as far as we can. In the end we may arrive at distinctions that agree with what philosophers from Aristotle to Strawson have called "category-differences," and there is no harm in using the label if we mean only that the distinctions are ultimate in the analysis we have given and not also that they have to be supported by a hypothesis about a special subject matter. We can hardly make the additional claim without passing beyond the point where we can hope for help from philosophical analysis.

HISTORICAL NOTES

Stoics and Neoplatonists. In place of Aristotle's ten categories the Greek Stoics substituted four "most generic" notions or concepts: substratum, or subject; quality, or essential attribute; state, or accidental condition; and relation. The Stoic view, as well as the Aristotlelian doctrine, was criticized by the Neoplatonist Plotinus. In his *Sixth Ennead* Plotinus argued that the ultimate categories are neither the Aristotelian ten nor the Stoic four but correspond to the five "kinds" listed in Plato's *Sophist:* being, rest, motion, identity, and difference. The central point for Plotinus was that different categories apply to the intelligible and sensible worlds, the ultimate categories applying only to the former. Plotinus' views on categories figured prominently in medieval discussions only as they were considerably modified by his pupil Porphyry. In Porphyry's short commentary on Aristotle's *Categories*, generally known as the *Isagoge* (Εἰσαγωγή, "Introduction"), he accepted Aristotle's list of ten but raised Plotinian questions about the way they exist. He noted that categories are genera and asked whether genera and species subsist (exist outside the understanding) or are in the naked understanding alone; whether, if they subsist, they are corporeal or incorporeal; and finally, whether they are separated from sensibles or reside in sensibles. He remarked that these questions are too deep for an introductory treatise, and we have no record of how he thought they should be answered.

Boethius. Boethius translated the *Isagoge* into Latin, along with Aristotle's *Categories* and *On Interpretation.* He also wrote a commentary on the *Isagoge*, offering answers to Porphyry's unanswered questions, and thus began a tradition, which persisted throughout the medieval period, of accepting Porphyry's questions as presenting the fundamental issues for any account of categories. Since genera and species appear most prominently as genera and species of substances, the issues centered first of all in the signification of common nouns taken as names of kinds of substances. The medieval "problem of universals" thus arose from Porphyry's questions about Aristotle's categories, and prominent medieval philosophers, such as Abelard, Aquinas, Duns Scotus, and Ockham, are known as conceptualists, realists, or nominalists because of their answers to these questions. The important point for a history of theories of categories is that the discussion of the problem of universals by major figures in medieval philosophy occurred within an unquestioned framework provided by Aristotle's theory of categories—in particular, within a framework that presupposed the basic Aristotelian interrelation of substance and accident and essential and accidental predication.

Locke and Hume. The Aristotelian framework broke down in modern pre-Kantian philosophy. Signs of the breakdown were evident in Hobbes and Descartes, but its full force appeared in Locke and Hume. With Locke's account of substance as an "unknown something" underlying appearances, essential predication in the category of substance becomes impossible, and the signification of common nouns supposed to name kinds of substances can be fixed only by "nominal essences," by conventional factors, rather than by Ockham's "natural signs in the soul." Essential predication, and hence necessary truth, remains possible only when the subjects are things of our own creation ("mixed modes") and not when they are substances in the real world.

The full consequences of Locke's departure from an Aristotelian framework were drawn by Hume. If it is impossible to know what something in the real world necessarily (essentially) is, it is also impossible to know that any one thing in the real world is necessarily connected with another or that any state of a thing at one time is necessarily connected with its state at another time. In other words, not only substance but also causality—an equally if not more fundamental notion (though not recognized as a category by Aristotle)—is made a matter of habit and custom. The stage was set for Kant to answer Hume with a radically new theory of categories.

Hegel. Despite the radical differences between Kantian and Aristotelian categories, two basic points of similarity remain: (1) Categories provide form but not content for cognitive discourse about the world and thus serve to distinguish what we can meaningfully say in such discourse from what we may seem to say when we make category-mistakes or misapply categories. (2) Categories presuppose the substance–accident (subject–predicate) form basic to Aristotelian logic. Hegel's philosophy retains neither of these points of similarity, although he adopted the Kantian view that the clue to a system of categories is to be found in logic. But instead of turning to logic as a study of forms of reasoning without regard for content, Hegel turned to logic as a dialectical process in which form and content are inseparable. The essential nature of this process is seen not in the forms under which subject and predicate are brought together in the premises of reasoning to make affirmative, negative, disjunctive, hypothetical, and other types of judgment but in the basic stages through which the process itself repeatedly moves. These stages Hegel called "thesis," "antithesis," and "synthesis," and he took them as interrelating the basic ideas, notions, or principles of reason, which he also called "categories." This interrelation of categories constitutes both Hegel's system of philosophy and what he held to be the "system of reality." The categories, then, are many, and their exact number cannot be determined until the system of reality is fully articulated. Hegel thus marked the beginning of a tradition in modern philosophy, in which "category" means simply any basic notion, concept, or principle in a system of philosophy.

This use of "category" is standard not only among Hegel's progeny of absolute idealists but also among metaphysicians generally, who dissociate themselves from analytical philosophy. The use remains even when there is no vestige of Hegel's threefold pattern of thesis, antithesis, and synthesis as a means of ordering the principles of speculative philosophy. The categorial scheme in Whitehead's *Process and Reality*, for example, is readily understood as dealing with the sort of notions Hegel called "categories" but hardly with categories in the Aristotelian–Kantian sense of setting limits of cognitive meaning, a sense that still survives in analytical philosophy.

Peirce. The collapse of Kant's theory of categories is inevitable, according to Peirce, as logic advances beyond the subject–predicate form recognized by Aristotle. So long as statements like "John gave the book to Mary" are not seen as possessing a logical form fundamentally different from and coordinate with the simple subject–predicate form of statements like "John is tall," categories are determined by what may be taken as different forms of this one-subject–one-predicate relation. Aristotle and Kant analyzed the forms differently, but the relation analyzed was the same. With the development of logic beyond Aristotle (a development to which Peirce made significant contributions), statements like "John gave the book to Mary" are recognized as statements with three-place predicates (x gave y to z) and are different in logical form from statements with one-place predicates (x is tall). Peirce claimed to have demonstrated in his "logic of relatives" that although one-place, two-place, and three-place predicates are basically different in logical form, predicates with more than three places have no features of logical form not already found in three-place predicates.

The demonstration remains one of the more questionable parts of his logic, but Peirce accepted it as proof that in formal logic there are but three fundamentally different types of predicates and hence that there are but three categories. He sometimes referred to his categories as the "monad," the "dyad," and the "polyad," but he preferred the more general expressions "firstness," "secondness," and "thirdness." As genera (or modes) of being, the categories are designated as "pure possibility," "actual existence," and "real generality." A pure possibility stands by itself, determined by nothing but conditions of internal consistency; what actually exists stands in relation to other existences and to some extent both determines and is determined by them; a true generalization is a representation related to other representations, to actually existing things, and to pure possibilities. In his philosophical cosmology Peirce had three universes corresponding to the three modes of being, and in his semeiotic theory, or theory of signs, he developed an extensive classification of signs, with the main divisions triadic, each triad comprising a firstness, a secondness, and a thirdness. Although Peirce's categories thus function architectonically somewhat as Hegel's thesis, antithesis, and synthesis, they serve, as Hegel's triad does not, to set limits of cognitive meaning. Though Peirce did not use the phrase "category-mistake," he said repeatedly in his later writings that nominalism, which he regarded as the great error in the history of philosophy, arises from the failure to recognize real generality as a mode of being distinct from actual existence. In arguing that universals have no actual existence, the nominalist has failed to see that to ask in the first place whether they have such existence is a category-mistake. In his final years Peirce labored to show that the pragmatic criterion of meaning, which he propounded early in his career, is not only consistent with but actually necessitated by his theory of categories.

Husserl. The role of categories in setting limits of cognitive meaning figures prominently in the philosophy of Husserl. To determine "primitive forms" or "pure categories" of meaning is the first task of a "pure philosophical grammar." The fundamental form is that of propositional meaning, and other primitive forms, such as the nominal and adjectival, are forms of meaning that belong to constituents of a proposition. After determining these pure categories of meaning, pure logical grammar turns to primitive forms or categories of the composition and modification of meaning (forms such as those exhibited by propositional connectives and modal expressions). In addition to a pure logical grammar, Husserl held, there are a pure logic of consistency (noncontradiction) and a pure logic of truth. The picture is further complicated in that pure logic may be taken as giving rise to a formal ontology and, again, developed into a transcendental logic. A full account of categories requires the full development of logic in all its phases, and in this respect Husserl's view of categories seems reminiscent of Hegel. But at no point (even in formal ontology) did categories cease for Husserl to be purely formal and become inseparable from content. Husserl was careful to distinguish the kinds of nonsense precluded by his categories from nonsense of content (*inhaltlich Unsinn*). A phrase like "if–then is round" is nonsense because it violates a category-difference, a condition of meaningfulness established by logic alone; a phrase like "the seat of the table is hard" violates no such condition, and its nonsense arises from a material, not a formal (logical), incompatibility. While at times Husserl's language may suggest what Carnap and others have since called "syntactical categories," it should be noted that Husserl had nothing like Carnap's technical distinction between syntax and semantics and that the "syntactical categories" of Husserl's pure logical grammar are in Carnap's sense neither purely syntactical nor semantical.

Frege and Wittgenstein. In their philosophies of mathematics and logic both Peirce and Husserl remained close enough to Kant not to accord set theory the fundamental role it has come to play in logic and the foundations of mathematics. Frege, although he did not present any of his views under the heading "a theory of categories," did far more than Peirce or Husserl to shape the discussion of categories in the twentieth century. Frege analyzed sense and reference, concept and object (notions fundamental to Peirce's and Husserl's theories of categories) in a way that permitted him to take set theory as basic in mathematics and to define cardinal numbers as classes of classes. Russell's efforts to cope with the contradictory notion of the class of all classes not members of themselves (a notion one seems forced to admit with Frege's analysis) produced the theory of types.

The conclusion suggested by the difficulties encountered in the theory of types, that categories as setting limits of cognitive meaning are not proper subject matter for a theory, was first advanced by Wittgenstein. In his early work, *Tractatus Logico-philosophicus*, Wittgenstein spoke of the limits of cognitive meaning as the ineffable, as what can be shown but not said. In his later writings he repudiated the suggestion that the limits constitute an ineffable subject matter, something to be unveiled but not articulated as a theory by philosophical analysis. However, with the assumption of such subject matter philosophical clarity is to be achieved by the construction of an ideal language, a language is stripped of all superfluous symbolism and is hence unable to give the illusion of transcending the ineffable limits of cognitive meaning. But if this assumption is itself an illusion, as Wittgenstein later held, if we can no more show than we can state the limits of *all* language, then philosophical clarity can be achieved only piecemeal, context by context; there is no short cut via an ideal language. And a fortiori there is no universal scheme of categories to be unveiled, let alone to be established by a theory. Wittgenstein's influence may be seen in the hesitation of Ryle, Strawson, and other present-day analytical philosophers to claim that categories should (or can) have the absolute universality claimed in theories of categories from Aristotle's to the theory of types.

Bibliography

STANDARD HISTORIES

Ragnisco, P., *Storia critica delle categorie dai primordi della filosofia greca fino al Hegel*, 2 vols. Florence, 1871.

Trendelenburg, A., *Historische Beiträge zur Philosophie*, Vol. I, *Geschichte der Kategorienlehre*. Berlin, 1846.

RECENT WORKS

Ackrill, J. L., *Aristotle's Categories and De Interpretatione*. Oxford, 1963. A new translation, written for the serious student of philosophy who does not read Greek. Copious notes, constituting over half the volume, provide an excellent scholarly commentary.

Anscombe, G. E. M., and Geach, P. T., *Three Philosophers.* Ithaca, N.Y., 1961. Contains penetrating but difficult discussion applying recent techniques of analysis to problems of categories in Aristotle, Aquinas, and Frege.

Black, Max, "Russell's Philosophy of Language," in P. A. Schilpp, ed., *The Philosophy of Bertrand Russell.* Evanston, Ill., 1946. Pp. 229–255. Difficulties with the original theory of types as a theory of categories. See also Russell's reply on pp. 691–695.

Cross, R. C., "Category Differences." *PAS* (1958–1959), 255–270.

Hall, Everett W., "Ghosts and Categorical Mistakes." *Philosophical Studies,* Vol. 7 (1956), 1–6.

Hall, Everett W., *Philosophical Systems: A Categorial Analysis.* Chicago, 1960. Sketchy survey of different philosophical systems as different categorial schemes.

Harrison, Bernard, "Category Mistakes and Rules of Language." *Mind,* Vol. 74 (1965), 309–325.

Hillman, D. J., "On Grammars and Category Mistakes." *Mind,* Vol. 72 (1963), 224–234.

Pap, Arthur, "Types and Meaninglessness." *Mind,* Vol. 69 (1960), 41–54.

Passmore, John, *Philosophical Reasoning.* New York, 1961. Difficulties of maintaining a theory of categories are discussed in Ch. 7.

Popper, Karl R., *Conjectures and Refutations.* New York and London, 1962. Chs. 11–14 offer criticisms of the view that limits of meaningfulness can be set by discovery of types or categories.

Quine, W. V., *Word and Object.* New York and London, 1960. Presents a skillful defense of the view that categories are relative to language.

Rorty, Richard, "Pragmatism, Categories, and Language." *Philosophical Review,* Vol. 70 (1961), 197–223.

Ryle, Gilbert, *The Concept of Mind.* London, 1949.

Ryle, Gilbert, "Categories," in A. G. N. Flew, ed., *Logic and Language,* Second Series, Oxford, 1953. Pp. 65–81.

Ryle, Gilbert, "Systematically Misleading Expressions," in A. G. N. Flew, ed., *Logic and Language,* First Series. Oxford, 1951. Pp. 11–36.

Shwayder, D. S., *Modes of Referring and the Problem of Universals.* Berkeley and Los Angeles, 1961. Technical discussion of points crucial to a theory of categories, especially Strawson's.

Smart, J. J. C., "A Note on Categories." *British Journal for the Philosophy of Science,* Vol. 4 (1953), 227–228.

Sommers, Fred, "Types and Ontology." *Philosophical Review,* Vol. 72 (1963), 327–363.

Strawson, P. F., *Individuals.* London, 1959.

Thompson, Manley, "On Category Differences." *Philosophical Review,* Vol. 66 (1957), 468–508.

Warnock, G. J., "Categories and Dilemmas," in *English Philosophy Since 1900.* London and New York, 1958. Ch. 7.

MANLEY THOMPSON

CATEGORIES, SYNTACTICAL AND SEMANTICAL. *See* SYNTACTICAL AND SEMANTICAL CATEGORIES.

CATHARSIS. *See* KATHARSIS.

CATTANEO, CARLO (1801–1869), possibly the most interesting Italian philosopher of the nineteenth century, and a distinguished scholar in history, economics, linguistics, and geography. Born in Milan, he received a law degree from the University of Pavia, where for some years afterward he taught Latin and the humanities. In 1839 he founded the journal *Il Politecnico,* which he described as "a monthly repertory of studies applied to culture and social prosperity." Cattaneo led the 1848 Milanese insurrection against Austrian rule, the story of which he related in a masterly booklet, *L'insurrezione di Milano nel 1848* (in *Scritti storici e geografici,* Vol. IV, Florence, 1957; first published in French in Paris, 1848). When the first Italian war of independence ended in failure, in 1849, Cattaneo went into exile, first in Paris and then in Lugano, Switzerland, where for several years he taught philosophy in the local lyceum. Although he was appointed a deputy to the Italian parliament in 1860, he refused to enter the parliament house in order not to have to swear allegiance to the king. He continued to spend most of his time at Lugano, where he edited a new series of *Il Politecnico* from 1860 to 1863, the first series having been suspended in 1844.

The main influence on Cattaneo was the Lombard Enlightenment philosophy espoused by his teacher G. D. Romagnosi, which was interested in scientific inquiry as related to the well-being of society and concerned with progressive government—facets visible in the work of Alessandro Volta and Cesare Beccaria. Cattaneo blended this inheritance with reflection on his own research in fields other than philosophy but generally disregarded philosophical tradition. He developed an original though unsystematic body of ideas that can best be described as an empirical, scientifically minded phenomenology of history or a nonidealistic historicism. The contemporary reader may catch a Marxian ring or occasionally find a resemblance to such thinkers as Wilhelm Dilthey, G. H. Mead, and John Dewey.

For Cattaneo the philosopher's task consists in clarifying objective current historical problems rather than subjective difficulties. There is no single problem to be made the center of systematic speculation, nor any logical or genetic "first truth" on which the chain of deductive reasoning may be hung. There is instead a plurality, itself subject to change, of well-determined and interrelated problems. There are no final solutions to problems, but only a body of perfectible solutions, which are discovered not by absolute reason but by general human reasonableness. Logic is the theory of scientific research; in philosophy, too, the experimental method, which unites men, must supersede metaphysics, whose continuous veerings divided men.

We know in order to act. The aim of all intellectual endeavor is to change the face of earth for the good of mankind: both nature and society must be "transformed" by man-invented techniques. Insofar as he brings about a knowledge that is public and beneficial, the philosopher is "a craftsman" who works "for the common people"—"we are all workmen if we supply something useful to mankind." To such philosophy Cattaneo contrasted "the philosophy of the schools," whose "ontological hammer" generated "a hidden, priestly wisdom scorning the common people," drawing on "fantastic hypotheses and imaginary intuitions," and "consuming itself in the repetition of empty formulae"—with the result of "throwing wide-open an immeasurable gap between doctrine and fact about man." In saying such things Cattaneo had in mind particularly Antonio Rosmini-Serbati, who was then trying to reconcile philosophical Catholicism with the subjectivism of modern philosophy.

For Cattaneo thought is social action, and it must be studied in the various human activities. There is no essence of thought to be reached directly. To become acquainted with his own nature, man must not recede into himself but rather must go out into the world to collect information. A complete science of thought amounts to knowledge of all that mankind has produced. By "mankind" Cattaneo meant empirical men in their finite world; while professing to be a follower of Giambattista Vico (who was at the time almost unknown), he was highly critical of Vico's oversimplified principles of interpretation, especially of the notion of historical cycles ("Su la *Scienza nova* del Vico," 1839; "Considerazioni sul principio della filosofia," 1844).

Cattaneo intended the phenomenology of history to overcome in a new way the traditional opposition of appearance and reality. What appears to us is what there is—all the reality we can or must cope with—and we cannot reach it outside the social development of mankind (see especially "Un invito alli amatori della filosofia," 1857). This must be construed methodologically, according to what Cattaneo labeled the "psychology of associated minds." The "solitude of the new-born in front of *things*" is a philosophical myth. "Even sensation is from the beginnings a social fact," and "whatever idea one comes to conceive is never the operation of a solitary mind but rather of several associated minds." (*Psicologia delle menti associate,* 1859–1863, unpublished; quotations taken from *Scritti filosofici,* Vol. II, p. 14; Vol. I, p. 448; Vol. II, p. 16). To help us understand the varieties of human history, a social psychology supported by scientific method must replace individual psychology as connected with that "lobby of theology" which was "Descartes' solitude of consciousness."

Additional Works by Cattaneo

In addition to the essays mentioned in the article, Cattaneo's main philosophical work consists of studies on Romagnosi, Campanella, Humboldt, and others, the forewords to the annual volumes of *Il Politecnico,* and the lectures (*Lezioni*) delivered at the Lugano Lyceum on cosmology, psychology, ideology (see the pages on categories and language), logic, and law and morals. Students of Cattaneo's philosophy, however, should take into account also many of his writings in other fields.

There are several anthologies of Cattaneo's papers, especially the philosophical ones, the best being those edited by Gaetano Salvemini (Milan, 1922) and Franco Alessio (Florence, 1957). A complete edition of Cattaneo's works, divided into five sections according to subject matter, appeared in 1956 in Florence; the philosophical section, edited by N. Bobbio, comprises three volumes.

Works on Cattaneo

On Cattaneo's life, see the Salvemini introduction. On his historical position, see Mario Fubini, *Il romanticismo italiano* (Bari, 1953), *passim.* On his thought, see the introductions by Alessio and Bobbio, and also Bruno Brunello, *Cattaneo* (Turin, 1925); Alessandro Levi, *Il positivismo politico di Carlo Cattaneo* (Bari, 1928); and Luigi Ambrosoli, *La formazione di Carlo Cattaneo* (Milan and Naples, 1959).

FERRUCCIO ROSSI-LANDI

CAUSATION. A cause has traditionally been thought of as that which produces something and in terms of which that which is produced, its effect, can be explained. That which is caused might be either some new substance or simply a change in something that already exists. This appears to be only a relative distinction, however, for outside Christian theology philosophers have usually taken for granted that no new substance can be produced out of nothing by a cause. A statue, for example, results from imposing changes on something that already exists. The most general idea of a cause, then, is that which produces, and thus accounts for, some change. If the change is sufficiently striking to warrant applying a new name to what results, then it is natural to speak of the cause as producing a new substance. A moth, for instance, is simply the result of the change in a pre-existing caterpillar, but the change is so striking that the thing is now called a moth rather than a caterpillar. This is what Aristotle called "generation." A leaf, on the other hand, which turns from green to red is still called a leaf. This is what Aristotle called, simply, qualitative "motion," wherein no new substance results. The distinction is plainly a relative one.

Aristotle's four causes. Aristotle, drawing upon the traditions of his predecessors, distinguished four quite different kinds of causes or explanatory principles. These he called the "efficient" cause (*causa quod*), or that by which some change is wrought; the "final" cause (*causa ut*), or end or purpose for which a change is produced; the "material" cause, or that in which a change is wrought; and the "formal" cause, or that into which something is changed. Thus, for example, a statue is produced by a sculptor (its efficient cause) by his imposing changes upon a piece of marble (its material cause) for the purpose of possessing a beautiful object (its final cause), the marble thereby acquiring the form, or distinctive properties, of a statue (its formal cause).

Aristotle believed his predecessors had utilized all these principles of explanation but criticized them for emphasizing some to the neglect of others. The early Milesians, for example, were concerned too much with material causes, believing they could explain the world by discovering some basic matter—water, air, or the like—which all things are composed of. The concept of an efficient cause of change emerged with Empedocles, who postulated two motive forces, poetically called "Love" and "Strife," to account for the evolutionary changes in the world. Plato, on the other hand, often spoke as if the explanation of all things would be achieved simply by discovering their forms, or formal causes, a procedure which Aristotle considered highly one-sided.

The concepts of material and formal causes are archaic and now have little significance outside aesthetics. Final causes have likewise long since been expurgated from physics. They are occasionally invoked, especially at the common-sense level, for the understanding of biological or developmental phenomena, but most biologists profess a deep abhorrence for them. In the anthropological sciences, particularly psychology, the role of final causes—that is, goals or purposes—is still highly controversial. It would seem that voluntary human behavior would sometimes be quite unintelligible except in terms of men's goals or purposes. There are, nevertheless, many experimental psychologists in whose work this idea professedly plays no part whatever and others for whom it is but a derivative concept. This is largely because such investigators have insisted on modeling their science after physics, where the idea of purpose or goal is manifestly out of place. It is also due, however, to a widespread misconception of what a final cause or purpose is supposed to be. It is often, but erroneously, supposed that such a cause could be nothing but an efficient cause occurring after its effect, whereas, in fact, it is the purpose or goal of an activity or process and not, in the usual sense, the cause of it.

Modern conceptions of cause. Philosophers have distinguished other kinds of causes, many of which overlap each other as well as the four of Aristotle. An "immanent" cause, for instance, is one which produces a change within itself, as in the case of a man who produces his own voluntary motions and thoughts; it is distinguished from a "transeunt" cause, which produces a change in something else. This distinction was made by Spinoza and others but is seldom made now. The Scholastics distinguished between a *causa cognoscendi,* the reason or ground for a truth, and a *causa fiendi,* the cause of the existence of something, but the term "cause" is rarely used in the first sense any more.

John Stuart Mill, following Thomas Reid, distinguished efficient causes from what he called "physical" causes, delimiting the former to the causation of a voluntary act by an agent, but he considered the concept of an efficient cause, as thus conceived, to be esoteric—capable of being confirmed only by oneself.

R. G. Collingwood distinguished three senses of a cause, the first being the causation of a voluntary act by an agent, the second being something which can be used by a man to bring about or prevent something in nature, and the third being a condition or set of conditions in nature which are invariably accompanied by some change, whether these conditions are within men's control or not. Collingwood considered the second sense to be the primary one and referred to causes thus conceived as "levers"—that is, as means to ends. A similar conception has been persuasively advocated by Douglas Gasking.

Partly because of the rise of physical science and the accompanying demise of Aristotelian modes of thought, the concept of a cause is now generally that of an efficient cause or, more specifically, what Mill called a "physical" cause. The remainder of this discussion will, accordingly, be devoted to this concept.

TRADITIONAL PROBLEMS OF EFFICIENT CAUSATION

The utility of the concept of a cause. Modern science arose in opposition to Aristotelian thought, which had in the late Middle Ages become allied with Christian theology, and there has since been a pronounced tendency, already noted, to eschew Aristotelian concepts wherever possible. There have not been wanting scientists and philosophers who have insisted that the very concept of a cause is quite worthless, being "anthropomorphic" in origin and in any case replaceable by such less esoteric concepts as concomitant variation, invariable sequence, and so on. Bertrand Russell declared the concept of cause a "relic of a bygone age," and many writers have noted that the word "cause" seldom occurs in the vocabulary of physicists.

Nevertheless, it is hardly disputable that the idea of causation is not only indispensable in the common affairs of life but in all applied science as well. Jurisprudence and law would become quite meaningless if men were not entitled to seek the causes of various unwanted events such as violent deaths, fires, and accidents. The same is true in such areas as public health, medicine, military planning, and, indeed, every area of life. No one doubts that the battle against malaria began with the search for the cause of it, and measures then taken against it have all been aimed at eliminating its cause or moderating its effects by the introduction of other causal factors. This is typical of the way men manage their practical affairs, great and small, in dealing with their environment. It is true that the concept of causation is a theoretically difficult one, beset with many problems and the source of much metaphysical controversy, but the suggestion that it can be dispensed with is extreme.

Causation and change. It is quite common to refer to objects or substances as causes. Thus, one says that malaria is caused by certain mosquitoes, that the earth is warmed by the sun, and so on. Most writers on the subject agree, however, that causes and effects are ordinarily changes in the states of things or substances or, less commonly, unchanging persistences of the states of substances. Succumbing to malaria, for instance, is a change, and it is caused, not by a mosquito as such, but by being bitten by a certain mosquito, which is also a change or event. More precisely, it is caused by the changes wrought in the body by certain microscopic organisms transmitted by mosquitoes. The earth is not warmed by the sun as such, but, rather, certain parts of the earth are warmed by becoming turned toward the sun, and these again are changes or events. The unchanging persistence of a state, such as a constant fever, might be explained by another persistent state, such as the continuing presence of malarial organisms in the blood, and this, too, would be a causal explanation.

Universality and uniformity. To assert that causation is universal is to assert that no change ever occurs without some cause—in short, that every event has a cause. To affirm, on the other hand, that causation is uniform is to affirm that the causal relations between changes or states can be expressed in the form of general laws or, in short, that similar causes always produce similar effects. David Hume, J. S. Mill, and others have expressed the principle of uniformity in the dictum, "the future will resemble the past." Although this statement is, of course, ambiguous, it is intended to mean that the laws of nature that prevailed heretofore will continue to hold in the future.

Universality. It should be noted that the universality and the uniformity of causation are two entirely different claims. Either could be true without the other's being true. The universality of causation has throughout the history of philosophy, until very recent times, usually been regarded as very obvious, sometimes even self-evident. There are many thinkers today, however, who consider it quite possible that certain changes involving the minutest constituents of matter simply have no causes at all. There are also philosophers who consider it doubtful whether all voluntary human acts are caused in any generally accepted sense. Thus, what was once considered quite obvious is now at least controversial. There is, in any case, no philosophical way of proving the universality of causation, for such a proof would have to demonstrate some absurdity in the denial of it. It is not the least difficult to imagine a change occurring without anything causing that change, and there is no contradiction whatever in asserting that this sometimes happens, although, of course, it may be false. It is obvious, too, that there is no scientific or empirical way to prove either the universality or the nonuniversality of causation. If some change occurs and no cause of that change is observed—as often happens, of course, even in one's ordinary daily experience—then one can say that no such cause exists or, upon the same negative evidence, fall back upon the supposition that there is such a cause but that it has eluded discovery. J. S. Mill maintained that the universality of causation is "coextensive with human experience," but this is inaccurate. The causes of many events that men have experienced have never been experienced at all. If the reverse were true, there would be no such thing as an unsolved murder. Causes are in such cases assumed to exist or inferred from other causal connections that men have experienced, but they are not experienced.

Uniformity. The doctrine of the uniformity of causation, on the other hand, is relatively recent in philosophy and arose, more or less, with the development and growth of science and its increasing emphasis upon laws of nature. Of course, philosophers have always been aware of certain uniformities of nature, but there was little emphasis upon the absolute uniformity of causation before the rise of experimental science. There seemed, moreover, to be certain causes—such as the sun, for instance—whose effects were so numerous and diverse that there appeared to be almost no similarity between them at all. It was at first thought that causes produced their effects by virtue of their power or efficacy to do so. (Such is, in fact, part of the original meaning of an efficient cause.) This easily gave rise to the idea that a cause must be at least as great as its effect, that the lesser cannot produce the greater, a claim that was made, and considered self-evident, even by Descartes. The supposition that a given kind of cause could have but one kind of effect was seldom considered obvious, however.

The idea of power. An example of cause as power is a sculptor, who has not only the physical equipment but also the power or ability to convert marble to a statue. Lacking either he could not make a statue. The sun, similarly, has the power to make things grow and the power to do all the other things it does. It was in terms of this concept that God was thought of as the cause of the world and, accordingly, as a being who is all-powerful. Bishop Berkeley considered it so obvious that a cause cannot be thought of apart from the idea of power that he used this as an important argument to prove that our "ideas" (sensations) cannot be caused either by matter or by other ideas, both being, as he put it, "inert" or passive and, hence, lacking the power to produce anything (*A Treatise Concerning the Principles of Human Knowledge*, Sections 25–29, 69). A man's ideas must accordingly, he thought, be caused by some "active" being or, literally, an agent, such as himself or God. Prior to John Locke and the rise of empiricism, the very movements of men and animals were thought to be the expressions of the power of such creatures over their own bodies. Aristotle accordingly described animals as "self-moved." When philosophers finally addressed themselves to the understanding of the concept of power within the framework of empiricist presuppositions they became involved, of course, in enormous difficulties since this idea does not seem to correspond to any idea either of sensation or "reflection" (introspection) or to be analyzable in terms of such ideas. Many writers have suggested that it is derived from the feeling of effort or will that is involved in voluntary action. The longest part of Locke's *Essay Concerning Human Understanding* is devoted to a tortuous and inconclusive discussion of the idea of power (Book II, Ch. 21).

In *An Enquiry Concerning Human Understanding*, David Hume finally proposed to eliminate this idea from the conception of causation altogether, maintaining essentially that causes and effects are merely changes that we find constantly conjoined (Sections 4–7). We should not, according to Hume, explain changes in terms of causes having the power to produce them. We should instead simply note that certain changes are, in fact, found to be invariably conjoined with others. It is only because we find such uniformities and thereby come to expect them that we come to speak of power in the first place. Very many philosophers since Hume have believed that he was essentially right, at least with respect to his elimination of the idea of power from the concept of causation, and, in fact, the association is seldom referred to any more in philosophical literature.

A noteworthy exception to Hume's resolution was taken by Thomas Reid, who maintained that the idea of the active power of a cause is everywhere presupposed in any description of deliberate and voluntary human behavior, even though no philosopher can define this concept in terms of any others. Reid held that the causation of voluntary actions by an agent is, moreover, the paradigm example of causation, and he often suggested in his writings that the relations between the states and changes of inanimate things can be called "causal" only in a loose and metaphorical sense. There has recently been an increasing tendency in philosophy, particularly in philosophical psychology and in discussions of the will, to defend similar views. Human beings, and perhaps other animals, are claimed by an increasing number of philosophers to be the causes of certain of the motions of their own bodies in a way that uniquely distinguishes them as "agents," or beings who act and are thus possessed of what Reid called "active power." Such a view has the effect of rendering quite irreducible the difference between human behavior and the behavior of inanimate things, and it is accordingly almost universally rejected in experimental psychology.

The idea of necessary connection. Prior to David Hume's analyses, it was also generally supposed by philosophers that there is a certain necessary or inherent connection between any cause and its effect. By this is meant that the joint occurrence of both is not "accidental"—that a cause is something which is such that, once given, its effect cannot fail to occur—and that a cause compels the occurrence of its effect—that the effect must happen in case the cause exists. These are all ways of saying essentially the same thing. If the sun shines upon a rock under certain conditions, for example, then it is not merely true that the rock becomes warm; it must become warm, these two states being so related that one cannot fail to occur if the other occurs. Similarly, if a man insults another, it is not merely true that the insulted man becomes angry; he cannot, normally, help becoming angry, or, in other words, the insult makes him angry.

It was one of Hume's important claims that there is, in fact, no such necessary connection between any cause and its effect. Just as the idea of power cannot be traced to any sense experience and hence must, in case we have any such idea at all, be the fabrication of our own minds, so also the idea of a necessary connection between cause and effect cannot be traced to any sense impression. Hume's main argument for this negative conclusion was that the idea of any cause is perfectly separable in our minds from its effect; that is, we can easily, and without any absurdity or contradiction, imagine any cause whatever without its accustomed effect or with some effect which, in fact, never accompanies it. There is, accordingly, no absurdity or contradiction in saying of some cause that it does not have the particular effect that it does have. There is no contradiction, for example, in affirming that water solidifies instead of boiling when heated, that a man thrives instead of suffocating under water, or that when a rolling ball strikes another of the same weight, it simply stops or both move on together, instead of the first stopping and the other moving. We learn from experience that such things do not happen, but no experience teaches us that they cannot happen. There is, accordingly, no necessary connection between a cause and its effect. Anything might cause anything according to Hume. For the same reason, Hume insisted, no one can ever infer any effect simply from a description of a cause. Experience alone teaches us what follows upon what, and this is all that it teaches us. "One event follows another," he said, "but we never can observe any tie between them. They seem *conjoined*, but never *connected*."

It should be noted that Hume did not deny that men have an idea of a necessary connection between cause and effect or that this idea was part of what men mean by a causal connection. He only denied that any such connection exists between causes themselves and their effects. He traced the idea of a necessary connection to certain habits of expectation within our own minds. That is to say, men become accustomed to finding certain changes more or less constantly conjoined with others—for example, finding certain experiences, such as putting one's finger into a flame, followed by pain—and the associations thus established in men's minds lead to a habitual expectation of certain impending events upon the experiencing of others. It is this habit of expectation or "customary transition of the imagination" to which Hume traced the idea of a necessary connection between cause and effect. What this means, of course, is that the necessary connections between causes and their effects are read into our experience or imputed to causes and effects when in fact no such connection exists.

The priority of causes to their effects. Philosophers who once spoke so freely of causes as things having the power to compel the occurrence of effects always took for granted that the power or efficacy of a cause never extends to things past or that causes cannot occur after their effects. This priority of a cause to its effect was, moreover, considered to be a metaphysical necessity and not a mere convention of speech. It was generally assumed that nothing past is within the power of anything. Things past are unalterable; they are and must forever remain whatever they have been. Things present, on the other hand, are sometimes alterable. They can be changed in numerous ways, depending upon what causes act upon them. Contemporary philosophers, who have wanted to insist that the causal relation can be analyzed without invoking any idea of power, have nevertheless, for the most part, agreed that causes cannot occur after their effects. However, this is generally considered to be not a metaphysical truth depending on the efficacy of causes but simply a consequence of customary linguistic usage. That is, it is generally thought to be simply part of the usual meaning of "cause" that a cause is something temporally prior to, or at least not subsequent to, its effect.

The direction of necessitation. Just as the power or efficacy of causes was thought never to extend to past things, so also it was always assumed that causes necessitate their effects in a special way in which effects can never be said to necessitate their causes. Indeed, the concepts of power and necessary connection were sometimes treated as if they were one and the same, and Hume himself sometimes referred to power, force, and necessary connection synonymously. Thus, it was thought that a man, in vanquishing his foe, makes him die or does something that renders it impossible for him to live, that subjecting water to a certain temperature makes it boil, and so on. However, despite the fact that such a cause can be certainly inferred from such an effect, given a sufficiently detailed description of the latter, it was never supposed that the effect necessitated such a cause. The sun might shine upon a stone and thus make it become warmer, but in a sense in which it could not be said that the stone, in becoming warmer, makes the sun shine upon it. It is in the sense illustrated by these examples that causes generally were thought to necessitate their effects in some way in which it would be absurd to speak of effects necessitating their causes. However, many recent philosophers have pointed out that if there is any necessary connection between causes and their effects, that connection has no more direction from cause to effect than from effect to cause, that the states of any thing at any given time determine its past states in the same way that they determine its future states, or, in epistemological terms, that the same principles of inference that enable one to predict its future states also enable one to retrodict its past states.

This is a question that has not been satisfactorily resolved in philosophy, for while it is certainly true that, according to any customary interpretation of necessitation, the present state of anything necessitates or determines its past states no less than its future ones, the application of this principle results in paradoxical assertions. It permits us to say, for example, that a given man, by dying at a certain time and place and in a certain way, determines or compels another man to have vanquished him, in the same sense that one can plausibly say that a man, in vanquishing another, compels that other to die or that a stone, in becoming warmer in just the way it does, makes the sun shine upon it, in the same way that the sun, in shining upon it, makes the stone become warmer.

MAIN CONTEMPORARY PROBLEMS OF CAUSATION

As already noted, there appears to be no philosophical way of determining whether causation is universal—that is, whether every occurrence has a cause—or whether it is uniform—that is, whether the same or similar causes always have the same or similar effects. Both the universality and the uniformity of causation are widely held, but many writers (A. E. Taylor, for example) consider them to be only practical postulates or maxims. Of course, it would beg the question to *define* causal concepts in such a way as to entail the truth of either thesis. There is, on the other hand, no experimental way of proving them, since occurrences which at least appear to constitute exceptions to one or the other of those theses are quite common. To treat such apparent exceptions as merely apparent and not real is, of course, only to indicate that the thesis to which it appears to be an exception is regarded as a postulate or maxim or, in any case, something for which no disconfirmation will be permitted. No one, for example, has ever shown experimentally that all the simple voluntary actions of men are caused or that similar such actions always have similar causes, and the opinions of philosophers are, in fact, divided on these questions. Similarly, no one has shown experimentally that the changes in the minutest constituents of matter are all caused or that similar such changes have similar causes, and on these questions, too, divergent views are held by learned men.

There remain two important philosophical questions concerning causation that have not been satisfactorily resolved. These are (1) whether the concept of power or causal efficacy is, after all, essential to the understanding of causal connections and (2) whether there is, after all, any kind of necessary connection between a cause and its effect. A third question, which is derived from these, is whether the causal relation has a temporal direction—whether causes must precede their effects, and if so, why.

Necessity versus invariable sequence. It is useful at this point to consider obvious individual instances of causation—that is, to begin with commonplace examples of changes that are causally related and then ask, as Hume did, precisely what is meant by saying that one is the cause of the other.

Suppose, for example, we let *A* stand for the beheading of Anne Boleyn and *B* for her subsequent death and we assume that the first of these changes was, in fact, the cause of the second. What, then, does that mean? Does it mean simply that these changes are constantly conjoined, that the one never occurs without the other? Of course, it does not, for each of these changes occurred only once in the history of the universe and each of them is, accordingly, also "constantly conjoined" with any other change that has ever occurred.

It is to avoid this obvious difficulty that many philosophers, following the suggestions of Hume, have preferred to speak of similar things and to say that *A* was the cause of *B* provided *A* was immediately followed by *B* and that things similar to *A* are always followed by things similar to *B*. This is essentially Hume's conception. Not only was the beheading of Anne Boleyn followed by her death, but all beheadings are followed by death. It seemed to Hume and to J. S. Mill, too, that we can then define the causal relation simply in terms of such invariable sequence. According to this suggestion, two changes or sets of changes, *A* and *B*, are respectively the cause and the effect of each other if *A* was immediately followed by *B* and if things similar to *A* are always immediately followed by things similar to *B*. Mill added the qualification that the two must be "unconditionally" conjoined—that is, conjoined under all "imaginable" circumstances, but that introduces another consideration to which we shall return later. For Hume, in any case, this conception had the merit of being entirely empirical—that is, a description of the causal relation which does not involve any ideas which do not have their source in observation or experience. Whether two changes are such that one immediately follows the other, for example, is something that can be tested in experience, and whether other similar changes likewise succeed one another in the same way can also be checked and confirmed by experience. There is in this conception of causation no reference to any necessary connection between cause and effect, and, Hume thought, no such connection can be experienced, nor is it needed for a complete description of the causal relationship.

The question of similarity. There is a difficulty in Hume's account, however, which Russell noted but which Hume and many others did not sufficiently appreciate. It has to do with the notion of "similarity." What does "similar" mean in this context? Does it mean exactly similar? If so, then we would appear to be back where we started, for the only thing exactly similar to any event is that event itself. Thus, the only thing in the history of the universe that is exactly similar to the beheading of Anne Boleyn is the beheading of Anne Boleyn, and the only thing exactly similar to her death is her death. Other similar events are only more or less similar—similar in some respects but not in others.

If, however, we understand this similarity to be one of degree, then the statement that things similar to *A* are always followed by things similar to *B* may not be true, even in cases where *A* is the cause of *B*. One could, for example, arrange a clever and realistic dramatization of Anne's beheading which might be rather similar to that historical execution but which is not, in fact, followed by anything at all similar to Anne's death.

Relevant similarities. When Hume and so many others noted that similar causes have similar effects and then attempted to define the causal relation in terms of the *de facto* invariability of things similar to one another being followed by other things similar to one another, they obviously did not mean that this similarity must be exact. Similar causes must, in order to have similar effects, be similar only in certain crucial or relevant respects. A dramatization of the beheading of Anne Boleyn, for example, is similar to the historical execution of that queen, but in certain crucial or relevant respects it is not similar, and that is why it is not followed or need not be followed by any similar effect.

There is, however, the great difficulty of defining "relevance" in this context without spoiling the whole analysis. One cannot say, for example, that similar events must be similar in all causally relevant respects in order to have similar effects, for that would amount to utilizing the idea of a causal relation in analyzing that relation itself.

This point can be illustrated as follows. Suppose one had two pairs of matches. Suppose that the first pair were similar to each other in all respects except that one was red and the other blue. Suppose that the second pair were similar to each other in all respects except that one was wet and the other dry. Now the degree of similarity between the members of each pair would be the same, each would differ from its partner in only one respect. One of these differences, however, is relevant to the question whether the matches ignite when struck in the same way on a rough surface, and the other is not. The color of the match is irrelevant, but whether it is wet or dry is not. All this means, however, is that the dryness of a match is causally connected with its igniting when struck, while its color is not.

If, then, one suggests that those changes which are similar in relevant respects are always followed by other changes which are similar in relevant respects, his analysis of the causal relationship becomes worthlessly tautological. It means only that those changes that are similar in the respects that causally connect them with their effects have similar effects.

Laws of nature and the concept of causation. Many modern philosophers, seeking, like Hume and Mill, to analyze the causal relation within a framework of empiricism, have sought to avoid the foregoing difficulties by appealing to the concept of a law. There is, obviously, a close connection between statements expressing causal connections and those expressing laws of nature, and it is therefore natural to suppose that the former might be explained in terms of the latter.

Laws as necessities. Laws of nature were once commonly thought of as necessary or inviolable principles. The formulation of such laws would thus be statements of what must invariably happen, and ordinary people still tend to think of natural laws in this way, as in some sense governing nature. Examples of very simple laws of nature, according to this conception, would be that water, when heated to 100° C. at sea level, must boil, or cannot fail to boil; that unsupported bodies near the surface of the earth must fall, or cannot fail to fall; and so on.

Of course, it would not be difficult to analyze the causal relation in terms of this conception of a law of nature. One could simply say that a statement of the form "*A* was the cause of *B*" means that both *A* and *B* occurred and that there is a law of nature according to which, or from which it can be deduced, that whenever *A* occurs, *B* must occur also.

Such a conception of causation is considered quite worthless by empiricists and scientists generally, however, for it is obvious that it preserves the very notion of a necessary connection between cause and effect which Hume sought to avoid. To think of laws of nature as inviolable principles concerning what must happen is simply another way of saying that the things related by those laws are connected by a kind of necessity. If, for example, one construes the statement "This water was caused to boil by being heated" to mean that the water was heated to a certain point and boiled and that it is a law of nature that when water is so heated, it must boil, then it immediately follows that this water could not fail to boil when so heated —which is simply to affirm the necessary connection between cause and effect which empiricists have always wanted to deny.

Laws as uniformities. Some philosophers, such as Mill, McTaggart, and Russell, endeavor to defend the view that laws of nature are in no sense inviolable rules but, rather, are mere uniformities expressed by statements of what does, as a matter of fact, invariably happen. Instead of saying that water must boil when heated in a certain way or that unsupported bodies near the earth must fall, according to this view we should say that water does in fact invariably boil when so heated and that such unsupported bodies do in fact fall.

Few thinkers have any fault to find with this conception of a law of nature, but some philosophers (for example, A. C. Ewing and Brand Blanshard) have seriously doubted whether causation can be analyzed in terms of it. The chief reasons for this are that not all purely *de facto* uniformities are recognizable as instances of causal connection and that those which do involve a causal relationship seem intuitively also to involve, in A. C. Ewing's words, "an intrinsic or inherent connection."

One could not, for example, analyze any statement of the form "*A* was the cause of *B*" by saying simply that *A* occurred and was followed by *B* and that it is a law of nature that whenever *A* occurs in certain circumstances, it is followed by *B*. There can be no law of nature connecting merely two particular things. It is no law, for instance, that whenever Anne Boleyn is beheaded, she dies. If, on the other hand, the needed law is expressed by saying that whenever things similar to *A* occur in certain circumstances, they are followed by things similar to *B* for instance, that whenever any water is heated, it boils—then one is again faced with the difficulties of specifying those respects in which the things in question must be similar. Any two or more things are dissimilar in some respects.

This difficulty might be overcome by specifying in the statement of a law of nature those respects in which things must be similar in order to have similar effects and, further, by specifying the circumstances as well. For example, there might be a law to the effect that when any substance of such and such precisely stated chemical composition is treated in a certain specified way under certain specified conditions, it ignites. A match, for example, whose head was of a certain description would be similar to any other match of the same description, and any other similarities and differences between such matches could be disregarded as irrelevant—that is, as not mentioned in the law.

Critics of this approach maintain, however, that no matter how elaborately the statement of any law is formulated, it is always possible to find examples of things which behave according to such a law but which are nevertheless not causally connected. The *de facto* uniformity of their behavior is, according to this view, purely accidental, implying that in any genuine causal relationship there is an element of that intrinsic or inherent connection to which Ewing referred or, in other words, of a necessary connection. Thomas Reid, for example, noted in a famous passage in *Essays on the Active Powers of the Human Mind* (Essay 4, Ch. 9) that day is invariably followed by night and night by day and yet neither is the cause of the other. Ducasse has similarly noted that in infants the growth of teeth invariably follows, but is not caused by, the growth of hair.

The point at issue here can perhaps be made in the following way. Suppose one took a quantity of matches—a thousand—and gave them a set of properties which uniquely distinguished them from all other matches that have, in fact, ever existed and presumably ever will exist. Suppose, for example, one decorated the sticks in a certain elaborate way so that all were similar with respect to those decorations, and suppose further that, as a matter of fact (although not of necessity), no other match so decorated has ever existed or ever will exist. Now, if all those matches were struck in a similar way, it might be true that every match (in the history of the universe) having those properties ignites when struck. If a law of nature is a true general statement of how certain things which are similar in certain specified respects invariably do behave under specified conditions, then that statement would qualify as a law of nature. Obviously, however, it would be false to analyze the causal relation involved in terms of that statement, for it is a purely accidental connection. The decorations on the matchsticks have nothing to do with how the matches behave when struck, even though it might be true that every match in the history of the universe which is so decorated does, in fact, ignite when struck. If, contrary to fact, another match were to have those properties but lacked the property of being dry, then it might not ignite when struck. There is some connection between a match's being dry and igniting when struck, and there is no such connection between its being decorated in the way we have supposed and igniting when struck, in spite of the fact that every match which is so decorated does, in fact, ignite. This, however, seems to mean only that there is no necessary connection between the decorations on a matchstick and the behavior of the match when it is struck, in spite of the fact that the invariance here is complete, while there is some such connection between its being dry and its igniting.

Necessary connection reconsidered. Hume evidently had some notion of the kind of difficulty elicited in the above example, for having defined a cause as "an object, followed by another, and where all objects similar to the first are followed by objects similar to the second," he immediately added, "in other words where, if the first object had not been, the second never had existed." The second statement, however, far from being equivalent to the first, is not even implied by it. The first expresses a *de facto* constancy of sequence between things that do, at some time, exist, whereas the second expresses what would be true if something else, which is not true, were true. Hume here has made an inference from constancy of conjunction to some sort of connection stronger than mere constancy of conjunction—the very sort of inference which he had previously said could never be made.

It was to take account of the same point that Mill introduced the qualification of unconditionality. In order for certain changes or states to be causally connected, it is not enough, Mill said, that they should be invariably conjoined, as day and night are. They must be "unconditionally" conjoined, meaning that they must be conjoined under all imaginable as well as all actual circumstances. Day and night are, to be sure, constantly conjoined, but we can imagine circumstances in which they would not be —circumstances in which there would be perpetual day, for example. They are therefore not causally connected.

It is evident that with this qualification the fundamental point of the empirical analysis has been abandoned. "Under all imaginable circumstances" obviously means under all circumstances, both actual and possible. The very point of the empirical analysis, however, was to set forth a conception of causation, not in terms of what can and cannot happen, not in terms of what is and is not possible, but solely in terms of what does happen. Worse than that, it was one of Hume's main arguments, purporting to show that there is no necessary connection between causes and their effects, that we can always perfectly easily imagine that those *de facto* sequences that we have discovered should be quite different. We can easily imagine that water solidifies instead of evaporating when heated, that men thrive under water instead of suffocating, that men live as easily after being shorn of their heads as after being shorn of their hair, and so on. In this he was obviously right. Such suppositions are contrary only to our experience, not to what we can conceive and imagine. The introduction of Mill's unconditionality therefore has the result that there is no such thing as a causal connection, that no changes or states are ever causally related; we can always imagine circumstances in which the one occurs and the other does not, which is enough, in Mill's terms, to show that they are not unconditionally conjoined.

Causes as necessary conditions. There seems to be a need, then, to distinguish the causal conditions from the other conditions under which a given change occurs, even in cases in which some of these other conditions accompany changes of the kind in question as invariably as those which cause it. In the light of this many recent and contemporary philosophers (for example, H. L. A. Hart and A. M. Honoré, A. J. Ayer, and R. G. Collingwood) are quite willing, contrary to the fundamental point of view inaugurated by Hume, to speak of the causal conditions of any change as those which were in some sense necessary for its occurrence, or *conditiones sine quibus non*—that is to say, those conditions which were such that, had any of them not occurred, the change in question would not have occurred either. Most contemporary philosophers agree with Hume, however, that the kind of necessity involved here is not logical necessity, since there is never any logical contradiction in affirming, of any two events that can be described independently of each other, that one occurred and the other did not. Two exceptions are A. C. Ewing and Brand Blanshard, both of whom have suggested that causes imply their effects and are therefore not logically independent of them. Those who reject this claim of logical necessity and also the empiricist claim that there is no necessary connection whatever sometimes introduce such concepts as physical, nomological, or etiological necessity, as C. J. Ducasse did.

A given change that is caused, then, according to the last

view, occurs under a set of indefinitely numerous conditions, some of which might be such that events like the one in question always, in fact, occur in their presence. Among these, however, some are such that the event in question would not have occurred had they not been present, given all the other conditions exactly as they were, whereas others are such that it would have made no difference whether they were present or not. It is quite possible, for instance, that no match ever has ignited except in the presence of some gravitational force, yet the presence of such a force is not necessary for the ignition of a match.

An expression of the form "*A* was the cause of *B*" means, then, according to this view, that both *A* and *B* occurred and that *A* is that set of conditions, among all those that occurred, which was such that each of them was necessary for, but logically independent of, the occurrence of *B*, given only the other conditions that occurred. More loosely, this means that a causal condition of any event is any condition which is such that, had it not occurred, the event in question would not have occurred, given only those other conditions that occurred, and that the totality of these conditions is the cause of the event.

Some writers, in deference to ordinary usage and practical considerations, prefer to reserve the expression "the cause" for some causal condition of an event that is conspicuous or novel or, particularly, one that is within someone's control. H. L. A. Hart and A. M. Honoré have illustrated with numerous examples the practical advantages of doing so, and R. G. Collingwood has argued persuasively that nothing can be called a cause, in its original and significant sense, which is not within the control of an agent. This seems, however, as Mill maintained, to be essentially a practical and terminological rather than a philosophical question. Philosophically, according to Mill, the cause of an event is a whole set of conditions, as we have "no right to give the name of cause to one of them, exclusively of the others." Ordinarily, for instance, one would not mention the presence of oxygen in describing the cause of some fire, even though it might, in fact, have been a necessary condition for the occurrence of that fire, but this is only because it is a normal condition, normally not within anyone's control, and is therefore presupposed. If, as Hart and Honoré have pointed out, one were dealing with some substance that suddenly ignited upon accidentally coming into contact with oxygen, then it would be natural to speak of the presence of oxygen as the cause of its igniting. Logically, however, it makes no difference whether one says that, given certain other conditions, an event is caused by some further condition that is novel or within someone's control or whether one says that this further condition was, together with those other necessary conditions, the cause of the event in question.

Causes as sufficient conditions. According to the foregoing and now fairly widely held conception, a *causal condition* of an event is any *sine qua non* condition under which that event occurred or any condition which was such that, had the condition in question not obtained, that event (its effect) would not have occurred, and *the cause* of the event is the totality of those conditions. If this is so, however, then it at once follows that the cause—that is, the totality of those necessary conditions—is also sufficient for the occurrence of the event in question. Once one has enumerated all the conditions necessary for the occurrence of a given event, that totality of conditions will at once be sufficient for its occurrence or such that no further conditions will be necessary. To say, however, that a given set of conditions was sufficient for the occurrence of a given event, which was their effect, is only to say that those conditions were such that, all of them having occurred, the effect in question could not fail to occur.

In the light of the foregoing, then, a cause might be defined loosely—as A. J. Ayer has defined it—as being either a necessary condition or a sufficient condition or both. More precisely, the cause of a given event (its effect) can be defined either as (1) that set of conditions, among all the conditions that occurred, each of which was necessary and the totality of which was sufficient for the occurrence of the event in question or (2) some one or more conditions within that set which were novel, unusual, or controllable. The first definition is philosophically simpler and more useful for the understanding of causal connections, but the second reflects ordinary usage better.

The plurality of causes. J. S. Mill maintained that many events are such that they can be produced in a variety of ways. A match can be ignited by friction, but also by being heated, and perhaps in other ways, too. Similarly, a man's death can be caused by bacteria, by a bullet, by a fall, and in numberless other ways. There is some sense in which this claim is obviously true, and it presents a difficulty for defining causes and effects in terms of necessary and sufficient conditions. If, for example, one claims that a given match's being struck was a causal condition of its igniting and one construes this to mean that it was a necessary condition, then it can be replied that the match could have ignited just as well even if it had not been struck—it might have been thrust into a flame, for instance. Alternatively, it can be claimed that no totality of conditions can ever be considered sufficient for the occurrence of any event, such as a match's igniting, for it might not have ignited even in the presence of those conditions—it might suddenly have been made wet, for example, or otherwise been prevented from igniting. This claim could be construed as a doctrine of "the plurality of effects."

This line of criticism can apparently be overcome by limiting the application of the definition to things that actually occur, excluding those which do not. Thus, it has been suggested that a statement of the form "*A* was the cause of *B*" means that *A* was that set of conditions, *among those and only those that occurred,* which were individually necessary and jointly sufficient for *B*. If, accordingly, a match was ignited by friction and not by being thrust into a flame, then the latter condition, being not something that occurred, can be disregarded as not being a cause or any part of a cause of the event in question. From this point of view, there is never any plurality of causes or of effects for things that actually occur.

Causation and induction. It is often claimed, as it was claimed by Hume, that any statements about what is physically necessary, sufficient, or impossible are nothing but empirical generalizations or inductions. To say, for example, that a given event would not have occurred had not some other event also occurred only means, according to this criticism, that we have never found the one occurring without the other. Thus, the only reason one can give for saying that a man cannot live after being beheaded is that no one has ever seen it happen, and this, according to philosophers faithful to the suggestions of Hume, is all that such statements mean in the first place. McTaggart pointed out that except for our experience we would have no more reason for saying that a man must die if he loses his head than if he loses his hair.

This is a highly controversial issue, involving all the unresolved problems of inductive inference, but at least the issue itself is perfectly clear and can be expressed in these two alternative questions: Do we discover from experience only what does invariably happen or fail to happen under certain conditions and then incorrectly or falsely express this by speaking of what can and cannot happen under those conditions? Or do we discover from experience what does invariably happen or fail to happen under certain conditions and then reasonably and at least sometimes correctly or truly infer from this what can or cannot happen under those conditions? Either position is beset with difficulties of the severest kind. Those who, like Blanshard and Ewing, maintain that we sometimes correctly infer certain necessary conditions can challenge their opponents to show some other way of distinguishing causal from other invariant conditions, while those who, like Hume and Russell, maintain that this is an incorrect inference can challenge their opponents, as Hume did, to produce the reasoning by which it is made.

The distinction between cause and effect. Any adequate analysis of the causal relation should enable one to distinguish analytically between causes and effects. It should not obliterate the difference between them. That is, any analysis of a true statement of the form "*A* was the cause of *B*" should be such that it does not equally entail that *B* was the cause of *A* or that it is arbitrary which one regards as the cause and which the effect. The concepts of cause and effect, if they have any proper use at all, have different uses; they are not one and the same concept. Some writers, notably Russell and McTaggart, have suggested the extreme view that there is no theoretical difference between causes and effects, that it is arbitrary which one calls which, but this appears to ignore a clear distinction that all men easily make.

If causes are regarded as necessary and sufficient conditions, however, in accordance with the foregoing suggestions, then the distinction between a cause and its effect is not maintained. For concerning any event or set of events *A* and any event or set of events *B*, if *A* is necessary and sufficient for *B* and therefore the cause of *B* according to the definition suggested, then it logically follows that *B* is necessary and sufficient for *A* and therefore, by the same definition, the cause of *A*. Most persons would reject this as absurd. Few persons would want to say that a match's igniting is a cause of its being struck, that a stone's becoming warm is a cause of the sun's shining upon it, or that a man's intoxication is a cause of his having alcohol in his blood.

It was once taken for granted in philosophy, as previously noted, that the difference between a cause and its effect was one of power or efficacy, or that a cause compels or acts upon its effect in a manner in which the effect does not act upon the cause, or that a cause produces its effect, in a manner that cannot be described simply in terms of the concepts of necessary and sufficient conditions. Alcohol, for example, has the power to produce feelings of intoxication, but a man cannot produce alcohol in his blood just by having such feelings.

Modern philosophers, on the other hand, have for the most part tried to distinguish causes from their effects either in terms of the distinction between means and ends or in terms of temporal considerations. These two views will be considered in turn.

Causes as "levers." According to the conception of causes as means to ends, which has been persuasively argued by both R. G. Collingwood and Douglas Gasking, causes and their effects differ essentially in that causes are always certain conditions within the control of agents, by means of which they can bring about or prevent certain other conditions. Collingwood accordingly refers to them as "levers," and Gasking calls them "recipes." Heating water, for example, is a means to making it evaporate, whereas one cannot make water become hot by evaporating it. Heating a metal wire will make it glow, but we have no way of making metal glow and thereby making it become hot. Gasking has argued that if it were otherwise—that is, if there were some way of making metal glow other than by heating it (by exposing it to light, for example)—and if we found that whenever it was thus made to glow, it also became hot, then we would regard its glowing as the cause of its getting hot, since its glowing would then become the means, within our control, for heating it.

This conception of the unique relation of a cause to its effect fits certain examples very well, and the conception of causes as means or levers doubtless is, as these and other writers have maintained, the original notion of a cause. Unfortunately, however, there are other clear examples of causation that this conception does not fit at all and in which it is nevertheless possible to distinguish between cause and effect. Ice is caused to melt from a river in the spring by the increased heat of the sun. It is clearly the heat of the sun that causes the ice to melt, in some sense in which it would seem very absurd to say that the melting of the ice causes the heat of the sun upon it. Yet neither of these conditions is a means, within the control of any agent, for attaining any end. Similarly, the causes of certain diseases do not come to be thought of as causes only after they become controllable by men. If in some part of the world men should quite inexplicably become ill and perish and it should then be discovered that this was due, say, to certain unusual radiations from the sun, those radiations would still be considered the cause even if there were no way at all of controlling them. The tides, similarly, are caused by gravitational forces of the moon. Here it is perfectly easy to distinguish cause from effect even though neither is within anyone's control and neither is, therefore, a means for bringing about or preventing the other.

Causation and time. Most philosophers have supposed that causes should be distinguished from their effects in terms of time, the cause always occurring before its effect, and that if this is done, there is no need to speak of any special power or efficacy of the cause in relation to its effect. Ducasse offers this suggestion. If, then, the foregoing conception of causation, in terms of necessary and sufficient conditions, is modified to take this into account, then a statement of the form "*A* was the cause of *B*" will be taken to mean that *A* was that condition or set of conditions, among those that occurred, which was both necessary and sufficient for the occurrence of *B* and which preceded *B* in time.

It has lately been doubted, however, whether an analytical distinction between causes and effects can be drawn quite so easily without reference to such notions as power or efficacy. There has, in fact, been considerable discussion of the question why a cause might not follow its effect in time or why causes must precede their effects, and this question has been expressed in such a way that it is not answered merely by pointing out the ordinary meaning of the word "cause." For if one grants that, according to the ordinary usage of English, nothing is ever called the cause of any event that precedes it, it can still be asked why the words "cause" and "effect" are so used. Many persons find it singularly unsatisfying to suppose that usage here is arbitrary or that it reflects no difference resting on some natural distinction. There is an evident absurdity in speaking of a man's death as the cause of his having been shot, but philosophers are far from agreed as to what kind of absurdity it is—whether, that is, it reflects only an inept choice of words or whether it is a metaphysical absurdity which would remain even if the meanings of "cause" and "effect" were modified. Prior to Hume most philosophers would have simply affirmed that the power of a cause does not extend to the past. Few persons now would question the truth of this statement. The question, then, is whether the statement expresses a truth about language—that is, about how the word "cause" is used by persons who speak English—or whether it expresses a truth of metaphysics.

The problem at issue here can be illustrated as follows. Suppose a given match is dry, is struck in the presence of oxygen at a given time T_1, and that it is hot, charred, and brittle shortly after, at T_2. Call the first set of conditions *A*, the second *B*, and assume that, given exactly the other conditions that then occurred but only those, the three conditions constituting *A* were individually necessary and jointly sufficient for *B*, and assume that the three conditions constituting *B* were individually necessary and jointly sufficient for *A*. The relationship of *A* to *B*, then, is exactly the same as the relationship of *B* to *A*, with the single exception that *A* precedes *B* in time. The philosophical problem is simply this: Why should *A* be considered the cause, rather than the effect, of *B*? Is this simply a question of meaning—that is, of the way the words "cause" and "effect" are ordinarily used? Granting that the words are used this way, is that usage arbitrary, rendering the distinction between causes and effects an arbitrary one? Or is there some metaphysical difference between causes and effects which ordinary usage of words takes account of?

Contemporaneous causes and effects. Some philosophers (A. E. Taylor, for example) who defend the older metaphysical conception of causation maintain, with Thomas Reid and others, that causes cannot be properly conceived except as things having the power or efficacy to produce certain changes in other things and that it is this element of efficacy rather than any mere accident of temporal position that distinguishes causes from their effects. According to this view, the conception of power is a metaphysical notion that cannot be analyzed in terms of necessary and sufficient conditions and one which is not simply derivative from any linguistic usage.

This view finds considerable support from the often noted fact that some causes and their effects appear to be contemporaneous, neither occurring before the other. Indeed, it has often been maintained (for example, by Russell, Taylor, and Collingwood) that all causes and effects are contemporaneous, that there is never any real temporal succession of events that are causally connected. If this is true, then it at once follows that the difference between causes and their effects is not merely a temporal difference and that one cannot distinguish, between two events causally connected with each other, which is the cause and which is the effect merely by asking which occurs first in time since neither of them occurs first.

Examples of causes and effects which appear contemporaneous are not difficult to cite. Consider, for instance, a locomotive that is pulling a caboose, and to make it simple, suppose that this is all it is pulling and that the two are tightly connected. The motion of the locomotive is sufficient for the motion of the caboose, the two being connected in such a way that the former cannot move without the latter's moving with it. But so also, the motion of the caboose is sufficient for the motion of the locomotive. Given that the two are connected as they are, it is physically impossible that the caboose should be moving without the locomotive's moving with it. From this it logically follows that the motion of either is likewise a necessary condition for the motion of the other, given, of course, that other conditions are such as they are—both objects being in motion, no obstructions to motion being present, no other movers present, and so on. There seems, however, to be no temporal gap between the motion of the one object and the motion of the other; they move together, the motion of neither being followed by the motion of the other.

Of course, it is tempting in such an example to suppose that the locomotive must begin moving before the motion of the caboose can begin, but this is not relevant. The effect under consideration is not the caboose's beginning to move but its being in motion. Moreover, if the two are tightly connected, as we are supposing, then it is false that either must begin moving before the other moves. Moreover, even if they were not tightly connected, the motion of neither could be considered the cause of the motion of the other until both were moving, which again reduces the temporal interval between these two motions to zero.

Again, consider the relationships between one's hand and a pencil one is writing with. It is surely true that the motion of the pencil is caused by the motion of the hand and not vice versa. This, we can suppose, means in part that the motion of the hand is sufficient for the motion of the pencil under the circumstances assumed to obtain. Given those circumstances, however, the motion of the pencil is also sufficient for the motion of the hand, for under the circumstances assumed—that the fingers are grasping the pencil in a certain way, and so on—neither the hand nor the pencil can move without the other's moving with it. It logically follows, then, that under the conditions assumed to obtain the motion of either is also a necessary condition for the motion of the other. It further appears that the motions are contemporaneous; the motion of neither is followed by the motion of the other. They move together. And in that case one cannot distinguish cause from effect by any consideration of which occurs first. It would be clearly false to say that the hand moves and then, after it stops moving, the pencil begins to move, and it would be hardly less plausible to suppose that the hand moves in quick jerks, each such brief motion of the hand then being followed by a brief motion of the pencil. There appears to be no temporal gap at all between cause and effect.

From the foregoing considerations it is apparent that some of the main philosophical problems of causation do not yield to any easy solution. The idea of a necessary connection between cause and effect may be, as Hume thought, an esoteric and metaphysical one, but it is doubtful whether anyone can render an adequate analysis of the causal relation without it. The idea of causal power or efficacy is perhaps more esoteric still, and yet there is no obvious way of eliminating it from the concept of causation. Considerations of means and ends or of time do not help to eliminate this concept. If, however, one professes to find no difference between the relation of a cause to its effect, on the one hand, and of an effect to its cause, on the other, he appears to contradict the common sense of mankind, for the difference appears perfectly apparent to most men, even in cases where neither cause nor effect can be represented as a means or end and even when both occur contemporaneously. Here, then, as in so many areas of philosophy, our advances over our predecessors appear more illusory than real.

Bibliography

Two recent and very thorough studies of causation are Mario Bunge's *Causality* (Cambridge, Mass., 1959) and H. L. A. Hart and A. M. Honoré's *Causation and the Law* (Oxford, 1958). Both works deal extensively with numerous problems of causality, the first with special reference to science and the second with reference to questions of jurisprudence. Briefer general discussions are found in A. E. Taylor's *Elements of Metaphysics* (London, 1903; paperback ed., New York, 1961), Ch. 5, of which there have been many editions; J. M. E. McTaggart's *Philosophical Studies* (London, 1934), Ch. 7; Richard Taylor's "Causation," in *Monist*, Vol. 47 (1963), 287–313; and Bertrand Russell's "On the Notion of Cause," first published in *PAS* (1912–1913) and reprinted in *Mysticism and Logic* (London, 1917), Ch. 9. Russell's essay has been particularly important in formulating contemporary problems of causation and is frequently cited. An independent recent discussion of some of these issues is Max Black, "Making Something Happen," in Sidney Hook, ed., *Determinism and Freedom in the Age of Modern Science* (New York, 1958).

Aristotle's well-known discussion of the four kinds of causes is given in *Metaphysics* I.3. Although historically interesting, this work sheds no light on contemporary problems. Hume's celebrated discussion, perhaps the most significant in the philosophical literature on this subject, is found in *An Enquiry Concerning Human Understanding*, Sections 4–7; see also Hume's *Treatise of Human Nature*, Book I, Part 3. Theories fundamentally like Hume's have been defended and elaborated by many other authors, among them John Stuart Mill, in his *System of Logic*, Vol. I, Book 3, Chs. 4–6, and Vol. II, Book 3, Ch. 21. A recent thoroughgoing and very clear analysis along essentially the same line is given by C. J. Ducasse in *Nature, Mind and Death*, Part II (La Salle, Ill., 1951), although this writer considerably modifies certain Humean positions and greatly expands upon others. Hume's theory was searchingly criticized by his contemporary Thomas Reid in his *Essays on the Active Powers of the Human Mind*, especially Essay 4. A more recent defense of certain concepts rejected by Hume, particularly that of a necessary connection between cause and effect, is given by A. C. Ewing in *Idealism: A Critical Survey* (London, 1934), Section 3, Ch. 4. A somewhat similar approach is represented in Brand Blanshard's *The Nature of Thought*, Vol. II (New York, 1940), Sections 10–20. A. N. Whitehead's objections to Hume's regularity theory are most fully stated in *Symbolism, Its Meaning and Effect* (New York, 1928) and *Process and Reality* (New York, 1929). Other important criticisms of Hume's theory are C. D. Broad, *The Mind and Its Place in Nature* (London, 1925), Ch. 3, and *Examination of McTaggart's Philosophy*, Vol. I (Cambridge, 1933); and Wolfgang Köhler, *Gestalt Psychology* (London, 1929).

Contemporary defenses of the regularity view of causation are found in A. J. Ayer, *Foundations of Empirical Knowledge* (London, 1951), Ch. 4; R. E. Hobart, "Hume Without Scepticism," in *Mind*, Vol. 39 (1930); John Hospers, *Introduction to Philosophical Analysis* (Englewood Cliffs, N.J., 1953); Arthur Pap, "Philosophical Analysis, Translation Schemas and the Regularity Theory of Causation," in *The Journal of Philosophy*, Vol. 49 (1952), 657–666, and *Analytische Erkenntnistheorie* (Vienna, 1955), Ch. 4; Hans Reichenbach, *The Rise of Scientific Philosophy* (Berkeley, 1951), Ch. 10; and Moritz Schlick, "Causation in Everyday Life and in Recent Science," in Herbert Feigl and Wilfrid Sellars, eds., *Readings in Philosophical Analysis* (New York, 1949), pp. 515–533.

The best-known defense of the claim that causes are essentially means to ends and hence must be conceived in relation to human activity is given in R. G. Collingwood's *An Essay on Metaphysics* (Oxford, 1940), Part 3-c. A very similar idea is defended by Douglas Gasking in a highly perceptive article, "Causation and Recipes," *Mind*, Vol. 64 (1955), 479–487.

Apart from consideration of language, the question whether causes must precede rather than follow their effects has been raised several times in recent literature. See Michael Dummett and Antony Flew, "Can an Effect Precede Its Cause?," in *PAS*, Supp. Vol. 28 (1954), and Dummett's "Bringing About the Past," in *Philosophical Review*, Vol. 73 (1964), 338–359; A. J. Ayer's *The Problem of Knowledge* (London, 1956), Ch. 4; and R. M. Chisholm and Richard Taylor's "Making Things to Have Happened," in *Analysis*, Vol. 20 (1960), 73–78.

RICHARD TAYLOR

CELSUS, Middle Platonist (Origen wrongly called him an Epicurean) critic of Christianity who wrote the *Alethes Logos* ("True Doctrine") about A.D. 178. We know the work—whose title derives from a Platonic expression (*Meno* 81a)—only through quotations in Origen's reply, *Contra Celsum*, composed seventy years later. Celsus began his work by assuming the character of a Jew and attacking Christian views from this standpoint. Then he proceeded on his own to demonstrate their inadequacy in relation to the basic axioms of contemporary philosophical theology, especially with regard to the doctrines of God and providence and poetic–philosophical inspiration; as a Platonist he found the Christian idea of the Incarnation both impossible and immoral. At the end of his work he urged the Christians to abandon their irrational faith and join him in upholding the state and its religion. After Christianity was recognized by the Roman government, Celsus' work was destroyed.

The theology of Celsus is based, in his own view, on an ancient tradition handed down, especially among oriental wise men, from remote antiquity. This tradition, the "true doctrine," informed him of the existence of one god known by many names and worshiped by all pious men. Such a "polytheistic monotheism," he believed, had been perverted or misunderstood, first by the Jews and then by the Christians. If they were to return to the tradition, they would abandon their irrational exclusiveness and would recognize the divine right of the one emperor. His work thus culminates in a theology of politics.

Origen's reply is important not only because in it his philosophical theology, developed earlier, is clearly expressed in relation to Celsus' views, but also because it shows the extent to which he agreed with Celsus in opposing more literal religious conceptions. Each held, for example, that his own authoritative traditions are to be understood symbolically, whereas the other's traditions must be meant literally. But Origen finally took his stand on the particularity of the Hebrew–Christian tradition, which Celsus found totally unacceptable.

Bibliography

Bader, R., *Der Ἀληθὴς λόγος des Kelsos*. Stuttgart and Berlin, 1940. Critical edition of Greek text.

Chadwick, Henry, *Origen: Contra Celsum.* Cambridge, 1953. Translation with introduction and very full notes.

ROBERT M. GRANT

CERTAINTY. Certainty (Latin *certus*, sure) has been taken in philosophical usage either as a state of mind or as a relational property of statements or propositions. The former has usually been called "assurance" or "psychological certainty" (its opposite, "doubt" or "skepticism"), and the latter, "logical certainty" or "propositional certainty" (its opposite, "probability" or "doubtfulness"). Psychological certainty may be justified or unjustified, as in the belief that the moon reflects light or is made of green cheese. But propositional certainty is never justified or unjustified; it simply obtains or does not obtain. Usage follows the rule, however, that for certainty of a proposition to obtain, someone must have made sure or become justifiably certain of the proposition. Thus, certainty of propositions requires psychological certainty plus its justification.

Of course, it is to be understood here that justification pertains to a truth claim rather than to a deed or action like someone's pouring the soup down the sink or repeating an incantation. And this introduces a matter which must be noted if only to be put clearly out of the way—namely, the alleged certainties which do not or might not pertain to statements or propositions. Mystics, some metaphysicians, and highly imaginative people have claimed certainties where on any proper canons of propositional significance there seems to be nothing at issue to be believed, doubted, or disbelieved. Usage outside of philosophy may allow to such cases psychological certainties—for instance, as persons' attitudes toward sets of words. But the prevailing usage among philosophers does not stretch this far.

Usage of terms. Certainty must be distinguished from truth, for the two terms function in differing contrasts. It makes literal sense to speak of a statement as certainly true, certainly false, or probably true, but it does not make literal sense to speak of it as falsely certain or truly or falsely probable. It is scarcely intelligible to speak of a statement as even probably certain, except when a guess is being made as to how the evidence or grounds will shortly turn out.

It has become apparent that there is a connection between certainty and knowledge in that whatever is certain is known. But usage does not require, conversely, that whatever is known is certain. Not only may some forms of knowledge—for example, knowledge by acquaintance and know-how—occur unexpressed in statements, but also some of what is commonly called knowledge—for instance, hypotheses or expert opinions—is less than certain. Admittedly some philosophers, notably Plato and Locke, have refused to label as knowledge that which is only probable. By dominant usage now, however, that which is certain forms a subclass of things known.

Yet certainty is not so narrow as the a priori. Convention generally has the distinction between certainty and probability cut across that between the a priori and the a posteriori or that between the necessary and the contingent. For instance, that one random throw of an unweighted die (theoretically conceived) will produce a result above two is both probable and a priori; the judgment of probability itself is a priori and necessary. Again, some certainties are often allowed to be empirical or a posteriori.

Despite Cartesian doctrine, certainty is not coextensive with clarity. Usage does not wholly settle that there are degrees of certainty, as there are of clarity, and as we all recognize to our regret, some of the very clearest statements are uncertain. Nor is the certainty of a statement always its self-evidence; a statement may become certain without becoming self-evident. Nor, finally, is certainty the same as infallibility, if for no other reason than that infallibility can be predicated of persons or devices only.

PRINCIPAL DOCTRINES

What kinds of statements, if any, admit of certainty? The main doctrine among philosophers has been that only two kinds can be certain—namely, those asserting claims of reason and those expressing immediate experience. Yet not only has this doctrine been held with differences of detail; it is one in a whole spectrum of doctrines ranging from the wholly categorical skepticism traditionally associated with Pyrrho and Timon in the days of Aristotle to such relatively unskeptical positions as those of Aristotle, Aquinas, Descartes, Spinoza, Locke, Leibniz, Berkeley, Hume, Kant, and Mill. Of course, it would be strange if any philosopher were so categorically antiskeptical as the Pyrrhonists were skeptical. For to insist not only that certainty is achievable in every type of statement but also that it attaches to every single statement that can be entertained would be to scuttle logic and the concept of evidence and the difference between sense and nonsense. There may be a paradox in the Pyrrhonists' position at the opposite extreme, but at least it is not so obvious. Their position, although withholding certainty from every statement, can allow probability to some and improbability to their contradictories, and thus it does not obviously amount to a sweeping rejection of the law of contradiction.

But far more plausible than either extreme are those

positions which withhold certainty from only some kinds of statements and not from all. They allow at least some statements to be certain and thereby satisfy our understanding that the term "certain" may mark a difference between some statements and others. Positions of this sort do not so obviously run the risk of using the term vacuously. This is no small point of principle, for if no conceivable statements are certain, then within what class are the terms "certain" and "uncertain," in any clear use, to mark a difference? If a person does not understand such a difference, does he understand the terms?

Thus, there would appear to be a principle by which universal skepticism becomes unintelligible, as does the doctrine of universal certainty. This principle is one of predicative contrast or of sense-in-contrast. Holding apparently of all predicates, it requires in the case of the term "certain" and its contradictory that there be an understood class of statements within which they both apply in marking a difference. Briefly, some statements must be certain, and some must fail to be. If this is so, then neither Pyrrhonism nor a doctrine of universal certainty makes proper sense. (This is to say nothing of the difficulty of self-reference raised by the statement "Every statement is uncertain," of which Pyrrho himself apparently had no clear notion.)

Some of the variations among historical doctrines may be traced, of course, to varying conceptions of what constitutes a statement. One could go through the writings of major philosophers picking out sentences each of which has been taken by some to express a statement that is certainly true, by others to express one that is very doubtful, and by still others as expressing no statement at all. The second position, unlike the first, is skeptical as to the truth of the statement. The third, however, is skeptical as to its sense or genuineness—that is, as to the possibility of something being said that is either true or false. Very roughly, history has shown a tendency for prolonged truth-skepticism to convert into sense-skepticism, and today, after progressive refinements of the notion of propositional sense, many traditional doctrines look very strange indeed as candidates for sense. It would be thought spectacular, for example, that a present-day philosopher should say, as Aristotle once did (*Posterior Analytics*, I, 1), that every predicate may be truly affirmed or denied of every subject. To take an instance from common life, we need not reflect long to see that there is no question of the tone middle C being soluble or not being soluble in water, for a tone is not the sort of thing about which one may ask in reference to solubility.

Evidently, the Pyrrhonists suffered in part from this confusion of questions of truth with questions of sense.

SKEPTICISM AS TO REASON

Turning to the familiar doctrine that both claims of reason and statements of immediate experience are certain and that no others can be, we may first consider claims of reason. These statements, testable by reason only, can have no empirical evidence one way or the other. Experience may provide illustration but not evidence—that is, it may provide visual aids or pointers for the understanding but not data or grounds. Among claims of reason those which are tested by the meaning of terms and the laws of logic are most important to consider. By accepted usage such statements, if true, are tautologies; if false, self-contradictions. Thus, the skeptical question here might be put in the form "Are any putative tautologies ever tautologies for sure?" It might also be in the form "Are any statements made certain simply by the meaning of their terms and the laws of logic?"

Little reflection is required to see that skepticism concerning even the simplest of such claims is indefensible. For instance, "$2 + 2 = 4$," "If he is a father, he is a parent," and "If all *A*'s are *B*'s, then no *A*'s are non-*B*'s" are plainly logical truths, and their logical certainty is not controversial, given the familiar definitions or use of the words and symbols expressing them. To hold otherwise would be either to pretend that there are crucial obscurities here or to reject the most fundamental principles of logic, principles which are required even by skepticism itself. Any seeming denial of the law of contradiction, for instance, fails to be an example at all, for to the *seeming* denial "It is *not* the case that the law of contradiction holds," we would be invited on its own showing to respond, "Oh, then it *may be* the case?"

Certainty as simplicity. Concerning the less obvious claims of logic something more must be said. Suppose we are given a complicated claim, one which, if logically true, would be a complicated tautology not readily evident as tautological. We now might have a problem which no simple claim would illustrate. If a skeptic tells us that no logical claims at all are sure to be tautologies and if he rejects as irrelevant the above defense of simple tautologies, then his point is apparently one about complexity or abstruseness. Thus, he is perhaps saying that many-step deduction is inferior to one-step logical inference or recognition. A similar point is sometimes put in traditional terminology by saying that "demonstration" is less certain than "intuition" (see Descartes's *Regulae*, Rule XI, or Locke's *Essay*, Book IV Chs. 2 and 17). Of course, this new thesis about demonstration and intuition would not be skepticism solely about complicated or obscure logical claims as opposed to the relative certainty of simple or obvious or easy ones. Here a new difficulty arises, for some demonstrations are at least as reliable as corresponding intuitions. If this were not so, it would never be possible to check up on an intuition as a simple claim—never possible, that is, to test a one-step inference by an inference of two or more steps, never possible to check a two-step inference by one of three or more steps, and so on. How could we then tell whether simplicity in itself were reliable or unreliable? Actually, the notion of a simple recognition which is not implanted in a system in a manner allowing many steps to certify it is a myth.

Certainty through repetition. The skeptic, however, need not yet be satisfied. While all demonstrations, he may say, are systematic, they are also cumulative in the sense that the proof of a claim of reason is more reliable after it is thrice rehearsed than after it is gone through once. His notion may be that as creatures who can make logical mistakes and who make countless perceptual (nonlogical) judgments in the process of reading, figuring, and so on, we are not infallible. He may say that the approximation to certainty increases under repeated check but that we never reach a limit.

This argument has been suggested in remarks by A. J. Ayer (*The Problem of Knowledge*, Ch. 2). It is difficult to assess, but it has at least two weaknesses. First, it actually presupposes, in its induction from cases of error and correction, that we can identify logical and other errors and also their corrections. This is decisive against the skeptical argument unless it purports to start only from probable errors and probable corrections and concludes only that perhaps or probably we never have certainty—in which case, however, its whole terminology is obscure and perhaps vacuous. Second, even if all logical reasoning were subject to corroboration through repeated check, there seems to be no clear sense in treating deductive corroboration as interminable. If from tomorrow on, everyone who multiplied 659 by 437 got 286,983 instead of 287,983, we would have vastly better courses open to us than simply to doubt whether 287,983 were correct. We would, rather, accept almost any other view of this new phenomenon. But even if, from tomorrow on, we found enough of our figuring and reasoning so chaotic that the skeptic seemed to have a point, only a moment's reflection would show that his thesis falls victim as well. A logical system is essentially something which has certainties possible within it; any quite pervasive indecision would concern whether to adhere to the given system or to some other instead.

Uncertainty in logic. Skepticism as to all claims of logic is therefore not easy to make out. More plausible is the view that given the position from which we speak, some claims of logic are certainly true and at least some others are certainly false. Does this leave us with the implication that no claims of logic are permanently uncertain? Not necessarily. But even if it did, there is no apparent reason to consider this possibility a disaster. For we retain a contrast between claims checked and claims not yet checked, between a logical formula that has been established as a theorem and one that has not been. Thus, certainty and uncertainty retain a contrast in questions of logic as elsewhere. In some parts of logic, moreover, we can draw the contrast between an a priori certainty and an a priori probability, as noted above.

SKEPTICISM AS TO THE SENSES

Prevailing doctrine, as we noted, not only defends claims of reason against the skeptic but also pronounces on two other kinds of statements. It maintains that statements about objects and other persons are incapable of certainty. It maintains that statements about one's own immediate experience, however, at least to oneself, are radically different in that they are immune to uncertainty. It is thus a skeptical doctrine in only a limited way. It purports to make sense by contrasting ordinary empirical statements—which we may call "objective statements" even if some are about persons—with claims of logic on the one hand and on the other with one's statements about one's own sensations, thoughts, or the like—which we may call "sense statements."

Sense statements. Perhaps some notion like that of sense statements is as old as common sense. But although it was important in medieval philosophy, its importance today is due largely to Descartes. At one stage in his exposition Descartes ventured that he might be mistaken in thinking that he was sitting in front of a blazing fire but that he could not be mistaken about its seeming true to him. He could not, as he put it, be mistaken about the idea itself. This notion, taken over by Locke, Hume, and others, has been elaborated in slightly varying ways, usually with pains, sensations, images, and other so-called objects of inner sense being included. According to this theory, it is absurd for a person to say, "I believe I am in pain, but perhaps I am not," just as it is usually absurd to say, "I said it seemed so-and-so to me, but I was not sure whether it really did"—absurd, that is, unless the experience itself is indeterminate or borderline. Accordingly, sense statements (presumed to be sincere) are sometimes said to be "incorrigible" on the ground that one who makes such a statement cannot possibly be mistaken about his experience even though he may deceive others.

Plausible though this theory may seem on first reading, many difficulties have been discovered in it. If such statements could not conceivably be mistaken, then are they properly statements? Are they the same as what a person asserts by identical words when he is known by others to be lying? Do such assertions have inferential relations to objective statements, as is usually supposed? If the theory is true, then how may we find out whether in the case of someone else such an utterance is faithful to his experience? These difficulties come out more plainly when we proceed to consider the other theory which has usually been conjoined with it, the theory that objective statements, unlike sense statements, are never certain.

Objective statements. It is with respect to statements about other persons and objects that the orthodox doctrine on certainty may be called skeptical. The reasoning is that because an objective statement can be grounded only in some finite set of sense statements describing experience up to some given time, because the objective statement always overreaches those sense statements by indefinitely implying further ones, and because the given ones never give us a guarantee as to further ones, every objective statement must be uncertain to everyone.

The striking thing is that such a view of objective statements has been combined with the foregoing view of sense statements. These two views, together with a view of logical statements as (usually) certain, have been held by a considerable number of philosophers, from the Middle Ages (for example, Nicholas of Autrecourt) to the present (for example, Russell, Carnap, and others in the Vienna circle and Ayer and C. I. Lewis), although it is worth noting that it was not the final view of either Descartes or Hume. The historical prominence of this combined doctrine is remarkable because if sense statements in one's own case are exactly those statements certain to oneself and if objective statements can never be certain to anyone, then how could theorists have known these two things to obtain together in the case of anyone at all? If person *A* cannot have certain knowledge about another person *B* and thus not about his immediate experience, then how may *A* or anyone else be in a position to hold the incorrigibility doctrine of sense statements for the case of *B*? Plainly, by hypothesis, *A*'s claim that *B*'s sense statements are incorrigible would be an objective statement and hence not a certainty. Even if *B* were supposed to know that his sense statements were incorrigible, he could not possibly establish that they were. Neither he nor anyone else would know what it would be like to establish this or to establish the opposite. Thus, in principle it would be impossible to check up on the combined hypothesis, and it is impossible to see how it could even be understood if it were supposed true.

Yet can even the single thesis about the incorrigibility of sense statements be held? Sense statements, if they are to be understood at all, must permit the usual translations in grammatical person. (If "It seems to me that *p*," said by me, is true, then so must "It seems to him that *p*," said by another of me, be true.) But if sense statements do permit such translations and are also incorrigible, then all corresponding objective statements are incorrigible. And this is absurd on any defensible view. Is the translatability of sense statements then to be denied? This again would be unacceptable. Evidently, then, sense statements, if they are statements, are like objective statements in being subject to error; that is, some, not all, of them are. Some of each sort, then, are certain, and some are not.

Fallibilism concerning objective statements. But what of the doctrine that all objective statements are uncertain? If the above remarks are correct, it will not suffice to argue, as the orthodox theorists do, that the relations of objective statements to sense statements and the allegedly unstructured character of immediate experience make all objective statements into hypotheses which can never be finally verified. Instead, some other reasoning would be required. That reasoning could not be from ordinary usage, for as Hume, Reid, Moore, and others have noted, usage acknowledges paradigms of certainty in the objective class and distinguishes some statements there that are certain from others that are not. As Hume noted, we can all be sure that the sun will rise tomorrow, despite the puzzle he raised concerning how induction can in principle be justified. We all recognize that we are often in circumstances in which simple statements like "Here is a sheet of paper" or "There is a table in this room" are lacking nothing for certainty. If usage, then, will not support the skeptical doctrine, what can be found to support it?

A fallibilist argument reminiscent of the orthodox one cited above but not committed to the notion of sense statements is the bare argument that all empirical statements are predictive without limit and that future observation may overturn them or lead us to revise them. (This view has been held by Reichenbach and others.) A position of this sort is common among philosophers of science, and it may be inspired, if not supported, by a comparison of common language with the language of physics or chemistry. If we ask on what grounds the claim is made that future observations always may overturn accepted statements, we usually find two reasons. One is that surprises in observation are logically possible. (However, as Norman Malcolm has made clear, this does not imply that they are, actually, possible.) The other reason is a historical one: As the history of science goes, empirical statements are indeed occasionally revised. But this historical reason would at least equally support a different conclusion, that as our knowledge grows and our needs alter, we may choose to give an empirical sentence an altered range of application—that is, we may choose to modify its use or meaning. To revise the use of an empirical sentence is not the same as to come upon new and contrary evidence relevant to what it asserted in the former use. These have been confused, and their confusion is one of the most common sources of fallibilism.

To provide a concept of uncertainty that saves the fallibilist thesis from triviality, one might try saying that no objective statement is a safe bet when the stakes are the highest imaginable, that to risk the greatest conceivable stakes on any such statement would not be rationally justified. And the reason is that even the logical possibility of error opens up room for reasonable doubt.

Such an attempt fails, however, to show that putative tautologies are safe by contrast—that is, that we can ever bet the utmost on our having taken, correctly, a given formula as tautological. It also fails to show that the mere logical possibility of error in the empirical case amounts to the actual possibility of error. Moreover, an inquiry into the implications of judging a bet to be a winning one or a losing one would seem to turn up a paradox, since to judge a person's bet is, among other things, to make an empirical commitment about what he actually did, even when he bet on a tautology.

Empirical certainty has had its main defense in the sort of case built up by Moore, Lazerowitz, Wisdom, Malcolm, and others. But still another argument can be added against some fallibilists. As Arthur Pap has said (*Mind*, 1946 and 1950), some of them have also held that some of our empirical predicates—for example, red—have been ostensively defined, and this thesis entails that there are or have been some things having those predicates—for example, some red things. Still, this argument counts against only one type of fallibilism. The important consideration for most types will remain that of contrast between certainty and uncertainty and the rule of usage that to call some objective statements uncertain must be to say not just that they are objective statements but that they have been discovered to be unlike other objective statements with respect to available grounds.

Bibliography

For a survey see the entry "Certainty" in J. O. Urmson, ed., *Concise Encyclopedia of Western Philosophy and Philosophers* (London, 1960), or in J. M. Baldwin, ed., *Dictionary of Philosophy and Psychology* (New York, 1901–1905). For a provocative, streamlined sketch see Bertrand Russell, *The Problems of Philosophy* (London, 1912), Chs. 1, 5, and 13.

For classic discussions prior to the twentieth century see René Descartes, *Meditations*, especially the first, second, and sixth meditations, and David Hume, either *An Enquiry Concerning Human Understanding*, Chs. 6 and 12, or *Treatise of Human Nature*, Book I, Parts 3–4. Also useful are John Locke, *Essay Concerning Human Understanding*, Book IV, Chs. 1–4 and 15–17, and J. S. Mill, *A System of Logic*, Book II, Chs. 5–7, and Book III, Ch. 1.

For relatively nontechnical recent discussions see G. E. Moore, "Certainty," "A Defence of Common Sense," and "Proof of an External World," all in his collection *Philosophical Papers* (London, 1959); Norman Malcolm, "Certainty and Empirical Statements," in *Mind*, Vol. 51 (1942), 18–46, reprinted in his *Knowledge and Certainty* (Englewood Cliffs, N.J., 1963); O. K. Bouwsma, "Descartes' Evil Genius," in *The Philosophical Review*, Vol. 58 (1949), 141–151; and A. J. Ayer, *The Problem of Knowledge* (London, 1956), especially Ch. 2.

For recent systematic treatments see Moritz Schlick, "Is There a Factual A Priori?" translated in Herbert Feigl and Wilfrid Sellars, eds., *Readings in Philosophical Analysis* (New York, 1949); Hans Reichenbach, *Experience and Prediction* (Chicago, 1938), especially Chs. 2 and 5; and C. I. Lewis, *An Analysis of Knowledge and Valuation* (La Salle, Ill., 1946), especially Chs. 2, 5, and 10 (this modifies his earlier position in *Mind and the World Order*, New York, 1929).

For recent critical comments upon well-known views see M. Lazerowitz, "Strong and Weak Verifications," in *Mind*, Vol. 48 (1939), 202–213, and Vol. 59 (1950), 345–357; Norman Malcolm, "The Verification Argument," in Max Black, ed., *Essays in Philosophical Analysis* (Ithaca, N.Y., 1950), and in *Knowledge and Certainty, op. cit.;* Arthur Pap, "Ostensive Definition and Empirical Certainty," in *Mind*, Vol. 59 (1950), 530–535; John Wisdom, *Philosophy and Psycho-analysis* (Oxford, 1953), especially the essay "Philosophical Perplexity" and the discussion of Ayer; and H. G. Frankfurt, "Philosophical Certainty," in *The Philosophical Review*, Vol. 71 (1962), 303–327.

C. D. Rollins

CHAADAEV, PYOTR YAKOVLEVICH (1794–1856). Although Russia had previously had some theologians and some secular philosophers and social critics, Pyotr Yakovlevich Chaadaev can correctly be called the first Russian philosopher, since his work was the first to reflect a distinctively Russian outlook. The son of a wealthy landowner, Chaadaev began his studies at Moscow University but left to serve as an officer in the army, taking part in the campaigns against Napoleon. He resigned his commission in 1821 and traveled abroad from 1823 to 1826. During this time he met Schelling, with whom he later corresponded. Chaadaev had met Pushkin in 1816, and they remained close friends until Pushkin's death.

In 1829, Chaadaev began his main philosophical contribution, the *Lettres philosophiques*, and within two years he completed all eight. The publication of the First Letter, dated December 1, 1829, in the journal *Telescop* in 1836 marked the start of Russian philosophy and the end of Chaadaev's publishing career. The storm raised by the publication of the First Philosophical Letter is indicative of the difficult climate in which Russian intellectuals had to work throughout the nineteenth century, especially during the reign of Nicholas I. Censorship forbade any further writing by Chaadaev, or the publication of any comment, favorable or unfavorable, on the Letter. Chaadaev was declared insane and kept under house arrest for a year. In 1837 he wrote *L'Apologie d'un fou* ("The Apology of a Madman"), which was first published in Paris in 1862.

Chaadaev's philosophical outlook lay, like Russia, between East and West. Leaning far to the West in the First Letter, Chaadaev swung back to a more sympathetic view of Russia, of Russian thought and Russian Orthodoxy, in later Letters and in the "Apology."

Chaadaev's philosophy gave intellectual expression to Russia's long struggle for political and cultural unity. "The totality of all beings," Chaadaev wrote in the Fifth Letter, "forms an absolute unity, but this view has nothing in common with the kind of pantheism proposed by most modern philosophers." It is a dynamic ideal unity that makes the moral world one as nature is one; it makes history one, all human generations one man, the process progressing according to one rational–moral law, which directs human events through the one Christian church. History is thus the history of ideas, incomprehensible without Christianity, and Christianity itself is revealed in history. The goal of history is the kingdom of God, incarnate on earth through the church. The basic stuff of reality is not the individual or the individual intellect, but a God-given "ocean of ideas" to which we are united metaphysically and historically. Chaadaev's metaphysics and theology thus become an idealistic philosophy of history.

The unity of history is broken, however, by egoism. It is not clear whether Chaadaev held that the unity is in fact broken or merely appears broken, but, owing to Chaadaev's idealism, it could consistently be both. Egoism is original sin and leads to both moral and logical error, and only by overcoming it can we find salvation and truth. Thus altruism acquires a logical ground. The capacity for salvation and for the furtherance of history and its predestined end lies in the nature of man as a social being. Sympathy, love, compassion are our spiritual characteristics. Society awakens our spiritual powers and preserves and transmits them as well. Providential reason guides history, but man is free and responsible in that, as essentially a moral being, he can and should submit to universal moral reason.

Chaadaev's First Letter raised the storm it did because in it Chaadaev accused Russia of egoism, of making no attempt to join the society of nations, and pointed out the characteristic evil ways into which Russia had fallen as a result of its egoism. Russia had contributed nothing to history; it was like an illegitimate child having no inheritance. Russians were restless, more homeless than nomads; having no past, they were unable to see a future or to find any meaning in their individual and national lives. In the "Apology," and even in the later Letters, Chaadaev showed signs of finding a place for Russia in history. Russia, lacking in culture, was less prejudiced than Europe. Russian minds were free and for this reason could, if a serious effort to overcome isolation were made, take over the conduct of human affairs. This was Russia's divine mission.

In his concern with unity—of man with society, of societies with one another, of history—in his universalism, in his condemnation of egoism as simultaneously immoral and illogical, and in his sense of Russia as having a divine mission, Chaadaev embodied the main characteristics of Russian thought, which were developed by the Slavophiles and westernizers that immediately succeeded him and became an integral part of Russian philosophy.

Works by Chaadaev

Sochineniya i Pisma ("Works and Letters"), M. O. Gershenzon, ed., 2 vols. Moscow, 1913–1914. Includes the first, sixth, and seventh philosophical letters as the first, second, and third letters, in Russian translation and in French.

Literaturnoye Nasledstvo ("Literary Heritage"), Vols. XXII–XXIV. Moscow, 1935. Includes the second, third, fourth, fifth, and eighth letters in Russian translation.

Russian Philosophy, James M. Edie, James P. Scanlan, and Mary-Barbara Zeldin, eds., with the cooperation of George L.

Kline, pp. 101–154. Chicago, 1965. The first and selections from the third, fifth, sixth, and eighth letters, translated by Mary-Barbara Zeldin.

Works on Chaadaev

Falk, Heinrich, S. J., *Das Weltbild Peter J. Tschaadajews nach seinen acht "Philosophischen Briefen."* Munich, 1954.

Gershenzon, M. O., *P. I. Chaadaev: Zhizn i Myshlenie.* St. Petersburg, 1908.

Moskoff, Eugene A., *The Russian Philosopher Chaadayev, His Ideas and His Epoch.* New York, 1937.

Quenét, Charles, *Tchaadaeff et les lettres philosophiques.* Paris, 1931.

Zenkovsky, V. V., *Istoriya Russkoi Filosofii,* 2 vols. Paris, 1948–1950. Translated by George L. Kline as *A History of Russian Philosophy,* 2 vols. London and New York, 1953. See Vol. I, pp. 148–170.

MARY-BARBARA ZELDIN

CHAIN OF BEING. *See* LOVEJOY, ARTHUR ONCKEN.

CHAMBERLAIN, HOUSTON STEWART (1855–1927), Anglo-German race theorist and philosophical and historical writer. Chamberlain was born in Southsea, near Portsmouth, England. Despite his English birth and family, his early indifference toward England and all things English developed into a lifelong hatred. Chamberlain was brought up by relatives in France. After being forced to attend schools in England, he returned to England only briefly, in 1873 and 1893. A nervous breakdown determined the course of his physical and mental development. (Frequently ill, hypersensitive, neurotic, he was crippled during the last 13 years of his life by an incurable paralysis.) He traveled in western and central Europe for nine years seeking a cure. A German tutor inspired him to turn his mind to German literature and philosophy, and eventually he chose Germany as his home. As early as 1876 he wrote, "My belief that the whole future of Europe—that is, of world civilization—is in Germany's hands has become a certainty" (*Lebenswege meines Denkens,* p. 59).

Chamberlain's intellectual development began with the study of botany and other natural sciences; this was soon completely supplanted by a preoccupation with philosophy, literature, theology, art, and history. The turning point of his life was his meeting his future father-in-law, Richard Wagner, "the sun of my life," whom Chamberlain considered the greatest poet and musician of all time. Goethe inspired the central concept of Chamberlain's picture of the world and his "theory of life," the concept of *Gestalt* ("form") as the expression of all that is timeless and unchangeable. The *Gestalt* is encountered as the primary concept in the intuition of everything living (*Anschauung*) and must be grasped and interpreted in thought. It is the key to metaphysics and art, two fields which Chamberlain passionately defended against rationalism and "the coarsely empirical theory of evolution."

Race. Chamberlain's "Lebenslehre" ("Theory of Life"), which he first drafted in 1896 (it was not published until 1928 and was then titled *Natur und Leben*—"Nature and Life"), presented the position of most of his later writings, a position to which he frequently sacrificed historical truth in *Die Grundlagen des 19. Jahrhunderts* (*Foundations of the Nineteenth Century*), his weakest but best-known work. Chamberlain upheld "Life," intuition, metaphysics, "holy art" in the Wagnerian sense, and antidemocratic thought against rationalism, biological materialism (of Jewish origin), the superficial belief in progress, and moral decadence. His *Weltanschauung*—a favorite word of Chamberlain's—is closely related to Wagner's theory of decadence and regeneration. It carries with it the urge to improve the world, and Chamberlain felt himself called into the battle for moral renewal not of humanity in general (he spoke derogatorily of "the ghost, humanity"), but of the Teutonic culture and people. To save culture from the threat of materialism was also the declared aim of his books on Kant and Goethe.

In the *Grundlagen* Chamberlain represented history as a conflict of opposing philosophies of life, represented by the Jewish race on the one hand and by the Germanic–Aryan race on the other. The application of the biological idea of race to the study of cultural phenomena was widespread around the turn of the twentieth century. Under the influence of Darwin, it was used by anthropologists, ethnologists, religious historians, and others. It could serve both as a basis for scholarly interpretation and as a vehicle for racism, following the example of Gobineau. It was natural for Chamberlain to take over the concept of race from his scientific studies, but the significance he gave to it went beyond what was tenable in the light of the scientific knowledge then available and even denied the relevance of scientific criticism: "Even if it were proved that there had never been an Aryan race in the past, we are determined that there shall be one in the future; this is the decisive point of view for men of action" (*Grundlagen,* 1st ed., Vol. I, p. 270). Intuition and instinct, an overwhelming irrationalism, the capacity to sweep away logical contradictions—these are the major characteristics of this "historical" work.

Without ever giving a precise definition of "race," Chamberlain considered it to be the "*Gestalt* in particular, transparent purity" (*Natur und Leben,* p. 152) "Only thoroughbred 'races,'" he held, "accomplish the extraordinary" (*Rasse und Persönlichkeit,* p. 75). In connection with his race theory, Chamberlain emphasized the significance of nations: "It is almost always the nation as a political entity that creates the conditions for the formation of a race, or at least for the highest expressions of the race" (*Grundlagen,* 1st ed., Vol. I, p. 290). The awareness of racial identity, not physical characteristics, determined a race. Thus Chamberlain could speak of the English or Japanese "races" and also employ the term in a very broad sense, as when he included the Slavs and Celts among the Teutonic peoples.

Race was always dominant in Chamberlain's thought, whether he was describing the "heritage of the old world" as Hellenic art and philosophy, Roman law, and the coming of Christ; the cultureless chaos of peoples which separated the ancient from the modern world; or the role of the Jews and the Teutonic peoples, who entered Western history as "pure" races and whose antagonism shaped the modern world. He recognized the existence of other historical forces, such as religion or the desire for power, but he placed them far below race in importance. He was thus led to the paradox of trying to prove that the historical

Jesus, whose birth he regarded as "the most important date in the entire history of humanity," was not a Jew. Chamberlain denied that the Jewish people possessed any metaphysical inclinations or philosophical tendencies. Their outstanding characteristics in his view were materialism and rationalism. They were thus incapable of religion and could not have produced the man Jesus. The Jews served Chamberlain as a dark foil for the image of the Germanic peoples, whom he celebrated as the creators of "all present culture and civilization" and whose standard-bearers were the Germans. Paul Joachimsen, in a memorial article, described the aim of the *Grundlagen* as "to demonstrate the elements of Western cultural development in the light of an Aryan theodicy." But whereas Joachimsen considered Chamberlain's work as a document already belonging to the past, we know today what terrible consequences his ideas had when they were translated into reality after his death. The chief ideologist of National Socialism, Alfred Rosenberg, showed himself to be Chamberlain's disciple in his *Mythus des 20. Jahrhunderts* ("Myth of the Twentieth Century").

Goethe and Kant. One must not interpret Chamberlain's personality exclusively by the *Grundlagen*. His philosophical books on Kant and Goethe provide a far more solid basis for judgment and are more representative of his inclination and his intellectual position. His *Goethe* (1912) is a milestone in studies of the poet. Chamberlain was concerned to present "a clear, enthusiastic, and at the same time a critically reflective, grasp of this great personality in its essence and effect." Chamberlain found in Goethe the same polarities which he found in himself: nature and freedom, intuition and concept, poet and scholar, Christian and pagan—in brief, "the juxtaposition of opposed vocations." Jean Réal rightly described *Goethe* as "full of originality, of depth, and of prejudice" ("Houston Stewart Chamberlain et Goethe").

Chamberlain interrupted his studies of Goethe, which he pursued for more than twenty years, in order to write his *Immanuel Kant* (1905). Through Kant's limitation of the possibility of metaphysics Chamberlain came to realize the place of religion in human life. This side of Kant's thought appealed to Chamberlain's antirationalistic, vitalistic tendencies.

During World War I, Chamberlain composed fanatical anti-English propaganda. He was an intimate of Kaiser Wilhelm II from 1901 until well into the Kaiser's exile in the Netherlands. He was quite naturally unable to come to terms with the Weimar Republic and turned his sympathies to Hitler, whom he first met in 1923. *Mensch und Gott* ("Man and God"), written in Chamberlain's old age, is an impressive attempt at a philosophical synthesis but casts no light on his personality as a whole. One can agree with the judgment of Friedrich Heer in *Europa—Mutter der Revolutionen* (Stuttgart, 1964, p. 6): "H. S. Chamberlain presents himself as a highly significant symbol combining high culture and barbarism."

Works by Chamberlain

Richard Wagner, Munich, 1896. Translated by G. Ainslie Hight as *Richard Wagner;* revised by the author. Munich, 1897.

Die Grundlagen des 19. Jahrhunderts, 2 vols. Munich, 1899; 28th ed., 2 vols., Munich, 1942. Translated by John Lees as *Foundations of the Nineteenth Century*, 2 vols. London and New York, 1910.

Immanuel Kant. Die Persönlichkeit als Einführung in das Werk. Munich, 1905; 5th ed., Munich, 1938. Translated by Lord Redesdale, 2 vols. London, 1914.

Goethe. Munich, 1912; 5th ed., Munich, 1931.

Deutsches Wesen. Ausgewählte Aufsätze. Munich, 1916.

Lebenswege meines Denkens ("My Thought's Path Through Life"). Munich, 1919; 3d ed., Munich, 1942.

Mensch und Gott. Betrachtungen über Religion und Christentum. Munich, 1921; 6th ed., Munich, 1943.

Rasse und Persönlichkeit. Aufsätze. Munich, 1925.

Natur und Leben, Jakob von Uexküll, ed. Munich, 1928.

Briefe 1882–1924 und Briefwechsel mit Kaiser Wilhelm II, Paul Pretzsch, ed., 2 vols. Munich, 1928.

Works on Chamberlain

Chamberlain, Anna, *Meine Erinnerungen an Houston Stewart Chamberlain.* Munich, 1923.

Joachimsen, Paul, "Houston Stewart Chamberlain." *Zeitwende*, Vol. 3 (1927), 347–361, 430–439.

Réal, Jean, "Houston Stewart Chamberlain et Goethe." *Études germaniques.* Vol. 5 (1950), 154–166.

Réal, Jean, "La Lettre à l'amiral Hollmann (1903) ou Guillaume II à l'école de Houston Stewart Chamberlain." *Études germaniques*, Vol. 6 (1951), 303–312.

Réal, Jean, "The Religious Conception of Race: Houston Stewart Chamberlain and Germanic Christianity," in *The Third Reich.* Published under the auspices of the International Council for Philosophy and Humanistic Studies with the assistance of UNESCO. London, 1955. Pp. 243–286.

Seillière, Ernest, *Houston Stewart Chamberlain, le plus récent philosophe du pangermanisme mystique.* Paris, 1917.

Stolberg-Wernigerode, Otto Graf zu, "Houston Stewart Chamberlain," in *Neue deutsche Biographie.* Edited by Historische Kommission bei der Bayerischen Akademie der Wissenschaften. Berlin, 1957. Vol. III, pp. 187–190.

Ziegenfuss, Werner, "Houston Stewart Chamberlain," in Werner Ziegenfuss, ed., *Philosophen-Lexikon.* Berlin, 1949. Vol. I, pp. 181–186.

ANTONIA RUTH SCHLETTE
Translated by *Tessa Byck*

CHANCE. There are various possible definitions of the term "chance." Bertrand Russell, following Laplace, defines a chance event as one whose cause is unknown. Antoine Augustin Cournot, following Aristotle and J. S. Mill, defined a chance event as the concurrence of two independent causal chains. These and other similar definitions of the term do not grant chance events a distinct and separate ontological status but distinguish them from other events on the basis of whether or not men can predict their occurrence. This typically leads to theories of probability that, it is claimed, provide an explanation of chance.

Pure chance events. The line of argument that defines chance in terms of predictability tends to obscure a metaphysical meaning of "chance" as denoting *uncaused* events. The existence of such events, sometimes called "pure" chance events, has been defended by Epicurus, Charles Peirce, and William James.

Epicurus claimed that atoms, the ultimate constituents of matter, fall vertically through space at equal velocities but that sometimes one makes an uncaused swerve (*clinamen*) and thus comes into collision with other atoms. This produces a cluster of atoms and thus a material object. Man's free will consists of just such an uncaused swerve of atoms occurring in his mind. Epicurus thus attempted to refute Democritus' assertion that all events are causally determined and that therefore nothing is contingent. It is important to note that the swerve envisioned by Epicurus is not due either to an external force or to a change in the atom itself but is entirely uncaused. It is not just that men cannot discover the cause because of its obscurity. There is simply no cause to be discovered.

Peirce believed that universal determinism is a mere postulate of science and that empirical evidence, rather than confirming this postulate, tends to disconfirm it. The more precisely scientific observations are made, he thought, the more numerous are the irregular departures from scientific laws. Peirce claimed that it is only by granting the occurrence of chance events that one can account for the diversity of the universe. To the charge that the notion of a chance event is unintelligible (a charge made by F. H. Bradley), Peirce replied that it is only on the assumption of universal determinism that chance is unintelligible. It is, he said, no argument against chance to assume that no chance exists and then deduce from this that no chance exists.

James espoused a doctrine of chance as a way out of the logical conflict between determinism and free will. He described chance as a purely negative concept, being simply the negation of necessity. He gave as an example his decision to walk down one street rather than another on his way home. No matter what he decided, James claimed, after the occurrence of the event determinists would assert that his decision was the only possible one. However, James claimed this was dogmatic and arbitrary, since either decision was a real possibility and consistent with the plan of the universe. James did not believe that the existence of such chance events could be either proved or disproved, since the fact that a certain event occurs provides no evidence as to whether or not certain other events might possibly have occurred instead. A belief in the existence of such possible events was for James an instinctive feeling that allows one to view the future as "other and better" than the past, and only an appeal to feelings can decide the question. Faced with a possible contradiction between a belief in chance and a belief in God's omniscience, James concluded that God knows the ends he wishes achieved but not necessarily the exact means to these ends. At various points in God's plan ambiguous possibilities exist, and it is here that man's free will comes into play, deciding on means to already determined ends.

Difficulties in the theory of chance. There seem to be three main reasons for the unpopularity of the idea of pure chance.

First, the principle of determinism is a useful scientific hypothesis. To abandon it would, it has seemed to some, be to give up the scientific enterprise itself.

Second, the positing of chance events does not really help to solve the problem of free will. It has been pointed out by many writers—including Hume and Mill, and in more recent years by Moritz Schlick, C. D. Broad, and Richard Taylor—that, if a man's actions are the result of pure chance, then his actions have no rhyme or reason and it makes no sense to hold him responsible for what he does. The claim that men's free actions result from chance thus seems to be no improvement over the belief that they are determined.

Third, as Ernest Nagel has pointed out, the entire notion of an absolutely unqualified disorder of events seems self-contradictory, since for any sequence of events whatsoever a mathematical function can be constructed that states a correspondence between these events and the times at which they occur. This is not to say that each event might not be an uncaused event but that the disorder predicated of the entire series of events must be relative to a specified set of laws. Thus, a series of events that is random relative to one set of laws may be ordered relative to another set of laws. The difficulty is, then, to specify that set of laws in relation to which a sequence is to be considered a chance sequence. It should be noted, however, that neither Epicurus, Peirce, nor James spoke of chance sequences but rather of individual pure chance events, and this is consistent with the existence of a complex mathematical function that orders these events.

Quantum mechanics. The development of quantum mechanics has led some thinkers to claim, on the basis of Heisenberg's principle of uncertainty and von Neumann's theorem, that certain subatomic events are inherently unpredictable and that the principle of universal determinism has thus been proved false on the subatomic level. Whether this be true or not—and physicists themselves cannot seem to agree—one must carefully distinguish between these two very different questions: (1) Are events on the subatomic level uncaused? or (2) Are the causes of these events simply too complex for men to grasp?

The first of these questions can never be conclusively answered affirmatively, since no matter how much evidence there might be to suggest that a given occurrence is uncaused, no certainty can be afforded that new evidence might not be uncovered which does determine the cause of the event. In addition, the second question cannot be conclusively answered affirmatively until the cause of the event in question has actually been uncovered. It would thus appear that any event whose cause has not yet been discovered may be viewed either as a pure chance event that possesses no cause or as a complex event whose cause is as yet unknown but may be eventually discovered. It is this difficulty—that one situation can be so interpreted as to support two contradictory theses—that lies at the heart of the philosophical problem of chance.

Bibliography

An excellent general treatment of all the various notions of chance is Ernest Nagel, *The Structure of Science* (New York, 1961), Ch. 10. For a comparison of Epicurus' views with those of his contemporaries, see Cicero's *De Fato* (Loeb Classical Library). Peirce's views are given in his "The Doctrine of Necessity Examined," originally published in *The Monist*, Vol. 2, No. 3 (1892), 321–337, and reprinted in Justus Buchler, ed., *Philosophical Writings of Peirce* (New York, 1955). James's views are stated in his "The Dilemma of Determinism," which is included in numerous editions of his essays.

A critical survey of arguments in support of determinism is contained in Sidney Hook, "Determinism," in *The Encyclopaedia of the Social Sciences* (New York, 1935). A classic treatment of determinism and chance is Philipp Frank, *Das Kausalgesetz und seine Grenzen* (Vienna, 1932). These same subjects are discussed with reference to certain Marxian themes in Mario Bunge, "What Is Chance?," in *Science and Society,* Vol. 15, No. 3 (1951), 209–231.

The relationships between chance, determinism, and moral responsibility are examined in C. D. Broad, "Determinism, Indeterminism, and Libertarianism," in his *Ethics and the History of Philosophy* (London, 1952), and Richard Taylor, *Metaphysics* (Englewood Cliffs, N.J., 1963), Ch. 4.

For a discussion of the relevance of quantum mechanics to the question of chance, see Max Planck, *The Philosophy of Physics* (New York, 1936), a lucid book demanding little knowledge of science; Max Born, *Natural Philosophy of Cause and Chance* (Oxford, 1949), a more technical book that discusses the principle of determinism in various fields of physics; and David Bohm, *Causality and Chance in Modern Physics* (Princeton, N.J., 1957), an excellent recent treatment, meant for physicist and nonphysicist alike, of all the various issues in this field.

Two essays on chance by modern physicists are Percy Bridgman, "Determinism in Modern Science," and Alfred Landé, "The Case for Indeterminism," both in Sidney Hook, ed., *Determinism and Freedom in the Age of Modern Science* (New York, 1958), a symposium. Illuminating comments by both Sidney Hook and Ernest Nagel on these two essays appear in the same volume.

STEVEN M. CAHN

CHANGE. The word "change" designates one of the most conspicuous and most pervasive features of our sensory and introspective experience—only the related feature of plurality or diversity is equally so. Change, indeed, is so pervasive that only after the antithetical concept of changelessness or immutability was developed in the earliest period of Greek philosophy did change become a problem for philosophical thought.

GREEK AND MEDIEVAL PHILOSOPHY

In the Milesian school the claim was made that there is a single unchanging ground: water for Thales, the Indeterminate for Anaximander, air for Anaximenes. The appearance of change and diversity was not denied, but various explanations were proposed for it: condensation and rarefaction by Anaximenes, probably following Thales, and "the separation of the opposites" by Anaximander.

Denial of change. Far more abstract and radical was the view of Parmenides of Elea, who denied both change and diversity in the name of the unity and immutability of the First Principle. This principle, according to him, is Being, or abstract corporeality filling space; Nonbeing, or the void, does not exist. Change is impossible because it would require a self-contradictory conversion of Being into Nonbeing; nor can the absolute continuity of Being be broken into "many" by the nonexisting void.

But if change and diversity are unreal, how can the illusion of their existence arise? If Being is immutable and one, it can appear changing and many only in a finite human perspective; this implies that such finite perspectives must exist alongside the eternal One. But in conceding the existence of anything apart from a single ontological principle, the unity of this principle is sacrificed; similarly, it is impossible to speak of a complete denial of change as long as one continues to speak of changing appearances. Thus, neither change nor diversity is completely eliminated; at the same time they both remain logically underivable from the Eleatic One. This pattern of thought underlies the logic of all forms of static monism, which face the same difficulties as their Eleatic prototype.

Parmenides' disciple Zeno, irritated, according to Plato, by those who ridiculed his master, tried to point out absurdities in any view upholding the reality of change and motion. His four famous arguments against motion—the argument of Achilles and the tortoise, of dichotomy, of the flying arrow, and of the stadium—are still being discussed.

Change as change of place. The reaffirmation of change and plurality subsequent to Zeno was couched in language strongly influenced by the central Eleatic ideas. According to Empedocles and Anaxagoras, the elements are qualitatively diverse but persist immutably through their various combinations: ". . . of no one of all things is there any birth, nor any end in baneful death. There is only a mingling and a separation of what has been mingled" (Empedocles, Fr. 8). "We Greeks are wrong in using the expressions 'to come into being' and 'to be destroyed,' for nothing comes into being or is destroyed. Rather, a thing is mixed with or separated from already existing things" (Anaxagoras, Fr. 17). In other words, diversity was upheld, but qualitative change was denied, or rather reduced to change of place.

This became more obvious in the atomists, who were closer to Parmenides in upholding the qualitative unity of the primordial matter, which filled space, though not continuously. But unlike Parmenides, they accepted the reality of the void in order to explain motion. Thus, their homogeneous matter was divided into an infinite number of fragments moving through empty space. Both qualitative change and qualitative diversity were denied, or rather reduced to changes in position and configuration of elements, each of which retained the properties of the Parmenidean Being—absolute homogeneity, indivisibility, and immutability—on a minute scale. Atomism was a synthesis of Eleatic monism and Pythagorean pluralism. As John Burnet said, "Leucippus . . . gave the Pythagorean monads the character of the Parmenidean One." Change was admitted by the atomists only as a change of position, which affected neither the void nor the atoms but only their external relations in space. By this view of change, as well as by their anticipation of the law of constancy of matter, the atomists greatly strengthened substantialist modes of thought.

Becoming as qualitative change. The antisubstantialist trend in Greek philosophy was represented by Heraclitus of Ephesus. Instead of Parmenides' reasoning—"All change is contradictory, therefore it does not exist"—Heraclitus argued: "All change is contradictory; therefore contradiction [the unity of opposites] is the very essence of reality." Thus the world of Heraclitus was still one, but in a sense quite different from that of Parmenides; it was the dynamic unity of process, in which each momentary phase was continuously transformed into its "opposite," that is, into a subsequent qualitatively different phase. The inadequacy of the ordinary conceptual treatment of change was suggested by Heraclitus' statement: "We step and we do not step into the same river; we are and we are not" (Fr. 81), which clearly anticipated the future Hegelian view of becoming as a synthesis of being and nonbeing. This conception of becoming as qualitative change, as a perpetual transformation of one phase into another, was altogether different from the motion of atoms. Heraclitus, in insisting on the fluidity of everything, virtually rejected the existence of any unchanging substrate or vehicle of motion: "All things flow; nothing abides." Heraclitus also held that becoming is irreversible: "You cannot step twice into the same river" (Fr. 41), although he also shared with the majority of pre-Socratic thinkers a seemingly incompatible belief in the periodicity of successive worlds.

The primacy of Being. The subsequent development of Greek, medieval, and, to a considerable extent, modern philosophy was dominated by the antinomy of Being and Becoming. In most, though not in all, philosophical systems Being was given prominence while Becoming was placed in an inferior and subordinate role. This is clearly true of Plato's thought: the basic reality is constituted by the immutable logical essences (Ideas), while the realm of change, synonymous with that of generation and decay, has an inferior status intermediate between Being and Nonbeing. In the *Timaeus* Plato contrasted "that which always is and has no becoming" with "that which is always becoming and never is." To this metaphysical dichotomy there corresponds the epistemological dichotomy between knowledge and mere opinion. Because only opinions are possible concerning the realm of change, no true science of the physical world is possible. In the *Sophist* Plato admitted that it is intolerable to claim that perfect reality is "devoid of change and life"; but this concession to Heraclitus hardly modified the historical impact of his thought.

Aristotle compressed, so to speak, Plato's immutable Ideas into a single entity, his God, whose immutability was most closely imitated by the uniform and everlasting orbits of the celestial bodies and the imperishability of the ethereal stuff of which they were made. Although the Unmoved Mover had the attributes of the Eleatic One, Aristotle's conception of the physical world was close to that of Heraclitus. He rejected the atomistic explanation of qualitative change and diversity by the displacement of the homogeneous and immutable elements, denied the existence of atoms and the void, and asserted the reality of qualitative change and diversity. He regarded the four sublunar elements as mutually transformable in a way analogous to the Heraclitean transformation of opposites. Every change, including that of position, implied the passage from potentiality to actuality. In introducing the concept of not-yet-existing possibility and in insisting on the contingency of the future, Aristotle came very close to the idea of an "open future," which is the central theme of modern process philosophy.

Plotinus tried to make the puzzling relation between the timeless realm of Being and the restless flux of phenomena more intelligible by his idea of emanation. According to him, the realm of change proceeds from that of Being (which for Plotinus again had the attributes of the Eleatic One) by means of degradation or diminution. This idea was implicitly present in Plato's view of the realm of change as that which "never truly is," forever oscillating between Being and Nonbeing. According to Plotinus, change and succession appear on the second level of emanation with the World Soul in which individual souls are contained. Unlike the Divine Intellect at the first stage of emanation, the souls are unable to grasp the timeless truth at once, in a single instantaneous act, but only gradually, step by step, by a laborious process of reasoning. Succession and change are thus mere results of our inability to grasp everything at once. As in Plato, time is "the moving image of eternity," an imperfect (because moving) imitation of the perfect timeless reality; but in this context "motion" is understood in a psychological sense as "movement of soul." Thus the thought of Plotinus foreshadowed two modern, though radically opposed, trends: one, that time is a mere infirmity of the human mind which prevents us from seeing things *sub specie aeternitatis;* and the other, that there is a close correlation between temporality and mentality (temporalistic panpsychism).

The Greek doctrine of the contrast between the timeless realm of perfection and the changing realm of corruption, together with the corresponding contrast between the timeless divine insight and man's temporal, and therefore fragmentary, knowledge dominated medieval theology —Christian, Jewish, and Islamic. Nearly all the theologians accepted predestination as an inevitable consequence of the timeless divine insight that embraces the totality of all successive events in one act, *totum simul.* Thus, Thomas Aquinas, who stressed the immutability of God (*Summa Theologica,* Q. 9) and who applied to God Boethius' definition of eternity ("the complete and perfect possession of unending life"), accepted complete predestination (Q. 22, 23, 24). In eliminating uncertainty from the future, the medieval thinkers faced the difficult problem of reconciling predestination with the freedom of will postulated on ethical grounds. The protestant reformers of the sixteenth century (Luther, and especially Zwingli and Calvin) were more consistent when they flatly denied freedom in the name of divine omniscience.

MODERN PHILOSOPHY

Static monism. In modern philosophy the Greek and medieval pattern of two realms, eternal and temporal, was retained in various systems of pantheistic monism. The transcendent eternity of the medieval God was replaced by an impersonal immanent order of nature that was as devoid of change as the Paremenidean Being, Aristotle's God, Plato's Ideas, and Plotinus' One. From Giordano Bruno to F. H. Bradley this basic pattern remained the same. Thinkers like Spinoza still recognized that the unchangeability of God, or the eternal order of nature, implied the strictest determinism. But neither Bruno nor Spinoza denied change on the "lower," or phenomenal, level. Post-Kantian idealistic monism continued the same trend. It was greatly influenced by Kant's view of time as a mere form of sensibility, applicable only to phenomena and not to "the intelligible world." This explains why J. G. Fichte's "Absolute Ego," despite his verbal emphasis on becoming (*Werden*) and activity (*Urtätigkeit*), is outside of time (see his *Grundlage der Gesammten Wissenschaftslehre,* in *Sämmtliche Werke,* Berlin, 1845, p. 217: "For pure reason everything is at once; time exists only in imagination"). This also explains why Schelling's philosophy was so close to that of Bruno and Spinoza.

The position of Hegel was more ambiguous. His emphasis on the historical character of reality and his explicit agreement with Heraclitus are well known, but at the same time he insisted on the timelessness of the Absolute Idea. This ambiguity has led to two opposite interpretations of Hegel: a dynamic one, interpreting dialectic as a historical process (Benedetto Croce, J. N. Findlay), and a static one (J. M. E. McTaggart), according to which the Absolute Idea ("Infinite End") is timelessly realized—"It is only a delusion on our part which makes us suppose otherwise. And the only real progress is the removal of the delusion. The universe is eternally the same and eternally perfect. The movement is only in our minds" (McTaggart, *Studies in the Hegelian Dialectic,* 2d ed., Cambridge, 1922, p. 171).

Schopenhauer's view of change was much less ambiguous. His Universal Will, despite the dynamic connotation of the term, was a static principle, explicitly posited beyond time and space, and assimilated to the Eleatic ἕν καὶ πᾶν. The same distinction between temporal appearances and the timeless ground of phenomena is found in F. H. Bradley, the most outspoken defender of static monism in the twentieth century; in *Appearance and Reality* he tries to show the contradictory and consequently unreal character of change and time; the transphenomenal Absolute must be free of these contradictions.

Static pluralism. Denial of change is not always coupled with denial of diversity, as various instances of static pluralism show. That the dynamic character of Leibniz' pluralism is more apparent than real is evident from his own definition of a monad as a substance containing in itself all its future states. The deterministic implications of preestablished harmony led Leibniz to anticipate Kant, Fichte, and Laplace by saying that "if someone could have a sufficient insight into inner parts of things . . . he would be a prophet and would see the future in the present as in a mirror" ("Von dem Verhängnisse," in *Hauptschriften zur Grundlagen der Philosophie,* Ernst Cassirer and A. Buchenau, eds., 5 vols., Leipzig, 1904–1906, Vol. II, p. 129). While in Leibniz the elimination of change and succession was only implicit, in the pluralism of J. F. Herbart and McTaggart it was explictly stated. For Herbart the ultimate elements of being, *die Realen,* were absolutely immutable, and the illusion of change arose because to our accidentally shifting attention the *Realen* appear in different aggregations. Herbart's atoms were immaterial. As in physical atomism, every change was reduced to change of relations between unchangeable units; but unlike physical atoms, Herbart's units were qualitatively different and placed in "intelligible space." In McTaggart's system the reality of time (and consequently of change) was explicitly denied. For him the temporal series were mere perspective representations of the timeless series; only the latter are ultimately real.

Change, perception of change, and time. Other thinkers, more interested in concrete empirical features of change than in its ultimate ontological status, began to explore psychologically the perception of change, which could not be separated from the problem of temporal awareness in general. Before the British empiricists only Aristotle, Plotinus, and Augustine approached the problem of change from a similar viewpoint. A number of problems emerged, all closely related—the relation of change to time, that of change to duration, and of change to succession, and the problem of continuity and discontinuity of change which is closely related to that of temporal threshold. The most important problem, on whose solution the solutions of the others largely depend, is that of the relation of change to time. That change requires succession was generally recognized; but there was much less agreement as to whether the converse was true. The absolute theory of time, represented by Isaac Newton, whose predecessors were Isaac Barrow, Pierre Gassendi, and Bernardino Telesio, claimed that time is independent of change; even empty time would flow, and did flow before the creation of the world. Berkeley and Leibniz adhered to Aristotle's view that time is inseparable from its concrete changing content and that to speak of empty time as "flowing" is meaningless. (This was one important point of dispute between Leibniz and Newton's disciple, Samuel Clarke.) But while Berkeley claimed that the infinite divisibility of change and time (both being inseparable) is a mere fiction because mathematical instants are never perceived and consequently are unreal, Leibniz, influenced by his own discovery of the infinitesimal calculus, applied the concept of infinite divisibility to change and time.

Berkeley's idea of the indivisible moments (*minima sensibilia*) was adopted by Hume, while Kant followed Leibniz in accepting the infinite divisibility of all phenomenal changes. Thus the close union of time and change led to two different results: For Berkeley and Hume time shared the discreteness of perceptual change, while for Leibniz and Kant concrete changes shared the infinite divisibility of the mathematical time. The intermediate solution of Locke distinguished between immediately experienced qualitative duration and the homogeneous Newtonian duration of the physical world (*Essay Concerning Human Understanding,* Book II, Ch. 14). This solution became the basis of the widely accepted distinction between the mathematical durationless present of the objective world of matter and the durational "specious present" of psychology, challenged only in recent decades.

Another motive behind Berkeley's and Hume's idea of *minima sensibilia* was their attempt to explain the variety of introspective experience by the combination and recombination of minute unchangeable elements, "psychological atoms"—"impressions" in Hume, "sensations" in Condillac and Taine, *Vorstellungen* in Herbart and German psychology, *Empfindungen* or "elements" in Mach, "atomic facts" in Wittgenstein, "logical atoms" in Russell—characterized by distinctness and substantiality. As Hume said, "They [perceptions] are also distinct and separable, and may be considered as separately existent, and have no need of anything else to support their existence. They are therefore substances, as far as this definition explains substance" (*A Treatise of Human Nature,* Book I, Part IV, Sec. 5). Hume's impressions were, so to speak, immutable Cartesian substances on a minute scale.

CHANGE IN CLASSICAL AND CONTEMPORARY SCIENCE

Static determinism. Psychological atomism borrowed its model from the revived physical atomism that in various degrees influenced nearly all the founders of modern physics. The basic mechanistic goal of explaining the diversity and change in nature by the changing configurations of the homogeneous bits of matter was fully accepted. It was of secondary importance whether this matter was regarded as made of tiny indivisible grains (Gassendi) or of infinitely small points (*atomi non quanti* of Galileo), or as filling space continuously (Descartes). The basic principle of the kinetic theory of matter—to reduce apparently qualitative changes to mere displacements of immutable units—was accepted by all, even though a full elaboration and empirical verification of the principle had to wait until the end of the nineteenth century. By 1900, after the spectacular triumphs of the corpuscular-kinetic models in physics (the verification of the atomistic structure of matter and electricity, the kinetic theory of gases, the discovery of Brownian motion, the mechanical models of ether, the configurational models of the organic compounds), the final victory of Democritus over Aristotle and Heraclitus seemed assured. At the same time the law of conservation of matter and energy was hailed by Spencer, Taine, Ostwald, Haeckel, and others as an empirical confirmation of the traditional idea of permanence of substance; the equality of cause and effect was seen as a mere consequence of the equivalence of successive forms of energy, whose permanence in successive transformations provided the causal link for which Hume had looked in vain. This tendency to reduce the successive causal relation to the identity of a single basic stuff revealed the affinity between modern classical science and the static monism of traditional metaphysics. Change exists only on the surface and does not affect the immutability and unity of the underlying substrate. This disbelief in the ultimate reality of change and succession was clearly expressed by Laplace, Du Bois-Reymond, T. H. Huxley, John Tyndall, and Friedrich Paulsen. To all of them the apparent absence of the future was a mere illusion caused by the limitations of human knowledge.

Recent dynamic trends. After 1900 physics seemed to point in the very opposite direction. Although the existence of elementary particles was verified beyond doubt, it was also shown that their properties are altogether different from those of the classical Lucretian atom. They were deprived of all the intuitive features with which they had been endowed from the time of Democritus to that of Lorentz—even constancy of their mass, their precise locations, and their permanence (identity through time). The very distinction between "full" and "empty" on which the classical concept of corpuscle was based was challenged by the general theory of relativity, while the close association of mass and energy prevents us from regarding the mass total of an aggregate as a mere sum of its constituent parts. Moreover, the elements of matter combine in a paradoxical way the properties of particles and waves, so that they are neither particles nor waves in the traditional sense; and the word "events," which is free of the substantial connotations of "elements," is much more appropriate to them. This is consonant with the general dynamic trend in physics. Not only was mass fused with energy but space was merged with time into space-time. The latter fusion means, contrary to popular misunderstanding, a dynamization of space rather than a spatialization of time, as Einstein himself agreed in a discussion with Émile Meyerson; and both space-time and mass-energy are fused into a single, though heterogeneous, dynamic entity or, rather, process. Space and time cease to be immutable containers of motion, and matter ceases to be its substantial vehicle; thus the whole classical concept of motion as a displacement of a substantial entity in static space yields to a more comprehensive and less intuitive notion of change that has some affinities with the Heraclitean concept of irreversible change without vehicle and without container. The twentieth-century criticism of Laplacean determinism and of its virtual elimination of becoming and succession fits into the over-all dynamic trend of contemporary physics.

CHANGE IN CONTEMPORARY PHILOSOPHY

Process philosophy. The reaffirmation of change and the exploration of its structure is a salient feature of contemporary thought. The inadequacy of the atomistic interpretation of change was first recognized in the realm of introspection. James Ward's article "Psychology" in *Encyclopaedia Britannica* (1886) was preceded by William James's article, "On Some Omissions of Introspective Psychology" (*Mind*, 1884), largely reprinted in *The Principles of Psychology* (1890), in which the atomistic "mind-dust theory" was severely criticized and the concept of permanently existing "idea" or *Vorstellung*, periodically reappearing before the footlights of consciousness, was labeled "as mythological an entity as the Jack of Spades" (*Principles*, Vol. I, p. 316). The continuity of the concretely experienced "stream of thought" was stressed against the discontinuity resulting from its artificial conceptualization. In the same year the term *Gestalt* was used for the first time by Christian Ehrenfels in his article "Über Gestaltqualitäten" (*Vierteljahrschriften für wissenschaftliche Philosophie*, Vol. 14, 1890, 249–292), and fruitfully applied to the perception of melody, which, according to Ehrenfels, is a dynamic unity despite the diversity of its successive tones. A conclusion similar to that of Ehrenfels had been reached by Henri Bergson a year before (*Essais sur les données immédiates de la conscience*). In his later books Bergson applied the results of his introspective analysis of psychological duration to duration in general. Every "true duration" (*durée réelle*), he held, is essentially incomplete in the sense that each of its moments introduces an element of novelty which was not contained in the past. In ignoring novelty (an element stressed earlier by Boutroux in his contingentism and by C. S. Peirce in his tychism), radical determinism virtually (and sometimes explicitly) claims that everything is given at once, which is absurd. Equally false is radical indeterminism, which, in positing the *creatio ex nihilo* of each moment, ignores the dynamic continuity of change and makes impossible both memory and causation. While mathematical continuity (infinite divisibility) is merely discontinuity infinitely repeated, duration is a continuum of successive heterogeneous phases that excludes the discontinuity of any externally related units, whether of durationless instants or of the Humean atomic segments. This implies that the mathematical present is a fiction both in psychology and in physics; even physical processes are pulsational in nature, though their temporal span is much shorter than that of mental events (*Matter and Memory*, Ch. 4).

Whitehead's metaphysics of events, with its emphasis on "the creative advance of nature" and on "the immortality of the past" (from which the irreversibility of becoming follows), as well as its denial of durationless instants, was very close to Bergson's views. Various other aspects of the historical character of reality were stressed by John Dewey, Samuel Alexander, C. Lloyd Morgan, C. D. Broad, and Benedetto Croce.

Process philosophy aroused much hostility among those who confused classical Laplacean determinism with rationality in general; to them the idea of novelty, especially in the physical world, appeared throroughly irrational despite the recent discussion of the principle of indeterminacy in physics. Similarly, the existence of mathematical instants was defended by those who failed to realize that the deceptive clarity of the concept is based on a questionable analogy between time and a geometrical line. Even some mathematicians today question the empirical applicability of the concept of mathematical continuum, especially to the quantum phenomena (see Herman Weyl, *Das Kontinuum*, 1918, pp. 69–71; Karl Menger, "Topology Without Points," *Rice Institute Pamphlets*, Vol. 17, 1940, p. 107).

It is true that it is very difficult to synthesize conceptually the continuity of becoming and the individuality of events. This antinomy is probably a new form of the Heraclitean "unity of opposites" and may be related to the present "wave-corpuscle" antinomy. In most instances resistance to a genuine acceptance of change and novelty stems from the failure to overcome the deeply ingrained habits of spatialization and from the often unconscious commitment to traditional patterns of thought, especially to the metaphysics of Being. Although the dialogue between Parmenides and Heraclitus is still going on, the former is now much less favored than the latter. However, a systematic exploration of various aspects of the problem of change has only begun.

Bibliography

The bibliography dealing with the problem of change is practically inseparable from that dealing with time, and the latter is so vast that only very limited selection is given here.

Modern restatements of the Eleatic denial of change are F. H. Bradley, *Appearance and Reality*, 2d ed. (New York, 1908), esp. Chs. 4 and 18; J. M. E. McTaggart, "The Unreality of Time," in *Mind*, N.S. Vol. 17 (1908); and Donald Williams, "The Myth of Passage," in *Journal of Philosophy*, Vol. 58 (1951).

Reaffirmations of the reality of change are F. C. S. Schiller, "Metaphysics of the Time-Process," in *Mind*, N.S. Vol. 4 (1895), 36–46, and "Novelty," in *PAS*, Vol. 22 (1922–1923); William James, *A Pluralistic Universe* (New York, 1910), and *Some Problems of Philosophy* (New York, 1911); Henri Bergson, *Oeuvres complètes* (Geneva, 1945); A. N. Whitehead, *The Concept of Nature* (Cambridge, 1920), "Time," in *Proceedings of the Sixth International Congress of Philosophy* (1927), and *Process and Reality* (Cambridge, 1929); C. D. Broad, *Scientific Thought* (London, 1923), esp. Ch. 2; Charles Hartshorne, "Contingency and the New Era in Metaphysics," in *Journal of Philosophy*, Vol. 29 (1932), 421–431 and 457–469; Paul Weiss, *Reality* (Princeton, N.J., 1938); Richard Taylor, "Pure Becoming," in *Australasian Journal of Philosophy*, Vol. 38 (1960); and Nicholas Rescher, "The Revolt Against Process," in *Journal of Philosophy*, Vol. 59 (1962).

On the status of change in the physical world, see Hans Reichenbach, *The Philosophy of Space and Time* (New York, 1958), and *The Direction of Time* (Los Angeles, 1956); *Bulletin de la Société française de philosophie* (Apr. 6, 1922), the discussion between Einstein, Meyerson, and Bergson; Émile Meyerson, *La Déduction relativiste* (Paris, 1925), esp. Ch. 7, and *Identité et réalité*, 5th ed. (Paris, 1951), esp. Ch. 6; G. J. Whitrow, *The Natural Philosophy of Time* (London and Edinburgh, 1961); Milič Čapek, *The Philosophical Impact of Contemporary Physics* (Princeton, N.J., 1961); and Richard Schlegel, *Time and the Physical World* (Ann Arbor, Mich., 1961).

On the psychological aspects of change, see William James, *The Principles of Psychology*, 2 vols. (New York, 1890), Vol. I, esp. Chs. 9 and 15; L. W. Stern, "Die psychische Präsenzzeit," in *Zeitschrift für die Psychologie und die Physiologie des Sinnesorganen*, Vol. 13 (1897), 325–349; and Bertrand Russell, "On the Experience of Time," in *The Monist*, Vol. 25 (1915). Paul Fraisse, *Psychologie du temps* (Paris, 1957), contains a very complete bibliography.

On the relation of continuity to discreteness, see Henri Bergson, "La Perception du changement," in *La Pensée et le mouvant* (Paris, 1934); W. Gotschalk, "The Nature of Change," in *The Monist*, Vol. 40 (1930), 363–380, and "Concepts of Continuity," in *PAS*, Supp. Vol. 4 (1924); the symposium "Continu et discontinu," in *Cahiers de la nouvelle journée*, Vol. 15 (1929), especially the article by Louis de Broglie, "Continuité et individualité dans la physique moderne."

On the relation of change to eternity, see Josiah Royce, *The World and the Individual*, 2 vols. (New York, 1901–1902), Vol. I, chapter entitled "The Temporal and Eternal"; E. S. Brightman, "A Temporalist View of God," in *Journal of Religion*, Vol. 11 (1932); A. O. Lovejoy, "The Obsolescence of the Eternal," in *The Philosophical Review*, Vol. 18 (1909), 479–502; and J. A. Leighton, "Time and the Logic of Monistic Idealism," in *Essays in Honor of E. J. Creighton* (New York, 1917), pp. 151–161.

MILIČ ČAPEK

CHANNING, WILLIAM ELLERY (1780–1842),

America's most famous Unitarian minister, was described by Emerson as "one of those men who vindicate the power of the American race to produce greatness." Channing, born in Newport, Rhode Island, graduated from Harvard in 1798. The following two years he spent as a tutor in Richmond, Virginia, and in private study. During this period he underwent a profound religious experience, and in 1801 he returned to Harvard for theological study. He was ordained the minister of Boston's Federal Street Congregational Church in 1803 and held this pastorate throughout his life. He died in Bennington, Vermont.

Channing was not an original or profound thinker, a systematic philosopher, or a great writer. His significance in the history of ideas lies in his representative influence, his achievement in expressing and synthesizing the diverse strands of thought that appeared in America at the end of the eighteenth and the beginning of the nineteenth centuries.

Although Channing was celebrated in his own lifetime as a man of letters (his critical essays on Milton, Napoleon, and Fénelon were widely read both here and abroad), his lasting reputation stands on his attempt to develop an "enlightened" religious faith for the Americans of his generation. Jonathan Edwards had responded to the spirit of the Enlightenment by employing the ideas of Locke and Newton to revitalize Calvinist dogma. Channing employed the liberating spirit of eighteenth-century thought to free Christianity from an outmoded theology. "God has given us a rational nature," he said in his famous sermon "Unitarian Christianity" (1819), "and will call us to account for it." Without denying the authority of Scripture, Channing argued that men should "reason about the Bible precisely as civilians do about the Constitution under which we live." This rational approach to revelation led Channing to reject the "irrational and unscriptural doctrine of the Trinity." Substituting the moral perfection of God for the Calvinist conception of divine sovereignty, Channing also repudiated such doctrines as natural depravity and predestination. "It is not because his will is irresistible but because his will is the perfection of virtue that we pay him allegiance," Channing asserted. "We cannot bow before a being, however great and powerful, who governs tyrannically."

As a religious thinker Channing was liberal but not radical. Eighteenth-century skepticism had no place in his thinking. He was influenced considerably by Scottish "common-sense" philosophers, such as Adam Ferguson and Richard Price, and in his discourse "The Evidences of Revealed Religion" (1821) he relied heavily on the traditional arguments of William Paley in attempting to refute David Hume and assert the validity of miracles.

Channing is also important for his influence on the New England transcendentalists. Like Rousseau, whose writings he admired, he was partly an Enlightenment figure and partly a romantic. Channing's romanticism is most apparent in the sermon "Likeness to God" (1828), in which he asserted that man discovers God not only through Scripture and rational inquiry but also through consciousness. Long before Emerson's famous essays were published, Channing was preaching that in all its higher actions the soul had "a character of infinity" and describing sin as "the ruin of God's noblest work." Despite the fact that Channing never professed enthusiasm for the "new views," the similarity between his conception of the divine potential in human nature and the later pronouncements of Emerson and Theodore Parker is unmistakable. The path to transcendentalism lay through Unitarianism, and it was Channing who helped to pave the way.

Finally, Channing is significant for his humanitarian influence. His belief in the parental character of God and the dignity of man provided an ideological base for humanitarian efforts, and he spoke out in favor of most of the reform causes of his day. His pamphlet against slavery, written in 1835, attracted wide attention. Although Channing always shied away from radical solutions to social disorder, no one was more influential in articulating the gospel of human dignity that nourished most American reformers before the Civil War.

Bibliography

The most usable edition of Channing's works is a one-volume edition (Boston, 1886). There are several full-length studies of Channing, including David Edgell's *William Ellery Channing: An Intellectual Portrait* (Boston, 1955); Arthur Brown's *Always Young for Liberty* (Syracuse, N.Y., 1956); and Robert L. Patterson's *The Philosophy of William Ellery Channing* (New York, 1952).

Irving H. Bartlett

CHAOS AND COSMOS. According to the forerunners of pre-Socratic speculation, Chaos denoted a state of affairs that preceded the emergence of the world. Cosmos, according to later natural philosophers from Pythagoras to Archimedes, described the world order that was thought to manifest itself in the totality of natural phenomena.

According to surviving evidence, Hesiod was the first Greek speculative thinker to use Chaos in his account of the birth of the world (*Theogony*, 116). He referred to it in conjunction with the ideas of Earth, the Heavens, and Eros, and he appears to have derived its existence from much older Greek mythical speculations about the genesis of the universe. In his description he made no attempt to explain the causes of Chaos' existence. He insisted on the temporal priority of Chaos over everything else, but nowhere did he claim that Chaos came out of nothing. Rather, he implied that it coexisted with the undifferentiated state of the universe (from eternity) and that it manifested itself as the gap produced the moment the Heavens were separated from the Earth. According to this story—variants and elaborations of which are also to be found in the so-called Orphic theogonies of the sixth and early fifth centuries B.C.—once Heaven and Earth had been separated, the dark and windy chasm of Chaos was transformed, through the appearance of Eros, into the background against which the world was created. This fertilizing force of Eros brought back Heaven and Earth into a productive embrace, and the resulting rain helped to separate the Wet and the Dry, the Cold and the Hot. Fire exhalations then created the stars; waters surrounded the land; and the starry sky, like a hollow hemisphere, covered the Earth. The rest of the universe was viewed as a complication of these elements. How these complications (such as the shape of the Earth, the regularity of heavenly motions, the nature of physical change or permanence) were supposed to have developed, we are never told. (The gross anthropomorphism of mythical cosmogonies make such questions unanswerable.) In their attempts to preserve the usefulness of Chaos as a cosmological notion—Plato (*Timaeus*) and Aristotle (*Physics*, 208b29) identifying it with space, and Zeno of Citium with water—later speculative philosophers dissociated Chaos from cosmogonical thinking. In doing so, they did not succeed in answering more plausibly Hesiod's cosmogonic question, How can we account for the most pervasive differentiations of the universe? But they did reach a new realization: before an attempt is made to explain the birth of the world (assuming that the world was born), it is necessary that we know what the world is and how we can construe it as a cosmos.

According to a reliable tradition, Aetius' *Placita* (2, 1, 1), the first natural philosopher to use the word Cosmos to refer to the general world order was Pythagoras. According to other evidence (Diogenes Laërtius, 8.48), Parmenides restricted the term to the Heavens; Empedocles, to the combination of the four elements; and Democritus, to the physical structure of the world. While these speculators' use of the Cosmos concept did not prevent them from either claiming or denying the genesis of the world from something unformed and pre-existing, it did provide them with a test for the reasonableness of their theories. Henceforth, they would have to fit these theories into a broader account of the nature of the world's constitutive elements; the old cosmogonies would have to pass the test of the new cosmologies. With the resulting shift in emphasis, questions about the constitution of the world—its evolution, location, status, and animation—proved more interesting than the old genealogical accounts. To be sure, in all these speculations something of the initial meaning of the word Cosmos, namely, order (or ornament), lingered on. But at best it was a hopeful expectation rather than an incontrovertible fact.

The new cosmologists, from Pythagoras to Epicurus, had to argue for their theories. In order to draw a comprehensive but creditable picture of the world and to explain in what sense the world could be shown to be a Cosmos, they had to philosophize about their data, as well as guard themselves against inconsistency and inadequate evidence. Thus, some speculative thinkers, such as the Pythagoreans, concentrated on the rational form of the world manifesting itself in numbers. While the Pythagorean approach went a long way toward both generality and precision in physical explanations, it left much to be desired in the area of empirical observation and sense confirmation. Similarly, by trying to debunk physical change in the world, Parmenides provided hardly any distinction between a physical Cosmos and a logical construct. His approach lent support to the idea of rational demonstration, but it disastrously undermined the belief in the usefulness of natural description. Later, the post-Eleatic pluralists (Empedocles, Anaxagoras, the Atomists), by acknowledging the complexity of physical change, were forced to compromise the uniqueness and identity of the Cosmos. Still later, when Plato and Aristotle again tackled the cosmological question, they had no rational option but to subsume it in the broader issues of metaphysics, epistemology, and logic. The outcome was a more self-conscious cosmology, but also a less empirical study of the general structure of nature. Finally, although Stoicism and Epicureanism worked out many original ideas in their natural philosophies (such as their ideas of *pneuma*, the all-pervasive cosmic tension; *tonos*, force or intensity; and *soma*, physical body or material thing) as a reaction to the logical criticism of pre-Socratic thought, their positive views on the Cosmos were contrary to physically observable or even imaginable phenomena.

The end of Greek philosophy was historically preceded by the bankruptcy of philosophical cosmologies. Henceforth, all important cosmological theories were to be found in the mathematical and astronomical studies of the Alexandrian and early Christian scientists. A remarriage between cosmology and philosophy was not effected before the sixteenth and seventeenth centuries.

Bibliography

Burnet, J., *Early Greek Philosophy*. London, 1930.

Cornford, F. M., "Innumerable Worlds in Presocratic Cosmogony." *Classical Quarterly*, Vol. 28 (1934), 1–16.

Cornford, F. M., *Principium Sapientiae*. Cambridge, 1952.

Diels, H., *Die Fragmente der Vorsokratiker*, 10th ed. Berlin, 1961.

Gigon, O., *Grundprobleme der antiken Philosophie*. Bern, 1959.

Guthrie, W. K. C., *A History of Greek Philosophy*, Vol. 1. Cambridge, 1962.

Jaeger, W., *The Theology of the Early Greek Philosophers*. Oxford, 1947.

Kirk, G. S., and Raven, J. E., *The Presocratic Philosophers*. Cambridge, 1957.

Tannery, P., *Pour l'histoire de la science hellène*, A. Dies, ed., 2d ed. Paris, 1930.

Vlastos, G., "Presocratic Theology and Philosophy." *Philosophical Quarterly* (1952), 97–123.

P. DIAMANDOPOULOS

CHARDIN, PIERRE TEILHARD DE. *See* TEILHARD DE CHARDIN, PIERRE.

CHARRON, PIERRE (1541–1603), skeptical philosopher and theologian, was born in Paris, in a family of 25 children. He studied at the universities of Paris, Bourges, Orléans, and Montpellier, receiving a law degree from Montpellier in 1571. Sometime during his student years he became a priest. He was a very successful preacher and theologian in southern France, serving as preacher in ordinary to Queen Margaret of Navarre and as a theological adviser and teacher in various dioceses in the *Midi.* In spite of his many worldly successes, he tried to retire to a monastic order in 1589 but was refused admittance because of his age.

During the 1580s Charron met Michel de Montaigne in Bordeaux and became his close friend and disciple. Montaigne made Charron his intellectual heir, adopting Charron as his son. After Montaigne's death, in 1592, Charron wrote his major works, *Les Trois Veritez* (Bordeaux, 1593), *Discours chrestiens* (Bordeaux, 1601; Paris, 1604), *De la Sagesse* (Bordeaux, 1601), and *Le Petit Traicté de la sagesse* (written in 1603, published posthumously in Paris, 1606). These works were very popular and were republished often in the seventeenth century, especially the very skeptical *De la Sagesse*, which was highly influential in disseminating skeptical views and arguments into philosophical and theological discussions and played an important role in the development of modern thought, libertinism, and fideism.

Serious efforts to suppress and reject Charron's skeptical views were made by such figures as the Jesuit Father François Garasse, who in 1623 accused Charron of having supplied *le brèviare des libertins* and of having been a secret atheist trying to destroy religion. His work, which was first condemned in 1605, was seen as more dangerous than Montaigne's, partly because Charron was a professional theologian, partly because he wrote more didactically. A Protestant medical doctor, Pierre Chanet, published *Considerations sur la Sagesse de Charon* (1643), an attempted Aristotelian refutation of Charron's skepticism about the possibility of knowledge.

Although Charron, like Montaigne, was attacked on many sides, his views were also defended and advanced by the so-called *libertins érudits*—Gabriel Naudé, Guy Patin, François de La Mothe Le Vayer, and Pierre Gassendi—and were supported in varying degrees as theologically orthodox by various French Counter Reformation leaders. Pierre Bayle considered Charron an excellent and prime representative of fideistic Christian thought. Interest in and concern with Charron's views diminished in the eighteenth century, and he came to be considered a second-rate and derivative Montaigne whose style lacked the freshness and literary quality of his mentor's. In the light of recent criticism suggesting that Montaigne was or might have been a sincere believer and that his skepticism was part of a theological movement of the period, Charron, too, has begun to be re-examined and re-evaluated.

The first statement of Charron's views was the *Trois Veritez*, a tract against Calvinism and the views of its French leader, Philippe Duplessis-Mornay. The three truths Charron sought to establish were that God exists, that Christianity is the correct view of God, and that Catholicism is the true statement of Christianity. Most of this enormous work deals with the last claim. However, the work begins with a brief discourse on knowledge of God, developing skepticism about the possibility of human knowledge in this area, on the basis of both human rational limitations and the nature of God. Our own capacities are so limited and unreliable that it is doubtful that we could really know anything in either the natural or the supernatural realm. God's nature is infinite and therefore surpasses all attempts to define or limit it. Hence, we cannot know, in rational terms, what he is. Thus the greatest theologians and philosophers know as much or as little about God as do the humblest artisans. Our knowledge consists only of negative information, what God is not. In fact, Charron announced, "the true knowledge of God is a perfect ignorance about Him" (*Trois Veritez*, Paris, 1595, p. 26).

Charron combined the skeptic's views about the inadequacy and unreliability of human knowledge with the mystic's and negative theologian's view that God is unknowable because he is infinite and then utilized this combination to attack atheism. The denial that God exists proceeds from some definition of God, from which absurd conclusions are then drawn. Such a definition can only be the result of human presumption, the attempt to measure divinity by human means, and, as such, is worthless, since the atheist does not, and cannot, know what he is talking about.

Throughout the *Trois Veritez* Charron argued principally in a negative way, trying to show that it is unreasonable not to believe in God, Christianity, and Catholicism and that the evidence adduced by opponents is unreliable or dubious. He often contended that opponents, usually Calvinists had to base their case on the results obtained by the weak and miserable human capacities, employing these defective results as measures of divine truth.

Charron's skeptical defense of the faith was made more explicit in *De la Sagesse* and in his defense of that work, *Le Petit Traicté de la sagesse*. His major thesis was that since man cannot discover any truth except by revelation, morality should be based on following nature, except when guided by divine light. To support this thesis, Charron first put forth most of Montaigne's skeptical views in an organized fashion. We must first know ourselves ("The true science and the true study of man is man," *De la Sagesse*, Book I, Ch. 1), and this involves knowing the limitations on what we can know. Charron presented the traditional skeptical critique of sense knowledge, questioning whether we possess the requisite senses for gaining knowledge, whether we can distinguish illusions and dreams from veridical experience, and whether we can, in view of the enormous variability of sense experiences, determine which ones correspond to objective states of affairs. Next, he raised skeptical questions about our rational abilities, contending that we possess no adequate or certain criteria that enable us to distinguish truth from falsehood. He pointed out that in fact we believe things mainly as a result of passions and social pressures, not reasons and evidence. We actually function as beasts and not as rational beings. Hence, we should accept Montaigne's contention that men possess no genuine principles unless God reveals them. Everything else is only dreams and smoke.

The second book of *De la Sagesse* presents a discourse on the method for avoiding error and finding truth, in view of the human predicament. Charron's method closely resembles the one Descartes set forth later: examine all questions freely and dispassionately, keep prejudice and emotions out of all decisions, develop a universality of mind, and reject any decisions that are in the slightest degree dubious. This skeptical method, Charron claimed, is of greater service to religion than any other there may be. It leads us to reject all dubious opinions until our minds are "blank, naked and ready" to receive the divine revelation on faith alone. The complete skeptic will never be a heretic, since if he has no opinions, he cannot have the wrong ones. If God pleases to give him information, then he will have true knowledge. Until the skeptic receives the revelation, he should live by a *morale provisoire*, following nature. The last book of *De la Sagesse* presents this theory of natural morality, showing how one ought to live as a skeptic and a noble savage if one has no divine guidance.

De la Sagesse was one of the first important philosophical works to be written in a modern language and to present a moral theory apart from religious considerations. Some considered the work a basic didactic statement of Pyrrhonian skepticism, challenging both traditional philosophical claims to knowledge and religious ones and thus preparing the ground for a thoroughly naturalistic view of human nature and conduct. Charron claimed that the argument in *De la Sagesse* only represented part of his view, dealing with the human situation apart from divine guidance.

The over-all theory stated in his various works, his ecclesiastical career, and the piety expressed in his *Discours chrestiens* suggest that he was a sincere fideist, who saw skepticism as a means of destroying the enemies of the true faith while preparing the soul for salvation.

The problem of interpreting Charron's views involves a larger issue, that of assessing the purport of the revival of skepticism in the Renaissance and the relation of this revival to Reformation and Counter Reformation thought. Skeptical thought, perhaps, played several different and possibly incompatible roles in the period. Both then and now, skeptics like Charron could provide the "rationale" both for antirational fideism and for irreligious naturalism.

Works by Charron

There are no definitive modern editions of Charron's writings. The only edition of his complete works is *Toutes les oeuvres de Pierre Charron* (Paris, 1635). There are many editions of *Les Trois Veritez* up to 1625, several of the *Discours chrestiens* up to 1622, and a large number of *De la Sagesse* up to 1880. The earliest translations of *De la Sagesse* are those by Sam Lennard (London, 1st ed., 1615; 2d ed., 1697) and G. Stanhope (*Of Wisdom*, 1st ed., 1697; 2d ed., 1707). A bibliography of editions and translations of Charron's works appears in Jean Charron's *The "Wisdom" of Pierre Charron*, pp. 147–151 (see below).

Works on Charron

Bayle, Pierre, "Charron (Pierre)," in *Dictionnaire historique et critique*, 2 vols. Rotterdam, 1702.

Bremond, Henri, "La Folle 'Sagesse' de Pierre Charron." *Le Correspondant*, Vol. 252 (1913), 357–364.

Busson, Henri, *La Pensée religieuse française de Charron à Pascal.* Paris, 1933.

Charron, Jean, "Pierre Charron," in Nathan Edelman, ed., *A Critical Bibliography of French Literature*, Vol. III, *The Seventeenth Century*, pp. 476–478. Syracuse, N.Y., 1961. Annotated bibliography of works about Charron.

Charron, Jean, *The "Wisdom" of Pierre Charron, an Original and Orthodox Code of Morality.* University of North Carolina Studies in the Romance Languages and Literatures, No. 34. Chapel Hill, N.C., 1961.

Gray, Floyd, "Reflexions on Charron's Debt to Montaigne." *French Review*, Vol. 35 (1962), 377–382.

Julien-Eymard d'Angers, "Le Stoïcisme en France dans la première moitié du XVIIe siècle. Les Origines (1575–1616)." *Études franciscaines*, n.s. Vol. 2 (1951), 389–410.

Julien-Eymard d'Angers, *L'Apologétique en France de 1580 à 1670: Pascal et ses précurseurs.* Paris, 1954.

Popkin, Richard H., "Charron and Descartes: The Fruits of Systematic Doubt." *Journal of Philosophy*, Vol. 51 (1954), 831–837.

Popkin, Richard H., *The History of Scepticism from Erasmus to Descartes.* Assen, Neth., 1960 and 1963. See especially Ch. 3.

Rice, Eugene F., Jr., *The Renaissance Idea of Wisdom.* Harvard Historical Monographs, XXXVII. Cambridge, Mass., 1958. See also R. H. Popkin's review of this work in *Renaissance News*, Vol. 12 (1959), 265–269.

Sabrié, Jean B., *De l'Humanisme au rationalisme; Pierre Charron (1541–1603), l'homme, l'oeuvre, l'influence.* Paris, 1913.

Strowski, Fortunat, *Pascal et son temps*, Vol. I, *De Montaigne à Pascal*, pp. 159–210, Paris, 1907.

RICHARD H. POPKIN

CHARTRES, SCHOOL OF. A cathedral school existed at Chartres as early as the sixth century but did not become famous until the eleventh and twelfth centuries. Under Bishop Fulbert (d. 1028), a pupil of Gerbert of Aurillac, students, among them Berengar of Tours, flocked to Chartres to study the *trivium* and *quadrivium*, medicine and theology. Later, Bishop Ivo brought renown in canon law. The high point was reached in the early twelfth century under Bernard of Chartres and his brother Theodoric (Thierry) and their pupils Gilbert of Poitiers (de la Porrée), William of Conches, and Clarembald of Arras. Also associated with the school in various ways were Bernard of Tours, Adelard of Bath, Alan of Lille, and John of Salisbury. The Chartrains of this period were humanists who loved the literature and philosophy of classical antiquity. The richness of their program of studies is evident in Theodoric's *Heptateuch*, a handbook of the seven liberal arts and a collection of the authors who were read. In the early twelfth century Chartres was the center of Latin Platonism. Plato himself was known only indirectly through a fragment of the *Timaeus* in the translation and commentary of Chalcidius and through Macrobius, Apuleius, Seneca, and Boethius, whose *Opuscula Sacra* and *Consolatio Philosophiae* were much commented on. Devotion to Platonism produced realist interpretations of the problem of universals, speculations about the Ideas, matter and form, cosmological thought, and discussions about the world soul. Aristotle was generally less highly esteemed. The Chartrains knew only his logical writings (the *Organon*), including the *logica nova* (the rediscovered *Prior Analytics, Topics,* and *Sophistic Refutations*), which makes an early appearance in Theodoric's *Heptateuch.* Under the inspiration of Boethius, attempts were made to reconcile Aristotelianism and Platonism. Theology was presented largely in philosophical clothing. Confident of the harmony of faith and learning, the Chartrains attempted to establish the existence of God by numerical speculations, to synthesize Platonic cosmology and biblical revelation, and to compare the Platonic world soul with the Holy Spirit, as in William of Conches. God was considered to be the form of all being, a view which has been called pantheistic by some historians. Greek and Arabian writings on medicine, astronomy, and mathematics, including works by Hippocrates, Galen, Ptolemy, Euclid, al-Khwarizmi, Johannitius, and others were circulated and read in translation. In the early twelfth century Chartres was without a peer as a school of classical and humane learning and of Platonism, and it was rivaled in philosophy only by Paris. The bloom was fading fast by mid-century, but the influence of the school continued to be marked among the disciples of Gilbert of Poitiers, in thirteenth-century writings on natural philosophy, and still later in the works of Nicholas of Cusa.

Bibliography

Clerval, A., *Les Écoles de Chartres au moyen âge.* Paris, 1895.

Geyer, B., *Die patristische und scholastische Philosophie.* Basel, 1927, Pp. 226–252.

Gregory, T., *Anima Mundi. La filosofia di Guglielmo di Conches.* Florence, 1955.

Parent, J., *La Doctrine de la création dans l'école de Chartres.* Paris and Ottawa, 1938.

Wulf, M. de, *History of Mediaeval Philosophy*, translated by E. C. Messenger. London, 1952. Vol. I, pp. 173–188. Translation of *Histoire de la philosophie médiévale.* Louvain, 1934.

DAVID LUSCOMBE

CHATEAUBRIAND, FRANÇOIS RENÉ DE (1768–1848), French author, was born at Saint-Malo in Brittany and educated at Dol-de-Bretagne and Rennes in preparation for studying for the priesthood at the Collège de Dinan. Finding that he had no vocation, he followed the tradition of his social class and became an army officer instead. In 1788 he joined the order of the Knights of Malta, went to Paris, and began to associate with men of letters. From then on literature was his chief interest in life, though his literary career was paralleled by a career in diplomacy and politics. In 1803 he was appointed an attaché at the French embassy in Rome, and upon the return of Louis XVIII to power he played a role in politics in the Ministry of the Interior. His main diplomatic post was that of French plenipotentiary at the Congress of Verona, an account of which he published in 1838.

Chateaubriand's political as well as his religious views

were in a state of constant flux. As a young man he had been favorable to the revolution, but he was soon disillusioned and in 1792 went into voluntary exile in London. There he published his *Essai historique, politique et moral sur les révolutions*, which he later retracted. This work was clearly influenced by the Philosophes, especially Rousseau, and, though far from atheistic, was definitely favorable to deism and opposed to Christianity. As Sainte-Beuve showed a half century later in his *Causeries du Lundi*, the printed version of Chateaubriand's views was much less extreme than what he really thought. Having undergone a personal crisis when he learned of the death of his mother, he returned from exile in 1800 and began the preparation of one of his most famous works, *Le Génie du Christianisme*. The aim of the volume was to persuade the public that Christianity had as many themes worthy of artistic expression as paganism. It produced, said Sainte-Beuve, "a whole army of parlor Christians." This was precisely the goal of its author, to make Christianity fashionable.

In September 1816, Chateaubriand published his pamphlet *De la Monarchie selon la Charte*, which preached political liberalism in a constitutional monarchy. This brought on his temporary political ruin, but he soon recovered and was utilized by the government in various diplomatic posts. Toward the close of his life he developed an intimacy with Mme. Récamier and her circle but withdrew from politics and devoted himself to the preparation of his memoirs, the *Mémoires d'outre-tombe* (published posthumously in 1849).

Chateaubriand's contributions to French philosophy were indirect. The early *Essai sur les révolutions* made it clear that he considered any type of philosophy to be antireligious and religion to be a substitute for philosophy. In it he attempted to show that no philosophy could ever hope to reach the truth, for truth was discovered not by reasoning but by some inner light, a kind of feeling (*sentiment*), perhaps what Pascal called the heart. It was this belief that appeared in such works as *Atala*, where the theme of the Noble Savage is developed. Though Atala is herself a Christian, she is a Christian by sentiment, not by reason, and her form of Christianity was believed by her inventor to be higher and nobler than that deduced by argument.

Similarly, Chateaubriand anticipated Wordsworth in maintaining even as a young man that in the contemplation of nature, in the sense of the landscape, there is a spontaneous revelation of the truths of morality and religion. The famous passage "Night Among the American Savages," which terminates the *Essai* and was reprinted in part in the *Génie du Christianisme*, is not only a description of a moonlight scene near Niagara Falls but also an evocation of the nobility of soul which belongs only to men who have lived in a state of cultural primitivism far from the contamination of society. Like Rousseau, Chateaubriand pitted nature and society against each other, and it is significant that in this passage the Indians are only two women, two small children at the breast, and two warriors. There is no mention of a tribe or village. The sole contact these people have with anything outside themselves is with the "ocean of trees." But it is to be noted that far from reinforcing the sense of individuality, this contact, on the contrary, induces an absence of all distinct thoughts and feelings, a kind of mystical union with that God who is nature itself.

This type of anti-intellectualism reappeared in the *Génie du Christianisme*. Chateaubriand said in the preface to this work that he turned away from eighteenth-century liberalism when he learned of his mother's death. He was in exile in London at the time. "I wept," he wrote, "and I believed." The evidence of tears was proof of the truths of Catholicism, as in the *Essai* the feelings aroused by natural scenery were proofs of the truth of deism. But Catholicism is hardly a religion spontaneously kindled in the hearts of all men. It is a religion initiated and developed in society. Hence, Chateaubriand found himself aligned with the Traditionalists, a group as far from Rousseauistic sentimentalism as can be imagined. For whereas Joseph Marie de Maistre and the Vicomte de Bonald believed reason was the faculty that united men, the sentimentalists believed it was what divided them into conflicting sects.

It was perhaps for this reason that Chateaubriand emphasized the gifts Christianity had made to European culture. He wrote at the height of the Neoclassical movement, when the masters were Jacques Delille in poetry, Antonio Canova in sculpture, and Jacques Louis David in painting. They, of course, found their inspiration in classical mythology and history. Chateaubriand tried to prove that there was more to be found in the Catholic tradition. However true this may have been, the point he was making was that to the extent that any set of beliefs increases the amount of beauty and goodness in the world, that set of beliefs is true. There is a concealed pragmatic test here that is of interest historically and would probably not be able to resist criticism. But at a time when men had lived through a period of horror brought on by the suppression of religion, it was understandable that they should attribute the horrors to the philosophy they believed had generated the antireligious practices. To Chateaubriand at this time the one alternative to philosophy was Catholicism, not that natural religion which he had lauded in the *Essai*. And this belief he never abandoned. He was not the type of writer to set down a body of premises from which he would deduce certain inferences. On the contrary, his hatred of philosophy was such that he simply stated his conclusions as his heart dictated; it remained for others to disentangle the form of his argument. He established a cultural atmosphere rather than a set of doctrines, and his works are more properly viewed as long poems of a purely lyrical nature than as doctrinal treatises.

Works by Chateaubriand

Oeuvres complètes, 20 vols. Paris, 1858–1861. Introduction by C. A. Sainte-Beuve.

Essai historique, politique et moral sur les révolutions. London, 1797.

Le Génie du Christianisme. Paris, 1802. See especially the preface.

Les Martyrs. Paris, 1809.

Works on Chateaubriand

Bertrin, Abbé Georges, *La Sincérité religieuse de Chateaubriand*. Paris, 1899.

Chinard, G., *L'Exotisme américain dans l'oeuvre de Chateaubriand.* Paris, 1918.

Sainte-Beuve, C. A., "Chateaubriand, anniversaire du Génie du Christianisme," in *Causeries du Lundi*, Vol. X, pp. 74–90. Paris, 1855.

Sainte-Beuve, C. A., *Chateaubriand et son groupe littéraire sous l'Empire.* Paris, 1869.

GEORGE BOAS

CH'ENG HAO (1032–1085), also called Ch'eng Ming-tao, was cofounder, with his brother Ch'eng I, of the Neo-Confucian school of Nature and Principle (*li*). He held some minor official posts but devoted most of his life to teaching.

By making principle the foundation of his philosophy and identifying it with the nature of man and things, Ch'eng Hao and his brother set the pattern for the Neo-Confucian philosophical movement known since the eleventh century as the school of Nature and Principle. To Ch'eng Hao principle was the principle of nature (*t'ien li*), a concept which he evolved himself; it was the natural law. It had all the characteristics of principle as conceived by Ch'eng I, but as the principle of nature it was self-existent and unalterable. Whereas Ch'eng I stressed the doctrine that principle is one but its manifestations are many, Ch'eng Hao emphasized more strongly the principle of production and reproduction as the chief characteristic of nature. To him the spirit of life was in all things. This creative quality was *jen*, the highest good. In man, *jen* becomes humanity, or love, which makes him the moral being he is. It enables him to embrace all things and heaven and earth as one body.

Whatever is produced in man, that is, whatever is inborn in him, is his nature. In its original, tranquil state, human nature is neither good nor evil. The distinction arises when human nature is aroused and manifested in feelings and actions and when these feelings and actions abide by or deviate from the mean. The chief task of moral and spiritual cultivation is to calm one's nature through absolute impartiality and the identification of internal and external life. To achieve this end Ch'eng Hao advocated sincerity and seriousness.

There can be no denying that Ch'eng Hao was the more idealistic and his brother the more rationalistic. Ch'eng Hao more or less concentrated on self-cultivation, whereas his brother advocated both seriousness and learning. Under the influence of Buddhism Ch'eng Hao also advocated quietism. The two brothers had vastly different temperaments and therefore showed divergent tendencies, but it is not true, as some scholars claim, that one was monistic and the other dualistic.

Bibliography

Chan, Wing-tsit, *A Source Book in Chinese Philosophy.* Princeton, N.J., 1963.

Fung Yu-lan, *A History of Chinese Philosophy*, translated by Derk Bodde, Vol. II. Princeton, N.J., 1953.

Graham, A. G., *Two Chinese Philosophers, Ch'eng Ming-tao and Ch'eng Yi-ch'uan.* London, 1958.

WING-TSIT CHAN

CH'ENG I (1033–1107), or Ch'eng I-ch'uan, was the most outstanding Chinese teacher of his time, a lecturer to the emperor on Confucian classics, and cofounder, with his brother Ch'eng Hao, of the Neo-Confucian school of principle (*li*) that dominated Chinese thought for many centuries.

The central concept of the school is principle. The concept, negligible in ancient Confucianism, had been developed by the Neo-Taoists and Buddhists, but the Ch'eng brothers were the first to build their philosophy primarily on it. To them, principle is self-evident and self-sufficient, extending everywhere and governing all things. It is laid before our very eyes. It cannot be augmented or diminished. It is many, but it is essentially one, for "definite principles" are but principle. "Principle is one but its manifestations are many." It is universal truth, universal order, universal law. Most important of all, it is the universal principle of creation. It is dynamic and vital. Man and all things form one body because all of them share this principle. It is identical with the mind and with the nature of man and things. Since principle is principle of creation and since life-giving is good, principle is the source of goodness. To be good is to obey principle. Thus, principle is both natural and moral and both general and specific. It has meaning as an abstract reality, but more so as the moral law of man.

The relation between principle and material force, which actualizes things, is not a dualistic one. Although Ch'eng I said that "material force exists after physical form and is therefore with it whereas the Way [principle] exists before form and is therefore without it," he also said that "what makes yin and yang [material force] is the Way." Material force is the physical aspect of principle. In the process of creation each operation is new, for material force is perpetually generated by Origination. (Origination is comparable to creation, except that it is natural and self-caused and is not an act of any being.)

To understand principle one can study one thing intensively or many things extensively. One can also read books, study history, or handle human affairs, for all things and affairs, including blades of grass, possess principle. This intellectual approach makes Ch'eng's system strongly rationalistic. The approach, however, is balanced by the moral, for whereas "the pursuit of learning depends on the extension of knowledge," "self-cultivation requires seriousness." This dual emphasis reminds one of the Buddhist twofold formula of meditation (dhyana) and wisdom (prajna).

Bibliography

The works of Ch'eng I are in *Erh-Ch'eng ch'üan-shu* ("The Complete Works of the Two Ch'engs"). Translations of some of them appear in Wing-tsit Chan, *Source Book in Chinese Philosophy* (Princeton, N.J., 1963), Chs. 31–32.

For secondary sources treating Ch'eng I and Ch'eng Hao together, see the bibliography for CH'ENG HAO.

WING-TSIT CHAN

CH'ENG MING-TAO. *See* CH'ENG HAO.

CH'ENG YI-CH'UAN. *See* CH'ENG I.

CHERNYSHEVSKI, NIKOLAI GAVRILOVICH (1828–1889), Russian literary and social critic, was the guiding spirit of Russian nihilism and a major representative of positivistic materialism in nineteenth-century Russian philosophy.

Chernyshevski was born in Saratov, Russia. The son of an Orthodox priest, he attended a theological seminary before entering the University of St. Petersburg in 1846. After his graduation in 1850, he taught secondary school in Saratov until 1853, when he returned to St. Petersburg, secured a master's degree in Russian literature, and began writing for leading reviews. He soon became a principal editor of *Sovremennik* ("The Contemporary"), and by the early 1860s was the foremost spokesman of radical socialist thought in Russia. Arrested in 1862, he was banished to Siberia in 1864 and passed the remaining 25 years of his life in forced exile. He was permitted to return to Saratov, in failing health, a few months before his death.

In his student days Chernyshevski was attracted to the writings of the French socialists and of Hegel and the left-wing Hegelians. In 1849 he read Ludwig Feuerbach's *Essence of Christianity* and by 1850 had formed an allegiance to Feuerbach that was decisive in his philosophical development. He was also influenced by the English utilitarians, notably John Stuart Mill, whose *Principles of Political Economy* he translated into Russian in 1860.

Chernyshevski's master's dissertation and first philosophical work, *Esteticheskiye Otnosheniya Iskusstva k Deystvitelnosti* ("The Aesthetic Relation of Art to Reality," St. Petersburg, 1855), is a critique of Hegelian aesthetics "deduced" (as Chernyshevski later expressed it) from Feuerbach's naturalistic principles. Chernyshevski argued that art is an aesthetically inferior substitute for concrete reality. The essential purpose of art is to reproduce the phenomena of real life that are of interest to man, compensating for his lack of opportunity to experience the reality itself. The derivative purposes of art, which give it a moral dimension, are to explain this reality for the benefit of man and to pass judgment upon it. Chernyshevski developed his aesthetic views further, emphasizing the social context of art, in his *Ocherki Gogolevskovo Perioda Russkoy Literatury* (St. Petersburg, 1855–1856; translated as *Essays on the Gogol Period of Russian Literature*).

In his chief philosophical work, a long essay entitled *Antropologicheski Printsip v Filosofii* ("The Anthropological Principle in Philosophy," 1860), Chernyshevski exhibited his acceptance of Feuerbach's anthropologism and adopted the materialistic position he retained throughout his life. By "the anthropological principle" Chernyshevski meant the conception of man as a unitary organism whose nature is not bifurcated into "spiritual" and "material" elements. He argued that philosophical questions can be resolved only from this point of view and by the methods of the natural sciences. Indeed, in all their essentials such questions had already been resolved by the sciences, according to Chernyshevski: man is a complex chemical compound whose behavior is strictly subject to the law of causality, who in every action seeks his own pleasure, and whose character is determined by the features of the environment within which he is obliged to act.

On this basis Chernyshevski advocated "rational egoism"—an ethical theory of enlightened egoistic utilitarianism—and maintained that radical reconstruction of the social environment is needed to create happy and productive individuals. He portrayed these "new people" and the socialist order of the future in a novel, *Chto Delat* (*What Is to Be Done?*, St. Petersburg, 1863), which was the principal literary tract of Russian nihilism and was for decades enormously influential in the radical movement. In his socioeconomic thought in general Chernyshevski emphasized the peasant commune and the artel and is considered an important forerunner of Russian Populism.

Chernyshevski was a severe critic of Neo-Kantian phenomenalism. In a number of letters and in the essay *Kharakter Chelovecheskovo Znaniya* ("The Character of Human Knowledge," Moscow, 1885), written in exile, he espoused epistemological realism and condemned the skepticism and "illusionism" (as he called it) of such scientists as Virchow and Du Bois-Reymond.

Works by Chernyshevski

Izbrannyye Filosofskiye Sochineniya ("Selected Philosophical Works"). 3 vols. Moscow, 1950–1951.

Polnoye Sobraniye Sochineni ("Complete Works"). 16 vols. Moscow, 1939–1953.

Selected Philosophical Essays. Moscow, 1953.

What Is to Be Done?, translated by Benjamin R. Tucker. Boston, 1886; abridged, New York, 1961.

Works on Chernyshevski

Plekhanov, G., *N. G. Tschernischewsky.* Stuttgart, 1894.

Steklov, Y. M., *N. G. Chernyshevsky, Yevo Zhizn' i Deyatel'nost'.* 2 vols. Moscow, 1928.

Venturi, Franco, *Il populismo russo.* 2 vols. Turin, 1952. Translated by Francis Haskell as *Roots of Revolution.* New York, 1960.

Zenkovsky, V. V., *Istoriya Russkoi Filosofii.* 2 vols. Paris, 1948–1950. Translated by George L. Kline as *A History of Russian Philosophy.* 2 vols. New York and London, 1953.

JAMES P. SCANLAN

CHICHERIN, BORIS NIKOLAYEVICH (1828–1904), Russian philosopher, was educated at Moscow University, where he studied under both K. D. Kavelin and T. N. Granovsky. Until 1868 he was a professor at Moscow University; he also served briefly as tutor to the royal family and as mayor of Moscow (1881–1883). He was cautiously liberal in politics and, after an early period of agnosticism, devoutly Russian Orthodox in religion.

Chicherin wrote substantial critical studies of Vladimir Solovyov (1880) and Auguste Comte (1892), as well as several works on philosophy of law and on the state. His ethical individualism, like that of N. I. Kareyev, was close to Kant's, but, unlike Kareyev, Chicherin was an orthodox Hegelian in logic, ontology, and philosophy of history. This eclecticism generated an unresolved tension in his thought. On the one hand Chicherin asserted that great men are merely "organs and instruments of a universal spirit" and that, under certain conditions, a nationality (*narodnost*) "may become an individual person." On the other hand he insisted that man as a rational creature and "bearer of the Absolute" is an end in himself and must not be "treated as a mere instrument."

Chicherin asserted, with N. K. Mikhailovski, that "not society, but individuals, think, feel, and desire"; he opposed the "monstrous notion" that society is a higher organism, an all-devouring Moloch, whose function is "to make mankind happy by putting it in chains." Chicherin was alert to encroachments by the social and political spheres on the private and personal realm; he saw the individual—the "foundation-stone of the entire social edifice"—as a single spiritual substance, possessed of reason and free will, and hence of a moral worth and dignity that demand respect.

Chicherin saw the dialectical movement of both thought and being as a passage from initial unity to final multiplicity, through the two intermediary stages of relation and combination. Thus, more explicitly than Hegel, he converted the dialectical triad into a tetrad.

Bibliography

Two of Chicherin's works, *Polozhitelnaya Filosofiya i Yedinstvo Nauki* ("Positive Philosophy and the Unity of Science," Moscow, 1892) and *Osnovaniya Logiki i Metafiziki* ("Foundations of Logic and Metaphysics," Moscow, 1894), have been translated as *Philosophische Forschungen* (Heidelberg, 1899). Chicherin's *Filosofiya Prava* ("Philosophy of Law") was published in Moscow in 1900.

For discussion of Chicherin, see V. V. Zenkovsky, *Istoriya Russkoi Filosofii,* 2 vols. (Paris, 1948 and 1950), translated by G. L. Kline as *A History of Russian Philosophy,* 2 vols. (London and New York, 1953), pp. 606–620.

GEORGE L. KLINE

CHINESE PHILOSOPHY. In its 2,500 years of evolution Chinese philosophy has passed through four periods: the ancient period (until 221 B.C.), when the so-called Hundred Schools contended; the middle period (221 B.C.–A.D. 960), when Confucianism emerged supreme in the social and political spheres, only to be overshadowed in philosophy first by Neo-Taoism and then by Buddhism; the modern period (960–1900), when Neo-Confucianism was the uncontested philosophy, although by no means without variety or conflicts of its own; and the contemporary period (from 1912), when Neo-Confucianism, having become decadent and being challenged by Western philosophy, first succumbed to it, then was revived and reconstructed, but at mid century was overwhelmed by Marxism.

ANCIENT PERIOD: HUNDRED SCHOOLS (UNTIL 221 B.C.)

The Hundred Schools, which included individual agriculturalists, diplomatists, military strategists, and other independent thinkers, had one thing in common, their primary concern with man both as an individual and as a member of society. This humanistic note was dominant from the earliest times and characterized all schools. The most prominent of the schools were the Confucianists, the Taoists, the Moists, the Logicians, the Yin Yang school, and the Legalists.

Chinese thought at the dawn of civilization was dominated by the fear of spiritual beings. During the Shang dynasty (1751–1112 B.C.) the Chinese would do nothing important without first finding out, through divination, the pleasure of the spirits. But when the Chou overthrew the Shang, in 1112 B.C., human talent was needed to consolidate the newly established kingdom and to fight the surrounding barbarians. Human skill in irrigation proved to be more effective than praying to the spirits for rain. And the tribal anthropomorphic Lord (*ti*), who controlled human destiny at his whim, was now replaced by impartial and universal Heaven (*T'ien*). The Mandate of Heaven (divine election) for the House of Chou to rule rested on the moral ground that rule belongs to the man of virtue. In the final analysis, it was man's ability and virtue that counted. Humanism had reached a high pitch.

Confucian school. The person who elevated humanism to the highest degree was Confucius (551–479 B.C.). His central concerns were the "superior man" and a well-ordered society. Up to his time the ideal man was the aristocrat, the *chun-tzu* (literally, "son of a ruler") a perfectly natural concept in a feudal society. In a radical departure from the past, Confucius formulated an entirely new ideal, the superior man, one who is wise, humane, and courageous, who is motivated by righteousness instead of profit, and who "studies the Way [Tao] and loves men." This conception of the superior man has never changed in the Confucian tradition.

Nature of the individual. Confucius never explained how it is possible for one to become a superior man. He seemed to imply that man is good by nature, but he said only that "by nature men are alike but through practice they have become far apart." It was necessary to explain how we know that man can be good. Mencius (c. 372–c. 298 B.C.), one of his two major followers, supplied that explanation. From the facts that all children know how to love their parents and that a man seeing a child about to fall into a well will instinctively try to save him, Mencius concluded that man's nature is originally good, possessing the "Four Beginnings"—humanity (*jen*), righteousness (*i*), propriety (*li*), and wisdom—and the innate knowledge of the good and the innate ability to do good. Evil is due not to one's nature but to bad environment, lack of education, and "casting oneself away." The superior man is one who "develops his mind to the utmost" and "nourishes his nature."

Hsün Tzu (c. 313–c. 238 B.C.), although holding essentially the same idea of the superior man, contended that the original nature of man is evil. He argued that by nature man seeks for gain and is envious. Because conflict and strife inevitably follow, rules of propriety and righteousness have been formulated to control evil and to train men to be good. Propriety and righteousness are not native moral characteristics of man but the artificial efforts of sages. Thus, Hsün Tzu was directly opposed to Mencius. Nevertheless, both were truly Confucian because their central objective was the good man.

Nature of society. Confucius wanted a society governed by men of virtue who, through personal examples and moral persuasion rather than law or punishment, would bring about the people's welfare and social order. Mencius, applying his theory of original goodness, reasoned that if a ruler applies his originally humane mind to the administration of his government, he will have a humane government, and what Confucius desired will naturally ensue. Hsün Tzu, on the other hand, felt that since man's nature is evil, he needs rulers to regulate him by law and teachers to guide him by rules of propriety and righteousness. Once more he and Mencius were opposed, but again they aimed at the same thing—namely, a well-ordered society.

Relation of the individual and society. The Confucian school, then, is devoted to the harmonious development of the individual and society. This theme is systematically presented in the little classic *The Great Learning,* traditionally ascribed to the Confucian pupil Tseng Tzu (505–c. 436 B.C.). It consists of eight successive steps: the investigation of things, the extension of knowledge, the sincerity of the will, the rectification of the mind, the cultivation of the personal life, the regulation of the family, national order, and world peace. The goal is a harmonious world in which man and society are well developed and adjusted.

The harmony of the individual and society rests on several basic ideas. Foremost of these is humanity (*jen*). Confucius discussed humanity more than any other subject, and throughout history it has remained one of the key concepts in Confucianism. Previously the term connoted particular virtues, such as kindness, benevolence, and affection. Confucius interpreted it to mean the general virtue, the foundation of all particular virtues. Humanity is the moral character, which enables man to attain true manhood. The moral character is developed in oneself and in one's relations with others. A man of *jen,* "wishing to establish his own character, also establishes the character of others." Thus, *jen* has two aspects, conscientiousness (*chung*) and altruism (*shu*).

Following Confucius, Mencius stressed humanity. But he almost always mentioned humanity and righteousness (*i*) together, the first in the Confucian school to do so. By this time a clear distinction between what is good, correct, or proper and what is evil, incorrect, or improper had to be made. He wanted the innate sense of correctness fully exercised. Hsün Tzu felt the same necessity to define correctness, but he sought to achieve this end through the precision of and distinctions made in law, rules of propriety, and music.

Another idea behind the harmony of the individual and society is the rectification of names. For Confucius it meant verifying or implementing an exact correspondence between titles of rank and actual fulfillment of responsibilities. Mencius, however, took "rectification" to mean correcting errors in one's heart (moral errors). Hsün Tzu gave it a logical interpretation. To him rectification was distinguishing the concepts of names and actualities, similarities and differences, and particularity and generality. In doing this he developed the only logical aspect, in the formal sense, of ancient Confucianism. Confucius, Mencius, and Hsün Tzu all believed that when names are rectified the positions of the individual and society will be well adjusted.

The third concept basic to social harmony is the mean (*chung-yung*). By this Confucius chiefly meant moderation as a guide to human action, but he implicitly referred to the ideals of centrality and harmony as well. The reference to centrality and harmony was greatly elaborated in the classic *The Doctrine of the Mean,* traditionally ascribed to Confucius' grandson Tzu-ssu (492–431 B.C.). Centrality (*chung*) consists in not deviating from the mean, and harmony (*yung*) exists in the common, the ordinary, and the universal. Centrality in the individual is the state of equilibrium in one's mind before the feelings are aroused, and harmony is the state after they are aroused. In society centrality and harmony together mean complete concord in human relations. Ultimately, through the moral principle, heaven and earth will attain their proper order and all things will flourish in a harmonious universal operation. At this point the doctrine of the mean assumed metaphysical significance, which made it a profound influence on Neo-Confucianism.

When the individual behaves correctly and society operates in the right manner, the Way is said to prevail. The Way (Tao) is the moral law, or moral order. It is the Way of Heaven. Heaven was no longer conceived of as the anthropomorphic Lord (*ti*), the greatest of all spiritual beings. To Confucius, Heaven was the origin of all things the Supreme Reality, whose purposive character is manifested in the Way. The Supreme Being only reigns, leaving the Way to operate by itself. But no one can be separated from this Way, and for the Way to be meaningful it must be demonstrated by man. "It is man that can make the Way great," Confucius said. The note of humanism was sounded again.

Taoist school. To the Confucian school Tao was a system of moral truth, the expression of Heaven. To the Taoist school, however, it was Nature itself. Lao Tzu (c. sixth century B.C.), the founder of the school, equated Tao with Heaven, the "self-so" (*tzu-jan*), and the One. It is eternal, spontaneous, nameless, and indescribable, at once the beginning of all things and the way in which they pursue their course. It is nonbeing, not in the sense of nothingness but in the sense of not being any particular thing. It is absolute and mystical. When it is possessed by an individual thing, it becomes that thing's character or virtue (*te*). The ideal life of the individual, the ideal order of society, and the ideal type of government are all based on it and guided by it. As the way of life it denotes simplicity, spontaneity, tranquillity, weakness, and, most important of all, nonaction (*wu-wei*), or, rather, letting Nature take its own course. Lao Tzu's concept of Tao was so radically different from those of other schools that his school alone eventually came to be known as the Taoist school (Tao-chia).

Chuang Tzu (born c. 369 B.C.), Lao Tzu's chief follower, took a step forward and interpreted Tao as the Way of unceasing transformation. In so doing he gave Tao a dynamic character. In the universal process of constant flux all things are equalized from the point of view of Tao. At the same time, since everything transforms in its own way, its individual nature is to be respected. Thus, in the ideas of Chuang Tzu there is a curious combination of universality and particularity, a point that had far-reaching effect on later Taoist developments.

Although the Taoist school was definitely more transcendental than the Confucian, its chief concern, like that of the Confucian school, was man. Lao Tzu discoursed mainly on government, and Chuang Tzu discussed at great length the way to find spiritual freedom and peace. There is no desertion of society or the individual in Taoism.

The dominant notes in the Taoist school were, however, oneness and naturalness. It is not surprising that the Taoists strongly attacked other schools, particularly the Confucian, for making distinctions of all kinds. But so far as interest in man and society was concerned, the school agreed with the Confucian and other schools.

Moist school. The Taoist school in time became strong enough to compete with Confucianism, but in the ancient period it was the Moist school, founded by Mo Tzu (c. 468–c. 376 B.C.), that rivaled Confucianism in prominence. In practically all its major doctrines it stood opposed to Confucianism. The most serious and irreconcilable issue was that between the Moist doctrine of universal love and the Confucian doctrine of love with distinctions. Mo Tzu wanted people to love other people's parents as they love their own, whereas the Confucianists, especially Mencius, insisted that although one should show love to all, one should show special affection to his own parents. Otherwise there would be no difference between other people's parents and one's own, and family relationships would collapse.

In further opposition Mo Tzu condemned religious rites and musical festivals as economically wasteful; the Confucianists held that ceremonies and music are necessary to provide proper expression and restraint in social behavior. This conflict on the practical level stemmed from the fundamental opposition of utilitarianism and moralism. In this issue, as in the issue of universal versus graded love, Mo Tzu justified his doctrines on the basis of "benefits to Heaven, to spiritual beings, and to all men."

Mo Tzu also attacked the Confucianists' teaching of humanity (*jen*) and righteousness (*i*), for advocating them but for failing to recognize that humanity and righteousness originated with Heaven. As he repeatedly said, it is the will of Heaven that man should practice humanity and righteousness, be economical, and practice universal love, and it is man's duty to obey the will of Heaven. Of all the ancient schools only the Moist placed ethics on a religious basis.

Logicians. The Moist doctrine of universal love was subscribed to by the Logicians. Their main interest, however, lay in a discussion of names and actualities. The school was small and has left little imprint, if any, on subsequent Chinese intellectual history. But it was the only school devoted to such metaphysical problems as existence, relativity, space, time, quality, actuality, and causes. Its most outstanding scholars were Hui Shih (c. 380–c. 305 B.C.) and Kung-sun Lung (born 380 B.C.). To Hui Shih things were relative, but to Kung-sun Lung they were absolute. The former emphasized change, whereas the latter stressed universality and permanence. The Logicians employed metaphysical and epistemological concepts that were primitive and crude, but they were the only group in ancient China interested in these concepts for their own sake.

Yin Yang school. While the schools mentioned above were thriving, the Yin Yang school prevailed and influenced all of them. We know nothing about its origin or early representatives, but its ideas are simple and clear. Basically, it conceived of two cosmic forces, one yin, which is negative, passive, weak, and disintegrative, and the other yang, which is positive, active, strong, and integrative. All things are produced through the interaction of the two. Associated with the theory of yin and yang is that of the five agents, or elements (*wu-hsing*)—metal, wood, water, fire, and earth. According to this theory things succeed one another as the five agents take their turns. Originally the two doctrines were separate. It is generally believed that Tsou Yen (305–240 B.C.), the representative thinker of the Yin Yang school, was the one who combined the interaction of yin and yang with the rotation of the five agents.

Yin and yang were at first conceived as opposed to each other, succeeding each other, or complementary to each other. The five agents, too, were conceived as overcoming one another or producing one another. Eventually all alternatives were synthesized so that harmony reigns over conflict and unity exists in multiplicity. Yin, yang, and the five agents are forces, powers, and agents rather than material elements. The whole focus is on process, order, and laws of operation. Existence is viewed as a dynamic process of change obeying definite laws, following definite patterns, and based on a pre-established harmony.

One implication of this doctrine is the correspondence and at the same time the unity of man and Nature, for both are governed by the same process. Another is that the universe is a systematic, structural one, determinate, describable, and even predictable. Still another implication is that the universe is a perpetual process of rotation. Just as the five agents rotate, so history proceeds in cycles, and just as yin and yang increase and decrease, so things rise and fall. The Yin Yang school, more than any other, put Chinese ethical and social teachings on a cosmological basis. Generally speaking, its ideas have affected every aspect of Chinese life, be it metaphysics, art, marriage, or even cooking. Wherever harmony is sought or change takes place, the forces of yin and yang are at work.

Legalist school. Philosophically the Legalist school is the least important because it had no new concept to offer. In fact, it did not concern itself with ethical, metaphysical, or logical concepts, as other schools do. Its chief objective was the concentration of power in the ruler. Within the Legalist school there were three tendencies—the enforcement of law with heavy reward and punishment, the manipulation of statecraft, and the exercise of power. The school, called Fa-chia (meaning school of law) in Chinese, had many representatives, some of them prime ministers, but the most outstanding was Han Fei Tzu (died 233 B.C.), who combined the three tendencies of his school.

The Legalist school assumed the evil nature of man and rejected moral values in favor of concrete results. In insisting that laws be applicable to all, it unwittingly subscribed to the doctrine of the equality of all men, and in insisting that assignments be fulfilled with concrete results, it strengthened the doctrine of the correspondence of names and actualities. There is no doubt that compared to other schools, it looked to circumstances rather than principles and to the present rather than the past. It agreed with them in one respect, that life is in a process of constant change.

The Legalists helped the Ch'in to liquidate the feudal states and establish a new dynasty in 221 B.C. The Ch'in enforced the Legalists' totalitarian philosophy, suppressed other schools, and burned their books in 213 B.C. The contest of the Hundred Schools now came to an end.

MIDDLE PERIOD (221 B.C.–A.D. 960)

The Legalists ruled the Ch'in with absolute power and tolerated no other schools, but other schools were by no means totally absent from the scene. When the dynasty was overthrown by the Han in 206 B.C., some of these schools re-emerged, carrying with them a crosscurrent of thought. The result was a syncretic movement.

Syncretic Confucianism. Confucianism became the state ideology in 136 B.C. It was supreme in government, society, education, and literature and remained so until the twentieth century. But philosophically it was almost overwhelmed by the doctrine of yin and yang. This can readily be seen in the philosophies of the *Book of Changes* and Tung Chung-shu.

The *Book of Changes* (*I Ching*) is a Confucian classic, but the Taoists also made much use of it. (Tradition ascribes part of the work to Confucius, but it was most probably composed several centuries later, although portions may have been in existence in Confucius' lifetime.) It shows the strong impact of the Yin Yang school. According to the *Book of Changes* creation of the world begins with the Great Ultimate (*t'ai-chi*), which engenders yin and yang. Yin and yang, in their turn, give rise to the four forms of major and minor yin and yang. The four forms produce the eight elements (*pa-kua*), which, through interaction and multiplication, produce the universe. The cosmogony is naive and elementary, but it introduced into Confucianism the strong features of Taoist naturalism and the interaction of yin and yang. Since then the Confucianists have viewed the universe as a natural and well-coordinated system in which the process of change never ceases.

The syncretic spirit was also strong in Tung Chung-shu (176–104 B.C.), the most outstanding Confucian philosopher of the period. He combined the Confucian doctrines of ethics and history with the ideas of yin and yang. Greed and humanity, the two foremost moral qualities, he correlated with yin and yang, respectively. Likewise, he equated human nature and feelings with yang and yin and thereby with good and evil. All things are grouped into pairs or into sets of five to correspond to yin and yang and the five agents. Ultimately they are reduced to numbers. In this arrangement historical periods parallel the succession of the five agents, and man, the microcosm, corresponds to Nature, the macrocosm. But Tung went beyond the idea of mere correspondence. To him, things of the same kind activate each other. There is the universal phenomenon of mutual activation and influence that makes the universe a dynamic, organic whole.

Unfortunately, this doctrine soon degenerated into superstition. Early in the Han dynasty (206 B.C.–A.D. 220) there was a wide belief in prodigies, which were taken to be influences of Nature on man or vice versa. Wang Ch'ung (A.D. 27–c. 100), an independent thinker, revolted against this. He declared that Heaven (Nature) takes no action and that natural events, including prodigies, occur spontaneously. Man is an insignificant being in the vast universe, and he does not influence Nature or become a ghost at death to influence people. In addition, Wang Ch'ung insisted that any theory must be tested by concrete evidence, and he supported his own theories with numerous facts. Thus, he raised rationalistic naturalism to a height never before reached in Chinese history and prepared for the advent of rationalistic and naturalistic Neo-Taoism, which was to replace Confucian philosophy.

Neo-Taoism. Under the influence of the doctrine of the correspondence of man and Nature and the belief in prodigies, Han dynasty thinkers were chiefly concerned with phenomena. Thinkers of the Wei-Chin period (220–420), however, went beyond phenomena to find reality behind space and time. They were interested in what is profound and abstruse (*hsüan*), and consequently their school is called Hsüan-hsüeh ("profound studies") or the Metaphysical school. They developed their doctrines in their commentaries on the *Lao Tzu*, the *Chuang Tzu*, and the *Book of Changes*, the "three profound studies." To Wang Pi (226–249), the most brilliant Neo-Taoist, ultimate reality is original nonbeing (*pen-wu*). It is not nothingness but the pure being, original substance, which transcends all distinctions and descriptions. It is whole and strong. And it is always correct because it is in accord with principle (*li*), the universal rational principle that unites all particular concepts and events. The note of principle was a new one. It anticipated Neo-Confucianism, which is based entirely on it.

Kuo Hsiang (died 312), another famous Neo-Taoist, developed his theory in his comments on Chuang Tzu's doctrine of self-transformation. To Kuo Hsiang, things transform themselves according to principle, but each and every thing has its own principle. Everything is therefore self-sufficient, and there is no need for an over-all original reality to combine or govern them, as Wang Pi believed. Whereas Wang Pi emphasized nonbeing, the one, and transcendence, Kuo Hsiang emphasized being, the many, and immanence.

As a movement Neo-Taoism did not last long, but its effect on later philosophy was great. It raised the Taoist concepts of being and nonbeing to a higher level and thereby formed the bridge between Chinese and Buddhist philosophies.

Buddhism. In the first several centuries Buddhism existed in China as a popular religion rather than as a philosophy. When Buddhists came into contact with the Chinese literati, especially the Neo-Taoists, in the third century, they matched Buddhist concepts with those of Taoism, identifying *Tathatā* (Thusness, *Nirvāṇa*) with the Taoist "original nonbeing," for example. Under Neo-Taoist influence, early Buddhist schools in China all engaged in discussions on being and nonbeing.

Middle Doctrine and Dharma Character. The problems of being and nonbeing largely characterize the two major Buddhist schools that developed in China in the sixth century, the Middle Doctrine (Chung-lun), or Three Treatise (San-lun), school and the Dharma Character (Fa-hsiang), or Consciousness Only (Wei-shih), school. The Middle Doctrine school, systematized by Chi-tsang (549–623), was based on three Indian scriptures—the *Mādhyamika Śāstra* ("Treatise on the Middle Doctrine"), by Nāgārjuna (c. 100–200), the *Dvādaśamikāya Śāstra* ("Twelve Gates Treatise"), also by Nāgārjuna, and the *Śata Śāstra* ("One Hundred Verses Treatise"), by Āryadeva (exact dates unknown), a pupil of Nāgārjuna. This school regarded both being and nonbeing as extremes whose opposition must be resolved in a synthesis. The synthesis, itself a new extreme with its own antithesis, needs to be synthesized also. In the end all oppositions are dissolved in the True Middle or emptiness. The school was essentially nihilistic and is often called the school of Nonbeing.

In contrast, the Consciousness Only school, which was founded by Hsüan-tsang (596–664), regarded all dharmas (elements of existence) and their characters—that is, the phenomenal world—as real, although only to a certain degree because they are illusory, apparent, and dependent. The school divides the mind into eight consciousnesses, the last of which contains "seeds" or effects of previous deeds and thoughts that affect future deeds and thoughts. Future deeds and thoughts are "transformations" of present ones, and present ones are "transformations" of past ones. When an individual attains perfect wisdom all transformations are transcended. In these transformations dharmas are produced. Some, the products of imagination, have only illusory existence. Others have dependent existence because they depend on causes for their production. But those of the "nature of perfect reality" have true existence. Since the school accepts dharmas and their character as real, it is often called the school of Being.

In spite of the fact that their basic problems of being and nonbeing are Chinese, the two schools were essentially no more than Indian schools transplanted to Chinese soil. They lacked the spirit of synthesis and were too extreme for the Chinese, and they declined after a few centuries, a relatively short time compared to other schools. In the meantime the Chinese spirit of synthesis asserted itself, notably in the T'ien-t'ai (Heavenly Terrace) and Hua-yen (Flower Splendor) schools.

T'ien-t'ai. According to the T'ien-t'ai school, which was founded by Chih-i (538–597) in the T'ien-t'ai Mountains, dharmas are empty because they have no self-nature and depend on causes for production. This is the Truth of Emptiness. But since they are produced, they do possess temporary and dependent existence. This is the Truth of Temporary Truth. Thus, dharmas are both empty and temporary. This is the Truth of the Mean. Each truth involves the other two so that three are one and one is three. This mutual identification is the true state of all dharmas. In the realm of temporary truth—that is, the phenomenal world—all realms of existence, whether of Buddhas, men, or beasts, and all characters of being, such as cause, effect, and substance, involve one another, so that each element, even an instant of thought, involves the entire universe. This all-is-one-and-one-is-all philosophy is expressed in the famous saying "Every color or fragrance is none other than the Middle Path."

Hua-yen. In the same spirit of synthesis, the Hua-yen school, established by Fa-tsang (596–664), propagated the doctrine of the universal causation of the realm of dharmas. This realm is fourfold. It contains the realm of facts, the realm of principle, the realm of principle and facts harmonized, and the realm of all facts interwoven and mutually identified. Principle is emptiness, static, the noumenon, whereas facts are specific characters, dynamic, constituting the phenomenal world. They interact and interpenetrate and in this way form a perfect harmony. This doctrine rests on the theory of the six characters, which states that each dharma possess the six characteristics of universality, speciality, similarity, difference, integration, and disintegration. Thus, each dharma is both one and all. The world is in reality a perfect harmony in all its flowery splendor.

Ch'an. Whereas Buddhist philosophy in the sixth and seventh centuries came to be more and more Chinese with the T'ien-t'ai and Hua-yen schools, Confucian philosophy remained dormant. In the eighth and ninth centuries its very life was threatened by the growth of Ch'an, or the Meditation school (Zen in Japan).

The Meditation doctrine, introduced from India by Bodhidharma (fl. 460–534), aimed at the realization of the Ultimate Reality through sitting in meditation. Its emphasis was on concentration to the point of absence of thought in order to get rid of attachments. As the Meditation school developed it conceived of the mind as split into the true mind, which does not have thought or attachments to the characters of dharmas, and the false mind, which has them. Sitting in meditation was the effort to get rid of them.

Hui-neng (638–713), an aboriginal from the south, rose in revolt against the tradition. He and his followers refused to divide the mind but maintained that it is one and originally pure. Erroneous thoughts and erroneous attachments are similar to clouds hiding the sun. When they are removed the original nature will be revealed and great wisdom obtained. The way to discover the original nature is calmness and wisdom. Calmness does not mean not thinking or having nothing to do with the characters of dharmas. Rather, it means not being carried away by thought in the process of thought and being free from characters while in the midst of them. Sitting in meditation is useless, and external effort, such as reciting scriptures or worshiping Buddhas, is futile. When the mind is unperturbed by selfishness or deliberate effort and is left to take its own course, it will reveal its pure nature, and enlightenment will come suddenly. Instead of assuming a dualistic nature of the mind, ignoring the external world, and aiming at uniting with the Infinite, as Indian meditation did, Chinese meditation assumed the original goodness of nature, took place in the midst of daily affairs, and aimed at self-realization.

Chinese influences on Ch'an are obvious. Buddhism had become characteristically Chinese, with its interest in the here and now. It swept all over China. The Confucian Way was in imminent danger of disappearance. Han Yü (768–824), the greatest Confucianist of the T'ang dynasty (618–907), had to defend the Confucian Way and demanded that Buddhist and Taoist books be burned. His contribution to Confucian philosophy is negligible, but he paved the way for Confucian awakening.

MODERN PERIOD: NEO-CONFUCIANISM (960–1912)

The combination of the wide spread of Ch'an and the attractiveness of the Hua-yen and T'ien-t'ai metaphysics, as well as the Ch'an psychology, woke the Confucianists from a long slumber. For centuries, within the Confucian school itself, efforts had been confined to textual studies and flowery compositions. Reaction, long overdue, now set in. Consequently in the early years of the Sung dynasty (960–1279) Confucianists raised new problems and attempted to find solutions.

Since the *Book of Changes* had exerted tremendous influence throughout the ages, the Confucianists naturally turned to it for inspiration and support. But instead of using it for divination, as the Taoists did, they used it for a study of human nature and destiny on the basis of principle. This new movement eventually came to be known as the school of Nature and Principle (Hsing-li hsüeh or, in English, Neo-Confucianism).

The man who opened the vista and determined the direction of Neo-Confucianism was Chou Tun-i (also called Chou Lien-hsi, 1017–1073). Elaborating on the cosmogony of the *Book of Changes*, he held that in the evolution of the universe from the Great Ultimate through the two material forces of yin and yang and the five agents to the myriad things, the five agents are the basis of the differentiation of things, whereas yin and yang constitute their actuality. The two forces are fundamentally one. Consequently the many are ultimately one and the one is actually differentiated in the many. Both the one and the many have their own correct states of being. The nature and destiny of man and things will be correct in their differentiated state if they all follow the same universal principle. This was the central thesis of Neo-Confucianism for the next several centuries. The influence of the Buddhist one-in-all-and-all-in-one philosophy is unmistakable.

Rationalistic Neo-Confucianism. Neo-Confucianism developed in two different directions, the rationalistic school of Principle and the idealistic school of Mind.

Ch'eng–Chu philosophy. The central figures in the rationalistic movement were Ch'eng I (Ch'eng I-ch'uan, 1033–1107), who formulated the major concepts and provided the basic arguments, and Chu Hsi (1130–1200), who supplemented and refined them and brought Neo-Confucianism into a systemic, rationalistic whole.

At the center of the school is its concept of principle (*li*); its other major concepts are the Great Ultimate, material force, the nature of man and things, the investigation of things, and the moral quality of humanity, or *jen*.

The idea of principle, virtually absent in ancient Confucianism, probably came from Neo-Taoism and Buddhism. If so, it was employed to oppose them. In the view of the Neo-Confucianists of the Sung dynasty both Taoist nonbeing and Buddhist emptiness are too abstract, but their principle is concrete. Ch'eng I repeatedly said that for a thing to exist there must first be its principle, the law according to which it will exist. Principle is definite, correct, self-evident, and self-sufficient. It is in each and every thing. Put differently, the principle for each particular thing is a definite one.

Since the possible number of things in the world is infinite, the number of actual and potential principles is infinite. As new things appear, new principles are realized. In the production and reproduction in the universe the process of daily renewal never ceases. This is a principle in itself, and there is always a new principle to make a new thing possible. But all principles are at bottom one, called the Great Ultimate. As substance the Great Ultimate is one, but as it functions it is manifested in the many, or the innumerable concrete things. The Great Ultimate is both the sum total of all principles and principle in its oneness.

The manifestations of the Great Ultimate depend on material force, which actualizes things. Operating as yin and yang, material force provides the stuff that makes a thing concrete. Things differ from one another because of their material endowments, and they resemble one another because of principle. Principle as the Great Ultimate exists before physical form (*hsing-erh-shang*), whereas material force exists after physical form (*hsing-erh-hsia*). Logically speaking, principle is prior to material force, but as Chu Hsi emphasized, they are never separate. Without material force principle would be neither concrete nor definite, and without principle there would be no law by which material force could operate. In the universe there has never been any material force without principle or principle without material force.

When principle is endowed in man it becomes his nature. Man's nature is originally good because principle is good, and principle is good because it is the source of all goodness. Evil arises when feelings are aroused and deviate from principle. In this respect Neo-Confucianism retains the traditional Confucian doctrine that Nature is good whereas feelings are sources of evil. The Sung Neo-Confucianists made a sharp distinction between the principle of Nature and selfish human desires.

Through moral cultivation selfish desires can be eliminated and the principle of Nature realized. To the rationalistic Neo-Confucianists the first step toward cultivation was the investigation of things (*ko-wu*). According to Ch'eng I every blade of grass and every tree possesses principle. Therefore, all things should be investigated. One can investigate by studying inductively or deductively, by reading books, or by handling human affairs. When things are investigated, as *The Great Learning* taught, one's knowledge will be extended, one's will sincere, one's feelings correct, and one's personal life cultivated. When this is done one will have fully developed one's nature and fulfilled one's destiny.

The development of human nature, according to the Ch'eng–Chu philosophy, does not stop with personal perfection but involves all things. This is where the concept of *jen* comes in. To Ch'eng I and Chu Hsi, as to previous Confucianists, *jen* is humanity, the moral quality that makes man a true man. But under the influence of the century-old Confucian doctrine of the unity of man and Nature and also the cosmological scale of Buddhist ethics, the Neo-Confucianists applied the concept of *jen* to all things and said that through it man can "form one body with heaven, earth, and all things." Furthermore, they added a new note to *jen* by interpreting the word in its other sense, that of seed or growth. *Jen* was then understood to be the chief characteristic of heaven and earth, the production and reproduction of things. This life-giving character is the highest good. It is inherent in man's nature. Man's duty is to develop it and put it into practice. Neo-Confucianism returned to the chief topic and fundamental ethical concern of Confucius and gave it new meaning.

As has been indicated, Chu Hsi and Ch'eng I were the chief figures of rationalistic Neo-Confucianism. However, Ch'eng I's older brother Ch'eng Hao, their uncle Chang Tsai, and Shao Yung, who with Ch'eng I and Chou Tun-i are called the Five Masters of early Sung Neo-Confucianism, also contributed substantially to it.

Ch'eng Hao. Ch'eng Hao (Ch'eng Ming-tao, 1032–1085) shared many ideas with his brother. The two were really the twin leaders of the school in its formative stage. Whereas Ch'eng I stressed the idea of principle as one and its manifestations many, Ch'eng Hao stressed principle as production and reproduction. He saw the spirit of life in everything, which impressed him much more than the rational character of things. Furthermore, to Ch'eng Hao the highest principle was the principle of Nature, a concept he evolved himself. He believed that principle is more than the rational basis of being. It is the principle of Nature, the self-evident universal truth that carries with it the dictate to distinguish right from wrong and the imperative to do good. Instead of focusing his attention on the investigation of things, he directed it to the calmness of mind. Only when the mind is calm—that is, free from selfishness, cunning, and deliberate effort—can it be peaceful. One can then respond to things as they come and naturally maintain a balance between the internal and the external. Ch'eng Hao considered understanding the nature of *jen* to be of the greatest importance. The man who has such an understanding will be free from all opposition between the self and the other and will be able to form one body with all things. It can easily be seen that although he differed from his brother on many points, Ch'eng Hao strengthened Neo-Confucianism by providing it with warmth and spirituality.

Chang Tsai. Unlike the Ch'eng brothers, Chang Tsai (Chang Heng-ch'ü, 1020–1077) regarded principle not as above or different from material force but as the law according to which material force operates. He identified material force with the Great Ultimate and considered yin and yang as merely the two aspects of material force. As substance, before consolidation takes place, material force is the Great Vacuity (*t'ai-hsü*). As function, in its activity and tranquillity, integration and disintegration, and so forth, it is the Great Harmony. But the two are the same as the Way (Tao). In its ultimate state material force is one, but in its contraction and expansion and the like it is manifested in the many. Similarly, in ethics *jen* is one, but in its application in the various human relations, as filial piety toward parents, brotherly respect toward brothers, and so on, it is many. Chang Tsai's advocacy of the concept of vacuity was too Taoistic to be attractive to his fellow Neo-Confucianists, but in making the doctrine of the one and the many the metaphysical foundation of Confucian ethics, he made "a great contribution to the Confucian school," in Chu Hsi's description.

Shao Yung. Shao Yung (1011–1077) agreed with his contemporaries that there are supreme principles governing the universe, but he added that they can be discerned in terms of numbers. In his cosmology change is due to spirit; spirit gives rise to number, number to form, and form to concrete things. Since the Great Ultimate engenders the four forms of major and minor yin and yang, Shao Yung used the number 4 to classify all phenomena. In his scheme there are the four seasons, the four heavenly bodies, the four kinds of rulers, the four periods of history, and so on. Since the structure of the universe is mathematical, elements of the universe can be calculated and objectively known. The best way to know is to "view things as things." All these are new notes in Neo-Confucianism that set Shao Yung apart from the rest. He was as much interested in the basic problems of principle, nature, and destiny as were other Neo-Confucianists. However, he hardly discussed social and moral problems, and his whole metaphysical outlook was too near Taoist occultism to be considered part of the main current of rationalistic Neo-Confucianism.

Idealistic Neo-Confucianism. In spite of the fact that the rationalistic Neo-Confucianists tried to maintain a balance between principle and material force in metaphysics and between the investigation of things and moral cultivation in the way of life, they tended to be one-sided in their emphasis on principle and the investigation of things.

Lu Hsiang-shan. Opposition to these trends arose in Chu Hsi's own time, notably from his friend and chief opponent, Lu Hsiang-shan (Lu Chu-yüan, 1139–1193). Ch'eng I and Chu Hsi had regarded mind as the function of man's nature, which is identical with principle. To Lu mind *was* principle. It is originally good and endowed with the innate knowledge of the good and the innate ability to do good, as Mencius had taught long before. It is one and indissoluble. There is no such distinction as that between the moral mind, which is good, and the human mind, which is liable to evil, a distinction made by Chu Hsi. Both the principle of Nature and human desires are good, and they should not be contrasted, as they were by Chu Hsi. The mind fills the whole universe. Throughout all ages and in all directions there is the same mind. It is identical with all things, for there is nothing outside the Way and there is no Way outside things. In short, the mind *is* the universe. To investigate things, then, is to investigate the mind. Since all principles are inherent and complete in the mind, there is no need to look outside, as did Ch'eng I and Chu Hsi.

This thoroughgoing idealism shows not only the influence of Mencius but also the impact of Buddhism. However, Lu was no less a critic of Buddhism than were other Neo-Confucianists. Actually, he criticized Chu Hsi not to promote Buddhism but to uphold Confucianism. In his opinion the way of Chu Hsi led to a divided mind, aimless drifting, and devotion to isolated details that meant little to life. Lu advocated instead a simple, easy, and direct method of recovering one's originally good nature. It consisted in having a firm purpose, "establishing the nobler part of one's nature," and coming to grips with fundamentals. In short, Chu's way was "following the path of study and inquiry," whereas Lu's way was "honoring the moral nature."

Lu's opposition did not have any immediate effect, for rationalistic Neo-Confucianism was too strong to be checked. It dominated the Chinese intellectual world for several hundred years. By the fifteenth century, however, it had degenerated into concern only with isolated details and had lost touch with the fundamentals of life. There was no longer any intellectual creativity or moral vigor in it.

Wang Yang-ming. Opposition rose again, this time from Wang Yang-ming (Wang Shou-jen, 1472–1529), who pushed the idealistic movement to its highest point in Chinese history. Wang reiterated most of Lu Hsiang-chan's ideas but carried some of them to new heights. Like Lu, he said that the mind is principle and that things are in the mind, but he emphasized the direction of the mind—that is, the will. To him a thing (or affair) was nothing but the mind determined to realize it. There is no such thing as filial piety, for example, unless one is determined to put it into practice and actually does so. Like Lu, Wang said that the investigation of things is the investigation of the mind; however, he added that since the most important aspect of the mind is the will, the sincerity of the will must precede the investigation of things, an idea diametrically opposed to Chu Hsi's contention that as things are investigated, one's will becomes sincere. Going beyond Mencius' doctrine of the innate knowledge of good, Wang held that because of one's innate ability to do good, one necessarily extends the innate knowledge into action. Knowledge and action are really identical; one is the beginning and the other the completion. Here are two original doctrines, the extension of the innate knowledge and the unity of knowledge and action, both of which represent new steps in Chinese thought.

Wang Fu-chih. For 150 years the idealistic philosophy of Wang Yang-ming dominated China, putting Chu Hsi's rationalism on the defensive. A number of philosophers attempted compromise, without much success. In the seventeenth century Wang's idealism declined, and Chu Hsi's rationalism reasserted itself. But rationalism enjoyed neither monopoly nor prominence, for revolts arose one after another. From the seventeenth century on, Confucianists regarded both Chu and Wang as too speculative. The spirit of the time demanded the evident, the concrete, and the practical.

One of the first to rebel was Wang Fu-chih (Wang Ch'uan-shan, 1619–1692). He rejected the central Neo-Confucian thesis that principle is a universal, transcending and prior to material force. Instead, he contended that principle is identical with material force. It is not a separate entity that can be grasped but the order and arrangement of things. The Great Ultimate and the principle of Nature are no transcendent abstractions. They, along with the mind and the nature of things, are all within material force. Wang Fu-chih boldly declared, "The world consists only of concrete things." He also refused to accept either the distinction between the principle of Nature and human desires or the subordination of human desires.

Tai Chen. In the same spirit, Tai Chen (Tai Yung-yüan, 1723–1777) attacked the Neo-Confucianists, particularly those of the Sung dynasty, for their conception of principle. He said that they looked upon principle "as if it were a thing." To him principle was nothing but the order of things, and by things he meant daily affairs, such as drinking and eating. The way to investigate principle, he thought, is not by intellectual speculation or by introspection of the mind but by critical, analytical, minutely detailed, and objective study of things based on concrete evidence. Tai Chen's conception of principle led him to oppose vigorously the Neo-Confucianists' view of human feelings and desires, which he thought they had undermined. In his belief principle can never prevail when feelings are not satisfied, for principles are merely "feelings that do not err." Tai Chen perpetuated the Neo-Confucian doctrine that the universe is an unceasing process of production and reproduction, except that to him Nature, like principle, was but an order.

K'ang Yu-wei. By the end of the nineteenth century there was a swing back to the philosophy of Wang Yang-ming. The sad situation in China called for dynamic and purposive action that only an idealism like Wang's could provide. All of these factors conditioned the thought of K'ang Yu-wei (1858–1927), the greatest Confucianist of the time. In an attempt to translate Confucian philosophy into action he enunciated the extraordinary theory that Confucius was first and last a reformer. K'ang himself engineered the abortive political reform of 1898. Obviously influenced by the Christian concepts of utopia and progress, he envisaged the Age of Great Unity. In his theory of historical progress history proceeds from the Age of Chaos to the Small Peace and finally to the Great Unity, when nations, families, classes, and all kinds of distinctions will be totally abolished. The philosophical basis for this utopia is his interpretation of *jen*. He equates it with what Mencius called "the mind that cannot bear" to see the suffering of others. It is compassion. It is also the power of attraction that pulls all peoples together. As such it is ether and electricity, which permeate all things everywhere.

K'ang was philosophically superficial but historically important. He showed that at the turn of the twentieth century China was at a philosophical crossroad.

CONTEMPORARY PERIOD (FROM 1912)

Philosophy in twentieth-century China has indeed been confusing and chaotic, but certain tendencies can clearly be seen. There was first of all importation from the West. In the first three decades Darwin, Haeckel, Nietzsche, Schopenhauer, Bergson, Kant, Descartes, James, Dewey, Marx, and others were introduced, each with his champion. Of these, James and Dewey were the most influential, since pragmatism was advocated by Hu Shih, leader of the intellectual revolution. However, only Marxism has remained strong, and it has become the established state philosophy.

Under the stimulation of Western philosophy both Confucianism and Buddhism resurged from a long period of decadence. In the 1920s and early 1930s, Ou-yang Ching-wu (1871–1943), strongly impressed by Western idealism, sought to revive Buddhist idealism as it was centuries ago, and his opponent, Abbot T'ai-hsü (1889–1947), attempted to transform Buddhist idealism in the light of Western philosophy. Since neither knew Western philosophy or was really a philosopher, their movements, though extensive and vigorous, resulted more in religious reform than in intellectual advancement, and in the late 1930s their work quickly disappeared from the philosophical scene.

The renewal of Confucian philosophy, however, was different. Fung Yu-lan (born 1895) developed his philosophy on the basis of rationalistic Neo-Confucianism, and Hsiung Shih-li (born 1885) built his on the foundation of idealistic Neo-Confucianism. Since the 1930s they have been the two most prominent philosophical thinkers in China. While importation from the West and reconstruction of traditional philosophy were going on, certain philosophers tried to evolve their own systems out of Western thought. The most successful of these has been Chang Tung-sun (born 1886), who alone has produced a comprehensive and mature philosophy.

Fung Yu-lan. Trained in philosophy at Columbia University, Fung Yu-lan (born 1895) derived his rationalism from the Neo-Confucianism of Ch'eng I and Chu Hsi and has converted Neo-Confucian concepts into formal logical concepts. According to him, his "new rationalistic Confucianism" is based on four main metaphysical concepts —principle, material force, the substance of Tao, and the Great Whole. The concept of principle is derived from the Ch'eng–Chu proposition "As there are things, there must be their specific principles." A thing must follow principle, but principle does not have to be actualized in a thing. It belongs to the realm of reality but not actuality and is purely a formal concept. The concept of material force is derived from the Ch'eng–Chu proposition "If there is principle, there must be material force" by which a thing can exist. Material force is basic to the concept of existence but does not itself exist in the actual world. It is only a formal logical concept. The concept of Tao means a "universal operation," the universe of "daily renewal" and incessant change. Finally, the Great Whole, in which one is all and all is one, is also a formal concept, being the general name for all, not an assertion about the actual world. It corresponds to the Absolute in Western philosophy.

Basically, Fung's philosophy is a combination of Neo-Confucianism and Western realism and logic. Fung calls his own system a "new tradition." It is new not only because it has interpreted Neo-Confucian ideas as formal concepts. In addition, Fung's system has replaced Neo-Confucianism, which is essentially a philosophy of immanence, with a philosophy of transcendence. To Fung the world of actuality is secondary.

In 1950, Fung repudiated his philosophy because it "neglects the concrete and the particular," but in 1957 he still maintained that Confucius was an idealist rather than a materialist. This suggests that he was not entirely Marxian in his interpretation of Chinese thought. He has remained the most important Chinese philosopher of the last thirty years—the most original, the most productive, and the most criticized.

Hsiung Shih-li. Hsiung Shih-li (born 1885) calls his philosophy the "new doctrine of consciousness-only." According to his main thesis reality is endless transformation of closing and opening, which constitute a process of unceasing production and reproduction. The original substance is in perpetual transition at every instant, continually arising anew and thus resulting in many manifestations. But reality and manifestations, or substance and function, are one. In its closing aspect original substance has the tendency to integrate, resulting in what may temporarily be called matter, whereas in its opening aspect it has the tendency to maintain its own nature and be its own master, resulting in what may temporarily be called mind. This mind itself is one part of the original mind, which in its various aspects is mind, will, and consciousness.

Hsiung's terminology comes from the *Book of Changes* and the Buddhist Consciousness Only school, but his basic ideas—the unity of substance and function and the primacy of the original mind—come from Neo-Confucianism, especially that of Wang Yang-ming. He has avoided Chu Hsi's bifurcation of principle and material force and Wang's subordination of material force to the mind and has provided the dynamic idea of change in Neo-Confucianism with a metaphysical foundation.

Chang Tung-sun. The theory of Chang Tung-sun (born 1886) has been variously called revised Kantianism, epistemological pluralism, and panstructuralism. Chiefly formulated between 1929 and 1947, it is derived from Kant but rejects Kant's bifurcation of reality into phenomena and noumena and Kant's division of the nature of knowledge into the a posteriori and the a priori. To Chang knowledge is a synthesis of sense data, form, and methodological assumptions. Perception, conception, mind, and consciousness are all syntheses, or "constructs," and constructs are products of society and culture. He maintains that although he has combined Western logic with modern psychology and sociology, his system is his own. During World War II he shifted more and more from metaphysics to the sociology of knowledge and thus has been drawn closer and closer to Marxism.

During the years since World War II neither Hsiung's, Fung's nor Chang's philosophy has become a movement, although Hsiung has exercised considerable influence on a number of young philosophers. While Chang is keeping silent, Hsiung maintaining his position, and Fung still reconsidering his philosophy, Marxism has become the triumphant and official system of thought. It demands that philosophy be practical, scientific, democratic, and for the masses. Traditional philosophy is being studied and will survive, but it is being interpreted in a new light.

(See also BUDDHISM, COMMUNISM, PHILOSOPHY UNDER; and MYSTICISM, HISTORY OF. For the writings of Mao Tse-tung, see DIALECTICAL MATERIALISM. See Chinese Philosophy in Index for articles on figures important to Chinese philosophy.)

Bibliography

GENERAL WORKS

Chan, Wing-tsit, *A Source Book in Chinese Philosophy.* Princeton, N.J., 1963. Chapters from the writings of most of the outstanding Chinese philosophers.

Chan, Wing-tsit, *An Outline and an Annotated Bibliography of Chinese Philosophy,* enl. ed. New Haven, 1965.

Creel, H. G., *Chinese Thought: From Confucius to Mao Tse-tung.* Chicago, 1953.

Fung Yu-lan, *The Spirit of Chinese Philosophy,* translated by E. R. Hughes. London, 1947.

Fung Yu-lan, *A Short History of Chinese Philosophy,* Derk Bodde, ed. New York, 1948.

Fung Yu-lan, *A History of Chinese Philosophy,* translated by Derk Bodde, 2 vols. Princeton, N.J., 1952–1953.

Hou Wai-lu et al., *A Short History of Chinese Philosophy,* translated by Wang Cheng-chung. Peking, 1959.

Needham, Joseph, *Science and Civilisation in China,* Vol. II, *History of Scientific Thought.* Cambridge, 1956.

ANCIENT PHILOSOPHY

Hu Shih, *The Development of the Logical Method in Ancient China*, 3d ed. Shanghai, 1928.
Hughes, E. R., *Chinese Philosophy in Classical Times*, rev. ed. London, 1954.
Waley, Arthur, *Three Ways of Thought in Ancient China*. London, 1939.

CONFUCIANISM

The Four Books, translated by James Legge, in *The Chinese Classics*, 3d ed., 5 vols. Oxford, 1960.
Liu, Wu-chi, *A Short History of Confucian Philosophy*. Baltimore, Md., 1955.
Wang Ch'ung, *Lun-Heng*, translated by Alfred Forke, 2 vols. London, 1907–1911.
The Yi King (Book of Changes), translated by James Legge. Sacred Books of the East, Vol. XVI. Oxford, 1899. The second edition has been reprinted by Dover as a paperback under the title *The I Ching*.

NEO-CONFUCIANISM

Chang, Carsun, *The Development of Neo-Confucian Thought*, 2 vols. New York, 1957–1962.
Chow, Yi-ching, *La Philosophie morale dans le Néo-Confucianisme (Tscheou Touen-Yi)*. Paris, 1953.
Chu Hsi, *Reflections on Things at Hand*, translated by Wing-tsit Chan. New York, forthcoming.
Forke, Alfred, *Geschichte der neueren chinesischen Philosophie*. Hamburg, 1936.

TAOISM

Huai-nan Tzu, *Tao, the Great Luminant*, translated by Evan Morgan. Shanghai, 1934.
Lieh Tzu, *The Book of Lieh Tzu*, translated by A. C. Graham. London, 1962.

BUDDHISM

Hsüan-tsang, *Vijñaptimātratāsiddhi, le siddhi de Hiuan-Tsang*, translated into French by Louis de La Vallee Poussin, 2 vols. Paris, 1928–1929.
Hui-neng, *The Platform Scripture: The Basic Classic of Zen Buddhism*, translated by Wing-tsit Chan. New York, 1963.
Seng-chao, *The Book of Chao*, translated by Walter Liebenthal. Peking, 1948.
Shen-hui, "Entretiens du maître de Dhyāna Chen-houei du Ho-tsö," translated into French by Jacques Gernet. *Publications de L'École Française d'Etrême-Orient*, Vol. 51 (1949), 1–126.

CONTEMPORARY PHILOSOPHY

Brière, O., *Fifty Years of Chinese Philosophy, 1898–1950*, translated by Laurence Thompson. London, 1956.
Chan, Wing-tsit, *Chinese Philosophy, 1949–1963: An Annotated Bibliography of Mainland Chinese Publications*. Honolulu, Hawaii, forthcoming.
Day, Clarence Burton, *The Philosophers of China, Classical and Contemporary*. New York, 1962.

WING-TSIT CHAN

CHOICE. *See* CHOOSING, DECIDING, AND DOING.

CHOICE, AXIOM OF. *See* SET THEORY.

CHOOSING, DECIDING, AND DOING. There are at least three groups of philosophical problems whose solutions depend on adequate explications of the concepts of choosing, deciding, and doing. The first group consists of problems about the relation between minds and bodies. Some philosophers maintain that some words we ordinarily think of as describing private mental acts or events can nevertheless be intelligibly explicated without mentioning mental acts. The theory that maintains this of *all* mental-concept words is sometimes called philosophical behaviorism, and this theory must be able to show that "choosing" and "deciding" do not stand for mental events. It must be able to show that such concepts as "choose," "decide," and "intend" can be explicated either in terms of the occurrence of publicly observable physical events or in terms of tendencies for publicly observable events to occur. Thus, a correct understanding of these concepts is relevant to the controversy over philosophical behaviorism.

The second group of problems are those in ethical theory. We make moral judgments of actions, and therefore any adequate ethical theory must be able to answer the following questions: How do we determine the boundary between an action and what precedes it, as well as between an action and what follows it? Where does an action begin, and where does it end? Are intentions, decisions, choices, "acts of will," muscle contractions, or nerve impulses actions, or are they not actions but preliminaries to actions which nevertheless stand in certain important relations to actions? If all or some of the above are actions, then is whatever follows them not an action but instead a consequence? How does one determine where an action ends and its consequences begin? The answer to this last question is of crucial importance to any attempt to resolve the famous dispute between formalist ethical theories, which judge individual actions by rules alone, and teleological (or utilitarian) ethical theories, which judge individual actions by consequences alone.

The problem of "freedom of the will" is the central problem of the third group. Here the relevant questions are the following: Are decisions and choices in principle capable of being caused and capable of causing actions? Are actions identical with sets of events that in principle can be predicted on the basis of antecedent conditions and relevant causal laws? If an action is more than a set of events, does this preclude causal determination of actions? Finally, we must add to the above groups of problems that some philosophers seek to understand, for understanding's sake alone, what it means to choose, decide, and act.

CHOOSING AND DECIDING

Preliminary considerations. The following are some views which have been held about the nature of choice: (1) Choices are mental acts or mental events that precede and perhaps cause actions. (2) Choices are never mental acts but overt actions done in a context of alternatives. (3) Choices, when distinct from decisions, are overt actions done in a context of alternatives, and when they are not overt actions they are identical with decisions. (4) Choices may or may not involve mental acts and fundamentally are overt actions for which certain sorts of explanations in terms of purposes can be given. Each of these theories of choice will be examined in turn. We shall treat the last three as progressive attempts to meet the difficulties encountered in, and to improve upon, the first view.

We shall begin by explaining some characteristics of

choice with which none of the above views take issue and with a preliminary distinction between choice and decision. First, choices, unlike beliefs, are neither true nor false. We rate choices by calling them good or bad, wise or foolish, and correct or incorrect when "correct" and "incorrect" mean that a choice is suitable or unsuitable for the attainment of some end, but we never rate choices by calling them true or false. This is so when we choose things, such as an apple or a martini, as well as when we choose actions and policies. The same can be said of decisions, in one of two sharply distinct senses of that term: Sometimes we *decide that* something is the case, for example, that cigarettes cause cancer, and such decisions are either true or false; we also *decide to* do something, for example, to buy a car, and such decisions are neither true nor false. It is clear that "choose" can never mean "decide that," although we have yet to see if in some contexts it means "decide to." Some of the more plausible views we shall examine will suggest that although choosing is sometimes the same as deciding, in most contexts choosing is more closely related to action than is deciding, and deciding is more closely related to intending than is choosing.

Statements *about* choices are true or false, such as "Jones chose (is choosing, will choose) an apple," and these include first-person past-tense statements, for example, "I chose an apple." However, some first-person future-tense statements of choice and all first-person future-tense statements of decision appear to be unintelligible, for example, "I will choose (or decide to buy) a 1965 Ford tomorrow." Saying that one has not yet chosen or decided appears to entail that one has not yet made up one's mind what to buy and, hence, that one does not yet know what one will choose or decide tomorrow (for a discussion of this point, see SELF-PREDICTION). Of course, "I will choose a 1965 Ford tomorrow" is intelligible if this is a statement about a choice one will make among various 1965 Fords, for in this case, presumably, one has already chosen (decided) to buy *a* 1965 Ford and has yet to choose *which* 1965 Ford. The reason for saying that only *some* first-person future-tense statements of choice are unintelligible is that we have yet to examine the view that there are two senses of "choice," one identical with decision and incompatible with foreknowledge and another distinct from decision and compatible with foreknowledge. First-person present-tense statements of choice have peculiarities of a different sort, and we shall discuss such statements later, in the context of a particular theory of choice.

Choice as a kind of action. Let us suppose that a choice is a kind of action and that it is distinct from the overt action which is chosen. If a philosopher maintains that all actions are produced by antecedent choices, an infinite regress arises. For if choices are actions, they must be preceded by choices, which, because they are also actions, must be preceded by still other choices; thus, we are led to the absurdity that no one can act until he performs an infinite number of choices. If a philosopher instead maintains merely that any action which we believe we are able to perform is an action which we are able to choose, then a different difficulty arises when we suppose that choices are actions: If Jones believes he can do x, it follows that he can choose to do x, and, if he reasons logically, it also follows that he believes he can choose to do x; since, on the theory we are considering, "choosing to do x" is itself an action, it follows that he believes that he can choose to choose to do x. In other words, if we admit (1) that we believe that we are able to perform some actions, and (2) that we are able to choose any actions which we believe we are able to perform, and (3) a hypothesis that choosing is an action, then it follows that we are able to choose to choose (as well as choose to choose to choose) some actions. Many philosophers have argued that "choosing to choose" makes no sense; if they are correct and if (1) and (2) are true, then choosing is not an action. Finally, it appears that any action for which we can be held morally accountable is one we can choose. We *are* held morally accountable for our choices. Therefore, if choosing is an action it again follows that we can choose to choose.

These arguments, if sound, tell against any theory that maintains that choosing is an action. For example, let us suppose that Jones chooses a martini from a tray of various kinds of drinks. The theory we have been considering maintains that Jones's choosing is a mental action that precedes and perhaps causes his physical action of taking the drink; another view maintains that Jones's choosing is simply the physical action of taking the drink. A difficulty with both these views is that they appear to entail that Jones can choose to choose. One way out of this difficulty is to maintain that choices are not actions.

Choice as "doing x rather than y." Some philosophers maintain that choosing to perform an action is the same as performing one action in a range of alternatives and that choosing an object is the same as taking or getting one object from among alternatives: to choose x is to do x (or what gets x) rather than y (see P. H. Nowell-Smith for a discussion of this theory). This theory requires explanation and qualification before it can be plausible. It appears to face the objection that has been raised against all views which maintain that choosing is a kind of doing, namely, that if the view is true we can choose to choose. But it is obvious for other reasons, too, that this theory cannot plausibly maintain that choosing is *merely* an overt action, for example, taking a martini from a tray of different kinds of drinks, for the action can be done when one has no choice or when one merely picks a drink, without preference, from the tray. The theory we are now considering can maintain, at most, that choices are overt actions done in a particular way. We must now consider three classes of objections which have been raised against this theory.

Sometimes we choose to do something long before we do it, for example when Jones chooses to attend college x while he is still in high school or when Jones chooses now the car he will buy next month. Therefore, choosing cannot be the same as doing. In answer to this objection it can be argued that one meaning of "choosing" is "doing x rather than y" but that the word has another meaning when we "choose in advance," one which is more or less the same as the meaning of "deciding." Evidence for this claim is that in some contexts doing is a necessary condition for choosing, whereas doing is never a necessary condition for deciding, and that in other contexts where doing is not a necessary condition for choosing, we are able, with varying degrees of success, to substitute "decide" for "choose." Thus, this modification of the theory says that "doing x rather than y" is the *fundamental* meaning of "choose" because, unlike the other sense of "choose," it is not interchangeable with "decide."

These claims are best defended in the light of examples. If Jones is offered a tray of different kinds of drinks and chooses a martini, is it necessary that any mental acts of choice pass through his mind before he can correctly be said to choose? He may say to himself "I choose the martini," but it does not appear to be necessary that he do so. It is necessary that he should see the tray, believe that there are alternatives before him, and recognize the martini among the other drinks, but these states or activities do not constitute choosing. He chooses when he reaches out and takes the martini rather than a different drink, and if at the same time he is occupied in conversation, it is unlikely that any thoughts pass through his mind which we could plausibly say constituted his choosing. The theory we are considering rejects the view that there *must* be a mental act of choice prior to the action; it appeals to experience and introspection and maintains that very often in such cases of "habitual choice," nothing goes on which can be called the choice in addition to the physical act of taking one drink rather than another.

The difference between choice and decision. In the preceding example Jones did not *decide* to take a martini because decision is more closely tied to deliberation and intention than is choice. That is, if Jones decided to take a martini, then we expect that prior to the action there was deliberation, or at least preference and resolution, and that between the time he decided and the time he acted we could correctly say that he intended to take a martini. Moreover, Jones can know that he always chooses martinis in preference to other kinds of drinks and still choose one when it is offered, but he cannot know that he always takes martinis and still decide to take one when the tray is offered: decisions cannot be known in advance, but choices, in this sense of "choice," can. Hence, if what Jones does when the tray is offered is decide, he cannot know that he always takes martinis. Again, it makes sense to speak of habitual choices, but less sense to speak of habitual decisions. And we can sometimes say truly "Jones decided to choose a martini," which shows several things: It shows that decision can precede choice and hence inform Jones of exactly what he will take from the tray before the tray appears and he makes his choice. It also shows that all acts of deliberation and resolution can be completed before he chooses, which is further evidence that the choice is the action itself. On the other hand, it does not even make sense to say "Jones chose to decide on a martini," for here "chose" appears to have the same meaning as "decided," where "decide" carries its usual sense of "make up one's mind about some future course of action."

So far, the theory maintains that whenever we choose in advance, and hence whenever choosing is not "doing *x* rather than *y*," choosing is deciding. It is this latter sense of "choose" that is at work when we speak of "difficult choices," when we maintain truly that no one can possibly know what he will choose before he makes his choice, and when we say things like "Jones chose what car he will buy next month." Yet there can still remain nuances of difference between "choosing" in this sense and deciding, and these differences depend on an affinity which remains between "choosing in advance" and "choosing" in its fundamental sense of "doing *x* rather than *y*." If we wish to discover whether "Jones decided what car he will buy" or "Jones chose what car he will buy" is more appropriate, we must find out how close Jones came to actually picking out and buying a car, and the closer he came to actually picking a car, the more appropriate is "chose." In a car lot with a salesman or at home with brochures before him, Jones chooses a car, for the overt action of pointing to or checking off a car in a brochure is a stand-in for choosing a car on a lot. But if he does nothing besides make up his mind, it would be more appropriate to say that he decides than that he chooses. A more clear-cut case is "Jones chose a martini from the not-yet-arrived tray of drinks": This use of "chose" is incorrect, not merely unusual. "Decided," not "chose," is correct when Jones neither takes a drink nor does some stand-in action such as saying to his neighbor, "I'm going to have a martini."

Action as a condition of choice. Is doing *x* ever a necessary condition for choosing *x*? That is, in cases where we choose to do something at once, such as take a drink from a tray of drinks, it follows from the theory that it is logically impossible to have chosen if one does not in fact perform the action, but this does not appear to be logically impossible. Let us imagine that Jones's arm suddenly becomes paralyzed before he can take a martini from the tray. Did he nevertheless choose a martini? Some philosophers would answer negatively. If there was antecedent deliberation or mental selecting, then he had decided to take a drink, and he also chose in the sense of "chose" that is difficult to distinguish from "decided." But he did not *choose a drink* in the sense of "choose" for which "decide" cannot be substituted. If, on the other hand, there was no antecedent deliberation—if it was to be a "habitual choice"—then he neither chose nor decided.

Choices and reasons. The theory so far leaves unexplained the meaning of "rather" in "choosing is doing *x* rather than *y*" and hence fails to explain how this qualification enables the theory to escape the preceding objections to the view that choices are actions. When we say that choosing is doing or taking from among alternatives, we exclude cases where it makes no difference what the alternatives are. If a person takes a cigarette from a pack of cigarettes, an unknown card from a deck, or a drink from a tray when he does not care which kind of drink he gets, he does not choose a particular item. He chooses to take one rather than refrain from taking one, but *which* one he takes or picks is not a matter for choice if there is no basis for choice. Hence, to say that one does *x rather* than *y* implies that there is a connection between *which* action one performs and some preference, intention, principle, antecedent resolution, or habit. To explain this connection is to give a reason why one does *x* rather than *y*. If one chooses, there is a basis for choice, and if there is a basis for choice, there is a reason why one does *x* rather than *y*; hence, if no reason can be produced, there was no choice. This last claim can also be supported by appeal to the fact that choices can be good or bad. The sentence "*x* is good" entails that there is a reason why *x* is good. It is part of the meaning of any evaluative concept that there are reasons for evaluative differences between things, these reasons being appeals to other differences between those things. Consequently, if one asserts "*x* is good," one must have in mind some feature of x that distinguishes it from other things which are not good. The kinds of differences between choices which make some of them good and some of them bad are suitability or unsuitability to goals, principles, or habits, and to appeal to the success or failure of a choice to suit some goal is to give a reason why it is a good or a bad choice. If every choice is good or bad, it follows that every choice aims, with or without success, to suit a goal, principle, or habit.

Choices, reasons, and causes. Reasons for actions are explanations of them in terms of goals, principles, or habits. A peculiarity of reasons, as distinct from causes, is that the time at which a putative reason is produced, or at which it is entertained by some mind, is irrelevant to whether or not it is a reason. C cannot possibly be the cause of x if it occurs later than x, but R can be a reason for x quite regardless of whether it is stated before or after the occurrence of x; R can be a reason for x even if it is never actually produced but is merely producible. Of course, the time at which one gives a causal explanation is also irrelevant to whether or not something is the cause of x. But the point is that reasons, as distinct from statements of reasons, are not datable, whereas causes as well as statements of causes are datable. When we say that Jones chose x for the sake of z, or in order to obtain z, we are not saying that some event preceded and caused x. What we are asserting is that Jones considered x to be more suitable than y for the attainment of z. It may be the case that some set of events precedes and causes action x, but that is not anything we assert when we give a reason for x. Choices, if they cause actions, must be events temporally prior to actions, but it is just this causal model of intelligent human behavior that this theory, as well as the views of many philosophers (see Ryle, Hampshire, and Melden), rejects (see REASONS AND CAUSES for elaboration of this distinction).

This is why antecedent events play no logical role in the explication of the concept of choosing. If a person chooses x, he does what he believes to be better suited to his purposes than any of the alternatives before him. There must, of course, be evidence, in addition to the fact that one does x, that x is believed to be suitable to a purpose or habit. This evidence most typically consists in saying, either before or after the action, why one does x, but it also may include antecedent mental acts of preference or resolution, as well as the frequency with which such acts were done in the past or will be done in the future. Reasons are necessary conditions for choices, but the time at which evidence for the existence of a reason shows itself is not part of this necessary condition. Therefore, even if every choice were preceded by a mental act of selection, this would be only a contingent fact about choices, not part of the meaning of "choice."

Aristotle's remarks about choice are similar in some respects to the theory we have been examining. Aristotle seeks to explain deliberate choice and offers reasons why deliberate choice cannot be identical with desire, passion, wish, or opinion. He points out that we appraise opinions according to whether they are true or false or arrived at in the right way; but we never appraise choices for these reasons but rather because they are good or bad or fail or succeed in attaining an end. Aristotle concludes that a choice is "a voluntary act preceded by deliberation." He also speaks of choice as the function of practical intellect or purposive thought. And Aristotle's implication seems to be that deliberate choices are actions whose reasonableness depends on how they are directed toward goals.

Avowals of choice. We are now in a position to say something about first-person present-tense statements of choice, such as "I choose that one." If such statements are *about* choices, it follows that they are always either true or false and that the choice which the statement of choice truly or falsely reports is distinct from the act of uttering the words "I choose that one." However, is it in all contexts possible to say falsely to a clerk, "I'll have that one," or to a waiter, "My choice is the steak"? Can a person be mistaken when he says this to a clerk—mistaken in the sense that he merely *thought* he was choosing a violet necktie, not mistaken in the sense that he made a bad choice, or thought he was choosing a blue necktie, or immediately regretted his choice? This kind of mistake does not appear to be possible. Therefore, if "My choice is that one," said to a waiter, clerk, or official, reports an occurrence which is the choice, then this report is an infallible report. But how can a report which is plainly not an analytic statement be infallible? It does not help to appeal to what some philosophers believe is the certainty of introspective reports and maintain that "My choice is x," like "I believe that y," cannot be false unless one is lying. For in certain contexts it is not even possible to lie when one says "My choice is x," whereas it is always possible to lie when one says "I believe that y."

The problem, then, is that if "My choice is x" reports a choice, it is always possible that it is false, and this does not appear to be always possible. There are, however, some contexts in which such utterances can be false, namely, those in which a person is choosing in advance; for it is always possible that an announcement of a *decision* should be false. Thus, when President Coolidge said "I do not choose to run . . . ," it was possible that he nevertheless had secretly decided to run again for president.

One answer to our difficulty is to maintain that first-person present-tense statements of choice *are* choices, rather than assertions that choices have taken place. For it is sometimes the case that nothing else need occur besides the act of uttering the words "My choice is x," for it to be true that one has chosen. Such utterances are not fallible because they are neither fallible nor infallible. They are actions performed with words, and we engage in such actions, instead of simply taking things, in part because civilization requires such politeness and in part because (as in a restaurant or before an official) we require the assistance of others. Utterances of the form "I choose . . . " and "My choice is . . . " are used primarily in more or less formal situations in which they are established and generally accepted conventions, or social practices, applying to both the person who expresses a choice and his listener, relations such as those between customer and clerk, patient and doctor, citizen and an official offering alternatives to him. In these situations, if a person says "I choose that one" and later says that he did not mean it or that he lied or mistakenly reported his thoughts, we understand this (if we understand it at all) to be a request that he be allowed to make a different choice, and by no means do we take it to be evidence that, as a matter of fact, he did not make a choice.

It may be objected that such choices fail to fit the pattern of "doing *x* rather than *y*." For in a store Jones chooses a tie by saying "My choice is that one," not by simply reaching out and taking the tie. It is very likely that this objection requires that the theory be qualified further. The qualification is that when one chooses by uttering a first-person present-tense statement of choice, one succeeds in choosing even if one does not get what one chooses. One can choose a steak in a restaurant or a tie in a store without ultimately receiving either item. These cases, however, still satisfy the most general requirement of the theory because *saying* "my choice is the steak" rather than "My choice is the lobster" is an instance of *doing x* rather than *y*. But of course, in this case *what* one does is not necessarily the act of taking or getting *x* but a verbal action which one believes is a means to *x*. And here an important difference emerges between choosing by uttering words and choosing by simply taking. In each case choosing requires *doing* something. However, in situations where social practices prohibit simply taking *x*, uttering a particular form of words is not merely a means to *x* but a convention which has the same function as taking *x* in other situations where verbal expressions are not required. This is why reaching for a martini on a tray without succeeding in getting the drink is not a choice, whereas saying to a host "I'll have a martini" without receiving a martini *is* a choice.

Because first-person present-tense expressions of choice are primarily used in social contexts in which we are dependent on the assistance of others, these utterances are usually also requests or commands. Could it plausibly be argued that "My choice is the steak," uttered to a waiter, is neither true nor false insofar as it is an order but is true or false insofar as it also reports the occurrence of a choice? Although a person can request, or order, without also choosing, he often does both. When he both chooses and requests, must anything occur which is the choice in addition to his uttering the words? To this question the theory has already given its answer.

When a person utters the words "My choice is the red one" in an appropriate social context, there are conditions relevant to its being true or false that he chooses, but there are no conditions relevant to whether the sentence he utters in choosing is true or false. We must admit that if a man is play acting, talking in his sleep, or hypnotized, he can utter the words "My choice is the red one" when it is not the case that he chooses anything. But this does not entail that what he says is false; it entails instead that the action he performed, namely, uttering the words "My choice is the red one," failed to satisfy certain necessary conditions of choice, conditions having to do with goals, purposes, and appropriate contexts, and which were discussed above.

DOING

Let us begin our discussion of the concept of doing by simply listing, in apparent temporal order, everything that may be involved in the occurrence of a voluntary action. There will be deliberation, decision or choice, intention (and brain processes, nerve messages, and muscle contractions), bodily movement, and a series of further occurrences, for example, words uttered and a lie told, which extend indefinitely into the future and which appear to be causally related. We must attempt to discover which of these items are only preliminaries or necessary conditions for actions, which of them are actions, and which of them are consequences of actions.

Preliminaries of action. We shall begin with the "early" items on the list. Very often a person does *y* by doing *x* —for example, he saves a life by telling a lie. We shall now consider the view that what this person really or actually does is *x* and that *y* is not an action but a consequence of an action. But it may also be the case that he does *x* by doing *w*, in which case, on this view, *x* and *y* would be consequences of *w*. It is necessary that we be able to do some things directly, without their being more appropriately called "results" of something else we do, for otherwise we could not avoid the infinite regress of doing *y* by *x*, and *x* by *w*, etc., and there would be no actions at all. Hence, the view we are considering maintains that what we really do is what we do directly and that all other occurrences are more accurately described as consequences of these direct actions. And it implies that the most plausible candidates for "direct actions" are choices, acts of will, muscle contractions, or whatever it appears can logically be an action and which may be causally first in the sequence of occurrences produced by Jones. We shall examine some of these possibilities and then question an underlying assumption on which the general view depends, namely, that there is only one action description which applies with strict correctness to what Jones does, whereas what he does may have many consequences.

We have already criticized the view that choices are actions separate from overt actions, as well as the view that decisions are actions of any kind. "acts of will," however, are not instances of doing anything at all (see O. S. Franks and D. F. Pears, ed., *Freedom and the Will*). Choices, in the fundamental sense of "choice," and acts of will are both ways in which we act, not actions themselves. One can do something with effort, take effort trying to do something, and resolve to do something; each of these cases deserves a thorough explication, but it is clear that these efforts and resolves are not themselves anything which can be done with effort or resolve, nor can they be chosen. Moreover, they cannot be done alone and are not even intelligible apart from actions which they modify in various ways. This final point can serve to distinguish many kinds of accompaniments of actions from actions themselves. One can raise one's arm *simpliciter*, but an intention is always an intention *to do* something, a choice is always a choice *of some action*, and we cannot exert will unless it is the will *with which we act* or try to act.

Could muscle contractions be direct actions? On this hypothesis, Jones stops the car by stepping on the brake, and he steps on the brake by contracting his muscles, where stopping the car and stepping on the brake are both more correctly describable as consequences of a muscle contraction. However, there are reasons for believing that in most contexts muscle contractions are not actions, although they may be actions in certain unusual contexts. For example, imagine a person whose arm is removed, save the muscles and the minimally necessary nerves and vessels. In this case he could, upon request, contract his brachia radialis, perhaps at a medical demonstration. Suppose that one goes on to say "He contracted his muscles by sending nerve impulses." Here too it is possible to imagine a context in which a person could *do* such a thing, for example, if only the nerves remained, strung out to a machine sensitive to nerve impulses. The point is that contracting one's biceps is an action, but contracting one's brachia radialis and sending nerve impulses are not actions, although they could be actions in special contexts, such as those described. It is true that nerve impulses and muscle contractions, as well as many other events, are necessary conditions for overt actions. But there are loose and complex criteria for correctly distinguishing actions from preliminaries and accompaniments of actions, and muscle contractions, in most contexts, do not satisfy these criteria. In the cases of muscle contractions and nerve impulses, it is relevant that normally no one is interested in such goings-on, that one cannot contract muscles without moving one's limbs—our interest normally being in the latter to the exclusion of the former—and that one cannot, in ordinary contexts, choose or intend to send a nerve impulse or contract a certain muscle. What we correctly call an action, as distinct from mere events, is in important ways dependent on what we can easily imagine to interest or concern a person or to form part of some intelligible policy, plan, or aim. It is this condition that muscle contractions at a medical demonstration satisfy and that most muscle contractions and nerve impulses fail to satisfy. The existence of such criteria makes implausible the view that actions, *par excellence*, are what stand first in a causal sequence of events produced by a person.

Actions and consequences. We must also seek criteria for distinguishing actions from the consequences which follow them, and in so doing we must question the assumption, mentioned earlier, that only one action description applies correctly to what one does. Let us suppose that Jones speaks and in so doing tells a lie that saves a life. One way to divide this into action and consequences is to say that Jones told a lie and that a consequence of his action was that a life was saved. But it is equally appropriate to say that Jones told a life-saving lie, which in turn had various consequences. Therefore, it will be useful to be able to refer to "a life being saved" in a way that is neutral in regard to the categories "action" and "consequences." To this purpose we shall consider everything that Jones produces, when he acts, to comprise a temporal series of occurrences or "characteristics" extending indefinitely into the future. Thus, the example we are considering includes the characteristics "words being uttered," "a lie being told," "a life being saved," "grief being prevented," and countless others. We shall soon see why we must resist temptations to call all the elements of this action–consequence sequence "events" rather than merely "characteristics" and to assume that they are causally related to one another. Our immediate claim is that most of the characteristics of interest to us in such a sequence can be described by either action descriptions or result descriptions. If "telling a lie" is the action description we find convenient, then we are free to classify the characteristic "a life being saved" as a consequence; but if we employ the action description "saving a life," then only characteristics that in the situation presuppose saving a life can be described by result descriptions, for example, "grief being prevented." There is, we are suggesting, no rigid distinction between action and consequence, and we are free to construe many characteristics either as results or as constitutive of an expanded version of the action.

We do, of course, have criteria for classifying occurrences as constitutive of actions and as results or consequences. Intention is one such criterion: we often say that what a person does is what he intends and that what he does not intend is a mere result. But it cannot be a sufficient criterion, for if it were there could be neither unintentional actions nor intended results. When a person is intentionally conquering a nation, eliminating a disease, or reforming a penal code, it is sometimes more appropriate, because of the indirectness with which such things are brought off, to call them goals and, when they are achieved, to call them results and reserve the term "action" for the various means to these goals. Similarly, it is indisputable that people sometimes shoot other people unintentionally. The temptation in both kinds of case may be to restrict "action" to what is causally anterior. But then either we allow as actions only the "earliest" and simplest occurrences which meet the criteria we have discussed earlier, namely, simple bodily movements, or we grant that some "later" occurrences are classifiable *either* as actions *or* as consequences of bodily movements. If we choose the first alternative, we are obliged to maintain that no one ever *does* anything except make simple bodily movements. If we choose the second alternative, then we cannot classify occurrences as results rather than as actions solely on the grounds that what precede and produce them can also be classified as actions.

There is a difference between incorrect and merely unusual uses of action descriptions. The weak criteria we employ to classify occurrences under action descriptions or result descriptions—intention, interest, causal remoteness, etc.—most often determine only that one type of description is more unusual than another. For example, in ethics there is no logical obstacle to adopting a utilitarian rule, "One ought to maximize happiness," rather than the utilitarian principle, "One ought to do whatever produces happiness." And this is so notwithstanding that it is more unusual to speak of maximizing happiness as something one *does* rather than as something which *results from* prior actions. Frequently, however, the above criteria tell us nothing about the relative appropriateness of action descriptions and result descriptions, for example, in many situations in which we choose between classifying "stopping a car" or "saving a life" as something Jones does or instead as a result of something simpler that Jones does.

The apparent impossibility of drawing a sharp distinction between actions and consequences of actions is relevant to a famous controversy in ethical theory. The controversy is between formalists, who maintain that the rightness of an individual action is wholly determined by the kind of action it is, and teleologists, who maintain that the rightness of an individual action is wholly determined by the goodness or badness of its consequences. Each type of theory faces apparent counterexamples: sometimes expected consequences appear to morally require that we make exceptions to moral rules, and sometimes actions with good consequences nevertheless appear to be immoral. Each theory has attempted to avoid counterexamples and save the appearances by exploiting the reciprocal translatability of action descriptions and result descriptions. If an occurrence produced by Jones, such as "a life being saved," is deemed morally relevant or "right-making" by the formalist, he classifies it as a kind of action and hence as the proper subject matter of a rule. If the same occurrence is considered morally relevant by the teleologist, he classifies it as a result and hence as something that can be good or bad. If our analysis of the distinction between actions and consequences is correct, these two metaethical theories are compatible, and because their importance for ethics has rested on their supposed incompatibility, each is trivial.

The preceding claims about actions, consequences, and ethics can be summarized in the following argument: Let us suppose that Jones's action involves (*a*) the characteristic "being a lie" and (*b*) the characteristic "saving a life," and that both the formalist and the teleologist agree that what Jones does is morally right because it involves characteristic (*b*).

(1) We are free to classify (*b*) either as a consequence of the action "lying" or as specifying part of the kind of action Jones does.

(2) If (*b*) is classified as a consequence, then what he does is a morally right action because it has "good consequence (*b*)."

(3) If (*b*) is classified as specifying a kind of action, then what he does is a morally right action because it falls under applicable "rule (*b*)," where (*b*) specifies the content of the rule.

(4) Therefore, we are free to appeal either to "good consequence (*b*)" or to "rule (*b*)" to justify the rightness of what Jones does.

(5) How we classify (*b*) is of no moral significance.

(6) Therefore it is of no moral significance whether we justify what Jones does by appeal to rules or instead by appeal to consequences.

Actions and causes. It may appear that the action–consequence relation is an instance of cause and effect, but nevertheless there are some important dissimilarities between these two relations. First, not everything which is caused by an action is correctly called a consequence of an action. The effects of Jones's action extend indefinitely into the future, but we limit the consequences of what he does by considering, among other things, what is important, of interest to us, not too temporally distant, and explicable by reference to intentions or to intentions gone wrong. Not all these limitations apply all the time, but some or other of them do when we mean by "consequences" the products of human action rather than merely the effects of a cause.

Second, *y* can be a consequence of *x* when *y* is not at all caused by *x*, for example, when a consequence of extending one's arm from a car window is that a turn signal is given, when a consequence of delivering posters is being a political campaigner, or when a consequence of moving Q to Kt6 is that one's opponent is checkmated. In none of these three examples is *y* caused by *x*, because in each case there are no events constitutive of *y* that are not also constitutive of *x*. If *x* causes *y*, we know that two sets of physical (or perhaps mental) events take place, yet in each of our examples only one set of physical (or mental) events takes place. These examples stand in apparent contrast with other sorts of actions, such as "the car's stopping is a consequence of stepping on the brake," where there is an obvious causal relation between events constitutive of the action and other events constitutive of its consequence. Thus, it is useful to distinguish between "doing *y by* doing *x*" and "doing *y in* doing *x*" (see G. E. M. Anscombe) and to allow the latter formula to characterize cases where doing *x* is part of what we mean by doing *y*. To say that extending one's arm and moving Q to Kt6 are part of what we mean by signaling and checkmating, respectively, is to say that given statements of certain other necessary conditions which we shall describe shortly, "Jones extended his arm" *entails* "Jones signaled." We should add that in all the preceding examples *y* can be correctly construed either as a consequence of action *x* or as something one *does*.

So far we have suggested that Jones may or may not be signaling when he extends his arm but that the events he produces are in either case the same. Some philosophers, moreover, have maintained (see Stuart Hampshire and A. I. Melden) that other and *mutually exclusive* action descriptions, in addition to "extending one's arm" and "signaling," are compatible with a single set of events produced by Jones. For example, when Jones extends his arm from a car it is possible that Jones be pointing at something, or not pointing but stretching, or neither pointing nor stretching but signaling, and that in each of these three cases the events produced by Jones can be identical. Since, by hypothesis, *which* of these three actions Jones actually performs does not depend on events he produces, it behooves us to seek elsewhere for criteria that justify the application of one action description rather than another. And we must see whether it makes sense to say that these criteria *cause* his action to be of one sort rather than another.

Practices and intentions. Two possible criteria for identifying the correct action description are the applicability of social practices or conventions and the intention with which the action is done. We shall discuss each briefly, and we shall offer some evidence for the view that actions such as signaling, pointing, and making chess moves are logically dependent on applicable social practices and intentions. This means that given other conditions, the existence of an intention or applicable practice logically entails, and does not cause, a given action. But the issue is complicated by the fact that given an appropriate bodily movement, it appears to be sometimes sufficient and sometimes merely necessary for an action to take place that one intend it. Similarly, it appears to be sometimes sufficient and sometimes merely necessary for an action to take place that a practice or convention apply to it, and sometimes the convention and the practice will be jointly sufficient. It will be evident that which of these alternatives holds depends not only on the kind of action in question but also on the circumstances in which the action is to be done.

If signaling a turn with one's arm were not a generally accepted convention, it would be impossible to signal in this manner. One must have learned to signal with one's arm in a setting of general agreement that this is the way to do it. Otherwise, extending one's arm is no more a turn signal than is dumping debris from the window of the car, and this is so regardless of what one intends to do and, in most situations, regardless of what the other driver interprets one to be doing. It is possible for one to intend to signal and nevertheless fail to do so solely because one failed to exploit any available accepted conventions. This does not rule out inventing signals in peculiar situations or when in distress, for all such signaling succeeds, if it does, by analogy with other, already existing conventions. For similar reasons, although less obviously, an applicable convention may be a necessary condition for one to be pointing. Dogs, cats, and infants give their whole attention to the outstretched arm, not to the object which is "pointed to," and it is not obvious that they are simply not sufficiently intelligent to "infer" both that something is meant and what is meant. By contrast, there is no convention that is a necessary condition for stretching.

If Jones extends his arm from the car, then whether he stretches, points, or signals often depends on which of these he intends to do. Intending to point is usually a necessary condition for pointing, and if we assume the applicability of a convention as well as the correct bodily movement, it is a sufficient condition for pointing. Given the proper background conditions, intending to point or signal logically entails that one points or signals. Hence, the presence of the intention is, in some contexts, part of what we mean by "Jones is pointing (or signaling)." If this is true, then there are actions which, at least in certain specifiable contexts, cannot possibly be done unintentionally and other kinds of actions which in any context can be done unintentionally (see Anscombe). One can break, kick, or kill something unintentionally, but one cannot point out something unintentionally. Signaling is perhaps a more difficult case than pointing because it appears that in some circumstances for Jones to signal it is sufficient that he make the appropriate bodily movement in a situation in which a signaling convention applies. If so, it is sometimes possible to signal unintentionally.

It is often argued, however, that there cannot be different intentions without there being different events either before or at the time of the action. That is, because when one signals rather than points there need be no overt difference between the two actions, there then must be different mental events produced when one signals and when one points. These events would constitute an intention, distinct from and temporally prior to the overt action. We cannot now discuss in detail the concept of "intention." However, some philosophers have maintained (see Hart, in *Freedom and the Will,* and Melden and Anscombe) that intentional actions are essentially actions that are explainable in terms of the agent's purposes, goals, or plans. They have maintained that the occurrence of relevant prior mental events is not a necessary condition for the concept of intention to apply, although it is a contingent fact that many intentions can be identified by means of prior mental events (see INTENTION for further discussion).

Freedom of the will. It may be seen that this theory of intention is not unlike the theory of choosing that has been sketched earlier in this article. That is, intentional actions and choices are each construed to be actions which are explainable in certain kinds of ways, rather than as actions which are necessarily preceded by mental events called "intentions" and "choices." If this account of "intention" is true, and if it is also true that intentions and applicable practices are necessary conditions for performing certain kinds of actions, then it follows that no set of antecedent events produced by the agent can be a sufficient condition for the performance of an action of this kind. Moreover, if applicable practices and intentions are never causes of actions but nevertheless necessary for some actions, then no set of causes can be sufficient for the occurrence of certain actions. And if this is so, then it would appear that the determinists' hypothesis, namely, that there is some set of antecedent conditions causally sufficient for the occurrence of every human action, is false. Several recent philosophers employ arguments similar to the above (see Hampshire) and thus maintain that a correct elucidation of the concepts of "action," "choice," and "intention" lends support to libertarianism.

The view that there cannot be causal conditions sufficient for the occurrence of every action, and its supposed antideterministic implications, are fraught with obscurities and difficulties. It can be expected that in the near future philosophers will progress toward a better understanding of events, causes, actions, practices, intentions, noncausal conditions, and of the relations between them. We shall conclude with a brief account of some of these difficulties.

First, let us suppose that in doing any of several different actions, exactly the same events would be produced by Jones, for example, the events involved in extending his arm from the window of a car. And suppose also that every event in the universe is causally determined, that whether Jones signals or points depends on what he intends, and that his intention is not an event and hence can neither cause what he does nor itself be caused. Some philosophers (see Warnock in *Freedom and the Will*) have questioned the relevance of these claims to libertarianism. Even if it follows from the above suppositions that Jones is free, in some sense of "free," to either point or signal, nevertheless it does not follow that Jones is free to do any action incompatible with the events which do occur. His arm does extend from the car: that is determined; a small number of action descriptions compatible with these events may apply "freely," but the vast number of actions which libertarians wish to believe Jones can do—for example, keeping both hands on the wheel or not driving at all—are causally impossible for him to do. Can it be that the arena of free action, if there is any, should be so sharply limited?

Second, the antideterministic position we have discussed relies, as far as we have gone, on the claim that causal conditions cannot be sufficient for the occurrence of every action and hence that noncausal conditions are necessary for certain actions. But from the mere fact that a condition necessary for an action is not caused, it does not follow that the existence or applicability of that condition is in any way within the power of the agent. An applicable signaling convention may be a logically necessary condition for an arm movement to be a turn signal, but it is surely not up to the agent whether this convention exists and applies to his arm movement. It is important to see that logically necessary conditions usually need not be mentioned in discussions of determinism: No libertarian, who believes that he is free to write or not write a valid argument on a blackboard, believes that it must also be up to him whether there be applicable rules of logic. A libertarian believes that what he writes is up to him, but he does not believe that it is up to him whether a *given* argument that he writes is valid; so, too, no one should believe that it is up to him whether a given arm movement is a signal, if what determines its being a signal is a convention which is no more up to him than are the rules of logic. Thus, the fact that there are noncausal necessary conditions for actions does not by itself constitute an obstacle to determinism.

Third, can intentions be caused, if intentional actions essentially are actions explainable in terms of ends? It is clear that to state a reason is not to state a cause, any more than a rule of chess is a cause of a chess move. But what a person intends must be discoverable in terms of his dispositions to act and to utter certain words. If there are causes sufficient for every event constitutive of this evidence for his having a certain intention, are these causes then sufficient for his acting with one intention rather than another? For the sake of argument we may grant three things: (1) that all bodily events produced by a person are causally determined, (2) that an intention is a kind of reason and not a set of events, and (3) that if a given set of events occurs, it is quite settled what intention a person has. None of these diminishes the absurdity of saying that intentions can be caused, for we granted that they are not events but reasons. What can be doubted is the relevance of these considerations to libertarianism, for reasons similar to those offered in the preceding discussion of logically necessary conditions. Chess rules and laws of logic, and perhaps intentions, are necessary conditions for certain action descriptions to apply correctly. When a rule applies, it does not *cause* an action to take place, but, given that there is a particular rule, *that* it applies may well be inferable from a statement of causally sufficient conditions.

Fourth, some philosophers (see Melden) deny that simple bodily movements, as well as those more complex actions for which intentions and applicable conventions are necessary conditions, can be identified with sets of overt events. There does seem to be a difference between the action of moving one's arm and the physical motion of one's arm, but accounts of this difference are subject to many difficulties. One such account is that human actions, as distinct from bodily events, such as twitches and visceral motions, are explainable by reference to goals or purposes. That is, if we wish to know whether an occurrence is an action, in addition to being a bodily event that has causal antecedents, we should discover whether it can be made intelligible in terms of reasons, as well as be accounted for causally. This is not to say that all actions are purposeful or intentional. An action is equally intelligible to us when it is shown to be intentional, or the by-product of an intentional action, or the result of intentions gone wrong. Many of the difficulties with this view have to do with whether simple wants, unconscious desires, habits, whimseys, etc., can all *explain* in the requisite way and hence supply reasons for actions.

Past attempts to solve the free-will problem have been largely confined to the questions of whether concepts related to human action name events which result wholly from antecedent causal chains of the sort described by physical science and, if so, whether this fact is compatible with moral responsibility. What has recently been questioned is this presupposition, found in nearly all past views about the problem, that any concept which is related to human action is the name of an event or set of events. Thus, it is likely that the free-will problem must be rethought and reformulated in view of elucidations by contemporary philosophers of such concepts as "choosing," "deciding," and "doing."

Bibliography

Aristotle, *Nichomachean Ethics*, Bk. III.

Anscombe, G. E. M., *Intention.* Oxford, 1958.

Bennett, D., "Action, Reason, and Purpose." *Journal of Philosophy*, Vol. 62, No. 4 (1965).

Black, Max, "Making Something Happen," in Sidney Hook, ed., *Determinism and Freedom in the Age of Modern Science.* New York, 1958.

Danto, Arthur, "What Can We Do?" *Journal of Philosophy* (July 18, 1963).

Daveney, T. F., "Choosing." *Mind* (October 1964).

Davidson, D., "Actions, Reasons, and Causes." *Journal of Philosophy* (November 7, 1963).

Evans, J. L., "Choice." *Philosophical Quarterly* (1955).

Franks, O. S., "Choice." *PAS* (1933–1934).

Glasgow, W. D., "On Choosing." *Analysis* (1957).

Glasgow, W. D., "The Concept of Choosing." *Analysis* (1960).

Hampshire, Stuart, *Thought and Action.* London, 1959.

Hart, H. L. A., and Honoré, A. M., *Causation in the Law.* Oxford, 1959.

Melden. A. I., *Free Action.* London, 1961.

Nowell-Smith, P. H., *Ethics.* London, 1954.

Nowell-Smith, P. H., "Choosing, Deciding, Doing." *Analysis* (January 1958).

Pears, D. F., ed., *Freedom and the Will.* London, 1963.

Peters, R. S., *The Concept of Motivation.* London and New York, 1958.

Ryle, Gilbert, *The Concept of Mind.* London, 1949.

Vesey, G. N. A., "Volition." *Philosophy*, Vol. 36, No. 136 (1961). Reprinted in D. Gustafson, ed., *Essays in Philosophical Psychology.* New York, 1964.

ANDREW OLDENQUIST

CHRISTIANITY. The present article is restricted to Christian belief and scarcely touches on the origins of Christianity or its history and institutional forms. Among Christian beliefs only a few can be treated; certain others, such as the existence and attributes of God, are discussed in other articles (see, for example, GOD, CONCEPTS OF).

CHRISTIAN BELIEF

Perhaps the first thing that should be said about Christian belief is that it does not constitute a philosophy. That is to say, it is not a metaphysical system comparable, for example, to Platonism or the systems of Aristotle and Spinoza. Although the body of Christian doctrine does consist largely of metaphysical beliefs, in the sense that they are beliefs whose scope transcends the empirical world, it differs from what are usually identified as philosophical systems by its essential relation to and dependence on particular historical events and experiences. Such systems as Platonism begin with philosophical concepts and principles and seek by means of these to construct a comprehensive mental picture of the universe. Christianity, on the other hand, begins with particular, nonrecurrent historical events that are regarded as revelatory and on the basis of which Christian faith makes certain limited statements about the ultimate nature and structure of reality.

The relationship between experience and discursive reflection in Christianity can be brought out by distinguishing two orders of Christian belief. There is a primary level, consisting of direct reports of experience, secular and religious, and a secondary level, consisting of theological theories constructed on the basis of these reports.

At the primary level Christian literature affirms a number of both publicly verifiable historical facts and "religious facts," or "facts of faith." The latter consist of incidents in the history of Israel as understood and participated in by the prophets and in the life of Jesus as he was responded to by the apostles, these events being seen by faith as revelatory of God. The resulting testimonies of the prophets and apostles are not formulations of theological doctrine but direct expressions of moments of intense religious experience. The four New Testament gospels are writings on this primary level, recording events that occurred either within the purview of secular history or within the religious experience of the early Christian community.

Within this primary stratum of Christian belief certain facts of faith have always stood out as being pre-eminently important. By means of these Christianity has defined itself in distinction to other religions. Among the total body of those who have called themselves Christians there is no universally agreed-on list of these defining facts of faith, except insofar as such lists have been adopted, locally or more widely, by particular Christian communions, sects, or movements. However, it is safe to say that the main streams of contemporary Christianity, claiming continuity of faith with the first Christian generation, affirm at least the following: the reality of God and the propriety of speaking of him in a threefold manner, as Father, Son, and Spirit; the divine creation of the universe; human sinfulness; divine incarnation in the person of Jesus, the Christ; his reconciliation of man to God; his founding of the Christian church and the continuing operation of his Spirit within it; and an eventual end to human history and the fulfillment of God's purpose for his creation. Stated in this general form these are facts of faith that cumulatively define Christianity. Many further tenets are regarded as essential by different subgroups within Christianity, but the above probably constitute the permanent core that is acknowledged by virtually the whole of Christendom, past and present.

The second order of Christian belief consists in theological theories or doctrines that seek to explain these facts of faith and to relate them to one another and/or to human knowledge in general. The formulation of doctrines is essentially a discursive and speculative activity, differing from theory construction in secular philosophy only in that the theologian includes in his data, and indeed accords a central and determinative importance to, the special facts of Christian faith.

This distinction can now be illustrated by reference to some of the central Christian themes, noting both the relevant facts of faith and the theological theories that have been developed about them.

Creation. The doctrine of creation (which Christianity holds in common with Judaism) stands somewhat apart from the other doctrines to be described below. The others have arisen out of reflection on specific historical phenomena, but belief in the divine creation of the universe, although connected with the religious experience of absolute dependence on God, has presumably been arrived at primarily as an implicate of the monotheistic understanding of God as the sole ultimate reality.

The doctrine of the divine creation of the universe out of nothing stands in contrast to other conceptions of its origin. This doctrine denies that the universe is eternal, although the denial does not entail the belief that it was created at some moment in time—Augustine, for example, taught that time is itself an aspect of the created world. The doctrine also excludes the Platonic notion of a Demiurge fashioning the world out of a formless matter and the Neoplatonic notion of the physical universe's coming to be by emanation from the Absolute. In distinction to these ideas the doctrine of *creatio ex nihilo* asserts that the universe has been summoned into existence out of nothing (that is, not out of anything) by the creative will and purpose of God.

Incarnation. Jesus was born about 5 B.C. in Palestine and was executed by crucifixion at Jerusalem probably in A.D. 29 or 30. There immediately arose a conviction among his disciples, reflected in all the New Testament documents, that he had been raised by God from the dead, and under the compulsion of this conviction the Christian church came into existence, witnessing to both the divine status and the saving power of Jesus, now proclaimed as the Christ.

The beliefs of Jesus' disciples about him are reflected in the four memoirs, or gospels, which were produced in different centers of the apostolic church during the second half of the first century. On the one hand, these depict him as fully and authentically human, subject, like other men, to temptation, hunger, pain, fatigue, ignorance, and sorrow. But at the same time they affirm that he is Lord, Messiah (*Christos*), the Son of God. This extremely exalted view reaches its highest expression in the Fourth Gospel, which claims in its prologue to Jesus' life that the Word (Logos), which was in the beginning with God, and was God, and through which all things were made, "became flesh, and dwelt among us, full of grace and truth; and we have beheld his glory, glory as of the only Son from the Father" (John 1.14; the conception of the Logos in the Fourth Gospel derives both from the Word and the wisdom of God in the Old Testament and from the Logos as the universal principle of reason in Greek philosophy). The faith that Jesus was the Christ apparently arose out of a practical acceptance of his status as one who had authority to forgive sins, to declare God's mind toward man, to reveal the true meaning of the divine Law, to heal diseases, and to assume that men's eternal destiny and welfare was bound up with their responses to him. This practical acknowledgment of his unique authority probably crystallized into conscious conviction as to his deity under the impact of the resurrection events.

In the gospels these two beliefs, identifying Jesus both as a son of man and as the Son of God, occur together without any attempt to theorize about the relationship between them. Thus, this primary stratum of Christian literature contains, as data for theological reflection, reports of (*a*) the publicly observable fact that Jesus was a man, and (*b*) the fact of faith that he was divine, in that "in him all the fullness of God was pleased to dwell" (Colossians 1.19).

During its first four centuries of life these data provided the church with its chief intellectual task. The eventual outcome of the Christological debates, formalized by the Council of Chalcedon (451), was not to propound any definitive theory concerning the relationship between Jesus' humanity and his divinity but simply to reaffirm, in the philosophical language of that day, the original facts of faith. The various views that were from time to time branded as heretical came under this condemnation because directly or by implication they denied one or the other of the two fixed points of Christian thought in this field, the human and divine natures of Christ.

The first of the Christological heresies, the Docetism of some of the Gnostics in the first and second centuries, denied the real humanity of Christ, suggesting that he was a human being in appearance only. The motive behind this theory was to exalt his divine status, but the effect was to deny one of the foundation facts of Christianity as historically based faith. The next great heresy, Arianism, in the fourth century, went to the opposite extreme, denying continuity of being or nature between the Godhead and Christ and regarding him as a created being, so that "there was a time when he was not" (ἦν ὅτε οὐκ ἦν). It was in the controversy with Arianism that the notion of substance (οὐσία, *substantia*) became a key category in the Christological debates. Arius declared that the Son was ὁμοιούσιον τῷ πατρί (of *like* substance with the Father), whereas the Council of Nicea (325), excluding Arianism as a heresy, insisted that the Son was ὁμοούσιον τῷ πατρί (of the *same* substance as the Father). It was made clear by Athanasius, the champion of orthodoxy, that the iota's difference between these formulations involved an immense religious difference, for only a savior who came from the Godward side of creation could offer man an ultimate salvation. This Homousian Christology was reaffirmed by the Council of Chalcedon and has ever since been the position of the main streams of historic Christianity.

During the last hundred years a number of theologians (for example, the Ritschlian school and H. R. Mackintosh) who accept the Nicene and Chalcedonian affirmations of the full humanity and real deity of Christ have questioned the adequacy of the category of substance in terms of which that affirmation was made. They have pointed out that it belongs to the thought-worlds of Plato and Aristotle and that it is a static notion, contrasting in this respect with such characteristically dynamic Biblical categories as purpose and action. Accordingly there is now a fairly widespread tendency to describe the incarnation as a complex event constituting God's self-revealing action in man's history. In the New Testament records we see God at work in and through a human life, dealing with human beings in a way that makes plain the divine nature in its relation to man. The acts and attitudes of Jesus toward the men and women with whom he had to do were God's acts and attitudes in relation to those particular individuals, expressed in the finitude of a human life. Along these and other lines Christological discussion continues.

The Trinity. The Trinitarian doctrine is a second-order Christian belief. It was gradually developed within the church both to take account of certain data at the experiential level and to aid the development of the general system of Christian doctrine, some of the key points of which are related by the Trinitarian framework.

The New Testament basis for this doctrine was the Christian community's threefold awareness of God, first as the transcendent moral creator witnessed to in the prophetic tradition received from Judaism; second, as having been at work among them on earth in the person of Christ; and third, as the Holy Spirit, which was referred to apparently indiscriminately as the Spirit of God and the Spirit of Christ, inspiring and guiding both individuals and the Christian community.

The doctrine of the Trinity developed in close conjunction with Christology and made possible the completion of the church's thought concerning the person of Christ. For it had never been the accepted Christian conception that God, simply as such and in his totality, became man in the incarnation. The belief that "God was in Christ" (2 Corinthians 5.19) was held in conjunction with the belief that God was also and at the same time sustaining and governing the universe. The God who was incarnate in Christ was the God who had created heaven and earth. This was expressed by the affirmation that God is both Father and Son; and the reality of the Spirit, operating in the world both before and after the thirty or so years of the incarnation, required the further expansion into a Trinitarian formulation. Thus, the doctrine of the Trinity (*a*) asserts the full deity of Christ as the second person of the Trinity; (*b*) prohibits a too simple conception of incarnation (as one branch of the theological tradition has put it, Christ is *totus deus*, wholly God, but not *totum dei*, the whole of God); and (*c*) recognizes the universal presence and activity of God in the world as the divine Spirit. This latter point is of great practical importance because it entails a Christian message not only about God's actions in the past but also about a divine activity in the present that can directly affect the individual today.

In the Trinitarian discussions that accompanied the Christological debates one of the main questions concerned the issue of equality versus subordination within the Trinity. Is the Son subordinate to the Father, or the Spirit to both? The answer that was eventually embodied in the *Quicunque vult*, or "Athanasian" Creed, of the sixth century was that the members of the Trinity are coeternal and have an equal divine status; the Son is eternally begotten by the Father, and the Spirit eternally proceeds from the Father and the Son. (The latter point was the occasion of the rift in the sixth century between the Eastern church, with its center at Constantinople, and the Western church, with its center at Rome. In its original form the Nicene Creed described the Spirit as proceeding (only) from the Father. Later the Western church added the famous *filioque*—"and the Son"—an insertion that Eastern Christianity rejected as an unwarrantable tampering with the creed.)

In the accepted Trinitarian language the Father, the Son, and the Holy Spirit are spoken of as three "Persons," the Latin *persona* having been used to translate the Greek *ὑπόστασις* (which had displaced *πρόσωπον*—literally, "face"—in this context). *Persona* is not, of course, the equivalent of "person" in the modern sense of an individual center of consciousness and purpose. Originally a persona was the mask worn by an actor, then his part in the play, and then by further extension any part a person might play in life. Thus, whereas *τρεῖς ὑπόστασεις* suggests three divine entities, *tres personae* suggests three roles or functions of the deity. These two different conceptions have each been developed in Christian thought, leading to what have been called respectively "immanent," or "ontological," and "economic" theories of the Trinity.

According to the ontological theories the doctrine of the Trinity is an affirmation about the transcendent metaphysical structure of the Godhead. It asserts that God in his inner being consists of three divine realities that are individually distinct and yet bound together in a mysterious unity—"three in one and one in three." The extreme form of this view is the "social" conception of the Trinity as comprising three consciousnesses. According to the economic theories, on the other hand, the doctrine is about God specifically in his relation to the world. It asserts that the one God has acted toward mankind in three distinguishable ways—in creation and providence, in redemption, and in inner guidance and sanctification. God must indeed, in his inner being, be such as to become related in these ways to his creation, but this does not necessarily require the postulation of three distinct and yet intimately related divine realities.

Redemption. That human beings are sinful is a theological statement of the observable fact that men and women are persistently self-centered and that even their highest moral achievements are quickly corrupted by selfishness. Yet although we thus fail, exhibiting a chronic moral weakness and poverty, our failure is not inevitable; we are ourselves, at least in part, responsible for it. The Biblical story of the fall of man depicts this situation by means of the myth that man was originally created perfect but fell by his own fault into his present state, in which he is divided both in himself and from his fellows and God.

At its primary level of belief Christianity claims that by responding to God's free forgiveness, offered by Christ, men are released from the guilt of their moral failure (justification) and are drawn into a realm of grace in which they are gradually re-created in character (sanctification). The basis of this claim is the Christian experience of reconciliation with God and, as a consequence, with other human beings, with life's circumstances and demands, and with oneself. The "justification by faith" of which Paul spoke, and which represented the main religious emphasis of the Reformation of the sixteenth century, means that men are freely accepted by God's gracious love, which they have only to receive in faith. In Paul Tillich's contemporary restatement, a man has only to accept the fact that although unacceptable even to himself, he is accepted by God.

In this case, work at the secondary level of theological reflection did not begin seriously until the church had been preaching the fact of divine reconciliation and atonement for about a thousand years. Anselm, in the eleventh century, taught that the death of Christ constituted a satisfaction to the divine honor for the stain cast upon it by man's disobedience, and this remains the core of Catholic atonement doctrine. Luther and Calvin, in the sixteenth century, spoke of Christ's death as a substitutionary sacrifice by which Christ suffered in his own person the punishment that was justly due mankind, and this remains the core of official Protestant atonement doctrine. In the nineteenth century, however, the thought was developed (going back to Anselm's contemporary Abelard) that God's forgiveness does not need to be purchased by Christ's death, but that this brings home to the human heart both man's need for divine forgiveness and the reality of that forgiveness. There are in the twentieth century continuing efforts to understand Christ's redeeming work in a way that would bring together the valid insights in these and other traditional views, each of which by itself has seemed one-sided.

Heaven, hell, and judgment. Jesus impressed upon his hearers in the strongest possible terms the absolute importance of decisions made and deeds performed in this present life. He regarded men and women as free and responsible persons on whose daily choices depended their own final good and happiness or irretrievable loss and failure. In doing this he used the traditional language of heaven and hell, which were understood until comparatively recently in terms of a prescientific cosmology, with heaven located in the sky above our heads and hell in the ground beneath our feet. Heaven is now generally conceived of as the enjoyment of the full consciousness of God's presence and participation in the divine "kingdom," which represents the final fulfillment of God's purpose for his creation; and hell is viewed as self-exclusion from this.

There are many perennially debated questions in this area. Are men divinely predestined, some to eternal salvation and others to eternal damnation ("double predestination"), as Augustine and Calvin taught? Does "hell" signify an eternal state, or is it a temporally bounded purgatorial experience that might lead to eventual salvation? (The adjective *αἰώνιος*, which is used in the New Testament, can mean either "eternal" or "for the aeon, or age"). Or does "hell" perhaps signify sheer annihilation? Can the final frustration of God's purpose by the loss of part of his human creation be reconciled with his ultimate sovereignty, and does the idea of never-ending torment, as a form of suffering out of which no good is finally brought, rule out the possibility of a Christian theodicy? Are all men to be finally saved ("universalism"), or only some?

In relation to such questions it is perhaps useful to distinguish between two standpoints from which eschatological statements may be made. There is the existential standpoint of "real life," in which we exercise a fateful responsibility in our moral choices and are confronted with the tremendous alternatives of spiritual life and death, symbolized by heaven and hell. There is also the detached standpoint of theological reflection, in which it seems possible to deduce from the two premises of the sovereignty and the love of God that although damnation is abstractly conceivable and is known in existential experience as a dread possibility, God's saving purpose in relation to his creatures will nevertheless in the end be triumphant, and eternal loss will remain an unrealized possibility.

The church. Although Christianity as historically institutionalized lies outside the narrow scope of this article, it must be added that Christian faith has always drawn people together into a community of faith, or church. The largest Christian institution, the Roman Catholic church, holds that the authentic Christian community is defined by its visible continuity, manifested in a succession of bishops and popes, with the earliest church. Protestantism holds that the Christian community is defined by a different continuity, that of faith, and affirms that the external institutions associated with Christian faith are continually in need of reformation in the light of the original Christian data embodied in the scriptures.

Bibliography

THE BIBLE

Old Testament, R. Kittel, ed., 7th ed. Stuttgart, 1951. Hebrew text.

New Testament, G. D. Kilpatrick, ed., 2d ed. London, 1958. Greek text.

American Revised Standard Version. New York, 1952–1957. Old and New Testaments and Apocrypha in translation.

New English Bible, Vol. 1, New Testament. London, 1961. Translation.

COLLECTIONS OF CHRISTIAN LITERATURE

Baillie, John, McNeill, John T., and Van Dusen, Henry P., eds., *Library of Christian Classics*, 26 vols. London and Philadelphia, 1954—.

Migne, J. P., ed., *Patrologia Latina*, 221 vols. Paris, 1844–1864.

Migne, J. P., ed., *Patrologia Graeca*, 162 vols. Paris, 1857–1866.

Roberts, Alexander, and Donaldson, James, eds., *The Ante-Nicene Fathers*, 10 vols. Grand Rapids, Mich., 1951.

Schaff, Philip, et al., eds., *Nicene and Post-Nicene Fathers of the Christian Church.* Grand Rapids, Mich., 1952–1956. Two series, each in 14 vols.

ENCYCLOPEDIAS

Campenhausen, H. F. von, et al., eds., *Die Religion in Geschichte und Gegenwart*, 3d ed., 6 vols. Tübingen, 1957–1962.

Hastings, James, ed., *Encyclopedia of Religion and Ethics*, 13 vols. Edinburgh, 1908–1926.

Vacant, A., et al., eds., *Dictionnaire de Théologie catholique*, 3d ed., 15 vols. Paris, 1923–1950.

HISTORY OF CHRISTIANITY

Latourette, K. S., *A History of the Expansion of Christianity*, 7 vols. New York and London, 1937–1945.

HISTORY OF CHRISTIAN THOUGHT

Harnack, Adolf von, *Lehrbuch der Dogmengeschichte*, 4th ed., 3 vols. Tübingen, 1909–1910. Third ed. translated by Neil Buchanan as *History of Dogma*, 7 vols. London, 1894–1899; New York, 1958.

Kelly, J. N. D., *Early Christian Doctrines.* London, 1958.

Seeberg, Reinhold, *Lehrbuch der Dogmengeschichte*, 4th ed., 4 vols. Basel, 1953–1954. Translated by C. E. Hay as *Textbook of the History of Doctrines.* Grand Rapids, Mich., 1952.

Wolfson, H. A., *The Philosophy of the Church Fathers.* Cambridge, Mass., 1956—.

ROMAN CATHOLICISM

Aquinas, Thomas, *Summa Contra Gentiles*, Editio Leonina Manualis. Rome, 1934. Translated by A. C. Pegis, J. F. Anderson, V. J. Bourke, and C. J. O'Neil as *On the Truth of the Catholic Faith*, 4 vols. New York, 1955–1957.

Aquinas, Thomas, *Summa Theologica*, Editio altera Romana, 6 vols. Rome, 1894. Translated by the English Dominican Fathers. London, 1911–1922; New York, 1947–1948.

Denzinger, H. J. D., *Enchiridion Symbolorum Definitionum et Declarationum de Rebus Fidei et Morum*, 29th ed. Freiburg, Germany, 1952. Translated by R. J. Defarrari as *The Sources of Catholic Dogma.* St. Louis, Mo., 1957.

Schmaus, Michael, *Katholische Dogmatik*, 5 vols. Munich, 1948–1958.

Smith, G. D., ed., *The Teaching of the Catholic Church*, 2 vols. London, 1948; New York, 1949.

PROTESTANTISM

Barth, Karl, *Kirchliche Dogmatik.* Munich, 1932—. Translated as *Church Dogmatics*, G. W. Bromiley and T. F. Torrance, eds. Edinburgh, 1936—.

Calvin, John, *Institutio Christianae Religionis.* Basel, 1536. Critical ed. by P. Barth and W. Niesel. Munich, 1926. Translated by F. L. Battles as *Institutes of the Christian Religion*, J. T. McNeill, ed., 2 vols. London and Philadelphia, 1961.

Luther, Martin, *A Commentary on St. Paul's Epistle to the Galatians*, Philip Watson, ed. and translator. London, 1953.

Luther, Martin, *Lectures on Romans*, translated by W. Pauck. London and Philadelphia, 1961.

Luther, Martin, *Werke*, 58 vols. Weimar, 1883–1948.

Schleiermacher, Friedrich, *Der Christliche Glaube*, critical ed. by M. Redeker. Berlin, 1960. Translated as *The Christian Faith*, H. R. Mackintosh and J. S. Stewart, eds. Edinburgh, 1928.

Tillich, Paul, *Systematic Theology*, 3 vols. Chicago and London, 1951–1964.

EASTERN ORTHODOXY

Bulgakov, Sergei N., *L'Orthodoxie.* Paris, 1932. Translated by E. S. Cram as *The Orthodox Church.* London, 1935.

Tsankov, Stefan, *Das orthodoxe Christentum des Ostens.* Berlin, 1928. Translated by D. A. Lowrie as *The Eastern Orthodox Church.* London, 1929.

Zernov, Nicholas, *Eastern Christendom.* New York, 1961.

CONTEMPORARY ECUMENICAL MOVEMENT

Bell, G. K. A., ed., *Documents on Christian Unity*, 4 vols. London, 1924–1958.

Neill, Stephen C., and Rouse, R., eds., *A History of the Ecumenical Movement, 1517–1948.* Philadelphia, 1954.

CREATION

Gilkey, Langdon B., *Maker of Heaven and Earth.* Garden City, N.Y., 1959.

THE PERSON OF CHRIST

Baillie, D. M., *God Was in Christ.* London and New York, 1948.

Hendry, G. S., *The Gospel of the Incarnation.* Philadelphia, 1958.

Knox, John, *Jesus: Lord and Christ.* New York, 1958.
Mackintosh, H. R., *The Doctrine of the Person of Jesus Christ.* London and New York, 1912.
Pittenger, W. Norman, *The Word Incarnate.* London and New York, 1959.

ATONEMENT

Anselm, *Cur Deus Homo?*, F. S. Schmitt, ed. Bonn, 1929. Also in F. S. Schmitt, ed., *Opera Omnia*, Vol. II. Anonymous translation in Ancient and Modern Library of Theological Literature. London, 1889. "Satisfaction" theory.
Aulen, Gustaf, *Christus Victor.* Translated by A. G. Hebert. London, 1931. "Christus Victor" theory.
Denney, James, *The Christian Doctrine of Reconciliation.* London, 1918. "Penal-substitutionary" theory.
Mozley, J. K., *The Doctrine of the Atonement.* London, 1915 Historical.
Rashdall, Hastings, *The Idea of Atonement in Christian Theology.* London, 1919. "Moral influence" theory.

TRINITY

Franks, R. S., *The Doctrine of the Trinity.* London, 1953. Historical.
Hodgson, Leonard, *The Doctrine of the Trinity.* London, 1943.
Welch, Claude, *In His Name.* New York, 1952. Welch and Hodgson represent the two types of theory described in this article.

ESCHATOLOGY

Althaus, Paul, *Die letzten Dinge*, 4th ed. Gütersloh, 1933.
Cullmann, Oscar, *Christus und die Zeit.* Zurich, 1946. Translated by F. V. Filson as *Christ and Time.* Philadelphia, 1950; rev. ed., London, 1962.
Hügel, F. von, *Eternal Life.* Edinburgh, 1912.

CHRISTIANITY AND OTHER RELIGIONS

Farmer, H. H., *Revelation and Religion.* London, 1954.
Kraemer, H., *Religion and the Christian Faith.* London, 1956.

JOHN HICK

CHRYSIPPUS (c. 279–206 B.C.), Stoic philosopher born at Soli, in Cilicia, became the third leader of the Stoa at Athens upon the death of Cleanthes, in 232 B.C. This post he held until his own death. Because of his defense of the Stoa against the attacks of Arcesilaus and the skeptical Academy, and undoubtedly also on the basis of his voluminous writings, it was said in antiquity "if there had been no Chrysippus, there would be no Stoa." He wrote 705 books, about half of which, judging from the catalogue preserved by Diogenes Laertius, dealt with logic and language. None of his works is extant, though quotations from his books and assessments of some of his views have survived in the works of other ancient authors.

Chrysippus' epistemology is empirical. Presentations of objects are produced in the ruling part of the soul by movements engendered in the sense organs of the percipient. Illusory presentations can be distinguished from those that are veridical by deliberation, which consists in checking any given presentation against a fund of common notions, i.e., families of remembered similar presentations; if the presentation is found to be sufficiently like some common notion, one may assent to it, thus acknowledging its veridical character.

Propositions are either simple or nonsimple. The truth condition of a simple proposition is the occurrence of the fact it conveys. The truth conditions of nonsimple propositions are functions of the truth-values of their ingredient propositions.

Chrysippus formulated five undemonstrated argument forms whose variables are to be specified by propositions. Among them are forms of the *modus ponens* and the *modus tollens* arguments. Arguments of varying complexity can be constructed by combining two or more of these basic forms. Chrysippus enjoyed a particular renown for his competence as a dialectician.

The moral philosophy of Chrysippus is concerned primarily with a statement of the final end of life and the relation of other things to it and with a consideration of the emotions and therapy for those enslaved by them. The final good is "to live in accordance with one's experience of the things which come about by nature." This is equivalent to living in accordance with reason, which in man supervenes upon instinct as a guide in life. The excellence of reason is wisdom, or knowledge of what is really good and what is really bad. Chrysippus' view in regard to the source of this knowledge is ambivalent. On the one hand—and this is obviously the doctrine that coheres best with his epistemology—it derives from generalizations made upon particular experiences. On the other hand, there are fragments implying that his knowledge is innate.

Emotions are great obstacles to happiness and are to be totally eradicated. In keeping with his monistic psychology, which rejects the Platonic doctrine of a tripartite soul, Chrysippus conceived of an emotion as a recently formed false judgment about the goodness or badness of something; such a judgment causes "a forceful and excessive impulse." Therapy for the emotions consists in persuading their victims that the judgments constituting the emotions are false.

The dominant motifs of the natural philosophy of Chrysippus are monism and determinism. The one substance that converts periodically into an elaborately structured universe has two constant aspects, a passive one and an active one. The passive is matter; the active is identified variously as reason, pneuma (spirit or breath), and God. Chrysippus regards so-called individual substances not as discrete units of matter but rather as "parts" of one primary substance. Everything that occurs is controlled unexceptionably by fate, which is "the continuous causal chain of the things that exist." Nothing comes about except in accordance with antecedent causes. Even in the case of states of affairs that might seem to be of a spontaneous or uncaused nature, "obscure causes are working under the surface." Chrysippus believed that men were responsible for their conduct, and he sought in several ways to show that such a belief was not undermined by the rigorously deterministic view he espoused.

Bibliography

Arnim, Hans V., *Stoicorum Veterum Fragmenta.* Leipzig, 1903.
Bréhier, E., *Chrysippe et l'ancienne Stoïcisme.* Paris, 1951.
Mates, B., *Stoic Logic.* Berkeley, Calif., 1953.
Pohlenz, M., *Die Stoa*, Göttingen, 1948.

JOSIAH B. GOULD, JR.

CHUANG TZU (b. 369 B.C.), the greatest Taoist next to Lao Tzu, was also known by his private name, Chou. Not much is known about his life except that he was a minor government official at one time and that he later declined a prime ministership in the state of Ch'u to retain his freedom. Although Chuang Tzu and Mencius were contemporaries, they were not acquainted with each other's teachings. Chuang Tzu advanced the concept of Tao and gave Taoism a dynamic character. To him, Tao as Nature is not only spontaneity but also a constant flux, for all things are in a state of perpetual "self-transformation," each according to its own nature and in its own way. If there is an agent directing this process, there is no evidence of it. Things seem to develop from simple to higher life and finally to man, but man will return to the simple stuff, thus completing a cycle of transformation.

In this unceasing transfiguration, things appear and disappear. In such a universe "time cannot be recalled" and things move like "a galloping horse." They seem to be different, some large and some small, some beautiful and some ugly, but Tao equalizes them as one. This is Chuang Tzu's famous doctrine of the "equality of all things." According to it, reality and unreality, right and wrong, life and death, beauty and ugliness, and all conceivable opposites are reduced to an underlying unity. This is possible because all distinctions and oppositions are merely relative, because they are the result of a subjective point of view, because they mutually cause each other, and because opposites are resolved in Tao. By the doctrine of "mutual causation" Chuang Tzu meant that a thing necessarily produces its opposite; for instance, "this" implies "that," life ends in death, construction requires destruction, and so forth. By the resolution of opposites Chuang Tzu meant that a thing and its opposite, both being extremes, need to be synthesized. But the synthesis is itself an extreme which requires a synthesis. At the end Tao will synthesize all, in a dialectic manner not unlike that of Hegel.

In Chuang Tzu's philosophy the pure man abides in the great One, wherein he finds purity and peace. He becomes a "companion of Nature" and does not substitute the way of man for the way of Nature. He rejects all distinctions and seeks no self, fame, or success. He seeks "great knowledge," which is all-embracing and extensive, and discards "small knowledge," which is partial and discriminative. He "fasts in his mind" and "sits down and forgets everything"—especially the so-called humanity and righteousness of hypocritical society; he "travels in the realm of infinity." In this way he cultivates "profound virtue," and achieves a "great concord" with Tao. Herein he finds spiritual peace and "emancipation."

Both the mystical and fatalistic elements are obvious, and in these Chuang Tzu went beyond Lao Tzu. He was also more transcendental, for while Lao Tzu's chief concern was how to govern, Chuang Tzu's primary interest was to "roam beyond the mundane world," in spite of the fact that his ideal being is "sagely within" and "kingly without," that is, both transcendental and mundane. Nevertheless, Chuang Tzu stresses the individual more than does Lao Tzu. To be in accord with Tao, everything must nourish its own nature and follow its own destiny. The eagle should rise to the clouds, but the dove should hop from treetop to treetop. If a man were to shorten the crane's neck because it is long or to lengthen the duck's leg because it is short, that would be interfering with Nature. Spiritual freedom and peace can be achieved only through knowing one's own nature and capacity and being able to adapt oneself to the universal process of transformation. Although the ultimate goal is oneness with Tao, one's individuality is to be clearly recognized. Individual differences are not to be taken as basis for discrimination, but neither are they to be denied or ignored. This respect for individual nature and destiny eventually led to the emphasis on the particular nature in Neo-Taoism.

Bibliography

Available in English is *Chuang Tzu*, translated by Herbert A. Giles (London, 1961); the authorship of this work is a very controversial matter. Most scholars accept the first seven chapters, the so-called inner chapters, as authentic and the remaining 26 chapters as later additions, either partly or in whole dating from the third to the first century B.C. Selections have been translated in Wing-tsit Chan, *A Source Book in Chinese Philosophy* (Princeton, N.J., 1963). See also Fung Yu-lan, *A Short History of Chinese Philosophy* (New York, 1948).

WING-TSIT CHAN

CHUBB, THOMAS (1679–1746), English Arian and deist, was born at East Harnham, near Salisbury, the son of a maltster. Receiving little formal education, he read widely in geography, mathematics, and theology while working as apprentice to a glovemaker and, later, as a tallow chandler. At one time he lived in the house of Sir Joseph Jekyll, master of the rolls, in the capacity, it is alleged, of a sort of superior servant. Through the kindness of friends (one of whom was the celebrated surgeon William Cheselden) and the sales of his candles, his last years, spent at Salisbury, were largely devoted to study and to the presidency of a debating society. Chubb's importance, frequently overlooked, lies in the fact that a self-educated and humble artisan developed a good style of writing and mastered the prevalent rationalistic thinking sufficiently well to compete on equal terms with highly educated upper-class scholars and divines. He was the first, and one of the few, leading English deists of poor circumstances (only Peter Annet and Thomas Morgan shared this humble background). With Chubb it was apparent that deism had filtered down to the level of the common people and had become widespread.

Chubb's first publication was an Arian tract, *The Supremacy of the Father Asserted*, inspired by William Whiston's *Primitive Christianity Revived* of 1711 and published in 1715 upon the recommendation of Whiston.

Although Chubb went through an early phase of Arminianism and was always hard pressed to reconcile Jehovah with the rationalistic concept of a Supreme Being, he nevertheless became and remained a "Christian deist." Skeptical of the Jewish revelation, he was less so of the Islamic and openly accepted the Christian, at least as he understood it. In *The True Gospel of Jesus Christ asserted* (1732) and *The True Gospel of Jesus Christ Vindicated* (1739) he identified the essence of Christianity with the few simple principles of natural religion as found, for example, in Lord Herbert of Cherbury. He openly compared the propagation of primitive Christianity with the then current spread of Methodism and thereby rejected the claims of supernatural power associated with the early church. He defended his sort of rationalistic Christianity against some of the aspersions of that formidable deist Matthew Tindal. Although Voltaire had some kind words to say about Chubb, it is unlikely that he had read many of Chubb's tracts and certainly did not accept the concept of "Christian deism."

Chubb, like the general run of deists, found reason sufficient to guide man to God's favor and the happiness of another world; he was suspicious of mystery and of miracles and critical of some passages in the Scriptures; he regarded revelation not as divine but as the work of honest men who gave a fair and faithful account of matters of fact; he was dubious about a particular providence and, therefore, of prayer; he argued against prophecy and miracle and believed in the dignity of human nature and in free will. Among the multitudinous answers to Chubb from the more orthodox, the foremost came in 1754 from Jonathan Edwards of Massachusetts. *A Careful and strict Enquiry into The modern prevailing Notions of the Freedom of Will, Which is supposed to be essential To Moral Agency, Vertue and Vice, Reward and Punishment, Praise and Blame,* Edwards' chief claim to philosophical fame, devotes no fewer than 19 pages to the refutation of Chubb on free will. Chubb, it may reasonably be inferred, was widely read in America.

In fine, though adding little constructive thought to the deistic movement, this humble and least formally educated of the English deists was definitely one of its most valuable and popular spokesmen. In the nonpejorative sense of the term he was a candid freethinker.

Bibliography

Chubb was prolific in publication, and his ardent deism was expressed in the titles of a few of his chief works: *The Comparative Excellence and Obligation of Moral and Positive Duties* (1730); *A Discourse Concerning Reason, With regard to Religion and Divine Revelation* (1731); *The Sufficiency of Reason In Matters of Religion Farther Considered* (1732); *The Equity and Reasonableness of the Divine Conduct, In Pardoning Sinners upon their Repentence Exemplified* (1737), which was directed against Bishop Butler's famous *Analogy of Religion* of the previous year; *An Enquiry Into the Ground and Foundation of Religion. Wherein is shewn, that Religion is founded in Nature* (1740); and *A Discourse on Miracles, Considered as evidence to prove the Divine Original of a Revelation* (1741).

Other works by Chubb include *Four Tracts* (1734) and *Some Observations Offered to Publick Consideration. . . . In which the Credit of the History of the Old Testament is particularly considered* (1735). The posthumous *Works of Mr. Thomas Chubb,* 2 vols. (London, 1748) contains the valuable "Author's Farewell to his readers."

See also Sir Leslie Stephen's *History of English Thought in the Eighteenth Century* (London, 1876; the paperback, 2 vols., New York, 1963, follows the revised edition of 1902) and the general bibliography under DEISM.

ERNEST CAMPBELL MOSSNER

CHU HSI (1130–1200), Neo-Confucianist, was the most important Chinese philosopher in the Christian era. He gave Neo-Confucianism its final complexion, and his influence extended to Japan and Korea. Chu Hsi spent nine years in public life, mostly as a guardian of temples, but he preferred poverty and freedom. He was a teacher, and he attracted all the prominent scholars as pupils; he was the author of many works.

Practically all major Neo-Confucian doctrines were synthesized by Chu Hsi into a harmonious whole. He combined the doctrine of Chou Tun-i (1017–1073) on the Great Ultimate, which generates all things through the interaction of yin and yang, or tranquillity and activity, and the doctrine of principle of Ch'eng I. (The closest parallel to the concept of principle in Western philosophy is a Platonic Idea.) Chu Hsi held that the Great Ultimate has no physical form but consists of *li*, or principle in its totality. All actual and potential principles are contained in the Great Ultimate, so that the supply of new principles is never exhausted. The Great Ultimate is complete in all things as a whole, but it is also in each thing individually. The relation between the Great Ultimate in the universe and the Great Ultimate in each individual thing is not that of whole and part, but that of moonlight and moonlight-shining-on-objects. The moonlight on each object is different; but moonlight, after all, is moonlight as a whole.

That the principle of things is to be actualized accounts for the phenomenal world. Actualization requires principle as its substance and material force as its actuality. Thus the Great Ultimate involves both principle and material force. Principle is necessary to explain the reality and universality of things. It is incorporeal, one, eternal and unchanging, uniform, constituting the essence of things; it is always good, and it is the reason for creation. Material force is necessary to explain physical form, individuality, and the transformation of things. It is physical, many, transitory and changeable, unequally present in things; it constitutes their physical substance and involves both good and evil. It is the agent of creation.

Only seemingly dualistic, principle and material force are never separate. Principle needs material force to have something to inhere in, and material force needs principle as its own law of being. They always work together because they are directed by the mind of the universe. In man this mind is mixed with physical nature and human desires, and it needs to be transformed through the investigation of things and an understanding of their principles.

Works by Chu Hsi

Chu Hsi's *Chin-zzu lu* has been translated by Wing-tsit Chan as *Reflections on Things at Hand* (New York, 1966). An anthology of Chu Hsi's sayings and excerpts from his letters and essays, in translation by J. Percy Bruce, is entitled *The Philosophy of Human Nature* (London, 1922).

Works on Chu Hsi

For works on Chu Hsi see J. Percy Bruce, *Chu Hsi and His Masters* (London, 1923); Wing-tsit Chan, *A Source Book in Chinese Philosophy* (Princeton, N.J., 1963), Ch. 34; Carsun Chang, *The Development of Neo-Confucian Thought* (New York, 1957), Vol. II, Chs. 11–12; Fung Yu-lan, *A History of Chinese Philosophy,* translated by D. Bodde (Princeton, N.J., 1953), Vol. II, Ch. 13.

WING-TSIT CHAN

CHURCH FATHERS. *See* PATRISTIC PHILOSOPHY.

CHWISTEK, LEON (1884–1944), Polish mathematical logician, philosopher, aesthetician, essayist, and painter, was a lecturer at the University of Cracow and from 1930 a professor of mathematical logic at the University of Lvov.

Theory of realities. The central problem of Chwistek's philosophy was a criticism of the idea of a uniform reality. It had been shown by Bertrand Russell that in logic admission of the totality of all functions of *x* produces contradictions; Chwistek claimed that in philosophy, likewise, many obscure and misleading thoughts result from the assumption of a single all-inclusive reality.

The results of this criticism led Chwistek to the thesis of a plurality of realities. Out of many possible realities four are particularly important to philosophy. The first, the reality of natural objects, is assumed by common sense; natural objects are of a given form regardless of our perception. Chwistek's defense of natural reality and our knowledge of it is reminiscent of the British common-sense philosophy of the nineteenth century. The objects studied in physics are not natural; the telescopic and microscopic worlds, matter, and the particles upon which the forces are supposed to act form a second reality. They are constructions, not something naturally given. The third reality, that of impressions, the elements of sensation, as studied by Hume or Mach, forms the world of appearances. The fourth reality is that of images, produced by us and dependent on our will, fantasy, and creative processes.

All four of these realities are necessary to account for our knowledge. In addition, when we reflect that we speak about a reality, we cannot include ourselves or our reflection in this reality. Such a reflection must be a part of a higher reality. Otherwise confusions and contradictions arise. The act of discourse cannot be a part of the universe of discourse.

Aesthetics. Chwistek applied the doctrine of plurality of realities to investigations in many areas—aesthetics, for example. Natural reality is dealt with by primitive art. In primitive art each object is given one color only, and perspective is not obeyed. The primitivist paints not as he sees but as things are supposed to be by themselves. He uses his vision, but mainly he uses his knowledge about the world. Realism in art depicts the physical reality as it is conceived at a given time. Impressionism is the art of the reality of impressions; it flourished in a society that had developed psychological research and made psychologism its fundamental scientific method. Futurism is the art of free images, of an actively created reality of fantasy and mental constructions.

In each style of art the artist tries to give a perfect form to his creation independent of the kind of reality he is working with. The form is the common feature of all works of art. Thus, Chwistek justified all styles by relating them to different realities, and he advocated formism: evaluation of form, not of reality, is the proper aesthetic evaluation.

Mathematics and semantics. Chwistek extended his pluralism to mathematics. There is no one system of mathematics, but there are many mutually exclusive systems. Various geometries coincide only in part. When we build analysis based on logic, we can accept, reject, or accept the negations of some extralogical existence axioms, such as the axiom of choice, the axiom of infinity, and the assumption of the existence of transfinite cardinal numbers. Logic itself should not decide any existence problem.

This restrained program for logic was paired with the requirement that logic be understandable in a nominalistic manner and deal with expressions in a constructive, mechanically computable way. Among principles often accepted as logical are some propositions questionable from the constructivist point of view—for example, the axiom of reducibility and the axiom of extensionality. The axiom of reducibility has to do with the distinction between predicative and impredicative concepts. An impredicative concept is a concept definable only by a definiens containing a quantifier that accepts as one of its values the very concept being defined. Russell and Chwistek ruled out such definitions as involving a vicious circle.

As was incisively pointed out by Kurt Gödel (in *The Philosophy of Bertrand Russell*, P. A. Schilpp, ed. [Evanston, Ill., 1946], pp. 135–138), impredicative definitions involve a vicious circle only if one takes, as Chwistek did and Russell did not, a nominalistic attitude toward logic. Only if the quantifier is understood as a summary reference (infinite conjunction) to all of its values that are expressions and if one of the values of a quantifier that occurs in the definiens is the expression that is the definiendum do we presuppose what we want to define. Russell was not a nominalist. His exclusion of impredicative definitions was a way of avoiding antinomies. By differentiating between ranges of values of variables according to the way the quantifier binding a variable occurs, Russell constructed the ramified theory of logical types. This is a somewhat awkward theory. In analysis we want to speak about, for example, the real number that is the least upper bound of a set of real numbers that has a bound. To introduce this concept we must quantify over real numbers greater than all real numbers of a class that includes the least of them. Russell's theory avoids this impredicativeness by setting the least upper bound in a different logical type from the starting real numbers. But then the least upper bound and the real numbers involved cannot be values of the same variables, and several statements about particular sets of real numbers (for example, that a given function is continuous) are impossible.

To overcome this difficulty Russell accepted the axiom of reducibility, which says that every propositional function is coextensive with a predicative one. In many cases we cannot construct such a predicative function, and therefore constructivists, such as Chwistek, cannot accept this axiom. Moreover, for a nominalist, that two propositional functions are coextensive is not a sufficient guarantee of their identity. Thus, Chwistek attempted the task, which Russell called "heroic," of forming a purely constructivist system of the foundations of mathematics without impredicative definitions, the axiom of reducibility, or the axiom of extensionality. He observed, as F. P. Ramsey did, that results similar to Russell's can be obtained by the simple theory of types (where one distinguishes only between variables ranging over individuals, properties of individuals, properties of such properties, etc.) instead of the more complicated ramified theory. But simple type theory is inconsistent with the axiom of intensionality, which Chwistek wanted to be free to accept and which asserts the nonidentity of the concepts defined by two different propositional functions (even if they are coextensive).

The systems Chwistek constructed for the foundations of mathematics were such that they answered the philosophical needs of their author. They were admittedly more complicated than Russell's. "But it may be erroneous to think that clear ideas are never complicated; while we must agree that many simple ideas are, as a matter of fact, very obscure." Chwistek presented several formulations of his attempts at a constructivist theory, all of them too sketchy to be judged definitive. The relation to other constructivist systems is hard to establish. The last few versions were called "rational metamathematics." This theory deals with expressions, some of which are theorems.

A principal part of rational metamathematics, the fundamental system of semantics, uses two specific primitive signs, *c* and *, about which we stipulate that *c* is an expression and that if *E* and *F* are expressions, then **EF* is an expression. These formation rules assign a definite tree (or grouping) structure to each finite expression as well as to any two expressions written one after the other. Some of the allowed combinations of *c* and * may have no meaning—in this Chwistek was a formalist. To some other expressions we assign meaning, and in accordance with this assignment we accept proper axioms. We take 0 to be an abbreviation of **cc*. The fundamental substitution pattern (*EFGH*)—which is read "*H* is the result of substituting *G* for every occurrence of *F* in *E*"—is taken to be an abbreviation of ****EE*FF*GG*HH*. The Sheffer stroke function, |*EF*, is regarded as an abbreviation of ***EE**EE*EE***FF**FE*FF*. Identity = *EF* stands for (*EOOF*).

Selected Works by Chwistek

Wielość Rzeczywistości ("Plurality of Realities"). Cracow, 1921.

"The Theory of Constructive Types." *Annales de la Société Polonaise de Mathématique*, Vol. 2 (1924, for 1923), 9–48, and Vol. 3 (1925, for 1924), 91–141.

"Fondements de la métamathématique rationnelle." *Bulletin de l'Académie Polonaise des Sciences et des Lettres*, Series A (1933), 253–264. Written with W. Hetper and J. Herzberg.

"Remarques sur la méthode de la construction des notions fondamentales de la métamathématique rationnelle." *Bulletin de l'Académie Polonaise des Sciences et des Lettres*, Series A (1933), 265–275. Written with W. Hetper and J. Herzberg.

Granice Nauki. Lvov and Warsaw, 1935. Rev. ed. translated by H. C. Brodie and A. P. Coleman as *The Limits of Science*. London, 1948.

Wielość Rzeczywistości w Sztuce ("Plurality of Realities in Art"), K. Estreicher, ed. Warsaw, 1960.

Pisma Filozoficzne i Logiczne ("Philosophical and Logical Writings"), K. Pasenkiewicz, ed., 2 vols. Warsaw, 1961–1963.

A reformulation of Chwistek's system of semantics by John Myhill appears in the *Journal of Symbolic Logic*, Vol. 14 (1949), 119–125, and Vol. 16 (1951), 35–42.

H. Hiż

CICERO, MARCUS TULLIUS (106–43 B.C.), of Arpinum, Roman orator and statesman, had a lifelong interest in philosophy and wrote a number of philosophical works during periods of forced retirement from public life. He was well acquainted with the four main Greek schools of his time and counted among his friends and teachers the Epicureans Phaedrus and Zeno, the Stoic Posidonius, the Peripatetic Staseas, the Academics Philo and Antiochus, and many others. He identified himself primarily with the Academy, though he found much to admire also in the Stoa and Lyceum. He rejected Epicureanism.

In a famous passage in a letter to Atticus (xii, 52, May 21, 45 B.C.), with reference to some of his books on philosophy, Cicero calls them copies ("apographa"), written with little effort; he supplied only the words ("Verba tantum adfero, quibus abundo"). A week earlier he had written: "It is incredible how much I write, even at night; for I cannot sleep" (*Ad Atticum* xiii, 26). Modern scholars have found in such passages support for the view that these writings are chiefly valuable for the reconstruction of lost Greek originals, which Cicero in his haste sometimes misunderstood or jumbled together. The search for sources has been a major preoccupation of Ciceronian scholars for almost a century.

A more generous view is that in spite of his own statements Cicero's philosophical writings are more than hasty copies of Greek originals; they present a fairly coherent and modestly original system of thought. At a minimum Cicero took from the Academy a framework for his views. The Platonism of the New Academy had abandoned the search for truth and was occupied, rather, with the confrontation of conflicting opinions. Carneades, its leading spokesman, had even devised criteria for preferring one opinion to another. Within such a framework Cicero examines alternative views and makes his selection (though not necessarily in terms of Carneades' criteria). The views examined extend to all three commonly accepted branches of philosophy—logic, physics, ethics—and the presentation follows an orderly plan. Within this broad coverage, however, are many unresolved conflicts; clearly, Cicero's primary purpose was to offer to his Roman readers a wide range of philosophical opinions rather than to construct a well-integrated system.

Philosophy and rhetoric. Whatever originality Cicero's views possess is not in their components (he believed that the Greeks had already exhausted the varieties of possible opinions) but in their combination. The most conspicuous feature of his thought is the union of philosophy with rhetoric. This union carries with it some criticism of Socrates, who was blamed for their separation (see *De Oratore* iii, 61), and appears to align Cicero with Isocrates rather than Plato; yet he does not consider the union incompatible with Platonism. Carneades had prepared the way for a reconciliation between rhetoric and the Academy when he made philosophy a contest between opinions, and Greek theoretical rhetoricians had long since sought to implement Plato's prescription in the *Phaedrus* for a scientific rhetoric. Cicero could also point to the literary excellence of the dialogues as evidence that Plato was a master of the rhetorical art (*ibid.* i, 47).

The union of rhetoric and philosophy gave Cicero the materials for construction of his humanistic ideal. The highest human achievement lies in the effective use of knowledge for the guidance of human affairs. Philosophy and the specialized disciplines supply the knowledge, and rhetorical persuasion makes it effective. Each is useless without the other, and the great man is master of both. Cicero associates this ideal with a free society—that is, a constitutional republic in which persuasion rather than violence is the instrument of political power. He believes that Rome has the essential features of such a state but that unless a great man is found to guide it, its freedom is in jeopardy.

Commitment to the union of eloquence and knowledge led Cicero to the view that if the statesman-philosopher is to speak persuasively on all subjects, he must have knowledge of all subjects. But recognizing the impossibility of such a requirement, Cicero advocated liberal education as the best approximation. An important part of liberal education is the study of philosophy, and Cicero's philosophical works provided materials for this study. Thus, in his philosophical writings no less than in his great public orations, he was combining wisdom and eloquence in the service of the Roman people.

Philosophical works. The literary form that Cicero used emphasizes his didactic intent. Most of the philosophical works are dialogues, preceded by an introduction in defense of philosophical studies. The speakers are distinguished Romans, including Cicero himself, and frequently the listeners are young men just beginning their political careers. Conflicting views are presented in long speeches, with few interruptions. Sometimes the clash of opinions leads to insult and denunciation, especially when Epicureans are involved, but personal abuse of one speaker by another is avoided. There is hardly a vestige of dramatic conflict in such dialogues as *Tusculanae Disputationes*, where the conversation is between a young man and his preceptor. In two late works, *De Officiis* (*On Duties*, addressed to Cicero's son) and *Topica* (addressed to a young lawyer, Trebatius), the dialogue form is discarded.

In logic Cicero wrote *Academica*, in two versions (45 B.C.), on the dispute between dogmatists and Academic skeptics about the criterion of truth; only portions of these are extant. *Topica* (44 B.C.), though usually grouped with the rhetorical works, is also on logic. The title is from Aristotle, but the treatment is not. Cicero compiles a single exhaustive list of kinds of argument without distinction between the philosophical and the rhetorical.

There are three works, planned as a unit, on physics: (1) *De Natura Deorum*, (2) *De Divinatione*, and (3) *De Fato* (45–44 B.C.). They present Epicurean, Stoic, and Academic arguments and counterarguments about religion and cosmology. Cicero himself was inclined to accept the Stoic arguments for a divine providence, but he rejected the Stoic doctrine of fate.

The major ethical writings are *De Finibus Bonorum et Malorum* (45 B.C.), in which Epicurean, Stoic, and Peripatetic ethical views are examined; *Tusculanae Disputationes* (45 B.C.), on fear of death, on pain, on distress of mind, and on other matters; and *De Officiis* (44 B.C.), a practical ethics based on Stoic principles.

On political theory Cicero wrote two dialogues with titles taken from Plato. There is *De Re Publica* (51 B.C.), from which the famous "Dream of Scipio" is an excerpt. The subject matter of the "Dream" ensured its preservation; it portrays the virtuous soul enjoying a more perfect existence after death in the region above the moon. The rest of the work is fragmentary. The other political dialogue, *De Legibus* (date uncertain), depicts Roman law as a very nearly perfect realization of Greek (chiefly Stoic) theory.

Some of the rhetorical works, especially the first book of *De Oratore* (55 B.C.), discuss the relation of philosophy to rhetoric and present the ideal of the great man in whom both are united.

Minor works on philosophical themes include *Paradoxa Stoicorum, De Senectute, De Amicitia,* and the lost *Consolatio* and *Hortensius*. Cicero also translated two Platonic dialogues, *Protagoras* (lost) and *Timaeus* (W. Ax, ed., Leipzig, 1938).

Bibliography

Editions and translations of all the extant philosophical and rhetorical works except the *Timaeus* have been published by the Loeb Classical Library (Cambridge, Mass., London, and New York, 1914–1949). Four—*Brutus, On the Nature of the Gods, On Divination, On Duties*—were translated by H. M. Poteat, with an introduction by R. P. McKeon (Chicago, 1950). The extant portions of the *Academica* were edited, with an excellent introduction and notes, by J. S. Reid (London, 1885); Reid also published a translation (London, 1880). *De Re Publica* has been translated, with an excellent introduction, by G. H. Sabine and S. B. Smith (Columbus, Ohio, 1929; reprinted, Indianapolis, Ind., and New York, n.d.).

For further information see R. Philippson, "M. Tullius Cicero, die philosophische Schriften," in A. Pauly and G. Wissowa, *Real-Encyclopädie der classischen Altertumswissenschaft*, W. Kroll, ed., Vol. VII A (Stuttgart 1939), Cols. 1104–1192, and H. A. K. Hunt, *The Humanism of Cicero* (Melbourne, 1954). For publications since 1939 see S. E. Smethurst's bibliographical reports in *Classical World*, Vol. 51 (1957–1958), 1–4, 24, 32–41; Vol. 58 (1964–1965), 36–45.

P. H. DeLacy

CIVILIZATION. *See* CULTURE AND CIVILIZATION.

CLANDESTINE PHILOSOPHICAL LITERATURE IN FRANCE. The body of clandestine literature in France which deals with philosophy, religion, ethics, and social problems is impressive. It can be traced back to the sixteenth century, and the diffusion, particularly wide between 1714 and 1740, of the allegedly atheistic treatise *La Béatitude des Chrétiens ou le fléau de la foy*, published by Geoffroy Vallée in 1572, and of other tracts of early date bears witness to the continuity and vitality of the tradition of free thought in France. The term "Clandestine philosophical literature" usually refers to works known to have circulated in manuscript form during the first half of the eighteenth century and the importance of the subject lies in the fact that the circulation of these works provided one of the sources of the French encyclopedic movement and a solid foundation for liberalism. For the period between 1700 and 1750, I. O. Wade has listed 392 extant manuscripts of 102 different treatises, including 15 translations from other languages. Many more are known to have been in circulation.

The technique of the clandestine manuscript essay was used to circumvent the severe censorship and was most common between 1710 and 1740, when the activities of copyists, colporteurs, and the police were particularly vigorous. Works that found their way into print were often impounded, but they were copied and distributed until the French Revolution. Occasionally authors whose identities could be established were incarcerated. This happened to Fourcroy in 1698 for his *Doutes sur la religion proposées à Mss. les Docteurs de Sorbonne,* but he soon secured his release from the Bastille. Most often the police found it futile to make arrests and concentrated on preventing the diffusion of the tracts. Public burning, usually in effigy, of works condemned by the Parlement of Paris did not prevent reprints and manuscript copies from being made in the Low Countries, one of the centers of the clandestine trade. After 1750, however, covert circulation became increasingly unnecessary, owing to the breakdown of the censorship, and a number of the more important treatises were printed, many with the indication of a false place of publication.

Voltaire, Henri-Joseph Dulaurens, Holbach, and Jacques-André Naigeon, in their desire to foster deism or atheism, prolonged the life of the anonymous tracts by including them in collective volumes, such as *Nouvelles Libertés de penser* (Amsterdam, 1743, 1770), *Recueil nécessaire* (by Voltaire; Geneva, 1765, 1766, 1768, 1776), *L'Évangile de la raison* (by Voltaire; Geneva, 1764, 1765, 1767, 1768), *Recueil philosophique* (by Naigeon; "Londres," 1770), and *Bibliothèque du bon sens portatif* (by Holbach; "Londres," 1773). The treatises constituted one of the main sources from which the *philosophes* drew their polemics.

Through the records preserved in the Archives de la Bastille and from statements appearing in manuscripts and letters by Dubuisson, Fréret, de Bure, and Charles-Marie de la Condamine, we know something of the organization and diffusion of these manuscripts. Le Coulteux, Charles Bonnet, Lépine, and a certain Mathieu or Morléon (who was incarcerated in 1729) are known to have specialized in the works of Henri de Boulainvilliers and his friends. These works were distributed often in the vicinity of the Procope and other cafés to listed patrons and initiates, including members of the clergy and the Parlement. Copies such as those of Meslier's *Testament* were made by professionals, occasionally the personal secretaries of men like the comte de Boulainvilliers, the comte d'Argenson, and Malesherbes, and the practice of employing copyists was continued throughout the century. The price of such copies varied greatly. A sum as prohibitively high as twenty pistoles is known to have been asked for Mirabaud's *Examen critique du Nouveau Testament.*

The clandestine movement, fed by new discoveries in science, reflected the climate of world opinion, an attitude to life and society, man and his welfare, God and the universe which, although not new, was reinforced by new arguments and gained an ever-increasing audience. Although the tracts appeared sporadically and were mostly anonymous, they share a few common characteristics and must be judged as a stage in the history of free thought, which goes back to the Renaissance in France and has its deepest roots in the works of Epicurus and Lucretius.

"Theophrastus Redivivus." The *Theophrastus Redivivus* (1659) is significant in that it establishes a link between the atheism of men of the Renaissance and that of men of the seventeenth century (it refers, for example, to Lucilio Vanini and Cyrano de Bergerac) and also of the eighteenth century, when it was secretly circulated. The author, possibly a regent in one of the Parisian colleges, wrote in Latin a 2,000-folio-page compendium of historical references. He developed the arguments that if God exists he is the Sun and that the world is eternal. For the author all religions are false, and miracles, oracles, prophecies, and revelations are man-made. The resurrection of the dead and the immortality of the soul are absurdities; happiness is to be found only in living according to nature, which is revealed to us through experience; there is no absolute good or evil, as we may deduce from the multiplicity of customs and laws; man is a species of animal endowed with speech and reason. Animals, however, are not totally devoid of these faculties. The author referred neither to Gassendi nor to Descartes, but he did mention the treatise *De Tribus Impostoribus,* attributing to Frederick II the proposition that Moses, Christ, and Muhammad were three remarkable impostors (see BOULAINVILLIERS).

Background. Throughout the seventeenth century the *libertins* in the wake of Rabelais and Montaigne became erudite skeptics, radical naturalists, associating freedom of morals and freedom of belief. As freethinkers they were prompted more by a feeling of revolt against asceticism and scholasticism than by any convincing argument. Gassendi contributed to the rehabilitation of Epicurus and Lucretius. Emmanuel Maignan, too, in his *Cursus,* evolved a philosophy that bridged Aristotle and Epicurus, linking matter and thought, sensationism and the spiritual world, and developing the idea of a scale of being. But it was from Descartes that the movement of free thought gained its greatest impetus. Cartesian rationalism and mechanism provided freethinkers with a new certainty and their systems with a new coherence. Long after his philosophy had been adopted by the Jesuits and had consequently grown unpopular, Descartes continued to exercise a determining influence on free thought through the method he advocated. His philosophy, however, was commonly misunderstood by freethinkers and with La Mettrie it culminated in an extreme mechanistic materialism that Descartes would have decried.

Spinoza's influence on the clandestine literature was considerable but rather indirect. His work was largely known through the writings of other thinkers, like Bayle and Boulainvilliers, and his philosophy was commonly distorted by Cartesian misrepresentation. The *Ethics* was little known, and frequently its views were reconstituted through refutations. The *Tractatus Theologico politicus* was of interest on account of its Biblical criticism, and in Holland, Jean Leclerc, professor of philosophy and Hebrew at the University of Amsterdam, was allowed to carry on this critical work. In France, however, the uncompromising attitude of Bossuet stifled Biblical criticism. Richard Simon, a well-known teacher at the Oratorian school at Juilly who had admitted in his *Histoire critique du Vieux Testament* (1678) the truth of much of Spinoza's exegesis while recognizing the authority of the Bible, succeeded in offending both Catholics and Protestants and was expelled from the Oratorian congregation in 1678. He retired to continue his rational critique in two *instructions pastorales* (1702, 1703), *Histoire critique du texte du Nouveau Testament* (1683), *Histoire critique des versions du Nouveau Testament* (1690), and *Histoire critique des principaux commentateurs du Nouveau Testament* (1692).

Disputes that reached the general public—such as those over the authorship of the Pentateuch, in which La Peyrère, Hobbes, Spinoza, Simon, Jean Leclerc, and others held different views—led to much perplexity. The body of anonymous treatises that continued such discussions and in many cases rejected revelation is naturally large. These include the *Examen de la religion*, the *Analyse de la religion* (written after 1739), and the *Militaire philosophe* (composed between 1706 and 1711).

Hobbes's *Leviathan* (1651) seems to have been little known in France. Bayle's *Dictionnaire*, however, enjoyed great authority, and his *Lettre sur la comète de 1680* popularized the ideas that the conception of Providence did not rest on rational premises and that atheists could be good men. Bayle's views were those of a protestant, but his argument was such that his articles could easily be used to develop anti-Christian ideas. The anonymous writers also read Fontenelle and knew something of the English deists whose thought developed along parallel lines. There were translations of works by Bernard Mandeville, Lord Bolingbroke, John Toland, Anthony Collins, and Thomas Woolston, but it was only after the publication of Voltaire's *Lettres anglaises* (1734), which discussed Newtonian physics and philosophy and the ideas of Locke, that the English influence became significant. Leibniz' influence, too, was felt only at a late stage, partly because he was known primarily through Bayle and also through de Maupertuis, whose ideas served to link the *Monadology* with Diderot and materialism.

The coterie of Boulainvilliers. The only group of writers known to have been involved in concerted action was that centered in the comte de Boulainvilliers and closely linked with d'Argenson, the duc de Noailles, and the Académie des Inscriptions. This coterie included Nicolas Fréret, Jean-Baptiste de Mirabaud, César Dumarsais, and J.-B. Le Mascrier. Voltaire, in his *Dîner du comte de Boulainvilliers* (1767), attested to the important influence of this group, which was especially responsible for the diffusion of Boulainvilliers's *Esprit de Spinoza* (known to have existed by 1706 and first published in 1719 in Holland).

Fréret. Nicolas Fréret (1688–1761), a student of law, joined the coterie of Boulainvilliers at the age of 19. Fréret appended to copies of the *Histoire ancienne* an account of Boulainvilliers's life and works. In 1714 he was admitted to the Académie des Inscriptions; in 1715 he was imprisoned for some months in the Bastille, where he read Bayle's *Dictionnaire* and wrote a Chinese grammar. From 1720 to 1721 he was preceptor of the duc de Noailles.

The *Lettre de Thrasibule à Leucippe* (written c. 1722 and published in London, probably in 1768; also published in *Oeuvres de Fréret*, Vol. IV, London, 1775) is generally attributed to him. Systematic and Cartesian in its presentation, this treatise combines sensationist psychology and naturalist ethics. Thrasibule, a Roman, describes the early Christians as combining Jewish beliefs with Stoicism and as influenced by both monotheist and polytheist currents. He argues that knowledge is acquired through our senses and has only relative validity. Only the truths of mathematics and reason are universal. Religious beliefs however, do not spring from reason; it is reason alone that should guide man in regulating his life, establishing society and laws, and achieving happiness. This work can be seen as an early essay in comparative religion, and it sharply reflects the growing interest in the science of law and social philosophy. It perhaps influenced Montesquieu, and Rousseau annotated it while engaged in writing the *Discours sur l'inégalité*.

Fréret is also reputed to be the author of an *Examen critique des apologistes de la religion chrétienne* (composed after 1733), which introduces the historical method adopted by Voltaire in, for example, the *Essai sur les moeurs* and the *Dictionnaire philosophique*, in which Voltaire acknowledged his debt. Fréret was held in high esteem as a savant. He was a chronologist, a geographer, an orientalist, and a philologist as well as a philosopher, and he delivered papers on a wide variety of subjects to the Académie des Inscriptions, becoming its permanent secretary in 1743. These *Mémoires de l'Académie* outline new methods for the study of prehistory and geography as well as history. Fréret specialized in mythology, opposing the *évhéméristes*, who believed that all myths had a basis in historical fact. A pioneer in comparative philology, he made known the Chinese linguistic system. His *Oeuvres complètes* were published by Leclerc de Septchênes in Paris, 1796–1799, but about half his works were omitted (many of his manuscripts bequeathed to the Académie des Inscriptions have never been published), and a few of the treatises included cannot be attributed to him.

Mirabaud. Jean-Baptiste de Mirabaud (1675–1760) was educated by the Oratorian congregation and entered a military career. He then became secretary to the duchess of Orléans and preceptor of her two youngest daughters. In 1724 he translated *Gerusalemme liberata* by Tasso. He was elected to the Académie Française in 1726, becoming its secretary in 1742. Mirabaud read his manuscripts to select groups of friends. He was probably the author of four essays (described below), often to be found together, that threw new doubts on Biblical chronology and promoted Fontenelle's method of oblique attack on miracles. Many of Mirabaud's notes recall ideas expressed in *La Religion chrétienne analysée* (a popular post-1742 tract attributed by Voltaire and Claude François Nonnotte to César Dumarsais). The *Opinion des anciens sur le monde* (c. 1706–1722) challenges the story of Genesis. In the *Opinions des anciens sur la nature de l'âme* (composed before 1728, published in *Nouvelles Libertés de penser*) Mirabaud pointed out that the Jews, the Greeks, and the Romans envisaged the soul as material and that the Egyptians introduced the belief in the immortality of the soul as a restraining influence on public morals. The *Opinion des anciens sur les Juifs* (c. 1706–1722), based on Jacques Basnage's *Histoire des Juifs* (1706), tries to prove that the Jews had no right to claim to be a "chosen" people. The *Examen critique du Nouveau Testament* (c. 1706–1722), which deals with the canonical and the noncanonical gospels, stresses that neither Philo nor Josephus mentioned Christ and that Christian morality conflicts with natural morality. Much of our information on Mirabaud is derived from the *Notice sur Jean-Baptiste de Mirabaud* (Paris, 1895), by Paul Mirabaud.

Dumarsais. César Chesneau Dumarsais (1676–1756), a grammarian, was personally known to Fontenelle and Voltaire and was associated with the *Encyclopédie* until his death. For a time he was preceptor in the family of John Law. Dumarsais edited, with Le Mascrier, some of the deistic works of Mirabaud and wrote a defense of Fontenelle's *Histoire des oracles* and probably the deterministic essay *Le Philosophe* (written before 1728); edited by Herbert Dieckmann in 1948). He was probably responsible for *La Religion chrétienne analysée* (also known as *Examen de la religion* and *Doutes*, in which inconsistencies in the Bible are shown up, the doctrine of original sin is attacked, and the doctrine of the Trinity is stated to be contrary to reason. It is argued that God should be worshiped without ceremony and that man must follow his reason, which is his *lumière naturelle*, and adopt a social morality incompatible with Christian dogma.

Meslier. The most interesting of the clandestine authors was no doubt Jean Meslier (1664–1729), a priest who was directly or indirectly influenced by Spinoza. (Reading Fénelon's *Démonstration de l'existence de Dieu* and R.-J. de Tournemine's *Réflexions sur l'athéisme* helped Meslier clarify his ideas.) He identified nature with matter, which he saw as eternal and as endowed with movement. He favored a mechanical interpretation of nature, rejecting the arguments of those who believed in chance and in a divine design. In his 1,200-page *Testament*, Meslier listed the errors, illusions, and impostures of Christianity. His attack on Christianity is one of the most detailed and comprehensive ever written, and his materialistic system is particularly interesting in that it foreshadows many aspects of Diderot's thought (see MESLIER).

Voltaire is known to have acquired a copy of the *Testament* and to have made extracts, which he dated 1742 and published in 1761 or 1762 under the title *Extrait*. The first edition sold out immediately and was followed in the same year by an edition of 5,000 copies. In 1772 Holbach published extracts under the title *Le Bon Sens du curé Meslier*, and in 1789 Sylvain Maréchal published *Le Cathéchisme du curé Meslier*.

Meslier's social ideas were remarkable for the time. He claimed in very general terms that all men are equal and have the right to live, to be free, and to share in the fruits of the earth. He divided mankind into workers and parasites and saw in revolt the best hope of better conditions. He dreamed of a class struggle, not reconciliation.

Other works. Among other anonymous works that cast doubts on the proofs of the truth of Christianity and allege contradictions in the Bible are five manuscript volumes of the *Examen de la Genèse* and the *Examen du Nouveau Testament* (probably written in the late 1730s or early 1740s), which are attributed to Mme. du Châtelet, Voltaire's mistress. She purports to have proved that the stories of the Bible relate barbarous and cruel events and cannot have been inspired by God. No doubt she received some help from Voltaire, but she relied chiefly on the work of Jean Meslier and Thomas Woolston and especially on the *Commentaire littéral sur tous les livres de l'Ancien et du Nouveau Testament* (23 vols., Paris, 1707–1716) by Augustin Dom Calmet.

Among other manuscripts whose authorship is now known is *Le Ciel ouvert à tous les hommes* (also entitled *Le Paradis ouvert* and *Nouveau Système de la religion chrétienne*), by the priest Pierre Cuppé, which must have been in draft in 1716. The tract never assails orthodoxy, but Cuppé submitted the Scriptures to scrutiny and preached toleration and brotherly love, concluding that all men are saved by God's love. Cuppé's stress on his respect for reason, as well as his deistic beliefs, led to his being considered a forerunner of French deism.

The author of *Le Militaire philosophe* (1706–1711; published in London by Naigeon in 1768) is unknown. It is first a commentary of Malebranche's views on religion. It gives a frank exposition of deism, which won Voltaire's commendation. After a strongly worded criticism of the Old and the New Testaments, the work rejects Christianity and develops the doctrine of natural religion, stressing the roles of reason and instinct. Man, who is both body and soul, is free and immortal, and his behavior should be governed by reason and by conscience. Man must worship God and abide by the golden rule. The author foreshadowed Montesquieu in his insistence on the absolute character of justice and the relative nature of civil laws and in his treatment of chance, which he rejected as an explanation of events. He anticipated Voltaire in his use of the figure of a watchmaker to explain the function of God. His idea that truth is to be found in the individual soul was later developed by Rousseau.

A widely disseminated treatise was *Israël vengé*, by Isaac Orobio, a Spanish Jew who escaped from the Inquisition to France and then to Holland and died in 1687 or 1688. His originally unpublished critical attack on the Christian religion was translated by Henriquez and published in London in 1770. It was circulated by Lévesque de Burigny.

The *Jordanus Brunus Redivivus* is a materialistic compilation. The author believed in the Copernican system (and the existence of other solar systems with living beings) and in the eternity of matter. There are no innate ideas, no objective good or evil. Man is motivated by pain and by pleasure. Experience can deceive us. Reason alone is valid but must not be thought infallible. The laws of nature are eternal, but everything is in a state of flux. Certain passages of this work bring to mind Diderot's *Rêve de d'Alembert*. Other manuscripts whose authorship is uncertain include *Lettre d'Hypocrate à Damagette* (1700 at latest), *Recherches curieuses de philosophie* (1713), *Suite des Pyrrhoniens: qu'on peut douter si les religions viennent immédiatement de Dieu ou de l'invention des politiques pour faire craindre et garder les préceptes de l'homme* (c. 1723), *Traité de la liberté* (a determinist and materialist tract, probably by Fontenelle, c. 1700), *Essai sur la recherche de la vérité*, and *Dissertation sur la formation du monde* (1738), which was inspired by Lucretius and formulates transformist theories while upholding the conception of fixed species.

Influence. It will be seen that the clandestine tracts fall into two main categories, those written from the standpoint of critical deism and those that are atheistic, deterministic and materialistic. The outstanding eighteenth-century literary works based on this movement can be similarly characterized. Montesquieu's adoption of the letter form for *Les Lettres persanes* (1731) may owe something to the *Lettre à Damagette*, and the views expressed in *Lettre persane 46* reflect those expressed in *La Religion chrétienne analysée*. Voltaire, who adopted the form for his *Lettres philosophiques*, published anonymously in 1734, wrote in the same year a *Traité de métaphysique* (which Mme. du Châtelet kept under lock and key), which embodied his own deism as well as many of the ideas expressed in the clandestine literature.

Toward the middle of the century atheism gained ground, no doubt encouraged by such treatises as *Lettre sur la religion, sur l'âme et sur l'existence de Dieu*. Diderot's *Pensées philosophiques*, published anonymously in 1746, allegedly at the Hague but actually in Paris, and condemned to be burned by the Parlement of Paris, is characteristic of this tendency. Although based on a translation of Shaftesbury, the work succeeds in presenting an original and vividly expressed atheism side by side with more commonplace arguments in favor of natural religion. In particular it challenges Christian belief in miracles, outlining the principles of the new Biblical criticism. In the eighteenth century alone the *Pensées philosophiques* ran to twenty editions (some with crude interpolations) and reprints. It was translated into German, Italian, and English and was the subject of long and heated controversy. Twelve signed or anonymous refutations by Protestants, Catholics, parliamentarians, and others were published, some of them, together with Diderot's text, being circulated in manuscript form.

As government policy wavered and censorship grew slack, an increasing number of the manuscripts of earlier date were published, and anonymity became a thin veil, if not a mere convention. The main current of what has become known as clandestine literature, which many have identified with the tradition of free thought, came to an end with the advent of Montesquieu, Voltaire, Rousseau, and Diderot. In their works it found its finest literary expression, and thanks to them it became integrated into coherent patterns that have won it a place in the history of ideas.

Bibliography

The most important reference works in the field are I. O. Wade, *Philosophical Ideas in France From 1700 to 1750* (Princeton, N.J., 1938), and J. S. Spink, *French Free-thought From Gassendi to Voltaire* (London, 1960). The following works are also very important: W. H. Barber, *Leibniz in France* (Oxford, 1955); A. Vartanian, *Diderot and Descartes* (Princeton, N.J., 1953); and P. Vernière, *Spinoza et la pensée française avant la Révolution* (Paris, 1954).

The reader should also consult E. R. Briggs, "L'Incrédulité et la pensée anglaise en France au début de XVIIIe siècle," in *Revue d'histoire littéraire de la France*, Vol. 41 (1934), 497–538; E. R. Briggs, "Pierre Cuppé's Debts to England and Holland," in Theodore Besterman, ed., *Studies on Voltaire and the XVIII Century*, Vol. VI (Geneva and New York, 1958), pp. 37–66; Pierre Brochon, *Le Livre de colportage en France depuis le XVIe siècle, sa littérature, ses lecteurs* (Paris, 1954); Herbert Dieckmann, ed., *Le Philosophe: Texts and Interpretation*, Washington University Studies, New Series, Language and Literature, No. 18 (St. Louis, Mo., 1948); Herbert Dieckmann, "The Abbé Jean Meslier and Diderot's *Eleuthéromanes*," in *Harvard Library Bulletin*, Vol. 7 (Spring 1953), 231–235; J. P. Free, *Rousseau's Use of the Examen de la religion and of La Lettre de Thrasibule à Leucippe*, unpublished doctoral dissertation (Princeton, N.J., 1935); A. D. Hole, *Mirabaud's Contribution to the Deistic Movement and His Relation to Voltaire*, Princeton doctoral dissertation *Abstracts* (Princeton, N.J., 1952); G. Lanson, "Questions diverses sur l'histoire de l'esprit philosophique en France avant 1750," in *Revue d'histoire littéraire de la France*, Vol. 19 (1912), 1–29, 293–317; A. R. Morehouse, *Voltaire and Jean Meslier* (New Haven, 1936); R. R. Palmer, *Catholics and Unbelievers in Eighteenth Century France* (Princeton, N.J., 1939); Renée Simon, "Nicolas Fréret, académicien," in Theodore Besterman, ed., *Studies on Voltaire and the XVIII Century*, Vol. XVII (Geneva and New York, 1961); J. S. Spink, "La Diffusion des idées matérialistes et anti-religieuses au début de XVIIIe siècle: Le *Theophrastus Redivivus*," in *Revue d'histoire littéraire de la France*, Vol. 44 (1937), 248–255. See also Diderot's *Pensées philosophiques*, Robert Niklaus, ed. (Geneva, 1950).

ROBERT NIKLAUS

CLARKE, SAMUEL (1675–1729), theologian and philosopher, was born in Norwich, England. The son of Edward Clarke, an alderman and member of Parliament for Norwich, he was educated in the free school of Norwich and in Caius College, Cambridge. He studied Newton's physics independently, as it was a subject largely beyond his tutors, and became a convinced Newtonian. The accepted physics textbook at Cambridge was a Cartesian work, *The System of Natural Philosophy* of Jacques Rohault. While still an undergraduate Clarke produced an improved Latin translation of Rohault's work, which replaced the current, inferior version, and added to his translation a set of footnotes that expounded Newton's physics in opposition to Rohault's doctrines. Thus, he struck a subtle first blow for the displacement of Cartesian by Newtonian physics in the English universities. Clarke became a friend and associate of Newton, and he later translated Newton's *Opticks* into Latin.

Upon graduating Clarke was ordained in the Established Church and became the protégé of John Moore, bishop of Norwich. Through Moore's patronage Clarke became successively rector of Drayton, near Norwich, rector of St. Bennet's at Paul's Wharf in London, and chaplain in ordinary to Queen Anne. She made him rector of St. James, Westminster, where he served for 20 years, until his death.

Clarke was much admired as a preacher, and several volumes of his collected sermons have come down to us. His fame as a philosopher and theologian rests on the two series of Boyle lectures that he delivered at St. Paul's, in 1704 and 1705. He is also remembered for his last task as a Newtonian, an exchange of letters with Leibniz, who was critical of Newton's physics.

Existence and attributes of God. In *The Works of Samuel Clarke* the two sets of Boyle lectures were published under the joint title "A Discourse Concerning the Being and Attributes of God, the Obligations of Natural Religion, and the Truth and Certainty of the Christian Revelation in Answer to Mr. Hobbes, Spinoza, the Author of the Oracles of Reason, and Other Deniers of Natural and Revealed Religion." In his presentation of these topics Clarke promised to use a method as near to mathematical as the nature of such a discourse would allow.

The first set of Boyle lectures is entitled "A Demonstration of the Being and Attributes of God." While acknowledging that many arguments to prove God's existence have been offered before, Clarke chose to repeat none of them and offered instead what he referred to as "one argument in a chain of propositions." There are eight propositions in the chain. The first three are the most important, for by them Clarke hoped to establish the existence of a god. The remainder establish the attributes of the divine being.

Clarke's first proposition is: "It is absolutely and undeniably certain that something has existed from all eternity." In defense of this proposition Clarke argued that there is something now, and since something cannot come from nothing, there must always have been something. The second proposition is: "There has existed from eternity some one, unchangeable and independent being." This proposition is a refinement of the first. Not only has there always been something, but that something is a being, single, unchangeable, and independent. Clarke made the slide from "something" to "being" without apology. He argued for a single, persistent being because an endless succession of beings dependent on one another appears to leave open the possibility that the succession could be broken off. But it is not clear why a succession defined as endless is any less plausible than an eternally existent being. The conceptual advantage to Clarke is clear enough, however.

The third and crucial proposition is: "That unchangeable and independent being, which has existed from eternity without any external cause of its existence, must be self-existent, that is necessarily existent." This proposition was meant to be the clinching step in the demonstration, but Clarke's defense of it appears to go in two directions. On the one hand, there is the issue of whether the unchangeable, independent, and eternal being is self-existent. On the other hand, if this being is self-existent, is it necessarily existent? It looks as though self-existence might be an interesting fact about this being, and Clarke argued that it follows from his account of this being, as having existed from eternity without any external cause, that this being is self-existent. But there remains the question whether "self-existent" must mean "necessarily existent." Clarke passed over this question and chose to equate the two notions. Thus, in the defense of his third proposition he said that the only true idea of a self-existent being is the "idea of a being the supposition of whose non-existence is an express contradiction." But we need to have the equation of self-existent and necessarily existent clarified. Why is it that a self-existent being must necessarily exist? Why is it an absolute contradiction to think of a self-existent being as not existing? On this transition from self-existence to necessary existence Clarke's natural theology appears to founder. In succeeding propositions he endeavored to establish that the self-existent being is infinite, omnipresent, intelligent, free, omnipotent, wise, good, and just.

Moral philosophy. The Boyle lectures for 1705 are entitled "A Discourse Concerning the Unchangeable Obligations of Natural Religion, and the Truth and Certainty of the Christian Revelation." The lectures are an exposition of 15 propositions. Propositions V–XV are devoted to Clarke's defense of the truth and certainty of Christianity. In these propositions he claimed that simple and uncorrupted Christian doctrines must be agreeable to reason. The first four propositions devoted to "The Unchangeable Obligations of Natural Religion" are the statement of Clarke's moral philosophy.

Clarke wrote in answer to Hobbes's contention that nothing is simply and absolutely good or evil. For Hobbes there was no common rule of good and evil to be taken from the nature of objects themselves. Rather, before a commonwealth has been established every man is his own rule of good and evil. After the commonwealth all men defer to the decisions of an agreed-upon judge (*Leviathan*, Part I, Ch. 6). Clarke attacked Hobbes's relativism by arguing that if murder is evil after men have made a compact against it, why was it not evil before? How can a compact add to the character of something?

Clarke's statement of his own position was shaped to answer Hobbes's claim that good and evil are not to be discovered by consulting the nature of objects themselves. Clarke held that different things bear necessary and eternal relations to one another. From these different relations there necessarily arises an agreement or disagreement of some things with other things. With regard to persons, from the different relations of different persons to one another there necessarily arises a fitness or unfitness of certain kinds of behavior between persons. Clarke endeavored to establish these propositions by appealing to analogies with mathematical reasoning. For instance, he said that the fitness of certain kinds of behavior between persons ". . . is as manifest, as that the properties which flow from the essences of different mathematical figures have different congruities or incongruities between themselves. . . ."

From these fitting relations between persons Clarke derived "the eternal law of righteousness." With respect to our fellow creatures this law is: ". . . so deal with every man as in like circumstances we could reasonably expect he should deal with us, and that in general we endeavor, by an universal benevolence to promote the welfare and happiness of all men." The eternal law of righteousness is also spoken of as the Law of Nature and the right reason of things. Clarke appealed to right reason to account for someone's obligation to follow the law of righteousness. Right reason distinguishes men from beasts and enables us to see that there is a natural and necessary difference between right and wrong and between just and unjust. It follows that a vicious person is someone whose reason has been either clouded by education or bad habits or overborne by selfish desires. Clarke's system of moral philosophy rested heavily on reason as the faculty that discerns the fitness of actions and impels our obligation. But at the same time he admitted that the role of reason in speculative matters and the role of reason in morality are not wholly similar. In mathematics, for example, as soon as one understands the terms and the conditions of their compatibility, one immediately assents to those propositions in which the terms are properly combined. But morality is a matter of both reason and will, and despite a person's knowledge of the right reason of things he might nonetheless withhold his will from conforming to it.

In founding morality on the fitness and unfitness in the

relations of things Clarke was careful to claim that the fitness is independent of the will of God. God must discover the fitness and conform his will to it just as any other moral agent must. But Clarke's use of "fitness" and "unfitness" here is not without its difficulties. These are normative terms, and some feelings are required to back them up. By his appeal to reason Clarke hoped to have given these terms a purely descriptive use. Whether he succeeded in doing so is one of the problems of his moral philosophy.

Defense of Newton. Clarke's correspondence with Leibniz was carried on under the sponsorship of Caroline, the princess of Wales, who had known Leibniz in Germany before she married George I's only son. She met Clarke when she came to the English court. Caroline was much impressed by Clarke, but according to Voltaire, Edmund Gibson, bishop of Lincoln, prevented Clarke's appointment as archbishop of Canterbury by telling Caroline that Clarke was the most learned and honest man in her dominions but had one defect—he was not a Christian. The correspondence consists of five letters by Leibniz and five replies by Clarke. The exchange of letters took place during 1715 and 1716 and was terminated by the death of Leibniz. Clarke immediately prepared an edition of the correspondence, which was published in 1717.

The occasion of the correspondence was Leibniz' remarking in a letter to Caroline that Newtonian physics had contributed to a decline of natural religion in England. This charge was taken seriously by Newton and his followers because they believed that Newtonian physics showed God to have a decisive role in the conservation of the universe. As they also held that the acceptability of Christianity could be deduced from the reasonableness of natural theology, it was of the greatest importance that Leibniz be fully and satisfactorily answered before the princess. Clarke was chosen to answer Leibniz as the one man in England qualified by sufficient knowledge of both theology and physics.

Leibniz attacked Newton at two main points: the notions of absolute space and time, and the concept of gravity. In order to distinguish real from apparent motion Newton required some fixed point against which real motion could be measured. He saw that if he picked out an actual object in space against which to measure the movement of other objects, any movement of the first object would give the appearance of motion to the other objects. To ensure that in his physics he was giving an account of a real, and not an apparent, motion he postulated an absolute space through whose parts real motion takes place in an absolute time. Newton then went on to enhance this conceptual scheme with the theological dictum that it is as if space were God's sensorium.

Leibniz called the idea of God's having a sense organ absurd. Newton was ascribing parts to God, a suggestion that is inconsistent with the simplicity of God's being. Clarke parried this criticism by explaining that Newton meant by "sensorium" not an organ but the place of sensation. He stressed that Newton had said only that it is *as if* space were God's sensorium and had intended only to refer to God's omnipresent apprehension of all things. As for the notions of absolute space and time, Leibniz found Newton to be making things of space and time. He argued that space is correctly understood as the order in which things coexist and that time is an order of successions. Leibniz found that absolute space, conceived as separated from all things, would have parts indistinguishable from one another. Thus, no part of space would be any different from another, and there would be no accounting for why things are in one place rather than another. However, when space is regarded as an order of coexistence the order can be accounted for by Leibniz' Principle of Sufficient Reason: God has chosen to order things as they are because this order makes for the best of all possible worlds. Clarke replied by arguing that God's will alone is sufficient reason to account for things being where they are.

Leibniz attacked the concept of gravity as a revival of the abhorred scholastic notion of action at a distance, without any intervening means. He argued that gravity must be accounted for either as the operations of some quality in created bodies or as an act of will on the part of their Creator, an instance of pre-established harmony. To argue otherwise would be to make gravity a continuing miracle, a view that is insulting to the intelligence of God. Clarke replied that as the operation of gravity is regular and constant, it is certainly a natural, not a miraculous, phenomenon. All Newton claimed is that there is such a phenomenon and that its operation can be shown experimentally. On these grounds alone the existence of gravity ought to be acknowledged, even though the Newtonians made no attempt to account for its cause. As for appealing to pre-established harmony to account for physical phenomena, Clarke saw that taking such an appeal seriously would mean the end of arguing from phenomena and experiments, the end of all that Newton had accomplished.

Bibliography

The *Works of Samuel Clarke* is a collected edition of four volumes (London, 1738–1742), prefaced by a short biography by Benjamin Hoadley, bishop of Salisbury. Volume II of *The British Moralists*, edited by L. A. Selby-Bigge (Oxford, 1897), reproduces, with slight deletions, the whole of Clarke's arguments for the opening propositions of the "Discourse on the Unchangeable Obligations of Natural Religion"; a fair view of Clarke's moral philosophy can be obtained by consulting this work. For Clarke's correspondence with Leibniz, see *The Leibniz–Clarke Correspondence; Together With Extracts From Newton's Principia and Opticks*, edited by H. G. Alexander (Manchester, 1956); in this edition Leibniz' letters, which were originally written in French, are offered only in Clarke's English translations. In the original edition of 1717, prepared by Clarke, and in Clarke's *Works*, French and English versions of the correspondence are printed *en regard*. See also "Samuel Clarke," by Bernard Peach, in *Encyclopedia of Morals*, edited by V. Ferm (New York, 1956).

ELMER SPRAGUE

CLASSIFICATION. *See* DEFINITION; LOGICAL TERMS, GLOSSARY OF.

CLAUBERG, JOHANNES (1622–1665), German Cartesian philosopher. He was born in Solingen and studied at Bremen and at Groningen, the Netherlands, until

1647; during this time he also traveled to France and England. In 1648 and 1649 he attended the lectures of the Cartesian philosopher Johan de Raey in Leiden, and from 1649 to 1651 he was professor of philosophy and theology at the Calvinist university of Herborn. He became professor of philosophy at the Calvinist gymnasium in Duisburg in 1651, and after this institution became a university in 1655, he also lectured in theology there.

In 1647 Clauberg published at Groningen his *Elementa Philosophiae Sive Ontosophia*, which conformed to the German-Dutch Aristotelian tradition. He rejected such basic Aristotelian notions as matter and form, power and act, but he retained the Aristotelian doctrine that knowledge is obtained through the senses alone.

Under the influence of de Raey, Clauberg was partially converted to Cartesianism. His theory concerning the connection of soul and body was called occasionalism, but it was not the same as Malebranche's occasionalism. In spite of his conversion, Clauberg did not reject the substance of his earlier philosophy. In a new edition of his *Ontosophia*, entitled *Ontosophia Nova, quae Vulgo Metaphysica* (Duisburg, 1660), the structure of the work was left unaltered, although at several points Clauberg tried to reconcile his former doctrines with the Cartesian tenets, following the examples of Andriaan Heereboord and Lambert van Velthuysen. The most significant change was the rejection of Aristotelian empiricism on the basis of Cartesian gnosiology. In some of his other works Clauberg followed the Cartesian method of geometrical demonstration.

In his *Ontosophia* Clauberg distinguished three different meanings of "being"—a more general sense as "intelligible" (*intelligibile*), a less general sense as "something" (*aliquid*), and a particular sense as "real being" (*ens reale*), or being outside the intellect. Attributes are either original or derived. The original attributes are essence existence, and production. Production originates the derived attributes.

In natural philosophy Clauberg followed Descartes and de Raey. God is the primary cause of motion, and the quantity of motion in the universe is constant. The planets are moved by vortices in the ethereal substance.

Works by Clauberg

Opera Omnia Philosophica. Amsterdam, 1691.

Defensio Cartesiana Contra Jac. Revium et Cyr. Lentulum. Amsterdam, 1652.

Initiatio Philosophi, seu Dubitatio Cartesiana. Leiden and Duisburg, 1655.

Metaphysica de Ente, quae Rectius Ontosophia. Amsterdam, 1664, 3d ed. of *Ontosophia*.

Physica Contracta. Amsterdam, 1664.

Works on Clauberg

Balz, A. G. A., *Cartesian Studies*. New York, 1951. Pp. 159-194.

Bohatec, J., *Die Cartesianische Scholastik in der Philosophie und Theologie der reformierten Dogmatik des 17. Jahrhunderts*. Leipzig, 1912.

Brosch, Pius, *Die Ontologie des Johannes Clauberg*. Greifswald, 1926.

Müller, Hermann, *Johannes Clauberg und seine Stellung im Cartesianismus*. Jena, 1891.

Thijssen-Schoute, C. L., *Nederlands Cartesianisme*. Amsterdam, 1954. Pp. 141 ff.

Wundt, Max, *Die deutsche Schulmetaphysik des 17. Jahrhunderts*. Tübingen, 1939. Pp. 93 ff.

GIORGIO TONELLI

CLEANTHES (c. 331-232 B.C.), Stoic philosopher and second head of the Stoic school. Born in Assos in the Troad, he came to Athens, where he attended first the lectures of Crates the Cynic and later those of Zeno of Citium, founder of the Stoa, or "Porch," whose teachings Cleanthes afterward followed. Renowned for his industry and limitless patience, he was esteemed for his high moral qualities and complete lack of arrogance. Ancient opinion tended to discount any originality of mind in him, describing him as a plodder and awarding him the title of "the Ass." Under his leadership the fortunes of the Stoic school seem to have faltered but were revived by its "second founder," Chrysippus. Yet, one may question so low an estimate of his capabilities; after all, his famous pupil, Chrysippus, held him in reverence. Gentle in his dealings with opponents, choosing to see the cogency (rather than the failings) of their arguments, he is said to have written fifty works, only fragments of which are extant.

He is best remembered for his *Hymn to Zeus*, fine poetry which admirably summarized the leading tenets of early Stoicism: wonder and submission to the world order; fate blended with free will. Carrying forward Zeno's assimilation of the Heraclitean doctrine of flux and transforming his dualism of fire (God?) and formless matter (the active and passive principles), Cleanthes created the lofty pantheism so strikingly expressed in his famous *Hymn*.

He also stressed the materialistic temper of Zeno's doctrine: whatever is, is at once capable of acting and of being acted upon. For all that is, there is an antecedent cause, and since *cause* means cause of the motion of any body and since only body can act on body, it follows that the antecedent cause is as corporeal as the matter upon which it acts. The two principles are thus coextensive. Cleanthes coupled this pansomatism with the physical property of *tonos*, tension, to formulate the Stoic explanation of the structure of the universe, thus accounting for the destinies of all particulars: the tension of the one omnipresent substance is the cause of the universal flux. Application of the concept of *tonos* to natural philosophy (Zeno and the Cynics restricted it to ethics) is largely due to Cleanthes; it is his contribution to the elaboration of Stoic physics.

For the early Stoics, investigation into man's destiny turned on their conception of the *summum bonum:* true happiness is the morally honorable life derived from nature's recommendation; "live according to nature" has ever since been a Stoic hallmark. With Cleanthes the emphasis on nature (ambiguous with Zeno) was first marked out, taking the nature of the universe alone as that with which man's life ought to be in accord (without adding the nature of man, an elaboration of Chrysippus).

Bibliography

Arnim, J. von, *Stoicorum Veterum Fragmenta*. Leipzig, 1905. Vol. I, pp. 552-588, "Cleanthis Assii Fragmenta. . . ."

Pearson, A. C., *Fragments of Zeno and Cleanthes.* Cambridge, 1891.

Verbeke, G., *Kleanthes von Assos.* Brussels, 1949.

Zuntz, G., "Zum Hymnus des Kleanthes." *Rheinisches Museum für Philologie* (1951), 337–341.

JASON L. SAUNDERS

CLEMENT OF ALEXANDRIA, Titus Flavius Clemens (c. 150–c. 213), Christian theologian of the Alexandrian school, was born of pagan parents, probably in Athens. Clement learned from several teachers in the Mediterranean world before he came to Alexandria, where he studied under the Christian philosopher Pantaenus, a converted Stoic who was the head of the catechetical school. Clement remained in Alexandria from 175 to 202, writing and teaching, until he fled during the persecution of the emperor Septimius Severus. He died in Palestine. Alexandria's heritage of learning, culture, syncretism, and religious mystery may be seen in his writing. His three major works form a trilogy that leads from paganism to mature Christianity. In the *Protrepticus* ("Exhortation") he attacks the absurdities of pagan deities and exhorts his readers to turn to Christianity. In the *Paedagogus* ("Tutor") he instructs Christians in the good life. In his chief work, the unfinished *Stromateis* ("Patchwork"), he sets down his philosophical opinions in unsystematic notes—"Gnostic notes concerning the true philosophy." This work, which represents the final stage of instruction, includes much material that he had learned from his teachers but hesitated to write about because of its difficult and sacred nature. He regards obscurity, compression of style, and haphazard arrangement as safeguards against the abuse of sophistry. Clement used the word "gnostic" because he wanted to show that there was a true Christian *gnosis*, or knowledge, which developed out of faith and which was better than the boasted knowledge of the heretical Gnostics. Gnosticism was especially strong in Alexandria. Clement put forward an attractive alternative to it and attacked what he considered to be its peculiar tenets of esoteric knowledge, dualism, and ethical determinism. Knowledge, he said, grows out of faith and is not distinct from it. There is one God who made all things. Men are free to choose the way they will go.

Clement wrote against the background of Middle Platonism, of Antiochus of Ascalon, Maximus of Tyre, Albinus, and Numenius, whose thought was governed by the problem of defining the relation between the one and the one-many, and of deriving the latter from the former. The difference between a one and a one-many, or between simple and complex unity, is like the difference between the unity of a pinpoint and the unity of a spider's web. In Middle Platonism these two unities were developed into divine entities. Simple unity is divine and transcendent, while complex unity is divine and immanent. Clement was influenced by the Alexandrian Jewish Platonist Philo, for whom God is a simple, bare unity and the Logos an all-embracing cosmic whole. Clement's thought is governed by the pattern of simple and complex unity; and his accounts of God, goodness, and truth are expressed in these terms.

God is the transcendent one, a simple unity, the ultimate first principle and cause of all things. The categories of logic cannot be applied to him. "Nor are any parts to be ascribed to him, for the one is indivisible." God cannot properly be named. The good names we give him are supports to our minds to stop us from erring. Taken separately, these names do not say what God is like, but together they show his power. While God cannot be known, the Son, or the Logos, is wisdom, knowledge, and truth. He unites in himself the world of Platonic forms, or "powers," as they are also called in later Platonism. "The Son is not simply one thing as one thing nor many things as parts, but one thing as all things. All things come from him. For he is the circle of all the powers rolled into one and united." Within this unity of the Son the individual believer is saved. Faith is union in him, while disbelief is separation, estrangement, and division. Paganism is wrong because it multiplies the nature of divinity, and Marcion, the Christian heretic, is wrong because he divides the supreme God from the Creator of the world, making two Gods instead of one.

God's goodness is perfect and unique. God does not prevent evil and suffering from taking place, but when they do, he turns them to good account. He may use suffering as a form of correction for sinners. After death, imperfect souls may be sanctified by an intelligent nonmaterial fire. The complex goodness of men is always assimilation to God—growing like him by participation in his goodness. Clement constantly refers to Plato's statement in the *Theaetetus* concerning assimilation to God. All men, says Clement, receive the image of God at their birth and all may then, as they choose, become assimilated to him and receive his likeness. In the *Paedagogus*, Clement gives detailed instruction for Christian behavior. From Plato came the emphasis on self-knowledge, and the conception of evil as ignorance and virtue as knowledge. Virtue comes through discipline and the pursuit of goodness, without thought of ulterior gain. The harmony of the soul is aided by the harmony of the body. From Aristotle, Clement draws the notion of virtue as the fulfillment of man's function and the achievement of his end. This fulfillment is found in pursuing the mean between extremes and in possessing right reason. Clement draws heavily on Stoic ethics, commending what is in accord with nature and in harmony with reason. There is a class of things intermediate between good and evil. One should recognize the things which are in one's power and the things which are not, and avoid being dominated by one's irrational passions.

Clement speaks of truth in two ways. The simple elements of Christianity are true, and heresy is to be rejected as false. Truth is one and unique, powerful and strong in delivering men from error. It comes from God and is preserved within the tradition of the church. Second, Clement speaks of truth as including all that is consistent with basic Christian truth. This truth is a whole composed of many parts. It is one body from which each of the philosophical sects has torn a limb, or part, falsely imagining it to be the whole of truth. The many parts must be brought together, so that the perfect Logos, the truth, may be known. The truth of philosophy was partial, but real. It was for the Greeks, as the Law was for the Jews, a schoolmaster to bring them to Christ. Clement shared with others the quaint notion that the Greeks stole their ideas from the Hebrews.

Faith is an act not a process. Faith is the acceptance from God of an indemonstrable first principle from which all other truth may be deduced. It is a judgment of the soul, an Epicurean *preconception*, and a Stoic *assent*. Knowledge (*gnosis*) is both logical and spiritual, joining things together either by logical reasoning or by spiritual vision. The eighth book of the *Stromateis* is a notebook of logic composed of materials from various sources. It deals with demonstration and definition in an Aristotelian way, gives a Stoic refutation of the skeptical suspension of judgment (that is, if one must suspend judgment, then one should suspend judgment concerning suspense of judgment), and treats of cause, using both Stoic and Aristotelian terms. Causes may be original, sufficient, cooperating, and necessary. Spiritual knowledge is growth in Christ, awareness of God's universal presence, and union with him in love. Symbolism reveals hidden connections and points to unity. Knowledge is always a complex unity, while faith is a simple unity.

Clement achieved the first real synthesis of classical philosophy and Christianity. The Apologists had used particular ideas to bridge the gap between philosophy and Christianity. In Justin's writings, for example, God is described in terms of the Platonic ineffable being, and the divine reason implanted in men is expounded along Stoic lines; but there is no comprehensive conceptual framework which enables these and other ideas to modify one another. Clement's synthesis was developed by Origen, and the result was the theology of the fourth-century Greek Fathers and of Augustine.

Bibliography

Clement's works are to be found in O. Stahlin, *Die griechischen christlichen Schriftsteller der ersten drei Jahrhunderte*, Vols. 12, 15, 17, and 39 (Leipzig, 1905–1936), and in J. P. Migne, *Patrologia Graeca*, Vols. 8–9 (Paris, 1857). A translation of his writings is W. Wilson, *Clement of Alexandria*, Ante-Nicene Christian Library, Vols. 4 and 12 and parts of Vols. 22 and 24 (Edinburgh, 1882 and 1884). Sections of Clement's works are translated by H. Chadwick in the Library of Christian Classics, Vol. II (London, 1954). The *Protrepticus*, with a parallel translation by G. W. Butterworth, has been published in the Loeb Classical Library (London, 1919).

For literature on Clement, see C. Bigg, *The Christian Platonists of Alexandria*, 2d ed. (Oxford, 1913); J. Patrick, *Clement of Alexandria* (Edinburgh and London, 1914); R. B. Tollinton, *Clement of Alexandria*, 2 vols. (London, 1914); C. Mondésert, *Clément d'Alexandrie* (Paris, 1944); W. Völker, *Der wahre Gnostiker nach Clemens Alexandrinus* (Berlin and Leipzig, 1952); E. F. Osborn, *The Philosophy of Clement of Alexandria* (Cambridge, 1957).

E. F. OSBORN

CLIFFORD, WILLIAM KINGDON (1845–1879), English mathematician and philosopher, was born in Exeter, the son of a justice of the peace. At the age of 15 he went to Kings College, London. There he gained a minor scholarship to Trinity College, Cambridge, to which he went in 1863. He began to exhibit powers of originality in mathematics, publishing a number of mathematical papers during the year in which he first entered Cambridge.

At the university Clifford distinguished himself not only by his intellect but also by his singular character. As one of the most prominent undergraduates, he was soon invited to join the Apostles, an exclusive Cambridge club made up of the 12 most distinguished undergraduates of the time. Here he exhibited some of that breadth of learning and clarity of mind for which he was to be noted all his life. It appears that he was highly concerned about religious questions because he studied Aquinas and learnedly supported the Catholic position. Later, however, he became an agnostic and turned against religion; Spencer and Darwin became the most important influences upon his thinking in many areas.

Clifford was elected a fellow of Trinity in 1868. In that year he began the practice of giving public lectures, a source from which most of his published work stems. He participated in a scientific expedition, which was wrecked off the coast of Catania, Sicily. In 1870 he was appointed professor of applied mathematics at University College, London. Soon after, he became a member of the most distinguished intellectual society of the day, the Metaphysical Society, as well as of the London Mathematical Society. Tragically, his life was drawing to a close, for he had contracted tuberculosis. His condition worsened, until by 1878 it was evident that the disease was far advanced. In 1879 he traveled south to try to counteract the disease, but he died on March 3 of that year.

During Clifford's lifetime he published only a textbook on dynamics and some scattered technical and nontechnical papers based on his lectures. It remained for a number of his friends to gather together his work. H. J. S. Smith edited the mathematical papers, F. Pollock the philosophical ones. The young Karl Pearson edited and completed his popular work on science, *The Common Sense of the Exact Sciences*.

Scientific epistemology. Clifford's philosophical views must be placed within the context of several major influences upon his thought: the Kantian frame in epistemology, the Riemannian frame in geometry, and the Darwinian frame in biology. On the basis of these and other influences, Clifford constructed a scientific epistemology and attempted to construct a scientific metaphysic. A discussion of his epistemology is first in order, since out of it grew his metaphysics. Clifford conceived of knowledge as a biological response to the world. Its structure, therefore, is determined by that adjustment. However, any analysis of knowledge as such reveals that within it the form and the content of knowledge are distinguishable from each other. Kant believed that he had determined a method to make this distinction in all cases. Clifford, taking his cue from Kant, believed that he too could make this distinction, but in a way that took into account the ultimately biological character of knowledge. He thought that an analysis of the foundations of science, and in particular of the axioms of geometry, would reveal that these axioms are forms of experience in the life of any particular individual. Thus, since the biological adaptation of the race has crystallized three-dimensional Euclidean space, this spatial framework has become the one in which individuals see spatially locatable objects. Clifford went even further in this direction by claiming that such a construction is ultimately a growth of experience which has been transformed into neural capacities. Thus, Clifford conceived of the form–content distinction of knowledge as one relative to the biological development of the race. What is at one time the content of experience is later, through a biological process, transformed into a form of experience.

The principles of geometry and arithmetic serve, for individuals, to structure their experience. They are or correspond to ways in which our sense data are "spatially" or "numerically" organized. Their logical status is therefore closely akin to the one that Kant assigned to them. They are a priori, for no experience is capable of verifying or falsifying them, whereas at the same time they are synthetic, since the predicate term is not contained in the subject term.

Within this framework of thought it is intelligible to discuss Clifford's concrete epistemological ideas. He offered analyses of what might be called (1) perceptual statements, (2) geometric, arithmetical, and even physical principles, and (3) belief statements in general.

Perceptual statements. In various essays Clifford offered an analysis of perceptual statements concerning objects, persons, and the spatial aspects of objects and persons. In general, he refused to admit a phenomenalist analysis of such statements. In all cases some ideal conception, be it of "an eject" (a technical term which will be explained later) or of "a form of experience"—in other words, a conception which is not itself definable in terms of a set of sense experiences—enters into the meaning of the statement, either explicitly or implicitly. This is true with the qualification that Clifford sometimes suggested that statements about physical objects are reducible to statements about sense experiences.

Geometric, arithmetical, and physical principles. The analysis which Clifford provided of the several kinds of statements differed somewhat from one another, and it would be wise to examine them in sequence. As has already been indicated, the statements of geometry and arithmetic state universal and therefore formal characteristics of experience. In the case of geometric statements, Clifford asserted that they are universally true about the objects of our perceptions, in the sense that all perceptions of spatial relationships must conform to them. Furthermore, they are necessary, since the perceptions compatible with the negations of such statements are impossible. Clifford contended that Kant had established the necessary properties of space by a subjective method, a method of introspection, whereas Clifford attempted to demonstrate such properties by a consideration of the neurological bases of perception. The limits of what is perceptible, given man's neurological structure, were, for Clifford, what is known a priori to the individual, while those perceptions whose contradictions are not imperceivable, again given man's neurological structure, are known a posteriori. Clifford proceeded to demonstrate, to his satisfaction, that at this level of analysis both Euclidean and non-Euclidean space are compatible with the neurological structure of perception, and that it is a matter of the general explicatory value of a geometric theory as to which of the various geometries is to be accepted. Of course, man's neurological structure evolves over a period of time, so that what is necessary at one time is not necessary at another—this indicates that Clifford used the term *necessary,* in this context, in a relative sense.

Clifford's analysis of arithmetical statements differs somewhat from his analysis of geometric statements. He thought that their validity depended upon several factors: (1) the tautological character of certain parts of language, (2) the acceptance of a general principle of the uniformity of nature of the kind that J. S. Mill suggested, and (3) the acceptance of an analysis of arithmetical operations in terms of the physical operation of counting. Numerals are assigned in a one-to-one correspondence with standard sets of objects, each set containing one member more than the preceding set. The operations of addition, multiplication, and, by implication, subtraction and division are next defined in terms of the physical operations of juxtaposition of sets of objects. Clifford then claimed that if the meaning of "distinct objects" were granted, along with the assumption that all objects maintain their identity through space and time (the uniformity of nature), then the laws of arithmetic can be seen to hold for all objects. On the basis of the natural numbers, he sketched the development of the more complex number systems.

Clifford did not have much to say about the status of physical laws and theories, except to suggest that there are some principles of physics that are, like the principles of geometry and arithmetic, rules for the ordering of sense impressions.

Belief statements. Clifford's examination of the basis of belief in the natural sciences led him to a more general analysis of belief. Indeed, it was this general analysis of belief and the agnostic and antireligious conclusion to which it led that occasioned great opposition on the part of William James and others. Clifford claimed that no statement is worthy of belief unless all the possible evidence points to the truth of the statement. He recognized that in practice it is impossible to have available all the possible evidence about the truth or falsity of a proposition. Failure of memory, the expenses of collecting information, and a host of other factors contribute to this impossibility. But he claimed that an acceptance of the principle that similar causes have similar effects (another version of the principle of the uniformity of nature) permits our acceptance of many beliefs in cases where the standard of all possible evidence is not met. Such a principle permits an inductive inference from known facts to unknown ones, and thus permits us to make up for evidence we do not possess. These ideas are contained in his essay "The Ethics of Belief," to which James's famous essay "The Will to Believe" is a reply. In that essay James claimed that a belief is worthy of acceptance in some cases where there is no empirical evidence either for or against the content of the belief. And this criterion permitted James to believe in the existence of God.

Scientific metaphysics. Clifford's epistemological views were the occasion for his speculative metaphysical ideas. He had been wrestling with the problem of whether the existent world is wholly phenomenal in character or whether there are entities of a nonphenomenal character which go to make it up. In earlier essays—for example, "The Philosophy of Pure Sciences"—he inclined toward a purely phenomenalist view, but in his more mature and well-known essay "On the Nature of Things-in-themselves" he reversed his former stand. Not all existence is phenomenal in character. He was clear, for example, that the ego cannot be analyzed in purely phenomenal terms. Clifford thus postulated the existence of what he termed "ejects" as well as of phenomenal "objects." An eject is distinguished from an object in the following way: an object can be an object of *my* consciousness, an eject is something *outside* my consciousness. Thus, another's ego (and this holds for all persons) is an eject; it is never in my consciousness. Clifford postulated that there are nonpersonal as well as personal entities that are ejects. The elements of ejects are themselves what Clifford called feelings. They are constituents of everything, he claimed, since the fact that there is a continuity of forms in nature gives assurance that, at least to some degree, any entity in nature possesses the same qualities that all others have. Since feelings are elements of consciousness, all entities therefore have this aspect of consciousness to a certain extent, although it is only to more complex entities that we ascribe consciousness. The elementary entities that are called "feelings" were considered by Clifford to be absolute existents and therefore things-in-themselves. Clifford then named these elementary entities mind-stuff, since they participate somehow in the character of the mental. Their necessarily incomplete representation in the mind of man is what is known as the material world. There exists a complex mirroring relation—indeed, Clifford used the image of two reflecting mirrors—between the external world and its representation in knowledge. Thus, Clifford's speculative metaphysic ultimately postulated a Spinozistic world in which the mental and physical are really two different ways of looking at the same world. Another possible interpretation of his thought is that all existence is ultimately infused with a psychic aspect, that is, that panpsychism is the most correct view of reality.

In conclusion, it is worthwhile mentioning several areas of thought in which Clifford was ahead of his time:

(1) Clifford recognized the fact that scientific laws are always "practically inexact." By this notion he wished to point out that a scientific law is never exactly confirmed by the evidence for it but rather is confirmed within the limits of experimental error. A law is accepted on the basis of experimental evidence even if that experimental evidence does not exactly coincide with what, on the basis of deductions from the law, one might expect to be confirming evidence. This is so simply because all measurement of evidence in modern scientific practice involves taking into account errors of measurement, and such errors of measurement must be "factored out" before a definite conclusion is reached as to the relevance of the evidence.

(2) Clifford, in the brief note "On the Space-theory of Matter," declared himself to be in the geometric tradition that holds that the determination of the truth or falsity of geometrical axioms is empirical. Clifford saw that through a change in the basic assumptions of microgeometry (geometry of the infinitesimally small) he could work out a system of geometry and physics which would clear up the anomalies in physical theory that existed in his day. He saw that a reformulation of microgeometry in non-Euclidean terms could achieve this result, and in this respect he anticipated, at least in part, Einstein's program. However, he never carried through this program on his own; he merely suggested that such a program was feasible.

(3) Clifford showed the possibility, at least in principle, of constructing a wholly empirical geometry in the following special sense: Geometry is considered to be a set of statements about the relations between geometrical objects such as points, lines, planes, and volumes. However, these geometrical objects and relations are themselves characterized in a completely empirical way, not as ideal objects, as they are usually characterized in most treatments of geometry. That is, they are identified with the physical objects or apsects of physical objects. The principles of geometry are then empirical statements whose truth or falsity is a matter of observation. This point of view is close to a geometric operationalism. Clifford's account of it is found in his book *The Common Sense of the Exact Sciences*.

Bibliography

For works by Clifford, see *The Common Sense of the Exact Sciences*, Karl Pearson, ed. (London, 1885), reissued with a preface by Bertrand Russell and a new introduction by James R. Newman (New York, 1955); *Lectures and Essays*, F. Pollock, ed., 2 vols. (London, 1879); and *Mathematical Papers*, H. J. Smith, ed. (London, 1882).

For literature on Clifford, see George S. Fullerton, *A System of Metaphysics* (New York, 1914), which contains a criticism of Clifford's theory of mind-stuff; and A. S. Eddington, *The Nature of the Physical World* (Cambridge, 1929).

HOWARD E. SMOKLER

COHEN, HERMANN (1842–1918), Neo-Kantian philosopher, was born at Coswig, Anhalt, Germany. His father, Gerson Cohen, was a teacher and precentor at the synagogue; his mother was Friederike née Salomon. In 1878 Hermann married Martha Lewandowski, the daughter of Professor Louis Lewandowski, who was also a precentor at the synagogue and a composer of Jewish ritual songs. In 1853 Hermann went to the gymnasium of Dessau, which he attended for some years. He left there prematurely and went to the Jewish Theological Seminary at Breslau. Later, as a student at the University of Breslau, he wrote the essay "Über die Psychologie des Platon und Aristoteles," which won the prize of the philosophical faculty in August 1863. On August 5, 1864, he took the bachelor's examination as an extramural pupil at the Breslau Matthias Gymnasium. In the fall of the same year he went for further university studies to Berlin. He wrote an essay, "Philosophorum de Antinomia Necessitatis et Contigentiae Doctrinae" and entered it for a university prize. Since the prize was not awarded to him, he submitted the work (somewhat altered) to the philosophical faculty at Halle. On the basis of this work he was awarded the doctorate of philosophy by this faculty on October 27, 1865.

On his return to Berlin he published several studies, some of them in *Zeitschrift für Völkerpsychologie und Sprachwissenschaft*. Steinthal, the coeditor of this periodical, who was warmly interested in the very gifted young man, had stimulated his interest in social psychology. It was not until 1870 that his publications disclosed a special interest of their author in Kantian philosophy. In that year Cohen intervened in the Homeric struggle that had broken out between Adolf Trendelenburg and Kuno Fischer over Trendelenburg's criticism of the Kantian transcendental aesthetic. Trendelenburg agreed with Kant that the concepts of space and time are a priori, but he denied their exclusion from things-in-themselves, which was, in Kant's opinion, an unavoidable consequence of their intuitive apriority. According to Trendelenburg, a third possibility was left, namely the validity of space and time with regard to all existing objects *in spite of* the apriority of their *concepts*. Kuno Fischer, defending Kant against the charge of leaving this "gap," insisted that Kant's assignment of both space and time to human sensibility, in the Transcendental Aesthetic, was irrefutable. Cohen, a pupil of Trendelenburg, but not a favorite one, in an essay published in the above periodical (Vol. 7, No. 3, pp. 239–296) gave the Solomonic judgment. Trendelenburg was right in criticizing Kuno Fischer, but wrong in criticizing Kant.

Philosophical teaching. This judgment already contained in germ the whole of Cohen's future philosophical achievement. In the following year his first philosophical book, *Kants Theorie der Erfahrung* (Berlin, 1871) made it clear why, in his opinion, both Trendelenburg and Fischer were wrong. The teaching of the transcendental aesthetic, which showed space and time to be forms of our sensibility, had to be complemented by the teaching of the transcendental logic, where these forms are shown to be a priori conditions of possible experience. Possible experience, as Kant said throughout the *Critique*, is the only object of a priori knowledge. Therefore, the exclusive subjectivity of space and time, assumed by both parties to be Kant's complete view, disappears entirely if one takes into account the methodological difference between a psychological classification of space and time among native ideas and the Kantian transcendental theory of their being the a priori conditions of the possibility of experience.

By thus extending the matter in question to the whole of Kant's theory of a priori knowledge, Cohen gave evidence of the philosophical turn of his gifts. In 1873 he presented to the philosophical faculty of Marburg a treatise entitled *Die systematischen Begriffe in Kants vorkritischen Schriften* (Berlin, 1873) with an application for the *venia legendi* (lectureship). On the recommendation of F. A. Lange, Cohen's application was accepted. Lange died two years later, and in January 1876 Cohen, proposed by the faculty, was appointed to the vacant chair. He devoted his work to the fortification and extension of his new interpretation of Kant, which from the beginning had aroused admiration for the author's energy and devotion, though many doubted the compatibility of Cohen's interpretation with Kant's real opinion.

In any case, Cohen found himself confronted with a serious problem. If the objectivity of space and time consisted in their being a priori conditions of the possibility of experience, the question remained from what principle experience itself derived its validity. There was no identity between the conditions of experience and the conditions of things-in-themselves. This was unquestionably Kant's teaching. But, as Cohen observed, Kant had a new concept of experience. Actually, the innovation—if there was one—was Hume's not Kant's. Experience, according to Hume, is a statement on matters of fact presupposing some connection of these matters by general rules. The difference between Kant and Hume is not in the concept of experience but in the question of whether it is possible to justify the universality of that intellectual presupposition with regard to the objects of sense perception. Hume claimed it is not possible; those a priori assumptions are not a matter of intelligence at all. Man is driven to them by the laws of nature, which make him believe automatically in the possibility of experience.

This might not be a satisfactory answer. But Cohen's solution to the question—to derive the objectivity of those presuppositions (including space and time) from their being a priori conditions of experience—was not only not satisfactory—it was no answer at all. It was an answer that answered by what was the subject of the question. If, therefore, Cohen wished neither to accept the unconditioned subjectivity of Kant's possibility of experience nor to fall back on Hume's skepticism—which way was left to him?

It was the way of a crypto-positivism. The objectivity of doubtful a priori assumptions, such as space, time, and the categories, was demonstrable, according to Cohen, by means of the "fact of science" (*das Faktum der Wissenschaft*). Surely it was a historical fact that Newton had used these assumptions as principles in establishing his mathematical theory of the phenomena of nature. It was also a fact that Newton was far from justifying the assumption of these principles by deriving them from experience. But this by no means made the fact of their use as nonempirical principles of natural science equivalent to the fact of an existing a priori knowledge of nature. It was, on the contrary, evident that none of Newton's mathematical laws of natural phenomena, formulated in differential equations, could be called a knowledge of those phenomena if it was not verifiable by experience. How, then, could those principles presupposed by Newton's physics assume the character of a priori requirements for the cognition of nature by the mere fact of being presupposed by Newton, if the cognitive character of these presuppositions with regard to natural phenomena was demonstrable only by experience?

Despite this unanswerable question, Cohen boldly proclaimed that Newtonian science demonstrated by its own historical facticity the possibility of an a priori knowledge of nature by means of the concepts of space, time, and the Kantian categories. He called the manner of this demonstration the "transcendental method." It proved to be an enormous success. Cohen's pupils vied with each other in showing that modern science would not have been possible if its promoters had not presupposed what they actually had—that is, space, time, and the principles assigned by Kant to pure understanding. This, if it was meant to be a legitimation of a priori knowledge of natural phenomena by means of those principles, was clearly a vicious circle.

The desire to escape this consequence determined Cohen's philosophical development and the fate of Neo-Kantianism in general. Cohen realized eventually that his transcendental method, if it were to prove effective with regard to a priori knowledge of nature, required the tearing down of the insurmountable barrier Kant had fixed between a priori and empirical knowledge by means of his distinction between sensibility as receptivity and understanding as spontaneity. Therefore Cohen posited a kind of thinking that originated by its own act the whole field of principles of our knowledge ("Denken des Ursprungs"). Thus, all human knowledge must be in principle a priori knowledge.

In *Die Logik der reinen Erkenntnis* (Berlin, 1902) Cohen elaborated this puzzling idea. He explained by abundant historical comments that the real task of metaphysics was the thinking of the origin. If this is to be regarded as more than an utter triviality, it testifies that the author, in order to escape the deadly embrace of Hume, fled into the arms of Fichte and Hegel. Once more he fell victim to the ancient illusion of being able to understand Kant better than Kant himself by dropping the conditions essential to the very problem of transcendental philosophy. Thus Cohen, however unintentionally, encouraged a new movement from Kant to Hegel in German Neo-Kantianism. Even Heideggerian existentialism claimed some kinship with the critique of pure reason by proclaiming the search for the "common root" of sensibility and intelligibility, necessarily problematical with Kant, as a way of salvation from all possible transcendental problems.

Practical philosophy. Cohen similarly interpreted Kant's moral philosophy according to the maxim that to interpret Kant one must go beyond him in his *Kants Begründung der Ethik* (Berlin, 1877). He inherited from Trendelenburg's Aristotelianism the idea of virtue as the supreme problem of moral philosophy. Combined with the Kantian assumption of an a priori principle of morals, this idea generated the problem of ethics as the problem of an a priori science of virtue. Here again Aristotle intervened by his teaching that all other virtues are implied in justice. Thus, the problem of morals presented itself to Cohen as the problem of an a priori knowledge of justice. All a priori knowledge, according to Cohen's transcendental method, required some factual science to justify it. Kant did not presuppose any such factual science in his *Critique of Practical Reason.* In this Cohen believed Kant to be mistaken. According to him, morals does have a basic science, jurisprudence, because the idea of justice is the constitutional law of this science. If there were no a priori law of justice, the sort of systematic knowledge of the laws that the Romans assigned to *iurisprudentia* would not be possible. In identifying *iurisprudentia* with *scientia iusti*, Cohen found that the a priori character of Kant's categorical imperative was justified by the factual existence of jurisprudence.

Politics. It is easy to observe that autonomy as conditioned by the categorical imperative is by no means the principle of a society that, like the state, is realizable under the conditions of experience. And it is no less easy to see that the positive laws of a given state, the objects of jurisprudence, in spite of the possibility of their being systematically treated by jurisprudence, do not necessarily agree with some a priori idea of justice. Nevertheless, the idea of a human society constituted by the law of autonomy meant a quite personal engagement to Cohen, above and beyond all philosophical subtleties concerning its meaning or its justification. This engagement drove him from the field of transcendental deductions into politics. It made him a public champion of those whose personal dignity granted by the law of autonomy was infringed upon by society. He eventually found himself among them. Some years after he settled at Marburg, anti-Semitism appeared on the German political stage. The famous historian Heinrich von Treitschke published in his *Preussische Jahrbücher* (Vol. 1879, No. 11) an article in which he called attention to an attitude allegedly adopted by a good many Jewish writers, whom he accused of being antinational and anti-Christian. He held that they should respect the feelings of the majority. The weak point in Treitschke's pleas was the authority that he assigned to what in his romanticism he called Christian German culture.

Cohen in his *Eine Bekenntnis in der Judenfrage* (Berlin, 1880), without attacking Treitschke's romantic idea of a law given by Germano-Christian feeling, boldly announced that the Jews already belonged to the German nation—not *in spite of* their being Jews, but *because* they were Jews. This, of course, was too much for both parties. But to Cohen the philosopher and learned Jewish theologian it seemed quite simple to demonstrate. The Germans, he argued, are the nation of Kant. The Jews are a nation whose creed has been purified by the prophets. The teachings of the prophets, as Cohen's learnedness interpreted them, were identical with Kant's ethical idealism. Therefore, whoever tells a Jew that he can belong to the German nation only at the cost of his religion denounces him as having no true morality of his own. From that time on, Cohen continued as a collaborator in the interpretation of Jewish tradition by adapting it to his philosophy. His writings in this field were edited by Bruno Strauss and published with an introduction by Cohen's admirer Franz Rosenzweig as *Hermann Cohens jüdische Schriften* (3 vols., Berlin, 1924).

Besides the startling historical and ideological identifications of his Germano-Jewish patriotism, there was yet another reason for Cohen's reputation as a political outsider. It was not unusual to support the workingman's longing for a decent living according to the law of humanity. All the so-called *Katheder-Sozialisten*, among them some of the most influential professors of the German Empire, did it. But the mixture of philanthropy and justice that Cohen considered the supreme principle of his moral philosophy made him believe in a basic accordance between the doctrine of Karl Marx and his own. Thus, he became responsible for the legend of a kinship between Kant and Marx. This was enough to color the politician Cohen with a red tinge—and if his true patriotic German feeling separated him from Jewish orthodoxy and Zionism, his rather innocent socialism did not make him a favorite with either his government or his faculty.

Hence, his retirement in 1912 brought a great disappointment with it. The faculty, not very fond of intricate transcendental deductions that were admired by students but doubted by philosophers, refused to give his chair to the man of his choice, Ernst Cassirer. The choice of his colleagues, Paul Natorp dissenting, was a young experimental psychologist.

Later religious views. Deeply hurt, Cohen left Marburg and retired to Berlin. There he devoted himself to a lectureship at the Lehranstalt für Wissenschaft des Judentums, of which he was already a member of the board of trustees. Thus, he was again a theologian. Meanwhile, his philosophy had dissolved theology into a transcendental deduction of the eternity of cultural progress governed by the "social ideal"; namely, the community of autonomous beings. But in actual fact there was no solid deduction even of this eternity. The question of whether religion had any meaning at all arose again. Cohen answered it in two books, *Der Begriff der Religion im System der Philosophie* (Giessen, 1915) and *Die Religion aus den Quellen des Judentums* (Leipzig, 1919). In both of these works the point of departure lies in the observation that the belief in the eternity of cultural progress is of little comfort to the individual in his personal sufferings. Therefore, an empty space has been left by philosophy. This space may be filled by God as a savior bringing personal consolation to all men. Cohen found this idea of the Divine Being splendidly expressed by the prophets and the Psalmist. But the mere idea of a powerful personal Helper does not cause that Helper to exist; and since this idea, according to Cohen himself, could not be justified by his philosophical system, the question of a savior's existence was left entirely to personal conviction. To the great satisfaction of his religious friends, Cohen, when he died, seemed to be in full possession of this conviction.

Aesthetics. The manner in which Cohen addressed religious problems in his last writings was prepared by his aesthetics. Aesthetics had been treated by Kant within the frame of what he called the critique of judgment. Cohen's comment, published under the title *Kants Begründung der Ästhetik* (Berlin, 1889), once again disclosed the author's difficulty in harmonizing his own ideas in this field with the peculiar but at bottom simple Kantian theory of aesthetic pleasure.

In spite of the stock of questions left unanswered by Cohen's principles, he continues to live in the memory of philosophers as a Kantian who dominated to a great extent the philosophical discussions of his time. But if Cohen's own interpretation was attractive, it did not make Kant attractive; and his school of Neo-Kantianism eventually expired. The unbearable viciousness of the famous gnosiological circle, wrongly imputed to Kant himself but inextricably woven into Cohen's own omnipresent transcendental method, drove the younger generation to the worship of new gods. But even so, Cohen has left a stimulus to study "that Kant" whom, as one of his pupils is reputed to have said, "nobody ever knew." The feeling expressed by these words was precisely Cohen's own feeling when he began his work.

Works on Cohen

Cassirer, Ernst, "Hermann Cohen." *Social Research*, Vol. 10, No. 2 (1943), 219–232.

Kinkel, Walter, *Hermann Cohen, Einführung in sein Werk.* Stuttgart, 1928.

Natorp, Paul, *Hermann Cohen als Mensch, Lehrer, und Forscher.* Marburg, 1918.

Rosmarin, T. W., *Religion of Reason, Hermann Cohen's System of Religious Philosophy.* New York, 1936.

Vuillemin, J., *L'Héritage kantien et la révolution copernicienne.* Paris, 1954.

JULIUS EBBINGHAUS

COHEN, MORRIS RAPHAEL (1880–1947), American naturalistic philosopher, was born in Minsk, Russia. When 12 years old, he was brought to New York City by his parents, who immigrated to America in search of greater opportunity and freedom. In his early youth he came under the influence of the Scottish free-lance scholar Thomas Davidson. Cohen graduated from the College of the City of New York (City College) in 1900 and received his Ph.D. in philosophy from Harvard University in 1906. At Harvard he studied under Josiah Royce, William James, and Hugo Münsterberg.

From 1912 to 1938, Cohen taught philosophy at City College. He was an outstanding teacher, and some of his students became eminent teachers, philosophers, and lawyers. He was a visiting lecturer in philosophy at Johns Hopkins, Yale, Stanford, and Harvard and from 1938 through 1941 was a professor at the University of Chicago. For years he gave courses at the New School for Social Research. He was also a lecturer at the law schools of St. John's University, Columbia, Yale, Harvard, Cornell, the University of Buffalo, and New York University. Although an agnostic, he had been a dedicated Jew. His wit, his critical spirit, his erudition, and his interest in a wide range of friends made him a colorful and animating person.

Cohen's philosophic interests included the philosophy of science, metaphysics, logic, social philosophy, legal philosophy, and the philosophy of history. His contribution to legal philosophy has been especially widely recognized.

Metaphysical and logical principles. Cohen's general philosophic outlook is naturalistic. There is no place in his philosophy for the extranatural and no place for extrascientific methods to attain knowledge. His outlook is also rationalistic, for he assumed that rationality is inherent in nature. His philosophy is based on three principles: rationality, invariance, and polarity. These three principles, coherently interwoven, provide his view of reality.

Rationality. In its long history the concept of rationality has acquired a variety of meanings. It has meant logical order, inductive generalization, and wisdom. Each of these meanings has been significant. Cohen did not offer an inclusive definition of rationality, but in his philosophy of nature the first meaning is dominant and in his ethical and legal philosophies the third meaning is central.

Rationality as logical order may be considered methodologically or ontologically. Methodologically, it is a procedure to order our objects of thought in a logical way. Most philosophers, except for mystics and irrationalists, feel the necessity of such a procedure. Yet Cohen went beyond the methodological use of rationality and insisted on its ontological status. The rules of logic and pure mathematics "may be viewed not only as the principle of inference applicable to all systems but also as descriptive of certain abstract invariant relations which constitute an objective order characteristic of any subject matter" (*Reason and Nature*, p. 142).

For Cohen, as a logical realist, the formal aspects of logic apply to everything. As against idealists, positivists, and pragmatists, he was firm in insisting that the rational order is independent of human or superhuman mind. Idealists, according to him, deny the objectivity of logical order by giving it only a psychological status, but the psychological description of reasoning as a mental event cannot determine, according to him, whether a given logical argument is valid. Positivists, his arch philosophic enemies, fall short in a similar way. As sensations are considered the only deliverance of the external world, for positivists logical connections are mere fictions. Pragmatists, he argued, similarly depreciate the status of rational order. In their attempt to interpret the truth of judgment in terms of practical consequences, they consider logical relations as merely practical tools of thought without any ontological standing.

However, Cohen admitted an element of contingency in nature. "By no amount of reasoning," he wrote, "can we altogether eliminate all contingency from our world" (*ibid.*, p. 82). The universe is ultimately what it is, and contingency cannot be eliminated. And by contingency Cohen meant that the world contains an irrational element in the sense that "all form is the form of something which cannot be reduced to form alone" (*Studies in Philosophy and Science*, p. 11).

Invariance. Science is not, as Cohen rightly pointed out, a mere observation of particular facts; it is never satisfied with stating only what has occurred. The aim of science is to determine the universal, invariant relations of particular events. To say that sulfur has melted at 125° C. is a mere statement of fact similar to the statement that Russians for generations have used the Cyrillic alphabet, but to say that sulfur always melts at 125° C. means that if ever anything conforms to the category of sulfur, it melts at this temperature. The second statement expresses not only a historical event but also an invariant relation which belongs to "the eternal present."

Although the essence of particular things is their invariant relations, our knowledge of these is only probable. Only in logic or in mathematics can we attain certainty; in the world of facts our knowledge is only probable, for we cannot prove that the opposite of a given factual statement is absolutely impossible.

Polarity. According to the principle of polarity, opposites involve each other. As Cohen expressed it in *Reason and Nature*, "Opposites such as immediacy and mediation, unity and plurality, the fixed and the flux, substance and function, ideal and real, actual and possible, etc., like the north (positive) and the south (negative) poles of a magnet, all involve each other when applied to any significant entity" (p. 165).

In addition to its methodological value as a guide to the clarification of ideas, the principle of polarity, like the principle of rationality, has ontological status. Empirical facts, such as the existence of the north and south poles, are said to be resultants of opposing tendencies. Cohen generalized this alleged fact as the principle of "the necessary copresence and mutual dependence of opposite determinations."

Ethics. Historically, there have been two major opposing theories of morality—the absolutist and the relativist. Cohen examined both of these theories and found them unsatisfactory. The absolutist is too rigid and uncritical; the relativist is too chaotic, without guiding principles. Cohen thought the principle of polarity could reconcile the two opposing views. Actually, these two views provide a vantage point for arriving at the truth. Concretely, every issue of life involves choice. The absolutist is right "in insisting that every such choice logically involves a principle of decision," and the relativist is right "in insisting on the primacy of the feeling or perception of the demands in the actual case before us" (*ibid.*, p. 438). We may thus have an ethical system that is rigorously logical and at the same time richly empirical. Such an ethics must be grounded in what human beings desire and believe, and yet its primary condition must be the logical analysis of judgment as to what constitutes right and wrong, good and evil—an ethic that is the rational formulation of our ends.

Law. Cohen was a pioneer in introducing legal philosophy as a significant study to universities and law schools. As Leonora Cohen Rosenfield wrote, "His philosophical treatment of the law in relation to man and the social order may prove in time to be his foremost influence."

For Cohen law is essentially a system for the orderly regulation of social action. Jurisprudence must avoid the extremes of positivism and formalism. "Law without concepts or rational ideas, law that is not logical is like prescientific medicine—a hodge-podge of sense and superstition," yet law without reference to the actual facts of human conduct would be empty. A law is both stable and dynamic; it is a balance between prevailing customs and the emerging demands of society. Cohen was especially critical of what he called the "phonograph theory of law," the theory that the judge arrives at his decision in a mechanical way, according to unchanging laws. Cohen effectively argued that the judge's opinions on social and economic questions deeply influence his decisions. One of the chief merits of his analysis of law is his insistence on the interdependence of the factual and the normative. As he maintained, "Justice and the law, the ideal and the actual are inseparable, yet identifiable."

Works by Cohen

Reason and Nature: An Essay on the Meaning of Scientific Method. London, 1931. Cohen's major work.

Law and the Social Order: Essays in Legal Philosophy. London, 1933. Important work.

An Introduction to Logic and Scientific Method. New York and London, 1934. Written with Ernest Nagel.

A Preface to Logic. Toronto and New York, 1945. Important work.

The Meaning of Human History. La Salle, Ill., 1947. Important work.

A Dreamer's Journey. Chicago, 1949. Autobiography.

Studies in Philosophy and Science. New York, 1949.

Reason and Law: Studies in Juristic Philosophy. Chicago, 1950.

Works on Cohen

Baron, Salo W.; Nagel, Ernest; and Pinson, Koppel S., eds., *Freedom and Reason: Studies in Philosophy and Jewish Culture in Memory of Morris Raphael Cohen.* Glencoe, Ill., 1951. See Part I.

Cairns, Huntington, "The Legal Philosophy of Morris R. Cohen." *The Vanderbilt Law Review*, Vol. 14 (1960).

Kuhn, M. A., *Morris Raphael Cohen: A Bibliography.* 1957. Available in the City College library.

Rosenfield, Leonora Cohen, *A Portrait of a Philosopher: Morris R. Cohen.* New York, 1962.

YERVANT H. KRIKORIAN

COHERENCE THEORY OF TRUTH. The coherence theory is one of the two traditional theories of truth, the other being the correspondence theory. The coherence theory is characteristic of the great rationalist system-building metaphysicians Leibniz, Spinoza, Hegel, and Bradley; but it has also had a vogue with several members of the logical positivist school, notably Neurath and Hempel, who were much influenced by the systems of pure mathematics and theoretical physics. According to the coherence theory, to say that a statement (usually called a judgment) is true or false is to say that it coheres or fails to cohere with a system of other statements; that it is a member of a system whose elements are related to each other by ties of logical implication as the elements in a system of pure mathematics are related. Many proponents of the theory hold, indeed, that each member of the system implies every other member. To test whether a statement is true is to test it for coherence with a system of statements. The system with which all true statements must cohere is said by its logical positivist supporters to be that accepted by the scientists of the contemporary culture. The metaphysical supporters of coherence, on the other hand, insist that a statement cannot properly be called true unless it fits into the one comprehensive account of the universe or reality, which itself forms a coherent system. In either case, no statement can be known to be true until it is known to cohere with every other statement of the system; where the system consists of all true statements, such knowledge is unattainable.

It is not altogether possible to give a plausible exposition of the theory independently of its close historical links with rationalist and idealist metaphysics, but the account might go something like this.

In practice, we sometimes reject as false an ordinary person's assertions—for instance, that he saw a ghost—or even a scientist's results—for instance, in experiments on extrasensory perception—on the ground that they do not cohere with the other common-sense or scientific views that we also hold as true.

Meaning of truth. In the exact and reputable science of pure mathematics, the logical test for the truth or acceptability of any proposition is whether it coheres with some of the other propositions, and ultimately with the axioms, of its system. In this test, which is not merely a practical one, for a proposition to cohere with other propositions is for it to be logically deducible from them. Further, this coherence is what we mean by calling such a proposition true.

Internal relations. It is characteristic of the parts of a logical system like that of pure mathematics that no part would be what it is if its relations to the other parts were different from what they are. Thus, 2 would not be the number we associate with the numeral 2 if it were the third of 4 instead of the half of 4 or the cube root of 27 instead of the cube root of 8. Hence, it is said, the meaning and the truth of, for instance, "$2 + 2 = 4$" are bound up with the meaning and the truth of all the other statements in the arithmetical system; and our knowledge of its meaning and its truth is bound up with our knowledge of their meaning and their truth. This principle that nothing would be what it is if its relations to other things were different—which is called the doctrine of internal relations—holds, say the metaphysical supporters of coherence, for every element, whether in thought or in reality. For example, they argue that we would not even understand, much less know the truth or falsity of, a statement about something blue if blue were "divorced in our thought from all the colours in the spectrum to which it is related by likeness and difference, all the shades within its own range, and all the definition it possesses in virtue of being thought as a quality rather than as a substance or a relation" (Brand Blanshard, *The Nature of Thought*, Vol. II, p. 316). Further, not only would we not know the meaning or truth of such a statement, but it also cannot properly be said to have its meaning or truth-value independently of its relations to other statements. The statement "Caesar crossed the Rubicon in 49 B.C." is said to be pregnant with a meaning "owing to the concrete political situation within which it took place" that it would not otherwise have.

Degrees of truth. A corollary of the principle of internal relations and of the coherence theory in general is the doctrine of degrees of truth. If the truth of any given statement is bound up with, and can only be seen with, the truth of all the statements of the system and thus is bound up with the whole system, it is argued that individual statements as such are only partly true—and, therefore, partly false—while only the whole system is wholly true. "Truth," said Bradley, "must exhibit the mark of expansion and all-inclusiveness."

Criterion of truth. Coherence theorists might admit that their arguments hitherto have been drawn from the nature of the a priori reasoning typical of mathematics and metaphysics; but some have also claimed that an examination of the a posteriori reasoning of the empirical sciences and ordinary life also supports the theory, not only as giving the meaning of "truth" but also as giving the test of truth (*ibid.*, pp. 226–237). In testing for truth it is obvious, runs the claim, that coherence is our only criterion when dealing with statements about the past. No one can now compare the statement that the battle of Hastings was fought in 1066 with anything else than other statements, such as those that occur in documents, history books, or works of art. However, we can contrast with this a statement about something present, such as "There is a cat on the mat." If asked how you would test this, your reply might be "I would look and see. If what I saw corresponded to what was asserted, I would call the judgment true." However, you are assuming that "there is some solid chunk of fact, directly presented to sense and beyond all question, to which thought must adjust itself" (*ibid.*, p. 228). What you take and use as a fact is really "another judgement or set of judgements, and what provides the verification is the coherence between the initial judgement and these" (*ibid.*). Consider how much of your previous experience and education, how great an exercise of your powers of conceptualization, has gone into your perception of the cat on the mat; how much, in a word, your supposed perception of fact is really a judgment, since, without a stock of judgments, what is seen could never be identified as a cat and a mat, respectively. Your test of the truth of the judgment that there is a cat on the mat or your comparison with what was there turns out to be a comparison of the original judgment with another judgment. This example, in addition, shows not only that coherence is the test or criterion of truth, but also that it gives the meaning of "truth," for it shows that the truth of the tested judgment consists in its coherence with other judgments and not with something other than a judgment.

ASSUMPTIONS OF THE THEORY

The arguments used by supporters of the coherence theory rest on various assumptions about meaning, fact, thought, and judgment that are linked partly with the impression made on them by the a priori reasoning of mathematics and logic and partly with their theory of knowledge.

A priori as paradigm of truth. Metaphysics is traditionally nonempirical; its conclusions are a priori deductions from certain tenets, such as Berkeley's "To be is to be perceived" or Zeno's analysis of infinity. The conceptual statements typical of philosophy—such as that no one can know what is false, that no one can know what has not yet been proved, or that no one can know what is going to be—are true or false because of logical relations between such concepts as knowledge, truth, proof and the future. Further, ever since Plato, mathematics has been the metaphysician's ideal; Leibniz' system was based on certain principles which he held to characterize logic and mathematics, and Spinoza's famous book on ethics is subtitled "proved in geometrical order." Some of the logical positivists, because of their training in mathematics and theoretical physics, sought to establish all knowledge as a vast system of logically interrelated statements expressed in the language of physics. In such systems, the criterion of truth is indeed the coherence of the statement under consideration with at least some other members of the system.

Criticism. Coherence of a statement with other members of the system is not sufficient to prove the coherence theory of truth. First, the a priori statements typical of pure mathematics, unlike the empirical statements of science and everyday life, serve not to give information about characteristics of objects in the world but to show the various conclusions that can be derived from a given set of axioms and a given set of rules for operating on them. It is no objection to the truth of a given mathematical statement that there are or may be other systems with whose members it does not cohere or that it is a member of a system with no application to the world.

However, it is an objection to coherence as the meaning of "truth" or as the only criterion of truth that it is logically possible to have two different but equally comprehensive sets of coherent statements between which there would be, in the coherence theory, no way to decide which was the set of true statements. To reject a particular empirical statement like "He saw a ghost" because it conflicts with the body of our beliefs is not to assimilate the judgments of everyday life to those of mathematics, since this rejection, unlike the analogous one in mathematics, is made only because we think the body of our everyday beliefs has already been shown to be true of the world. Coherence of one judgment with another is accepted as a practical test of truth only because the second judgment is independently accepted as true.

Metaphysical supporters of the coherence theory distinguish their comprehensive system from particular systems such as those of mathematics by linking it to experience by means of their theory of knowledge, which assimilates what is thought, what is experienced, and what is. This appeal to experience and reality is indeed an inconsistency in the metaphysical version of the coherence theory, but it is more sensible than the position of the logical positivist supporters of the theory, who, in the name of consistency, allow that mutually incompatible but internally coherent systems of statements differ not in truth but only in the historical fact that our contemporaries have adopted one of the systems.

Second, there is in the a priori statements typical of mathematics and philosophy a close connection between meaning and truth. Such statements as "Twice two is half of eight" or "What is known cannot be false" are true in virtue of the meanings of the words that express them; it is because the meanings of the words are internally related as they are that these statements are true. It is not because of the relations between the meanings of "knowledge" and "breakfast," however, that it is true that no one knows what Pompey had for breakfast on the day he was murdered, nor is it because of the relations between the meanings of "two" and "four" that it is true that I made two mistakes on page four of my typescript.

Third, even within mathematics coherence gives the criterion, not the meaning, of truth. Mathematical statements are true in virtue of the criterion of coherence with each other, whereas it would seem that empirical statements are true in virtue of the criterion of correspondence with the nature of the world. However, to say that either kind of statement is true is to say that what it asserts is a fact. Whether "X is Y" is a mathematical or an empirical statement, if "X is Y" is true, then it is a fact that X is Y.

Fourth, even when confined to mathematics, the coherence doctrine of degrees of truth does not seem tenable. The fact that a given statement in mathematics is not true unless it coheres with some (or even all) other statements in the system does not imply that it is not itself wholly true; it could at most imply that it does not give the whole truth.

Ambiguities in degrees of truth. It is worth pointing out here how the theory of degrees of truth depends for its plausibility and its air of paradox on various ambiguities. There are at least three different ways in which we may qualify truth. First, we commonly ask how true something is, meaning how much truth is there in it, and commonly reply that it is partly, entirely, or perfectly true. For example, the report that Negroes in Alabama have been deprived of their right to vote might be said to be not quite true, either on the supposed grounds that they have been denied the opportunity to exercise their right rather than been deprived of it or that, although there has been a deprivation of the right, it extends only to women.

Second, instead of asking how much truth there is in something, we may quite differently ask how much of *the* truth there is in it. To ask how much truth there is in something is to ask how much of what is not true is included; to ask how much of *the* truth there is in something is to ask how much of what is true is not included. A particular statement could be perfectly true without containing more than a minute proportion of the whole truth. Being wholly true is not the same as being the whole truth, nor is being partly true the same as being part of the truth. What is only partly true is necessarily partly false, but what is part of the truth may be entirely true.

Third, we can, in the case of general statements like "Water boils at 100° C," ask how far or under what conditions is it true. It may, for example, be true of water at sea level but not at high altitudes.

When coherence theorists say that every statement is only partly true, they usually seem to mean that every statement is only part of the truth, since nothing but the whole system of statements can give the whole of the truth. What they mean, therefore, is quite correct but wrongly expressed, because they have confused the first and the second of the above qualifications of truth. A typically ambiguous assertion is Blanshard's remark that "the trueness of a proposition is indistinguishable from the amount of truth it contains." At other times, as in their discussion of mathematical statements, by "degrees of truth" they mean "true in certain conditions." Thus, the statement "$2 + 2 = 4$" is said to be only partly true, as it is true in pure mathematics but not necessarily in all applied fields. Here again, what is meant is correct enough—not that such statements are not perfectly true, but that they are not universally true. The main reason, however, for the coherence theorists' belief in degrees of truth is based on a mistaken deduction from their doctrine of internal relations. Because each statement is, according to this doctrine, logically connected with other statements, it follows both that the truth of each statement is dependent on the truth of other statements and that our knowledge of its truth depends on our knowledge of the truth of these other statements. What appears to be true might turn out to be false when its further connections become known. Hence, it is said, "a given judgement is true in the degree to which its content could maintain itself in the light of a completed system of knowledge." This conclusion, however, is mistaken. A statement can be perfectly true in itself even though it would not have been true unless it had been connected in certain ways with other true statements; and it can be perfectly true whether we know this or not.

Epistemological assumptions. The second main influence in the usual defense of the coherence theory—that of a particular theory of knowledge—can be seen most prominently in the argument for transforming the common-sense belief that a statement (or judgment) is true if and only if it corresponds to facts into the doctrine that the judgment is true if and only if it coheres with another judgment or set of judgments. The first move in this transformation is from (*a*) " 'There is a cat on the mat' is true if and only if it corresponds to the fact that there is a cat on the mat" to (*b*) " 'There is a cat on the mat' is true if and only if it corresponds to the situation described as 'There is a cat on the mat.' " This is an illegitimate move, however, since a fact is not a situation, an event, or an object; otherwise we would have to postulate negative and conditional situations, events, and objects, to be described by such statements as "It is a fact that no one has yet succeeded in doing this" and "It is a fact that anyone who did succeed would be munificently rewarded." Hence, even if the moves designed to show that the situations, events, and objects we discover are not independent of our method of discovering them were valid, they would not show that facts are not independent of our methods of discovering them.

The second move in the transformation is from (*b*) " 'There is a cat on the mat' is true if and only if it corresponds to the situation, event, or object describable as 'There is a cat on the mat' " to (*c*) " 'There is a cat on the mat' is true if and only if it corresponds to what is verified to be a cat on the mat." This is illegitimate, however, since (*b*) is an explanation, although a false one, of the meaning of "true," whereas (*c*) contains the reason why someone might hold that there is a cat on the mat. Something can be true without anyone's knowing it to be true, although, of course, no one would sincerely say it was true unless he thought he knew it was. Idealist supporters of the coherence theory, like Bradley, move easily from (*b*) to (*c*) because they tend to identify reality with experience and knowledge, what is with what is experienced or with what is known. Further, they move distractingly to and fro between assertions about truth and assertions about *the* truth (the whole truth, the ultimate truth, a part of the truth), from assertions about the notion of truth to assertions about that which actually happens to be true. Thus, they speak of the identity of reality and truth when they mean the identity of reality and *the* truth, that is, what is true.

The third move in the transformation is from (*c*) " 'There is a cat on the mat' is true if and only if it corresponds to what is verified to be a cat on the mat" to (*d*) " 'There is a cat on the mat' is true if and only if it corresponds to a verification, or an experience, that would be expressed in the judgment (or, in logical positivist language, "the observation statement") 'I see (or there is) a cat on the mat.' " Because of this move they rule out the correspondence theory as a test of the truth of statements about the past, since there can be no verifying experience about what happened in the past. This move, too, is illegitimate because it assimilates what is verified, or experienced, to the verification, or experience, of it—the cat on the mat that I perceive to my perception of the cat on the mat. Such an assimilation is a standard part of the theory of knowledge of the Idealist metaphysicians, but an analogous assimilation is made by some logical positivists who, in their talk about observation statements, do not carefully distinguish between the report of what is discovered and that of which it is a report. Having reached (*d*), the coherence theorist then emphasizes how much our previously acquired powers of judgment are exercised in this experience. He concludes that the second term with which our original judgment that there is a cat on the mat corresponds is not, as we thought, a fact; it is really another judgment or set of judgments.

Whether the whole argument is designed to show that correspondence is really coherence when the correspondence is put forward as giving the nature of truth or only when it is put forward as giving the criterion of truth, it seems equally invalid.

What the coherence theory really does is to give the criteria for the truth and falsity of a priori, or analytic, statements. Any attempt to change the meaning of "coherence" from coherence with other statements to coherence with fact (or reality of experience) is to abandon the theory. A merit of the theory is that it sees that the reasons for calling an analytic statement true or false are not those which some correspondence theorists, primarily thinking of empirical statements, try to fasten on all statements. When it sets itself up as the theory of truth, its mistake is twofold. First, it suggests that the criteria appropriate to a priori, or analytic, statements apply to every kind of statement; what the metaphysicians really did was to suppose all statements to be a priori.

Second, it confuses the reasons, or criteria, for calling a statement true or false with the meaning of "truth" or "falsity." As far as the criteria of truth are concerned, we can say only of a priori, or analytic, statements that they are true because they cohere with each other, and only of empirical statements that they are true because of what the world is like; however, as far as the meaning of truth is concerned, we can say of any kind of statement that it is true if it corresponds to the facts. Thus, as well as saying that a true a priori statement coheres with other statements in the system, we can also say that it corresponds to the a priori facts. It may be a fact that the sum of the angles of a Lobachevskian triangle is less than two right angles and also that the field of Waterloo is a mile square. What we must remember is that although both sorts of statements, if true, state the facts—tell us how things are—this amounts to something different in the two cases; the size of the angles of a Lobachevskian triangle is not something in the world in the way that the size of the field of Waterloo is.

Bibliography

Ayer, A. J., "The Criterion of Truth." *Analysis*, Vol. 3 (1935–1936), 28–32. Reprinted in M. Macdonald, ed., *Philosophy and Analysis*. Oxford, 1954. Attacks the coherence theory as put forward by the logical positivists.

Blanshard, Brand, *The Nature of Thought*. London, 1939. Vol. II, Chs. 25–27.

Bradley, F. H., *Appearance and Reality*. Oxford, 1893. Chs. 15 and 24.

Bradley, F. H., *Essays on Truth and Reality*. Oxford, 1914. Chs. 7 and 11.

Ewing, A. C., *Idealism: A Critical Survey*. London, 1934. Ch. 5.

Hempel, C. G., "On the Logical Positivists' Theory of Truth." *Analysis*, Vol. 2, No. 4 (1935), 49–59.

Joachim, H. H., *The Nature of Truth*. Oxford, 1906.

Khatchadourian, Haig, *The Coherence Theory of Truth: A Critical Evaluation*. Beirut, 1961.

Russell, Bertrand, *An Inquiry Into Meaning and Truth*. London, 1940. Ch. 10.

Schlick, Moritz, "Facts and Propositions." *Analysis*, Vol. 2, No. 5 (1935), 65–70. Reprinted in M. Macdonald, ed., *Philosophy and Analysis*. Oxford, 1954. Attacks the coherence theory as put forward by the logical positivists.

Woozley, A. D., *Theory of Knowledge*. London, 1949. Pp. 146–169.

ALAN R. WHITE

COLDEN, CADWALLADER (1688–1776), the ablest representative of Newtonian materialism in eighteenth-century colonial America, was born in Ireland of Scottish parents. He studied for the practice of medicine and immigrated to America in 1710. Eventually, he entered politics and became lieutenant-governor of New York, a position he held for 15 years, until his death at the outbreak of the Revolutionary War. Had his name not been so closely identified with the Tory cause, his accomplishments might have been appreciated earlier.

Colden wrote much, corresponding with Linnaeus, Leonhard Euler, Franklin, and Samuel Johnson, but he published little. He was known for his experimental work in botany, cancer, and the control of epidemic diseases and for his book *The History of the Five Indian Nations Depending on the Province of New York* (London, 1727; New York, 1927). His most important philosophical inquiries were contained in *An Explication of the First Causes of Action in Matter, and of the Cause of Gravitation* (New York, 1745), the first scientific work of its kind printed in America, and in *The Principles of Action in Matter* (London, 1751).

Colden was not an original thinker, but he was alive to current intellectual crosscurrents. If he had any claim to distinction, it was his attempt to go beyond Newton by suggesting an explanation for gravitation. For Newton, the mutual attraction of bodies was an effect of some unknown cause. Colden attributed the cause of gravitation to the joint action of the various powers of matter. Although material substances are unknowable, we can know the actions of bodies—their resisting, moving, and elastic properties. Colden here anticipated a dynamic and energized view of matter.

Colden was not a pure materialist; indeed, he allowed the existence of "intelligent being," which is also known by its action and effects but differs from material being in its essential nature. The intelligent being, however, never acts in contradiction to material being, and matter fulfills the purposes of intelligent being. Colden was sympathetic to deism; he believed that God as First Cause gave direction to the actions of matter but does not interfere in its orderly operations.

Many of Colden's philosophical manuscripts remain unpublished at the New York Historical Society. "The First Principles of Morality" presents a utilitarian scheme: The test of goodness is pleasure, and knowledge is virtue. The "Enquiry into the Principles of Vital Motion" suggests a theory of physiological atomism; "Reflections" proposes a theory of psychological hylozoism; "The Introduction to a Study of Physics" presents a phenomenalistic occasionalism; and "A Treatise on the Animal Oeconomy" attempts to explain the properties of animals "according to the laws of matter in motion." "An Introduction to the Study of Philosophy Wrote in America for the Use of a Young Gentleman" (in Joseph L. Blau, ed., *American Philosophical Addresses, 1700–1900*, New York, 1946) contains an attack on scholastic philosophy and the appeal to authority; it is a summary of many of his ideas.

Although conservative in politics, Colden was in science, religion, and philosophy devoted to the ideals of the Age of Reason.

Works by Colden

The Letters and Papers of Cadwallader Colden, 9 vols. New York, 1917–1935.

Kurtz, Paul, ed., *American Thought Before 1900: A Sourcebook From Puritanism to Pragmatism*. New York, 1965. See pp. 101–

121 for selections from Colden's writings; there is an introduction by the editor.

Works on Colden

Anderson, P. R., and Fisch, M. H., *Philosophy in America From the Puritans to James.* New York, 1939. Pp. 97–124.

Blau, Joseph L., *Men and Movements in American Philosophy.* New York, 1952. Pp. 27–36.

Keys, Alice M., *Cadwallader Colden. A Representative Eighteenth Century Official.* New York, 1906.

Riley, I. W., *American Philosophy: The Early Schools.* New York, 1907. Pp. 323–373.

PAUL KURTZ

COLERIDGE, SAMUEL TAYLOR (1772–1834), critic, romantic poet and philosopher, was born four years before the publication of Bentham's *Fragment on Government,* and died only two years before the death of Bentham's most influential disciple, James Mill, at a time when the young John Stuart Mill was making a brilliant success in political journalism. The striking fact about Coleridge's place in English intellectual history, however, is that he developed a form of idealism in virtual isolation from the main stream of empirical philosophy. In developing his own philosophical insights, Coleridge turned to Kant. He had two reasons for doing this. First, he was deeply dissatisfied with the mechanistic theory of mind still flourishing in English philosophy, since he was unable to formulate within its terms certain views about poetic imagination; while Kant's *Critique of Judgment* (1790) had, however, set out with great rigor, and within a much more tractable conceptual framework, views essentially similar to Coleridge's own. Second, Coleridge thought he saw in Kant's Transcendental Dialectic a way of combating the chronic latitudinarianism in English theology that had predominated throughout the eighteenth century and continued until the time of the Oxford Movement. But it must be remembered that although Coleridge was a serious student of Kant and one of Kant's earliest and ablest English interpreters, he was not a systematic or academic philosopher. His philosophical writings are always disorganized, eclectic, aphoristic. Philosophy became for him what poetry had always been: a necessary means for self-analysis, for the objectification of his personal engagement with life.

Philosophical development. What can be very schematically called the first stage in Coleridge's philosophical development was a highly enthusiastic acceptance in 1794 of David Hartley's theory of association and the "necessitarianism" which that doctrine seemed to imply. Also at this time, after an intense study of Locke and of William Godwin's *Inquiry concerning Political Justice* (1793), Coleridge became strongly inspired by the Enlightenment ideal of social perfectibility. So inspired was he that in December of that year, having had these enthusiasms reciprocated by Robert Southey, he left Cambridge without taking his degree. In January 1795 he lectured at Bristol on religion and politics and became preoccupied with Southey on the project of a pantisocracy, an ideal socialist community consisting of twelve young men and their wives, which was to be established on the banks of the Susquehanna. This project never really got under way; but its rather serious practical outcome for Coleridge was his marriage on October 4, 1795, to the uncomplicated Sara Fricker, sister of Southey's pantisocratic fiancée. Coleridge's early marriage was unfortunate because it prevented his developing what would have been in every way a more compatible relationship with Sara Hutchinson, whom he met through the Wordsworths in 1799 and whose inaccessibility he spent the greater part of his life lamenting. (Thus the celebrated *Dejection: An Ode,* written in 1802, should be considered more as a crescendo in this lament than as a statement of any alleged conflict between imagination and metaphysics.)

Despite his temporary acquiescence in Hartley's psychology, it was in fact Hartley's theology that most of all appealed to Coleridge. In particular, Hartley's idea of an ascending scale of affections, from primary sensations of pleasure and pain through new complexes of association to self-interest and eventually to sympathy, moral sense, and theophany (*Religious Musing,* 1794–1796) made a lasting impression on him. To this idea, conceived of mechanistically by Hartley, Coleridge later found an organically conceived analogue in Schelling's *Naturphilosophie.* Possibly in 1795, and certainly in 1796, Coleridge read Berkeley. The next important stage of his philosophical development consisted in the replacement of Hartley's passive concept of mind by Berkeley's never consistently expressed notion of finite mind being actually creative in perception and imagination when it is considered as participating in the infinite, all-productive mind of God. Once more it was the place of God in the philosophy of Berkeley that most concerned Coleridge; and Berkeley's view of nature as purposive, as divine language, found expression in a number of poems written between 1796 and 1800 (for instance, *Destiny of Nations,* ll. 18–20; *Frost at Midnight,* ll. 59–62; *Apologia pro Vita Sua*).

By 1797 the Godwin-Hartley-necessity phase was over. It is probably significant that Coleridge emancipated himself from the mechanical theory of mind at the same time that he lost his once firmly held belief in the ideals of the French Revolution (*France: An Ode,* 1798). In September 1798, Coleridge accompanied the Wordsworths to Germany. After a short meeting in Hamburg with the poet F. G. Klopstock, Coleridge left the Wordsworths to see the countryside and settled himself at the University of Göttingen in order to improve his German and to collect material for a biography of Lessing. At Göttingen he attended the biological lectures of J. F. Blumenbach and had theological arguments with disciples of the rationalist J. G. Eichhorn. He returned to England in July 1799, transporting £30 worth of German philosophy books "with a view to the one work, to which I hope to dedicate in silence the prime of my life." This work was his never-completed *Opus Maximum.* Thus, the third period of Coleridge's philosophical development was a long assimilation of Kant and the German romantic philosophers, particularly Schelling, which he began in earnest in 1801 and continued well beyond 1816, when he was settled in the London house of James Gillman and able to write his most important philosophical works.

Philosophy and faith. That "seminal" quality of mind which J. S. Mill detected in Coleridge and praised so highly needs, as we shall see, slight re-evaluation. Mill was perhaps right in claiming that the "Germano-Coleridgean" school had done more for the philosophy of human culture than any of their predecessors could have done. Yet, in stressing the great contributions made to social theory by a series of Continental thinkers from Herder to Michelet and in attributing to Coleridge simply a share in those contributions, Mill tended to ignore the less philanthropic and more personalistic aspects of European romanticism. For Coleridge was a post-Kantian "philosopher of life" in the tradition of Heine's *Die romantische Schule*. For example, the closeness in particular doctrines and virtual identity in general philosophical orientation between Coleridge and Friedrich Schlegel is remarkable. Both thinkers are essentially religious critics of the Enlightenment's secular anthropology. That man is a "fallen creature . . . diseased in his will" is a principle as axiomatic to Coleridge and Schlegel as it is self-dramatizing and even morally pernicious to the philosophical radicals.

Where Bentham and his followers write primarily as social reformers seeking, in the manner of Hume and Helvétius, a means of harmonizing individual egoism with the general good of society, the "Germano-Coleridgeans" take man's tragic alienation from God to be the fundamental datum not only of religion but also of philosophy. For the Benthamites the area of moral significance is in socioeconomic relationships, the external actions of everyday public association. For Coleridge, on the other hand, almost as much as for Kierkegaard, the locus of reality is in the individual's experience of God. Thus, with thinkers like Coleridge philosophy inevitably becomes a form of theosophy. Religion is the highest exercise of the human spirit, and philosophy is a kind of rational prolegomenon that prepares the way for man's fuller appreciation of his relationship with God. Philosophy does this by trying to ascertain "the origin and primary laws (or efficient causes) either of the world man included (which is Natural Philosophy)—or of Human Nature exclusively, and as far as it is human (which is Moral Philosophy)." The remaining branch of philosophy, according to Coleridge, is epistemology, which deals with "the question concerning the sufficiency of the human reason to arrive at the solution of both or either of the two former problems.

Reason and understanding. The core of Coleridge's epistemology is contained in his distinction between Reason and Understanding and his insistence that these differ not in degree but in kind. Although the terminology Coleridge uses here is decidely Kantian, Kant's distinction between understanding (*Verstand*) and reason in the narrow sense (*Vernunft*) is only superficially similar to Coleridge's. Like his parallel distinctions between Imagination and Fancy, Genius and Talent, Symbol and Allegory, Coleridge's contrast between Reason and Understanding is more evaluative than descriptive and well illustrates his characteristic attempt to keep empiricist and associationist concepts in a subordinate position within a larger idealist framework. Understanding is "the faculty of judging according to sense . . . the faculty by which we reflect and generalize," which roughly corresponds to Locke's definition of it as "the power of perception." In other words, it is what Coleridge takes to be the pragmatic reasoning faculty of the empiricists.

The Coleridgean Reason, however, is a higher and more esoteric faculty that has at least three not very clearly differentiated functions. In its "speculative" aspect, Reason (1) provides us with basic logical rules of discourse, the so-called "laws of thought"; (2) is the origin of synthetic a priori truths in mathematics and science; and, in its most important "practical" aspect (3) is "the source of ideas, which . . . in their conversion to the responsible will, become ultimate ends." Reason produces Ideas or ideals that, although not capable of demonstration, are nevertheless not self-contradictory and may have a clear and distinct form. But they can also, says Coleridge, be more like an instinct or longing: "a vague appetency towards something which the Mind incessantly hunts for . . . or the impulse which fills the young Poet's eye with tears, he knows not why." What Coleridge's distinction amounts to is this: "Understanding" is a pejorative blanket term for the negative aspects of eighteenth-century logic and science, while "Reason" is an approbatory label for those personal ideals and religious beliefs that are psychologically foreign to, or at least not logically entailed by, scientific empiricism. "Reason" thus is clearly allied with Christian faith. Coleridge is not, then, doing a piece of straight conceptual analysis in making this distinction, even though he often writes as if he thinks he is. Instead, he is persuasively psychologizing in an attempt to reorient contemporary philosophical attitudes into unison with contemporary Christian ideals. The barely disguised function of Coleridge's distinction is to give metaphysical respectability to those Ideas of God, freedom, and immortality that Kant had rightly regarded as merely regulative rather than constitutive elements of knowledge.

Mind and nature. Philosophy must begin, says Coleridge, with a primary intuition that can be neither merely speculative nor merely practical, but both in one. Here Coleridge significantly modifies the views of Schelling. If the existence of external nature is taken to be the primary intuition, as in natural philosophy, then it becomes necessary to explain how mind or consciousness can be related to it. If, conversely, mind is taken to be primary, as in the Cartesian *Cogito*, we must account for the existence and significance of nature. The only satisfactory way to do either of these things is to suppose that there is in fact no dualism between nature and mind. Nature appears as extrinsic, alien, and in antithesis to mind. The difference is not absolute, however, but merely one of degree of consciousness and, consequently, of freedom. Nature is mind or spirit slumbering, unconscious of itself. It is representable under the forms of space and time, subject to the relations of cause and effect, and requires an antecedent explanation. Mind, however, originates in its own (that is, God's) acts and exists in a realm of freedom. But if in its turn this qualitative difference between nature and mind is to be accounted for, a first cause must be postulated that is itself neither exclusively mind nor exclusively nature, subject or object, but the identity of both. Such a first cause or unconditional principle could not be a natural thing or object because each thing is what it is in consequence of some other thing. Nor can this principle be mind as such, because mind exists only in antithesis to nature. (Rather than indulging in tautology here, Coleridge seems to be making the phenomenologist's point that consciousness is always intentional; i.e., is consciousness *of* something.) The unconditioned must be conceived, apparently, as a primeval synthesis of subject and object, consciousness and nature, in the self-consciousness of God. In God or Spirit lies the identity of the two, of being and knowing in the "absolute I AM."

Thus nature and mind seem to be conceived by Coleridge as two dialectical opposites resulting from God's free act of self-alienation in becoming self-conscious. On this last point, however, he is in his published works particularly (and perhaps necessarily) obscure. Unlike Fichte and Schelling, Coleridge wishes to combine the dialectics of the Identity–Philosophy with the traditional Christian concept of dualism between creature and creator. In the unpublished *Opus Maximum* and other manuscripts, he elaborates this point of divergence from the Germans by distinguishing the "personeity" of God from the "personality" of man and goes to great lengths in accounting for the problem of evil. What is important and seminal in Coleridge's metaphysics, however, is not its details or conclusions, but the rich suggestiveness of its basic categories applied to certain problems in aesthetics and social theory.

Imagination and fancy. From the formal dialectics of his idealism Coleridge drew a living description of how the artist's mind works. Since conscious life exists only through contradiction, or doubleness, the whole of nature out of which conscious life develops must exhibit opposing forces in the reconciling and recurrence of which "consists the process and mystery of production." Art is produced through that same dialectical struggle for the reconciliation of opposites that takes place between mind and nature. Art is not, then, merely imitative, but symbolic of reality. Like all symbols (as Coleridge defines them), it is consequently an inherent part of the process it represents; and the artist as creator, his consciousness being the focus of nature and Idea, matter and form, becomes symbolic of God. So, like God, the artist or Genius must suffer alienation in order to create. He needs to be in a special sense disinterested, emotionally aloof for a while from his subject matter and from himself. For in the joy of creation "individuality is lost." He must first "eloign himself from nature in order to return to her with full effect." Just as in the cosmic struggle for synthesis, so in the microcosm of art and the individual artist's mind, there is an attempted fusion of conscious and unconscious forces.

The artist (Coleridge usually considers the case of the poet) achieves such fusions in virtue of his special psychological make-up; that is, through his having the power of Imagination. Coleridge's theory of Imagination, however, does not neatly reflect any of the everyday uses of "imagination" distinguished by modern linguistic analysts. His poet does not create through merely imaginary (unreal) fantasy, nor does he imagine in the sense of making to himself or his reader a kind of supposal, veridical or false. And although it is of course true that the poet is imaginative in being creative or inventive, it is not the case, according to Coleridge, that it is in this fact alone that the poet's Imagination consists. Nor is Imagination "invention" in the sense that it adds to the real, as common usage might suggest. Instead, as we have seen, Coleridge's view is that the poem and the poet are microcosmic analogues, indeed symbolic parts, of reality. His theory is not concerned, then, with an elucidation of ordinary senses of "in imagination" or even with ordinary senses of "with imagination." It is, typically, a piece of speculative (though not therefore unempirical) psychology that is the rather overweighted vehicle for a value judgment. In this and certain other respects, Coleridge's theory of Imagination has interesting affinities with J. P. Sartre's theory in which imagination is related to the notion of nihilation of consciousness. Needless to say, Sartre is borrowing from a later development of the same German tradition to which Coleridge was indebted.

Coleridge considers three things: primary Imagination, secondary Imagination, and Fancy. The power of primary Imagination is not peculiar to poets, but is standard psychological equipment for all men. It is Coleridge's term for what he considers to be finite mind's repetition in perception of God's creative act. His view seems to be that by synthetically perceiving and categorizing things that are not me, I become conscious of myself, and that this state of human self-consciousness is analogous to God's own creative schizophrenia. Secondary Imagination is the specialized poetic faculty. Differing only in degree and in its mode of operation from primary Imagination, it is the poet's power of unifying chaotic experience into the significant form of art. Thus, secondary or poetic Imagination "dissolves, diffuses, dissipates, in order to recreate . . . it struggles to idealize and to unify. It is essentially *vital*, even as all objects (*as* objects) are essentially fixed and dead."

Fancy, on the other hand, differs in kind from Imagination. While poetic Imagination is organic in its operation, producing true analogues of God's creation, Fancy is merely mechanical, aggregative; it is at best imitative rather than symbolic and the instrument of Talent, as opposed to Genius. Fancy is in fact that lower-grade imagination that Locke and Hume set beside sense and memory as a third, nonreferential, source of ideas. Thus Fancy is allied to Understanding, while Imagination, in its ability to transcend and transform the phenomenal, is allied to Reason. It embodies in works of art that inner struggle between nature and mind within which art and Genius are temporary points of resolution. Despite Coleridge's unhelpful talk about Imagination and Fancy being mental faculties, there is no doubt that the concrete application of these essentially evaluative concepts leads to a highly practical literary criticism. To mention only one instance, Coleridge's conception of the work of art as in some degree analogous to a biological organism and his distinction between mechanical regularity and organic form in poetry has had the greatest possible influence on modern criticism. Largely through the far-reaching implications of his distinction between Imagination and Fancy, Coleridge became the first English writer on poetry since the Renaissance to embody the highest powers of critical response within a framework of philosophical concepts that seemed to explain and reinforce that response rather than to inhibit or destroy it.

Morals and politics. Although Coleridge was in his ethical theory a follower and acute critic of Kant, he is interesting today not so much for his own positive views as for his attack upon utilitarianism. Coleridge launches this attack in two ways. First, he tries to demonstrate the logical absurdity of the greatest happiness principle by *reductio ad absurdum* techniques; second, he "postulates the Will," which involves the claim that the utilitarian notion of personality is psychologically inadequate. On the logical side, Coleridge opens fire with the surprisingly modern assertion that the whole of moral philosophy is contained in one question: "Is *Good* a superfluous word . . . for the pleasurable and its causes—at most a mere modification to express degree and comparative duration of pleasure?" His reply is that the meaning of "good" can be decided only by an appeal to universal usage, for the distinction between "good" and "pleasurable," which, he holds, is common to all languages of the civilized world, must "be the consequent of a common consciousness of man as man."

Then, avoiding the error J. S. Mill was soon to make, Coleridge distinguishes between things that are good because they are desired, and things that are or ought to be desired because they are good. This leads him to conclude that "good" cannot be defined simply in terms of pleasure or happiness. Against the Benthamite view that the agent's motive has nothing to do with the morality of his action, Coleridge makes two points, partly logical and partly psychological. The utilitarian position cannot generally hold, he says, because it follows from it that I could do a morally right act by sheer chance. But such complete lack of inward, conscious participation on my part could never be a sufficient criterion for my acting morally. The utilitarian principle therefore confounds morality with law. Moreover, it is no defense here to say that the principle was put forward as a criterion for judging the morality of the action and not that of the agent, because this last distinction is "merely logical, not real and vital." Acts cannot be dissociated from an agent any more than ideas from a mind.

In his social philosophy, Coleridge writes in the tradition of Burke. His mature views are contained in *On the Constitution of the Church and State*, which was begun as an attempt to formulate objections to various bills for Catholic emancipation and finished as an idealist treatise containing the whole logomachy of organism and the reconciliation of opposites. In any society there are always two antithetical forces at work. Since, dialectically speaking, "opposite powers are always of the same kind, and tend to union," Coleridge's idea of a well-functioning society is the nonrevolutionary reconciliation of forces working for permanence with forces working for progression. These he identifies with, respectively, the aristocratic, landed interest and the bourgeois, commercial interest of early Victorian England; a monarch also being required to maintain cohesion. Coleridge's habit of generalizing from the history and the contemporary pattern of British political institutions rather than, as he alleges, drawing a description of the idea of a state, should at least make suspect his application of these largely a priori principles. This habit leaves Coleridge, like Hegel, wide open to the charge of surrounding the constitution of his own country with an aura of metaphysical sanctity to which it has no claim. Despite such ruinous methodology, however, what Coleridge has to say about the intelligentsia and the part it has to play in the dissemination of culture has been influential. Coleridge contrasts *cultivation* with *civilization*. Civilization he takes to denote external, material social progress, while cultivation is more inward and personal: the "harmonious development of these qualities and faculties that characterize our humanity." So that cultivation can take place, Coleridge proposes the formation of a state-endowed class, the "clerisy" or "national church," which would effectively consist of professors of liberal arts officially established throughout the country. The national church would, however, be in no sense identical with the Church of England or with any purely religious organization. Its purpose would be to preserve the results of learning, to "bind the present with the past" and to give every member of the community an understanding of his social rights and duties. The almost limitless possibilities for authoritarianism in such an arrangement are, again, obvious. Nevertheless, in Coleridge's *Church and State* the idea of culture as something independent of material progress was first systematically introduced into English thinking, and was from then onward available in various forms, not merely to influence society but also to judge it.

Conclusion. Though it is no doubt true that Coleridge was, with Bentham, one of the great seminal minds of England in his age, it is not true without qualification that the cultural powers wielded by Bentham and Coleridge were "opposite poles of one great force of progression." Here Mill was surely indulging in public-spirited wish fulfillment rather than relating the facts. Coleridge and his German contemporaries undoubtedly brought to social consciousness those deeper insights into the nature of the individual and the organic complexities of human associations that were classically synthesized by Hegel in the *Philosophy of Right* (1821). Yet the inherent ambiguity of these insights has today become a disturbing commonplace. Mill inevitably overlooked the darker side of romanticism. For once the romantic artist or philosopher ceases to believe in God, he tends either to find a new object of veneration in history or hero worship or, more recently, to relinquish his very inwardness and imagination in solipsistic nausea. It was Coleridge's curious fortune that he never lost his belief in God.

Bibliography

The Complete Works of S. T. Coleridge, edited by W. G. T. Shedd, 7 vols. (New York, 1853 and 1884), was very far from complete. Fortunately, Professor Kathleen Coburn is now in the process of preparing the first scholarly and really comprehensive edition of practically everything Coleridge wrote, apart from the *Collected Letters*, E. L. Griggs, ed., 4 vols. (Oxford and New York, 1956–1958). Miss Coburn has already brought out two volumes of Coleridge's *Notebooks* (London and New York, 1957 and 1962) and his *Philosophical Lectures* (London and New York, 1949). Miss Coburn's *Inquiring Spirit: A new presentation of Coleridge from his published and unpublished prose writings* (London and New York, 1951) gives an exciting foretaste of what is to come.

Among the prose works essential for a study of Coleridge as a thinker, note particularly the following: *Biographia Literaria* (London, 1817), John Shawcross, ed., 2 vols. (Oxford, 1907); *The Friend*, 3 vols. (London, 1818); *Aids to Reflection* (London, 1825); *On the Constitution of the Church and State, According to the Idea of Each* (London, 1830); *Coleridge on Logic and Learning*, A. D. Snyder, ed. (London, 1929); *S. T. Coleridge's Treatise on Method*, A. D. Snyder, ed. (London, 1934); *Coleridge's Shakespearean Criticism*, T. M. Raynor, ed. (London, 1930); *Specimens of the Table Talk of the late S. T. Coleridge*, H. N. Coleridge, ed., 2 vols. (London, 1835).

On Coleridge's general philosophical position, see especially John H. Muirhead, *Coleridge as Philosopher* (London, 1930) and Elizabeth Winkelmann, *Coleridge und die Kantische Philosophie* (Leipzig, 1933). Both these works are reliable but philosophically very old-fashioned. Among the very large number of articles on Coleridge's thought, A. O. Lovejoy, "Coleridge and Kant's Two Worlds," reprinted in *Essays in the History of Ideas* (Baltimore, 1948) deserves special attention. James D. Boulger, *Coleridge as a Religious Thinker* (New Haven, Conn., 1961) gives a good account of the later Coleridge.

On the theory of imagination, see especially James V. Barker, *The Sacred River* (Baton Rouge, La., 1957); I. A. Richards, *Coleridge on Imagination* (2d ed., London, 1950); René Wellek, *A History of Modern Criticism* (London, 1965), Vol. 2, Ch. 6; J. M. Cameron, "Poetic Imagination," in *Proceedings of the Aristotelian Society*, n. s. Vol. 62 (1961–1962), 219–240. The best short work in this field is Gordon McKenzie, *Organic Unity in Coleridge*, University of California Publications in English, Vol. 7, No. 1 (1939), 1–108. R. H. Fogle, *The Idea of Coleridge's Criticism* (Berkeley, 1962) is suggestive if not always epistemologically acute.

A reliable account of Coleridge's political thought is given in John Colmer, *Coleridge: Critic of Society* (Oxford, 1959). J. S. Mill, "Bentham" and "Coleridge," in *London and Westminster Review* (1838 and 1840) will always remain great classics. Also see F. R. Leavis, *Mill on Bentham and Coleridge* (London, 1950) and Raymond Williams, *Culture and Society, 1780–1950* (London, 1958), Part II, Ch. 3. Justus Buchler, *The Concept of Method* (New York and London, 1961) contains an interesting analysis of the *Treatise on Method* and compares Coleridge's views with those of other thinkers, including Bentham.

MICHAEL MORAN

COLET, JOHN (1466–1519), Christian humanist and English educator, was the founder of St. Paul's School for Boys, leader of the "Oxford Reformers" Sir Thomas More and Erasmus, and chief transmitter of Florentine Platonism from Italy to such English Renaissance figures as Spenser, Donne, and Milton. The son of a London lord mayor, Colet took a master's degree from Oxford (1490) and then explored Plato, Plotinus, and Origen in Latin translation. From 1493 to 1496, he traveled in France and Italy. The appealing tradition that he studied in Florence under Marsilio Ficino was shattered in 1958 when Sears Jayne discovered correspondence between Colet and Ficino in a copy of Ficino's *Epistolae* (1495) at All Soul's College, Oxford. This correspondence shows that Colet never visited Florence or met Ficino.

Upon his return to Oxford in 1496, Colet delivered Latin lectures on St. Paul's Epistles to the Romans and Corinthians. The visiting Erasmus and others applauded as Colet, frequently quoting the Florentine Platonists, propounded a new "historical approach" to the study of Scripture. In 1504 Colet was appointed dean of St. Paul's Cathedral, where, contrary to custom he preached frequently and in English. His congregation included the young lawyer Thomas More.

Colet's penchant for controversy is illustrated by his *Convocation Sermon* (1512), in which he wrathfully condemned his own bishops for their moral laxness. Charges of heresy provoked by this sermon were dismissed by his friend Archbishop Warham, but Colet was soon again involved in controversy. He attacked the war policy of Henry VIII and was summoned to court; but Henry, after hearing Colet's arguments, was so dazzled that he made the dean a royal chaplain.

Colet's chief contribution to philosophy was his remarkably successful attempt to blend pagan and Christian thought. In practice Colet followed the approach of St. Augustine, who argued that pagan philosophy, when properly controlled, is a useful handmaiden for Christianity. By pagan philosophy, Colet understood especially Florentine Platonism, a weird conglomeration of original Platonism, later Neoplatonism, and private Florentine speculation on man, love, beauty, and mystical union. Much of this speculation came to Colet through Ficino's *Theologia Platonica* (1482) and Pico della Mirandola's *Heptaplus* (1489), both of which he admiringly quoted or paraphrased in his scriptural treatises.

Despite his debt to the Florentines, Colet avoided the heretical Florentine approach which proclaimed that pagan philosophy and Christianity are equal and even identical. Instead, Colet was careful, as was his model Augustine, to purge pagan views of heretical "errors" before merging them with Christian doctrine. For example, Colet favored the Platonic soul–body terminology over Paul's spirit–flesh, but rejected Plato's dictum that the soul alone comprises the total personality. Again, Colet accepted the Neoplatonic view that Creation was a merging of form and matter, yet he was careful to emphasize that this form is not an emanationist overflow from God's essence, but rather an entity created by God outside himself. In the realm of redemption, Colet accepted Plato's position that only a harmonized soul can govern the body, but he deviated from Plato in insisting that such harmonization can come only from the Holy Spirit's infusion of sanctifying grace. Even in the delicate area of mysticism, Colet borrowed from the *Symposium* the view that love transforms the lover into the object loved.

Whether Colet was as successful in adhering to Catholic as to generally Christian doctrine is a controversial issue. A doctrinal cleavage between Colet and More would seem to be reflected in the *Dialogue on Tyndale* (1529), where More strongly rebuts a form of religion (described in words almost identical to Colet's *Exposition of Romans*), which condemns, as mere shadows, all types of external religion such as sacraments, vestments, and ritual. A comparative study of Colet and More suggests that Colet might have found himself in grave difficulty with Catholic authorities had he lived until the doctrinal reformation of 1534.

Bibliography

During the period 1867–1876, Joseph Hirst Lupton issued five volumes in which he edited Colet's *Treatise on Sacraments* and translated the remainder of Colet's extant Latin works: two treatises on the Hierarchies of the pseudo-Dionysius (c. 490–550); the lectures on St. Paul's First Epistle to the Corinthians; a similar series on the Epistle to the Romans; a Genesis commentary in the form of *Letters to Radulphus*; an exposition (never given as lectures) on the first five chapters of Romans; and *On Christ's Mystical Body, the Church*. Lupton's translations have been out of print since 1893, but Bernard O'Kelly has begun modern translations with *John Colet's Enarratio Primum S. Pauli Epistolam ad Corinthios* (Oxford, 1963). Colet's only English works, the *Convocation Sermon* and the *Right Fruitful Monition* pamphlet, are printed in the Appendix to Lupton's *A Life of John Colet* (London, 1887), still the indispensable biography. Another biographical classic is Frederic Seebohm's *The Oxford Reformers* (London, 1867). Colet's influence as educator is detailed in M. F. McDonnell's *The History of St. Paul's School for Boys* (London, 1909).

Since World War II there has been a revival of interest in

Colet's thought, as evidenced by Eugene Rice, Jr., "John Colet and the Annihilation of the Natural," in *Harvard Theological Review*, Vol. 45 (July 1952), 141–163; Albert Duhamel, "The Oxford Lectures of John Colet," in *Journal of the History of Ideas*, Vol. 14 (October 1953), 493–510; Ernest William Hunt, *Dean Colet and His Theology* (London, 1956); Leland Miles, *John Colet and the Platonic Tradition* (La Salle, Ill.), 1961; London, 1962), and Sears Jayne, *John Colet and Marsilio Ficino* (London, 1963).

LELAND MILES

COLLIER, ARTHUR (1680–1732), English idealist philosopher, was born at Langford Magna, Wiltshire, where his father was rector. In 1697 he entered Pembroke College, Oxford, but transferred in 1698 to Balliol. He took orders and in 1704 succeeded to the family living at Langford Magna. Such events as mark his life were of a private character. He was in constant financial difficulties, arising, it is said, from his own impracticality and the extravagance of his wife; his writings did nothing to bring him into contact with a wider world since scarcely anybody read them. He was buried at Langford on September 9, 1732.

Collier makes no mention of Locke. He read Berkeley (with whose views his own partly coincide), but only after the publication of Collier's major work, *Clavis Universalis* (1713). Descartes, Malebranche, and Collier's neighbor John Norris were the philosophers who particularly interested Collier, although he was also considerably influenced by Suárez and other late scholastic philosophers.

Malebranche and Norris had argued that perception provides us with no direct evidence for the existence of an external world. They did not deny, however, the existence of such a world, even though it is an embarrassment to their metaphysics. They retain it for theological reasons. Collier agreed with them in rejecting the view that perception reveals an external world to us but went on to argue that the very conception of an external world is self-contradictory.

Philosophical views. In the Introduction to *Clavis Universalis* Collier begins by explaining just what he wishes to assert and what to deny. His starting point is that what we perceive is "in the mind"; the objects of perception, that is, depend upon the mind for their existence. In denying their externality Collier is denying their independence or self-subsistence; he is not at all denying that they exist. "It is with me a first principle," he writes, "that whatsoever is seen, is." Indeed, even what is imagined must exist, since it is an actual object of mind. Collier does not deny, either, that what we perceive seems to us to be independent of our minds. But, he suggests, this "quasi-externeity" also characterizes what we imagine as much as what we see. The difference between types of objects of perception lies only in the degree of vividness with which they are perceived.

Collier is not, of course, alleging that our mind causes the ideas which it has. Ideas, he says, exist in the mind qua perceiver, not qua voluntary agent. Nor is he asserting that the ideas which other people perceive are internal to my mind. "The world which John sees is external to Peter, and the world which Peter sees is external to John." Peter's world and John's world may be similar, but they are numerically different. The crucial point for Collier is that every object must be "in-existent" to some mind; every object has existence, but no object has "extra-existence."

To establish his main conclusions, Collier makes use of two main lines of argument, to each of which a book of the *Clavis Universalis* is devoted. In the first book he sets out to show that we have no good reason for believing that objects exist externally to mind. It is generally supposed that we directly perceive them to be external, but the "quasi-externeity" of objects is no proof, he argues, that they are really external. Everybody admits that in hallucinations, for example, we can suppose objects to be external which are not in fact external. As for the Cartesian argument that there must be an external world because otherwise God would have deceived us when he implanted in us so strong an inclination to believe that there is, Collier points out that according to Descartes himself we are constantly mistaken about what is and what is not a property of the external world. If we can be mistaken about the externality of colors, for example, without God's veracity being impugned, why not about the existence of objects?

Thus far, Collier's argument has been in some measure an *argumentum ad hominem*; he has supposed it to be an intelligible hypothesis that there is an external world and has argued only that there is no good reason for accepting that hypothesis. In the second book he goes further. The concept of an external world is, he says, riddled with contradictions. To establish this point, he calls upon the commonplace skeptical arguments of his time, which had ordinarily been used, however, to demonstrate that the concept of the physical world is as full of mysteries and obscurities as are the concepts of theology rather than to show that it does not exist. Philosophers have demonstrated, Collier argues, that an external world must be finite and that it must be infinite, that it must be infinitely divisible and that it cannot be infinitely divisible, that it is capable of motion and that it cannot be capable of motion. Faced with this situation, we have no alternative but to declare that the very concept of an external world is self-contradictory. Finally, he argues, no intelligible account can be given of the relation between an external world and God. Stress its dependence on God's will, and its externality vanishes; stress its externality, and it takes on the attributes of God.

In a letter to the publisher Nathaniel Mist, Collier pushes his argument slightly further. The subtitle of *Clavis Universalis* was, he now says, misleading insofar as in it he professed to provide "a demonstration of the non-existence or impossibility of an external world." This suggests that the existence of an external world is a possibly true, even if in fact a false, hypothesis. The correct account of the matter is that the doctrine that an external world exists is "neither true nor false"; it is "all-over nonsense and contradiction in terms," the very concept of an external world being self-contradictory.

Religious views. Collier's other publications consist of *A Specimen of True Philosophy, in a Discourse on Genesis* (1730), which is designed as a preliminary essay to a complete commentary on the Bible, and a series of seven sermons published as *Logology* (1732). These works are primarily theological. Collier's metaphysical views are more clearly formulated in the brief "Confession" he wrote in 1709 but did not publish. There is, he says, one substance,

God, which is "being itself, all being, universal being." The existence of everything else is dependent upon the existence of God not only causally but also in the sense that particular things have no substance of their own. However, although everything but God is ultimately dependent on him, everything except Christ is also relatively dependent on something else; qualities "in-exist" in objects, objects in the mind, and the mind in Christ, through whom God made the transition from universality to particularity. Not unnaturally, Collier was accused of Arianism. He thought of himself, however, as reconciling the Arians and the orthodox by admitting Christ's dependence on God but asserting his priority to all created things and even to time, Christ's begetting being "the first pulse of time."

In Great Britain attention was first drawn to Collier's work by Thomas Reid and Dugald Stewart, but he has never exerted any real influence, being overshadowed by Berkeley. In Germany he attracted some attention as a result of an abstract of the *Clavis Universalis* published in the *Acta Eruditorum* (1717) and a German translation by John Christopher Eschenbach in 1756. He is quoted by Christian Wolff, and it is sometimes supposed, without any real evidence, that the Kantian antinomies derive from his work.

Bibliography

For *Clavis Universalis* see Ethel Bowman's edition (Chicago, 1909) or Samuel Parr, *Metaphysical Tracts of the Eighteenth Century* (London, 1837), which also includes *A Specimen* and a brief précis of *Logology*. Antonio Casiglio has translated *Clavis Universalis* into Italian, with notes (Padua, 1953), and has included as an appendix to an article on Collier's *True System* an Italian translation of that work in *Sophia*, Vol. 23, No. 3–4 (1955), 302–321. Collier's "Confession" is in Robert Benson, *Memoirs of the Life and Writings of the Rev. Arthur Collier* (London, 1837).

See also John Henry Muirhead, *The Platonic Tradition in Anglo-Saxon Philosophy* (London and New York, 1931); Georges Lyon, *L'Idéalisme en Angleterre au XVIIIe siècle* (Paris, 1888). On Collier and Berkeley see George Alexander Johnston, *The Development of Berkeley's Philosophy* (London, 1923), Appendix I; for Collier and Kant see A. O. Lovejoy, "Kant and the English Platonists," in *Essays Philosophical and Psychological in Honor of William James . . . by His Colleagues at Columbia University* (New York, 1908), and H. J. de Vleeschauwer, "Les Antinomies kantiennes et la *Clavis Universalis* d'Arthur Collier," in *Mind*, Vol. 47, No. 187 (1938), 303–320.

JOHN PASSMORE

COLLINGWOOD, ROBIN GEORGE (1889–1943), English philosopher and historian, was born in Coniston, Lancashire. His father, W. G. Collingwood, friend and biographer of John Ruskin, educated him at home until he was old enough to enter Rugby and imbued him with a Ruskinian devotion to craftsmanship and art and an adult attitude toward scholarship. Although Collingwood later wrote contemptuously of most of his teachers at Rugby and praised Oxford chiefly for leaving him to himself, his undergraduate work in Greek and Latin was excellent and in *literae humaniores* (philosophy and history from Greek and Latin texts), brilliant. He was elected to a fellowship at Pembroke College in 1912, and to the Waynflete professorship in 1934. Except for a period of service with the admiralty intelligence during World War I, he remained at Oxford throughout his career, until in 1941 illness compelled him to retire.

Although he always considered philosophy his chief vocation, Collingwood was a pupil of the great Romano-British archeologist F. J. Haverfield. Since he alone of Haverfield's pupils both survived the war and remained at Oxford, Collingwood considered it his duty to transmit Haverfield's teachings to others. Although he was a competent excavator, most of Collingwood's work was theoretical. Both in suggesting questions that excavation might answer and in drawing together and interpreting the results of others' excavations, he was brilliant. The final monuments to his historical labors are his sections on Roman Britain in the first volume of the *Oxford History of England* (1936; 2nd ed. 1937) and in Tenney Frank's *An Economic Survey of Ancient Rome* (5 vols., New York, 1933–1940). To these must be added his extensive contributions to the revised edition of the British section of Theodor Mommsen's *Corpus Inscriptionum Latinarum*, begun by Haverfield, for which Collingwood drew each inscription from his own accurate rubbings.

The consensus of present-day archeologists appears to be that Collingwood's "imperishably accurate" work on inscriptions will prove more valuable than his works of synthesis and interpretation. Collingwood himself expected that his interpretations would be superseded, but he was convinced that first-rate thinking in history, as in natural science, remains valuable even if further evidence requires that its conclusions be revised. In most of his work his willingness to propose hypotheses was fruitful. He knew something that cautious historians often forget—that nothing is evidence except for or against some hypothesis.

Collingwood's philosophical work falls roughly into three periods: (1) 1912–1927, his acceptance of idealism; (2) 1927–1937, his mature philosophy of the special sciences, conceived as resting on an idealist foundation; and (3) 1937–1943, his rejection of idealism. His ethical and political views will be discussed separately.

ACCEPTANCE OF IDEALISM

In his first book, *Religion and Philosophy* (London, 1916), Collingwood maintained three doctrines familiar to readers of his later work: (1) that creations of the human mind, no matter how primitive, must be studied historically, not psychologically; (2) that historical knowledge is attainable; and (3) that history and philosophy are identical. What he meant by this third doctrine depends on what he meant by "history" and by "philosophy"; in subsequent years he changed his mind about both.

In his *Autobiography* (London, 1939) Collingwood related that in 1917 a publisher rejected a manuscript, *Truth and Contradiction*, in which he had reached conclusions about truth and about the relation between history and philosophy that are characteristic of his thought at a much later period. Those conclusions are that truth or falsity does not belong to propositions but to complexes of questions and answers; that all such complexes rest on "absolute presuppositions" that are neither true nor false; and that since the business of philosophy is to elicit the absolute presuppositions held by different people at different times, philosophy is really a branch of history.

Since Collingwood destroyed the manuscript of *Truth and Contradiction* after writing his *Autobiography*, it is impossible to ascertain how closely the earlier work anticipated the later. However, in *Ruskin's Philosophy* (London, 1920), a lecture delivered in 1919, he asserted that a man's philosophy is "the [set of] principles which . . . he assumes in all his thinking and acting"; and he went on to maintain that since most men do not know what their philosophy is, "it is the attempt to discover what people's philosophy is that marks the philosopher." At least until 1919, therefore, Collingwood conceived of philosophy as a historical investigation of men's ultimate and largely unacknowledged principles, but it may be doubted whether Collingwood at that time denied that ultimate principles are either true or false. In *Ruskin's Philosophy* he sympathized with Hegel's refusal to accept as ultimate any dualism, whether of reason and understanding or of theory and practice. And two years later, in an essay, "Croce's Philosophy of History" (*Hibbert Journal*, Vol. 19, 1921, 263–278), he attacked Benedetto Croce for holding that philosophy was being "absorbed" into history, so that it is "cancelled out entirely as already provided for" by history. Collingwood did not then think that either history or philosophy in the ordinary sense could absorb the other but rather that each, if seriously pursued, leads to the other. He agreed with the "idealistic" Giovanni Gentile that they are "poised in equilibrium."

"Speculum Mentis." *Speculum Mentis* (Oxford, 1924) was Collingwood's first attempt to construct a philosophical system. In it he critically reviewed five "forms of experience," ordered according to the degree of truth each attains.

Art. Art, the lowest form of experience, Collingwood defined after Croce as pure imagination, which he distinguished from sensation, on the one hand, assertion, on the other. Unlike sensation, imagination is active and has its own guiding principle, beauty. "Beauty," however, must be defined in terms of imagination and not vice versa. As a form of experience, the deficiency of art is that while in itself a work of art is neither true nor false, it inevitably suggests assertions: it is expressive. Despite Croce's definition, then, imagination in art is in conflict with expression in art, and their conflict shows that art alone cannot satisfy the human spirit.

Religion. Art gives rise to religion, in which something imagined is affirmed as real. Like art, religion has its own guiding principle, holiness. The artistic consciousness does not affirm that what it imagines is real; but religion, even Christianity, which Collingwood considered its highest form, affirms something imagined—a Father in heaven, the Real Presence in the sacrament, the resurrection of the dead—as real. These affirmations, Collingwood held, symbolize something true; but religion requires that they be affirmed in their symbolic form: "A philosopher would not be regarded as a Christian for subscribing to a statement which he declared to be a mere paraphrase of the Apostles' Creed in philosophic terms."

Christianity, by affirming the incarnation and atoning death of God, symbolizes the overcoming of the opposition between man and God. This unity of man with God symbolizes man's capacity to attain nonsymbolic, direct knowledge.

Science. Theoretical science is the first form of experience in which man tries by reason to grasp truth. But theoretical science, whether a priori as in mathematics or empirical as in natural science, is abstract. Natural science is the application of mathematics to the empirical world, conceived as subject to laws (mechanism) and composed of an ultimate undifferentiated stuff (materialism). But the world, as we experience it, is not merely mathematical, mechanical, and material. Theoretical science is therefore only supposition: its truths are hypothetical. It can say truly, "If there were an *S*, there would be *P*," where *S* and *P* are events in a material world specified in mechanistic terms; but mechanistic terms are not unconditionally applicable to the world of experience. They are abstract; and to abstract is to falsify.

History. History appears to offer a way of escape from the abstractness of theoretical science; for it treats of the world of experience as a concrete temporal process. In their highest development, all theoretical sciences—physics and biology no less than the social sciences—assume a historical form. But history, too, has its characteristic deficiency. At bottom it is an extension of the historian's perception; and a perceived world is alien to its perceiver: a spectacle. Perception can never be knowledge because it can never grasp the whole historical process, and what is beyond the perceiver's ken may have implications for what is within it. Every specialist in a period is ignorant of a large part of what came before it, and his ignorance "introduces a coefficient of error into his work of whose magnitude he can never be aware." Even if this were not true, he could not escape the limitation of all attempts at knowledge in which subject and object are distinct. Since what is merely object is alien, it is falsified by the very process of appropriating it.

Philosophy. But one form of experience, philosophy, yields truth. Philosophy is self-knowledge. In it the distinction between knowing subject and known object vanishes. The self that is known is that which has attained all the subordinate forms of experience—art, religion, science, and history—and corrected their distortions. Philosophy has no positive content of its own: it is the awareness of what is true in those subordinate forms. In knowing their limitations it transcends them. Hence the absolute mind exists in the life of each individual mind to the extent that the individual mind raises and solves problems in any form of experience; as long as this process goes on, each mind is infinite. "The truth is not some perfect system of philosophy: it is simply the way in which all systems, however perfect, collapse into nothingness on the discovery that they are only systems."

MATURE PHILOSOPHY

Philosophy of religion. From 1924 to 1930, Collingwood further explored the positions of *Speculum Mentis*, especially those in aesthetics and religion. For the most part he remained content with his earlier theory of art, but in an essay, "Reason Is Faith Cultivating Itself" (*Hibbert Journal*,

Vol. 26, 1927, 3–14), and a pamphlet, *Faith and Reason* (London, 1928), he abandoned the doctrine of *Speculum Mentis* that religion is essentially symbolic. Religion, he argued, can rid itself of superstition. Christianity correctly insists that there is a sphere of faith that transcends reason and is its basis. Neither the belief that the universe is rational nor that life is worth living can be established by scientific or ethical inquiry, yet they underlie natural science and rational ethics. Popular Christianity expresses those beliefs symbolically; but symbolizations are not essential to it. The ignorant believer who denounces philosophical or scientific paraphrases of Christian dogmas has no right to speak for Christianity.

Philosophy of history. In his *Autobiography* Collingwood recorded that during the summer of 1928 he finally perceived the flaw that had vitiated his philosophy of history in *Speculum Mentis.* He presented his revised views in a pamphlet, *The Philosophy of History* (London, 1930). In 1936 he wrote the lectures that are the fullest statement of these views and that make up the greater part of his *Idea of History* (Oxford, 1946). The error he detected in *Speculum Mentis* was that the historical past is a spectacle, an object alien to the historian's mind. It has two roots: the realist error that knowing is fundamentally like perceiving; and the idealist error that the same thought cannot exist in different contexts. Against the realists, Collingwood maintained that every thought is an act that may be performed at different times and by different minds. A historian can know that Caesar enacted a certain thought if he can reconstruct that thought in his own mind (so re-enacting it) and demonstrate by evidence that his reconstruction is true of Caesar. Against the idealists, he maintained that, while some contexts change the character of a thought, others do not. The fact that, with my knowledge of modern geometry, I rethink one of Euclid's thoughts, for instance, the forty-fifth proposition of his first book, does not entail that my thought is different from Euclid's.

The key to Collingwood's conception of historical verification is his repeated declaration that historical method is "Baconian," a matter of putting evidence to the question. Given any piece of evidence, more than one reconstruction can be made of the action of which it is a relic. But each reconstruction, taken together with other knowledge, will entail consequences different from those of its fellows. A given reconstruction is established if no consequence that can be drawn from it conflicts with the evidence and if every other reconstruction has some consequence that does conflict with it. If a historian cannot show that one reconstruction, and only one, can be reconciled with the evidence, he must suspend judgment.

Historians must not only show what happened but also explain it. Collingwood proved that the two tasks are accomplished together. The past happenings that historians are concerned to discover are acts; and an act is a physical event that expresses a thought. To discover that an act took place includes discovering the thought expressed in it; and discovering that thought explains the act.

Natural science. Just as in *The Idea of History* and in the writings that preceded it Collingwood had demolished the historical skepticism of *Speculum Mentis,* so in a set of lectures written in 1933–1934, which became *The Idea of Nature* (Oxford, 1945), he renounced his earlier skepticism about natural science and confessed that since "the knowledge acquired for mankind by Galileo and Newton and their successors . . . is genuine knowledge," philosophy must ask "not whether this quantitative material world can be known but why it can be known." His answer to that question, however, was equivocal. Collingwood named three constructive periods in European cosmological thought: the Greek, the Renaissance, and the modern, each with its characteristic view of nature. But he said curiously little about the question, "Why is one view of nature replaced by another?" In his introduction to *The Idea of Nature* he declared that "natural science must come first in order that philosophy may have something to reflect on," which suggests that views of nature change only as scientific thought changes; but in his exposition of the change from the Renaissance to the modern view of nature and in his criticisms of modern views, he often wrote as though philosophy might decide what is or is not a tenable view of nature without referring to natural science at all.

Metaphysics. Abandoning his earlier view that philosophy is no more than awareness of the limitations of subordinate forms of experience, Collingwood, in his *Essay on Philosophical Method* (Oxford, 1933), assigned philosophy the task of "thinking out the idea of an object that shall completely satisfy the demands of reason." He no longer rejected natural science and history as offering false accounts of such an object. Instead, he described each as limited in its aims. Natural science attempts to find true universal hypothetical propositions; history seeks true categorical propositions, but only about individuals in the world. The propositions of philosophy must be both categorical (about something existent) and universal (about everything existent). Hence, its object can only be the *ens realissimum,* the being that comprehends all being, of which all finite beings are appearances.

Although distinct from history, philosophy is nevertheless closely allied to it. Just as the various definitions that have been proposed for any philosophical concept constitute a scale of forms, of which the lower are appearances of the higher, so do the various metaphysical systems that purport to give an account of the *ens realissimum.* The way to knowledge in metaphysics is through critical reflection on its history.

REJECTION OF IDEALISM

Aesthetics as theory of language. In 1937 Collingwood was invited to revise or to replace his *Outlines of Philosophy of Art* (London, 1925), in which he had largely followed the theory of art in *Speculum Mentis.* He chose to replace it; and his new book, *The Principles of Art* (Oxford, 1938), moved closer to Croce, whose article "Aesthetic" Collingwood had translated for the 1929 edition of the *Encyclopaedia Britannica.* Collingwood began by assuming that an aesthetic usage of the word "art" has been established in the modern European critical tradition and that it is the business of aesthetics to define what "art" so used means. The classical definition of art as representation (*mimesis*), in all its varieties, confounded art with craft (*techne, ars*), that is, with the production of something preconceived. Analysis shows that none of the classical definitions state either a necessary or a sufficient condition of art. Works of art may be, and commonly are, also works of craft. But what makes something a work of art and determines whether it is a good or a bad one is not what makes it a work of craft.

A work of art is an imaginative creation; the function of imagination is to raise what is preconscious (for instance, mere feeling) to consciousness by giving it definite form. Since this activity is expression, Collingwood repudiated his earlier stand and accepted Croce's doctrine that imagination and expression are identical. He also accepted Croce's view that all expression, in any medium, is linguistic; for any form by which the preconscious is raised to consciousness is linguistic. Language thus begins in the cradle. Children speak before they learn their mother tongues.

The primitive language of the cradle is too narrow in range to serve the purposes of any but infants; it must be enriched by "intellectualizing" it so that it can express thoughts as well as feelings. An intellectualized language is one containing "conceptual" terms, and all conceptual thinking is abstract.

An intellectualized language does not cease to be expressive; rather its range of expressiveness is increased. Art is, therefore, not an activity cut off from, say, science. Every fresh linguistic utterance is imaginative and can be considered a work of art. Hence Croce was right when he said that there is poetry without prose, but no prose without poetry. And since it is the nature of art to be expressive, good art is successful expression. Bad art is the malperformance of the act of bringing preconscious thoughts and feelings to consciousness, a malperformance that misrepresents what is thought and felt. It can arise only in a corrupt consciousness. Critics can detect bad art, works of corrupt consciousness, by comparing them with successful works.

Philosophy of mind. In his last book, *The New Leviathan* (Oxford, 1942), Collingwood amplified and corrected the philosophy of mind he had outlined in *The Principles of Art.* Mind is consciousness, and while every act of consciousness has an object, no act of consciousness involves consciousness of itself. The various functions of consciousness are stratified into orders. The most primitive of them is consciousness of feeling. An act involving consciousness of a primitive act belongs to a higher order. Collingwood distinguished five such orders: primitive consciousness, appetite, desire, free choice, and reason. In principle, there is no upper limit to the orders of consciousness; for in reasoning about an act of reason a higher-order act is brought into being.

Holding that feeling (that is, sensation with its emotional charge) is not an act of consciousness, Collingwood denied that one can become conscious of an act of consciousness by introspection or inner sense. All acts of consciousness are linguistic; mind is the child of language. In analyzing the various forms of language, Collingwood reiterated his conclusion in *The Principles of Art* that conceptual thinking is abstract, and he expressly repudiated the idealist doctrine that to abstract is to falsify.

All theories of the relation between body and mind betray a philosophical misconception. Body and mind are not two related substances: they are man as investigated in two different ways, physiologically and historically. There is no conflict between physiology and history. To hold that Brutus' movement in stabbing Caesar can be investigated and explained physiologically does not imply that Brutus' act cannot be investigated historically nor does it detract from the value of a historical explanation of that act. Here Collingwood strikingly anticipated Gilbert Ryle's view as expressed in *The Concept of Mind* (New York, 1950).

Later metaphysics. In his *Autobiography* Collingwood reaffirmed his adherence to the conception of metaphysics as a historical science of absolute presuppositions which he claimed to have reached in *Truth and Contradiction.* In the *Essay on Metaphysics* (Oxford, 1940) he amplified this position. Every science, whether theoretical or practical, consists in asking and answering questions; and every sequence of questions rests ultimately on absolute presuppositions that are not answers to questions. Since truth or falsity belongs only to answers to questions, absolute presuppositions are neither true nor false. The task of metaphysics is to ascertain what is absolutely presupposed in a given society and how one set of absolute presuppositions has come to be replaced by another. Metaphysicians, however, must not criticize the absolute presuppositions they discover; for criticism presupposes that they are either true or false. A society does not consciously change its absolute presuppositions. Since most men are quite unconscious of their absolute presuppositions, any change in them is unconscious too and comes about because of internal strains.

Collingwood did not acknowledge what must have been obvious to his readers, that in the *Autobiography* and in the *Essay on Metaphysics* he had jettisoned the metaphysics of the *Essay on Philosophical Method.* His views in the *Essay on Metaphysics* are so incoherent that some sympathetic critics have ascribed his change of mind to illness. (Both the *Autobiography* and the *Essay on Metaphysics* were written while he was recovering from a series of strokes.) However, his conception of metaphysics in the *Essay on Philosophical Method,* no less than his earlier conception in *Speculum Mentis,* rested on idealist doctrines from which he had been gradually freeing himself. He still believed that philosophical concepts are not abstract. The doctrine that philosophical propositions are both categorical and universal cannot be detached from the idealist theory of the concrete universal. But both in *The Principles of Art* (written before his illness) and in *The New Leviathan* Collingwood explicitly declared that all concepts are abstract.

Although in his *Autobiography* Collingwood repudiated his earlier idealist conception of philosophy, his views about religion, natural science, and history remained virtually intact. Nor were his views on art altered by his later historicism in metaphysics. This suggests that his change of mind in 1938 may be less fundamental than has been thought. After 1924 the main direction of Collingwood's thought was opposed to skepticism in the special sciences. His earlier skepticism had sprung from his idealistic rejection of abstract thinking and his conviction that philosophical thought is not abstract. By 1938 his work on the philosophy of art and the special sciences had overthrown both these errors, and it became clear that he could no longer hold the idealistic metaphysics of the *Essay on Philosophical Method.* It is natural that in seeking something to put in its place he reverted to his youthful historicism, and that it in turn proved inadequate. His inability to find a substitute for idealism does not show that he was mistaken in rejecting it; nor does it prejudice his achievements in aesthetics, philosophy of history, and philosophy of mind.

ETHICS AND POLITICS

In *Speculum Mentis* Collingwood recognized three forms of ethics: utilitarian, in which action is conceived as a means to an end; duty or concrete ethics, in which action is conceived as determined by the will to act in accordance with the moral order of the objective world; and absolute ethics, in which the distinction between the individual and society, and with it the sense of abstract law, disappears. The first form was held to be characteristic of science, the second of history, and the third of philosophy. Both in *Speculum Mentis* and in the *Essay on Philosophical Method* he represented the forms of ethics on a scale in which the higher forms complete and correct the lower.

Collingwood never renounced this triadic scheme, although in *The New Leviathan* he proposed a new view of the connection between morality and theoretical science, namely, that theoretical science reflects moral practice. Telelogical science reflects utilitarian morality; "regularian" science reflects a morality of law; and history reflects the concrete morality of "duty."

In *The New Leviathan* Collingwood set out to bring the "classical politics" of Hobbes and Locke up to date. He accepted the classical conception of politics as bringing men out of a state of nature into a state of civil society. Essentially, political life is a process in which a nonsocial community (i.e., the state of nature) is transformed into a social one. This cannot happen unless the rulers understand that social life is a life in which men freely engage in joint enterprises. Civilization is "a process whereby a community undergoes a change from a condition of relative *barbarity* to one of *civility.*" Barbarism is hostility to civilization; but although barbarous communities always strive to destroy civilized ones, in the long run the defeat of barbarism is certain.

Bibliography

The obituary essays by R. B. McCallum, T. M. Knox, and I. A. Richmond in *Proceedings of the British Academy*, Vol. 29 (1943), 463–480, together with T. M. Knox's editorial preface to Collingwood's *The Idea of History*, are indispensable and contain full bibliographies. E. W. F. Tomlin, *R. G. Collingwood* (London, 1953) is useful but elementary. Alan Donagan, *The Later Philosophy of R. G. Collingwood* (Oxford, 1962) treats of Collingwood's work after 1933.

ALAN DONAGAN

COLLINS, ANTHONY (1676–1729), English deist, freethinker, theologian, and philosopher, was born at Hounslow, near London, the son of Henry Collins, a well-to-do gentleman. Collins was educated at Eton and at King's College, Cambridge, and for a while was a student in the Temple. This training in the law later enabled him to maintain an excellent reputation for many years as justice of the peace and deputy lieutenant in Middlesex and in Essex. He was married twice to daughters of the landed gentry. A devoted admirer of Locke both as philosopher and as writer on religion, Collins, aged 27, made the pilgrimage to Oates early in 1703 to meet the master, then aged seventy. They were strongly attracted to one another. Later that year Locke wrote poignantly to Collins: "You complain of a great many defects [in yourself] and that complaint is the highest recommendation I could desire to make me love and esteem you and desire your friendship. And if I were now setting out in the world, I should think it my great happiness to have such a companion as you, who had a true relish of truth . . . and, if I mistake not you have as much of it as I ever met with in anybody." In his will Locke left Collins a legacy of £110 and some books and maps, and named him one of three trustees of his estate. Collins arranged tributes to the master that appeared in 1708 as *Some Familiar Letters between Mr. Locke and several of his friends* and in 1720 as *A Collection of Several Pieces of Mr John Locke, published by M. Des Maizeaux under the direction of Mr Anthony Collins.*

By that time Collins had made a lasting, if at the time a notorious, name for himself through a series of outspoken yet restrained publications, all of which were anonymous (although most sophisticated readers were aware of the author's identity). The more important include *An Essay Concerning the Use of Reason in Propositions, the Evidence whereof depends upon Human Testimony* (1707); *Priestcraft in Perfection: Or, A Detection of the Fraud of Inserting and Continuing this Clause (The Church hath Power to Decree Rites and Ceremonys, and Authority in Controversys in Faith) In the Twentieth Article of the Articles of the Church of England* (1710); *A Discourse of Free-Thinking, Occasion'd by the Rise and Growth of a Sect call'd Free-Thinkers* (1713; actually published late in 1712); *A Philosophical Inquiry concerning Human Liberty* (1715).

In 1711 Collins made the first of many visits to Holland, where he met numerous men of intellect. Soon after the appearance of the *Discourse of Free-Thinking*, with accompanying public uproar, Collins visited Holland briefly, possibly for reasons of prudence. His later major works include *A Discourse of the Grounds and Reasons of the Christian Religion* (1724), which elicited 35 replies within two years and which Bishop Warburton later named one of the most plausible books ever written against Christianity, admitting that the replies might have been left to confute one another; *The Scheme of Literal Prophecy Considered* (The Hague, 1725; London, 1726), a sequel to the *Discourse; A Discourse concerning Ridicule and Irony in Writing* (1727); and the *Dissertation on Liberty and Necessity* (1729). This last, together with the earlier *Philosophical Inquiry concerning Human Liberty*, constitutes a powerful statement of the doctrine of necessitarianism. By and large, it is to be noted, the English deists upheld the freedom of the will.

During all this time Collins carried on vigorous, frequently witty, controversies with—to name but a few—Henry Dodwell the elder, famous nonjurist; and such clerical antagonists as Richard Bentley, the classical scholar;

Samuel Clarke, the rationalist; and William Whiston, the Biblical literalist. His health weakened by repeated attacks of the stone, Collins died late in 1729 and was buried in Oxford chapel. It is said that despite a lifetime of controversy, he was never attacked on the basis of his character. Collins represents the philosophical skeptic in the true sense of the word.

FREETHINKING

The right and the necessity to inquire freely and fearlessly into all subjects, especially religion, was Collins' constant and fundamental thesis. Its master statement is the *Discourse of Free-Thinking*, but it was adumbrated in two earlier works. The *Essay Concerning the Use of Reason* makes the point that reason is "that faculty of the Mind whereby it perceives the Truth, Falsehood, Probability or Improbability of Propositions." Truth and falsehood are known rationalistically and are certain. Probability may take the form of opinion when discovered by reason or of faith when perceived by testimony. Testimony is the foundation of much of our knowledge but can never impugn the natural (rationalistic) notions implanted in the mind of man. The Bible, consequently, is not to be taken seriously when it portrays God in human terms; certain parts of the Bible are to be accepted, while others are to be rejected. Thus, Collins combined Locke's arguments for the reasonableness of Christianity and morality and religious principles with the rationalistic Common Notions of Lord Herbert of Cherbury. *Priestcraft in Perfection* carried the attack, common to most deists of the eighteenth century, against the dogmas of established churches. Such dogmas, Collins argued, must be viewed as fraudulent when contrary to reason. The appeal to mystery and to things above reason simply will not do.

The title page of the *Discourse of Free-Thinking* is embellished with several quotations: one from the Old Testament, one from the New Testament, one from Cicero, and one from Shaftesbury. The influence of Shaftesbury is apparent throughout, but Collins was less hesitant to employ the method of ridicule (as is fully attested in the *Discourse Concerning Ridicule and Irony in Writing*). The general definition of the right to think freely was applied mainly to religion. Collins pointed out that the new science and the new philosophy had exposed many errors of the past; the Reformation was the result of fearless thinking on the part of a few leaders; the abundant literature of travel exposed the superstitions of peoples throughout the world and also the infinite numbers of pretenders to divine revelation. Freedom had exorcised the witches that so plagued James I and Charles I: ". . . great numbers of witches have been almost annually executed in England, from the remotest antiquity to the late Revolution; when the liberty given and taken to think freely, the Devil's power visibly declin'd, and England as well as the United Provinces ceas'd to be any part of his Christian territories." (The "Witches Act" of 1603 was to be repealed in 1736.)

With tongue in cheek, Collins suggested that the Society for Propagating the Gospel in Foreign Parts was really a freethinking organization because infidels must be asked to examine and to reject their native traditional religions in order to accept true religion. He further suggested that such zealous divines as Francis Atterbury, George Smalridge, and Jonathan Swift be drafted annually for this enterprise in the same manner as "military missionarys." The argument then turned against the priests of all ages who are responsible for quibbling about Biblical interpretations and end up calling one another atheists. The Bible, Collins continued, is clearly replete with corrupted texts—30,000 in the New Testament alone, according to one authority. Its text, therefore, is to be examined in the same scholarly and critical manner as the texts of all ancient books. The *Discourse* concluded with a refutation of the standard objections to freethinking. Atheism is not, after all, the worst of all evils; enthusiasm and superstition hold that title, according to Bacon. Cicero was quoted to confute the claim that some false ideas are necessary for the good of society (an early version of the Marxian notion of religion as the opiate of the people). A long list of freethinkers was given, including Socrates, Plato, Aristotle, Epicurus, Plutarch, Cicero, and Seneca among the ancient pagans; Solomon and the prophets of the Old Testament; Josephus, the Pharisee; Origen, the Church Father; and, among the moderns, Bacon, Hobbes, and Archbishop Tillotson ("whom all English free-thinkers own as their head"). Collins then asserted that he might well have added other names, such as Montaigne, Descartes, Hugo Grotius, Richard Hooker, Lord Falkland, Lord Herbert of Cherbury, Milton, Ralph Cudworth, Sir William Temple, and the master, Locke. All enemies of freethinking were branded crack-brained and enthusiastical, malicious, ambitious, inhumane, ignorant, or brutal—or courters of priests, women, and the mob.

BIBLICAL CRITICISM

The Discourse of the Grounds and Reasons of the Christian Religion and the *Scheme of Literal Prophecy Considered* follow the rational, scholarly methods for Biblical criticism described earlier, but concentrate on the question of the fulfillment of Old Testament prophecies in the New Testament. The most cogent attacks are on the virgin prophecy in the book of Isaiah and the unusually specific prophecies in the book of Daniel. In both works Collins pursued the theme of the necessity of thinking freely and went out of his way to defend the right of William Whiston, one of his chief adversaries, to think freely—although wrongly, as he saw it—about prophecy. Whiston was a literalist, and Collins had no great difficulty and no little sport in pointing out the absurdities to which Whiston was driven. Collins himself had promised to investigate the miracles of the New Testament but was unable to do so before his final illness and death, and the task fell to Thomas Woolston.

Like John Toland before them, Collins and Woolston forced the issue of the scriptural canon upon the orthodox and opened the way in England for historical criticism.

Bibliography

Bibliotheca Anthony Collins. London, 1732.

Broome, J. H., "Une Collaboration: Anthony Collins et Desmai-

zeaux." *Revue de littérature comparée*, Vol. 30 (1956), 161–179.
Cranston, Maurice, *John Locke, A Biography*. London, 1957. Pp. 460–477. The Collins–Locke friendship.
Disraeli, Isaac, *Curiosities of Literature*. Boston, 1860. Vol. III, pp. 333–343.
Hahn, Joseph, *Voltaires Stellung sur Frage der menschlichen Freiheit in ihrem Verhältnis sur Locke und Collins*. Borna and Leipzig, 1905.
Nichols, John, *Illustrations of the Literary History of the Eighteenth Century*. London, 1817. Vol. II, pp. 148–150.
Thorschmid, Urban G., *Critische Lebensgeschichte Anton Collins*. Dresden and Leipzig, 1755.
Torrey, Norman L., *Voltaire and the English Deists*. New Haven, 1930. Ch. 3, "Voltaire and Anthony Collins: Metaphysics and Prophecies."
See also the general bibliography to DEISM.

ERNEST CAMPBELL MOSSNER

COLORNI, EUGENIO (1909–1944), Italian methodologist and philosopher of science. After graduating in philosophy from the State University of Milan under Piero Martinetti, Colorni taught for some years in secondary schools while doing independent research. Because of his anti-Fascist activity, he was put in political confinement in 1938, but was nevertheless able to carry on his studies in the foundations of physics. In 1943 he escaped to Rome, where he was shot by the Nazis a few days before the arrival of the Allied troops. Colorni was a founder of the European federalist movement, and as a leader of the Italian Socialist party he organized its clandestine troops. He received posthumously a gold medal for bravery.

Colorni was one of the most original Italian thinkers, after Benedetto Croce, Giovanni Gentile, and Giovanni Vailati. His posthumously published papers supply a link between Italian methodology, philosophy of science, and analytical philosophy before World War I and after World War II. His position was quite exceptional in Italy between the wars. A supporter of common sense and painstaking analyses, Colorni rejected the thesis that there are nonnatural, superscientific truths while denying that there are natural laws and data formed before the human process of formulating them. He examined such issues as ontological dualism, anthropomorphism, the reification of concepts, the a priori of scientific research, the psychological material which often goes into the formulation of problems, and the distinction between knowing that (*conoscere*) and knowing how (*saper fare*), all from the standpoint of a renewed, pragmatically corrected Kantianism close in character to the operationalism of Percy W. Bridgman and Hugo Dingler. His remarks on the logic of physical constants, such as the velocity of light, were especially keen.

Bibliography

Colorni published a critical analysis of Croce's aesthetics, *L'estetica di Benedetto Croce* (Milan, 1932), and a number of historical essays, mainly on Leibniz. Some of his manuscripts on methodology and the philosophy of science were published soon after the war in short-lived journals: "Filosofia e scienza," in *Analysis* (Milan), Vol. 2 (1947), 71–81; "Apologo," in *Sigma*, Vol. 1 (1947), 28–39; "I dialoghi di Commodo," *ibid.*, 40–51 and 87–106; "Critica filosofica e fisica teorica," in *Sigma*, Vol. 2 (1948), 261–292.

The unpublished material consists of further essays on Leibniz, an analysis of philosophy as a psychological and linguistic disease (1939), some papers in theoretical physics (on relativity, 1938; on electromagnetism, 1941), and an essay on the logic of economic theory (1942?). A complete collection of Colorni's papers is forthcoming.

Works on Colorni include Alessandro Levi, "Eugenio Colorni," in *Rivista di filosofia*, Vol. 38 (1947), 142–146; Vittorio Somenzi, "I fondamenti della fisica in alcune critiche moderne," in *Sigma*, Vol. 2 (1948), 517–526; Ferruccio Rossi-Landi, "Sugli scritti di Eugenio Colorni," in *Rivista critica di storia della filosofia*, Vol. 7 (1952), 147–153; and, for the historical framework, Ferruccio Rossi-Landi and Vittorio Somenzi, "La filosofia della scienza in Italia," in *La filosofia contemporanea in Italia* (Rome, 1958).

FERRUCCIO ROSSI-LANDI

COMBINATORY LOGIC. *See* LOGIC, COMBINATORY.

COMEDY. *See* HUMOR.

COMENIUS, JOHN AMOS (1592–1670), also called Komensky, Czech philosopher of education and theologian, was born in Uhersky Brod. Comenius was a member of the Community of the Moravian Brethren (*Unitas Fratrum*) and studied Protestant theology at the universities of Herborn and Heidelberg. Shortly after his return to Moravia, the Thirty Years' War broke out. The Protestant Czechs were defeated by the Catholic Hapsburg monarchy, and Comenius became a permanent exile. Elected bishop of the *Unitas* in 1632, he considered it his main mission as a pastor and as a theological writer to preserve the faith and unity of the dispersed Moravian brethren.

In his writings, which range from such topics as theology, politics, philosophy, and science (as he understood science) to linguistics and education, as well as in his personal life, he combined such contradictory strands of thought as world immanence and world transcendence, interest in science and dependence on false prophets, progressivism, and apocalyptic expectations. In order to understand this mingling of ideas, we must project ourselves into the baroque age, when so many illustrious minds were wandering from one extreme to another. Thus, despite scholastic and Calvinist influences during his years of study, Comenius' concept of the divine regime contained a notable admixture of Neoplatonic, evolutionary, mystical, and pantheistic ideas. God was for him the God of Nature as well as the God of Heaven. However, all these pantheistic leanings did not shake the foundations of Comenius' faith, and throughout his life he clung to the fundamentals of the Christian dogma. Nevertheless, it was the cosmic curiosity in Comenius' religion which opened his mind to the unfolding of the natural and humanistic sciences. Yet Comenius lacked any real understanding of science in the Newtonian sense. The generic concept under which he subsumed the new scientific pursuits was that of "Light," to be understood as both the "Light of God" and the light of reason that God has kindled in man in order to guide him on his way toward eternal truth.

No doubt a certain utopian chiliasm inspired Comenius, but he also shared with the greatest minds of his time the enthusiasm about a new discovery, the discovery of "method," understood as a form of systematic and empirical inquiry which would guarantee the harmonization between man's reason and the natural—and perhaps even the supernatural—universe. The man who impressed Comenius most of all was Francis Bacon. Through Bacon, he became convinced that the new inductive method would shed light not only on the *arcana naturae* but also on the mysteries of the human mind and of human learning. The long title of Comenius' *Great Didactic* (*Didactica Magna*) tells the reader that the author believes he has found a system to teach "all things to all men." Comenius was one of the first to grasp the significance of a methodical procedure in schooling, to project a plan of universal education, and to see the significance of education as an agency of international understanding. Often quoted are the eight principles of teaching which Comenius expounds in Chapter 9 of the *Great Didactic*, in strange analogy to what he supposes to be the economy and order of the sun's functioning in the universe. Still valid in these principles is the emphasis on the interrelation between mental maturity and learning, on the participation of the student, and on the logical interconnection of the subjects in the curriculum.

Education—to be extended to both sexes, all men, and all peoples—should be crowned by a *pansophia* (encyclopedic synthesis of universal knowledge), with the aim of a *dilucidatio* (systematic interpretation) of the order of all things within the cosmic order. For the promotion of the great and world-wide mission of education, Comenius recommended a "Universal College" of the great and wise men of the whole world, and an easily constructed international language for the peace and "for the reform of the whole world" and as an "antidote to the confusion of thought."

In 1668 he dedicated a treatise, *The Way of Light* (*Via Lucis*), "to the torch bearers of this enlightened age, members of the Royal Society of London, now bringing real philosophy to a happy birth." He expressed the "confident hope" that through their endeavors "philosophy brought to perfection" would "exhibit the true and distinctive qualities of things . . . for the constantly progressive increase of all that makes for good to mind, body, and estate."

Works by Comenius

The Great Didactic, translated by M. W. Keatinge. London, 1923.

The Way of Light, translated by E. T. Campagnac. Liverpool, 1938.

The Labyrinth of the World and the Paradise of the Heart, translated by Matthew Spinka. Chicago, 1942.

John Amos Comenius, Selections, Jean Piaget, ed. New York, 1957. Contains references to recent Czech literature.

Works on Comenius

Kozik, František, *The Sorrowful and Heroic Life of John Amos Comenius*. Prague, 1958.

Kvacala, J., *J. A. Comenius*. Berlin, 1914. Contains a large bibliography.

Laurie, S. S., *John Amos Comenius*. Boston, 1885.

Ulich, Robert, *History of Educational Thought*. New York, 1950.

Ulich, Robert, *Three Thousand Years of Educational Wisdom*. Cambridge, Mass., 1959.

ROBERT ULICH

COMMON CONSENT ARGUMENTS FOR THE EXISTENCE OF GOD. Numerous philosophers and theologians have appealed to the "common consent" of mankind (the *consensus gentium*) as support for certain doctrines. Richard Hooker, for example, in his *Treatise on the Laws of Ecclesiastical Polity* appeals to this common agreement of mankind in justifying his view that the obligatory character of certain moral principles is immediately evident. Most frequently the conclusions supported in this way were those asserting the existence of God and the immortality of the human soul. In the present article we shall confine ourselves to common consent arguments for the existence of God.

Among those who favored arguments of this kind were Cicero, Seneca, Clement of Alexandria, Herbert of Cherbury, the Cambridge Platonists, Gassendi, and Grotius. In more recent times these arguments were supported by numerous distinguished Protestant and Catholic theologians. Hegel did not accept the argument, but he thought that it contained a kernel of truth. Rudolf Eisler, in his *Wörterbuch der philosophischen Begriffe*, ranks the argument fifth in importance among so-called proofs of the existence of God, and this seems an accurate estimate of its place in the history of philosophy. At the same time, Mill was probably right when he observed that, as far as the "bulk of mankind" is concerned, the argument has exercised greater influence than others which are logically less vulnerable. Although there are hardly any professional philosophers at the present time who attribute any logical force to reasoning of this kind, it is still widely employed by popular apologists for religion.

Some supporters claim relatively little. "In no form," wrote the nineteenth-century theologian Robert Flint, "ought the argument from general consent to be regarded as a primary argument. It is evidence that there are direct evidences—and when kept in its proper place it has no inconsiderable value—but it cannot be urged as a direct and independent argument" (*Theism*, p. 349). Cardinal Mercier similarly regarded the argument as "indirect or extrinsic." It does not by itself prove the existence of God, but it is a "morally certain indication that there are proofs warranting the assertion that God exists" (*A Manual of Modern Scholastic Philosophy*, Vol. II, p. 55). Father Bernard Boedder and G. H. Joyce claim a great deal more. Boedder (*Natural Theology*, p. 63) regards it as an "argument of absolute value in itself." The universal consent "of nations in the recognition of God must be deemed the voice of universal reason yielding to the compelling evidence of truth." Later, however, he admits that it is not "absolutely conclusive, except when taken in conjunction with the argument of the First Cause" (*ibid.*, p. 75). Joyce, a twentieth-century writer to whom we owe one of the fullest and clearest statements of one version of the argument, is far more sanguine. He calls it without any qualification a "valid proof of the existence of God" and seems to regard the conclusion as established with "perfect certainty."

The argument has rarely been stated by any philosopher in the form of a simple appeal to the universality of belief in God. In this form it is patently invalid and invites Pierre Bayle's comment that "neither general tradition nor the unanimous consent of all men can place any injunction upon truth." There is, on the face of it, no reason why the whole of mankind should not have been as wrong on a speculative topic as it has been on some more empirical questions on which, history teaches, it has been mistaken. The actual versions of the argument advanced by philosophers are more complicated and can be conveniently grouped into two classes. In the first we have arguments in which the universality of belief, for reasons peculiar to this particular case, is taken as evidence either that the belief itself is instinctive or that it is due to longings or needs which are instinctive. It is then concluded, for a variety of reasons, that the belief must be true. In the second group we have arguments according to which the universality of the belief, in conjunction with the claim that believers used reason in arriving at their position, is treated as evidence for the existence of God. We shall refer to arguments of the first kind as "biological" versions and to those of the second kind as the "antiskeptical dilemma." Whatever the shortcomings of these arguments may be, they cannot be dismissed simply on the ground that the whole of mankind may well be mistaken.

Although no doubt some of the disputes in which philosophers and others have engaged in this connection are antiquated and sometimes have a slightly preposterous ring to modern ears, other related issues are still very much with us. For example, it is still maintained by a number of influential philosophers and psychologists that man is "by nature" religious, so that the spread of skepticism and atheism is likely to lead to highly undesirable results. "It is safe to say," writes Jung about his patients, "that every one of them fell ill because he had lost that which the living religions of every age have given their followers" (*Modern Man in Search of a Soul*, p. 254). Nor are attempts lacking even in our own day to show that everybody "really" believes in God, no matter what he may say or think. In the course of evaluating various forms of the Argument from Common Consent, we shall have occasion to say something about these more contemporary issues as well.

BIOLOGICAL FORMS OF THE ARGUMENT

Instinctive belief in God. A familiar version of the biological form of the Argument from Common Consent is found in Seneca's *Epistulae Morales* (Letter 117):

> We are accustomed to attach great importance to the universal belief of mankind. It is accepted by us as a convincing argument. That there are gods we infer from the sentiment engrafted in the human mind; nor has any nation ever been found, so far beyond the pale of law and civilization as to deny their existence.

Seneca did not elaborate on the nature of the "sentiment" that is "engrafted in the human mind," but later writers did, especially when replying to criticisms such as Locke's. In the course of his polemic against the theory of innate ideas, Locke had rejected the initial premise of the argument as plainly false. His reasons were twofold. First, he noted with regret that there were atheists among the ancients, and also, more recently, "navigation discovered whole nations among whom there was to be found no notion of a God" (*Essay Concerning Human Understanding*, Book I, Sec. IV). Aside from questioning the prevalence or even the existence of unbelief, the usual reply to this kind of criticism has been to make a distinction between two senses in which an idea or a belief may be said to be innate or instinctive. Such an assertion may mean that the idea or the belief is present in the human mind at birth as an image or some other actual "content," or it may amount to the much milder claim that it is present as a disposition to arrive at the belief when noticing certain things in the world or in oneself (usually this is stated very strongly to the effect that, when noticing the things in question, the person cannot help coming to believe in God). It is then explained that belief in God is instinctive in the latter or dispositional sense only. To avoid the charge of triviality, the defenders of the argument usually insist that because of this disposition, teaching or indoctrination is not required. Thus Charles Hodge, who makes it clear that he advocates a doctrine of the innateness of belief in God in the dispositional sense, adds that ". . . men no more need to be taught that there is a God, than they need to be taught that there is such a thing as sin" (*Systematic Theology*, Vol. I, p. 199). "Adam," he also writes, "believed in God the moment he was created, for the same reason that he believed in the external world. His religious nature, unclouded and undefiled, apprehended the one with the same confidence that his senses apprehended the other" (*ibid.*, pp. 200–201).

Several comments are in order here. To begin with, the theory that belief in God is innate does not become vacuous when it is stated in this way, so long as we are told what the facts are in the presence of which a human being cannot help coming to believe in the existence of God. However, when these facts are specified as the adjustments of organisms to their environment or as our experiences of duty and obligation (and these are the ones most frequently mentioned), Locke's objection seems to be fundamentally intact. For, apart from the question of primitive tribes, a great many of the unbelievers in Western culture appear to have been fully exposed to these facts. But this does not usually move the proponents of the argument. Aside from certain rejoinders which will be discussed later, their formulations usually contain highly elastic words which make possible a speedy disposition of apparent negative instances. The unbeliever may have been exposed to the relevant facts but not "adequately"; or he may have been exposed to them adequately, but his religious nature may have been "clouded" or "defiled"; or, contrary to outward appearances, the unbeliever may really believe, but the belief may be so faint as to be barely perceptible. This last method was adopted by Hodge when faced with the negative evidence drawn from the observations of blind deaf-mutes. Unbelievers like Büchner had pointed to several famous cases, including that of Laura Bridgman, who either could not be brought to form an idea of God at all or who reported that, prior to instruction, no such idea had entered their minds. As far as is known, Hodge never made any empirical studies of blind deaf-mutes, but this did not prevent him from replying with full confidence. "The knowledge obtained by Christian instruction so much surpasses that given by intuition," he assures us, that the purely intuitive knowledge of the blind deaf-mute "seems as nothing" (*ibid.*, p. 197).

At this stage one must raise the following questions: Under what circumstances would a human being *not* possess an innate belief in God? More specifically, let us suppose that a person observes the facts of organic adjustment and experiences a sense of duty and obligation but nevertheless maintains, with all appearance of sincerity, that he does not believe in God. Under what circumstances would it be true to say that he had observed the facts adequately, that his religious nature was not clouded or defiled, but that he nevertheless had no belief in God? Unless these questions are satisfactorily answered, the argument does not really get off the ground. For it is meant to be based on an empirical premise, and the premise will not be empirical if it is retained no matter how human beings may respond to the stimuli that are supposed to activate the innate disposition to believe in God.

Waiving this difficulty, and granting that the distinction between the two senses in which a belief may be instinctive circumvents the first of Locke's objections, the argument would still be open to his second criticism, namely, that the universality of an idea or a belief does not establish its innateness. It may well be possible, Locke argued, to account in other ways for the universal occurrence of an idea or the general agreement on a topic. The ideas of the sun and heat, he wrote, are also universal without being "natural impressions on the mind" (*op. cit.*, Book I, Sec. 2). Locke, who was primarily concerned with the origin of the *idea* of God rather than with any question of the universality of belief in God, claimed that he could give an adequate account of how this idea arose in the human mind without an appeal to innate ideas, and John Stuart Mill later offered a detailed account of how belief in God might be universal without being instinctive. Reasons for rejecting such accounts would have to be offered before one could infer the innateness of belief in God from its universality.

Mill, one of the few great philosophers of recent times to discuss this argument in detail, objected to it on several other grounds as well. Assuming a belief to be innate or instinctive, he asked why this should be any reason whatsoever for regarding it as true. The only justification for this transition that Mill could think of he dismissed as begging the question. This is "the belief that the human mind was made by a God, who would not deceive his creatures" (*Three Essays on Religion*, p. 156), which of course presupposes what is to be proved. Whether this is in fact the only possible justification of the inference from the innateness of a belief to its truth, Mill's observation that the former does not by itself afford evidence for the latter seems to be very well taken. The force of his point, however, may be obscured because instinctive beliefs are frequently referred to as a priori and because this and related expressions are ambiguous. In this present context, calling a proposition a priori simply means that it was not affirmed as the result of instruction. In other contexts, and more commonly, to say that a proposition is a priori logically implies that it is a necessary truth and hence requires no empirical confirmation. It should be clear that if a proposition is a priori in the former sense, it does *not* automatically follow that it is a necessary truth or a truth at all. If an empirical or, more generally, a nonnecessary proposition were instinctively entertained, it would stand just as much in need of proof or confirmation as any other; and, except for a few defenders of the Ontological Argument, believers and unbelievers alike are satisfied that "God exists" does not express a necessary proposition.

Flint and others complained that Mill was unfair because there are versions of the argument which cannot be accused of circular reasoning. It will become clear in the next section that the antiskeptical form of the argument is in fact immune from such a criticism (and Mill was probably not familiar with it). However, it is difficult to see how the version of the biological argument which we have been discussing can bridge the transition from the instinctiveness of belief to its truth without introducing God as guarantor of the instinct's trustworthiness.

Innate yearning for God. There is, however, another version of the biological argument which can perhaps be stated in such a way as to avoid the charge of circular reasoning. This version, moreover, has certain additional advantages over the one considered previously. "All the faculties and feelings of our minds and bodies," writes Hodge, "have their appropriate objects; and the possession of the faculties supposes the existence of those objects." Thus the eye, "in its very structure, supposes" that there is light to be seen, and the ear would be "unaccountable and inconceivable" without the existence of sound. "In like manner" our religious feelings and aspirations "necessitate" the existence of God (*op. cit.*, p. 200). "The yearning for some kind of God," in the words of Chad Walsh, a contemporary defender of the argument, "does point toward an in-built hunger in each of us—a hunger for something greater than we are." But every other hunger has its normal gratification. This is true of physical hunger, of love and sex, and of our craving for beauty. If, similarly, our religious hunger did not have its proper gratification, it would be difficult to see "how it got built into our natures in the first place. What is it doing there?" (*Atheism Doesn't Make Sense*, p. 10).

This version of the argument escapes one of the difficulties of the version considered earlier. It can very plausibly be argued that absence of belief in God does not prove absence of a yearning for God; and in fact there are undoubtedly unbelievers who wish they could believe. But, granting that the existence of unbelievers does not prove that the wish for God's reality is not universal, this version of the argument nevertheless appears to be open to a number of fatal or near fatal objections. To begin with, there seem to be exceptions here also. There seem to be people who not only do not believe in God but who are also devoid of any hunger for God. Furthermore, even if this hunger were universal, it might, as before, be possible to explain it on some basis other than that it is innate; or, putting the point differently, one would have to be satisfied that all such explanations are inadequate before one could conclude that it is innate. More seriously and waiving such objections as that the analogy between "religious hunger" and either physical hunger or having organs like eyes and ears is more than dubious, statements to the effect that we have eyes because there is light are objectionable on several grounds. Neither the observed facts nor contemporary biological theory warrants any such assertion. We are entitled to say that we have eyes and that there is light and that the eyes are useful because there is light, so that, other things being equal, organisms with eyes are likely to win out in the struggle for survival against organisms without eyes. Many kinds of biological variations are not similarly useful, but these are rarely noticed by proponents of the argument. When reading the teleological formulations of these writers—Walsh's question "How did the longing get *built into* [italics added] our nature in the first place?" or Hodge's remark that "possession of the faculties *supposes* [italics added] the existence of the appropriate objects"—one can hardly avoid the suspicion that although God is not explicitly brought into the premise of the argument, these authors surreptitiously introduce a designer who supplied organisms with their native equipment in order to fit them to their environment. It might indeed be possible to establish the existence of a designer on other grounds, but in the present context the defender of the argument is guilty of circular reasoning and thus would not escape Mill's stricture. No such circularity is involved if the instinctive desire is made the basis of an argument for *immortality* after the existence of a beneficent deity has been independently established. Dugald Stewart, in his *Philosophy of the Active and Moral Powers of Man* (Edinburgh, 1828, Book III, Ch. 4), offered such an argument, observing, "whatever desires are evidently implanted in our minds by nature, . . . we may reasonably conclude, will in due time be gratified under the government of a Being infinite both in power and goodness." Stewart was not guilty of circular reasoning, since he thought that he had previously proved the existence of God by means of the Design Argument.

THE ANTISKEPTICAL DILEMMA

Joyce's argument. One of the most carefully developed statements of the second main form of the Common Consent Argument is found in G. H. Joyce's *The Principles of Natural Theology*. There are three stages to this form of the argument. (1) As in the biological versions, it is contended that practically all human beings, past and present, can be counted as believers in God. However, here it is not maintained that there are innate tendencies in human beings to believe in God. If anything, the opposite is true: men crave liberty of action and resent any being with superior authority. If, nevertheless, nearly all human beings are "perfectly certain" of the existence of their "absolute Master," this can be so only because "the voice of reason" is so clear and emphatic: "All races, civilized and uncivilized alike, are at one in holding that the facts of nature and the voice of conscience compel us to affirm this [the existence of God] as certain truth" (*op. cit.*, p. 179). (2) If the whole of mankind were mistaken in a conclusion of this kind, it would follow that something is amiss with man's intellect, that "it is idle for man to search for truth." In that event, pure skepticism would be the only alternative. (3) However, all of us, unless we wish to be perverse, realize that "man's intellect is fundamentally trustworthy —that, though frequently misled in this or that particular case through accidental causes, yet the instrument itself is sound" (*ibid.*). Since reason is fundamentally trustworthy, universal skepticism is not a serious alternative to the acceptance of mankind's conclusion that God exists.

Some writers, though not Joyce, are concerned to add that on this topic great men are at one with the masses of believers. "Even for the independent thinker," writes John Haynes Holmes, "there is such a thing as a consensus of best opinions which cannot be defied without the weightiest of reasons" ("Ten Reasons for Believing in Immortality," in Paul Edwards and Arthur Pap, eds., *A Modern Introduction to Philosophy*, New York, 1965, p. 241). If there were no God and no afterlife, the deceived would include, in the words of James Martineau, "the great and holy whom all men revere." Whom are we to reverence, he goes on, "if the inspirations of the highest nature are but cunningly-devised fables?" (*ibid.*).

Joyce is aware that the "common consent" of the human race on this subject has been challenged from two sides. To the criticism that there are unbelievers at the present time and that the history of Western countries records instances of other unbelievers, he replies that these are so few in comparison with the number of believers that they do not affect the "moral unanimity of the race," and he adds that he never meant to claim that literally everybody who ever lived has affirmed the existence of God. To the criticism that there are primitive peoples without a belief in God or at least in one God, Joyce replies that there is in fact no race without religion and that even where there is belief in a plurality of gods, it is invariably found that "the religion recognizes a supreme deity, the ruler of gods and men" (p. 182). Joyce concedes that the supreme deity of primitive religions often lacks some of the characteristics attributed to God by Christian and Jewish monotheists. But this does not affect the argument, since "an idea of God does not cease to deserve that name because it is inadequate" (p. 181). A person may be said to believe in God if he believes in a "Supreme Being, personal and intelligent, to whom man owes honor and reverence" (*ibid.*), regardless of what else he also believes or fails to believe.

Objections to Joyce's argument. The claim that belief in God is practically, if not indeed strictly, universal in the human race is shared by defenders of both forms of the Common Consent Argument. We shall discuss the difficulties of such a position in some detail in the next section. Meanwhile, it should be pointed out that even if the moral unanimity of mankind on this subject is not questioned, the argument, as presented by Joyce, appears to be open to two powerful objections.

To begin with, it presupposes that all or most believers in God arrive at their belief by means of reason or the intellect. If this is not the case, then the argument clearly fails, since nothing derogatory about reason would follow if it was not the source of the mistaken conclusion. In actual fact, it seems more than doubtful that the majority of men use reason in any significant sense in arriving at belief in God or even in fortifying their belief after their original acceptance of it. In making this observation, "reason" is not used in any specially narrow sense. A person may, in a perfectly familiar and proper sense, be said to have arrived at a conclusion by means of reason without having set out any formal arguments. However, there seems to be a good deal of evidence that the majority of human beings came to their belief in God by traditional indoctrination. Nor is it particularly plausible to maintain that originally this belief was the product of reason. If reason had anything to do with it, its role, in the opinion of most contemporary psychologists, was probably quite subsidiary. Joyce's view that man's natural inclinations would lead to denial rather than to belief in God seems highly doubtful. There is a good deal of disagreement about the exact psychological mechanisms involved, but the majority of psychologists seem to think that man's loneliness and helplessness, as well as his animistic propensities, incline him to belief in protective (and also hostile) cosmic powers. This does not, of course, mean that such beliefs cannot also be adequately supported by rational considerations, but it does undermine Joyce's argument.

It should be emphasized that the view just outlined is by no means confined to antireligious psychologists. Fideistic theists would most certainly endorse these observations, as would many believers who have stressed the evil and suffering in the observable world. Indeed, most of the defenders of the biological form of the Common Consent Argument would be opposed to Joyce's account. "Our own consciousness," in the words of Charles Hodge (*op. cit.*, pp. 199–200), "teaches us that this is not the ground of our own faith. We do not reason ourselves into the belief that there is a God; and it is very obvious that it is not by . . . a process of ratiocination, that the mass of the people are brought to this conclusion."

However, even if this difficulty could be overcome and if it were granted that human beings arrive at their belief in God by reason, Joyce's argument would still be in trouble. If "universal skepticism" stands for the view that human beings can never find the true answer to *any* question, then it is not implied by the rejection of the universal belief of mankind in God. All kinds of other explanations of the "universal error," short of "the radical untrustworthiness" of human reason, seem possible and cannot be ruled out without further ado. It has, for example, been widely held by Kantians, nineteenth-century positivists, and fideists that human reason, while trustworthy as long as it deals with empirical and purely formal issues, is not fit to handle questions transcending experience.

As for the observations of Martineau and Holmes, several points are in order. To begin with, "appeals to the best opinion" are of logical force only in areas in which there are experts, as there are in physics or dentistry, for example. In this sense there is no such thing, either for the independent thinker or for anybody else, as a "consensus of best opinion" when we come to such questions as the existence of God or the immortality of the soul. Furthermore, just as there have been great men and great philosophers who believed in God, so there have also been great men and great philosophers who did not. Since presumably both groups cannot be right, we will be left with the conclusion that men who deserve to be "reverenced" are occasionally mistaken—no matter which view is taken on this subject. Finally, there is nothing about the loftiness of an "inspiration" that guarantees its truth. People whose loftiness makes them believe the best about their neighbors are probably as often mistaken as those whose lack of loftiness makes them believe the worst.

IS BELIEF IN GOD UNIVERSAL?

Let us now turn to a discussion of the detailed objections to the premise which all forms of the Common Consent Argument share, namely, that all or practically all human beings are believers in God.

Anthropological objections. To begin with, there is a series of objections based on what is known or allegedly known about primitive tribes and about religions which are not monotheistic. We have already seen that Locke believed, on the basis of the reports of travelers, that there were whole nations without the notion of God. This view was widely advocated by anthropologists and sociologists in the nineteenth century, many of whom did not rely on the reports of others but spent long periods studying the beliefs and habits of primitive peoples at first hand. It was developed in considerable detail by Sir John Lubbock in his pioneering work, *Prehistoric Times,* and it had the unqualified endorsement of Charles Darwin, who, in *The Descent of Man* (Ch. 3), reported confirmations in his own experience with the Fuegians. The denial that belief in God is universal was an essential part of the position of the so-called evolutionary anthropologists. They maintained that there was a gradual transition from animism, via fetishism, to a belief, first, in many gods and then, finally, in a single God. Several of these writers, however, used the word "religion" very broadly to include belief in any unseen spiritual agencies, and in this sense both E. B. Tylor (the eminent evolutionary anthropologist) and Darwin were ready to admit that *religious* belief appeared to be universal among the less civilized tribes. The philosopher Fritz Mauthner, who followed this tradition, expressed himself very strongly on the subject. In *Der Atheismus und seine Geschichte im Abendlande* (Vol. IV, Ch. 10) he accused Christian missionaries of "translation impertinence" in dragging out of aborigines the confession that they believed in a heavenly Father, when more careful investigation revealed that they did not mean anything of the kind. He also protested against the trick, as he called it, by advocates of the *consensus gentium,* of using the word "religion" ambiguously—at first in the broad sense of Tylor and Darwin, in which it may be plausible to maintain the universality of religion, and then shifting to the narrower sense, required by their argument, in which it implies belief in God or gods.

Critics of the argument have also pointed out that there are numerous tribes believing in polytheism without having in their theology one supreme deity. Hence, even if the argument were otherwise sound, it could not prove the existence of a single Supreme Being.

Finally, it has been maintained that there are religions, of which Buddhism is the most notable instance, which have no belief in God at all.

To the last of these criticisms, the customary answer is that, while the founder of such a religion may indeed not have believed in God or gods, once these religions spread, they acquired theologies—and sometimes exceedingly extravagant ones at that. Joyce, who was familiar with this objection, regarded the example of Buddhism as highly favorable to his argument. It was his contention that no religion or philosophical system which rules out belief in God "has ever succeeded in maintaining a prominent hold on any people" (p. 197). In China, Buddhism flourished, but there it became a polytheistic religion. In India, on the other hand, where the original agnostic teachings were not substantially changed, the Buddhist creed could not hold its own and had to give way to modern Hinduism.

The existence of polytheistic religions is not, of course, questioned by defenders of the Common Consent Argument. Some, indeed, like Flint and Mercier, are willing to concede that the argument, by itself, does not favor a stronger conclusion than that God *or* gods exist. This, however, is not the usual reaction. Recent advocates of the argument have commonly challenged the entire scheme of the evolutionary anthropologists. Basing their argument largely on the work of the Austrian anthropologist Father Wilhelm Schmidt (1868–1954) and others belonging to the "theological school," they deny that polytheism antedates monotheism and insist, furthermore, that in every polytheistic religion there is one supreme deity. According to Schmidt, the simplest peoples are also the oldest, and they are believers in a very pure monotheism. Their God possesses all the main attributes of the God of Christianity and Judaism: he is the creator of reality, he supplies the foundation of morality, and he is also omnipotent, omniscient, and supremely good. As societies became more complex, this monotheism became transformed into various kinds of animism, polytheism, and ancestor worship. Even among these later cultures, Schmidt finds "a clear acknowledgment and worship of a supreme being," while all other "supernormal beings" are regarded as far inferior and subject to him.

It would be idle to get involved here in the controversies between Schmidt's school and other schools of anthropology, especially since there are objections to the Argument from Common Consent which can be evaluated without taking sides on anthropological issues. Perhaps the only comment worth making is that while contemporary anthropologists are willing to credit Schmidt and other members of the theological school with some sound criticisms of the evolutionary anthropologists and with a good deal of impressive field work, the great majority of them regard his basic theories as quite unsupported by the available evidence.

Unbelievers in the Western world. The other main challenge to the claim that belief in God is universal consists in pointing to the unbelievers in Western culture. It is admitted that unbelievers are a minority, but it is argued that they are and have for some time been too significant a minority not to affect the "moral unanimity of mankind" on this subject. This challenge and the various attempted rebuttals deserve, but have very rarely received, extended discussion.

"Belief" redefined. One way in which the significance of individual unbelievers may be discounted is apparent in the tendency of some Protestant writers to define "belief in God" or "religion" or both so broadly as to make it virtually impossible for a human being not to be a believer or to be religious. In our own day such writers frequently follow Paul Tillich's definition of an atheist as someone who believes that "life is shallow" and of an irreligious person as someone who has "no object of ultimate concern." However, the use of such definitions to do away with unbelievers achieves a victory which is purely illusory. It will now indeed be possible to call a man like Diderot a believer and religious. But in the sense in which there was a dispute about the existence of unbelievers, namely, whether there are people who do not believe in the existence of what is usually understood by "God," Diderot and countless other people will still have to be classified as unbelievers. Moreover, if the premise of the Common Consent Argument is now a true proposition, with "believer" used in the *new* sense, the conclusion established, if any, would not be the one originally aimed at. It would not show that God exists but rather, using Tillich's redefinitions, that life is not shallow and that there are objects of ultimate concern.

Unbelievers discounted as abnormal. One of the favorite devices used to defend the *consensus gentium* against irritating exceptions has been the charge that unbelievers are in effect too morally or mentally defective to count as representative of human opinion. Strangely enough, this tactic was used by Pierre Gassendi, who was highly critical of Herbert of Cherbury's argument and from whom, in view of his own independence of thought, one might have expected something better. In the course of expounding his version of the argument, Gassendi minimized the number and importance of atheists, declaring that they are either "intellectual monstrosities" or "freaks of nature." More recently this defense was adopted by some eminent nineteenth-century Protestant theologians. Thus A. H. Strong, in a text which was widely used in Protestant seminaries, observed that just as the oak must not be judged by the "stunted, the flowerless specimens on the edge of the Arctic Circle," so we must not take account of unbelievers in judging the nature of man (*Systematic Theology*, Vol. I, p. 56). One of the rivals of Strong's book was Hodge's *Systematic Theology*. Hodge was not to be outdone. A man's hand, he reminds us, may be so hardened as to lose the sense of touch, but this does not prove that the hand is not "normally the great organ of touch." Similarly, it is possible that "the moral nature of a man may be so disorganized by vice or by a false philosophy as to have its testimony for the existence of God effectually silenced" (*op. cit.*, p. 198). Human beings cannot abandon belief in God "without derationalizing and demoralizing their whole being" (p. 201); and the belief, or rather lack of belief, of such a "derationalized" and "demoralized" individual does not count.

Perhaps two brief comments will be sufficient here. First, Hodge at least is begging the question when he refers to the "false philosophy" that silences the testimony for the existence of God. The question is precisely whether this is a false philosophy. If this were already known, there would be no need for the Argument from Common Consent. Second, and more important, anybody having the slightest familiarity with the history of unbelief must surely protest that many of the outstanding thinkers of the last two centuries were avowed unbelievers. Like other mortals, they may have been frequently in error, but to dismiss them as freaks, to compare them to stunted, flowerless oaks, or to regard their moral nature as disorganized by vice is surely outrageous nonsense.

Unbelief discounted as an illusion. Some of those who regard the unbeliever as "unnatural" or "monstrous" do not, perhaps, wish to refer to any actual human being. This may be so because some of them also maintain that *really* everybody is a believer in God even though he may say the opposite and believe that he believes the opposite. (The strategy here is rather different from the redefinitional maneuver described above.) Hodge, for example, offers two reasons in support of such a position. First, unbelief is such an unnatural state that it cannot last. "Whatever rouses the moral nature, whether it be danger, or suffering, or the approach of death, banishes unbelief in a moment (*ibid.*, p. 198). There seems to be an obvious answer to this. It is true that unbelievers have become converted or reconverted on occasions, but it is equally true that others have remained unbelievers right to the end of their lives. Furthermore, those who became converted must *really* have been unbelievers before their change of position, or else there would have been no conversion. To this it must be added that there are also shifts in the opposite direction, and if a person does not count as an unbeliever *at all* because he ultimately becomes a believer, then those who change from belief to unbelief will have to be counted as unbelievers exclusively.

Hodge's second reason would probably have a much wider appeal. "It is hardly conceivable," he writes, "that a human soul should exist in any state of development, without a sense of responsibility, and this involves the idea of God. For the responsibility is felt to be not to self, nor to men, but to an invisible Being, higher than self and higher than man" (*ibid.*, p. 197). Hodge is certainly not alone in taking the line that if a person is a moral creature and not lacking in sensibility, then he must be a believer in God. Even at the present time there are many people who seem to rule out a priori the possibility that a good person can be an unbeliever. To give just one illustration, Justice William O. Douglas wrote a highly laudatory preface to a recent collection of the court pleas of Clarence Darrow (*Attorney for the Damned*). Darrow had repeatedly stated and defended his agnosticism, and he never once retracted this position. Nevertheless, seeing that Darrow was such a kind and compassionate man, Douglas remarks: "Darrow met religious bigotry head-on . . . but he obviously believed in an infinite God who was the Maker of all humanity."

There are several confusions in reasoning of this kind. To begin with, the criteria which all of us employ to determine that a man is kind, that he does not lack sensibility, that he shows responsibility in his relations with other human beings—that, in short, he is a "moral person" or a good man—are quite distinct from those which we employ when determining that he is a believer in God. This at any rate must be so if the statement that all believers in God and only believers in God are good is to be, as it is usually taken to be (both by those who accept it and by those who deny it), a factual claim and not a tautology.

Second, the claim that responsibility is invariably felt not to oneself or to other men but to an invisible Being is unwarranted. Assuming that some people do on occasions feel responsibility to an invisible Being, this is certainly not true of all. If people who assure us that they feel responsible, but not to an invisible Being, are to be discounted or disbelieved, why should we count and accept the assurances of those who say that they feel responsible to the invisible Being? Moreover, it appears that the attitude, even of religious believers, is not generally in accord with Hodge's account. If a believer borrows money and considers himself obligated to return it, he surely, like an unbeliever, regards himself as obligated to the person who lent him the money and not to anybody else. Suppose believers were asked the following question in such a situation: "If an atheistic philosopher persuaded you that God does not exist, but if otherwise the situation remained exactly the same—you needed the money badly, your friend helped you without hesitation, you promised to repay him as soon as possible, and so on—would you still consider yourself obligated to repay the loan?" It seems very doubtful that more than a handful of believers would reply that they no longer regarded themselves as obligated.

Questions about whether a person who says that he believes or disbelieves a proposition and who is apparently not lying, does really believe or disbelieve it, are complicated by the fact that "belief" is an ambiguous word. Without entering into any subtleties or attempting an elaborate analysis, it may be granted that there is nothing absurd in the suggestion that a person may sincerely regard himself as an unbeliever when in fact he is a believer, or vice versa. It is helpful in this connection to distinguish belief in terms of verbal responses and positions adopted in purely theoretical contexts from belief insofar as it is exhibited in actions and in involuntary responses, especially to critical situations.

Bertrand Russell discusses this question in a little-known essay entitled "Stoicism and Mental Health." He points out that people who say, with all appearance of sincerity, that they believe in an afterlife seem to fear their own death or regret the death of their friends as much as those who say that they do not believe in an afterlife. He explains this "apparent inconsistency" by remarking that the belief in the afterlife is in most people "only in the region of conscious thought and has not succeeded in modifying unconscious mechanisms" (*In Praise of Idleness*, paperback ed., London, 1960, pp. 133–134). Many of us, like Russell, are inclined to regard the latter, the sense in which belief is expressed in involuntary responses and not merely in theoretical contexts, as the "deeper" sense. We say that a man has reached and avows a certain conclusion, but "deep down" he really believes the opposite. It must be conceded to the defender of the Argument from Common Consent that there are people who are unbelievers in the verbal and theoretical sense but who in a deeper sense do believe in God. This is notoriously true of some who are brought up in a religious home and much later come under the influence of skeptical thinkers.

Nevertheless, the Common Consent Argument is not really helped by this admission. For, in the first place, there can be no reasonable doubt that a good many people are unbelievers in both senses; and second, not a few cases are known of believers, that is, people who sincerely believe in God in terms of their verbal and theoretical responses whose actions show them to be unbelievers "deep down." This fact has been repeatedly stressed by religious writers when castigating some of the members of their own groups as "practical atheists."

Unbelief seen as a negligible influence. Some defenders of the argument are quite ready to admit the existence of highly educated unbelievers. In other words, they question neither the genuineness of the lack of belief nor the intellectual standing of unbelievers. However, they add to this the fact that unbelievers have failed and are bound to fail to make any major inroads on mankind at large. "We find a disposition on the part of some few philosophers to dispute the validity of the belief," writes Boedder (*op. cit.*, p. 68), "but nevertheless the belief has proved to be persistent and indestructible in the mass of mankind. It is this persistency among the mass of men, retained even in the teeth of skeptical opposition, on which our argument is based."

Sometimes a comparison is made between the unbelievers and the philosophers who deny the existence of an external world or the reality of space and time but are rightly laughed off by ordinary people whose common sense is intact. Granting that the ordinary person is in some sense right as against the philosopher who denies the reality of time, to confine ourselves to one such case, the comparison seems to be very weak in more ways than one. For one thing, unbelief in matters of religion is not at all confined to professional philosophers or to people who are naturally referred to as intellectuals. Furthermore, as G. E. Moore has pointed out, the philosophers who *say* such things as "time is unreal" and who presumably in some sense also believe this, also say things and cannot help saying things which indicate that *they also do not believe it.* The very philosophers who say that time is unreal nevertheless use clocks, complain when their students are late, plan for the future, and engage in the same activities which the ordinary man regards as presupposing the reality of time. Nothing even remotely comparable can be found in the case of unbelievers as a class.

However, returning to the original question, it is not at all certain that unbelieving philosophers and other critics of belief in God have not significantly affected the masses. There seems to be a good deal of evidence to the contrary; but even if it were true and the impact has in fact been negligible, this could be explained quite plausibly without supposing either that belief in God is inherent or, as Boedder claims, that reason, properly used, is certain to lead to a theological conclusion.

ARE MEN BY NATURE "GOD-SEEKERS"?

There are philosophers and psychologists of influence who either do not believe in God at all or who, at any rate, do not favor the enterprise of buttressing belief in God by means of "proofs" but are nevertheless concerned to maintain that human beings are by nature religious—that they are, in Max Scheler's phrase, "God-seekers." They would point out that it is this question of "philosophical anthropology," and not any question about the validity of the Common Consent Argument, which is of real interest and human importance. Though perhaps invalid as a proof of the *existence of God,* the Common Consent Argument does embody an important insight about the *nature of man.*

These writers are a great deal more sophisticated than most of the traditional defenders of the argument, whose views we considered in preceding sections. They do not at all deny that, in the most obvious sense, the world is full of unbelievers, but they would add that a great many of these unbelievers feel a strong urge to worship something or somebody and therefore invent all kinds of surrogate deities. Man's "gods and demons," writes Jung, "have not disappeared at all; they have merely got new names." Those, in the words of Unamuno, "who do not believe in God or who believe that they do not believe in Him, believe nevertheless in some little pocket god or even devil of their own." "Religious agnosticism," writes Scheler, "is not a psychological fact, but a self-deception . . . it is an essential law [*ein Wesensgesetz*] that every finite spirit believes either in God or in an idol. These idols may vary greatly. So-called unbelievers may treat the state or a woman or art or knowledge or any number of other things as if they were God" (*Gesammelte Werke,* Vol. V, pp. 261–262). Scheler adds that what needs explanation is not belief in God, which is original and natural, but unbelief or, rather, belief in an idol. The situation is not infrequently compared with the sexual instinct and what we know about the consequences of its suppression. If the sexual instinct does not find natural gratification, it does not cease to be operative but becomes diverted into other and less wholesome channels. The worship of institutions and human deities is said to be a similarly pathological phenomenon.

An evaluation of this position, which amounts in effect to an endorsement of the theory of the religious instinct without inferring the existence of God from it, is not possible here because it would involve elaborate discussions of child psychology and the causation of neurosis and "alienation." Here we can only observe that in the opinion of many contemporary thinkers there is no reason whatever to suppose that human beings are "by nature" religious. In their opinion the "hunger for God," in its orthodox no less than in its newer "substitute" expressions, is invariably the result of certain deprivations and traumatic experiences. People who suffer from insufficient contact with other human beings and who do not find the natural world satisfying will tend to experience longings for something supernatural or feel a need to endow human beings with supernatural attributes. Some of these writers would go further and maintain that traditional religion, through its life-denying morality and irrational taboos, is itself in no small measure responsible for the existence of the type of personality that displays the hunger for God. Freud, who took this position, conceded that those in whom the "sweet—or bitter-sweet—poison," as he called religion, had been instilled early in life were unable to dispense with it later on. The same, he added, is not true of others who have been brought up more soberly. "Not suffering from neurosis," they will "need no intoxicant to deaden it.

Bibliography

There is no full-length study in any language of the different forms of the Common Consent Argument. The major reference works contain either no entries or else very brief and unhelpful ones. Even Rudolf Eisler's "Consensus Gentium," in *Wörterbuch der philosophischen Begriffe*, 3 vols., 4th ed. (Berlin, 1930), devotes less than a page to this subject.

The fullest defenses of the argument are found in Charles Hodge, *Systematic Theology*, 3 vols. (New York, 1871–1873), Vol. I; Bernard Boedder, *Natural Theology* (London, 1896); and G. H. Joyce, *The Principles of Natural Theology* (London, 1923). Briefer discussions also favoring the argument are contained in A. H. Strong, *Systematic Theology*, 3 vols. (Philadelphia, 1907), Vol. I; Robert Flint, *Theism* (London, 1877); Hermann Ulrici, *Gott und die Natur*, 3 vols., 3d ed. (Leipzig, 1875), Vol. I; and Cardinal Mercier, *A Manual of Modern Scholastic Philosophy*, translated by T. L. and S. A. Parker, 2 vols., 3d ed. (London, 1926), Vol. II. The famous nineteenth-century biologist G. J. Romanes, in "The Influence of Science Upon Religion," which forms Part I of his *Thoughts on Religion* (Chicago, 1895), defends the biological form of the argument as proving not that there is a God but that *if* "the general order of nature is due to Mind," then the character of that Mind is "such as it is conceived to be by the most highly developed form of religion."

A popular contemporary statement of the biological version of the argument is advanced in Chad Walsh, *Atheism Doesn't Make Sense* (Cincinnati, n. d.). Among earlier writers, Cicero defended the argument in *De Natura Deorum*, Book II, Sec. II, translated by C. D. Yonge as *The Nature of the Gods* (London, 1892); by Herbert of Cherbury in *De Veritate*, translated by M. H. Carré (Bristol, 1937); and by Pierre Gassendi in *Syntagma Philosophicum*, in his *Opera Omnia*, H. L. H. de Montmorency and F. Henri, eds., Vol. I (Lyons, 1658).

One of the earliest criticisms of the argument was by Locke, in *Essay Concerning Human Understanding* (London, 1690), Book I. There are brief and unsystematic critical discussions in several of the works of the freethinkers of the seventeenth, eighteenth, and nineteenth centuries, including Bayle, Holbach, and Büchner, but the first detailed and systematic critique is found in J. S. Mill, *Three Essays on Religion* (London, 1874). More recently, the argument has been attacked in John Caird, *Introduction to the Philosophy of Religion* (Glasgow, 1880); Fritz Mauthner, *Der Atheismus und seine Geschichte in Abendlande*, Vol. IV (Stuttgart, 1923); and in two books by Josef Popper-Lynkeus: *Das Individuum und die Bewertung menschlicher Existenz* (Dresden, 1910) and *Über Religion* (Vienna, 1924). Popper-Lynkeus' criticisms are, for the most part, an elaboration of Hume's remark that "the conviction of the religionists, in all ages, is more affected than real." Hume's discussion of this topic occurs in Sec. XII of *The Natural History of Religion* (London, 1757; critical ed. with introduction by H. E. Root, London, 1956), a work which also anticipates many of the conclusions of the evolutionary anthropologists of the nineteenth century. There is a discussion, at once critical and sympathetic, in Miguel de Unamuno, *The Tragic Sense of Life in Men and in Peoples*, translated by J. E. Crawford Flitch (New York, 1921).

Two recent works surveying the evidence concerning the religious beliefs of primitive tribes are G. E. Swanson, *The Birth of the Gods* (Ann Arbor, Mich., 1960), and W. J. Goode, *Religion Among the Primitives* (Glencoe, Ill., 1951). Wilhelm Schmidt's theory is stated in his *The Origin and Growth of Religion*, translated by H. J. Rose (London, 1931). A view similar to Schmidt's was expressed by Andrew Lang in various works, including *The Making of Religion* (London, 1898) and *Magic and Religion* (London, 1901). The *Anthropological Review*, Vol. 2 (1864), 217–222, contains an interesting summary of an address by the Reverend F. W. Farrar, "On the Universality of Belief in God and in the Future State," in which a great deal of evidence is presented to the effect that neither belief in God nor belief in an afterlife is universal. The discussion following Farrar's address is also reported, and most of the participants, including W. R. Wallace, fully supported Farrar's negative conclusion.

J.-H. Leuba, *The Belief in God and Immortality* (New York, c. 1915), presents evidence concerning belief and unbelief among academic groups in the United States in the early years of the twentieth century. Unfortunately, there has been virtually no study in depth of religious belief and unbelief in the general population of any country.

Jung's views on the natural religious needs of human beings and the sickness of modern men who have lost their religion are stated in *Psychology and Religion* (New Haven, 1938) and *Modern Man in Search of a Soul*, translated by W. S. Dell and C. F. Baynes (New York, 1933). Scheler's similar views are found in his *Vom Ewigen im Menschen*, in *Gesammelte Werke*, 4th rev. ed., Vol. V (Bern, 1954). The opposite position is defended by Sigmund Freud in *The Future of an Illusion*, translated by W. D. Robson-Scott (London and New York, 1927), and Wilhelm Reich, in *The Mass Psychology of Fascism*, translated by T. P. Wolfe (New York, 1946). The views of Freud and Reich are foreshadowed in Ludwig Feuerbach, *The Essence of Christianity*, translated by George Eliot (London, 1853).

PAUL EDWARDS

COMMON SENSE. Several things can be learned about common sense from Dr. Johnson's attempt to refute Berkeley by kicking the stone. Its philosophical incompetence is not one of them. Dr. Johnson of course misunderstood Berkeley, and his misunderstanding was not a collapse of common sense. He thought that if stones had, as Berkeley said, no "material substance" and were collections of "ideas," a boot ought to go through them without resistance. And if Berkeley had been maintaining that solid objects were only apparently solid and were really collections of what we would ordinarily call ideas, the refutation would have been an appropriate reaction of common sense.

THE NOTION OF COMMON SENSE

Whatever other aspects of meaning the word "sense" may retain in the compound "common sense," it has prominently the force of sense as opposed to nonsense. In what is contrary to common sense there is always something more or less—but obviously—nonsensical. It produces the feeling, varying in strength according to circumstances, that argument is only precariously in place in dealing with it. For to deploy arguments at all *directly* against the manifestly absurd is to invest it with some intellectual dignity and to muffle its self-annihilating character. It is, moreover, to invite the suspicion that one has failed to recognize absurdity, and such failure has a very foolish look. As a man of redoubtable common sense, Dr. Johnson kept dialectic for the right occasion. He did not kick the stone formally in the name of common sense, but his action has traditionally been praised and condemned as a piece of common-sense behavior. Yet he was demonstrating against a philosopher who was also determined to be on the side of common sense.

Berkeley. Berkeley's notebooks contain the reminder to himself: "To be eternally banishing Metaphisics &c & recalling Men to Common Sense" (*Philosophical Commentaries*, No. 751). Confident that he could always secure the neutrality of common sense when he could not have its assistance, Berkeley went about his own metaphysical enterprise, which was to exhibit the dependence of physical objects on their being perceived. His *Three Dialogues* (1713) is studded with references to common sense: to opinions that are "repugnant" or "shocking" to it, to its "dictates," to the judgment of men of "plain common sense." The objections that have to be most carefully answered are those which appear to proceed from common sense. Since the issues concern mainly the world of perception, the man of common sense in the *Dialogues* is eminently the man who "trusts his senses," who will not tolerate the suggestion that the things he sees and handles are not real things but their mere representations.

The eighteenth century also brought into existence, in France and Scotland, philosophies of common sense—philosophies, to a greater or lesser degree, centered on this notion. They safeguarded what they held to be the beliefs (or "truths") of common sense by defending its authority and—in the Scottish philosophy—by exposing contraries of these beliefs to its blunt rejection.

Common-sense beliefs. It may be asked whether common sense had beliefs until philosophers engaged in its defense ascribed them to it. The *Oxford English Dictionary* lists a variety of meanings for the expression. Three of these, referring to a mental endowment, might be taken together: ordinary understanding—without which a man is out of his mind, or feeble-minded (an early meaning); ordinary, practical, good sense in everyday affairs; and the "faculty of primary truths." Ordinary understanding is not obviously, and practical, good sense is obviously not, the sort of thing that could stamp a set of beliefs with a special character. The third of these meanings is marked "philosophical." A further meaning must be noticed: "the general sense, feeling, or judgement of mankind . . . ." Here common sense seems to be a cluster of beliefs or persuasions, somehow "felt" to be true by most people. An argument drawn from common sense, in this case, would amount to an appeal to an ancient tribunal of opinion, common consent. (The most absolute modern proponent of this tribunal has probably been Lamennais, in his *Essai sur l'indifférence,* Paris, 1817–1823.)

Philosophers have frequently meant by common sense an intuitively based common consent. And the philosophers, during and after the eighteenth century, who have argued from common sense and for its beliefs have often thought of common sense in this way. They have, however, as often thought of it in a more ordinary way, as the common sense that is opposed—always at first sight, sometimes irreconcilably—to high and obvious paradox.

Can the common sense that is opposed to gross paradox properly be thought of as having beliefs, however strong? If there is some artificiality in saying that common sense has beliefs, there is none in speaking of its rejection of an opinion; the reason—it might be suggested—is that common sense does not declare itself in advance of attack upon it. The man of plain, ordinary common sense cannot readily be said, for instance, to believe that the things around him continue to exist in his absence—the idea of their not doing so does not cross his mind. But when he encounters the contrary opinion, his common sense asserts itself. On the supposition that the declarations of common sense are essentially reactive, to ascribe to it beliefs specified by what it rejects—and this the philosophers who have maintained its beliefs seem often to have intended—would be a minor linguistic innovation, justified in that it makes its commitments explicit. The supposition would have to be modified in some cases. It does not come naturally to us to speak of a *belief* in our personal identity through time, because this identity is something of which we are aware. Nevertheless, it can be argued that here also common sense has commitments which are not apparent before its reaction to various assertions.

Reaction to skepticism. A philosophy of common sense is a natural reaction to the fact, or to the threat, of philosophical paradox or skepticism. The French Jesuit Claude Buffier (1661–1737) saw us as threatened, since Descartes, with skepticism about all matters of fact beyond the range of our consciousness, the states of which cannot be doubted. What we need is unimpeachable authority for the fundamental convictions shared by all normal men about matters of fact with respect to which consciousness can give no guarantees. Common sense supplies it. It puts us into assured possession of such "first truths" as that there is an external world, that our minds are incorporeal, that we are capable of free agency. First truths have characteristic marks: No attack upon them, and no attempt to prove them, can operate from premises that surpass them in clarity or evidence. They are, and always have been, acknowledged by the vast majority of mankind. Those who imagine they reject them act like other men in conformity with them.

Hume. Hume's work *A Treatise of Human Nature* (1739–1740) produced by reaction a more important philosophy of common sense than Buffier's. In parts of the *Treatise*—to isolate what gave the book its most generally "shocking" aspect—things were reduced to the contents of the mind and the mind to its contents. While many of Hume's conclusions are capable of a milder interpretation than they were given by his readers, Hume himself did not pretend that a number of them were anything but profoundly disturbing to our natural beliefs. At the same time he thought these beliefs had us too tightly in their grip for reasoning to be able to pry us loose. In the *Treatise* "nature" has the last word, but its meaning is left uncertain. We must submit, but whether in submitting to nature we are also submitting to truth is quite another matter. In Hume's later *An Enquiry Concerning Human Understanding,* "common sense and reflection" are mentioned as correcting, in some degree, the indiscriminate doubt of an extreme skepticism, but nature and reasoning are still seen as coming into conflict. However, it should be remarked that there is another side to Hume in which these skeptical tendencies are in abeyance.

THE "SCOTTISH SCHOOL"

Reid. A central purpose of Thomas Reid's *An Inquiry into the Human Mind on the Principles of Common Sense* (1764), and of his two later books, was, with Hume kept steady in view, to defend common sense against philosophical paradox and skepticism. It was for Reid a doubly difficult undertaking; if, as he held, the truths of common sense were self-evident, how could they be denied? And again, if they were self-evident, how could they be made evident when denied?

The great source of paradoxical or skeptical repudiations of common sense, Reid thought, was an innocent-looking theory that he believed philosophers had very generally adopted in order to explain the possibility of our awareness of anything beyond the present contents of our minds.

According to this theory, such awareness is secondhand, necessarily mediated by "ideas" within our minds that are representative substitutes for external things. As its implications were drawn out, the theory, Reid maintained, committed philosophers to a steadily increasing range of conflict with common sense, with no stopping before "ideas," losing their representative character, monopolize existence. The "theory of ideas" is to be found in Locke, needing only, Reid believed, an unsparing logic such as Hume's to produce Hume's world. (Locke's *An Essay Concerning Human Understanding* [1690], has a deceptively common-sense air; its tone is down-to-earth, and experience is set up as the source of knowledge. Locke wanted no paradoxes, and when they were approached by what he said, he was not very efficient at drawing conclusions.)

The truths of common sense cannot be made evident by deductive proofs, but, Reid maintained, there is always absurdity in opinions contrary to its dictates. His most general procedure in defending common sense was to remind us of its command over us. Common sense has so fundamentally determined the scaffolding of ordinary language that the philosopher, in trying to word an opinion which is against common sense, is liable to need another language; and his utterance is continually threatened with incoherence between its structure and its content. The beliefs of common sense govern the behavior even of those who repudiate them in opinion, and they are only fitfully repudiated even in opinion; the paradoxical or skeptical philosopher is no sooner off his guard than he is believing with, as well as acting like, other men. Reid stressed a truism about matters of common sense: They lie within "the reach of common understanding." If this were not so, the judgment of the great bulk of mankind would carry no weight against a philosopher's superior competence. But in "a matter of common sense, every man is no less a competent judge than a mathematician is in a mathematical demonstration" (*Intellectual Powers,* Essay VI, Ch. 4). Whether or not something is a matter of common sense may well have to be investigated—prejudices shamming common sense must be exposed; what Reid denied is that the philosopher is in a better position than anyone else to pronounce on the truth of what really comes from common sense.

Many of the opinions that Reid rejected as contrary to common sense do not appear to be in conflict with the necessities of action he held common sense to impose. Thus, he attacked Berkeley as having denied the existence of a material world, but Berkeley denied that the truth of his opinion would make any changes in our experience; stones, for instance, would remain the solid objects we find them to be. Reid's limited success in vindicating the beliefs of common sense by pointing to inconsistencies between the profession and the practice of dissenters was connected with his interpretation of many of these beliefs; they presented themselves to him as containing an element that lies beyond verification by experience and that might therefore be called metaphysical. He construed, for example, our belief in the existence of a material world as disallowing any phenomenalistic account of the nature of material things, our belief in personal identity as involving a reference of all our experience to its (immaterial) subject, our belief in the freedom of our will as involving indeterminancy of choice.

Reid's followers. The notion of an appeal to common sense in great matters of philosophical dispute was crudely taken up by two of Reid's contemporaries, James Beattie (the poet) and James Oswald. When they were regarded as its representatives, the school that became associated with Reid's name could easily be spoken of as appealing to "the judgment of the crowd." Dugald Stewart (1753–1828), teaching and writing with Reid's moderation, though without his penetrating simplicity, consolidated the school's position in Scotland, and his books helped to make the influence of the ideas he shared with Reid strongly felt in France and America.

Sir William Hamilton. Sir William Hamilton (1788–1856) produced a philosophy in which doctrines of Reid and Kant were fused into an unstable compound. It proclaimed the sovereignty of common sense and compromised its deliverances, which for Reid were necessarily objective, with an ambiguous assertion of the "relativity" of knowledge. According to Hamilton, the convictions of common sense come to us with the backing of our entire cognitive nature. They are tests of other truth; their own must be presumed, for they are too elementary to have antecedents from which they could be derived. The only possible falsification of common sense would be demonstrated inconsistency in its deliverances, and this would bring in epistemological chaos. J. S. Mill's *An Examination of Sir William Hamilton's Philosophy* (1865) gave a reactionary, obscurantist look to the authority that Reid and Hamilton claimed for common sense. The "psychological" method, which Mill opposed to their "introspective method," was damagingly designed to show how a belief—such as everyone's belief in an external world—had grown up, taking on in the process the appearance of obviousness; the psychological method would undermine the doctrine that a belief is a dictate of nature by exhibiting its natural history.

"CRITICAL COMMON SENSE"

Reid and Hamilton both thought that criticism is or may be necessary in order to determine whether a belief is in fact a belief of common sense. They also held, however, that once this fact is established, it follows that the belief is true. The label "critical common sense" might be used, not too misleadingly, to distinguish from this position those philosophical views which combine the greatest respect for common sense with the insistence or admission that at least some of its beliefs are open to critical revision.

Aristotle. If common sense is identified with what is commonly believed and its criticism is thought of as designed to elicit and defend the truth in common beliefs, then Aristotle may be called the first common-sense philosopher. "We must," Aristotle said, "as in all other cases, set the observed facts before us and, after first discussing the difficulties, go on to prove, if possible, the truth of all the common opinions about these affections of the mind, or, failing this, of the greater number and the most authoritative; for if we both refute the objections and leave the common opinions undisturbed, we shall have proved the case sufficiently" (*Nicomachean Ethics,* 1145b2–7; cf. 1172b35–1173a2, *Eudemian Ethics* [attributed to Aristotle], 1216b26–35).

C. S. Peirce. The "Critical Common-sensism" argued for by the American philosopher C. S. Peirce (1839–1914) was largely defined in relation to the views held by the Scottish school. It saw the beliefs of common sense, Peirce said, as changeless, the same for all men at all times. It rightly thought of them as having a kind of instinctive character—but instincts can undergo modification. Peirce was sure that these beliefs show some modification as men become civilized and civilization develops. They are not, as ordinarily held, beliefs that have been up for acceptance or rejection; they exist as lifelong "belief-habits." And they possess a logical feature in virtue of which they are doubt-resistant when criticized: They have an essential vagueness. Peirce illustrated this with "our belief in the Order of Nature." Let an attempt be made to give this belief precision, and what results will be found disputable. "But who can think that there is *no* order in nature?" (*Collected Papers,* Vol. V, p. 359).

The "Critical Common-sensist," Peirce said, tries to "bring all his very general first premisses to recognition" and to develop "every suspicion of doubt of their truth" (*ibid.,* p. 363). But the doubt he is looking for must be the real thing, not "paper" doubt; we can no more induce genuine doubt by an act of will than we can give ourselves a surprise by deciding to. "Strong thinkers" are "apt to be great breath-holders," but holding one's breath against belief is not doubting. In claiming "indubitability" for a belief of common sense, Peirce was not declaring its truth—"propositions that really are indubitable, for the time being" may "nevertheless be false" (*ibid.,* p. 347). The future holds possibilities of surprise for all our beliefs. Yet Peirce seems to have held that though any one of our indubitable beliefs might turn out to be false, they could not all do so.

Henry Sidgwick. "Common sense organised into Science," Henry Sidgwick (1838–1900) remarked, "continually at once corrects and confirms crude Common Sense" (*Lectures on the Philosophy of Kant,* p. 425). Sidgwick saw common sense as a great mass of ore, rich in valuable metals, that needs philosophical smelting. It must have removed "inadvertencies, confusions, and contradictions" (*ibid.,* p. 428). However, the procedures by which this is done—rigorous reflection, the adjustment of its beliefs to the assured results of science—are not alien to it. Sidgwick's *Methods of Ethics* (1874) contains a detailed examination of the "morality of common sense," directed toward showing its frequent vagueness, its areas of indecision, its compromises between conflicting ideas, and also toward showing how its fundamental convictions can be taken up into a form of utilitarianism that can reasonably claim the acquiescence of common sense.

G. F. Stout. For G. F. Stout (1860–1944), common sense has been self-correcting in its evolution and it is still to some extent modifiable. The man in the street is not to be taken as its representative; the common sense of philosophical importance resides in the consensus of ignorant and educated belief. This unanimity is the result of a long development, during which idiosyncrasies of opinion have been worn down by mutual attrition, and mistakes—which common sense itself can see to be such—have been corrected. Common sense is less a matter of particular beliefs than "the persistence of plastic tendencies to certain most general and comprehensive views" (*Mind and Matter,* p. 11). These include such strongly metaphysical dispositions as "the tendency to find Mind in Nature generally" (*ibid.,* p. 14). When a conflict arises between common sense and some scientific or philosophical opinion, the final decision, Stout maintained, rests with common sense, "however indirectly"; for common sense must either be provided with reconciliatory explanations or be brought to see that the considerations in favor of the opinion more than cancel the presumption against it.

Russell and Broad. It is convenient to mention here two contemporary philosophers who have thought that there are philosophical opinions which can be described as common-sense but who have thought that some of these opinions are quite radically mistaken. Science takes common sense as its starting point, Bertrand Russell says; it has arrived at results with regard to the nature of physical things and their relation to perception that are incompatible with parts of the "metaphysic" of common sense. One does what one can for common sense, but, according to C. D. Broad, sometimes not much is possible; nor should a philosopher feel disturbed at a break with common sense that results from seeing together facts which the plain man notices only separately and from taking into account other facts of which he is altogether ignorant.

COMMON SENSE AND ORDINARY LANGUAGE

G. E. Moore. G. E. Moore (1873–1958) did not think that common sense never errs. He seems often to have treated universal, or very general, acceptance as the identifying mark of a common-sense belief, and, as he mentions, things that everybody once believed have turned out to be false. He was prepared to allow that, for all he knew to the contrary, there might be many false propositions included within the vague boundaries of "the Common Sense view of the world." Moore had no special interest in critically sifting the beliefs of common sense for truth and falsity. He was primarily interested in its massive certainties.

Moore's paper "A Defence of Common Sense" (1925) lists sets of propositions that are as obviously true as almost any imaginable: for instance (with considerable paraphrase for the sake of brevity), propositions stating that the earth has existed for many years; that its inhabitants have been variously in contact with, or at different distances from, one another and other things; and that these facts are matters of common knowledge. According to Moore, these "truisms," taken together, imply the truth of the common-sense view of the world in certain of its "fundamental features," for they imply that there are material things, space, time, and other minds besides one's own—in a clear meaning of each of the expressions "material thing," "space," "time," etc. The abstract words contain ambiguities that are absent from, for example, "The earth has existed for many years," but Moore thought that some philosophers who have denied the existence of material things, of space, of time, or of other minds besides their own are to be understood as having expressed views incompatible with such banally obvious truths. He thus regarded them as paradoxically uttering opinions inconsistent with what they themselves know to be true. They constantly reveal this knowledge in its incompatibility with their opinions; a solipsistic philosopher, for example, sets himself to persuade others that he alone exists.

There is very great doubt, Moore thought, about the correct "analysis," in some important respects, of propositions of common sense that are quite certainly true. (Roughly, for Moore, the analysis of a concept or a proposition lays bare its structure by indicating the concepts it implicitly contains and the way they are combined.) Moore did not think that a phenomenalistic analysis of the concept of a material thing could be ruled out as absolutely impossible. It follows that, in his judgment, a philosopher who was using the sentence "Material things do not exist" simply to word a phenomenalistic doctrine and to repudiate its alternatives would not be repudiating a conviction of common sense that is manifestly true. And if this is so, it is hard to see what a philosopher could have in mind in using the words that would constitute such repudiation. By contrast, denials of the "reality" of space and time on the ground that their concepts are self-contradictory do appear to be in irreconcilable conflict with the most commonplace facts about position and distance, and about past, present, and future.

Norman Malcolm. The philosophical paradoxes that Moore attacked on many different occasions are construed in Norman Malcolm's essay "Moore and Ordinary Language" as disguised, variously motivated rejections of common language, and Moore's defense of common sense is construed as its vindication. A philosopher declares, for instance, "We can never know for certain the truth of any empirical statement." As interpreted by Malcolm, he is saying that it is never right to say "I know for certain" when it is *logically* possible that one is mistaken, that the words are always improperly used in this situation. Moore's reply, characteristically translating from the abstract to the concrete, pointed out the absurdity of anyone's suggesting, when he is sitting on a chair, that he believes he is, that he very probably is, but that he does not know it for certain. What Moore's reply did, on Malcolm's interpretation, was "to appeal to our language-sense," "to make us feel how queer and wrong" it would be to speak here in the way the philosopher proposes and substitute "believe" for "know for certain" or to turn to such words as "probable" ("Moore and Ordinary Language," p. 354).

"A philosophical paradox," Malcolm says (*ibid.*, pp. 359–360), "asserts that, whenever a person uses a certain expression, what he says is false." However, from the fact that the expression has a use in ordinary language, it follows, Malcolm argues, that it is free from self-contradiction (since a self-contradictory expression necessarily has no use) and therefore that it *can* be employed to make true statements. And this is enough to refute the paradox. Whether or not people always say something false when using these expressions becomes a matter to be settled by matter-of-fact evidence, and the paradoxical philosopher does not deal in evidence of this sort.

In Malcolm's essay a stronger claim is made in effect for Moore's refutations: They produce indisputably true statements employing the expressions that the paradoxes reject, for they present *paradigms* of the correct application of these expressions. And it is maintained that we could not learn the meaning of some expressions without such paradigms or standard cases; that we could not learn, for example, the meaning of "material thing" without being shown examples of material things, or the meaning of spatial and temporal expressions without acquaintance with spatial and temporal relations, or the meaning of "certain," "probable," "doubtful" without being introduced to the contrasted situations to which they apply. Thus, a statement denying that there is anything answering to one of these expressions must be false. Scrutiny of "the argument from paradigm cases" has been an incident in the recent shift of philosophical interest from common sense (at least under that name) to ordinary language (see PARADIGM CASE ARGUMENT).

Ludwig Wittgenstein. The way to philosophical paradox is opened, according to Ludwig Wittgenstein (1889–1951), when some feature of ordinary language is misconstrued as only philosophers are likely to misconstrue it. This disorder, along with such other characteristic philosophical aberrations as directionless bafflement, is to be got rid of by bringing words back from their alienation in metaphysical discourse to the familiar surroundings from which they have been abstracted and watching them at work there. Philosophers have not carelessly misunderstood ordinary language; it is waiting for them with "bewitchment" and "illusion." In the emancipation that is achieved when one is able to "command a clear view" of the functioning of language, everything is left, but seen to be, "as it is." Wittgenstein rarely mentioned common sense. He referred in *The Blue Book* (Oxford, 1958, p. 48) to the "common-sense philosopher" (such as Moore or Reid) who, "*n.b.*, is not the common-sense man." The common-sense man, Wittgenstein may be taken to suggest, is man before the philosophical Fall

Bibliography

THE NOTION OF COMMON SENSE

Berkeley, George, *Three Dialogues Between Hylas and Philonous.* London, 1713.

Buffier, Claude, *First Truths,* translated anonymously. London, 1780.

Isaacs, Nathan, *The Foundations of Common Sense.* London, 1949.

Lewis, C. S., "Sense," in *Studies in Words.* Cambridge, 1960.

Also see the works listed below by Grave, Reid, Stewart, Peirce, Stout (*Mind and Matter*), Malcolm, Moore (*Philosophical Papers,* Ch. 2), and Woozley.

THE "SCOTTISH SCHOOL"

Beattie, James, *An Essay on the Nature and Immutability of Truth.* Edinburgh, 1770.

Chastaing, Maxime, "Reid, la philosophie du sens commun." *Revue philosophique de la France et de l'étranger*, Vol. 144 (1954), 352–399.

Grave, S. A., *The Scottish Philosophy of Common Sense.* Oxford, 1960.

Mill, John Stuart, *An Examination of Sir William Hamilton's Philosophy.* London, 1865. Chs. 3, 8–14.

Reid, Thomas, *Works*, Sir William Hamilton, ed., 2 vols. Edinburgh, 1846–1863. Hamilton's appendices include a long historical and expository dissertation on the notion of common sense.

Stewart, Dugald, *Works*, Sir William Hamilton, ed., 11 vols. Edinburgh, 1854–1860. Vol. III, Ch. 1.

"CRITICAL COMMON SENSE"

Broad, C. D., *The Mind and Its Place in Nature.* London, 1925. Chs. 2–4.

Broad, C. D., "A Reply to My Critics," in P. A. Schilpp, ed., *The Philosophy of C. D. Broad.* New York, 1959. Pp. 803–805.

Peirce, C. S., *Collected Papers*, Charles Hartshorne and Paul Weiss, eds., 6 vols. Cambridge, Mass., 1931–1935. Vol. V, pp. 293–313, 346–375.

Russell, Bertrand, "Reply to Criticisms," in P. A. Schilpp, ed., *The Philosophy of Bertrand Russell*, 2d ed. Evanston, Ill., 1946. Pp. 700–705.

Russell, Bertrand, *Human Knowledge.* London, 1948. Part III; Part IV, Ch. 10.

Sidgwick, Henry, *The Methods of Ethics*, 6th ed. London, 1901.

Sidgwick, Henry, "The Philosophy of Common Sense," in *Lectures on the Philosophy of Kant*, J. Ward, ed. London, 1905. Pp. 406–429.

Stout, G. F., *Studies in Philosophy and Psychology.* London, 1930. Ch. 6.

Stout, G. F., *Mind and Matter.* Cambridge, 1931.

COMMON SENSE AND ORDINARY LANGUAGE

Campbell, C. A., "Common-sense Propositions and Philosophical Paradoxes." *PAS*, Vol. 45 (1944–1945), 1–25.

Chappell, V. C., "Malcolm on Moore." *Mind*, Vol. 70, No. 279 (July 1961), 417–425.

Chisholm, R. M., "Philosophers and Ordinary Language." *Philosophical Review*, Vol. 60 (1951), 317–328. Malcolm's reply follows immediately.

Duncan-Jones, A. E., and Ayer, A. J., "Does Philosophy Analyse Common Sense?" *PAS*, Supp. Vol. 16 (1937), 139–176. Symposium.

Flew, A. G. N., ed., *Essays in Conceptual Analysis.* London, 1956. Chs. 1 and 6. Discusses paradigm cases.

Malcolm, Norman, "Moore and Ordinary Language," in P. A. Schilpp, ed., *The Philosophy of G. E. Moore.* Evanston and Chicago, 1942. Pp. 345–368.

Malcolm, Norman, "Defending Common Sense." *Philosophical Review*, Vol. 58 (1949), 201–220.

Moore, G. E., "A Reply to My Critics," in P. A. Schilpp, ed., *The Philosophy of G. E. Moore.* Evanston and Chicago, 1942. Pp. 660–675.

Moore, G. E., *Some Main Problems of Philosophy.* London, 1953. Chs. 1, 5–7, 11.

Moore, G. E. *Philosophical Papers.* London, 1959. Ch. 2, "A Defence of Common Sense," and Ch. 7, "Proof of an External World."

Passmore, J. A., *Philosophical Reasoning.* London, 1961. Ch. 6. Discusses paradigm cases.

Wittgenstein, Ludwig, *Philosophical Investigations.* Oxford, 1953.

Woozley, A. D., "Ordinary Language and Common Sense." *Mind*, Vol. 62, No. 247 (July 1953), 301–312.

S. A. GRAVE

COMMUNISM is a system in which the land, buildings, implements, and goods are held in common. Property is vested in a community, with the members left to work according to their capacities and to draw on the common stock according to their needs.

Social systems approaching communism have been said to have existed in ancient China, Persia, and the Peru of the Incas and among various primitive peoples. However, the evidence is scanty and dubious. One must lay aside as not being communist societies (1) forms of work-organization imposed on subject populations by rulers exempt from the requirements of communism (for example, the regime of the Incas), (2) temporary sharing of booty during violent uprisings, when communism is the cover for pillage (for example, communist episodes in ancient Persia and during the Peasants' War in Germany), (3) parasitical, or economically dependent, organizations within which joint consumption is the rule (for example, many religious communities and military castes). If, apart from these communist corporations, integral communist societies have existed, it has not been at any higher level than nomads jointly owning their herds.

Motivation of communist projects. Sound information played no role in the many communist projects. Their authors were content with tenuous legends (the Atlantis of Plato's *Critias* or the Sparta of Plutarch's *Lycurgus*) or with scraps of misinformation ("noble savages" in the New World). Communism, in other words, is a speculative idea, not a historical datum. That idea has recurred, in essentially identical form, ever since men became cultivated enough to deplore gross inequity and to conceive its suppression in a society subject to rational symmetry (uniformity of rights, duties, and status) or to a static ethic of distributive justice (equal quanta of pains and pleasures for all). The rational motive is uppermost in the bulk of utopias, which are communist only incidentally, for the sake of simplicity. The ethical motive is stronger in those more passionate constructions where the abolition of private property is seen as the only cure of human vices and miseries, or at least of political instability and injustice. In tracing the history of these projects (if recurrence of an unchanging idea can be said to constitute a history), one must keep in view the contrast between plans for a caste or fraternity that will live communally in order to attain political or religious goals in a noncommunist society (like Plato's rulers or Christian and Buddhist orders) and plans for an integral communist economy. The latter are quite rare and are often based on a misunderstanding about the former: the planner of a communist economy assumes that the communal life of a brotherhood was meant to be extended to all men. This happened when Plato was cited as an integral communist and when heretics hoped to apply the regime of convents to secular society. At the risk of complicating the distinction between communist corporations and communist society, it must be said that projects for the communist society that rely on the existence of slaves should be classed (not only by the humanitarian, but by the economist too) as aiming only at a limited, parasitical community of friends or rulers.

History of the concept. Although, according to Aristotle, Phaleas of Chalcedon was the first to urge equality of possessions and Hippodamus of Miletus anticipated some of Plato's scheme, Plato's *Republic* (about 370 B.C.) is considered the archetype of communistic literature. In that social allegory of the human soul, Plato commended holding things in common, not by all men (that would be his despised democracy, which "dispenses equality to equals and unequals alike"), but by an aristocratic minority of rulers and their aids. His object was to separate politics from economic life, public responsibility from private property, because he held egoism (owning goods, making money, founding a family) incompatible with high civic virtue, just as, later, Christians held those same things incompatible with the highest forms of religious life. Integral communists could at least claim Plato's authority for two basic tenets: the egoism evident in getting and spending is the root of all evil, and static perfection can be attained by a polity that curbs it. Aristotle therefore criticized them in advance when he argued against Plato that "seditions have for cause not only inequality of goods but inequality of honors. Vulgar men object to inequality of goods; superior men to inequality of honors." That is, hedonism is not an adequate political psychology.

Other ancient and medieval conceptions. There are fragmentary reports of other Greek and Hellenistic communists, such as Antisthenes, Diogenes, and Zeno of Citium. Vastly more influential than their writings were Plutarch's lively (in fact, burlesque) account of Sparta under a half-fabulous Lycurgus and zealous Christian readings of certain passages in the Acts of the Apostles. The communism of the first Christian community was little else than the mutual aid of poor Galileans, isolated in Jerusalem and expecting the end of the world at any moment (and hence instant reward for their renunciation). Yet it was given as an example by some fathers of the church in communist sermons that were taken literally by some listeners. Thereafter, dozens of medieval heresies included projects for communism, especially when sponsored by monks who, having lived in communist corporations, envisaged making the whole world a monastery. In this tradition Joachim of Fiore (c. 1135–1202) forecast a "Third Age" of peace and communism, and the Joachimites' Eternal Gospel was kept alive by Franciscan extremists. Several crusades were needed early in the fourteenth century to exterminate the Apostolic Brethren, whose leader, Fra Dolcino, preached through northern Italy "the community of goods and women." Religious communism appeared again, mixed up with rational political demands and with the pillaging that is inseparable from plebeian uprisings, in the Hussites and Anabaptists and in Thomas Münzer, ideologist of the German Peasants' War.

Renaissance. Noble, rational savages replaced Spartans and apostles as models for communism when the voyages of discovery began. Thomas More's *Utopia* (1516) described a communism that was no longer the sacerdotal condition of an aristocracy of education or of righteousness, but the lot of most citizens—though there were still slaves for the "uneasy, sordid tasks." Tommaso Campanella, a Neapolitan Dominican contemporary with Francis Bacon (whose own *New Atlantis,* published posthumously in 1627, retained private property in the first technocrat, science-fiction utopia), imagined a communist City of the Sun, where economic equality was merely one aspect of the regimentation of work and sex in a fantastic theocracy.

Eighteenth century. There were only a few other seventeenth-century communists, but eighteenth-century France produced them by the score. Novels and poems about far-off communist lands abounded, and the theory was provided by the enemies of the Physiocrats and by disciples of the Rousseau of the *Discours sur l'inégalité,* such as Gabriel Bonnet de Mably's *Les Doutes proposés aux philosophes économiques sur l'ordre naturel et essentiel des sociétés* (1768). Brissot de Warville deserves to be remembered among them for coining the exclamation "Property is theft!" Above all, there was Morelly, an obscure figure whose *Code de la nature* (1755) was long attributed to Diderot, even by Babeuf, who during the French Revolution tried to implement the code in the Conspiracy of Equals. Morelly was the most meticulous, rational, and naive of all the communists.

Decline of pure communist theories. The proliferation of such projects in the late eighteenth century is significant. Communism had ceased to be intermittent speculation by isolated thinkers separated by ages and now reflected (in the distorting mirror held up by a class of intellectuals) genuine social aspirations. The social movements of egalitarian democracy and of socialism were just over the horizon. Plato, Lycurgus, and the Jesuits' sensible Paraguayans were regularly invoked, but communism's credentials were now thought to be better than that—they were believed to be inscribed in Natural Law. Of course, the Physiocrats had already claimed Nature as endorsing private property, but the communists reclaimed her: community of goods was not only a hypothetical remedy for all moral ills but a positive requirement of natural society. In reality, when the democratic and socialist movements did arise, they had little time for communist revery. Their objectives went far beyond arranging equitable distribution in communal refectories and free public shops, and they had much else to do first. For social thinkers communism ceased to be a separate subject of speculation and became a decorative myth, at best an optional extra for the far-distant future. So Étienne Cabet's *Voyage en Icarie* (Paris, 1840), certain unhappy experiments in "co-operative communities" in the United States, and Edward Bellamy's *Looking Backward* (Boston, 1888) were the last flickers of a millennial tradition. As for the unrepentant utopians (and counterutopians, such as Aldous Huxley), they have been too busy with the biological and psychological mutations in store for the species to worry about such minor matters as how property is owned.

Elements of communism. All communist projects have common features, not only because they always quote their predecessors, but also because they are restatements of a simple theme. Competition for private property is the origin of every vice, crime, and disorder. So economic activities must be restricted and, above all, separated from politics. They easily can be, because "the world is a table sufficiently well stocked for all the guests" (Morelly); only unequal distribution, luxury, idleness, and wasteful family kitchens make it seem otherwise. The economic problem, therefore, is not *production*, but simply the fair distribution of a fixed stock of goods *assumed as given*—given by a minimum of congenial labor (six hours a day, according to More; four hours, according to Campanella). Communism starts when the economic problem is taken as already solved, on the supply side by slavery or, in more humane times, by unspecified but wonderful inventions, and on the demand side by the frugality and restraint of consumers.

Consumption. The demand side is the more characteristic in the communist equation, and it is this that distinguishes the system from socialism. It expresses the consumer ethic as against the producer ethic of socialism and other industrial attitudes. Production being ignored or summarily dismissed (as it could plausibly be by parasitical corporations, which were all most communists had in view), economics becomes the organization of consumption. Of course, it has to be ascetic consumption, but that is welcomed on moralistic grounds. It is confessed that not all men would be content with so little, so the assumption is added that citizens become "philosophers." Plato, Zeno, Plutarch, and Campanella were explicit on the point that communism is for philosophers, and all the other projects presupposed an equivalent moral regeneration. Even philosophers' demands, however modest, must stay fixed if the economic problem is to remain solved, so everything that is liable to make demands evolve must be outlawed. Thus, the community is isolated, it practices no foreign trade and little other external intercourse, its population size is frozen, fashions never vary, technology is rigorously regulated, and even philosophy itself (ever inclined to call for a revaluation of values) is curbed in, if not banished from, this society of philosophers.

The family. Gnawing doubt lingers: is not the family the ultimate origin of competition for and perpetuation of private property? So the dissolution of monogamy and family life is often demanded. The reason is still economic (or rather antieconomic), not sexual. None of the communists contemplate sexual license, and when they institute the community of women, sexual relations are rationed frugally—just as food is at the common table, that "school of sobriety." The family has to be destroyed, or at least weakened (More and Morelly retained monogamy but took children from parents) to get at the roots of cupidity, such as inheritance customs. State regulation of sex life has the added advantage, for Plato and Campanella, of permitting eugenics.

Society without laws. Self-disciplined, abstemious philosophers, it is felt by naive psychologists, would need no laws over them. So a regular feature of communism after Plato (who was an incontinent legislator) is the absence of external legal obligation. Plutarch's Lycurgus forbade written laws and prohibited lawsuits; More's Utopia had "few laws and no lawyers" and no fixed penalties; the City of the Sun had "but few laws and those short and plain"; Morelly said written law came only after the Golden Age, and he composed a brief, immutable code for his utopia; Cabet's Icarie knew no judges or police. The yearning to have done with law is one of the keys to communism. It is the vision of a *life without conditions*, free from all external constraints, for most of the conditions of social existence are expressed in the multitude and complexity of written laws and of customary procedures backed by laws. Lack of laws and economic sufficiency have the same significance in this respect, the disappearance of all external "limitation." There is present, too, the tautology that law makes crime. Abolish private property and there will be no more theft; prohibit marriage and there will be an end to adultery; institute equality and there will be no envy or insolence.

Communism and socialism. Though recurrently confused (both by socialist "deviationists" and by antisocialists), communism and socialism are in important respects contraries. Communism is the timeless, abstractly moral wish to regulate individual consumption so that it is everywhere equal and frugal and to separate morally dangerous economic activities from the ethical state. Socialism is a specifically modern movement that favors the promotion and coordination of productive activities under the direction of the state. Confusion arises because socialism seems to include, as a means, the whole substance of communism, holding things in common. But both the "things" and the "holding" are very different. The communists' "things" were consumer goods; producer goods in their day were few and simple farm tools and artisans' kits, which they mostly left in private hands (the exceptions among communists being those, like More, who forgot even to specify who would own the instruments of production). Naturally, then, holding in common meant equal access for all. The socialists' "things," in contrast, are the vast stock of producer goods previously accumulated by capitalism. "Holding in common" for socialists obviously cannot mean equal access or sharing out. It means centralized direction of the economy, sometimes speciously called "people's ownership." Such a doctrine can better be, and usually is, expounded without using the language of communism.

Why then is part of the socialist movement known as communism? First, because in 1847 and 1848 the socialists whom Marx opposed were utopian but not communist, so Marx could revive the older name for his *Communist Manifesto*, though he had no more patience with communist projects than they. Once Marxism had won leadership in the socialist movement, that unsuitable label was dropped. By 1900 socialists called themselves socialists, seldom "communists." Then, in 1914, the movement split. Lenin held that the socialist parties had betrayed the cause, so he too deliberately revived the older word to distinguish his "true" socialism. Meantime, the term had suffered another vicissitude. In 1875 Marx had condemned, in the *Critique of the Gotha Program*, communist fantasy in the movement by saying that fair and equal shares could become a socialist slogan only in the distant future, after socialism had solved the economic problem and after men had undergone the required moral transformation. Lenin, in his *State and Revolution*, picked up this aside and made of it the dogma that communism is the second, higher stage of socialism. So while continuing to be denounced in the present as dangerous revery by all socialist leaders, communism gained a new, though shadowy, existence, as the remote myth of a life without external limitations that is in store for men who are (as the Soviet theorist S. Strumilin said in words that might have been Plato's or More's) "instructed, cultivated socialists who do not abuse the chance to get consumer goods [and] whose needs approximate fixed norms"—that is, for perfect philosophers in a society that has banished philosophy.

Bibliography

H. Morley's *Ideal Commonwealths* (London, 1885) collects some of the main primary sources: Plutarch's *Lycurgus*, More's *Utopia*, Bacon's *New Atlantis*, and Campanella's *City of the Sun*.

Almost all modern books about "communism"—see R. N. Carew Hunt, *Books on Communism* (London, 1959)—refer to Marxist socialism and Soviet Russia and thus have no relevance to communism as here discussed. For that, see J. Stammhammer, *Bibliographie des Sozialismus und Communismus*, 3 vols. (Jena, 1893–1908); G. Walter, *Histoire du communisme* (Paris, 1931); T. D. Woolsey, *Communism and Socialism* (London, 1880); and, for the French communists, A. Lichtenberger, *Le Socialisme au XVIIIe siècle* (Paris, 1895). The subject overlaps that of utopias; hence consult L. Mumford's *The Story of Utopias* (New York, 1922); J. O. Hertzler's *The History of Utopian Thought* (New York and London, 1923); R. Ruyer's *L'Utopie et les utopies* (Paris, 1950). (See also UTOPIAS AND UTOPIANISM.) For the distinction between communism and socialism, see E. Durkheim, *Le Socialisme* (Paris, 1928), translated by Charlotte Sattler as *Socialism and Saint-Simon* (Antioch, Ohio, 1958) and as *Socialism* (New York, 1962); V. Pareto, *Les Systèmes socialistes* (Paris, 1902); and P. Sweezy, *Socialism* (New York, 1949).

NEIL MCINNES

COMMUNISM, PHILOSOPHY UNDER. Communism as a political movement regards itself as resting upon and implying the philosophy of dialectical materialism. In all countries under communist rule, dialectical materialism and its social application, historical materialism, are presented as the official philosophy, deviation from which is at best an error and at worst a counterrevolutionary act.

The politicalization of philosophy by communist parties and governments cannot be overstressed. Lenin's principle of *partiinost* (partisanship or party-mindedness) presented dialectical materialism as a weapon in the struggle for communism. The repression of non-Marxist philosophies became a matter of defending and strengthening the dictatorship of the proletariat. Communist countries have put enormous stress on teaching and propagating the popular conclusions of dialectical materialism to the widest possible audience—Soviet primers of Marxist–Leninist philosophy have been published in editions of 250,000 and 500,000 copies—and philosophers have been expected to make their philosophic activity an integral part of such education, in order to carry out the dialectical principle of the unity of theory and practice.

The Russian Bolsheviks after 1917 transformed communist philosophy into a dogmatic theology with sacred texts (the works of Marx, Engels, Lenin, and, for a period, Stalin), an ecclesiastical authority that may not be challenged (the Communist party), official teachers (the approved party ideologists), and innumerable heresies suppressed and persecuted as such. Under Stalin this dogmatism forced communist philosophers for their own safety to consistently reduce any position they were arguing against to one which the classics had denounced. It also led them to emulate the dogmatic style of Lenin, with its abusive expressions, its readiness to reduce philosophical positions to simple issues, and its quickness to ascribe unworthy political motives to any opponent. The Marxist view of philosophy as a reflection of economic and political interest led communist philosophers to merge the concepts of philosophy and ideology. Finally, the combination of dogmatism and of Marxist belief in unilinear progress and the class nature of philosophy led to a conception of philosophic education as the teaching of attested conclusions and the denial of perennial philosophical puzzles.

Since the Soviet Union was the first, and for some thirty years, the only, communist country, the main lines of communist philosophy were laid down there. Soviet philosophy may be divided into three periods: a period of discussion, 1917–1931; a Stalinist period of rigid dogmatism, 1931–1947; and a period of renewed discussion and growing professionalization, beginning in 1947.

SOVIET PHILOSOPHY 1917–1931

The teachers of philosophy in Russian universities at the time of the Bolshevik revolution were for the most part religious philosophers, Hegelians, and Neo-Kantians. During the disorganization of the war-communism period (1917–1921), many of them were permitted to continue their teaching. In 1921 a campaign to remove non-Marxist professors was inaugurated, together with an ideological campaign to expose religious and "idealist" views. More than a hundred leading intellectuals were arrested in August 1922 and were banished from Russia a few months later. These included virtually all the leading figures in Russian academic philosophy: N. A. Berdyaev, S. N. Bulgakov, S. L. Frank, I. A. Ilyin, L. P. Karsavin, N. O. Lossky, and the Neo-Kantian I. I. Lapshin. From that time on, anti-Marxist philosophical activity became a clandestine, illegal political act.

Among Marxists, however, an official dogma and authoritarian control were not fully established until the consolidation of the Stalinist dictatorship in the years 1929–1931. The huge Russian editions of the works of Marx, Engels, and Lenin begun early in the 1920s were increasingly appealed to as doctrinal authority; but there were important disagreements about the respective importance of dialectic and materialism in the Marxist system of dialectical materialism. Both sides were published by official publishing houses and in the newly founded communist philosophical journal *Pod Znamenem Marksizma* ("Under the Banner of Marxism"), and some quasi-Marxist philosophers were able to issue books bearing the imprint "published by the author."

Mechanism. While the tradition established by G. V. Plekhanov and supported by Lenin insisted that philosophy was a crucial part of Marxism and rested on a creative, materialist development of Hegelian dialectic, a group consisting largely of natural scientists claimed that Marxism meant the overcoming of all philosophy and its supersession by science. This group of "mechanists" consisted of S. K. Minin, I. M. Skvortsov-Stepanov, A. I. Variash, A. K. Timiriazev (son of the famous Russian physiologist K. A. Timiriazev), Z. A. Tseitlin, V. N. Sarabianov, and, in some respects, N. I. Bukharin and L. I. Akselrod-Ortodoks.

The most extreme of the antiphilosophical views held by members of this group was expressed in Minin's 1922 article "Filosofiya za Bort" ("Overboard with Philosophy"), but even Stepanov in his *Istoricheskii Materializm i Sovremennoe Estestvoznanie* ("Historical Materialism and Contemporary Natural Science," 1927), wrote: "The Marxist recognizes no special field of 'philosophical activity' distinct from that of science; for the Marxist, materialist philosophy consists in the latest and most general findings of modern science. To understand any organic phenomenon is to trace it back to relatively simple chemical and physical processes" (G. A. Wetter, *Dialectical Materialism*, translated by Peter Heath). Bukharin proposed transcribing the "mystical" language of Hegelian dialectics into the language of modern mechanics by treating the theory of equilibrium as a more general formulation, "purged of idealist elements," of the laws governing material systems in motion.

The mechanists argued that the dialectic is merely a method and is not present in reality; there is, therefore, no special science of dialectic. They attributed all motions to impulses from without: while they recognized "contradiction" within a system, they saw such contradiction as the conflict of two separate forces within that system. The mechanists also argued that quality can be completely deduced from and reduced to quantity. They denied that there were basic dialectic "leaps" from the inorganic to the organic and from the organic to consciousness. In the social field the mechanists relied on a rigid economic determinism (*stikhiinost'*), according to which socialism is fated and comes about by gradual numerical changes in social forces. Freedom, they argued, is not a true dialectical counterpart to necessity; rather, it is an illusory concept expressing the fact that we do not know all the operative causes.

Deborinism. The mechanist school was strongly opposed by a number of Soviet philosophers under the leadership of A. M. Deborin, including Milonov, Perelman, S. I. Hessen, G. S. Tymianski, N. A. Karev, I. K. Luppol, Y. E. Sten, Dimitriev, and Markovski. The Deborinists emphasized the importance and integrity of the philosophy of dialectical materialism, basing their view to a considerable extent on the work of Plekhanov.

The general tendency of the Deborinist view was to reject both the a priori philosophy of nature and a purely empirical conception of natural science that rejects philosophy altogether. Science, which investigates individual facts, must make use of the dialectical method, which alone enables it to weld these facts into a single whole. The Deborinists, in opposition to Bukharin, emphasized the internal contradiction of the truly Hegelian dialectic, in which the antithesis is presupposed by the thesis, brought into being by it, and held in a single system with it. The Deborinists also stressed the law of the transformation of quantity into quality and therefore the leaps and the emergence of new forms. The naive mechanists, the Deborinists argued, neglected the specific character of the definite levels or stages of development of matter (being, life, consciousness) and the character of these stages as particular "nodes" or categories of being. The origin of the organic can be derived from the inorganic, but its form cannot.

Condemnations of 1929 and 1931. Until 1925–1926 the mechanists were the dominant force in Soviet cultural life, even though in 1922 Lenin had written to the journal *Under the Banner of Marxism*, advising Bolshevik philosophers to regard themselves as a society of materialist friends of the Hegelian dialectic. The first publication (1925) of Engels' *Dialectics of Nature* (written 1872–1886) lent his support to the proposition that higher forms cannot be reduced, without residue, to lower forms; and further support came from the publication (1929) of Lenin's *Philosophical Notebooks*, which treated philosophy as a central and creative field of Marxist endeavor.

In 1929 the Second All-Union Conference of Marxist–Leninist Scientific Institutions adopted a resolution condemning mechanism as "carrying on what was in essence a struggle against the philosophy of Marxism–Leninism, not understanding the foundations of materialist dialectics, substituting for revolutionary materialist dialectics a vulgar evolutionism, and for materialism, positivism, preventing . . . the penetration of the methodology of dialectical materialism into the realm of natural science." Deborin was confirmed in his position as editor-in-chief of *Under the Banner of Marxism*, and the Timiriazev Scientific Institute, a stronghold of mechanism, was reorganized under the Deborinist Y. Y. Agol.

Mechanism was condemned both as a departure from the tradition of Marxism and as being out of step with the developments of contemporary science. The Deborinist victory, however, was short-lived. On September 27, 1929, Stalin condemned the mechanists but at the same time complained that theoreticians generally had not kept pace with practical developments in the Soviet Union. The speech was a signal for an attack on two fronts, spearheaded by two new figures, M. B. Mitin and P. F. Yudin, directors of the communist cell in the Moscow Institute of Red Philosophers. Mechanism was accused of being a right-wing deviation and the theoretical foundation of the kulak agents within the party (Bukharin had opposed Stalin's plans for forced collectivization on the ground that the wealthier peasants would in any case "inevitably" be drawn into socialism), of leading to economism and to Neo-Kantian and other revisionist doctrines.

The Deborinists, on the other hand, were accused of overemphasizing leaps (just as the mechanists had overemphasized evolutionary continuity) and of thus giving ideological support to Trotsky's "left-wing deviation," or what Stalin had labeled as Menshevizing idealism. They had taken over the Hegelian dialectic without transforming it into a materialist dialectic, they had separated form and content, and they had taken from Plekhanov his "erroneous" discounting of Lenin's copy theory of knowledge and his Feuerbachian attempt to solve the subject–object relation in epistemology in purely metaphysical terms without regard for historical and revolutionary reality. Above all, the Deborinists were accused of being "abstract," of divorcing theory from practice, philosophy from politics.

On January 25, 1931, after a speech by Stalin, the central

committee of the Communist party condemned both mechanism and "the idealist distortion of Marxism on the part of Comrades Deborin, Karev, Sten and others." Deborin recanted and publicly thanked the central committee and especially Comrade Stalin for having "restrained him just in time." Since then he has continued to live in Moscow, taking a modest part in the work of the Academy of Sciences and occasionally writing uncontroversial philosophical articles.

SOVIET PHILOSOPHY 1931–1947

The decree of January 25, 1931, was a turning point in the history of Soviet philosophy. Stalin was quickly elevated to the status of all wisdom; controversy was directed solely against bourgeois ideology; internal discussions quickly degenerated into the "routing out" of heresies or errors.

The new official philosophy remained close to the positions that Deborin had preached against the mechanists. The status and importance of philosophy as a discipline continued to be upheld, and Soviet philosophers continued to insist that phenomena of higher orders could not be reduced to those of lower orders. The law of the conflict and interpenetration of opposites was maintained as a fundamental law of dialectics distinguishing "true" Marxist philosophy from vulgar mechanistic materialism, but it was interpreted in a less Hegelian spirit.

The main difference between the new movment and Deborinism was one of spirit rather than of dogma. The Stalinist philosophers made themselves entirely subservient to the day-to-day requirements of party policies; they gave the impression that there was only one creative philosopher in the Soviet Union, Joseph Stalin. The leading official philosopher, M. B. Mitin, wrote in his *Dialekticheskii Materializm* ("Dialectical Materialism," Moscow, 1933): "The further advancement of Marxist–Leninist theory in every department, including that of the Philosophy of Marxism, is associated with the name of Comrade Stalin. In all Comrade Stalin's practical achievements, and in all his writings, there is set forth the whole experience of the world-wide struggle of the proletariat, the whole rich store-house of Marxist–Leninist theory." The main effort went into compiling official textbooks and into revising textbooks that had been outdated by new denunciations and shifts in the party line. Mitin and Razumovski published a two-volume textbook on dialectical and historical materialism (*Dialekticheskii i Istoricheskii Materializm*, Moscow, 1933), and other textbooks and monographs laying down the "correct" Marxist view on various philosophical questions were published. Few productions of the period were as philosophical as P. Dosev's *Teoriya Otrazheniya* ("*The Copy Theory*," Moscow and Leningrad, 1936).

The constitution and the purges. The new Stalin constitution adopted in 1936 was proclaimed as marking the end of the period of the construction of socialism. Socialism had now been achieved; there was much talk of socialist legality, of the creative role of socialist law, and of the rights and importance of human personality. The philosophical works published by Mitin and his colleagues between 1931 and 1935 were accused of abstract and scholastic presentation and of "political illiteracy," that is, of mentioning the writings of Trotsky and Zinoviev, who were about to be exposed in the great purge trials. Mitin acknowledged his error and promised to follow the party line on the philosophical front, so no action was taken against him. However, the purges of 1936–1938 and the atmosphere of terror that swept over the Soviet Union, followed by the destruction of World War II, enormously reduced the volume of philosophical production and almost completely removed any incentive for independent or original work even within the narrow confines of the new Stalinist philosophy.

A collectively written history and a dictionary of philosophy were begun, but there was virtually no original work of even slight significance done after 1936. In 1944, at the height of the war effort, the central committee complained of shortcomings in the work done by philosophers but criticized "serious errors" in the third volume of the history of philosophy, error which consisted of passing over in silence Hegel's reactionary attitudes, his nationalism, and his deification of the Germans as a chosen people.

Stalin's works had to be treated as authoritative and as displaying, on every occasion, unexampled signs of incredible genius. His short pamphlet *Dialekticheskii i Istoricheskii Materializm* (*Dialectical and Historical Materialism*, Moscow, 1938), initially published as part of *The History of the CPSU (B) Short Course*, was hailed by Mitin as a "creation . . . marking an epoch in the development of Marxist–Leninist philosophy, and of world historical significance." But to the professional philosopher there is not one sentence of Stalin's work that displays any philosophical competence or insight.

SOVIET PHILOSOPHY SINCE WORLD WAR II

With the end of World War II philosophical activity in the Soviet Union received a powerful new impetus. In 1946 it was decreed that logic should be taught in the upper grades of secondary school and that by 1948 a sufficient number of specialists should be trained for this purpose by the universities. However, the stress on *partiinost* was re-emphasized. *Istoriya Zapadno-evropeiskoi Filosofii* ("The History of Western European Philosophy," Moscow, 1946), by one of the most important Soviet philosophers, G. F. Aleksandrov (who in 1942 had won the Stalin prize for his work on Aristotle), was denounced by Stalin's commissar for culture, A. A. Zhdanov, as displaying the vice of "bourgeois objectivism." Before an audience of ninety leading "workers in philosophical science" from all over the Soviet Union, brought together by the central committee in June 1947, Zhdanov criticized Aleksandrov's work for the abstract neutrality of its style, for its failure to show Marxism as a revolutionary and qualitative leap in the history of philosophy, for not linking philosophical ideas with the material conditions of life, and especially for omitting Russian philosophy and thus giving tacit support to the "bourgeois" belittlement of Russian philosophy and the "bourgeois" distinction between Western and Eastern culture. Zhdanov went on to say that generally Stalin was dissatisfied with the timidity, abstractness, and laziness of Soviet philosophers, and that the time for a serious expansion of philosophical activity had come.

Liberalization under Stalin. There is some disagreement among Western writers whether the revival of Soviet philosophical discussion is best dated from 1947 or from the death of Stalin in March 1953. A number of factors making for philosophical improvement had begun to build up in the latter part of Stalin's regime but could not make themselves fully evident till his death and the comparative loosening of dogmatic control. The 1920s and the early 1930s had been periods of educational crash programs designed to maximize literacy and basic skills. By the late 1930s a more stable educational system producing better-trained people had emerged, but its impact on Soviet society was interrupted by the war. In the early postwar period there was once again the need for an enormous expansion of education, but this time at a much higher level. The sophistication of Soviet society had enormously increased, and so had the absolute numbers of people capable of reading serious work.

The postwar movement of Stalinist society toward the ethos of advanced industrial civilization also has its effects on the position of philosophy and ideological work in Marxist–Leninist dogma. In the 1920s and early 1930s the dialectic had been seen primarily as a weapon of criticism, connected with class struggle. From 1936 on, however, Stalin had begun to convert the dialectic into the basis for a stable ideology of Soviet rule. Its task now was not to sharpen class struggle but to help create consensus. The economic reductionism implicit in the materialist interpretation of history was modified. In his *Dialectical and Historical Materialism*, Stalin stressed the capacity of the ideological superstructure for reacting on the economic base. In 1950, in his *Marxism and Questions of Linguistics*, Stalin stressed the comparative independence of the ideological superstructure and the fact that there were certain cultural phenomena, such as language, which transcended class divisions and were therefore ideologically neutral. A similar independence was later ascribed to formal logic.

In line with this stress on the importance of ideology, the philosophers' discussions of 1947 were used to inaugurate a period of renewed philosophical activity. *Under the Banner of Marxism* had ceased publication in 1944, so in 1947 the journal *Voprosy Filosofii* ("Problems of Philosophy") was launched as a biannual; by 1957 it was a monthly. A second philosophical journal, *Filosofskie Nauki* ("Philosophical Sciences"), appeared under the auspices of the Ministry of Higher Education in 1958. The number of philosophical books published annually quadrupled in the decade 1948–1958; so did the number of *kandidat* theses in philosophy submitted in three leading Moscow institutions between 1947 and 1954. The number of graduate students of philosophy rose from about 1,000 in 1951 to 2,000 in 1954. In 1947 only three of the thirty universities (Moscow, Leningrad, and Kaunas) had full faculties of philosophy; in 1951 the editors of *Voprosy Filosofii* complained that such outlying philosophical institutes as those in the Ukraine, White Russia, and Georgia "confine themselves exclusively to the history of philosophy in their respective countries and are content to leave the working-out of contemporary problems of Marxist philosophy as a monopoly to the Philosophical Institute of the Academy of Sciences of the U.S.S.R. . ." (in Moscow). Since then the number of philosophical faculties at universities has been greatly increased, philosophical work outside Moscow and Leningrad has been greatly intensified, and in the University of Tiflis in Georgia, an extremely active philosophical center has emerged under the leadership of Professor K. S. Bakradze.

Nevertheless, during the final years of Stalin's rule the party continued as an active arbiter of philosophical and scientific questions. Criticism of contemporary "bourgeois" philosophy was carried on in the crudest and most vindictive terms. In 1948 the central committee organized a conference for the purpose of condemning orthodox genetics and announcing that the Michurin–Lysenko school, with its rejection of genes and its belief in the heritability of acquired characteristics, was the correct Marxist–Leninist view of biology. A. A. Maksimov and a group of philosophers of science attacked the physicists for using and defending the "subjective–idealist" theory of relativity but were successfully repelled. In 1950 Stalin's shattering blow to Marxist linguistics led to two years of hasty philosophical activities to bring the philosophical dogma into line with Stalin's new pronouncements.

Death of Stalin. The death of Stalin brought two new elements into the renewed philosophical activity. Within a year references to Stalin as a great philosophical genius disappeared from the journals, and demands for a certain respect for professional competence and integrity began to be heard. In 1956, at the 20th Congress of the CPSU, N. S. Khrushchev inaugurated a campaign for liquidating the cult of personality in Soviet cultural life. In 1961, at the 22d Congress, Stalin's errors, including the error of dogmatically laying down positions in fields in which he was not competent, were exposed to the world. By 1958 the leading Soviet philosopher, P. N. Fedoseev, was emphasizing the importance of concrete analysis in philosophy and the impropriety of importing methods appropriate to the struggle against hostile ideology into scientific discussions.

Weakening of dogmas. The trend toward professionalization and professional integrity in Soviet philosophical discussion has been accompanied by the relinquishing of some important dogmas. In 1955 discussions on the philosophy of science led to the acceptance of the theory of relativity as fully compatible, in its physical formulations, with the doctrines of dialectical materialism—it was taken to confirm the dialectical materialist view that geometry is a branch of physics, that space and time cannot be abstracted from matter, and that matter is not just inert material but can also be energy. (The materialist part of dialectical materialism thus came to mean no more than the proclamation that processes in or of "reality" were objective and existed independently of any observer.) The following year, cybernetics (previously condemned as a bourgeois pseudo science) was accepted as the science of computers, which brings out certain important analogies with human thinking. In connection with the acceptance of cybernetics, the development of mathematical logic and the truth-table technique were accepted by an increasing number of Soviet philosophers. At the same time the regime of Lysenko in biology was overthrown in favor of orthodox genetics.

Studies in the dialectic. The above developments have produced significant signs of a new atmosphere in considerable areas of Soviet philosophy. There is much emphasis on problems within dialectical materialism—the relation of formal and dialectical logic, the philosophy of physics, the relationship and coordination of the categories of dialectical materialism, and so on. An increasing number of works on these questions are being published by university presses. The standard argument in such works is still by deduction from unquestioned fundamental principles of dialectical materialism, but opponents are not necessarily abused, and the use of quotations from the classics increasingly looks beyond the literal words to the context and spirit in which they were written. In the fairly serious discussion that has been proceeding on the law of contradiction and Zeno's paradoxes, at least one writer has regarded the solution proffered by Engels as quite inadequate.

Criticism and history of philosophy. In the history of philosophy as well as in the criticism of contemporary Western philosophy there have been similar changes in style and seriousness of content. *Voprosy Filosofii*, especially in 1955, objected to the nihilistic denial of the value of the history of philosophy, to improper attacks on "objectivism," to the overvaluation of the role of Russian philosophy, and to false conceptions that the philosophy of Marxism did not build on previous achievements. A five-to-six-volume encyclopedia of philosophy (Vol. I, Moscow, 1960), under the editorship of F. V. Konstantinov, presents a fair and reasonably accurate account of the work of contemporary Western philosophers and of such condemned philosophers of the 1920s as L. I. Akselrod-Ortodoks and Deborin. (The politically controversial Bukharin is simply omitted.) The new *Philosophical Dictionary* edited by M. M. Rosenthal and P. F. Yudin in 1963 displays an enormous improvement over their earlier *Short Philosophical Dictionary* (1951) in range, technicality, and fairness of entries. The serious, unabusive tone of K. S. Bakradze's book on contemporary bourgeois philosophy (*Ocherki po Istorii Noveishei i Sovremennoi Burzhuaznoi Filosofii*, Tiflis, 1960), of A. S. Bogomolov's studies in contemporary bourgeois theories of evolution and development, especially his *Ideya Razvitiya v Burzhuaznoi Filosofii* (Moscow, 1962), and of two papers by B. V. Biriukov on Gottlob Frege has no parallel in Soviet philosophy before 1955. Articles by A. J. Ayer, Niels Bohr, Wilfrid Sellars, and Mario Bunge have been published in *Voprosy Filosofii* (although always with dialectical materialist comment or reply).

Ethics, aesthetics, social philosophy. The increasing stress placed by the party on the role of ideology as an educator for the conditions of the new life has produced, since 1951, a growing concern with the problems of Marxist–Leninist ethics, a field in which A. F. Shishkin has become a leading representative of the official view. The tendency has been to weaken or reject altogether the end-directedness of Marxist ethics and also to emphasize the categories of ethical living as expressions of commonly accepted rules of social life, although in rather conventional terms that ignore the philosophical analysis of ethical concepts. The reaction against Stalinism has produced a climate in which the integrity of aesthetic and ethical qualities are stressed, as reflected in a recent work by the Leningrad professor V. P. Tugarinov, *O Tsennostiakh Zhizni i Kultury* ("On the Values of Life and Culture," Leningrad, 1960). While Soviet theorists reject as "revisionist" the Marxian humanism which emphasizes alienation as a fundamental category going deeper than mere economic exploitation, recent Soviet writing has put more emphasis on the early works of Marx and on the logical structure and philosophical presuppositions of Marx's work in general. In law there have been some studies on truth and the judicial process. Sociology, previously rejected as a bourgeois substitute for Marxism, now has a number of defenders and limited research is being undertaken. There is an increasing number of articles on Indian, classical Chinese, Latin American, Korean, and other philosophies, although the result is to increase the blurring of the distinction between technical philosophy and mere proclamation of outlooks.

General characteristics. The fundamental principles of dialectical materialism are still treated as attested assumptions that cannot be challenged, but they are being reinterpreted with specific problems in mind. In ontology and logic there is a serious awareness of problems; there have been some serious studies on evolution and emergence; there is a steady, intelligent concern with the philosophy of physics. In all these fields, however, problems can still be dealt with only in the framework of dialectical materialism which often involves the shirking or glossing over of problems. Soviet philosophers have not developed the precision of language, the skepticism about large-scale metaphysical answers, and the habit of examining limited problems, utterances, and concepts in depth. In the fields that come closer to social questions—in ethics, aesthetics, and the historical aspects of the history of philosophy—work is still rather poor and uncritical. The philosophy of society in any serious sense does not exist.

PHILOSOPHY IN OTHER COMMUNIST COUNTRIES

When other communist states were established after World War II, they universally acknowledged the "leading role" of the Communist party of the Soviet Union. The official philosophy implemented by each ruling Communist party thus became the philosophy of dialectical materialism in the Soviet form of that period, and the later Soviet revisions were incorporated when made, with the aim of eradicating all other philosophical views as erroneous or counterrevolutionary. In practice certain differences arose, depending on the state of philosophy in the particular country before the take-over and on political developments since the take-over. These differences related to the force of unorthodox views in the country, to the tone of philosophical discussion, and to the sophistication forced on the dialectical materialists in dealing with opposition. They did not relate to the content of the official view, which has on the whole been entirely parasitic on Soviet Marxism–Leninism and has made no independent contributions to it. The official institutes of philosophy, like those in the non-Russian states of the Soviet Union in the time of Stalin, have seen their task as being primarily the development of a Marxist interpretation of the history of philosophy in their own countries and the combating of heresies with which they are confronted. This, generally, is the position in East Germany, Czechoslovakia, Rumania, Bulgaria, and even Hungary, where the independent and important philosophical work of Georg Lukács, vacillating between original philosophic contributions and orthodox but cultured Stalinism, has on the whole produced only dogmatic reactions from communist philosophers (such as the poor and barely philosophical work of the director of the Philosophical Institute, Josef Szigeti). Recent discussions in the Soviet Union, have, however, spread to these countries. In Hungary, György Tamas is currently preparing an encyclopedia of logic that will attempt to tackle the problem of the relationship between formal and dialectical logic. In Czechoslovakia there has been some work on questions of methodology. In East Germany the development of sociology is beginning and there has been some interest in ethics, but the Marxist work of Ernst Bloch and his disciples has been condemned.

Philosophy in Communist China, Poland, and Yugoslavia is less directly parasitic on that of the Soviet Union. Since the first translations of Western philosophers, made between 1889 and 1910, and the New Renaissance movement of 1917, Marxism has been one of the philosophical trends in westernizing Chinese thinking. Ch'en Tu-hsia, Li Ta-chao and Yeh Ch'ing wrote on philosophy from a Marxist standpoint in the 1920s and 1930s, drawing increasingly on the work of Plekhanov, Lenin, and Bukharin. In the 1940s dialectical materialism in China became Maoism. Mao Tse-tung followed the Stalinist textbooks in philosophy, although his works, like much of Chinese Marxist writing, mix traditional Chinese conceptions with Soviet Marxism–Leninism. Mao's essay "On Practice" (1937) links dialectical materialism, in part unconsciously, with traditional Chinese conceptions of knowledge as a guide to action and of cyclical patterns arising from the waxing and waning of opposites. Since the formation of the Chinese People's Republic, Chinese communist philosophy has been noted mainly for its emphasis on practical activity. The Chinese communists have carried the Leninist–Stalinist doctrine of *partiinost* to new lengths. While there has been philosophical work done in the institutes and universities, it is mainly Marxist reinterpretation of traditional Chinese philosophy and is generally done by collective effort; this work must be carried out in an atmosphere of constant denunciation for ideological errors. China's best-known philosopher, Fung Yu-lan, who remained in communist China and accepted Marxism, has promised to rewrite his works but has several times had to recant new errors following denunciations by his students.

In Poland the general precommunist sophistication of philosophical work has even affected the work of official communist dogmatists. Yugoslav philosophy, despite Yugoslavia's breach with Russia, remained until 1957 fairly orthodox dialectical materialism, largely because past philosophical traditions were weak. Since 1957 there has been a growing tendency among Yugoslav philosophers toward Marxist humanism. This tendency emphasizes the ethical aspect of Marxist doctrine and the overcoming of alienation through social praxis, and sees in the Yugoslav form of communism the realization of, or at least the willingness to work toward, such humanism.

Bibliography

Blakeley, T. H., *Soviet Theory of Knowledge.* Dordrecht, 1964. A good exposition.

Bocheński, J. M., ed., *Studies in Soviet Thought* (1961—) The best-informed periodical on Soviet and east European philosophy. See also the Sovietica series of books published at Dordrecht under the general editorship of Bocheński.

Joravsky, David, *Soviet Marxism and Natural Science.* London, 1961.

Jordan, Z. A., *Philosophy and Ideology. The Development of Philosophy and Marxism–Leninism in Poland Since the Second World War.* Dordrecht, 1963.

Müller-Markus, S., *Einstein und die Sowjetphilosophie.* Dordrecht, 1960. Describes Soviet discussions on relativity.

Somerville, John, ed., *Soviet Studies in Philosophy.* A journal of translations from Soviet philosophical periodicals.

Wetter, G. A., *Der dialektische Materialismus. Seine Geschichte und sein System in der Sowjetunion.* Vienna and Freiburg, 1953. Translated by Peter Heath as *Dialectical Materialism: A Historical and Systematic Survey of Philosophy in the Soviet Union.* London, 1958. The best general survey.

EUGENE KAMENKA

COMPUTING MACHINES. The process of calculation has frequently engaged the attention of students of mental processes, perhaps because of its seeming simplicity and freedom from certain complicating emotional factors. Calculating machines have, in fact, existed for centuries, although they lacked certain essential features that characterize the modern computing machine.

To do even the simplest kinds of calculation with a machine, we must have a way of representing numbers. The word "calculate" comes from the Latin word for "stone" or "pebble," for in ancient times (and in some places even today) simple calculations were often done using piles or rows of pebbles, or *calculi*, to represent the numbers. The process of calculation involved translating the starting numbers, or "inputs" in modern terminology, into appropriately representative piles of stones, performing the desired manipulations on the piles of stones, and translating the resulting piles of stones into the final numbers, or "outputs." Over the centuries numerous ingenious ways were found to facilitate the manipulation of the stones or to substitute other forms of representation that were simpler to manipulate, such as the wired beads of the abacus.

History of computing machines. From the seventeenth century on, geared mechanisms were frequently used as calculating devices and held the attention of such noted mathematicians as Pascal and Leibniz. The representation of numbers by positions of toothed wheels was a great step forward, for it permitted part of the manipulation of the representation to be done automatically by geared mechanisms, thus redefining the relationship between the man and his computing machine. In addition to merely aiding the human calculator by holding numbers for him in a reliable way, the machine became involved in the actual algorithms, or manipulation procedures. Whereas an abacus operator must move his stones according to the proper procedure to perform an addition, the operator of a simple geared calculating machine merely enters the two numbers to be added and presses a button which causes the machine to perform the addition algorithm by rotating gears appropriately.

There are, of course, more complex arithmetic procedures in which addition, multiplication, and so forth are merely elementary steps themselves. Thus, if we possess a machine that has the ability to perform addition algorithms automatically, we can build higher-level algorithms for use with that machine, thus putting the operator back in the position of a manipulator, an executor of algorithms. As long as the calculating machine is rather slow at performing its algorithms, the speed of the machine will be the limiting factor in the speed of the entire calculation, for a human operator will rarely have to intervene to perform his tasks. With the advancement of technology, however, the ability of machines to perform the simple algorithms of arithmetic was improved to the point where the slowness of the human operator in linking together the subalgorithms into larger algorithms prevented further improvements. Attention became focused on the problem of putting the entire algorithm under the control of a machine, a problem first seriously examined by Charles Babbage in the early nineteenth century.

The notion of algorithms. We are all familiar with simple algorithms, mostly involving written representations of numbers. In an early grade we are taught an algorithm for adding two numbers; in the next grade, an algorithm for multiplying; in the next, an algorithm for long division; and, finally, an algorithm for taking square roots. Essentially, an algorithm specifies a sequence of operations which, when carried out on numerical representations, yields the numerical representation of the results—or answer, in school terminology. ("Write the addend on the paper; write the augend under the addend, being careful that the decimal points are in line"; and so forth.) The specification of an algorithm can be made explicit in terms of the basic operations a machine can perform rather than in terms of what a second-grader can perform. Once made explicit, the algorithm itself can be "coded" into some representation that can be sensed by the machine. If we so code our algorithms, we need only attach to the machine the algorithm it needs for interpreting the coded operations in sequence and using them to direct its step-by-step execution of its basic algorithms. Here, then, is the essential formulation of an automatic computing machine: The basic machine has built into it the ability to accept coded numbers as input (perhaps written on punched cards, as Babbage envisioned, or on a tape that the machine can move back and forth); the ability to accept coded specifications, or "programs" (perhaps written on another tape); the ability to manipulate the input numbers according to that specification; and the ability to write output numbers (perhaps on yet another tape).

The Turing machine. In 1936 A. M. Turing initiated a line of theoretical investigation that is still very active today: Given a particular computing machine of this type—that is, a particular representation of numbers, a particular set of algorithms, a particular arrangement of its tapes, and a particular way of specifying a program for it—just what computations could the machine perform? One surprising result of this investigation of computability is that even though machine characteristics might vary widely, most machines that could do any computations at all could do no better than the rather simple configuration which Turing originally proposed. Thus, the Turing machine became a sort of standard of computational power and limitations. Turing also showed that it was possible to build a universal machine, universal in the sense that it could perform any calculation that any other Turing machine could perform. Finally, he showed that there were some numbers that such a universal machine could not compute.

At about the same time Turing was working, efforts began toward the realization of an automatic computing machine in practical form—first primarily electromechanical (using relays and switches to represent numbers) and then electronic (using vacuum tubes). A century earlier Babbage had tried to use geared mechanisms, but he never quite succeeded in overcoming the technical difficulties. As the new electromechanical and electronic machines came into use, it was quickly realized that the limitations proved by Turing were far less strict than the practical limitations imposed by the physical form of the devices themselves. For instance, Turing did not attempt to distinguish between the abilities of two machines on the basis of the time it took each one to perform a certain algorithm. Also, Turing's idealized machines did not make errors. Real devices made errors, however, and often computations could not be made because they would take too long. Only recently have mathematical machine theorists turned to the problems of speed and error, and few, if any, of their theorems have any practical bearing on real computing problems.

Computer organization. The problems of speed and error are inextricably intertwined. On a machine with a finite probability of error at each step, the more steps an algorithm takes, the less likely it is to produce a correct result (though there are certain partially self-correcting algorithms). Conversely, the less likely a machine is to make an error, the more steps between errors there are in which to execute longer error-free algorithms. Even with self-correcting algorithms, the more frequently errors occur, the more time the machine will spend upon the part of the algorithm that does the correcting (and upon the corrections of the correcting part ad infinitum). Ultimately, the machine may not be able to keep up and thus may never return to the task of progressing through the useful part of the algorithm.

In practice, the problem of errors and speed is attacked by trying to increase the speed and reliability of components, by organizing the machine so as to perform more computation with fewer steps, and by building self-correcting procedures into the machine and its programs. The first approach is essentially a matter of technology, except for the philosophical question of whether perfect components can ever be fabricated. The second and third approaches, however, are of considerable philosophical interest but require further investigation into the way real machines are built.

Memory. The first practical improvement in organization over a simple Turing-type machine is the addition of a store, or "memory," for holding intermediate results. Since the simple Turing machine may use the same tape for input and output, the machine with a separate memory has no logical advantage—in the sense of computability—over it, for any intermediate results may be written on the tape as output and read back as input whenever needed. In actual machines, since the main memory is usually limited in size because of cost and engineering considerations, the input and output tapes are often used in exactly this way, as an intermediate store. Such practices are avoided whenever possible, however, for the serial nature of the tape makes it necessary to spend large amounts of time scanning over tape that has no significance to the current stage of the algorithm. Thus, a memory capable of storing only a few numbers—where any number can be obtained in a single step—could decrease computation steps by factors of thousands or millions over the simple Turing machine, depending, of course, on the problem at hand.

There seems to be a highly suggestive empirical law that the more storage available for use on a given problem, the faster the computation can be carried out. Keeping all the answers in the store, classified according to the input that produces them, provides a particularly fast and simple universal algorithm. With a big enough memory a machine can store all possible inputs together with their outputs and thus solve any problem by "table-look-up." One way of charactering the complexity of a computation task, then, is to describe the size memory that would be needed on a "table-look-up" machine. The size is often surprisingly small.

In the game of ticktacktoe, for example, there are only 9 possible positions (not all of them unique) after the first move and no more than 72 possible positions after the second move. In fact, the simplest calculation shows that there are no more than 9! (or 362,888) possible games of ticktacktoe, a number that makes it quite possible to store all possible games in the memory of a computer in such a way that it will become a perfect (barring mechanical errors) ticktacktoe player. A similar analysis for the game of three-dimensional ticktacktoe (in which four in a row must be obtained) indicates that no more than 64! (or about 10^{89}) games are possible, a number far beyond the capacity of any known or contemplated computer memory. This does not mean that a computer cannot be built to play three-dimensional ticktacktoe very well or even perfectly. As a matter of fact, such programs have been written (but not using a simple "table-look-up" technique) to enable rather small computers to beat any human opponent at the game. Such programs take advantage of the structure of the game to a far greater extent than does the simple "table-look-up" technique, recognizing, for example, that certain positions are identical if the board is simply rotated in space.

Specialized algorithmic structures. The recognition of regularities over a large class of problems and the incorporation of special facilities to manipulate them directly are a second way in which computers can be organized to show speed improvements over simple Turing machines, though again no logical advantage is introduced. In arithmetic, for example, efficient algorithms for taking square roots, finding trigonometric functions, and so forth might be built into the "hardware." There is, of course, a limit to the amount of structure that can be extracted from a class of problems and built into a computer. We do not, however, have a theory, even for mathematical problems, that can come close to estimating such a limit. Empirical observation shows that the narrower the class of problems, the more efficient the algorithms that can be built into the machine. In a way, the memory can be thought of as merely another special structure, one which is useful for an extremely wide class of problems. On the other hand, we could think of the special algorithmic structures as specialized forms of memory, for they are often realized in actual machines by using tables in parts of the memory.

Detection and self-correction. The possibility of self-correcting procedures was first seriously examined by C. E. Shannon for information transmission and by John von Neumann for computations of a more general nature. Many of the important results they reached can be appreciated by rather simple intuitive arguments, though they are supported by difficult mathematical arguments. For example, it is easy to see that we can improve our confidence in a given computation by performing it independently on different machines and comparing results. If, say, a given machine has a probability of .9 of producing an errorless computation, we can raise the probability of a correct answer to about .97 by using three machines and a two-out-of-three rule. We will also have a number of cases where, since we get three different results, we know that we cannot choose any of the results with confidence. Only very rarely will we make the mistake of choosing a wrong answer and thinking it is right because two wrong answers were the same. By an extension of this technique, we can raise the probability of a correct answer to an arbitrarily high level (though not to 1) at the expense of a vast amount of equipment. A problem of great practical importance is how to achieve high levels of reliability without this expense.

Many algorithms, although not self-correcting, have checkpoints in them at which an error in an earlier stage can be detected. For example, in calculating a square root by successive approximations, the approximation at each stage can be checked by squaring it and comparing its square with the number whose square root we are seeking. If the computer's error is not due to a permanent failure of one of its components (so that it would repeat the same error endlessly), such an error-detecting algorithm can always be turned into an error-correcting algorithm. To the original algorithm we add checkpoints at which the current result is checked and, if correct, stored for possible future use. If a checkpoint is reached at which the current result does not check, the algorithm is returned to the earlier correct stage, and the correct results for that stage are restored. In this manner actual computations can be made highly independent of the intermittent malfunctioning of the machine's parts.

When a component in a computer fails permanently, different procedures are required. Such a component can be repaired or replaced by human operators, but it has been shown both theoretically and practically that machines can be built which continue to work correctly in spite of such permanent failures or which can actually locate and repair or replace their own defective components. Von Neumann also showed how to build a machine, with the computational power of a Turing machine, that will reproduce itself given an environment containing an adequate supply of simple building materials. The theoretical—and, even more strikingly, the practical—demonstration of machines with the ability to correct their own errors, repair their broken components, or even reproduce themselves has laid to rest a number of classical philosophical problems about differences between biological organisms and machines. It has also opened up an even larger number of new problems and suggested fruitful lines of investigation for their solution.

A few cautionary words on terminology are in order at this point. In both the practical and theoretical work with computing machines, a number of new concepts arise that must be given names. In any developing field we are always between the Scylla of creating entirely new technical terms and the Charybdis of using suggestive but imprecise old words. The relationship between the work of computers and the mental work of men has led to the adoption of a large number of highly controversial terms, such as "memory," "language," "read," "write," and "decide." Such words were chosen to simplify the work of professionals working with computers and not to guide or mislead philosophers in assessing the computer's real or potential powers. Philosophical arguments must be settled on the basis of the facts of the matter, not the words chosen to present those facts.

Nonnumerical computations. Error-correction, self-repair, and self-reproduction are all conspicuous properties of biological organisms, but the properties that seem to distinguish man from other biological species have always been of more intense interest to philosophers. Investigations of the behavior of nonhuman species indicate that most, if not all, of these distinguishing properties stem from or are related to man's ability to use symbols. What light can computing machines throw in this dark corner?

Nonarithmetic procedures. It is frequently said that computers are limited in their abilities because they can perform only simple arithmetic operations, such as addition and multiplication. We have seen, however, that algorithms of extreme complexity can be executed because of the computer's ability to integrate sequences of algorithms into more complex algorithms. Furthermore, such comments overlook the computer's ability to perform decision algorithms—that is, to choose among two or more alternative paths of a program, basing that choice on the appropriate properties of previously computed quantities. For example, a program might contain three alternative paths to use, depending on whether a number in memory were positive, negative, or zero. And, just as in the case of arithmetic algorithms, such simple decisions can be compounded to gain the effect of enormously complex decision procedures.

Furthermore, it is not true that computers are restricted to working with numbers, though even if it were true, the arithmetization of formal systems, as introduced by Gödel, shows that a machine with strictly arithmetic powers can work in other symbolic domains by a suitable coding in terms of numbers. As a practical matter, such an arithmetization would not be efficient, so computing machines are built with much more general abilities to represent and perform algorithms on symbolic information. Thus, if we examine a portion of the memory of a computer and find, for example, 100110010100001101001000001000101000011111000111000100000000101 in the basic "bit" (binary digit) code, we cannot tell without examining in detail the program that manipulates this information what it is supposed to represent. It might be a number, three numbers, ten numbers, someone's name, part of a map, an entry in a Russian–English dictionary, the statement of a geometric theorem, some instructions from the program, a position in a chess game, three bars of the viola part in a string quartet, instructions telling a milling machine how to cut a turbine blade, or the second line of a rhyming couplet. It might even be a combination of some of these things or one thing part of the time and something else later. In fact, it could also represent nothing at all, being merely waste symbols left over from unknown previous operations. And if the computer can represent so many things symbolically, it has at least the possibility of performing some extremely sophisticated tricks of symbol manipulation, such as punning, rhyming, composing *double-entendres,* drawing cartoons and caricatures, solving puzzles, or writing music.

Verbal ability. The most obvious type of nonnumerical symbol processing is written language, and, as we might expect, most of the practical applications of computers involve the processing of language data of all types. The simplest programs deal with processes common to everyday business operations, such as arranging names in alphabetical order, looking up information in alphabetical directories, or selecting items from files of information according to simple matching criteria. On higher levels are programs that can correct spelling errors, break cryptographic codes, search legal decisions for applicable precedents to cases, and so forth. At an even higher level, encroaching perhaps on things that, if done by human beings, would be said to involve "thought," are programs that do simple but effective translations from one language to another, identify the author of manuscripts of unknown origin according to their "style," perhaps fill in missing words or phrases (as was done with the Dead Sea Scrolls), or "abstract" articles by extracting important sentences. In these applications there is a great deal of controversy over just how "good" a job the computer is actually doing, but there has always been controversy about what constitutes a good translation or abstract.

Game playing. The subjective nature of so many verbal tasks has perhaps provided much of the impetus for attempts to program computers to play games. A competitive game—be it checkers, go, or ticktacktoe—has, whatever else its complications, a simple criterion for excellence of performance: The better player wins, or at least the winning player is better. Thus, a computer program for playing checkers that enables the machine to beat its own inventor and most other people (including checker champions) is of some philosophical interest. Other nonverbal tasks, such as the control of chemical plants and other industrial processes, are handled by computers in ways that are, without much doubt, superior to the job that human beings can do.

What is the significance of a computer's ability to outstrip a human being, even in a task where there is little or no controversy about who (or what) is doing the better job? In trying to answer such a question, the philosopher immediately faces two complementary pitfalls that he can avoid only by having a certain amount of knowledge about computer technology. Both these pitfalls are based on the well-known fact that people are easily fooled by appearances. For example, when we say that a computer can play checkers, we do not necessarily mean that the computer actually moves the pieces on the board, for we are satisfied that once we have a program that can designate the winning moves, it is merely a matter of engineering to attach a mechanical "hand" that will pick up checkers and move them according to the computer's directions. In other words, the essence of the game of checkers as a human task is in the abstract play, not in the physical movement of pieces. Unfortunately, it is much easier to impress people with a checker-playing machine if it actually does move the checkers—and the more anthropomorphic the process, the better. A certain amount of showmanship in the output device can definitely be substituted for a certain amount of quality of play, at least as far as initial impressions are concerned. But output devices are becoming more impressive as the technology advances—computers can respond with speech, drawings, moving pictures, music, and other striking acts—so that ever more caution must be exercised in the analysis of what the essential symbolic difficulty is in a particular performance.

We may, of course, err with equal ease on the other side of such questions. Since we are posing the questions, we must beware of setting criteria so specific to human idiosyncrasies that they rule out a priori the possibility of any machine's performance being judged significant. We may be surprised to find how little mystery is left to human thought processes after the idiosyncrasies are eliminated. Observations of people interacting with computers indicate that we tend to attach the appellation thinking to some extremely simple behaviors as long as we forget or do not know we are interacting with a machine. When people play games with computers, for example, they often begin by referring to the machine with a rather self-conscious "it," but as they become involved in the intricacies of the competition, they quite unconsciously switch to a more comfortable "he." As such interactions become an increasingly common experience—and even today many people are dealing with computers over the telephone or teletype or by mail without ever suspecting this—we shall have a new standard by which to measure the complexity of symbolic behavior.

Programming. In the wake of some spectacular performance by a computer, we often hear the performance discounted with the words, "The machine is only doing what it was programmed to do." This remark may be taken to imply either that a machine cannot do anything it is not explicitly programmed to do or that for the behavior of an organism to be worthy of note, it must be incapable of being programmed. To answer the questions raised by such a remark, we should know precisely which performances can be programmed and which, if any, cannot.

Although it is possible to build a machine that is capable of executing only a single program, actual machines are built with the capacity to execute a vast number of programs, the choice being left to the user of the machine rather than to its designer. In a very real sense a computing machine is not a complete machine until it is provided with a program to execute; another way of thinking about a computer is as a chameleon-like device capable of being any one of a number of machines according to the program given to it. Most computing machines today are "stored-program" machines, which means that the specification of the program is coded and stored in the memory of the machine just as a set of numbers, letters, or any other symbolic information might be stored. Thus, if we know the size of the memory of the machine, we can begin to estimate the number of different programs it can execute—that is, the number of different machines it can be.

Surprise and creativity. An important theorem in the theory of machines shows that it is possible to perform experiments in which the behavior of a machine is observed and its internal state—the program it is currently executing—is deduced. Since the program explicitly determines the behavior of a machine for all sequences of inputs, this theorem tells us, in effect, that after we have observed the machine for a while, we can know all about its future performance; there will be no surprises in its behavior. What this seems to say, then, is that a machine with a program cannot possibly "create" anything new, but this argument merits a more careful examination. First, errors may occur; thus, the program does not quite explicitly determine the future behavior of the machine. Because we have built computers primarily for the task of eliminating the types of errors flesh is heir to, the probability of errors is low, and we will not often be surprised by the machine in this manner. We might, however, build machines with error rates comparable to man's and see how often we found unexpected, or "creative," results—but there is not much economic demand for such fallible computers.

The second weakness in this argument has to do with speed. How long must an experiment be that tells us what program is in the machine? Roughly, the experiment involves reading a tape that has as many symbols on it as there are possible programs. But, as we have observed, we can estimate this number according to the memory size of the machine. To demolish the argument, then, we need note only that for a typical machine there might be any one of $10^{1000000}$ different programs stored in its memory, thus requiring a tape that could not conceivably be read by the machine using all of recorded time. And if that were not enough, we need observe only that the tapes attached to a machine can be thought of as an extension to its main memory; indeed, it is common for programs several times as large as the main memory to be stored on tape and called into the main memory in pieces. Such a machine might have $10^{10^{10}}$ or even more possible programs and could be counted on to supply a long series of surprises to its human operator.

We do not, of course, ordinarily program computers by filling them with huge sets of randomly generated instructions. On the contrary, the process of programming a computer is filled with checks and safeguards, each of which is intended to help prevent the programmer from getting anything unknown or unintended into his final program, precisely because we do not want surprises from a computer. Nevertheless, in spite of all safeguards and precautions experience tells us that any program can be counted on to surprise its own programmer many times. Most of those surprises, naturally, produce nothing useful—from our point of view, at least—but in the few experiments with programs that were supposed to surprise their programmers (by proving theorems, for example), the density of useful surprises was much higher. Thus, even the existence of a programmer does not imply the predictability of machine performance.

Machines and human beings. In a way those who argue for the existence of tasks performable by people and not performable by computers are forced into a position of never-ending retreat. If they can specify just what their task involves, then they admit the possibility of programming it on some machine. If they specify the task only according to procedures for recognizing it, they stand in danger of being fooled by a clever simulation. Worst of all, however, even if they construct proofs that a certain class of machines cannot perform certain tasks, they are vulnerable to the possibility of essentially new classes of machines being described or built. Furthermore, they bear the burden of proof that people can indeed perform the task in question—where again they stand in danger of being fooled by a clever simulation.

"Man is the measure of all things," says man. At the very least, computers have forced man to reinterpret the meaning of the measurements. Either the yardstick is not so long as we had thought or the things to be measured are growing longer every day. (See CYBERNETICS.)

Bibliography

Buchholz, Werner, ed., *Planning a Computer System.* New York, 1962. A collection of articles on the philosophy and designing of the (then) largest computing machine, examining many alternative organizations of a real computing machine.

Davis, Martin, *Computability and Unsolvability.* New York, 1958. A formal but understandable development of computability theory, drawing together a number of alternative lines of development.

Leeds, H. D., and Weinberg, Gerald M., *Computer Programming Fundamentals*, 2d ed. New York, 1965. An introduction to the functions of computers, their programming, the testing of programs, and the obstacles to the conception and execution of computer programs.

Shannon, C. E., and McCarthy, J., eds., *Automata Studies.* Princeton, N.J., 1956. The best collection of articles about investigation into such problems as operation in the face of error, syntheses of theoretical machines, and relationships between machines and psychological problems.

Trakhtenbrot, B. A., *Algorithms and Automatic Computing Machines*, translated by Jerome Kristian, James D. McCawley, and Samuel A. Schmitt. Boston, 1963. A translation and adaptation of the second Russian edition (1960), this book is a fairly simple explanation of computation theory which attempts to relate theoretical and practical developments.

GERALD M. WEINBERG

COMTE, AUGUSTE (1798–1857), French positivist philosopher. Positivism may be viewed as either a philosophical system and method or as a philosophy of history. In the latter aspect, Comte's work was almost an early history of science. He has a good claim to having originated the new science of sociology; certainly, he coined the term. His political philosophy, elaborated on the basis of his positive sociology, was a noteworthy attempt to reconcile science with religion, and the ideals of the Revolution of 1789 with the doctrine of the counter-revolution of his own time. His influence on nineteenth-century thought was strong; he had numerous disciples, such as Émile Littré, and sympathetic supporters, such as John Stuart Mill. His ideas still have important meaning and interest.

LIFE

Comte was born in Montpellier, France. Although his family were ardent Catholics, he announced at the age of 14 that he had "naturally ceased believing in God." At this time he also seems to have abandoned his family's royalism and to have become a republican.

Comte's relations with his family were strained throughout his life. His mother, 12 years older than her husband, clutched at the son. She once wrote asking for word from him "the way a beggar asks for bread to sustain life" threatening that he would know what he had lost only when she was dead. His father and sister constantly complained of ill health; the latter appears to have suffered from hysteria. Comte portrayed them all as covetous and hypocritical and accused them of keeping him in financial distress. The facts, however, suggest that they did what they could for the son and brother whom they loved and admired but found so strange. It is necessary, in order to understand Comte's philosophy and polity, to comprehend his family's compelling influence on him. Although he rejected the ties to his parents and sister (he also had a brother), with their Catholic royalism and their strong emotional demands, these ties reasserted themselves in altered form in his later life and thought. These same family bonds also become important in understanding his nervous breakdown.

Education. Two events are outstanding in Comte's early life: his attendance at the École Polytechnique and his service as secretary to Saint-Simon. The École Polytechnique, founded in 1794 to train military engineers and rapidly transformed into a general school for advanced sciences, was the product of both the French Revolution and the rise of modern science and technology, and it became the model for Comte's conception of a society ordered by a new elite. Although he was there for only a short period, from 1814 to 1816, he immersed himself in the scientific work and thought of such men as Lazare Carnot, Lagrange, and Laplace. Indeed, it was Lagrange's

Analytical Mechanics that inspired Comte to expound, by means of a historical account, the principles animating each of the sciences.

Expelled from the École at the time of its royalist reorganization, Comte remained in Paris instead of returning home, as his parents desired. He came under the influence of the *idéologues* (Volney, Cabnis, and Destutt de Tracy) and, through his wide reading, of the political economists Adam Smith and J. B. Say, as well as of such historians as David Hume and William Robertson. Of major importance was Condorcet, whom Comte called "my immediate predecessor," and whose *Sketch for a Historical Picture of the Progress of the Human Mind* provided an outline of history in which developments in science and technology played a prominent role in mankind's rise through various stages to a period of enlightened social and political order. Then, in August 1817, he became secretary to Henri, comte de Saint-Simon. This crucial relationship lasted seven years, until it dissolved in acrimony.

Comte and Saint-Simon. The question of what Comte owed his patron, and what he added to the latter's ideas, is vexed. Both men were responding to the same intertwined challenges of the French, scientific, and industrial revolutions. Both sought a science of human behavior, called social physiology by Saint-Simon, and both wished to use this new science in the effort to reconstruct society. Saint-Simon, the older man, had priority in some of the ideas: he was first to announce the law of the three stages, talked of organic and critical periods, and called for a new industrial–scientific elite. Moreover, Comte's early work, including the fundamental opuscule, "Prospectus des travaux scientifiques nécessaires pour réorganiser la société," appeared as the last part of a work that also included two of Saint-Simon's writings.

However, Comte's development of the ideas—for example, the encyclopedic range of data with which he supported the idea of the three stages—went far beyond Saint-Simon and ultimately established a qualitative difference in their systems. Further, where Saint-Simon hoped to deduce his new social science from existing knowledge, such as the law of gravitation, Comte saw each science as having to develop its own method. Comte also perceived that such a development came historically; that is, only in the course of the progress of the human mind. And whereas Saint-Simonianism evolved toward a vague socialism, Comte's thought emerged as a philosophical or scientific position.

Later life. After the angry break with Saint-Simon, Comte, who could never obtain a satisfactory university post, supported himself primarily by tutoring in mathematics. Gradually, beginning in 1826, he also lectured on his new philosophy to a private audience composed of many of the outstanding thinkers of his time: Henri Marie de Blainville the physiologist, Jean Étienne Esquirol the psychologist, Jean Baptiste Joseph Fourier the mathematician, and others. From these lectures came Comte's major work, the six-volume *Cours de philosophie positive* (1830–1842).

Meanwhile, Comte entered into connubial arrangements, which were only later formalized in a macabre religious ceremony (Comte was then in the midst of his nervous breakdown) insisted upon by his mother. Although Comte was nursed back to health by his wife, the marriage was unhappy and was finally dissolved in 1842. Two years later, Comte met Mme. Clothilde de Vaux and fell deeply in love, and from this love may have come his new emphasis on a universal religion of humanity. In any case, after the *Cours*, which forms the core of Comte's positivism—the part that had the most influence on subsequent philosophers—came such various attempts to set up the religion of humanity as the *Système de politique positive* (1851–1854), and the *Catéchisme positiviste* (1852). In 1857, worn out from his labors, Comte died in wretchedness and isolation. Behind him he left only his monumental attempts at synthesis of many of the most important intellectual strands of his period.

POSITIVE PHILOSOPHY

Comte's positive philosophy emerged from his historical study of the progress of the human mind—the western European mind. India and China, he claimed, had not contributed to the development of the human mind. Indeed, by mind he really meant the sciences: astronomy, physics, chemistry, and physiology (biology). Mathematics, for Comte, was a logical tool and not a science.

The three stages. The history of the sciences shows that each goes through three stages: the theological, the metaphysical, and the positive. The progress of each field through the three stages is not only inevitable but also irreversible; it is, in addition, asymptotic—that is, we always approach, but never obtain, perfect positive knowledge.

Briefly, Comte's view of each of the three stages is as follows: In the theological stage, man views everything as animated by a will and a life similar to his own. This general view itself goes through three phases; animism, or fetishism, which views each object as having its own will; polytheism, which believes that many divine wills impose themselves on objects; and monotheism, which conceives the will of one God as imposing itself on objects. Metaphysical thought substitutes abstractions for a personal will: causes and forces replace desires, and one great entity, Nature, prevails. Only in the positive stage is the vain search for absolute knowledge—a knowledge of a final will or first cause—abandoned and the study of laws "of relations of succession and resemblance" seen as the correct object of man's research.

Each stage not only exhibits a particular form of mental development, but also has a corresponding material development. In the theological state, military life predominates; in the metaphysical state, legal forms achieve dominance; and the positive stage is the stage of industrial society. Thus, Comte held, as did Hegel, that historical development shows a matching movement of ideas and institutions.

According to Comte, the first science to have gone through the triadic movement was astronomy, whose phenomena are most general and simple, and that affects all other sciences without itself being affected. (For instance, chemical changes on the earth, while they affect physiological phenomena, do not affect astronomical or physical phenomena.)

Methodology. In the *Cours*, Comte attempted to demonstrate, by a mass of detail, that each science is dependen on the previous science. Thus, there can be no effective physics before astronomy, or biology before chemistry. Further, the history of the sciences reveals the law that as the phenomena become more complex (as biological phenomena are more complex than astronomical), so do the available methods by which those phenomena may be treated—for example, the use of comparative anatomy in contrast to simple observation of planetary movement.

In this part of his work, Comte demonstrated the real power and flexibility of his approach. In contrast to Descartes, who saw only one right method of conducting the reason—the geometrical method—Comte believed that each science develops by a logic proper to itself, a logic that is revealed only by the historical study of that science. He explicitly named Descartes as his predecessor and claimed to have fulfilled Descartes's work by studying the mind historically instead of merely abstractly. In Comte's view, the logic of the mind cannot be explained in a priori fashion, but only in terms of what it has actually done in the past. In this respect, Comte's position implies a fundamental revolution in philosophy.

Himself a mathematician, Comte objected to the overextended use of mathematics. In his view, mathematics was simply one tool among many. He admitted that while in principle all phenomena might be subject to mathematical treatment, in practice those phenomena far up the scale in complexity, such as biology or his hoped-for new science of sociology, were not amenable to such an approach. On the other hand, Comte sharply dissociated the positive method from the inquiry into first causes; as we have seen, this would be metaphysical, not positive, knowledge.

Observation. The first means of scientific investigation, according to Comte, is observation. We observe facts, and Comte would agree with the logical positivists of our day that a sentence that is not either a tautology or an assertion of empirical facts can have no intelligible sense. However, by the observation of a fact, Comte—perhaps more sophisticated than many of his latter-day followers—did not mean having a Humean sensation or a complex of such sensations. He meant an act of sensing that was connected, at least hypothetically, with some scientific law. Comte admitted that the simultaneous creation of observations and laws was a "sort of vicious circle" and warned against the perverting of observations in order to suit a preconceived theory. However, he insisted that the task of the scientist was to set up hypotheses about invariable relations of phenomena, concomitantly with their verification by observation.

Experimentation. After observation, understood in this sense, experimentation is the next available method. Since it can be resorted to only when the regular course of a phenomenon can be interfered with in an artificial and determinate manner, the method is best suited to physics and chemistry. In biology, interestingly enough, Comte suggested that disease—the pathological case—while not determined beforehand, could serve as a substitute for experimentation.

Comparison. For the more complex phenomena of biology and sociology, the best available means of investigation is comparison. In biology this might be comparative anatomy. In social science, the method might take the form of comparing either coexisting states or consecutive states: the first method anticipated anthropology; the latter comprised historical sociology.

Sociology. Comte described the study of consecutive social states as a "new department of the comparative method." This "new department" was the final science to be developed by man, and the only one that had not yet entered the positive stage: sociology. As the last phenomena to be considered as falling under invariant laws, social phenomena were the ones that would give meaning to all the rest. Only by perceiving through the new science of sociology that man is a developing creature who moves through the three stages in each of his sciences could we understand the true logic of his mind.

Comte acknowledged both Montesquieu and Condorcet as his predecessors in the science of sociology, for they, too, had perceived that social phenomena appear to obey laws when correctly considered. However, the task of bringing sociology into the positive stage, or at least up to its threshold, was performed by Comte alone. He officially announced the advent of the new science in the fourth volume of the *Cours*, 47th lesson, when he proposed the word *sociologie* for what Quételet had named *physique sociale*.

Statics and dynamics. Comte divided sociology into two parts: statics and dynamics. Social statics is the study of political–social systems relative to their existing level of civilization; that is, as functioning cultural wholes. Social dynamics is the study of the changing levels of civilization; that is, the three stages. The division into statics and dynamics is merely for analytic purposes: the distinction is one between two different ways of organizing the same set of social facts (just as, for example, in biology students of comparative anatomy and of evolution classify the same facts in different ways).

Order and progress. Statics and dynamics, then, are branches of the science of sociology. To this classification, Comte added a division between order and progress, which he conceived as abstractions about the nature of the society studied by sociology. (He further complicated the matter by using the terms "organic" and "critical" or "negative" to describe various periods.) Thus, order exists in society when there is stability in fundamental principles and when almost all members of the society hold similar opinions. Such a situation prevailed, Comte believed, in the Catholic feudal period, and he devoted numerous pages to analyzing the ideas and institutions of medieval social structure.

In contrast to the concept of order, and using images that remind one of the Hegelian dialectic, Comte posited what he called the idea of progress. He identified this progress with the period bounded by the rise of Protestantism and the French Revolution. What was now needed, Comte told his readers, was the reconciliation or synthesis of order and progress in a scientific form. Once a science of society had been developed, opinions would once again be shared and society would be stable. According to Comte, people did not argue over astronomical knowledge, and, once there was true social knowledge, they would not fight over religious or political views. Liberty of conscience, Comte declared, is as out of place in social thought as in physics, and true freedom in both areas lies in the rational submission to scientific laws.

The gradual becoming aware of and understanding of these invariable laws was what Comte meant by progress. (One of these invariable laws, incidentally, was that society *must* develop in a positive direction.) Thus, in the Middle Ages, when society found its order in terms of shared religious ideas, sociology was in the theological stage, and the French Revolutionary period witnessed the emergence of the metaphysical stage. As has been explained, Comte denigrated the *period* of progress, from the rise of Protestantism to the French Revolution, while from the point of view of social dynamics, he had to praise the *progressive movement* toward positivism that took place during this "negative" period. Comte's classification was neither always clear nor consistent.

Political philosophy. Comte's sociology was overly intertwined with his conception of the right polity. In Comte's view, society had broken down with the French Revolution. The Revolution had been necessary because the old order, based on outdated "theological"—Catholic—knowledge, no longer served as a respectable basis for shared opinions; it had been undermined by the progress of the sciences. The Revolution itself offered no grounds for the reorganization of society because it was "negative" and metaphysical in its assumptions. The task, therefore, was to provide a new religion, and a new clergy, that could once again unify society. Comte's solution was a science on which all could agree. In place of the Catholic priesthood, Comte proposed a scientific–industrial elite that would announce the "invariable laws" to society. It was a bold effort to synthesize the old regime (as conceived by Comte) and the Revolution, and to meet the problems of a modern industrial society with the insights about the need for order and shared certainty that were revealed in the theological–feudal period. These insights, religious in nature and intuitive in form, were now to be reformulated by Comte and his followers in terms of positive science.

Positive religion. Comte, in responding to the actual problems of his time, was also working out a synthesis of two bodies of thought. Montesquieu and Condorcet have already been mentioned as the sources of Comte's conception of social statics and social dynamics. Comte's views on organic and critical periods, and his dislike of Protestantism as negative and productive only of intellectual anarchy, were undoubtedly derived from the Catholic counterrevolutionary thinkers Bonald and de Maistre, whom he began to read around 1821. It was Bonald, in fact, who first announced that one did not argue over social truths any more than one argued over the fact that 2 plus 2 equals 4, and de Maistre stated that Protestantism is a negative ideology. Comte rewarded de Maistre by putting his name in the calendar of positivist saints.

Now the positivist calendar was a product of Comte's increasing turn from his earlier mainly philosophical and scientific interests to a form of mysticism. Comte appointed himself the high priest of a new religion of humanity. The new "religion"—based on Comte's positive science—had its holy days, its calendar of saints (which included de Maistre, Adam Smith, Frederick the Great, Dante, and Shakespeare), and its positive catechism. It was nontheistic, for Comte never reverted to a belief in God or in Catholic dogma. As an effort to replace the Catholic religion with a new version of the cult of reason of 1793, it is of great interest, but it was not this aspect of Comte's work that influenced such important figures as Littré and J. S. Mill and it is not what is generally meant when one speaks of Comte's Positivism.

Educational theory. It was on the basis of the earlier, rather than the later, parts of his work that Comte sought to regenerate education. To know a given science, Comte believed, one must know the sciences anterior to it. According to this scheme, the sociologist must first be trained in all the natural sciences, whose knowledge has already gone through the three stages and become positive. (A by-product of this approach to education was Comte's conviction that the proposed method of studying would aid each science by suggesting answers to its problems from other fields.) Positive education was a necessary foundation for the positive polity, as well as for the positive sociology.

Comte and socialism. To round off this presentation of Comte's thought, a brief word is in order on the relationship of his views to the emerging proletarian movement. The goal of Comte's polity was never the affluent society, although he believed that every social measure ought to be judged in terms of its effect on the poorest and most numerous class. He sought, instead, a moral order, with the positive religion enjoining everyone "to live for others." The two classes from which Comte expected the greatest moral influence were women and proletarians, and he relied on their respective charms and numbers to soften the selfish character of the capitalists. In this way, class conflict would be abolished, and the owners of industry would be moralized instead of eliminated. Comte was against the abolition of private property; on the other hand, he joined Marx in attacking the individualist attitudes and behavior of the property-owning classes. In this context, it is interesting to note that Marx, who claimed not to have read Comte until 1866, when he judged his work "trashy," had as a friend the Comtian Professor E. S. Beesly, who chaired the 1864 meeting establishing the International Workingmen's Association.

CRITICISM AND ASSESSMENT

Against Comte's entire system, various criticisms may be lodged. J. S. Mill took Comte to task for not giving a place in his series of sciences to psychology (instead, Comte concentrated on phrenology) and commented that this was "not a mere hiatus in M. Comte's system, but the parent of serious errors in his attempt to create a Social Science."

Perhaps there is a connection between Comte's disregard of introspective psychology and his unquestioned faith in the possibility of an ultimate positive stage of society and knowledge. For example, Comte did not even consider the question of how we can be sure that the positive stage is the last one. Since the human mind and its logical procedures, in Comte's own view, can be known only in terms of experience, it is at least theoretically possible that another stage might be reached. And how can we be sure that, although the positive method has been extended to all natural phenomena, it can be extended to human phenomena? Even if we grant this—and admittedly it is an appealing and useful assumption—does the discovery of laws regulating human phenomena put us in possession of a final science of humanity? At this point, are we not still without a science of ethics, a science that will tell us with complete positive certainty what end to pursue? Comte considered none of these questions, nor, with his neglect of introspective psychology, the further question of whether man's moral disposition is necessarily improved by the pursuit of science.

On another level, both Comte's sociology and his political philosophy can be criticized as embodying a wrong view of scientific procedure. In his best moments, he knew that science proceeds by free inquiry and constant redefinition of its "laws." However, in setting up a scientific elite, who were to announce fixed and stable laws to society, he betrayed his own insight. The polemic needs of his polity—ordered, organic, and positive—triumphed over the philosophic and scientific method he had so painstakingly elaborated in the *Cours*.

Along this same line of criticism, Comte can be charged with serious errors of fact. His anti-Protestant, pro-Catholic feelings led him to make sweeping and unexamined statements, such as that Protestantism was "anti-scientific" (a conclusion supported, perhaps, by Luther's views, but undermined, for example, by the Puritan involvement in the Royal Society) and that Catholicism was a nonaggressive religion. Thus, speaking of the Crusades, Comte asserted, as a matter of fact: "All great expeditions common to the Catholic nations were in fact of a defensive character." Throughout his work, especially in the last three volumes of the *Cours*, which are devoted to his sociology rather than to the natural sciences, similar remarks are to be found.

Yet, with all the criticisms of either a conceptual or factual nature that can be leveled against Comte's position, one must not lose sight of his essential contributions. He did grasp the notion that knowledge in the various sciences is unified and related. His law of the three stages, while too rigid and schematized, did point to the different ways of viewing the world and to the fact that men at different stages of history have emphasized one way of ordering society more than another. And, most important, Comte did prepare the way for a new science, sociology, that would help study the interrelations of men in society and how these interrelations change in the course of history.

(For the development of positivist thought after Comte, see POSITIVISM.)

Bibliography

There is no critical edition of Comte's works. His most important writings, all published in Paris unless otherwise stated, are as follows: *Opuscules de philosophie sociale 1819–1828* (1883), which includes the 1822 "Plan des travaux scientifiques nécessaires pour réorganiser la société"; *Cours de philosophie positive*, 6 vols. (1830–1842), and Harriet Martineau's English condensation of *Cours*, *The Positive Philosophy of Auguste Comte*, 2 vols. (London, 1853), which was personally approved by Comte; *Discours sur l'esprit positif*, prefixed to the *Traité philosophique d'astronomie populaire* (1844); *Discours sur l'ensemble du positivisme* (1848); *Calendrier positiviste* (1849); *Système de politique positive*, 4 vols. (1851–1854), translated by J. H. Bridges, Frederic Harrison, and others as *The System of Positive Polity*, 4 vols. (London, 1875–1877); *Catéchisme positiviste* (1852), translated by Richard Congreve as *The Catechism of Positive Religion* (London, 1858); *Appel aux conservateurs* (1855); and *La Synthèse subjective* (1856).

In addition, see P. Valat, ed., *Lettres d'Auguste Comte à M. Valat* (1870); *Lettres d'Auguste Comte à John Stuart Mill, 1841–1846* (1877); *Testament d'Auguste Comte* (1884); *Lettres à des positivistes anglais* (London, 1889); *Correspondance inédite d'Auguste Comte*, 4 vols. (1903–1904); and *Nouvelles Lettres inédites. Textes présentés par Paulo E. de Berredo-Carneiro* (1939).

The most important work on Comte, essential to a study of his intellectual development, is Henri Gouhier, *La Jeunesse d'Auguste Comte et la formation du positivisme*, 3 vols. (Paris, 1933–1941). The same author's *La Vie d'Auguste Comte* (Paris, 1931) is the best biography. For an analysis of Comte's philosophical ideas, J. S. Mill, *Auguste Comte and Positivism* (London, 1865) is still obligatory. See also Thomas Whittaker, *Comte and Mill* (London, 1908); Lucien Lévy-Bruhl, *La Philosophie d'Auguste Comte* (Paris, 1900), translated by Kathleen de Beaumont-Klein as *The Philosophy of Auguste Comte* (New York, 1903); Émile Littré, *Auguste Comte et la philosophie positive* (2d ed., Paris, 1864); J. Delvolvé, *Reflexions sur la pensée comtienne* (Paris, 1908); and Pierre Ducassé, *Méthode et intuition chez Auguste Comte* (Paris, 1939).

On Comte's religious attitudes, see George Dumas, *Psychologie de deux Messies positivistes: Saint Simon et Auguste Comte* (Paris, 1905).

Jean Lacroix, *La Sociologie d'Auguste Comte* (Paris, 1956) is one of the most interesting books on Comte. For a critical view of Comte's sociology in relation to morality, H. B. Acton, "Comte's Positivism and the Science of Society," in *Philosophy*, Vol. 26 (October 1951) is valuable.

Treating Comte as a historian of science are Paul Tannery, "Comte et l'histoire des sciences," in *Revue générale des sciences*, Vol. 16 (1905), and George Sarton, "Auguste Comte, Historian of Science," in *Osiris*, Vol. 10 (1952). In this connection, John C. Greene, "Biology and Social Theory in the Nineteenth Century: Auguste Comte and Herbert Spencer," in Marshall Clagett, ed., *Critical Problems in the History of Science* (Madison, Wis., 1959) is interesting. Frank Manuel, *The Prophets of Paris* (Cambridge, Mass., 1962), Ch. 6, and F. A. Hayek, "Comte and Hegel," in *Measure*, Vol. 2 (1951), are rewarding; the Hayek article treats Comte as a historicist.

BRUCE MAZLISH

CONCEPT is one of the oldest terms in the philosophical vocabulary, and one of the most equivocal. Though a frequent source of confusion and controversy, it remains useful, precisely because of its ambiguity, as a sort of passkey through the labyrinths represented by the theory of meaning, the theory of thinking, and the theory of being. Logic, epistemology, and metaphysics have all accordingly found use for it in one capacity or another. A preliminary impression of these uses can most readily be gathered, not by premature attempts to discover or define the meaning of the term, but by considering what is implied in such expressions as "having a concept," "acquiring the concept of . . . ," and so on. What tale do these expressions tell? To have a concept '*x*' is, we may say (with some exceptions), (*a*) to know the meaning of the word "*x*"; (*b*) to be able to pick out or recognize a presented *x* (distinguish non-*x*'s, etc.), or again to be able to think of (have images or ideas of) *x* (or *x*'s) when they are not present; (*c*) to know the nature of *x*, to have grasped or apprehended the properties (universals, essences, etc.) which characterize *x*'s and make them what they are. These descriptions of conceptual use are neither exclusive nor exhaustive, nor even particularly clear. In a sense, however, they are indisputable. No one denies that we can do such things as identifying specimens of a kind or learning the meanings of words. But philosophers have differed long and often violently on two questions: (1) as to which (if any) of these conceptual uses is the fundamental one; (2) as to what sort of detailed account is to be given of them. The meaning of the term "concept" fluctuates accordingly. The answer given to question (1) determines (roughly) whether "having a concept" is to be given a nominalistic, mentalistic, or realistic interpretation. The answer to question (2) comes down (again roughly) to a decision as to whether the chosen model of conceptual use is to be construed as (*a*) a cognitive relation of some kind between a subject and an object or (*b*) the exercise of a function. Depending on this, the concepts involved, when disentangled from the having of them, will come to be regarded either as entities or objects (of which the word is the name), or, alternatively, as dispositions (capacities, tendencies, etc.). Internecine disputes are therefore possible on this issue, even among those who agree on the answer to (1).

The term "concept" is thus essentially a dummy expression or variable, whose meaning is assignable only in the context of a theory, and cannot be independently ascertained. The chief advantage of employing it is that, once given determinate status within a theory, it enables the theorist to move systematically from one type of conceptual use (*a*, *b*, or *c* above) to another, explaining the nonpreferred modes as manifestations of the preferred one. If having a concept is having intuitive or implanted knowledge of a real universal (1*c*), and this is taken to mean acquaintance with a supersensible individual Form (2*a*), then to know the meaning of the associated word is to have been given the (proper) name of that individual. This is Platonism, if not necessarily of a kind endorsed by Plato. Similarly, if having a concept is knowing the meaning of a word (1*a*), and if knowing the meaning is being able to use the word correctly (2*b*), then the employment of concepts in thinking becomes explicable, not as a mental manipulation of more or less shadowy "ideas," but as a mere subvocal manifestation of the primary capacity for using words. This, for reasons which will appear, is a contemporary favorite, generally traced to the later Wittgenstein.

The last example illustrates a further reason for the continuing tendency to debate these issues in terms of concepts. Despite its ambiguities, it is a more conveniently abstract word than those needed to describe how concept-using is actually carried on. The use of a word, for example, is always the use of an item in a given natural language. But this is an unwanted restriction here. Even if concepts be no more than verbal capacities, the concept 'horse' is not a capacity for using the *word* "horse"; for Frenchmen have the concept without the capacity. Again, if concept-using be thinking, a thought is always a thought in somebody's head; but whose head, and in what fashion it appeared there, are questions of no interest in the present connection. The concept terminology enables us to dispense with irrelevant concreteness of this kind, and hence to talk of word meanings without doing linguistics, of ideas without doing empirical psychology, and of kinds or properties without doing natural history or natural science.

The foregoing analysis in terms of "having a concept" has yielded no more than a broad classification of prevailing theories into substantival and functional versions of the three main patterns of explanation, focused, respectively, on words, thoughts, and things. No historical light is thereby thrown, of course, on the actual origins of such theories, nor has any reason been given for preferring one theory to another. Nevertheless, if the underlying mechanism is as stated, it may serve to suggest points at which strains are likely to be felt concurrently in all theories of a given type, and reasons, indeed, of a more general kind, why any theory whatsoever, generated according to this pattern, is doomed to frustration in its purpose of explaining what concepts are.

Entity theories. As an illustration of the points at which strains are likely to be felt concurrently, it is worth pointing to some standard obstacles confronting the group of entity theories. These are the theories that identify concepts with individual entities of one kind or another, typical examples in each mode being subsistent word meanings, abstract ideas in the mind, and externally located unitary Forms. Every theory of this sort is open to weighty and familiar objections on its own account, but the short answer to all of them is that the abstractions they postulate are not observed, but calculated into existence (or rather, subsistence); that there is no other reason, beyond the demands of theory, for believing them to exist; and that even if they did, they would provide no answer to the problems they are invoked to solve. The reasons for this are again familiar. Many concepts (though not all) are general, which is to say (*inter alia*) that a word such as "horse" (or its equivalents) can be used to talk of many different individuals, of the class of horses as a whole, and of the conjoint properties which distinguish horses, say, from cows or sheep; that many different images of horses can be produced, either in or out of association with the word; that many different examples of horses can be recognized or identified, with or without the help of images, and that many different dealings can be undertaken with horses, in this context or that; and that so far as any or all of these activities are correctly, appropriately, or successfully accomplished, they *all* count as evidence of possessing the concept of 'horse.' It seems obvious that possession of these varied and interchangeable skills does not require, and would not be explained by, acquaintance with an abstract general entity, even if such entities were possible, which they are not. Locke's infamous multiform triangle (*Essay* IV, vii, 9) is the classic illustration, alike of the absurdity and the explanatory uselessness, of any such attempt to determine what concepts are.

It might be replied, on behalf of conceptualism, at least, that ideas, if not general, can still be recurrent; the same abstract idea '*x*,' recurring in the mind with each repetition of the word "*x*," could still be the concept that endows it with meaning. But this is no improvement; for if the recurrent conceptual series 'x_1,' 'x_2' · · · is to perform its allotted function, some guarantee is needed that it is the *same* '*x*' on each occasion, and for this we should have to call on the superconcept ''*x*,'' which itself is subject to the same difficulty; and so ad infinitum.

The root of all modern objection to entity theories of

concepts is that they rely implicitly on a fallacious view of meaning, whereby all words, other than logical connectives, are taken to be names, and general or abstract words to be names of general or abstract things and characteristics—which must at least subsist, therefore, in order for their names to have designata, and so meaning. Carried to its extreme, this theory construes sentences as lists of abstract objects, peoples the universe with subsistent self-contradictions and fictions (for these, too, can be meaningfully spoken of, even in denying them to exist), and in general obscures the fact—palpable enough once recognized—that words have many other functions besides naming, and mostly do not name at all. Removal of this fixation on a single pattern of word use removes also the temptation to go continually in search of conceptual nominees for words, in the shape of meanings, "objects of thought," or real universals. It is the more curious that they should have been sought at all in this fashion when it is remembered that proper names (which all words are, in effect, according to the naming theory) are one of the few classes of words that are generally supposed to be *without* meaning, and therefore to need no concepts to animate them.

Dispositional theories. If, for the above and other reasons, subsistent concepts now have none to praise and not many left to love them, the way seems clear for a theory of the dispositional kind, and many philosophers, following a tradition whose sources are to be found in Berkeley, Hume, and Kant, have in fact favored, though with the usual divisions, some version of this view. They have held, that is, that concepts are essentially habits or capacities for the right use of words, or for the production of suitable conditioned responses, or for recognition, or for image formation, or again for a discursive acquaintance with distributed *universalia in rebus* on the Aristotelian model. In all these cases the habit or propensity is generally thought of as acquired—at least as regards the more elementary empirical concepts—by some process of comparison, selection, and abstraction. Recurrent elements in experience are taken to engender, modify, and reinforce the disposition, which then operates in its turn as a principle for the ordering of subsequent experience, the guidance of action, or the control of thought and talk. A similar account of concept formation is, of course, given by some entity theorists, who tend likewise to explain the more complex concepts as due to further processes of abstraction, composition, and so on performed upon the elementary concepts already obtained in this way.

Concepts, in this dispositional sense, are still subjective and peculiar to the individual. It is assumed, however, that exposure to a common environment, plus the customary processes of education and social attrition, will normally lead to a sharing of concepts and to the eventual acquisition of a standard repertory of concepts held in common by virtually all members of a given cultural or linguistic group. By some writers, following Kant, it would indeed be claimed that certain concepts of high generality are native and necessary to members of any culture whatsoever, since they are prerequisite to any judgment about objects and are thus intrinsic to the recognition of anything as belonging to an objective, common world. These are categories, or a priori concepts, so called because they are not got by abstraction from experience—for any such process would already presuppose the use of them. Whether there are concepts of this kind is a question too large for discussion here, nor is it proposed to argue, what some have denied, that empirical concepts are themselves obtained by abstraction. Questions as to the origin of concepts are not peculiar to the dispositional view of them; but neither is that view committed in advance to answering such questions in one way rather than another.

It will be evident, then, that on the present account of the matter, concepts no longer figure as things or inferred entities, named by words, but are to be treated merely as logical constructions out of the actual or possible occasions of their employment. And thus far at least, by the very modesty of their claims, the dispositional theories enjoy an obvious advantage over their rivals. But this they tend to forfeit as soon as it is asserted—which it often is—that some one particular type of disposition is primary or fundamental, and the remainder merely secondary manifestations thereof. For this is to mistake one subset or another of the sufficient conditions of having a concept for necessary or necessary-and-sufficient conditions, and thereby to generate a pseudo-explanatory theory of the real nature of concepts which immediately exposes itself to refutation. A man able to use the word "horse" correctly certainly has the concept 'horse,' but is not forthwith deprived of it if stricken with aphasia; so long as he can still manage horses, he has the concept—as he would scarcely have it if, even while retaining the use of the word, he were unable to distinguish horses from cattle or sheep. A blind man, similarly, has a concept of 'red' if able to use the word appropriately, though he cannot identify its instances; or at least he has a better notion of it than other blind men who do not even have the use of the word. His employment of it, in practice, is not unlike that of the physicist, whose theoretical concepts refer to entities or processes ('field' or 'radiation,' for instance) which in fact or in principle are unobservable to him. And if concepts such as these are not invalidated by the absence of recognition capacities, there seems equally little reason to argue that the absence of verbal capacities precludes the possession of concepts by young children, animals, or even computers. The attribution is at all events harmless; for if concepts be, not mental entities, but mere multifarious capacities for intelligent saying, thinking, and doing, nothing follows from their possession as to the presence of 'mind' or 'consciousness' in what is said to possess them.

It should be noted, in conclusion, that the term "concept" is at times used in senses different from (though not unrelated to) that described above. Logicians in particular, when analyzing propositions, find it a convenient abbreviation for the connotation or sense of words and phrases as such, or for the defining properties of a class (and are liable to be led by this into the defiant postulation, guilty admission, or indignant rejection of "abstract entities"). Their use of the term is at all events an abstract or impersonal one, and the same can be said of those writers of general treatises who speak of "The Concept of God," ". . . of Law," ". . . of Mind," and the like. Here the reference is merely to the variety of beliefs, theories, and practices associated with the key word in question, without regard to the dispositions of particular persons. It is in this sense, too, that philosophers practice that description and analysis of concepts of which specimens will be found on nearly every page of this encyclopedia, and of which the present discussion of the concept of concept is but one more humble example.

Bibliography

The older literature on concepts, though very extensive, is largely coincident with that on universals (see bibliography to UNIVERSALS). For an unusually full discussion of the subject, see Thomas Reid, *Essays on the Intellectual Powers of Man*, in his *Works*, Sir William Hamilton, ed., Vol. I (Edinburgh, 1846), Essays 4 and 5. The most useful modern treatments are R. I. Aaron, *Theory of Universals* (Oxford, 1952); I. M. Copi, in Paul Henle, ed., *Language, Thought, and Culture* (Ann Arbor, Mich., 1958); Peter Geach, *Mental Acts: Their Content and Their Objects* (London, 1957); Gilbert Ryle, "Thinking Thoughts and Having Concepts," in *Thinking and Meaning* (Louvain, 1962); and, above all, H. H. Price, *Thinking and Experience* (London and Cambridge, Mass., 1953).

P. L. HEATH

CONDILLAC, ÉTIENNE BONNOT DE (1715–1780), French philosopher, was born in Grenoble and died in the abbey at Flux near Beaugency. Although his family was in the legal profession, Condillac studied theology at Saint-Sulpice and at the Sorbonne, receiving holy orders at Paris in 1740. However, he was more interested in science than in sacerdotalism, and developed that interest with the help of his cousin Jean Le Rond d'Alembert (mathematician, physicist, astronomer, and a key writer with Diderot of *L'Encyclopédie*). Such people as Helvétius, Fontenelle, and Diderot also encouraged him in the direction of scientific researches, and he was a friend of Jean-Jacques Rousseau. It is said that although he wore the cassock of a priest until the end of his life, he celebrated Mass only once. Whether or not this is true, the fact remains that rather early in life he became convinced that a secular, rational systematization of human experience was his primary task.

By 1734, when Voltaire published his *Lettres philosophiques* extolling English civilization, the two great Englishmen, Newton and Locke, whom he praised in those letters were already greatly admired in France. Isaac Newton's *Philosophiae Naturalis Principia Mathematica* had come out in 1687, and Pierre Coste in 1700 had published his masterful translation (reviewed by Locke himself) of Locke's *An Essay Concerning Human Understanding*. However, it was Voltaire's *Lettres*, and his *Eléments de la philosophie de Newton* (1738), that helped clarify for Condillac (who apparently read little or no English) the English antimetaphysical, experience-centered way of thinking that he had felt lacking in Descartes. Locke's scrupulous tracing of ideas to their origin in experience, combined with Newton's dazzling simplification of our understanding of terrestrial and celestial motion through his law of gravitation, had seized Condillac's allegiance and imagination by 1740. These two accomplishments embodied the dominant ideal of Condillac's whole philosophic life: empirico-logical economy and rigor.

Condillac's *Traité des sensations*, which he published in 1754, established him as the great French *métaphysicien*, or clarifier of ideas by reference to experience. In 1758 he was appointed teacher of the young Ferdinand of Parma. He returned to France in 1767 and the next year was elected to the Académie Française. In 1776 he published *Le Commerce et le gouvernement considérés relativement l'un à l'autre*, which on the whole, was a popularization of the physiocratic doctrines of François Quesnay and Du Pont de Nemours. Like them, he believed in agriculture as the fundamental source of wealth, in free trade (as against mercantilism), and in the power of reason to discover civil laws that would preserve each man's right to enjoy the fruits of his labor. He spent his last few years away from Paris, where the current atheism and materialism had begun to irritate him; he himself believed in the existence of God and also in a deep distinction between matter and spirit or mind. He died peacefully at the abbey that was his benefice.

Method. In his study of the human mind, Condillac wanted to elucidate certain basic terms (like "attention," "judgment," "reasoning") by analyzing them down to one type of primary fact, or *première vérité*. He was among other things a logician seeking to construct a system whose postulates were few—actually only one in number—a system that was a straight-line proof that moved cautiously from one postulate to more and more complex claims.

From Locke, Condillac had learned the importance of determining the limits of human knowledge before making claims about matters of fact or of value. And from Locke—as well as Descartes—he had learned that such a project can best be carried out by means of analysis, by breaking down our notions about the human mind into simples and then recomposing or ordering those parts into a whole that is clearer, more articulate because this double movement has occurred. To understand a machine thoroughly, we take it apart (in our minds at least) and put it back together, dealing sequentially with elements that in the machine are simultaneous and coexistent. Condillac contended that all thinking persons perform such a two-stage process when they are seeking exact understanding of anything. He believed that if we scrupulously perform it on such notions as "understanding," we shall learn precisely and completely the nature and limitations of our mental powers.

This analysis should move, according to Condillac, in a way analogous to the way mathematical analyses proceed, by way of identities. The movement from the *première vérité* to broad asseverations about the human mind must display the following form: $w=x$; $x=y$; $y=z$; therefore, $w=z$. As in mathematics, these identities, although they are clear, are not trivial or pointless; what we learn from them is that despite superficial differences of form (w does not look like x, for instance) there is a plain identity of meaning; different forms mean the same thing. For instance, "exclusive sensation" (intently smelling a gardenia) is the same as "attention." The perception of odor *is* our attention or attentiveness at that time. No mysterious inward spotlight, no "medium" in which the odor is perceived, is involved in our understanding of the meaning of "attention." "Exclusive sensation" and "attention" are identical terms with different superficial forms, and by way of a sequence of such identities we analyze (break down and recompose) the constituent meanings of our most important and complex terms. By moving from simple, narrow notions to broader ones by way of logically transitive identities, Condillac hoped to secure an exact understanding of the nature and limitations of the human mind.

Behind this method lay Condillac's notion of *une langue bien faite.* He was convinced that a lucid, well-constructed language, simple in its elements and at the same time complete and comprehensive, was the basic desideratum of human thought. Indeed, he often said that language is itself our method; and if language is not *bien faite,* not lucid and complete, then *ipso facto* our way of understanding things is not adequate. He was, for instance, convinced that a question well posed is a question nearly solved; its language guides the mind to its answer. And in all his writings Condillac was trying to construct a well-made language.

System. The main themes of Condillac's lifelong philosophy were presented in his first work, the *Essai.* Here he pointed out that since the Fall the soul of man depends upon the body for its knowledge, and specifically upon the interaction of external things with the body's sense organs. In innocence or after death this may not be the case, but now we learn all we know by way of our bodies. There are two elements to every perception: an object acting on an organ, and an "impression" that is spiritual or mental and is occasioned, not caused but triggered, by that action. There are various forms that these impressions take: in mere perception the impression is not vivacious, and therefore does not leave a trace; in attention, however, the impression is vivacious and persists, becoming memory. Memory does not involve an active mind; it is simply the prolonging of an impression by virtue of its own vivacity. Abstraction occurs when certain parts of a vivacious impression are not so prolonged.

Judgment occurs when two impressions appear together (for instance, we judge "This rose and that rose are white"). When there is a chain of such judgments, such that later judgments presuppose earlier ones and earlier ones bring about the later ones, reasoning (*raisonnement*) takes place. The word "understanding" (*entendement*) refers to all the operations of the mind that thus arise automatically from our impressions: mere perceiving, attending to, remembering, abstracting, judging, reasoning, and others. Crucially involved in this whole process is language; signs help us to recall, vivify, and refine these operations.

In 1749 Diderot published his *Lettre sur les aveugles,* which pointed out that Condillac's analysis of understanding was strikingly similar to Berkeley's subjective idealism; Diderot, in effect, invited Condillac to dissociate himself from such idealism by refuting Berkeley's contention that all experience is a modification of our own mind. Thus, it suddenly became necessary for Condillac to prove what he had previously assumed with Locke—that there is an external world, a material world that causes our impressions or our sensations. He had to do this because Berkeley's reduction was anathema to his dualistic convictions.

The famous *Traité des sensations,* then, had a double purpose: to show how modifications of the mind (*modifications de l'âme*), or impressions received by way of the senses, could give rise automatically, without reference to unobservable spirits or innate ideas, to all our mental operations, and at the same time to defend the existence of an external, material world. The first purpose was familiar; the second required a new approach, the rejection of the assumption that sensations or impressions are images occasioned by external material things. Condillac could not assume what he had to prove. By means of purely mental sensations he had to prove the existence of a material world external to the mind.

To accomplish this double purpose, he hypothesized a marble statue internally constituted like a living human being, having a mind deprived of all ideas, and with all of its senses closed, so that it would be possible to open them one at a time and to analyze the relationships between the various sensations. The marble of the statue, its initial rigidity and lack of interaction with the environment, was hypothesized to maintain the subjectivity of the statue's experience, since to assume a being that interacted with its environment was to assume a being that had an environment and had objects with which it could interact.

The desire to avoid begging the question in favor of the existence of an external world dictated Condillac's choice of the first sense organ to open. He chose the olfactory organ because odor involves no danger of being thought of as an image of an external object but is plainly a modification of the mind. Odor, aside from illustrating the familiar rise from mere perception to attention to memory, also involves or induces an affective reaction, agreeableness or disagreeableness. For example, from the experience of the odor's agreeableness, associated with the sensation of smell itself, desires arise by a process similar to the way judgment and reasoning arise; and from the momentary desires longer passions come to be. Vivacious agreeableness is remembered as associated with certain remembered olfactory or other impressions and is compared with them, and thus we desire to continue, for example, to smell a rose. The sum total of our desirings and our more lasting passions constitutes the will (*volonté*) of man, just as the sum total of his sensations, memories, judgments, and reasoning constitutes his understanding. The will of man is intimately involved with sensation automatically induced by the all-important *première vérité,* just as his understanding is.

However, the second purpose of the *Traité* was not yet fulfilled. How do we get from modifications of the soul to the belief in an external world? In attempting to answer this question Condillac thought that if he could show the origin within experience of our awareness of the outthereness or exteriority of sensations, he would at the same time be demonstrating that there is a cause that produces these sensations, a cause independent of the mind's functionings. Because of this confusion he did not refute Berkeley, but he did give an ingenious explanation of the perception of phenomenological exteriority, an explanation that was to be importantly developed by the *idéologues* of the nineteenth century, particularly Destutt de Tracy, and in a very special way by Maine de Biran.

To show how the perception of phenomenological exteriority arises, Condillac added the statue's sense of touch. The term *le toucher,* or "tactile sensation," covers kinesthesia (our own felt breathing and other felt bodily movements) as well as the felt pressure of the body against an outward object. By opening the sense of touch, Condillac permitted the statue to move itself, mechanically, by the confusedly felt contraction of its muscles. (Previous to this, hearing, taste, and even sight had been opened and had not revealed exteriority. In saying that sight reveals only impressions "in the eye" and not "out there," Condillac was accepting the English surgeon William Cheselden's account of having removed cataracts from the eyes of a person born blind and finding that this person saw objects as if they were against his eyeballs.) The sense of touch opened, the statue first experienced double contact by, for example, touching its own chest. This gave him two feelings of solidity or resistance, one located in one place (the hand) and another located in another place (the chest), and two feelings of exclusion; both feelings were part of the same self or consciousness. Then Condillac had the statue press its hand against an object other than its own body; this object also excluded the hand from its (the object's) place, but now there was only one feeling of exclusion or resistance. By comparing double contact with single touch, the statue came to the awareness that there is an outward world, a world not felt from the inside but felt only as an obstacle outside the body. At this point he had discovered exteriority, and by way of attention, judgment, and reasoning was able to transform this discovery into the notions of space and matter.

While this transformation and generalization is going on, our memories of touch become associated with our sensations of sight, hearing, and such; in that intimate association, in moving away from or toward objects seen, heard, and such, these latter sensations are made more subtle as far as our capacity to differentiate between them is concerned, and they are located in space with respect to each other. The "teacher" of our other senses is the sense of touch.

Condillac then gave the statue language; and with language (which had somewhat less importance in the *Traité* than it had in the *Essai*) the chain of identities that extends from the most elementary sensations to the most broad intellectual arguments and operations of the will was complete.

The method and conclusions Condillac presented in the *Traité* were employed in his essays on liberty, on animals, and on the existence of God (showing how man rises to a belief in a God who is the providential cause of persons and things). In these essays he also showed how morality arises as a refinement of volitional or affective operations; and he completed his philosophy with the assertion that God is the ultimate source from whom morality and understanding derive their force.

Bibliography

The first edition of the *Oeuvres complètes de Condillac,* competently edited by G. Arnoux and Condillac's brother, Gabriel Bonnot, abbé de Mably, appeared in 23 volumes (Paris, 1798). The latest edition, in three volumes, of his philosophical works, *Oeuvres philosophiques,* was edited by Georges Le Roy (Paris, 1947–1951).

Following are the first editions and Condillac's re-editings of his important essays: *Essai sur l'origine des connaissances humaines* (Paris, 1746; re-edited 1771); *Traité des systèmes* (Amsterdam and Leipzig, 1746; re-edited 1771); *Traité des sensations,* with *Dissertation sur la liberté* (Paris, 1754; re-edited 1778); *Traité des animaux,* with *Dissertation sur l'existence de Dieu* (Amsterdam, 1755; re-edited 1766); *Le Commerce et le gouvernement considérés relativement l'un à l'autre* (Amsterdam, 1776).

His posthumously published works are *La Logique* (Paris, 1792) and *La Langue des calculs* (Paris, 1798).

Not much of value has been written about Condillac. For his life, see Baguenault de Puchesse, *Condillac, sa vie, sa philosphie, son influence* (Paris, 1910); this is not definitive, but it is the fullest account available. An exposition of Condillac's philosophy is Georges Le Roy, *La Psychologie de Condillac* (Paris, 1937). The best book on Condillac—lucid, scrupulous, and very useful—this eschews criticism in favor of sympathetic exposition.

PHILIP P. HALLIE

CONDITIONAL STATEMENTS. *See* CONTRARY-TO-FACT CONDITIONAL; IF.

CONDORCET, MARQUIS DE (1743–1794), Marie-Jean-Antoine-Nicolas Caritat, French mathematician, historian of the sciences, political theorist, and social reformer. Condorcet was one of the youngest of the Encyclopedists and the only prominent one to participate actively in the French Revolution. He was born in Ribemont in Picardy and was educated by the Jesuits at the Collège de Navarre. Admitted to the Académie des Sciences in 1769 on the basis of his early mathematical writings, he was elected its perpetual secretary in 1776 and ably depicted the progress of the sciences to a wide public in the customary eulogies (*Éloges*) of deceased academicians, which he presented in this position. A protégé of d'Alembert, for whom Condorcet's election to the Académie Française in 1782 was regarded as a personal triumph, and of Turgot, who called him to the directorship of the mint during his abortive reforming ministry, Condorcet was active in the prerevolutionary campaigns for economic freedom, religious toleration, legal reform and the abolition of slavery. After his marriage to Sophie de Grouchy in 1786 their salon became one of the most brilliant and influential of the prerevolutionary period. He took part in the opening debates of the French Revolution as a member of the municipal council of Paris and was a convinced republican by the time he was elected to the Legislative Assembly in 1791. Prominent in this assembly, he directed his most sustained efforts toward the elaboration of a project for public education which had great influence on the eventual establishment of the French educational system. In the National Convention, Condorcet's opposition to the death penalty led him to cast his vote against the execution of Louis XVI (he voted for the supreme penalty short of death). He then undertook the task of drawing up a draft constitution for the new republic, but although accepted by the committee on the constitution, his liberal constitutional scheme—commonly known as the Girondin constitution of 1793—shared the unfortunate fate of the group with which it was associated. In July 1793, Condorcet's indignant defense of his constitution against that prepared by the Jacobins led to his denunciation and flight into hiding. He spent his remaining months of life secluded in Paris, working on the *Sketch for a Historical Picture of the Progress of the Human Mind* (*Esquisse d'un tableau historique des progrès de l'esprit humain*), published posthumously in 1795. He left his asylum in March 1794 and was arrested and imprisoned at Bourg-la-Reine, near Paris. He died during the first night of his imprisonment, either from exhaustion or from a self-administered poison.

Probability and social science. It has often been assumed that Condorcet's increasing preoccupation with social and political affairs, if not the result of a sense of frustration with his mathematical investigations, was at least accompanied by a waning interest in them. Quite the reverse is true. Condorcet's experience at the Académie des Sciences fostered a sense of the power of science to elucidate even the realm of social behavior. His mathematical endeavors were intimately bound up with his fundamental intellectual concern. He aimed to bring to social questions the attitudes and methods of the physical sciences, thereby welding the broken elements of the moral and political sciences into a new social science, which he regarded as the necessary condition of a rational political and social order. Condorcet seized upon the calculus of probabilities as the essential epistemological connection between the physical sciences and the science of man. All the truths of experience are merely probable, he argued. In the social sciences the observation of facts may be more difficult and their order less constant. The results of the social sciences may therefore be less probable than those of the physical sciences. But Condorcet maintained that the probability of all statements of experience can be expressed and evaluated mathematically within probability theory. Thus, while the statements attained by the social sciences may on occasions be less probable than those of the physical sciences, in Condorcet's view the mathematical estimate of their respective probabilities is equally certain. The meteorologist cannot be certain that it will rain tomorrow, for example, but if on the basis of his observations he can estimate the probability of its doing so as x:1, then he can be certain that there is a probability of x:1 that it will rain tomorrow. Similarly, the economist, who cannot be certain that the standard of living will continue to rise, can in theory arrive at a certain mathematical estimate of the probability of its doing so.

The significance of this argument can be best assessed in terms of the earlier epistemological claims to certainty made by Descartes on behalf of the mathematical and physical sciences. Condorcet accepted the skeptic's evaluation of the physical sciences as being merely probable. But in arguing that probabilities in the physical sciences (like those in the social sciences) can be evaluated with mathematical certainty, he remained in a sense fundamentally Cartesian. Not only did he hold to the idea of certainty as the criterion of acceptable knowledge, but he also accepted mathematics as the paradigm of certain knowledge (although even this certainty is based in the last analysis, he was occasionally prepared to argue, on the observed constancy of the operation of the human mind). Condorcet's argument in this respect ranks with that of Giambattista Vico as one of the major eighteenth-century attempts to establish the validity of social science. But whereas Vico turned away from the mathematical and physical sciences in search of a historical and organic conception of his new science, Condorcet's probabilistic evaluation of the physical sciences served to integrate them with the science of man in an essentially mathematical conception of science. For Condorcet, the mathematician was able, by using the calculus of probabilities, to subject to the certain evaluation of mathematics even those areas of knowledge condemned by Descartes as untrustworthy. The calculus of probabilities provided a sure means of estimating the validity of our opinions and the probability of our expectations; it bound the moral and physical sciences together on a sliding scale of probabilities which could at all stages be evaluated with mathematical certainty.

Condorcet developed this conception in two very different works. In the first, the *Essay on the Application of Analysis to the Probability of Majority Decisions* (*Essai sur l'application de l'analyse à la probabilité des décisions rendues à la pluralité des voix*, 1785), he set out to discover by means of the calculus of probabilities under what conditions there will be an adequate guarantee that the majority decision of an assembly or tribunal is true. In one of its applications he envisaged such an analysis as the means of solving a perennial problem of liberal thought, that of reconciling the claims of an elite to exercise special responsibilities in the process of decision making with the general principle of universal or majority consent. But the obscure mathematics of the essay and its inevitable reliance on unverifiable assumptions as to the probable truth or error of the opinions of individuals composing social bodies have left it largely ignored by those interested in Condorcet's political theory. More recently, social mathematicians interested in elucidating the relationship between individual and collective choice (whether political or economic) have been able to disengage from the probabilistic framework of this work a theoretical model of collective decision making that is remarkably modern in its implications and approach. (See the works of Black and Granger, cited below.)

The *Essai sur l'application de l'analyse* was intended to convince academicians of the validity of Condorcet's contention that the moral and political sciences can be treated mathematically. The unfinished "General View of the Science Comprising the Mathematical Treatment of the Moral and Political Sciences" ("Tableau général de la science, qui a pour objet l'application du calcul aux sciences morales et politiques") was meant for a different audience. It appeared in 1793 in a popular journal that sought to initiate citizens of the new French republic into the social science, or the art of the rational conduct of politics. Condorcet saw the new social mathematics ("mathématique sociale") as a common, everyday science of conduct ("une science usuelle et commune," *Oeuvres*, Vol. I, p. 550) which would provide the essential foundation of a democratic, but rational, politics. He viewed man in all his conduct as a gambler. Each individual automatically and instinctively balances the probability of one opinion against that of another, the desired goal of a proposed action against its probable results. The mathematical science of man was intended not only as an objective description of social behavior but also as a scientific basis for individual conduct which would enable men to substitute for habitual and instinctive modes of thought and action the precise evaluation of reason and calculation. Social mathematics, coupled with an exact language based on precise philosophical analysis of our ideas, would free men from instinct and passion and restore the empire of reason in social affairs. It formed the essential link between scientific advance and moral progress, for evil, as Condorcet remarked, was far more often the result of an erroneous calculation of interest than the product of violent passion.

Idea of progress. In the *Sketch for a Historical Picture of the Progress of the Human Mind,* Condorcet turned to history for a demonstration of the power of reason and calculation in social affairs. The *Sketch* was only the hastily written introduction to a larger work on the history of science and its impact upon society which Condorcet had been contemplating for many years. Some of the fragments of this unfinished work are of considerable philosophical interest. One outlined a project for a universal, symbolic language of the sciences; another elaborated a decimal system of classification addressed to the much-debated problem of scientific classification. But it is with the *Sketch* itself that Condorcet's name and influence have been chiefly associated, and it is with that work—often regarded as the philosophical testament of the eighteenth century—that Condorcet bequeathed to the nineteenth century the fundamental idiom of its social thought, the idea of progress.

The aim of the *Sketch* was to demonstrate man's progressive emancipation, first from the arbitrary domination of his physical environment and then from the historical bondage of his own making. Condorcet shared with other eighteenth-century theorists a view of progress that depended ultimately upon man's cumulative ability to combine sensations and ideas (in the manner revealed by sensationalist psychology) to his own satisfaction or advantage. This Promethean psychological capacity functioned in the same manner in the human race as in the individual; it proceeded by way of a natural, self-revealing logic or "method," from the fundamental data of sense experience to the most general principles of the moral and physical sciences. Condorcet's main concern, therefore, was less to explain the growth of reason in itself—this growth was posited as natural—than to point to the destruction of the obstacles which had inhibited that growth or diverted the historical development of the mind from the natural logic of ideas.

Condorcet's hopes for future progress rested on two conclusions. First, he was convinced that the obstacles which had in the past threatened the advance and dissemination of reason—elitism and tyranny on the one hand; popular prejudice, ignorance, and social and political subjection, on the other—were finally being destroyed under the joint impact of scientific, technological, and political revolution. Second, he believed that the discoveries of sensationalist psychology had made it possible to articulate the natural and fundamental principles of the social art, or science, and he drew from the doctrine of the rights of man—grounded upon the "facts" of man's sensate nature—a comprehensive outline of the principles of liberal democracy that it would be the purpose of the social art to implement.

Although this belief in indefinite future progress was based on the general assertion that observation of past events warrants extrapolation as to the probable future, Condorcet was not a strict historical determinist. Man is subject to the general laws of physical nature, he maintained in an unpublished introduction to the *Sketch,* but he has the power to modify these laws and turn them to his own advantage. Although this power is feeble in the individual, when exercised by mankind collectively and over a long period of time, it can balance the forces of nature and can even be regarded as the work of nature itself. For if nature has endowed man collectively with the capacity to learn from experience, to understand its laws, and to modify their effects, the progressive emancipation of man from nature is itself natural, and the growth of freedom is a natural law. The *Sketch* not only demonstrated the power of the social art but also made clear that it could succeed only as a communal and democratic art. It is this emphasis upon the collective experience and achievements of mankind, this concern with the "most obscure and neglected chapter of the history of the human race" (*Sketch,* Barraclough translation, p. 171)—namely, the progress of the mass of the people in society—that links Condorcet's view of history with his conception of social science.

Bibliography

The standard edition of Condorcet's works is A. Condorcet-O'Connor and F. Arago, eds., *Oeuvres de Condorcet,* 12 vols. (Paris, 1847–1849). The *Essai sur l'application de l'analyse à la probabilité des décisions rendues à la pluralité des voix* (Paris, 1785) and Condorcet's many other mathematical writings are not included in this edition. For a bibliography of these mathematical works see Charles Henry, "Sur la Vie et les écrits mathématiques de Jean-Antoine-Nicolas Caritat marquis de Condorcet," in *Bulletino di bibliografica e di storia delle scienze matematiche e fisiche,* Vol. 16 (1883), 271–324. See also Charles Henry, ed., *Correspondance inédite de Condorcet et de Turgot (1770–79)* (Paris, 1883); Léon Cahen, "Condorcet inédit: Notes pour le Tableau des progrès de l'esprit humain," in *La Révolution française,* Vol. 75 (1922), 193–212; Gilles-Gaston Granger, "Langue universelle et formalisation des sciences: Un Fragment inédit de Condorcet," in *Revue d'histoire des sciences,* Vol. 7 (1954), 197–219; Alberto Cento, "Dei manoscritti del 'Tableau' di Condorcet," in *Rendiconto del Istituto Lombardo di Scienze e Lettere: Classe di Lettere e Scienze Morali e Storiche,* Vol. 88 (1955), 311–324; K. M. Baker, "An Unpublished Essay of Condorcet on Technical Methods of Classification," in *Annals of Science,* Vol. 18 (1962), 99–123. For a modern translation of the *Esquisse,* see *Sketch for a Historical Picture of the Progress of the Human Mind,* translated by June Barraclough, with an introduction by Stuart Hampshire (London, 1955).

For reference see Franck Alengry, *Condorcet, guide de la Révolution française, théoricien du droit constitutionnel et précurseur de la science sociale* (Paris, 1904); Duncan Black, *The Theory of Committees and Elections* (Cambridge, 1958); Janine Bouissounouse, *Condorcet: Le Philosophe pendant la Révolution* (Paris, 1962); Léon Cahen, *Condorcet et la Révolution française* (Paris, 1904); Alberto Cento, *Condorcet e l'idea di progresso* (Florence, 1956); Gilles-Gaston Granger, *La Mathématique sociale du marquis de Condorcet* (Paris, 1956); Frank E. Manuel, *The Prophets of Paris* (Cambridge, Mass., 1962); and J. Salwyn Schapiro, *Condorcet and the Rise of Liberalism* (New York, 1934).

KEITH MICHAEL BAKER

CONFIRMATION: QUALITATIVE ASPECTS.

Most statements about matters of empirical fact cannot be conclusively established, or verified, by the observational or experimental evidence available at a given time. This is especially obvious when the statement, or hypothesis, in question has the form of an unlimited generalization, such as "All ravens are black" or "Any metal object expands with rising temperature." For evidence can be available on no more than a finite number of relevant cases—a finite number of actually observed ravens and their color, a finite number of data concerning volume changes in metal pieces at rising temperature—whereas the hypothesis also pertains to all unexamined instances, whether in the past, the present, or the future. Hence, such generalizations are not logically implied and thus conclusively verified by the evidence. The same is true of hypotheses having the form of mixed universal and existential generalizations, such as "For any chemical compound there exists a range of temperature and pressure in which the compound is solid" or "Some chemical compounds do not dissolve in any substance." And it is true even of many hypotheses which ostensibly assert just one particular fact, for often such assertions are of implicitly general character, as is, for example, the statement that a given object is soluble in water, which implies that if at any time and place the object is placed into any body of water, it will dissolve. Finally, it is true of statements about the "unobservable" objects and occurrences postulated in scientific theories.

The evidential relationship in which a finite set of observational or experimental data can stand to a hypothesis of any of the kinds just mentioned is therefore at best that of providing partial support for, or confirmation of, the hypothesis. To explicate this concept of confirmation more precisely is an important task of any theory of empirical knowledge in general and of scientific knowledge in particular; it is also one of the principal objectives of a theory of induction. Such explication calls for the formulation of general principles that govern the concept; these might be presented systematically as postulates and theorems of a formalized theory of confirmation, and they might even include an explicit definition of that concept. Some of the efforts made toward such systematic clarification will now be briefly surveyed.

Qualitative and quantitative analyses. Generally, confirmation may be viewed as a relation between a body of actual or potential evidence, formulated in an evidence sentence *e*, and a hypothesis, represented by sentence *h*. In logical studies confirmation is often construed as a relation between the sentence *e* and the sentence *h*. This interpretation parallels and generalizes the formal conception of logical implication as a relation between sentences (rather than, say, between propositions); indeed, logical implication may then be regarded as a subrelation of confirmation.

Even with this general understanding, confirmation may still be conceived of in formally different ways—for example, as a purely qualitative concept or as a quantitative one. In the latter construal, confirmation allows of different degrees which are indicated by sentences of the form "$c(h,e)=r$"—that is, of the form "The degree of confirmation of *h* on *e* is *r*." Frequently, this quantitative concept of confirmation is assumed to satisfy the basic laws for probabilities, and it is thus identified with the concept of the logical or inductive probability of *h* on *e*. This is done explicitly in Rudolf Carnap's system of inductive logic. Other theories of inductive probability—such as that of J. M. Keynes, which allows for both numerical and nonnumerical probabilities—may also be regarded as bearing on the quantitative concept of confirmation. On the other hand, Karl Popper, who rejects an inductivist view of scientific method in favor of a falsificationist one, holds that what should be considered in this context is the extent to which a hypothesis has been able to withstand serious efforts to refute it by rigorous scientific tests and that this extent is properly represented by his quantitative concept of "degree of corroboration," which does not satisfy all the principles of probability theory.

The qualitative interpretation forgoes distinctions of degree and treats confirmation as a relation *C* which an evidence sentence either does or does not bear to a given hypothesis. Thus, to say that $C(e,h)$—that is, that *e* confirms *h*—is simply to assert that the evidence *e*, as far as it goes, supports, bears out, or accords with the hypothesis *h*. The idea thus vaguely characterized is much in need of precise explication, but thus far it has not received as much attention as the quantitative concept of confirmation. That it is nonetheless important is suggested by the observation that the paradigm case of qualitative confirmation—namely, the confirmation of a generalization by its "positive instances," which is frequently invoked in philosophical discussions of induction—gives rise to what are called the paradoxes of confirmation.

Paradoxes of confirmation. Consider a hypothesis of the universal conditional form "For any *x* if *x* is *P*, then *x* is *Q*" or "All *P* are *Q*"—for example, "All ravens are black." It seems entirely reasonable to say that an individual object *i* affords a positive (confirming) or a negative (disconfirming) instance of such a hypothesis according to whether *i* is both *P* and *Q* or is *P* but not *Q*. More precisely, an evidence sentence of the type "*i* is *P*, and *i* is *Q*" should count as confirming the given hypothesis, and an evidence sentence of the type "*i* is *P*, and *i* is not *Q*" should count as disconfirming (indeed, as logically invalidating) it. A criterion to this effect, which may be considered as setting down at least sufficient conditions of qualitative confirmation and disconfirmation, was proposed by Jean Nicod, who suggested that the two "elementary relations" of confirmation and invalidation afford perhaps the only way in which particular facts can affect the probability of universal propositions.

The same universal proposition can be expressed in any number of logically equivalent sentences, and if an evidence sentence confirms one formulation of a proposition, then surely it must count as also confirming any equivalent formulation of it; this is the "equivalence condition" for confirmation. Thus, the following sentences, which are logically equivalent and hence express the same hypothesis, must be confirmed by the same evidence sentences: (*a*) "All ravens are black"; (*b*) "All nonblack things are nonravens"; (*c*) "Any particular thing is not a raven and/or is black."

Now, by Nicod's criterion, (*b*) is confirmed by any evidence sentence stating that a certain object, say *i*, is not black and not a raven—which is true, for example, when *i* is a white crow or a red rose; (*c*) is confirmed by any evidence sentence stating of some object *i* that it is not a raven and/or is black—which is true, for example, when *i* is a crow, a rose, or a shoe of any color and also when *i* is any black object, such as a lump of coal. Any object that is both a raven and black and thus affords confirmation for (*a*) will thus give rise to confirmatory instances for the hypothesis that all ravens are black.

This result is paradoxical. It is paradoxical not in the sense of involving a logical contradiction but, rather, in the sense of being a counterintuitive logical consequence of two requirements—Nicod's criterion and the equivalence condition—that seems to be reasonably, and, indeed, necessarily imposed upon the qualitative concept of confirmation.

Carl G. Hempel, who called attention to these consequences, has argued that the two requirements from which they follow are indeed unexceptionable and that the consequences lose the appearance of paradox if we observe that the sentence "*e* confirms *h*" means only that if the hypothesis *h* is judged exclusively by the information included in *e*, then it is borne out or supported. For example, an evidence sentence that confirms, in Nicod's sense, formulation (*b*) of the raven hypothesis tells us no more about the world than that a certain object *i* is neither black nor a raven; it does not indicate any further characteristics of *i* (to refer to *i* as a white crow or as a red rose is therefore to violate the understanding in question by suggesting additional information), nor does it indicate whether there are any objects other than *i* in the world. Considering this, it is clear that our evidence bears out even the hypothesis that nothing in the world is a raven and hence, by logical implication, that all ravens are black. Essentially the same view on this issue has been taken by Nelson Goodman and by Israel Scheffler, who has dealt in detail with some dissenting opinions.

Several writers have argued that by means of a suitable quantitative theory of confirmation or inductive probability and on the basis of certain presumably reasonable assumptions such as the assumption that the probability of an object's being nonblack greatly exceeds that of its being a raven, it is possible to establish an objective logical difference, at least in degree, between positive instances of the paradoxical and of the nonparadoxical kinds; the difference being that a nonparadoxical positive instance increases the prior probability of the generalization much more than a paradoxical one. This general idea, which in most variants is compatible with the recognition of paradoxically positive instances as confirmatory, was first advanced by Janina Hosiasson-Lindenbaum; more or less similar views have been taken by other writers, among them I. J. Good, D. F. Pears, and G. H. von Wright.

General definition. Hempel has proposed an explicit general definition, in purely formal or syntactical terms, for the case where the evidence sentence and the hypothesis are expressed in a formalized language with the logical structure of a first-order predicate calculus without identity. The definition is constructed to ensure the fulfillment of certain "conditions of adequacy"; these include the equivalence condition mentioned earlier and some others. These are that (1) logical implication is to be a subrelation of confirmation—that is, if *e* logically implies *h*, then *e* must confirm *h*; (2) if *e* confirms every sentence in a class *K*, then *e* must also confirm every sentence logically implied by *K*; (3) any logically consistent evidence sentence *e* should be logically compatible with the class of all hypotheses it confirms.

To the assumption that any adequately construed concept of qualitative confirmation must meet these requirements, Carnap and Popper have rightly objected that (3) is too restrictive, since the same evidence may well bear out two incompatible hypotheses. Carnap has also questioned conditions (1) and (2) on the ground that they are demonstrably incompatible with an additional condition of adequacy, proposed by him, which connects the qualitative concept of confirmation with the quantitative one of degree of confirmation or inductive probability: On at least one adequate definition of logical probabilities, it should generally be the case that an evidence sentence *e* qualitatively confirms a hypothesis *h* only if the probability of *h* on *e* exceeds the "a priori probability" of *h*, that is, the probability of *h* on tautological, or null, evidence. The task of constructing a more satisfactory definition of qualitative confirmation that does not use a quantitative concept of confirmation is still uncompleted.

Goodman's problem. Even with further refinements the concept of confirmation cannot be adequately defined in purely formal or syntactical terms. This has become especially clear through Nelson Goodman's studies of induction, which show that some hypotheses of the form "All *P* are *Q*" cannot derive any evidential support at all from information of the type "*i* is *P*, and *i* is *Q*." For example, let "*x* is *P*" stand for "*x* is an emerald" and "*x* is *Q*" for "*x* is grue," where an object is said to be grue if it has been examined before a certain time *t* and is green or has not been examined before *t* and is blue. Then any emerald *i* examined before *t* and found to be green affords a formally confirming instance, in Nicod's sense, of the generalization "All emeralds are grue." Yet however many such instances may be in hand, they will not count as confirming that generalization, for the latter implies that all emeralds which are not examined before *t*—in particular, all those which may be examined after *t*—are blue, and this consequence must surely be regarded as disconfirmed rather than confirmed by the evidence. Thus, whether a hypothesis of universal form admits of confirmation by particular instances, whether it can be "projected," in Goodman's phrase, from observed to unobserved cases, will depend on what predicates are used in its formulation. The use of the predicate "grue," for example, precludes "projectibility." Thus, there arises the problem of characterizing those predicates that can occur in "projectible" generalizations. Goodman does this by means of the pragmatic (rather than purely syntactic or semantic) notion of the "entrenchment" of a predicate—that is, of the extent to which the predicate, or any predicate coextensive with it, has been used in previously projected generalizations; "grue," for example, is much less well entrenched than "green," which has figured in many previous inductive generalizations. By reference to the relative entrenchment of the constituent predicates, Goodman then formulates a number of criteria for the relative "projectibility" of generalizations and thus also for their susceptibility to confirmation by positive instances.

Bibliography

Carnap, Rudolf, *Logical Foundations of Probability*. Chicago, 1950; 2d ed., 1962. Presents, at a fairly technical level, the most fully developed quantitative theory of confirmation. On confirmation in general, see Secs. 1–6; on the qualitative concept, see Secs. 46, 86–88.

Good, I. J., "The Paradoxes of Confirmation," Parts I and II. *The British Journal for the Philosophy of Science*, Vol. 11 (1960), 145–148; Vol. 12 (1961), 63–64.

Goodman, Nelson, *Fact, Fiction, and Forecast*. Cambridge, Mass., 1955. Chs. 3–4.

Hempel, Carl G., "Studies in the Logic of Confirmation," Parts I and II. *Mind*, Vol. 54 (1945), 1–26, 97–121. Develops in detail the paradoxes of confirmation and offers a general definition of qualitative confirmation for certain formalized languages.

Hosiasson-Lindenbaum, Janina, "On Confirmation." *The Journal of Symbolic Logic*, Vol. 5 (1940), 133–148. On the paradoxes, see especially Sec. 4.

Keynes, J. M., *A Treatise on Probability*. London and New York, 1921; 2d ed., 1929. One of the classical quantitative approaches.

Kyburg, Henry E., "Recent Work in Inductive Logic." *American Philosophical Quarterly*, Vol. 1 (1964), 249–287. A compact critical survey with extensive bibliographical references.

Nicod, Jean, *Foundations of Geometry and Induction*. New York and London, 1930. The author outlines his general conception of confirmation on pp. 219–220.

Pears, D. F., "Hypotheticals." *Analysis*, Vol. 10 (1950), 49–63. Deals with the paradoxes.

Popper, Karl, *The Logic of Scientific Discovery*. London, 1950. On the author's concept of degree of corroboration, see especially Ch. 10 and the concluding "New Appendices," Secs. *vii and *ix.

Scheffler, Israel, *The Anatomy of Inquiry*. New York, 1963. Part III offers a lucid and detailed analysis of qualitative confirmation.

Wright, G. H. von, *The Logical Problem of Induction*. Oxford, 1957. On the paradoxes of confirmation, see particularly Ch. 6, Secs. 5–6.

CARL G. HEMPEL

CONFIRMATION: QUANTITATIVE ASPECTS. The most straightforward of the current analyses of the quantitative aspects of confirmation construes the degree of confirmation of a hypothesis on a given body of evidence as simply a measure of the extent to which that evidence inclines us to believe the hypothesis. Most contemporary subjectivists, as those who hold this view are called, also subscribe to some version of behaviorism. They maintain a behavioral interpretation of degrees of belief or adopt behavioral criteria for their identification. Whatever the version of behaviorism they support, a consideration of the characteristics of rational behavior enables subjectivists to establish conditions which sets of degrees of belief must satisfy if they are to be conjointly rational. All the principles of probability theory can in this manner be proved to hold for degrees of confirmation.

The subjectivist position is, however, too weak to serve all our purposes. Providing no analysis of the rationality of degrees of belief considered independently of one another—of what our degrees of belief *ought* to be—it permits us to consider any hypothesis to be confirmed to any degree by any body of evidence. Knowing what we do in fact know, we are not at liberty to think it likely to be hot next winter. Subjectivist analyses are thus in need of supplementation.

Frequentist analyses. An obvious course is to point out that we ought to think it likely to be cold next winter because we know that winters have usually been cold. Elaborating on this truism, we might go on to maintain that on evidence reporting that m out of n X's have been Y's, the *objective* degree of confirmation of an X being a Y is m/n. Frequentist analyses, as they are called, can be formulated in a variety of ways, but basic to them all is the concept of the likelihood of some randomly selected X being a Y. What often concerns us, however, is how likely a particular X is to be a Y. A man considering some specific course of conduct will ask himself how likely it is to succeed. It may appear that all he need do is determine the relative frequency of successes in the appropriate reference class. But what reference class would be appropriate? The class of all the courses of conduct ever pursued would be too inclusive, and each of the countless narrower classes of courses of conduct to which the project he is contemplating belongs may have yielded a different relative frequency of successes. The problem of the single case has thus far resisted all frequentist attempts at solution.

An analogous difficulty arises if we ask for the degree of confirmation of some specific unrestricted generalization. For to seek to determine the proportion of generalizations of the sort in question that have been found to hold without exception is to encounter the problem of classifying the generalization, the problem of determining the reference class of the proposed frequency analysis.

Carnap's analysis. The frequentists' difficulties suggest that what is needed is a more comprehensive theory that permits the determination of degrees of confirmation of hypotheses, whatever their logical form. The importance of Rudolf Carnap's analysis derives from the fact that it serves this purpose. Carnap develops his position in terms of a set of simplified models of the language we ordinarily use. But conclusions reached with respect to one of Carnap's artificial languages can readily be applied to statements couched in the vernacular, the advantage of this indirect procedure being that it enables him to establish some impressive results that are not otherwise demonstrable.

An artificial language of Carnap's sort is identified in part by its stock of names and of primitive predicates, predicates designating psychologically simple properties subject to sensory discrimination. A primitive predicate and its complement—a predicate true of all those and only those objects of which the primitive predicate is false—constitute what Carnap calls a basic pair. A Q-predicate is a compound predicate formed by conjoining one of the two components from each of the basic pairs of the language. A Q-state description is a conjunction of n statements, each ascribing some one of the Q-predicates to a different one of the n individuals that can be named in the language.

Only one of the various Q-state descriptions constructible in a given language describes the actual state of affairs—only one, that is, is true. We do not usually know which one this is, but Carnap contends that a consideration of the various epistemic options to which we are obliged to be indifferent will enable us to assign to each Q-state description a measure of initial or a priori credibility.

He maintains two theses in this connection. The first is that there are no rational grounds for inclining a priori to the possibility that x objects are characterized by Q-predicate A, y objects by Q-predicate B, and so on, over the possibility that v objects are characterized by A, w by B, and so on. These various structural possibilities, or rather the *structure descriptions* describing them, may, of course, accommodate different numbers of Q-state descriptions. (A structure description tagging each nameable object with the same Q-predicate accommodates only one Q-state description; any other structure description accommodates a greater number.)

Carnap refers to the Q-state descriptions included under a single structure description as isomorphic to one another, and maintains, as his second indifference thesis, that there is no rational way of choosing a priori between isomorphic Q-state descriptions. His two theses on a priori indifference lead him to suggest that the measure of initial credibility of any given Q-state description be set at the reciprocal of the product of τ, the number of structure descriptions constructible in the language, and ζ, the number of Q-state descriptions isomorphic to the one at issue—that is, at $1/\tau\zeta$.

A moment's reflection will establish that as our body of information grows, the number of Q-state descriptions remaining compatible with that information grows progressively smaller. Of those that remain at any one occasion, only some, as a rule, will also be compatible with any given hypothesis not itself ruled out by our information. Carnap proposes to identify the degree of confirmation of hypothesis h relative to evidence e with the ratio of the sum of the respective initial credibility measures of the various Q-state descriptions compatible with both h and e to the sum of the respective measures of those compatible with e alone.

Difficulties. However, Carnap's theory leaves the problem of the single case unsolved. His theory determines degrees of confirmation for statements only, and what often concerns us is how likely this or that event is to occur. Nevertheless, although Carnap does not solve the problem of the single case, he does enable us to outflank it. The degree of confirmation of a statement describing an event can be construed as the degree of confirmation of that event under the given description, and a relativized assessment along these lines suffices for all practical purposes. The concept of the degree of confirmation of an event per se can safely be left unexplicated.

But a greater difficulty confronts Carnap's analysis. Suppose that in a million tosses of a die, the faces other than the two have fallen uppermost about five-sixths of the time. Using Carnap's analysis, the degree of confirmation of the hypothesis that the next toss will not yield a two would as a rule be quite high. Suppose, however, we had chosen to describe our experience with this die by recording that about five-sixths of the tosses were either both among the first million recorded and other than a two, or both not among the first million recorded and a two. Parity of reasoning would oblige us to assign a high degree of confirmation to the hypothesis that the next toss, the millionth-and-first, will instantiate this compound property and thus will yield a two—an assessment conflicting with the one above.

This problem was introduced and first discussed by Nelson Goodman. It is not unique to Carnap's analysis but can be raised in connection with every theory of confirmation assigning evidential relevance to the relative frequencies recorded. The moral Goodman draws is that not all predicates are such that the recorded relative frequencies associated with them are always indefeasibly relevant to the degree of confirmation of a hypothesis in which they occur, that not all predicates are always equally "projectible." His discussion makes it clear that a logic of the quantitative aspect of confirmation must establish a criterion for the comparison of degrees of "projectibility." He himself proposes such a criterion, but the issue is not yet fully resolved.

Confirmation of generalizations. Carnap's theory avoids the second of the two difficulties of the frequentist analysis, but only at the cost of embracing a paradox. The degree of confirmation of an unrestricted generalization is readily determinable, but if such a generalization is phrased in a language containing a number of names sufficient to enable us to formulate factually exhaustive Q-state descriptions, its degree of confirmation is invariably almost nil.

However, this perplexing result is also not unique to Carnap's theory. A generalization can be construed as the conjunction of all its instances, and in accordance with the special multiplication theorem (which states that the degree of confirmation of a conjunction of logically independent statements is equal to the product of their respective degrees of confirmation), the degree of confirmation of a conjunction of this sort is the product of the degrees of confirmation of its various conjuncts. Thus every theory assigning degrees of confirmation to singular hypotheses and subscribing to the special multiplication theorem—to which the subjectivist analysis of the corationality of degrees of belief is committed—is bound to establish that the degree of confirmation of an unrestricted generalization approaches zero as the number of its instances approaches infinity. Carnap contends that although this may be an unexpected result, it does not jeopardize the acceptability of his analysis. He argues that an investigation of the extent to which our information supports some generalization is never, in fact, concerned with its degree of confirmation proper but, rather, with either its degree of instance confirmation (the degree of confirmation of a randomly selected instance of that generalization) or its degree of qualified instance confirmation (the degree of confirmation of the consequent of such an instance given the truth of the corresponding antecedent), and he maintains that his analysis establishes altogether plausible results in these two connections. It is debatable, however, whether his argument does justice to every variety of research program.

Hypotheses and degree of confirmation. The impossibility of determining a degree of confirmation significantly higher than zero for any generalization has led some authors to conclude that degrees of confirmation cannot really be at issue in the assessment of hypotheses. Karl Popper is the principal spokesman for this point of view. Popper demonstrates that the scientific significance of hypotheses is not a function solely of their degrees of confirmation, and his discussion is highly suggestive. In order to invalidate our concern with degrees of confirmation, he would, however, have to prove that the significance of hypotheses is independent of their degree of confirmation. Popper has not proved this, nor is it likely that any other analysis of the significance of hypotheses can.

The concept of degree of confirmation refuses to be ignored. Thus far, it has also been intractable to adequate analysis, but current awareness of the difficulties involved enhances the prospects of further study.

Bibliography

Carnap, Rudolf, *The Logical Foundations of Probability*, 2d ed. Chicago, 1962.

Goodman, Nelson, *Fact, Fiction, and Forecast.* Cambridge, Mass., 1955.

Popper, Karl R., *The Logic of Scientific Discovery.* London, 1959.

Reichenbach, Hans, *The Theory of Probability*, 2d ed. Berkeley and Los Angeles, 1949. A frequentist analysis.

Savage, Leonard J., *The Foundations of Statistics.* New York, 1954. A subjectivist analysis.

FREDERIC SCHICK

CONFUCIUS (551–479 B.C.) is the most influential and most revered person in Chinese history. A descendant of a noble family, he grew up in poor circumstances but became a self-educated man and one most learned for his time. In his early twenties he served as keeper of the granary and later as supervisor of flocks in his native state of Lu. He also began to teach and showed a keen interest in politics. A decade later he was in the neighboring state of Ch'i for several years and was consulted on government, but he returned home when opposition threatened his life.

Both a high official and a rebel of Lu solicited his support, but he refused them. Some years later he made a trip to the capital of Chou to consult Lao Tzu on the details of ceremonies. At 51 he became a magistrate and then minister of justice, probably in the same year, perhaps having served as assistant minister of public works between the two appointments. As minister of justice he succeeded at a diplomatic meeting, in recovering the land taken by Ch'i. He also destroyed the walled cities of three powerful barons in order to restore power to the ruler of Chou. At 56, finding the ruler no longer interested in his ideas, he left Chou and spent almost 13 years traveling, with some of his pupils, through nine states. Unable to influence their rulers, he returned to Lu at 68 to continue teaching and perhaps to work on the documents and songs that eventually formed part of the *Spring and Autumn Annals*, the *Book of Changes* (*I Ching*), and four other classics, the *Book of History, Book of Odes, Book of Rites*, and *Book of Music.*

He said he was only a transmitter and looked to ancient sage-kings as models, but he was the first in China to become a professional teacher, to teach people literature and principles of conduct instead of vocational statecraft, and to open the doors of education to all. He radically changed traditional concepts of Heaven, the superior man, and humanity (*jen*) (see CHINESE PHILOSOPHY). He departed from the traditional "*ju* (literati) of the weak" emphasizing submission, taking no action, etc., and became a "*ju* of the strong," emphasizing an active life, etc., thus starting a new class of intellectuals. He also inaugurated the tradition of wandering scholars.

Raising the growing humanistic tendency to a greater height than before, he talked about life instead of death and about man rather than spiritual beings. He declared that "it is man that can make the Way great and not the Way that can make man great." For him the ideal is the harmony of the perfect individual and a well-ordered society based on the mutual moral obligations of the five human relations between ruler and minister, father and son, elder brother and younger brother, husband and wife, and one friend and another, with filial piety and brotherly respect as the two fundamental virtues. Government is to be conducted through the ruler's moral examples, and religious ceremonies are to fulfill moral duties. Confucius sharply contrasted the superior man, whose standard is moral principle, with the inferior man whose standard is profit. In short, his whole doctrine can be summed up as ethical humanism.

Bibliography

See *The Analects of Confucius*, translated by Arthur Waley (London, 1938).

For literature on Confucius, see Wing-tsit Chan, *A Source Book in Chinese Philosophy* (Princeton, N.J., 1963), and H. G. Creel, *Confucius, the Man and the Myth* (New York, 1949), which also appeared in a paperback edition entitled *Confucius and the Chinese Way* (New York, 1960).

WING-TSIT CHAN

CONSCIENCE. Doubtless from the earliest times in which groups established social customs, or mores, and enforced them, members of such groups who were tempted to violate these mores could almost feel the disapproval of their fellows and hear in their own minds a protesting outcry, perhaps some primitive equivalent of "No!" or "Don't!" In the early eighteenth century such inner voices or feelings were described as edicts of one's moral sense or of one's conscience. This kind of account of these restraining influences became explicit with the development of faculty psychology, which involved the view that there are different faculties of the human mind responsible for different capacities or abilities which the mind seems to exhibit. Reason was thought of as the rational faculty, emotion as a passional one, and volition as a faculty that enables us to reach decisions and make choices. The moral faculty was thought by some, Shaftesbury and Francis Hutcheson, for example, to operate through feelings. For instance, a feeling of repugnance would tend to be aroused by the thought of doing anything immoral—anything in violation of the mores—and a feeling of approval by the thought of acting virtuously.

In contrast with this moral-sense type of theory, Samuel Clarke and Richard Price, among others, thought that it must be something akin to reason or the understanding which enabled us to distinguish right from wrong. Joseph Butler termed this faculty of the mind "conscience," and in more recent times this term has become the common one.

Modern behaviorists, to be sure, would not write of conscience as a mental faculty; they refer instead to "learned modes of reaction to stimuli." When one has been conditioned to respond in certain standard ways which are widely and strongly approved, one tends to find that one can break with such approved behavioral norms only after a genuine struggle and a stiff volitional conflict. In any case, whether we speak of the voice of conscience or of the voice of our group or of learned blockage and interference patterns, we often find that there are inhibitions to be overcome before we can break with the mores of our peers.

It has been suggested that a policeman, upholding the law, functions as a kind of government-supported externalized conscience. His mere presence in uniform suffices to warn us not to break, for example, the speed law that we are already bending a bit. Even animals below the human level can be trained to feel the force of such an externalized conscience. Cats, for example, can be trained not to sleep on the couch when humans are in the room. But it is difficult, to say the least, to teach them not to do so when no human observer is present to their senses. With human children and adults, by contrast, it is possible to develop an internalized conscience, which, even in the absence of all enforcers, will remind them, and even stimulate them strongly, not to do certain prohibited actions and to do certain required ones. The driver who stops his car at red traffic lights only when he sees or suspects that an officer is nearby has, like the cat, only an externalized conscience about this type of act, whereas one who habitually stops is, as we say, acting conscientiously—obeying, perhaps unconsciously, his internalized conscience.

That "the voice of conscience" is often effective seems clear, but it is also clear that it can and often does lose its effectiveness. A dutiful son may well adopt many of the mores of his father for a time and then gradually abandon them. If a person persists in violating his conscience, it will grow decrepit, bother him less and less effectively, and it may soon cease to deter him at all.

Conscience as a reliable guide. As children many of us were taught that the voice of conscience is the voice of God and, hence, completely reliable. Some would claim, in more sophisticated terms, that although God gave us free will and does not infringe upon our freedom of choice, he nevertheless continues to lend us moral support. He gives us, through conscience, a means for distinguishing right from wrong. If we follow the guidance of conscience, we shall do our duty and act rightly. If we act contrary to its deliverances, we shall surely act wrongly.

There are, however, many difficulties with this kind of account and, indeed, with any other which claims that conscience is a sufficient guide to moral conduct.

First, the consciences of different people, whether members of the same or of different societies, often differ radically. Conscientious objectors to war and volunteers for wartime service usually disagree strongly as to the rightness of a given war. Cannibals do not share the conscientious objections to eating human flesh that vegetarians do, and both these groups differ from those who feel it is morally permissible to eat animal but not human flesh.

Second, there seem to be exceptions to all the edicts of conscience. Even within groups whose members share, say, a conscientious prescription against deliberately taking a human life, the exceptions that the various consciences allow to individuals vary greatly from one person to another. Tolstoy, and presumably some Quakers, would insist that his conscience forbids the taking of a human life under any conditions. By contrast, although many of us verbally would fully accept the commandment not to kill, we would be likely in practice to find ourselves approving some acts of killing, for example in self-defense or in defense of others, and disapproving of some avoidances of killing, for example in a very deserving mercy case.

Third, conscience fails to provide guidance for many important and even some crucial moral questions. Many problems that we confront are so complex that we frankly have very little idea, and certainly no confirmed judgment or deliverance of conscience, as to which alternative is most worthy of being chosen. In many such cases, where getting adequate knowledge in the time available before a decision must be reached is impossible, we know in advance that we would be only too happy to do what is right if we could identify, with some reasonable degree of probability, the right alternative. A situation of this sort must frequently arise for people who cannot pass the decision on to someone else. The president of the United States, for example, cannot avoid the responsibility for important decisions that must be made—very often on vastly less evidence than he would like to have. Similarly, there are many difficult problems to be decided by those of us who are less highly placed, problems where the decision will not indeed be world-shaking but where it will affect a number of lives in important ways. We often sweat with the desire to solve a difficult problem in the right way but are unable, in the time available before a decision must be taken, to find out which way is the right way. In complicated cases the relatively simple prescriptions of conscience tend to prove quite inadequate.

It is not that the prescriptions of our conscience are worthless; they are often of value in reminding us of the moral views which have been taken by other members of our peer group. Awareness also of the edicts which spring from the consciences of others with different backgrounds not infrequently throws light on our own problem. But in complicated and novel cases, the edict of another's conscience cannot provide us with certain knowledge as to what ought to be done.

Sources of deliverances of conscience. Psychologists, anthropologists, and other social scientists have gathered empirical evidence as to various sources of the deliverances of conscience. Many of the edicts of our conscience seem to have come to us while we still rested at our mother's knee. These were usually simple in form but quite effective for many years. Others came from our fathers, from teachers, from preachers, from lecturers and writers, from friends whom we respected. This wide variety of the sources of the edicts which now emanate apparently from our own consciences explains many things about them: their vagueness, their variability, their changing authority over us. As suggested by behaviorists, at least some of them rest on conditioned responses instilled in us at an early age by repetitions we no longer remember.

Examination of a particular edict of conscience throws significant light on "our inner voices." Suppose we warn our sons, ages four and six, to stay off a railway trestle near our home. We say with great emphasis, "*Never* go out on that trestle, no matter what." One day the younger boy pursues his gay red ball onto the trestle. The older boy rushes to him and pulls him off the trestle just before a train crosses it. Will we punish him for breaking our "absolute" rule? Obviously not. Our consciously instilled rule, now a command of conscience, has its values, positive and negative. It needs supplementation as soon as increasing maturity permits rational consideration. And to this phase anyone who has attained knowledge and discretion should surely move on.

Universalizability of moral prescriptions. Since the edicts of conscience have pedestrian empirical sources and are subject to exceptions, it was natural for Immanuel Kant to insist, through his categorical imperative, that every valid moral principle must hold universally: "So act that you can will the maxim or principle of your action to be a universal law, binding on the will of every rational being." This requirement has two facets. First, for an act to be moral it must be done not on whim or impulse or as a mere reflex response to stimuli, but in accordance with some moral principle or maxim. Second, this principle must be one that the agent is willing to have universally adopted. This requirement that a person should act only on a principle that he is *willing* to have universally adopted seems to introduce undesirable psychological factors that might tend to vary radically from one person to the next. Thus, a pessimist like Schopenhauer might approve of universal suicide and be willing to have everyone else do so, whereas an optimist might be willing to have everyone work toward increasing the population. Such a formulation of the universalizability principle would thus lead to incompatible moral edicts.

To eliminate such psychological factors and to state the principle in a way closer to Kant's intent, R. M. Hare urges that a moral principle, to be applicable to a person *A*, must also be applicable in like circumstances to any similar person *B*. Although Hare's intent seems clear, he does not specify the degree of similarity required. Complete identity would make the principle useless. On the other hand, it seems clear that Hare was not suggesting, for example, that because it is right for *A* to make love to his wife, it is also proper that *B*, who is like *A* in various respects, should also make love to Mrs. *A*. Perhaps the universalizability thesis is best stated as follows: If it is right for *A* to do an act of kind *X* in a set of circumstances *C*, then it is right for any *B* who is like *A* in all relevant respects to do an act of kind *X* in circumstances like *C* in all relevant respects. So stated, the principle is analytically and thus necessarily true. But whether we can ever know in practice that both sets of circumstances and both agents are alike in all relevant respects is highly doubtful. It would be difficult, if not impossible, even to specify these respects. But we do know what is meant by this prescription, and we sometimes know with a fair degree of probability that the required likenesses are present.

Because the universalizability principle is analytic, it is necessarily true. But it is an "If . . . then . . ." statement: If *A* should do *X* in *C*, then *B* should do *Y* in *D*, where the similarities between *A* and *B*, *C* and *D*, and *X* and *Y* meet the requirements previously mentioned. Quite aside from the difficulties of knowing whether or not these requirements are met, the statement tells us only that if its antecedent is true, its consequent is also true. But to know the antecedent to be true—that *A* ought to do *X* in *C*—we must turn to experience for an answer. To know anything to be good on the whole, we must know if its existence (or occurrence) is preferable to its nonexistence. To know any act to be right, we must know that no possible alternative is preferable to it. Such preferability presupposes empirical knowledge of values. The possibility of such knowledge is a matter of controversy, but many, including the present writer, believe it to be attainable.

Bibliography

WORKS OF HISTORICAL INTEREST

Balguy, John, *The Foundation of Moral Goodness.* Part I, London, 1728; Part II, London, 1729.

Butler, Joseph, *Fifteen Sermons.* London, 1726.

Clarke, Samuel, *A Discourse Concerning the Unchangeable Obligations of Natural Religion and the Truth and Certainty of the Christian Revelation.* 2d corrected ed., London, 1706.

Hutcheson, Francis, *An Inquiry Into the Original of Our Ideas of Beauty and Virtue.* London, 1725.

Kant, Immanuel, *The Moral Law, or Kant's Groundwork of the Metaphysics of Morals*, translated with analysis and notes by H. J. Paton. London, 1948.

Price, Richard, *A Review of the Principal Questions and Difficulties in Morals.* London, 1758.

Shaftesbury, 3d earl of (Anthony Ashley Cooper), *An Inquiry Concerning Virtue or Merit.* London, 1699.

RECENT WORKS

Broad, C. D., "Some Reflections on Moral-sense Theories in Ethics," *PAS*, Vol. 45 (1944–1945), 131–186.

Raphael, D. Daiches, *The Moral Sense.* London, 1947.

Ross, W. David, *The Right and the Good.* London, 1930.

Ross, W. David, *Foundations of Ethics.* Oxford, 1939.

Smith, T. V., *Beyond Conscience. A Critical Examination of Various Doctrines of Conscience.* New York, 1934.

CHARLES A. BAYLIS

CONSCIOUSNESS. The term "consciousness" occurs in philosophy, psychology, and common speech with a variety of different meanings. In this article those meanings will be discussed which are relevant to the formulation of several recurrent philosophical problems.

SELF-KNOWLEDGE

In *An Essay Concerning Human Understanding* Locke defined consciousness as "the perception of what passes in a man's own mind" (II, i, 19). Consciousness or reflection is a person's observing or noticing the "internal operations" of his mind. It is by means of consciousness that a person acquires the ideas of the various operations or mental states, such as the ideas of perceiving, thinking, doubting, reasoning, knowing, and willing and learns of his own mental states at any given time. It "might properly enough be called 'internal sense'" because "the understanding turns inwards upon itself, reflects on its own operations, and makes them the object of its own contemplation" (II, i, 4 and 8). Locke's use of "consciousness" was widely adopted in British philosophy. In the late nineteenth century the term "introspection" began to be used. G. F. Stout's definition is typical: "To introspect is to attend to the workings of one's own mind" (*A Manual of Psychology*, New York, 1899, p. 14).

According to Thomas Reid consciousness is only of the present state of mind. It has become customary to distinguish introspection, or the observation of a present state, from retrospection, or the recollection of a state in the immediate past. Few writings make the further distinction between the act of observing or attending to one's present states for the purpose of acquiring knowledge of them and the actual achieving of or coming to possess such knowledge. In this article "introspection" will refer to the act of observing one's mental states and "self-knowledge" or "knowledge" to the achievement of that knowledge. In the history of philosophy a number of questions have been raised.

Introspection and self-knowledge. Do introspection and self-knowledge accompany every mental state? According to Locke it is necessary that a person know or be conscious of his own mental state (*Essay*, II, i, 19, and xxvii, 9). Both Thomas Reid and Sir William Hamilton, among others, have agreed with Locke. Leibniz, however, pointed out that Locke's view leads to an infinite regress, for if every mental state is accompanied by self-knowledge, then, because self-knowledge is also mental state, it too must be so accompanied, *ad infinitum* (*New Essays Concerning Human Understanding*, II, i, 19). The regress is harmful only if there is a difference between one's knowing something and one's knowing that one knows it. But there does seem to be a difference. It seems possible for a person to believe that he does not know whether, for example, a certain geometrical theorem is true and then for him to remember having proved it true. It seems reasonable to claim that he knew it to be true all the time, but since he did not believe he knew it, he did not know he knew it.

The regress may be avoided by defining a first-order mental state as one which is not about any mental state. Locke's thesis may be reformulated as the claim that it is necessary that self-knowledge accompany every first-order state. There is now a further difficulty. In order for someone who is perceiving a tree to know that he is perceiving a tree, it is necessary that he possess the concepts of a tree and of a perception, that he know what a tree is and what perception is. But it is possible for some creatures, for example, animals and young children, to perceive without possessing the relevant concepts. In general, it is possible that the concepts used in the description of a mental state are not possessed by the individual who is in that state. In such a case the individual could not possess self-knowledge.

Another reformulation which avoids this difficulty is: If a person is in a first-order mental state and possesses the concepts entering into its description, then it is necessary that he know he is in that state. A number of thinkers (for example, Leibniz, Freud, and Russell) who believe that there are or can be unconscious first-order states would reject even this claim, and with good reason, for it seems possible for a person to make erroneous judgments about his motives or his desires or his beliefs.

Does introspection ever occur? Many philosophers have denied the possibility of introspection. One reason, given by Auguste Comte, is that introspection implies the absurdity that a person could divide himself in two, one part reasoning and the other observing the first reasoning. Another common objection is that attending to an experience modifies that experience, so that the only way to grasp an experience unaffected by attention is through retrospection.

A more fundamental objection has been raised by those who are skeptical of the traditional dualism between mind and body. On the traditional account, introspection has been thought to be analogous to perception; it has been understood as a nondiscursive process by which the mind contemplates its own acts. Just as one can distinguish between seeing an object and making judgments about what one sees, so one can distinguish between introspecting a mental state and making judgments about it. But perceiving involves the use of the sensory organs, the eyes, ears, etc. What is the organ of introspection? There is no physical organ to do the job, so, on the traditional theory, it must be the mind or one of its parts. It would seem, then, that the standard account of introspection presupposes that the mind is a nonphysical entity capable of having quasi-sensory experiences. This presupposition is rejected by behaviorists and by materialists (see MIND–BODY PROBLEM). According to them there can be no inner sense.

In opposition to the critics of introspection, Thomas Reid argued that with respect to mental states, "consciousness is the evidence, the only evidence, which we have or can have of their existence" (*Essays on the Intellectual Powers of Man*, Bk. I, Ch. 2). Retrospection is not sufficient for knowledge of past states, for we can retrospect only what we have been previously conscious of. Reid's view leads to a dilemma. If a person is justified in asserting that he is in pain only if he has introspected his experience of being in pain, what justifies him in asserting that he has introspected the experience? If it is answered that what justifies him is that he has introspected his introspection, then he could not be justified in asserting that he is in pain unless he were justified in asserting an infinite number of other propositions. If, on the other hand, it is answered that his first introspection itself justifies the assertion that he has introspected his experience of pain, one can reply that his experience of pain itself justifies his assertion that he is in pain. The dispensability of introspection for self-knowledge has been thus argued by Sydney Shoemaker: "It is a distinguishing characteristic of first-person-experience statements . . . that it is simply their *being* true, and not the observation that they are true, or the possession of evidence that they are true, that entitles one to assert them" (*Self-knowledge and Self-identity*, Ithaca, N.Y., 1963, p. 122).

Since the existence of introspection as traditionally conceived is not a necessary condition of self-knowledge, and since its being such a condition has been a primary reason for thinking it exists, it is now doubtful whether the traditional theory is acceptable. Recently the claim that there are many types of facts about mental states and behavior which can be known without observation has been much discussed. But even if the traditional theory is wrong, something like introspection often takes place. It is a common, everyday phenomenon to think about one's experiences at the time they are occurring. For example, a person looking at a painting may wonder whether he is enjoying his experience or whether he is enjoying it more than some previous experience. The main difficulty with the traditional theory was its attempt to categorize the process of self-reflection as a form of sense perception or of direct awareness.

Is introspection fallible? That introspection can yield erroneous beliefs about one's own mental states has been asserted on many occasions in the history of philosophy. On the other hand, in his *Philosophical Investigations* Wittgenstein said, ". . . it makes sense to say about other people that they doubt whether I am in pain; but not to say it about myself" (Sec. 246).

Perhaps a clearer formulation of the question is: Is it possible for a person to have false beliefs about his mental states at the time he is supposedly in those states? The following cases are among those in which false beliefs are clearly possible: (1) There is a type of mental state which is cognitive, which is such that a person's being in that state entails that he knows that something is the case; examples are perceiving and remembering. If a person claims to perceive or remember that something is the case, and if the proposition expressing what is supposedly perceived or remembered is false, then the person merely thinks or believes he perceives or remembers. Hence, it is possible for a person to believe falsely that he is in a cognitive state. (2) It is possible for a person to have false beliefs about his own motives, desires, and personality traits. (3) With respect to sensations, a person can be mistaken about their location (for example, he might think he has a pain in his leg after it has been amputated) or about their cause (for example, he might think he has a toothache when in fact the pain is not caused by an infection in the tooth).

The question now arises whether there is a type of mental state such that it is necessary that if a person believes his mind is in that state, then his belief is true. If there are any, let them be called immediate experiences. Some philosophers have claimed that such events as being in pain or thinking or imagining something are immediate experiences, on the grounds that there is no difference between the experiences and the belief that one is having them. Shoemaker suggests a principle on which this view is based when he says that statements about immediate experiences "are incorrigible in the sense that if a person sincerely asserts such a statement it does not make sense to suppose, and nothing could be accepted as showing, that he is mistaken" (p. 216). The principle seems to be: It is necessary that if a person has a belief for which there can be no disconfirming evidence, then his belief is true. Other philosophers have disagreed on the grounds that any statement may be withdrawn for the sake of consistency in our beliefs. (See Nelson Goodman, "Sense and Certainty," *Philosophical Review*, Vol. 61, 1952, 160–167).

Source of our ideas of the mind. Is introspection the source of our concepts of mental states? According to Locke, consciousness provides us with our ideas of the various operations of the mind. No person can know what perception is unless he has observed a case of perception, and his own perceptions are the only ones he can observe. This theory is merely a special case of a fundamental psychological principle of traditional empiricism, which states that all ideas are abstracted from or compounded out of what is observed. Now the problem of how people do get ideas or concepts is very much up in the air and certainly cannot be solved without a great deal of psychological investigation. But this much can be said about the traditional theory: If introspection is best characterized not as inner sense or direct observation but as thinking and judging about one's mental states, then it cannot be an original source of concepts. For thinking is an activity in which a person is already exercising the concepts he possesses; he cannot think about anything unless he already has an idea of it. Locke's thesis, which is doubtful, must be distinguished from one which it entails and which is less problematic, namely, that a person cannot have the concept of certain mental states unless he has been in those states, that, for example, a person cannot know what pain is unless he has been in pain.

STATES OF CONSCIOUSNESS

The term "consciousness" has a broad use to designate any mental state or whatever it is about a state which makes it mental. "Consciousness includes not only awareness of our own states, but these states themselves, whether we have cognisance of them or not. If a man is angry, that is a state of consciousness, even though he does not know that he is angry. If he does know that he is angry, that is another modification of consciousness, and not the same" (Stout, *Manual of Psychology*, p. 8). G. E. Moore, in an important and influential essay, "The Refutation of Idealism," claimed to have discovered something common to the various mental states:

> The sensation of blue differs from that of green. But it is plain that if both are *sensations* they also have some point in common. . . . I will call this common element "consciousness" . . . . We have then in every sensation two distinct terms, (1) "consciousness," in respect of which all sensations are alike; and (2) something else [the object], in respect of which one sensation differs from another. (*Philosophical Studies*, London, 1922)

It is consciousness which makes a fact a mental fact. How are we to understand the distinction between consciousness and the object? On this point Moore was ambiguous, giving two apparently incompatible analyses. According to the first—let it be called the constituent analysis—a mental fact consists of at least two terms or constituents—consciousness and the object—and a unique relation between them, called knowing. According to the second—the relational analysis—consciousness does not have this relation of knowing to the object; it *is* this relation. What the other term of the relation is, Moore did not say, but let it be called the subject. Moreover, consciousness has or is an external relation in the sense that the object, when the subject is conscious of it, is what it would be if the subject were not conscious of it. Moore did not clearly state what he meant by describing knowing as unique; we may surmise that he meant that knowing is not further analyzable, that it is not, to use Bertrand Russell's term, a "logical construction" out of other things.

An important consequence of both the constituent and relational analyses is that what makes one mental fact different from another is the difference of their objects, since consciousness is the common element. But in order for something to be a distinguishing constituent, it must exist; consciousness, therefore, is always of an existing object. What, then, can one say about those states of consciousness which consist of thinking about or imagining something which, apparently, does not exist (for example, thinking about Mr. Pickwick)? There seem to be two alternatives open to the theory. First, the object does always exist, but some exist in an unusual manner or in a manner not characteristic of objects of that species (for example, Mr. Pickwick exists in Dickens' imagination rather than in the physical world). Second, the ostensible object does not always exist, but the state of consciousness can be so analyzed as to imply the existence of something else of which the subject is conscious (for example, an image of or the concept of Mr. Pickwick or the name "Mr. Pickwick"). A third choice is to deny that there must always be an object of a state of consciousness and to affirm that different states are distinguished by their intrinsic features (see INTENTIONALITY).

A position that at first appears to be in conflict with Moore's view is stated by William James, who wrote: "I believe that 'consciousness' . . . is the name of a nonentity, and has no right to a place among first principles" ("Does 'Consciousness' Exist?" *Essays in Radical Empiricism*, London, 1912). But he immediately qualified his assertion to mean that consciousness is not a term but a relation that exists between two terms when one knows the other. It appears that James was here advocating the relational analysis. He gave the analysis a form which later became known as neutral monism: "If we start with the supposition that there is only one primal stuff or material in the world, a stuff of which everything is composed, and if we call that stuff 'pure experience,' then knowing can easily be explained as a particular sort of relation towards one another into which portions of pure experience may enter." No term is intrinsically a subject or object of consciousness; it is a subject if it occurs in one context or arrangement of terms and an object if it occurs in another. Russell later developed neutral monism in detail in his *Analysis of Mind:* "The stuff of which the world of experience is composed is . . . neither mind nor matter, but something more primitive than either." The claim of Russell and James that there is a primal nonmental stuff out of which all particulars are composed seems rather obscure. On the level of common sense, two objects made out of wood or iron are made of the same stuff; then what is the stuff which is the same in all experiences? James contradicted his initial claim when, in answer to this question, he wrote: ". . . there is no *general* stuff of which experience at large is made. There are as many stuffs as there are 'natures' in the things experienced." The "stuff" of a thing is simply the properties it has. As James admits, some particulars have the property of being conscious of others, and hence consciousness is part of their stuff. The opposition between neutral monism and the constituent analysis is more apparent than real.

In any case, the concepts in terms of which these issues have been formulated and debated—stuff, relation, term, property—need further analysis and clarification. In recent years the problem has been given a new form in the claim that consciousness *is* a process in the brain, where "is" designates a relation of composition. Brain processes are the "stuff" of which consciousness is composed (U. T. Place, "Is Consciousness a Brain Process?" *British Journal of Psychology*, Vol. 47, 1956). However, a brain process is a "stuff" in a different sense from that in which cotton is the stuff out of which a piece of cloth is made, for the brain process is an event and cotton is a material. It is not clear in what sense the word "is" could be used when it is said that consciousness is a brain process. At any rate, some critics have questioned whether the very statement that consciousness is a brain process is intelligible.

The term "state of consciousness" has become a technical term in philosophy whose meaning is most often conveyed by such examples as thinking of or imagining or believing something, or having a certain feeling or emotion or motive or sensation. It is logically possible that there is no one thing—whether stuff or property or relation—which all the standard examples have in common, although certain criteria have been proposed (for example, privacy, intentionality) which seem to mark off some states from others. It may be possible to sort the various states into groups, each distinguished by some defining property. If this can be accomplished, then the term "state of consciousness" can be defined as designating the disjunction of all these properties. Even if such a definition can be formulated, it may have little philosophical interest.

The chief thesis of philosophical behaviorism is the assertion that states of consciousness are behavioral dispositions, not inner events or occurrences, or stated more fully, that propositions which, on older views, were interpreted as referring to inner states of consciousness can be fully translated into statements about behavioral dispositions. The question of the validity of this thesis has occupied the center of the stage in recent philosophy of mind. There have been numerous attempts to analyze the various states in terms of the categories of disposition and event. Moreover, the concept of behavior has been much discussed, and many philosophers have argued that for the purpose of understanding distinctively human behavior, the concept must be construed as referring not to mere physical motions but to actions resulting from intentions. As a result, the concepts of intention, motivation, desire, and others referring to the immediate determinants of action have been the subject of a large number of articles and books.

Bibliography

There are full discussions of introspection in C. D. Broad, *The Mind and Its Place in Nature* (London, 1925), Ch. 6; C. A. Campbell, *On Selfhood and Godhood* (London, 1957), Lecture 7; Sir William Hamilton, *Lectures on Metaphysics* (Boston, 1859), Lectures 11–19; William James, *The Principles of Psychology* (New

York, 1890), Ch. 7; C. A. Mace, "Introspection and Analysis," in Max Black, ed., *Philosophical Analysis*, (Englewood Cliffs, N.J., 1963); Bertrand Russell, *The Analysis of Mind* (London, 1921), Ch. 6; and Gilbert Ryle, *The Concept of Mind* (London, 1949), Ch. 6.

On the topic of unconscious mental states, see C. D. Broad, *op. cit.*, Chs. 8–10, and A. C. MacIntyre, *The Unconscious* (London, 1958).

A clear statement of the relational analysis of states of consciousness is found in Bertrand Russell, "On the Nature of Acquaintance," in R. C. Marsh, ed., *Logic and Knowledge, Essays 1901–1950* (New York, 1956).

For a defense of the view that states of consciousness differ in their intrinsic properties, see Wilfrid Sellars, *Science, Perception, and Reality* (London, 1963), Ch. 2. Gilbert Ryle, *op. cit.*, Ch. 5, contains a now classical discussion of dispositional concepts.

A number of excellent analyses of particular states of consciousness are reprinted in Donald F. Gustafson, ed., *Essays in Philosophical Psychology* (New York, 1964).

For discussions of the concepts of action and intention, see R. S. Peters, *The Concept of Motivation* (London, 1958), and Charles Taylor, *The Explanation of Behaviour* (London, 1964).

CHARLES LANDESMAN, JR.

CONSENSUS GENTIUM. *See* COMMON CONSENT ARGUMENTS FOR THE EXISTENCE OF GOD.

CONSERVATION PRINCIPLES. *See* ENERGY.

CONSERVATISM. Conservatism refers both to men's attachment to the customs and institutions which have long surrounded them and to the doctrines by which such an attachment is explained and defended. No attitude has been more common in human history. Change has generally been regarded with suspicion, and innovators have frequently been forced into the position of insisting that they merely seek to restore what has been temporarily lost. Under these conditions, laws are not "made," but must be declared by the ruler, sometimes after they have been coaxed from some divine source. Conservatism is therefore the preference for what has grown up over a long period of time in contrast to what has been made by deliberate human contrivance.

Background. "Before the Reformation," wrote Lord Hugh Cecil, "it is impossible to distinguish conservatism in politics, not because there was none, but because there was nothing else" (*Conservatism*, p. 25). But from the time of the Reformation, it has been possible in most political struggles to discern one party which seeks "reform" and another which resists it—or at least the particular reforms in question. Even this familiar dichotomy is an anachronism if we use it to explain anything that happened much before the eighteenth century. Priests may have preached the folly of man's pride, and Swift may have railed against "projectors," but the issue had not yet arisen in its modern form. Conservative attitudes which steadily developed in reaction to the rationalist notion that man could scientifically control all human life, finally crystallized when rationalist optimism turned into the revolutionary ideology of the French Revolution. It is the convention to date conservative philosophy from the publication of Edmund Burke's *Reflections on the Revolution in France*, in 1790, although Burke, revered by many as the greatest of conservative thinkers, was technically a Whig. The actual name "conservatism" developed in London and Paris around 1830 and was adopted after 1835 by growing numbers of British Tories.

Conservatism became philosophically self-conscious in response to the comprehensive challenge to existing institutions associated with the French Revolution. It did not, of course, lack deep philosophical roots, and it could provide itself with an extensive intellectual genealogy in which such writers as Lord Bolingbroke, Hume, Swift Richard Hooker, and Aquinas, as well as Plato and Aristotle, deserve mention. Inevitably, conservatism deployed the arsenal of arguments provided by the work of these writers according to the political situation of the moment. The purest examples of conservative thinking are perhaps to be found less in formal philosophical writings than in the speeches and pamphlets of conservative statesmen, most notably those of Disraeli. We often find conservatives defending monarchical and patriarchal institutions, since the main impetus of reform has come from democrats and egalitarians. But the actual content of what is to be conserved is logically independent of the more philosophical arguments of conservative thought.

Conservatism most precisely denotes a hostility to radical social change, particularly social change that is instituted by the force of the state and justified by an appeal to abstract rights or to some utopian aim. Conservatives believe that governments are limited by the nature of their instruments to maintaining peace and order: any attempt to go beyond these functions is likely to create a disproportionate amount of misery and disruption. This is a barren little flower of doctrine which can grow in any kind of soil, from the sandy wastes of fearful privilege to the lush richness of artistic or religious sensibility. Philosophically, it is merely a prescriptive implication of a structure of thought whose main emphasis often lies elsewhere.

All conservatives are united in the belief that human affairs are extremely complicated and that the details of human behavior are unpredictable: this we may call the complexity thesis. It is historically important because it was used by Burke in the *Reflections* as a gambit for blocking revolutionary projects founded upon reason and natural rights. "The nature of man is intricate; the objects of society are of the greatest possible complexity: and therefore no simple disposition or direction of power can be suitable either to man's nature or to the quality of his affairs." Political judgment therefore cannot be based on the deductive application of metaphysical principles to problems arising in the sphere of government. Conservatives regard ruling as a special kind of skill, possibly arcane and certainly not universally distributed among members of the human race. It is learned by practice and example and therefore is likely to be most highly developed among members of a long-established ruling class. These beliefs explain the caution, indeed often hostility, with which conservatives have contemplated the growth of democracy. They have preferred slow and gradual extensions of the franchise (as in Great Britain) to the rapid enfranchisement of whole populations, because they believe that time and experience are necessary to acquire the habits (particularly those of moderation and compromise) that sound political judgments demand. Conservative politicians have, indeed, carried out rapid enfranchisements in colonial affairs—not because they believe such policies to be right in an abstract sense, but because they are following the expedient principle of gracefully opening a door to assailants who in any case are certain to break it down.

Reason and instinct. Some conservative writings appear to exalt instinct and habit over reason. Indeed, in ethical matters, conservatives generally believe that good comes more often out of habit and a sound moral training than from utilitarian calculations. But in political matters, the conservative attitude is less one of dislike for philosophy than for *philosophes:* to the conservative it has generally been reason-intoxicated man who has produced those grandiose social blueprints (such as the collectivization of agriculture or the "thousand-year *Reich*") whose operation in politics has in recent centuries produced so much misery. For conservatives, politics is an inexact art, and political principles are no more than practical maxims that contribute to our understanding of difficult situations. If this point is ignored, political principles turn into either dogmas or slogans, evoking utopian hopes in the politically ignorant.

The complexity thesis, developed in another direction, yields a particular view of human nature. Many conservatives have accepted some version of the doctrine of original sin and have taken the Augustinian view that government is ordained by God as a remedy for human defects. Others have merely insisted on the prudential reminder that men are frail, unstable, and unpredictable. Most have agreed that virtue, stability, and civilization depend on the continuity of long-established institutions. Political stability is founded on state, church, and family, while moral stability rests upon a strong sense of duty, preferably buttressed by religious belief. These views may be described as classical and should be distinguished from the romanticism that has had an enormous vogue in the last two centuries. "Classical" and "romantic" are vague terms, but their use may be justified by the fact that one significant group of conservative thinkers (including T. E. Hulme, Percy Wyndham Lewis, and T. S. Eliot) were posing political questions in precisely those terms around the year 1914.

Conservative accounts of the nature of man may emphasize either his enduring sinfulness or his frailty. The only position conservatives cannot take without ceasing to be conservative is the belief that men are fundamentally good and perhaps ultimately perfectible. For in answer to the question "What is the root cause of political and social problems?" conservatives will point immediately to the nature of man, while liberals and socialists will point to man's environment. Within the field of social contract theory, for example, Hobbes is conservative in attributing social conflict to the essential nature of man, while Locke is liberal in locating the cause in the accidental depredations of a few men who are tempted to violate the laws of nature. Disagreement about the cause of social and political problems has important consequences, for if we find the cause in man's environment, we will be disposed to study that environment scientifically in an effort to discover the means of improvement. If, for example, we come to believe that poverty and emotional maladjustment are the root causes of human evils, we will find a possible cure in technology or in psychological therapy. The conservative, however, is distinguished by the belief that the usefulness of such measures is strictly limited and that if improvement can occur at all, it will result from moral changes in the way men behave. Conservatives stress moral characteristics such as cruelty, greed, charity, and integrity as irreducible determinants of human life.

This moral stress has often been associated with strong religious beliefs, and in this respect Burke was both typical and pre-eminent. He saw the course of human affairs as a providential sequence of events. The hand of God is everywhere, both in what survives and in what is destroyed. History is not a sequence of accidents but (in Hegel's phrase) "the march of God in the world." The history of human institutions exhibits not the brilliance of reason in a few men, but the wisdom of the species in slowly fashioning habits of behavior, particularly habits of command and subordination, to fit the changing human situation. These institutions require maintenance rather as a garden requires weeding: they must be protected against the fanatics who would plow up the whole garden each season and replant it according to the season's fashions. What we inherit from the past is a trust to be used, replenished, and transmitted to our descendants. The ruler must be guided by what is good for his subjects. These subjects, however, include not only the living but those now dead and those yet to be born. This position, which is stated by Burke in many places (perhaps most extensively in the *Reflections*), is basically mystical; it arises from a profound love of the familiar, which mingles easily with practical maxims on wise government. Conservatism of this kind is most at home in countries that have an established state religion and is summed up in the trinity of God, king, and country. It will seldom be found in countries that have not experienced a long continuity of rule. Modern France, for example, having been subject to frequent revolutionary changes of government, provides only a caricature of this kind of conservatism—the kind of caricature that dominated the Vichy regime during World War II.

Skeptical conservatism. Conservatism need have no connection at all with religious belief. There is another tradition, that of realistic skepticism, in which conservative political conclusions are reached by a quite different route. Doubting the existence of any universal human nature about which we can validly generalize, realistic skepticism limits itself to the dispositions of men as they are known in the modern world. One form of this attitude is found in Swift, who wrote, "I hate and detest that animal called Man, although I heartily love John, Peter, Thomas, and so forth." Modern man, then, is distinguished by his individuality, which he expresses in his disposition to make his own choices. Each man is passionate about his own projects and is primarily interested in cultivating them with the minimum outside interference. To some extent, modern men are capable of governing themselves, but their individual resources are insufficient. In order to prevent constant collision and frustration, some agency is required which will supervise a set of rules that is designed simply to serve this limited purpose. The image of the ruler is therefore that of the umpire or referee who controls the game without participating in it himself.

The political skeptic warns against the tendency of the specific activity of government to turn into something more grandiose and quite different. For there are many who dream of a perfectly harmonious condition of affairs and who deplore the waste and lack of planning in modern life. Such people regard government as a vast reservoir of powers that are to be captured and guided in the direction of their own particular dream. Politics thus becomes an encounter of dreams, and the umpire abandons his position and begins to play the game on his own account. Yet for the skeptical conservative, one dream is on a par with any other. Governments are not, and cannot be expected to become, repositories of truth: any such claims are impostures. A government that actually governs, rather than imposing some dream or other upon its subjects, will be guided, not by a vision of truth, nor by the attempt to impose one project upon its subjects, but by the evolution of the society it rules. Social life constantly generates new situations: some activities decline and new ones arise, a process which requires an adaptation of the rules governing the society. But changes in the rules should always grow out of, rather than be imposed upon, the life which they regulate. Further, changes should be made economically or else they may lose their effectiveness. Rules (i.e., the laws and procedures of institutions, the habits of personal behavior) are most useful when they are most familiar. Frequent changes are deplorable in that they give rise to feverish hopes and disappointments which encourage further dreams of taking over the resources of government.

Skeptical conservatism is a long-standing tradition in Western thought and is found in such writers as Montaigne, Hobbes, Swift, Pascal, Hume, and, among contemporary thinkers, Michael Oakeshott. Its brand of conservatism is strictly political; it allows the possibility of being conservative in politics but in little else. A skeptical conservative in politics may be a revolutionary innovator in art or a libertarian in his sexual life—a combination seldom found among traditional conservatives. Both its political consequences and its use of the image of the umpire might seem to assimilate skeptical conservatism to nineteenth-century laissez-faire liberalism, which owed much to Locke and is still vigorously maintained by such contemporary writers as Friedrich von Hayek. What distinguishes the skeptical conservative from the classical liberal is the former's refusal to elevate such key institutions as human choice, private property, and diversity of belief into a metaphysic whereby they are assigned some sort of absolute value. A skeptical conservative is likely to believe that political doctrines, as well as governments, must recognize their limitations.

Two versions of tradition. All varieties of conservatism place a high value on tradition, but the term "tradition" is radically ambiguous. Liberals see in tradition only that human inertia which leads to static repetition from generation to generation. According to them, tradition is a barrier to improvement and an impediment to the growth of efficiency. It clutters purposive behavior with rituals and customs unnecessary to the work in hand. Progress, therefore, is to be found in the shift from traditional to rational ways of acting. Conservatives, on the other hand, regard tradition as the heritage of skill and attainment on which our present achievements must be founded. Many traditional ways of acting are no doubt habitual and unthinking and thereby economize our efforts. What is more important, however, is that traditions are fertile and adaptable. At this point in the argument, the conservative defense of tradition is likely to become an attack upon the inflated claims that have been made for reason. The tradition of any activity includes not only the conscious reasoning which goes into that activity, but also the dispositions, habits, sensibilities, and sympathies out of which the activity can grow and develop. Reason attempts to make an activity self-conscious by making its principles of operation explicit. What is summed up in the principles, however, is only a part of the activity—the upper part of the iceberg. All activities call upon resources in the individual of which he is only imperfectly conscious. Further, the attempt to rationalize activities is not only incomplete but also brings with it the threat of decline in the tradition; for once these rational principles have been elicited, they constitute an ideology that is likely to turn into a set of inflexible dogmas. Rational principles are often useful—in teaching and in philosophy, for example—but reason cannot, and should not be allowed to, monopolize our approach to practice.

A favorite political example of this argument is the idea of natural rights, which conservatives take to be a rationalized (and therefore inferior) abridgment of the traditional rights of Englishmen under common law. While the traditional rights of Englishmen under common law can change and develop within a system of great subtlety and flexibility, the rights of man must be declared by reason once and for all. Because of this, natural rights are intellectually vague and function in some political traditions as little more than an agreeable camouflage over government actions that are determined by considerations very different from an allegiance to reason. In answer to the question "What lies behind the stability of political affairs?" conservatives will reply, "Tradition." For conservatives, reason is an impossible answer, because both the content and operations of reason must be shaped by the concrete tradition within which it arises.

Conflicting accounts of tradition issue in conflicting accounts of authority. The liberal contemplating authority demands that it should justify itself, preferably by gaining the consent of its subjects. Conservatives regard the consent of the subject as being one among a number of valuable guides to a wise government, but they resist the elevation of the principle of consent into an unqualified political criterion. They take the view that authorities are the fallible (because human) custodians of long-established traditions. All human achievements have been made (and sustained) in the face of great difficulties: authorities exist to guard such achievements and traditions against the continual threat of human folly, laziness, blindness, and stupidity. This point of view accounts for many of the connotations of conservatism—its stress on duties rather than on rights; its concern with discipline in contrast to the indulgent and permissive strain of modern liberalism; its patriarchal support for authority and "due degree" rather than for indiscriminate equality; and its pessimistic skepticism about grandiose political projects promising the ultimate arrival of heaven on earth.

Conservatism is the repository of a number of political truths that are presented with a unique subtlety and elaboration, as well as of a set of preferences. As a doctrine it imposes its own limits, for if it is pressed in any direction it leads to skepticism or mysticism, and in some cases to both. The main danger besetting the conservative is that he may become so enchanted with the particular things that he finds suitable for conservation at his particular time that he will begin to construct a fixed ideology—a static blueprint of a good society. As with all political doctrines, the philosopher is first tempted to construct political principles in order to explain his position and then finds himself in danger of being trapped by them. The step from conservatism to some kind of antiliberal ideology is a small one: even Burke was provoked into taking it by his hatred of the Jacobins. Those who take this step, however, begin to move away from conservatism, for the actual content of a conservative's preferences must be determined by his time and situation. The moment he begins to regard *any* particular institution as absolutely good, he moves outside the tradition of conservative thought.

Bibliography

Among many good general introductions to conservatism, the reader might consult Lord Hugh Cecil, *Conservatism* (London, 1912); Keith Feiling, *What Is Conservatism?* (London, 1930); Quinton Hogg, *The Conservative Case* (Harmondsworth, 1959); and Russell Kirk, *The Conservative Mind* (Chicago, 1953). R. J. White, *The Conservative Tradition* (London, 1950) is a useful anthology of conservative opinions. Recent vigorous American conservative thinking is described in Clinton Rossiter, *Conservatism in America* (New York, 1955). Edmund Burke's *Works*, F. Lawrence and W. King, eds. (London, 1803–1827) or T. W. Copeland, ed. (Chicago, 1958 ff.), especially perhaps the *Reflections on the Revolution in France*, are the fountainhead of much modern conservative speculation. The best modern statement of the skeptical position is Michael Oakeshott, *Rationalism in Politics* (London, 1962).

KENNETH MINOGUE

CONTINGENT AND NECESSARY STATEMENTS. The distinction between necessity and contingency is an ancient and prima facie obvious one, at least as applied to events. In this form it is a distinction between what must occur and what may or may not occur and is clearly allied to the distinction between what is necessary and what is merely possible. The distinction between necessary and contingent statements or truths is less obvious. The necessity of events by no means entails that there are necessary truths—statements whose truth is necessary, as opposed to those whose truth is only contingent, that is, those which merely happen to be true. It is also less clear that if a statement is said to be contingently true, it may also be said to be merely possibly true, for there is an obvious sense in which even a contingent truth must, on occasion, actually hold. It is a contingent truth that flowers bloom in the spring, but it would be wrong to say that it is merely possibly true; it *is* true. An examination of the notion of necessary truth might therefore profitably begin with a consideration of what we are saying when we say that some statement must be true.

Relative necessity. In ordinary circumstances the assertion "That statement must be true" is likely to be made at the conclusion of an argument, and the use of the words "That must be true" invites completion with "because. . . ." The argument in question may be one of a number of different kinds; it need not be purely deductive. An inductive argument or an appeal to evidence may lead to the conclusion "So it must be true," and so may an appeal to authority. In all such cases we invoke reasons, whatever their nature. This is so often the case that to say in any context "It must be true" is to invite the question "Why?," a question that can be answered only by providing the relevant reasons. In other words, a statement that must be true may be taken as one whose truth is in an important sense necessitated by the reasons adduced in its support. This might be expressed by saying that the necessity of necessary truths is not really a property of theirs *simpliciter* but exists only in relation to the supporting reasons. To maintain this categorically would be to maintain that necessary truth, as such, is relative. A conclusion of an argument is necessary if the premises are to be maintained; it is necessary *to* them.

Absolute necessity. The notion of relative necessity, whose prototype instance can be seen in the use of "so necessarily" in stating the conclusion of an argument, stands in complete contrast to the usually accepted philosophical concept of necessary truth. The conclusion of an argument that follows necessarily from the premises is conditional upon them, but in the philosophical sense necessary truths have generally been taken to be unconditional. They are universally and unconditionally true and thus do not depend upon any argument for their justification. Their necessity belongs to them as such, and not merely in relation to the supporting arguments. It is only in the absolute sense that necessary truths can be opposed to contingent truths.

The situation is different with relative necessities. When a set of premises in an argument does not fully justify the conclusion, and we cannot say that they necessitate the conclusion or that the truth of the conclusion is necessary to their truth, we may on occasion be able to say "It is probably true." Generally speaking, however, all that we are entitled to claim is that the conclusion is possibly true. In this sense, necessity stands in opposition to mere possibility. Some of the relations between these notions and analogous ones were charted by Aristotle in his *De Interpretatione*.

MAJOR CONCEPTIONS OF NECESSARY STATEMENTS

Aristotle. Besides distinguishing between necessity and possibility, Aristotle also distinguishes between absolute and relative necessity (or necessity on a hypothesis). The conclusion of an argument may, of course, be necessary in relation to the premises or merely possible relative to them. But in demonstration, the argument is not only a valid deductive one in itself; it also proceeds from premises that are necessarily true or are true in themselves. The necessity that belongs to such propositions is the kind of absolute necessity most often expressed as "that which cannot be otherwise than it is." This notion is contrasted with the notion of "that which *can* be otherwise and is so for the most part, only or sometimes, or as it happens." Since the latter corresponds to our notion of contingency, Aristotle apparently would have thought of the contingent in terms of what is possible in an absolute sense. That is to say, the contingent is just what *can* be otherwise in an absolute sense, without reference to anything else.

Essential truths. For Aristotle, those propositions which are absolutely necessary or true in themselves are "essentially true." They provide the axioms from which the truths of any particular science are derived; they express the essences of objects that form the province of that particular science. In addition to the axioms and theorems of particular sciences, there are principles, such as the principle of contradiction, that are common to all the sciences. Just as it is impossible to demonstrate the first principles of any particular science, so it is impossible to demonstrate these common principles. Their justification belongs to dialectic. We come to see the truth of the axioms of particular sciences through a form of induction that may be called intuitive; we see their truth in particular instances. The justification of principles such as that of contradiction is provided by an appeal to what *anyone* would say. If someone denies the principle, we convict him out of his own mouth by showing that his very denial presupposes its truth.

In Aristotle's view, then, absolutely necessary truths express insights into the essences of things, or into the nature of being, as represented, for example, in the principle that something cannot both be and not be. These principles are the sphere of what has since become known as metaphysics. There are, on the other hand, relative necessities, where something is necessary relative to a given end or on a given hypothesis, and in this sense a proposition following deductively from given premises would be necessary to them. There are analogous senses of "possible." Insofar as we are concerned with a world in which there is matter, in which things are more than their essences, we may say that some features of things are only possible, since those features are not entailed by the essence of the things in question. This is what is meant by contingency, and a contingent proposition for Aristotle would thus be a proposition whose truth is not determined simply by the essence of the thing about which it is asserted.

The concept of essence. The Aristotelian conception of the difference between necessity and contingency and between necessary and contingent propositions clearly presupposes a certain metaphysical point of view, namely, that things have real essences. When the realm of necessary truth has been restricted to relations between ideas or concepts (as it tended to be in the empiricism of the seventeenth and eighteenth centuries), the propositions opposed to necessary truths have not been those which are merely possibly true, but contingent truths, those which depend on circumstances, that are not true in themselves. The rejection of the Aristotelian scheme of essences eliminates absolutely necessary truths about the world; contingent truths are now identified with truths that state facts about the world.

The theory about essences is thus replaced by a theory about concepts, and the factual and the contingent are identified with each other. It remains true that there are really two distinctions—the essential/contingent and the necessary/possible. Or, rather, the essential/contingent distinction is equivalent to the necessary/possible distinction *only* when the latter terms are taken in their absolute sense. The rejection of essences allowed the opposition of the necessary to the contingent *simpliciter,* but in an important sense it is an incorrect opposition, widely accepted though it is. Similarly, the restriction of necessity to relations of ideas made possible the identification of the contingent and the factual. This also is, strictly speaking, incorrect.

Leibniz' criteria for necessary truth. The transition to the position which embraces the distinction between the necessary and contingent and which identifies the contingent and the factual can best be seen in Leibniz' distinction between truths of reason and truths of fact, a distinction that is akin to Hume's distinction between relations of ideas and matters of fact. But, despite making the distinction, Leibniz also held that in every true proposition the predicate is contained in the subject. Hence, everything that is true of a thing is part of that thing's essence, and everything that happens to a thing follows from that thing's nature. This is, in effect, to say that nothing simply happens to a thing; there is no real contingency. Leibniz attempted to avoid the unpalatable consequences of this view by saying that it is so for God. We, on the other hand, because of our finitude and consequent ignorance, can know only that if a proposition is true, it is necessarily true; we cannot tell with certainty which propositions are true. Contingency is preserved by the fact that God has to choose, out of all possible worlds, that world, that arrangement of essences, which is the best. The notion of an essence remains in Leibniz' philosophy in what he called complete concepts or concepts of individuals. This metaphysical view fits very uneasily with the distinction between truths of reason and truths of fact, or the necessary and the contingent in more or less the contemporary sense.

Principle of contradiction. According to Leibniz' distinction, truths of reason are such that their denial involves a contradiction, which is not so of truths of fact. While truths of reason depend on the principle of contradiction, truths of fact depend on something less, the principle of sufficient reason. Leibniz also explained the matter by saying that truths of reason are reducible to identical propositions via chains of definitions of the terms involved. If this is so, their basis can also be seen in another of the so-called laws of thought: the principle of identity. It has been pointed out by others, such as Frege, that, in fact, more than this is required if the reduction is to be fully acceptable. Leibniz' proof that "$2+2=4$" is reducible to an identical proposition makes use not only of the definitions of numbers in terms of the notion of "successor" but also of the associative law for addition: $a+(b+c)=(a+b)+c$. This, however, reveals a defect in

Leibniz' conception of proof, rather than in his account of truths of reason as such, and it may still be valid to say that truths of reason are truths whose denial involves a contradiction. Indeed, this conception was taken up by Kant and handed down to his successors.

It can scarcely be maintained, however, that by a necessary proposition is *meant* one whose denial results in a contradiction, for it is at the best a theory that all necessary truths fit this description. But it is certainly not true of merely relatively necessary truths, and it is not clear that it is true of Aristotle's essential truths, if any of these exist. It is Leibniz' ambiguous position on both of these that creates the unhappy relationship between his general metaphysics and the acceptance of the distinction now under consideration. Even if it is denied that there are any essential truths in this sense, the reference to the principle of contradiction could be, at the most, a criterion for deciding whether any proposition constitutes a necessary truth. A possible criticism of this point of view is that the criterion involves extralogical considerations; it is not formal because it involves the performing of operations on the proposition in question and a determination of the results. But this feature is unobjectionable in a criterion for deciding on the status of the proposition, although it would be objectionable as an account of what is *meant* in speaking of a proposition as necessary.

It might also be objected that the reference to the principle of contradiction does not by itself explain the necessity of a truth of reason. Russell has, in his *Introduction to Mathematical Philosophy*, made similar objections to the view that what makes the axioms of a formal system necessary is that their denial involves a contradiction. He maintains that this view is unsatisfactory because it merely shifts the question of necessity to the principle of contradiction and because the principle itself can appear as a theorem in the formal system, and one fairly remote from the axioms at that. This is partly true and partly a misconception. It is undoubtedly true that reference to the principle of contradiction in turn provokes a question concerning its status. On the other hand, the fact that the formula $\sim(p \cdot \sim p)$, which Russell supposes to express the principle of contradiction, can be proved as a theorem of the propositional calculus by no means directly bears on the status of the principle. The proof of the formula shows that *it* is valid under all truth conditions; but the formula is not actually the principle, which may be presupposed by all discourse and, hence, by any system of logic that has anything to do with discourse. If the principle that a proposition cannot be both true and false is valid in this sense, it is not surprising that the formula $\sim(p \cdot \sim p)$ appears as a theorem in the system; and where it does not, as in systems of many-valued logic, the interpretation of analogous formulas that do appear may show that the principle is presupposed just the same. Such interpretation tends to show that such terms as "not" receive a different meaning in such systems, and the principle remains valid on the original meaning of the terms.

The other point, that reference to the principle of contradiction provokes the question of its status, remains. This, however, matters less if the principle is referred to as a criterion of decision than if it is invoked in order to explain the necessity of a truth of reason. In the latter case it would be necessary to account in turn for the necessity of the principle, and this clearly cannot be done in the same way. Although the problem will be discussed further, it is important to note now that, even if the points so far raised are waived, it remains a *theory* that all necessary truths are such that their denial involves a contradiction.

Analytic truths. The theory that the denial of necessary truths always involves a contradiction restricts the field of necessary truth to those truths which Kant called analytic and excludes those truths which Kant called synthetic a priori. If any of the latter exist, their denial does not involve a contradiction. There is, in all events, no contradiction in the idea that a proposition may be necessary without being guaranteed by the principle of contradiction. The supposition that necessary truths are restricted to analytic truths explains the connection, so often encountered in seventeenth and eighteenth century empiricism, between the idea that necessary truths are such that their denial involves a contradiction and the idea that necessary truths express only relations of ideas. The point is explicit in Kant's account of analytic judgments, according to which the concept of the predicate is already, in these judgments, contained in that of the subject. If this is so, it is impossible to deny without contradiction that the predicate belongs to the subject.

Linguistic theory of necessary truth. The view that necessary truth always concerns relations of ideas does not quite entail the thesis that all necessary truths are analytic, for the relations in question may not be logical relations. Yet the supposition that the view does entail the thesis is fundamental to seventeenth- and eighteenth-century empiricism and has its counterpart in the theories of twentieth-century empiricists, where it is given a linguistic dress. According to this linguistic theory, necessary truths are those which hold owing to linguistic convention. In some of the earlier and more radical positivist formulations of the thesis, it was even maintained that necessary propositions are merely verbal. A. J. Ayer, in *Language, Truth and Logic,* said that analytic statements (these being the only necessary statements) reveal our determination to use words in a certain way. Other positivists said that they were rules for the transformation of one set of words into another. In sum, necessary propositions had something to do with words and words alone. There are several conclusive objections to this thesis.

Necessary truths as verbal propositions. The most extreme version of the linguistic thesis—that necessary propositions are verbal propositions—now seems so obviously false as to be ludicrously so, for it is tantamount to the thesis that necessary propositions are empirical propositions about the use of words. The temptation for a positivist to hold this view is obvious enough, for it removes the need to accept nonempirical truths. It may be true that the only result achieved by asserting an analytic statement is a revelation about the speaker's use of words, but this cannot be the main function of the statement itself. Similar considerations apply to the view that necessary propositions are really rules. Apart from the fact that propositions, but not rules, can be true or false, an analytic proposition may be true in virtue of such rules but cannot itself be the expression of the rules. Hence, the thesis was modified to the view that necessary propositions are true in virtue of linguistic conventions. Behind every analytically true proposition there is some other proposition that states the conventions for the use of the terms involved, and this latter proposition gives the necessary and sufficient conditions for the necessity of the former.

Necessity determined by verbal propositions. As it stands, the view stated above suggests that the necessity of an analytic proposition is conveyed by the proposition about linguistic conventions; these explain the necessity of the analytic proposition. But in fact the linguistic conventions alone do not do this. At the most, they provide a reason for saying that a particular sentence expresses a necessary proposition; they do not explain what it is to say that a proposition is necessary but only help to determine whether a given proposition is necessary. They do not even provide the complete reasons for saying that a proposition is analytic, since these reasons also entail reference to logical principles, to which, given the meaning of the terms involved, they may be reduced (see ANALYTIC AND SYNTHETIC STATEMENTS).

A further criticism is that the reference to conventions for the use of expressions makes the matter sound far too arbitrary and seems to restrict necessary propositions to those expressed in a given language. The meaning of words is not just a matter of agreement between users of them, and what they can be applied to seems to be determined by what they mean, rather than vice versa. But, however plausible it may be to say that the use of words in a given language is determined by how the users propose to use them, this cannot explain the common meaning possessed by different words in different languages. Nor can it do anything to explain the necessity of propositions, when by "proposition" is meant what is expressed, in different languages, by sentences with the same meaning. Rudolf Carnap has, in effect, claimed that notions like that of L-truth (logical truth or, in effect, analyticity) must be restricted to a given language, on the grounds that semantic rules apply to a given language. This is unacceptable because truth is not a property of sentences in a given language but of the use of such sentences—that is, of statements or propositions—and sentences in different languages may have the same use and express the same propositions. This applies a fortiori to logical or analytic truth.

The final criticism of the linguistic theory of necessary truth is that it applies, at the very most, only to analytic truth. It neglects the possibility of other kinds of truth that are necessary for other reasons. Empiricists, of course, have claimed that there are no such necessary truths, but as it stands this claim is a mere dogma. The claim that there are necessary truths of this kind can only be assessed on its own merits. On the face of it, even logical truths must be excepted from the theory, for the analysis of the backing of analytic truths makes reference not only to the meaning of the terms involved but also to logical principles or truths. Can it be plausibly maintained that logical truths are also true by linguistic convention? The answer must be "No." Logic is prior to language; even if it is admitted that there is something conventional about the use of words, this can scarcely be said about logic. Our acceptance of and conformity to logical principles is not a matter of linguistic habit.

BASIS AND CHARACTER OF NECESSARY TRUTH

Nature of logical truth. What, then, is a truth of logic? This is a question of some difficulty and, even if it can be answered, there is a further question of how it can be necessary.

Tautologies. Ludwig Wittgenstein, in his *Tractatus Logico-philosophicus*, tried to give a criterion, if not an elucidation, of logical truth in terms of the notion of tautology, that is, a proposition which is true for all truth-values of its constituent propositions and true under all truth conditions, as revealed by truth tables. But this view assumes that all propositions are or can be reduced to propositions of the calculus of truth-functions. If there are propositions of other forms that are logical truths, then the notion of a logical truth cannot be equated with that of a tautology. The problem here is equivalent to the decision problem for logical calculi. What means can be provided for determining all logical truths? It is now known, thanks to Alonzo Church, that this problem cannot be solved generally for all calculi. Hence, there cannot be a single criterion for logical truth. The one that Wittgenstein offered for truth-functions was roughly equivalent to one of Leibniz' criteria for truths of reason—that they are true in all possible worlds.

Notion of L-truth. An extended version of the thesis that logical truths are tautologies, provided for the notion of L-truth by Carnap, offers a similar but generalized criterion and in its application to language makes the same assumption—that it is possible to isolate atomic, or simple, propositions into which complex propositions may be broken down. But the aim of Carnap's theory is to give an account of something like analyticity by providing a basis for L-true statements as found in language; it is not meant to explain logical truth as such. Nor could it do so, since the fundamental objection to any account derivative from Leibniz' notion of "true in all possible worlds" is that the sense of "possible" involved is "logically possible." To know what is logically possible, the notion of logical truth would have to be already presupposed; hence, any definition of logical truth in terms of possible worlds or similar notions must be circular.

Function of logical constants. Willard Quine has tried to elucidate logical truth in terms of the essential role played by logical constants, that is, the logical nondescriptive terms on which the properties of a logical calculus are based and which may be opposed to variables. A logical truth is a proposition whose truth depends solely on the logical constants employed and not on the descriptive terms, which are inessential and dispensable (as in "All men are men," whose truth does not depend on the fact that it contains a reference to men). Quine's aim here is to distinguish logical truths from analytic statements, in which the descriptive terms do play a role. On the commonly accepted view of analytic statements, logical truths result from them when definitional equivalents are substituted for the appropriate terms. Quine thinks that insofar as their necessity is concerned, logical and analytic statements are on a par. He holds that they are merely the most entrenched statements, those which we are least willing to surrender in the face of apparently falsifying circumstances. (See ANALYTIC AND SYNTHETIC STATEMENTS for a discussion of Quine's view of analyticity.) Hence, the reference to the essential role of logical constants does not explain the necessity of these truths, nor is it meant to; it merely explains why we speak of them as logical. It is doubtful, however, whether it does even this. What counts as a logical constant? Can any general account be given of these, or must we rely simply on enumeration of them?

Function of topic-neutral concepts. Gilbert Ryle has attempted to give a general account of logical constants in terms of what he calls topic-neutral concepts, concepts that are neutral for any particular subject matter—for instance, "some," "all," "and," and "not." Logical truths are those which depend only on the logical powers of such concepts. But the logical power of a concept is defined by the entailments of the statements in which the corresponding expression figures, and since the notion of entailment presupposes that of logical necessity, this conception cannot explain logical necessity. It is also insufficient as an account of logical *truth*. Ryle would hold against formal logicians, such as Quine, that there is no particular reason to give preference to those topic-neutral concepts which are selected by them as logical constants and that it would be equally reasonable to pick others. Any formal system is merely the working out of the logical powers of a certain set of such concepts by determining which arguments are to be counted as valid and which are not. It is, of course, true that different logical systems are constructed for different purposes and therefore turn on different notions. It can hardly be denied, however, that some notions of this sort are more fundamental than others. The propositional calculus, for example, is concerned with arguments whose validity turns on the relative truth and falsity of propositions; hence, notions like that of negation and the so-called material implication are fundamental to it (negation, for instance, because if a proposition must be either true or false, then either it or its negation must be true).

Traditional laws of thought. The decision on which logical constants are to be fundamental turns on what is thought to be fundamental to logic. Merely to appeal to extant logical systems is of no use until it has been decided why they are to be called *logical* systems. Certainly they will be logical if they provide the principles of valid argument, but what principles are fundamental in this respect? It has been noted that in the propositional calculus the fact that notions like that of negation are fundamental depends on the fact that a proposition must be either true or false. This, the law of excluded middle, is basic to the whole system. Likewise, since an argument will be invalid if, and only if, the premises are true and the conclusion false, it is vital that a proposition cannot be both true and false—the law of contradiction. It seems, after all, that the traditional laws of thought have a special role to play and that the force of logical truths depends upon them.

The purpose of this discussion has been to indicate that the view that all necessary truths are analytic does not explain logical truths. Moreover, since it has generally been maintained that the necessity of analytic truths depends on their reducibility to logical truths, it is clearly important to establish the source of the latter's necessity. But the problem of giving a completely general account of logical truth is a problem of great difficulty; and the same is true of the problem of explaining the necessity of logical truths, except in terms of already accepted notions like entailment and validity, which themselves may presuppose the notion of logical necessity. At the same time, it seems that whatever is, in a particular system, counted as a logical truth depends for its validity on more fundamental principles, such as the laws of excluded middle and contradiction. Indeed, these laws are even presupposed in our conceptions of entailment and validity, for an argument is valid only if the premises entail the conclusion, and one statement entails another only if it is contradictory to assert the antecedent and deny the consequent. The fundamental importance of the law of contradiction, which Leibniz pointed out, remains. If it is implausible to say that logical truths in general are analytic, it is even more implausible to say that the laws of contradiction and excluded middle are analytic. It is clear, therefore, that there must be necessary nonanalytic truths.

Are analytic and logical truths necessary? Nothing in the discussion so far explains in what sense any of the truths discussed can be said to be necessary. It has been assumed, following Leibniz' distinction between truths of reason and truths of fact, that necessary truths may be opposed to contingent truths and that the necessity in question is an absolute and unconditional one. This, however, may be disputed. If analytic and logical truths were truths about concepts, it would perhaps be possible to oppose contingent truths about the world to necessary truths about concepts. But analytic and logical truths are not about concepts; rather, they are, given the principle of contradiction, true in virtue of the nature of the concepts involved. The analytic proposition "All bodies are extended" is, as Kant insisted about the corresponding judgments about bodies, not the concept of a body. Such truths must, therefore, be necessary truths about things and may be opposed to contingent statements about things, but if this is so, they are not like Aristotle's essential truths, for they are, as has often been pointed out, trivial. To say that it is a contingent fact about men that they are intelligent, but a necessary fact about them that they are human, sounds like a bad joke. It sounds similarly odd to say that men cannot be otherwise than human. It is, perhaps, because of this that philosophers have tended to say that such statements do, after all, tell us something about the concepts involved, or even about the use of the terms involved.

All in all, it is more plausible to say that logical and analytic truths are only relatively necessary—their necessity derives from the fact that their truth is necessary to something else. There is a clear sense in which such a statement as "All men are human" could be other than true—if "human" meant other than it does, or if our concepts of man and humanity were other than they are. This provides a reason for rejecting the idea that the statement's truth is absolutely necessary and for claiming that it is relatively necessary—necessary to the use to which we put the words "men" and "human." The point is that if we do use these words or the corresponding concepts in the way we do, the statement in question must be true. This would make its necessity a form of what Aristotle called necessity *ex hypothesi.*

We have seen, however, that in Aristotle the necessary *ex hypothesi* was opposed to the absolutely necessary, and that this made sense in application to truths because of his belief in essential truths. If the last are rejected on the grounds that things do not have essences (what is improperly spoken of as the essence of a thing being properly spoken of as how we conceive it), the question may be raised whether there are any absolutely necessary truths at all. It might be replied that the substitution of statements about concepts for statements about essences means that absolute necessity can have a place in statements about concepts or about connections between concepts. Even if "Man is a rational animal" is not essentially true, it may be analytic; and its analyticity is due to the fact that our concept of man includes that of rational animal, or that being a man entails being a rational animal. Is the statement of this conceptual connection or entailment absolutely necessary? It has certainly been generally maintained that entailment statements are themselves necessary statements, for it seems odd to say that it is contingent that, for instance, redness entails coloredness. This has been denied (for example, Strawson) on the grounds that an entailment statement asserts that a necessary connection holds and for this reason is not itself necessary. It is perhaps questionable whether this is, in fact, what an entailment statement asserts, but in any case it implies a false dichotomy. The truth of an entailment statement is certainly necessary to our employment of the relevant concepts. This, however, does not show that the entailment statement is necessary in an absolute sense, as opposed to being contingent. If this is the case, it would seem that all statements may be contingent, in that if true, they could still be other than true.

A possible objection to this view of entailment statements is that it involves a confusion between concepts and the words expressing them, or between sentences and propositions. It might be said that the word "red" might have been used to express a concept different from our present concept of redness; the sentence "Being red entails being colored" or "Whatever is red is colored" might have been used to express a proposition different from the one that it normally expresses. On the other hand, our *concept* of redness could not have been so different that it did not include the concept of being colored. Similarly, the proposition that whatever is red is colored could not be otherwise than true.

The question of connections between concepts raises large issues in connection with the criteria of identity for concepts and propositions. (And there is a connection between these two, since the concepts a man has in a certain context can be seen by the propositions he takes to be analytic, as Quine has, in effect, indicated in respect of the association between synonymity and analyticity.) As things are, our concept of redness is such that the concept of being colored is already presupposed. But such need not be the case, since we might not have a concept of being colored at all. In that case, our concept of redness would be different from what it now is. Still, it might be objected, if we did have a concept of being colored, our concept of redness would be analytically connected with it. But this is already to state a hypothesis that is an indispensable basis of the proposition's necessity. Such a hypothesis must be involved when the necessity is relative to concepts. As long as necessary connections can be held to exist in the nature of things, they can be conceived to hold absolutely. Similar connections between concepts hold only on the assumption that we have such concepts.

In any case, it is surely possible for our concepts to change or to be different from what they are now. It is conceivable, for example, that people should see a radical difference between what we sometimes call warm and cool colors, to such an extent that they find it natural to say that there is nothing in common between them. The concept of color might be restricted to cool colors, and in these circumstances it would be false to say that whatever is red is colored. It will not do here to say that a mere shift in language has taken place and that even for those people who accept only cool colors it would be true to say that whatever is red is what *we* mean by "colored," since, for them, there is nothing corresponding to what *we* mean by "colored." What would have taken place under these conditions would be a shift in people's conception of things. It remains true that as long as necessity is a function of connections between concepts, it is relative to the system of concepts that is in operation. Necessity is thus contingent on the existence of that system of concepts. Entailments only hold relative to a given system of thought.

Nonanalytic necessary truths. It has been admitted in recent times (although Kant and some of his successors insisted on it, too) that there are connections between concepts which are less than entailments. Their existence may be indicated by the type of argument that Kant called transcendental.

Transcendental truths. Kant's argument for the principle that every event has a cause in the "Second Analogy" (*Critique of Pure Reason*) states, in effect, that the connection between cause and event is, while not an analytic one, a necessary one in relation to possible experience. The truth of the principle that every event has a cause is a necessary condition for the application of the concept of objective experience. Any event that is the object of a possible objective experience must be so caused. Although it is impossible here to assess it in detail, this argument has some kind of plausibility. Its type is that a connection between two concepts must be taken as a necessary condition of their application to any instance of a certain kind of thing. It is not necessary *simpliciter*, or necessary to the system of concepts from which those in question are drawn, but only to a certain application of them. If the connection can be substantiated by argument (and only argument will show whether there is such a connection), then a refusal to admit it can be met with the reply "I agree that it would make sense to suppose that an event might be uncaused, but such an event could not be one that could be an object of objective experience; hence, if you do not accept the connection here, you must give up talking of such experience."

Laws of thought. There may be various necessary connections between concepts analogous to that holding in the Kantian example. One example may be Wittgenstein's point in the *Philosophical Investigations* that there must be a general connection between the notions of an inner process and an outer expression for the inner to be intelligible. However, perhaps the strongest candidates for this status are the laws of thought, which we saw as underlying even logical truths. Indeed, we might say that logical truths are necessary relative to them, so that given that we accept them, we must accept the logical truths. Does this mean that the laws of thought themselves have an absolute necessity? The answer seems to be "No." That a statement cannot be both true and false, or must be either true or false, is not an absolute necessity but is necessary only in relation to the goal of intelligible discourse or thought. A statement is not definable as that which is either true or false and cannot be both. The attainment of truth and the eschewing of falsity are functions of discourse; but such functions are not always performed, and people may utter expressions that, if they express anything, do not state anything true or false. It would be wrong in such circumstances to say that the people concerned do not assert statements, for they may have intended to state something and there would be nothing wrong in referring to their statement in this context. On the other hand, they would clearly not have succeeded in saying anything intelligible. Hence, it is plausible to say that saying something true or false, and not both, is a necessary condition of saying something intelligible. It is a necessary condition of significant thought. The connection between the concepts of a statement and truth-or-falsity is necessary to their application to what is conceived as constituting intelligible discourse or thought.

Since the so-called laws of thought are such that they cannot be intelligibly denied, it might be thought that they are for that reason absolutely necessary. This is not so, for someone could reject them, at the cost of being unintelligible in the long run. If no one wanted to be intelligible, it might come about that language would lose the function in which truth is its end. It is, perhaps, difficult to see why language should persist at all in such circumstances, but it is nevertheless conceivable that it should and that it should never be intelligible. In such circumstances it would be wrong to insist that such principles as that of contradiction must apply to it. These principles remain relatively necessary, although of course they are absolutely, and not merely relatively, a priori. Their justification must be, as Aristotle saw, dialectical; and their only justification consists in showing that anyone who tries to deny them intelligibly must presuppose them.

Necessary truth and the a priori. It has been assumed throughout the preceding discussion that all necessary truth is a function of concepts. Given this, it might seem that it is all a priori, but this view depends upon the rejection of knowledge of essences in the Aristotelian fashion. Something like the Aristotelian view, however, is held by some philosophers who wish to maintain that natural laws are statements of necessary connections within nature, and these connections would, of course, be absolute. Few philosophers of this persuasion would hold that knowledge of laws of nature is a priori.

To this position, however, it may be replied that connections in nature are matter-of-fact and contingent. Nature might not have been as it is; it might have been otherwise. If we wish to attribute a necessity to natural laws, it must be a necessity contributed by the system of concepts in terms of which natural laws are expressed, the theory of which they are part. The truth of statements of law is necessary to the application of this system of concepts, and the necessity is once again relative. Natural laws provide no exception to the thesis that all necessary truth is a priori.

Necessary truth and certainty. Necessary truths have appealed to some philosophers because they have seemed a possible exception to universal skepticism of knowledge, for if a truth is necessary, it seems that it must be certain. There is some plausibility in this point of view, for while it is not the case that if a truth is certain (if we are entitled to be certain about it), it must be necessarily true, it nevertheless seems that the converse must be so. Yet there is an obvious difference in function between the concepts of necessity and certainty; the latter concept has a direct connection with knowledge that the former has not. It may seem that the difference can be bridged, since if one knows that a statement is necessarily true, then one is entitled to be certain of it. Yet it is also clear that if one knows that a statement is true at all, one is equally entitled to be certain of it; moreover, all truths are eternal in the sense that once true, they are always true. Hence, the only bearing that necessity has on the issue of certainty is that if a statement is necessarily true, it must be true; and any statement that is known to be necessarily true is certain. Yet if everything that has been said is true, this does very little to answer the skeptic.

The restriction of necessary truth to relative necessity means that what can be known with certainty in this context is that something must be so on a given hypothesis. No straightforward matters of fact can be necessary, for they are all contingent. At the same time, although they are contingent matters of fact, they may be certain because a truth need not be necessary to be certain.

Bibliography

Historical background may be found in the following portions of *The Works of Aristotle*, W. D. Ross, ed. (Oxford, 1908–1931): *De Interpretatione*, translated by E. M. Edghill, 12 ff.; *Metaphysics*, translated by W. D. Ross, V.5 and VI.2; *Physics*, translated by R. P. Hardie and R. K. Gaye, II.9; and *Posterior Analytics*, translated by G. R. G. Mure, I.1 ff., especially I.6. Also see David Hume, *Treatise of Human Nature*, I.iii.1; Immanuel Kant, *Critique of Pure Reason*, Introduction; and Gottfried Leibniz, *Discourse on Metaphysics; Correspondence with Arnauld; Monadology*, translated by G. R. Montgomery, revised by A. R. Chandler, 2d ed. (La Salle, Ill., 1945).

Criticisms of Leibniz' explanation of necessary truth are Gottlob Frege, *Foundations of Arithmetic* (Oxford, 1950), Sec. 6, and Bertrand Russell, *Introduction to Mathematical Philosophy* (London, 1919), Ch. 18.

Further information on the linguistic theory of necessary truth is contained in A. J. Ayer, *Language, Truth and Logic* (London, 1947), Ch. 4; A. C. Ewing, "The Linguistic Theory of A Priori Propositions," in *PAS*, Vol. 40 (1939/40), 207–244; and Norman Malcolm, "Are Necessary Propositions Really Verbal?," in *Mind*, Vol. 49 (1940), 189–203.

Logical truth is discussed in Rudolf Carnap, *Introduction to Semantics* (Cambridge, Mass., 1948); W. C. Kneale, "Truths of

Logic," in *PAS*, Vol. 46 (1945/46), 207–234; W. V. Quine, "Truth by Convention," in Herbert Feigl and W. S. Sellars, eds., *Readings in Philosophical Analysis* (New York, 1949); Gilbert Ryle, *Dilemmas* (Cambridge, 1954), Ch. 8; Alfred Tarski, *Logic, Semantics, Metamathematics*, translated by J. H. Woodger (Oxford, 1956), pp. 409 ff.; and Ludwig Wittgenstein, *Tractatus Logico-philosophicus*, translated by D. F. Pears and B. F. McGuinness (London, 1961), 4.3 ff.

Necessary truth in general is covered in D. W. Hamlyn, "On Necessary Truth," in *Mind*, Vol. 70 (1961), 514–525; W. C. and Martha Kneale, *The Development of Logic* (Oxford, 1962), Ch. 10; Arthur Pap, *Semantics and Necessary Truth* (New Haven, 1958); P. F. Strawson, "Necessary Propositions and Entailment Statements," in *Mind*, Vol. 57 (1948), 184–200; and Ludwig Wittgenstein, *Philosophical Investigations* (Oxford, 1953), especially Vol. I, pp. 242 ff., which shows the connection between inner states and outer criteria, and *Remarks on the Foundations of Mathematics*, translated by G. E. M. Anscombe (Oxford, 1956), Part I.

D. W. HAMLYN

CONTINUITY. The problem of continuity arises first of all at the level of perception. Some objects, movements, and qualitative changes are perceived as continuous, while others exhibit breaks or gaps. Perceptual continuity is subjective in the sense that a thing or process that appears continuous to one observer may appear discontinuous to another. This dependence on an observer's aided or unaided discriminatory powers suggests, at least for the purposes of mathematics and the natural sciences, the need for a notion of continuity that is not so dependent. If such an objective notion of continuity is to be provided, it may turn out to be no longer something instantiated in perception, and the question of its relation to perception will have to be examined. One must, therefore, distinguish three interrelated problems: the analysis of perceptual continuity, the construction of an objective notion of continuity, and the analysis of the relation that this notion bears to experience.

The continuity problem is intimately related to that of infinity. One of the questions that inevitably arises in the analysis of any continuous transition is whether the number of its phases is finite or infinite. At a stage of mathematical development at which various types of infinite sets are distinguished, one must further examine the type of infinity involved. Except for a brief remark on the problem of the application of the mathematical notion, the present exposition will follow the general course of historical development without going into detail.

From the Pythagoreans to Aristotle. The discovery that the side of a unit square is incommensurable with its diagonal, and therefore that $\sqrt{2}$ is irrational—that is, that it cannot be expressed as a fraction—is credited to Pythagoras (sixth century B.C.) or a member of his school. If the rational points of a line segment (the points on it that stand in one–one correspondence to the series of rational numbers in their natural order) form an infinite totality, and if the rational and irrational points of the segment also form an infinite totality, then the second totality includes, but is not included in, the first; and the first is not continuous because it contains gaps. Without a clearer understanding of the notion of infinity, the notion of the continuity of a line segment, and of anything being moved through it, is liable to be seen as paradoxical.

The earliest exposition of such paradoxes was that of Zeno (fifth century B.C.), who put them forward as arguments in support of the metaphysical views of his teacher Parmenides, who held reality to be changeless and the appearance of motion to be an illusion. The following paradox (reported in Aristotle's *Physics*, VI, 9) is characteristic of Zeno's point of view and method: Between any two points on the path of a moving object, however near they may be to each other, there lies at least one other point and, therefore, an infinite number of points. Since the movement from one point to another takes some time, however little, and since an infinite number of intervals must be crossed in order to get from one point to another, a movement between any two points would take an infinite time. It is concluded, therefore, that motion along a continuous path, or indeed any motion, is impossible.

The attempt of Aristotle (384–322 B.C.) to resolve Zeno's paradoxes was based on his rejection of the notion of an actual or complete infinite totality, and consequently of any idea of dividing a line segment into an infinite number of indivisible elements—that is, an infinite number of unextended points. For Aristotle, a class may be only potentially infinite. Its membership may be increased without limit, but it is never given as a complete totality. According to him, a continuous connection occurs when the extremes of two things that touch each other become the same for both. This characterization was meant to apply to mathematical, as well as to perceptual, continuity, since for Aristotle mathematical relations were abstracted from perceptual situations.

Although Aristotle's conceptions of infinity and continuity remained dominant until the middle of the nineteenth century, they were never unanimously accepted. Philosophers of the Platonic tradition, including Augustinian theologians, always regarded the notion of infinite given totalities, whether they are continua or not, as legitimate. They were not troubled by the inapplicability of such a notion to sense experience, since for them mathematics was not an abstraction from—much less a description of—sense experience, but a description of reality; and reality was not apprehended by the senses, but by reason. Democritean atomism also survived as a strong philosophical undercurrent and encouraged attempts to explain a continuum as a type of ordering in an actually infinite class of indivisible elements.

From Aristotle to Newton and Leibniz. A revival of Platonic and Democritean ideas was a feature of the early development of modern science, and it also affected the notion of continuity. Thus, Galileo Galilei (1564–1642) rejected Aristotle's arguments against the possibility of a continuum consisting of an infinite number of indivisible elements. Among these arguments was the one that the addition of one indivisible element to another could not produce a divisible quantity because, if it could, the indivisible would become divisible. Galileo held that although a continuous quantity is not constructible by adding a finite number of indivisibles to each other, it can be conceived as consisting of an actual infinity of such elements.

Galileo brought out with great clarity some of the difficulties involved in the notions of an actual infinity and of a continuum, especially in regard to the application of such attributes as "equal," "greater," and "smaller" to infinite totalities. In so doing he anticipated some of the paradoxes to which Bernhard Bolzano (1781–1848) and later writers drew attention. Galileo, however, was not able to resolve them. He had to resort to metaphors, such as the comparison of a continuum to a solid that has been reduced to the finest powder consisting of an infinite number of infinitely small atoms.

The creation by Newton (1643–1723) and Leibniz (1646–1716) of the differential and integral calculus was the outcome both of original work by them and their predecessors and of a deepened understanding of Greek mathematics, especially the work of Eudoxus (fourth century B.C.) and Archimedes (287–212 B.C.). It led inevitably to a new stage in the philosophical approach to the problem of continuity. Leibniz distinguished sharply between the mathematical and the physical continua. Thus, he argued (for example, in a letter to Varignon of February 2, 1702) that one can, and should, make the analysis of the mathematical continuum independent of metaphysical assumptions, which presumably include his own "law of continuity." This principle of continuity, according to which everything in nature happens by degrees and according to which there are no discontinuous changes, dominated modern science from its inception until the advent of quantum mechanics at the beginning of the twentieth century.

Mathematical continuity was for Leibniz an ideal notion defined in terms of infinitely small or more precisely, "incomparably small," quantities, in the sense that they can be assumed to be as small as one needs to assume them to be in the context involving them. In particular, if anyone denies the validity of a chain of mathematical reasoning conducted in terms of incomparably small quantities, then it can be shown in the calculus of infinitesimals that the error resulting from the employment of such quantities is smaller than any quantity chosen, however small. Leibniz' mathematical theory contains—explicitly, according to some scholars; implicitly, according to others—the definition of a continuous function, as found in the standard textbooks of the twentieth century. (A function $f(x)$ is continuous in the interval $a \leq x \leq b$ if, and only if, for every point ξ of the interval and for every real number $\epsilon > 0$ there exists a real number $\delta > 0$ such that $|f(x) - f(\xi)| < \epsilon$ whenever $|x - \xi| < \delta$.)

Mathematically, Newton's and Leibniz' conceptions are similar enough to explain the bitter struggle for priority waged between them and between succeeding generations of scholars on their behalf. Newton conceived, at least at first, infinitesimals as quantities in process of vanishing or originating (*incrementa modo nascentia*). Side by side with statements that seem obscure from the point of view of present-day mathematics, Newton gave many clear analyses of continuous and differentiable functions. Thus, in the *Principia* he stated expressly that the ultimate ratios in which quantities vanish are not ratios of ultimate quantities, but limits to which the ratios of decreasing quantities approach. (In modern terminology, $y' = dy/dx$ is not a ratio of two infinitesimals, but the limit of a series of difference quotients; that is,

$$\lim_{\Delta x \to 0} \frac{\Delta y}{\Delta x}.)$$

Newton's and Leibniz' ideas were acutely criticized by George Berkeley (1685–1753), both from the point of view of his metaphysics and from a purely logical point of view. His logical objections, although unsympathetic and naturally directed to the weak points of the new theories, were largely justified. He was quick to object to reasoning in which "nothings," his derogatory term for infinitesimals, seemed to be considered proportional to real quantities and which at times bore a close resemblance to proving that 2 equals 5 by dividing both sides of the equation $2 \cdot 0 = 5 \cdot 0$ by 0. Berkeley stood at the beginning of a period of conceptual clarification that culminated in the continuum theories by Richard Dedekind (1831–1916) and Georg Cantor (1845–1918).

From Newton and Leibniz to modern times. Among the conditions that made the Dedekind–Cantor continuum theories possible were, on the one hand, a sharpening of the axiomatic method by axiomatizing not only mathematical theories but also the logic underlying them, and on the other, the creation of the theory of sets (see CANTOR, GEORG; SET THEORY). The key notions are those of an infinite set and of a nondenumerable set. Dedekind defined a set as infinite if, and only if, a one–one correspondence can be established between its members and the members of a proper subset of it. An infinite set is denumerable if, and only if, it can be mapped in a one–one manner on the set of natural numbers; otherwise, it is nondenumerable. A continuum is a nondenumerably infinite set, say K, the elements of which constitute a series that, apart from its serial order, also conforms to the following postulates, as given by E. V. Huntington in his *The Continuum* (1917): (1) If K_1 and K_2 are any two nonempty parts of K, such that every element of K belongs either to K_1 or K_2 and every element of K_1 precedes every element of K_2, then there is at least one element X in K such that any element that precedes X belongs to K_1, and every element that follows X belongs to K_2. (2) If a and b are elements of the class K and a precedes b, then there exists at least one element x in K such that a precedes x and x precedes b. The continuum is linear if in addition (3) the class K contains a denumerable subclass R in such a way that between any two elements of the class K there is an element of R. For example, the class of real numbers between 0 and 2 is a continuum. It is, moreover, a linear continuum with R the class of rational numbers and $\sqrt{2}$ an element of the continuum but not of R.

The Cantor–Dedekind theory of continuity was originally put forward within the framework of an intuitive or "naive" set theory. As a consequence, it was affected by the discovery of antinomies in set theory. Attempts to avoid these antinomies have led to a multiplicity of set theories and thus of theories of continuity. In this connection, reference should be made to Kurt Gödel's incompleteness theorems and to the Löwenheim—Skolem theorem. These discoveries have renewed in the minds of many philosophers and mathematicians the Aristotelian suspicions about the concept of actually infinite totalities and of any definition in terms of this concept. In the first half of the twentieth century, intuitionist mathematicians developed a mathematics and logic admitting only potential infinity and accepting the concept of a continuum as only a medium of free becoming.

The metaphor of the continuum as a medium of free becoming can be made precise only after an explanation of various key concepts of intuitionist mathematics, such as the notion of an infinitely proceeding sequence and of the notions of a spread and a species. The last two terms replace the notion of a set or class used in the classical theory of sets. (For details, see MATHEMATICS, FOUNDATIONS OF.)

One of the most important problems that arises in theories of continuity of the Cantor–Dedekind type is the so-called continuum problem: If $\aleph$ is the cardinal number of the set of all natural numbers $\{1,2,3, \cdots\}$—that is, the set of all sets equivalent to it—then it can be shown that the cardinal number c of the set of all subsets of $\{1,2,3, \cdots\}$ is also the cardinal number of the set of all real numbers and that, with a suitable definition of exponentiation, $c=2^{\aleph}$. Cantor showed by his diagonal argument that $\aleph < c$ and conjectured that there is no cardinal number x such that $\aleph < x < c$. The conjecture that c is the next higher cardinal number after $\aleph$ is known as the continuum hypothesis. In 1938 Gödel demonstrated that the continuum hypothesis cannot be disproved in the standard set theoretical systems. In 1963 Paul Cohen showed that the continuum hypothesis also cannot be proved. The recognition that the continuum hypothesis is independent of the axioms of set theory may well become as fertile a source of new developments as did the recognition that the parallel postulate is independent of the other postulates of Euclidean geometry.

The problem of application. Mathematical continuity, at least in the versions of Dedekind, Cantor, and their successors, is clearly not instantiated in experience. This raises the question of the relation of mathematical continuity to experience, especially since it occurs as an essential part of the mathematical framework of physics. Various types of answers to this question have been suggested. One might agree with Plato that no mathematical concept is applicable to experience and that empirical situations merely "participate" in the nonempirical reality of the Forms. Again, one might agree with Kant and David Hilbert that mathematical infinity and continuity, unlike the notions of elementary or constructive mathematics that are applicable to experience, are merely auxiliary notions, with regard to which no more can or need be shown than that their adjunction to elementary mathematics does not lead to contradictions. Lastly, one may hold with Henri Poincaré that the notion of mathematical continuity arises through a step-by-step modification of an empirical notion, with which it may for certain purposes and within certain contexts be identified.

Although the problem of the applicability of a mathematical notion of continuity to perceptual continua seems to presuppose an analysis of the notion of a perceptual continuum, such analyses are rarely undertaken. Poincaré regarded the notion of perceptual continuity as internally inconsistent. Henri Bergson and William James considered any attempt at analyzing the notion of perceived continuity as doomed to failure, because any such analysis merely exemplifies the irreconcilable clash of intellectualist logic with sensible experience. Bertrand Russell, on the other hand, seems to have regarded the distinction between mathematical and empirical continuity as illegitimate, and to have seen no difficulty in the assumption that perceptual space and time consist of points and instants that in any finite interval constitute actually infinite totalities.

Bibliography

Aristotle, *Physics*. Book VI.

Bergson, Henri, *L'Évolution créatrice*. Paris, 1907. Translated by Arthur Mitchell as *Creative Evolution*. New York, 1911.

Berkeley, George, *The Analyst, or a Discourse addressed to an Infidel Mathematician*. London, 1734.

Cantor, Georg, *Gesammelte Abhandlungen*, E. Zermelo, ed. Berlin, 1932.

Cohen, Paul, "Independence of the Continuum Hypothesis." *Proceedings of the National Academy of Sciences*, Vol. 50 (1963) and Vol. 51 (1964).

Dedekind, Richard, *Stetigkeit und irrationale Zahlen*. Brunswick, 1888.

Galilei, Galileo, *Discorsi intorno a due nuove scienze*. Leiden, 1638. Translated by H. Crew and A. De Salvio as *Dialogues Concerning Two New Sciences*. New York, 1914.

Gödel, Kurt, *The Consistency of the Continuum Hypothesis*. Princeton, 1940.

Heath, T. L., *Mathematics in Aristotle*. Oxford, 1949.

Heyting, Arend, *Intuitionism, An Introduction*. Amsterdam, 1956.

Huntington, E. V., *The Continuum*. Cambridge, Mass., 1917.

James, William, *A Pluralistic Universe*. London, 1912.

Leibniz, G. W., "Nouveaux Essais sur l'entendement humaine," in R. E. Raspe, ed., *Oeuvres philosophiques*. Leipzig and Amsterdam, 1765. Translated by A. G. Langley as *New Essays Concerning Human Understanding*. London and New York, 1896.

Newton, Isaac, *Philosophiae Naturalis Principia Mathematica*. London, 1687. Translated by Alexander Motte as *The Mathematical Principles of Natural Philosophy*. London, 1727. Revised and edited by Florian Cajori. Berkeley, 1946.

Poincaré, Henri, *La Science et l'hypothèse*. Paris, 1912. Translated by W. J. Greenstreet as *Science and Hypothesis*. London, 1905.

Quine, W. V., *Set Theory and Its Logic*. Cambridge, Mass., 1963.

Russell, Bertrand, *Our Knowledge of the External World*. London, 1914. Ch. 5.

Weyl, Hermann, *Das Kontinuum*. Leipzig, 1918.

S. KÖRNER

CONTINUUM PROBLEM. The celebrated continuum problem arose with Georg Cantor's theory of sets. A set is to be thought of as any collection of objects whatsoever. A set A is said to be a subset of a set B (in symbols, $A \subseteq B$) if every element of A is also an element of B. By the power set of A, written $\mathcal{P}(A)$, is meant the set of all subsets of A. Two sets A and B are said to be similar, or to have the same cardinality, if A can be put into a one-to-one correspondence with the elements of B (as, for example, the fingers of one's left hand can be put into a one-to-one correspondence with the fingers of one's right hand). We say that A has lower cardinality than B, or that B has higher cardinality than A, if A can be put into a one-to-one correspondence with a subset of B but not with the whole of B. We let ω be the set of natural numbers $\{0,1,2,3,\cdots\}$. A set is called denumerable (or countable) if it can be put into a one-to-one correspondence with ω.

Is every infinite set denumerable? Cantor showed that many sets which at first sight appear to be nondenumerable (such as the set of all rational numbers) are actually denumerable. Indeed, Cantor first conjectured that every infinite set is denumerable and spent many years trying to prove this. Then he made the basic discovery that his conjecture was false. He showed that the set $\mathcal{P}(\omega)$ has higher cardinality than ω—more generally, that for any set A, $\mathcal{P}(A)$ has higher cardinality than A. Cantor's famous argument is as follows: Consider a one-to-one correspondence that assigns to each element a of A a certain subset S_a of A. Let S be the set of all a that do not belong to S_a. Then S is distinct from each S_a (because a belongs to one of S, S_a but not to the other). Therefore, the one-to-one correspondence is not onto the whole of $\mathcal{P}(A)$ (because no element a corresponds to S). On the other hand, it is obvious that there is a one-to-one correspondence from A onto a subset of $\mathcal{P}(A)$; just assign to each a the one-element set whose only member is a. Thus, $\mathcal{P}(A)$ has higher cardinality than A. It can be shown that $\mathcal{P}(\omega)$ has the same cardinality as the set of all real numbers or as the set of all points on a straight line. For this reason $\mathcal{P}(\omega)$ is said to have the cardinality of the continuum.

The continuum problem is this: Does there exist a set of higher cardinality than ω but lower cardinality than $\mathcal{P}(\omega)$? The continuum hypothesis asserts that there is no such intermediate set. And the generalized continuum hypothesis asserts that for every set A, there can never be a set of higher cardinality than A but lower cardinality than $\mathcal{P}(A)$.

So far no attempts have been the slightest bit successful in indicating whether the continuum hypothesis is true or false. Today many principles are known to be consequences of the generalized continuum hypothesis, and many principles are known to be equivalent to this hypothesis (see Wacław Sierpiński, "L'Hypothèse généralisée du continu et l'axiome du choix"). But we have no idea whether the continuum hypothesis holds. Another question not to be confused with the truth or falsity of the continuum hypothesis is whether the continuum hypothesis can be formally proved or disproved from the present axioms of set theory. This question is now completely settled.

We use the term "present axioms of set theory" to mean the system ZFS (Zermelo–Fraenkel–Skolem), which is the system currently in most widespread use. (A closely related system is VNB, von Neumann–Bernays. We will soon give some idea of the axioms of VNB.) In 1938, Kurt Gödel proved the famous result that the generalized hypothesis is formally consistent with the axioms of ZFS (assuming, of course, that ZFS is itself consistent, which we will assume throughout this article). And in 1963, Paul Cohen settled the matter in the other direction; he showed that the negation of the generalized continuum hypothesis (in fact, even the negation of the special continuum hypothesis) is consistent in ZFS. Thus, the continuum hypothesis is independent of the axioms of ZFS—that is, it can be neither proved nor disproved in ZFS. So the axioms of ZFS are not strong enough to settle the continuum problem.

Another important independence result concerns the axiom of choice. This axiom says (in one form) that given any nonempty collection Σ of nonempty sets, there exists a function f—a so-called choice function for Σ—which assigns to each member S of Σ some element of S. Gödel has shown that the axiom of choice is not disprovable in ZFS, and Cohen has shown that it is not provable in ZFS. Thus, the axiom of choice is also independent of the axioms of ZFS. Cohen's most remarkable result has been to show that even if we add the axiom of choice to the other axioms of set theory (that is, to ZFS), it is still not possible to prove the continuum hypothesis.

Significance of the results. There has been a remarkable diversity of opinion concerning the significance of the independence results. These results have been proved for the particular axiom systems ZFS and VNB (though the arguments hold for many related systems). There are, however, very different formal axiom systems of set theory in which the arguments of Gödel and Cohen do not hold. But it is highly questionable whether these other systems really describe the notion of "set" as used by the working mathematician. (In W. V. Quine's system, for example, the axiom of choice is provably false.) For those who regard all these alternative systems as on an equal footing (and these include many so-called formalists) the independence results may well seem insignificant; they could be construed as merely saying that the continuum hypothesis comes out positive in one system and negative in some other, equally good system. On the other hand, there are those who concede that ZFS is the more "natural" set theory but who cannot understand what could be meant by mathematical truth other than provability in ZFS. They would therefore construe the independence results as saying that the continuum hypothesis is neither true nor false. A slightly modified viewpoint in effect maintains that the only propositions we can ever know to be true are those provable in ZFS and hence that we can never know whether the continuum hypothesis is true or false.

The so-called mathematical realists, or mathematical Platonists (and these seem to include a large number of working mathematicians), look upon the matter very differently. We can describe the realist viewpoint as follows: There is a well-defined mathematical reality of sets, and in this reality the continuum hypothesis is definitely either true or false. The axioms of ZFS give a true but incomplete description of this reality. The independence results cast no light on the truth or falsity of the continuum hypothesis, nor do they in any way indicate that it is neither true nor false. Rather, they highlight the inadequacy of our present axiom system ZFS. New principles of set theory may one day be found which, though not derivable from the present axioms, are self-evident (as the axiom of choice is to most mathematicians) and which might settle the continuum problem one way or the other. Indeed, Gödel—despite his own proof of the formal consistency of the continuum hypothesis—conjectured in "What Is Cantor's Continuum Problem?" that when such a principle is found the continuum hypothesis will be seen to be false.

In the present exposition we will adopt a realist viewpoint.

Axiomatic set theory. The following is an intuitive account of present-day set theory.

For any two sets x and y, by $\{x,y\}$ we mean the set whose only elements are x and y. By $\cup x$ (read "union x") is meant the set of all elements which belong to at least one member of x. We have already mentioned the power set $\mathcal{P}(x)$. By 0 is meant the empty set, that set which has no members. By the ordered pair $\langle x,y \rangle$ is meant the set $\{\{x,x\},\{x,y\}\}$.

We also speak of properties of sets (or conditions on sets). We write $P(x)$ to mean that the property P holds for the set

x. We say that a property P is coextensive with a set x if P holds for every y if and only if y is a member of x. By a class A we mean either a set or a property that is not coextensive with any set. For any set x and class A, we write $x \in A$ to mean that x is a member of A if A is a set or that A holds for x if A is a property; in either case we say that x belongs to, or is a member of, A. We let V be the class of all sets. It turns out that V is not a set but a property (the property of being a set). Classes which are not sets are sometimes called proper classes.

A class A is called a (binary) relation if every element belonging to A is an ordered pair. By a function F is meant a relation such that for every set x there is at most one element y for which $\langle x,y \rangle \in F$ (also written "$F(x)=y$"). By $F''x$ is meant the set of all elements $F(y)$ where y is a member of x.

How do we know that the sets $\{x,y\}$, $\cup x$, $\mathcal{P}(x)$, 0, and $F''x$ exist? They all follow from one principle, the unlimited abstraction principle, which states that every condition determines a set—that is, given any property, we can form the set of all elements having that property. (Thus, for example, $\cup x$ is the set of all elements satisfying the condition of belonging to at least one member of x, and $\mathcal{P}(x)$ is the set of all y satisfying the condition of being a subset of x.) Unfortunately this tempting principle is unsound; it leads quickly to contradictions, such as Russell's famous paradox of the set of all sets that do not belong to themselves. (Such a set must belong to itself if and only if it does not.)

One of Ernst Zermelo's contributions was to replace this unsound principle with the limited abstraction principle, or separation principle (also known as the *Aussonderungsprinzip*), which states that given any property P and any set x, we may form the set of all elements of x which have the property P. This principle has never been known to lead to any contradiction; indeed, it is a principle in constant use by the everyday working mathematician (who speaks, for example, of the set of all numbers having a given property or the set of all real-valued functions having a given property). As a price for having given up the unlimited abstraction principle Zermelo had to take the existence of the sets 0, $\{x,y\}$, $\cup x$, and $\mathcal{P}(x)$ as separate axioms. He also took an axiom of infinity, which in effect provides for the existence of ω. The axiom providing for the existence of $F''x$, known as the axiom of substitution or of replacement, was added later by A. A. Fraenkel. This axiom, incidentally, implies the separation axiom and also (together with the power axiom) gives the existence of $\{x,y\}$. The axiom of infinity implies the existence of 0. Hence, the only axioms we need for set existence are those for $\cup x$, $\mathcal{P}(x)$, ω, and $F''x$. We also need the so-called axiom of extensionality, which says that two sets containing the same members are identical—that is, they satisfy the same conditions.

We might also wish to state axioms providing for the existence of various properties (or conditions). Zermelo did not do this—indeed, his system was not really a formal axiom system in the modern sense of the term. It was Thoralf Skolem who proposed to identify properties with first-order properties, by which is meant conditions defined by first-order formulas—that is, well-formed expressions built from the set-membership symbol "$\in$," the variables x, y, · · · ranging over all sets, the connectives of propositional logic, and the quantifiers for the set variables x, y, · · ·. In Skolem's version it was necessary to formulate Zermelo's separation principle as an infinite number of axioms (one for every first-order formula). And in the theory ZFS the axiom of substitution is likewise formulated as infinitely many axioms. (In contrast, only finitely many axioms are needed in VNB.)

Zermelo protested vigorously against this interpretation by Skolem. Zermelo thought of properties as all meaningful conditions, not just those conditions given by first-order formulas (or higher-order formulas, for that matter). Skolem replied that Zermelo's notion of property was too vague to be satisfactory.

There are many realists who feel that Zermelo's system, despite its nonformal character, comes far closer to the true Cantorian set theory. Of course, there is no harm in laying down formal axioms which force at least the first-order properties into the picture, but there is no reason to identify all properties with those properties whose existence is forced by the axioms. In this connection we should mention the stronger theory VNB* (see the Appendix to John L. Kelley, *General Topology*), in which there are axioms providing for the existence of second-order properties as well—that is, properties given by formulas in which we quantify over properties as well as sets. The realists feel that VNB* provides a more complete description of Cantorian set theory than does VNB (or ZFS), but it still should not be thought of as the whole of Cantorian set theory, since there is no reason to identify properties with second-order properties either.

Cantorian versus first-order universes. We wish to clear up another misunderstanding, but to do this we need a little more technical background.

A class A is called transitive or complete if every member of A is itself a set of members of A. A class A is called supercomplete if it is transitive and contains, with every element x, all subsets of x as well. Important examples of transitive sets are the ordinal numbers, which we will define shortly. Examples of supercomplete sets are the sets R_α (which will soon be discussed) and all transitive sets of the form $\mathcal{P}(x)$.

We say that a subclass B of A is first-order definable over A if B is the class of all elements of A that satisfy some first-order formula (perhaps with some constants in A), interpreting the quantifiers as ranging over just the elements of A. We shall say that A is first-order supercomplete if it is transitive and contains, with every element x, all subsets of x which are first-order definable over A. (Obviously, first-order supercompleteness is far weaker than true supercompleteness. Examples of first-order supercompleteness will arise later.)

By a Cantorian universe C we shall mean a transitive class satisfying the following four conditions: (1) for every $x \in C$, $\cup x \in C$; (2) $\omega \in C$; (3) for every $x \in C$, $\mathcal{P}(x) \in C$; (4) for every $x \in C$ and every function F from C into C, $F''x \in C$.

By contrast, we define a transitive class C to be a first-order universe if C satisfies (1) and (2) and, in place of (3) and (4), the following weaker conditions: (3*) for every $x \in C$, the set of all subsets of x which are first-order definable over C is a member of C; (4*) for every $x \in C$ and every function F which is first-order definable over C, $F''x \in C$.

A Cantorian universe is necessarily supercomplete, and a first-order universe is necessarily first-order supercomplete.

To say of a transitive class C that it is a first-order universe is to say nothing more or less than that C is a model for (the axioms of) ZFS—that is, that these axioms are true—when the quantifiers are interpreted as ranging over C. Thus, the formal axioms of ZFS can never force a model C to be a genuine Cantorian universe; they only force C to be a first-order universe. It is precisely this fact which is exploited in various independence proofs.

Indeed, Gödel obtained his consistency results by showing the existence of a certain first-order universe L (the class of constructible sets, which we will soon define) in which both the axiom of choice and the continuum hypothesis are true, when we interpret the quantifiers as ranging over L. It is unknown whether L is a true Cantorian universe. (Moreover, from the axioms of ZFS it cannot be proved either to be or not to be one.) On the other hand, Cohen constructed a first-order universe in which the continuum hypothesis is false. This universe is definitely not a true Cantorian universe. (Indeed, it is a denumerable set.) But the existence of even a first-order universe in which a statement is false is enough to guarantee that the statement can never be formally proved from the axioms of ZFS.

Thus, there are first-order universes in which the continuum hypothesis is true and first-order universes in which the continuum hypothesis is false. But for true Cantorian universes the continuum hypothesis is either true in all of them or false in all of them (and this fact is provable in ZFS, as subsequent discussion will show). It is this which the mathematical realist means when he asserts that the continuum hypothesis is definitely either true or false (but we do not yet know which).

Ordinals and cardinals. For any set x, by x^+ is meant the set of all elements which either belong to x or are identical with x.

By an ordinal (also called ordinal number) is meant a set x that belongs to every class A satisfying the following three conditions: (1) $0 \in A$; (2) for every y in A, $y^+ \in A$; (3) for every subset y of A, $\bigcup y \in A$. (This definition involves quantifying over all classes, but it can be replaced by a first-order condition; hence, the existence of the class of ordinals can be established in VNB.) It can be shown that every element of an ordinal is an ordinal. Also, for any two distinct ordinals, one of them is a member of the other. We use Greek letters—"α," "β," "γ," and "λ"—for ordinals. If $\alpha \in \beta$, then we also say that α is less than, or smaller than, β and write $\alpha < \beta$. It turns out that every nonempty class of ordinals contains a smallest one. By a limit ordinal is meant an ordinal which is neither 0 nor α^+ for any α. (Ordinals of the form α^+ are called successor ordinals.) The finite ordinals are just the ordinals 0, 0^+, 0^{++}, 0^{+++}, etc.—these are taken for the "natural numbers" in modern set theory. And the set ω of finite ordinals is an ordinal; it is the first (smallest) infinite ordinal—and the first limit ordinal.

By a cardinal is meant an ordinal that cannot be put into a one-to-one correspondence with any smaller ordinal. If α is a cardinal and x can be put into a one-to-one correspondence with α, we say that α is the cardinal of x, or that x has cardinality α. Using the axioms of substitution and choice, we can show that every set x has a unique cardinality; this cardinal is usually written $\overline{\overline{x}}$.

It can be proved that there exists a unique one-to-one correspondence which assigns to every ordinal α an infinite cardinal ω_α such that for any α and β, we have $\alpha < \beta$ if and only if $\omega_\alpha < \omega_\beta$. We call ω_α the αth infinite cardinal (in order of increasing magnitude). Thus, ω_0 is the first infinite cardinal, which is simply ω. Then comes ω_1, which is the first nondenumerable cardinal. For any cardinal k, by 2^k is meant the cardinality of the power set of k. Thus, 2^{ω_0} is the cardinality of the continuum, and the continuum hypothesis is equivalent (in the presence of the axiom of choice) to the assertion that $2^{\omega_0} = \omega_1$. And the generalized continuum hypothesis is equivalent (in the presence of the axiom of choice) to the assertion that for every α, $2^{\omega_\alpha} = \omega_{\alpha+1}$.

Rank. Using a basic tool of set theory known as the transfinite recursive theorem, we can show that there is a unique way of assigning to every ordinal α a set R_α such that (1) R_0 is the empty set; (2) for every α, R_{α^+} is the power set of R_α; (3) for every limit ordinal λ, R_λ is the set of all elements belonging to some R_α for $\alpha < \lambda$. A set x is called regular if it belongs to some R_α, and by the rank of a regular set is meant the first α such that $x \in R_{\alpha^+}$. (It turns out that every ordinal α is regular and of rank α.)

The statement that every set is regular is known to be equivalent to the axiom of foundation, which asserts that every nonempty class A contains an element x that has no members in common with A. This axiom is consistent in VNB because the class of all regular sets turns out to be a first-order universe—indeed, even a true Cantorian universe—in which the axiom of foundation is true. It is usual to take the axiom of foundation as an additional axiom (although its negation is also known to be consistent in VNB).

For some α, every set R_α is supercomplete, and every supercomplete model of ZFS is of the form R_α. Under the union operation R_α is always closed. Under the power-set operation R_α is closed if and only if α is a limit ordinal. For any limit ordinal α beyond ω, $\omega \in R_\alpha$. Thus, for every limit ordinal α beyond ω, R_α satisfies the first three of the four conditions defining a Cantorian universe. If the fourth condition is also satisfied, α is called a (strongly) inaccessible ordinal (according to one of several equivalent definitions).

Richard Montague and R. L. Vaught have proved that the existence of an inaccessible ordinal implies the existence of an ordinal α less than the first inaccessible ordinal such that R_α is a first-order universe. Stated otherwise, if there exists any set which is a Cantorian universe, then there exists a supercomplete first-order universe which is not a Cantorian universe.

We remarked earlier that given any two Cantorian universes C_1 and C_2, the continuum hypothesis is true in one if and only if it is true in the other. Roughly, the idea is this: First, one Cantorian universe—say C_1—must be a subclass of the other (indeed, any one Cantorian universe either is one of the sets R_α or is the class V of all sets, and whenever $\alpha < \beta$ the $R_\alpha \subseteq R_\beta$). Second, the definitions of ω and 2^{ω_0} do not alter if we reinterpret "set" to mean "element of C_1" or "element of C_2." Last, the elements ω and 2^{ω_0} of C_1 (or, indeed, any two sets x and y of C_1) can be put into a one-to-one correspondence in C_1 if and only if they can be so put in C_2 (that is, any one-to-one correspondence between them must lie in C_1 and C_2). A similar argument works for the generalized continuum hypothesis.

Constructible sets. Again using the transfinite recursion theorem, it is possible to assign to every α a unique set M_α such that (1) $M_0 = 0$; (2) for every α, M_{α^+} is the set of all subsets of M_α which are first-order definable over M_α; (3) for limit ordinals λ, M_λ is the union of all M_α for $\alpha < \lambda$.

A set x is called constructible if it belongs to some M_α. The class of all constructible sets is denoted by "L." We have already remarked that L is a first-order universe in which the axiom of choice is true.

It is worth noting that L can alternatively be characterized as the intersection of all first-order universes which are not sets (just as the class R of regular sets can be characterized as the intersection of all Cantorian universes which are not sets). Thus, x has rank if and only if it belongs to all proper Cantorian universes; x is constructible if and only if it belongs to all proper first-order universes.

Is every set constructible? No one knows. But Gödel has shown that it is consistent to assume so. His proof of the consistency of $V = L$ uses an idea of "absoluteness" which we might describe as follows:

All notions in set theory are defined ultimately in terms of "set" (and the membership relation ϵ). If we reinterpret "set" to mean constructible set, the resulting notion may change in meaning. If the notion does not change, then it is called absolute. It turns out that many of the notions in set theory are absolute, such as the notions that $y = \cup x$, that x is an ordinal, that x is finite, that $z = \{x,y\}$. (On the other hand, the notions that x is a cardinal and that y is the power set of x are not known to be or not to be absolute.) It turns out that the very notion of constructibility is absolute. This means that if in the definition of "constructible" we everywhere replace "set" with "constructible set," every element of L is constructible in the new sense. In other words, the so-called axiom of constructibility, which states that every set is constructible, is true in the model L. Thus, L is a model for ZFS, the axiom of choice, and the axiom of constructibility.

Gödel's most remarkable discovery is that there are at most ω_1 constructible sets of integers (and, more generally, there are at most $\omega_{\alpha+1}$ constructible subsets of M_{ω_α}). This means that the hypothesis $V = L$ implies the continuum hypothesis. Suppose every set is constructible. Then there are at most ω_1 sets of integers—that is, $2^{\omega_0} \leq \omega_1$. But obviously $\omega_1 \leq 2^{\omega_0}$, so we have $2^{\omega_0} = \omega_1$. Indeed, $V = L$ implies the generalized continuum hypothesis because it happens that ω_α is the cardinality of M_{ω_α}, and there are at most $\omega_{\alpha+1}$ constructible subsets of M_{ω_α}. Since $V = L$ is consistent and $V = L$ implies the generalized continuum hypothesis, the latter is also consistent in the theories ZFS and VNB and, by a modified argument, in VNB*.

We might also remark that Gödel has shown that for any inaccessible ordinal α, the set M_α is a first-order universe satisfying the axiom of choice and the generalized continuum hypothesis. He also showed that the set M_{ω_ω} satisfies all the axioms of ZFS except the axiom of substitution—in particular, it is first-order supercomplete (though again it is unknown whether it is truly supercomplete).

Relative strengths of the hypotheses. Consider the following hypotheses:

(1) The axiom of constructibility.

(2) The generalized continuum hypothesis.

(3) The axiom of choice.

We have discussed how (1) implies (2). It is also well known that (2) implies (3). One might ask whether (1) is genuinely stronger than (2), in the presence of the axioms of ZFS, and whether (2) is stronger than (3). One might also ask whether the negation of the axiom of constructibility is consistent relative to ZFS.

First, Paul Cohen constructed a first-order universe in which the axiom of constructibility fails. This (with Gödel's result) shows that the axiom of constructibility is independent of the axioms of ZFS.

Second, Cohen constructed a model of ZFS in which the axiom of constructibility is false but the generalized continuum hypothesis is nevertheless true. Thus, the generalized continuum hypothesis does not conversely imply the axiom of constructibility; the latter is genuinely stronger.

Third (and most striking of all), Cohen constructed a model of ZFS in which the axiom of choice is true but the generalized continuum hypothesis—indeed, even the special continuum hypothesis $2^{\omega_0} = \omega_1$—is false. So the generalized continuum hypothesis is genuinely stronger than the axiom of choice.

Thus, Cohen has completely settled the relative strengths of (1), (2), and (3) with respect to the formal system ZFS.

Measurable cardinals. New light has recently been thrown on the axiom of constructibility by the consideration of the existence of measurable cardinals.

By a two-valued measure μ on a set M is meant a function which assigns to every subset x of M one of the two values 0 and 1 and is such that given any finite or denumerable collection Σ of pairwise disjoint subsets of M, if every member of M receives the value 0 (under μ), so does $\cup\Sigma$. (This is also expressed by saying that the function μ is countably additive.) The measure is called nontrivial if μ assigns to M itself the value 1 and to every finite subset of M the value 0. Moreover, M is called measurable if there exists a nontrivial measure on M. Whether M carries a nontrivial two-valued measure depends only on the cardinality $\overline{\overline{M}}$ of M. If M carries a nontrivial measure, then one says that $\overline{\overline{M}}$ is measurable. We let MC denote the proposition "there exists a measurable cardinal." For the moment assume MC and let m be the least measurable cardinal. It is known (assuming the axiom of choice) that m must be very large. S. Ulam has shown that m is strongly inaccessible. Recently, H. J. Keisler and Alfred Tarski proved that for any ordinal α less than m, there is a strongly inaccessible ordinal less than m but greater than ω_α.

The first important relation between the hypothesis MC and the axiom of constructibility was discovered by Dana Scott. He obtained the extremely surprising result that MC implies the existence of nonconstructible sets. Subsequently, Rowbottom sharpened Scott's result and showed that the existence of a measurable cardinal implies the existence of a nonconstructible set of natural numbers—in other words, he showed that MC implies that there are only countably many constructible sets of natural numbers.

Since *MC* succeeded in throwing light on the axiom of constructibility, there naturally arose hopes that *MC* might throw light on the continuum hypothesis. This hope has very recently been dispelled. In late 1964, Azriel Levy in Jerusalem and Robert Solovay in Princeton independently showed (using techniques similar to Cohen's) that even when we add *MC* and the axiom of choice to the axioms of ZFS, if the resulting system is consistent it is still not possible to prove or to disprove the special continuum hypothesis. (It is not known whether this holds for the general continuum hypothesis.)

The consistency of *MC* itself (in ZFS or VNB) remains an unsolved problem.

Bibliography

Cantor, Georg, *The Theory of Transfinite Numbers*, translated by P. E. B. Jourdain. La Salle, Ill., 1941.

Cohen, Paul, *The Independence of the Axiom of Choice*. Stanford, Calif., 1963. Mimeographed.

Cohen, Paul, "The Independence of the Continuum Hypothesis," I and II. *Proceedings of the National Academy of Sciences*, Vol. 50 (1963), 1143–1148, and Vol. 51 (1964), 105–110.

Gödel, Kurt, "Consistency-proof for the Generalized Continuum Hypothesis." *Proceedings of the National Academy of Sciences*, Vol. 25 (1939), 220–224.

Gödel, Kurt, *The Consistency of the Axiom of Choice and of the Generalized Continuum-hypothesis With the Axioms of Set Theory*. Princeton, N.J., 1940. Uses system VNB.

Gödel, Kurt, "What Is Cantor's Continuum Problem?" *American Mathematical Monthly*, Vol. 54 (1947), 515–525.

Keisler, H. J., and Tarski, Alfred, "From Accessible to Inaccessible Cardinals." *Fundamenta Mathematicae*, Vol. 53 (1964), 225–308.

Kelley, John L., *General Topology*. Princeton, N.J., 1955.

Montague, Richard, and Vaught, R. L., "Natural Models of Set Theories." *Fundamenta Mathematicae*, Vol. 47 (1959).

Quine, W. V., *Mathematical Logic*. New York, 1940.

Scott, Dana, "Measurable Cardinals and Constructible Sets." *Bulletin de L'Académie Polonaise des Sciences:* Series of *Mathematical, Astronomical and Physical Sciences*, Vol. 9 (1961), 521–524.

Sierpiński, Wacław, "L'Hypothèse généralisée du continu et l'axiome du choix." *Fundamenta Mathematicae*, Vol. 34 (1947), 1–5.

Ulam, S., "Zur Masstheorie in der allgemeinen Mengenlehre." *Fundamenta Mathematicae*, Vol. 16 (1930), 140–150.

RAYMOND M. SMULLYAN

CONTRARY-TO-FACT CONDITIONAL.

The terms "contrary-to-fact," "counterfactual," and "unfulfilled" all have the same meaning when applied to conditional statements. Applied to categorical statements, they would mean "false in fact," but when applied to conditionals, they mean that the antecedent, or protasis, is false. This falsity is not explicitly stated; it is implicitly stated, or suggested, by context or by use of the subjective mood. "If the vase had fallen, it would have broken" implicitly asserts, or suggests, that the vase did not fall. Such statements are normally proposed as true and as an appropriate and natural way of expressing some part of knowledge.

They are used in explicating disposition terms. Talk about dispositions, capacities, tendencies, and so on, commits one to accepting as true, statements about what certain things or persons would have done in circumstances that have not occurred. To take a simple case: anyone who says that a given salt is soluble in water is committed to accepting the statement that a sample of it would have dissolved if at any time it had been placed in water.

Counterfactual statements are often used by historians to sum up, or to give emphasis to, an argument or the presentation of a case. The statement, "If Hitler had invaded England in 1940, he would have conquered the country," is of a kind that could be so used in an account of World War II.

It is also said that counterfactuals are sustained by scientific laws. A law of the form, "All *A* are *B*," for example, is said to sustain the claim that if *X* had been an *A*, whatever *X* might be, then it would have been a *B*. Many philosophers have concluded from this that an analysis of the concept of scientific law is satisfactory only if it also provides an analysis of contrary-to-fact conditionals.

The occasions for asserting, or assenting to, such conditionals in the sciences and in ordinary life are numerous, and they include occasions when the consequences of a *supposition* are considered. A scientist who had occasion to suppose, contrary to fact, that the earth has no satellite, or that there is another planet in the solar system, naturally uses such conditionals.

In the doctrine of phenomenalism conditionals should also play a crucial role. According to this doctrine, statements about physical objects must, in principle, be reducible to statements about the sense experiences of actual or hypothetical observers. Phenomenalists should be concerned to provide an analysis of conditional statements such as "If there had been an observer present, then he would have had such and such sense experiences." Few, if any, philosophers, however, have come to investigate such conditionals as a consequence of their wish to defend phenomenalism.

For philosophers, such conditionals raise certain problems, although these problems are normally thought to belong to a wider field of conditional statements than that of counterfactuals as just described. Subjunctive conditionals, such as "If the vase were to fall, it would break," where the falling or not falling is left open, and factual conditionals—to use the term suggested by N. Goodman—such as "Since the vase fell, it broke," have been said to raise most of the major problems as well. Most writers have, in fact, said that none of the terms used to describe the relevant conditionals is adequate, since, for example, not all of them are contrary-to-fact, nor are they all expressed in the subjunctive mood.

The problem of analysis. The general problem has been taken to be that of providing an analysis of such statements that satisfactorily accounts for the conditional element in them, this being common to the various forms. There are some problems peculiar to those that are strictly counterfactual because they involve "belief-contravening suppositions," as N. Rescher terms them, but discussion of these has been thought to be of value in illuminating the general problem.

R. M. Chisholm, with his paper "The Contrary-to-Fact Conditional" (1946), and N. Goodman, with "The Problem of Counterfactual Conditionals" (1947), have been chiefly responsible for more recent considerations of the issues, although they did not discover them. Chisholm refers, among others, to F. H. Bradley, C. I. Lewis, R. Carnap,

C. D. Broad, C. G. Hempel, F. P. Ramsey, and W. V. Quine as having raised relevant issues in one context or another. Bradley, for example, speaks of counterfactual suppositions as "ideal experiments," or thought experiments. In the judgment, "If you had not destroyed the barometer, it would now forewarn us," he said that "we assert the existence in reality of such circumstances and such a general law of nature as would, *if we suppose* some conditions present, produce a certain result." This conclusion is very similar to that arrived at by more recent writers, although they probably would not share his views on other logical matters. The reference to law does indicate one topic that most later philosophers have taken to be central to the problem, that of the distinction between lawlike and accidental universal statements.

Chisholm considers that counterfactuals have been overlooked by modern logic, which has not provided any way of interpreting them so as to bring out their logical peculiarity. Because of the large number of uses for such conditionals in philosophy, science, and ordinary discourse, he wants to remedy this omission. For Goodman, they raise a set of problems in the philosophy of science, and he believes that a satisfactory definition of scientific law, a satisfactory theory of confirmation and of disposition terms, would largely provide a solution. He says, indeed, that lack of means for interpreting counterfactuals amounts to lack of an adequate philosophy of science, and Chisholm would find no quarrel with this. There is sufficient agreement between them, about the nature both of the problem and of the way in which it is to be solved, for the one outline to be given.

First, however, a statement of the problem is needed. Let "If *A*, then *C*" represent a counterfactual, where *A* and *C* are antecedent and consequent respectively; and let them be statements in the indicative mood, such as "The vase falls" and "The vase breaks," when taken by themselves, with suitable provision for subjunctive mood or modal expressions when put into the conditional form. There is held to be no problem where *A* entails or strictly implies *C*. The problem arises only (1) when the assertion is that *C* in some sense follows from *A*, in the absence of a relation of strict implication between them; and (2) when the question of truth or falsity is settled by finding out whether some connection obtains, other than strict implication.

The problem, as it has been generally discussed, is this: How can an analysis of counterfactuals be provided such that both their import and what is involved in determining their truth and falsity can be made clear, when neither a simple truth-functional analysis of them nor one that uses irreducible or nonexplicable modal notions, is allowable?

The simple truth-functional analysis is rejected since, taken as a material implication, "If *A*, then *C*" would be true just because *A* is false. So too, however, would be "If *A*, then not-*C*." (Similar remarks apply also if such a conditional were taken to be equivalent to the conjunction, "Not-*A* and if *A*, then *C*.") When a counterfactual is asserted, what is normally conveyed is that, given *A*, only one of *C* or not-*C* is the case. Thus, two counterfactuals of the forms just given are contraries, and not subcontraries, as they are in a simple truth-functional interpretation.

A nonexplicable modal notion would be equivalent to the necessary connection that Hume attacked and so a major difficulty for empiricism. Most accounts of counterfactuals have sought to provide an interpretation that is compatible with empiricism.

Some attempts to solve the problem. Chisholm says that the analysis of counterfactuals consists in rendering a subjunctive conditional of the form, "$(x)(y)$, if x were ϕ and y were ψ, y would be χ," into an indicative statement that will say the same thing, although the form of particular statements may be more or less complex than this. This translation is to bring out the proper logical form of such conditionals, and he compares his task with that of Russell in the theory of definite descriptions. Following suggestions of Ramsey and Quine, both Chisholm and Goodman hold that counterfactuals or subjunctive conditionals can be analyzed as asserting a strong relation, like formal implication, between the statements *A* and *C* and that this strong relation should be made explicit in the proposed translation or explication of such assertions.

The proposed analysis is this: that any subjunctive or contrary-to-fact conditional, not analytically true, is equivalent to the statement that there is a set of statements, *S*, taken to be true, which, conjoined with *A*, entails or strictly implies *C*. The set of statements, *S*, is not specified in the assertion of any counterfactual; but anyone making such an assertion implicitly commits himself to holding that there is such a set of statements and that they are true. They are taken to be statements of relevant circumstances or conditions. For example, where the counterfactual is "If this match had been struck, it would have lit," there could be among the statements of *S*, such statements as "The match is dry," "Sufficient oxygen is present," and so on.

Goodman sees two main problems in this analysis or interpretation. The first is to define the relevant conditions, or to specify the kinds of propositions that are admissible in *S*. The second problem is the definition of scientific laws, because the main propositions in *S*, justifying the connection of *A* and *C*, are laws. For the first of these, however, there are two kinds of questions to be distinguished. One is a substantive question with different issues raised for different cases: for example, a conditional beginning with "If the vase had been dropped" raises different questions concerning relevant conditions from one beginning with "If this match had been struck." This is of interest to philosophers only in so far as it throws light upon the second kind of question, namely, the formal question concerning the logical requirements of *S*. Goodman states that the problem here is "to define the circumstances under which a given counterfactual holds while the opposing conditional with the contradictory consequent fails to hold." In order to secure this, restrictions must be placed upon statements admissible in *S*. What is required is a set of conditions such that *C* follows from the conjunction of *S* and *A*, and not-*C* does not follow. The statements of *S* should be "cotenable."

Both Chisholm and Goodman have tried to formulate some of the restrictions needed: for example, given that *A* is false, it would not be possible to say that *S* is the totality of true statements, since this would include not-*A*, so that from the conjunction of *S* and *A* any conclusion trivially follows. Chisholm suggests various other restrictions: for example, *S* should not contain vacuous truths; therefore, every universal statement in *S* must have existential import; and, again, no statement in *S* can be an accidental universal. Goodman, although not directing his argument against these restrictions, in fact, showed that even when the universal statements in *S* have existential import and are not accidental, freedom from trivial implications is not guaranteed.

Indeed, F. L. Will has shown that the restrictions upon *S* proposed by Chisholm can, with ingenuity, be met and yet allow this trivialization. The proposed conditions are, thus, inadequate, and since a consequence of Will's argument is that any adequate set of restrictions would be extraordinarily complex, this strongly suggests that the original proposal needs revising.

S. Hampshire has said that the conditionals in question raise difficulties for three classes of philosophers: those wanting a truth-functional analysis of all compound statements; those who support a view of truth as correspondence with fact; and those who support the verifiability theory of meaning. The general assumption is that counterfactuals are properly described as true or false and that any of the three views confronts the difficulty of saying how such conditionals can be *statements* able to be accommodated to the theory in question. Chisholm and Goodman belong to the first group here referred to, and they overcome the main difficulty, that concerning the vacuous truth of conditionals with false antecedents, by stating, as already indicated, that they are more complex statements than a prima facie account suggests. H. Hiż has brought out explicitly what is involved in such a view when he describes counterfactuals as metalinguistic statements, or statements about other statements, a view very briefly suggested by Quine. In particular, Hiż's view is that they are statements about what can be deduced from a system of statements, *S*, when *A* is added to the system as a supposition. Adding *A* as a supposition means that nothing turns upon *A*'s truth or falsity, unless *A* and *S* are an inconsistent conjunction. This account has been endorsed by Chisholm and is a highly favored view, being advanced in one form or another by R. B. Braithwaite, E. Nagel, K. R. Popper, J. Weinberg, and others. The most favored system of statements is that of scientific laws or sets of such laws.

Chisholm in pursuing this later development of his views speaks of the assertion of such conditionals on certain presuppositions, these being the statements of *S*. The peculiar problem for the strictly counterfactual cases is now to take into account the fact that the assertor must exclude some of his beliefs if he is to be consistent. This point about excluding beliefs, once a counterfactual assumption has been made, has been hinted at in many discussions of the problem, but its significance has not often been clearly seen. Rescher, taking counterfactuals to involve belief-contravening suppositions, has brought out its significance, independently of Chisholm. He argues, as others have done for counterfactual antecedents, that every such supposition is by nature ambiguous: for example, asked to suppose that Caesar is alive today, one could not decide upon one state of affairs as the only possible one in accord with the supposition. Whichever interpretation is chosen, it will conflict with some other beliefs. Thus, anyone supposing *A* or entertaining the possibility of *A* must make changes in the other relevant beliefs that he holds.

Plausible and implausible counterfactuals. The outcome of Rescher's discussion is that there can be no logical resolution of the problem of counterfactuals: it is from extralogical resources, or the dialectical setting, that resolution comes. As with all belief-contravening suppositions, anyone, including ourselves, asking us to make a belief-contravening supposition must be prepared to interpret and select, when considering the bearing of the supposition on other relevant beliefs. Rescher nevertheless distinguishes between nomological, or law-governed, counterfactuals, on the one hand, and purely hypothetical counterfactuals, on the other. He holds that we can adjudicate, in any case of disputes where the first kind are concerned, between plausible and implausible counterfactuals. In the case of the second, he says that perplexity results if we are asked to resolve a case where counterfactuals seem to compete. We can, for example, distinguish plausible from implausible counterfactuals, each beginning with "If Jones had eaten arsenic." But the distinction is not clear where they are purely hypothetical counterfactuals, each beginning, for example, with "If Hume and Voltaire had been compatriots." This analysis, Rescher concludes, removes the logical problem of counterfactuals, but nomological conditionals nevertheless create real problems for the understanding of the concept of scientific law.

One way of showing the consequences of making a belief-contravening assumption is the following, suggested by Rescher and by J. L. Mackie: when such a supposition, *A*, is made, there are at least two other true statements or statements believed to be true, *P* and *Q*, which are in some way relevant to the supposition and which form an inconsistent set. An inconsistent triad is the minimum set. Three statements forming such a set are "Jones has eaten arsenic" (*A*), "All persons who eat arsenic die" (*P*), and "Jones is still alive" (*Q*). Since the point of a strictly counterfactual conditional is to suppose *A* true or to introduce *A* as a supposition into the context of statements believed to be true, some means must be found of excluding some statements of the inconsistent set as ones that would not be accepted as true if *A* were accepted as true. Given *PQA* as such a set, some means must be found for excluding *P* or *Q* when *A* is supposed true.

There are cases where no plausible case could be made out for preferring one statement to another. For example, suppose that Bizet and Verdi were compatriots, and one were asked to say what would be the consequence of the supposition. It is not likely that one would have any ground for saying that Bizet would be Italian rather than that Verdi would be French. In this purely hypothetical case, the supposition, taken with "Bizet is French" and "Verdi is Italian," forms an inconsistent triad. Anyone who asserts that if Bizet and Verdi had been compatriots, then Verdi would have been French, leaves no doubt about what he is assuming as true or, in other words, about what he is taking as fixed and what he is rejecting. But the case is still a purely hypothetical one.

Chisholm, discussing a similar example in 1946, "If

Apollo were a man, then" (1) "he would be mortal," or (2) "one man would be immortal," says that the choice of which of these is asserted depends upon whether our beliefs about Apollo or about men, are false, given the assumption. But such a case seems to be as purely hypothetical a case as the other, and there is equally little ground for preferring one of the alternatives over the other. Chisholm says that the context usually determines which of the beliefs are taken as false, and he adds that, in a logically adequate language, the antecedents of the conditionals would be so formulated that misunderstanding would not arise.

Even if it were the case, however, that the language were adequate to make fully explicit the statements of *S* assumed by any assertor, this still would not prevent disputes over whether or not such and such statements are the appropriate ones for particular suppositions. It is this kind of dispute that has attracted considerable attention in the discussion of the problem and that has led to consideration of laws and accidental universals. The point is that, in these cases of competing counterfactuals, where it has made sense to say that one can plausibly be asserted and the other cannot, it has usually been because one is grounded upon a lawlike universal, the other upon an accidental universal. Such a pair of competing counterfactuals would be "If wood were denser than water, it would not float" and "If wood were denser than water, it would float." The first would be preferred as true because it is grounded upon the lawlike universal statement, "Nothing denser than water floats in water." The second would be rejected as false because it is grounded upon the accidental universal statement, "All wood floats in water." Another way in which very much the same point has sometimes been put is this: laws of science or lawlike statements sustain counterfactuals, whereas accidental universals do not. It is this question of the character of laws that Rescher says remains.

Counterfactuals as incomplete arguments. J. L. Mackie argues that a more detailed account of the meaning and use of counterfactuals in general also resolves the problems that they raise for understanding the concept of a law. He denies the commonly held assumption that a counterfactual or other nonmaterial conditional, "If *A*, then *C*" is a statement that can be said to be true or false or implied by other statements. It is, rather, a condensed or incomplete argument, and to advance it is not even to say that there are premises available to complete it. A set of statements, *S*, could as before complete the argument, and any such set *sustains*, but does not imply, the conditional. Thus, he says, "All defeated presidential candidates are disappointed" and "Kennedy was a presidential candidate" sustain, but do not imply, "If Kennedy had been defeated, he would have been disappointed." This account avoids the difficulties of those mentioned above that try to reduce conditionals to certain sorts of statements and interpret them truth-functionally.

Mackie also mentions that all universal statements sustain open and factual conditionals but that, while lawlike universals sustain strict counterfactuals or subjunctive conditionals, accidental universals do not. "All the coins in my pocket are silver," for example, sustains "If *x* is a coin in my pocket, it is silver," but not "If *x* had been a coin in my pocket, it would have been silver." With these conditionals there is no question of finding truth-criteria on the account he gives, so that the two problems he has to consider are: (1) When are we prepared to advance a counterfactual? and (2) Why are we justified in doing so?

In brief, the conclusion he arrives at is that we advance a counterfactual when we have good reasons for accepting *S*, the sustaining statement, and when these reasons are not undermined by the supposition, *A*. The problem of deciding when we have good reasons for accepting statements is precisely the problem of induction. In asking the question why accidental universals do not sustain counterfactuals that appropriate lawlike universals would sustain, the problem is to find the deficiency of accidental universals, not an extra virtue in the lawlike ones. The deficiency consists in the fact that the reasons we have for accepting accidental statements are such that the supposition that there are instances of the subject term not included in the evidence undermines them, whereas no such undermining occurs with laws. In this way, the distinction between plausible and implausible counterfactuals can be accounted for.

Counterfactual as an act of assertion. Only one set of views in the extensive literature since 1946 has been considered. One other view that should be mentioned is that of G. H. von Wright, who argues for an interpretation of the nonmaterial conditional, "If *p* then *q*," not as a statement, nor as an incomplete argument, but as an act of asserting *q* on the condition *p*. He distinguishes potential and contrary-to-fact modes of asserting, and one conclusion that he draws is that the contrary-to-fact conditional is irreducible, but indispensable for the interpretation of laws.

Bibliography

Bradley, F. H., *The Principles of Logic*. Oxford, 1883. Pt. 1, Ch. 2.

Braithwaite, R. B., *Scientific Explanation*. Cambridge, 1953. Chs. 1, 9.

Broad, C. D., *Examination of McTaggart's Philosophy*. Cambridge, 1933. Vol. I, Ch. 14, Sec. 3.

Carnap, R., "Testability and Meaning." *Journal of the Philosophy of Science*, Vol. 3 (1936), 419–471; Vol. 4 (1937), 1–40.

Chisholm, R. M., "The Contrary-to-Fact Conditional." *Mind*, Vol. 55 (1946), 289–307. Amended in H. Feigl and W. Sellars, eds., *Readings in Philosophical Analysis*. New York, 1949.

Chisholm, R. M., "Law Statements and Counterfactual Inference." *Analysis*, Vol. 15 (1954/1955), 97–105.

Goodman, N., "The Problem of Counterfactual Conditionals." *Journal of Philosophy*, Vol. 44 (1947), 113–128. Reprinted in his *Fact, Fiction, and Forecast*. London, 1954.

Hampshire, S., "Subjunctive Conditionals." *Analysis*, Vol. 9 (1948/1949), 9–14. Also in M. Macdonald, ed., *Philosophy and Analysis*. Oxford, 1955.

Hempel, C. G., "Studies in the Logic of Confirmation," *Mind*, Vol. 54 (1945), 1–26, 97–121.

Hiż, H., "On the Inferential Sense of Contrary-to-Fact Conditionals." *Journal of Philosophy*, Vol. 48 (1951), 586–587.

Kneale, W. C., "Natural Laws and Contrary-to-Fact Conditionals." *Analysis*, Vol. 10 (1949/1950), 121–125. Also in M. Macdonald, ed., *Philosophy and Analysis*. Oxford, 1955.

Lewis, C. I., *An Analysis of Knowledge and Valuation*. La Salle, Ill., 1946. Ch. 8.

Mackie, J. L., "Counterfactuals and Causal Laws," in R. J. Butler, ed., *Analytical Philosophy*. Oxford, 1962. Pp. 66–80.

Nagel, E., *The Structure of Science*. London, 1961. Ch. 4.

Pap, A., *An Introduction to the Philosophy of Science*. New York, 1962. Pt. 4.

Popper, K. R., *The Logic of Scientific Discovery*. London, 1959. New Appendix 10.

Quine, W. V., *Mathematical Logic*, rev. ed. Cambridge, Mass., 1951. Ch. 1.
Ramsey, F. P., *The Foundations of Mathematics*. London, 1931. Ch. 9 B.
Reichenbach, H., *Nomological Statements and Admissible Operations*. Amsterdam, 1954.
Rescher, N., "Belief-contravening Suppositions." *Philosophical Review*, Vol. 70 (1961), 176–196.
Walters, R. S., "The Problem of Counterfactuals." *Australasian Journal of Philosophy*, Vol. 39 (1961), 30–46.
Will, F. L., "The Contrary-to-Fact Conditional." *Mind*, Vol. 56 (1947), 236–249.
Wright, G. H. von, *Logical Studies*. London, 1957. Pp. 127–165.

R. S. WALTERS

CONVENTION. *See* CUSTOM.

CONVENTIONALISM is the name usually given to any view that scientific laws and theories are conventions that depend upon our more or less free choice from among alternative ways of "describing" the natural world. The chosen alternative is said to be no truer than others, only more convenient. The view involves more than the recognition that the way in which we describe the world depends on our linguistic conventions and more than the belief that the statements of pure mathematics and logic are "true" by virtue of these conventions. It involves also the assertion that *any* coherent system of mathematics or logic can be applied to nature. It is easy to misinterpret conventionalism, and its critics have often done so by regarding it as making scientific conclusions the results of *arbitrary* decisions. It is doubtful that this is fair to any actually held conventionalistic theory.

Conventionalism owes much to Kant, although he was not a conventionalist. He regarded the nature of our descriptions as depending mainly upon universal properties of the human mind rather than upon individual choice. Nevertheless, he paved the way for conventionalism with the idea that the order we find in the world is not independent of the character of our minds. The origin of conventionalism is usually traced to Henri Poincaré, who admitted a debt to Kant. There are connections also with the work of Ernst Mach and Pierre Duhem.

Both Mach and Duhem distinguished between a "pictorial" or "explanatory" element and a relational element in scientific theories; the first element is relatively unimportant and the second is essential. For Mach, theories were merely tools for prediction, constructed in such a way as to make prediction as simple and powerful as possible. Those parts of theories which appear to be descriptive of hidden events are, in fact, not so. It is the mathematical relations contained in theories that enable us to predict. Even the relational parts of theories cannot be verified directly, and the pictorial parts cannot be verified at all, so that we are left with considerable freedom of choice in constructing theories. Whichever "picture" we accept is conventional and inessential; what is essential is that the mathematical relations will allow correct predictions. Duhem held a similar view and added that when we use mathematics in the sciences, we represent measurable properties in a purely conventional way by mathematical symbols that we connect with one another arbitrarily in "hypotheses." These hypotheses are combined according to the methods of pure mathematics, and the consequences are retranslated into physical terms to become predictions.

POINCARÉ'S CONVENTIONALISM

Poincaré arrived at his conclusions about the nature of scientific laws and theories by considering mathematics, especially different systems of geometry, both in its pure state and as used in scientific theories. It was at one time thought that Euclid's parallel postulate, the postulate that through one point only one line can be drawn parallel to a given straight line, was deducible from his axioms. Early in the nineteenth century this deduction was shown to be impossible by Nikolai Lobachevski and Farkas Bolyai.

If Euclid's postulate were deducible from his axioms, then contradictions would result from accepting the axioms and rejecting the postulate. The work of Lobachevski and Bolyai encouraged mathematicians to develop coherent systems of geometry starting from Euclid's axioms, or some selection from them, and the denial of the parallel postulate. It also cast doubt on the possibility of constructing any geometry without postulates, which led to the idea that there is no one true geometry of physical space. Several systems of non-Euclidean geometry were developed in a completely abstract way simply by exploring the implications of different postulates, with no thought for their application.

In *Science and Hypothesis* Poincaré gave a popular exposition of Lobachevskian and Riemannian geometries in order to bring out sharply the differences between various systems. As he said, "The sum of the angles of a triangle is equal to two right angles in Euclid's geometry, less than two right angles in that of Lobachevski, and greater than two right angles in that of Riemann." He then explained that it is possible to construct a "dictionary" of geometrical terms used in these systems that will enable us to "translate" theorems in one system into theorems in another. Since Euclidean geometry leads to no contradictions, neither will the other systems.

This led Poincaré to say that the axioms of geometry are not synthetic a priori, for then Euclidean geometry would be necessary and non-Euclidean geometries impossible; they cannot be experimental truths, for then geometry would be open to continual revision. He had already dismissed the view that axioms are analytic a priori, since consistent alternative geometries are possible. The only remaining possibility is that they are *conventions*, or "definitions in disguise."

Poincaré did not intend to imply that our choice of conventions for physical geometry is arbitrary. He explicitly denied this. We accept certain conventions because experiment has shown us that they are convenient. The only necessary limitation on our choice is the avoidance of contradiction but, for the sake of convenience, we allow our choice to depend on our observations. Our postulates are thus more precise, and more firmly held, than the approximate experimental laws from which they spring.

We can no more ask whether Euclidean geometry is *true* than we can ask whether the metric system is true. For our ordinary, everyday purposes of dealing with "natural solids"; that is, "those bodies which we can compare and measure by means of our senses," Euclidean geometry will always be the most convenient. It is simplest in itself, as a polynomial of the first degree is simpler than one of the second degree, and it "sufficiently agrees with the properties of natural solids." In fact, it deals with "ideal solids," which are "simplified images" of natural solids.

Between our perceptual space and the space of any geometry there are differences that we tend to ignore, owing to our established habits of thinking about our perceptions. If we had been brought up to think of perceptions as organized according to some non-Euclidean geometry, we should tend to regard *this* geometry as the true description of physical space. Our experience would not be organized geometrically unless we fitted to it some particular geometrical system. Geometrical space is not imposed on our minds by the world; our minds impose a geometry on the world. Our conceptions of space are based on the laws by which our sensations succeed one another; these laws prevent our descriptions from being merely arbitrary, but they are consistent with different geometries. Thus, descriptions of the world in terms of non-Euclidean geometries are intelligible to us.

No geometry can be refuted by experience because each depends upon conditions that we may choose to regard as fulfilled or not in any particular application. If Lobachevski's geometry were true, the parallax of a very distant star would be finite; but if Riemann's were true, it would be negative, which might seem to provide a basis for empirical refutation. But this depends on the assumption of a straight-line path for light, which, in this context, is not open to verification. We can insure that different geometries will apply by making different assumptions about this path. In considering an experiment whose results appear to conflict with Euclidean geometry, we have the choice of saying that light travels in Euclidean nonstraight lines or in non-Euclidean straight lines.

Poincaré urged that in the sciences we distinguish between experiment, mathematical reasoning, convention, and hypothesis. In physics we tend to confuse conventional elements with experimentally testable results. Although experiment provides some basis for Newton's three laws, it cannot invalidate them in their most general meaning, in which they are definitions or conventions. Like other scientific laws, they might take different forms because "every proposition may be generalized in an infinite number of ways." We accept the familiar generalized forms of these laws because they are simplest, and we work *as if* the simplest law were the most probable, even if this can never be established.

Geometry and mechanics differ logically in that the conventions of geometry and the experiments leading to them are about different sorts of things, ideal and natural solids respectively, whereas the conventions of mechanics and the experiments leading to them are about the same sort of things, natural solids.

Poincaré denied that he saw the whole of science as conventional. He distinguished between *principles*, such as the law of inertia, which *are* conventions, and *experimental laws*, which are not. A law is related to a principle as follows: We discover experimentally an approximate relation, R, between two terms and then introduce, by definition, new terms that are exactly related by R. The relation "pv = a constant" holds approximately for actual gases but exactly for ideal gases. We then describe the behavior of actual gases, summarized in laws, by reference to departures from the behavior of ideal gases, summarized in principles. We may be forced to revise laws but not principles. The more advanced theories of physics, such as the kinetic theory and the modern atomic theory, contain principles and are not, therefore, open to experimental refutation against our will. They may be rejected, not because they are refuted, but because some more useful theory has been found. Moreover, we may simultaneously hold two contradictory theories that are useful for dealing with different ranges of phenomena. There is no objection to this if the theories are not claimed to be *true*.

OTHER CONVENTIONALIST THEORIES

A. S. Eddington's view can also be regarded as conventionalistic. He called his general account of science "selective subjectivism" and expounded it with the help of his famous "fish-net" analogy. It has close connections with his claim to deduce certain physical quantities from what he called "epistemological principles"; that is, principles related to the methods of acquiring knowledge.

Suppose that an ichthyologist is investigating marine life by examining the fish caught in a certain net. He reaches two generalizations: (1) No sea creature is less than two inches long. (2) All sea creatures have gills. These differ logically as genuine scientific conclusions differ. Someone considering the first may object that many fish in the sea are not catchable by this net just because they are under two inches long; the ichthyologist replies that he is interested only in the fish that are catchable in his net. He is not dismayed by the fact that the generalization is a function of the properties of the net; he defines the ichthyologically interesting in terms of these properties. Similarly, the physical scientist regards as physically interesting only what is discoverable by his observationally based methods. What is conventional, here, is the acceptance of observation as the basis of physical science.

The second generalization is different. The fact that the net has brought up only fish with gills does not imply that it will do this always and everywhere. Because this conclusion is not a function of the properties of the net, it is open to revision in the light of further evidence. This should not, however, lead the ichthyologist to doubt his first generalization. "Generalizations that can be reached epistemologically have a security which is denied to those that can only be reached empirically." The former are fundamental laws of physics and wholly subjective, while the latter consist of a vast amount of special information about the particular objects surrounding us and are at least partly objective. One of these "special facts" is that space is largely empty, with matter scattered about in it in relatively small islands. The physicist begins with such special information as this and eventually works up to fundamental laws.

Eddington was perhaps misled by his analogy. It is true that whether all the creatures caught in the net have gills does not depend upon the structure of the net; but the corresponding empirically derived generalizations appear to depend upon observation just as much as, or even more than, the fundamental, "wholly subjective" laws and therefore to depend just as much on the characteristics of our sensory equipment. It is difficult for this account to sustain the distinction between subjective and objective in the sciences.

C. I. Lewis argues that the a priori enters into science in definition and classification and in the tacit acceptance of a criterion of scientific reality. "Mind contributes to experience the element of order, of classification, categories and definition." There is no knowledge without interpretation; but if all interpretation is to be subject to the check of further experience, we are involved in an infinite regress and no knowledge is possible. Interpretation depends upon the a priori, the ascription of a particular order to experience in advance of experience. The a priori does not compel acceptance but represents the relatively freely chosen activity of the mind; its necessity is "its character as legislative act." The real is the given seen in the order prescribed by the a priori; that is, categorially interpreted.

Arthur Pap, in *The A Priori in Physical Theory*, attempts to develop Lewis' "conceptual pragmatism" and substantiate it by the procedures of physics. The basis of his account is dissatisfaction with a hard and final distinction between analytic and synthetic propositions. If we examine the sciences as developing systems, rather than as completed structures, we see that a proposition may function at one stage as experimental law and at a later stage as an analytic rule or convention. This is clearly seen in the construction of measuring instruments according to some law that thereby becomes a priori.

CRITICS OF CONVENTIONALISM

Moritz Schlick rejected conventionalism in its usual form but shared its skepticism about the correctness of calling laws "true" or "probable." For him laws were not statements but prescriptions, or rules of conduct, that guide our predictive activities. They set out instructions for forming true (singular) propositions about the world. Because laws have unrestricted generality, they are unverifiable and so, if considered as statements, are meaningless. It has been suggested by W. C. Kneale that this prescriptive view of laws is the only one consistent with positivism. For Poincaré a law determines the kind of statement to be taken as true, whereas for Schlick it determines the method by which true statements are to be reached.

Schlick asserts that conventionalism rests on a logical mistake. The conventionalist concentrates excessively on the equations in terms of which scientific laws are expressed. By neglecting the "definitional explications" through which these expressions are given meaning, he mistakes the equation for the whole law and sees the law as a tautology. Scientific laws are not expressions in pure mathematics.

K. R. Popper also criticizes conventionalism, regarding as its source the inability of some philosophers to believe that the simplicity of nature revealed by physics can be anything but a human creation. He gives a description of conventionalism that is difficult to recognize as the view of anyone usually considered a conventionalist. For the conventionalist, he says, laws of nature are our own free creations and are arbitrary. Theoretical science is not a picture of the world but a logical construction that is not determined by the properties of the world. Popper holds that the determined conventionalist can construct an account of science that is impervious to criticism, but he rejects it as embodying an implausible idea of science. The only way to avoid conventionalism is by deciding not to apply its methods.

Ernest Nagel has some more pointed criticisms. He holds that Poincaré does not distinguish clearly between pure and applied geometry, so that part of his argument shows no more than the formal intertranslatability of the statements of three systems of pure geometry. It follows only that the choice of notation for a geometry is a convention, which can hardly be denied. However, the rest of the argument for the conventionality of applied geometry, and so for part of science is, according to Nagel, far from clear. Physical geometry results from a particular kind of interpretation of a system of pure geometry. Is physical geometry *therefore* no more than a set of concealed definitions? This does not follow. However, this may not be a fair criticism of Poincaré, since it was at this point that he argued that our choice is influenced by empirical evidence. Moreover, he held that we can always choose between retaining a simple geometry by making the rest of our laws more complex and accepting a more complex geometry while retaining the simplicity of the rest of our laws. When he made the much-criticized statement that "Euclidean geometry is, and will remain, the most convenient" he was talking about natural solids; he would perhaps not have been surprised to find that for a different context a different geometry was more convenient. Nagel is doubtless correct, however, when he says that Poincaré, and other conventionalists, give too naive an account of simplicity, especially in relation to scientific theories.

Hans Reichenbach argues that the choice of a geometry for physical description is arbitrary only as long as no definition of congruence is specified and that, although the choice of definition is arbitrary, once such a definition is specified, it becomes an empirical matter that geometry holds for physical space. This is in line with Nagel's argument, and it may similarly be said that although some conventionalists have neglected this, it is doubtful that Poincaré did so; he held that experience teaches us that some definitions of congruence are more convenient than others, so that the choice is not entirely arbitrary.

Bibliography

Bonola, R., *Non-Euclidean Geometry*, translated by H. S. Carslaw. New York, 1955. Contains reprints of original papers by Lobachevski and Bolyai and an account of the development of non-Euclidean systems.

Bridgman, P. R., *The Logic of Modern Physics*. New York, 1927.

Campbell, N. R., *Physics, the Elements*. Cambridge, 1926.

Cohen, L. J., *The Diversity of Meaning*. London, 1962. Contains an interesting discussion of conventionalism and a considerable amount of related material.

Dingler, H., *Das Experiment*. Munich, 1928.

Dingler, H., *Der Zusammenbruch der Wissenschaft und der Primat der Philosophie.* Munich, 1931. Dingler's works are written from the point of view of a conventionalist.

Duhem, Pierre, *The Aim and Structure of Physical Theory,* translated by P. P. Weiner. Princeton, 1954. One of the classical expressions of conventionalism.

Eddington, A. S., *The Nature of the Physical World.* Cambridge, 1928. Shows the development of Eddington's version of conventionalism.

Eddington, A. S., *The Philosophy of Physical Science.* Cambridge, 1949. Shows the development of Eddington's conventionalism and gives a concise account of his "selective subjectivism."

Einstein, Albert, *Sidelights of Relativity,* translated by C. B. Jeffery and W. Perrett. London, 1922. Reprinted in H. Feigl and M. Brodbeck, eds., *Readings in the Philosophy of Science.* New York, 1953.

Einstein, Albert, "Reply to Criticisms," in P. A. Schilpp, ed., *Albert Einstein, Philosopher–Scientist.* Evanston, Ill., 1949. P. 676 f.

Frank, P., "Einstein, Mach and Logical Positivism," in P. A. Schilpp, ed., *Albert Einstein, Philosopher–Scientist.* Evanston, Ill., 1949. P. 269.

Frank, P., *Modern Science and Its Philosophy.* Cambridge, Mass., 1949. Contains a brief historical account of conventionalism.

Frank, P., *Philosophy of Science.* Englewood Cliffs, N. J., 1957. Ch. 3.

Grünbaum, A., "Conventionalism in Geometry," in L. Henken, P. Suppes, and A. Tarski, eds., *The Axiomatic Method.* Amsterdam, 1959.

Hanson, N. R., *Patterns of Discovery.* Cambridge, 1958.

Helmholtz, Hermann von, "On the Origin and Significance of Geometrical Axioms," in *Popular Scientific Lectures.* London, 1881.

Helmholtz, Hermann von, *On Counting and Measuring.* New York, 1930.

Hutten, E. H., *The Language of Modern Physics.* London, 1956.

Kneale, W. C., *Probability and Induction.* Oxford, 1949.

Lenzen, V., *The Nature of Physical Theory.* New York, 1931 An interesting discussion of the place of the a priori and the conventional in physical science.

Lenzen, V., "Procedures of Empirical Science," in *International Encyclopedia of Unified Science.* Chicago, 1938.

Lewis, C. I., "The Pragmatic Conception of the A Priori" (1922), in H. Feigl and W. Sellars, eds., *Readings in Philosophical Analysis.* New York, 1949. Pp. 286 ff.

Lewis, C. I., *Mind and the World Order.* New York, 1929. An important modern version of conventionalism.

Mach, Ernst, *Popular Scientific Lectures,* 3d English ed., translated by T. J. McCormack. Chicago, 1898. See especially "On the Economical Nature of Physical Inquiry" and "On the Principle of Comparison in Physics." This is an early account having features in common with that of Poincaré.

Mach, Ernst, *The Analysis of Sensations,* translated by C. M. Williams and S. Waterlow. Chicago, 1914.

Mach, Ernst, *The Science of Mechanics,* 6th English ed., translated by T. J. McCormack. La Salle, Ill., 1960.

Nagel, Ernest, *The Structure of Science: Problems in the Logic of Scientific Explanation.* New York, 1961. Contains interesting critical discussions of conventionalism.

Pap, Arthur, *The A Priori in Physical Theory.* New York, 1946. A development of the views of C. I. Lewis. Contains a useful bibliography.

Pap, Arthur, *An Introduction to the Philosophy of Science.* New York, 1962. Contains a discussion of Poincaré's view of physical geometry.

Pearson, Karl, *The Grammar of Science,* 2d ed. London, 1900. A development of Mach's views.

Poincare, Henri, *Science and Hypothesis,* translated by W. J. Greenstreet. London, 1905. Often regarded as the *locus classicus.*

Poincaré, Henri, *The Value of Science,* translated by B. G. Halsted. London, 1907.

Poincaré, Henri, *Science and Method,* translated by F. Maitland. London, 1914. Both this and *The Value of Science* contain further reflections on conventions in science.

Popper, K. R., *The Logic of Scientific Discovery.* London, 1959. Highly critical of conventionalism.

Quine, W. V., "Truth by Convention" (1922), in H. Feigl and W. Sellars, eds., *Readings in Philosophical Analysis.* New York, 1949. Pp. 250 ff.

Ramsey, F. P., *The Foundations of Mathematics.* London, 1931.

Reichenbach, Hans, *Experience and Prediction.* Chicago, 1938.

Reichenbach, Hans, "The Philosophical Significance of the Theory of Relativity," in P. A. Schilpp, ed., *Albert Einstein, Philosopher–Scientist.* Evanston, Ill., 1949. P. 287. Some telling criticisms of conventionalism.

Reichenbach, Hans, *Philosophy of Space and Time.* New York, 1958.

Russell, Bertrand, *Foundations of Geometry.* Cambridge, 1897

Schlick, Moritz, *Space and Time in Contemporary Physics,* translated by H. L. Brose. Oxford, 1920.

Schlick, Moritz, *Gesammelte Aufsätze.* Vienna, 1938. Contains Schlick's near-conventionalist account of science.

Schlick, Moritz, "Are Natural Laws Conventions?" in H. Feigl and M. Brodbeck, eds., *Readings in the Philosophy of Science.* New York, 1953. P. 181. Critical of Poincaré.

Toulmin, S. E., *The Philosophy of Science.* London, 1953. For a brief discussion of the Ramsey–Schlick view.

Whittaker, E., *From Euclid to Eddington.* New York, 1958.

Wittgenstein, Ludwig, *Philosophical Investigations,* translated by G. E. M. Anscombe. Oxford, 1953.

Wittgenstein, Ludwig, *Remarks on the Foundations of Mathematics,* translated by G. E. M. Anscombe. Oxford, 1956.

Wittgenstein, Ludwig, *The Blue and Brown Books.* Oxford, 1958.

Wittgenstein, Ludwig, *Tractatus Logico-philosophicus,* translated by D. F. Pears and B. F. McGuinness. London, 1961. Wittgenstein's works contain many discussions of, and scattered remarks about, rules, definitions, and conventions.

PETER ALEXANDER

COOK WILSON, JOHN. *See* WILSON, JOHN COOK.

COPERNICUS, NICOLAS (1473–1543), or Mikolaj Kopernick, Polish clergyman, physician, and astronomer, and the propounder of a heliocentric theory of the universe. Copernicus was born at Torun (Thorn) on the Vistula. He studied liberal arts, canon law, and medicine at the universities of Cracow (1491–1494), Bologna (1496–1500), and Padua (1501–1503) and received a doctorate in canon law from the University of Ferrara in 1503. Through the influence of his uncle, the bishop of Ermland, Copernicus was elected *in absentia* as a canon of the cathedral of Frauenburg in 1497. By 1506 he had returned to Poland, serving as physician to his uncle until 1512, when he took up his duties as canon. Copernicus' duties as canon involved him in the complex diplomatic maneuverings of the time and in the administration of the cathedral's large estates. In his own day he was more widely known as a physician than as an astronomer. He was one of the few persons in northeastern Europe to have a knowledge of the Greek language, and the one book he published without the urging of colleagues was a Latin translation of the poems of Theophylactus Simocatta, a seventh-century Byzantine poet. Copernicus' competence in economics was shown in some reports on money, presented to the Prussian diet, in which he anticipated a form of Gresham's law.

Copernicus' interest in astronomy was probably aroused at Cracow by the mathematician Wojciech Brudzewski and spurred on at Bologna by the astronomer Domenico Maria da Novara. Copernicus' first documented astronomical observation was made in Bologna in 1497. Twenty-seven such observations were used in his major treatise; others he recorded in the margins of books in his library. By 1514 he was so well known as an astronomer that he was asked by Pope Leo X to assist in the reform of the calendar, a task he declined because the motions of the sun and the moon had not yet been sufficiently determined.

Although Copernicus' major work, *De Revolutionibus Orbium Coelestium Libri IV,* was not published until 1543, the year of his death, he had been developing his theories at least from about 1512, the approximate date of his *Commentariolus* (a short outline of his system which he gave in manuscript copies to a few trusted friends). The first published account of his system was the *Narratio Prima* of his disciple and biographer (the biography is no longer extant), Georg Joachim Rheticus, in 1540. It was Rheticus who finally induced Copernicus to allow the publication of his major work.

Late medieval astronomy. The difference between Copernicus' theory and the then prevailing Ptolemaic system of astronomy can be stated briefly. The Copernican system was heliocentric rather than geocentric and geostatic; it placed the sun close to the center of the universe and the earth in orbit around the center, rather than postulating an immobile earth at the center of the universe. But the full significance of this statement can be understood only via an examination of the *ad hoc* character of late medieval astronomy. Such late scholastic thinkers as Grosseteste, Bradwardine, Buridan, Oresme, and Cusa had perceived the theoretical virtues and explanatory power of the heliocentric principle, as had Ptolemy himself long before. They understood the imperfections of the Ptolemaic techniques; yet they conceded that observational evidence did not clearly favor either theory—as was the case until the late sixteenth century. On scriptural grounds these thinkers accepted orthodox geocentrism; but they aired, more fully and deliberately than any of their predecessors, the arguments in support of terrestrial movement. They played *advocatus diaboli* with precision and imagination.

But prior to Copernicus astronomy was a piecemeal undertaking. Such problems as the prediction of a stationary point, or of an occultation, were dealt with one at a time, planet by planet. There was no conception that one planet's current stationary point might be related to another planet's later occultation. Techniques were employed as needed, and problem-solving was not systematically integrated. Copernicus' theory changed this piecemeal approach forever. He effected a Kantian revolution in astronomy perhaps even more than Kant effected a Copernican revolution in philosophy. Copernicus relocated the primary observational problem, that of explaining the apparent retrograde motions of the planets, by construing the motions not as something the planets "really" did "out there," but as the result of our own motion. The earth's flight around the sun makes other circling objects sometimes appear to move backward in relation to the fixed stars. Although either the Ptolemaic or the Copernican theory could be reconciled with sixteenth-century observations, Copernicus' view did not require investing those planets with queer dynamical properties, such as retrogradations-in-fact; a planet which actually halted, went into reverse, halted again, and then proceeded "forward" would be a strange physical object indeed. Rather, in Copernicus' view, all planets, including the earth, had the same kind of motion—a simple motion that explained the observed retrogradations.

It had been clear even to the ancients that the view that the earth was in the exact center of the universal system and that all celestial bodies moved about the earth in perfect circles could not generate predictions and descriptions even remotely close to the observed facts. In order to generate the right predictional numbers as well as tractable orbital shapes, the Ptolemaic astronomers made a number of *ad hoc* assumptions. They moved the earth from the exact center of the planetary array; they used the geometrical center of the system as a reference point from which to calculate planetary distances; and they invented a third point, the *punctum aequans* (a mere computational device without physical significance, a device that Copernicus described as "monstrous"), around which the centers of the planetary epicycles described equal angles in equal times. No mechanisms known in nature or in art, however, have one center from which distances are determined, another from which velocities are determined, and a third from which observations are made. Moreover, the location of all these points and the choice of angular velocities around them were fixed arbitrarily and *ex post facto* simply to cope with each new observation as it turned up.

Even had Ptolemaic astronomy achieved perfection in predicting and describing, it was still powerless to explain planetary motion. One might ask how a theory that could describe and predict perfectly could in any way lack explanatory power; but Copernicus would have distinguished between the mere capacity of a theory to generate accurate numbers, and its further ability to provide an intelligible foundation for comprehending the phenomena studied. Even had the Ptolemaic system been able to predict accurately any future position of each moving point of light, Copernicus would still have asked what these points of light were, and what systematic mechanical interconnections existed between them.

An imaginative scholar, aware of the many difficulties posed by the Ptolemaic system as it had been developed over the years, and knowing (as Copernicus did) the accounts of ancient heliocentric theorists, might have only been expected to continue to seek improvements within the Ptolemaic system by incorporating promising heliocentric devices from his Scholastic predecessors (if he knew them) and from the ancients. Any gifted astronomer of Copernicus' day bent on improving astronomy "from the inside" would thus have had to take heliocentrism seriously.

In fact, Copernicus' books and Rheticus' summary might be viewed as an articulate and systematic expression of much late medieval planetary thinking. The ties with fifteenth-century Scholastic thought are everywhere apparent. But the primary insight of *De Revolutionibus,* although not novel, was boldly carried out and very much sharpened in detail. It was a comprehensive attempt to make the science of that day work better; it was not explicitly a plan for a new science of tomorrow. The dramatic consequences, largely unanticipated by Copernicus, are a tribute to his thoroughness as a student of nature and not to any self-conscious desire to level the orthodoxy around him.

The Copernican alternative. Copernicus was led to conclude that, in view of the plethora of epicycles required by the Ptolemaic system to account for the observed motion of the heavenly bodies, it must contain some basic error. He found that the assumption of a moving earth, however absurd and counterintuitive it appeared, led to a much simpler and aesthetically superior system. Imagine yourself on the outer edge of a merry-go-round, sitting in a swivel chair. The constant rotation of the chair, when compounded with the revolution of the chair around the center of the merry-go-round, would generate—to say the least—complex visual impressions. Those impressions are compatible either with the motion as just described or with the supposition that it is the chair which is absolutely fixed and that all of the visual impressions stem from the motion of the merry-go-round about the chair-as-center and of a like motion of the walls of the building in which it is housed. The actual observations could be accounted for by either hypothesis. But what is easy to visualize in this example was extraordinarily difficult to comprehend in astronomical terms. That it was the earth that rotated and twisted, and revolved around the sun, seemed contrary to experience, common sense, and Scripture. Yet it was this simple alternative hypothesis that, for reasons demanded by astronomy, Copernicus espoused.

Copernicus' revolution. Fundamentally, then, Copernicus argued that the observational intricacies of planetary motion were not real, but merely apparent. This argument made planetary motion simpler to comprehend but our own motion more intricate and therefore harder to believe. That was the fundamental objection to Copernicus' innovation.

But one must be quite clear about the nature of the theory. It was not a celestial dynamics, even in the sense that Kepler's theory of the causes of planetary motion (in terms of primitive spokes of force radiating from the sun) was a celestial dynamics. Copernicus, like his predecessors, was no astrophysicist; he was concerned with positional astronomy—the kinematics of planetary appearances, the motions of stellar lights against the black bowl of the sky and the underlying geometry that would, with a minimum of *ad hoc* assumptions, make those motions intelligible. So, both the *Almagest* and the *De Revolutionibus* were concerned with plantetary kinematics exclusively—the latter in a systematic way, the former in the manner of a recipe-collection. And even as a kinematic theory, Copernicus' theory was less adequate than those of Tycho Brahe and Kepler. He believed that the planets moved in perfect circles, an assumption shattered by Kepler's discovery of elliptical orbits. There is nothing in Copernicus to compare with Kepler's second law—that planets sweep out equal circumsolar areas in equal times. Nor is there anything to compare to Kepler's third law, correlating the time a planet requires to circle the sun with its distance from the sun. (And only when Kepler's three laws were added to the Galileo–Descartes law of inertia, and Newton's law of universal gravitation, was there developed a genuine celestial mechanics.) Copernicus' contributions consisted in a redeployment of the established elements of Ptolemaic positional astronomy. It is in this sense that he has been, and should be, viewed as the last great medieval astronomer.

Simplicity of Copernicus' theory. Copernicus' theory was not psychologically simpler than competing systems. A moving earth, and a sun and stars that do not "rise" and "circle" us, seemed contrary to experience. Also, a theoretical apparatus that linked all astronomical problems instead of leaving them to be faced one at a time could not constitute an easier system of calculation. Indeed, in the sixteenth century, heliocentrism was psychologically far more complex than the theories men were accustomed to.

Was Copernicus' conception perhaps simpler in that, as a formal theoretical system, it did not require primitive new ideas for each new problem or for the times when old problems led to difficulties? It invoked nothing like a *punctum aequans;* that is, it invoked fewer independent conceptual elements (primitive terms) merely to explain aberrant calculations than did other astronomies. But this point is insufficient to explain the sense in which Copernicus' system manifests "simplicity." Computational schemes had been proposed by Caelio Calcagnini and Geronimo Fracastoro that were simpler in that they were built on smaller sets of primitive notions. But they were so inadequate to the observational tasks of astronomy that it would have been as idle to stress their simplicity as it would be today to press for the theoretical adoption of Dalton's atom because of its simplicity; the issue of simplicity does not arise except between theories that are comparable in explanatory and predictional power.

It has been urged that Copernicus' theory was numerically simpler, in that it required only 17 epicycles to the Ptolemaic 83. But the Ptolemaist, because he addressed his problems singly and without regard for the configurational complexities of taking all planets at once, never had to invoke 83 epicycles simultaneously. The number was usually no more than 4 or 5 per individual calculation.

This error is analogous to that involved in referring to a Ptolemaic "system" at all. Such a system results only from taking all individual calculating charts for the separate planets, superimposing them, running a pin through the centric "earthpoint," and then scaling the orbits up or down so they do not collide. This scaling is determined by a principle of order wholly unconnected with any part of the Ptolemaic epicycle-on-deferent technique. In contrast, Copernicus' system locates the planets in a circumsolar order such that their relative distances from, and their angular velocities around, the sun are in themselves sufficient in principle to describe and predict all stationary points, retrograde arcs, occultations, and the brightening and dimming of the planetary lights. Thus, since Copernicus linked all planets, and invented systematic astronomy, he had to invoke all the epicycles his theory needed en bloc. The number of epicycles in any calculation would tend to be greater, not less, than that required in a corresponding Ptolemaic problem.

Copernicus' scheme is systematically simpler. It required more independent concepts than some others, but these were deductively interlocked. Copernicus was astronomy's Euclid. He constructed out of the disconnected parts of astronomy as he found it a systematic monument of scientific theory. The *De Revolutionibus* is psychologically and quantitatively more complex than anything that had gone before, but it was deductively simpler. What Euclid had done for geometry, and what Newton was later to do for physics, Copernicus did for positional astronomy.

Importance of the theory. It has been argued that, as formalizations, the Copernican and Ptolemaic theories were strictly equivalent (D. J. de S. Price), geometrically equivalent (A. R. Hall), even "absolutely identical" (J. L. E. Dreyer). But characterizing the theory as no more than "an alternative frame of reference plus some anti-Aristotelian philosophy" obscures the sense in which the heliocentric system and the geocentric systems of the sixteenth century were really equivalent. They were not equivalent in the sense that every consequence of the one was also derivable from the other. Even when construed as mere geometrical calculations on paper, what the Ptolemaist would generate within his theory as corresponding to a stationary point in Mars's orbit is not congruent with what the Copernican would generate. The orbits were accorded different shapes in both theories, so points on those shapes, although viewed at the same angle from the earth, will not be superimposable. Nonetheless, every line-of-sight observation inferable within the one theory is completely inferable in the other. As positional astronomy, the two theories were observationally equivalent; no astronomer then could distinguish the two by comparing them with known facts. (Even today the Nautical Almanac is virtually a textbook of geocentric observation-points.) But the theories were neither formally equivalent nor physically equivalent, and certainly not absolutely identical. This is a difference that should make a difference to a philosopher.

With Freud, man lost his Godlike mind; with Darwin his exalted place among the creatures on earth; with Copernicus man had lost his privileged position in the universe. The general intellectual repercussions of this fact are more dramatic than any consequences within technical astronomy, where one can speak of the Keplerian "revolution" but of not more than a Copernican "disturbance."

For the broad history of ideas, however, the implications of Copernicanism can hardly be exaggerated. Even religious revolutionaries such as Luther and Melanchthon came to view Copernicus' position with abhorrence. His views challenged the literal interpretation of Scripture, the philosophical and metaphysical foundations of moral theory, and even common sense itself. The result was a massive opposition, learned and lay, to the reported ideas of Copernicus. It was the slow, sure acceptance of the technical *De Revolutionibus* by natural philosophers that ultimately quieted the general clamor against heliocentrism. Without the riotous reaction against it, Copernicus' book might have been but a calm contribution to scholarship somewhat like Laplace's *Mécanique céleste*. In the sixteenth and seventeenth centuries, however, the name Copernicus became a battle cry against the establishment in religion, in philosophy, and in natural science. It was a cry amplified in the world of wider scholarship and theology—far beyond Copernicus' original pronouncements. For Copernicus epitomized the well-trained, thorough, and rigorous sixteenth-century natural philosopher. He sought to make the theories he had inherited work better than when he found them. The history of ideas is charged with such figures. The difference is that Copernicus was presented with a theory that was incapable of further internal revision and improvement. The only recourse was fundamental overhaul—the consequences of which we still feel today.

Works by Copernicus

Edward Rosen is the editor and translator of *Three Copernican Treatises* (New York, 1939), which contains a translation of the *Commentariolus*, a "Letter Against Werner," and Rheticus' *Narratio Prima*.

De Revolutionibus Orbium Coelestium Libri IV is available in a facsimile text and a Latin printed text edited with notes by S. Kubach (1944). The translation by C. G. Wallis in *Great Books of the Western World*, Vol. 16 (Chicago, 1952) is to be used with caution.

Works on Copernicus

Armitage, Angus, *Copernicus, the Founder of Modern Astronomy*. London, 1938.

Hanson, N. R., "Contra-Equivalence." *Isis*, Vol. 55 (1964).

Hanson, N. R., "The Copernican Disturbance and the Keplerian Revolution." *Journal of the History of Ideas*, Vol. 22 (1961), 169–184.

Kuhn, Thomas, *The Copernican Revolution*. Cambridge, Mass., 1957.

Mizwa, S. P., *Nicholas Copernicus, 1543–1943*. New York, 1943.

Price, D. J. de S., "Contra-Copernicus," in Marshall Clagget, ed., *Critical Problems in the History of Science*. Madison, Wisc., 1959.

Prowe, Ludwig, *Nicolaus Coppernicus*, 3 vols. Berlin, 1883–1885.

Rudnicki, J., *Nicholas Copernicus*, translated by B. W. A. Massey. London, 1943.

NORWOOD RUSSELL HANSON

CORDEMOY, GÉRAUD DE, French historian and philosopher, was born in Paris early in the seventeenth century and died there in 1684. After 1667, he lived in almost complete retirement as reader (*lecteur*) to the dauphin, a post that he held by favor of Bossuet. During this period, he was engaged, at Bossuet's order, on a biography of Charlemagne, a work that he never finished, for he understood his task as involving a complete history of the French monarchy. Nevertheless, Cordemoy found time to write a number of short philosophical treatises, important as critical studies of Cartesianism.

Accepting the ultimate duality of the soul and the body, Cordemoy argued that if body is extension, then it cannot be self-moved, nor, in contrast to Galileo, can motion be one of its essential attributes. For since a body can come to rest and still remain corporeal, and since nothing can lose an essential attribute without changing its nature, a body at rest is either no longer corporeal or motion is not part of its essence. Therefore, if a body moves, it can move only because of the imposition of an immaterial, or spiritual, force. There is no other possibility. Since we know that many bodies are in a state of motion, there must be a spiritual force to account for their remaining in motion.

This confronted Cordemoy with the common sense observation that sometimes bodies collide; and when they do so, they change their velocity and direction. But this change cannot be attributed to their bodily nature. Moreover, all that we observe is their proximity and contiguity; we cannot observe the transfer of any force from one to the other. The material contact therefore must be no more than the occasion on which the spiritual force operates.

A second problem left by Descartes was that of the interaction between the soul and the human body in both sensation and volition. Cordemoy argued that just as we cannot observe the exchange of force between two bodies, so we cannot observe it between soul and body. Moreover, there are four types of facts that are evidence of the will's inefficacy: (1) bodily motions that occur before we have any will and also death, which the will would normally not allow to happen if it were omnicompetent; (2) the termination of motions that appear to be initiated by will; (3) the impossibility of extending our lives indefinitely by an act of will; (4) the discrepancy between the motions of the young and the old while the will remains no less strong. The first of these is familiar in the ordinary involuntary motions of pulse and respiration. The third is in conflict with all human desires, since no man wants to shorten his life, nor can we die just by an act of will. The fourth is based on the observation that the volition of the aged is frustrated by their corporeal weakness. Cordemoy not only anticipated Geulincx and Malebranche, but to some extent Hume.

Having made a sharp distinction between matter and soul in the Cartesian manner, Cordemoy tried to explain the four Aristotelian kinds of change on the basis of local motion alone. Although all motion is qualitatively homogeneous, local motion may be fast or slow, and its differences are observable. Consequently, all that one has to do to explain why a body disintegrates, to take but one example, is to point out that its constituent particles move so slowly as no longer to cohere.

Though Cordemoy was a careful analytical thinker, his fame was obscured by that of his younger contemporaries. Yet their theses exist in germ in their predecessor.

Works by Cordemoy

Les Oeuvres du feu M. de Cordemoy, 1704. Of most interest for philosophers: *Le Discernement du corps et de l'âme*, *Discours physique sur la parole*, and *Deux Petits Traités de métaphysique*, in *Oeuvres*.

Works on Cordemoy

Bouillier, F., *Histoire de la philosophie cartésienne*. Paris, 1854.

Balz, A. G. A., *Cartesian Studies*. New York, 1951. Ch. 1 is the best, and indeed a unique, essay on the totality of Cordemoy's doctrines.

Boas, George, *Dominant Themes of Western Philosophy*. New York, 1947. Pp. 163 ff.

GEORGE BOAS

CORDOVERO, MOSES BEN JACOB (1522–1570), Jewish legalist and mystic, was the outstanding systematizer of the cabala. The place of his birth is not known; his father probably was among the Jews expelled from Cordova, Spain. Cordovero's career centers in Safad, the little town in Palestine that had a period of glory in the sixteenth century. Here, after studying with three distinguished rabbinical teachers—Joseph Caro, Jacob Berab, and Moses di Trani—he was ordained at an early age and became one of the leading figures of the community. His cabalistic studies were begun at the age of 20, under the direction of his brother-in-law, Solomon Alkabez, and became the major concern of the remainder of his life. Isaac Luria, who was to become the key figure in a new, more theosophic version of cabalistic teachings, was originally a pupil of Cordovero.

Cordovero wrote at least ten important cabalistic books, of varying lengths, during his lifetime. From the philosophic point of view, the greatest of these was *Pardes Rimmonim* ("A Garden of Pomegranates," first printed at Cracow, 1591). This large book attempted to present a systematic exposition of cabalistic ideas and to justify them by deductive rational argumentation instead of the usual methods of cabalistic exegesis. The word *Pardes* (*PRDS*) in the title acrostically represents the four modes of interpretation of Scripture: *peshat*, literal interpretation; *remez*, allegorical, or hinting, interpretation; *derash*, homiletical interpretation; and *sod*, mystical interpretation. Among the subjects emphasized by Cordovero in his treatment are God's unity, God's will, God's knowledge and thought, God's wisdom and goodness, God's many names, and God's relation to creation; the emanations (*sephirot*), both individually and collectively, the reason for there being precisely ten emanations, and the mystery of their multiplicity in unity; the Shekinah; angels; soul; being; prophecy; the relation of correspondence between the upper and lower worlds and the necessity of each to the other; the Law and the commandments; the mysteries of the Law; the secrets of the Hebrew alphabet; man and Israel; righteousness; time; freedom and bondage; the service of God. Cordovero was one of the first writers to stress the idea of *zimzum*, the voluntary self-shrinkage of God to make room for the material world.

Because of his rational discussion of all these subjects and his successful philosophic justification of them, in terms of his own presuppositions, Cordovero may well be regarded as the climactic figure of the earlier period of cabalistic speculation. To what extent he was also intrigued by the more practical or "magical" aspects of cabala, we cannot tell.

Bibliography

There is no English translation of any of Cordovero's works. There is a revised edition of a Hebrew chrestomathy, S. A. Horodezky, ed., *Torath Ha-Kabbala shel Rabbi Mosheh Cordovero* (Jerusalem, 1950/1951), with a full introduction.

Gershon Scholem, *Major Trends in Jewish Mysticism* (New York, 1941 and 1946), contains the only significant discussion in English.

J. L. BLAU

CORRESPONDENCE THEORY OF TRUTH. The term "correspondence theory of truth" has circulated among modern philosophical writers largely through the influence of Bertrand Russell, who sets the view (which he himself adopts) that "truth consists in some form of correspondence between belief and fact" against the theory of the absolute idealists that "truth consists in *coherence*," that is, that the more our beliefs hang together in a system, the truer they are.

ANCIENT AND SCHOLASTIC VERSIONS OF THE THEORY

The origins of the word "correspondence," used to denote the relation between thought and reality in which the truth of thought consists, appear to be medieval. Aquinas used *correspondentia* in this way at least once, but much more often he used other expressions and preferred most of all the definition of truth which he attributed to the ninth-century Jewish Neoplatonist Isaac Israeli: *Veritas est adaequatio rei et intellectus* ("Truth is the adequation of things and the intellect"). At one point he expanded this to *adaequatio intellectus et rei, secundum quod intellectus dicit esse, quod est, vel non esse, quod non est.* This is an echo of Aristotle's "To say of what is that it is not, or of what is not that it is, is false; while to say of what is that it is, and of what is not that it is not, is true." Other Scholastics sometimes said that a proposition is true when and only when *ita est sicut significat* ("the thing is as signified"); this too is in line with the Aristotelian account, in which "is" is not restricted to the meaning "exists"—the definition also covers the point that to say of what is so that it is not so, or of what is not so that it is so, is false; while to say of what is so that it is so, and of what is not so that it is not so, is true. This simple statement is the nerve of the correspondence theory; we shall continually return to it.

Plato. Aristotle did not originate the correspondence theory but took it over from Plato's *Sophist.* There it was developed with an eye on a rejected alternative—not the coherence theory, which is a comparatively late invention (G. E. Moore is probably correct, in his "Truth" article in Baldwin's *Dictionary*, in tracing its vogue to Kant), but one that we may call the existence theory, which also crops up in the *Theaetetus.* In this latter dialogue Socrates tries to find what differentiates true from erroneous belief, and the first suggestion he considers is that whereas true belief is directed toward what is, false belief is directed toward what is not. This view is rejected on the ground that just as to see or hear what is not is to see or hear nothing, and to see or hear nothing is just not to see or hear at all, so to "think what is not" is to think nothing, and that is just not to think at all, so that erroneous thought, on this view, would just not be thinking at all.

The same theory is considered in the *Sophist*, but here an alternative is put forward. Thought is compared with speech (it is the soul's dialogue with itself), and the important thing about speech is that in order to be true or false it must be complex—only complete statements are true or false, and these must consist of both nouns and verbs. (These points are also stressed by Aristotle.) As simple examples of complete statements, Plato gives "Theaetetus is-sitting-down" and "Theaetetus is-flying." The first of these is true because Theaetetus is sitting down, and the second is false because he is not flying. This escapes the difficulties of the existence theory because it abandons the suggestion that thinking is a simple direction of the mind toward an object—if it were that, its verbal expression would not have to be a complete sentence but could be just a name—and so opens up the possibility for thinking to be erroneous even though what is thought about, such as Theaetetus, is perfectly real.

The existence theory, however, dies hard and has continued to maintain itself, not merely as a rival to the correspondence theory but even more as something which that theory is in constant danger of becoming. (The two views continually oscillate, for example, in the early work of Russell and Moore.) It is easy to equate the complexity of thinking with its having a complex object—for instance, Theaetetus'-sitting-down or Theaetetus'-flying—which exists if the thought is true and does not if it is not.

Aristotle. There is no trace of the above slide or degeneration in Aristotle, nor even of a conscious resistance to it, but he has passages which have some bearing on it and which in any case develop a little further the correspondence theory itself. For example, having said that the distinguishing mark of a substance or individual thing is that it may have opposite qualities at different times, he resists a suggestion that statements and opinions would count as things by this criterion, since they may be at one time true and at another time false—for example, the statement or opinion that a person is sitting down will be true while he is doing so but false when he stands up. This, Aristotle suggests, is unfair, because what is in question here is not any genuine alteration in the statement or opinion itself, but rather in the facts outside it by which its truth or falsehood is measured. "For it is by the facts of the case, by their being or not being so, that a statement is called true or false."

Sometimes Aristotle represents the verification of statements by facts as a kind of causation. Causation, he says, differs from implication because even where implication is reciprocal we can distinguish the cause from the effect:

> The existence of a man, for instance, implies the truth of the statement in which we assert his existence. The converse is also the case. For if he exists, then the statement in which we assert his existence is true, and conversely, if the statement in which we assert his existence is true, he exists. But the truth of the statement is in no way the cause of his existence, though his existence is in a way the cause of the truth of the statement. For we call the statement true or false according as he exists or not. (*Categories* 14b15–20)

(What Aristotle calls a cause here is perhaps something more like a criterion.)

Megarian "liar" paradox. The Platonic–Aristotelian correspondence theory was not long formulated when a distressing consequence, or apparent consequence, of it was pointed out by Eubulides, a member of the school of Megara, which seems to have conducted constant warfare against various basic Platonic–Aristotelian positions. Eubulides invited his hearers to consider a man who says "I am lying" or "What I am now saying is false." According to the Platonic–Aristotelian view, this is true if what the man is saying *is* false—it is true if it is itself false—and false if what he is saying is *not* false—false if it is true. Therefore, in at least this one case, that view leads to the position that whatever we say about the truth or falsehood of an utterance entails its own opposite. We may note, too, that in this instance the Aristotelian one-sided dependence of the truth or falsehood of a proposition on the related matter of fact does not hold, since the related matter of fact in this instance *is* precisely the truth or falsehood of the proposition. This "paradox of the liar" was much discussed by both ancient and medieval writers and still presents a serious problem to anyone attempting to give a satisfactory general account of truth and falsehood.

Stoics. What is substantially the Platonic–Aristotelian account of truth is also found among the Stoics, but with modifications. The Stoics held that truth in the primary sense is a property of statements or *axiomata,* not in the sense of sentences but in the sense of what the sentences state or mean. These *axiomata* exist independently of their being expressed by sentences, and the "meanings" of false sentences exist just as much as the meanings of true ones—that is to say, *axiomata* include objective falsehoods as well as objective truths. (This is not, therefore, the existence theory.) Describing the Stoics' account of truth from this point on, Diogenes Laërtius says that the *axioma* expressed by "It is day" is true if it is day and false if it is not. This is an example rather than a general theory; Sextus Empiricus says that the kind of *axioma* called simple and definite—the kind that would be expressed by a sentence of the form "This *X Y*'s" (for instance, "This bat flies")—is true when the predicate belongs to the object denoted by the demonstrative. This, however, only defines "true" for the simplest type of proposition. For other types we know that the Stoics laid down such rules as that an *axioma* of the form "Some *X Y*'s" is true if and only if there is some true *axioma* of the form "This *X Y*'s," and one of the form "*p* and *q*" is true if and only if both of its components are; but we do not know whether they regarded such rules as actually defining "true" for these forms. It is scarcely likely that they saw them as parts of a single "recursive" definition of truth, such as is found in Tarski, but they laid the foundations for such a development.

Medieval logicians. Such statements of truth conditions, as we now call them, were also laid down and discussed by the logicians of the later Middle Ages, although they generally treated truth as a property not of abstract *axiomata* but of spoken and written sentences. Besides the truth conditions of sentences containing "not," "or," and "some," they considered those of sentences containing expressions like "possibly" and verbs in the past and future tenses (see MODAL LOGIC). They observed, for example, that while in general a past-tense statement *is* true if and only if the corresponding present-tense statement *was* true, and a statement that something *could have been* so *is* true if and only if the statement that it *is* so *could have been* true, there are exceptions to such rules. For example, "Something white *was* black" *is* true, but "Something white *is* black" was never true. The rule here is that a past-tense predication *is* true if the corresponding predication *was* true of the individuals to which the subject term now applies; for instance, "Something white was black" is true if "It is black" could have been truly said in the past of a thing that is now white. "It could have been that no proposition is negative" is true, since God might have annihilated all negative propositions; but "No proposition is negative" could in no circumstances have been true, since the mere existence of this sentence (which is itself negative) falsifies it. The rule is rather that a sentence *de possibili* is true if and only if things could have been as the corresponding unqualified sentence says they are.

The later medieval logicians also implicitly modified the Platonic–Aristotelian theory in order to cope with the "liar" and similar paradoxes. Buridan, for example, although he preserved the formula that a sentence is true when *ita est sicut significat,* gave a somewhat un-Aristotelian twist to the meaning of *significat.* According to Buridan, the man who says "I am saying something false," and says nothing else, really is saying something false, not because things are otherwise than as his sentence *significat formaliter* but because they are otherwise than as his sentence *significat virtualiter.* A sentence "virtually" signifies whatever follows from itself together with the circumstances of its utterance, and what follows from this particular sentence together with the circumstances of its utterance is that it is both true and false; since this is never the case, things are not as it "virtually" says they are, and it is false.

MOORE'S CORRESPONDENCE THEORY

In the twentieth century a particularly extended and fruitful discussion of the correspondence theory is found in a series of lectures given by G. E. Moore in 1910–1911. Here truth and falsehood first appear as properties of what are called propositions. Moore uses the term "proposition" to mean not an indicative sentence but what such a sentence *means,* an *axioma* in the Stoic sense. When we both hear and understand a spoken sentence, and both see and understand a written one, there is something apprehended by us over and above the sentence, and while this apprehension or understanding is the same kind of act in all cases, what is apprehended is in general different when different sentences (such as "Twice two are four" and "Twice four are eight") are involved and therefore is distinguishable from the act of apprehending. We also "constantly think of and believe or disbelieve, or merely consider, propositions, at moments when we are neither hearing nor seeing any words which express them"; for example, when we "apprehend a proposition, which we desire to express, before we are able to think of any sentence which would express it." In this lecture Moore is quite confident that "there certainly are in the Universe such things as propositions," and that it is propositions rather than sentences or acts of belief which are true or false in the primary sense. We often say that beliefs are true or false, but this is only because the word "belief" is often used not for an act of believing but for what is believed; for instance, if we say that two different people have the same belief, we mean to identify what they believe rather than their respective acts of believing, and what is believed is simply a proposition in Moore's sense. Acts of believing and sentences could, however, be said to be true or false in a secondary sense, when what is believed or expressed is a true or false proposition.

Moore's later position. Moore returns to the subjects of true and false beliefs and the nature of propositions in later lectures in the series, but now he seems to move somewhat away from the position outlined above. He leads up to them with a problem which he states as follows: "Suppose a man believes that God exists; . . . then to say that his belief is true seems to be exactly equivalent to saying that it *is a fact* that God exists or that God's existence is a fact" (*Some Main Problems in Philosophy*, p. 250). Quite generally it seems that "the difference between true and false beliefs is . . . that where a belief is true, there what is believed is a fact; whereas where a belief is false, there what is believed is not a fact" (*ibid.*). Even where a belief is false, however, there does seem to be something that is believed.

> A man believes in God's existence and it seems quite plain that he is believing in something—that there is such a thing as what he believes in, and that this something is God's existence. It seems quite plain, therefore, that there *is* such a thing as God's existence, *whether* his belief is true or false. But we have just seen that if his belief is false, then God's existence is *not* a fact. And what is the difference between saying that there is such a thing as God's existence and (saying) that God's existence is a fact? (*ibid.*)

This is the problem of the *Theaetetus* all over again—if a false belief has no real object, how can it be a belief at all?

Denial that propositions exist. Moore raises the above question with regard to a more certainly false proposition, namely, that the hearers of his lecture were at that time hearing the noise of a brass band; and he then restates, but no longer with conviction, his earlier theory. We *could* say that there was indeed such a thing as their hearing a brass band then but that this was a proposition, not a fact. But, Moore argues, this theory admits in the case of the phrase "the fact that they are hearing a brass band" that what looks like the name of a real object of a possible belief is not one, so why should we not say this also of the phrase "the proposition that they are hearing a brass band"? Moore is thus led to the view that the subject–verb–object form of assertions about beliefs is misleading. His new theory, he says, "may be expressed by saying that there simply are no such things as *propositions.* That belief does *not* consist . . . in a relation between the believer, on the one hand, and another thing which may be called the proposition believed" (*ibid.*, p. 265). He cannot give any satisfactory alternative analysis of belief statements to supplant the one he has abandoned, but he thinks he can give an account of the truth and falsehood of beliefs without one.

False belief and facts. In developing the account of truth and falsehood of beliefs, Moore considers the case of a friend believing that he has gone away for his holidays, and begins in a thoroughly Aristotelian vein. "If this belief of his is *true* then I *must* have gone away . . . and, conversely, . . . *if* I *have* gone away, then this belief of his certainly *is* true" (*ibid.*, p. 274). And similarly, "if this belief is *false*, then I *can't* have gone away . . . and conversely, *if* I have not gone away, then the belief that I *have* gone away certainly *must* be false" (*ibid.*, p. 275). However, this statement of necessary and sufficient conditions does not constitute a definition of truth and falsehood, for "when we assert: 'The belief that I have gone away is true,' we mean to assert that this belief has some property, which it shares with other true beliefs," whereas "in merely asserting 'I have gone away,' we are not attributing any property at all to this belief" (*ibid.*, p. 276). For "Plainly I might have gone away without my friend believing that I had; and if so, his belief would not be true, simply because it would not exist." This objection, however, suggests that Moore's having gone away would not after all be a sufficient condition, but only a necessary one, of his friend's belief being true; and it could be met by defining the truth of his friend's belief, not simply as Moore's having in fact gone away but as this together with his friend's believing it.

The problem remains, however, of generalizing this to cover all cases, which Moore goes about solving as follows: "We can see quite plainly," he says, "that this belief, if true, has to the fact that I have gone away a certain relation which that belief has to no other fact," a relation which cannot be defined in the sense of being analyzed, but with which we are all perfectly familiar and which "is expressed by the circumstance that the name of the belief is 'the belief that I have gone away,' while the name of the fact is 'that I have gone away' " (*ibid.*). Moore proposes to call this relation correspondence, and "To say that this belief is true is to say that there is in the Universe *a* fact to which it corresponds, and to say that it is false is to say that there is *not* in the Universe any fact to which it corresponds" (*ibid.*, p. 277).

Facts rather than propositions. It is essential to Moore's final account that although there are no propositions, there are facts. A belief, even if true, does not consist in a relation between a person and a fact, but the truth of a belief does. He is also at pains to insist that facts "are" or exist in the very sense in which, say, chairs and tables do. He concedes that as a matter of usage we find it natural to say "It is a fact that bears exist," while we do not find it at all natural to say "That bears exist, is" (or "That bears exist, exists"; or even "The existence of bears exists"), but he thinks this simply reflects our acute sense of the difference in kind between facts and other things—they are real objects but objects of a very special sort. We also express their character by calling them truths, or by prefixing "It is true that" to them as an alternative to "It is a fact that." This property of *being* a truth or fact is to be carefully distinguished from the "truth" which is possessed by some beliefs and which consists, as previously explained, in correspondence to a truth or fact.

RUSSELL'S CORRESPONDENCE THEORY

In Moore's account of truth and falsehood, it will be seen, there are two elements which are a little mysterious and which he is reluctantly compelled to leave in that condition—the correct analysis of belief statements and the nature of the correspondence which entitles us to use the same form of words in describing the content of a belief and in asserting the fact to which, if true, it corresponds.

Shortly before Moore gave these lectures, Russell had made an attempt to elucidate just these points. In the concluding section of a paper he gave before the Aristotelian

Society in 1906, there is a hint of this explanation, which is more fully developed in various writings of the period 1910–1912. He suggests in the 1906 paper that a belief may differ from an idea or presentation in consisting of several interrelated ideas, whose objects will be united in the real world into a single complex or fact if the belief is true, but not otherwise, so that a false belief is indeed "belief in nothing, though it is not 'thinking of nothing,' because it is thinking of the objects of the ideas which constitute the belief." In the later versions this is expanded to the view that a belief consists in a many-termed relation, the number of terms always being two more than that occurring in the fact to which, if true, the belief corresponds. For example, if it is a fact that Desdemona loves Cassio, then in this fact the two terms Desdemona and Cassio are "knit together" by the relation of loving, while if it is a fact that Othello believes that Desdemona loves Cassio, then the four terms Othello, Desdemona, the relation of loving, and Cassio are "knit together" in this fact by the relation of believing. The correspondence between the belief and the fact, when the fact exists and the belief is therefore true, consists in a certain characteristic semiparallelism between the ordering of the last terms of the belief relation and the ordering of the terms by their ordering relation in the fact. Knowing and perceiving, on the other hand, really are relations between the knower or perceiver and the fact known or perceived (which of course must *be* a fact for knowledge or perception to occur).

Criticisms. The above theory is open to a number of objections, some of which have recently been particularly well stated by P. T. Geach, and one of which, due in essence to Wittgenstein, had already led Russell to abandon the theory, in a course of lectures on logical atomism delivered in 1918.

Belief and what is the case. Russell's 1906–1912 theory—and indeed even Moore's more vague theory, of which it is a possible filling out—makes it altogether too mysterious that the very same words should be used to express what is believed and what is actually the case if the belief is true. (At most, there is in some languages a slight but regular formal alteration when the latter is put into *oratio obliqua* to give the former.) As Wittgenstein puts it (*Philosophical Investigations*, Para. 444), "One may have the feeling that in the sentence 'I expect he is coming' one is using the words 'he is coming' in a different sense from the one they have in the assertion 'He is coming.' But if it were so how could I say that my expectation had been fulfilled?"—that *the very thing* I expected had come to pass?

This severance of the senses of the *oratio obliqua* and *oratio recta* forms of the same sentence is exacerbated in Russell's account, as Geach points out, by its consequence that believing is not one relation but several, since the number of terms it requires differs with the number of terms required by the relation which occurs among its objects (for instance, while Othello's believing that Desdemona loves Cassio is a 4-termed relation, his believing that Desdemona gave Cassio a certain ring would be a 5-termed one). This difference arises even when we are only considering beliefs of which the apparent objects are simple relational propositions; still more radical differences would have to be admitted with believings apparently directed toward compound and general propositions. This point was, indeed, stressed by Russell himself from the outset and seems never to have been regarded by him as a serious objection to the theory, since in his 1918 lectures, even when he had abandoned the view which necessitated it, we find him saying that "belief will really have to have different logical forms according to the nature of what is believed" (*Logic and Knowledge*, p. 226), so that "the apparent sameness of believing in different cases is more or less illusory."

There is here, it seems, a remnant of the ramified theory of types which Russell at first thought necessary to deal with such paradoxes as that of the "liar." According to this theory, propositions are not only of different logical forms but also of different logical types, and "truth" and "falsehood" must be differently defined for each type; indeed, even such ordinary logical functions as negation and conjunction must be understood differently according to the types of propositions to which they are attached. Even by the time he was exercising the influence acknowledged in Russell's 1918 lectures, Wittgenstein had definitely abandoned this theory: "*Any* proposition can be negated. And this shews that 'true' and 'false' mean the same for all propositions (in contrast to Russell)" (*Notebooks 1914–1916*, p. 21).

Verbs in judgments. What Russell did successfully assimilate from Wittgenstein at this period was that in such judgments as that Othello believes that Desdemona loves Cassio, "both verbs have got to occur as verbs, because if a thing is a verb it cannot occur otherwise than as a verb." He also says:

> There are really two main things that one wants to notice in this matter that I am treating of just now. The *first* is the impossibility of treating the proposition believed as an independent entity, entering as a unit into the occurrences of the belief, and the *other* is the impossibility of putting the subordinate verb on a level with its terms as an object term in the belief. That is a point in which I think that the theory of judgment which I set forth once . . . was a little unduly simple, because I did then treat the object verb as if one could put it as just an object like the terms. (*Logic and Knowledge*, p. 226)

"Every right theory of judgment," as Wittgenstein puts it, "must make it impossible for me to judge that 'this table penholders the book' (Russell's theory does not satisfy this requirement)" (*Notebooks 1914–1916*, p. 96).

Propositions in judgments. Russell's objection ties up in two ways with Wittgenstein's that "a proposition itself must occur in the statement to the effect that it is judged." In the first place, it is by inserting the "proposition itself" into the "statement to the effect that it is judged" that we enable the subordinate verb to occur as a verb and not disguised as an abstract noun. (It looks, in fact, as if these "two main things" that Russell says we must notice cannot be observed together.) We might put the two objections together thus: Because the use of abstract nouns is *always* something to be explained, it is more illuminating to say that "Othello ascribes unfaithfulness to Desdemona" (where "ascribes" is apparently a 3-termed relation with "unfaithfulness" as one of its terms) means exactly what is meant by "Othello believes that Desdemona is-unfaithful" than it is to say that the second means exactly what is meant by the first.

Facts as objects. The second way in which the two objections come together is more complicated, and it can be gathered from an extended discussion of what may at first seem another point: that Russell's 1906–1912 theory, like Moore's of 1910, still takes "facts" seriously as a special sort of object. On this point Russell's 1918 view is a little obscure. He seems not to have changed at all on this subject, and describes it as one of those truisms which "are so obvious that it is almost laughable to mention them," that "the world contains *facts*, . . . and that there are also *beliefs*, which have reference to facts, and by reference to facts are either true or false" (*Logic and Knowledge*, p. 182). He sharply contrasts facts with propositions in this respect. "If we were making an inventory of the world, propositions would not come in. Facts would, beliefs, wishes, wills would, but propositions would not" (*ibid.*, p. 214). This last remark occurs in a criticism of an attempt by Raphael Demos to eliminate the *negative* fact that a certain piece of chalk is not red from the "inventory of the world" by equating it with the fact that the chalk has some other positive but incompatible color (see NEGATION). "Even if incompatibility is to be taken as a sort of fundamental expression of fact," Russell says to this, "incompatibility is not between facts but between propositions. . . . It is clear that no two *facts* are incompatible" (*ibid.*). And since propositions do not have being independently, this "incompatibility of propositions taken as an ultimate fact of the real world will want a good deal of treatment, a lot of dressing up before it will do." However, Russell's own alternative, that there are irreducibly negative facts—for instance, the fact that it is not the case that this piece of chalk is red—equally involves the consequence that there are facts which contain real falsehoods as constituents. This Russell himself pointed out in his 1906 paper, and it led him then to be more hesitant than he was later about dismissing the notion of objective falsehoods. Even if, he says in this paper, we can remove the suggestion that false beliefs have objective falsehoods for their objects:

> There is . . . another argument in favour of objective falsehood, derived from the case of true propositions which contain false ones as constituent parts. Take, e.g., 'Either the earth goes round the sun, or it does not.' This is certainly true, and therefore, on the theory we are considering, it represents a *fact*, i.e. an objective complex. But it is, at least apparently, compounded of two (unasserted) constituents, . . . of which one must be false. Thus our fact seems to be composed of two parts, of which one is a fact, while the other is an objective falsehood. ("On the Nature of Truth," pp. 47–48)

The real moral of all this is surely that if propositions must go, facts must go, too; but Russell seems to shrink from this step.

Elsewhere in the 1918 lectures, however, he says that facts, although apparently real in a way in which propositions are not, have the extraordinary property that they cannot be named. In the first place, they are not named by propositions (sentences). For this he has a rather strange argument, taken from Wittgenstein. Whereas Moore thought of a false belief as one which corresponds to no fact at all, Wittgenstein held that a false statement does correspond to a fact, but in the wrong way. Hence, to quote Russell's exposition of the theory:

> There are *two* propositions corresponding to each fact. Suppose it is a fact that Socrates is dead. You have two propositions: "Socrates is dead" and "Socrates is not dead." And those two propositions corresponding to the same fact, there is one fact in the world, that which makes one true and one false. . . . There are two different relations . . . that a proposition can have to a fact: the one the relation that you may call being true to the fact, and the other being false to the fact. (*Logic and Knowledge*, p. 187)

This means that a proposition does not name a fact, since in the case of a name, there is only one relation that it can have to what it names. Further,

> You must not run away with the idea that you can name facts in any other way; you cannot. . . . You cannot properly name a fact. The only thing you can do is to assert it, or deny it, or desire it, or will it, or wish it, or question it. . . . You can never put the sort of thing that makes a proposition to be true or false in the position of a logical subject. (*ibid.*, p. 188)

RAMSEY AND THE LATER WITTGENSTEIN

Russell's whole position, as it stands, is difficult to maintain. If there are really individual objects to which the common noun "fact" applies, and we can sometimes actually perceive them (Russell continued to hold this in the 1918 lectures), then if at the time of our perceiving one our language has no name for it, why can we not invent one and christen the thing on the spot? However, there is not just superstition, but something true and important, behind the statement of Russell and Wittgenstein that facts cannot be named, and they both identify it in the end. "When I say 'facts cannot be named,'" Russell admitted in 1924, "this is, strictly speaking, nonsense. What can be said without falling into nonsense is: 'The symbol for a fact is not a name.'" Or better, perhaps: to state a fact is not to name an object. Whatever may be the case with "that" clauses, *sentences* aren't names of anything; just as, whatever may be the case with abstract nouns, verbs are not names of anything—they are not names at all, but have other functions; naming is one thing, saying or stating another. Even Plato saw that this distinction was important.

But can we not *name what a sentence says*, for instance, by the corresponding "that" clause? Not really—"*what* a sentence says," although a good sense can be given to it, is a misleading expression; when it means anything, it means "*how* a sentence says things are" or, better, "how *we* say things are" when we use the sentence in question. To *name* what we are saying is to *say* what we are saying, and to name what we are thinking or wishing is similarly to say what we are thinking or wishing. "I think that bears exist" is, therefore, not to be analyzed as "I think (that bears exist)," which suggests that "that bears exist" is one term of the relation expressed by "think " but rather as "I think that (bears exist)," where "bears exist" does not even look like a name (it looks like, and is, a sentence) and "think that" does not look like the expression of a relation. If Othello thinks that Desdemona loves Cassio, there is indeed a 3-termed relation between Othello, Desdemona, and Cassio (not, as Russell thought, a 4-termed one between Othello, Desdemona, Cassio, and loving), but this relation consists in his *thinking that she loves him*, that is, the relation is expressed by the whole complex verb "—— thinks that——loves——," not by the simple"——thinks that——," which does not express any relation at all, since its second gap is not filled by the name of an object but by a sentence, which does not name but ***says*** what he thinks (how he thinks things are). The plain "thinks," without the "that," means nothing at all. I may, indeed, use forms of expression like "I think something that Jones doesn't think" or "Something that Jones thinks is not true," but the "thing" in this "something" is no more to be taken seriously than the "what" in "what I say"—these sentences respectively mean simply "For some *p*, I *think that p* and Jones does not think that *p*" and "For some *p*, Jones thinks that *p* but it is not the case that *p*." The correspondence theory can now assume the simple form: "*X* says (believes) truly that *p*" means "*X* says (believes) that *p*, and *p*"; and "*X* says (believes) falsely that *p*" means "*X* says (believes) that *p*, and not *p*."

Ramsey. The above position was very lightly sketched in 1927 by F. P. Ramsey, who says in effect that the words "fact" and "true" in their primary use are inseparable parts of the adverbial phrases "truly," "in fact," "it is a fact that," and "it is true that"; and these, attached to some sentence, say no more than this sentence says on its own. "It is false that *p*" or "That *p*, is contrary to fact" similarly says no more than the simple "Not *p*." Thus there are not only no falsehoods but no facts or truths either, any more than there is an entity called "the case" involved in the synonymous phrase "It is the case that." This part of Ramsey's view has led some writers to set it in opposition to the correspondence theory as a "no truth" theory, but Ramsey also discusses more complex uses of "true" in which there is something more like a juxtaposition of what a man says and what is so. In particular he considers the statement "He is always right"—"Whatever he says is true"—and renders this as "For all *p*, if he says that *p*, it is true that *p*," and this in turn as "For all *p*, if he says that *p*, then *p*." This may seem to require a further verb in its second clause, but there is already a "variable verb" implicit in the variable *p*.

Wittgenstein. We may expand Ramsey's discussion of the more complex uses of "true" by taking up a suggestion of the later Wittgenstein (which, indeed, we have already used a bit). In the *Tractatus*, Wittgenstein says that "the general form of propositions is: this is how things are." In the *Investigations*, criticizing this identification, he reminds us that "This is how things are" is itself a proposition, an English sentence applied in everyday language, as in "He explained his position to me, said that this was how things were, and that therefore he needed an advance." "This is how things are" can be said to stand for any statement and can be employed as a propositional *schema*, but only because it already has the construction of an English sentence. Wittgenstein continues, "It would also be possible here simply to use a letter, a variable, as in symbolic logic. But no one is going to call the letter '*p*' the general form of propositions."

"This is how things are," although a genuine proposition, is nevertheless being employed only as a propositional variable. "To say that this proposition agrees or does not agree with reality would be obvious nonsense." "This is how things are" is a propositional variable in ordinary speech in much the same way that a pronoun is a name variable in ordinary speech. In Wittgenstein's example, the "value" of this "variable" is given by a specific sentence uttered earlier, much as the denotation of a pronoun may be fixed by a name occurring earlier. "I'm desperate—that's how things are" is like "There's Jones—he's wearing that hat again." "This (that) is how things are" is a prosentence. But we may also obtain a specific statement by "binding" this variable, as in "However he says things are, that's how they are," that is, Ramsey's "For all *p*, if he says that *p*, then *p*." We speak truly whenever things are as we say they are, and falsely when they are not. There was a hint of this way of putting things when the later Scholastics equated *est vera*, said of a sentence, with *ita est sicut significat* or *qualitercumque significat, ita est*—"*however* the sentence signifies (that the case is), *thus* it is"—avoiding the possibly misleading "*What* the sentence says is so."

These "misleading" forms, however, *need* not mislead us, once the whole picture has been spread out, and we can soften our earlier skepticism by agreeing that after all there *are* facts, and that there are falsehoods, if all that is meant by "There are facts" is "For some *p*, *p*" and by "There are falsehoods" "For some *p*, not *p*." We can say, too, that there are both facts and falsehoods that have never been either thought or asserted, that is, we can insist on the objective or mind-independent character of propositions, if by this we mean that for some *p*, both *p* and it has never been thought or said that *p*. (We cannot, of course, give examples of such facts or falsehoods, for to do so would be to state them, and then they would not be unstated; but this is no more strange than that there should be people—as there certainly are—whose names we do not know, although we cannot in the nature of the case name any specific examples.) It is significant that Moore in his last years contrived to assimilate a Ramsey-like account of truth without losing any of his earlier sense of the mind-independent and speech-independent character of what is so. Propositions about propositions, he said in effect, are *not* propositions about sentences precisely because the words "proposition," "true," and "false" are eliminable—just because "The proposition that the sun is shining is true" is equivalent to and perhaps identical with the plain "The sun is shining," it neither says anything about sentences nor entails that there are such things, since the sun could obviously *be* shining even if no one ever said so.

TARSKI'S SEMANTIC THEORY

In the theories of Ramsey and the later Moore, truth is a quasi property of a quasi object. What is really defined in them is not a property of anything, but rather what it is to say with truth that something is so; it is an account of the adverbial phrase "with truth" rather than of the adjective "true." The late medieval treatment of "true" as a straightforward adjective applying to straightforward objects—sentences—was revived in the twentieth century, and developed with extraordinary precision, elegance, and thoroughness, in a paper by Alfred Tarski which is one of the classics of modern logic.

"True" as a metalinguistic adjective. A sentence, Tarski points out, is true or false only as part of some particular language. The Schoolmen were sensitive to this point also; Buridan, for example, observed that if we neglect it, we will be trapped by such arguments as the following: "A man is a donkey" is a true sentence if and only if a man is a donkey; but "A man is a donkey" could have been a true sentence (since we could have used it to mean what we now mean by "White is a color"); *ergo* it could have been that a man is a donkey. Moore was fond of making similar points.

Further, Tarski argues, a sentence asserting that some sentence *S* is a true sentence of some language *L*, cannot itself be a sentence of the language *L*, but must belong to a metalanguage in which the sentences of *L* are not used but are mentioned and discussed. He is led to this view by the paradox of the "liar" which he presents, after Łukasiewicz, as follows: He uses the letter *c* as an abbreviation for the expression "the sentence printed on page 158 [of his paper], line 5 from the top," and the sentence printed there is "*c* is not a true sentence." By the ordinary Aristotelian criterion for the truth of sentences, we may say "'*c* is not a true sentence' is a true sentence if and only if *c* is not a true sentence." But "*c* is not a true sentence" is precisely the sentence *c*, so we may equate the preceding with "*c* is a true sentence if and only if *c* is not a true sentence," which is self-contradictory. The contradiction is eliminated if we put "of *L*" after "true sentence" throughout and deny the principle "'*c* is not a true sentence of *L*' is a true sentence of *L* if and only if *c* is not a true sentence of *L*" on the ground that *c* is not a true sentence of *L* under any conditions whatever, because it is not a sentence of the language *L* at all but of its metalanguage *M*.

Similar paradoxes lead to similar conclusions about terms like "is a name of" or "signifies"—in fact, all terms which concern the relations between the expressions of a language and the objects which this language is used to describe or talk about. All such semantic terms must occur, not in the language which they concern, but in the associated metalanguage. This metalanguage must contain names for expressions in the object language and may also contain descriptions of the structure of such expressions; for instance, we might be able to say in it that one sentence is the negation of another, meaning by this that it is formed from that other by prefixing the expression "It is not the case that" to it. Tarski is attempting to state the conditions under which, for a given language *L*, we can define the term "true sentence" (and perhaps other semantic expressions) in terms of this basic metalinguistic apparatus, and in such a way as to entail all sentences, in the metalanguage *M*, of the form "*x* is a true sentence if and only if *p*," where *x* is a *name* of some sentence of *L* (we need not write "sentence of *L*" in the formula, since in *M* this is what "sentence" means), and *p* is the *translation* into *M* of this same sentence. (*M* could include *L* as a part of itself, in which case the sentences of *L* would be their own translations into *M*.) Note that this criterion of a satisfactory definition of truth, which Tarski calls the Convention *T*, is not itself such a definition in *M* of truth in *L*, since it talks *about* expressions of *M*, and about their relation to what they mean (they "name" sentences of *L*), and so is itself not in the metalanguage *M* but in the metametalanguage.

Since in many (meta)languages we form the name of an expression by putting that expression in quotation marks, the following might seem to meet Tarski's criterion: "For all *p*, '*p*' is a true sentence if and only if *p*." This, one might think, would immediately yield such individual cases as "'Snow is white' is a true sentence if and only if snow is white" (given, of course, that "Snow is white" is a sentence of *L*). This will not do, however, for by enclosing the fourteenth letter of the alphabet in quotation marks (however we use that letter elsewhere) we simply form the name of the fourteenth letter of the alphabet. Hence, what we get by instantiation of the proposed definition are, for example, the sentences "The fourteenth letter of the alphabet is a true sentence if and only if snow is white" and "The fourteenth letter of the alphabet is a true sentence if and only if snow is not white," which together entail that snow is white if and only if snow is not white, a contradiction.

"Recursive" definition of truth. If the language *L* contained only the two simple sentences "Snow is white" and "Grass is green," plus such compounds as could be formed by prefixing "It is not the case that" to a sentence and by joining two sentences by "or," we might offer the following "recursive" definition of "true sentence":

(1) "Snow is white" is a true sentence if and only if snow is white, and "Grass is green" if and only if grass is green.

(2) The sentence formed by prefixing "It is not the case that" to a given sentence *S* is true if and only if *S* is not true.

(3) The sentence formed by placing "or" between the two sentences S_1 and S_2 is true if and only if either S_1 or S_2 is true.

There is a mathematical device for turning such "recursive" definitions into ordinary ones, so this feature of the above need not worry us; but we are clearly not very far along if we have to begin by listing all elementary sentences and defining "true" for each of them.

Suppose we enrich *L* by adding "Snow is green" and "Grass is white" to the elementary sentences, and enrich *M* by calling "snow" and "grass" names and "is green" and "is white" predicates, and defining an elementary sentence as a name followed by a predicate. We may then alter (1) above to "For any name *X* and predicate *Y*, the sentence *XY* is true if and only if the predicate *Y* applies to the object named by *X*." This, however, assumes that the metalanguage already contains the semantic expressions "names" and "applies to"; if it does not, we can only "define" them by saying that "snow" names snow, "grass" names grass, "is white" applies to X if and only if X is white, and "is green" applies to X if and only if X is green.

This is still not very satisfactory, but it is Tarski's basic procedure, except that for his simplest L he takes a language in which there is only one predicate, the relative or two-place predicate "is included in," and no names at all, but only variables standing for names of classes; sentences are formed from "sentential functions" by prefixing a sufficient number of universal quantifiers ("for all x," "for all y") to "bind" all the variables in the function. That is, the sentences in this language are ones like "For all x, x is included in x," and ones in which "not" and "or" are used either inside or outside the quantifiers or both—"For all x and y, either x is included in y or y is included in x" or "It is not the case that for all x, it is not the case that x is included in x" (this last can be abbreviated to "For some x, x is included in x"). Tarski so defines "sentential function" as to cover sentences as special cases (they are simply those sentential functions in which all the variables are bound by quantifiers) and defines the "satisfaction" of a sentential function by a class or classes (a notion very like that of a predicate's "applying to" an object) in such a way that the truth of a sentence becomes the satisfaction by *all* classes and groups of classes of the function which "is" the sentence in question.

To develop this in a little more detail: Tarski defines "sentential function" recursively, by saying that a variable followed by "is included in" followed by a variable is a sentential function, and so are expressions formed by joining sentential functions by "or" or by prefixing "It is not the case that" or a universal quantifier to a sentential function. "Satisfaction" is more complicated, for Tarski wishes to run together such cases as that the function "x is included in x" is satisfied by the class A if and only if A is included in A; "For all y, x is included in y" is satisfied by A if and only if for all y, A is included in y; "x is included in y" is satisfied by the pair of classes A and B if and only if A is included in B; "x is included in y or y in z" by the trio of classes A, B, and C if and only if A is included in B or B in C; and so on. To cover all such cases he introduces the notion of an infinite numbered sequence of classes, numbers his variables, and says that the sequence f satisfies the function "v_m is included in v_n" if and only if the mth member of f is included in the nth; the rest is done recursively—f satisfies the negation of a function Φ if and only if it does not satisfy Φ itself, the disjunction of Φ and Ψ if and only if it satisfies either Φ or Ψ, and the universal quantification of Φ with respect to the nth variable if and only if Φ is satisfied both by f itself and by all sequences which are like f except in having a different nth term.

This last part of the definition is difficult but crucial. How it works can best be seen by considering a simple example. The function "v_1 is included in v_2" is satisfied by all sequences such that the first member is included in the second. The function "For any v_2, v_1 is included in v_2" is satisfied by a sequence f if and only if f is one of the sequences satisfying the preceding function and the preceding function is still satisfied if we replace f by any sequence otherwise like it but with a different second term. This means, in view of what sequences satisfy the first function, that a sequence will satisfy the second function if and only if its first member is included in its second, whatever class that second member may be. Finally, consider the function "For all v_1, for all v_2, v_1 is included in v_2." This is satisfied by a sequence f if and only if f satisfies the preceding function (the second) and if the preceding function is still satisfied if we replace f by any sequence otherwise like it but with a different *first* term. This means, in view of what sequences satisfy the second function, that a sequence will satisfy the third only if its first member is included in its second, whatever class either of them may be, that is, if and only if every class is included in every class. It is clear that if this function were satisfied by any sequence at all, it would be satisfied by every sequence whatever. (In fact, of course, it is not satisfied by all, and therefore not by any.) In some cases a sentential function will be satisfied by any sequence whatever, even though it contains free variables—as is the case with "v_1 is included in v_1"—but if it is thus satisfied and has all its variables bound—that is, is not merely a sentential function but a sentence—it will be, in Tarski's sense, "true."

Truth and correspondence. Tarski goes on to consider a more complicated language in which there are variables of two logical types, and an ingenious extension of the notion of a sequence enables him to define "true sentence" for this language also; but when he comes to consider "languages of infinite order," in which there are variables of an infinity of logical types, he has a proof (very similar to Gödel's proof of the incompletability of arithmetic) that any definition of either "truth" or "satisfaction" in terms of the basic material he allows himself would result in the provability of some sentence contravening his Convention T, that is, of the negation of some sentence of the form "x is a true sentence if and only if p," in which x is a name in the metalanguage of a sentence in the language studied and p is the translation into the metalanguage of the same sentence. Even with such a language, however, it is possible to introduce into the metalanguage the undefined semantic expression "true sentence" and so to axiomatize the metalanguage, thus enriched, that all sentences of the form indicated in the Convention T will be provable in it, and also desirable general theorems about truth, such as that "For any sentence x, either x is a true sentence or the negation of x is a true sentence." "Truth," introduced in this way, has something of the mysteriousness of the "correspondence" introduced without analysis by Moore, but Tarski has not merely a suspicion but a proof that, where "truth is understood as a property of sentences of the language in question, such acceptance of a semantic term without definition is inevitable.

Bibliography

Aristotle's definition of truth is in his *Metaphysics* 1011b26 ff., and there are further discussions in *Categories* 4a10–4b19 and 14b12–23, and *De Interpretatione* 16a10–19. As to Aristotle's Platonic sources, Plato states in the *Theaetetus* 188E–189A the problem solved in the *Sophist* 240D and 260C–263D.

Aquinas' echoes of Aristotle are in his *De Veritate*, Q. 1, A. 1, and *Summa Contra Gentiles*, Book I, Ch. 59. Buridan's *Sophismata* unfortunately has not been reprinted in modern times, but there are accounts of his treatment of the "liar" and similar paradoxes in E. A. Moody, *Truth and Consequence in Medieval Logic* (Amsterdam, 1953), and A. N. Prior, "Some Problems of Self-Reference in John Buridan," in *Proceedings of the British Academy*, Vol. 48 (1962), 115–126.

G. E. Moore's 1910–1911 lectures were published under the title *Some Main Problems in Philosophy* (London, 1953); see especially Chs. 6 and 13–16. Bertrand Russell's multiple relation theory of truth is developed in his "On the Nature of Truth," in *PAS* (1906–1907), 28–49; *Philosophical Essays* (London, 1910), Ch. 7; the Introduction to the first edition of *Principia Mathematica* (Cambridge, 1910), pp. 42–45; and *Problems of Philosophy* (London, 1912). P. T. Geach's criticisms of the multiple relation theory are in his *Mental Acts* (London, 1957), Sec. 13; Wittgenstein's, in his *Notebooks 1914–1916* (Oxford, 1961), pp. 21 and 96–97. Russell's recantation is in his 1918 lectures on *The Philosophy of Logical Atomism* (edited by R. C. Marsh), which is included in the collection *Logic and Knowledge*, also edited by R. C. Marsh (London, 1956); see especially pp. 182, 187–188, 214, 218, 225–226. His "double correspondence" theory is in *The Analysis of Mind* (London, 1921), Lecture 13. The more subtle views of the later Russell and Wittgenstein on propositions and facts appear in Russell's 1924 paper "Logical Atomism," included in his *Logic and Knowledge* and in Wittgenstein's *Blue and Brown Books* (Oxford, 1958), pp. 30–38, and *Philosophical Investigations* (Oxford, 1953), Paras. 134 and 444.

The key passage from F. P. Ramsey is in his paper "Facts and Propositions," included in R. B. Braithwaite, ed., *The Foundations of Mathematics* (London, 1931), pp. 142–143. For later views of G. E. Moore, exhibiting some influence from Ramsey, see R. B. Braithwaite, ed., *The Commonplace Books of G. E. Moore* (London, 1962), pp. 228–231, 319, and especially 374–377. For the use of a Ramsey-type definition in the handling of paradoxes, see A. N. Prior, "On a Family of Paradoxes," in *Notre Dame Journal of Formal Logic*, Vol. 2 (1961), 16–32, and J. L. Mackie, "Self-Refutation—A Formal Analysis," in *The Philosophical Quarterly* (July 1964), 1–12.

Alfred Tarski's "The Concept of Truth in Formalized Languages" was first printed as a paper in 1931, then modified and enlarged in a German translation in 1935, of which there is an English version in his *Logic, Semantics, Metamathematics* (Oxford, 1956), Paper 7. Tarski states its main ideas less formally in "The Semantic Conception of Truth and the Foundations of Semantics," in *Philosophy and Phenomenological Research*, Vol. 4 (1944), 341–376. Notable comments on it include Max Black, "The Semantic Definition of Truth," in *Analysis*, Vol. 9 (Mar. 1948), 49–63, and J. F. Thomson, "A Note on Truth," in *Analysis*, Vol. 9 (Apr. 1949), 67–72.

A. N. PRIOR

COSMOGONY. *See* COSMOLOGY.

COSMOLOGICAL ARGUMENT FOR THE EXISTENCE OF GOD. "The Cosmological Argument" is the name given to a group of interrelated arguments that claim to prove the existence of God from premises asserting some highly general fact about the world, such as that it exists contingently.

It does not attempt (as the Ontological Argument does) to derive the existence of God from an analysis of his essential nature alone, nor does it argue from particular manifestations of orderliness or apparent design in the world's structure to a divine designer. It is enough that there is a world—a world of conditioned objects and events. To explore their conditions is to be led toward something unconditioned; to be aware of the regress of causes behind any given event is to become aware that there must be a First Cause of all; to realize the contingency of things in the world is to be impelled to acknowledge a being whose existence is uniquely necessary. This unconditioned, necessary source of the world's being is to be identified with the God of theism.

A list of a few defenders and attackers of the Cosmological Argument may help to indicate its importance in the history of ideas and its extraordinary resilience under criticism. Its defenders include Plato, Aristotle, Thomas Aquinas, Descartes, Leibniz, Locke, and most contemporary Roman Catholic theologians. Among its critics have been Hume, Kant, and J. S. Mill, from whom present-day attackers—Russell and Broad, for instance—derive most of their logical ammunition. Kant himself testified to the lasting importance of the argument for any natural theology. "It . . . sketches the first outline of all the proofs in natural theology, an outline which has always been and always will be followed, however much embellished and disguised by superfluous additions" (*Critique of Pure Reason*, A604;B632).

A natural theologian, disillusioned with the Ontological Argument because it never emerges from the circle of concepts, will probably decide that an argument for the existence of God must start with empirical premises. He will expect the argument to show that the world can be as it is only on the assumption that a God exists in addition to the world. Even if he started with an argument from design to its explanation in a designer, the impetus of his quest for complete explanation will surely carry him on to ask, "Why does a world exist at all?" and in raising this question, he will have moved across to the territory of the Cosmological Argument. There is doubtless still a gulf between the First Cause and Sustainer of the world on the one hand and the God of Christianity and Judaism on the other; nevertheless, the gulf is not quite so vast as that between mere designer, planner, or architect and the God of religion.

But what if one is not a natural theologian? Many Protestant theologians accept the criticisms of Hume and Kant, accept the impossibility of any philosophical arguments for God, and put their trust in revelation alone. It does not follow, however, that their own theologies are now invulnerable to all the criticisms aimed at the Cosmological Argument. Certain of these criticisms question the intelligibility of theism in general—not merely whether it can be established in some way by unaided reason. Any theistic theologian must be able to speak meaningfully of a divine being who transcends the world entirely and yet in some way is related to it as the ultimate ground of its being. But it is precisely the meaningfulness of this language that is denied in some criticisms of the Cosmological Argument. Thus the importance of the continuing debate over this argument is not limited to champions of natural theology.

COSMOLOGICAL ARGUMENTS

Plato. In *The Laws* (Book X) Plato asks how one can account for the existence of motion in the world. Two kinds of motion are distinguished, motion that is imparted to an entity from other entities, and self-originated motion. To Plato, it is only living beings, beings with souls, that can originate movement. Imparted motion must ultimately depend upon self-originated motion; hence, Plato argues, all motion in the world is ultimately due to the activity of soul. Scientific studies (particularly astronomy) detect orderly movement in the cosmos, and it is inferred that the cosmos-controlling soul must be perfectly wise and good. (Plato is aware that in lesser degree disorder also exists in the world; in the theology of *The Laws* this is accounted for by the activity of another soul or souls.)

Aristotle. In *Metaphysics* (Book XII) Aristotle used a form of the Cosmological Argument in his attempt to explain motion—in the first instance, the eternal circular motion of the heavens. He thought that the only intellectually satisfying explanation would be in terms of a mover that was not itself moved and that was not merely passing on motion derived from some other source. Since that which is moved, as well as moving things, is intermediate, there must be something that moves things without being moved; this will be something eternal, it will be a substance, and it will be an actuality. But the Unmoved Mover, the deity at whom Aristotle thus arrived, did not move the heavens physically (for physical movement involves mutual contact, and the moved reacts upon the mover), but moved them by being the object of aspiration and desire. Since Aristotle described matter as eternal, his cosmological argument was not an account of its origin or creation. Whereas Plato's supreme deity is represented as purposing, planning, and acting vis-à-vis the cosmos, Aristotle's supreme deity enjoys a wholly contemplative (indeed *self*-contemplative) activity.

Thomas Aquinas. In the *Summa Theologica* (I, 2, 3), Aquinas set forth five "Ways," or rational approaches, to belief in God. Of these, the first three are forms of the Cosmological Argument. The First Way argues from change or motion, the Second Way from efficient causality, and the Third Way from contingency, to God as a necessary being.

(1) If a thing which imparts motion to another thing is itself in motion, it must have been set in motion by something else, and so on. An infinite regress is ruled out, for unless there were a first mover, there could be no subsequent movers.

(2) "Among phenomena we discover an order of efficient causes." The regress of cause behind cause cannot be infinite, for if there were not a first efficient cause, there could be no intermediate causes.

(3) Things in our experience can be or not be; there is no necessity about their existence. They are generated and corrupted. But if everything were like this, "once there would have been nothing at all"; hence, "nothing in existence even now." There must be, therefore, something the existence of which is necessary. "Necessary reality is always actual; it is never poised between existence and nonexistence." The necessity of necessary beings cannot, in every case, be caused by some other being; therefore there must exist some being that has "of itself its own necessity," namely, God.

Descartes. In the "Third Meditation" Descartes asks, "from whom could I . . . derive my existence" were there no God? "The conservation of a substance, in each moment of its duration, requires the same power and act that would be necessary to create it . . . ." But I am not aware of possessing any power by which to insure that my existence should continue from moment to moment; and therefore I "know that I am dependent upon some being different from myself." Since a cause must contain "as much reality" as its effect, this ultimate cause must be a "thinking being" and must possess "the idea and all the perfections I attribute to Deity."

Locke. Locke formulated the argument thus: "If . . . we know there is some real being, and that nonentity cannot produce any real being, it is . . . evident . . . that *from eternity there has been something;* since what was not from eternity had a beginning; and what had a beginning must be produced by something else." Further, certain beings such as ourselves are "knowing, intelligent" beings. It is "impossible that things wholly void of knowledge . . . should produce a knowing being . . ." (*Essay Concerning Human Understanding*, Book IV, Ch. 10). And so the argument deduces God.

The Neo-Scholastics. Neoscholastic theologians continue to lean most heavily upon Aquinas' Five Ways; the Third Way, the argument from contingency, has been especially stressed. There is a strong tendency, however, to see in the Ways a single thrust of argument that aims to show the derivative and dependent nature of the world as we experience it, and at the same time to lead to an awareness of the wholly different mode of being of the God who (necessarily) upholds it. To some proponents of the argument, it has the power of a conclusive reasoned proof; to others, it is a preparation for an intuition of transcendence—an intuition or insight that cannot properly be verbalized as a discursive, step-by-step demonstration.

CRITICISMS OF COSMOLOGICAL ARGUMENTS

Plato. Plato's version of the Cosmological Argument has been challenged in various ways. Its most vulnerable assumption is that motion and rest are not equally natural or original, that the existence of motion needs explanation in a way that the existence of rest does not. As we shall see in several examples, the possibility of an infinite series of past events, the possibility that there never was a beginning to motion, tells against a formidable number of cosmological arguments. In Plato's own day, the atomist Democritus denied that motion was derivative from soul or from anything else. For him, motion was eternal. (See the neat discussion of this by Walter Kaufmann in *Critique of Religion and Philosophy*, London, 1959, Sec. 44.)

Aristotle. Aristotle's cosmology and conception of the Unmoved Mover are both so far from current science or metaphysics that his version of the argument seems rather unconvincing and remote to us. The God of Aristotle's *Metaphysics* neither made nor sustains the world's being; he only elicits motion in it. He has no knowledge of the world and cannot be said to act upon it. Aristotle's importance to the development of the Cosmological Argument comes chiefly through the Christian reconstructions of Thomas Aquinas.

Descartes. Two remarks may be made on the quotations from Descartes. First, let us consider the claim that something must "conserve" objects in being from moment to moment, since they have no power in themselves to do so.

This might simply be a way of drawing attention to the causal interdependence of objects. If so, the argument would stand or fall with the possibility of causal arguments to God in general. But it might be that objects and organisms are being tacitly understood as derivative and dependent in a more radical—and philosophically questionable—way: as the note of a flute is dependent upon the player's continuing to blow, as a shadow or a projected film is dependent upon the continuance of a light supply. But we have no reason to believe that all existents are like this, that they are dependent for their very being upon continual behind-the-scenes activity. Changes in environment may produce changes of state in the entities within it; but even dramatic changes of state—for example, the death of an organism—are not identical with absolute loss of being. (For a fuller discussion of the dependence of the world on God, see CREATION, RELIGIOUS DOCTRINE OF.)

Second, the path of argument from First Cause, or Necessary Being, to a Christian personal God must be a complex and problematic one. Proponents of the Cosmological Argument have sometimes improperly shortened it, as Descartes does in the quotations presented here, and as Locke did by similar tactics. Descartes wrote, "There must at least be as much reality in the cause as in its effect"; Locke held that it is "impossible that things wholly void of knowledge . . . should produce a knowing being."

For a rejoinder we can turn to John Stuart Mill. "Where is the proof that nothing can have caused a mind except another mind?" asked Mill in his article "Theism," in *Three Essays on Religion.* "From what except from experience can we know what can produce what—what causes are adequate to what effects?" Mill argues against the assumption "that no causes can give rise to products of a more precious or elevated kind than themselves." Our knowledge of nature bears out the opposite view—that higher organisms can emerge from lower. Since Mill's day our thinking about nature has become progressively less mechanistic and anthropocentric and more deeply evolutionary. The task of the apologist to imbue his First Cause with life and mind has become correspondingly more arduous.

ANALYSIS OF THE COSMOLOGICAL ARGUMENT

The Cosmological Argument contains two key concepts—necessity and causality. In the argument's various forms one or the other may be dominant, or both may play an equally important role. We shall consider each of these three possibilities in turn.

Necessity. If there exists "contingent being," it is argued, there must also exist "necessary being." Necessary in what sense? If the "causally necessary" is relegated to the second heading, what senses remain? Logical necessity has been a tempting option, but against it the criticisms of Hume, Kant, and their successors have been particularly crushing. Necessity in the logical sense is a characteristic not of beings but of propositions. To speak of a necessary being is as crude a category mistake as to speak of a "contradictory sheep" or a "self-evident frying pan"—and for exactly the same reasons.

Could we not, however, agree with this judgment and speak of the proposition "God exists" as necessarily true? The difficulty now arises that this is an existential proposition, not one affirming connections between concepts; and it is very difficult to see how such an existential proposition can ever be logically necessary. If we were to treat it as if it did concern relations between concepts, we should have to treat existence as a predicate. The proposition would then assert that among the elements that make up the complex concept of deity, existence is necessarily included. That would indeed make the proposition "God is nonexistent" contradictory and the proposition "God exists" logically necessary. But it would sadly mishandle the logic of existence. We can describe some being as good, powerful, and wise; but if we add to our list "existent," we have ceased to describe, to add new predicates, and are doing something logically quite different. "That's what it's like," we say, ending our description: "and there is one of them." Kant's way of expressing this was to accuse the Cosmological Argument of secretly relying upon the Ontological Argument, although professing to be an independent demonstration of God's existence. In essence, Kant's criticism is justified, though the detail of his argument contains certain logical slips. (See J. J. C. Smart, "The Existence of God," in *New Essays in Philosophical Theology*, London, 1955, pp. 28 ff.).

Hume pithily stated that "there is no Being, whose existence is demonstrable"; and that "whatever we conceive as existent, we can also conceive as nonexistent" (*Dialogues Concerning Natural Religion*, Sec. IX). If we are confining ourselves to the issue of logical necessity alone, and if we ask ourselves "Is God's nonexistence conceivable?" the answer is plainly "yes." Suppose the rejoinder were made: "God's nonexistence is not conceivable. Were there no God, there could be no world and no one able to do any conceiving." It could be replied that this brings in causal issues which for the moment were being set aside. Even if God's nonexistence entailed the world's nonexistence, we can meaningfully entertain a proposition asserting the nonexistence of both. (To do that, we do not have to be able to imagine this possibility in the sense of visualizing it or experiencing it vicariously.) As C. B. Martin points out in *Religious Belief* (Ithaca, N.Y., 1959), if we want to maintain that "the statement 'There was and will be nothing' [is] either meaningless or self-contradictory . . . [we should be forced to judge that the statement 'There was and will be something' is] . . . either meaningless or tautological." It is surely neither.

Causality. Many recent defenders of the Cosmological Argument agree that whatever is meant by "necessary being" (or the "necessity" with which God exists), it cannot be logical necessity. There remain, however, other possibilities—causal necessity or (more generally) various kinds of factual necessity. One can interpret the pair of contrasting terms "contingent" and "necessary" without any reference to logical necessity. The contingent is the finite, that which has a beginning in time; the necessary is the independent, incorruptible, and indestructible. It is unconditioned in the sense that no conceivable event could cause it not to be or to become other than it is. It is also the condition of the existence of anything else—of the contingent and dependent. (*Cf.* John Hick, "God as Necessary Being" and T. Penelhum, "Divine Necessity.") We must now ask if a valid cosmological argument can be constructed using the idea of factual necessity.

Thomists give the argument an empirical appearance: "It is evident to our senses . . . that . . . some things are in motion." The world we know is a structure of causally dependent objects; none of them is ontologically self-sufficient. Now, mere prolongation of the lines of causal dependence cannot, even in theory, lead to a complete, satisfying explanation of the existence of any object. Therefore, something quite different has to be done, namely, to posit an ontologically self-sufficient being, the inaugurator and sustainer of the world's processes.

The critics, led once more by Hume and Kant, argue that if we are talking of causality, then our discourse must remain within the sphere in which alone the concept of cause has been given its meaning and role, that is to say, the relating of event to event in the spatiotemporal world of experience. If the concept is used outside that context which confers meaning upon it, we shall utter mystifying nonsense. But exactly this occurs when the causal process is said to require an initiator or maintainer which is not itself an event or events in the world of experience. Even if all events in nature do have causes, that does not entitle us to demand a nonnatural cause for nature as a whole or for any events in nature. We may compare Kant in the *Critique of Pure Reason:* "[the] principle whereby from the contingent we infer a cause . . . is applicable only in the sensible world; outside that world it has no meaning whatsoever." The Cosmological Argument not only assumes that we can infer to some kind of First Cause but also that we may look for it "beyond this world in a realm into which [the causal] series can never be extended."

If one wishes to be consistently empiricist, one has to admit that the universe, the sum of things, has not been examined and found to have, or not to have, a First Cause. In this sense of "universe" there is necessarily only one universe and no possibility of inductive arguments based on observations of universes other than our own. (See Hume, *Enquiry Concerning Human Understanding*, Sec. XI; also A. G. N. Flew, *Hume's Philosophy of Belief*, London, 1961, Ch. 9.)

Someone might choose at this point to stop being empirical or Kantian but to retain the principle that everything must have a cause—retain it as a metaphysical insight, a demand of reason. The principle would be construed as a quite general one, able to include the universe itself as well as individual events within it. But what now of God? Will he not also require a cause in this interpretation? Neither God nor any other being could now halt the regress of causes; unless God is made to do so by definition, which would be a purely verbal, arbitrary solution.

J. S. Mill, indeed, found a similar difficulty in his own rather different treatment of the First Cause argument. "The cause of every change," he argued, "is a prior change; and such it cannot but be; for if there were no new antecedent, there would not be a new consequent." As far as our experience goes, therefore, "the causes as well as the effects [have] a beginning in time, and [are] themselves caused. . . . Our experience, instead of furnishing an argument for a first cause, is repugnant to it."

One of the chief hazards for a causal argument to God is the possibility that the causal process is itself infinite, that it has no beginning in time. Aquinas tried to rule this out. He denied that one could "go on to infinity with efficient causes, for in an ordered series the first is the cause of the intermediate and the intermediate is the cause of the last." "Take away the cause, and the effect also goes. Therefore if there were not a first among efficient causes . . . there would be no intermediate causes nor an ultimate effect."

But what exactly are we doing if we take away the First Cause and posit instead an infinite succession of causes and effects? There is no specific cause whose existence or efficacy as a cause is being removed: no phenomenon is being robbed of its cause and thus robbed of its being. For all that is being said is that no matter what phenomenon you mention, that phenomenon will have a cause, which itself has a cause.

To insist that there must be a First Cause of all is not really to render the causal process intellectually transparent; it is, rather, to put into it a profound element of obscurity. For it is to say that one entity exists for whose existence no explanation can be found. But the believer in an infinite causal process can claim that no phenomenon whatever is, in theory, beyond explanation. "But how did it all start?" says the objector, "What of the beginning?" "It did not start," comes the answer; "There was no beginning." If this answer is held to be unintelligible, a reply at least *ad hominem* can be made to the theist. He may be reminded that he wishes to say identical things about God. (See, on these arguments, Paul Edwards, "The Cosmological Argument," in *The Rationalist Annual*, London, 1959, pp. 63 ff.)

In the Third Way, Thomas Aquinas argued: "All things cannot be . . . contingent, for what is able not to be may be reckoned as once a nonbeing, and were everything like that once there would have been nothing at all . . . " and thus "nothing would ever have begun."

Critics have observed that although every entity may be "able not to be," it does not follow that all of them must exercise this ability at any one instant. Even if we take "contingent" to mean "actually beginning to exist at some moment in time," we could not rule out the possibility that the universe might consist of an infinite series of temporally overlapping entities. No living species is composed of immortal members, yet species continue—or if they disappear, it is not simply because of their contingency. Locke tried to argue that since "nonentity cannot produce any real being, it is an evident demonstration that *from eternity there has been something.*" "Something," yes; but not necessarily always one and the same something. (See J. F. Ross and C. J. F. Williams, "God and 'Logical Necessity,'" *Philosophical Quarterly*, Vol. 11, 1961, 22 ff. and 356 ff.)

Even if we might "go on to infinity" in this direction—backward in time—a defender of the argument will deny that this is possible in that other and most important direction—where we search for the conditions which allow an entity to remain in being or in a particular state of being, or allow an event to occur now. This does not involve a regress into the past but into the hierarchy of contemporary causal factors necessary and sufficient to account for the entity or event. An explanation of a cloudburst over London, for instance, may be given in terms of cloud, wind, and temperature conditions. These we may explain in terms of larger systems of atmospheric pressure, due in turn to air movements in the upper atmosphere. To explain the movements, we refer to many still wider factors like the effect of the earth's rotation, its position relative to the sun, and so on; and we need not stop there. Surely, then, a presently existing First Cause must be operating for all this to be possible, or else how could the dependent causes themselves operate?

But the same rejoinder can be made. Think of any one of these necessary and contemporary causal factors. If one denies that there exists a First Cause, then one is not denying that *this* causal factor exists, nor is one denying it any of the causes necessary to maintain it in being.

It might be sensible at this stage for the defender of the argument to reflect whether factual necessity must be construed as causal necessity. We have been seeing how the causal versions fare little better under criticism than those that turn upon logical necessity. But there are still other considerations which prompt one to look for some third possibility. If God, for instance, is related to the world as its efficient cause, as the initiator and maintainer of its causal processes, that comes perilously near to robbing him of his divine otherness. That any member of the series of causes and effects in nature could be directly identified with God or the activity of God derogates from his status as the one who infinitely transcends nature. This is a major difficulty for a sophisticated theism: It may indeed find that its doctrine of transcendence has virtually excluded any possibility of an intelligible relation between God and world. But that is too general a problem for the present article to explore. It is enough to note that there may be religious as well as philosophical objections to thinking of God as the world's cause.

We might follow up the suggestion that the relation between God and world (call it the cosmological relation) is an utterly unique relation, only adumbrated, never exemplified, in the various relations of dependence that obtain between things and events in the world itself. "First Cause," "Creator," "Author," and other such concepts no more than hint in the direction of this quite unconceptualizable relation of thoroughgoing ontological dependence. If an argument for the existence of God is based on the assumption that he must be, if anything, a cause in the literal sense, of course an impasse is reached. Failure shows only that the cosmological relation has been crudely misconceived.

If someone now goes on to say that he sees or intuits that the world is in fact dependent upon God in this thoroughgoing and unique way, can there be any argument for or against his claim? For it, one might argue that certain basic religious experiences—experiences of the numinous, the *mysterium tremendum et fascinans*—are constantly described, even if stammeringly, in terms that fit in very neatly with the claim about God's relation to the world. Numinous experience is experience of a being too "other" for our concepts to grasp, but beyond doubt a being before whom our derivativeness and our insufficiency are borne in upon us in a weird and momentous way.

Yet there is no compulsion being laid here upon a reluctant and skeptical reason. Numinous experience is not immune in principle from attempted naturalistic and noncognitive explanations. The question may be asked: Have we adequate reasons for believing that this so-called elusive cosmological relation is a relation at all and not merely the ghost of those relations (cause–effect, artist–artifact, parent–child), which we have in fact whittled away to nothing in our hopeless attempt to apply them to God and the world? We may not have sharpened the cosmological relationship to a fine point but—in our nervousness—sharpened it away altogether.

A tantalizing new difficulty is that although the straightforward causal argument to God clearly did have some empirical impetus, the same is not true of the revised version that we are discussing. If the cosmological relation is altogether unique, we are no longer being led along a regress of familiar terms, linked by a familiar relation, to a final term in God. It looks as if we cannot eliminate the two weaknesses simultaneously. Either we have the empirical basis and impetus—and the weakness that God becomes too much like a nonmysterious part of nature—or else we can restore the mystery and ineffability and lose the empirical thrust.

Necessity with causality. There are many presentations of the argument in which the strands of necessity and causality are intertwined, both vocabularies being used simultaneously. Here is their general pattern.

In the study of nature we seek intelligible structure. A certain degree of intelligibility is achieved when we manage to subsume events under natural laws; and we may subsume these laws again under still more general laws. But even the most general laws we know are intellectually unsatisfying in that they are still mere statements of how things in fact happen. There is no intrinsic necessity about them; they still cry out for further explanation. The final step is to say that an ultimate explanation must be one that eliminates all mere happening—that is, one that shows how all mere happenings are derived from a completely rational (or suprarational) divine mind. Such ultimate explanation must be possible in theory; otherwise even partial explanations would fail.

The last point may be considered first. One could argue against it by insisting that the criteria used for a successful explanation are multiple, that they vary immensely from one field of investigation to another, and (most pertinently) that explanation does not always generate infinite regresses. If an explanation is not ultimate or cosmically comprehensive, it does not have to be judged an unsatisfactory explanation. Chains of explanation can come to natural endings when the specific problem requiring explanation has been solved. Suppose, for instance, that my typewriter disappears. If my wife reminds me that I had given a colleague permission to borrow it that day, an explanation has been furnished and I need probe no further. If I do need to probe further, that will be only if a complication, a new problem, reveals itself—say, if my colleague denies that he had in fact borrowed it.

There are important parallels here with the problem of the meaning of life. The theist sometimes assumes, or argues, that if a person's life does not have a meaning or purpose as a whole (presumably a God-conferred purpose), then that life is wholly meaningless and futile. But a person may infuse his life with a variety of overlapping purposes, thus making his life eminently purposeful, although it has no over-all total purpose or meaning. So, too, limited explanations can be of the utmost value in dealing with problems of practice and theory, although no overarching total explanation of the world is attainable.

The ideal of comprehensive explanation, if taken as the eliminating of all but necessary truths, is quite certainly a spurious ideal. It derives from the intellectual impressiveness of logical and mathematical systems that do have this structure; but such systems are not, unfortunately, accounts of the world. Unless we were to identify God with the sum of things (thus abandoning theism for pantheism), we should always have the existence of God itself as a fact that could not be rendered necessary. But we have seen reason to deny that any existential proposition can be logically necessary, whether about world or God or the two taken as identical. So pantheism would really be in no better state. (Compare C. D. Broad, *Religion, Philosophy and Psychical Research*, pp. 183 ff.; C. B. Martin, *Religious Belief*, Ch. 9; and Paul Edwards, *Rationalist Annual*, 1959, pp. 63 ff.)

Some of the Cosmological Argument's keenest critics—Kant most memorably—have testified to the extraordinary hauntingness of the argument even while they expose and explode its logical confusions.

> Unconditioned necessity, which we so indispensably require as the last bearer of all things, is for human reason the veritable abyss. Eternity itself, in all its terrible sublimity . . . is far from making the same overwhelming impression on the mind; for it only *measures* the duration of things, it does not *support* them. We cannot put aside, and yet also cannot endure, the thought that a being, which we represent to ourselves as supreme amongst all possible beings, should as it were, say to itself: "I am from eternity to eternity, and outside me there is nothing save what is through my will, *but whence then am I?*" All support here fails us . . . . (*Critique of Pure Reason*, A613;B641)

The metaphysical pathos, the expressive tone, of the argument is a product of many factors, some philosophical, some religious. There is ontological astonishment at there being a world at all; ontological anxiety at our individual dependence and precariousness, our being poised between existence and nonexistence; and a vertiginous awareness of the limits of thought. Those elements of religious experience that prompt belief in a transcendent, numinous deity can add their peculiar contribution. These are all powerful ingredients; their presence together in reflection and meditation upon the cosmological line of argument can certainly yield a "terrible sublimity." It can also make most difficult the task of sober philosophical appraisal.

Bibliography

STATEMENTS AND CRITICISMS

The works of historically important philosophers are mentioned in the text of the article. For the Cosmological Argument as defended, revised, or otherwise sympathetically discussed by twentieth-century philosophers, see C. A. Campbell, *Selfhood and Godhood* (London, 1957), Lectures 18–19, an idealist version owing much to F. H. Bradley; M. C. D'Arcy, *The Nature of Belief* (London, 1931); A. Farrer, *Finite and Infinite* (London, 1943); E. L. Mascall, *Existence and Analogy* (London, 1949), and *He Who Is* (London, 1943); and Dom Illtyd Trethowan, *An Essay in Christian Philosophy* (London, 1954).

FURTHER TWENTIETH-CENTURY STUDIES

In addition to the works mentioned in the text, the following may be consulted. Many of the logical complexities discussed in this article can be found exemplified or analyzed in these; and in some cases (notably in Smart's *Reasons and Faith* and Lewis' *Our Experience of God*) the religious experience out of which cosmological reasoning emerges is also analyzed: C. D. Broad, *Religion, Philosophy and Psychical Research* (London, 1953), pp. 175–201; A. C. Ewing, *The Fundamental Questions of Philosophy* (London, 1951), Ch. 11; R. L. Franklin, "Necessary Being," in *Australasian Journal of Philosophy*, Vol. 35 (1957), 97 ff.; Ronald W. Hepburn, *Christianity and Paradox* (London, 1958), Chs. 9 and 10, and "From World to God," in *Mind*, Vol. 72 (1963), 40–50; John Hick, "God as Necessary Being," in *Journal of Philosophy*, Vol. 57 (1960), 725 ff.; H. D. Lewis, *Our Experience of God* (London, 1959); T. Penelhum, "Divine Necessity," in *Mind*, Vol. 69 (1960), 175 ff.; Bertrand Russell and F. C. Copleston, "The Existence of God—A Debate," in Bertrand Russell, *Why I Am Not a Christian*, Paul Edwards, ed. (London, 1957); and Ninian Smart, *Reasons and Faiths* (London, 1958), and "Paradox in Religion," in *PAS*, Supp. Vol. 33 (1959), 219 ff.

Since this article was written, there has appeared a study by Patterson Brown, "St. Thomas on Necessary Being," in *Philosophical Review*, Vol. 73 (1964), 76–90. This points to some inadequacies in recent criticism of Aquinas' thought (by, for instance, C. B. Martin, Paul Edwards, F. C. Copleston, and the present writer). Brown reminds his readers that for Aquinas there was a plurality of "necessary beings," beings that do not have in themselves a principle of corruption. Of these, however, all but one are derivative, in that they are created *ex nihilo* by God and are capable of being annihilated. God alone is underivatively necessary.

RONALD W. HEPBURN

COSMOLOGY. The term "cosmology" stands for a family of related inquiries, all in some sense concerned with the world at large. Two main subgroups of uses may be distinguished: those belonging to philosophy and those belonging to science.

"Cosmology" has received wide currency as a name for a branch of metaphysics, ever since Christian von Wolff, in his *Discursus Praeliminaris de Philosophia in Genere* (1728), gave cosmology a prominent place in his classificatory scheme of the main forms of philosophical knowledge and distinguished this branch from ontology, theology, and psychology. (See *Discourse on Philosophy in General*, translated by R. J. Blackwell, Indianapolis, 1963, Para. 77). Despite the severe strictures that Kant leveled against the pursuit of rational cosmology in his *Critique of Pure Reason*, the term has continued to enjoy a standard use among many philosophers. For example, it occupies a central place in the manuals of scholastic philosophy; these adhere, for the most part, to the Wolffian scheme of classification of the branches of metaphysics. The term has been used, too, by many philosophers not in the scholastic tradition; for example, A. E. Taylor in his *Elements of Metaphysics* (London, 1903) assigns to cosmology the task of considering "the meaning and validity of the most universal conceptions of which we seek to understand the nature of the individual objects which make up the experienced physical world, 'extension,' 'succession,' 'space,' 'time,' 'number,' 'magnitude,' 'motion,' 'change,' 'quality,' and the more complex categories of 'matter,' 'force,' 'causality,' 'interaction,' 'thinghood,' and so forth" (p. 43). Cosmology is sometimes understood even more broadly, as being synonymous with speculative philosophy in its most comprehensive sense. Thus in Whitehead's *Process and Reality* (New York, 1929), whose subtitle is "An Essay in Cosmology," the attempt is made to construct a categorial scheme of general ideas "in terms of which every element of our experience can be interpreted" (p. 4).

In its second major use, the term "cosmology" designates a science in which the joint efforts of the observational astronomer and the theoretical physicist are devoted to giving an account of the large-scale properties of the astronomical or physical universe as a whole. The task of constructing models of the universe that are suggested by and tested by appeals to the observational findings of the astronomer distinguishes the enterprise of scientific cosmology from the a priori investigations of rational cosmology (as a branch of metaphysics) and the purely conceptual and categorial analyses of the speculative philosopher. Nevertheless, even scientific cosmology poses a number of philosophical questions. The sum of these—and they are principally methodological and epistemological in character—constitutes the philosophy of scientific cosmology. The present article is concerned with the philosophy of cosmology in this sense. Attention will be focused on a central theme in this area: the question whether cosmology must employ a method different from that employed in other empirical sciences because of its distinctive subject matter, namely, the universe as a unique system.

DESCRIPTION OR EXPLANATION?

Is the familiar distinction between description and explanation (or the corresponding one drawn between sciences still in the early stages that are primarily descriptive, and those that have progressed to the predominating use of the explanatory aspects of theory) a distinction that can be profitably applied in giving an account of the logic of cosmology? No simple and unqualified answer can be given. For, on the one hand, cosmology, in attempting to gain knowledge of the universe as a whole, certainly is not content to rest with the observational reports of the astronomer, and therefore cannot be classed with the descriptive sciences. On the other hand, in advancing to the level of theory, as cosmology in a qualified sense certainly does, it is not primarily concerned with the explanation of laws—as is the case with other explanatory sciences.

If by description is meant giving an account of some single event or object in observational terms, or (in an extended sense of "description") formulating a generalization (law) in observational terms which refers to the observable or measurable properties and relations of a class of events, then cosmology, which is interested in giving an account of the universe as a whole, is not engaged in description. Even if we recognize, as we must, the descriptive activities of observational cosmology as a branch of observational astronomy, these fall short of giving us an adequate account of the universe as a whole. All that astronomy can give us is a description of the domain of objects and events within the range of its most powerful instruments. At the present time, however, these instruments, have not reached the limit, if there is a limit, to what is in principle observable. Moreover, even if the universe were in some sense finite and wholly explorable by actually or theoretically available instruments, the statement that what is thus observationally explored is in fact the universe as a whole would not be warranted by observational evidence alone. Such a statement could not, therefore, be part of the description of the universe, insofar as this description is a report of what is found. The claim that the universe is open to complete inspection requires the support of theory. It is a statement which is not included *in* the description, but is a rider *to* the description—to the effect that the description as given is of the universe as complete; considerations other than purely observational ones are needed to support this claim.

If cosmology is not content with description, does it then aim at giving explanations? Here our answer must be qualified. In the case of ordinary empirical generalizations, where there are multiple instances of some phenomenon of which we have examined a limited number, we say that the law supported by this evidence may be used as a reliable rule of inference. Since the law applies to a kind of subject matter, or a type of phenomenon, it can be upheld as a useful means for predicting and explaining those instances that can be brought within its scope. But in cosmology, the primary goal is not to establish laws. The universe, by definition, is a unique object or system. Cosmology does not undertake to establish laws about universes; at best one can establish laws about the constituents of the universe. The relation which the observable portion of the universe bears to the universe is that of part to presumed whole, rather than that of instance to law. Hence, if to explain means to bring an instance under a law, this mode of explanation, which is a characteristic concern of other branches of physical science, does not characterize cosmology.

Can it be said, then, cosmology aims at giving explanations in the sense in which theories are employed to explain laws? Here our answer, once more, cannot be a straightforward "yes" or "no." The characteristic device employed by theoretical cosmology is a model of the universe, and a model in many respects functions precisely as a theory does. It is a conceptual construction that cannot be said to be a mere report of what is already found in observation, nor even an anticipated description of what might be found in future observations. Rather, it is a means for making the observational data themselves intelligible. However, the facts which the cosmologist wants to explain are not laws in the ordinary sense of the term, and so in this respect the purpose of a model of the universe is not identical with that of a theory in the ordinary sense.

Consider, for example, the question "Why is the apparent magnitude of galaxies correlated with their red shift?" This question asks for an explanation of an important datum of observation. The observed fact is sometimes called Hubble's "law," but it is a law only in the peculiar sense in which we refer to Kepler's laws as "laws." That is, Hubble's law tells us something about a particular distribution or process of a unique set of objects, namely the system of galaxies, just as Kepler's laws tell us something about the orbits of the planets in our solar system, not in any solar system. In general, however, laws of science are characterized by their universal form. They are unrestricted in scope and are not ostensibly tied to objects or events specifically located in some particular space-time region. Thus Newton's law of gravitation, for example, says that for *any* two bodies, the gravitational force that holds between them is inversely as the square of their distance apart and proportional to their masses. Now when we deal with the system of bodies and processes that constitute the unique configuration we call the universe, we are not dealing with *any* configuration of events and objects; we are dealing with the configuration actually observed and given.

An interesting and important question that can be raised here, however, is whether the unrestricted laws of ordinary physics are not themselves, in a more profound sense, relatively restricted, since they apply to bodies or phenomena within the ultimately unique configuration that constitutes the physical universe. From this point of view, the study of cosmology sets the environment and limiting framework for all other branches of physical science. Hence it is not unreasonable to expect—as E. A. Milne, D. W. Sciama, and others have pointed out—that one may hope to understand the laws of physics themselves in terms of the unique background making up the universe studied in cosmology. However, such a claim is associated only with certain specific models, namely, the kinematic model as worked out by Milne and the steady state model as sketched by Hermann Bondi and Sciami, and therefore this idea of explaining all laws by a cosmological model cannot be held up as a working goal for all cosmological models. In fact, the majority of models developed within the framework of general relativity theory have not been designed to embody this feature.

OBSERVATION AND THEORY

The study of cosmology has two lines of attack, that of the observational astronomer and that of the theoretical physicist. One might say that both the observational astronomer and the theoretical cosmologist are studying the universe, though from different vantage points, or that one supplies observational data about the universe that the other undertakes to interpret; but this is, at best, only a sketch of the situation and is in some ways seriously misleading. For it will not do to say that both the astronomer and the theoretical cosmologist are studying the universe, as if the universe is laid out for identification before them and the only difference between them is in approach and method. If we look more closely at the study of cosmology, the situation is rather different.

The observational astronomer is not confronted with the universe as an observationally complete whole. Instead, he obtains observational clues from various instruments about a large population of identifiable subsystems—namely, individual galaxies and clusters of galaxies. This population of observable entities is sometimes referred to as "the observable universe." However, this phrase is not to be understood in the sense that we have independent means for identifying the universe and that we wish to refer to it insofar as it is being observed. "The observable universe" is not the same as "the universe observed." What the astronomer reports on of relevance to cosmology is an observable population of galaxies and clusters of galaxies. These observational reports have to do with such matters as the spatial distribution of galaxies, their systematic motions, density, spectroscopic patterns, individual shapes, and stellar composition. The population of subsystems that makes up the observable universe is now, as in a sense it must always be, a finite population. With the advance in the power and sensitivity of instruments, knowledge of the extent of this population and the refinement in the details of the reports about this population are improved. Although it is regarded as likely that further advances in observational resources will disclose a wider population of subsystems similar to those already observed, it must be remembered that it is always possible for further observations to disclose as basic constituents of the universe astronomical units of a higher degree of inclusiveness than galaxies or clusters of galaxies, or even entities of an altogether different type from those heretofore disclosed. Whatever may be the case in the future, it certainly is the case at present that what comes within the observational reaches of the astronomer is definitely not the universe as an absolute whole, if there is in fact such a whole.

When we say that the theoretical cosmologist studies the universe in order to understand it or make it intelligible, what is it that he studies? He does not study the universe in any direct way, if that means having before him a readily identified object which he tries to comprehend, for example by subsuming it under some law. Nor, as we have just seen, does the universe he studies consist of a complete population of entities about which the observational astronomer furnishes him detailed reports. The theoretical cosmologist is not given information about the universe as a whole, nor even about what lies beyond the immediate range of the astronomer's instruments.

What then does he study? A brief and simple answer is to say that he constructs a model of the universe and that he studies the way in which this model may be used to interpret the observational data already available. The cosmologist will use his model to interpret the data assembled by the observational astronomer and to guide the astronomer in the search for further data. Insofar as the use of theoretical models proves satisfactory, we may say that cosmology has helped us to understand the universe and to make it intelligible. This is not to be understood, however, as meaning that even at the end of a relatively successful course of inquiry, the cosmologist has been able to confront the universe directly as some kind of readily identifiable object, system, or class of objects. What is to be understood by "the universe," in short, can only be approached and identified through the use of models, not independently of them.

THE MODEL AND ITS CONSTRUCTION

The kind of model that the cosmologist constructs is wholly conceptual rather than material. It consists of different sorts of symbols including ordinary language, mathematical language, diagrams, and charts, all of which will normally be employed in presenting a given model. A model of the universe is not something that can be directly visualized or completely represented in a pictorial diagram. Consider, for example, a typical model in which use is made of a geometric mode of representation according to which the galaxies are treated as a set of mathematical points that trace out a set of geodesic curves in space time. In this case, the metric of this set of points is given by the general Robertson–Walker expression for the space-time interval (ds):

$$ds^2 = dt^2 - \left(\frac{R^2(t)}{c^2}\right)\left\{\frac{dr^2 + r^2\,d\theta^2 + r^2\sin^2\theta\,d\phi^2}{(1 + kr^2/4)^2}\right\}$$

where $R(t)$ is the expansion factor, k is a constant whose value determines whether space is Euclidean or non-Euclidean, c is the velocity of light, and r, θ, and ϕ are spatial coordinates. In addition to the specification of purely geometric or kinematic features, which are specified by introducing appropriate values for the curvature constant (k) and the expansion factor ($R(t)$), a model will also require some assignment of specific dynamic or gravitational properties to the entities thus represented. Additional formulas will then be required, and these will normally involve relativity theory or some equivalent branch of physics. It is clear that however much a simple diagram making use of dots and lines may serve to give us a visual representation of what we are talking about, this hardly suffices to encompass all those additional features of the model not included in the diagram.

Although the cosmologist cannot inspect the original, the universe itself, he nevertheless undertakes to make a model of it. How is this done? The answer is to be found by noting the various clues and sources to which the cosmologist appeals in determining the properties to be assigned to his model. These are of two principal types: observational clues provided by the astronomer, and theoretical principles thought to be of relevance to the cosmologic problem.

Observational clues. In general, the observational data the astronomer gathers aid the cosmologist by suggesting ways of assigning certain idealized properties to the model, by providing empirically ascertained values for the constants and variables in the model, and by offering tests for the adequacy of the model as a tool for predicting observable matters of fact.

Idealized properties. The kinds of entities and their properties that the astronomer observes suggest to the cosmologist the lines to follow in developing a simplified and idealized conception of the universe. Let us take some examples. The galaxies, though of enormous physical bulk, may be considered for purposes of the model as particles making up a continuous and perfect fluid. The advantage of treating the galaxies in this fashion is that it permits a great simplification of the problem, to which readily available mathematical tools of representation and calculation may be applied. Here, of course, the cosmologist adopts a technique which is universally adopted in other branches of physical science and with similar justification. If necessary, suitable corrections to this idealization can always be introduced when application is made of the model to "describe" the actual universe.

An important feature of the domain of galaxies already observed is their spatial distribution. The actual spatial distribution of the galaxies is roughly homogeneous and isotropic when fairly large volumes of space are considered. On a smaller scale, departures from homogeneity become more noticeable, in the clustering of the galaxies, for example. When still smaller volumes of space are investigated, homogeneity breaks down altogether. In general, then, the claim to the uniformity of distribution of galaxies can be upheld only if one takes a sufficiently large unit of volume, say 3.5×10^8 parsecs in diameter. Yet in constructing his model, and as a first approximation, the cosmologist will assign a complete homogeneity to his model of the universe. The expression "cosmological principle" is commonly used to designate this feature of spatial homogeneity. Models that satisfy this cosmological principle, and thus possess the feature of spatial homogeneity, are known as uniform model universes. When put into mathematical language, a uniform model universe is one possessing a constant curvature at a given moment of time. In the language of general relativity theory, since the density and pressure of material that make up the model are the same in all volumes of space at a given time, whatever their size, a geometric representation of this fact will involve the use of one or another of the spaces of constant curvature. All segments of space of the entire universe will have the same curvature. Such a model clearly requires a process of idealizing and simplifying the spatial distribution of bodies actually observed. For if we were to use the language of geometry to describe the actually observed spatial distribution, we should have to note the actual local departures from homogeneity or constancy of curvature.

In constructing a model of the universe that embodies the feature of spatial homogeneity or constancy of curvature, it is not enough to specify what that curvature is at the present moment of cosmic time. A fully determined model requires (in addition to other features) that the spatial properties of the universe be specified for any point in its past or future. Here there are, broadly speaking, two possibilities. According to one, the spatial properties of the universe remain the same at all times; this view is upheld by those who adhere to the "perfect cosmological principle" and use it to define the properties of the steady state model. A second alternative is to adopt the cosmological principle in its more restricted form as designating merely spatial uniformity, as is the case with the orthodox cosmological models of general relativity. For such models, the entire history of the universe, from a spatial point of view, could be specified if one knew just one thing—the rate at which the distance between any two galaxies changes with time. In a universe characterized simply by the cosmological principle, since an observer would always find a spatially isotropic distribution of particles about him, the only basic feature subject to change is a temporally noticeable feature, namely, changes in the density of the distribution of particles. Such changes in the density might then serve to define a cosmic "clock."

Empirically obtained values. A second important function which the appeal to observational data serves in the construction of cosmological models is that of yielding empirically obtained values for some of the constants and variables of theory. For example, in relativistic uniform models of the expanding universe, the defining characteristics of a particular model need to be specified by assigning values for the following quantities: the cosmological constant (λ), the temporal pattern of the universe as determined by evaluating the function $R(t)$, the values for the velocity factor and the acceleration factor in the velocity–distance relation which specify how the galaxies are moving, the density (ρ) and the pressure (p) of the material and energetic content that fills the universe, and the curvature constant (k). Observational evidence is, at present, either not available at all or not accurate enough to give sufficiently precise determinations for all of these terms. The cosmologist must, therefore, use whatever data is available to eliminate those models that are incompatible with present observations and to suggest lines of inquiry that will help to narrow the field down to those models that can be further tested by observation.

One over-all condition for the acceptance of a model is, of course, the consistency of the empirically obtained values it proposes. In a particular model, a particular combination of empirically assigned curvature and density values, for example, may lead to a calculated "age of the universe" that will be inconsistent with an independently obtained estimate for the lower bound of such an "age"; the estimated time scale of the universe will be too short. In general what is sought is a model all of whose empirically ascertainable values are mutually consistent within the available limits of accuracy.

Empirical tests. Finally, as a natural extension of the point just made, we see how the data obtained by the astronomer serve to test the calculated numerical values for quantities appearing in the cosmologist's equations or other qualitative predictions made on the basis of a given model. Thus whether the extremely remote galaxies at the horizon of the now observable population of galaxies have roughly the same characteristics as those that are nearer is an important question much discussed at the present time as a means for evaluating the rival claims of the steady state and evolutionary theories. The steady state theory claims that galaxies which are at the outer limits of observability should have roughly the same characteristics as those at lesser distances. According to various "evolutionary" models, those same remote galaxies, from which we receive light and other forms of radiation emitted billions of years ago, could, in effect, tell us about the earlier stages of the evolution of the universe. Since conditions at the time of emission were presumably different from what they are now, these very remote galaxies should display differences from those that are nearer to us in at least some of their properties, and these differences should give us valuable clues about the course of development of the universe as a whole. In this regard a number of delicate questions that are the subject of much controversy have arisen in current research.

Theoretical ideas. A second major source of ideas in the construction of cosmological models is to be found in the conceptual resources of mathematical physics. Here there are two broad possibilities that confront the cosmologist.

Use of established principles. As a first possibility, the cosmologist may turn to some already established body of physical theory as expressed in fundamental principles and derived laws. Such theory will normally have already been found to be successful in dealing with a variety of physical problems of lesser scope than, and wide differences from, the purely cosmological problem. The cosmologist will nevertheless propose to see to what extent the same general body of ideas may be used when applied to the distinctive subject matter of cosmology. He will investigate to what extent the universe as a physical system has a detailed structure that may be articulated and specified by means of the selected physical theory. For example, he may use Newtonian mechanics to construct a model of the universe. Newton himself drew, in a general qualitative way, the cosmological consequences of using the inverse square law of gravitation as a guide. He argued that the universe, throughout its infinite space, must be filled by a more or less evenly distributed matter. For if all the matter that exists were to be confined to a finite "island" in an infinite "ocean" of space, it would have a center of mass toward which, in time, all matter would move by gravitational attraction. The fact is that no such motion is found, and Newton concluded, therefore, that matter is distributed uniformly throughout an infinite space.

At the present time, the primary and predominant source to which the cosmologist turns is the general theory of relativity as expressed in Einstein's general field equations. These equations specify the relations between the space–time metric of any physical domain and its material or energetic content. The discovery of solutions to those field equations that are of special relevance to the cosmologic situation has led to the construction of several varieties of relativistic models. The other major use to which the field equations of general relativity have been put takes the form of the Schwarzschild solution. It was this solution which first afforded the opportunity for testing the predictive and explanatory powers of the theory as a whole. Schwarzschild's solution is particularly applicable to a physical system such as we encounter in the solar system, namely, a single massive particle (the sun) in whose neighborhood we may study the behavior of much smaller masses (the planets) and light rays. The success of its predictions and explanations has been the primary basis for the confidence placed in the general theory. To return then to cosmology: Within the broad class of homogeneous, or uniform, model universes we may distinguish the nonstatic models and the static models. Among the static models is Einstein's original model of 1917, which pictured the universe as finite and unbounded; in the light of the subsequent discovery of the mutual recession of the galaxies, it is no longer considered adequate. The nonstatic models include the ever-expanding-universe models that originate from zero or in some finite volume, and oscillating models that undergo alternate contractions and expansions. Within each of these groups, individuating characteristics for a particular model are to be found in the choice of values for the curvature, age, density, and cosmological constant. No single model has as yet been universally adopted.

Creation of new principles. The other broad possibility for furnishing theoretical ideas for cosmologic models is one in which the cosmologist, instead of appealing to already established principles or laws, for example those of relativistic mechanics, undertakes to create afresh basic principles thought to be of special relevance to the cosmologic problem. By way of illustration, there is the conflict of the 1930s and 1940s between the way in which E. A. Milne sought to establish his kinematic model and the more orthodox procedures of relativistic cosmology. Although Milne did use the formulas of special relativity, he did not take these over directly from Einstein's own presentation; Milne attempted instead to derive them from what he thought of as more basic and primitive postulates. These postulates, he claimed, state the conditions for the measurement of time and for the communication of results by different timekeepers and observers. A more recent example of the same sort of procedure is the steady state model of the universe proposed by Bondi and Thomas Gold in 1948. In support of this model, it is argued that since the universe is unique, there is no reason to believe that the laws which apply to smaller-scale physical phenomena, for example in laboratory terrestrial physics, or even in the domain of gravitational phenomena in the solar system, need be expected to apply to the universe as a whole. Therefore, instead of taking such laws as the point of departure in investigating the physical properties of the universe as a whole, it is suggested that the cosmologist can actually enjoy a far greater freedom than is believed possible in orthodox relativistic cosmologies. Let the cosmologist adopt any "laws" or principles which he believes are appropriate to the study of the universe as a whole, even though these may not have been established or confirmed in other (smaller-scale) areas of physical phenomena. The important thing is to see whether using these laws and principles leads to confirmable empirical results and whether they help to increase and deepen our understanding of the universe.

Those who favor this view (Bondi and Gold among others) determine some of the major features of the steady state model by appeal to the specially introduced postulate known as the perfect cosmological principle. This principle was not in prior use in other branches of physics but was introduced because of its special relevance to cosmology. (Hoyle's model of the steady state universe proceeds along more conventional lines, at least in this respect. Although it differs from the expanding universe models of general relativity in abandoning the principle of the conservation of matter—in order to make possible the idea of the continuous creation of matter—it appeals for its basic physical principles, although in modified form, to the field equations of general relativity.)

One general motive that seems to inspire the setting up of specially devised principles for cosmologic models is the desire to show that the science of cosmology is basic to all other physical sciences. Instead of appealing to other branches of physics for principles to be used in describing the features of the universe as a whole, it is thought desirable that one should be able, eventually, to show that the laws of ordinary physics can be linked with the properties of the universe as a whole. The universe would then disclose itself to be a unitary physical system within which it would be possible in principle to deduce ordinary physical laws from the principles of cosmology. Milne undertook to show how, for example, the inverse square law of gravitation, among other things, could be deduced from such more fundamental cosmological ideas. Similarly, within the framework of a steady state model, Sciama attempts to show how the local inertial properties of matter can be linked (as Ernst Mach originally proposed) with the distribution of masses in the universe at large.

From a logical point of view, there is no reason to discourage such efforts. On the contrary, the realization of such a goal would be of immeasurable significance for all of science, and one should in logic suspend judgment until such a program can be carried through with some fair degree of success.

Meanwhile, it is necessary to point out that some of the writers who favor this approach put methodological interpretations on the use and warrant for the specially devised principles that are not acceptable, whatever the eventual success or promise of the program as a whole. Thus Milne and Bondi, who support different models, are each concerned to stress what they take to be a special method for cosmology—as contrasted with other branches of physics. Milne, for example, thought of ordinary physics as employing an inductive method, whereas cosmology, he believed, should be based on a deductive method. Cosmology, he argued, should not employ the laws of ordinary physics to the extent that these are inductively warranted. This was his major complaint against what he took to be the faulty procedure of relativistic cosmologies founded on the "inductively established" principles of general relativity. In making this claim, Milne was in error, since the principles of general relativity theory are not, as he thought, ordinary inductive generalizations. In fact, Milne's own appeal to "self-evidence" as the warrant for introducing his preferred cosmological principles must be rejected, for the appeal is groundless and fails to support the certainty and uniqueness which he claimed for his principles. In constructing a model of the universe, the cosmologist is engaged in setting up a theoretical tool for dealing with the facts of observation. Whether he gets his theoretical principles by "borrowing" them from some other branch of physics or whether he creates them especially for the problem at hand is of secondary importance to what he does with these principles once he has them and how he evaluates the results he achieves. There is a common method which characterizes cosmology regardless of the particular model being proposed or favored, and it is precisely the same method which is employed in other branches of physics. Moreover, the same criteria of evaluation need to be brought to bear in the appraisal of results in cosmology as in other areas of science. Far from including any appeal to self-evidence or to similar rationalistic demands, a satisfactory model requires the constant support provided by observational evidence.

COGNITIVE WORTH OF MODELS

Consideration of the goals set by scientific cosmology gives rise to a central philosophical question, that of determining the cognitive worth of any cosmological model. This is an epistemological question and may be put in terms of the traditional issues separating the realist and the conceptualist (or the instrumentalist). Should we say with the realist that cosmological models offer us an account of the structure of the independently existing universe, or, rather, should we say with the conceptualist that these models are simply useful means of presenting and interpreting observational data?

As a basis for clarifying the issue at hand, it will be helpful to point out a fundamental ambiguity in the use of the term "universe" itself. Employed without the qualifying adjectives "observed" or "observable," it may have at least two quite distinct senses. One meaning of "universe" is "that to which the observed universe belongs"; another is "that which is characterized by a cosmological model." So far as the realist is concerned, the two meanings are equivalent; in his view the universe defined by a cosmological model will be the same universe as the one described by the expression "that to which the observed universe belongs." But the realist's view of cosmological models cannot be assumed in advance to be the only tenable one. Thus the distinction suggested here has the merit of permitting us to keep this question open. If later a realist philosophy is accepted, the appropriate modifications can be made. Clearly, we do not need to commit ourselves to the position that everything properly said of "the universe" in the sense of "that which is characterized by a cosmological model" can also be said of "the universe" in the sense of "that to which the observed universe belongs." For example, we might want to attribute the property of being "a whole" or "an absolute totality" to the universe as characterized by a particular model, but not to the universe in the sense of that to which the observed universe belongs.

Cosmology aims at articulating the character of the universe *as* a whole. To that extent, then, it rests on the methodological postulate that the universe *is* a whole. The specific character of the whole will, of course, be variously described by various models. What remains fixed, however, is the assumption that the goal of cosmology is to characterize the universe *as* a whole. Therefore the statement "The universe is a whole" is in this context an analytic statement, a matter of definition. But note that it is a definition in which "the universe" is used to signify "that which is characterized by a cosmological model." Not only does cosmology require that, as a matter of definition, the universe be thought of as a whole (in the sense of being intelligible in the way that mathematical classes, geometrical relations, or physical systems are); it also postulates that the universe as a whole is unique or absolute. This means that there is just one such class, pattern, or system, and that all other physical processes or systems of lesser duration or spatial extent are to be taken only as parts of this all-embracing whole. Since each model will so define the universe, it would be a misuse of language to speak of a plurality of universes. Again, of course, the precise structure of this unique or absolute whole will, at least in some respects, vary from model to model.

But what if "the universe" means "that to which the observed universe belongs"? Is the statement "The universe is an absolute, unique whole" still analytic? To this the answer must be no. For when we use "the universe" in this sense, we move from methodology to ontology. In contrast to the case of the universe as defined by a cosmological model, we are no longer committed by the basic methodological postulate of cosmology to saying that the universe *is* a whole. True, in setting up a science, it may be necessary to presuppose the existence of some pervasive structure as the object of study. Yet such a presupposition need not be binding on what the universe is existentially. So long as "the universe" means simply "that to which the observed universe belongs," nothing in this meaning contains analytically the notion of its being a "whole" or an "absolute whole." Indeed, even if we grant that the observed universe is structured in some manner, this does not entail that the wider universe of which it is a part is also pervasively structured. Nor does the fact that we describe the observed universe as "part of" or "that which belongs to" something else require us to say that the universe to which it belongs is a unique or absolute whole. For our reliance on such terms as "part," "whole," and "belong" reveals merely that the mind, in reaching into the unfamiliar, must use analogies in order to relate the unfamiliar to what it already knows.

The universe as the "something more" than the observed universe may well be a complete, unique and intelligibly structured whole. But the claim that we are able to say so is something to which we need not commit ourselves. It is better left as an open question, since, strictly speaking, it is one on which we neither have nor can have any knowledge. Stipulating an affirmative answer by definition does not, of course, establish such knowledge.

Bibliography

HISTORICAL SURVEYS

De Sitter, W., *Kosmos.* Cambridge, Mass., 1932.

Koyré, A., *From the Closed World to the Infinite Universe.* Baltimore, 1957.

Kuhn, T. S., *The Copernican Revolution.* Cambridge, Mass., 1957.

Munitz, M. K., ed., *Theories of the Universe From Babylonian Myth to Modern Science.* Glencoe, Ill., 1957.

SYSTEMATIC SURVEYS

Bondi, H., *Cosmology*, 2d ed. Cambridge, 1960.

Bondi, H., and others, *Rival Theories of Cosmology.* London, 1960.

Bonnor, W. B., *The Mystery of the Expanding Universe.* New York, 1964.

Couderc, P., *The Expansion of the Universe*. London, 1952.
Eddington, A., *The Expanding Universe*. Cambridge, 1933.
Hubble, E. A., *The Realm of the Nebulae*. New Haven, Conn., 1936.
Hubble, E. A., *Observational Approach to Cosmology*. Oxford, 1937.
Lemaitre, G., *The Primeval Atom*. New York, 1950.
McVittie, G. C., *Fact and Theory in Cosmology*. London, 1961.
Milne, E. A., *Relativity, Gravitation, and World-Structure*. Oxford, 1935.
Milne, E. A., *Modern Cosmology and the Christian Idea of God*. Oxford, 1952.
Sciama, D., *The Unity of the Universe*. London, 1959.
Tolman, R. C., *Relativity, Thermodynamics and Cosmology*. Oxford, 1934.
Whitrow, G. J., *The Structure and Evolution of the Universe*. London, 1959.

PHILOSOPHICAL PROBLEMS

Bondi, H., "Fact and Inference in Theory and in Observation," in A. Beer, ed., *Vistas in Astronomy*. London, 1955. Vol. I.
Bondi, H., "Philosophical Problems of Cosmology," in C. A. Mace, ed., *British Philosophy in the Mid-Century*. London, 1957.
Davidson, W., "Philosophical Aspects of Cosmology." *British Journal of the Philosophy of Science*, Vol. 13, No. 50 (August 1962).
Dingle, H., "The Philosophical Aspects of Cosmology," in A. Beer, ed., *Vistas in Astronomy*. London, 1955. Vol. I.
Finlay-Freundlich, E., "Cosmology," in *International Encyclopedia of Unified Science*, Vol. I, No. 8. Chicago, 1951.
Harré, R., "Philosophical Aspects of Cosmology." *British Journal of the Philosophy of Science*, Vol. 13, No. 50 (August 1962).
Johnson, M., *Time, Knowledge and the Nebulae*. London, 1945.
McVittie, G. C., "Rationalism and Empiricism in Cosmology." *Science*, Vol. 133, No. 21 (April 1961).
Monist, Vol. 47, No. 1 (Fall 1962). Entire issue.
Munitz, M. K., *Space, Time, and Creation*. Glencoe, Ill., 1957.
Munitz, M. K., *The Mystery of Existence*. New York, 1965.
Toulmin, S., "Contemporary Scientific Mythology," in S. Toulmin, R. W. Hepburn, and A. MacIntyre, *Metaphysical Beliefs*. London, 1957.

MILTON K. MUNITZ

COSMOS. *See* CHAOS AND COSMOS; COSMOLOGICAL ARGUMENT FOR THE EXISTENCE OF GOD; COSMOLOGY; MACROCOSM AND MICROCOSM.

COSTA, URIEL DA, or Gabriel Acosta (1585–1640), an opponent of traditional religion, was born in Portugal to a New Christian family, that is, one forced to convert to Catholicism from Judaism. After completing studies at Coimbra, he held a minor church office. According to his autobiography, Biblical studies led him back to Judaism, which he then expounded to his family as he deduced it from the Bible. The family fled to Amsterdam to escape the Inquisition and to practice their religion freely. Da Costa soon found that his Biblical Judaism was in conflict with actual practices, which he claimed were too rigid and ritualistic. He attacked "the Pharisees of Amsterdam" and wrote a book arguing that the doctrine of the immortality of the soul was doubtful and un-Biblical. The next year da Costa completed his *Examen dos tradiçoens Phariseas conferidas con a ley escrita* ("Examination of the Traditions of the Pharisees Compared with the Written Law," 1624), a work considered so dangerous that the author was excommunicated by the Jews and arrested by the Dutch authorities as a public enemy of religion. He was fined, and the book was publicly burned. (Its contents can be reconstructed from a reply by Samuel da Silva.) In 1633 he sought readmission to the Jewish community. Though he had not changed his views, he needed the communal life, and so, he said, he would "become an ape among apes," and submit to the synagogue. However, he soon found himself doubting whether the Mosaic law was really God's law, and asking whether all religions were not human creations. He transgressed all sorts of Jewish regulations and observances, and finally was condemned for discouraging two Christians from becoming Jews. He was again excommunicated. In 1640 he submitted once more and underwent the most severe penance, first recanting before the whole synagogue, then receiving 39 lashes, and finally lying prostrate while the congregation walked over him. He then went home, wrote his autobiography (*Exemplar Humanae Vitae*), and shot himself.

Da Costa's tragic career has made him a symbol of the dangers of religious intolerance, as well as a precursor of modern naturalism and higher criticism. One romantic painting shows him as a kindly scholar, holding young Spinoza on his knee, teaching him.

Almost all our information about da Costa comes from his autobiography, published in 1687 from a Latin manuscript. It is not known if it is the original text or an altered version. Very little other data has turned up concerning his actual relations with Amsterdam Jewry or Spinoza. I. S. Révah's recent study, based on Portuguese Inquisition records, indicates that da Costa's initial conversion was not, in fact, from Catholicism to Biblical Judaism, but rather to a peculiar Iberian form of crypto-Judaism. Then, Révah suggests, in Amsterdam da Costa developed first a Biblical Judaism, and later a variety of deism or natural religion.

Da Costa's influence, from the eighteenth century onward, has been mainly on religious liberals opposing traditional orthodoxies. It is his martyrdom, rather than his doctrines (which we hardly know), that has affected people. Considering the many intellectuals gruesomely killed by Protestants and Catholics, it is odd that da Costa has stood out as *the* example of a freethinker destroyed by religious bigotry. Possibly Enlightenment and romantic thinkers could better accept a hero victimized by Judaism than one victimized by their own previous Christian traditions.

Works by da Costa

Die Schriften des Uriel Da Costa, with introduction, translation, and index. Carl Gebhardt, ed. Amsterdam, 1922. Bibliotheca Spinozana Tomus II.
Une Vie humaine. Translated, with a study of the author, by A.-B. Duff and Pierre Kann. Paris, 1926.

Works on da Costa

"Acosta, Uriel," in *Jewish Encyclopedia*, Vol. I, pp. 167–168.
Bayle, Pierre, "Acosta," in *Dictionnaire philosophique et critique*. Rotterdam, 1695–1697.
Révah, I. S., "La Religion d'Uriel da Costa." *Revue de l'histoire des religions*, Vol. 161 (1962), 45–76.

RICHARD H. POPKIN

COUNTERFACTUALS. *See* CONTRARY-TO-FACT CONDITIONAL.

COURNOT, ANTOINE AUGUSTIN (1801–1877), French mathematician, economist, philosopher, and educator. Cournot was born in Gray, Haute Saône. He was educated at *collèges* at Gray (which now bears his name) and Besançon, and at the École Normale Supérieur in Paris. In addition to teaching at the universities of Lyon and Paris, he was head of the *Académie* at Grenoble and rector of the *Académie* at Dijon and succeeded André Marie Ampère as inspector general of studies. An able student of mechanics (including astronomy) and of mathematics, he applied probability theory to problems in both the physical and the social sciences. His work in economics early secured his reputation in that field, and he is now generally regarded as a founder of econometrics; as a philosopher he remains much less known.

Cournot is identified by Jean de la Harpe as a critical realist. This designation would be peculiarly appropriate were it not for the fact that this name has been taken by a group of American philosophers whose position is notably unlike that of Cournot in important respects. Since the term "critical realist" is equivocal, it may be advisable to refer to Cournot as a critical rationalist. Cournot is a realist of sorts in his metaphysics and more rationalist (albeit critically so) than empiricist or positivist in his epistemology. For him knowledge is a function of reason. The senses furnish neither the basis nor the criteria of knowledge, which not only can but does extend beyond their limits. Yet the senses do make important contributions to knowledge, especially by restraining its claims by challenging overextended speculations by confronting them with what William James aptly called "brute facts." Cournot rejects all dogmatic philosophies, whether rationalist or empiricist. Knowledge requires a continuing appraisal of all principles to determine both their grounds and the range of their legitimate applications. Specifically, he examines the established sciences to see whether they have any basic concepts in common. He discovers three such concepts—order, chance, probability. These three concepts lie at the heart of Cournot's philosophy and suffice to account for his rejection of many earlier and contemporary alternative positions. He rejects the idealistic basis and implications of Kant's philosophy, but he accepts the critical intent of the Kantian program.

For Cournot, order is a basic category which, as "objective reason," relates to the nature of things and, as "subjective reason," to the means through which we apprehend that nature. The major function of philosophy is to examine and criticize the efforts of subjective reason to know objective reason, making sure among other things that such closely related and often confused principles as "reason" and "cause," "rational order" and "logical order," are clearly differentiated in both their meaning and their function. We have knowledge when we apprehend the objective reason of things, but such knowledge is rarely complete and certain. Therefore, our knowledge is relative and probable, not absolute and apodictic, but it nonetheless rests on objective grounds, not on forms or categories native to the mind itself.

Cournot's unusual and cogent use of probability draws attention to a fundamental moderating element in his philosophy. His treatment of probability is developed most extensively in his *Exposition* (1843) and is used ingeniously and productively in his *Essai* (1851), *Traité* (1861), and *Matérialisme, vitalisme, rationalisme.* Long before putting these views to philosophic use, Cournot had applied them to problems in astronomy and in various fields of social studies, notably in economics, where he applied them with lastingly important results.

The calculus of probabilities is related to both order and chance. Both order and probability have plural meanings. Order as a category of the objective reason of things must not be confused either with logical order—that is, with the order essential to a formal system of ideas—or with causal order, by which Cournot means essentially what Aristotle called "efficient cause." The reason for a phenomenon must be distinguished from its cause, from the conditions or circumstances which give rise to it. *Cause* is related to the particular and unique; *reason* is related to the universal and abstract aspects of phenomena which are the ground for laws of general and fundamental relations among them, relations which are necessary, but not in themselves sufficient, conditions for the production of specific phenomena. Probability is of two sorts, mathematical and philosophical. Mathematical probability applies to those relatively rare situations in which the number and relative frequency of various possibilities can be numerically determined. Philosophical probability—which may attain practical, but never demonstrable, certainty—applies to the vastly more numerous cases in which such numerical determination is not possible. It involves an appraisal of evidence in terms of rational cogency where probabilities persuade and win the acquiescence of reasonable persons even though the relevant evidence is neither quantifiably manipulatable nor conclusive. We live continuously and inescapably with such probabilities; philosophical criticism is also largely concerned with them. In either case probability is a function of objective factors and conditions and not solely of our ignorance or other subjective factors, although these do contribute to our need to deal with probabilities of both types.

Of Cournot's three basic ideas, that of chance is least adequately developed. It is unfortunate that there is no specific and clear definition of this concept in its theoretical function, yet what the concept refers to is not at all unclear. Numerous examples leave no doubt about the meaning of the term as Cournot uses it. A chance occurrence is one in which there is an unpredictable conjunction of independent series of events, each series being internally related and having a determinable nature. However complete our knowledge of each independent series, events resulting from unpredictable conjunctions among them are contingent, unpredictable, fortuitous. Such events have causes, but they are not reducible to laws. The absence of reasons for such events is irreducible, chance, like order, being an objective feature of the nature of things. This doctrine is one source of the pluralism in Cournot's philosophy. In it he anticipates Émile Boutroux and suggests certain aspects of the philosophies of C. S. Peirce (for example, his "tychism") and M. R. Cohen (whose general philosophical position is not unlike Cournot's critical rationalism).

Another pluralistic aspect of Cournot's thought is indicated in the title of his last philosophic work, *Matérialisme, vitalism, rationalisme.* Countering the principles of Darwinian evolution, Cournot holds to the principle that living beings are distinguished from nonliving things by a unity and form suggestive of finality and by a vital principle inexplicable in physical and chemical terms. Here Cournot anticipates both Henri Bergson and the emergent evolutionists, notably Samuel Alexander and C. Lloyd Morgan.

In his consideration of such concepts as form, unity, simplicity, and symmetry, Cournot moves toward a transrationalism—that is, toward a view in which ideas that go beyond normal rational analysis and use, such as finality, purpose, and God, find a place. This development is consistent with, indeed perhaps it is a consequence of, his pluralism and his implied doctrine of levels and with his rejection of any reductionist view as these are evidenced by his assertion that the phenomena of life involve something not present in nonliving phenomena. Such ideas as simplicity and symmetry are relevant to rational investigation, to the discovery of the order and reason of things, as in the probabilistic assessment and choice between otherwise equally adequate alternative hypotheses. In this sense such concepts are regulative ideas of reason. But Cournot argues that they are more than this, and in his treatment of these concepts he moves from a logic of reason toward an aesthetic of reason, in which the concept of order has a connotation more extensive than reason can explore. What effect does such a transrationalism have on the claimed objective existence of chance, the second concept so fundamental to Cournot's philosophy as a whole? None. Why this is the case is not adequately developed in Cournot's works, although a hint is found in *Exposition:* God lays out the laws or rational elements of reality and leaves to objective and inexpugnable chance the details of fortuitous occurrences. Therefore, even such a superior intelligence would, like man, be unable to foresee contingent events, although unlike man its assessment of what is contingent would not be complicated by subjective factors of the sort which inescapably limit and affect human judgment.

In developing his philosophy, Cournot deals with the nature of language, ethics, and aesthetics and with various social institutions and factors which contribute to civilization. He also discusses the nature of science, history, and philosophy and considers at some length the irreducible distinctions between them. His *Considérations* is a peculiarly interesting account of his handling of various historical matters.

Works by Cournot

Mémoire sur le mouvement d'un corps rigide soutenu par un plan fixe. Paris, 1829.

Recherches sur les principes mathématiques de la théorie des richesses. Paris, 1838. Translated into English by N. I. Bacon as *Researches into the Mathematical Principles of the Theory of Wealth.* Economic Classics series. London, 1877.

Traité élémentaire de la théorie des fonctions et du calcul infinitesimal, 2 vols. Paris, 1841; 2d ed., revised and corrected, 1857.

Exposition de la théorie des chances et des probabilités. Paris, 1843.

De l'Origine et des limites de la correspondance entre l'algèbre et la géometrie. Paris, 1847.

Essai sur les fondements de nos connaissances et sur les caractères de la critique philosophique, 2 vols. Paris, 1851; 2d ed., 1912; 3d ed., 1 vol., 1922. Translated into English by Merritt H. Moore as *An Essay on the Foundations of Our Knowledge.* New York, 1956.

Traité de l'enchaînement des idées fondamentales dans les sciences et dans l'histoire, 2 vols. Paris, 1861; 2d ed., 1 vol., 1911; 3d ed., 1 vol., 1922. The 1911 and 1922 editions include a Foreword by L. Lévy-Bruhl.

Principes de la théorie des richesses. Paris, 1863.

Des Institutions d'instruction publique en France. Paris, 1864.

Considérations sur la marche des idées et des événements dans les temps modernes, 2 vols. Paris, 1872; republished with Introduction by M. Mentré, 2 vols., Paris, 1934.

Matérialisme, vitalisme, rationalisme: Études sur l'emploi des données de la science en philosophie. Paris, 1875, 1923.

Revue sommaire des doctrines économiques. Paris, 1877.

Souvenirs: 1760 à 1860. Paris, 1913. Written in 1859; published with Introduction and notes by E. P. Bottinelli.

Works on Cournot

Bottinelli, E. P., *A. Cournot métaphysicien de la connaissance.* Paris, 1913.

Darbon, A., *Le Concept du hasard dans la philosophie de Cournot.* Paris, 1911.

Harpe, Jean de la, *De l'Ordre et du hasard: Le Réalisme critique D'Antoine Augustin Cournot.* Memoirs of the University of Neuchâtel, Vol. IX. Neuchâtel, 1936.

Lévêque, R., *L' "Élément historique" dans la connaissance humaine d'après Cournot.* Publications of the Faculty of Letters of the University of Strasbourg, No. 82. Paris, 1938.

Mentré, F., *Cournot et la renaissance du probabilisme au XIXe siècle.* Paris, 1908.

Milhaud, G., *Études sur Cournot.* Paris, 1927.

Revue de métaphysique et de morale, Vol. 13, No. 3 (1905), 293–543. A special number dedicated to A. Cournot, with portrait. Articles by H. Poincaré, G. Milhaud, G. Tarde, C. Bouglé, A. Anpetit, F. Faure, A. Darlu, F. Vial, D. Parodi, R. Audierne, H.-L. Moore.

Ruyer, R., *L'Humanité de l'avenir d'après Cournot.* Paris, 1930.

Segond, J., *Cournot et la psychologie vitaliste.* Paris, 1911.

MERRITT HADDEN MOORE

COUSIN, VICTOR (1792–1867), French philosopher and historian, was born in Paris and educated at the Lycée Charlemagne and the École Normale, where he studied under Pierre Laromiguière. He began his teaching career in 1815, assisting Pierre Paul Royer-Collard in his course on the history of philosophy at the University of Paris. Cousin studied German and read Kant and F. H. Jacobi; but he was especially attracted to the works of Schelling, whose thought had a permanent influence upon him. A trip to Germany in 1817 brought him into personal contact with both Schelling and Hegel, a fact which was later responsible for the accusation that he had rejected French philosophy in favor of Germany's. In 1821 Cousin was removed from his position because of his supposed antigovernmental views, and he used his freedom to make another trip to Germany. While there he was imprisoned, on charges which have never been entirely clear, but was freed after six months. Returning to France, he spent his time writing his philosophical and historical works and editing the works of other philosophers, including Proclus (6 vols., 1820–1827) and Descartes (1826, 11 vols.), and beginning his translation of Plato (13 vols., 1822–1840). In

1828 he was restored to his post and from then on had an influential career as lecturer. He became a spokesman for the *juste milieu*, as he called it, which in philosophy meant eclecticism. Cousin's power increased when in 1840 he became minister of public instruction, director of the École Normale, and a member of the Institut de France. He was not only the most famous French philosopher of his time but also supreme dictator of who should teach philosophy and what should be taught. He had become, moreover, a power in the whole educational system of France when he published a report on Prussian education (1833). (This report was later translated into English in 1834 and distributed to the schools of Massachusetts by an act of the legislature.) At the advent to power of Louis Napoleon in 1848 Cousin retired from active teaching and spent his time in literary studies.

Eclecticism. Though Cousin started his career as a pupil of Laromiguière, it was the common-sense philosophy of Thomas Reid, as interpreted by Royer-Collard, that was the source of his own doctrine. To Cousin common sense was a fusion of the best that had been done in philosophy, combining the empiricism of sensationalism in epistemology with the spiritualism of religion. The epistemology of Condillac and his school, Cousin felt, because it made the spirit of man a simple passive victim of external forces, had led them to atheism and materialism, both of which were to be condemned. Atheism and materialism could not give men those permanent principles which would guide their moral life. Such principles were to be found only if men realized that their minds were active as well as passive, their activity consisting in their use of their a priori categories of substance and causality.

Though it is likely that Cousin got the idea of the complementary active and passive aspects of mentality from Schelling, he himself attributed it to Maine de Biran's self-scrutiny. This gave him a French origin for doctrines which were to guide French professors. Maine de Biran's active will, Cousin maintained, was balanced by sensibility, which "implies" the existence of an external world. Sensibility and active will were accompanied by reason, and thus Cousin revived the traditional threefold analysis of the mind. Corresponding to the three faculties was a threefold division of philosophical problems into that of the good, the beautiful, and the true. In his book *Du Vrai, du beau et du bien* (1853) Cousin argued that these problems were united in a whole which absorbed what was valid in sensation (Locke), reason (Plato), and the heart (for which he named no sponsor). These three parts of the soul are not independent of one another. Reason requires both sensation and the heart, sensation requires reason and the heart, and the heart requires both reason and sensation. By analogy epistemology, ethics, and aesthetics are all intertwined and inseparable except for purposes of exposition.

Political philosophy. The political philosophy of Cousin was expressed in *Justice et charité*, a brief tract which he wrote as one of a series published by members of the Académie des Sciences Morales et Politiques in 1848. This tract is based on the same metaphor of the interdependence of separate things. The purpose of all the tracts in this series was to substantiate the right to property, the well-being of family life, popular freedom, and progress. Cousin opposed the idea of equality, the right to work, and governmental aid. Justice is the protection of natural rights, but every right implies a complementary duty. Men are all free, but their freedom resides only in the search for truth, in religious beliefs and practices, and in property. Justice demands that these rights be respected and protected by the state. On the other hand, charity demands that we abuse none of these rights, that we individually seek the truth and not perpetuate error, that we give others the religious freedom that we demand for ourselves, that we respect others' property as we would have them respect ours. In short, law is futile if it is not obeyed, and we cannot obey a law which is not enforced. Respect for the law is like charity in that it has no limits; for charity extends to all men and to liberty in all its forms.

Aesthetics. Cousin was a strong believer in absolute beauty. His ideal work of art was the Apollo Belvedere. Art, he believed, is neither an imitation of nature (sensationalism) nor edification (moralism), but rather a vision of "the infinite." Though all arts utilize matter, they communicate to it "a mysterious character which speaks to the imagination and to the soul, liberates them from the real, and bears them aloft either gently or violently to unknown regions." These unknown regions are the country of God, the world of the ideal. Though this passage might seem to ally Cousin with the Romantic school, in fact it led him to give highest praise to the classicists of the seventeenth century. He was clearly under the influence of J. J. Winckelmann, who also admired the Apollo Belvedere as the *summum* of all ideal beauty and believed that all praiseworthy artists put into their works of art the ideal beauty of Plotinus. Cousin saw in beauty, as did Hegel, a sensuous manifestation of the Absolute, though he expressed it in different language.

At the same time Cousin admitted that one must not exaggerate the idealism of a work of art. All works of art speak to the senses as well as to the heart. The ideal must be presented to us in sensible form and it must also be agreeable to our feelings. A work of art which is beautiful was for Cousin a concrete presentation of the unity he found in eclecticism. Consequently, art that did not realize the potentialities of the sensuous, the rational, and the sentimental would not be of as high a rank as art that did. The conclusion was that poetry was the highest of all the arts. Its power of words is such that it can stimulate images, feelings (affections), and thoughts at one and the same time. It is thus a synthesis of all human powers.

Historiography. The pioneering editorial work of Cousin, mentioned above, made accessible to the public manuscripts that had been previously hidden in libraries. His eclecticism served him well in this field, for with the exception of the sensationalists of the eighteenth century, there were few philosophers of the past in whom he could not find some truth. Cousin's *Philosophie sensualiste au XVIIIe siècle* (1819), a course of lectures, is the most biased of his historical studies, but still treats of Locke, Condillac, Helvétius, Saint-Lambert, and Hobbes in an interesting manner. His criticism of Locke, that Locke was unable by the very nature of his epistemology to account for universal and necessary ideas, Cousin's analysis of Condillac's notion that deduction is always tautological, and even Cousin's attacks on Helvétius are carefully based on the texts and are far from superficial. Fundamentally his objection to these thinkers was the pragmatic, moral, and religious consequences of their premises, an objection which obviously sprang from his own moral and religious convictions. His *Cours de l'histoire de la philosophie* (1829) was considered a work serious enough to be analyzed and commented upon by Sir William Hamilton in the *Edinburgh Review*, and, indeed, its exposition of the technique of historiography was thorough and based on a perception of genuine historical problems. Cousin made the mistake of dividing all possible philosophies into four kinds—sensualism, idealism, skepticism, and mysticism—and thus helped to influence his successors in this area toward thinking of philosophies as always productive of systems. This division led Cousin to look for a unitary idea pervading each system, though the idea in question might be a simple metaphor or a theory of the origin of ideas which exfoliated into an ethics, aesthetics, theology, or other theoretical construct. Like Hegel, Cousin was given to envisioning philosophical systems as "expressive" of ages and peoples, as if an age or a people were homogeneous. Yet at the same time he admitted the heterogeneity of what he called populations as distinguished from peoples, the latter being unified in their beliefs and outlooks on the world's problems, the former being diversified or, as he would put it, not yet unified. Where there was diversity, there was nevertheless a predominant idea in every epoch, but alongside of it existed other ideas "playing a secondary but real role." Each people, Cousin maintained, was given, presumably by God or by the inevitable course of history, an idea to represent, and its history was the realization of this idea. This idea expresses itself in all human concerns—in philosophy, religion, science, art, and morals. It is almost certain that Hegel was the source of this theory, though Cousin made no mention of his influence. He was willing, however, to give great credit to J. J. Brucker, Dietrich Tiedemann, and W. G. Tennemann; these last two, he believed, expressed a history of philosophy associated with Locke and Kant respectively. As for the nineteenth century, Cousin held that it would not have its own history of philosophy until it had a representative philosophy. That philosophy would be a union of the two traditions referred to by Cousin as the nucleus of a "vast and powerful eclecticism."

It is customary to treat Cousin with patronizing disdain, and it is true that he was always ready to compromise with political power and adjust his conclusions and, indeed, his methods of research to what he believed to be expedient. He succeeded in excluding from his "regiment," as he called it, philosophers whose views were not harmonious with his own. Thus neither Auguste Comte nor J. G. F. Ravaisson-Mollien nor Charles Renouvier, to cite but three names, were able to become members of the teaching staff of the University of Paris. On the other hand, Cousin did stimulate research into the classics of philosophy, and his very chauvinism turned men's attention to such neglected figures as Maine de Biran. His eclecticism was not real, for he rejected any philosophy whose supposed religious and ethical effects he thought were undesirable. Yet his notion that every philosophy contained some truth induced his pupils to look into them all and gave them a catholicity of interest that was unusual and almost unique.

Bibliography

With the omission of his editions of classical authors and literary studies, Cousin's works include *Fragments philosophiques* (Paris, 1826); *Cours de l'histoire de la philosophie*, 3 vols. (Paris, 1829), which together with *Cours de l'histoire de la philosophie moderne*, 5 vols. (Paris, 1841) contains many titles also published separately; *Justice et charité* (Paris, 1848); and *Du Vrai, du beau et du bien* (Paris, 1853).

For literature on Cousin, see P. F. Dubois, *Cousin, Jouffroy, Damiron, souvenirs publiés avec un introduction par Adolphe Lair* (Paris, 1902); Paul Janet, *Victor Cousin et son oeuvre* (Paris, 1885); and Jules Simon, *Victor Cousin* (Paris, 1887), which has been translated under the same title by M. B. Anderson and E. P. Anderson (Chicago, 1888). For a generally hostile approach, from a positivistic point of view, see Lucien Lévy-Bruhl, *History of Modern Philosophy in France*, translated by G. Coblence (Chicago and London, 1924), Ch. 12; for a favorable account see John Veitch and X, "Cousin, Victor," in *Encyclopaedia Britannica*, 11th ed. (Chicago, 1910).

GEORGE BOAS

COUTURAT, LOUIS (1868–1914), French philosopher and logician, studied at the École Normale Supérieure and earned an agrégé in philosophy and a licentiate in mathematics. He taught philosophy at the universities of Toulouse and Caen but soon gave up teaching in order to devote all of his time to his own researches.

Couturat first attracted attention with his important doctoral thesis, *L'Infini mathématique* (Paris, 1896). At a time when the mathematicians were still questioning the validity of Cantor's theories and when the majority of French philosophers, led by Charles Renouvier, were resolute advocates of finitism, Couturat presented a vigorous case in behalf of an actual infinite. In opposition to the formalist theories of number of Julius Dedekind, Leopold Kronecker, and Hermann Helmholtz, he bases number on magnitude—not on a strictly spatial intuition but on magnitude considered as the object of a "rational intuition." This is why, of the various generalizations of number—the arithmetical, the algebraic, the geometrical—he regards the geometrical as the most rational. His reasoning consisted of offering the actual infinite as a new generalization of number, analogous to those that resulted in signed numbers, fractions, irrationals, and imaginaries. All of these numbers at first seemed to be arithmetical nonsense, but they took on meaning once they were recognized as suitable for representing new magnitudes and for allowing various operations on them that were hitherto impossible. The justification for infinite numbers is that they are indispensable for maintaining the continuity of magnitudes.

From this point on, Couturat's studies proceeded in three areas closely associated in his mind—the history of philosophy, logic and the philosophy of mathematics, and the development of a universal language.

After writing an essay (his Latin complementary thesis) on the myths of Plato, he devoted himself to Leibniz, the great infinitist, whose reinterpretation he undertook independently of Russell but at the same time and in the same sense. As indicated by the title of his book *La Logique de Leibniz* (Paris, 1901), Couturat had at first intended simply to study the precursor of modern logistic. He soon perceived, however, that Leibniz' "logic was not only the heart and soul of his system, but the center of his intellectual activity, the source of all his discoveries, . . . the obscure or at least concealed hearth from which sprang so many *fulgurations*." The manuscripts he discovered at Hanover, a copious collection of which he published in *Opuscules et fragments inédits de Leibniz* (Paris, 1903), further strengthened Couturat in this conviction. Considering only Leibniz' known, celebrated works, if we wish to find the real root of his system, we must look not to the *Monadology* or the *Theodicy* but to the *Discourse on Metaphysics*, together with the *Correspondence With Arnauld*, which is, as it were, a commentary on the *Discourse*. Taking the old formula *praedicatum inest subjecto* in all its rigor, Leibniz held that every true proposition can be resolved into identities provided one pursues its analysis to the end. Contingent or factual truths differ from the necessary truths of reason only in respect to the infinite length of the analysis, an analysis which God alone is able to complete. Couturat showed, with supporting texts, that all the theses of the Leibnizian metaphysics are obtained from this position and derive their unity from it. The system thus appears as a panlogism.

It is likewise to his interest in Leibniz that we may ascribe, indirectly, Couturat's important study "La Philosophie des mathématiques de Kant," published in the *Revue de métaphysique* (1904) on the centennial of Kant's death. In *L'Infini mathématique* Couturat had already criticized the Kantian antinomies which claim to establish the impossibility of an actual infinite. He now concluded that "the progress of logic and mathematics in the nineteenth century has invalidated the Kantian theory and decided the issue in favor of Leibniz" and his ideal of a completely "intellectualized" mathematics. The majestic edifice of the three *Critiques* lacks the indispensable basement of a logic on a level with science. "The brass colossus has feet of clay."

Deploring the fact that Gerhardt, in editing Leibniz, had separated the mathematical writings from the philosophical, Couturat could not but associate himself with the task assumed by the newly founded *Revue de métaphysique* of working for a *rapprochement*, unfortunately broken off in the nineteenth century, between philosophers and scientists. After the establishment of the *Revue* in 1893, scarcely a year passed when he did not publish one or more articles in this spirit (some thirty at the time of his death, plus three that appeared posthumously). Rather than present original views, he dedicated himself with great disinterestedness to making known the views of others, mainly foreigners. He explained to French philosophers the mathematical logic of Peano, the universal algebra of Whitehead, and the foundations of geometry and the principles of mathematics according to Russell. He vigorously defended both the new logic (to whose diffusion he contributed with his *L'Algèbre de la logique*, Paris, 1905) and the Russellian logistic. This involved him in a celebrated controversy with his former teacher Henri Poincaré. Although at the time Poincaré was often able to score against his opponent, subsequent developments in logic and mathematics have been more favorable to Couturat on many points.

Couturat's admiration for Leibniz, who dreamed of a universal language; his adherence to logistic that he saw as the source of an algorithm disengaged from the contingencies and irregularities of the natural languages; his participation in the organization of the first International Congress of Philosophy (Paris, 1900); his active collaboration with André Lalande in the preparation of the *Vocabulaire technique et critique de la philosophie* (Paris, 1926); and his rationalism, which one may characterize as militant in the sense that his purpose was less to rediscover reason in things than to work to make it rule among men—all these converging concerns led him to devote himself more exclusively to a task which became a veritable apostolate for him—the creation and adoption of an international auxiliary language by the rationalization of Esperanto and Ido. He prepared himself for this mission first by studying and then by publishing, in collaboration with Léopold Léau, the *Histoire de la langue universelle* (Paris, 1903). After 1900, Couturat was the moving spirit of the Délégation Pour l'Adoption d'une Langue Auxiliaire Internationale, initiated by Léau, and later of the Akademie di la Lingue Internaciona Ido. In 1908 he founded and directed until his death the monthly review *Progreso*, written in the reformed language and designed to propagate it. The opposition of many Esperantists and the death of Couturat, which happened to come at the very moment when a war that exacerbated national particularisms was breaking out, caused the abandonment of the project. His friends and admirers have often regretted that Couturat should have expended so much effort in vain and sacrificed his wide talent to a noble dream.

Works by Couturat

L'Algèbre de la logique. Paris, 1905. The 1914 edition (Paris) was republished at Hildesheim, Germany, in 1965, Georg Olms edition.

Les Principes des mathématiques. Paris, 1905. Republished under the same title with the addition of the article "La Philosophie des mathématiques de Kant" in Hildesheim, Germany, in 1965.

La Logique de Leibniz, Georg Olms edition. Hildesheim, Germany, 1961.

Works on Couturat

Cassirer, Ernst, "Kant und die moderne Mathematik. Mit Bezug auf Russells und Couturats Werke über die Prinzipien der Mathematik." *Kantstudien* (1907).

Lalande, André, "L'Oeuvre de Louis Couturat." *Revue de métaphysique*, Vol. 22 (1914), 644–688. Includes a detailed bibliography.

ROBERT BLANCHÉ

Translated by *Albert E. Blumberg*

CRAIG'S THEOREM is a result in mathematical logic, formulated by William Craig, professor of philosophy at the University of California, Berkeley. It has attracted some attention from philosophers of science, as allegedly showing that theoretical entities are in principle unnecessary for deriving the observational consequences of a scientific theory.

The theorem applies to any of a large class of formal systems or "axiom systems." A formal system is here understood to consist of the following: (1) a vocabulary consisting of a finite or infinite supply of primitive (undefined) symbols, divided into logical and nonlogical symbols; (2) rules of combination for generating certain finite sequences of the primitive symbols—the so-called well-formed formulas (wffs); (3) a finite or infinite selection of the wffs, designated as axioms; and (4) rules of inference for deriving further wffs from the initial axioms.

A sequence of wffs, each of which is either an axiom or has been derived from previous wffs in the sequence of application of the rules of inference of the system, is called a proof; the last wff of a proof is called a derived formula; axioms and derived formulas together are called the theorems of the system.

In this description of a formal system it is understood that all the rules in question are "effective"; that is, they are such that they determine in a finite number of steps whether a given configuration of symbols is an instance of the various categories specified (primitive symbol, wff, proof, etc.). Thus, given a finite sequence of primitive symbols belonging to the system in question, the rules must suffice to determine, in a finite number of steps, whether the sequence begins with an axiom; which rule of inference, if any, derives the next wff of the sequence from that initial axiom; and so forth. In short, the rules must provide an effective decision procedure for identifying proofs belonging to the system.

It is a well-known fundamental result of metamathematics, however, that many formal systems do not and cannot have an effective decision procedure for identifying *theorems*. That a given string of primitive symbols is well-formed can indeed be determined effectively, but in order to establish that such a wff is derivable by means of a proof, there is usually nothing better to do than actually to hit upon such a proof. Insistence upon the effectiveness of the rules of combination and rules of inference seems inescapable; for were this condition waived, it would sometimes be impossible to know whether a given sequence of symbols constituted a proof, which would be contrary to the general purpose of rendering the notion of a rigorous mathematical argument by means of the concept of a formal system.

A sketch of Craig's proof. Let the nonlogical primitive symbols of a given formal system, S, be divided in any way into two sets, consisting of "preferred" symbols and the remaining nonpreferred symbols. Let a wff all of whose nonlogical symbols are preferred be called a preferred formula; and let a theorem that is a preferred formula be called a preferred theorem. Consider that the problem is to derive from a given formal system, S, another formal system, S′, satisfying the following conditions: (1) the primitive symbols of S′ shall consist exclusively of the preferred symbols of S; (2) the theorems of S′ shall consist exactly of the preferred theorems of S, that is, of just those theorems of S in which the only nonlogical symbols are the preferred ones.

The following solution suggests itself. It is well known that all the proofs of S can be arranged in advance in a single infinite series so that each proof, *P*, can be assigned its rank, *n*, in this "enumeration." Suppose this enumeration has been performed. Consider each of the proofs of S in the order $P_1, P_2, \cdots$. If the proof examined terminates in a preferred formula, adopt that theorem as an axiom for S′; otherwise, proceed to the next proof in the series; and continue thus indefinitely. In this way, it seems, we might be able to select from S the preferred theorems, and by treating them as the axioms of S′, provide a trivial solution of the set task. That the axioms thus provided will be infinite in number is no objection, since the relevant conception of a formal system allows for infinitely many axioms to be generated in accordance with a definite rule of procedure; nor is it an objection that the proposed system S′ is trivial in the sense of requiring no rules of inference, since the task did not stipulate that the solution should be in some sense interesting. However, the following is a decisive objection to the proposed solution: The suggested procedure for determining the axioms of S′ is not effective; for given a wff of the proposed S′, the question whether or not it is an axiom of S′ can be answered only by indefinitely prolonged scrutiny of successive terms of the series $P_1, P_2, \cdots$ (or by the lucky accident of finding a proof for the formula in question). If the formula in question is in fact a preferred theorem of S, the scrutiny will indeed determine in a finite number of steps that the formula is an axiom of S′; but if the formula is not a preferred theorem of S, there will be no way of discovering that. (Never finding a proof is not an effective procedure.)

Craig's main idea is an ingenious modification of this first abortive attempt at solution. Suppose P_n, the *n*th proof in the enumeration of proofs of S, does terminate in a preferred theorem; in that case, choose as an axiom of S′, not the theorem, *T*, in question, but rather the logical conjunction $T \cdot T \cdot \cdots \cdot T$, consisting of exactly *n* occurrences of *T*. (Thus, if a preferred theorem, T_1, is proved by the 100th proof of S, the corresponding axiom of S′ will be a conjunction of 100 terms, each of them being T_1.) It is easily seen that this procedure, unlike that first considered and rejected, has the essential merit of being effective. For, given a wff of the proposed S′, we can certainly determine in a finite number of steps whether it is a reiterated conjunction of the form $F \cdot F \cdot \cdots \cdot F$. If it is, we can then count the number of occurrences of the reiterated constituent *F*; if this number is *n*, looking at the *n*th proof of the enumerated series of proofs in S will at once determine whether *F* is indeed the terminal formula of P_n and, thus, whether the original formula should be counted as an axiom of S′. It seems, accordingly, that in this way the task has been solved, by generating from the initial system S another formal system whose theorems are just the preferred theorems of S.

The construction. The following points are relevant to the alleged philosophical implications of the theorem. (1) The only rule of inference needed in the constructed S′ is one permitting passage from a reiterated conjunction of the form $F \cdot F \cdot \cdots \cdot F$ to its elementary constituent *F*. (2) For any axiom of S′ having the form F_n (a conjunction of *n* *F*'s), there will be infinitely more axioms of the form $F_{n'}$, with the same *F*, but with different values of *n*. (This is so because a proof of a given formula *F* in S can always be extended in trivial ways to yield other proofs terminating in the same formula.) (3) The rules for generating the axioms of S′ involve direct or indirect reference to the system S. (As sketched above, the procedure for generating S′ presupposes that S has been specified and is available for examination together with a procedure for enumerating the proofs of S. This feature of the procedure might be concealed, however, by offering some equivalent procedure for scrutinizing candidates for axiomhood in S'. A human computer might be offered a complex arithmetical rule for effectively deciding whether a given wff of S' should count as an axiom, without realizing the provenance of that rule in some undisclosed formal system S.)

Philosophical implications. Craig's theorem has been held to show that theoretical terms are in a certain sense dispensable in science. Imagine a branch of science (or the whole of science, if it could be unified) presented as a formal system whose primitive nonlogical symbols are either "observational" or "theoretical." Treat the observational symbols as preferred symbols and apply Craig's construction: it seems that in this way we can obtain a subtheory whose theorems are just the observational theorems of the original scientific theory. The high degree of redundancy of the proposed purely observational system (see point 2 of the previous section) and its triviality when considered as a deductive system (see point 1 of the same section) are in principle irrelevant: in codifying the known data and the observational predictions or retrodictions derived from them, we could, by relying upon the reconstructed theory, avoid reference to theoretical entities entirely.

To this argument the following answer seems sufficient. Manipulation of the reconstructed theory, allegedly purged of theoretical reference, still requires a covert appeal to the original theory (see point 3 of the previous section) with its full panoply of theoretical entities. To be sure, derivations of proofs in the original S may now be viewed as marginal groundwork, merely preparatory to inclusion of a given formula as an axiom in S'. Yet substantially the same processes of manipulation are needed for handling S' as were required for the original system S. (This statement can be illustrated as follows. If we want to determine whether a particular formula F occurs as a theorem in S', we must look for a "reiterated conjunction" having the form F_n. To this end, we can do nothing better than to check successively upon $F_1, F_2, \cdots$ by reference to the original S; that is, to look for a proof of F in S. This procedure is not effective, of course. S' does not provide a decision procedure apart from S; at most, it is a plausible way of thinking about what is done in S.) Thus the appearance of our having dispensed with S and the theoretical symbols it contains is an illusion. Of course, a philosopher might choose to consider the theoretical symbols of the original system as merely auxiliary devices for generating purely observational statements, somewhat in the manner of Craig's construction. But this inclination could equally be served by his leaving the original system unreconstructed and regarding all theoretical symbols as merely incomplete or auxiliary, reserving ultimate or full significance only to formulas containing no theoretical terms.

Craig's theorem is merely an ingenious way of showing how, in effect, certain favored theorems of a given system might be selected out of a given formal system without violating the mathematician's conception of a formal system. The moral to be drawn might be that this conception of a formal system does not fully meet the requirements of what a scientist would recognize as a theory. Apart from this, the theorem seems to have no philosophical significance at all.

Bibliography

A careful, nontechnical sketch of Craig's theorem can be found in his "Replacement of Auxiliary Expressions," in *Philosophical Review*, Vol. 65 (1956), 38–55. See also his "On Axiomatizability Within a System," in *Journal of Symbolic Logic*, Vol. 18 (1953), 30–32, which contains the full argument.

A useful discussion of the role of theoretical terms in formal scientific theory is Carl Gustav Hempel, "The Theoretician's Dilemma," in H. Feigl, M. Scriven, and G. Maxwell, eds., *Concepts, Theories, and the Mind–Body Problem*, Vol. II in the Minnesota Studies in the Philosophy of Science (Minneapolis, Minn., 1958), pp. 37–98, including a discussion of Craig's theorem, pp. 76–80.

MAX BLACK

CRATYLUS, an Athenian, was contemporary with Socrates but was probably considerably younger. He was, according to Aristotle, a follower of the doctrines of Heraclitus, and Plato, in his youth, was closely associated with him. Aristotle implies that this was before he came under Socrates' influence, although later sources put the influence of Cratylus upon Plato after the death of Socrates.

Cratylus took as his starting point the doctrine of the flux of phenomena (here assumed to have been a genuine doctrine of Heraclitus, despite G. S. Kirk's objections), and he capped Heraclitus' saying that one cannot step twice into the same river by adding "nor once either." His reason clearly was his contention that the river is changing even as you step into it. He ended by coming to the view that one ought not to say anything, but only move the finger, since no true statement can be made about a thing that is always changing. According to Aristotle, upon whose evidence the above account rests, Plato took from Cratylus the belief, which he maintained even in later years, that all sensible things are always in a state of flux and that there is no knowledge about them.

Plato in the *Cratylus* attributes to him the doctrine that everything has a right name of its own, fixed by nature, and somehow or other this one right name will point to the nature of the thing named.

At an early stage it became clear to modern critics that the contention that there is a right name that indicates the true nature of a thing is apparently inconsistent with the doctrine of a Heraclitean flux in phenomena, since this flux would prevent a thing from having an abiding nature. Attempts to explain this contradiction in Cratylus' position have been numerous. Frequently it has been supposed that Cratylus either did not have a doctrine of words at all or else did not believe in the flux doctrine.

All such explanations seem misguided. Aristotle makes it clear that the final step—the refusal to use words—came after a previous period when Cratylus was already a Heraclitean. The implications of Plato's account are also clear; Cratylus at the time of the dialogue had long been interested in the doctrines of Heraclitus, and he also held the theory of words attributed to him. It might be that he failed to realize the inconsistency at the stage represented by the dialogue, and, when the inconsistency became clear, subsequently proposed to abandon speech. More probably, at the time of the dialogue he inclined to the view to which he is clearly attracted when Socrates mentions it, namely, that words themselves in some sense flow, and so point to the flowing nature of the objects to which they refer (*Cratylus*, 437D).

Bibliography

Testimonia in Diels-Kranz, *Fragmente der Vorsokratiker*, Vol. II, 10th ed. (Berlin, 1961). See also V. Goldschmidt, *Essai sur le Cratyle* (Paris, 1940); G. S. Kirk, "The Problem of Cratylus," in *American Journal of Philology*, Vol. 72 (1951), 225–253; D. J. Allan, "The Problem of Cratylus," *ibid.*, Vol. 75 (1954), 271–287; H. Cherniss, "Aristotle, Metaphysics 987a32–b7," *ibid.*, Vol. 76 (1955), 184–186.

G. B. KERFERD

CREATION, RELIGIOUS DOCTRINE OF. Not all cosmogonies are specifically creation theories, and not all accounts of creation are accounts merely of the "beginning of things." Stories of how the world began have often described not its creation but its birth from primordial parents, such as Oceanus or Chaos. They have also used the language of creation—of construction, craftsmanship—with regard to the structure of the world but not with regard to its original matter. The matter is thought of as "given" and perhaps even as recalcitrant to the divine craftsman. The Christian doctrine of creation is primarily about the ontological dependence of the world upon God; and it is of only secondary interest whether that world had a literal beginning, a first moment.

Since the Christian account of creation is distinctive in its thoroughness (creation *ex nihilo*) and in its impact upon both philosophy and science, this article will be chiefly concerned with it.

THE CHRISTIAN DOCTRINE OF CREATION

The doctrine of creation is remarkably rich in the evaluative and evocative overtones characteristic of religious doctrines. If God, as Christianity conceives of him, is the author and sustainer of the world, then the world is a planned and purposed enterprise. It will not do to speak of life as "absurd," as the atheist existentialists do. It will make sense to ask "Why am I here? What is the purpose God has for my life?" The questions may not be readily answerable, but they will at least be meaningful and proper.

Since the God of Genesis "saw every thing that he had made, and, behold, it was very good," Thomas Aquinas could say, "To hold creatures cheap is to slight divine power." The fitting attitude toward nature as God's handiwork is one of respect and reverence. Arrogant exploitation of nature's resources, callousness, and cruelty toward the animal world are forms of contempt for their divine maker. The doctrine works equally against those types of spirituality that despise, and seek eventual escape from, the body. The body is no tomb; the very fact that it has been created indicates that its activities can be directed to good ends.

To affirm that in confronting nature we confront the divine handiwork is not, however, to affirm that nature is itself God. The creation doctrine has the negative function of preventing an idolatrous worship of nature and of reminding one that although God is unchangeable, incorruptible, and all-sufficient, nature is none of these things. As contingent, created, derivative, it is a theater of change and instability. Evil is not a possibility for God, but it is a possibility for nature and an actuality for man.

Man is able only intermittently and dimly to see the world *as* God's world, to discern the creator's splendor in his works. Nonetheless, the doctrine of creation has valuably stimulated the religious imagination and the arts, particularly poetry and painting, to recapture such glimpses and visions. It has also—in more philosophical but equally imaginative ways—prompted believers to see the world as a contingent, derivative world. The incompleteness of explanations, the endless ramifications of causal dependence, the intellectual opacity of space and time—these and many other features of the world can be dwelt upon in such a way as to give force to the claim that the world has a creaturely status.

In common with all the other central Christian doctrines, the doctrine of creation directs the attention to two very different quarters—the this-worldly and the otherworldly. It carries the imagination toward the idea of a transcendent Creator of nature, and it also compels one to take seriously certain aspects of the natural world itself. Two of these aspects are particularly noteworthy: the world seen as historical process and the world seen as the subject matter of a natural science.

To one who accepts the creation doctrine, time is not a mere illusion; nor is temporal process something essentially bad, something from which deliverance alone is to be sought. One of Augustine's criticisms of Neoplatonism was that its view of time could not allow any historical events to have unique and ultimate importance. The Christian, with his claims about the unique redemptive work of Christ, must repudiate that view; and the doctrine of creation helps to articulate a contrasting account. Time is as much a God-created (therefore real and good) feature of the world as are the substances the world contains. And however we interpret the words "In the beginning God . . . ," they clearly announce a linear, not a cyclical, notion of time. Thus room is left for real progress, real regress, real novelty.

Francis Bacon introduced the second of these aspects, the relevance of the creation doctrine to the scientific study of nature. "Whatever deserves to exist," wrote Bacon, "deserves also to be known." Whatever is worth God's trouble to create is worth man's trouble to understand. Natural philosophy can make visible "the footsteps of the Creator imprinted on his creatures." Here the creation doctrine is providing a support for the timid and unsure of foot, a theological "banister" against vertigo before the new and uncharted. The presence of God's imprints and footsteps is a guarantee that nature will be found, to an encouraging extent, rational and intelligible. Mysteries will also be encountered; the design of nature must not be expected to be transparent to the finite intellect of man. God's ways are not our ways. The mysteries, the seeming anomalies, are mysteries of God; and in Bacon's writing they take on the tone not of deplorable, intractable obstacles to understanding nature but of God's sublime "otherness."

In general, the doctrine of divine creation helped to steer the natural sciences between two hazards. On one side lay the danger of imagining that science could be constructed a priori, as a system of necessary truths. If the world had been identical with God, or with God's thinking, this might have been possible. In fact, however, the world is utterly distinct from God; it does not emanate from him by any necessity but receives its being by his free act of will. It is a contingent world whose nature and laws will certainly display that contingency to the scientist. Science, in short, must be empirical.

The risk on the opposite side was that science might be judged altogether impossible, that nature might turn out to be too complex or chaotic to admit of any theory-building. But, although the exploration of nature was not identical with the exploration of the divine mind, it would be made possible and would be furthered by the orderliness and coherence that such a mind would certainly stamp upon any of its works.

The emphasis on creation as freely willed by God, as in no way necessitated, allows the doctrine to express the central Christian affirmation about God: that his nature is love, ἀγάπη (agapē). There is no lack or insufficiency in God that needs the creating of the world to remedy it. Love demands society and community, but the divine society of the Trinity is itself thought of as supplying this scope for love, from eternity. It is possible, therefore, to see the creation of the world as a wholly gratuitous exercise of love.

The Christian claims about creation are thus part of a closely related system of doctrines, and they can by no means be reduced to the single assertion that God is the First Cause or sustaining power of the world. Some theologians will allow that the core of the doctrine is indeed the world's ontological dependence upon God, and that we can grasp the fact of this dependence by natural reason. Others (notably Karl Barth) deny that rational reflection and speculation about the world's contingency can even begin to establish the doctrine. Barth affirms that the doctrine can be known only by faith, and that its content is not expressible in the language of metaphysics but only in that of Christian theology. These two claims are closely related. The God in whom the Christian believes is the God who revealed himself through the specific events of Hebrew history and in the no less historical life, death, and resurrection of Christ. Thus the Christian conception of deity is very different from the conception of a mere timeless "something" beyond the world, upon which the world depends. Reason alone could never establish a link between such a metaphysical something and the God of the Christian creeds. Reason could hardly prove that creation was wholly *good*, sheer "divine benefit," as Barth calls it. Apart from the revelation of God in Christ, this goodness cannot be known.

Revealed or not, the doctrine of creation was clearly developed in and through a sustained polemic with its rivals, both earlier and contemporary. Against the Platonic account of a Demiurge shaping a pre-existent matter after the pattern of the Forms, Christianity affirmed that God created out of nothing whatever. Against Aristotle, the eternity of the world had to be denied, as being incompatible with its derivativeness. This denial, however, begets a new problem. Ought we to conceive God as existing (temporally) before the world, and then "suddenly" creating it at a particular (arbitrary?) moment of time? Not at all, said Augustine and the main theological tradition after him; God's eternity is not an endless temporal succession, nor did time exist until the world existed. Agreeing here with Plato's *Timaeus*, it must be said that time and the world began together. This answer at least has the merit of blocking the questions "What did God do before creating?" "Why did he create just when he did create?" "How could there be time before there were events?"

Since the creation of the world could not literally be taken as an event or events occurring in time, the chief emphasis in the doctrine falls upon the world's constant dependence upon God, a dependence that is alleged to be no less entire today than at any mythologically envisaged "beginning." This interpretation provided a weapon against deism, for the deist naively imagines the world as being once fabricated by God—set up in being, as it were—and then left to manage itself by its own resources. The creation doctrine, without blurring the God–nature gulf, can and does insist on a much more intimate, thoroughgoing, and sustained dependence of the world upon the Creator.

GROUNDING OF THE DOCTRINE

The Christian doctrine of creation is not merely parable or poetry—it makes claims not only to aesthetic and moral impressiveness but also to internal logical coherence and to truth. Even if one were to claim that its truth is to be accepted "on authority," on faith, or by revelation (or all three), the question of its internal coherence would remain crucial. If the doctrine could not be intelligibly stated, there could be no discussion about its truth or falsity.

Time and the creation of the world. The Christian doctrine bypasses certain formidable difficulties by affirming that the world was created *along with*, not *in*, time. It does not force upon us the notion of a time without events. God's eternity is not to be taken as endless temporal duration but as something qualitatively different—a completeness and changelessness that knows none of the successiveness of temporal experience with its "not yet" and "no longer." It becomes very hard, however, if not impossible, to see how the eternal and nontemporal God can *act upon* the temporal and noneternal world; and if it is objected that such a relationship must of course remain mysterious and opaque to us, we must (while receiving the objection with great sympathy) judge the doctrine to be so much the less intelligible—and that at a critical point.

The expression "the whole universe." If the Christian doctrine of creation asserts that the whole universe is created and sustained by God, it presupposes that the expression "the whole universe" is logically in order. Yet it is a notoriously obscure expression, one that may always generate antinomies or paradoxes. Perhaps a reformulation of the doctrine could avoid the difficulty: "given any particular entity or any particular event, were it not for the activity of God, that entity or event would not be or would not happen." This seems to free us from the conception of the universe as a given, limited whole, which it certainly is not.

But we are still forced into thinking of it in just this illegitimate way when we amplify our claim about the created status of the particular entities themselves. The statement that their creation is performed by a deity whose being is not circumscribed by the universe, who works upon it but transcends it, is still logically perplexing. It is perplexing in the same way that such phrases as "beyond the universe" and "outside the universe" are perplexing: all of these consider the world as a somehow completed and somehow limited totality. When in everyday contexts one says "beyond the bushes," "beyond the city boundary," "outside working hours," "beyond the normal life-span," we know in what dimension the "beyondness" lies. The difficulty with the "beyond" of divine transcendence is that all clearly specifiable dimensions are ruled out in advance. All such dimensions belong exclusively to the world and not to God, and we cannot apply them to the relation between God and world.

Ontological dependence. The concept of ontological dependence contains difficulties analogous to those above. This concept is made prima facie intelligible, and given at least some measure of support, by analogies drawn from various familiar dependence relations. A heavy body, if not held up, will fall; a living body, without sustenance, will die. Once a builder has finished a house, said Augustine, he can go away and leave it without the risk of its collapse; but if God were to cease "supporting" the world, even momentarily, it would altogether cease to be. Aquinas quoted this approvingly against "those who argue as though a thing did not need an active cause except while it was in process of being made." The movement of thought here is toward a heightened sense of the instability of things, and hence to the need for constant divine upholding. Although complete *ontological* instability is *sui generis*, it is at least adumbrated in instances of unstable equilibrium and in the instability of living processes.

However, even if much of the observable world is unstable, what is observed are, strictly, instabilities of state, not of being. To say of an organism that it has ceased to be is not to deny that the matter of which it was composed still exists in a changed form. Is the theologian, then, justified in extending to the notion of existence itself the precariousness that attends all the off-balance phenomena, the instabilities of state, position, and the like? The analogies themselves can scarcely serve as proofs; and yet, besides these, little independent argument is forthcoming.

There seems to be no clear and decisive way of discriminating between two very different possibilities. The first is that the world does depend ontologically upon God and that the analogies from familiar dependence relations suffice to suggest this unique and unconceptualizable God–world relation. The second possibility is that the alleged relation of ontological dependence is no relation at all—that it is illusion. All the instabilities of state and situation are irrelevant to the question "Is there instability of *being*?" Persuasively deployed, the instabilities can make us feel that the world is "poised between being and nonbeing," held in being by God, as a car balanced on the edge of a precipice may (for a time) be held from falling by the exertions of bystanders. But neither observation and experience nor strict rational argument seems able to show that the world has this sort of precariousness.

Although this discussion of ontological dependence has been more critical than constructive, it should be acknowledged, in fairness, that certain forms of religious experience can give a far greater impressiveness to the elusive claim of the world's dependence on God than any of the analogies or arguments could by themselves suggest; and they may survive the philosophical criticism of these arguments. The life of a devoted Christian centers worshipfully upon an unseen focus. The moral and aesthetic ideals of such a person are not satisfiable by any this-worldly attainments and fulfillments; and he traffics in symbols and rituals which constantly remind him that on earth he has no continuing city but seeks one to come. An imagination so nourished in a sense of the "beyond" and the "wholly other" has no difficulty in giving an experiential "filling" to the notion of the world's dependence on God.

If one can have such a lively sense of dependence, does that entail the truth of the doctrine? Is this "sense" necessarily illusion-free? Is it genuinely cognitive, or could it be ultimately, though disguisedly, emotive? The pursuit of these questions cannot be undertaken here, but the very possibility of raising them and, more so, the difficulties of knowing how to set up decision procedures for settling them, warn us that the appeal to religious experience, relevant though it is, does not by itself settle all our conceptual and epistemological problems.

Relations between God and the world. There is a rather uneasy tension between the idea of the world's dependence upon God as creator and the idea of God's transcendence. Insofar as we can point clearly and confidently to cases of instability and incompleteness in nature, so far also we can conceive appropriate this-worldly, natural stabilizings and completings. If we conceive God as supplying the stability and completion, we are conceiving him as, basically, a *natural* entity. On the other hand, insofar as we try to think through what is meant by his transcendence and "otherness," we make ourselves quite unable to conceive of his acting upon the world, whether to create it or to sustain it.

This tension can be relieved momentarily by saying that God is not only transcendent but immanent as well. No more than momentarily, however, because the problem at once reappears in a new and equally unyielding form. How can one and the same deity have what seem to be incompatible characteristics, namely immanence and transcendence? If the divine "otherness" is taken seriously, it not only forbids intelligible, direct relating of world and God; it also forbids *indirect* relating. Between utter incommensurables there can be no mediation; there can be no mediation, therefore, between transcendence and immanence, if by "immanence" we mean an aspect of deity that is in *rapprochement* with the world. The problem reappears within the concept of deity itself as a danger of inner disunity, the conflict between the immanent and transcendent aspects of God's nature.

Theism is here in a serious dilemma. The creator's transcendence entails his utter difference from the created world; therefore, the language we use for describing that world is quite inapplicable to him. Yet in order to enunciate its central doctrines, theism must speak of God's activity vis à vis the world, and of man's response to God. That is to say, it must attempt the logically impossible. Whether one can make a legitimate appeal to a doctrine of analogy is too intricate a question for brief discussion. It would be necessary to show by minute analysis whether the analogically modified senses of the particular words employed retained any distinct meaning at all, or whether meaning had indeed been retained but only at the cost of betraying the absolute otherness of God (see ANALOGY IN THEOLOGY).

Creation as planned and purposed by God. The Christian doctrine of creation makes explicit reference to God as freely willing or purposing to create and sustain the world. If the doctrine is to be intelligible, the notions of God as willing, planning, and purposing must be intelligible. These notions cohere perfectly well with certain claims Christians wish to make about God—notably, that he is "personal"—but they clash most vehemently with other and equally important claims.

Willing and purposing are concepts learned in the context of everyday human existence, where men desire, want, and lack, and where they deliberate on practical means and policies for attaining their goals. Willing and purposing are logically connected with such concepts as the anticipating and overcoming of difficulties, the calculating of the probable course of future events, and the possession of a limited standpoint from which alone one's planning can be done, a standpoint from which some features of one's situation can be seen or known better than others, and others not seen or known at all.

A concept of God as planning or purposing or willing to create the world could not include one single facet of that normal conceptual background. God is not limited, ignorant, or in any way insufficient. Moreover, since he is *necessarily* none of these things, the background logically cannot apply; it cannot even survive in a set of such counterfactual statements as "God might have been, but happily is not, in need. . . ." Any being who "might have been in need" cannot be God.

Since God created the world and time together, his creative and sustaining act must be said to fall outside the temporal dimension, and likewise his "purposing" and "willing." Certainly the words "timeless, eternal purposing," "nontemporal, willing" will consent to lie together on the page. But what do they mean? Even the most alluring analogues to eternal existence—the "timeless moments" of aesthetico-mystical experience, or extrapolation from experiences of a "specious present"—shed little or no light upon the concept of a timeless willing or purposing to create. Nor do they illuminate the conception of God as sustaining the world from moment to moment—the eternal and nontemporal supporting a world existing in time.

Certainly, we can imagine our timeless moments as being progressively enriched, as coming to constitute a larger and larger part of our total experience. We could think of these as the first rungs of a ladder, as terms in a series, which we then extrapolate out of our experience; and we might claim to locate at the remote and hidden terminus of that series the eternal mode of being proper to God. But we could not rely on such a scale and its extrapolations with any real confidence. The guiding human experiences (even imaginary ones) give us pathetically few clear terms of the series for us to be able to say with assurance that we see its principle of construction, and that we can extrapolate safely and boldly to the limit. To trust in these operations would be rather like using a weapon with a very short barrel to hit a very distant target.

CREATION IN THE CONTEXT OF SCIENTIFIC COSMOLOGICAL THEORIES

Surely the currently flourishing field of scientific cosmology, in which there is a relatively high measure of logical rigor and an insistence upon empirical grounding, ought to be considered in a study of creation. Certain theories of scientific cosmology postulate a "beginning" to the universe, a unique creation; others speak of "continuous creation." At the time of writing, these two groups of theories coexist in vigorous rivalry, neither having thus far shown itself decisively superior to the other.

One of the chief arguments for the "unique creation" type of theory turns upon the Second Law of Thermodynamics and claims that the process (the increase of entropy) with which that law is concerned could not have gone on from a limitless past or continue to a limitless future. If there is now a steady tendency toward "uniformity" and "homogeneity," we must posit both a beginning to the world—a finite time ago—and an eventual "heat death," a final attainment of complete uniformity. The recession of the galaxies, the "expanding" of the universe, has seemed to some cosmologists also to imply a "beginning," a primordial state of immense density, the center from which expansion and dispersion subsequently took place.

In contrast, the "continuous creation" theorists try to account for these same facts of recession within a "steady-state" theory of the universe. According to this, new matter in the form of hydrogen atoms is "created" in quantity sufficient to maintain the cosmic *status quo*, despite the scattering and receding of galaxies. Both groups of theories are attempts to interpret data obtained by observation and experiment; but in the nature of the case neither group can be verified or falsified in any observationally direct manner. The present interest, in any case, is not in the correctness of a particular theory but in the cosmological use of the concept of creation. Is it a legitimate use? (For further discussions of these theories, see COSMOLOGY.)

If "creation" involves intelligent "bringing into being," the alleged "beginning" posited by the first of the theories mentioned above cannot count as creation. It is quite *non*-theistic in its strict interpretation; the most it is entitled to assert is that the world just "started to be. . . ." Furthermore, the Second Law of Thermodynamics applies, originally and strictly, to closed thermal systems; and it is most dubious whether the whole universe can with any propriety be considered such a system. To consider it so would involve viewing it as a limited whole, existing in an environment. What the "environment" could be, if not simply more universe, it is difficult to imagine; and we cannot interpret it as more universe if we are seeking the environment of the universe as a whole.

Turning to the astronomical arguments about the receding galaxies, is the idea of a creation of the world really supported by the notion of a primordial state out of which the great cosmic expansion came? It would be supported if, and only if, it were shown that this was a real beginning, not merely the start of a new phase in a process that already had passed through earlier phases. It must be shown to be not only the start of "the universe as we know it" but also the start of the universe *as such.* Yet to discriminate between these possibilities does not seem to be in the power of the theory itself. The use of the word "creation" in its context is therefore scientifically and philosophically obfuscating.

Finally, in the "continuous creation" theory, theistic implications are again eliminated. The atoms come into being spontaneously—no agency prompts their appearance; the language of purposing, fashioning, forming does not apply. If "creation" is deprived of all these strands of meaning, it is left with scarcely any meaning at all. Worse than that, because of the place "creation" has had in theological explanation, it retains the tone and weightiness of an "ultimate explanation" concept. It stops further questioning. In cosmological theory it is clearly inappropriate to suggest that explanation must end here. If explanations do end in science, they end only "for the moment," or "because of the present limits of experimentation and understanding"—limits that science hopes to push back and never properly regards as metaphysically ultimate.

This article has taken for its theme the main philosophical and religious roles played by the concept of creation in the history of ideas. In spite of the difficulties, the incoherences in the uses of the concept, it does not follow that there is no useful function for "creation." "Creation," "creativity," and related concepts are indispensable in any adequate moral and aesthetic philosophy. In those contexts they are logically connected with the ideas of human freedom, moral vision, moral criticism, ideas of inventiveness, originality, and the life of imagination. Indeed, a significant part of the metaphysical and theological discussion of creation can be translated or "demythologized" into moral and aesthetic terms, and it has been indirectly relevant to the development of moral philosophy and aesthetic theory.

Bibliography

In view of the immense wealth of material on the topic, the bibliography is confined to recent studies.

Barth, Karl, *Church Dogmatics*, Vol. III, Part I, *Doctrine of Creation*, translated by J. W. Edwards and others. Edinburgh, 1959.

Brunner, Emil, *Dogmatics*, Vol. II, *The Christian Doctrine of Creation and Redemption*, translated by Olive Wyon. London and Philadelphia, 1952.

Dingle, Herbert, *Through Science to Philosophy*. Oxford, 1937. Ch. 11.

Dingle, Herbert, *The Scientific Adventure*. London, 1952. Both Dingle works are relevant to the discussion of scientific cosmology and creation.

Foster, M., "The Christian Doctrine of Creation and the Rise of Modern Natural Science." *Mind*, Vol. 43 (1934), 446–468; Vol. 44 (1935), 439–466; Vol. 45(1936), 1–27.

Garrigou-Lagrange, Réginald, *Dieu, sa nature, son existence*. Paris, 1934; 11th ed., 1950.

Mackinnon, D. M., and Flew, A. G. N., "Creation," in A. G. N. Flew and Alasdair MacIntyre, eds., *New Essays in Philosophical Theology*. New York, 1956.

Mascall, E. L., *He Who Is*. New York, 1943.

Mascall, E. L., *Christian Theology and Natural Science*. New York, 1957.

Munitz, M. K., "Creation and the 'New' Cosmology." *British Journal for the Philosophy of Science*, Vol. 5 (1954–1955), 32–46. The brief discussion of scientific cosmology in the present article is indebted to that of Munitz.

Passmore, J. A., *Philosophical Reasoning*. New York, 1962. Ch. 3. Highly relevant to the problem of the God–world dualism and therefore to "creation."

Scriven, Michael, "The Age of the Universe." *British Journal for the Philosophy of Science*, Vol. 5 (1954–1955), 181–190.

Tillich, Paul, *Systematic Theology*, Vol. I. Chicago, 1951; London, 1953. Especially Ch. 11.

Toulmin, Stephen, and others, *Metaphysical Beliefs*. New York, 1957. Contains interpretations of the Second Law of Thermodynamics.

RONALD W. HEPBURN

CREIGHTON, JAMES EDWIN (1861–1924), American idealist philosopher, was born in Pictou, Nova Scotia. Creighton was educated at Dalhousie College, Halifax (A.B., 1887), where one of his teachers was Jacob Gould Schurman, whom he later followed to Cornell University. He was appointed fellow in philosophy there in 1888 and studied in Leipzig and Berlin, returning to Cornell in 1889 as an instructor. He received his Ph.D. in 1892 with the thesis, "The Will; Its Structure and Mode of Operation," and became associate professor. In 1895 he was elected Sage professor of logic and metaphysics, succeeding Schurman, and held that chair until his death. He received LL.D. degrees from Queens University (1903) and from Dalhousie (1914). While Creighton was dean of the graduate school at Cornell from 1914 to 1923, his flexible policies stimulated student initiative, but the administrative demands on his time limited his literary output. He was coeditor of the *Philosophical Review* from 1892 until 1902, when he became sole editor, and he was American editor of *Kantstudien* from 1896 until his death.

Convinced that the intellectual life is a social venture, Creighton was a cofounder of the American Philosophical Association and in 1902 became its first president. His vigorous instruction influenced the development of philosophy in American education through the efforts of his students, 22 of whom honored him with a volume of articles, *Philosophical Essays* (New York, 1917), commemorating 25 years of his teaching.

Creighton's "speculative idealism" grew out of his view that philosophical inquiry must occur in the context of the history of ideas and must begin with "the standpoint of experience." But experience is not a simple, isolated particular which can be understood by analysis. Finite individuality has system implicit in it, and can be understood as a part of the order of the universe. It is unity in plurality and identity in difference. It is permeated with meaning. In short, Creighton identified it as the "concrete universal." Thus, with Bernard Bosanquet, Creighton held that philosophical judgments are ways in which experience progresses toward its goal of intelligibility, and the task of such judgments is to disclose the implications of the dynamic coordinates of experience: mind, nature, and other selves. Reality cannot be identified with mind, will, or personality but must be comprehended as a system in which each entity plays a part as an individual and as a significant function of the purposeful whole. Epistemological problems traceable to Kant's emphasis on the centrality of the knowing subject are artificial because mind by its very nature is already in touch with reality. Subject and object cannot be viewed as ontologically discrete but are correlative. Accordingly, Creighton dissociated himself from neorealism, which regards truth as a quality of single propositions; from pragmatism, which fails to see that thought modifies the internal structure of experience itself; and from Berkeleianism and other "mentalistic" idealisms, which interpret nature as a phase of mind, thereby transforming experience unnecessarily into an order of ideas instead of accepting objective reality as a direct intuition. Such idealisms, even Royce's absolutism, issue in subjectivism and thus deny the objective world. Creighton maintained that this conclusion would render all thought chaotic because the objective order is the presuppostion of all rationality.

Appointed to the Carus lectureship in 1924, Creighton planned to develop his views on historical method in philosophy, but death intervened. He wrote virtually nothing on ethics, aesthetics, or religion, unlike his idealist contemporaries, but certain details of his system can be inferred from his excellent critical discussions of competing movements.

Works by Creighton

Cotranslator with E. B. Titchener of Wundt, W., *Lectures on Human and Animal Psychology*. London, 1894.

Cotranslator with A. Lefevre of Paulsen, F., *Immanuel Kant*. New York, 1902.

An Introductory Logic. New York, 1908. The fifth edition (New York, 1932) was revised by one of Creighton's colleagues, H. R. Smart.

Studies in Speculative Philosophy, Smart, H. R., ed. New York, 1925. Fourteen of his 38 major articles were posthumously published in this volume, which is the best single source for his views, containing a select bibliography and his most representative essay, "Two Types of Idealism."

Works on Creighton

Blau, Joseph L., *Men and Movements in American Philosophy*. New York, 1952.

Cunningham, G. Watts, *The Idealist Argument in Recent British and American Philosophy*. New York, 1933.

Townsend, Harvey G., *Philosophical Ideas in the United States*. New York, 1934.

Critical discussions of Creighton's work can be found in the three books listed above.

WARREN E. STEINKRAUS

CRESCAS, HASDAI (1340–1410), Spanish rabbi and philosopher. Crescas was born in Barcelona, the scion of a distinguished family. He exercised considerable influence both in the Jewish community and at the Aragonese court. After the 1391 persecution of the Jews, in which his only son perished, Crescas moved to Saragossa, where he engaged in literary activity until his death.

Crescas' purpose was to defend Judaism from both internal and external subversion. To this end he composed his Spanish "Refutation of the Principles of Christianity" (extant only in Hebrew translation), a rational critique of Christian dogmatic theology, and his masterwork, *The Light of the Lord* (*Or Adonai*), conceived as an introduction to a legal code which was never composed. Crescas wrote in the tradition of those thinkers, such as Judah Halevi and Nahmanides, who rejected the rationalistic compromising of Judaism with the teachings of Aristotle, but he differed from them in that he chose to combat the philosophers on their own ground. In this respect his position may be compared with that of al-Ghazali in Islamic philosophy. The *Light* is arranged as a dogmatic treatise, beginning with an exposition of the primary concept of God's existence and unity and followed by expositions of certain fundamental and subordinate doctrines. The first section, in which Crescas presents and criticizes the 26 basic propositions of physics which Maimonides (*Guide*, Part II, Introduction) culled from Aristotle, is concerned less with advancing a new system than with indicating the inadequacy of those of his forerunners. Crescas conceived of time as duration independent of motion and insisted on the possibility of a vacuum based on a conception of space as extension independent of body. These two notions enabled him to establish the existence of infinite time and space, thereby destroying the concept of the Aristotelian prime mover. Furthermore, the debate over creation *ex nihilo* is dismissed as futile since, in any event, all is derivative from God, who is the only necessary existent.

Crescas maintained both the literalness of the Biblical attributes and God's unity by advancing the Kalam-like theory of essential attributes compatible with God's absolute simplicity. These attributes are related to the subject as light rays are to the source of luminescence, one being inconceivable without the other, and are bound together by the unifying principle of the divine goodness. It is this goodness or perfection which characterizes the Divinity, rather than the Aristotelian concept of self-thinking thought.

The return of Crescas to the Biblical conception of God is best exemplified in his treatment of the problem of the conflict between divine foreknowledge and man's free will. Maimonides had taken refuge in the notion that God's knowledge has nothing in common with man's, while Gersonides sacrificed divine knowledge of the future and the particulars to man's unconditional free will. Rejecting both points of view, Crescas felt it unnecessary to reconcile divine knowledge (which he considered absolute) with free will but rather free will with causality. Definitely inclined toward determinism, he maintained that an act is contingent when considered in relation to itself but necessary in relation to its causes and to God's knowledge. Man's consciousness of free will consists in the pleasure or disapproval felt when an act is committed.

Divine providence, prophecy, and immortality are not dependent on intellectual perfection, as in Maimonides and Gersonides, but rather on love and reverence for God, which is the purpose of the Divine Law and the universe. It is the substance of the soul itself, rather than the acquired intellect, which survives death.

Crescas' independence of Aristotle helped pave the way for such Renaissance thinkers as the younger Pico della Mirandola and Giordano Bruno. Of particular interest is Crescas' influence on the thought of Spinoza, who knew his work well.

Bibliography

The *editio princeps* of the *Or Adonai* (*Light of the Lord*) appeared at Ferrara in 1556 and has since been published several times. The first section, which deals with the 26 propositions, has been edited and translated into English by H. A. Wolfson in *Crescas' Critique of Aristotle* (Cambridge, Mass., 1929). The section on free will was rendered into German by Philipp Bloch in *Die Willensfreiheit von Chasdai Crescas* (Munich, 1879).

Crescas' thought has been surveyed in M. Waxman, *The Philosophy of Don Hasdai Crescas* (New York, 1920) and M. Joel, *Don Hasdae Crescas' religionsphilosophische Lehren in ihrem geschichtlichen Einflusse dargestellt* (Breslau, 1866). His influence on Spinoza has been discussed by Joel in *Zur Genesis der Lehre Spinozas* (Breslau, 1871) and by D. Neumark in "Crescas and Spinoza," in *Essays in Jewish Philosophy* (Cincinnati, Ohio, 1929). For a full bibliography, see *Encyclopedia Judaica* (Berlin, 1928), Vol. V, pp. 698 ff., 708.

FRANK TALMAGE

CRITERION. The word "criterion" and its equivalents have been employed by many philosophers. Giambattista Vico used "criterion of truth" as a technical expression in the discussion of Descartes's philosophy; and in *The Critique of Pure Reason* Kant has an argument to show that there can be no general such criterion. The Louvain scholastics at the beginning of the twentieth century made much of the concept, so that *critériologie* became almost a synonym for epistemology. The present article will be restricted to the discussion of the notion of *criterion* which became influential in Anglo-American philosophy as a result of the use of the term as a philosophical tool by Wittgenstein.

Wittgenstein's usage in *The Blue and Brown Books* has been discussed at length by Rogers Albritton. The dominant conception of *criterion of X* in those books, he says, is something that may be described as "X" under certain circumstances, something in which *X* may consist. In the *Philosophical Investigations*, however, the sense has changed: "A criterion for a given thing's being so is something that can show the thing to be so and show by its absence that the thing is not so; it is some thing by which one may be justified in saying that the thing is so and by whose absence one may be justified in saying that the thing is not so"—all this by logical necessity.

Albritton's account of *criterion* in *The Blue and Brown Books* is disputable: its exegesis of *Philosophical Investigations* seems certainly wrong. For it follows from his definition that there can only be a single criterion for a given state of affairs. If that criterion is present, the thing is so, no matter what else may be absent; and if that criterion is absent, the thing is not so, and there is no room for any other criterion which might show the thing to be so after all. But on several occasions in the *Investigations* Wittgenstein considers the possibility that there may be more than one criterion for the same state of affairs. He says, for instance, that in different circumstances we apply different criteria for a person's reading (Sec. 164), and he speaks of the great variety of criteria for personal identity (Sec. 404).

In the *Philosophical Investigations* a criterion of *p*'s being the case is something by which we can tell whether *p* is the case. A criterion for somebody's understanding an algebraic formula is something by which we tell whether he understands it: for instance, the application he makes of it (Sec. 146). A criterion of identity for a sensation is something which could tell us which sensation it was (Sec. 253); a criterion of identity for two processes is something which could tell us whether the two processes are the same (Secs. 376–377). A criterion of correctness for a memory would be something which could tell us whether the memory was correct (Secs. 56, 258; Part II, p. 222).

This, however, is not enough. For any evidence about *p*'s being the case is something by which we can tell whether *p* is the case. But not all evidence that *p* is a criterion for *p*'s being the case.

Criteria and symptoms. In *The Blue Book* Wittgenstein made a distinction between criteria and symptoms. He wrote:

> To the question: "How do you know that so-and-so is the case?" we sometimes answer by giving "*criteria*" and sometimes by giving "*symptoms.*" If medical science calls angina an inflammation caused by a particular bacillus, and we ask in a particular case "why do you say this man has got angina?" then the answer "I have found the bacillus so-and-so in his blood" gives us the criterion, or what we may call the defining criterion of angina. If on the other hand the answer was "His throat is inflamed," this might give us a symptom of angina. I call "symptom" a phenomenon of which experience has taught us that it coincided, in some way or other, with the phenomenon which is our defining criterion. Then to say "A man has angina if this bacillus is found in him" is a tautology or it is a loose way of stating the definition of "angina." But to say "a man has angina whenever he has an inflamed throat" is to make a hypothesis. (p. 25)

One conclusion which we might draw from this passage is that a criterion differs from a symptom in being a decisive piece of evidence. After all, if it is a tautology that when a man has a certain bacillus in his blood, he has angina, then the finding of such a bacillus settles beyond appeal the question whether he has angina. The equation of *criterion* with *decisive evidence* is sometimes made by Norman Malcolm, who says that the application of a criterion must be able to yield either an affirmative or a negative result (*Dreaming*, pp. 24 and 60); and Hilary Putnam, in his attack on Malcolm's theory of *criterion*, makes it an essential step in his argument that criteria should be "ways of settling a question with certainty" ("Dreaming and 'Depth Grammar,'" in *Analytical Philosophy*, Ronald Butler, ed., first series, p. 213).

Criterion as decisive evidence. Is this notion of criterion Wittgenstein's? Some passages in the *Investigations* might suggest so. At one point Wittgenstein raises the question:

what do we regard as the criterion for remembering a color right? It is possible, he reminds us, for a color to strike one as brighter on one day than on another, and yet for one to have reason to believe that one must be wrong and that the color is, despite appearances, the same. "This shews us," he concludes, "that we do not always resort to what memory tells us as the verdict of the highest court of appeal" (Sec. 56). From this we may conclude that, for Wittgenstein, a criterion for *p*'s being the case is "the highest court" to which we might appeal to settle whether *p*.

But the equation of *criterion* with *decisive evidence* must face the difficulty which refuted Albritton's account. If a criterion is conclusive evidence on a topic, how can there be more than one criterion on a single topic? For if there are two independent criteria for a single state of affairs, it is possible that the two criteria may conflict; and in that case, at least one of them is not decisive. This consideration can be urged also against a weaker thesis which is sometimes put forward—that a criterion, while not being necessarily conclusive evidence, is nonetheless the best possible evidence for the state of affairs for which it is a criterion. For it does not seem possible that two independent pieces of evidence could each be better than all other pieces of evidence on the same topic.

It might be replied that while there cannot be two independent pieces of evidence which each settle a question in the affirmative (by their presence) and in the negative (by their absence), yet it is quite conceivable that there should be two pieces of evidence, the presence of either of which would settle the question conclusively in the affirmative but the absence of neither of which would settle it conclusively in the negative. This is certainly so: however, many of the pieces of evidence listed in the *Philosophical Investigations* as criteria for states of affairs are not pieces of evidence which would provide even a conclusive affirmative answer on the topic to which they relate. What a man says, for instance, is a criterion for what mental images he has; but his saying that he has a certain image does not establish that he has, for he may be lying (Sec. 377; *cf.* Part II, p. 222). In the passage cited above (Sec. 56), Wittgenstein's argument was not that memory was not a criterion for change of color but that memory was not always decisive, since there are also criteria for the correctness and incorrectness of memories. All this is elsewhere realized by Malcolm, who wrote in his review of *Philosophical Investigations:* "Do the propositions that describe the criterion of his being in pain *logically imply* the proposition 'He is in pain?' Wittgenstein's answer is clearly in the negative" (*Knowledge and Certainty*, p. 113).

Criterion and definition. There is, it seems, a difference concerning the decisiveness of criteria between *The Blue Book* and the *Investigations.* In *The Blue Book* Wittgenstein does indeed point out that it is not commonly clear which phenomena are criteria and which are symptoms. "It may be practical to define a word by taking one phenomenon as the defining criterion, but we shall easily be persuaded to define the word by means of what, according to our first use, was a symptom." But although there are passages (such as the consideration of criteria of identity on p. 61) which point forward to the *Investigations*, "criterion" in the *Blue Book* seems often equated with "defining criterion"; and a defining criterion is a phenomenon which is conclusive.

In the *Investigations* Wittgenstein returned to the distinction between criteria and symptoms:

> The fluctuation in grammar between criteria and symptoms makes it look as if there were nothing at all but symptoms. We say, for example: "Experience teaches that there is rain when the barometer falls, but it also teaches that there is rain when we have certain sensations of wet and cold, or such-and-such visual impressions." In defence of this one says that these sense-impressions can deceive us. But here one fails to reflect that the fact that the false appearance is precisely one of rain is founded on a definition. (Sec. 354)

Here it is clear that the sense impressions which are the criteria for rain are not conclusive evidence for rain. The difference between criteria and symptoms is that the evidential value of symptoms is something taught by experience, while the evidential value of criteria is something "founded on a definition." If *X* is a criterion of *Y*, then it is a necessary truth that *X* is evidence for *Y*. This leaves open the possibility that there can be more than one criterion for the same state of affairs: there is nothing contradictory in more than one kind of thing's being, by logical necessity, evidence for one and the same state of affairs.

This notion of criterion is well expounded by Sydney Shoemaker:

> We may characterize the criteria for the truth of a judgment as those states of affairs that are (whose existence would be) direct and noninductive evidence in favor of the truth of the judgment. (*Self-Knowledge and Self-Identity*, p. 3)

Shoemaker observes that the term "criteria" is sometimes used also to refer not to the evidential phenomena themselves but to the necessarily true propositions stating the evidential relationship between these phenomena and the judgments of whose truth they are evidence, not only to critical evidence but also to critical rules. Shoemaker's account seems to fit excellently the use of "criterion" in the *Investigations.*

The necessary connection between a criterion and that for which it is a criterion is, for Wittgenstein, the result of human choice: criteria are things which "we fix" (Sec. 322; Part II, pp. 212, 222). The connection is brought about by definition or by the less formal processes of teaching and learning:

> When I say the ABC to myself, what is the criterion of my doing the same as someone else who silently repeats it to himself? It might be found that the same thing took place in my larynx and in his . . . . But then did we learn the use of the words: "to say such-and-such to oneself" by someone's pointing to a process in the larynx or the brain?" (Sec. 376)

X is not a criterion for *Y* if someone could learn the meaning of "*Y*" without having grasped the connection between *X* and *Y*.

Uses of the concept. Wittgenstein uses the concept of *criterion* especially to clarify certain problems in the philosophy of mind. Most commonly, in the *Investigations*, a criterion is an observable phenomenon which is, by logical necessity, evidence for a mental state or process which is not itself observable. Thus, the criterion for the color of someone's mental image is what he says and does: I cannot observe the color of his image, but I can hear what he says and see what he does (Sec. 377).

> . . . there are certain criteria in a man's behaviour for the fact that he does not understand a word, that it means nothing to him; that he can do nothing with it. And criteria for his "thinking he understands," attaching some meaning to the word, but not the right one. And, lastly, criteria for his understanding the word right. (Sec. 269)

In general, "An 'inner process' stands in need of outward criteria" (Sec. 580).

It is, perhaps, necessary to insist that it does not follow, because the criteria for the application of a concept are behavioral, that the concept itself is behavioral. To say that *X* is the criterion for *Y* is not—in the *Investigations*—to say that *X* is the definition of *Y* or that "*Y*" means *X*. Pain behavior may be a criterion for pain, but "pain" does not mean pain behavior. It is a necessary truth that pain behavior is evidence for pain; but this does not imply that "pain" denotes crying. "On the contrary," says Wittgenstein, "the verbal expression of pain replaces crying and does not describe it" (Sec. 244).

A criterion for a mental event need not always be something which is itself directly observable. How do we tell whether someone meant such-and-such by a particular mathematical rule? "The fact that he has, for example, mastered a particular technique in arithmetic and algebra . . . is such a criterion" (Sec. 692). But to have mastered a technique is to possess a capacity; and a capacity is not observed but is inferred on the basis of criteria, most obviously on the basis of exercises of the capacity. Wittgenstein compares the relationship of understanding to its exercise with the relationship between fitting a hollow space and being stuck into a hollow space (Sec. 182). As this last example shows, mental states and processes are not the only unobservable states of affairs which must be inferred from criteria.

Opposition to private language. Wittgenstein's most famous use of the concept of *criterion* is in the course of his argument against private languages. He argues that it would be impossible to give a private ostensive definition of a sensation; for a definition, if successful, must bring it about that in future the sign defined is correctly associated with the thing signified. But if a sensation were a private and incommunicable event, there could be no criterion of correctness for the association of a sign with a sensation (Sec. 258). Memory cannot provide such a criterion, unless we have some further criterion for distinguishing correct from incorrect memories (Sec. 265). But where what is remembered is a private object, we have no way of distinguishing between an accurate memory of an unchanging object and a deceptive memory of a changing one (Part II, p. 207). Hence, a private ostensive definition is impossible.

It appears implicit in the argument against private language that a concept is vacuous if there is no criterion for its application. This doctrine does not lead to verificationism without the added thesis that a criterion is a piece of conclusive evidence. It leads to the weaker conclusion that a concept is vacuous unless there is something which counts as a noninductive evidence for its application. There are difficulties about understanding and accepting this thesis as applying to the concepts of logic and mathematics; it appears more acceptable within the field to which Wittgenstein applies it in the *Investigations*. For if there cannot be noninductive evidence for the application of a concept, then it seems there cannot be inductive evidence for its application either, since inductive correlations presuppose the possibility of noninductively identifying the phenomena to be correlated.

But why cannot there be concepts which apply to reality directly, and not on the basis of criteria? Do we not recognize the application of concepts in this way whenever we say things on the basis of observation rather than inference? It is not part of Wittgenstein's thesis that a concept which has criteria is always employed on the basis of those criteria. The concepts of pain, of mental images, and of personal identity have criteria which Wittgenstein discusses at length; but none of these criteria, he says, are applied when a man says of himself that he has a pain or an image (Secs. 239, 290, 377, 404). An observation statement, of course, differs from a first-person report of a sense impression. It may be made without inference; but unlike the report of a sense impression, it can be justified only by an appeal to evidence, and in the last analysis to criteria. These criteria may themselves be sense impressions; in that case, the subject himself will not recognize these by criteria, but his employment of the concepts involved in reporting sense impressions, as the argument against private languages shows, must itself be subject to control by criteria.

Criterion and concept change. Can the criteria for a concept change without the concept's changing? This has been hotly debated. If "criterion" is equated with "conclusive evidence," then it seems that any change in criteria must involve a change of sense: thus, Malcolm argues that if a physiological criterion for dreaming were introduced, a new concept would arise for which the name "dreaming" could not be rightly used (*Dreaming*, p. 81). Putnam, on the contrary, has argued that it is only in a very restricted sense that the sense of the term "acid" changed when a new theoretical definition replaced the rough-and-ready criteria of eighteenth-century chemists ("Dreaming and 'Depth Grammar,'" pp. 220–221).

If "criterion" is defined as in the quotation above from Shoemaker, we can make a distinction here. Shoemaker observes:

> A test of whether something is one of the criteria for the truth of judgments of a certain kind is whether it is conceivable that we might discover empirically that it is not, or has ceased to be, evidence in favor of the truth of such judgments. (*Self-Knowledge and Self-Identity*, p. 4)

If this is correct, then it is not possible to subtract one of the criteria for a concept without changing that concept. But it does not follow that it is impossible to add to the criteria without so doing. To take Malcolm's example: if new criteria were added to the concept of dreaming so that the dreamer's waking reports ceased to be evidence for his dream, then the concept would have changed. This is clear, but it is not so clear that criteria could not be added so that the dreamer's reports ceased to be the only noninductive evidence for his dream. To discover, in this and other similar cases, what kind of criteria could be added without changing the concept in question seems to call for detailed investigation and fine discernment.

Bibliography

Albritton, Rogers, "On Wittgenstein's Use of the Term 'Criterion.'" *Journal of Philosophy*, Vol. 56, No. 22 (1959), 845–857.

Buck, R. C., "Non-other Minds," in Ronald Butler, ed., *Analytical Philosophy*. Oxford, 1962. Pp. 187–210.

Hare, R. M., *The Language of Morals*. Oxford, 1952. Pp. 94–110.

Kant, Immanuel, *Critique of Pure Reason*, translated by Norman Kemp Smith. London, 1933. Pp. 97 ff.

Malcolm, Norman, *Dreaming*. London, 1959.

Malcolm, Norman, *Knowledge and Certainty*. Englewood Cliffs, N.J., 1963. Pp. 112–117.

Mercier, Desiré, *Critériologie*, 8th ed. Louvain, 1923.

Putnam, Hilary, "Dreaming and 'Depth Grammar,'" in Ronald Butler, ed., *Analytical Philosophy*. Oxford, 1962. Pp. 211–235.

Shoemaker, Sydney, *Self-Knowledge and Self-Identity*. Ithaca, N.Y., 1962.

Vico, Giambattista, *De Antiquissima Italorum Sapientia* (1710), in Fausto Nicolini, ed., *Opere*, 8 vols. Bari, 1911–1941. Vol. I.

Wellman, Carl, "Wittgenstein's Conception of a Criterion." *Philosophical Review*, Vol. 71, No. 4 (1962), 433–447.

Wittgenstein, Ludwig, *Philosophical Investigations*. Oxford, 1953. Part I, Secs. 51, 56, 141, 146, 149, 160, 164, 182, 190, 239, 253, 258, 269, 288, 290, 322, 344, 354, 376–377, 385, 404, 573, 580, 625, 633, 692; Part II, pp. 177, 181, 185, 198, 203, 222.

Wittgenstein, Ludwig, *The Blue and Brown Books*. Oxford, 1958. Pp. 24–25, 49–50, 55, 57, 61, 63–64.

ANTHONY KENNY

CRITICAL PHILOSOPHY. *See* GERMAN PHILOSOPHY; KANT, IMMANUEL; NEO-KANTIANISM.

CRITICAL REALISM. *Critical Realism* is the title of a book by Roy W. Sellars published in 1916. The name was adopted by a group of philosophers who shared many of his views on the theory of knowledge. *Essays in Critical Realism: A Cooperative Study of the Problem of Knowledge* by Durant Drake, A. O. Lovejoy, J. B. Pratt, A. K. Rogers, George Santayana, Roy W. Sellars, and C. A. Strong was published in 1920.

Background. Much of the epistemological debate since the seventeenth century stems from the matter–mind dualism of Descartes, who argued that what we know first and most surely is not a physical world but the existence of our own minds, and of Locke, who argued that we are immediately acquainted only with our own ideas. Starting from these assumptions, how can one know a physical world external to the mind, if, indeed, such a world exists at all? Critical Realism is a chapter in this long debate. Some philosophers, finding it impossible to bridge the gap from a mental world to a material reality that transcends it, turned to some form of subjectivism or idealism; at the beginning of the twentieth century the dominant philosophy in Britain was the Neo-Hegelian idealism of F. H. Bradley and Bernard Bosanquet, and in America it was the voluntarism of Josiah Royce, the personalism of George H. Howison and Borden Parker Bowne, or the pragmatism of William James. But idealism, uncongenial to common sense and to ordinary interpretations of physical science, was followed by a reaction. Scientific knowledge seemed to support philosophical realism rather than idealism.

Shortly before the emergence of Critical Realism a group of philosophers, calling their view the New Realism, argued that even if it is true that whenever something is being perceived, it is an object for a mind, it does not follow that it has no existence except by being perceived. Hence, the idealist commits a fallacy if he concludes that the whole world is nothing but ideas from the truism that when something is known, it is an object for a mind. The American new realists, then—and here they could claim the support of such important British thinkers as G. E. Moore and Bertrand Russell—maintained that elements in perception can at the same time be elements in the physical world. Things do not cause ideas in us, as Locke would have said, so that we first know only ideas and then try to infer from them the nature of the real world which is never directly perceived. Rather, knowing is more akin to selecting, or throwing a light upon, aspects or parts of a world already there to be selected or illuminated by the light of consciousness.

The critical realist position. The critical realist agrees with the new realist in holding that there is an objective physical world; their disagreement is chiefly on the question of the relation of the datum of knowledge to its object. Physical things, or parts of them, cannot be directly presented to us in perception. Considering the great variety of what is perceived—the double image, the partially submerged bent stick, the toe that is felt after the leg has been amputated—under various conditions by both normal persons and those who are, for example, inebriated or color-blind, are we to say that the real world actually contains all that is disclosed in all these circumstances? And is there no such thing as error? The trouble is that the "direct" realist, by identifying the immediate data of knowledge with elements of the physical world, is trying to account for the universe with an insufficient number of categories or kinds of entities. The knower, whether he is conceived as an organism and a part of nature or as a mind, does not "take in" the physical world. According to Santayana, the datum is an essence, a Platonic universal, which has an identity by being just the character it is, whether it characterizes one or many things in nature or characterizes no existent whatsoever. The datum, the immediately intuited evidence of reality, cannot be numerically identical with any part of that reality.

It is on this epistemological point that the critical realist opposes both the idealist and the direct realist. Whatever exists and whatever its character may be, no datum, or essence, given in experience exists, at least not in the sense in which we say that the objects of perception exist. As Santayana says in *Scepticism and Animal Faith*, "Existence is never given." When the astronomer talks about the moon, he does not mean by "the moon" the yellow disk image that may come to your mind; no doubt, a different image will come to the mind of your companion. If both of you understand the astronomer, "the moon" will mean to both of you, and to the astronomer, the same object to which your thoughts or perceptions are referred—namely, the distant satellite of the earth to which you ascribe certain physical properties. The words or images are the symbols of a meaning, but the essence of the word or image is not, in general, the essence of its meaning. The essence of the meaning is intended to be, but in cases of error will not be, the essence of the actual moon in the sky. This distinction, perhaps difference, between the nature of an image or sense datum and the nature of the object known by means of it is still more obvious when we consider feelings instead of visual images. When sympathizing with a person who has a toothache, we do not say, "I feel the way you feel"; we say, "I know how you feel." Knowing about another person's toothache is not having a toothache.

In perception, as distinguished from thought or conception, there is a tendency to identify image with meaning, so that an effort of analysis is required to separate image, meaning, and object. Paradoxically, the meaning is often psychologically prior to the image. For example, we may perceive a penny as round and as "out there" before noting that in the given perspective it presents an elliptical image. We can then analyze the situation into the image (elliptical), the meaning (round), and the belief that a round object was out there. Error is possible because there may be no object having the same essence as that contemplated in the meaning we have given to the elliptical image that was presented to us. A resolute skeptic who doubts all existence cannot be proved to be mistaken, but if he is consistent, he should be as skeptical of the existence of other minds and even of his own living self as he is of a physical world. Since the idea of change is no guarantee of actual change or process, he should arrive at an inarticulate solipsism of the present moment.

Yet there is no doubt that philosophers as well as laymen normally believe in the existence of themselves and other minds and ascribe at least some of the characters they intuit to things that exist in space at present or past times. In memory and in the belief in history, the referent of present thoughts is a world of things and events believed to be existentially real and independent of any intuitions, present or past. An actual past or future is not given in any datum, but when one speaks, as David Hume did, of having or of being a succession of perceptions, one posits the existence of a temporal series of events and thereby instantiates in existence one or more essences. To ascribe existence to an essence as such would be a logical or categorial error; it would equally be a logical error to assert that an essence had been intuited by some mind or that some event or perception had occurred and at the same time deny that there is any factual temporal existence. The ontological status proper to essences is timeless subsistence. Actual intuitions come to exist on particular occasions, but knowledge of what they mean, says Santayana, "involves a leap of faith and action from the symbol actually given in sense or thought, to some ulterior existing object."

In *Essays in Critical Realism* Santayana argued that a child reaching for the moon is in quest of an object deployed in a physical world along with the outstretched arm and other bodies. If the moon did not transcend experience, if what is experienced were itself the object striven for, it would already be attained, and there would be no biological need to employ the presently intuited essence as a symbol for an existence still to be reached. There would be no knowledge about anything nor any need for it. If there is any validity in our scientific and common-sense beliefs, our intuitions are engendered in a biological organism by a natural environment. Matter in flux embodies now one essence, now another, and the set of propositions that describes all that exists at all times constitutes the realm of truth. Truth is therefore that part of the realm of essence that happens to characterize existence, and to have knowledge is to believe what is true.

But believing a proposition does not guarantee its truth, beyond the truth of the fact that it is believed. The terms of our beliefs are, in general, symbolic rather than literal representations of nature. Does it make any difference, then, if we clothe nature with intuited essences that are more fanciful than true as long as they are signals for successful action? If a pragmatist at this point suggests that truth means no more than the verification in later experience of the anticipated result of action guided by the earlier experience, the realist cannot agree. The pragmatist does agree with the realist that in knowing there is a reference beyond the immediate having of perceptions, but for the pragmatist the consummation of knowing, the successful working of an idea, does not go beyond experience; the referent of an idea is another experience. This avoids the problems of a mind–matter dualism and avoids the unanswerable question: How can we know when our ideas correctly represent external things? But the realist sees the pragmatist position as a reversion to idealism and subjectivism and will have none of it. If the pragmatist, to escape idealism, speaks in naturalistic terms, he admits all that the realist asks for. Lovejoy quotes William James: "Practically our minds meet in a world of objects which they share in common" (*Essays in Radical Empiricism*, New York, 1912, p. 79) to show that the practical man, going about his business of solving problems, must assume the existence of an external world; it is important that he discover what its properties were antecedent to and independent of the inquiry in which that discovery is made. Phenomenalism and positivism, sharing with pragmatism the view that the referent of all that can be meaningfully said about real existence must be, in principle, capable of being found in direct experience, are likewise rejected by the critical realist.

How, then, is knowledge of an external reality possible? The critical realist maintains that Locke erred in taking his own ideas to be the objects of knowledge. Knowledge, Locke said, is nothing but the perception of the agreement or disagreement of our ideas. When he comes to a discussion of "knowledge of real existence," however, he is forced to abandon his own definition, and true knowledge becomes the correspondence between ideas and external things. The critical realist argues that Locke should have recognized that when ideas are used in knowing, as distinguished from being merely entertained or had as an experience, there is always reference to an object other than themselves. But merely insisting that data have a referent beyond themselves does not tell us why we should believe one interpretation of them to be a truer description of the facts than any other interpretation. In his more skeptical mood Santayana tells us that knowledge is only faith mediated by symbols, yet in *The Realm of Matter* he sets forth what he takes to be the "indispensable properties of substance." Presumably, he means literally true properties. Substance has parts external to one another and, being in flux and unequally distributed, constitutes a spatial and temporal field of action. These are very nearly those primary qualities which Locke had said resemble the ideas the mind has of them, and if the critical realist seems to have a better case for his position than Locke had, it is chiefly because the sciences have supplied us with a detailed account of the mechanism of perception.

The scientist finds by actual experiment that the date of emission of light from the star, the distorting intervening media between the star and the observer, and the physiological peculiarities of the observer's body all condition what turns up at what time in the experience of the observer. But this scientific account cannot be used by the critical realist to support his position without begging the question. What is proved is that whenever something is found in our world, we can also find something else related to it; scientific knowledge consists of finding what is related to what. This supports the critical realist's thesis that experience depends upon a reality outside all possible experience only if it is assumed from the outset that the experimental data used by the astronomer and by the physiologist are experienced effects of a physical star and a physical organism. The scientist could interpret his explanatory theories on idealist or pragmatist, instead of on critical realist, assumptions. Hence, it is not what the scientist finds, but the epistemology he happens to assume, that supports critical realism. The best that can be said for this realist assumption is that it may be the most economical way to predict and control our experiences and that it may even be the truth about reality.

Differences among critical realists. Some of the critical realists, including Sellars, believe that their position is not best interpreted, even by some within their own camp, when a curtain of essences, ideas, or sense data is drawn between the perceiver and the objects he wants to know by means of such data. For in that case, as in Locke's representative perception theory, the essences or ideas are themselves the only possible objects of knowledge. Sellars would escape this difficulty by what he believes to be a more adequate account of perceiving. When a biological organism has sensations—that is, is affected by an object in the environment with which it must come to terms—the sensation functions as information about the object that caused it. Perception is a response; it is an act of taking the sensation as the appearance of the external object. It is not the sensation or the sense datum that appears; it is by means of the sensation that the object appears. A sophisticated analyst might make the qualities of the sensation the object of his study, but then he is no longer using them to decipher things.

Sellars finds an ally in the English philosopher Gilbert Ryle, who follows common sense in the belief that we perceive trees and hands, not sense data. Here it would seem that Sellars has left the critical realists to join the direct realists, but he would insist that he is not taking either a direct presentational view or a Lockean representational view. The mediating role of sensation, which determines how the object will look, is not to be ignored. We look *with* our sensations but not *at* them.

In addition to some differences about the role of essences and of sense data, the critical realists are not all in accord on questions of metaphysics. Sellars and Santayana could be called metaphysical monists because for them only one kind of substance—matter—exists. The psyche of which Santayana speaks is the conscious material organism. Sellars thinks of the so-called mental functions not as being carried on by a substantial mind but as ways in which biological organisms, after a long evolutionary development, have learned to respond to stimuli.

Lovejoy, on the other hand, maintains that only a psychophysical dualism is a tenable corollary of an epistemological dualism; only a mind could have sensations and thoughts and intend or mean objects by them.

There has, then, been considerable divergence in the views of thinkers who were, and many who still are, called critical realists. Some have drawn closer to the positions of the direct realists in America or in Britain, and it may be that the label will cease to characterize a definite epistemology.

Bibliography

Drake, Durant, *Mind and Its Place in Nature*. New York, 1925.

Drake, Durant, et al., *Essays in Critical Realism: A Cooperative Study of the Problem of Knowledge*. London, 1920.

Lovejoy, A. O., *The Revolt Against Dualism*. La Salle, Ill., 1930.

Murphy, A. E., "The Fruits of Critical Realism." *Journal of Philosophy*, Vol. 34 (1937), 281–292.

Pratt, J. B., *Personal Realism*. New York, 1937.

Santayana, George, *Scepticism and Animal Faith*. New York, 1923.

Santayana, George, *Realms of Being*, 4 vols. New York, 1927–1940.

Schilpp, Paul A., ed., *The Philosophy of George Santayana*. Evanston, Ill., 1940.

Sellars, Roy W., *Critical Realism*. Chicago, 1916.

Sellars, Roy W., *The Philosophy of Physical Realism*. New York, 1932.

Sellars, Roy W., "American Critical Realism and British Theories of Sense Perception." *Methodos*, Vol. 14, Nos. 55–56 (1962), 61–108.

A. G. RAMSPERGER

CROCE, BENEDETTO (1866–1952), the best-known Italian philosopher of this century. His universally and justly celebrated book on aesthetics, *Estetica come scienza dell'espressione e linguistica generale* (1902), which became the first volume of his systematic "philosophy of the spirit," was a foundation stone in the great revival of historical idealism in Italy between 1900 and 1920. In a long and diligent life devoted almost entirely to scholarly studies, Croce gained an international reputation in the fields of aesthetics, literary criticism, cultural history, and historical methodology; and he exercised in these areas an influence so pervasive that it cannot yet be definitively estimated.

Life and works. Born at Pescasseroli, in the Abruzzi, of a family of wealthy landowners, Croce never needed to earn a living. He displayed an early bent for literary and historical research but never seriously entered on an academic career, preferring to be master of his own course of study. From 1883—when his parents were killed, and he himself buried and injured, in an earthquake—until 1886 he lived with his uncle Silvio Spaventa (brother of the philosopher Bertrando) in Rome, and for a time he attended the university there. At the university he came under the influence of Antonio Labriola, who led him to the study of Johann Friedrich Herbart and, later, of Karl Marx. These studies left a lasting mark on his philosophy. After 1886 he lived permanently in Naples.

In 1893 Croce published his first philosophical essay, "La storia ridotto sotto il concetto generale dell'arte" ("History Brought Under the General Concept of Art"), a title that foreshadowed the main concerns of his mature thought. In 1898, while working on a book on Marx (*Materialismo storico ed economia marxista*), he entered into correspondence with his younger contemporary, Giovanni Gentile, who was similarly occupied. Thus began a friendly collaboration that lasted 25 years. In 1900 came the first sketch of Croce's *Aesthetic.* In 1903 he founded the journal *La critica*, and in 1904 he became an editorial adviser to the publishers Laterza of Bari. For the rest of his life he exercised an ever-increasing influence on the literary and academic world through these two channels.

Even as the volumes of Croce's philosophy of spirit were being published, his association with Gentile was leading him to a re-examination of Hegel. He published his results in 1907 (*Ciò che è vivo e ciò che è morto nella filosofia di Hegel*) and made appropriate revisions in his *Estetica* and in his *Logica come scienza del concetto puro* (1905). *Filosofia della pratica, economia ed etica* appeared at Bari in 1909. In 1911 he published *La filosofia di Giambattista Vico*—Vico was the other major influence on his thought—and in the succeeding years he wrote the essays that appeared at Bari in 1917 as the culminating volume of his system, *Teoria e storia della storiografia.*

In 1910 Croce was made a life member of the Italian senate, but he was not then actively involved in politics. He was a neutralist prior to Italy's entry into World War I in 1915; and in the postwar crisis, he became minister of public instruction in Giovanni Giolitti's last cabinet (1920–1921). With Gentile's help, Croce drafted a reform of the school system, rejected at the time but later incorporated in the fascist *Riforma Gentile* of 1923–1924. Naturally, therefore, he regarded the first fascist administration with some benevolence. His breach with fascism (and with Gentile) came with the establishment of an overt dictatorship in January 1925. He drafted a celebrated "Protest" against Gentile's "Manifesto of Fascist Intellectuals" and thus became identified as the chief antifascist intellectual, a role he worthily maintained through more than 15 years of almost complete political isolation and retirement. He emerged briefly in 1929 to speak in the senate against the concordat with the Vatican. After the fall of fascism he became a leader of the revived Liberal party and served once more as a cabinet minister for a short period in 1944.

During his years of isolation, Croce wrote voluminously and his thought developed significantly. His aesthetics reached its final form only in *La poesia* (1936). His opposition to fascism is often apparent in his literary criticism, but it expressed itself more naturally in his historical writing and in theoretical reflection on politics and history, where it led to vital developments in his thought.

Croce celebrated his eightieth birthday by founding and endowing the Institute for Historical Studies, which is still located in his former home. In spite of a serious stroke in 1950, he went on working right up to his death.

Aesthetics. When Croce's philosophical interests were first aroused in 1893, he was a historical and literary scholar who accepted most of the assumptions of the French positivism then dominant in the circles in which he moved. But controversy led him to ask himself whether history was an art or a science, and he made a decisive choice in favor of the idealist view of the great Hegelian philosopher of art and literary historian Francesco De Sanctis (1817–1883). Initially, his idealist aesthetics was set in a context of a realistic metaphysics, of which there were still some signs in the *Aesthetic* of 1902; but the attempt to expound his view systematically, combined with his discovery of Vico and rediscovery of Hegel, led to the development of his full-fledged idealism. Thus, his aesthetic theory was the original foundation of his philosophy of spirit, although it might fairly be argued that the theory of moral judgment became more fundamental in the final form of his system. Croce himself distinguished four phases in his reflections on aesthetics. Some critics have held one or more of the later phases to be inconsistent with his system as a whole, but they will here be viewed as part of a continuous and essentially consistent evolution.

Aesthetic intuition. It is characteristic of idealist aesthetics to regard aesthetic experience as a kind of cognition. Following Vico and De Sanctis, Croce regarded it as the primitive form of cognitive experience. Intuition is a nonconceptual form of knowledge; it is the awareness of a particular image either of outward sense (a person or a thing) or of inner sense (an emotion or a mood). Intuitions possess a kind of ideal being and validity that is independent of and ontologically prior to any question of existence or nonexistence. Croce's use of the term "intuition" derived directly from Kant's use of *Anschauung*, and he originally thought of the external world as a Kantian manifold of sensation, which we organize into distinct perceptions through the intuitive faculty of imagination. Thus, history was initially "subsumed under the general concept of Art," as the subform of art that is concerned with the ordering of intuitions of actual existence. He soon abandoned this position, but if Kant's theory of space and time as the "forms of intuition" through which the sensible manifold is organized is recalled, it can be seen how Croce's view applies to the plastic arts, which he often seemed to ignore. His own background and interests were predominantly literary, and his theory frequently seems specifically devised to meet the needs of literary critics who have to deal with poems, which are uniquely individual entities created in the conceptual (or logically universal) medium of language. Croce himself fostered this illusion by insisting that aesthetics was "the general science of language." This is a very Pickwickian contention on his part, since the conceptual function of words and symbols in factual communication—which must surely be regarded as fundamental in a general theory of *language*—is specifically excluded from his "science of expression"; and all forms of nonconceptual communication—even nonverbal ones—are included in it.

Lyrical intuition. If it had not been for his overriding concern with poetry, Croce might never have advanced to the second phase of his aesthetics, the theory that all intuition is "lyrical" in character. The problem he faced was essentially one of defining what it is that is nonconceptually communicated in poetry by way of language. His answer was that poetry communicates emotions and moods, it expresses for cognitive contemplation different aspects of the practical personality of man. Here the "circle of the spirit," the doctrine that man's theoretical activity has his practical reality as its one and only object, comes into view. By means of this doctrine, Croce was able to dispense with the last residues of naive realism present in his basically Kantian epistemology. Some doctrine of this sort was certainly needed if the view that art is nonconceptual cognition was to be maintained. As Croce said in 1908, in his lecture announcing the doctrine, "An image that does not express a state of mind has no theoretical value." But the need might well have appeared less pressing, and the solution less natural and obvious, if he had not always thought primarily about poetry.

It is easy—especially if one reads only the *Breviary of Aesthetics* (1912), as many English-speaking students do—to misinterpret Croce's theory that all art is lyrical as a type of romanticism, which he was, in fact, absolutely opposed to. His doctrine was that art is the expression of emotion, not just for its own sake but as a special kind of cognitive awareness. He was seeking a middle way between the intellectualist errors of classical theorists, with their artificial canons, rules, and genres (all of which he categorically rejected), and the emotional excesses of the romantics, with their glorification of immediate feeling. His critique of classical intellectualism is easily grasped; but it is a mistake to think, as some critics have, that his "lyricism" is radically inconsistent with his own systematic rationalism. Unlike Gentile, Croce always refused to identify intuitions as "feelings" or to formulate his theory in terms of "feeling" at all, because he held that "feeling" was an ambiguous concept which when clarified referred to the practical impulse that is the content of intuition.

Cosmic intuitions. How can the expression of emotion produce cognitive awareness? This was the problem that Croce faced in the third phase of his thought—his theory that all intuition has a "cosmic" aspect. Again, some doctrine of the sort was required by his basic thesis that intuition is cognitive of particulars without reference to their existential status. Simply as images they provide experience of the universal human spirit. This self-validating character, this reference to universal humanity (not as an abstract nature or essence but as the activity of the spirit revealing itself in personal experience and in history as a whole) is what Croce called the cosmic aspect of genuine intuition. Some intuitions, however, are more directly cosmic than others and are hard to characterize in terms of specific emotions; this was the classical counterweight against lyrical romanticism in Croce's thought. It was apparently suggested to him by an essay of Wilhelm von Humboldt on Goethe, and he applied it in critical studies of such masterpieces as *Faust* and the *Divine Comedy*. Oddly enough, however, it was neither Dante nor Goethe, but Ariosto, who served as Croce's paradigm of the cosmic poet. Croce earnestly desired to avoid confusion between the proper lyrical unity of a poem and the logical coherence of a philosophical system. His own critical practice even provides some justification for the view that the whole cosmic phase of his theory was an aberration. The truth is rather that it was an inescapably necessary complement of his general view and that his critical practice suffered from an antiphilosophical bias.

Literature and art. The final phase of Croce's aesthetic theory is the theory of literature in *La poesia*, which forms the negative corollary of his theory of intuition. Much that is ordinarily classified as art was, in Croce's view, not properly art at all because in it the purity of intuitive cognition is subordinated to various practical ends, such as entertainment or intellectual and moral instruction. For instance, he declared the *De Rerum Natura* to be a work of literature, not of art; and although this is an extreme case of his critical bias, it is easy to see what led him to it, since the passionate conviction and practical aim of Lucretius are evident in every line of the poem.

Logic of history and the sciences. As aesthetics is the science of pure intuition, so logic is the science of pure concept; and as pure intuition is the form in which we imaginatively express some particular aspect of the human spirit, so pure conception is the form in which we rationally evaluate these particular manifestations and relate them to one another and to the spirit as a systematic unity. Thus on the one hand, conceptual cognition presupposes intuition because it requires intuitions as its material; and on the other hand, aesthetics, the science of intuitive cognition, is only a subdivision of logic because beauty is a form of the pure concept. Concepts presuppose intuitions but are not derivable from them; and any evaluation or correlation of intuitions—even the categorizing of them as intuitions—presupposes concepts. This is the "dialectic of the distincts," which Croce insisted was more ultimate and fundamental than the Hegelian dialectic of opposites. His model here was Kant, rather than the often-cited Vico. For Vico, as for Hegel, poetic cognition was already an immature form of reason, or, in other words, reason develops out of it; whereas for Croce, as for Kant, the two functions were quite distinct and interdependent, although not equally primitive. Croce's aesthetics was a new transcendental analytic, and his logic was a new deduction of the categories.

Knowledge. For Croce, however, the words "reason" and "knowledge" meant something very different from what they meant to Kant. Croce's work was a "critique of historical reason," and the knowledge that he regarded as genuine was historical knowledge. It is only to historical judgments that the predicates "true" and "false" are properly applicable. According to Croce, the scientific knowledge of Kant's *Critique* was a myth, and belief in this myth was one type of logical error. (Croce offered an exhaustive analysis of the types of logical error as a sort of negative proof of his own deduction.) Science and scientific investigation are forms of practical activity, not of cognition. They cannot be genuinely cognitive because they are founded on pseudo concepts, not on the genuine forms of the pure concept.

Thus, for example, if a child reports that "the cat is on the mat," this is a statement of historical fact and its truth or falsity can be established. But if a scientist says, "The cat is a mammal with such and such properties," the words "cat" and "mammal," together with all the property-terms, are abstract universals, artificial summaries of actual aesthetic and historical experience. These abstractions are enormously useful in practical experience—indeed, they are vital to the intelligent planning of our lives—but they could only be the basis of genuine knowledge if we were endowed with the kind of rational intuition into the "real essences" of things that is described in Plato's myths.

The forms of the pure concept are the distinct forms of the spirit itself, since only a proof that some form of the spirit is "distinct" in Croce's sense could establish the a priori validity of a proposed category or standard of judgment. There are four such forms and, hence, four ways in which our experience can be cognitively categorized and evaluated. Any proper element of experience can be considered from two theoretical and two practical points of view; it can be evaluated intuitively, rationally, economically, or morally.

Error. In his theory of error, Croce followed Descartes and Antonio Rosmini. He regarded all genuine error as caused by the intrusion of practical motives into theoretical contexts. He was primarily concerned with philosophical errors, such as the belief that science is knowledge or the belief in myth (a historical narrative possessing absolute significance), which he took to be the origin of religion. About mistakes in historical interpretation, his view appears to have been that (if the historian advances his hypotheses in a properly tentative spirit) they are not really errors but stages in the development of truth.

Philosophy and history. Under the influence of Gentile, Croce accepted the Hegelian identification of philosophy with the history of philosophy and reduced even the a priori judgments of his own logic (for example, that there are four forms of the spirit) to the status of historical judgments. He did this because he held that no one could "close the gates of truth" against further progress. Yet he never accepted Gentile's view that this formal concession to the future meant that all deductions of "the forms of the spirit" were mistaken; he remained convinced that his logic possessed an eternal validity. In his view, the unity of philosophy and history was a unity of distincts.

Economics and law. The most fundamental of all distinctions in Croce's philosophy is the distinction between theory and practice. Goaded by the actual idealists who sought to unify theory and practice in the "pure act," Croce tried to justify this distinction by arguments that were largely wasted, because his opponents did not really deny the distinction any more than he denied the unity. The only point at issue was the more general question of whether the unity arose from a dialectic of opposed moments or of distinct forms.

Economic utility and vitality. It has already been shown how the circle of the spirit first appeared when Croce recognized practical impulse as the presupposed content of intuition. It would seem to follow that the practical manifestation of the spirit is somehow more primitive than the spirit's theoretical functions; but the implication is, at best, only a partial truth, for Croce claimed also that the primitive form of practical activity—economic volition—presupposes both forms of theoretical activity. He had learned from his long study of Marx and of the English classical economists that the calculation of economic utility is a rational process and that economic action involves historical judgment. The practical impulse that intuition presupposes, considered in itself, is not yet the conscious action of the spirit; it is only the blind urge of organic life out of which the spirit emerges. But the origin of volition in vitality is what accounts for the independence that Croce always ascribed to economic utility as a distinct spiritual form. Critics objected from the beginning that there was a paradox involved in treating utility as an autonomous form of value. There is no such thing as simple usefulness; there is only usefulness for some purpose. It is really life or vitality that is the primitive category of action. In later writings Croce recognized this, but he continued to hold that economic action is the first form of action in the true sense.

In spite of Croce's insistence that the "utility" of the economists is a fundamental philosophical category, his logic does not allow the admission of economics itself as a genuine philosophical science. The work of economists, like that of all other scientists, belongs to the category of utility itself, not to that of truth. "Economic man" is a paradigm case of a pseudo concept.

Law and utility. It is more surprising, perhaps, to find the concept of law subsumed under that of utility in Croce's system. The Kantian model, which we have appealed to several times, might lead us to expect moral law as the universal form of practical consciousness. Law in fact functions as a transitional notion in Croce's system because it may be obeyed either from motives of duty or from motives of expediency. Croce held, however, that in the making and execution of law we should be guided strictly by considerations of social utility, since no one can make a genuinely moral judgment about what is right for a whole class of cases defined abstractly. Laws are of necessity framed in terms of the pseudo concepts of economics and social science; even the moral habits and rules we adopt as our own guides are similarly abstract. They belong among the instruments of life, not among its purposes. Because so much of the work of government is also instrumental, Croce tried at first to formulate a purely economic theory of political action in general. This view he subsequently abandoned.

Ethics and politics. Moral action and moral judgment are the distinct universal forms of practical consciousness corresponding to economic action and economic rationality. The dialectic of the distinction is closely analogous to that of the two theoretical forms. There can be economic acts which are not moral (for example, historical explanation of an *im*moral act is bound to be at the economic level); but there cannot be moral acts that have no vital utility (asceticism or abstract moralism is a moral error). On the other hand, practical activity cannot concretely achieve rationality at the economic level without superseding that level. There can be no theory of economic life except from an independent ethical point of view. This is shown by the inconsistency of utilitarian ethics, which attempts to justify individual self-sacrifice by smuggling in moral principles that have not themselves been accounted for. Confined strictly to the economic level, rational men would live in the Hobbesian state of nature, and all the consequences of Hobbesian philosophy would follow.

Moral, as distinct from economic, consciousness is the awareness of some definite act as a duty overriding private inclinations. Moral judgment declares the act to be a duty because it embodies some universal spiritual value (which may fall under the category of beauty, truth, or social utility or be a distinctively moral good). Whatever category the value belongs to, if the act is a moral duty, there is always a sense of "harmony with the Universe." The moral point of view is the final all-embracing awareness of the spirit as a whole, in its wholeness; hence this is the point of view from which true history can be written.

Freedom. Because he held that all true judgment is historical, Croce could do little except offer historical illustrations of his view. Reflection on the nature of history itself and on the reason for rejecting scientific concepts as pseudo concepts, however, throws further light on goodness as a distinct category of the spirit. Science fails to be genuine knowledge because the spirit in all its forms always exhibits spontaneity and individual uniqueness. At the moral level, this spontaneity becomes conscious freedom and self-possession. History is "the story of liberty," and freedom is another name for the good as a distinct form of value.

Ethico-political history. Gentile buttressed an ethical theory similar to Croce's with the Hegelian conception of the national state as an ethical organism and as the bearer of the spirit in history. Croce admitted that if one interpreted the concept "state" broadly enough, this was a legitimate way of viewing it. But he was initially more inclined to think of politics as an economic art or technique of directing selfish passions into orderly channels (as if there were no conflicting moral ideals in political life). The advent of fascism taught him that both of these extreme views were mistaken. Politics does involve moral consciousness, but the absorption of all morality into the "ethical state" is a "governmental concept of morality" unacceptable in a society of free men. The true bearer of the spirit is the individual moral agent, and the state contains the dialectic of practical life as a whole (economics and ethics). The ethical universal is only fully revealed in the history of the state so conceived. Political life, as the unity in which all spiritual activities (even poetry) have a place, is raised to the ethical level in the consciousness of the historian who writes ethico-political history. This is the complete expression of the spirit in which philosophy and history are unified. Croce's work as a historian, particularly in *La storia del regno di Napoli* ("History of the Kingdom of Naples," 1925), illustrated how this concept applies to periods of decadence as well as periods of progress.

The "circularity of the spirit" might seem to require that this form of historical consciousness become the content of poetic intuition. But Croce never made this point, and he does not seem to have held this view. The circle of the spirit, as he describes it, closes by returning from vitality to poetry. Ethico-political history transcends the circle altogether because it is the perfected consciousness of the spirit in its circularity.

Works by Croce

Croce's *Opere complete* as of 1965 consists of 67 volumes.

La storia ridotto sotto il concetto generale dell'arte. Naples, 1893.

Materialismo storico ed economia marxista. Palermo, 1900. Translated by C. M. Meredith as *Historical Materialism and the Economics of Karl Marx.* New York, 1914.

Estetica come scienza dell'espressione e linguistica generale. Bari, 1902. Translated by Douglas Ainslie as *Aesthetic.* New York, 1909; 2d complete ed., 1922.

Logica come scienza del concetto puro. Naples, 1905. Translated by Douglas Ainslie as *Logic.* New York, 1917.

Ciò che è vivo e ciò che è morto nella filosofia di Hegel. Bari, 1907. Translated by Douglas Ainslie as *What Is Living and What Is Dead in the Philosophy of Hegel.* London, 1915.

Filosofia della pratica, economia ed etica. Bari, 1909. Translated by Douglas Ainslie as *Philosophy of the Practical.* New York, 1913.

La filosofia di Giambattista Vico. Bari, 1911. Translated by R. G. Collingwood as *The Philosophy of Giambattista Vico.* New York, 1913.

Breviario di estetica. Bari, 1913. Translated by Douglas Ainslie as *The Essence of Aesthetic.* London, 1921. First published in *The Book of the Opening of the Rice Institute.* Houston, Texas, 1912.

Teoria e storia della storiografia. Bari, 1917. Translated by Douglas Ainslie as *History—Its Theory and Practice.* New York, 1921.

Contributo alla critica di me stesso. Naples, 1918. Translated by R. G. Collingwood as *Autobiography.* Oxford, 1927.

Frammenti di etica. Bari, 1918. Translated by Arthur Livingston as *The Conduct of Life.* New York, 1924.

Goethe. Bari, 1919. Translated by E. Anderson. London, 1923.

Ariosto, Shakespeare, Corneille. Bari, 1920. Translated by Douglas Ainslie. New York, 1920.

La poesia di Dante. Bari, 1921. Translated by Douglas Ainslie as *The Poetry of Dante.* New York, 1922.

Elementi di politica. Bari, 1922. Translated by Salvatore Castiglione as *Politics and Morals.* London, 1946.

La storia del regno di Napoli. Bari, 1925.

Aesthetica in nuce. Bari, 1928. Translated by R. G. Collingwood as "Aesthetics," in *Encyclopaedia Britannica*, 14th ed. New York and London, 1929. Vol. VII.

Storia d'Italia dal 1871 al 1915. Bari, 1928. Translated by Cecilia M. Ady as *History of Italy 1871–1915.* Oxford, 1929.

Storia d'Europa nel secolo XIX. Bari, 1932. Translated by Henry Furst as *History of Europe in the Nineteenth Century.* New York, 1933.

La poesia. Bari, 1936.

La storia come pensiero e come azione. Bari, 1938. Translated by Sylvia Sprigge as *History as the Story of Liberty.* London, 1941.

My Philosophy. London, 1949. Essays selected by R. Klibansky and translated by E. F. Carritt.

Works on Croce

Borsari, Silvano, *L'opera di Benedetto Croce.* Naples, 1964.

Caponigri, A. R., *History and Liberty.* London, 1955. A study of the historical works.

Nicolini, Fausto, *Benedetto Croce.* Turin, 1962. A definitive biography.

Orsini, G. N. G., *Benedetto Croce, Philosopher of Art and Literary Critic.* Carbondale, Ill., 1961. A masterly survey of Croce's aesthetic writings.

Piccoli, R., *Benedetto Croce.* London, 1922. Still the best general introduction to Croce, but it covers only the period from 1893 to 1920.

H. S. HARRIS

CRUSIUS, CHRISTIAN AUGUST (?1715–1775), German Pietist philosopher and theologian, was born at Leuna, Saxony. Educated in Leipzig, he was appointed extraordinary professor of philosophy there in 1744, and professor of theology in 1750. Crusius initiated the third wave of Pietist attacks on Wolffianism by a series of dissertations (1739–1745), and continued it in his four main philosophical works (1744–1749). He later turned to theological studies, lost interest in philosophy, and founded a new theological school, the Biblicoprophetic school, which partially diverged from Pietism. He later became *canonicus* at the Meissen Theological Seminary.

Crusius' reputation in his own time and his influence on his contemporaries was second among Pietist philosophers only to Christian Thomasius. The collaboration of his close follower, A. F. Reinhard, with Maupertuis and the Berlin Academy in their polemics against Wolffianism established a link between Wolff's Pietist and academic opponents. Several later philosophers acknowledged Crusius as their teacher, although they combined a Crusian background with more advanced trends of French and English origin. These thinkers contributed considerably to the renewal of German philosophy after the dissolution of the Wolffian school. In theology Crusius' influence was even stronger.

Crusius' importance was forgotten or suppressed soon after his death, especially among theologians, and has not yet been fully re-established because of the hostility of the subsequently dominant rationalist and philological schools to the trend of his theology. As a philosopher, Crusius was nearly voted into oblivion, along with most other minor eighteenth-century philosophers, by idealistic historiographers. He was rediscovered by the new philological historiographers, chiefly in connection with his influence on Kant.

Origin of Crusius' thought. After 1730, Wolff and his school began to recover from his expulsion from Halle University in 1723, and from the loss by most of his pupils of their professorships, an attack launched for personal and political reasons by his Pietist opponents. The Pietists were gradually deprived of official support and were more and more restricted to theoretical controversy with Wolff. However, Wolf's system of philosophy was a much more modern, comprehensive, and technically refined body of doctrines than those in the obsolete and clumsy treatises of Christian Thomasius, Franz Budde, and Andreas Rüdiger. A far-reaching reform in the doctrine and quality of Pietist philosophy was needed for it to face the Wolffian doctrine and counteract it successfully. Crusius' teacher, A. F. Hoffman (1703–1741), developed the logical doctrines of Thomasius and Rüdiger, taking into account Wolff's new philosophical techniques and achievements and accepting some of his doctrines, in his own *Vernunft-Lehre* (Leipzig, 1737). Crusius' own logic was inspired by Hoffman's refined and comprehensive handbook, whose quality and thoroughness substantially met the most modern requirements. Hoffman's early death prevented him from publishing the treatises on the other branches of philosophy that he had announced in 1734, but Crusius proceeded along Hoffman's lines, both improving and completing his lifework. Crusius provided the Pietist school with a renewed, efficient, and modern theoretical platform that temporarily assured its philosophical survival, outlived orthodox Wolffianism, and led to a far-reaching change in German philosophy.

Methodology and logic. Crusius' methodology, the foundation of his philosophical attitude, was based on two central ideas, both originating in the Pietist tradition. Philosophy is not, as it was for Wolff, a pure "science of possible things insofar as they are possible," but is based on existing things. Second, human understanding has very narrow limits; theoretical certainty is impossible concerning many fundamental points whose only foundation is moral certitude or revelation. The mysteries of religion are not only beyond human reason, as Wolff claimed, but also contradict it. Something may be unthinkable for human reason that is not so for God or in itself.

Crusius held that the most general principle of human knowledge is neither the principle of identity nor the principle of contradiction, but a principle concerning what we can and cannot think: What cannot be thought at all is false, and what cannot be thought of as false is true. Our notions of identity and contradiction are based on this principle, which he called the principle of *cogitabilitas*. It is an inner criterion, depending on the nature of the human understanding.

Crusius further held that human reason cannot reach ultimate truth. Knowledge begins with experience, both inner and outer, and in many cases is stopped in its analysis of an order of facts by certain notions that, although they are not simple in themselves, cannot be further analyzed by man. Even if an analysis is completed and man does reach some simple basic notion, this notion cannot be demonstrated or deduced from a unique source. Each notion must be intuited singly by connecting it with concrete examples.

It is therefore impossible, according to Crusius, to assume that the method of philosophy is identical with the method of mathematics. Mathematics deals with very simple properties of things and its objects are exhaustively defined, whereas many notions relating to objects of philosophical thought can neither be known with intuitive distinctness nor analyzed by man. Again, mathematics proceeds only by demonstration and solely on the basis of the principle of identity. Philosophy, on the other hand, frequently must revert to moral certainty and is based on several different principles and on the knowledge of fact.

The main characteristics of Crusian logic, as expounded in his *Weg zur Gewissheit und Zuverlässigkeit der menschlichen Erkenntnis* ("Way to Certainty and Reliability of Human Knowledge," Leipzig, 1747), follow from these views. Crusius connected logic with methodology. His logic contained much empirical psychology and many informal concrete and practical rules for obtaining or verifying knowledge, including rules for experimentation. Because Crusius so limited the field of theoretical demonstration, he presented a highly developed logic of probability (which he called moral certitude), covering, among other topics, induction, hypothesis, and the reliability of testimony. The last was essential in the justification of revelation.

Both for Crusius and for Wolff, knowledge derived only from the senses, but the main characteristics of Crusius' methodology allowed his successors to be much more receptive to English and French empiricism, sensationalism, and common-sense philosophy than were orthodox Wolffian rationalists. This receptivity was partially due to Locke's strong influence on Christian Thomasius, but the ethical and mystical sources of these Pietistic attitudes was most important.

Metaphysics. Crusius, in his *Entwurf der nothwendigen Vernunftwahrheiten* ("Sketch of Necessary Rational Truths," Leipzig, 1745), divided metaphysics into ontology, theology, cosmology, and pneumatology, in explicit opposition to Wolff's ordering of the metaphysical sciences.

Ontology. Ontology begins, not with first principles, but with the notion of a thing in general, directly connected with the notion of a "really given thing." Only after introducing these notions did Crusius discuss essence, existence, and causality. Crusius regarded existence as indefinable and as a primary notion arising from sensation.

In his discussion of causality, Crusius expounded a principle of determining reason, his version of Leibniz' principle of sufficient reason. Crusius held, against Wolff, that a sufficient reason suffices only for free actions insofar as they are free. Rational truths and natural events not depending on free causes need a more cogent foundation, a determining reason. This principle does not derive from the principle of identity, but rather from what we must conceive or what we cannot conceive as united or separate, and thus from a new case of the principle of *cogitabilitas*. Crusius, aiming at a sharper distinction between mechanism and free actions, held that the real nature of causality is unknown and that our knowledge of causal connections is based on the constant conjunction of two events in experience. This, of course, cleared the path for the members of his school to accept the Humean critique of the causal connection.

Crusius' ontology reveals a general characteristic of his metaphysics. His was not a monolithic system beginning with a single principle and deducing from it all subsequent notions and propositions, as was Wolff's. Rather, it was founded both on several independent principles and on a multitude of elementary notions that could be defined only by an appeal to reality (by their concrete representation)—notions such as existence, space, time, and force; or, in psychology, the particular powers of the soul, some mental faculties, and pleasure and pain. Through Hoffman Crusius derived this view from Locke's doctrine of simple ideas, but he supposed that the number of elementary notions (which he once called categories) could be infinite.

Theology. Rational theology followed immediately after ontology, instead of being—as for Wolff—the final section of metaphysics, because Crusius held that God's existence is a necessary foundation for cosmology and pneumatology. Crusius denied the Ontological Argument: God's existence can be proved by moral evidence only, and his attributes cannot, properly speaking, be understood by man—among other things, positive infinity is beyond man's reason. The human notion of God is partially relative and partially negative; nevertheless, it is certain. God is different from created beings both in degree and in essence. Among the attributes of God, Crusius stressed his free will, which is limited by the principle of contradiction and by his goodness. In God and God alone, intellect and will are a single power.

Cosmology. Crusius held that matter is composed of a multitude of simple substances. Simple material substances are extended, and the infinite divisibility of matter is impossible. Simple substances have an essential, though not absolutely necessary, force. They act upon each other only by motion and contact. Physical space and time are real, but they are neither independent beings (substances), nor properties, nor relations (all of these concern the metaphysical essence of things). Space and time are intimately connected with existence; they are conditions of things insofar as such things exist. There is no real space or time without substance to fill it; outside the real world there is only possible (not sensible) space or time, which is infinite and filled by God. There are empty spaces in the world (otherwise movement would be impossible), but they are only physically—and not metaphysically—empty, because they are filled with God's presence. Mathematical space and time are distinct from physical space and time, and are abstracted from the relations of things.

Crusius was trying to offer a new set of solutions to the difficulties of the traditional doctrines of substance, of space and time and their limits, and of the void, while avoiding the concepts of *res extensa*, Leibnizian monads, and atoms, as well as the contradictions presented by the real space and time of Descartes and Newton and the ideal space and time of Leibniz and Wolff. His doctrine resembled that of Locke, but it was a mixture of well-chosen elements of the traditional views connected by doubtful subtleties.

Pneumatology. In his pneumatology, or rational psychology, Crusius rejected Thomasius' spiritual materialism but retained some of its characteristics. He held that finite spirits are simple unextended substances, but that they fill a space and share with material substances the power of motion. Thus, a real interaction between spiritual and material substances is possible, and the doctrines of pre-established harmony and occasionalism are unnecessary. The human soul is an independent substance with two fundamental powers, thinking and willing, both of which are a complex of several independent lesser powers.

Crusius was, in general, very cautious in his pneumatology, and frequently appealed to the limitations of human reasoning. For instance, he held that the immortality of the soul could be proved only if God's existence were presupposed—that is, by an appeal to moral certitude.

Natural philosophy. Crusius' treatise on natural philosophy, *Anleitung, über natürliche Begebenheiten ordentlich und vorsichtig nachzudenken* ("Introduction to Regular and Prudent Reflections on Natural Events," 2 vols., Leipzig, 1749), was by far the least original of his works. Nevertheless, he was the first important Pietist philosopher to accept mechanism. In this work, Pietist philosophy finally renounced animism and adopted the more modern Cartesian and Leibnizian views, although it was still opposed to Newton's theory of gravitation. Crusius stressed the difficulties of physics and the purely hypothetical character of much of our knowledge of the particular laws of nature.

Ethics. Crusius' first major work was a treatise on ethics, *Anweisung, vernunftig zu leben* ("Instructions for a Reasonable Life," Leipzig, 1744). Hoffman's influence on Crusius is clear. Ethics, for Crusius, is not based on reason alone, but also on revelation. Natural duties have been imposed on man through God's free choice.

The will. Crusius split Wolff's empirical psychology into two parts. He incorporated the first part, concerned with the cognitive power, into logic. The second, concerned with the will, he placed in ethics. Moral goodness consists in the conformity of the human will with God's will. The human will is a power to act on the understanding, on the body, and on the will itself, but its connection with the understanding is not altogether clear. We are immediately conscious of freedom, which is the main property of the human will. The will is moved by sufficient reason, which does not necessitate, and therefore the will is free.

Duty. The second section of the *Anweisung*, on ethics proper, discusses human duties. An action is moral if it is done out of obligation only, and not in quest of happiness. Virtue is formally conditioned by a coincidence of human will and divine law, and is materially conditioned by love for God. Divine law is known through conscience, which is an immediate power of moral judgment founded on a sort of common sense called moral taste. Evil originates in a wrong use of free will, which, when it submits to unreasonable impulses, corrupts human understanding and the true representation of goodness.

A third section of the *Anweisung* was devoted to moral theology; a fourth, to natural law; and a fifth, to prudence, which was closely studied in Thomasius' school and partially corresponded to Kant's technical imperatives.

Revealed theology. In his revealed theology Crusius united orthodox Pietist doctrines with those of a dissident Pietist, J. A. Bengel (1687–1752). Bengel and Crusius carried to an extreme the Pietist belief that the Bible is an organic whole inspired by God and historically true throughout. The Pietists held that Scripture is the only source of theological truth, and rejected all exegetical developments, even those of Protestant divines. No rational criticism of the Bible was permitted; its meaning could be penetrated only by a kind of empathy or inner light. Crusius stressed a theology of history, founded on Biblical prophecies, that tried to explain the whole history of Christianity and to reveal its future aim in a second coming of Christ.

Crusius' influence on Kant. Recent historical scholarship has stressed Crusius' importance in Kant's development, and the view that Kant's philosophy was rooted in Wolff's system has been more and more questioned. Recent research has shown that Kant, educated in the Pietistic, eclectic, and anti-Wolffian milieu of Königsberg University, was mainly trying in his precritical development (1745–1768)—despite the nonorthodox Wolffian influence of his teacher, Martin Knutzen—to counteract Wolffian philosophy in an increasingly original way. He therefore appealed both to recent anti-Wolffian trends—to Maupertuis and his Berlin circle and through Maupertuis to Newton—and to Crusius, the new leader of Pietist philosophy and only nine years his senior, whose reputation grew tremendously from 1744 on.

Crusius' influence on Kant consists in six main points, some of which were also held by other Pietist philosophers or by Maupertuis. Crusius stressed the limits of human understanding, a theme that recurs in Kant's writings under different forms from 1755 on. He rejected the Ontological Argument, as did Kant after 1755, and he later rejected all theoretical proofs of God's existence. He assumed a multiplicity of independent first principles; Kant did so after 1755. He denied the importance of formal logic, and simplified it. He rejected the possibility of defining existence, and accepted a multiplicity of simple notions. He rejected the mathematical method as applied to philosophy. Kant adopted these last three positions in 1762.

Kant's Crusianism reached its climax in his *Untersuchung über die Deutlichkeit der Grundsätze der naturlichen Theologie und der Moral* ("Investigations Concerning the Distinctness of the Fundamental Principles of Natural Theology and Morals," Berlin, 1764), written in 1762. By 1763 Kant's enthusiasm for Crusius' philosophy was waning, but he did not reject the six tenets above and was still influenced by Crusius on individual points as late as the 1770s. Bohatec has claimed that Crusius' doctrines in revealed theology exerted some influence on Kant's late works in religion.

Additional Works by Crusius

Die philosophischen Hauptschriften, Giorgio Tonelli, ed. Hildesheim, 1964——.

DISSERTATIONS

De Corruptelis Intellectus a Voluntate Pendentibus. Leipzig, 1740.

De Appetitibus Insitis Voluntatis Humanae. Leipzig, 1742.

De Usu et Limitibus Principii Rationis Determinantis, Vulgo Sufficientis. Leipzig, 1743.

Opuscula Philosophico-Theologica. Leipzig, 1751. Reprint of above three dissertations.

THEOLOGICAL WORK

Hypomnemata ad Theologiam Propheticam. Leipzig, 1764–1778.

Works on Crusius

Adickes, Erich, *Kantstudien*. Kiel and Leipzig, 1895.

Bohatec, J., *Die Religionsphilosophie Kants*. Hamburg, 1938.

Campo, Mariano, *La genesi del criticismo kantiano*. Varese, 1953.

Delitzsh, Fr., *Die biblisch-prophetische Theologie, ihre Fortbildung durch Christian August Crusius, und ihre neueste Entwicklung seit der Christologie Hengstenbergs*. Leipzig, 1845.

Festner, C., *Christian August Crusius als Metaphysiker*. Halle, 1892.

Heimsoeth, Heinz, "Metaphysik und Kritik bei Chr. Aug. Crusius" (1926), reprinted in his *Studien zur Philosophie Immanuel Kants*. Cologne, 1956.

Marquardt, A., *Kant und Crusius*. Kiel, 1885.

Schmalenbach, H., *Leibniz*. Munich, 1921. Pp. 553–560.

Schmucker, J., *Die Ursprünge der Ethik Kants*. Meisenheim an der Glan, 1951.

Seitz, A. von, *Die Willensfreiheit in der Philosophie des Christian August Crusius*. Würzburg, 1899.

Tonelli, Giorgio, "Kant, dall'estetica metafisica all'estetica psicoempirica." *Memorie della Academia delle scienze di Torino*. Series 3, Vol. 3, Part 2 (1955).

Tonelli, Giorgio, "La Question des bornes de l'entendement humain au XVIIIe siècle." *Revue de metaphysique et de morale* (1959), 396–427.

Tonelli, Giorgio, *Elementi in Kant precritico*. Turin, 1959. Vol. I.

Tonelli, Giorgio, "Der Streit über mathematische Methode in der Philosophie in der ersten Hälfte des XVIII Jahrhunderts." *Archiv für Philosophie*, Vol. 9 (1959).

Wundt, Max, *Kant als Metaphysiker*. Stuttgart, 1924. Pp. 60–81.

Wundt, Max, *Die deutsche Schulphilosophie im Zeitalter der Aufklärung*. Tübingen, 1945. Pp. 254–264.

GIORGIO TONELLI

CUDWORTH, RALPH (1617–1688), the most systematic metaphysician of the Cambridge Platonist school. He was born at Aller, Somerset; his father, rector of Aller, had been a fellow of Emmanuel College, Cambridge, and chaplain to James I. After his father died in 1624, Cudworth was privately educated by his stepfather, Dr. Stoughton, until he entered Emmanuel College in 1632. There he came under the influence of Benjamin Whichcote. He was elected a fellow of Emmanuel in 1639. For his bachelor of divinity degree in 1646, he defended, against Calvinism, Whichcote's thesis that good and evil are eternal, immutable, and founded on reason.

Cudworth's sympathy with Puritanism—insofar as it attacked ecclesiastical pretension—at first told against him in his career at Cambridge. But in 1645, with the victory of the Puritan cause, he was appointed, against the wish of the fellows, master of Clare College and, with unanimous approval, Regius professor of Hebrew. Active in the affairs of the Commonwealth, he served on a number of parliamentary committees. However, when Cudworth was invited on March 31, 1647, to preach to a House of Commons which was bitterly divided on questions of church government, he expounded Whichcote's doctrine that Christianity is essentially a way of life and that men should be free to choose the form of ritual and methods of church government which suit their individual temperament. This sermon, first published in 1647 and many times reprinted, is the clearest and most eloquent expression of Cudworth's religious and moral ideals.

As master of Clare College, Cudworth was not a success. Unlike his fellow Platonists he was a "difficult" man who made many enemies. In 1650 he left Cambridge to become rector of North Cadbury, Somerset, but was recalled to Cambridge in 1654 to be master of Christ's College, where Henry More was a fellow. In that year Cudworth married. His daughter Damaris (1658–1708) was, as Lady Masham, an intimate friend and correspondent of John Locke. She published in 1696 *A Discourse Concerning the Love of God*, directed against John Norris, and did much to communicate and defend her father's ideas in both England and France. After the Restoration, which Cudworth welcomed, his enemies attempted to secure his dismissal from his Cambridge posts. They were unsuccessful; Cudworth remained at Christ's College until his death in 1688.

Metaphysics. Although he wrote continually, Cudworth published slowly and reluctantly. *The True Intellectual System of the Universe* (1678, imprimatur 1671) is, for all its massiveness, only the first segment of the work he meant to publish. It was to have contained three parts, the first directed against atheistic determinism, the second against Calvinism, the third expounding a theory of free will. Only the first part was ever published, and although Cudworth's biographer, Thomas Birch, writing in 1743, was able fully to describe them, neither Part II nor Part III now exists in manuscript.

In its present form *The True Intellectual System* is primarily a critique of what Cudworth took to be the two principal forms of atheism—materialism and hylozoism. The materialist Cudworth had especially in mind is Thomas Hobbes. Cudworth attempts to show that Hobbes had revived the doctrines of Protagoras and is therefore subject to the criticisms which Plato had deployed against Protagoras in the *Theaetetus*. On the side of hylozoism Strato is the official target. However, Cudworth's Dutch friends had certainly reported to him the views which Spinoza was circulating in manuscript. Cudworth remarks in his Preface that he would have ignored hylozoism had he not been aware that a new version of it would shortly be published.

Cudworth hoped to destroy hylozoism and materialism with a single blow by drawing out the consequences of an atomic theory of matter. This is at first sight a surprising method of procedure, since atomism is ordinarily regarded as a variety of materialism and had been associated with atheism. But Cudworth set out to show, in the dreariest sections of *The True Intellectual System*, that atomism was originally theistic, having been first formulated by Moses, identified by Cudworth with that Phoenician "Moschus" to whom legend had ascribed the origins of atomism. Fortunately, however, Cudworth's philosophical arguments are independent of such Florentine aberrations. (He was, all the same, a notable scholar. *The True Intellectual System* served for generations as the principal source book of Greek philosophy.)

The Aristotelian–Scholastic doctrine of substantial forms left open the possibility, Cudworth thought, that mind is a property of material objects, and it cannot rule out hylozoism. If, however, material objects are simply collections of inert space-filling atoms, it is at once obvious that minds cannot be material objects. For by their very nature, according to Cudworth, minds are centers of activity. Nor is there then any ground for supposing that, as hylozoists maintain, all material objects are possessed of life. Thus, the atomic theory of matter, far from being hostile to theism, is, in fact, the best possible foundation for a theistic distinction between matter and spirit.

Similarly, Cudworth suggests, the atomists' theory of perception leads inevitably to the conclusion that mind is incorporeal. A sensation, considered as a purely physical process, can be nothing but a variety of pressure. But the atomist admits that the sensation of color as we experience it is not merely a species of pressure. The difference between physical pressure and sensation as apprehended can be accounted for only by supposing the intervention of a mind which is not itself a material object. Furthermore, Cudworth argues, unless there is a mind which is capable of looking beyond its immediate sensations, we could never even discover that there are material objects, nor could we fall into error. A passive recipient of pushes could neither develop a theory nor make a mistake. Thus, once more, mind cannot be a material object as material objects are defined by atomists.

Although Cudworth's epistemology is largely Cartesian, he rejects the Cartesian dualism of consciousness and extension in favor of a dualism of activity and passivity. In addition to conscious minds and material objects, there are at work in the universe, he argues, "spiritual plastic powers," which are capable, like minds, of acting and of having purposes but not of being conscious. They operate, he thinks, even in the human soul, as is particularly clear in our dreams; the activities of organisms derive wholly from them. God works through such powers, although he does not directly govern their day-to-day activities, and it is by virtue of their presence in nature that nature can properly be described as spiritual.

This was the side of Cudworth's metaphysics which particularly interested his contemporaries. The biologist John Ray, in his *The Wisdom of God in the Works of Creation* (1691), expressed his approval of Cudworth's theory; it played a large part in philosophical biology until the time of Darwin. John LeClerc, in his *Bibliothèque choisie* (1703–1713), summarized and analyzed *The True Intellectual System.* This provoked a long controversy with Pierre Bayle, who argued, in a number of articles and letters (1704–1707) brought together in his *Oeuvres diverses* (1731), that the doctrine of plastic powers was atheistic in tendency, since it made it unnecessary to suppose that wherever purpose is exhibited, God must be directly at work. Denis Diderot and Jean d'Alembert's *Encyclopédie* (1751–1772) devoted a good deal of attention to Cudworth's theory of plastic powers. Revised by Paul Janet in 1860, Cudworth's theory is very likely continuous with modern doctrines of the unconscious.

Moral philosophy. Cudworth's best-known contribution to moral theory is *A Treatise Concerning Eternal and Immutable Morality*, published from the British Museum Cudworth manuscripts in 1731 by Edward Chandler, bishop of Durham. This, however, is more an epistemological propaedeutic to moral philosophy than a direct contribution to ethics. Sensation, Cudworth argues, can never give us knowledge. Knowledge is possible only when mind has itself as its object, whereas in sensation the mind is remote from its object. Furthermore, sensation cannot make us aware of such general concepts as cause, effect, means, end, order, and proportion, which are essential to knowledge. By their nature sensations are incomplete and fragmentary. They arouse concepts in us, by which we systematize them, but the concepts, not the sensations, are the true objects of knowledge.

The objects of knowledge, then, are modifications of mind. But knowledge is of eternal truths, the existence of which is quite independent of our existence. Eternal truths must, Cudworth concludes, relate ideas in the mind of an eternal and immutable being—God. But how are we to tell that we have achieved knowledge, since we have no access to God's mind? The only criterion, Cudworth argues, is the clarity and distinctness of our ideas. Descartes was inevitably involved in circularity when he set out to demonstrate the reliability of the criterion of clarity and distinctness by proving the existence of a God whose nature is such that he would not deceive us; nothing can be more certain than that what we clearly and distinctly perceive must be true.

"Things are what they are not by Will but by Nature"; this doctrine links Cudworth's epistemology to his ethics. Not even God, let alone a merely human sovereign, can, Cudworth argues, make an act good merely by willing it, for it is either eternally true or eternally false that acts of a certain kind are good. Even though it is, in fact, the case that God wills only what is good, the goodness of what he wills is not constituted by his willing it; on the contrary, he wills what is good because it is good. (Cudworth was fully conscious of his debt to Plato's *Euthyphro.*) No doubt, Cudworth admits, an act which is in its own nature morally indifferent can come to be good—although only in a derivative, "formal" sense—because God has commanded it. But this is only by virtue of the general principle that obedience to God is good, and we cannot without circularity suppose that the goodness of such obedience is founded on its being commanded.

We can obtain some notion of Cudworth's moral psychology, as distinct from his epistemology, from *A Treatise on Free Will*, edited from the British Museum manuscripts by John Allen in 1838. This work would seem to have been written at a relatively early date; to appreciate Cudworth's position fully we have to join it to his many subsequent manuscript writings on the same theme. Cudworth's argument is directed partly against Hobbes's *Of Liberty and Necessity* (1654) and partly against Calvinism. Much of what he says is conventional; what is original is his rejection of the traditional doctrine of faculties.

To Cudworth "It is really the man or soul that understands and the man or soul that wills," as it is also the man, not the will, that is free. The faculties are ways in which the mind acts, not entities within the mind. Every act, he argues, is at once an act of will, the expression of an instinct or inclination, and an intellectual act. As firmly as Hume after him, Cudworth denies that reason is ever a motive to action; the instincts and inclinations, he says, "set the wheels at work" and "employ the thinking, consulting and speculative power." The conflicts in our soul, he suggests, are not between faculties but between opposing ways of life—the animal, egoistic life and the spiritual life, with its concern for the common good.

Freedom, according to Cudworth, does not consist in "indifferency"—that is, in exercising a quite arbitrary act of power; it lies in our capacity to prefer the spiritual to the animal life. Free will, in his view, is not a source of sin. We sin through failure to choose the best, not by freely choosing the worst. But what about our freedom to choose the best? Is this a purely arbitrary power, or is it determined by the general nature of the soul which chooses? This was the question on which, as he admits, Cudworth could never come to a satisfactory conclusion. He hoped to leave room for free choice without admitting arbitrariness; he never succeeded in persuading himself that he had done so.

Cudworth's ethics is only sketched in his manuscripts. In direct opposition to the sort of position Kant was to adopt, he argues that we act well only when we act out of love, not out of a sense of duty. The good life is free, disinterested, above egoism, harmonious, concordant, and therefore beautiful. All vice is a variety of self-love.

To what degree Cudworth's manuscripts were read by his contemporaries is uncertain. Both Locke and Shaftesbury may have obtained access to them by way of Lady Masham, for they were certainly influenced by Cudworth's general ethical position. So, later, was Richard Price, but only by *Eternal and Immutable Morality*, from which his moral epistemology largely derives.

Bibliography

The best edition of *The True Intellectual System* is John Harrison's English translation (London, 1845) of Mosheim's Latin edition (Jena, 1733); this also includes the *Treatise on Eternal and Immutable Morality*. Thomas Birch's edition (London, 1743) contains Birch's life—the main biographical source—Cudworth's principal sermons, and his *Discourse on the Lord's Supper*. For a detailed bibliography see John Arthur Passmore, *Ralph Cudworth* (Cambridge, 1951), and the bibliography under CAMBRIDGE PLATONISTS, especially the books by Tulloch, Muirhead, and Raven. See also Meyrick Heath Carré, "Ralph Cudworth," in *Philosophical Quarterly*, Vol. 3, No. 12 (1953), 341–352. For Damaris Cudworth see Florence Ada Keynes, *Byways of Cambridge History* (Cambridge, 1947).

JOHN PASSMORE

CULTURE AND CIVILIZATION. The word "civilization" was derived from an actual social condition, that of the citizen (Latin, *civis*). The word "culture" in its social, intellectual, and artistic senses is a metaphorical term derived from the act of cultivating the soil (Latin, *cultura*). In the case of "civilization" there was an apparently simple contrast with "barbarism," another social condition, which was originally a description of the life of a foreign group. In the case of "culture" there was no such simple contrast. The cultivation of the mind was seen as a process comparable to the cultivation of the soil; hence, the early meanings of "culture," in this metaphorical sense, centered on a process, "the *culture of* the mind," rather than on an achieved state. The first important development from this metaphorical use of "culture" was a description of certain men as "cultivated" and then as "those who are cultivated." In this use the meaning is very close to "civilized."

Modern development of "culture." The important modern development of the concept of "culture" took place between the late eighteenth and the late nineteenth centuries. The early stages are very difficult to trace because there is often only a slight difference between the older use, which refers to a process, and the early modern use, which refers to a condition. As early as Milton, there is a use of the concept that can be read either way, and there are many instances that can be read either way in Kant's writings. However, from the late eighteenth century on in both English and German social thought, the modern usage became more common. Broadly, the concept was developed in four ways, all of which still affect its meaning. First, "culture" came to mean "a general state or habit of the mind," with close relations to the idea of human perfection. Second, it came to mean "a general state of intellectual and moral development in a society as a whole." Third, it came to mean "the general body of the arts and intellectual work. Fourth, it came to mean "the whole way of life, material, intellectual, and spiritual, of a given society.

This complex development represents an attempt to think in new ways about man's social, moral, and intellectual life at a time of profound and many-sided change. In one important respect it was part of a general reaction against the mechanistic philosophy and against what were regarded as its social consequences in the emerging industrial civilization. Samuel Taylor Coleridge, in 1830, distinguished between the cultivation of general humanity and a merely external civilization in which progress is calculated by reference to things other than man himself. Thomas Carlyle and, later, Matthew Arnold made the same distinction. The fact that "culture" was a metaphor derived from natural growth probably had an important effect on this meaning. During this period the contrast between "natural" and "mechanical" was frequently pointed out, and members of the romantic movement, in describing intellectual and social phenomena, generally turned to biology rather than to physics and mechanics for their analogies. Another aspect of the romantic movement that undoubtedly contributed to the modern meanings of "culture" was its high valuation of folk life and national tradition. This was not only a contrast with what was often seen as a merely sophisticated "civilization" but also an emphasis on the particular and distinctive customs and arts of different people—what would later be called their national cultures, as distinct from what was still seen as the general and uniform development of "civilization." It is also possible that the concept was affected by the growing knowledge of the non-European civilizations of India and Persia and, later, China, which possessed elaborate and quite different social organizations with long-standing artistic and intellectual traditions. Although many Europeans saw these societies as merely backward in comparison to their own, with its highly developed technology and politics, others saw them as distinctive shapings of the human mind that could not easily be assimilated to a simple, unilinear idea of civilization. Finally, during this period there was an important development in relating the arts and different forms of thought to particular kinds of social organization. A new emphasis was placed on the strong connections between the ways of ordinary social and material life and the styles and assumptions of imaginative and intellectual work. The concept of a specific "culture" was an obvious way of expressing these relations.

Three concepts of culture. In view of the above it is possible to see the close relations between the modern meanings of "culture" and a whole range of reactions to the great social and political changes in Europe between the late eighteenth and nineteenth centuries. Since these changes were in themselves controversial, however, and since the new meanings drew upon so many responses, the concept of "culture" was from the beginning controversial and often confused. Three main emphases can subsequently be traced. First, there is the idealist emphasis, which survives (albeit with scant support) in very much its original form. "Culture" is here seen as a process and a state of cultivation that should be a universal idea. This usage is ethical and, indeed, spiritual and expresses an ideal of human perfection. It can easily conflict with the emphasis on particular "cultures," which stresses the differences in the ways in which men find meaning and value in their lives and, indeed, conceive of perfection itself. This latter emphasis, now widespread in anthropology and sociology, is necessarily relative and comparative, whereas the surviving idealist emphasis tends to be absolute and is most commonly associated with the classical and Christian heritage of Europe.

Standing uneasily between these emphases is what is still probably the most common popular meaning of the word "culture"—namely, a body of actual artistic and intellectual work. There is an inevitable tension between this meaning and the other two. Actual artistic and intellectual work often fails to conform to the idea of a perfect or perfecting state of mind already associated with known, traditional meanings and values. It becomes necessary, in this middle position, to distinguish "high culture" from "mass culture" or "mid-culture" and other similar twentieth-century coinages. On the other hand, if culture is viewed as a body of artistic and intellectual work to which great, and at times supreme, value is attached, it is difficult, from such a position, to accept the anthropological and sociological uses of the word "culture." In this respect these uses are mainly neutral, since they refer to what different peoples do and make and think, without regard to any artistic or intellectual merit. In any case these uses include elements of social and economic life (especially institutions) that do not seem to be culture in the artistic and intellectual sense at all. There is, as will be shown, an important controversy within anthropology and sociology concerning the concept of culture. But beyond this dispute, and at times overlapping it, are the radical differences between "culture" as a social concept, "culture" as an artistic and intellectual classification, and "culture" as an embodiment of universal and absolute values.

When such differences in usage refer, as in this case, to real and important differences in viewpoint and belief, it would be merely arbitrary and dogmatic to distinguish the one "proper" meaning of "culture" and to condemn all others. Rather, the immense and complicated argument that has centered on this idea should be seen as an index of the issues to which it refers. And, indeed, the idea of culture raises many of the fundamental issues of Western civilization and has become a major point of division between idealist and materialist conceptions of civilization and between idealist and historical methods in intellectual and artistic criticism. It has also been a focus of the attempt to see societies as wholes, in new ways and with new interests in their various aspects. In this respect the emphasis on culture has been an attempt to redefine the nature of society and of civilization itself.

Culture in the social sciences. The larger controversy over culture has been reflected within anthropology and sociology. The first use of "culture" in English as a precise scientific term is generally credited to E. B. Tylor in his *Primitive Culture* (London, 1871). But the concept was familiar in German ethnology at least a generation earlier, and the basis for extending the term to "a whole way of life" was already present in the work of the English romantics. "That complex whole," Tylor's definition of "culture" began, the emphasis being on that relation between elements in a whole way of life which was described above. The real anthropological controversy arose when relationships within this whole were analyzed and interpreted. It is worth noting, however, that Tylor used "culture" and "civilization" virtually as synonyms; since his subject was "primitive culture," this usage is at once startling and important. His full definition was, "Culture or Civilization . . . that complex whole which includes knowledge, belief, art, morals, law, customs, and any other capabilities and habits acquired by man as a member of society" (*Primitive Culture*, Vol. VII, p. 7). It is in this sense that all human societies have a "culture" and a "civilization." However, there are two bases for dispute. Is social evolution in general to be regarded as a universal and even unilinear process? If so, it may be reasonable to reserve "civilization," with its root meaning of living in cities, to the later stages of this process. In this sense all societies have a culture, but only some have reached civilization. Within civilization (in this instance regarded as a general stage in social evolution), different societies will still have different cultures. But this definition of civilization as an attained stage in social evolution at once precipitates the second dispute. The effect of the work of Karl Marx and of the many non-Marxists who were influenced by him was to posit a definite relation between "that complex whole" of meanings and values "acquired by man as a member of society" and particular types of social and economic institutions. In general, types of organization of material life were held to determine systems of meanings and values, although the process by which this determination was established was often very complex. According to this view, "culture" inevitably includes the material organization of life and cannot be confined to the area of meanings and values. Many anthropologists and sociologists have accepted this assumption, although the word "society," a relatively modern term with a general meaning, then becomes virtually identical with "culture" and is the more widely used term within the authentic Marxist tradition.

To many social thinkers, however, this primacy of the organization of material life was not acceptable. They pointed to the extraordinary cultural variations between peoples at comparable economic stages and rejected both the doctrine of economic primacy and the theory of unilinear social evolution. Some retained the emphasis of the concept of culture as the "complex whole," although they denied the primacy of economic factors within it. The material and economic elements would be included among other elements in the description of the "complex whole." Others, notably Alfred Weber and R. M. MacIver, in conformity with uses of "culture" outside the field of anthropology, reserved the concept of culture for the area of values and meanings while using "civilization" for the area of material organization. Weber regarded civilization as the product of science and technology and as universal and accumulative in that it relates primarily to nature rather than to man. Culture, on the other hand, was the human interpretation, expressed in meanings and values—in philosophy, religion, and art—of the purposes of life and society. MacIver, particularly in his earlier work, made a broadly similar distinction; he related culture to ends and civilization to means and viewed the technological order of civilization as determined within the cultural order of meanings and values.

Methodological problems. In the social sciences there is thus a fundamental theoretical dispute that is perhaps more often conducted as a dispute over terminology than in any more general and abstract way. The degree of variation that can actually be found, even when it is masked by the ordinary currency of a disputed term like "culture," is large enough to show very forcibly the present difference between the social and the physical sciences. In social studies scientific method is ordinarily a secondary discipline, concerned with the handling and presentation of evidence, and within these limits it is important. But it is difficult for any science to attain maturity when there is so basic a theoretical dispute about the nature of the evidence itself. It would be theoretically possible to resolve the disputes on the nature of social evolution and on the relative effect of different elements in a culture by repeated case studies. It is significant, however, that in each case a historical perspective would be necessary; neither question can be resolved when a particular culture or group of cultures is investigated as if it were isolated in space and time.

Cultural relativity. In the above context the modern emphasis on cultural relativity acquires a critical importance. The emphasis on relativity is most marked in work done since the 1920s. It is a reaction against both a theory and an unconscious prejudice. The prejudice was correctly diagnosed as ethnocentrism. It was evidently wrong to interpret all cultural phenomena in terms of categories applicable to European societies, and it was arbitrary and dangerous to attempt to evaluate very diverse cultures by references to a fixed value system that was likewise derived from European tradition. The terminological transition from "culture" to "a culture" was thus very important. A particular complex whole should be studied as far as possible in its own terms, rather than assimilated to the observer's terms. But the advantage of this emphasis was more limited than it first appeared to be. However sympathetic and objective such a study might be, the very undertaking of it placed it outside the terms of most cultures. Also, the motives for such study tended to originate within European or European-influenced societies, and these motives included not only scientific curiosity but also, it can be argued, motives governed by reactions to such societies. It has never been wholly possible to separate such interests from the primitivism that has taken many forms in modern industrial societies. It also seems to be the case that the demonstration of relativity, not so much as a method of study but as a conclusion about human nature, is directly related to a liberal ideology that has also taken very varied forms in modern industrial societies. In any case the fundamental disputes about social evolution and about the determinative effect of different elements within a culture reflect, more or less directly, contemporary arguments about the nature, control, and development of our own societies. It is thus always possible that an ethnographic prejudice has been replaced by an ideological prejudice that in its turn requires cultural analysis.

Influence of general senses. It is possible, as we have seen, to relate contemporary theories of culture to fundamental materialist or idealist positions. It would be rash to suppose that even if there were a commonly recognized method of collecting and presenting evidence, these positions do not enter cultural studies at the crucial point of deciding what evidence to look for—whether oral and literary traditions (the original romantic emphasis), kinship systems (now much influenced by psychological theory and speculation), or economic organization (much influenced by divided theories of political economy). The definition of "culture" as "a complex whole" can sometimes promote, but sometimes merely mask, the crucial question about the ways in which these areas relate and interact. At the simplest level we can look at the "complex whole" in order either to understand it or simply to describe it, and this in itself is a cultural decision. There is thus a reciprocal relation between the original definitions and the actual studies, and this is only rarely transcended.

Culture and history. The critical area in this continuing argument seems to be the relation of cultural studies to history. Historical study itself contains much the same variation and dispute, but it is nevertheless only in a historical dimension that the critical questions of culture can be properly studied. The alternative to the older kind of unilinear theory of cultural development cannot be a static relativism. The only real alternatives are a better unilinear theory or some new kind of multilinear theory. The isolation of the "complex whole" at a particular point in time is only partially possible. Such terms as "culture," "civilization," and "society" were responses, in their modern uses, to particular kinds of social change. It would be ironic if these terms should themselves become hypostatized, as undoubtedly happened in the development of the literary usage of "culture."

The essential inquiry, which these terms aid, is into the shaping of human experience. It is a condition of their continuing usefulness that the idea of "shaping" should remain dynamic and that "a complex whole" should also be seen as complex in time. It is within the scope of these considerations that we can best follow the active and continuing inquiry, both inside and outside the social sciences, into the meaning of "culture" and "civilization."

Bibliography

Arnold, Matthew, *Culture and Anarchy*. London, 1869.

Bidney, David, *Theoretical Anthropology*. New York, 1953.

Elias, Norbert, *Über den Prozess der Zivilisation*. Basel, 1939.

Eliot, T. S., *Notes Towards the Definition of Culture*. London, 1949.

Kroeber, A. L., *The Nature of Culture*. Chicago, 1952.

Kroeber, A. L., and Kluckhohn, Clyde, *Culture: A Critical Review of Concepts and Definitions*. Cambridge, Mass., 1952.

Mann, Thomas, *Betrachtungen eines Unpolitischen*. Berlin, 1918.

MacIver, R. M., *Society: Its Structure and Changes.* New York, 1931.
Weber, Alfred, "Kultursoziologie," in *Handwörterbuch der Soziologie,* Alfred Vierkandt, ed. Stuttgart, 1931. Pp. 284–294.
Williams, Raymond, *Culture and Society.* London, 1958.

RAYMOND WILLIAMS

CULVERWEL, NATHANAEL (1618?–1651?), religious and moral philosopher commonly if rather misleadingly described as a Cambridge Platonist. Culverwel was probably a son of Richard Culverwel, rector of St. Margaret's, in London, although neither his parentage nor the date of his birth is certain. He certainly grew up in a Calvinist atmosphere. In 1633 he was admitted to Emmanuel College, Cambridge, where he encountered the teachings of Benjamin Whichcote, the spiritual leader of Cambridge Platonism. Ralph Cudworth was slightly junior to him as an undergraduate at Emmanuel but was elected to a fellowship three years before Culverwel's election in 1642. John Smith was of the same generation. Culverwel's contemporaries refer in somewhat obscure terms to troubles which beset him in later life; these may have included some sort of mental breakdown. He died not later than 1651.

Culverwel published nothing during his lifetime. Shortly after his death, however, William Dillingham prepared for publication a discourse entitled, in Culverwel's typically metaphorical style, *Spiritual Opticks: or a Glasse discovering the weaknesse and imperfection of a Christians knowledge in this life* (1651). This was sufficiently successful to encourage Dillingham to proceed to the publication of a manuscript by Culverwel, composed, Dillingham says, about 1646, which was obviously intended, although incomplete, to be a book—*An Elegant and Learned Discourse of the Light of Nature.* In the same volume Dillingham included a number of Culverwel's sermons. Prefixed to the *Discourse* is an essay by Culverwel's brother Richard which asserts that in its present form the *Discourse* is somewhat misleading, since the praise of reason which it contains was to have been followed by another section in which the limitations of reason would have been more strongly insisted upon. That judgment is borne out by the tone of Culverwel's sermons, which are severely Calvinist.

The *Discourse,* as it stands, is an elaboration of Whichcote's favorite quotation (from *Proverbs* 20.27), which Culverwel translates as "The understanding of a man is the candle of the Lord." Insofar as it is critical of those who "blaspheme reason," the *Discourse* is written in Whichcote's spirit. However, its philosophical tone is in many respects Aristotelian rather than Platonic; Culverwel sharply criticizes the "fanciful ideas" of "the Platonists," under which heading he almost certainly includes his Emmanuel colleagues. (None of them had yet published, so that although—unusually for his time—Culverwel makes precise references to such near-contemporaries as Lord Herbert of Cherbury, Lord Brooke, and Sir Kenelm Digby, he could not refer to the Cambridge Platonists in similarly definite terms.) When Culverwel speaks with enthusiasm of Plato, it is of the *Laws* or the *Republic* rather than of John Smith's favorite, the *Phaedo;* quite unlike Smith or Cudworth he rarely pays any attention to the Neoplatonists. On the other hand, he writes with great approval not only of Aristotle but also of the Scholastics, especially Aquinas and Suárez, and even of Francis Bacon, to whom the Platonists were generally strongly opposed.

He differs from the Platonists on four crucial points. The first is epistemology; he disagrees with them, as he puts it, about "the time at which the candle of the Lord is lighted." It is true that at an early stage in the *Discourse* (Ch. 7) he writes: "There are stamped and printed upon the being of man some clear and indelible principles, some first and alphabetical notions, by putting together of which it can spell out the law of nature," a passage which it is natural to read as a defense of innate ideas. Later, however, in Chapter 11, he argues quite explicitly against the doctrine of innateness, even in the modified form in which Platonists like Cudworth held it. First principles—which he describes as having "so much of certainty in them, that they are near to a tautology and identity"—arise, he argues, "from the observing and comparing of objects"; these principles are not inherent in our minds. He strongly criticizes Plato and Descartes in Chapter 14 for "too much scorning and slighting" of sensations. Sensation, he admits, is no more than "the gate of certainty," but only through this gate can certainty enter the soul. Otherwise, the soul would remain "a blank sheet."

Second, he criticizes the Platonist tendency to diminish the gap between human and divine by treating the human soul as having a degree of divinity, as being, insofar as it is rational, an ingredient in divine reason. The candle of the Lord, he argues, is lit by God but is no part of God's light. God's light is like the sun; a candle is but a wavering, imperfect light even when it is at its brightest. Men cannot hope to be godlike, the ideal the Platonists set before themselves.

This is connected with the third point of difference. Culverwel continued to be a Calvinist; he continued to believe, therefore, that no human being is worthy of salvation. In a sermon entitled "The Act of Oblivion," addressed to a congregation presumed to belong to the elect, he says that God "might have written thy name in his Black Book, with fatal and bloody characters, and made his justice glorious in thy misery and damnation"; God had chosen otherwise because he so chose, not because any members were deserving of a higher destiny. If God has chosen to save Socrates, he argues, this can only be because God gave a private revelation to him, not because Socrates was a worthy man. God may well have chosen to save Aristophanes rather than Socrates. God's decrees, Culverwel insists, are absolute; it is ridiculous to suppose that a man can save himself from the damnation decreed for him merely by exercising an act of choice, by choosing to be good. Nothing could be further from the spirit of Cambridge Platonism than Culverwel's unmitigated Calvinism.

Finally, and this again is connected with his Calvinism, Culverwel's emphasis as a moral philosopher is on law rather than on reason. He agrees with the Platonists, it is true, that some acts are good in their own nature and that some relationships are peculiarly just and rational; however, the performance of such acts, he argues, does not constitute a moral good. Essentially, he says, morality is a matter of obedience to rule, and there can be rules only when there is a lawgiver. The obligatoriness of moral laws depends upon the fact that they are commanded by God. Even though the lawgiving is itself a rational act, even though moral laws are based upon the lawgiver's apprehension of "the eternal relations of things," even though it is by our reason that we discover their nature, command, not reason, is still the foundation of morality. A capacity for obeying rules, he suggests, is the distinguishing mark of a rational being; moral rules apply to men, not to animals, just because men are capable of following rules. But human rationality does not in any way constitute the obligatoriness of the rules.

Following Hugo Grotius, Culverwel devotes a great deal of attention to the concept of a natural law and its relation to the laws of nations. In the *Discourse*, as his argument proceeds, the importance of law comes more and more to the fore, and the importance of reason recedes, although Culverwel takes the two to be intimately connected. For Culverwel, as for so many of his antirationalist successors, Abraham's sacrifice of Isaac is the crucial case. This was decreed, and the decree had to be obeyed, he argues, even though it goes against all our concepts of a rational morality; "the candle durst not oppose the sun."

One can discern a tension in Culverwel's work between his Calvinism and the Platonism he had learned from Whichcote. A very similar tension between empiricism and rationalism, between the concept of law and the concept of reason, is manifest in Locke, and it is more than likely that Locke was strongly influenced by Culverwel's *Discourse*, most obviously, but by no means exclusively, in the *Essays on the Law of Nature*, which he wrote in 1660.

Bibliography

The best edition of the *Elegant and Learned Discourse of the Light of Nature* is edited by John Brown, with a critical essay by John Cairns (London, 1857). The sermons, including *Spiritual Opticks*, can be read in the 1652 edition of the *Discourse* (London; reprinted, 1654). There are extracts in John Wesley, *Christian Library*, Vols. IX–X (London, 1819–1827); and Ernest Trafford Campagnac, *The Cambridge Platonists* (Oxford, 1901).

See also William Cecil de Pauley, *The Candle of the Lord, Studies in the Cambridge Platonists* (London, 1937); A. C. Scupholme, "Nathanael Culverwel—a Cambridge Platonist," in *Theology*, Vol. 38, No. 225 (1939); Wolfgang von Leyden, *John Locke: Essays on the Law of Nature* (Oxford, 1954); and the bibliography to CAMBRIDGE PLATONISTS.

JOHN PASSMORE

CUMBERLAND, RICHARD (1631–1718), bishop and moral philosopher, was born in London, the son of a London citizen. Educated at St. Paul's School, in 1648 he entered Magdalene College, Cambridge, where, distinguishing himself both by his scholarship and by his capacity for friendship, he was elected a fellow in 1656. He first studied medicine, but he finally decided to enter the church, accepting preferment in 1658 to the rectory of Brampton, Northamptonshire, and in 1667 to the rectory of All Hallows at Stamford, Lincolnshire. In 1661, Cambridge appointed him one of its 12 official preachers, and he kept in close touch with Cambridge intellectual life. Cumberland earned the reputation of being an exceptionally staunch Protestant. Report has it that the attempt of James II to reintroduce Roman Catholicism into England produced in him a dangerous fever. Such zeal did not go unrewarded under William III, and although quite without personal ambition, Cumberland was consecrated as bishop of Peterborough on July 5, 1691. He performed his episcopal duties with diligence until his death in 1718.

Jewish history was Cumberland's main interest. In 1686 he published *An Essay towards the Recovery of the Jewish Measures and Weights*. His domestic chaplain and son-in-law Squier Payne published in 1720 *Sanchoniatho's Phoenician History*, translated with a commentary by Cumberland. This monument of misplaced scholarly ingenuity derived its immediate inspiration from Hugo Grotius. With no qualms about the authenticity as history of Sanchoniatho's cosmogony, Cumberland devoted himself to identifying its personages with characters in the Old Testament. A sequel, *Origines Gentium Antiquissimae; or Attempts for Discovering the Times of the First Planting of Nations*, appeared in 1724.

Cumberland's sole philosophical work, *De Legibus Naturae* (1672), was designed, as the subtitle explains, as a refutation of Hobbes—the first full-length philosophical reply to Hobbes to be published. Written in an inelegant Latin, badly printed, ill-organized, intolerably diffuse, Cumberland's treatise did not attract much contemporary attention. In 1692, with Cumberland's approval, James Tyrrell prepared an abridgment and translation as *A Brief Disquisition of the Law of Nature*, hoping to draw attention to Cumberland's main ideas. But the abridgment was a poor one (in addition, Tyrrell's own views were mingled with Cumberland's) and failed in its main purpose. Eighteenth-century philosophers were more interested in Cumberland's work than his contemporaries had been; he anticipated their ambitions and preoccupations. A complete English translation was prepared by John Maxwell in 1727, and what has become the standard translation was published, with copious annotations by John Towers, in 1750. A French translation by Jean Barbeyrac (1744) ran into two editions.

Cumberland's point of departure is Grotius' *De Iure Belli et Pacis* (1625). Grotius, or so Cumberland interprets him, had based his demonstration of the existence and binding force of natural laws upon the consensus of civilized opinion. Very conscious of Hobbes, Cumberland sets out to supplement Grotius by demonstrating that natural laws are founded on "the nature of things," as distinct from the commands of sovereign rulers. To that extent Cumberland's aims coincide with Ralph Cudworth's, but unlike Cudworth he does not base his argument on Platonic metaphysics. Nor does he criticize, as did the Cambridge Platonists, the mechanical world view; indeed, he wholeheartedly accepts it. He thinks of his approach as scientific and nonmetaphysical. He sets out to construct an ethics which, although Christian, is independent of revelation and, although demonstrating that morality is eternal and immutable, is based on "the evidence of sense and experience." These were to be the typical eighteenth-century specifications for a satisfactory moral theory.

Cumberland begins by arguing that there is a single

natural law from which all moral laws can be derived—the law, namely, that an agent secures his own good by the promotion of the good of the whole to which he belongs. If this single law is based on "the nature of things," if its truth can be demonstrated from experience, then, he thinks, morality rests secure. And, he argues, experience reveals to us—he draws upon his medical training to illustrate the point—that the parts of a whole secure their own welfare only when they work for the good of the whole to which they belong. A bodily organ, for example, is at its healthiest when it is most effectively securing the health of the body. This truth men could recognize, so Cumberland argues against Hobbes, even in a state of nature. Thus, the foundation of moral laws is not the will of the sovereign.

Benevolence, Cumberland further maintains, is natural to mankind. Even brute animals, indeed, devote themselves to the welfare of their fellow brutes. A state of nature, therefore, would not be, as Hobbes suggested, a war of all against all; their human instincts, not the pressure of a sovereign will, lead men to cooperate with their fellow men in society. Certainly, Cumberland admits, men sometimes act in opposition to the good of the whole, just as an organ of the body will sometimes infect, rather than work toward the health of, the organism of which it forms a part. The fact remains, however, that the "natural impetus of man" is toward securing the common good, just as the general tendency of a bodily organ is to make the body healthier. The legislator's rewards and punishments, like medicine, are directed toward correcting abnormalities; they are not the original springs of moral action.

All moral concepts, Cumberland tries to show, are definable in terms of the single natural law that men secure their own welfare by pursuing the common good. An act is "naturally good" if by virtue of its own nature it tends toward the common good; it is "right" if it is the shortest way to that end; it is "morally good" if it conforms to the natural law. Particular virtues are similarly deducible from the obligation of pursuing the common good; to show that the common good ought to be our objective is at the same time to show that we ought to be law-abiding, just, temperate, and obedient to God.

Most of what were to be the leading eighteenth-century moral theories can be found somewhere suggested, if nowhere fully worked out, in *De Legibus Naturae*. Cumberland argues in detail that moral principles are analogous to the propositions of mathematics, and Samuel Clarke learned much from him on this point. Cumberland also sketches a moral calculus of the sort Francis Hutcheson was to employ; there are many resemblances between his moral philosophy and the third earl of Shaftesbury's; he has been described as the first systematic utilitarian; the organic theory of morality and of the state is conspicuous in his work; resemblances between Cumberland and Spinoza are easy to detect.

Accounts of his moral philosophy differ widely, depending on which of the manifold tendencies in his thinking commentators stress. In Cumberland's own eyes, however, the crucial points are (1) there is a law of nature, defined as a proposition of "unchangeable truth and certainty . . . which lays firm obligations upon all outward acts of behaving, even in a state of nature"; (2) this law enjoins upon us the pursuit of the common good and assures us that by pursuing the common good we achieve happiness and personal perfection; (3) observation of the world, including man's nature, demonstrates the truth of this law; (4) all other moral precepts are applications of the law of nature to particular forms of human action.

Bibliography

The best edition of Cumberland's *De Legibus Naturae* is John Tower's 1750 translation (Dublin), which also includes, as Appendix IV, Squier Payne's *Life of Cumberland*, the main biographical source. For commentaries, see Frank Elsworth Spaulding, *Richard Cumberland als Begründer der englischen Ethik* (Leipzig, 1894); Ernest Albee, *A History of English Utilitarianism* (London, 1902); Frank Chapman Sharp, "The Ethical System of Richard Cumberland, and Its Place in the History of British Ethics," in *Mind*, Vol. 21, No. 83 (1912), 371–398.

JOHN PASSMORE

CUSANUS. *See* NICHOLAS OF CUSA.

CUSTOM. There is obviously some sort of intrinsic relation between social customs and morality, yet philosophical discussions of the relation are practically nonexistent. This article will present the outlines of a logical analysis of the concept of custom that treats it as a normative concept occurring as part of practical, ethical discourse. This may not be the only correct analysis of custom, and it may not faithfully reflect all of the possible uses of this fuzzy concept. However, the recognition of custom as a practical rather than as a theoretical, descriptive category will help untangle some of the traditional puzzles and, in particular, will provide a better understanding of the relation between customs and morality. Much of the confusion about customs is due to the failure to see that persons employing the term "custom" are more interested in conveying a moral message than in advancing social scientific inquiry.

Definition. "Custom" may be tentatively defined as a norm of action (precept, rule of conduct) generally accepted and practiced by a group of people who regard it as sanctioned by the general tradition of the group. Of custom one says, "It is the way our ancestors did it, and it is our way" or "That's the way it has always been done by us." Each of the three parts of this definition requires explanation.

First, a custom is an explicitly recognized dictate concerning what should or should not be done; it is not simply a general habitual pattern of behavior (an observed regularity), but a norm used to guide and justify action. Customs belong to the explicit part of a group's culture, its ideology, and represent ideals of conduct that are expressly acknowledged and taught and that cannot be transgressed.

Second, a custom is a rule for which only limited validity is claimed; it is considered binding only on members of the group concerned and not on others. In this sense customs are relative to a community.

Third, a custom is a precept whose claim to validity is based solely on the contention that it is generally acknowledged and practiced by the community and is of ancient origin. For customs, as W. G. Sumner said, the tradition alone is their warrant. In order to have the status of custom, a precept must be held to be anonymous, whatever its origin actually is.

Essential, then, to the present conception is that customs are justified by reference to tradition alone. This rationale differentiates customs from other kinds of precepts, like technological precepts. If, therefore, some reason other than general practice and tradition is given for accepting and conforming to a prevailing practice, it cannot be considered a custom. In a sense customs are irrational, for by definition they are not based on reasons that hold for men generally, regardless of the group to which they belong.

Whether a precept is to be classified as a custom depends on one's view as to why it is binding. A certain precept may be taken by some of its practitioners to be a custom and by others to have a more general, rational basis. Accordingly, the concept of custom is doubly relative. The validity of the custom depends on one's belonging to the group whose custom it is, and its categorization as a custom depends on one's view of the source of its validity.

It can now be seen why it is so easy to succumb to the temptation of describing the practices of other societies, particularly "primitive" ones, as customs, while refusing to do so for our own practices with regard to the same matters. When we do not understand the reason for a procedure or practice, we assume that it must be just a custom, that it has no reason except tradition.

There are practical consequences of calling a norm of action a "custom." Since customs claim only limited validity—that is, membership in the group concerned is a necessary as well as a sufficient condition of being bound to observe them—it follows that the recognition of a precept as a custom of a certain group functions differently for the group member and the outsider. To describe to a fellow member a practice as "one of our customs" calls attention to a requirement to which he is subject and to a course of conduct with which he is expected to conform. To describe it as such to an outsider not only explains to him why we act as we do but also informs him that he is not expected to act in the same way since an outsider is immune from the requirements of our customs.

It should now be clear why the term "custom" has fallen into disrepute among contemporary anthropologists. To begin with, "custom" is not a neutral term but reflects the speaker's own rational evaluation of the practice so named. Hence, almost any use of the term will represent an ethnocentric classification. More importantly, deeper knowledge of nonliterate cultures has caused increasing interest in the reasons—explicit and implicit—for practices that we would otherwise have classified as irrational customs. Finally, the contemporary trend has been to examine practices in their functional interrelationship with other institutions of the society and in the cultural pattern as a whole; hence, the old-fashioned ethnological treatise that simply listed and catalogued "customs" is no longer popular. (For a critique of this "method of isolation" see A. Macbeath, *Experiments in Living.*)

Customs and morality. One view of the relationship of customs to morality, sometimes called "relativism," identifies morals with customs. The argument is simple: If customs are relative to a group and acquire their validity only from group tradition and if morals are identical with customs, then morals—that is, the principles of right and wrong—are relative to a group and acquire their validity only from group tradition. Consequently, it is argued, morality has no rational basis other than group tradition. As with customs each community has its own morality, and the validity of each of these moralities is limited to the members of the group concerned. Therefore, just as we must respect and tolerate the customs of others, so we must respect and tolerate their moralities.

Although some relativists hold that their position is based on empirical evidence, the position is essentially a logical doctrine concerning the nature of morality. As such, however, it is inconsistent with any ordinary conception of morals, for in order to identify morals with customs, it would be necessary to show not only that every moral principle concerning what is right and wrong has no basis other than custom but also that all such principles ground their claim to validity on the tradition of the group. This is, of course, absurd, for no existing (or possible) system of morality would admit that being a custom is either a necessary or a sufficient condition of a moral principle. The purpose of a moralist's role would be lost if morals were identified with customs.

The opposite extreme, which may be called "absolutism," asserts that customs have no more connection with true morality than superstitions have with science. This position goes back at least to Plato and is held by most ethical intuitionists. Against this position it can be argued that dissociating customs from morals either places morals in a vacuum or else elevates precepts that have validity only as customs into unquestioned eternal principles. A modified version of this epistemologically oriented theory maintains that customs are really only traditional popular beliefs concerning right and wrong; as such they represent, if valid, a lower-grade knowledge ("opinion"), embodying wisdom accumulated from generations of experience. From this conception it follows that customs are theoretically dispensable (in the ideal society) and that their only authority, like that of other popular beliefs, depends on the degree to which they approach true morality. Thus, there is no place in moral theories of this kind for customs in the strict sense defined earlier.

Neither the view that morals and customs are identical (relativism) nor the view that they are entirely distinct and separable (absolutism) is acceptable. Nevertheless, there must be some kind of relation between morals and customs. What is it? In order to find out, we must begin by asking what customs do and how they function.

The functions of customs. In every society customs are pervasive, covering almost every aspect of life, yet many are concerned with describing how to do something rather than with dictating that we should do it. They determine the right ways of doing things. For instance, custom does not tell us that we must eat but tells us only when, where, and how to eat. This suggests that custom may, perhaps, serve the same function with regard to morality by telling us how to do what morality tells us to do. Recognizing this, utilitarians, among others, have emphasized the utility of customs as a means for standardizing behavior so that we will be able to know what to expect from our fellow men. The function of laying down standardized action patterns is, of course, not exclusively fulfilled by custom. It is also a function of law, of professional and social organizations, and even of advertising.

Other functions of customs can be seen if we examine how customs affect the individual. What reasons are there for an individual to conform to the customs of his group? The traditional answer has been that failure to conform will incur social disapproval. One of the reasons why an individual is disapproved by society for not conforming to its customs is that conformity as such is considered a sign of loyalty to the group. Conformity to its customs is often taken as a mark of group membership and makes the individual "one of us." Conversely, failure to conform stamps the individual as an outsider or, perhaps, a heretic or rebel. The use of customs to signify and affirm membership in a group is especially obvious when a subgroup in a society—for example, a religious sect, a military order, a social caste, or a professional clique—wants to differentiate itself from the rest. On the other hand, a nonconformist may refuse to follow the customs of a group simply in order to express defiance of the group.

In both cases customs are used to communicate with others in order to establish, or to deny, "identities"—that is, relationships, limits, powers, and claims. More generally, customs operate to confer a significance on acts that they would not otherwise have. Actions like saluting or genuflecting, under certain circumstances, have a significance that is derived entirely from custom. In one important way, therefore, customs function like a language—they enable us to use our actions as a means of communicating with one another. To a large extent it is only by means of customs that we are able to relate to one another, pro or con, and to express our attitudes and feelings toward one another. How crucial customs are for communal living becomes apparent if one tries to imagine what it would be like to be thrown into a society where one knew everything except its customs. Without knowledge of customs one would not be able to fulfill some of the simplest of moral injunctions, like the injunction to love and respect others. One would not know what his commitments were or how to honor them. He would not know how to show gratitude or solicitude for others, how to be decent and honest, or how to avoid hurting the feelings of others. Then, general requirements of morality transcend every particular group, but they cannot be executed apart from customs. We have to operate within the context of custom.

Bibliography

Benedict, Ruth, *Patterns of Culture*. Boston, 1934.

Ladd, John, *The Structure of a Moral Code*. Cambridge, Mass., 1956.

Macbeath, Alexander, *Experiments in Living*. London, 1952.

Malinowski, Bronislaw, *Crime and Custom in Savage Society*. London, 1926.

Monist, Vol. 47 (1963). See articles on ethics and anthropology.

Montaigne, Michel de, "On Custom," in *Essays*, Book I, Ch. 23.

Sapir, Edward, "Custom," in *Encyclopaedia of the Social Sciences*, Vol. IV (New York, 1930), pp. 658–662.

Sumner, W. G., *Folkways*. Boston, 1907.

Tönnies, Ferdinand, *Die Sitte*. Frankfurt, 1909. Translated by A. F. Bornstein as *Custom*. New York, 1961.

JOHN LADD

CYBERNETICS. The word "cybernetics" comes from the Greek κυβερνήτης, meaning "steersman." In choosing the term, Norbert Wiener and Arturo Rosenblueth paid their respects to Clerk Maxwell's paper "On Governors," which is generally cited as the first significant treatment of feedback mechanisms. (The word "governor" comes from a Latin derivative of κυβερνήτης.)

W. R. Ashby, in *An Introduction to Cybernetics*, construes the subject matter of cybernetics to be the domain of all possible machines; he sees cybernetics as a field of study standing to the real machine—whether it be electronic, mechanical, neural, or economic—much as geometry stands to a real object in terrestrial space.

Thus, cybernetics does not, strictly speaking, constitute an area of philosophical inquiry. Relative to philosophy, however, it may be viewed as a background of scientific and technological methods, achievements, and speculation that prompts certain philosophical inquiries. More specifically, the relevance of cybernetics to philosophy, in particular to the philosophy of mind, may be found in the reasons why and the ways in which the following questions and many other related ones have been discussed: Could a machine exhibit purposive behavior? Could a machine think? Could a robot be conscious? Could a machine be creative? Are human beings highly complicated automata? Are computer (and computer program) models useful in psychological theory? and—a somewhat more unusual query—What do certain metamathematical results tell us about minds and machines?

The questions which explicitly mention computers or metamathematics were not, of course, raised prior to the twentieth century, but some of the other questions are old ones being asked in new contexts.

Historical parallels. In the seventeenth century Descartes argued that animals were mere machines devoid of thought or feeling (although he was somewhat equivocal in his treatment of animal feelings). The seemingly eccentric character of this doctrine was overshadowed by its compelling suggestion that the behavior of at least some organisms could be fully explained mechanistically. In the eighteenth century La Mettrie saw himself as having extended Descartes's doctrine of animal automatism to man in *L'Homme machine* (1747). Tacit in Descartes's writings is the assumption that any subject that is simply a machine is thereby a subject that lacks thought or feeling. La Mettrie, on the other hand, ignored such a restriction on the use of the word "machine" and argued that both animals and men are machines, albeit conscious and cognitive ones. Views that in many respects resembled those found in *L'Homme machine* were later propounded in the nineteenth century by T. H. Huxley, W. K. Clifford, Morton Prince, and others, who argued that man was a conscious automaton. Huxley, in an essay of 1874, paid elaborate tribute to Descartes's physiological notions and doctrine of animal automatism, claiming to find in his notions many of the essentials of late nineteenth-century physiological psychology. And it is common for historians of psychology to find the genesis of the doctrine of reflex action in the mechanistic features of Cartesianism and to see its full-blown application to human organisms in the writings of La Mettrie, Holbach, Cabanis, and others, up through modern behaviorists.

Disputes over the accuracy of the mechanistic portrait of intelligent behavior have persisted intermittently from the seventeenth century through the advent of cybernetics itself. Such disputes frequently involved discussions of whether machines could display certain capacities and capabilities usually ascribed only to intelligent organisms. In the late nineteenth century William James and William McDougall both quarreled with mechanistic psychology on the ground that machines were incapable of purposive self-adaptive movement and, hence, always fell short as models of intelligent behavior.

Though different in origin, controversies that had much in common with the above disputes were conducted during the same periods in both theoretical biology and chemistry. In the early twentieth century such mechanists as Jacques Loeb and Joseph Needham and such vitalists as Hans Driesch and Eugenio Rignano argued whether the principles of living matter could be explained mechanistically without reference to vital forces or entelechies. Suggestive of the ways in which the issues were sometimes posed are the titles of two books published in the 1920s, Eugenio Rignano's *Man Not a Machine: A Study of the Finalistic Aspects of Life* (London, 1926) and Joseph Needham's *Man a Machine, in Answer to a Romantical and Unscientific Treatise Written by Sig. Eugenio Rignano & Entitled "Man Not a Machine"* (New York, 1928).

More detailed comparisons between men and machines took place in psychology in the 1930s, when such behaviorists as Clark L. Hull and others designed electrochemical parallels to the conditioned reflex and when actual maze-"learning" machines were constructed. A similar use of real machines to illustrate or establish a thesis came to be one of the most prominent features of cybernetics only a few years later.

Advent of cybernetics. The true beginnings of cybernetics, as distinct from its historical parallels, can be found in a number of activities which took place in the 1940s. There were significant technological advances, such as the development of electronic computers and the invention and proliferation of highly ingenious negative feedback mechanisms and machines all of which have in common the ability to use inputs so that outputs are restricted and regulated to attain certain goals. (A simple example of negative feedback is provided by the way in which a certain constancy of coldness is maintained in a refrigerator through the use of a thermostatic control that turns the unit off or on whenever certain temperature levels are exceeded.) Also, there were the studies in the early 1940s by W. R. Ashby ("Adaptiveness and Equilibrium") and Arturo Rosenblueth, Norbert Wiener, and Julian Bigelow ("Behavior, Purpose, and Teleology"). Both these articles suggest that negative feedback mechanisms are basic to the workings of the central nervous system. This suggestion has come to be called "the hypothesis of cybernetics." (The above speculation gained currency at about the same time the analytic techniques of propositional logic were being applied to the organization of neural events by Warren S. McCulloch and Walter Pitts; see "A Logical Calculus of the Ideas Immanent in Nervous Activity.") The international conferences of cybernetics began in 1944, with the first published transactions appearing in 1950. And major texts on cybernetics, such as Wiener's *Cybernetics—or Control and Communication in the Animal and the Machine* and Ashby's *Design for a Brain* (New York, 1948), appeared. All these activities led to a noticeable reawakening of philosophical interest in the topic of mentality and machines.

Mechanism and vitalism. Many antimechanistic claims to the effect that machines, unlike intelligent organisms, could never exhibit teleological (purposive) behavior have come to be seen as far less persuasive when machines solve mazes, learn, play chess, prove theorems, and so on. At least it seems clear that if one accepts the criteria which had been proposed by antimechanists for distinguishing teleological from nonteleological behavior, many of the new machines appear to behave teleologically. A semantically interesting feature of this development in the mechanist–vitalist controversy is that the issue of whether machines could behave teleologically has not been settled in the affirmative through a stipulation of new meanings for either the word "machine" or the terms "teleological," "goal-seeking," or "purposive." Instead, the issue has been settled (at least for the moment) by constructing new machines. Hence, mechanists are apparently in a position to claim a nontrivial victory over vitalists on this point. It remains to be seen, however, whether there is some way of strengthening the distinction between teleological and nonteleological behavior so that it marks an important difference between men and machines. Of late, however, there has been a notable lack of effort in this direction, and even to admit the need for such a strengthening of criteria indicates a retreat from earlier vitalist claims. This retreat, however, does not in itself establish the mechanist's case; it simply weakens a position that competes with it.

Can a machine think? The most explicit and influential treatment of the question Can a machine think? is that of the late British logician and mathematician A. M. Turing. In his article "Computing Machinery and Intelligence" (1950), Turing argued that if we could make a machine that was capable of certain highly sophisticated outputs and that could not, under certain conditions, be distinguished by its output from an intelligent human being, we should then concede that machines could think. Furthermore, Turing believed that it would soon be possible to build such machines and that only prejudice would prevent our attributing thought and intelligence to them.

The most frequently raised objection to Turing's argument is that we cannot determine whether a machine can think simply on the basis of outputs, for the outputs might have been brought about in some nonthinking manner. Whether we could accurately characterize a subject as intelligent would seem to depend not only on what it does but at least in part on how it does it. Even if one acknowledges the cogency of this reply, however, the type of argument used by Turing seems to retain some interest if it is construed more broadly, as a way of opting for a behavioristic account of mentality. In short, Turing's challenge may be seen as stating that any well-defined task may be mechanized and that intelligent behavior consists of nothing more than a set of potentially well-defined tasks. But this counterchallenge raises, in turn, the question of whether the execution of certain tasks would require a certain sort of conscious subject and, hence, whether a machine capable of such tasks really would still be a machine. If it is alleged that consciousness itself may be explained in terms of specifiable behavior, then this must be shown, for to many it would seem that such features of mentality as having a pain or feeling fear are not easily construed solely in terms of behavior, although it may readily be admitted that they have important and obvious effects on it.

Consciousness, behavior, and robots. Acceptance of the last-mentioned point has led a number of philosophers to suppose that even if we constructed a robot which was able to simulate all of human behavior, it would not thereby be a robot that was conscious and had feelings and the like. But even if it were not thereby a conscious robot, it can still reasonably be asked whether a robot could be conscious. The quick answer to this has been that such a robot would not be a robot at all but some sort of man or living organism. This answer, in turn, provokes the question of how we could know that this would have to be the case. If someone had said that if a machine were to exhibit self-adaptive behavior, it would not be a machine but a living organism of some kind, that someone, it now seems, would have been wrong. And might not someone be wrong in saying something similar about robots and consciousness? Could there be any way of justifying a claim that future technology could never show them to be compatible? Philosophers who have believed there is a way of justifying such a claim have usually been philosophers who have supposed that the statement "Robots could not be conscious" can be shown to be a logical or "analytic" truth that necessarily follows from an analysis of the meanings of the words "robot" and "conscious." But it has always seemed possible to quarrel with such an analysis itself, and the very notion of analytic truth has proved to be a highly problematic one. At any rate, this "quick answer" does not in itself settle anything but leads into a tangle of complicated problems in the philosophy of language.

Another issue that has some bearing on most of those already discussed is the claim that robots (or machines) do only what they are programmed to do. This claim has usually been put forward to impugn either the ascription of certain deeds or the ascription of credit for certain deeds to robots (or machines). It hardly seems sufficient, however, just to say the robot (or machine) did not really do *X* or should not really get credit for doing *X* because it did only what it was programmed to do. No one has yet shown that there is any opposition between "being programmed to do" and "really doing." To decide in some general fashion which sorts of deeds a robot (or machine) could in principle be programmed to do is no easy matter. A number of tasks have come to be programmable that once might have seemed "in principle" impossible. Moreover, it will not do simply to say that a robot (or machine) should in no case get credit for doing what it does because credit for what it does belongs to the designer and programmer. In some cases it seems more reasonable to credit a machine with a certain original output than it would be to credit the designer or programmer of the machine with that output. (If a fisherman uses a fish-finding device to find fish and does actually find some, he does not say that the designer of his fish-finding device was good at finding those fish; he says the fish-finding device was good at finding those fish.)

Nevertheless, the precise manner in which and the degree to which a particular robot (or machine) could be said to go beyond its designer or programmer in given cases constitute a cluster of issues that deserve more attention. The outcome of disagreements concerning the possible creative abilities of machines will probably depend on the outcome of such issues. Here, too, questions about minds and machines and questions about free will and responsibility intersect. If it is proposed that ascriptions of credit and responsibility be withheld from robots (or machines) on the ground that their behavior is completely determined and predictable—grounds which have themselves been disputed—then it proves interesting to ask whether similar ascriptions should be withdrawn from human agents in the event that we discover their behavior to be determined and predictable.

"Mechamathematics." An important metamathematical result, Gödel's theorem, has been seen by certain mathematical logicians and philosophers to have a bearing on controversies concerning minds and machines. The statements to this effect, however, have on the whole been highly compressed. A number of writers have suggested or hinted that Gödel's theorem can be used to show that minds are essentially different from machines. It is not clear from their remarks exactly how they would develop their defense of this claim or whether once they did so, they would agree with one another. Thus, no summary of these arguments will be attempted.

A glimpse of the controversy with respect to Gödel's theorem may be provided by the following sketch. Gödel proved that for any formal system which is (1) consistent and (2) contains elementary number theory, there will be some "undecidable" formula, *f*, such that neither it nor its negation will be provable within the system. (This is a strengthened form of Gödel's theorem stated by J. B. Rosser.) Any machine, *m*, may be looked upon as an instantiation of some formal system; therefore, for any machine that is the instantiation of a consistent formal system of a certain strength, there will be an undecidable *f*. Hilary Putnam ("Minds and Machines") construes a remark of Ernest Nagel and J. R. Newman in their *Gödel's Proof* (New York, 1958) to support the claim that if we were to suppose that a given machine, *m*, represented a mind, *M*, in that *m* could prove just the mathematical statements that *M* could prove, there would always turn out to be an undecidable *f* which *m* could not prove but which *M* could. Hence, no machine can be an adequate model of the mind. Putnam replies that for a given *m* all we can do is find some *f* such that we can prove that if *m* is consistent, *f* is true where *f* is such that it cannot be proved by *m* if *m* is consistent. But *m* can find this, too. If consistent, it cannot prove *f*. But neither can we unless we could establish the consistency of *m*, which we might not be able to do.

The most extensive effort to meet objections to antimechanistic arguments based on Gödel's proof is to be found in J. R. Lucas' "Minds, Machines and Gödel." Lucas blends arguments similar to the one disputed by Putnam with others of a more informal character, such as the assertion that only a conscious being could consider both itself and its performance without thereby becoming something other than that which did the performance. It is claimed that a machine could not do this without becoming a different machine.

In *Philosophy and Scientific Realism* (London, 1963), J. J. C. Smart devotes a number of pages to these topics. In the course of this he raises the question of whether machines could come to prove theorems using the techniques that human beings use. He disputes the claim that human problem-solving techniques (whatever they are like) are beyond the pale of mechanization. Certainly, there seems to be no a priori reason why elective guessing procedures, various strategies, and so on could not be programmed into a machine. The more we learn about human problem-solving techniques, it has been said, the easier it will be to program a machine to apply similar techniques. Conversely, it has been suggested that in attempting to program a machine to apply such techniques, we will further our understanding of human intellectual processes. In fact, extensive research has been based on this suggestion.

Computer simulation of cognitive processes. Research into computer simulation of cognitive processes compares the behavior of a computer programmed in a certain way with the behavior of human subjects who are engaged in such intellectual activities as making choices, playing games, proving theorems, and so on. The computer program supposedly provides a precise language for expressing theories of mental processes. Whereas some cybernetic research has concentrated on attempting to explain human thinking in terms of electrical and chemical processes in the brain or in terms of neural organization, computer simulation studies have concentrated on explanations in terms of information processes. This procedure gives rise to a cluster of methodological or quasi-philosophical problems that differ somewhat from those mentioned previously. These might be called evaluation problems or comparison problems, problems that center on any attempt to provide criteria for deciding when a particular simulation is a "good" or close simulation of human behavior and whether even if it is a good simulation, it is thereby useful in theorizing about that behavior. Insofar as the use of such models does provide some clarification of mental activity, it would be expected that certain general philosophical views about minds (and machines) will find reinforcement in such models and other philosophical views may find that they have to be made to square with the models.

It is sometimes alleged that even if we were to develop machines or robots to which it seemed reasonable to ascribe thoughts and feelings, this would not help us solve any of the traditional mind–body questions since all the old problems of dualism versus materialism would arise for the machines and robots in the same way that they have arisen for human beings. But no argument seems to have been presented that could show that this would necessarily be the case. Although it may now be difficult to spell out how a machine or robot could have thoughts or feelings without our remaining puzzled by the relationship between its mental states and its physical states, it also seemed difficult at one time to spell out how a machine could behave adaptively without our ascribing an entelechy or vital force to it. This is no longer the case. Perhaps no current conceptual analysis will give us the final insight into the future development of machines; the future development of machines, however, may well yield some insight into our current concepts.

Bibliography

HISTORICAL PARALLELS AND BACKGROUND

Baernstein, H. D., and Hull, C. L., "A Mechanical Model of the Conditioned Reflex." *Journal of General Psychology*, Vol. 5 (1931), 99–106.

Boring, Edwin G., *A History of Experimental Psychology*, 2d ed. New York, 1957.

Driesch, Hans, *The History and Theory of Vitalism.* New York, 1914.

Fearing, Franklin, *Reflex Action: A Study in the History of Physiological Psychology.* Baltimore, 1930.

Hull, C. L., "Mind, Mechanism, and Adaptive Behavior." *The Psychological Review*, Vol. 44 (1937), 1–32.

Huxley, T. H., "On the Hypothesis That Animals Are Automata, and Its History," in his *Essays*, Vol. I, *Methods and Results.* New York, 1911.

James, William, "Are We Automata?" *Mind*, Vol. 4 (1879), 1–22.

James, William, *Principles of Psychology*, 2 vols. New York, 1890; paperback ed., 1950.

Lange, F. A., *The History of Materialism*, translated by E. C. Thomas, 3d ed. London, 1950.

Loeb, Jacques, *The Mechanistic Conception of Life.* Chicago, 1912.

Maxwell, Clerk, "On Governors." *Proceedings of the Royal Society*, Vol. 16 (1868), 270.

McDougall, William, *An Introduction to Social Psychology.* London, 1908; New York, 1961.

Rosenfield, Leonora, *From Beast-Machine to Man-Machine: Animal Soul in French Letters From Descartes to La Mettrie.* New York, 1941.

Stephens, J. M., "A Mechanical Explanation of the Law of Effect." *American Journal of Psychology*, Vol. 41 (1929), 422–431.

Vartanian, Aram, *Diderot and Descartes: A Study of Scientific Naturalism in the Enlightenment.* Princeton, N.J., 1953.

Vartanian, Aram, *La Mettrie's L'Homme machine: A Study in the Origins of an Idea.* Princeton, N.J., 1960.

GENERAL WORKS

Ashby, W. R., *An Introduction to Cybernetics.* London, 1956.

Borko, Harold, ed., *Computer Applications in the Behavioral Sciences.* Englewood Cliffs, N.J., 1962.

Culbertson, James T., *The Minds of Robots.* Urbana, Ill., 1963.

Feigenbaum, Edward A., and Feldman, Julian, eds., *Computers and Thought.* New York, 1963.

Foerester, Heinz von, ed., *Cybernetics, Circular Causal, and Feedback Mechanisms in Biological and Social Systems: Published Transactions of the Sixth, Seventh, Eighth, Ninth, and Tenth Conferences*, 5 vols. New York, 1950–1955.

George, F. H., *The Brain as a Computer.* Oxford, 1962.

McCulloch, Warren S., and Pitts, Walter, "A Logical Calculus of the Ideas Immanent in Nervous Activity." *Bulletin of Mathematical Biophysics*, Vol. 5 (1943), 115–133.

Miller, G. A.; Galanter, Eugene; and Pribram, K. H., *Plans and the Structure of Behavior.* New York, 1960.

National Physical Laboratory, *Mechanisation of Thought*

Processes. Symposium No. 10, Vols. I–II, London, 1959. Contains papers by W. R. Ashby, D. M. MacKay, Marvin Minsky, and others.

Neumann, John von, "The General and Logical Theory of Automata," in L. A. Jeffress, ed., *Cerebral Mechanisms in Behavior.* New York, 1951.

Neumann, John von, *The Computer and the Brain.* New Haven, 1958.

Newell, A., and Simon, Herbert, "Computer Simulation of Human Thinking." *Science*, Vol. 134 (1961), 2011–2017.

Newell, A.; Simon, Herbert; Shaw, J. C., *The Processes of Creative Thinking.* P-1320, rev., Santa Monica, Calif., 1959. RAND Corporation, mimeographed.

Rosenblatt, F., "The Perception: A Probabilistic Model for Information Storage and Organization in the Brain." *Psychological Review*, Vol. 65 (1958), 368–407.

Shannon, C. E., and McCarthy, J., eds., *Automata Studies.* Princeton, N.J., 1956.

Sluckin, W., *Minds and Machines*, rev. ed. London, 1960. A clear, well-written general introduction.

Walter, W. Grey, *The Living Brain.* New York, 1953.

Wiener, Norbert, *Cybernetics—or Control and Communication in the Animal and the Machine.* New York, 1948.

Yovits, Marshall C., and Cameron, Scott, eds., *Self-Organizing Systems: Proceedings of an Interdisciplinary Conference, May 5th and 6th, 1959.* New York, 1960.

PHILOSOPHICAL AND MISCELLANEOUS WORKS

Ashby, W. R., "Adaptiveness and Equilibrium." *Journal of Mental Science*, Vol. 86 (1940), 478–483.

Anderson, Alan Ross, ed., *Minds and Machines.* Englewood Cliffs, N.J., 1964. Includes articles by A. M. Turing, Hilary Putnam, and J. R. Lucas discussed in text.

George, F. H., "Could Machines Be Made To Think?" *Philosophy*, Vol. 31 (1956), 244–252.

Gödel, Kurt, "Über formal unentscheidbare Sätze der Principia Mathematica und verwandter Systeme I." *Monatshefte für Mathematik und Physik*, Vol. 38 (1931), 173–189.

Hook, Sidney, ed., *Dimensions of Mind.* New York, 1960.

Kemeny, John G., *A Philosopher Looks at Science.* Princeton, N.J., 1959.

MacKay, D. M., "Mindlike Behavior in Artefacts." *British Journal for the Philosophy of Science*, Vol. 2 (1951), 105–121. Also see volumes of this journal from 1951 on for numerous philosophical discussions of minds and machines.

Mays, Wolfe, "The Hypothesis of Cybernetics." *British Journal for the Philosophy of Science*, Vol. 2 (1951), 249–250.

Mays, Wolfe, "Can Machines Think?" *Philosophy*, Vol. 27 (1952), 148–162. Also see volumes of this journal from 1952 on for numerous philosophical discussions of minds and machines.

PAS, Supp. Vol. 26 (1952). Includes a symposium by J. O. Wisdom, R. J. Spilsbury, and D. M. MacKay on mentality in machines.

Rogers, H., *Theory of Recursive Functions and Effective Computability.* Cambridge, Mass., 1957. Massachusetts Institute of Technology, mimeographed.

Rosenbloom, Paul, *The Elements of Mathematical Logic.* New York, 1950. See especially pp. 206–208.

Rosser, J. B., "Extensions of Some Theorems of Gödel and Church." *Journal of Symbolic Logic*, Vol. 1 (1936), 87–91.

Rosenblueth, Arturo; Weiner, Norbert; and Bigelow, Julian, "Behavior, Purpose, and Teleology." *Philosophy of Science*, Vol. 10 (1943), 18–24.

BIBLIOGRAPHIES

Minsky, Marvin, "A Selected Descriptor-indexed Bibliography to the Literature on Artificial Intelligence." *IRE Transactions on Human Factors in Electronics*, Vol. HFE-2 (1961), 39–55. Also in Feigenbaum and Feldman, *op. cit.*, pp. 453–523.

Simmons, P. L., and Simmons, R. F., "The Simulation of Cognitive Processes: An Annotated Bibliography," *IRE Transactions on Electronic Computers*, Vol. EC-10 (1962), 462–483; Vol. EC-11 (1962), 535–552.

KEITH GUNDERSON

CYNICS, the "dog philosophers" of the Greek and Roman world, so called almost certainly from the nickname of Diogenes of Sinope, were not a continuous school of theoretical philosophy but an erratic succession of individuals who from the fourth century B.C. to the sixth century A.D. preached, through ascetic practice and mordant denunciation of established convention, a more or less similar way of life designed to lead to the happiness of the individual. Consequently there is no established doctrinal canon by which to define an "orthodox" Cynic, and the ancient but still lively debate as to whether Antisthenes or Diogenes was the founder of Cynicism is an unreal one. Nevertheless, despite marked variations of stress and tone in individual exponents, Diogenes was always regarded as the arch-Cynic, and a sufficient number of characteristic attitudes recur to identify the movement.

The nature of the existing evidence of Cynicism is highly unsatisfactory. The written works with which Diogenes was credited have not survived, and doxographies are few and of uncertain origin (for example, Diogenes Laërtius, Bk. 6, 70–73). Since Diogenes' life was his main testament, the largest class of evidence is anecdotal, with all the uncertainties and elaborations of an oral tradition. Information of his pupils and of Cynics of the third century B.C. is tantalizingly fragmentary. Even the comparatively abundant material on contemporary Cynicism from the first century A.D. comes from outside the movement, from sympathizers of such diverse interests as Epictetus, Dio Chrysostom, and Julian, or from satirists like Lucian.

Teaching. The Cynics believed that happiness was found in "virtuous" action, which was the practical expression of self-realization (*arete* and "know thyself"). This state was in turn produced by a rational awareness of the distinction between natural and artificial values. External and physical goods such as wealth, reputation, pleasure, conventional duties arising from family, property, or state, and all traditional inhibitions, whether social or religious, were condemned as unnatural tyrannies which fettered a man through desire, indulgence, and the ignorance of a confused and corrupt society—the three causes of human misery. Freedom was secured by "following nature" by means of self-discipline whose end was self-sufficiency (*autarkeia*); since man was vulnerable and perverted through his emotions and desires, happiness could be guaranteed only by the understanding and strength of mind to want nothing, lack nothing. And since the artificial currency of human standards was thought to be, not an indifferent factor, but an active corruption to be eradicated, Cynics wished not merely to devalue the coin (like Socrates and the Stoics), but to deface it (*paracharattein*); hence, the most characteristic feature of Cynicism was an asceticism which sought to reduce physical wants to a minimum, as in the case of the animals after which Cynics were named, and to achieve spiritual independence like gods. Independence was not to be achieved, however, by the withdrawal of a hermit; the Cynic engaged in an active crusade which required a continual training (*askesis*) to harden the body and temper the spirit in the very face of temptation, and thus to free the natural "perceptions" and capacities for virtuous actions. The toiling, painful effort of this moral struggle (*ponos*) was categorized as a good, the steep short cut to virtue, which evoked the only natural pleasure; and the legend of Herakles' life of service spent in successfully overcoming labors was sanctified as an ideal of freedom and self-fulfillment. He and the Cynic, whether slave or oppressed, ruled himself as his own master and, therefore, was the ideal king among men. Essentially individualistic and largely antisocial in advocating independence from any community, Cynicism was the most radical philosophy of spiritual security offered to fill the social and moral vacuum created in the fourth century B.C. by the dissolution of the city–state political organism. Yet there was a strong philanthropic impulse in the movement in the sense that the gospel of Herakles, the ideal king, was a spiritual evangel for all men, to be preached by personal example. The Cynic saw himself as "scout and herald of God," dedicating his own labors as a reconnaissance for others to follow; he was the "watchdog of mankind" to bark at illusion, the "surgeon" whose knife sliced the cancer of cant from the minds of others. Cynics deliberately adopted shamelessly shocking extremes of speech and action to jolt the attention and illustrate their attack on convention.

Fearlessness in criticism was a virtue, useful to further Cynic ideals, but it was also open to abuse, as was the license of affected shamelessness. There was always a real danger that the negative, denunciatory side of Cynicism would predominate, the more so since happiness was most often described as freedom from misery, and virtue, practical wisdom, and right reason remained somewhat nebulous terms. The Cynics did not offer arguments to intellectuals, whose theories they despised as useless. Rather, they offered the ideal practical example of autonomy of will through their own actions, bringing by the very vilification of luxury and sensual indulgence and by the justification of poverty, spiritual hope to the poor, disenchanted and oppressed. Thus the more formal types of philosophical instruction were abandoned and three new literary genres fostered: the *chreia*, or short anecdotal quip with a pungent moral tang; the diatribe, or popular sermon in conversational style; and Menippean satire.

History of the movement. The most influential of Diogenes' converts was Crates of Thebes. Joined by his wife in a life devoted to Cynic ideals, he earned by his humanity and good works the affectionate name of "Door-Opener." He wrote philosophical tragedies and poetry about a Cynic paradise named the island of Pera. In the third century B.C. Bion of Borysthenes, a wandering preacher, was "the first to tart up philosophy" by popularizing the diatribe; Menippus of Gadara initiated a new type of satire mingling seriocomic themes in prose and verse (his works are lost); Cercidas of Megalopolis applied Cynic ideas to practical politics by proposing reforms attacking social inequalities in the refounding of his city; the fragments of Teles, a dull Megarian schoolmaster, throw some light on Bion and earlier Cynics. After a quieter, although not dormant, period Cynicism revived in the first century A.D. with some encouragement from Stoicism: Demetrius was prominent in the Stoic-flavored opposition to the emperor in the seventh decade; Dio Chrysostom found solace for his exile in an amalgam of Cynic and Stoic practice; Epictetus, the Stoic, admired Diogenes. The second century records the apogee of Cynic influence and extravagance. The leading figures differed sharply. The philanthropy and popularity of Demonax of Cyprus contrasted with the brutal scorn of Oenomaus of Gadara. Peregrinus Proteus, a convert from Christianity, was an irrepressible radical with a touch of the mystic; he burned himself to death before huge crowds at the Olympic festival. These were men of ideals; but Lucian and Julian also record with disgust a riffraff of confidence tricksters and professional beggar-preachers masquerading under the Cynic uniform of cloak, knapsack, and stick. The peculiar animal–divine polarity of Cynicism attracted both saints and rogues. In the history of Greek thought Cynicism was most influential on the development of Stoicism, first through Zeno and then much later with Epictetus, who gave noble expression (3.22) to the most uncompromisingly radical ethic that anyone attempted to put into practice in the ancient world.

It is tempting to recognize Cynic traits in other civilizations, as Onesicratus, the admiral and historian of Alexander, did on encountering the gymnosophist Indian fakirs. In medieval times, the mendicant friars are more apposite than anchorites, especially when one considers the complementary virtues of Franciscans and Dominicans (*Domini canes*).

Bibliography

A selection of ancient evidence on the Cynics is to be found in Diogenes Laërtius, *Lives*, Bk. 6; Dio Chrysostom, *Orations*, 4, 6, 8, 9, 10, 32, 72; Epictetus, *Discourse*, 3.22; Lucian, *Demonax, Peregrinus, Runaways, The Cynic, The Fisher;* Julian, *Orations*, 6, 7; and *Teletis Reliquiae*, edited by O. Hense (Tübingen, 1909).

Three very different approaches to Cynicism are to be found in D. R. Dudley, *A History of Cynicism* (London, 1937); R. Höistad, *Cynic Hero and Cynic King* (Uppsala, Sweden, 1949); and F. Sayre, *The Greek Cynics* (Baltimore, 1948). (All three include detailed bibliographies.) Dudley's book is organized as a historical account of the movement. Höistad is concerned with the development, within the context of philosophy in the fourth century B.C., of those Cynic views pertaining to the ideal human or king and with the subsequent influence of those ideas. Sayre attempts a composite picture of the Cynic, which emerges as an extreme and hostile account of the disreputable side of Cynicism, a distortion owing to a somewhat uncritical handling of anecdotal material. His book contains, however, a generous amount of evidence in translation.

I. G. Kidd

CYRANO DE BERGERAC, SAVINIEN DE (1619–1655), soldier, man of letters, and freethinker, was born in Paris, where he died 36 years later; he resembled only superficially the hero of Rostand's romanticized drama (1897). Hostile to the formal authoritarian education to which he had been subjected at the Collège de Beauvais, he was persuaded to serve in the army, where he gained a considerable reputation as a duelist and writer of verses. His military career came to an end when he was wounded at the siege of Arras in 1640. Between 1642 and 1651 he studied philosophy assiduously, with special stress on Pierre Gassendi and Descartes, and was, according to some, a pupil of Gassendi himself. Descartes' principle of methodical doubt, Gassendi's rehabilitation of Epicurus, and the attendant influence of a newly translated Lucretius were all forces providing a common philosophical denominator which drew Cyrano closer to his fellow *libertins*—Gabriel Naudé, La Mothe Le Vayer, and Molière, among others. At the same time he was emerging as a burlesque poet of consequence and a redoubtable political writer who first attacked and then defended the Machiavellian statecraft of Cardinal Mazarin. In 1652 he entered the service of the duc d'Arpajon under whose protection he brought out in 1654 his *Oeuvres diverses*, which included the boldly rational *Lettre contre les sorciers* and a farcical comedy, *Le Pédant joué*, from which Molière borrowed two passages for *Les Fourberies de Scapin*. In 1654 Cyrano also published an intellectually challenging and ideologically daring tragedy, *La Mort d'Agrippine*. A falling beam, dislodged by accident—or perhaps intentionally—brought death a year later.

Cyrano's reputation as an intellectual libertine, propagator of subversive ideas, satirist of man and his foibles, and as a figure in the vanguard of scientific thought—already firmly established before 1655—received increased notoriety with the posthumous appearance of *L'Autre Monde, ou Les États et empires de la lune et du soleil*, which described imaginary voyages to the moon and the sun, respectively. The first of the two parts of this work was made public in truncated form by the author's friend Le Bret in 1657. The second part, either unfinished or censored (the original manuscript has vanished), was published in 1762.

Despite borrowings and suggestions from a variety of sources, Cyrano's work, particularly when compared with that of many of his contemporaries, is strikingly original. Subscribing to the still little known and highly controversial Copernican theory, he adhered to the principle that all is relative in the universe and attacked religious and philosophical anthropocentrism. In fact he was the first to link closely together a criticism of the religion of Moses and the philosophy of Aristotle. In the man-machine–beast-machine debate, he stressed the idea of continuity among all living creatures. A forerunner of Diderot's materialism, he outlined a calculation of probability according to which atoms, by means of chance and infinite time alone, could, in their innumerable combinations, create the organized world known to man. Furthermore he demonstrated an awareness of the forces of gravitation, the laws of which Newton was to discover and define several decades later. But he did not have Gassendi's gift for observation and experimentation or Descartes' aptitude for mathematics. He was more a popularizer of science than a true scientist. Indeed, he was the originator of science fiction.

The chief significance of Cyrano lies in the fact that he epitomized the general mental attitudes among the freethinkers of his period: enmity toward tradition, interest in ethical and scientific progress, and fondness for philosophical abstractions. As such he was eminently representative of those engaged in a protracted intellectual struggle which revealed the great trend of the French critical spirit—a spirit that was to gain increased momentum in the eighteenth century and to approach fulfillment with the publication of Diderot's Encyclopedia.

Works by Cyrano

Modern editions of de Bergerac's works include F. Lachèvre, ed., *Les Oeuvres libertines de Cyrano de Bergerac* (Paris, 1921); H. Weber, ed., *Cyrano de Bergerac. L'Autre Monde* (Paris, 1959); and Richard Aldington, ed. and transl., *Voyages to the Moon and Sun* (New York, 1962).

Works on Cyrano

See P.-A. Brun, *Savinien de Cyrano de Bergerac. Sa vie et ses oeuvres* (Paris, 1893); René Pintard, *Le Libertinage érudit dans la premiere moitié de XVIIIe siècle* (Paris, 1943); J.-J. Bridenne, "A la recherche du vrai Cyrano de Bergerac," in *Information littéraire* (Nov.–Dec. 1953).

OTIS FELLOWS

CYRENAICS, a school of hedonistic philosophy active in the second half of the fourth century B.C. and the first quarter of the third century B.C. The name was applied to followers of Aristippus of Cyrene, the friend of Socrates but the standard formulation of doctrine shows later influences and was probably due to Aristippus' grandson, also named Aristippus and nicknamed "Mother-taught." Further developments were introduced at the end of the fourth century by Hegesias, Annikeris, and Theodorus, who gave their names to subordinate sects.

Cyrenaics concentrated on practical ethics, rejecting physics and mathematics as offering no contribution to a life of happiness. They discussed ethics under the headings: (1) objects of pursuit and avoidance; (2) sensations; (3) actions; (4) causes; (5) proofs. Happiness was dependent on pleasure, and the particular sensation of pleasure of the moment was regarded as the goal of action, the only good desirable for its own sake, and the criterion of right and wrong. This ethical hedonism was illogically supported by natural observation that all living things were attracted by pleasure and that human beings from childhood were instinctively so attracted. It was also defended by an epistemology, possibly stimulated by Plato's *Theaetetus* and based on the fallibility of perception, which restricted knowledge to the field of sensations: The taste of sweetness and feeling of cold are real; it is impossible to know that the honey is sweet or the hail cold. Thus, all vain opinion, envy, and superstition were dismissed as illusory; only active physical sensations, described as rough and smooth movements—the one painful and repellent, the other pleasant and attractive—were sure guides and criteria for action. Pleasure was a positive sensation, not mere absence of pain. Cyrenaics also claimed that only immediate stimulus set in motion strong sensations and thus discounted memory of past and anticipation of future pleasures and pains. The Cyrenaic lived for the enjoyment of the moment.

We are told that one pleasure does not differ in worth from another pleasure, nor is one more pleasant than another. In later controversy (probably with Epicureans) Cyrenaics held the physical pleasures and pains were better (stronger?) than mental ones. The skill of the philosopher lay in his exercise of choice. Wealth and luxury, while capable of producing pleasure, were not pleasant in themselves; it might be "better to lie on a paillasse and have no fears than be wealthy and choked with cares." So Cyrenaics were forced to take into consideration the consequences of an act. Above all, the philosopher was the man who had rational control over his pleasures and pains by self-adaptation to circumstances and by the manipulation of situations and people for his own hedonistic ends, for all acts were indifferent in value except in their utility to the agent. This stress on rational control as a key to freedom of action is a Socratic legacy which dominated philosophies of conduct in a troubled age. The Cyrenaic interpretation should be contrasted with the abstinence advocated by contemporary Cynicism. Aristippus had said (presumably against Antisthenes) that "the man who controls pleasure is not he who stays away from it, but he who uses it without being carried away by it; just as the master of a ship or horse is not one who does not use them, but he who guides them wherever he wishes."

Nevertheless, the stimulus of pleasure as a physical sensation was external and not completely under human control, and a pessimistic side of the school was revealed by Hegesias, who had a poor opinion of the world ("We must not hate men," he said, "but teach them better"). Pains outnumbered pleasures in our lives, and so he conceded that happiness was in practice unattainable. Also by stressing the indifference of poverty, wealth, slavery, freedom, and the rest, rather than their capacity of producing pain or pleasure, he saw the philosopher's art as the avoidance of evils rather than the choice of goods. His difference from Aristippus is best illustrated by his lectures on suicide and the indifference of life and death, which were so effective that they had to be banned by Ptolemy I (Soter).

Annikeris, on the other hand, allowed the philosopher happiness even with few pleasures accruing to him, repeating that the end was the enjoyment of each single pleasure as it came, not the accumulation of pleasures. He also reacted against the iron rule of self-interest imposed by his predecessors by admitting altruistic acts of friendship, gratitude, respect for parents, and patriotism, for the sake of which the philosopher might even endure deprivation of pleasure.

Theodorus finally redefined the end of action not as the physical sensation of pleasure but as the mental emotion of joy brought about by practical intelligence (as grief was the product of folly), thereby guaranteeing self-sufficiency by putting the end under the agent's control. He displayed a marked Cynic contempt for all conventional rules and values, holding absolutely to the simple criterion of utility to the doer. Thereafter the school appears to have disintegrated before the advance of the more successful hedonistic philosophy of Epicurus.

Bibliography

G. Giannantoni, *I Cirenaici* (Florence, 1958), and E. Mannebach, *Aristippi et Cyrenaicorum Fragmenta* (Leiden and Cologne, 1961), contain collections of the fragments with commentary. See also Vol. II, Part 1, of Eduard Zeller, *Die Philosophie der Griechen*, translated by O. J. Reichel as *Socrates and the Socratic Schools* (London, 1885).

I. G. KIDD

CZECHOSLOVAK PHILOSOPHY. The tempestuous political history of the territory of contemporary Czechoslovakia—Bohemia, Moravia, and Slovakia—is reflected in the irregularity and lack of continuity in its philosophical development.

Aristotle was discussed and lectures on logic were delivered by Master Bohumil in 1271, even before the founding of King Charles University of Prague in 1348 (the first institution of its kind north of the Alps and west of the Rhine). At the end of the fourteenth century the moral and religious treatises of Thomas of Štítné (c. 1333–1401) were written in the vernacular instead of in Latin. About the same time the influence of the ideas of John Wyclyf on Czech students at Oxford played an important role in the birth of the Czech Reformation movement. The significance of Wyclyf's disciple Jan Hus (c. 1369–1415), the rector of the University of Prague, lay less in his originality than in the courage with which he challenged the authority of the medieval church. His refusal to recant at the Council of Constance in 1415 was aptly characterized as "the declaration of the rights of individual conscience" (Ernest Denis, *Huss et la guerre hussite*, Paris, 1930, p. 176). The principle of free inquiry was thus implicitly formulated, but since it was applied only to the interpretation of the Scriptures, its philosophical significance was not grasped.

More genuine philosophical activity was aroused in the next century by the combined impact of humanism and the Reformation. A number of philosophical books, classical as well as modern, were translated into the native tongue. Erasmus' *Encomium Moriae* was translated in 1511, only two years after its original publication. The first book on logic by a Czech author, Petrus Codicillus' *Praecepta Dialectices* (1590), reflected the influence of Ramus and Melanchthon. About the same time Giordano Bruno found a temporary refuge at Prague, where he dedicated his *Articuli Centum et Sexaginta Adversus Huius Tempestatis Mathematicos et Philosophos* to Rudolf II, Holy Roman emperor and king of Bohemia, whose capital was at Prague. The liveliness of Prague as an intellectual center at that time is also shown by Kepler's and Tycho Brahe's sojourns there. When Brahe was buried in Prague in 1601, the funeral sermon (later published by Gassendi in his *Tychonis Brahei Vita* in 1654) was given by Jan Jesenský (Jessenius), a professor of Slovak origin who was later rector of the University of Prague. Before editing Savonarola's *Universae Philosophiae Epitome* (1596), Jessenius wrote *Zoroaster, Nova Brevis, Veraque de Universo Philosophia*, which contained a mixture of Neoplatonic ideas, astral hylozoism, and ideas derived from Patrizzi and Copernicus.

The development of philosophy was interrupted by the success of the Counter Reformation; Jessenius himself was one of its first victims in 1621. He was the second rector of the University of Prague to die for his convictions.

Jessenius' death symbolized the intellectual death of the whole nation for 150 years. Philosophical interest survived only among Protestant refugees abroad and in some Lutheran colleges in eastern Slovakia, which remained (temporarily, at least) under the rule of the Calvinist princes of Transylvania. It was in Slovakia that a discussion took place in 1667 between Isac Zaban, professor at Prešov, who defended a qualitative atomism (*Existentia Atomorum*), and his opponent Elias Ladiver (*De Atomis, Contra Zabanium*).

Among refugees the most famous was Jan A. Komenský, or Comenius (1592–1670), whose great significance as a pioneer of modern methods in education is generally known. However, his philosophical insight was severely limited by his Protestant orthodoxy, and he opposed both

Descartes and Copernicus in his *Refutatio Philosophiae Cartesianae et Astronomiae Copernicanae* (1656; the manuscript was not preserved). Faint anticipations of the kinetic view of matter in his *Disquisitiones de Calore et Frigore* (1659) were due to the influence of Francis Bacon.

The restoration of religious freedom and the abolition of serfdom in 1781 created the conditions for the revival of philosophical interest and intellectual life in general. The deistic philosophy of the Enlightenment inspired the philologians and historians who resurrected the native tradition and language. In philosophy the creation of suitable terminology was the first task. The Hegelian Augustin Smetana (1814–1851), an excommunicated priest, still wrote in German, but the historian František Palacký (1798–1876) wrote a book and several articles on aesthetics in Czech. Ludovít Štúr (1815–1856) used Hegel's doctrine of national spirit to justify the distinctness of the Slovak language from Czech. The influence of Hegel was superseded by that of Herbart, whose ideas dominated the University of Prague until the death of Professor Josef Durdík (1837–1902). Durdík's Herbartism did not prevent him from having a lively interest in English thought and the science of his time, as is clear from his two German works, *Leibniz und Newton* (Halle, 1869) and the posthumously published *Kant und Darwin* (1906). Nearly all his other books, most of them on aesthetics and the history of philosophy, are in Czech.

After 1900, and especially after the attainment of Czech political independence in 1918, the liveliness of discussion and the diversity of points of view in Czechoslovak philosophy reached their height. The most important representative of positivism was František Krejčí (1858–1934), who defended the double-aspect theory of Wundt and Spencer, notably in his six-volume *Psychologie* (Prague, 1897–1926). Thomas Garrigue Masaryk (1850–1937) was also greatly influenced by the positivists and by David Hume; however, partly under the influence of Brentano's theism, he reacted critically against positivism (see especially his *Modern Man and Religion*, London, 1938). This philosophical attitude is present in all his works, whether they deal with methodology, social philosophy, or philosophy of history; most of them also appeared in other languages, especially English and German. More opposed to positivism under the combined influence of Masaryk and Hans Driesch was Emmanuel Rádl (1873–1942). Of his numerous writings only *Geschichte der biologischen Theorien* (Leipzig, 1905; Czech edition, Prague, 1909) and *Neue Lehre vom zentral Nervensystem* (Leipzig, 1912) are accessible to the foreign reader. Ferdinand Pelikán (born in 1885) was influenced by Fichte and the contingentism of Boutroux in his *Entstehung und Entwickelung des Kontingentismus* (Berlin, 1915). It is regrettable that the excellent studies of the philosopher and mathematician Karel Vorovka (1879–1929)—*Úvahy o nazory v matematice* ("Reflections on Intuition in Mathematics"; Prague, 1917), *Kantova filosofie ve svých vztazích k vědam exaktním* ("Kant's Philosophy in Its Relations to the Exact Sciences"; Prague, 1924), and *Americká filosofie* ("American Philosophy"; Prague, 1929)—are inaccessible to the majority of foreign readers.

The promising development of Czechoslovak philosophy was interrupted by the Nazi occupation from 1939 to 1945 and again by communist rule in 1948. Since 1948 Marxism–Leninism has been the official philosophy; no other views are tolerated even now, although the polemic against them has lost some of its original violence.

(See Czechoslovak Philosophy in Index for articles on Czechoslovak philosophers and other figures important to Czechoslovak philosophy.)

Bibliography

Čyževski, Dmytro, *Hegel bei den Slaven*. Reichenberg, Czechoslovakia, 1934; 2d ed., Bad Homburg, Czechoslovakia, 1961.

Patočka, Jan, "La Philosophie en Tchécoslovaquie et son orientation actuelle." *Etudes philosophiques*, Vol. 3 (1948), 63–74.

Pelikán, Ferdinand, "Die tschechische Philosophie," in Friedrich Ueberweg, *Grundriss der Geschichte der Philosophie*, 12th ed. Berlin, 1928. Vol. V, pp. 289–298.

Silberstein, L., "Le Travail philosophique et sociologique en Tchécoslovaquie." *Le Monde slave*, Vol. 12, No. 1 (1935), 286–315.

Zába, Gustav, "Slavische Philosophie in Böhmen," in Friedrich Ueberweg, *Grundriss der Geschichte der Philosophie*, 11th ed. Berlin, 1916. Vol. IV, pp. 726–734.

MILIČ ČAPEK

CZOLBE, HEINRICH (1819–1873), German naturalist philosopher, was born near Danzig and died in Königsberg, where from 1860 to 1868 he had been a high-ranking army doctor. Czolbe's philosophy was a positivistic naturalism that developed from an early, materialist view to a later, Spinozist view.

Czolbe's thought, which is not free from paradoxes and is somewhat overburdened with hypotheses, was developed under two influences. On one hand, he was deeply impressed by Friedrich Hölderlin's elegiac novel *Hyperion*, with its striving for a pantheistic synthesis of nature and mind. On the other, he was stimulated by Rudolf Hermann Lotze's critique of the concept of a "vital force," and by the works of Ludwig Feuerbach, D. F. Strauss, and Friedrich Ueberweg.

Czolbe held, with Feuerbach, that philosophical thought should "be satisfied with the world as given"—that is, that it should not assume any supersensible forces or essences and that, in explaining phenomena, it should use only concepts grounded in experience and intuition. This strict rejection of any mystical metaphysics was based less on epistemology than on ethics, for Czolbe regarded it as man's moral obligation to acquiesce in the natural order of the world. His optimistic belief in the superiority of the given world order was also the root of his moral philosophy. He adhered to a form of eudaemonism, holding that the ultimate meaning of existence lies in the greatest possible harmonious, spiritual, and material happiness of all feeling creatures.

Czolbe's world view, which he improved and reconstructed unremittingly, exhibits traits of naive realism and uncritical materialism. Nothing exists except material events; sensory qualities are properties of things and rest, as does consciousness, on the motion of atoms. Czolbe later despaired of explaining psychical processes (which for him consisted solely of sensations and feelings) and organic events in a purely mechanistic and physical manner. He therefore postulated, in addition to matter, two independent kinds of being—an organic reality irreducible to the inorganic and a spatially extended "world mind" (as a foundation for mental happenings). The latter is constructed from the elements of sensuous intuition—that is, out of sensations.

Czolbe developed a monistic concept of the world by taking infinite, empty space, conceived of as having real objective existence (with time as its fourth dimension) as the primitive foundation of the universe and the one explanatory principle of reality. Thus, "recasting Spinozism in an empiricist manner and returning to the philosophy of the Greeks," he said, toward the end of his life, that he had come to regard "space and time as the sole substance among the innumerable attributes of the world."

Principal Works by Czolbe

Neue Darstellung des Sensualismus ("New Statement of Sensationalism"). Leipzig, 1855.

Entstehung des Selbstbewusstseins ("Genesis of Self-Consciousness"). Leipzig, 1856.

Die Grenzen und der Ursprung der menschlichen Erkenntnis ("The Limits and Source of Human Knowledge"). Jena and Leipzig, 1865.

Grundzüge einer extensionalen Erkenntnistheorie ("Main Features of an Extensional Theory of Knowledge"), E. Johnson, ed. Plauen, Germany, 1875.

For criticism on Czolbe, see P. Friedmann, *Darstellung und Kritik der naturalistischen Weltanschauung Heinrich Czolbes* ("Exposition and Critique of the Naturalistic World Outlook of Heinrich Czolbe"). Bern, 1905.

FRANZ AUSTEDA
Translated by *Albert E. Blumberg*

D

D'ALEMBERT, JEAN LE ROND. *See* ALEMBERT, JEAN LE ROND D'.

DANTE ALIGHIERI (1265–1321), the author of the *Divine Comedy,* was born in Florence of a middle-class family with some pretensions to nobility. It is likely that he frequented the church schools, and he probably spent a year at the University of Bologna. He fought in the battle of Campaldino (1289) and a few years later married Gemma Donati, by whom he had at least three children. He took part in the government of his native city, serving on various city councils (1295–1297, 1301), as prior (1300), and as ambassador to San Gimignano (May 1300) and later to Rome (October 1301), where his mission was to negotiate with the pope to bring about a just peace between the warring factions of White Guelphs and Black Guelphs. Aided by the intervention of Charles of Valois, the Blacks took over the city and Dante, a White, went into exile. He wandered from court to court of medieval Italy, with especially long sojourns at Verona and at Ravenna, where he spent the last three years of his life. He seems to have served his patrons as adviser and on occasion specifically as ambassador; it was after an embassy to Venice on behalf of Guido da Polenta, lord of Ravenna, that the poet died.

By choice Dante might well have devoted himself to political life: circumstance deprived him of this opportunity and constrained him to put his great gifts to the service of letters; his masterpiece, the *Divine Comedy,* is generally regarded as the supreme poetic achievement of the Western tradition and has assured his fame. His *Vita Nuova* is the story of his idealistic love for Beatrice, presumably of the Portinari family, who married Simone de' Bardi and died in 1290. The *Convivio,* composed after the author went into exile, is a didactic work; the *De Vulgari Eloquentia* is a milestone in the history of linguistics, being the first serious study of a vernacular tongue; and the *De Monarchia* is the vehicle for Dante's expression of his political theory. Mention should also be made of his *Rhymes,* a collection of verses of varying kinds—some purely lyrical, some moralistic, and some, one might say, philosophical.

To what extent Dante may properly be considered a philosopher depends on one's definition of the term. Richard McKeon does not consider him such "by the crucial test that, despite the philosophic doctrines that crowd his poems, scholars have been unable to agree concerning what his attitude toward the philosophers he uses is." But this is to make a very special category of philosophers. The best statement of Dante's attitude is found at the beginning of the *Convivio* ("Banquet"), where he represents himself not as one of the great (scholars and philosophers) who actually sit at the banquet table but rather as one who, sitting at their feet, passes on to others the crumbs that he is able to pick up. This would make him on the one hand at least an eager student of philosophy and on the other what we should now call a popularizer, if the term may be used without disparagement. And within the great area of philosophy his major interest was in ethics and politics. Let us concede that in the field of pure speculation his mind was alert and curious rather than original. Like his contemporaries he was for the most part content to follow Aristotle as interpreted by Aquinas, with recourse to what he thought of as "Platonic" where it suited him. His use of his authority, his stature as a poet, and his influence, which still endures, make it worthwhile to study his philosophical posture in some detail.

The "Vita Nuova" and "Convivio." If a drive to seek eternal truth, permanent universals, and order in things is the proper attribute of a philosopher, as it would seem to be, then Dante's claim to the cherished title is reasonable. Perhaps his first work, the *Vita Nuova,* is the most dramatic example of this precisely because, paradoxically, it is not a philosophical work at all. It is a love story of intimate and personal nature, grounded, it would seem, in historical fact but taking on the air of a spiritual parable; its immediate sources are not in works of philosophy but in the love cult of the Middle Ages. Yet the construction and the apparatus betray a disciplined intent; the prose and poetry are mingled in a strict architectural pattern; and each of the poems is followed by an analysis composed in the tradition of Scholasticism. Digressions on the nature of personification and the meaning of certain terms are evidence of what one might fairly call the philosophical manner. Beatrice herself becomes in the course of the confessional narrative something very close to a theological and thus a quasi-philosophical concept.

It is, however, the *Convivio* that is the most purposefully "philosophical" of Dante's canon. It was inspired, the author tells us, by the reading of Cicero and Boethius, and Dante in fact seems to see himself as having much in common with the latter, also a victim of political injustice, and as turning to the same source for consolation. It is noteworthy, too, that Dante attempts, as did Boethius—consciously, one suspects—to set philosophy free from its entanglement with Christian theology. His definition of philosophy in the third tractate goes back to Pythagoras, and in Book IV, in the course of enumerating the virtues appropriate to the successive ages of man, he turns to the pagans (such as Aeneas and, very strikingly, Cato), to exemplify such virtues. All but startling is his eulogy: "And what earthly man was more worthy than Cato to signify God? Truly none." Such an attitude toward the "ideal pagan" dramatizes the author's celebrated exposition of the two beatitudes (II, 4): one in speculation and contemplation, the other in proper conduct of the active life; the former is "higher" than the latter, which, however, clearly is not "subordinate": "It is typical of Dante," says Étienne Gilson, "to base the autonomy of an inferior order on its very inferiority."

In this connection the plan of the *Convivio* (if it may be called a plan, for, unlike most of Dante's works, the book seems to have grown of itself) is very revealing of the author's concept of the uses, if not the nature, of philosophy. The first tractate is highly personal, stating that the genesis of his interest was his need for consolation in his exile and, quite frankly, his feeling that his "image" in Italy had suffered somewhat from the youthful and impassioned portrait that emerged from the pages of the *Vita Nuova*. In the second tractate he avows that in effect philosophy, "the fairest and noblest daughter of the universe," is the new lady who has replaced Beatrice in his heart. In the third tractate he discusses the meaning of philosophy, which he finds to signify "love of and zeal for wisdom," adding that philosophy has "as its subject understanding and as its form an almost divine love of the thing understood." Presumably "understanding" can be applied to the various fields of study which Dante had enumerated in the second tractate, composing an ingenious correlation between the sciences and the heavens of the Ptolemaic system. Of these branches the highest for any medieval theologian (theology itself is in the empyrean, beyond the physical cosmos) would be metaphysics, but it is significant that Dante brackets it with physics in the starry heaven and puts ethics in the loftiest physical sphere, the *primum mobile*, morality being "the science that disposes us rightly for the other sciences" even as the crystalline heaven sets in motion all the other spheres. In fact, the largest part of the work, the fourth treatise, is given over to a study of true nobility, its source and its effects.

Dante finds this human excellence not to be the Aristotelian "inherited wealth and good manners" but rather to be a God-given grace, the nature of which is evident in its fruits. The fruits, which are enumerated in chronological order, are all of such a nature as to be properly called social virtues. Dante's ideal is not a mystic or a visionary but, in the best sense of the term, a man of the world, living in a community and serving it to the best of his ability—certainly an Aristotelian concept. Only in the stage of "decrepitude" does Dante say that the good man's thoughts should turn to God and the afterlife, and even this passage, beautiful as it is, has about it a tone more pagan than Christian. It is noteworthy that all the men chosen to exemplify the appropriate virtues are men of action, in many cases pagans but also including such ambiguous characters as Lancelot and Guido da Montefeltro, the *condottiere*. Thus the *Convivio*, dedicated to the glorification of philosophy, ends by being a rule of good living, high-minded, to be sure, but practical as well. Noteworthy too is the rather lengthy excursus of Book IV (Chs. 4–5) which is inserted to justify the Roman Empire. Dante finds historical correspondences between the empire and the church, affirms that Christ chose to come to earth at the time the world was best governed and at peace (that is, under Augustus), and concludes with a panegyric to Rome. This is the more interesting because some of his data are traceable to St. Augustine, whose view of imperial Rome was quite opposite.

The "De Monarchia." The *De Monarchia*, developing the latent and the tentative attitudes of the *Convivio*, may well contain Dante's most original contribution to philosophical thought. Written, it seems likely, either during or shortly after Henry VII of Luxembourg's descent into Italy (c. 1313), it is an eloquent defense of the imperial cause or, more accurately, principle. The work is divided into three parts: in the first Dante shows the necessity for the rule of one monarch in temporal affairs; in the second he argues that for historical reasons such a monarch should be the Roman emperor; and in the third he defends the thesis that the emperor, although he owes deference to the pope, should not be subordinate to the pontiff in temporal matters.

It is the first book that is the most fascinating to the student of Dante the philosopher. Briefly, the main argument is that peace is a necessity if humanity is to actualize its potential intellect in the highest degree; and there can be no assurance of peace, national rivalries being what they are and greed being as strong as it is, unless the world is governed by one prince, supreme above all nations and beyond the temptations of *cupiditas*. In the course of defining the collective potential intellect, Dante invokes the name of Averroës, thus laying himself open to a charge of heresy (and indeed the *De Monarchia* was solemnly burned and remained on the Index for many years).

However, Gilson has well made the point that the collective potential intellect of humanity as conceived by Dante was not a "being," as was the "possible intellect" (or kind of oversoul) of Averroës, but rather a "community." Indeed, in the course of his arguments in the first book Dante follows Thomistic reasoning, but unlike Thomas, who never so much as mentioned the word "emperor," he applies it to secular purposes. Conceding the superiority of contemplation over action and, by inference, of the spiritual over the temporal, he nevertheless stresses the importance of the machinery necessary to perfect the fulfillment of man's proper endowment in the active life and his happiness in this world. So too at the end he readily concedes that the emperor owes the pope the respect of a younger brother, but while thus indicating that the spiritual life is superior, he seems also to imply that it is separate and independent; both pope and emperor would, in his theory, derive their authority directly from God. The result is in fact a kind of political facet of the Averroistic double truth, as contemporary critics were quick to point out. Gilson, for whom Dante is no Averroist, nevertheless commends him for seeing clearly "that one cannot entirely withdraw the temporal world from the jurisdiction of the spiritual world without entirely withdrawing philosophy from the jurisdiction of theology" and adds that Dante's perception of this fact gives him "a cardinal position in the history of mediaeval political philosophy." In this sense and with a practical intent characteristic of Dante, the *De Monarchia* reaffirms the underlying thesis of the *Convivio.*

The "Divine Comedy." It has been argued by some critics that the *Divine Comedy* is in essence a repudiation of the secular and independent *Convivio* and *De Monarchia* and is evidence of a kind of "Conversion" of the poet, resulting either from some inner crisis or from his despair at the defeat of Henry VII. Perhaps if we say that in the *Comedy* the substance of the earlier works is utilized as a preparation for the vision, a basis for the mystic superstructure rather than as a finality in itself, we may speak of "conversion," but not, in the opinion of this writer, if the word carries any suggestion of rejection. It is true that the devotional element is novel and important: the intercession of the Virgin Mary makes it possible for the poet to undertake the supernatural journey and to enjoy the vision which crowns it. The vision itself is of a mystical nature, adumbrated perhaps in the *Vita Nuova* but totally absent from the "philosophical" works. Concern with purely theological matters—the Incarnation, predestination, divine justice, and the like—bulk large in the *Comedy*, which also contains (in *Paradiso* XI) a very interesting example of the *contemptus mundi* posture, otherwise quite uncharacteristic of Dante. The poet is also very careful to point out the error of the belief in Averroistic oversoul (*Purgatorio* XXV). Such elements have led to discussion of Dante's Augustinianism as opposed to his Thomism. (T. K. Swing has argued that in his manipulation of these doctrines "Dante is the first to accomplish a consistent elucidation of the teleological destiny of the Christian soul through a metaphysical scheme.") It is true that the presence of St. Bernard as Dante's last guide and, as it were, sponsor for his ultimate vision, gives dramatic emphasis to the Neoplatonic or Augustinian strain. But if the substitution of rapture for reason represents the victory of Augustine over Aquinas, it also carries us beyond the limits of philosophy and perhaps out of the area of our proper concern here.

We may yet affirm, in the face of all such elements as noted, that the *Comedy* is, in the author's intent, primarily an exposition of ethics; the letter to Can Grande specifically defines it as having for its subject "man, liable to the reward or punishment of Justice, according as through the freedom of the will he is deserving or undeserving." And in this area the frame of reference is, as it was in the *Convivio*, Aristotelian and Thomistic—not without some original sallies of Dante's own. The presence in the *Paradiso* of the Latin Averroist Siger of Brabant, for example, may be interpreted as an affirmation of the autonomy and dignity of the "contemporary profane science" (Pierre Mandonnet) of Aristotelian philosophy. But from the point of view of ethical investigation, the *Inferno* is the most interesting part of the work, for here, dealing not with the way of salvation, which is no longer possible to the damned, nor with the ultimate doctrines, interesting only to saints, Dante is in a sense free to formulate his own code of morality. Clearly his inclusion of pagans and other non-Christians in hell indicates his intent to establish a code of behavior for all men; his hell is nonsectarian, broadly speaking. His main divisions of incontinence, violence, and fraud are ingeniously worked out from a combination of Aristotle, Cicero, and Aquinas; interesting too is his creation of the "vestibule" for the lukewarm spirits and his peopling of the limbo with the souls of the virtuous pagans. Nor does the "converted" Dante abandon his appreciation of the second beatitude; not only do the pagans in limbo enjoy quite a comfortable immortality but Cato, so much revered in the *Convivio,* reappears as the guardian of purgatory, where he symbolizes free will; and, most startling of all, in the heaven of Jupiter the Trojan Ripheus is shown as an example of the "baptism of desire" that would make it possible for a good man, totally ignorant of the Mosaic or Christian message, to win salvation. To be sure, this is rare and does not avail to save Vergil or Aristotle, but on the other hand salvation in Christian terms also is ultimately a matter of predestined grace: without being unorthodox, Dante, in the example of Ripheus, has revealed his deep concern for ultimate justice. Indeed, the analysis of sin in the *Inferno,* as Kenelm Foster has pointed out, has its genesis in a conception of justice and presupposes society. The souls in the *Inferno* have "injured" others, have broken the social fabric in one way or another; even the heretics seem to be there because they have misled their followers rather than because of their own arrogant pride (a sin not specifically classified in the *Inferno*). We may also remark that Dante's concern for the good life on earth does not desert him: the theory of the two "suns" necessary for the proper illumination of mankind reappears in the *Purgatory;* the emperor is glorified (a reserved seat awaits Henry VII in the celestial rose); and certain cabalistic prophecies indicate Dante's hope for a *dux* who will lead the temporal world back to order and sanity. "The *Divine Comedy* is as much a political as it is a religious poem," says Passerin d'Entrèves, and surely in that climactic work both politics and religion are seen *sub specie philosophiae.* If Dante is not a true philosopher, he is certainly a magnificent amateur.

Works by Dante

Le opere di Dante. Florence, 1921; 2d ed., 1960.

Convivio, translated by Philip Wicksteed. London, 1903.

Epistolae, with English translation by Paget Toynbee. Oxford, 1920.

The Portable Dante, Paolo Milano, ed. New York, 1947. Selected translations.

Divine Comedy, translated by H. R. Huse. New York and Toronto, 1954. A useful, prose, line-for-line version, easily available.

Monarchy, translated by Donald Nicholson. London, 1954.

Works on Dante

Davis, C. T., *Dante and the Idea of Rome.* Oxford, 1957.

Entrèves, A. P. d', *Dante as a Political Thinker.* Oxford, 1952.

Foster, Kenelm, "The Theology of the 'Inferno,'" in *God's Tree.* London, 1957.

Gilson, Étienne, *Dante et la philosophie.* Paris, 1939. Translated by David Moore as *Dante the Philosopher.* New York, 1949.

Mandonnet, Pierre, *Dante le théologien.* Paris, 1935.

Mazzeo, J. A., *Structure and Thought in the Paradiso.* Ithaca, N.Y., 1958.

Mazzeo, J. A., *Medieval Cultural Tradition in Dante's Comedy.* Ithaca, N.Y., 1960.

McKeon, Richard, "Poetry and Philosophy in the Twelfth Century," in R. S. Crane and others, eds., *Critics and Criticism: Ancient and Modern.* Chicago, 1952.

Nardi, Bruno, *Dante e la cultura medievale.* Bari, 1949.

Santayana, George, *Three Philosophical Poets.* Cambridge, Mass., 1910; New York, 1953. Latter edition is paperback.

Swing, T. K., *The Fragile Leaves of the Sybil: Dante's Master Plan.* Westminster, Md., 1962.

THOMAS GODDARD BERGIN

DARWIN, CHARLES ROBERT (1809–1882), British biologist whose theory of organic evolution revolutionized science, philosophy, and theology. Darwin was born at Shrewsbury. He attended the universities of Edinburgh and Cambridge but was not attracted by his medical studies at the first or by his theological studies at the second. Near the end of his undergraduate days he formed a friendship with J. T. Henslow, professor of botany at Cambridge, "a man who knew every branch of science" (*Autobiography of Charles Darwin*). This association, together with an enthusiasm for collecting beetles and a reading of works by Humboldt and Herschel, generated in him "a burning zeal to contribute to the noble structure of Natural Science." The opportunity to do so on a large scale arose when Henslow secured for him the post of naturalist "without pay" aboard H.M.S. *Beagle,* then about to begin a long voyage in the Southern Hemisphere. Thus, between 1831 and 1836 Darwin was able to make extensive observations of the flora, fauna, and geological formations at widely separated points on the globe. This experience determined the course of his life thereafter and laid the foundation for many of his fundamental ideas. On his return he lived in London for six years, where he became acquainted with leading scientists of the day. Sir Charles Lyell, Sir Joseph Hooker, and T. H. Huxley were among his most intimate friends. In 1842 he took up residence at Down, a secluded village in Kent. Here, during the forty years until his death, he conducted the researches and wrote the works which made him famous. He was buried in Westminster Abbey close to the grave of Sir Isaac Newton.

Darwin's productivity, despite recurrent bouts of illness, was prodigious. His publications ranged over such diverse subjects as volcanic islands, coral reefs, barnacles, plant movement, the fertilization of orchids, the action of earthworms on the soil, the variation of domesticated animals and plants, and the theory of evolution. Even if he had never written *The Origin of Species* (1859) and *The Descent of Man* (1871), he would still be regarded as one of the great biologists of the nineteenth century. Of course, it was these two books which made him the initiator of a revolution in thought more far-reaching than that ushered in by Copernicus. He established beyond reasonable doubt that all living things, including man, have developed from a few extremely simple forms, perhaps from one form, by a gradual process of descent with modification. Furthermore, he formulated a theory (natural selection), supporting it with a large body of evidence, to account for this process and particularly to explain the "transmutation of Species" and the origin of adaptations. As a result, the biological sciences were given a set of unifying principles, and man was given a new and challenging conception of his place in nature.

It was characteristic of Darwin that he came to these conclusions by his own observations and reflections. When he embarked on the *Beagle,* his outlook was "quite orthodox." He accepted without question the fixity of species and their special creation as depicted in Genesis. Doubts began to arise in his mind during the ship's visit to the Galápagos Archipelago in 1835, when he noticed that very small differences were present in the so-called species inhabiting separate islands. The doubts were reinforced by his observation of fossils on the Pampas and the distribution of organisms on the South American continent as a whole. He was "haunted" by the idea that such facts "could be explained on the supposition that species gradually became modified." In July 1837 he "opened his first notebook" to record additional facts bearing on the question, but it was not until he happened to read Malthus' *Essay on Population* in October 1838 that he found an explanatory theory from which the above "supposition" followed. He then proceeded to formulate the principle of natural selection, which is simply "the doctrine of Malthus applied with manifold force to the whole animal and vegetable kingdoms." Darwin never professed to have invented the idea of organic evolution, of the mutability of species, or even of natural selection. What he did profess was to have produced the first scientific proof that these ideas apply to the living world.

Unlike some lesser men of science, Darwin was not inclined to rush into print in order to establish a proprietary right to his theory. His modesty and single-minded desire to find out the truth forbade any such action. Accordingly, the theory underwent several preliminary formulations. It was first set down in a short abstract in 1842 and two years later was expanded into an essay which both Lyell and Hooker read. Early in 1856 Lyell advised Darwin to write a full-length account of his views. It was when this manuscript, which would have been "three or four times as extensive" as *The Origin of Species,* was about half finished that Alfred Russel Wallace's paper, which contained virtually the same ideas that Darwin was working out, arrived at Down from the Malay Archipelago. The resulting crisis was resolved by having a joint communication from the two men read at a meeting of the Linnaean Society on July 1, 1858. Between September of that year and November 1859, Darwin "abstracted" the large manuscript and produced his classic. *The Origin of Species* appeared on November 24 in an edition of 1,250 copies, all of which were sold on the first day. Ultimately, six editions containing many revisions were published.

Despite the interest which *The Origin of Species* excited, it was by no means universally approved at first. In the scientific world support for it came from Darwin's friends, but others expressed opposition which often took the form of objections to the modes of explanation and proof employed in the work. Darwin's use of historical or genetic explanations, his implicit adoption of statistical conceptions ("population thinking," as it is now called), and his practice of introducing conjectures or "imaginary illustrations" to buttress his argument were repugnant to biologists who held that scientific explanation must consist in bringing directly observed phenomena under general laws. Believers in this oversimplified model also disliked his notion of "chance" variations and his repudiation of "any law of necessary development." Before long, however, the cumulative force of Darwin's arguments, augmented by the case put forward in *The Descent of Man*, convinced the great majority of biologists, so that opposition from this quarter had disappeared by 1880.

The popular reaction to Darwin's theory focused on its religious and ideological implications. These were recognized to be hostile to the Establishment. Hence, Darwin found himself enthusiastically supported by radicals, rationalists, and anticlericals and vehemently attacked by reactionaries, fundamentalists, and priests. He shrank from entering into this controversy, which was altogether distasteful to him, but T. H. Huxley, who enjoyed crossing swords with theologians, took a different stand. Appointing himself "Darwin's bulldog," he relentlessly pursued such antievolutionists as Bishop Wilberforce and W. E. Gladstone. His efforts had a good deal to do with creating the image of Darwin as an enemy of the Bible, the church, and Christianity.

This image was, in fact, fairly close to the truth. Darwin's religious beliefs, as he relates in his *Autobiography*, underwent a change from naive acceptance of Christian doctrines to reluctant agnosticism. In the two years following his return from the voyage of the *Beagle* he was "led to think much about religion." Doubts were engendered in his mind about the historical veracity of the Gospels, the occurrence of miracles, and the dogma of everlasting damnation of unbelievers (which he calls "a damnable doctrine"). By reflection on such matters he "gradually came to disbelieve in Christianity" and wondered how anybody could wish it to be true.

A similar erosion occurred in connection with his belief in the existence of a personal God. When he wrote *The Origin of Species*, Darwin accepted a vague theism or deism. In the last chapter he speaks of laws having been "impressed on matter by the Creator" and of life's powers "having been breathed by the Creator into a few forms or into one." He was thus able at the time to deny that it was his intention "to write atheistically." Yet it was also clear to him that the theory of natural selection exploded the old argument for theism based on the presence of design in the organic world. The vast amount of suffering and misery which exists seemed to him a strong argument against any belief in a beneficent First Cause. He had moods in which it seemed difficult or impossible to conceive that "this immense and wonderful universe, with our conscious selves, arose through chance." In the end, however, he concluded "that the whole subject is beyond the scope of man's intellect. . . . The mystery of the beginning of all things is insoluble by us; and I for one must be content to remain an Agnostic."

Darwin's reflections on religion, although not systematic, provide a good example of his intellectual integrity. "I have steadily endeavored," he wrote in his *Autobiography*, "to keep my mind free, so as to give up any hypothesis, however much beloved (and I cannot resist forming one on every subject), as soon as facts are shown to be opposed to it." That statement might well serve as his epitaph.

Works by Darwin

The Autobiography of Charles Darwin (London, 1958) was edited by his granddaughter Nora Barlow, who restored the material omitted from the original. The original *Autobiography* was first published in 1887 as part of the *Life and Letters of Charles Darwin*, but many passages of the manuscript were omitted because they contained candid and caustic judgments of persons and of the Christian religion. These omitted passages, amounting to nearly six thousand words, were restored in the 1958 edition.

The *Life and Letters of Charles Darwin* (2 vols., New York, 1959) was edited by Francis Darwin. The 1959 edition has an introduction by George Gaylord Simpson.

Among the many editions of *On the Origin of Species* are a facsimile of the first edition, with an illuminating introduction by Ernst Mayr (Cambridge, Mass., 1964), and a variorum text of the six editions, edited by Morse Peckham (Philadelphia, 1959). The *Origin* is also available in paperback with a foreword by Gaylord Simpson (New York, 1962).

For the voyage of the *Beagle* see *Charles Darwin's Diary of the Voyage of H.M.S. Beagle* (Cambridge, 1933), which was edited from the manuscript by Nora Barlow, and Nora Barlow's edition of *Charles Darwin and the Voyage of the Beagle* (London, 1945), for which she has written an introduction.

Darwin and Wallace's *Evolution by Natural Selection* (London, 1958) has been edited, with an introduction, by Gavin De Beer. This volume contains the Linnaean Society papers.

Works on Darwin

For works on Darwin see Alvar Ellegård's *Darwin and the General Reader* (Göteborg, Sweden, 1958) and Gavin De Beer's excellent *Charles Darwin: Evolution by Natural Selection* (London, 1963).

T. A. Goudge

DARWIN, ERASMUS (1731–1802), English physician, man of science, and poet, was the grandfather of Charles Darwin, whose evolutionary views he partly anticipated, and of Francis Galton. Like Charles he was educated at Cambridge, where he took the M.B. degree in 1755. For more than forty years he practiced medicine at Lichfield and Derby and gained a wide reputation for his skill, intellectual vigor, and originality of character. Among his friends were Rousseau, whom he met in 1766, and Joseph Priestley. He corresponded with both men. In 1784 he founded the Philosophical Society at Derby to stimulate interest in the sciences. He wrote copiously, with varying degrees of success. His chief prose works are *Zoonomia or the Laws of Organic Life* (2 vols., London, 1794–1796) and *Phytologia or the Philosophy of Agriculture and Gardening* (London, 1799). Two long poems embodying his views about the origin and development of life, *The Botanic Garden* (London, 1789) and *The Temple of Nature* (London, 1803), were not taken seriously by his contemporaries, although Darwin himself was rather proud of them. Coleridge likened the poems to "mists that occasionally arise at the foot of Parnassus" and coined the word "darwinizing" to describe their biological speculations. After his death Erasmus Darwin was forgotten until interest in his ideas revived as a result of the fame of his grandson Charles.

An important feature of Erasmus Darwin's work is the relation it establishes between early evolutionary theory and the embryological controversy of the preformationists and the epigenesists. In "Of Generation," Chapter 39 of *Zoonomia,* Darwin argues against the doctrine that each new individual is already "preformed" on a minute scale in the reproductive cell from which it is developed. He defends an epigenetic position according to which new individuals develop by utilizing material from the environment to generate new parts. Hence, there is a transformation of a relatively undifferentiated egg into a complex organism. From this position it is only a short step to the view that life in general has evolved by a similar transformation.

Darwin actually took this step but did not provide a systematic justification of it. His writings are a curious mixture of observed facts, sober scientific judgments, and extravagant speculations, all designed to support the conclusion that living things, different from one another as they now are, originated from one "primal filament" which existed long ago. Through the ages organisms have altered to meet altered conditions of life. The result has been a continuous perfecting of their capacities. "This idea of the gradual formation and improvement of the animal world accords with the observations of some modern philosophers" (*Zoonomia,* Vol. I). An evolution of life has undoubtedly occurred.

Among the items of evidence adduced to support this contention are some which anticipate matters later embodied in *The Origin of Species.* Thus, Erasmus Darwin calls attention to such phenomena as the metamorphosis of tadpoles into frogs, the changes produced by the domestic breeding of animals, the specialized adaptations to climatic conditions, and, above all, "the essential unity of plan in all warm-blooded animals." These things oblige us to believe that all organisms have been derived from "a single living filament."

Embedded in Darwin's work are the rudiments of a theory about the causes of evolution. What he says foreshadows the more finished theory of Lamarck. Environmental stimuli act on organisms which are endowed with the unique power of "irritability or sensibility." The organisms respond in accordance with their wants, desires, and dislikes. Thus, the bodily characteristics required to satisfy the organisms' demands are produced. These characteristics are inherited by some members of succeeding generations and favor them in the struggle for existence, which is depicted in lurid terms by Darwin in *The Temple of Nature.*

The facts that man's body bears traces of his evolution from lower forms of life and that the earth itself appears to have come into being gradually by the operation of natural processes in no way led Darwin to doubt the existence of "the Great Architect" of the cosmos. His solid and complacent deism enabled him to regard God as simply "the Great First Cause," who infused spirit and life into the primal filament and gave it the potentiality to evolve. "The whole of nature may be supposed to consist of two essences or substances, one of which may be termed spirit and the other matter"(*Zoonomia,* Vol. I, Section 1). The "whole of nature" was designed by the Great Architect. Indeed, God "has infinitely diversified the works of His hands, but has at the same time stamped a certain similitude on the features of nature, that demonstrates to us, that the whole is one family of one parent."

Darwin's views mark the close of the era of romantic speculation about natural history and the advance into an era of systematic observation and generalization. He did not, however, succeed in formulating any enduring principles. Perhaps his major achievement was acquiring the characteristics of scientific curiosity, independence of mind, and intellectual power which were transmitted to his descendants.

Bibliography

For material bearing on the once notorious controversy between Charles Darwin and Samuel Butler, in which the assessment of Erasmus Darwin's ideas played a part, see Charles Darwin, *Life of Erasmus Darwin: An Introduction to an Essay on His Works by Ernst Krause* (London, 1879), and Samuel Butler, *Evolution, Old and New* (London, 1879), Chs. 12–14. The complex story of the controversy is given in the complete edition of *The Autobiography of Charles Darwin,* Nora Barlow, ed. (London, 1958), Appendix, Part 2, pp. 167–219.

See also Hesketh Pearson, *Doctor Darwin: A Biography* (London, 1930), and Desmond King-Hele, *Erasmus Darwin* (New York, 1964).

T. A. GOUDGE

DARWINISM. The term "Darwinism" has both a narrow and a broad meaning. In the narrow sense, it refers to a theory of organic evolution presented by Charles Darwin (1809–1882) and by other scientists who developed various aspects of his views; in the broad sense, it refers to a complex of scientific, social, theological, and philosophical thought that was historically stimulated and supported by Darwin's theory of evolution. Biological Darwinism—the first sense—was the outstanding scientific achievement of the nineteenth century and is now the foundation of large regions of biological theory. Darwinism in the second sense was the major philosophical problem of the later nineteenth century. Today, Darwinism no longer provides the focus of philosophical investigation, largely because so much of it forms an unquestioned background to contemporary thought.

Darwin's theory is an example of scientific innovation that has had reverberations into the farthest reaches of human thought. It is fair to say that every philosophical problem appears in a new light after the Darwinian revolution. In order to outline the connections between biological and philosophical Darwinism, it will first be necessary to describe Darwin's own views and to discuss various criticisms that were directed against them. It will then be possible to describe Darwinism in the broader sense, and to distinguish the various ways in which the scientific theory has afforded material for philosophical inquiry.

DARWIN'S THEORY

The theory of the origin of species by means of natural selection was the discovery of Darwin and Alfred Russel Wallace (1823–1913). (See articles on DARWIN and WAL-

LACE for the circumstances of the codiscovery.) Both Darwin and Wallace had stated the theory in a series of papers delivered before the Linnaean Society on July 1, 1858. The members of the Linnaean Society listened without enthusiasm and apparently without much understanding, but in fairness to them, it should be observed that Wallace and Darwin did not present their theory forcefully on this occasion. Some of the shattering implications of the theory were not drawn in detail, and the evidence in its support, which Darwin in particular had amassed, was barely hinted at. Wallace's paper "On the Tendency of Varieties to depart indefinitely from the Original Type" was a discussion of a widely accepted argument in favor of the "original and permanent distinctness of species," namely, that the varieties that are produced by artificial selection in domesticated species never vary beyond the limits of the original wild species, and that whenever artificial selection is relaxed, the domesticated varieties revert to the ancestral form. These facts were interpreted by naturalists as evidence for an innate conservative tendency in nature that kept all variation within the bounds defined by the unbridgeable gaps between species.

But, Wallace argued, the view that artificial selection can produce only new varieties, never new species, rests on the false assumption that naturalists possess a criterion for distinguishing the species from the variety. Moreover he stated, "This argument rests entirely on the assumption that *varieties* occurring in a state of nature are in all respects analogous to . . . those of domestic animals, and are governed by the same laws as regards their permanence or further variation. But it is the object of the present paper to show that this assumption is altogether false. . . ." Overproduction, together with heritable variations, some of which are better adapted to the circumstances of life, will tend to make varieties depart indefinitely from the ancestral type, bringing about changes that will eventually amount to the origin of a new species. Wallace accounted for the reversion of domestic varieties by pointing out that the ancestral type is better adapted to life "in a state of nature," and consequently the *very same* principles that bring about progress in nature also bring about the reversion of domestic varieties.

Wallace aimed his argument precisely at the philosophical presupposition that for so long had stood in the way of a proper interpretation of natural selection, namely, that the species—being the exemplar of a divine archetype—is as well adapted as it could be and, consequently, that variation away from the type will automatically be selected *against.* Natural selection, according to this interpretation, is an agency of permanence, not change. One of Wallace's, as well as Darwin's, most original contributions consisted in breaking the hold of this idea.

Wallace's argument is implicit in Darwin's Linnaean Society papers, but the focus is different. Instead of challenging accepted opinion, Darwin added up well-known facts. With great eloquence he described the prevalent overproduction of animals and plants: "Nature may be compared to a surface on which rest ten thousand sharp wedges touching each other and driven inwards by incessant blows." The wedges are held back by large numbers of "checks" which bring about the death, or prevent the mating, of individuals. "Lighten any check in the least degree, and the geometrical powers of increase in every organism will almost instantly increase the average number of the favored species." He called attention to the extreme heritable variability of animals under domestication. In nature there is also variation, although no doubt not as much. Some variants will be better adapted to their environments than others and will tend to survive and propagate. "Let this work of selection on the one hand, and death on the other,' go on for a thousand generations, who will pretend to affirm that it would produce no effect . . . ?" To the effects of this natural selection, Darwin added the effect of "the struggle of males for females."

Both Wallace and Darwin had stated the essence of the theory of the *Origin of Species* (1859). The *Origin* itself is mainly a sober, scrupulously fair and thoroughly documented elaboration and defense of the doctrine of natural selection presented in the Linnaean Society papers. Darwin set out to accomplish three things: (*a*) to show that evolution has in fact occurred; (*b*) to describe the mechanism of evolution; and (*c*) to account for the major facts of morphology, embryology, biogeography, paleontology, and taxonomy on the evolutionary hypothesis.

The fact of evolution. Darwin freely admitted that we do not directly observe the process of evolution. The time needed even for the origin in nature of a new variety is far too long. Consequently, the case for the occurrence of evolution is simply the same as the case for its scope and mechanism, and since Darwin did not have access to direct evidence for the efficacy of natural selection—a gap that was not filled until the twentieth century. Darwin argued that life is too short for direct evidence but that certain facts force the conclusion upon us that there *must* be evolution; and if we adopt the hypothesis, a wide range of hitherto unconnected facts may be given a uniform explanation.

The mechanisms of evolution. Darwin described three mechanisms that tend to effect the evolution of populations. These are natural selection, sexual selection, and the inheritance of characteristics acquired during the lifetime of the individual organism.

Natural selection. In the *Origin* Darwin placed the greatest weight on evolution by natural selection. It operates in conjunction with sexual selection and the inheritance of acquired characters and, Darwin argued, there are some features of organisms that could have developed *only* by natural selection. Indeed, it seems that the theory of natural selection was partially inspired by his observations on the *Beagle* voyage (1831–1836) of local variations, particularly in the islands of the Galápagos Archipelago, that could not be accounted for on Lamarckian grounds.

The theory of natural selection as Darwin presented it may be summarized as follows: (1) Populations of animals and plants exhibit variations. (2) Some variations provide the organism with an advantage over the rest of the population in the struggle for life. (3) Favorable variants will transmit their advantageous characters to their progeny. (4) Since populations tend to produce more progeny than the environment will support, the proportion of favorable variants that survive and produce progeny will be larger than the proportion of unfavorable variants. (5) Thus, a population may undergo continuous evolutionary change that can result in the origin of new varieties, species, genera, or indeed new populations at any taxonomic level. Darwinian natural selection may accordingly be defined as a differential *death rate* between two variant subclasses of a population, the lesser death rate characterizing the better-adapted subclass.

Darwin was careful to present evidence for every hypothesis in his account of natural selection. It was especially necessary to argue that natural populations do exhibit the requisite amount of variation and that the variation is heritable. He cited, among other things, the extreme variability of domestic plants and animals and the well-known fact that new varieties can be propagated. He admitted that the causes of variation were unknown; but he argued that changing environmental conditions greatly increase variability by action on the reproductive system, thereby providing material for natural selection when it is most needed. This is "indefinite variability." In addition, there is "definite variability," due to the direct action of the environment on the body of the organism. "Definite variations" are heritable; they provide material for natural selection and, being responsive to the environment, are more likely than chance variations to be adaptive.

"The laws governing inheritance," he remarked, "are for the most part unknown." This lack of knowledge turned out to be the most serious obstacle to the further development of the theoretical foundations of selection theory in the nineteenth century; but, as Darwin noted, although the laws of inheritance were unknown, a number of the phenomena of inheritance were known, and those were probably all that were required for the theory of natural selection. Most important is the obvious fact that progeny bear an overwhelming resemblance to their parents, although they differ in some degree. In addition, Darwin was familiar with the intermittent appearance of hereditary characters, with sex-linked and sex-influenced characters, and with the tendency for a character to appear in the progeny at the same developmental stage that it appears in the parents.

For natural selection to be an agency of change rather than an agency of permanence, it is necessary that some variations from the ancestral type represent better adaptations. Darwin pointed out that, in fact, every organism could be better adapted to its ordinary environment; and that, moreover, environments change.

Pre-Darwinian taxonomy ascribed a very special significance to the species, as against varieties, genera, and the higher taxonomic groups. The species was regarded by the pious as the unalterable work of God; the limits laid down by the diagnostic features of any species established the limits of possible variation within the species. Thus, although any biologist would be willing to countenance the origin of new varieties or subspecies, brought about by the operation of biological laws, most were unwilling to admit the possibility of the origin of new species by natural processes. The title of Darwin's book was aimed precisely at this conception. Like Wallace, he argued that there is no difference in principle between the diagnostic characters of varieties and species; therefore, to admit the origin of new varieties amounts to admitting the possibility of new species—and if new species appear, so may new genera, families, and so on. He cited the existence of "doubtful species"—groups that cannot be definitely placed at either the variety or species level—and the general inconsistency of taxonomists in the identification of species.

Sexual selection. In the Linnaean Society papers Darwin described the second mechanism of evolution as the "struggle of males for females." The theory was developed further in the *Origin*, and it occupied some two-thirds of the pages of his *Descent of Man and Selection in Relation to Sex* (1871). In these later statements of the theory, the struggle of males for females is a special case of a more general phenomenon. Suppose that a population is divided in some proportion between males and females and suppose for the sake of simplification that all of the males and females are equally well endowed for the struggle for survival. Now, Darwin argued, it may happen that either the males or females are unequally endowed with some characteristic that will increase their propensity to leave progeny. There will then be selection in favor of that characteristic, even though it will not be favored by natural selection. All such cases Darwin calls "sexual selection." It is clear that different sorts of characteristics can influence the probability of having offspring. Some individuals, for example, may possess behavior patterns that lead to the fertilization of a larger percentage of eggs or have more efficient organs of copulation. Or they may have some advantage in the competition for mates—migratory male birds may arrive early at the breeding grounds and be ready to receive the more vigorous females, leaving the culls for their tardy brothers; or the females may for some reason prefer plumage or displays of a certain character; or some males may aggressively drive away other males; and so on. Finally, some characteristics that are also useful in the struggle for survival might also be useful in the competition for mates; for example, the antlers of male deer may do double duty against both rivals and predators.

Darwin appeals to sexual selection in order to account for the evolution of such things as mating rituals and secondary sexual characteristics, such as breeding plumage in birds. He regards it as especially significant in the evolution of man. The loss of body hair, for example, is attributed to systematic choice among man's ancestors of mates that exhibited large regions of bare skin.

The inheritance of acquired characters. Darwin's work was plagued by ignorance and misinformation concerning the laws of heredity. The principles of segregation and independent assortment, which form a cornerstone of contemporary evolution theories, were discovered by Gregor Mendel in 1864; but his paper remained unnoticed until 1900. Moreover, although "sports" were well known to biologists, the concept of mutation had not been clearly formulated. Consequently, the modern theory of the origin of genetic variation in populations was not available to Darwin; instead, he suggested that some variations are due to the action of the environment on the germ plasm and that others are due to the effects of use and disuse. For example, if an animal's skin is tanned by sunlight, this may induce changes in its germ plasm that will result in its progeny possessing pretanned skin; or if a wolf develops his muscles by chasing rabbits, his pups may inherit larger muscles. These mechanisms, if they exist, would account for some variability. But they would also account for some evolutionary change even in the absence of natural or sexual selection. Since, accordingly, there seemed to be no sound reason for rejecting the inheritance of acquired characters and since the doctrine would aid in explaining both variability and evolutionary change, Darwin was led to adopt it and to give it increasing weight in his later years. This aspect of Darwin's views is often labeled Lamarckism, but Lamarck himself, although he did accept the inheritance of the effects of use and disuse, did not accept the doctrine of the direct action of environmental factors on the germ plasm.

The scope of evolutionary theory. It is clear that Darwin regarded his theory as revolutionary. He believed that all the traditional branches of biology would be transformed and deepened; familiar phenomena would take on a new significance; apparently unconnected facts could be regarded as mutually related. Even the vocabulary of the older biology would acquire new meanings: "The terms used by naturalists, of affinity, relationship, community of type, paternity, morphology, adoptive characters, rudimentary and aborted organs, etc., will cease to be metaphorical, and will have a plain signification." Natural history would acquire the fascination, not of a catalogue of *curiosae*, but of a labyrinth that may be charted.

> When we no longer look at an organic being as a savage looks at a ship, as something wholly beyond his comprehension; when we regard every production of nature as one which has had a long history; when we contemplate every complex structure and instinct as the summing up of many contrivances, each useful to the possessor, . . . when we thus view each organic being, how far more interesting—I speak from experience—does the study of natural history become!

And not only would the old biology be put on a new foundation; whole new fields of research would become possible. For example, "Psychology will be securely based on the foundation . . . of the necessary acquirement of each mental power and capacity by gradation. Much light will be thrown on the origin of man and his history."

The major part of the *Origin* is devoted to the detailed application of the theory of natural selection to a range of biological phenomena. It is impossible to give more than a general impression of the thoroughness, detail, and diversity of Darwin's evidence. The modern reader cannot fail to be impressed not only by Darwin's immense learning but also by his subtlety of insight—his ability to locate those phenomena which lend his theory the most striking support.

The *Origin* as a whole provides, on the one hand, a sweeping portrait of the history and biology of living things, a portrait whose internal balance and consistency are easily discernible. On the other hand, Darwin fills selected regions of his portrait with careful detail, exhibiting the applicability of his theory to a variety of phenomena. These two aspects of his work constitute both the argument for the fact of evolution and the argument for the truth of his account of its mechanisms.

In the broad portrait Darwin shows how the main facts of known fossil successions, the relation of living fauna and flora to recent fossil forms, the geographical distribution of species, the connection between morphology and function, and the major features of embryological development are explicable by his theory. He applies it in detail to such phenomena—to mention only a few—as rudimentary organs, insect metamorphosis, the divergence of island and mainland forms, and sexual dimorphism. He provides us with a discussion of taxonomy that is philosophically superior to many contemporary accounts, arguing, among other things, in favor of the special significance for the taxonomist of embryological and phylogenetic studies.

Darwin was always sensitive to the effect that his views might have on the general public. In composing the *Origin* he decided to avoid the whole topic of man's evolution; the book would be a sufficiently bitter pill without explicitly treating a subject that was "so surrounded with prejudices." His only explicit reference to man was the remark quoted above, that "light will be thrown on the origin of man and his history." Darwin's successors, however, were not so cautious. Sir Charles Lyell (1797–1875) discussed the question in 1863. Shortly thereafter, Wallace published his paper "The Origin of Human Races and the Antiquity of Man Deduced from the Theory of Natural Selection." T. H. Huxley (1825–1895) and a number of Continental morphologists, particularly Ernst Haeckel (1834–1919), produced a series of studies aimed at showing the similarity of man and the anthropoid apes and giving speculative reconstructions of man's ancestry. Thus, by the date of Darwin's *Descent of Man* (1871), the controversy over man was in full swing; and there were already a number of alternative theories that Darwin had to consider, such as whether the races of men are distinct species.

Darwin showed a wise unwillingness to acknowledge any known nonhuman species, living or extinct, as ancestral to man. We have so far examined, he argued, only animals that have diverged from the prehuman stock. For instance, the anthropoid apes and man have a common ancestor, but its remains have not been found. Nor did he identify species that are ancestral to the primates, the mammals, or even the vertebrates. He did trace a general line of descent: Old World ape, a lemurlike animal, some "forms standing very low in the mammalian series," marsupials, and monotremes. No true reptile is an ancestor of man. All the classes of vertebrates may have been derived from a remote ancestor similar to the larvae of the tunicates. With a flash of romanticism, Darwin wrote: "In the lunar or weekly recurrent periods of some of our functions we apparently still retain traces of our primordial birthplace, a shore washed by the tides."

In the *Descent of Man* evolution by the inheritance of acquired characters and by sexual selection plays a larger role than in the *Origin*. Darwin admitted that he had been accused of overrating the importance of natural selection, but added, "whether with justice the future will decide." His relative retreat from natural selection was probably occasioned by two factors: first, his doubts as to whether the earth is old enough for evolution by natural selection without substantial help from faster mechanisms; second, his belief that man is in many ways less the child of violent nature than his ancestors, a belief that requires considerable appeal to sexual selection and to the development of moral and spiritual qualities through social usage.

CRITICISMS OF DARWIN'S THEORY

In spite of the resistance that Darwin's theory aroused on other than scientific grounds, the weight of his arguments was largely—but with many notable exceptions—sufficient for the younger generation of biologists. In 1872, in the sixth edition of the *Origin*, Darwin was in a position to write, "At the present day almost all naturalists admit evolution under some form." It was, like any novel and important theory, carefully scrutinized for empirical weaknesses. We shall describe the major ones and indicate how they were dealt with.

The most damaging scientific objections were the following.

(1) Darwin had no direct evidence for the effectiveness of natural selection, let alone for the origin of new species.

(2) Darwin could not show a single species that was transitional between two known species.

(3) Complex organs, such as the vertebrate eye, could not have evolved by stages, since they would have been useless at any preliminary stage and hence would have given their possessor no selective advantage.

(4) If evolution has taken place, then some evolutionary trends must have continued past the point of usefulness to the organism. Such trends could not be accounted for by Darwinian selection.

(5) The earth is not old enough for evolution to have taken place.

(6) Evolution by natural selection is incompatible with the laws of inheritance.

(7) There is no inheritance of acquired characters.

The first two objections were commonly raised in the nineteenth century; they are genuine questions that require some sort of answer. However, Darwin was not in a position to answer them in a way that would satisfy everybody, since the weight that one assigns to them depends in part upon personal preference.

Indirect evidence. With regard to the first objection Darwin pointed out that natural selection cannot be directly observed; we can only present indirect evidence in its favor. On this point he was mistaken. Natural selection has been directly studied in the twentieth century, both experimentally (in fruit fly populations, for example) and in nature (for instance, the development of so-called industrial melanism). But even today Darwin's and Wallace's contention that evolution by natural selection can pass the species limit has no *direct* support. Darwin recognized, however, that it is no fatal objection to a theory if some of its components are not subject to direct verification.

Transitional species. On the second criticism—the absence of forms intermediate between species—Darwin had a double-barreled answer. He admitted that, for instance, we know of no forms intermediate between man and the apes. But we have innumerable examples of species that are in process of giving rise to new species, namely, those that have varieties or subspecies. These polytypic species (as they are now called) are intermediate between other species which, to be sure, have not yet evolved, but which are in process of evolving.

When it was further objected that we ought to have better examples of demonstrable ancestors of existing species, Darwin appealed to the incompleteness of the fossil record. This is the correct answer, but one which is hardly satisfying to a skeptic. Again, the weight that one would assign to the objection depends upon personal preference.

Development of complex organs. Darwin was well aware of the difficulty in accounting for the origin of structures which would be useless, even deleterious, until they were essentially complete. The eye, he wrote, gave him "a cold shudder." However, in such cases as the eye he had no alternative but to appeal to natural selection. Therefore, he was compelled to argue that in point of fact all the earlier stages in the evolution of the eye were useful in the struggle for survival. Darwin himself provided us with the standard textbook example: he constructed a plausible sequence of stages that could have led to the human eye. Each stage is a functional eye; and something similar to each stage does exist in one or another living species. The criticism has the form, "Such and such *could not* have happened." It can be countered piecemeal, by showing in a variety of cases how it *could* have happened.

Orthogenetic trends. A great many of Darwin's critics accepted the fact of evolution but entered reservations concerning his account of the mechanisms of the process. The reservations were of several types. Some rejected "Lamarckism," by which they meant simply the inheritance of acquired characters; they were known as the Neo-Darwinians. Others doubted that there was such a process as sexual selection. Still others, however, believed that there must be an evolutionary process that Darwin had not identified at all. The evidence consisted in the existence of apparently nonfunctional evolutionary trends. Trends that continue over long periods and that are relatively straight-lined—for example, increasing size in horses and increasing length of sabers in the saber-toothed cat—came to be called orthogenetic trends. The question was whether orthogenetic trends could be accounted for on Darwinian principles.

Wallace argued (in "Geological Climates and the Origin of Species," *Quarterly Review*, 1869) that the development of man's brain could not be so accounted for. Man's apelike ancestors, he argued, had reached a certain stage of evolution and then, over a period of some ten million years, remained largely unchanged except for a steady orthogenetic increase in the size and complexity of the brain. This was an unprecedented episode in the history of life, for it freed man from those ordinary pressures of natural selection that so often led to close specialization and ultimate extinction. Moreover, the brain acquired abilities that could not have been exercised in a primitive environment, such as the power to construct speculative systems of ideas or the insight into spiritual reality. These are present in modern man, but would have been useless in man's primitive ancestors. Natural selection operates only on abilities that are actually so exercised as to give an advantage in the struggle for life. "An instrument," Wallace concluded about the brain, "has been developed in advance of the needs of its possessor." Later he wrote: "A superior intelligence has guided the development of man in a definite direction, and for a special purpose, just as man guides the development of many animal and vegetable forms." Thus we avoid the "hopeless and soul-deadening belief" that man is the product of "blind eternal forces of the universe."

Darwin looked upon this as a failure of nerve, a hankering after miraculous origins for man. "I can see no necessity for calling in an additional and proximate cause in regard to man," he wrote in a letter to Wallace. Nevertheless, Wallace's position, fitting as it did the efforts of many theologians to come to grips with Darwinism, gained a number of adherents, and although the main line of evolutionary theory has bypassed it, even now versions of Wallace's position turn up from time to time.

Wallace had argued that the evolution of the brain was an orthogenetic trend that outstripped its usefulness. Others argued that trends sometimes continued even after they had become positively deleterious. A favorite example was the teeth of the saber-toothed cat, which, it was alleged, were valuable as weapons up to a certain length, but which finally became detrimental by interfering with feeding. There would be selection *against* increased tooth length under these conditions; consequently, it was argued, some cause other than natural selection must have operated. A variety of theories were proposed—for example, those of Karl Nägeli (1817–1891) and E. D. Cope (1840–1897). These theories posited an otherwise unknown internal principle of change, which was compared to the laws of embryological development, to the principle of inertia, or, as with Henri Bergson, to creative spiritual activity. Since the theories accounted for nothing other than the alleged orthogenetic trends, they have always had a peripheral position in the history of evolutionary thought. Moreover, subsequent analysis of orthogenesis has shown that in most cases the trends are in fact adaptive; and in those cases where they are not adaptive, contemporary theory provides various possible sorts of explanation compatible with the doctrine of natural selection, such as the explanation that if a trend affects only adults past the breeding age, it will not be selected against.

Age of the earth. In 1865 William Thomson, Lord Kelvin, published a paper entitled "The Doctrine of Uniformity in Geology Briefly Refuted." Its argument was aimed at Lyell and his followers, who had maintained that the earth as we now find it is not the result of a series of catastrophes, but is the outcome of the ages-long operation of geological processes that we can still observe. This viewpoint, known as uniformitarianism, was widely accepted among geologists even before the publication of the *Origin*, having been impressively established in Lyell's *Principles of Geology* (1834). It was in fact an earlier application of the idea of evolution. But uniformitarianism required vast reaches of time; consequently, Kelvin was prodding its weakest point when he argued that the earth could not be as old as the geologists supposed. Grant, Kelvin argued, that the earth was once a molten sphere; then it could not have solidified much over twenty million years ago, or it would now be cooler, through dissipation of its heat, than we actually find it. The biological consequences were clear: there was not enough time for evolution to have produced the forms we now see.

Darwin was deeply concerned by this reasoning. As far as he could tell, it was perfectly sound; on the other hand, he was perfectly convinced that the earth had supported life for a much longer time. His later emphasis on Lamarckism was probably an attempt to provide an evolutionary process that was swifter than natural selection. But this was a half measure; in fact, Darwin simply swallowed what he believed to be a contradiction—a not uncommon occurrence in the history of science. It turned out that Kelvin's argument was mistaken, since he was unaware of an additional source of heat within the earth, namely radioactive decay.

Laws of inheritance. As noted above, the evolutionists of the nineteenth century worked in ignorance of the principles of genetics discovered by Mendel; this lack was by far the most serious theoretical gap in the Darwinians' arguments. It now appears that no fundamental innovation in evolutionary theory was possible until the gap was filled. Biologists of the nineteenth century accepted a rough theory of blending inheritance, that is, the view that the characteristics of the progeny of sexual crosses were intermediate between the characteristics of the parents. This theory was seldom explicitly defended, since everyone was familiar with a variety of phenomena that were incompatible with it, for example, blue-eyed children of brown-eyed parents. Nevertheless, when biologists theorized at all on the subject, the theory produced was ordinarily a vague and suitably guarded version of the theory of blending inheritance.

In 1867 Fleeming Jenkin ("The Origin of Species," *North British Review*) pointed out that the blending theory was incompatible with the theory of natural selection as ordinarily presented by the Darwinians. He argued that if favorable variations appeared in a population, their characteristics, even if favored by natural selection, would soon be lost in the vast population pool by crossing with individuals of the normal type. Assume, for instance (as Jenkin did), that a white man is greatly superior to a Negro and that a white man is shipwrecked on a Negro island. "He would kill a great many blacks in the struggle for existence; he would have a great many wives and children. . . . But can anyone believe that the whole island will gradually acquire a white, or even a yellow population?" Jenkin's argument in essence is this: the white man's children will be darker than their father; and it is impossible on the blending theory that their descendants could become lighter, whatever the effects of natural selection might be.

Again, Darwin was forced to admit the strength of a powerful objection which he was unable to counter directly. At best, he could only argue that natural selection would be effective if adaptive variations were sufficiently common; the Negro island could become white, for example, if there were a steady influx of shipwrecked sailors. He actually had no evidence that adaptive variations were sufficiently common; instead, he retreated more and more to the Lamarckian theory that variation is due to the effects of activity in the environment and would accordingly be largely adaptive.

Unlike the answer to Kelvin's objection, which could not have been offered in the nineteenth century, the answer to Jenkin was available but remained unknown except to a few, who did not see its significance. Mendel's paper on plant hybridization established an alternative to the blending theory of inheritance. Mendel showed that there were discrete genetic factors that pass unchanged from generation to generation and are hence not subject to Jenkin's swamping effect. Mendel had established that the character of these factors (genes) is not changed by other factors in the germ plasm and that the factors segregate independently of one another in gamete formation. (He was unaware of the phenomenon of linkage.) Researchers of the literature on heredity recovered Mendel's work in 1900; and in 1904 William Bateson (1861-1926), in *Genetics and Evolution*, applied Mendel's laws to the theory of natural selection, thus answering Jenkin's objection.

The new genetics turned out to be far more significant for the theory of evolution than merely answering Jenkin's objection. The history of scientific Darwinism in the twentieth century is mainly the story of a series of advances in genetics, and the working out of their consequences for evolution. Mendel's laws were correlated with the behavior of the chromosomes in meiosis; the concepts of chromosome and gene mutation were introduced; linkage was discovered and understood; and statistical methods were employed in the analysis of the dynamics of genetic change in natural populations. One major gain of these developments was a systematic understanding of the origin and maintenance of genetic variability—the question that was so troublesome for Darwin. Another was the final decline of the Lamarckian aspect of Darwinism.

Acquired characters. The Neo-Darwinians had already denied the inheritance of acquired characters, but their evidence against it, like the Neo-Lamarckians' evidence in its favor, was largely anecdotal. August Weismann (1834-1914) had presented the theory that life is essentially a continuous stream of germ plasm that from time to time gives rise to whole organisms; the organisms die but the germ plasm is immortal. The stream can divide (gamete formation) and merge (fertilization), thus accounting for variability. This view was employed by Weismann and others as a theoretical argument against the inheritance of acquired characters, for it is an easy step from the continuity of the germ plasm to its independence of somatic influences. The emergence of Mendelism shed a new light on Weismann's theory. The mechanism of "immortality"—self-replication of chromosomes—was elucidated, and evidence accumulated that the chromosomes were indeed uninfluenced, or influenced only randomly, by somatic factors.

PHILOSOPHICAL DARWINISM

We have considered Darwinism as a biological theory; we may now consider its wider intellectual connections. These are many and complex, so it will be necessary to select the most important—those which now seem to be enduring ingredients of speculative thought or those which struck the people of the later nineteenth century with the greatest force. The differences between the climate of opinion—the ordinary presuppositions, ideas about the proper pattern of argument, assumptions as to proper method, in short, the world view—of the men of the mid-nineteenth and mid-twentieth centuries is large, comparable in degree to the differences between the Middle Ages and Renaissance. Of course the change had many causes, but the advent and absorption of Darwinism, while in part an effect of other currents, was also one major cause.

We shall consider the connections of Darwin's theory in three major regions: scientific cosmology, theology, and social doctrine.

Scientific cosmology. Scientists have general views about the way things are. The scientists of any historical period are likely to share a common set of views, with, of course, individuals differing over one or another point to some degree. These general views, insofar as they concern a subject matter of professional scientific interest and insofar as they are capable of influencing method, methodology, or empirical formulations, may be called cosmological. They differ from the ordinary statements of a science (for example, "organisms overproduce," "acquired characters are not inherited") in degree of determinateness. They are so formulated that they are exempt from immediate verification and falsification but subject to specification, by means of a series of semantical decisions, into determinate, verifiable propositions. A good example of such a cosmological proposition is "Nature makes no jumps," or "Nature has no gaps." Darwin, unlike many of his contemporaries, was fond of making this remark (in Latin); he employs it in the Linnaean Society papers and subsequently quotes it again and again. It constitutes part of Darwin's cosmology and is a point on which the nineteenth century was deeply divided. It is clear that the sense of the proposition is not sufficiently determinate, as it stands, for verification. But it can be construed to mean, for instance, that evolution is gradual or that the apparent gaps between living species can be filled if we consider a sufficient stretch of history.

These properties of cosmological belief have important implications. First, it is possible to arrive at a cosmology by a process akin to generalization—an empirical statement can be *construed as* the determinate form of an indeterminate proposition, which in turn can be applied to new subject matters. This is the formal pattern of the influence of science on cosmology. Second, the precise verbal formulation of a cosmological belief is relatively unimportant; indeed, it can affect thought without being explicitly formulated at all. For cosmological beliefs do not function as premises of empirical arguments; rather, they impart color to empirical argument, affecting its form and conceptual materials.

Darwin's biological theory was itself supported by prior developments in cosmological belief. The theory of evolution by natural selection did not occur to Darwin in an intellectual vacuum. Most important of these cosmological beliefs was uniformitarianism, the belief that nature operates everywhere and always by the same sorts of law. This view Darwin had imbibed from Lyell's *Principles of Geology*; it became cosmological by construing the geological theory as exhibiting a general truth about the way things, including livings things, are. This particular belief is already a powerful stimulus to look at organic nature as the outcome of a historical process, although, to be sure, the belief does not *entail* this conclusion.

A second belief, which Darwin inherited and was seen to support, was the necessity of taking time seriously. This meant, among other things, that the past is long. By the date of the *Origin* there was little actual evidence on the age of the earth, let alone the age of the universe. Outside scientific circles, the prevailing view was that the earth and universe were the same age, something on the order of thousands of years. As long as this is accepted, evolution is evidently most improbable. Some geologists, in particular James Hutton (1726–1797), had, on the other hand, argued that the earth is infinitely old—an important argument, since it helped to accustom scientists to the possibility of vast stretches of time and change. Geologists after Hutton were willing to help themselves to as much time as they needed, and Darwin gladly followed suit.

Taking time seriously, however, gained a deeper meaning after the publication of the *Origin,* namely, that change is a fundamental feature of nature. This constituted part of the cosmology of every Darwinian. It meant that the process of change is not merely the reshuffling of pre-existing materials in accordance with physical law but that the materials themselves are subject to alteration. For instance, as applied to biology it meant that the fundamental form, the species, did not merely exhibit eternal law but changed in such a way that new regularities of behavior replaced the old. In the favored terminology of the nineteenth century, we may say that taking time seriously meant that the laws of nature are subject to change.

Structures and patterns of behavior, then, have to be regarded as historically conditioned. This is the cosmological aspect of the most characteristic post-Darwin view of method, the insistence upon the investigation of origins, together with the view that such investigation can be scientific. Thus, we find the development of the idea of a human prehistory, the application of elaborate schemes concerning, as they were called, stages of development—spiritual, social, political, moral—and the belief that, at least in outline, the future of man may be successfully charted.

Pre-Darwinian biological theory was strongly influenced by the view that all living things are patterned after an eternal idea or archetype. This was held not only for the species but also for other taxonomic categories and for anatomical structures as well. Taxonomists were fond of describing, for example, the ideal vertebrate or mollusk; and morphologists described the ideal organ. One of the achievements of Darwinism was to break the hold of this notion on taxonomic and anatomical theory. Darwin was finally able to write in *Descent of Man,* "A discussion of the beau ideal of the liver, lungs, kidneys, etc., as of the human face divine, sounds strange to our ears."

Theology. The expressed doctrines of theology are related to empirical propositions as cosmological doctrines are related to the natural sciences. The role of Darwin's theory as a generator of such indeterminate beliefs naturally is well exemplified in theology. On the one hand it was immediately taken to be in prima facie opposition to a number of theological doctrines, especially the following: the uniqueness of man as God's supreme creation; the importance of natural theology; and the dominant theory, in Protestant circles, that the Bible is an authoritative source of beliefs about the natural world.

The first theological reaction to Darwinism can only be described as one of outrage; but by the close of the century, theologians having decided that since they must live with Darwinism, they ought to love it, the outlines of a reconciliation had been sketched. Even further, Darwinism was allowed to guide the formation of a new brand of theology. We shall consider first the reaction.

As we have seen, Darwin's readers were quick to grasp the consequences of the *Origin* for man himself. These consequences immediately aroused the most intense feelings. These feelings were quite justified, for Christian theology demands that man be considered unique; and his uniqueness was universally interpreted as ontological separateness from the rest of creation. The geologist Adam Sedgwick (1785–1873), for example, spoke no more than common opinion when he wrote in 1850 that man is a barrier to "any supposition of zoological continuity—and utterly unaccounted for by what we have any right to call the laws of nature." The Darwinians argued that man is not only continuous with the animal kingdom and subject to the laws of nature; they also asserted that his mental, moral, and spiritual qualities evolved by precisely the same processes that gave the eagle its claws and the tapeworm its hooks. Such opinions were a threat to the deepest level of Christian doctrine, and were bound to be, until man's uniqueness could be given a new theological interpretation.

Moreover, the furor over the animal nature of man was heightened, especially in Britain, by local circumstances. T. H. Huxley compared man and the ape with endless zest, knowing how the comparison annoyed his opponents. For apes and monkeys were thought to be oversexed and rather obscene; in addition, the British took very seriously the principle that a man's standing in the world is dependent on the standing of his ancestors. Thus the literature of the period is enlivened by comic remarks, such as, "Are you descended from an ape, Mr. Huxley, from your mother's or your father's side?" (Bishop Wilberforce) and "You can't wash the slugs out of a lettuce without disrespect to your ancestors" (John Ruskin). But the symbol of the ape squatting in one's family tree was no more than an expression of dismay at being swallowed up in the infinite forms of nature. The twentieth century has not fully regained its equanimity on this point. Pius XII wrote that a Catholic may accept a doctrine of evolution, but he should beware of doubting that there was a first man and woman. And consider this passage from the speech of William Jennings Bryan at the Scopes trial (1925): "We are told just how many species there are, 518,900. . . . and then we have mammals, 3,500, and there is a little circle and man is in the circle, find him, find man."

The edifice of traditional theology was touched at other points. Early nineteenth-century theologians placed heavy weight on the cooperation of science and religion. The clergyman–naturalist was a familiar figure. It was thought that the intricacy and systematic interconnections of nature exhibited the handiwork of God; to study them was an act of piety. More specifically, natural teleology was the mainstay of natural theology. William Paley's *Natural Theology* (1802) is a good example. He holds that God's creation is totally good, that the organs of living things are almost perfect, that all animals have their just share of happiness, and that all this demonstrates with thousandfold certainty the existence and beneficence of God. An older natural theology tended to see evidences of God's design throughout nature; but Paley, and others after him, such as Thomas Chalmers in the *Bridgewater Treatises* (1834), rest their case on the structure of living things: consider, they suggest, the hand, the heart, the eye (especially the eye); they are complex and adapted for their functions to a degree that transcends all possibility of chance correlation.

By hindsight this attitude appears curiously self-defeating as well as vulnerable. The religiously inspired examination of organic adaptation was precisely one factor that led to Darwin's account of the origin of adaptation. His theory made the last citadel of divine teleology in nature untenable except, of course, for a few holdouts; but it was also widely interpreted as refuting all natural teleology, especially by the German materialists. "Chance" had been defined by Paley as "the operation of causes without design," and on this definition Darwinism leaves the origin of species to chance.

Theology in the middle half of the nineteenth century was especially vulnerable to Darwinism on a second point, namely, its extreme Biblicism and, even further, its literalism in Biblical interpretation. It hardly needs saying that Darwinism is incompatible with any literal construction put upon either the Old Testament or the New Testament. The laity and most of the clergy, however, insisted upon such constructions. Matthew Arnold quotes the following as prevailing opinion in England: "Every verse of the Bible, every word of it, every syllable of it, every letter of it, is the direct utterance of the Most High"—a view Coleridge describes as "Divine ventriloquism." The matter was not so extreme outside of Britain, but the fact remains that Protestant education and practice relied heavily on the study and interpretation of the Bible.

The intellectual compromise that gradually emerged seems obvious today; the problem was not to think of it but to accept it. It consists in admitting that man is part of nature and that he is indeed, even in his spiritual aspects, the outcome of an evolutionary process. But lowly origins do not detract from a unique present. And the process of evolution is either guided, as Wallace suggested, or is itself the mode and manner of God's creation. Indeed, it was sometimes argued that Darwinism provides us with an elevated conception of God. Canon Charles Kingsley, for example, wrote to Darwin as follows: "I have gradually learnt to see that it is just as noble a conception of the Deity to believe that he created primal forms capable of self-development . . . , as to believe that He required a fresh act of intervention to supply the *lacunas* which He Himself had made." This passage is quoted by Darwin with some changes in later editions of the *Origin.* As Kingsley also put it, Darwin allows us to get "rid of an interfering God—a master-magician, as I call it" in favor of a "living, immanent, ever-working God."

The final step in this direction was to give God an even more intimate metaphysical connection with natural process. This step had been taken by previous philosophers—Spinoza and Hegel, for example; but it was repeated under the aegis of Darwinism by Bergson, Whitehead, and a number of Protestant thinkers. The problem of a divine nature that is both perfect and yet incomplete is one contemporary heritage of Darwinism.

Social doctrine. The social thought of the later nineteenth century drew so heavily from the theories of evolution that its major ideas became known as social Darwinism. The 1850s were a period of revolutionary fervor in the streets as well as the academies, and political ideologists seized on Darwin as their major intellectual spokesman. His views, or rather selected aspects of them, presented ideal material for application to ethical, economic, and political problems.

It is convenient to divide social Darwinism into a political right and left, using these terms in their rough, contemporary editorial-page sense. In adopting Darwinism to social questions, it must be admitted that the right wing had the best of the bargain. In Europe these were the men whose interests were vested in hereditary privilege and in the factories and institutions of the industrial revolution. On the grounds of these interests they defended themselves against any attempt to justify social revolution, governmental control, unionism, or socialism in any of its many nineteenth-century forms. The ideology that was developed, with the help of Darwinism, in order to facilitate this defense also committed them, in various combinations, against such things as child-labor legislation, poor laws, compulsory safety regulations, and public education. A similar ideology provided the United States with its justification for the undisturbed economic expansion, speculation, and competition that we associate with the Robber Barons.

On the other hand, Darwinism was employed by the social reformers. Karl Marx wanted to dedicate the first volume of *Das Kapital* to Darwin. George Bernard Shaw, although he criticized the theory of natural selection, defended his socialism with the help of his version of Bergson's creative evolutionism. The reformers saw Darwinism as the final demonstration that no particular economic or political institution—however hallowed by tradition or supported by existing theories—need be regarded as unalterable. The forms of society, like the forms of life, are local, temporary, and functional and may accordingly be changed (for the better) without shaking the foundations of the cosmos.

In short, the biology and cosmology of Darwinism was capable of being all things to all men. It enjoyed this status by virtue of its ability to inspire and lend a measure of apparent scientific support to the following major ideas:

(1) The vision of a science that was historical, and at the same time a rigorous application of natural law, inspired a new vision of a science of society. Herbert Spencer (1820–1903), whose evolutionism antedated the *Origin,* became the symbol of this ideal wedding of history and sociology. He drew elaborate comparisons between social structures and the forms of living organisms and saw societies as undergoing a progressive evolution in which egoism would be gradually replaced by altruism through a mechanism analogous to the inheritance of acquired characters. Sociology stood in relation to society as evolutionary biology stood to the phenomena of organic nature.

(2) The process of natural selection, interpreted as the survival of the fittest, provided a means for explaining social process. The American political economist William Graham Sumner (1840–1910), for example, saw society as the outcome of a social struggle in which each man, in

pursuing his own good, can succeed only at the expense of others. The fittest in this social struggle are the ruthless, the imaginative, the industrious, the frugal. They climb to the top, and it is right that they should do so. The idle, infirm, and extravagant are losers, not adapted to the realities of their world, and thus legitimately subject to elimination by "social selection." Sumner presents society with an alternative: either "liberty, inequality, survival of the fittest," or "not-liberty, equality, survival of the unfittest." Self-made millionaires are the paradigm of the fittest. They are "a product of natural selection, acting on the whole body of men to pick out those who can meet the requirement of certain work to be done."

This doctrine of the financially successful as the cream of the universe naturally had a sympathetic audience. John D. Rockefeller, Andrew Carnegie, and Theodore Roosevelt were supporters, although Roosevelt believed that the unfit were entitled to some protection.

(3) Darwinism provided a rationale for Adam Smith's doctrine of the "Invisible Hand." Smith had supposed that while each man follows his innate tendency to "truck, barter, and trade," men's efforts would automatically dovetail in such a way that the economic good of society as a whole would be served. And Darwin had shown that the net result of each organism's engaging in a struggle for its own welfare was continuous evolution of the species as a whole in the direction of better adaptation to its environment. The political implications of this viewpoint are clear.

The central ethical question raised by the social Darwinists is this: granted that man is subject to natural law, and even granted further that he is subject to some form of natural or social selection, can one legitimately derive from this such policies as laissez-faire? Alfred Russel Wallace had argued that with the advent, under divine guidance, of man's brain, the evolution of man was no longer controlled by natural selection, so that inference from the doctrine of natural selection to ethical policy would be illegitimate. Huxley provided a similar argument: man represents an island of cultural evolution in a sea of Darwinian change. These issues have largely passed into history, however, due to the philosophical point that whether or not to support a law of nature is not a question for decision. (See also ETHICS, HISTORY OF, section on Evolutionary Ethics.)

The fate of Darwinism in the twentieth century has been mixed. Social Darwinism is of no more than historical interest. It is rightly regarded as philosophically naive and, moreover, as concerned with social questions that are not of contemporary interest. The same is largely true of the theological battles over the significance of evolution. Current theology exhibits a sublime indifference to the questions that agitated Huxley and Bishop Wilberforce. It must be pointed out, however, that modern theology is free to pursue other problems because of the clarification of the status of man and of the relation of science to theology that emerged from the Darwinian debate.

In biological theory proper, Darwin's theory remains secure. His Lamarckism is no longer accepted, if we discount some periodic revivals in the Soviet Union; and the doctrine of sexual selection is still a matter of some debate. But the major theory of the *Origin*, evolution by natural selection, is the framework of modern evolutionary theory. This modern account—sometimes called the synthetic theory and sometimes, rather confusingly, Neo-Darwinism—accepts *in toto* the doctrine of natural selection as described above but develops it in a manner that Darwin himself could not have envisaged. The Synthetic Theory may fairly be described as Darwin's theory of natural selection, deepened by the absorption of twentieth-century genetics and systematically applied to the whole range of biological phenomena.

The absorption of genetics accounts for the novel developments in the doctrine of natural selection itself. Darwin thought of natural selection fundamentally as differential *survival*, and he regarded the organism as the natural unit that is subjected to selective pressures. With the advent of Mendelian genetics, and especially of the statistical study of the genetics of populations, these two Darwinian conceptions underwent a significant change. From the geneticist's point of view, differential survival is subordinate to differential *reproduction* of genetic materials; evolution is simply temporal change in the genetic constitution of a population. The simplest model of evolutionary change would be the following: suppose that we have in a population two alleles, a_1 and a_2, of a gene a, and that a_1 is present in the proportion p, and a_2 in the proportion $1-p$. Then any temporal change in the value of p would be a case of reproductive differential between a_1 and a_2; and it would be an evolutionary change in the population. Some biologists simply identify such differential reproduction with natural selection, in which case sexual selection is a special case of natural selection. The natural unit of selection becomes the gene rather than the whole organism.

This conception of natural selection is not incompatible with Darwin's. Differential survival is still the major cause of differential reproduction of genes; and there is still a clear and obvious sense in which the organism is the fundamental unit of natural selection. But the new conception of natural selection facilitates the discussion of a large range of questions, for example, the roles of isolation and migration in evolution; the effectiveness of very small selective advantages; the roles of gene mutations, sex-linkage, and dominance; and so on. The modern theory has much to say on these topics that could not have been foreseen by Darwin, but nothing that he could not readily endorse.

Bibliography

DARWIN AND WALLACE

Darwin, Charles Robert, *On the Origin of Species by means of Natural Selection, or the Preservation of Favoured Races in the Struggle for Life*. London, 1859. The latest variorum text, Morse Peckham, ed. (Philadelphia, 1959), is also available in paperback with an introduction by G. G. Simpson (New York, 1962). There is also a Modern Library edition (New York, 1949).

Darwin, Charles Robert, *The Descent of Man, and Selection in Relation to Sex*. London, 1871.

Darwin, Charles Robert, *The Voyage of the Beagle*. London and New York, n.d. A reissue by J. M. Dent and E. P. Dutton of their 1906 edition of the *Journal of Researches Into the Geology and Natural History of the Various Countries Visited by H. M. S. Beagle, 1832–1836*.

Darwin, Charles Robert, and Wallace, Alfred Russel, *Evolution by Natural Selection*. Cambridge, 1958. This contains Darwin's sketch of 1842, his essay of 1844, and the Darwin and Wallace papers read before the Linnaean Society in 1848.

Wallace, Alfred Russel, "The Origin of Human Races and the Antiquity of Man Deduced From the Theory of Natural Selection." *Journal of the Anthropological Society of London* (1864).

Wallace, Alfred Russel, *Contributions to the Theory of Natural Selection.* London, 1870.

Wallace, Alfred Russel, *Darwinism.* London, 1889.

CULTURAL ASPECTS OF DARWINISM

Dewey, John, *The Influence of Darwinism on Philosophy.* New York, 1910.

Eiseley, Loren, *Darwin's Century; Evolution and the Men Who Discovered It.* New York, 1958. Contains many illuminating discussions of the interplay of philosophical and scientific theories.

Fothergill, Philip, *Historical Aspects of Organic Evolution.* London, 1952. A history of evolutionary theories.

Goudge, T. A., *Ascent of Life; a Philosophical Study of Evolution.* Toronto, 1961.

Gray, Asa, *Natural Science and Religion.* New York, 1880. A topical discussion of the way theism looked to an evolutionist.

Himmelfarb, Gertrude, *Darwin and the Darwinian Revolution.* New York, 1959.

Hofstadter, Richard, *Social Darwinism in American Thought, 1860–1915.* Philadelphia, 1944.

Huxley, Thomas Henry, *Evolution and Ethics, and Other Essays.* New York, 1898.

Schneider, Herbert, "The Influence of Darwin and Spencer on American Philosophical Theology." *Journal of the History of Ideas*, Vol. 6 (1945).

MODERN EVOLUTIONARY THEORY

Darlington, C. D., *The Evolution of Genetic Systems.* Cambridge, 1939.

De Beer, Gavin, *Embryology and Evolution.* Oxford, 1930.

Dobzhansky, Theodosius, *Genetics and the Origin of Species*, 3d ed. New York, 1951.

Fisher, R. A., *The Genetical Theory of Natural Selection.* Oxford, 1930. This is the classic application of statistical methods to the dynamics of evolving populations; together with the Darlington and Dobzhansky works, it affords a good introduction to the crucial relations between evolution and population genetics.

Mayr, Ernst, *Systematics and the Origin of Species.* New York, 1942.

Ross, H. H., *A Synthesis of Evolutionary Theory.* Englewood Cliffs, N.J., 1962.

Simpson, G. G., *The Meaning of Evolution.* New Haven, 1951. The best general introduction to the modern synthetic theory, this is a revised and abridged paperback edition of *The Meaning of Evolution: A Study of the History of Life and Its Significance for Man.* New Haven, 1949.

Simpson, G. G., *The Major Features of Evolution.* New York, 1953. This and the above work by Simpson are the best nontechnical introductions for the general reader.

MORTON O. BECKNER

DAVID BEN MERWAN AL-MUKAMMAS. *See* MUKAMMAS, DAVID BEN MERWAN AL-.

DAVID OF DINANT, materialistic pantheist of the Middle Ages, taught at Paris near the beginning of the thirteenth century. Apart from this fact, almost nothing is known of his life. It is uncertain whether he derived his name from Dinant in Belgium or Dinan in Brittany. His major work, *De Tomis, Hoc Est de Divisionibus*, is probably identical with the *Quaternuli* condemned at a provincial council in Paris in 1210, and his writings were among those banned at the University of Paris in 1215 by the papal legate, Robert de Courçon. Our knowledge of his ideas is largely derived from Albert the Great, Thomas Aquinas, and Nicholas of Cusa.

David developed his philosophy at a time when Latin Christian thought was facing an almost unprecedented challenge from rival world views. Neoplatonism, introduced into the medieval West by John Scotus Erigena and popularized in the twelfth century by numerous translations of Arabic works, was the first great non-Christian system to impress the medieval mind, but by the early thirteenth century Aristotelianism loomed large, and other Greek philosophies were not unknown. Attempts were made to blend the Christian doctrine of creation with these doctrines, notably with the Neoplatonic theory of emanation, with the result that the distinctive character of the Biblical conception of the relation between the world and God was at least occasionally obscured.

The title of David's *De Tomis* suggests some indebtedness to Erigena's *De Divisione Naturae*, and David's pantheism may well have been inspired to some extent by his reading of Erigena's work. His thought seems, however, to have been more strongly influenced by ancient Greek materialism, as described in Aristotle's *Physics* and *Metaphysics*, and by certain Aristotelian ideas dialectically manipulated in the manner of the early medieval logicians.

David's interpretation of reality was essentially monistic. He first divided the objects of knowledge into three classes and then presented individual objects within each class as mere modes of a primary reality. Thus, bodies are modes of matter (*hyle*), souls are modes of mind (*nous*), and eternal substances or separated forms are modes of God. Furthermore, these three primary realities are themselves essentially one being or substance.

David supported this doctrine by a dialectical argument based on the logical notion of a "difference" (*differentia*) which, when added to a genus, forms a species. Such *differentiae*, he argued, can be predicated only of composite beings. God, mind, and prime matter, however, are all simple realities, and can therefore include no *differentiae.* Consequently, they must be substantially identical.

David's monism may be further characterized as materialistic. In his view, neither God nor matter possesses form, since beings determined by form are individual, composite substances. God and matter, therefore, cannot be known by an assimilation of their forms through abstraction. If in fact the intellect knows both God and matter, the explanation must be that it is already identical with them. Furthermore, if both God and matter are unformed, they are nothing but being in potentiality. Being in potentiality, however, is the definition of prime matter. Properly speaking, then, the ultimate reality, which is at once God, mind, and matter, is best described as matter.

Bibliography

Gabriel Théry, *David de Dinant. Étude sur son panthéisme matérialiste* (Paris, 1925), is the only book on David of Dinant. See also A. Birkenmajer, "Découverte de fragments manuscrits de David de Dinant," in *Revue néo-scolastique de philosophie*, Vol. 35 (1933), 220–229, which does not, however, affect the accepted picture.

EUGENE R. FAIRWEATHER

DA VINCI, LEONARDO. *See* LEONARDO DA VINCI.

DEATH. Although most of the great philosophers have touched on the problem of death, few have dealt with it systematically or in detail. Frequently, as in the case of Spinoza, an author's views on the subject are known to us from a single sentence; and at almost all stages in Western history we are likely to discover more about the topic in the writings of men of letters than in those of technical philosophers. Whether this relative reticence on the part of philosophers should be attributed to a general lack of interest or to other causes is a moot point. Schopenhauer, who was the first of the major philosophers to deal extensively with the subject, declared that death is the muse of philosophy, notwithstanding that the muse is seldom avowed. And the existentialist philosophers from Kierkegaard to the present have more or less consistently endorsed Schopenhauer's contention; Camus's declaration in *The Myth of Sisyphus* (1942) that suicide is the only genuine philosophical issue is an extreme but notable case in point. On the other hand, most contemporary Anglo-American analytic philosophers probably regard the paucity of materials on death as evidence of the subject's resistance to serious philosophical inquiry. In general, they wish to exclude the subject of death from the area of legitimate philosophical speculation, either as a part of their campaign against metaphysics or on the grounds that the subject can be more adequately dealt with by psychologists and social scientists. The psychologists and social scientists have, in fact, recently given signs of a willingness to explore the question. One such indication was a symposium on the psychology of death at the 1956 American Psychological Association Convention, which resulted in the publication in 1959 of an anthology including contributions from scholars in a wide variety of fields. Unfortunately, as several of the contributors to this volume lamented, the number of experimental studies actually undertaken has been disappointingly small.

THE KNOWLEDGE OF DEATH

The primary concern of most philosophers who have dealt with the question of death has been to discover ways in which men may mitigate or overcome the fear it tends to inspire. There are, however, several other loosely related problems that have also tended to excite interest or controversy and that it will be advisable to discuss first. How does man learn of death? Is death a natural phenomenon, or does it require explanation in nonnatural terms? What specific psychological or social conditions tend to heighten the awareness and fear of death?

Awareness of death. The clearest and simplest answer to the first of these questions was given by Voltaire, who stated: "The human species is the only one which knows it will die, and it knows this through experience" (*Dictionnaire philosophique*). Although some persons have questioned whether man is the only animal who knows he will die, arguing that certain of the lower animals appear to show some vague presentiment of approaching extinction, it appears to be unquestioned that man alone has a clear awareness of death and that man alone regards death as a universal and inevitable phenomenon. The interesting question is how man knows he will die. The view that experience alone gives knowledge of death derives support from the ignorance of death displayed by many children and from anthropological data indicating that many primitive peoples refuse even as adults to regard death as necessary or universal. However, a number of twentieth-century philosophers have contested this view, especially Max Scheler and Heidegger, who argue that the awareness of death is an immanent, a priori structure of human consciousness. Although neither of these authors offers anything in the nature of scientific evidence for his position, it is not easily refuted; for, if one grants current notions about levels of consciousness, apparent ignorance of death may be interpreted as merely superficial and attributed to some form of repression. Moreover, the imperfect knowledge of death among primitive peoples is a fact that could be used against those who argue that the knowledge of death comes from experience, since the hazards of their lives expose primitive peoples to an earlier and greater experience of death than is common among civilized men. At the very least it must be granted that the knowledge of death depends not only upon experience but also upon a level of mental culture that makes it possible to interpret experience accurately.

Ironically, Freud, who more than anybody else has habituated us to think in terms of levels of consciousness and has thereby rendered credible the idea that knowledge of death may exist despite apparent ignorance, stated that the consciousness, not the apparent ignorance, of death is merely superficial, the unconscious being firmly convinced of its immortality. How Freud could reconcile this belief, which dates from the period of World War I, with his later belief in the unconscious death wish is not clear.

Death: a natural phenomenon? Is death a natural phenomenon? Most persons today tend to find this question a bit foolish. It is noteworthy, however, that most primitive peoples attribute death to the agency of gods or demons who are jealous of human achievements. Equally significant is the Christian explanation of death as punishment for the sins of Adam. It should also be observed that if by a "natural" phenomenon one means a fact that can be fully understood and explained by empirical inquiry, death is not a natural phenomenon for Heidegger or Scheler. This reluctance to explain death in terms of natural causes has an interesting parallel in the reluctance to explain life itself naturalistically, and the religious or metaphysical perspectives which give rise to nonnaturalistic interpretations of life tend also to occasion nonnaturalistic interpretations of death.

Variations in consciousness of death. Are there great variations in the awareness or fear of death from person to person, from epoch to epoch, from culture to culture? If so, how are these variations to be explained? Surprisingly, very little attention has been given to these questions. The most interesting and almost the only hypothesis on this topic is that of Huizinga and Paul-Louis Landsberg, who, each in his own way, link the consciousness of death to individualism. According to these authors, the consciousness of death has been most acute in periods of social disorganization, when individual choice tends to replace automatic conformity to social values; they point especially to classical society after the disintegration of the city-states; to the early Renaissance, after the breakdown of feudalism; and to the twentieth century. This hypothesis has yet to be fully confirmed or disconfirmed by careful historical and anthropological study. However, it is true that late antiquity, the early Renaissance, and the twentieth century have made unusually great contributions to the literature on death.

THE FEAR OF DEATH

With respect to the fear of death, the great divide is between those who argue that only the hope of personal immortality will ever reconcile men to death and those who argue that the fear of death may be mitigated or overcome even when death is accepted as the ultimate extinction of the individual person. The second group, which is remarkably heterogeneous, may be subdivided according to the techniques recommended for allaying fears.

The Epicureans. One of the oldest of the "solutions" to the fear of death was that of Epicurus and his followers. According to Epicurus, the fear of death is based upon the beliefs that death is painful and that the soul may survive to experience pain or torture in an afterlife. Since both of these beliefs are mistaken, it suffices to expose them as such. Although death may be precipitated by painful disease, death itself is a perfectly painless loss of consciousness, no more to be feared than falling asleep. And since the soul is merely a special organization of material atoms, it cannot survive physical destruction. "Death," Epicurus said, "is nothing to us. . . . It does not concern either the living or the dead, since for the former it is not, and the latter are no more" (*Letter to Menoeceus*). It is hardly necessary to point out that many persons have questioned Epicurus' conception of the soul and consequently have rejected his views with respect to its immortality. The principal criticism, however, is that the Epicureans have falsely diagnosed the cause of mankind's fear of death. Death terrorizes us, not because we fear it as painful, but because we are unwilling to lose consciousness permanently. The twentieth-century Spanish existentialist philosopher Miguel de Unamuno reports that "as a youth and even as a child, I remained unmoved when shown the most moving pictures of hell, for even then nothing appeared to me quite so horrible as nothingness itself."

The Stoics. The later Stoics, especially Seneca, Epictetus, and Marcus Aurelius, offered a more complicated and elusive view of death. Seneca said that to overcome the fear of death we must think of it constantly. The important thing, however, is to think of it in the proper manner, reminding ourselves that we are but parts of nature and must reconcile ourselves to our allotted roles. He recurrently compared life to a banquet from which it is our obligation to retire graciously at the appointed time, or to a role in a play whose limits ought to satisfy us, since they satisfy the author. The fear of death displays a baseness wholly incompatible with the dignity and calm of the true philosopher, who has learned to emancipate himself from finite concerns. Essential to the Stoic outlook was the Platonic view that philosophizing means learning to die; that is, learning to commune with the eternal through the act of philosophic contemplation.

Although much of Stoic thinking on death crept into later Christianity, the contemporary Christians saw in this thinking a sinful element of pride. Death, Augustine said, is a punishment for human sin, and the fear of death cannot be overcome except through divine grace. Others find it highly questionable whether one can reasonably accept the metaphysical underpinnings of the Stoic view, most especially the belief in a providential order of Nature.

Spinoza. A third solution is that of Spinoza. He wrote: "A free man thinks of nothing less than of death, and his wisdom is not a meditation upon death but upon life" (*Ethics*, Prop. LXVII). Since Spinoza did not elaborate, it is possible to argue almost endlessly about the precise import of this famous remark. Most often, however, it is interpreted to mean that men can and should allay the fear of death simply by diverting their attention from it, and some persons have argued that by his nature man tends to—perhaps must—follow this advice. La Rochefoucauld, for instance, averred that man can no more look directly at death than he can look directly at the sun. One fundamental criticism of this position comes from the Stoics and the existentialists, both of whom maintain that the fear of death can be allayed only by facing it directly. A second criticism consists in pointing out that the fear of death is frequently an involuntary sentiment that cannot be conquered by a merely conscious decision or a bare act of will. It is not enough to tell people not to think of death; one must explain how they can avoid thinking of it.

Death and the good life. This brings us to a fourth view on death, a view that was felicitously put by Leonardo da Vinci. Just as a day well spent brings happy sleep, so, he said, a life well spent brings happy death. Painful preoccupation with death has its source in human misery; the cure is to foster human well-being. A happy man is not seriously pained by the thought of death, nor does he dwell on the subject. This view was held by many Enlightenment thinkers, most notably Condorcet. It also appears to be the view of most pragmatists and of Bertrand Russell.

There are two counterarguments. The first is the theme prevalent in several branches of Christianity concerning the total impossibility of attaining happiness on earth. The second is the even more familiar and prevalent Christian theme that in order to achieve happiness in this life, one must first conquer the fear of death. Happiness, therefore, is not a cure; it is a consequence of the cure.

Death without consolation. In sharp contrast to this last position is that of a long line of nineteenth-century and twentieth-century philosophers, from Schopenhauer to contemporary existentialists. For them human well-being or happiness, at least as traditionally conceived, is totally impossible to achieve; and if the individual is to experience such rewarding values as life does permit, he must uncompromisingly embrace the tragedy of the human condition, clearheadedly acknowledging such evils as death. Like the Stoics, these authors would have us think constantly of death. Unlike the Stoics, however, they do not offer us the consolation of belief in a providential order of nature. From the standpoint of Being or Nature, the death of the individual is totally meaningless or absurd.

For Schopenhauer the finite, empirical self is a manifestation of a cosmic will that has destined man to live out his life in suffering or painful striving. The only remedy is to achieve a state of indifference or pure will-lessness—a state best known in moments of pure aesthetic contemplation but to which the awareness of death substantially contributes.

According to Nietzsche, the superior man will not permit death to seek him out in ambush, to strike him down unawares. The superior man will live constantly in the awareness of death, joyfully and proudly assuming death as the natural and proper terminus of life.

Heidegger and Sartre, like most existentialists, urge us to cultivate the awareness of death chiefly as a means of heightening our sense of life. The knowledge of death gives to life a sense of urgency that it would otherwise lack. The same point has been made by Freud, who compared life without the consciousness of death to a Platonic romance or to a game played without stakes.

Heidegger makes the additional claim, although here Sartre parts company with him, that the awareness of death confers upon man a sense of his own individuality. Dying, he says, is the one thing no one can do for you; each of us must die alone. To shut out the consciousness of death is, therefore, to refuse one's individuality and to live inauthentically.

(See also "MY DEATH.")

Bibliography

Jacques Choron, *Death and Western Thought* (New York, 1963), is a fairly comprehensive review of what Western philosophers have had to say on the subject of death. It is especially recommended for its wealth of quotations. Herman Feifel, ed., *The Meaning of Death* (New York, 1959), is an anthology containing many contemporary essays by psychologists, sociologists, and workers in allied fields.

Russell's views on death may be found in "The Art of Growing Old," in his *Portraits from Memory and Other Essays* (London and New York, 1956) and in "What I Believe," in his *Why I Am not a Christian* (London and New York, 1957).

Heidegger's views will be found in his *Being and Time* (New York, 1962), Part II, Ch. 1; Sartre's in his *Being and Nothingness* (New York, 1956), pp. 531–553.

An interesting work by a Roman Catholic existentialist is Paul-Louis Landsberg, *Essai sur l'experience de la mort* (Paris, 1951).

Freud's views are expressed in "Thoughts for the Times on War and Death," in James Strachey and Anna Freud, eds., *Standard Edition of the Complete Psychological Works of Sigmund Freud* (London, 1957), Vol. XIV, pp. 288–317.

Johan Huizinga, *The Waning of the Middle Ages* (London, 1952), provides the best account of that author's reflections.

For an analysis of primitive attitudes toward death, see Lucien Lévy-Bruhl, *Primitive Mentality*, translated by Lilian A. Clare (London, 1923).

ROBERT G. OLSON

DEATH: THE PROBLEM OF ONE'S OWN DEATH. *See* "MY DEATH."

DEBORIN, ABRAM MOISEEVICH (1881–1963), Russian Marxist philosopher. Born to a poor Russian Jewish family (named Ioffe), Deborin left manual labor to become a revolutionary philosopher. After the revolution of 1905, under the influence of Plekhanov and philosophical training at the University of Bern, he turned from Bolshevism to Menshevism and began an outpouring of Marxist articles; this became a flood after 1917, when Deborin quit the Mensheviks and offered his services to the Communist regime. He became the chief teacher and editor of Soviet Marxist philosophy during the period when the political chiefs allowed the philosophers considerable autonomy. In 1928 he was accepted into the party and in 1929 presided over a conference that elevated his interpretation of dialectical materialism to semiofficial status. Only a year later, however, he was sharply attacked by young Stalinists—his former students, for the most part. To describe Deborin's suddenly discovered heresy, Stalin coined the term "Menshevizing idealism"—the separation of philosophy from "practice"—a very loose term which in this context signified the policies and views of the Communist party's political chiefs. Deborin did not suffer the fate of his major lieutenants, N. A. Karev and I. A. Sten, who were condemned as "enemies of the people," but he lost his important educational and editorial posts and virtually ceased philosophical publication from 1931 until Stalin's death in 1953. During this period he busied himself with minor editorial and administrative tasks in the Academy of Sciences. After Stalin's death Deborin resumed his former rate of publication and completed two volumes of a history of social thought before illness and death cut him off.

Deborin is remembered most for his polemics and for his emphasis on Hegel as the chief source in the elaboration of Marxist philosophy. His polemics were occasionally directed against non-Marxist thinkers but much more frequently against unorthodox Marxists—for example, those who tried to bring ideas of Mach or Freud into Marxism. Mechanistic and positivist views were dominant among Soviet Marxists when Deborin became their chief philosopher; he organized a vigorous campaign against such views—"a social movement in support of dialectics," as he called it.

The Second Conference of Marxist–Leninist Scholarly Institutions in April 1929 formally endorsed Deborin's interpretation of mechanistic materialism and positivism as "incorrect" and "un-Marxist." This was the first important instance in Soviet history of the legislation of philosophical truth by decrees of conferences. The practice became a regular feature of Soviet philosophy, with the added specification (by a decree of January 1931 condemning Deborin's views as "incorrect" and "un-Marxist") that the Communist party's Central Committee is the ultimate source of philosophical truth, "the Areopagus in which the wisdom of our Party is concentrated" (Stalin). Deborin's philosophy was condemned not only for its stress on Hegel but even more for its failure to go all the way from the earlier, or Leninist, to the later, or Stalinist, understanding of *partiinost'* (variously and awkwardly translated as "party spirit," "partyness," "partisanship"). In the earlier version *partiinost'* included a sociological proposition and a moral injunction: (1) philosophical views are determined by class interests and (2) the philosopher should discover and uphold the views that correspond to the interests of the lower classes. Since 1931 two Stalinist corollaries have been stressed: (3) the Central Committee of the Soviet party is the unanswerable judge not only of class interests but also of the philosophical views that correspond to them and (4) the philosopher's primary duty is to follow the lead of the Central Committee. Deborin never disputed the third and fourth points, but he was reluctant in his acquiescence to them, and the bulk of his writings antedated the announcement of them, when the tone of Soviet philosophy was much freer than it has been since. Although some Soviet intellectuals in the post-Stalin era have indicated repeated dissatisfaction with the third and fourth points, they show no signs of Deborinite inspiration. Deborin's Hegelian studies seem turgid and derivative to many, and they have had little influence on the Hegelian revival in the post-Stalin Soviet Union, much less, certainly, than the works of Georg Lukács, which Deborin and all subsequent officials of Soviet philosophy have condemned.

Bibliography

Deborin's chief works are *Vvedenie v Filosofiiu Dialekticheskogo Materializma* ("Introduction to the Philosophy of Dialectical Materialism," Petrograd, 1916) and several collections of his articles: *Lenin kak Myslitel'* ("Lenin as a Thinker," Moscow, 1924), *Filosofiia i Marksizm* ("Philosophy and Marxism," Moscow, 1926), *Dialektika i Estestvoznanie* ("Dialectics and Natural Science," Moscow and Leningrad, 1928), and *Filosofiia i Politika* ("Philosophy and Politics," Moscow, 1961). See also his *Sotsial'no-politicheskie Ucheniia Novogo Vremeni* ("Sociopolitical Doctrines of Modern Times"), Vol. I (Moscow, 1958); a posthumous edition of the second volume was promised at the time of his death.

For studies of Deborin see René Ahlberg, *"Dialektische Philosophie" und Gesellschaft in der Sowjetunion* (Berlin, 1960), and David Joravsky, *Soviet Marxism and Natural Science, 1917–1932* (New York, 1961).

D. JORAVSKY

DECISION. *See* CHOOSING, DECIDING, AND DOING.

DECISION THEORY. The fundamental problem of decision theory may be characterized in the following way: A person, or group of persons, is faced with several alternative courses of action but has only incomplete information about the true state of affairs and the consequences of each possible action. The problem is to choose an action that is optimal or rational relative to the information available and in accord with some definite criteria of optimality or rationality. The main branches of decision theory may be characterized by the accompanying table of examples.

	INDIVIDUAL DECISIONS	GROUP DECISIONS
NORMATIVE THEORY	Classical economics Statistical decision theory Moral philosophy	Game theory Welfare economics Political theory
DESCRIPTIVE THEORY	Experimental decision studies Learning theory Surveys of voting behavior	Social psychology Political science

The discussion of the philosophical significance of decision theory will be broken down here according to the four entries in the table. The emphasis will be on normative rather than on descriptive theory.

INDIVIDUAL NORMATIVE THEORY

Criteria of rationality. A common problem confronting the theory of induction and moral philosophy is that of giving an adequate account of the concept of rationality. The normative theory of individual decision making has been concerned with explicating the notion of rationality in what is in some respects a very thorough fashion. However, an essential difficulty has arisen that is of considerable philosophical importance. Recent work in decision theory has shown that there is no simple coherent set of principles capable of precise statement which correspond to naive ideas of rationality. Just as research in this century in the foundations of mathematics has shown that we do not yet know exactly what mathematics is, so the work in decision theory shows that we do not yet understand what we mean by rationality. Even in highly restricted circumstances it turns out to be extremely difficult to characterize in a nonparadoxical fashion a rational choice among alternative courses of action.

Principle of utility. In setting forth the difficulties of individual normative theory it will perhaps be clearest to approach the subject historically. A good place to begin is the definition of utility given in the first chapter of Jeremy Bentham's *The Principles of Morals and Legislation:*

> By utility is meant that property in any object, whereby it tends to produce benefit, advantage, pleasure, good or happiness (all this in the present case comes to the same thing), or (what comes again to the same thing) to prevent the happening of mischief, pain, evil, or unhappiness to the party whose interest is considered: if that party be the community in general, then the happiness of the community; if a particular individual, then the happiness of that individual.

Bentham interpreted his maxim of "the greatest good for the greatest number" as meaning that utility is maximized, and he spent considerable effort in formulating a program for measuring utility. From the standpoint of decision theory the rationale proposed by Bentham is clear enough: always choose that action which maximizes utility. Unfortunately, Bentham's ideas on how to measure utility were vaguely formulated, to say the least.

In the tradition of Bentham and within the framework of classical economics, one of the biggest steps forward was taken by Vilfredo Pareto (1906), who showed that only a very weak theory of measurement was needed for the classical theory, namely, that the individual or group be able to say which of any two actions or decisions had the greater utility (in terms of its consequences). This ordinal theory of Pareto, which dominated the economic theory of utility from the beginning of the twentieth century to the publication of John von Neumann and Oskar Morgenstern's treatise on the theory of games in 1944, rested squarely on the assumption that the individual who is choosing among alternatives has no uncertainty about the consequences of these alternatives. Once uncertainty in the consequences is admitted, no ordinal theory of decision can be satisfactory. A simple example will suffice to make this fact clear: A typical middle-class member of our society now has insurance coverage for a wide variety of contingencies. In each case the taking out of this insurance depends on a theory of decision that goes beyond ordinal considerations.

Theory of expected utility. The expected utility hypothesis, which apparently was first clearly formulated by Daniel Bernoulli in 1738, is the most important approach that has yet been suggested for making decisions in the context of uncertain outcomes. The central idea is extremely simple: The individual must choose between several possible decisions. The possible decisions may have a variety of consequences, and ordinarily the consequences are not simply determined by the decision taken but are also affected by the present state of affairs, or, as it is often termed, the present state of nature. It is supposed that the individual has a utility function on the possible consequences and that he has a probability function on the possible states of nature which expresses his beliefs about the true state of nature. According to the expected utility hypothesis a decision maker should then select a decision or course of action that maximizes his expected utility. It will perhaps be useful to consider a simple example that illustrates these ideas. Suppose that an individual must decide whether to go in uncertain weather to a special lecture on phenomenology. Let the set S of states of nature have as members the two possible states of raining, s_1, and of not raining, s_2. Let the set C of possible consequences be those of going to the lecture and not being rained on, c_1, of staying home, c_2, and of going to the lecture and being rained on, c_3. The two decisions are going to the lecture, d_1, and not going to the lecture, d_2. Formally, d_1 and d_2 are functions from S to C such that

$$d_1(s_1)=c_3, \quad d_1(s_2)=c_1, \quad d_2(s_1)=d_2(s_2)=c_2.$$

Suppose now that the individual assigns a subjective probability of .4 to s_1 and .6 to s_2 and that he prefers consequence c_1 to c_2 to c_3. It should be evident, as was already remarked, that the merely ordinal preference for c_1 over c_2 over c_3 is insufficient to lead to a rational decision between d_1 and d_2. We must suppose also that the individual assigns numerical values to the consequences; in particular, let his utility function u be such that

$$u(c_1)=10, \quad u(c_2)=5, \quad u(c_3)=-10$$

(and we suppose u is unique up to a choice of unit and zero). Then the expected utility hypothesis leads him to compute the expectation (in the ordinary sense of random variables) for both d_1 and d_2, using the numerical utility function to define the values of the random variables, and then to choose the decision that has the greater expected utility. Let $E(d_1)$ be the expected utility of decision d_1, and similarly for $E(d_2)$. In our particular example the individual finds that

$$E(d_1)=(.4)(-10)+(.6)(10)=2,$$
$$E(d_2)=(.4)(5)+(.6)(5)=5,$$

so he should elect not to go to the lecture; that is, he should take decision d_2.

Utility and probability. A central problem for both normative and descriptive decision theory is to state axioms of behavior that lead to a numerical representation of utility and probability so that decisions are based on maximization of expected utility. A little reflection on this problem suggests two different ways to proceed. One is to attempt to state axioms in such a way that we first obtain a measure of utility, which is then used to obtain a measure of subjective probability. The other approach proceeds in the reverse order: we state axioms that permit us first to obtain a measure of subjective probability, which is then used to measure utility. The earliest approach, that of F. P. Ramsey (1931), follows the first course—that is, utility is measured first. Ramsey's essential idea was to find a random event of subjective probability 1/2, to use this event to determine the utilities of outcomes or consequences, and finally to apply the constructed utility function to measure the subjective probabilities of the states of nature. This approach has been used extensively in descriptive studies of decision theory since 1957.

The approach that begins with a consideration of probability rather than of utility was originated by Bruno de Finetti, although its historical antecedents go back to the famous work of Thomas Bayes (1763, 1764). The most important recent work on these matters is L. J. Savage, *The Foundations of Statistics.* Savage extends de Finetti's ideas by paying greater attention to the behavioral aspects of decisions. He postulates a single primitive relation of weak preference on the set of decisions; it is called a relation of weak preference because the individual may be indifferent about two distinct decisions and not strictly prefer one to the other. Even a rough gloss of Savage's axioms is too technical for the present context. As might be expected, he does require that the relation of preference among decisions be transitive and that it be connected—that is, given any two decisions, one must be weakly preferred to the other.

Criticisms of expected utility theory. From the viewpoint of the general theory of rational decisions, there are two points to be emphasized about the rule enjoining the decision maker to maximize his expected utility. The first is that the adoption of this rule of behavior as an important part of one's concept of rationality does not in any sense commit one to a hedonistic calculus of pleasure, as might be thought if Bentham's definition of utility were too systematically associated with the application of the rule. No material doctrine of pleasure enters in formulating the expected utility theory, and the theory could in principle be adapted without change to a calculus of obligation and a theory of expected obligation. This material indifference means that the theory of expected utility offers a rather incomplete theory of rationality from the standpoint of moral philosophy.

The second point to be made about adopting the rule of maximizing expected utility concerns a charge that the theory is too complete. It is too much, it is said, to demand the existence of a subjective probability distribution representing beliefs about the true state of nature and a utility function on consequences. Decisions, even rational decisions, are taken on the basis of a much less complete analysis of the alternative courses of action. Evaluation of the general merits of this criticism is difficult and will not be gone into thoroughly, but it is important to recognize that a good deal of the modern theoretical literature about decisions made in uncertain situations concentrates on principles other than the Bayesian one of maximizing expected utility. The basic motivation for this work is the recognition that often a decision maker does not have adequate information to assign probabilities to the possible states of nature. This is especially a problem when the uncertainty arises not only from random factors in the environment but also from the more or less rational decisions taken by other people.

Weaker principles. If the decision maker is unable, or unwilling, to act as though he knows the probability of occurrence of each event, then he must invoke some weaker decision principle than the maximization of expected utility. The formulation and mathematical development of such principles is the focus of the theory of games and of much of statistical decision theory, which is a well-developed branch of mathematical statistics.

The simplest and least controversial of these principles is the sure-thing principle. This principle asserts that if two decisions are such that for each possible state of nature the consequences of choosing the first decision are at least as desirable as those of choosing the second, then the first one should be weakly preferred to the second. The obvious central weakness of the sure-thing principle is that it can rarely be applied. In general, neither of two given decisions is better than the other in the sense of the sure-thing principle.

Another thoroughly explored principle is the maximin or minimax principle of von Neumann. Suppose that for each of his possible decisions an individual determines what is the worst (minimum) consequence that can occur. He then selects the decision for which the worst consequence is as good as possible; that is, he selects the decision which has the largest value for its worst consequence. For obvious reasons such a decision is called a maximin decision. (The minimax terminology of von Neumann originates from a slightly different way of formulating the problem—in terms of minimizing the maximum loss instead of, as we have put it here, maximizing the minimum gain.) The famous result of von Neumann is that for a very wide class of two-person, zero-sum games each player has a minimax strategy; moreover, if both players are rational, neither can do better than to adopt his minimax strategy. In this context a two-person, zero-sum game is defined by a set of strategies for each of the two players and a payoff function for any pair of strategies used such that the numerical payoff to one player is the negative of that to the other. On the other hand, for situations that are not gamelike in character the principle underlying maximin decisions is conservative in the extreme. Concern is focused exclusively on the worst possible consequence of any course of action, no matter how improbable that consequence may be. For many practical decisions the maximin principle does not lead to intuitively acceptable results.

A third example of a principle of decision is Savage's principle (1951) of minimizing the maximum regret that can arise from making one decision rather than another. Still another is the concept of equilibrium, particularly as applied to nonzero-sum games. In this case the basic idea is that if a single player changes his strategy and all other players hold to theirs, then any change will make the first player worse off.

Axiomatic decision theory. In view of the difficulty of fixing upon any one principle as clearly satisfactory in all situations, several authors, most notably John Milnor, have attempted an axiomatic approach to a better understanding of what is involved in the concept of a rational decision. The basic idea of this line of attack is to list intuitively appealing criteria that a decision principle should satisfy and then to ask what principles do indeed jointly satisfy the criteria proposed. The results of Milnor's investigation have particular bearing on the remarks made earlier about the indefiniteness at present of the concept of rationality. Milnor proposes nine criteria that any acceptable principle of decision should satisfy. He goes on to show that none of the standard decision principles proposed satisfy all nine. More generally, his results, like those of Russell's paradox for the foundations of set theory, yield an impossibility theorem and show that the naive theory of rationality, like the naive theory of sets, cannot easily be systematically reconstructed.

Randomization. An important concept for the theory of rational decisions appeared with the work of von Neumann and others on optimal strategies in gamelike situations. This was the idea that the most rational decision may be one that has a random component. In general, the minimax strategies for players in a game are probabilistic rather than deterministic in character. Without doubt this is a genuinely new and surprising idea in the theory of rational or prudent behavior. Again, it is a result at variance with naive intuition, which urges us to deliberate and to use all possible information available in making a decision. Unfortunately, the reconciliation of this approach with the Bayesian rule of maximizing expected utility is still far from being reached.

GROUP NORMATIVE THEORY

The table shown earlier lists three disciplines in the quadrant for group normative theory: game theory, welfare economics, and political theory. The relations of game theory to the concept of a rational decision have already been discussed. From the standpoint of decision theory perhaps the most important element is the widening of the concepts of welfare economics to include the more general concepts of social decision appropriate to political theory. The classical central problem of welfare economics has been the Benthamite one of devising and analyzing schemes for the distribution of economic goods. It is now increasingly recognized that the restriction to economic goods can be dropped and that the problem may be regarded as the more general one of deciding social and political policy. The over-all aim of this work is to analyze and propose schemes for making social and political decisions in what seems to be a just and equitable manner.

Arrow's results. As in the case of the normative theory of individual decisions, the results of perhaps the greatest philosophical significance are negative results that call into question the naive concept of rationality as applied to the decision-making procedures of a group. The best-known impossibility theorem in this connection is that of Kenneth J. Arrow, which is concerned with the existence of a just or equitable method of social decision. Arrow presupposes a number of possible social states, with each member of the society having a preference ordering for these states. The problem is to construct an intuitively reasonable social preference ordering from the given individual orderings.

One simple proposal is the method of majority decision. Social state *A* is preferred to social state *B* by the group as a whole if a majority of the members of the group prefer *A* to *B*; otherwise it is not preferred. Unfortunately, there are intuitively desirable axioms that are violated by the method of majority decision. Perhaps the easiest way to illustrate the difficulties is to describe the so-called paradox of voting, which apparently was first noted by E. J. Nanson in 1882. Suppose there are three issues *A*, *B*, and *C* and three people voting on these issues. Let us assume that the first person prefers *A* to *B* to *C*, the second person prefers *B* to *C* to *A*, and the third person prefers *C* to *A* to *B*. The issues are voted on in pairs. It is easily checked that if the first choice is between *A* and *B*, the selected issue will be *C*; if between *A* and *C*, the outcome will be *B*; and if between *B* and *C*, the outcome will be *A*. In other words, the outcome chosen is completely dependent, in this symmetrical situation, on the arbitrary choice of which issues are to be voted on first. That the order of voting on bills and their amendments can seriously affect the outcome is part of the folklore of practical politics and indicates that the paradox of voting reflects a relatively deep problem for any defense of the rationality of simple majority voting.

What Arrow has done is to present four reasonable axioms that any social decision method should satisfy and then to ask if there exist any methods satisfying the axioms. The first axiom postulates a positive association of social and individual values. In particular, if one among alternative social states rises in the ordering of every individual without there being any other change in the orderings, it is natural to postulate that it rises, or at least does not fall, in the social ordering.

The second axiom states the independence of irrelevant alternatives. If, for instance, a set of candidates is being considered for an office and the voters' preferences for these candidates are known, then the removal of one candidate from the list will not affect the relative preferences for the other candidates. It should be emphasized that this postulate takes no account of strategic considerations. Its concern is with the actual preferences of the group members, not with their behavioral use of a strategy in situations where they feel their first choice could not possibly be elected.

The third axiom asserts that the social decision method is not to be imposed. A decision method is said to be imposed when there is some pair of alternative social states *X* and *Y* such that the community can never express its preference for *Y* over *X*, no matter what may be the preferences of all the individuals concerned. Outmoded cultural and religious taboos furnish examples violating this condition.

The fourth axiom asserts that the social decision method shall not be dictatorial; that is, the preferences shall not simply correspond to those of one individual in the social group. Arrow proved that if there is any degree of variety in the individual preference orderings, then there exists no social decision method satisfying the axioms.

Positive group decision principles. Duncan Black's work on the theory of committees and elections shows that simple positive results very close to the framework developed for Arrow's negative results can be established when some fairly sharp restrictions are imposed on the variety of individual preferences. Necessary and sufficient conditions on the group decision function in order that individual preferences may be satisfied by the simple majority decision functions were given by Kenneth O. May in 1952. In general, the negative and positive results on group decision principles would seem to hold promise for the renascence of systematic political theory.

DESCRIPTIVE THEORY

The descriptive theory of decision has less direct philosophical relevance than the normative theory, but a few points may be mentioned. Among descriptive theories the main division is between algebraic and probabilistic theories. The algebraic theories are the natural extensions of the theories discussed earlier to empirical studies of actual behavior. Perhaps the most intensive study has been of the algebraic theory of maximizing expected utility. The postulate involved here is that when one decision has a greater expected utility than another, it is certain which decision the individual will choose.

Probabilistic theories, on the other hand, make this choice a matter of probability rather than a certainty. The probabilistic theories have arisen in a natural way from the familiar psychological observation that in highly similar situations individuals will on one occasion make one choice and on another occasion another choice. Empirical observation of such "inconsistencies" has been the main impetus to the study of probabilistic theories. These theories all assume that when a set X of alternatives is presented, there exists a probability $p(x)$ that any particular member x of X will be chosen. Each of these probabilities is, of course, nonnegative, and the sum of the probabilities over the set X is equal to 1. The theoretical problem is to investigate what mathematical constraints individuals impose on the probabilities beyond those automatically implied by probability theory. It is to be emphasized that the probabilities in question here have a different significance from those involved in the deliberate use of a randomizing device to select a minimax strategy. The probabilities of choice studied in descriptive theories do not arise from deliberate computations on the part of the individual but are characteristic above all of his nonverbalized actual choices.

Although connections between decision theory and learning theory are being explored in the current literature, it is impossible to consider them here. (A probabilistic utility theory, for example, is derived from learning theory in Patrick Suppes, "Behavioristic Foundations of Utility.") Their promise for the future is a stronger psychological foundation for decision theory.

Bibliography

Arrow, Kenneth J., *Social Choice and Individual Values*. New York, 1951; 2d ed., 1964.

Bayes, Thomas, "An Essay towards solving a Problem in the Doctrine of Chances." *Philosophical Transactions of the Royal Society*, Vol. 53 (1764), 370–418. Written in 1763.

Bayes, Thomas, "A demonstration of the second rule in the

essay towards the solution of a Problem in the Doctrine of Chances." *Philosophical Transactions of the Royal Society,* Vol. 54 (1765), 296–325. Written in 1764.

Bentham, Jeremy, *The Principles of Morals and Legislation.* London, 1789.

Bernoulli, Daniel, "Specimen Theoriae Novae de Mensura Sortis." *Commentarii Academiae Scientiarum Imperiales Petropolitanae,* Vol. 5 (1738), 175–192. Translated by L. Sommer in *Econometrica,* Vol. 22 (1954) 23–36.

Black, Duncan, *The Theory of Committees and Elections.* Cambridge, 1958.

Davidson, Donald; Suppes, Patrick; and Siegel, Sidney, *Decision-making: An Experimental Approach.* Stanford, 1957.

Finetti, Bruno de, "La Prévision: Ses Lois logiques, ses sources subjectives." *Annales de l'Institut Henri Poincaré,* Vol. 7 (1937), 1–68. Translated by Henry E. Kyburg, Jr., as "Foresight: Its Logical Laws, Its Subjective Sources" in Henry E. Kyburg, Jr., and Howard E. Smokler, eds., *Studies in Subjective Probability.* New York, 1964. Pp. 93–158.

Luce, R. Duncan, and Raiffa, Howard, *Games and Decisions: Introduction and Critical Survey.* New York, 1957.

Luce, R. Duncan, and Suppes, Patrick, "Preference, Utility, and Subjective Probability," in R. Duncan Luce, Robert R. Bush, and Eugene Galanter, eds., *Handbook of Mathematical Psychology,* Vol. III. New York, 1965.

May, Kenneth O., "A Set of Independent, Necessary and Sufficient Conditions for Simple Majority Decisions." *Econometrica,* Vol. 20 (1952), 680–684.

Milnor, John, "Games Against Nature," in Robert M. Thrall, Clyde H. Coombs, and Robert L. Davis, eds., *Decision Processes.* New York, 1954. Pp. 49–59.

Nanson, E. J., *Transactions and Proceedings of the Royal Society of Victoria,* Vol. 19 (1882), 197–240.

Pareto, Vilfredo, *Manuale d'economia politica.* Milan, 1906.

Ramsey, Frank P., "Truth and Probability," in *The Foundations of Mathematics and Other Logical Essays.* London and New York, 1931. Pp. 156–198.

Savage, Leonard J., "The Theory of Statistical Decision." *Journal of the American Statistical Association,* Vol. 46 (1951), 55–67.

Savage, Leonard J., *The Foundations of Statistics.* New York, 1954.

Suppes, Patrick, "Behavioristic Foundations of Utility." *Econometrica,* Vol. 29 (1961), 186–202.

Von Neumann, John, "Zur Theorie der Gesellschaftsspiele." *Mathematische Annalen,* Vol. 100 (1928), 295–320. Translation in Albert W. Tucker and R. Duncan Luce, eds., *Contributions to the Theory of Games,* Vol. IV. Princeton, 1959. Pp. 13–42.

Von Neumann, John, and Morgenstern, Oskar, *Theory of Games and Economic Behavior.* Princeton, 1944.

PATRICK SUPPES

DEDUCTION. *See* FORMAL SYSTEMS AND THEIR MODELS; LOGIC, MODERN.

DEFINITION. The problems of definition are constantly recurring in philosophical discussion, although there is a widespread tendency to assume that they have been solved. Practically every book on logic has a section on definition in which rules are set down and exercises prescribed for applying the rules, as if the problems were all settled. And yet, paradoxically, no problems of knowledge are less settled than those of definition, and no subject is more in need of a fresh approach. Definition plays a crucial role in every field of inquiry, yet there are few if any philosophical questions about definition (what sort of thing it is, what standards it should satisfy, what kind of knowledge, if any, it conveys) on which logicians and philosophers agree. In view of the importance of the topic and the scope of the disagreement concerning it, an extensive re-examination is justified. In carrying out this conceptual re-examination, this article will summarize the main views of definition that have been advanced, indicate why none of these views does full justice to its subject, and then attempt to show how the partial insights of each might be combined in a new approach.

All the views of definition that have been proposed can be subsumed under three general types of positions, with, needless to say, many different varieties within each type. These three general positions will be called "essentialist," "prescriptive," and "linguistic" types, abbreviated as "E-type," "P-type," and "L-type," respectively. This classification is not intended as a precise historical summary, but merely as a useful schema for stating some of the problems and disputes. Thus, some outstanding philosophers may very clearly belong to one of these types. Others who, for the purposes of this article, are placed in a certain class hold positions varying considerably from the presentation to be given. It must therefore be borne in mind that not all the criticisms that will be made apply to all philosophers included in the class being criticized. Writers whose accounts of definition fall largely under the E-type include Plato, Aristotle, Kant, and Husserl. Those who support P-type views include Pascal, Hobbes, Russell, W. V. Quine, Nelson Goodman, Rudolf Carnap, C. G. Hempel, and most contemporary logicians. Supporters of L-type views include John Stuart Mill (in part), G. E. Moore (in part), Richard Robinson, and most members of the school of linguistic analysis.

According to essentialist views, definitions convey more exact and certain information than is conveyed by descriptive statements. Such information is acquired by an infallible mode of cognition variously called "intellectual vision," "intuition," "reflection," or "conceptual analysis." Prescriptive views agree with essentialism that definitions are incorrigible, but account for their infallibility by denying that they communicate information and by explaining them as symbolic conventions. Although linguistic views agree with essentialism that definitions communicate information, they also agree with prescriptivism in that they reject claims that definitions communicate information that is indubitable. The linguistic position is that definitions are empirical (and therefore corrigible) reports of linguistic behavior.

ESSENTIALISM

An essentialist account was first proposed by Socrates and Plato. Socrates is renowned for having brought attention to the importance of definitions. His favorite type of question, "What does (virtue, justice, etc.) mean?," became the characteristic starting point of philosophical inquiry. But Socrates did not make clear what kind of answer he was looking for. In Plato's *Euthyphro* Socrates is reported to have said that the kind of answer he expected to his question "What is piety?" was one giving an explanation of "the general idea which makes all pious things to be pious" and "a standard to which I may look and by which I may measure actions." He did not explain, however, what he meant by "idea" and "standard" nor how one produces an "idea" or a "standard" when one is defining a term. Richard Robinson, in his book *Plato's Earlier Dialectic* (p. 62), has suggested that the question "What is *X*?" is more ambiguous than Socrates realized and that it may be answered in all sorts of ways, depending on the context in which it is asked.

Plato. Plato's attempts in his later dialogues to explain the meaning of the Socratic question "What is *X*?" constitute the celebrated Theory of Forms, the trademark of Platonic metaphysics and epistemology. In a passage of central importance (***Republic VI***), Plato distinguished two kinds of objects of knowledge (sensible things and forms) and two modes of knowledge (sense perception and intellectual vision). Sensible things are objects of opinion, while abstract forms are objects of philosophical knowledge. Physical objects, shadows, and images are imperfect and ephemeral copies of forms; our perceptual knowledge of them is an inaccurate approximation to our knowledge of their abstract archetypes. Definitions describe forms, and since forms are perfect and unchanging, definitions, when arrived at by the proper procedure, are precise and rigorously certain truths. Empirical statements describe objects of perception and are therefore only more or less reliable approximations to truth.

Models and copies. Plato's analogy between definitions and empirical descriptions—an analogy upon which all E-type theories of definition rest—is supplemented by a second analogy between the relation of a model to a copy and the relation of a definition to an individual predication. This analogy was suggested by Socrates when he asked for "a standard to which I may look and by which I may measure actions." Plato describes the process of coming to know as if it were like the procedure of a craftsman producing a piece of sculpture or a house. The sculpture is a "copy" of the subject who models for it; the house is in one sense a "copy" of the architect's blueprint, in a somewhat different sense a "copy" of a small-scale model, and in still a third sense a "copy" of the idea in the mind of the builder. Plato's frequent references to the arts and crafts in his exploration of conceptual problems indicate that the analogy of the model – copy relation plays a central role in his theory of knowledge.

Thus, Platonic essentialism provides two sets of answers (both of which rest on metaphors) to the questions "What kind of statements are definitions?" "What purpose do they serve?" and "How are they to be judged as good or bad?" It suggests primarily that definitions are descriptions of objects that are somehow analogous to tables, chairs, and other familiar things, that these definitions serve the purpose of providing descriptive information about their objects; and that they are confirmed by a mode of cognition somehow analogous to sense perception, yet independent of the sensory organs. Secondarily, Platonic essentialism specifies the relation between the objects of definitions and those of empirical descriptions by characterizing the former as models of which the latter are "copies."

Adequacy of the model metaphor. Metaphors are apt or inapt, illuminating or misleading, according to two criteria: (1) the number and importance of the known points of resemblance between the things compared and (2) the number and importance of previously unnoted facts suggested by the metaphor. To what extent does Plato's metaphor of the unseen model satisfy these criteria?

The primary term of comparison in Plato's metaphor is the abstract form or universal that a definition allegedly describes. The secondary term is the model for a painting or, alternatively, a tailor's pattern. As the painter looks to his model and the tailor to his pattern, the philosopher can look to the forms for the specifications that identify things as instances of one class rather than another, as well as for exact information about the properties of that class.

What are the known points of resemblance between forms and models, on which this metaphor is grounded? Merely to ask this question is already to see that the metaphor is defective from the start, since there cannot possibly be *any* literal points of comparison. The Platonic forms, unlike models and patterns, have no observable properties by virtue of which they can be said to "resemble" anything at all. Thus, if the model metaphor has any value, it must lie entirely in what the metaphor suggests, rather than in its literal grounds.

Primarily, the model metaphor suggests that definitions and their corollaries constitute all there is to knowledge. Whenever a question of fact or of judgment is raised in the Platonic dialogues, it is treated as a problem of definition. For example, when, in the *Euthyphro,* Socrates and Euthyphro argue about the propriety of a son's prosecuting his father for murder, Socrates proceeds as though the issue could be settled by arriving at a clear definition of piety—as though one could then look at the definition, look at the action, and decide whether they coincide. We can identify a portrait or a garment by comparing it with its model or its pattern, but we cannot classify and judge an action in the same way. Description and evaluation are seldom matters of identification by comparison with a pattern. In this respect Plato's essentialism is misleading rather than illuminating.

The metaphor of the unseen model also suggests that definitions provide us with precise and rigorous knowledge in the way that blueprints make possible a high degree of uniformity and precision in productive arts such as architecture. But definitions increase precision only when they change the original meanings of words for technical purposes. Generally speaking, a definition can be no more precise than the concept it defines, at the risk of shifting to a different concept. Our concept of what constitutes an adult is vague; if we try to make it precise by specifying an exact age at which childhood is divided from adulthood, we merely lose sight of what we started out to talk about by replacing the concept of maturity with that of having passed a certain birthday.

The model metaphor is not entirely misleading; it suggests at least one genuine resemblance between the terms it compares. The relation between definitions and empirical descriptions is, in one respect, rather similar to the relation between portraits and their models. We judge a portrait (to some extent) by noting whether the portrait looks like the model; we verify the empirical description "This table is round" by looking at the table to see whether it has the properties definitive of tables and of roundness. But if we are asked, "Is that person a good model?" or "Is that definition a good definition?" we cannot look toward anything of which the model is himself a portrait, and we cannot look at a definitional form of which the particular definition is itself an instance. Definitions are not evaluated in the same way as empirical descriptions, just as models are not judged in the same way as their portraits. Thus the analogy between definitions and empirical descriptions from which Platonic essentialism starts eventually contradicts itself.

Aristotle. One can find in Aristotle's works anticipations of every later theory of definition, but he gave high priority to his own brand of essentialism, whereby he explained the nature of "real" as distinguished from "nominal" (that is, prescriptive or linguistic) definition. Like Plato, Aristotle stressed the similarity between definitions and statements of fact, and he assumed that definitions convey precise and certain information. But Aristotle employed a different supporting metaphor to explain the special nature of definitions. The most noteworthy feature of his many discussions of definition is his insistence that a real definition should provide a causal explanation of the thing defined. In the *Physics,* Aristotle distinguished four types of causes—formal, material, final, and efficient. He characterized the first three types as "internal," while efficient causes are (usually) "external" to their effects. Internal causes are not available to public inspection, but must be discovered in abstract intuition. The causal explanation provided by a real definition is in terms of one or more of these three internal types of cause.

Definition and causality. It is not easy to explain just what Aristotle meant by "internal cause." Part of what he seems to have meant is that, unlike "incidental" causes, internal causes are necessary for their effects. But it is by no means clear what sense of necessity is involved in this instance. To explain this necessity as causal would be a case of circular reasoning. On the other hand, to say that the necessity is logical seems only another way of saying that the effect is definable in terms of its cause, which is again circular reasoning. As an example of a causal definition, Aristotle defined a lunar eclipse as the privation of the moon's light because of the interposition of the earth between the moon and the sun (*Posterior Analytics* 90a). This example confirms the suggestion that for something to be an internal causal is for it to be part of a definition. But the difficulty then arises that definition has been explained by internal causality, internal causality by necessity, and necessity by definition. Thus, Aristotle's eclipse leaves us in the dark about definition.

Classification and explanation. The trouble is that the idea of internal causality is a metaphor. An essential cause is not "internal" to the thing defined as a kernel is inside a nut, but only metaphorically "inside."

This metaphor suggests two important but dubious principles: that scientific knowledge consists entirely of definitions and their corollaries and that systematic classification is identical with theoretical explanation. If to define a term is, at the same time, to provide a causal explanation of what it denotes and if the classification of a thing in terms of its species and differentia is sufficient for deducing the laws of its behavior, then the work of scientific inquiry is completed when a comprehensive system of classification has been constructed. Thus, Aristotle wrote in the *Posterior Analytics* (90b) that "Scientific knowledge is judgment about things that are universal and necessary, that the conclusions of demonstration *and all scientific knowledge* follow from the first principles" and that "the first principles of demonstration are definitions" (italics added).

That scientific knowledge is not entirely derivable from a set of definitions and that systematic classification is only one small aspect of scientific procedure need hardly be argued. Aristotelian concepts of causality and explanation have been almost completely expunged from modern science, and causes are conceived of in quite different ways. But it is not the archaic character of Aristotle's use of "cause" and "explanation" that concerns us here. It is largely a matter of terminological convenience whether we continue to use these words in the Aristotelian manner or confine them to the procedures of modern physical science. In regard to the problem of clarifying the functions and criteria of definitions, however, Aristotle's claim that definitions reveal the internal causes of their definienda must be criticized not as a false, but as a misleading, metaphor, for it dissolves the very distinctions which it is intended to explain—namely, the distinction between definitions and empirical statements of fact, that between the method of evaluating definitions and the method of confirming factual hypotheses, and that between the distinctive functions of definition and the general aims of scientific inquiry.

Ideas and concepts. A third metaphor that has been employed in the support of E-type views of definition originated in Cartesian dualism. Descartes himself leaned toward a prescriptive account of definition, which will be considered later. But Locke, Kant, Husserl, and other philosophers who accepted the Cartesian division between the "inner world" of the mind and the "outer world" of physical events took the essentialist position that philosophical inquiry should provide information about a special set of objects ("ideas" for Locke, Hume, and Husserl; "concepts" for Kant, Heinrich Rickert, and G. E. Moore) discoverable by an infallible mode of cognition ("reflection" for Locke and Husserl; "analysis" for Hume, Kant, Rickert, and Moore).

According to Locke, the outer world of material objects and their motions is describable by the laws of physics, while the inner world of ideas is describable by the laws of psychology that are discovered by reflection on the contents of the mind. These contents are simple and complex ideas; the task of philosophy is to analyze complex ideas into their simple elements and to describe their mode of combination.

Kant distinguished between "analytical" and "synthetic" definitions, regarding the former as the identification of the simple elements (predicates) out of which concepts are formed by the understanding and the latter as the formation of rules of serial order that provide the synthetic a priori postulates of mathematics and physics.

The philosophers under consideration, like their predecessors, assumed that definitions convey knowledge of objects (ideas, images, essences, concepts, or meanings) whose special nature guarantees precision and certainty and that this remarkable kind of knowledge is acquired through a special mode of cognition (reflection, introspection, intuition, or conceptual analysis). The literal content of the private-world metaphor thus seems to be identical with that of the essentialist metaphors already considered. The differences between the private-world and essentialist metaphors (other than terminological ones) must be sought in the suggestive implications of the metaphor. But there is an important difference between philosophers such as Locke, Hume, and Husserl, who reserve the word "definition" for conventions of word usage and do not consider their introspective analyses of ideas to be definitions, and those such as Kant, Rickert, and C. I. Lewis, who regard philosophical definitions as products of conceptual analysis.

Both groups employ the Aristotelian distinction between real and nominal definitions, except that members of the first group avoid calling the results of their introspective studies "definitions" because they think of them as descriptions of the workings of the mind analogous to descriptions of a clock that has been taken apart for inspection. They think of the special mode of cognition by means of which they discover how simple ideas are organized into complex ideas as inner vision or grasp, which is analogous to sight and touch. But members of the more abstractly minded group compare the special faculty by which real (or analytic or explicative) definitions are discovered to the experience (familiar to logicians and mathematicians) of recognizing logical relation, rather than comparing it to any type of sense perception. They speak of "understanding the meanings of words," of "logical analysis," of "understanding what is contained in a concept," rather than of seeing or grasping the "contents of the mind." There are, then, two kinds of world imagined by these theorists: a world of privately visible or tangible ideas, sense data, secondary qualities, and so forth and a world of abstract concepts or meanings. Some, like Kant, Husserl, and, most systematically, C. I. Lewis, posit both kinds of worlds.

What then do these two metaphors suggest, and how illuminating are their implications? The metaphor of the private world of sense data that is allegedly described by definitions of complex ideas suggests that such definitions, like reports of hallucinations, dreams, and other private experiences, must be taken at face value (provided that they are sincerely and consistently expressed), since they cannot be checked by public observation. This would account for the unchallengeable character of definitions and their analytic corollaries, in contrast to the corrigibility of empirical statements. But this view deprives definitions of any claim to objective validity and entails that every person has a right to his own definitions, in the same way that everyone has a right to his own dreams.

The metaphor of the world of concepts and meanings also attributes a self-certifying character to definitions but fares better with respect to the common-sense fact that we balk at some definitions and accept others—for the recognition of logical relations, no matter how intuitive, is a socially shared experience. We immediately and privately understand, see, or grasp that a statement of the form $P \cdot Q$ implies a statement of the form Q, but we can also argue the fact and summon evidence (in the form of postulates of a logical system) to prove it. But this metaphor, which of all those we have considered comes closest to not being a metaphor at all and blends imperceptibly into a prescriptive concept of definition, suggests both too much and too little. It suggests that definitions are logical truths and possess logical certainty. But although some definitions are worse than others, all logical truths are normatively equal. Moreover, the metaphor fails to indicate how definitions can be evaluated other than by their formal consistency (the standard by which we confirm a system of logical truths). Yet a definition of a cow as a three-legged animal would be universally rejected on grounds having nothing to do with inconsistency. The denial of a logical truth can be shown to involve a contradiction, but the denial of a definition leads to contradiction only if one has already accepted the definition. Although consistency is a sufficient condition for a system of logical truths, it is merely a necessary condition for sound definitions; yet no additional conditions are provided by logistic phenomenalism.

PRESCRIPTIVISM

E-type views claim that definitions are statements and that they make assertions that can be pronounced true or false. Essentialists, however, have difficulty explaining how and why definitions differ from ordinary statements of fact, and hence they fall back on metaphors. P-type theories avoid this trouble by denying that definitions are statements of any kind. The prescriptivist assimilates definitions to imperative sentences rather than to declarative sentences and endows them with the function of syntactic or semantic rules for prescribing linguistic operations.

There are two main varieties of prescriptivism. The nominalist variety explains definitions as semantic rules for assigning names to objects, while the formalist variety regards definitions as syntactic rules for abbreviating strings of symbols. P-type views of definition can be traced back to the Greek Sophists and Skeptics, but this article will concentrate on the modern sources of these views. The rebirth of science in the seventeenth century was accompanied by a sweeping rejection of medieval thought, in particular the medieval concept of definition as the penetration by metaphysical intuition into a realm of changeless forms. The nominalist theories of language employed by Sophist and Cynic contemporaries of Plato to undermine belief in the objectivity of knowledge, and again by the more radical medieval Scholastics to subvert the control of theology over science, became, in the seventeenth century, a cornerstone of the reconstruction of knowledge on a new scientific foundation.

Seventeenth-century writings on definition are not entirely free of the influence of classical essentialism. Seventeenth-century prescriptive theories of definition try to avoid the obscurities of essentialism by repudiating the informative role of definitions, but they cannot provide adequate criteria for distinguishing good definitions from bad without presupposing some sort of informative role for them.

Nominalism. For Bacon and Hobbes, definitions possessed a therapeutic function, as a means of clearing up or avoiding ambiguous, vague, and obscure language. Regarding semantic confusion as the main source of intellectual trouble, they proposed to clear the way for a new system of knowledge by subjecting existing concepts to the test of definitional reduction to observable and measurable properties. Definition was thus a surgical knife for cutting away metaphysical encrustations, as described by Bacon in paragraph 59 of the *Novum Organum:*

> But the idols of the market-place are the most troublesome of all: idols which have crept into the understanding through the alliances of word and names, and this it is that has rendered philosophy and the sciences sophistical and inactive. Whence it comes to pass that the high and formal discussions of learned men end oftentimes in disputes about words and names: with which it would be more prudent to begin, and so by means of definitions reduce them to order.

Thomas Hobbes also stressed the clarifying role of definitions, taking geometry as his model. In the *Leviathan* he wrote:

> Seeing then that truth consists in the right ordering of names in our affirmations, a man that seeketh precise truth had need to remember what every name he useth stands for . . . or else he will find himself entangled in ffords as a bird in lime twigs. And therefore in geometry, which is the only science which it hath pleased God hitherto to bestow on mankind, men begin at settling the significations of their words: which settling of significations they call *definitions,* and place them in the beginning of their reckoning.

Definitions thus clear up ambiguities and "settle significations," rather than communicate information about a realm of essences. They are introduced at the beginning of inquiry, as in geometry, rather than at the culmination of inquiry, as in metaphysics and Aristotelian natural science.

According to Hobbes, all knowledge consists in the "right ordering of names in affirmation." A proposition connects one name to another, and an inference adds or subtracts one proposition from another. The structure of scientific thought thus maps the structure of the physical world. It would seem then that, for Hobbes, all scientific knowledge is derivable from definitions. Yet Hobbes also stressed the role of perception in knowledge. The solution to this paradox lies in Hobbes's conception of naming. All inquiry is deductive except for the assignment of names to things, and it is to the assignment of names that we must look for the empirical sources of knowledge. But it follows that definitions as assignments of names must be as informative for Hobbes as they are for Plato or Aristotle. This conclusion leads to a further paradox, for, according to Hobbes, definitions provide no information at all; they express conventional decisions to use particular signs as names of particular objects.

There is an ambiguity in Hobbes's account of definitions that must hamper any attempt to reduce definitions to assignments of names. In order to make definitions entail all the propositions of scientific knowledge, Hobbes had to include, in the notion of naming, all the cognitive functions that we ordinarily distinguish from naming. He first compared the highly abstract and sophisticated definitions of concepts in mathematics and natural science to simple naming procedures such as baptism. Then, in order to account for the conspicuous differences between the two kinds of procedures, he was compelled to reinject into the notion of naming the very distinctions he set out to eliminate. The reduction of definitions to assignments of names only *appears* to solve the problem of whether definitions are informative: It first suggests that definitions are as arbitrary as acts of naming and then suggests that naming is, after all, not always arbitrary.

Early formalism. Although the language used by the Cartesians of the seventeenth century in discussing definitions was similar to that of Bacon and Hobbes, their emphasis and direction of interest was different. Bacon and Hobbes were primarily concerned with the role of definitions in achieving semantic clarity, the Cartesians were more interested in the role of definitions in deductive inference. They developed a conception of definitions as theoretically dispensable abbreviations whose value lies solely in the notational economy they make possible. Cartesian references to "names" are rather misleading since, unlike Hobbes, the Cartesians did not regard assignment of names as the initial and fundamental process of inquiry from which the rest of knowledge is derived. This role was taken over by axioms and postulates which relate "simple" (i.e., indefinable) terms to each other, definitions then being introduced as rules for substituting brief expressions for logical complexes of simple terms.

Descartes did not give much attention to the subject of definition. In rejecting classical syllogistic logic as the framework of scientific inference, he abandoned the emphasis on terms or classes as the basic units of inference in favor of propositional units. The simplest inference became, for Descartes, the intuitive recognition of the implication of one proposition by another. Consequently, postulates replaced definitions as the foundation of deductive science, and essential definitions ceased to represent the highest goal of knowledge.

Pascal's analysis of the nature and function of definitions made explicit the view of definition implicit in Descartes's theory of knowledge. The main elements of Pascal's discussion are formalistic. However, it is not free of ambiguity with respect to the purely notational role of definitions as against the informative role ascribed to them by essentialists.

Pascal's theory of definition is expounded in a brief essay, *De l'Esprit géométrique* (*Oeuvres,* 14 vols., Léon Brunschvicg and E. Boutroux, eds., Paris, 1904–1914). He began by distinguishing two types of definition, *définitions de nom,* which he claimed to be the only type appropriate in science, and an unnamed type which seems to be what Aristotle called "real," the type favored by essentialists, about which he thereafter says nothing more.

Définitions de nom are said to be "mere impositions of names upon things that have been clearly indicated in perfectly intelligible terms," as, for example, the definition of "even number" as "number that can be divided by two without remainder." Such definitions, Pascal claimed, are conventional labels that need have nothing in common with the things they name. They communicate no information about their *nominata*, expressing merely the decision of the writer to use them in the prescribed manner. The sole limitation on *définitions de nom* is that they be internally and mutually consistent.

When he discussed the methodology of definition, Pascal no longer regarded the relation between language and reality as purely conventional. We must make sure "not to define things that are clear and are understood by everyone." Geometry provides the model for definitional procedure. "It does not define such things as *space, time, motion, number, equality* . . . because these terms so naturally designate the things to which they refer, for those who understand the language, that the intended clarification would be more likely to obscure them than to instruct." One might think that, in saying "space naturally designates" its referent, Pascal meant that the word "space" is so familiar that everyone understands what it signifies. But why, then, should he interdict any definition of "space"? If definitions are notational conventions, there could be no objection to stipulating a new use of the word. Indeed, the ordinary use of "space" is quite different from its technical use in mathematics. Why, then, is it improper to define either the ordinary or the mathematical use? Surely, Pascal was not thinking of the word "space," but of space itself as an irreducible entity that cannot be analyzed into simpler components, and if so, then he was thinking of definition not as a notational convenience, but as an informative mode of analysis.

The Cartesian theory of knowledge by which Pascal was guided conceives of the world as a system of elements combined according to mathematical laws to form complex objects and events. While Descartes stressed the analytical reduction of complex propositions to simple ones (i.e., axioms), Pascal joined definitions to axioms as the basis from which the deductive reconstruction of science should start. But common to all the Cartesians is the assumption that knowledge is a mathematical mapping of the structure of nature. In the light of this epistemological atomism, the conventional character attributed to definitions contrasts sharply with the requirement that they correspond to an antecedent natural order—a requirement that leads back to essentialism.

Modern formalism. The formalistic conception of definitions as rules of notational abbreviation was only vaguely anticipated by seventeenth-century philosophers, who failed to separate this purely syntactic procedure from epistemological considerations such as mapping the order of nature. Only in recent times have formalistic discussions of definition been purified of epistemological assumptions, by (among others) Russell, Whitehead, W. V. Quine, Rudolf Carnap, C. G. Hempel, and Nelson Goodman. But it remains doubtful whether this purely formalistic view either is or can be consistently maintained.

Russell and Whitehead, in *Principia Mathematica* (Vol. I, p. 11), define a definition as follows:

> A definition is a declaration that a certain newly introduced symbol or combination of symbols is to mean the same as a certain other combination of symbols of which the meaning is already known . . . . It is to be observed that a definition is, strictly speaking, no part of the subject in which it occurs. For a definition is concerned wholly with the symbols, not with what they symbolize. Moreover, it is not true or false, being the expression of a volition, not of a proposition.

This characterization of definition is not consistently syntactical. It defines "definition" in terms of sameness of meaning, while claiming that a definition "is concerned wholly with the symbols, not with what they symbolize." Later in the same passage, Russell and Whitehead declare:

> In spite of the fact that definitions are theoretically superfluous, it is nevertheless true that they often convey more important information than is contained in the propositions in which they are used. This arises from two causes. First, a definition usually implies that the *definiens* is worthy of careful consideration. . . . Secondly, when what is defined is . . . something already familiar . . . , the definition contains an analysis of a common idea. (*Ibid.*, p. 12)

The first and last sentence in the passage above express a nonsyntactical attitude toward definitions. Definitions turn out to be highly informative, and we seem to have returned to an essentialist view of the matter. But a further qualification has been attached, namely, "when what is defined is . . . something already familiar." In fact, two types of definition are being considered, one being a rule of notational abbreviation and the other an "analysis of an idea." But if some definitions are "analyses of ideas" and are highly informative, then these are the important kinds of definitions, and the formalist view proclaimed at the outset loses its force.

Similar difficulties attend the efforts of other modern logicians to deal with the problem of definition from a purely formal point of view. Thus, W. V. Quine, after asserting that "a definition is a convention of notational abbreviation," qualified his statement as follows:

> Although signs introduced by definition are formally arbitrary, more than such arbitrary notational convention is involved in questions of definability; otherwise any expression might be said to be definable on the basis of any expressions whatever. . . . To be satisfactory . . . a definition . . . not only must fulfill the formal requirement of unambiguous eliminability, but must also conform to the traditional usage in question. ("Truth by Convention," in H. Feigl and W. Sellars, eds., *Readings in Philosophical Analysis*, New York, 1949, p. 252)

Nelson Goodman took the same position and fell into the same difficulties:

> In a constructional system . . . most of the definitions are introduced for explanatory purposes. . . . In a formal system considered apart from its interpretation, any such definitional formula has the formal status of a

> convention of notational interchangeability once it is adopted; but the terms employed are ordinarily selected according to their usage, and the correctness of the interpreted definition is legitimately testable by examination of that usage. (*The Structure of Appearance*, p. 3)

In common with many other logicians, Quine and Goodman distinguish between the function of definitions "in a formal system" and their function when the system is interpreted—that is, when definite meanings are assigned to the symbols of the system. But this distinction overlooks the fact that from a purely formal standpoint, there is no such thing as a definition at all. Before it is interpreted, the formula which we interpret as a definition is just a string of marks. From a "purely formal standpoint," not only is there no difference between a definition and a notational abbreviation, but there is no difference between a definition and *any* other kind of formula. There are only various strings of marks, some permitted by the rules of formation of the system, others excluded by these rules. Consequently, the distinction made by Quine and Goodman between definitions in a formal system and those in an interpreted system is seriously misleading.

Rudolf Carnap and C. G. Hempel have tried to clarify the difference between informative definitions and mere notational abbreviations by distinguishing between "old" and "new" concepts. Definitions of old concepts are called "explications" by Carnap and "rational reconstructions" by Hempel, while both call definitions of new concepts "notational conventions." When we are "explicating" or "reconstructing" a concept, our definitions are subject to evaluation by the criteria of conformity to usage and increase of precision (Rudolf Carnap, *The Logical Syntax of Language*, p. 23). When definitions are introduced solely for the purpose of abbreviation, only the criterion of consistency applies. One must therefore wonder why Carnap and Hempel should bother to call notational abbreviations "definitions," since they have nothing whatever in common with explications.

Perhaps the answer to this question lies in the logical difficulties lurking within the notion of explication. What does it mean to "reconstruct" or "explicate" a concept, and what precisely is the difference between "old" and "new" concepts? If definitions of old concepts must conform to established usage, are they not true or false statements about language usage, in which case the distinction between definitions and empirical statements disappears? These problems lead naturally into the linguistic theory of definition.

LINGUISTIC THEORIES

Anticipations of a linguistic view of definition may be found in classical writings (for example, in Aristotle's discussion of "nominal definition") and in the nominalist and formalist positions previously considered. But while early nominalism, attempted to reduce all the varied functions of words to that of proper names and thus to reduce meaning to the arbitrary assignment of a name to an object, formalism added linguistic considerations as an inessential afterthought. The first step from nominalism to an L-type view proper was taken by John Stuart Mill, although his formulations are permeated with elements of both nominalism and essentialism. A further step was taken by G. E. Moore, but Moore's discussion also contains a heavy strain of essentialism. The clearest formulation of the lingustic view was provided by Richard Robinson in his book *Definition*, which has the distinction of being the only book in the English language devoted to this subject.

In his *System of Logic*, J. S. Mill defined "definition" as follows: "The simplest and most correct notion of a Definition is, a proposition declaratory of the meaning of a word: namely, either the meaning which it bears in common acceptation, or that which the speaker or writer . . . intends to annex to it" (10th ed., p. 86).

Mill then explained that a definition is a "verbal proposition" that "adds no information to that which was already possessed by all who understood the name (defined)"—a tautology that Mill mistook for an important observation. But, unlike the thoroughgoing prescriptivist, Mill did not regard definitions as purely conventional stipulations, at least insofar as terms in general use are concerned:

> It would, however, be a complete misunderstanding of the proper office of the logician in dealing with terms already in use, if we were to think that because a name has not at present an ascertained connotation, it is competent to anyone to give it such a connotation at his own choice. The meaning of a term actually in use is not an arbitrary quantity to be fixed, but an unknown quantity to be sought. (*Ibid.*, p. 91)

At this point, Mill conceded that some definitions are not mere "declarations" but convey some kind of information about "unknown quantities to be sought." Mill gave two reasons for this departure from prescriptivism. The first consideration involves him in a tug of war between nominalist and linguistic theories. "Since names and their significations are entirely arbitrary, such (verbal) propositions are not, strictly speaking, susceptible of truth or falsity, but only of conformity or disconformity to usage or convention; and all the proof they are capable of is proof of usage" (*ibid.*, p. 92).

In this instance, Mill first denied and then asserted that definitions are informative. If "all the proof they are capable of is proof of usage," then they *are* capable of proof after all, despite his initial disclaimer of this possibility.

Mill's second reason for ascribing at least a quasi-informative function to some definitions resembles, to some extent, the phenomenalist conception of definition as analysis of complex ideas into simple constituents. Mill wrote:

> A name, whether concrete or abstract, admits of definition, provided we are able to analyze, that is, to distinguish into parts, the attribute or set of attributes which constitutes the meaning both of the name and of the corresponding abstract. . . . We thus see that to frame a good definition of a name in use is not a matter of choice but of discussion . . . not merely respecting the usage of language, but respecting the properties of things, and even the origin of these properties. (*Ibid.*, p. 91)

The source of Mill's shifts of emphasis and inconsistencies lies in the ambiguity of his notion of meaning. At times he identified the meaning of a term with the object it "names," at other times with the customary usage of the word, and at still other times with an abstract object or "idea" capable of being divided into simpler parts. Thus, depending on which conception of meaning he had in mind, he thought of a definition as the stipulation of a name, a report of linguisitc usage, or the analysis of a complex idea into its constituent parts.

G. E. Moore. The extent to which G. E. Moore's approach to definitions can properly be called "linguistic" is debatable. Moore placed less stress on the linguistic aspect of definition than later philosophers such as Ryle, Strawson, and Robinson, who were influenced by Moore's analytical method. For Moore, as for Socrates, the clarification of language was only a means toward the discovery of deeper philosophical truths. But there can be no doubt that Moore inspired others to concern themselves with language and that his painstaking attention to the nuances of words was the most distinctive feature of his work.

In his *Principia Ethica,* Moore characterized "analytical" definitions (the kind produced by philosophical analysis) as follows: "Definitions of the kind that I was asking for, definitions which describe the real nature of the object or notion denoted by a word and which do not merely tell us what the word is used to mean, are only possible when the object or notion is complex" (p. 7).

In order to indicate the kind of descriptive information that he expected philosophical definitions to provide, Moore offered an example that is as misleading as it is famous: "When we say . . . 'The definition of horse is "a hoofed quadruped of the genus Equus"' . . . we may mean that a certain object, which we all of us know, is composed in a certain manner: that it has four legs, a head, a heart, a liver, etc., all of them arranged in definite relations to one another" (*ibid.,* p. 8).

This passage is curious; it suggests that an analytical definition lists the physical parts of the thing defined. The example, however, gives the species and differentia of the class of horses but does *not* mention any physical parts. In commenting on this passage in his *Reunion in Philosophy* (p. 184), Morton White has observed that Moore shifted inadvertently from logical to physical complexity.

In later writings, Moore maintained that concepts are the proper subject matter of definition. "To define a concept," he wrote, "is the same thing as to give an analysis of it" ("Reply to My Critics," in *The Philosophy of G. E. Moore,* pp. 664–665). It is not easy to tell just what Moore meant by "concept analysis." For the analysis of a concept, he offered three criteria which add up to the relation of synonymity of expressions. Thus, despite his explicit effort to find an informative function for definitions that goes beyond the explanation of how words are used, it is not unreasonable to conclude that all that his obscure notion of "analyzing a concept" finally comes to is linguistic clarification. In denying that analytic definitions "merely tell us what the word is used to mean," Moore was rejecting the view that definitions are generalizations about common usage and suggesting that they have a more explanatory function. But he never made clear what that function is.

In the only full-length volume in English devoted to the study of definition, Richard Robinson formulated a purely linguistic account of definitions as reports of word usage. But he thought it necessary to supplement his main view with a "stipulative," or prescriptive, account. The reasons for his vacillation are that reports of usage are empirical generalizations, while definitions are, if acceptable at all, necessary truths, and that stipulations are uninformative, while definitions are highly informative. Thus, neither the linguistic nor the prescriptive interpretation accounts for all features of definitions. But the mere juxtaposition of the two can hardly overcome the defects of each taken separately.

A PRAGMATIC–CONTEXTUAL APPROACH

Linguistic theories of definition brought needed attention to the close relation between definitions and the meanings of words, but they erred in identifying meanings either with objects or concepts allegedly denoted by words or with linguistic usage. A correct theory of definition would unite the partial insights of E-type, P-type, and L-type views without relying on misleading metaphors, denying the obvious informative value of definitions, or reducing definitions to historical reports of linguistic behavior.

Why should essentialists and linguistic philosophers claim that definitions convey knowledge, while prescriptivists deny that they do? In some sense of the word "knowledge," anyone would agree that definitions communicate knowledge. The problem is to identify a special sense of "knowledge" that is appropriate to definitions but does not require us to postulate obscure essences or to reduce definitions to historical reports. This special kind of knowledge may be knowledge of how to use words effectively. Use, unlike usage, is functional. As Gilbert Ryle has observed, there are misuses and ineffective uses, but there is no such thing as a misusage or ineffective usage ("Ordinary Language," in *Philosophical Review,* Vol. 42 1953). Usage is what people *happen* to do with words and is determined by habits, while use is what *should* be done with words and is governed by rules. To explain the right use of a word, as distinct from merely reporting its usage, a definition must give the rules that guide us in using it. In this respect definitions are rules, rather than descriptions or reports.

All three traditional theories of definition assume, mistakenly, that if definitions convey knowledge, then the knowledge they convey is of the same type as that conveyed by ordinary statements of fact. Essentialists conclude that the knowledge conveyed by definitions is descriptive knowledge of essences, linguistic philosophers conclude that it is descriptive knowledge of language usage, while prescriptivists maintain that definitions do not convey knowledge of any kind. There has been a strikingly similar three-way dispute over the status of value judgments: nonnaturalists hold that value judgments convey knowledge of an abstract realm of "values"; naturalists maintain that they convey knowledge of observable causal relations; and emotivists assert that they convey no knowledge whatsoever. Arguments about whether definitions and value judgments convey true or false information mistakenly presuppose that all information must be of the descriptive type, thus overlooking the fact that cookbooks, military manuals, Sunday sermons, and do-it-yourself instruction sheets all convey, in various ways, the kind of normative information that Ryle has called "knowledge-how" in *The Concept of Mind* (Ch. 2). Practical or ethical advice may be regarded as stating rules that inform us how to act effectively, while definitions provide rules that inform us how to speak or write effectively. In either case it may be said that the information conveyed is subject to being evaluated as good or bad, but not to being verified as true or false.

Applications of a contextualist view. The three views of definition distinguished above fail to provide adequate criteria for distinguishing good definitions from bad ones. The assume that the criteria of a good definition can be stated independently of the specific context in which the definition is offered and the purpose it is intended to serve. But no brief list of criteria can be given that would enable us to judge at sight whether a definition is adequate. The most we can do on a general level is to classify the kinds of rules of use that definitions provide, the kinds of discursive purposes they serve, and to say generally that definitions are good if and only if they serve the purpose for which they are intended.

Thus, an evaluation of a definition must begin with the identification of the point or purpose of the definition, and this requires knowledge of the discursive situation in which the need for the definition arises. We use words to incite ourselves and others to action, to express and share emotions, to draw attention to things, to memorize, to make inferences, to evoke and enjoy images, to perform ceremonies, to teach, to exercise, and to show off. It is when we are unsure of the most effective use of an expression for one of these purposes, that we seek a definition.

Linguistic rules. Rules governing the uses of words can be sorted into three main types: (1) referring rules, which aid us in identifying the things or situations to which a word may be applied; (2) syntactical rules, which govern the ways in which a word may be combined with other words to form phrases and sentences; and (3) discursive rules (the most difficult to formulate), which indicate when we may use language metaphorically (as in poetry) and when we must use it literally (as in science), as well as indicating differences of category or logical type (for example, the rule that one cannot predicate human qualities such as intelligence of inanimate things such as machines) and indicating when a word should be used in one sense rather than another (for example, "space" in mathematics as distinguished from physics). Discursive rules are the genuinely philosophical rules.

Rules for defining. The practical value of any account of the nature of definition is to be found in the clarity of the standards it provides for judging when a definition is good or bad. How does the pragmatic–contextualist account fare in this respect?

A number of rules of thumb for evaluating definitions have become canonical in the literature on the subject despite the fact that they make no clear sense in terms of any of the traditional views. The following rules can be found in practically every textbook on logic. They were first suggested by Aristotle in his *Topica* and have survived without change by sheer weight of tradition:

(1) A definition should give the essence or nature of the thing defined, rather than its accidental properties.

(2) A definition should give the genus and differentia of the thing defined.

(3) One should not define by synonyms.

(4) A definition should be concise.

(5) One should not define by metaphors.

(6) One should not define by negative terms or by correlative terms (e.g., one should not define north as opposite of south, or parent as a person with one or more children).

Significance of the rules. Rule 1, which makes sense only according to the essentialist theory, is nevertheless accepted by many writers who hold a prescriptive or linguistic view of definition, although these writers usually mean that a definition should indicate the properties that *define* the meaning of the term in question rather than those that just happen to hold true of the objects to which the term applies. But in such a case, the rule is vacuous; it asserts only that a definition should define rather than describe.

Rule 2 deserves its high status only if one accepts Aristotle's extension of biological classification to metaphysics, but it retains a limited value when it is reinterpreted in linguistic terms. We may understand "genus" to mean what Ryle has called the logical grammar of a term. The term defined need not be the name of any natural species or, for that matter, any object whatsoever. In defining words like "function," we do not identify a class of objects. We define a function as a certain type of relation, thus indicating that whatever can be said about relations in general can also be said about functions in particular. We thus provide a rule of syntax governing the word "function," indicating with what other words it may be combined. The differentia of function—namely, that the relation is many–one between two variables—is a referring rule (criterion of identification) that helps us to identify the situations or formulas to which the term "function" may be applied. But it is wrong to think that the genus and differentia are necessary for a good definition. What must be stated in a definition varies with the definition's purpose. The genus may already be known and only the differentia needed or vice versa. Moreover, there are types of definition, such as contextual and recursive definition, that cannot be expressed in genus–differentia form. Contextual and recursive definitions provide rules for substituting a simpler expression for each of an infinite number of complex expressions of a given type.

Synonyms. The rule that forbids defining by a synonym makes sense only on the contextualist view of definitions as rules of use, although it has long been cited by supporters of the traditional views. The same books that cite this rule also insist that the definiendum must be logically equivalent to the definiens. But a synonym is just an expression that is logically equivalent to a given expression. The trouble seems to be that the term "synonym" is employed in a vaguely restricted sense to signify not just any logically equivalent expression, but a very brief one. Thus, we often find the injunction, "Do not define a word by a single other word." But this formulation, while sufficiently clear, is misleading. Is a two-word definition, such as "phonograph disc" for "record," a case of defining by a synonym or not? Just how many words may the definiens contain if it is not to violate this rule?

To make matters worse, the prohibition of synonyms is inconsistent with rule 4, which demands that a definition be concise; indeed, the more concise the definiens, the more it looks like a synonym. However, we can understand a rule only if we know what specific purpose the rule is intended to serve. A contextualist view of definitions provides the following solution to the conflict between conciseness and nonsynonymity.

Single-word definitions are seldom useful because if a person does not know the rules governing the definiendum, he is not likely to know the rules governing the definiens. The more words there are in the definiens, the more likely it is that those for whom the definition is offered are familiar with some of the words and thus understand some of their rules of use. Everyone has experienced the frustration of looking up a word in a dictionary and being confounded by some equally unfamiliar synonym.

But why should definitions be concise if the greater the number of words, the greater are our chances of at least partial comprehension? One obvious answer is that brief explanations are easier to remember. A second answer is that a lengthy definiens is more likely to suggest some rules of use that are inessential to the definiendum. But the most important consideration has to do with the kind of discursive context in which the definition is employed. In mathematics and in other formal contexts such as jurisprudence and contractual language, the purpose of most definitional equations is to abbreviate discourse or notation. In such cases it is a virtue rather than a defect for the definiens to be long and complicated, since it is precisely this fact that makes the definiendum worth introducing as an abbreviation. Moreover, the complexity of the definiens is less likely to produce confusion in technical contexts because of the great pains taken to preserve consistency and precision of language. In contrast, the rule of conciseness is more appropriate to informal discourse, in which definitions are intended to translate or otherwise clarify an expression unfamiliar to some of the participants. In informal discourse, the definiens should be brief, while in formal contexts, the longer and more complicated the definiens, the more useful the definition. Clearly, one can make little sense of criteria of good definitions without specifying the context in which and the purpose for which a definition is needed.

Figurative language. Why should a definition avoid figurative language? This traditional injunction is probably a result of the concentration of classical philosophy on formal discursive contexts such as mathematics and natural science, in which figures of speech are usually out of place. But in informal contexts such as conversation, literature, public debate, and even the less technical discussions of scientists, figurative language may well be the most effective way of getting a point across, and it is certainly the only way to define expressions whose meaning is essentially figurative (for example, "fathead" may be defined as "a fool puffed up with vanity"). No literal definiens can do justice to the nuances of natural discourse, as every translator knows from bitter experience.

Negative and correlative terms. Why not define by the use of negative or correlative terms? This injunction, in contrast to rule 5, holds for informal discourse and becomes senseless when applied to formal discourse. It is perfectly proper in mathematics or logic to define "$-p$" as "the negation of p" or to define "$F^{-1}(x)$" as "the inverse of the function $F(x)$." The reason for prohibiting negative and correlative definitions in informal contexts is that a person who is unclear about the rules of use of the definiendum would be just as puzzled about the rules of use of a negative or correlative definiens.

Meaning equations. In the light of the preceding discussion, it is advisable to look again at the problem of synonymity. It has already been noted that every meaning equation—that is, every definition of the form "E" means (or means the same as) "x, y, z"—provides a definiens that is synonymous with its definiendum. The very point of the definition is to assert this synonymity and thus to transfer the rules of use already known to govern the definiens to the presumably less familiar definiendum. In order to make sense of the traditional injunction against synonymous definitions, we found it necessary to interpret the synonymity in question as a special and restricted subtype of synonymity, measured by the number of words in the definiens. But although it is absurd to require that a meaning equation must not offer synonyms (in the general sense of "synonym"), it is quite sensible to cast doubt on the usefulness of meaning equations. Meaning equations provide a kind of definition misleadingly called "explicit," in contrast to axioms and postulates, which are frequently regarded as "implicit" or "partial" definitions.

It is unfortunate that meaning equations have come to be called "explicit" definitions, because their function, as we have seen, is to transfer rules of use from definiens to definiendum without articulating the rules in question, so that the rules remain implicit. The most explicit kind of definition, the kind that actually states the rules governing the use of an expression, is a very complicated matter. Outside of technical contexts, it is doubtful whether complete definitions of this kind can ever be provided. On the other hand, it is just as doubtful whether a complete articulation of all the rules of use of the definiendum need be given. We seldom, if ever, require more than one or a few rules of reference, logical grammar, or relevant discourse that happen to be obscure to us in a particular context. Thus, meaning equations are frequently neither the most valuable nor the most appropriate kind of definition. In technical discourse, contextual, recursive, and operational definitions play a far more important role than mere notational abbreviations. And in nontechnical contexts, such as teaching a child or a foreigner the use of a word, definitions by illustration, by enumeration of instances or enumeration of subclasses, and by an indefinite number of other devices (depending on the ingenuity and linguistic sensitivity of the parties concerned) are usually more appropriate and effective than meaning equations. The evaluation of specific definitional procedures remains an important task for philosophically minded experts in each field of discourse and inquiry.

Bibliography

Aristotle, *Works,* W. D. Ross, ed. Oxford, 1928. See especially *Physics* 192–195, *Metaphysics* 982–984, *Posterior Analytics* 90, *Topics.*

Ayer, A. J., *Language, Truth, and Logic,* 2d ed. London, 1946. Chs. 3 and 4.

Bacon, Francis, *Novum Organum,* in *Works,* J. Spedding, ed. London, 1901. Vol. IV.

Black, Max, *Problems of Analysis.* Ithaca, N.Y., 1954. Ch. 2.

Carnap, Rudolf, "Testability and Meaning." *Philosophy of Science,* Vol. 3 (1936), 419–471 and Vol. 4 (1937), 1–40.

Carnap, Rudolf, *Introduction to Semantics.* Cambridge, Mass., 1942. Secs. 6, 24.

Carnap, Rudolf, "The Two Concepts of Probability." *Philosophy and Phenomenological Research,* Vol. 5 (1945), 513–532.

Carré, M. H., *Realists and Nominalists.* Oxford, 1946.

Church, Alonzo, "Definition," in D. D. Runes, ed., *Dictionary of Philosophy.* New York, 1942.

Copi, I. M., *Introduction to Logic.* New York, 1948. Ch. 4.

Descartes, René, *Rules for the Direction of the Understanding,* in *Works,* translated by E. S. Haldane and G. R. T. Ross. Cambridge, 1911. Vol. I.

Dewey, John, and Bentley, A. F., "Definition." *Journal of Philosophy,* Vol. 44 (1947), 281–306.

Dubs, Homer H., *Rational Induction.* Chicago, 1930.

Frege, Gottlob, *Translations from the Writings of Gottlob Frege,* P. T. Geach and Max Black, eds. Oxford, 1952.

Goodman, Nelson, *The Structure of Appearance.* Cambridge, Mass., 1951. Ch. 1.

Hempel, C. G., *Fundamentals of Concept Formation in Empirical Science.* Chicago, 1952. Ch. 1, Parts 2–4.

Hobbes, Thomas, *Leviathan.* Book I, Secs. 3–5.

Husserl, Edmund, *Ideas,* translated by W. R. Boyce Gibson. New York, 1931. Vol. I.

Husserl, Edmund, *Erfahrung und Urteil.* Hamburg, 1948. Pp. 410 ff.

Kant, Immanuel, "Introduction," in *Critique of Pure Reason,* translated by Norman Kemp Smith. London, 1929.

Kaplan, Abraham, "Definition and Specification of Meaning." *Journal of Philosophy,* Vol. 43 (1946), 281–288.

Lenzen,Victor, "Successive Definition," in *Procedures of Empirical Science.* Chicago, 1938.

Lewis, C. I., *An Analysis of Knowledge and Valuation.* La Salle, Ill. 1946. Pp. 105 ff.

Locke, John, *Essay Concerning Human Understanding,* A. C. Fraser, ed. Oxford, 1894. Vol. I.

Maritain, Jacques, *Philosophy of Nature,* translated by I. Byrne. New York, 1951.

Mill, John Stuart, *A System of Logic.* London, 1879. Pp. 72 ff., 436 ff.

Moore, G. E., *Principia Ethica.* Cambridge, 1913. Ch. 1.

Moore, G. E., "Reply to My Critics," in P. A. Schilpp, ed., *The Philosophy of G. E. Moore.* Evanston, Ill., 1942. Pp. 660–667.

Pepper, S. C., "The Descriptive Definition." *Journal of Philosophy,* Vol. 43 (1946), 29–36.

Plato, *The Dialogues of Plato,* translated by Benjamin Jowett. See especially *Charmides, Euthyphro, Meno, Republic, Sophist,* and *Theaetetus.*

Quine, W. V., "Truth by Convention," in *Philosophical Essays for A. N. Whitehead.* London and New York, 1936.

Rickert, Heinrich, *Zur Lehre von der Definition.* Tübingen, 1929.

Robinson, Richard, *Plato's Earlier Dialectic.* Ithaca, N.Y., 1941.

Robinson, Richard, *Definition.* Oxford, 1954.

Russell, Bertrand, and Whitehead, A. N., *Principia Mathematica.* Cambridge, 1910. Vol. I.

Scriven, Michael, "Definitions in Analytical Philosophy." *Philosophical Studies,* Vol. 5 (1954).

Scriven, Michael, "Definitions, Explanations, and Theories," in H. Feigl, G. Maxwell, and M. Scriven, eds., *Minnesota Studies in the Philosophy of Science,* Vol. II. Minneapolis, 1958. Pp. 99–195.

Wittgenstein, Ludwig, *Philosophical Investigations,* translated by G. E. M. Anscombe. New York, 1953.

RAZIEL ABELSON

DEGREES OF PERFECTION, ARGUMENT FOR THE EXISTENCE OF GOD. The proof for the existence of God from degrees of perfection, sometimes called the Henological Argument, finds its best-known expression as the fourth of Thomas Aquinas' "Five Ways" in his *Summa Theologiae* Ia, 2, 3. It is here quoted in full:

> The fourth way is based on the gradation observed in things. Some things are found to be more good, more true, more noble, and so on, and other things less. But comparative terms describe varying degrees of approximation to a superlative; for example, things are hotter and hotter the nearer they approach what is hottest. Something therefore is the truest and best and most noble of things, and hence the most fully in being; for Aristotle says that the truest things are the things most fully in being. Now *when many things possess some property in common, the one most fully possessing it causes it in the others: fire,* to use Aristotle's example, *the hottest of all things, causes all other things to be hot.* There is something therefore which causes in all other things their being, their goodness, and whatever other perfections they have. And this we call God.

Comparatives and superlatives. A distinctive feature of the Fourth Way is the principle that "comparative terms describe varying degrees of approximation to a superlative; for example, suppose "whiter than" is such a comparative term. The judgment that bond paper is whiter than newsprint would then be more adequately expressed as "The color of bond paper is closer to *pure white* than is the color of newsprint." However, the new comparative term "closer to" (that is, "more closely resembles," "more similar to") is used in exactly the same sense when none of the things compared is a superlative, for example, in "The color of bond paper is closer to the color of newsprint than the color of newsprint is close to the color of lemons," and here "closer to" obviously does not describe a degree of approximation to pure white. If "closer to," used to compare colors, does describe degrees of approximation to a superlative, the superlative must be the greatest possible similarity between colors, that is, qualitative identity of colors. Perhaps the initial judgment should then be expressed "The similarity between the color of bond paper and pure white is closer to the *greatest possible similarity* than is the similarity between newsprint and pure white." But here there is still a comparative term, "closer to," used to compare similarities between colors. It seems impossible to define a comparative term by means of a superlative without using another comparative term, and we are on our way to an infinite regress. If all comparative terms describe degrees of approximation to a superlative, then any comparative judgment implicitly refers to infinitely many superlatives.

But perhaps not all comparative terms describe degrees of approximation to a superlative. Suppose "closer to" (as used to compare colors) does not, and therefore the infinite regress can be cut short. Then "closer to" can be used to define "whiter than," and the definition need not refer to pure white, or to any other superlative. This is a reason for denying that "whiter than" describes a degree of approximation to a superlative. The definition runs as follows:

First it must be given, perhaps simply by fiat, that color *B* is whiter than color *A*. *B* need not be pure white, or superlatively white. Then any color *X* is between *A* and *B* if and only if both *X* is closer to *A* than *A* is close to *B* and *X* is closer to *B* than *B* is close to *A*. If *X* is between *A* and *B*, then *X* is whiter than *A*, and *B* is whiter than *X*. If *X* is different from both *A* and *B* and is not between *A* and *B*, then (1) *X* is whiter than *B* if and only if *X* is closer to *B* than *X* is close to *A* and (2) *A* is whiter than *X* if and only if *X* is closer to *A* than *X* is close to *B*. Two colors, *X* and *Y*, can be compared with respect to whiteness by (1) comparing *X* with the initially given pair in the manner just described and (2) by similarly comparing *Y* with either the pair *A* and *X* or the pair *B* and *X*.

Superlative terms can be defined by means of comparatives more easily than comparative terms can be defined by means of superlatives. For example, "Brand *X* is the whitest bond paper if and only if Brand *X* is whiter than any other bond paper." Or "Brand *X* is the whitest bond paper if and only if no other bond paper is whiter than Brand *X*." On the second definition there can be more than one whitest bond paper. On the first definition there can be only one; and it is therefore possible that nothing satisfies the first definition. Such nonequivalent forms of definition are possible whatever the kind of superlative term defined; either form may be used if it is not confused with the other. Both definitions above define a *relative superlative term.* "Whitest" is defined with respect to a certain class, the class of bond papers. Since not only bond paper is white, neither definition rules out the possibility that something other than bond paper is whiter than the whitest bond paper. A *universal superlative* term is defined with respect to the class of everything of which the corresponding comparative term is predicable. For example, "*X* is the whitest thing if and only if nothing is whiter than *X*." Both relative and universal superlative terms can be *absolute superlative terms.* An absolute superlative term is defined by means of a modal term like "possible" or "can." "*X* is pure white if and only if it is not *possible* for anything to be whiter than *X*." There are as many senses of an absolute superlative term as there are relevant senses of "possible."

Any comparative term can be used to define some superlative term. For example, "greater than" can be used to define "greatest prime number": *n* is the greatest prime number if and only if *n* is a prime number and there is no prime number greater than *n*. But it has been proved that there is no greatest prime number—that the predicate "greatest prime number" cannot be truly predicated of any number. This raises a general question: How can we know whether a particular superlative term could possibly be truly predicated of something? One can define "pure white," but this gives no assurance that there might possibly be something which is pure white. Perhaps we do not know what we are talking about when we talk about "pure white"; for perhaps there can be nothing to talk about, just as there can be nothing to talk about when we talk about "the greatest prime number." A superlative term should be suspected of not being truly predicable of anything possible unless there is a reason to think otherwise, and such a reason is not provided by the fact that the superlative term can be defined by a perfectly understandable comparative term.

Such a reason is sometimes provided when the superlative term can be defined without using any corresponding comparative or superlative terms. Definitions of this sort will usually, perhaps always, employ a universal quantifier. For example, "An object is (absolutely) *pure gold* if and only if *all* its atoms are atoms of gold. A *perfect* reflector is one that reflects *all* the light falling on it." Definitions of the form "Something is pure _____ if and only if it contains *no* impurities" or "something is a perfect _____ if and only if it has *no* imperfections" will not do by themselves. The terms "contains *no* impurities" and "has *no* imperfections" are as problematic as the particular superlative terms they define and should be used without qualms only if they can be characterized independently. "Absolutely pure minestrone soup" can be defined as "minestrone soup completely free of impurities," but this is no help until we have a complete list of possible impurities. Aniline dyes are definitely impurities in soups. Some batches of minestrone soup are therefore definitely purer than others. But starting from an incomplete list of possible impurities, there is no obvious way, other than by arbitrary stipulation, of making a complete list. It seems that "absolutely pure minestrone soup" can therefore be given a clear sense only by stipulation. We do not *need* to give it a clear sense in order to talk sensibly about some batches of soup being purer than others.

A comparative term is often much clearer than the corresponding superlative term; one can often know how to use a comparative term without at all knowing how to use the corresponding superlative term. It seems reasonable to deny that such comparative terms describe degrees of approximation to a superlative.

Perfections. Aquinas stated his principle quite generally, but presumably he would have been willing to qualify it. He argued himself that there can be nothing which is unlimited in size (*Summa Theologiae* Ia, 7, 3) and he would deny, reasonably, that the comparative term "longer than," for example, describes degrees of approximation to a superlative. The argument from degrees of perfection does not lead to the heretical conclusion that God is pure white or pure red. Still less does it lead to the impossible conclusion that God is both pure white and pure red or that God is both perfectly circular and perfectly triangular. The argument is concerned only with perfections whose predication does not imply any sort of imperfection. If a thing is white, it must be extended; if extended, it must be divisible; and if divisible, it must be perishable. Perishability is an imperfection, and therefore whiteness, like all other properties which exist only in something extended, can exist only in things less than completely perfect. Perfections which involve absolutely no imperfection are sometimes called "transcendental perfections." The traditional list includes being, unity, truth, goodness, nobility, and sometimes beauty and intelligence. Aquinas thought that anything, a member of any genus, and God, who is not a member of any genus, could have these perfections. For Aquinas' argument the principle about comparison need be true only of the transcendental perfections.

The principle about comparison is generally dubious, and it is particularly dubious with the transcendental perfections. Goodness, for example, is sensibly predicated of something only when it is understood as being of some kind. One who asserts of something "It is good" should be prepared always to answer the question "A good *what?*" Things of a certain kind are good in virtue of having certain characteristics; things of another kind in virtue of having others. Thus, if comparisons of goodness describe degrees of approximation to a superlative, then comparison with respect to any of the different characteristics admitting of degrees in virtue of which different kinds of things are good must also describe degrees of approximation to a superlative. The restriction of the comparative principle to transcendental perfections is not much of a restriction.

Those who do not subscribe to a Thomistic metaphysics, or to one like it, will not find any reason to accept the principle that comparisons of perfections describe degrees of approximation to a superlative. It is not surprising that Aquinas' philosophy contains enough material to construct more arguments for God's existence than he formulated explicitly. Some of these back up the Fourth Way. For example, Aquinas' philosophical theology makes great use of the Aristotelian distinction between act and potency: "Each thing is perfect according as it is in act, and imperfect as it is in potency" (*Summa Contra Gentiles* I, 28, 6). Furthermore, something whose actuality is less than complete must be caused by something else with at least as much actuality (*ibid.*, I, 28, 7). Bearing these two principles in mind, the argument from degrees of perfection can be reformulated as follows:

> Some things are found to be more perfect than others. Thus, some things have less than the superlative degree of perfection. Since a thing's perfection is its actuality, these things have less than the superlative degree of actuality. Something whose actuality is less than complete must be caused by something else with at least as much actuality. The resulting hierarchy of causes cannot be infinite, so there must be a first cause whose actuality is complete, who is pure act, and who therefore has all perfections in a superlative degree. And this we call God.

Thus reformulated, the Fourth Way resembles the First Way, the argument from efficient causality, and the Second Way, the argument from change. And it is susceptible to the same sorts of familiar objections raised against them. These objections, however, may seem less forceful against the Fourth Way than against the other arguments. A modern reader who is untroubled by the idea of an infinite hierarchy of efficient causes may well balk at the idea of an infinite hierarchy of increasing perfection. And one who claims that a proof of a first cause does not prove *God's* existence may admit that a proof of an absolutely perfect being does. However, this does not make the argument from degrees of perfection more convincing than the other proofs. The argument is now generally neglected, and a modern nonbeliever is not likely to be much influenced by it. For its premises will seem plausible only to one who accepts metaphysical principles, which in turn will seem plausible only to one who has a prior belief in the existence of God.

The reformulation of the Fourth Way given earlier brings out the relevance of the relation between comparative and superlative to other parts of Aquinas' system. A central doctrine of Aquinas' philosophical theology is that God is *pure act*, that there neither is nor could be any potency in him. Even if it is granted that we can learn, from Aristotle's and Aquinas' examples, how to compare some things as being more or less in act, this gives us no reason to suppose that the superlative term "pure act" is intelligible or that it could possibly apply to something.

Bibliography

The Fourth Way seems the most Platonic of Aquinas' Five Ways. See, for example, Plato, *Phaedo*, 100–101. Two books in English on Aquinas' relation to Plato are Arthur Little, *The Platonic Heritage of Thomism* (Dublin, 1950), and R. J. Henle, *Saint Thomas and Platonism* (The Hague, 1956). The Fourth Way is the major topic of Little's book. Henle's book has a very complete bibliography.

The principle that comparative terms describe varying degrees of approximation to a superlative appears several times in Aquinas' *Summa Contra Gentiles* (I, 28, 8; I, 42, 19; I, 62, 5). It does not, however, appear in the very compressed argument for God's existence (I, 13, 34), where an argument from degrees of truth is attributed to Aristotle. Aristotle's *Metaphysics* II, 993b25–30, a passage mentioned in both the *Summa Theologiae* and the *Summa Contra Gentiles* versions of the argument, does seem adaptable to Aquinas' purposes. *Metaphysics* IV, 1008b31–1009a5, mentioned only in the *Summa Contra Gentiles* version, does not. Aristotle probably should not be counted among the philosophers who employed or would be willing to employ the argument from degrees of perfection to prove the existence of a perfect being.

Several arguments from degrees of perfection appear in the writings of Augustine; see, for example, Bk. V, Sec. 11, and Bk. VIII, Secs. 4 and 5, of *De Trinitate*, the work of Augustine's referred to in the preface of Anselm's *Monologion*. Anselm's arguments from degrees of perfection appear in the first four chapters of the *Monologion*.

The Blackfriars edition of Aquinas' *Summa Theologiae* (New York, 1964—; only a few of the projected 60 vols. have been published so far) has the Latin text, along with a new English translation. The second volume, Ia. 2–11 (New York, 1964), translated by Timothy McDermott, contains appendices by Thomas Gilby, "The Fourth Way" and "Perfection and Goodness."

Aquinas' doctrine of "analogical" predication is usually invoked to explain the notion of a transcendental perfection. This, as well as the act–potency distinction, is discussed in Knut Tranøy, "Thomas Aquinas," in D. J. O'Connor, ed., *A Critical History of Western Philosophy* (New York, 1964), and further references are given.

The Fourth Way is the least widely accepted of Aquinas' proofs for the existence of God. References to the disputes are given in Étienne Gilson, *The Christian Philosophy of St. Thomas Aquinas* (New York, 1956). See also Gilson's *Elements of Christian Philosophy* (New York, 1960).

Descartes presented a proof for the existence of God from the degrees of perfection found in *ideas*. See his *Third Meditation*, his *Principles of Philosophy*, I. xviii., Objection II of the second set of *Objections to the Meditations*, and his *Reply* to this objection.

DAVID SANFORD

DEISM (Lat. *deus*, god) is etymologically cognate to theism (Gr. *theos*, god), both words denoting belief in the existence of a god or gods and, therefore, the antithesis of atheism. However, as is customary in the case of synonyms, the words drifted apart in meaning; theism retained an air of religious orthodoxy, while *deism* acquired a connotation of religious unorthodoxy and ultimately reached the pejorative. Curiously, however, the earliest known use of the term deist (1564) already had this latter intent, although it was by no means consistently retained thereafter. The situation is complicated by a late eighteenth- and nineteenth-century technical metaphysical interpretation of deism, in which the meaning is restricted to belief in a God, or First Cause, who created the world and instituted immutable and universal laws that preclude any alteration as well as divine immanence—in short, the concept of an "absentee God." A further complication has been the acceptance of natural religion (religion universally achievable by human reason) by many eminent Christian theologians throughout the course of many centuries. Such theologians also believed in revelation and in personal divine intervention in the life of man, a position that had been made clear and authoritative by St. Thomas Aquinas. No sharp line can be drawn between the doctrines of such rationalistic theologians and those of deists, especially those who termed themselves "Christian deists." Nor is it accurate to maintain that the historical deists (mainly of the seventeenth and eighteenth centuries), like the philosophical deists, altogether denied the immanence of God, even though they did tend to become more and more critical of the necessity of any revelation and of the Hebraic–Christian revelation in particular. It is therefore necessary to distinguish between the two types of deists. The remainder of this article will be devoted to a survey of historical deism.

Early history of deism. To attempt to disentangle the antecedents of historical deism—intertwined as they are with rationalistic natural religion on the one hand, and with skepticism on the other—would indeed be foolhardy. Skepticism itself might end in Pyrrhonism or atheism or fideism. It is safe to generalize, however, that any tendency away from religious dogmatism, implicit faith and the mysterious, and in the direction of freedom of thought on religious matters, was in some measure a premonitory symptom of deism.

The earliest known use of the word "deist" was by Pierre Viret, a disciple of Calvin, in his *Instruction chrétienne* (Geneva, 1564), Vol. II, "Epistre" (signed, Lyons, December 12, 1563). Viret regarded it as an entirely new word that (he claimed) the deists wished to oppose to "atheist": according to him, the deist professes belief in God as the creator of heaven and earth but rejects Jesus Christ and his doctrines. Although those unidentified deists were learned men of letters and philosophy, they were bitterly attacked by Viret as monsters and atheists. This definition and commentary was given wide circulation through Pierre Bayle's citation in his article on Viret in the *Dictionnaire historique et critique* (1697; English translation, 1710). The word "deist" remained unknown in England until 1621, when it appeared in Burton's *Anatomy of Melancholy* (III. iv. II. i). After discussing atheists and near-atheists, Burton continues: "Cousin-germans to these men are many of our great Philosophers and Deists," who, although good and moral, are yet themselves atheists. These "great Philosophers and Deists" likewise remain unidentified. A century and a half later, Hume, in his *History of England*, ventured to name James Harrington, Algernon Sidney, and Sir John Wildman, among others, as the reputed leaders of the deists under the Commonwealth. The first interpretation of "deist" in both French and English as a euphemism for "atheist" was not followed by Dr. Samuel Johnson, who, in his *Dictionary* (1755), defined "deist" as "a man who follows no particular religion but only acknowledges the existence of God, without any other article of faith."

The first appearance of "deism" seems to have been in Dryden's preface to his poem *Religio Laici* of 1682, where he equated it with natural religion. Dr. Johnson agreed: "The opinion of those that only acknowledge one God, without the reception of any revealed religion." Neither Dryden nor Johnson, evidently, regarded deism as disguised atheism. The notion of deism, however, if not the word itself, is to be found in one form or another throughout the Renaissance until, in the late seventeenth century, the Englishman Charles Blount openly acknowledged that he was a deist.

Beginning in the early sixteenth century, general contributions to the development of deism include such broad movements as anti-Trinitarianism, Unitarianism, secularism, anticlericalism, Erastianism, Arminianism, and Socinianism, the rise of the sects, and the general revolt against authority. It may be argued that all of these currents and undercurrents were united in the increasing trend away from religious persecution and toward religious toleration, the glorification of the natural powers of man, and the endorsement of the right to think and to publish freely on all religious and political subjects.

DEISM IN BRITAIN

The British deists constituted no conspiracy and formed no school of thought; they were highly individualistic, frequently unknown to one another, and sometimes at odds with one another. They were less systematic philosophers than thoughtful writers on practical moral, religious, and political issues. In 1704 the rationalist Anglican theologian Samuel Clarke distinguished four varieties of deists: those who denied providence; those who acknowledged providence in natural religion but not in morality; those who, while denying a future life, admitted the moral role of the deity; and finally, those who acknowledged a future life and the other doctrines of natural religion. The following summary of the leading deists will testify to the general truth of Clarke's subtle distinctions.

Lord Herbert of Cherbury. Lord Herbert (1583–1648) never called himself a deist and had but a single acknowledged disciple, Charles Blount; nevertheless, he exerted considerable influence and deserves the title of "the father of English deism" bestowed on him in 1714 by Thomas Halyburton in *Natural Religion Insufficient.* Lord Herbert's *De Veritate, Prout Distinguitur a Revelatione, a Verisimili, a Possibili, et a Falso* was published in Paris in 1624, in London in 1633, and again in 1645. The first edition, therefore, postdated Burton's avowal of the existence of many deists by three years. In the expanded London edition of 1645, Herbert laid down the religious Common Notions that constitute the rationalistic basis of deism and that were to be assumed, if not always acknowledged, by virtually all succeeding deists. These principles are (1) that there is one supreme God; (2) that he ought to be worshiped; (3) that virtue and piety are the chief parts of divine worship; (4) that man ought to be sorry for his sins and repent of them; (5) that divine goodness dispenses rewards and punishments both in this life and after it. These truths, he argued, are universal, and may be apprehended by reason. Revelation is not openly repudiated, but by implication is rendered supererogatory. (Somewhat incongruously, however, Herbert prayed for a sign from Heaven that would grant permission to publish *De Veritate*, and was satisfied that he had received it.) Herbert treated Scripture as ordinary history, ridiculed bibliolatry, and overtly attacked priestcraft, and disavowed faith as a basis for religion. His *De Religione Gentilium* (1663) is one of the earliest studies of comparative religion.

Propagation of deism. Although precise documentation is not available, deism was ripening between the time of Herbert and Charles Blount, through such various and overlapping influences as humanism in general, the philosophy of Hobbes, the idealism of James Harrington, the naturalistic Biblical exegesis of Spinoza and others, the corruption of the clergy, the widespread religious rationalism of the Cambridge Platonists and other Latitudinarians, the "sweet reasonableness" of Locke, and the scientific approach of Newton—all of which were contributing to religious and political toleration. By the close of the seventeenth century, a new and memorable influence was added—the pervasive presence of the skepticism of Bayle. The first direct attack on British deism, Bishop Stillingfleet's *Letter to a Deist* (1677), acknowledges that owning to the being and providence of God but expressing "a mean esteem" of the Scriptures and the Christian religion had become a common theme.

Charles Blount. Beginning in 1679, Blount (1654–1693) was an indefatigable propagandist who, in the battle for freedom on all fronts, learned to resort to indirect methods in order to keep clear of the law. His *Summary Account of the Deist's Religion* (1693), which appeared posthumously during the same year in which he committed suicide, is his most outspoken work.

The year 1610 marks the last burning of heretics in England. Yet the matter of legal suppression of heterodox works is of vital importance in understanding and assessing the writings of the deists. The strict Press Licensing Act of 1662 was allowed to drop by 1695, but the blasphemy laws were still in effect. The ecclesiastical courts had the power to imprison heretics for a period of six months; in 1676 Lord Chief Justice Hale ruled that through common law the Court of King's Bench had jurisdiction over blasphemy, because Christianity is "parcel of the laws of England"; and finally, in 1698 a vicious statute was enacted under which any acknowledged Christian who made any accusation whatsoever against the Christian religion could be rendered incapable of holding office, of taking legal action, of purchasing land, and, if the blasphemy was repeated, would be made to suffer three years' imprisonment without bail. Such repressive measures drove the heterodox into various evasive techniques. Irony, innuendo, ridicule, raillery, allegorical interpretation of the Scriptures, fictitious analogies, frequent use of the dialogue and epistolary forms, the claim to be "Christian deists," pseudonymity, and anonymity not only successfully hampered legal prosecution but also made it difficult for modern historians to ascertain the genuine beliefs of the writers.

After Herbert and Blount, the foremost British deists were John Toland, Anthony Collins, and Matthew Tindal, and of somewhat less consequence, William Wollaston, Thomas Woolston, Thomas Chubb, Thomas Morgan, Henry, Lord Bolingbroke, and Peter Annet. Others, such as Shaftesbury and Mandeville, have been labeled deists with some justification, and many others without justification, even including orthodox clergymen who emphasized natural religion, expressed scruples about specific Biblical passages or voiced doubts about specific Biblical miracles.

John Toland. Toland (1670–1722) produced in 1696 his most famous deistical work, the very title of which spells out its major thesis: *Christianity not Mysterious: Or a treatise Shewing That there is nothing in the Gospel Contrary to Reason, Nor above it: And that no Christian Doctrine can be properly call'd a Mystery*. The treatise is basically rationalistic and is reminiscent of Herbert's *De Veritate*. It opposes not only Biblical mysteries, but also challenges the validity of the Biblical canon and points out corruptions in Biblical texts. It mocks the implicit faith of the Puritans and their bibliolatry, and severely censures the vested interests of priests of all denominations. Philosophically, Toland was in the tradition of Bruno, Descartes, Spinoza, Leibniz, and, to a lesser extent, of Locke. Eclectic and somewhat inconsistent in his opinions, he was a freethinker and a deist, a materialist and a pantheist (the first use of the word "pantheist" is found in 1705 in his *Socinianism truly stated*). With his great learning, Toland became a figure of international renown, for the first time bringing deism to a wide reading public through a profusion of bold controversial publications.

Anthony Collins. Collins (1676–1729) was a well-to-do and well-educated gentleman and magistrate. At the age of 27 he earned the respect and friendship of Locke. Two early works, *An Essay Concerning the Use of Reason* (1707) and *Priestcraft in Perfection* (1709), prepared the way for the more famous *Discourse of Free-Thinking* (1713), in which the right to think and publish freely is examined chiefly as it pertains to religion. Enthusiasm and superstition are considered more evil than atheism; modern science and the Protestant Reformation are presented as examples of courageous freethinking that have relieved many from age-old errors, including witchcraft; and priests are blamed for trivial quarreling among themselves over Biblical interpretations and are held responsible for many corrupt texts. An impressive list of freethinkers is furnished from the ancient Greeks, Romans, and Hebrews; from the Church Fathers; and from the moderns, ranging from Montaigne to Tillotson and Locke.

Collins defended his style of writing in *A Discourse concerning Ridicule and Irony in Writing* (1727); his philosophical doctrine of necessitarianism (wherein he differs from the doctrine of free will espoused by most deists) is developed in a *Philosophical Inquiry concerning Human Liberty* (1715) and a *Dissertation on Liberty and Necessity* (1729); and his Biblical criticism, mainly of the supposed fulfillment of Old Testament prophecies in the New Testament, in the *Discourse of the Grounds and Reasons of the Christian Religion* (1724) and the *Scheme of Literal Prophecy Considered* (1725). Collins is unquestionably the most readable and urbane of the British deists.

Matthew Tindal. (1657?–1733) A law fellow at All Souls College, Oxford, and advocate at Doctors' Commons, Tindal was the most learned of the British deists, as well as the most significant historically. His *Christianity as Old as the Creation: Or, The Gospel A Republication of the Religion of Nature* (1730), composed in dialogue form, was at once recognized as "The Deist's Bible," and elicited over 150 replies, the most famous of which is Bishop Butler's *The Analogy of Religion* (1736). Although a declared admirer of Locke, Tindal deduces the being and attributes of God by a priori reason. As man reasons downward from the knowledge of the attributes of God to knowledge of himself, the religion of nature, including all the moral precepts requisite for leading the life of virtue and achieving ultimate salvation, then follows. Scripture, replete with ambiguities, is not only unnecessary but is actually confusing to men of reason; and according to Tindal, all men of whatever education or status in life are capable of Right Reason. Some Old Testament heroes are inspected in detail and are found wanting in virtue; even some New Testament parables are subjected to critical comment. Tradition is repudiated as a basis for Christianity, since it can be used equally as the basis for any and all religions. The customary deistical castigation of priestcraft is combined with this repudiation of tradition. Tindal, a rationalist, always maintained the title of "Christian deist."

Lesser English deists. The remaining British deists, already named, each made some personal contribution to the movement, however small.

William Wollaston. A graduate of Sidney Sussex College, Cambridge, Wollaston (1660–1724) took holy orders, but through the unexpected inheritance of a large fortune he was able to devote himself to moral philosophy and general learning. His *The Religion of Nature Delineated* (1724) was well received by Queen Caroline the Illustrious, as well as by the public at large. It was attacked, however, by the American deist Benjamin Franklin and was subjected to ridicule by Lord Bolingbroke, the British deist. Unlike most deistical treatises, it contains no Biblical criticism of any sort. Almost purely rationalistic, it has obvious affinities, in a simplified form, with Herbert of Cherbury's religious Common Notions. Man knows truth (that is, things as they are) by means of reason; vice, or the denial of things as they are, is a lie. To seek happiness is man's duty, because happiness, or the excess of pleasure over pain, is part of man's approach to truth. Man is by nature not fundamentally selfish; his search for truth must take into account the happiness of others. It is altogether likely that Bishop Butler, in *The Analogy of Religion*, had Wollaston at least partly in mind when he reproved extreme religious rationalism as "that idle and not very innocent employment of forming imaginary models of a world, and schemes of governing it."

Thomas Woolston. Woolston (1670–1731), fellow of Sidney Sussex College, Cambridge, and Christian divine, was a deist of another stamp. A disciple of Anthony Collins, who had spearheaded the assault on Biblical prophecies, Woolston extended the assault to Biblical miracles. Influenced by the writings of the Greek Church Father Origen, he interpreted Scripture allegorically, was subsequently deemed out of his mind by his adversaries and, as a result, in 1720 was deprived of his fellowship. In 1705 he first employed the allegorical method in *The Old Apology for the Truth of the Christian Religion against the Jews and Gentiles Revived*, and later published a series of anticlerical tracts against those who spurned it. But it was a series of six *Discourses On the Miracles of our Saviour, In View of the Present Contest between Infidels and Apostates* (1727–1729) that brought prosecution by the government, ending in 1729 with a conviction of blasphemy. Sentenced to a fine of £100, imprisonment for one year, and security for good behavior during life, he died in jail in 1731, unable to pay the fine. A fighter for freedom of thought and publication for all, Woolston ironically fell the victim of his own principles. The six *Discourses* take a colloquial and frequently witty dialogue form, with a fictitious learned Jewish rabbi presenting Woolston's queries concerning 15 New Testament miracles. Woolston's madness may possibly have been real (in which case his sentence was truly infamous), but his tracts read more like the strong convictions of a strong mind. He was one of two of the leading British deists (the other being Peter Annet) to suffer punishment by the government.

Thomas Chubb. An Arian and "Christian deist," Chubb (1679–1746) was a self-educated and humble artisan. Writing for the common people, Chubb was also able to hold his own with the educated upper classes, divines, and scholars. He mastered the widespread rationalism of the early eighteenth century and propagated its basic ideas through prolific publication, as is observable in such works as *A Discourse Concerning Reason, With Regard to Religion and Divine Revelation* (1731) and *An Enquiry Into the Ground and Foundation of Religion. Wherein is shewn, that Religion is founded in Nature* (1740). Another approach is taken in *A Discourse on Miracles, Considered as evidence to prove the Divine Original of a Revelation* (1741), a work influenced by Toland and Woolston. Although he is skeptical of the Hebrew revelation, Chubb is never skeptical of the Christian, as is manifested in *The True Gospel of Jesus Christ asserted* (1732) and *The True Gospel of Jesus Christ Vindicated* (1739). In these two tracts, Chubb employs natural religion as proof of Christian religion. He defends the miraculous propagation of primitive Christianity against the aspersions of the deist Matthew Tindal. A believer in free will, Chubb was answered at considerable length by the eighteenth-century American theologian Jonathan Edwards in *A Careful and Strict Enquiry into The modern prevailing Notions of the Freedom of Will* (1754).

Thomas Morgan. A Welsh "Christian deist," divine, and medical doctor, Morgan (d. 1743) came from a poor family (as did Chubb and Annet). Morgan combined the religious Common Notions of Lord Herbert with some of the principles of historical Biblical criticism found in the writings of Toland and Chubb. He opposed Chubb, however, on the question of free will. Morgan's chief contributions to the deistical controversy are to be found in *The Moral Philosopher, in a Dialogue between Philalethes, a Christian Deist, and Theophanes, a Christian Jew* (1737), and its two sequels. His general historical criticism of Scripture stresses the many ambiguities that permit many different interpretations of Biblical texts by believers who truly attempt to understand their significance. All history, therefore, is simply probability, and infallibility is fostered by priestcraft for selfish purposes. Toleration, reasonableness, and freedom are necessary to combat superstition and persecution.

Henry St. John, Viscount Bolingbroke. Tory statesman, historian, deist, and wit, Bolingbroke (1678–1751) left his philosophical and religious compositions to be published posthumously in 1754 by David Mallet. Regarded by Dr. Johnson as a "blunderbuss" against religion and morality, Bolingbroke's *Works* were regarded by Hume as unoriginal and feeble. In the twentieth century, Voltaire's long-alleged great indebtedness to Bolingbroke has been discredited, and the claim that Pope's *Essay on Man* was founded on Bolingbroke's *Fragments or Minutes of Essays* has been vigorously challenged. As a philosopher Bolingbroke is a rationalist, but a curiously inconsistent one. In one passage he states that only Right Reason can demonstrate the Being of Deity, yet in another, that only empiricism can prove the Being of Deity. Paradoxes abound: no universal revelation has ever been made, but modern religion can benefit by the study of primitive religions—for example, of China and Egypt. Like all the deists, Bolingbroke regarded the baneful influence of priestcraft as a major cause of the corruption of religious texts and religious traditions. With Bolingbroke, the course of British rationalistic deism, stemming from that of Lord Herbert in the middle of the seventeenth century, up to the middle of the eighteenth century, had been pretty well played out, but there was always opportunity for remorseless repetition and intensified publicity.

Peter Annet. Schoolmaster Annet (1693–1769) may be regarded as the last of the old-line deists. An outspoken freethinker, Annet advocated the freedom to divorce and, in a long series of tracts, attacked the Resurrection of Jesus and the character and conversion of St. Paul. His truculent assault on the credibility of all miracles in general, and those of the Old Testament in particular, carried on in *The Free Enquirer* of 1761, brought a governmental charge of blasphemous libel to which Annet pleaded guilty. The inhumane sentence against a man aged 70 included imprisonment for a month, two pilloryings, hard labor for a year, a fine, and bonds of security for good behavior during life. Annet survived this flagrant miscarriage of justice with its attendant humiliation and returned to schoolmastering until his death. The ascription to him of the authorship of the notorious *History of the Man after God's own Heart* (1761) has been disproved by modern scholarship. Although he contributed little fresh to the deistical movement, Annet, like Chubb, wrote directly to the people in their own language.

The rationalistic climate of opinion. Little has been said so far about the rationalistic "orthodox" of the seventeenth and eighteenth centuries, those Latitudinarians, who were closely akin to the deists, except on the one crucial point of raising objections against Christian revelation. Nevertheless, both groups were united in a contemptuous rejection of Tertullian's dictum, *credo quia impossibile est;* in this respect, there was no warfare between reason and religion. In a 1670 defense of the orthodox rationalists, a Latitudinarian was succinctly defined as "a gentleman of a wide swallow."

Ralph Cudworth. Cudworth (1617–1688) may be taken as representative of the small but important band of Cambridge Platonists who sought to synthesize the spirit of Christianity with that of Greek philosophy by affirming that reason is spiritual as well as intellectual. Cudworth distinguishes between fundamental and nonfundamental religious doctrines: "I perswade myself, that no man shall ever be kept out of heaven, for not comprehending mysteries that were beyond the reach of his shallow understanding; if he had but an honest and good heart, that was ready to comply with Christ's commandments" (*A Sermon before the House of Commons, March 31, 1647.*) In *The True Intellectual System of the Universe* (1678), Cudworth argues cogently against fatalism. His posthumous *Treatise concerning Eternal and Immutable Morality* (1731) derives morality from natural law rather than from the positive precepts of revelation. Another member of the group, Benjamin Whichcote, states their position admirably: "If you would be religious, be rational in your religion." In short, the Cambridge Platonists stood for reason and moderation.

John Tillotson. Tillotson (1630–1694), archbishop of Canterbury and great champion of Anglicanism, employed rationalistic arguments against the Catholic use of tradition and authority. Observing that these same arguments could be turned against Christianity itself, the deists frequently seized upon Tillotson's authority and quoted his arguments in this new context. Collins went so far as to name him the man "whom all English free-thinkers own as their head."

The New Science. It might be expected that the New Science, which had made such great strides from Copernicus to Newton, would have precipitated warfare between science and religion as it did in the nineteenth century, following Darwin's *Origin of Species* (1859). But insofar as Britain was concerned, such was not the case, for Bacon had enunciated the principle of a rigid dichotomy between science and religion which, on the whole, was adhered to during the seventeenth century. Indeed, science was more generally used as a bulwark for Christianity than the reverse—notably, in the case of the Latitudinarians. Newton himself was a student of Old Testament prophecies and believed in the Scriptures as inerrant guides.

The "skeptical chemist" Robert Boyle wrote orthodox religious tracts, one of which had the ancillary purpose of proving that by being "addicted" to experimental philosophy, a man is assisted rather than indisposed to being a good Christian. In 1691 Boyle endowed a lectureship for the proof of the Christian religion against the attacks of infidels. Great efforts were made to replace a priori reasoning with the argument from design. Richard Bentley, the first Boyle lecturer, corresponded with Newton in preparing *The Folly of Atheism and what is now called Deism* (1692). William Derham's two lectures, *Physico-Theology* (1713) and *Astro-Theology* (1715), continued the effort. Nevertheless, the bulk of the Boyle lectures, from the beginning to 1732, are almost purely rationalistic, as, for example, Samuel Clarke's *Demonstration of the Being and Attributes of God* (1704) and *Discourse Concerning the Unchangeable Obligations of Natural Religion, and the Truth and Certainty of the Christian Religion* (1705). Collins gibed that until Clarke's "demonstration" of the existence of God, nobody had doubted the fact; and Benjamin Franklin, in his autobiography, acknowledged that he became a deist after reading some of the Boyle lectures. The New Science, in effect, had relatively little influence on the course of the deistical controversy, since neither side squarely faced the problem of the relationship of science to religion.

The decline and fall of reason. Rationalistic refutations of deism were prolific and formidable but achieved relatively little because they had so much in common with those of deism. Tindal had forced upon the apologists acceptance of the natural sufficiency of reason in theology. Thus, if deism was to be defeated, it had to be from a citadel other than that of an infallible and universal reason. One of the infrequent replies to Tindal's direct challenge, "Dare any say that God is an Arbitrary Being, and His laws not founded on the eternal reason of things?" (*Christianity as Old as the Creation*) was *The Case of Reason, Or Natural Religion Fairly and Fully Stated* (1731). Its pietistic author, William Law (1686–1761), better remembered for his *A Serious Call to a Devout and Holy Life* (1729) and as a forerunner of John Wesley, totally disavowed Right Reason in the areas of morality and religion, and argued for historical evidence and implicit faith.

Bishop Joseph Butler (1692–1752) offered in the *Rolls Sermons* (1726) an important revaluation of the authority of conscience and in the *Analogy of Religion* (1736) a matter-of-fact defense of Christianity; he sought to prove by analogy that all deistical objections against revelation were equally applicable to natural religion. The danger of this argument (which employed some of the methods of science and of Lockean empiricism) was that it might conceivably drive readers to become skeptical of both kinds of religion, to espouse atheism, or to retreat into implicit faith.

Bishop George Berkeley's (1685–1753) *Alciphron, or the Minute Philosopher* (1732), with its subtitle "Containing an Apology for the Christian religion against those who are called Freethinkers," is a brilliant series of polemical dialogues, but it contains little of his highly controversial and much misunderstood philosophical denial of abstract ideas and of "matter," for which Berkeley was frequently accused of being a skeptic. His *The Analyst* (1734), addressed to an "infidel mathematician" (presumably Edmund Halley), adopts the hazardous method of defending orthodoxy by asserting that the axioms of mathematics are as irrational and incomprehensible as the mysteries of Christianity.

Law and Butler had paved the way for antirationalistic assults on deism, the former through faith, the latter through matter of fact. The argument for faith was implemented in *Christianity Not Founded on Argument* (1742) by Henry Dodwell ("the younger"), who had as little use for historical proofs as for intellectual proofs. According to Dodwell, the Boyle lectures, like all rationalistic efforts, had only succeeded in spreading infidelity; external proofs have no real evidential value; probability reigns; so in the final analysis, there is no other way to approach religion, than to believe because you wish to believe. With Dodwell's appeal to emotionalism, the "enthusiasm" of Wesley was just around the corner.

Conyers Middleton (1683–1750), Anglican clergyman, and equally antirationalistic, pressed the historical argument against external proof of the validity of religious claims in his *Free Inquiry into the Miraculous Powers which are supposed to have subsisted in the Christian Church from the Earliest Ages through several successive Centuries* (1749). Professedly denying the supernatural powers associated with the growth of Catholicism, Middleton could scarcely have been unaware that the same arguments could also be used to attack Gospel miracles, and that there is in actuality no breach between sacred and profane history.

Fatal blows to the Age of Reason (as differentiated from the Age of Enlightenment) came simultaneously on two levels—intellectually, from David Hume (1711–1776) and emotionally, from John Wesley (1703–1791). What might be termed the deistical side of Hume can most readily be seen in "Of Miracles" and "Of a Particular Providence and of a Future State" (1748), "The Natural History of Religion (1757), and *Dialogues Concerning Natural Religion* (1779), the last of which comes to the purposefully lame conclusion "that the cause or causes of order in the universe probably bear some remote analogy to human intelligence." Natural religion, whether of the rationalistic or matter-of-fact variety, can lead only to doubt, uncertainty, and suspension of judgment. In reality, of course, Hume was no deist, but rather an antideist, a skeptic who destroyed the vulnerable a priori basis of deism.

At about the same time, John Wesley attacked deism through "enthusiasm," the doctrine of continuous personal inspiration and inner conversion of the soul: "By grace are ye saved through faith." The fatal blows had been delivered; the Age of Reason had fallen and deism was dead. Or was it? The question will be taken up after brief considerations of deism in France, Germany, and America.

DEISM ON THE CONTINENT

The term "Enlightenment" was unknown in Britain during the eighteenth century, although its spirit was plainly manifest. When it did appear in the nineteenth century, it was employed in the derogatory sense of shallow and pretentious intellectualism coupled with unreasonable contempt for tradition and authority. In eighteenth-century France and Germany, on the contrary, full-fledged movements of *Éclaircissement* and *Aufklärung* were under way and were winning important intellectual and political victories. The present section will confine itself, insofar as possible, to religion and will deal with only a few predominant thinkers.

Voltaire. Without stopping to investigate such sixteenth-century precursors as Jean Bodin, Rabelais, Pierre Charron, and Montaigne, or such seventeenth-century precursors as Descartes, Gassendi, Fontenelle, and Bayle, it is well to proceed directly to Francois-Marie Arouet, universally known as Voltaire (1694–1778), the greatest of the French deists. Banishment to England (1726–1729) by order of the *ancien régime* put the already widely known poet, playwright, *philosophe* (and later, historian and novelist) into the scientific atmosphere of Newton, the philosophical and religious atmosphere of Locke and some of the earlier deists (Voltaire had already known Bolingbroke in France), and the literary neoclassical atmosphere of Swift and Pope. Much impressed by the relatively tolerant attitudes of the English as compared to the rigid censorship of the *ancien régime*, Voltaire published in London in 1733 *Letters Concerning the English Nation.* A surreptitiously arranged French version of 1734, *Lettres philosophiques*, speedily burned by the common hangman, was Voltaire's first bombshell against governmental and church tyranny. Thereafter, his remorseless battle cry of *Écrasez l'infâme!* was to be heard throughout a long life of polemic.

Although he consistently used the word "theist" in reference to himself, Voltaire was a deist in the tradition of the British deists, never attacking the existence of Deity but always the corruptions of church and priestcraft. As late as 1770, in a letter to Frederick the Great voicing strong disapproval of the avowed atheism of many of the *philosophes*, Voltaire repeated his conviction that if God did not exist, it would be necessary to invent him. The *Lettres philosophiques* eulogizes the Quakers as ideal deists for their freedom of thought and their freedom from dogmatism and clericism; attacks Pascal's Pyrrhonism, which leaves man only the alternative of implicit faith; praises the philosophical empiricism and religious reasonableness of Locke; and seeks to convert the scientists of France to the Newtonian system. Other writings on religion and morality, *Poème sur la loi naturelle* and *Poème sur le désastre de Lisbonne*, both of 1756, as well as the famous novel *Candide* (1759), assail the doctrine of philosophical optimism and, indeed, of divine benevolence. Believing as he did in a natural religion based on reason, Voltaire's chief onslaughts were upon dogmatism, superstition, fanaticism, and tyranny. His *Traité sur la tolérance* (1763), a classic denunciation of oppression, occasioned by the infamous Calas *affaire* of 1762, was followed in 1764 by the witty and effective *Dictionnaire philosophique.* Like most of the so-called deists, Voltaire was fundamentally a humanist seeking to better the condition of mankind.

Jean-Jacques Rousseau. Novelist, political writer, deist, *philosophe* and anti-*philosophe*, Rousseau (1712–1778) remains one of the most inscrutable literary and philosophical geniuses of all time—a supreme individualist doting upon his own uniqueness. Born a Protestant, he became a Catholic, and finally a deist. His *Confessions* reveals that it was the reading of Voltaire's *Lettres philosophiques* that first incited him to study, to think, and to become a dedicated man of letters.

In touching solely upon Rousseau's role as a deist, it is fitting to examine the "Profession of Faith of a Savoyard Vicar," part of the fourth book of *Émile, ou de l'éducation* (1762). The first book had opened with the affirmation that everything is good as it comes from the Author of all things, but that everything degenerates in the hands of man. The fourth book seeks to develop and clarify this thesis, using, for prudential purposes, a vicar as spokesman. Jettisoning metaphysical proofs of God and subscribing to no strict system, the vicar simply feels God within himself, as a world governor of will, intelligence, power, and goodness. This beneficent deity is to be worshiped from the heart, and not through artificial forms. Yet it is paradoxically evident that while mere animals are happy, superior man is miserable. Why? asks the vicar. He replies to his own question that far from being a simple uncompounded creature, man is actually a being of contradictions. Self-love is natural to him, but a sense of justice or conscience or inner light is innate; he has the power to will things, but does not always exert this power to enforce his will. Man, therefore, is the author of evil: born good, he acquires vice. God, infinitely powerful, is infinitely good and supremely just. To emulate God in seeking justice is man's only source of happiness. In this respect, natural religion, learned through conscience, is sufficient. Christian revelation, on the one hand, is fraught with difficulty, mystery, obscurity, and dogma. Its majesty, sublimity, and beauty, on the other hand, bear witness to its divinity: it is not a man-made invention; indeed, it remained Rousseau's "pillow-book" throughout life. Rousseau, in brief, is a sentimental and primitivistic, rather than a "hard," rationalistic deist. Yet, in substance, his "soft" sentimental deism is actually not far removed from the religious Common Notions of Lord Herbert or even from Spinoza's Doctrines of Universal Faith.

Rousseau's device of using the Savoyard vicar as spokesman for his own deism was unsuccessful; *Émile* was publicly burned and an order was issued for the arrest of the author, who was forced to flee the country. Except for his much later autobiographical writings, *Émile* was Rousseau's last major work.

Atheism. Aside from Voltaire, who subscribed to "hard" deism, and Rousseau, who dispensed the "soft" variety, the *philosophes* were not deists at all. To them, deism was but the starting point on the road to atheism. Their militant atheism, as well as their dogmatic belief in constant and inevitable progress and the perfectibility of man, shocked Gibbon and Hume, and greatly disturbed both Voltaire and Rousseau. The names of d'Alembert and Diderot (editors of the *Encyclopédie*), Baron d'Holbach (and his "atheistical club"), Helvétius, Grimm, La Mettrie, Condillac, and Condorcet can hardly be excluded from the list of atheistical *philosophes* or, at least, those well on the road to atheism. Deism in France, although considerably influenced by deism in England, was much more extreme both religiously and politically, simply because England had already made considerable social progress. In France, deism was part and parcel of the general move toward materialism, freedom of thought and publication, freedom from the tyranny of the *ancien régime* in the affairs of state and church, that ultimately exploded in the Revolution.

Deism in Germany. The course of the *Aufklärung* differed in major respects from the analogous movements in Britain and France, and developed later. Under the domination of the earlier Leibniz–Wolff philosophy, rational supernaturalism generally prevailed. After 1740 (the year of the accession of Frederick the Great, the first modern freethinking king), numerous translations of the British deists and of their orthodox refuters (as indicated in G. W. Alberti's *Briefe betreffend den allerneusten Zustand der Religion und der Wissenschaften in Gross-Brittannien* of 1752–1754, J. A. Trinius' *Freydenker-Lexicon* of 1759, and U. G. Thorschmid's *Freidenker-Bibliothek* of 1765–1767) introduced a new influence. Although the German *philosophes* were widely read, there was little of French radicalism in either their religious or political thinking. Among out-and-out deists (called *Freidenkers*, or Freethinkers), the names of Karl Bahrdt, Johann Eberhard, Johann Edelmann, and Reimarus must be mentioned.

Hermann Samuel Reimarus. The apology of Reimarus (1694–1768) for natural religion as opposed to atheism and materialism, written in 1755, was Englished in 1766 as *The Principal Truths of Natural Religion Defended and Illustrated.* His direct attacks on Christianity, through a painstaking study of New Testament texts, included "On the Object of Jesus and His Apostles" and "On the Story of the Resurrection," and were published posthumously (1774–1778) by Lessing as *Fragments of an Anonymous Work found at Wolfenbüttel.*

Gotthold Ephraim Lessing. Lessing (1729–1781), distinguished man of letters and author of the *Laokoon* (1766) and *Nathan the Wise* (1779), was a freethinker in the nonabusive sense of the term. He should probably not be classified as a typical deist, since he professed belief in natural revelation in his last publication, *The Education of the Human Race* (1780), and at the close of his life he is said to have privately acknowledged pantheistic beliefs. Lessing's lifelong friend Moses Mendelssohn (1729–1786), a Jewish freethinker, is customarily classified as a deist in the loose usage of the term.

Immanuel Kant. The case of Immanuel Kant (1724–1804), the greatest of the German philosophers, is highly instructive. Born and educated as a religious Pietist, he came under the influence of Newtonian physics and always remained interested in science. In theology his three most famous critiques, stimulated by the "mitigated scepticism" of Hume, agree with Hume in principle. The *Critique of Pure Reason* (1781) presses beyond Hume in criticizing proofs of the existence of God; the *Critique of Practical Reason* (1788) is concerned with moral experience in natural religion; and the *Critique of Judgement* (1790), in a sense, mediates between the first two. Kant's position as a "Christian deist," however, is best expressed in *Religion within the Limits of Reason Alone* (1792–1794). The limits of religion, basically naturalistic, are set in conscience or practical religion. Christianity is stripped of mystery and tradition and is treated as a purely moral religion—in fact, the only purely moral one; God is the moral Creator of the world, and it is the duty of the good man to worship him. Kant's transcendental philosophy is beyond the scope of this article, but it is relevant to say that Kant was the leader of the *Aufklärung*, which he defined as the freeing of man from the self-imposed bondage of the mind, and proclaimed as its motto *sapere aude* ("dare to know").

DEISM IN THE UNITED STATES

The works of the British deists, as well as those of the defenders of the faith, were well known in American intellectual circles, commencing with the second quarter of the eighteenth century. In the latter half of the century, Voltaire's "hard" deism and, especially, Rousseau's "soft" deism were widely disseminated; but the atheism of the *philosophes* made little headway. The Great Awakening, triggered by the preaching of Jonathan Edwards in 1734 and bolstered by the preaching of the English Methodist George Whitefield, militated against orthodox Puritanism and in favor of republicanism both in religion and politics, but the atmosphere of rationalism still prevailed. Before the Revolution, however, deism made relatively little progress. Among the intelligentsia at Harvard, nevertheless, the Dudleian lectures were established in 1755 for the purpose of explicating natural religion. Alarms sounded by the orthodox that deism was sweeping the country were unjustified. However, the Treaty of Paris in 1763 and the French alliance at the time of the Revolution undeniably quickened the spread of radical Gallic ideas.

Benjamin Franklin. Franklin (1706–1790), man of letters, scientist, and diplomatist, as early as 1723 acknowledged himself a deist to intimate friends but circumspectly continued church attendance throughout life, thereby setting the conservative pattern followed by most of the leaders of the colonial and Revolutionary periods. In London in 1725 Franklin published his *Dissertation on Liberty and Necessity, Pleasure and Pain* in opposition to the free-will doctrine of the British deist Wollaston. However, Franklin shortly repudiated and suppressed this juvenile work. When he was about 22, he drafted "Articles of Belief and Acts of Religion," a creed not unlike Lord Herbert of Cherbury's religious Common Notions and one which sustained him for life. Prudence and practicality characterize all of Franklin's publications and actions. *Poor Richard's Almanack* (1732–1757) is the essence of common sense, or how to get along in the world without unduly disturbing society; his list of virtues by no means coincides with the Christian virtues.

Thomas Jefferson. Framer of the Declaration of Independence, diplomatist, vice president and twice president of the United States, and member of the Episcopal church, Jefferson (1743–1826) was in reality a deist, rationalist, and, above all, a humanitarian. He compiled but never published what later came to be known as *The Jefferson Bible, being The Life and Morals of Jesus Christ of Nazareth.* This little work, a cento of clippings from the Gospels of Matthew, Mark, Luke, and John pasted in a blankbook, extols Jesus as a man for his moral teachings, omits ambiguous and controversial passages, and, while rejecting many of the supernatural elements, presents the core of Christian morality and is genuinely religious in tone. Religion, for Jefferson as well as for Franklin, was essentially a utilitarian moral code.

George Washington. Washington (1732–1799), general and first president of the United States, was a deist of a similar stripe. Although he always maintained a church pew, he was one of the leading statesmen who advocated total separation of state and church and who saw to it that no reference to Christianity or even to Deity was made in the Constitution. In answer to a direct question from a Muslim potentate in Tripoli, Washington acquiesced in the declaration of Joel Barlow, then American consul in Algiers, that "the Government of the United States of America is not in any sense founded on the Christian religion."

Thomas Paine. Born in England, Paine (1737–1809) arrived in America in 1774, bearing a letter of introduction from Franklin. A political theorist, diplomatist, and man of letters, Paine was a deist, but not overtly until the publication in Paris of his *The Age of Reason: Being an Investigation of True and Fabulous Theology* (1794–1796). The first of its two books, intended to rescue deism from the reigning French atheism, is a more or less scientific assault upon revealed religion in general as being supererogatory to natural religion. The second book carries the attack directly to both the Old and New Testaments, arguing that the Bible is not the word of God and depicting Christianity as a species of atheism. Paine wrote vigorously and extensively and was outspoken in carrying his message to the common people, whose battles he had fought on the political, social, and economic fronts as well. In *The Age of Reason* the battleground was not new but was considerably enlarged from that of any earlier British deist. The work offended readers in France and shocked many in England and America who were laboring under the delusion that the deistical controversy was over and that orthodoxy had triumphed. Paine was rewarded for his efforts by banishment from England and by social obloquy in America. The patriot who throughout a long and turbulent career had accomplished so much for the new country, the man who had so vigorously combated atheism, was held to be an atheist, infidel, radical, and drunkard.

Lesser American deists. Paine was not the first acknowledged American deist, for the year 1784 produced *Reason the Only Oracle of Man, or a Compendious System of Natural Religion.* Its author, Ethan Allen (1738–1789), Revolutionary hero and leader of the Green Mountain Boys, had acquired his deism through early reading of the British deists. His book is flagrantly anticlerical and anti-Christian; he argues that a rationalistic universal religion of nature which provides the fundamentals of morality is all-sufficient and needs no supplementation. Both the Hebraic and the Christian testaments are subjected to ridicule. Like Paine, Allen was not so much an original thinker as a fearless propagandist.

Beginning in 1793, the blind ex-Baptist preacher Elihu Palmer (1764–1806) led a fiery deistical campaign from the lecture platform and by publication against the divine authority of the Bible. In 1794 he rushed to the defense of Paine's *Age of Reason* and in 1801–1802 published *Principles of Nature; or, a Development of the Moral Causes of Happiness and Misery among the Human Species.* From 1803 to 1805 he edited a weekly deistical paper, *Prospect; or, View of the Moral World.* Palmer also organized the Deistical Society of New York. With his many speeches and tracts designed to disseminate deism among the lower classes, Palmer was a most unusual deist, in that he was deliberately leading a popular crusade.

Philip Freneau (1752–1832), writer of patriotic verse, was also the American poet of the religion of nature and humanity, and his ideas were close to those of Paine. The very titles of such poems as "Belief and Unbelief: Humbly recommended to the serious consideration of creed makers," "On the Uniformity and Perfection of Nature," "On the Religion of Nature," tell their own story, without need of commentary.

Decline of deism. During the eighteenth century, Puritanism in America had begun to crumble under the combined attacks of the Great Awakening, Methodism, and deism. "The Triumph of Infidelity" (1788), the poem by Timothy Dwight, orthodox president of Yale University, bears weak witness to the strength of deism. Shortly after 1800 deism became submerged in a revival of enthusiastic evangelism, particularly in the frontier areas, where intellectual attainments were hardly predominant. In New England, Unitarianism began making headway under the influence of Joseph Priestley, who in 1794 had immigrated from England. But elsewhere emotionalism, conservatism, reaction, and fideism were triumphant.

THE LEGACY OF DEISM

Historical deism, a term of many connotations, was essentially rationalism applied to religion, and as such was the counterpart to literary neoclassicism. Deism and neoclassicism flourished at approximately the same time, both stressing universality and shying away from particularity. In deism, this cardinal point meant that from the very beginning the Hebraic and Christian revelations were suspect, if not invariably attacked. Deism primarily put forth the view that the aim of religion is morality and that anything traditionally taught beyond morality is superfluous. The widely accepted distinction between constructive deism and critical deism, or, as it has also been put, deism before Locke and deism after Locke, or humanistic deism as opposed to scientific deism, will not survive the careful scrutiny and evaluation of leading deistical texts. Yet the prime position of Right Reason in deism did not prevent empiricism, in the form of scholarly examination of Scriptural texts and historicism, from assuming increasingly important roles. Edward Gibbon's purely naturalistic investigation into the early progress and establishment of the Christian religion in the famous (or infamous) fifteenth and sixteenth chapters of his *Decline and Fall of the Roman Empire* (Vol. I, 1776) was manifestly influenced, not only by the philosophical skepticism of Hume, but also by the somewhat crude historical investigations of a number of the deists themselves. One general development of the deistical movement, therefore, was the rise of "the higher criticism": the Bible was no longer deemed sacrosanct, and its verbal inspiration no longer dogmatically assumed. A second development was the greatly intensified study of comparative religion. A third development was the rise of "the philosophy of religion," spurred on by Hume's demonstration that no matter of fact, including the existence of God, can be proved a priori.

In actuality, deism did not die; it did not even fade away, and it still exists in fact, though perhaps not in name, for those who say (with Voltaire) that there must be a God and those who say (with Rousseau) that they know there is a God. Nor was deism vanquished, as has so often been asserted, by the superior talents of its orthodox opponents, by the exhaustion of the subject, or by the incapacities of its protagonists: certainly, among the English, at least, Toland, Collins, and Tindal were the intellectual equals of most of their adversaries. By and large, both orthodox and heterodox alike were rational theists of a somewhat naive variety. Charles Leslie's *Short and Easy Method with the Deists* of 1696 proved, in actuality, neither short nor easy. The deists were long subjected to the *odium theologicum*, and the historians of the movement have almost without exception downgraded or slandered them socially as well as intellectually since the time of John Leland in the mid-eighteenth century. Even the foremost rationalists of the nineteenth century, Mark Pattison and Leslie Stephen (the latter produced the most complete and erudite history to date) are condescending. Rarely have the achievements of deism been acknowledged and appreciated, and then only in passing, in brief comments from specialized monographs, articles, and encyclopedia entries. No really satisfactory, complete, impartial, and scholarly account of the significance of the movement has as yet appeared.

Deism had somewhat different effects in different countries, depending on the different national cultural situations. By the close of the eighteenth century in England, it seemed, superficially at least, to have disappeared or gone underground. Yet in 1790, when Burke triumphantly asked, "Who born within the last forty years has read one word of Collins and Toland, and Tindal, and Chubb, and Morgan, and that whole race who called themselves Freethinkers? Who now reads Bolingbroke? Who ever read him through?" he was historically mistaken and premature in his inference. For in the nineteenth century, radical publishers such as William Benbow, William Hone, and, most notably, Richard Carlile (1790–1843), all of whom were political as well as religious reformers, flooded the popular market with periodicals (for example, *The Deist; or Moral Philosopher*, 1819–1820), pamphlets, and cheap reprints and excerpts from freethinkers of all ages, including the whole range of the British deists, the skeptical Hume, Voltaire and Rousseau of France, and Paine and Elihu Palmer of America. The campaign was continued by others throughout the nineteenth century and survives in the present century on a higher intellectual level by affiliations with Unitarianism, Fabian socialism, and rationalist and humanistic societies, among others.

In France, the true deism of Voltaire and Rousseau was overwhelmed by the atheism of most of the *philosophes*, a doctrine which inevitably contributed to the upheaval of the French Revolution. The course of these eighteenth-century developments may be said to be paralleled today, on the one hand, by widespread atheism and, on the other, by the militant anticlericism of even many of the devout. In Germany, early intellectual deism was followed by both the fideism of Friedrich Heinrich Jacobi and a new post-Humean variety of rationalism which began with Kant and the romanticists of the following century.

In America, deism was long submerged by evangelism among the semiliterate masses and by Unitarianism among the well educated. An aggressive antireligionism resurged in the 1870s with Robert Ingersoll, "the great agnostic," and a host of followers, such as William Brann in Texas in the 1890s with his world-famous newspaper *Brann's Iconoclast*. Today, rationalist and humanistic societies and Unitarianism are omnipresent.

With few exceptions, deists in all countries have been interested in political and social reform, and with the passage of time it has become virtually impossible to isolate the purely religious aspects. Deism remains a symptom of revolt against orthodoxy and dogmatism.

By way of summary and possible oversimplification, deism is the individual's affirmation of his right to think for himself on all subjects and to communicate his thoughts to others for the general welfare. It is the affirmation of the principle of the oneness of humanity. It marks the rise of secularism and the beginning of modernity in theology. In this sense it is still viable, and although freethinking today claims a philosophical substratum different from the simple rationalism of the seventeenth and eighteenth centuries, it is akin in spirit to historical deism. The early rise of deism in all countries was strongly abetted by the growth of the spirit of toleration, and deism, in its turn, has strongly contributed to the continued growth and acceptance of toleration of other views. Perhaps, in the most universal sense, this is the major legacy of historical deism to the modern world.

Bibliography

USEFUL ANTHOLOGIES

Berlin, Isaiah, ed., *The Age of Enlightenment*. New York, 1956.

Brinton, Crane, ed., *The Portable Age of Reason Reader*. New York, 1956.

Creed, John M., and Smith, John S. Boys, eds., *Religious Thought in the Eighteenth Century*. Cambridge, 1934.

Fellows, Otis E., and Torrey, Norman L., eds., *The Age of Enlightenment*. New York, 1942.

Hampshire, Stuart, ed., *The Age of Reason: The 17th Century Philosophers*. New York, 1956.

Torrey, Norman L., ed., *Les Philosophes*. New York, 1960.

GENERAL HISTORIES

Lechler, Gotthard V., *Geschichte des englischen Deism*. Stuttgart, 1841.

Leland, John, *A View of the Principal Deistical Writers that have appeared in England in the last and present Century*, 3d ed., 3 vols. London, 1754–1756. Early, voluminous, and vituperative apologetics.

Orr, John, *English Deism: Its Roots and Its Fruits*. Grand Rapids, Mich., 1934. Discursive, not too sound.

Sayous, Edouard, *Les Déistes anglais et le christianisme, 1696–1738*. Paris, 1882.

Stephen, Leslie, *English Thought in the Eighteenth Century*, 2 vols. London, 1876; revised, 1902; paperback, New York, 1963. Vol. I is most scholarly study available but with a curious personal animus.

GENERAL HISTORICAL BACKGROUND

Abbey, C. J., and Overton, J. H., *The English Church in the Eighteenth Century*, 2 vols. London, 1878.

Becker, Carl L., *The Heavenly City of the Eighteenth-Century Philosophers*. New Haven, 1932. Becker's brilliant paradox has dimmed over the years.

Bury, J. B., *A History of Freedom of Thought*. New York, 1913.

Cassirer, Ernst, *The Philosophy of the Enlightenment*. Princeton, 1951 and Boston, 1955.

Colie, R. L., *Light and Enlightenment: a Study of the Cambridge Platonists and the Dutch Arminians.* Cambridge, 1957.

Cragg, G. R., *From Puritanism to the Age of Reason.* Cambridge, 1950.

Farrar, A. S., *Critical History of Free Thought.* London, 1862.

Hall, Thomas C., *The Religious Background of American Culture.* Boston, 1930.

Havens, George R., *The Age of Ideas.* New York, 1955.

Hazard, Paul, *La Crise de la conscience européenne,* 3 vols. Paris, 1935.

Hazard, Paul, *La Pensée européenne au XVIIIe siècle,* 3 vols. Paris, 1946. Both of Hazard's works are brilliantly comprehensive.

Humphreys, A. R., *The Augustan World.* London, 1954. Useful survey.

Hunt, John, *Religious Thought in England from the Reformation to the End of the Last Century,* 3 vols. London, 1873.

Jordan, Wilbur K., *Development of Religious Toleration in England,* 4 vols. Cambridge, Mass., 1932–1940. Highly important.

Lecky, W. E. M., *History of the Rise and Influence of Rationalism in Europe,* 2 vols. in one. London, 1910. Valuable.

Martin, Kingsley, *French Liberal Thought in the Eighteenth Century.* Boston, 1929.

M'Giffert, Arthur C., *Protestant Thought Before Kant.* London, 1919.

Parrington, Vernon L., *Main Currents in American Thought,* 3 vols. New York, 1927.

Robertson, J. M., *A History of Freethought in the Nineteenth Century,* 2 vols. London, 1929.

Robertson, J. M., *A Short History of Freethought Ancient and Modern,* 3d ed., 2 vols. London, 1915. Both works are indispensable.

Smith, Preserved, *A History of Modern Culture,* 2 vols. New York, 1930–1934. Wide coverage.

Tulloch, John, *Rational Theology and Christian Philosophy in England in the Seventeenth Century,* 2 vols. Edinburgh and London, 1872.

Urwin, Kenneth, *A Century for Freedom,* London, 1946.

Willey, Basil, *The Eighteenth Century Background.* London, 1940. Somewhat superficial.

SPECIALIZED STUDIES

Aldridge, Alfred O., "Shaftesbury and the Deist Manifesto." *Transactions of the American Philosophical Society,* new ser. Vol. 41, Part 2 (1951), 297–385.

Boller, Paul F., Jr., *George Washington & Religion.* Dallas, Texas, 1963.

Cole, G. D. H., *Richard Carlile.* London, 1943.

Courtines, Leo P., *Bayle's Relations with England and the English.* New York, 1938.

Hefelbower, S. G., *The Relation of John Locke to English Deism.* Chicago, 1918.

Koch, G. Adolf, *Republican Religion: The American Revolution and the Cult of Reason.* New York, 1933. Indispensable.

Lovejoy, A. O., "The Parallel of Deism and Classicism." *Modern Philology,* Vol. XXIX (1932), 281–299. Important.

Luke, Hugh J., Jr., *Drams for the Vulgar: A Study of some Radical Publishers and Publications of Early Nineteenth-Century London.* Unpublished Ph.D. dissertation. The University of Texas, 1963.

Morais, Herbert M., *Deism in Eighteenth Century America.* New York, 1934.

Mossner, Ernest C., *Bishop Butler and the Age of Reason.* New York, 1936.

Noack, Ludwig, *Die Freidenker in der Religion,* 3 vols. Bern, 1853–1855.

Pattison, Mark, "Tendencies of Religious Thought in England," in *Essays and Reviews.* London, 1860.

Popkin, Richard H., "Scepticism in the Enlightenment," *Studies on Voltaire and the Eighteenth Century,* Geneva, xxiv/xxvii (1963), 1321–1345.

Russell, Bertrand, *Why I Am Not a Christian and Other Essays on Religion and Related Subjects,* Paul Edwards, ed. London, 1957.

Salvatorelli, Luigi, *From Locke to Reitzenstein: the Historical Investigation of the Origins of Christianity.* Cambridge, Mass., 1930.

Stromberg, Roland N., *Religious Liberalism in Eighteenth-Century England.* Oxford, 1954. Sound survey.

Tennant, F. R., *Miracle and Its Philosophical Presuppositions.* Cambridge, 1925.

Torrey, Norman L., *Voltaire and the English Deists.* New Haven, 1930. Indispensable.

Webb, Clement C. J., *Studies in the History of Natural Theology.* Oxford, 1915.

Winnett, A. R., "Were the Deists 'Deists'?" *Church Quarterly Review,* Vol. CLXI (1960), 70–77. Makes distinction between philosophical and historical deists.

Yolton, John W., *John Locke and the Way of Ideas.* Oxford, 1956.

ERNEST CAMPBELL MOSSNER

DEL VECCHIO, GIORGIO, Italian legal philosopher, was born in Bologna in 1878, the son of the economist Giulio Salvatore Del Vecchio. He studied in Italy and Germany and taught in Ferrara, Sassari, Messina, Bologna, and at Rome, where he was a professor from 1920, rector of the university from 1925 to 1927, and dean of the faculty of law from 1930 to 1938. He was dismissed by the fascists in 1938 because of his Jewish background. He resumed teaching in 1944 but was dismissed again in 1945, this time as a former fascist; he taught again from 1947 to 1953. He was named professor emeritus in 1955. Del Vecchio founded the *Rivista internazionale di filosofia del diritto* in 1921 and was its editor; he founded the Istituto di Filosofia del Diritto of the University of Rome in 1933 and the Società Italiana di Filosofia del Diritto in 1936.

Del Vecchio was influential in turning Italian legal thought from nineteenth-century positivism. His own position has been described as Neo-Kantian idealism and as humanist ethical idealism. According to Del Vecchio, the thinking subject is necessarily conscious of the *other,* not merely as object, but as itself a subject. Hence, mutual recognition and respect are necessary, and it is possible to deduce for the mutual relations of subjects not merely a logical form but also an ideal content of justice based on respect for personality. Law is the objective coordination of possible actions between subjects according to an ethical principle, which in its highest expression is the principle of justice. Psychologically, the idea of justice is a necessary aspect of consciousness, found in rudimentary form even among animals. Historically, the idea has been realized with varying degrees of positivity in human societies, and continual effort is needed to realize it in the changing specific conditions of life. There are instances of "involution" (regression), but history on the whole shows a progressive evolution toward the understanding and realization of justice. These main ideas, stated in Del Vecchio's early writings, were developed with a wealth of historical learning in his *Lezioni di filosofia del diritto* and *La giustizia;* in other writings he has applied them to particular problems of legal and political philosophy.

Del Vecchio, like other veterans of World War I, joined the fascist movement when it arose because he saw it as a defense against Bolshevism, and it is unjust to consider him a representative of fascist philosophy. For a time he did hope, mistakenly, that the fascist "strong state" might realize the "ethical state" that, by harmonizing individual freedoms, would enhance individual personality. Throughout the fascist period, however, Del Vecchio's fundamental teaching was unchanged; and he continued to assert the validity of natural law and to defend individual freedom against the statolatry of official fascist doctrine.

Works by Del Vecchio

LONGER WRITINGS

La giustizia. Rome, 1922–1923. Expanded in later editions; 5th ed., Rome, 1959. Translated by Lady Guthrie as *Justice.* Edinburgh, 1952.

Lezioni di filosofia del diritto. Milan, 1930; 11th ed., Milan, 1962. Translated from 8th ed. by T. O. Martin as *Philosophy of Law.* Washington, D.C., 1953.

SHORTER WRITINGS

Del Vecchio's shorter writings (since 1902) have been collected and republished.

Studi sul diritto, 2 vols. Milan, 1958. "Sui principii generali del diritto," republished in this volume, was translated by Felix Forte as *General Principles of Law.* Boston, 1956.

Studi sullo stato. Milan, 1958.

Presupposti, concetto e principio del diritto. Milan, 1959. Translated by John Lisle as *The Formal Bases of Law.* Boston, 1914; 2d ed., Boston, 1921.

Studi su la guerra e la pace. Milan, 1959.

Contributi alla storia del pensiero giuridico e filosofico. Milan, 1963.

Humanité et unité de droit. Paris, 1963.

Works on Del Vecchio

Orecchia, Rinaldo, *Bibliografia di Giorgio Del Vecchio,* 2d ed. Bologna, 1949.

Vidal, Enrico, *La filosofia giuridica di Giorgio Del Vecchio.* Milan, 1951.

A. H. CAMPBELL

DEMIURGE, an anglicized form of δημιουργός, the ordinary Greek word for a workman, craftsman, or artificer, is commonly used in Greek literature from Homer onward. In Homer it is applied to heralds, soothsayers, and physicians as well as to manual workers; but in later Greek it primarily means a craftsman or maker, such as a carpenter or a smith. Its importance in the history of philosophy derives almost entirely from Plato's *Timaeus,* in which a Demiurge, or Craftsman, is represented as ordering and arranging the physical world and bringing it as far as possible into conformity with the best and most rational pattern. In two other places (*Republic* 530A and *Sophist* 265C) Plato uses the word δημιουργος, or the corresponding verb, in connection with divine creation; and it occurs in one passage in Xenophon's Socratic discourses (*Memorabilia* 1.4.9), but these are all casual and isolated references. For our understanding of Plato's conception of creation we must rely almost exclusively on the *Timaeus.*

The *Timaeus* is, in fact, Plato's only substantial essay in physical theory and cosmology. There is disagreement about the date of the dialogue and about its place in the chronological order of Plato's writings; but it is generally agreed to be later than the great group of middle dialogues, from the *Phaedo* and *Symposium* to the *Republic* and *Phaedrus,* in which Plato expounds his most characteristic metaphysical and ontological doctrines. The substance of these doctrines is repeated and underlined in the *Timaeus* itself, which makes a sharp division between the eternal, transcendent, intelligible, unchanging world of true being or reality and the temporal, phenomenal, sensible, unstable world of mere becoming. It was this very contrast between the world of Forms and the world of sense that had led Plato to neglect physical research and speculation; and when he does turn to this subject in the *Timaeus,* he repeatedly insists that even his own best efforts in this field cannot produce more than an εἰκὼς μυθός—a "likely tale"—falling far short of the certainty and exactness that can be sought in mathematics and pure philosophy. He speaks of the whole doctrine of the *Timaeus* in the provisional, tentative manner in which he presents the eschatological myths of the *Gorgias, Phaedo, Republic,* and *Phaedrus.*

Against this background it may appear surprising that Plato ventured on these topics at all. His motives become plainer if we remember his own comments in the *Phaedo* (97C–99D) on the cosmology of Anaxagoras. Socrates first praises Anaxagoras for holding that νοῦς—Intelligence or Reason—ordered and arranged the world, imposing a rational plan on a pre-existing chaos. He then complains that Anaxagoras did not pursue this line of thought to its proper conclusion: he uses Reason as a mere *deus ex machina* to explain the origin of the cosmic process as a whole but does not give detailed teleological explanations of particular things and events, showing that everything is arranged for the best. Anaxagoras resorts instead to the purely physical explanations that had been used by his Ionian predecessors, which is like trying to explain why Socrates does not escape from prison wholly in terms of bones and sinews, without reference to intelligence, intention, motive, and morality. Aristotle makes a similar comment in *Metaphysics* I,3: Anaxagoras stands out among his contemporaries and predecessors "like a sober man among drunkards," but he does not make proper use of his concept of cosmic νοῦς.

The *Timaeus* is Plato's attempt to carry out the program of rationalist cosmology that Anaxagoras had promised but had failed to fulfill. The Demiurge is portrayed as the agent who turns the initial chaos into a cosmos. Like a human craftsman, he arranges existing materials and does not create them. The conception of creation *ex nihilo* is foreign to the whole tradition of Greek thought. The Demiurge shapes his materials to conform as much as possible to the eternal intelligible model of the Forms. First, he makes other gods, the world soul that the cosmos requires as its motive principle, and the immortal part of the human soul. The created gods then complete the work by making physical things, including human bodies. The Demiurge's success is necessarily limited: the Reason that constitutes his pattern is opposed by a recalcitrant Necessity (ἀνάγκη) that hinders his work in something like the way in which a human craftsman may be frustrated by intractable materials—and no material is perfectly tractable. This obstacle to a faultless achievement by the Demiurge is also the main reason why Plato cannot hope to give more than a "likely tale" of the Demiurge's work.

It has been widely believed, from ancient times to the present day, that the Demiurge is a mythical figure and that Plato did not believe in the literal existence of such a creator-god. He is a personification of the Reason whose requirements he is represented as trying to embody in the nature of the cosmos. Even if he is literally meant, he must still be sharply contrasted with the creator-god of the Judaeo-Christian tradition, not only because he is not in that sense a creator, but also because he is in no sense an object of worship.

It is more difficult to decide whether the process of creation is also mythical; whether Plato believed that the imposition of order on the physical world was a definite event that took place at some time in the past, or whether the narrative of the *Timaeus* is a presentation in chronological form of Plato's views about the relative value and ontological priority of the various elements in the universe. According to this latter view, the story that bodies were created after souls would be a pictorial way of marking the inferiority of the body to the soul. Aristotle reports (*De Caelo* 279b33) that this was the tradition in Plato's Academy. The chronological picture is said to be used only for purposes of exposition, like a figure in geometry. Aristotle himself took the chronology literally, and he was followed in this by Plutarch; but the ancient authorities were nearly all on the other side.

Most modern scholars have disagreed with Aristotle, but he has had some notable supporters; and the question is still being debated. In support of the usual interpretation one may quote the parallel case of the *Republic*, where the building and dissolution of the ideal community is a pictorial means of presenting a logical analysis in chronological terms. Defenders of the opposite view point out that the word *γέγονεν* ("it came into being") gives an emphatic answer to the crucial question "Has the cosmos always been, or has it come to be, starting from some beginning?" (28B). However, the imagery of the *Republic* is equally emphatic. Once a man has chosen to represent one thing by painting a picture of another, the fact that he uses firm brush strokes and bright colors does not destroy its claims to be a picture.

The concept of the Demiurge was taken over by the Neoplatonists and by some Gnostic writers. To the Gnostics he was the evil lord of the lower powers, creator of the despised material world, and entirely separate from the supreme God. Their parody of the Demiurge as a clumsy imitator is blended with hostile satire of the Old Testament creator-God. Plotinus protested against their conception of the Demiurge as a source of positive evil in the world.

There is no clear case of any notable modern thinker whose teaching has been closely or directly influenced by the concept of the Demiurge, although there are hints of a similar idea in J. S. Mill's essay "Theism," where the word "Demiurgos" is applied to a God whose creative power is limited by the nature of his materials.

Bibliography

Archer-Hind, R. D., *The Timaeus of Plato.* London and New York, 1888. Text, translation, introduction and notes.

Bury, R. G., *Plato, Timaeus, Critias, Clitopho, Menexenus, Epistulae.* Loeb Classical Library. London and New York, 1929. Text and translation.

Cornford, F. M., *Plato's Cosmology.* London, 1937. Translation of the *Timaeus*, with a running commentary.

Crombie, I. M., *An Examination of Plato's Doctrines.* London and New York, 1963. Vol. II, *Plato on Knowledge and Reality*, Ch. 2.

Grube, G. M. A., *Plato's Thought.* London, 1935. Ch. 5.

Hackforth, R., "Plato's Cosmogony." *Classical Quarterly*, N. S. Vol. 9 (1959), 17–22.

Taylor, A. E., *A Commentary on Plato's Timaeus.* Oxford, 1928. Prolegomena and notes.

RENFORD BAMBROUGH

DEMOCRACY. "Democracy" is difficult to define, not only because it is vague, like so many political terms, but more importantly, because what one person would regard as a paradigm case another would deny was a democracy at all. The word has acquired a high emotive charge in the last hundred years; it has become good tactics to apply it to one's own favored type of regime and to deny it to rivals. The most diverse systems have been claimed as democracies of one sort or another, and the word has been competitively redefined, to match changes in extension by appropriate changes in intention. However, there is still this much agreement: democracy consists in "government by the people" or "popular self-government." As such, it would still be universally distinguished from, say, a despotism that made no pretense of popular participation—the despotism of Genghis Khan or of Louis XIV, for instance—or from a theocracy, like the Vatican. There remains plenty of room for disagreement, however, about the conditions under which the people can properly be said to rule itself.

In the first place, what is "the people"? In ancient Greece, the *demos* was the poorer people; democracy meant rule of the poor over the rich. This is still the usage of those who identify the people with the proletariat and democracy with the rule of the working class. However, the word "people" is often used to differentiate the subject mass from the ruling elite, as, for instance, when Locke speaks of a tyrannical government putting itself into a state of war with the people. In this sense, "the people" necessarily means the ruled. Can the people, however, be said *to rule itself* in the same sense as it is said to be ruled by monarchs, oligarchs, and priests? To rule is, generally, to prescribe conduct for someone else. There is a sense, it is true, in which moralists speak of ruling oneself, when by a kind of metaphor they speak of reason governing the passions. Again, a former colony becomes self-governing when its people is no longer ruled by outsiders; but this is not inconsistent with its still being ruled by *native* masters.

The usual paradigm of a people governing itself is the direct democracy of ancient Athens. Admittedly, citizenship was a hereditary privilege, excluding slaves and metics, and it is very doubtful whether, without this limitation, the citizen body would have been small enough for it to have operated as it did. Aside from this, however, the Athenian people governed itself in the sense that every individual could participate personally in policy decisions by discussion and voting, in a face-to-face situation. Athenian procedures are held to have been democratic in the sense that everyone was supposed to have an equal opportunity to state a case and influence decisions, even if, in some cases, individuals had ultimately to accept decisions that they had previously resisted. So today, in a similar sense, if a school or a department is said to be democratically run, we should expect its head to consult his staff on important issues and to concur in decisions to which he himself is opposed when the weight of opinion is against him. Self-government for a small group consists in general participation in the deliberative process, in which each person's voice carries a weight appropriate not to his status but to the merits, in the judgment of others, of what he has to say. If, despite continuing disagreement, a decision is essential, then it must be arrived at by majority vote. For it is not consistent with equal participation in decision making for any one individual to be privileged to say in advance that regardless of the distribution of opinions, his own or that of his group must prevail. That privilege excluded, decisions may be reached by lot or by vote; and if by vote, the opinion of either the lesser or the greater number may prevail. Deciding by lot was in fact used in Athens to fill certain public offices; it is a way of giving everyone an equal chance where advantages or privileges cannot be equally and simultaneously enjoyed; but to decide policy by lot would make nonsense of the procedure of public discussion, which is as integral to the democratic process as the idea of equality. The same would apply to a rule whereby whatever opinion received the fewest votes would prevail; for what point would there be in persuasion if it had no effect on the outcome or, still worse, if it actually reduced the chance of one's view being implemented? If a democratic decision is thought of, then, as the result of a fair confrontation of opinions, it must, at best, be generally agreed upon, and at worst, agreed upon by the majority.

Conditions of political democracy. Obviously, the conditions of face-to-face democracy, with direct participation, cannot be fulfilled within the political structure of modern states, both because of the size of their populations and because of the specialized knowledge needed to govern them. So although everyone may agree on what makes a small group democratic, when it comes to applying the concept to mass organizations, there is plenty of room for different interpretations of the principles to be applied and of the way to realize them under these very different conditions. Democracy now becomes representative government, that is, government by persons whom the people elect and thereby authorize to govern them.

"Election" and "representation" are themselves complex notions, however. In one sense, to be representative of a group may mean no more than to possess salient characteristics common to and distinctive of most of its members. In another, quasi-legal sense, one person may be said to represent another if, according to some code of rules, the consequences attached to an act of the representative are precisely those that would be attached to the act had it been performed by the principal himself; the representative can, in this case, *commit* the represented. In yet a third sense, one may represent another by looking after his interests, with or without his authorization (for example, the representation of infants in law). Now, democratic representation need not imply representation in the first sense, that of resemblance. Since an elected member of a legislature is taken to represent those who voted against as much as those who voted for him, he need not resemble those he represents, even in his opinions. Nor does he commit them as if they themselves had acted; the fact of their having legal duties does not depend on the fiction that, if their representative votes for a law, they have personally agreed to it. Their legal duties remain even if their representative voted against it. Nor must we necessarily accept moral responsibility for what is done by those who politically represent us, for in voting against them, we may have done the only thing open to us to disavow them.

Political representation is closer to the third sense of the term—the representation of interests; a democratic representative is usually thought to have the duty to watch over either the interests of his constituents or, as a member of an assembly representing the whole people, the interests of the people at large. Nevertheless, he could still represent the interests of a group of people without their having had any part in choosing him. Some members of colonial legislatures in Africa used to be nominated by the governor to represent the interests of the unenfranchised native population. Precisely analogous, from the standpoint of the liberal democrat, is the case of a single-party system, where the ruling party invites the electors to endorse the candidate it has chosen to represent them. No matter how zealously the representative watched their interests, this would not count as democratic representation, precisely because the electors had had no part in selecting him. This view of democracy, therefore, is not compatible with tutelage; it implies the possibility not only of rejecting but also of freely proposing candidates, if none put forward by others is acceptable. Choosing and rejecting representatives is, indeed, the central act of participation by the citizens of a mass democracy, from which any effectiveness that they might have in other respects derives.

Closely related to election is the notion of the *responsibility* of the democratic representative. This means, in practice, that representatives must submit themselves periodically for re-election and, as a corollary, that they must be prepared to justify their actions and to attend to the experience and needs of their constituents, whose good will they must retain so long as they wish to remain in office.

Democracy and popular sovereignty. It is often said that in a democracy the people's will is sovereign. But can the people be said to have a will? Opinions are divided on most things; there may be ignorance and apathy; on many questions only sectionally interested groups may have any clear opinions at all. Small groups, like committees, may reach agreed policies to which everyone feels committed; or in time of grave national danger, whole nations may discover a collective devotion to a single objective, overriding all conflicts of interests. However, although it might be intelligible to speak of a collective will in such cases, they are too limited or too rare to provide a framework for a general theory of democratic government. Such cases apart, one may speak of action, will, or decision in relation to collectivities only if their collective acts can be identified by some more or less formal procedure or if there are rules authorizing some identifiable individual to act *in the name of* the whole group. Thus, "Parliament has decided . . ." presupposes rules determining who are members of Parliament, defining their roles, and giving their several actions a collective significance and validity as "legislation." Are there analogous procedures, by virtue of which the people can be said to act or to express a will? Only by voting and by applying the majority principle in elections and referenda. And of course, applied to any particular collection of individual votes, different systems of voting or different arrangements of constituency boundaries can yield quite different results, each in its own rule context expressing "the people's will." Nevertheless, some people consider a system democratic to the extent that it approximates to government by referendum, though they would agree that this could not work as a day-to-day procedure. The doctrine that a government ought not to initiate policy changes without putting them to a vote in a general election (or, in a stronger form, that having done so, it is entitled—or obliged—to implement them forthwith) is a practical application of the popular-sovereignty view of democracy. A possible corollary sometimes derived from this last view is that it is undemocratic to oppose or impede any government acting with the people's mandate. Moreover, since the people is sovereign, the traditionally important safeguards against the abuse of power become otiose; for, in Rousseau's words, "the sovereign, being formed wholly of the individuals who compose it, neither has nor can have any interest contrary to theirs." Popular-sovereignty theory is always, therefore, on the brink of totalitarianism, since—as the French Jacobin party showed—it is only a short step from proclaiming the sovereignty of the people to claiming the unlimited authority of its elected representatives, to proscribing opposition, and to denying individuals any rights other than those which the government with majority support deems fit.

There is, of course, another view, closer to the tradition of liberal individualism, which sees democracy as a way of safeguarding and reconciling individual and group interests. For James Madison, the virtue of the new constitution of the United States was that it permitted no faction, not even a majority, to deprive minorities of their natural rights, since it demanded the concurrence in action of independent authorities. The constitution was designed to balance diverse interests against one another, so that none might ever become a dominant and entrenched majority. Recent pluralistic accounts of democracy (or of what R. A. Dahl calls "polyarchy"), while more sophisticated, follow a similar approach. To be democratic, policy-making agencies must be sensitive to a wide range of pressures, so that no interest significantly affected by a decision will be left out of account. Popular participation consists not merely in voting, but also in wide consultation with interest groups and in the whole process of public criticism and governmental self-justification. Democracy, according to this view, requires the dispersal, not the concentration, of power; every voter has his quantum, making him worth the attention of those who want to govern. The people is not homogeneous, but a highly diversified complex of interest groups with crisscrossing memberships. It rarely makes sense to talk of the majority, except with reference to the result of a particular election or referendum, to describe how the votes were cast. A sectional majority, if there were one, would have no intrinsic claim to rule. To govern, a party would have to piece together an electoral majority; but every elector would have his own reasons for voting as he did, and no party could say in advance that, since it had no potential supporters among the members of some particular group, that group could, therefore, be safely neglected. Admittedly, wherever group divisions coincide over a wide range of interests (as, for instance, in many polyethnic societies), these conditions might not be fulfilled, and there might be a built-in majority and minority. In such a case, no party aiming at majority support could afford to uphold a minority interest, and democracy would tend to give way to majority tyranny. Thus, where popular-sovereignty theorists see the majority as the expression of the supreme will of the people, writers like Madison, Alexis de Tocqueville, J. S. Mill and, more recently, Walter Lippmann and the pluralists have seen it as either a myth or a potential tyrant.

The possibility of democracy. According to elitist sociologists like Vilfredo Pareto, Gaetano Mosca, and Robert Michels, there is always, behind the democratic facade, an oligarchy, even though its members take turns at playing the key governing roles. Now obviously, in every organization leaders initiate action and followers concur, but the power relations between leader and led are not on that account always the same. Precisely because democracy is a form of political organization, it *must* also be a pattern of leadership; nevertheless, the way leaders gain and retain their authority; the extent to which their initiatives respond to the interests of those they lead; their need to listen to and answer criticism—these things distinguish a democracy in important ways from what we usually mean by an oligarchy.

For the Marxist, bourgeois democracy is a sham because equal political rights cannot equalize political power where economic power is unequal. This does not amount to saying that democracy is *necessarily* impossible, only that economic equality and a classless society are necessary conditions for it.

According to other critics, popular self-government is delusory because government calls for expertise which few voters possess. Most accept the directions of some party, to whose image they are irrationally committed, and are incapable of a rational choice of policy. However, except in the popular-sovereignty variant, democracy does not require the electors to choose policies. Their role is merely to choose governors whom they trust to deal fairly and efficiently with problems as they emerge, and to look for new governors when they are disillusioned. A party's public image need not be an irrational construct; it may accurately epitomize deep-rooted tendencies and traditional preferences and be a reliable guide to the spirit in which the party would govern.

Justification of democracy. Democracy, it is sometimes said, asks too much of ordinary men, who would never be prepared to maintain the lively and informed interest in politics that ideally it demands. This, however, presupposes a particular view of the purpose and justification of democratic government. For some writers, as J. S. Mill, men and women cannot be fully responsible, adult, moral persons unless they are "self-determining," that is, concerned about the ways in which their lives are to be controlled. This view is a development from an older natural-rights theory of democracy, according to which (in the words of Colonel Rainborough, the Leveller), "Every man that is to live under a government ought first by his own consent put himself under that government," this being a condition for preserving his natural autonomy as a rational being. Or again, for democrats in the tradition of Rousseau, men achieve moral fulfillment only as participants in the collective self-governing process, helping to give expression to the "General Will" for the "Common Good"; failure in this constitutes failure in one's moral duty as a citizen.

There is, however, a more strictly utilitarian theory, sketched by Bentham and James Mill and implicit in a good deal of the work of democratic political scientists today. According to this view, the test of the adequacy of a political system is whether it tends to provide for the interests of the governed and protect them against the abuse of power. Democracy, they maintain, is likely to do this better than other systems. Active participation has no intrinsic virtue. James Mill would have limited the franchise to men over 40, on the grounds that the interests of women and younger men would be adequately safeguarded by their husbands and fathers, and therefore universal suffrage would be an unnecessary expense. For many modern writers, politics is a second-order activity: if things are going well, there is really no reason for people who prefer to spend their time on other things to devote it to politics. Political activity, indeed, is often most vigorous, as in Germany before 1933, when passions are high and democracy is in imminent danger of collapse. Apathy may be a sign of political health, indicating that there are no irreconcilable conflicts nor serious complaints. If there is ground for disquiet, it is only that apathy may become so habitual that democracy's defenses may be found unmanned in the face of some future attack.

This is a prudential model of democracy, in which satisfaction is maximized and conflicts reconciled by pressures bringing countervailing pressures into operation. It leaves out of account, perhaps, the sense in which democracy moralizes politics. Because decisions have to be publicly justified, political debate is conducted in moral terms, reviewing the impact of decisions on all interests affected, not just on this or that pressure group. Moreover, the quantum of power one has as a citizen can be represented not simply as a lever for personal or sectional protection or advantage, but also as a public responsibility; for even when one's own interests are not affected, one is still a member of a court of appeal. The bystanders in a democracy are, in a sense, the guarantors that a political decision shall not simply register the strongest pressure but shall be a reasoned response to diverse claims, each of which has to be shown to be *reasonable*, in the light of whatever standards are widely accepted in the community.

Bibliography

GENERAL

Benn, S. I., and Peters, R. S., *Social Principles and the Democratic State.* London, 1959. Reissued as *Principles of Political Thought.* New York, 1964.

Dahl, R. A., *Preface to Democratic Theory.* Chicago, 1956. A formal analysis of types of democratic theory.

De Grazia, A., *Public and Republic.* New York, 1951. On theories of representation, with useful annotated bibliography.

Mayo, Henry B., *An Introduction to Democratic Theory.* New York, 1960.

Pennock, J. R., *Liberal Democracy: Its Merits and Prospects.* New York, 1950. Includes an extensive bibliography.

Sartori, G., *Democrazia e definizione*, 2d ed. Bologna, 1958. Translated by the author as *Democratic Theory.* Detroit, 1962. Notes include extensive bibliographical references.

Wollheim, R., "Democracy." *Journal of the History of Ideas*, Vol. 19 (1958), 225–242. Includes brief history and bibliographical references.

ON THE SEMANTICS OF "DEMOCRACY"

McKeon, R., ed., *Democracy in a World of Tensions.* Chicago, 1951. Edited for UNESCO.

Naess, A., Christopherson, J. A., and Kvalø, K., *Democracy, Ideology, and Objectivity.* Oslo, 1956. A semantic analysis of the McKeon volume.

ON THE HISTORY OF DEMOCRATIC IDEAS

Crosa, E., *La sovranità popolare dal medioevo alla rivoluzione francese.* Bocca, 1915.

Glover, T. R., *Democracy in the Ancient World.* Cambridge, 1927.

Gooch, G. P., *English Democratic Ideas in the Seventeenth Century*, H. J. Laski, ed. Cambridge, 1927.

Mill, James, *Essay on Government.* London, 1821; Cambridge, 1937.

Mill, John Stuart, *Considerations on Representative Government.* London, 1861. Recent edition by R. B. McCallum. Oxford, 1946.

Rousseau, J. J., *Political Writings of Jean-Jacques Rousseau*, C. E. Vaughan, ed. Oxford, 1962. In French.

Rousseau, J. J., *Rousseau: Political Writings*, translated and edited by F. Watkins. London, 1953.

Spitz, D., *Patterns of Antidemocratic Thought.* New York, 1949.

Talmon, J. L., *Origins of Totalitarian Democracy.* London, 1952.

Tocqueville, Alexis de, *De la Démocratie en Amérique*, 2 vols. Brussels, 1835–1840. Translated by H. Reeve as *Democracy in America*, P. Bradley, ed., 2 vols. New York, 1945.

Woodhouse, A. S. P., *Puritanism and Liberty.* London, 1938.

STANLEY I. BENN

DEMOCRITUS. *See* LEUCIPPUS AND DEMOCRITUS.

DE MORGAN, AUGUSTUS (1806–1871), British mathematician and logician, was born at Madura, India, where his father was an army officer. After early education in the west of England, he entered Trinity College, Cambridge, in 1823 and graduated fourth wrangler in 1827. His refusal to subscribe to the religious tests then in force precluded him from further advancement at Cambridge, but he was fortunate enough to be appointed first professor of mathematics at the newly opened University of London. Because of his habit of resigning on matters of principle, he twice vacated this chair, once at the beginning and once at the end of his career; but he enjoyed, in the interval, the highest repute and affection as a teacher and had many pupils who later achieved distinction.

In addition to numerous important papers on the foundations of algebra and the philosophy of mathematical method, De Morgan was the author of several excellent elementary textbooks; a standard bibliography, *Arithmet-*

ical Books (London, 1847); a large treatise on the calculus (London, 1842); and an enormous quantity of learned journalism, mostly in the shape of review articles in the London *Athenaeum* and contributions on mathematical and astronomical subjects to the *Companion to the Almanac* (1831–1857) and to the *Penny* (later *English*) *Cyclopaedia*. His best-known work in this line is the posthumously assembled *Budget of Paradoxes* (London, 1872), a still-diverting miscellany from the lunatic fringes of science and mathematics, originally serialized in the *Athenaeum*. Despite many years' service as secretary of the Royal Astronomical Society, De Morgan was in general suspicious of official bodies and distinctions, never sought membership in the Royal Society, and declined an Edinburgh LL.D. Indifferent to politics and society—and professedly hostile to the animal and vegetable kingdoms as well—he nonetheless maintained an extensive scientific correspondence with such friends as William Whewell, George Boole, Sir John Herschel, Sir William Rowan Hamilton (the mathematician), and John Stuart Mill. His crotchets did little to disguise his exceptional benevolence and firmness of character or to inhibit his talents as a humorist and a wit.

De Morgan's outlook was that of a philosophical mathematician and historian of science; he did not claim to be a philosopher in any narrow sense of the term. He admired Berkeley and followed him to the extent of holding the existence of minds to be more certain, as a fact of experience, than that of a material world. But his general attitude to such questions may be gathered from his remark that, while he would not dissuade a student from metaphysics, he would warn him, "when he tries to look down his own throat with a candle in his hand, to take care that he does not set his head on fire."

In common with other mathematicians of his time, De Morgan realized that algebra could be conceived as a system of symbols whose laws could be codified independently of any arithmetical or other interpretation that might be given to them. His logic (see LOGIC, HISTORY OF) had a similar aim. Deeply versed in the history of logic, he was able to freshen and illuminate the subject by generalizing its traditional principles along mathematical lines. In this respect he ranks as the chief precursor of Boole; but his views attained notice chiefly through the controversy that arose when Sir William Hamilton (of Edinburgh) accused him of plagiarizing the doctrine of a quantified predicate.

De Morgan's *Formal Logic* (London, 1847) represents the best-known, though by no means the most mature, statement of his logical views. Among its many excellences, the chapter on fallacies is worthy of mention. De Morgan's later work is dispersed in pamphlets and periodicals, most notably in five memoirs contributed to the *Cambridge Philosophical Transactions* (Vols. 8–10, 1847–1863) and in his *Syllabus of a Proposed System of Logic* (London, 1860, reprinted in *On the Syllogism* (London, 1964). Though too largely concerned with polemics against Hamilton, and hampered by a notation that found no acceptance, these writings display much originality in the handling of negative terms, compound propositions, and numerous unorthodox varieties of syllogistic reasoning. Apart from the well-known "De Morgan laws" for the negation of conjunctions and disjunctions (or logical sums and products), the most important development was the recognition that the copula performs its function in the syllogism solely by virtue of its character as a transitive and convertible relation. De Morgan was led by this to examine the logic of relations in general and so paved the way not only for Peirce's "logic of relatives" but for all that has since been done in this branch of the subject.

As a skilled actuary, who was often in demand as a consultant to insurance companies, De Morgan was not unnaturally interested in the mathematical theory of probability and the problems of applying it to the hazards of mortality and other types of experience. His treatise, "Theory of Probabilities," in the *Encyclopaedia Metropolitana* (London, 1837) and the more popular *Essay on Probabilities* (London, 1838) were among the earlier discussions of this topic in English (see further relevant chapters of *Formal Logic* and the papers on the evaluation of argument and testimony attached to the first two Cambridge memoirs above). De Morgan's conception of probability was largely derived from Laplace, whose ideas (and errors) he was thus instrumental in propagating among his nineteenth-century successors. His method of approach was to construe the theory as an extension of formal logic, that is, as an investigation of the rules whereby propositions not absolutely certain affect the certainty of other propositions with which they are connected. He also employed the "inverse" procedures founded on Bayes's theorem, whereby, from known factual premises, it is sought to conjecture the probabilities of their likely or possible antecedents. In attempting to quantify the degree of uncertainty involved, De Morgan identified it with the amount of belief that is, or rather, that ought to be attached to it by a rational person, and proceeded on this basis to discuss the compounding and derivation of partial beliefs in accordance with the mathematical rules of the calculus of chances. His view of the matter was thus both a priori and subjective, though not in the objectionably psychological sense that has sometimes been ascribed to him. There are better reasons for censuring the technical errors he fell into through uncritical reliance on the Laplacean "rule of succession" and "principle of indifference"; even here, however, his confidence in the mathematical apparatus was often less blindly trusting than that of the writers who preceded him.

De Morgan's conception of scientific method may be gathered primarily from a review of Bacon's works inserted in the *Budget of Paradoxes*. He there embraced what is essentially the modern "hypothetico-deductive" view of the subject; but one has to go to Whewell before him or to W. S. Jevons after him to see it worked out in full.

Bibliography

Apart from the works mentioned under LOGIC, HISTORY OF, there is not much literature on De Morgan. The best general accounts are in A. Macfarlane, *Ten British Mathematicians* (New York, 1916) and J. A. Passmore, *A Hundred Years of Philosophy* (London, 1957). The *Memoir* by his wife, Sophia Elizabeth De Morgan (London, 1882), contains an excellent account of him. The details of the quarrel with Hamilton may be found in Hamilton's

Letter to Augustus De Morgan (Edinburgh, 1847) and De Morgan's *Statement in Answer* (London, 1847) or more readily in the appendices to De Morgan's *Formal Logic*.

P. L. HEATH

DEONTIC LOGIC. *See* LOGIC, DEONTIC.

DEONTOLOGICAL ETHICS. The term "deontology" derives from the Greek words *deon* (duty) and *logos* (science). Etymologically it means the science of duty. In current usage, however, its meaning is more specific: A deontological theory of ethics is one which holds that at least some acts are morally obligatory regardless of their consequences for human weal or woe. The popular motto "Let justice be done though the heavens fall" conveys the spirit that most often underlies deontological theories.

The first of the great philosophers emphatically to enunciate the deontological principle was Immanuel Kant. According to Kant objectively right behavior may be inspired by prudence, by benevolence, by respect for the moral law, or by still other motives, but the highest and the only unqualifiedly moral motive is respect for the moral law. If, therefore, considerations based on concern for one's own well-being or the well-being of others indicate a course of action at odds with that dictated by respect for the moral law, respect for the moral law should prevail. Kant went so far as to argue that it is wrong to tell a lie even to save another man's life. Moral rules, he claimed, are universally valid and admit of no exceptions.

The most distinguished twentieth-century exponent of deontological ethics is W. D. Ross. Ross does not insist on the universal validity of moral rules. The fact that an act violates a moral rule is, he says, a prima facie reason for not performing that act. It can and does happen, however, that one moral rule conflicts with another. In such cases we are obliged to choose between them, and our behavior will necessarily constitute an exception to the rule that we deem less applicable in the concrete situation. Like Kant, however, Ross refuses either to derive moral rules from considerations based on prudence and sympathy or to allow such factors to determine their relative ranking in cases of conflict. For Ross any statement relating either to moral rules or to our concrete duty in a specific case must be justified by an act of intellectual intuition.

More recently a number of authors have tended to favor a modified version of deontological ethics called "rule utilitarianism." This is the view that although any moral rule must be justified by showing that its adoption has humanly desirable consequences, an act violating a moral rule cannot itself be morally justified in the same manner. The usual argument for rule utilitarianism is that except in cases where moral rules conflict, one would be committing a linguistic impropriety by referring to an act that violates a moral rule as right or just.

Bibliography

Broad, C. D., *Five Types of Ethical Theory*. London, 1930.
Carritt, E. F., *The Theory of Morals*. London, 1948.
Ewing, A. C., *The Definition of Good*. New York, 1947.
Kant, Immanuel, *Lectures on Ethics*, translated by Louis Infield. London, 1930.
Kant, Immanuel, *Critique of Practical Reason and Other Writings in Moral Philosophy*, translated by Lewis White Beck. Chicago, 1949.
Kant, Immanuel, *Fundamental Principles of the Metaphysic of Morals*, translated by Thomas Abbott. New York, 1949.
Prichard, H. A., *Moral Obligation*. Oxford, 1949.
Ross, W. D., *The Right and the Good*. Oxford, 1930.
Ross, W. D., *The Foundations of Ethics*. Oxford, 1939.
For rule utilitarianism, see UTILITARIANISM.

ROBERT G. OLSON

DE SANCTIS, FRANCESCO (1817–1883), Italian liberal politican and political and literary critic. De Sanctis was born near Naples. Although trained for the law, he turned to the study of Italian culture. He taught at the Military School of Naples, but his participation in the Revolution of 1848 led to his dismissal, a three-year prison sentence, and banishment. He taught and lectured in Turin and Zurich, and returned to Naples in 1860 as governor of the province of Avellino. As director of the Ministry of Public Instruction he brought scholars of great repute to the University of Naples and fought for the secularization of the public schools. After becoming editor of the newspaper *Italia* in 1863, he continued to champion reforms and helped to establish the modern Italian tradition of combining philosophy and worldly affairs. In 1868 De Sanctis returned to literary criticism. Several years later he completed his *History of Italian Literature*. He accepted the chair of comparative literature at the University of Naples in 1872, but in 1877 he resumed his political career as organizer of a liberal opposition party, vice-president of the Chamber of Deputies, and minister of public instruction.

De Sanctis developed no systematic aesthetics or political philosophy. His principles of criticism are implicit in his essays. Literary truth, for De Sanctis, is realized in form, but literature's connection with political and social life is the substance of its meaning and the true source of formal beauty. Form transforms an idea into art and is the instrument by which artistic truth is achieved; it is art itself. Content and ideas are, for artistic purposes, without truth. Form provides truth, artistic integrity, the capacity to project an experience or idea so as to bring it subjectively alive for an observer. It does so successfully when it is naturally wedded to the content and seems fused with it. Successful form is derived from the concrete vision of the poet as he reflects on a living experience of the language and forms of his age. This tie between the artist and his immediate image is the deepest source of true art. The language and ideas of art spring from and are shaped by the social and historical events against which they act in the mind of the artist. De Sanctis sought, by grasping history and language, to grasp the work of art as conceived by the artist. History, and specifically political history, provides the framework in which ideas are tested against each other and find concrete representation in artistic form.

Traditional criticism saw technical skill as the essence of poetry, but poetry is involved with the values of the moral, historical, and social orders it expresses and reflects. The philosophical commitments of the poet, his moods and personal objectives, are the stimuli, the raw materials from which an ordered piece of art is shaped. The essence of art is form, but form into which content has passed and fulfilled itself.

De Sanctis believed that the poet must be immersed in the life of his national community. The subject and object of art is the human being. The artist must study man, exhort him, laugh at him, understand him. The artist's manner of picturing human life gives art its truth; this truth is gained by mastery of the language of the age and absorption of its combinations and formal possibilities.

Although art is measured by aesthetic criteria, as a historical phenomenon it is subject to social and moral considerations. Therefore, De Sanctis was led from literary criticism to literary history to the history of Italian culture and ultimately to the relation and debt of Italian culture to Italian politics.

Politics, De Sanctis believed, is a reflection of the moral fiber of a nation. Political activities reflect a wider cultural context and have a special responsibility for that culture, through the power to stimulate or repress it. Politics is a national dialogue between the various sectors of the population. The capacity of the popular classes to participate in and guard a national political organism, to preserve its morality in the face of the tasks of national destiny, to absorb the style and content of past national leaders imprints the national style and goal on political behavior.

Many of De Sanctis' political essays are exhortations, expressions of concern over apathy and loss of morality in political life, as well as attempts to express the inner urgings of Italy. For De Sanctis morality and culture were intimately connected. Moral political activity carried out Italy's destiny, which its previous culture had marked for restored greatness. The politics of a great nation reflects its culture and is perpetually open to self-renewal through the participation of the bearers of that culture. If they cease to participate in the nation's political activity, the culture breaks down, and politics becomes immoral, politicians self-aggrandizing, and the people apathetic.

Works by De Sanctis

Saggi critici. Naples, 1866; Bari, 1957.

Storia della letteratura italiana, 2 vols. Naples, 1870–1871. Translated by Joan Redfern as *History of Italian Literature,* 2 vols. New York, 1931.

Scritti politici. Naples, 1895.

Scritti rarii inediti o rari. Naples, 1898.

La scuola liberale e la scuola democratica. Bari, 1953.

Works on De Sanctis

Cione, Edmondo, *Francesco De Sanctis,* 2d ed. Milan, 1944.

Croce, Benedetto, *Estetica,* 5th rev. ed. Bari, 1922. Translated by Douglas Ainslie as *Aesthetics,* 2d ed. London, 1922. Part II, Ch. 15.

Holliger, Max, *Francesco De Sanctis: Sein Weltbild und seine Ästhetik.* Freiburg, 1949.

Landucci, Sergio, *Cultura e ideologia in Francesco De Sanctis.* Milan, 1964.

Montanari, Fausto, *Francesco De Sanctis.* Brescia, 1949.

Russo, Luigi, *Francesco De Sanctis e la cultura napoletana.* Venice, 1928.

Irving Louis Horowitz

DESCARTES, RENÉ (1596–1650), was one of the founders of modern thought and among the most original philosophers and mathematicians of any age. He was born at La Haye, a small town in Touraine, France. Educated at the Jesuit college of La Flèche, he retained an admiration for his teachers but later claimed that he found little of substance in the course of instruction and that only mathematics had given him any certain knowledge. In 1618 he went to Holland to serve in the army of Maurice of Nassau, and in this capacity he traveled in Germany and perhaps elsewhere; in the following year he was at Ulm, Germany. There, on the night of November 10, after a day of concentrated reflection, he had certain dreams which he interpreted as a divine sign that it was his destiny to found a unified science of nature based (it would seem) on mathematics. At this time his interest was largely in physics and mathematics, in which he was stimulated by contact with the mathematician Isaac Beeckman. He did not, however, set himself at once to write works of philosophy or science but continued to travel widely. His first substantial work was the never-completed treatise *Regulae ad Directionem Ingenii* ("Rules for the Direction of the Mind"), which was written in 1628 or 1629 but was not printed until 1701. The *Regulae* reveals that Descartes was already preoccupied with method as the clue to scientific advance—a method of basically mathematical inspiration, though it is intended to be the method of rational inquiry into any subject matter whatsoever. This concern with method appears in the *Regulae* in a form that is both more detailed and less metaphysically committed than the form that appears in Descartes's later philosophical works.

In November 1628 Descartes was in Paris, where he distinguished himself in a famous confrontation with Chandoux, whose view that science could be founded only on probabilities he eloquently attacked, claiming both that only absolute certainty could serve as a basis of human knowledge and that he himself had a method of establishing this basis. As a result of this incident he was urged to develop his system by Cardinal Bérulle, an Oratorian. (Descartes's close association with the Augustinian and Scotist outlook of the Oratory is significant to his philosophy.) In the same year he retired to Holland, where he remained, with brief interruptions, until 1649.

In Holland, Descartes worked at his system, and by 1634 he had completed a scientific work called *Le Monde.* When he heard, however, of the condemnation of Galileo for teaching the Copernican system, as did *Le Monde,* he immediately had the book suppressed. This incident is important in Descartes's life, for it reveals that spirit of caution and conciliation toward authority which was very marked in him (and which earned the disapproval of some, including Leibniz and Bossuet). The suppression also affected the subsequent course of his publications, which were from then on strategically designed to recommend his less orthodox views in an oblique fashion. In 1637 he published a book containing three treatises on mathematical and physical subjects—the *Geometry,* the *Dioptric,* and the *Meteors*—prefaced by *Discours de la méthode* (*Discourse on the Method*). This celebrated work is remarkable for a number of things: for its autobiographical tone, for its very compressed exposition of the foundations of the Cartesian system, and for the fact that it was written in French. By writing in French, Descartes intended (as Galileo also did, by writing in Italian) to aim over the heads of the academic community and to reach educated men of *bon sens,* among whom he hoped to get a favorable hearing. The French style that Descartes developed for this purpose has always been regarded as a model for the expression of abstract thought in that language.

Descartes followed this book in 1641 with a more purely metaphysical work, the six *Meditationes de Prima Philosophia* (*Meditations on First Philosophy*), which were published together with six (later seven) sets of *Objections* from various persons, including Thomas Hobbes, Antoine Arnauld, and Pierre Gassendi, and also with Descartes's *Replies to the Objections;* together these form one of the most important texts of Descartes's philosophy. The exposition of the *Meditations* is heuristic and almost dramatic in tone. A more formal treatise, the *Principia Philosophiae* (*Principles of Philosophy*), followed in 1644. It contains, besides philosophical matter, a cautious exposition of Descartes's views on cosmology; he expressed the hope that it could "be used in Christian teaching without contradicting the text of Aristotle," an aspiration that, despite his efforts at concealing his real opinions, was optimistic.

In 1649 Descartes yielded, after much hesitation, to the requests of Queen Christina of Sweden that he join the distinguished circle she was assembling in Stockholm and instruct her in philosophy. In this year he also published *Les Passions de l'âme* (*The Passions of the Soul*). The next year, however, as a result of the Swedish climate and the rigorous schedule demanded by the queen, he caught pneumonia and died.

THE METHOD OF DOUBT

In Part II of the *Discourse on the Method* Descartes gives an account of four rules that, he says, he had found adequate to express his method:

> The first of these was to accept nothing as true which I did not clearly recognize to be so: that is to say, carefully to avoid precipitation and prejudice in judgements, and to accept in them nothing more than was presented to my mind so clearly and distinctly that I could have no occasion to doubt it.
>
> The second was to divide up each of the difficulties which I examined into as many parts as possible, and as seemed requisite for it to be resolved in the best manner possible.
>
> The third was to carry on my reflections in due order, beginning with objects that were the most simple and easy to understand, in order to rise little by little, or by degrees, to knowledge of the most complex, assuming an order, even if a fictitious one, among those which do not follow a natural sequence relative to one another.
>
> The last was in all cases to make enumerations so complete and reviews so general that I should be certain of having omitted nothing. (*The Philosophical Works of Descartes*)

It is immediately obvious that, taken by themselves, these rules are so general, and several of their key terms so vague, that they provide little positive guidance. Thus, there is some justice in a famous sneer of Leibniz' that Descartes's celebrated rules added up to saying "Take what you need, and do what you should, and you will get what you want." To some extent, at least, Descartes was probably willing to admit that the rules, regarded merely as abstract prescriptions, had no great content, for it is a repeated emphasis of his work that it is only in the actual application of the mind to specific problems that a man will come to recognize what it is to see something "clearly and distinctly," will realize that his ideas have been insufficiently analyzed, and so forth. The problem of the meaning of "clear and distinct perception" is really the central issue of the interpretation of the method, and it will be seen that it recurs at the heart of Descartes's philosophy.

Whatever the difficulties of interpreting the rules, there are two features of Descartes's method that stand out clearly. One is that the method is intended as an analytical or (what Descartes regarded as the same thing) heuristic method; it applies to the situation of one who is confronted with a problem and proceeds to answer it by resolving the situation into a number of constituent elements or ideas. Descartes's model here is in some part that of the resolution of a complex curve or curvilinear motion by use of coordinate geometry, a branch of mathematics whose discovery by Descartes (announced in an obscure and not very general form in the *Geometry* of 1637) is still marked by the use of the expression "Cartesian coordinates." Descartes thought that the great merit of his method, as opposed to the traditional logic, was precisely that it was a method of discovery and not merely a device for the presentation of discoveries already made; in this he represents a characteristic seventeenth-century concern that is also found, for instance, in Bacon and Galileo. Consistent with this concern, he thought that the most illuminating way of expounding his more purely philosophical doctrines was by "the order of discovery," as he expounds them in the *Meditations;* this is indeed the most effective way of understanding Descartes's approach and his problems, and the path of his *Meditations* will, for the most part, be pursued in this article. He opposes to this "analytical" type of exposition a "synthetic" type, a formal deductive exposition on Euclidean lines; in response to a request, he offers such an exposition of his system in the *Second Set of Replies to Objections,* with remarks to the effect that synthetic exposition is inferior to the method he has previously used. Yet in some later developments of rationalism, most notably in Spinoza, the "synthetic" or deductive method of exposition came to be favored as a paradigm of the luminously intelligible.

The second outstanding feature of Descartes's method is that it is intended as a method not only of scientific inquiry, nor only of philosophical inquiry, but of any rational inquiry whatsoever. In any such inquiry the intellectual power of the mind that the method is supposed to guide is the same; and Descartes indeed had a vision of the unity of all knowledge, philosophical and scientific, that he expressed in an image of the Tree of Knowledge, whose roots were metaphysics, whose trunk was physics, and whose branches were the other sciences (including medicine and morality). Such an image suggests the continuity of metaphysics and science, and much of Descartes's writing implies just such an ideal, with philosophy and the natural sciences unified in one a priori inquiry. However, at other times he seems prepared to admit that one cannot expect the same sorts of arguments to be possible in natural science as in metaphysics.

The method, then, is not a peculiarly philosophical method; it becomes such when it is applied to philosophical issues, in particular to highly general questions about the foundations of knowledge. When it is so applied, the first rule—that nothing should be accepted as true unless it is so clearly and distinctly perceived that there could be no occasion to doubt it—takes on a special character as the chief weapon of Descartes's philosophical inquiry—the famous method of doubt. Descartes proclaims that he intends to doubt as much as possible, in order to see whether anything may then be left which will resist the doubt. If there is, this will constitute an indubitable certainty, from which he may be able to proceed to find other certainties and thus construct his system on solid foundations.

This metaphor of "solid foundations" constantly reappears in Descartes's explanations of his procedure; and it embodies at the very outset a presupposition of Descartes's philosophy (though it was perhaps not consciously seen by him as such) that it is the ideal of knowledge to be systematic, an ordered body of propositions dependent on one another. The same presupposition is present, rather more subtly, in another image that Descartes appeals to in explaining the method of doubt: that he is acting like a man who has a barrel of apples and takes them out one by one to remove any rotten ones, lest they infect the others (*Seventh Set of Replies*). This presupposition, however, does not serve by itself to explain a peculiar feature of Descartes's procedure that has too often gone unquestioned: that while he often states that his aim is merely to discover what is true, he actually sets himself the task of discovering things that are indubitable and, in a strong sense, certain. He apparently regards it as a simple dictate of reason that he should pursue the first by way of the second, but it is not immediately obvious why this should be so. In some part, no doubt, he is influenced by mathematics as a paradigm of knowledge; but this explanation scarcely goes very deep, for Descartes claims that what makes mathematics a paradigm of knowledge is precisely its certainty, and the question remains of why he should think this. Some explanation is to be found in the historical circumstances: a revival of skeptical considerations from ancient sources, notably Sextus Empiricus, was playing a considerable role in contemporary arguments about religious certainty and authority; and some play was made with the idea that all propositions could be rendered equally improbable, so that there was no knowledge at all.

Apart from these considerations, however, some motivation for Descartes's preoccupation with the indubitable must be sought; and it can be argued that this preoccupation is already implicit in the egocentric approach which is one of the most characteristic features of his philosophy and which, with its related insistence on epistemology as the starting point of philosophy, serves to distinguish it and much that follows it from most philosophy that preceded it. Descartes's basic question is "What do I know?" and he hopes to be able to answer this question by reflection on the beliefs that he finds himself disposed to hold. One necessary condition of a belief's constituting knowledge is that it is true; but it is difficult to see how any reflection on my beliefs could serve to identify those of them that are true, since the fact that I have these beliefs means that I already suppose them to be true. At this point the only procedure that seems to offer hope of being able to segregate the true beliefs through reflection will be that of selecting just those beliefs whose truth is in some way guaranteed by the fact that they are believed; this is essentially the first rule of the method, the pursuit of the indubitable. Another and slightly different way of putting this is to say that Descartes's task will not have been satisfactorily carried out so long as, for anything I claim to know, it is possible to ask whether I know that I know it; to eliminate this question, genuine knowledge has to be self-guaranteeing—a point emphasized by Spinoza.

Descartes proceeds to apply the method of doubt by suspending his belief in anything in which he can find, or indeed imagine, the slightest ground of doubt. In this way he succeeds (or so he claims) in suspending belief in the entire physical universe, including his own body; in God; in the past; and even in the truth of simple propositions of mathematics (although, as will be seen, some perceptions of logical consequence have to be regarded as immune to the doubt). The arguments by which Descartes so rapidly extends the doubt are sketchy and have given rise to considerable disagreement. In part, he relies on invoking actual occasions of error—for instance, by recalling false judgments based on illusions of the senses; in particular, he refers frequently to the "illusions" of dreams. Yet evidently there can be no very direct route from these considerations to the universal skepticism concerning the physical world that he proceeds to entertain. For, first, if the extension of the doubt involved his claiming to know that he had actually been deceived in the past, it would rest on claims to knowledge of a kind that it itself goes on to disavow; and, second, even if these considerations of past error were allowed to show that *any* occasion of supposed perception might be illusory (because, for instance, I might be dreaming), there would be no valid inference from this to the supposition that *every* supposed occasion of perception might be illusory.

It seems, in fact, doubtful that Descartes did wish to proceed by any direct route from such considerations as illusion and dreaming to the universal skepticism; rather, he is to be taken as invoking those considerations to weaken the reliance on any supposed experience of perception and then going on to entertain the notion of universal illusion. His point is the more immediate one that in this notion he can, at least at this stage of reflection, see no inherent absurdity. Indeed, in the *Meditations* (though not in his earlier writings) he uses a device that seems to make it plain that the universal skepticism has no direct dependence on an appeal to actual types of illusion: he feigns, for the sake of his argument, the existence of a malicious demon, an extremely powerful agency devoted to deceiving him. His question then becomes "If there were such an agency, how many of my normal beliefs could conceivably be the product of his deceit?" To this question Descartes gives the very large-scale answer already indicated, and his reasons for giving this answer seem to come down essentially to the claim that he can see no evident absurdity in supposing that he is so broadly deceived.

Descartes's skepticism has received much attention, but it is fair to say that at no point of his argument is Descartes in any serious sense a skeptic; rather, he is one who uses skeptical arguments as an instrument of analysis. He repeatedly emphasizes—not only in the last of the *Meditations* but also in the *First Meditation*, where the doubt is being invoked—that the extravagant doubts are unreal. He regards the "hyperbolical" doubt, as he sometimes calls it, as running counter to something that is actually the case: that even among our beliefs that are not indubitable, some are, in fact, much more probable than others. The hyperbolical doubt is a device for identifying the indubitable.

"COGITO ERGO SUM"

The doubt comes to a halt, and the first indubitable proposition is identified, when Descartes reflects that one thing, at least, he cannot doubt: his own existence. For if he is to doubt anything, if indeed he is to have any thought at all, then certainly he must exist. In the terms of the *Discourse* (Part IV):

> I noticed that while I was trying to think everything false, it must needs be that I, who was thinking this, was something. And observing that this truth, *I am thinking, therefore I exist* [*Je pense, donc je suis;* Latin version, *cogito ergo sum*] was so solid and secure that the most extravagant suppositions of the sceptics could not overthrow it, I judged that I need not scruple to accept it as the first principle of [the] philosophy that I was seeking. (*Descartes: Philosophical Writings*)

The formulation of the argument in the *Second Meditation* differs from that in the *Discourse* in three respects: (*a*) there is less suggestion that the particular form of thought that reveals the existence of the thinker is that of doubting—any form of thought will have the same result; (*b*) the famous formula *cogito ergo sum* is not actually employed, Descartes preferring the formulation "'I am, I exist' is necessarily true whenever I utter it or conceive it in my mind"; (*c*) an additional expression of the basic idea is given in terms of the malicious demon—"there is no doubt that I exist, if he is deceiving me; let him deceive me as much as he likes, he can never bring it about that I am nothing, so long as I think I am something." Although a good deal has been made of the second point, notably by F. Alquié, who inclines to an "existentialist" interpretation of Descartes, these differences from the *Discourse* seem to be of minor importance.

Descartes was, on the whole, content to leave the peculiar certainty or indubitability of the *cogito* unanalyzed, regarding it as a primitive datum that the mind can recognize only when it encounters it. Some modern discussions, however, have sought to give an explanation of the indubitability involved: Ayer, for instance, suggests that the sense of "indubitable" involved here is one by which p is indubitable if, and only if, "p is true" follows from "I doubt whether p is true"; this yields "I exist," "I am doubting," and "I am thinking" (where this last is taken as following from "I am doubting") as indubitable. A more elaborate logical analysis, involving appeal to a "performatory" element, is offered by Hintikka. Such analyses certainly bring out one logical feature of Descartes's basic propositions: a feature that may also be illustrated, in the spirit of these analyses, by remarking that "I do *not* exist" and "I am *not* thinking" (at least where "thinking" is taken in a sufficiently broad sense, to cover any intelligent and meaningful assertion, as Descartes intended) are necessarily paradoxical assertions that, while not formal contradictions (as, again, Descartes realized), could not possibly be true because their truth would defeat the conditions of their own assertibility.

While these points undoubtedly illuminate certain aspects of the nature of the *cogito*, they are not adequate to bring out all that Descartes intended. For him, *cogitatio* or *pensée* covered more than the modern English term "thought" naturally covers, including not merely ratiocination but also any form of conscious state or process or activity whatsoever; for him, such phenomena as willing and having images are equally forms (in his technical term, *modes*) of *cogitatio*. He makes it clear that the certainty of the *cogito* applies to any mode of *cogitatio;* what can be indubitable is not merely the bare proposition "I am thinking" but also more determinate statements about my states of consciousness—that I am doubting this or that, that I am imagining certain things, that it seems to me (at least) that I am seeing certain physical objects, and so on. All such statements of "immediate experience" are recognized as being, if true, indubitably so. The admission of such statements clearly requires a sense of "indubitable" or "certain" different from that which emerged from the previous analyses of the bare statement "I am thinking"; for the denials of the statements of "immediate experience," unlike the denials of "I am thinking," "I exist" previously considered, are not inherently paradoxical—for instance, they can be used to tell a lie. Here Descartes is disposed to use a model of the mind's states as immediately evident to itself.

A question that has been much discussed is whether Descartes regards *cogito ergo sum* as expressing an inference. His remarks on this issue—as rather often on questions raised by objectors—are not evidently consistent and are quite difficult to interpret. The most probable view of his outlook is that, first, he wishes to deny that the *cogito* presents itself to the mind psychologically as involving an inferential step; and that, second, he wishes to deny that the *cogito* is a *syllogistic* inference resting on the major premise "Everything that thinks, exists" while nevertheless admitting that it does presuppose the rather different principle "In order to think, it is necessary to exist," which he says is merely an "eternal truth" (*vérité éternelle*) that "does not give us knowledge of any existent thing" (see *Principles* I, 10 and a letter to Claude Clerselier, 1646). This last point is one of the clearest indications that Descartes was prepared to admit that there were at least some simple conceptual or a priori truths which must be immune to the doubt and which he must be able to rely on in order to take any step out of the doubt.

THE REAL DISTINCTION

Many correspondents pointed out to Descartes that the argument of the *cogito* was to be found in several passages of Augustine. To one such correspondent, Andreas Colvius (letter of November 14, 1640), he writes: "I find that it is employed [by Augustine] to prove the certitude of our being, and further to show that there is some image of the Trinity in us . . . in place of the use that I make of it in order to show that this *I*, which thinks, is an immaterial substance which has nothing corporeal about it."

What Descartes here claims to have derived from the *cogito* are in fact two central and closely related doctrines of his: (1) that this "I" whose existence he has proved is a substance whose whole essence is to think and (2) that this substance is "really distinct" from any physical body that he has. It is remarkable that in the passage just quoted Descartes is prepared (in effect) to associate both these doctrines so closely with the *cogito*, for the following year, in replying in the *Third Replies* to some remarks of Hobbes, he is very insistent that in the *Meditations* the "real distinction" is not proved until the *Sixth Meditation* (the last) and not in the *Second Meditation*, where the *cogito* is offered. But while this is literally true, it is difficult to see that much weight can be attached to it or that anything underlies the "real distinction" which is not implicit in the procedure of the *cogito;* and the idea that the essence of the "I" is to be a thinking being or substance is certainly intimately related to both. It will suffice to examine the argument for the "real distinction," together with some comments on Descartes's use of the terms "substance" and "essence."

This "real distinction" between mind and body is regarded by Descartes as one of the two central doctrines of the *Meditations,* as is shown by the full title of the work: "Meditations on First Philosophy, in which the Existence of God and the Real Distinction between Mind and Body are Demonstrated"—a title that Descartes substituted in the second edition for that of the first, which had read ". . . in which the Existence of God and the Immortality of the Soul are Demonstrated." He was moved, most probably, by the consideration that the immortality of the soul is not mentioned in the *Meditations,* let alone demonstrated. The argument for this "real distinction" comes essentially to this: Descartes can be certain of his existence as a thinking thing while still in doubt that he has a body—hence, he and his body (if he has one) must be really distinct one from another. An obvious objection, skillfully pressed by Arnauld in the *Fourth Objections,* is that this argument seems to refer only to a psychological fact about Descartes's understanding, which may depend on Descartes's being confused about the possibilities. In reply, Descartes makes it sufficiently clear that he is here appealing to a clear conception of what is objectively possible, so that his argument is, in effect, that he clearly perceives that it is actually possible that he should exist as a mind or thinking thing without existing as a body—thus, mind and body are really distinct. The weakness of this seems to be that even if the premise is granted, it yields a less strong conclusion than Descartes wanted. The most that this argument could prove is that it is not necessarily the case that, existing as a mind, he must exist also as a body: it does not prove either that mind and body cannot be one and the same, or that they are not, as a matter of fact, one and the same. Yet Descartes quite certainly supposed that in proving mind and body to be "really distinct" in this sense, he had thereby shown them to be actually nonidentical substances.

Even weaker appear to be such independent arguments as Descartes offers for his essence being that of a merely thinking being. Though his treatment is obscure, he is under suspicion of moving directly from the consideration of the *cogito*—that he cannot truly think that he is not thinking, nor that he does not exist—to the stronger claim that thought is his essential property; the latter entails, among other things, that he cannot exist without thinking (see a letter to Guillaume Gibieuf, January 19, 1642).

The considerable difficulties and obscurities involved in Descartes's arguments on these points are most economically explained by recognizing that one is here dealing with a fundamental element of his metaphysical outlook, which is assumed rather than proved. The basic premise, the foundation of his celebrated dualism, is that there are only two essential attributes, thought and extension (though this has not yet been reached at the present stage of Descartes's argument). Thus, all created substances (and Descartes holds that the term "substance" is used univocally of all such substances, both mental and physical, though it is used in a slightly different sense in referring to the uncreated or self-created substance, God) must have their nature explained in terms of one of these essential attributes; indeed, Descartes says that a substance is different from its essential attribute "only by a distinction of reason." Moreover, any other property that a substance possesses must be a *mode* of its essential attribute: all properties of thinking things are (roughly speaking) *ways* of thinking; all properties of physical things, *ways* of being extended. From these premises it immediately follows that if the "I" thinks at all, it cannot also be true of that same thing that it has any physical property—mind and body must be nonidentical. (For this approach to the "real distinction," see particularly the *Third Replies*). What is not shown by any satisfactory (or even clearly identifiable) argument is that thought must be accepted as an essential attribute in this heavily committal sense: the dualism implicit in this conception appears to be the real starting point, as well as the culmination, of Descartes's metaphysics.

THE EXISTENCE OF GOD

The next step of Descartes's return from the doubt illustrates an essential feature of his thought, very significant to later developments in the history of philosophy. Having established so far only that he exists as a thinking being, he must in order to prove the existence of anything else—and in particular of an "external" physical world—proceed entirely from the contents of his own consciousness. The characteristic feature of Descartes's system is that he proceeds to do this by a transcendental route, by proving next the existence of God, and only from God the existence of other contingent beings. The historical significance of this is that while Descartes's epistemological problem of "working out" from the data of consciousness remained central, his transcendental solution to it rapidly ceased to carry conviction. This is a primary way in which the Cartesian system, which is in itself a religious and dualistic metaphysics containing many scholastic elements, was the true ancestor of many later skeptical, subjectivist, and idealist developments.

Descartes's arguments for the existence of God proceed, as his system demands, only from the contents of his own consciousness and indeed from one item that he claims to find in his consciousness—an idea of God, of a Perfect and Infinite Being. It is essential for Descartes's outlook that an idea (which he defines, *Second Replies* Def. 2, merely as "the form of any thought, that form by the immediate awareness of which I am conscious of that said thought") does not necessarily take the form of an image: he intends, rather, the purely intellectual and rational comprehension of the nature of a thing. Such is his idea of God.

His first and main argument proceeds by applying to this idea a version of a traditional causal principle that he holds to be self-evident, to the effect that the cause of anything must contain at least as much reality or perfection as the effect. This is an entirely general principle, but it has a special application to things, such as ideas, that have a representational character: every idea is an idea of something or has an object (whether that object actually exists or not), and the causal principle just mentioned applies in such cases not merely to the existence of the idea qua idea—on which level all ideas have the same degree of reality or perfection—but also to the idea qua having a certain kind of object: on this level, ideas possess different degrees of reality as their respective objects have different degrees of reality.

In the degenerate scholastic terminology that Descartes employs, the cause of any idea must possess at least as much reality as the idea possesses, not only *formally* (intrinsically, qua idea) but also *objectively* (in respect of its having a certain sort of object). If the cause has just as much reality as the effect, the reality of the effect is said to be present in it *formally;* if the cause has a greater degree of reality, it is said to contain the effect *eminently*. The argument then proceeds that alone among the ideas that Descartes has, the idea of God possesses objectively a supreme degree of reality because it is the idea of a Perfect Being; hence its cause must possess formally a similar degree of reality. But this cause is evidently not Descartes himself: among other things, he is in a state of doubt and ignorance, which he clearly recognizes to be imperfections. Hence, there must exist a Being independent of Descartes who is indeed perfect: God.

There are two criticisms of this argument that Descartes himself tries to anticipate. The first is that he might have formed the idea of the infinitely Perfect Being merely by considering his own imperfect state and thinking away its limitations. To this he replies that his idea of God is not that of a being merely negatively infinite—one such that we cannot conceive of limits to his excellence—but of a being actually infinite—such that we know that there are no limits to his excellence. To put the distinction another way, God's excellence is not merely indefinitely, but infinitely, great (*Principles* I, 26 *et seq.;* for a slightly different explanation of these terms, see *First Replies*). The other criticism is that the various perfections of God might actually exist but in different subjects, so that, in fact, there would be no Perfect Being containing them all. To this Descartes replies that "the unity, simplicity or the inseparability of all God's attributes, is itself one of the chief perfections that I conceive him to have" (*Third Meditation;* cf. *Second Objections and Replies*).

Two features of the argument are particularly worth remarking in the general context of Descartes's thought. First, there is an obvious tension produced by the fact that on the one hand the argument seems to presuppose an idea of God notably clear and determinate, while on the other hand it turns on the contrast between the infinitude of God and the finite imperfection of Descartes's own mind (an emphasis possibly influenced by Nicholas Cusanus); this can only add force to the traditional view that the human conception of God must necessarily be extremely limited and imperfect. This tension is more generally present in Descartes, and indeed in much seventeenth-century thought, a genuine sense of contingency and limitation being in conflict with a tendency to regard the power of the rational mind as virtually limitless (a peculiar and poignant form of this tension is to be found in Blaise Pascal). Second, the conception of degrees of reality or perfection that Descartes so straightforwardly invokes is not only a very obvious traditional incursion into Descartes's supposedly presuppositionless inquiry but is also more particularly a feature of traditional thought that his own system, it might be supposed, did a great deal to undermine; its ultimately Aristotelian inspiration fits awkwardly into the Cartesian picture of essentially rational minds enjoying equally the "natural light," as against a purely mechanically unified world of matter.

Descartes also uses considerations that introduce God as the cause of Descartes's own existence. He could not have created himself, since it takes greater perfection to create substance than to create any attributes whatsoever. Thus, if he had had the power to create himself as a thinking substance, he would have been able to give himself the perfect attributes which, in the previous argument, he noted that he lacked. (This point depends on a slightly different application of the idea of degrees of perfection, introducing a scale of perfection between the metaphysical categories of substance, attribute, and mode, not a scale of perfection between substances.) Nor can he suppose that he has existed from all eternity, for it takes as much power to conserve a substance in being from moment to moment as it does to create it in the first place. This argument illustrates how strongly the creative activity of God is involved in the created world, offering as it does (in contrast, for instance, with the outlook of Leibniz) a picture of created things tending constantly to slip out of existence if it were not for God's sustaining activity. Nor, lastly, can he suppose that he has been created merely by his parents or some other contingent being: they also would have to have the idea of God that has been implanted in them, and this, as in the previous argument, must go back to the creative power of God. The use of this last consideration shows that the arguments which refer to the creation of Descartes himself are not, in fact, independent of the first argument, which refers to his idea of God—and Descartes makes it entirely clear that he does not intend them to be independent. In particular, he makes it clear that he does not wish to argue to the existence of God from the mere existence of a contingent being such as himself; for, he says, he can see no evident repugnance in the idea of an infinite series of contingent beings in causal relations—he rejects the traditional Cosmological Argument, which sought to demonstrate the existence of a Necessary Being merely from the existence of contingent beings. It is the presence of the idea of God—"the mark of the workman on his work"—that is the foundation of all of Descartes's reasonings here.

He does, however, have another and independent argument for the existence of God, which he offers in the *Fifth Meditation*. This starts once more from the idea of God, but in this case merely from the content of the idea without reference to the possession of the idea by an imperfect being. The argument relies on the notion that Descartes can discover the attribute of existence to be one of the chief perfections contained in the idea of God. Hence, it is necessary that God exists, just as it is necessary that the angles of a plane triangle add up to two right angles. Thus, this argument is merely an extremely simple version of the Ontological Argument for God's existence, a slightly different version of which was originally propounded by Anselm and had been rejected by Aquinas. Descartes, though he is himself entirely satisfied with the validity of the argument, is aware that it may present an appearance of sophistry; and this is why (he says) he places it second rather than as his leading argument. Later philosophy, particularly after the criticism offered by Kant, has largely agreed in rejecting this argument as based on a false conception of existence.

There are two views that Descartes holds about the nature of God that are worth noting because they have attracted contemporary criticism; the first, in particular, exemplifies the Scotist and Augustinian influences on his outlook. Descartes holds that the omnipotence of God requires that he should be able to do even what we would understand as being logically impossible, and thus that the "eternal truths" are dependent on God's will. God could have brought it about that two and two did not equal four; although, since God has not chosen that this should be so, it must be beyond our finite comprehension how it might have been so (it remains obscure how, on Descartes's view, we can be certain that it is not so, at least in some cases). The second point is of less importance: Descartes, contrary to many theologians, wished to hold that God was the *efficient* cause of himself. Descartes does not wish to press this rather mystifying view too hard, for fear, he says, of "verbal difficulties"; his motive in offering it seems to have been to emphasize that in saying that God was the cause of himself, one was not merely saying something negative—that God had no cause—nor merely that to understand the essence of God is to have a sufficient explanation of his existence (though this indeed follows from Descartes's use of the Ontological Argument). He wishes to stress, in some sense, the dependence of God's existence on God's own activity.

GOD AND THE FOUNDATIONS OF KNOWLEDGE

There is a property of God that is central to the further construction of Descartes's epistemology: "God . . . is liable to no errors or defect. From this it is manifest that he cannot be a deceiver, since the light of nature teaches us that fraud and deception necessarily proceed from some defect" (*Third Meditation*). This characteristic of God—that he would not deceive us—Descartes is also on occasion disposed to connect with God's benevolence—that he would not wish to lead us, his creatures, into error. It is central to Descartes's system because he founds on it the possibility of knowledge of the external world and of the past. Both of these are matters in which the way of "clear and distinct ideas" does not by itself enable Descartes to reach any certainty from the indubitable contents of consciousness; the mere existence of images and sensations leaves open the possibility, on which the doubt fastened, that there may be neither a past nor an independently existing physical world corresponding to them. At this point, the essence of Descartes's argument is to say that while this possibility remains open, so far as the "natural light" or reason is concerned, we nevertheless have a very strong tendency to believe that there is a reality corresponding to these ideas. This tendency survives the closest scrutiny in the light of reason—while the "natural light" reveals no inherent necessity for a corresponding reality, it reveals no inherent impossibility of it either. This being so, Descartes argues that our very strong natural tendency to believe in the reality would be misleading if no such reality existed, and God would then be responsible for our being creatures who, despite the best efforts of their reason, were systematically misled. This would, in effect, make God a deceiver. But God is no deceiver; hence, we may conclude that we are not systematically misled with respect to those things which we have a strong natural tendency to believe and that, accordingly, we are not misled in supposing that there is both a past and an external world.

An essential feature of this argument is that it extends the warrant of God's not being a deceiver only to those beliefs, our strong tendency to hold which survives the scrutiny of reason; the warrant cannot be invoked to support mere "prejudices"—this would obviously frustrate the method of doubt. If one is to avoid error, one must, in effect, do one's own part first by clarifying one's ideas. The result of this activity may well be that the proposition to which one may eventually assent under God's warrant will be different from that to which one was tempted to assent when in the state of prejudice (as in the case of physical objects). Thus, the avoidance of error under God's dispensation involves the correct use of both the understanding and the will; for Descartes, belief is a matter of assent, and assent is something that is given or withheld—it is, in fact, a mode of the will. In this respect there is, of course, a close parallel, consciously sustained by Descartes, between intellectual and moral correctness and error—in both cases God guides the agent toward (respectively) "the true" and "the good," but correct willing on the agent's part is a necessary condition. In both cases, moreover, there exist "temptations" to fall into error—in the pursuit of the good, the tendencies of bodily desire; in the case of the true, the influence of misleading sensations, again a bodily function. Although Descartes seeks to qualify the opposition of rational intellect and misleading bodily sensations implicit in this picture, it plays a prominent part in his philosophy; and the influences of Augustine and, ultimately, of Plato are clearly seen in it.

It appears to be Descartes's doctrine that all belief is a matter of assent and hence depends on the will; and if this doctrine is to have any content, it must imply that, for any proposition, the mind must be able to (though it may not wish to) withhold its assent. However, when the doctrine is applied to the basic propositions of the Cartesian construction, in particular the *cogito* and the proofs of God's existence, two difficulties follow, one inherent in these issues and one systematic. The inherent difficulty emerges when due weight is given to Descartes's rule, repeatedly appealed to in the construction of the system, that one should give one's assent to all—and only—those ideas which one "clearly and distinctly perceives." Insofar as Descartes expresses himself in these terms, as he sometimes does, it emerges that some of the "ideas" in the mind are of a *propositional* character, besides those ideas that are ideas of various substances, accidents, and modes; this point makes it not altogether easy to apply universally his definitions of clarity and distinctness, by which, he says:

> I term that "clear" which is present and apparent to an attentive mind, in the same way that we see objects clearly when, being present to the regarding eye, they operate upon it with sufficient strength. But the "distinct" is that which is so precise and different from all other objects that it contains within itself nothing but what is clear. . . . Perception may be clear without being distinct, but cannot be distinct without also being clear. (*Principles* I, 45–46)

The difficulty that emerges is this: the sense of "clearly and distinctly perceiving" a proposition in which one ought to give one's assent only to propositions so perceived must also be the sense in which what one clearly and distinctly perceives is that the proposition is *true;* and this indeed emerges from many of Descartes's formulations. But if this is so, there will be no room for a separate function of assent: one who has clearly and distinctly perceived a proposition to be true must thereby already believe it. Thus, the distinction between understanding and will in matters of belief seems to break down at the level of the basic certainties.

This question is connected with the systematic difficulty, which consists in the fact that if assent can always be withheld, even from propositions as compulsive as the *cogito,* it is unclear what could ever suffice to prevent the assent from being withheld. What Descartes needs is something absolutely indubitable, and if assent can always be withheld, nothing will be absolutely indubitable. Here, as his general theory of assent might imply, Descartes finds himself in difficulty and responds to it with considerable ambiguity. On occasion he is disposed to suggest that one might withhold assent from clear and distinct perceptions, but that after God's existence has been proved, we can see an overwhelming reason for not doing so: God's benevolence assures us that our clear and distinct perceptions are really true. But since the proofs of God's existence depend on clear and distinct perceptions, to argue in this way is to argue in a circle, as contemporary critics were quick to point out. (See the *Second Set of Objections, Fourth Set of Objections,* and *Fifth Set of Objections.*)

Descartes's "official answer" (as it might be called) to the charge of circularity is that he applies the justification drawn from God only to those considerations which are not at present clearly and distinctly perceived but are retained in memory. This is consistent with the general structure and ties in with a distinction drawn in the *Regulae* between "intuition" and "deduction," the latter consisting of intuitions held together by memory. However, it cannot be denied that there are many passages, including some of those in which the "official answer" is given, in which the more ambitious and invalid use of God's justification seems to recur (for an example even after the arguments with the critics of the *Meditations,* compare *Principles* I, 13—the "official answer"—with *ibid.,* 30). It is doubtful whether any fully consistent view on this issue can be extracted from Descartes's works.

MATTER AND PHYSICAL SCIENCE

The conception of physical matter that God ultimately validates is rather different from that which would come to mind before philosophical reflection. Matter, according to Descartes, has the essential attribute of extension, and all genuine properties of matter, must be (quantitative) modes of extension. These modes include duration, which Descartes holds to be necessarily contained in our conception of an existing material thing, since to conceive of it as existing is to conceive of it as continuing to exist. He further holds—none too clearly—that the notion of time adds to that of duration "only a mode of thinking," by which he seems to mean that it introduces a measure of the durations of different things by relating them to some selected reference class of notions (see *Principles* I, 55 and 57).

Descartes's conception of matter is a pure idea of reason, which, like the other fundamental Cartesian ideas of mind and God, is innate. He first introduces this idea of matter early in the heuristic order of the *Meditations*—in connection with the famous argument of the piece of wax in the *Second Meditation.* The aim of this argument—which turns on the fact that a piece of wax can be recognized to be present although all its sensible qualities have undergone change—is not to prove at this stage what the essential property of matter must be but to draw attention to an intellectual conception of matter latent in the mind that, reflection shows, is what is being used in forming judgments about matter undergoing sensible change. That this intellectual conception correctly expresses the essence of matter is stated only at a later stage, in the *Fifth Meditation.* It is Descartes's final doctrine that no knowledge of the material world is, save in an indirect manner, derived from the senses. The pure intellectual conception of matter as extension is not derived from the senses, nor (and this for Descartes is a closely related point) can it be adequately represented in images: a favorite argument is that we have a rational comprehension of infinite variations in extension, and this comprehension cannot be adequately expressed in images. Further, not only is the concept of matter intellectual but any perceptual judgment also involves intellectual inference—an inference, ultimately grounded in God's not being a deceiver, from our sensations to the presence of matter that causes them. This representational and causal theory of perception is not only held unquestioningly by Descartes but is also implicit in many of the initial formulations of the doubt and in the approach to the proof of the "external world" as something outside and independent of the mental data certified in the *cogito*.

The conception of matter as extension has a number of important consequences. It implies that the material causes of sensations are not, in fact, as sensation suggests they are to the unreflective mind; in particular, the nature of our sensations may promote the confused—and for Descartes unintelligible—belief that the material world is actually colored, whereas all that is intelligible, and thus can be guaranteed by God's warrant, is that variations in the modes of extension are parallel, but not similar, to variations of perceived color. Thus, Descartes holds the distinction between primary and secondary qualities that is a commonplace of much seventeenth-century scientific thought and is found notably in Galileo and in Locke. There are other consequences of Descartes's views, however, that are more distinctive, following from the fact that his conception of the physical world is totally kinematic and involves no concept that cannot be explained in terms of pure geometry together with time. His physics, in fact, contains no physical (as opposed to mathematical) concept at all; the only departure from a totally abstract geometrical picture is the principle, itself sufficiently abstract, that matter excludes other matter from the place that it occupies.

This excessively geometrical concept of matter has unfortunate results for Descartes's physics. The quantity that is conserved in his system is *motion*, where this is defined as the product of a body's speed and its size, the "size" being understood as the continuous volume of the body, omitting matter found in its interstices (as water is found in the pores of a sponge). The consequences that Descartes draws from this principle are, not surprisingly, in error, his laws of impact in particular being fundamentally mistaken. But there appear to be striking conceptual difficulties as well, when the question is raised of what is meant in the Cartesian system by the distinction between a body and its environment, or between a body and the contents of its interstices. Descartes does not believe in a void, as will indeed be apparent from his virtual equation of matter and space, an equation that makes plausible for him his basic argument for the impossibility of a void—if there is nothing between two bodies, then they must be contiguous.

Since the material world is a plenum and is continuous, there are no ultimate atoms; Descartes in fact employs atomistic forms of explanation, as in his theories of light, but his conception of the particles involved is merely that of small volumes of matter, each of which, as a matter of fact, moves as a whole. Again, since there is no void for any displaced body to move into, any movement must involve a simultaneous movement of matter in some closed curve; this principle (which was similarly derived by Aristotle from the belief in the plenum) is an important element in the theory of *vortices* that figures in Descartes's physics, notably in his explanations of planetary motion. Thus, the picture of the material world is of one, infinite, three-dimensional, continuous, and homogeneous extended body in the terminology of substance, it seems that while there are indefinitely many thinking substances, there is, strictly speaking, only one extended substance that constitutes the whole material universe. But now it becomes extremely unclear how any body is to be distinguished from its environment. Certainly the Cartesian physics seems to have no room for any concept of *density:* no more matter can ever be put into any volume—the volume must already be full of matter, and matter necessarily excludes other matter from the place it occupies—and thus any quantitative conception of density seems to be ruled out. Related difficulties are to be found with other physical concepts essential for the vortex theory, such as *viscosity*. In fact, the only principle that Descartes can consistently appeal to in distinguishing any body from its environment is differential motion of volumes of the continuous matter with respect to different places; it is not surprising that his explanations do not, in fact, succeed in conforming to this ideal.

It will be evident from Descartes's conception of the physical world that his aims for scientific explanation are that it should be entirely mechanical, with final causation totally excluded, and that mathematical physics should emerge as the fundamental science. However, beyond this point there are certain obscurities about his intentions on two related questions: the connections between physics and metaphysics and the extent to which scientific reasoning was supposed to be pure deduction from evident premises. On the first issue, the model of the Tree of Knowledge suggests that Descartes regards physics as continuous with metaphysics, and the second part of the *Principles* offers supposed derivations of certain fundamental physical laws from the properties of God. Yet elsewhere Descartes writes rather as though metaphysics were to be regarded only as a preliminary to scientific thought, offering foundations in an epistemological rather than an axiomatic sense for the truths of physics. On the question of whether physics can proceed by rigorous deduction from self-evident (or, possibly, metaphysically demonstrated) principles, it is very hard to render Descartes's professions consistent. Two quotations will suffice to illustrate the difficulties:

> . . . I only consider [in physics] the divisions, shapes and movements [of quantity, regarded geometrically]; and I do not want to receive as true anything but what can be deduced from these with as much evidence as will allow it to stand as a mathematical demonstration. (*Principles* II, 64)

> To demand of me geometrical demonstrations in a matter which depends on physics is to want me to do the impossible. If one will call "demonstrations" only the proofs of geometers, one will have to say that Ar-

chimedes never demonstrated anything in mechanics. . . . One is content in such matters if the authors, having presupposed certain things which are not manifestly contrary to experience, go on to speak consistently and without producing any paralogism, even if their suppositions were not entirely true. . . . Those who are content to say that they do not believe what I have written because I deduce it from certain suppositions which I have not proved, do not know what they are asking, nor what they should ask. (Letter to Mersenne, May 27, 1638)

Closely connected with this question is that of the role of experiment and observation in Descartes's science. He was always prepared to admit a place for experiment, but his accounts of why it is needed suffer from ambiguities parallel to those just noticed. His favored formulation is to say that there are many different ways in which a phenomenon can be "deduced" from his principles and that experiment is necessary to decide between them; the weakness of this is obviously that if "deduction" is meant strictly, and the principles are consistent, then there is no decision to be made—all routes of deduction must be equally valid. In this connection, it seems clear that a less strict sense of "deduction" is intended and that Descartes has in mind a method of postulating hypotheses within the general framework of his principles; these hypotheses can then be decided upon by experiment.

In the philosophy of science, it is fair to say that Descartes never arrived at so clear a picture of scientific inquiry, nor as effective scientific results, as Galileo. This may be ascribed to the pervasive effect on his science of some of his metaphysical conceptions (more noticeable in his later work, perhaps, than in his early discussions with Beeckman) and to the drastic assimilation of physics and geometry, which had the paradoxical result that Cartesian physics did not actually admit of the essential type of abstraction performed by Galileo—it cannot isolate a particular force (such as gravity) in terms of how a body would move if free from resistance, for to imagine it moving without any resistance is to imagine it in a void, and this, for Descartes, involves a logical impossibility and is incomprehensible. Nevertheless, it should be added that "ce roman de la physique," as Christian Huygens called it, provided not only certain important results—such as the sine law of refraction and at least an obscure approximation to the law of rectilinear inertia—but also a framework of scientific and cosmological ideas robust enough still to be regarded in the early eighteenth century as a real rival to the Newtonian system; Newton himself considered it worthy of painstaking refutation.

MIND AND BODY

A human being must be, for Descartes, some kind of union of two distinct things: a soul, or mind, and a body. The body is part of mechanical nature; the mind, a pure thinking substance. Since the body is a mechanical system, the soul is not (as in the opinion of the ancients) the principle of life: live bodies differ from dead ones as stopped watches differ from working ones; the body does not die because the soul leaves it, but the converse (*Passions of the Soul* I, 5 and 6). Moreover, there are many actions that the bodily machine performs on its own, without any intervention of the soul.

Nevertheless, there is a close union between soul and body—what Descartes is sometimes prepared to call, with an utterly misleading use of a traditional scholastic phrase, a "substantial union." He does suggest that this union is in fact a primitive and unanalyzable notion (see letter to Princess Elizabeth, June 28, 1643); but there is a good deal he is prepared to say about it, and in the late work *Passions of the Soul,* he gives a thoroughgoing causal account of the relations involved. Before reaching this account, Descartes has stressed the idea that "my soul is not in my body as a pilot in a ship," meaning by this that the soul is able to move the body "directly" and also that the soul feels pains and other sensations "in" the body; it does not merely appreciate the body's needs and other states intellectually from outside. In the account of the *Passions of the Soul,* this concern is preserved only rather weakly by saying that in a sense the soul is joined to all parts of the body; but, Descartes continues, there is one part in which "it exercises its functions more particularly than elsewhere"—the pineal gland, a structure near the top of the brain. Descartes particularly selected this organ because it appeared unique in the brain in being single and also because he falsely believed that it did not occur in other animals, for which the question of the relations of soul and body did not arise.

The picture Descartes offers is that of the soul directly moving the pineal gland and thus affecting the "animal spirits" which he considered the hydraulic transmission system of mechanical changes in the body; consonant with his views on the conservation of motion, it is only the direction, and not the speed, of movement of these spirits that is affected by the soul. This is the direction of action of the *will.* In the opposite direction, changes in the body—such as the effect of external objects on the sense organs—are transmitted to the pineal gland by the spirits and can there affect the soul by causing sensations in it. The further details of this theory need not be pursued here, except to mention that Descartes incorporated into this view a theory that he held before: that in the case of visual sensation, at least, and with visual imagery, a physical picture or representation was formed in the brain, and it was this that the soul was conscious of. There are certain difficulties in understanding exactly how Descartes envisages this consciousness and to what extent a pictorial element recurs at the purely mental level (on this question, see Norman Kemp Smith, *New Studies,* Ch. 6).

The pineal gland theory offered in the earlier parts of the *Passions of the Soul* (a work that also contains other matter, on the emotions and on certain moral issues, which will not be discussed here) was not a part of the Cartesian system that found wide favor; its conception of a local mechanical interaction between two entities, one of which had precisely been defined as having no extended or mechanical properties, seems almost as awkward for the Cartesian system itself as it does to any other point of view. The rejection of Descartes's account led to many important developments in the history of rationalism, notably to the occasionalism of Malebranche and to the theory of pre-established harmony that is particularly associated with Leibniz.

It has already been remarked that in Descartes's view there are certain actions which the body performs "without the intervention of the soul," acting as a purely mechanical system; it is important that these also include certain relations between perception and action or reaction, as when we by reflex throw out our hands to save ourselves from falling or react to certain stimuli by behavior expressive of emotion. In all these cases the body is acting as a reactive machine, the perceptual stimuli producing bodily change merely through the mechanisms of the brain and the nervous system. It is Descartes's view that the behavior of all animals other than man is reactive; and it seems to be his view, further, that while men may have at least some consciousness of the occurrence of these processes—in the form, for instance, of experienced emotions—this is not so with the other animals, which have no soul or mind, and hence no consciousness, at all. This is the famous Cartesian doctrine that animals are machines, a doctrine that aroused particular opposition from two of his English correspondents, Henry More and William Cavendish, the marquess of Newcastle.

Descartes is not always verbally consistent in his accounts of this view, but on the whole it does seem that he held the strong thesis that has usually been ascribed to him; it entails, for instance, that the only sense in which one can hurt an animal is that one can damage it. If this is so, it throws an interesting light on the Cartesian view of the mind or consciousness. Descartes's main grounds for ascribing the possession of mind uniquely to man are grounds concerned with *ratiocination*, particularly that man has a language, which (he supposes) no machine or animal could have; however, free will—again with special reference to conscious intellectual deliberation—is also cited. These distinctions by themselves would seem to have little force in denying that animals possess consciousness of pain or some other kinds of feelings and sensations; and what appears to be Descartes's wholesale rejection of all forms of consciousness in their case is an expression of his concept of the unity of mind under the primary aspect of pure intellect. Totally abandoning any Aristotelian conception of degrees or orders of "soul," he fastens on an intellectual conception that carries all other modes of consciousness with it. This conception emerges also in a certain tendency to regard sensation and feeling, in their purely mental aspects, as confused forms of (intellectual) thought, a tendency that plays some role in his account of perception, for instance, even though it is not consistently carried through either there or in the original descriptions of consciousness given in the *cogito*.

The influence of Descartes has been enormous. The Scottish philosopher Thomas Reid wrote that Malebranche, Locke, Berkeley, and Hume shared "a common system of the human understanding" that "may still be called the Cartesian system," and this very true remark could be extended through the history of philosophy into modern times. As Reid observed, Descartes's influence worked as much on empiricist philosophers as on those of his own rationalist temper; however, different parts of his outlook had these several effects. The influence on empiricism was perhaps the deeper of the two; one can see there, in the particular form of starting with the supposedly indubitable data of the individual consciousness, the effects of Descartes's enterprise of making epistemology the starting point of philosophy. Many postempiricist developments center in the same interest, sometimes (as in the case of Edmund Husserl) with an explicit attempt to recapture the Cartesian approach. The problems posed by Descartes's dualism remain at the heart of much contemporary philosophical inquiry, the work of Gilbert Ryle and Ludwig Wittgenstein, for example, being aimed directly against what are still very powerful Cartesian conceptions.

Bibliography

The standard edition of Descartes's works is *Oeuvres de Descartes*, Charles Adam and Paul Tannery, eds., 12 vols. (Paris, 1897–1910; Index général, Paris, 1913).

English translations of the philosophical works, or of selections from them, include the following; there are no extensive translations from the correspondence: *The Philosophical Works of Descartes*, translated by E. S. Haldane and G. T. R. Ross, 2 vols. (Cambridge, 1911–1912; corrected ed., 1934; paperback, New York, 1955), is very useful, though the translation is a little heavy and diffuse; selections from the correspondence are included in Vol. II. A vigorous but free translation is found in *Descartes: Philosophical Writings*, selected, translated, and edited by G. E. M. Anscombe and P. T. Geach (Edinburgh, 1954); it also contains brief, useful notes and a good bibliography. Also see *Descartes' Philosophical Writings*, selected and edited by Norman Kemp Smith (London, 1952).

In a special class among the numerous editions of particular works is *Discours de la méthode*, text and commentary by Étienne Gilson, 2d ed. (Paris, 1930), which sheds great light on the *Discourse*.

There are many expository, critical, and historical works on all aspects of Descartes; the following is but a brief selection: Norman Kemp Smith, *Studies in the Cartesian Philosophy* (London and New York, 1902) and *New Studies in the Philosophy of Descartes* (London, 1952); Étienne Gilson, *Études sur le rôle de la pensée médiévale dans la formation du système cartésien* (Paris, 1930); J. Laporte, *Le Rationalisme de Descartes*, 2d ed. (Paris, 1950); G. Milhaud, *Descartes savant* (Paris, 1920); F. Alquié, *La Découverte métaphysique de l'homme chez Descartes* (Paris, 1950); L. J. Beck, *The Method of Descartes. A Study of the Regulae* (Oxford, 1952); and M. Guéroult, *Descartes selon l'ordre des raisons*, Vol. I (Paris, 1953).

Two articles on the *cogito* from an analytical point of view are A. J. Ayer, "Cogito ergo sum," in *Analysis*, Vol. 14 (1953), 27–31, and J. Hintikka, "Cogito, ergo sum: Inference or Performance?" in *Philosophical Review*, Vol. 71 (Jan. 1962), 3–32.

BERNARD WILLIAMS

DESCRIPTIONS. *See* PROPER NAMES AND DESCRIPTIONS.

DESCRIPTIONS, THEORY OF. *See* ANALYSIS, PHILOSOPHICAL; EXISTENCE; REFERRING.

DESSOIR, MAX (1867–1947), German philosopher and theorist of aesthetics, was born in Berlin. His advanced studies there led to a doctorate in philosophy (1889) and his studies in Würzburg to a doctorate in medicine (1892). On the University of Berlin faculty he rose to an assistant professorship in 1897 and to a full professorship in 1920.

In Berlin Dessoir enjoyed a rich life of close association with many scholars and artists of international reputation. In 1906 he founded the *Zeitschrift für Ästhetik und allgemeine Kunstwissenschaft*, which he edited for many years. In 1909 he organized the Gesellschaft für Ästhetik und allgemeine Kunstwissenschaft and was long its director.

With the advent of the National Socialist government in 1933, Dessoir encountered growing harassment and frustration until finally Propaganda Minister Goebbels debarred him from all teaching, public speaking, and publication. By August 1943, Berlin life had become so difficult that he and his wife left the city, soon settling with a friend at Bad Nauheim. Dessoir died four years later at Königstein in Taunus.

Dessoir's philosophical outlook is that of a Neo-Kantian critical idealist, humanized and enriched by a broad and detailed knowledge of psychology and the arts.

Early in life he developed an interest in parapsychological phenomena, approaching this subject with the liberal objectivity of a philosophically emancipated scientist, who avoids both the bias against a field hardly reputable in professional psychology and the uncritical enthusiasm for unbridled, fanciful theories. The unconscious speech and writing of mediums, for Dessoir, are merely more extreme cases of a condition at least potentially present even in the normal person, that is, a split in personality with the separate persistence of each part. The recessive self, being unable to express itself through the dominant self, finds independent modes of expression. This interpretation has important bearings on the common belief that the creative artist is an inspired medium, controlled by some transcendent spiritual power.

Dessoir was also concerned to show how deep, pervasive human needs lead to the intellectually less disciplined *Weltanschauungen*, which more rigorous philosophical schools, while resisting, should nevertheless understand. Such *Weltanschauungen* often retain vestiges of primitive magic, such as the belief that a word contains the essence of the thing to which it refers, or the excessive confidence in a self-sufficient, intuitive certainty.

Dessoir's writings on aesthetics and on what he called a general science of art rest on a basic distinction. The field studied by aesthetics, broadly understood as the whole realm of aesthetic objects, attitudes, and categories, includes natural objects and even certain aspects of intellectual and social structures. Hence, this field is much wider than the arts. But the arts, in turn, though more limited in extent, are richer in content and relevance, having their roots and fruits in many phases of man's physical, intellectual, social, and religious nature.

Dessoir felt that a general science of art was urgently needed to study the similarities, differences, and systematic interconnections of the various arts in regard to conditions of origin and growth, mental characteristics and stages of the creative process, epistemological assumptions, media and techniques, and functions in human life. But the creative artist was too much concerned with his own productive activity; the art critic, with the particular work under examination at the moment; the historian and theorist of any one art, with his own special area. Hence it devolved upon the philosophical aesthetician to develop aesthetics and the general science of art as one unitary discipline.

In his account of the aesthetic object, attitude, and categories Dessoir proposed to find, study, and characterize them *in* the concrete aesthetic situation, rejecting the futile attempt to derive them either from some metaphysical absolute *above* or from some psychological elements *below.* He considered versions of aesthetic objectivism (which defines the aesthetic situation in terms of the object) and aesthetic subjectivism (which defines it in terms of the attitude), finding each of them in turn an inadequate abstraction. "Whereas in the realm of truth the subject has no place and in the realm of morality the object is regarded only as something to be overcome, aesthetic subject and object are inseparable" (*Ästhetik und allgemeine Kunstwissenschaft*, 2d ed., p. 19).

The scope of aesthetic objects is not merely the scope of beautiful objects, for beauty is by no means the only aesthetic value. Nor does the scope of aesthetic objects coincide with nature as a whole; this view ignores the selective and interpretative function of art. Aesthetic objects are rather those objects of nature or technology, those intellectual or social constructs in which whole and part, part and part are felt to necessitate one another beyond the minimal degree requisite for ordinary experience.

Aesthetic objects (both spatial and temporal, visual and auditory) show harmony and proportion, rhythm and meter, size and degree. By size and degree is meant the extensive and intensive magnitude of an object as a whole, in distinction from ratios of magnitudes among its component parts. The more important the theme, the greater should the magnitudes be, though the possibility of empathy sets lower and upper limits.

Concerning the successive stages and general nature of the aesthetic attitude, both experimental and less strictly controlled introspections yield a wide variety of reports, depending on the observer and the object observed. But there is general agreement concerning the alternation of more active and more passive stages and the presence of periods of marked tension. In the broad sense of the term *pleasure*, which permits degrees and kinds, Dessoir held that the aesthetic attitude is pervasively pleasant.

Dessoir found five primary aesthetic forms: the beautiful, the sublime, the tragic, the ugly, and the comic. Only in beauty are moderation and harmony essential. The other four forms can contain grotesque and even monstrous features.

"The ideally beautiful is an intuitively apparent formal unity which coincides with the natural course of inner activities and likewise with an harmonious co-existence of inner states" (*op. cit.*, p. 140). Purposiveness is always an aspect of the beautiful, unobtrusively imparting an organic unity to the component elements. In connection with beauty, Dessoir considered the derivative concepts: gentility, ornament, prettiness, and grace.

Sublimity involves such overpowering might in the object that petty feelings of personal fear vanish from the soul. This self-forgetfulness can occur most easily in the presence of artistic sublimity, for the negative condition necessary for self-forgetfulness is the more or less subconscious feeling of security when confronting superior might. Whoever has a real sense of sublimity cannot feel himself a harmonious being in a harmonious world. That man as man is an infinite being we learn through the experience of the sublime and the similar experience of the tragic.

"The tragic consciousness is the recognition of the inescapable suffering destined for all good men, and the power to win from this suffering an ultimate state of exaltation" (*op. cit.*, p. 151). Genuine tragedy leaves the conflict unresolved, proving that in the world and in life there are oppositions which nothing can remove. Above the forgiving generosity of deity stands inexorable fate.

The ugly is only the polar opposite of the beautiful, whether one takes it to be a value or a disvalue. Akin to the tragic and the comic, it is distinguished from the beautiful by its instability and inconsistency.

Insofar as the ugly is a deviant from the norm, it can under certain conditions pass into the comic, two principal subforms of which are the witty and the humorous. Wit is a clever use of terse language to express unexpected similarities, often as a satirical thrust. A sense of humor is an awareness of human significance and insignificance. Humor unites the finite and the infinite, teaching us how to conquer fate with a smile.

The three chief theories of artistic creation (illumination, intensification, and good technical judgment) are quite compatible and may refer to the successive stages of creative activity: the productive mood, the moment of conception, the sketch, and the execution. In this scheme, good technical judgment applies to both sketch and execution. The productive mood usually seizes the artist unexpectedly—an ecstatic surge of various feelings. In the moment of conception some relatively definite form appears in sensory imagination, but is still rather nebulous and provisional. Even now the artist cannot say with absolute certainty what will become of it. In a small work the sketch may be the final stage. In a large work the sketch usually reacts upon the artist, releasing in him the full-fledged vision, the organic whole whose details are worked out in the execution.

After indicating certain rudiments of art in the child and in primitive people of the present and of the remote past, Dessoir turns to the systematic classification of the arts, acknowledging that their interpenetration makes this task very difficult. Ignoring all secondary considerations and concentrating on the main traditional points of view, we get the following four intersecting groups: (1) spatial, figurative arts (of rest and juxtaposition)—plastic art, painting, architecture; (2) temporal, musical arts (of movement and succession)—mimetic art, poetry, music; (3) arts of imitation, definite associations, and real forms—plastic art, painting, mimetic art, poetry; (4) free arts of indefinite associations and unreal forms—architecture, music.

Culture is a whole of distinct, autonomous, but mutually involved elements—economy, law, morality, religion, science, art—in which spiritual values are discovered and realized. So "art merely for art's sake" is a fatuous and futile maxim. A thorough study of art necessarily includes its relevance to other cultural areas.

Both science and art select their materials from experience and organize them in their characteristic ways, science structuring an indefinitely extended spatiotemporal continuum in terms of logical, mathematical, and causal necessities, art combining its elements through felt necessities, to form finite, discrete wholes, enjoyed in detachment from their contexts. Yet science and art are often closely interwoven, as in historiography and artistic scientific exposition.

Extremely democratic views concerning the proper social function of art are seriously misguided. To claim that art should permeate every social group and human activity is to forget that art is only one of many expressions of human nature, that exclusive stress on art in any culture has led to artistic degeneration, that only a relatively few persons have the sensitivity and training for fine artistic creation or appreciation. The justification of high art lies in what it gives to those persons. Its kingdom is not of this world.

The moral function of art is pervasive. It educates artist and critic in integrity and courage; it sensitizes and deepens the appreciative recipient. "A glimpse of the beauty created by man can leave us in a state of long-echoing emotion, mellowing and calming; humor can bring lasting consolation and reconciliation; tragedy can rouse and raise us into a greater life. Wherever the persuasive power of art is allied with the imperative power of the good, a lasting result can appear" (*op. cit.*, p. 422). But the supreme and absolute moral function of art is to show that outer and inner, the earthly and the divine, in their ultimate ground are one.

Works by Dessoir

Bibliographie des modernen Hypnotismus. Berlin, 1888.
Karl Philipp Moritz als Ästhetiker. Naumburg, 1889.
Geschichte der neueren deutschen Psychologie. Berlin, 1894.
Ästhetik und allgemeine Kunstwissenschaft. Stuttgart, 1906.
Abriss einer Geschichte der Psychologie. Heidelberg, 1911. Translated by Donald Fisher as *Outlines of the History of Psychology.* New York, 1912.
Kriegspsychologische Betrachtungen. Leipzig, 1916.
Vom Jenseits der Seele. Stuttgart, 1917.
Vom Diesseits der Seele. Berlin, 1923. Revised as *Psychologische Briefe.* Berlin, 1948.
Einleitung in die Philosophie. Stuttgart, 1936.
Die Rede als Kunst. Munich, 1940.
Buch der Erinnerung. Stuttgart, 1946.
Das Ich, der Traum, der Tod. Stuttgart, 1947.

Works on Dessoir

Herrmann, Christian, *Max Dessoir: Mensch und Werk.* Stuttgart, 1929.
See also bibliography on Dessoir in *Zeitschrift für Ästhetik und allgemeine Kunstwissenschaft,* 1927.

STEPHEN A. EMERY

DESTUTT DE TRACY, ANTOINE LOUIS CLAUDE, COMTE (1754–1836), French philosopher and propounder of the doctrine of Ideology, was born in Paris. Educated at the University of Strasbourg, he entered the army and served later as deputy of the Bourbonnais nobility to the States-General. Despite his noble rank he was a fervent partisan of reform in monarchical government, but by 1792 he had become disgusted with the extremists among the revolutionaries and retired from politics to Auteuil, where he joined the celebrated group of philosopher-scientists which found its center at the home of Mme. Helvétius. Among his intimates were Cabanis and Condorcet, Volney and Garat. Imprisoned for a year under the Terror, he began to study the works of Condillac and John Locke, the result of which was his elaboration of the discipline he called Ideology. The group associated with Destutt de Tracy took the name *Idéologues* from his doctrine. They became influential in 1795 in two new institutions, the École Normale and the Institut National, especially in the Second Class of the Institut National.

Ideology, according to Destutt de Tracy, is the analysis of ideas into the sensory elements of which he believed them to be composed. Training in this new science would replace classical logic, and, he maintained, if a man learned how to analyze his ideas, he would then discover which of them were founded in experience and which were groundless. Destutt de Tracy held that Ideology was a branch of zoology; all ideas had a physiological determinant. The child, with his weak sense organs, has nothing but sensation and memory; the adult, whose sense organs have become strengthened through use, has the powers of judgment and intelligence. It was therefore to be asked what the effect of habit would be on judgment. This question was put to the Second Class of the Institut National on 15 Vendémiaire, An VIII (October 6, 1799). The winning *mémoire* was that of Maine de Biran, at that time a young disciple of the *Idéologues*, and his *Mémoire sur l'habitude* (1802) formed the link between the French epistemological tradition of the eighteenth century and that of the nineteenth-century "spiritualists."

The word "thinking" in the works of Destutt de Tracy means, as it did for Descartes, all conscious processes. Any immediate apprehension is called "feeling," whether it be sensory, emotional, or intellectual. Even memory and the perception of relations were "felt." But the feelings were not images; they were merely the awareness of whatever content might be before one. Destutt de Tracy called these contents ideas, following Locke. They were of four kinds: sensations, memories, judgments, and desires.

The question which puzzled Destutt de Tracy and, for that matter, most of the philosophers of this period in France was whether all consciousness is passive or whether some is active. If all were passive, then we should have no reason to believe in the existence of an external world. There is, however, according to Destutt de Tracy, one idea which gives us an intimation of a reality beyond ourselves, the idea of touch. When we put pressure upon an object, it resists. We cannot, at the same time, desire both a feeling and its annihilation. The feeling of resistance annihilates the desire to penetrate. Therefore, when we feel resistance, we are forced to conclude that there is a resisting object. In this way an element of activity was introduced into Destutt de Tracy's epistemology, an element which was to form the logical nucleus of the theories of his successors, Maine de Biran and Laromiguière.

Destutt de Tracy thought that the analysis of general ideas into elementary feelings would destroy the analyzer's faith in many of the teachings of religion. For if an idea could not be found to be either an elementary feeling or to be composed of such, it must be discarded. But many religious ideas cannot be so analyzed and therefore must be discarded.

Although the *Idéologues* had favored Napoleon's coup d'état of 1799, they soon opposed him, and in 1803 Napoleon suppressed the Second Class of the Institut. Destutt de Tracy's antireligious views, which directly clashed with Napoleon's re-establishment of religion, were a major factor in Napoleon's act of suppression. The soon-to-be emperor, moreover, could not tolerate Destutt de Tracy's view that every man has the power to determine the truth and falsity of his ideas without recourse to authority and that among those ideas are those of right and wrong, both moral and political.

Works by Destutt de Tracy

Quels sont les moyens de fonder la morale chez un peuple? Paris, 1798.

Observations sur le système d'instruction publique. Paris, 1801.

Eléments d'idéologie, 4 vols. Paris, 1801–1815.

Grammaire générale. Paris, 1803.

Logique. Paris, 1805.

Traité de la volonté et de ses effets. Paris, 1805.

Commentaire sur l'esprit des lois de Montesquieu. Liège, 1817. First published in an English translation by Thomas Jefferson as *A Commentary and Review of Montesquieu's Spirit of Laws.* Philadelphia, 1811.

De l'Amour, Gilbert Chinard, ed. Paris, 1926.

Works on Destutt de Tracy

Boas, George, *French Philosophies of the Romantic Period.* Baltimore, 1925. Ch. 2, esp. pp. 24–31.

Chinard, J., *Jefferson et les idéologues.* Baltimore, 1925.

Picavet, François, *Les Idéologues.* Paris, 1891. Chs. 5 and 6. Still the classic work.

Van Duzen, C., *The Contributions of the Idéologues to French Revolutionary Thought.* Baltimore, 1935.

GEORGE BOAS

DETERMINABLES AND DETERMINATES. The terminology of determinables and determinates existed in scholastic philosophy, but the modern use of these terms originated with the Cambridge (England) philosopher and logician W. E. Johnson, who revived the terminology in his *Logic* (1921). Johnson said, "I propose to call such terms as colour and shape *determinables* in relation to such terms as red or circular which will be called *determinates.*" Some other determinables are size, weight, age, number, and texture. The terminology has since passed into philosophical currency and is now used to mark both the relation between determinate and determinable qualities and the relation between the corresponding words.

The chief features of this relation which Johnson and his successors have found interesting are:

(1) It is logically distinct from the relation of genus to species. The denotation of a species term is marked off within the denotation of a genus term by the possession of properties known as differentia. The species is thus to be construed as formed by the conjunction of two logically independent terms, either of which can, depending on the purposes at hand, be construed as genus or differentia. For

example, the species term "man" is defined as the conjunction of the terms "rational" and "animal." However, the determinate term "red" is not definable by conjoining the determinable term "color" with any other independent term. To put this point another way: whereas we can say, "All humans are animals which are rational," no analogous statement can be made beginning, "All red things are colored things which are . . . ." Any term which could fill the gap would have to be synonymous with "red." Red things do not possess some trait other than their redness which, when conjoined with their coloredness, makes them by definition red. Both the genus-species relation and the determinable-determinate relation are relations of the less specific to the more specific; but in the former case the specification is provided by some property logically independent of the genus, whereas in the latter case the determinate cannot be specified by adding additional independent properties to the determinable.

This characteristic has been emphasized by Johnson, Cook-Wilson, Prior, and Searle; and it is this feature which chiefly justifies the introduction of this terminology as an addition to the traditional arsenal. Attempts have been made—by Searle, for example—to give a rigorous formal definition of the determinable relation utilizing this feature; but it is not clear to what extent they have succeded.

(2) Determinates under the same determinable are incompatible. For example, the same object cannot be simultaneously red and green at the same point; and a man six feet tall cannot be simultaneously five feet tall. It might seem that counterexamples could be produced to this point since, for example, an object can be both red and scarlet, and red and scarlet are both determinates of color. However, such counterexamples are easily disposed of on the basis of the fact that scarlet is a shade of red, and hence red is a determinable of scarlet.

We must distinguish the relation in which red stands to scarlet from the relation in which color stands to either red or scarlet. Both are cases of the determinable relation, but they are significantly different. We may think of color terminology as providing us with a hierarchy of terms, many of which will stand in the determinable relation to each other as the specification of shades progresses from the less precise to the more precise. But at the top of the hierarchy stands the term "color," which we may describe as an absolute determinable of all the other members of the hierarchy, including such lower-order determinables as "red" and their determinates, such as "scarlet."

Our original point can then be restated by saying that determinates under the same determinable are incompatible unless one of the determinates is a lower-order determinable of the other. In the literature of this subject, the counterexamples are usually avoided by saying that any two exact determinates—for example, exact shades of color—are incompatible. However, it is not clear what "exact" is supposed to mean in this context.

(3) Absolute determinables play a special role vis-à-vis their determinates. This role may be expressed by saying that, in general, for any determinate term neither that term nor its negation is predicable of an entity unless the corresponding absolute determinable term is true of that entity. For example, both the sentence "The number seventeen is red" and the sentence "The number seventeen is not red" sound linguistically odd because numbers are not the sort of entities which can be colored. Lacking the appropriate absolute determinable, neither a determinate term nor its negation is true of the entity in question.

To have a convenient formulation of this point, we may say that the predication of any determinate term or its negation of an object *presupposes* that the corresponding absolute determinable term is true of that object. We define presupposition as follows: a term A presupposes a term B if and only if it is a necessary condition of A's being either true or false of an object x that B is true of x. Thus, in short and in general, determinates presuppose their absolute determinables. No doubt certain qualifications would have to be made to account for the operation of this principle in a natural language. For example, perhaps what is presupposed by "red" is more accurately expressed by "colorable" rather than by "colored."

Aside from the intrinsic interest of these distinctions, they have proved useful in other areas of philosophy. Locke's very puzzling discussion of primary and secondary qualities can be illuminated by pointing out that he fails to make sufficient use of the distinction between determinable and determinate qualities. When, for example, he says the primary qualities of a material body are inseparable from it in whatever state it may be, he clearly does not mean that a body must have this or that determinate shape or size as opposed to some other shape or size, but rather that it must have the absolute determinables of the primary qualities: it is a necessary condition of something's being a material object that it have some shape or other, some size or other, and so on.

Again, it is useful to point out that absolute determinables are closely related to categories. The notion of a category (or at least one philosophically important notion of a category) is the notion of a class of objects of which a given term can be significantly predicated. Thus, for example, correlative with the notion of "red" is the notion of things which can significantly be called red; these things are the members of the category associated with "red." But a necessary condition of something's being a member of the class of things which can be significantly called "red" is that the absolute determinable of "red" must be true of that thing since, as we saw above, determinates presuppose their absolute determinables. Because a category (of the sort we are considering) is always a category relative to a certain term, and because a determinate term presupposes its absolute determinable, the absolute determinables provide a set of necessary conditions for category membership relative to the determinate terms.

Where the absolute determinable provides not only a necessary but also a sufficient condition of predicability of the determinate term, the absolute determinable will simply denote the members of the category associated with the determinate term. Thus, assuming "colored" (or "colorable") is the only presupposed term of "red," the category associated with "red," and with any other determinate of "color," is only the class of objects which are (or could be) colored.

Bibliography

Johnson, W. E., *Logic*. Cambridge, 1921.

Körner, S., and Searle, J. R., "Determinables and the Notion of Resemblance: Symposium." *PAS* Supp. (1959), 125–158.

Prior, A., "Determinables, Determinates, and Determinants." *Mind*, Vol. 58 (1949), 1–20, 178–194.

JOHN R. SEARLE

DETERMINISM is the general philosophical thesis which states that for everything that ever happens there are conditions such that, given them, nothing else could happen. The several versions of this thesis rest upon various alleged connections and interdependencies of things and events, asserting that these hold without exception.

There have been many versions of deterministic theories in the history of philosophy, springing from diverse motives and considerations, some of which overlap considerably. We shall consider these in the order in which they have been historically significant, together with certain alternative theories that philosophers have proposed. There are five theories of determinism to be considered, which can for convenience be called ethical determinism, logical determinism, theological determinism, physical determinism, and psychological determinism.

ETHICAL DETERMINISM

Advocates. It seemed to Socrates that every man always chooses what seems to him best, that no man can set as the object of his choice something that seems evil or bad to him. Plato had much the same view, arguing that no man who knows what is good can possibly choose anything else. They drew the obvious corollary that wrongdoing or the pursuit of evil must always be either involuntary or the result of ignorance.

A thirsty man, for example, might choose to drink from a certain cup in ignorance of the fact that it contains poison, or knowing its contents, he might be forced to drink from it. But he could not, knowing that it contained poison and that this would bring upon him a great evil, voluntarily drink from it. Socrates and Plato thought that similar reasoning applies to any choice whatsoever. Hence, the Socratic doctrine that virtue is knowledge and vice ignorance. If one knows the good, he automatically seeks it; if one seeks something else, it can only be because he is pursuing an apparent, but specious, good—in other words, because he is ignorant of what is in fact good. An obvious corollary to this, and one that was drawn by Plato, is that the best commonwealth would be one governed by philosophers—that is, by men who know the good and can intellectually distinguish it from its counterfeits.

It is evident that in this ethical intellectualism, which is so central to Platonism, there is a theory of determinism. Men's voluntary actions are invariably determined by an apparent good; hence, all their actions are determined by this, if by nothing else. Philosophers who have been convinced by this teaching have nevertheless without exception insisted that it enhances rather than debases man's freedom. Freedom, they have maintained, is precisely the determination of the will by what is good. To have one's will or choice determined by what is bad is to be enslaved; to have it determined by something less than the highest good is, to that extent, to be less than perfectly free. Thus, Plato described the wicked tyrant, who pursues what is evil because he is ignorant of the true good, as enslaved and an object of pity.

Descartes believed that no man who knew his true "end" or highest good could reject it in favor of something less and maintained that man's freedom consisted precisely in knowing that good and being thereby determined to seek it. St. Thomas Aquinas spoke similarly, with qualifications, concerning man's knowledge of his true "end" or highest good. Leibniz similarly took for granted the fact that God could not possibly be guided by anything except the true good, which he must surely know, and that in creating a world, for example, he therefore could not create any but the best possible world. Still, Leibniz maintained, this is no derogation of God's freedom; on the contrary, it is the most perfect freedom to have one's will thus determined.

Opponents. Aristotle rejected this theory of ethical determinism, mostly because it conflicts with what he took to be the evident fact of incontinence. It seemed clear to him that sometimes a man's desires or appetites are in conflict with his reason, precisely in the sense that he desires something bad even while knowing that it is bad, which is the very essence of incontinence. John Locke took the same position. A drunkard, Locke pointed out, well knows that his use of spirits is bad for him, but the mere knowledge of this cannot be depended upon to extinguish his desire for them.

Most contemporary thinkers incline to the same view. The moral and intellectual determination of men's choices and the consequent impossibility of genuine incontinence are no longer considered a plausible view by very many. Nevertheless, it is not easy to see just what is wrong with it. Surely, men do prefer the better to the worse in some sense—not what is absolutely better, perhaps, but what at least seems better; otherwise, why would any man choose it? It is the very nature of things bad to be shunned, and that is precisely why they are called bad.

Perhaps the real issue here is the more general opposition between rationalism and voluntarism. If one assumes the primacy of man's reason and supposes his will, or what the Greeks called his appetite, to be naturally subordinate to it, then the Socratic thesis of the determination of the will by the reason is difficult to refute. If, on the other hand, one presupposes the primacy of man's will or appetite and assumes the intellect to be at least sometimes subordinate to the will, then there is no difficulty in accounting for incontinence. Furthermore, there have been many philosophers—for example, Spinoza, Hobbes, and William James—who have insisted that all it means to describe something as good is that it is the object of one's will—that is, of his desire or interest. If this is so, then the Socratic thesis becomes utterly trivial. It amounts to saying nothing more than that the object of a man's will is always an apparent good—that is, something that is the object of his will. This is certainly true but not significant.

LOGICAL DETERMINISM

Very early in the development of Western philosophy it occurred to certain thinkers that logic alone suggests that men's wills are fettered, that nothing is really in their power to alter. This thesis was developed by Diodorus Cronus and others of his school, whom Aristotle sometimes referred to as "the Megarians," and more importantly by the highly influential school of the Stoics. Such views were associated by the ancients with the idea of fate, an idea which has, however, the same implications as certain forms of determinism with respect to human freedom. Thus, if no man's destiny is in any degree up to him, if everything that he ever does is something he could never have avoided, then in the clearest sense it is idle to speak of his having a free will. The Stoics thought that the most elementary consideration of logic shows this to be true.

The consideration in question is simply the supposition that every statement whatsoever is true or, if not true, false. This ultimately came to be expressed in the dictum *tertium non datur,* meaning that no third truth-value, besides true and false, can be assigned to any statement. If this is so, then it must hold for statements about the future as well as any others, for statements about individual men's future actions and even for statements or propositions that are never asserted. It must also, of course, apply to statements believed by the gods. The last idea eventually became very important when the belief in an omniscient and infallible god became theological dogma.

What apparently led certain ancients, such as Chrysippus, Posidonius, and the Stoics generally to take the idea of logical determinism seriously was a consideration of signs, omens, and portents, which were then widely believed in. If there are signs from which it can be discovered what is going to happen, especially what a certain man is going to do at a certain time, and if, moreover, such signs are vouchsafed to men by gods, then it seems that such predictions must unavoidably, in the fullness of time, be fulfilled. Any such prediction which was not fulfilled could not have been true when made, contradicting the supposition that it was true. If such a prediction must be fulfilled, then it seems to follow that it is not within anyone's power to confute it. The extension of this thought to all actions of all men leads quite naturally to the view that no man's actions are ever free or that nothing any man ever does was ever avoidable, it having always been true that he was going to do whatever he eventually did.

Aristotle's opinion. A penetrating discussion of this problem is contained in some much disputed passages of Aristotle's *De Interpretatione.* Aristotle there considers the question of whether every true proposition, asserting that a certain event has occurred at a certain time, was true before the event in question took place and whether every false proposition, asserting that a certain event has occurred at a certain time, was false before the event failed to take place at that time.

Suppose, for example, a naval battle took place yesterday. This would seem to entail that it was already true, prior to yesterday, that it was going to occur. If anyone had said a thousand years earlier that such a battle was going to occur that day, then it would seem that his prediction was true, and if anyone had denied it a thousand years earlier, then the events of that day would have shown him to have been wrong. Aristotle, however, seemed reluctant to make this seemingly obvious inference. He suggested that it is inconsistent with the fact that men sometimes deliberate about whether to make certain things happen and with the belief all men have that it is sometimes up to them whether the events about which they deliberate will occur. If it is true a thousand years before a naval battle occurs that it is going to occur on a certain day, then whether or not anyone actually makes the prediction, it is difficult to see how, when that day arrives, it can still be up to the naval commander whether the battle will occur or what point there could be in anyone's deliberating about whether to precipitate it. The same difficulty arises if one supposes it to have been false a thousand years earlier that a naval battle would later occur. Aristotle therefore seems to suggest that some propositions—namely, those which assert or deny the future occurrence of certain deliberate actions of men or of events which are dependent upon these—are sometimes neither true nor false until the actions have either occurred or failed to occur.

Subsequent controversy. This whole question was highly vexing to the early thinkers who followed Aristotle. It was even more troublesome to the Scholastics, many of whom felt bound to affirm the freedom of the human will but also bound to affirm that God knows from the beginning of time everything that will ever happen in his creation. Most of the Stoics, whose philosophy was highly fatalistic anyway, embraced the view of logical determinism or fatalism, while many of the Epicureans, who from moral considerations had always set themselves against any theories of fatalism, sometimes defended the view that statements about the future need not be either true or false and hence could not be known in advance even by the gods.

Diodorus Cronus was perhaps the most polemical of the early advocates of logical determinism. His fundamental principle, which is obviously a very strong one, was that it always follows from the fact that something *has* happened that it was *going* to happen and, hence, that it was true that it was going to happen before it did happen. Applying this seemingly incontestable dictum, Diodorus concluded that nothing is ever possible except what actually happens, from which it follows that it is never within any man's power to do anything except what he actually does.

Among the problems to which this conclusion gave rise was one called "the idle argument," which states that there is never any point in any man's ever taking any precautions or making any preparations. If, for example, a man is ill, then it follows from Diodorus' principle that he is either going to recover or he is not going to recover. If he is going to recover, then he will recover whether or not he summons a physician; similarly, if he is going to perish, then he will perish whether or not he summons a physician. Hence, there is no point in his summoning a physician in either case because the outcome is already inevitable. The philosopher Chrysippus sought to resolve this evident absurdity by inventing the notion of "condestinate" facts, facts whose truths are dependent upon one another. Thus, it may be true that a man is going to recover from his illness and also true that he is going to recover only if he summons a physician, from which one cannot conclude that he will recover whether or not he summons a physician. The two facts are, in this case, "condestinate."

Contemporary analytical distinctions. Contemporary philosophers have for the most part tried to resolve the problems of logical determinism by distinguishing between modal concepts, such as necessary, impossible, and so on, and the nonmodal concepts of true and false and by refusing to make certain inferences from one kind of concept to the other. Thus, from the fact that something happens of necessity, it follows that it happens, and from the fact that it is impossible for something to happen, it follows that it does not happen. The reverse of these inferences cannot be made, however; something might happen without being necessary, and something might fail to happen without being impossible. This permits one to say without contradiction that it is true, without being necessary, or false, without being impossible, that a certain man is going to perform a certain action.

The difficulty that some writers have found in this seemingly obvious solution is that "necessary" and "impossible," as applied to human actions, do not mean logically necessary and impossible. (As Gilbert Ryle and others have noted, the only things that can be logically necessary or impossible are propositions, not events or actions.) When the ancients described an event or action as necessary, they simply meant that it was unavoidable, and when they described it as impossible, they meant that it was not within the power of an agent to bring it about. This is still what men mean by such locutions. It is surely not obvious how an action can be avoidable on the supposition that it has been true from the beginning of the world that it would be performed by a certain man at a certain time and place, and it is not obvious how it can be within the power of an agent to perform a given action on the supposition that it is eternally false that he will. Still, as critics of this line of thought have forever pointed out, we must take for granted that men are often able to do many things which they never do and to forgo many things which they do all the time. It is perhaps just this that has always been at issue.

Following the suggestions of Aristotle, some contemporary philosophers, such as Charles Hartshorne, have maintained that predictions concerning a man's future voluntary actions are always false, the truth being expressed only by a statement to the effect that he might and might not perform them. Others have argued that such predictions are neither true nor false when made, though they eventually become either true or false. In this connection Ryle has suggested that "correct" and "incorrect," as applied to predictions of this sort, are more like verdicts than descriptions and thus convey more the idea of "fulfilled" and "unfulfilled" than of "true" and "false." It would be always wrong to call a prediction fulfilled as long as it is a prediction, and similarly, Ryle suggests, it is misleading to speak of predictions as having been true. Ryle and others have also noted the error of thinking of predictions as the causes of the events they predict, though essentially the same error was pointed out by St. Augustine and many of the Scholastics, who noted that God's prescience is never by itself the cause of anything.

Perhaps the most significant upshot of this whole problem, however, has been the considerable contemporary philosophical discussion concerning the status of future things, particularly future contingent or undetermined things. Do they exist "in the future," awaiting only the lapse of time in order to become present, or do they have the more nebulous status sometimes referred to as possible existence? Ryle has suggested that predictive statements are not true or false in the same way that statements about past things are, precisely because the things to which they ostensibly refer do not have the same determinate existence, that some descriptive statements therefore cannot make sense until the things ostensibly described really do exist. He thus compares certain predictive statements, such as the statement that a given man is going to cough at a certain future time, with statements about "past" things which might have been but never were—for example, certain automobile accidents that were prevented. All these suggestions have raised some of the most vexatious questions in contemporary metaphysics, and they are very far from being resolved.

THEOLOGICAL DETERMINISM

With the development of Christian theology there arose the concept of a God who is, among other things, perfectly good, omniscient, and omnipotent and upon whom, moreover, the entire world and everything in it, down to the minutest detail, are absolutely dependent for existence and character. This idea is obviously loaded with possibilities for deterministic theories, and there have been many philosophers and theologians who have developed them into extensive systems, some of which have formed the basis for theological doctrines having an extremely wide and abiding influence.

Moral determination of God's will. If, for example, we consider first the absolute goodness of God, it seems incongruous not only to think of him as choosing or by his action inflicting evil, but equally of his being able to choose, inflict, or even permit evil. Since, moreover, the world is the result of his act of creation, it seems to follow that it is the only world that was ever possible, being of necessity the best that was possible. Many of the Stoics affirmed this conception, identifying the world or "nature" with God or Zeus and also with fate. The world, they thought, is the only possible world, and nothing in it could be different from what it is. It is nevertheless good, and so the aim of a wise man should simply be to find and accept his place in it. Spinoza's philosophy contains essentially the same idea. In the first book of his *Ethics* he affirms that nothing in nature is contingent, that there is no free will in God, and, hence, that things could not have been produced by God in any other manner, though Spinoza was led to these conclusions by considerations other than the mere goodness of God.

Perhaps it was Leibniz who tried hardest to reconcile the moral determinism implied by God's absolute goodness with the existence of alternative possibilities. Leibniz distinguished two senses of necessity, which he called absolute and hypothetical. Given the absolute goodness of God, he said, then the world that exists must be the only possible world, because it is of necessity the best possible one. But this is only on the hypothesis that God is good; hence, the exclusive necessity of this world is only hypothetical. In the absolute sense, not taking into account God's goodness, this world is only one of many possible worlds, contrary to what Spinoza maintained. Something is necessary in an absolute sense only if its negation involves a contradiction, and in this sense neither God's acts nor men's are necessary. The actions of men are necessary only in the sense that there is a sufficient reason for them, as for everything else. This is consistent with their being free, considered in themselves, Leibniz thought, since in no absolute sense are they necessary.

It is doubtful, however, whether Leibniz' distinctions supply more than a verbal solution to the problem of theological determinism. One can grant that this must be the only possible world given the hypothesis that it is the creation of an absolutely good creator and thus agree that apart from that hypothesis it is not the only possible world. But as soon as one affirms God's goodness, which traditional theology considered beyond doubt, then it is difficult to see in what sense alternative worlds are still "possible." Leibniz' concept of hypothetical necessity has nevertheless had the most far-reaching significance in the subsequent development of the ideas of determinism and free will, for it became a cornerstone for generations of later philosophers, like David Hume, in their attempted reconciliations of physical and psychological determinism with free will.

Divine omniscience and determinism. The omniscience of God has likewise seemed to many thinkers to imply the inevitability of everything that happens. The philosophical arguments involved in this kind of determinism, resting on the idea that all truths are eternal, are essentially the same as those which led Diodorus and others to assert fatalism, but the addition of the premise that there is a being who knows all truths from the beginning of time gives these arguments an especially powerful appeal to the imagination.

St. Augustine. An omniscient being knows everything. St. Augustine and virtually every other theologian who contributed greatly to the development of Christian thought assumed without question that God, as thus conceived, must know in advance every action that every man is ever going to perform, including, of course, every sin he will ever commit. If this is so, then the question arises of how men can behave otherwise than God knows they will—how, for example, a man can forgo those sins which God, when he created the man, knew he would commit. The strongest concise way of expressing this point is to say that (1) if God knows that I shall perform a certain act at a certain time and (2) if I am nevertheless able to forgo that act when the time for performing it arrives, then (3) it follows that I am at least able to confute an item of divine knowledge, whether or not I actually do so. That conclusion, of course, is absurd. The second premise, accordingly, must be false if the first is true.

Carneades, a pre-Christian defender of human self-determination and freedom, maintained that even Apollo could not know in advance what men were going to do. Such a view, however, seemed so inconsistent with the notion of omniscience that hardly any Christian thinker entertained it. St. Augustine, in considering this question independently of the idea of God's power, maintained that God's foreknowledge constitutes no threat whatsoever to man's free will. God, according to St. Augustine, foresees all events because they are going to occur; they do not occur just because he has foreseen them. Thus, he compared God's prescience to a man's memory. The fact that someone remembers an event does not render that event necessary or involuntary, and the same is true with respect to God's foreknowing an event. Again, St. Augustine pointed out, there is no difficulty in the notion of God's foreknowing that someone will be happy, from which one can hardly conclude that such a man must therefore be happy against his will. And whether or not we do anything else voluntarily, it can hardly be denied that we *will* things voluntarily, and this constitutes no reason why God should not know what we are going to will. Many of the other events God foreknows are things which, as God knows, depend upon our wills for their happening, from which it follows that they are both foreknown and willed—that is, voluntary. Most of the apparent difficulties in reconciling divine prescience with human freedom seemed to St. Augustine to evaporate in any case as soon as one comprehends the nature of God's eternity. The distinctions of "before" and "after," which are essential to the formulation of this kind of theological determinism, have no application to God, according to St. Augustine. His eternity is not an everlastingness but, rather, an existence that is altogether independent of time. God therefore sees the whole of history in a manner similar to that in which we view the present, and from this point of view one is not easily tempted to suppose that God's knowledge imposes any determination on things to come.

Subsequent views. St. Augustine's reflections on this problem have for the most part been followed by subsequent thinkers. St. Thomas Aquinas, for example, similarly emphasized the eternity of God's vision and argued that God's knowledge is not by itself the cause of anything. Boethius, in *The Consolation of Philosophy*, defended the same view, adding numerous analogies to increase the plausibility of his arguments. Thus, he noted, a sign shows that to which it points without thereby producing it. In the same way God knows what will come to pass, but his knowing does not cause anything to happen. Again, a man might at one and the same time see another man walking and the sun rising; yet the man's walking can be voluntary, whereas the sun's rising is not. This, Boethius maintained, is the manner in which God views all things from the perspective of eternity. Boethius was thus led to his famous definition of eternity as "the simultaneous and complete possession of infinite life." In such a conception there is no suggestion of succession in time, and God must thus see all things in a manner similar to that in which we view things spread out in a given moment.

This Augustinian solution to the problem, echoed so often in the subsequent history of thought, has not been without dissenters, however. In the fourteenth century Peter Aureol reaffirmed what he took to be the arguments of Aristotle, maintaining that propositions concerning particular future contingent events, such as men's acts of free will, cannot be either true or false. This would seem to imply, of course, that God cannot foreknow them, but Peter Aureol seemed reluctant to draw that heterodox conclusion. He observed that God's foreknowledge does not make anything true or false and is to that extent consistent with the lack of either truth or falsity in some such propositions. He apparently did not observe that in order to be known by God, a proposition must nevertheless be true when foreknown, since God obviously cannot know something to be true which is in fact neither true nor false. William of Ockham expressed similar doubts but, unlike Peter Aureol, was unwilling to reject either the law of the excluded middle or the doctrine of divine omniscience. God, according to William of Ockham, is omniscient and hence knows all future contingent events. In the case of any disjunction to the effect that a given contingent event either is going to occur at a given time or is not going to occur at that time, God knows which of the mutually inconsistent propositions is true since he is omniscient. It follows that one of them is true and the other one false. But, according to this thinker, no one knows how this is possible, and no philosophical arguments, such as St. Augustine's, can render it really intelligible. Ockham's position thus consisted essentially of simply affirming what he thought was required by both logic and faith and refusing to render either intelligible in terms of the other.

The attempts of St. Augustine and many others to reconcile God's omniscience with the indetermination of men's actions were entirely rejected by the eighteenth-century American theologian Jonathan Edwards, who maintained that divine prescience imposes the same necessity upon things as does predestination, a doctrine which had been taught by St. Augustine. Foreknowledge, Edwards agreed, does not cause those things which are foreknown, but it nonetheless renders them certain and therefore inevitable. Indeed, such foreknowledge could not exist if determinism were not true, for there can be no certainty with respect to any contingent things. To say that things are foreknown with certainty by God and are nevertheless contingent and thus uncertain struck Edwards as an evident absurdity.

Similar doubts are expressed, among contemporary philosophers, by Charles Hartshorne. Hartshorne has defended indeterminism and free will, and defending also the belief in God, he has proposed an exceedingly interesting revision of the idea of omniscience. An omniscient being, according to him, is one who knows everything that it is possible to know. There can, however, be no antecedent truth with respect to particular future free actions of men other than that they might and might not occur. God, accordingly, cannot know whether they will be performed until the time for the performance arrives. He is nevertheless omniscient, since only those things that are inherently unknowable are unknown to him. It is significant and rarely noted that this is precisely the position taken by St. Thomas Aquinas with respect to God's omnipotence. God, according to St. Thomas, is omnipotent not in the sense that he can do anything whatsoever but, rather, that he can do anything that it is possible to do.

Divine power and predestination. It was earlier noted that the three chief sources of theological determinism are God's presumably unlimited goodness, knowledge, and power. It is undoubtedly the third of these alleged attributes which has been the richest source of such theories. Even St. Augustine, although he defended human freedom on other grounds, felt obliged to relinquish it in the light of his conception of God's power. Thus arose the doctrine of predestination and all the baneful consequences it has wrought in the history of Christendom.

A man's power, St. Augustine thought, is nothing in comparison to that of his maker. Indeed, a man is helpless to do anything except sin unless he is assisted by the power and grace of God—"God worketh in us both to will and to do." Adam, our first ancestor, was, to be sure, free and, hence, free not to sin, but he sinned anyway and thereby cast the entire race of men into a morass of sin from which it is unable to lift itself by its own power. God as well as the blessed are unable to sin, but men are unable to avoid it. Accordingly, no man can be saved by the exercise of his own will, which can lead him only to damnation. He can be saved only by being chosen by God.

The same opinions were promulgated by Martin Luther and John Calvin, particularly in Luther's dispute with Erasmus and Calvin's dispute with the Arminians on the issue of man's free will; they formed a considerable part of the theological basis of the Protestant Reformation. Both Luther and Calvin stressed the power, sovereignty, and righteousness of God, subordinating to these the belief in his love and mercy. God, according to Luther, does not merely foreknow what will happen. He foreknows, purposes, and does everything according to his eternal, changeless, and infallible will. To affirm any power or freedom on man's part, particularly any freedom to perform meritorious actions, seemed to both Luther and Calvin to compromise the power of God and even to set men in competition with him. Without God's grace everything we do is evil and therefore determined. It is not within any man's power to do any good thing. Even actions which would otherwise be right and proper, such as acts of charity, are, according to Luther, without merit if not accompanied by faith and prompted by grace. Luther thus compared the human will with the will of a beast of burden, which is ridden by either God or Satan. If ridden by God, it goes where God wills, and if by Satan, where Satan wills; in neither case, however, does it choose the rider. The riders, God and Satan, vie over who shall control it. Such views as these were once, of course, the source of persecutions and upheavals, but they are rarely enunciated with seriousness now, even by theologians, for the idea of divine power no longer has the reality in men's minds that it once had.

PHYSICAL DETERMINISM

Modern theories of determinism were inspired mainly by the development of physical science, particularly in the seventeenth and eighteenth centuries. Scientists then discovered that the motions of the heavenly bodies were not only regular but also "obeyed" certain laws which could be expressed with mathematical exactness. Gradually, the whole approach to the study of nature, which had been philosophical, speculative, and heavily influenced by Aristotle, gave way to observation, experiment, and the search for laws. The idea slowly took hold that all things in nature, men included, behave according to inviolable and unchanging laws of nature. In the philosophical tradition there was a great deal that made this idea plausible, reasonable, and almost inevitable. Theories of determinism were about as old as philosophy. The rise of physical science only prompted philosophers to revise somewhat the content of deterministic theories to which they were already thoroughly accustomed. They more or less ceased thinking of human actions and other events as determined by moral considerations or by an eternal and immutable God and began thinking of them as determined by eternal and immutable laws of nature.

The Epicureans. Of course, this idea was by no means new. The view that everything is composed of matter or, more precisely, of minute and impenetrable atoms or invisible material particles had been elaborated by Leucippus and Democritus before the Christian era and had been perpetuated in the teachings of the Epicureans for centuries. Such a conception of nature gave rise to the idea that if everything that happens is resolvable into the motions and combinations of atoms, then men's behavior, too, must be reducible to and understandable in terms of the motions of atoms. The early atomists assumed that this must be true even of men's thoughts and desires, since, according to them, even the "soul" is composed of atoms. The behavior of atoms, in turn, was thought to be a function of their speed, direction of motion, and sometimes their shapes. Atoms changed the direction of their motion simply by being struck by other atoms. Material bodies arose from the combination of atoms into groups or clusters and perished as a result of their dispersion. The atoms themselves, however, were individually indestructible and indivisible.

The Epicureans who took over this theory of nature were not long in discovering its implications with respect to human freedom. These philosophers were concerned mostly with discovering the means to the attainment of the highest good for man, which they took to be happiness and freedom from pain. It would be idle, however, to work out the means for the attainment of this if men had no freedom to choose those means. If the theory of atomism were true, then it would seem that what became of a man and whether he attained a good life were simply matters of how physical bodies and, ultimately, the atoms of which all bodies are composed behaved, and no man would have any hand in what became of him. The Epicureans accordingly modified the theory by claiming the atoms to have the power of occasional spontaneous motion, which they referred to as the capacity to swerve. Ordinarily, an atom would change its direction only by being driven from its path by impact with another atom, but occasionally, they maintained, an atom alters its path spontaneously, without any cause for this change at all. This enabled the Epicureans to maintain that there is an element of contingency and uncertainty in nature, that not everything is determined by physical laws, and that men can therefore intelligibly be thought of as free to some extent or, in modern terms, as having free will. The Epicureans' opponents never tired of waxing merry with the doctrine of the swerve, however. Indeed, that doctrine did enable the Epicureans to avoid determinism, but there appeared to be nothing else in its favor, and it seemed, moreover, to be plainly irrational.

Hobbes's materialism. Perhaps the best example of physical determinism in modern philosophy is the system of Thomas Hobbes. His philosophy represents a thoroughgoing attempt to interpret human nature according to the basic presuppositions of the science of bodies—that is, physics—and although it is no longer novel, it is probably fair to say that the generations of thinkers since Hobbes who have shared his aim and purpose have not significantly modified or improved upon his fundamental ideas. Modern materialistic theories differ from Hobbes's basic system only in details and mode of expression and share equally with it such purely philosophical merits and defects as it may possess.

Hobbes denied the existence of any immaterial soul or spirit in men, maintaining, as do some contemporary materialists, such as J. J. C. Smart, that ideas, sensations, and all psychological processes are motions or modifications of matter in the brain. From this it at once follows that human behavior is the behavior of matter and is to be understood according to the same general principles that we apply to matter. The idea that men might be the original sources of their own voluntary motions or that acts of will might arise without causes was rejected as unintelligible; nothing, Hobbes said, "taketh a beginning from itself." Whatever happens, whether in the realm of human behavior, human thought, or elsewhere is caused and hence causally determined by changes of material particles. Voluntary actions are therefore no less necessitated than anything else.

Hobbes nevertheless insisted that such complete physical determinism is consistent with human liberty, for he defined liberty as simply the absence of external restraint or impediment and, hence, as something that even inanimate things can possess. He said that, properly understood, liberty is simply the "absence of all the impediments to action that are not contained in the nature and intrinsical quality of the agent." Hobbes concluded that any unobstructed moving body can be considered free. The unobstructed water of a flowing stream, for example, descends freely, though it is not at liberty to ascend or to flow across the river bed. It is part of the "nature and intrinsical quality" of water to flow downward, and it flows freely.

Hobbes interpreted human nature according to such analogies. All voluntary human action, he thought, is caused by the alternate operation of the general motives of desire and aversion, which he took to be similar to, and, indeed, varieties of, physical forces. The proximate or immediate cause of a voluntary motion is an act of the will, but an act of the will is never free in the sense of being uncaused. It is caused by some kind of desire or aversion. Deliberation was described by Hobbes as an alternate succession of contrary appetites, a kind of vacillation between competing impulses, in which the appetites are of such approximately equal force that neither immediately overcomes the other. Deliberation ceases when one of them comes to outweigh and thus to prevail over the other. An "act of will," accordingly, is simply the "last appetite"—that is, the desire or aversion upon which one finally acts. To speak of an agent's act of will as "free" would be equivalent to saying that the agent is able to perform it if he wills to perform it, and this Hobbes dismissed as an "absurd speech." To say a man is free to do a given action means only that he can do it if he wills—that is, that his will or "last appetite" is sufficient to produce that action—but it is obviously nonsense to speak of an act of will itself being free in any such sense. Any other sense of freedom, however, seemed to Hobbes inherently incoherent. It is, for example, a fairly common conception of liberty among the advocates of free will that a free agent is one who, when all things necessary to produce a given action are present, can nevertheless refrain from that action. This, according to Hobbes, is equivalent to saying that conditions might be sufficient to produce a given effect without that effect's occurring, which is a contradiction.

It is noteworthy that Hobbes, though he claimed all human behavior to be physically determined and necessitated, did not conclude that men are not responsible for their actions. In this his theory represents an important departure from some of his predecessors. The Epicureans took for granted that behavior that is physically determined is unfree, and they therefore denied, in the face of their own presuppositions, that all human behavior is physically determined. But Hobbes maintained that a voluntary act is simply one that is caused by an act of will. It is rendered no less voluntary by the fact that acts of will are caused. Generations of philosophers, while for the most part rejecting Hobbes's materialism, have nevertheless followed him in this and in his conception of liberty. Arthur Schopenhauer, for example, declared it nonsense to ask whether acts of will are free, giving the same reason that Hobbes had given; defined freedom as the absence of impediments and constraints; and, like Hobbes, found no incongruity in speaking of inanimate bodies, such as a flowing stream, as acting freely. In the twentieth century Moritz Schlick, A. J. Ayer, and many others have made the point that freedom is not opposed to causation but to constraint. The significance of these ideas is enormous, for they appear to offer the means of once and for all reconciling the apparent opposition between determinism and freedom, thus dissolving the whole problem of free will. Many philosophers are still convinced that this insight is entirely correct and that there really is therefore no problem of free will.

PSYCHOLOGICAL DETERMINISM

Most philosophers since Socrates, and even those before him, have, unlike Hobbes, distinguished between men's minds and their bodies, taking for granted that men are not just collections of material particles. Descartes distinguished minds and bodies as two entirely distinct, substances whose essential properties are utterly different. Most philosophers since have rejected much of Descartes's philosophy but have nevertheless preserved the distinction between minds and bodies. In contemporary philosophy minds and bodies are not often described as distinct substances, but an absolute distinction is nevertheless often drawn between "psychological" predicates and verbs, on the one hand, and "physical" ones, on the other, and this amounts to much the same thing. Because of this, most modern theories of determinism, as applied to human behavior, can suitably be called theories of psychological determinism. Most of these theories are in complete agreement with Hobbes's concept of free and voluntary behavior as the unconstrained and unimpeded behavior that is caused by an act of will, a motive, or some other inner event. The only significant difference is that acts of will and other inner causes are conceived of as psychological or mental events within the mind of the agent rather than as modifications of matter in his brain.

Cartesian indeterminism. Descartes stands out in modern philosophy as a defender of free will, which is conceived of as indeterminism with respect to the voluntary operations of the mind. In his *Meditations* he described such freedom as infinite, meaning that no limitation whatsoever is put upon the mind's power of choice. His theory was essentially that willing consists of assenting or dissenting to some conceived object of choice or to some proposition. By the understanding one is enabled to entertain certain propositions, but understanding by itself neither affirms nor denies, neither chooses nor rejects. This role is reserved for the will. Accordingly, human understanding can be of limited scope, as it is, without in any way limiting the freedom of the will. The understanding sometimes represents things in an obscure and confused manner, sometimes even falsely, as in the case of various illusions and deceptions, but it sometimes represents them clearly and distinctly. Intellectual error results from the precipitous use of the will—that is, from assenting to things that are not clearly and distinctly perceived by the understanding. Moral error results from a similar unrestrained use of free will—that is, from men's assenting to or choosing objects that are only speciously good, without a clear and distinct apprehension of their true worth. Thus, error is always avoidable. To know what is true, attain genuine knowledge, and choose rightly, one needs only to confine the assent of the will to what is clearly and distinctly perceived by the understanding as true or good. God cannot therefore be blamed for men's errors. He endowed men with understanding adequate for the perception of truth and with a will that is absolutely unlimited in its freedom to accept what is true and reject what is doubtful or false.

This way of conceiving of the human will has provided what is virtually a standard solution to the problem of moral evil—that is, to the problem of reconciling the occasional turpitude of men with the presumed goodness of their creator—but beyond that hardly any philosophers have agreed with it. Probably no other indeterminist, for example, has described the freedom of the human will as unlimited. The theory was also quickly subjected to criticism on epistemological grounds. With great perception Spinoza, for example, challenged the basic distinction between the understanding and the will. It is quite impossible, Spinoza said, to have a clear and distinct understanding of some truth without at the same time assenting to it. The perception of truth is one and the same thing with the knowledge of it, and one cannot therefore have a true idea without at the same time knowing that he has a true idea.

Much more important, however, were the implications of Descartes's idea of a "free" will, conceived of as a will that is not determined by anything else. It appeared to imply that men's choices are completely random and capricious, utterly mysterious and inexplicable. In fact, this has always been the overwhelming stumbling block for all theories of indeterminism, whether in the Epicurean notion of spontaneous swerves of atoms or Descartes's notion of uncaused assents, dissents, and choices. If such things are really free in the sense of being causally undetermined and if human behavior is to be explained in terms of such things, then human behavior itself would have to be random, capricious, and utterly inexplicable. Since, however, human behavior does not appear to be exactly what these theories suggest, there has always been a powerful incentive to reject indeterminism in favor of some conception of determinism which does not do violence to men's conceptions of liberty.

Innumerable philosophers have thought that this is accomplished in the manner suggested by Hobbes—that is, by conceiving of a voluntary action as one that is caused by such an inner event as volition, motive, desire, choice, or the like; conceiving of an involuntary action as one that is caused by some state or event external to the agent; and then defining a free action not as a causally undetermined one but as one that is not involuntary or constrained. This kind of determinism has been advocated by so many philosophers, including many contemporary writers, that it would be tedious to list them. The basic idea was suggested by Aristotle, although Aristotle did not discuss the problem of free will as such. It was lengthily defended by John Locke, who was, however, aware of some of the difficulties in it, which he never entirely resolved except by enormous equivocations. Probably the most famous classical defense of it was presented by David Hume, who is still thought by many to have solved the problem of free will.

Locke's theory of liberty. Locke, like Descartes, distinguished between a man's mind and his body and described both as substances. Changes in a man's body, including voluntary motions, are, he thought, all caused, but the causes are within the mind in the case of voluntary motions. Unlike Descartes, however, Locke did not suppose that anything within the mind is causally undetermined, nor did he think it necessary to suppose this in order to preserve the belief in human freedom, which he thought misleading to label "freedom of the will."

Locke defined liberty or freedom as "a power in any agent to do or forbear any particular action, according to this determination or that of the mind, whereby either of them is preferred to the other." One acts freely, then, provided he is acting according to the preference of his own mind, and this is perfectly consistent with his action's being causally determined. It might, for instance, be determined by that very preference. Locke also defined freedom as "being able to act or not to act, according as we shall choose or will," and this again, far from implying that free actions are uncaused, implies that they are caused by the agent's choice or will. In the light of this, Locke, like Hobbes, dismissed the question of whether men's wills are free as "improper" or meaningless, like asking whether a man's sleep is swift or whether virtue is square. Liberty, he said, is something that can be possessed only by agents, not by their wills.

That an action can be perfectly voluntary and nevertheless unavoidable was, Locke thought, borne out by clear examples. Suppose, for instance, that a man went to a certain room because there was someone he had a strong desire to see and suppose that while he was there conversing with him, someone secretly bolted the door behind him so that he could not leave. Now, Locke pointed out, his action of remaining in the room, entirely in accordance with his own preference and desire, would not cease to be voluntary just because he could not, unbeknown to him, leave if he wanted to.

One acts voluntarily and freely, then, in doing what he wills, prefers, or chooses. Locke distinguished, however, between desires or preferences and volitions, noting that men can prefer certain things which they can be no means will. Thus, a man might prefer to fly than to walk, but he cannot will it. Locke defined a volition as "an act of the mind knowingly exerting that dominion it takes itself to have over any part of the man, by employing it in, or withholding it from, any particular action." Elsewhere he defined a volition as "an act of the mind directing its thought to the production of any action, and thereby exerting its power to produce it." A volition, then, is a psychological act which sometimes figures causally in the production of voluntary motion. It is itself causally determined by the mind, and the mind, in the determination of its volitions, is, Locke thought, causally determined by the satisfaction of doing or continuing a given action or by feeling uneasy in doing or continuing it.

There is, then, throughout Locke's involved, tortuous, and sometimes equivocating discussion the general presupposition that determinism is true and that indeterminism is irrational and unintelligible. The philosophical problem, as he understood it, is simply that of showing that determinism is compatible with what all men believe concerning human liberty. He seemed to believe that once certain crucial concepts, such as "voluntary," "free," and the like, are rightly defined and understood, the problem of free will would evaporate.

Hume on freedom and necessity. The defining of the concepts was, in any case, precisely what David Hume set out to do in his celebrated discussion of liberty. According to Hume, all men have always been of the same opinion on this subject, believing both that men are free and that all their actions are causally determined. There is therefore no philosophical problem of free will, and the whole dispute, he thought, has heretofore been purely verbal in character, involving only confusions in the meanings of words.

It was a fundamental point of Hume's philosophy that causation is essentially constant succession, that there is no necessary connection between causes and their effects.

Causes, therefore, do not compel the occurrence of their effects; they only precede them. The question of whether human actions are caused, then, is simply the question of whether there is anything with which they are constantly joined. Hume claimed that no one has ever been in any doubt about this. Throughout history certain actions have always been associated with certain motives with the same constancy and regularity that one finds between any causes and their effects. Human actions are caused, then, in the same way that everything else is caused.

Far from concluding from this, however, that no human actions are free, Hume concluded the opposite, for he considered it the very nature of a free action that it springs from the motive of the agent. He therefore defined freedom as being able to act according to the determinations of one's own will—that is, of one's motives—a definition that presupposes that one's free actions are caused. One's actions are not unfree if they are caused but if they are caused by something other than the determinations of one's own will.

Nor does this conception of liberty, according to Hume, vitiate a man's responsibility for what he does. On the contrary, responsibility depends upon the causation of actions by motives. All laws are based on rewards and punishments and thus rest on the assumption that men's motives can be relied upon to have a regular influence on their behavior. There would be no point in appealing to such motives as fear and hope if nothing could be predicted from their operation. Justice, moreover, requires such an operation of motives, for no man can be a fit object of punishment if his actions are in no way traceable to his motives. Indeed, if one could not rely upon the constant and predictable operation of motives, all intercourse with one's fellows would be hazardous or impossible. One could not even invite a guest to his table with any confidence of not being robbed by him, for the knowledge of his honesty and friendliness would in that case provide no assurance. Sometimes, to be sure, men are robbed or murdered when they had every reason to expect otherwise; however, men are also sometimes destroyed by earthquakes and the like when they had no reason to expect it. No one concludes from this that earthquakes are without any causes. Determinism, then, does not imply that all human behavior is predictable in the most straightforward sense of the term, for many unpredictable things are nevertheless causally determined. A man might not know why his watch has stopped and might not have been able to predict that it was going to stop, but this is only because the cause is hidden from him. He does not suppose that there was no cause at all. Similarly, a normally genial man might on occasion be peevish, but this is only due to some cause—some intestinal disorder, for instance—that is hidden from others and perhaps even from himself.

The important question for Hume, then, was not whether all human actions are causally determined, since all men have always been convinced that they are, or whether any human actions are free, since all men have always been of the same opinion on this, too. It is simply the question of how these two beliefs, so universally shared, can both be true, and Hume found the answer to this in analyzing what is meant by saying that one's action may be caused and also free.

Determinism and responsibility. What is essentially Hume's argument has been repeated by other philosophers and is still vigorously pressed by many of them. There have nevertheless always been doubters who have contended that this is a superficial conception of liberty, that the actions of a causally determined agent can be "free" only in a technical sense which does not at all correspond with the notion of freedom that men in fact have and that moral responsibility requires. A genuinely free action, according to this point of view, is not merely one that is in keeping with one's preferences, desires, and volitions, but one that is avoidable or, in C. D. Broad's terminology, "substitutable." To say that a given action was free means at least, according to these writers, that the agent could have done otherwise given the very conditions that obtained, not just that he could have done otherwise if something within him had been different. This thought was expressed by Kant, who rendered it in the formula "ought implies can." What Kant had in mind was that whenever one rightly judges that a given agent is morally obligated to perform a certain action, he must logically presuppose that the agent can perform it—not just that he can if he wants, prefers, or wills to, but that he can in some absolute sense. This kind of freedom has been aptly called "categorical," as opposed to the "hypothetical" freedom defended by Hume and others, for it is a freedom both to do and to forbear doing a certain action under the same set of conditions.

The difficulty in deterministic theories that all these critics have felt can perhaps be illustrated with an example. Suppose that a given man is often motivated to steal and that in accordance with determinism he always does steal when, prompted by that motive, his efforts to do so meet with no impediment. According to the determinist theory, these actions are then free and voluntary, and he is responsible for them. Suppose further, however, still in keeping with determinism, that he has no control over the occurrence of this motive, that it arises, let us suppose, as a result of an abominable background and deprivation in his youth, that, in short, he is the product of precisely those influences that nourish and perpetuate that motivation. One's inclination may be to say that even given such a background, he did not have to become a thief, but that would not be in keeping with the thesis of determinism. According to that thesis, it was causally determined and, hence, inevitable and unavoidable that he should become whatever he is. It follows from these suppositions, then, that he cannot help being whatever he is and performing just the actions he does perform. We can indeed still say that if he were not the kind of man he is or if he were motivated otherwise than he is or if something had been different, he could then act otherwise than he does; however, any point to ascribing this merely hypothetical kind of freedom to him seems to vanish when we add, as the determinist must, that nothing could have been different, that he could not have been any other kind of man, that he could not have been motivated differently, and that, hence, he could not have acted otherwise than he did.

It was with this sort of thing in mind that Kant, contrary

to what he acknowledged to be the requirements of reason, postulated what he called a "causality of freedom" and insisted that the theory of determinism cannot be applied to men. Their freedom, he thought, must be categorical or such that their actions are not entirely determined by factors over which they have no control. The same point was pressed by G. W. Fichte, Thomas Reid, Samuel Clarke, and William James, and among contemporary writers it has been eloquently urged by C. A. Campbell and many others. It was essentially the point that was skillfully made by Henry Mansel in his criticisms of J. S. Mill's determinist theories. Mill defended a theory that was in all basic respects identical with Hume's—that causation is constant conjunction; that men, when acting voluntarily, always act in accordance with their strongest desires or aversions; that justice, morality, and the administration of laws all require such causal determination of behavior, and so on. Mansel argued that when pressed to its ultimate conclusions, this theory did not differ in its consequences from what he called "Asiatic fatalism," or the view that all men are helpless to do anything except what they actually do. Mill denied this by arguing that although one's actions are determined by his will, his will by his desires, his desires by his motives, and his motives by his character, his character is itself amenable to his will. Mill did not, however, succeed in explaining how, according to his theory of determinism, a man's character, which he evidently thought of as the ultimate determinant of his conduct, could be "amenable" to or within the control of his "will," which is merely the expression of his character.

"Hard" and "soft" determinism. William James is among the relatively few philosophers who, impressed by the kind of argument Mansel directed against determinism, have defended a theory of outright indeterminism or chance. He was, like the Epicureans, led to do so by what he thought were the requirements of morals. Determinism, he said, implies that the world we have is the only possible world and that nothing could have been other than it was; he declared this to be incompatible with the reasonableness of regret and other basic moral sentiments. In the course of his argument he drew a very useful distinction between what he called "hard" and "soft" determinism. By soft determinism he meant all those theories, like those of Hobbes, Hume, and Mill, which affirm that determinism is true and then, by means of what he considered sophistical and contorted definitions, somehow manage to preserve a semblance of certain moral notions like liberty, responsibility, and so on that, according to James, are plainly obliterated by any theory of determinism. Hard determinists, on the other hand, are those who affirm what their theory entails—namely, that no man can help being what he is and doing what he does and that moral distinctions are therefore irrational and ought never to be applied to men or anything else.

There have been relatively few defenders of hard determinism, most philosophers preferring instead to try reconciling determinism with morals. Certain materialist philosophers of the French Enlightenment, such as Baron d'Holbach, are exceptions, for they did maintain that men are only helpless products of an impersonal nature who govern neither themselves nor anything else but are simply carried along to whatever destinies the circumstances of their lives inflict upon them. Arthur Schopenhauer sometimes defended the same thought, emphasizing the irrational forces that govern human behavior. The American lawyer Clarence Darrow applied this hard determinism in courts of law with the most devastating effect, saving many men from the gallows not by pretending they were legally innocent but by the simple and eloquent plea that they could not help being what they were and doing what they had done. Among contemporary philosophers the claim that men are not morally responsible, as an implication of determinism, has been vigorously defended by John Hospers, and many others have pointed out the dubious character of soft determinism. The standard "solution" to the problem of free will, embodied in the writings of Hume, Mill, and many others, is as a result no longer considered to be as obvious as it once was, and a decreasing number of philosophers are now willing to speak blithely of free and voluntary behavior's being caused by motives, desires, volitions, and the like.

Determinism and modern psychiatry. Contemporary psychiatrists are for the most part highly impatient with theories of human freedom, particularly the theories with which philosophers are familiar. Whether all or most human behavior is causally determined is, after all, an empirical question of fact, and psychiatrists profess to know with considerable assurance not only that it is but to some extent what the causal factors are, particularly in cases of deviant behavior. Philosophers have largely been content to speak in general terms of motives, volitions, desires, and the like as the springs of action, but psychiatrists speak of specific unconscious fears, defenses, and hostilities. One finds in their writings, in fact, an extensive and elaborate terminology for the identification and description of hitherto undreamed of forces which are supposed to be the real determinants of behavior, including certain typical human behavior that both the learned and unlearned have long been accustomed to thinking of as rational, deliberate, and free. Philosophical speculations on the problem of free will have, as a result, come to appear rather superficial to many of those who are familiar with psychiatry.

Hospers' opinion. Perhaps no contemporary philosopher has done more toward viewing these problems in the light of modern psychiatry than John Hospers. One can, according to this writer, agree with the philosophers who maintain that freedom is opposed not to causality but to restraint and compulsion and also think of human behavior as being typically caused by human desires and even volitions. He nevertheless advances impressive empirical evidence, drawn from typical cases of the kind long familiar to psychiatry, to show that our very desires, volitions, and even deliberations are the product of unconscious forces, compromises, and defenses which are not only not within our control but whose very existence is usually unsuspected by those—all of us—who are their victims; that they were for the most part implanted in us in our earliest years, to which our memory does not even extend; and that our after-the-fact explanations or reasons for our behavior are mostly illusions and wishful thinking. "It is not," Hospers claims, "as if man's will were standing high and serene above the flux of events that have moulded him; it is itself caught up in this flux, itself carried along on the current." Spinoza compared a man with a conscious stone which thinks it moves freely through the air only because it does not know the cause of its motion, and Baron d'Holbach compared him with a fly riding on a heavy wagon and applauding itself as the driver. Hospers similarly says that a man is "like the hands on the clock, thinking they move freely over the face of the clock," a comparison which is particularly apt in the light of the psychiatrists' claim that the forces which move us lie within us and are normally deeply hidden.

Philosophers almost entirely agree that if a man's behavior is the effect of a neurosis or inner compulsion over which he has no control and of which he usually has no knowledge, then in a significant sense he is not morally responsible, and in any case he certainly is not free. The most common illustration of this is kleptomania. What is philosophically significant about kleptomania is that its victim does act according to his own volition and desire but that the volition and desire are themselves the product of a neurosis. The profound significance of Hospers' view lies in his claim, which with considerable justification he believes is empirically supported by psychiatry, that virtually all significant behavior is of the same order as kleptomania and other familiar compulsions, having its sources in the unconscious. The issue is accordingly not a philosophical one but an empirical one. It is simply whether, in fact, as Hospers graphically expresses it, "the unconscious is the master of every fate and the captain of every soul." His defense of this claim is an array of fairly typical cases which are quite well understood by psychiatrists—the compulsive gambler who always plays until he loses, the man who inwardly loves filth and so washes his hands constantly, the mother who lets her child perish of illness on the train because she "must get to her destination," and so on. In case histories like these, Hospers believes, we can, if we are honest and sophisticated, see our own lives and conduct partially mirrored and perhaps begin to have some inkling of the unconscious, deeply hidden but powerful forces which almost entirely determine what we are and what we do. If Hospers is right and if psychiatrists do actually know what they confidently claim to know—and it would be very rash to suggest that they really do not—then the problem of determinism versus free will is not, as Hume thought, resolved in a way that accommodates both views. It is, rather, solved, and it is solved on the side of hard determinism with all the enormous and, to some minds, shocking implications which that theory has for morals and law.

The theory of self-determination. The great difficulty of indeterminism, as previously noted, is that it seems to imply that a "free" or causally undetermined action is capricious or random. If one's action is strictly uncaused, then it is difficult to see in what sense it can be within the control of an agent or in any way ascribable to him. The difficulty with determinism, on the other hand, is that it seems to render every action ultimately unavoidable. The implications of determinism do not therefore significantly differ from those of pure fatalism.

It is partly in order to meet both of these difficulties that some philosophers have defended a theory of self-determination or agency. The essential elements of all such theories are that men are the sources or causes of their own actions; that their being the source or cause distinguishes those bodily motions that are actions from those that are not, the latter being caused by something other than themselves; and that free actions are those that an agent performs or produces but which he is not caused by anything else to perform or produce. This theory thus distinguishes "action," or "agency," as a basic philosophical category, treating actions as different in kind from other events and as not in any way describable in terms of the latter.

The theory of self-determination is most fully and clearly set forth by Thomas Reid in his *Essays on the Active Powers of Man,* though he does not call his theory by that name. The basic idea, however, was, according to Cicero's essay *On Fate,* advocated by Carneades. It has also been defended by G. W. Fichte and Samuel Clarke. Aristotle seems to have had some such conception in mind when he spoke of men and other animals as self-moved, and Kant also seemed to when he ascribed to men a special causality of freedom and distinguished this sharply from ordinary causality. Perhaps its best-known advocate among contemporary philosophers is C. A. Campbell, who ascribes a "creative activity" to "selves"—that is, to minds or persons—and argues that men are capable of originating their own actions in opposition to the inclinations of their characters.

Carneades on causality and freedom. Carneades, in trying to resolve the problems begotten by the Epicurean theory of uncaused swerves of atoms, on the one hand, and the fatalism of their opponents, on the other, suggested that the idea of being uncaused is ambiguous, like the idea of something's being empty. When one describes a vessel as empty, he does not ordinarily mean that it is absolutely empty—that it does not contain even air, for example. He means only that it does not contain oil or wine or whatever one might expect. Similarly, when one says that a man's action was uncaused, he does not mean that it was without any cause at all but only that it had no antecedent cause. This is compatible with its having been caused by the agent himself. Carneades noted, moreover, that the Epicureans themselves ascribe the power of motion to atoms, giving no account or cause of why they should be in motion other than that it is their nature to move. Why, then, may not men be thought of as having a similar original power of motion without supposing that some antecedent force must set them going? When men act freely, he thought, they are simply the sources of their own behavior, which is therefore caused, though not caused by anything external to themselves. One acts unfreely when he is caused to act as he does by some antecedent and external force. This way of viewing the matter, Carneades suggested, does not imply any fatalism, nor does it imply that a man's actions are random, like the swerves of the atoms. To say that a man is the cause of his own action does not imply that he was unable to cause any other action, nor does it imply that his action was uncaused.

Reid's theory. Reid developed many arguments against determinism, which he sarcastically called "the glorious system of necessity," but his own positive theory is remarkably similar to that of Carneades. Reid argued that determinism is inconsistent with a whole range of beliefs that are shared by all mankind and maintained that we have far more reason for adhering to these than for affirming any philosophical theory with which they are inconsistent. In particular, he maintained that determinism is incompatible with deliberation, with morality, and with the pursuit of ends. When, for example, a man deliberates about some possible course of action, he assumes that the proposed end, as well as the means to its attainment, is within his power to accept or reject—that is, that it is up to him whether the end shall be sought and if so, how. Without this belief he could not deliberate. The belief itself, however, is incompatible with determinism, for determinism entails that no act that is performed was avoidable and that in this sense it is never up to any man what he does. Again, all men believe that a basic distinction can be made between acts that are blameworthy, praiseworthy, and neither. Determinism, however, implies that every act that is performed is ultimately unavoidable and, hence, that no such basic distinction can be made. Finally, all men believe they can pursue, sometimes over a long period of time, certain ends that they have previously conceived. This implies, however, that their actions in pursuit of such ends are within their own power and control, which is inconsistent with determinism.

Reid therefore defined the liberty or freedom of a moral agent as "a power over the determinations of his own will," a definition that contrasts interestingly with Hume's definition of freedom as "a power of acting or not acting according to the determinations of the will." In rejecting determinism, Reid did not, however, affirm that human actions are uncaused. On the contrary, he maintained that nothing happens without a cause, that everything that changes is changed either by some other thing or by itself. Not all causes, then, are antecedent and external causes. Some things, such as men, are sometimes the causes of their own behavior. Indeed, Reid took this to be the very reason for calling a man an agent—namely, that he is a being who acts, not merely one that is acted upon. To speak of an agent being caused to act by something other than himself was for Reid a contradiction, so that acting and acting freely amount to the same thing, whereas the idea of a necessary agent amounts to a contradiction.

It is evident that Reid employed the concept of causation differently from Hume. A cause, he said, is not merely some change that always accompanies another. It is always something that has the power to produce a change, whether in itself or in something else, and no man can define it beyond this. In fact, he maintained that no man would even understand any philosophical definition of a cause if he did not first have the idea of causation from the awareness of himself as an agent. There is, then, no reason why men may not be the original causes of their own voluntary actions, which is precisely what all men believe themselves to be. This way of viewing the matter permits us to say that determinism, defined as the thesis that everything that happens is the result of some antecedent cause or causes, is false and, further, that nothing occurs without any cause whatsoever. Reid's philosophy thus overcomes the chief difficulties of both determinism and simple indeterminism. It accomplishes this, however, only by introducing what many philosophers have thought to be an enormous difficulty of its own—namely, understanding how anything can be the cause of its own changes. One is reminded of Hobbes's dictum, "Nothing taketh a beginning from itself." Alexander Bain pressed this difficulty in both Reid's and Samuel Clarke's philosophies, maintaining that it rendered their claims quite unintelligible, and Patrick Nowell-Smith has recently made the same point against C. A. Campbell's similar views. The idea of something's being self-moved in the sense understood by Carneades, Reid, Clarke, and Campbell is obviously entirely unlike any concept of physics. Accordingly, Nowell-Smith has suggested that it should be understood in the way such physical concepts as self-regulating, self-propelled, self-starting, and the like are understood, thus rendering it less esoteric. It was Reid's view, however, that this seeming difficulty is only a fact, that all men really do consider themselves to be the causes of their own voluntary actions in a sense in which no inanimate things are ever causes, and that we should be guided in our opinions not by what this or that system of philosophy requires but by what the common sense of mankind universally affirms.

The "strongest motive." It is fairly common to suppose that a man invariably acts—in fact, must act—in response to his "strongest motive" and that voluntary behavior is therefore always causally determined by such motives. Philosophical determinists frequently fall into this line of thought, sometimes substituting "strongest desire" for "strongest motive," though it is now less common than it once was. It is well illustrated in one of Alexander Bain's discussions of the free will controversy, in which he writes that "in the absence of prohibition, [an agent's] decision follows the strongest motive; being in fact the only test of strength of motive on the whole." Again, Bain notes that "any supposition of our acting without adequate motive leads at once to a self-contradiction; for we always judge of strength of motive by the action that prevails" and, further, that the action which follows upon deliberation "testifies which motive has in the end proved the strongest."

It is to the credit of Thomas Reid, with whose writings Bain was familiar, that he exhibited both the source of the considerable persuasiveness of such reflections as these and at the same time their fallaciousness. The reason this kind of claim has seemed so compelling to so many philosophers is that it has functioned as an analytic statement or one that is rendered true by definition of the concept of a "strongest motive." As such, it sheds no light whatsoever on any fact of human nature and leaves entirely unanswered the question of whether voluntary actions are really caused.

What, Reid asked, is the test of whether the motive that is strongest is the one acted upon? It is simply the motive that prevails. The claim that a man acts upon his strongest motive therefore means, Reid noted, only that he acts upon that motive upon which he acts, which is hardly a significant philosophical claim. If, however, we apply any other criterion for distinguishing which motive is strongest, then there is nothing at all to suggest that we always act on our strongest motives. On the contrary, it is a fairly common experience to feel strongly motivated to do some things from which we nevertheless refrain from purely rational considerations, for example, or perhaps from moral ones. The temptation here, of course, is to say that the fact that one refrains from a given action only shows that some contrary motive is "stronger," but this indicates that we are again using as our concept of the strongest motive the motive that prevails and saying nothing more than that a man acts upon the motive upon which he acts.

Reid, however, went farther than this by denying that motives can be likened to forces and that varying "strengths" can be ascribed to them in the first place. A motive, he said, is not a cause but a rational consideration of a reason. As such, it is something purely abstract, which has "strength" or "weakness" only in the sense of expressing wisdom, prudence, or the opposites. A "conflict of motives" is nothing at all like the conflict of opposing forces, one of which overcomes the other by superior force. It is more to be likened to the conflicting pleas of contending attorneys. One of these can be "stronger" or have more "force" or "weight" than the other only in the sense that it is more reasonable and persuasive. When, accordingly, we speak of rational or intelligible considerations as having "force," "weight," or "strength," we are not using these notions in the sense they have for physics but as metaphors borrowed from physical nature. It is, Reid thought, largely from mixing these literal and metaphorical meanings that some persons are led into theories of determinism and into supposing that human nature bears a greater resemblance to inanimate bodies than it actually does.

CONTEMPORARY PROBLEMS

The problems of determinism are still very lively in philosophy and have recently gained powerful momentum from detailed philosophical analyses of peripheral questions. Most current philosophical discussion bearing on the problem of free will is not aimed directly at whether men have free will, but at a whole host of questions that have been begotten by this long controversy. Ludwig Wittgenstein's reflections have made it evident, for example, that philosophers do not even know what it means to call something an action in the first place or just how some of men's bodily motions qualify as actions while others do not. It is an elementary distinction which is constantly made by common sense, but philosophers have thus far been unable to analyze it. Obviously, as long as this ignorance prevails, there is little point in discussing whether men's actions are ever free. Certain recent writers, such as Arthur Danto, have suggested that the concept of an action is basic and unanalyzable and that it corresponds to nothing that is found in physical science. Previous generations of philosophers often took for granted that an action is a bodily motion caused by some such inner episode as a volition, motive, desire, or choice, but these terms are now used with much greater care.

Gilbert Ryle, in his *The Concept of Mind,* declared volitions to be a fabrication of philosophy, corresponding to nothing that has ever existed, and since his devasting critique of this whole notion there has been great reluctance among scholars even to employ the word. The concepts of desire, motive, choice, and kindred notions have been similarly subjected to criticism, so that fewer philosophers are still willing to speak blithely of them as causes. A. I. Melden, for example, has maintained that no particular motive can be described at all independently of the action of which it is allegedly the cause and that its connection with an action is therefore a logical one, not, as Hume and so many others supposed, a causal one. Moreover, Melden has pointed out that if an action is conceived of as a bodily motion together with its motive in order to distinguish actions from bodily motions that are not actions, then it is plainly impossible to explain any action in terms of its motive, as philosophers were once so ready to do.

The interpretation of statements expressive of human ability as either disguised or incomplete conditional statements has likewise been considerably unsettled by the precise and detailed analyses of the late J. L. Austin. In his celebrated essay "Ifs and Cans" this writer maintained that statements involving the locution "I can" cannot possibly require, for their complete sense, the addition of some such hypothetical as "if I choose" but are, instead, to be understood in some absolute sense. Accordingly, they do not, as so many philosophers since Hume have supposed, express the idea of a causal condition at all. "I could have if I had chosen," is similarly claimed by Austin to express a past indicative rather than a conditional despite its grammatical form, for it normally expresses the idea of having had an opportunity or ability rather than the idea of a causal connection between one's choice and his action. In statements involving the locution "I shall if I choose," the word "shall," according to Austin, is normally expressive of an intention rather than a simple future tense and thus also differs essentially from other conditionals in the future tense. Such painstaking analyses as Austin's, although not pursued with the explicit aim of supporting or disconfirming any theories of determinism or free will, have nevertheless considerably weakened some of the strongest defenses of determinism since so many of them have more or less presupposed that statements expressive of human ability, which are so central to any discussion of free will, are simply disguised statements of causal conditions and thus are not only consistent with, but actually imply, a theory of determinism for the very understanding of them.

The highly refined and critical inquiries of contemporary philosophy have brought into further question the whole concept of the will. Is willing to do something an act, for instance, or not? If it is, then how does it shed any light on the concept of acting? If it is not, then how does an action differ from any other bodily change having an inner psychological cause? Clearly, no difference is marked merely by applying different names to such things. Furthermore, if there are such things as acts of will, do they or do they not require antecedent causes? If not, then why should any action require an antecedent cause? If so, then how are deliberate or willed actions to be distinguished from simple compulsions?

Closely associated with the notion of the will is that of intending. Doing something intentionally is now seldom thought of as merely undergoing some change as the result of an inner intention, intentions currently being thought of more in the manner in which Reid described motives—

namely, as reasons and purposes having a rational content. Again, it is fairly common practice among contemporary philosophers to distinguish sharply, as Reid did, between the causes of an action and the reasons for it. If this is a real distinction, then it follows that whether some human acts are reasonable and intelligible is quite independent of whether they are caused, and there is no absurdity in describing an action as both free, in the sense of being avoidable and not the effect of antecedent conditions, and rational. This line of thought has raised anew the whole problem of understanding purposeful behavior. Men often do certain things in order to achieve certain results, and this appears to distinguish human behavior from the behavior of inanimate things in a fundamental way. When philosophers were more eager than they are now to interpret human behavior within the framework of determinism, many of them assumed that purposeful behavior was simply behavior that is caused by purposes, desires, or intentions, but this conception harbors the same difficulties as the volitional conception of action that Ryle, Melden, and others have so severely criticized. If one is acting in acting purposefully and if action can be distinguished from such other bodily behavior as digestion, perspiration, and the like only in terms of concepts like purpose, desire, or intention, then one can hardly explain purposeful activity as action that is caused by one's purpose, desire, or intention. The connection is conceptual rather than causal. Desires, purposes, and intentions are, moreover, desires for this or that, purposes or intentions to do this or that, and their objects or aims may never be realized. Thus, they are what we sometimes call "intentional" concepts, and there seems to be nothing that completely corresponds to them in the realm of physical science. No inanimate thing, for example, can without metaphor be spoken of as behaving as it does in response to its desire for something which perhaps never has and never will exist, and no engineer who spoke in that manner of even the most sophisticated machine would ever suppose that he had thus given a causal explanation of anything.

More and more philosophers are inviting attention to certain fundamental differences between the way men view the past and the future. The future, some have wanted to suggest, is a realm of possibilities in a sense in which the past is not. This idea is at least as old as Aristotle's philosophy, but the renewed interest in whether men's actions might be free in some sense not countenanced by determinism has quickened interest in it. It is, for example, sometimes contended that there is a fundamental difference between finding that something is true and making something become true, a contention that renders the concept of action more fundamental than it was once supposed to be and raises anew the question of what is meant by acting freely.

The question, then, of whether determinism is true or of whether men have free will is no longer regarded as a simple or even a philosophically sophisticated question by many writers. Concealed in it is a vast array of more fundamental questions, the answers to which are largely unknown.

Bibliography

The literature on determinism and free will is so vast that only a sampling can be given here.

A good though not recent critical history of the controversy is outlined in Alexander Bain's *Mental and Moral Science* (London, 1872), Book IV, Ch. 11. More recent general studies include Sidney Hook, ed., *Determinism and Freedom in the Age of Modern Science* (New York, 1958), which is a collection of papers by contemporary philosophers, and Sidney Morgenbesser and James Walsh, eds., *Free Will* (Englewood Cliffs, N.J., 1962), which brings together carefully selected discussions from classical and modern writers and is intended mainly for students. A widely read but superficial discussion of the problem is contained in D. F. Pears, ed., *Freedom and the Will* (New York, 1963), which is in part the transcription of a series of discussions by contemporary philosophers most of whom are connected with Oxford University.

ETHICAL DETERMINISM

The ethical determinism associated with Plato and Socrates is a theme of Plato's *Protagoras* and *Gorgias,* and certain elements of this theory are treated rather unsatisfactorily in his *Hippias Minor.* Aristotle discusses the theory and related problems in the *Nichomachean Ethics,* Book VII, Ch. 2.

LOGICAL DETERMINISM

The most frequently cited reference in discussions of logical determinism is the ninth chapter of Aristotle's *De Interpretatione.* Among the many recent discussions of the problems arising from those passages are A. N. Prior's "Three-Valued Logic and Future Contingents," in *Philosophical Quarterly,* Vol. 3 (1953), 317–326; R. J. Butler's "Aristotle's Sea Fight and Three-Valued Logic," in *Philosophical Review,* Vol. 64 (1955), 264–274; G. E. M. Anscombe's "Aristotle and the Sea Battle," in *Mind,* Vol. 65 (1956), 1–15; Richard Taylor's "The Problem of Future Contingencies," in *Philosophical Review,* Vol. 66 (1957), 1–28; R. Albritton's "Present Truth and Future Contingency," *ibid.,* 29–46; and C. Strang's "Aristotle and the Sea Battle," in *Mind,* Vol. 69 (1960), 447–465.

One of the best sources for the ancients' views on both determinism and fatalism and the only source for some of them is Cicero's *De Fato,* translated by H. Rackham for the Loeb Classical Library (London, 1942). The problem of fatalism, conceived of essentially as it was by ancient philosophers, has been extensively discussed in recent literature—for example, in Gilbert Ryle's provocative essay "It Was to Be," which is Ch. 2 of his *Dilemmas* (Cambridge, 1954), and by A. J. Ayer, "Fatalism," the concluding chapter of his *The Concept of a Person* (New York, 1963). Richard Taylor's "Fatalism," in *Philosophical Review,* Vol. 71 (1962), 56–66, was followed by many critical discussions by various British and American authors in subsequent issues of the same journal and in *Analysis,* Vol. 23 (1962) and Vol. 24 (1963), and in the *Journal of Philosophy,* Vol. 61 (1964) and Vol. 62 (1965).

THEOLOGICAL DETERMINISM

Leibniz' claim that God could create no world except the best one possible and the implications he drew from this are found in his *Discourse on Metaphysics* and his *Theodicy.* St. Thomas Aquinas' opinions on the moral determination of God's will are set forth in the *Summa Theologica,* Part I, Q. 19, especially Articles 9 and 10.

The question of whether determinism and fatalism follow from the conception of God as an omniscient being has been discussed by countless authors. St. Augustine's views, for example, are reproduced in a selection entitled "On Free Will," in Morgenbesser and Walsh, *op. cit.,* and also in *The City of God,* Book XI, Ch. 21. Boethius' famous treatment of the problem is given in *The Consolation of Philosophy,* Book V. St. Thomas Aquinas discusses it in the *Summa Theologica,* Part I, Q. 14, Article 13. His views and the views of various other Scholastics are given in Frederick Copleston's excellent *History of Philosophy,* Vols. II–III (London, 1950–1953). An extensive defense of theological determinism and predestination on various grounds is given by Jonathan Edwards in his famous *Freedom of the Will,* edited by P. Ramsey (New Haven, 1957). Charles Hartshorne's rather novel and perceptive reconciliation of free will with certain theological presuppositions is found in Ch. 3 of his *Man's Vision of God* (Chicago, 1941). Although some of the foregoing sources raise the question of predestination, this doctrine, developed specifically as an implication of God's power, is more fully developed in St. Augustine's *Treatise on the Predestination of the Saints,* in the Nicene and Post-Nicene Fathers, first series, Vol. V, edited by Philip Schaff (New York, 1902); see also Augustine's *Enchiridion on Faith, Hope and Love,* edited by Henry Paolucci (Chicago, 1961). Martin Luther's uncompromising denial of human free will is set forth in his polemic with Erasmus, under the title *Discourse on Free Will,* translated by Ernst F. Winter (New York, 1961). John Calvin's defense of the same doctrine can be found at the close of the third book of his *Institutes of the Christian Religion.*

PHYSICAL DETERMINISM

The materialism of the Epicureans and the manner in which they tried to reconcile this with free will are beautifully exhibited in Lucretius' *On the Nature of Things;* an excellent source for earlier Epicurean arguments is Cicero's *De Fato.* Thomas Hobbes's materialism and arguments in favor of determinism are most fully expressed in *On Human Nature.* A more readily available source of Hobbes's important writings on this question is a paperback book of selections edited by Richard S. Peters, *Body, Man and Citizen* (New York, 1962). Arthur Schopenhauer, though he was not a materialist, defended a theory very similar to that of Hobbes in his *Essay on the Freedom of the Will,* translated by K. Kolenda (New York, 1960).

PSYCHOLOGICAL DETERMINISM

Most discussions of determinism and free will in modern philosophy have been within the framework of psychological determinism, which assumes that human behavior has its origins in psychological causes of various kinds. Descartes's defense of free will within this context is expressed in the fourth of his *Meditations* and also in *The Principles of Philosophy,* Part I, Sections 32–39. John Locke's extremely vacillating but influential discussion is found in *Essay Concerning Human Understanding,* Book II, Ch. 21, where he discussed at length the idea of power. The classical attempt to reconcile determinism and liberty was achieved by David Hume in Section 8 of his *Enquiry Concerning Human Understanding.* A defense along similar lines has been given, among numberless others, by C. J. Ducasse, in Ch. 11 of *Nature, Mind and Death* (La Salle, Ill., 1951). A now famous essay expressing essentially the same view was written by Dickinson Miller under the name R. E. Hobart and entitled "Free Will as Involving Determinism and Inconceivable Without It," in *Mind,* Vol. 43 (1934), 1–27. J. S. Mill defended Hume's theory in his *Examination of Sir William Hamilton's Philosophy,* the relevant excerpts from which are reprinted in Morgenbesser and Walsh, *op. cit.*

Problems of moral responsibility are involved in almost every discussion of determinism and are central to most of them. Immanuel Kant's treatment of the problem and his defense of the idea of a causality of freedom are given in his *Critique of Pure Reason,* under the section "Transcendental Dialectic," particularly in his discussion of the third "antinomy," and, more fully, in his *Critique of Practical Reason.* C. D. Broad's influential and highly elaborate analysis, "Determinism, Indeterminism and Libertarianism," appears in his *Ethics and the History of Philosophy* (London, 1952) and has been reprinted in Morgenbesser and Walsh, *op. cit.* Problems of determinism and responsibility are discussed by several authors in Hook, *op. cit.,* particularly in the essays by Paul Edwards, "Hard and Soft Determinism," and John Hospers, "What Means This Freedom?" Both authors vigorously defend determinism and the claim that determinism and moral responsibility cannot be reconciled with each other.

William James's essay "The Dilemma of Determinism," in which the distinction between hard and soft determinism was first made, is included in almost all of the many collections of his popular essays. Most modern and contemporary writers who have defended deterministic theories have also defended some version of soft determinism, though they have seldom used the term itself. Examples, in addition to most of those already mentioned, are Patrick Nowell-Smith, in the last two chapters of his *Ethics* (Baltimore, Md., 1954), and A. J. Ayer, in Ch. 12 of his *Philosophical Essays* (London, 1954).

The most thoroughgoing defense of the theory of self-determinism was given by Thomas Reid, in his *Essays on the Active Powers of Man,* of which there have been many editions. A contemporary defense of what is essentially the same theory is given by C. A. Campbell, in Ch. 9 of *Selfhood and Godhood* (London, 1957). The same book contains an appendix in which the opinions of Patrick Nowell-Smith are subjected to a most thoroughgoing criticism. A similar concept is defended by Richard Taylor, "Determinism and the Theory of Agency," in Hook, *op. cit.* The same theory underlies Taylor's "I Can," in *Philosophical Review,* Vol. 69 (1960), 78–89, reprinted in Morgenbesser and Walsh, *op. cit.* Another recent article which indirectly suggests such a view is Arthur Danto's "What We Can Do," in *Journal of Philosophy,* Vol. 60 (1963), 435–445. Determinism is also attacked at great length in Konstantin Gutberlet, *Die Willensfreiheit und ihre Gegner* (Fulda, Germany, 1893), and in Ch. 9 of M. Maher, *Psychology* (London, 1940). These two works are written from a Catholic point of view.

A. I. Melden's *Free Action* (London, 1961) offers fairly elaborate and penetrating analyses of a wide range of concepts that have always been central to the free will controversy, such as those of wants, motives, actions, and so on; although the author does not try to prove directly that men have free will, he attacks the bases of certain widely held determinist theories. Gilbert Ryle's *The Concept of Mind* (London, 1949) contains a chapter, "The Will," which amounts to a devastating critique of the idea that voluntary actions are caused by volitions. J. L. Austin's "Ifs and Cans," which is included among his *Philosophical Papers,* J. O. Urmson and G. J. Warnock, eds. (Oxford, 1961), is a painstaking inquiry into what is meant by saying of an agent that he could have done otherwise; although it is directed at claims made specifically by G. E. Moore and Patrick Nowell-Smith, it actually attacks the foundations of theories that have been widely held for over a century.

A detailed and annotated bibliography of works on determinism and free will can be found in Paul Edwards and Arthur Pap, eds., *A Modern Introduction to Philosophy,* 2d ed. (New York, 1965).

RICHARD TAYLOR

DETERMINISM IN HISTORY. Philosophical reflection upon history has always been impressed by the limited extent to which individuals and groups seem to be able to mold events to their purposes. In the case of some events at least, there seems to be an inexorable necessity—an inevitability or unavoidability—about what happens. The "necessity" of historical events, however, has been asserted by historians and philosophers of history in at least three fundamentally different senses.

SENSES OF DETERMINISM

Fate and providence. The first sense is the notion that events are "fated" to occur, a notion familiar to Greek as well as Oriental thought. The central concept is of an agency external to the historical process itself, sometimes, but not always, personified, determining events somewhat in the way a human agent may be said to determine, through his will, what happens in a process he monitors and manipulates. It is generally assumed, however, that the means by which fated events are brought about lie outside the mechanism of ordinary causal connection: they are "transcendent." This clears the way for a characteristic expression of fatalism—the assertion that what is fated will occur no matter what we do to try to prevent it. To many critics, such a claim has appeared unintelligible. For historical events are surely, in some sense at least, constituted by what we do. A revolution, for example, could hardly occur if nobody revolted. The fatalist claim thus looks self-contradictory. What fatalism really denies, however, is the preventive efficacy of anyone's actions prior to the fated event, a refinement that leaves the claim coherent, if unbelievable. Nor is the doctrine necessarily involved in the incoherence of representing prior actions as both within our power to have performed otherwise and, at the same time, fated in their turn. For fatalism, unlike some other forms of historical determinism, has generally been asserted selectively. It is the doctrine that certain things will necessarily come to pass, not that everything happens necessarily.

Many theological philosophies of history are fatalistic in the indicated sense because of the role they assign to the will of God in their accounts. Unlike most of their pagan predecessors, however, these accounts generally make some attempt to rationalize and even to moralize interventions hitherto conceived as arbitrary, and usually also as menacing. In this way a fatalistic conception of history becomes "providential." Theological interpretations, of course, leave little for philosophers to argue about; for the workings of Divine Providence can be discerned only through some extrarational insight or source of revelation. And as Hegel complained about providential theories generally, the overarching purpose or plan is usually conceded, even by those who claim insight into it, to be partly "concealed from our view." Some theological interpretations have tried to meet this sort of objection by identifying the workings of providence, tentatively at least, with certain standing conditions and even with historical laws. A comparison between Reinhold Niebuhr's twentieth-century *Faith and History*, with its confidence in the "providential structure of existence," and Bishop Bossuet's seventeenth-century *Discourse on Universal History*, which still envisages God ruling the course of empire by "decree," is instructive in this connection. Yet even Niebuhr confessed in the end that, to a finite human mind, both the plan and mode of operation of God in history remain mysterious.

Historical inevitability. Any attempt to make fate or providence immanent in the ordinary processes of history is a move toward a second major conception of the necessity of historical events, one often referred to in contemporary discussion as the doctrine of "historical inevitability." In this conception, the course of history has a necessary over-all direction, whether it be attributed to an active but impersonal "force," a nisus toward some ultimate goal, or a "dynamic" law of development. The necessary direction of history has been variously conceived by various philosophers. Thus the Greeks tended to envisage it as cyclical and repetitive, while most philosophers of the Enlightenment found an equally simple but linear pattern of inevitable progress. According to Giambattista Vico, history traces a spiral path as civilization after civilization, each in its own unique way, follows the curve from heroic age to neobarbarism. According to Hegel, the spiral proceeds dialectically toward the actualization of a potential human freedom, each regress contributing to an ultimate spiritual synthesis. Just how deterministic such interpretations of history's direction were actually intended to be is, in fact, a disputable matter. Almost none assert that every historical event happens necessarily; the claim is usually limited to the main trend or the more significant events. And many speculative theorists do not seem to claim even that much. Oswald Spengler, for example, in his *Decline of the West* left the origin, by contrast with the development, of historical cultures unaccounted for; Hegel's lectures on the philosophy of history can be interpreted as having held that the stages of freedom succeed each other only with "rational," and not with "natural" necessity; and Toynbee's *Study of History* discovered historical "laws" so accommodating that they appear to be compatible with an almost indefinite number of exceptions.

Yet the discovery of inevitability is generally taken to be a major goal of speculative theories of history. And historians themselves often refer to "underlying tides and currents" (A. L. Rowse) or "great social forces" (E. P. Cheyney) in a way which seems to call for a more literal interpretation than the references they also occasionally let slip to the "fate" or "destiny" of historical individuals. Recent polemical works like K. R. Popper's *The Poverty of Historicism* and Isaiah Berlin's *Historical Inevitability* certainly assume that the doctrine of inevitability is still a live option for many people. Like fatalism, it is regarded by its critics as morally and politically dangerous. But it has also been subjected to a logical and conceptual critique, the major complaint of which is that insofar as historical inevitability is asserted on empirical grounds, the notion of "necessity" is employed in a way that is scientifically indefensible. According to Popper, inevitability theories confuse genuine laws, which assert conditional and hypothetical necessities, with statements of historical *trends,* which are not necessities, but facts. Laws license prediction whenever the conditions specified in their antecedent clauses are satisfied. The lack of corresponding empirical justification for the social "prophecies" obtained by merely extrapolating trends is often obscured by the "force" metaphors characteristically used in describing them.

A speculative theorist who wished to claim metaphysical rather than scientific status for his conclusions might perhaps remain unmoved by such considerations. Yet almost all inevitability theorists at some point cite empirical evidence; and in the nineteenth century particularly, such theories were often thought to provide models for social science itself. The belief that the extrapolation of trends is a scientifically respectable procedure, Popper observed, may well be traceable to the fascination that untypical sciences like astronomy have had upon philosophers of history. The temptation is to say that if eclipses can be predicted by projecting the observed behavior of the solar system, then revolutions and the like ought similarly to be predictable by projecting the tendencies of the social system. Such reasoning ignores the fact that the cyclical "direction" of the solar system is not just observed; it is explained. And the explanation is in terms of initial conditions obtaining, together with laws of motion that are conditional and hypothetical. The same could be said of the so-called directional "law" of evolution in biology, which is sometimes cited as a paradigm for linear theories of historical inevitability. No corresponding attempt is usually made to derive the alleged necessity of observed historical trends from more fundamental considerations. For to represent the large-scale pattern as "resultant" in such a way, especially if the relevant initial conditions included individual human actions, might undermine the thesis of unavoidability.

Scientific determinism. The notion of explaining historical trends in terms of the operation of scientific laws brings us to a third generic conception of necessity in history, the "scientific" sense. To put it most simply, an event might be said to be determined in this sense if there is some other event or condition or group of them, sometimes called its cause, that is a sufficient condition for its occurrence, the sufficiency residing in the effect's following the cause in accordance with one or more laws of nature. The general assertion of historical determinism then becomes the assertion that for every historical event there is such a sufficient condition. Whether, in consequence, history manifests a unitary pattern or direction is a further and separate question.

Race and climate. Many historical determinists who would claim to be "scientific" in the above sense have gone a step further. Like the inevitability theorists, they have sought a simple clue to the historical process, in this case in causal factors of a limited range. Typical of such single-factor theories are those that fasten on certain biological or psychological conditions, such as the alleged racial characteristics of certain groups, or on features of the physical environment, such as topography, climate, soil, or natural resources. The writings of Joseph Arthur de Gobineau and of Houston Stewart Chamberlain, with their concept of Aryan superiority, are notorious examples of the first of these, although few serious attempts have been made to write detailed and scholarly histories (rather than propaganda) on their principles. The search for geographical determinants, on the other hand, has a reputable record going back at least to Montesquieu and Bodin, and it received classic expression in the work of Henry Thomas Buckle in the nineteenth century and of Ellsworth Huntington in the twentieth. Both types of theory, however, oversimplify the diversity of history. It is one thing to point out that civilizations originated in river valleys or that the decline of Rome was accompanied by race-mixing. It is quite another—even if some features of events can properly be ascribed to such factors—to say that all significant historical change is determined by geographical or biological causes.

Social causes. Racial and environmental interpretations locate the explanatory factors outside the course of historical events themselves. Social interpretations offer single-factor accounts that seek causes in one kind of historical condition by contrast with others. According to Marx, for example, the explanation of political, religious, legal, and other "ideological" features of a society is to be found in that society's mode of economic life and in the relations of production that its human elements consequently take up toward each other. In extreme forms of the theory at least, a one-way causal relation is asserted to hold at any time between economic and noneconomic factors, as well as between economic conditions at different times. Such an economic interpretation of history, with its more variable explanatory factor, has a far richer potential than racial or environmental ones for explaining the details of historical change. Like all single-factor theories, however, any attempt to defend its monistic causal claims generally either fails to carry conviction or runs afoul of a basic distinction between sufficient (determining) and merely necessary (conditioning) conditions. Thus, in a crude but revealing lapse, often cited, Engels argued that because a man cannot engage in politics, science, religion, and art if he lacks the basic material conditions of life, the latter *determine* the former.

Multiple-factor theories. More considered statements of single-factor theories try to provide for a degree of interaction between the chosen factor and others. This leaves the difficult problem of explaining the sense, if any, in which the special factor is the fundamental one. It also leave's the problem—which bedeviled inevitability theories as well—of the relation between large-scale social causes and effects and the actions of participating individuals. "Great man" theories like Carlyle's are rightly out of fashion, but it is difficult to deny the historical importance of a Lenin or a Napoleon. Plekhanov's classical Marxist discussion of this problem, in *The Role of the Individual in History,* adopts the uneasy compromise that individual causes can make a difference to a historical outcome, but only to its less significant features or to its timing. Such legislation as to the "spheres of influence" of various sorts of conditions, all conceded to be necessary, often seems highly arbitrary; and under pressure, single-factor theories tend to develop into "interpretations" only in the sense of directing attention to one factor in historical change that is deemed especially noteworthy, often for pragmatic reasons. The claim that historical events are determined then ceases to have any special connection with the claims made for the chosen factor. It reverts simply to the assertion that for every event there is a sufficient condition, no matter how disparate the causal elements that may sometimes be required to constitute it.

In the broad sense thus indicated, the contention that historical events are all determined may seem quite unproblematic. And when one considers the thoroughly causal language of historical accounts, the contention may seem also to be in accordance with historical practice. It is true that what historians actually call a cause is seldom itself a sufficient condition. But it is generally assumed by determinists that its claim to be a cause depends upon its completing a sufficient set of such conditions, some of which may not have been overtly specified. Yet the assumption of scientific determinism in history has been disputed on a number of grounds, the three set forth below being among the most frequently cited. These arguments have a common feature: all claim that this assumption contradicts others that the historian normally and properly makes. In consequence, the notion is represented as importing an incoherence into historical thinking as a whole.

OBJECTIONS TO DETERMINISM

Chance. It has been objected, first, that history is a realm in which events sometimes occur "by chance"—it being assumed that what happens by chance cannot happen of necessity. Certainly, historians often report what happened in such terms. And chance has been regarded by some of them almost as a principle of historical interpretation. Thus J. B. Bury, in his *Later Roman Empire*, represented the success of the barbarians in penetrating the Roman Empire as due to a succession of coincidences—the "historical surprise" of the onslaught of the Asiatic Huns, which drove the Goths west and south; the lucky blow that killed a Roman emperor when the Goths engaged a Roman army that just happened to be in their way; the untimely death of that emperor's talented successor before he had arranged for the assimilation of those tribesmen who had settled within the imperial border; the unhappy fact that the two sons who subsequently divided the empire were both incompetent, and so on. Bury's example does at least afford a strong argument against the notion that history is a *self*-determining system—one of the assumptions of the doctrine of historical inevitability. It illustrates the intrusion of nonhistorical factors into the historical process—an untimely death, for example—Bury's awareness of which led him to object to any search for what he called "general" causes. Bury's example makes clearer, too, the inappropriateness of a science like astronomy as a model for social and historical explanation. For the solar system, unlike human society, is virtually isolated from such external influences. This makes it possible for us to make astronomical predictions without taking into account anything but the description of the state of the system itself at any time and to predict accurately for long periods ahead. In history the situation is very different. The sufficient conditions of historical events are seldom to be found in other historical events.

But does the admission of chance, as Bury described it, count against the whole doctrine of historical determinism in the scientific sense? In support of their claim that it must, historical indeterminists sometimes cite parallels in physical inquiry. Modern subatomic physics, for example, whether correctly or not, has often been said to be indeterministic precisely because it regards certain aspects of the behavior of single electrons as matters of chance. Yet it may be questioned whether any of the contingencies, accidents, or unlucky "breaks" mentioned by Bury were matters of chance in the physicist's sense. For there is no reason to think of any of them as uncaused. What is peculiar about them is that they occur (to use a common phrase) at the intersection of two or more relatively independent causal chains. But there is nothing in such coincidences, determinists will maintain, that enables us to say that what occurs at the "intersections" could not be deduced from prior statements of conditions and appropriate laws, provided we took all the relevant conditions into account.

In practice, of course, a historian may not be in a position to explain why a given coincidence occurred; at least one relevant chain—the biological one leading to the emperor's death, for example—may be beyond the scope of his kind of inquiry. What happened may consequently be represented by him as something unforeseen—perhaps even as the intrusion of the "irrational" into the course of events. Here the notion of chance is extended from the paradigm case where an event is said to have no cause at all to one where the cause is simply unknown because nonhistorical.

The notion is commonly extended further (as Bury's example illustrates) to events whose causes, although not beyond the range of historical inquiry, are beyond the immediate range of the historian's interests—the appearance of the Huns, for example. This makes it misleading to define "chance event" in history, as some have done, as an event that has historical effects but lacks historical causes. The causes of the invasion of the Huns simply lie outside the story the historian is telling. The judgment that a historical event happened by chance is thus a function of what the historian (and his readers) are concerned about. (This also covers the case where "by chance" seems chiefly to mean "unplanned.") It follows that, from one standpoint, an event may properly be judged to be a chance occurrence, while from another it clearly could not be: the activities of the Huns, for example, were scarcely a matter of chance from their own standpoint. Speculative philosophers of history, if they aim to take the additional standpoints of God or "History" into account, will obviously have further problems when deciding whether something was a chance occurrence. The issues thus raised are doubtless of considerable interest for a general account of the logic of historical narration. It is difficult to see, however, that they have any important bearing on the acceptability of historical determinism.

Novelty. A second consideration often advanced against the determinist assumption is that history is a realm of novelty and that its course must therefore remain not only unforeseen but unforeseeable, even if we take into account the broadest possible range of antecedent conditions. The fact that what the historian discovers is often surprising is thus held to have an objective basis in human creativity, from which periodically there emerge events and conditions with radically novel characteristics. Such "emergence," it is often claimed, rules out the possibility of scientific prediction before the event because prediction is necessarily based on laws and theories that relate types of characteristics already known. In this connection it is interesting to note a "proof" offered by Popper that some historical events at least are unpredictable in principle. If we accept the common assumption that some historical events are dependent in part on the growth of human knowledge, Popper pointed out, then it is logically impossible that we should be able to predict them before they occur. For *ex hypothesi*, one of their conditions must remain unknown to us.

Confronted by such an argument, determinists would want to make clear that, as they conceive it, determinism does not entail predictability, even though it has, unfortunately, sometimes been defined in terms of predictability. An event can be determined even though it is not known to be so. Popper himself did not regard the argument cited above as counting against historical determinism; indeed, his own statement of it strongly suggested that the unpredictability of the events in question actually follows from their being determined in a certain way, that is, by a set of conditions that are less than sufficient in the absence of as yet unattained human knowledge. All that is required by the doctrine of determinism, however, is that events *have* sufficient conditions, whether or not they can be known before the fact. It would thus be better, perhaps, to define the notion in terms of explicability rather than predictability. Determinists often point out that the emergent characteristics of natural things can be explained in the scientific sense, although they could not have been predicted before they first emerged. In his "Determinism in History," Ernest Nagel cited the emergence of the qualities of water out of a combination of hydrogen and oxygen. These are emergent and novel in the sense of not being possessed by the original elements and not being deducible from information about the behavior of these elements in isolation. Yet we have been able to frame laws governing the emergence of these originally novel attributes under specifiable conditions that allow us to deduce and now even to predict the attributes.

A likely reply is that whereas the emergence of the characteristics of water is a recurring, experimentally testable phenomenon, the emergence of novelty in the course of history is not. At least some historical events and conditions, it may be said, are unique and hence not subject to scientific explanation even after the fact. In considering this rejoinder, however, it is important not to misunderstand the claims of scientific determinism. For these do not include the deducibility in principle of the occurrence of historical events "in all their concrete actuality." Only events as historians represent them in their narratives are said to be so deducible. And their descriptions of events, it will be argued, are necessarily phrased in terms that apply, although not necessarily in the same combinations, to events at other times and places.

It may of course be doubted that we shall ever actually discover the determining conditions of such historical novelties as Alexander's use of the phalanx, Caesar Augustus' imperial policy, or the organization of the medieval church, under descriptions as highly detailed as historians customarily apply to them—a problem scarcely touched by the consideration, advanced by Nagel, that social science has sought, with some measure of success, to discover the conditions under which men act creatively. Yet determinists will regard these as merely "practical" difficulties, not bearing on the basic issue. That issue, they will maintain, is whether the novelties that can be recognized by historical inquiry are such as to rule out their subsumability under laws "in principle." Unless historians' knowledge can be said to go beyond any description of such novelties in terms of a unique conjunction of recurring characteristics, the argument from historical novelty will be deemed to have missed its mark.

In fact, this further, and highly debatable claim is one that some historical theorists would be quite prepared to make. They would point out, for example, that we can *listen* to Mozart's music and *read* Newton's scientific writings—two examples of creativity cited by Nagel—and, by thus enjoying direct acquaintance with radical historical novelty, discover more than could be conveyed by any description in terms of recurring characteristics. Ordinary historical knowledge of novel military tactics, imperial policies, or institutional organizations, they would maintain, would similarly go beyond what could be expressed without reference, either explicitly or implicitly, to named individuals, groups, or periods. They would consequently represent historical narrative as employing concrete universals—like "Renaissance" or "Gothic"—as well as abstract ones. And since scientific laws can be framed only in terms of abstract universals, they would claim that warranted assertions of novelty expressed in terms of concrete universals do undermine the assumption of determinism.

Freedom. A third and even more common argument against accepting a determinist view of historical events turns on the claim that history is a realm not only of chance and novelty but of human freedom. The subject matter of history, it is sometimes said, is not mere "events" but human "actions," in a distinctive sense quite familiar to plain men who deliberate and decide what to do. If the historian is not to misrepresent such a subject matter, the argument goes, then he must take seriously the notion of choosing between alternatives. As Johan Huizinga expressed it, in his "Idea of History" (in Fritz Stern, ed., *The Varieties of History*), "the historian must put himself at a point in the past at which the known factors still seem to permit different outcomes. If he speaks of Salamis, then it must be as if the Persians might still win." In *Historical Inevitability*, Isaiah Berlin gave a further and even more familiar reason for adopting the standpoint of "agency." "If determinism were true, . . ." he wrote, "the notion of human responsibility, as ordinarily understood, would no longer apply." For an ascription of responsibility requires the assumption that the agent was "in control," that he could have acted otherwise than he did. Historical accounts, in other words, like the moralistic ones plain men ordinarily give of their own and others' actions, presuppose "freedom of the will." And this is held to be incompatible with the assumption of determinism.

Few philosophical problems have been discussed as exhaustively (or as inconclusively) as the problem of freedom of the will, and it is quite impossible in this context to do justice to the subtleties involved. There are, however, two chief ways of handling the present objection. Historical determinists can try to explain away the problem of freedom by arguing that, although moralistic accounts properly regard historical agents as free, the sense in which they must do so is quite compatible with the deterministic assumption. Libertarians, correspondingly, can try to give an account of historic causation that does not rule out an action's being both caused and undetermined. For historians, either of these ways out of the difficulty would presumably be more acceptable than the outright denial of the legitimacy of either moral appraisal or causal explanation in historical accounts. For, with no obvious sign of strain, historians generally offer both.

The determinist case often turns on the contention that the sense of freedom involved in attributing responsibility to a moral agent is not the "could have done otherwise" of absolute indeterminism; that sense implies only that the agent would have done otherwise if certain antecedents—his circumstances or his character, for example—had been a little different. Indeed, it is often argued that the test of whether the agent is really "in control," and hence responsible, is whether he acts differently on another occasion when the conditions have been changed—say, by his having been praised or blamed, rewarded or punished. It is therefore not the agent's freedom in the sense of his action's being uncaused that is at stake. The determinist, in arguing this way, conceives himself, furthermore, as accepting, not rejecting, the notion that the moral categories the historian uses are those of the plain man. What is denied is that the "ordinary" sense of "free" is the unconditional "freedom of the will" of the metaphysicians. As for Huizinga's claim that the historian must think of the agent's problem as if there were real possibilities open to him, this would be regarded as a purely methodological point. What is brought out thereby is the applicability to actions of a concept of understanding that requires us, quite properly, to view them in relation to what the agents thought about their situations, including any illusions they may have had about them.

Many libertarians might accept the latter contention. But most would surely repudiate the claim that responsibility requires freedom only in a sense compatible with determinism. To ascribe responsibility to a person whose actions necessarily follow from antecedent events, Berlin declared, is "stupid and cruel," and he meant rationally incoherent, not just foolish. In a sense alleged to be central to our notion of responsibility, such a person could *not* have done otherwise. Must a libertarian who takes such a stand, then, abandon the possibility of explaining actions causally? Some, at least, would say, No, provided we recognize that the term "cause," when applied to human actions, bears a special sense. Thus, according to R. G. Collingwood, the causes (in a distinctively historical sense) of "the free and deliberate act of a conscious and responsible agent" are to be sought in the agent's "thought" about his situation, his reasons for deciding to act (*Essay on Metaphysics*). What a libertarian will deny is that any combination of such "rational" causes that excludes the agent's decision to act—since the latter falls into the historian's explanandum, not his explanans—is a sufficient condition of his action. Such causes become "effective," it might be said, only through an agent's deciding to act upon them. Yet when he does so, reference to them as his "reasons" will explain what he did in the sense of making it understandable. What such reference will not and need not do is explain his action in the sense of showing its performance to be deducible from sufficient antecedent conditions.

It is generally agreed that the conflict between historical determinists and indeterminists cannot be resolved by the offering of proofs or disproofs. Modern scientific determinists, in any case, seldom state their position dogmatically. According to Nagel, for example, all that can be claimed is that the principle of determinism has "regulative" status as a presupposition of the possibility of scientific inquiry—a principle which must therefore govern the scientific study of history as well. What is particularly interesting about theories of rational causation is the conceptual foundation they offer for denying that the principle of determinism is a necessary presupposition even of seeking explanations when the subject matter is human action: they show at least the conceivability of explanatory inquiry on libertarian principles. It must be conceded, however, that few contemporary philosophers regard indeterminism as an acceptable assumption to carry into historical or social investigation.

Bibliography

For examples of determinist or near-determinist views of history, see H. T. Buckle, *A History of Civilization in England* (London, 1899) or E. Huntington, *Mainsprings of Civilization* (New York, 1945). The works of various speculative and single-factor theorists mentioned above may also be consulted: Patrick Gardiner's *Theories of History* (Glencoe, Ill., 1959) contains relevant extracts from the works of Vico, Hegel, Marx, Plekhanov, Buckle, Tolstoy, Spengler, Toynbee, Croce, and Collingwood. For a contemporary attack on deterministic views, both of the scientific and metaphysical kinds, see Isaiah Berlin, *Historical Inevitability* (London, 1954) and the reply offered by E. H. Carr in *What Is History?* (London, 1961). For a moderate defense of the deterministic assumption against such attacks, see Ernest Nagel, "Determinism in History," *Philosophy and Phenomenological Research*, Vol. 20 (1960), 291–317. The viability of indeterministic historical and social scientific inquiry is argued for in Alan Donagan, "Social Science and Historical Antinomianism," *Revue Internationale de Philosophie*, Vol. 11 (1957), 433–449. The role of the individual in history is discussed in Sidney Hook, *The Hero in History* (New York, 1943). Johan Huizinga's "Idea of History" is included in English translation in Fritz Stern, ed., *The Varieties of History* (New York, 1956), pp. 290–303. The claim that historians use "cause" in a special sense is developed by R. G. Collingwood in *An Essay on Metaphysics* (Oxford, 1940), which should be read in conjunction with his *The Idea of History* (Oxford, 1946). See further the bibliography to GREAT MAN THEORY OF HISTORY.

W. H. DRAY

DEUSSEN, PAUL (1845–1919), German philologist and philosopher, was the son of a Protestant clergyman in the village of Oberdreis in the Westerwald. He received a thorough classical training in the old secondary school of Pforta, where he developed a close friendship with Friedrich Nietzsche. Both Deussen and Nietzsche enrolled in the theological faculty at the University of Bonn, but Nietzsche soon shifted to classical philology and followed his teacher Ritschl to Leipzig. Deussen remained in Bonn for four semesters, then also shifted to classical philology and earned his doctorate at Berlin in 1869 with a dissertation on Plato's *Sophist.* After a brief period of teaching in secondary schools, he became the tutor for a Russian family in Geneva in 1872. There he intensified his study of Sanskrit, began a study of the Indian philosophical classics, and became an enthusiastic follower and interpreter of Schopenhauer (after having long resisted Nietzsche's enthusiastic endorsements). In 1881 he qualified to lecture in Berlin under Eduard Zeller on the basis of his work *The System of the Vedanta*, and became an extraordinary professor in 1887. Appointed full professor in Kiel in 1889, he retained this post until his retirement.

Deussen's major work, on which he labored for more than twenty years, was the *Universal History of Philosophy*, consisting of two large volumes in six parts. The first volume was devoted to Indian thought and the second to the thought of the West from the Greeks to Schopenhauer, with a section on the philosophy of the Bible.

For Deussen the history of philosophy was a discipline indispensable not only for the understanding of life but for its religious interpretation as well. Its task was to strip off the "mythical vestments" or "hulls" of the various philosophical and religious systems in order to discover the single unified truth that all share.

This unified, permanent truth was made clear in the philosophy of Kant as completed by Schopenhauer, but it also embraced insights from the Vedanta, Plato's doctrine of Ideas, and Christian theology. Schopenhauer, Deussen said, had "freed the essentials of Kant from the weight of traditional misunderstanding" and offered "the completion of a unified doctrine which is grounded in experience, internally coherent in its metaphysics, and which appears, in its practical part, as a Christianity renewed throughout its whole depth on scientific foundations, and which will become, and for the predictable future remain, the foundation of all human scientific and religious thought" (*Geschichte der Philosophie*, Vol. I, Part 1, p. 22). Rightly understood, Schopenhauer was the *philosophus Christianissimus* (the most Christian philosopher). The affirmation of the will to live is the egoism of our natural existence; its denial is "disinterested righteousness, the love of man, and the willingness to sacrifice for great causes—all great, heroic, overindividual striving and creating" (*Erinnerungen an Friedrich Nietzsche*, p. 105). But the divine, in this synthetic conception, cannot be understood theistically. The highest Being is beyond all personality, and all will eventually confess, "I believe in one living, but not one personal God."

Deussen was one of the early interpreters of Jakob Boehme (1897). He edited a critical edition of Schopenhauer in 14 volumes (Munich, 1911), and he founded the Schopenhauer Society and edited its yearbook from 1912 until his death.

Bibliography

Deussen's chief work was *Allgemeine Geschichte der Philosophie, mit besonderer Berücksichtigung der Religionen*, 2 vols. (Leipzig, 1894–1917); Vol. I, Part 2 was translated by A. S. Geden as *The Philosophy of the Upanishads* (Edinburgh, 1906). *Die Elemente der Metaphysik* (Aachen, 1877), was translated by C. M. Duff as *The Elements of Metaphysics* (London, 1894).

Deussen was the first Western philosopher to include Eastern thought in a general history of philosophy in any scientific way. Among his publications in this field are *Das System des Vedanta* (Leipzig, 1883), translated by Charles Johnston as *The System of the Vedanta* (Chicago, 1912); *Die Sūtra des Vedānta*, translated from the Sanskrit (Leipzig, 1887), translated by H. Woods and C. B. Rumble as *The Sutras of the Vedanta With the Commentary of Cankara* (New York, 1906); *Sechzig Upanishads des Veda*, which he translated from the Sanskrit (Leipzig, 1897); *Vier philosophische Texte des Mahâbhâratam* (Leipzig, 1906); *Bhagavadgītā. Der Gesang des Heiligen* (Leipzig, 1911); and *Die Geheimenlehre des Veda* (Leipzig, 1907–1909).

Three volumes of an autobiographical nature are *Mein Leben* (Leipzig, 1927); *Erinnerungen an Friedrich Nietzsche* (Leipzig, 1901); and *Erinnerungen an Indien* (Leipzig, 1904). Bound together with the *Erinnerungen an Indien* is a lecture, "On the Philosophy of the Vedanta in Its Relations to Occidental Metaphysics," delivered and first published in Bombay in 1893.

On Deussen, see "Erinnerungen an Paul Deussen," which is Vol. 20 of *Jahrbuch der Schopenhauergesellschaft* (1920).

L. E. Loemker

DEUSTUA, ALEJANDRO O. (1849–1945), Peruvian educator, aesthetician, and philosopher, was born in Huancayo. He was a professor at the University of San Marcos, rector of the University, and director of the National Library in Lima. Deustua contributed greatly to the development of Peruvian education at all levels. His philosophical writing was done at an advanced age. It reflected the influence of K. C. F. Krause and Henri Bergson.

Running through the thought of Deustua are the polar ideas of liberty and order. Their interplay extends to a philosophy of civilization, but it is most clear in his major interest, aesthetics. It may be introduced through his definitions of beauty and art. Beauty is "a conciliation of liberty and nature, through the mediation of an ideal order created by the imagination." Since an internal image is not sufficient, external forms are created by art, which is the "graceful expression of the conciliation between nature and liberty, a conciliation imagined by the artist and translated by means of adequate or expressive forms."

The element of nature is furnished by human sensibility, including sensation and emotion. Liberty is found in absence of resistance, which in turn allows development from within to take place. It belongs to spirit and is paramount in that function of spirit called imagination, which is defined not as imaginal but as creative. Liberty is manifest only in an order, and it is fully realized only in an order entirely of its own making, an artistic order or harmony. This order is created by the imagination, using sensuous elements and acting in close relation with emotion. Harmony is a unity in variety: aesthetic pleasure is opposed to monotony and to excessive complexity. Types of harmony are symmetry and rhythm. Related to these are an outward order of parts and whole in space, characteristic of classical art, and an inward order of causes or purposes in time, characteristic of romantic art. When liberty is realized in order, the result is grace.

In addition to beauty there are several other types of value, to all of which imagination can contribute in one degree or another. These values may in turn contribute to the aesthetic experience, but they fall below beauty in freedom. Logical truth is characterized by demonstrative necessity. Economic value is subject to the imperative of desire, in contrast to the disinterestedness of aesthetic experience. Although moral value presupposes a free agent, it requires that the will submit to duty and law. Religious revelation and myth are aesthetic in nature; but they demand submission to the divine will. Only in the aesthetic sphere is liberty sovereign, unbound by orders or norms external to it. For this reason, aesthetic value is "the value of values."

Works by Deustua

"Las ideas de orden y libertad en la historia del pensamiento humano" ("The Ideas of Order and Liberty in the History of Human Thought"). *Revista universitaria* (Lima), 1917–1922.

Estética general ("General Aesthetics"). Lima, 1923.

Estética aplicada. Lo bello en el arte: escultura, pintura, música ("Applied Aesthetics. The Beautiful in Art: Sculpture, Painting, Music"). Lima, 1935.

Works on Deustua

Salazar Bondy, Augusto, *La filosofía en el Perú* and *Philosophy in Peru*. Washington, 1954. This is a single book, in both Spanish and English, published by the Pan American Union. The Spanish text is on pp. 35–40 and the English on pp. 77–82.

ARTHUR BERNDTSON

DEWEY, JOHN (1859–1952), American philosopher, educator, and social critic. Dewey was born in Burlington, Vermont. A shy youth, he enjoyed reading books and was a good but not a brilliant student. He entered the University of Vermont in 1875, and although his interest in philosophy and social thought was awakened during his last two years there, he was uncertain about his future career. He taught classics, science, and algebra at a high school in Oil City, Pennsylvania, from 1879 to 1881 and then returned to Burlington, where he continued to teach. He also arranged for private tutorials in philosophy with his former teacher, H. A. P. Torrey. Encouraged by Torrey and W. T. Harris, the editor of the *Journal of Speculative Philosophy* who accepted Dewey's first two philosophical articles, Dewey applied for the graduate program at the newly organized Johns Hopkins University. He was twice refused fellowship aid, but he borrowed $500 from an aunt to begin his professional philosophical career.

The external events of Dewey's Vermont years were relatively unexciting, and there is very little to indicate that he would become America's most influential philosopher and educator as well as one of the most outspoken champions of social reform. Yet the New England way of life left a deep imprint on the man and his thought. His modesty, forthrightness, doggedness, deep faith in the workings of the democratic process, and respect for his fellow man are evidenced in almost everything that he did and wrote.

Under the imaginative guidance of Daniel Gilman, the first president of Johns Hopkins, the university had become one of the most exciting centers for intellectual and scholarly activity. Dewey studied with C. S. Peirce, who taught logic, and with G. S. Hall, one of the first experimental psychologists in America. However, the greatest initial influence on Dewey was G. S. Morris, whose philosophical outlook had been shaped by Hegel and the idealism so much in vogue on the Continent and in England.

Dewey was an eager participant in the controversies stirred up by Hegelianism. He dated his earliest interest in philosophy to a course in physiology that he took during his junior year at the University of Vermont, where he read T. H. Huxley's text on physiology. Dewey discovered the concept of the organic and developed a sense of the interdependence and interrelated unity of all things. He tells us that subconsciously he desired a world and a life that would have the same properties as had the human organism that Huxley described. In Hegel and the idealists, Dewey discovered the most profound philosophical expression of this emotional and intellectual craving. From this organic perspective, which emphasized process and change, all distinctions are functional and relative to a developing unified whole. The organic perspective could be used to oppose the static and the fixed and to break down the hard and fast dichotomies and dualisms that had plagued philosophy.

Dewey's writings during his Hegelian period are infused with an evangelical spirit and are as enthusiastic as they are vague. Whatever issue Dewey considered, he was convinced that once viewed from the perspective of the organic, old problems would dissolve and new insights would emerge. Long after Dewey had drifted away from his early Hegelianism, his outlook was shaped by his intellectual bias for a philosophy based on change, process, and dynamic, organic interaction.

After completing his doctoral studies at Johns Hopkins with a dissertation on the psychology of Kant, Dewey joined Morris at the University of Michigan in 1884. He remained there for the next ten years, with the exception of one year (1888) when he was a visiting professor at the University of Minnesota. At Michigan, Dewey worked with G. H. Mead, who later joined Dewey at Chicago. During his years at Michigan, Dewey became dissatisfied with pure speculation and sought ways to make philosophy directly relevant to the practical affairs of men. His political, economic, and social views became increasingly radical. He agreed to edit a new weekly with a socialist orientation, to be called *Thought News*, but it never reached publication. Dewey also became directly involved with public education in Michigan. His scientific interests, especially in the field of psychology, gradually overshadowed his interest in pure speculation. He published several books on theoretical and applied psychology, including *Psychology* (New York, 1887; 3d rev. ed., 1891), *Applied Psychology* (Boston, 1889), and *The Psychology of Number and Its Applications to Methods of Teaching Arithmetic* (New York, 1895). The latter two books were written with J. A. McLellan.

Dewey's appointment in 1894 as chairman of the department of philosophy, psychology, and education at the University of Chicago provided an ideal opportunity for consolidating his diverse interests. In addition to his academic responsibilities, Dewey actively participated in the life of Hull House, founded by Jane Addams, where he had an opportunity to become directly acquainted with the social and economic problems brought about by urbanization, rapid technological advance, and the influx of immigrant populations. Dewey mixed with workers, union organizers, and political radicals of all sorts. At the university, Dewey assembled a group of sympathetic colleagues who worked closely together. Collectively they published the results of their research in a volume of the Decennial Publications of the University of Chicago entitled *Studies in Logical Theory* (Chicago, 1903). William James, to whom the book was dedicated, rightly predicted that the ideas developed in the *Studies* would dominate the American philosophical scene for the next 25 years.

Shortly after Dewey arrived in Chicago, he helped found the famous laboratory school, commonly known as the Dewey School, which served as a laboratory for testing and developing his psychological and pedagogic hypotheses. Some of Dewey's earliest and most important books on education were based on lectures delivered at the school: *The School and Society* (Chicago, 1900) and *The Child and the Curriculum* (Chicago, 1902). When Dewey left Chicago for Columbia in 1904 because of increasing friction with the university administration concerning the laboratory school, he had already acquired a national reputation for his philosophical ideas and educational theories. The move to Columbia, where he remained until his retirement in 1930, provided a further opportunity for development, and Dewey soon gained international prominence. Through the Columbia Teachers College, which was a training center for teachers from many countries, Dewey's educational philosophy spread throughout the world.

At the time that Dewey joined the Columbia faculty, *The Journal of Philosophy* was founded by F. J. E. Woodbridge, and it became a forum for the discussion and defense of Dewey's ideas. There is scarcely a volume from the time of its founding until Dewey's death that does not contain an article either by Dewey or about his philosophy. As the journalistic center of the country, New York also provided Dewey with an opportunity to express himself on pressing political and social issues. He became a regular contributor to the *New Republic*. A selection of Dewey's popular essays is collected in *Characters and Events*, 2 vols. (New York, 1929).

Wherever Dewey lectured he had an enormous influence. From 1919 to 1921, he lectured at Tokyo, Peking, and Nanking, and his most popular book, *Reconstruction in Philosophy* (New York, 1920), is based on his lectures at the Imperial University of Japan. He also conducted educational surveys of Turkey, Mexico, and Russia. Although he retired from Columbia in 1930, he remained active and wrote prolifically until his death. In 1937, when Dewey was 78, he traveled to Mexico to head the commission investigating the charges made against Leon Trotsky, during the Moscow trials. After a careful investigation, the commission published its report, *Not Guilty* (New York, 1937). In 1941 Dewey championed the cause of academic freedom when Bertrand Russell—his arch philosophical adversary—had been denied permission to teach at the City College of New York, Dewey collaborated in editing a book of essays protesting the decision.

Although constantly concerned with social and political issues, Dewey continued to work on his more technical philosophical studies. M. H. Thomas' bibliography of his writings comprises more than 150 pages. Dewey's influence extended not only to his colleagues but to leaders in almost every field. The wide effects of his teaching did not depend upon the superficial aspects of its presentation, for Dewey was not a brilliant lecturer or essayist, although he could be extremely eloquent. His writings are frequently turgid, obscure, and lacking in stylistic brilliance. But more than any other American of his time, Dewey expressed the deepest hopes and aspirations of his fellow man. Whether dealing with a technical philosophical issue or with some concrete injustice, he displayed a rare combination of acuteness, good sense, imagination, and wit.

Experience and nature. The key concept in Dewey's philosophy is experience. Although there is a development from an idealistic to a naturalistic analysis of experience and different emphases in his many discussions of experience, a nevertheless coherent view of experience does emerge. In his early philosophy Dewey was sympathetic to the theory of experience developed by the Hegelians and the nineteenth-century idealists. He thought of experience as a single, dynamic, unified whole in which everything is ultimately interrelated. There are no rigid dichotomies or breaks in experience and nature. All distinctions are functional and play a role in a complex organic system. Dewey also shared the idealists' antipathy to the atomist and subjectivist tendencies in the concept of experience elaborated by the British empiricists. But as Dewey drifted away from his early Hegelian orientation he indicated three major respects in which he rejected the idealistic concept of experience.

First, he charged that the idealists, in their preoccupation with knowledge and knowing, distorted the character of experience. Idealists, Dewey claimed, neglected the noncognitive and nonreflective experiences of doing, suffering, and enjoying that set the context for all knowing and inquiry. Philosophy, especially modern philosophy, had been so concerned with epistemological issues that it mistook all experience as a form of knowing. Such bias inevitably distorts the character of both man's experience and his knowing. Man is primarily a being who acts, suffers, and enjoys. Most of his life consists of experiences that are not primarily reflective. If we are to understand the nature of thought, reflection, inquiry, and their role in human life, we must appreciate their emergence from, and conditioning by, the context of nonreflective experience. There is more to experience, Dewey believed, than is to be found in the writings of the idealists and, indeed, in the writings of most epistemologists.

The second major departure from his early idealism is to be found in Dewey's rejection of the idea of a single unified whole in which everything is ultimately interrelated. In this respect, he displayed an increasing sympathy with the pluralism of the British empiricists. He insisted that life consists of a series of overlapping and interpenetrating experiences, situations, or contexts, each of which has its internal qualitative integrity. The individual experience is the primary unit of life.

The third shift is reflected in Dewey's increasingly naturalistic bias. The Hegelians and the nineteenth-century idealists did have important insights into the organic nature of experience, but they had overgeneralized them into a false cosmic projection. Dewey discovered in the new developing human sciences, especially in what he called the anthropological–biological orientation, a more careful, detailed, scientific articulation of the organic character of experience.

Dewey thought of himself as part of a general movement that was developing a new empiricism based on a new concept of experience, one that combined the strong naturalistic bias of the Greek philosophers with a sensitive appreciation for experimental method as practiced by the sciences. He was sympathetic with what he took to be the Greek view of experience, which considers it as consisting of a fund of social knowledge and skills and as being the means by which man comes into direct contact with a qualitatively rich and variegated nature. But Dewey was just as forceful in pointing out that this view of experience had to be reconstructed in light of the experimental method of the sciences. One of his earliest and clearest discussions of the nature of experience as an organic coordination is to be found in "The Reflex Arc Concept in Psychology" (*Psychological Review*, Vol. 3, 1896).

Dewey's interest in developing a new theory of experience led many critics to question the exact status of experience within nature, and some objectors charged him with excessive anthropomorphism. Sensitive to this type of criticism, Dewey, particularly in *Experience and Nature* (Chicago, 1925; 2d ed., New York, 1929), attempted to deal with this criticism and to sketch a metaphysics, "the descriptive study of the generic traits of existence."

Nature, according to Dewey, consists of a variety of transactions that can be grouped into three evolutionary plateaus, or levels. Transaction is the technical term that Dewey used to designate the type of action in which the components and elements involved in the action both condition and are conditioned by the entire coordination. The elements of a transaction play a functional role in the developing coordination. The three plateaus of natural transactions are the physicochemical, the psychophysical, and the level of human experience. There are no sharp breaks or discontinuities within nature. But there are distinctive characteristics of the different levels of natural transactions that are reflected in their patterns of behavior and in their consequences. From this perspective, human experience consists of one type of natural transaction, a type that has been the latest to evolve. The distinguishing characteristics of this level of natural transaction are to be located in the type of language, communication, and social living that humans have developed. Experience is all-inclusive in the sense that man is involved in continuous transactions with the whole of nature, and through systematic inquiry he can come to understand the essential characteristics of nature. Some of the more specific areas of Dewey's philosophy can be investigated against this panoramic view of experience and nature.

Art and experience. The ideas contained in Dewey's *Art as Experience* (New York, 1934) provided a surprise for many readers. Popular versions of his philosophy had so exaggerated the role of the practical and the instrumental that art and aesthetic experience seemed to have no place in his philosophical outlook. More perceptive commentators realized that Dewey was making explicit a dimension of his view of experience that had always been implicit and essential to an understanding of his philosophy. The meaning and role of art and aesthetic quality are crucial for understanding Dewey's views on logic, education, democracy, ethics, social philosophy, and even technology.

Dewey had persistently claimed that knowing, or more specifically, inquiry, is an art requiring active experimental manipulation and testing. Knowing does not consist of the contemplation of eternal forms, essences, or universals. Dewey argued that the "spectator theory of knowledge," which had plagued philosophy from its beginnings, is mistaken. He also objected to the sharp division between the theoretical sciences and the practical arts that had its explicit source in Aristotle and had influenced so much later philosophy. Dewey maintained that Aristotle's analysis of the practical disciplines is more fruitful for developing an adequate theory of inquiry than is his description of the theoretical sciences of knowing. Not only is inquiry an art, but all life is, or can be, artistic. The so-called fine arts differ in degree, not in kind, from the rest of life.

Dewey also gave a prominent place to what he called immediacy, pervasive quality, or aesthetic quality. This immediacy is not restricted to a special type of experience but is a distinctive feature of anything that is properly called "*an* experience." The primary unit of life, we have mentioned, is *an* experience, a natural transaction of acting, suffering, enjoying, knowing. It has both temporal development and spatial dimension and can undergo internal change and reconstruction.

But what is it that enables us to speak of an individual experience? Or, by virtue of what does an experience, situation, or context have a unity that enables us to distinguish it from other experiences? Dewey's answer is that everything that is an experience has immediacy or pervasive quality that binds together the complex constituents of the experience. This immediacy or pervasive quality can be directly felt or had. But this qualitative dimension of experience is not to be confused with a subjective feeling that is somehow locked up in the mind of the experiencer. Nor is it to be thought of as something that exists independently of any experiencer. These qualities that pervade natural transactions are properly predicated of the experience or situation as a whole. Within an experiential transaction we can institute distinctions between what is subjective and what is objective. But such distinctions are relative to, and dependent on, the context in which they are made. An experience or a situation is a whole in virtue of its immediate pervasive qualities, and each occurrence of these qualities is unique. As examples of such pervasive qualities, Dewey mentions the qualities of distress or cheer that mark existent situations, qualities that are unique in their occurrence and inexpressible in words but capable of being directly experienced. Thus, when one directly experiences a frightening situation, it is the situation that is frightening and not merely the experience.

These pervasive, or "tertiary," qualities are what Dewey calls aesthetic qualities. Aesthetic quality, is thus an essential characteristic of all experiences. Within an experience, the pervasive quality can guide the development of the experience, and it can also be transformed and enriched as the experience is reconstructed. Aesthetic quality can be funded with new meaning, ideas, and emotions. A situation that is originally indeterminate, slack, or inchoate can be transformed into one that is determinate, harmonious, and funded with meaning; this type of reconstructed experience Dewey called a consummation. Such experiences are reconstructed by the use of intelligence. For example, when one is confronted with a specific problematic situation that demands resolution, one can reconstruct the situation by locating its problematic features and initiating a course of action that will resolve the situation. Consummations are characteristic of the most mundane practical tasks as well as the most speculative inquiries. The enemies of the aesthetic, Dewey claimed, are not the practical or the intellectual but the diffuse and slack at one extreme and the excessively rigid and fixed at the other. The type of experience that philosophers normally single out as aesthetic is a heightened consummation in which aesthetic qualities dominate.

Dewey viewed human life as a rhythmic movement from experiences qualified by conflict, doubt, and indeterminateness toward experiences qualified by their integrity, harmony, and funded aesthetic quality. We are constantly confronted with problematic and indeterminate situations, and insofar as we use our intelligence to reconstruct these situations successfully we achieve consummations. He was concerned both with delineating the methods by which we could most intelligently resolve the conflicting situations in which we inevitably find ourselves and with advocating the social reforms required so that life for all men would become funded with enriched meaning and increased aesthetic quality.

Logic and inquiry. Early in his career, Dewey started developing a new theory of inquiry, which he called instrumental or experimental logic. Dewey claimed that philosophers had lost touch with the actual methods of inquiry practiced by the experimental sciences. The function of instrumental logic is to study the methods by which we most successfully gain and warrant our knowledge. On the basis of this investigation, instrumental logic could specify regulative principles for the conduct of further inquiry.

The central themes of Dewey's conception of logic were outlined in *Studies in Logical Theory* (Chicago, 1903), applied to education in *How We Think* (Boston, 1910), and further refined in *Essays in Experimental Logic* (Chicago, 1916). Dewey also wrote numerous articles on various aspects of logic, but his most systematic and detailed presentation is in *Logic: The Theory of Inquiry* (New York, 1938), in which he defines inquiry as "*the controlled or directed transformation of an indeterminate situation into one that is so determinate in its constituent distinctions and relations as to convert the elements of the original situation into a unified whole*" (p. 104). By itself, this definition is not sufficient to grasp what Dewey intends. But his meaning can be understood when the definition is interpreted against the background of what we have said about the individual experience or situation and the way in which it is pervaded by a unifying quality.

We find ourselves in situations that are qualified by their indeterminateness or internal conflict. From the perspective of the experiencer or inquirer, we can say that he experiences a "felt difficulty." This is the antecedent condition of inquiry. Insofar as the situation demands some resolution, we must attempt to articulate the problem or problems that are to be solved. Formulating the problems may be a process of successive refinement in the course of the inquiry. The next logical stage is that of suggestion or hypothesis, in which we imaginatively formulate various relevant hypotheses for solving the problem. In some complex inquiries we may have to engage in hypothetico-deductive reasoning in order to refine our hypotheses and to ascertain the logical consequences of the hypothesis or set of hypotheses. Finally, there is the stage of experimental testing in which we seek to confirm or disconfirm the suggested hypotheses. If our inquiry is successful, the original indeterminate situation is transformed into a unified whole. Knowledge may be defined as the objective of inquiry. Knowledge is that which is warranted by the careful use of the norms and methods of inquiry. When "knowledge" is taken as an abstract term related to inquiry in the abstract, it means warranted assertibility. Furthermore, the knowledge gained in a specific inquiry is funded in our experience and serves as the background for further inquiry. By reflecting on this general pattern of inquiry, which can be exhibited in common-sense inquiry as well as the most advanced scientific inquiry, we can bring into focus the distinctive features of Dewey's logic.

First, this pattern of inquiry is intended to be a general schema for all inquiry. But the specific procedures, testing methods, type of evidence, etc., will vary with different types of inquiry and different kinds of subject matter. Second, a specific inquiry cannot be completely isolated from the context of other inquiries. The rules, procedures, and evidence required for the conduct of any inquiry are derived from other successful inquiries. By studying the types of inquiry that have been most successful in achieving warranted conclusions, we can abstract norms, rules, and procedures for directing further inquiry. These norms may themselves be modified in the course of further inquiry. Third, all inquiry presupposes a social or public context that is the medium for funding the warranted conclusions and norms for further inquiry. In this respect, Dewey agrees with Peirce's emphasis on the community of inquirers. Inquiry both requires such a community and helps to further the development of this community. Dewey attempted to relate this idea of a community of inquirers to his view of democracy. The essential principle of democracy is that of community; an effective democracy requires the existence of a community of free, courageous, and open-minded inquirers. Fourth, inquiry is essentially a self-corrective process. To conduct a specific inquiry, some knowledge claims, norms, and rules must be taken as fixed, but no knowledge claim, norm, or rule is absolutely fixed; it may be criticized, revised, or abandoned in light of subsequent inquiry and experience.

Dewey's theory of inquiry as an ongoing self-corrective process and his view of knowledge as that which is warranted through inquiry both differ radically from many traditional theories of inquiry and knowledge. Dewey thought of this theory as an alternative to the views of those philosophers who have claimed that there is an epistemological given that is indubitable and known with certainty. According to this epistemological model, some truths are considered to be absolutely certain, indubitable, or incorrigible. They may be considered self-evident, known by rational insight, or directly grasped by the senses. On the basis of this foundation, we then build or construct the rest of our knowledge. From Dewey's perspective, this general model that has informed many classical theories of knowledge is confused and mistaken. There are no absolute first truths that are given or known with certainty. Furthermore, knowledge neither has nor requires such a foundation in order to be rational. Inquiry and its objective, knowledge, are rational because inquiry is a self-corrective process by which we gradually become clearer about the epistemological status of both our starting points and conclusions. We must continually submit our knowledge claims to the public test of a community of inquirers in order to clarify, refine, and justify them.

Democracy and education. Dewey is probably best known for his philosophy of education. This is not a special branch of his philosophy, however, for he claimed that all philosophy can be conceived of as the philosophy of education. And it is certainly true that all the concepts we have discussed inform his thinking about education. He returned again and again to the subject of education, but the essential elements of his position can be found in *My Pedagogic Creed* (New York, 1897), *The School and Society* (Chicago, 1900), *The Child and the Curriculum* (Chicago, 1902), and especially in his comprehensive statement in *Democracy and Education* (New York, 1916).

It is essential to appreciate the dialectical context in which Dewey developed his educational ideas. He was critical of the excessively rigid and formal approach to education that dominated the practice of most American schools in the latter part of the nineteenth century. He argued that such an approach was based upon a faulty psychology in which the child was thought of as a passive creature upon whom information and knowledge had to be imposed. But Dewey was equally critical of the "new education," which was based on a sentimental idealization of the child. This child-orientated approach advocated that the child himself should pick and choose what he wanted to study. This approach also was based on a mistaken psychology, which neglected the immaturity of the child's experience. Education is, or ought to be, a continuous reconstruction of experience in which there is a development of immature experience toward experience funded with the skills and habits of intelligence. The slogan "Learn by Doing" was not intended as a credo for anti-intellectualism but, on the contrary, was meant to call attention to the fact that the child is naturally an active, curious, and exploring creature. A properly designed education must be sensitive to this active dimension of life and must guide the child, so that through his participation in different types of experience his creativity and autonomy will be cultivated rather than stifled.

The child is not completely malleable, nor is his natural endowment completely fixed and determinate. Like Aristotle, Dewey believed that the function of education is to encourage those habits and dispositions that constitute intelligence. Dewey placed great stress on creating the proper type of environmental conditions for eliciting and nurturing these habits. His conception of the educational process is therefore closely tied to the prominent role that he assigned to habit in human life. (For a detailed statement of the nature and function of habit, see *Human Nature and Conduct*, New York, 1922.) Education as the continuous reconstruction and growth of experience also develops the moral character of the child. Virtue is taught not by imposing values upon the child but by cultivating fair-mindedness, objectivity, imagination, openness to new experiences, and the courage to change one's mind in the light of further experience.

Dewey also thought of the school as a miniature society; it should not simply mirror the larger society but should be representative of the essential institutions of this society. The school as an ideal society is the chief means for social reform. In the controlled social environment of the school it is possible to encourage the development of creative individuals who will be able to work effectively to eliminate existing evils and institute reasonable goods. The school, therefore, is the medium for developing the set of habits required for systematic and open inquiry and for reconstructing experience that is funded with greater harmony and aesthetic quality.

Dewey perceived acutely the threat posed by unplanned technological, economic, and political development to the future of democracy. The natural direction of these forces is to increase human alienation and to undermine the shared experience that is so vital for the democratic community. For this reason, Dewey placed so much importance on the function of the school in the democratic community. The school is the most important medium for strengthening and developing a genuine democratic community, and the task of democracy is forever the creation of a freer and more humane experience in which all share and participate.

Ethics and social philosophy. In order to understand Dewey's moral philosophy, we must again focus on his concept of the situation. Man is a creature who by nature has values. There are things, states of affairs, and activities that he directly enjoys, prizes, or values. Moral choices and decisions arise only in those situations in which there are competing desires or a conflict of values. The problem that a man then confronts is to decide what he really wants and what course of action he ought to pursue. He cannot appeal to his immediate values to resolve the situation; he must evaluate or appraise the situation and the different courses of action open to him. This process of deliberation that culminates in a decision to act is what Dewey calls "valuation." But how do we engage in this process of valuation? We must analyze the situation as carefully as we can, imaginatively project possible courses of action, and scrutinize the consequences of these actions. Those ends or goods that we choose relative to a concrete situation after careful deliberation are reasonable or desirable goods. Our choices are reasonable to the extent that they reflect our developed habits of intelligence. Choices will be perverse or irrational if they are made on the basis of prejudice and ignorance. Dewey is fully aware that there are always practical limitations to our deliberations, but a person trained to deliberate intelligently will be prepared to act intelligently even in those situations that do not permit extended deliberation. When we confront new situations we must imagine and strive for new goals. As long as there is human life, there will always be situations in which there are internal conflicts that demand judgment, decision, and action. In this sense, the moral life of man is never completed, and the ends achieved become the means for attaining further ends. But lest we think that man is always striving for something that is to be achieved in the remote future, or never, Dewey emphasized that there are consummations—experiences in which the ends that we strive for are concretely realized.

It should be clear that such a view of man's moral life places a great deal of emphasis on intelligence. Dewey readily admitted his "faith in the power of intelligence to imagine a future which is a projection of the desirable in the present, and to invent the instrumentalities of its realization." It should also be clear that ethics conceived of in this manner blends into social philosophy. Valuation, like all inquiry, presupposes a community of shared experience in which there are common norms and procedures, and intelligent valuation is also a means for making such a community a concrete reality. Here, too, ends and norms are clarified, tested, and modified in light of the cumulative experience of the community. Furthermore, it is the objective of social philosophy to point the way to the development of those conditions that will foster the effective exercise of practical intelligence. The spirit that pervades Dewey's entire philosophy and finds its perfect expression in his social philosophy is that of the reformer or reconstructor, not the revolutionary. Dewey was always skeptical of panaceas and grand solutions for eliminating existing evils and injustices. But he firmly believed that with a realistic scientific knowledge of existing conditions and with a cultivated imagination, men could improve and ameliorate the human condition. To allow ourselves to drift in the course of events or to fail to assume our responsibility for continuous reconstruction of experience inevitably leads to the dehumanization of man.

Philosophy and civilization. Dewey presented a comprehensive and synoptic image of man and the universe. The entire universe consists of a multifarious variety of natural transactions. Man is at once continuous with the rest of nature and exhibits distinctive patterns of behavior that distinguish him from the rest of nature. His experience is also pervaded with qualities that are not reducible to less complex natural transactions. Thus, Dewey attempted to place man within the context of the whole of nature. In addition, Dewey was sensitive to the varieties of human experience. He sought to delineate the distinctive features of different aspects of experience, ranging from mundane practical experience to the religious dimension of experience. Within the tradition of philosophy Dewey may be characterized as a robust naturalist or a humanistic naturalist. His philosophy is both realistic and optimistic. There will always be conflicts, problems, and competing values within our experience, but with the continuous development of "creative intelligence" men can strive for and realize new ends and goals.

This synoptic view of man and the universe is closely related to Dewey's conception of the role of philosophy in civilization. Philosophy is dependent on, but should attempt to transcend, the specific culture from which it emerges. The function of philosophy is to effect a junction of the new and the old, to articulate the basic principles and values of a culture, and to reconstruct these into a more coherent and imaginative vision. Philosophy is therefore essentially critical and, as such, will always have work to do. For as the complex of traditions, values, accomplishments, and aspirations that constitute a culture changes, so must philosophy change. Indeed, in pointing the way to new ideals and in showing how these may be effectively realized, philosophy is one of the means for changing a culture. Philosophy is continually faced with the challenge of understanding the meaning of evolving cultures and civilizations and of articulating new projected ideals. The motif of reconstruction that runs throughout Dewey's investigations dominates his conception of the role of philosophy in civilization. He epitomized the spirit of his entire philosophical endeavor in his "plea for casting off of that intellectual timidity which hampers the wings of imagination, a plea for speculative audacity, for more faith in ideas, sloughing off a cowardly reliance upon those partial ideas to which we are wont to give the name facts." He fully realized that he was giving philosophy a more modest function than had been given by those who claimed that philosophy reveals an eternal reality. But such modesty is not incompatible with boldness in the maintenance of this function. As Dewey declared, "a combination of such modesty and courage affords the only way I know of in which the philosopher can look his fellow man in the face with frankness and humanity" (*Philosophy and Civilization*, p. 12).

Bibliography

The most exhaustive bibliography of John Dewey's writings is M. H. Thomas' *John Dewey: A Centennial Bibliography* (Chicago, 1962). This excellent guide includes a comprehensive listing of Dewey's writings, translations and reviews of his works, and a bibliography of books, articles, and dissertations about Dewey.

A less comprehensive bibliography of Dewey's writings can also be found in *The Philosophy of John Dewey*, P. A. Schilpp, ed. (Chicago, 1939).

The following secondary sources are helpful as general introductions to Dewey's life and philosophy. Richard J. Bernstein, *John Dewey* (New York, 1966) focuses on the concept of experience and nature. George R. Geiger, *John Dewey in Perspective* (New York, 1958) stresses the role of aesthetic experience as the key to Dewey's philosophy. Sidney Hook, *John Dewey: An Intellectual Portrait* (New York, 1939) captures both the spirit and letter of Dewey as a man, social reformer, and philosopher. Robert J. Roth, S. J., *John Dewey and Self-Realization* (Englewood Cliffs, N. J., 1962) shows the importance and meaning of religious experience for Dewey.

RICHARD J. BERNSTEIN

DIALECTIC. The term "dialectic" originates from the Greek expression for the art of conversation (διαλεκτικὴ τέχνη). So far as its great variety of meanings have anything in common, it is perhaps that dialectic is a method of seeking and sometimes arriving at the truth by reasoning, but even this general description, which to fit the variety of cases is so vague as to be valueless, fails to do justice to the Hegelian and Marxist notion of dialectic as a historical process. However, among the more important meanings of the term have been (1) the method of refutation by examining logical consequences, (2) sophistical reasoning, (3) the method of division or repeated logical analysis of genera into species, (4) an investigation of the supremely general abstract notions by some process of reasoning leading up to them from particular cases or hypotheses, (5) logical reasoning or debate using premises that are merely probable or generally accepted, (6) formal logic, (7) the criticism of the logic of illusion, showing the contradictions into which reason falls in trying to go beyond experience to deal with transcendental objects, and (8) the logical development of thought or reality through thesis and antithesis to a synthesis of these opposites. Meaning (2) is notably still current, and the term is often used in a pejorative sense.

In the following discussion the different kinds of dialectic will be elucidated in their historical order.

Socrates and his predecessors. Dialectic perhaps originated in the fifth century B.C., since Zeno of Elea, the author of the famous paradoxes, was recognized by Aristotle as its inventor (Diogenes Laërtius, *Lives* VIII, 57). Aristotle presumably had Zeno's paradoxes in mind, as they are outstanding examples of dialectic, in the sense of refutation of the hypotheses of opponents by drawing unacceptable consequences from those hypotheses. For example, it is unacceptable that Achilles never overtakes the tortoise; therefore, the hypothesis that leads to this conclusion must be rejected. Insofar as this method relies on the law of formal logic known as *modus tollens* (if p implies q, and q is false, then p is false), Zeno was a pioneer of logic, but there is no evidence that he could formulate the law itself; it was left to Aristotle later to state explicitly the principles that underlie this kind of dialectic, and thus to create the science of formal logic.

Dialectic as the use of such indirect logical arguments to defeat an opponent seems to have been used by Zeno for serious philosophical purposes, but it later became, in the hands of the Sophists, a mere instrument for winning a dispute. For example, the Sophist Protagoras claimed that he could "make the worse argument appear the better"; such an aim belongs rather to rhetoric than to logic or philosophy. This degenerate form of dialectic was named "eristic" by Plato (for example, in *Sophist* 231E) and others, from the word ἔρις (strife). Eristic came to make deliberate use of invalid argumentation and sophistical tricks, and these were ridiculed by Plato in his dialogue *Euthydemus,* which takes its name from an actual Sophist who appears in it as a user of eristic arguments. Aristotle, too, thought the Sophists worth answering in his book *De Sophisticis Elenchis* ("Sophistical Refutations"), although he sharply distinguished eristic from dialectic, dialectic being for him a respectable activity.

If, however, the lost work of Protagoras did begin, as several subsequent writers attest, with the claim that on every subject two opposite statements (λόγοι) could be made, and if the book continued with a content of statement and counterstatement, then Protagoras deserves to be considered the ancestor of the medieval or of the Hegelian dialectic rather than the father of eristic.

Socrates stands in contrast to the Sophists. Unlike them, he professed to be seeking the truth. But he was not above winning the argument, and what is called the *elenchus* was a major element in dialectic as practiced by him, if we are to accept as accurate the presentation of him in Plato's earlier dialogues. The Socratic *elenchus* was perhaps a refined form of the Zenonian paradoxes, a prolonged cross-examination which refutes the opponent's original thesis by getting him to draw from it, by means of a series of questions and answers, a consequence that contradicts it. This is a logically valid procedure, for it corresponds to the logical law "if p implies not-p, then not-p is true (that is, p is false)." Dialectic seems to have been, for Socrates, literally the art of discussion, a search for truth by question and answer; but the definition of a concept is the sort of truth that was typically sought by him, and he supplemented his *elenchus* with another technique, later called epagoge (ἐπαγωγή) by Aristotle. This consisted in leading the opponent on to a generalization by getting him to accept the truth of a series of propositions about particular cases. It may now be seen why, in discussing dialectic, Aristotle says "there are two innovations that may justly be ascribed to Socrates: epagogic arguments and universal definition" (*Metaphysics* M 4, 1078b). For Aristotle had a different conception of dialectic, and since *elenchus* goes back to Zeno, the two features he mentions are the only contributions made by Socrates to dialectic as Aristotle understood it. The Socratic irony, or pretense not to know anything and not to be conducting a refutation, was a personal feature of Socrates' dialectic and contributed nothing to later developments.

Plato. In the middle dialogues of Plato there occurs a development of the notion of dialectic beyond what we take to be typical of the historical Socrates. Even though Socrates is the protagonist, the views he is portrayed as putting forward are presumably those of Plato. Dialectic is regarded there as the supreme philosophical method, indeed the highest of human arts: it is "the coping-stone, as it were, placed above the sciences" (*Republic* 534E). In the *Cratylus* Plato had described the dialectician as "the man who knows how to ask and answer questions" (390C), and this view of dialectic as question and answer is the Socratic element which forms the single thread running through his altering conceptions of the method. Furthermore, dialectic always had the same subject matter: it sought the unchanging essence of each thing. But the kind of reasoning that Plato regarded as involved in dialectic seems to change: In the middle dialogues it was some kind of operation on hypotheses, whereas in the later ones (for example, *Phaedrus* and *Sophist*) there is, instead, an emphasis on division (διαίρεσις) as a method. Division in effect consists of a repeated analysis of genera into species, of more general notions into less general ones, as a way of arriving at a definition when no further division is possible. This process is complemented by the opposite process of synthesis or collection (συναγωγή).

Although Plato always spoke of dialectic in an extremely favorable manner, his discussion of it in *Republic* VI–VII marks a high point, as it is there made to be the distinguishing feature in the education of the philosopher-kings and is to be concerned eventually with the supreme Form, that of the Good. It is to reach certainty and overcome the need for hypotheses (*Republic* 511B). But the elevation of the sentiments expressed is matched by suitable vagueness as to the exact process involved, and the interpretation of the few words that are at all precise has been greatly disputed.

It may seem that if dialectic is a process of discussion, then it cannot be of any use for private thought. For Plato, however, there was no difference between the two: "Thought and speech are the same thing, but the silently occurring internal dialogue of the soul with itself has been specially given the name of thought" (*Sophist* 263E; see also *Theaetetus* 189E). However, Plato's most important pupil, Aristotle, was already taking a different view of the nature of thought and hence assigning a merely secondary role to dialectic: "Deception occurs to a greater extent when we are investigating with others than by ourselves, for an investigation with someone else is carried on by means of words, but an investigation in one's own mind is carried on quite as much by means of the thing itself" (*De Sophisticis Elenchis* 169a37). Dialectic was no longer to be the method of science.

Aristotle. The practice of dialectic was probably a major activity in Plato's Academy, to which Aristotle belonged from 367 B.C. until Plato's death in 347. Aristotle's *Topics* was apparently intended as an aid to this dialectical debate. It is a handbook for finding arguments to establish or demolish given positions, or *theses*, such as "Every pleasure is good," and while the particular theses used as examples in the *Topics* are no doubt borrowed from the debates in the Academy, the methods provided for dealing with them are completely general, that is, applicable to any thesis of the same form. The *Topics* is therefore the first systematic account of dialectic, and Aristotle indeed boasted that prior to his own treatment of the subject "it did not exist at all" (*De Sophisticis Elenchis* 183b36), and criticized the Sophists for giving teaching that was unsystematic (ἄτεχνος). His own trend toward generality and system had the effect that in the *Topics* Aristotle discovered many basic principles of formal logic, including some in the propositional calculus and in the logic of relations, but he hardly reached an explicit formal statement of them. A large part, at least, of this work was written before his discovery of the (categorical) syllogism, a type of argument for which he developed, in his *Analytics,* an elaborate system—the earliest system of formal logic—that superseded dialectic as a theory of demonstration. But even if Aristotle's formal logic developed as an alternative to his dialectic, it may still have arisen out of dialectic in some sense, since it has been argued that he discovered the syllogism as a result of reflection on Plato's method of division.

The distinguishing feature of dialectic for Aristotle was not so much the type of reasoning as the epistemological status of the premises. Reasoning is dialectical if its premises are opinions that are generally accepted by everyone or by the majority or by philosophers; if the premises merely *seem* probable, or if the reasoning is incorrect, then it is "eristic." Aristotelian dialectic is thus quite respectable; it has even been called a "logic of probability," a name which could be misleading because dialectic does not in fact involve inductive reasoning. However, dialectic is not good enough, Aristotle believed, to be a method of acquiring knowledge proper, or science. For that we require demonstration, which is valid reasoning that starts out from true and self-evident premises. The value of dialectic, according to Aristotle, is threefold: It is useful for intellectual training, for discussions with others based on their own premises, and for examining the unprovable first principles of the sciences. "Dialectic, being a process of criticism, contains the path to the principles of all inquiries" (*Topics* 101b3).

Stoics and medievals. Euclides of Megara (a contemporary of Plato) and his successors in that town were logicians of note, and the Megarian tradition in logic was continued by the Stoics. The Stoic logic was known as dialectic, perhaps because the initiators of their tradition had an interest in the Zenonian paradoxes and related reasoning. Under the headship of Chrysippus, who lived from 280 to 206 B.C., the Stoic school reached its zenith, and it was still going strong four centuries later. A saying is recorded from this period, that "if the gods had dialectic, it would be the dialectic of Chrysippus" (Diogenes Laërtius, *Lives* VII, 180). By "dialectic" the Stoics primarily meant formal logic, in which they particularly developed forms of inference belonging to what we now call the propositional calculus. But they applied the term "dialectic" widely: for them it also included the study of grammatical theory and the consideration of meaning-relations and truth. This widened scope, reflecting the special interests of the early Stoics, remained typical of the school; it was accepted by Cicero and perhaps overemphasized by Seneca, who wrote that dialectic "fell into two parts, meanings and words, that is, things said and expressions by which they are said"—*διαλεκτική in duas partes dividitur, in verba et significationes, id est in res quae dicuntur et vocabula quibus dicuntur* (*Epistulae Morales* 89, 17).

In the Middle Ages "dialectic" continued to be the ordinary name for logic: for example, the first medieval logical treatise was the *Dialectica* of Alcuin. But the word *logica* was also used; in fact, Abelard wrote a *Dialectica* and more than one *Logica.* As the works of Plato and Aristotle became known, the Scholastics took over various conceptions of dialectic, and the medieval disputation, by which university degree examinations were conducted, can be regarded as a remote descendant or revival of the debates in the Platonic Academy. The disputants maintained theses and antitheses, arguing mainly in syllogisms; the most significant difference from ancient practice was that the class of unacceptable consequences now included those propositions that were inconsistent with divine revelation.

Kant and his successors. In his *Critique of Pure Reason* (A61, B85) Kant asserted rather sweepingly that the actual employment of dialectic among the ancients was always as "the logic of illusion (*Logik des Scheins*)." He explained that he applied the term to logic as a critique of dialectical illusion. He entitled the second division of his Transcendental Logic "Transcendental Dialectic." This new kind of dialectic was concerned with exposing the illusion of transcendental judgments, that is, judgments which profess to pass beyond the limits of experience; but the illusion can never, he thought, be dispelled entirely, as it is natural and inevitable.

Although Kant, in his Transcendental Dialectic, had set out the antinomies of pure reason as four sets of thesis and antithesis, he did not call his resolution of the antinomies a synthesis. It was his successor Johann Gottlieb Fichte who, in his *Grundlage der gesamten Wissenschaftslehre* (Jena and Leipzig, 1794), first introduced into German philosophy the famed triad of thesis, antithesis, and synthesis. In this he was followed by Schelling, but not in fact by Hegel. Fichte did not believe that the antithesis could be deduced from the thesis; nor, on his view did the synthesis achieve anything more than uniting what both thesis and antithesis had established.

Hegel and his successors. Hegel is commonly supposed to have presented his doctrines in the form of the triad or three-step (*Dreischritt*) of thesis, antithesis, and synthesis. This view appears to be mistaken insofar as he did not actually use the terms; and even though he evinced a fondness for triads, neither his dialectic in general nor particular portions of his work can be reduced simply to a triadic pattern of thesis, antithesis, and synthesis. The legend of this triad in Hegel has been bolstered by some English translations which introduce the word "antithesis" where it is not required.

However, there is indeed a Hegelian dialectic, involving the passing over of thoughts or concepts into their opposites and the achievement of a higher unity. But if it is a process that arrives at a higher truth through contradictions, it does not constitute a new conception of dialectic. Hegel actually showed his awareness of the traditional notion by paying tribute to "Plato's *Parmenides*, probably the greatest masterpiece of ancient dialectic." And even the doctrine that dialectic is a world process—not merely a process of thought but also found in history and in the universe as a whole—was not wholly new, but goes back to Heraclitus and the Neoplatonist Proclus. Here again Hegel, with his interest in the history of philosophy, was aware of his predecessors. What seems to be genuinely new in Hegel's view of dialectic is the conception of a necessary movement. Dialectic was said to be "the scientific application of the regularity found in the nature of thought." The "passing over into the opposite" was seen as a natural consequence of the limited or finite nature of a concept or thing. The contradictions in thought, nature, and society, even though they are not contradictions in formal logic but conceptual inadequacies, were regarded by Hegel as leading by a kind of necessity, to a further phase of development.

Hegel has had an enormous influence not only on willing disciples but even on thinkers nominally in revolt against him, such as Kierkegaard (see HEGELIANISM). One of the most important offshoots of the Hegelian dialectic was the Marxist dialectic, in which, of course, "matter" was substituted for Hegel's "spirit" (see DIALECTICAL MATERIALISM).

Bibliography

GENERAL DISCUSSIONS

For general discussions of dialectic, see Paul Foulquié, *La Dialectique* (Paris, 1949); Eduard von Hartmann, *Ueber die dialektische Methode* (Berlin, 1868; 2d ed. 1910); Karl Dürr, "Die Entwicklung der Dialektik von Plato bis Hegel." *Dialectica*, Vol. 1 (1947); and Jonas Cohn, *Theorie der Dialektik* (Leipzig, 1923).

SOCRATES AND HIS PREDECESSORS

On Zeno, see H. D. P. Lee, *Zeno of Elea* (Cambridge, 1936); G. E. L. Owen, "Zeno and the Mathematicians," in *PAS*, Vol. 58 (1957–1958), 199–222; and John Burnet, *Early Greek Philosophy* (London, 1892; 4th ed., 1930). For the period before Socrates as a whole, see Burnet's *From Thales to Plato* (London, 1914). For criticisms of the Sophists, see Plato, *Euthydemus*, and Aristotle, *De Sophisticis Elenchis*, translated by W. A. Pickard-Cambridge in *The Works of Aristotle*, Vol. I (Oxford, 1928). On this whole phase of dialectic, see the extremely reliable work of William and Martha Kneale, *The Development of Logic* (Oxford, 1962), Ch. 1.

PLATO

The most helpful book on Plato's use of dialectic is Richard Robinson, *Plato's Earlier Dialectic* (Ithaca, N.Y., 1941; 2d ed., Oxford, 1953), but the word "earlier" occurs in its title because it contains no examination of the methods of division and synthesis which appear in some of Plato's later dialogues. For the original descriptions of the Platonic dialectic, see the Dialogues of Plato, *passim* (in any translation), but above all the *Republic*, Books VI–VII, especially 510–540 in the standard numbering. See also James Adam, *The Republic of Plato*, Vol. II (Cambridge, 1902; reissued, 1963), pp. 168–179; Richard Lewis Nettleship, *Lectures on the Republic of Plato* (London, 1901), pp. 277–289; Julius Stenzel, *Studien zur Entwicklung der Platonischen Dialektik von Sokrates zu Aristoteles* (Breslau, 1917; 2d ed., 1931), translated by D. J. Allan as *Plato's Method of Dialectic* (Oxford, 1940; reissued, New York, 1964); Francis M. Cornford, "Mathematics and Dialectic in the *Republic* VI–VII," in *Mind*, Vol. 41 (1932), 37–52, 173–190; R. S. Bluck, "ὑποθέσεις in the *Phaedo* and the Platonic Dialectic," in *Phronesis*, Vol. 2, No. 1 (1957), 21–31; D. W. Hamlyn, "The Communion of Forms and the Development of Plato's Logic," in *The Philosophical Quarterly*, Vol. 5 (1955), 289–302; Georges Rodier, "Les Mathématiques et la dialectique dans le système de Platon," in *Archiv für Geschichte der Philosophie*, Vol. 15 (1902), 479–490, and his "L'Évolution de la dialectique de Platon," in *Année philosophique* (1905), 49–73; D. S. Mackay, "The Problem of Individuality in Plato's Dialectic," in *University of California Publications in Philosophy*, Vol. 20 (1937), 131–154; and Juan A. Nuño Montes, *La dialéctica platónica* (Caracas, 1962).

ARISTOTLE

For the original account, see Aristotle, *Topica*, translated by W. A. Pickard-Cambridge in *The Works of Aristotle*, Vol. I (Oxford, 1928). The most accessible scholarly discussion of this phase is Ernst Kapp, *Greek Foundations of Traditional Logic* (New York, 1940). Important treatments of the controversial issues involved are Friedrich Solmsen, *Die Entwicklung der Aristotelischen Logik und Rhetorik* (Berlin, 1929), his "The Discovery of the Syllogism," in *Philosophical Review*, Vol. 50 (1941), 410–421, and his "Aristotle's Syllogism and Its Platonic Background," in *Philosophical Review*, Vol. 60 (1951), 563–571; and Paul Wilpert, "Aristoteles und die Dialektik," in *Kant-Studien*, Vol. 68 (1956), 247–284. There is also Livio Sichirollo, *Giustificazioni della dialettica in Aristotele* (Urbino, 1963).

STOICS AND MEDIEVALS

For a discussion of Stoic use of dialectic, see Benson Mates, *Stoic Logic* (Berkeley and Los Angeles, 1953). For a general account of the medieval phase and references to particular works, see William and Martha Kneale, *op. cit.*, Ch. 4. For the postmedieval rejection of dialectic, see Duane H. Berquist, "Descartes and Dialectics," in *Laval théologique et philosophique*, Vol. 20, No. 2 (1964), 176–204.

KANT AND HIS SUCCESSORS

Kant and his successors are discussed in Graham H. Bird, *Kant's Theory of Knowledge* (London, 1962); John E. Llewelyn, "Dialectical and Analytical Opposites," in *Kant-Studien*, Vol. 55 (1964), 171–174; and Richard Kroner, *Von Kant bis Hegel*, 2 vols. (Tübingen, 1921–1924).

HEGEL AND HIS SUCCESSORS

For general discussions of the Hegelian phase, see K. R. Popper, "What Is Dialectic?," in *Mind*, Vol. 49 (1940), 403–426, reprinted in Popper's *Conjectures and Refutations* (London, 1963); Sidney Hook, "What Is Dialectic?," in *Journal of Philosophy*, Vol. 26 (1929), 85–99, 113–123, his *From Hegel to Marx* (London, 1936), and his "Dialectic in Social and Historical Inquiry," in *Journal of Philosophy*, Vol. 36 (1939), 365–378; and Siegfried Marck, *Die Dialektik in der Philosophie der Gegenwart*, 2 vols. (Tübingen, 1929–1931). On dialectic in Hegel, see John M. E. McTaggart, *Studies in the Hegelian Dialectic* (Cambridge, 1896); G. R. G. Mure, *An Introduction to Hegel* (Oxford, 1940); and above all, John N. Findlay, "Some Merits of Hegelianism," in *PAS*, Vol. 56 (1955–1956), 1–24, and his *Hegel: A Re-examination* (London, 1958), and a valuable chapter by him on Hegel in D. J. O'Connor, ed., *A Critical History of Western Philosophy* (London, 1964). See also Gustav E. Mueller, "The Hegel Legend of Thesis–Antithesis–Synthesis," in *Journal of the History of Ideas*, Vol. 19 (1958), 411–414; Carl J. Friedrich, "The Power of Negation: Hegel's Dialectic and Totalitarian Ideology," in D. C. Travis, ed., *A Hegel Symposium* (Austin, Tex., 1962), pp. 13–35; and Walter Kaufmann, *Hegel* (New York, 1965). On Marx, see Harold B. Acton, *The Illusion of the Epoch: Marxism–Leninism as a Philosophical Creed* (London, 1955).

ROLAND HALL

DIALECTICAL MATERIALISM. Marxism–Leninism is the name given to the form of Marxist theory that is accepted and taught by the Russian and Chinese Communist parties and the Communist parties associated with them. Marxism–Leninism is both a view of the world as a whole and of human society and its development. The view of human society is called historical materialism, the name bestowed upon it by Friedrich Engels. The view of the world as a whole is called dialectical materialism, a title devised by G. V. Plekhanov, the Russian Marxist, and first used by him in an article published in 1891. Marxist–Leninists regard dialectical materialism as the basis of their philosophy and generally begin comprehensive expositions of that philosophy with an account of it. One might say that dialectical materialism constitutes the logic, ontology, and epistemology of Marxism–Leninism, and historical materialism its ethics, politics, and philosophy of history. Sometimes, however, the term "dialectical materialism" is used for the fundamentals of Marxism–Leninism as a whole. When dialectical materialism is thus conceived, the natural sciences are the working-out of dialectical materialism in the nonhuman sphere and historical materialism its working-out in the sphere of human society. But these slight differences do not affect the content of the theory.

MARX'S MATERIALISM

Approving references to materialism are prominent in Marx's writings, especially in the early works. In *The Holy Family* (1845), for instance, he argued that one branch of eighteenth-century French materialism developed into natural science and the other branch into socialism and communism. Thus he regarded "the new materialism," as he called it, as a source of the social movement which he believed was destined to revolutionize human life. Materialism, as Marx understood it, was very closely connected with social criticism and social development. One aspect of materialism that Marx supported was its rejection of idealist attempts to undermine and belittle sense experience. He held that there is something dishonest and irresponsible in philosophies which deny that sense experience reveals the existence of an independent material world; hence his view of knowledge was realist, both on philosophical and moral grounds. In taking this view he was much influenced by Ludwig Feuerbach. Like Feuerbach, Marx rejected speculative philosophy, or metaphysics, as we should call it today, on the ground that the truth about the world and society can only be discovered by the use of empirical scientific methods. In a broad sense of the term, therefore, Marx was a positivist, in that he denied the possibility of any knowledge of the world that is not based on sense experience. Hence, Marx's view of the world was naturalistic and opposed to any form of religion or supernaturalism. Again under the influence of Feuerbach, Marx held that belief in God, in an afterlife, and in heaven and hell cannot be rationally justified, but may be explained (indeed, explained away) in terms of the unfulfilled needs and hopes of men whose lives are frustrated by an oppressive social order. Marx held, too, that men are not immaterial souls conjoined with material bodies. In his view, psychophysical dualism is a relic of supernaturalism and must be rejected with it. Marx did not systematically develop this view as part of a philosophical argument but took it as the basis of his view, expressed in *The Holy Family* and in *The German Ideology* (1845–1846), that repression of the instincts and natural desires is bad. Marx, therefore, thought that thinking is inseparable from acting and that scientific advance and practical improvement are in principle bound up with one another. Marx's materialism, therefore, is very wide in scope, combining empiricism, realism, belief in the use of scientific methods pragmatically conceived, rejection of supernaturalism, and rejection of mind–body dualism. Animating these aspects of his view is the conviction that they support and justify the socialist diagnosis of social ills and the prediction that a communist form of society must come.

Marx was very much influenced by the philosophy of Hegel. For example, in *The Holy Family* he borrowed almost verbatim some arguments from Hegel's *Encyclopedia* against abstract and unrealistic thinking, and his earliest, unfinished sketch of his theory of man and society, the so-called *Economic and Philosophical Manuscripts* (1844), was both a critique of political economy and a critique of the philosophy of Hegel. Marx's interest in Hegel continued throughout his life. In a letter to Engels in 1858 Marx wrote that he had been looking at Hegel's *Logic* and would like, if he had time, to write a short work setting out what was wrong and what was valuable in Hegel's method. Later, in the Preface to the second edition of Volume I of *Capital*, Marx referred to "the rational kernel" of Hegel's dialectical method and said that in *Capital* he had "toyed with the use of Hegelian terminology when discussing the theory of value." This sentence does not indicate a very strong attachment to Hegel's dialectic, for "toyed with" (*kokettierte sogar hier und da*) is appropriate to a superficial liaison, and the word "terminology" (*Ausdrücksweise*) might be meant to contrast with the substance of what is being said. But although Marx was as much opposed to the speculative element in Hegelianism as any professed positivist could have been, he was deeply influenced by the Hegelian dialectical method. Jean Hippolyte has shown in his *Études sur Marx et Hegel* (Paris, 1955) how very closely the structure of *Capital* is linked with Marx's earlier, more consciously Hegelian writings, so that some of the Hegelian substance persists, although the Hegelian terminology is less apparent. One important Hegelian legacy is the view that social development takes place through struggle and opposition. Another is that the transition from one important form of society to another is by means of sudden leaps rather than by merely gradual stages. Thus Marx considered that different social laws applied at different historical epochs. Again, Marx shared Hegel's aversion to abstraction and his predilection for total views, but in this he was at one with Comte as well as with Hegel. These views of Marx's, however, related to the theory of human society. He showed little inclination to linger over questions of ontology. There is a reference in Volume I of *Capital* to the "law discovered by Hegel in his *Logic*, that at a certain point what have been purely quantitative changes become qualitative," and at this point Marx said that some chemical changes take place in accordance with this law. However, Marx left it to Engels to pursue the matter.

ENGELS AND DIALECTICAL MATERIALISM

Engels took up the law of quantity and quality in his *Herr Eugen Dühring's Revolution in Science* (1878), generally known as *Anti-Dühring*, which had appeared as a series of articles in the Leipzig *Vorwärts* in 1877. Engels' work was directed against Eugen Dühring, a well-known non-Marxist socialist and publicist, who had vigorously criticized some Hegelian features in Marxist writers as being speculative, metaphysical, and unscientific. Thus Engels, like Marx, felt called upon to defend the Hegelianism of his youth, although, again like Marx, he claimed to have purged it of its speculative and idealist elements. In the Preface to the second edition of *Anti-Dühring* (1885) Engels stated that he had read the whole of the manuscript to Marx before it was printed and that Chapter 10 of Part II (on economics and its history) had been written by Marx himself and abridged by Engels. This chapter has no direct relevance to dialectical materialism and thus has some significance as an indication of Marx's own interests.

Philosophy of nature. Engels apologized in a general way in the Preface to the second edition of *Anti-Dühring* for inadequacies in his knowledge of theoretical natural science, although he retracted nothing. He also spoke with approval of "the old philosophy of nature." By this he meant a philosophical examination of the phenomena of the natural world claiming to be more fundamental and general in scope than the particular researches of individual men of science. Such inquiries were more frequent at a time when the term "philosopher" was applied to philosophers and scientists alike and the role of the natural scientist was less definitely specified than it became in the nineteenth and twentieth centuries. Engels alluded to Hegel's contributions to the philosophy of nature in the second main triad of the *Encyclopedia* and called attention in particular to Section 270 in which Hegel criticized Newton's theory of forces. Hegel, like Goethe and Schelling (and William Blake), was highly critical of Newton's cosmological theories, and Engels believed that Hegel, at any rate, was being justified by subsequent researches. It should be noted, therefore, that Engels had no objection to the practice of philosophizing about the nature of the physical world but, on the contrary, was consciously reviving an older, and apparently abandoned, intellectual tradition. By doing this, he introduced into the Marxist theory of nature one of its most characteristic features: the claim that the specialized sciences of nature need to be supplemented by a unified philosophy of nature and that as they develop, the natural sciences are constantly verifying the views first propounded by Hegel in his *Logic* and in his *Encyclopedia.*

From 1873 onward Engels had been studying the natural sciences with a view to writing a comprehensive work on the dialectical characteristics of the material world. Part of what he did was incorporated into *Anti-Dühring*, but much of his more detailed work remained unpublished until 1925, when an edition of the surviving manuscripts was published by the Marx–Engels Institute in Moscow under the title *Dialectics of Nature.* This edition was found to be faulty in various ways, and corrected versions were subsequently published and translated. The work contains, *inter alia*, an essay on electricity (a subject much favored by Schelling and other romantics), in which Engels says that the basic thought of Hegel and Michael Faraday is the same; an attack on parapsychology as "the shallowest empiricism" and a proposal that it be rejected outright on general grounds of theory; notes on infinite series and infinite numbers, which he takes to prove that the world is both infinite and contradictory; and sketches for an attack on Ludwig Büchner and other nonsocialist, nondialectical materialists popular during the second half of the nineteenth century. Engels' criticism of Büchner is particularly interesting since, among a series of passages probably intended to document *Anti-Dühring*, there is a quotation from Büchner's *Kraft und Stoff* in which, while attacking supernaturalism and idealist philosophy, Büchner wrote: "It is needless to observe that our expositions have nothing in common with the conceptions of the old 'philosophy of nature.' The singular attempts to construe nature out of philosophy instead of from observation have failed, and brought the adherents of that school into such discredit that the name 'philosopher of nature' has become a byeword and a nickname." Engels regarded this as an "attack on philosophy" and accused Büchner of "shallow materialist popularisation." Engels made his own attitude quite clear by appending passages from Hegel's "Philosophy of Nature."

Engels on Marxist materialism. After Marx's death in 1883 Engels was occupied in editing the unpublished parts of *Capital*, but in 1886, in some articles that appeared in the Social Democratic journal *Die Neue Zeit*, he turned his attention once more to fundamental philosophical issues. These articles were published in 1888 in book form under the title *Ludwig Feuerbach and the Outcome of Classical German Philosophy.* In this work Engels set out to explain what sort of materialism Marxist materialism is and to show how it is related to the Hegelian philosophy. Engels renewed his support for the dialectical structure of Hegel's philosophy, although, of course, he rejected its idealist aspects. There is an account of Engels' epistemology, in which a pragmatistic point of view is emphasized.

Mind and matter. According to the argument of *Ludwig Feuerbach* there are two and only two fundamental but opposing philosophical alternatives: idealism, according to which mind is primary in the universe and matter is created by, or dependent upon, mind; and materialism, according to which matter is the primary being and mind the subordinate and dependent feature of the world. It will be seen that in stating this view Engels extended the term "idealism" beyond its usual philosophical meaning to comprise not only such views as Berkeley's immaterialism and Hegel's absolute idealism but also any form of theism.

Thus, in Engels' classification, St. Thomas Aquinas and Descartes would both be regarded as idealists because they both held that an immaterial deity created the material world. It should be noted that in this view mind is held to be secondary but not nonexistent. Engels took the widely held natural-scientific point of view that there was once a time when only matter existed and that mind evolved from it and must remain dependent upon it. He did not hold the theory of reductive materialism, according to which mind is just a form of matter.

Knowledge and perception. In *Ludwig Feuerbach* Engels also gave a brief account of knowledge and sense perception. He considered that in sense perception the material things in the neighborhood of the percipient's body are somehow "reflected" in his brain "as feelings, instinct, thoughts, volitions." Engels recognized that the theory that in perception the immediate object of awareness is a "reflection" could lead to agnosticism or idealism, for a skeptic could question whether we can ever know of the existence of material things at all if all that we directly apprehend are reflections of them. This, indeed, is a line of thought that Berkeley developed in criticizing Locke's theory that it is ideas, not physical things, that are directly apprehended. Engels' answer was that what must dispel any such doubts is "practice, viz. experiment and industry." His discussion is vague, but he appears to have thought that skeptical doubts about the existence of material things are rendered untenable by a consideration of what we do to and with things. A skeptic's or idealist's practice belies his theories. Furthermore, Engels held that the truth of scientific theories about the material world is established by the power they give men to manufacture new substances and things and to bring the forces of nature under human control. "If we are able to prove the correctness of our conception of a natural process by making it ourselves, bringing it into being out of its conditions and using it for our own purposes into the bargain, then there is an end of the Kantian incomprehensible 'thing-in-itself'" (*Ludwig Feuerbach*, pp. 32–33). Engels appears to have conflated the problem of our perception of the external world with the problem of how scientific laws are established, but it is clear that he believed that the notion of practice can help to solve them both. In the Preface to *Ludwig Feuerbach* Engels printed for the first time, under the title *Theses on Feuerbach*, some jottings made by Marx in 1845. The doctrine of the philosophical importance of practice is stated in these theses, particularly in the first, second, fifth, and eleventh. One of the things that Marx appears to have been asserting in them is that perception is a deed or activity of the perceiving corporeal man and not merely a passivity of an immaterial mind. In 1892, in the Introduction to some chapters from *Anti-Dühring* published separately under the title *Socialism: Utopian and Scientific*, Engels developed this view, arguing that perception is a more or less successful action on the world.

Attack on "vulgar materialists." Another feature of Engels' materialism is its opposition to the theories of those whom he called in *Ludwig Feuerbach* "vulgarising pedlars," and who, in later Marxist philosophy, are called "vulgar materialists." These were a group of German writers and lecturers, of whom Büchner was one, who argued that materialism was the inevitable consequence of natural science in general and of physiology in particular. Engels objected that they wasted too much time arguing that God does not exist. He also objected that they identified thought with brain processes. Furthermore, they failed to recognize the social, indeed the socialist, implications of materialism. But primarily he objected that theirs was a mechanical materialism. A consideration of this objection brings us to a central feature of Engels' dialectical materialism.

By mechanical materialism Engels meant the type of materialism current in the eighteenth century, when the most highly developed natural science was mechanics. According to this view, all the most complex phenomena of nature, including life and mind, can be reduced to the arrangement and rearrangement of material particles. The most complex beings can be nothing but arrangements of the ultimate simple ones, so that chemical combination, life, mind, and thought are no more than increasingly elaborate applications of mechanical principles. According to Engels, in saying that everything is reducible to the interaction of forces, the vulgar materialists were anachronistically upholding this eighteenth-century view, whereas the natural sciences of the nineteenth century, in developing chemistry and biology, went beyond those of the eighteenth century. In merely mechanical mixtures the original components remain side by side with each other, but in chemical combinations new substances result from the joining of their ingredients. The theory of biological evolution showed that new forms of life have emerged from the simpler forms, not merely more complex ones.

Mechanical materialism itself is a form of what Engels, following Hegel, called the "metaphysical" attitude of thought. Engels' source in Hegel is the phrase "the former metaphysics," by which Hegel referred to the philosophical method used by Christian Wolff and others in the eighteenth century in trying to prove important truths about the world and the human soul by the use of definitions and axioms and allegedly strict deductions. Engels agreed with Hegel that this quasi-mathematical method was inappropriate in philosophy and added that it was inappropriate in science too. In *Anti-Dühring* Engels said that in the the metaphysical mode of thinking, "things and their mental images, ideas" are regarded as isolated and fixed; things either exist or do not exist; and positive and negative exclude one another. But this, he held, is to overlook the changefulness and interconnections of things. Collecting distinct items of information and neglecting the aspect of process helped natural science to get started but was only a preliminary stage toward grasping the world in all its interconnections, processes, beginnings and endings, and contradictions. Mechanical materialism is a fruit of metaphysical thinking. Metaphysical thinking was, in the Hegelian philosophy, and then in the writings of Marx, superseded by dialectical thinking; and this was, in Engels' view, another way of saying that mechanical materialism must be superseded by dialectical materialism. Engels believed that nineteenth-century biology and chemistry had developed along lines that Hegel had foreseen and required. In particular, he referred to passages in Hegel's *Logic* and *Encyclopedia* according to which a fuller understanding is gained when the category of mechanism is left behind and replaced by the higher categories of life. In Hegel's "Philosophy of Nature," to which Engels' *Dialectics of Nature* so often refers, the mechanical forms are succeeded by physical ones that include "chemical process" and electrical phenomena, and these by "the organic." It is this sequence that provided the framework for Engels' philosophy of nature.

Engels on dialectics. Since dialectical thinking is, in Engels' view, opposed to metaphysical thinking, it is thinking which attempts to grasp things in their interrelationships and in the totality to which they belong, in the process of change, of being born and of dying, in their conflicts and contradictions. Furthermore, it is thinking which recognizes the emergence of novelty and which sees such emergences as sudden, even catastrophic. Dialectical thinking, he also held, was becoming more and more apparent as the natural sciences progressed. Scientific discoverers were dialecticians without knowing it.

Contradictions in nature. In *Anti-Dühring* Engels expounded his dialectical philosophy of nature in some detail. Dühring had criticized the Hegelian elements of Marx's thought. In particular he had argued that contradiction is a logical relationship and that it is absurd to suppose that it can be a relationship between things or events in the natural world. In Part I, Chapter 12 of *Anti-Dühring* Engels endeavored to defend the dialectical theory against this objection. First, he said that the view that there could be no contradictions in nature rests upon the assumption of "the former metaphysics" that things are "static and lifeless." Then he argued that when we consider things in movement and in their effects upon one another, the dialectical view has to be adopted. "Movement itself," he wrote, "is a contradiction: even simple mechanical change of place can only come about through a body at one and the same moment of time being both in one place and in another place, being in one and the same place and also not in it. And the continuous assertion and simultaneous solution of this contradiction is precisely what motion is." Engels also maintained that what is true of mechanical change of place is "even more true of the higher forms of motion of matter, and especially of organic life and its development." Engels had argued in Part I, Chapter 8 that in absorbing and excreting nutriment living matter at each moment is "itself and at the same time something else." Engels also held that there are real contradictions in "higher mathematics," where straight lines and curves may be identical. (He probably had in mind Section 119 of Hegel's *Encyclopedia.*) Similarly, Engels said that the square root of minus one is not only a contradiction but "a real absurdity."

Engels' claim that movement is in itself contradictory is based on a passage from Hegel's *Science of Logic* in which it is argued that it is not sufficient, if something is to move, for it to be *here–now* and then, after that, *there–then,* for this would merely be for it to be at rest first in the one place and then in the other. For it to move, Hegel concluded, a body must be "here and not here in the same now" and must "be and yet not be in the same here" (*Science of Logic,* Book II, Sec. 1, Ch. 2, C). Hegel was discussing Zeno, who had argued that since movement is contradictory, what is real cannot move. Hegel in this passage accepted Zeno's arguments that movement is contradictory, but unlike Zeno concluded that since there is movement, movement "is an existing contradiction." Hegel's views on contradiction are difficult to understand and have been interpreted in various ways. If intended to argue that contradictory propositions could both be true, that "both p and not-p," then he was wrong and so was Engels in following him. For it can be proved that from any pair of contradictory propositions any conclusion we like can be deduced and hence that if contradictories are true, *anything* can be true. In this logical sense the term "contradiction" has its appropriate use in thought or discourse, as Dühring had argued. In saying that something both is and is not in the same place at the same time, that it is true both that it is in P at time t and that it is not in P at time t, the whole negating force of the word "not" is lost. Either, then, Hegel's philosophy has no value or he must have meant by "contradiction" something different from what formal logicians mean by it. It is likely enough that it is the second alternative that is correct. In attacking Dühring, Engels seems to have committed himself to the first alternative. He adopted a speculative, nonempirical thesis, for whereas movement is something that can be observed in natural things and events, contradiction is not observable in them. What Engels did in his argument about contradiction in the nature of things was to provide one of Zeno's paradoxes with a merely verbal, and indeed absurd, "solution."

It appears that Engels' doctrine on this matter is now being reinterpreted or abandoned. This process began with an article on Zeno's paradoxes by the famous Polish logician Casimir Ajdukiewicz. When this article appeared in Poland in 1948, dialectical materialists were forced to take account of his arguments. In order to do so they granted that "contradiction" does not mean "logical contradiction" when applied to what exists in nature. This view is adopted by the Russian authors of *The Fundamentals of Marxism–Leninism: Manual* (English translation, Moscow, no date, but later than 1960), who write: "Contradictions due to incorrect thinking should not be confused with objective contradictions existing in objective things. Although the word 'contradiction' is the same in both cases, it means different things" (pp. 99–100).

Quantity and quality. Another dialectical law of nature that Engels made much of in his *Anti-Dühring* is that according to which certain of the changes in nature take place suddenly and abruptly rather than by gradual accretion. The simplest instances of this sort of change are the changes of water into ice as its temperature is lowered to the freezing point and into steam as its temperature is raised to the boiling point. The ice and steam do not come into existence gradually and *pari passu* with the gradual lowering and raising of the temperature, but appear all at once as soon as the freezing or boiling point has been reached. Other examples of the principle were given by Engels: the sudden transformation of one chemical substance into another in the course of chemical combination; the melting points of metals; the transformation of mechanical motion into heat; the necessity for a sum of money to exceed a certain amount before it can become capital; the fact, reported by Napoleon, that whereas two Mamelukes were more than a match for three Frenchmen, a thousand Frenchmen were more than a match for fifteen hundred Mamelukes. One very general idea in all this is that gradual alterations in the quantity of something are not necessarily accompanied by a merely gradual alteration in its characteristics. Apart from this, Engels had in mind the evolutionary scheme of development from simpler forms of matter, like gases, to more distinctive and varied forms, like the many kinds of solids, plants, and animals. This development is not a mere rearrangement of otherwise unchanging particles or elements but is the emergence of new features out of the old, even though the later qualities could not have emerged unless the earlier and simpler ones had first existed. The emerged qualities, however, are not reducible to those from which they have emerged. The point at which changes in a single quality transform it into a new one Engels called a "nodal line." He also said that there is a "leap" from one quality to another.

Once again Engels was following Hegel very closely. The account in *Anti-Dühring* is based upon Sec. 108 of the *Encyclopedia* and Book I, Division 3, Chapter 2, *B* of the *Science of Logic*, where Hegel discussed the category of "measure." In these passages Hegel tried to show the part played by proportion in the constitution of things. He gave the examples of water turning, at critical points or nodal lines, into ice or steam, and of chemical combinations and constant proportions, which Engels and Marx repeated later. He also instanced birth and death, the acquisition of new properties by numbers as the series of natural numbers develops, and the acquisition of new features by the notes of a musical scale. He gave a moral example, based on Aristotle, of slight changes that turn virtues into vices, carelessness into crime, and so on. He even gave a political example, borrowed from Montesquieu, of the relation of a type of constitution to the population of a state. In the *Encyclopedia* Hegel also referred to the ancient Greek puzzles about the point at which a man becomes bald or at which a number of grains of wheat become a heap. Interesting as these examples are, they are extremely disparate. The grains of wheat example is partly a question of how many grains we shall *call* a heap, and this is to some extent a matter of decision. The concepts of a heap or of baldness are rather vague. The examples of a series of gradual physical changes succeeded by a total transformation of quality are clearly of interest to Engels because of the analogy to revolutionary social change by contrast with gradual alteration. Undoubtedly the social examples had impressed Hegel, who had called attention to the gradual steps that lead up to an explosive revolutionary break in the Preface to the *Phenomenology of Mind*, where he wrote: "This gradual disintegration which did not alter the general look and aspect of the whole is interrupted by the sunrise which, in a single flash, brings to view the form and structure of the new world."

In itself, whether there are or are not nodal lines and constant proportions in the physical world would seem to have no logical connection with the way in which the social order changes, unless, indeed, it is held that human society really is, or is reducible to, physical events—and this is in conflict with Engels' general rejection of reductive materialism. If, then, this law is not an expression of a view that is inconsistent with Engel's main view, it would seem to serve an almost animistic purpose. Sudden revolutionary change, he seems to be suggesting, is a fundamental character of the universe as a whole, so that when we urge revolution, we have the universe behind us. That the view at any rate serves this purpose may be seen from Stalin's subsequent impatience with it. When socialism is established, it is natural for the socialist leaders not to wish to think in terms of their own disappearance and of the emergence of still further social revolutions. Hence, Stalin, in his famous article on linguistics, wrote scornfully of "comrades who have an infatuation for explosions."

Interpenetration of opposites. In addition to the law of transformation of quantity into quality, Engels mentioned two other laws of dialectics, the law of the interpenetration of opposites and the law of the negation of the negation. The first of these laws was already touched upon in the exposition of the theory of contradictions in nature and of the deficiencies of the metaphysical point of view. Although Engels mentioned it in the *Dialectics of Nature*, he did not discuss it as such, and in *Anti-Dühring* his emphasis was on the other two laws, to each of which he devoted a chapter. The law of the interpenetration of opposites (which was later called the law of the unity and struggle of opposites) seems to have been intended to provide an explanation of why there is any change or development at all. An idea behind it is that in the absence of all tension everything would remain exactly as it is, since there would be nothing to provoke any change. Change takes place because the world does not consist of isolated, self-sufficient, independent particulars, but of opposing forces overcoming or being overcome. Contradiction, or opposition, is in this view the motive force both of natural and of human history.

Negation of the negation. The law of the negation of the negation was more specifically emphasized by Engels. He was able to quote from a passage in Marx's *Capital* in which it is said that when, as a result of competition between capitalists, the few remaining giant capitalist enterprises find themselves confronted by a poverty-stricken proletariat, the latter will rise and expropriate the former, the expropriators will be expropriated. "Capitalist production," wrote Marx, "begets, with the inexorability of a Law of Nature, its own negation. It is the negation of the negation." According to Engels in *Anti-Dühring*, the law of the negation of the negation is "an extremely general—and for this reason extremely comprehensive and important—law of development of nature, history and thought, a law which . . . holds good in the animal and plant kingdoms, in geology, in mathematics, in history and in philosophy." The law is illustrated, according to Engels, by every case in which a plant has seeds that germinate and result in the growth of further plants. "But what is the normal life-process of this plant? It grows, flowers, is fertilised and finally once more produces grains of barley, and as soon as these have ripened the stalk dies, is in its turn negated. As a result of this negation of the negation we have once again the original grain of barley, but not as a single unit, but ten, twenty or thirty fold" (*Anti-Dühring*, p. 152). One idea in this very famous passage is that out of what looks like death and destruction there arises something better and more various. (Engels in fact wrote of "qualitatively better seeds which produce more beautiful flowers.")

In his early book *The Poverty of Philosophy* (1847) Marx had quoted the Latin phrase *mors immortalis*, that is, "deathless death," and Engels similarly regarded progress as taking place through continual destruction and amplified renewal. What holds for plants obviously holds for animals. Geology illustrates the law, too, for it describes "a series of negated negations, a series arising from the successive shattering of old and depositing of new rock formations." The same law appears in mathematics. A is negated by $-A$, and "if we negate that negation by multiplying $-A$ by $-A$ we get A^2, i.e., the original positive magnitude but at a higher degree, raised to its second power" (*Anti-Dühring*, p. 153). Engels even found the law operating in the history of philosophy. In early philosophy, he held, there is a simple, natural form of materialism according to which matter is the source of everything. This form of materialism was negated by idealism, which rightly showed that mind is not the same as matter, but wrongly held that matter is dependent upon mind. In its turn, idealism is negated by "modern materialism, the negation of the negation," which contains in itself two thousand years of philosophical development. Engels believed that in "modern materialism," i.e., dialectical materialism, philosophy as previously understood is destroyed and yet preserved in the positive sciences.

This law, like the law of the transformation of quantity into quality, draws together some extremely disparate types of being. Is it likely, indeed, does it make sense to say, that the same principle is exemplified in a rule for operating on algebraical symbols and in the relationship of natural materialism, idealism, and dialectical materialism? One instance of the law that has given rise to much discussion is that of the grain of barley. What is it that negates what, and what is comprised in the negation of the negation? This problem was discussed by the Russian Marxist G. V. Plekhanov in his *The Development of the Monist View of History* (1895), in which he defended Engels' view against the criticisms of another Russian, N. K. Mikhailovski, who had made fun of the idea that, as he put it, "oats grow according to Hegel." In his account of Engels' argument, Mikhailovski took it that it is the stalk which negates the seed, and Plekhanov accused him of misquotation and asserted that it is the whole plant which does the negating. Plekhanov argued further that Engels' account of this botanical negation of the negation was supported by an authoritative textbook of botany, Van Tieghem's *Traité de botanique* (Paris, 1891), which had recently appeared. The whole discussion is entertaining but ludicrous. For the main difficulty about the law of the negation of the negation is that it can be made to fit almost anything by carefully choosing what are to count as the negating terms. The prime interest in the law is that it is intended to give support to the view that human progress is by means of destruction that leads to better things.

Engels' philosophical legacy. Engels was deeply interested in the advances of the sciences and believed that as a result of them nineteenth-century materialism had to be very different from earlier types of materialism. But Engels was drawn in two different directions. On the one hand, he sought to establish a naturalistic, scientific view of the world, and this led him in the same direction as the positivists. On the other hand, he was attracted by Hegel's dialectical method and by the romantic dream of a philosophy of nature, and this led him to regard the positivist outlook as thin and unadventurous. Like Marx, he deplored the conservative social tendencies of Auguste Comte and considered Hegel by far the better philosopher. Nevertheless, Engels did adopt one important positivist thesis, the thesis that knowledge of the world can be obtained only by the methods of the special sciences, so that all that can survive of philosophy is logic and the philosophy of the sciences. Thus, at the beginning of *Anti-Dühring* he wrote: "What still independently survives of all former philosophy is the science of thought and its laws—formal logic and dialectics. Everything else is merged in the positive science of nature and history." It should be noted that Engels here used the very adjective "positive" that had been formerly used by Saint-Simon and Comte. Although the positivists said nothing of "dialectics," Engels' point of approach from Hegelianism to positivism was his claim that the positive sciences make use of the dialectical method. But Engels, as we have seen, searched the sciences for examples of the dialectic and so applied his terms that he could not fail to find them there. This association of a positivist view of philosophy with what positivists would describe as a "metaphysical" view of the sciences was to remain a permanent feature of dialectical materialism.

Engels also bequeathed a problem about the nature of logic. Was formal logic disproved or rendered nugatory by the dialectical logic that was coming to fruition in the nineteenth century? In holding that there are existent contradictions Engels seemed willing to go against formal logic, but he also thought that formal logic would remain as a part of philosophy alongside dialectics. His position was complicated by the fact that in *Dialectics of Nature* he criticized formal logic as being "metaphysical" in the Hegelian sense already considered. As a result, controversy among exponents of dialectical materialism about the status of formal logic—by which they generally mean traditional Aristotelian logic—has been constantly renewed.

LENIN'S CONTRIBUTIONS

Lenin's great political achievements, as well as his deep philosophical interest, secured a respectful acceptance for his own philosophical views. And there is some appropriateness in the fact that Lenin's name, rather than Engels', accompanies that of Marx in the name of the whole doctrine of Marxism–Leninism, since Lenin absorbed and re-emphasized Engels' views before superseding him as a founding father.

Lenin's main contributions to dialectical materialism are the doctrine of *partiinost* ("party spirit" or "partisanship"), his elaborations of the Marxist theory of knowledge and of matter, and his renewed emphasis upon dialectics.

"Partiinost." Lenin briefly formulated the doctrine of *partiinost* as early as 1895, in the course of a controversy with the nonorthodox Marxist reformer Peter B. Struve, who had said that philosophical views were not a matter of controversy between parties but could be shared by members of opposing parties. Lenin wrote that *partiinost* is included in materialism and that no genuine adherent of materialism could remain uncommitted to the proletarian cause. In this particular context Lenin seems to have been thinking primarily of historical materialism; it is clear from his later writings, however, that he thought that the Marxist should never approach philosophical theories with detachment but should adopt or reject them in the light of their effects on the attainment of socialism. There are several points to be noted in Lenin's view. In the first place he held that dialectical materialism is not merely a theory but a form of action for the establishment of socialism. Thus, a dialectical materialist is necessarily a socialist, and his view of the world is inseparable from his efforts to promote the proletarian cause. In the second place, Lenin held that a socialist intellectual cannot be indifferent to philosophical matters. He is not a complete socialist unless he is a materialist, and a materialist of the right kind. Hence, the leaders of the socialist movement must always be on the alert to protect its doctrines against contamination by philosophical idealism. (This last is a doctrine which Stalin strictly enforced.) A fourth point on which Lenin laid great stress is that idealism is fundamentally supernaturalistic, however tenuous the connection between certain forms of it and religion may appear to be on the surface. In attacking idealism, wherever and however it appears in the socialist literature, what is really being attacked is religion and the antisocialist class forces that uphold it.

The doctrine of *partiinost* derives from Marx's and Engels' theory of ideologies. Ideologies, in their view, are systems of ideas whose function is to defend and to justify the class interests of those who believe in them and teach them, and philosophical systems are ideologies in this sense. Bourgeois ideologies serve to promote bourgeois interests, and the way to criticize them is not primarily by intellectual refutation—this will have little or no effect as long as bourgeois class interests remain—but by unmasking the motives behind them. This view is supported by the Marxist doctrine of the unity of theory and practice. In writing a philosophical book a man is taking part in the social struggle, and in a society divided into classes he is of necessity promoting or endeavoring to promote some class attitude. Lenin considered that Marxists, who understand what is going on in the ideological sphere, should do deliberately and consciously what is so often done unknowingly. This attitude was powerfully expressed in his *Materialism and Empirio-Criticism* (1909). Lenin thought that certain members of the Russian Social Democratic party were spreading what were essentially idealist philosophical views, and he set out to put them right. These Marxists (false Marxists, as Lenin thought) were adopting, under the title of empiriocriticism, the phenomenalist theories of Ernst Mach and Richard Avenarius. In doing so, according to Lenin, they were adopting a cryptoidealist philosophy which could weaken the Marxist movement by dissipating its materialism. "Marx and Engels," wrote Lenin, "were partisans in philosophy from start to finish; they were able to detect the deviations from materialism and concessions to idealism and fideism in each and every 'new tendency'" (p. 352). Thus, *Materialism and Empirio-Criticism* was largely a diatribe intended to crush a view held to be dangerous to the party.

Knowledge and matter. Lenin's *Materialism and Empirio-Criticism* is not only a partisan polemic but also the book in which Lenin expounded his views about knowledge and the nature of matter. It was pointed out above that some Russian social democrats had taken up ideas from the writings of Mach and Avenarius. Mach and Avenarius had tried to put forward as consistently empiricist a view as possible. Mach sought to eliminate from physics all notions that were not capable of direct or indirect verification in sense experience, and Avenarius sought for the terms in which the simplest and most economical explanations can be given. They both concluded that fundamentally the statements of science are statements of what people do experience or will experience and that scientific laws state how such experiences are correlated with one another. To the most elementary of these experiences Mach gave the name "sensations," and empiriocriticism amounted to phenomenalism, the view that material things are actual or possible sensations. Mach's theory of scientific knowledge is not unlike that of the idealist philosopher George Berkeley, who also sought to eliminate from the body of scientific knowledge any conceptions that could not be referred to sensations, or "ideas" (as he called sensations). Mach recognized the similarity between his view of science and that of Berkeley but pointed out that his view differed from Berkeley's in that he did not hold, as Berkeley did, that sensations were produced by God.

Lenin made the most of the fact that Mach's phenomenalist theory had affinities with that of Berkeley. Berkeley, Lenin said, was honest about his religious aims, whereas "in our time these very same thoughts on the 'economical' elimination of 'matter' from philosophy are enveloped in a much more artful form . . . ." Lenin objected that these phenomenalistic views run counter to our everyday practice, in which we come across material things and act upon them. We might call this the argument from common sense. He also objected that the theory that the material world is an orderly correlation of sensations is incompatible with the well-established scientific theory that there was once a time when matter existed but beings capable of having sensations did not. Berkeley, if he had known of this argument, could have countered it by saying that God could somehow have experienced the material world. If Mach had taken this course, Lenin claimed, he would have revealed his idealism.

Having rejected idealism and phenomenalism, Lenin had to give his own account of the material world and of our knowledge of it. He adopted Engels' theory that in perception material objects are "reflected" in the percipient and produce "copies" there. From this it would seem that the material world is much as we see and hear it to be, and Lenin seems to have emphasized this. Plekhanov, following Herrmann von Helmholtz, had argued that sensations are not exact copies of objects outside us but that they possess the same structure and might more accurately be termed "symbols" or "hieroglyphs." Lenin claimed, however, that Helmholtz's view undermines its materialist basis, "for signs or symbols may quite possibly indicate imaginary objects, and everybody is familiar with the existence of such signs and symbols" (p. 239). Lenin did not see that a similar objection applies to "copies" or "reflections" as well, for unless we have independent knowledge of that from which the copy is made, we cannot know that it is a copy. Furthermore, Lenin held (*Materialism and Empirio-Criticism*, Ch. 5, Sec. 7) both that sensations copy what is in the physical world and that what is in the physical world is shown by science to be very different from what it appears to be. Thus, he wrote that sensations of red reflect "ether vibrations" of one frequency and sensations of blue, "ether vibrations" of another frequency, but he did not say how sensations can copy or be like the vibrations. Elsewhere he said that it is "beyond doubt that an image cannot wholly resemble the model" and went on to say that "the image inevitably and of necessity implies the objective reality of what it 'images' " (p. 240). By putting "images" in quotation marks, he seems to have been denying its literal force, and by saying that the images "cannot wholly resemble the model," he raised doubts about what it was he really meant to assert.

The basic thing that Lenin wanted to say about the nature of matter was that it exists objectively and independently; therefore, he actually defined matter as "that which, acting upon our sense-organs, produces sensations." This would apply to Berkeley's God as well as to material objects. Still, Lenin called this his "philosophical" account of matter, contrasting it with the "scientific" conception of matter, which changes as scientific knowledge advances. In Lenin's view, the philosophical conception of matter remains unaffected as the scientific view of it changes from atomist theories to theories of electromagnetism. In *Materialism and Empirio-Criticism* Lenin argued, probably correctly, that the electromagnetic theory of matter is no less materialistic than atomic theories. Indeed, he held that it is in closer accord with dialectical materialism. "Modern physics is in travail," he wrote, "it is giving birth to dialectical materialism" (pp. 323–324). Like Engels, he was attracted to theories of matter that "dissolve" the rigid substances and hard atoms of the older views. He believed that such theories were substituting dialectical concepts for metaphysical and mechanistic ones.

Dialectics. In 1894, in *What the "Friends of the People" Are*, Lenin quoted approvingly from Engels' *Anti-Dühring*. In *Materialism and Empirio-Criticism* he frequently referred to dialectics, without, however, making it the center of his discussion. But while he was in exile in Switzerland during World War I, he renewed his study of philosophy, particularly of its dialectical aspects. His *Philosophical Notebooks* (first published in 1933) show the wide extent of his reading during those years, particularly his detailed study of Hegel's *Science of Logic*, in which he noted some germs of historical materialism. Lenin's reading of this book led him to conclude that it was not so much opposed to materialist modes of thought as had previously been supposed. On the one hand, Lenin approved of the Marxist commonplace that Hegel's system is materialism turned upside down. On the other hand he wrote that in the final chapter of the *Science of Logic*, on the Absolute Idea, there is scarcely a mention of God and that "it contains almost nothing that is specifically *idealism*, but has for its main subject the dialectical method" (*Collected Works*, Moscow, 1961, Vol. 38, p. 234). It is apparent from Lenin's notes that his respect for the *Science of Logic* increased as he read it. Not only did he conclude that it transcended idealism but also that idealism itself has virtues. Two notes in particular may be referred to. Among his comments on Hegel's *Lectures on the History of Philosophy* he said: "Intelligent idealism is closer to intelligent materialism than stupid materialism" (p. 276). And at the end of a short paper entitled "On the Question of Dialectics," written in 1915, he wrote that idealism "is a *sterile flower* undoubtedly, but a sterile flower that grows on the living tree of living, fertile, genuine, powerful, omnipotent, objective, absolute human knowledge" (*Philosophical Notebooks*, p. 363). Many of Lenin's jottings in his *Notebooks* are of this character, in marked contrast to the rancorous anti-idealism of *Materialism and Empirio-Criticism*, in which any approach toward idealism is regarded as treachery. Perhaps it is of significance that the one thesis common to Berkeley and Lenin is the thesis that nothing is substantial that is not active.

MAO TSE-TUNG

Mao Tse-tung's writings on dialectical materialism are referred to here mainly because of the political eminence of their author. Apart from his poems, his writings are mostly on political subjects, and his chief excursions into philosophy are two short articles written in 1937, "On Practice" and "On Contradiction." It has been suggested that Mao has introduced an empiricist element into dialectical materialism, but this is not borne out by a study of these two writings. In the first, it is true, Mao stated that knowledge begins with sense perception in practical contexts, passes on to rational knowledge, which enables the world to be "molded" for human purposes, and then leads to more rational knowledge at a higher level. It is not clear from the article whether the author was thinking of induction or of the testing of hypotheses or of both. But it is clear that, in Mao's view, in passing to this higher level "a leap" is made. In thus utilizing the law of the transformation of quantity into quality Mao was asserting that certain sorts of rational knowledge are different in kind from sense knowledge, and this can hardly be described as empiricism.

In "On Contradiction" Mao Tse-tung argued that in a contradiction each contradictory aspect "finds the presupposition of its existence in the other aspect and both aspects co-exist in one entity." As examples of this he mentioned life and death, above and below, misfortune and good fortune, landlords and tenant-peasants, bourgeoisie and proletariat, imperialists and colonies. He also argued that "each of the two contradictory aspects, according to given conditions tends to transform itself into the other," and as examples of this he cited the revolutionary proletariat becoming the rulers instead of the ruled, peace and war, landlords becoming landless tenants and landless tenants becoming smallholders.

It is easy to see the incongruities in both sets of examples. The opposition between life and death, for instance, is different from those between above and below and misfortune and good fortune, for there is nothing intermediate between life and death, whereas between above and below there is the relation of being at the same level and between good and bad fortune there is the condition of having neither the one nor the other. As to the second set of examples, the transformation of revolutionaries into rulers is not a logical transformation, but something that sometimes happens and sometimes does not. The example of peace and war is trivial. Mao wrote: "War and peace transform themselves into each other. War is transformed into peace; for example, the First World War was transformed into the postwar peace. . . . Why? Because in a class society such contradictory things as war and peace are characterised by identity under certain conditions." We know, of course, that wars end and that peace is often followed by war, but nothing is added to this by saying that a contradictory aspect transforms itself into its opposite, as if peace were one entity and war another. These writings of Mao Tse-tung's are, in fact, mainly concerned with immediate practical issues and contribute little to the philosophy from which they derive. It is in Soviet Russia that dialectical materialism has been most fully elaborated since Lenin died (see COMMUNISM, PHILOSOPHY UNDER).

Marxist Works

MARX

"Oekonomische–philosophische Manuskripte," in D. Riazanov and V. Adoratski, eds., *Marx–Engels Gesamtausgabe*, Berlin, 1927–1932. Division I, Vol. III. Translated by Martin Milligan as *Economic and Philosophic Manuscripts of 1844*. Moscow and London, 1959.

"Theses on Feuerbach," appended to *The German Ideology*, R. Pascal, ed. London, 1938.

Misère de la philosophie. Brussels and Paris, 1847. Translated by H. Quelch as *The Poverty of Philosophy*. Chicago, 1910.

MARX AND ENGELS

Die heilige Familie. Frankfurt, 1845. Translated as *The Holy Family*. Moscow and London, 1956.

Die deutsche Ideologie, V. Adoratski, ed. Vienna, 1932. Translated as *The German Ideology*, R. Pascal, ed. London, 1964.

ENGELS

Herr Eugen Dührings Umwälzung der Wissenschaft. Leipzig, 1878. Translated by E. Burns as *Herr Eugen Dühring's Revolution in Science*. London, 1934.

Die Entwicklung des Sozialismus von der Utopie zur Wissenschaft. Zurich, 1883. Translated by E. Aveling as *Socialism: Utopian and Scientific*. London, 1892.

Ludwig Feuerbach und der Ausgang der klassischen deutschen Philosophie. Stuttgart, 1888. Translated as *Ludwig Feuerbach and the Outcome of Classical German Philosophy*. London, 1935.

Dialektika Prirody. Moscow, 1925. Translated as *Dialectics of Nature*, with an introduction by G. B. S. Haldane. London, 1940; new translation, London, 1954.

PLEKHANOV

Selected Philosophical Works. Moscow and London, 1961. Vol. I.

K Voprosu o Razvitii Monisticheskago Vzglyada na Istoriyu. St. Petersburg, 1895. Translated by Andrew Rothstein as *In Defense of Materialism: The Development of the Monist View of History*. London, 1947.

LENIN

Materializm i Empiriokrititsizm. Moscow, 1908. Translated by A. Fineberg as *Materialism and Empirio-Criticism*. Moscow and London, 1948.

"Karl Marx," in his *Collected Works*. Moscow and London, 1960—. Vol. 21, 1964.

Filosofskie Tetradi. Moscow, 1933. Translated as *Philosophical Notebooks*, in his *Collected Works*. Moscow and London, 1960—. Vol. 38, 1962.

OTHERS

Cornforth, Maurice, *Dialectical Materialism*, 3 vols. London, 1954.

Kedrov, B. M., *Classification of Sciences. Book I: Engels, His Predecessors*. Moscow, 1961.

Stalin, Joseph, *Dialectical and Historical Materialism*. First published as Chapter 4 of Stalin's *History of the Communist Party of the USSR*. Moscow, 1939.

Works by Non-Marxists

Acton, H. B., *The Illusion of the Epoch: Marxism–Leninism as a Philosophical Creed*. London, 1955.

Acton, H. B., "Karl Marx's Materialism." *Revue internationale de philosophie*. Nos. 45–46 (1958), 265–277.

Bochenski, J. M., *Der sowjetrussische dialektische Materialismus (Diamat)*. Bern and Munich, 1950. Translated by Nicolas Sollohub as *Soviet Russian Dialectical Materialism*. Dordrecht, Netherlands, 1963.

Hook, Sidney, *Reason, Social Myths, and Democracy*. New York, 1950. Contains an excellent discussion of Engels' dialectical laws.

Joravsky, David, *Soviet Marxism and Natural Science*. London, 1961. Important on "mechanism" and the relation of dialectical materialism to positivism.

Jordan, Z. A., *Philosophy and Ideology. The Development of Philosophy and Marxism–Leninism in Poland Since the Second World War*. Dordrecht, Netherlands, 1963.

Paul, G. A., "Lenin's Theory of Perception." *Analysis*, Vol. 5 (1938), 65–73.

Wetter, Gustav, *Der dialektische Materialismus: seine Geschichte und seine Systeme in der Sowjetunion*. Vienna and Freiburg, 1953. Translated by Peter Heath from the fourth German edition as *Dialectical Materialism. A Historical and Systematic Survey of Philosophy in the Soviet Union*. London, 1958. Discusses Marx, Engels, Plekhanov, Lenin, and later Soviet writers.

H. B. ACTON

DICTIONARIES. *See* PHILOSOPHICAL DICTIONARIES AND ENCYCLOPEDIAS.

DIDEROT, DENIS (1713–1784), French encyclopedist, philosopher, satirist, dramatist, novelist, literary and art critic, was the most versatile thinker of his times and a key figure in the advancement of Enlightenment philosophy.

LIFE

Born in Langres, son of a master cutler, Diderot was a brilliant student in the local Jesuit schools. He was sent to college in Paris and received his master's degree at the age of nineteen. Afterward, he refused to adopt a regular profession and, when his allowance was cut off, lived for many years in poverty and obscurity. His great ambition was to acquire knowledge. In this he was eminently successful, for he emerged from this period of self-education with an excellent command of mathematics and considerable proficiency in the Greek, Italian, and English languages. He first came into public notice as a translator of

English works—a history of Greece, Shaftesbury's *Inquiry concerning Virtue and Merit* (1745), and Robert James's *Medicinal Dictionary* (1746–1748). He was secretly married in 1743; and his wife bore him a number of children, all of whom died in childhood except a daughter, Angélique, who lived to perpetuate the memory of her distinguished father.

In 1746 he published his first original work, the bold and controversial *Pensées philosophiques.* In that year, too, he became associated with the *Encyclopédie*, the greatest publishing venture of the century, of which he soon became editor-in-chief, with the aid of d'Alembert for the mathematical parts. This enterprise was his chief occupation and source of income until 1772. The boldness of his thought, in spite of the dexterity with which he attempted to conceal it, met almost instant opposition, resulting in the seizure of manuscripts, censorship, and temporary suppression. Only a man of Diderot's indomitable courage and determination could have brought the project to a successful conclusion.

In 1749, while manuscripts for the *Encyclopédie* were being prepared for the printer, Diderot published his *Lettre sur les aveugles* ("Letter on the Blind"), in which he questioned the existence of purpose or design in the universe. For this and other suspect works he was seized by the police and spent a few uncomfortable months in the prison of Vincennes. His reputation in his parish as a materialistic atheist was catching up with him. The subsequent *Lettre sur les sourds et muets* ("Letter on the Deaf and Dumb," 1751), equally original, was mild enough to escape persecution. His *Pensées sur l'interprétation de la nature* (1754) was both a plea for strict adherence to the scientific method and an exposition of results of that method, including definite evidence in support of evolutionary transformism.

After the official suspension of the *Encyclopédie* in 1759, Diderot prudently withheld his most important philosophical works for the use of posterity. The *Rêve de d'Alembert* ("D'Alembert's Dream"), written in 1769, and the *Réfutation de l'ouvrage d'Helvétius* ("Refutation of Helvétius") first became public in the nineteenth century. *Le Neveu de Rameau* (*Rameau's Nephew*), a scathing satire of eighteenth-century society, and the novels *La Religieuse* ("The Nun") and *Jacques le Fataliste* (*Jacques the Fatalist*), which saw the light of day only after the French Revolution, as well as various short stories and dialogues, were all of ethical import. Two bourgeois dramas, *Le Fils naturel* ("The Natural Son," 1754) and *Le Père de famille* ("The Father of the Family," 1758), accompanied by critical essays, could, however, be safely published, though the *Paradoxe sur le comédien* ("The Paradox of the Actor"), important for its aesthetic insights, was withheld. Diderot's *Salons*, replete with brilliant criticism of art and literature, were also published posthumously, although in manuscript copy they formed an important part of Friedrich Grimm's *Correspondance littéraire*, written only for foreign consumption. Diderot knew that his ideas were too advanced for his own generation, but he maintained the conviction that he would some day be appreciated at his true value.

When, in 1772, his long labors on the *Encyclopédie* were ended, Diderot set off for St. Petersburg by way of Holland and spent some months in 1773 in intimate conversations with Catherine the Great. Persuaded of his merit through Grimm, she had not only paid in advance for his library (he desperately needed the money as a dowry for his daughter) but also gave him a salary as its custodian until his death. Holbach's *System of Nature* (1770), frankly atheistic and materialistic, had sharply drawn the line between atheism and deism, and both Catherine and Frederick II took the side of the less revolutionary Voltaire. Since Diderot supported Holbach in this controversy, his political *Observations* on Catherine's plan to recodify Russian law were doomed too radical and suppressed by his royal patron.

Returning to France in 1774, Diderot spent the remaining years of his life in semiretirement, enjoying at least a semblance of domestic felicity. His letters to his mistress, Sophie Volland, form, next to Voltaire's, the most interesting correspondence of the century. His final work, the *Essai sur les règnes de Claude et Néron* ("Essay on the Reigns of Claudius and Nero," 1778–1782), was a eulogy of Stoic virtue, as illustrated by Seneca, and also a reply to charges of treachery and immorality made against Diderot in the *Confessions* of Rousseau, his former friend and coworker.

Diderot died in Paris six years after Voltaire and Rousseau, with whose names his is inextricably linked as a leader of the French Enlightenment.

GENERAL PHILOSOPHICAL ATTITUDES

Diderot's philosophy was remarkably undogmatic. He advocated the open mind and believed that doubt was the beginning of wisdom and often its end; he continually questioned his own theories and conclusions, developed extreme theses, or paradoxes, in ethics and aesthetics, and decided that "our true opinions are those to which we return the most often." Nevertheless, after passing briefly through a period of deistic belief (a deist, he finally concluded, was a man who had not lived long enough—or wisely enough—to become an atheist), he became an unabashed and enthusiastic materialist and developed a theory of materialism much less vulnerable than that of his forebears. His main contribution was a philosophy of science which looked far into the future and upon which his aesthetic and ethical theories were firmly and inseparably founded.

Sensationalism. Like Voltaire, Rousseau, and Condillac, Diderot was early preoccupied with the theory of sensationalism. At weekly dinners with the latter two, Locke's psychology was thoroughly discussed. Between Diderot and Condillac influence was undoubtedly mutual. But Condillac, having taken holy orders and being therefore more circumspect, worked out a more systematic and more abstract philosophy and left it to Diderot to direct French sensationalism into definitely materialistic channels.

Diderot's philosophical thought was clarified by his constant distrust of abstractions. Abstractions, he declared in "D'Alembert's Dream," are linguistic signs, which are useful in speeding up discourse and upon which the abstract sciences are built; but as symbols emptied of their ideas, they are obstacles to clear thinking. Those who use abstractions must have constant recourse to examples, thus giving them perceptibility and physical reality. The mind is nothing but the brain functioning; the will is the latest impulse of desire and aversion. The naming of things is purely conventional.

Diderot's early philosophical publications were especially concerned with problems of communication. His empirical mind could not be satisfied with speculative studies, such as Condillac's theoretical experiment of endowing a statue with one sense at a time. He chose rather to study the actual cases of individuals deprived of the sense of sight or the sense of hearing. His *Lettre sur les aveugles* (1749) dealt first with case histories and the problems of "reading" through touch, illustrated by the methods of Nicholas Saunderson, the blind professor of mathematics at Oxford. This first truly scientific study of blindness led to Diderot's imprisonment. The passage that provoked the authorities was an imaginary deathbed conversation, in which the blind professor, unable to appreciate the alleged perfection of the order and beauties of nature, expressed his consequent doubts as to the existence of an intelligent God. The treatise on the deaf and dumb, two years later, was also based on scientific observation, but proceeded to discuss aesthetic theories, especially the importance of gesture to communication. In his later posthumous works, sensationalism played an important role in the development of his materialistic monism.

Empiricism. As early as 1748, in the libertine novel *Les Bijoux indiscrets* ("The Indiscreet Toys"), Diderot showed himself a pronounced empiricist, a firm believer in the efficacy of the scientific method. In an important chapter of that work, Experience (the word meant both observed fact and experiment) figures first as a growing child, who discovers with the aid of a pendulum the velocity of a falling body, calculates the weight of the atmosphere with a tube of mercury, and with prism in hand, decomposes light. The child visibly grows to colossal stature and, like a Samson, crumbles the pillars of the Portico of Hypotheses.

Diderot's "Thoughts on the Interpretation of Nature" (1754), taking its title and inspiration from Francis Bacon, again extolled the experimental method above purely rationalistic theory. Following the work of Maupertuis and Buffon—and especially in studying Louis Daubenton's anatomical comparison of the foot of the horse and the hand of man—Diderot arrived at principles of transformism and natural selection that were to influence greatly his mature philosophy. He surmised that "there had never been but one animal, prototype, through differentiation, of all other animals." The dawning of the age of biological science, he believed, would usher in the great discoveries of the future.

Imagination. Observation and the classification of natural phenomena was the first and essential step, but the great scientist must perceive relationships and form hypotheses, subject to experimental verification. Diderot closely associated the poetic imagination with the scientific, both in theory and practice. This theory is clearly expounded in the first of the three "conversations" of "D'Alembert's Dream." This section discusses the role of analogy, which is merely the working out of the rule of three by the feeling instrument that is man. To the genius, whether poet or scientist, will come the sudden perception of a new relationship, resulting in poetic metaphor or useful hypothesis.

Style. Diderot's own mind worked in sudden flashes of perception. His best philosophical works are random or loosely associated thoughts or observations—or dreams. His satirical narrative, *Rameau's Nephew*, and his novel, *Jacques the Fatalist*, are apparently loosely constructed, much given to dialogue, with digressions and intercalated stories after the manner of Sterne. They follow the pattern of general conversation, in which one idea gives birth to another, and so on, until the thread is difficult to retrace. The theory of associationism was firmly based, however, on his theories of sensationalism and memory (to be discussed below).

Scientific background. Diderot's inquisitive and encyclopedic mind equipped him admirably to comprehend the great advances that the sciences were making in the middle of the century. From mathematics he turned to chemistry and for three years studied assiduously under Guillaume-Francois Rouelle, forerunner of Lavoisier. He was well acquainted with the work of the Dutch biologists Niklaas Hartsoeker and Bernard Nieuwyntit, who laid the foundations for the still unknown science of genetics. He was familiar with Abraham Trembley's experiments with the fresh-water polyp, and with Joseph Needham's discovery of Infusoria, in apparent proof of the theory of spontaneous generation. These experiments influenced his development of the concepts of the sensitivity of matter and the essential identity of its organic and inorganic forms.

As translator of Robert James's *Medicinal Dictionary*, Diderot was well informed in the science of medicine. Characteristically, he sought (in vain), before writing his "Letter on the Blind," to be admitted to an operation for cataract, and he consorted with doctors, many of whom were contributors to the *Encyclopédie*. While in prison at Vincennes, the recently published first three volumes of Buffon's *Natural History* received his careful scrutiny, and from all possible sources he collected case histories of injuries to, and surgical operations on, the brain.

By 1769, when he composed "D'Alembert's Dream," Diderot was adequately prepared to develop an original philosophy of science, a monistic theory that has been described as naturalistic humanism and dynamic, or "energetistic," materialism, which far surpassed the mechanistic theories of his forebears, from Lucretius to La Mettrie, and foreshadowed Darwin. In this work, first published in 1830, Diderot showed himself at once a great and an imaginative philosopher and writer. In its pages, his mature philosophy, presented fantastically but seriously, was best illustrated.

MATERIALISM–MATTER IN MOTION

Diderot adopted the Heraclitean theory of flux. The universe, for him, was a single physical system, obeying the immutable laws that Descartes assigned to matter in motion; it was dynamic or "becoming," rather than static or created. Unlike Descartes, however, Diderot followed John Toland in believing that motion was not added but was essential to matter. He gave the idealistic monad of Leibniz a positive content. Diderot maintained that not only are bodies affected by external force but that the atom contains internal forces, a form of kinetic or potential energy. All things carry with them their opposites; being and not-being are part of every whole. "Living," he wrote, "I act and react as a mass; dead, I act and react in the form of molecules. Birth, life, decay, are merely changes of form." No knowledge was gained, no solution reached, in postulating a Creator or supernatural agency to account for material phenomena. All change, including the transformation of the universe from chaos to order, was to be explained by the interaction of the elementary material particles. What man perceives as order is simply his apprehension of the laws of motion as enacted by material bodies.

Sensitivity of matter. An additional and very important hypothesis upon which Diderot's construction was built was the sensitivity of all matter, both inorganic and organic. By postulating both motion and sensitivity as inherent in matter, he felt that the entire range of natural phenomena (both physical and mental) and the full variety of experience could be adequately explained. All that nature contains is the product of matter in motion, subject to the processes of fermentation produced by heat; through eons of time growth, increasing complexity, and specialization have occurred.

Diderot believed that there were no inexplicable gulfs between the various kingdoms. The known facts concerning the inorganic, the organic, plant, animal, and man, were like islands jutting out of a sea of ignorance. As the waters receded through scientific investigation, the missing links would be discovered. "How d'Alembert differs from a cow," he admitted, "I cannot quite understand. But some day science will explain." He nevertheless attempted to trace the development of his friend, from the earth mold to mathematician, from the unconscious through the subconscious to the conscious life.

BIOLOGY AND EVOLUTION

During Diderot's lifetime the biological sciences were in their infancy. The scope and profundity of his insights are therefore all the more amazing. When scientific facts failed him, he had recourse to hypotheses that he was convinced would some day be verified. It was in consideration of this conviction that he presented his mature philosophy as a dream, a dream which, with the passage of time, can truly be called prophetic.

The crucial problem that confronted Diderot was to account for the emergence and behavior of the living individual. The coordinated behavior and continuous identity that characterize the organism seemed to transcend any possible organization of discrete material particles. It was difficult to see how merely contiguous material parts could form an organic whole capable of a unified and purposeful response to its environment. Traditionally, the existence of unique species and individuals was explained by recourse to supernatural design and metaphysical essence.

Contemporary science offered Diderot a choice between preformation, a Lucretian theory accepted at times by La Mettrie, and epigenesis, which explained organic formation in terms of juxtaposition and contiguity. Diderot rejected preformation, and in support of epigenesis he developed the concept of molecular combinations endowed with specialized functions and organic unity. In "D'Alembert's Dream," Diderot employed the image of a swarm of bees in an attempt to bridge the gap between contiguity and continuity in the production of a whole that is qualitatively unique and different from the sum of its parts. He pointed out that although the swarm consists simply of numerous separate individuals in physical contact, it does, as a whole, possess the characteristic of purposeful, unified behavior that is associated with the individual organism. It is possible to mistake the swarm of thousands of bees for a single animal. The unity of the organism is derived from the life of the whole, and Diderot thus affirmed the continuity of the kingdoms and refuted the metaphysical principle of essences. A half century later the discovery of the organic cell and the principles of cell division confirmed his views.

Diderot found support for his theories in the embryological ideas that he had gathered from his reading, especially of Albrecht von Haller's *Elements of Physiology*, and from Dr. Bordeu, his friend and the protagonist in the conversations of the "Dream." In the conversation with d'Alembert, which gives rise to the dream, Diderot attempts briefly to trace d'Alembert from the parental "germs." He then describes how, under the influence of heat, the chicken develops within the egg. Excluding all animistic hypotheses, he declares that this development "overthrows all the schools of theology; . . . from inert matter, organized in a certain way and impregnated with other inert matter, and given heat and motion, there results the faculty of sensation, life, memory, consciousness, passion, and thought."

Heredity. Diderot's conviction of the importance of hereditary factors constitutes the main argument of his refutation of Helvétius' work *On the Mind*, in which education and law, purely environmental factors, were proposed exclusively as causes of the development of a moral society. Diderot agreed with Bordeu ("organs produce needs, and reciprocally, needs produce organs") on the Lamarckian principle of the inheritability of acquired characteristics. Moreover, he clearly stated his belief that the individual recapitulates the history of the race and that certain hereditary factors may crop up after many generations.

To explain how parental factors are inherited (cells and genes were as yet unknown), Diderot resorted to a hypothesis of organic development through a network or bundle of threads (or fibers or filaments), which strongly suggested the nervous system. Any interference with the fibers produced abnormalities, or "monsters." (He was one of the first to seek to understand the normal through the abnormal, both in embryology and psychology.) In his careful description, in the "Dream," of the embryological differentiation between the male and female sex organs, he was led to surmise that man is perhaps the "monster" of the woman, and vice versa. His theories clearly foreshadow not only the phenomena of recessive genes but also the fundamental role of chromosomes. One of his chief arguments against design in the universe was nature's prolific production of "monsters," most of which were too ill adapted to their environment to survive. Their elimination was the closest he came to the principle of natural selection.

MATTER AND THOUGHT

Diderot believed that once it is granted that sensitivity is a property of matter and that matter thereby develops increasing complexity and specialization, it then follows that thought can best be understood as a property of that highly complex and specified material organ, the brain. He accepted Bordeu's theory of the individual life of the various bodily organs. All were linked, however, through the nervous system to the central organ, which, depending upon circumstances and temperaments, exerted more or less control over them. Personal identity, the unified self, was thus assured by the nervous system, and the brain played the role of both organ and organist.

Memory. Self-awareness, however, depends entirely on the remembering function of the human brain. Quite characteristically, Diderot assigned a neural mechanism to Locke's theory of the association of ideas. In his investigations of the physical substrata of memory, he read all he could find on the anatomy of the brain and injuries to the brain and consulted doctors and specialists in brain surgery. A number of case histories were reported in the "Dream." In the preliminary conversation with d'Alembert, however, he used La Mettrie's metaphor of vibrating strings and harmonic intervals to explain the association of images and memory, the passage from sense perceptions to comparisons, reflection, judgment, and thought. Memory furnishes the continuity in time, the personal history that is fundamental to self-consciousness and personal identity. In Diderot's mind, memory was corporeal, and the self had only material reality. He thus attempted to give psychology a scientific, physiological basis, which was further developed in the nineteenth and twentieth centuries.

In the midst of notes taken mostly from his reading and published later as the *Éléments de physiologie*, Diderot included an eloquent passage in support of his theory: "I am inclined to believe that all we have seen, known, perceived, or heard—even the trees of a great forest . . . all concerts we have ever heard—exists within us and unknown to us." He could still see in his waking hours the forests of Westphalia, and could review them when dreaming—as brilliantly colored as if they were in a painting. Moreover, "the sound of a voice, the presence of an object . . . and behold, an object recalled—more than that, a whole stretch of my past—and I am plunged again into pleasure, regret, or affliction."

Dreams and genius. The concept of the greater or lesser control exerted by the central organ over the other organs of the body was applied by Diderot not only to dreams but also to the phenomenon of genius. In sleep, control is relaxed and anarchy reigns. A random recall in the central organ may then be referred to the subordinate organ, or the procedure may be reversed, from organ to brain. In dreams, random combinations may be formed and dragons created. Only personal past experience is available, however, for such imaginings. The one impossible dream is that the dreamer is someone else.

Applied to genius, the explanation of which was of great concern to Diderot and an important aspect of *Rameau's Nephew*, the concept of central control ran into difficulties. In the early *Pensées philosophiques*, in opposition to Pascal, he championed the strong emotions as the chief source of the good, the true, and the beautiful. Later, his acquaintance with David Garrick led him to write a paradox on the acting profession, in which he claimed that the great actor, with complete command of his emotions, makes his audience laugh or weep by coolly calculated gesture and intonation; he must register the emotions, but not feel them at the same time. In "D'Alembert's Dream" he explained that dominating control by the center produced wise and good men but that genius was the result of the strongest emotions under almost complete control, a theory that could be illustrated by the horseman, Hippolytus, in firm command of the most spirited horses that Greece produced. In Diderot's hands, genius was not a mere talent produced, as Helvétius had claimed, by education and chance, but a psychophysiological phenomenon, and in that respect akin, when central control is lost, to madness.

ETHICS

The fundamental principles of Diderot's ethics may be found most readily in "D'Alembert's Dream." Will and liberty (free will) he described as senseless terms, abstractions that obscured the facts. The will of the waking man is the same as that of the dreamer: "the latest impulse of desire and aversion, the last result of all that one has been from birth to the actual moment." "There is only one cause . . . and that is a physical cause." But Diderot clearly distinguished between fatalism and determinism. Man is not, like the lower animals, a prey to the bombardment of the senses. The self, the brain with its properties of memory and imagination, intervenes between the external stimulus and the act.

Diderot was tempted, but refrained from writing a treatise on ethics. Many critics have attributed this failure to the moral dilemma posed by his determinist convictions. It is more probably that he felt his ideas were too advanced for the age and society in which he lived. Moral problems were foremost in his mind throughout his career. A letter of 1756 stated clearly his deterministic beliefs. Heredity played a dominant role, for some, happily, are endowed with moral or socially acceptable propensities, while others, unfortunately, are not. Moral monsters must be eliminated, but in general, man is modifiable. *Rameau's Nephew* is, among other things, the story of the dilemmas that confront moral man in an immoral society, in which honesty is not necessarily the best policy.

Diderot's imaginary *Supplément au voyage de Bougainville* (1796) describes and extols the primitive customs of Tahiti. Unlike Rousseau's, Diderot's "primitivism" was not a plea for a return to a less civilized society. Not nature or natural law, but the fundamental laws of nature, were uppermost in Diderot's mind. The conventions of modern society, it seemed to him, unnecessarily restricted the basic biological needs of man. Before Freud, he sensed the dangers of sexual repression, a theme developed in the final section of the "Dream" and fundamental to his novel "The Nun." Celibacy, in his view, led too often to mental or sexual aberration. He ended his Tahitian tale, however, with the admonition that, though we should try to change bad, or "unnatural," laws, we must obey the laws that our society has imposed.

Diderot frankly admitted his enjoyment of sensual pleasures—books, women, pictures, friends, and toasting his toes before a fire. But in the preface of *Le Père de famille,* addressed to the princess of Nassau, he declared that "he who prefers a voluptuous sensation to the conscience of a good act is a vile man." He felt certain that through education and knowledge we could recognize what was good, and that virtue, or beneficence, was the one and only path to happiness. There are intimations in his works of a belief that the good and wise man, in a corrupt society, should at times rise above a bad law, a theme illustrated in his last play, *Est-il bon? Est-il méchant?*

Toward the end of his life, in his praise of Seneca, he extolled the Stoic concept of virtue as its own reward. He summed up his natural, humanistic ethics in a brief pronouncement: "There is only one virtue, justice; one duty, to be happy; one corollary, neither to overesteem life nor fear death."

AESTHETICS

In the theory and practice of the arts dependent on the imagination—literature, music, and the fine arts—Diderot also introduced innovations. His approach to the theory of beauty was through the perception of relationships and the arts of communication. An unusual perception of relationships, through analogy and associative memory, was the mark of the genius, whether scientist or poet. The artist first experiences an emotional or aesthetic stimulus strong enough to fire his imagination. A second moment of enthusiasm, which comes from the ability to communicate his vision through his special technique, sounds, colors, lines, or words, is essential, however.

His *Encyclopédie* article "Beau" (1751) gave evidence of a thorough acquaintance with French and English aestheticians. That same year he launched out on his own in his "Letter on the Deaf and Dumb." Here he discussed the importance of gesture and expression in communication. The great actor is one who paints in gestures what he expresses in words, just as the great poet paints in sounds and rhythms what he means in words. Likewise, the beauty of a painting depends on its inner rhythm and structure. The sublime in painting and poetry is derived from the emotions imparted through the harmonies of sound and color, the wedding of sense and sound. Poetry, he declared, is therefore essentially untranslatable.

Art and morality. A strong moralistic tone pervaded Diderot's aesthetic theories and criticism. The painter must have morals as well as perspective. The bourgeois drama, a genre which he originated and illustrated, though not very successfully, should compete with the law in persuading us to love virtue and hate vice.

There was more than a touch of sentimentality in the art criticisms of the *Salons,* which he wrote biennially from 1759 to 1781. For a period, the bourgeois pathos of Greuze held a strong appeal for him. A notable connoisseur of the arts, he was not, however, fooled. He recognized the masterly compositions of François Boucher, but condemned his allegorical subjects and depiction of the loves of the gods. Chardin's use of color, he knew, was far superior to that of Greuze, though his subject matter was too often "ignoble." Yet Chardin taught him that painting was not, as the classical theorists long held, the imitation of beautiful nature. He stood in awed amazement before Chardin's painting of the skate and called it magic.

Criticism. Diderot created modern art criticism as a literary art. The *Salons,* especially of 1765 and 1767, still make fascinating reading and contain the best of his literary criticism. That he was himself a great writer is now at last being generally recognized. First and foremost, he was a master of dialogue; written for the ear, his dialogues are artistic transpositions of reality. His dislike of abstractions made him an early champion of realism. He never ceased to admire Molière and Racine—and Shakespeare—but believed that the theater was destined to follow new paths. His romantic spirit was revealed by his advocacy of strong emotions and his streak of sentimentality. He therefore foreshadowed the romantic–realistic revolt against classicism, delayed in France until the nineteenth century by the political revolution.

Diderot's trinity was truth, goodness, and beauty. In his aesthetic order, first place was given to that which was both useful and agreeable; second, to the merely useful; and third, to the purely agreeable. Since the essence of the arts was not subject matter, but the perception and communication of relationships, he felt it was advantageous to add a moral subject, the useful, to technical beauty.

SOCIETY AND POLITICS

Diderot made his *Encyclopédie* a major weapon for upsetting the social and political institutions of the Old Regime. In the first volume his article "Autorité politique" boldly proclaimed, before Rousseau's *Contrat social,* that sovereignty resided in the people, who alone should determine how and to whom it should be delegated. There, too, appeared the first discussion of the "general will." In an often vain effort to evade censorship, he chose out-of-the-way places, sometimes seemingly harmless definitions of terms, to point out the danger that lay before both the state and the church unless they were strictly separated.

In his *Observations* on the instructions of Catherine II to her deputies in the recodification of Russian law, he was even more forthright: "The only true sovereign is the nation," he wrote; "there can be no true legislator except the people." He also chided Catherine for submitting political institutions to religious sanction: "Religion is a support that in the end almost always ruins the edifice." He did not hesitate to call her a tyrant and refuted her arguments in favor of benevolent despotism. Her suppression of his manuscript was so thorough that parts of it are coming to be known only in the present century.

Rameau's Nephew was a sweeping satire of French

eighteenth-century society, especially of the often ignorant and very wealthy general tax collectors, who, with their hordes of parasites, were a menace to the development of the arts, as well as powerful enemies of the *Encyclopédie*. In a dialogue with Diderot, the parasitic nephew of the great Rameau defended his debasement and moral corruption, quite shocking to his moralistic interlocutor, as the only means of satisfying the pangs of hunger in a thoroughly corrupt society. Throughout Diderot's works—in his dramas, his short stories and novels, in his art and literary criticism, as well as in his social and political theories—his sympathies were with the Third Estate.

Because he was forced to withhold his best and most forthright works for publication by future generations, the growth of Diderot's fame has been a very slow process. Rousseau declared that it would take two centuries for the realization that he was the great genius of his century. His first enthusiasts were also men of genius, Goethe, Balzac, Baudelaire, and Hugo.

It can hardly be a cause for wonder that Diderôt is receiving special attention in Marxist societies and that many excellent editions and translations have come from Marxist presses. Yet it was to the scientist and philosopher in Engels, rather than the social economist, that Diderot's work most greatly appealed. His philosophical determinism was in no sense economic determinism; his sturdy bourgeois qualities give small comfort to Marxist sociology; and his views of the importance of hereditary traits are in sharp opposition to behavioristic theory. He would seem to qualify most readily as a naturalistic humanist.

Works by Diderot

Oeuvres complètes, Assezat-Tourneux, ed., 20 vols. Paris, 1875–1877.

Oeuvres, A. Billy, ed. Paris, 1935. Essential works in one volume.

Correspondance, G. Roth, ed. Paris, 1955—.

Le Rêve de d'Alembert, Jean Varloot, ed. Paris, 1962.

ENGLISH TRANSLATIONS

Diderot's Early Philosophical Works, translated and edited by Margaret Jourdain. Chicago and London, 1916.

Dialogues, translated and edited by Francis Birrell. New York, 1927.

Diderot, Interpreter of Nature; Selected Writings, translated and edited by Jean Stewart and Jonathan Kemp. London, 1937; New York, 1938. Best translations of "D'Alembert's Dream," etc.

Rameau's Nephew and Other Works, translated by Jacques Barzun and Ralph H. Bowen. New York, 1956.

Jacques the Fatalist and His Master, translated by J. Robert Loy. New York, 1959 and 1961.

Selected Works of Diderot, translated and edited by Lester G. Crocker. New York, 1965.

Works on Diderot

Crocker, Lester G., *Diderot, the Embattled Philosopher*. Ann Arbor, Mich., 1954. Good general introduction to Diderot's life and works.

Fellows, Otis E., et al., eds., *Diderot Studies*. Geneva, 1949—. Critical essays and monographs in English and French by contemporary scholars. Five volumes had been published as of 1965.

Wilson, Arthur M., *Diderot: The Testing Years (1713–1759)*. New York, 1957. Best biography to date and best critical studies of early works. The first of two volumes.

BIBLIOGRAPHY

Cabeen, D. C., ed., *A Critical Bibliography of French Literature*, Vol. IV. Syracuse, N.Y., 1951. Especially valuable for researchers.

NORMAN L. TORREY

DILTHEY, WILHELM

DILTHEY, WILHELM (1833–1911), German philosopher. In Dilthey's "philosophy of life" the influence of Kant, of the idealist and romantic philosophies of Hegel, Schelling, and Schleiermacher, and of British empiricism can be traced. His most distinctive contribution to philosophy is his epistemological analysis of the *Geisteswissenschaften*, or human studies, and of history in particular.

Dilthey's life, externally uneventful, was that of a university professor wholly dedicated to scholarship. Born at Biebrich, the son of a clergyman of the Reformed church, he went to the grammar school at Wiesbaden and from there to Heidelberg to study theology. After a year he moved to Berlin, where he became increasingly absorbed in history and philosophy. In 1864 he took his doctorate and obtained the right to lecture. He was appointed to a chair in Basel in 1866; calls to Kiel, in 1868, and Breslau, in 1871, followed. In 1882 he became the successor of Lotze at the University of Berlin, where he taught until 1905.

The range of Dilthey's work, the width of his interests, and the depth of his knowledge are awe-inspiring. He contributed to metaphysics, moral philosophy, and the theory of knowledge; but in addition he was an original historian of ideas who wrote illuminatingly on the Renaissance, the Reformation, the German Enlightenment, and the development of German idealism. He surveyed the changing conceptions of human nature and the function of psychology and produced influential studies in literary criticism.

Dilthey's intense appreciation of the wealth and variety of human life and his ability to draw on a vast store of historical and biographical material to document it made his works stimulating and refreshingly undogmatic, but they also frustrated his ambitious attempts to achieve a final ordering of his ideas. Most of his works remained in fragments; a mass of incomplete drafts filled his cupboards. This, together with his loose, repetitive, and somewhat involved style, limited the extent of his influence during his lifetime. Only after his death—when his friends and disciples edited a collected works that included many unpublished manuscripts and expounded and systematized his thought—did the full magnitude of his achievement emerge.

PHILOSOPHY OF LIFE

The essential quality of Dilthey's thought is best appreciated by an examination of his "philosophy of life" (*Philosophie des Lebens*). For Dilthey, life is not merely the biological fact man shares with other animals, but human life, experienced by us in all its distinctive complexity. It is the agglomeration of innumerable individual lives which constitutes the social and historical reality of the life of mankind. The hopes and fears, the thoughts and acts of individuals, the institutions which men have created, the laws by which they guide their conduct, the religions they believe in, all art, all literature, and all philosophy are part of that life. So is all science, because although it considers inanimate nature, it is still a human activity. If life is so comprehensively defined, any philosophy must be a philosophy of life, even though it concentrates on one or another aspect of life. However, Dilthey's "philosophy of life" has a more specific meaning.

To start with, Dilthey explicitly asserted that life was not only the proper, but also the sole, subject matter of philosophy. A strict empiricist, he rejected any form of transcendentalism. There is nothing behind life, no thing-in-itself, no metaphysical ultimate or Platonic heaven of forms of which life is only a phenomenon, imitation, or hieroglyph. It follows that the knowing subject and, for that matter, the philosopher, is part of life and can know it only from within. There is no absolute starting point for thought, no body of absolute standards outside experience that can be reached by pure speculation. All reflections on life, all valuations and moral principles, are the product not of a pure knowing mind but of particular individuals living at a particular time in a particular place, determined by circumstances, influenced by the opinions around them, and bound by the horizons of their age. All such reflections and valuations are, therefore, tinged with relativity.

Second, Dilthey asserted that what we actually experience is life in its whole wealth and variety. He considered the positivist view that we "experience" only sensations and impressions a metaphysical dogma that, by abstracting from our real experience, narrows our channels of knowledge. We see things and people, listen to music and poetry, observe the workings of the law, experience religious awe, patriotic enthusiasm, or aesthetic satisfaction. All these, not merely the sensation of blobs of color or twinges of pain, are part of the experience from which the true empiricist must start—although he may later analyze it into its components.

In spite of his resolve to be true to experience and his sense of its irreducible variety, Dilthey was not content—as many empiricists are—with examining individual problems only. He strove for a comprehensive vision of reality. How can the philosopher, confronting the almost infinite diversity of life without any absolute norms, perceive any meaning or pattern in it? Dilthey replied that life is not a mass of disconnected facts; it is encountered everywhere as already organized, interpreted, and therefore meaningful. The philosopher starts from the meanings that human beings have given to their world. That the philosopher is part of life, a human being affected by the circumstances of his age like his fellows, becomes an asset. The processes by means of which life becomes organized and meaningful are familiar to him from his own experience. He is aware of the working of his mind, of how ideas give rise to feelings and feelings turn into intentions; he is familiar with the temporal quality of our lives, with the succession of moments in which the present is filled with experience and colored by recollection of the past as well as with anticipation of the future. In common with his fellow men, the philosopher also uses principles for the organization of his experience. These Dilthey called the categories of life. His analysis of them is a keystone of his philosophy.

The categories. Kant had shown that what we call experience is already intellectualized, that is, thought processes have gone into the organization of its raw material. The principles of this organization he called categories. Causality is an example of such a category, or a rule according to which we order our sense impressions. Kant confined his analysis to our experience of physical reality, but Dilthey extended this approach to the experience of life as meaningful. (He also, incidentally, rejected the transcendental deduction and considered the categories the result of empirical generalizations.) The principles by means of which we thus organize our experience are the categories of life. They are ways of interpreting events in terms of some relationship. Dilthey produced a list of these categories; however, it had to remain incomplete because categories, according to him, are arrived at by empirical generalizations.

One category Dilthey defined in terms of the relation of inner and outer, by which he referred to mental content and its physical expressions. This is the principle that lies at the base of symbolization and governs our experience of the frown as an expression of anger and of the railway signal as an intelligible instruction to the driver. Another of Dilthey's categories is "power." It is in terms of this category that we experience our own impact on things and people and their effect on us, helping our plans or frustrating our desires. It is thus the category that corresponds to that of causality in the understanding of the physical world. Other categories Dilthey listed are those of part and whole, means and ends, and development. Of particular significance in his original scheme were the following three categories: value, through which we experience the present; purpose, through which we anticipate the future; and meaning, through which we recall the past. In his later writings, Dilthey emphasized the special role of meaning. "How is meaningful experience possible?" became his central question, and he conceived the categories as different ways in which meaning is constituted in various contexts.

These organizing principles, or categories, operate primarily below the level of conscious deliberation. It is not that we see the rose, the frown, or the wall and then infer that the rose is beautiful, the man angry, or the wall an obstruction. We "see" the beautiful rose, the angry man, or the obstacle. But we do not stop there; impelled to make experience meaningful, and using the categories by which this can be accomplished, we organize and interpret life consciously and deliberately. Religions, myths, proverbs, works of art, and literature are such interpretations; moral principles, constitutions, and legal codes are explicit formulations of our valuations and purposes.

Weltanschauungen. There is in mankind a persistent tendency to achieve a comprehensive interpretation, a *Weltanschauung*, or philosophy, in which a picture of reality is combined with a sense of its meaning and value and with principles of action. These philosophies, like the more limited interpretations, are subjective and relative. We are pursuing a phantom if we try to give them objective validation. However, because they are themselves parts of life, they reveal one-sided but quite genuine aspects of that life.

The philosopher of life proceeds, therefore, from the analysis of the ways in which ordinary life becomes meaningful to the interpretations of that meaning in literature, religion, and other manifestations and finally to the philosophy of philosophy, or a critical survey of the various philosophic systems. These *Weltanschauungen* Dilthey classified into three basic types: positivism (for example, Hobbes), the idealism of freedom (for example, Kant), and objective idealism (for example, Hegel). A final synthesis of these different interpretations must elude the philosopher—it would, once again, be a step into one-sidedness. But in his sovereign view of the pageant of life and the various meanings attributed to it, he has become aware of all the meaning there is. This awareness, combined with the consciousness of the relativity of all interpretations and valuations, liberates the spirit for open-minded acceptance of reality and for creative endeavor.

GEISTESWISSENSCHAFTEN

Dilthey's persistent concern with the nature and methodology of the human studies is closely related to his philosophy of life. If the philosopher based his reflections merely on the life within and around him he would become parochial. He would, as Dilthey warned, mistake his corner for the world. A true philosophy of life must be based on the broadest possible knowledge of life's manifestations, and it is the human studies—psychology, history, economics, philology, literary criticism, comparative religion, and jurisprudence—that can provide this. The philosopher must absorb the conclusions of these disciplines, and, indeed, Dilthey's own philosophic work was enriched by his historical, biographical, and literary research. But the philosopher, in turn, has something to offer to these disciplines from which they can derive methodological strength. From the philosophy of life an epistemology can be derived. Its development was a central theme of Dilthey's philosophy.

The human studies have a common subject matter: man, his doings, and his creations. They deal with the whole socially organized and historically evolving human world. Within this body of disciplines Dilthey distinguished between the systematic studies, which aim at the formulation of general laws, and history, which is concerned with the temporal succession of individual events. They are, however, interdependent, for history provides the systematic disciplines with evidence, in such forms as case histories and records of economic developments; the systematic disciplines, together with common-sense generalizations and the findings of physical science, provide the laws in terms of which the connections between individual events in history can be explained.

Historicism. The problem of historiography—or in Dilthey's words, of a "critique of historical understanding"—was particularly close to his heart. Dilthey applied his general epistemology to this problem; he also made detailed suggestions about the use of sources, the role of philology, and other matters of technique in history. But, more generally, he formulated three principles that form an important aspect of what has come to be known as historicism:

(1) All human manifestations are part of a historical process and should be explained in historical terms. The state, the family, even man himself cannot be adequately defined abstractly because they have different characteristics in different ages.

(2) Different ages and differing individuals can only be understood by entering imaginatively into their specific point of view; what the age or the individual thought relevant must be taken into account by the historian.

(3) The historian himself is bound by the horizons of his own age. How the past presents itself to him in the perspectives of his own concerns becomes a legitimate aspect of the meaning of that past.

Das Verstehen. In all the human studies, general intellectual procedures and methods shared with all the sciences, or borrowed from particular ones, are employed. These include observation, description, classification, quantification (where possible), induction and deduction, generalization, comparison, the use of models, and the framing and testing of hypotheses. However, the human studies cannot achieve the knowledge they seek without also using the method of understanding—*Das Verstehen*—which in fact characterizes them as a group and distinguishes them from the physical sciences. For Dilthey, *Das Verstehen* is a technical term with a definite meaning that must be clearly distinguished from its general use as a synonym for any kind of comprehension. It is the comprehension of some mental content—an idea, an intention, or a feeling—manifested in empirically given expressions such as words or gestures.

What we understand from an expression is the meaning that human beings perceive in, or attribute to, a single situation or their whole lives. That men experience life as meaningful, that they tend to express that meaning, and that this expression can be understood are the three central tenets of Dilthey's epistemology; on them he based his methodology of the human studies.

As part of this epistemological analysis, Dilthey considered three conditions which made understanding possible. First, he argued, we must be familiar with the mental processes through which meaning is experienced and conveyed. If we did not know what it was to love or abhor something, to have an intention, or to express something, we could not begin to understand anything; of course we need not abhor spiders to understand Miss Muffet's abhorrence of them. Because we are human beings and because all expressions ultimately derive from the activity of individual human beings, this requisite of familiarity with mental processes is always at least partially fulfilled. It can be fulfilled more adequately through the study of biographies and descriptive psychology. Insofar as Dilthey's earlier writings emphasized this aspect of understanding, they have been both criticized as "psychologism" and described sympathetically as methodological individualism. However, in his later years he placed increasing emphasis on two additional conditions.

The first of these two conditions for understanding expressions is knowledge of the particular concrete context in which they occur. A word is better understood, sometimes only understood, in its verbal setting; an action, in the situation that gave rise to it. For this condition Dilthey derived the methodological principle that to understand an expression we must systematically explore the context in which it stands. For example, to understand a religious movement or a philosophic doctrine better, we must relate it to the climate of opinion and the social conditions of the time. For example, the philosophy of Spinoza can be better understood against the background of the rise of science and the conflict between different religious sects in the sixteenth and seventeenth centuries.

The second of these conditions is knowledge of the social and cultural systems that determine the nature of most expressions. To understand a sentence we must know the language; to understand a chess move, the rules of the game.

Two problems arise about the way we understand such systems. First, we are theoretically involved in a circle. To understand a word we must understand the language, yet to understand a language we must have come to understand the words that constitute it. In practice we solve this problem by a kind of shuttlecock movement. From approximate knowledge of individual words an understanding of the language grows; this, in turn, makes our understanding of individual words more precise; and so on. This procedure is characteristic of the human studies.

The second problem in understanding cultural systems is more general; understanding a legal code is different from and more complex than understanding what Aunt Emily feels. Dilthey parted company with methodological individualism on this point. Legal systems or works of literature are, of course, the products of individual minds, empirically given in physical signs (such as marks on paper) and in the psychological experiences that they precipitate. Yet it is methodologically convenient, as well as in conformity with common usage, to treat them as independent entities belonging to a sphere of their own and confronting the individual: Brown's life, we say, has been affected by Milton's poetry. This sphere Dilthey called the objectifications of life (*Die Objektivationen des Lebens*) or the objective mind (*Der objektive Geist*).

Thus, according to Dilthey, understanding and interpretation, used systematically in the human studies, disclose to us the features of life. Philosophy assists the human studies in the achievement of methodological clarity and receives from them, in return, the factual insights into life which are grist to its mill.

Dilthey's theories are not only of historical interest but also contain ideas of continuing relevance, and the long-term influence of his work has been considerable. His conception of philosophy as the systematic interpretation of human experience and as the effort toward greater awareness of our presuppositions provides a corrective to the two extremes of metaphysical dogmatism and resignation to piecemeal investigation. Heidegger acknowledged his own and his generation's indebtedness to Dilthey's analysis of temporality. Jaspers and Ortega y Gasset were influenced by his ideas. His theory of meaning elaborated in terms of the categories of life and his analysis of understanding and expressions made a valuable contribution to epistemology and methodology in the human studies. German educational theory and practice remain dominated by his views. Historicism continues to be a live issue among historians, and his suggestions on psychology, taken up and developed by Eduard Spranger, can be traced in the works of contemporary psychologists. Above all, Dilthey's theory of understanding became the basis of Max Weber's methodology and thus influenced modern sociological theory. Contemporary sociologists have drawn on these ideas in their polemics against behaviorism and positivism.

Works by Dilthey

Dilthey's works have been collected in 12 volumes as *Gesammelte Schriften* (Leipzig and Berlin, 1914–1936; 2d ed., Stuttgart and Göttingen, 1957–1960). The second edition is the first complete one; Volume X, on moral philosophy, did not appear in the first edition. Vols. I–IV, VI, IX, and XII contain extensive contributions to the history of philosophy and of ideas, notably on the changing religious and philosophic conceptions of man (Vols. I and II), the history of German idealism (Vol. IV), the German Enlightenment (Vol. III), the history of pedagogic ideas (Vol. IX). Vols. V and VI are devoted to the philosophy of life. The section "Das Wesen der Philosophie" from Vol. V has been translated by S. A. and W. T. Emery as *The Essence of Philosophy* (Chapel Hill, N.C., 1954). Vol. IX contains Dilthey's typology of philosophic systems. Vols. I and VII develop the theory of the human studies; Vol. VII contains Dilthey's final and most original contributions to this subject. About one hundred pages of selected passages representing the central thought of Vol. VII have been translated and edited by H. P. Rickman (*Meaning in History: Dilthey's Thought on History and Society*, London, 1961; New York, 1962).

Some of the 12 volumes contain useful introductions by the editors. Georg Mirsch's introduction to Vol. V is of particular importance.

Among the writings not in the *Gesammelte Schriften* are *Das Leben Schleiermachers* (Vol. I, Berlin, 1870; Vol. II, Berlin and Leipzig, 1922, enlarged from unpublished notes of Dilthey's by Herman Mulart); *Das Erlebnis und die Dichtung* (Leipzig and Berlin, 1905; 13th ed., Stuttgart, 1957); *Von Deutscher Dichtung und Musik* (Leipzig and Berlin, 1933; 2d ed., Stuttgart, 1957); *Die Grosse Phantasiedichtung* (Göttingen, 1954).

Various collections of Dilthey's correspondence are also available.

Works on Dilthey

From several hundred German books and articles the following can be recommended: Georg Mirsch, *Lebensphilosophie und Phänomenologie: Eine Auseinandersetzung der Diltheyschen Richtung mit Heidegger und Husserl* (Bonn, 1930; 2d ed., Leipzig and Berlin, 1931), which is extremely involved and difficult but contains the most profound discussion of the philosophic implications of Dilthey's mature thought; O. F. Bollnow, *Dilthey: Eine Einführung in seine Philosophie* (Leipzig and Berlin, 1936), which is clear and helpful.

Among the English works are H. A. Hodges' *Wilhelm Dilthey: An Introduction* (London, 1944), containing a brief account of Dilthey's teaching, historical place, and significance, an extensive bibliography, and about fifty pages of English translations of selected passages; Hodges' *The Philosophy of Wilhelm Dilthey* (London, 1952), which is a comprehensive account of the different stages and aspects of Dilthey's philosophy; and the preface to

H. P. Rickman's translation, *Meaning in History*, which is an exposition of Dilthey's theory of the human studies and its relevance today.

H. P. RICKMAN

DINGLER, HUGO (1881–1954), German philosopher of science, was the most important representative of Continental operationism, as distinguished from the operationalism of the American physicist P. W. Bridgman. Dingler was also a main contributor to *Grundlagenforschung* (research on the foundations of the exact sciences). After studying under such teachers as David Hilbert, Edmund Husserl, Felix Klein, Hermann Minkowski, Wilhelm Roentgen, and Woldemar Voigt at the universities of Erlangen, Munich, and Göttingen, Dingler received a Ph.D. in mathematics, physics, and astronomy in 1906 and became *Privatdozent* in 1912. He was appointed professor at the University of Munich in 1920 and at the Technische Hochschule in Darmstadt in 1932. In 1934 he was dismissed on charges of philosemitism. He later resumed teaching but soon rebelled again against the political situation, and eventually he was put under the continuous watch of a Gestapo agent "who unfortunately"—as Dingler told the present writer—"was not gifted for philosophy and did not profit from my compulsory daily lessons." Such difficulties in the German political situation during Dingler's life contributed to the lack of awareness of his work, despite his some twenty books and seventy essays in exceptionally clear German. Perhaps a more decisive factor was Dingler's independence of all the main schools and trends in contemporary philosophy of science—positivism and empiricism, Neo-Kantianism, phenomenology, intuitionism, and formalism.

From the juvenile *Grundlinien einer Kritik und exakten Theorie der Wissenschaften, insbesondere der mathematischen* ("Essentials of a Critique and Rigorous Theory of the Sciences, Especially of the Mathematical Ones," Munich, 1907) to the posthumous *Die Ergreifung des Wirklichen* ("The Grasping of Reality," Munich, 1955), Dingler's main concern was to give a new answer to the Kantian question "How is exact science possible?" He regarded arithmetic, analysis, geometry, and mechanics as the exact sciences *par excellence;* he called them "mental" (*geistige*), meaning that they cannot be derived from experience and must be synthesized operationally from a few univocal ideas used as "building stones" (*Bausteine*). In this way scientific inquiry was to be made continuous with everyday life and viewed in terms of practical activity. The operational reconstruction of the foundations of science was to abolish the field of foundations as an independent territory open to philosophical disagreement or mystification. Dingler came to consider the given itself, as expressed in protocol, or basic, sentences, as a highly complicated kind of result.

To prevent any residues of previous theories from entering into the operational reconstruction, we must start from a "zero situation" in which we suppose only that the world is "simply there" and that we can operate on it. This is a methodological principle, not a metaphysical denial of reality: it is a voluntary suspension of rational processes which can be brought about at any moment. After 1907, under Husserl's influence, Dingler labeled the zero situation "the standpoint of freedom from presuppositions." In 1942 he described it as *das Unberührte*, the intact or untouched—"that which has not yet been operated upon."

The first univocal step out of the zero situation consists in entertaining an idea in which the sheer relation of difference (with equality and similarity as its special cases) is present, and is applied (*anwendet*) only once, as in the idea "something distinct without further specification," that is, the idea of an entity as distinguished from all the rest, as standing out from a background. This idea is not the description of anything existing in the world but rather is the first requirement for any such description. All we can say about it is that it is present and limited; we can then specify it as constant or variable, and in either case we can also give special attention to its limits. In this way we reach a purely qualitative fourfold scheme which precedes the concepts of number, space, and time. To this scheme correspond four rules of operation, which afford the starting points of the exact sciences: (1) something distinct without further specification, and constant, for arithmetic; (2) the same, but variable, for analysis (more generally for the doctrine of time and variables); (3) the same, but constant, considered with respect to its limits, for geometry; and (4) the same, but variable, considered with respect to its limits, for kinematics and mechanics.

By means of complications of this basic scheme Dingler was able to operationally derive and prove the axioms of the exact sciences and to construct their whole fabric. This painstaking and original construction is to be found chiefly in *Philosophie der Logik und Arithmetik* (1931), *Die Grundlagen der Geometrie* (1933), *Die Methode der Physik* (1938), and *Lehrbuch der exakten Naturwissenschaften* (1944).

Works by Dingler

WORKS ON "GRUNDLAGENFORSCHUNG"

Philosophie der Logik und Arithmetik. Munich, 1931.

Geschichte der Naturphilosophie. Berlin, 1932. A history of the development of the idea of *Grundlagenforschung* in experimental science.

Die Grundlagen der Geometrie. Stuttgart, 1933.

Die Methode der Physik. Munich, 1938.

Lehrbuch der exacten Naturwissenschaften. Berlin, 1944. Only thirty copies printed. Parts reprinted with Italian translation and a commentary by Enrico Albani in *Methodos,* Vol. 7 (1955), 277–287, and Vol. 8 (1956) 29–30, 122–137, 191–199.

OTHER WORKS

Metaphysik als Wissenschaft und der Primat der Philosophie. Munich, 1926.

Das System. Munich, 1933.

Das Handeln im Sinne des höchsten Zieles. Munich, 1935.

Von der Tierseele zur Menschenseele. Leipzig, 1941.

Grundriss der methodischen Philosophie. Füssen, 1949. A crystal-clear summary of Dingler's main views, but of lower technical quality than his main treatises.

ESSAYS

"Methodik statt Erkenntnistheorie und Wissenschaftslehre." *Kant-Studien,* Vol. 41 (1936), 346–379.

"Über die letzte Wurzel der exakten Naturwissenschaften."

Zeitschrift für die gesamte Naturwissenschaft, Vol. 8 (1942), 49–70.

"Das Unberührte. Die Definition des unmittelbar Gegebenen." *Zeitschrift für die gesamte Naturwissenschaft,* Vol. 8 (1942), 209–224.

"Die philosophische Begründung des Deszendenztheorie," in Gerhard Hebener, ed., *Die Evolution der Organismen.* Jena, 1943.

Works on Dingler

Benini, Giorgio, *I concetti fondamentali della filosofia metodica di Hugo Dingler.* Unpublished dissertation, Catholic University of the Sacred Heart, Milan, 1953.

Ceccato, Silvio, "Contra Dingler, pro Dingler." *Methodos,* Vol. 4 (1952), 223–265, with English translation 266–290 and reply by Dingler, 291–296, translated into English 297–299.

Kramps, Wilhelm, *Die Philosophie Hugo Dinglers.* Munich, 1955. The main study.

Kramps, Wilhelm, ed., *Hugo Dingler Gedenkbuch zum 75. Geburtstag.* Munich, 1956. Contains 14 essays by various authors and a bibliography.

Sandborn, Herbert, "Dingler's Methodical Philosophy." *Methodos,* Vol. 4 (1952), 191–220.

FERRUCCIO ROSSI-LANDI

DIOGENES LAËRTIUS, called Laërtius Diogenes in the manuscripts and older scholarship, was the author of the only extant continuous account of the lives and doctrines of the chief Greek philosophers. He probably lived in the early part of the third century, for his work mentions no author later than Saturninus and omits Neoplatonism altogether. His book, variously called *The Lives of Philosophers, History of Philosophy,* and *Lives and Opinions of Famous Philosophers,* is chiefly important for some of its biographical material and for fragments from the works of the philosophers and poets. Diogenes' own poems (occasionally quoted in his *History of Philosophy*), of which he published a complete collection (not extant) in more than one book (I.39), are miserable stuff.

His work begins with an introduction on barbarian schools of thought (Magi, Chaldeans, Gymnosophists, and Druids), followed by an account of some of the sages of early Greece (Book I). He followed an Alexandrian procedure in arranging the philosophers in two "successions," an Ionian, or Eastern (Books I.22–VII), and an Italian, or Western (Book VIII); to these he appended his so-called Sporadics, important philosophers who did not, in his opinion, found successions (Books IX–X). This arrangement scatters the pre-Socratics through Books I, II, VIII, and IX. The work is probably as finished as Diogenes intended (see X.138, where he spoke of giving the finishing touch to his entire book) and was written, at least in part, for a woman interested in Platonism (III.47; cf. X.29, where he again addresses a single reader).

Diogenes was an industrious, curious, and at times credulous compiler, mostly from secondary sources, which he interwove in a manner that is sometimes confused and confusing: for example, the account of Plato's education in Book III.5–17, where Diogenes continually broke up his narrative by inserting irrelevant comments from a variety of sources. Excerpts are occasionally inserted in the wrong place, as at IX.18, where a note probably referring to Xenophon is applied to Xenophanes, who could hardly have been a pupil of the rhetorician Boton of Athens. He took the material on Epicurus word for word from Epicurus' own writings, inserting marginalia and scholia in the text, sometimes so that he disturbs the sense. The work is a tissue of quotations but at least has the merit of usually naming Diogenes' sources: over two hundred authors and three hundred works are named specifically. Since most of his favorite sources (such as Antigonus of Carystus, Hermippus, Sotion, Apollodorus of Athens, Sosicrates of Rhodes, Demetrius and Diocles of Magnesia, Pamphila, and Favorinus) were themselves masters of the art of making one new book from many old ones, Diogenes' material often comes to us at several removes from the original. Though he did not go to the primary documents, he was seldom content to copy just one handbook but would combine them, and his originality consists almost exclusively in his selection of materials. Such a method naturally produces contradictions and repetitions: for example, the frequent references to Heraclitus' *megalophrosyne* (arrogance), which no doubt was mentioned in all the handbooks.

Since this is so, the value of any section of Diogenes depends on the value of its sources. For instance, the account of Stoic doctrine (VII.39–160) is reliable; the direct quotations from Epicurus are valuable; the lives of Pythagoras and Empedocles contain good material drawn, respectively, from Timaeus and Alexander Polyhistor; and the lives of Plato, Aristotle, the leading Stoics, and some others are good literary portraits when the extraneous notes are removed. But the treatment of the earlier philosophers is perfunctory: Heraclitus, for example, is reduced to a mere caricature, and the summary of Aristotle's doctrines shows Stoic, perhaps even Epicurean, influence.

Diogenes nowhere stated that he had studied philosophy, nor is it clear to what school he may have belonged. He included an encomium of Epicurus and panegyrics on the Cynics; he treated both Skepticism and Epicureanism with sympathetic interest; in IX.109 he used a phrase ("*our* Apollonides," referring to a Skeptic) that would, if not derived from his source, indicate that he was himself a Skeptic; and he addressed at least part of his work to a Platonist. Sextus Empiricus' similar impartiality to all schools of philosophy suggests that Diogenes too may have been a Skeptic, but this has not been proved.

Works by Diogenes

Diogenes Laertius: Lives of Eminent Philosophers, 2 vols. Loeb Classical Library. London and New York, 1925. With a translation by R. D. Hicks.

Diogenis Laertii Vitae Philosophorum, H. S. Long, ed., 2 vols. Oxford Classical Texts. Oxford, 1964. Critical text.

Works on Diogenes

Biedl, A., "Zur Textgeschichte des Laertios Diogenes," in *Studi e Testi,* 184. Biblioteca Apostolica Vaticana. Vatican, 1955. Good bibliography.

Hope, R., *The Book of Diogenes Laertius, Its Spirit and Its Methods.* New York, 1930.

Schwartz, E., "Diogenes (40)," in A. Pauly, G. Wissowa, and W. Kroll, eds., *Real-Enzyklopädie der classischen Altertumswissenschaft,* Vol. V, cols. 738–763. Stuttgart, 1905.

HERBERT S. LONG

DIOGENES OF APOLLONIA, natural philosopher of the second half of the fifth century, seems to have done most of his work in Athens. Ancient evidence suggests that he was acquainted with Ionian speculation, was influenced by Anaxagoras' doctrine of Mind, and was indebted to the atomists' view that coming to be and passing away were caused by the mixing or separating of elements of the same kind. Following Anaximenes, he proposed the physical theory that all things in the world are modifications (*heteroioseis*) of the same basic stuff, air (*aer*).

Theophrastus described Diogenes as an eclectic. More sympathetic studies of Diogenes' thought show him to be an elegant systematizer of ideas. In a period of transition in Greek thought, he attempted to reconcile ancient insights with new discoveries, to bring pre-Socratic speculations in line with the details of biological observation. He was the author of a book, *On Nature*. Reports also associate him with the lost treatises *Meteorology*, *Against the Sophists*, and *Nature of Man*.

The assertion that everything in the universe is a modification of a single basic substance was made by Diogenes on the force of two related considerations. According to the first, physical interaction would be impossible if each individual thing were radically and substantially different from everything else. According to the second, the uniformly exhibited harmony of nature would be a mystery if an underlying, all-pervasive intelligence did not control and guide everything. To deny these considerations would be equivalent, Diogenes thought, to ignoring the ways in which things mix or help or harm each other, the ways things depend on each other (as in nutrition and growth). Moreover, such a denial would overlook the balance, measure, and intelligible structure that characterize every aspect of nature. Diogenes boldly asserted that air is the basic cosmic substance, since it is the life principle and intelligence of the whole animate world. Air is the source and guiding power of every physical change. It is the most versatile and adaptable substance. Its capacity to manifest itself in a wide variety of forms, and under every conceivable condition—as hot, as cold, as wet and then dry—is evidence of its rationality and divinity. To the extent that there is air in all animation, a part of God is in every living creature.

The implications of this general claim led Diogenes to the problem of perception. Following an empirical approach, he attempted to explain sensing, feeling, and cognizing by means of the "mechanical"-spiritual properties of air. With patient references to details of anatomy, physiology, and embryology Diogenes tried to show how sensation and perception were brought about, and why air in each case was crucial. While his adherence to this general principle was consistent, Diogenes' respect for observation kept him free from earlier pre-Socratic dogmatism. His cosmological views amply bear this out. Here again he insists on the importance of air in explaining the formation of celestial bodies through condensation and rarefaction; but specific explanations of the nature of the stars, of their motions, of the earth's constitution, of the sun's fire, of the presumed infinity of worlds are carefully backed up by empirical evidence.

Diogenes was one of the earliest Greek natural philosophers to acknowledge the usefulness of "theoretically" guided observation. Sadly, few of his contemporaries were able to appreciate the implications of this.

Bibliography

Beare, J. I., *Greek Theories of Elementary Cognition*. Oxford, 1906.

Burnet, John, *Early Greek Philosophy*, 4th ed. London, 1930. Pp. 352–358.

Diels, H., and Kranz, W., *Fragmente der Vorsokratiker*, 7th ed. Berlin, 1954. Vol. II, pp. 51–69.

Diller, H., "Die philosophiegeschichtliche Stellung des Diogenes von Apollonia." *Hermes*, Vol. 76 (1941).

Jaeger, Werner, *The Theology of the Early Greek Philosophers*, translated by E. S. Robinson. Oxford, 1947. Pp. 155–171.

Kirk, G. S., and Raven, J. E., *The Presocratic Philosophers*. Cambridge, 1957. Pp. 427–445.

P. DIAMANDOPOULOS

DIOGENES OF SINOPE, fourth century B.C., prototype of the Cynics, who probably were so called from Diogenes' Greek nickname, the Dog (*kuon*; adjective form, *kunikos*). Tradition held that on coming to Athens in exile, he was influenced by Antisthenes' teaching; Diogenes' ascetic distortion of Socratic temperance gives some point to Plato's supposed remark that he was a "Socrates gone mad."

It is not easy to recover the philosopher from, on the one hand, the lurid fog of anecdotal tradition that represents the stunts of an eccentric tramp at Athens and Corinth defacing conventional human standards—as he or his father, Hicesias, was supposed to have defaced in some way the currency of Sinope—or, on the other, the idealized legend that grew after his death. But doxographic traces (for example, Diogenes Laërtius, VI.70–73) and, indeed, the tradition as a whole presuppose a serious teacher who, in disillusioned protest against a corrupt society and hostile world, advocated happiness as self-realization and self-mastery in an inner spiritual freedom from all wants except the bare natural minimum; and who, in a bitter crusade against the corrupting influence of pleasure, desire, and luxury, extolled the drastic painful effort involved in the mental and physical training for the achievement of a natural and inviolable self-sufficiency.

The anecdotes illustrate Diogenes' philosophy in action. Since for Diogenes virtue was revealed in practice and not in theoretical analysis or argument, the stories of, for example, his embracing statues in winter and his peering with a lantern in daytime for a human being, the tales of his fearless biting repartee and criticism of notables such as Alexander, however embroidered or apocryphal, correctly reflect his pointed teaching methods, which encouraged the development of a new didactic form, the *chreia*, or moral epigram. Some exaggeration here is due to the "dog-cynic" shamelessness pedagogically employed to discount convention, and some is no doubt inherent in the uncompromising extremes of Diogenes' doctrines.

He is credited with tragedies illustrating the human predicament and with a *Republic*, which influenced Zeno the Stoic, that was notorious for its scandalous attack on convention. His famous remark that he was a citizen of the world is more probably antinational than international, for he was concerned with the individual rather than the community. Diogenes sought to make any man king, not of others, but of himself, through autonomy of will, and his own life was his main philosophical demonstration to this end.

Works on Diogenes of Sinope

Crönert, W., *Kolotes und Menedemos*. Leipzig, 1906.
Diogenes Laërtius, *Lives*, VI. 20–81.
Dudley, D. R., *History of Cynicism*. London, 1937.
Höistad, R., *Cynic Hero and Cynic King*. Uppsala, Sweden, 1949.
Sayre, F., *The Greek Cynics*. Baltimore, 1948.

I. G. KIDD

DIOGENES THE CYNIC. *See* DIOGENES OF SINOPE.

DIONYSIUS THE PSEUDO-AREOPAGITE. *See* PSEUDO-DIONYSIUS.

DIRECT REALISM. *See* REALISM.

DOGMA. The Greek word of which "dogma" is a transliteration means "that which seems good." It was applied by Greek authors to the decrees of public authorities and to the tenets of various philosophical schools. In English the word can be used for any fixed and firmly held belief on any subject, but it usually suggests that the belief is a condition, or at least a sign, of belonging to either a secular or (more frequently) a religious group. The word can also imply that the belief rests on a special—often divine—authority; that any member of the group who attenuates or changes the belief is thereby a "heretic"; and that heresy is a moral, and perhaps also legal, offense that merits the strongest condemnation (and perhaps also punishment).

The clearest example of religious dogma in ancient philosophy comes from Plato. In the *Republic* (376E ff.) he lays down two "ways in which God is to be spoken of" (*tupoi theologias*). The first is that God is good and the cause of good alone; the second is that God is true and incapable of change. In the *Laws* (887E–888D) he actually uses "dogma" to mean a correct "belief" about the gods. Everyone must believe that the gods are concerned with human affairs and that they cannot be appeased by sacrifice. Those who reject these beliefs must be duly punished by the state.

The primary sense of "dogma" is the one it has acquired in Christianity. Other religions have their distinctive tenets, but Christianity alone deserves attention on three grounds. First, its dogmas are far more numerous and complex than those of other faiths: Judaism requires only the recitation of the *Shema*, and Islam requires only assent to the *Kalima*. (Both these short creeds affirm the unity of God.) Second, Christian dogma has had many important points of contact with Western secular philosophy. Third, Christian theologians have given to the word "dogma" itself a technical, precise significance. (There is nothing that can properly be called dogma in the religions of the East. The Eightfold Path of Buddhism is a nontheistic way of salvation, not a creed. In Hinduism there are many divergent views of God and the Absolute, but none of them is "orthodox.")

All the main Christian bodies are agreed that dogma is essentially the formulation of belief on the basis of the Scriptures. God revealed himself both in the events to which the Bible testifies and in the Biblical interpretation of them. The role of dogma is to express the meaning of this revelation in conceptual terms.

All would also agree that dogma does not add to the revelation which was complete with the apostles. Dogma merely makes explicit what is implicit in apostolic teaching. Hence, St. Vincent of Lérins affirms that the development of dogma is an "advance" (*profectus*), not a change (*permutatio*). Although a dogma can always be restated in a form that is either more exact per se or more comprehensible to a particular audience, its substance is immutable.

This point is clearly made by Hans Küng in his important book on the second Vatican Council, *The Council and Reunion* (London, 1961). On the one hand, "dogmatic definitions express the truth with infallible accuracy and are in this sense unalterable (as against Modernism)" (p. 163). On the other hand, "one and the same truth of faith can always be expressed in a still more complete, more adequate, better formula" (*ibid.*).

All Christian bodies, finally, would agree that the *ultimate* object of assent is not any statement about God, but God himself. Furthermore, dogmas do not render God intelligible; they symbolize a mystery that surpasses understanding. Therefore, we cannot assent to them without the gift of faith.

However, Christians differ in their views on both the number of and the authority for dogmatic definitions. Roman Catholic theologians hold that the definitions given by twenty ecumenical councils of the church are inerrant. They further hold that the pope alone, when he speaks *ex cathedra*, is infallible in matters of faith and morals. Finally, they hold that a dogma (for example, the dogma of the Immaculate Conception) can be justified as a logical "development" even though it lacks any scriptural support.

Non-Roman Christians oppose these claims. The Orthodox church holds that only seven councils are ecumenical and inerrant. Both Luther and the Anglican reformers said that all councils are capable of error. All Protestants and Anglicans agree in denying both the infallibility of the pope and the validity of dogmas that are not explicitly supported by the Bible.

From the beginning, dogma has been stated through the terms of secular philosophy. One need mention only the use made of "substance" and "relation" in the doctrine of the Trinity. Such philosophical expressions were required both to make the faith intelligible and to safeguard it against heresy. Even those Protestants who reject scholastic terminology are forced to substitute other concepts (for example, those of existentialism).

In the theology of Aquinas, and in conciliar definitions, philosophy is instrumental. The content and authority of dogma are derived wholly from revelation, although some theologians have attempted to place dogmas in the context of a speculative system that is alien to the basic principles of Christian theism. Inevitably, the dogmas then lose their original, distinctive, and (above all) supernatural significance. Thus Hegel and his disciples held that Christ merely exhibits in a supreme mode the natural coinherence of the finite and the infinite.

At the other extreme, some post-Kantian thinkers, while remaining in the church, have denied that dogmas state objective truths concerning God. But we are to act "as if" they were true, and in so acting we shall find that the moral life is given both a meaning and a power which it cannot otherwise possess. This reduction of dogmas to the status of pragmatic postulates is the 26th proposition condemned by the decree *Lamentabili* (1907).

Bibliography

Bettenson, Henry, *Documents of the Christian Church.* Oxford, 1947.

Brunner, Emil, *The Christian Doctrine of God*, translated by Olive Wyon. London, 1949. Chs. 1–11.

Journet, C., *What Is Dogma?*, translated by Mark Pontifex. London, 1946.

Newman, J. H., *An Essay in Development.* Several editions since 1845.

H. P. OWEN

DOING. *See* CHOOSING, DECIDING, AND DOING.

DOSTOYEVSKY, FYODOR MIKHAILOVICH (1821–1881), Russian novelist and essayist, is considered a forerunner of existentialist thought. He was born in Moscow and attended school there and in St. Petersburg (at the School of Military Engineers). In 1849 he was arrested for membership in a utopian socialist, clandestine organization, the Petrashevsky Circle, and sent to Siberia for eight years. The arrest and imprisonment interrupted his career for almost ten years. After his return, and for the remainder of his life, he was very conservative in political belief, a rabid defender of the autocracy, and a firm defender of the Russian Orthodox faith. Several trips to western Europe in the 1860s reinforced a bitter hatred for the West that he carried throughout his life. Much of his work was concerned with demolishing the pretensions of the scientific, rational humanitarianism of the nineteenth century and with justifying the necessity of faith and of God as conditions of true freedom. His most important works are *Poor Folk* (1846), *The Double* (1846), *The House of the Dead* (1860), *The Insulted and the Injured* (1861), *Notes From the Underground* (1864), *Crime and Punishment* (1866), *The Idiot* (1869), *The Possessed* (1871–1872), *The Adolescent* (1875), and *The Brothers Karamazov* (1879–1880).

Thought. At the center of all Dostoyevsky's writing is the problem of freedom. What is permitted and what is not permitted is a question that Dostoyevsky dramatizes again and again, and one can regard the development of his work as a dramatic testing of the limits of freedom and a progressive refinement of what he meant by the concept of freedom.

Man, for Dostoyevsky, is limited by society, economic conditions, laws, history, the church, and especially by God. He is classified, defined, and fixed by a hundred institutions and a thousand conditions. Man, however, does not want to be defined and limited; he wants to be free and he wants to be totally free. According to Dostoyevsky he is right in wanting to be free, for freedom is the essential attribute of his identity.

Dostoyevsky's free man must be a revolutionary. He must refuse what society, economics, religion, other people, and his own past have made of him. Golyadkin, the hero of the early tale *The Double* (1846), refuses to be what society and economic conditions and his own acts have made of him: a civil servant of a certain rank, living on Shestilavochnaya Street with a servant named Petrushka; someone not poor and not rich; something of a bootlicker, a bit of a hypocrite, and a social bore. He revolts against this Golyadkin by creating a double. By giving all his undesirable traits to the double, he is able to make in his mind a new identity: good, brave, intelligent, and heroic. The Golyadkin others see is a mistake; the Golyadkin he carries in his mind is the true one. When the two come into conflict, he defends unto madness his freedom to reject what the past and conditions have made of him and his right to create himself.

The Double, Dostoyevsky's best and most representative early work, clearly looks forward to *Notes From the Underground*, where Dostoyevsky's conception of freedom and man's search for identity are fully and explicitly treated. This is a key work and the best source for Dostoyevsky's mature philosophical views. It has been rightfully hailed as the great philosophical prelude to the dramatic triumphs of the great novels that follow. The underground man is Dostoyevsky's totally free man. He carries revolt against limitation to its extreme and raises it to a philosophical principle. Like the existentialists who were to follow three-quarters of a century later, he is *en marge;* he is in revolt not only against society but also against himself, not once, not only today or tomorrow, but eternally.

Dostoyevsky's radical contemporaries, particularly N. G. Chernyshevski in "The Anthropological Principle in Philosophy" (1860), asserted that it was merely a matter of time until the laws of man's moral nature were discovered. Then the rational man would necessarily choose according to these laws. The underground man is Dostoyevsky's bitter answer to these assertions of the rational organization of man's happiness. The underground man refuses to accept the laws of nature. Against science, against the laws of reason, against the whole movement of man's systematic accumulation of knowledge, against the ideal of Chernyshevski's "Crystal Palace," against all that man pursues and dreads, the underground man opposes his unique, whimsical, subjective world: wish, dream, hope, cruelty, suffering, pettiness, viciousness. If the laws of nature (defined by reason) really exist, then "free will" is an illusion that will be dispelled by reason. But the underground man asserts that man will reject the laws of nature and the rational organization of happiness because he will prefer to follow his whims and stick gold pins into others or have them stuck into himself. If his subjective revolt is really the pledge of a reality that is full, complex, and true—of which reason is only a small part and not the whole—then the laws of reason are an illusion, a dream that has arisen like a mist over the scientific infancy of man. Which is the dream and which the reality in this weird dialectic?

Do the laws of nature exist? Is man a function of some infinite calculus, or is he free to follow the sweet curve of his foolish will? Whatever the answer may be, we know that the underground man and Dostoyevsky do not believe that the laws of nature exist. For Dostoyevsky these laws do not exist because reason itself, as an objective entity, does not exist. There is no "reason" in Dostoyevsky's world, only reasoners. Behind every rational formula there is a formulator, and behind every generalization there is a generalizer. In Dostoyevsky's world there are no "ideas" apart from the men who carry them. An idea for Dostoyevsky is always someone's idea, and reason is always someone's reasoning. Every act of reason is a covert act of will. Man is totally subjective and totally free.

However, this freedom implies an implacable and terrible truth about the actions of men and their treatment of others. If there are no laws to one's nature—and there cannot be if one is to be free—then man alone is his own law. And if he is his own end, he will make everything else serve that end, including other people. Even more, every a priori truth becomes illusion. Otherwise, the truth would be prior to our choices, and our choices would be determined by it. Truth as something absolute, timeless, and pre-existent to our choices is impossible in Dostoyevsky's concept of freedom. Truth, like everything else in his world, depends on our wills. The implications of this are terrifying: every action of principle, every act of unselfishness, every good, beautiful, virtuous, reasonable act is so only in appearance. No matter how much naive and tender romantic souls may want to believe in them, they are really deceptions, for the reality is man's free will and his deadly duel with other free wills.

The total freedom of the underground man brought Dostoyevsky to the total terror of a universe without truth or principle, good or evil, virtue or vice. This nihilistic vision of the universe was to send philosophers like L. I. Shestov and Nietzsche into dark ecstasy over the naked power of the will, and it was also to bring Dostoyevsky to what seemed to be an irresolvable dilemma: Freedom is the supreme good because man is not man unless he is free, but freedom is also a supreme evil because man is free to do anything, including illimitable destruction.

The problem that Dostoyevsky faced after finishing *Notes From the Underground* was how to preserve freedom while restraining its destructive implications. In his next novel, *Crime and Punishment,* he attempted to dramatize a solution. *Crime and Punishment* treats the consequences of a "free will" unleashed on society, and, at the same time, it attempts to find a force to restrain the free will. This force is God, but God in turn poses a contradiction. As the rational organization of human happiness met the destructive aspects of the existing social structure by destroying free will, so God threatens to restrain the destructive aspects of free will by destroying freedom. This dilemma and a search for some resolution dramatically inform the great novels that follow *Crime and Punishment.*

In characters like Nastasya Filipovna in *The Idiot,* Nicholas Stavrogin and Kirilov in *The Possessed,* and Ivan Karamazov in *The Brothers Karamazov,* Dostoyevsky explored with incredible creative skill and dramatic power the destructive implications of free will. Nicholas Stavrogin succeeds in living his freedom to its extreme: He triumphs over fear, moral principles, and public opinion, and his triumphs end in suicide. Kirilov exposes the logical implications of total freedom with terrifying clarity, and he kills himself as a consequence of his logic. Total freedom leads to total destruction. The freedom that kills life is not the only possibility, for there is a freedom that gives life. Dostoyevsky attempted to embody the life-giving freedom unsuccessfully in the converted Raskolnikov of *Crime and Punishment,* with ambiguous success in Prince Myshkin of *The Idiot,* and most successfully in Alyosha and Father Zossima of *The Brothers Karamazov.*

The two kinds of freedom are most fully embodied and brought into conflict in the persons of Christ and the Grand Inquisitor in "The Legend of the Grand Inquisitor." (This passage in *The Brothers Karamazov* is one of the greatest pieces of prose literature ever written.) Christ's freedom is that of conditionless faith, given by man in fearful and lonely anxiety and without the reassurance of rational proof, miracles, or the support of the crowd. The Grand Inquisitor's freedom is the freedom of the superior will, presented in its most attractive form. He loves man, even though he knows him to be weak, and works for his physical and spiritual comfort, even though he is convinced that man faces a void beyond the grave. So powerfully did Dostoyevsky dramatize the Grand Inquisitor's argument against Christ and his freedom that critical opinion has split since that time in choosing Christ or the Grand Inquisitor as the bearer of truth. Dostoyevsky was without doubt on the side of Christ, but he meant to have each reader decide in free and lonely anxiety where to place his own belief.

Bibliography

The most complete Russian edition of Dostoyevsky's works is the thirteen-volume *Polnoe Sobranie Khudozhestvennykh Proizvedenii* (Moscow and Leningrad, 1926–1930). There is no complete English edition of Dostoyevsky's works, but there are many translations of his major novels; the translations by Constance Garnett and David Magarshack are most widely used.

Dostoyevsky's letters have been translated in full into French by Dominique Arban and Nina Gourfinkel as *Correspondance de Dostoievsky,* 4 vols. (Paris, 1951, 1959, 1960, 1961), but only a small number of his letters have been translated into English. Dostoyevsky's journal has been translated by Boris Brasol as *The Diary of a Writer,* 2 vols. (New York, 1949), and translations of the notebooks to the major novels will soon be published in four volumes (1966–1968) under the editorship of Edward Wasiolek.

There is an extensive bibliography of commentary and interpretation of Dostoyevsky's philosophical views in Russian and most major languages. The most important works available in English are Nicolas A. Berdyaev, *Dostoevsky,* translated by Donald Attwater (New York, 1957); René Fülöp-Miller, *Fyodor Dostoevsky: Insight, Faith and Prophecy,* translated by Richard and Clara Winston (New York, 1950); Vyacheslav Ivanov, *Freedom and the Tragic Life: A Study in Dostoevsky,* translated by Norman Cameron (New York, 1957); L. I. Shestov, *In Job's Balances,* translated by Camilla Coventry and C. A. Macartney (London, 1932); and Leon Zander, *Dostoevsky,* translated by Natalie Duddington (London, 1948).

EDWARD WASIOLEK

DOUBLE TRUTH, DOCTRINE OF. *See* AVERROISM.

DOUBT. To be in doubt about a proposition is to withhold assent both from it and from its contradictory. Although people sometimes withhold assent with no reason for doing so and persist in this even after conceding that they have no reason, doubt is rational only when one has a reason for it and reasonable only when the reason is a good one. Doubt may be accompanied by various feelings, but it seems unlikely that there are specific feelings uniquely associated with it; in general, the feelings associated with doubt are anxiety or hesitation, which are identified as feelings of doubt when they arise in contexts involving questions of belief. In any case, philosophers are not ordinarily concerned with psychological characterizations of a doubter's state of mind. Their attention is primarily devoted to understanding the conditions under which doubt is reasonable and to defining the limits of reasonable doubt.

Evidence and reasonable doubt. Whether it is reasonable for a person to doubt a proposition cannot always be decided solely by considering the evidence which the person possesses relevant to the proposition or, in a situation in which there is purportedly noninferential knowledge, by considering his ground for assent. Doubts that are unreasonable or absurd in one situation may be quite reasonable in another, although the available evidence or ground is the same in both cases. For example, special caution is appropriate when the penalties for error are particularly great; hence, an ordinarily acceptable basis for assent may be inadequate if much depends upon avoiding error, although the gravity of the risk does not in itself constitute evidence. Moreover, a basis for assent that would be entirely compelling in normal circumstances may be insufficient if otherwise remote possibilities of error must be taken seriously because of threats posed by a resourceful deceiver.

From the fact that someone has no reason to doubt a given proposition, therefore, it does not follow that the evidence he possesses is sufficient to render unreasonable *all* doubts concerning the proposition. It would seem quite worthwhile to explore the ways in which the reasonableness of doubt is affected by considerations other than the available evidence or ground for assent. However, philosophers, on the whole, are interested only in very general principles that are not affected by contingencies of any sort. For this reason, perhaps, philosophical studies of doubt have usually been concerned with limiting cases in which the reasonableness of doubt depends only on the available evidence or ground for assent. In other words, they have dealt mainly with what is *indubitable*—with what it is never reasonable to doubt regardless of contextual variables of the sort described above. Accordingly, a philosopher's designation of certain propositions as *dubitable* is not generally to be understood as a denial that there are circumstances in which doubting these propositions would be absurd. The designation means only that given the evidence or ground for the propositions, there are conceivable circumstances in which doubt would be reasonable.

Conditions of indubitability. Toward the end of the First Meditation, Descartes invokes the distinction between what is indubitable and what, in normal circumstances, is open to no reasonable doubt. In defense of his decision to regard as dubitable many propositions which, in practice, it is unreasonable to doubt, he declares, "I cannot at present yield too much to distrust, since it is not now a question of action but only of meditation and of knowledge." In their usual concerns, men are not often required to decide whether a proposition is indubitable, as distinct from deciding whether there is any reason to doubt it. Questions of indubitability are theoretical: they concern only the relation between a proposition and the evidence or ground for it, and take no account of the other concrete circumstances in which a proposition is evaluated.

Limits of relevant evidence. When is one entitled to regard a proposition as indubitable? It might be maintained that one is not entitled to do so as long as anything which can serve as evidence relevant to the proposition remains unexamined, on the ground that when this evidence comes to be examined, it may turn out to require an alteration of belief. But by virtue of the empirical and logical connections among facts, the truth-value of any proposition affects the truth-values of an unlimited number of others: hence, the truth-values of an unlimited number of propositions are relevant to that of any proposition and may serve as evidence concerning it. Since it is impossible to examine each of these other propositions, no proposition could ever be regarded as indubitable if it were first necessary to examine everything that may serve as evidence relevant to its truth-value. On the other hand, it seems that this impasse can be avoided only if it is possible to settle in advance the import of matters that have not been examined.

Immediate experience. That it is in fact possible to settle the import of matters that have not been examined may be brought out as follows. The impossibility of checking all the consequences of an empirical proposition is often cited to support the view that empirical propositions must always remain dubitable. Nonetheless, many philosophers who employ this argument concede the indubitability of so-called "basic propositions," or a person's current reports of the immediate contents of his consciousness (for example, pains, sense data, thoughts). But however fragmented and ephemeral immediate experiences may be, they are not without innumerable conditions and consequences. Like those of empirical propositions (statements of fact about the world outside immediate consciousness), the truth-values of basic propositions are connected with those of an unlimited number of other propositions which may be construed as evidence relevant to them. Hence, if a person's current reports of the immediate data of his own consciousness are indubitable, it is not because he has surveyed everything that may serve as evidence relevant to them: rather, it is because his ground for making the report is such that he cannot reasonably acknowledge that any evidence could supersede it. Indeed, it is reasonable for him to require that all evidence be interpreted so as to be consistent with his report.

Incorrigibility. When one proposition serves as evidence relevant to a second, it does so by virtue of certain other empirical or logical propositions (laws or rules) by which the two are connected. The connection may be broken or its nature altered, however, if the intermediary propositions upon which it depends are rejected or revised. Thus, the possibility of coming upon contrary evidence can be excluded by requiring that this alternative be adopted whenever necessary.

But under what conditions is it reasonable to make such a requirement of incorrigibility—to arrange that nothing count as evidence against a certain proposition? In some cases (for instance, when a mathematical proposition is supported by a well-understood proof, or when a basic proposition is grounded in immediate experience) it may seem fairly clear that the conditions are satisfied. However, philosophers have failed to provide a general account of these conditions; instead, they have usually limited themselves to identifying particular instances of their satisfaction. Some philosophers have claimed with considerable plausibility that certain elementary mathematical propositions (such as that $2 + 2 = 4$) may be regarded as indubitable without proof, but they have done little to explain systematically why this should be so. With regard to empirical propositions, neglect of the problem of clarifying the conditions in which they may be accepted as indubitable has resulted in part from widespread controversy over whether the problem properly arises at all. That there are no such conditions is frequently maintained by philosophers (for example, Russell, Ayer, Peirce, C. I. Lewis) who subscribe to certain popular epistemological doctrines—in particular, the doctrines that every empirical proposition is to be construed on the model of a scientific hypothesis, or that it is to be interpreted phenomenalistically as equivalent to an unlimited number of predictions.

Logical contingency and necessity. A more general obstacle to a sound understanding of the basis of indubitability lies in a tendency to look for it in the wrong place. A proposition is indubitable when there could be no reason to doubt it, but this impossibility is not in general inherent in the logical character of the proposition itself. Indubitability is an epistemic property which depends on the relation between a proposition and the evidence or ground for assent with which it is considered. In particular, dubitability and indubitability must not be confused with logical contingency and logical necessity. The logical contingency of a proposition does not as such entail that no one has conclusive evidence or ground for it, and a logically necessary proposition may reasonably be doubted by someone who is not in a position to appreciate its necessity and who therefore must concede the possibility that further inquiry will uncover evidence against it.

Moreover, it is a mistake to suppose that evidence for a proposition is not conclusive unless its conjunction with the denial of the proposition is self-contradictory. To be sure, a proposition is indubitable if and only if no basis for assenting to its alternative is conceivable, but something may be inconceivable even though it contradicts neither itself nor what has already been established.

Conditions of rational inquiry. The claim that a basis for doubt is inconceivable is justified whenever a denial of the claim would violate the conditions or presuppositions of rational inquiry. Avoidance of self-contradiction is perhaps the most familiar of these conditions, but it is not the only one. For instance, since inquiry is fundamentally an attempt to discriminate between what is to be accepted and what is to be rejected, nothing can rationally be conceived which involves denying the necessity for making these discriminations or undermining the possibility of making them.

A systematic explanation of dubitability and indubitability awaits, therefore, a general theory of the nature of rationality which illuminates the presuppositions and conditions that rationality requires. Furthermore, it awaits an account, developed from this theory, of the particular conditions in which propositions of various sorts must be regarded as indubitable if the possibility of rationality is to be preserved. Even if this were done, however, a further problem would remain. While an adequate theory of rationality would give a clear account of the conditions in which a proposition may reasonably be regarded as indubitable, it cannot of course guarantee that these conditions are correctly identified in any given case. To support the claim that a certain proposition is indubitable, it is not sufficient to understand the conditions in which such claims are justified; it is also necessary to know that the conditions are fulfilled in the particular case in question.

The indubitability regress. A disturbing pattern of argument seems to develop, however, in considering the proposition that a given proposition is indubitable. The proposition that the conditions for the indubitability of a certain proposition have been satisfied cannot itself be regarded as beyond doubt unless the conditions for *its* indubitability have been satisfied; but the satisfaction of *these* conditions is dubitable unless . . . , and so on.

But acknowledging this regress does not require one to concede that it is never reasonable to regard a proposition as indubitable. Rather, the view to which the regress leads appears to be that while there are occasions on which it is reasonable to regard a proposition as indubitable, it is never altogether indubitable just which occasions these are. There is an air of paradox here, perhaps, but there is no logical difficulty. The regress does not interfere with the possibility of there being satisfactory logical relations between indubitability claims and judgments establishing that these claims are reasonable. It only interferes with our confidence in ourselves, suggesting that there is always room for doubt as to whether we are being reasonable. Or, to put the matter a bit differently, the regress supports no more than the mordant comment that it is never reasonable to insist that the question of whether one is being reasonable is entirely closed.

Bibliography

In addition to *loci classici* in Descartes, *Meditations on First Philosophy;* Hume, *An Enquiry Concerning Human Understanding;* and Kant, *Critique of Pure Reason*, there are particularly interesting and relevant discussions in the following more recent works: A. J. Ayer, *The Problem of Knowledge* (London, 1956); C. I. Lewis, *An Analysis of Knowledge and Valuation* (La Salle, Ill., 1946); N. Malcolm, "Knowledge and Belief," in *Knowledge and Certainty* (Englewood Cliffs, N.J., 1963); G. E. Moore, "Four Forms of Scepticism," in *Philosophical Papers* (London, 1959); and C. S. Peirce, *Collected Papers* (Cambridge, Mass., 1935).

HARRY G. FRANKFURT

DRAMA. *See* GREEK DRAMA; TRAGEDY.

DREAMS. Almost all men have had dreams, yet few could say with confidence what they are, beyond agreeing that they occur during sleep and have some likeness to waking experience. Yet most people would in all probability accept the kind of definition given by philosophers, for example Plato's "visions within us, . . . which are remembered by us when we are awake and in the external world" (*Timaeus*, 46A) or Aristotle's "the dream is a kind of imagination, and, more particularly, one which occurs in sleep" (*De Somniis*, 462a). Indeed, such notions seem to be summarized in the *Oxford Dictionary*'s definition: "A train of thoughts, images, or fancies passing through the mind during sleep; a vision during sleep." Dreams are striking phenomena, and the more superstitious see in them signs and portents of what is to happen; even today divination by dreams has not lost its popularity. A more sophisticated way of looking at dreams is to regard them as revealing something about the sleeper, either about his physical condition or about his mental state. An example of the former can be seen in the diagnostic technique used in the temple of Aesculapius; patients seeking a cure had to sleep all night in the temple precincts and would experience a "vision" that would indicate the disease or its cure. Many writers had suggested that mental states were revealed by dreams, but there was little serious study of the idea until the work of Sigmund Freud and his followers. Freud's doctrine of the unconscious, and the way in which it is revealed in dreams and other less rational activities, is important for psychiatry; but he had little to say about the nature of dreams which is of interest to the philosopher, though the fact that they had been found worthy of study may have resulted in an increase in philosophic concern about the problems they raise.

While we are having them, dreams often appear to be as real as waking experience; children have to be told that the object of their terror "was only a dream," hence not part of the world. William James expressed this well in his *Principles of Psychology:* "The world of dreams is our real world whilst we are sleeping, because our attention then lapses from the sensible world. Conversely, when we wake the attention usually lapses from the dream-world and that becomes unreal." This similarity has led philosophers to pose the question, "How can you prove whether at this moment we are sleeping, and all our thoughts are a dream; or whether we are awake, and talking to one another in the waking state?" (Plato, *Theaetetus*, 158). In perhaps the most famous example of the difficulty of distinguishing dreams from reality, Descartes introduced his method of universal doubt. He concluded, "I see so manifestly that there are no certain indications by which we may clearly distinguish wakefulness from sleep that I am lost in astonishment" (*First Meditation*). Descartes finally resolved his doubts in this respect by appealing to a criterion of consistency: "For at present I find a very notable difference between the two, inasmuch as our memory can never connect our dreams with one another, or with the whole course of our lives, as it unites events which happen to us while we are awake" (*Sixth Meditation*). Such a consistency criterion has been adopted by several more recent writers on the topic. Unfortunately, this will not do the task required, for consistency can only be used as a test of a particular experience by waiting to see what happens in the future. It would enable me to tell that I had been dreaming, not that I am now dreaming; for however confident I am of the reality of my surroundings, something may happen in the future that will reveal them to be part of a dream. Further, the problem remains whether any consistency discovered is a real or a dreamed one. The failure of consistency to provide a test need not be worrying, for the times in which genuine doubt arises are normally those involving memory—I am not sure if this event actually happened or whether I dreamed it. In such a case I would normally try to remember some part of the event which would have left a mark in the physical world, and then see if there is such a trace of the event; if there is nothing, I conclude that I had dreamed the occurrence. In spite of Descartes' remark, it is rare that we are in doubt about whether we *are* dreaming. The expression "I must be dreaming" is normally used in circumstances when I am quite sure that I am not dreaming, to express surprise at some pleasant occurrence, for example the arrival of a friend whom I thought to be somewhere distant. There are times when we are aware that we are dreaming, though normally a dream presents itself as real and no questions about its genuineness arise. It seems that the conviction that one is dreaming does not come from a previous doubt within the dream about the status of the experience, it just occurs, though sometimes accompanied with a feeling of relief. But in most cases the dream convinces us that it is reality, in that no doubt or questioning arises during its course. The difference between dreams and hallucinations lies in the fact that there is nothing external to dreams with which they can be compared, no tests that can be applied. For if we did apply a test in a dream, the result would be to confirm its reality. Philosophers have sought for some mark or test that would solve this problem, but there is none available. Any suggested sign of reality could be duplicated in the dream, and if all dreams bore marks of unreality, then there could not even be confusion over the remembering of them.

It has been generally agreed that dreams are due to the workings of the imagination no longer under the control of the intellect or the senses, as can be seen from the quotations at the beginning of this article; but it would seem that in such contexts the meaning of the word "imagination" had been left vague, serving rather as an indication of puzzlement than as a solution to a problem. Some recent work by physiologists has led to the suggestion (by W. Dement and N. Kleitman) that dreaming is correlated with rapid eye movements during sleep. Such a suggestion would seem to confirm Aristotle's remark that "dreaming is an activity of the sensitive faculty, but of it as being imaginative" (459a). The use of a physiological criterion for dreams has been challenged by Norman Malcolm in his book *Dreaming* (1959), which is clearly the most important contemporary discussion of the whole topic. In the course of it he challenges virtually all the assumptions made by previous philosophers. In criticism of the physiological work, he asserts that waking testimony is the sole criterion of dreaming (p. 81). The obvious difficulties that arise from the common belief that external stimuli can cause or influence the course of a dream, or that observers can sometimes tell from bodily movements that a sleeper is having a violent dream, he dismisses by means of a definition that dreams can take place only when the subject is sound asleep and that a person who is sleeping cannot respond to external stimuli (pp. 25–26). It might be thought that Malcolm was here doing the same thing for which he criticizes the physiologists, namely introducing a new concept of dreaming, for surely the ordinary unsophisticated notion includes the possibility of our recognizing that someone asleep is having a dream, in some cases at least, as well as the possibility of the dreamer being aware that he is dreaming. If both of these beliefs are ruled out by a philosophical argument, then it would appear that the concept of dreaming held by most people has been changed in important ways. Most of the points made in the earlier part of this article would be understood by those with an unsophisticated notion of dreaming.

Malcolm's arguments are, however, powerful and subtle, and his critics, of whom A. J. Ayer is perhaps the most eminent, have found it not at all easy to refute them. Malcolm bases his reasoning on Wittgenstein's *Philosophical Investigations*, in particular on the dictum that "an 'inner process' stands in need of outward criteria" (I. § 580). Malcolm argues that we can come by the concept of dreaming only by learning it from descriptions of dreams, "from the familiar phenomenon that we call 'telling a dream' " (II, p. 55). To talk of "remembering a dream" is to use the word "remember" in a sense different from the normal, for there is no external criterion by which we can check our memory, as there is in the paradigm cases of remembering, that of remembering an event in the public world, which can be checked by ourselves and others. What is told sincerely on waking *is* the dream, because there is no other way of finding out what, if anything, occurred while the teller slept. (This can be compared with Freud's reliance on the narration of the dream, but this was essential for its use in diagnosis. Nevertheless, Freud was willing to evaluate critically the veracity of actual dream accounts on the basis of his theory or as a result of previous analysis of its dreamer. For most purposes, it made no difference whether the dream account or the dream itself was being considered; Freud's concern was with different problems.) Yet Malcolm rejects Ayer's suggestion that this theory amounts to saying that "we do not dream, but only wake with delusive memories of experiences we have never had." Malcolm is clearly correct in stressing the importance of the report of a dream and its difference from reports of public events; what the dreamer says on waking is final. Though we must learn the use of the word "dream" in the way Malcolm indicates, this does not rule out the possibility of its use being extended by further experience, for instance, correlating dream reports with observations of the dreamer, as Dement and Kleitman have done. The trouble is Malcolm's use of the term "criterion," which is never clearly explained, and which seems to lead him into a crude verificationism; he even talks of "the senselessness, in the sense of the impossibility of verification, of the notion of a dream as an occurrence . . ." (p. 83). A further consequence of Malcolm's use of the dream report as a criterion for dreaming is that it becomes impossible to talk of children having dreams before they have learned to speak (p. 59). If, as Malcolm apparently wishes to maintain, words can be used only if their application can be strictly verified, then many ordinary uses will be cut out. That we now have a particular concept of some mental activity does not make it impossible that further experience will lead us to introduce a modification of it, in which case the way in which we first learned it may have no bearing on the criterion of its use. For example, many words used in the sciences are first learned in an approximate way and their criteria of application refined in the course of education. Malcolm claims that his argument applies only to words that refer to "inner" processes. What he seems to do, however, is to extend Wittgenstein's argument, valid in the area Wittgenstein intended it for, beyond its legitimate sphere. The primary use of the word "dreaming" depends upon the notion of telling a dream, but this does not prevent an extended use. Peter Geach remarks that Wittgenstein mentioned in a lecture Lytton Strachey's description of Queen Victoria's dying thoughts: "He expressly repudiated the view that such a description is meaningless because 'unverifiable'; it has meaning, he said, but only through its connexion with a wider, public, 'language-game' of describing people's thoughts" (*Mental Acts*, p. 3). In fact it is only because we know what it is to dream that we can understand the difficulties raised by talk of "verifying" reports of dreams.

Ayer also criticizes Malcolm's denial that one can make assertions while asleep, but in this case with less effect. It does seem clear that the words "I am asleep" cannot be used to make a genuine assertion, because such an utterance would contradict what was asserted, just as the only possible truthful reply to the question, "Are you asleep?" is "No." An absence of reply is what would lead the questioner to assert that the man was really asleep.

In spite of Malcolm's statement (p. 66) that there is no place for an implication or assumption that a man is aware of anything at all while asleep, many would claim, and understand others' claims, that they had become aware that they were dreaming. This also implies that they were aware that they were asleep. As part of a dream narrative, such awareness could be reported by the words, "I suddenly realized that it was all a dream." Clearly, such an assertion could not be taught by ostensive means. However, there seems no reason why, having learned how to use the ordinary concept of dreaming and expressions such as "I suddenly realized that," we should not combine the two into an assertion that would be commonly understood to apply to a possible experience. Malcolm's claim that a person must be partially awake to be aware that he is dreaming (pp. 38–44) seems, as suggested above, a redefinition of the term for which no adequate reason is advanced.

Malcolm wishes to say that the problem of what dreams are is a pseudo problem; he refuses to allow that they can be called experiences, illusions, workings of the imagination, or anything else they have been thought to be by previous philosophers. Ayer concludes his criticism of *Dreaming* by maintaining that dreams are experiences and mostly illusions, and "are found to be so by the same criteria that apply to illusions in general." This remark is difficult to understand; here Malcolm's stress on the report of the dream comes into its own; in recounting it I am not claiming that these things happened. Because while dreaming there is no possibility of making assertions about my experiences to other people, to describe dreams as illusions makes no sense. Malcolm has clearly made out his case in this respect. On the other hand, it seems difficult to deny that dreams are experiences, if only because the description is sufficiently vague to cover almost any "mental" phenomena. The same may be said of talking of dreams as being composed of images; here dreaming is being used as one of the examples of mental imagery, a vague concept. In spite of Malcolm's work, the problem of the nature of dreaming is still open for philosophic discussion, but any future examination of the problem will have to take his book fully into account. Many philosophers would still wish to assert that dreams occur, that they take place during sleep, while admitting that the meaning and justification of such claims is by no means clear.

Bibliography

HISTORICAL WORKS

Aristotle, *De Somniis* (*On Dreams*). Translated by J. I. Beare, in *Works of Aristotle*, Vol. III. Oxford, 1931.

Aristotle, *De Divinatione per Somnum* (*On Prophesying by Dreams*). *Ibid.*

Bradley, F. H., "On My Real World," in *Essays on Truth and Reality*. Oxford, 1914.

Descartes, René, *Meditationes de Prima Philosophia*. Translated by E. S. Haldane and G. R. T. Ross, in *The Philosophical Works of Descartes*, Vol. I. Cambridge, England, 1934.

Freud, Sigmund, *Introductory Lectures on Psycho-analysis*. Translated by J. Riviere. London, 1949.

Freud, Sigmund, *The Interpretation of Dreams*. Edited and translated by James Strachey. New York, 1963.

James, William, *The Principles of Psychology*. New York, 1950.

Malcolm, Norman, *Dreaming*. London, 1959.

Plato, *Theaetetus* (158A). Translated by B. Jowett. Oxford, 1871.

Plato, *Timaeus* (46A). *Ibid.*

Russell, Bertrand, *Our Knowledge of the External World*. London, 1949.

Sartre, Jean-Paul, *L'Imaginaire. Psychologie phénoménologique de l'imagination*. Paris, 1940. Translated by B. Frechtman as *The Psychology of the Imagination*. London, 1949.

Wittgenstein, L., *Philosophical Investigations*. Translated by E. Anscombe. Oxford and New York, 1953. Especially pp. 184, 222–223. Also relevant is Malcolm's review of this work in *Philosophical Review* (October 1954), 530–559.

ARTICLES

Ayer, A. J., "Professor Malcolm on Dreams." *Journal of Philosophy*, Vol. 57 (1960), 517–535. Malcolm's reply and Ayer's rejoinder in *Ibid.*, Vol. 58 (1961), 294–299.

Chappell, V. C., "The Concept of Dreaming." *Philosophical Quarterly*, Vol. 13 (July 1963), 193–213.

Dement, W., and Kleitman, N., "The Relation of Eye Movements During Sleep to Dream Activity: An Objective Method for the Study of Dreaming." *Journal of Experimental Psychology*, Vol. 53 (1957), 339–346.

MacDonald, M., "Sleeping and Waking." *Mind*, Vol. 62 (April 1953), 202–215.

Manser, A. R., and Thomas, L. E., "Dreams." *Proceedings of the Aristotelian Society*, Suppl. Vol. 30 (1956), 197–228.

Putnam, H., "Dreaming and 'Depth Grammar,' " in R. J. Butler ed., *Analytical Philosophy*. Oxford, 1962.

A. R. MANSER

DREWS, ARTHUR CHRISTIAN HEINRICH (1865–1935), German metaphysician and philosopher of religion, was born at Ütersen in Holstein. In 1898 he was appointed professor at the Technische Hochschule in Karlsruhe, and most of his life was divided between his teaching duties there and an intensive program of writing.

Drews's principal ideas derived from Eduard von Hartmann's philosophy of the unconscious. Drews believed that modern philosophy had been led astray by Descartes' stress on the primacy of the thinking subject. What is primary is not consciousness but unconscious will or striving; and this unconscious will in its friction with matter is said to generate consciousness. Thus, consciousness is a secondary phenomenon in which the world process becomes aware of itself. The metaphysic Drews constructed from these ideas he called "concrete monism." It is a pantheistic world view, for the unconscious striving whose history is the world process is identified with an immanent God. This points to the religious dimension of Drews's philosophy, for religion is itself the coming to self-awareness of the divine world process in the life of humanity, so that this life of humanity is itself the divine life and the suffering of humanity is the passion of God himself. In the religious consciousness of man, the divine life is experienced as suffering, dying, and overcoming.

Drews saw a parallel to this in Christianity's ideas of the redemptive sufferings of Christ, but before Christianity could be absorbed into his monistic system it had to be drastically dehistoricized. In order to do this Drews advocated a "Christ myth" theory that is perhaps more influential today than is his pantheistic metaphysic. Taking up the early form-critical theories of the New Testament scholar Johannes Weiss, Drews argued that we know nothing of a historical Jesus, but only of the Christ figure in whom the primitive church believed; he claimed that this Christ figure was a purely mythical invention, and indeed a new version of the astral mythology that had been the religion of the Near East from time immemorial. Christ is the timeless mythical symbol that points to the process of striving and overcoming by the divine life that is immanent in the world and in humanity. The truth concealed in Christianity can be seen only when it is separated from a particular historical figure and understood as a timeless symbol of this universal process. Drews supported these views by elaborate attempts to work out in detail the identification of the New Testament characters with the mythical figures of the celestial cults, Jesus being the sun-god, the twelve apostles the signs of the zodiac, and so on.

Principal Works by Drews

Eduard von Hartmanns Philosophie und der Materialismus in der modernen Kultur. Leipzig, 1889.

Die deutsche Spekulation seit Kant, 2 vols. Berlin, 1893.

Kants Naturphilosophie als Grundlage seines Systems. Berlin, 1894.

Die Religion als Selbst-Bewusstsein Gottes. Jena, 1906.

Plotin und der Untergang der antiken Weltanschauung. Jena, 1907.

Die Christusmythe, 2 vols. Jena, 1909–1911. Translated by C. Delisle Burns as *The Christ Myth*. London, 1910–1912.

Das Markus-Evangelium als Zeugnis gegen die Geschichtlichkeit Jesu. Jena, 1921.

Der Sternhimmel in der Dichtung der alten Völker und des Christentums. Jena, 1923.

Psychologie des Unbewussten. Berlin, 1924.

Die Entstehung des Christentums aus dem Gnostizismus. Jena, 1924.

Die Leugnung der Geschichtlichkeit Jesu in Vergangenheit und Gegenwart. Karlsruhe, 1926.

At present there is no satisfactory secondary source for Drews's philosophy.

JOHN MACQUARRIE

DRIESCH, HANS ADOLF EDUARD (1867–1941), perhaps the outstanding representative of neovitalism, was born at Bad Kreuznach, Germany. His father, Paul Driesch, was a merchant in Hamburg. From 1877 Hans Driesch attended the Johanneum (a humanist gymnasium) in his native city, graduating with honors in 1886. He then studied zoology, first under A. Weismann at Freiburg, then at Munich, and finally under Ernst Haeckel at Jena, receiving his Ph.D. in 1889; his dissertation was entitled "Tektonische Studien an Hydroidpolypen" ("Tectonic Studies of Hydroid Polyps").

Development of Driesch's thought. Reacting to arguments advanced by G. Wolff, W. His, and A. Goette, Driesch early became skeptical of Haeckel's mechanistic interpretation of the organism. The work of Wilhelm Roux, in particular, induced him to explore the whole vitalism–mechanism issue. Driesch's first publication, *Die mathematisch-mechanische Behandlung morphologischer Probleme der Biologie* ("Mathematico-mechanical Treatment of Morphological Problems of Biology"; Jena, 1890), led to a break with Haeckel. Then, following Roux's example, Driesch put the embryogenetic theory of His and Weismann to an experimental test. His and Weismann had held that morphogenetic development of the living organism could be explained by assuming that a specifically organized yet invisible structure of great complexity is contained in the nucleus of the germ cell and that the gradual unfolding of this structure, through nuclear division, determines the course of every ontogeny. Roux's experiments, in 1888, had seemed to confirm this theory of "tectonic preformation." When he destroyed one of the blastomeres at the two-cell stage, the remaining one would develop into a half embryo—either the left half or the right half, depending on which blastomere had been destroyed. Driesch merely intended to provide further confirmation of these facts. But where Roux had experimented with the egg of a frog, Driesch used eggs of the sea urchin. Against all expectations he found that each blastomere of the two-cell stage of a sea urchin egg developed into a whole embryo half the normal size. This was the opposite of Roux's results and was irreconcilable with the His–Weismann theory.

While at the Marine Biological Station in Naples, from 1891 to 1900, Driesch continued his experimental investigations, confirming and reconfirming in startling ways his earlier findings, and began to formulate his own theory. Relevant to the development of his ideas was a study of Otto Liebmann's book *Analysis der Wirklichkeit* ("Analysis of Reality") and of the writings of Kant, Schopenhauer, Descartes, Locke, and Hume. Alois Riehl's *Kritizismus* ("Criticism") provided the springboard for Driesch's own theoretical efforts. The first results were published in 1893 under the title *Die Biologie als selbständige Grundwissenschaft* ("Biology as an Independent Basic Science"; Leipzig). This book was followed by *Analytische Theorie der organischen Entwicklung* ("Analytic Theory of Organic Development"; Leipzig, 1894), which contains the first formulation of Driesch's own teleologically oriented embryological theory. But as yet this was a theory of "preformed teleology," not a vitalistic interpretation of embryological development. Only in 1895 did it dawn on Driesch that mechanistic principles could not account for his experimental findings.

Up to this time Driesch had accepted a "machine" theory of organismic development. Now he realized that such a theory would not do. In an essay entitled "Die Maschinentheorie des Lebens" ("The Machine Theory of Life," in *Biologisches Zentralblatt*, Vol. 16 [1896], 353–368) he formulated as precisely as possible the view he had held so far, a view that he did not yet regard as vitalism. His first formulation of a dynamically teleological, and therefore genuinely vitalistic, theory was published under the title *Die Lokalisation morphogenetischer Vorgänge, ein Beweis vitalistischen Geschehens* ("The Localization of Morphogenetic Processes, a Proof of Vitalistic Developments"; Leipzig, 1899). In this book Driesch introduced the concept of the "harmonious equipotential system" and the proof that such a system cannot be accounted for in terms of mechanistic principles. The publication of 1899 thus marked the end of one period in Driesch's intellectual development and the beginning of another.

Gradually his interest in experimental work ceased. He now searched the literature in the field of physiology for possible proof that a "machine" theory could provide an adequate explanation of the phenomena of life. He found none, as his two books *Die organischen Regulationen* ("Organic Regulations"; Leipzig, 1901) and *Die "Seele" als elementarer Naturfaktor* ("The 'Soul' as Elementary Factor of Nature"; Leipzig, 1903) show. However, the conception of the "autonomy" of life had now to be justified within the broader framework of natural science. Driesch provided this justification in a book entitled *Naturbegriffe und Natururteile* ("Concepts of Nature and Judgments of Nature"; Leipzig, 1904). In 1905 he published *Der Vitalismus als Geschichte und als Lehre* (*The History and Theory of Vitalism*), in which he summed up his position against a historical background. That same year he "resolved to become a philosopher." His Gifford lectures at the University of Aberdeen in 1907–1908, published in 1908 as *The Science and Philosophy of the Organism*, provided a splendid opportunity to present his position in systematic form.

From 1908 on, Driesch was concerned exclusively with philosophical problems. In 1909 he became a *Privatdozent* at Heidelberg and in 1912 a member of the university's philosophical faculty. In 1912, also, he published his basic philosophical work, *Ordnungslehre* ("Theory of Order"). This was followed by *Die Logik als Aufgabe* ("Logic as a Task"; Tübingen, 1913) and, in 1917, by *Wirklichkeitslehre* ("Theory of Reality"). These three books together—ranging as they do over the fields of epistemology, logic, and metaphysics—embody the whole of Driesch's philosophical system, but they do not mark the end of his intellectual development. In *Leib und Seele* ("Body and Soul"; 1916) Driesch set forth his definitive arguments against every "psycho-mechanical parallelism," and in *Wissen und Denken* ("Knowing and Thinking"; Leipzig, 1919) he clarified and expanded his epistemological position.

In 1919 Driesch accepted a chair of systematic philosophy at the University of Cologne and in 1921 assumed a similar post at the University of Leipzig. During 1922–1923 he was a visiting professor in China. In 1926–1927 he lectured in the United States and in Buenos Aires. Being out of sympathy with the Nazi regime, ideologically and politically, he was retired in 1933. Hitler could not tolerate a thinker who fervently believed that nationalism was but "an obstacle to the realization of the *one* State of God." During the time of changing appointments, Driesch became interested more and more in problems of psychology and parapsychology. Books published in 1932 and 1938 reflect this development.

Driesch's philosophy. Although known primarily as one of the leading neovitalists, Driesch was also a critical realist and an "inductive" metaphysician. His system as a whole is developed most fully and most systematically in his *Ordnungslehre* and his *Wirklichkeitslehre.*

In his Gifford lectures Driesch had evolved the argument that the phenomena of ontogenetic development, as revealed in his own experimental work, can be explained only when we assume the existence and the efficacy of some nonmechanistic and "whole-making" factor in nature, which Driesch called *entelechy.* This entelechy, "lacking all the characteristics of quantity," is not some special kind of energy, not a "constant" or a "force." It is not in space or in time but acts into space and into time. Entelechy, Driesch confessed, is "entelechy, an elementary factor sui generis" that "acts teleologically." But even Driesch could not blind himself to the fact that such a definition of his key concept is essentially meaningless because it is defined only negatively. He therefore tried, in his *Ordnungslehre*, to show that the conception of entelechy is logically legitimate after all.

Starting with the "irreducible and inexplicable primordial fact" that "knowing about my knowledge, I know something," Driesch found in his experience "primordial concepts of order the meaning of which I, as the experiencing subject, grasp only 'intuitively'" (*Bedeutungsschau*), and that the experience as a whole presses on toward our "seeing everything in order." The method through which this "order" is revealed is that of "positing" or "discriminating" "objects of experience." It is necessary, however, to distinguish between "positing" (*setzen*) and "implicitly positing" (*mitsetzen*). What is "posited" may, in turn, "implicitly posit" something else. The whole procedure implies that the "object" is always "my" object (since I "posit" it), not some "thing-in-itself." To postulate an "objectivity" as a reality independent of, and separated from, "my" experience would involve a fallacy. Still, we must somehow transcend this "methodological subjectivism" by attempting to obtain a complete view of the totality of experience, actual and possible. In constructing this "whole" we are to be guided by the principle of economy: Only necessary steps should be taken, for "order" is perfect only when it includes everything necessary but nothing more. Now, upon inspection, I find that the experience I have is such that I can always select some specific part of it and identify it as "this," or as *A*. But as soon as I have posited a "this," all the rest of my experience has become a "nonthis," and the basic principle of noncontradiction—"this is not nonthis"—emerges. Moreover, when I posit a "this" and define it as *A*, I have before me (1) the *concept* *A* and (2) the *judgment* "*A* is there" or "*A* exists" (at least as an object for me). But let us now assume that some particular object *A* has the discernible attributes *abcd*, whereas some other object *A′* has the attributes *acd*. The objects are clearly different, but *A* includes *A′*, or "*A* implicitly posits *A′*." Thus, the posit "wolf" implicitly posits "beast of prey," and any existing wolf implicitly posits an existing beast of prey. By extension, we obtain "*A* posits *A′*, and *A′* posits *a;* therefore, *A* posits *a*." The principles of logic, thus, have their basis in our intuitive experience of order. The same is true, of course, of arithmetic and geometry. In fact, it is the aim of Driesch's general theory of order to disclose all the primordial elements of order first given in basic intuition.

Among "my" experiences there are some that I "have had before"; I "remember" them. This fact opens up an entirely new dimension of experience. But given this new dimension, I can now establish a remarkable order in my experience if I regard some of the objects of my immediate experience as an indication of the "being" or the "becoming" of an *X* that behaves as if it were independent of my experience of it; i.e., it behaves as if it were a self-sufficient "realm of nature" in which the bipolar "cause–effect" relationship prevails. However, since, on the one hand, the effect cannot be richer in content than is its cause but, on the other hand, the living individual is a "whole" that is more than the sum of its parts, a close scrutiny of experience led Driesch to distinguish between a "merely mechanical causality" (*Einzelheitskausalität*) and a "whole-making causality" (*Ganzheitskausalität*) that involves more than merely additive changes. In ontogenetic development, for example, a mere sum of "equipotentialities" is thus transformed into the "wholeness" of the mature organism. "Restitution" and "adaptations," experimentally demonstrable, are manifestations of this "whole-making" causality. The living organism itself, in its indisputable wholeness, is the most obvious result of *Ganzheitskausalität.* Thus, vitalism finds its justification within Driesch's epistemology.

At the psychological and cultural levels, "whole-making causality" predominates, and Driesch posited "my soul" as "the unconscious foundation" of my conscious experience. The "soul," therefore, is also "posited in the service of order." "My primordial knowing of the meaning of order and my primordial willing of order . . . indicate . . . a certain primordial state and dynamics of my soul." "The *working* of 'my soul' [which guides my 'actions'] and certain *states* [of my soul] are 'parallel' to 'my conscious havings.'" "This sounds very artificial," Driesch admitted, "but logic is a very artificial instrument." When Driesch took up this theme again, in his *Wirklichkeitslehre*, he argued that "metaphysically," "my soul and my entelechy are One in the sphere of the Absolute." And it is at the level of the Absolute only that we can speak of "psychophysical interaction." But the Absolute, so understood, transcends all possibilities of our knowing, and it is "an error to take, as did Hegel, the sum of its traces for the Whole."

All considerations of normal mental life lead us only to the threshold of the unconscious; it is in dreamlike and certain abnormal cases of mental life that we encounter "the depths of our soul." And in parapsychological phenomena—especially in telepathy, mind reading, clairvoyance, telekinesis, and materialization (all of which Driesch accepted as proved facts)—we find traces of a supra-individual wholeness. More important, however, our sense of duty also points toward a supra-personal whole, which, in the course of history, is continuously evolving. "In my experience of duty I am participating in the supra-personal whole of which I am an empirical embodiment, and it is *as if* I had some knowledge about the final outcome of the development of that whole." That is to say, my sense of duty indicates the general direction of the supra-personal development. The ultimate goal, however, remains unknown. From this point of view, history took on its particular meaning for Driesch.

Throughout his work Driesch's orientation is intended to be essentially empirical. Any argument concerning the nature of the ultimately Real will therefore have to be hypothetical only. It starts with the affirmation of the "given" as consequent of a conjectural "ground." His guiding principle in the realm of metaphysics amounts to this: The Real that I posit must be so constituted that it implicitly posits all our experience. If we can conceive and posit such a Real, then all laws of nature, and all true principles and formulas of the sciences, will merge into it, and our experiences will all be "explained" by it. And since our experience is a mixture of wholeness (the organic and the mental realms) and nonwholeness (the material world), Reality itself must be such that I can posit a dualistic foundation of the totality of my experience. In fact, there is nothing—not even within the ultimately Real—to bridge the gap between wholeness and nonwholeness. And this means, for Driesch, that ultimately there is either God and "non-God," or a dualism within God himself. To put it differently, either the theism of the Judeo-Christian tradition or a pantheism of a God continually "making himself" and transcending his own earlier stages is ultimately reconcilable with the facts of experience. Driesch himself found it impossible to decide between these alternatives. He was sure, however, that a materialistic–mechanistic monism would not do.

Additional Works by Driesch

Der Vitalismus als Geschichte und als Lehre. Leipzig, 1905. Translated as *The History and Theory of Vitalism.* London, 1914. Rev. German ed., *Geschichte des Vitalismus.* Leipzig, 1922.

The Science and Philosophy of the Organism, 2 vols. London, 1908. Translated into German as *Philosophie des Organischen.* Rev. ed., Leipzig, 1921.

Zwei Vorträge zur Naturphilosophie. Leipzig, 1910.

Die Biologie als selbständige Grundwissenschaft und das System der Biologie. Leipzig, 1911.

Ordnungslehre, ein System des nichtmetaphysischen Teiles der Philosophie. Jena, 1912; rev. ed., 1923.

The Problem of Individuality. London, 1914.

Leib und Seele, eine Prüfung des psycho-physischen Grundproblems. Leipzig, 1916; rev. ed., 1920; 3d ed., 1923. Translated as *Mind and Body.* New York, 1927.

Wirklichkeitslehre, ein metaphysischer Versuch. Leipzig, 1917; rev. ed., 1922.

Das Problem der Freiheit. Berlin, 1917; rev. ed., Darmstadt, 1920.

Das Ganze und die Summe. Leipzig, 1921. Inaugural address at the University of Leipzig.

"Mein System und sein Werdegang," in R. Schmidt, ed., *Die Philosophie der Gegenwart in Selbstdarstellung,* Vol. I. Leipzig, 1923. One of the more than 100 articles that Driesch published.

Metaphysik. Breslau, 1924.

The Possibility of Metaphysics. London, 1924.

Relativitätstheorie und Philosophie. Karlsruhe, 1924.

The Crisis in Psychology. Princeton, 1925.

Grundprobleme der Psychologie. Leipzig, 1926.

Metaphysik der Natur. Munich, 1926.

Die sittliche Tat. Leipzig, 1927.

Biologische Probleme höherer Ordnung. Leipzig, 1927; rev. ed., 1944.

Der Mensch und die Welt. Leipzig, 1928. Translated as *Man and the Universe.* London, 1929.

Ethical Principles in Theory and Practice. London, 1930.

Philosophische Forschungswege. Leipzig, 1930.

Parapsychologie. Leipzig, 1932; 2d ed., 1943.

Philosophische Gegenwartsfragen. Leipzig, 1933.

Alltagsrätsel des Seelenlebens. Leipzig, 1938; 2d ed., 1939.

Selbstbesinnung und Selbsterkenntnis. Leipzig, 1940.

Lebenserinnerungen; Augzeichnungen eines Forschers und Denkers in entscheidender Zeit, Ingeborg Tetaz-Driesch, ed. Basel, 1951. Posthumous.

Works on Driesch

Child, C. M., "Driesch's Harmonic Equipotential Systems in Form-regulations." *Biologisches Zentralblatt,* Vol. 28 (1908).

Fischel, A., review of Driesch's Gifford lectures, *The Science and Philosophy of the Organism,* Vol. I. *Archiv für Entwicklungs-Mechanik,* Vol. 26 (1908).

Griffith, O. W., review of *The Problem of Individuality* and *The History and Theory of Vitalism. The Hibbert Journal,* Vol. 13.

Haake, W., "Die Formphilosophie von Hans Driesch und das Wesen des Organismus." *Biologisches Zentralblatt,* Vol. 14 (1894).

Heinichen, O., *Driesch's Philosophie.* Leipzig, 1924.

Jenkinson, J. W., "Vitalism." *The Hibbert Journal* (April 1911).

Jourdain, E. B. P., review of *Ordnungslehre. Mind,* Vol. 23 (1914).

Morgan, T. H., review of *The Science and Philosophy of the Organism,* Vol. I. *Journal of Philosophy,* Vol. 6 (1909).

Oakeley, H. D., "On Professor Driesch's Attempt to Combine a Philosophy of Life and a Philosophy of Knowledge." *PAS,* N.S. Vol. 21 (1920–1921).

Oakeley, H. D., review of *Wirklichkeitslehre. Mind,* Vol. 30 (1921).

Russell, L. J., review of *Die Logik als Aufgabe. Mind,* Vol. 23 (1914).

Schaxel, J., "Namen und Wesen des harmonisch-äquipotentiellen Systems." *Biologisches Zentralblatt,* Vol. 36 (1916).

Schaxel, J., "Mechanismus, Vitalismus und kritische Biologie." *Biologisches Zentralblatt,* Vol. 37 (1917).

Schneider, K. C., "Vitalismus." *Biologisches Zentralblatt,* Vol. 25 (1905)

Secerov, Slavko, "Zur Kritik der Entelechielehre von H. Driesch." *Biologisches Zentralblatt,* Vol. 31 (1911).

Spaulding, E. G., "Driesch's Theory of Vitalism." *Philosophical Review,* Vol. 15 (1906).

Spaulding, E. G., review of *The Science and Philosophy of the Organism,* Vols. I and II. *Philosophical Review,* Vol. 18 (1909).

Vollenhoven, D. H. T., "Einiges über die Logik in dem Vitalismus von Driesch." *Biologisches Zentralblatt,* Vol. 41 (1921).

Wagner, A., "Neo-Vitalismus," I, II. *Zeitschrift für Philosophie und philosophische Kritik,* Ergänzungsband, Vol. 136 (1909).

William H. Werkmeister

DU BOIS-REYMOND, EMIL (1818–1896), German physiologist and philosopher of science. He was born in Berlin and in 1846 qualified as a *Privatdozent* in physiology at Berlin University. He was named associate professor of physiology at the university in 1855 and became full professor three years later. Du Bois-Reymond made important contributions to physiology through his extensive studies in animal electricity, muscle and nerve action, and the processes of metabolism. Later he engaged in discussion of philosophical problems as well, notably in his widely reprinted works *Ueber die Grenzen des Naturerkennens* ("On the Limits of the Knowledge of Nature," 1872) and *Die sieben Welträtsel* ("The Seven Riddles of the Universe," 1880).

Du Bois-Reymond's point of view was a relativistic positivism founded on natural science. He regarded knowledge of the transcendental, or supersensible, as impossible and metaphysical problems as insoluble. In particular, with respect to seven such mystifying questions that are raised again and again and yet are never answered in a generally convincing way, he took the skeptical and agnostic position indicated in his widely quoted words *ignoramus et ignorabimus* ("we do not know and we shall never know"). Three questions he held to be transcendental and therefore in principle insoluble; these relate to the nature of matter and force (which for him were nothing more than abstractions), the origin of motion, and the origin of sensation and consciousness. Three other problems he termed very difficult but in principle solvable: those having to do with the origin of life, the adaptiveness of organisms, and the development of reason and language. With regard to the seventh and final "riddle of the universe," the problem of freedom of the will, he was undecided.

Ernst Haeckel, in his well-known *Welträtsel*, published in opposition to Du Bois-Reymond's views in 1899, acknowledged only a single "riddle of the universe"—the "problem of substance." Du Bois-Reymond's three "transcendental" riddles Haeckel disposed of by means of his monistic conception of substance. The three "very difficult" riddles, in his opinion, had been solved by the modern theory of evolution. And the problem of the freedom of the will he regarded as a pseudo problem because free will "as a pure dogma rests on mere illusion and in reality does not exist at all."

As a natural philosopher Du Bois-Reymond forcefully raised the demand that the whole of nature be interpreted in an exclusively mechanistic fashion in the sense of Laplace's "ideal spirit." He held that the mechanistic, quantitative explanation of nature, despite its deficiencies and difficulties (which he conceded), was the only possible and fruitful one. On the other hand, he rejected as worthless such metaphysical concepts as "vital force." At the same time he was quite clear about the insuperable limits of the mechanistic approach. While he uncompromisingly stressed the necessity of an approach to nature that conceives of the world as describable by means of a single mathematical formula determining all that happens, he explicitly admitted that mental phenomena cannot be derived from and understood in terms of the physical and physiological processes in the brain and nervous system. As to what mental phenomena are, Du Bois-Reymond held, we remain in doubt. At this point his mechanistic conception of nature joined with his agnosticism.

Bibliography

Works by Du Bois-Reymond are *Ueber die Grenzen des Naturerkennens* (Leipzig, 1872); *Die sieben Welträtsel* (Leipzig, 1880); and *Reden* (Leipzig, 1885–1887; 2d ed., 1912). *Reden* includes both of the other books, as well as Du Bois-Reymond's works on Copernicus, Leibniz, Maupertuis, Voltaire, La Mettrie, Diderot, Goethe, Chamisso, Darwin, Helmholtz, and others.

A work on Du Bois-Reymond is Heinrich Boruttau, *Emil Du Bois-Reymond* (Vienna, 1922).

FRANZ AUSTEDA
Translated by *Albert E. Blumberg*

DUCASSE, CURT JOHN, philosopher and educator, was born in 1881 in Angoulême, France. After attending schools in France and England, he came to the United States in 1900. He received his B.A. and M.A. degrees from the University of Washington and, in 1912, his Ph.D. from Harvard University, where he had served as an assistant to Josiah Royce. He taught philosophy at the University of Washington from 1912 until 1926, at Brown University from 1926 until his retirement in 1958, and elsewhere as visiting professor. He is a former president of the Association for Symbolic Logic (1936–1938), which he helped to found, and of other learned societies. He has published extensively in all fields of philosophy.

Philosophical method. Ducasse's views on method are worked out in detail in *Philosophy as a Science: Its Matter and Method* (New York, 1941), in his Carus lectures, published as *Nature, Mind, and Death* (La Salle, Ill., 1951), and elsewhere.

He holds that philosophy is a science and that it differs from other sciences not in the generic features of its method but by virtue of its subject matter, which consists of "spontaneous particular appraisals" (1941) or "standard evaluative statements" (1951) made by some person or group. The primitive problems of philosophy are to define the value predicates "good," "valid," "real," and so on, and their opposites, as used by the person or persons whose standard evaluative statements are taken as data. In the definitions will appear such terms as "necessary," "fact," "possibility," which are also in need of analysis, giving rise to derivative problems. Both sorts of problems are essentially semantical. Ducasse is thus squarely in the analytical tradition. However, he has argued more explicitly than other contemporary analysts that a proposed analysis of a term as used in paradigm statements has the status of a hypothesis, and that it can be confirmed or disconfirmed by observing whether it is substitutable for the analysans in the paradigm statements without altering any of their standard implications.

Causation. Ducasse had adumbrated the above views and had applied his method to the concept of causality in *Causation and the Types of Necessity* (Seattle, 1924). Ducasse has always regarded causality as a "fundamental category," and in subsequent works he continued to refine his original analysis.

According to Ducasse, causality is a relation between

events, is essentially triadic, and is correctly defined in terms of Mill's method of difference. That "method" is not in fact a method for discovering causal connections but a description of the causal relation itself. If, in a state of affairs *S*, only two changes occur, one the change *C* at time T_1 and the other the change *E* at time T_2, *C* is the cause of *E*. Ducasse asserted that despite Hume's definition of causation as regularity of sequence, Hume actually thought of it in terms of the advent of a single difference in a given state of affairs, as is proved by the way he formulated his rules for ascertaining causal connections by a *single* experiment.

Given the above definition, the supposition that some events have no cause implies a contradiction. Hence, indeterminism, the view that some events are matters of objective change, is self-contradictory, although men are "free" in the sense that, and to the extent that, they can do what they will to do.

Mind and nature. In *Nature, Mind, and Death*, Ducasse went on to assert that nature is the material world, comprising all the things, events, and relations which are publicly perceptible. The mental, which is directly observable only through introspection, is not part of nature. Substances are analyzed as systems of properties and their relations. A property is a causal capacity. Thus,

> to say of carborundum that it is *abrasive* means that, under certain conditions, friction of it against certain other solids causes them to wear away. . . . More generally, to say that a substance *S* has a property or capacity *P* means that *S* is such that, in circumstances of kind *K*, an event of kind *C*, occurring in *S* or about *S*, regularly causes an event of kind *E* to occur in or about *S*. (*Nature, Mind, and Death*, p. 165)

Since *C* and *E* may stand for either a physical or a mental event, there are four kinds of properties: physicophysical, if *C* and *E* are both physical events; physicopsychical, if *C* is physical and *E* psychical; psychophysical; and psychopsychical.

The relation of a mind, a mental substance, to "its body," a material substance, is that of causal interaction. This is an analytic truth, for by "its body" can only be meant "the body with which that mind directly interacts." Many of the usual objections to interactionism presuppose a mistaken conception of causality.

In the case of physicopsychical properties ("bitter," "blue") it is important to distinguish between the sense quality in terms of which the property is defined and the property itself. "Bitter," for example, is equivocal. As applied to quinine, it is a disposition term designating the capacity of quinine to cause a certain taste experience when one places it on one's tongue. As applied to the experience itself, it is the name of a quality. With respect to the properties of material things, Ducasse is a realist. Quinine is bitter and roses are red, in the dispositional sense, even if the properties are not being exercised. Of properties, it is false that *esse* is *percipi*. But in the case of sense qualities, it is true that *esse* is *percipi*.

Now G. E. Moore, in his "Refutation of Idealism," had argued that since we can distinguish the sensum blue that is the object of a sensation from the sensing itself, sensa might exist without consciousness of them, and they might therefore be nonmental. Against Moore, Ducasse argues in *Nature, Mind, and Death* that a sensum is not an "object" of sensation but the "content" of it. When one sees some lapis lazuli, the lapis lazuli is the object seen. But the relation of the lapis lazuli to the seeing of it when "I see some lapis lazuli" is true is not the same as the relation of blue to the seeing of it when "I see blue" is true. (Compare "I taste quinine" with "I taste bitter," or "I am jumping a ditch" with "I am jumping gracefully.") After a meticulous examination of various hypotheses on what the relation of sensa to sensing might be, Ducasse concludes that sensa are species of experience. "I sense blue" means "I sense bluely," or, alternatively, "I sense in the manner blue," just as "I am dancing a waltz" means "I am dancing waltzily (in the manner of dancing called 'dancing a waltz').' Just as a waltz could not conceivably exist apart from the dancing of it, a sensum could not exist apart from the sensing of it.

On the basis of this analysis, Ducasse submits that the basic criterion of the mental may be expressed by saying that *"if something being experienced is connate with the experiencing of it, then it is a mental primitive."*

Aesthetics. In *The Philosophy of Art* (New York, 1929), *Art, the Critics, and You* (New York, 1944), and many articles, Ducasse formulates and defends an emotionalist theory of art and aesthetic experience. His principal contentions are that art in the broadest sense is skilled activity; that fine or aesthetic art consists in the skilled objectification of feeling; that the fine artist judges the adequacy of the work he creates not by the degree to which it approximates to beauty but by the faithfulness with which it reflects back to him the feeling to which he attempted to give objective expression; that in the aesthetic attitude one "throws oneself open" to the advent of feelings; and that judgments of aesthetic value are relative to the taste of the critic.

Philosophy of religion. In *A Philosophical Scrutiny of Religion* (New York, 1953), Ducasse defines religion as essentially any set of articles of faith, with the observances, feelings, and so on, tied thereto, that has the social function of motivating altruism in individuals and the personal function of giving the believer inner peace and assurance. According to this definition, belief in a God or gods is not essential to religion. Ducasse himself is not a theist. He holds that orthodox theism is contradicted by the existence of evil, and that polytheism is more plausible than monotheism conceived in the orthodox manner.

Paranormal phenomena. Throughout his career, Ducasse has been interested in and has written about the "wild facts" of mental telepathy, clairvoyance, precognition, and so on. His interest in them is manifold. If paranormal phenomena do occur, received theories about the mental and the physical must be revised to account for them. It is a gratuitous assumption that any theory capable of taming the wild facts would have to postulate supernatural entities or "spooks." It could well be as scientific as are current theories about hypnotism, which have more or less tamed the wild facts of mesmerism. One of the troubles of psychical research is the lack of a fruitful theory.

If paranormal phenomena do occur, there would be

important implications for philosophy. How would philosophers have to conceive of time, causality, perception if there were such a thing as precognition?

It is a logical possibility that a mind survives the death of its body (or, to allow for reincarnation, bodies), even when due account has been taken of current science. But is there any evidence that it does? If there is, it is likely to be found by objective sifting of the reports concerning paranormal phenomena. In *A Critical Examination of the Belief in a Life After Death* (Springfield, Ill., 1961), Ducasse states that the conclusion about survival seemingly warranted at present is that "the balance of the evidence so far obtained is on the side of the reality of survival," but that the evidence is not conclusive.

Bibliography

A complete bibliography of Ducasse's writings up to December 31, 1951, is available in *Philosophy and Phenomenological Research,* Vol. 13, No. 1 (September 1952), 96–102. This issue also contains "Symposium in Honor of C. J. Ducasse" by seven philosophers, a biographical note, and a portrait.

For George Santayana's response to Ducasse's views on causation, "ontological liberalism," art, and properties, see Daniel Cory, ed., *The Letters of George Santayana* (New York, 1955), pp. 213–215, 234–235, and 287–288. For a careful review of *Nature, Mind, and Death* by H. H. Price, see *The Journal of Parapsychology,* Vol. 16, No. 2 (June 1952).

VINCENT TOMAS

DUHEM, PIERRE MAURICE MARIE (1861–1916), was noted for his original work in theoretical physics, especially thermodynamics, and in the history and philosophy of science. He was born and studied in Paris; at the age of 25 published an important book on thermodynamics. In 1887 he went to the faculty of sciences at Lille University, where he taught hydrodynamics, elasticity, and acoustics. He married but his wife soon died, leaving him with a daughter. In 1893 he moved to Rennes and in 1895 to a chair at Bordeaux University, which he held until his death. Throughout his life he was a Catholic and a conservative.

His approach to physics was systematic and mathematical, and his interest in axiomatic methods undoubtedly determined to some extent the nature of his philosophical account of scientific theories, contained mainly in his book *La Théorie physique: son objet, sa structure* (*The Aim and Structure of Physical Theory*), first published in 1906. He wrote a great deal on the history of science, especially in the fields of mechanics, astronomy, and physics, largely because he believed that a knowledge of the history of a concept and of the problems it was designed to meet was essential for a proper understanding of that concept. For the scientist, the history of his subject should be not a mere hobby but an essential part of his scientific work. Duhem's most important works in this field are *Les Origines de la statique,* published in 1905–1906, and *Le Système du monde,* an account of various systems of astronomy, in eight volumes, published between 1913 and 1958.

Science and metaphysics. Duhem's account of physical theory is positivistic and pragmatic, having clear connections with those of Ernst Mach and Henri Poincaré. It begins with, and takes its character largely from, his views on explanation. Indeed, one might say that it begins with a dogmatic and unsupported presupposition about the nature of explanation. He says that to explain is "to strip reality of the appearances covering it like a veil, in order to see the bare reality itself."

But the sciences depend upon observation, and observation shows us no more than the appearances: it cannot penetrate to the reality beneath. This reality is the province of metaphysics; only metaphysics can explain. Science merely deals with the relations between, primarily, our sensations (or the appearance of the world to us) and, ultimately, our abstract ideas of these appearances. A physical theory is somehow an abstract representation of the relations between appearances and not a picture of the reality lurking behind them.

Thus, as far as science alone is concerned, Duhem is as antimetaphysical as Mach and more so than Heinrich Hertz. But, in general, he is not antimetaphysical at all. In a sense, metaphysics is the most important of all studies because it penetrates to the reality of things and explains the appearances; but when we are doing science, we must never import into it metaphysical aims or ideas. Science and metaphysics are both highly respectable, but they are utterly distinct and must be kept so on pain of confusion.

We may, Duhem thinks, penetrate to reality, not by the methods of science, but by pure reason. He attaches great importance to the doctrine that man is free, a statement which cannot conflict with any of the conclusions of science. His metaphysical views, which he did not work out in detail, are Aristotelian; properly understood—that is, stripped of its outmoded science—the Aristotelian physics contains an accurate picture of the cosmological order, whose appearance to human beings is studied by the sciences.

Scientists, according to Duhem, have seldom made the distinction between science and metaphysics, with the result that many theories have been seen as attempted explanations and so have been garnished with strictly superfluous "pictorial" and explanatory elements. These theories can be divided into two parts, called by Duhem "representative" and "explanatory." What is valuable in such theories, and hence what survives and what may be common to apparently different theories, is the representative part.

The uses of theories. This conception of the representative nature of theories is linked with the various ways in which theories are useful to us. First, they promote economy by connecting large numbers of experimental laws deductively under a few hypotheses or principles; we need remember only these principles instead of a large number of laws. Second, by classifying laws systematically they enable us to select the laws we need on a particular occasion for a particular purpose. Third, they enable us to predict, that is, to anticipate the results of experiments. These are functions which can be performed by the representative parts of theories, which merely link general statements derived from observation and experiment in a practically convenient way, rather than in a way that corresponds to the underlying reality of things.

The construction of theories. Duhem's account of the way in which theories are constructed exhibits his conception of the nature of physical theories. There are four fundamental operations in their construction.

(1) Among the observable, measurable properties that we wish our theory to represent, we look for a few that can be regarded as simple and as combining to form the rest. Because they are measurable, we can represent them by mathematical symbols. These symbols have no intrinsic connection with the properties they represent: they are conventional signs for these properties. For example, temperature measured in degrees centigrade is a conventional and quantitative representation of the felt warmth and cold of sense experience.

(2) We construct a small number of principles, or "hypotheses," which are propositions arbitrarily connecting our symbols in a manner controlled only by the requirements of convenience and logical consistency. We may give as an example the definition of "momentum" as the product of mass and velocity.

(3) We combine these hypotheses according to the rules of mathematical analysis; again there is no question of representing the real relations between properties, and convenience and consistency are still our guides.

(4) Certain of the consequences drawn out by our third operation are "translated" back into physical terms. That is, we arrive at new statements about the measurable properties of bodies, our methods of defining and measuring these properties serving as a kind of "dictionary" to assist us in the translation. These new statements can now be compared with the results of experiments; the theory is a good one if they fit, a bad one if they do not.

The nature of laws and theories. Thus, a physical theory, for Duhem, is always mathematical and is a conventional system of linkages between propositions "representing" general statements or laws arrived at by experiment or observation. It is a device for calculating, and nothing matters except that the results of the calculations square with our observations. We might illustrate this in the following way. There are various routes by plane from city *A* (the known laws) to city *B* (the new laws), and it does not matter which route we take as long as we arrive at *B*: We are flying blind; the plane has no windows, and we cannot see the landscape, the sun, or even the clouds during the journey; we must not suppose that the interior of the plane resembles *A* or *B* or the country in between.

The idea that physical characteristics are analyzable into basic elements which are simple and ultimate has figured largely in empiricist and positivist accounts of the sciences. This idea involves numerous difficulties, not the least among them being that of giving any precise meaning to simplicity. Duhem avoids some of the difficulties. Because physical theories do not explain, his simple elements need not be ultimate in nature; they need not be *incapable* of further analysis. They may merely be properties which we *take to be* fundamental and which we have not succeeded in analyzing.

Duhem distinguishes between "practical facts" and "theoretical facts." A description of a phenomenon in ordinary ("observational") language states a practical fact, and its translation into the symbols of the theory states a theoretical fact. But the theoretical fact, as should now be obvious, is a "fact" only in a very odd sense; it has some kind of formal correspondence with the practical fact, but it is always an approximation or an idealization and always has many alternatives.

There is a similar relation between empirical or "common-sense" laws and scientific laws. Scientific laws state the relations between symbols that derive their meanings from the theories of which they are a part. These laws are approximations and idealizations and do not state the relations between actual physical properties. As an example, Duhem cites Boyle's law. This states the relations, not between pressures that may be felt and volumes that may be seen, but between their ideal representatives in a complex theory of gases. The same word "pressure" may stand for different concepts in different theories, and in its common-sense, everyday use it stands for a concept or concepts different again from all these.

A common-sense law, such as "Paper is inflammable," is correctly said to be either true or false. No scientific law, however, can be said to be true or false because every accepted scientific law has equally acceptable alternatives. None of these alternatives is any more correct than any of the others. There are two points here. To call the law we actually accept "true" is to suggest that the acceptable alternatives are false, which is misleading. Moreover, all the possible alternatives are idealizations: there is nothing of which they can be said to be strictly true. The symbols used in scientific laws are always too simple to represent completely the phenomena and their connections; hence, the laws must always be provisional.

Duhem distinguishes between observation and interpretation in a way which would now be questioned by certain philosophers. An observer looking at a spot of light on a scale *may* be merely observing this spot, or he may be doing this *and* interpreting it as the final step in measuring the resistance of a coil. Here, observing needs only attentiveness and reliable eyesight, but interpreting requires a knowledge of electrical theory as well. A boy who knew nothing whatever about electrical theory could be given the task of recording the movements of the spot on the scale; a physicist who had not seen these movements but who knew the theory and was prepared to rely on the boy could interpret the records appropriately.

It follows from Duhem's account that scientific laws and theories are not arrived at by induction. No experiment in physics involves mere generalizing from observations because the description of the experiment and its result, in the appropriate terms, involves the use of our physical symbols and, therefore, an interpretation of the phenomena depending upon the acceptance of a particular theory.

Duhem has important things to say about the testing of scientific hypotheses and theories. An empirical generalization of the form "All *A*'s are *B*" can never be conclusively established, because we can never be sure that we have examined all the *A*'s, but it may be conclusively falsified by finding one *A* which is not *B*. Thus, if we take such a generalization to be the pattern of scientific hypotheses, we must say that these hypotheses are open to conclusive refutation. But this is too simple, for a scientific hypothesis can never be tested independently of other hypotheses. This is a point which probably has to be made for any adequate account of scientific theorizing, but it is clearly an essential part of Duhem's account. For him, a hypothesis is always part of a theory, and it is used to make predictions only along with other parts of the theory and perhaps other theories. The failure of a prediction, then, indicates some inadequacy in the hypothesis in question *or* in some other hypothesis of the theory *or* in another theory that has been assumed in making the prediction, but it does no more than this to locate the inadequacy. It shows conclusively that something is wrong, but it tells us neither where to look for that something nor what we must reject or modify.

Thus, there can be no crucial experiments in physics. The pattern of a crucial experiment is this: we have two conflicting hypotheses about a given phenomenon and we design an experiment which will give one specifiable result if one hypothesis is acceptable and the other not, and another specifiable result if the other is acceptable and the first not. But hypotheses are not, as this suggests, independent and isolable. In fact, we must always confront a whole theory, of which one hypothesis is a part, with another whole theory, of which the other hypothesis is a part. It is much more difficult to devise an experiment to choose between theories, and even if we could, it might be that a theory which conflicts with the experiment could be squared with it by making minor modifications whereby it would become as acceptable as the other theory under test.

This view may be criticized on the grounds that it is logically possible to find a crucial experiment that would enable us to choose between two *theories.* Of course, a theory which conflicts with experimental results may be capable of modification so that it does not conflict, but if it then gives exactly the same deductions as its rival, it is doubtful that they can be regarded as different theories, in Duhem's view. On the other hand, if they give different deductions covering the same field, it remains logically possible to devise a conclusive experiment to choose between *these two theories.* Popper objects to Duhem's view on the grounds that the only reason Duhem thought crucial experiments impossible was because he stressed verification rather than falsification. It is not clear that Popper's objection is valid, for Duhem seems to have noticed the obvious fact that the aim of a crucial experiment is to eliminate one of the theories.

Although there is much in common between Duhem's and Poincaré's accounts of scientific theories, Duhem uses this last point about theory modification in criticism of part of Poincaré's view. According to Poincaré and others, certain important hypotheses of physical theory cannot be refuted by experiment because they are *definitions.* For example, the statement that the acceleration of a freely falling body is constant really defines "freely falling"; if an experiment appears to conflict with this, the most we can say is that the body was not falling freely. Nothing we observe can compel us to reject the original statement because it is not an empirical statement. Duhem, in reply, gives a different reason why we sometimes treat scientific statements in this way. It is not that the hypotheses we treat in this way are definitions but that they cannot be tested in isolation; thus, we are usually free, in the face of an unfulfilled prediction, to keep any given hypothesis and reject some other. This does not mean that we shall never be forced to reject that given hypothesis in consequence of some other modification we make to the theory, but only that the odds are against this happening on any given occasion.

Works by Duhem

Le Potentiel thermodynamique et ses applications à la mécanique chimique et à la théorie des phénomènes électriques. Paris, 1886. His first book.

Le Mixte et la combinaison chimique. Essai sur l'évolution d'une idée. Paris, 1902.

Les Théories électriques de J. Clerk Maxwell: Étude historique et critique. Paris, 1902.

L'Évolution de la mécanique. Paris, 1903.

Les Origines de la statique. Paris, 1905–1906.

La Théorie physique, son objet et sa structure. Paris, 1906. Second edition with new appendix (1914) translated by P. P. Wiener as *The Aim and Structure of Physical Theory.* Princeton, 1954. This book contains Duhem's most important philosophical work.

Études sur Léonard de Vinci, ceux qu'il a lus et ceux qui l'ont lu. Paris, 1906–1913.

"Physics—History of," in *Catholic Encyclopedia.* New York, 1911. Vol. 12, pp. 47–67.

Le Système du monde. Histoire des doctrines cosmologiques de Platon à Copernic, 8 vols. Paris, 1913–1958. An enormous historical work of considerable importance.

Works on Duhem

Agassi, J., "Duhem *versus* Galileo." *British Journal for the Philosophy of Science,* Vol. 8 (1957), 237–248.

Duhem, H.-P., *Un Savant français: P. Duhem.* Paris, 1936.

Frank. P., *Modern Science and Its Philosophy.* Cambridge, Mass., 1949.

Ginzburg, B., "Duhem and Jordanus Nemorarius." *Isis,* Vol. 25 (1936), 341–362.

Jammer, M., *Concepts of Force.* Cambridge, Mass., 1957.

Launay, L. de, "Pierre Duhem." *Revue des Deux Mondes* (1918), 363–396.

Lowinger, A., *The Methodology of Pierre Duhem.* New York, 1941. See also a review of this work by B. Ginzburg. *Isis,* Vol. 34 (1942), 33–34.

Picard, E., *La Vie et l'oeuvre de Pierre Duhem.* Paris, 1922.

Poincaré, H., "Sur la Valeur objective des théories physiques." *Revue de métaphysique et de morale,* Vol. 10 (1902), 263–293.

Popper, K. R., *The Logic of Scientific Discovery.* London, 1959.

Popper, K. R., *Conjectures and Refutations.* London, 1963.

Rey, A., "La Philosophie scientifique de M. Duhem." *Revue de métaphysique et de morale,* Vol. 12 (1904), 699–744.

Roy, E. le, "Science et philosophie." *Revue de métaphysique et de morale,* Vol. 7 (1899), 503.

Roy, E. le, "Un Positivisme nouveau." *Revue de métaphysique et de morale,* Vol. 9 (1901), 143–144.

PETER ALEXANDER

DÜHRING, EUGEN KARL (1833–1921), German philosopher and political economist, was born in Berlin and died in Nowawes, near Potsdam. Dühring practiced law in Berlin from 1856 to 1859, but an eye ailment, eventually leading to total blindness, forced him to abandon this career. In 1861 he took his doctorate in philosophy at the University of Berlin, with a dissertation entitled *De Tempore, Spatio, Causalitate Atque de Analysis Infinitesimalis Logica.* He became university lecturer in 1863, but his feuding with colleagues and his attacks on the university led to his dismissal in 1877. From then until his death he lived the life of a private scholar. In his later years, Dühring's attacks on religion (*Asiatismus*), militarism, Marxism, the Bismarck state, the universities, and Judaism became more and more virulent. Nevertheless, he retained a small group of loyal followers who founded a journal primarily devoted to his essays, the *Personalist und Emanzipator* (1899). Three years after Dühring's death, E. Döll founded the Dühring-Bund.

Dühring's early views, expressed in his *Natürliche Dialektik*, were Kantian. Eventually, however, he came to reject Kant's phenomena–noumena distinction, with its corollary that we do not apprehend reality as it is in itself. Dühring maintained that the mind does grasp reality directly, and that the laws of thought are in some sense also laws of being.

Knowledge and reality. While denouncing metaphysics and every sort of supernaturalism, Dühring formulated a theory of reality that is no less metaphysical than that of the philosophers whom he attacked. Philosophy, according to Dühring, should aim at a comprehensive account of reality, an account that will be consonant with the natural sciences. A complete knowledge of reality is possible if we restrict ourselves to what is given, utilizing the "rational imagination" that is the organ for philosophizing. (This constructive imagination is used also in mathematics, Dühring held.) The outcome of this activity, an activity of passion guided by the understanding, will be a coherent and comprehensive world picture. Dühring praised Schopenhauer, Feuerbach, and Comte for their efforts in this direction.

The fundamental law that we are to use in apprehending reality is the Law of Determinate Number. This law provides an easy solution to the antinomies in which reason finds itself when seeking knowledge beyond the realm of possible experience. It states that all thinkable numbers are complete or determined, and that the notion of an infinite or undetermined number is therefore impossible. Dühring suggested that the conception of an infinity of events or of units is somehow logically contradictory, as if one were to speak of a countless number that had been counted. For the theory of reality, the consequences of Dühring's law are that the number of events in time that preceded the present moment must be finite, and so too must be the number of objects in space. The history of the universe must have had an absolute beginning, and every object that exists or has existed must be divisible into a finite number of parts. It is nevertheless possible, Dühring maintained, that time and space extend infinitely from here and now.

A "primordial being" lies beyond the first event in time, though this being can be defined only by negating the properties of objects and events in time. Still, we can say of it that it contains the "roots" of every event and object, though it does not consist of events and is not an object. History develops out of this primordial being by an evolutionary process, from the more homogeneous to the more diversified.

What is actual must be here and now. The past is no longer real. The primordial condition of being no longer exists, though its traces are still evident. The laws of the physical universe, the atoms that make up matter—these are the unchanging aspects of the world, the persistent traces of the primordial being.

Change and evolution. The evolution of the universe involves the coming into being of genuinely new forms, and there exists the possibility that further novelty will emerge with the passage of time. The coming into being of motion, and of living creatures and conscious agents, are examples of new phenomena in the transition from the original condition of the world to its present state. Productive, creative activity is an essential fact about the universe, yielding new existences, new phenomena. The laws that describe such changes are nevertheless constant. We do not clearly understand how such genuine novelty occurs, and we ought not to construct speculative hypotheses. An honest philosopher will simply confess his ignorance.

How the world may evolve in the future is also beyond our knowledge. Either natural processes will continue mechanically without ever coming to an end or, what is more probable, there will emerge something radically different. Dühring accepted the latter alternative for the reason that he believed differentiation is a basic law of nature. However, since the number of possible changes is finite, there must be either an eternal recurrence of the world process, as Nietzsche suggested, or an end.

Mind and consciousness. Dühring's philosophy of mind is at first glance dualistic. Conscious activity is totally different from inanimate processes. The former is, however, an outcome of the clash of mechanical processes or forces. The sensation of resistance is the most basic sort of consciousness, and it reveals very clearly that its origin is the antagonism of physical forces.

While Dühring's position is positivistic in its emphasis on the limitation of human knowledge to the world described by natural science, and in its rejection of any independent philosophical knowledge of reality, he differs from some nineteenth-century positivists, such as Mach, in rejecting phenomenalism as the only valid basis for knowledge. Dühring maintained that although no disembodied spirits or souls exist, the world that is given to consciousness is one that contains not only matter and physical forces but also life and activity. Furthermore, he did not repudiate the concepts of cause and force or approve of a reductionism that would restrict intelligible discourse to phenomena, a restriction that he called "a morbid and skeptical aberration."

Religion. In his passionate opposition to religion and to every form of mysticism, Dühring is reminiscent of Lucretius. Religion is "a cradle of delusions," he maintained, and it is only by becoming free from its superstitions that man can become truly noble. The idea of an "other world" is a stumbling block to the proper appreciation of the real world that we encounter directly. We must find our values in this world.

Dühring's teleological optimism led him to reject Darwin's theory that a struggle for existence is necessitated by the insufficiency of means to satisfy natural needs. The conditions for happiness are not impossible, he said. Even pain exists as an enhancement of our appreciation of pleasure. Only man-made institutions stand in the way of human happiness; religion is one of these institutions. Science, as carried on in the nineteenth century, is equally pernicious, since it involves "a hodge-podge of superstition, skepticism and apathy."

Ethics and economics. Dühring held that the feeling of sympathy is the foundation of morality. In applying this theory to the field of economics, Dühring came to a conclusion that Engels and other Marxists have found highly objectionable. The interests of capitalist and worker, Dühring maintained, are not really opposed. By means of free competition there could be an ultimate harmony and compatibility between the two classes. Dühring's economic doctrines also supported the idea of a "national" political economy. He advocated tariff protection of national industries as a means of promoting the culture and morality of all citizens in the state. This goal could be realized most effectively when the economy of a nation was self-sufficient.

Nationalism and racism. Dühring was an ardent German patriot, and some of the enormous popularity that his writings enjoyed in the latter part of the nineteenth century can be traced to this. He worshiped Frederick the Great. Along with his nationalistic zeal, however, Dühring betrayed a generous amount of prejudice, denouncing Jews, Greeks, and even Goethe, who was too cosmopolitan for Dühring's taste. Some conjecture that Nietzsche was influenced by Dühring's *Wert des Lebens.* But the joyous affirmation of life that Dühring shared with Nietzsche stands in sharp contrast to the vicious, embittered tone of many of Dühring's writings, and Nietzsche's rejection of pessimism stands on quite other grounds than that of Dühring.

Works by Dühring

Kapital und Arbeit. Berlin, 1865.

Der Wert des Lebens. Breslau, 1865.

Natürliche Dialektik. Berlin, 1865.

Kritische Geschichte der Philosophie. Berlin, 1869.

Kritische Geschichte der Nationalökonomie und des Sozialismus. Berlin, 1871.

Kritische Geschichte der allgemeinen Prinzipien der Mechanik. Berlin, 1873.

Kursus der National- und Sozialökonomie. Berlin, 1873.

Kursus der Philosophie. Leipzig, 1875. Later editions are entitled *Wirklichkeitsphilosophie.*

Logik und Wissenschaftstheorie. Leipzig, 1878.

Die Judenfrage. Karlsruhe and Leipzig, 1881.

Sache, Leben und Feinde. Karlsruhe, 1882. Autobiography.

Der Ersatz der Religion durch Vollkommeneres. Karlsruhe, 1883.

Works on Dühring

Albrecht, G., *Eugen Dührings Wertlehre.* Jena, 1914.

Döll, E., *Eugen Dühring.* Leipzig, 1892.

Druskowitz, H., *Eugen Dühring.* Heidelberg, 1888.

Engels, F., *Herrn Eugen Dührings Umwälzung der Wissenschaft.* Leipzig, 1878. Translated by E. Burns as *Herr Eugen Dühring's Revolution in Science.* London, 1935. Commonly known as *Anti-Dühring.* Attacks Dühring's philosophy, politics, and economics.

Reinhardt, H., ed., *Dühring and Nietzsche.* Leipzig, 1931.

Vaihinger, H., *Hartmann, Dühring und Lange.* Iserlohn, 1876.

ARNULF ZWEIG

DUNS SCOTUS, JOHN (c. 1266–1308), medieval theologian and philosopher. As with many of the medieval Schoolmen, little is known of the early life of John Duns, the Scot (or Scotus). From the record of his ordination to the priesthood by Bishop Oliver Sutton at Northampton on March 17, 1291, it is inferred that he was born early in 1266. Rival traditions, neither of which can be traced to medieval sources, link him with each of the two main branches of the Duns family in Scotland. According to one account, he was the son of Ninian Duns, a landowner who lived near Maxton in Roxburghshire, received his early schooling at Haddington, and in 1277 entered the Franciscan convent at Dumfries, where his uncle was guardian. Another popular tradition, however, states that his father was the younger son of the Duns of Grueldykes, whose estate was near the present village of Duns in Berwickshire. As a bachelor of theology, Scotus lectured on the *Sentences* of Peter Lombard at Cambridge (date unknown), at Oxford about 1300, and at Paris from 1302 to 1303, when he and others were banished for not taking the side of King Philip the Fair against Pope Boniface VIII in a quarrel over the taxation of church property for the wars with England. The exile was short, however, for Scotus was back in Paris by 1304 and became regent master of theology in 1305. In 1307 he was transferred to the Franciscan study house at Cologne, where he died the following year.

Works. Scotus' early death interrupted the final editing of his most important work, the monumental commentary on the *Sentences* known as the *Ordinatio* (or in earlier editions as the *Commentaria Oxoniensia* or simply the *Opus Oxoniense*). An outgrowth of earlier lectures begun at Oxford and continued on the Continent, this final version was dictated to scribes, with instruction to implement it with materials from his Paris and Cambridge lectures. A modern critical edition of the *Ordinatio,* begun by the Typis Polyglottis Vaticanis (Vatican Press) in 1950, is still in progress. Though less extensive in scope, Scotus' *Quaestiones Quodlibetales* are almost as important; they express his most mature thinking as regent master at Paris. Also authentic are the *Quaestiones Subtilissimae in Metaphysicam* on Aristotle's *Metaphysics;* some 46 shorter disputations held in Oxford and Paris and known as *Collationes;* and a series of logical writings in the form of questions on Porphyry's *Isagoge* and on Aristotle's *Categories, De Interpretatione* and *De Sophisticis Elenchis.* The *Tractatus de Primo Principio* is a short but important compendium of natural theology; drawing heavily upon the *Ordinatio,* it seems to be one of Scotus' latest works. Like the *Theoremata,* a work whose authenticity has been seriously questioned, the *Tractatus* was apparently dictated only in an incomplete form and left to some amanuensis to finish.

Theology and philosophy. Like the majority of the great thinkers of the late thirteenth and early fourteenth centuries, Scotus was a professional theologian rather than a philosopher. One of the privileges accorded mendicant friars like the Franciscans and Dominicans was that of beginning their studies for a mastership in theology without having first become a Master of Arts. The philosophical courses they took in preparation were pursued in study houses of their own order and were, as a rule, less extensive than those required of the candidate for an M.A. As a consequence of this educational program their commentaries on the philosophical works of Aristotle were usually written later than those on Biblical works or on the *Sentences* of Peter Lombard; also, the most important features of their philosophy are frequently found in the context of a theological question. This does not mean that they confused theology with philosophy in principle, but only that in practice they used philosophy almost exclusively for systematic defense or explication of the data of revelation. But in so doing, these theologians assumed that philosophy as a work of reason unaided by faith played an autonomous role and had a competence of its own, limited though it might be where questions of man's nature and destiny were at issue.

This critical attitude concerning the respective spheres of philosophy and theology became more pronounced around the turn of the fourteenth century. Thus, we often find Scotus not only distinguishing in reply to a particular question the answers given by the theologians from those of the "philosophers" (Aristotle and his Arabic commentators) but also pointing out what the philosophers could have proved had they been better at their profession. On the other hand, the genuine interest in the logical structure of "science" (*episteme*), as Aristotle understood the term, led to an inevitable comparison of systematic theology with the requirements of a science such as Euclid's geometry.

Paradoxically, it is in the attempt of the Scholastics to show to what extent theology is or is not a science that we find the most important expressions of their ideas of a deductive system. This is particularly true of the lengthy discussions on the nature of theology in the Prologue of Scotus' *Ordinatio*. Similarly, if we look for the origin of some important and influential philosophical concepts that lie at the heart of Galileo's mechanics, we find them in the medieval discussions of "the intension and remission of forms" (that is, how qualities like hot and white increase in intensity). It was in his analysis of how a man might grow in supernatural charity, for instance, that Scotus introduced his theory of how variations in the intensity of a quality might be treated quantitatively. This key notion, developed by the Merton Schoolmen and extended to the problem of motion, made possible Galileo's description of the free fall of bodies.

Scotus was most concerned with what philosophy has to say about God and the human spirit. Though his ethical views and philosophy of nature are not without interest, Scotus was primarily a metaphysician.

METAPHYSICS

Scotus was thoroughly familiar with the writings of Avicenna, whose concept of metaphysics Scotus brought to the service of theology. Avicenna agreed with Averroës that Aristotle's metaphysics was meant to be more than a collection of opinions (*doxa*) and had the character of a science (*episteme*) or body of demonstrated truths, where "demonstration" is understood in the sense of the *Posterior Analytics*. They also agreed that this science was in great part concerned with God and the Intelligences responsible for the movement of the planetary spheres. But Averroës believed that the existence of God is proved by physics or natural science (by Aristotle's argument for a prime mover), whereas Avicenna developed a causal proof within the framework of metaphysics itself. Scotus argued that the Averroistic view subordinates Aristotle's "first philosophy" to physics when it should be autonomous. Moreover—and more important—one needs a metaphysician to prove that the "prime mover" is the First Being, and metaphysics provides more and better arguments for God's existence than this particular physical proof. Part of the difficulty with the physical proof stems from Aristotle's axiom that "whatever is moved is moved by another." Scotus did not regard this as intuitively evident or deducible from any other such principles. Furthermore, he saw numerous counterinstances in experience, such as man's free will or a body's continued motion after external force is removed.

The transcendentals. Scotus saw metaphysics as an autonomous science concerned with the transcendentals, those realities or aspects of reality that transcend the physical. Its subject matter, as Avicenna rightly maintained, is being as being and its transcendental attributes. In contrast with St. Thomas, who restricted transcendental to such notions as have the same extension as "being," Scotus treated any notion applicable to reality but not included in one of Aristotle's ten categories as transcendental. At least four classes of such can be enumerated. Being (*ens*) is the first of the transcendental notions. It is an irreducibly simple notion of widest extension that is used to designate any subject whose existence implies no contradiction. "Existence" refers to the real or extramental world. Next come the three attributes coextensive with being—"one," "true," and "good"—for to be capable of existing in the extramental world, the subject must have a certain unity and be capable of being known and being desired or willed. Third, there are an unlimited number of attributes such as "infinite-or-finite," "necessary-or-contingent," "cause-or-caused," and so on, that are coextensive with being only in disjunction. Finally, there are many other predicates whose formal notion or definition contains no hint of imperfection or limitation. These are known as pure or unqualified perfections. In addition to being (*ens*), its coextensive attributes, and the more perfect member of each disjunction, this class of transcendentals includes any attribute that can be ascribed to God, whether it pertain to him alone (such as omnipotence or omniscience) or whether it also is characteristic of certain creatures (such as wisdom, knowledge, free will).

Disjunctive attributes. Like Avicenna, Scotus regarded the disjunctive transcendentals as the most important for metaphysics, but being Christian, he conceived these supercategories of being somewhat differently. Avicenna held that creation proceeded from God by a necessary and inevitable process of emanation, whereas for Scotus creation was contingent and dependent on God's free election. Therefore, for Scotus the less perfect member of each disjunction represents only a possible type of real being, whereas for Avicenna these possible types must all eventually be actualized, and therefore the complete disjunction is a necessary consequence of "being." Scotus expressed this difference in what might be called his "law of disjunction":

> In the disjunctive attributes, while the entire disjunction cannot be demonstrated from "being," neverthe-

less as a universal rule by positing the less perfect extreme of some being, we can conclude that the more perfect extreme is realized in some other being. Thus it follows that if some being is finite, then some being is infinite, and if some being is contingent, then some being is necessary. For in such cases it is not possible for the more imperfect extreme of the disjunction to be extentially predicated of "being" particularly taken, unless the more perfect extreme be existentially verified of some other being upon which it depends. (*Ordinatio* I, 39)

The task of the metaphysician, then, is to work out the ways in which the various transcendental concepts entail one another. One of the more important conclusions that will emerge from such an analysis is that there is one, and only one, being in which all pure perfection coexists. Such an infinite being we call God.

Proof for God's existence. Scotus suggested that the metaphysician might use any pair of disjunctives to prove God exists (and here he seems to be in the tradition of William of Auvergne and the "second way" of St. Bonaventure). However, the one metaphysical proof he chose to work out in any detail seems to be a synthesis of what he considered the best elements of all the proofs of his predecessors. Henry of Ghent, whose writings so often served as the springboard for Scotus' own discussion of any problem, had tried to bring some order into the many proofs advanced during the Middle Ages by grouping them under two general headings, the way of causality and the way of eminence. The first drew its inspiration from Aristotelian principles, whereas the second was Augustinian in tone and stemmed from the School of St. Victor and the *Monologion* of St. Anselm. The way of causality was further divided by Henry accordingly as God is treated as the efficient, the final, or the exemplar cause of creatures.

Scotus simplified the causal approach by eliminating the exemplar cause as a distinct category. He treated it as merely a subdivision of efficiency and implied that the cause in question is intelligent and does not act by a blind impulse of nature. As for the way of eminence, it was treated not simply in terms of its Platonic or Augustinian origins but as having a foundation in Aristotelian principles as well. The proof was developed in two principal parts, one dealing with the relative attributes of the infinite being—efficiency, finality, and eminent perfection—and the second with the absolute property of his infinity. Given the infinity of God, Scotus essayed to show there can be but one such being. Each section is a concatenation of closely reasoned conclusions, some thirty-odd in all.

The argument was perhaps one of the most elaborate and detailed proofs for God's existence constructed during the Middle Ages, and apart from any intrinsic merit as a whole it is of considerable historical interest. From the time Scotus first formulated it, he subjected the proof to several revisions, mainly in the direction of greater conceptual economy and logical rigor. In what seems to be the final version (in the *Tractatus de Primo Principio*), the proof is prefaced by two chapters that represent an attempt to formalize what a Schoolman at the turn of the fourteenth century must have regarded as the basic axioms and theses of the science of metaphysics. Other interesting aspects of the argument appear in answer to possible objections to the proof. One anticipates Kant's causal antinomy. Aristotle and his Arabic commentators maintained that the world with its cyclic growth and decay had no beginning. How, then, can one argue to the existence of an uncaused efficient cause? Scotus' solution reveals the influence of Avicenna. On the ground that whatever does not exist of itself has only the possibility of existence as something essential to itself, Avicenna argued that this holds not only of the moment a thing begins to be but of every subsequent moment as well. The true cause of any effect, then, must coexist with and conserve the effect and therefore must be distinguished from the ancillary chain of partial causes that succeed one another in time.

Scotus developed this distinction in terms of what he called an essential versus an accidental concatenation of causes. A series of generative causes such as grandparent, parent, and child, or any sequence of events such as those later analyzed by Hume, would be causes only accidentally ordered to one another in the production of their final effect. Where an essential ordering or concatenation exists, all the causal factors must coexist both to produce and to conserve their effect. This is true whether they be of different types (such as material, formal, efficient, and final) or whether they be a chain of efficient or final causes, such as Avicenna postulated for the hierarchy of Intelligences between God and the material world. While infinite regress in accidentally ordered causes may be possible, Scotus said, the chain as a whole must be essentially ordered to some coexisting cause that guarantees the perpetuity of what is constant or cyclic about such repetitive productivity. But no philosopher postulates an infinite regress where the concatenation of causes is essential and all must coexist. One does not explain how any possible effect is actually conserved, for instance, by assuming an infinity of links upon which it depends.

Technical demonstration. How is any proof that begins with factual propositions demonstrative or scientific in Aristotle's sense of demonstrative? Are not all such premises contingent? With Avicenna obviously in mind, Scotus explained that pagan philosophers could admit that every factual proposition is necessarily true because of the deterministic chain of causes that links it to the first creative cause, God. According to pagan philosophers, this is true not only of eternal entities like primary matter or the inferior or secondary Intelligences but also of all temporal events brought about by the clockwork motions of the heavenly bodies that these Intelligences cause. Empirical explanations of temporal events are required only because the human mind is unable to trace all the intricate links of causal efficacy that make any given event a necessary and inevitable consequence of God's essential nature.

If such a theory were true, Scotus argued, it would eliminate all genuine contingency from the world and thus conflict with one of the most manifest truths of human experience, namely, that we are free to act otherwise than we do. Should one deny such an obvious fact, it is not argument he needs but punishment or perception. "If, as Avicenna says, those who deny a first principle should be beaten or exposed to fire until they concede that to burn or not to burn are not identical, so too ought those who deny that some being is contingent be exposed to torments until they concede that it is possible for them not to be tormented" (*Ordinatio* I, 39). If true contingency exists, however, it can only be because the first cause does not create the world by any necessity of nature. But if the whole of creation depends upon God's free will, then every factual or existential statement about it will be radically contingent. How, then, can any proof from effect to cause satisfy Aristotle's demand that demonstration begin with necessary premises? One could argue legitimately, but not demonstratively, from such an obvious fact as contingency. Yet, Scotus maintained, it is possible to convert the argument into a technical demonstration by shifting to what is necessary and essential about any contingent fact, namely, its possibility. For while one cannot always infer actuality from possibility, the converse inference is universally valid. What is more, Scotus added, statements about such possibilities are necessary; hence, he preferred to construct the proof from efficiency in the mode of possibility thus: Something can be produced, therefore something can be productive; since an infinite regress or circularity in essentially concatenated causes is impossible, some uncaused agent must be possible and hence actual, since it cannot be both possible and incapable of being caused if it is not actually existing.

One can argue similarly of the possibility of a final cause or of a most perfect nature. (Scotus' argument in this connection bears a curious parallel to Wittgenstein's about simple objects in the *Tractatus Logico-Philosophicus*.) Scotus saw God as the necessary or a priori condition required to make any contingent truth about the world possible; these possibilities must be a part of God's nature, "written into him from the beginning"; as source of all possibility, he himself cannot be "merely possible." It is in God's knowledge of, and power over, these limitless possibilities that we discover what is fixed, essential, and noncontingent about not only the actual world but about all possible worlds as well. Since God is the fixed locus in which all possibilities coexist, he must be infinite in knowledge, in power, and therefore in his essence or nature. Since contradictions arise if one assumes that more than one such infinite mind, power, or being exists, there can be but one God.

THEORY OF KNOWLEDGE

After establishing the existence of an infinite being to his own satisfaction, Scotus undertook an analysis of the concepts that enter into statements about God, and in so doing he threw considerable light upon his own theory of knowledge, particularly upon how he considered notions that transcend the level of sensible phenomena to be possible.

Univocity and the transcendentals. Some of the earlier Schoolmen like Alexander of Hales, St. Bonaventure, and Henry of Ghent fell back upon various theories of innatism or illuminationism (in which elements from St. Augustine and Avicenna were grafted upon the Aristotelian theory of knowledge) to account for such knowledge as seems to have no foundation in the data of the senses. These hybrid interpretations of Aristotle had this in common: his theory was used to explain only how general or universal concepts applicable to the visible world are abstracted from sense images. But where any notion applicable to God was involved, some illumination from a transcendent mind was thought to be required. Not only did this hold for notions obviously proper to God—such as "necessary being" and "omnipotence"—but also for such seemingly common transcendentals as "being," "true," and "good." Although the latter terms were predicated of creatures as well as of God, their meaning was not univocal. Associated with each term were two similar, and hence often indistinguishable, meanings, both simple and irreducible to any common denominator. One was believed to be proper to creatures and to be abstracted from sensible things by the aid of an agent intellect; the other was proper to God, and since it transcended in perfection anything to be found in creatures, it must be given from above. It was maintained that these innate ideas, impressed upon the soul at birth, lie dormant in the storehouse of the mind, to be recalled like forgotten memories when man encounters something analogous in sensible experience. The discovery of God in created things, then, was explained much like Plato's account of how man recalls the transcendent world of ideas.

As Aristotle's own writings became better known, however, the popularity of such theories diminished. More and more Scholastics followed Aquinas in rejecting any special illumination theory to explain man's knowledge of God, but like Aquinas they failed to see that this required any modification of the traditional doctrine of the analogy of being and other transcendental terms. Scotus seems to have been the first to see the discrepancy between the two positions. He pointed out that if all of our general notions (including those of being and its transcendental attributes) are formed by reflecting upon sensible things, as Aristotle explained, then some notions such as being must be univocally predicable of God and creatures, or all knowledge of God becomes impossible. Arguing specifically against Henry of Ghent, who claimed we have either a concept of being proper to God or one common to finite creatures, Scotus insisted on the need of a third or neutral notion of being as a common element in both the other concepts. This is evident, he said, because we can be certain that God is a being while remaining in doubt as to whether he is an infinite or a finite being. When we prove him to be infinite, this does not destroy but adds to our previous incomplete and imperfect notion of him. The same could be said of other transcendental notions, such as wisdom or goodness. Indeed, every irreducibly simple notion predicable of God must be univocally predicable of the finite and created thing from which it was abstracted. Any perfection of God is analogous to its created similitude, but we conceive such a perfection as something exclusive or proper to God through composite concepts constructed by affirming, denying, and interrelating conceptual elements that are simple and univocally predicable of creatures. For even though every such element is itself general, certain combinations thereof may serve to characterize one, and only one, thing. Although such concepts are proper to God, they retain their general character and do not express positively the unique individuality of the divine nature. Hence the need for proving that only one God exists.

Scotus also held that the transcendental notion of being

(*ens*) is univocal to substance and accidents as well as to God and creatures. We have no more sensible experience of substance than we do of God; its very notion is a conceptual construct, and we would be unable to infer its existence if substance did not have something positive in common with our experiential data.

The formal distinction. The concept of the formal distinction, like univocity of being, is another characteristic metaphysical thesis connected with Scotus' theory of knowledge. Though usually associated with his name, the distinction did not originate with him. It represents a development of what is sometimes called the "virtual distinction" or "conceptual distinction with a foundation in the thing." The latter is an intermediate between the real distinction and that which is merely conceptual. The difference between the morning star and evening star, for example, is purely conceptual. Here one and the same thing, the planet Venus, is conceived and named in two different ways because of the different ways or contexts in which it appears to us. The real distinction, on the contrary, concerns two or more individual items, such as Plato and Socrates, body and soul, or substance and its accidents. Though two such things may coexist or even form a substantial unity or accidental aggregate, it is logically possible that one be separated from the other or even exist apart from the other. The Scholastics generally recognized the need of some intermediary distinction if the objectivity of our knowledge of things is to be safeguarded. How is it possible, they asked, to speak of a plurality of attributes or perfections in God when the divine nature is devoid of any real distinction? How is it possible for a creature to resemble God according to one such attribute and not another? Similarly, if the human soul is really simple, as many of the later Scholastics taught, how can it lack all objective distinction and still be like an angel by virtue of its rational powers and unlike the angel by reason of its sentient nature? All agree that it is possible for the human mind to conceive one of these intelligible aspects of a thing apart from another and that both concepts give a partial insight into what is objectively present to the thing known.

To put it another way, there is a certain isomorphism between concept and reality, in virtue of which concept may be said to be a likeness (*species*) or picture of reality. This "likeness" should not be construed in terms of the relatively simply way a snapshot depicts a scene, but perhaps something more akin to Wittgenstein's "logical picture," being based upon what shows itself in both the world of facts and our thoughts about the world. In virtue of this intelligibility of form, we can speak of *ratio* (the Latin equivalent of the Greek *logos* or the Avicennist *intentio*) either as in things or as in the mind. To the extent that this *ratio* or intelligible feature is a property or characteristic of a thing, we are justified in saying that the individual possessing it is a so-and-so. Though such *rationes* can be conceived one without the other because their definitions differ and what is implied by one is not necessarily implied by the other, nevertheless, as characteristic of a specific individual, they constitute one thing. They are not separable from that individual in the way the soul can be separated from the body, or a husband from his family. Not even the divine power can separate a soul from its powers or the common features of the individual from what is unique (his *haecceity*).

Aquinas spoke of this nonidentity as conceptual, with the qualification that it does not arise merely in virtue of thinking mind but "by reason of a property of the thing itself." Henry of Ghent called it an intentional distinction, but he added that the distinction is only potential prior to our thinking about it. Scotus, however, argued that if something has the native ability to produce different concepts of itself in the mind, each concept reflecting a partial but incomplete insight into the thing's nature, then the distinction must be in some sense actual. Put in another way, there must be several "formalities" in the thing (where "form" is understood as the objective basis for a concept and "little form" or formality as an intelligible aspect or feature of a thing that is less than the total intelligible content of a thing). Here again Scotus argued (on a line later followed by Wittgenstein) that a thing's possibilities, unlike their actualization, are not accidental but are essential to it and must have some actual basis. If a thing is virtually two things inasmuch as it is able to be grasped in two mutually exclusive ways, this nonidentity of intelligible content must be prior to our actually thinking about the thing, and to that extent it exists as a reality (*realitas*) or in other words, objectively. This nonidentity of realities, or formalities, is greatest in the case of the Trinity, where the peculiar properties of the three divine persons must be really identical with, but formally distinct from, the divine nature they have in common. This formal nonidentity holds also for the divine attributes, such as wisdom, knowledge, and love, which although really one are virtually many.

The formal distinction was also used by Scotus to explain the validity of our universal conceptions of individuals, a Scotistic thesis that influenced C. S. Peirce. Unlike the "nominalists," Scotus did not believe that the common features of things can be accounted for fully in terms of their being represented by a common term or class concept. Some objective basis for this inclusion is required, and this similarity or aspect in which one individual resembles another he called its common nature (*natura communis*). This common nature is indifferent to being either individualized (as it invariably is in the extramental world) or being recognized as a universal feature of several individuals (as it is when we relate the concept of this "nature," such as "man," to Peter or Paul). The common nature is individualized concretely by what Scotus called its thisness (haecceity), which is a formality other than the nature, a unique property that can characterize one, and only one, subject. Scotus consequently rejected the Aristotelian–Thomistic thesis that the principle of individuation is identified somehow with matter by reason of matter's quantitative aspect. This thesis would seem to make individuality something extrinsic to the thing itself, or at least the effect of something really other than the thing itself, since matter or matter signed with quantity is really distinct from the form. The requirement of haecceity is a logical one, according to Scotus, for in practice we do not differentiate individual persons or objects because we know their respective haecceity (that is, their Petrinity, Paulinity, their "thisness," or "thatness"), but because of such accidental differences as being in different places at the same time, or having different colored hair or eyes. However, this individuating difference, he insisted, is known to God and can be known by man in a future life, where his intellect is not so dependent upon sense perception.

Knowing as an activity. Though Scotus rejected illumination in favor of what is basically an Aristotelian theory of knowledge, his teaching on the subject shows the influence of some other of Augustine's ideas, notably the active role of the intellect in cognition. Scotus' position is midway between the Aristotelian passivism (the "possible intellect" as a purely "passive potency" receives impressions from without) and Augustine's activism (the intellect as spiritual can act on matter, but matter cannot act upon the spirit or mind). Scotus believed that the so-called possible intellect actively cooperates in concept formation and other intellectual operations. This activity is something over and above that which is usually ascribed to the "agent intellect." Intellect and object (or something that is proxy for the object, such as the intelligible *species* where abstract knowledge is involved) interact as two mutually complementary principles (like man and woman in generation) to produce concepts. Since these concepts reflect only common or universal characteristics of individuals rather than what is uniquely singular about them, it cannot be the singular object itself that directly interacts with the mind, but an intelligible likeness (species) that carries information only about the "common nature" of the object and not its haecceity. The formation of such a likeness or species is the joint effect of the agent intellect and sense image working together as essentially ordered efficient causes. It is in this way that Scotus interpreted the Aristotelian distinction of agent and possible intellect.

Intuitive versus abstractive cognition. Although the above description accounts for man's abstract intellecutal knowledge, Scotus believed that man's mind is capable of intuitive knowledge as well. By this he understood a simple (nonjudgmental) awareness of an object as existing. Where abstract cognition leaves us unable to assert whether a thing exists or not, one can assert that it exists from intuitive cognition of anything. In such a case no intelligible species of the object need intervene, for the mind is in direct contact with the thing known. While most Scholastics limited intuitive knowledge to the sense level, Scotus argued that if man's intellect is capable only of abstract cognition—what can be abstracted from sense encounters in the way described by Aristotle—then the face-to-face vision of God promised to us in the afterlife becomes impossible. Consequently, our ideas of the proper object of the human intellect must be expanded to account for this.

Scotus thought that rational considerations also require us to admit some degree of intuitive power in man even if the full ambit of this power cannot be established by a philosopher. There are many primary contingent propositions of which we are absolutely certain (such as "I doubt such and such" or "I am thinking of such and such"). Since this certitude cannot be accounted for by any amount of conceptual analysis of the propositional terms, we must admit some prior simple awareness of the existential situation that verifies the proposition. This cannot be mere sensory knowledge, since the existential judgment often involves conceptual or nonsensory meanings, as in the examples given above. It is not clear that Scotus wished to assert that in this life we have intuitive knowledge of anything more than our interior acts of mind, will, and so on. This would seem to limit intellectual intuition to reflective awareness and would be consistent with his statements that we have no direct or immediate knowledge of the haecceity of any extramental object. However, he believed that in the afterlife man by his native powers will be able to intuit any created thing, be it material or spiritual, and to that extent man's mind is not essentially inferior to that of the angel. On the other hand, it is not merely because of man's lapsed state that his mind is at present limited to knowing the intelligible features of sense data but also because of the natural harmony of body and mind that would obtain even in a purely natural state.

Certitude. Man's capacity for certitude was also discussed, with Henry of Ghent as the chief opponent. Henry, Scotus explained, appealed to illumination, not for the acquisition of our everyday concepts about the world, since these are obtained by abstraction, but for certitude of judgment. Although the "mechanics" of the process are not fully clear, two "mental images" or species are involved, one derived from creatures, the other imparted by divine illumination from above. Since both the human mind and the sensible object are subject to change, no species or likeness taken from the sensible object and impressed upon the mind will yield invariant truth. Something must needs be added from above. Scotus made short shrift of this theory. If the conclusion of a syllogism is no stronger than its weakest premises, neither does a blending of an immutable and a mutable species make for immutability. Furthermore, if the object is so radically mutable that nothing is invariant under change, then to know it as immutable is itself an error. By way of contrast, Scotus set out to show that certitude is possible without any special illumination. This is certainly the case with first principles and the conclusions necessarily entailed by them. Such necessary truths assert a connection or disconnection between concepts that is independent of the source of the concepts. It is not, for example, because we are actually in sense contact with a finite composite that we can assert that a "whole" of this kind is greater than a part thereof. Even if we erroneously perceive white as black and vice versa, a judgment like "white is not black" precludes any possible error because it depends only on a knowledge of the terms and not on how we arrived at that knowledge.

A second type of certitude concerns internal states of mind or actions. That we are feeling, willing, doubting are experiential facts that can be known with a degree of certitude equal to that of first principles or the conclusions they entail.

A third category concerns many propositions of natural science where a combination of experience and conceptual analysis gives us certitude. Reposing in our soul is the self-evident proposition: "Whatever occurs in a great many instances by a cause that is not free is the natural effect of that cause." Even if the terms are derived from erring senses, we know this to be true, for the very meaning of nature or natural cause is one that is neither free nor acts haphazardly. If experience reveals recurrent behavior patterns where no free intelligent agent is involved, then we are evidently dealing with a natural cause. If the same situation recurs, we can be certain at least of what *should* result therefrom. That the effect expected actually does occur depends upon two further conditions: that the natural course of events is not interrupted by some unforeseen causal factor and that God does not miraculously intervene. Even sensory perception can be analyzed critically to exclude any reasonable doubt. Conflicting sense reports produce such illusions as the stick immersed in water that feels straight yet appears to be bent. Yet there is always some self-evident principle possessed by our mind that enables us to decide which sense perceptual information is correct. Here it is the proposition "Any harder object is not broken by something soft that gives way before it." There are many areas of knowledge, then, where man is perfectly well equipped to arrive at certitude without any special divine enlightenment.

THE DOMAIN OF CREATURES

Exemplar ideas. Scholastics generally accepted Augustine's theory that before creatures are produced, they pre-exist in God's mind as archetypal ideas. Scotus differed from Bonaventure and Aquinas, however, by denying that God knows creatures through such ideas. Every creature is limited and finite as to intelligible content. To make God's knowledge of a creature dependent upon this limited intelligibility of any given idea denigrates the perfection of his intellect; if there is any dependence of idea and intellect, it must be the other way round. Only the infinitely perfect essence can be regarded as logically, though not temporally, antecedent to God's knowledge of both himself and possible creatures. Since possible creatures are written into the divine nature itself, in knowing his nature God knows each possible creature, and in knowing the creature he gives it intelligibility and existence as an object of thought. Like the creative painter or sculptor who produces an idea of his masterpiece in his mind before embodying it in canvas or stone, God, if he is not to act blindly but intelligently, must have a guiding idea or "divine blueprint" of the creature that is logically prior to his decision to create it. Creatures, then, are dually dependent upon God; they depend upon his infinitely fertile knowledge for their conception as exemplar ideas, and they depend upon the divine election of his omnipotent will for their actual existence. This tendency to distinguish various "logical moments" in God, and in terms of their nonmutual entailment to set up some kind of order or "priority of nature" among them, is characteristic of much of Scotus' theological speculation and became a prime target for Ockham's subsequent criticism.

Theory of matter and form. The hylomorphic interpretation formerly attributed to Scotus was based on the *De Rerum Principio*, now ascribed to Cardinal Vital du Four. Scotus, unlike most of his Franciscan predecessors, did not accept the view of ibn-Gabirol (Avicebrón) that all creatures are composed of matter and form. He considered both angels and human souls as simple substances, devoid of any real parts, though they differ in the formal perfections they possess.

Since Scotus did not equate matter with potency (as did St. Bonaventure), nor did he consider it in any way a principle of individuation (as did St. Thomas), there was no reason to postulate it in spiritual creatures either to explain why they are not pure act like God or to account for the possibility of a plurality of individuals in the same species. Hence, against Aquinas, Scotus argued that even though angels lack matter, more than one individual of the same species may exist. More important, Scotus, like John Peckham and Richard of Middleton before him, insisted that matter must be a positive entity. Peckham's view grew out of his Augustinian theory of matter as the seat of the "seminal reasons," but Scotus rejected this germinal interpretation of inchoate forms and argued that if matter is what Aristotle thought it to be, it must have some minimal entity or actuality apart from form. It is true that primary matter is said to be pure potency, but there are two types of such passive potency; one is called objective and refers to something that is simply nonexistent but that can be the object of some productive creation. Matter as the correlative of form, however, is a "subjective" potency or capacity; it is a neutral subject able to exist under different forms and hence is not really identical with any one of them. Absolutely speaking, God could give matter existence apart from all form, either accidental or substantial. In such a case, matter would exist much like a pure spirit or the human soul.

Ockham followed Scotus on this point, as well as in his view that the primary matter of the sun and planetary spheres is not any different from that found in terrestrial bodies, though the substantial form in question may be superior to that of terrestrial elements and compounds.

The human soul as form. From man's ability to think or reason, Scotus argued that the intellective soul is the substantial form that makes man precisely human. But to the extent that reason can prove the soul to be the form of the body, it becomes correspondingly more difficult to demonstrate that the soul will survive the death of the body. While the traditional arguments for immortality have probabilistic value, only faith can make one certain of this truth. On the other hand, if the soul must be a spiritual substance to account for the higher life of reason, at least one other perishable "form of corporeity" must be postulated to give primary matter the form of a human body. Though to this extent Scotus agreed with the pluriformists against St. Thomas, it is not so clear that he would postulate additional subsidiary forms. A virtual presence of the lower forms (elements and chemical compounds) in the form of corporeity would seem to suffice. The form of corporeity has dimensive quantity, that is, it is not the same in each and every part of the body, as is the human soul. The same may be said of the "souls" of plants and animals. Though the human soul has the formal perfections of both the vegetative and the animal souls, these components are not really distinct parts. A formal distinction between the soul's faculties or powers suffices to account for this.

Free will. Particularly in his conception of free will, Scotus departed in many respects from contemporary positions. The will is not simply an intellective appetite, a motor power or drive guided by intelligence rather than mere sense perception. Freedom of will, in other words, is not a simple logical consequence of intelligence but is unique among the agencies found in nature. All other active powers or potentialities (*potentiae activae*) are determined by their nature not only to act but to act in a specific way unless impeded by internal or external causes. But even when all the intrinsic or extrinsic conditions necessary for its operation are present, the free will need not act. Not only may it refrain from acting at all but it may act now one way, now another. The will has a twofold positive response toward a concrete thing or situation. It can love or seek what is good, or it can hate or shun what is evil. Moreover, it has an inborn inclination to do so. But unlike the sense appetites, the will need not follow its inclination. Scotus rejected Aquinas' theory that man is free only if he sees some measure of imperfection or evil in a good object and that the will is necessitated by its end (the good as such), though it is free to choose between several means of attaining it.

But Scotus saw a still more basic freedom in the will, one that Aristotle and Plato failed to recognize. Their theory of man's appetites and loves can be called physical in the original sense of that term. All striving, all activity stems from an imperfection in the agent, whose actions all tend to perfect or complete its nature. *Physis* or "nature" means literally what a thing is "born to be" or become. Since what perfects a thing is its good, and since striving for what is good is a form of love, we could say that all activity is sparked by love. The peculiarity of such "love," however, is that it can never be truly altruistic or even objective. It is radically self-centered in the sense that nature seeks primarily and above all else its own welfare. If at times we find what appears to be altruistic behavior, it is always a case where the "nature" or "species" is favored at the cost of the individual. But nature, either in its individual concretization or as a self-perpetuating species, must of necessity and in all that it does seek its own perfection. This is its supreme value, and the ultimate goal of its loves. Such a theory presents a dual difficulty for a Christian. How can one maintain that "God is love" (I John 4.16) and how can man love God above all things if self-perfection is his supreme value? Aquinas tried to solve the problem within the general framework of the Aristotelian system by making God the perfection of man. In loving God as his supreme value, man is really loving himself. Love of friendship becomes possible to the extent that he loves another as an "other self." This solution had its drawbacks, for certain aspects of Christian mysticism must then be dealt with in a Procrustean way. It leaves unexplained certain facets of man's complex love life. Finally, the theory commits St. Thomas, as it did Aristotle, to maintain that the intellect, rather than free will, is the highest and most divine of man's powers—a view at odds with the whole Christian tradition and particularly with Augustine.

Scotus tried another tack, developing an idea suggested by St. Anselm of Canterbury. The will has a twofold inclination or attraction toward the good. One inclination is the affection for what is to our advantage (*affectio commodi*), which corresponds to the drive for the welfare of the self described above. It inclines man to seek his perfection and happiness in all that he does. If this tendency alone were operative, we would love God only because he is our greatest good, and man's perfected self (albeit perfected by union with God in knowledge and love) would be the supreme object of man's affection; it would be that which is loved for its own sake and for the sake of which all else is loved. But there is a second and more noble tendency in the will, an inclination or affection for justice (*affectio justitiae*), so called because it inclines one to do justice to the objective goodness, the intrinsic value of a thing regardless of whether it happens to be a good for oneself or not. There are several distinguishing features of this "affection for justice." It inclines one to love a thing primarily for its own sake (its absolute worth) rather than for what it does or can do for one (its relative value). Hence, it leads one to love God in himself as the most perfect and adorable of objects, irrespective of the fact that he happens to love us in return or that such a love for God produces supreme delight or happiness in man as its concomitant effect. Third, it enables one to love his neighbor literally as himself (where each individual is of equal objective value). Finally, this love is not jealous of the beloved but seeks to make the beloved loved and appreciated by others. "Whoever loves perfectly, desires co-lovers for the beloved" (*Opus Oxoniense* III, 37). Recall the tendency to make others admire the beautiful or the sorrow felt when something perfectly lovely is unloved, desecrated, or destroyed. If the *affectio commodi* tends to utter selfishness as a limiting case, the first checkrein on its headlong self-seeking is the *affectio justitiae*. Scotus wrote:

> This affection for what is just is the first tempering influence on the affection for what is to our advantage. And inasmuch as our will need not actually seek that towards which the latter affection inclines us, nor need we seek it above all else, this affection for what is just, I say, is that liberty which is native or innate in the will, since it provides the first tempering influence on our affection for what is to our own advantage. (*Ibid.*, II, 6, 2)

The will's basic liberty, in short, is that which frees it from the necessity of nature described by Aristotle, the need to seek its own perfection and fulfillment above all else. Here is the factor needed to account for the generous and genuinely altruistic features of human love inexplicable in terms of the physicalist theory.

Scotus therefore distinguished between the will with respect to its natural inclinations and the will as free. The former is the will considered as the seat of the affection for the advantageous. It views everything as something delightful, useful, or a good for oneself and leads to the love of desire (*velle concupiscentiae*). As free or rational (in accord with right reason), the will is the seat of the affection for justice that inclines us to love each thing "honestly" or as a *bonum honestum*, that is, for what it is in itself and hence for its own sake. Since only such love recognizes the supreme value and dignity of a person and finds its highest and most characteristic expression when directed toward another, it is usually called the love of friendship (*velle amicitiae*) or of wishing one well (*amor benevolentiae*).

ETHICAL AND POLITICAL PHILOSOPHY

Although not primarily an ethicist, Scotus did solve enough specific moral problems from the standpoint of his general system of ethics to make it clear that his ethical system falls well within the accepted code of Christian morality of the day. Yet it does have some distinctive features, most of them growing out of the theory of the will's native liberty. Without some such theory, Scotus did not believe a genuine ethics is possible. If man had only a "natural will" (a rational or intellectual appetite dominated by the inclination for self-fulfillment), he would be incapable of sin but subject to errors of judgment. On the other hand, if the will's freedom is taken to mean nothing more than simple liberation from this inclination of nature, its actions would become irrational and governed by chance or caprice. What is needed is some counterinclination that frees man from this need to follow his natural inclination yet is in accord with right reason. This is precisely the function of man's native freedom. Man's reason, when unimpeded by emotional considerations, is capable of arriving at a fairly objective estimate of the most important human actions in terms of the intrinsic worth of the goal attained, the effort expended, the consequences, and so on. By reason of its "affection for justice" the will is inclined to accept and to seek such intrinsic values, even when this runs counter to other natural inclinations of self-indulgence. But being free to disregard the inclination for self-indulgence and to follow the higher dictates of justice, man becomes responsible for the good or evil he foresees will result from either course of action. It is the exercise of this freedom that is a necessary, though not a sufficient, condition for any action to have a moral value.

The other requisite conditions become apparent if we consider the nature of moral goodness. An action may be called good on several counts. There is that transcendental goodness coextensive with being which means simply that, having some positive entity, a thing can be wanted or desired. But over and above this is that natural goodness which may or may not be present. Like bodily beauty, this accidental quality is a harmonious blend of all that becomes the thing in question. Actions also can have such a natural goodness. Walking, running, and the like may be done awkwardly or with a certain grace or beauty. More generally, an activity or operation of mind or will can be "in harmony with its efficient cause, its object, its purpose and its form and is naturally good when it has all that becomes it in this way" (*Opus Oxoniense* II, 40). But moral goodness goes beyond this natural goodness. "Even as beauty of body is an harmonious blend of all that becomes a body so far as size, color, figure and so on are concerned," Scotus wrote, "so the goodness of a moral act is a combination of all that is becoming to it according to right reason" (*ibid.*). One must consider not only the nature of the action itself but also all the circumstances, including the purpose of its performance. An otherwise naturally good action may be vitiated morally if circumstances forbid it or if it is done for an evil end.

Right reason tells us there is one action that can never be inordinate or unbecoming under any set of circumstances: the love of God for his own sake. "God is to be loved" is the first moral principle or ethical norm. This and its converse, "God must never be hated or dishonored," are two obligations from which God himself can never grant dispensation. He is the one absolute intrinsic value, which cannot be loved to excess; but "anything other than God is good because God wills it and not vice versa" (*ibid.* III, 19).

Scotus argued here as in the case of the divine intellect. The intelligibility of a creature depends upon God's knowing it, and not the other way around. So too its actual value or goodness depends upon God's loving it with a creative love and not vice versa. This obviously applies to transcendental goodness, which is coextensive with a thing's being, but it also holds for natural and moral goodness as well. If the infinite perfection of God's will prevents it from being dependent or necessitated by any finite good, it also insures that creation as a whole will be good. God is like a master craftsman. For all his artistic liberty, he cannot turn out a product that is badly done. Yet no particular creation is so perfect, beautiful, or good that God might not have produced another that is also good; neither must all evil or ugliness be absent, particularly where this stems from a creature's misuse of his freedom. Nevertheless, there are limits to which God's providence can allow evil to enter into the world picture. He may permit suffering and injustice so that mankind may learn the consequences of its misbehavior and through a collective sense of responsibility may right its social wrongs.

While certain actions may be naturally good or bad, they are not by that very fact invested with a moral value; they may still be morally indifferent even when all circumstances are taken into consideration. Only hatred and the "friendship-love" of God are invested with moral value of themselves, and as the motivation for otherwise naturally good or indifferent actions they may make the actions morally wrong or good. Otherwise, the action must be forbidden by God to be morally wrong or commanded by him to be morally good. To that extent, moral goodness too depends upon the will of God. However, it is important to know that some actions are good or bad only because God commands or forbids them, whereas he enjoins or prohibits other actions because they are naturally good or bad, that is, they are consonant or in conflict with man's nature in the sense that they tend to perfect it or do violence to it. Such are the precepts of the natural law embodied in the Decalogue and "written into man's heart." But note that what makes obedience to this instinctual law of moral value is that it be recognized and intended as something willed by God; otherwise, good as it may be naturally, the action is morally indifferent. This too is a consequence of man's native liberty, which can be bound only by an absolute value or the will of its author. To the extent that the first two commandments are expressions of the first moral principle and its converse, God can never make their violation morally right or a matter of indifference; the same does not hold of the last seven, which regulate man's behavior to his fellow man. God granted genuine dispensations from natural law, permitting polygamy to the patriarchs so that the children of God might be multiplied when believers were few. This might be permitted again if plague or war so decimated the male population that race survival was threatened. In such a case, God would reveal this dispensation to man, probably through his church.

Human society. Although Scotus wrote little on the origin of civil power, his ideas of its origin resemble Locke's. Society is naturally organized into families; but when they band into communities they find some higher authority necessary and agree to vest it in an individual or a group, and decide how it is to be perpetuated—for example, by election or hereditary succession. All political authority is derived from the consent of the governed, and no legislator may pass laws for private advantage or that conflict with the natural or divine positive law. Private property is a product of positive rather than natural law and may not be administered to the detriment of the common good. More striking, perhaps, than Scotus' social philosophy was his theological theory (which influenced Suárez and, more recently, Teilhard de Chardin) that the second person of the Trinity would have become incarnate even if man had not sinned. Intended as God's "firstborn of creatures," Christ represents the alpha and omega not only of human society but of all creation.

Known to posterity as the "subtle doctor," Scotus is admittedly a difficult thinker. Almost invariably his thought develops through an involved dialogue with unnamed contemporaries. Although this undoubtedly delighted his students and still interests the historian, it tries the patience of most readers. His style has neither the simplicity of St. Thomas' nor the beauty of Bonaventure's, yet as late as the seventeenth century he attracted more followers than they. Like students who unconsciously mimic the worst mannerisms of their mentor, many of Scotus' disciples seemed bent more on outdoing him in subtlety than in clarifying and developing his insights, so that for both the humanist and reformer "dunce" (a Dunsman) became a word of obloquy. Yet there have always been a hardy few who find the effort of exploring his mind rewarding. Even a poet like Gerard Manley Hopkins regarded his insights as unrivaled "be rival Italy or Greece," and the philosopher C. S. Peirce considered Scotus the greatest speculative mind of the Middle Ages as well as one of the "profoundest metaphysicians that ever lived." Even existentialists, who deplore the efforts to cast his philosophy in Aristotle's mold of science, find his views on intuition, contingency, and freedom refreshing. Scotus' doctrine of haecceity, applied to the human person, invests each individual with a unique value as one wanted and loved by God, quite apart from any trait he shares with others or any contribution he might make to society.

Despite his genius for speculation, Scotus considered speculation merely a means to an end: "Thinking of God matters little, if he be not loved in contemplation." Against Aristotle, he appealed to "our philosopher, Paul," who recognized the supreme value of friendship and love, which, directed to God, make men truly wise.

Bibliography

EDITIONS AND TRANSLATIONS

Opera Omnia, L. Wadding, ed., 12 vols. (Lyons, 1639), reprinted with L. Vivès, ed., 26 vols. (Paris, 1891–1895), contains most authentic and some spurious works, with commentaries by seventeenth-century Scotists. The seven volumes of the critical Vatican edition, edited by C. Balić and others (Vatican City, 1950—), contain only the first book of the *Ordinatio* and seven distinctions of the Oxford lectures. The edition may run to thirty or forty volumes.

For *Tractatus de Primo Principio,* see M. Mueller's edition (Freiburg im Bresgau, 1941) and new editions with English translations by Evan Roche (St. Bonaventure, N.Y., 1949) and Allan Wolter (Chicago, 1965); the latter is entitled *Duns Scotus: A Treatise on God as the First Principle.*

Wolter's book contains translations of two questions from the first Oxford lectures; his *Duns Scotus: Philosophical Writings* (Edinburgh and London, 1962) is in Latin and English, and the paperback reprint (Indianapolis, Ind., 1964) appears without Latin. The question translated in S. Morgenbesser and J. Walsh, eds., *Free Will* (Englewood Cliffs, N.J., 1962), is Scotus' earlier view, which he modified slightly; cf. C. Balić, "Une Question inédite de J. D. Scot sur la volonté," in *Recherches de théologie ancienne et médiévale,* Vol. 3 (1931), 191–208. A translation of a question on the need for theology appears in Herman Shapiro, ed., *Medieval Philosophy* (New York, 1964), and in Nathaniel Micklem, *Reason and Revelation* (Edinburgh, 1953); on Christ as alpha and omega of creation in C. Balić, *Theologiae Marianae Elementa* (Sibenik, Yugoslavia, 1933), a Latin edition, and Allan Wolter, "D. Scotus on the Predestination of Christ," in *The Cord* (St. Bonaventure, N.Y.), Vol. 5 (Dec. 1955), 366–372, an English translation.

STUDIES AND BIBLIOGRAPHIES

The best introduction to the vast literature of the nineteenth and twentieth centuries is O. Shäfer, *Bibliographia de Vita, Operibus et Doctrina I. D. Scoti Saecula XIX–XX* (Rome, 1955); also see A. B. Emden, *A Biographical Register of the University of Oxford to A.D. 1500,* Vol. I (Oxford, 1957), pp. 607–610, and the annual *Bibliographia Franciscana* (Rome), especially Vol. XI (1962) on.

Most general histories and studies as late as C. R. S. Harris, *Duns Scotus* (Oxford, 1927), use the inauthentic *De Rerum Principio* or other spurious works. Recommended are the following more recent histories of medieval philosophy: P. Böhner and Étienne Gilson, *Christliche Philosophie von ihren Anfängen bis Nikolaus von Cues,* 3d ed. (Paderborn, 1954); Frederick Copleston, *A History of Philosophy,* Vol. II, Part II (Westminster, Md., 1950); Armand Maurer, *Medieval Philosophy* (New York, 1962); and Julius Weinberg, *A Short History of Medieval Philosophy* (Princeton, N.J., 1964).

See Franciscan Institute Publications, Philosophy Series (St. Bonaventure, N.Y.): Allan Wolter, *Transcendentals and Their Function in the Metaphysics of Duns Scotus* (1946), for his metaphysics; P. Vier, *Evidence and Its Function According to Duns Scotus* (1947), and Sebastian Day, *Intuitive Cognition* (1947), for his theory of knowledge; and R. Effler, *J. D. Scotus and the Principle "Omne Quod Movetur ab Alio Movetur"* (1962), for his theory of motion and of the will.

W. Hoeres, *Der Wille als reine Vollkommenheit nach Duns Scotus* (Munich, 1962), on the will; J. F. Boler, *Charles Peirce and Scholastic Realism* (Seattle, Wash., 1963), on Peirce's relation to Scotus; and especially the volume of essays commemorating the seventh centenary of Scotus' birth, J. K. Ryan and B. Bonansea, eds., *Studies in Philosophy and the History of Philosophy* (Washington, 1965), Vol. III, may also be consulted.

ALLAN B. WOLTER, O.F.M.

DURANDUS OF SAINT-POURÇAIN (c. 1275–1334),

scholastic philosopher and theologian, bishop, and author (*Doctor Modernus, Doctor Fundatus*), was born in Saint-Pourçain-sur-Sioule in Auvergne, France. He entered the

Dominican order at Clermont at the age of 18, and his philosophical studies were probably completed in his own priory of Clermont. By 1303 he was assigned to St. Jacques, Paris, to study theology at the university. There, according to some historians, he was influenced by his confrere James of Metz. The first version of Durandus' commentary on the *Sentences* of Peter Lombard represents his lectures as bachelor (1307–1308). In these lectures he strongly opposed certain views of Thomas Aquinas, whom the Dominican order had in 1286 commanded its members to study, promote, and defend. At Paris the nominalistic views of Durandus were immediately attacked by Hervé Nédellec and Peter of La Palu. Consequently, between 1310 and 1313 Durandus prepared a revision of his commentary, in which he mitigated many of his previous statements and omitted the more offensive passages. However, this was neither satisfactory to the order nor in accord with his own convictions. Nevertheless, he was granted a license by the university to incept in theology, succeeding Yves of Caen. Before completing his first year as master (1312–1313), he was called to Avignon by Pope Clement V to lecture in the papal *Curia,* replacing Peter Godin. Toward the end of that year the master general of the Dominicans, Berengar of Landorra, appointed a commission of nine theologians, headed by Hervé Nédellec, to examine the writings of Durandus. The commission singled out 93 propositions that were contrary to Thomistic teaching. Between 1314 and 1317, Durandus was continuously attacked in Paris by Hervé Nédellec, Peter of La Palu, John of Naples, James of Lausanne, Guido Terreni, and Gerard of Bologna. He replied to these in his *Excusationes* and in his Advent disputations *de quolibet* at Avignon (1314–1316). In the first *Quodlibet* he inveighed against "certain idiots" who charged him with Pelagianism or semi-Pelagianism.

Consecrated bishop in 1317, Durandus prepared a third and final version of his commentary on the *Sentences*, now free from all control by his order. He expressed regret that the first version had been circulated outside the order against his wishes, "before it had been sufficiently corrected" by him, insisting that only this new version was to be recognized as definitive. However, while some views are closer to the "common teaching" of the schools, the final version contains much that was taken verbatim from the first draft and from the first Avignon *Quodlibet.* It is, perhaps, not surprising that the final version, completed in 1327, abounds in compromises and contradictions.

In the jurisdictional dispute between Pope John XXII and Philip VI of France, Durandus sided with the pope in the treatise *On the Source of Authority* (1328), a work that later was published by Peter Bertrandi as his own composition. However, Durandus' reply to the pope's theological opinion concerning the beatific vision (1333) was promptly submitted to a commission of theologians, who found 11 objectionable statements. The reply of "the blessed master Durandus" was later vindicated by Benedict XII. But Durandus did not live to see himself vindicated, for he died at Meaux in 1334.

In philosophical matters Durandus manifested an independence of spirit more influenced by Augustine and Bonaventure than by Aristotle and Aquinas. He has often been called a precursor of Ockham, but the similarities are only incidental; and it is most unlikely that either philosopher influenced the other. Besides denying the Thomistic distinction between essence and existence in creatures (as did Hervé Nédellec), he rejected the reality of mental species and the distinction between agent and possible intellect. For him, only individuals exist, receiving their individuality not from matter but from their efficient cause. Thus, in the act of knowing, the possible intellect is sufficiently active of itself to grasp individual existents directly and to create universal concepts by eliminating individual differences from consideration. In theology he manifested certain nominalist and Pelagian tendencies typical of the *moderni* of his day, tendencies that were to assume a more radical form in the teaching of Ockham.

In the later Middle Ages the prestige of Durandus was considerable. In the sixteenth century his final *Commentary on the Sentences* enjoyed an extraordinarily high reputation, particularly after its first printing (Paris, 1508). At Salamanca it was one of the alternative texts in the faculty of theology, the others being the *Summa* of Aquinas and the *Sentences* of Peter Lombard, and the chair of Durandus rivaled those of Aquinas and Scotus.

Later writers have sometimes confused this Durandus with William Durand, Durandus Petit, or Durandus Ferrandi.

Works by Durandus

De Jurisdictione Ecclesiastica et de Legibus. Paris, 1506. Published under the name of Peter Bertrandi.

Commentaria in Quatuor Libros Sententiarum. Paris, 1508, 1515, 1533, 1539, 1547, 1550; Lyons, 1533 and 1569; Antwerp, 1567; Venice, 1571 and 1586.

Works on Durandus

Glorieux, P., *Répertoire des maîtres en theologie.* Paris, 1933. Vol. I, No. 70, pp. 214–220. The bibliography is relatively complete up to 1933.

Koch, Joseph, *Durandus de S. Porciano.* Beiträge zur Geschichte der Philosophie des Mittelalters. Münster, 1927.

Quétif, J., and Échard, J., *Scriptores Ordinis Praedicatorum Recensiti.* Paris, 1719. Vol. I, pp. 586–587.

Stella, Prospero T., "Le 'Quaestiones de libero arbitrio' di Durando da S. Porciano." *Salesianum*, Vol. 24 (1962), 450–523. Additions and corrections to Koch's work.

JAMES A. WEISHEIPL, O.P.

DURATION. *See* BERGSON, HENRI; TIME.

DURKHEIM, ÉMILE (1858–1917), French sociologist and philosopher. He was born in Épinal (Vosges). At an early age Durkheim decided not to follow the rabbinical tradition of his family. On leaving the Collège d'Épinal Durkheim went to Paris, first to the Lycée Louis-le-Grand, and then, in 1879, to the École Normale Supérieure. He was dissatisfied with what he saw as a too literary, unscientific style of education, connected with a superficial dilettantism in contemporary philosophy. On graduating in 1882, he decided to devote his career to sociology with the aim of establishing an intellectually respectable, positive science of society to replace, or at least supplement, speculative philosophy and provide an intellectual foundation for the institutions of the Third Republic. At an early stage, then, Durkheim developed a preoccupation which was to dominate his whole intellectual life—to establish a genuine science of social life, which would include a science of ethics and thus provide a reliable guide to social policy.

Influences and intellectual development. From 1882 to 1887 he was professor of philosophy at *lycées* in Sens, Saint-Quentin, and Troyes, during which time various intellectual influences helped him to fill out his conception of a social science. His study of Herbert Spencer instilled in him a predilection for biological models, which was most pronounced in his early work. His reading of Alfred Espinas, and later personal contact with him, led him to his central conception of the "collective consciousness" of a society and the related conviction that the laws of social life are *sui generis* and not reducible, for instance, to laws of individual psychology. In "Individual and Collective Representations" (1898) he argued that we should not attempt to infer social laws from biological laws, but that the findings of biology should be compared subsequently with independently established social laws on the assumption that "all organisms must have certain characteristics in common which are worth while studying." His conception of a positive science of ethics received a powerful new impetus from a visit to Wundt's psychophysical laboratory in Leipzig while on a leave of absence during the school term of 1885/1886. In 1887 he was appointed *chargé de cours* at the University of Bordeaux, becoming the first to teach social science at a French university; he also taught pedagogy and thus began to develop an enduring interest in the relevance of sociology to educational questions.

In 1896 Durkheim was promoted to professor of social science at Bordeaux. In 1898 he founded and became editor of *L'Année sociologique*, a journal designed to unify the social sciences and encourage specific research projects. He moved to the University of Paris as *chargé de cours* in 1902, becoming professor of education in 1906 and professor of education and sociology in 1913. The outbreak of war in 1914 moved Durkheim to write a number of pamphlets with a strongly nationalistic tone, not always easy to reconcile with the views developed in his earlier, more scholarly works.

The collective conscience. Durkheim's determination to establish an autonomous, specialized science of sociology led him to investigate the possibility of viewing human societies as irreducible, *sui generis*, entities. From there he was led to the central conception in his work, that of "collective representations," whose system in a given society constitutes its "collective conscience." Collective representations have both an intellectual and an emotional aspect. As examples Durkheim offered a language, a currency, a set of professional practices, and the "material culture" of a society; but he also included the phenomenon of group emotions, such as may be generated, for example, at a lynching, and which cannot be accounted for as a mere summation of the individual emotions of the several participants. Durkheim said that collective representations are "collective" rather than "universal"; they "exist outside the individual consciousness," on which they operate "coercively." It is possible to determine collective representations directly—not merely via the thoughts and emotions of individuals—by examining their permanent expressions in, for instance, systems of written law, works of art, and literature, and by working with statistical averages. Thus, in *Suicide* Durkheim said that the "social fact" was the statistical suicide rate, not the circumstances attending individual suicides. His treatment of the relations between collective and individual representations, however, was often obscure, and he would pass from statements about the social determinants of the suicide rate to statements like this: "Human deliberations . . . are often only purely formal, with no object but confirmation of a resolve previously formed for reasons unknown to consciousness." His important conception of social forces thus took on a questionable, metaphysical complexion.

Normal and pathological social types. The conception of "social solidarity" went with that of collective representations and provided Durkheim with a means of distinguishing social types. The simplest form of social group is the "horde," which exhibits a "mechanical" solidarity in which individuals are attached directly to the group by adherence to a common set of powerful collective sentiments. The "clan" is the horde considered as an element in a more extensive group, and the most primitive form of durable social group is the segmental society organized in clans. More complex societies exhibit "organic" solidarity with extensive division of labor: the collective conscience is weak and individuals are attached to functional groups, while the society's cohesion is to be seen in the complex interdependence of these groups.

The distinction between social types led to a conception of "normal" and "pathological" forms, which provided a basis for Durkheim's account of the practical, ethical relevance of sociology. The normal is so only relative to a given social type at a particular stage of development. It may thus be difficult to determine, particularly during transitional phases. But once we have determined it in a particular case, the normal will merge with the average, though the sociologist must also attempt to show how the normal condition of a species follows logically from its nature. Durkheim believed that we can thus distinguish between social "health" and "disease" by means of "an objective criterion, inherent in the facts themselves"; for, he argued, on Darwinian lines, the dissemination of a characteristic throughout a species would be inexplicable if we did not suppose it to be on the whole advantageous. The sociologist, like the physician, should try "to maintain the normal state."

Durkheim applied this precept in the practical conclusions he drew from his study of suicide. It is important to maintain collective sentiment against suicide, at least those types of suicide most characteristic of organic solidarity, since the general ideal of humanity is the sole remaining strong collective sentiment, and the practice of suicide offends this sentiment. He advocated making use of the special nature of societies with organic solidarity in order to counteract suicide, by strengthening occupational groups and allowing them to take a firmer grip on the lives of individuals.

Durkheim's most influential discussion of a pathological

social situation concerned "anomie." Anomie is characteristic of advanced organic societies and comes about when diverse social functions are in too tenuous or too intermittent mutual contact. Anomic division of labor exhibits itself in commercial crises, conflicts between capital and labor, and the disintegration of intellectual work through specialization. In relation to individuals the result of anomie is that "society's influence is lacking in the basically individual passions, thus leaving them without a check-rein." Durkheim used this concept to explain such phenomena as the high correlation between suicide and widowhood and between the suicide rate and the divorce rate.

Function and cause. Closely connected with his position on suicide and collective sentiments is Durkheim's concept of "function" as a mode of sociological explanation. He defined "function" as a relation between a system of vital movements and a set of needs. The prime need of any social collectivity is solidarity among its members, and Durkheim's main attempts at functional explanation, as in his treatments of the social division of labor, punishment, and primitive religion, were designed to show how such institutions or practices contribute to the type of solidarity peculiar to the societies in which they occur. The function of a practice is not to be confused with any aims of its practitioners; this would be to confuse sociology with psychology. But neither did Durkheim identify the function of a practice with its cause. The function of a fact does not explain its origin or nature: that would imply an impossible anticipation of consequences. Explanations of origins require the concept of an "efficient cause," though the persistence of a practice may be explained by the fact that its function helps to maintain a pre-existing cause.

The causes of social facts are always to be found in preceding social facts, in the "internal constitution of the social group," or "social milieu." This concept, Durkheim held, is what makes sociology possible, by facilitating the establishment of genuinely social causal relations. Without it there could be only historical explanation, showing how events were possible, but not how they were predetermined. The social milieu was defined in terms of the volume of the group, the degree of communication between its members, and their concentration. Durkheim used this last concept to explain the development of the division of labor. Greater density of population brings with it a sharpened struggle for existence between individuals and this, in turn, makes necessary a greater degree of specialization. The division of labor is thus a "mellowed dénouement" of the struggle for existence.

Durkheim regarded causation as a species of *logical* relation; it was J. S. Mill's failure to recognize this, Durkheim held, that led him to speak erroneously of a possible plurality of causes. The most important method of establishing causal relations in sociology is that of concomitant variations, which can establish a genuine "internal bond" between phenomena as opposed to a merely "external" relation.

Primitive religion and categories of the intellect. In his treatment of primitive religion Durkheim was more immediately interested in functional than in causal questions, though he did not distinguish these as carefully as in *The Division of Labor in Society*, using apparently interchangeable phrases like "respond to the same needs" and "depend on the same causes." He also seems to have confused questions about the function of religions with questions about their meaning and truth. All religions "hold to reality and express it"; all "are true in their own fashion; all answer, though in different ways, to the given conditions of human existence." Durkheim rejected both the animistic account of primitive religions offered by Spencer and E. B. Tylor and the naturistic account originating with Max Müller; both went astray, he felt, in making such religions vast systems of error. Durkheim saw totemism as the most fundamental feature of primitive religions; he tried to show that the totem symbolizes not merely the totemic principle (or "god"), but also the clan itself, and this is possible because "the god and society are only one." Religion is "primarily a system of ideas with which the individuals represent to themselves the society of which they are members, and the obscure but intimate relations which they have with it." He thus regarded the explicit content of religious ideas as relatively unimportant. The reality they express is a sociological one, concealed from the worshipers themselves.

Durkheim regarded religion as the mother of thought. The categories of the intellect, such as "class," "force," "space," and "time," originate with religion. Moreover, since the reality expressed by religion is a social one, these categories themselves originally correspond to forms of social organization and activity. Because totemism involves the idea of forces permeating both the natural and the human realms, it solves the Kantian problem of how men can apply these categories to nature. The a priori necessity of these categories is a reflection of society's coercive insistence on the ritual performances in terms of which such concepts are originally used.

Works by Durkheim

De la Division du travail social. Paris, 1893. Translated by G. Simpson as *The Division of Labor in Society.* Glencoe, Ill., 1952.

Les Règles de la méthode sociologique. Paris, 1895. Translated by S. A. Solovay and J. H. Mueller as *The Rules of Sociological Method.* Glencoe, Ill., 1950.

Le Suicide. Paris, 1897. Translated by J. A. Spaulding and G. Simpson as *Suicide.* Glencoe, Ill., 1951.

Les Formes élémentaires de la vie religieuse. Paris, 1912. Translated by J. W. Swain as *The Elementary Forms of the Religious Life.* London, 1915; Glencoe, Ill., 1954.

Education et sociologie. Paris, 1922. Translated by Sherwood D. Fox as *Education and Sociology.* Glencoe, Ill., 1956.

Sociologie et Philosophie. Paris, 1924. Translated by D. F. Pocock as *Sociology and Philosophy.* London and Glencoe, Ill., 1953. Includes "Individual and Collective Representations."

L'Éducation morale. Paris, 1925. Translated by Herman Schnurer and Everett K. Wilson, ed., as *Moral Education.* Glencoe, Ill., 1961.

Leçons de sociologie: physique de moeurs et du droit. Paris, 1950. Translated by C. Brookfield as *Professional Ethics and Civic Morals.* London, 1957. The last three books, published posthumously, contain the ideas developed in Durkheim's university lectures.

Works on Durkheim

Alpert, Harry, *Émile Durkheim and His Sociology.* New York, 1939.

Parsons, Talcott, *The Structure of Social Action.* New York, 1937; Glencoe, Ill., 1949.

Wolff, Kurt H., ed., *Émile Durkheim, 1858–1917; a Collection of Essays, with Translations and a Bibliography.* Columbus, Ohio, 1962.

PETER WINCH

DUTCH PHILOSOPHY. From its beginning, philosophical thought in the Netherlands has been open to foreign influences; at the same time, it has also shown some signs of a national character of its own. The most striking of these signs is a tendency toward eclecticism, accompanied by a tendency toward skepticism of too positive affirmations, a critical attitude toward official pronouncements, and reservations about system building. On the whole, Dutch philosophy has avoided far-reaching abstractions. Religious tendencies, which have always been prevalent among the Dutch people, have often affected rational reflection in philosophy.

Medieval period. In the Middle Ages, the southern provinces unquestionably led the cultural and scientific life of the Netherlands. Originally, Liége was the main center of philosophy. From the eighth to the eleventh centuries, Dutch philosophy underwent influences from England and Ireland; in the twelfth century these were superseded by French influences, particularly from the School of Chartres, Bernard of Clairvaux, and Hugh and Richard of St. Victor. Dutch philosophy reflected all the struggles of the Scholasticism of the Christian West. Following a period of ultrarealism, defended by Odo of Tournai at the end of the eleventh century, came a period of moderate realism in the spirit of Abelard. Major thinkers of this period were Rupert of Deutz (c. 1070–1135) and William of St. Thierry (c. 1085–1147). Simon of Tournai (c. 1130–1201) is considered a founder of the Scholastic method, and the first traces of Aristotelianism can be seen in his work. Alanus de Insulis (Alain de Lille, c. 1128–1203), *doctor universalis,* combined philosophical speculation with poetry. At the beginning of the thirteenth century, a monistic undercurrent in the spirit of John Scotus Erigena was represented in the materialistic pantheism of David of Dinant and the formal pantheism of Amalric of Bena.

In the Netherlands, as elsewhere, the triumphal progress of Aristotelianism began in the thirteenth century. More than any other formulation, Aristotelianism, which suited the Dutch preference for concreteness and realism, came to dominate Dutch scholastic thought, whereas Augustinianism had little effect during this period.

A great figure of the thirteenth century, and the greatest Dutch thinker of the Middle Ages, is Siger of Brabant (c. 1235–c. 1281). Influenced by the Arabs, especially by Averroës, he developed Aristotelian doctrines in what he maintained was a purely historical interpretation. He was fully aware of the discrepancies between his Aristotelianism and Christian doctrine, but could not reconcile the contradictions and pretended to set aside the conclusions of logical reasoning, represented by Aristotle, in favor of Christian revelation. Thomas Aquinas opposed him, not only on account of Siger's theory of a general cosmic intellect, which the latter defended for a time, but also in behalf of his own conception of an Aristotelianism guaranteed against all suspicion of heterodoxy.

The Netherlands produced two more important thinkers of the thirteenth century, Henry of Ghent (d. 1293) and Godfrey of Fontaines (d. after 1303). They may be considered representative of Dutch thought in this period because of their independent views of both Augustinianism and Aristotelianism, and their critical casts of mind.

In the fourteenth century, nominalism had its effect in the Netherlands, but Dutch nominalists such as Marsilius of Inghen (d. 1396) and Hendrik Totting of Oyta (end of the fourteenth century) never went as far in the rejection of metaphysics as William of Ockham.

The trend among the numerous Dutch scholars at the University of Cologne (founded in 1389) was toward Albertism and also toward the special Neoplatonic theories of Albertus Magnus, which were preferred to the Aristotelianism of Thomas Aquinas. The foremost representative of this point of view was Heymeric van de Velde, or à Campo (d. 1460); against him, Henry of Gorcum (d. 1431) and Gerard ter Steghen (d. 1480) defended Thomism. The mystic Dionysius the Carthusian (1402/3–1471), who lived at Roermond, was also connected with Albertism.

In 1425 a national university for the whole of the Netherlands was established at Louvain, where realism in the Aristotelian spirit was thereafter dominant. At Louvain, too, occurred the first meeting on Dutch ground between Scholasticism and what was called the "Biblical humanism" of Wessel Gansfort (1419–1489), Rodolphus Agricola (1444–1485), and, above all, Erasmus of Rotterdam (1469–1536). From the conjunction of these two modes of thought arose the typically Dutch characteristics of self-control, self-reliance, moderation, and toleration, which for centuries were unmistakable elements in Dutch cultural life. The spiritual legacy of Erasmus, together with Scholasticism, was strong in the northern Netherlands, while the humanist tradition was later strengthened by Dirck V. Coornhert (1522–1590).

Renaissance. The Reformation and the division between the northern and southern provinces made no difference in the form and content of philosophical instruction. At the University of Leiden (founded 1575), and at the northern universities founded later—Franeker (1585), Groningen (1614), Utrecht (1634), and Harderwijk (1648)—philosophy was taught according to the standard medieval schema and the principles of Aristotle. An outstanding figure in Protestant Scholasticism in the Netherlands was Franco Burgersdijck (1590–1635), a professor at Leiden, whose handbooks were used for more than two hundred years. Hugo de Groot, or Grotius (1583–1645), was educated at Leiden in the Aristotelian tradition.

The rise of Cartesianism in the mid-seventeenth century brought new life into Dutch philosophy. Even during his stay in the republic, Descartes acquired some convinced followers but also strenuous opponents. Opposition to Cartesianism was embodied in the work of Gisbert Voetius (1589–1676), professor at Utrecht. Both ecclesiastical and secular powers armed themselves against the new philosophy's pretensions to an independent and original world view. Nevertheless, Cartesianism quickly gained prominence at all the universities; under the influence of the new ideas, Aristotelian Scholasticism gradually became Cartesian Scholasticism. At Leiden this movement was chiefly represented by Andriaan Heereboord (1614–1661), Jan de Raey (1622–1702), and Burchard de Volder (1643–1709). Aristotelianism was maintained in the universities along with this *philosophia novantiqua* until well into the eighteenth century.

The most original thinker in this period was Arnold Geulincx (1624–1669), professor at Louvain and later at Leiden. His occasionalism formed a bridge between Descartes and Spinoza.

The philosophy of Baruch de Spinoza (1632–1677) was influenced by Descartes, Renaissance Platonism, Jewish philosophy, and Scholasticism. Presented in the *Ethics*, it is a closed system of ideas in which the essential unity of God and nature is stressed. According to Spinoza's intention, however, it is an attempt to express in the language of rational ideas what he had himself mystically experienced. However rationalistic its appearance, Spinoza's system finds not only its condition, but also its ultimate end, in an intuitive knowledge of God which leads toward mystical vision.

The vast majority of Spinoza's contemporaries, and almost all philosophical and theological writers of the eighteenth century, saw in him simply an "atheist" who must be fought not only by spiritual but also by temporal weapons, that is, by the full power of church and state. Beneath the surface of philosophical thought, however, Spinoza's theories continued to exercise an influence.

Eighteenth century. Aristotelianism and Cartesianism gradually gave way to the "experimental philosophy" of Isaac Newton, introduced into the Netherlands by William J. 's-Gravesande (1688–1742). In the philosophy of Leibniz, systematized by Christian Wolff, others found a guarantee of a spiritualistic world view which could be reconciled with that of orthodox Christianity. Enlightenment ideas also came into currency from England and France, their way having been prepared by the work of Pierre Bayle (1647–1706), a French refugee living in Rotterdam. Finally, philosophical speculation was chaneled in the stream of common-sense philosophy; this, according to the conviction held by some influential figures of the time, was best suited to the Dutch temperament. François Hemsterhuis (1721–1790), a significant exception to the rationalism of this spiritually impoverished period, combined a revived Platonism with the common-sense philosophy. Philip W. van Heusde (1778–1839), professor at Utrecht, added a new splendor to Hemsterhuis' combination; his ideas were influential chiefly in the field of theology.

Toward the end of the eighteenth century, the Kantian critical method was introduced by Paul van Hemert (1756–1825) and Johannes Kinker (1764–1845); their work, however, met with more opposition than sympathy and had no lasting effect, although the fundamental ideas of Kantianism and of German speculative idealism had further influence within the country.

Nineteenth century. The empiricism of Cornelis W. Opzoomer (1821–1892), professor at Utrecht, left its mark upon mid-nineteenth century Dutch philosophy. Arrayed against empiricism (which had originated particularly in the positivism of John Stuart Mill), and defenders of incipient critical philosophy, were Jan P. N. Land (1834–1897), professor at Leiden, and Bernard H. C. K. van der Wyck (1836–1925), professor at Groningen and later Opzoomer's successor at Utrecht. With Cornelis Bellaar Spruyt (1842–1901), professor at Amsterdam, they paved the way for the revival of Kantianism in the twentieth century.

In the meantime, a Spinoza renaissance was effected through Johannes van Vloten (1818–1883), who interpreted Spinozism in a rationalistic and naturalistic sense and used it as a means to combat every form of religion. In the second phase of this renaissance, which occurred about the turn of the century, Spinoza was offered as the representative of a new world view for modern man.

In the nineteenth century, Dutch Catholicism in general embraced a spiritualistic philosophy, deriving from Cartesianism and connected, through Malebranche, with Augustinian ideas. The encyclical of Pope Leo XIII, *Aeterni Patris* (1879), again drew attention to the principles of Scholastic philosophy, particularly those of Thomas Aquinas.

Toward the end of the nineteenth century, philosophical interest was awakened once more through the work of Spruyt, Heymans and Bolland. Cornelis Belaar Spruyt, like Kant, chose the critical method, but turned away from the Kantian approach to favor the realistic aspect of the critical philosophy, represented by J. F. Fries. Gerard Heymans (1857–1930), professor at Groningen, was responsible for the construction of a complete system of inductive metaphysics (related to that of Gustav Fechner) which he announced as the hypothesis of psychic monism from a critical point of view. Gerard J. P. J. Bolland (1854–1922), professor at Leiden, gave a strong impetus to the revival of Hegelianism.

Twentieth century. In the first decades of the twentieth century, Dutch philosophy took several new directions. Marburgian Neo-Kantianism found disciples in Bernard J. H. Ovink (1862–1944), professor at Utrecht, and his numerous students. Arthur J. de Sopper (1875–1960), Bolland's successor at Leiden, and Hendrik J. Pos (1898–1955), professor at Amsterdam, were originally influenced by the Baden school of Neo-Kantianism, but later both were emancipated from it. De Sopper came to a theonomous realism, while Pos arrived at a Marxist realism via absolute idealism. Spinozism moved in two directions, one rationalistic and the other religious and mystical, with Willem G. van der Tak (1885–1958) and Johan H. Carp (b. 1893) as the representatives and leaders of the "Rijnsburg" and the "The Hague" schools respectively. Related to Spinozism, but independent of any particular school, was the work of Johannes D. Bierens de Haan (1866–1943; not to be confused with the psychologist), who offered an idealistic monism which, unlike all others, culminates in the intellectual contemplation of the ultimate ground of reality, unreachable by rational thought. Philip Kohnstamm (1875–1951), professor at Amsterdam and Utrecht, presented a personalistic philosophy based upon the Bible. Among Dutch Catholics, Johannes V. de Groot (1848–1922), professor at Amsterdam, and Josephus Th. Beysens (1864–1945), professor at Utrecht, developed a critical realism in accord with the principles of Thomas Aquinas and directed toward the solution of modern problems. In Calvinist circles, under the leadership of Hendrik

Dooyeweerd and Dirk H. Vollenhoven, both professors in the Free University at Amsterdam, a "philosophy of the idea of law" was developed, which denied autonomy to philosophical thinking and sought for the origins of philosophy in the special revelation of God.

After World War II, this picture of philosophical thought in the Netherlands was radically altered. Neo-Kantianism was no longer heard of; Hegelianism practically died out with Bolland's students; Neo-Thomism in large part lost its attraction for younger Catholics; Heymans' students moved away from him in several directions; and Spinozism vanished from the philosophical scene.

The phenomenological method and existential way of thinking took over in all philosophical circles; only the Calvinist "philosophy of the idea of law" seemed immune to these new influences. Reinier F. Beerling had introduced German existentialism before World War II, but later abandoned it and turned toward Hegel. Christian existentialism was embraced, among Catholics, by Remigius C. Kwant, professor at Utrecht; Bernard Delfgaauw, professor at Groningen; and Willem Luypen; and among Protestants, by Arnold E. Loen, professor at Utrecht, and Cornelis A. van Peursen, professor at Leiden and at the Free University at Amsterdam. Neopositivism and analytic philosophy, particularly under American and British influence, also attracted followers. The names of Luitzen E. J. Brouwer and Arend Heyting, both professors at Amsterdam, are significant in regard to research into the bases of mathematics. The work of Evert W. Beth (1908–1964), professor at Amsterdam, extends also to philosophy of science and logic; that of Andrew G. M. van Melsen, professor at Nijmegen and at Groningen, and that of Henry P. van Laer, professor at Leiden, cover the same field and are inspired by Neo-Thomist principles. Of Dutch Catholics, C. Schoonbrood is the nearest to English and American analytic philosophy, without accepting the metaphysical implications of logical atomism and logical positivism. In the 1950s and 1960s, the weight of Dutch philosophy seems to have shifted toward positivism.

(See Dutch Philosophy entry in Index for articles on Dutch philosophers.)

Bibliography

Antal, G. v., *Die holländische Philosophie im neunzehnten Jahrhundert.* Utrecht, 1888.

Faber, W., *Wijsgeren in Nederland.* Nijkerk, 1954.

Land, J. P. N., *De wijsbegeerte in de Nederlanden.* 's-Gravenhage, 1899.

Land, J. P. N., *Philosophy in the Dutch Universities.* Leiden, 1877.

Poortman, J. J., *Repertorium der Nederlandse wijsbegeerte,* 2 vols. Amsterdam, 1948–1958.

Sassen, F., *Geschiedenis van de wijsbegeerte in Nederland tot het einde der negentiende eeuw.* Amsterdam and Brussels, 1959.

Sassen, F., *Philosophical Life in the Netherlands,* Library of the Xth International Congress of Philosophy. Amsterdam, 1948. Vol. II, pp. 9–20.

Sassen, F., *Wijsgerig leven in Nederland in de twintigste eeuw,* 3d ed. Amsterdam, 1960.

F. L. R. SASSEN
Translated by *R. L. Colie*

DUTY. In practical reasoning of an informal sort, the concept of duty plays a limited, relatively unproblematic role. In thinking about what to do, a reasonable man tries to see his wants in relation to his interests and to the interests of others; he evaluates alternatives in the light of his previous commitments and bears in mind his obligations and responsibilities. Duty is one among other factors to be taken into account. The reason is obvious: a man's duties are the things he is expected to do by virtue of having taken on a job or assumed some definite office. One could say (although it sounds somewhat redundant) that believing that one's duties entail doing something or other is a reason, though not a conclusive one, for doing that thing, and believing that a possible line of action would count as a neglect of duty is a reason against adopting that line of action. How much weight such considerations have depends on what duties are in question and on the agent's obligations as they affect the particular situation. Duties, then, are counted as one of the considerations which guide and constrain rational choice.

The concept of duty in theoretical ethics is quite a different matter. Some moral philosophers (F. H. Bradley would be one example, Cicero another) have concerned themselves with duties of the everyday sort, those that go with being a parent, voter, teacher, or whatever. But many philosophers use "duty" quite indiscriminately to refer to particular obligations, moral principles, or indeed to anything which is held to be a requirement of conscience. "Duty" is a technical term in ethics and the rules for its use vary from one writer to another. For the most part, these differences are of no theoretical interest, but there is one important exception, the doctrine of Kant. His views, set forth in the *Critique of Practical Reason* and in the *Foundations of the Metaphysics of Morals,* mark a radical break with traditional ethics, and since what he takes to be the central concept of morals he calls "duty," it is worthwhile finding out what he means by it.

Ordinary duties. As noted above, ordinary duties are tasks or assignments for which a man becomes responsible as a result of holding a particular job or office. When the tasks are intricate and have to be done just right, for example, the duties of an airplane pilot, then they are spelled out in detail; thus also for tasks that are relatively simple but for which applicants are unlikely to be highly motivated or imaginative, for example, the duties of a night watchman. In contrast, the duties that go with being a parent or with the practice of a profession are not codified, and responsibility for deciding what should be done is assigned to the individual.

Someone who neglects his duties deserves blame. Censure, if reasonable, is graduated to accord with the degree of neglect and with the importance of the task. A host who fails in his duties to his guests is inconsiderate but does not deserve to be pilloried. Negligence on the part of a pharmacist or a bus driver is a more serious matter. A characteristic of duties, as distinct from other constraints on conduct, is that a man who is delinquent loses, at some point, his title to the office which his duties define. He is court-martialed, unfrocked, disbarred, or fired (compare the euphemism "relieved of his duties"). Ceremonial dismissals are appropriate, of course, only when the duties in question are, in a broad sense, institutional and have been formulated explicitly. Not all duties fit this pattern; a man may become unfit for an office without being declared to be so, without his dereliction being so much as noticed by anyone, including himself. Someone who fails in the duties of friendship is simply no longer a friend, no matter what he or anyone else may think.

Legal penalties attach to neglect of duties where such neglect is held to be seriously detrimental to human welfare. Where a verdict has to be reached, an offense must be clearly defined. Parents, physicians, and legislators are among those to whom the greatest measure of discretion is granted in discharging their duties. It is an odd consequence that in matters of the greatest human importance only gross and flagrant derelictions of duty are punishable by law. Of course there are extralegal sanctions, and the threat of contempt and blame, of ostracism from one's group, may be a strong incentive to duty. The penalties of social disapproval, however, are distributed in a capricious and often unreasonable way, and a man may neglect all sorts of duties and yet, given discretion and a certain amount of luck, escape criticism altogether. Appreciation of this fact is what leads those concerned with moral education to try to instill in their charges a sense of duty. The attempt succeeds to the extent that the subject becomes habitually conscientious and carries out his duties without thinking about whether he might neglect them with impunity. A more primitive strategem is to introduce the fiction of an all-seeing Providence in the hope of making the subject believe that no lapses go unnoticed and that all who neglect their duties will, on some unspecified future date, be punished.

Since duties are required minimal performances, no special merit accrues to someone who does his duty. A hero, one who does something that is both worthwhile and hazardous, acts "beyond the call of duty." A modest hero disclaims credit by saying that he did no more than his duty required. A man may be praised for carrying out some particular duty under difficult conditions. Such praise is sometimes justified and sometimes not; the claims of any duty may on occasion be outweighed by the claims of obligation or moral principle.

Although being conscientious is a virtue, it is not the only one, and unless it is mediated by intelligence and moral sensitivity, it may do more harm than good. A man must learn, for example, how to deal with conflicting duties. If he is a jobholder, a parent, and a citizen, then he holds three offices concurrently. Even if his life is well organized, situations are likely to arise in which he has to determine which of two duties takes precedence. Such questions have to be worked out in particular cases; there is no formula or principle of ranking that can be applied. Moreover, as noted earlier, questions about duties are not independent of broad moral issues: if, as seems likely, there are offices which one ought not, as a matter of moral principle, to hold, then there are duties which no one ought to perform, even when called upon to do so.

Kant's doctrine. The idea of taking duty (*die Pflicht*) as the central moral concept originates with Kant. There are earlier doctrines which appear, especially when paraphrased, to be analogous, but the similarities are inconsequential in contrast with the differences. Kant himself maintained that his basic thesis is neither original nor esoteric and that, on the contrary, it is self-evident to the plain man. Everyone, he held, recognizes the difference between doing something because one wants to do it and doing something because one feels that one is morally obligated to do it. Moreover, it is universally acknowledged that only what is done from a sense of moral obligation is meritorious. Kant's theory is an exposition of what he took to be the consequences of these premises. He did not claim that the *theory* is easy and familiar. (In fact, he is often obscure and difficult to follow.) He did claim that his theory is the one which philosophers must eventually accept if they are consistent and if they take seriously the intimations of the plain man.

The views which Kant ascribed to common sense appear to be correct: people do not deserve credit unless they act from reasons of conscience, and we do believe that such reasons are, somehow or other, distinctive. Kant used the word "duty" (and here he diverged, at least from ordinary English usage) to refer very generally to features he took to be distinctive of conscientious conduct. At times this practice leads to rhetorical vagueness, and "duty" becomes synonymous with "whatever ought to be done." However, he also gave it a more precise sense, one which appears in the set of interdependent definitions which, taken together, provide the framework of his theory. In brief, he held that the only unqualified good is the "good will" and that to have a good will is always to act from a sense of duty.

Duty involves recognition of and submission to the "moral law" which is the "supreme principle" of morality. Since what the moral law prescribes goes (more or less) against the grain, that is, runs counter to inclinations, the law is expressed as an imperative. The imperative is described as being "categorical" and "unconditioned," and Kant meant these modifiers to reinforce the distinction mentioned earlier: objects of desire are variable and evanescent, and thus strategies for achieving such objects are applicable under some conditions and not under others. The moral law, however, applies to everyone and is unrestricted with respect to times, places, and particular situations.

The "categorical imperative" is formulated in three ways that Kant seems to have regarded as equivalent. They are as follows: "So act that the maxim of your will could always hold at the same time as a principle establishing universal law"; "Act so as to treat humanity, whether in your own person or in that of another, always as an end and never as a means only"; "Act according to the maxims of a universally legislative member of a merely potential kingdom of ends." Apart from the question of how to collate these formulas, difficult problems of interpretation arise for each of them taken separately. Nonetheless, one can see in a general way what Kant had in mind: a man is dutiful to the extent that he is seriously concerned with being equitable and fair, with treating other people like human beings and not like machines, and with trying to govern his own behavior by standards that could be adopted by everyone.

Kant believed that the concepts of duty, the good will, and the moral law are all such as can be apprehended a priori. Part of what he meant (and what is certainly true) is that no conclusions about what ought to be done can be derived directly from compilations of facts about what people do or have done. Although Kant was much concerned with distinguishing actual laws which depend on external sanctions from the moral law which the individual imposes on himself, he characterized the moral life by means of a set of juristic metaphors. The righteous man, for example, is said to "accuse himself before the bar of his conscience." This device suggests that Kant believed the "kingdom of ends" invoked in the third version of the categorical imperative to be an ideal beyond the hope of achievement. Human inclinations are apt to be anarchic, and as duty is a kind of inner law, so conscience is prefigured as a stern magistrate.

Pre-Kantian doctrines. It is customary to cite the Stoics as the earliest philosophers to elevate duty to the status of a first principle. However, as far as one can tell from their writings, which tend to vagueness, and from sketchy accounts of what they were reputed to believe, their views were quite different from Kant's. In fact, their word *kathēkon,* usually translated as "duty," appears to mean "what it would be suitable or fitting to do." At any rate, the supreme duty is to live "in accord with nature," but it is not clear what that entails or how, if at all, one could avoid living in accord with nature. Particular maxims have to do with ways of avoiding anxiety and frustration, a goal which Kant would have regarded as morally unworthy. The one genuine point of contact, and also the most interesting contribution of Stoic thought, is the idea that morality transcends national boundaries and class distinctions. The cosmopolitanism of the Stoics marks an advance over the views of Plato and Aristotle, both of whom thought that the demands of morality can be satisfied without taking any account of the claims of barbarians, slaves, or foreigners. On the other hand, the Stoic one-world concept ought, perhaps, to be seen not so much as a moral ideal but rather as an implicit recognition of the changes brought about by the conquests of Alexander and, in later writings, as an aspect of the ideology of Roman imperialism.

Theological ethics attaches importance to the concept of duty, and, in this context, what is meant is, unlike Kantian or Stoic duty, something parallel to the ordinary notion. To be a believer or a member of a congregation is to hold a particular office, often one that is defined by clearly formulated rules of conduct and ritual observance. In some religions the faithful are told that they are in some sense children of God, and to the extent that this belief is taken seriously, a set of quasi-filial duties with respect to the deity will come to seem important. Kant, despite his Pietistic background, was clearly opposed to such a view. It is crucial to his doctrine that men should regard themselves and others as adults rather than as hapless children.

Anticipations of particular Kantian theses can be made out in a number of earlier writers: Richard Cumberland, Ralph Cudworth, Samuel Clarke, and Richard Price maintained (in opposition to Hobbes) that moral duty is based on self-evident axioms and that the requirements of duty are universally binding. Rousseau had much to say about conscience, which he regarded as a sort of inner voice—one which speaks with unique authority on questions of duty. Hume explicitly remarked on the logical gap between the concept of what is done and the concept of what ought to be done. Nonetheless, it is not clear that anyone before Kant succeeded in holding in focus the idea of a morality which is not, in some indirect way, dependent on considerations of prudence.

In his paper "Does Moral Philosophy Rest on a Mistake?" (1912), H. A. Prichard argued that traditional ethics (for example, the doctrines of Plato, Aristotle, Hume, Bentham, and Mill) goes astray in trying to work out some general answer to the question of why it is reasonable or worthwhile to do one's duty. Prichard's point is that the question itself is the result of a confusion. That something is a duty is (or may be) a sufficient reason for doing that thing, and *if* it is, then no further reason is called for. If Prichard's historical thesis is right, and it seems quite plausible, then there is a sense in which Kantian doctrine and common sense agree and are jointly opposed to traditional ethics. Ordinary duties are not hierarchically ordered under a supreme moral principle; nor do the claims of duty (individually or collectively) provide a unique determination of morally right action. Nonetheless, and despite their untidy array, ordinary duties are "unconditioned" in that they provide us with reasons for acting such that if the reasons are accepted, there is no need for, indeed no room for, further justification.

Bibliography

For a discussion of prima facie duties, see ROSS, W. D.

For the Stoic conception of duty, see Cicero's *De Oficiis,* which has been translated by H. M. Poteat as *On Duties* (Chicago, 1950), and W. J. Oates, ed., *The Stoic and Epicurean Philosophers* (New York, 1940).

See also Immanuel Kant, *Critique of Practical Reason and Other Writings in Moral Philosophy,* translated by L. W. Beck (Chicago, 1949), which contains *Foundations of the Metaphysics of Morals;* H. A. Prichard, "Does Moral Philosophy Rest on a Mistake?" in *Mind,* Vol. 21 (1912), 121–152, also included in his *Moral Obligations* (Oxford, 1949), pp. 1–17; G. E. Moore, *Ethics* (London, 1912), Ch. IV; G. E. Hughes, "Motive and Duty," in *Mind,* Vol. 53 (1944), 314–331; W. D. Ross, *Foundations of Ethics* (Oxford, 1947), pp. 14–27; and W. K. Frankena, "Obligation and Ability," in Max Black, ed., *Philosophical Analysis* (Ithaca, N.Y., 1950).

MARY MOTHERSILL

DYNAMISM designates the view that all phenomena of nature, including matter, are manifestations of force. Although it is generally recognized that dynamism was first formulated by Rudjer Boscovich (1711–1787), his thought would have been impossible without the previous scientific and philosophical work of Newton and Leibniz. Newton gave the first accurate definition of force as the product of mass and acceleration and established the all-important role that the force of gravity plays in the overall fabric of the universe. His definition of inertia, the most fundamental property of matter, as *vis insita* ("residing force") prepared the way for Boscovich's view that even the very core of matter should be interpreted dynamically. On the other hand, Newton still showed definite mechanistic leanings; like Gassendi and other atomists he accepted the existence of absolutely hard and indivisible particles that, although very small, still possessed volume. He also did not exclude the possibility that gravitation could be mechanically explained by the pressure of ether.

Leibniz, by pointing out the difficulties inherent in the concept of extended atoms and by stressing the impossibility of reducing matter to mere extension, also anticipated Boscovich. In a sense, Leibniz' monad was an ancestor of Boscovich's atom. On the other hand, in all concrete physical explanations Leibniz favored Cartesian mechanistic models. He opposed the Newtonian concept of attractive force acting at a distance as a thinly disguised return to the occult qualities of the Scholastics. The monad was for him a metaphysical, not a physical, entity. The substance of matter should be conceived by analogy with the activity of man's mind—or in Leibniz' terminology, with the activity (*appétition*) of man's own monad. The monads were units of psychic or quasi-psychic activity that constituted both other minds and matter. Nevertheless, matter as a phenomenon should be interpreted in a strictly mechanistic way. Briefly, although Leibniz was a metaphysical dynamist, as a physicist he was a Cartesian mechanist.

Boscovich. Boscovich was essentially correct when he insisted that the similarity of his ideas to those of Newton and Leibniz was incidental rather than essential. His atoms were unextended and without volume, being nothing but pointlike centers of forces. His rejection of atomic volumes was based on the law of continuity; if an atom were extended, then its surface would represent a discontinuous transition from zero density of the surrounding vacuum to infinite density ("complete fullness") of the atomic volume. Second, the velocities of the atoms bouncing off one another would also have to change abruptly. According to Boscovich, the only way to preserve the existence of atoms and to respect the law of continuity was to assume that when atoms collide, their velocities are gradually reduced before they change direction; and this is possible only if we abandon the idea of a rigid atomic surface and, by implication, the classical idea of impenetrable atomic volume. Impenetrability was to be superseded by repulsive force, which increases asymptotically toward infinity in inverse ratio to the distance from the center of the atom. Thus, in Boscovich's view, the centers of atoms are those points in the dynamic field at which repulsive force is infinitely large; impenetrability is replaced by the field of repulsive force; and the boundary of this field supersedes the rigid surface of the classical Democritean atom. Beyond this boundary, force becomes attractive; in this way the phenomena of cohesion are accounted for. Force becomes alternately attractive and repulsive at various distances from the center, finally becoming the attractive force of gravity, which decreases with distance according to Newton's law.

Dynamism in Germany. The influence of both Leibniz and Boscovich on the subsequent development of dynamism was profound and lasting. In general, Boscovich's influence was greater in France and England; Leibniz', in Germany. Sometimes the influence of both thinkers was felt, as probably was the case with Christian Wolff and Immanuel Kant. Leibniz' influence on Wolff is well known, but Wolff's claim that the unextended units of nature were devoid of perception (*Cosmologia Generalis*, Sec. 223; *Psychologia Rationalis*, Sec. 644) and that they were finite in number was akin to Boscovich's similar views.

Kant's *Monadologia Physica* (1756) reflected Leibniz' influence in its title. However, it appeared after Boscovich's early exhibition of dynamism in *De Viribus Vivis* (1745), and thus the possibility of Boscovich's influence on Kant, either directly, or indirectly through Wolff or Moses Mendelssohn, is not excluded. Indeed, similarities are striking. Like Boscovich, Kant accepted pointlike atoms endowed with two kinds of forces—repulsion, decreasing with the cube of the distance, and attraction, decreasing with the square of the distance. Repulsive force produces apparent impenetrability; points at which repulsion and attraction are in equilibrium constitute the apparent "surface" of an atom; the space outside this surface is filled by the gravitational field where attraction prevails. Kant's scheme lacks Boscovich's alternating zones of attraction and repulsion. However, there are more important differences. While Boscovich, in the best atomistic tradition, insisted on the homogeneity of his dynamic atoms and rejected Leibniz' principle of identity of indiscernibles, Kant's monads were heterogeneous, "intensively diverse," like the monads of Leibniz and Wolff (*Monadologia Physica*, Prop. XII).

Kant's view of matter in his later thought became more complex and more ambiguous. In the *Critique of Pure Reason* he regarded space as a necessary condition of every sensory experience. Therefore, if space was infinitely divisible, matter was infinitely divisible (mathematically continuous). Thus, the monadology of his early period seemingly was definitely abandoned. But in the second antinomy Kant tried to show that the discrete monadic character of matter (thesis) and its infinite divisibility (antithesis) could both be demonstrated. Kant apparently did not realize that the concept of extensionless monad was entirely compatible with the infinite divisibility of extended matter. This explains why his *Metaphysical First Principles of Natural Sciences* (1786) retained elements of his early monadological view despite its repeated emphasis on the continuity of matter. Matter was again constructed from repulsion and attraction; but since these forces were central, the concept of a pointlike center from which the continuous dynamical field emanates was implicitly present.

Kant's influence on German philosophy of nature continued throughout the nineteenth century. Johannes Friedrich Herbart, whose pluralism of simple unextended units showed a certain affinity with that of Leibniz, constructed matter, as Kant did, from the equilibrium of attractive and repulsive forces. The dynamic atomism of Gustav Theodor Fechner, upholding the existence of pointlike centers of force, was more empirical. In the second edition of his *Physikalische und philosophische Ato-*

menlehre (Leipzig, 1864), Fechner acknowledged the influence of Boscovich. He was also aware that Justus von Leibig in his *Chemische Briefe* (4th ed., Leipzig, 1859) had defended the concept of a dynamic pointlike atom. Similar views were held by Wilhelm Eduard Weber and by Hermann Lotze, who defined atoms as "immaterial existences that from a fixed point in space control by their forces a definite extent without in the strict sense occupying it" (*Microcosmus*, 1885; translated by E. Hamilton and E. E. C. Jones, New York, 1886, Vol. I, p. 35).

The influence of Schopenhauer strengthened the dynamic view of reality, but it favored a dynamic atomism only after his intellectual descendants (Julius Bahnsen, Eduard von Hartmann, and Friedrich Nietzsche) departed from his extreme monism by substituting individual centers of will (Nietzsche's *Machtquanten*) for the undifferentiated unity of his cosmic Will. Nietzsche made the plurality of the dynamic centers from which expansive forces radiate and mutally clash in never-ending antagonism the basis of his metaphysics of "Will to Power." Robert Hamerling, another philosopher influenced by Schopenhauer, in his *Atomistik der Wille* (Hamburg, 1891) insisted, like Boscovich, that "not the atom itself, but merely its sphere of action is extended" (p. 169).

France and England. The influence of Boscovich in France and England was more direct than in Germany, and the resulting dynamism was much less metaphysical and more scientific.

In France such physicists as André Ampère, Augustin Cauchy, Siméon Poisson, A. Barré de St. Venant, and the Abbé Moigno upheld the reality of rigorously pointlike dynamic atoms. Only in the second half of the nineteenth century did this view gain ground among some philosophers, notably in the neocritical school headed by Charles Renouvier. Renouvier effected a transformation of the extensionless atom of dynamism similar to that done by the pluralistic disciples of Schopenhauer: it became a monad, a unit of perception and will.

In England interest in dynamism was confined mostly to physicists and philosophers of science. One exception was Dugald Stewart (*Works*, Edinburgh, 1854, Vol. I, p. 423 f.), who admired Boscovich's philosophy as much as did the philosopher–chemist Joseph Priestley. But most significant was the attitude of Michael Faraday. In his frequently quoted article "A Speculation concerning Electric Conduction and the Nature of Matter" he accepted Boscovich's rejection of any distinction between the material nucleus and the surrounding dynamic field. The atom thus became a simple mathematical center of the dynamic field; and since it could not be separated from this field, which pervaded the fields of other atoms, each atom pervaded the whole universe. This idea exerted a great influence on both Bergson's and Whitehead's views of matter. According to Bergson, the difference between a "thing" and its "effects"—more specifically, between the material nucleus and its surrounding field—was of a merely practical origin without ontological significance. Bergson quoted the same passage from Faraday that inspired Whitehead to his famous criticism of "the fallacy of simple location." The attitude of James Clerk Maxwell toward Boscovich's views was more critical than that of Faraday, as was that of William Thomson, who nevertheless at the end of his life characterized his view as "Boscovichianism pure and simple." A sympathetic reference to Boscovich's view of matter can also be found in J. J. Thomson's *Corpuscular Theory of Matter* (1907). Although Herbert Spencer referred to Boscovich's dynamism in *First Principles* (4th ed., New York, 1896, pp. 54–57, 61), dynamism was a monism of energy because the term "force" meant for him, as for many other nineteenth-century thinkers, "energy." Spencer thus was a link between classical dynamism and the energetism propounded by Wilhelm Ostwald.

In the era of classical physics, dynamism was the only philosophy of nature that could seriously compete with mechanism. By its criticism of mechanism it helped to free scientific imagination from domination by naive and crudely sensory models of matter, and thus indirectly prepared the way for the abstract and nonintuitive models of contemporary physics. But dynamism was too deeply steeped in classical thought to be entirely consistent or to avoid the very assumptions for which it criticized mechanism. The pointlike atoms of dynamism were still endowed with an inertial mass that persisted through time; as Maxwell observed, Boscovich's atoms possessed continuity of existence through space and time like the atoms of Democritus, Gassendi, and Newton. Dynamism assumed direct instantaneous action at a distance, contrary to the growing evidence that all physical interactions are time-consuming. The assumption of the zero radius of atoms implied the difficult notion of an infinitely large repulsive force at the very center of a force field. The discovery of the finite, though very small, radius of the electron and other microphysical "particles" was in direct opposition to the basic postulate of pointlike atoms. Thus dynamism, in its classical form at least, was as clearly outdated as mechanism.

Bibliography

Adickes, Erich, *Kant als Naturforscher*, 2 vols. Berlin, 1924–1925. Vol. I.

Andler, Charles, *La Maturité de Nietzsche jusqu'à sa mort*. Paris, 1928. Pp. 403–411.

Boscovich, R. J., *Theoria Philosophiae Naturalis*. Venice, 1763. Translated by J. M. Child in a Latin–English edition. Chicago, 1922.

Buek, Otto, "Die Atomistik und die Faradaysche Begriff der Materie." *Archiv für die Geschichte der Philosophie*, Vol. 18 (1905).

Čapek, Milič, *The Philosophical Impact of Contemporary Physics*. Princeton, 1961. Ch.7.

Faraday, Michael, "A Speculation concerning Electric Conduction and the Nature of Matter." *Philosophical Magazine*, Vol. 24 (1844), 136.

Hesse, Mary B., *Forces and Fields*. London, 1961.

Jammer, Max, *Concepts of Force*. Cambridge, Mass., 1957. Ch. 9.

Kant, Immanuel, *Metaphysische Anfangsgründe der Naturwissenschaft*, in Arthur Buchenau, ed., *Werke*. Berlin, 1912. Vol. III, pp. 367–478.

Kant, Immanuel, *Monadologia Physica*, in Arthur Buchenau, ed., *Werke*. Berlin, 1912. Vol. I, pp. 485–500.

Mittasch, Alwin, *Nietzsche als Naturphilosoph.* Stuttgart, 1952. Ch. 11.

Oster, Melchior, *Roger Joseph Boscovich als Naturphilosopher.* Cologne, 1909. Especially pp. 72–77.

Renouvier, Charles, *Essais de critique générale. Troisième essai, Les Principes de la nature.* Paris, 1864. Pp. 20–31. Bibliography of Cauchy, Ampère, Poisson, and Moigno.

Simmel, Georg, *Das Wesen der Materie nach Kants physischer Monadologie.* Berlin, 1881.

Whyte, Lancelot Law, ed., *Roger Joseph Boscovich, S. J., F.R.S., 1711–1787.* London, 1961. Contains complete bibliography of works by and on Boscovich.

MILIČ ČAPEK

E

EBERHARD, JOHANN AUGUST (1739–1809), German theologian and "popular philosopher," was born in Halberstadt. He studied theology at Halle, and became a preacher at Halberstadt in 1763 and at Charlottenburg in 1774. In 1778 Frederick II of Prussia appointed him professor of theology at Halle. Eberhard became a member of the Berlin Academy in 1786 and a privy councilor in 1805. He wrote on theology, epistemology, ethics, aesthetics, philology, and the history of philosophy.

Eberhard received a Wolffian education, but, under the influence of Moses Mendelssohn and C. F. Nicolai, he soon developed a personal point of view. As a popular philosopher, Eberhard was averse to abstract speculation and interested in natural theology, psychology, ethics, and aesthetics. He opposed enthusiasm, sentimentalism, and occultism, and favored the empirical approach.

In his *Neue Apologie des Socrates* ("New Apology of Socrates," 2 vols., Berlin, 1772–1778) Eberhard denied that salvation depended on revelation, and asserted that there is no original sin and that a heathen could go to heaven. He rejected eternal punishment as a contradiction of its aim—the moral improvement of the sinner.

Eberhard's *Allgemeine Theorie des Denkens und Empfindens* ("General Theory of Thinking and Feeling," Berlin, 1776) was dominated by the thought of Locke, and by Leibniz' *Nouveaux Essais*. Like Kant and J. N. Tetens, Eberhard vindicated sensation against the earlier tendency to stress reason; and like Kant, Tetens, and J. H. Lambert, he developed a thoroughgoing phenomenalism. He held that sensation is passive and supported Locke's view that all ideas derive from sensation. He claimed that sensing is a transition from thinking to acting.

Eberhard held that beauty is not an objective characteristic of things, but an adequacy of the object to the representative power of the subject (a view he called—as Kant did later—"subjective finalism"). Beauty excites this activity, and the aim of art is therefore the awakening of pleasurable passions (a doctrine rejected by Kant and later German aestheticians). The first appearance of aesthetic activity in man is represented, according to Eberhard, in children's play (a foreshadowing of Schiller's aesthetics of play).

Eberhard, as editor of the *Philosophisches Magazin* from 1788 to 1791 and of the *Philosophische Archiv* from 1792 to 1795, published a large number of articles critical of Kant's *Kritik der reinen Vernunft*, most of them written by himself. He claimed that Kant's views were entirely derived from Leibniz, and that they were only a special kind of dogmatism. Kant answered Eberhard in his *Ueber eine Entdeckung, nach der alle neue Kritik der reinen Vernunft durch eine ältere entbehrlich gemacht werden soll* (Königsberg, 1790). It was one of the few times Kant deigned to answer unjustifiable criticism.

Additional Works by Eberhard

Sittenlehre der Vernunft. Berlin, 1781.
Theorie der schonen Künste und Wissenschaften. Berlin, 1783.
Vermischte Schriften, 2 vols. Halle, 1784–1788.
Allgemeine Geschichte der Philosophie. Berlin, 1788.
Handbuch der Aesthetik, 4 vols. Halle, 1803–1805.

Works on Eberhard

Draeger, G., *J. A. Eberhards Psychologie und Aesthetik*. Halle, 1915.
Ferber, E. O., *Der philosophische Streit zwischen I. Kant und J. A. Eberhard*. Giessen, 1884.
Lungwitz, K., *Die Religionsphilosophie Eberhards*. Erlangen, 1911.
Nicolai, C. F., *Gedächtnisschrift auf J. A. Eberhard*. Berlin, 1810.

Giorgio Tonelli

ECKHART, MEISTER (c. 1260–1327/1328), German mystic, was born Johannes Eckhart at Hochheim in Thuringia. After entering the Dominican order at an early age, he pursued higher studies at Cologne and Paris. He became successively provincial prior of the Dominican order of Saxony, vicar-general of Bohemia, and superior-general for the whole of Germany (in 1312). During the last part of his life Eckhart became involved in charges of heresy. In 1329, 28 of his propositions were condemned by Pope John XXII, 11 as rash and the remainder as heretical. Nevertheless, Eckhart was to have a lasting influence upon medieval mysticism.

Eckhart's account of God and the universe depended not only on theology and metaphysical speculation but also on his interpretation of mystical experience. Thus, he distinguished between *Deus* or God, as found in the three Persons of the Trinity, and *Deitas* or the Godhead, which is the Ground of God but is indescribable. The Godhead, through an eternal process, manifests itself as the Persons. In the same way, Eckhart distinguished between faculties of the soul, such as memory, and the *Grund* or "ground" of the soul (also called the *Fünklein, scintilla* or "spark"). By contemplation it is possible to attain to this *Grund*, leaving aside the discursive and imaginative activities which normally characterize conscious life. In doing this, one gains unity with the Godhead. Although Eckhart gave some sort of explanation for the ineffability of the Godhead (namely, that it is a pure unity and thus not describable), the main motive for his doctrine lay in a feature of mystical experience—that it involves a mental state not describable in terms of thoughts or images.

The need to give an account of contemplative knowledge led Eckhart to evolve a complex psychology. The soul operates at the lowest level, through the body; thus it has powers of digestion, assimilation, and sensation. At a higher level the soul functions through the powers of anger, desire, and the lower intellect (the *sensus communis* or "common sense," which combines what is given through the various senses in perception). At a third level the soul works through memory, will, and the higher intellect. At the fourth level it is possible in principle to know things in total abstraction, that is, as pure forms, which is therefore to know them as they pre-exist in God's intellect. Finally, the spark of the soul can possess a kind of knowledge in which God is known as he is.

In the development of these ideas, Eckhart certainly spoke in ways which might have offended his more orthodox contemporaries. The notion of the spark within the soul seemed to imply that the soul is uncreated. The notion of God's birth within the soul, through mystical experience, seemed to present the sacraments of the church as mere means of preparing for such experience, rather than as efficacious in themselves. Likewise, Eckhart's language of deification could easily have been construed to mean that the historical Christ has only an exemplary and symbolic value. Eckhart's teaching that God creates the world in the same "eternal now" in which the emanation of the divine Persons from the Godhead takes place could be understood as implying the eternity of the world—a doctrine that conflicts with the literal sense of Biblical revelation. His statement that all creatures are a "mere nothing" could be held to imply a kind of monism. Recently, however, among Catholic historians of philosophy an attempt has been made to show that his theology is less unorthodox than the above doctrines might suggest, and as a Dominican, Eckhart certainly employed the language of Thomism.

This recent discussion serves to underline the degree to which Eckhart permitted changes and inconsistencies in the formulation of his ideas. Thus, at one time he held that the divine essence is *intelligere*, or understanding (a thesis original to Eckhart, and one which reinforced the doctrine of similarity of the soul to God), and only secondarily is God *esse*, or being. Later, however, he held, in accordance with Thomist doctrine, that God's essence is *esse*. Various other fluidities and antinomies can be detected in Eckhart's thought; these were partly caused by the shifting way in which he used key terms. For example, he asserted that God is above being and yet also, that he *is* being. The first use of "being" could be taken to refer to finite existence; the second use could be taken in a Thomistic sense. At times he spoke of God as both Godhead and God, and at other times he spoke of God as distinguished from the Godhead.

Although on occasion Eckhart used the term "emanation" to describe the creation of the world, he in fact adhered to an orthodox account of creation out of nothing. But he stressed the continuous creativity of God, and in this and other respects he was influenced by Augustine. Even though his language about creation could be misinterpreted to imply the eternity of the cosmos, Eckhart was at pains to evolve a two-level theory of time. In a sense all events are simultaneous for God, who is timelessly eternal (so that to speak of a temporal gap between the procession of the Trinity and the creation of the world makes no sense). Temporal concepts, however, are properly applied within the created order, and therefore the creation can be dated retrospectively. Eckhart's two-level theory of time corresponded to his two-level theory of truth. The truths that we assert are limited and partial (or, as Eckhart asserted, there is untruth in them), but there is an absolute truth which can be realized existentially, namely, the pure being of the Godhead.

The general shape of Eckhart's beliefs, if we except his doctrines of the Godhead and of the soul, was fully in accord with contemporary belief (for example, in regard to angels and purgatory). What made his sermons and teachings popular was the way in which he reiterated the need to penetrate beneath the externals of religion, while his free use of homely, striking, and sometimes paradoxical examples and similes effectively conveyed his message.

There is a remarkable parallel between some of Eckhart's central ideas and the doctrines of the Indian theologian Śankara (died c.820)—a parallel first expounded by Rudolf Otto. In Śankara's system, too, there is a distinction between the Absolute and God conceived as personal and a similar claim that the divine can be found within the soul. The comparison may give a clue to the reason for the shape of Eckhart's teachings. It certainly suggests that there are experiential reasons for this kind of doctrine, even though they may be complicated reasons. They seem to be as follows. The experience of the introvertive mystic includes a state of consciousness in which there is both a sense of illumination and an absence of distinction between subject and object; that is, the contemplative is not having an experience like that of ordinary perception, where the thing perceived can be distinguished from the percipient. Consequently, if the mystic connects his experience with God (whom he believes in for independent reasons), he may be inclined to speak of merging with God. But since his experience is without differentiation and since the notion of God—and especially that of a Trinitarian God—includes the idea that he has attributes, it is not unnatural, although it appears unorthodox, to treat the entity experienced by the mystic as being "beyond" God conceived personally. Indeed, Eckhart maintained that the true aristocrat (that is, the spark or ground of the soul) reaches beyond God, to the Godhead. It is likewise natural, in the Christian context in which Eckhart lived, to interpret this simple undifferentiated unity found in the

Godhead as being the basis out of which the Persons of the Trinity proceed. In this way mystical experience, for Eckhart, was connected with the God of ordinary religion. Nevertheless, Eckhart endeavored to express himself in accordance with orthodox belief, despite the difficulties which he found in trying to do justice both to his experience and to the ordinary language of theism. Certainly, he did not seriously intend to deny orthodoxy.

Despite the papal condemnation of some of his propositions, Eckhart had a wide influence. Johannes Tauler, Heinrich Suso, Jan van Ruysbroeck, and the group known as the Friends of God were in different ways indebted to his teachings and example.

Works by Eckhart

Meister Eckhart, F. Pfeiffer, ed., 4th ed. Göttingen, 1924. Includes sermons, treatises, and fragments.

Meister Eckhart, a Modern Translation, translated and edited by R. B. Blakney. New York, 1957. Includes bibliographical notes and the more important writings.

Selected Treatises and Sermons, J. M. Clark and J. V. Skinner, eds. London, 1958.

Works on Eckhart

Clark, J. M., *The Great German Mystics.* Oxford, 1949. A good introduction.

Clark, J. M., *Meister Eckhart.* London, 1957. A biography.

Gilson, Étienne, *Christian Philosophy in the Middle Ages.* New York, 1955.

Otto, Rudolf, *Mysticism East and West.* London, 1932.

Wulf, Maurice de, *Histoire de la philosophie médiévale*, Vol. III. Louvain, 1947.

NINIAN SMART

ECONOMICS AND ETHICAL NEUTRALITY. The problem of value judgments has attracted relatively little attention in English writings on economics. The predominant, "orthodox" view has been that economics can be as ethically neutral, or value-free (*wertfrei*), as the natural sciences. On the other hand, in Germany, for example, this view has never found general acceptance and has been the subject of a continuous but seemingly fruitless debate (the *Werturteilsstreit*) since it was advocated by Max Weber. Independently of the German debate, the issue of value judgments has gained some prominence in recent English writings.

The critics of the orthodox view seem to claim that economics, and the social sciences in general, cannot be *wertfrei.* Perhaps this claim was prompted by the fact that the principle of *Wertfreiheit* has been interpreted in a variety of senses. According to T. W. Hutchinson, for example, it has sometimes been deemed to imply that economics can "be kept free from . . . bias and 'persuasiveness' " (*'Positive' Economics and Policy Objectives*, p. 108), which would indeed render the principle suspect. However, it is pertinent to consider whether the various claims that *Wertfreiheit* is impossible touch the formulation of the principle which has been most consistently employed in orthodox writings.

Description versus prescription. The orthodox view among economists rests on the principle adduced by David Hume that norms or proposals cannot be deduced from descriptive statements alone, a descriptive statement being defined as a statement which has truth-value, whether or not its truth can be ascertained. Logically, descriptive statements have no ethical implications and are value-free. Since the scientific part of economics consists exclusively of descriptive statements, it is value-free.

Despite arguments which purport to criticize this view, some of which will be considered below, no successful criticism of it has emerged. This does not seem surprising; if one denies the distinction between descriptive statements and value judgments, then "value impregnation" would presumably have to be regarded as universal, and not a special problem of the social sciences. Yet this is rarely, if ever, suggested. Inevitable value impregnation seems to be regarded as characteristic only or mainly of the social sciences. Prima facie, this seems a strange claim. To say that in discussing problems of economics we necessarily imply value judgments suggests that it is the nature of the subject which dictates how we talk about it. But this is clearly false: Whether or not we choose to utter sentences with truth-value depends on us. In this respect the social sciences do not differ from the physical sciences.

It is not clear whether those who cavil at the idea of a *wertfrei* economics and insist on the inevitable value impregnation of the discipline would necessarily dispute that economics can be *wertfrei* in the sense explained. Some criticisms of *Wertfreiheit,* at any rate, do not seem necessarily incompatible with the claim that there is a scientific, value-free part of economics.

Propaganda versus argument. Before examining the alleged sources of inevitable value impregnation, it is necessary to guard against a possible misunderstanding. The claim that economics is inevitably value impregnated has been advanced ostensibly as a theoretical criticism of the orthodox position. Yet its purpose may have been to draw attention to, and criticize, the "ideologically biased" and "emotive" public pronouncements of economists, especially on matters concerning public policy. Thus, it has been suggested,

> the distinction between the logic of economic science and the practice of economists lies at the heart of the perennial dispute between the opponents and the defenders of orthodox . . . economics, for while the former have been chiefly concerned with the economists' practice, the latter have presented the case for the defence largely in terms of methodological principle. (A. W. Coats, "Value Judgments in Economics," pp. 53–54)

If this be the correct interpretation of the claim of value impregnation there is little to be said about it at the methodological level. If some economists' practice involves faulty reasoning, such as supposed inferences of prescriptions from descriptions, that reasoning may be criticized in the usual way. However, if it is claimed that in public pronouncements some economists deliberately or inadvertently express themselves in a manner that misleads the public, then the claim amounts simply to a charge of conscious or unconscious dishonesty. Whether or not this charge is justified, it cannot be the subject of methodological discourse. Propaganda is not the province of methodology.

METHODOLOGICAL CONSIDERATIONS

We must, therefore, treat the claim of value impregnation as a methodological argument. This article will consider four strands of argument that have been used in support of the contention that economics cannot be *Wertfrei.* These strands are ably summarized in Gunnar Myrdal's *Value in Social Theory* (pp. 1–2).

Truth and values. Those who emphasize value impregnation are often concerned to stress considerations such as the following.

(*a*) We can no longer hold that science develops by the inductive method, according to which the scientist's mind is the passive undistorting recipient of scientific truths. We now realize that, on the contrary, the scientist has to select the questions he attempts to answer, and that this selection may be influenced by such factors as his values or ideology. In this sense, scientific work may be said to depend on values.

(*b*) Just as the selection of questions may be ideologically biased, so also may what we accept as true answers to those questions. Indeed, the hypothesis that what is regarded as a true answer is a function of ideology might well hold for economists. Thus, left-wing economists have tended to "infer" from a set of statistics that progressive taxation has no disincentive effects; right-wing economists have tended to "infer" the opposite. Again, some economists, favoring direct controls, have thought that international elasticities of supply and demand were too small for devaluation to correct a balance-of-payments deficit, in which case direct controls might have to be imposed; others, being against direct controls, have thought the elasticities were sufficiently large for devaluation to work, thus making direct controls unnecessary.

(*c*) Since our values may affect our search for and our view of empirical truth, they may also affect our view of what is practically possible. This view, in turn, helps to shape our policy aims. Hence it may be said that the idea of an ideologically or ethically neutral economics is illusory.

Although these considerations are often mentioned with the vague suggestion that they invalidate the principle of *Wertfreiheit,* they do not. With regard to the claim that there is ideological bias in the selection of topics for investigation, it has been pointed out that:

> those who adhere to the postulate of *Wertfreiheit* have seldom wished to deny the influence of human values on research and theoretical development in the social sciences. They would hardly deny that the acquisition of all knowledge is selective, and that this selection may be influenced by values which thus influence the direction of research. . . . But this state of affairs is without any logical-methodological relevance. (Hans Albert, "Das Wertproblem in den Sozialwissenschaften," p. 338)

The problem of selection, which relates to the motives for discussing certain sets of statements, can have no bearing on the logical status of these statements. Yet this problem does suggest a possible reinterpretation of the claim of value impregnation.

Predictions made on the basis of economic hypotheses are, like all scientific predictions, made subject to the fulfillment of certain conditions. A change in these conditions may imply that a particular prediction no longer follows from the theory. Yet these conditions (for example, economic institutions) are often amenable to alteration by deliberate policy decisions. This suggests two important consequences. First, in the construction of theories, an economist has considerable discretion regarding the conditions he chooses to treat as given (that is, as parameters) and those he chooses to treat as variables. For example, he may choose to investigate models in which money wagerates are regarded as fixed or as affected by market forces; the effects of any given monetary and fiscal policy may differ considerably for each model. Second, it is sometimes suggested that some particular aim is unachievable. Yet an aim which may be unachievable under one set of assumed conditions may well be achievable under an alternative set.

The reinterpretation of the claim of value impregnation suggested by these considerations is simply this: Economics has been influenced by values and ideology in the sense that there has been a failure to ask important questions which might have been asked and hence possibly a failure to suggest new possibilities for economic policy. The claim, thus reinterpreted, cannot be easily appraised. However, to confuse or identify this line of argument with that purporting to demonstrate the impossibility of *Wertfreiheit* may produce unfortunate consequences. It sometimes leads to insisting, as F. Croner does, that in the social sciences a so-called value premise which allegedly "determines the content, concepts, and direction of research" must be formulated explicitly as a preliminary to theoretical discussion. Although values and extrascientific interests may be part of the problem situation and therefore a topic of interest, this insistence tends to direct the focus of discussion from the original problem toward psychological questions concerning the motivation for the inquiry. As Gottlob Frege put it in another context, the discussion then tends to become "psychologically infected."

Similarly, in regard to the point that what we accept as true answers may be biased, it is sufficient to point out that the motives for regarding a statement as true or false can in no way affect its logical status; nor, of course, can they affect its truth.

Regarding the claim that economics is not neutral because our views of practical possibilities affect our policy aims, it is sufficient to point out that the notion of neutrality implicit in this claim has nothing to do with the neutrality required by the principle of *Wertfreiheit.* This principle merely states that we cannot deduce policy prescriptions solely from descriptive statements; it does not require that policy prescriptions be independent of factual considerations. This is an untenable requirement under which factual arguments would have no place in the discussion of policy aims.

Yet this view of neutrality may have led to the confusion between ethical utterances and persuasive utterances that has occurred in discussions of the ethical content of economics. Thus, I. M. D. Little apparently wanted to define value judgments as persuasive utterances. Yet he was aware that purely descriptive statements could be persuasive. There was, therefore, the danger of arriving at the conclusion that all statements could be value judgments. To avoid this dilemma, he suggested a clarification:

> We may add that it is not sufficient that a value judgment should influence people. One can influence people by pointing out the consequences of the moral or aesthetic attitudes which they have to certain facts. A value judgment is one which tends to influence them by altering these beliefs or attitudes. (*A Critique of Welfare Economics,* p. 70)

Evidently this suggestion cannot clarify the alleged distinction between persuasive utterances which are value judgments and those which are not. Moreover, such a distinction is not required; one need merely remember both that descriptive statements cannot entail prescriptions and that descriptive statements in economics may be persuasive.

Emotive language. Another argument in favor of the view of value impregnation is the claim that economics bristles with emotive concepts which cannot be denuded of their evaluative components.

This claim can be disposed of briefly. The notion of emotive language and persuasive definitions may be relevant and interesting in the context of substantive problems in social science, for example in psychology or sociology. But these notions, which relate to the motives for and the psychological or sociological effect of using certain words, are utterly irrelevant to metascientific, methodological, problems.

Consider, for example, the statement, "A reduction in import duties will increase the level of unemployment." The proponent of this statement may regard an increase in unemployment as undesirable, and so may those to whom the statement is addressed. Thus all may attach emotive significance to the phrase "an increase in unemployment." Indeed, the statement may have been made in order to persuade the audience that a reduction in import duties is undesirable; and it may have succeeded in this. These facts may be of interest to a psychologist or sociologist, but they clearly have no bearing on the truth or falsity of the statement.

Economic counsel. The orthodox position has often been summed up in the statement that the economist as economist cannot give imperative advice. This formulation seems an inept restatement of the point that prescriptions cannot be deduced from descriptions, and echoes the confusion between questions of valid inference, which are relevant to the discussion, and questions regarding the capacity in which a given individual may make different kinds of utterances, which are irrelevant.

The point which is of concern here is that, according to the orthodox position, it is possible to give advice scientifically on a hypothetically imperative basis. This is often expressed by saying that, if the ends are given, it is possible to state scientifically, without intruding value judgments, the best means for their realization.

This view has been criticized by Myrdal on the ground that it requires the possibility of a clear-cut separation between means and ends, whereas such a separation is usually impossible, and hence, as a rule, the recommendation of appropriate means will entail value judgments.

To appraise this claim it is first necessary to state the logical requirements for value-free, conditional advice, which are usually not stated explicitly in discussions of this problem. Then there is the altogether different question whether it is reasonable to expect that an expert economic adviser may confine himself to the tendering of value-free advice.

The logical requirements for value-free advice may be simply stated: We require a set of policy aims, which in conjunction with empirical hypotheses and initial conditions, enable us to deduce a prescription. If such a deduction is possible, the resulting advice will be value-free. Since, in economics, the problem is usually to state optimal choices, these requirements may in most cases be rephrased thus: We require a given utility-function (the given ends) for which, subject to given constraints, we are able to find a maximal solution. If such a solution exists, it will provide a value-free indication of optimal choices. This procedure does not require a clear-cut dichotomy between means and ends, and hence the absence of that clear-cut dichotomy does not logically preclude the possibility of value-free advice.

Can an economic adviser, for example to governments, expect to be furnished with the data, especially the utility-function, which would enable him to find a solution for the optimal choices? The answer is surely No. Ends of policy are not simply given but are elicited and modified in the course of discussion. In such a discussion the participants, including the experts, must be expected to behave persuasively, since the purpose is to persuade someone to adopt certain policy aims.

Thus, the apparent denial of the logical possibility of value-free advice is misplaced. But the contention that the advice tendered in the course of discussions of economic policies will generally be persuasive and value loaded must be granted readily. Here, too, there seems to have been a confusion between two distinct sets of questions.

Interpersonal comparisons of utility. The arguments so far examined purporting to show the value impregnation of economics have come mainly from "unorthodox" sources. However, a charge of illegitimate intrusion of value judgments into certain parts of economics was made by the orthodox writer L. C. Robbins. The charge was connected with a problem related to that of value-free advice, namely with the question whether it is possible to make scientific statements about social welfare. Briefly, Robbins' argument was that statements such as "a more equal distribution of income would raise social welfare" rested on a comparison of the utilities of different individuals. Such comparisons—although usually unavoidable in any appraisal of alternative economic policies—were untestable and were based on arbitrary and conventional assumptions, and hence were value judgments which had no place in economic science.

This view of interpersonal comparisons, which has been widely accepted among economists, invites two comments. First, although interpersonal comparisons are not, and apparently cannot be, rendered testable, it is not clear why they should be regarded as value judgments. The second point is more important. The distinction between value judgments and synthetic statements, and, within the latter class, between testable and untestable statements, is admittedly crucial for methodology; but, as Robbins himself realized, it must not be regarded as setting limits to the permissible scope of professional discussion.

Both value judgments and synthetic statements are inextricably involved in discussions of economic policy. Yet it has often been suggested that economists, as economists, must refrain from uttering value judgments. This suggestion seems to have arisen from a confusion between problems of valid inference and the question of demarcating what economists may properly say, but the attempt to restrict the scope of argument in this way can only have stultifying consequences.

Bibliography

Albert, Hans, "Das Wertproblem in den Sozialwissenschaften." *Schweizerische Zeitschrift für Volkswirtschaft und Statistik,* Vol. 94 (1958), 335–340.

Albert, Hans, "Wertfreiheit als methodisches Prinzip," *Schriften des Vereins für Sozialpolitik,* New Series, Vol. 29 (1963), 32–63. A thorough discussion of the principle of *Wertfreiheit* as part of scientific methodology, with references to the German debate.

Archibald, G. C., "Welfare Economics, Ethics and Essentialism," *Economica,* New Series, Vol. 26 (1959), 316–327. A criticism of the view that certain parts of economics, especially welfare economics, are necessarily ethical.

Coats, A. W., "Value Judgments in Economics." *Yorkshire Bulletin of Economic and Social Research,* Vol. 16 (1964), 53–67.

Croner, F., "Wissenschaftslogik und Wertproblematik," *Kölner Zeitschrift für Soziologie und Sozialpsychologie,* Vol. 16 (1964), 327–341.

Hutchison, T. W., *'Positive' Economics and Policy Objectives.* London, 1964. A historical survey of views, mainly English, on the relationship between economics and value judgments; a discussion of how value judgments impinge on economics and of the relation between economics and economic policy.

Klappholz, Kurt, "Value Judgments and Economics." *The British Journal for the Philosophy of Science,* Vol. 15 (1964), 97–114. A more detailed discussion, with additional references, of the arguments presented here.

Little, I. M. D., *A Critique of Welfare Economics,* 2d ed. Oxford, 1957. See especially Ch. 5. Influential in introducing the notion of persuasive definitions into the discussion of the status of economics.

Myrdal, Gunnar, *Value in Social Theory,* with introduction by P. Streeten, ed. London, 1958. Myrdal is the most prominent exponent of the doctrine of value impregnation.

Robbins, L. C., *An Essay on the Nature and Significance of Economic Science,* 2d ed. London, 1935. See especially Ch. 6. The most influential recent English statement of the principle of *Wertfreiheit* in economics.

Weber, Max, *The Methodology of the Social Sciences,* translated by E. A. Shils and H. A. Finch, eds. Glencoe, Ill., 1949. See especially Chs. 1 and 2. Weber is the most celebrated German exponent of *Wertfreiheit* in the social sciences; his views found much greater acceptance in English-speaking countries than in his native land, where they gave rise to the *Werturteilsstreit.*

KURT KLAPPHOLZ

ECONOMICS AND RATIONAL CHOICE. Economists nowadays might hesitate to claim for their subject the philosophical generality implied by its onetime occasional title, "the science of value." Even in the days when philosophers like John Stuart Mill and Henry Sidgwick (following the glorious example of Adam Smith) played an important part in economic theorizing, economics was preoccupied with value in exchange rather than with value in general or value per se. Yet the specialized study of value in exchange, which is to say, of price determination, has led among other things to one of the most elaborate constructions of sustained philosophical reasoning in existence. The pure theory of price determination embodies a general theory of choice; this theory explicates concepts that enter into the definition as well as into the regulation of decisions and actions and extends to the terms on which the preferences of a plurality of agents can be consistently accommodated to one another in systems of social interaction.

Economics shares methodological problems with other sciences; but it is this theory of choice and accommodation that constitutes its distinctive claim to philosophical attention. How fruitful the theory is as a guide to empirical investigations is problematical, and in fact a great deal of economics contrives to make little use of it. Even studies of markets and prices often rely on correlating statistics without attempting to apply the details of the theory; and perhaps the theory holds its place alongside more fashionable topics (macroeconomic aspects of inflation, depression, and economic growth) chiefly because of its received prestige. There is also a question, which requires cautious handling, about how relevant the theory is to prescriptions for policy—or even to prescriptions for policy-making. It does not reckon seriously enough with the limitations of information under which agents in the real world almost always operate.

The theory nevertheless illuminates a number of perennial topics of philosophical analysis: the meaning of intentional actions; the intelligibility of utilitarianism; the explication of justice. Furthermore, its demonstration that prices are determined by the accommodation of preferences supplies a general model for social harmony, which is subtly responsive to multiple personal choices freely made. If economics as represented in this model does not transcend the notion of value in exchange, it does at any rate generalize that notion far enough to embrace every possible subject of social policy.

Rational personal choice. To appreciate the economic theory of choice in a suitably generalized form, one may begin by considering an individual agent who already possesses some good things, renewable in subsequent periods of time so far as they need to be replaced or recontracted for. The goods may be material or immaterial: a stock of raw materials; equipment; finished products; agreeable features of social arrangements; an equable climate; bodily energy; acquired skills; money. Assume that all of these things are divisible and (in various degrees) substitutable for one another; the agent, for instance, can increase his skills by moving farther north for training. Assume that none of the goods are free: To enjoy any of them the agent is already forgoing some alternative goods (for example, hours of leisure); and none of them, so far as they are subject to increase or decrease, can be replenished or increased without giving up some others. The general question that economic analysis now poses is, Can the agent improve his situation (in his own eyes)?

The obvious (tautological) answer is that he can, so long as by rearranging the quantities of his different goods he can achieve a new combination of goods which he prefers to the old one. Rearrangement may heighten pleasures which he has not had enough of; it may remedy conditions which he has objected to. The incentive to make rearrangements will disappear only when diminished quantities of goods x and others cease to be more than compensated for in his own eyes by increased quantities of goods y and others. If he continues to make rearrangements up to this point, the agent will achieve an optimum combination of goods—though optimum only relative to his own preferences, which may not be laudable, and to the limits of his own resources, which may not be deserved.

Utility. Transforming one combination of goods into a preferred combination may be said to involve an increase in utility, or satisfaction, for the agent. The optimum combination, once reached, would afford him maximum total utility. If one treats utility as at least in principle measurable, the criterion for maximizing utility within a given budget of resources may be stated in this way: The utility derived from the final or marginal unit of any good taken into the agent's combination (at the cost of forgoing some quantities of other goods) must be the same as the final utility obtained from any other kind of good at the same marginal cost or sacrifice. If it were not, then a reduction in the total quantity taken of one kind of good could be more than compensated for by an increase in the total quantity taken of some other kind.

The criterion has the apparent advantage of guaranteeing that the agent will reach an optimum combination if he pays due heed simply to marginal comparisons between different kinds of goods considered (with their costs) two kinds at a time. But will he in fact be able to make even these particularized calculations? Can he (or anyone else) measure his utilities? By an application of the theory of games, measurements of intensity of preference can be built up for individual agents taken separately; but it is doubtful whether detours through this system of measurement (which requires protracted experiments) are practical in ordinary life; it is also doubtful how far the resulting measurements, which are affected by tastes or distates for gambling, correspond to the riskless utilities of received economic theory.

Measurable or not, the concept of utility seems redundant anyway. It suffices for the purposes of the criterion that the agent distinguish the marginal substitutions that he wishes to make from those that he does not. The "utility" of neoclassical economists (Alfred Marshall and his contemporaries) figures in this connection as nothing more than a quantitative metaphor for speaking of orders of preference.

Moreover, by drawing upon the indifference curve technique of analysis developed by F. Y. Edgeworth, Vilfredo Pareto, and J. R. Hicks, a criterion can be supplied that dispenses with the metaphor and yet realizes the advantages of proceeding by marginal comparisons. Assume that the rate at which giving up quantities of any good results in increases in the quantities of another good is fixed; let it be called the objective rate of exchange between the two goods. Unless he is already at an optimum, the agent—starting with given quantities of both goods (or of either)—will prefer substituting successive amounts of one good for successive amounts of the other. As he does this, it may be assumed, he will find himself desiring greater amounts of increase in one good to compensate him for given amounts of decrease in the other. (This assumption bears a partial analogy to the assumption, commonplace in neoclassical economics, of diminishing marginal utility.) The criterion for reaching an optimum combination now becomes: the agent's marginal rate of substitution between the two goods is to be brought into equality with the objective rate of exchange. For, again, if it is not, an opportunity exists for the agent to make substitutions that will give him a preferred combination of those two goods, that is to say, with a larger proportion of the good that (in his present position) he rates higher than the objective rate does.

Extending the economic conception. Analogous treatment can be given to the choices of an agent acting as a producer rather than as a consumer—seeking to maximize physical output by substituting one factor of production for another within the limits of his budget of resources; or seeking to maximize profits from the simultaneous operation of several alternative lines of production. Although it applies in finer detail as the alternatives considered are more precisely and completely quantified, the basic scheme of analysis is designed to embrace prudential considerations of all kinds. It applies to organizations as well as to persons; to people acting on behalf of other persons as well as to people acting on their own behalf; to housewives, businessmen, philanthropists, and racketeers.

The theory succeeds in defining a philosophically instructive ideal of rational choice, since it extracts from ordinary language essential principles common to rationality and its cousin-concepts—thrift, prudence, providence, efficiency, and the like. It is wasteful—unthrifty—to use further resources for any purpose when more urgent needs go unsatisfied; imprudent to choose ephemeral goods without providing for persistent needs; inefficient to obtain any goods at costs exceeding their benefits.

The philosophical reach of the theory does not stop with the exhibition of these principles, however. Since the theory embraces alternatives of all kinds, it embraces actions of every sort. Every action represents a choice among alternatives. But no action is fully intelligible unless the choice of it accords with the agent's preferences at the time, in the circumstances given. That people's actions should accord with their preferences, so far as they consider their preferences and perceive opportunities for heeding them, is a necessary condition for establishing a minimum of consistency and intelligibility in their actions, including actions done under duress. The theory of rational choice developed in economics offers an explication of this necessary condition; and thus explicated, the condition provides all the room imaginable for crude and casual schemes of preference to give way on reflection to subtler and more comprehensive ones.

The market: collective rationality without collective planning. The objective rate of exchange may be identified for some goods and in some connections with rates of physical transformation available to current technology.

However, generally speaking, it is fixed for producers as well as consumers by the terms of trade, or prices, the terms on which an agent can increase some of his goods by directly or indirectly trading others for them in the market. But the prices that the market establishes for given goods in terms of others, while fixed for any single agent (fixed, as to range of discretion, even if the agent enjoys some degree of monopoly over the goods that he is prepared to trade), register the combined effects of many agents' bids and offers. They may be regarded as devices for reconciling the needs and preferences of many different agents with limitations of time, of resources (natural and human), and of technology.

In their turn the prices furnished by the market have the effect of encouraging rational calculation on the part of individual agents. The encouragement redoubles with the use of a monetary standard for reckoning prices, to which marginal comparisons between any sorts of goods can be referred and accomplished, if the agent so desires, with something like the precision envisaged in the theory of choice. The agent's task in choosing between any two sorts of goods may then be said to be to equate the marginal rate of substitution between them with the ratio of their prices. Max Weber teaches that money makes calculation more precise—and by doing so it refines the possibilities and extends the scope of rational action; rationality has developed as a pervasive feature of Western civilization with the wider and wider use of money as a standard means of reckoning.

How well does the market accommodate the preferences of different agents? The answer—worked out in intricate detail by pure economic theory, in abstraction from the rigidities of actual market institutions—depends upon how thoroughly agents calculate their preferences (and on certain assumptions about benefits being divisible and marketable). The market does, especially on the production side, put people under some pressure to calculate thoroughly, since competition among the participants tends to make errors of judgment ruinous. Given a distribution of property and of productive talents favorable to competition, and technological conditions likewise favorable, it can be proved a priori that market processes will settle into equilibrium only when the offers of goods and services that people are prepared to make have been assorted in kind and quantity to correspond with the preferences that people are prepared to express for acquiring them. Once there, the economy will also have reached a Pareto optimum: no further marginal change will be possible either in production or distribution that would make anyone better off (according to his own preferences, whatever these might be) without making someone else worse off. But free activity rationally conforming to individual preferences, it has been held, automatically generates processes that lead to such an optimum. To invoke Adam Smith's famous metaphor, every agent will be led by "an invisible hand," doing what is rationally best for himself, to contribute his share to the best for everybody.

Advantages of the market. The arguments for making the market the prescribed general form for economic arrangements emerge in the very course of working out the assumptions from which the automatic processes follow. For a Pareto optimum is not only a state of equilibrium; it is a stopping place for the reasoning undertaken by welfare economics, the nearest to best that an economy can be supposed to do proceeding from a given initial distribution of claims on resources, without judging among the preferences of different participants.

As a general ideal, the classical liberal conception of the market has been politically discredited—perhaps before all its philosophical lessons were drawn. Is it not in some respects a subtler and farther-reaching ideal for collective rationality than, for example, Kant's kingdom of ends, in which every legislator has the same moral tastes and assents to exactly the same way of life? The market ideal offers a collective means for harmonizing a great diversity of tastes—even of ways of life—with minimum recourse to prohibitory legislation and minimum use of coercion.

Might not the market accomplish, moreover, at least a major part of justice? It seems unjust to give some people's preferences precedence over others' unless there are moral grounds for doing so; the market ideal (in spite of its traditional silence regarding unequal property) shows how equally valid preferences can be treated equally. As a means of expressing many people's preferences simultaneously and obtaining some attention for all of them, the market can handle much more complex information than any practical system of voting. The findings of economists converge on this point with the findings of those political scientists who would defend democracies not by their clumsy provisions for popular mandates but by the degree to which the competitive interaction of political parties, pressure groups, and constitutional agencies exemplifies some sort of "invisible hand" process.

Objections to the market. Yet the market ideal has notorious drawbacks. The objection that individual agents are not very rational in intention or very knowledgeable in fact might be softened, like the objection that their tastes may be ignoble and even vicious, by citing the possibilities of educating them or by dwelling on the moral dangers of alternative arrangements. More explosive politically has been the objection pressed by Marx and never shaken off by academic economics: To adopt the market ideal without questioning the initial distribution of claims on resources betrays an ideological bias, which sanctions market processes working out to an economic optimum contingent not merely on the given tastes of the participants but also on differential advantages conferred by the institution of inheritable private property. The justice achieved by the market ideal is in these respects a very qualified kind of justice.

The market is so liable in so many ways to monopolistic distortions that it is impossible to make the market in practice a perfectly fair game for every participant. If the market were a fair game, it would not necessarily be an attractive one. For market processes to work out to their promised end, any given participant must be ready to change his job, his habitation, and his way of life at a moment's notice; he must not hold out for customary wages or customary status when the terms of the market change against him. Should he be expected to submit so readily? Should community life be upset, some communities or community-supporting relationships even destroyed, in order to facilitate market adjustments? In fact, there are a number of good things that market processes cannot easily deal with, and some that the market tends to destroy.

Historically there has been so much social resistance to thoroughgoing fulfillment of market arrangements that one may say the experiment of carrying them out has not been undertaken, much less allowed to work its way to equilibrium. The approximations that have been tried—for example, in the capitalistic economies of Britain and the United States—have failed to cope smoothly with large-scale technological changes, which have been so frequent as to make the idea of a beneficent equilibrium continually obsolescent anyway. They have also failed to cope smoothly with large-scale failures in investment incentive, which have suggested that equilibrium of a sort may be identical with stagnation. Only during transitory booms have these economies been able to keep people and resources fully employed without planning; much of the time they have left great numbers of people languishing in idleness while urgent social needs have gone unattended. In practice, and in theory, too, the market ideal has been discounted in favor of increased measures of social planning, not merely by people who do not understand the ideal but also by many who do.

Collective rationality through planning. The government is the favored agent of social planning. If one abstracts from the political processes that determine what governments actually do, a government may be treated as a rational economic agent with the task of allocating resources so that total benefits, socially assessed, are maximized. But how are benefits to be assessed socially? Bentham's project for interpersonal measurements of utility remains unrealized; it has been natural, nevertheless, for economists to keep personal utilities in view and thus to assume that assessment should consult the preferences of the people affected. Recent theoretical thinking has gravitated around the idea of a welfare function, into which people's personal preferences for various combinations of goods would enter and, however assorted, there aggregate under some rule for ranking over-all policies. If people's preferences are to be consulted in detail, however, people must be given a chance to express their preferences in detail for alternative assignments of goods; and the simplest way—indeed, the only practical way—of doing this is to allow them some scope for demonstrating their preferences in a market. This point is conceded by socialist economists. Social planning, on this view, would not seek to abolish the market, but would make at least limited use of it as a sensitive means of registering preferences.

Unsuspected difficulties have been discovered, however, in fixing upon any rule for passing from personal preferences to the social rankings of a welfare function. Kenneth J. Arrow has shown that no rule—including rules for voting as well as the rule that the market shall operate—will satisfy certain apparently reasonable conditions, for instance, that of responding democratically to changes in personal preferences and at the same time generating transitive social rankings. The full implications of this finding have not been worked out, though various ways of minimizing its bearing on practical politics have been suggested. One theoretically significant way out is to assume that the variation between different people's preferences is limited by common principles of ordering; principles of political division suffice (for example left or right agreeing which of a set of policies are more or less leftish).

Perplexities about preferences may be reduced by basing planning on needs instead. There is a limited social agreement that needs take precedence over preferences, and perhaps even that some needs take precedence over other needs—an agreement that is embodied in ordinary conception, as distinguished from economists' conceptions, of welfare. But there are many needs, as there are many degrees of preference; and in the absence of anything like a felicific calculus no straightforward technique exists for calculating the comparative weights of either needs or preferences for the community as a whole. Even if society agrees that some needs take precedence over others, the agreement is hardly likely to indicate which should be served further in the myriad different situations where both are already served to some extent. Sooner or later, resort to preferences—somebody's or a group of somebodies'—is unavoidable.

But limited information would, except in extremely simple cases, obstruct planners from actually filling out a welfare function as a means of identifying maximum social benefits. Detailed information about people's preferences cannot be collected without suspending the ordinary business of society. In practice, the information would be too costly to be forthcoming.

In the face of these limitations, is it not sensible to scale down the requirements of rationality in government planning? Instead of blindly trying to reach a goal that cannot be identified—maximizing total social benefits by choosing among all available combinations of policies—a community, considered as a complex of policy-making institutions, will find it more efficient to proceed in the manner of Karl Popper's "piecemeal planning," hoping to find step by step satisfactory small remedies for outstanding inadequacies of policy. Given changing tastes and other complications, such a process will prove unending; but under changing and complicated conditions should it be expected to end?

The concept of personal rationality can be usefully revised along the same lines. The room that the economic theory of choice leaves for people to perfect their choices is not room that they are going to use up. Persons no more than societies can be expected to finish the comprehensive surveys of their preferences for various goods that would assure them of calculating optimum combinations. It has been suggested that economic theory might advance in realism by paying more attention to the cutoff points at which calculation ends in observed practices of "satisficing" (H. A. Simon's term). Instead of pursuing the vain ideal of maximizing, agents typically make limited searches among readily perceived alternatives and settle for one that meets minimum standards of acceptability.

The idea of marginal comparisons, however, need not be sacrificed in the interests of realism, since it is well suited to interpreting incremental choices—and incrementally varying series of choices—within realistically limited ranges of information. People can be expected to make marginal improvements when they perceive them. Moreover, much of the theory of market accommodation can be adapted to the assumption that agents choose with limited aims and limited information; for prices will have incentive and deterrent effects in the same directions as before. If the theory were not adaptable, it would remain a permanent acquisition of philosophy, a touchstone for evaluating discussions of social choice; just as the marginal analysis of maximization remains a touchstone for evaluating treatments of choices by single agents. (See DECISION THEORY.)

Bibliography

A good first book, or refresher, to read about economic theory is William Fellner's *Emergence and Content of Modern Economic Analysis* (New York, 1960). The history of the subject can be pursued further in Joseph A. Schumpeter's inexhaustibly rich *History of Economic Analysis* (New York, 1954). For the neoclassical treatment of marginal utility, see Alfred Marshall, *Principles of Economics* (8th ed., London, 1920); or perhaps even better, Philip H. Wicksteed, *The Common Sense of Political Economy* (London, 1910), where the bones of the argument are more clearly exposed and its relations with philosophical analysis more visible.

Axiomatic treatments of utility along lines suggested by the theory of games, together with an extensive bibliography, can be found in R. Duncan Luce and Howard Raiffa, *Games and Decisions* (New York, 1957). J. R. Hicks, in the first chapter of *Value and Capital* (2d ed., Oxford, 1946), elucidates the shift from marginal utility theory to theories based on indifference curves and marginal rates of substitution (a shift foreshadowed in Wicksteed). The pure theory of economic choice reaches an even more advanced level of sophistication in the first of *Three Essays on the State of Economic Science* by Tjalling C. Koopmans (New York, 1957); philosophers with a taste for logic and set theory will find this book especially clear and rewarding. Joan Robinson, in *Economic Philosophy* (London, 1962), gives a pungent and irreverent account of the limitations of pure theory of the neoclassical type and its successors as a guide to major issues of public policy.

The drawbacks of the liberal market-ideal are presented with admirable objectivity by Frank H. Knight in a famous essay on "The Ethics of Competition" (the second of two by that name reprinted in a book of the same title, London, 1935). A lively book by J. de V. Graaff, *Theoretical Welfare Economics* (Cambridge, 1957), offers a comprehensive view of intricate technical issues. For a treatment of the market as a technique to be used in conjunction with social planning, see Robert A. Dahl and Charles E. Lindblom, *Politics, Economics, and Welfare* (New York, 1953); for a socialist's view, see Oskar Lange, "On the Economic Theory of Socialism," reprinted in a book of the same title by Lange and Taylor (Minneapolis, 1938).

Kenneth J. Arrow's *Social Choice and Individual Values* (2d ed., New York, 1963) is remarkable not only for its thesis about the difficulties of finding a rule for aggregating personal preferences, but also for its use of mathematical logic and its attention to philosophical ethics. Karl R. Popper's views on policy-making can be found both in *The Open Society and Its Enemies* (2 vols., London, 1945) and in *The Poverty of Historicism* (2d ed., London, 1960). The concept of satisficing is introduced by Herbert A. Simon in Part IV of his *Models of Man* (New York, 1957); see also Ch. 6, "Cognitive Limits on Rationality," in James G. March and Herbert A. Simon, *Organizations* (New York, 1958). For Max Weber's views on rationality, see *The Theory of Social and Economic Organizations,* translated by A. M. Henderson and Talcott Parsons (New York, 1947), among other works.

DAVID BRAYBROOKE

EDDINGTON, ARTHUR STANLEY (1882–1944), was an English astronomer who was educated at Owens College, Manchester, and Trinity College, Cambridge, where he was Plumian professor of astronomy from 1913 to 1944. He never married, was socially rather diffident, and lived the quiet life of a Cambridge academic. He was elected a fellow of the Royal Society in 1914 and was knighted in 1930.

Eddington was one of the most brilliant theoreticians of his day, possessing an outstanding ability to survey complex and highly ramified subjects as wholes. His report to the Physical Society (1918) on the general theory of relativity, expanded into *The Mathematical Theory of Relativity* (London, 1923), contained important original contributions to the theory. Eddington's discovery of the mass–luminosity relation in stars and his explanation of white dwarf stars, which made possible the modern theory of stellar evolution, were published in *The Internal Constitution of the Stars* (London, 1926). These two books are considered to be his most substantial contributions to physics and astronomy. His interpretation of relativity theories led him to a belief in the profound importance of epistemology for physics. At first in semipopular books on modern physics—*Nature of the Physical World* (London, 1928) and *New Pathways in Science* (London, 1935) being the most important—Eddington argued for the view that physics could be almost entirely based upon investigations into the nature of sensation and measurement. A more elaborate and purely philosophical defense of his view was given in *The Philosophy of Physical Science* (London, 1939). Formal attempts actually to produce physics as derived in this way were presented in *Relativity Theory of Protons and Electrons* (London, 1936) and *Fundamental Theory* (London, 1946), published posthumously.

Eddington's real contributions to philosophy, if any, lie in his work on the epistemology of physics. However, he also defended idealism and mysticism, and he claimed that the indeterminacy of quantum physics solved the traditional philosophical problem of free will versus determinism in favor of free will. Particularly in his semipopular writings, Eddington was betrayed into philosophical excesses and, at times, gross confusion by a play of analogy and paradox, which, while part of his equipment as an immensely entertaining and brilliant writer, also served his love of mystery and obscurantism.

Selective subjectivism. Eddington gave to his epistemological view the two names "selective subjectivism" and "structuralism." He accepted the causal theory of perception, and with this theory Eddington's own system stands or falls. From this theory it follows, first, that we know directly only the contents of our own consciousness (sense data) and, second, that these contents cannot be claimed to resemble elements of the objective world in any qualitative way. Our sensory apparatus selects from objective reality what we are able to observe and what is therefore the material for physical knowledge, just as, to use Eddington's own analogy, a net of a certain size mesh selects fish only of a size greater than the mesh. Just as we could generalize, prior to examining any catch of fish, about the size of fish the net would yield, so we can generalize in physics prior to the results of observation, merely by reflecting upon observational procedure, especially metrical procedures.

Despite distortions, mostly qualitative, in the picture that our senses thrust upon us, we may conclude that the picture has a structure in common with the unknowables that stimulate the senses. We notice patterns of recurrence in sensation, and it is the task of physics to elaborate the structure of these patterns. In particular, the structure of pointer-reading observations should be studied, since pointer readings—being merely observed coincidences—are minimally corrupted by the qualitative veils cast by our senses. However, Eddington denied the pointer readings directly represent anything objectively real.

Apriorism. Like Kant, to whose system Eddington admitted that his own was distantly similar, he claimed that knowledge must conform to certain primitive rational patterns if it is to be intelligible. One of these forms of thought is that we believe in the existence of minds other than our own. The recognition of a common structure in the experience of many minds leads to a belief in an objective reality independent of these minds. There is no primitive belief in an objective reality. This route to the existence of an external world is an unobtrusive but significant part of Eddington's idealistic metaphysics.

Using the notion of structure as defined in the mathematical theory of groups, Eddington was able, out of highly generalized material from epistemology (for example, the claim that only relations between things are observable) and from the forms of thought, to build quite intricate group structures, for example, the structure found in Dirac's mathematical specification of an elementary particle in an elementary state giving charge and spin. In addition to this a priori derivation of the formal structure of laws, Eddington also exploited the theory of groups in deducing a priori the basic natural constants, such as the gravitational constant and the fine structure constant, from various features of the group structure of the type of mathematics employed. In this, he compared himself with Archimedes, who deduced the nature of π from the axiom of Euclid, whereas previous determinations of its nature had relied upon merely empirical methods.

On this basis Eddington claimed that the mind fits nature into a pattern determined by the nature of the mind itself; that the discoveries made by the physicist are just what his sensory, intellectual, and metrical processes dictate that he shall find.

It is difficult not to share the general view that Eddington vastly overstated the extent to which convention enters into theory construction. Extensive criticism in this article without more extensive elaboration of the complexities of his group structure derivations would be unjust. Some brief comments must suffice.

Eddington's view was that observation was required only for the purpose of identifying, on the one hand, the elements of the group constructed by pure mathematics with, on the other hand, the theoretical terms of, say, electromagnetism. It is far from clear where he thought the complete theoretical structure then stood from the point of view of its a priori status. If such "identification" demands that it be fully observed that the electromagnetic field is properly (that is, truly) described by Maxwell's equations, which have the group structure in question, then Eddington was requiring "observation" to add a very great deal more than he seems to have been prepared to admit.

Eddington fell into confusion that illustrates well his mistakes in general. This was his claim that the basis of the special theory of relativity may be deduced a priori because it depends on the fact that simultaneity of events at a distance from each other is not observable, that is, that it depends upon an epistemological fact. It is true that to decide a question about the simultaneity of spatially separated events, one must make assumptions as to the speed of the signals which inform one that the events have occurred. And it is also true that in the last resort these assumptions could be checked only if one could decide independently on the simultaneity of events spatially distant from each other. But this epistemological circularity is an insufficient basis for relativity theory. Moreover, further contingent facts, not deducible a priori (for example, the fact that in any inertial system light takes the same time round any closed paths of the same length, whatever their orientation) are required. Eddington claimed that the result of the Michelson–Morley experiment could have been foreseen on a purely epistemological basis. It seems quite clear that he was wrong.

Idealism. "To put the conclusion crudely—the stuff of the world is mind-stuff," Eddington wrote in *Nature of the Physical World.* The idealist conclusion was not integral to his epistemology but was based on two main arguments.

The first derives directly from current physical theory. Briefly, mechanical theories of the ether and of the behavior of fundamental particles have been discarded in both relativity and quantum physics. From this Eddington inferred that a materialistic metaphysics was outmoded and that, in consequence—the disjunction of materialism or idealism being assumed exhaustive—an idealistic metaphysics is required.

The second and more interesting argument was based on Eddington's epistemology and may be regarded as consisting of two parts. First, all we know of the objective world is its structure, and the structure of the objective world is precisely mirrored in our own consciousness. We therefore have no reason to doubt that the objective world, too, is "mind-stuff." Dualistic metaphysics, then, cannot be evidentially supported. (The conclusion appears to be a valid deduction from its premises.)

But, second, not only can we not know that the objective world is nonmentalistic, we also cannot intelligibly suppose that it could be material. To conceive of a dualism entails attributing material properties to the objective world. However, this presupposes that we could observe that the objective world has material properties. But this is absurd, for whatever is observed must ultimately be the content of our own consciousness and, consequently, nonmaterial. This last argument confuses, among other things, the supposition that the objective world has certain properties with the supposition of our observing that it has them.

(For some of Eddington's views on the existence of God, see the article POPULAR ARGUMENTS FOR THE EXISTENCE OF GOD. See also the article STEBBING, LIZZIE SUSAN.)

Additional Works by Eddington

Space, Time, and Gravitation. London, 1920.
Science and the Unseen World. London, 1929.
The Expanding Universe. London, 1933.

Works on Eddington

Dingle, H., *Sources of Eddington's Philosophy*. London, 1954.
Stebbing, S., *Philosophy and the Physicists*. London, 1937.
Whittaker, E. T., *Eddington's Principles in the Philosophy of Science*. London, 1951.

G. C. NERLICH

EDUCATION, PHILOSOPHY OF. See PHILOSOPHY OF EDUCATION, HISTORY OF and PHILOSOPHY OF EDUCATION, INFLUENCE OF MODERN PSYCHOLOGY ON.

EDWARDS, JONATHAN (1703–1758), Puritan theologian and philosopher, was born in East Windsor, Connecticut. He was the only son of Timothy Edwards, the pastor of the Congregational Church at East Windsor; his mother was the daughter of Solomon Stoddard, pastor at Northampton, Massachusetts. About the age of 12 or 13 he wrote several essays in natural science which reveal remarkable powers of observation and deduction. "Of Insects" describes the habits of spiders. Another essay, on the rainbow and colors, shows an acquaintance with Newton's *Opticks*. Around the same time Edwards wrote a short demonstration of the immateriality of the soul. These writings are the work of a precocious mind, deeply interested in nature and finding in it the marks of a provident God.

In 1716, Edwards entered Yale, where the world of philosophy opened up to him. For a short time his tutor was Samuel Johnson, who introduced him to the new philosophical ideas coming from England, especially those of Locke. He read Locke's *Essay Concerning Human Understanding*, from which, he claimed, he derived more enjoyment "than the most greedy miser finds, when gathering up handfuls of silver and gold, from some newly discovered treasure." His precocity in philosophy is proved by his notes "Of Being" and "The Mind," both probably written before his graduation in 1720.

There followed two years of graduate study in theology at Yale, in preparation for the ministry. During this period Edwards had a profound religious experience, which he described later, in his *Personal Narrative* (1739), as having given him a new awareness of the absolute sovereignty and omnipresence of God and of complete dependence on him. Edwards' religious philosophy grew out of this transforming experience.

In 1722 he became pastor of a Scotch Presbyterian congregation in New York, but the life of study and teaching attracted him, and two years later he was back at Yale as senior tutor. In 1727 he was ordained assistant minister to his grandfather Solomon Stoddard, and when Stoddard died, in 1729, Edwards took over the Northampton parish.

For almost twenty years Edwards preached and wrote in this parish. During that time he continued his boyhood custom of jotting down his reflections, which he called "Miscellanies" or "Miscellaneous Observations." They fill nine volumes and contain 1,360 entries. These journals, most of which are still unedited, were intended to be a first draft of a monumental book provisionally entitled "A Rational Account of the Main Doctrines of the Christian Religion Attempted." This proposed *summa* of Calvinist theology was not completed.

Edwards' pervasive theme was the Calvinist doctrine of God's sovereignty and the complete helplessness of man to effect his own salvation by good works. In a famous sermon preached in Boston in 1731, entitled "God Glorified in Man's Dependence," he opposed Arminianism—a doctrine derived from the Dutch theologian Jacobus Arminius (1560–1609) and then gaining ground in the colonies—which granted to men some part in their salvation through benevolence and good works. Edwards played a vigorous role in the revivalist movement known as the Great Awakening, which swept through New England in the 1740s, reaching hysterial peaks of religious enthusiasm. His own conception of religious experience is found in *A Treatise Concerning Religious Affections* (1746).

Through sternness of doctrine and lack of prudence Edwards alienated his parishioners, and in 1748 he was dismissed from his parish. His next post was the missionary parish at Stockbridge, Massachusetts, where he preached to a small group of Indians and a few whites. He had plenty of leisure to write, and a major work, *Freedom of the Will*, defining and defending his Calvinist doctrine of human freedom, appeared in 1754. The sequel, *The Nature of True Virtue* (1765), places virtue in the emotions rather than in the intellect. His last completed work, "Concerning the End for Which God Created the World," is a speculative theological work on God's purpose in creation.

At Stockbridge, Edwards began a vast synthesis of theology called *The History of the Work of Redemption*, but this was interrupted by his election, in 1757, to the presidency of New Jersey College, now Princeton University. He died at Princeton the following year.

Philosophical orientation. In the language of the day, Edwards was a "philosophizing divine." His primary interests were religious, and his main writings were theological. Apart from his college notes he produced no purely philosophical works. However, his theological treatises abound in philosophical reflections, all of which were intended to clarify and defend his theological positions. For him the arts, sciences, and philosophy ideally had no status separate from theology; as they become more perfect, he said, they "issue in divinity, and coincide with it, and appear to be as parts of it."

Edwards' philosophical views reflect his college training in Puritan Platonism, itself an offshoot of Cambridge Platonism and the Platonism of Peter Ramus. He attempted to synthesize with this Christian Platonism elements from the English empiricists, especially Locke, Newton, and Hutcheson, whose works were introduced into New England in the early 1700s. Puritan Platonism taught Edwards that the spiritual world alone is real, that the visible universe is but its shadow, created to lead the mind, under the divine illumination, to an awareness of the presence of God. Into this general idealistic philosophy he wove strands of doctrine from the empirically minded Locke and the scientist Newton, whose works were beginning to make a stir in the colonies. From Locke he took the notion that all our ideas originate in sensation; from Newton, the conception of space as the divine sensorium.

Being. In his notes "Of Being," Edwards took up the Parmenidean thesis of the necessity of Being, arguing the impossibility of absolute nothingness on the ground that it is a contradictory and inconceivable notion. Since pure nothingness is an impossibility, he held, there never was a time when Being did not exist. In short, Being is eternal. He also established the omnipresence of Being, arguing that we cannot think of pure nothingness in one place any more than we can think of it in all places. Thus, Being possesses the divine attributes of necessity, eternity, omnipresence, and infinity. Consequently, Being is God himself.

Further attributes of Being deduced by Edwards are nonsolidity and space. Solidity, he argued, is resistance to other solids, and since there are no beings outside of Being, Being itself, or God, cannot be conceived as solid. That Being, or God, is identical with space Edwards proved by the impossibility of conceiving the nonexistence of space. We can suppress from thought everything in the universe but space itself. Hence, space is divine. Following the Cambridge Platonists and Newton, Edwards conceived of God's mind as the locus in which material things spatially exist.

Nature of mind. Edwards' notes entitled "The Mind" are heavily indebted to Locke. Like the English philosopher, he distinguished between two faculties of the mind, understanding and will. Understanding he defined as the faculty by which the soul perceives, speculates, and judges. Its first operation is sensation, for without the activity of the senses there can be no further mental operations. The mind needs the senses in order to form all its ideas. The objects of the senses are not real qualities of bodies but impressions and ideas given to us by God. Edwards agreed with Locke that secondary qualities, such as colors, sounds, smells, and tastes, do not inhere in bodies but are mental impressions. Every intelligent philosopher, Edwards wrote, now grants that colors are not really in things any more than pain is in a needle.

Idealism. Edwards went beyond Locke in applying to primary qualities, such as solidity, extension, figure, and motion, the arguments against the reality of secondary qualities. All the primary qualities, he insisted, can be reduced to resistance. Solidity is simply resistance; figure is the termination of resistance; extension is an aspect of figure; motion is the communication of resistance from one place to another. Hence, a visible body is composed not of real qualities but of ideas, including color, resistance, and modes of resistance. Resistance itself is not material; it is "nothing else but the actual exertion of God's power." Consequently, the visible universe has only a mental existence. It exists primarily in God's mind, where it was designed by a free act of the divine will. It also exists in our minds, communicated to us by God in a series of united and regularly successive ideas.

Historians have debated whether Edwards owed his idealistic philosophy to Berkeley or to his own precocious genius. At the time he formulated it, Berkeley's works were not yet available at Yale. Although it is possible that he heard reports of Berkeley's idealism, it is more likely that he arrived independently at his idealistic conclusions.

According to Edwards, minds alone are, properly speaking, beings or realities; bodies are only "shadows of being." Goodness and beauty belong to anything in proportion to its intensity of being. Hence, minds alone are really good and beautiful; the visible world has but a shadow of these perfections. Its value is to lead the mind to the enjoyment of spiritual and divine goodness and beauty.

Creation. The created world depends entirely on God for its existence and preservation. He freely created it, and he constantly holds it in existence, as colors are continually renewed by the light of the sun falling on bodies. The universe constantly proceeds from God as light shines from the sun. Under the activity of God the universe is a revelation of the divine mind to created minds; it is a panorama of shadows and images exhibiting the divine mind and will. Edwards, in his notebook entitled *Images or Shadows of Divine Things*, described nature as a symbol of God. God, he said, revealed himself in the Bible and also in the visible universe and the souls of men, which are made in the image of God. In order to interpret correctly the symbols of God in the created world, the mind has to be purified by a divine illumination. To Edwards there is no more sublime or delightful activity than to discover and to contemplate the traces of God in nature.

The will. The second faculty of the mind described by Edwards is the will. The importance of the will lies in the fact that it is the seat of the passions or affections, the chief of which is love. According to Edwards, all the other passions originate in love and are for its sake. Love is the excellence and beauty of minds. In *A Treatise Concerning Religious Affections* he argued that all human activities, especially those of religion, arise from affection. The affections, he said, are the "very life and soul of all true religion." The essence of religion lies in holy love, especially the love of God. Although Edwards' doctrine of religious experience, under the influence of pietism, gives ample scope to the emotions, and he appealed to them in his sermons, he generally maintained a Puritan sobriety of expression and avoided the sensationalism that marked the Great Awakening. He insisted that religion be centered in what he called the "gracious affections" that spring from the awareness of God and divine things.

Religion and ethics. Religious experience is possible, according to Edwards, through a supernatural sense that the elect receive by divine grace. This new sense, which is different from the five bodily senses, gives man, reborn by grace, a new kind of sensation or perception by which he passively receives from God ideas and truths about divine things. By a kind of sense experience the elect enjoy an inward, sweet delight in God, which unites them to God more closely than all rational knowledge of him. The way to God is through the heart rather than through the head.

Problem of freedom. Edwards regarded the will, like the intellect, as an essentially passive power, moved to action by external forces. As the intellect passively receives impressions and ideas from God, so the will is inclined to agreeable objects and repelled by disagreeable objects. The will is not a self-determining power; its actions are determined by causes. God alone is free in the sense that he can determine his own volitions. The principle of causality, according to which everything that happens has a cause, applies to the movements of the human will as it does to everything created. Of course, the will is moved not by physical causes but by motives or moral causes. These motives are presented to the will by the understanding, and the strongest of them determines the movement of the will.

Edwards opposed the Arminians of his day, who attributed to the human will an inner spontaneity and power of self-determination. In his view this kind of freedom is a divine prerogative; the human will does not have this kind of inner freedom. Its actions are determined not by being physically coerced but by being morally necessitated. A man cannot help willing as he does, given the motives presented to him. And since these motives are determined by God's providence, the movements of man's will are entirely within the divine power.

Although Edwards denied that the human will has freedom of self-determination, he granted that in a sense man is free. Like Hobbes and Locke, he defined human liberty as the ability to carry out what the will inclines man to do. Liberty is the absence of impediments to action. This denial of the essential freedom of the will harmonizes well with Edwards' Calvinist belief in the total depravity of man and in predestination.

Virtue. Shaftesbury (1671–1713) and Francis Hutcheson (1694–1746) influenced Edwards' ethics. With them he denied that true virtue consists in the selfish pursuit of pleasure or in the utility of human actions. Rather, virtue is disinterested benevolence or affection; it is the intrinsic beauty of the dispositions of man's heart. An action is good not because it is advantageous to ourselves or to others but solely because it springs from a beautiful disposition of will. Virtue is a spiritual beauty or excellence that commends itself to us for its own sake. Any other motive for acting is based on self-love and consequently does not measure up to true virtue.

Edwards did not think that man has a natural impulse to such disinterested virtue. In his view man, owing to original sin, is totally depraved and given over to self-love. Only by the election of God and the gift of efficacious grace can man rise above his "dreadful condition" and perform truly virtuous actions. Without supernatural aid seemingly disinterested affections, such as the natural love of parents for their children, are accompanied by self-love and hence are not truly virtuous. At most they are secondary virtues or the shadows of true virtue.

Edwards was the most gifted and articulate theologian–philosopher in the New England colonies and perhaps in American history. He supported a losing cause in his defense of Puritanism, but for a while he gave it new life and spirit. The liberal theology that he combated all his life finally won the day; in the form of Unitarianism it dominated New England culture in the nineteenth century. But Edwards' powerful religious and philosophical stimulus remained. New England transcendentalists, such as Emerson, although rejecting all systematic theology and proclaiming the divinity of man, continued the Puritan's passionate search for the divine in the communion with nature.

Works by Edwards

Works, S. Austin, ed., 8 vols. Worcester, 1808–1809; reprinted in 4 vols., New York, 1844, 1847. An old but useful edition, found in some libraries.

Works, S. E. Dwight, ed., 10 vols. New York, 1829–1830. This is the standard and best edition of Edwards' works, except for those newly edited. Vol. I contains a "Life of Edwards" by Dwight.

Works, P. Miller, ed. New Haven, 1956—. Vol. I, *The Freedom of the Will*, P. Ramsey, ed. Vol. II, *Religious Affections*, J. E. Smith, ed. A new edition which will supersede Dwight's.

Representative Selections, C. H. Faust and T. H. Johnson, eds. New York, 1935; rev. ed. (paperback), with rev. and updated bibliography, 1962. Useful selections from Edwards' works and a good bibliography.

Images or Shadows of Divine Things, P. Miller, ed. New Haven, 1948.

Puritan Sage: Collected Writings of Jonathan Edwards, V. Ferm, ed. New York, 1953. Useful selection of Edwards' works.

The Nature of True Virtue. Ann Arbor, Mich., 1960. Foreword by W. Frankena. Best edition of this work.

Works on Edwards

Miller, P., *Jonathan Edwards*. New York, 1949; paperback ed., 1959. Both this and *Errand Into the Wilderness* (below) are first class.

Miller, P., *Errand Into the Wilderness*. Cambridge, Mass., 1956.

Schneider, H. W., *The Puritan Mind*. New York, 1930; paperback ed., Ann Arbor, Mich., 1958.

Schneider, H. W., *A History of American Philosophy*. New York, 1946; 2d ed., 1963. Pp. 11–31.

Winslow, O. E., *Jonathan Edwards, 1703–1758*. New York, 1940; paperback ed., 1962. Pulitzer Prize-winning biography—excellent and fascinating account of Edwards' life and times, with good bibliography.

ARMAND A. MAURER

EGOCENTRIC PARTICULARS. See INDEXICAL SIGNS, EGOCENTRIC PARTICULARS, AND TOKEN-REFLEXIVE WORDS.

EGOISM AND ALTRUISM. Why do we sometimes prefer to consult the interests of others rather than our own interests? What is the relationship between selfishness and benevolence? Is altruism merely a mask for self-interest? At first sight these may appear to be empirical, psychological questions, but it is obviously the case that even if they are construed as such, the answers will depend on the meaning assigned to such key expressions as "self-interest," "benevolence," "sympathy," and the like. It is in connection with elucidating the meaning of such expressions that philosophical problems arise—problems which are of particular interest because we cannot understand such expressions without committing ourselves, in some degree, to some particular conceptual schematism by means of which we can set out the empirical facts about human nature. That there are alternative and rival conceptual possibilities is a fact to which the history of philosophy testifies.

The problems with which we are concerned do not appear fully-fledged until the seventeenth and eighteenth centuries. That they do not is a consequence of the specific moral and psychological concepts of the Greek and of the medieval world. In neither Plato nor Aristotle does altruistic benevolence appear in the list of the virtues, and consequently the problem of how human nature, constituted as it is, can possibly exhibit this virtue cannot arise. In the *Republic* the question of the justification of justice is indeed raised in such a way as to show that if Thrasymachus' account of human nature were correct, men would find no point in limiting themselves to what justice prescribes, provided that they could be unjust successfully—and Thrasymachus' account of human nature is certainly egoistic. But Plato's rejoinder to Thrasymachus is a statement of a different view of human nature in which the pursuit of *good as such* and the pursuit of *my good* necessarily coincide.

In the medieval world the underlying assumption is that man's self-fulfillment is discovered in the love of God and of the rest of the divine creation. So although Aquinas envisages the first precept of the natural law as an injunction to self-preservation, his view of what the self is and of what preserving it consists in leads to no special problems about the relation between what I owe to myself and what I owe to others. It is only when Hobbes detaches the doctrines of natural law from their Aristotelian framework that the problem emerges in a sharp form.

Initial Hobbesian statement. Hobbes is the first major philosopher, apart from Machiavelli, to present a completely individualist picture of human nature. There are at least three sources of Hobbes's individualism. First, there is his reading of political experience. His translation of Thucydides reveals his preoccupation with the topic of civil war, with the struggle of one private interest against another. Second, there is Hobbes's commitment to the Galilean resoluto-compositive method of explanation: to explain is to resolve a complex whole into its individual parts and to show how the individual parts must be combined in order to reconstruct the whole. To explain the complex whole of social life is, therefore, to resolve it into its component parts, individual men, and to show how individuals must combine if social life is to be reconstructed. Since the individuals in terms of whose coming together social life is to be explained must be presocial individuals, they must lack those characteristics which belong to the compromises of social life and be governed only by their presocial drives. Third, there is the detail of the Hobbesian psychology, which insists that such drives must be competitive and aggressive because of the will to power over other men which ceaselessly and restlessly drives men forward.

Thus, from all three sources arises a picture of human nature as essentially individual, nonsocial, competitive, and aggressive. From this view it follows that the apparent altruism and benevolence of men in many situations need to be explained; the Hobbesian explanation is simply that what appears to be altruism is always in fact, in one way or another, disguised self-seeking. Undisguised, unmodified self-seeking leads to total social war. The fear of such war leads to the adoption of a regard for others from purely self-interested motives. John Aubrey in his sketch of Hobbes in *Brief Lives* tells of an exchange between Hobbes and a clergyman who had just seen Hobbes give alms to a beggar. The clergyman inquired whether Hobbes would have given alms if Jesus had not commanded it; Hobbes's reply was that by giving alms to the beggar, he not only relieved the man's distress but he also relieved his own distress at seeing the beggar's distress. This anecdote compresses the central problem into a single point: Given that human nature is competitive and self-seeking, why and how can altruism and benevolence be treated as virtues? One's immediate response to this brief and cryptic statement of the problem may well be to inquire why—if one does not share Hobbes's premises—one should take it as given that human nature is essentially self-seeking. To this one replies by posing another question: How can any actual or possible object or state of affairs provide me with a motive, appear to me as good or desirable, unless it appears to be what will satisfy some desire of mine? If the (necessary and sufficient) condition of an object's providing me with a motive is that it satisfy some desire of mine, then it will surely be the case that all my actions will have as their goal the satisfaction of my desires. And to seek only to satisfy my own desires is surely to have an entirely self-seeking nature.

Eighteenth-century restatements. The root of the problem lies in the apparently egoistic implications of the psychological framework within which the questions of moral philosophy have been posed by a whole tradition of British thinkers from Hobbes on. Within this framework philosophers have oscillated between two positions: the Hobbesian doctrine of altruism as either a disguise or a substitute for self-seeking and the assertion of an original spring of altruistic benevolence as an ultimate and unexplained property in human nature.

On the one side we find, for example, Shaftesbury, who argues that men are so contrived that there is no conflict, but an identity, between what will satisfy self-interest and what will be for the good of others; the practice of benevolence is what satisfies man's natural bent. Bernard Mandeville, in *The Grumbling Hive, or Knaves Turn'd Honest* (later retitled *The Fable of the Bees: or, Private Vices, Public Benefits*), argues by contrast that the only spur to action is private, individual self-seeking and that it is for the public and general good that this is so. Francis Hutcheson, who treats benevolence as constituting the whole of virtue, provides no argument to back up his view, nor does he explain why we approve of benevolence rather than of self-interest.

Butler. Bishop Butler's position is at once more complex and more interesting than Hutcheson's or Mandeville's. Butler believes that we have a variety of separate and independent "appetites, passions and affections." Of these, self-love is only one, and it is not necessarily opposed to benevolence. We satisfy the desire for our own happiness in part, but only in part, by seeking the happiness of others. A man who inhibits those desires of his which find their satisfaction in achieving the happiness of others will not in fact make himself happy. By refusing to be benevolent, he damages his own self-interest and disobeys the call of self-love. Cool and reasonable self-love consists in guiding our actions by reference to a hierarchy of principles; supreme among these is moral reflection or conscience, by means of which human nature is defined and the good that will satisfy it discerned. Thus, self-love itself refers us to the arbitration of conscience, which in turn prescribes that extent and degree of benevolence which will satisfy the needs of self-love.

The chief objection to Butler is likely to arise from the apparently self-enclosed character of his account. In Butler's system the harmony between self-love and benevolence appears to reign by definition rather than in fact, that is, in human nature itself. But this criticism misconstrues Butler's stand, although we can deduce from Butler's psychology empirical consequences of a testable kind which at first sight render it liable to refutation by the facts. For if Butler is correct, those who are benevolent to the required degree do not find their benevolence at odds with their self-interest. In this sense, at least, virtue and happiness may be required to coincide, and if they do not coincide, Butler's view of human nature is false. But Butler allows himself an escape clause. He concedes that in the world as we know it, the pursuit of self-interest and devotion to benevolence may not appear to coincide, but, he says, the divergence seems to exist only if we do not allow for divine providence, which ensures that the world to come will be such as to ensure that self-interest and altruistic benevolence required the same actions of us.

Theology and the long run. In contrast with Hobbes's view that altruistic behavior (or at least just behavior) is in our immediate interest as a means of preserving ourselves from the war of all against all and in contrast with Butler's view that benevolence and self-interest are two distinct springs of action that move us to the same actions, there is the view that benevolence is to our long-term, as opposed to our short-term, self-interest. Butler, as already noted, uses something like this view to supplement his basic position, but it is the stock in trade of a form of theological egoistic utilitarianism to be found in Abraham Tucker and William Paley.

In both writers the crucial psychological premise is that men are so constructed that they always pursue their own private and individual satisfaction. In both writers the fundamental moral rule is an injunction to universal benevolence, which is equated with the promotion of the greatest happiness of the greatest number. The problem is how, given the character of human nature, a motive can be found for obeying the fundamental moral rule. The solution is to say that God has so contrived the afterlife that only if we obey the fundamental moral rule will we in the long run, that is, in the eternal run, secure our own happiness. In Paley it is clear that we could find no good reason to be moral if God did not exist, but God's function in bridging the gulf between self-interest and morality is veiled in conventional theological terms. In Tucker's *The Light of Nature Pursued* the account of how God bridges the gulf is more explicit. God has arranged that all the happiness that men either have enjoyed or will enjoy is deposited in what he calls "the bank of the universe." By working to increase the happiness of others, I increase the amount of happiness so deposited. But by increasing the general stock of happiness, I also increase my own happiness, for God has arranged to divide this stock of happiness into equal shares, to be allotted one to a person, and so by increasing the size of the general stock, I also increase the size of my own share. I am, as it were, a shareholder in a cosmic bank of which God is at once the chairman and the managing director.

Tucker's absurdities, though unimportant in detail, do bring out how impossible is the task of reconciling an egoistic theory of human nature with a moral theory of benevolent utilitarianism. Of such impossibilites are absurdities born; to this the secular utilitarianism of Hume, Bentham, Mill, and Sidgwick is as much a witness as is the theological utilitarianism of Tucker and Paley.

Hume and the utilitarians. Hume's initial approach to the problem is as flexible and undogmatic as that of any philosopher. In the ***Treatise of Human Nature*** Hume poses the question why we approve and obey rules which it is often in our interest to break. He makes no assumptions of the kind found in other eighteenth-century writers (men are entirely ruled by self-interest). He merely remarks, apparently on empirical grounds, that it is often the case that self-interest would, if it were followed, lead us to disregard the rules of justice. Nor does he invoke any compensating natural regard for the interests of others. We do have some regard for the interests of others, but it varies with the closeness of their ties to us, and we have by nature no regard for the public interest as such. "In general, it may be affirm'd that there is no such passion in human minds as the love of mankind, merely as such, independent of personal qualities, of services, or of relation to oneself" (***Treatise,*** Bk. III, Part II, Sec. i).

If, then, self-interest would lead us to disobey the rules of justice and if we have no natural regard for the public interest, how do the rules come into existence, and what fosters our respect for them? The crucial fact is that did we not have respect for the rules of justice, there would be no stability of property. Indeed, the institution of property could not and would not exist. Now the existence of property and its stability is to all our interests, and we are always conscious of how much we are injured by others failing to observe the rules. So we have become conscious that although our immediate and short-term benefit rests in breaking the rules on a given occasion, our long-term benefit resides in insisting upon a universal observance of the rules.

By the time Hume came to write the *Enquiry Concerning Human Understanding,* he had shifted his ground. He now sees self-interest and "a tendency to public good, and to the promoting of peace, harmony, and order in society" as two independent, coexistent springs of action; he sees the independent power of sympathy and of a sense of the public good, rather than a rational view of what is of long-term benefit to self-interest, as moving us to benevolence and altruism.

Bentham, Grote, Mill, Sidgwick. The utilitarians present the problem in terms differing somewhat from those of Hume because they were more rigidly committed to a psychology derived from Hartley, according to which only pleasure and pain ever move us to action. In this psychology both "pleasure" and "pain" are the names of sensations. Clearly in this view the only pleasure whose prospect attracts me is *my* pleasure, and the only pain the prospect of which repels me is *my* pain. It seems to follow that all action is egoistically motivated, yet all four utilitarian writers make "the greatest happiness of the greatest number" either the only criterion of action or at least a central criterion. How can so egoistically motivated an agent as the utilitarians assume consult the general happiness? That he will have to learn to do so is what Bentham takes for granted in his legal and political writings. Bentham provides for inducements which will counteract the self-interest of legislators, for example. He affirms expressly that "the only interest which a man is at all times sure to find adequate motives for consulting is his own." But in the *Deontology* he seems by contrast to take it for granted that the pursuit of *my* pleasure and the pursuit of the greatest happiness of the greatest number will always as a matter of fact coincide.

This assumption of coincidence is abandoned by John Grote, who tries to minimize the difficulties by reducing our obligation to consult the general happiness to an injunction to consult the general happiness insofar as to do so will ensure our own happiness. Yet even Grote presupposes that, for the most part and generally, my happiness and that of the greatest number will not conflict.

J. S. Mill's arguments are of two kinds. He first argues that pleasure and the absence of pain are desired by all; here what is meant is clearly that each desires his own pleasure. The proof, and the only possible proof, that pleasure is desirable is that all men desire it, and since all men do desire it, it must be admitted to be desirable. Hence, everyone must acknowledge that it is desirable to produce as much pleasure as possible, and here what is clearly meant is that each ought to desire the pleasure of all. The fallacy in the transition from the premise that each desires his own pleasure to the conclusion that each ought to desire the pleasure of all is usually thought to reside in the transition from fact to value, but it lies, rather, in the transition from an assertion about the agent's *own* pleasure to conclusions about the *general* happiness.

However, elsewhere in *Utilitarianism* Mill faces the difficulties in such a transition explicitly. He reproduces familiar arguments in an interesting form. The feelings of sympathy which Hume stressed in the *Enquiry* reappear as a man's "feeling of unity with his fellow-creatures." A man who has this feeling has a "natural want" to live in harmony with others. It is often overshadowed by selfish emotions, but those who do possess it know that they would be worse off if they did not possess it. The reason for this conviction is that the best prospect of realizing such happiness as is attainable is a willingness to sacrifice the prospects of one's own present and immediate happiness to an ascetic devotion to altruism and benevolence. Henry Sidgwick became conscious of the difficulties which Mill brushes aside in this account. In the *Methods of Ethics,* however, Sidgwick could find no way to make the transition from the desire for one's own pleasure to that for the general happiness, and these remain for him independent goals, as they had been for some eighteenth-century philosophers.

The problem in empirical psychology. The philosophers from Hobbes to Sidgwick who analyze the concepts of egoism, altruism, and sympathy often write as if they were empirical students of human nature, disputing the facts of human action and motivation. But it is more illuminating to read them as offering conceptual accounts of what it is to have a good reason for action and of what the limits upon the range of possible good reasons are. But so closely allied are conceptual and empirical issues at this point in the argument that it is not surprising to find that the would-be empirical accounts which psychologists claim to have derived from observation should sometimes turn out to be a rendering of conceptual schemes which have already been encountered in philosophy. So it is with Freud, most strikingly in his earlier writings. The important place in Freudian theory held by the pleasure principle, the concepts of gratification and of libido, and the consequent view of socialization all lead to a theory in which the gratification of the self is primary and in which altruism and benevolence are interpreted as secondary phenomena which acquire the regard that they do because they are originally associated with forms of self-gratification. Freud's genetic account differs in detail from that given by J. S. Mill, but the form of the account is the same. Nor is this accidental; the pre-Freudian psychologies of Hartley, who influenced Mill, and of Bain, Mill's contemporary offer associationist accounts in which the genetic order is the same as it is in Freud. There is, therefore, not only the task of clarifying the concepts involved in these accounts, but also the task of settling how far the issues raised are genuinely empirical and how far genuinely conceptual. The concepts in need of clarification are of five kinds: the nature of desire; self-interest; altruism and benevolence; motives, actions, and sympathies; and the genetic fallacy.

Nature of desire. If I want something, it does not follow that I want it because it will give me pleasure to have it or because it is a means of getting something further which will give me pleasure. It is, of course, true that if I get what I want, I have thereby satisfied one of my wants. Having any of my wants unsatisfied is certainly less satisfactory than having them satisfied, but it is not necessarily painful or even unpleasant. So it is neither true that I necessarily desire pleasure nor true that in seeking to satisfy my desires, I necessarily seek pleasure or the avoidance of pain.

Moreover, if I do something, it does not follow that I do it because I want to, let alone that I do it because I shall get pleasure from it. It has sometimes been suggested that the performance of an action is itself an adequate criterion of the agent's wanting to do whatever it is, and those who hold this view interpret such an expression as "doing what one does not want to do" when it is applied in cases of action under duress as meaning that the agent would not want to perform that particular action normally but does want to do it on this occasion rather than endure the threatened consequences of not doing it. This contention is less than self-evident. Moreover, if there is a sense of "want" such that if I do something, it is thereby true that I want to do it, that sense is a weaker and a different one from that given when I explain what I do by citing as a, or the, reason that I want to do it. For it is precisely because we have independent criteria for asserting that the agent did or did not want to do what he did that the want can be cited as an explanation for the action.

Action, desire, and pleasure, then, do not stand in so close a conceptual relationship that we cannot ask as a matter of contingent fact on any given occasion whether a man acted to get pleasure or whether he did what he did because he wanted to or not. To understand this is a necessary preliminary to understanding the notion of self-interest.

Self-interest. What is to my interest depends upon who I am and what I want. This elementary but too often unnoticed truism underlies one of Socrates' implied answers to Thrasymachus in Plato's *Republic*. The question "Is justice more profitable than injustice?" will, as Plato makes clear, be answered differently depending upon whether it is answered by a just man or an unjust man. For what the just man wants is not what the unjust man wants. Thus, there is not a single spring of action or a single set of aims and goals entitled "self-interest" which is the same in every man. "Self-interest" is not in fact the name of a motive at all. A man who acts from self-interest is a man who allows himself to act from certain motives in a given type of situation. The same action done from the same motive in another type of situation would not be correctly characterized as done from self-interest. So if I eat to sate my hunger or do my job well in order to succeed, I do not necessarily act from self-interest. It is only when I am in a situation where food is short or my rising in the world requires a disregard for the legitimate claims of others that to consult only my hunger or my ambition becomes to act from self-interest. The notion of self-interest therefore has application not to human behavior in general but to a certain type of human situation, namely, one in which behavior can be either competitive or noncompetitive. Equally, in this type of situation alone can the notions of benevolence and altruism have application. Therefore, it is to the elucidation of these that we must next turn.

Altruism and benevolence. The question canvassed in the eighteenth century whether benevolence might not be the whole of virtue could have been raised only in an age in which the concept of virtue had been greatly narrowed or the concept of benevolence had been greatly widened or both. For in most of my dealings with others of a cooperative kind, questions of benevolence or altruism simply do not arise, any more than questions of self-interest do. In my social life I cannot but be involved in reciprocal relationships, in which it may certainly be conceded that the price I have to pay for self-seeking behavior is a loss of certain kinds of relationships. But if I want to lead a certain kind of life, with relationships of trust, friendship, and cooperation with others, then my wanting their good and my wanting my good are not two independent, discriminable desires. It is not even that I have two separate motives, self-interest and benevolence, for doing the same action. I have one motive, a desire to live in a certain way, which cannot be characterized as a desire for my good rather than that of others. For the good that I recognize and pursue is not mine particularly, except in the sense that I recognize and pursue it.

We can now diagnose one major cause of confusion in the whole discussion. All too often from Hobbes on, a special type of human situation has been treated as a paradigm of the whole moral life—that is, a situation in which I and someone else have incompatible aims and my aims are connected only with my own well-being. Of course, such situations do arise, but the clash between self-interest and benevolence which characterizes them is only one case out of many in which incompatible aims have to be resolved.

Motives, actions, and sympathy. We can now understand that at the root of the confusions lies a belief in the possibility of a purely a priori characterization of human motives. From Hobbes on there has been a tradition, shared by empiricists as well as by their critics, which seeks to discuss human motivation almost entirely in the light of general conceptual considerations about desires, the passions, and pleasure and pain. What evades this tradition is not only the variety of aims and motives which can inform action, a variety to be discovered only by empirical inspection, but also the specific and particular character of certain motives.

The difficulties in the notion of sympathy, for example, are such that one cannot inquire straightforwardly whether there is or is not a sympathy for mankind as such. To say that a man acted from sympathy is always to refer to a set of particular occasions when sympathy was aroused for particular people in some particular plight. How wide the range of a man's sympathies is, is an empirical fact, and there is no conceptual limit to the possibilities. But it is a conceptual point that just as a generalized ambition can be manifested only in particular aspirations, so a generalized sympathy can be manifested only in particular acts of charity and benevolence. Now, suppose a man to perform a charitable and benevolent action; we would be wrong to suppose that we can always answer the question whether he was sympathetic to them because they were his relations (or his countrymen or his next-door neighbors) or whether he would have been equally sympathetic if they had been strangers or foreigners. A man can act out of sympathy without the range of his sympathies being determinate. Thus, the eighteenth-century question whether there is, as such, a general benevolence toward mankind implanted in human breasts is misleading.

Genetic fallacy. The question of innate benevolence toward mankind is also misleading because the eighteenth-century view disregards both the variety and the variability of human nature. Philosophers discuss what passions men have and not what passions they might acquire. Learning is, at best, peripheral to their inquiry; insofar as it does enter, there is another fallacy in writers from Hobbes on—that of confusing the question of what motives there were originally (for Hobbes, in the state of nature; for Freud, in early childhood) with the question of what the fundamental character of motives is now, in adult life. Because the instinctual drives and desires of young children have to be socialized, it does not follow that adult attitudes and emotions are only masks for such drives and desires. This is not to say that they cannot be such masks, but if the notion is to have any content, whether they are must be an empirical question.

Bibliography

Broad, C. D., "Certain Features in Moore's Ethical Doctrines," in Paul A. Schilpp, ed., *The Philosophy of G. E. Moore*. Evanston, Ill., 1942. Pp. 43–57.

Broad, C. D., *Five Types of Ethical Theory*. London, 1930. Pp. 161–177.

Brunton, J. A., "Egoism and Morality." *Philosophical Quarterly*, Vol. 6 (1956), 289–303.

Ewing, A. C., *Ethics*. London, 1953. Ch. 2.

Medlin, B., "Ultimate Principles and Ethical Egoism." *Australasian Journal of Philosophy*, Vol. 35 (1957), 111–118.

Moore, G. E., *Principia Ethica*. Cambridge, 1903; paperback, 1959.

Rashdall, Hastings, *Theory of Good and Evil*. Oxford, 1924. Vol. I, pp. 44–63.

Sharp, F. C., *Ethics*. New York, 1928. Chs. 22–23.

ALASDAIR MACINTYRE

EHRENFELS, CHRISTIAN FREIHERR VON (1859–1932), Austrian psychologist and philosopher, was born in Rodaun near Vienna. He studied at the University of Vienna under Franz Brentano and Alexius Meinong, and took his doctorate at Graz in 1885. He taught at Vienna as a *Privatdozent* from 1888 to 1896, when he became extraordinary professor at the German University of Prague. He was a full professor at Prague from 1900 until 1929. Besides his professional work, Ehrenfels wrote two essays on Richard Wagner and several plays.

Gestalt psychology. In psychology, Ehrenfels is best remembered for inaugurating gestalt psychology in his article "Über Gestaltqualitäten" (1890). Starting from Ernst Mach's thesis in his *Beiträge zur Analyse der Empfindungen* (Jena, 1886), that we can sense (*empfinden*) spatial and temporal forms ("wholes," *Gestalten*), Ehrenfels argued that sensing is limited to the present but that the apprehension of a complex datum requires recollection and so seems to lack the immediacy of sensing. This is particularly evident in the case of acoustic data, but it also holds for visual data perused successively. The immediate apprehension of a melody or a figure must therefore be otherwise accounted for than by sensing. Discussing acoustic complexes, Ehrenfels showed that what is in fact apprehended differs from the complex or sum of the component elements, since these vary while the gestalt remains unchanged. This is corroborated by the fact that acoustic forms (melodies) are more easily remembered than are tonal intervals or absolute pitch. Similarly, figures do not depend for their apprehension on absolute location. This implies that gestalt qualities are positive representational contents bound up with the occurrence in consciousness of complexes consisting of separable elements. In Meinong's language (adopted by Ehrenfels in a later paper), they are "founded contents" (*fundierte Inhalte*).

Ehrenfels' notion of gestalt was essentially developed from a differential analysis of data, complex, and unity, unity being regarded as a quality. The phenomenological account of a gestalt in terms of contrast, background, and poignancy—features essential to subsequent gestalt psychology—was secondary in Ehrenfels' analysis, although he did mention such features.

Ehrenfels extended the notion of gestalt to numbers and to the field of logic. He viewed the contradiction in such concepts as that of a round square as a temporal gestalt quality of the psychic process of attempting to form a representation of the concept, an attempt that proves unfeasible. Ehrenfels also used the notion of gestalt in cases, such as phenomena of style and behavior, in which an analysis into component elements is practically impossible. In general, a gestalt is a novel and creative feature with respect to its component elements (in contrast to Hume, who admitted only the composition of impressions or ideas and imaginative interpolation within the continuum of sensory qualities).

Value theory. Ehrenfels made important contributions to value theory and ethics. His series of articles, "Werttheorie und Ethik," although inspired by Meinong's lectures, was published before Meinong's ethical works and possessed at least partial originality. Ehrenfels' subsequent *System der Werttheorie* (1897–1898) discussed points of difference with Meinong's first publications on value theory. Ehrenfels defined value as "the relation, erroneously objectified by language, of a thing to a desire directed towards it" ("Werttheorie und Ethik," in *Vierteljahrsschrift für wissenschaftliche Philosophie*, Vol. 17, p. 89) or to a disposition of desire or feeling (*ibid.*, pp. 209–210). "The value of a thing is its desirability" (*System der Werttheorie*, Vol. I, p. 53). Ehrenfels took value not simply as instrumental to the promotion of one's happiness but insisted that instrumental value (*Wirkungswert*) is valuable only relative to intrinsic value (*Eigenwert*). We desire the existence or nonexistence of something, and do not necessarily strive for its possession as a means to our happiness. The valuable object is not bound up with utility (*Nutzen*) but possesses a more general fittingness (*Frommen*) for us. Ehrenfels adapted the economic theory of marginal utility to explain the strength of any desires possessing a fittingness for us (*Grenzfrommen*). He thus introduced a quantitative element of valuation: Values and valuation are conditioned by the prior existence of other value objects.

In view of their dependence on emotional dispositions, values have a certain relativity, but there exists wide agreement among human beings as to the value of pleasure and pain and of certain other psychic phenomena, both in ourselves and in others. We value those valuational dispositions of others that are directed toward objects valued by us. In fact, Ehrenfels restricted intrinsic values to psychic realities.

The relativity of values is also apparent in changes in valuation brought about by various causes. Ehrenfels also distinguished trends of valuation, for which he offered a theoretical scheme. Means may turn into ends, as when the satisfaction of feelings of hunger replaces nourishment as the end of eating. By contrast, superior values may feature as ends, as when in the interest of nourishment we suppress our feelings of hunger in the presence of poisonous food. A third factor in trends of value is survival, which is best assured if the object serving it coincides with it. Ends transcending mere survival are exemplified in cultural progress, in which values become nonindividualistic. Superior nonindividualistic values are transmitted through example and suggestion, and cause further value promotion in a value milieu. Ehrenfels found reason to believe that with the increasing integration of human knowledge an upward trend toward superior values could be expected.

Social ethics. Ehrenfels' theory of value formed the basis for his ethics, which he subdivided into social and individual ethics. Social ethics is concerned with ethical valuation, that is, valuation of psychic (or supposedly psychic) objects that are causally related to certain actions. These objects are intrinsic values, and we demand that a plurality of individuals coincide in their valuation of them. The ultimate object of ethical valuation is not action, or its means or ends, but the desiderative and emotional disposition behind it. It is then called moral (or immoral) disposition, and its valuation moral (or immoral) valuation. (Accordingly, morality is distinguished from law and custom, which do not consider disposition.) Moral dispositions are the emotional dispositions of taking pleasure in others as intrinsic values, that is, as individuals themselves possessing a disposition toward actions serving intrinsic values, particularly the dispositions of love of one's neighbor, of mankind, of God. Such pleasure in others psychologically depends on an awareness of them in thought or in more or less vivid representation. There is a perspective of comparative closeness or distance in valuation. Among other moral dispositions are justice, constancy, and honesty, and their negative counterparts.

Individual ethics. Individual ethics is concerned with man's response, through "mystical" or "tragic elevation," to his fate as a finite body. The craving for such elevation is the source of the valuations (ethical sanction, conscience) of whatever goes to promote it. These private valuations do not strictly encompass the socioethical ones, but do as a matter of fact coincide with them. Ehrenfels' individual ethics thus was a separate strain centering on an aesthetic desire for psychic harmony. To reach such a state, belief in God or metaphysical convictions are helpful though not indispensable.

Sexual and racial views. Ehrenfels' tendency to emphasize biological factors led him in later writings ("Sexuales Ober- und Unterbewusstsein," 1903/04; *Sexualethik*, 1907; "Sexualmoral der Zukunft, 1930; *cf.* the earlier statement in "Werttheorie und Ethik," *Vierteljahrsschrift für wissenschaftliche Philosophie*, Vol. 17, p. 354) to question moral restraint on sexuality and to advocate greater frankness, honesty, and delicacy in marital relations. He won Freud's praise for his pioneering work in this field. His biological tendency also led him to recommend selective breeding practices for man (*cf.* "Die sexuale Reform," 1903/04) and to embrace ideas bordering on race prejudice ("Leitziele zur Rassenbewertung," 1911).

Metaphysics. In his *Kosmogonie* (1916) Ehrenfels contributed to metaphysics a theory of the origin of the world. Rejecting a monism which admits only the cumulative effects of accidental events, he regarded the origin of the world as the result of the interaction of two principles, a principle of chaotic disorder and a principle of psychoid unity of gestalt that, with infinite improbability but with infinite time to allow for its incipience, has been solicited by the opposing principle. Once the principle of unity has been engaged, the resulting gestalt survives because it is infinitely improbable that chaos is capable of continuous destructive action of its own even in infinite time. The gestalt principle, in turn, is credited with creativity, making for further development. Ehrenfels' cosmogony can be taken as a speculative abstraction intended to put the theory of evolution on a new footing in that it tries to give a plausible account of emerging nonrandomness in the universe.

Works by Ehrenfels

"Über Gestaltqualitäten." *Vierteljahrsschrift für wissenschaftliche Philosophie*, Vol. 14 (1890), 249–292.

"Werttheorie und Ethik." *Vierteljahrsschrift für wissenschaftliche Philosophie*, Vol. 17 (1893), 26–110, 200–266, 321–363, 413–425; Vol. 18 (1894), 22–97. Five consecutive articles.

System der Werttheorie, 2 vols. Leipzig, 1897–1898.

"Sexuales Ober- und Unterbewusstsein." *Politisch-anthropologische Revue*, Vol. 2 (1903/04), 456–476.

"Die sexuale Reform." *Politisch-anthropologische Revue*, Vol. 2 (1903/04), 970–994.

Sexualethik. Wiesbaden, 1907.

"Leitziele zur Rassenbewertung." *Archiv für Rassen- und Gesellschaftsbiologie*, Vol. 8 (1911), 59–71.

Kosmogonie. Jena, 1916.

"Sexualmoral der Zukunft." *Archiv für Rassen- und Gesellschaftsbiologie*, Vol. 22 (1930), 292–304.

Works on Ehrenfels

Eaton, Howard O., *The Austrian Philosophy of Values.* Norman, Okla., 1930.

Meister, Richard, "Ehrenfels," in *Neue deutsche Biographie.* Berlin, 1959. Vol. IV, pp. 352–353.

Orestano, Francesco, *I valori umani* (Vols. XII and XIII of his *Opere complete*), 2 vols. Milan, 1942. Vol. I, pp. 69–102, 123–126; Vol. II, pp. 46–101.

Varet, Gilbert, *Manuel de bibliographie philosophique.* Paris, 1956. Vol. II, p. 877, note.

KLAUS HARTMANN

EINSTEIN, ALBERT (1879–1955), creator of the special and general theories of relativity and one of the greatest natural philosophers of all time, was born of Jewish parents in Ulm, Germany. When he was a year old, his family moved to Munich, where Einstein's father and uncle ran a small electrochemical factory. In 1894 this business collapsed, and the family moved to Milan. Einstein had already begun to study theoretical physics seriously, and on his father's advice to enter a technological institute he sought admission to the Swiss Federal Polytechnic in Zurich. He failed the entrance examination but passed it a year later (1896) and was admitted as a student of mathematics and physics.

After graduating, Einstein had great difficulty in obtaining employment, although he had become a Swiss citizen, but in 1902 he was appointed to a post in the patent office in Bern. Soon afterward he married Mileva Maritsch, who had been a fellow student at Zurich.

Einstein's move to Bern was a turning point in his life. At the patent office his work consisted mainly in determining the basic ideas involved in applications for patents, and it may well have been this training that developed his remarkable faculty for seeing to the heart of a problem. The work was not arduous and left him with ample time for his own researches. In 1905 he published in *Annalen der Physik* four papers of major importance, including his first memoirs on special relativity, which attracted widespread attention. As a result, attempts were made to obtain a university appointment for him, but it was not until 1909 that he was elected to a professorship in the University of Zurich. A year later he accepted a chair in the German University of Prague. In 1912 he was appointed professor of theoretical physics in the Federal Polytechnic in Zurich.

By this time Einstein was regarded as the rising star of theoretical physics. At the end of 1913 he was invited to Berlin as a member of the Royal Prussian Academy of Sciences and of the Kaiser Wilhelm Gesellschaft, which had recently been founded as a center of research institutes. He was also offered a chair at the University of Berlin with no obligations, so that he could concentrate on research. On moving to Berlin he separated from his wife, and after their divorce in 1919 he married his cousin, Elsa Einstein.

Soon after his arrival in Berlin, Einstein published his general theory of relativity (the main paper being "Die Grundlage der allgemeinen Relativitätstheorie," in *An-*

nalen der Physik, August 1916, 769–822). This marked a major advance beyond the classical gravitational theory of Newton. One of the predictions of the new theory concerned the deflection of light in a gravitational field. In particular, a ray of light coming from a star and passing near the sun should be deflected through an angle of about 1.75 seconds of arc. This prediction was tested by two British eclipse expeditions during the solar eclipse of May 1919, and the results appeared to be in good accord with Einstein's theory. The report of the British astronomers to the Royal Society in London later that year laid the foundations for Einstein's world fame. In November 1922 he was awarded a Nobel prize.

Despite his great reputation, there were occasional expressions in Germany of hostile feeling against Einstein because he was a Jew and a pacifist. Nevertheless, he acquired German citizenship. In the early 1930s he spent the winters as visiting professor at the California Institute of Technology, and so he was abroad when Hitler came to power in Germany in January 1933. Later that year Einstein accepted a permanent appointment at the Institute for Advanced Study at Princeton. He became an American citizen in 1941 and remained in the United States for the rest of his life.

Photons and molecules. Although best known for his work in relativity, Einstein made other important contributions to theoretical physics. In 1905 he extended Planck's hypothesis (first made in 1900) of the discontinuous character of the emission and absorption of radiation by atoms to the nature of radiation itself ("Einen die Erzengen und Verwandlung des Lichtes betreffenden heuristischen Gesichtspunkt," in *Annalen der Physik,* Vol. 17, 1905, 132–148). He showed that radiation has a corpuscular as well as a wavelike aspect; thus, he can be regarded as the discoverer of the photon, or light corpuscle.

In another paper ("Die von der molekularkinetischen Theorie der Warme geforderten Bewegung von in ruhenden Flüsigkeiten suspendierten Teilchen," in *Annalen der Physik,* Vol. 17, 1905, 549–560) Einstein turned his attention to the Brownian motion. This is named for the Scottish botanist Robert Brown, who in 1828 had observed that even in the absence of currents and other external disturbances, pollen grains suspended in water can be seen under the microscope to be continually moving in an irregular zigzag fashion. Einstein showed how this motion can be used as direct evidence for the existence of molecules, a question still in dispute at that time. He argued that although the velocity of a suspended particle caused by collisions with the molecules of the liquid is unobservable, the effect of a succession of irregular displacements can be detected with a microscope, as Brown had observed. From the philosophical point of view, Einstein's investigation is of interest because it helped to convince physicists of the importance of probability in relation to natural laws. Nevertheless, Einstein always believed that the ultimate laws are essentially causal and deterministic and that it is only our inability to deal with large numbers of particles in any other way that compels us to use statistical methods.

Special relativity. Important as these papers were, they were overshadowed by two other papers of the same year in which Einstein set forth the subject that is now known as the special theory of relativity ("Zur Elektrodynamik bewegter Körper," in *Annalen der Physik,* Vol. 17, 1905, 132–148; "Ist die Tragheit eines Körpers von seinem Energieinhalt abhängig?" in *Annalen der Physik,* Vol. 18, 639–641). Newtonian dynamics was based on the assumption that the laws of motion are the same with respect to all inertial frames of reference. (These frames are all in uniform relative motion, including relative rest.) Associated with this postulate is the experimental fact that no mechanical experiment can be performed to determine the absolute velocity of any inertial frame. Maxwell's theory of electromagnetism, however, introduced a special velocity—namely, the velocity c of electromagnetic waves (which include light waves) in "empty space." In accordance with the prevailing mechanistic philosophy of physics, these waves were regarded as oscillations in a peculiar universal medium called the ether, and this medium seemed to provide a standard of absolute rest. In particular, it should have been possible by an optical experiment to determine the motion of the earth through the ether. A famous experiment with this object was made by A. A. Michelson and E. W. Morley in 1887, but a null result was obtained. Attempts were made to explain this result, but it was Einstein who first went to the heart of the matter.

Einstein realized that the trouble was due to having introduced the idea of the ether as the medium of the transmission of light, for the laws of electromagnetism, like the laws of dynamics, must be the same in all frames of reference in uniform relative motion and therefore do not permit us to measure an absolute velocity. The French mathematician Henri Poincaré had already introduced this principle of (special) relativity in 1904, but he did not go on to construct a theory of relativity. Unlike Einstein, he failed to realize that this principle implied the rejection of the ether concept, which he thought must still be retained as a mechanical basis for the transmission of light.

Einstein unconditionally accepted the principle of relativity as a fundamental general law of physics and regarded it as a more suitable starting point for the study of physical phenomena than Newton's laws. It was this attitude toward relativity more than anything else that made Einstein's theory so difficult for older physicists to accept. Instead of reducing optics to mechanics, Einstein sought to base both on the same general law. According to the principle of relativity, light should have the same properties for all observers in uniform relative motion, and, as Einstein realized, its velocity (*in vacuo*) should therefore be the same for all such observers. This conclusion, however, was not compatible with the traditional idea of relative motion.

Einstein decided that the difficulty could be overcome only by abandoning the Newtonian concept of time. This assumed that a meaning could be automatically attached to the idea that two events in different places are simultaneous. Instead, Einstein argued that the only events that we can directly judge to be simultaneous occur in our immediate neighborhood. When we observe a distant event, we can infer its time of occurrence only by invoking assumptions concerning its distance and the velocity of light. The concept of world-wide simultaneity is therefore not a primitive idea like local simultaneity but an idea that depends on a postulate concerning light and our rules of measurement.

The reasoning that led Einstein to recognize this fundamental point was stimulated by his interest in philosophy. The philosophers who helped him most to develop his critical powers were Hume and Mach. Hume impressed Einstein by his penetrating criticism of traditional common-sense assumptions and dogmas. Mach's influence was more complex. Einstein did not accept his view that the laws of physics are only summaries of experimental results, for he believed that these laws also involve factors contributed by the human mind. He was, however, in sympathy with Mach's critical examination of Newtonian mechanics and his rejection of Newton's belief that space and time are absolute, existing in their own right irrespective of all physical phenomena. In particular, he agreed with Mach that it was not necessary to invoke the idea of absolute space to explain the existence of inertial systems and to account for the difference between rotating and nonrotating bodies, since all motion could be regarded as occurring relative to the stellar universe. Mach's criticism of Newton's absolute space contributed to Einstein's rejection of the luminiferous ether.

Einstein's theory implies that observers in uniform motion relative to one another will, in general, assign different times to the same event and that a moving clock will appear to run slow compared with an identical clock at relative rest. Also, a body in relative motion will be regarded as having a shorter length in the direction of its motion than it has for an observer for whom it is at relative rest. These effects, however, become appreciable only when the relative velocity is a significant fraction of the velocity of light. Nevertheless, they imply that all statements concerning space and time have a meaning only when referred to a definite observer.

Moreover, Einstein discovered that Newton's laws of mechanics must be modified for rapidly moving bodies. The inertial mass of a body must increase when its velocity increases, with the result that no particle of matter can ever attain the velocity of light. (Indeed, the velocity of light plays the role of a limiting velocity in Einstein's theory, signifying the fastest rate at which information can be conveyed.) The dependence of mass on velocity led Einstein to conclude that mass and energy are both manifestations of the same fundamental entity. This hypothesis has received impressive confirmation in nuclear physics and has resolved the problem of the origin of the sun's radiation.

General relativity. Einstein's original restriction of the principle of relativity to observers in uniform relative motion was in accordance with the Newtonian idea that there is a fundamental difference between accelerated and uniform motion, the former being associated with the action of force and the latter with the absence of force. However, the only way in which a meaningful distinction could be drawn between accelerated and uniform motion as such was by reference to absolute space, a concept that Einstein wished to eliminate from physics. He therefore sought to extend the principle of relativity to frames of reference (and observers) in all types of relative motion. In his "The Foundation of the General Theory of Relativity," published in 1916, he asserted that the laws of nature should be expressed in a form that is the same for any choice of space and time coordinates. An infinity of laws can be so expressed, but Einstein's object was to find the laws that in this general covariant form are the simplest possible.

At the same time, Einstein also sought to eliminate the concept of force and was successful in the case of gravitation, for which he was able to devise a purely geometrical theory. The peculiarity of a gravitational field is that locally (in a small region where it can be regarded as uniform) all bodies fall with the same acceleration and so are unaccelerated relative to one another. Motion in a uniform gravitational field is therefore equivalent to uniform motion with respect to a frame of reference that has the corresponding acceleration. It had been shown in 1908 by the mathematician Hermann Minkowski that all uniform motions can be described purely geometrically by straight lines in a particular four-dimensional type of space, known as "flat" space time, which plays a role in special relativity similar to that of absolute three-dimensional Euclidean space in Newton's theory. Einstein found that he could depict accelerated motions caused by gravitation as the analogues of straight lines in a "curved" space time with a geometry of a nonuniform type first studied by the mathematician Georg Riemann. The precise form of this geometry was determined by the distribution of matter and energy in each region of space time according to a particular law of general covariant form (Einstein's field equations).

Influence on modern physics. Einstein showed that general relativity could account for three small effects, not obtainable with Newton's theory, concerning planetary motion and the effect of gravitational fields on the transmission of light. In 1917 he applied his theory to cosmology and devised a world model that was finite but unbounded (the Einstein universe). This paper ("Kosmologische Betrachtungen zur allgemeinen Relativitätstheorie," in ***Sitzungsberichte der Preussischen Akademie der Wissenschaften***, 1917, 142–152) was the origin of modern theoretical cosmology.

Einstein regarded special relativity as the limiting form of general relativity in situations where gravitational effects are negligible. Owing to the weakness of most gravitational fields, the special theory is applicable to a wide class of phenomena, and modern elementary particle physics is based on it. The outstanding achievement of the general theory is the reduction of gravitation to geometry. In his later years Einstein devoted much effort to devising a still more general unified field theory, incorporating both gravitational and electromagnetic forces, but it is now generally believed that a totally different line of approach is required.

Einstein had no sympathy with the general view of Niels Bohr and other quantum physicists that the ultimate laws of nature are not causal or deterministic. Instead, he believed that physical reality is a four-dimensional space-time continuum in which events are already determined, the passage of time applying only to the human consciousness as it becomes aware of different events. His greatest contribution to scientific method was his recognition of the importance in physical theory of invariant quantities—that is, quantities that are unaltered by transformation formulas from one frame of reference to another; examples are the velocity of light (in special relativity) and the space-time interval between two events. Einstein was also very influential in discrediting the naive empiricism that was the dominant philosophy of physics before the advent of general relativity. In his view although the consequences of a physical theory must be tested empirically, its axioms are not automatic inferences from experience but are free creations of the human mind, which is guided by considerations of a mathematical nature.

Additional Works by Einstein

On the Method of Theoretical Physics. Oxford, 1933. The Herbert Spencer lecture delivered at Oxford, June 10, 1933.

Relativity, the Special and the General Theory: A Popular Exposition, translated by Robert W. Lawson, 15th ed. London, 1954.

Works on Einstein

Cassirer, Ernst, "Einstein's Theory of Relativity," translated by William and Marie Collins Swabey in *Substance and Function and Einstein's Theory of Relativity*. Chicago and London, 1923.

Frank, Philipp, *Einstein, His Life and Times*. London, 1948.

Reichenbach, Hans, *The Philosophy of Space and Time*, translated by Maria Reichenbach and John Freund. New York, 1958. Contains introductory remarks by Rudolf Carnap.

Schilpp, Paul Arthur, ed., *Albert Einstein: Philosopher-Scientist*. Evanston, Ill., 1949.

Törnebohm, Håkan, *A Logical Analysis of the Theory of Relativity*. Stockholm, 1952.

G. J. WHITROW

ELIOT, GEORGE, the assumed name of Marian (or Mary Ann) Evans (1819–1880), English novelist, poet, essayist, and translator. She was reared near Coventry and in her early years attended a school run by a fervent evangelical mistress. From this woman she acquired intense religious beliefs, but she gradually lost her faith. In 1842 she wrote that she thought Christian dogmas "dishonorable to God" and pernicious to human happiness. However, within a few months she had come to regard the dogmas in themselves as of little importance. "Speculative truth begins to appear but a shadow of individual minds, agreement between intellects seems unattainable, and we turn to the *truth of feeling* as the only universal bond of union," she wrote in a letter in October 1843; a belief in the importance of feeling remained central to her life and work.

In Coventry she had a group of friends with literary and philosophical interests, and under their influence she undertook, in 1844, a translation of D. F. Strauss's *Das Leben Jesu;* the translation was published in 1846. She went to London in 1851 to work for John Chapman as assistant editor of the *Westminster Review*. She published occasional essays and read much. Among her numerous friends in London were Herbert Spencer, to whom she was falsely rumored to be engaged, and George Henry Lewes, the philosopher and critic. Lewes was married but separated from his wife. In October 1854 George Eliot and he decided to live together. They never married, but they lived a life of exemplary domesticity until Lewes's death, in 1878. On May 6, 1880, to everyone's surprise, she married John W. Cross, long a family friend. She died that same year, after a short illness.

In 1854 George Eliot's translation of Ludwig Feuerbach's *Das Wesen des Christentums* was published. She also translated Spinoza but did not publish the translation. Upon Lewes's urging, she tried writing fiction; her first story was published in *Blackwood's Magazine* in 1857. She was immediately successful as a writer of fiction. To her fiction—notably *Adam Bede* (1859), *The Mill on the Floss* (1860), *Silas Marner* (1861), *Middlemarch* (1871–1872), and *Daniel Deronda* (1876)—rather than to her poetry or her essays, she owed her fame and her considerable influence as a moral teacher.

George Eliot's views on moral, religious, and metaphysical problems pervade and profoundly shape her writings, but they are never presented in abstract, systematic form. She had no faith in general moral principles: "to lace ourselves up in formulas," she wrote, is to repress the "promptings and inspirations that spring from growing insight and sympathy." Like Strauss, Feuerbach, and Comte, she thought of religious and metaphysical doctrines as projections and symbols of feelings, and as valuable only to the degree that the feelings they express and reinforce are valuable. Her "most rooted conviction," she told a friend in 1859, was that "the immediate object and the proper sphere of all our highest emotions are our struggling fellow-men in this earthly existence," and she declared that one of her main aims in her writing was to show that human fellowship does not depend on anything nonhuman. Christianity can foster many valuable emotions, she held, but the insistence of some Christians that all action must be for the glory of God stifles benevolence and love and directs feelings away from men. The idea of God has been beneficial only insofar as it has been "the ideal of a goodness entirely human."

George Eliot thus belongs with those Victorian writers who tried, in different ways, to work out a humanistic morality capable of satisfying the deep human needs that they thought the older, religiously based morality could no longer satisfy. Her view is naturalistic and deterministic; men are seen as being as much under the dominion of the laws of nature as are other parts of the world, though the comparisons are usually with organic growth and decay rather than with purely mechanical processes. Hereditary and social influences on character are heavily emphasized, as is the effect one's repeated actions or evasions will have on one's own character and hence on one's future actions.

The morality that springs from this view is primarily one of sympathy and compassion. The complexity and obscurity of motives and the mixture of good and evil in personality and in deed are constantly displayed in the novels. It is usually difficult, George Eliot suggested, to know what one ought to do in particular cases; one must rely ultimately on one's deepest feelings when these are enlightened by sympathy and by knowledge of circumstances and consequences. Wrongdoing is usually traced to stupidity, callousness, or thoughtlessly excessive demands for personal satisfaction, rather than to deliberate malice or conscious selfishness. Vice and crime are shown as eventually bringing retribution, but the reward of virtue is at best the peace that comes with acceptance of one's lot. George Eliot saw quiet renunciation and patient selflessness as the chief virtue. She frequently traced the career of an unusually sensitive and intelligent person who hopes to do great things for others but after painful defeats ends by settling into a life of unheroic and routine benevolence. She suggested that this is the only feasible way of achieving lasting good. In the thought that what we do will have some good effect on future generations and we shall be remembered by them with love, she held, there was a sufficient motive to virtue and a sufficient replacement of the belief in personal immortality and personal reward.

Bibliography

Two essays reprinted in George Eliot's *Essays and Leaves From a Notebook*—"Evangelical Morality: Dr. Cummings" (1855) and "The Poet Young" (1857)—are especially relevant to her moral views.

The standard biography is John W. Cross, *The Life of George Eliot*, 3 vols. (London, 1885–1887); it is composed mainly of her letters, heavily censored. *Marian Evans and George Eliot*, by Lawrence and Elisabeth Hanson (London, 1952), is more accurate and contains a good bibliography. *The George Eliot Letters*, Gordon Haight, ed., 7 vols. (New Haven, 1954–1955), is a masterpiece of scholarship. Two essays by R. H. Hutton, reprinted in his *Modern Guides to English Thought* (1887), give an assessment by a younger contemporary from an orthodox Christian standpoint.

There are numerous studies of George Eliot's life, intellectual development, and writings. See especially Joan F. Bennett, *George Eliot: Her Mind and Her Art* (New York, 1948); Gordon Haight, *George Eliot and John Chapman* (New Haven and London, 1940); Barbara Hardy, *The Novels of George Eliot* (Oxford, 1959); and Leslie Stephen, *George Eliot* (London, 1902).

J. B. SCHNEEWIND

ELIOT, THOMAS STEARNS (1888–1964), is best known as a poet and literary critic (he received the Nobel Prize for literature in 1948), but his work in social and cultural theory has also been widely influential. His principal works of this kind are *After Strange Gods* (London, 1934), *The Idea of a Christian Society* (London, 1939), and *Notes Towards the Definition of Culture* (London, 1949).

Eliot was born in St. Louis but lived in London from 1915 on and became a British subject in 1927. He graduated from Harvard University in 1909 and engaged in advanced studies in philosophy there, at the Sorbonne, and at Oxford until 1915. In the year 1913/1914 he served as an assistant in philosophy at Harvard, studying methodology with Josiah Royce and logic with Bertrand Russell. Eliot and Russell, despite enormous differences in political, social, and religious outlooks, became close friends. Eliot's Harvard doctoral dissertation, completed at Oxford in 1915, has recently been published as *Knowledge and Experience in the Philosophy of F. H. Bradley* (London and New York, 1964). Bradley's idealism influenced Eliot's critical doctrines, and in 1926 Eliot published an essay on Bradley, reprinted in *Selected Essays* (London, 1951). In this essay he praised especially Bradley's critique of utilitarianism: "He replaced a philosophy which was crude and raw and provincial by one which was, in comparison, catholic, civilized, and universal." But even before completing his studies, Eliot had finished some of his finest early poems, and he never produced any technical philosophical studies aside from his thesis.

In his early poetry and criticism, Eliot was a considerable innovator, but it was a main goal of his experiments to try to recover the sense of a fruitful tradition. In particular, this meant rejecting the literary theory and practice of romanticism and finding earlier sources. In a famous comment in 1921, he argued that there had been, in the seventeenth century, a major change in the English mind, which he called the "dissociation of sensibility"—the separation of feeling and thought. He came later to stress a loss of a sense of order, both internal and external, and to associate it with the decline of the Christian and classical cultural framework. To counteract this loss, the poet and critic must strive to recover a sense of the whole European tradition. At the end of this phase of his development Eliot described himself as a classicist, and he was to write henceforward as a declared and orthodox Christian.

After Strange Gods is the bridge from his mainly literary to his mainly social and cultural criticism. The book's subtitle is *A Primer of Modern Heresy*. Its argument is that modern writers, deprived of tradition, have constructed private or esoteric systems of belief, and, deprived of a common language and imagery, they have been forced to experiment. The struggle for common meanings, always difficult, is now even more difficult. This failure of communication is profoundly damaging to the whole society. The writer's task is to develop the full potential maturity of the language of his society. Paradoxically, therefore, the most creative work is that which begins from and is most aware of the full tradition and history of the language in which it is written. The loss of this tradition makes the modern writer's task overwhelmingly difficult.

In *The Idea of a Christian Society*, Eliot applied and extended this argument to social questions. He argued that the Western democracies, although nominally Christian, in fact live by quite other values. The idea of a Christian society is at best an understanding of the social ends which would deserve the name of Christian, but in the modern world there is an unusually wide gap between such ends and the main principles of social organization. Many of the driving forces of modern society—especially its false emphasis on profit, its substitution of exploitation of men and things for right use, and its general adoption of commerce as the central human concern—are in fact hostile to any Christian life in the world. It is therefore not surprising, Eliot claimed, that society is far from being Christian; what is surprising is that people retain as much Christianity as they do.

In *Notes Towards the Definition of Culture*, Eliot's most substantial theoretical work, he distinguished three senses of "culture"—the culture of the individual, of the group, and of the whole society. He argued that it is false to set as the goal of the group what can be the aim of the individual alone, and to set as the goal of the whole society what can only be the aim of a group. This argument became Eliot's main theoretical justification for what is ordinarily called "minority culture," and for his critique of egalitarian doctrines in education: It is false to educate the whole society to perform the cultural tasks of a particular group. At the same time, culture in each sense is necessarily connected with culture in the other senses. The group depends on the whole way of life of the society, as social organization depends upon tradition. Likewise, the culture of the individual cannot be isolated from the culture of the group.

Eliot further emphasized the extent to which the culture of a whole society is a matter of custom and behavior and is often unconscious: It is all the characteristic interests and activities of a people, whether or not some of these are thought of as "culture" in the narrower sense. What is often called "culture"—religion, arts, laws, and intellectual activity—is the conscious expression of the total culture, the whole way of life.

It follows from this, Eliot argued, that the maintenance and extension of the conscious culture of a society cannot be delegated to an elite, a group of specialists selected by merit. However skilled an elite may be in the special activities themselves, its members will necessarily lack the continuity with the rest of the society which is ultimately necessary for the health of the conscious culture. An elite, newly selected in each generation, will inevitably lack a sense of tradition. Eliot therefore saw no alternative to the maintenance of classes in society, and in particular to the maintenance of a governing class with which the specialists will overlap and interact. The need for continuity in culture, and for a tradition as opposed to a group of specialists with unrelated skills, argues, finally, for a social conservatism that will keep a proper relationship between continuity and change. This last phase of Eliot's social thinking has been especially influential since World War II.

Bibliography

Gardner, Helen, *The Art of T. S. Eliot*. London, 1949.

Leavis, F. R., *The Common Pursuit*. London, 1952. See "Mr. Eliot, Mr. Wyndham Lewis and Lawrence" and "Approaches to T. S. Eliot."

Lucy, Sean, *T. S. Eliot and the Idea of Tradition*. London, 1960.

Rajan, B., ed., *T. S. Eliot: A Study of His Writings by Several Hands*. London, 1947.

Williams, Raymond, *Culture and Society*. London, 1958. Part 3, Ch. 3.

RAYMOND WILLIAMS

EMANATIONISM explains the origin and structure of reality by postulating a perfect and transcendent principle from which everything is derived through a process called emanation (Greek *aporroia, probolē, proodos;* Latin *emanatio*) which is comparable to an efflux or radiation. Emanation is timeless and thus can be called a process only figuratively. It leaves its source undiminished, so that the source remains transcendent; but as the process continues, each of its products is less perfect.

In these three respects emanationism is opposed to evolutionism because evolution is a temporal process in which the principle itself is involved (immanent) and in which an increase in perfection is usually conceived. Emanationism is also opposed to creationism, according to which the principle creates the rest of reality (from which it differs absolutely), either out of nothing or by transforming a pre-existing, chaotic matter into a cosmos. There is some affinity between emanationism and pantheism, except that the latter teaches the immanence of the principle in its product. Some philosophers characterize emanationism as panentheism.

Emanationism forms an important part of several philosophic and religious doctrines, though it is somewhat elusive in the latter.

Philosophic emanationism. A theory of emanation can be found to a certain extent in the philosophy of Plato and the Old Academy as presented by Aristotle. Out of two highest principles (usually called the One and the Indefinite Dyad), ideas, in some way identified with or comprising mathematicals (numbers; geometrical entities, i.e., point, line, plane, solid) evolve; out of solids, the physical world evolves. But the nature of the process (for which Aristotle used the term *genesis*) remains unclear. The Stoa, Neo-Pythagoreanism, and Philo contributed some ideas to emanationism, but the philosophy first appears in full clarity in the system of Plotinus. His supreme principle, because it is transcendent, ineffable, and absolutely simple (One), must "overflow," just as what is mature must beget. The first product of this overflowing is intelligence (*nous*), which roughly corresponds to Plato's idea. From intelligence emanates psyche (corresponding to Plato's mathematicals) which becomes, by degrees, less and less perfect, more and more multiple. From the psyche emanates matter that, when "illuminated" by the psyche, becomes the physical world.

Often, although not always, Plotinus describes emanation as a necessary, involuntary, "natural," and therefore blameless process, somewhat like a point of absolutely intense light which emits a cone of light without any loss of its own substance. As the cone of light expands in volume, it grows dimmer, finally passing into complete darkness, on which the light produces images as on a screen. But just as the ontic status of darkness is ambiguous (Is it a minimum of light or its complete absence and therefore not its product?), so the status of matter in Plotinus is never quite clear.

The emanationism of Plotinus was taken over by all Neoplatonists, but among them, Proclus deserves particular mention. By subdividing Plotinus' emanative steps, Proclus made the process more continuous; and to the "vertical" emanation he added something like a "horizontal" one, fully articulating the realms of intelligence and psyche. From Neoplatonism, emanationism passed into the Christian, Muslim, and Jewish philosophies of the Middle Ages (Dionysius the Pseudo-Areopagite, John Scotus Erigena, Nicholas of Cusa, al-Farabi, Avicenna, Averroës, the book of Zohar), often with pantheistic or creationistic modifications. In modern times, evolutionism has obliterated the emanationist philosophy.

Religious emanationism. In religion, emanationism appears in many Gnostic systems, most conspicuously in *Pistis Sophia* ("Faith-Wisdom") and in some writings of Valentinus. But in neither of these is it the exclusive principle explaining the origin of everything outside the highest principle. Furthermore, emanation appears in these writings as the result of some reflection and will. It produces, not abstract principles, as in Plotinus, but a host of mythological characters—the first products of emanation according to Valentinus are thirty Aeons—performing a cosmic drama. In addition, what remains entirely in the background in Plotinian theory becomes prominent in Gnosticism; namely, that some acts of the will, which produce emanations, are the result of error or shortcomings. The physical world is created by one of the products of emanation, the Demiurge (identified with the Mosaic creator, the Platonic divine craftsman). The Demiurge is evil himself, and his creation, the world, is an evil place in which man finds himself entrapped and from which gnosis shows the elect ones a way to salvation. Although soteriology plays some part in Plotinian theory, it does not occupy a central place in the system. According to Plotinus, the efflux is balanced by a reflux, which takes place *pari passu* with the efflux. For man, the enactment of this reflux remains the most important task; and every man is, by nature, capable of performing it. Gnostic emanationism is ultimately motivated by a feeling of complete hostility to and estrangement from the material world—a feeling which the emanationism of Plotinus, in spite of some ascetic and pessimistic strains, explicitly refuses to countenance.

Bibliography

Dodds, E. R., "Proclus," in *The Elements of Theology*, 2d ed. Oxford, 1963; pp. 212–214, 230.

Eisler, R., *Wörterbuch der philosophischen Begriffe*, 3 vols., 4th ed. Berlin, 1927–1930; pp. 321–322.

Faggin, G., "Emanatismo," in *Enciclopedia filosofica*. Venice and Rome, 1957; pp. 1861–1864.

Heinze, M., "Emanation," in *Schaff-Herzog Encyclopedia of Religious Knowledge*. New York and London, 1909; pp. 117 ff.

Mora, J. Ferrater, "Emanación," in *Diccionario de filosofía*, 4th ed. Buenos Aires, 1958; pp. 400–401.

Ratzinger, J., "Emanation," in *Reallexikon für Antike und Christentum*. Stuttgart, 1959; pp. 1219–1228.

PHILIP MERLAN

EMERGENT EVOLUTIONISM is a doctrine first brought into prominence by C. Lloyd Morgan as an interpretation of the history of nature. It was designed in part to cope with the influence of Darwinism on philosophy by providing a way of interpreting evolution without having recourse to mechanistic, vitalistic, reductionist, and preformationist ideas. In its most restricted form the doctrine deals only with the history of living things on the earth. A more inclusive version deals with the history of the spatiotemporal universe. The most comprehensive version of the doctrine becomes a speculative cosmogony encompassing the totality of existence. Throughout, the central problem is to describe or explain how a temporal succession of phenomena marked by an increase of variety, diversity, and complexity has come about. The main concepts employed are emergence, levels, and novelties. Their import and interrelations will first be sketched.

Emergence. Classical Darwinism assumed that all changes in living things take place gradually. "Natural selection," Darwin wrote in the *Origin of Species*, "will banish the belief in the continued creation of new organic beings, or in any great and sudden modifications of their structure." This assumption of the continuity of organic changes made it difficult to understand how any single modification or group of coadapted modifications could first arise. Emergent evolutionists maintain that such events must be discontinuous with what went before. Whatever comes to be for the first time must do so suddenly or abruptly. One function of the concept of emergence is to express this contention.

Another function is to provide a more acceptable interpretation than has hitherto been offered of the evolution of organic variety, diversity, and complexity. Four interpretations of these phenomena are rejected: (1) the vitalistic attribution of them to the action of a unique, undetectable life force; (2) the mechanistic attribution of them to the operation of physicochemical laws alone; (3) the preformationist contention that organic variety, diversity, and complexity are simply actualizations of potentialities contained all along in living substances; and (4) the reductionist contention that whatever has happened in evolution is at bottom a reshuffling of certain fundamental units, which themselves remain unchanged. In opposition to these views the concept of emergence implies that the variety, diversity, and complexity engendered by evolution are irreducible, cumulative features of the creative advance of nature. From time to time the evolutionary process has produced items the like of which had never been previously exemplified anywhere in its history.

Levels. When the concept of emergence is used in cosmogony, it is closely connected with the concept of levels. A level is defined as a portion of the world that is marked by a set of closely related characteristics (qualities, regularities, structures) peculiar to it and emergent from other levels that existed previously. Thus, living things form a level that emerged a couple of thousand million years ago from the nonliving, physicochemical level. Artifacts form a level that emerged from human culture in relatively recent times. The general scheme of levels is not to be envisaged as akin to a succession of geological strata or to a series of rungs in a ladder. Such images fail to do justice to the complex interrelations that exist in the real world. These interrelations are much more like the ones found in a nest of Chinese boxes or in a set of concentric spheres, for according to emergent evolutionists, a given level can contain other levels within it. Hence, it is unnecessary to suppose that there must be some bottom level out of which everything has evolved, and it is misleading to think that the scheme as a whole is a static hierarchy like the Aristotelian scale of nature or the Plotinian great chain of being.

Levels are usually distinguished as higher and lower. One way of making the distinction is provided by Lloyd Morgan's concepts of involvement and dependence. Suppose that level A with characteristics a_1, a_2, a_3 exists alone at time t_1 and that at t_2 level B with characteristics b_1, b_2, b_3 supervenes on A to form the system AB. Since B involves the coexistence of A but not vice versa, B is said to be higher than A. Suppose, further, that at t_2 a new characteristic, a_4, arises in A because B has supervened on A. Then the set of characteristics a_1, a_2, a_3, a_4 depends on B, and A is therefore lower than B. Likewise, if level C supervenes on AB at t_3, C is higher than A and B. If at least one new characteristic, b_4, arises in B at t_3, then B is lower than C, and so on. This simplified model shows that characteristics can emerge at both higher and lower levels, for b_1, b_2, b_3 are emergent with respect to a_1, a_2, a_3 on lower level A, but a_4 is emergent with respect to the characteristics of the higher level B. The model also shows that the two-level system AB has more characteristics than level A, just as the three-level system ABC has more characteristics than AB. However, it sometimes happens that one or more characteristics of a given level may be lost when another level supervenes upon it. Thus, high-energy characteristics found at the level of nonliving matter are not exhibited at the level of living matter.

Emergent evolutionists disagree among themselves on the question of how many levels there are. Those who distinguish a small number do so by using very broad categories. Thus, Lloyd Morgan lists four successive emergent levels (psychophysical events, life, mind, and spirit or God), and Samuel Alexander lists five levels (space time, matter, life, mind, and deity). These categories are construed in a highly metaphysical sense. Paul Oppenheim and Hilary Putnam use nonmetaphysical categories to distinguish six levels (elementary particles, atoms, molecules, cells, multicellular organisms, and social groups). Other emergentists object to such classifications as being at best ideal sections abstracted from the vast, ramifying systems that occur in nature. Life and mind, for instance, "are so amazingly complex and comprise so many heterogeneous processes that their blanket designation as two emergent levels cannot seem very illuminating" (Wheeler, *Emergent Evolution,* p. 17). It is more in accord with the evidence to regard life and mind as the final accumulative stages of a long series of minimal emergences rather than as abruptly occurring saltations. "The insistence on levels becomes, therefore, largely a matter of descriptive emphasis, and should not conceal the necessity for detailed scientific knowledge of every emergence and the peculiar constellations and interactions of the parts which immediately determine it" (*ibid.*, p. 18).

Novelty. Every genuine emergent introduces novelty into the world. To say that an emergent characteristic is novel means that (1) it is not simply a rearrangement of pre-existing elements, although such rearrangement may be one of its determining conditions; (2) the characteristic is qualitatively, not just quantitatively, unlike anything that existed before in cosmic history; and (3) it was unpredictable not only on the basis of the knowledge available prior to its emergence but even on the basis of ideally complete knowledge of the state of the cosmos prior to its emergence. These points permit a distinction to be made between what is new in the sense of being a fresh combination of old factors—the only sort of newness that can occur in the world dealt with by physics—and what is novel in the sense of being qualitatively unique and unpredictable—which occurs only in the theory of emergent evolution. Such philosophers as Peirce, Bergson, and F. C. S. Schiller have used the word "novelty" to designate what they take to be a feature of the course of events at each instant of time or a feature of each moment of conscious, waking life. However, this use of the word is not adopted by emergent evolutionists.

The unpredictability of novel characteristics has been taken to imply that their occurrence is unintelligible, something to be simply accepted with "natural piety," as Lloyd Morgan and Alexander have said. Since these characteristics cannot be predicted, they cannot be explained, for prediction and explanation are two sides of the same coin. Some have declared that novel characteristics are causally disconnected from antecedent conditions. Hence, the appearance of novelty is a sign of radical contingency in nature. Others have declared that novel characteristics always attach to organic wholes, which are more than the sum of their parts and that the existence of these wholes is either an inexplicable fact or is due to a primordial "whole-making" agency at work in the cosmos. Such assertions have tended to surround the emergence of novelties with an aura of mystery.

Criticisms and answers. Because of this aura of mystery, critics have argued that the notion of emergence is exposed to serious objections. When it encourages an appeal to inexplicable factors, it blocks the path of rational inquiry and leads to irrationalism. Furthermore, rational inquiry is based on the principle that whatever happens has a cause from the knowledge of which the effect can be deduced. This is taken to mean that there cannot be more in the effect than there is in the cause. But the emergence of novelty contravenes this principle and thus is unacceptable. Even if one does not subscribe to that interpretation of the causal principle, there are other objections. Thus, Stephen Pepper has argued against the notion of emergence on the ground that it implies that all novel characteristics are epiphenomena. Since epiphenomena are devoid of causal efficacy, however, they can contribute nothing to the creative advance of nature. Hence, the doctrine of emergent evolution cannot account for the increase of variety, diversity, and complexity that has come about in the history of the cosmos.

Emergent evolutionists have sought to meet these criticisms in various ways. Thus, it has been contended that the doctrine is purely descriptive and affirms only that novelties have occurred in biological and cosmic evolution. This descriptive interpretation of the doctrine detaches it from the question of the predictability of those novelties. Those defenders of the doctrine who hold that it must have some explanatory force seek to detach it from a preformationist view of causality. There is no reason, they assert, why effects must previously have existed in some way in their causes or why an effect cannot contain more than its cause or be "higher" than its cause. Such medieval views of causality are outmoded. Nor is there any reason why the causal relation should be construed on the model of logical inference, so that the effect must be discernible to the "eye of reason" when it contemplates the cause alone. A more empirical version of causality enables us to understand how an emergent may be theoretically unpredictable and yet be explicable. For we can be said to explain the characteristics of emergent level *B* provided we can show that they follow from pre-existing conditions of level *A*, according to a rule that is itself formulable only after *B* has supervened on *A*. Causal explanation in this sense is "entirely compatible with the belief in emergence" (Lovejoy, "The Meaning of 'Emergence' and Its Modes," p. 30).

Another way of dealing with the issue of the ineligibility of emergents is to distinguish causal from other modes of determination. It can be argued that although the emergence of novelties may be unintelligible (inexplicable) on the basis of causation alone, it is understandable, at least in principle, "with the help of the totality of categories of determination, not excluding causation" (Bunge,

Causality, p. 211). According to this approach, the distinction introduced by G. H. Lewes (*Problems of Life and Mind*, Vol. II, p. 412) between resultant and emergent properties can be adopted. Resultant properties are wholly determined by causation; they are repetitive and predictable in principle. Weight is a typical example of such a property. Emergent properties are novel and unpredictable. They are not unintelligible, however, because they can be accounted for in terms of the categories of determination that supplement causation, such as functional interdependence, structural or holistic determination, and quantitative self-determination (Bunge, *Causality*, pp. 17 ff.).

It has been argued that emergent evolutionists make a mistake in treating predictability as a predicate that applies or fails to apply to characteristics *simpliciter*. This mistake is revealed in frequently cited examples of emergence. Thus, it is said that some of the properties of water, like translucence, are emergent, since they cannot be predicted on the basis of knowledge of the properties of its chemical constituents, oxygen and hydrogen. What such a statement overlooks is that predictability is a complex relation between a characteristic and a body of evidence, a system of logic, a particular language, a hypothesis, and above all, a covering theory. Hence the question of whether a characteristic is predictable in principle can be answered by ascertaining whether the term referring to that characteristic occurs among the terms of the relevant theory. If it does, the characteristic is predictable; if not, it is not predictable. In other words, to say that water has the emergent characteristic of translucency is to say that the statement "Water is translucent" cannot be deduced from any set of statements about oxygen and hydrogen that does not contain the term "translucent." An extension of this line of argument has been made by Arthur Pap, who contends that although many emergents are relative in the sense just indicated, it is possible to provide a satisfactory account of absolute emergence by limiting that expression to cases where characteristics are only definable ostensively. Thus, the disposition of a chemical substance, ammonia for example, would be an emergent provided that the expression "pungent smell" can only be defined by experiencing the sensation it denotes. Another extension of the argument has been made by Paul Henle, who defines the concept of emergence in terms of his notion of logical novelty rather than the concept of unpredictability.

Locus of novelty. Every version of emergent evolutionism is committed to the claim that novel characteristics have come to exist in the history of the universe. Some versions limit these characteristics to new qualities that attach to entities already in existence. Other versions postulate the emergence of new processes, new patterns of events, and new integrated structures or wholes. Still other versions hold that where a new level of being has emerged, there must also be an emergence of new laws. The claim in the last case is not simply that fresh theoretical formulations of laws are made, but that novel modes of determination among existents have emerged and that these modes constitute the objective counterpart of the fresh formulations. Thus, if we grant that living organisms are, relatively speaking, late arrivals on the cosmic scene and if we reject reductionism, then we must agree that distinctively biological laws are emergents. Before the appearance of life they might have been formulated theoretically by some "mathematical archangel," but they would then have applied to nothing.

Possibilities of verification. It is now generally agreed that emergent evolutionism cannot be validated or invalidated on a priori grounds. No one has shown that every version of the doctrine is logically incoherent or that some version applies necessarily to the world. The only tests that can be used are empirical and inductive, but such tests yield different results when brought to bear on different versions. The most favorable case appears to be that of biological evolution, for it has certainly given rise to innumerable new types of living things during the past two thousand million years. Yet these new types will not be novelties in the strict sense unless they have no counterparts anywhere in the spatiotemporal universe. To establish this condition, it would have to be demonstrated that biological evolution as we know it could not have occurred except on the earth. An empirical demonstration of that conclusion is not to be expected and, indeed, a considerable presumption now exists that the physical conditions at many other points in the cosmos are such that historical processes identical or very similar to terrestrial evolution may have taken place there. Furthermore, the new types of life that have arisen on the earth will not be emergents unless it can be established that they involve discontinuities in the evolutionary process. Here again, it is difficult to find uncontroversial supporting evidence, for even the presence of permanent gaps in the fossil record is not a conclusive sign of discontinuity. Finally, the contention that some biological laws are emergents always faces the countercontention that such "laws" merely reflect the lack of a deeper understanding on our part of invariant modes of determination among physical events.

The more comprehensive versions of emergent evolutionism that purport to apply to the whole spatiotemporal universe or to the totality of existence remain speculative possibilities at best. As such their main defect is a tendency "to lump into one category of 'emergent properties' items which require radically different treatment, e.g., *sense-qualities, life, purpose, value, thought*" (Meehl and Sellars, "The Concept of Emergence," p. 247). Another defect of the comprehensive versions is a failure to distinguish the logical thesis about novel characteristics and their unpredictability from the historical thesis about their occurrence in the creative advance of nature. But even the removal of these defects would not make the speculative versions of emergent evolutionism more than possible maps of the universe.

Bibliography

Alexander, S., *Space, Time and Deity*. London, 1920.

Broad, C. D., *The Mind and Its Place in Nature*. London, 1925.

Bunge, M., *Causality*. Cambridge, Mass., 1959. Ch. 8.

Bunge, M., *Metascientific Inquiries*. Springfield, Ill., 1959. Ch. 5.

Garnett, A. C., "Scientific Method and the Concept of Emergence." *The Journal of Philosophy*, Vol. 39 (1942), 477–485.

Henle, P., "The Status of Emergence." *The Journal of Philosophy*, Vol. 39 (1942), 486–493.
Lewes, G. H., *Problems of Life and Mind*. London, 1874. Vol. II.
Lovejoy, A. O., "The Meanings of 'Emergence' and Its Modes." *Proceedings of the Sixth International Congress of Philosophy*. New York, 1926. Pp. 20–33.
MacDougall, W., *Modern Materialism and Emergent Evolution*. London, 1929.
Meehl, P. E., and Sellars, W., "The Concept of Emergence," in H. Feigl and M. Scriven, eds., *Minnesota Studies in the Philosophy of Science*, Vol. I. Minneapolis, Minn., 1956. Pp. 239–252.
Morgan, C. Lloyd, *Emergent Evolution*. London, 1923.
Nagel, E., *The Structure of Science*. New York, 1961. Ch. 11.
Needham, J., *Integrative Levels: A Revaluation of the Idea of Progress*. Oxford, 1937.
Noble, E., *Purposive Evolution*. London, 1926.
Oppenheim, P., and Putnam, H., "Unity of Science as a Working Hypothesis," in H. Feigl and M. Scriven, eds., *Minnesota Studies in the Philosophy of Science*, Vol. II. Minneapolis, Minn., 1958. Pp. 3–36.
Pap, A., "The Concept of Absolute Emergence." *British Journal for the Philosophy of Science*. Vol. 2 (1951–1952), 302–311.
Pepper, S. C., "Emergence." *The Journal of Philosophy*, Vol. 23 (1926), 241–245.
Russell, E. S.; Morris, C. R.; and MacKenzie, W. L., "The Notion of Emergence." *PAS*, Supp. Vol. 6 (1926), 39–68. A symposium.
Wheeler, W. M., *Emergent Evolution and the Development of Societies*. New York, 1928.

T. A. GOUDGE

EMERSON, RALPH WALDO (1803–1882), American author, leader of New England transcendentalism. Emerson was born in Boston, Massachusetts. His father, a locally distinguished Unitarian clergyman, died in 1811 leaving Emerson and five other children in the care of a pious mother and a very learned aunt on the father's side. From 1813–1817 Emerson attended the Boston Latin School; then, after four undistinguished years at Harvard, he became a schoolmaster while he continued to study extramurally at Harvard Divinity School. "My reasoning faculty is proportionally weak," he confessed in his *Journal* in 1824, on deciding to become a minister, "nor can I ever hope to write a Butler's Analogy or an Essay of Hume. . . . [But] the preaching most in vogue at the present day depends chiefly on *imagination* [italics added] for its success, and asks those accomplishments which I believe are most within my grasp." Made just before he was 21, this acute piece of self-analysis marks the stage in Emerson's life when he really began to understand himself and gain a genuine premonition of his future role as literary artist. For Emerson is, more than anything else, an imaginative writer. (Thus Nietzsche, who was at an early stage influenced by Emerson—admiring his "manifoldness" and "cheerfulness"—recognized him as one of the nineteenth century's few great masters of prose.)

Formative experiences. Unitarianism was at first the main formative influence on Emerson, but it was not the most far-reaching, and the sort of preaching he was eventually to excel in had little to do with any established church or, for that matter, with Christianity as such. A trip to Florida for health reasons, in the winter of 1826–1827, brought about a chance meeting with the aristocratic Achille Murat, whose "consistent Atheism" Emerson found combined, to his surprise, with moral perspicuity. By the late 1820s the young theological student had already got through a prodigious regimen of philosophical and occult reading that included (as the most important authors for his maturer orientations) Zoroaster, Confucius, Muhammad, the Neoplatonists, Jakob Boehme, Leibniz, Montesquieu, Rousseau, Edmund Burke, the Scottish philosophers, Swedenborg, Johann von Herder, and—above all—Madame de Staël (the *De l'Allemagne*). Emerson's attention was being irresistibly drawn to the new cultural movement in Germany. The disturbing advances in German Biblical criticism were beginning to penetrate to him via his brother William's enthusiastic letters from Göttingen (William had also met and talked with Goethe). Soon Emerson was absorbed in Carlyle's pioneering essays on German literature, and in Coleridge's *Aids to Reflection* (1825)—in which Emerson discovered the pseudo-Kantian distinction between "Reason" and "Understanding."

In 1829 Emerson was appointed pastor of the Second Church of Boston; shortly afterward he married Ellen Louisa Tucker. Ellen's tragic death of tuberculosis early in 1831 had a deeply anguishing and yet strangely liberalizing effect upon Emerson. He questioned himself about immortality; preached sermons which expounded embryonic versions of his own later doctrines of "self-reverence" (or self-reliance," as he sometimes called it), "compensation," and "correspondence"; found he was bored with weekday Bible classes; and eventually gave up his pastorate.

On January 2, 1833, he sailed for Europe. This first European tour (he made two more, one in 1847–1848 and one in 1872–1873) was crucial in helping him shape into something like a whole the new philosophical outlook he had been consciously groping toward since at least 1824 and to which he ultimately gave poetic expression in his major works. During a short stay in Britain he managed to get an interview with Coleridge at Highgate, met Wordsworth, and spent 24 hours with the Carlyles at Craigenputtock. Carlyle immediately became a lifelong friend.

The conversations with Coleridge and Carlyle, the two men who were to the disenchanted young American living embodiments of all that was viable in contemporary European culture, had simply the effect of confirming Emerson's old belief: As a guide to solving the problem of life's meaning, there is "really nothing external, so I must spin my thread from my own bowels." He reasoned to himself that "the purpose of life seems to be to acquaint a man with himself" and "the highest revelation is that God is in every man." In his *Journal* entry for September 8, 1833, written while sailing back to America, Emerson included with the above affirmation of his maxim of "self-reverence" two other by then quite explicit convictions: (1) "There is a *correspondence* [italics added] between the human soul and everything that exists in the world," and (2) since "a man contains all that is needful to his government within himself," it must be that "nothing can be given to him or taken from him but always there is a *compensation* [italics added]." Here were brought together the key notions that Emerson was to elaborate for the rest of his life, first in his original transcendentalist manifesto, *Nature* (1836), and then in practically all the later works, including *Essays* (First Series, 1841; Second Series, 1844), *Representative Men* (1850), *English Traits* (1856), *Conduct of Life* (1860), *Society and Solitude* (1870), and *Letters and Social Aims* (1875).

In 1835 Emerson married Lydia Jackson, with whom, he soberly remarked to William, he had found a "quite unexpected community of sentiment and speculation." Soon he was settled in unusual domestic serenity with his wife and his mother in Concord, which remained his home for the rest of his life. Emerson's writings, his sagelike personality, and his roles as the leader of New England transcendentalism and the editor of the *Dial* gradually brought him an international reputation as perhaps America's leading man of letters.

Mature writings. If propounded by a philosopher, Emerson's assertions concerning "correspondence" and "compensation" would demand further explication and defense. But to expect anything resembling epistemological lucidity, or even concern, in a writer like Emerson would be to approach him with misconceptions. Indeed, those who read him as one would a philosopher like Kant, Schelling, Hegel, or even Coleridge (all of whom certainly had a great influence upon Emerson), largely miss the peculiar merits and significance of his works. For Emerson was neither a critical philosopher nor an idealist metaphysician, but an intuitive sage-poet: "In Emerson," wrote Nietzsche to Overbeck, "*we have lost a philosopher.*"

Like his artistic models Montaigne, Pascal, and the Goethe of the *Maximen und Reflexionen*, Emerson was a virtuoso of the *pensée*, in which style and content, symbol and "meaning," are inseparably conjoined. His meditations are exploratory rather than defining or definitive, and the nonpropositional, revelatory use of language with which Emerson alternately enraptures and ensnares his reader renders inappropriate the conventional task of giving a systematic conspectus of his leading ideas. The analysis to be applied to any work by Emerson is that of the literary critic rather than the philosopher. His method of exploration consists in the cumulative and often dialectical juxtaposition and attempted coalescence of *aperçus* relating to a single broad theme—"Nature," "Friendship," "Wealth," "Immortality"—usually in the form of an essay, lecture, or address. In fact, all Emerson's prose works are homiletic: They are secular sermons that differ from the sermons of his ancestors, the New England Puritan divines, largely by virtue of a greater breadth and subtlety of message and the intense personalism of their inner soliloquy.

Yet, despite the epistemological imprecision of his views, Emerson is philosophically interesting in at least two ways. First, because of the very full *Journal* he kept throughout his life, he affords an extremely well-documented record of a major writer who found it urgently necessary to struggle with philosophical ideas in order to achieve personal (and artistic) integration in an age "destitute of faith, but terrified at scepticism," as Carlyle characterized it. (The ideological perplexities of his age, moreover, lead directly to our own.) Emerson strove to discover for himself "an original relation to the universe": a kind of personal *Weltansicht* which would somehow keep vital his essentially religious sensibilities and give succor to his pressing emotional needs. Since Christianity could no longer do either of these things, he meditated upon his own experience in the light of those pieces of philosophy that seemed most accommodating. That Emerson found the Germanic philosophical tradition more to his liking than the Anglo-Saxon was the natural result of his individualism, his belief in the primacy of personality, and his closely related admiration for the hero, genius, or great man, in which he joined Fichte, Carlyle, and Nietzsche (see especially *Representative Men*). He expressed these fundamentally anthropocentric and aristocratic orientations quite succinctly: "No object really interests us but man, and in man only his superiorities; and though we are aware of a perfect law in nature, it has fascination for us only through its relation to him, or as it is rooted in the mind."

Both Schelling and Hegel influenced Emerson in profound and clearly traceable ways—Schelling first, through Coleridge, and Hegel later, particularly through W. T. Harris and the St. Louis School of Hegelians, with whose *Journal of Speculative Philosophy* Emerson was closely associated in the late 1860s and early 1870s. The primacy of "personality," or "self-consciousness," as it was usually called, was already an established axiom with the Germans. And if the all-embracing dichotomy between mind and nature—with its innumerable manifestations in the trouble-making divisions of "reality and illusion," "religion and science," "moral law and physical law," "the eternal and the temporal," in effect, the division of "the transcendental ideal and the banal actual"—could be shown to be only an immature stage in the development of Absolute Spirit whose final blossoming would exhibit all as one: then, indeed, there would be not only "a correspondence between the human soul and everything that exists in the world" but, even better, a coalescence. Much in the manner of Hegel, Emerson came to see History, or God, or the Oversoul as a kind of primordial schizophrenic, originally split into mind and nature and now victoriously struggling to personal integration in and through the creative achievements of human culture. Metaphysically speaking, human culture is identical with mind's reintegration with nature. Indeed for Emerson science itself becomes the handmaiden of transcendentalism: Man's conquest of the material environment shows nature to be not alien but fully transparent to mind, and since whatever is intelligible must somehow be itself intelligence, mind and nature are in reality one. But in such a panspiritualistic universe every apparent evil can only be for the greater universal good; the "compensation" for evil lies in the ultimate self-harmony of mind. This is the tortuous metaphysical hallucination that forms the basis of Emerson's optimism. As far then as it can be discerned, his *philosophia prima* is that of the German idealists, and one sympathetic way of characterizing him would be to say that where Schelling and the rest made the fundamental mistake of attempting to give rational and systematic expression to the mythology of romanticism, Emerson put the whole thing into poetry—which was exactly where it belonged.

But Emerson's individualism had a further and more

practical consequence. He could never reconcile himself to the values of a civilization which, as he saw it, was "essentially one of property, of fences, of exclusiveness"; and the incisive manner in which this dissatisfaction with the prevailing social reality found expression in his writings gives Emerson a special place in the great line of romantic critics of mass society from Rousseau to Jaspers. Brilliantly critical of emergent American commercialism, which necessarily seemed to involve cultural superficiality, Emerson was particularly virulent against the species of democracy that in fact often demands only conformity to depersonalizing custom, and a consequent sacrifice of individual autonomy, of "self-reliance." He did not limit his criticism to America; *English Traits* is still, among other things, a major indictment of European cant, Philistinism, and materialism by an American.

The second reason why Emerson is philosophically interesting is his influence on philosophers. Nietzsche has been mentioned; so also should be Bergson. A number of Bergson's fundamental concepts often seem in part to be systematizations of Emerson's eclectic intuitions (compare, for example, the *élan vital* with Emerson's "vital force" in the essay "Experience"); perhaps the most noteworthy is the decided interest in Emerson shown by the pragmatists James and Dewey.

Emerson's most pervasive influence, however, was not so much on professional thinkers or writers, but on the public, through the great popular sale of his works. His highly personal yet persuasive and accessible form of romanticism insinuated itself into the general intellectual consciousness of America, and to a lesser extent into that of Europe. "His relation to us is . . . like that of the Roman Emperor Marcus Aurelius," said Matthew Arnold in *Discourses in America* (published in 1885, three years after Emerson's death); "he is the friend and aider of those who would live in the spirit."

Bibliography

The Complete Works of Ralph Waldo Emerson in the 12-volume Centenary Edition (Boston, 1903–1904) is the standard edition of Emerson's works. Emerson's *Journals* were originally edited by E. W. Emerson and W. E. Forbes (Boston, 1909–1914). A more recent version is *Journals and Miscellaneous Notebooks of Ralph Waldo Emerson*, William H. Gilman and others, eds., 3 vols. (Cambridge, Mass., 1960–1963). For more bibliographical details consult *Eight American Authors: A Review of Research and Criticism*, Floyd Stovall, ed. (New York, 1956; reprinted with a bibliographical supplement extended to 1962, New York, 1963). An informed and brilliantly perceptive account of the role of German thought in Emerson's intellectual development is contained in H. A. Pochmann's *German Culture in America* (Madison, Wis., 1961), pp. 153–207). Among recent studies of Emerson's mind and art, the most illuminating is Jonathan Bishop, *Emerson on the Soul* (Cambridge, Mass., and London, 1965).

MICHAEL MORAN

EMOTION AND FEELING. Since philosophy has always been concerned, in one way or another, with human nature, and since emotions obviously play a large role in human experience and behavior, philosophers have devoted considerable attention to the topic. They have raised questions about the place of emotion in the good life, about the extent to which conduct is or must be emotionally determined, about the place of emotion in aesthetic expression and experience, about the ways in which emotions are aroused. More recently, Continental philosophers have been inclined to base ontology on the phenomenology of such emotional states as dread and anguish. Fundamental to all these problems, whether dealt with by philosophers or psychologists, is the task of clarifying the concept of emotion. This task may be thought of as involving such questions as (1) What kind of an entity is an emotion? Is it a kind of feeling, sensation, cognition, physiological condition, behavior pattern, tendency, or some combination of these? (2) How does one distinguish one emotion from another, in oneself and in another? This article will be confined to a consideration of various positions on these questions.

Demarcation of the topic. What does and does not belong in the category of emotion ("passion," "affection") is one of the subjects of controversy between different schools of thought. For the purposes of this article we shall delimit the problem area in the following way. To begin, we shall take certain terms as cases of emotion-terms: fear, anger, indignation, remorse, embarrassment, grief, distress, joy, craving, disgust (the list is not intended to be complete). Emotions are what are designated by such terms in *some* of their uses. The qualification is important. We must distinguish an emotion as a kind of temporary state of a person (the term "emotional state" could be used for greater specificity here) from more or less long-term dispositions to various states, including emotional states, and activities. Such dispositions include:

(1) Attitudes toward particular objects: admiration, contempt, gratitude, resentment, jealousy, hate, sympathy.

(2) Dispositions to act and feel in certain ways toward objects of certain kinds under certain kinds of circumstances: generosity, friendliness, benevolence, humility.

(3) Liabilities to emotional states: irritability, excitableness, fearfulness.

Psychological factors of all three sorts have often been lumped together with what we would call emotions under the heading of "emotion" or "passion." Many emotion-terms can be used to designate dispositions as well as temporary emotional states. Thus one can be said to have a fear of snakes, to have been angry at one's brother for several years, or to have a craving for oysters. In saying these things, we are not reporting a condition the person is in at some particular time; rather we are attributing to him a general set of dispositions and tendencies. To be afraid of snakes, in this sense, is to be disposed to be in an emotional state of fear when in the presence of snakes, as well as to have other dispositions, such as a disposition to avoid places where snakes are thought to be frequent. To have been angry at (resentful toward, grateful to) one's brother for several years is to have had a number of dispositions, including the disposition to get into an emotional state of anger toward him under certain conditions.

It is noteworthy that typical uses of the general term "emotion" have to do with emotional states rather than attitudes or other general dispositions or liabilities. One is not termed an "emotional person" because of having a lot of admiration, contempt, or gratitude toward other people, but rather because of frequently getting into states of anger, indignation, grief, or joy and expressing them freely. When someone is said to give way to his emotions or control his emotions, it is emotional states which are in question. The same is true of getting emotional over something and being emotionally upset. Emotional attitudes like hate and gratitude constitute an important and complicated problem of analysis, but this article will be restricted to the problem of clarifying the notion of emotional states, a notion which is involved, along with other things, in concepts of attitudes.

There are a number of typical features of emotional states which most thinkers agree are connected with emotion in one way or another. Consider the following case of marked fear. A man sees a funnel-shaped dark cloud approaching and realizes that it is a potentially destructive tornado. He feels frightened. Various bodily changes ensue, including increased strength and rate of heartbeat, paling, goose flesh, and dryness of the throat. These changes are reflected in his bodily sensations, which also include such things as a sinking sensation in the stomach and sporadic local chills. He has strong tendencies to run away and to protect his goods and loved ones, tendencies which may or may not find expression, depending on circumstances. He finds it difficult to think about anything else or to concentrate on the work at hand.

Generalizing from this example, we may list the following factors, each of which has been considered by many thinkers to be essential to emotions:

(1) A cognition of something as in some way desirable or undesirable.

(2) Feelings of certain kinds.

(3) Marked bodily sensations of certain kinds.

(4) Involuntary bodily processes and overt expressions of certain kinds.

(5) Tendencies to act in certain ways.

(6) An upset or disturbed condition of mind or body.

Theories of emotion differ as to which of these items they take to constitute the emotion itself and which they take to be causes, effects, or concomitants of the emotion. The presentation of theories that follows is organized in terms of these differences.

Feeling theory. One strong tradition takes the conscious feeling to be the emotion. This view has a number of versions, differing according to the general psychological scheme in terms of which it is stated. Thus Descartes conceives of a "passion of the soul" as a "perception" (in other words, a conscious state) in which the soul is passively affected, as in sense perception, but in which what is perceived is attributed to the soul itself, rather than to some physical body. For Hume, passions are "impressions of reflection," unique kinds of experience which arise as a result of sense perceptions (including sensations of pleasure and pain) and thoughts. For thinkers in the tradition of faculty psychology, such as Kant and William Hamilton (1788–1856), emotions are modes of feeling, where feeling is taken to be one of the ultimate faculties of the mind, along with cognition and will; so conceived, feeling is the faculty of being affected positively and negatively by objects cognized. For elementaristic psychologists like Wilhelm Wundt (1832–1920) and Edward B. Titchener (1867–1927), emotions are compounds of feelings, where feelings are taken to be mental elements somewhat like sensations, but differing from them in not being localizable, in not being directly dependent on sensory receptors and in having certain special properties like pleasantness and unpleasantness.

What is common to all these views is the conviction that what makes a condition an emotion, and what makes it the particular emotion it is, is the presence in consciousness of a certain felt quality which, like sensory qualities (redness, smell of burning wood), is completely accessible to introspection and accessible in no other way. The one and only way to know what fear, anger, joy, or remorse is, is to actually experience the feeling that *is* fear, anger, etc. Thus the emotion is only contingently connected with the other factors, including the cognitions which give rise to it and its expressions, whether voluntary or involuntary. It is conceivable that human nature might have been such that the emotion called "fear" would have been associated with cognitions of objects as friendly rather than as dangerous and with tendencies to approach rather than tendencies to flee. Hume considers it an inexplicable fact that the emotion of pride should regularly be induced by the awareness of things which belong to us rather than by consideration of objects which have no connection with us.

Motivational theory. According to another powerful tradition, what makes a state an emotion is that it occurs at some stage of a motivational process conceived as the process of apprehending something as desirable or undesirable and then taking steps to acquire it or to avoid it, or at least having a tendency to do so. This involves taking a cognition of something as desirable or undesirable (1) and/or tendencies to act in a certain way (5) as defining what the emotion is. Different motivational theories differ as to their emphasis on one or the other of these factors. They were both made central by the Stoics, who conceived a "passion" as an excessive or overpowering impulse which is based on an ill-founded judgment of good or evil. (The qualifications "overpowering" and "ill-founded" reflect the Stoic low evaluation of passion in contrast with calm reason.) Thomas Aquinas seems to stress (5) in defining a "passion" as "a movement of the sense appetite resulting in a corresponding change in the body," but in his detailed account he also stresses the initial judgment of good or evil on which the movement of the appetite is based.

A more exclusive emphasis on goal-directed endeavor is to be found in Juan Luis Vives (1492–1540), who defined "affections" as "acts of the faculties by which our minds are endowed by nature for seeking good and avoiding or combating evil" and in Thomas Hobbes, who regarded all passions as forms of appetite and aversion. Vives' classification illustrates the way in which different "affections" or "passions" were distinguished in terms of the different stages of pursuit of the desirable and the avoidance of the undesirable. To tend toward something is love or liking; when the object is future this takes the form of desire; when present, joy or delight. To tend to avoid something is to hate it; when the object is future this takes the form of fear; when present, sorrow. To tend to remove something which is blocking a tendency toward the desirable is anger.

This conception of the passions can also be found in

John Locke and in those inspired by him to develop a "sensationist" psychology. Since Locke termed the passions "modes of pleasure and pain," pleasure and pain being simple ideas (ultimate qualities of consciousness) obtained both from sensation and from the mind's awareness of its own operations, his account might appear to be a form of the feeling theory. But in fact it turns out that the various passions are distinguished not as so many different immediately felt qualities but as so many ideas of the causes and effects of pleasant and unpleasant sensations. It is difficult to distinguish this from feeling theory, since according to sensationist principles ideas themselves are copies of sensations, and complexes thereof, and as such are themselves qualified by pleasantness and unpleasantness. Nevertheless when we follow out the development of this view, for instance in James Mill, we find that joy is an idea of a pleasant sensation in the future, with a certainty of its occurrence, whereas fear is an idea of an unpleasant sensation, uncertain to occur in the future. This is clearly a motivational theory, with emphasis on the first aspect, cognition of an object as desirable or undesirable, translated into a sensationist, hedonistic psychology.

The motivational conception is alive, though not dominant, in contemporary psychology. Thus Magda B. Arnold defines emotion (in part) as "the felt tendency toward anything intuitively appraised as good (beneficial), or away from anything intuitively appraised as bad (harmful)" (*Emotion and Personality*). Emphasis on action tendency can be found in behaviorists like E. C. Tolman, who defines emotions as "a drive or tendency toward a particular type of behavior result."

Since feeling was not recognized as a distinctive category before the eighteenth century, it is not entirely clear whether such thinkers as Aquinas and Hobbes wanted to identify passions with cognitions and action tendencies themselves, or with a state of feeling resulting from them, or with both. It seems likely that they at least wanted to include feeling; it is doubtful that they would attribute a passion to one who was not consciously affected by the apprehensions and inclinations of which they speak. In any event, one can include states of feeling in his concept of an emotion and still take factors (1) and (5) as determining when a feeling can be said to figure in an emotion. Thus William McDougall took emotions to be the immediately felt aspects of the operations of instincts.

Critically reviewing the different forms of a motivational view, we can see that a given emotion cannot be identified with either a particular behavior pattern or a tendency thereto. It cannot be identified with a particular behavior pattern because it is quite possible, for example, to be afraid and yet not engage in any sort of "running away" behavior. Even if we could describe a behavior pattern of such generality that it covered physically running away from a bear, running away from a disliked person by changing jobs, and mentally running away from a problem by refusing to think of it or repressing it, it is clear that one can be afraid and yet deliberately refuse to run away. Of course this does not show that a *tendency* to run away is not part of what fear is. But there are other emotions which are not so closely associated with distinctive reaction tendencies, for example, grief, joy, remorse, and embarrassment. There is not one special kind of purposive activity in which we expect a man to engage just because he is overjoyed or embarrassed. (It required considerable dialectical ingenuity for Aquinas to maintain that the repose of the sense appetite in joy is really a motion of the sense appetite.) There are typical overt expressions of these emotions such as broad expansive movements and squirming, respectively; but that is another matter. Hence, the version which stresses the antecedent factor, recognition of something as desirable or undesirable, is in a stronger position. Thus we are not afraid of x unless we take x to be dangerous; we are not angry at x unless we take x to be acting contrary to something we want; we do not have remorse over having done x unless we regard it as unfortunate that we did x; we are not grief-stricken over x unless we see x as the loss of something we wanted very much; we do not have pity for x unless we take x to be in an undesirable state; and so on.

Before proceeding further let us standardize our terminology for the cognitive factor. Many theorists employ terms like "judgment," "appraisal," or "evaluation." These can be misleading if they are taken to imply a conscious formulation of a judgment; after all, one can be frightened by something without having time to say to oneself, "That is dangerous." On this count, terms like "apprehension" or "recognition" are preferable. Perhaps the most judicious choice would be "perceive x as . . ." or "take x to be . . . ," with the understanding that "perceive" is being used in a wide sense in which it is not restricted to sense data, but can involve memory, belief, and intellectual realization as well. For a general characterization of what the subject of an emotion takes x to be, we have slipped into the terms "desirable" and "undesirable." These seem preferable to the more traditional contrast of "good" and "evil," which today has too narrow a connotation, or such terms as "beneficial" and "harmful," which are not sufficiently wide. (I can be suffering remorse over something which I take to have been morally wrong without regarding it as either beneficial or harmful. But I will still be taking it to be contrary to one of my desires, the desire to act morally.) Since the term "evaluation" can be used for taking something to be desirable or undesirable, we shall henceforth refer to this factor as a perceptual evaluation of something, or, to be still more concise, simply an evaluation of something; further discussions of motivational theories will be confined to this "evaluational" form.

Bodily upset theory. Thinkers who have conceived emotion primarily in one or the other of the two ways already presented often also take note of the fact that emotions typically involve a "perturbation," "disturbance," or "agitation" of the person. So long as the emphasis was on perturbations of the soul or mind, this was likely to be regarded as merely one of the felt qualities which is typical of emotions. However, with increased emphasis on the physiological aspects of human behavior and experience, the way was opened for a more objective conception of the disturbance involved in emotion. Physiological studies have revealed certain disturbances in normal bodily functioning as regular features of emotional states. These include increased adrenalin secretion, increased heartbeat, alteration of the distribution of blood to various parts of the body, changes in pattern of respiration, suspension of digestive activities, and increases in red corpuscles in the blood. It is these changes which are manifested in the involuntary overt expressions of emotion which have long been noted—paling, blushing, panting, trembling, and so on. And it is the sensation of these changes or some of their results which constitutes the felt disturbance or perturbation characteristic of emotion.

Moreover, there is a more behavioral sense in which these states constitute disturbances; when sufficiently intense, they interfere with activities which require a high degree of coordination or control. Thus Gilbert Ryle takes it as a criterion of what he calls "agitations" that it make sense to speak of them as interfering with thinking or concentrating on tasks. A person can be too grief-stricken to think about what he is doing, too overjoyed to concentrate on his work, or too frightened to notice what is happening around him. Psychologists, seeking an objective criterion for the term "emotion," have tended to identify emotion with bodily states which are disturbances in this double sense. Thus: "Emotion is activity and reactivity of the tissues and organs innervated by the autonomic nervous system" (Marion A. Wenger, as quoted in Robert Plutchik, *The Emotions: Facts, Theories, and a New Model*, p. 175).

Difficulties in the feeling theory. There are several reasons for the attractiveness of feeling theories. First, an emotion can occur without its typical overt expressions. One can be afraid or angry or annoyed or overjoyed without anyone else realizing it. Thus it seems that the emotion itself is something inner which may or may not issue in overt behavior. Second, it seems to be an inner mental rather than an inner bodily state, since it is the sort of thing of which one can have the same kind of immediate infallible knowledge one has of one's sensations and thoughts, a kind of knowledge open to no one else. If I am angry at someone, then I, but no one else, know that I am angry just by virtue of my being angry; nothing further is required. Thus an emotion has to be identified with something of which such knowledge is possible, and this is restricted to states of consciousness. Third, that the state of consciousness in question is a feeling is suggested by the fact that there is no important difference between feeling angry and being angry, between feeling annoyed and being annoyed.

All of these claims have been challenged. As for the first: It has been pointed out that although one can inhibit all overt manifestations of an emotional state—if one is sufficiently motivated to make the necessary effort and has a high degree of self-control and if the emotion is not too strong—there will still be the tendencies to those manifestations. Moreover, apart from overt expression, it remains to be shown that one can be angry or overjoyed without the occurrence of typical internal bodily processes. As for the second, psychoanalysis has forced on our attention cases in which one misinterprets or misidentifies one's emotional state. For example, I might feel quite tense around a certain acquaintance; I may be aware of this simply as tenseness, without understanding its source, whereas in fact I am quite angry with him about something. The evidence for this interpretation would be such things as (*a*) my involuntary expressions and gestures when off guard, (*b*) a regular pattern of getting consciously angry over such things with other people with whom I have no reason to repress my true reaction, (*c*) indirect expression (in dreams) of my anger with him.

If the second claim falls, the third suffers the same fate. For, assuming that I cannot be mistaken about what I am feeling at the moment, if I can be mistaken about whether I am angry, then being angry cannot be just feeling angry. To be sure, some claims that an emotion does not necessarily involve the usual state of feeling depend on using an emotion term in the attitudinal rather than the emotional-state sense, as when it is pointed out that being afraid of heights (as a long-lasting characteristic of a person) does not consist of some feeling the person has continuously. And it does seem that any claim that there are *occurrent* emotional states that do not include the usual feelings will rest on indirect and complex methods for identifying the emotional state, such as the psychoanalytic procedures mentioned above.

In addition to these challenges to its evidential grounds, the feeling theory has been judged inadequate in several respects. Its current unpopularity is due largely to a generalized suspicion of states of consciousness and data of introspection. Many analytical philosophers, under the influence of Wittgenstein, have maintained that no term can have an intersubjectively shared meaning if it simply functions as a name for objects that are necessarily private; hence emotion words, as terms in a public language, cannot be so functioning. Psychologists have found introspection as a method to be unreliable and sterile. And behaviorists regard states of consciousness as outside the pale of science. However, these considerations do not have crucial importance for our present concerns. If emotions had the same status as sensations, however that status is finally interpreted and however sensation terms get intersubjective meaning, most feeling theorists would be satisfied. Hence we shall concentrate on arguments to the effect that emotions do not have the same kind of status as feelings and sensations.

Philosophers who have recently attacked the feeling theory most vigorously have held some form of an evaluational view, and their main point has been that it is essential to an emotion to have an "object" of a certain kind. If one is remorseful, one is remorseful over past misdeeds; if one is annoyed, one is annoyed at something. A feeling is only contingently connected with such an object; it is logically possible that the feeling typically involved in remorse could be aroused by drugs or by thinking about next year's world series baseball competition rather than by reflection on one's past misdeeds. But in that case it would not be a feeling of remorse. Therefore remorse cannot be identified with a kind of feeling. This lack of identity is further manifested by the impossibility of making the distinctions we do make between emotions solely on the basis of the feelings involved. Annoyance does not seem to feel markedly different from indignation; what distinguishes them is the way the person apprehends the situation—whether he thinks some rightful expectation has been violated. Finally, one will not be able to distinguish emotions from other mental states if one identifies them with feelings. How can one distinguish emotional feelings from other feelings, such as feeling contented, feeling refreshed, or feeling restless, except by saying that emotional feelings arise from the recognition that something is desirable or undesirable in some way?

The nature of feeling. In order to make an intelligent judgment on these issues, we shall have to look further into the nature of these feelings which one side affirms, the other denies, to constitute emotional states. The term "feel" is a protean one. Some of the uses which seem prima facie quite distinct are the following:

(1) Perceptual: feel a cool breeze on one's cheeks.

(2) Exploratory: feel for the light switch.

(3) Localized bodily sensation: feel a shooting pain in the foot, a lump in the throat, a tingling in one's hand.

(4) General bodily condition: feel sleepy, tired, feverish, refreshed.

(5) Hedonic tone: feel good, contented, satisfied.

(6) Emotional: feel distressed, embarrassed, homesick, depressed, enthusiastic.

(7) Tendency: feel like taking a walk.

(8) Epistemic: feel that a certain team will win, that things are improving.

(9) Attitudinal: feel sorry for him, unsure of myself, drawn to her.

The first seven are all occurrent states, which have to do, at least in part, with the conscious state of the individual at a single moment. On the other hand, the last two, the epistemic and the attitudinal, are more or less long-term dispositions or liabilities. In saying about a particular person that he feels that a certain team will win a competition, or that he feels unsure of himself, one does not imply that he is in any particular conscious state at any particular time. We have the same distinction between temporary states and attitudes in emotional feeling terms that we have in emotion terms which do not make explicit reference to feeling. Thus, I might have felt acutely sorry for someone at the moment he made a horrible blunder, or I might have felt sorry for someone for years. Within the class of occurrent states, we shall concentrate on (6), which comprises the kinds of feelings that have been thought to constitute emotions, although an important part of our task will be the examination of the relations of this subclass to other subclasses of the occurrent group, particularly bodily feelings of various kinds.

The first point to be made is that if we take terms like "feel angry" and "feel indignant" in their ordinary senses, then identifying being angry with feeling angry does not commit one to the feeling theory rather than a motivational theory. This is because, as such terms are ordinarily used, we distinguish between one feeling and another, at least in part, in the ways stressed by evaluational theorists. Feeling annoyed and feeling indignant, just as being annoyed and being indignant, differ as to what the person takes the situation to be. Hence if we identify feelings in the ordinary way, then the fact that we distinguish between emotions in terms of the subject's evaluations does nothing to show that we do not distinguish between emotions in terms of the feelings involved. But it is clear that a feeling theorist like Hume or Titchener means to be using "feeling" in a more stripped-down sense. He wants to identify an emotion with some "pure" feeling-element which can be distinguished from any associated perceptions, thoughts, beliefs, judgments, tendencies, and other cognitive or conative factors. But to specify this unambiguously is no easy task.

Let us begin by noting that there are many ϕ's which are such that one can be ϕ without feeling ϕ. One can be tired without feeling tired, be under pressure without feeling under pressure, be disturbed without feeling disturbed. We can then ask what is added when in addition to being under pressure I also *feel* under pressure, in addition to being tired I also feel tired. An answer to these questions will specify the nature of the "feeling element" in feelings ordinarily so called.

Answers given to this kind of question have tended to gravitate to one of two poles: The extra element in each case (1) consists of a certain quality of consciousness which is just as immediate and unanalyzable as a sensory quality but is distinct from all sensory qualities, or (2) is a complex of bodily sensations. The first position can be held in a more or less extreme form. The more extreme form is found in Hume, who posits a distinct unanalyzable quality for each distinguishable "passion." Wundt and Titchener are more economical; they attempt to analyze particular emotions into constituent elementary feelings, which have only a few basic unanalyzable dimensions of qualitative variation (pleasantness–unpleasantness and excitement–quiescence, for example).

Some forms of the first reply involve relating feeling to a special faculty of the mind or positing mental elements, termed "feelings," as carriers of the unique feeling-qualities. To assess these moves would lead this discussion into a general discussion of types of conceptual frameworks for thinking about the mind. Here we must stick to questions which bear specifically on the nature of feeling. It does not seem that the issue between (1) and (2) can be decisively settled by just introspecting and seeing what is there, unlike, for example, the question as to whether sounds have different qualities than colored expanses have. Generations of investigators have introspected in order to determine whether the feeling element in, for example, feeling excited includes more than bodily sensations, but the answers given on this basis have shown no tendency to convergence. Probably this is because we do not have the effective stimulus control over bodily sensations that we have over sensations from the external senses. If we want a subject to determine introspectively whether feeling excited includes any noncognitive element of immediate consciousness other than bodily sensations, we would first have to teach him what would and would not fall within the category of bodily sensations. However, we are unable to do this because it is not possible to produce in the subject samples from the entire range of bodily sensations.

Hence the question of the nature of the feeling element will have to be settled more indirectly. Assuming that bodily sensations accompany feelings anyway, it is clearly a more economical hypothesis to assume that the "feeling" component in feelings is nothing but a complex of bodily sensations than it is to posit special unanalyzable qualities for each distinguishable kind of feeling. If the former hypothesis does not contradict any firm data, the latter choice could only reflect a general predilection for multiplying ultimate qualities. When defenders of special feeling-qualities have been pressed hard, they have retreated, as with Titchener, to regarding pleasantness and unpleasantness as the only qualities that distinguish feelings from sensations. But instead of positing special feeling-elements as bearers of pleasantness and unpleasantness, these elements being such that they can accompany any state of consciousness, we can account for the same facts by taking pleasantness and unpleasantness as qualifying any state of consciousness. Moreover, there are reasons for treating pleasantness and unpleasantness as functions of one's preferences rather than as ultimate qualities of consciousness. (See PLEASURE.)

Let us be clear on what we are and are not committing ourselves to in holding that the feeling element in feelings consists of a pattern of bodily sensations. This thesis does not imply that whenever one knows that he feels morose, nostalgic, embarrassed, relieved, or ill at ease, he could restate his report in explicit bodily sensation terms, that is, in terms which denote bodily sensations that could occur outside this kind of context. To be sure, people can generally do something toward specifying what bodily sensations are involved in feelings of the sort just mentioned; thus, feeling morose involves a sensation of generally diffused heaviness and feeling relieved involves a sensation of muscular relaxation. If no specification of this sort were possible, our hypothesis would be much less plausible. Nevertheless a person may have learned to respond verbally to a certain pattern of bodily sensations only by the "diagnostic" labels, "feel morose," "feel relieved," and so on, each of which labels the pattern as the sort that normally occurs in a kind of situation designated in evaluative terms. Thus on this hypothesis, when one says that he feels morose he is to be interpreted as informing us (in part) that he is having a pattern of bodily sensations of the sort he typically has when he is brooding over reverses and frustrations, when he is disinclined to initiate vigorous activity, and so on. It can be true that this is (in part) the informational content of his statement, and correlatively it can be true that a pattern of bodily sensations is part of the basis on which he makes his report, without his being able to reformulate his information in terms of an analysis of the pattern into elements like sinking sensations, relaxations, a lump in the throat, shivers, and so on, each of which can occur in other patterns. Indeed, the position might be put by saying that phrases such as "feel morose," or, perhaps better, "feel just as I do when I am morose" *are* descriptions of bodily sensation that differ from what are ordinarily called descriptions of bodily sensation in that they denote complex patterns of sensation rather than relatively elementary sensations; they also differ in that they appear to have been learned in connection with types of situations defined in terms of the relation of certain external facts to the person's desires, attitudes, and aversions. One learns what it is to feel relieved (what "feels relieved" means) by learning to recognize a pattern of bodily sensations as the pattern that typically occurs when one discovers that a possible danger has been removed.

What the bodily sensation-pattern view does commit us to is the functional dependence of reports of feelings on the stimulation of internal sensory receptors. For unless we take as a criterion of something's being a sensation (bodily or otherwise) that it can be reliably produced by the stimulation of nerve endings, we have no distinctive concept of bodily sensations. Hence according to this view a person reports feeling one way rather than another (apart from his beliefs about the situation he is in) because of a certain kind of pattern of stimulation of sense receptors within the body. Insofar as the psychophysiology of bodily sensation can be developed beyond its present rudimentary state, the bodily-sensation hypothesis will be capable of interesting empirical tests.

There are other recommendations for this view of feelings. For one thing, it helps us to see connections between apparently very diverse uses of "feel." Feeling a lump in the throat or feeling a cold chill run down the spine differs from feeling a cool wind on the cheek only as internal bodily sensation differs from external tactile sensation; again, feeling twitchy, sleepy, or energetic differs from the preceding only in a lesser degree of localization. Similarly, on the present hypothesis, feeling morose, relieved, ill at ease, or lonely will differ from the bodily sensations just mentioned, apart from cognitive and motivational components, only in that they each involve a more complex pattern of bodily sensations. We might even try to bring "feeling like going for a walk" into the same camp by claiming that to feel like going for a walk, as contrasted with just being prepared or willing to go for a walk, essentially involves a distinctive pattern of bodily sensations of incipient muscular tendencies. In linking together these various uses of "feel," the theory also helps us to see what is distinctive about feeling vis-à-vis other mental states. On this account we can see what distinguishes feelings from thoughts and intentions, without positing mysterious entities or ultimate qualities, just by pointing out the way in which feelings do, whereas thoughts and intentions do not, essentially involve bodily sensations.

Reconsideration of feeling theory of emotion. If we adopt the theory of feeling as bodily sensation, the identification of emotions with "pure" feeling reduces to William James's position that an emotion is to be identified with sensations of the bodily changes which make emotion an upset or disturbed state. Thus in its most intelligible and plausible form the feeling theory becomes closely connected with the bodily upset theory, the one being the psychic shadow of the other, and the choice between them depending more on one's metaphysical inclinations than on any factual differences. Of course one could identify emotions with bodily sensations of incipient action tendencies, rather than with bodily sensations of organic upset. This position is taken by the psychologist Nina Bull, who takes emotion on its conscious side to consist of sensations of postural sets and preparatory motor attitudes. Such a view would be a psychic shadow of the action-tendency form of the motivational theory. As such, it would be subject to the already mentioned objections to supposing that there are distinctive action tendencies for each emotion. We shall confine our attention to James's form of the position.

We can now sharpen the question as to whether it is possible to distinguish between any two emotions by reference to the feelings involved. The question now becomes one as to whether there is a distinctive pattern of bodily sensations for each distinguishable emotion. A negative answer is often given on the basis of the fact that people are generally unable to provide different analyses of, for example, feeling annoyed and feeling indignant into bodily sensations like thrills and tensions that could occur in any context. But, as the foregoing discussion indicates, this inability is quite compatible with its being the case that the terms "feel annoyed" and "feel indignant" are used to report complex patterns of bodily sensations for which we have no other available designation. Physiological researches have disclosed no patterns of glandular secretion, cardiac functioning, respiratory patterns, and so on, which are distinctive of fear, anger, joy, and other distinguishable emotions. But since the available techniques of objective measurement are quite crude by comparison with the fineness of discrimination of conscious sensation, this evidence is far from conclusive.

A stronger argument against the identification of feeling with bodily sensation is that any bodily processes or sensations which are typical of a certain emotion could occur in such a context that the person would not attribute that emotional state to himself. Thus bodily changes typical of fear have been induced by suddenly tipping a chair in which the subject was seated. When this was unexpected the subject reported having been frightened, but when he was warned in advance what would happen, he reported not being frightened. Nevertheless the recorded bodily upset in heart action, respiration, glandular and digestive secretions, and so on, was indistinguishable in the two cases. In an ingenious experiment, Stanley Schachter and J. E. Singer injected subjects with a drug which induces changes typical of emotional upset ("Cognitive, Social, and Physiological Determinants of Emotional States," *Psychological Review*, Vol. 69, 1962, 379–399). Among subjects receiving the same injection, the reported emotional states varied widely in accordance with (1) whether the subject was told what to expect from the drug and (2) whether he was then exposed to a frivolous or an aggressive companion. Because of obvious limitations of available techniques of measurement and control we cannot be sure that bodily sensations were exactly, or even approximately, the same for all subjects in this experiment. Nevertheless the results of this and similar experiments strongly suggest that a person's cognitions of motivationally relevant features of his situation play an essential role in his identification of his emotional state.

Again, emotions are appraised as reasonable or unreasonable, justified or unjustified. We say things like, "It's unreasonable of you to be so afraid of him" or "There is no justification for your being so indignant." But it is difficult to see how either involuntary bodily processes or organic sensations could be subject to such appraisals.

Finally, the feeling and bodily upset theories give us no basis for drawing the line between emotion and nonemotion. What is the difference between bodily upsets and/or bodily sensations that enter into emotions and those that do not? On what basis do we say that a startled reaction and a sensation of an upset stomach are not emotions? The fact that we do make these distinctions seems to show that some other criterion is being employed.

Insufficiency of evaluational theory. All the criticisms so far advanced against the feeling theory point in the direction of the evaluational theory. It seems that we do distinguish between shame and embarrassment, for example, by reference to how the subject perceives the object of the emotion. Even if there are in fact subtle differences in the patterns of bodily sensation associated with the two, it seems that what in fact forms the basis of the distinction is that it is necessary for shame but not for embarrassment that the subject take the object to be something which is his fault. Such evaluations can obviously be judged as more or less reasonable, realistic, or justified. And the presence of such evaluations seems to be what makes bodily states and sensations emotional. Some sinkings in the stomach are emotional, because they stem from an evaluation of something as dangerous; other sinkings are not emotional, because they stem from indigestion. Nevertheless we cannot identify emotions with evaluations alone without completely losing contact with such phrases as "emotional reaction," "getting emotional over it," and "controlling one's emotions." An evaluation can be either emotional or unemotional. Two people can see a snake as equally dangerous, both can take the same sorts of steps to meet the dangers, and yet one is gripped with fear while the other is calm. Again, two people can see what a third person is doing as violating someone's rights, yet one is very indignant, the other is untouched. Even if it should be claimed that no perceptual evaluation of the appropriate sort can be completely unemotional, it will still remain true that two persons can see a situation as equally dangerous yet one be much more frightened than the other. That is sufficient to show that being frightened cannot consist only in seeing something as dangerous, since the degree of fright can vary without a variation in the perceptual evaluation.

It is neglect of this consideration that is largely responsible for the fact that systematists have typically included in the category of passions not only emotions, but attitudes like love and hate, dispositions like desire and aversion, and qualities of character like benevolence and courage. What binds these together is that they all, in various ways, involve evaluations of objects.

Comprehensive view. Since none of the factors we have been considering is sufficient by itself to constitute an emotion, the obvious move would be to construe an emotion as some complex of evaluation, bodily upset, and sensation thereof. It is important that we make the connection between these three factors causal, rather than a mere contiguity. Otherwise the fact that the same bodily upset can be contemporaneous with two evaluations, one of an object as dangerous, the other of the same object as beautiful, might lead us to include both evaluations in the emotion of fear. Proceeding along this line we arrive at a definition of an emotional state as a more or less disturbed state of the organism, together with the bodily sensations produced by this state, arising from a perceptual evaluation of something. Such a conception has been put forward by the psychologists P. T. Young and Magda B. Arnold, although most psychologists who emphasize bodily upset are inhibited by behaviorist or physicalistic prejudices from taking full account of the central importance of evaluations, and most philosophers who are impressed by the latter are too unwilling to go beyond what is obviously involved in common-sense concepts to allow themselves to appreciate the significance of bodily upset as a criterion.

The difficulties that remain concern the question whether each of the factors specified in this definition is necessary for the occurrence of an emotional state. We have already seen that there are some reasons for thinking that it is possible for a person to be angry or frightened without having the feelings typically associated with these states. That an evaluation of an object is not strictly necessary is suggested by the phenomenon of "objectless emotions," such as a nameless dread, a vague apprehension of some impending disaster, or a general irritation at nothing in particular. One may try to save the necessity of this condition by positing an unconscious repressed evaluation of something as the source of the emotional condition in each of these cases. Thus it may be said that what a person is really afraid of in a particular case of nameless dread is his own repressed impulses, which he has unconsciously evaluated as dangerous. But it is not clear that such an imputation can be justified for every objectless emotion. The remaining factor, a disturbed state of the organism, seems to evoke the fewest objections. It seems impossible to envisage a clear case of an emotional state which does not involve such a disturbance, along with sensations of it. Even the cases discussed earlier, in which the person does not feel as one generally does when in the grip of the emotion in question, for instance anger, still involve some awareness of a disturbed state of the body, for example, a felt tenseness.

We are in a dilemma. If we exclude from our compound criterion every factor that is not a necessary condition (in the absence of which an emotional state can occur) we will be left only with bodily upset and, as we have seen, this is not by itself a sufficient condition; one's body can be upset, as in illness, without one's thereby having any recognizable emotion. But how can we include in our criterion any condition that is not necessary for the occurrence of an emotion?

We may find a way out by noting that the cases of emotion without typical feelings and without conscious evaluations of objects are not clear cases. They are not the cases a person would give if he set out to explain to someone what an emotion is. One would not evince lack of understanding of the concept if he should raise a doubt as to whether these cases are cases of anger, fear, or whatever. This suggests the hypothesis that these applications of the term are derivative from its application to more full-blooded cases in which all these factors are present. It may be that the concept of emotion is like many other concepts, such as religion, poetry, and science, in that we cannot explicate it without making a distinction between central (paradigm) cases and cases which deviate from the paradigm in lacking some central feature but do not deviate sufficiently to completely inhibit the application of the term. Thus the full range of cases exhibits what Wittgenstein called "family resemblances." There is a list of typical features, such that some are present in all cases, no one feature is present in all cases, and only the paradigm cases exhibit all the features. If we can agree that the concept of emotion must be elucidated by this more complex pattern of analysis, there will be good reason for including in our list of typical features all those contained in our initial list. For, now that we have seen that every feature, with the possible exception of bodily upset, is absent in some cases, we cannot justify exclusion of, for example, typical involuntary expressions like gaping and dilation of the eyes, on the ground that one may have the emotion in question without exhibiting it in the normal way. Thus we may take the original list of typical features as bringing out what sort of thing an emotion is. This way of viewing the matter would seem to accommodate most fully the various considerations presented in this article.

Bibliography

PHILOSOPHICAL WORKS

An excellent survey of the history of the subject is to be found in H. M. Gardiner, R. G. Metcalf, and J. G. Beebe-Center, *Feeling and Emotion, A History of Theories* (New York, 1937). More recent developments are surveyed in J. G. Beebe-Center, "Feeling and Emotion," in Harry Helson, ed., *Theoretical Foundations of Psychology* (New York, 1951).

Important historical treatments are to be found in Thomas Aquinas, *Summa Theologica*, II, 2, 22–48; René Descartes, *The Passions of the Soul;* John Locke, *An Essay Concerning Human Understanding*, Book II, Ch. 20; Thomas Hobbes, *Leviathan*, Part I, Ch. 6; Benedict Spinoza, *Ethics*, Part III; David Hume, *A Treatise of Human Nature*, Book II.

Recent discussions by analytical philosophers include Gilbert Ryle, *The Concept of Mind* (London, 1949), Ch. 4; Errol Bedford, "Emotions," *PAS*, New Series, Vol. 57 (1965–1957), 281–304; R. S. Peters and C. A. Mace, "Emotions and the Category of Passivity," *ibid.*, Vol. 62 (1961–1962), 117–142; and Anthony Kenny, *Action, Emotion and Will* (London, 1963).

PSYCHOLOGICAL WORKS

William James's classic theory can be found in William James and C. G. Lange, *The Emotions* (Baltimore, 1922). Useful summaries and integrations of psychological thought on the subject can be found in P. T. Young, *Emotion in Man and Animal* (New York, 1943), M. B. Arnold, *Emotion and Personality*, 2 vols. (New York, 1960), and Robert Plutchik, *The Emotions: Facts, Theories, and a New Model* (New York, 1962).

WILLIAM P. ALSTON

EMOTIVE MEANING. The concept of emotive meaning became prominent as a result of attempts by members of the Vienna circle and their followers to establish the verifiability criterion of meaningfulness and attempts by other philosophers to analyze moral and poetic discourse.

Factual and emotive meaning. The philosophers who advocated the verifiability criterion were convinced that it is futile to argue over matters for which it is in principle impossible to give empirical evidence. They sought to develop a criterion of meaningfulness that would rule out such questions as whether universals exist independently of their exemplifications and whether it is objectively true that pleasure is a good thing. The verifiability criterion recognizes a sentence as meaningful only if it is in principle possible to cite empirical evidence which would count for or against it. However, they were forced to admit that people say many things for which it makes no sense to look for empirical evidence but which are clearly not devoid of meaning—for example, lines of poetry such as "Life's but a walking shadow" and expressions of emotional reaction such as "How disgusting!" They took this point into account by reformulating the criterion so that it stated a requirement for a *kind* of meaning, variously termed "cognitive," "factual," or "scientific"; it was then allowed that utterances which did not satisfy the verifiability criterion but were still not lacking in sense had "emotive" meaning.

However, philosophers animated primarily by such concerns have done little or nothing to give any positive account of emotive meaning. The assumption embodied in the use of "emotive" seems to be that whereas sentences satisfying the requirement can be used to state facts, those which fail to satisfy it, and are not pure nonsense, all have the function of expressing (and perhaps evoking) emotion. But it is on the face of it quite implausible to regard such a mixed group as moral judgments, requests, and the variety of utterances we have in poetry and fiction as all essentially expressions of emotion. It seems clear that among the sentences which do not pass the verifiability test one will have to distinguish a number of different functions, of which expressing emotion is only one.

Symbolic and emotive functions. More serious attempts to arrive at a positive conception of emotive meaning have developed out of the concern to discover and formulate the peculiarities of moral and poetic discourse. The most influential work in this tradition has been *The Meaning of Meaning*, by C. K. Ogden and I. A. Richards. There a distinction is drawn between the symbolic (referential) and emotive functions of language. The symbolic function is a statement's referring to something and putting forward an assertion about it as true. The emotive function is the expression and evocation of feelings and attitudes. Thus, if we say, "Ann Arbor is in Michigan," we are using words to "communicate a reference"; we are making a statement which can be evaluated as true or false in a straightforward sense of those terms. However, if I say, "Rats!" or "That's splendid!" or "Life's but a walking shadow," I am not using my words (primarily) to record or communicate references to anything, and what I say cannot properly be assessed as true or false. On the contrary, I am using such sentences primarily to express my annoyance at something or enthusiasm for something or sense of futility and/or to evoke or strengthen such feelings and attitudes in my auditors. It is quite compatible with the distinction between symbolic and emotive functions to hold that generally, or even invariably, what we say has functions of both kinds. Nevertheless, particular stress was put on this distinction because it was felt that certain areas of discourse, especially poetry and moral discourse, had suffered from its neglect. According to Richards, once we realize that the primary function of poetry is emotive—the inculcation of "fitting attitudes to experience"—we will cease trying to force poetry into a scientific mold by looking for a kind of truth embodied in it. Similarly, once we see that moral judgments such as "You ought to pay more attention to your children" have the primary function of expressing and evoking positive and negative attitudes toward lines of conduct, we will abandon the futile attempt to find ways of showing them to be true or false in the way that statements of fact are true or false and will concentrate attention on such more rewarding enterprises as a study of the nature and determinants of attitudes.

As continuing discussion has brought out, this innocuous-looking distinction conceals a host of complexities. To the extent that we succeed in uncovering these, we may well come to doubt that there is any distinction which exactly meets the specifications laid down by Ogden and Richards. Of course, it is only to be expected that a dichotomous division of linguistic functions will yield very broad classes which have many subdivisions. But the trouble with the distinction in question is that the classes specified, insofar as any definite specification is given, are without any clear principle of unity; each contains members which seem to have little to do with one another and which have quite different relations to members of the opposing class. This difficulty attaches to both sides of the supposed dichotomy.

ANALYSIS OF SYMBOLIC AND EMOTIVE USES OF LANGUAGE

Problems concerning "referential." Ogden and Richards characterize the "symbolic" function both as the "symbolization of references" and as the making of statements; they seem to regard these characterizations as interchangeable, and many have followed them in this. Yet the characterizations do not seem to be very closely associated. To clear this up we have to decide how we are going to interpret "reference" and "statement." The latter is a bit easier. A statement is something that can be assessed as true or false. Thus, "My car is in the garage" (given a normal context for such an utterance) will count as a statement, whereas "Would you bring me a glass of water?" will not. But other cases are not so clear. Is "You did the right thing" true or false? "True" and "false" are in fact applied to such utterances. But it is claimed that when we apply them we are not using "true" and "false" in the "literal" or "scientific" sense they have when applied to statements of empirical fact. The matter is controversial; nevertheless, although we may not be able to settle all cases, there remain many clear cases of statements and nonstatements.

With "reference" and allied terms the situation is more difficult. There is a clear sense of "refer" in which I *refer* to what I am talking about in an utterance, as contrasted with what I am saying about it. Thus, in saying "My car is in the garage" I would be referring to my car and to the garage, but not to myself or to the relation of one thing being in another. Following this line, one might speak of language as being used referentially when a linguistic expression is used to refer to something. Thus, in the above sentence "my car" and "the garage" are used referentially, but "is" and "in" are not, nor is "my" or "the" by itself, nor is the whole sentence. This is a narrower sense of "referential" than the one Ogden and Richards want; if their distinction is accepted, the sentence "My car is in the garage" would be called referential, rather than emotive. Ogden and Richards' theory of reference states that making a reference to something, x, is taking something else, y, to be a sign of x, as when I take a certain noise to be a sign of an improperly seated valve. But this account is not generally accepted, and for very good reasons. If in the course of thinking about or discussing the nature of scientific explanation I were to say, "Explanation is very different from prediction," that would be a paradigm of what they call the symbolic or referential use. However, I need not be taking anything to be a *sign* of explanations and predictions, although I am referring to them.

Perhaps the best that can be done to explain the sense of "referential" needed for the distinction between symbolic and emotive meaning is to say that a linguistic expression is used referentially when it is used to call an auditor's attention to something. (Here the use of language is restricted to interpersonal communication. Consideration of the use of language in talking to oneself would further complicate matters.)

If this is what "referential use" means, it is clearly not restricted to statements, as Ogden and Richards suggest. If I make a request ("Please bring me a drink of water") I am using words to call something to the attention of the auditor *just as much* as I would be in making a statement ("I already have a glass of water"). Similar comments apply to other clearly nonstatemental utterances—promises, questions, denunciations, exhortations. It cannot even be claimed that statements are distinguished by the fact that in their case the referential function is *primary*. Attending to the notion of my reading your paper is just as much a necessary condition of my communicating with you when I promise to read your paper as it is when I tell you that I have read your paper. The "referential" function is as essential in the one case as in the other. In fact, it is basic to any linguistic communication, with the possible exception of pure interjections, such as "Splendid!," "Ugh!," "Hello." If one does take interjections to be exceptions, it is probably because the *words* involved do not present any objects to the mind of the auditor. But to this there are two possible replies: (1) Such expressions are always used in a context which serves, more or less, to indicate the object of the feeling or attitude expressed. If I say "Ugh!" shortly after entering a room, while curling my upper lip slightly, I depend on the context of my utterance to convey the idea of something unpleasant or distasteful in the room. This does not seem vastly different from using the context to convey the content of my statement when I make a statement by saying "Yes" to a question. (Here the relevant feature of the context is the question just asked.) (2) Apart from this, it seems that the use of interjections does ordinarily serve to call attention to the feeling or attitude being expressed—disgust, enthusiasm, or whatever. It may even present the idea of the speaker's having such a feeling or attitude. To this it can be replied that even so, the interjection does not *refer to* the feeling but expresses it. Undoubtedly it serves to express the feeling, but if it does not also refer to the feeling, then "refer" is being used in the narrower sense, in which "went out" in "He went out" does not refer to anything. It would seem, then, that in any sense of "referential" broad enough to cover the cases Ogden and Richards want it to cover, it is much too broad, in that it plays the (same sort of) essential role in all linguistic communication.

Problems concerning "emotive." The emotive function of language is often said to be the expression and evocation of feelings and attitudes. One might ask why feelings and attitudes together should constitute one function of language, rather than, say, feelings and beliefs, or ideas and attitudes. Obviously the reason is that feelings and attitudes are thought to be noncognitive, in contrast to beliefs, conceptions, etc. However, it is doubtful that a concept of the cognitive that both is important and yields the desired distinctions can be clearly formulated.

Definition of "cognitive." According to one analysis, the cognitive is equivalent to the intentional, which means, roughly, having an object as an essential characteristic. An idea or a belief is intentional: we cannot specify what idea we are talking about without specifying it as the idea *of* something, and in order to identify a belief we have to make explicit that it is the belief that such-and-such is the case. A sharp pain is not intentional; it is what it is by virtue of its intrinsic characteristics rather than by virtue of its "pointing to" something outside itself. But by this criterion attitudes are clearly cognitive also, for any given attitude is what it is partly because it is an attitude *toward* one thing rather than another, such as my distrust of a certain politician. Some feelings can be nonintentional, as when we feel depressed without feeling depressed over anything in particular. But other feelings (perhaps this involves another sense of "feeling") are intentional—for instance, feeling resentment *at* something you have done or feeling satisfied *with* the job I have done. The expression of these intentional feelings constitutes the major part of "emotive language."

A much stronger definition, etymologically supported, would restrict the cognitive to cases of knowledge. But in that sense mere beliefs and the entertaining of possibilities would be ruled out. A satisfactory solution might be to define a cognitive mental element as one that is appropriately judged in terms of its relation to something outside itself. Thus, the intentionality of the element would be a criterion in its assessment. This would clearly include mere beliefs and the consideration of possibilities, for even if they do not qualify as knowledge they can be appropriately assessed as corresponding with or failing to correspond with the facts. However, attitudes, too, can be evaluated in terms of how appropriate they are in the light of certain facts. Thus one might criticize *X* for feeling resentment toward *Y* by pointing to the fact that *Y* had done nothing to *X* that could serve to justify resentment. It may be claimed that the sense in which attitudes might or might not conform to the facts is very different from the sense in which beliefs might or might not conform, but a specification of this difference would undoubtedly turn into a very long story.

Definition of "emotive." Perhaps more headway could be made by attempting to give a positive characterization of emotive states of mind rather than by first characterizing the cognitive and then specifying the other side as the negation of it. Thus, it might be thought that feelings and attitudes are distinct from purely cognitive states in that they essentially contain an element of immediate feeling and perhaps embody a direct tendency to act in a certain way. One would not have to deny that resentment toward *Y* involved a cognitive aspect, but the claim would be that a genuine case of resentment also has to include certain distinctive kinds of immediate feeling and tendencies to act toward Y in certain ways rather than others. Something might be done with this approach, but it would turn out that on the basis of this criterion, the range of feelings and attitudes is narrower than we had supposed. For example, I may have quite a definite and well-formed attitude of disapproval toward teen-age beach parties without any noticeable affective states ever being connected with it and without my having any more tendency to do anything about it than I have in connection with many beliefs. In fact, there are many beliefs about matters of practical importance, such as the belief that my furnace is not working, which have action tendencies associated with them as firmly as with many attitudes.

Expressing and evoking. The conjunction of "express" and "evoke" presents some difficulties. To be sure, the emotive theorist need not saddle himself with the assumption, sometimes made, that generally an expression which is suited to express a feeling will also be well suited to evoke it. I may quite adequately express my annoyance by saying "Damn!" but unless my auditor strongly disapproves of swearing, I am not likely to evoke annoyance in him. It is also easy to avoid the error committed by Ogden and Richards when they include "the promotion of effects intended" among the emotive functions of language. It would certainly wreck the whole scheme to class the production of all effects—for example, conveying information to someone—among the emotive functions. A more restricted class of effects is what is needed. But serious problems would remain. The fact is that expression and evocation belong to quite different dimensions of functioning. One cannot be said to have *evoked* a feeling of contempt unless his utterance had a certain effect, whereas this is not true of *expressing* a feeling of contempt. There is no effect such that if one did not produce it he did not express contempt.

We may, using terminology introduced by John Austin, describe evocation as "perlocutionary" (done *by* saying something) and expression as "illocutionary" (done *in* saying something). Both kinds of acts involve something more than a "locutionary" act (the utterance of a sentence or sentence surrogate). For the perlocutionary act it is the occurrence of a certain effect of the utterance. For the illocutionary act we are able to see that something beyond the utterance of an appropriate sentence is involved. The sentence "Have you learned nothing in all these years?," which can be used to express contempt for someone, can also be uttered without expressing contempt for anyone; one would do this if he used the sentence to give an example, as has just been done here. But it is difficult to make explicit what the something extra of illocutionary acts is. One view is that what enters into a given illocutionary act over and above the utterance of an appropriate sentence is the subjection of the utterance to certain rules which forbid the utterance of the sentence unless certain conditions hold. Thus, the above sentence can be used to express contempt for someone when its utterance is subject to the *requirement* that the speaker actually has contempt for the person in question. To put the matter differently, I express contempt for someone when, in uttering an appropriate sentence, I take responsibility for its being the case that I have contempt for the person in question. Again, I advise you to take another course in chemistry when, in uttering an appropriate sentence, I take responsibility for the existence of such conditions as that you have already had a course in chemistry, that it is not impossible for you to take another one, and that I believe that it would be in your best interests to do so. Other examples of illocutionary acts are telling someone that the plane is late, admitting that one accepted a bribe, remarking that there is a good crowd for the meeting, asking someone to turn down the radio, and promising someone to meet him at a certain time and place. Examples of perlocutionary acts are getting someone to realize that ____, frightening someone, getting someone to do something, and arousing enthusiasm in someone for something.

Reflecting on the fundamental character of this distinction, we can begin to appreciate one of the reasons it is so difficult to make sense of the distinction between the symbolic (referential, cognitive) and emotive functions. The emotive side of the distinction, as usually formulated, contains functions that enter into quite different contrasts. Evoking feelings and attitudes contrasts with other effects (on auditors) which our utterances have and for whose sake we speak as we do. In looking for fundamental distinctions in this area it is natural to concentrate on differences between types of psychological states, such as cognition, emotion, feeling, etc., since psychological states are usually among the effects we seek to produce through speech. In looking for contrasts to *expressing* feelings and attitudes it is also relevant to attend to distinctions between kinds of psychological states, for one can express opinions, convictions, and intentions as well as more purely emotional states. But expressing feelings also contrasts in a more fundamental way with other kinds of illocutionary acts, such as making promises, predictions, and requests. In view of this heterogeneity, the difficulty in finding a clear principle of division is hardly surprising.

Asserting and expressing. Taking advantage of the insights gained above, let us see what clear distinctions can be made among uses of language. It is with illocutionary uses, if anywhere, that we must seek to find whether anything can be salvaged from the dichotomy between expressing feelings and making statements that can be evaluated as true or false. As used by philosophers, "statement" and "assertion" are technical terms which cover much more than statements or assertions in any ordinary sense. The terms are generally applied to anything said which can be assessed as true or false. If so, the position usually taken by emotivists, that expressing a feeling and asserting that one has the feeling are mutally exclusive, does not seem to be borne out by the facts. Presumably this position has seemed plausible because people have been preoccupied with the expression of feelings by interjections. It is undoubtedly true that when I express enthusiasm for something by saying "Capital!" or express annoyance at something by saying "Damn!" I have not (explicitly) said anything which can be evaluated as true or false. But I can equally express enthusiasm for something by saying "I'm terribly enthusiastic about that" and can equally express annoyance at something by saying "That annoys me no end." In these cases my utterances could also be reported by saying that I had *told* someone I was enthusiastic about something or was annoyed by something; these seem to be clear cases of statements in the philosopher's sense. Thus, it seems that although expressing a feeling and stating that one has it are not identical, they coincide in an important range of cases. If so, the distinction between them could hardly be as fundamental as emotivists make it out to be.

Psychological function. The position that expressing a feeling and asserting that one has the feeling may coincide could be challenged in several ways. The emotivist might reply by claiming that even if there are cases where one is both expressing a feeling and stating that one has it, the activities are still quite distinct; it is just that one is doing both simultaneously. This claim would have to be supported by an account of what it is to express a feeling that (1) is distinct from an account of what it is to state that one has the feeling and (2) applies to the cases in question.

Sometimes expressing a feeling is thought of as a kind of release of emotional tension; one *presses out* the feeling through one's utterance; it is a kind of "letting off steam." But this conception seems plausible only if one has restricted his attention to the use of expletives. Saying "Damn!" in a violent manner does sometimes serve to reduce tension. But there are many contexts in which one expresses appreciation for something or expresses interest in something or expresses delight at something where the utterance neither has, nor is intended to have, the function of reducing emotional tension because there was no significant quantity of tension to be reduced. The most that could plausibly be claimed along this line is that an utterance will not count as an *expression* of a feeling unless it is delivered with a certain amount of feeling (with "expression"). It may be that saying in a flat tone of voice, after considerable deliberation, "Yes, that annoys me" would not count as an expression of annoyance. But even this is questionable.

Natural-sign function. Ogden and Richards suggest that expressing a feeling or attitude consists in performing an utterance which could be taken as a natural sign of that state, just as a certain hum in an amplifier can be taken as a sign of a defective tube. To say that x is a natural sign of y is to say that they have in fact occurred together in a sufficient proportion of cases to enable one to infer the presence of the latter from the presence of the former. (Natural signs are explained more fully in SIGN AND SYMBOL.) By contrast, when I *assert* that I have a feeling, my utterance is connected with the feeling (if any) via the conventional rules of the language; it *symbolizes* the feeling. Thus, according to Ogden and Richards' position, expressing a feeling and asserting that one has that feeling differ fundamentally with regard to the kind of word–world relation involved, even though there are cases in which both kinds of relations are involved.

There is no doubt that this natural-sign relationship exists between facial expressions and tones of voice, on the one hand, and the feelings and attitudes they are said to express, evince, manifest, or betray, on the other. One takes a certain look on the face as a manifestation of contempt because he believes that as a matter of fact such a look often accompanies a contemptuous attitude toward something. But it does not seem that this kind of account applies to expressing x by *saying* something. Whether I say "Damn!" or "That annoys me no end," my utterance counts as an expression of annoyance (just as in the second case it counts as a statement that I am annoyed) only because the words I utter (and the grammatical constructions I employ) have the significance they have in the language, and this is a matter of conventional rules. The assumption often made by emotivists that sentences serve to express feelings in basically the same way as involuntary gestures, looks, and intonations is quite unjustified. Expressing a feeling, as an illocutionary act, is rule-governed in just the same way as making a statement or making a request.

Thus, we are faced with two salient facts: (1) In a large range of cases what one is doing can be specified either as expressing one's feeling toward something or as asserting that one has that feeling toward something. (2) No one has succeeded in giving an analysis of expressing feelings (as a linguistic activity) which would sharply differentiate it from asserting that one has a feeling. It is difficult to avoid the conclusion that the assertion–expression distinction does not represent a major division in the field of illocutionary acts.

Types of illocutionary acts. The question remains whether, within the great diversity of illocutionary acts, one can draw any distinctions that correspond at all to the intentions of those who feel there is a fundamental distinction between cognitive and emotive uses of language. There are two distinctions which may fulfill those intentions. One can distinguish between statements (to which questions of truth or falsity are appropriate) and nonstatements, and one can distinguish between cases of expressing something and all other illocutionary acts. But this is a long way from what the emotivists were after, for several reasons. First, there is no appreciable correlation between the distinctions. As we have seen, many cases of expressing feelings are such that what is said can be evaluated as true or false ("That annoys me no end"), and if we had extended the discussion to expressions of belief and intention we would have even more reason to think so. The above two distinctions divide the field of illocutionary acts in quite different ways. Second, there is no justification for considering either side of either of these distinctions to be characteristically "emotive." There is none in the distinction between expressing something and all other illocutionary acts because of the fact that "cognitive" states like belief can be expressed as well as feelings and attitudes. Emotivists may claim that beliefs are not expressed in the same sense as feelings, but this claim will presumably rest on one of the inadequate accounts of the expression of feelings examined above. The nonstatement side of the first distinction contains an enormous diversity of items—promises, verdicts, suggestions, commands greetings, congratulations, interrogations. Greetings and promises, for instance, seem to differ from each other as much as either differs from statements. There seems to be little prospect of finding any positive feature shared by all. Certainly they do not all involve feelings or attitudes in any common or distinctive way. Third, there is no reason to attach the labels "cognitive" and "referential" to one side of these distinctions rather than the other. Whenever we perform any illocutionary act, with the possible exception of one-word interjections, we use words in such a way as to get across to a suitably trained auditor what it is we are talking about. In that sense what we say has "cognitive content" or "conceptual content," whether we are expressing something, making a statement, or making a request, promise, or demand.

Emotive force. Insofar as we can obtain a clear sense of "cognitive" that fulfills our requirements, we can distinguish between producing cognitive states in a hearer and producing effects of other sorts. But once again the noncognitive side of this distinction will be very diverse, even more diverse than the cognitive side. In addition to feelings and attitudes, among the presumably noncognitive effects we seek to produce through speech are actions, tendencies to action, amusement, reassurance, and boredom. One might claim that one or more of the last three are feelings and/or attitudes. The fact that this is controversial points up the need for tightening these terms.

Actually there are two parallel distinctions here, one between effects which utterances actually have and the other between intended effects of utterances. (People rarely say something for the purpose of boring an auditor, though that effect is often produced.) Neither distinction has any strong correlation with the illocutionary act distinctions just discussed. A nonstatemental utterance can have various cognitive effects; for example, in asking you who the American League batting champion in 1912 was, I may, in addition to putting certain objects before your mind, lead you to realize that I am interested in baseball and that the American League existed as long ago as 1912. And speakers may exploit these potentialities. I may deliberately set out to get a certain piece of information across to you by asking a question or making a request. Again, statements can have a variety of noncognitive effects, and these potentialities can be exploited. Thus, I may tell you that a burglar tried to get into the house last night, in order to frighten you. Analogous remarks could be made about the distinction between expressing and other kinds of illocutionary acts.

Nevertheless, the notion that an utterance is liable to have emotive effects is not an unimportant one (assuming we can satisfactorily clarify the concept of the emotive). Rhetoricians have had occasion to note the probable emotive effects of various locutions on various types of audiences. Pairs of terms such as "stool pigeon" and "informant for the police" or "bureaucrat" and "official in a large organization" differ markedly in this respect for large classes of audiences; the term "emotive force" is sometimes used to mark the difference. Philosophers who greatly value the notion of emotive language typically suppose that an adequate understanding of poetry and ethical discourse requires a great deal of attention to the emotive force of some of the terms employed therein. No doubt this is an interesting topic. But it would seem to be a mistake to suppose that this consideration could tell us anything about the content of ethical or poetic utterances or shed any light on *what* is being said when such utterances are issued. When I have said something, I have said it regardless of what effects my utterance has or does not have. If we supposed that the content of what I said could be constituted by my success or failure in bringing about certain effects, we would be supposing that the future can influence the past. Of course, that still leaves open the possibility that what I say when I utter a given sentence is a function of the sorts of effects the sentence usually, or often, has. But that is rather implausible. Rip Van Winkle was quite unprepared for the effect his utterance had when he said on awakening (after having slept through the American Revolution), "I am a loyal subject of the King," and he was unprepared because he did not know what effects an utterance of the sentence usually had in the contemporary setting. But assuming that he knew what the words meant, he knew perfectly well what he had said. Thus, although emotive force may be an interesting topic in its own right, it seems a mistake to suppose that its study will throw light on the content of what we say in various areas of discourse.

Emotive force and cognitive meaning. There has been considerable controversy over whether emotive force can vary independently of the "descriptive" or "cognitive" meaning of expressions. (These discussions have generally used the term "emotive meaning," but in fact they have concerned what we are now calling "emotive force.") The basic question is whether it is possible for two terms to differ in emotive force without differing at all in cognitive meaning or whether, on the contrary, a difference in emotive force always depends on a difference in cognitive meaning. Clearly, many emotive differences are so dependent. "Blackguard" differs in emotive force from "saint" because of the difference in what we are attributing to someone when we apply one or the other term to him. Whether such dependence holds in every case partly depends on how we analyze "descriptive meaning" or "cognitive meaning." Do "cheap" and "inexpensive," or "stool pigeon" and "informant for the police," differ in descriptive meaning as well as cognitive force? Let us suppose that "cheap" differs from "inexpensive" (apart from emotive force) only by typically calling up ideas of shoddiness, unattractiveness, unreliability, etc. If we take a hard line and refuse to call anything part of the meaning of "cheap" unless it would be strictly implied by an application of the term, then, since *ex hypothesi* when we call something cheap we do not strictly imply that it is shoddy, etc., we would not be able to find any difference in descriptive meaning behind the difference in emotive force. If, on the other hand, we admit ideas typically elicited by a word into its "descriptive meaning," we would make the opposite decision. It seems clear that any two terms which differ noticeably in emotive force will differ at least in the ideas they typically call up, but many pairs will not exhibit any other relevant difference. Hence, a decision on the original question will depend on a decision as to what counts as "meaning."

EMOTIVE MEANING

Thus far little has been said about emotive *meaning.* This is a reflection of the fact that although many writers on the subject make free use of the phrase, they in fact talk mostly about kinds of uses or functions of language and do little or nothing to exhibit any basis for using the term "emotive" to label a special kind of *meaning.* It is not clear that any of the distinctions between uses we have been examining implies a corresponding distinction in types of meaning. The illocutionary act distinctions could be reflected directly only in differences in the meanings of *sentences*, for a word or a phrase is too small a unit with which to perform an illocutionary act. One might say that insofar as a sentence can be used to express something, it has "expressive meaning," and insofar as a sentence can be used to make a statement, it has "assertive meaning," or "cognitive meaning." But to do this would only be to rechristen the distinctions between different illocutionary acts.

Emotive force and meaning. The notion of meaning has a much more important application to words than to sentences; we rarely speak of what a sentence means. There are good reasons for this, the chief one being that the primary reason for saying what a linguistic element means is to help someone gain a more complete mastery of a language, and it is obviously more economical to teach a language word by word than sentence by sentence. The number of words is relatively limited; given a finite number of words, plus some rules of grammatical construction, a person can form and understand an indefinite number of sentences. In dealing with words the perlocutionary dimension would *seem* to have a more direct connection with meaning. And, in fact, those who speak of emotive meaning generally have in mind something like what we have called "emotive force." Whether we agree that the emotive force of a word is any part of its meaning depends on the theory of meaning we adopt. (See MEANING.) If we have a referential theory, according to which the meaning of a word is what the word refers to, or perhaps the relation between the word and what it refers to, we would deny that emotive force has anything to do with meaning. Insofar as the protagonists of emotive meaning proceed on the basis of any explicit account of meaning, it is a "perlocutionary" account in terms of the effects of utterances on auditors.

Stevenson's conception of meaning. Charles Stevenson has made the most determined attempt to develop a conception of emotive meaning. He construes meaning in general as the disposition of a linguistic expression to elicit psychological effects in hearers. He then proposes that we distinguish between cognitive and emotive meaning on the basis of the nature of the effects produced. This will, of course, get us back into the problem of distinguishing between cognitive and noncognitive psychological states and processes.

Stevenson does not quite identify emotive meaning with emotive force. He stipulates that a word's power to affect listeners in a certain way is not to be classed as part of its meaning unless it gained that power through a process of conditioning which attended its use in communication. This would clearly exclude any emotive force a word has by virtue of the physical characteristics of its sound. But it is not clear what else would be included or excluded. What about transfer phenomena? Suppose that the word "dough" arouses a warm feeling in one because it sounds like the name of a town, Deauville, where he spent many happy summer vacations as a child? We would not be inclined to say on this basis that he attached a (somewhat) different meaning to the word "dough." Would this be a case of the word's gaining a certain power "through a process of conditioning which attended its use in communication"? Perhaps the conditioning did not involve the use of that word, but presumably it involved the use of the name of the town in communication. However the line is drawn, it will undoubtedly let many things into the meaning of words which we would not ordinarily put there. If hearing the word "salesman" tends to elicit feelings of hostility and contempt in me, we would not ordinarily say that I attach a different meaning to the word (or understand it to mean something different) from a person in whom it arouses no such response. And this would be the case no matter how clear it is that I got into this state through a process of conditioning involving the use of the word in communication. Even if this reaction were very widespread among members of the language community, one would not expect to find any mention of the fact in a dictionary which listed the meanings of the word "salesman." However, this is true in only one of the senses of that protean word "meaning," the sense we are employing when we tell someone who is unfamiliar with a word what it means, or when we tell someone to look up the meaning of a word in the dictionary. It may be that in another sense of the term it would be correct to say that the word "salesman" has a special meaning (or significance) *for* me. A disenchanted wife might say to her husband, "When you say 'I love you' it doesn't mean anything to me any more," even though her mastery of the English language had not diminished a whit. *This* sense of meaning is roughly equivalent to emotive force. But it seems that those who make a point of stressing emotive meaning think of themselves as supplementing the lexicographer, bringing out aspects of meaning, in his sense of the term, which have been unduly neglected, rather than pointing out that there is a sense of "meaning" in which it is synonymous with "emotive force."

Meaning and effects. The difficulty with Stevenson's approach to meaning extends beyond the boundaries of the emotive. He has at least as much difficulty in his treatment of "cognitive meaning." In general it would seem that no aspect of the lexicographical sense of "meaning" can be equated with the powers words have to produce effects. "Procrastinate" means—to put things off. How is this to be analyzed as a statement concerning the disposition of the word to produce cognitive states in hearers? Perhaps the best analysis is as follows: When "procrastinate" is uttered in the hearing of a fluent speaker of English, it tends to call up the idea of putting things off. There are many problems about this formulation. What sort of an entity is an idea of putting things off? How do we tell when such an idea has been elicited? In what proportion of cases does such elicitation have to take place if we are to be justified in saying that this is what "procrastinate" means? The interesting thing is that although it is very dubious whether this formulation in terms of cognitive effects is correct, it is quite certain that "procrastinate" means—to put things off. Hence, we cannot equate the two.

A new approach to emotive meaning. It would seem that there is no hope of developing a full-blown concept of emotive *meaning* so long as we concentrate on the emotive *effects* of words. However, if we take a different approach to meaning in general, more might be accomplished. Suppose we take a meaning of a word to consist in the constant contribution it makes to the illocutionary act potential of sentences in which it occurs. If, as suggested above, we analyze an illocutionary act in terms of the conditions for the satisfaction of which a person takes responsibility in performing the act, we can attempt to bring out the sense in which "stool pigeon" has a different emotive meaning from—though the same descriptive meaning as—"informant for the police." It can be pointed out that if we experiment with substituting one of these expressions for the other in a variety of sentences, we will find a characteristic difference in illocutionary act potential resulting from the substitution, which can be illustrated by the following example: If I use "He's a stool pigeon" in the normal way, among the conditions for the satisfaction of which I am taking responsibility is the condition of my having an unfavorable attitude toward the activities I am attributing to him. However, I take responsibility for no such condition if I use instead the sentence "He's an informant for the police." Otherwise the illocutionary act force of the two sentences seems to be the same. For example, in both cases I take responsibility for its being the case that he is regularly engaged in providing information to a certain police force. Generalizing from this pair of terms, we can say that a given expression has an emotive meaning if its presence in a sentence serves to contribute to the illocutionary act potential of the sentence some condition having to do with the existence of a particular feeling or attitude on the part of the speaker. Another way to put this is to say that a word has emotive meaning provided its presence in a sentence is sufficient to give that sentence the potentiality of being used to express some feeling or attitude.

By proceeding along these lines, we can avoid any objection based on the discrepancy between meaning and effects (or potentialities to produce effects). The fact that the presence of a word in a sentence will give the use of that sentence the force of an expression of a feeling or attitude is a fact which is logically independent of the effect which the utterance of the word has on this or that occasion, or even the effects which its utterance generally has. To apply this distinction to a particular case, let us suppose that in contemporary America when someone is referred to as a communist an unfavorable impression of him tends to be generated but that there is no rule of our language which lays it down that one takes responsibility for having an unfavorable attitude toward the person referred to when he uses the sentence "He's a communist." In that case we would say that "communist," unlike "stool pigeon," does not have emotive meaning (at least on these grounds—there may be other grounds for attributing emotive meaning to it), but it does have emotive force. This concept of emotive meaning incorporates at least part of what those who introduced the term were trying to get at. The rest will have to be accommodated under the other concepts introduced in this article.

Bibliography

The pioneering contribution of C. K. Ogden and I. A. Richards is set forth in *The Meaning of Meaning*, 10th ed. (London, 1949). C. L. Stevenson's fullest presentation of the concept of emotive meaning is to be found in Ch. 2 of *Ethics and Language* (New Haven, 1944); further elaboration can be found in his essays "The Emotive Meaning of Ethical Terms," "Relativism and Nonrelativism in the Theory of Value," and "Meaning: Descriptive and Emotive," all reprinted in *Facts and Values* (New Haven, 1963). See also the "Retrospective Comments" in that volume.

For critical discussion of these positions, consult William Frankena, "'Cognitive' and 'Noncognitive,'" in Paul Henle, ed., *Language, Thought, and Culture* (Ann Arbor, Mich., 1958); Max Black, "Some Questions About Emotive Meaning," in *Language and Philosophy* (Ithaca, N.Y., 1949); H. D. Aiken, "Emotive 'Meanings' and Ethical Terms," *Journal of Philosophy*, Vol. 41 (1944); and Carl Wellman, *The Language of Ethics* (Cambridge, Mass., 1961), Chs. 4 and 7.

The best source for the logical positivist use of the concept is A. J. Ayer, *Language, Truth and Logic*, 2d ed. (London, 1946). The dispute over the dependence of emotive force on "descriptive meaning" is carried on in a series of articles: R. B. Brandt, "The Emotive Theory of Ethics"; C. L. Stevenson, "Brandt's Questions About Emotive Ethics"; and R. B. Brandt, "Stevenson's Defense of the Emotive Theory." All are in Vol. 59 (1950) of the *Philosophical Review*. (See also the bibliography for EMOTIVE THEORY OF ETHICS.)

WILLIAM P. ALSTON

EMOTIVE THEORY OF ETHICS. The "emotive theory" of ethics (here understood broadly as synonymous with "noncognitive theory") is a systematic answer to the questions: What is it to have an ethical conviction or an opinion about values? What is the meaning of words (like "right" or "good") characteristically used to express such convictions or opinions? What kind of justification or reasoning can support them? As such, this theory is a part of critical ethics, or metaethics, not a substantive theory in ethics, like hedonism or utilitarianism. In this respect it is like philosophical theories about the meaning and justification of scientific statements, in contrast to theories *in* science, like Darwin's theory and the theory of gases.

The main contentions of the emotive theory may be described, by way of preliminary summary, as consisting of a negative and a positive claim. (1) The negative claim (directed against naturalist and intuitional theories) is that ethical judgment and reasoning are drastically different from judgment and reasoning in science: ethical convictions are a kind of thing wholly different from scientific beliefs; words like "wrong" and "good," unlike scientific predicates, do not name properties, or at least do not do so primarily; ethical convictions can neither be demonstrated, like propositions of arithmetic, nor tested by observation or experiment, in the manner possible in the empirical sciences. (2) The positive claim is that ethical words function rather like interjections ("Alas!") or optatives ("Would that . . . !") or performatives. (A performative verb is one which, like "condemn" and "promise," can be used to do something, like condemn or promise, as well as to describe an action. Ethical expressions may be thought to function like the performing uses of such verbs or even to be substantially synonymous with some, for example, "I condemn you for. . . .") Different types of emotive theory exhibit wide variations of the positive claim and also some variations of the negative one. All types agree in denying that naturalism and nonnaturalism, or intuitionism (see ETHICAL NATURALISM and ETHICAL OBJECTIVISM), are adequate theories of ethics. What follows is primarily a discussion of the second, positive claim.

Some parts of the theory are old: the Greeks recognized that ethical statements, unlike those of science, are expressions of praise or derogation and that they influence conduct. Moreover, the metaethical theories of Francis Hutcheson and David Hume, in the early eighteenth century, are most reasonably construed as forms of emotive theory. But it was not until the 1930s that the plausibility of a theory of this sort was intensively examined by philosophers. The logical positivist theory of meaning, which was influential in the 1930s, was a strong motive for attention to the emotive theory, but the emotive theory is logically independent of this theory of meaning, which is today accepted by few if any writers on ethics.

Positive content of emotive theory. Some forms of the emotive theory suggested in the 1930s have hardly any supporters today. Such forms would include the suggestion (made, for example, by R. Carnap) that to say a person "ought" to do something is to issue a disguised command and the proposal (by A. J. Ayer, for example) that ethical terms function typically to express emotion. The more influential types of theory after 1950 agree on some variant of five major contentions (to be discussed below), an agreement which permits a wide spectrum of difference. All five contentions build on the noncontroversial assumption that there are conative-emotional dispositions (different from cognitive frames of mind, like belief or expectation), such as being in favor of something; being committed to a policy (or having decided on a policy); having a preference or interest; being disposed to become emotionally aroused about various types of situation (for instance, being ready to feel guilty about doing a certain thing or to be indignant about someone else doing a certain thing). The generic term "attitude" may be used to refer to such dispositions. It is further generally agreed by philosophers that whereas attitudes cannot contradict one another in the way in which beliefs may (when one belief cannot be true if the other is), they may conflict in the sense that the goal of behavior to which one attitude tends to lead is incompatible with the realization of the aim of behavior to which another attitude tends to lead. Thus, if one attitude tends to lead to voting for something and another attitude tends to lead to voting against it, it is helpful to speak of the attitudes as clashing or conflicting. The emotive theory, accepting these points, goes on as described below.

Attitude and ethical conviction. The first main contention of the emotive theory is that an attitude toward something is either all there is to, or is a necessary constituent of, an ethical conviction (or conviction about the value of something). (This does not mean, however, that every sort of attitude is a constituent of some ethical conviction: for example, the attitude of being an Anglophile would not necessarily be a part of, much less constitute, an ethical conviction.) Furthermore, the existence of conflicting attitudes is a necessary element in every ethical disagreement. Some writers (e.g., C. L. Stevenson) appear to think that this alleged relation between attitudes and ethical convictions can be confirmed by observation: they assume that an ethical conviction is whatever state of mind is expressed by characteristic uses of ethical language ("is wrong," "is a good thing") and that what is expressed by ethical utterances clearly includes some kind of attitude. In this case it is assumed that an instance of "ethical language" can be identified without knowing what specific state of mind it expresses. Other writers (e.g., A. Duncan-Jones, R. M. Hare) think the relation is logically necessary, for they think an utterance would not be counted as "ethical" or as expressing an "ethical conviction" unless it expressed an attitude.

Meaning of ethical statements. The next thesis is about the meaning of ethical words. One might incline, on the basis of the foregoing point, to view ethical statements as *reports* about the speaker's attitudes ("*A* is wrong" meaning something like "I disapprove of *A*") and, hence, as expressions of the speaker's belief about his own attitudes. This view is repudiated by advocates of the emotive theory on the ground that it implies something that is not true, namely, that ethical statements can be established as true or false by observation of the speaker's attitudes. Rather, the ethical statements are thought to *express* the speaker's attitudes (at least this is part of what they do); this view avoids the above objectionable implication, since an ethical statement is not taken just to *say* that the speaker has a certain attitude. Statements of the emotive theory, however, employ different senses of "express," and none is ideally precise. Some sophisticated types of the theory (e.g., C. L. Stevenson's) suggest that ethical utterances express attitudes in the sense in which the scientist's factual statements express his beliefs. More particularly, these suggest that an utterance "expresses" a certain state of mind (*a*) if it does not explicitly *say* that the speaker has that state of mind; (*b*) if use of an expression would normally elicit, among those in the cultural tradition of the speaker, a belief that he had a certain state of mind (provided they did not think him intent on deception), either because of a known rule of the language to that effect or because the state of mind is always or almost always present when the expression is sincerely used; and (*c*) if the expression arises from the state of mind more spontaneously and the auditor's passage to the belief about it is more intuitive and perceptual than would be the case if the speaker explicitly said he had the attitude.

Imperative or prescriptive force. The third main contention is that an adequate account of the meaning of ethical utterances must emphasize their imperative or prescriptive force. (Not every statement with imperative or prescriptive force need be ethical, of course.) According to some writers (e.g., C. L. Stevenson), this force consists in a capacity, causally dependent on the auditor's language training, to mold the attitudes of auditors after the pattern of the attitude expressed, independently of any beliefs the utterance may produce in the mind of the auditor. Thus, "Adultery is wrong" is supposed to make one tend to disapprove of adultery without mustering any reasons, such as the probable consequences. Others (e.g., R. M. Hare) say that ethical utterances prescribe or tell what to do (something common to advising, requesting, exhorting, and commanding) and that prescribing is a basic form of discourse which can hardly be analyzed further. By way of partial explanation, it is sometimes said that to accept a prescription is to be or become ready to behave as prescribed. (One can understand a prescription, however, without accepting it). Since people will presumably prescribe only what they favor in some way or to some degree, a person's prescriptions are a clue to his attitudes and perhaps necessarily express them in the sense of "express" just indicated.

Cognitive content. In most forms, the emotive theory makes the fourth major assertion that ethical statements have some cognitive content, in some sense or other. When a person expresses his attitude toward something, it is often said, he may thereby incidentally also convey information concerning his beliefs about what the world is like. Thus, if a person says there is nothing wrong in doing so-and-so, it may be possible to infer that he thinks so doing will not injure anyone seriously. Various emotive theorists have also thought that the use of ethical words may *imply* certain things, in the sense of authorizing auditors to believe them, although they are not strictly entailed by what is said. The use of ethical language may imply that the attitude expressed is a considered one or that the attitude is not peculiar or even that it is shared by all other persons (or at least, *would* be in ideal circumstances, such as others knowing all the facts); or the implication may be that the speaker is prepared to support a singular ethical statement ("You ought to do *A*!") by a relevant universal ethical principle which he is prepared to live by himself, and that he would not make such a statement unless he were so prepared. Some writers (e.g., H. O. Aiken) maintain that the speaker is expressing the attitudes of the community or is prescribing in the name of the community, rather than expressing strictly his own attitudes or prescribing on his own account. This last interpretation is thought to permit a relation of contradiction between differing ethical statements. (For example, in the same community under the same circumstances, if one person says, "It's all right to abandon one's old father in the wilderness," and another person says, "No, it's wicked," it cannot be the case that both statements are true.) This interpretation also permits a kind of "objectivity" that many people feel must be permitted by an adequate account of ethical thought and reasoning.

Reasons in ethics. On the fifth issue, the nature and force of "reasons" in ethics, rather different views are implied by different forms of the general themes discussed above. Some writers (e.g., C. L. Stevenson) hold that a "reason" in ethics is simply any consideration, knowledge of which will affect the relevant attitudes of somebody. A reason, then, does not entail or confirm (in the sense of inductive logic) an ethical judgment, its force is causal and is contingent on the basic attitudes of the individual. Producing reasons thus may reduce disagreement in ethics but need not lead toward "ideal truth," a concept which is not used. (There may be second-order attitudes toward the process of reasoning itself, so that introduction of some considerations into ethical debate or reflection is disapproved of and condemned as "irrational.") For example, one may disapprove of using veiled threats in an ethical discussion, however effective this may be in moving an opponent's attitudes. Other writers (e.g., R. M. Hare) assert a somewhat closer parallel between moral and scientific reasoning. Such writers hold that since a person's singular moral judgment (prescription) commits him to some universal prescription which, given the facts of the case, logically entails the particular judgment, a person is therefore debarred from applying moral terms in their ordinary sense to a particular action or situation unless he is prepared to issue (and accept for himself) a corresponding universal prescription. As a consequence, any facts adduced which convince a person that he does not wish to commit himself to the relevant universal prescription necessarily also make it impossible for him any longer sincerely to assert the particular moral judgment. Accordingly, there is a logic of ethical reasoning, although the ultimate appeal, in support of fundamental universal prescriptions (principles), is to what a person can commit himself (can want) to prescribe universally, in view of what it would be like for the prescription to be generally adopted: thus the appeal is not solely to observation but partly to a person's fundamental attitudes.

Other writers (e.g., J. N. Findlay, Jonathan Harrison) of the above-mentioned (supposed) implications of moral words, or else on a theory of the meaning of "justified" for moral contexts, say that one can present a logically coercive reason against a moral judgment by showing that other persons—perhaps other persons in ideal circumstances—do not share the attitude expressed by the judgment. If this account is accepted, moral judgments can be justified in a way that is hardly distinguishable from that recognized by ethical naturalism, namely, that of scientific reasoning. However, even if the first, most extreme viewpoint about ethical reasoning is accepted, there is more parallel between the logic of ethical reasoning and that of empirical science than is usually recognized.

Reasons for and against the emotive theory. Some form of emotive theory must be adopted if neither naturalism nor nonnaturalism is acceptable. Since most philosophers today are dissatisfied with the rationalist epistemology (involving a kind of intuitive insight unlike anything in science) required by nonnaturalism, the choice is between some form of naturalism and some form of emotive theory. Historically, many advocates of the emotive theory have thought that naturalism in all forms was refuted by G. E. Moore (in *Principia Ethica*, Cambridge, 1903) through his "open question argument." This was a mistake: the open question argument at most shows that moral words are somewhat vague or that people are not exactly clear what they mean by them or that they are used in different senses in different contexts or that their meanings are not easy to formulate. Furthermore, even if no definitions proposed by naturalists correspond to what people ordinarily mean by ethical words, such definitions may well represent what educated people would use them to mean if they took a broad view of human society and human nature and the possible role of moral discourse in living and based a decision concerning the meaning of ethical words on such a view. Thus, naturalism might still be a live option, even if the open question argument were correct in its conclusion about the meaning of moral words as ordinarily used.

Another mistaken argument, historically relied upon by some advocates of the emotive theory, is to the effect that moral statements could not, if they had a purely descriptive meaning, as naturalists think, be typically used to give advice or guide conduct. This reasoning seems mistaken: witness the guiding force of "If you do *A*, it will hurt!" In any case, it is far from clear that moral terms are most typically used for some practical end, such as directing action.

There are, however, more cogent reasons for adopting the emotive theory, such as those discussed below.

Support for the emotive theory. Most philosophers do think that the sincere application of a favorable ethical term to something is always accompanied by some corresponding ethical attitude toward that thing. This provides at least some support for the emotive theory. (It seems, however, not to be a rule of language that ethical terms are used correctly only in this circumstance: instructions in the use of ethical words, as they are given to children, seem not to restrict the use of, say, "wrong" only to cases where one has some unfavorable attitude.)

A second point in favor of adopting some form of the theory is that discovery of what one wants or can approve—the formation or discovery of practical attitudes—does not play an essential role in intelligent moral reflection. The emotive theory allows for this (as, however, do subjective or attitudinal forms of naturalism). Personal attitudes do not have the same role in scientific reflection, except when it is specifically about personal attitudes, and the emotive theory has the virtue of underlining this fact.

The emotive theory also has a simple explanation of why a person's actions and choices are excellent indicators of his real ethical beliefs; for, according to the theory, attitudes are a necessary constituent of ethical convictions, and attitudes may be expected (by definition) to be manifest in choices. The emotive theory must, however, avoid too simple a form at this point, for people sometimes think a given action would be wrong but succumb to the temptation to perform it.

Difficulties in the emotive theory. Since the emotive theory has many forms, no one difficulty is likely to be serious for all possible types. Some difficulties, however, are worth mentioning. The first is that the emotive theory is mistaken if it is offered as an account of the meaning of words like "good" and "right" in all their ordinary ethical uses. For instance, in a conditional sentence ("If it is right to . . . , then . . .") the word "right" seems to be used in an ordinary way, but it is hardly prescribing or expressing the speaker's attitudes. Again, an ethical statement apparentley does not have exactly the same meaning as any pure imperative or optative or performative statement; something must be added to an imperative in order to come close to the force of an ethical statement. In order to provide for this, some emotive theorists as mentioned above, speak of ethical statements as "implying" or "expressing" various things. When such complexities are introduced, the question arises whether the conceptual apparatus of naturalism is not equally adequate to characterize moral language and convictions, and simpler besides. Perhaps a more important question is whether, irrespective of how close the emotive theory comes to rendering the meanings of ethical terms as actually used, it outlines the most useful meaning for the key terms of practical discourse. What people on reflection want to know, when they raise moral questions, might be more helpfully phrased if the questions used the conceptual apparatus of naturalism. Thus it might be helpful if everyone understood "Is it wrong to do this?" as meaning "Would doing this be forbidden by the kind of conscience I should want developed in everyone if I knew all the relevant facts?" It should be conceded in favor of the emotive theory that what question a person wants answered for the purpose of action is itself a matter of attitudes. Nevertheless, it is possible that there are considerations that would necessarily lead reflective persons to agree that certain factual questions are the only ones that need be answered for the purposes of intelligent action. In this case, a naturalistic definition of ethical terms could be a correct rendering of good or ideal or clarified meanings for ethical terms. Such a conclusion would not necessarily be inconsistent with the emotive theory, however; for, as indicated above, naturalism in some forms differs little from some forms of the emotive theory.

Bibliography

The most influential formulations of the emotive theory are R. M. Hare, *The Language of Morals* (Oxford, 1952) and *Freedom and Reason* (Oxford, 1963); P. H. Nowell-Smith, *Ethics* (Baltimore and London, 1954); and C. L. Stevenson, *Ethics and Language* (New Haven, 1944). Other presentations of the theory are A. J. Ayer, *Language, Truth, and Logic* (London, 1936); H. N. Castaneda and G. Nakhnikian, eds., *Morality and the Language of Conduct* (Detroit, 1963); Paul Edwards, *The Logic of Moral Discourse* (Glencoe, Ill., 1955); J. Ladd, *The Structure of a Moral Code* (Cambridge, Mass., 1957); and P. B. Rice, *On the Knowledge of Good and Evil* (New York, 1955).

Criticisms of the theory have mostly been in article form and in reviews. Many of these are summarized in R. B. Brandt, *Ethical Theory* (Englewood Cliffs, N.J., 1959), Ch. 9.

RICHARD B. BRANDT

EMPEDOCLES, Greek poet, prophet, and natural philosopher, originator of the doctrine of four elements which dominated Western cosmology and medical thought down to the Renaissance. Empedocles was born in Acragas (Agrigento), Sicily, in the early fifth century B.C. and died sometime after 444 B.C. He played a political role in his native city, apparently as a democratic leader, was later exiled, and traveled through other Greek colonies in southern Italy. In one of his poems he describes himself as a "deathless god, no longer a mortal," surrounded wherever he goes by admiring crowds asking for advice, for prophecy, and for a "healing word" to cure them from disease (Fr. 112). A number of anecdotes illustrate his reputation for supernatural powers (including the raising of the dead), and the legend that he died by throwing himself into the crater of Etna gives us an idea of the charismatic impression he left behind in the popular imagination. Modern scholars have often found it difficult to reconcile the scientific and the religious sides of Empedocles' thought. He expounded his views in powerful hexameters, of which considerable fragments are preserved from two distinct poems, *On the Nature of Things* (*Peri Physeōs*) and *Purifications* (*Katharmoi*).

Natural philosophy. Theophrastus said that Empedocles was much influenced by Parmenides and even more by the Pythagoreans. Pythagorean influence must be seen in his religious teaching and probably also in the role which he assigns to numerical proportion in the natural combination of the elements. From Parmenides he accepted the fundamental principle that nothing can arise out of nothing, nor can anything perish into nonentity. But whereas for Parmenides this meant that all motion and change must be illusory, Empedocles admits that there is real process in nature: "the mixture and separation of things mixed."

By accepting four distinct elements, or "roots of all things," in place of Parmenides' monolithic Being, Empedocles is able to explain natural change as a result of the combination, separation, and regrouping of indestructible entities. There remains, of course, something illusory about the kaleidoscopic appearance of change. Since there can be no generation or annihilation of anything real, Empedocles insists that to describe natural processes in terms of birth and becoming or death and destruction is to follow a linguistic usage which is systematically misleading (Frs. 8–12). In reality there is only the mixing, unmixing, and remixing of permanent entities.

One generation later a similar view of the discrepancy between the appearance of continual change and the reality of unchanging entities led Democritus to distinguish between primary (or true) and secondary (or conventional) sense qualities. However, there is no reason to believe that Empedocles envisaged any such distinction. He assigns the qualities of color, heat, and moisture to the elements themselves and describes the formation of compounds by analogy with the action of a painter mixing his colors. He seems not to have faced the difficult question posed by such analogies: In what does the indestructibility of the elements consist if their essential properties are those which are seen to change?

Nevertheless, the simplicity of this tetradic scheme and its direct application to the great cosmic masses of land, sea, atmosphere, and celestial fire (that is, sun, stars, and lightning) led Plato, Aristotle, and most of their successors to adopt the doctrine of four elements in variously modified forms. Empedocles himself developed the doctrine in a grandiose cosmology which can be reconstructed only in part. The four elements interact under the influence of two cosmic powers, Love (or Aphrodite), on the one hand, and Strife (or Quarrel), on the other. These powers function respectively as forces of attraction and repulsion, but they are also conceived of concretely as ingredients in the mixture. They operate as a kind of dynamic fluid, comparable in some respects to the concept of phlogiston in early modern science. The power of Love or attraction acts first by bringing like together with like—for instance, earth to earth, fire to fire—but it also assimilates the elements to one another, so that what were originally unlikes become like and are united in a new, homogeneous compound (Fr. 22). Love thus represents the power of organic unity and creative combination.

The process of world formation occurs in a cycle which may be said to begin with a totally homogeneous fusion of the elements in a primordial sphere under the exclusive influence of Love. The process of differentiation is set off when Strife makes its entry into the sphere, in accordance with some fixed periodic scheme. It would seem that the cosmic sphere is always saturated with one or the other of these powers or, more frequently, with both of them in a variable ratio; the quantity of Love present in the world varies inversely to that of Strife (Frs. 35 and 16). The life cycle of the universe thus oscillates between the poles of unity and diversity: "Now there grows to be one thing alone out of many; now again many things separate out of one; there is a double generation of mortal beings, a double disappearance" (Fr. 17). This has generally been taken to imply that the creation of things occurs twice, first in the passage from unity under Love to complete diversity under Strife and again in the reverse process from separation of all things to total fusion. (The standard interpretation has recently been challenged by Bollack, who denies that Empedocles intended a double cosmogony. See Bibliography.) The present phase of the world cycle is apparently regarded as one of the increasing prevalence of Strife.

Empedocles gave some account of the structure of the heavens and also of the phenomena of earth, sea, and atmosphere which the Greeks studied under the title of meteorology, but the remains of his physical poem show an equal or greater concern with zoology and botany. In the microcosm of plants and animals he discovered the same principles of elemental mixture, harmony, and separation at work. Following up an idea of Anaximander's, he imagined several phases in the emergence of living things from the earth (in combination with other elements), plants preceding animals, and he describes earlier, monstrous forms of animal life. As in Anaximander sexual reproduction appears only in the latest phase of the development. But the details of his doctrine are obscure, and it is difficult to say how far there is any significant anticipation of the theory of evolution.

Physiology and psychology. Empedocles shows a keen interest in embryology and physiology, explaining the structure of the eye by analogy with that of a lantern (Fr. 84) and comparing the process of respiration (including the movement of the blood) with the siphon effect of the clepsydra or water pipe, which retains or releases fluid by means of air pressure (Fr. 100). The notion of elemental combination is specified in numerical terms for certain living tissues. Bones are formed by earth, water, and fire in the ratio 2:2:4. The blend of the elements is most equal in flesh, especially in blood (Fr. 98).

Physiology passes over into psychology without a break. (It is clear that as a doctor Empedocles would have practiced psychosomatic medicine.) Blood is the primary seat of thought and perception (Fr. 105) precisely because it is here that the elements are most equably blended. Fundamental in Empedocles' psychology, as in his physics, is the principle of like to like. We see earth with the earth that is in us, water with water, love with love, strife with strife (Fr. 109). This and other passages in Empedocles suggest a one-to-one correspondence between the corporeal elements as such and our conscious experience of them. More precisely, his view seems to be that of a radical panpsychism in which, on the one hand, all elemental bodies are endowed with thought and sensation (Frs. 102–103) and, on the other hand, knowledge itself is treated like a physical thing obeying the laws of combination, attraction, and repulsion. Thus, Empedocles announces that his own teachings, if carefully assimilated, will form part of the character and elemental composition of the student, whereas, if neglected, "they will leave you in the course of time, yearning to return to their own dear kind; for you must know that all things have intelligence and a share in thought" (Fr. 110). Hence, all our conscious thought and feeling has its direct counterpart in the elemental blend within us (Frs. 107–108), which is itself continually being altered by the stream of incoming and outgoing material (Frs. 89, 106).

Religious teaching. The religious views stated in the *Purifications* are so strange and so dogmatically presented that some scholars—Diels and Wilamowitz, for instance—have supposed that this poem dates from a later, less scientific period in Empedocles' life, reflecting some religious conversion after the bitter experience of exile. Now, the *Purifications* may, in fact, have been composed later than the physical poem, but no biographical development can resolve the alleged contradiction between the scientist and the mystic in Empedocles, for the physical work also presupposes a religious point of view.

In particular, *On Nature* proclaims the immortality and pre-existence of the soul (or life principle) as a special case of *ex nihilo nihil.* In Empedocles' view the Parmenidean law of conservation for all real entities guarantees the indestructibility of life in exactly the same way as it guarantees the imperishability of the elements. Hence, only fools can "imagine that men exist merely during what we call life, but that they are nothing at all before being composed or after they are dissolved" (Fr. 15; compare with Fr. 11). Since it is precisely the doctrine of immortality which is supposed to contradict the psychophysics of Empedocles, this contradiction, if it exists, must be located within the physical poem. Furthermore, the same poem implies a developed theology in the description of the primordial cosmic sphere as a "god" (*theos*, Fr. 31), in the reference to the four elements as immortal deities (*daimones*, Fr. 59; compare with Fr. 6), and in the apocalyptic pronouncement of the power of Love-Aphrodite (Fr. 17). Some readers might be inclined to discount such expressions as mere features of poetic style, but such a literary interpretation of theological language, which may be appropriate in the case of Lucretius, seems unconvincing for Empedocles, who appeals to principles of piety and purity throughout the poem (Frs. 3–5, 110, and so on).

The religious views thus alluded to in the physical poem receive emphatic statement in the *Purifications.* Here Empedocles proclaims his own divinity and traces his career as an immortal *daimōn,* banished from the company of the other gods for some prenatal crime; passing through a series of vegetable, animal, and human incarnations; at last attaining the purified life of "prophets, poets, doctors, and leaders"; and now ready to escape from human misery altogether and return once more to the blessed fellowship of the gods. Part of the process of purification consists in the ritual abstinence from meat and certain other foods, such as beans and laurel leaves. This joining of the belief in transmigration with the religious practice of vegetarianism is distinctly Pythagorean. If one adds Empedocles' notion that birth in human form means that the *daimōn* is clothed in an alien garment of flesh (Fr. 126) as a result of a lamentable fall from bliss (Fr. 118), one has a particularly striking example of that otherworldly tendency in Greek religion which is generally known as Orphic and which exercised such a profound influence on Plato as well as on the religious thought of late antiquity.

Remote as this view may seem from the biology and physics of the poem *On Nature,* Empedocles has taken care to preserve a sense of continuity between his religious teaching and his cosmology by a number of parallels, in particular by identifying the primeval sin of the *daimōn* (for which it is punished by incarnation in the cycle of rebirth) as "reliance on Strife." The fellowship of the purified spirits is conceived by contrast as a realm of Love and affection. Thus, the precosmic sphere of the physical poem is paralleled in the *Purifications* by an account of a bygone golden age in which war and bloodshed were unknown, affection prevailed between man and beast, and Aphrodite was queen (Frs. 128–129). Although both poems (which are addressed to different audiences) probably cannot be fitted together at every point, Empedocles clearly thought of the two as compatible, perhaps as complementary views of the world of nature (or physical transformation) and the world of spirit (or divine life). As a result of his panpsychism, Empedocles was able to conceive of nature and spirit as forming two aspects of a single whole rather than as constituting two entirely distinct realms. In any case the essential structure of both worlds is characterized by the same, almost Manichaean rivalry between the beneficent force of Love and the destructive power of Strife. If one sees Love in the physical poem as the cosmic counterpart of the immortal *daimōn* and his extramundane homeland, Empedocles' whole cosmology will appear as a construction designed to find a place for the Pythagorean doctrine of the transmigrating soul within the shifting and unstable world of elemental strife which had been described by the Ionian natural philosophers.

This reconciliation of the two poems is possible only if one admits the identification of the transmigrating *daimōn* with the element of divine Love—that is, with the unifying principle of intelligent organization present within each one of us but also present throughout nature. This identification has been accepted by Cornford and by others, and there is much to be said for it. But it is only fair to add that the identification cannot be proved from the extant texts and that some responsible scholars have denied that there is any possibility of reconciling the doctrine of immortality with the physical psychology of *On Nature.*

One should note Empedocles' clear statement—the first by any Greek—of the notion of an invisible, incorporeal, nonanthropomorphic deity, characterized as a "holy mind [*phrēn*] alone, darting through the whole cosmos with rapid thoughts" (Frs. 133–134). Before Empedocles, Xenophanes had insisted that the "greatest god" must be nonanthropomorphic, but he did not specify its incorporeality. On the other hand, Anaxagoras' principle of mind is clearly noncorporeal, but it is not described as a deity. Empedocles seems to have worked the Anaxagorean principle into his own theology. The phrasing of his account of the spiritual deity recalls the verses concerning Aphrodite as well as the description of the divine sphere. All three principles—the sphere in which the elements are joined, the attractive force of Aphrodite, and the "holy mind" of the cosmos—must somehow have been related in Empedocles' theology, perhaps as three different expressions of the universal power of Love. If so, Empedocles' theology forms the direct continuation of his psychology, since (on the interpretation offered above) it is this same power of Love which figures in the human microcosm as the transmigrating *daimōn*.

Bibliography

Remains of the poems and other ancient evidence are in H. Diels and W. Kranz, *Die Fragmente der Vorsokratiker,* Vol. I, 6th ed. (Berlin, 1951), Ch. 31.

There are two major studies of Empedocles: Ettore Bignone, *Empedocle* (Turin, 1916), and Jean Bollack, *Empédocle*, 3 vols. announced (Paris, 1962—).

See also Eduard Zeller, *Die Philosophie der Griechen,* Wilhelm Nestle, ed., Vol. I, 6th ed. (Leipzig, 1920), Part 2; John Burnet, *Early Greek Philosophy*, 4th ed. (London, 1930); F. M. Cornford, "Mystery Religions and Pre-Socratic Philosophy," in *Cambridge Ancient History*, Vol. IV (Cambridge, 1939), Ch. 15; W. K. C. Guthrie, *A History of Greek Philosophy*, Vol. II (Cambridge, forthcoming); Werner Jaeger, *Theology of the Early Greek Philosophers* (Oxford, 1947); and G. S. Kirk and J. E. Raven, *The Presocratic Philosophers* (Cambridge, 1957).

Special studies include J. Bidez, *La Biographie d'Empédocle* (Gand, 1894); Ulrich von Wilamowitz-Moellendorff, "Die *Katharmoi* des Empedokles," in *Berlin Sitzungsberichte* (1929), 626–661; Friedrich Solmsen, "Tissues and the Soul," in *Philosophical Review,* Vol. 59 (1950), 435–441; D. J. Furley, "Empedocles and the Clepsydra," in *Journal of Hellenic Studies,* Vol. 77 (1957), 31–34; Charles H. Kahn, "Religion and Natural Philosophy in Empedocles' Doctrine of the Soul," in *Archiv für Geschicte der Philosophie*, Vol. 42 (1960), 3–35; and E. L. Minar, Jr., "Cosmic Periods in the Philosophy of Empedocles," in *Phronesis,* Vol. 8 (1963), 127–145.

CHARLES H. KAHN

EMPIRICISM is the theory that experience rather than reason is the source of knowledge, and in this sense it is opposed to rationalism. This general thesis, however, can receive different emphases and refinements; hence, those philosophers who have been labeled empiricists are united only in their general tendency and may differ in various ways. The word "empiricism" is derived from the Greek ἐμπειρία (*empeiria*), the Latin translation of which is *experientia,* from which in turn we derive the word "experience." Aristotle conceived of experience as the as yet unorganized product of sense perception and memory; this is a common philosophical conception of the notion. Memory is required so that what is perceived may be retained in the mind. To say that we have learned something from experience is to say that we have come to know of it by the use of our senses. We have experience when we are sufficiently aware of what we have discovered in this way. There is another, perhaps connected, sense of the term "experience" in which sensations, feelings, etc., are experiences and in which to perceive something involves having sense experiences. These are experiences because awareness of them is something that happens to us. Indeed, the suggestion of passivity is common to uses of the word. To go into refinements here would not be relevant; one need only appreciate that the statement that experience is the source of knowledge means that knowledge depends ultimately on the use of the senses and on what is discovered through them. Sense experience may be necessary for the attainment of experience, but for present purposes that is unimportant.

The weakest form of empiricism is the doctrine that the senses do provide us with "knowledge" in some sense of the word. This could be denied only by one who had so elevated a conception of knowledge that the senses cannot attain to it. Plato, for example, held at one stage that because of the changeability of the world of sense, sense knowledge lacks the certainty and infallibility that true knowledge must possess. Hence, knowledge cannot be derived from the senses, but only from some other kind of awareness of what he called Forms. The most that sense perception could do would be to remind us of this genuine knowledge. This conception of knowledge demands an infallibility that sense perception cannot provide. Normally, we do not demand such high standards of knowledge, nor do we succumb to this kind of skepticism about sense perception. The common-sense view is that the senses do provide us with knowledge of some sort, and most people, when philosophizing, adopt this kind of empiricist view.

This weak form of empiricism can be generalized into the thesis that *all* knowledge comes from experience. The extreme form of this thesis would be the claim that no source other than experience provides knowledge at all. But this formulation is ambiguous, because there could be various reasons why all that we know might be dependent in some way upon experience. One reason might be that every proposition that we know is either a direct report on experience or a report whose truth is inferred from experience. A prima facie exception to such a thesis is provided by the propositions of mathematics; they have usually been thought to be a priori, not a posteriori—that is, we can know their truth independently of experience. There have, however, been philosophers who have denied the a priori nature of mathematical propositions. J. S. Mill, for example, maintained that the propositions of mathematics are merely very highly confirmed generalizations from experience and, consequently, all propositions are either reports on experience or generalizations from experience. This view has not been widely accepted.

A second reason for maintaining that all knowledge is dependent on experience would be that we can have no ideas or concepts which are not derived from experience, that is, that all concepts are a posteriori, whether or not the truths which can be asserted by means of these concepts are themselves a posteriori. It may be that we know some propositions without having to resort immediately to experience for their validation; for their truth may depend solely on the logical relations between the ideas involved. Yet these ideas may themselves be derived from experience. If all our ideas are so derived, then knowledge of any sort must be dependent on sense experience in some way. According to this thesis, not all knowledge is derived immediately from experience, but all knowledge is dependent on experience at least in the sense that all the materials for knowledge are ultimately derived from experience. St. Thomas Aquinas was an empiricist in this sense. He thought that all our concepts are derived from experience, in that there is "nothing in the intellect which was not previously in the senses" (a doctrine supposedly derived from Aristotle). He did not think, however, that all knowledge either consists of sense experience or is inferred inductively from experience. Similarly, Locke held and tried to show that all our ideas are derived from experience, either directly or by way of reflection on ideas of sense. He did not hold, however, that all knowledge was sense knowledge.

It is possible to argue an even more complex thesis. It may be held that while there are ideas which are not derived from experience—a priori ideas—and while there are a priori truths which may or may not involve a priori ideas, such ideas and truths only have application on the precondition that there is experience. That is to say that—for human beings at any rate—reason can function only by way of some kind of connection with experience; "pure" reason is impossible. This was, in effect, Kant's position, and although he did not call himself an empiricist *simpliciter*, he was certainly opposed to what he called dogmatic rationalism. He held that there is no place for forms of knowledge of reality which are derived from pure reason alone.

It is possible, then, to maintain a general empiricist thesis that all knowledge is derived from experience on the grounds either that (1) all that we know is directly concerned with sense experience or derived from it by strictly experiential means, that is, learning, association, or inductive inference; or (2) all that we know is dependent on sense experience in that all the materials for knowledge are directly derived from sense experience; or (3) all that we know is dependent on sense perception in that even though we can know some things a priori, this is only in a relative sense, since the having of experience is a general precondition for being said to have such knowledge. None of these theses demand any more than the ordinary conception of knowledge. They do not demand that the knowledge in question should possess absolute infallibility so that the possibility of error is logically excluded. For none of the theses in question is essentially designed to be an answer to skepticism.

Empiricism and skepticism. Some forms of rationalism, for example, the Platonic theory already referred to, are meant to be answers to skepticism. They presuppose that an adequate reply to philosophical skepticism can be given only by showing that reason can provide forms of knowledge where error is logically excluded. The search for certainty, so intimately associated with seventeenth-century rationalism in general and Descartes in particular, aimed at showing that knowledge is possible because there are some things about which we cannot be wrong. Empiricism can be a rival to rationalism, not just in the sense already noted—that it may reject the supposition that reason by itself, without reference to sense perception, can provide knowledge—but also in the sense that it proposes an alternate way of arriving at certainty. Empiricism, in this sense, is the thesis that the certainty required to answer the skeptic is to be found in the deliverances of the senses themselves and not in the deliverances of reason. Rationalism and empiricism, in this sense, are agreed that some such certainty must be found if skepticism is to be answered. They disagree about the sources of that certainty and about the method by which the rest of what we ordinarily call knowledge is to be derived from the primary certainties. Whereas rationalism seeks to derive knowledge in general from certain primary axioms (the truth of which is indubitable) by means of strictly deductive procedures, empiricism seeks to build up or construct knowledge from certain basic elements which are, again, indubitable. The clearest expression of this point of view is probably to be found in twentieth-century empiricism, especially that associated with the logical positivist movement. This point of view is also found in the British empiricists of the seventeenth and eighteenth centuries, Locke, Berkeley, and Hume, but in their case it is overladen with other elements and other forms of empiricism, some of which have already been noted. A short historical survey may serve to pinpoint the main issues.

EMPIRICISM IN GREEK AND MEDIEVAL PHILOSOPHY

It is often said that, in one sense, Aristotle was the founder of empiricism. Certainly Aquinas believed that he had Aristotle's authority for the view that there is nothing in the intellect which was not previously in the senses. It is not clear, however, that Aristotle ever raised this question. When he spoke of the relations between reason and the senses, he was concerned with issues in the philosophy of mind rather than with epistemology. Certainly Aristotle seems to have believed that knowledge is possible outside the immediate sphere of the senses and that reason can and does furnish us with necessary truths about the world. Aristotle's place in the development of empiricism, then, remains unclear.

Perhaps the first declared empiricist was Epicurus, who maintained that the senses are the only source of knowledge. Epicurus was an extreme atomist and held that sense perception comes about as a result of contact between the atoms of the soul and films of atoms issuing from the bodies around us. By this means *phantasiae* (appearances) are set up. These are all veridical. All sensations are true, and there is no standard other than sensation to which we may refer our judgments about the world. Sensations are set up in the soul by external stimuli, and for this reason Epicurus takes them to be "given." They constitute *phantasiae* when they occur in bulk. There is no further evidence that can be adduced in order that their veridicality may be assessed, either from other sensations or from reason. This is not to say that we cannot be in error concerning objects of perception; the films of atoms may become distorted in transit or the *phantasiae* caused by them may be fitted to the wrong *prolepsis* (conception). The last is a kind of abstract idea built up from successive sensations; the fitting of a *phantasia* to a *prolepsis* is what corresponds to judgment in Epicurus. It would appear that what Epicurus meant by his assertion that all sensations are true was that since they are caused in us, we can go no further in seeking information; they may not make us have true knowledge of objects, but in themselves they are incorrigible. Precisely how all knowledge was to be built up from these sensations is not clear, and it has often been remarked that the axioms on which Epicurus' metaphysical system rests are far from the data of sense and are often based on more or less a priori arguments. Nevertheless, Epicurus' ideal of knowledge is one which not only depends on experience for its materials but is based on basic truths of experience.

A theory of knowledge similar in many ways to that of

Epicurus may be found in St. Thomas Aquinas, although the main sources of Aquinas' philosophy are to be found in Aristotle. Aquinas was not a complete empiricist, for he did not think that all knowledge was derived from truths of experience. Knowledge of God, for example, could be obtained in other ways, and his existence could be proved by logical argument. Yet Aquinas did think that the materials for knowledge must be derived from sense experience, and he gave an account of the mechanism by which this comes about. Roughly, when the sense organs are stimulated, there also results a change in the soul, which is the form of the body; this is a phantasm, a kind of sensory image. In order for sense perception to occur, the universal character of the phantasm must be seen as such. For this purpose, Aquinas resorted to Aristotle's distinction between an active and a passive reason. The active reason has to make possible the acquisition by the passive reason of the sensible form of the object of perception by a process which Aquinas—probably adapting an analogy used by Aristotle—described as the illuminating of the phantasm. The active reason reveals the sensible form of the object by abstraction from the phantasm. This form is imposed upon the passive reason, which produces a *species expressa,* or verbal concept, which in turn is used in judgment. This process is called the *conversio ad phantasmata;* all concepts are arrived at in this way, by abstraction from phantasms. Hence, in applying them to entities which cannot be objects of perception, we must do so by means of analogies of various kinds with sensible objects. Aquinas' empiricism is, therefore, limited to concepts, and it is only in this limited sense that he held "there is nothing in the intellect which was not previously in the senses."

THE BRITISH EMPIRICISTS

When thinking of empiricism, one tends to think, above all, of the British empiricists of the seventeenth and eighteenth centuries.

Locke. John Locke was an empiricist in roughly the same sense that Aquinas was, and he set the tone for his successors. His "new way of ideas," as it was called, had as its purpose "to inquire into the original, certainty, and extent of human knowledge, together with the grounds and degrees of belief, opinion, and assent." The reference to certainty makes it appear that he was concerned with skepticism or with skeptical arguments similar to Descartes' method of doubt. Locke's solution to this problem, however, was by no means consistently empiricist. His main target for attack was the doctrine of innate ideas, the doctrine that there may be ideas with which we are born or, at any rate, which we do not have to derive from sense experience. The first book of his *Essay Concerning Human Understanding* is devoted to a biting attack on this doctrine. In the rest of the book he sets out a positive account of the way in which ideas are built up, explaining that by "idea" he means that which the mind "is applied about whilst thinking." Ideas may be either of sensation or of reflection upon those of sensation; there is no other source. Ideas are also classified as simple or complex, the latter being built up out of the former. The mind has a certain freedom in this process, which may lead to error. (Locke later admitted ideas of relation and general ideas alongside the simple and complex.) The second book of the *Essay* is an exhaustive account of the way in which all objects of the mind are built up from ideas of sense. In this respect, then, Locke's philosophy may be considered an attempt to show in detail the truth of the kind of view which Aquinas had embraced, without accepting the same view of the mechanism whereby ideas come into being.

But Locke wanted to assess the certainty of our knowledge as well as its extent. The mind's freedom in forming complex ideas is a source of error, but in the case of simple ideas the mind, to Locke, was like a great mirror, capable of reflecting only what is set before it. Nevertheless, he did not maintain that all our ideas reflect the exact properties of things nor that all knowledge is of this character. In the fourth book of the *Essay* he asserts that all knowledge consists of "the perception of the connection of and agreement, or disagreement and repugnancy, of any of our ideas," but he goes on to distinguish three degrees of knowledge—intuitive, demonstrative, and sensitive. We can have intuitive knowledge of our own existence, demonstrative knowledge of God's existence, and sensitive knowledge of the existence of particular finite things. Intuition and demonstration bring certainty with them; they provide in effect a priori knowledge. The question of how there can be a priori knowledge of the existence of anything and how this can be a matter of the agreement or disagreement between ideas presents many problems.

These problems become acute in connection with sensitive knowledge. Locke tried to argue at one point that knowledge of the existence of particular finite things is a matter of the perception of the agreement of our ideas with that of existence. This will not do; to know that something exists is not to know merely that the idea of it fits in with the idea of existence. Hence, Locke admitted that this knowledge has not the certainty of the other two, although he insisted that it goes beyond mere probability and is commonly thought of as knowledge. He also tried to argue for the claim that we do have knowledge of sensible things, maintaining that simple ideas are caused in us in such a way that the mind is passive in receiving them. Moreover, the senses may cohere in their reports. None of these considerations really show that we do have knowledge of sensible things, and Locke admitted that they did not amount to proof.

Locke did not claim that *all* our ideas correspond to the properties of things. He felt this claim was true in the case of the so-called primary qualities, for example, bulk, figure, and motion, qualities without which, he maintained, a thing could not exist. It was not true of secondary qualities—for example, color and taste. In this case, the properties of things cause us to have ideas that are not representative of those things; the term "secondary *quality*" is thus a misnomer. Locke's denial of the real existence of secondary qualities turns on his assimilation of our ideas of them to feelings like pain. (His acceptance of primary qualities was probably influenced by the success of physics in his time and its preoccupation with these properties of things.) As for things themselves, Locke maintained that we have little or no knowledge of their real essence, only of their nominal essence—their nature as determined by the way in which we classify them. This is due to the weakness of our senses. We cannot penetrate to the real essence of things, and our ideas of substances are mostly those of powers—the powers that things have to affect us and each other. It can be seen from all this that Locke was an empiricist in a very limited sense. In his view all the materials for knowledge are provided by sense perception, but the extent and certainty of sensible knowledge is limited, while on the other hand, there is nonempirical a priori knowledge of nonsensible things.

Berkeley. One aim of Berkeley, the second of the British empiricists, was to rid Locke's philosophy of those elements which were inconsistent with empiricism, although Berkeley's main aim was to produce a metaphysical view which would show the glory of God. According to this view, there is nothing which our understanding cannot grasp, and our perceptions can be regarded as a kind of divine language by which God speaks to us; for God is the cause of our perceptions. The *esse* of sensible things is *percipi*—they consist in being perceived and they have no existence without the mind. There exist, therefore, only sensations or ideas and spirits which are their cause. God is the cause of our sensations, and we ourselves can be the cause of ideas of the imagination.

Berkeley argued against those elements of Locke's philosophy which presupposed a physical reality lying behind our ideas. He attacked Locke's conception of substance and the distinction between primary and secondary qualities, pointing out that there was no distinction to be made between them in respect of their dependence on mind. He also attacked the doctrine of abstract ideas which Locke had held, the doctrine that we have general ideas of things abstracted from the conditions of their particular existence—Locke's theory of universals. This Berkeley did because he believed that Locke's theory might provide a loophole for asserting the existence of an idea of substance. The outcome of this was Berkeley's claim that there are no restrictions on the extent of our knowledge. We have knowledge of the existence of God and ourselves to the extent that we have notions of these spirits. We have knowledge of everything else, since the existence of everything else is a matter of its being perceived. There is nothing further beyond our ken. Even subjects like geometry, which might be supposed to involve knowledge of nonempirical matters, had to be limited in scope in order to rule out nonempirical objects of knowledge. Thus, Berkeley maintained that there is a least perceptible size; hence, there can be no ideas of infinitesimals or points.

In addition to claiming unrestricted scope for our knowledge, Berkeley asserted that knowledge is entirely dependent on sensations for all its materials other than the notions we have of God and ourselves. Berkeley claimed that this view "gives certainty to knowledge" and prevents skepticism. At the same time it defends common sense, he argued, because it does not involve the postulation of a reality behind ideas. His view gave certainty, he held, because sensations are by definition free from error; for error can arise only from the wrong use of ideas in judgment. The certainty of our sensations is due to the fact that there can be no question whether they actually represent a reality behind them; and this is the basis of Berkeley's claim to deal with skepticism. In general, all knowledge apart from that of our own existence and of God must, for Berkeley, ultimately be derived from sense perception. With these exceptions, therefore, Berkeley was an empiricist not only in respect of the scope and materials of knowledge but also in respect of its foundations. All truths must be founded on the truths of sense experience. The relations between ideas, which Locke had found a source of knowledge, were, for Berkeley, the result of the mind's own acts.

The mind operates upon the ideas given to it, comparing or contrasting them; it does not merely record what is there. Formal disciplines like mathematics, which might be thought to turn on the relations between ideas, thus depend on the ways in which the mind arbitrarily puts ideas together. Hence, to put the matter in terms more familiar today, mathematics is as much a matter of invention as discovery.

Hume. In respect to relations between ideas Hume perhaps went back to Locke, but in other respects much of Hume's philosophy may be represented as an attempt to rid empiricism of the remaining excrescences of nonempiricist doctrine in Berkeley. As to the materials for knowledge, Hume tried to improve on his predecessors with attempts at greater precision. He distinguished first between impressions and ideas, the former being the contents of the mind in perception, the latter those in imagination, etc. He further subdivided ideas into those of sense and those of reflection, and again, into those which are simple and those which are complex. Like Berkeley, he denied the existence of anything behind impressions, and a cardinal point of his empiricism, to which he returned again and again, was that every simple idea is a copy of a corresponding impression. The understanding is therefore limited to these mental contents. Hume's main method in philosophy was what he called the "experimental method," the reference in all philosophical problems to the discoveries of experience. In effect, the conclusions which he drew from this are the opposite of Berkeley's. They can produce only skepticism. No justification can be given for belief in the existence of the self and an external world, for example. Reason cannot justify such beliefs, for all that we are given is a bundle of impressions and ideas. Only a psychological explanation can be given to account for our having such beliefs. Hume gives such an explanation in terms of the constancy and coherence of our impressions and ideas, and the principles of the association of ideas.

Hume's theory of knowledge is based on a distinction between two kinds of relations of ideas. In the *Treatise of Human Nature* he makes the distinction between relations that depend completely on the related ideas and those that can be changed without changing the ideas. The former, in effect, constitute necessary connections, the latter factual ones. In the later *Enquiry Concerning Human Understanding* he short-circuited the discussion by distinguishing simply between relations of ideas and matters of fact. Mathematics depends entirely on relations of ideas and is thus concerned with necessary truths, the denial of which involves a contradiction. Matters of fact may rest simply on observation, but in the causal relation Hume finds the only case of a matter-of-fact relation which can take us from one idea to another. He shows that statements of causal connection cannot be logically necessary truths, in spite of the fact that we do attach some necessity to causal connections. After a long discussion he finds the explanation for this in the fact that causes precede their effects, are contiguous to them, and are such that there is a constant conjunction between them. As a result, the mind, through custom, tends to pass from one to the other. The feeling derived from this, which is an impression of reflection, constitutes the feeling of necessity which we find in the causal connection. Hume denied any real connection between cause and effect but tried to explain why we think that there is such. His demonstration that the causal connection is a contingent one is of the utmost importance, but his conclusions about it are skeptical. He held that there can be no real or objective justification for inference from cause to effect. He did allow, it is true, that certain rules can be provided which, when followed, will give some kind of probability to those inductive inferences which we actually do make. The aim of these rules is to make custom reliable and to avoid superstition. Hume has really no right, according to his own principles, to allow so much, and in doing so, he deserts skepticism in favor of a reductionist positivism, which seeks only to deny any necessary connection among things, while retaining belief in inductive inference. The concept of causal connection is thus in effect reduced to that of constant association of events contiguous in space and closely related in time. This is a position incompatible with his general skepticism. Apart from this, Hume's philosophy is of a piece. In Hume, then, extreme empiricism led to skepticism. Apart from relations of ideas, he held, the only *knowledge* we can have is of what we can directly observe, and any attempt to palliate this conclusion can produce only inconsistency.

In British empiricism, therefore, the gradual weeding out of anything inconsistent with empiricism, either in the form of the claim that the materials for knowledge must be derived from experience or in the form of the claim that knowledge cannot go beyond experience in its objects, resulted in skepticism about most of the things which we ordinarily claim to know. Kant proposed a reconciliation between this thesis and rationalism, maintaining that the rationalist claim of a priori knowledge about reality must be restricted to its application to experience. There is no room for a priori knowledge of anything which is not an object of experience. Pure reason can provide no real knowledge, despite the claims of rationalist metaphysicians. Such nonanalytic propositions as we do know a priori constitute principles that lay down the conditions to which experience must conform if it is to be objectively valid and not just a product of the imagination. A priori truths other than mere analytic truths have validity only in reference to experience; hence, while all knowledge is based on experience, it is not all derived from experience. This is scarcely empiricism in any recognized form, nor did Kant claim that it was; but it is a thesis that gives an important role to experience in knowledge.

One final point may be made about the British empiricists: They all employed a common method of trying to build up the body of knowledge from simple building blocks. The model for this method may have been the empirical science of the day. (Hume claimed to derive his experimental method from Newton.) The rationalists claimed more for reason and sought to reveal sources for knowledge and its materials other than experience; but they were also opposed to the empiricists in their choice of method, finding their inspiration in the method of axiomatic geometry.

John Stuart Mill. J. S. Mill, the main figure in nineteenth-century empiricism, followed directly in the tradition of Hume. Mill's account of our knowledge of the external world, for example, was in part phenomenalist in character; it maintained that things are merely permanent possibilities of sensation. But it was mainly an account of the way in which we come to believe in such a thing as an external world and thus followed Hume in its psychological character. In one respect, however, Mill was more radical than Hume. He was so impressed by the possibilities of the use of induction that he found inductive inference in places where we should not ordinarily expect to find it. In particular, he claimed that mathematical truths were merely very highly confirmed generalizations from experience; mathematical inference, generally conceived as deductive in nature, he set down as founded on induction. Thus, in Mill's philosophy there was no real place for knowledge based on relations of ideas. In his view logical and mathematical necessity is psychological; we are merely unable to conceive any other possibilities than those which logical and mathematical propositions assert. This is perhaps the most extreme version of empiricism known, but it has not found many defenders.

TWENTIETH-CENTURY EMPIRICISM

Empiricists in the twentieth century have generally reverted to the radical distinction between necessary truths, as found in logic and mathematics, and empirical truths, as found elsewhere. Necessity is confined by them, however, to logic and mathematics, and all other truths are held to be merely contingent. Partly for this reason and partly because it has been held that the apparatus of modern logic may be relevant to philosophical problems, twentieth-century empiricists have tended to call themselves "Logical Empiricists" (at least those who have been connected in one way or another with logical positivism). On the other hand, Bertrand Russell, who has derived something from the positivists, but who owes equally much to the British empiricists, has always claimed that there are limits to empiricism, on the grounds that the principles of inductive inference cannot themselves be justified by reference to experience.

In general twentieth-century empiricists have been less interested in the question of the materials for knowledge than in that of the empirical basis for knowledge. Insofar as they have considered the former question, the tendency has been, as in other matters, to eschew psychological considerations and to raise the problem in connection with meaning. All descriptive symbols, it is maintained, should be definable in terms of other symbols, except that ultimately one must come to expressions which are definable ostensively only. That is, there must ultimately be terms which can be cashed by direct reference to experience and to it alone; ostensive definition consists of giving the term together with some direct act of pointing, such that no other understanding of meaning is required. In regard to nondescriptive terms the situation is less clear, but the general tendency is to assume that the only possible source of ideas which might be called a priori is logic and mathematics. Following Russell, twentieth-century empiricists assumed that mathematical notions can be reduced to logical ones or can at least involve similar features amd that logical notions are concerned only with relations between symbols and can be defined accordingly. Russell, it is true, has suggested that terms like "or" might also be defined ostensively, for example, by reference to feelings of hesitation, but this suggestion has not been generally accepted.

If the views on the question of the materials for knowledge are not clear-cut, there has not been the same indefiniteness over the basis of knowledge. Although some positivists, the so-called physicalists, have maintained that the language of physics should be taken as providing the basic truths, most philosophers of positivist persuasion have gone to direct experience for the truths on which knowledge is taken to rest. These truths are to be found in sense-datum propositions—propositions which are a direct record of experience and which are for this reason incorrigible, consisting of ostensively definable terms, that is, names of sense data. It is not clear what would constitute an example of this. (Russell, for example, suggested "Red here now," where every expression is what he called a "logically proper name," such that its reference is guaranteed.) Nevertheless, it has been assumed that all propositions except logical ones must be reducible to these "basic propositions," which are about sense data. However, propositions about physical objects are not incorrigible. Yet to suppose that such propositions deal with entities which lie behind the immediate data of the senses and which can only be inferred from those data would be to suppose that there is a gap between us and physical objects, the crossing of which is problematical. This would allow an opening for the skeptic. An alternative view is phenomenalism, the doctrine that the meaning of our statements about physical objects can be analyzed in terms of propositions about sense data. Physical objects are logical constructions out of sense data ("logical" because the issue concerns the correct logical analysis of propositions about physical objects and not the question of how, as a matter of psychological fact, we construct our ideas of physical objects). In general, according to positivists, all propositions other than those which are logically necessary must be verifiable by reduction, either directly or indirectly, to propositions about sense data. Anything which is not so reducible is nonsense. In epistemological terms, any contingent truth which we can be said to know must be founded on and reducible to propositions concerning sense experience. Necessary truths, it is generally held, are true by convention or in virtue of the meaning of the words involved. They tell us nothing about the world as such.

This program has run into difficulties of two main kinds. First, there have been difficulties in actually carrying out the analysis demanded. It would be almost universally agreed that propositions about physical objects cannot be analyzed in terms of propositions about actual and possible sense data, since the analysis would have to be infinitely long. This is an objection of principle. Second, the criterion of verifiability tends to exclude some kinds of propositions which we ordinarily think that we understand. There have been difficulties in this respect, for example, over propositions of natural law, as well as propositions of ethics, etc. There has been widespread dissatisfaction with attempts to justify empiricism of this sort.

It should now be possible to offer some assessment of empiricism. As an answer to skepticism it claims that the certainty and incorrigibility that knowledge demands can (apart from logical truths) be found only in immediate experience and that the rest of knowledge must be built upon this. In this sense, the theory is misguided as well as unsuccessful in carrying out its program. The lack of success can be seen in the fact that eighteenth-century empiricism led to skepticism, while the twentieth-century program of reduction has been very widely admitted as a failure. The attempt was misguided in that knowledge does not require this kind of certainty and incorrigibility. Skepticism is not to be answered by providing absolutely certain truths, but by examining the grounds of skepticism itself. According to our ordinary conception of knowledge, what we claim to know must be true and based on the best of reasons. But by the best of reasons is not meant proof. Experience certainly provides justification for belief in, for example, physical objects, but if this belief is to amount to knowledge, it is not necessary that the justification should amount to proof. It is futile to argue whether experience or reason alone can provide proof of what we ordinarily claim to know. No one could have knowledge of the world unless he had experiences and could reason, but this does not mean that either experience or reason by themselves could provide the kind of absolute certainty which would constitute proof. Nor is it required that they should provide proof in order that knowledge may be possible.

What of the thesis that, whether or not experience can provide certainty, all knowledge is derived from experience? In Mill's sense, that all truths, of whatever kind, receive their validation from experience, the thesis is obviously false and need be considered no further. The thesis that all the materials for knowledge are derived from experience may seem more plausible. Yet, despite the number of philosophers who have maintained this thesis, it is not altogether clear what it means. The version of the doctrine held by Locke and Aquinas looks like a psychological account of the origin of our ideas; in logical dress it amounts to the view that all our concepts or all the words which we use are definable in terms of those which are ostensively definable. Whether or not there are any a priori notions outside logic and mathematics, it certainly seems implausible to say that logical and mathematical notions may ultimately be definable ostensively. More important, the notion of ostensive definition is itself suspect. How could one understand what was going on when a noise was made, accompanied by a pointing to something, unless one knew the kind of thing which was being indicated and, more important perhaps, was aware that it was *language* that was being used? In other words, much has to be understood before this kind of definition can even begin. The notion that words can be cashed in terms of direct experience without further presuppositions is, thus, highly suspect. This is not to say that there are no distinctions to be made between different kinds of concepts or words, but merely that the distinctions in question cannot be made by means of any simple distinction between empiricism and rationalism.

There remains the Kantian point that the having of experience is a condition for any further knowledge. This would certainly be the case for creatures of our kind of sensibility, as Kant would put it. Yet the logical possibility of the possession of knowledge by nonsensitive creatures remains, whether or not any such creatures exist in fact.

Bibliography

EPICURUS

Zeller, Eduard, *Stoics, Epicureans and Sceptics,* translated by O. J. Reichel. London, 1892.

Bailey, Cyril, *Epicurus, the Extant Remains.* Oxford, 1926. In Greek, with English translation.

Bailey, Cyril, *The Greek Atomists and Epicurus.* Oxford, 1928.

AQUINAS

Aquinas, St. Thomas, *Summa Theologica,* Ia, 78 ff., in Vol. IV of the English translation by the Fathers of the English Dominican Province. London, 1922.

Copleston, F. C., *Aquinas.* London, 1955.

THE BRITISH EMPIRICISTS

Ayer, A. J., and Winch, Raymond, eds., *British Empirical Philosophers.* London, 1952. A collection of writings by the British empiricists.

Mill, J. S., *System of Logic,* 8th ed. London, 1872.

See also Immanuel Kant, *Critique of Pure Reason,* the translation by Norman Kemp Smith. London, 1953.

TWENTIETH-CENTURY EMPIRICISTS

Anderson, John, *Studies in Empirical Philosophy.* Sydney, Australia, 1962.

Ayer, A. J., *Foundations of Empirical Knowledge.* London, 1940.

Ayer, A. J., *Language, Truth and Logic,* 2d ed. London, 1946.

Ayer, A. J., *Philosophical Essays.* London, 1954.

Ayer, A. J., *Problem of Knowledge.* London, 1956.

Ayer, A. J., ed., *Logical Positivism.* Glencoe, Ill., 1959.

Lewis, C. I., *Analysis of Knowledge and Valuation.* La Salle, Ill., 1946.

Price, H. H., *Thinking and Experience.* London, 1953.

Russell, Bertrand, *Inquiry into Meaning and Truth.* London, 1940.

Russell, Bertrand, *Human Knowledge.* London, 1948.

For other writings dealing with Empiricism, see the bibliographies to LOGICAL POSITIVISM; POSITIVISM; PRAGMATISM; and SENSATIONALISM.

D. W. HAMLYN

ENCYCLOPEDIAS. See ENCYCLOPÉDIE; PHILOSOPHICAL DICTIONARIES AND ENCYCLOPEDIAS.

ENCYCLOPÉDIE,

ENCYCLOPÉDIE, or the French Encyclopedia, a famous and controversial work of reference embodying much of what the French Enlightenment liked to call "philosophy."

Purpose, history, and influence. Begun simply as a commercial undertaking to translate and adapt Ephraim Chambers' *Cyclopaedia* (1728), the *Encyclopédie* was first entrusted to the Englishman John Mills and the German Godefroy Sellius, and then to the Abbé Gua de Malves of the French Academy of Sciences. Denis Diderot became chief editor in 1747 and, with Jean Le Rond d'Alembert as his principal colleague, greatly expanded the scope of the enterprise. Diderot's prospectus (1750) promised, as a principal and novel feature, a description of the arts and especially the crafts in France, with numerous illustrative engravings, and was accompanied by an elaborate "Chart of the Branches of Human Knowledge," which Diderot referred to as "the Genealogical Tree of All the Arts and Sciences." This *Système figuré des connoissances humaines* was avowedly inspired by the work of Francis Bacon, whose empiricism greatly influenced the entire work. Assuming that all knowledge comes originally from sensations, the *Système figuré* subsumed all branches of learning under either memory, reason, or imagination, to which corresponded, respectively, history, philosophy, and poetry. The correlation of philosophy with reason, while history was associated merely with memory, was very characteristic of the Enlightenment.

The first volume of the *Encyclopédie,* which included d'Alembert's influential "Discours préliminaire," was published in 1751, and revealed at once that the work would be carried on in the spirit of Locke's sensationalistic psychology and epistemology. Pierre Bayle, in addition to Bacon and Locke, also served as a model and inspiration for the *Encyclopédie,* though its editors rarely found it expedient to admit the fact. The *Encyclopédie* was greatly influenced by Bayle's skepticism, while falling short of his thoroughgoing Pyrrhonism. The work went much beyond him, however, in its attention to natural science, to the nascent social sciences, to economic processes, and to social reform.

The first volume established the *Encyclopédie* at once as a work that was both controversial and indispensable. It was much more comprehensive than previous works of reference, and even included copious articles on grammar, synonyms, and gazetteer-like articles concerning countries and cities. It constantly attempted to explode vulgar errors (see the article "Agnus Scythicus"), to be as precise in definition as possible, to make exact technological explanation an accepted part of the language, to suggest social reforms (see the article "Accoucheuse") or greater civil liberties (see "Aius Locutius"), and to weaken dogmatisms. In Biblical criticism (for example, see "Arche de Noé") or in articles touching upon political theory (for example, "Autorité politique") or materialism (for example, "*Âme*"), the *Encyclopédie* proved itself to be adventuresome and bold.

As a result, the *Encyclopédie* encountered much opposition and suspicion, especially from orthodox religious groups. In particular, the Jesuits, whom Diderot and d'Alembert suspected of wanting to take over the editing of the work for themselves, delighted in exposing plagiarisms in the *Encyclopédie* and in insinuating that it was subversive. In 1752, just after the publication of the second volume, the Royal Council of State prohibited further publication, although, a few months later, this decree was tacitly rescinded. Thereafter, the *Encyclopédie* was published at the rate of a volume a year until 1757, when it had reached through the letter G. By this time it was evident, as Diderot himself had stated in his remarkable article "Encyclopédie" in volume five, explaining the intentions and editorial policies of the work, that the object of the *Encyclopédie* was "to change the general way of thinking."

In 1757 there commenced a long and complicated crisis that resulted in d'Alembert's retiring from his part in the editing and finally in the suppression of the work by royal decree, on March 8, 1759.

Nevertheless, through the courage and tenacity of Diderot and the publishers, and as a result of the authorities studiously looking the other way, the work continued to be written, edited, and printed in secret, pending the time when it might once more be authorized. In 1765–1766, the rest of the alphabet (ten volumes of letterpress) was published. Meanwhile, the 11 volumes of plates were also being prepared and published under Diderot's supervision, the first appearing in 1762 and the last in 1772. About 4,225 sets of the original edition were sold, the price being 980 livres (326 for the 17 volumes of letterpress and 654 for the 11 volumes of plates). Inasmuch as the purchasing power of a livre was roughly equivalent to rather more than a dollar in current (1966) purchasing power, it is evident that this was a large commercial undertaking.

Each of the first seven volumes of the *Encyclopédie* had been subjected to previous censorship, but this was impossible with the last ten volumes, because they were edited secretly. There was, therefore, a considerable risk that the government might outlaw the whole edition if the articles were too forthright on theology and politics. In the end, there was little difficulty: by 1765–1766, when the final volumes were distributed, the Order of the Jesuits had been suppressed and public opinion generally was moving irresistibly toward the point of view represented by the *philosophes*. But Le Breton, the printer and chief publisher of the *Encyclopédie*, had meanwhile surreptitiously altered many of the most controversial articles after Diderot had edited them and read the proofs. Diderot discovered this treachery in 1764, too late to undo it. The recent discovery of a volume of proof sheets permits a before-and-after comparison of some of the articles mutilated by Le Breton; a study of these shows that the changes were substantial. The exact number of Le Breton's alterations is not known even yet, though Diderot always remained convinced that the publisher's depredations had been extensive. In spite of the maiming of the text, however, the articles in the last ten volumes are rather more sharp and critical about religious, social, and political topics than the first seven volumes had dared to be.

One of the novel features of the *Encyclopédie* was that it identified many of its contributors, the most famous being Diderot, d'Alembert, Voltaire, Rousseau ("Économie politique" and articles on music), Montesquieu ("Goût"), François Quesnay ("Fermiers," "Grains"), Turgot ("Étymologie," "Existence"), Jean-François Marmontel, Holbach, and Louis de Jaucourt. After the suppression of the work in 1759, many of the contributors (a total of 160 have been identified) discontinued their collaboration, thus greatly increasing the burden on Diderot. The *Encyclopédie* represented the greatest feat in the technology of printing and publishing up to that time. It was a symbol of the intellectual pre-eminence of France in the eighteenth century. But it was also the symbol of a new public philosophy; and its final publication, with editorial policies and practices consistent and unchanged, was a triumphant vindication of the energy and moral courage of Diderot and even, though to a lesser extent, of his publishers.

PHILOSOPHY IN THE ENCYCLOPÉDIE

The numerous and lengthy articles in the *Encyclopédie* concerning philosophers or schools of philosophy, from "Aristotélisme" to "Zend-Avesta," constituted in themselves a stage in the development of recording the history of philosophy. Most of these articles were written by Diderot himself. In the compilation of them, he avowedly relied upon works by Thomas Stanley and Boureau Deslandes and, very heavily, upon Johann Jacob Brucker's *Historia Critica Philosophiae* (Leipzig, 1742–1744). But Brucker's work, relaxed in style and blandly deistic, was changed by Diderot into a history of philosophy that was nervous and sometimes edgy in style and, in its implicit challenging of idealism and in its inclination toward materialism, very representative of the point of view of the Enlightenment in France. Some of the articles not written by Diderot are flabby or conformist in their thought (for example, "Aristotélisme," "Spinoza"), but Diderot's own most famous ones ("Chaldéens," "Cyniques," "Cyrénaique," "Éclectisme," "Éléatique," "Épicuréisme," "Hobbisme," "Leibnitzianism," "Platonisme," "Pyrrhonienne") substantiate the claim that through the *Encyclopédie* Diderot was one of the creators of the history of philosophy in France.

Ontology and epistemology. It was a favorite sport of the Encyclopedists to inveigh against "metaphysics." This criticism was primarily an expression of their dislike for the great rationalistic constructions of the seventeenth century, the systematic philosophy of Descartes, Malebranche, Spinoza, and Leibniz. In reality, since the Encyclopedists—like the logical positivists of the twentieth century—had a theory of being and a theory of knowledge, they were more metaphysical than they acknowledged or perhaps realized. The Encyclopedists predicated a real world of brute fact, and steadfastly resisted the Berkeleian philosophy, although they were familiar with it (see d'Alembert's article, "Corps"). This real world was knowable, according to the Lockean system of epistemology, through the testimony of the senses and reflection thereon. Diderot stated, for example, in the article "Inné" that "there is nothing innate except the faculty of feeling and of thinking; all the rest is acquired." Such reference to external reality interpreted by reason, led to the great emphasis given by the Encyclopedists to *expérience*, which in the French of their day had the double meaning of experiential and experimental (see d'Alembert's article, "Expérimental"). With this empirical approach to the problems of reality and knowledge, the

Encyclopédie contributed greatly to the strengthening of the rationale of scientific hypothesis and scientific method (see, for example, "Hypothèse"). In this respect, especially noteworthy in the articles written by d'Alembert (for example, "Cosmologie" and "Cartésianisme"), the *Encyclopédie* was a forerunner to the development of positivism. Nor were the Encyclopedists lamed by Humean skepticism. They knew Hume personally and loved him and had read his books, but they simply overlooked the implications of Hume's philosophy in respect to their own ontology and epistemology. The sensationalistic psychology of the Encyclopedists, in combination with their view of the world, strengthened them in their faith in reason, by which it was deemed possible to know and evaluate objective reality, while making it unnecessary for them to have much faith in faith. The philosophy of the *Encyclopédie* was about as far from fideism as it is possible to be.

Opposition to religious dogmatism. The *Encyclopédie* was often accused by its enemies of favoring a philosophy of materialism. This it never did outright, yet many of its articles pointed that way, especially those that had to do with the mind–body problem (for example, "Spinosiste," "Âme"). Moreover, the Encyclopedists were constantly eager to undermine dogmatic and intolerant religious orthodoxy. This function they considered as one of their most "philosophical," and it is in this connection that they helped to establish a new historiography. The Encyclopedists often wrote as though they were historical pessimists and indeed distrustful of history: "One can scarcely read history without feeling horror for the human race," wrote Voltaire in "Idole, idolatrie." Nevertheless, in their desire to shake religious dogmatism, they used criteria of historical criticism, for example, in trying to establish the correct chronology of the Bible (see "Chronologie sacrée"), and explored the nature of historical evidence (for example, as to miracles) in a way that secularized and modernized historical techniques. (In this respect the articles "Bible," "Certitude," "Mages," "Syncrétistes," are of particular interest.) As for the philosophy of history, the Encyclopedists' convictions regarding the spread of enlightenment led to a faith in progress which became one of the conspicuous features of eighteenth-century thought.

Ethics. The *Encyclopédie* was much concerned with ethics, especially because of its insistence, as expressed by Diderot in "Irréligieux," that "morality can exist without religion; and religion can coexist, and often does, with immorality." In ethical theory many of the articles still spoke in terms of *jus naturae*, and sometimes, as in "Irréligieux," identified this moral law as "the universal law that the finger of God has engraved upon the hearts of all." But this rather conventional ethics was constantly being blended with, or superseded by, utilitarianism. The articles in the *Encyclopédie* advanced a theory of ethics that was founded not so much in the will of God as in the nature of man. And inasmuch as man was conceived of as being by nature sociable, it logically followed that an ethic grounded in man's nature was also socially conscious and other-regardful. The *Encyclopédie* also endeavored to undermine notions of free will, teaching that man, precisely because he is modifiable and educable, is capable of virtue even in a deterministic universe (see "Liberté," "Modification," "Malfaisant").

Social and political theory. The social philosophy of the *Encyclopédie* was shaped in like manner by the conviction that man by his nature is sociable (see "Philosophe"). As a result, the *Encyclopédie* was much interested in theories of social origins, and devoted a good deal of attention to the ethnography of primitive peoples, using travel books as a principal source. The article on "Humaine espèce" is a remarkable exercise in physical anthropology; and articles such as "Laboureur," "Journalier," and "Peuple" are examples of a groping toward a recognizable sociology. Thus, the *Encyclopédie* figured importantly in the development of the social sciences, as well as in the dissemination of a utilitarian social philosophy. The *Encyclopédie* had a passion for improvement and constantly applied to institutions the criterion of social usefulness.

The *Encyclopédie* also possessed a quite clearly articulated political theory, even though it was difficult to discuss political philosophy critically in a country that was professedly an absolute monarchy and exercised censorship. This political philosophy was, as might be expected, greatly influenced by John Locke. Articles such as "Droit naturel" and "Égalité naturelle" spoke of "inalienable rights" and continued, as Locke and Samuel von Pufendorf had done, to explore the implications to political philosophy of new and emerging insights into the nature of man. In articles such as "Autorité politique" and "Loi fondamentale," the *Encyclopédie* praised limited monarchy and suggested that proper government rests upon consent (see "Pouvoir"). In the article "Représentants" a theory of representative government was advanced, and numerous articles suggested the guarantee of civil liberties (for example, "Habeas corpus," "Aius locutius," "Libelle") or advocated reforms ("Impôt," "Vingtième," "Privilège"). An English writer, reviewing the *Encyclopédie* in 1768, remarked that "whoever takes the trouble of combining the several political articles, will find that they form a noble system of civil liberty."

Linguistic theory. The *Encyclopédie* was much engrossed in theories regarding the origin of language, and devoted a great deal of space to articles on grammar and on synonyms. In part this was social philosophy, in the sense that it was hoped that such speculation would throw light upon social origins; even more, it was an early manifestation of scientific and philosophical interest in the nature of language. In articles such as "Étymologie," "Élémens de science," and "Encyclopédie," Turgot, d'Alembert, and Diderot, respectively, analyzed problems of definition, semantics, and nomenclature in the attempt to explore accurately the relationship between words, concepts, and things. The Encyclopedists were remarkable for realizing that knowledge itself depends upon the correct use of language.

Aesthetics. Aesthetic theory was not systematically developed in the *Encyclopédie*, although there were numerous articles on belletristic subjects, especially those contributed by Marmontel (see his article "Critique") and Voltaire. Special mention should be made of Diderot's articles "Beau" and "Beauté," which reviewed extensively the aesthetic theories current in the first half of the eighteenth century and argued that it is the perception of relationships that is the basis of the beautiful.

Humanism. The philosophy of the *Encyclopédie* was strongly humanistic in tone. Oriented toward science, and progressive (in the sense of believing in progress), the work was integrated by the particular philosophy of man that underlies the whole. It was a philosophy, Protagorean in savor, that made man the measure of all things. This point of view was summed up by Diderot in the article "Encyclopédie": "Man is the sole and only limit whence one must start and back to whom everything must return. . . ."

Bibliography

EDITIONS

Encyclopédie, ou dictionnaire raisonné des sciences, des arts et des métiers, par une société de gens de lettres . . ., 35 vols. in folio. Paris, 1751–1780. Diderot was editor-in-chief for 17 volumes of letterpress (1751–1766) and 11 volumes of plates (1762–1772); these 28 volumes were reprinted in folio at Geneva (1772–1776). The remaining volumes consist of four volumes of *Supplément*, one volume of supplementary engravings, and two volumes of index. Other editions, all published in French, appeared at Lucca (28 vols. in folio, 1758–1771), Livorno (33 vols. in folio, 1770–1779), Yverdon (58 vols. in quarto, 1770–1780), Geneva (45 vols. in quarto, 1777–1781), and Lausanne and Berne (36 vols. in octavo, 1778–1781). Reproductions of 485 of the original engravings are available in the admirably edited and inexpensive *Diderot, Denis, Pictorial Encyclopedia of Trades and Industry*, Charles C. Gillispie, ed., 2 vols. New York, 1959.

HISTORY OF THE ENCYCLOPÉDIE

Gordon, D. H., and Torrey, Norman L., *The Censoring of Diderot's Encyclopédie and the Re-established Text.* New York, 1947.

Grosclaude, Pierre, *Un Audacieux Message. L'Encyclopédie.* Paris, 1951.

Kafker, Frank A., "A List of Contributors to Diderot's Encyclopedia." *French Historical Studies*, Vol. 3 (1963/1964), 106–122.

Le Gras, Joseph, *Diderot et l'Encyclopédie.* Amiens, 1928.

Lough, John, "Luneau de Boisjermain v. the publishers of the *Encyclopédie.*" *Studies on Voltaire and the Eighteenth Century*, Vol. 13 (1963), 115–177.

Venturi, Franco, *Le origini dell'Enciclopedia.* Florence, 1946; 2d ed., 1963.

Wilson, Arthur M., *Diderot: The Testing Years, 1713–1759.* New York, 1957.

INTELLECTUAL AND PHILOSOPHICAL ASPECTS

Barker, Joseph E., *Diderot's Treatment of the Christian Religion in the Encyclopédie.* New York, 1941.

Delorme, Suzanne, and Taton, René, eds., *L'Encyclopédie et le progrès des sciences et des techniques.* Paris, 1952.

Havens, G. R., and Bond, D. F., eds., *A Critical Bibliography of French Literature*, Syracuse, N.Y., 1951. Vol. IV, *The Eighteenth Century*, pp. 139–141.

Hubert, René, *Les Sciences sociales dans l'Encyclopédie.* Paris, 1923.

"Numéro spécial à l'occasion du 2e centenair de l'*Encyclopédie.*" *Annales de l'Université de Paris*, October 1952.

Proust, Jacques, *Diderot et l'Encyclopédie.* Paris, 1962. Especially valuable.

Schalk, Fritz, *Einleitung in die Encyclopädie der französischen Aufklärung.* Munich, 1936.

Schargo, Nelly, *History in the Encyclopédie.* New York, 1947.

Weis, Eberhard, *Geschichtsschreibung und Staatsauffassung in der französischen Enzyklopädie.* Wiesbaden, 1956.

ARTHUR M. WILSON

ENDS AND MEANS. In *Darkness at Noon* Arthur Koestler presents a prison dialogue between two old Bolsheviks. The one, Ivanov, is the inquisitor of the other, Rubashov, who is to be charged with deviation into treason. Rubashov recalls the theme of Dostoyevsky's *Crime and Punishment:*

> As far as I remember, the problem is, whether the student Raskolnikov has the right to kill the old woman? He is young and talented . . . she is old and utterly useless to the world. But the equation does not stand. In the first place, circumstances oblige him to murder a second person. . . . Secondly, the equation collapses in any case, because Raskolnikov discovers that twice two are not four when the mathematical units are human beings.

Ivanov replies with a violent outburst: "Consider for a moment what this humanitarian fog philosophy would lead to, if we were to take it literally; if we were to stick to the precept that the individual is sacrosanct, and that we must not treat human lives according to the rules of arithmetic. That would mean that a battalion commander may not sacrifice a patrolling party in order to save the regiment." Ivanov proceeds through other examples to the conclusion that "the principle that the end justifies the means is and remains the only rule of political ethics." He boasts, "We for the first time are consequent—considering only the consequences of what we do." "Yes," replies Rubashov, "so consequent that in the interests of a just distribution of land we deliberately let die of starvation about five million farmers and their families in one year. So consequent were we in the liberation of human beings from the shackles of industrial exploitation that we sent about ten million people to do forced labor in the Arctic regions and the jungles of the East."

Here, as so often, the conflicts dramatized in a serious work of fiction can reveal to us the nature and the importance of a problem in moral theory. One of the great polarities of ethical thought is that between the teleological and the deontological. Ivanov, boasting of his concern with consequences only, represents the teleological extreme. (Some philosophers delight in employing for this the German term *Erfolgsethik.*) Rubashov's belated scruples are pulling him in the opposite direction, toward the idea that there are some classes of action which just are indefeasibly right or wrong, quite regardless of any good or bad consequences. (The favored Germanism in this case is *Gesinnungsethik.*) It is this clash between deontology and teleology that is epitomized, and often thought to be exhausted, by the question whether the end can or cannot justify the means.

The force and fascination of Ivanov's approach lies precisely in its compulsive rationality. Surely we must agree that sometimes it is not merely pardonable but morally imperative to tell lies to save a patient from demoralization or a public from panic; sometimes a commander ought to sacrifice a patrol to save a regiment, ought "to apply the laws of arithmetic to human beings"; sometimes it is a positive duty to assassinate a tyrant, to commit one murder to prevent a holocaust. Yet these premises once admitted, it seems that we become logically committed to conceding to Ivanov "that the end justifies the means is and remains the only rule of political ethics." As a principle this sounds like the negation of principle. Having led his whole life by it Rubashov himself is in the end disillusioned.

All the same, he can find no arguments to stay the relentless logic of his inquisitors. For the opposite view can be equally repellent. It seems to put whatever at any particular time and place happens to be the accepted morality beyond the reach of all criticism. Some of the rules sometimes and in some places in fact taught and accepted as moral are by any humane standards certainly cruel and unjust or vexatious and pointless. Often circumstances arise where what is enjoined by one accepted rule is forbidden by another. Sometimes people have to choose to accept either one rule or another. Yet if bad rules are ever to be criticized and rejected, if we are ever to make a rational choice between following one and following another which conflicts with it, if we are ever to be guided by reason in deciding what rules to adopt, then this can surely be done only by considering consequences. The sort of ethics represented by Ivanov has been described as the *reductio ad absurdum* of Benthamite utilitarianism. The distress of Rubashov's dilemma is not appreciated until it is seen that what is apparently being reduced to absurdity is the whole idea of reason in morals.

For it seems that if morality is to be more than a mere congeries of taboos, a disordered series of uniformly ultimate imperatives immune to criticism and not susceptible of any systematic rationale, then we must resort to teleology in some form or other. The crucial point is made as an eloquent protest by J. S. Mill in his essay "Bentham": "Whether happiness be or be not the end to which morality should be referred—that it be referred to an *end* of some sort, and not left in the dominion of vague feeling or inexplicable internal conviction, that it be made a matter of reason and calculation, and not merely of sentiment, is essential to the very idea of moral philosophy; is, in fact, what renders argument on moral questions possible" (*Westminster Review*, Vol. 24, 1838, 467–506).

The problem therefore seems to be to find some way of allowing an important place in ethical thinking to questions about consequences without having to concede as a general principle that the end justifies the means. One tempting first move is to slash at the Gordian knot by insisting that evil means can as a matter of fact never lead to good ends. Unfortunately, this is, except perhaps to the eye of faith, quite clearly untrue. Perhaps it would have been a better world if such were to have been a law of nature. But it is not. There is nevertheless something to be learned from this first false move. It can be used to bring out that any doctrine which insists that maxims for action are to be judged by their consequences has, as it were, a built-in mechanism of self-regulation. If ever it is found by experience that some particular application of such a doctrine leads in fact to consequences which are on balance bad, then this is by itself sufficient to show that that application was on its own terms mistaken. What such a discovery of the unfortunate consequences of trying to follow an ethic of consequences would actually show is: not that it is wrong to try to estimate consequences, but that the consequences have been in this case lamentably miscalculated. Indeed, to appeal in this way to what are or are supposed to be the actual consequences of applying an ethic of consequences is itself not to reject but rather yourself to apply some sort of ethic of consequences.

Another move, which may sometimes be tempting, is to insist that where evil means, or means thought evil, either do, or are believed to, lead to a good end, then that by itself is sufficient to show that these means are not on this occasion evil. This is a move usually made only by implication and with respect to some particular class of embarrassing cases. Suppose, for instance, one is committed to the rules that both murder and suicide are always, absolutely, and without exception wrong. Suppose too that one nevertheless wants to allow exceptions in favor of tyrannicide and of such sacrificial suicides as that of Captain Lawrence Oates, on the attractive, but inconsistent, ground that in these exceptional cases the actual or the intended consequences are good. (Captain Oates walked to his death in a blizzard in the vain hope that his snowbound companions might be rescued.) One may be tempted to say that tyrannicide is not really murder and that the Oates case, properly understood, is not one of suicide. However, unless one can think up some plausible nonconsequential ground for such apparently arbitrary distinctions, the move will be a mere evasion—an attempt to conceal teleological practice beneath a deontological disguise.

A more subtle move, one that promises more illumination, is to bring out and to inspect the model in terms of which all discussion about whether the end does or does not justify the means is necessarily conducted. If, as proves to be the case, this model seems not to fit in precisely those situations to which it is most typically applied, then the original dilemma will have lost the greater part of its force.

The conception of the explanatory model, in terms of which we try to interpret and to explain some group of phenomena, is one which is in the natural sciences and in some other fields both familiar and fundamental. Yet in ethical discussion it rarely becomes explicit. This is a dangerous situation. For if we are unaware that we are employing a model, then we cannot be on the alert to ensure that it makes a proper fit. A wrong model must necessarily distort our picture of the phenomena. It will lead us to formulate misguided questions and to debate issues misconceived. To use it will be like looking at the world through distorting lenses. We shall see all the facts forced into our unconscious matrix of misunderstanding.

Talk of ends either justifying or not justifying means, of achieving good ends by evil means, and so forth, presupposes that we are dealing with something analogous to a field game in which the objective is unitary and given. The problem is to find some way to reach it, or to select one or another of various alternative routes, all of which lead to the same place.

The first and most obvious way in which this model may be wrong is that its application presupposes that it is genuinely the same end that is reached by the different means, as one may go to the same town by different routes or by different methods—by road or across country, by bus or by train. Blinkered by this frame of thought, it is easy to overlook how limited is its application to the problems of ethics. In ethics the means used will usually affect the end achieved; the different routes most often lead to different places.

Two examples illustrate different aspects of this truth. Leaders in war may at some stage think, rightly, that there are several possible strategies, all of which would in the end bring victory. It might seem that here above all —where it has in fact so often been applied—this clear-cut soldierly model of objectives and methods must be entirely right. Yet it is surely not. For the various situations which would be produced by the execution of each of the alternative strategies might well be very radically different, notwithstanding the fact that they could all equally be characterized as the attainment of "Objective —Victory." Read, for instance, Chester Wilmot's *The Struggle for Europe,* and consider how very different the victory of 1945—the denotation of "victory" in the context of that year—might have been had the West adopted a rather different strategy earlier. By shifting weight from the front in France toward Italy and the Balkans, it might have been possible, at a price, to have won a significantly different victory. The Iron Curtain might then have enclosed less of Europe than it now does. The way you win a war determines the situation at the time of the victory. History books can be sliced into chapters; history cannot.

A second aspect of the same truth lies in the fact that people find it difficult to remain unaffected by what they do. In the end the reluctant inquisitor, Ivanov, of Koestler's *Darkness at Noon* may be transformed by the processes of habituation into the exultant O'Brien of George Orwell's appalling nightmare, *1984.* O'Brien boasts, "The Party seeks power entirely for its own sake. We are not interested in the good of others. We are interested solely in power . . . . Power is not a means, it is an end . . . . The object of persecution is persecution. The object of torture is torture. The object of power is power."

Though one must reject as a pious part-truth the thesis that good ends cannot as a matter of fact be achieved by evil means, it can at least be allowed that the real world is not in fact as hospitable to the objective and method model as is sometimes thought. What are supposed to be alternative means are often not means to the same end. In the words of Ferdinand Lassalle, quoted by Koestler, " . . . ends and means on earth are so entangled/That changing one you change the other too."

The first way in which this model may lead us astray in ethics is by giving us a distorted picture of the sorts of situations in which we have to act. The second is by garbling our understanding of the demands of morality. It suggests and presupposes that to lead a moral life is primarily, or even exclusively, a matter of achieving or attempting objectives; and that to find in any given situation what one ought to do is a matter of finding a way to bring into being some positive good. This is in two respects dangerously misleading, if not completely wrong. First, to do one's duty, or to discover what it is, is rarely if ever to achieve, or to find a way to achieve, an objective. Rather and typically, it is to meet, or to find a way to meet, claims; and also, of course, to eschew misdemeanors. Promises must be kept, debts must be paid, dependents must be looked after; and stealing, lying, and cruelty must be avoided.

Second, this model misleads in accentuating the positive in a way that is in this case wrong. Our primary duties are to fulfill fairly specific obligations and to assist in removing definite evils. If we do have any general duty to promote happiness or any other positive good, this duty is certainly always much less urgent than that of preventing suffering. It was one of the mistakes of classical Benthamite utilitarianism to have regarded pain as from the moral point of view symmetrical with pleasure. Morally, so long as hospitals are needed, hospitals must always have priority over amusement parks.

This is a mistake which can perhaps be best explained and excused by reference to the context of reforming interest from which that doctrine sprang. For it was to provide a rationale for the enlightened criticism of social institutions in general and of laws in particular that utilitarianism was originally developed. If you have in mind the production of a new system of law, it is very reasonable to ask of every existing law not only whether it does any harm but also whether it does any good; and there may be a temptation to attach equal weight to the answers to both questions.

It is again to this concern primarily with laws and with social institutions, rather than directly and immediately with moral ideas and with moral analysis as such, that we can attribute Bentham's concentration on actual and intended consequences. It was left to J. S. Mill to give more adequate attention to the point that the first question for the moral agent must always be deontological: "Is there something which I am by some accepted moral rule either required or forbidden to do?" The teleological, utilitarian questions about consequences arise only when there is a conflict between accepted rules, or when the acceptability of some present or proposed rule is at issue. Mill's labors, particularly in Chapter 2 of *Utilitarianism,* to make clear that he had no intention of advocating a policy of referring every moral question immediately to a utilitarian first principle, are too often overlooked. It is this policy, rather than a general concern with ultimate consequences, that Rubashov learned to fear; "As we have thrown overboard all conventions and rules of cricket morality our sole guiding principle is that of consequent logic . . . . We are sailing without ballast; therefore each touch on the helm is a matter of life and death." And, later, "Looking back over his past, it seemed to him now that for forty years he had been running amuck—the running amuck of pure reason. Perhaps it did not suit man to be completely freed from old bonds, from the steadying brakes of 'Thou shalt not' and 'Thou mayst not,' and to be allowed to tear along straight toward the goal."

(For further information, see DEONTOLOGICAL ETHICS; TELEOLOGICAL ETHICS; and UTILITARIANISM.)

Bibliography

Bentham, Jeremy, *Introduction to the Principles of Morals and Legislation.* London, 1789.

Butler, Joseph, *Fifteen Sermons.* London, 1726.

Butler, Joseph, "Dissertation of the Nature of Virtue." Appendix to *The Analogy of Religion.* London, 1736.

Koestler, Arthur, *Darkness at Noon.* London and New York, 1940.
Mill, J. S., *Utilitarianism.* London, 1863.
Orwell, George, *1984.* London and New York, 1949.

ANTONY FLEW

ENERGETICISM. See DYNAMISM; ENERGY; OSTWALD, WILHELM.

ENERGY, from the Greek *energeia* (*en*, in; *ergon*, work), originally a technical term in Aristotelian philosophy denoting "actuality" or "existence in actuality," means, in general, activity or power of action. In the physical sciences it is defined as the capability to do work, as accumulated work or, in the words of Wilhelm Ostwald, as "that which is produced by work or which can be transformed into work." Energy is measured in terms of units of work, to overcome a resisting force of one dyne over a distance of one centimeter. (The joule = 10^7 erg = the watt-second; the kilogram-meter = 9.81×10^7 erg. In atomic physics the unit is the electron volt; $ev = 1.6 \times 10^{-12}$ erg.

In physics, energy is either kinetic or potential. A body of mass m moving with a velocity v possesses, owing to its motion, the kinetic energy $\frac{1}{2}mv^2$, which is the work necessary to overcome the inertial resistance in accelerating the body from rest to its final velocity and which is again transformed into work if the body is brought to rest. The energy that a system of bodies possesses by virtue of the relative geometrical position of its constituent parts, if subjected to gravitational, elastic, electrostatic, or other forces, is its potential energy. If, for example, a stone is raised from the surface of the earth, the potential energy of the system stone-and-earth is increased; if an elastic spring is expanded, its potential energy increases with increase of length. The attribute "potential" thus merely characterizes the latency of temporarily stored energy and does not call into question the reality of this kind of energy. With the recognition of the principle of the conservation of energy, it became apparent that the concept of energy applies to all branches of physics and to all physical sciences. Because of the at least partial convertibility of any energy into mechanical work, the aforementioned units of work also serve as measures of thermal, electric, magnetic, acoustic, optical, etc. energy. For thermal energy (heat) it proved practical also to retain as a separate unit the caloric unit of heat, the calorie (equal to 4.18×10^7 erg).

HISTORY OF THE CONCEPT

In spite of its universality, the general notion of energy as a basic concept in science is a relatively recent result of a long and intricate conceptual process. From the scientific point of view this process may conveniently be divided into five consecutive stages: (1) early conceptions of energy as a source of force, (2) the rise of the concept of mechanical work, (3) the recognition of different forms of energy, of their interconvertibility, and of the conservation of their sum total, (4) the emancipation of energy as an autonomous existent, and (5) the mathematization of energy as an integral invariant. From the philosophical point of view—that is, with respect to the ontological and epistemological status of the concept of energy—one may speak of (1) accidental, (2) substantial, (3) relational, (4) causal, and (5) formal conceptions of energy.

Energy and force. Aristotle was the first to use *energeia* as a technical term in his conceptual scheme, where it often signified the progressive "actualization" of that which previously existed only in potentiality. He also seems to have formed, though in an implicit manner, the idea of energy in the sense of accumulated force or accumulation of force. Force, for him, was not only the cause of motion but also the factor determining the duration or extent of motion. In the *Physics* he formulated the fundamental law of his dynamics, which, in modern terminology, states that the velocity, D/T (distance divided by time), of a mobile is proportional to the ratio of the magnitude of the moving force, A, and the resistance, B, a relationship that he described by enumerating exhaustively all possibilities under which AT/BD remains constant (with the exception of doubling the distance, D, as well as the time, T). He argued that a given finite force cannot move a mobile over an infinite distance or for an infinite time. Aristotle thus associated with every force a capacitative limitation, or, in modern terms, an energy content.

The implications of this statement for cosmology—in particular, for the motion of the celestial spheres, which derive their eternal motion ultimately from the "first mover" in accordance with the axiom "all things that are in motion must be moved by something else"—called for further clarifications. Thus, for example, Averroës, in his "Commentary on the Physics," distinguished between the primary motive force, the *motor separatus,* and the secondary forces, the *motores coniuncti;* the latter, in direct contact with the spheres, corresponding to the medieval "intelligences," draw finite quotas of force from the inexhaustible supply of the former. By this process, according to which only finite amounts are subtracted from an infinite accumulation of force, Averroës thought he was able to explain both the eternity of celestial motion and the fact that this motion does not occur instantaneously (*in instanti*), as motion under the effect of an infinite cause should do. Considerations of this kind, which engaged Aristotelian commentators until the times of Thomas Aquinas, show clearly that the notion of force signified not only the immediate cause of motion or acceleration but also its cumulative determination, or energy content. Thomas Aquinas considered the possibility of a finite and yet invariable moving force, which, being immutable, acts always in the same manner (*vis infatigabilis*), and thus he conceived of force as a moving agent independent of and separated from a constantly rejuvenating source, a notion essential for the future conception of the universe as a clockwork in action without the need of a constant supply of additional energy. Early in the fourteenth century the nominalist Peter Aureoli, in *Liber Sententiarum*, distinguished explicitly between two different aspects of force: its velocity-determining property and its capacity of consumption, or measure of exhaustibility. His differentiation can rightfully be regarded as the first ontological distinction between force and energy.

This, of course, does not imply that allusions to particular forms of energy are not found in early scientific writings. In fact, already in the *Mechanica*, commonly ascribed to Aristotle, the notion of kinetic energy is clearly referred to when it is asked:

> How is it that, if you place a heavy axe on a piece of wood and put a heavy weight on the top of it, it does not cleave the wood to any considerable extent, whereas, if you lift the axe and strike the wood with it, it does split it, although the axe when it strikes the blow has much less weight upon it than when it is placed on the wood and pressing on it? It is because the effect is produced entirely by movement, and that which is heavy gets more movement from its weight when it is in motion than when it is at rest.

Mechanical work. The modern concept of energy, as the definition shows, is a generalization of the notion of work in mechanics. The concept of work can be traced back to the principle of virtual displacements, or virtual velocities, which, in turn, has its ultimate origin in Aristotelian dynamics. Aristotle's conclusions (in *De Caelo*) concerning one single force (under whose action "the smaller, lighter body will be moved farther . . . ; for as the greater body is to the less, so will be the speed of the lesser body to that of the greater") were soon generalized for the case of a force counteracting a load, as exemplified in simple machines such as the wheel and the axle. In particular, the study of the law of the lever, as mentioned in the *Mechanica*, in Archimedes' *On the Equilibrium of Planes*, in the writings of Hero of Alexandria, and in the *Liber Karastonis*, a Latin version of the ninth-century Arabic text by Thabit ibn-Kurrah, contributed to the gradual establishment of the principle of virtual displacements for which finally, in the thirteenth century, Jordanus Nemorarius tried to give a theoretical proof. The Renaissance formulation of this law—namely, that the ratio between force and load is reciprocal to that of the spaces (distances) traversed within the same time—as pronounced by Guidobaldo del Monte (*Mechanica*, 1577), by Simon Stevin (*Hypomnemata Mathematica*, Leiden, 1608, Book 3), and by Galileo (*Opere* 2), formed the basis for the definition of work as force times distance traversed.

Pierre Varignon, in his *Nouvelle Mécanique ou statique* (Paris, 1725), reported a letter from Johann Bernoulli, dated January 26, 1717, in which the term "energy" appears in this connection, apparently for the first time in the modern period: "For all equilibrium of forces in whatever manner they are applied to each other, whether directly or indirectly, the sum of the positive energies will be equal to the sum of the negative energies taken positively." Although some historians, referring to this letter, have ascribed to Bernoulli the definition of energy as "force times distance," a critical study of the text shows undoubtedly that he still defined energy as "force times virtual velocity." In spite of the fact that this notion and its derivative, namely, the notion of work defined as "force times distance," played at least implicitly an important part in the establishment of classical mechanics—Joseph Louis Lagrange saw in the principle of virtual velocities the fundamental basis for his *Mécanique analytique* (1788), the highlight of classical mechanics—energy considerations were rarely found in theoretical or even practical mechanics prior to the middle of the nineteenth century. Before the development of the steam engine and the rise of thermodynamics, industry had little interest in energy calculations: force, not its integrated form, counted in the use of simple machines. The primary object of theoretical mechanics, moreover, was still celestial dynamics, where, again, energetics was of little avail. This certainly is also one of the reasons why Newton's *Principia* contains practically no reference to the concept of energy or to any of its applications.

According to Ernst Mach, in *Die Mechanik in ihrer Entwicklung* (Leipzig, 1883; translated as *The Science of Mechanics*, La Salle, Ill., 1942), the delay of the development of energetics as compared with that of general mechanics stemmed from what he called "trifling historical circumstances," namely, the fact that in Galileo's investigations of free fall, the relationship between velocity and time was established before the relationship between velocity and distance, so that, as multiplication with mass shows, the notions of quantity of motion or momentum and force gained priority and were regarded as more fundamental than the concept of energy, which thus appeared as a derived conception. Whatever the reason for energetics' lagging behind Newtonian mechanics, it is an indisputable fact that the concept of energy became a subject of discussion among philosophers rather than among physicists or mechanicians.

The measure of "force." Foremost among the philosophical discussions was the controversy between the Cartesians and Leibniz over whether the true measure of "force" (i.e., energy) is momentum (the product of mass and velocity) or *vis viva* (as defined by Leibniz, the product of mass and the square of velocity). Descartes, having shown in his *Principles of Philosophy* that the (scalar) quantity of motion or momentum (the vectorial nature of this quantity was recognized only by Christian Huygens) is conserved, concluded that momentum is the measure of energy. Leibniz, in "A Short Demonstration of a Remarkable Error of Descartes" ("Brevis Demonstratio Erroris Memorabilis Cartesii," in *Acta Eruditorum*, 1689), opposed this view. Lifting a load of 1 pound, he claimed, to a height of 4 feet requires the same work as lifting 4 pounds to the height of 1 foot. Since, according to Galileo, the velocities (of free fall) are proportional to the square roots of the heights (of fall), the velocity of the first object is twice that of the second before reaching ground, or $v_1 = 2v_2$. Assuming that the "forces" (energies) are proportional to the masses (moles), Leibniz concluded that $m_1 \cdot f(v_1) = m_2 \cdot f(v_2)$, where $f(v)$ is an as yet unknown function of the velocity, v. Substituting $m_2 = 4m_1$ and $v_1 = 2v_2$ yields $f(2v_2) = 4 \cdot f(v_2)$, which shows that the unknown function is quadratic in its argument, v. What is conserved and hence is the measure of "force," Leibniz concluded, is mv^2. This controversy between the Leibnizians, among them Johann Bernoulli, Willem Jakob Gravesande, Christian von Wolff, Georg Bilfinger, and Samuel König, and the Cartesians, among them Colin Maclaurin, James Stirling, and Samuel Clarke, was essentially only a battle of words, since the Leibnizians considered force acting on bodies traveling over equal distances and the Cartesians considered force acting on bodies during equal intervals of time, as d'Alembert in *Traité de dynamique* (1743) and Lagrange in *Mécanique analytique* (1788) made clear.

Conservation of "force." The interesting aspect of the Leibnizian–Cartesian controversy is the fact that both sides argued on the basis of the conservation of their respective "measures": for the Cartesians it was the conservation of momentum, for the Leibnizians that of "living force" (kinetic energy). Both contentions, as we know today, were correct, since both measures are integrals of the equations of motion. One of the most ardent supporters of Leibniz was his desciple Christian von Wolff, who in the *Cosmologia Generalis* (1731) declared: "In all the universe the same quantity of living force is always conserved." Johann Bernoulli, in the essay "De Vera Notione Virium Vivarum" (in *Acta Eruditorum*, 1735), was probably the first to treat this statement of the *conservatio virium vivarum* as a fundamental principle in mechanics. The apparent loss of "living force" in inelastic collisions was usually explained away by the hypothesis that the invisible small parts of matter gain in *vis viva* just as much as the macroscopic bodies seem to lose, a view Leibniz had already expressed in *Essai de dynamique* and reaffirmed in a letter to Samuel Clarke (Fifth Letter, August 18, 1716), where he stated that "active forces are preserved in the world" and continued: " 'Tis true, their wholes (unelastic colliding bodies) lose it with respect to their total motion; but their parts receive it, being shaken by the force of the concourse. And therefore that loss of force is only in appearance. . . . the case here is the same, as when men change great money into small." Johann Bernoulli, in contrast, explained this apparent loss as an absorption of force required for the compression of the colliding bodies.

Transformation of potential energy. What Bernoulli had in mind was obviously the so-called latent force, subsequently to be called potential energy, and his is the earliest description of transformation of kinetic energy into potential. The idea of such "latent force" was soon generalized to nonmechanical processes. Already in 1738 Daniel Bernoulli, in his *Hydrodynamica, sive de Viribus et Motibus Fluidorum Commentarii*, spoke of the "latent force" of combustible coal, which "if totally extracted from a cubic foot of coal and used for the motion of a machine, would be more efficient than the daily work of eight or ten men." But the measure of this "latent living force" was still mv^2.

Strictly speaking, the notion of potential—that is, a function whose space derivatives yield the force components and which therefore equals the potential energy for a unit of mass, charge, etc.—preceded the idea of potential energy. For in 1777, Lagrange, in "Recherches sur l'attraction des spheroides homogènes" (*Mémoire de l'Académie*, Paris), calculated the potential for an arbitrary discrete distribution of mass particles, and in 1782, Pierre Simon de Laplace calculated the potential for a continuous distribution. Potentials were still spoken of as "force functions"; the term "potential function" was introduced for the first time in 1828 by George Green in his *Essay of the Application of Mathematical Analysis* and later (1840), independently, by Karl Gauss.

When, in 1788, Lagrange derived the principle of the conservation of mechanical energy, or what subsequently was generally called the "theorem of the living force," as an integral of the equation of motion, he asked himself how many such integrals exist and under what conditions. The question, however, whether a similar principle exists also for nonmechanical processes did not occur to him.

The first clear and consistent terminology of energy conceptions, still in the domain of mechanical processes, was used by the Paris school of practical mathematicians and mechanicians, not by the purely analytical school headed by Lagrange and Laplace. It was Lazare Carnot who, in his *Essai sur les machines en général* (1783; republished in 1803 in a revised and enlarged edition under the title *Principes fondamentaux de l'équilibre et du mouvement*), declared that the "living force" can manifest itself either as mv^2 or as Fd (force times distance), the second being a measure of the "latent living force." Jean V. Poncelet, in *Mécanique industrielle* (1829), finally introduced for this quantity the term "mechanical work" and stated distinctly that it is the inertia of masses that serves for the accumulation of work and thus enables the transformation of work into "living force" and vice versa. Poncelet also measured this quantity by the kilogrammeter, a unit of energy universally adopted since then.

We thus see how at the beginning of the nineteenth century the notions of work and living force and their transformability became firmly established within the confines of mechanics proper. Even the term "energy" was used in this connection. In *A Course of Lectures on Natural Philosophy* (London, 1807), Thomas Young, though an adherent of the Cartesian measure of force, admitted that "in almost all cases of the forces employed in practical mechanics, the labour expended in producing any motion, is proportional not to the momentum, but to the energy which is obtained." But it took another fifty years until the term "energy" in its present meaning acquired full citizenship within the vocabulary of the physical sciences. This was brought about from quite a different quarter. It derived from the study of those phenomena where heat and chemical change are the characteristic features.

Conversion processes. Although Francis Bacon, in his *Novum Organum*, had already stated that ". . . the very essence of heat, or the substantial self of heat, is motion, and nothing else," and although similar statements had been made even before the seventeenth century, the late eighteenth century, in general, interpreted heat as a fluidum, in the spirit of the phlogiston theory. Still Jean B. J. Fourier, in his *Théorie analytique de la chaleur* (1822) declared: "Thermal processes are a special kind of phenomena which cannot be explained by the principle of motion and of equilibrium." Although Joseph Black's doctrine of latent heat accounted for the disappearance of heat on the basis of the fluidum theory, the appearance of heat, as Count Rumford's experiments, at Munich in 1796 and 1798, with the boring of cannon clearly showed, was incompatible with this theory. Having eliminated all sources from which the heat produced during the boring could have originated, Rumford concluded that "it appears to be extremely difficult, if not quite impossible, to form any distinct idea of anything capable of being excited and communicated in the manner the heat was excited and communicated in those experiments, except it be motion." At the same time (1799) Humphry Davy performed at the Royal Institution in London his famous experiment in which two pieces of ice were rubbed together by a clockwork mechanism in a vacuum, the whole apparatus being maintained at the freezing point of water. Davy concluded that heat was "a peculiar motion, probably a vibration of the corpuscles of bodies" (*Essay on Heat, Light, and the Combinations of Light*, London, 1799). Rumford's and Davy's experiments, though in their quantitative aspects not yet fully explored, suggested the interchangeability of heat and motion and thus led to the more general idea of an interconvertibility, or "correlation," of the forces of nature, previously regarded as disparate and incommensurable.

Approaching this problem from a chemical and biological point of view, Justus von Liebig, one of the earliest investigators of the economy of living organisms, advanced the theory that the mechanical energy of animals, as well as the heat of their bodies, originated from the chemical energy of their food. Such physiological experiments as those carried out in Liebig's laboratory made possible the study of conversion processes and together with increased concern with engines and natural philosophical considerations, seem to have been responsible for the independent discoveries, between 1837 and 1847, of the principle of energy conservation. In fact, Liebig's pupil Friedrich Mohr, adopting the mechanistic view that all forms of energy are manifestations of mechanical force, wrote as early as 1837: "Besides the known fifty-four chemical elements there exists in nature only one agent more, and this is called 'Kraft' ['force']; it can under suitable conditions appear as motion, cohesion, electricity, light, heat, and magnetism."

Energy conservation principle. Robert von Mayer, a physician from Heilbronn, Bavaria, who had served on a ship in the tropics, had noted that the venous blood of his patients there was redder than it had been in Europe. He explained this difference by an excess of oxygen due to a reduced combustion of the food that provided the heat of the body. He thus concluded that chemical energy, heat of the body, and muscular work are interconvertible, an idea that he pursued upon his return by a quantitative investigation of the mechanical equivalent of heat. The first enunciation of the energy conservation principle, combined with the determination of the mechanical equivalent of heat, is found in Mayer's article "Bemerkungen über die Kräfte der unbelebten Natur" (in Liebig, ed., *Annalen der Chemie und Pharmacie*, 1842, Vol. XLII, pp. 233–240). His calculations, as explained in greater detail in his *Die organische Bewegung* (1845) were based on the difference of the specific heats of air at constant volume and at constant pressure, as measured by F. Delaroche and others, yielding, in modern units, 3.65 joule per calorie; had Mayer employed Henri Regnault's more accurate results he would have arrived at 4.2 joule per calorie, the currently accepted value. The amount of heat liberated by the expenditure of mechanical or electrical work was systematically measured by James Prescott Joule, a Manchester brewer and amateur scientist. In heating liquids by the rotation of paddle wheels, forcing water through narrow tubes, or compressing masses of air, Joule demonstrated that the expenditure of the same amount of work, irrespective of the manner in which this work was done, resulted in the development of the same amount of heat. His measurements of such conversion processes gave a firm quantitative support for the conservation principle.

The discovery of the physical principle of the conservation of energy was soon found to be in full agreement with the principal tenets of the prevailing natural philosophy, the German *Naturphilosophie*, whose early proponent, Friedrich Wilhelm Joseph von Schelling, had declared in 1799, in *Einleitung zu dem Entwurf eines Systems der Naturphilosophie*, "that magnetic, electrical, chemical, and finally even organic phenomena would be interwoven into one great association . . . [which] extends over the whole of nature." Mayer supported his own conclusions by the metaphysical argumentation that forces are essentially causes and "causes equal effects"; since causes are indestructible and convertible into effects, forces must likewise be indestructible and interconvertible. Even the experimentalist Joule, in an article "On the Calorific Effects of Magneto-electricity, and on the Mechanical Value of Heat" (*Philosophical Magazine*, Series 3, Vol. 23 [1843], 442), declared: "I shall lose no time in repeating and extending these experiments, being satisfied that the grand agents of nature are by the Creator's fiat indestructible." In another paper (in *Philosophical Magazine*, Series 3, Vol. 26 [1845], 382) he stated: "Believing that the power to destroy belongs to the Creator alone, I entirely coincide with Roget and Faraday in the opinion, that any theory which, when carried out, demands the annihilation of force, is necessarily erroneous." The conduciveness of the philosophical climate toward the enunciation of the energy principle can most clearly be recognized from the arguments of A. Colding, who arrived at the principle independently of Mohr, Mayer, and Joule:

> The first idea I conceived on the relationship between the forces of nature was the following. As the forces of nature are something spiritual and immaterial, entities whereof we are cognizant only by their mastery over nature, these entities must of course be very superior to everything material in the world; and as it is obvious that it is through them only that the wisdom we perceive and admire in nature expresses itself, these powers must evidently be in relationship to the spiritual, immaterial, and intellectual power itself that guides nature in its progress; but if such is the case, it is consequently quite impossible to conceive of these forces as anything naturally mortal or perishable. Surely, therefore, the forces ought to be regarded as absolutely imperishable. ("Nogle Soetninger om Kraefterne," 1843, in *Philosophical Magazine*, Series 4, Vol. 27 [1864], 56–64).

Even the classic paper of Hermann von Helmholtz, the physiologist turned physicist, "On the Conservation of Force" (*Über die Erhaltung der Kraft*, Berlin, 1847), shows clearly the impact of contemporaneous philosophy, with its renunciation of Hegelianism and its reversion to an idealistic rationalism, when it declares:

> The final aim of the theoretic natural sciences is to discover the ultimate and unchangeable causes of natural phenomena. Whether all the processes of nature be actually referrible to such—whether changes occur which are not subject to the laws of necessary causation, but spring from spontaneity or freedom, this is not the place to decide; it is at all events clear that the science whose object it is to comprehend nature must proceed from the assumption that it is comprehensible. . . .

The requirement of referring the phenomena of nature back to unchangeable final causes was interpreted by Helmholtz as reducing physical processes to motions of material particles possessing unchangeable moving forces that are dependent on conditions of space alone. Thus, Helmholtz, starting with the eighteenth-century dynamics of bodies acting under mutual attraction, generalized the Newtonian conception of motion to the case of a large number of bodies and showed that the sum of force and tension (what we now call kinetic and potential energies) remain constant during the process of motion. Applying conventional analytical mathematics, Helmholtz proved that the principle of the conservation of living force not only can be derived from Newtonian dynamics but may also serve as an equivalent point of departure for the deduction of theoretical mechanics.

This fundamental assumption may be formulated as the principle of the impossibility of a *perpetuum mobile.* When a system of particles acting under central forces passes from one configuration to another, the velocities acquired can be used to perform some work; in order to draw the same amount of work a second time from the system, one would have to restore its initial conditions by expending on it forces or energy from outside the system. The principle now requires that the amount of work gained by the transition from the first position to the second and the amount of work lost by the passage of the system from the second configuration to the first be equal, no matter in what way or at what velocity the change has been effected; otherwise a *perpetuum mobile* could be constructed on the basis of this cycle, contrary to the principle. So far Helmholtz' reasoning is but a paraphrase of the arguments used by Sadi Carnot and Benoît Clapeyron in their foundations of the thermodynamics of heat engines. By replacing the concept of work by that of "tensions" (*verbrauchte Spannkräfte*), which are equal but of opposite sign to the work performed, Helmholtz transformed the equation between living force (kinetic energy) and work into the statement that the sum of living force and tension is a constant, the tension being a function of the instantaneous state of the system. Although prima facie an insignificant change, this reformulation of the mechanical principle of the conservation of living force through the introduction of "tensions" opened up incalculable perspectives in that it could be applied to all branches of physics, not only to mechanics proper. Moreover, the new formulation was strikingly analogous to that of the principle of the conservation of matter, or mass, an accepted axiom in physical science since the times of Antoine Lavoisier. Exploiting the adaptability of the concept of "tension" to nonmechanical phenomena, Helmholtz not only reconciled the new doctrine of heat with the theory of mechanics, heat explicitly being treated as a form of energy, but also demonstrated the validity of the conservation principle for electrodynamics and other departments of physics. The recognition that mechanical work, heat, and electricity were only different forms of one and the same physical substratum—a result that can rightfully be considered the greatest physical discovery of the nineteenth century—found its analytical vindication in Helmholtz' paper.

At first, however, Helmholtz' memoir was hardly recognized, since its argumentation was based on mathematical reasoning, which at this time was accessible to but a small number of specialists. Another fundamental obstacle in the way of a just assessment of the new truth was the indiscriminate homonymous usage of the term "force" in both its Newtonian and its Leibnizian significations. Once the semantic difficulties had been removed, the principle of the conservation of energy found general acceptance and even popularity, owing to the writings of William Thomson (Lord Kelvin). In a discourse before the Royal Institution in 1856, Thomson distinguished carefully the significance of the Newtonian notion of force from what he called "energy." The term "energy"—apart from its early usage by Bernoulli and Young—had already been used three years earlier by William Rankine in his "On the General Law of the Transformation of Energy" (*Philosophical Magazine*, Series 4, Vol. 5 [1853], 106), but only Thomson's application led to its universal acceptance. "Any piece of matter or any group of bodies, however connected, which either is in motion, or can get into motion without external assistance, has what is called mechanical energy. The energy of motion may be called either 'dynamical energy' or 'actual energy.' The energy of a material system at rest in virtue of which it can get into motion, is called 'potential energy' . . ." (*On the Origin and Transformation of Motive Power*, 1856). In 1893, in a footnote to a reprint of his 1856 lecture (in *Popular Lectures and Addresses*, London, 1894, Vol. II), Thomson wrote: "Shortly after the date of this lecture I gave the name 'kinetic energy' which is now in general use. It is substituted for 'actual' and for 'dynamical.' . . ." Thus Helmholtz' "tension" was renamed "potential energy," and the sum total of kinetic and potential energies, the total energy of the system, was shown to be a constant that is characteristic of the system.

These innovations, however, had still to overcome some opposition. The Rankine-Thomson designation "potential energy" was rejected by John F. W. Herschel ("On the Origin of Force," in *Fortnightly Review and Familiar Lectures*, 1857) as "unfortunate," being too common a name for such a "great truth." Even the term "conservation" of force or energy was subjected to severe criticisms, particularly by T. H. Huxley and by Herbert Spencer in his *First Principles* (1862), on the ground that "conservation" implies a conserver and an act of conserving and therefore the assumption that without such an act, force (energy) would disappear—an idea at variance with the conception to be conveyed. But in addition to the terminology, the conception itself, particularly that of potential energy, was still a matter of debate. An interesting testimony to these difficulties is Michael Faraday's paper "On the Conservation of Force" (*Philosophical Magazine*, Series 4, Vol. 13 [1857], 225–239), in which the following problem is raised: Is there creation or annihilation of force if the distance between two gravitating bodies is changed and the attractive force varies inversely with the square of the distance? "Gravitation," Faraday continued, "has not yet been connected by any degree of convertibility with the other forms of force. . . . That there should be a power of gravitation existing by itself having no relation to the other natural powers, and no respect to the law of the conservation of force, is as little likely as that there should be a principle of levity as well as of gravity." Rankine's answer to Faraday's objection (*Philosophical Magazine*, Series 4, Vol. 17 [1859], 250) seems to have had little effect, for as late as 1876, James Croll, in his paper "On the Transformation of Gravity" (*Philosophical Magazine*, Series 5, Vol. 2 [1876], 242–254), attempted to solve Faraday's query with the assumption that "a stone when in the act of falling [may] be acted upon by gravity with less force at any given moment than it would be were the stone at rest at that instant."

The emancipation of energy. Although Croll's paper is full of misconceptions, which, interestingly, were clarified in an answer by the Viennese physiologist Ernst von Brücke, "On Gravitation and the Conservation of Force" (*Philosophical Magazine*, Series 4, Vol. 15 [1858], 81–90), it was of great importance for the subsequent development of the concept of energy. It connected the notion of energy for the first time with that of space. That space and change of position are necessary conditions for energy transformations Croll tried to demonstrate by the following consideration: four possibilities of energy transformations are conceivable—a change of potential energy into kinetic, of kinetic into potential, of kinetic into kinetic, and of potential into potential. Since, however, there "is evidently no such thing in nature, so far as is yet known, as one form of potential passing directly into another form" of potential energy and the existence of kinetic energy always implies change of position, the point is proved. Having thus associated energy with space, Croll went on to dissociate it from the material medium. "Our inability to conceive how force can exist without a material medium has its foundation in a metaphysical misconception," an idea he explained in greater detail in his book *Philosophy of Theism* (London, 1857). Croll's almost casual remarks, though scientifically rather objectionable and philosophically highly speculative, may be regarded as the earliest objection to the prevailing view, which still conceived of energy as an attribute, so to speak, of the dynamic system.

Meanwhile, James Clerk Maxwell's *Treatise on Electricity and Magnetism* (1873) appeared, opening the way for a field-theory treatment of electromagnetic phenomena. It showed, in particular, that the work necessary to build up an electromagnetic field can be regarded as equivalent to the energy produced in space with a certain density that depends on the squares of the magnitudes of the electric and magnetic fields. In the case of nonstatic fields these calculations lead to the conclusion, as was shown by J. H. Poynting in "On the Transfer of Energy in the Electromagnetic Field" (*Philosophical Transactions of the Royal Society*, Vol. 175 [1885], 343–361), that energy has to flow from one place in space to another in order to compensate for changes that occur in a particular region of space. A transfer of energy, it is true, had been associated with electricity before Poynting, but the energy flow was always considered as being confined to the conducting wires.

> But the existence of induced currents and of electromagnetic actions at a distance from a primary circuit from which they draw their energy, has led us, under the guidance of Faraday and Maxwell, to look upon the medium surrounding the conductor as playing a very important part in the development of the phenomena. If we believe in the continuity of the motion of energy, that is, if we believe that when it disappears at one point and reappears at another it must have passed through the intervening space, we are forced to conclude that the surrounding medium contains at least a part of the energy, and that it is capable of transferring it from point to point.

Thus the surrounding medium or empty space became the arena in which energy moves, and energy, disjoined from matter, was raised in its ontological status from a mere accident of a mechanical or physical system to the autonomous rank of independent existence: matter ceased to be the indispensable vehicle for its transport. Mechanics, with its restricted conception of transfer of energy by matter, could proceed only as far as Gaspard de Coriolis' notion of "energy currents," described in his *Traité de la mécanique* (1844). The complete emancipation or reification of energy could be achieved only by a theory of action-at-a-distance, such as Maxwell's theory of electromagnetism. Here energy could be labeled and traced in its motion or change of form just as a piece of matter is ticketed so that it can be identified in other places under other conditions.

The recognition of the new ontological status of energy led to a result of great philosophical importance: it strengthened the position of those who opposed the prevailing kinetic–corpuscular theory of nature, according to which all processes are reduced to motions of particles and motion is the fundamental concept for physical explanation. Referring to the demonstrated equivalence of all forms of energy, the opponents claimed that kinetic energy is only one of the forms in which this quantity appears. In their view, energy was a much more general conception than motion, a conception that should not be narrowed down to mean only energy of attraction and repulsion of gravitational or electrostatic nature or energy of various forms of motion. One of the earliest exponents of this school of "energetics" was G. Helm, who, in a treatise, *Die Lehre von der Energie* (Leipzig, 1887), revived the term "energetics," originally coined by Rankine, to characterize his position, according to which energy is the basic physical reality responsible for all natural phenomena. Helm referred to Gustav Zeuner, Ernst Mach, Josiah Gibbs, James Clerk Maxwell, A. J. von Oettingen, and Joseph Popper as advocating similar ideas. In particular, he claimed, energy can always be broken down into two factors, an intensity and an extensity factor, which characterize the quantity of energy as well as the direction in which changes of energy take place (the intensity factor always decreases). In spite of further expositions, Helm's ideas did not attract much attention until Wilhelm Ostwald incorporated Helm's "factorization of energy" into the second edition of his treatise on physical chemistry, *Lehrbuch der allgemeinen Chemie* (1893), as the foundation of his theory of chemical affinity. In the period between the first and second editions of his treatise Ostwald embraced the new doctrine of energetics, and with his address in 1895 to the German Congress of Naturalists at Lübeck, "The Conquest of Scientific Materialism" (*Die Überwindung des wissenschaftlichen Materialismus*), he became the principal speaker of the new movement. In his view, not only was energy the universal currency of physics, but all phenomena of nature were merely manifestations of energy and of its manifold transformations. In "Lectures on Natural Philosophy" (*Vorlesungen über Naturphilosophie*, Leipzig, 1901) he contended that since substance is by definition that which persists under transformations or changes, energy is substance. Methodological as well as epistemological considerations, Ostwald claimed, force us to see in energy the only substance—methodologically because the alternative view, scientific materialism, has failed to give an exhaustive explanation in even a single case of natural phenomena; epistemologically because "what we hear originates in work done on the ear drum and the middle ear by the vibrations of the air. What we see is only radiant energy which does chemical work on the retina that is perceived as light. . . . From this point of view the totality of nature appears as a series of spatially and temporally changing energies, of which we obtain knowledge in proportion as they impinge on the body, and especially upon the sense organs fashioned for the reception of the appropriate energies." Ostwald's conception of a physical object in terms of energy, of its volume in terms of compressibility, and of its shape in terms of elasticity is one of the final stages in a development that began with Locke's sensationalistic conception and eventually put an end to the substantial conception of matter.

The "dissolution of matter" into energy was particularly welcomed by the adherents of the monistic school of thought in their search for a unified conception of the universe. Gustave Le Bon, for instance, in his *L'Evolution de la matière* (Paris, 1905), spoke of the "dematerialization of matter into energy," a philosophical conclusion that in the same year found a far-reaching and profound scientific foundation. For in a paper entitled "Does the Inertia of a Body Depend Upon Its Energy Content?" ("Ist die Trägheit eines Körpers von seinem Energieinhalt abhängig?" in *Annalen der Physik*, Vol. 18 [1905], 639–641), Albert Einstein showed, on the basis of the Maxwell–Hertz equations of the electromagnetic field, that "if a body gives off the energy E in the form of radiation, its mass diminishes by E/c^2," where c denotes the velocity of light. Since then the mass–energy relation, $E=mc^2$, has been of fundamental importance, particularly in nuclear physics, where P. M. S. Blackett, G. P. S. Occhialini, O. Klemperer, and others showed that the total mass of a particle can be transformed into energy. Whereas in classical mechanics differences of energy alone were of physical significance, so that energy could be determined only up to an additive constant, in modern physics energy lost this indeterminateness and became a physical quantity of absolute magnitude. Moreover, in the theory of relativity the principles of the conservation of energy, or mass, and momentum, the latter being the basis of the Cartesian measure of "force," revealed themselves only as different aspects of one and the same conservation law, the conservation of the momentum–energy four-vector. On the basis of the Einstein equation $E=mc^2$ the problem of the source of solar (or stellar) energy could be solved, the "packing effect" in nuclear physics could be explained, and the release of nuclear energy could be predicted. Energy was released mass, and mass was frozen energy, or as Bertrand Russell, in *Human Knowledge: Its Scopes and Limits* (New York, 1948), summarized the situation: "Mass is only a form of energy, and there is no reason why matter should not be dissolved into other forms of energy. It is energy, not matter, that is fundamental in physics."

Conservation and invariance. Although the theory of relativity threw new light on the conservational aspects of energy, or mass, the relationship between conservation and invariance found its final elucidation in Emmy Noether's article "Invariant Variational Problems" ("Invariante Variationsprobleme," in *Göttinger Nachricten* [1918], pp. 235–257), which demonstrates the conservation of certain quantities (for example, the canonical energy–momentum tensor) for dynamic systems that are invariant under continuous transformations of the coordinates or, more generally, of the field functions involved. Conservation thus appeared as a consequence of symmetry properties, a fact that was in part known already from the Hamiltonian formulation of classical mechanics. In particular, if homogeneity of space and time is assumed, that is, if it is postulated that the system is invariant under translational transformations of the origins of space-coordinates and time-coordinates, then the conservation of momenta and of energy is but a mathematical consequence. The principle of the conservation of energy of a given dynamic system is therefore ultimately a consequence of the invariance (or symmetry) of the system under changes in the zero-point of the time scale, i.e., a consequence of the homogeneity of time. (See also FORCE.)

Bibliography

Duhem, P., *L'Évolution de la mécanique*. Paris, 1905.

Haas, A. E., "Die Begründung der Energetik durch Leibniz." *Annalen der Naturphilosophie*, Vol. 7 (1908), 373–386.

Haas, A. E., *Die Entwicklungsgeschichte des Satzes von der Erhaltung der Kraft*. Vienna, 1909.

Helm, G., *Die Energetik nach ihrer geschichtlichen Entwicklung*. Leipzig, 1898.

Hiebert, E. N., *Historical Roots of the Principle of Conservation of Energy*. Madison, Wis., 1962.

Jammer, M., "The Factorization of Energy." *The British Journal for the Philosophy of Science*, Vol. 14 (1963), 160–166.

Kuhn, T. S., "Energy Conservation as an Example of Simultaneous Discovery," in M. Clagett, ed., *Critical Problems in the History of Science*. Madison, Wis., 1959.

Mach, E., *Die Geschichte und die Wurzel des Satzes von der Erhaltung der Arbeit*. Prague, 1872.

Planck, M., *Das Prinzip der Erhaltung der Kraft*. Leipzig, 1st ed., 1887; 2d ed., 1908.

M. JAMMER

ENGELS, FRIEDRICH (1820–1895), the intellectual companion of Karl Marx, although generally considered inferior to his colleague as a thinker, contributed more than Marx to the development of the philosophical aspects of Marxism. Indeed he was the creator of orthodox Marxism as a system based on historical materialism and on dialectics. Engels was born in Barmen in the German Rhineland. His father was a textile manufacturer who had interests in England, and Engels went there to work in a cotton mill in Manchester, first as clerk, later as manager and part owner. Engels was a man of many talents, a scholar, linguist, pamphleteer, soldier, military commentator, and businessman. He was all those things with a thoroughness and distinction that would have brought him recognition in his own right, but it was his intellectual partnership with a man of genius that brought him fame. Engels met Marx briefly in Cologne in 1842, became acquainted with him in Paris in 1844, and worked actively with him before and during the revolutionary ferment of 1848, when they wrote the *Communist Manifesto.* In 1850 Engels reluctantly returned to his business in Manchester, in part because he saw that Marx needed financial support in order to continue his researches. This help Engels gave unstintingly throughout Marx's life and for years after his death, to his surviving children. Outliving Marx by 12 years, Engels edited his friend's manuscripts, notably the two volumes of *Das Kapital* left unfinished by Marx. He also served as official interpreter of Marxist doctrine during the years when it was beginning to attain world-wide influence over workingmen's movements.

Beginning with works written during Marx's lifetime and with Marx's express approval—e.g., *Anti-Dühring* (1878)—Engels emphasized the scientific, positivist component in their joint theories, which he compared with those of Darwin. Engels believed that he and Marx had discovered a rigid system of historical laws that would lead with inexorable necessity to socialism. These laws, Engels held, were dialectic rather than mechanical in character. That is, instead of being like the laws previously discovered in natural science and extrapolated to social studies by men whom Engels called vulgar materialists, they were laws that took account of the contradictions in reality and of the fact that development occurred in revolutionary leaps to higher levels. Engels took from Hegel the doctrine, which he called the law of the interpenetration of opposites, that objective contradictions exist in reality. He enunciated the law of the transformation of quantity into quality, which asserts that change occurs abruptly, after a period of gradual progression. The last dialectical law, the negation of the negation, states that progress takes place by a series of detours, from position *A* to the opposite, position –*A*, and then back to the opposite of that position, which turns out to be position *A* "raised to a higher power." To give one of Marx's own examples, the industrial bourgeoisie generates its opposite, the miserable proletariat, which then negates bourgeois capital in a revolutionary leap to the higher stage of classless industrial society.

Engels adumbrated these theories in *Anti-Dühring* and stressed them in a special excerpt from that work, *Socialism: Utopian and Scientific* (1892), but the extent to which he carried them was not known until his *Dialectics of Nature* was published in 1925. In this work he extended materialist dialectics to the natural sciences, with results that are often held to be ludicrous, and implied that dialectics would supersede formal logic. The lengthy controversies that these questions have provoked in Soviet philosophy arise, then, from the work of Engels rather than of Marx.

While it is certain that Engels stressed such questions more than Marx and that he lived on to formalize a Marxist tradition out of reverence for a friend who disliked just such formalism, one must be wary of attempts to set Engels, as a scientistic pedant, against Marx, as an existentialist or idealist. It is tempting for certain neo-Marxist philosophers, but in the end impossible, to purge Marxism of all its allegedly scientific content that has since been proven untrue and to lay all these errors at Engels' door, leaving only the "profound" (or ambiguous) speculations of the young Marx as true Marxism. For one thing, it was Engels who suggested those early speculations to Marx, in 1844. And decades later it was not Engels alone but the age and his own ambitions that led Marx to present his mature theory of history as a "scientific system" (decorated with some Hegelian flourishes). At all events, it was Marx's thought as understood by Engels that came to constitute Marxism and, in particular, Soviet dogma.

Works by Engels

Engels wrote many works jointly with Marx, and each had a hand in works published under the sole name of the other. Therefore, their complete works are published together: the most nearly complete edition is in Russian, *Sochineniya*, 32+ vols. (Moscow, 1955—), with a parallel German edition, *Werke*, 30+ vols. (Berlin, 1957—). An earlier incomplete edition was *Marx–Engels Gesamtausgabe,* 12 vols. (Berlin and Moscow, 1927–1935), In English there is Marx and Engels, *Selected Works,* 2 vols. (London, 1942; and, slightly different, 1951).

Of considerable historical and philosophical interest is Engels' voluminous correspondence: Marx and Engels, *Selected Correspondence 1846–1895* (London, 1934); *Die Briefe von Friedrich Engels und Eduard Bernstein* (Berlin, 1925); and E. Bottigelli, ed., *Friedrich Engels–Paul et Laura Lafargue, Correspondance, 1868–95*, 3 vols. (Paris, 1956–1959).

Engels' principal theoretical works published under his name alone are *Herr Eugen Dührings Umwälzung der Wissenschaft* (Leipzig, 1878), translated by E. Burns as *Herr Eugen Dühring's Revolution in Science* (London, 1934), also known as *Anti-Dühring; Ludwig Feuerbach und der Ausgang der klassischen deutschen Philosophie* (Stuttgart, 1888), translated as *Ludwig Feuerbach and the Outcome of Classical German Philosophy* (New York, 1934); *Dialektik der Natur,* translated by Clemens Dutt as *Dialectics of Nature* (New York, 1940); *Die Entwicklung des Sozialismus von der Utopie zur Wissenschaft* (Zurich, 1883), translated by E. Aveling as *Socialism: Utopian and Scientific* (New York, 1892); *Der Ursprung der Familie, des Privateigentums und des Staats* (Zurich, 1884), translated by E. Untermann as *The Origin of the Family, Private Property and the State* (Chicago, 1902); and *Grundsätze des Kommunismus,* E. Bernstein, ed. (Berlin, 1919), translated by Paul Sweezy as *Principles of Communism* (New York, 1952).

Works on Engels

All biographies of Karl Marx and commentaries on his work necessarily deal with Engels too. The only worthwhile biography of Engels alone is Gustav Meyer, *Friedrich Engels*, 2 vols. (The

Hague, 1934; an abridged English rendering, New York, 1936). For Engels' particular contributions to Marxism, see George Lichtheim, *Marxism* (London, 1964) and Sidney Hook, *Reason, Social Myths, and Democracy* (New York, 1950).

NEIL MCINNES

ENLIGHTENMENT is primarily a cultural historian's broad designation for a historical period, roughly the eighteenth century, in Western society. As a cultural period it is more closely linked with, indeed more dependent on, formal philosophical thought than any other in the West. "Enlightenment" and "Age of Reason" are, in customary usage, nearly interchangeable. There is, however, some tendency among historians of Western culture to use "Age of Reason" for the seventeenth and eighteenth centuries together, and to confine "Enlightenment" to the eighteenth century, when the characteristic ideas and attitudes of rationalism had spread from a small group of advanced thinkers to a relatively large educated public.

Sources. The eighteenth-century public acquired its Enlightenment less through direct contact with the work of philosophers than through what we should now call "popularizers"—journalists, men of letters, the bright young talkers of the *salons*. Especially on the Continent, this group of propagandists of the Enlightenment were known as *philosophes*, from the French term for philosopher, and in most Western languages Voltaire, Diderot, Condorcet, Holbach, Beccaria and their peers are called *philosophes*, not philosophers. The distinction is by no means wholly unjustified, for these writers were not systematic philosophers. They scorned "metaphysics" (though not epistemology), and their basic concepts were indeed derived from their seventeenth-century predecessors, notably Bacon, Descartes, and Locke. Yet it can be argued from their actual works that Diderot or Voltaire, for example, are perhaps as deserving of the title, "philosopher," as, say, Nietzsche.

Two major themes in the history of formal philosophy took on special importance as they were absorbed into the thinking of the educated public of the Enlightenment. First, in political philosophy, the development of the social contract theory from Hobbes through Locke to Rousseau was widely publicized, and became part of the vocabulary of ordinary political discussion both in Europe and in America, as did the concept of "natural rights." Some later historians have, of course, denied the importance of such ideas—as of all ideas—but the fact that they were widely used in the second half of the eighteenth century is undeniable. Second, in the theory of knowledge the classic sequence Locke-Berkeley-Hume-Kant by no means passed unnoticed among the general public. Here, however, it seems almost certain that Locke held his own among this public throughout the eighteenth century. Indeed, the importance of Locke for the world view of the Enlightenment can hardly be exaggerated. Historians have written of the "reception of Locke" on the Continent, using the analogy of the "reception" of Roman law in the Germanies.

Finally, in building the world view of the Enlightenment, the increasing prestige of natural science—then usually known as "natural philosophy"—played an important part. By the early eighteenth century, the achievements in mathematics, astronomy, and physics which culminated in Newton's *Principia* (1687) had penetrated widely if not deeply into the public mind of the West. That very modern phenomenon, "science made easy," began with a number of explanations of Newton's work, including a French translation of the *Principia* by Mme. de Châtellet with prefaces by Roger Cotes and Voltaire (Paris, 1759). Indeed Newton appears as the first of a line of culture heroes from among natural scientists that extends through Darwin to Einstein. No doubt the ladies and gentlemen who admired Newton were for the most part incapable of understanding the *Principia*, and, though some of them fashionably dabbled at home with scientific experiments, they had no very sophisticated concepts of scientific method. Science was for them, however, living, growing evidence that human beings, using their "natural" reasoning powers in a fairly obvious and teachable way, could not only understand the way things really are in the universe; they could understand what human beings are really like, and by combining this knowledge of nature and human nature, learn how to live better and happier lives.

The extent to which this learning process went on wholly outside formal educational institutions has often been exaggerated. The eighteenth century, for most universities, was indeed a low point, and secondary education too was often wholly "classical," much as it had been for centuries. Yet mathematics was always an important part of formal higher education, and as the eighteenth century wore on, the study of "natural philosophy" began to play an important part in the curricula of many secondary schools, notably in many of the schools of the Jesuits, of the English dissenters and in scattered institutions elsewhere in the West. Yet it is certainly true that academies like the British Royal Society (1662), the French *Académie des Sciences* (1666), the many local academies, literary clubs (*sociétés de pensée*), the *salons*, the Freemasons, Illuminati, Rosicrucians, circulating libraries, all nourished by an increasingly numerous periodical and book production, were the most effective agents in the spread of the Enlightenment. All this is confusedly and appropriately reflected in the hodgepodge of the libretto of Mozart's *Magic Flute* (1791).

Certainly, very specific and often very successful reform movements sprung directly from the works of the thinkers of the Enlightenment. Beccaria's *On Crimes and Punishments* helped set Bentham's mind to work on problems of law reform, and the two together, along with many others, inspired humane reforms in criminal law and in prisons, as well as efficient reforms in civil law, all over the Western world. Locke and Condillac's ideas on psychology bore fruit in the work of a man like the French physician Pinel, a reformer who, with help from kindred souls, began the modern treatment of insanity as a disease rather than as an act of God or Satan. Crime and insanity, no longer given theological explanations, could now be dealt with as mundane difficulties capable of empirical solutions. The list of such specific changes in attitudes, and consequent changes in institutions, could be made long indeed, and would also include many voluntary charitable societies and pressure groups—and the substantial beginnings, contrary to formal theories of laissez-faire, of government planning. The enlightened despots all over Europe, the French scientists of 1794 at work on research to improve weapons and logistics, the Benthamites devising punishments neatly tailored to fit the crime, all look forward over the nineteenth century to our twentieth century.

A MODEL OF ENLIGHTENMENT

"Enlightenment," like "humanism" or "romanticism," is a big general term through which we try to build up a mental construct out of a very great number of facts. No such construct can possibly include, without exception, all the facts of eighteenth-century culture. We might attempt to take a single real individual, and build from his life and work a man "typical" of the Enlightenment. Were we to do so, we could do much worse than to pick Thomas Jefferson. Even more representative would be a combination of Jefferson, Franklin, and Thomas Paine; in fact, the construction of a nonexistent but "typical" enlightened man is by no means a bad approach to this classic problem. (It should be noted that colonial and early national America was very much a part of the Enlightenment.) Here, however, we shall deal directly with ideas in order to construct a kind of "model" of the world view of the Enlightenment, fully aware that in fact we are not constructing a model even in the sense now fashionable in such social sciences as economics, but are using an old and well-tried literary device—that is, empirical, even commonsensical, generalization.

Three key clusters of ideas form our model of the world view of the Enlightenment: Reason, Nature, Progress.

Reason. Reason was to the enlightened man a kind of common sense sharpened and made subtler by training in logic and "natural philosophy" (science). Like any other physiological function, reason was held to work always and in substantially the same way in all human beings as Nature designed them. But—and this is important—in enlightened eyes, environmental conditions (institutional and cultural environment, rather than physical environment—in temperate climates at any rate), had in the West in the eighteenth century corrupted the normal physiological working of Reason in most human beings. For this corruption the eighteenth century held especially responsible the wider cultural environment. Church, state, social, and economic class, superstition, ignorance, prejudice, poverty, and vice all seemed to work together to impede the proper functioning of Reason. The *philosophes*, could they have been polled in the modern way, would probably have ranked the Roman Catholic church—indeed, all Christian churches—as the greatest single corrupting influence. Priests were selfish, cruel, intolerant. Voltaire's "crush the infamous thing" (*écrasez l'infâme*) rang through the century. But at bottom the great evil of the church, for the enlightened, was its transcendental and supernatural base, which put faith and revelation above reason.

In the great French *Encyclopédie*, under the article on *philosophe*, appears the revealing sentence, "Reason is to the *philosophe* what grace is to the Christian." And just as grace is available to the true Christian, so Reason, for the *philosophe*, is available to the truly enlightened, once the proper environmental conditions are achieved. The *philosophes* and their followers certainly held that the necessary environmental changes would take some time and effort, though Condorcet in his *Sketch for a Historical Picture of the Human Mind* (*Esquisse d'un tableau historique des progrès de l'esprit humain*, 1794) held that Western man was on the threshold of the final push into a wholly reasonable world. Moreover, in this reasonable world, if there might persist some inequalities in reasoning power among men, these would not be considerable. Helvétius, in his *Concerning the Mind* (*De l'Esprit*, 1758), is convinced that potentially all men have roughly equal powers of understanding.

Locke, in his *Essay Concerning Human Understanding* (1690), provided the philosophical and psychological foundation on which the *philosophes* constructed their faith in Reason. For Locke denied all "innate ideas," among which were the Christian truths of revelation, and held the mind to be a *tabula rasa* on which experience (that is, environment) inscribed a content. Obviously, if you can control this experience you can control the formation of the mind, the character—all that counts in a man. This sturdy faith in "cultural engineering," new, as a widespread one, in its assertion of the possibility of changing all human beings for the good by changing their environment, and in particular their education, from infancy on, has survived in diminished forms to this day.

Nature. Nature, the second great cluster of ideas in our model of Enlightenment, is closely meshed with that of Reason. In perhaps oversimple terms, Reason, properly working, enabled human beings to discover, or rediscover, Nature beneath the concealing corruptions of religion, social structure, convention, and indeed, beneath the often misleading impressions of sense experience not properly organized by Reason. Though the average enlightened man would not have admitted it, this Nature was in part a hypostatized conception of the beautiful and the good. It must be understood against two antitheses. First, there is the "super-" or "supranatural"—the miracle, the revealed truths of religion. For the enlightened, all these are simply figments of the imagination, nonexistent, indeed at bottom priestly inventions designed to keep men ignorant of the ways of Reason and Nature. Second, there is the "unnatural." Unlike the supernatural, the unnatural does indeed exist. The unnatural, the artificial, the burdens of irrational customs and traditions accumulated through historic time, are for the enlightened the form evil takes in this world. It must be noted that in simple naive logic the enlightened had as much trouble over the problem of the origin of evil as did the Christian. How the natural got to be unnatural was a question as difficult to answer as how an all-powerful, all-knowing, and all-good God allowed Adam to bite into the apple. Rousseau, for example, in the *Essay on the Origin of Inequality* (1754), blames the lapse from the state of Nature on the first man to fence in a piece of land and say, "This is mine." He does not explain why this natural man acted so unnaturally.

Nature, then, is quite simply the "good"—a set of ethical and aesthetic goals or standards. In specific content these standards were not in fact greatly different from those of the Judaeo-Christian tradition. There was no doubt a strong touch of Hellenism in the eighteenth, as in the sixteenth, century. The Enlightenment was this-worldly enough, and by no means ascetic. Its characteristic ethics (Helvétius again, or Jeremy Bentham, will do as samples) was hedonist and instrumentalist. Yet only among a few circles of court and nobility was the eighteenth century a time of moral looseness, cynicism, and corruption; and even in such circles, there often cropped up what we should call the strain of social consciousness. The enlightened despot (Joseph II of Austria), the enlightened nobleman (Lafayette), were hardly self-indulgent sensualists. There was, in fact, a touch of puritanism in the enlightened, as in almost all who really hope to make men over completely.

Some writers, especially in the second half of the century, were "primitivists." They held that there had once been on earth a state of Nature in which men lived free from evil. Some placed this state of Nature in a distant, semiclassical past, the Golden Age of Hellenistic tradition. Others found this state of nature in their own time, though far from Europe, in the South Seas, among those wise Chinese who believed in decency, not in a theistic God, and among those noble savages, the Red Indians of America. But for the most part, eighteenth-century writers seem to have had at most no more than a half belief in the historical reality of an idyllic state of nature; even Rousseau seemed aware that the state of nature is what we would now call a myth, a useful form of what we would now call propaganda for a new order. So too was that very popular political concept, the "social contract"; this device brought "natural" ethics into practical politics as the natural rights of man.

Progress. The third cluster of ideas is summed up in the word "Progress." Americans especially are so accustomed to accepting the notion of Progress as something self-evident that they find it hard to realize how new this doctrine really is. The central doctrine of development in the Judaeo-Christian tradition is that of a lapse from an original perfect state, that of the Garden of Eden; and in so representative a Christian view of world history as Augustine's *City of God*, a better state, though seen to be ahead as well as behind, is not one attained by the steady improvement of man's lot on this earth in the *civitas terrena*, but by a promise of a Second Coming of Christ. The Hellenistic tradition favored a variety of cyclical theories, with a Golden Age degenerating to a Silver Age and thence to an Iron Age before the process started all over again. The humanists of the Renaissance, as well as the leaders of the Protestant Reformation were trying to recapture a past they both believed much superior to their present.

The clearest beginnings of a belief that the present is better than the past came in the late seventeenth century in what in France was called the "quarrel of the ancients and the moderns" and in England the "battle of the books." The issue was a literary one: can a writer in the late seventeenth century achieve work equal to, perhaps better than, that of the great writers of Greece and Rome? At the moment the battle was no more than a draw, but in the early eighteenth century the moderns began to win out in public opinion. The French reformer and *philosophe* Turgot, in a speech at the Sorbonne "On the Successive Advances of the Human Mind" ("Discours sur les progrès successifs de l'esprit humain," 1750), outlined a complete doctrine of progress, which at the hands of his friend and disciple Condorcet in the above-mentioned *Sketch for a Historical Picture of the Human Mind* becomes an extraordinarily optimistic utopia of indefinite progress toward what has been called a doctrine of "natural salvation"—the attainment by everyone of immortality in this flesh on this earth.

The average man, even though enlightened, could hardly fly as high as did Condorcet. Moreover, the eighteenth century lacked what Darwin in the nineteenth century was to provide, a systematic theoretical explanation of the biological workings of an evolutionary process from "lower" to "higher," interpreted as Progress. The enlightened man tended toward a simple view that the agent of progress is the increasingly effective application of Reason to the control of the physical and cultural environment. Education became one of the major ways in which Reason was to do its work of reform. From Locke to Rousseau and Pestalozzi, the Enlightenment produced a series of very important writings on educational theory, and saw the beginnings of serious experimentation in the field.

This is hardly the place to attack the knotty problem of the relation between the key ideas of the Enlightenment and the complex currents of the full historical record of the period. There is clearly no single one-way "cause" involved, but many, among them the example of natural science, clearly cumulative and "progressive"; the beginnings of the extraordinary technological advances of our Western civilization; a very considerable and widespread economic growth—of course not evenly distributed as to class and geographical location, but still much greater, in France above all, than historians once believed; and reinforcing all, a "climate of opinion" favorable to enterprise. These factors, and many others which are by no means well understood, helped make the Enlightenment the take off point of modern Western civilization, so unique in its concrete material achievements.

MODIFICATIONS OF THE MODEL

This model—an optimistic, this-worldly belief in the power of human beings, brought up rationally from infancy on as nature meant them to be, to achieve steady and unlimited progress toward material comfort and spiritual happiness for all men on this earth—must be qualified and amended in many ways.

Christian survivals. First, in this extreme form Enlightenment is a repudiation, and in some respects an antithesis, of much of Christian belief. Enlightened denial of any kind of transcendence of the external world, of personal immortality, of the whole fabric of Christian sacraments, and enlightened rejection of the dogma of original sin, as well as much more in the Enlightenment, is quite incompatible with orthodox Christianity, Catholic and Protestant alike. In fact, most of our own contemporary world views which reject Christianity for some form of secularist faith—positivism, materialism (notably Marxism), rationalism, humanism, "ethical culture," and the rest—have their origin in the Enlightenment. Even in the eighteenth century, however, there was a wide spectrum of belief—from conventional Christianity hardly touched by the new ideas, through all sorts of compromises, to deism and unitarianism, which are only marginally theological beliefs. Probably our model of Enlightenment should include some form of belief in god, and almost certainly the fashionable deism of a Voltaire, a Thomas Paine, or even a Rousseau. This deist god was himself (or should one say, itself?) a highly rationalistic construct—the "clockmaker god" who had to exist in order to start this "Newtonian world machine" running, and guarantee that it would not run down, but who never interfered with it, and certainly never performed miracles. Voltaire was very proud of his aphorism, "If God did not exist, it would be necessary to invent him," hardly a Christian sentiment. Rousseau, in the episode of the Savoyard vicar in his treatise on education, *Émile* (1762), managed to instill some emotion into his deism, which was obviously the forerunner of Robespierre's worship of the Supreme Being of 1794.

There were outright atheists and materialists, especially in France in the second half of the century, whose doctrines were represented by Holbach's *Système de la nature* (1770) and La Mettrie's *L'Homme machine* (1748). Diderot himself seems to have been converted to atheism, but to a rather subtle and very modern existentialist atheism. Most of the *philosophes* who went as far as atheism, however, were convinced that such a belief (for it was a positive materialist belief, not a disbelief) was too strong medicine for the many, and that order and decency demanded Christian "superstition" for the present, at least to keep the lower orders down where they belonged. Atheistic doctrines were not put forward in the Holbach *salon* when the servants were about. Complete theological and metaphysical skepticism is rare indeed in the Enlightenment, which was at bottom an age of faith. Hume is the best example of a skeptic, but even Hume as a steady Scot betrayed some faith in common sense—his own, at least.

Christians were not at all passive when confronted with the challenge of the Enlightenment. The eighteenth century, in fact, saw the rise of the last of the great Protestant movements—Methodism in Britain and Colonial America, and the allied Pietism in Germany. These movements were by no means in conformity with our model. They were distrustful of reason, as understood by the *philosophes,* warmly evangelical, politically and socially conservative, reached down into the working classes, which were hardly touched by the Enlightenment, and are credited by such historians as William Lecky and Elie Halévy with having helped to preserve Britain from the contagion of the French Revolution. Even in France, the eighteenth century witnessed the rise of the quietism of Fénelon and Mme. Guyon and the persistence of Jansenism, a form of Catholic puritanism which was certainly not optimistic. A Jansenist episode in Paris throws light on the urban, sophisticated *esprit* characteristic of the Enlightenment. Crowds flocking to the grave of a Jansenist priest credited with miraculous healing powers actually ate dirt from the grave, and threatened to get out of hand. When the cemetery was barred off by the authorities, a sign appeared inscribed:

De par le roi défense à Dieu
De faire miracle en ce lieu

(By order of the king, God is forbidden to make miracles in this place.)

Historical pessimism. A second qualification must be made to the optimistic belief in Progress as being part of our model. It does not take much research to discover, even in the work of so great a culture hero of the Enlightenment as Voltaire, much backing and filling on the subject. Voltaire was convinced that his own time represented a decline from the Age of Louis XIV. One of his most famous works, *Candide* (1759) is a bitter attack on the "idealistic" doctrine of the philosopher Leibniz that all is for the best in the best of all possible worlds. There is a dark as well as a cynical side to the eighteenth century, as in Choderlos de Laclos' *Les Liaisons dangereuses* (1782); after all, de Sade, from whom "sadism" derives, was a child of the Enlightenment. The strain of pessimism, sometimes pushed to the edge of madness, runs through some of the greatest of British writers, from Swift to Samuel Johnson and William Cowper. The Italian, Vico, in this century of the rise of belief in unilinear Progress, produced in his *Scienza Nuova* (1725) a classic of the cyclical theory of history. In America, there was the uncomfortably Christian Jonathan Edwards, born in 1703, to balance the comfortably enlightened Benjamin Franklin, born in 1706.

Reform: from above or below? A third qualification must be made even about those who on the whole conform, in principle, to our model of the Enlightenment. On the great question (at bottom a political one) of how and how fast Reason was to get to work amending the present evil environment and paving the way for Nature's good environment, the enlightened by no means presented a united front. At one extreme (a well-populated one) there were the believers in enlightened despotism. Though some may have hoped that in the very long run the masses could perhaps become fully enlightened, these men were convinced that for the foreseeable future, ignorance and superstition had so far corrupted ordinary men and women that the only hope was to reform their whole environment from above, by the fiat of enlightened rulers coached by enlightened *philosophes.* There must be no nonsense about democracy, universal suffrage, reform from below, or reform by consent. Indeed, once the French Revolution had alarmed them enough, some of the once-hopeful reformers became convinced that the many were in fact on the side of the wicked old régime. Had not a Birmingham mob burned the house of Joseph Priestley, scientist, preacher, advanced thinker in all fields? Voltaire seems best classified as a believer in enlightened despotism, for he had the brilliant witty intellectual's contempt for the slow-witted, conformist "many." At their most kindly, such intellectuals thought of the many as sheep who would long need shepherds—good shepherds like themselves and their heroes Frederick the Great, Catherine the Great,

Joseph II, not bad shepherds like the run of the nobility and all those wicked schemers, the clergy.

At the other extreme were those who held that the common man, misled though he had long been, needed only to have the burdens which church and state had laid upon him lifted, in order to enter into his natural inheritance.

The extreme of the extreme is philosophical anarchism, the doctrine that men who obey their natural inner light need no authority over them. In spite of the belief that the state of nature had been a pleasantly free society, anarchism was by no means a common eighteenth-century doctrine. Toward the end of the century, however, anarchism was classically stated in William Godwin's *Political Justice* (1793).

For the most part, those of the enlightened who leaned toward a democratic or libertarian doctrine qualified it in various ways. Jeremy Bentham, who began in the hope that he could convert the English ruling classes to the idea of carrying out from above the reforms dictated by utilitarian ideas, was convinced by the 1790s that they would not do so, and turned to the job of getting the masses, or at least the middle classes, to achieve reform by democratic means. By the 1830s he and his disciples, the "philosophical radicals," had achieved a great deal, not as democratic leaders, actually, but rather as cultural engineers making their ideas acceptable to a limited but important public. Jefferson had still another political stance. He trusted the common man, but only the independent yeoman and small-town man, not the hopelessly corrupted man of the urban masses. Indeed, by and large the thinkers of the Enlightenment were at the least ambivalent toward democracy. From Rousseau's *Social Contract* (1762) some commentators have drawn support for libertarian theories of political action, and others have drawn support for authoritarian, even totalitarian, theories. Rousseau's famous phrase, "It may be necessary to compel a man to be free," is certainly hard for the libertarian to swallow or explain away, even in what may well be the purely "idealistic" context Rousseau meant for it. The analogy is obvious: as the dogmatic Christian feels that men are not really free when they are sinning, so the dogmatic enlightened feels that they are not really free when they are behaving contrary to the clear dictates of Reason.

In terms of political institutions, however, there can be no doubt that the foundations of modern Western democracy were strengthened by the Enlightenment. Notably, what Gaetano Mosca has called the doctrine of "juridical defense" (i.e. the principle that one set of agents of the government, usually the judiciary, can prohibit certain measures of other agents of the government, usually the administrators) emerged strengthened by eighteenth-century political theory, the doctrines of social contract and natural rights, and the specific bills of rights. In enlightened thought, there is indeed a strain of distrust of the government (at least of "big" government, and certainly of government as directed by the ruling classes of the old régime) and trust in the individual, well illustrated in Jefferson the theorist and speech-maker, though not in Jefferson the president. But in the Enlightenment there is hardly the kind of furious hatred for the state as such (that is, the government) that is found in Herbert Spencer's *The Man vs. the State* (1884). The second part of Thomas Paine's *Rights of Man* (1792), for instance, advocates a great deal of government action toward what we now call the welfare state.

Variations in time and place. A fourth qualification must take into account variations both in time and in place. The founders of the Age of Reason, philosophers (not *philosophes*) like Descartes, Spinoza, Leibniz, and Locke, were middle-of-the-roaders when they touched on practical affairs. It has been said that for Locke even God was a Whig. The thinkers of the early eighteenth century—the English Augustans, the French before the mid-century *Grande Encyclopédie* (Montesquieu, for example)—were moderates who carried neither their rationalism nor their opposition to the existing social and political order to radical extremes. The second half of the eighteenth century was different. Even in England the Benthams and the Priestleys were root-and-branch reformers. In France the second generation of *philosophes*, the men who made the *Grande Encyclopédie*, were as committed a set of intellectuals as ever lived—committed, in theory at least, to a thoroughgoing reform of the human environment, which of course is not at all to say that they planned the Revolution of 1789, let alone the Reign of Terror.

Even more important were the national variations. The Enlightenment was indeed cosmopolitan, and even as seen in our model, men from all over the West, save perhaps the Balkans, made some contribution to it. Yet this was a cosmopolitanism with a strong French stamp, so much so that resistance to many currents of thought in the Enlightenment took on an anti-French note, especially in Germany, and wholesale acceptance of the Enlightenment came close almost everywhere to being an imitation of all things French. In France itself, there is a striking difference between the strong Anglophilia of the first generation of *philosophes*, such as Montesquieu and the young Voltaire, and the near Anglophobia of the second generation of bright young radicals, such as Rousseau, Holbach, and many lesser figures, for whom England was just too full of medieval irrationalities.

Yet England and her American colonies (after 1776, the United States) were classic lands of the Enlightenment. The English, with Bacon, Locke, Newton, and the early deists like Toland and Tindal, have some claim to being the originators, the adventurers in ideas which the French did no more than develop and spread. Even in the second half of the eighteenth century, the English, with Bentham, Godwin, many minor reformers and "Jacobins," were active on the radical front; and in the United States, with Thomas Paine, Jefferson, on down to such minor anti-Christians as Ethan Allen (who wrote, or at least had ghostwritten for him, a work entitled *Reason the Only Oracle of Man*, 1784) we find our model of Enlightenment often fairly close to reality.

What most distinguished the English-speaking lands from France was the much stronger, and much more intellectually respectable, opposition to orthodox Enlightenment. Beyond a few crotchety defenders of the *noblesse* in France, there were hardly any striking conservative thinkers. England had a distinguished line of them, not mere conformists or mere opponents of any kind of change, but conservatives who did not accept the Enlightenment view of human rationality.

From Dean Swift and Samuel Johnson, to Hume, who, on questions of religion and philosophy was of course very much a man of the Enlightenment, British conservatives held their own in a way French conservatives did not. Edmund Burke, who became a major source for conservative political thought in Britain and the United States, bitterly opposed the orthodox enlightened view of the actual or potential rationality of mankind; yet the Burke who defended the American colonists, the Burke who would "reform in order to conserve" must not be listed as opposing root and branch (as did some later romanticists) the belief that human reason properly controlled can improve political institutions and the human lot.

Indeed, even though they were sympathetic with much of the program of the Enlightenment, the English moderates continued to refuse to follow Reason to the bitter, or merely Utopian, end. Adam Smith, founder of classical economics is a case in point. Compared with the French physiocrat, François Quesnay, Smith was a moderate indeed. *Laissez-faire, laissez-passer* may have become, even for the English in the nineteenth century, a dogma, an absolute, an abstraction. For Smith himself it was no more than a working principle subject to all sorts of modifications in practice. In the United States, the Jeffersonians never had it wholly their own way. John Adams, though not untouched in his youth by the advanced ideas of the Enlightenment, ended up as a picturesque, opinionated, ambivalent conservative, convinced that nothing very much could be done to make—or persuade—men to behave as the *philosophes* planned for them to behave.

Germany is the other important country in which very significant differences from the French model of Enlightenment appeared from the very start. Some of these differences are clearly of the sort to be treated immediately under our next qualification, one that centered on the romantic or pre-romantic attack on the Enlightenment—an attack that goes back certainly to the Rousseau of the 1750s. Some of the German uniqueness no doubt must be assigned to the vague but very real thing, the "national character," and some of it to so simple a nationalist feeling as patriotic German dislike of Frenchness; at the very least, it stemmed from the German desire to be different from the French. There were in the Germanies, however, authentic enlightened on the French model. Indeed, Frederick the Great of Prussia, as an intellectual, though not as a man of action, was a French *philosophe* indeed. C. F. Nicolai, a minor figure, was a fairly typical eighteenth-century rationalist. Once the French Revolution had given the signal, good Jacobins of the Enlightenment appeared as an active, even conspiratorial, minority from the Rhineland to Hungary. The Hungarian, Ignacs von Martinovics, condemned to death in 1794 for conspiring to make a revolution in Budapest, was an unfrocked monk, a violent anticlerical, a scientist and mathematician of dubious professional capacity, extraordinarily reminiscent of Marat.

Kant himself, who wrote an excellent little pamphlet in 1784 entitled "What Is Enlightenment?" (*Was ist Aufklärung?*), thought of himself as thoroughly in the mainstream of eighteenth-century thought and would, one suspects, have been astonished and displeased at what some of his nineteenth-century disciples, from Fichte to Hegel, made of him. In brief, much of the great age of German culture—including much of Lessing, Goethe, and even Herder—is stamped firmly as part of the Age of Prose and Reason.

Romanticism. But a good deal escapes this stamp, and sounds like what is usually called "romanticism." One of the hardest problems faced by the historian of culture is to disentangle from the work of writers and artists of the second half of the eighteenth century strands or clusters of ideas that must take some such label as "classic" or "enlightened" or "rationalist," from those that must take labels like "romantic," "sentimental," "transcendentalist." The generation that matured about 1800 felt for the Enlightened a contempt as deep as any on record. The Wordsworth who called Voltaire's *Candide* "that dull product of a scoffer's pen" summed it up in a well-known stanza from "The Tables Turned":

Enough of science and of art:
  Close up these barren leaves;
Come forth, and bring with you a heart
  That watches and receives.

Literary critics have long debated the now somewhat worn problem of the differences between the classical and the romantic outlook. For our purposes, it is perhaps sufficient to note that the romantics give a different content to the clusters of ideas—Reason, Nature, and Progress—of our model of Enlightenment. What was reason to the *philosophe* was, to the Germans and to their English disciple Coleridge, merely "understanding" (*Verstand*), the kind of thinking a bookkeeper does; the higher, better Reason (*Vernunft*) had a component of intuition, depth, transcendence, the kind of thinking a real philosopher does. Nature, to the eighteenth century, was calm, uniform (if really understood), the Golden Mean revealed, while to the romanticist it was wild, varied, unruly, and favored the unique, the individual. Progress was to the eighteenth century basically a physical, almost mechanical, process; to the romantic, who also usually believed in progress, it was a growth, an organic unfolding. The words of reproach are always important in these matters. For the romantic, his predecessors were guilty of holding a world view that was mechanistic, nominalist, atomistic, unfeeling, therefore unrealistic and inhuman.

Much of what we have above labeled romantic, of course, is to be found in Rousseau, in Vico, and in most of the great Germans—Lessing, Herder, Schiller, Goethe—all flourishing well before 1800. The strands are indeed mingled in all of them. If there is a chemically pure romanticism, it can hardly be found in men like these, all touched by the "climate of opinion" of the Enlightenment. And for the historian these two strands have one major element in common. Both worked as dissolvents of the complex of institutions, traditions, and ideas prevailing in the Europe of the old régime. Reason and Nature, however interpreted, found the existing order unreasonable and unnatural. Head and heart both condemned things-as-they-are.

Variation among the major figures. Finally, the obvious must be noted. If our model fits at all, it fits the minor thinkers, as well as the great audience of the enlightened, and not the major figures. Voltaire, Diderot, Rousseau, Montesquieu, Burke, Adam Smith, are by no means "terrible simplifiers." Each has a full awareness of the truth of the Baconian maxim, "The subtlety of nature is greater many times over than the subtlety of the senses and understanding." Of the major figures, Jeremy Bentham perhaps comes closest to fitting our model; but although Bentham carefully excluded anything mysterious, transcendental, or even just fuzzy from his mind, he was fully aware of the complexities and variety of the external world. The terrible simplifiers of the Enlightenment were the second-rate men—the Helvétiuses, the Holbachs, the Godwins, and, worst of all, the Robespierres.

Modern scholarship, in the hands of men like Ernst Cassirer, C. L. Becker, Paul Hazard, A. O. Lovejoy, Aram Vartanian, and a host of others, has indeed corrected, enriched, made closer to reality, the oversimple and in many ways hostile view of the eighteenth-century Enlightenment we have inherited from its nineteenth-century critics. We know the Enlightenment was not addicted to "pure" abstract and unrealistic thinking, nor to a rigorously static and mechanistic view of the universe, nor to a simple environmentalism based on belief in the natural goodness and/or reasonableness of man; we know that it was not lacking in depth and strength of thought and feeling. Yet we must not refine the Enlightenment into shreds. It did, after all, bring together from many sources and into sharp focus a new world view, itself much influenced by all of Western history, but still in important ways new—and in important ways still very much alive today. Poor Condorcet's "tenth epoch," his rationalist utopia, still looks very far away indeed, nearly two hundred years after he wrote about it. We have amended in many ways the optimistic, rationalistic, positivistic faith of the Enlightenment. We have preserved important elements of the Judaeo-Christian tradition that the Jacobins thought (as did Condorcet) were about to disappear forever. Nonetheless, Westerners, and especially Americans, are still spiritual children of the Enlightenment. Did not Adlai Stevenson, in the midst of an electoral campaign, in which the audience has to be told what it already believes, state that "Progress is what happens when inevitability yields to necessity. And it is an article of the democratic faith that progress is a basic law of life."? Surely this could never have been said so plainly at any time before 1700.

(See also CLANDESTINE PHILOSOPHICAL LITERATURE IN FRANCE; DEISM; and ENCYCLOPÉDIE. See Enlightenment in Index for articles on individuals who played a part in the Enlightenment.)

Bibliography

GENERAL BACKGROUND

Crane Brinton, ed., *The Age of Reason Reader* (New York, 1956), also in paperback, is an anthology with introductory survey and bibliographical suggestions. See also Preserved Smith, *A History of Modern Culture,* 2 vols. (New York, 1930 and 1934), a very complete, detailed survey, also available in paperback (New York, 1962). F. E. Manuel, *The Age of Reason* (Ithaca, N.Y., 1951) is an excellent brief survey.

NINETEENTH-CENTURY STUDIES

The following books will give a good cross section of nineteenth-century interpretations of the Enlightenment: H. A. Taine, *Origins of Contemporary France,* Vols. 1 and 2, *The Ancient Regime,* especially the section entitled "The Spirit and the Doctrine," English translation by John Durand (New York, 1876); John Morley, *Voltaire* (London, 1871), *Rousseau,* 2 vols. (London, 1873), *Diderot and the Encyclopaedists,* 2 vols. (London, 1878), all three books later reprinted; Leslie Stephen, *English Thought in the Eighteenth Century,* 2 vols. (London, 1876), later edition, paperback, 2 vols. (New York, 1962); Irving Babbitt, *Rousseau and Romanticism* (Boston, 1919), also paperback.

CONTEMPORARY STUDIES

Modern writers have considerably revised this nineteenth-century view. For a variety of critical estimates see Ernst Cassirer, *The Philosophy of the Enlightenment,* 2d ed., English translation by F. C. A. Koelln and J. P. Pettegrove (Boston, 1955); C. L. Becker, *The Heavenly City of the Eighteenth-Century Philosophers* (New Haven, 1932); R. O. Rockwood, ed., *Carl Becker's Heavenly City Revisited* (Ithaca, 1958); Paul Hazard, *The European Mind, 1680–1715* and *European Thought in the Eighteenth Century,* English translations by J. L. May (New Haven, 1953 and 1954); A. O. Lovejoy, *Essays in the History of Ideas* (Baltimore, 1952); J. B. Bury, *The Idea of Progress* (London, 1920); F. J. Teggart, ed., *The Idea of Progress* (Berkeley, 1925); F. C. Green, *Rousseau and the Idea of Progress* (New York, 1950); F. V. Sampson, *Progress in the Age of Reason* (Cambridge, Mass., 1956); L. I. Bredvold, *Brave New World of the Enlightenment* (Ann Arbor, 1961); H. N. Fairchild, *The Noble Savage* (New York, 1928); C. B. Tinker, *Nature's Simple Plan* (Princeton, 1922); Henry Vyverberg, *Historical Pessimism in the French Enlightenment* (Cambridge, Mass., 1958); Kingsley Martin, *The Rise of French Liberal Thought,* revised ed. (New York, 1954); F. E. Manuel, *The Eighteenth Century Confronts the Gods* and *The Prophets of Paris* (Cambridge, Mass., 1959 and 1962); A. Vartanian, *Diderot and Descartes* (Princeton, 1953); A. M. Wilson, *Diderot: The Testing Years, 1713–1759* (New York, 1957); Lester G. Crocker, *Age of Crisis: Man and World in French Eighteenth-Century Thought* (Baltimore, 1959); Ernst Cassirer, *Rousseau, Kant, Goethe* (Princeton, 1947); Elie Halévy, *Growth of Philosophic Radicalism* (Boston, 1945), also in paperback; John Plamenatz, *The English Utilitarians* (Oxford, 1958); G. P. Gooch, *English Democratic Ideas in the Seventeenth Century,* 2d ed. (Cambridge, 1919), also in paperback; Max Savelle, *Seeds of Liberty: The Genesis of the American Mind* (New York, 1948).

CRANE BRINTON

ENRIQUES, FEDERIGO (1871–1946), Italian mathematician and philosopher, graduated from the University of Pisa in 1891 and taught geometry at the universities of Bologna and Rome. In 1907, with the psychologist Eugenio Rignano, he founded the journal *Scientia.* Enriques belongs with Guido Castelnuovo and Francesco Severi in the Italian geometrical school, which dealt especially with algebraic geometry. He contributed to the European movement of "critique of science within science" that culminated in Einstein's theory of relativity. He did his main philosophical work before World War I; later he dealt mainly with the history of science.

As Giovanni Vailati stated, Enriques' lasting contribution to the philosophy of science was his clarification of the implicit conditions and restrictions upon the meaning and value of some basic notions of mathematics. Still valuable are his dialectical probing of the antitheses absolute–relative, knowable–unknowable, substance–appearance, objective–subjective; his analyses of the paradoxes of infinity and of time and its measurement, his comparison between insoluble problems in geometry and physics (such as the squaring of the circle and absolute motion) and insoluble problems in the theory of knowledge (*Problemi della scienza*, Bologna, 1906); and his criticism of the Ontological Argument and arguments derived from it (*Scienza e razionalismo*, Bologna, 1912).

Enriques rejected Peano's reduction of mathematics to logic and the formalistic approach to mathematics on the ground that they "neglected the psychological and realistic side to problems." He considered geometry as a branch of physics and topology as prior to projective and metric geometry. He had a taste for the critique of fundamentals as reduced to a few simple and deep-seated ideas rather than for analytical and technical developments; a purely methodological approach was not sufficient for him. Enriques wanted philosophy of science to be a part of a more comprehensive philosophy, but in constructing such a philosophy he wavered between divergent positions. Thus, he defended the role of hypotheses and models against the positivistic passivity toward facts and also criticized conventionalism and pragmatism in the name of the cognitive, "realistic" value of science. He halfheartedly accepted the Kantian approach of the legislating activity of thought and at the same time stated that in the phenomenal world, independent of whatever we do to it, there are invariants that make possible the logical principles of identity and noncontradiction.

Enriques waged a long war against Croce's and Gentile's restoration of idealism, insofar as it was restored at the expense of scientific culture and to counteract the escapism underlying the doctrines of Henri Bergson, Émile Boutroux, and Édouard Le Roy. No one in Italy did as much as Enriques to avoid that estrangement of science and philosophy that is still a drawback of Italian, and indeed, of Continental thought.

Works by Enriques

Problemi della scienza was translated into English by K. Royce, with a preface by Josiah Royce (Chicago, 1914). A complete list of Enriques' writings is appended to *Natura, ragione e storia*, an anthology of his essays edited by Lucio Lombardo-Radice (Turin, 1958).

Works on Enriques

On Enriques and recent Italian philosophy of science, see Lombardo-Radice's introduction to *Natura, ragione e storia*. See also Antonio Santucci, *Il pragmatismo in Italia* (Bologna, 1963), pp. 304–321; Ferruccio Rossi-Landi and Vittorio Somenzi, "La filosofia della scienza in Italia," in *La filosofia contemporanea in Italia* (Rome, 1958).

FERRUCCIO ROSSI-LANDI

ENTROPY. The concept of entropy is a mathematical measure of the disorganization of a system. The idea first arose as a part of the theory of heat, but a similar notion can be associated with probability distributions of any kind.

Entropy in thermodynamics. By the middle of the nineteenth century it was clear that two distinct principles were involved in the theory of heat. On the one hand, in any closed system—any system theoretically isolated from the rest of the universe—the total quantity of energy is constant. In other words, the quantity of heat that disappears in such a system is equivalent to the amount of other kinds of energy that appears, and vice versa. This law of conservation of energy (First Law of Thermodynamics) therefore asserts the invariance of the total *quantity* of energy in a system that is not interacting with its surroundings. On the other hand, the Second Law of Thermodynamics concerns the *quality* of this energy, that is, the amount of energy available in the system for doing useful work. It determines the direction in which thermodynamic processes occur and expresses the fact that, although energy can never be lost, it may become unavailable for doing mechanical work. This law, as formulated by Rudolf Clausius and William Thomson (later Lord Kelvin), was a refinement and generalization of the hypothesis that heat cannot, of itself, pass from a colder to a hotter body. Whereas we can get work out of the heat of a body which is hotter than surrounding bodies, we cannot get work out of a body which is colder than surrounding bodies. The less energy available for physical work, the higher the entropy of the system.

In 1854 Clausius restated the Second Law in terms of the concept of entropy. He derived this word from the Greek ἡ τροπὴ, "a transformation," and by it he meant what he called the transformation content of a body or a system. He defined it differentially: increase of entropy is equal to heat received divided by the temperature at which the heat is received, provided that the heat is insufficient to produce any appreciable change of temperature, which is measured on the absolute scale introduced by Kelvin. (Strictly speaking, no irreversible changes should occur in the body or system when this small quantity of heat flows into it.) The Second Law of Thermodynamics can then be stated: "The entropy of an isolated system never diminishes." Every reversible change occurring in a closed system will leave its total entropy unaltered, for the gain of entropy in one part of the system will be balanced by its loss in the other part. But every irreversible change in the system will increase its entropy. Irreversible changes occur when heat passes of its own accord from one part of a system to another that is at a lower temperature. In general, any spontaneous change in the physical or chemical state of a system will lead to an increase of its entropy. No spontaneous change will occur when the entropy is at maximum (that is, when no increase of entropy can occur without changing the conditions of the system), and the system will then be in a state of stable thermodynamic equilibrium.

Statistical theory of entropy. In thermodynamics, regarded as a subject *sui generis*, the statement that the entropy of an isolated system never diminishes spontaneously is a universal law justified by appeal to observation and experiment. But, because the thermodynamic concept of entropy does not represent anything which can be readily apprehended by the senses or grasped intuitively, theoretical physicists in the second half of the nineteenth century sought to explain it in terms of mechanical concepts. Since thermodynamic concepts such as heat, temperature, and entropy do not occur in mechanics, they have to be reinterpreted in mechanical terms. This was effected by appealing to the microscopic structure of matter. Consider, for example, the pressure exerted by a gas on the walls of the vessel that contains it. This pressure is produced by the cumulative force exerted by large numbers of molecules striking the walls and bouncing off again. The number of molecules involved is usually so enormous, however, that it would be hopeless to attempt to deal with them individually. Also, as they strike the walls, the mechanical force which they exert fluctuates erratically from point to point and from instant to instant. To overcome these difficulties in analyzing the behavior of gases, a new concept was needed as a link between mechanics and thermodynamics. It was provided by considering large numbers of molecules statistically.

The probability distribution of the velocities of molecules in a gas was obtained by James Clerk Maxwell in 1860. Some years later it was shown by Ludwig Boltzmann that a function can be derived from this probability distribution that has similar properties to entropy and can be regarded as its statistical analogue. Corresponding to a given macroscopic state of a gas—that is, a state defined by quantities which we are able to measure in the laboratory—there are a large number of so-called microscopic states, these being states in which each molecule has a specified velocity and position (and quantum state). The number of microscopic states that correspond to a given macroscopic state determines the probability of the latter. Boltzmann found that the entropy of a system in a given macroscopic state is proportional to the logarithm of the probability of that state. (The reason for the logarithmic function in this relation is that entropies are additive, whereas probabilities are multiplicative.) The Second Law of Thermodynamics was interpreted by Boltzmann as signifying that any closed system tends toward an equilibrium state of maximum probability, which is associated with equalization of temperature, pressure, and so forth. Since the probabilities of occurrence of ordered arrangements of molecules (for example, where the molecules in one part of the container are at one temperature and those in the other part are at another) are far less than those of random or disordered arrangements (where no sorting occurs), the law signifies that ordered arrangements tend to degenerate into disordered ones.

This explains why that part of the energy of a material system which is available for doing useful work should tend to diminish, since this energy is orderly energy, whereas heat, being associated with the random motion of large numbers of molecules, is disorderly energy. The energy of a system thus tends to become less and less available for mechanical work as more and more of it is converted into heat and the disorderliness of the molecules increases.

Boltzmann's interpretation meant, however, that the principle of the increase of entropy, now regarded as a measure of the disorder of a thermodynamic system, ceased to be an invariable law of nature and became a statistical one. From this point of view, the reverse process of a thermodynamical trend to a state of greater entropy (prohibited by the Second Law of Thermodynamics) was no longer impossible but only extremely improbable. Consequently, part of the water in a kettle on the fire could freeze while the rest boiled, although it is most unlikely that this would happen. Whether one takes this possibility seriously depends on whether one regards statistical mechanics as logically anterior to thermodynamics. Modern quantum theory, however, has led most physicists to regard probability as an irreducible feature of physical reality.

Paradoxes concerning entropy. Despite the power and cogency of Boltzmann's theory it was soon criticized as logically unsound. Thus, in 1876 Josef Loschmidt argued that the symmetry of the laws of dynamics with respect to past and future should imply a corresponding reversibility of molecular processes, contradicting the law of increasing entropy. In the course of time, separation processes should occur as frequently as mixing processes and the entropy of a system should tend to decrease as often as it tends to increase. Another objection was formulated some twenty years later by E. Zermelo, who appealed to a theorem in dynamics due to Poincaré which asserts that, under certain conditions concerning the finite nature of a system's motion, the initial state of the system will recur infinitely often. Zermelo claimed that molecular processes must therefore be cyclical, again in contradiction with the Second Law of Thermodynamics.

These difficulties were largely resolved by Paul and Tatiana Ehrenfest in 1907. They pointed out that Boltzmann's statistical proof of the Second Law of Thermodynamics concerned only the *average* variation of the entropy of an isolated system and did not preclude the possibility of decreases and increases in its value occurring with equal frequency. Nevertheless, a succession of decreases and increases is not incompatible with there being a high probability for an increase to occur following a given "initial" state of low entropy, provided that this initial state is at the trough of a fluctuation from thermodynamic equilibrium. The long-term behavior of a closed system is therefore characterized by a succession of fluctuations in the value of its entropy, with an almost certain return upward from any low value that it attains. Consequently, the apparent irreversibility in the entropic behavior of a closed system manifests itself as an overwhelming tendency for the system, starting from any nonequilibrium state, to move toward thermodynamic equilibrium.

Entropy and the universe. Clausius believed that his law of increasing entropy was not only a universal law but was also a law of the universe as a whole. He concluded that the universe is tending toward a state of "thermal death" in which the temperature, and all other physical factors, will be everywhere the same and all natural processes will cease. For many years this conclusion was widely accepted.

Doubt was thrown on it, however, by E. A. Milne, who in 1931 drew attention to a logical difficulty in applying the concept of entropy to the universe as a whole. He argued that in establishing the Second Law of Thermodynamics the following axiom is required: "Whenever a process occurs in the universe, it is possible to divide the universe into two portions such that one of the portions is entirely unaffected by the process." This axiom automatically excludes world-wide processes and means that we have no way of assessing change of entropy for the whole universe. Although we can calculate changes of entropy for isolated, or closed, systems with something outside them, the universe *ex hypothesi* has nothing physical outside it.

Although Boltzmann believed that at any time the most probable state of the universe was one of thermal equilibrium, he did not accept the idea of the complete thermal death of the universe, on the grounds that Clausius had overlooked the statistical nature of entropy. He advanced the hypothesis that there will always occur relatively small regions—which he suggested might be of the size of our galaxy—where significant fluctuations from equilibrium will arise spontaneously. Nevertheless, although the occurrence of a fluctuation would appear to be required for the development of biological organisms and hence for the existence of the observer, it need occur only on the scale of the solar system and would indeed be more probable on such a scale than on that of a galaxy. In fact, however, the entire universe of galaxies to the limits of present observation shows no indication whatsoever of thermodynamic equilibrium. The idea that the whole observable universe, and not merely our galaxy, should therefore be regarded as a gigantic fluctuation in a system which is normally in a state of equilibrium is difficult to accept. Rather, it would seem that not only is it difficult to formulate the concept of entropy for the whole universe but also that there is no evidence that the law of entropy increase applies on this scale. The systematic correlation of recessional motion with distance in the generally accepted interpretation of the red shifts in the spectra of the extragalactic nebulae is evidence to the contrary.

The various doubts that have arisen concerning the concept of world entropy have serious repercussions on any attempt to derive the irreversibility of time from the Second Law of Thermodynamics. Boltzmann himself believed that there are regions of the universe in which the direction of time, as given by the change of entropy, runs in the opposite sense to ours. He thought that in the universe as a whole the two directions of time are indistinguishable, just as in space there is nothing corresponding to our terrestrial distinction between up and down. Recent advances in cosmology have produced no evidence to support this hypothesis.

Entropy and information. The concept of entropy originated in phenomenological thermodynamics and the increase of entropy with time was at first regarded as an invariable law. The second stage in the history of the concept was concerned with its statistical reformulation. In the third and current stage, entropy has come to be associated with the modern quantitative concept of information and is no longer confined to physics.

The origins of these latest developments can be traced to Maxwell's introduction of the "sorting demon" in 1871. Maxwell considered what would happen if, in a vessel filled with gas and divided into two parts, *A* and *B*, by a division with a small hole in it, there were a being who saw the individual molecules and could open and close the hole so as to allow only the swifter molecules to pass from *A* to *B* and only the slower ones from *B* to *A*. In this way, without expenditure of work, the temperature of *B* would be raised and that of *A* lowered, contradicting the Second Law of Thermodynamics.

In an important paper, published in 1929, Leo Szilard showed that no such contradiction arises if due account is taken of the fact that the demon (who must be considered as part of the closed system involved) is acting on "information" concerning the detailed motion of the gas and is actually converting information into negative entropy. The following year G. N. Lewis considered the problem of separation and diffusion of gases and concluded that gain in entropy always means loss of information.

These investigations were remarkable for preceding the development of modern information theory by Claude Shannon in 1948. In this theory, information is not concerned with meaning but with the statistical character of a whole range of possible messages and is, in fact, a measure of the amount of freedom of choice we have in constructing messages. Shannon's investigation had an important bearing on Boltzmann's statistical analogue of entropy, for Boltzmann had left open the question of whether there might be an even more suitable statistical analogue. Shannon specified certain general mathematical properties which the required function must satisfy and found that the only possible function was Boltzmann's.

Entropy has already been described as a measure of the amount of disorder in a physical system, but it is now clear that a more precise statement is that entropy measures lack of information about the structure of a system. This lack of information is associated with the possibility of a great variety of microscopically distinct structures which, in practice, we cannot distinguish from one another. Since any one of these microscopic structures can occur at any given time, lack of information corresponds to actual disorder at that level and increase of entropy corresponds to progressive loss of information (for instance, by the attenuation of a sequence of pulses sent along an electric cable). The fact that *negative* entropy is identified with information is due to Clausius' unfortunate choice of the term "entropy" to denote the negative of the "availability for work" of the heat in a given system.

The importance of negative entropy in biology has been stressed by Erwin Schrödinger. Any living organism delays its decay into thermal equilibrium (death) by its capacity to maintain itself at a fairly high level of orderliness (and hence fairly low level of entropy) by continually absorbing negative entropy from its environment.

Since the development of information theory it has come to be realized that the statistical concept of entropy can be detached from thermodynamics and associated with any probability distribution whatsoever. In particular, it can be applied to a study of the statistical structure of language, and this has led to interesting results in the statistical characterization of literary vocabularies.

Bibliography

Bazarov, I. D., *Thermodynamics,* translated by F. Immirzi. Oxford, 1964.

Brillouin, Léon, *Science and Information Theory,* 2d ed. New York and London, 1962.

Dugas, R., *La Théorie physique au sens de Boltzmann et ses prolongements modernes.* Neuchâtel, 1959.

Grünbaum, Adolf, *Philosophical Problems of Space and Time.* New York, 1963.

Landsberg, P. T., *Entropy and the Unity of Knowledge* (inaugural lecture delivered at University College, Cardiff, Nov. 29, 1960). Cardiff, 1961.

Reichenbach, Hans, *The Direction of Time,* Maria Reichenbach, ed. Berkeley and Los Angeles, 1956.

Schrödinger, Erwin, *What Is Life?* Cambridge, 1944.

Shannon, C. E., and Weaver, Warren, *The Mathematical Theory of Communication.* Urbana, Ill., 1962.

Whitrow, G. J., *The Natural Philosophy of Time.* London, 1961; New York and Evanston, Ill., 1963.

G. J. WHITROW